The **Rough Guide** to

India

written and researched by

David Abram, Nick Edwards, Mike Ford, Daniel Jacobs, Shafik Meghji, Devdan Sen and Gavin Thomas

with additional contributions from

Edward Aves

Contents

Sacred spaces colour section following p.352

Bollywood and beyond colour section following p.624

Crafts to go colour section following p.1008

◀◀ Women sorting red peppers, Orissa ◀ Pilgrims at Sabarimala, Kerala

Metres
6000
5000
4000
3000
2000
1000
500
200
0

N

CHINA
TIBET
AUTONOMOUS REGION
NEPAL
BHUTAN
BANGLADESH
PAKISTAN
AFGHANISTAN

JAMMU & KASHMIR
Srinagar
Leh
Jammu Tawi
Dharamsala
Manali
Kullu
Pathankot
Amritsar
HIMACHAL PRADESH
Shimla
Chandigarh
PUNJAB
Mussoorie
Rishikesh
Haridwar
UTTARAKHAND
Nainital
CORBETT NATIONAL PARK
HARYANA
DELHI
UTTAR PRADESH
Mathura
Agra
Bharatpur
Ganges
Yamuna
Gwalior
Lucknow
Kanpur
Allahabad
Orchha
Khajuraho
Gorakhpur
Sarnath
Varanasi
Kushinagar
BIHAR
Patna
Gaya
Ganges
Darjeeling
SIKKIM
Gangtok
Kalimpong
JHARKHAND
BANDHAVGARH NATIONAL PARK
KANHA NATIONAL PARK
WEST BENGAL
KOLKATA (CALCUTTA)
MADHYA PRADESH
Jabalpur
Sanchi
Bhopal
Ujjain
Indore
Mandu
RAJASTHAN
Bikaner
Jaipur
Kota
Jodhpur
Jaisalmer
Udaipur
Mount Abu
GUJARAT
Ahmedabad
Vadodara
Gandhidham
Bhuj
Dwarka
ARUNACHAL PRADESH
Itanagar
ASSAM
Guwahati
NAGALAND
Kohima
MANIPUR
Imphal
MEGHALAYA
Shillong
MIZORAM
Aizawl
TRIPURA
Agartala

The International boundaries on this map are neither purported to be correct nor authentic by Survey of India directives. Publisher.

Introduction to India

India, it is often said, is not a country, but a continent. Stretching from the frozen summits of the Himalayas to the tropical greenery of Kerala, its expansive borders encompass an incomparable range of landscapes, cultures and people. Walk the streets of any Indian city and you'll rub shoulders with representatives of several of the world's great faiths, a multitude of castes and outcastes, fair-skinned, turbanned Punjabis and dark-skinned Tamils. You'll also encounter temple rituals that have been performed since the time of the Egyptian Pharaohs, onion-domed mosques erected centuries before the Taj Mahal was ever dreamt of, and quirky echoes of the British Raj on virtually every corner.

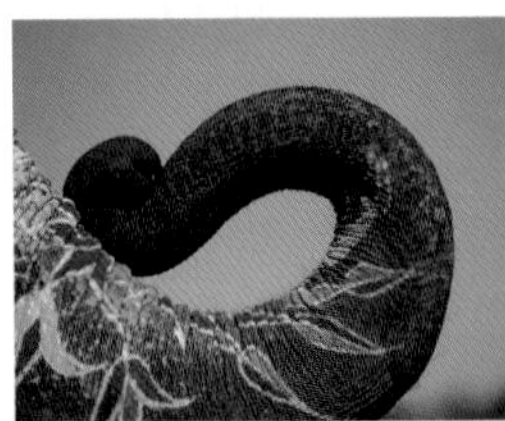

That so much of India's past remains discernible today is all the more astonishing given the pace of change since Independence in 1947. Spurred by the free-market reforms of the early 1990s, the **economic revolution** started by Rajiv Gandhi has transformed the country with new consumer goods, technologies and ways of life. Today the land where the Buddha lived and taught, and whose religious festivals are as old as the rivers that sustain them, is the second-largest producer of computer software in the world, with its own satellites and nuclear weapons.

However, the presence in even the most far-flung market towns of internet cafés and Japanese hatchbacks has thrown into sharp relief the **problems** that have bedevilled India since long before it became the world's largest secular democracy. Poverty remains a harsh fact of life for around a quarter of India's inhabitants; no other nation on earth has slum settlements on the scale of those in Delhi, Mumbai and Kolkata (Calcutta), nor so many malnourished children, uneducated women and homes without access to clean water and waste disposal.

Many first-time visitors find themselves unable to see past such glaring disparities. Others come expecting a timeless ascetic wonderland and are surprised to encounter one of the most materialistic societies on the planet. Still more find themselves intimidated by what may seem, initially, an incomprehensible and bewildering continent. But for all its jarring juxtapositions, intractable paradoxes and frustrations, India remains an utterly compelling destination. Intricate and worn, its distinctive patina – the stream of life in its crowded bazaars, the ubiquitous *filmi* music, the pungent melange of *beedi* smoke, cooking spices, dust and cow dung – casts a spell that few forget from the moment they step off a plane. Love it or hate it – and most travellers oscillate between the two – India will shift the way you see the world.

▶ Palace of the Maharawal, Jaisalmer

Fact file

- The Republic of India, whose capital is **Delhi**, is bordered by Afghanistan, China, Nepal and Bhutan to the north, Bangladesh and Myanmar (Burma) to the east and Pakistan to the west.
- It's the seventh-largest country, covering more than three million square kilometres, and second only to China in terms of population, at over **1.1 billion**. Hindus comprise eighty percent of the population, Muslims thirteen percent, and there are millions of Christians, Sikhs, Buddhists and Jains. **Twenty-three official languages** are spoken, along with more than a thousand minor languages and dialects; Hindi is the language of over forty percent of the population; English is also widely spoken.
- The **caste system** is pervasive and, although integral to Hindu belief, it also encompasses non-Hindus. It holds special sway in rural areas and may dictate where a person lives and what their occupation is.
- Seventy-three percent of males are literate, compared to 48 percent of females: 61 percent of the total population.

Where to go

The best Indian itineraries are the simplest. It just isn't possible to see everything in a single expedition, even if you spent a year trying. Far better, then, to concentrate on one or two specific regions and, above all, to be flexible. Although it requires a deliberate change of pace to venture away from the urban centres, rural India has its own very distinct pleasures. In fact, while Indian cities are undoubtedly adrenalin-fuelled, upbeat places, it is possible – and certainly less stressful – to travel for months around the Subcontinent and rarely have to set foot in one.

The most-travelled circuit in the country, combining spectacular monuments with the flat, fertile landscape that for many people is archetypally Indian, is the so-called **Golden Triangle** in the north: Delhi itself, the colonial capital; Agra, home of the Taj Mahal; and the Pink City of Jaipur in **Rajasthan**. Rajasthan is probably the single most popular state with travellers, who are drawn by its desert scenery, the imposing medieval forts and palaces of Jaisalmer, Jodhpur, Udaipur and Bundi, and by the colourful traditional dress.

▲ Flower market, Kolkata

East of Delhi, the River Ganges meanders through some of India's most densely populated regions to reach the extraordinary holy Hindu city of **Varanasi** (also known as Benares), where to witness the daily rituals of life and death focused around the waterfront ghats (bathing places) is to glimpse the continuing practice of India's most ancient religious traditions. Further east still is the great city of **Kolkata (Calcutta)**, the capital until early last century of the British Raj and now a teeming metropolis that epitomizes contemporary India's most pressing problems.

India's sacred geography

It's hard to think of a more visibly religious country than India. The very landscape of the Subcontinent – its rivers, waterfalls, trees, hilltops, mountains and rocks – comprises a vast sacred geography for adherents of the dozen or more faiths rooted here. Connecting the country's countless holy places is a network of pilgrimage routes along which tens of thousands of worshippers may be moving at any one time – on regular trains, specially decorated buses, tinsel-covered bicycles, barefoot, alone or in noisy family groups. For the visitor, joining devotees in the teeming temple precincts of the south, on the ghats at Varanasi, at the Sufi shrines of Ajmer and Delhi, before the naked Jain colossi of Sravanabelagola, or at any one of the innumerable religious festivals that punctuate the astrological calendar is to experience India at its most intense.

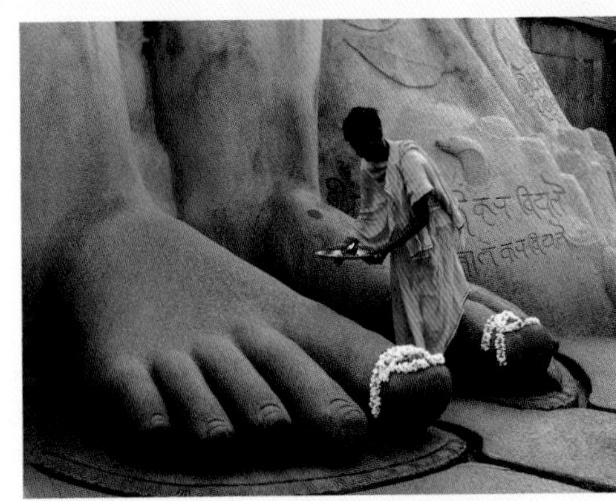

▲ The sacred Jain site of Sravanabelagola, Karnataka

The majority of travellers follow the well-trodden Ganges route to reach Nepal, perhaps unaware that the **Indian Himalayas** offer superlative trekking and mountain scenery to rival any in the range. With Kashmir effectively off the tourist map since the escalation of its civil war, **Himachal Pradesh** – where Dharamsala is the home of a Tibetan community that includes the Dalai Lama himself – and the remote province of **Ladakh**, with its mysterious lunar landscape and cloud-swept monasteries, have become the major targets for journeys into the mountains. Less visited, but possessing some of Asia's highest peaks, is the niche of **Uttarakhand** bordering Nepal, where the glacial source of the sacred River Ganges has attracted pilgrims for over a thousand years. At the opposite end of the chain, **Sikkim**, north of Bengal, is another low-key trekking destination, harbouring scenery and a Buddhist culture similar to that of neighbouring Bhutan. The **Northeast Hill States**, connected to eastern India by a slender neck of land, boast remarkably diverse landscapes and an incredible fifty percent of India's biodiversity.

Heading south from Kolkata (Calcutta) along the coast, your first likely stop is Konarak in **Orissa**, site of the famous Sun Temple, a giant carved pyramid of stone that lay submerged under sand until its rediscovery at

Prayer flags, Ladakh

the start of the twentieth century. Although it bore the brunt of the 2004 Asian tsunamis, **Tamil Nadu**, further south, has retained its own tradition of magnificent architecture, with towering *gopura* gateways dominating towns whose vast temple complexes are still the focus of everyday life. Of them all, Madurai, in the far south, is the most stunning, but you could spend months wandering between the sacred sites of the Cauvery Delta and the fragrant Nilgiri Hills, draped in the tea terraces that have become the hallmark of South Indian landscapes. **Kerala**, near the southernmost tip of the subcontinent on the western coast, is India at its most tropical and relaxed, its lush backwaters teeming with simple wooden craft of all shapes and sizes, and red-roofed towns and villages all but invisible beneath a canopy of palm trees. Further up the coast is **Goa**, the former Portuguese colony whose hundred-kilometre coastline is fringed with beaches to suit all tastes and budgets, from upmarket package tourists to long-staying backpackers, and whose towns hold whitewashed Christian churches that might have been transplanted from Europe.

North of here sits **Mumbai**, an ungainly beast that has been the major focus of the nationwide drift to the big cities. Centre of the country's formidable popular movie industry, it reels along on an undeniable energy that, after a few days of acclimatization, can prove addictive. Beyond Mumbai is the state of **Gujarat**, renowned for the unique culture and crafts of the barren Kutch region.

On a long trip, it makes sense to pause and rest every few weeks. Certain places have fulfilled that function for generations, such as the Himalayan resort of **Manali**, epicentre of India's hashish-producing area, and the many former colonial hill stations that dot the country, from **Ootacamund (Ooty)**, in the far south, to that archetypal British retreat, **Shimla**, immortalized in the writing of Rudyard Kipling. Elsewhere, the combination of sand and the sea, and a picturesque rural or religious backdrop – such as at **Varkala** in Kerala, **Gokarna** in Karnataka, and the remoter beaches of Goa – are usually enough to loosen even the tightest itineraries.

Indian railways

India's railways, which daily transport millions of commuters, pilgrims, animals and hessian-wrapped packages between the four corners of the Subcontinent, are often cited as the best thing the British Raj bequeathed to its former colony. And yet, with its hierarchical legion of clerks, cooks, coolis, bearers, ticket inspectors, stations managers and ministers, the network has become a quintessentially Indian institution.

Travelling across India by rail – whether you rough it in dirt-cheap second-class, or pamper yourself with starched cotton sheets and hot meals in an air-con carriage – is likely to yield some of the most memorable moments of your trip. Open around the clock, the stations in themselves are often great places to watch the world go by, with hundreds of people from all walks of life eating, sleeping, buying and selling, regardless of the hour. This is also where you'll grow familiar with one of the unforgettable sounds of the Subcontinent: the robotic drone of the chai-wallah, dispensing cups of hot, sweet tea. For the practical low-down on train travel see p.39.

When to go

India's weather is extremely varied, something you must take into account when planning your trip. The most influential feature of the Subcontinent's climate is the wet season, or **monsoon**. This breaks on the Keralan coast at the end of May, working its way north-east across the country over the following month and a half. While it lasts, regular and prolonged downpours are interspersed with bursts of hot sunshine, and the pervasive humidity can be intense. At the height of the monsoon – especially in the jungle regions of the north-west and the low-lying delta lands of Bengal – flooding

▲ Palolem Beach, Goa

Indian food

▲ Thali on banana leaf, Kerala

Indian cooking is as varied as the country itself, with dozens of distinctive regional culinary traditions ranging from the classic Mughlai style cuisine of the north to the feisty coconut- and chilli-infused flavours of the south; these are often a revelation to first-time visitors, whose only contact with Indian food will probably have been through the stereotypical Anglo-Indian dishes served up in the majority of restaurants overseas. Best known is the cuisine of North India, with its signature biryanis, tandooris and rich cream- and yoghurt-based sauces accompanied with thick naan breads, evidence of the region's long contact with Central Asia. The food of South India is light years away, exemplified by the ubiquitous vegetarian "meal" – a huge mound of rice served on a banana leaf and accompanied with fiery pickles – or by the classic masala dosa, a crisp rice pancake wrapped around a spicy potato filling. There's also a host of regional cuisines to explore – Punjabi, Bengali, Gujarati, Goan, Keralan and Kashmiri, to name just a few of the most distinctive – each of which has its own special dishes, spices and cooking techniques. For more information, see p.51.

can severely disrupt communications, causing widespread destruction. In the Himalayan foothills, landslides are common, and entire valley systems can be cut off for weeks.

By September, the monsoon has largely receded from the north, but it takes another couple of months before the clouds disappear altogether from the far south. The east coast of Andhra Pradesh and Tamil Nadu, and the south of Kerala, get a second drenching between October and December, when the "northwest" or "retreating" monsoon sweeps in from the Bay of Bengal. By December, however, most of the Subcontinent enjoys clear skies and relatively cool temperatures.

Mid-winter sees the most marked contrasts between the climates of north and south India. While Delhi, for example, may be ravaged by chill winds blowing off the snowfields of the Himalayas, the Tamil plains and coastal Kerala, more than 1000km south, still stew under fierce post-monsoon sunshine. As spring gathers pace, the centre of the Subcontinent starts to heat up again, and by late March thermometers nudge 33°C across most of the Gangetic Plains and Deccan plateau. Temperatures peak in May and early June, when anyone who can retreats to the hill stations. Above the baking Subcontinental land mass, hot air builds up and sucks in humidity from the southwest, causing the onset of the monsoon in late June, and bringing relief to millions of overheated Indians.

The best time to visit most of the country, therefore, is during the **cool, dry season**, between November and March. Delhi, Agra, Varanasi, Rajasthan and Madhya Pradesh are ideal at this time, and temperatures in Goa and central India remain comfortable. The heat of the south is never less than intense but it becomes stifling in May and June, so aim to be in Tamil Nadu and Kerala between January and March. From this time onwards, the Himalayas grow more accessible, and the trekking season reaches its peak in August and September while the rest of the Subcontinent is being soaked by the rains.

Average temperatures and rainfall

	Jan	Feb	Mar	Apr	May	Jun	Jul	Aug	Sep	Oct	Nov	Dec
Chennai (TN)												
Max/min °C	28/20	31/21	33/23	36/26	38/27	37/27	35/26	34/26	34/25	32/24	29/22	28/21
Max/min °F	83/68	87/70	91/74	96/79	100/81	99/81	95/78	94/78	93/77	89/75	85/72	83/70
Rainfall (mm)	28	33	5	13	38	71	122	137	160	157	152	152
Delhi												
Max/min °C	21/7	24/9	31/14	36/20	41/26	39/28	36/27	34/26	34/24	34/18	29/11	23/8
Max/min °F	70/63	75/48	88/57	97/68	106/79	102/82	97/81	93/79	93/75	93/64	84/52	73/46
Rainfall (mm)	23	18	13	8	13	74	180	173	117	10	3	10
Kolkata (Calcutta) (WB)												
Max/min °C	27/13	29/15	34/21	36/24	36/25	33/26	32/26	32/26	32/26	32/24	29/18	26/13
Max/min °F	81/55	84/59	93/70	97/75	97/77	91/79	90/79	90/79	90/79	90/75	84/64	79/55
Rainfall (mm)	10	31	36	43	140	297	325	328	252	114	20	5
Mumbai (M)												
Max/min °C	28/19	28/19	30/22	32/24	33/27	32/26	29/25	29/24	29/24	32/24	32/23	31/21
Max/min °F	82/66	82/66	86/72	90/75	91/81	90/79	84/77	84/75	84/75	90/75	90/73	88/70
Rainfall (mm)	3	3	3	0	18	485	617	340	264	64	13	3
Panjim (Goa)												
Max/min °C	32/19	32/21	32/23	33/25	33/26	30/24	29/24	28/24	29/24	32/24	33/22	32/21
Max/min °F	90/66	90/70	90/73	91/77	91/79	86/75	84/75	82/75	84/75	90/75	91/72	90/70
Rainfall (mm)	0	0	0	0	50	580	650	400	150	90	10	0

things not to miss

It's not possible to see everything India has to offer in one trip, and we don't suggest you try. What follows is a selective taste of the country's highlights: outstanding buildings, natural wonders, spectacular festivals and unforgettable journeys. They're arranged in five colour-coded categories, which you can browse through to find the very best things to see and experience. All highlights have a page reference to take you straight to the guide, where you can find out more.

01 Durga Puja Page **737** • An exuberant festival held in September or October, when every street and village erects a shrine to the goddess Durga. Kolkata (Calcutta) has the most lavish festivities.

02 Fatehpur Sikri Page **260** • The Mughal emporer Akbar's elegant palace complex now lies deserted on a ridge near Agra, but remains one of India's architectural masterpieces.

03 Boating on the backwaters of Kerala Page **1046** • Lazy boat trips wind through the lush tropical waterways of India's deep south.

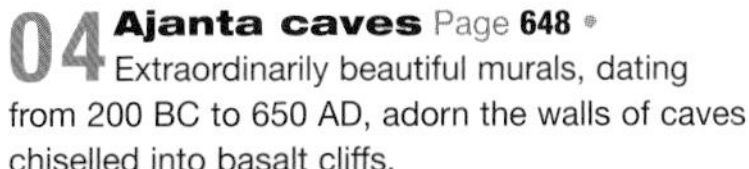

04 Ajanta caves Page **648** • Extraordinarily beautiful murals, dating from 200 BC to 650 AD, adorn the walls of caves chiselled into basalt cliffs.

05 Taj Mahal Page **250** • Simply the world's greatest building: Shah Jahan's monument to love fully lives up to all expectations.

06 Zanskar Page **515** • A barren moonscape with extraordinary scenery and challenging trails over the high passes.

07 National Museum, Delhi Page **107** • A splendid introduction to the culture and history of India, featuring outstanding sculpture, Mughal miniature paintings and much more.

08 Pushkar camel mela Page **185** • November sees the largest livestock market on earth, where 200,000 Rajasthani herders in traditional costume converge on the desert oasis of Pushkar to trade and bathe in the sacred lake.

09 Khajuraho Page **374** • Immaculately preserved temples renowned for their uncompromisingly erotic carvings.

10 Gangotri Page **323** • An atmospheric village on the Ganges that serves as a base for the trek into the heart of the Hindu faith – Gomukh, the source of the Ganges.

11 Orchha Page **370** • This semi-ruined former capital of the Bundela Rajas is an architectural gem, rising up through the surrounding forest.

12 Jaisalmer Page **196** • Honey-coloured citadel, emerging from the sands of the Thar Desert.

13 Manali–Leh Highway Page **467** • India's epic Himalayan road trip, along the second-highest highway in the world, is the most popular approach to Ladakh, and revered by motorbikers, cyclists and drivers alike.

14 Dharamsala Page **429** • Perched on the edge of the Himalayas, this is the home of the Dalai Lama and Tibetan Buddhism in exile.

15 Kochi Page **1059** • This atmospheric harbourside is strung with elegant Chinese fishing nets.

16 Keoladeo National Park, Bharatpur Page **170** • Asia's most famous bird reserve, where millions of migrants nest each winter. The perfect antidote to the frenzy and pollution of nearby Agra and Jaipur.

17 Cricket Page **62** • The nation's favourite sport is played everywhere, from the Oval Maidan in Mumbai to Eden Gardens in Kolkata (Calcutta), the hot cauldron of Indian cricket.

18 Gokarna Page **1123** • The beautiful beaches on the edge of this temple town are popular with budget travellers fleeing the commercialism of nearby Goa.

19 **Rath Yatra, Puri** Page **891** • Three colossal chariots with brightly coloured canopies are pulled by crowds of devotees through the streets of eastern India's holiest town.

20 **Konark** Page **896** • A colossal thirteenth-century temple, buried under sand until its rediscovery by the British.

21 **Madurai** Page **996** • Definitive South Indian city, centred on a spectacular medieval temple.

22 **Bandhavgarh National Park** Page **391** • Deep in the eastern tracts of Madhya Pradesh, this park is rich in animal and birdlife, including tigers and leopards.

23 **Hampi/Vijayanagar** Page **1129** • Deserted capital of the last great Hindu empire, scattered over a bizarre landscape of giant golden-brown boulders.

24 **Ellora caves** Page **641** • Buddhist, Hindu and Jain caves, and the colossal Hindu Kailash temple, carved from a spectacular volcanic ridge at the heart of the Deccan plateau.

25 **Rajasthani handicrafts** Page **150** • The teeming bazaars of the Pink City in Jaipur burst with vibrant cloth, jewellery, Persian- style pottery and semi-precious stones. Simply the best place to shop in the Subcontinent.

26 **Varanasi** Page **281** • City of Light, founded by Shiva, where the bathing ghats beside the Ganges teem with pilgrims.

27 Varkala Page **1037** • This pleasantly low-key Keralan resort boasts sheer red cliffs, amazing sea views and a legion of Ayurvedic masseurs.

28 Kathakali Page **1024** • Kerala is the place to experience Kathakali and other esoteric ritual theatre forms.

29 Mamallapuram Page **960** • A fishing and stone-carving village, with magnificent boulder friezes, shrines and the sea-battered Shore Temple.

30 Tikse Page **499** • The most architecturally impressive of the many dramatic monasteries within striking distance of Leh.

31 Meherangarh Fort, Jodhpur Page **190** • The epitome of Rajput power and extravagance, its ramparts towering above a labyrinthine, blue-painted old city.

32 Thrissur Puram Page **1074** • More than one hundred sumptuously caparisoned elephants march in Kerala's biggest temple festival, accompanied by ear-shattering South Indian drum orchestras.

33 **Udaipur** Page **214** • Arguably the most romantic city in India, with ornate Rajput palaces floating in the middle of two shimmering lakes.

34 **Amritsar** Page **528** • The largest city in Punjab, and site of the fabled Golden Temple, the Sikhs' holiest shrine.

35 **Palolem** Page **726** • Exquisite crescent-shaped beach in Goa's relaxed south, famous for its dolphins and local alcoholic spirit, *feni*.

Basics

Getting there

With most overland routes into India (except from Nepal) effectively blocked by closed or trouble-prone borders, the only practicable way of getting to India is by plane. There are numerous nonstop services from the UK, plus a few from North America and one from Australia. Most of these arrive at either Delhi or Mumbai, although there are also nonstop flights from the UK into Kolkata, Chennai and Bengaluru.

Fares worldwide always depend on the season, with the highest being roughly November to March, when the weather in India is best; fares drop during the shoulder seasons – April to May and August to early October – and you'll get the best prices during the low season, June and July. The most expensive fares of all are those coinciding with **Diwali** in November, when demand peaks as Indian emigrants travel home for holidays with their families.

For Goa, you may find it cheaper to pick up a bargain **package deal** from one of the tour operators listed on pp.28–30. Indian law prohibits the sale of flight-only tickets by charter companies, but operators sometimes get around this by tacking budget "bunk-house" accommodation to their tickets, which (if it exists at all) travellers ditch on arrival. Note also that the Indian government places a restriction of 28 days on the period of time a charter ticket can cover. If you wish to stay in the country for longer than that, you technically have to take a scheduled flight. Nor is it possible to fly in on a charter and out on a scheduled flight, or vice versa.

Packages

Lots of operators run **package holidays** to India, covering activities ranging from trekking and wildlife-watching through to general sightseeing or just lying on the beach, not to mention more specialist-interest tours focusing on anything from steam locomotives to food. In addition, many companies can also arrange **tailor-made tours** where you plan your own itinerary. Of course, any package holiday is a lot easier than going under your own steam, particularly if you only have a short time and don't want to use it up on making your own travel bookings. Nor do specialist trips such as trekking and tailor-made tours necessarily work out a lot more expensive than organizing everything independently. Tour operators pay a lot less for hotels and flights than you would, and if they're any good will also know the best hotels, routes and sights to feature, taking a lot of hassle out of the planning. On the other hand, a typical package tour can rather isolate you from the country, shutting you off in air-conditioned hotels and cars.

Flights from the UK and Ireland

It takes between eight and eleven hours to fly from the UK direct to India. A number of carriers fly nonstop from London Heathrow to Delhi and Mumbai; these currently include Air India, Jet Airways, Virgin Atlantic and British Airways (who also fly nonstop to Kolkata, Chennai and Bengaluru). Numerous other European and Middle Eastern carriers offer one-stop services via their home city in Europe or the Gulf. From elsewhere in the UK and Ireland you'll have to take an indirect flight, changing planes at either Heathrow or somewhere else in Europe, the Middle East or Asia. Both scheduled fares and flight-only charters usually start from around £400.

Flights from the US and Canada

India is on the other side of the planet from the US and Canada. If you live on the East Coast it's quicker to travel via Europe, while from the West Coast it's roughly the same distance (and price) whether you travel via Europe or the Pacific. There are currently nonstop flights from **New York** to Delhi and Mumbai on Air India and Continental (and also to Mumbai on Delta), and from **Chicago** to Delhi on American Airlines. Otherwise, you'll probably stop over somewhere in Europe (most often London), the Gulf, or both. Nonstop flights take around 15–16 hours, with fares from New York to Mumbai/Delhi starting at around $1000. There are currently no nonstop flights from the **West Coast**; count on a minimum 22 hours' travel time. Fares start at around $1400.

There are also no nonstop flights from **Canada** to India – you'll have to travel via a connecting city in the US, Europe or Asia with a minimum travel time of around 20 hours. Fares start at around CDN$1600 from Toronto and CDN$1800 from Vancouver.

Flights from Australia and New Zealand

The only nonstop flight to India from either **Australia** or **New Zealand** at present is

Six steps to a better kind of travel

At Rough Guides we are passionately committed to travel. We feel strongly that only through travelling do we truly come to understand the world we live in and the people we share it with – plus tourism has brought a great deal of **benefit** to developing economies around the world over the last few decades. But the extraordinary growth in tourism has also damaged some places irreparably, and of course **climate change** is exacerbated by most forms of transport, especially flying. This means that now more than ever it's important to **travel thoughtfully** and **responsibly**, with respect for the cultures you're visiting – not only to derive the most benefit from your trip but also to preserve the best bits of the planet for everyone to enjoy. At Rough Guides we feel there are six main areas in which you can make a difference:

- Consider what you're contributing to the **local economy**, and how much the services you use do the same, whether it's through employing local workers and guides or sourcing locally grown produce and local services.
- Consider the **environment** on holiday as well as at home. Water is scarce in many developing destinations, and the biodiversity of local flora and fauna can be adversely affected by tourism. Try to patronize businesses that take account of this.
- Travel with a purpose, not just to tick off experiences. Consider **spending longer** in a place, and getting to know it and its people.
- Give thought to how often you **fly**. Try to avoid short hops by air and more harmful night flights.
- Consider **alternatives to flying**, travelling instead by bus, train, boat and even by bike or on foot where possible.
- Make your trips "**climate neutral**" via a reputable carbon-offset scheme. All Rough Guide flights are offset, and every year we donate money to a variety of charities devoted to combating the effects of climate change.

Qantas's service from Sydney to Mumbai (with a flying time of around 13hr); otherwise, you'll have to make at least one change of plane in a southeast Asian hub city (usually Kuala Lumpur, Singapore or Bangkok). Fares start from around A$1500. Flying from New Zealand, the cheapest fares to India start at around NZ$2000 from Auckland; add on approximately NZ$150 for flights from Wellington or Christchurch.

Round-the-world tickets

If India is only one stop on a longer journey, you might want to consider buying a **Round-the-World (RTW) ticket**. Some travel agents can sell you an "off-the-shelf" RTW ticket that will have you touching down in about half a dozen cities (Delhi and Mumbai feature on many itineraries); others will have to assemble one for you, which can be tailored to your needs but is apt to be more expensive. Figure on between £1800/$3500 and £1500/$2500 for an RTW ticket including India, valid for one year.

Airlines, agents and operators

International airlines

Air Canada ⓦwww.aircanada.com.
Air France ⓦwww.airfrance.com.
Air India ⓦwww.airindia.com.
Alitalia ⓦwww.alitalia.com.
American Airlines ⓦwww.aa.com.
British Airways ⓦwww.ba.com.
Cathay Pacific ⓦwww.cathaypacific.com.
Continental Airlines ⓦwww.continental.com.
Delta ⓦwww.delta.com.
EgyptAir ⓦwww.egyptair.com.eg.
Emirates ⓦwww.emirates.com.
Etihad Airways ⓦwww.etihadairways.com.
Gulf Air ⓦwww.gulfair.com.
KLM (Royal Dutch Airlines) ⓦwww.klm.com.
Kuwait Airways ⓦwww.kuwait-airways.com.
Lufthansa ⓦwww.lufthansa.com.
Malaysia Airlines ⓦwww.malaysia-airlines.com.
Northwest/KLM ⓦwww.nwa.com.
PIA (Pakistan International Airlines) ⓦwww.piac.com.pk.
Qantas ⓦwww.qantas.com.
Qatar Airways ⓦwww.qatarairways.
Royal Jordanian ⓦwww.rj.com.
SAS (Scandinavian Airlines) ⓦwww.flysas.com.
Singapore Airlines ⓦwww.singaporeair.com.
South African Airways ⓦwww.flysaa.com.
SriLankan Airlines ⓦwww.srilankan.lk.
Syrian Airlines ⓦwww.syrianairlines.co.uk.
Thai Airways ⓦwww.thaiair.com.
United Airlines ⓦwww.united.com.

Domestic airlines

Air India ⓦwww.airindia.com.
Air India Express ⓦwww.airindiaexpress.in.
Go Air ⓦwww.goair.in.
IndiGo Airlines ⓦbook.goindigo.in.
Jet Airways/JetLite ⓦwww.jetairways.com.
Kingfisher Airlines ⓦwww.flykingfisher.com.
Paramount Airways ⓦwww.paramountairways.com.
Sahara Airways ⓦwww.saharaairlines.co.in.
SpiceJet ⓦwww.spicejet.com.

Travel agents

North South Travel UK ⓣ01245/608 291, ⓦwww.northsouthtravel.co.uk. Friendly, competitive travel agency, offering discounted fares worldwide. Profits are used to support projects in the developing world, especially the promotion of sustainable tourism.

STA Travel UK ⓣ0871/2300 040, US ⓣ1-800/781-4040, Australia ⓣ134 782, New Zealand ⓣ0800/474 400, South Africa ⓣ0861/781 781; ⓦwww.statravel.co.uk. Worldwide specialists in independent travel; also student IDs, travel insurance, car rental, rail passes, and more. Good discounts for students and under-26s.

Trailfinders UK ⓣ0845/058 5858, Ireland ⓣ01/677 7888, Australia ⓣ1300/780 212; ⓦwww.trailfinders.com. One of the best-informed and most efficient agents for independent travellers.

Travel CUTS Canada ⓣ1-866/246-9762, US ⓣ1-800/592-2887; ⓦwww.travelcuts.com. Canadian youth and student travel firm.

USIT Ireland ⓣ01/602 1906, Northern Ireland ⓣ028/9032 7111; ⓦwww.usit.ie. Ireland's main student and youth travel specialists.

Package holiday companies

Audley Travel UK ⓣ01993/838300, ⓦwww.audleytravel.com. Tailor-made and small-group tours that use interesting accommodation (homestays, tented camps and heritage properties); they're also strong on wildlife.

Bales UK ⓣ0845/057 1819, ⓦwww.balesworldwide.com. Wide range of group and tailor-made tours covering most of India.

Blazing Trails UK ⓣ01902/894009, ⓦwww.blazingtrailstours.com. Escorted motorcycle tours (on Enfields) in Goa, Kerala, Rajasthan and the Himalayas.

Butterfield & Robinson US & Canada ⓣ1-866/551-9090, ⓦwww.butterfield.com. Refreshingly unusual cycling and walking trips, including a varied supported tours of Rajasthan and Kerala by bike.

Cox & Kings UK ⓣ020/7873 5000, ⓦwww.coxandkings.co.uk, US ⓣ1-800/999-1758, ⓦwww.coxandkings.com. Established in India in 1758, with upmarket group and private tours, many featuring Rajasthan and Agra, plus the Palace on Wheels.

Culture Aangan ⓦwww.cultureaangan.com. Homestays in southern coastal Maharashtra. Profits go to support local communities and help preserve the area's traditional culture.

Exodus UK ⓣ0845 863 9600, Ireland ⓣ01/804 7153, US ⓣ1-800/843 4277, Canada ⓣ866/338 8735, Australia ⓣ1300 655 433, New Zealand ⓣ0800 838 747; ⓦwww.exodus.co.uk. Experienced specialists in small-group itineraries, treks and overland tours.

Explore Worldwide UK ⓣ0845/013 1537, US ⓣ1-800/486-9096, Australia ⓣ02/8913 0700, New Zealand ⓣ09/524 5118; ⓦwww.explore.co.uk. Wide range of small-group adventure holidays.

Geographic Expeditions US ⓣ1-800/777-8183, ⓦwww.geoex.com. Unusual tours, ranging from Tamil Nadu temple trips to Sikkim village walks.

High Places UK ⓣ0114/275 7500, ⓦwww.highplaces.co.uk. Sheffield-based trekking and mountaineering specialists; they also run an interesting 16-day tour through Kerala.

Insider Tours UK ⓣ01233/811771, ⓦwww.insider-tours.com. Some of the most original, "hands-on" and ethical itineraries on the market, taking visitors to wonderful off-track corners of Kerala, Goa, the Northeast and elsewhere.

Jewel in the Crown UK ⓣ01293/533338, ⓦwww.jewelholidays.com. Established Goa specialist, offering a wide range of holidays, as well as cheap flights.

Kerala Connections UK ⓣ01892/722440, ⓦwww.keralaconnect.co.uk. Itineraries in Kerala, as well as Tamil Nadu and Karnataka, for a wide range of budgets.

Lakshmi Tours UK ⓣ01985/844183, ⓦwww.lakshmitoursindia.com. Special-interest tours (drawing, textiles, Ayurveda) for small groups, mostly focusing on Rajasthan and Kerala.

Live India UK ⓦwww.liveindia.co.uk. Enfield motorcycle tours to locations well off the regular tourist trail, with stays in unusual hotels. The trips are led by experts with more than twenty years' experience of biking around India.

UK ⓣ01453/844400,
ns.co.uk. Quality treks
Pradesh, Ladakh and

ⓣ1-800/670-6984 or
hsandmountains.com.
nade or group) to some
g from tribal Chhattisgarh
e emphasis on culture,

36 0170, Australia
vw.peregrineadventures
ife and culture tours in
dia, plus trekking in Ladakh.
1892/515966, ⓦwww
nade holidays off the beaten track.
020/8903 3411, ⓦwww
by Indian rail experts, SD
ther itineraries for independent
o explore India by train, plus a
ap countrywide packages and
Kerala and Goa.

Steppes Discovery UK ⓣ01285/643333, ⓦ**www.steppesdiscovery.co.uk.** Nature-tour specialist offering small groups or tailor-made trips with an accent on conservation and ecology.

Trans Indus Travel UK ⓣ020/8566 3739, ⓦ**www.transindus.co.uk.** Fixed and tailor-made packages from various Indian cities, including wildlife, fishing and trekking tours.

Voyages Jules Verne UK ⓣ0845/166 7003, ⓦ**www.vjv.co.uk.** Classic heritage tours, including some by rail.

Western & Oriental Travel UK ⓣ0870/499 1111, ⓦ**www.westernoriental.com.** Award-winning, upmarket agency with tailor-made itineraries covering all of India but favouring Goa and Rajasthan.

Western & Oriental Travel UK ⓣ0845/277 3355, ⓦ**www.westernoriental.com.** Award-winning, upmarket agency with tailor-made itineraries ranging from Himalayan treks to southern temple tours, with the emphasis on culture, history and wildlife.

Entry requirements

st everyone needs a visa before elling to India. If you're going to study work, you'll need to apply for a special udent or business visa; otherwise, a andard tourist visa will suffice.

Tourist visas

Tourist visas are valid for six months from the date of issue (not of departure from your home country or entry into India), and usually cost £30/US$75. You're asked to specify whether you need a single-entry or a multiple-entry visa; as the same rates apply to both, it makes sense to ask for the latter just in case you decide to go back within six months. Note, however, that a ruling introduced in 2009 (in theory at least) prevents visitors on a tourist visa (or visas) from re-entering India within two months of their last visit other than in exceptional circumstances, and with pre-arranged clearance from your local embassy or consulate – although, again, whether or not this ruling is likely to be strictly enforced remains unclear at the time of writing.

Visas in the UK, US, Canada and Australia are no longer issued by Indian embassies themselves, but by various third-party companies (sub-contractors) – see opposite for details. The firms' websites give all the details you need to make your application. Read the small print carefully and always **make sure you've allowed plenty of time.** Applying in person it's possible to obtain your visa by the following working day – but don't bank on it; three to four working days is more common. **Postal applications** take a minimum of ten working days plus time in transit, and often longer.

Elsewhere in the world, visas are still issued by the relevant local embassy or consulate, though the same caveats apply. Bear in mind too that Indian High Commissions, embassies and consulates observe Indian public holidays as well as local ones, so always check opening hours in advance.

Visa agencies

In many countries it's possible to pay a **visa agency** (or "visa expediter" – see below) to process the visa on your behalf, which typically costs £60–70/$100–120, plus the price of the visa. This is worth considering if you're not able to get to your nearest Indian High Commission, embassy or consulate yourself. Prices vary from company to company, as do turnaround times. Two weeks is about standard, but you can get a visa in as little as 24 hours if you're prepared to pay premium rates. For a full rundown of services, check the company websites, from where you can usually download visa application forms.

Visa extensions

It is no longer possible to **extend a tourist visa** in India, though exceptions may be made in special circumstances. In addition, new rules introduced in late 2009 (see opposite) require that visitors travelling on a tourist visa must leave at least two months between visits to India. Thus, if your visa is about to elapse, it's no longer possible to pop over to a neighbouring country and then re-enter on a new visa a couple of days later

Indian embassies, high commissions, consulates and visa-processing centres abroad

Australia C/o VFS Global (Ⓦwww.vfs-in-au.net) which has offices in all states except Tasmania and NT; see website for contact details.
Canada C/o VFS Global (Ⓦin.vfsglobal.ca) which has nine offices countrywide – see website for details.
Ireland Embassy: 6 Leeson Park, Dublin 6 Ⓣ01/497 0843, Ⓦwww.indianembassy.ie.
Nepal C/o Indian Visa Service Centre (IVSC), House no.296, Kapurdhara Marg, Kathmandu Ⓣ01/400 1516, Ⓦwww.indianembassy.org.np.
New Zealand High Commission: 180 Molesworth St, PO Box 4045, Wellington Ⓣ04/473 6390, Ⓦwww.hicomind.org.nz.
South Africa 852 Schoeman St (corner of Eastwood St), PO Box 40216, Arcadia 0007, Pretoria Ⓣ012/342 2593, Ⓦwww.indiainsouthafrica.com; 1 Eton Rd, Parktown, PO Box 6805, Johannesburg 2000 Ⓣ011/482 8484 to 9; The Old Station Building (4th floor), 160 Pine St, PO Box 3276, Durban 4001 Ⓣ031/307-7020, Ⓦwww.indcondurban.co.za.
Sri Lanka High Commission: 36–38 Galle Rd, Colombo 3 Ⓣ011/232 7587, Ⓦwww.hcicolombo.org. Consulate: 31 Rajapihilla Mawatha, PO Box 47, Kandy Ⓣ081/222 4563.
UK C/o VFS Global (Ⓦin.vfsglobal.co.uk), which has offices in London, Birmingham, Manchester, Cardiff, Edinburgh and Glasgow – see website for contact details.
US C/o Travisa (Ⓦindiavisa.travisaoutsourcing.com), which has offices in Washington, New York, San Francisco, Chicago and Houston – see website for contact details.

Visa agencies

CIBT US Ⓣ1-800/929-2428, Ⓦwww.cibt.com. UK Ⓣ0844/736 0211, Ⓦwww.uk.cibt.com.
India Visa Office UK Ⓣ0844/800 4018, Ⓦwww.indiavisaheadoffice.co.uk.
India Visa Company UK Ⓣ020/8582 1117 Ⓦwww.skylorduk.com/gle_visa.htm.
India Visa 24 Ⓣ0800/084 5037, Ⓦwww.indiavisa24.co.uk.
Travel Document Systems US; Washington Ⓣ1-800/874-5100, New York Ⓣ1-877/874-5104, San Francisco Ⓣ1-888/874-5100, Ⓦwww.traveldocs.com.
Visa Connection US & Canada Ⓣ1-866/566-8472, Ⓦwww.visaconnection.com.
Visa Link Australia Ⓣ03/9673 1500, Ⓦwww.visalink.com.au.

Health

There are plenty of scare stories about the health risks of travelling in India, but in fact cases of serious illness are very much the exception rather than the rule. Standards of hygiene and sanitation have increased greatly over the past decade or so and, if you're careful, there's no reason you can't stay healthy throughout your trip – indeed many travellers now visit the Subcontinent without even experiencing the traditional dose of "Delhi belly". Having said that, it's still important to keep your resistance high and to be aware of the dangers of untreated water, mosquito bites and undressed open cuts.

It's worth knowing, if you are ill and can't get to a doctor, that almost any medicine can be bought over the counter without a prescription.

Precautions

When it comes to **food**, be wary of dishes that appear to have been reheated. Anything boiled, fried or grilled (and thus sterilized) in your presence is usually all right, though seafood and meat can pose real risks if they're not fresh; anything that has been left out for any length of time, or stored in a fridge during a power cut, is best avoided. Raw unpeeled fruit and vegetables should always be viewed with suspicion, and you should steer clear of salads unless you know they have been washed in purified water. The fruit-seller on the beach may have handled the peeled fruit, so make sure you douse your slice of pineapple or melon with safe water before eating it.

Be vigilant about **personal hygiene**: wash your hands often, especially before eating. Keep all cuts clean, treat them with iodine or antiseptic (a liquid or dry spray is better in the heat) and cover them to prevent infection.

Advice on avoiding **mosquitoes** is offered under "Malaria" on p.34. If you do get bites or itches, try not to scratch them: it's hard, but infection and tropical ulcers can result if you do. Tiger balm and even dried soap may relieve the itching.

Finally, especially if you are going on a long trip, have a **dental check-up** before you leave home.

Vaccinations

No **inoculations** are legally required for entry into India, but diphtheria, typhoid and hepatitis A jabs are recommended for travellers to many parts of the country, and it's worth ensuring that you are up to date with tetanus, polio and other boosters. Vaccinations for hepatitis B, rabies, meningitis, Japanese encephalitis and TB are also advised if you're travelling to remote areas, or working in environments with an increased exposure to infectious diseases.

Transmitted through contaminated food and water, or through saliva, **hepatitis A** can lay a victim low for several months with exhaustion, fever and diarrhoea. Symptoms include yellowing of the whites of the eyes, general malaise, orange urine (though dehydration could also cause that) and light-coloured stools. If you think you have it, get a diagnosis as soon as possible, steer clear of alcohol, get lots of rest – and try to avoid passing it on. More serious is **hepatitis B**, transmitted like AIDS through blood or sexual contact.

Typhoid fever is also spread through contaminated food or water, but is rare in most parts of India. It produces a persistent high temperature with malaise, headaches and abdominal pains, followed by diarrhoea.

Cholera, spread the same way as hepatitis A and typhoid, causes sudden attacks of watery diarrhoea with cramps and debilitation. Again, this disease rarely occurs in India, breaking out in isolated epidemics; there is a vaccination but it offers very little protection. Most medical authorities now recommend immunization against meningococcal **meningitis (ACWY)** too. Spread by airborne bacteria (through coughs and sneezes for example), it is a very unpleasant disease that attacks the lining of the brain and can be fatal.

Rabies is widespread throughout the country, and the best advice is to give dogs and monkeys a wide berth – do not play with animals at all, no matter how cute they might look. A bite, a scratch or even a lick from an infected animal could spread the disease; if you're bitten or scratched and it breaks the skin, immediately wash the wound gently with soap or detergent, apply alcohol or iodine if possible, and go immediately to the nearest hospital for an anti-rabies jab.

Medical resources for travellers

For up-to-the-minute information, make an appointment at a **travel clinic**. These clinics also sell travel accessories, including mosquito nets and first-aid kits.

Travel clinics and resources

International Society for Travel Medicine ⓦwww.istm.org. A full list of clinics worldwide specializing in travel health.

In the UK and Ireland

Hospital for Tropical Diseases Travel Clinic UK ⓣ020/7387 4411, ⓦwww.thehtd.org.

MASTA (Medical Advisory Service for Travellers Abroad) UK ⓣ0870/606 2782, ⓦwww.masta-travel-health.com. Forty clinics across the UK.

Nomad Pharmacy UK ⓦwww.nomadtravel.co.uk. Clinics in London, Southampton and Bristol.

Tropical Medical Bureau Republic of Ireland ⓣ1850/487674, ⓦwww.tmb.ie.

In the US and Canada

Canadian Society for International Health Canada ⓦwww.csih.org. Extensive list of travel health centres in Canada.

CDC US ⓣ1-877/394-8747, ⓦwww.cdc.gov. Official US government travel health site.

In Australia, New Zealand and South Africa

Netcare Travel Clinics South Africa ⓦwww.travelclinic.co.za. Travel clinics in South Africa.

Travellers' Medical & Vaccination Centre Australia ⓦwww.tmvc.com.au. Website listing travellers' medical and vaccination centres throughout Australia, New Zealand and South Africa.

Heat trouble

The sun and the heat can cause a few unexpected problems. Before they've acclimatized, many people get a bout of **prickly heat rash**, an infection of the sweat ducts caused by excessive perspiration that doesn't dry off. A cool shower, zinc oxide powder (sold in India) and loose cotton clothes should help. **Dehydration** is another

What about the water?

One of the chief concerns of many prospective visitors to India is whether the water is safe to drink. To put it simply, it isn't, even though you might see locals drinking it freely. **Bottled water**, available in all but the most remote places, is a much safer bet, though it has a major drawback – namely the **plastic pollution** it causes. Visualize the size of the pile you'd leave behind you after getting through a couple of bottles per day, imagine that multiplied by millions and you have something along the lines of the amount of non-biodegradable landfill waste generated each year by tourists alone.

The best solution from the point of view of your health and the environment is to purify your own water. **Chemical sterilization** using **chlorine** is completely effective, fast and inexpensive, and you can remove the nasty taste it leaves with neutralizing tablets or lemon juice.

Alternatively, invest in some kind of **purifying filter** incorporating chemical sterilization to kill even the smallest viruses. An ever-increasing range of compact, lightweight products are available these days through outdoor shops and large pharmacies, but pregnant women or those with thyroid problems should check that iodine isn't used as the chemical sterilizer.

possible problem, so make sure you're drinking enough liquid, and drink rehydration salts frequently, especially when hot and/or tired. The main danger sign is irregular urination (only once a day for instance); dark urine definitely means you should drink more (although it could also indicate hepatitis).

The **sun** can burn, or even cause sunstroke; a high-factor sun block is vital on exposed skin, especially when you first arrive. A light hat is also a very good idea, especially if you're doing a lot of walking around in the sun.

Finally, be aware that overheating can cause **heatstroke**, which is potentially fatal. Signs are a very high body temperature, without a feeling of fever but accompanied by headaches and disorientation. Lowering body temperature (taking a tepid shower for example) and resting in an air-conditioned room is the first step in treatment; also take in plenty of fluids, and seek medical advice if the condition doesn't improve after 24 hours.

Malaria

Malaria is one of the Subcontinent's big killers, and it's essential that you check with your doctor whether you'll need to take anti-malarial medication for your visit. The disease, caused by a parasite carried in the saliva of female Anopheles mosquitoes, can be found in many parts of India, and is especially prevalent in the northeast, although non-existent in the high Himalayan regions (there's a useful malaria map of the country at Ⓦwww.fitfortravel.scot.nhs.uk/destinations/asia-(east)/india/india-malaria-map.aspx, showing varying levels of risk across the country). Malaria has a variable incubation period of a few days to several weeks, so you can become ill long after being bitten – which is why it's important to carry on taking the tablets even after you've returned home.

Ideas about appropriate **antimalarial medication** tend to vary from country to country, and prophylaxis remains a controversial subject; it's important that you get expert medical advice on which treatment is right for you. In addition, resistance to established antimalarial drugs is growing alarmingly – none of the following provides complete protection, so avoiding being bitten in the first place remains important. Chloroquine- and proguanil-resistant strains of malaria are particularly prevalent in **Assam and the northeast**; travellers to this region might consider taking a course of malarone, doxycycline or mefloquine instead.

The most established regime – widely prescribed in Europe, but not in North America – is a combination of **chloroquine** (trade names Nivaquin or Avloclor) taken weekly either on its own or in conjunction with a daily dose of **proguanil** (Paludrine). You need to start this regime a week before arriving in a malarial area and continue it for four weeks after leaving. In India chloroquine is easy to come by but proguanil isn't, so stock up before you arrive. **Mefloquine**

A travellers' first-aid kit

Below are items you might want to take, especially if you're planning to go trekking – all are available in India itself, at a fraction of what you might pay at home:

- Antiseptic cream
- Insect repellent and cream such as Anthisan for soothing bites
- Plasters/Band-Aids
- A course of Flagyl antibiotics
- Water sterilization tablets or water purifier
- Lint and sealed bandages
- Knee supports
- Imodium (Lomotil) for emergency diarrhoea treatment
- A mild oral anesthetic such as Bonjela for soothing ulcers or mild toothache
- Paracetamol/aspirin
- Multi-vitamin and mineral tablets
- Rehydration sachets
- Hypodermic needles and sterilized skin wipes

(Lariam) is a newer and stronger treatment. As a prophylactic, you need take just one tablet weekly, starting two weeks before entering a risk area and continuing for four weeks after leaving. Mefloquine is a very powerful and effective antimalarial, though there have been widely reported concerns about its side effects, including psychological problems.

Doxycycline is often prescribed in Australasia. One tablet is taken daily, starting a day or two before entering a malarial zone and continuing for four weeks after leaving. It's not suitable for children under ten and it can cause thrush in women, while three percent of users develop a sensitivity to light, causing a rash, so it's not ideal for beach holidays. It also interferes with the effectiveness of the contraceptive pill. **Malarone** (a combination of atovaquone and proguanil) is the most recent drug to come on the market. The bonus is that you only have to start taking it on the day you enter a malarial zone and continue for just a week after leaving, meaning that, although it's expensive, it can prove economical for short trips.

Malarial symptoms

The first signs of malaria are remarkably similar to a severe flu, and may take months to appear: if you suspect anything go to a hospital or clinic for a blood test immediately. The shivering, burning fever and headaches come in waves, usually in the early evening. Malaria is not infectious, but some strains are dangerous and occasionally even fatal when not treated promptly, in particular, the chloroquine-resistant cerebral malaria. This virulent and lethal strain of the disease, which affects the brain, is treatable, but has to be diagnosed early. Erratic body temperature, lack of energy and aches are the first key signs.

Preventing mosquito bites

The best way of combating malaria is of course to avoid getting bitten: malarial mosquitoes are active from dusk until dawn and during this time you should use mosquito repellent and take all necessary precautions. Sleep under a mosquito net if possible, burn mosquito coils (widely available in India, but easy to break in transit) or electrically heated repellents such as All Out. An Indian brand of repellent called Odomos is widely available and very effective, though most travellers bring their own from home, usually one containing the noxious but effective compound DEET. DEET can cause rashes and a strength of more than thirty percent is not advised for those with sensitive skin. A natural alternative is citronella or, in the UK, Mosi-guard Natural, made from a blend of eucalyptus oils; those with sensitive skin should still use DEET on clothes and nets. Mosquito "buzzers" – plug-in contraptions that smoulder tablets of DEET compounds slowly overnight – are pretty useless, but wrist and ankle bands are as effective as spray and a good alternative for sensitive skin. Though active from dusk till dawn, female Anopheles mosquitoes prefer to bite in the evening, so be especially careful at that time. Wear long sleeves, skirts and trousers, avoid dark colours, which attract mosquitoes, and put repellent on all exposed skin.

Dengue fever and Japanese encephalitis

Another illness spread by mosquito bites is dengue fever, whose symptoms are similar to those of malaria, plus aching bones. There is no vaccine available and the only treatment is complete rest, with drugs to assuage the fever. Japanese encephalitis, a mosquito-borne viral infection causing fever, muscle pains and headaches, is most prevalent in wet, rural rice-growing areas. However, it only rarely affects travellers, and the vaccine isn't usually recommended unless you plan to spend much time around paddy fields during and immediately after the monsoons.

Intestinal troubles

Diarrhoea is the most common bane of travellers. When mild and not accompanied by other major symptoms, it may just be your stomach reacting to unfamiliar food. Accompanied by cramps and vomiting, it could well be food poisoning. In either case, it will probably pass of its own accord in

24–48 hours without treatment. In the meantime, it is essential to replace the fluids and salts you're losing, so take lots of water with oral rehydration salts (commonly referred to as ORS, or called Electrolyte in India). If you can't get ORS, use half a teaspoon of salt and eight of sugar in a litre of water, and if you are too ill to drink, seek medical help immediately. Travel clinics and pharmacies sell double-ended moulded plastic spoons with the exact ratio of sugar to salt.

While you are suffering, it's a good idea to avoid greasy food, heavy spices, caffeine and most fruit and dairy products. Some say bananas and pawpaws are good, as are *kitchri* (a simple dhal and rice preparation) and rice soup and coconut water, while curd or a soup made from Marmite or Vegemite (if you happen to have some with you) are forms of protein that can be easily absorbed by your body when you have the runs. **Drugs** like Lomotil or Imodium simply plug you up – undermining the body's efforts to rid itself of infection – though they can be useful if you have to travel. If symptoms persist for more than a few days, a course of antibiotics may be necessary; this should be seen as a last resort, following medical advice.

Sordid though it may seem, it's a good idea to look at what comes out when you go to the toilet. If your diarrhoea contains blood or mucus and if you are suffering other symptoms including rotten-egg belches and farts, the cause may be dysentery or giardia. With a fever, it could well be caused by **bacillic dysentery**, and may clear up without treatment. If you're sure you need it, a course of antibiotics such as tetracycline should sort you out, but they also destroy gut flora in your intestines (which help protect you – curd can replenish them to some extent). If you start a course, be sure to finish it, even after the symptoms have gone. Similar symptoms, without fever, indicate **amoebic dysentery**, which is much more serious, and can damage your gut if untreated. The usual cure is a course of Metronidazole (Flagyl) or Fasigyn, both antibiotics which may themselves make you feel ill, and must not be taken with alcohol. Symptoms of **giardia** are similar – including frothy stools, nausea and constant fatigue – for which the treatment is again Metronidazole. If you suspect that you have either of these, seek medical help, and only start on the Metronidazole (750mg three times daily for a week for adults) if there is definitely blood in your diarrhoea and it is impossible to see a doctor.

Finally, bear in mind that oral drugs, such as malaria pills and the Pill, are likely to be largely ineffective if taken while suffering from diarrhoea.

Bites and creepy crawlies

Worms may enter your body through skin (especially the soles of your feet) or food. An itchy anus is a common symptom, and you may even see them in your stools. They are easy to treat: if you suspect you have them, get some worming tablets such as Mebendazole (Vermox) from any pharmacy.

Biting insects and similar animals other than mosquitoes may also aggravate you. The obvious suspects are **bed bugs** – look for signs of squashed ones around beds in cheap hotels. An infested mattress can be left in the hot sun all day to get rid of them, but they often live in the frame or even in walls or floors. **Head** and **body lice** can also be a nuisance, but medicated soap and shampoo (preferably brought with you from home) usually see them off. Avoid **scratching bites**, which can lead to infection. Bites from ticks and lice can spread **typhus**, characterized by fever, muscle aches, headaches, and, later, red eyes and a measles-like rash. If you think you have it, seek treatment (tetracycline is usually prescribed).

Snakes are unlikely to bite unless accidentally disturbed, and most are harmless in any case. To see one at all, you need to search stealthily – walk heavily and they usually oblige by disappearing. If you do get bitten, remember what the snake looked like (kill it if you can), try not to move the affected part, and seek medical help: antivenins are available in most hospitals. A few **spiders** have poisonous bites too. Remove **leeches**, which may attach themselves to you in jungle areas, with salt or a lit cigarette: never just pull them off.

Ayurvedic medicine

Ayurveda, a Sanskrit word meaning the "knowledge for prolonging life", is a 5000-year-old holistic medical system that is widely practised in India. Ayurvedic doctors and clinics in large towns deal with foreigners as well as their usual patients, and some **pharmacies** specialize in Ayurvedic preparations, including toiletries such as soaps, shampoos and toothpastes.

Ayurveda assumes the fundamental sameness of self and nature. Unlike the allopathic medicines of the West, which depend on finding out what's ailing you and then killing it, Ayurveda looks at the whole patient: disease is regarded as a symptom of **imbalance**, so it's the imbalance that's treated, not the disease. Ayurvedic theory holds that the body is controlled by three forces, which reflect the forces within the self: *pitta*, the force of the sun, is hot, and rules the digestive processes and metabolism; *kapha*, likened to the moon, the creator of tides and rhythms, has a cooling effect and governs the body's organs; and *vata*, wind, relates to movement and the nervous system. The healthy body is one that has the three forces in balance. To diagnose an imbalance, the Ayurvedic **vaid** (doctor) responds not only to the physical complaint but also to family background, daily habits and emotional traits.

Imbalances are typically treated with herbal remedies designed to alter whichever of the three forces is out of whack. Made according to traditional formulae, using indigenous plants, Ayurvedic medicines are cheaper than branded or imported drugs. In addition, the doctor may prescribe various forms of yogic cleansing to rid the body of waste substances. To the uninitiated, these techniques will sound rather off-putting – for instance, swallowing a long strip of cloth, a short section at a time, and then pulling it back up again to remove mucus from the stomach. Ayurvedic **massage** with herbal oils is especially popular in Kerala where courses of treatments are available to combat a wide array of ailments.

Altitude sickness

At high altitudes, you may develop symptoms of **acute mountain sickness** (AMS). Just about everyone who ascends to around 4000m or more experiences mild symptoms, but serious cases are rare. The simple cure – descent – almost always brings immediate recovery.

AMS is caused by the fact that at high elevations there is not only less oxygen, but also lower atmospheric pressure. This can have all sorts of weird effects on the body: it can cause the brain to swell and the lungs to fill with fluid, and even bring on uncontrollable farting. The syndrome varies from one person to the next, but symptoms include breathlessness, headaches and dizziness, nausea, difficulty sleeping and appetite loss. More extreme cases may involve disorientation and loss of balance, and the coughing up of pink frothy phlegm.

AMS strikes without regard for fitness – in fact, young people seem to be more susceptible, possibly because they're more reluctant to admit they feel sick and they dart about more energetically. Most people are capable of acclimatizing to very high altitudes but the process takes time and must be done in stages. The golden rule is not to go too high, too fast; or if you do, spend the night at a lower height ("Climb High, Sleep Low"). Above 3000m, you should not ascend more than 500m per day; take mandatory acclimatization days at 3500m and 4000m – more if you feel unwell – and try to spend these days day-hiking higher.

The general symptoms of AMS can be treated with the drug acetazolamide (Diamox) but this is not advised as it will block the early signs of severe AMS, which can be fatal. It is better to stay put for a day or two, eat a high-carbohydrate diet, drink plenty of water (three litres a day is recommended), take paracetamol or aspirin for the headaches, and descend if the AMS persists or worsens. If you fly direct to a high-altitude destination such as Leh, be especially careful to acclimatize (plan for three days of initial rest); you'll certainly want to avoid doing anything strenuous at first.

Other precautions to take at high altitudes include avoiding alcohol and sleeping pills, drinking more liquid, and protecting your skin against UV solar glare.

HIV and AIDS

The rapidly increasing presence of **HIV/AIDS** has only recently been acknowledged by the Indian government as a national problem. The reluctance to address the issue is partly due to the disease's association with sex, a traditionally closed subject in India. As yet only NGOs and foreign agencies such as the WHO have embarked on awareness and prevention campaigns. As elsewhere in the world, high-risk groups include prostitutes and intravenous drug users. It is extremely unwise to contemplate casual sex without a condom – carry some with you (preferably brought from home as Indian ones may be less reliable; also, be aware that heat affects the durability of condoms), and insist upon using them.

Should you need an **injection** or a **transfusion** in India, make sure that new, sterile equipment is used; any blood you receive should be from voluntary rather than commercial donor banks. If you have a shave from a barber, make sure he uses a clean blade, and don't undergo processes such as ear-piercing, acupuncture or tattooing unless you can be sure that the equipment is sterile.

Getting medical help

Pharmacies can usually advise on minor medical problems, and most doctors in India speak English. Also, many hotels keep a **doctor** on call; if you do get ill and need medical assistance, take advice as to the best facilities around. Basic medicaments are made to Indian Pharmacopoea (IP) standards, and most medicines are available without prescription (always check the sell-by date). **Hospitals** vary in standard: private clinics and mission hospitals are often better than state-run ones, but may not have the same facilities. Hospitals in big cities, including university or medical-school hospitals, are generally pretty good, and cities such as Delhi, Mumbai and Bengaluru boast state-of-the-art medical facilities, but at a price. Many hospitals require patients (even emergency cases) to buy necessities such as medicines, plaster casts and vaccines, and to pay for X-rays, before procedures are carried out. Remember to keep receipts for insurance reimbursements.

However, **government hospitals** provide all surgical and after-care services free of charge and in most other state medical institutions charges are usually so low that for minor treatment the expense may well be lower than the initial "excess" on your insurance. You will, however, need a companion to stay, or you'll have to come to an arrangement with one of the hospital cleaners, to help you out in hospital – relatives are expected to wash, feed and generally take care of the patient. Beware of scams by private clinics in tourist towns such as Agra where there have been reports of overcharging and misdiagnosis by doctors to claim insurance money. Addresses of foreign consulates (who will advise in an emergency), and of clinics and hospitals, can be found in the Listings sections in the accounts of major towns in this book.

Getting around

Inter-city transport in India may not be the fastest or the most comfortable in the world, but it's cheap, goes more or less everywhere, and generally gives you the option of train or bus, sometimes plane, and occasionally even boat. Transport around town comes in even more permutations, ranging in Kolkata, for example, from human-pulled rickshaws to a state-of-the-art metro system.

Whether you're on road or rail, public transport or your own vehicle, India offers the chance to try out some classics: narrow-gauge railways, steam locomotives, the Ambassador car and the Enfield Bullet motorbike – indeed some people come to India for these alone.

By train

Travelling by train is one of India's classic experiences. The national rail network covers almost the entire country; only a few places (such as the mountainous regions of Sikkim, Ladakh, Uttarakhand and most of Himachal Pradesh) are inaccessible by train. Although the railway system might look like chaos, it does work, and generally better than you might expect. Trains are often late of course, sometimes by hours rather than minutes, but they do run, and when the train you've been waiting for rolls into the station, the reservation you made halfway across the country several weeks ago will be on a list pasted to the side of your carriage.

It's worth bearing in mind, with journeys frequently lasting twelve hours or more, that an **overnight train** can save you a day's travelling and a night's hotel bill, assuming you sleep well on trains. When travelling overnight, always padlock your bag to your bunk; an attached chain is usually provided beneath the seat of the lower bunk.

Types of train

There are three basic types of passenger train in India. You're most likely to use long-distance **inter-city trains** (called "express" or "mail") along with the speedier "**super-fast**" air-conditioned trains – these include the various "Rajdhani" expresses, which link Delhi with cities nationwide, and "Shatabdi" expresses, daytime trains that connect major cities within an eight-hour travelling distance. There are also painfully slow local "**passenger**" trains, which stop everywhere, and which you'll only use if you want to get right off the beaten track. In addition to these three basic types of train, there are also a few dedicated **tourist trains** and other special services, such as the famous Palace on Wheels and the toy train to Darjeeling – see p.43 & p.774 for more on these.

Classes of train travel

Indian Railways distinguishes between no fewer than seven **classes** of travel. Different types of train carry different classes of carriage, though you'll seldom have more than four to choose from any one service. The simplest and cheapest class, used by the majority of Indians, is **second-class unreserved** (or "second seating"). These basic carriages have hard wooden seats and often become incredibly packed during the day – bearable for shortish daytime journeys, but best avoided for longer trips and (especially) overnight travel, unless you're exceptionally hardy or unusually poor. On the plus side, fares in second-class unreserved are so cheap as to be virtually free. It also represents a way of getting on a train at the last minute if you haven't been able to secure a reserved seat.

Far more civilized, and only around fifty percent more expensive, is **second-class sleeper** ("sleeper class"), consisting of carriages of three-tiered padded bunks that convert to seats during the day. All seats in these carriages must be booked in advance even for daytime journeys, meaning that they don't get horrendously overcrowded like second-class unreserved, although there's usually still plenty going on, with itinerant chai- and coffee-sellers, travelling musicians, beggars and sweepers passing through the carriages. Overnight trips in second-class sleeper compartments are reasonably comfy. **First class** consists of non-a/c seating in comfortable if ageing compartments of two to four berths, though this class is being phased out and is now found on relatively few trains.

The other four classes are all air-conditioned (available only on inter-city and super-fast trains). **A/c chair car** (often denoted as "CC") is found almost exclusively on superfast services and consists of comfortable reclining seats; they're really designed for daytime travel, since they don't convert to bunks, and aren't generally found on overnight services. Shatabdi expresses are made up entirely of chair-car carriages (ordinary a/c chair car and, for double the price, an executive a/c chair car).

There are three classes of air-conditioned sleepers. The cheapest, **third-class a/c**, has open carriages with three-tier bunks – basically the same as second-class sleeper, except with a/c. Less crowded (and found on more services) is **second-class a/c**, which has two-tier berths. Most comfortable of all is **first-class a/c**, which consists of two-tier bunks in two- or four-person private compartments, complete with carpeting and relatively presentable bathrooms – although fares can work out only slightly cheaper than taking a plane.

Note that bed linen is provided free on most a/c services, while bottled water, snacks and simple meals are included in the ticket price of Rajdhani and Shatabdi services.

Ladies' compartments exist on all overnight trains for women travelling on their own or with other women; they are usually small and can be full of noisy kids, but can give untold relief to women travellers who otherwise have to endure incessant staring in the open section of the carriage. They can be a good place to meet Indian women, particularly if you like (or are with) children. Some stations also have ladies-only waiting rooms.

Timetables and fares

Fares, timetables and availability of berths can be checked online at Indian Railway's cumbersome website (Ⓦwww.indianrail.gov.in), or via the more streamlined, privately run Ⓦwww.cleartrip.com. Indian Railways' *Trains at a Glance* (Rs30; updated twice a year; also available online at Ⓦwww.indianrailways.gov.in/tag/index.htm) contains timetables of all intercity and superfast trains and is available from information counters and newsstands at all main stations.

Indrail passes

Indrail passes, sold to foreigners and Indians resident abroad, cover all fares and reservation fees for periods ranging from half a day to ninety days, but are considerably more expensive than buying tickets individually. The pass is designed for nationwide travel, so if you only use it, say, between Delhi, Agra and the cities of Rajasthan, you won't be getting your money's worth. The pass does, however, save you queuing for tickets, and it allows you to make and cancel reservations with

Rail records

Comprising 63,327km (39,316 miles) of track and 8,000 locomotives, which transport an average of 22 million passengers every day, India's **rail network** is the second largest in the world. It's also the biggest employer on the planet, with a workforce of around 1.6 million.

One record the country's transport ministers are somewhat less proud of, however, is the Indian Railways' **accident rate**. Four to five hundred crashes occur annually in India, causing between seven and eight hundred fatalities, which makes this the most dangerous rail network in the world, by a long chalk. Having said that, travelling by rail is considerably safer than using the buses. According to official statistics, an average of 233 people die on the country's roads every day – that's 85,000 annually.

impunity (and without charge), and generally smooths your way in. For example, if you need to find a seat or berth on a "full" train, passholders get priority for tourist quota places. Indrail passes are available in sterling or US dollars, at main station tourist counters in India, and outside the country at IR agents and sometimes at Air India offices. A seven-day pass costs US$80 in second class, US$135 in first, and US$270 in AC class. There's a full list of prices and overseas IR agents at ⓦwww.indianrail.gov.in/international_Tourist.html.

All rail fares are calculated according to the exact **distance** travelled. *Trains at a Glance* prints a chart of fares by kilometres, and also gives the distance in kilometres of stations along each route in the timetables, making it possible to calculate what the basic fare will be for any given journey.

Reserving tickets

It's important to plan your train journeys in advance, as demand often makes it impossible to buy a long-distance ticket on the same day that you want to travel (although the new Tatkal quota system – see below – has made life a little easier). Travellers following tight itineraries tend to buy their departure tickets from particular towns the moment they arrive to avoid having to trek out to the station again. At most large stations, it's possible to reserve tickets for journeys starting elsewhere in the country.

Online booking can be done through Indian Railways' official reservation site, ⓦwww.irctc.co.in, although the site only works during Indian opening hours and can be frustratingly difficult to use. A more dependable option is the privately run ⓦwww.cleartrip.com, which charges Rs100 per ticket to process purchases; major foreign credit cards are accepted. Bookings may be made from 90 days in advance right up to four hours before the scheduled departure time of the train. Cleartrip.com also handles **Tatkal tickets** which – for an extra charge of Rs75–150 – gives you access to a premium late-availability quota. Having booked your travel, you can then print out your own e-tickets, taking this along with some photo ID, such as a passport, when you board the train.

When **reserving a ticket in person** at a railway station, the first thing you'll have to do is fill in a little form at the booking office stating your name, age and sex, your proposed date of travel, and the train you wish to catch (giving the train's **name and number**, which should be displayed on a timetable in the booking hall). Most stations have computerized booking counters and you'll be told immediately whether or not seats are available. **Reservation offices** in the main stations are generally open from Monday to Saturday from 8am to 8pm, and on Sunday to 2pm. In larger cities, major stations have special tourist sections to cut queues for foreigners, with helpful English-speaking staff. Elsewhere, buying a ticket can often involve a longish wait, though women can often bypass this by simply walking to the head of the queue and forming their own "ladies' queue" (men may often find ladies pushing in front of them on the same principle). Some stations also operate a number system of queuing, allowing you to repair to the chai stall until your number is called. A good alternative to queuing yourself is to get someone else to buy your ticket for you. Many **travel agents** will do this for a small fee (typically around Rs30–50); alternatively, ask at your guest-house if they can sort it out.

Quotas and late-availability tickets

If there are no places available on the train you want, you have a number of choices. First, some seats and berths are set aside as a "**tourist quota**" – ask at the tourist counter of the reservations hall if you can get in on this, or else try the stationmaster. This quota is available in advance but usually only at major or originating stations. Failing that, other special quotas, such as one for "emergencies", only released on the day of travel, may remain unused – however, if you get a booking on the emergency quota and a pukka emergency or VIP turns up, you lose the reservation. Alternatively, you can stump up extra cash for a **Tatkal** ticket (see above), which guarantees you access to a special ten percent quota on most trains, though certain catches and conditions apply. Bookable online and at any computerized office, these are released from

8am two days before the train departs, and there's a surcharge of Rs75–150, depending on the class of travel.

RAC – or "Reservation Against Cancellation" – tickets are another option, giving you priority if sleepers do become available – the ticket clerk should be able to tell you your chances. With an RAC ticket you are allowed onto the train and can sit until the conductor can find you a berth. The worst sort of ticket to have is a **wait-listed** one – identifiable by the letter "W" prefixing your passenger number – which will allow you onto the train but not in a reserved compartment; in this case go and see the ticket inspector as soon as possible to persuade him to find you a place if one is free. Wait-listed ticket holders are not allowed onto Shatabdi and Rajdhani trains. You could **travel unreserved**, but if the train is full (as it will be on major routes) travel in second class will be extremely uncomfortable. If you get on where the train starts its journey, **baksheesh** may persuade an official to "reserve" you an unreserved seat (or even a luggage rack) where you can stretch out for the night (station porters may be able to act as middlemen in this regard, taking a cut themselves, of course). You could even fight your way on with everybody else and try to grab a seat yourself, but your chances are slim. For short journeys, or on minor routes you won't need to reserve tickets in advance.

Luxury tourist trains

Inspired by the Orient Express, Indian Railways offers high-end holiday packages aboard luxury **tourist trains**. The flagship of the scheme is the **Palace on Wheels** (Ⓦwww.palaceonwheels.net), with sumptuous ex-maharajas' carriages updated into modern air-conditioned coaches, still decorated with the original designs. An all-inclusive, eight-day whistle-stop tour (Sept–April weekly) starts at US$2350 per person for the full trip, with discounts off-season (Sept & April). Note that the train is often booked up for months ahead, so early reservations are advised.

The Palace on Wheels has proved so popular that it has spawned a number of similar heritage trains, including **Royal Rajasthan on Wheels** (Ⓦwww.royalpalaceonwheels.com) and the less expensive **Heritage on Wheels** (Ⓦwww.palaceonwheels.net/new/heritage.htm). All three trains can be booked through the Rajasthan Tourism Development Corporation (Ⓣ011/2338 1884, Ⓦwww.rajasthantourism.gov.in). Or you can call toll-free in North America (Ⓣ888/463-4299), the UK (Ⓣ0800/8456 201), Australia (Ⓣ1800/156 671), New Zealand (Ⓣ0800/442 510), or on line at Ⓦwww.palaceonwheels.net or www.indiarailtours.com.

Luxury tourist trains also operate in South India. **The Deccan Queen** (Ⓦwww.deccan-odyssey-india.com) takes in the highlights of Maharashtra, while the **Golden Chariot** (Ⓦwww.deccan-odyssey-india.com/golden-chariot) tours Karnataka. Rates and schedules are published online.

By air

Considering the huge distances involved in getting around the country, and the time it takes to get from A to B, **flying** is an attractive option, despite the cost – the journey from Delhi to Chennai, for example, takes a mere 2 hours 30 minutes by plane compared to 36 hours on the train. Delays and cancellations can whittle away the time advantage, especially over small distances, but if you're short of time and plan to cover a lot of ground, flying can be a godsend. There's also been a massive proliferation of privately run domestic airlines in India in recent years, with more planes covering more routes than ever before.

As with train tickets, **booking flights** is most easily achieved online via the airline's website. Larger carriers also have offices in major cities, as well as at the airports they fly to, listed in this book in the relevant Guide chapters. Children under twelve pay half fare and under-twos (one per adult) pay ten percent. See p.28 for a list of domestic airlines.

By bus

Although trains are generally the most characterful and comfortable way to travel in India, there are some places, particularly in the Himalayas, not covered by the rail network, or where trains are inconvenient. By contrast, **buses** go almost everywhere, usually more frequently than trains (though mostly in daylight hours), and are also sometimes faster (including in parts of Rajasthan and other places without broad-gauge track). Going by bus also usually saves you the bother of reserving a ticket in advance.

Services vary enormously in terms of price and standard. Ramshackle **government-run buses**, packed with people, livestock and luggage, cover most routes, both short- and long-distance. In addition, popular routes between larger cities, towns and resorts are usually covered by **private buses**. These tend to be more comfortable, with extra legroom, tinted windows and padded reclining seats. Note, however, that smaller private bus companies may be only semi-legal and have little backup in case of breakdown.

The description of the service usually gives some clue about the level of comfort. "Ordinary" buses usually have minimally padded, bench-like seats with upright backs. "Deluxe" or "luxury" are more or less interchangeable terms but sometimes the term deluxe signifies a luxury bus past its sell-by date; occasionally a bus will be described as a "2 by 2" which means a deluxe bus with just two seats on either side of the aisle. When applied to government services, these may hardly differ from "ordinary" buses, but with private companies, they should guarantee a softer, individual seat. It's worth asking when booking if your bus will have a video or music system (a "video bus"), as their deafening noise ruins any chances of sleep. Always try to avoid the back seats – they accentuate bumpy roads.

Luggage travels in the hatch of private buses – for which you will have to part with about Rs10–20 as "security" for the safekeeping of your bags. On state-run buses, you can usually squeeze it into an unobtrusive corner, although you may sometimes be requested to have it travel on the roof (you may be able to travel up there yourself if the bus is too crowded, though it's dangerous and illegal); check that it's well secured (ideally, lock it there) and not liable to get squashed. Baksheesh is in order for whoever puts it up there for you.

Buying a bus ticket is usually less of an ordeal than buying a train ticket, although at large city bus stations there may be twenty or so counters, each assigned to a different route. When you buy your ticket you'll be given the registration number of the bus and, sometimes, a seat number. As at railway stations, women can form a separate, quicker, "ladies' queue". You can usually only pay on board on most ordinary state buses, and at bus stands outside major cities. Prior booking is usually available and preferable for express and private services, and it's a good idea to check with the agent exactly where the bus will depart from. You can usually pay on board private buses too, though doing so reduces your chances of a seat.

By boat

Apart from river ferries, few **boat services** run in India. The Andaman Islands are connected to Kolkata and Chennai by boat – as well as to each other. Kerala has a regular passenger service with a number of services operating out of Alappuzha and Kollam, including the popular "backwater trip" between the two. The Sunderbans in the delta region to the south of Kolkata is only accessible by boat.

By car

It is much more usual for tourists to be driven in India than it is for them to drive themselves; **car rental** firms operate on the basis of supplying **vehicles with drivers**. You can arrange them through any tourist office or taxi firm, and local taxi drivers hanging around hotels and city ranks are also available for day hire. Cars will cost around Rs1500 (£22/$33) per day, which should include a maximum of 200km, with additional kilometres charged at around Rs6–7 per kilometre. On longer trips, the driver sleeps in the car, for which his firm may charge an additional Rs150–200. You should generally tip the driver Rs150–175 too.

Most tourists succumb to the romance of that quintessentially Indian automobile, the **Hindustan Ambassador** Mark IV, based on the design of the old British Morris Oxford. Sadly, however, the car's appalling suspension and back-breaking seats make it among the most uncomfortable rides in the world. Older models, in particular, can make for some gruelling journeys, with dashboards that become burning-hot and suffocating fumes plaguing the front seats. All in all, you'll be much better off in a modern two- or four-door hatchback – ask your rental company for the options. Air-conditioning adds considerably to the rate, and with larger cars such as SUVs, the daily rate of Rs1500 tends only to cover the first 80km, after which stiff additional per-kilometre charges apply.

A handful of big international chains offer **self-drive** car hire in India, but unless you've had plenty of experience on the country's notoriously dangerous roads, we strongly recommend you leave the driving to an expert. If you do drive yourself, expect the unexpected, and expect other drivers to take whatever liberties they can get away with. **Traffic** in the cities is particularly undisciplined; vehicles cut in and out without warning, and pedestrians, cyclists and cows wander nonchalantly down the middle of the road. In the country the roads are narrow, often in terrible repair, and hogged by overloaded Tata trucks that move aside for nobody, while something slow-moving like a bullock cart or a herd of goats can take up the whole road. It is particularly dangerous to drive at night – cyclists and cart drivers hardly ever have lights. If you are involved in an **accident**, it might be an idea to leave the scene quickly and go straight to the police to report it; mobs can assemble fast, especially if pedestrians or cows are involved.

To **import a car or motorbike** into India, you'll have to show a *carnet de passage*, a document intended to ensure that you don't sell the vehicle illegally. These are available from foreign motoring organizations such as the AA. It's also worth bringing a few basic spares, as parts for foreign makes can be hard to find in India, although low-quality imitations are more widely available. All in all, the route is arduous, and bringing a vehicle to India is something of a commitment.

By motorbike

Riding a **motorbike** in India is not for the faint-hearted. Besides the challenging road and traffic conditions (see above) with the resultant stress and fatigue, simply running an unfamiliar bike can become a nightmare.

Buying a motorbike in India is only for the brave. If it's an old classic you're after, the 350- or 500cc Enfield Bullet, sold cheapest in Puducherry, on the Tamil Nadu coast, leads the field, with models becoming less idiosyncratic the more recent they are. Low price and practicality may be your priorities so a smaller model from the likes of Bajaj, built in India but based on dependable old Japanese designs, may fit the bill if not the image. Delhi's Karol Bagh area is renowned for its motorcycle shops and rental agencies (see p.128). Obviously, you'll have to haggle over the price, but you can expect to pay half to two-thirds the original price for a bike in reasonable condition. Given the right bargaining skills, you can sell it again later for a similar price – perhaps to another foreign traveller – by advertising it in hotels and restaurants. A certain amount of bureaucracy is involved in transferring vehicle ownership to a new owner, but a garage should be able to put you on to a broker ("auto consultant") who, for a modest commission (around Rs1000–2000), will help you find a seller or a buyer, and do the necessary paperwork.

Motorbike **rental** is available in many tourist towns and can be fun for local use, but the condition can be hit and miss. However, unless you know your stuff, this is a better strategy than diving in and buying a machine. Unlike with sales, it's in a rental outfit's interest to hire you a bike that works. Mechanically, the important thing to establish is the condition of the chain and sprockets, whether the machine starts and runs smoothly and not least, whether both brakes and lights work (even so, riding at night is inadvisable). An in-depth knowledge of mechanics is not so necessary as every town has a bike mender who will be no stranger to Enfields.

A recommended firm in Delhi, both for purchasing bikes and for rental, is **Bulletwallas** (Ⓦwww.bulletwallas.com), at 7 Arakashan Rd, Multani Dhanda in the Paharganj district. An Aussie-run outfit, they specialize in Enfields, selling new, used, and customized machines with only quality parts.

Without doubt the least stressful way of enjoying India on a motorbike, especially a temperamental but characterful Enfield, is joining one of several **motorbike tours**. They focus on the best locales with minimal traffic and amazing landscapes: the Himalayas, Rajasthan and Kerala, and remove much of the stress from what is still an adventure.

Blazing Trails UK ⓣ01293/533338, ⓦwww.blazingtrailstours.com.
Classic Bike Adventure India Goa ⓣ0832/226 8467, ⓦwww.classic-bike-india.com.
Ferris Wheels Motorcycle Safaris Australia ⓣ02/9970 6370, ⓦwww.ferriswheels.com.au.
Himalayan Roadrunners US ⓣ802/738 6500, ⓦwww.ridehigh.com.
Live India UK ⓦwww.liveindia.co.uk.

By bicycle

In many ways a **bicycle** is the ideal form of transport in India, offering total independence without loss of contact with local people. You can camp out, though there are cheap lodgings in almost every village – take the bike into your room with you – and, if you get tired of pedalling, you can put it on top of a bus as luggage, or transport it by train.

Bringing a bike from abroad requires no *carnet* or special paperwork, but spare parts and accessories may be of different sizes and standards in India, and you may have to improvise. Bring basic spares and tools, and a pump. **Buying a bike** in India couldn't be easier, since most towns have cycle shops and even entire markets devoted to bikes. The advantages of a local bike are that spare parts are easy to get, locally produced tools and parts will fit, and your bike will not draw a crowd every time you park it. Disadvantages are that Indian bikes tend to be heavier and less state-of-the-art than ones from abroad; mountain bikes are beginning to appear in cities and bigger towns, but with insufficient gears and a low level of equipment, they're not worth buying. Selling should be quite easy: you won't get a tremendously good deal at a cycle market, but you may well be able to sell privately, or even to a rental shop.

Bicycles can be **rented** in most towns, usually for local use only: this is a good way to find out if your legs and bum can survive an Indian bike before buying one. Rates can be anything from Rs25 to Rs150 per day, and you may have to leave a deposit or your passport as security. Several adventure-tour operators offer bicycle tours of the country (see opposite), with most customers bringing their own cycles.

As for contacts, International Bicycle Fund in the US (ⓣ206/767-0848, ⓦwww.ibike.org) publishes information and offers advice on bicycle travel around the world and maintains a useful website. In India, the Cycling Federation of India, C-5A/262, DDA Flats, Janak Puri, New Delhi 110058 (ⓣ011/2255 3006, ⓦwww.cyclingfederationofindia.org), is the main cycle-sports organization.

City transport

Transport around towns takes various forms. City **buses** can get unbelievably crowded, so beware of pickpockets, razor-armed pocket-slitters and "Eve-teasers" (see p.83); the same applies to **suburban trains** in Mumbai (Chennai is about the only other place where you might want to use trains for local city transport). Any visitor to Delhi or Kolkata will be amazed by the clean efficiency of India's two **metro** systems.

You can also take **taxis**, usually rather battered Ambassadors (painted black and yellow in the large cities) and Maruti omnivans. With luck, the driver will agree to use the meter; in theory you're within your rights to call the police if he doesn't, but the usual compromise is to agree a fare for the journey before you get in. Naturally, it helps to have an idea in advance what the fare should be, though any figures quoted in this or any other book should be treated as being the broadest of guidelines only. From places such as main stations, you may be able to find other passengers to share a taxi to the town centre. Many stations, and certainly most airports, operate **pre-paid taxi schemes** with set fares that you pay before departure; more expensive pre-paid limousines are also available.

That most Indian of vehicles, the **auto-rickshaw** – commonly referred to as just an 'auto' – is the front half of a motor scooter with a couple of seats mounted on the back. Cheaper than taxis, better at nipping in and out of traffic, and usually metered (although again very few drivers are willing to use theirs and you should agree a fare before setting off), auto-rickshaws are a little unstable and their drivers often rather reckless, but that's all part of the fun. In major tourist centres rickshaw-wallahs can, however, hassle you endlessly on the street, often shoving themselves right in your path to prevent you from ignoring them, and once you're inside they may take you to several shops before reaching your destination. Moreover, agreeing a price before the journey will not necessarily stop your rickshaw-wallah reopening discussion when the trip is under way or at its end. In general it is better to hail a rickshaw than to take one that's been following you, and to avoid those that hang around outside posh hotels.

Some towns also have larger versions of auto-rickshaws known as **tempos** (or Vikrams), with six or eight seats behind, which usually ply fixed routes at flat fares. Here and there, you'll also come across horse-drawn carriages, or **tongas**. Tugged by underfed and often lame horses, these are the least popular with tourists.

Slower and cheaper still is the **cycle rickshaw** – basically a glorified tricycle. Foreign visitors often feel uncomfortable about travelling this way; except in the major tourist cities, cycle rickshaw-wallahs are invariably emaciated pavement-dwellers who earn only a pittance for their pains. In the end, though, to deny them your custom on those grounds is spurious logic; they will earn even less if you don't use them. As a foreigner you'll probably be quoted grossly inflated fares, but ask yourself if it's really worth haggling over tiny sums, which they could probably do with more than you.

Only in Kolkata do rickshaw-wallahs continue to haul the city's pukka rickshaws on foot.

If you want to see a variety of places around town, consider hiring a taxi, rickshaw or auto-rickshaw for the day. Find a driver who speaks English reasonably well, and agree a price beforehand. You will probably find it a lot cheaper than you imagine: the driver will invariably act as a guide and source of local knowledge, and tipping is usually in order.

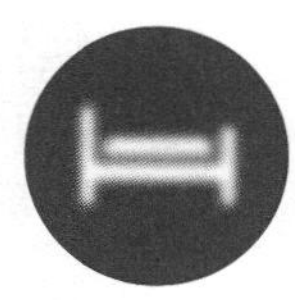

Accommodation

There are far more Indians travelling around their own country at any one time – whether for holidays, on pilgrimages, or for business – than there are foreign tourists, and a vast infrastructure of hotels and guesthouses caters for their needs. On the whole, accommodation, like so many other things in India, provides good value for money, though in the major cities, especially, expect to pay international prices for luxury establishments that provide Western-style comforts and service.

Budget accommodation

While accommodation prices in India are generally on the up, there's still an abundance of inexpensive **hotels** and **hostels**, catering for foreign backpackers, tourists and less well-off Indians. Most charge Rs300–400 for a double room, although rates outside big cities and tourist centres may fall below Rs200 (roughly £3/$4.50). The rock-bottom option is usually in a dormitory of a hostel or hotel, where you may pay as little as Rs100. Even cheaper still are **dharamshalas**, hostels run by religious establishments and pilgrim guesthouses (see p.51).

Budget accommodation varies from filthy fleapits to homely guesthouses and, naturally, tends to be cheaper the further you get off the beaten track. It's most expensive in Delhi, Mumbai, Goa and resorts

Accommodation price codes

All **accommodation prices** in this book are **coded** using the symbols below. The prices given are for a double room; in the case of dorms, we give the per-person price in rupees. Most mid-range and all expensive and luxury hotels charge a luxury tax of around ten to fifteen percent, and a local tax of around five percent. All taxes are included in the prices we quote.

Many parts of the country experience some seasonal variation and will be more expensive, or less negotiable, when demand is at its peak. For the hill stations, this will be in the summer (April–July); for Rajasthan, Goa and Kerala it'll be the winter, especially around Christmas and New Year. We've mentioned regional price fluctuations in the accommodation listings throughout the guide chapters. The price codes refer to high season, but not – in the case of resort areas such as Rajasthan, Goa & Kerala – the short 10–15-day peak over Christmas and New Year.

❶ Rs300 and under	❹ Rs701–1200	❼ Rs3001–4500
❷ Rs301–500	❺ Rs1201–2000	❽ Rs4501–7000
❸ Rs501–700	❻ Rs2001–3000	❾ Rs7001 and over

of Kerala, where prices are at least double those for equivalent accommodation in most other parts of the country.

The cheapest rooms usually have flimsy beds and thin, lumpy mattresses. Shared showers and toilets with only cold water are also the norm at the bottom of the range, although increasing numbers of places are offering en-suite bathrooms (or "attached" rooms, as they're known locally) and hot water, either on tap or in a bucket. Even so, it's always wise to check out the state of the bathrooms and toilets before taking a room. Bed bugs and mosquitoes are other things to check for – splotches of blood around the bed and on the walls where people have squashed them are tell-tale signs.

If a **taxi driver** or **rickshaw-wallah** tells you that the place you ask for is full, closed or has moved, it's more than likely that it's because he wants to take you to a hotel that pays him commission – added, in some cases, to your bill. Hotel touts operate in many popular tourist spots, working for commission from the hotels they take you to; this can become annoying, but sometimes paying the little extra can be well worth it, especially if you arrive alone in a new place at night.

Mid-range hotels

Even if you value your creature comforts, you don't need to pay through the nose for them. A large clean room, freshly made bed, your own spotless bathroom and hot and cold running water can still cost as little as Rs500 (£7.50/$11). Extras that bump up the price include local taxes, a TV, mosquito nets, a balcony and, above all, **air-conditioning**. Abbreviated in this book (and in India itself) as a/c, air-conditioning is not necessarily the advantage you might expect – in some hotels you can find yourself paying double for a system that is so dust-choked and noisy as to be more of a drawback than an advantage. Some offer **air-coolers** instead of a/c – these can be noisy and are less effective than full-blown a/c, but much better than just a fan. They're only found in drier climes as they don't work in areas of extreme humidity such as along the coasts of South India and the Bay of Bengal. Many medium-priced hotels also have attached restaurants, and also offer room service.

Most state governments run their own chain of hotels. They are usually good value, but far less well run than comparable places in the private sector. We've indicated such chain hotels throughout this guide by including the state acronym in the name – eg *MPTDC Palace* (standing for Madhya Pradesh Tourist Development Corporation). Bookings for state-run hotels can be made in advance through the state tourist offices throughout the country.

Upmarket hotels

The boom of the past decade has seen a proliferation in the number of luxury hotels throughout India. Roughly speaking they fall into two categories. Pitched primarily at visiting businessmen, smart, Western-style hotels with air-conditioning and swanky interiors are to be found predominantly in town and city centres. Because competition among them is rife, tariffs tend to represent good value for money, especially in the upper-mid-scale bracket. Formal five-star chains such as *Taj*, India's premier hotel group, charge international rates – as most of their guests are on expense accounts or staying as part of discounted tour packages. Note that many top-end hotels offer significant **reductions to their rack rates** if you **book online**.

Holding more appeal for foreign visitors are the **heritage properties** that have mushroomed all across the country in recent years. Rajasthan started the trend, with old forts, palaces, hunting lodges, havelis and former hunting camps converted for use by high-spending tourists. Brimming with old-world atmosphere, they deliver a quintessentially Indian "experience", often in the most exotic locations, with turbaned

Accommodation practicalities

Check-out time is often noon, but confirm this when you arrive: some expect you out by 9am, but many others operate a 24-hour system, under which you are simply obliged to leave by the same time as you arrived. Some places let you use their facilities after the official check-out time, sometimes for a small charge, others won't even let you leave your baggage after check-out unless you pay for another night.

Unfortunately, not all hotels offer **single rooms**, so it can often work out more expensive to travel alone; in hotels that don't, you may be able to negotiate a slight discount. It's not unusual to find rooms with three or four beds, however – great value for families and small groups.

In cheap hotels and hostels, you needn't expect any additions to your basic bill, but as you go up the scale, you'll find **taxes** and **service charges** creeping in, sometimes adding as much as a third on top of the original tariff. Service is generally ten percent, but taxes are a matter for local governments and vary from state to state.

Like most other things in India, the price of a room may well be open to **negotiation**. If you think the price is too high, or if all the hotels in town are empty, try haggling. You may get nowhere – but nothing ventured, nothing gained.

bellboys and antique automobiles adding to the colonial-era ambience. Other states were quick to get in on the act, and these days you can stay in fabulous Tamil mansions, colonial tea bungalows in the Nilgiris, wooden, gabled-roofed *tharavadaku* in the Keralan backwaters and Portuguese *palacios* in Goa. Quite a few wildlife sanctuaries also offer atmospheric, high-end accommodation in former hunting lodges, tented camps or tree houses, while down in Kerala, you can experience the lakes and lagoons of the backwaters on a converted rice barge. Reviews of the best heritage accommodation options appear in the relevant accounts.

Other options

Many railway stations have "**retiring rooms**": basic private rooms with a bed and bathroom (some stations also have dorms too). They can be handy if you're catching an early morning train and are usually amongst the cheapest accommodation available anywhere, but can be noisy. Retiring rooms cannot be booked in advance and are allocated on a first-come-first-serve basis; just turn up and ask if there's a vacancy.

In one or two places, it's possible to rent rooms in people's homes. In Rajasthan, Mumbai and Kerala the local tourist offices run "**paying guest**" or "homestay" schemes to place tourists with families offering lodging. Servas (Ⓦwww.servas.org), established in 1949 as a peace organization, is now devoted to providing homestays, representing some over six hundred hosts in India; you have to join before travelling by applying to the local Servas secretary (located via the website) – you then get a list of hosts to contact in the place you are visiting. Some people provide free accommodation, others are just day-hosts. There is no guarantee a bed will be provided – it's up to the individual.

Camping is generally restricted to wildlife reserves, where the Forest Department lay on low-impact accommodation under canvas for visitors, and to beach resorts in which building is restricted by local coastal protection laws. Except on treks, it's not usual simply to pitch a tent in the countryside.

YMCAs and **YWCAs**, confined to big cities, are plusher and pricier than mid-range hotels. They are usually good value, but are often full, and some are exclusively single-sex. Official and non-official **youth hostels**, some run by state governments, are spread haphazardly across the country. They give HI cardholders a discount, but rarely exclude non-members, nor do they usually impose daytime closing. Prices match the cheapest hotels; where there is a youth hostel, it usually has a dormitory and may well be the best budget accommodation available – which goes especially for the Salvation Army ones.

Finally, **religious institutions**, particularly Sikh *gurudwaras*, offer accommodation for pilgrims and visitors, and may put up tourists; a donation is often expected, and certainly appreciated, but some of the bigger ones charge a fixed, nominal fee. Pilgrimage sites, especially those far from other accommodation, also have **dharamshalas** where visitors can stay – very cheap and very simple, usually with basic, communal washing facilities; some charitable institutions even have rooms with simple attached bathrooms. *Dharamshalas*, like *gurudwaras*, offer accommodation either on a donations system or charge a nominal fee, which can be as low as Rs20.

Food and drink

Indian food has a richly deserved reputation as one of the world's great cuisines. Stereotyped abroad as the ubiquitous "curry", the cooking of the Subcontinent covers a wealth of different culinary styles, with myriad regional variations and specialities, from the classic creamy meat and fruit Mughal dishes of the north through to the banana-leaf vegetarian thalis of the south.

The basic distinction in Indian food is between the cuisines of the north and south. **North Indian food** (which is the style generally found in Indian restaurants abroad) is characterized by its rich meat and vegetable dishes in thick tomato, onion and yoghurt-based sauces, accompanied by thick breads. **South Indian food**, by contrast, is almost exclusively vegetarian, with spicy chilli and coconut flavours and lots of rice, either served in its natural state or made into one of the south's distinctive range of pancakes, such as the dosa, *iddli* and *uttapam*.

For **vegetarians**, in particular, Indian food is a complete delight. Some of the Subcontinent's best food is meat-free, and even confirmed carnivores will find themselves tucking into delicious dhals and vegetable curries with relish. Most religious Hindus, and the majority of people in the south, don't eat meat or fish, while some orthodox Brahmins and Jains also avoid onions and garlic, which are thought to inflame the baser instincts. **Veganism** is not common, however; if you're vegan, you'll have to keep your eyes open for eggs and dairy products. Many eating places state whether they are vegetarian or non-vegetarian either on signs outside or at the top of the menu. The terms used in India (and throughout our eating listings) are "veg" and "non-veg". You'll also see "pure veg", which means that no eggs or alcohol are served. As a rule, **meat-eaters** should exercise caution in India: even when meat is available, especially in the larger towns, its quality can be poor, except in the best restaurants, and you won't get much in a dish anyway – especially in cheaper canteens where it's mainly there for flavouring. Hindus, of course, do not eat beef and Muslims shun pork, so you'll only find those in a few Christian enclaves such as the beach areas of Goa, and Tibetan areas. Note that what is called "mutton" on menus is in fact goat.

For advice on **drinking water** in India, see p.33.
For a **glossary** of food terms, see pp.1194–1197.

Somewhat confusingly, places serving traditional meals in India frequently call themselves "hotels", even though they do not offer accommodation. This is particularly common in the south, where you'll often come across men waving signs on roadsides advertising a "hotel", when it's no more than a lunch stop.

Where to eat

Broadly speaking, eating establishments divide into three main types: cheap and unpretentious local cafés (known variously as *dhabas*, *bhojanalayas* and *udipis*); Indian restaurants aimed at more affluent locals; and tourist restaurants. **Dhabas** and **bhojanalayas** are cheap cafés, where food is basic but often good, consisting of vegetable curry, dhal (a kind of lentil broth), rice or Indian bread (the latter more standard in the north) and sometimes meat. Often found along the sides of highways, *dhabas* traditionally cater to truck drivers – one way of telling a good *dhaba* is to judge from the number of trucks parked outside. *Bhojanalayas* are basic eating places, usually found in towns (especially around bus stands and train stations) in the north and centre of the country; they tend to be vegetarian, especially those signed as "Vaishno". Both *dhabas* and *bhojanalayas* can be grubby – look them over before you commit yourself. The same is rarely true of their southern equivalent, **udipi** canteens, which serve cheap, delicious snacks such as masala dosa, *iddli, vada* and rice-based dishes, all freshly cooked to order and dished up by uniformed waiters.

There are all sorts of **Indian restaurants**, veg and non-veg and typically catering to Indian businessmen and middle-class families. These are the places to go for reliably good Indian food at bargain prices. The more expensive Indian restaurants, such as those in five-star hotels, can be very expensive by local standards, but offer a rare chance to try top-notch classic Indian cooking, and still at significantly cheaper prices than you'd pay back home – assuming you could find Indian food that good.

Tourist restaurants, found across India wherever there are significant numbers of western visitors, cater specifically for foreign travellers with unadventurous tastebuds, serving up a stereotypical array of pancakes, omelettes, chips, muesli and fruit salad, along with a basic range of curries. The downside is that they tend to be relatively pricey, while the food can be very hit and miss – Indian spaghetti bolognaise, enchiladas and chicken chow mein can be every bit as weird as you might expect. International-style **fast food**, including burgers (without beef – usually chicken or mutton) and pizzas, is also available in major cities.

Indian food

What Westerners call a "curry" covers a huge variety of dishes, each made with a different masala, or mix of **spices**. Curry powder does not exist in India, the nearest equivalent being garam masala ("hot mix"), a combination of spices added to a dish at the last stage of cooking to spice it up. Commonly used spices include chilli, turmeric, garlic, ginger, cinnamon, cardamom, cloves, coriander – both leaf and seed – cumin and saffron. These are not all added at the same time, and some (particularly cardamom and cloves) are used whole, so beware of chewing on them.

Chilli is another key element in the Indian spice cabinet, but the idea that all Indian food is fiery hot is a complete myth. North Indian food, in particular, tends to be quite mildly spiced, often more so than Indian food in restaurants abroad. South Indian food can be hotter, but not invariably so. If you don't like hot food, there are mild dishes such as korma and biriyani where meat or vegetables are cooked with rice. Indians tend to assuage the effects of chilli with chutney, *dahi* (curd) or raita (curd with mint and cucumber, or other herbs and vegetables). Otherwise, beer is one of the best things for washing chilli out of your mouth; the essential oils that cause the burning sensation dissolve in alcohol, but not in water.

Vegetarian curries are usually identified (even on menus in English) by the Hindi names of their main ingredients, such as *paneer* (cheese), *alu* (potatoes), *chana* (chickpeas) or *muttar* (peas). **Meat curries**

are more often given specific names such as *korma* or *dopiaza*, to indicate the kind of masala used or the method of cooking.

North Indian food

North Indian cooking has been heavily influenced by the various Muslim invaders who arrived in the Subcontinent from Central Asia and Persia and who gave Indian cooking many of its most popular dishes and accompaniments, such as the biriyani and the naan bread, as well as its relatively greater emphasis on meat compared to the south. The classic north Indian fusion of native and Central Asian influences (although it can be found as far south as Hyderabad) is so-called **Mughlai cooking**, the creation of the Mughal dynasty. Mostly non-veg, the food is mildly spiced but extremely rich, using ingredients such as cream, almonds, sultanas and saffron – the classic korma sauce is the best-known example.

The other big northern style is **tandoori**. The name refers to the deep clay oven (tandoor) in which the food is cooked. Tandoori chicken is marinated in yoghurt, herbs and spices before cooking. Boneless pieces of meat, marinated and cooked in the same way are known as tikka; they may be served in a medium-strength masala (tikka masala), one thickened with almonds (*pasanda*), or in a rich butter sauce (*murg makhani* or butter chicken). Breads such as naan and roti are also baked in the tandoor.

A main dish – which may be a curry, but could also be a dry dish such as a kebab, or a tandoori dish without a masala – is usually served with a dhal (lentils) and bread such as chapatis or naan. Rice is usually an optional extra in North India, and has to be ordered separately. Many restaurants also offer set meals, or **thalis**. This is a stainless-steel tray with a number of little dishes in it, containing a selection of curries, a chutney and a sweet. In the middle you'll get bread and usually rice. In many places, waiters will keep coming round with refills until you've had enough.

In North India, food is usually served with **bread**, which comes in a number of varieties, all of them flatbreads rather than loaves. **Chapatti** is a generic term for breads, but tends to refer to the simplest, unleavened type. It's usually made from wheat flour. The term **roti** is likewise generic, and a roti can be exactly the same as a chapatti, but the term tends to refer more to a thicker bread baked in a tandoor. **Naan** is a leavened bread, thick and chewy, and invariably baked in a tandoor; it's a favourite in non-veg restaurants as it best accompanies rich meaty dishes. You may also come across fried breads, of which **paratha** (or *parantha*) is rolled out, basted with ghee, folded over and rolled out again several times before cooking, and often stuffed with ingredients such as potato (*alu paratha*); it's popular for breakfast. **Puris** are little fried puffballs. **Poppadum** (*papad*) is a crisp wafer made from lentil flour and is typically served as an appetizer.

There's an enormous variety of regional cuisines across the north. **Bengalis** love fish and cook a mean *mangsho* (meat) curry as well as exotic vegetable dishes such as *mo-cha* – cooked banana flower. They also like to include fish bones for added flavour in their vegetable curries – a nasty surprise for vegetarians. **Tibetans** and **Bhotias** from the Himalayas have a simple diet of *thukpa* (meat soup) and *momo* (meat dumplings), as well as a salty tea made with either rancid yak butter (where available) or with ordinary butter. In **Punjab** and much of northern India, home cooking consists of dhal and vegetables along with roti and less rice than the Bengalis. Food in **Gujarat**, predominantly veg, is often cooked with a bit of sugar. Certain combinations are traditional and seasonally repeated, such as *makki ki roti* (fried corn bread) with *sarson ka sag* (mustard-leaf greens) around Punjab and other parts of North India. *Baingan bharta* (puréed roast aubergine) is commonly eaten with plain yoghurt and roti. In good Muslim cooking from the north, delicately thin *rumali roti* ("handkerchief" bread) often accompanies rich meat and chicken dishes.

South Indian food

The food of South India is a world away from that of the north. Southern cooking also tends to use a significantly different repertoire of spices, with sharper, simpler flavours featuring coconut, tamarind, curry leaves and plenty of dried red and fresh green chillies. **Rice** is king, not only eaten in its natural form, but also made into regional staples such as *iddlis* (steamed rice cakes) and dosas (fermented rice-batter pancakes), such as the ubiquitous masala dosa, a potato curry wrapped in a crispy lentil-flour pancake. The lavish naans, *parathas*, rotis and other breads that are such a feature of north Indian cooking aren't usually available, apart from the fluffy little *puri*. Meat is comparatively uncommon in the Brahmin-dominated temple towns of Tamil Nadu, but available throughout Kerala, where there are sizeable Christian and Muslim minorities.

Set meals are another common feature in the south, where they are generally referred to simply as "meals". They generally consist of a mound of rice surrounded by various vegetable curries, *sambar* dhal, chutney and curd, and usually accompanied by *puris* and *rasam*, a thin, hot, peppery soup. Traditionally served on a round metal tray or thali (also found in North India), with each side dish in a separate metal bowl, set meals are sometimes served up on a rectangle of banana leaf instead. In most traditional restaurants, you can eat as much as you want, and staff circulate with refills of everything. In the south even more than elsewhere, eating with your fingers is *de rigueur* and cutlery may be unavailable in cheap restaurants.

Wherever you eat, remember to use only your **right hand**, and wash your hands before you start. Try and avoid getting food on the palm of your hand by eating with the tips of your fingers.

Snacks and street food

India abounds in **snacks** and **street food**. *Chana puri*, a chickpea curry with a *puri* (or sometimes other type of bread, a Kulcha) to dunk, is a great favourite in the north; *iddli sambar* – lentil and vegetable sauce with rice cakes to dunk – is the southern equivalent. Street finger-food includes *bhel puris* (a Mumbai speciality consisting of a mix of puffed rice, deep fried vermicelli, potato and crunchy *puri* with tamarind sauce), *pani puris* (the same *puris* dunked in peppery and spicy water – only for the seasoned), *bhajis* (deep-fried cakes of vegetables in chickpea flour), samosas (meat or vegetables in a pastry triangle, fried), and pakoras (vegetables or potato dipped in chick-pea flour batter and deep-fried). In the south, you'll also come across the ever-popular *vada*, a spicy deep-fried lentil cake which looks rather like a doughnut.

Kebabs are common in the north, most frequently seekh kebab, minced lamb grilled on a skewer, but also shami kebab, small minced-lamb cutlets. Kebabs rolled into

Paan

You may be relieved to know that the red stuff people spit all over the streets isn't blood, but juice produced by chewing **paan** – a digestive, commonly taken after meals, and also a mild stimulant, found especially in the northeast, where it is fresh and much stronger.

Paan consists of chopped or shredded nut (always referred to as betel nut, though in fact it comes from the areca palm), wrapped in a leaf (which *does* come from the betel vine) that is first prepared with ingredients such as *katha* (a red paste), *chuna* (slaked white lime), *mitha masala* (a mix of sweet spices, which can be ingested) and *zarda* (chewing tobacco, not to be swallowed on any account, especially if made with *chuna*). The triangular package thus formed is wedged inside your cheek and chewed slowly, and, in the case of *chuna* and *zarda* paans, spitting out the juice as you go.

Paan, and paan masala, a mix of betel nut, fennel seeds, sweets and flavourings, are sold by paan-wallahs, often from tiny stalls squeezed between shops. Paan-wallahs develop big reputations; those in the tiny roads of Varanasi are the most renowned, asking astronomical prices for paan made to elaborate specifications including silver and even gold foil. Paan is an acquired taste; novices should start off, and preferably stick with, the sweet and harmless *mitha* variety, which is perfectly alright to ingest.

griddle-fried bread, known as *kathi* rolls, originated in Kolkata but are now available in other cities as well. With all street snacks, though, remember that food left lying around attracts germs – make sure it's freshly cooked. Be especially careful with snacks involving water, such as *pani puris*, and cooking oil, which is often recycled. Generally, it's a good idea to acclimatize to Indian conditions before you start eating street snacks.

You won't find anything called "**Bombay mix**" in India, but there's no shortage of dry spicy snack mixes, often referred to as *channa chur*. Jackfruit chips are sometimes sold as a savoury snack – though they are rather bland – and cashew nuts are a real bargain. Peanuts, also known as "monkey nuts" or *mumfuli*, usually come roasted and unshelled.

Non-Indian food

Chinese food is widely available in large towns. It's generally cooked by Indian chefs and isn't exactly authentic, except in the few Indian cities, most notably Kolkata, that have large Chinese communities, where you can get very good Chinese cuisine.

Tourist restaurants and backpacker cafés nationwide offer a fair choice of **Western food**, from unpretentious little bakeries serving cakes and sandwiches to smart tourist restaurants dishing up fine Italian cooking on candle-lit terraces. However, quality is very hit and miss. Delhi and Mumbai are also home to a range of specialist non-Indian restaurants featuring Tex-Mex, Thai, Japanese, Italian and French cuisines – usually in the restaurants of luxury hotels.

In addition to these places, international **fast-food** chains such as *Pizza Hut*, *Domino's*, *KFC* and *McDonald's* serve the same standard fare as elsewhere in the world at much cheaper prices.

Sweets

Most Indians have rather a sweet tooth and **Indian sweets**, usually made of milk, can be very sweet indeed. Of the more solid type, *barfi*, a kind of fudge made from milk which has been boiled down and condensed, varies from moist and delicious to dry and powdery. It comes in various flavours from plain creamy white to *pista* (pistachio) in livid green and is often sold covered with silver leaf (which you eat). Smoother-textured, round *penda* and thin diamonds of *kaju katli*, plus moist *sandesh* and the harder *paira*, both popular in Bengal, are among many other sweets made from *chhana* or boiled-down milk. Crunchier *mesur* is made with chickpeas; numerous types of gelatinous halwa, not the Middle Eastern variety, include the rich *gajar ka halwa* made from carrots and cream.

Jalebis, circular orange tubes made of deep-fried treacle and dripping with syrup, are as sickly as they look. *Gulab jamuns*, deep-fried spongy dough balls soaked in syrup, are just as unhealthy. Common in both the north and the south, *ladoo* consists of balls made from semolina flour with raisins and sugar and sometimes made of other grains and flour. Among Bengali sweets, widely considered to be the best are *rasgullas*, rosewater-flavoured cream-cheese balls floating in syrup. *Ras malai*, found throughout North India, is similar, but soaked in cream instead of syrup. Down south, *payasam* – a rice or vermicelli pudding flavoured with cardamom, saffron and nuts – is a popular dessert, with special versions served on major festivals.

Chocolate is improving rapidly in India and you'll find various Cadbury's and Amul bars. None of the various indigenous brands of imitation Swiss and Belgian chocolates are worth eating.

Among the large **ice-cream** vendors, Kwality (now owned and branded as Wall's), Vadilal's, Gaylord and Dollops stand out. Uniformed men push carts of ice cream around and the bigger companies have many imitators, usually quite obvious. Some have no scruples – stay away from water ices unless you have a seasoned constitution. Ice-cream parlours selling elaborate concoctions including sundaes have really taken off; Connaught Circus in Delhi has several. Be sure to try **kulfi**, a pistachio- and cardamom-flavoured frozen sweet which is India's answer to ice cream; bhang kulfi (popular during the festival of Holi) is laced with cannabis and has an interesting kick to it, but should be approached with caution.

Fruit

What **fruit** is available varies with region and season, but there's always a fine choice.

Ideally, you should peel all fruit including apples, or soak them in strong iodine or potassium permanganate solution for half an hour. Roadside vendors sell fruit which they often cut up and serve sprinkled with salt and even masala – don't buy anything that looks like it's been hanging around for a while.

Mangoes of various kinds are usually on offer, but not all are sweet enough to eat fresh – some are used for pickles or curries. Indians are very picky about their mangoes, which they feel and smell before buying; if you don't know the art of choosing the fruit, you could be sold the leftovers. Among the species appearing at different times in the season, which lasts from spring to summer, look out for Alphonso and Langra. Bananas of one sort or another are also on sale all year round, and oranges and tangerines are generally easy to come by, as are sweet melons and thirst-quenching watermelons.

Tropical fruits such as coconuts, papayas (pawpaws) and pineapples are more common in the south, while things such as lychees and pomegranates are very seasonal. In the north, temperate fruit from the mountains can be much like that in Europe and North America, with strawberries, apricots and even rather soft apples available in season.

Among less familiar fruit, the *chiku*, which looks like a kiwi and tastes a bit like a pear, is worth a mention, as is the watermelon-sized jackfruit, whose spiny green exterior encloses sweet, slightly rubbery yellow segments, each containing a seed. Individual segments are sold at roadside stalls.

Non-alcoholic drinks

India sometimes seems to run on **tea**, or chai, grown in Darjeeling, Assam and the Nilgiri Hills, and sold by chai-wallahs on just about every street corner. Tea is usually made by putting tea leaves, milk and water in a pan, boiling it all up, straining it into a cup or glass with lots of sugar and pouring back and forth from one cup to another to stir. Ginger and/or cardamom are often added. If you're quick off the mark, you can get them to hold the sugar. English tea it isn't, but most travellers get used to it. Sometimes, especially in tourist spots, you might get a pot of European-style "tray" tea, generally consisting of a tea bag in lukewarm water – you'd do better to stick to the pukka Indian variety, unless, that is, you are in a traditional tea-growing area.

Instant **coffee** is becoming increasingly common, and in some cases is more popular than tea, especially in the south. In the north, most coffee is instant, although increasing numbers of cafés and restaurants are now investing in proper coffee machines, especially in tourist centres. Café society has finally arrived in the major cities, and Delhi and Mumbai now have a fair share of trendy coffee shops serving real cappuccino and espresso. In the south, coffee is just as common as tea, and far better than it is in the north. One of the best places to get it is in outlets of the *India Coffee House* chain, found in every southern town, and occasionally in the north. A whole ritual is attached to the drinking of milky Keralan coffee in particular, poured in flamboyant sweeping motions between tall glasses to cool it down.

Soft drinks are ubiquitous. Coca-Cola and Pepsi returned to India in the early 1990s after being banned from the country for seventeen years and have now largely replaced their old Indian equivalents such as Campa Cola and Thums Up, although you'll still find the pleasantly lemony Limca (rumoured to have dubious connections to Italian companies, and to contain additives banned there). All contain a lot of sugar but little else: adverts for Indian soft drinks have been known to boast "Absolutely no natural ingredients!" None will quench your thirst for long.

More recommendable is **water**, either treated or boiled tap water (see box, p.33) or bottled water (though quality may be suspect). You'll also find cartons of Frooti, Jumpin, Réal and similar brands of **fruit juice** drinks, which come in mango, guava, apple and lemon varieties. If the carton looks at all mangled, it is best not to touch it as it may have been recycled. At larger stations, there will be a stall on the platform selling Himachali apple juice. Better still, green **coconuts**, common around coastal areas especially in the south, are cheaper than any of these, and sold on the street by vendors who will hack off the top for you with a machete and give you a straw to suck up the coconut water (you then scoop out the flesh and eat it). You will also find street stalls selling freshly made sugar-cane juice: delicious, and not in fact too sweet, but not always as safe healthwise as you might like.

India's greatest cold drink, **lassi**, is made with beaten curd and drunk either sweetened with sugar, salted, or mixed with fruit. It varies widely from smooth and delicious to insipid and watery, and is sold at virtually every café, restaurant and canteen in the country. Freshly made milkshakes are also commonly available at establishments with blenders. They'll also sell you what they call a fruit juice, but which is usually fruit, water and sugar (or salt) liquidized and strained; also, street vendors selling fresh fruit juice in less than hygienic conditions are apt to add salt and garam masala. With all such drinks, however appetizing they may seem, you should exercise great caution in deciding where to drink them: find out where the water is likely to have come from.

Alcohol

Prohibition, once widespread in India, is now only fully enforced in Gujarat and some of the northeastern hill states, although Tamil Nadu, Andhra Pradesh and some other states retain partial prohibition in the form of "dry" days, high taxes, restrictive licences, and health warnings on labels.

Most Indians drink to get drunk as quickly as possible, and this trend has had a terrible toll on family life especially among the working classes and peasantry. As a consequence, politicians searching for votes have from time to time played the prohibition card, but thereby deprive the state government of revenue in taxes, and can rarely point to evidence of reduced drinking. Kerala, the state boasting the highest rates of alcohol consumption, has achieved a kind of compromise by taking total control of liquor sales on the high street. Beer, wines and spirits are only sold through government shops.

Alcoholic enclaves in prohibition states can become major drinking centres: Daman and Diu in Gujarat, and Puducherry and Karaikal in Tamil Nadu are the main ones. Goa, Sikkim and Mahé (Kerala) join them as places where the booze flows especially freely and cheaply. Interestingly, all were outside the British Raj. Liquor permits – free, and available from Indian embassies, high commissions and tourist offices abroad, and from tourist offices in Delhi, Mumbai, Kolkata and Chennai, and even at airports on arrival – allow those travellers who bother to apply for one to evade certain restrictions in Gujarat.

Beer is widely available, if rather expensive by local standards. Price varies from state to state, but you can usually expect to pay around Rs75–125 for a 650ml bottle. A pub culture, not dissimilar to that of the West, has taken root amongst the wealthier classes in cities like Bengaluru and Mumbai and also in Delhi. Kingfisher, King's Black Label and Fosters are the leading brands, but there are plenty of others. All lagers, which tend to contain chemical additives including glycerine, are usually pretty palatable if you can get them cold. In certain places, notably unlicensed restaurants in Tamil Nadu and Kerala, beer comes in the form of "special tea" – a teapot of beer, which you pour into and drink from a teacup to disguise what it really is.

A cheaper, and often delicious, alternative to beer in Goa and Kerala and other southern states is **toddy** (palm wine). In Bengal it is made from the date palm, and is known as *taddy*. Sweet and non-alcoholic when first tapped, it ferments within twelve hours. In the Himalayas, the Bhotia people, of Tibetan stock, drink *chang*, a beer made from millet, and one of the nicest drinks of all – *tumba*, where fermented millet is placed in a bamboo flask and topped with hot water, then sipped through a bamboo pipe.

Spirits usually take the form of "Indian Made Foreign Liquor" (IMFL), although the recently legitimized foreign liquor industry is expanding rapidly. Some Scotch, such as Seagram's Hundred Pipers, is now being bottled in India and sold at a premium, as is Smirnoff vodka, amongst other known brands. Some of the brands of Indian whisky are not too bad and are affordable in comparison; gin and brandy can be pretty rough, while Indian rum is sweet and distinctive. In Goa, *feni* is a spirit distilled from coconut or cashew fruit. Steer well clear of illegally distilled *arak* however, which often contains methanol (wood alcohol) and other poisons. A look through the press, especially at festival times, will soon reveal numerous cases of blindness and death as a result of drinking bad hooch (or "spurious liquor" as it's called). Licensed country liquor, sold in several states under such names as *bangla*, is an acquired taste. Unfortunately, Indian **wine** – despite the efforts of a few pioneering vineyards such as Grovers (near Bengaluru) – is still generally of a poor quality, and also expensive, while foreign wine available in upmarket restaurants and luxury hotels comes with an exorbitant price-tag.

Smoking

One of the great smells of India is the *beedi*, the cheapest smoke, made of low-grade tobacco wrapped in a single *tendu* leaf and fastened with a tiny piece of coloured thread. Though free from chemical additives, it's worth knowing that *beedis* produce three times more carbon monoxide and nicotine than regular cigarettes, and five times more tar. *Beedis* are available at shops and from roadside kiosks – basically, anywhere which sells cigarettes. Paan-wallahs sometimes have a supply, too.

The media

With well over a billion people and a literacy rate approaching seventy percent, India produces a staggering 4700 daily papers in over three hundred languages, and another 39,000 journals and weeklies. There are a large number of English-language daily newspapers, both national and regional. The most prominent of the nationals are the Times of India, The Hindu, The Deccan Chronicle, The Hindustan Times, The Telegraph, The Economic Times and the New Indian Express (usually the most critical of the government). All are pretty dry and sober, and concentrate on Indian news; The Independent and Kolkata's Telegraph tend to have better coverage of world news than the rest. Asian Age, published simultaneously in India, London and New York, is a conservative tabloid that sports a motley collection of the world's more colourful stories. All the major Indian newspapers have websites (see opposite), with the Times of India, The Hindu and the Hindustan Times providing the most up-to-date and detailed news services.

India's press is the freest in Asia and attacks on the government are often quite outspoken. However, as in the West, most papers can be seen as part of the political establishment, and are unlikely to print anything that might upset the "national consensus".

There are also a number of *Time/Newsweek*–style **news magazines**, with a strong emphasis on politics. The best of these are *India Today* and *Frontline*, published by *The Hindu*. Others include *Outlook*, which presents the most readable, broadly themed analysis, *Sunday* and *The Week*. As they give more of an overview of stories and issues than the daily papers, you will probably get a better insight into Indian politics, and most tend to have a higher proportion of international news too. *Business India* is more financially oriented and *The India Magazine* more cultural. Film **fanzines** and gossip mags are very popular (*Screen* and *Filmfare* are the best, though you'd have to be reasonably *au fait* with Indian movies to follow a lot of it), but magazines and periodicals in English cover all sorts of popular and minority interests, so it's worth having a look through what's available.

Foreign publications such as the *International Herald Tribune*, *Time*, *Newsweek*, and *The Economist* are all available in the main cities, though it's easier (and cheaper) to read the day's edition for free online. For a read through the British press, try the British Council in Delhi, Mumbai, Kolkata and Chennai; the USIS is the American equivalent. Expat-oriented bookstalls, such as those in New Delhi's Khan Market, stock slightly out-of-date and expensive copies of magazines like *Vogue* and *NME*.

BBC World Service radio (Ⓦwww.bbc.co.uk/worldservice) can be picked up at 94.3FM in most major cities, on short wave on frequencies ranging from 5790–15310kHz, and on medium wave (AM) at 1413KHz (212m) between about 8.30am and 10.30pm (Indian time). It also broadcasts online. The Voice of America (Ⓦwww.voa.gov) can be found on 15.75MHz (19) and (75.75MHz (39.5m), among other frequencies. Radio Canada (Ⓦwww.rcinet.ca) broadcasts in English on 6165 and 7255KHz (48.6 and 41.3m) at 6.30–7.30am and on 9635 and 11,975 KHz (31 and 25m) at 8.30–9.30pm.

The government-run **TV company**, Doordarshan, which broadcasts a sober diet of edifying programmes, has tried to compete with the onslaught of mass access to **satellite TV**. The main broadcaster in English is Rupert Murdoch's Star TV network, which incorporates the BBC World Service and Zee TV (with Z News), a progressive blend of Hindi-oriented chat, film, news and music programmes. Star Sports and ESPN churn out a mind-boggling amount of cricket with an occasional sprinkling of other sports. Others include CNN, some sports channels, the Discovery Channel, the immensely popular Channel V, hosted by scantily clad Mumbai models and DJs, and a couple of American soap and chat stations. There are now several local-language channels as well.

News and media online

Ⓦwww.guardian.co.uk/world/india High-quality news features are the meat of this "Special Report" section of the *Guardian*'s award-winning website, which also has links to its archived India articles and an excellent dossier on Kashmir. Access is free.

Ⓦindiatoday.digitaltoday.in Homepage of India's best-selling news magazine.

Ⓦwww.samachar.com One of the best news gateway sites, featuring headlines and links to leading Indian newspapers.

Ⓦwww.tehelka.com Alternative news webzine, famous for exposing corruption scandals in government.

Ⓦtimesofindia.indiatimes.com, www.hinduonline.com, www.hindustantimes.com, www.deccanherald.com Websites of some of India's leading daily papers, with detailed national coverage.

Festivals and holidays

Virtually every temple in every town or village across the country has its own festival. The biggest and most spectacular include Puri's Rath Yatra festival in June or July, the Hemis festival in Ladakh, also held in June or July, Pushkar's camel fair in November, Kullu's Dussehra, Madurai's three annual festivals, and, of course, the Kumbh Mela, held at Allahabad, Haridwar, Nasik and Ujjain. While mostly religious in nature, merrymaking rather than solemnity are generally the order of the day, and onlookers are usually welcome. Indeed, if you're lucky enough to coincide with a local festival, it may well prove to be the highlight of your trip.

There isn't space to list every festival in every village across India here, but local festivals are listed throughout the body of the Guide. The following pages include details of the main national and regional celebrations. Hindu, Sikh, Buddhist and Jain festivals follow the Indian **lunar calendar** and their dates therefore vary from year to year – we've given the lunar month (Magha, Phalguna, Chaitra, and so on), where relevant, in the listings below. The lunar calendar adds a leap month every two or three years to keep it in line with the seasons. Muslim festivals follow the **Islamic calendar**, whose year is shorter and which thus loses about eleven days per annum against the Gregorian.

You may, while in India, be lucky enough to be invited to a **wedding**. These are jubilant affairs, always scheduled on auspicious days. A Hindu bride dresses in red for the ceremony, and marks the parting of her hair with red *sindur* and her forehead with a *bindi*. She wears gold or bone bangles, which she keeps on for the rest of her married life. Although the practice is officially illegal, large dowries often change hands. These are usually paid by the bride's family to the groom, and can be contentious; poor families feel obliged to save for years to get their daughters married.

Principal Indian holidays

India has only four **national public holidays** as such: Jan 26 (Republic Day); Aug 15 (Independence Day); Oct 2 (Gandhi's birthday); and Dec 25 (Christmas Day). Each state, however, has its own calendar of public holidays; you can expect most businesses to close on the major holidays of their own religion. The Hindu lunar calendar months are given in brackets below. **Key: B=Buddhist; C=Christian; H=Hindu; J=Jain; M=Muslim; N=non-religious; P=Parsi; S=Sikh.**

Jan–Feb (Magha–Phalguna)

H Pongal (1 Magha): Tamil harvest festival celebrated with decorated cows, processions and rangolis (chalk designs on the doorsteps of houses). Pongal is a sweet porridge made from newly harvested rice and eaten by all, including the cows. The festival is also known as Makar Sankranti, and celebrated in Karnataka, Andhra Pradesh and the east of India.

H Ganga Sagar: Pilgrims come from all over the country to Sagar Dwip, on the mouth of the Hooghly 150km south of Kolkata, to bathe during Makar Sankranti.

H Vasant Panchami (5 Magha): One-day spring festival in honour of Saraswati, the goddess of learning, celebrated with kite-flying, the wearing of yellow saris and the blessing of schoolchildren's books and pens by the goddess.

N Republic Day (Jan 26): A military parade in Delhi typifies this state celebration of India's republichood, followed on Jan 29 by the "Beating the Retreat" ceremony outside the presidential palace in Delhi.

N Goa Carnival: Goa's own Mardi Gras features float processions and feni-induced mayhem in the state capital, Panjim.

N International Kite Festival at Aurangabad (Maharashtra).

H Teppa Floating Festival (16 Magha) at Madurai (Tamil Nadu). Meenakshi and Shiva are towed around the temple tank in boats lit with fairy lights – a prelude to the Tamil marriage season.

N Elephanta Music and Dance Festival (Mumbai). Feb–March (Phalguna). Classical Indian dance performed with the famous rock-cut caves in Mumbai harbour as a backdrop.

B Losar (1 Phalguna): Tibetan New Year celebrations among Tibetan and Himalayan Buddhist communities, especially at Dharamsala (HP).

H Shivratri (10 Phalguna): Anniversary of Shiva's tandav (creation) dance, and his wedding anniversary. Popular family festival but also a sadhu festival of pilgrimage and fasting, especially at important Shiva temples.

H Holi (15 Phalguna): Water festival held during Dol Purnima (full moon) to celebrate the beginning of spring, most popular in the north. Expect to be bombarded with water, paint, coloured powder and other mixtures; they can permanently stain clothing, so don't go out in your Sunday best.

N Khajuraho (Madhya Pradesh) Dance Festival: The country's finest dancers perform in front of the famous erotic sculpture-carved shrines.

C Carnival (Mardi Gras): The last day before Lent, forty days before Easter, is celebrated in Goa, as in the rest of the Catholic world.

March–April (Chaitra)

H Gangaur (3 Chaitra): Rajasthani festival (also celebrated in Bengal and Orissa) in honour of Parvati, marked with singing and dancing.

H Ramanavami (9 Chaitra): Birthday of Rama, the hero of the Ramayana, celebrated with readings of the epic and discourses on Rama's life and teachings.

C Easter (movable feast): Celebration of the resurrection of Christ. Good Friday in particular is a day of festivity.

P Pateti: Parsi new year, also known as Nav Roz, celebrating the creation of fire. Feasting, services and present-giving.

P Khorvad Sal (a week after Pateti): Birthday of Zarathustra (aka Zoroaster). Celebrated in the Parsis' Fire Temples, and with feasting at home.
H Chittirai, Madurai (Tamil Nadu): Elephant-led procession.

April–May (Vaisakha)

HS Baisakhi (1 Vaisakha): To the Hindus, it's the solar new year, celebrated with music and dancing; to the Sikhs, it's the anniversary of the foundation of the Khalsa (Sikh brotherhood) by Guru Gobind Singh. Processions and feasting follow readings of the Granth Sahib scriptures.
J Mahavir Jayanti (13 Vaisakha): Birthday of Mahavira, the founder of Jainism. The main Jain festival of the year, observed by visits to sacred Jain sites, especially in Rajasthan and Gujarat, and with present-giving.
H Puram Festival, Thrissur (Kerala): Frenzied drumming and elephant parades.
B Buddha Jayanti (16 Vaisakha): Buddha's birthday. He achieved enlightenment and nirvana on the same date. Sarnath (UP) and Bodh Gaya (Bihar) are the main centres of celebration.

May–June (Jyaishtha)

H Ganga Dussehra (10 Jyaishtha): Bathing festival to celebrate the descent to earth of the goddess of the Ganges.

June–July (Ashadha)

H Rath Yatra (2 Ashadha): Festival held in Puri (and other places, especially in the south) to commemorate Krishna's (Lord Jagannath's) journey to Mathura.
H Teej (3 Ashadha): Festival in honour of Parvati to welcome the monsoon. Particularly celebrated in Rajasthan.
B Hemis Festival, Leh (Ladakh): Held sometime between late June and mid-July, this spectacular festival features chaam (lama dances) to signify the victory of Buddhism over evil.

July–Aug (Shravana)

H Naag Panchami (3 Shravana): Snake festival in honour of the naga snake deities. Mainly celebrated in Rajasthan and Maharashtra.
H Raksha Bandhan/Narial Purnima (16 Shravana): Festival to honour the sea god Varuna. Brothers and sisters exchange gifts, the sister tying a thread known as a rakhi to her brother's wrist. Brahmins, after a day's fasting, change the sacred thread they wear.
N Independence Day (Aug 15): India's biggest secular celebration, on the anniversary of independence from Britain.

Aug–Sept (Bhadraparda)

H Ganesh Chaturthi (4 Bhadraparda): Festival dedicated to Ganesh, especially celebrated in Maharashtra. In Mumbai, huge processions carry images of the god to immerse in the sea.
H Onam: Keralan harvest festival, celebrated with snake-boat races. The Nehru Trophy snake-boat race at Alappuzha (held on the 2nd Sat of Aug) is the most spectacular, with long boats crewed by 150 rowers.
H Janmashtami (23 Bhadraparda): Krishna's birthday, an occasion for fasting and celebration, especially in Agra, Mumbai, Mathura (UP) and Vrindaban (UP).
H Avani Mula festival, Madurai (Tamil Nadu): Celebration of the coronation of Shiva.

Sept–Oct (Ashvina)

H Dussehra (1–10 Ashvina): Ten-day festival (usually two days' public holiday) associated with vanquishing demons, in particular Rama's victory over Ravana in the Ramayana, and Durga's over the buffalo-headed Mahishasura (particularly in West Bengal, where it is called Durga Puja). Dussehra celebrations include performances of the Ram Lila (life of Rama). Best in Mysore (Karnataka), Ahmedabad (Gujarat) and Kullu (Himachal Pradesh). Durga Puja is best seen in Kolkata where it is an occasion for exchanging gifts, and every locality has its own competing street-side image.
N Mahatma Gandhi's Birthday (Oct 2): Solemn commemoration of independent India's founding father.

Oct–Nov (Kartika)

H Diwali (Deepavali) (15 Kartika): Festival of lights, and India's biggest, to celebrate Rama's and Sita's homecoming in the Ramayana. Festivities include the lighting of oil lamps and firecrackers, and the giving and receiving of sweets and gifts. Diwali coincides with Kali Puja, celebrated in temples dedicated to the wrathful goddess, especially in Bengal, and often accompanied by the ritual sacrifice of goats.
J Jain New Year (15 Kartika): Coincides with Diwali, so Jains celebrate alongside Hindus.
S Nanak Jayanti (16 Kartika): Guru Nanak's birthday marked by prayer readings and processions, especially in Amritsar and in the rest of the Punjab, and at Patna (Bihar).

Nov–Dec (Margashirsha, or Agrahayana)

H Sonepur Mela: World's largest cattle fair at Sonepur (Bihar).

N Pushkar (Rajasthan) Camel Fair. Camel herders don their finest attire for this massive livestock market on the fringes of the Thar Desert.
N Hampi Festival (Karnataka): Government-sponsored music and dance festival.

Dec–Jan (Pausa)

CN Christmas (Dec 25): Christian festival celebrated throughout the world, popular in Christian areas of Goa and Kerala, and in big cities.
N Posh Mela (Dec 27): Held in Shantiniketan near Kolkata (Calcutta), a festival renowned for baul music.

Movable

H Kumbh Mela: Major three-yearly festival held at one of four holy cities: Nasik (Maharashtra), Ujjain (MP), Haridwar (UP), or Prayag (Maharashtra) as well as at Allahabad (UP). The Maha Kumbh Mela or "Great" Kumbh Mela, the largest religious fair in India, is held every twelve years in Allahabad (UP); the next festival is due to take place in 2013 (Jan 27 to Feb 25; main bathing day Feb 10).
M Ramadan: The month during which Muslims may not eat, drink or smoke from sunrise to sunset, and should abstain from sex. Future estimated dates are: Aug 1–30, 2011; July 20 to Aug 18, 2012; July 9 to Aug 7, 2013;
M Id ul-Fitr: Feast to celebrate the end of Ramadan. The precise date of the festival depends on exactly when the new moon is sighted, and so cannot be predicted with complete accuracy. Estimated dates (though these may vary by a day or two) are: Aug 31, 2011; Aug 19, 2012; and Aug 8, 2013.

Sports

India is not perhaps a place that most people associate with sports, but cricket, hockey and football (soccer, that is) all have their place.

Cricket is by far the most popular of these, and a fine example of how something quintessentially British (well, English) has become something quintessentially Indian. Travellers to India will find it hard to get away from the game – it's everywhere, especially on television. Cricketing heroes such as the legendary batting maestro Sachin Tendulkar and superstar Indian captain Mahendra Dhoni live under the constant scrutiny of the media and public; expectations are high and disappointments acute. India versus Pakistan matches are especially emotive – the entire country received a fillip when India beat their arch-rivals in the final of the inaugural Twenty20 World Cup in 2007 by a nail-biting five runs. Besides spectator cricket, you'll see games being played on open spaces all around the country.

Test matches are rare, but interstate cricket is easy to catch – the most prestigious competition is the Ranji Trophy. Occasionally, in cities like Kolkata, you may even come across a match blocking a road, and will have to be patient as the players begrudgingly let your vehicle continue.

Horse racing can be a good day out, especially if you enjoy a flutter. The racecourse at Kolkata is the most popular, often attracting crowds of over fifty thousand, especially on New Year's Day. There are several other racecourses around the country, mostly in larger cities such as Mumbai, Delhi, Pune, Hyderabad, Mysore, Bengaluru and Ooty. Other (mainly) spectator sports include **polo**, originally from upper Kashmir, but taken up by the British to become one of the symbols of the Raj. Certain Rajasthani princes, such as the late Hanut Singh of Jodhpur, were considered to be the best polo players in the world between the 1930s and 1950s, but since the 1960s, when the privy purses were abolished, they have been unable to maintain their stables, and the tradition of polo has declined. Today, it's mainly the army who plays the game; the best place to catch a match is at the Delhi Gymkhana during the winter season. Polo, in more or less its original form, is still

India's Twenty20 vision

The whole global cricket scene has been massively shaken up by the creation of two new Indian Twenty20 leagues showcasing a mix of local talent and overseas cricketing stars. The controversial **Indian Cricket League (ICL)**, started in 2007, was the first venture of its kind, but soon became bogged down in litigation and was quickly overtaken by the razzmatazz of the rival India Cricket Board's **Indian Premier League** (Ⓦwww.iplt20.com), held for the first time in 2008. It features a mix of young up-and-coming locals, established Indian test-match players and international cricketing megastars such as Shane Warne, Ricky Ponting, Muttiah Muralitharan and Shoaib Malik. Each of the league's eight regional team "franchises" supplements their home-grown playing staff by signing up star "icon players", whose services are auctioned off via a series of sealed bids – the most expensive player, Mahendra Dhoni, went for a cool $1.5 million.

played on tiny mountain ponies in Ladakh; a good place to see a game played in traditional style is in Leh during the Ladakh Festival in early September.

After years in the doldrums, **Indian hockey**, which used to regularly furnish the country with Olympic medals, is making a strong comeback. The haul of medals dried up in the 1960s when international hockey introduced astro-turf – which was, and still is, a rare surface in India. However, hockey remains very popular, especially in schools and colleges and, interestingly, amongst the tribal girls of Orissa, who supply the Indian national team with a regular clutch of players.

Football (soccer) is similarly popular with a keenly contested national championship. The best teams are based in Kolkata and include three legendary clubs – Mohan Bagan, East Bengal and Mohamadan Sporting – who all command fanatical support. Unlike most of the league, these teams employ professional players and even include some minor internationals, mostly from Africa. International soccer tournaments are becoming increasingly common.

Tennis in India has always been a sport for the middle and upper classes. The country has produced a number of world-class players, such as the men's duo of Mahesh Bhupati and Leander Paes, who briefly achieved a world number-one ranking in the men's doubles in 1999, while the glamorous young Sania Mirza, the first ever Indian to break into the WTA's Top 50 ranked players, rivals the nation's cricketers in popularity.

Volleyball is very popular throughout India, especially in the resorts of Goa. Standards aren't particularly high and joining a game is quite easy. Since the arrival on the Formula 1 scene of Kingfisher tycoon Vijay Malia's Force India team, **motor racing has** also grown in popularity and there is a race-track on the outskirts of Chennai. Golf is widely followed, too, again amongst the middle classes; the second-oldest golf course in the world is in Kolkata, and one of the highest in the world is at Shimla.

One indigenous sport you're likely to see in North India is **kabadi**, played on a small (badminton-sized) court, and informally on any suitable open area. The game, with seven players in each team, consists of a player from each team alternately attempting to "tag" as many members of the opposing team as possible in the space of a single breath (cheating is impossible; the player has to maintain a continuous chant of kabadikabadikabadikabadi etc), and getting back to his/her own side of the court without being caught. The game can get quite rough, with slaps and kicks in tagging allowed, and the defending team must try to tackle and pin the attacker so as not to allow him or her to even touch the dividing line. Tagged victims are required to leave the court. Although still an amateur sport, kabadi is taken very seriously with state and national championships, and now features in the Asian Games.

Popular with devotees of the monkey god, Hanuman, **Indian wrestling**, or kushti, has a small but dedicated following. Wrestlers are known as *pahalwaans* or "strong men" and can be seen exercising early in the morning with clubs and weights along river *ghats* such as those in Varanasi or Kolkata.

Trekking and outdoor activities

India offers plenty of opportunities for adventure sports, including trekking, mountaineering, whitewater rafting, caving and diving – just make sure you've got comprehensive insurance (see p.78) before getting stuck in.

Trekking

Though trekking in India is not nearly as commercialized as in neighbouring Nepal, the country can claim some of the world's most spectacular routes, especially in the Ladakh and Zanskar Himalayas, where the mountain passes frequently top 5000m. Himalayan routes are not all extreme, with relatively gentle short trails exploring the Singalila range around Darjeeling, low-level forest walks through the rhododendron-clad hillsides of Sikkim and the well-beaten pilgrim trails of Garhwal. Trekking is also becoming more popular in the Western Ghats and Nilgiris of the south.

Hiring a **guide-cum-cook** is recommended whenever possible, especially on more difficult and less frequented routes, where the consequences of getting lost or running out of supplies could be serious. Porters (with or without ponies) can also make your trip a lot less arduous, and on longer routes where a week or more's worth of provisions have to be carried, they may be essential. You'll usually be approached in towns and villages leading to the trailhead by men touting for work. Finding out what the going day rate is can be difficult, and you should expect to have to haggle.

If the prospect of organizing a trek yourself seems too daunting, consider employing a **trekking company** to do it for you. Agencies at places like Manali, Leh, Darjeeling and Gangtok are detailed in the Guide, while specialist tour operators offering trips based around trekking are listed among those on pp.28–30.

Himachal Pradesh is the easiest state in which to plan a trek. Uttarkhand sees fewer trekkers, and there are plenty of opportunities to wander off the beaten track and either escape the hordes of pilgrims or, alternatively, to join them on their way to the sacred sites of Badrinath, Gangotri, Joshimath and Kedarnath. There are also exciting and exotic high-mountain trekking opportunities in the ancient Buddhist kingdoms of Ladakh and Zanskar, where trails can vary in length from relatively short four-day excursions to epics of ten days or more. At the eastern end of the Himalayas, Darjeeling makes a good base from which to explore the surrounding mountains. Neighbouring Sikkim has the greatest variations in altitude, from steamy river valleys to the third highest massif in the world. Shorter and less strenuous treks are available in the Ghats and the Nilgiri hills of southern India, with Munnar and Wayanad in Kerala, the Kodagu region of Karnataka and Ooty in Tamil Nadu proving the main springboards.

Having the right **equipment** for a trek is important, but hi-tech gear isn't essential – bring what you need to be comfortable but keep weight to a minimum. You can rent equipment in places such as Leh and Darjeeling, but otherwise, you'll have to buy what you need or bring it with you. Make sure everything (zips for example) is in working order before you set off. Clothes should be lightweight and versatile, especially considering the range of temperatures you might encounter: dress in layers for maximum flexibility.

Mountaineering

Mountaineering is a more serious venture, requiring planning and organization; if you've never climbed, don't start in the Himalayas. Mountaineering institutes at Darjeeling, Uttarkashi and Dharamsala run training courses. The one at Uttarkashi in Uttarakhand (Ⓦwww.nimindia.org) is popular with foreigners: you can learn rock- and ice-climbing skills and expedition techniques for a fraction of what you'd pay in the West, but the 28-day basic mountaineering course run by Siachen Glacier veterans of the Indian army is extremely gruelling. Permission for mountaineering expeditions should be sought at least six months in advance from the Indian Mountaineering Federation, Anand Niketan, Benito Juarez Road, New Delhi 110021 (T011/2411 1211, Wwww.indmount.org). Peak fees range from $1500 to $4000, according to height, and expeditions must be accompanied by an IMF liaison officer equipped to the same standard as the rest of the party. The IMF can also supply lists of local mountaineering clubs; climbing with such clubs enables you to get to know local climbers, and obtain permits for otherwise restricted peaks.

Skiing

Despite the mammoth spread of the Himalayas, skiing in India remains relatively undeveloped. The only options for organized skiing are the western Himalayas, in particular Uttarakhand, Himachal Pradesh and, political unrest permitting, Kashmir; the eastern Himalayas have unreliable snowfall at skiing altitudes.

The ski area at **Auli** (see p.327), near Joshimath in Uttarakhand, has had money poured into it but suffers from a short season, limited (though cheap) skiing and non-existent après-ski activity. In **Himachal Pradesh**, the skiing in the vicinity of Shimla is far too underdeveloped to warrant a detour, but the possibilities around Manali are more enticing because of the prospect of virgin powder: two or three surface tows operate in the Solang Nala for three months every winter. By far the most promising prospect at present, however, is **Gulmarg** in Kashmir. On a plateau at 2600m, the former British hill station boasts the highest ski lift in the world – and some of the most dependably fine powder snow to be had anywhere. Skiers are dropped at nearly 4000m by a French-built Gondola, from where the off-piste possibilities are truly world class. A New Zealand company is threatening to start heli-skiing in this area, but for the time being Gulmarg offers a refreshingly wild experience that's a world away from the lift queues and crowded après-ski bars of the Alps. Guided trips are organized by British, IMFGA-qualified team, Mountain Tracks (Wski-gulmarg.co.uk).

Whitewater rafting

Though not as well known as some of the mighty rivers of Nepal, the rivers Chenab and Beas in Himachal Pradesh, the Rangit and Teesta in Sikkim, the Zanskar and Indus in Ladakh, and the Ganges in Uttarakhand all combine exciting waters with magnificent scenery. Kullu, Manali, Leh, Gangtok and Rishikesh are among the main rafting centres. Prices start at around Rs750 per day including food, but it's worth sounding out a few agents to find the best deals. For more details see the relevant accounts in the Guide.

Caving

Meghalaya has the best caving potential of all the Indian states. The three main areas are the East Khasi hills, the South Garo hills and the Jainta hills (home to the 21.4km-long Krem Kotsati–Umlawan cave, the longest system in mainland Asia). For potholing contacts in Meghalaya, see p.852.

Diving and snorkelling

Because of the number of rivers draining into the sea around the Subcontinent, India's **coastal waters** are generally silt-laden and too murky for decent diving or snorkelling. However, in many areas abundant hard coral and colourful fish make up for the relatively poor visibility. India also counts two beautiful tropical-island archipelagos in its territory, both surrounded by exceptionally clear seas. Served by well-equipped and reputable diving centres, the Andaman Islands and Lakshadweep offer world-class diving on a par with just about anything in Asia. Don't come here expecting rock-bottom prices though. Compared to Thailand, India's dive schools are pricey, typically charging around $60–70 for a one-tank outing, to $400–450 for an open-water course.

For independent travellers, the most promising destination for both scuba-diving and snorkelling is the **Andaman Islands** in the Bay of Bengal, around 1000km east of the mainland. Part of a chain of submerged mountains that stretch north from Sumatra to the coast of Myanmar (Burma), this isolated archipelago is ringed by gigantic coral reefs whose crystal-clear waters are teeming with tropical fish and other marine life. Given the high cost of diving courses, most visitors stick to snorkelling, but if you already have your PADI permit, it's well worth renting equipment from one of the two dive schools in the capital, Port Blair, and joining an excursion to an offshore dive-site such as Cinque Island or the Mahatma Gandhi Marine Reserve. If you want to do an open-water course, book ahead as places tend to be in short supply especially during the peak season, between December and February.

Lakshadweep (see p.1070) is a classic coconut palm-covered atoll, some 400km west of Kerala in the Arabian Sea. The shallow lagoons, extensive coral reefs and exceptionally good visibility make this a perfect option for both first-timers and more experienced divers – though the one and only hotel there is an extremely pricey five-star.

PADI-approved dive schools also work out of a handful of resorts in Goa, including Palolem (see p.729). Although the waters off the Goan coast have poor visibility, these schools take clients further south to an island off the shores of neighbouring Karnataka where conditions are perfect.

As with other countries, qualified divers should take their current certification card and/or logbook; if you haven't used it for one year or more, expect to have to take a short test costing around Rs350 ($8).

Camel trekking

The way to experience the desert in style is from the top of a camel. The one-humped Arabian camel, or dromedary, common in desert regions of Rajasthan, is well adapted to the terrain, with long double eyelashes to keep sand out of its eyes, nostrils that it can close, and broad, soft, padded feet that are ideal for walking on sand. Riding on a camel is smoother than riding on a horse because the camel moves its left and then right legs together, rather than front and then back legs like a horse, giving it a more rolling gait. They are usually docile, good-tempered animals, but the male goes into rut in spring, when it becomes rather grumpy and can kick and bite, and spit its regurgitated stomach contents in anger.

Camel treks can be arranged at Jaisalmer (see p.196) and Bikaner (see p.210). Some treks stick to the beaten track, and take you to the popular tourist sights. Others specialize in heading off deep into the desert for a feeling of isolation and remoteness. Typically, camel treks include two days in the saddle and a night spent camping in the desert, but you can opt for longer or shorter trips.

Yoga, meditation and ashrams

The birthplace of yoga and the spiritual home of the world's most famous meditation traditions, India offers unrivalled opportunities for spiritual nourishment, ranging from basic yoga and pranayama classes to extended residential meditation retreats.

Yoga is taught virtually everywhere in India and there are several internationally known centres where you can train to become a teacher. **Meditation** is similarly practised all over the country and specific courses are available in temples, meditation centres, monasteries and ashrams. **Ashrams** are communities where people work, live and study together, drawn by a common, usually spiritual, goal.

Details of yoga and meditation courses and ashrams are provided throughout the

Guide chapters of this book. Most centres offer courses that you can enrol on at short notice, but many of the more popular ones, listed on pp.68–69, need to be booked well in advance.

Yoga

Yoga (meaning "to unite") aims to help the practitioner unite his or her individual consciousness with the divine. This is achieved by raising awareness of one's self through spiritual, mental and physical exercises and discipline. **Hatha yoga**, the most popular form of yoga in the West, is based on physical postures called *asanas*, which stretch, relax and tone the muscular system of the body and also massage the internal organs. Each *asana* has a beneficial effect on a particular muscle group or organ, and although they vary widely in difficulty, consistent practice will lead to improved suppleness and health benefits. For serious practitioners, however, hatha yoga is seen simply as the first step leading to more subtle stages of meditation which commence when the energies of the body have been awakened and sensitized by stretching and relaxing. Other forms of yoga include *raja* yoga, which includes moral discipline, and *bhakti* yoga, the yoga of devotion, which entails a commitment to one's guru or teacher. *Jnana* yoga (the yoga of knowledge) is centred around the deep philosophies that underlie Hindu spiritual thinking.

Rishikesh, in Uttarakhand, is India's yoga capital, with a bumper crop of ashrams offering all kinds of courses (see p.320 for more details). The country's most famous teachers, however, work from institutes further south. **Iyengar** yoga is one of the most famous approaches studied today, named after its founder, B.K.S Iyengar (a student of the great yoga teacher Sri Tirumalai Krishnamacharya), with its main centre, the Ramamani Iyengar Memorial Yoga Institute, in Pune, Maharashtra (Ⓦwww.bksiyengar.com). Lyengar's style is based upon precise physical alignment during each posture. With much practice, and the aid of props such as blocks, straps and chairs, the student can attain perfect physical balance and, the theory goes, perfect balance of mind will follow. Iyengar yoga has a strong therapeutic element and has been used successfully for treating a wide variety of structural and internal problems.

Ashtanga yoga is an approach developed by K Pattabhi Jois of Mysore (Ⓦwww.kpjayi.org), who also studied under Krishnamacharya. Unlike Iyengar yoga, which centres around a collection of separate *asanas*, Ashtanga links various postures into a series of flowing moves called *vinyasa*, with the aim of developing strength and agility. The perfect synchronization of movement with breath is a key objective throughout these sequences. Although a powerful form it can be frustrating for beginners as each move has to be perfected before moving on to the next one.

The son of Krishnamacharya, T.K.V. Desikachar, established a third major branch in modern yoga, emphasizing a more versatile and adaptive approach to teaching, focused on the situation of the individual practitioner. This style became known as Viniyoga, although Desikachar has long tried to distance himself from the term. In the mid-1970s, he co-founded the Krishnamacharya Yoga Mandiram (Ⓦwww.kym.org), now a flagship institute in Chennai, in neighbouring Tamil Nadu and, in 2006, an off-shoot now steered by his son Kausthub, called the Krishnamacharya Healing and Yoga Foundation (Ⓦwww.khyf.net).

The other most influential Indian yoga teacher of the modern era has been Swami Vishnu Devananda, an acolyte of the famous sage Swami Sivanda, who established the International Sivananda Yoga Vedanta Center (Ⓦwww.sivananda.org), with more than twenty branches in India and abroad. **Sivananda**-style yoga tends to introduce elements in a different order from its counterparts – teaching practices regarded by others as advanced to relative beginners. This fast-forward approach has proved particularly popular with Westerners, who flock in their thousands to intensive introductory courses staged at centres all over India – the most renowned of them at Neyyar Dam, in the hills east of the Keralan capital, Thiruvananthapuram.

Meditation

Meditation is often practised after a session of yoga, when the energy of the body has been awakened, and is an essential part of both Hindu and Buddhist practice. In both religions, meditation is considered the most powerful tool for understanding the true nature of mind and self, an essential step on the path to **enlightenment**. In Vedanta, meditation's aim is to realize the true self as non-dual Brahman or godhead – the foundation of all consciousness and life. *Moksha* (or liberation – the Nirvana of the Buddhists), achieved through disciplines of yoga and meditation, eventually helps believers release the soul from endless cycles of birth and rebirth.

Vipassana meditation is a technique, originally taught by the Buddha, whereby practitioners learn to become more aware of physical sensations and mental processes. Courses last for a minimum of ten days and are austere – involving 4am kick-offs, around ten hours of meditation a day, no solid food after noon, segregation of the sexes, and no talking for the duration (except with the leaders of the course). Courses are free for all first-time students, to allow everyone an opportunity to learn and benefit from the technique. Vipassana is taught in more than 25 centres throughout India including in Bodhgaya, Bengaluru, Chennai, Hyderabad and Jaipur.

Tibetan Buddhist meditation is attracting more and more followers around the world. With its four distinct schools, Tibetan Buddhism incorporates a huge variety of meditation practices, including Vipassana, known as *shiné* in Tibetan, and various visualization techniques involving the numerous deities that make up the complex and colourful Tibetan pantheon. India, with its large Tibetan diaspora, has become a major centre for those wanting to study Tibetan Buddhism and medicine. Dharamsala in Himachal Pradesh, home to the Dalai Lama and Tibetan government-in-exile, is the main centre for Tibetan studies, offering numerous opportunities for one-on-one study with the Tibetan monks and nuns who live there. Other major Tibetan diaspora centres in India include Darjeeling in West Bengal and Bylakuppe near Mysore in Karnataka. For further details of courses available locally, see the relevant Guide chapters.

Ashrams and centres

Ashrams can range in size from just a handful of people to several thousand, and their rules, regulations and restrictions vary enormously. Some offer on-site accommodation, others will require you to stay in the nearest town or village. Some charge Western prices, others local prices, and some operate on a donation basis. Many ashrams have set programmes each day, while others are less structured, teaching as and when requested. In addition to these traditional Indian places to learn yoga and meditation techniques, dozens of smaller centres open in the coastal resorts of Goa and Kerala during the winter, several of them staffed by internationally famous teachers. The more prominent of these are listed below.

Courses and ashrams

Ashiyana Tropical Retreat Centre Junasa Waddo, Mandrem, Goa Ⓦ www.ashiyana-yoga-goa.com. If you like your yoga retreats to be drop-dead gorgeous, look no further than here. Perched on the banks of a river facing the sea, the centre offers world-class yoga, massage, meditation and satsang tuition – from resident and visiting teachers – with accommodation in beautifully designed Indonesian-style tree houses. Daily and weekly rates include workshops.

Astanga Yoga Nilayam 235 8th Cross, 3rd stage, Gokulam, Mysore 570002, Karnataka Ⓦ www.kpjayi.org. Run by students of Pattabhi Jois, one of the great innovators of yoga in India, and offering tuition in dynamic yoga, affiliated with martial arts. Courses last between one and six months and need to be booked in advance.

Brahmani Centre *Grandpa's Inn*, Anjuna, Goa Ⓦ www.brahmaniyoga.com. Offers drop-in yoga classes – mainly ashtanga, with a few taster sessions in other styles, plus pranayama and bhajan devotional singing – by top-notch teachers. All levels of ability are catered for.

Divine Life Society PO Shivanandanagar, Muni ki Reti, Rishikesh, District Tehri Garhwal, Uttarakhand Ⓣ 0135/430040, Ⓦ www.sivanandadlshq.org. The original Sivananda ashram – well organized if institutional, with several retreats and courses on all aspects and forms of yoga.

Harmonic Healing & Eco Retreat Centre Patenem, Goa ⓣ9822/512814, ⓦwww.harmonicingoa.com. Yoga, pilates, reiki initiations, energy balancing and Thai massages from internationally acclaimed teachers, along with lessons in Bollywood dance and classical Indian singing, all against one of the loveliest beach panoramas in Goa.

International Society for Krishna Consciousness (ISKCON) 3c Albert Rd, Kolkata ⓣ033/247 3757; Bhaktivedanta Swami Marg, Raman Reti, Vrindavan ⓣ0565/442478, ⓦwww.iskcon.com. Large and well-run international organization with major ashrams and temples in Mayapur, north of Kolkata in West Bengal, Vrindavan in west UP and centres in several major Indian cities and abroad. Promotes bhakti yoga (the yoga of devotion) through good deeds, right living and chanting – a way of life rather than a short course.

Mata Amritanandamayi Math Amritapuri, Vallikkavu, Kerala ⓦwww.amritapuri.org. The ashram of the famous "Hugging Saint", Amma, visited annually by hundreds of thousands, who pass through for *darshan* and a hug from the smiley guru, whose charitable works have earned for her near-divine status in the south.

Osho Commune International 17 Koregaon Park, Pune, Maharashtra 411001 ⓣ020/612 6655, ⓦwww.osho.com. Established by the enigmatic Osho, who generated a huge following of both Western and Indian devotees, this "Meditation Resort" is set in 31 acres of beautifully landscaped gardens and offers a variety of courses in personal therapy, healing and meditation. For full details see p.671.

Prasanthi Nilayam Puttaparthi, Andhra Pradesh ⓣ08555/87236, ⓦwww.sathyasai.org. The ashram of Satya Sai Baba, one of India's most revered and popular gurus, who has a worldwide following of millions, despite the deaths of four followers in mysterious circumstances in 2000. The ashram is four or five hours by bus from Bangalore. Visitors sometimes comment on the strict security staffing and rigid rules and regulations. Cheap accommodation is available in dormitories or "flats" for four people. There is no need to book in advance though you should phone to check availability; see p.921 for more details. Sai Baba also has a smaller ashram in Bangalore and one in Kodaikanal.

Purple Valley Centre Assagao, Goa ⓦwww.yogagoa.com. Purple Valley has accommodation for up to 40 guests and what must be one of the most beautiful yoga shalas (practice areas) in India. Their teachers include Nancy Gilgoff and Sharath Rangaswamy, grandson of the illustrious Ashtanga Guru, Shri K. Pattabhi Jois.

Root Institute for Wisdom Culture Bodhgaya, Bihar ⓣ0631/400714, ⓦwww.rootinstitute.com. Regular seven- to ten-day courses on Tibetan Buddhism and meditation are held here from Oct to March, and there are facilities for individual retreats. Accommodation for longer stays should be booked well in advance. See p.803 for further details.

Saccidananda Ashram Thanneepalli, Kullithalai, near Tiruchirapelli, Tamil Nadu ⓣ04323/22260, ⓦwww.bedegriffiths.com. Also known as Shantivanam (meaning Peace Forest in Sanskrit), it is situated on the banks of the sacred river Cauvery. Founded by Father Bede Griffiths, a visionary Benedictine monk, it presents a curious but sympathetic fusion of Christianity and Hinduism. Visitors can join in the services and rituals or just relax here. Accommodation is in simple huts dotted around the grounds and meals are communal. Very busy during the major Christian festivals.

Sivananda Yoga Vedanta Dhanwantari Ashram Thiruvananthapuram, Kerala ⓣ0471/227 3093, ⓦwww.sivananda.org. An offshoot of the original Divine Life Society, this yoga-based ashram focuses on *asanas*, breathing techniques (*pranayama*) and meditation. They also run month-long yoga teacher-training programmes, but book well in advance. There are further branches in Madurai, Chennai, Delhi and Uttarkashi – see the website for details.

Tushita Meditation Centre McLeod Ganj, Dharamsala 176219, Himachal Pradesh ⓣ01892/21866, ⓦwww.tushita.info. Offers a range of Tibetan meditation courses. A ten-day course costs in the region of Rs3500; book well in advance.

Vipassana International Academy Runs a wide variety of 3- to 45-day courses in Vipassana meditation at around 25 centres across India. See ⓦwww.dhamma.org for details.

Culture and etiquette

Cultural differences extend to all sorts of little things. While allowances will usually be made for foreigners, visitors unacquainted with Indian customs may need a little preparation to avoid causing offence or making fools of themselves. The list of do's and don'ts here is hardly exhaustive: when in doubt, watch what the Indian people around you are doing.

Eating and the right-hand rule

The biggest minefield of potential faux pas has to do with **eating**. This is usually done with the fingers, and requires practice to get absolutely right. Rule one is: **eat with your right hand only**. In India, as right across Asia, the left hand is for wiping your bottom, cleaning your feet and other unsavoury functions (you also put on and take off your shoes with your left hand), while the right hand is for eating, shaking hands, and so on.

Quite how rigid individuals are about this tends to vary, with brahmins (who, at the top of the hierarchical ladder, are one of the two "right-handed castes") and southerners likely to be the strictest. While you can hold a cup or utensil in your left hand, and you can usually get away with using it to help tear your chapatti, you should not eat, pass food or wipe your mouth with your left hand. Best is to keep it out of sight below the table.

This rule extends beyond food. In general, do not pass anything4 to anyone with your left hand, or point at anyone with it either; and Indians won't be impressed if you put it in your mouth. In general, you should accept things given to you with your right hand – though using both hands is a sign of respect.

The other rule to beware of when eating or drinking is that your lips should not touch other people's food – *jhutha*, or sullied food, is strictly taboo. Don't, for example, take a bite out of a chapatti and pass it on. When drinking out of a cup or bottle to be shared with others, don't let it touch your lips, but rather pour it directly into your mouth. This custom also protects you from things like hepatitis. It is customary to wash your hands before and after eating.

Temples and religion

Religion is taken very seriously in India; it's important always to show due respect to religious buildings, shrines, images, and people at prayer. When entering a **temple or mosque**, remove your shoes and leave them at the door (socks are acceptable and protect your feet from burning-hot stone ground). Some temples – Jain ones in particular – do not allow you to enter wearing or carrying leather articles, and forbid entry to menstruating women. In the southern state of Kerala, most Hindu temples are closed to non-Hindus, but those that aren't require men to remove their shirts before entering (women must wear long dresses or skirts).

In a mosque, non-Muslims would not normally be allowed in at prayer time and women are sometimes not let in at all. In a Hindu temple, you are not often allowed into the inner sanctum; and at a Buddhist *stupa* or monument, you should always walk round clockwise (ie, with the *stupa* on your right). Hindus are very superstitious about taking photographs of images of deities and inside temples; if in doubt, desist. Do not take photos of funerals or cremations.

Funeral processions are private affairs, and should be left in peace. In Hindu funerals, the body is normally carried to the cremation site within hours of death by white-shrouded relatives (white is the colour of mourning). The eldest son is expected to shave his head and wear white following the death of a parent. At Varanasi and other places, you may see cremations; such occasions should be treated with respect, and photographs should not be taken.

Dress

Indian people are very conservative about dress. **Women** are expected to dress modestly, with legs and shoulders covered. Trousers are acceptable, but shorts and short skirts are offensive to many. **Men** should always wear a shirt in public, and avoid shorts (a sign of low caste) away from beach areas. These rules go double in temples and mosques. Cover your head with a cap or cloth when entering a *dargah* (Sufi shrine) or Sikh *gurudwara*; women in particular are also required to cover their limbs. Men are similarly expected to dress appropriately with their legs and head covered. Caps are usually available on loan, often free, for visitors, and sometimes cloth is available to cover up your arms and legs.

Never mind sky-clad Jains (see p.1174) or *naga sadhus*, **nudity** is not acceptable in India. Topless bathing is not uncommon in Goa (though it is in theory prohibited), but you can be sure the locals don't like it.

In general, Indians find it hard to understand why rich Westerners should wander round in ragged clothes or imitate the lowest ranks of Indian society, who would love to have something more decent to wear. Staying well groomed and dressing "respectably" vastly improves the impression you make on local people, and reduces sexual harassment for women too.

Other possible gaffes

Kissing and **embracing** are regarded in India as part of sex: do not do them in public. In more conservative areas (ie outside westernized parts of big cities), it is not even a good idea for couples to hold hands, though Indian men can sometimes be seen holding hands as a sign of "brotherliness". Be aware of your **feet**. When entering a private home, you should normally remove your shoes (follow your host's example); when sitting, avoid pointing the soles of your feet at anyone. Accidental contact with one's foot is always followed by an apology.

Indian English can be very formal and even ceremonious. Indian people may well call you "sir" or "madam", even "good lady" or "kind sir". At the same time, you should be aware that your English may seem rude to them. In particular, swearing is taken rather seriously, and casual use of the F-word is likely to shock.

Meeting people

Westerners have an ambiguous status in Indian eyes. In one way, you represent the rich sahib, whose culture dominates the world, and the old colonial mentality has not completely disappeared. On the other hand, as a non-Hindu, you are an outcaste, your presence in theory polluting to an orthodox or high-caste Hindu, while to members of all religions, your morals and your standards of spiritual and physical cleanliness are suspect.

As a traveller, you will constantly come across people who want to strike up a **conversation**. English not being their first language, they may not be familiar with the conventional ways of doing this, and thus their opening line may seem abrupt if at the same time very formal. "Excuse me good gentleman, what is your mother country?" is a typical one. It is also the first in a series of questions that Indian men seem sometimes to have learnt from a single book in order to ask Western tourists. Some of the questions may baffle at first ("What is your qualification?" "Are you in service?"), some may be queries about the ways of the West or the purpose of your trip, but mostly they will be about your family and your job.

You may find it odd or even intrusive that complete strangers should want to know that sort of thing, but these subjects are considered polite conversation between strangers in India, and help people place one another in terms of social position. Your family, job, even income, are not considered "personal" subjects, and it is completely normal to ask people about them. Asking the same questions back will not be taken amiss – far from it. Being curious does not have the "nosey" stigma in India that it has in the West.

Things that Indian people are likely to find strange about you are lack of religion (you could adopt one), travelling alone, leaving your family to come to India, being an unmarried couple (letting people think you are married can make life easier), and travelling second class or staying in cheap hotels when, as a tourist, you are relatively rich. You will probably end up having to explain the same things many times to many different people; on the other hand, you can ask questions too, so you could take it as an opportunity to ask things you want to know about India. English-speaking Indians and members of the large and growing middle class in particular are usually extremely well informed and well educated.

Shopping

So many beautiful and exotic souvenirs are on sale in India, at such low prices, that it's sometimes hard to know what to buy first. On top of that, all sorts of things (such as made-to-measure clothes) that would be vastly expensive at home are much more reasonably priced in India. Even if you lose weight during your trip, your baggage might well put on quite a bit – unless of course you post some of it home. For details on what to buy while in India, see the "Crafts to go" colour section.

Where to shop

Quite a few items sold in tourist areas are made elsewhere and, needless to say, it's more fun (and cheaper) to pick them up at source. Best buys are noted in the relevant sections of the Guide, along with a few specialities that can't be found outside their regions. India is awash with **street hawkers**, often very young kids. Although they can be annoying and should be dealt with firmly if you are not interested, do not write them off completely as they sometimes have decent souvenirs at lower than shop prices and are open to hard bargaining.

Virtually all the state governments in India run handicraft **"emporia"**, most with branches in the major cities such as Delhi, Mumbai, Chennai and Kolkata. These four cities also have **Central Cottage Industries Emporiums**. Goods in these emporiums are generally of a high quality, even if their fixed prices are a little expensive, and they are worth a visit to get an idea of what crafts are available and how much they should cost.

Bargaining

Whatever you **buy** (except food and cigarettes), you will almost always be expected to **haggle** over the price. Bargaining is very much a matter of personal style, but should always be lighthearted, never acrimonious. There are no hard and fast rules – it's really a question of how much something is worth to you. It's a good plan, therefore, to have an idea of how much you want to pay. Bid low and let the shopkeeper argue you up. If they'll settle for your price or less, you have a deal. If not, you don't, but you've had a pleasant conversation and no harm is done.

Don't worry too much about the first quoted prices. Some people suggest paying a third of the opening price, but it really depends on the shop, the goods and the shopkeeper's impression of you. You may not be able to get the seller much below the first quote; on the other hand, you may end up paying as little as a tenth of it. If you bid too low, you may be hustled out of the shop for offering an "insulting" price, but this is all part of the game, and you'll no doubt be welcomed as an old friend if you return the next day.

"Green" tourists are easily spotted, so try and look like you know what you are up to, even on your first day, or leave it till later; you could wait and see what the going rate is first.

Haggling is a little bit like bidding in an auction, and similar rules apply. Don't start haggling for something if you know you don't want it, and never let any figure pass your lips that you are not prepared to pay – having mentioned a price, you are obliged to pay it. If the seller asks you how much you would pay for something, and you don't want it, say so.

Sometimes rickshaw-wallahs and taxi drivers stop unasked at shops where they get a small **commission** simply for bringing customers. In places like Jaipur and Agra where this is common practice, tourists sometimes even strike a deal with their drivers – agreeing to stop at five shops and splitting the commission for the time wasted. If you're taken to a shop by a tout or driver and you buy something, you pay around fifty percent extra. Stand firm about not entering shops and getting to your destination if you have no appetite for such shenanigans. If you want a bargain, shop alone, and never let anybody on the street take you to a shop – if you do, they'll be getting a commission, and you'll be paying it.

Travelling with children

Travelling with kids can be both challenging and rewarding. Indians are very tolerant of children so you can take them almost anywhere without restriction, and they always help break the ice with strangers.

However the main problem with children, especially small children, is their extra vulnerability. Even more than their parents, they need protection from the sun, unsafe drinking water, heat and unfamiliar food. All that chilli in particular may be a problem, even with older kids, if they're not used to it. Remember too, that diarrhoea, perhaps just a nuisance to you, could be dangerous for a child: rehydration salts (see p.36) are vital if your child goes down with it. Make sure too, if possible, that your child is aware of the dangers of rabies; keep children away from animals, and consider a rabies jab.

For babies, nappies (diapers) are available in most large towns at similar prices to the West, but it's worth taking an additional pack in case of emergencies, and bringing sachets of Calpol or similar, which aren't readily available in India. And if your baby is on powdered milk, it might be an idea to bring some of that: you can certainly get it in India, but it may not taste the same. Dried baby food could also be worth taking – any café or chai-wallah should be able to supply you with boiled water.

For touring, hiking or walking, child-carrier backpacks are ideal; some even come with mosquito nets these days. When it comes to luggage, bring as little as possible so you can manage the kids more easily. If your child is small enough, a fold-up buggy is also well worth packing, even if you no longer use a buggy at home, as kids tire so easily in the heat. If you want to cut down on long train or bus journeys by flying, remember that children under 2 travel for ten percent of the adult fare, and under-12s for half price.

Travel essentials

Costs

For Western visitors, India is still one of the world's less expensive countries. A little foreign currency can go a long way, and you can be confident of getting good value for your money, whether you're setting out to keep your budget to a minimum or to enjoy the opportunities that spending a bit more will make possible.

What you spend obviously depends on where you go, where you stay, how you get around, what you eat and what you buy. Outside the tourist resorts of Kerala and Goa, you could just about survive on a **budget** of as little as Rs750 (£11/$17) per day, if you eat in local *dhabas*, stay in the cheapest hotels and don't travel too much. In reality, most backpackers nowadays tend to spend at least double that. On Rs2000 per day you'll be able to afford comfortable mid-range hotels, and meals in smarter restaurants, regular rickshaw or taxi rides and entrance fees to monuments. Spend around Rs5000 (£75/$110) per day and you can stay in smart hotels, eat in the top restaurants, travel first class on trains and afford chauffeur-driven cars. Although it is possible to travel very comfortably in India, it's also possible to spend a great deal of money, if you want to experience the very best the country has to offer, and there are plenty of hotels now charging $500 per night, sometimes a lot more.

Budget **accommodation** is still very good value, however. Cheap double rooms usually start from around Rs400 (£6/$9) per night, while a no-frills vegetarian **meal** in an ordinary restaurant will typically cost no more than Rs100. Long-distance **transport** can work out to be phenomenally good value if you stick to state buses and standard second-class non-a/c trains, but soon starts to add up if you opt for air-conditioned carriages on the superfast intercity services. The 200km trip from Delhi to Agra, for example, can cost anywhere from Rs78 (£1/$1.75) in second class unreserved up to Rs755 (£11.50/$17) in first-class a/c.

Where you are also makes a difference: Mumbai is notoriously pricey, especially for accommodation, and Delhi is also substantially more expensive than most parts of the country. Upscale visitor accommodation in Kerala costs almost as much as it does in Europe, although fierce competition tends to keep prices at the lower end of the budget spectrum down in the tourist towns of Rajasthan. Out in the sticks, on the other hand, and particularly away from your fellow tourists, you will often find things incredibly cheap, though your choice will obviously be more limited.

Don't make any rigid assumptions at the outset of a long trip that your money will last for a certain number of weeks or months. On any one day it may be possible to spend very little, but cumulatively you won't be doing yourself any favours if you don't make sure you keep yourself well rested and properly fed. As a foreigner in India, you will find yourself penalized by double-tier entry prices to museums and historic sites (see box below) as well as in upmarket hotels and airfares, both of which are levied at a higher rate and in dollars.

ASI entrance fees

The Archeological Survey of India (ASI), who manage many of India's most popular monuments, such as the Taj Mahal, currently operates a **two-tier entry system** at all its sites, whereby foreign visitors, including non-resident Indians, pay more (sometimes a lot more) than Indian residents; we've listed entrance fees for both foreigners and Indian residents throughout the Guide.

Some independent travellers tend to indulge in wild and highly competitive **penny-pinching**, which Indian people find rather pathetic – they have a fair idea of what you can earn at home. Bargain where appropriate, but don't begrudge a few rupees to someone who's worked hard for them: consider what their services would cost in your own country, and how much more valuable the money is to them than it is to you. Even if you get a bad deal on every rickshaw journey you make, it will only add a minuscule fraction to the cost of your trip. Remember too, that every pound or dollar you spend in India goes that much further, and luxuries you can't afford at home become possible here: sometimes it's worth spending more simply because you get more for it. At the same time, don't pay well over the odds for something if you know what the going rate is. Thoughtless extravagance can, particularly in remote areas that see a disproportionate number of tourists, contribute to inflation, putting even basic goods and services beyond the reach of local people.

Crime and personal safety

In spite of the crushing poverty and the yawning gulf between rich and poor, India is, on the whole, a safe country in which to travel. As a tourist, however, you are an obvious target for the tiny number of thieves (who may include some of your fellow travellers), and stand to face serious problems if you do lose your passport, money and ticket home. Common sense, therefore, suggests a few precautions.

Beware of crowded locations, such as packed buses or trains, in which it is easy for pickpockets to operate – slashing pockets or bags with razor blades is not

Drugs

India is a centre for the production of **cannabis** and to a lesser extent **opium**, and derivatives of these drugs are widely available. **Charas** (hashish) is produced all along the Himalayas. The use of cannabis is frowned upon by respectable Indians – if you see anyone in a movie smoking a chillum, you can be sure it's the baddie. Sadhus, on the other hand, are allowed to smoke **ganja** (marijuana) legally as part of their religious devotion to Shiva, who is said to have originally discovered its narcotic properties.

Bhang (a preparation made from marijuana leaves, which it is claimed sometimes contains added hallucinogenic ingredients such as datura) is legal and widely available in bhang shops: it is used to make sweets and drinks such as the notoriously potent bhang lassis which have waylaid many an unwary traveller. Bhang shops also frequently sell ganja, low-quality *charas* and opium (*chandu*), mainly from Rajasthan and Madhya Pradesh. Opium derivatives morphine and heroin are widespread too, with addiction an increasing problem among the urban poor. "Brown sugar" that you may be offered on the street is number-three heroin; Varanasi is becoming notorious for its heroin problem. Use of other illegal drugs such as LSD, ecstasy and cocaine is largely confined to tourists in party locations such as Goa.

All of these drugs except bhang are strictly controlled under Indian **law**. Anyone arrested with less than five grams of cannabis, which they are able to prove is for their own use, is liable to a six-month maximum, but cases can take years to come to trial (two is normal, and eight not unheard of). Police raids and searches are particularly common at the following places: Manali, the Kullu valley and Almora, and on buses from those places to Delhi, especially at harvest time; buses and trains crossing certain state lines, notably between Gujarat and Maharashtra; and the beach areas of Goa. "Paying a fine now" may be possible on arrest (though it will probably mean all the money you have), but once you are booked in at the station, your chances are slim; a minority of the population languishing in Indian jails are foreigners on drugs charges.

unheard of in certain locations, and itching powder is sometimes used to distract the unwary. Don't leave valuables unattended on the beach when you go for a swim; backpacks in dormitory accommodation are also obvious targets, as is luggage on the roof of buses. Even monkeys rate a mention here, since it's not unknown for them to steal things from hotel rooms with open windows, or even to snatch bags from unsuspecting shoulders.

Budget travellers would do well to carry a **padlock**, as these are usually used to secure the doors of cheap hotel rooms and it's reassuring to know you have the only key. You can also use them to lock your bag to seats or racks in trains, for which a length of chain also comes in handy. Don't put valuables in your luggage for bus or plane journeys: keep them with you at all times. If your baggage is on the roof of a bus, make sure it is well secured. On trains and buses, the prime time for theft is just before you leave, so keep a particular eye on your gear then, beware of deliberate diversions, and don't put your belongings next to open windows. Remember that routes popular with tourists tend to be popular with thieves too. Druggings leading to theft and worse are rare but not unheard of and so you are best advised to politely refuse food and drink from fellow passengers or passing strangers, unless you are completely confident it's the family picnic you are sharing or have seen the food purchased from a vendor.

However, **don't get paranoid**; the best way of enjoying the country is to stay relaxed but with your wits about you. Crime levels in India are a long way below those of Western countries, and violent crime against tourists is extremely rare. Virtually none of the people who approach you on the street intend any harm: most want to sell you something (though this is not always made apparent immediately), some want to practise their English, others (if you're a woman) to chat you up, while more than a few just want to add your address to their book or have a snap taken with you. Anyone offering wonderful-sounding moneymaking schemes, however, is almost certain to be a con artist.

If you do feel threatened, it's worth looking for help. **Tourism police** are found sitting in clearly marked booths in the main railway stations, especially in big tourist centres, where they will also have a booth in the main bus station. In addition, they may have a marked booth outside major tourist sites.

Be wary of **credit card fraud**; a credit card can be used to make duplicate forms by which your account is then billed for fictitious transactions, so don't let shops or restaurants take your card away to process – insist they do it in front of you or follow them to the point of transaction.

It's not a bad idea to keep $200 or so separately from the rest of your money, along with your travellers' cheque receipts, insurance policy number and phone number for claims, and a photocopy of the pages in your passport containing personal data and your Indian visa. This will cover you in case you do lose all your valuables.

If the worst happens and you get **robbed**, the first thing to do is report the theft as soon as possible to the local police. They are very unlikely to recover your belongings, but you need a report from them in order to claim on your travel insurance. Dress smartly and expect an uphill battle – city cops in particular tend to be jaded from too many insurance and travellers' cheque scams.

Losing your passport is a real hassle, but does not necessarily mean the end of your trip. First, report the loss immediately to the police, who will issue you with the all-important "complaint form" that you need to be able to travel around and check into hotels, as well as claim back any expenses incurred in replacing your passport from your insurer. A complaint form, however, will not allow you to change money or travellers' cheques. If you've run out of cash, your best bet is to ask your hotel manager to help you out (staff will have seen your passport when you checked in, and the number will be in the register). The next thing to do is telephone your nearest embassy or consulate in India. Normally, passports have to be applied for and collected in person, but if you are stranded, it is usually possible to arrange to receive the necessary forms in the post. However, you still have to go to the embassy or consulate to pick up your new passport.

"Emergency passports" are the cheapest form of replacement, but are normally only valid for the few days of your return flight. If you're not sure when you're leaving India, you'll have to obtain a more costly "full passport"; these can only be issued by embassies and larger consulates in Delhi or Mumbai, and not those in Chennai, Kolkata or Panjim (Goa).

Duty free allowance

Anyone over 17 can bring in one US quart (0.95 litre – but nobody's going to quibble about the other 5ml) of spirits, or a bottle of wine and 250ml spirits; plus 200 cigarettes, or 50 cigars, or 250g tobacco. You may be required to register anything valuable on a tourist baggage re-export form to make sure you can take it home with you, and to fill in a currency declaration form if carrying more than $10,000 or the equivalent.

Electricity

Generally 220V 50Hz AC, though direct current supplies also exist, so check before plugging in. Most sockets are triple round-pin (accepting European-size double round-pin plugs). British, Irish and Australasian plugs will need an adaptor, preferably universal; American and Canadian appliances will need a transformer too, unless multi-voltage. Power cuts and voltage variations are very common; voltage stabilizers should be used to run sensitive appliances such as laptops.

Gay and lesbian travellers

Homosexuality is not generally open or accepted in India, but in a landmark decision in July 2009, the High Court declared unconstitutional the Victorian ban on gay sex between consenting adults, as a result of which it is now legal. Prejudice is still ingrained however, especially in conservative areas such as Rajasthan.

For **lesbians**, making contacts is difficult; even the Indian women's movement does not readily promote lesbianism as an issue that needs confronting. The only public faces of a hidden scene are the organizations in Delhi listed on opposite. For **gay men**, homosexuality is no longer solely the preserve of the alternative scene of actors and artists, and is increasingly accepted by the upper classes, but Mumbai remains much more a centre for gay life than Delhi, let alone traditionalist Rajasthan. Following the High Court ruling however, there are now gay nights in several Delhi clubs, and *Time Out Delhi* has a section on gay and lesbian events.

One group of people you may come across are **hijras**, who look like transvestites and are accepted as a transitional "third sex" between male and female. Pukka hijras are born with genitals that are neither fully male nor female, but some are eunuchs, who undergo castration to become hijras because they are transsexuals (physically male but psychologically female). They live in their own "families" and have a niche in Indian society, but not an easy one. At weddings, their presence is supposed to bring good luck, and they are usually given baksheesh for putting in a brief appearance. Generally, however, they have a low social status, face widespread discrimination, and many make a living by begging or prostitution.

Gay and lesbian contacts and resources

You will need to contact the following places in advance for information as most addresses are PO boxes:

Campaign for Lesbian Rights (CALERI)/Shakhi PO Box 3526, Lajpat Nagar, New Delhi 110065 Ⓔ caleri@hotmail.com. Collective working for lesbian rights.

Gay Delhi Weekly social meetings and other events for gay men in Delhi; for information send a blank e-mail to Ⓔ gaydelhi-subscribe@yahoo.groups.com.

Humsafar Trust Ⓦ www.humsafar.org. Set up to promote safe sex among gay men, but the website has lots of links and up-to-date information.

Indian Dost Ⓦ www.indiandost.com/delhigay.php. The Delhi page of a website for gay men in India.

International Gay and Lesbian Human Rights Commission Ⓦ www.iglhrc.org. Latest news on the human rights situation for gay people worldwide, including regular bulletins on India.

Purple Dragon Lobby of the Tarntawan Place Hotel, 119/5-10 Suriwong Road, Bangkok 10500, Thailand Ⓣ +662/238-3227, Ⓦ www.purpledrag.com.

Thai-based gay-friendly tour operator covering India with tours of Delhi and the "Golden Triangle", and add-ons including Ranthambore and Udaipur.

Sangini PO Box 7532, Vasant Kunj, New Delhi 110070, Ⓦwww.sanginii.org. Lesbian information, support and contacts. Helpline Tues noon–3pm and Fri 6–8pm on Ⓣ011/5567 6450.

Timeless India 215–217 Somdutt Chamber-II, 9 Bhikaji Cama Place, New Delhi 110066 Ⓣ011/2617 4205 or 6, Ⓦwww.timelessexcursions.com. Tour operator offering a gay-oriented tour of Rajasthan, staying in gay-friendly heritage hotels.

Insurance

It's imperative that you take out proper **travel insurance** before setting off for India. In addition to covering medical expenses and emergency flights, travel insurance also insures your money and belongings against loss or theft. Before paying for a new policy, however, it's worth checking whether you are already covered: some all-risks home insurance policies may cover your possessions when overseas, and many private medical schemes include cover when abroad. In Canada, provincial health plans usually provide partial medical cover for mishaps overseas, while holders of official student/teacher/youth cards in Canada and the US are entitled to meagre accident coverage and hospital in-patient benefits. Students will often find that their student health coverage extends during the vacations and for one term beyond the date of last enrolment.

After exhausting the possibilities above, you might want to contact a specialist travel insurance company, or consider the travel insurance deal offered by Rough Guides (see box below). A typical travel insurance policy usually provides cover for the loss of baggage, tickets and – up to a certain limit – cash or cheques, as well as cancellation or curtailment of your journey. Most of them exclude so-called dangerous sports unless an extra premium is paid: in India this can mean scuba diving, whitewater rafting, windsurfing and trekking with ropes, though probably not jeep safaris. Many policies can be chopped and changed to exclude coverage you don't need – for example, sickness and accident benefits can often be excluded or included at will. If you do take medical coverage, ascertain whether benefits will be paid as treatment proceeds or only after return home, and whether there is a 24-hour medical emergency number. When securing baggage cover, make sure that the per-article limit – typically under £500 – will cover your most valuable possession. If you need to make a claim, you should keep receipts for medicines and medical treatment, and in the event you have anything stolen, you must obtain an official statement from the police.

Internet

All large cities and tourist towns now have at least a few (usually dozens) of places where you can get online, either at cyber cafés or your hotel or guesthouse. Prices typically range from around Rs20 to Rs60/hr. Unfortunately, connections are still poor in many places, with antiquated computers and maddeningly slow and unreliable dial-up connections, making it difficult to load complex websites or to perform online transactions (like booking a train ticket).

Laundry

In India, no one goes to the laundry: if they don't do their own, they send it out to a *dhobi*. Wherever you are staying, there will either be an in-house *dhobi*, or one very close by to call on. The *dhobi* will take your dirty washing to a *dhobi ghat*, a public clothes-washing area (the bank of a river for example), where it is shown some old-fashioned discipline: separated, soaped and given a damn good thrashing to beat the dirt out of it. Then it is hung out to dry in the sun and, once dried, taken to the ironing sheds where every garment is endowed with razor-sharp creases and then matched to its rightful owner by hidden cryptic markings. Your clothes will come back from the *dhobi* absolutely spotless, though this kind of violent treatment does take it out of them: buttons get lost and eventually the cloth starts to fray. If you'd rather not entrust your Savile Row made-to-measure to their tender mercies, there are dry-cleaners in large towns.

Living in India

It is illegal for a foreign tourist to work in India, and there's no shortage of English teachers, but you may consider doing some voluntary charitable work. Several charities welcome volunteers on a medium-term commitment, say over two months. People visiting India on business or with employment arranged in advance may apply for a business visa, and non-resident Indians are entitled to stay for up to five years.

If you want to spend your time working as a volunteer for an **NGO (Non-Governmental Organization)**, you should make arrangements well before you arrive by contacting the body in question, rather than on spec. Special visas are generally not required unless you intend to work for longer than six months. For information about which NGOs are operating across the country, log on to ⓦwww.indianngos.com and select options from a drop-down list.

Animal Aid 6900 37th Ave SW, Seattle, WA 98126, US; Badi Village, Across from T.B. Hospital. Main Road, Udaipur 313004, Rajasthan ⓣ0294/251 3359; ⓦwww.animalaidunlimited.com. Animal welfare group working to alleviate animal suffering in Udaipur, Rajasthan (see p.224). No special skills are required, though volunteers with veterinary knowledge are especially welcome.

Children Walking Tall, "The Mango House", House 148/3, near Vrundavan Hospital, Karaswada, Mapusa. Bardez, Goa 403526 ⓣ09822124 802, ⓦwww.childrenwalkingtall.com. A British-run operation that works with slum children in north Goa. Volunteers are needed to distribute clothes and fruit, sort through donations, teach or organize fundraising events.

Concern India Foundation A-52, 1st Floor, Amar Colony, Lajpat Nagar-IV, New Delhi 110024 ⓣ011/2622 4482 or 3, ⓦwww.concernindia.org. Charitable trust supporting grassroots NGOs working with disadvantaged people.

Darjeeling Children's Trust Rewang House, Dr. Zakir Hussein Rd, Darjeeling ⓣ09474 030016; ⓦwww.darjeelingchildrenstrust.com. Retired Major Pasang Wangdi helps run the UK-based charity, supporting eight primary schools, all within walking distance of the Chowrasta. Volunteers who are willing to give a week or more of their time are welcome.

DISHA Foundation Disha Path, near JDA Park, Nirman Nagar-C, Jaipur 302019, Rajasthan ⓣ0141/239 3319, ⓦwww.dishafoundation.org. Resource centre for children with cerebral palsy. Needs donations, sponsors, and volunteers with time or specific skills.

Friends of Shekhewati C/o Apani Dhani, Nawalgarh 333042, Rajasthan ⓣ01594/222 239, ⓦwww.apanidhani.com/friend. Conservation group aiming to save Shekhewati's art heritage; needs writers, photographers, architects and architecture students to volunteer their services.

Goa Animal Welfare Trust (GAWT) Old Police Station, Bansai, Cacora-Curchorem, Salcete, Goa 403706 ⓣ0832/265 3677, ⓦwww.gawt.org. GAWT does sterling work with stray and mistreated animals, and welcome volunteers in the respective centres around Goa.

Mandore Medical and Relief Society 10-D Near Government Bus Stand, Paota, Jodhpur 342006, Rajasthan ⓣ0291/254 5210, ⓦwww.mandore.com. Takes on volunteers for periods as short as a week to work in health awareness and education projects in rural areas around Jodhpur.

Salaam Baalak Trust 2nd Floor, DDA Community Centre, Gali Chandiwali, Paharganj, Delhi 110055 ⓣ011/2358 4164, ⓦwww.salaambaalaktrust.com. Charity working to help street children in Delhi's Paharganj (see p.106). Their website has an application form for volunteers.

Sambhali Trust *Durg Niwas Guesthouse*, 1 Old Public Park, Raika Bagh, Jodhpur 342001, Rajasthan ⓣ0291/251 2385, ⓦwww.sambhali-trust.org. Locally based NGO dedicated to providing education, training and empowerment to girls and women from underprivileged backgrounds in rural Rajasthan.

Seva Mandir Old Fatehpura, Udaipur 313004, Rajasthan ⓣ0294/245 1041, ⓦwww.sevamandir.org. NGO working in "tribal" villages in the Udaipur district; takes interns to help with development projects.

SOS Children's Villages of India A-7 Nizamuddin (West), New Delhi 110013 ⓣ011/2435 7299, ⓦwww.soscvindia.org. SOS has projects in different parts of India, including Delhi and Rajasthan, giving shelter to distressed children by providing a healthy environment and education including vocational training.

Left luggage

Most stations in India have "cloakrooms" (sometimes called parcel offices) for passengers to leave their baggage. These can be extremely handy if you want to go sightseeing in a town and move on the same day. In theory, you need a train ticket or Indrail pass to deposit luggage, but staff don't always ask; they may, however, refuse to take your bag if you can't lock it. Losing your reclaim ticket causes problems; the clerk will be assumed to have stolen the bag if he can't produce it, so there'll be untold running around to obtain clearance before you can get your bag without it. Make sure, when checking baggage in, that the cloakroom will be open when you need to pick it up. The standard charge is currently Rs10 per 24 hours.

Mail

Mail can take anything from six days to three weeks to get to or from India, depending on where you are and the country you are mailing to; ten days is about the norm. Most **post offices** are open Monday to Friday from 10am to 5pm and Saturday from 10am to noon, but town GPOs keep longer hours (usually Mon–Sat 9.30am–1pm & 2–5.30pm). **Stamps** are not expensive, but you'll have to stick them on yourself as they tend not to be self-adhesive (every post office keeps a pot of evil-smelling glue for this purpose). Aerogrammes and postcards cost the same to anywhere in the world. Ideally, you should also have mail franked in front of you

Sending a parcel from India can be a performance. First take it to a tailor to have it wrapped in cheap cotton cloth, stitched up and sealed with wax. Next, take it to the post office, fill in and attach the relevant customs forms, buy your stamps, see them franked and dispatch it. Surface mail is incredibly cheap, and takes an average of six months to arrive – it may take half, or four times that, however. It's a good way to dump excess baggage and souvenirs, but don't send anything fragile this way.

Maps

Getting good maps of India, in India, can be difficult. The government – in an archaic suspicion of cartography, and in spite of full, clear coverage of the country on Google – forbids the sale of detailed maps of border areas, which includes the entire coastline.

It therefore makes sense to bring a **full country map** of India with you. Rough Guides, in conjunction with the World Mapping Project, publishes one of the clearest and most up to date, as well as a regional map of South India (1:1,200,000) printed on untearable, water-resistant plastic paper and road-tested by the authors of this book. Nelles also covers parts of the country with 1:1,500,000 regional maps. These are generally excellent, but cost a fortune if you buy the complete set. Their double-sided map of the Himalayas is useful for roads and planning and has some detail but is not sufficient as a trekking map. TTK, a Chennai-based company, publishes basic state maps which are widely available in India, and in some specialized travel and map shops in the UK such as Stanfords; these are poorly drawn but useful for road distances. The Indian Railways map at the back of the publication *Trains at a Glance* (see p.40) is useful for planning railway journeys.

If you need larger-scale **city maps** than the ones we provide in this book – which are keyed to show recommended hotels and restaurants – you can sometimes get them from tourist offices, though the plans published free online at Google Maps are vastly superior (simply print them off at an internet café or before you leave home). Eicher has a series of glossy, A–Z-style books (Delhi, Mumbai, Kolkata, Chennai and

Bengaluru {Bangalore} only), produced in India and available at all good bookstores.

As for **trekking maps**, the US Army Map Service produced maps in the 1960s which, with a scale of 1:250,000, remain sufficiently accurate on topography, but are of course outdated on the latest road developments. Most other maps you can buy are based on these, and they're still the best available for most of the Himalayan regions. Leomann Maps (1:200,000) also cover the northwest Himalayan regions. These are not contour maps and are therefore better for planning and basic reference than for trekking. The Survey of India publishes a rather poor 1:250,000 series for trekkers in the Uttarakhand Himalayas – simplified versions of their own infinitely more reliable maps, produced for the military, which are absolutely impossible for an outsider to get hold of.

Money

India's unit of currency is the **rupee**, usually abbreviated "Rs" and divided into a hundred paise. Almost all money is paper, with notes of 5, 10, 20, 50, 100, 500 and 1000 rupees. Coins in circulation are 1, 2 and 5 rupees, and occasionally you'll see a 25 or 50 paise piece, though these are being phased out. Note that it's technically illegal to take rupees in or out of India (although they are widely available at overseas forexes), so you might want to wait until you arrive before changing money.

Banknotes, especially lower denominations, can get into a terrible state. Don't accept torn banknotes, since no one else will be prepared to take them and you'll be left saddled with the things, though you can change them at the Reserve Bank of India and large branches of other big banks. Don't pass them on to beggars; they can't use them either, so it amounts to an insult.

Large denominations can also be a problem, as change is usually in short supply. Many Indian people cannot afford to keep much lying around, and you shouldn't necessarily expect shopkeepers or rickshaw-wallahs to have it (and they may – as may you – try to hold onto it if they do). Paying for your groceries with a Rs100 note will probably entail waiting for the grocer's errand boy to go off on a quest to try and change it. Larger notes – like the Rs500 note – are good for travelling with and can be changed for smaller denominations at hotels and other suitable establishments. A word of warning – the Rs500 note looks remarkably similar to the Rs100 note.

At the time of writing, the **exchange rate** was approximately Rs67 to £1, or Rs45 to $1, and Rs60 to €1. You can check latest exchange rates online at ⓦwww.xe.com.

ATMs, cards and travellers' cheques

The easiest way to access your money in India is with **plastic**, though it's a good idea to also have some back-up in the form of cash or travellers' cheques. You will find **ATMs** at main banks in all major towns and cities, though your card issuer may well add a foreign transaction fee, and the Indian bank will also levy a small charge, generally around Rs25.

Your card issuer, and sometimes the ATM itself, imposes limits on the amount you may withdraw in a day – typically Rs10,000–20,000. Note, too, that the first time you try to take money out after arriving in India your request may be refused – a standard security procedure aimed at preventing fraud. Telephone your bank or credit card's 24 hour line for the block to be removed – or better still telephone your bank before you leave home to warn them.

Credit cards are accepted for payment at major hotels, top restaurants, some shops and airline offices, but virtually nowhere else. American Express, MasterCard and Visa are the likeliest to be accepted. Beware of people making extra copies of the receipt, in order to fraudulently bill you later; always insist that the transaction is made before your eyes.

One big downside of relying on plastic as your main access to cash, of course, is that cards can easily get lost or stolen, so take along a couple of alternatives if you can, keep an emergency stash of cash just in case, and make a note of your home bank's telephone number and website addresses for emergencies.

US dollars are the easiest **currency** to convert, with euros and pounds sterling not far behind. Major hard currencies can be changed easily in tourist areas and big cities, less so elsewhere. If you enter the country with more than US$10,000 or the equivalent, you are supposed to fill in a currency declaration form.

In addition to cash and plastic (or as a generally less convenient alternative to the latter), consider carrying some **travellers' cheques**. You pay a small commission (usually one percent) to buy these with cash in the same currency, a little more to convert from a different currency, but they have the advantage over cash that, if lost or stolen, they can be replaced. Not all banks, however, accept them. Well-known brands such as Thomas Cook and American Express are your best bet, but in some places even American Express is only accepted in US dollars and not as pounds sterling. Visa and American Express offer **pre-paid cards** that you can load up with credit before you leave home and use in ATMs like a debit card – effectively travellers' cheques in plastic form.

Changing money

Changing money in regular **banks**, especially government-run banks such as the State Bank of India (SBI), can be a time-consuming business, involving lots of form-filling and queuing at different counters, so it's best to change substantial amounts at any one time. You'll have no such problems, however, with **private companies** such as Thomas Cook or American Express. Major cities and main tourist centres usually have several **licensed currency exchange bureaux**; rates usually aren't as good as at a bank, but transactions are generally a lot quicker and there's less paperwork to complete.

Outside **banking hours** (Mon–Fri 10am–2/4pm, Sat 10am–noon), large hotels may change money, probably at a lower rate, and exchange bureaux have longer opening hours. Banks at Mumbai and Chennai airports stay open 24 hours, but neither is very conveniently located.

Wherever you change money, hold on to **exchange receipts** ("encashment certificates"); they will be required if you want to change back any excess rupees when you leave the country, and to buy air tickets and reserve train berths with rupees at special counters for foreigners. The State Bank of India now charges for tax clearance forms.

Opening hours

Standard shop opening hours in India are Monday to Saturday 9.30am to 6pm. Most big stores, at any rate, keep those hours, while smaller shops vary from town to town, religion to religion, and one to another, but usually keep longer hours. Government tourist offices are open Monday to Friday 9.30am to 5pm, Saturday 9.30am to 1pm, closed on the third Saturday of the month, and occasionally also the second Saturday of the month; state-run tourist offices are likely to be open Monday to Friday 10am to 5pm.

Phones

Since the cellphone revolution, privately run phone **international direct-dialling** facilities – **STD/ISD** (Standard Trunk Dialling/International Subscriber Dialling) places – have become a rarity in India – too few in number, in fact, to be relied upon. In addition, calling from them will cost more than dialling from a mobile if you have an Indian SIM card. Visitors therefore nearly all bring their own phones these days, and buy an Indian SIM to cover their trip. This is quick and cheap to do – though in the wake of the 2008 Mumbai terror attacks the government has threatened to clamp down on foreigners using them, which may well make the application process more complicated.

SIM cards are sold through most cellphone shops and network outlets. At the time of writing you merely had to take along a photocopy of your passport (photo and visa pages), fill in a form and pay a connection fee ranging from Rs25–250, depending on the dealer and network.

Coverage varies from state to state, but the largest national network providers are best – Vodaphone, Airtel and Idea. Once your retailer has unlocked your phone, you pay for an initial charge card, which can be topped up ("re-charged" as it's known); denominations range from Rs10–1000, though only by paying certain figures (for example Rs222 with Vodaphone) will you get the full amount in credits. Call charges to the UK and US from most Indian networks cost Rs2–3 per minute. Also, get your card supplier to turn on the "do not disturb" option, or you'll be plagued with spam calls and spam texts from the phone company.

Indian mobile numbers are ten-digit, starting with an 8 or (more common) a 9. However, if you are calling from outside the state where the mobile is based (but not from abroad), you need to add a zero in front of that.

Calling an Indian mobile from a UK or US landline, you can save a lot of money by dialling via a company such as Ratebuster (Ⓦwww.ratebuster.co.uk) or Best Minutes (Ⓦwww.bestminutes.co.uk). No sign-up is required; just check the firms' websites for their access number for India, wait for a connection, then key in the Indian number you want to reach.

Photography

Beware of pointing your camera at anything that might be considered "strategic", including airports and anything military, but even at bridges, railway stations and main roads. Remember too that some people prefer not to be photographed, so it's a good idea to ask before you take a snapshot of them. More likely, you'll get people, especially kids, volunteering to pose.

Most photo shops can now transfer **digital** images onto a CD – useful in order to free up memory space. **Camera film**, sold at average Western prices, is widely available in India (but check the date on the box, and note that false boxes containing outdated film are often sold). It's fairly easy to get films developed, though they don't always come out as well as they might at home. If you're after **slide film**, buy it in the big cities, and don't expect to find specialist brands.

Sexism and women's issues

India is not a country that provides huge obstacles to women travellers. In the days of the Raj, upper-class eccentrics started a tradition of lone women travellers, taken up enthusiastically by the flower children of the hippy era. Plenty of women keep up the tradition today, but few get through their trip without any hassle, and it's good to prepare yourself to be a little bit thick-skinned.

Indian streets are almost without exception male-dominated – something that may take a bit of getting used to, particularly if you find yourself subjected to incessant staring, whistling and name calling. This can usually be stopped by ignoring the gaze and quickly moving on, or by firmly telling the offender to stop looking at you. Most of your fellow travellers on trains and buses will be men, who may start up most unwelcome conversations about sex, divorce and the freedom of relationships in the West. These cannot often be avoided, but demonstrating too much enthusiasm to discuss such topics can lure men into thinking that you are easy about sex, and the situation could become threatening. At its worst in larger cities, all this can become very tiring. You can get round it to a certain extent by joining women in public places, and you'll notice an immense difference if you join up with a male travelling companion. In this case, expect Indian men to approach him (assumed, of course, to be your husband – an assumption it is sometimes advantageous to go along with) and talk to him about you quite happily as if you were not there. Beware, however, if you are (or look) Indian with a non-Indian male companion: this may well cause you harassment, as you might be seen to have brought shame on your family by adopting the loose morals of the West.

In addition to staring and suggestive comments and looks, **sexual harassment**, or "Eve teasing" as it is bizarrely known, is likely to be a nuisance, but not generally a threat. Expect to get groped in crowds, and to have men "accidentally" squeeze past you at any opportunity. It tends to be worse in cities than in small towns and villages, but anywhere being followed can be a real problem.

In time you'll learn to gauge a situation – sometimes wandering around on your own may attract so much unwanted attention that you may prefer to stay in one place until you've recharged your batteries or your male fan club has moved on. It's always best to dress modestly – a *salwar kameez* is perfect, as is any baggy clothing – and refrain from smoking or drinking in public, which only reinforces prejudices that Western women are "loose" and "easy".

Returning an unwanted touch with a punch or slap is perfectly in order (Indian women often become aggressive when offended), and does serve to vent a little frustration. It should also attract attention and urge someone to help you, or at least deal with the offending man – a man transgressing social norms is always out of line, and any passer-by will want to let him know it. If you feel someone getting too close in a crowd or on a bus, brandishing your left shoe in his face can be very effective.

Going to watch a Bollywood movie at the cinema is a fun and essential part of your trip to India but, at cheap cinemas especially, such an occasion is rarely without hassle. If you do go to the cinema, it's best to go to an upmarket theatre, or at least to go with a group of people and sit in the balcony area, where it's a bit more expensive but the crowd is much more sedate.

Violent sexual assaults on tourists are extremely rare, but the number of reported cases of rape is rising, and you should always take precautions: avoid quiet, dimly lit streets and alleys at night; if you find a trustworthy rickshaw/taxi driver in the day keep him for the night journey; and try to get someone to accompany you to your hotel whenever possible. While Indian women are still quite timid about reporting rape – it is considered as much a disgrace to the victim as to the perpetrator – Western victims should always report it to the police, and before leaving the area try to let other tourists, or locals, know, in the hope that pressure from the community may uncover the offender and see him brought to justice.

The **practicalities of travel** take on a new dimension for lone women travellers. Often you can turn your gender to your advantage. For example, on intercity buses the driver and conductor will often take you under their wing, and there will be countless other instances of kindness wherever you travel. You'll be more welcome in some private houses than a group of Western males, and may find yourself learning the finer points of Indian cooking round the family's clay stove. Women frequently get preference at bus and railway stations where they can join a separate "ladies' queue", and use ladies' waiting rooms. On overnight trains the enclosed ladies' compartments are peaceful havens (unless filled with noisy children); you could also try to share a berth section with a family where you are usually drawn into the security of the group and are less exposed to lusty gazes. In hotels watch out for "peep-holes" in your door (and in the common bathrooms), be sure to cover your window when changing and when sleeping.

Lastly, bring your own supply of **tampons**, which are not widely available outside main cities.

Time

India is all in one time zone: GMT+5hr 30min. This makes it 5hr 30min ahead of London, 10hr 30min ahead of New York, 13hr 30min ahead of LA, 4hr 30min behind Sydney and 6hr 30min behind NZ; however, summertime in those places will change the difference by an hour. Indian time is referred to as IST (Indian Standard Time, which cynics refer to as "Indian stretchable time").

Tipping and baksheesh

As a well-off visitor you'll be expected to be liberal with your **tips**. Low-paid workers in hotels and restaurants often accept lower pay than they should in the expectation of generous tips during the tourist season. **Ten percent** should be regarded as acceptable if you've received good service – more if the staff have really gone out of their way to be helpful. Taxi and auto-rickshaw wallahs will not expect tips unless you've made unplanned diversions or stops. What to **tip your driver** at the end of long tours, however, is a trickier issue, especially if you've been forking out Rs150–200 for their daily allowance, as well as paying for meals. The simple answer is to give what you think they deserve, and what you can afford. Drivers working for tour operators, even more than hotel staff and waiters, depend on tips to get through the off-season (many are paid only Rs200–300 per day because their bosses know that foreign customers tend to tip well).

Alms giving (baksheesh) is common throughout India; people with disabilities and mutilations often congregate in city centres and popular resorts, where they survive from begging. In such cases Rs5–10 should be sufficient. Kids demanding money, pens, sweets or the like are a different case: yielding to any request only encourages them to pester others.

Toilets

Western toilets are becoming much more common in India now, though you'll probably still come across a few traditional "squat" toilets – basically a hole in the ground. Paper, if used, often goes in a bucket next to the loo rather than down it. Instead, Indians use a jug of water and their left hand, a method you may also come to prefer, but if you do use paper, keep some handy. Some guesthouses and hotels do supply it, but don't count on it, and it's a good idea to stock up before going too far off the beaten track as it's not available everywhere. Travelling is especially difficult for women as facilities are limited or non-existent, especially when travelling by road rather than by rail. However, toilets in the a/c carriages of trains are usually kept clean, as are those in mid-range and a/c restaurants. In the touristy areas, most hotels offer Western-style loos, even in budget lodges. The latest development is tourist toilets at every major historical site. For Rs5 you get water, mirrors, toilet paper and a clean sit-down loo.

Tourist information

The main tourist website for India is Ⓦwww.incredibleindia.org. The Indian government also maintains a number of **tourist offices abroad**, whose staff are usually helpful and knowledgeable. Other sources of information include the websites of Indian embassies and tourist offices, travel agents (who are in business for themselves, so their advice may not always be totally unbiased), and Indian Railways representatives abroad see p.42.

Inside India, both national and local governments run tourist information offices, providing general travel advice and handing out an array of printed material, from city maps to glossy leaflets on specific destinations. The Indian government's tourist department, whose main offices are on Janpath in New Delhi and opposite Churchgate railway station in Mumbai (see p.95 & p.596), has branches in most regional capitals. These, however, operate independently of the state government information counters and their commercial bureaux run by the state tourism development corporations, usually referred to by their initials (e.g. MPTDC in Madhya Pradesh, RTDC in Rajasthan, and so on), which offer a wide range of travel facilities, including guided tours, car rental and their own hotels. A list of state tourist office websites is given on pp.128–129.

Just to confuse things further, the Indian government's tourist office has a corporate wing too. The Indian Tourism Development Corporation (ITDC) is responsible for the *Ashok* chain of hotels and operates tour and travel services, frequently competing with its state counterparts.

There's all sorts of information available about India **online** – we've listed the best websites in relevant places throughout the book. One particularly good general site is Ⓦwww.indiamike.com, a popular travel forum run out of a bedroom in New Jersey by inveterate India-phile Mike Szewczyk and featuring lively chat rooms, bulletin boards, photo archives and banks of members' travel articles.

India Tourism offices overseas

Australia Glasshouse Shopping Complex, 135 King St, Sydney NSW 2000 Ⓣ02/9555, Ⓔinfo@indiatourism.com.au.
Canada 60 Bloor St (West), Suite 1003, Toronto, ON M4W 3B8 Ⓣ1-416/962-3787 or 8, Ⓔinfo@indiatourismcanada.ca.
South Africa PO Box 412542, Craighall 2024, Hyde Lane, Lancaster Gate, Johannesburg 2000 Ⓣ011/325 0880, Ⓔgoito@global.co.za.
UK 7 Cork St, London W1S 3LH Ⓣ020/7437 3677, Ⓔlondon5@indiatouristoffice.org.
US 1270 Ave of Americas, Suite 1808 (18th floor), New York, NY 10020 Ⓣ1-212/586-4901, Ⓔny@itonyc.com; 3550 Wilshire Blvd, Suite 204, Los Angeles, CA 90010-2485 Ⓣ1-213/380-8855, Ⓔindiatourismla@aol.com.

Travel advice

Australian Department of Foreign Affairs Ⓦwww.smartraveller.gov.au.
British Foreign & Commonwealth Office Ⓦwww.fco.gov.uk.
Canadian Department of Foreign Affairs Ⓦwww.voyage.gc.ca.
Irish Department of Foreign Affairs Ⓦwww.foreignaffairs.gov.ie.

New Zealand Ministry of Foreign Affairs Ⓦwww.safetravel.govt.nz.
South African Department of Foreign Affairs Ⓦwww.dfa.gov.za
US State Department Ⓦwww.travel.state.gov.

Travellers with disabilities

Disability is common in India; many conditions that would be curable in the West, such as cataracts, are permanent disabilities here because people can't afford the treatment. Those with disabilities are unlikely to receive the best treatment available, and the choice is usually between staying at home to be looked after by your family, and going out on the street to beg for alms.

For the **traveller with a disability**, this has its advantages and disadvantages: disability doesn't get the same embarrassed reaction from Indian people that it does from some able-bodied Westerners. On the other hand, you'll be lucky to see a state-of-the-art wheelchair or a disabled loo, and the streets are full of all sorts of obstacles that would be hard for a blind or wheelchair-bound tourist to negotiate independently. Kerbs are often high, pavements uneven and littered, and ramps non-existent. There are potholes all over the place and open sewers. Some of the more expensive hotels have ramps for the movement of luggage and equipment, but if that makes them accessible to wheelchairs, it is by accident rather than design. Nonetheless, the 1995 Persons with Disabilities Act specifies access for all to public buildings, and is sometimes enforced. A visit to Delhi by the wheelchair-bound astro-physicist Stephen Hawking resulted in the appearance of ramps at several Delhi tourist sights including the Red Fort, Qutub Minar and Jantar Mantar. Following a 1997 court case, most major Indian airports have also been made a lot more accessible for chair users.

If you walk with difficulty, you will find India's many street obstacles and steep stairs hard going. Another factor that can be a problem is the constant barrage of people proffering things (hard to wave aside if you are, for instance, on crutches), and all that queuing, not to mention heat, will take it out of you if you have a condition that makes you tire quickly. A light, folding camp-stool is one thing that could be invaluable if you have limited walking or standing power.

Then again, Indian people are likely to be very helpful if, for example, you need their help getting on and off buses or up stairs. Taxis and rickshaws are easily affordable and very adaptable; if you rent one for a day, the driver is certain to help you on and off, and perhaps even around the sites you visit. If you employ a guide, they may also be prepared to help you with steps and obstacles.

If complete independence is out of the question, going with an able-bodied companion might be on the cards. Contact a specialist organization for further advice on planning your trip. In Delhi, Timeless India (Ⓣ011/2617 4205 or 6, Ⓦwww.timelessexcursions.com) offers "accessible tours" for wheelchair-bound visitors. Otherwise, some package tour operators try to cater for travellers with disabilities – Bales and Somak among them – but you should always contact any operator and discuss your exact needs with them before making a booking. You should also make sure you are covered by any insurance policy you take out.

For more information about disability issues in India, check the Disability India Network website at Ⓦwww.disabilityindia.org.

Guide

1

Delhi

* **Rajpath** The centrepiece of Lutyens' imperial New Delhi, this wide boulevard epitomizes the spirit of the British Raj. See p.105
* **Paharganj Bazaars** Frenetic market and hotel district opposite the New Delhi railway station. See p.106
* **National Museum** The country's finest museum, with exhibits from over five thousand years of Indian culture. See p.106
* **Red Fort** Delhi's most famous monument, this imposing sandstone fort is a ghostly vestige of Mughal splendour. See p.108
* **Jama Masjid** Shah Jahan's great mosque, with huge minarets offering bird's-eye views over the old city. See p.110
* **Humayun's Tomb** An elegant red-brick forerunner of the Taj Mahal, whose lovely gardens offer an escape from the heat. See p.113
* **Hazrat Nizamuddin** A Sufi shrine in a deeply traditional Muslim quarter, where hypnotic *qawwali* music is performed every Thursday. See p.114
* **Qutb Minar Complex** The ruins of Delhi's first incarnation, a thirteenth-century city dominated by an impressive Victory Tower. See p.117

▲ The Jama Masjid

Delhi is the symbol of old India and new...even the stones here whisper to our ears of the ages of long ago and the air we breathe is full of the dust and fragrances of the past, as also of the fresh and piercing winds of the present.

Jawaharlal Nehru

India's capital, **DELHI** is the hub of the country, a buzzing international metropolis which draws people from across India and the globe. Home to fifteen million people, it's big, sprawling and still growing. Yet tucked away inside Delhi's modern suburbs and developments are tombs, temples and ruins dating back centuries; in some places, the remains of whole cities from the dim and distant past nestle among homes and highways built in just the last decade or two. The result is a city full of fascinating nooks and crannies that you could happily spend weeks or even months exploring.

From a tourist's perspective, Delhi is divided into two main parts. **Old Delhi** is the city of the Mughals and dates back to the seventeenth century. It's the capital's most frenetic quarter, and its most Islamic, a reminder that for over seven hundred years Delhi was a Muslim-ruled city. While many of the buildings enclosing Old Delhi's teeming bazaars have a tale to tell, its greatest monuments are undoubtedly the magnificent constructions of the Mughals, most notably the mighty **Red Fort**, and the **Jama Masjid**, India's largest and most impressive mosque.

To the south, encompassing the modern city centre, is **New Delhi**, built by the British to be the capital of their empire's key possession. A spacious city of tree-lined boulevards, New Delhi is impressive in its own way. The **Rajpath**, stretching from **India Gate** to the Presidential Palace, is at least as mighty a statement of imperial power as the Red Fort, and it's among the broad avenues of New Delhi that you'll find most of the city's museums, not to mention its prime shopping area, centred around the colonnaded facades of **Connaught Place**, the heart of downtown Delhi.

As the city expands, however – which it is doing at quite a pace – the centre of New Delhi is becoming too small to house the shops, clubs, bars and restaurants needed to cater to the affluent and growing middle class. Many businesses are moving into **South Delhi**, the vast area beyond the colonial city. Here, among the modern developments, and new business and shopping areas, is where you'll find some of Delhi's most ancient and fascinating attractions. Facing each other at either end of Lodi Road, for example, lie the constructions marking two ends of the great tradition of Mughal garden tombs: **Humayun's Tomb**, its genesis, and **Safdarjang's Tomb**, its last gasp. Here too, you'll find the remains of six cities which preceded Old Delhi, most notably the **Qutb Minar** and the rambling ruins of **Tughluqabad**.

As a place to hit India for the first time, Delhi isn't a bad choice. The city is used to foreigners: hotels in all price ranges cater specifically for foreign tourists, and you'll meet plenty of experienced fellow travellers who can give you tips and pointers. And there's certainly no shortage of things to see and do while you acclimatize yourself to the Subcontinent. Quite apart from its historical treasures, Delhi has a host of **museums** and art treasures, cultural performances and crafts that provide a showcase of the country's diverse heritage. The city's growing **nightlife** scene boasts designer bars, chic cafés and decent clubs. Its auditoriums host a wide range of national music and dance events, drawing on the richness of India's great classical traditions. Smart new cinemas screen the latest offerings from both Hollywood and Bollywood, while its theatres hold performances in Hindi and in English. And if it's from Delhi that you're flying home, you'll find that you can buy goods here from pretty much anywhere else in India, so it's a good place to stock up with souvenirs and presents.

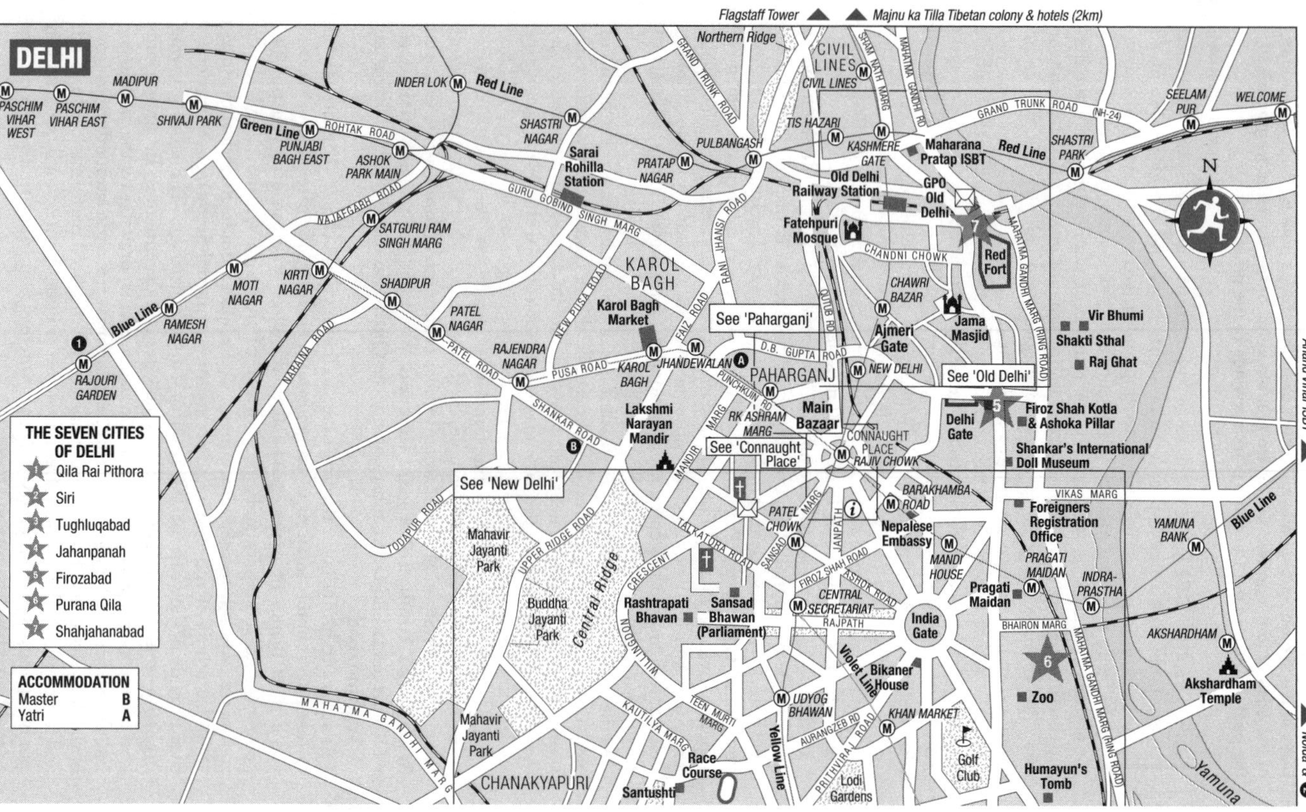
DELHI
Flagstaff Tower
Majnu ka Tilla Tibetan colony & hotels (2km)
Anand Vihar ISBT
Noida & 2
Sulabh Museum of Toilets (2km)
N
Northern Ridge
CIVIL LINES
CIVIL LINES
SHAM NATH MARG
MAHATMA GANDHI RD
GRAND TRUNK ROAD
GRAND TRUNK ROAD (NH-24)
SEELAM PUR
WELCOME
SHASTRI PARK
Red Line
Maharana Pratap ISBT
KASHMERE GATE
TIS HAZARI
PULBANGASH
PRATAP NAGAR
SHASTRI NAGAR
INDER LOK
Red Line
MADIPUR
PASCHIM VIHAR WEST
PASCHIM VIHAR EAST
SHIVAJI PARK
Green Line
ROHTAK ROAD
PUNJABI BAGH EAST
ASHOK PARK MAIN
Sarai Rohilla Station
GURU GOBIND SINGH MARG
NAJAFGARH ROAD
SATGURU RAM SINGH MARG
Old Delhi Railway Station
GPO
Old Delhi
Fatehpuri Mosque
CHANDNI CHOWK
Red Fort
MAHATMA GANDHI MARG (RING ROAD)
CHAWRI BAZAR
Jama Masjid
Vir Bhumi
Shakti Sthal
Raj Ghat
KAROL BAGH
Karol Bagh Market
RANI JHANSI ROAD
FAIZ ROAD
NEW PUSA ROAD
See 'Paharganj'
QUTUB RD
Ajmeri Gate
D.B. GUPTA ROAD
NEW DELHI
See 'Old Delhi'
MOTI NAGAR
KIRTI NAGAR
SHADIPUR
PATEL NAGAR
Blue Line
RAMESH NAGAR
RAJOURI GARDEN
1
RAJENDRA NAGAR
PATEL ROAD
PUSA ROAD
KAROL BAGH
JHANDEWALAN
A
PAHARGANJ
PUNCHKUIN RD
NARAINA ROAD
SHANKAR ROAD
B
Lakshmi Narayan Mandir
RK ASHRAM MARG
Main Bazaar
CONNAUGHT PLACE
RAJIV CHOWK
Delhi Gate
Firoz Shah Kotla & Ashoka Pillar
Shankar's International Doll Museum
See 'Connaught Place'
MANDIR MARG
See 'New Delhi'
BARAKHAMBA ROAD
VIKAS MARG
Foreigners Registration Office
YAMUNA BANK
Blue Line
PATEL CHOWK
JANPATH
Nepalese Embassy
MANDI HOUSE
PRAGATI MAIDAN
INDRA-PRASTHA
TODAPUR ROAD
UPPER RIDGE ROAD
Mahavir Jayanti Park
Central Ridge
Buddha Jayanti Park
CRESCENT
TALKATORA ROAD
SANSAD MARG
FIROZ SHAH ROAD
ASHOK ROAD
Pragati Maidan
Rashtrapati Bhavan
Sansad Bhawan (Parliament)
CENTRAL SECRETARIAT
RAJPATH
India Gate
BHAIRON MARG
AKSHARDHAM
Akshardham Temple
WILLINGDON
Violet Line
Bikaner House
Zoo
MAHATMA GANDHI MARG (RING ROAD)
TEEN MURTI MARG
KAUTILYA MARG
UDYOG BHAWAN
KHAN MARKET
Golf Club
Mahavir Jayanti Park
Race Course
Yellow Line
AURANGZEB RD
PRITHVIRAJ ROAD
Humayun's Tomb
Yamuna
CHANAKYAPURI
Santushti
Lodi Gardens
MAHATMA GANDHI MARG
THE SEVEN CITIES OF DELHI
1 Qila Rai Pithora
2 Siri
3 Tughluqabad
4 Jahanpanah
5 Firozabad
6 Purana Qila
7 Shahjahanabad
ACCOMMODATION
Master B
Yatri A

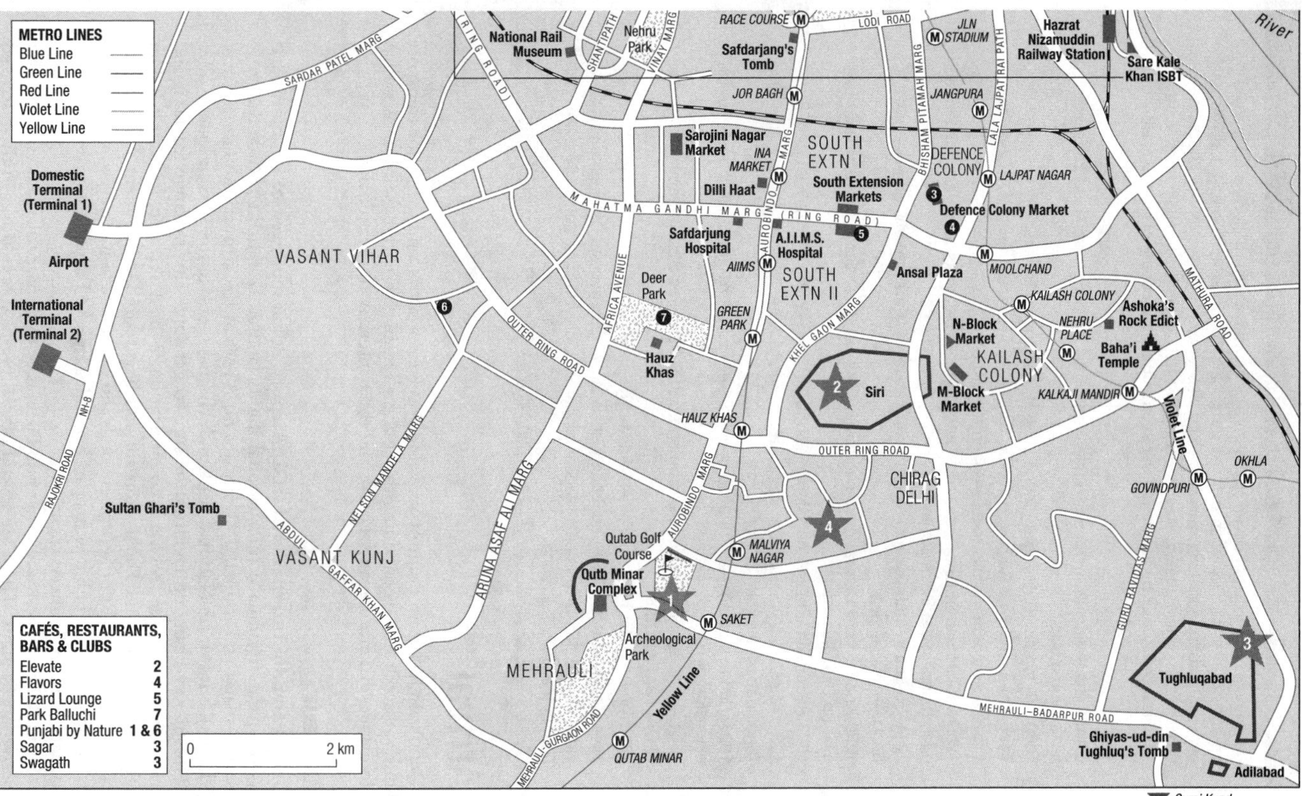
METRO LINES
Blue Line
Green Line
Red Line
Violet Line
Yellow Line
CAFÉS, RESTAURANTS, BARS & CLUBS
Elevate 2
Flavors 4
Lizard Lounge 5
Park Balluchi 7
Punjabi by Nature 1 & 6
Sagar 3
Swagath 3
0 2 km
Domestic Terminal (Terminal 1)
Airport
International Terminal (Terminal 2)
Gurgaon Funn Food Village
National Rail Museum
Nehru Park
Safdarjang's Tomb
Sarojini Nagar Market
Dilli Haat
Safdarjung Hospital
A.I.I.M.S. Hospital
South Extension Markets
Defence Colony Market
Ansal Plaza
Deer Park
Hauz Khas
Siri
N-Block Market
M-Block Market
Ashoka's Rock Edict
Baha'i Temple
Hazrat Nizamuddin Railway Station
Sare Kale Khan ISBT
River
Sultan Ghari's Tomb
Qutab Golf Course
Qutb Minar Complex
Archeological Park
Tughluqabad
Ghiyas-ud-din Tughluq's Tomb
Adilabad
Suraj Kund
VASANT VIHAR
VASANT KUNJ
MEHRAULI
SOUTH EXTN I
SOUTH EXTN II
DEFENCE COLONY
KAILASH COLONY
CHIRAG DELHI
RACE COURSE
JOR BAGH
INA MARKET
AIIMS
GREEN PARK
HAUZ KHAS
MALVIYA NAGAR
SAKET
QUTAB MINAR
JLN STADIUM
JANGPURA
LAJPAT NAGAR
MOOLCHAND
KAILASH COLONY
NEHRU PLACE
KALKAJI MANDIR
GOVINDPURI
OKHLA
Violet Line
Yellow Line
SARDAR PATEL MARG
SHANTIPATH
VINAY MARG
(RING ROAD)
LODI ROAD
BHISHAM PITAMAH MARG
LALA LAJPAT RAI PATH
MATHURA ROAD
MAHATMA GANDHI MARG (RING ROAD)
AUROBINDO MARG
AFRICA AVENUE
KHEL GAON MARG
OUTER RING ROAD
NELSON MANDELA MARG
ARUNA ASAF ALI MARG
ABDUL GAFFAR KHAN MARG
MEHRAULI-GURGAON ROAD
MEHRAULI-BADARPUR ROAD
GURU RAVIDAS MARG
NH-8
RAJOKRI ROAD

Delhi history

Delhi is said to consist of seven successive cities, with British-built New Delhi making an eighth. In truth, Delhi has centred historically on three main areas: Lal Kot and extensions to its northeast, where the city was located for most of the Middle Ages; Old Delhi, the city of the Mughals, founded by Shah Jahan in the seventeenth century; and New Delhi, built by the British just in time to be the capital of independent India.

Timeline

c.1450 BC Pandavas (heroes of the Mahabharata) have their capital at Indraprastha, near Purana Qila

1060 AD Tomars (Rajput clan) found Lal Kot, considered the first city of Delhi

1180 Chauhans (rival Rajput clan) oust Tomars and rename the city Qila Lal Pithora

1191 Qila Lal Pithora falls to the Afghan Muslim armies of Muhammad of Ghor

1206 Muhammad of Ghor's general, Qutb-ud-din Aibak, sets up as an independent ruler, founding the Delhi Sultanate

1211–36 Sultan Iltutmish makes Delhi the capital of lands stretching from Punjab to Bengal

1290 Khaljis, from Central Asia, overthrow Qutb-ud-din's "Slave Dynasty" and take over as Delhi sultans

1303 Sultan Ala-ud-Din Khalji commissions Siri, the second city of Delhi

1321 Ghiyas-ud-Din Tughluq ousts Khaljis, founds the Tughluq dynasty, and also Tughluqabad, the third city of Delhi

1326 Sultan Muhammad Tughluq founds Delhi's fourth city, Jahanpanah, as an extension of Lal Kot, joining it to Siri

1354 As the sultanate gradually disintegrates, Sultan Firoz Shah founds the fifth city of Delhi at Firozabad

1398 Timur the Lame (Tamerlaine) invades and sacks Delhi, founding Sayyid dynasty

1444 Sayyids ousted by Buhul Lodi, whose family take over as Delhi sultans

1526 First Battle of Panipat: Mughal emperor Babur defeats Sultan Ibrahim Lodi, ending the Delhi Sultanate

Arrival

Delhi is India's main point of arrival for overseas visitors, and the major transport hub for north India, containing the country's main international airport as well as four long-distance railway stations and three intercity bus terminals.

By air

Indira Gandhi International (IGI) Airport, 20km southwest of the centre, has two separate terminals: International flights land at Terminal 2, while domestic services land at Terminal 1. There are no ATMs at the airport (though this may change), but Punjab National Bank and Thomas Cook in the arrivals lounge offer 24hr money-changing facilities; be sure to get some small change for taxis and rickshaws. For those seeking accommodation, 24hr desks here, including Indian Tourism (ITDC) and Delhi Tourism and Transport Development Corporation (DTTDC), have a list of approved hotels and can secure you reservations. The two terminals are adjacent but 6km apart by road; a free AAI **shuttle** bus running every twenty minutes connects them.

From IGI the easiest way to get into Delhi is by **taxi**, particularly advisable if you arrive late at night. There are several official pre-paid taxi kiosks in the restricted

1541 Sher Shah Suri ousts Babur's son Humayun and founds the sixth city of Delhi at Purana Qila

1544 Humayun retakes Delhi but dies the following year

1565 Humayun's son Akbar shifts the Mughal capital from Delhi to Agra

1638 Akbar's grandson Shah Jahan shifts the capital back to Delhi, creating its seventh city at Shahjahanabad (Old Delhi)

1739 Persian emperor Nadir Shah sacks Delhi, slaughtering 15,000 of its inhabitants as Mughal power crumbles

1784 The Marathas (see p.1158) subdue Delhi, making the emperor their vassal

1803 In the Battle of Delhi, Britain's East India Company defeat the Marathas and take over as effective rulers

1857 In the great uprising (First War of Independence), Delhi supports the insurgents, but the British retake the city with bloody reprisals, deposing the Mughals and expelling Muslim Delhiites for two years

1911 The British decide on a new Indian capital at Delhi as opposition to colonial rule mounts in Calcutta

1931 New Delhi officially inaugurated as capital of the Raj

1947 British hand over power in Delhi to India's first elected government, but Hindu mobs drive many Muslims from the city, while Hindu and Sikh refugees flood in from Punjab and Bengal

1957 Delhi Development Authority (DDA) founded to plan the city's development

1975–77 Indira Gandhi's Emergency: forced evictions of Muslim slum-dwellers in Old Delhi

1984 Indira Gandhi's assassination, followed by sectarian riots targetting Delhi's Sikh population

1992 Delhi gains status of Capital Territory (CT), with its own government, but not full statehood; BJP take power in CT elections

1998 Congress Party wrests the CT from the BJP, holding power ever since

area outside the arrival hall; the fare will be around Rs250 to the city centre, with a 25 percent surcharge between 11pm and 5am; kiosk prices vary, so check a few first. Note that even these pre-paid taxi drivers may try to take you to hotels not of your choice (see p.94).

Alternatively there's a **bus** (Rs50; 40min), leaving every half-hour for Connaught Place, New Delhi Station (Ajmeri Gate side) and Maharana Pratap Inter-state Bus Terminal (ISBT) in Old Delhi; tickets are available from the Delhi Transport Corporation (DTC) counter in the arrival hall, and the bus travels via the domestic terminal too.

The **auto-rickshaws** that wait in line at the departure gate constitute the most precarious and least reliable form of transport from the airport, especially at night, though they're cheaper than a taxi; fares are around Rs150–180. Many hotels, including some of the Paharganj budget options, now offer **pick-up services** from the airport, where you will be met with a driver bearing your name on a placard. This presents the smoothest and most reliable method of getting to your hotel from the airport, though prices vary considerably, starting from around Rs250, but often twice as much or more.

At the time of writing, an **Airport Express Link** metro line was under construction and scheduled for completion in September 2010; when finished, it should speed travellers into central New Delhi in as little as sixteen minutes.

By train

Delhi has two major **railway stations. New Delhi station** is at the eastern end of Paharganj Main Bazaar, within easy walking distance of many of the area's budget hotels. The station has two exits: take the Paharganj exit for Connaught Place and most points south, and the Ajmeri Gate exit for Old Delhi. Cycle rickshaws ply the congested main bazaar toward Connaught Place – which is just 800m down the road – but cannot enter Connaught Place itself. Auto-rickshaws start at Rs20 for Connaught Place, or Rs40 to Old Delhi's Chandni Chowk – agree a price before getting in. **Old Delhi station**, west of the Red Fort, is also well connected to the city by taxis, auto-rickshaws and cycle-rickshaws; for autos there's a booth selling fixed-price pre-paid tickets – Connaught Place is Rs50, plus Rs5 per piece of baggage. Both stations are notorious for **theft**: don't take your eyes off your luggage for a moment. These stations are served by stops on the metro, but travelling on it with heavy

Delhi scams

Delhi can be a headache for the first-time visitor because of **scams** to entrap the unwary – one dodge is to dump dung onto visitors' shoes, then charge to clean it off. The most common wheeze, though, is for taxi drivers or touts to convince you that the hotel you've chosen is full, closed or has just burned to the ground so as to take you to one that pays them commission. More sophisticated scammers will pretend to phone your hotel to check for yourself, or will take you to a travel agent (often claiming to be a "tourist office") who will do it, dialling for you (a different number); the "receptionist" on the line will corroborate the story, or deny all knowledge of your reservation. The driver or tout will then take you to a "very good hotel" – usually in Karol Bagh – where you'll be charged well over the odds for a night's accommodation. To **reduce the risk of being caught out**, write down your taxi's registration number (make sure the driver sees you doing it), and insist on going to your hotel with no stops en route. Heading for Paharganj, your driver may try to take you to a hotel of his choice rather than yours. To avoid this, you could ask to be dropped at New Delhi railway station and walk from there. You may even encounter fake "doormen" outside hotels who'll tell you the place is full; check at reception first, and even if the claim is true, never follow the tout to anywhere he recommends. These problems can be avoided by **reserving in advance**; many hotels will arrange for a car and driver to meet you at your point of arrival.

New Delhi railway station is the worst place for touts; assume that anyone who approaches you here – even in uniform – with offers of help, or to direct you to the foreigners' booking hall, is up to no good. Most are trying to lure travellers to the fake "official" tourist offices opposite the Paharganj entrance, where you'll end up paying way over the odds, often for unconfirmed tickets. And don't believe stories that the foreigners' booking hall has closed. On **Connaught Place** and along **Janpath**, steer clear of phoney "tourist information offices" (which touts may try to divert you to), and never do business with any travel agency which tries to disguise itself as a tourist information office. For the record, India Tourism is at 88 Janpath and the DTTDC is at N-36, Middle Circle (in a street swarming with touts and look-alike agencies).

Finally, be aware that taxi, auto and rental-car drivers get a hefty commission for taking you to certain shops, and that commission will be added to your bill should you buy anything. You can assume that auto-wallahs who accost you on the street do so with the intention of overcharging you, or of taking you to shops which pay them commission rather than straight to where you want to go. Always hail a taxi or auto-rickshaw yourself, rather than taking one whose driver approaches you, and don't let them take you to places where you haven't asked to go.

baggage is prohibited. The other long-distance stations are **Hazrat Nizamuddin station**, southeast of the centre, for trains from Agra (except the Shatabdi Express); and **Sarai Rohilla station**, west of Old Delhi station, for some services from Rajasthan. Hazrat Nizamuddin has a pre-paid auto booth; Connaught Place is Rs60 (plus Rs5/ piece of baggage), slightly less from Sarai Rohilla, but you may find that no autos will accept the slip from the pre-paid booth at Hazrat Nizamuddin unless you pay Rs20–30 extra. There are occasionally local trains to New Delhi, but they tend to be sardine-can packed, and buying a ticket can be a real scrum.

By bus

State buses pull in at the **Maharana Pratap ISBT**, north of Old Delhi railway station. Auto-rickshaws to New Delhi or Paharganj take about fifteen minutes (R60, plus Rs5/piece of baggage), cycle rickshaws take twice that (and cost around Rs40). There's a pre-paid auto-rickshaw booth at the terminal, and also a metro station (Kashmere Gate). **Private buses** from all over India pull up in the street outside New Delhi railway station; some also drop passengers in Connaught Place. Some services from Uttar Pradesh and Uttarakhand leave you at **Anand Vihar ISBT**, across the Yamuna River towards Ghaziabad in east Delhi, which also has a pre-paid auto-rickshaw booth (Rs75 to Connaught Place, plus Rs5/piece of baggage), and is served by bus #73 or #85 to Connaught Place, and by the metro (though heavy baggage is not officially allowed). Buses from Agra and some from Rajasthan may leave you at **Sarai Kale Khan ISBT** by Hazrat Nizamuddin train station (cross over by the footbridge for pre-paid autos). Buses from Jaipur, Ajmer, Jodhpur and Udaipur may drop you at **Bikaner House** near India Gate, Rs40 from Connaught Place by auto.

Information

There are reasonably helpful tourist offices at the international and domestic airports, railway stations and bus terminals, and **India Tourism** at 88 Janpath, just south of Connaught Place (Mon–Fri 9am–6pm, Sat 9am–2pm; ⓣ011/2332 0005 or 8), is a good place to pick up information on historical sites, city tours, shopping and cultural events, as well as free city maps. **DTTDC** have an office at *Coffee House*, 1 Annexe, Emporium Complex, Baba Kharak Singh Marg, opposite Hanuman Mandir (daily 7am–9pm; ⓣ011/2336 5358, ⓦwww.delhitourism.nic.in), another at N-36 Connaught Place (daily 10am–5pm; ⓣ011/4152 3073), and others in the two airport terminals. Beware of any other firms that look like or claim to be tourist offices (see opposite) – DTTDC's office in Connaught Place is almost besieged by touts trying to divert you into dishonest look-alike travel agents, of which the street is full.

Exhibitions and cultural events are listed in local **magazines** such as the weekly *Delhi Diary*, fortnightly *Delhi City* and *Time Out Delhi* and monthly *First City*, all available from bookshops and street stalls; *Delhi Diary* can sometimes be found for free at big hotels or at the GOI tourist office. **Online**, apart from the DTTDC's website, it's worth checking the Delhi pages of India for You at ⓦwww.indfy.com/delhi.html for sightseeing information (click on "Places to see in Delhi"), the Delhi city government's tourism pages at ⓦdelhigovt.nic.in/page.asp for general information, and for current listings ⓦdelhi.clickindia.com or ⓦwww.delhilive.com.

City transport

Even with the addition of a metro system, **public transport** in Delhi is still inadequate for the city's population and size, and increased car ownership is adding to the general chaos. **Cows** have been banned from much of central Delhi, but not the more traditional districts. In an effort to reduce pollution, buses, taxis and auto-rickshaws have all now been converted from petrol and diesel to run on **Compressed Natural Gas** (CNG), but most inner-city thoroughfares are still choked with exhaust fumes and congested.

The metro

The construction of Delhi's **metro system** – which opened in late 2002 – is ongoing; it's being built in several phases, with work projected to continue until at least 2021. There are three lines: red, yellow and blue, all due to be extended in the near future, with a green line and a violet line also due to open shortly. For progress updates, ask at the tourist offices (see p.95) or visit Ⓦwww.delhimetrorail.com. The minimum fare is currently Rs8, while the highest fare from the centre is Rs23. The metro is wheelchair accessible, and each station should have an ATM. Children under 90cm (3ft) tall travel free if accompanied by an adult. Photography is prohibited, as in principle is baggage weighing more than 15kg, or measuring more than 60cm x 45cm x 25cm.

Buses

With auto- and cycle rickshaws so cheap and plentiful, only hardened shoestring travellers generally use Delhi's confusing and overcrowded **buses**, but they do prove useful from time to time. It's possible to check bus routes **online** at Ⓦdelhigovt.nic.in/dtcbusroute/dtc/Find_Route/getroute.asp, though the lists of bus stops do not always use location names that will be familiar to tourists (stops in Connaught Place, for example, are listed individually as "Regal Cinema", "Super Bazaar" and so on). Fares range from Rs10–20.

Auto-rickshaws and cycle rickshaws

Auto-rickshaws are the most effective form of transport around Delhi. There are pre-paid booths in Connaught Place and some transport terminals, but in general you'll need to negotiate a price before getting in; prices for foreigners vary according to your haggling skills, but as a sample fare, it should cost about Rs50

City and regional tours

The DTTDC tourist office (see p.95), daily except Monday, organizes a/c bus tours of New Delhi (9am–1.30pm; Rs150) and Old Delhi (2.15–5.45pm; Rs150), or a full-day tour which covers both (9am–5.45pm; Rs250). All start outside the DTTDC office opposite the Hanuman Temple on Baba Kharak Singh Marg. From the same place, depending on demand, they run a "Delhi by Evening" tour (Tues–Sun; Rs150), which includes sound and light shows at the Red Fort, and an Agra day-trip (Wed, Sat & Sun; depart 7am, return 10pm; Rs950). Delhi Transport Corporation (Ⓣ011/2884 4192, Ⓦwww.dtc.nic.in) runs one-day tours for Rs100, starting from New Delhi rail station at 9.15am, Scindia House in Connaught Place (corner of Janpath) at 9.30am, or the Red Fort at 9.45am. All the five-star hotels offer their own, door-to-door packages, and many hotels in and around Paharganj, such as *Namaskar* and *Metropolis*, can arrange city tours by taxi for Rs600–800, which is good value when shared between three or four people.

from Connaught Place to Old Delhi. In Connaught Place itself, there's a pre-paid auto-rickshaw kiosk, charging certified official fares.

Cycle rickshaws are not allowed in Connaught Place and parts of New Delhi, but are handy for short journeys to outlying areas and around Paharganj. They're also nippier than motorized traffic in Old Delhi. Rates should be roughly half that demanded by autos.

Taxis

Delhi's **taxis** (white, or black and yellow) cost around fifty percent more than auto-rickshaws. Drivers belong to local taxi stands, where you can make bookings and fix prices; if you flag a taxi on the street you're letting yourself in for some hectic haggling. A surcharge of around 25 percent operates between 11pm and 5am. Alternatively, radiocab firms such as Mega Cabs (Ⓣ011/4141 4141, Ⓦwww.megacabs.com) and Quick Cabs (Ⓣ011/4533 3333, Ⓦquickcabs.in) offer a 24-hour call-a-cab service with meters, though expect to pay a bit more than usual.

Car and cycle rental

For local sightseeing and journeys beyond the city confines, **chauffeur-driven cars** are very good value, especially for groups of three to four. Many budget hotels offer cars and drivers, as does the DTTDC (for enquiries round the clock contact their transport office on Aurobindo Marg at Kidwai Nagar West, by Dilli Haat Ⓣ011/2467 4153), and the booths at the southern end of the Tibetan Market on Janpath. DTTDC rates are Rs1495 for an eight-hour day within Delhi (more in an a/c vehicle), which includes 120km mileage. Alternatively, there's Kumar Tourist Taxi Service, K-14 Connaught Place (Ⓣ011/2341 5390, Ⓦwwwkumarindiatours com). Driving yourself in Delhi can be dangerous, so is not advisable.

Cycling in the large avenues of New Delhi takes some getting used to and can be hazardous for those not used to chaotic traffic. **Bicycle rental** is surprisingly difficult to come by; try Mehta Cycles (Ⓣ011/2358 9239) at 5109–10 Main Bazaar, Paharganj, a few doors from *Kholsa Cafe*, who rent bikes for Rs60 a day.

Accommodation

Delhi has a vast range of **accommodation**, from dirt-cheap lodges to extravagant international hotels. Bookings for upmarket hotels can be made at airport and railway station tourist desks; budget travellers will have to hunt around independently. Don't believe touts, taxi drivers or auto-wallahs telling you there are no rooms at your hotel, and avoid the places they recommend in Karol Bagh (see p.94).

Connaught Place and central New Delhi

You pay a premium to stay on **Connaught Place**, so if you want value for money, stay elsewhere. To its south, grander hotels on and around **Janpath** and along **Sansad Marg** cater mainly for business travellers and tourist groups, but there are some very good ones among them. Most upmarket hotels have plush restaurants and swimming pools, and some require non-Indian residents to pay in foreign currency. Only a couple of the budget travellers' lodges that once dotted the lanes off the northern end of Janpath remain, and they're often full, so book ahead. Unless otherwise stated, the hotels listed below are marked on the Connaught Place **map** on p.98.

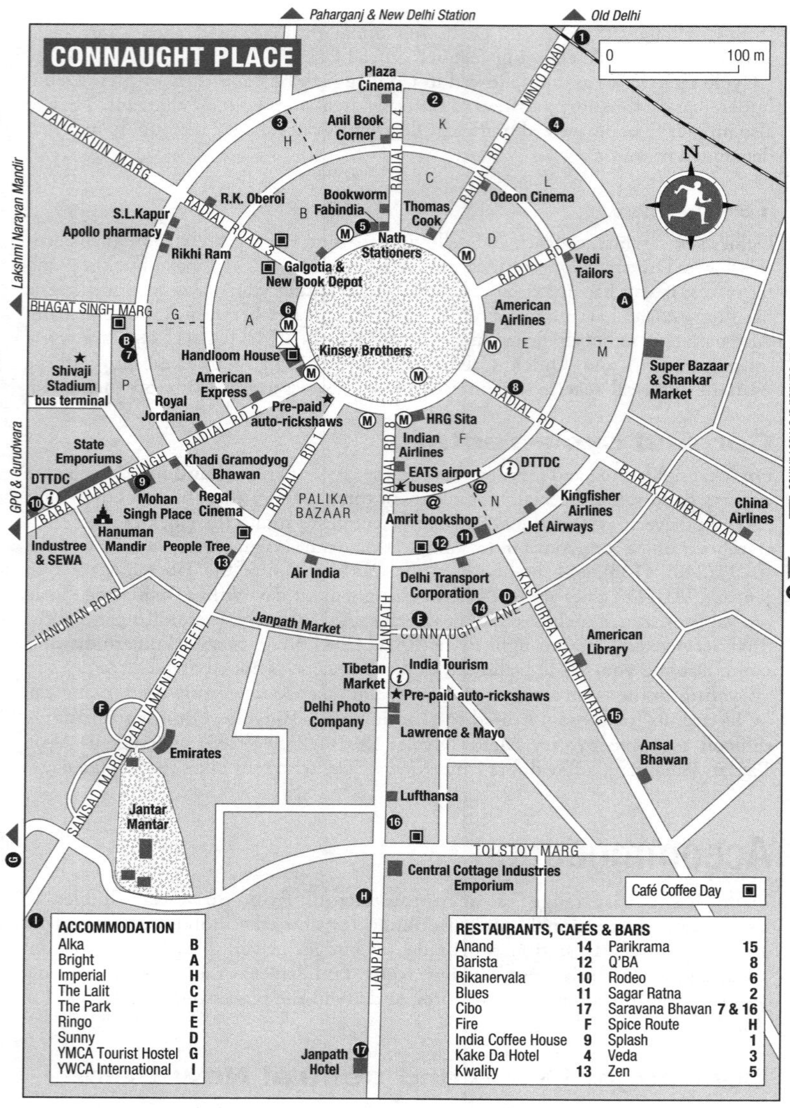

Alka P-16/90, Connaught Place ⓣ011/2334 4000, ⓦwww.hotelalka.com. "The best alternative to luxury", they reckon, but the rooms, though a/c and carpeted, are pretty poky – the cheaper ones don't even have a window, though they do try to make up for it with mirrors to create an illusion of more space. The staff, on the other hand, don't give out smiles to create an illusion of friendliness. On the plus side, there's a reasonable vegetarian restaurant, and an annexe on M-block for when the main hotel is full. ❽

Bright M-85, Connaught Place ⓣ011/4151 7766, ⓔhotelbright@hotmail.com. A mixed bag of rooms, some attached, at this city-centre hotel, which was under refurbishment when we last visited, but due to reopen in early 2010. The best room is no.11, spacious with big windows, but others are a bit on the dingy side, so try before you buy. Upstairs, *Blue* (T 011/2341 6666, E hotelbluedelhi@hotmail.com) has the benefit of a terrace and is a decent fallback option. 4–5

Imperial Janpath, Connaught Place end T 011/2334 1234, W www.theimperialindia.com. See also New Delhi map, p.104. Delhi's classiest hotel, in a beautiful 1933 Art Deco building set amid large, palm-shaded gardens. The rooms are stylish, as is the cool lobby done out in cream and gold, while corridors double up as galleries depicting fascinating eighteenth- and nineteenth-century prints of India. Staff maintain just the right degree of courteousness, and there are a number of excellent restaurants including the renowned *Spice Route* (see p.120). Doubles from US$525. 9

Le Meridien Windsor Place, Raisina Rd T 011/2371 0101, W www.lemeridien.com/newdelhi. See New Delhi map, p.104. Busy five-star with glass-walled elevators that take you up to bedrooms set around a massive atrium. The whole ensemble looks like a housing scheme in a sci-fi movie, though the rooms are spacious and comfortable within, and service is excellent. Facilities include a swimming pool, health club, choice of restaurants and bars, wheelchair access throughout, including a room adapted for wheelchair users. Rack rates start from US$374 per double. 9

Master R-500 New Rajendra Nagar T 011/2874 1089, W www.master-guesthouse.com. See Delhi map, p.90. A lovely little *pension*-style guesthouse, comfortable, secure and family-run, with four a/c double rooms of different sizes (a bathroom between each pair), free wi-fi and a secluded roof terrace. Located on the edge of the green belt only 10min by auto-rickshaw from Connaught Place (or bus #910 from Shivaji Terminal behind Block P) and not far from Karol Bagh metro. Vegetarian meals are available and rates include breakfast. Book ahead. 6

Ringo 17 Scindia House, Connaught Lane T 011/2331 0605, E ringo_guest_house@yahoo.co.in. An old backpacker favourite that's traded in its dorms for single and double rooms, which are plain but decent, some attached, and arranged around a central terrace that makes a pretty congenial little hangout. 1–2

Sunny 152 Scindia House, Connaught Lane T 011/2331 2909, E sunnyguesthouse1234@hotmail.com. Another former backpacker dorm hotel now offering cheap but rather box-like single and double rooms, some attached, with hot water at 20 minutes' notice. 1

The Lalit Off Barakhamba Rd and Tolstoy Marg, southeast of Connaught Place T 011/4444 7777, W www.thelalit.com. See also New Delhi map, p.104. Formerly the *Intercontinental*, now revamped into a stylish, modern hotel, with cool, elegant rooms and a spacious lobby decorated with some impressive works of art. When the hotel's at its busiest, doubles start from around Rs12,000, but prices are lower when business is slack. 9

The Park 15 Sansad Marg T 011/2374 3000 or 1800/117 275, W www.theparkhotels.com. See also New Delhi map, p.104. They don't come much snazzier than this place, from the super-cool lobby to the ultra-modern rooms, the decor is state-of-the-art, down to the LCD TV in each room and the frosted glass walls that screen off the en-suite bathrooms. Service is snappy, the atmosphere is relaxed, and all the facilities you'd expect are here, including a bar, a good restaurant and a pool. A cut above your run-of-the-mill five-star. Doubles from US$282. 9

YMCA Tourist Hostel Jai Singh Marg, southwest of Connaught Place T 011/2336 1915, W www.newdelhiymca.org. See also New Delhi map, p.104. A rather staid establishment popular with American budget travellers (though it isn't all that cheap), the institutional corridors belie the spacious if simple rooms, and there are good restaurants, a large swimming pool (open April–Oct only) and attractive gardens. Wheelchair friendly. Rates include breakfast and supper. 7

YWCA Blue Triangle Ashok Rd, southwest of Connaught Place T 011/2336 0133, W www.ywcaofdelhi.org. See New Delhi map, p.104. Open to men and women, rooms here are nice and big, with large attached bathrooms. The whole place is clean, quiet and respectable, with lawns outside to relax on. Rates include breakfast. 5

YWCA International 10 Sansad Marg, southwest of Connaught Place T 011/2336 1561, W www.ywcaindia.org. See also New Delhi map, p.104. Clean and airy a/c rooms with private bathrooms, though not as nice as at the *Blue Triangle* (but cheaper); set meals are available in the restaurant. Women are given priority but men can also stay. Rates include breakfast, and you get a free copy of *The Times of India* every morning. 5–8

Paharganj

Running west from New Delhi railway station, the **Paharganj** area is prime backpacker territory, with innumerable lodges offering inexpensive and mid-range accommodation. Some are extremely good value; others offer very little for very

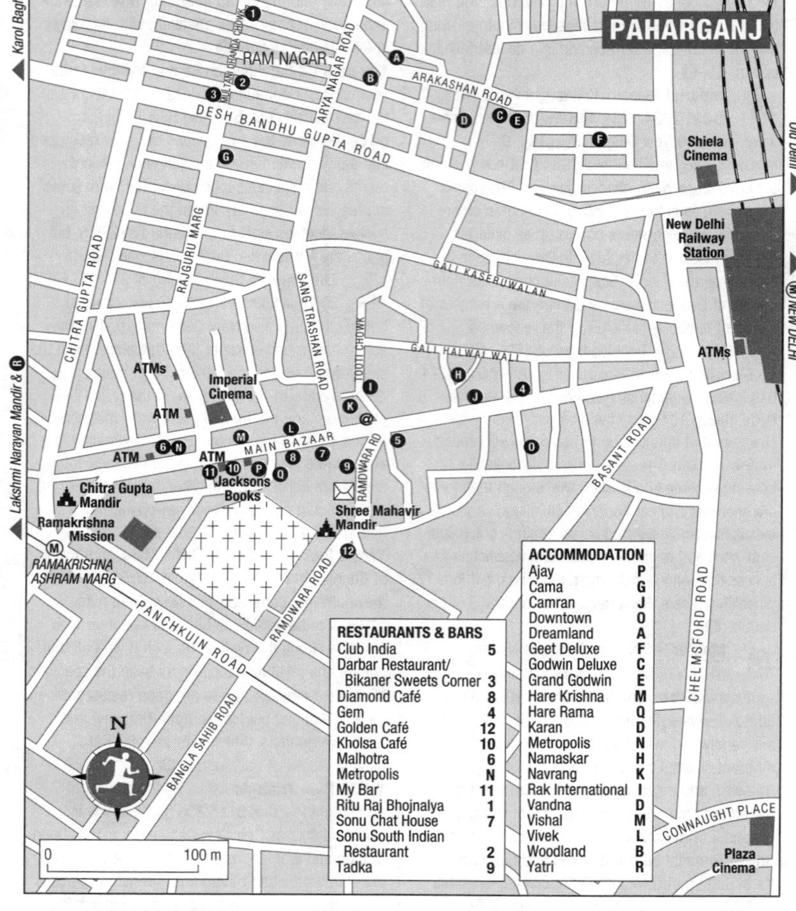

little, and most can suffer from slamming-door syndrome and people shouting till dawn (especially if windows face inwards onto the communal stairwell), so choose carefully if you value quiet. Some hotels here run a 24-hour checkout system, which means you check out at the same time you checked in – good if you arrived late, bad if you arrived early. Unless otherwise stated, the hotels listed below are marked on the Paharganj **map** above.

Ajay 5084-A Main Bazaar ⓣ011/2358 3125. Tucked away down an alley off the Main Bazaar, this well-run place with marble decor has clean rooms, some a/c, most with baths and TV, but not all with windows. There's a pool table, internet access and a 24hr bakery downstairs, next to a big café area for breakfast or snacks. 24hr checkout. ❷

Camran 1116 Main Bazaar ⓣ011/3297 4474, ⓔsubhashthakur@yahoo.com. A small run-down lodge in part of a late-Mughal period mosque, with some character and a panoramic rooftop terrace. There are very cheap box-like single rooms, of which some have attached bathrooms, but only shared bathrooms have hot water showers (otherwise it comes in a bucket). Dorm beds available (Rs100). ❷

Downtown 4583 Main Bazaar ⓣ011/4154 1529, ⓔltctravel@rediffmail.com. This friendly lodging, just off the Main Bazaar, is bright and breezy, and not bad value, but it's worth asking for a room with an outside window. There's also a dorm (Rs100). Minus points for its 11am checkout. ❶

Hare Krishna 1572–3 Main Bazaar ⓣ011/4154 1341. Rooms here are clean, the best are spacious, and most are attached. There's hot running water and a pleasant rooftop café-restaurant, but the lower floors can be pretty noisy. 24hr checkout. ❷

Hare Rama T-298 off Main Bazaar ⓣ011/3536 1301 or 2, ⓦwww.hareramaguesthouse.com. Attached rooms, reasonable cleanliness and low prices, but hard beds and iffy hot water at this busy hotel down an alley off the Main Bazaar. 24hr checkout. ❷

Metropolis 1634 Main Bazaar ⓣ011/2358 5766, ⓦwww.metropolistravels.com. Main Bazaar's most upmarket and comfortable hotel, though somewhat overpriced for what you get. A few double rooms have large windows and bathtubs; others don't have a window. All are a/c with a TV, fridge and balcony, and there's a good restaurant and bar, with seating downstairs or on the roof terrace. ❹–❺

Namaskar 917 Chandiwalan, Main Bazaar ⓣ011/2358 2233, ⓔnamaskarhotel@yahoo.com. Popular family-run budget hotel off the Main Bazaar with a variety of attached rooms, some with a/c, but not all the cheaper ones have hot showers or outside windows. The staff are very attentive and helpful, but they also run tours which they can be pushy about selling. ❶–❷

Navrang Tooti Chowk, 820 Main Bazaar ⓣ9818 243027. More like a down-at-heel lodge in a remote small town than a city hotel in the middle of Delhi, but it's very friendly, if somewhat basic. On the other hand, you get what you pay for, and at these rates it isn't bad value. Some rooms have bathrooms, but there's no hot running water (they'll bring you a bucket for Rs20). ❶

Rak International Tooti Chowk, 820 Main Bazaar ⓣ011/2356 2478, ⓦwww.hotelrakinternational.com. One of the most consistently popular Paharganj choices, in a small square off the Main Bazaar, with good value and large, cool rooms, a/c, TV, fridge and hot water. The rooftop is nice but could use a paint job. ❸

Vishal 1575–80 Main Bazaar ⓣ011/2356 2123, ⓔvishalhotel@hotmail.com. There's a choice here between rather bare, cheap rooms with outside bathroom, and much nicer large attached ones; check the sheets before you take a room. The good on-site restaurant is worth a try. ❷

Vivek 1534–50 Main Bazaar ⓣ011/4154 1436, ⓦwww.vivekhotel.com. A longstanding travellers' favourite, with a 24hr rooftop restaurant, and decent if unremarkable rooms, most with attached baths and hot water, some a/c; the best have windows facing the street. There's even room service. ❷

Yatri 3/4 Jhansi Rd, off Punchkuin Rd, by Delhi Heart and Lung Institute ⓣ011/2362 5563, ⓦwww.yatrihouse.com. See map, p.90. This guesthouse, tucked away up a small residential street ten minutes' walk from Paharganj, is like staying in a private home, with clean and quiet attached rooms, hot water, TV and a small enclosed garden for breakfast or just for relaxing, though it's a bit pricey for what you get. Book well in advance. ❼

Ram Nagar

Directly north of Paharganj, five minutes' walk from New Delhi railway station and just beyond the flyover section of Desh Bandhu Gupta Road, **Ram Nagar** is lined with hotels and a few restaurants. Accommodation tends to be slightly more expensive than in Paharganj, but the rooms are generally better. The hotels listed below are marked on the Paharganj **map** opposite.

Cama 3037 Chowk Chuna Mandi, Rajguru Marg ⓣ011/2358 0245, ⓔhotelcama@yahoo.com. The best-value hotel on this street between Paharganj and Ram Nagar. All rooms are attached with hot water. ❷

Geet Deluxe 8570 Arakashan Rd ⓣ011/2361 6140 to 43. A cut above the other mid-range options in this area, well kept with nice touches and a certain charm, and clean, decent-sized rooms, all with TV, and either a/c or air-cooled. ❹

Grand Godwin 8502/41 Arakashan Rd ⓣ011/2354 6891 to 8, ⓦwww.godwinhotels.com. Rooms start at merely "semi-deluxe" (on the ground floor and slightly smaller than the rest), but they're all well appointed and well kept, and there are super deluxe rooms and even suites, as well as a multi-cuisine restaurant. Rates include a buffet breakfast. The *Godwin Deluxe*, next door, has just been refurbished and offers even more deluxe rooms. ❺–❼

Vandna and **Karan** 47 Arakashan Rd ⓣ011/2362 8821 and 3. Two hotels next to each other and jointly run. The *Karan* has smaller and simpler rooms, while the *Vandna* – with mosaics of Krishna and the Qutb Minar flanking the doorway – has slightly larger rooms, though currently the same price; all the rooms in both hotels are attached with hot water and TVs, but mattresses are rather hard. ❷–❸

Woodland 8235/6 Multani Danda, Arakashan Rd ⓣ011/4154 1304 to 7, ⓦwww.hotelwoodland.com. Popular hotel with a choice of big a/c, or less expensive smaller, non-a/c rooms. If you want a cheaper room still, they'll send you to their sister establishment, the *Dreamland*, just across the street. ❸–❺

Old Delhi

Few tourists stay in **Old Delhi**: it's less central than Connaught Place and Paharganj, and it's dirtier, noisier and more crowded, with hotels geared mostly to Indian visitors rather than foreigners. The hotels around Old Delhi station in particular are bad value. Still, there are a couple of good upmarket options on the area's fringes and some reasonable budget hotels around the Jama Masjid. Of all the areas in town to stay in, this is by far the most colourful. The hotels listed below appear on the Old Delhi **map** on p.109.

Broadway 4/15A Asaf Ali Rd ⓣ011/4366 3600, ⓔbroadway@oldworldhospitality.com. On the southern edge of Old Delhi, close to Delhi Gate, this mid-range hotel has a lot of old-fashioned charm and an excellent restaurant specializing in Kashmiri feasts (see p.121), plus two bars. Rooms are a little bit sombre, but they're clean and well equipped, and some look out to the Jama Masjid. Tours through Old Delhi are available. ❼–❽

Duke 8 Netaji Subhash Marg ⓣ011/2327 1501, ⓔdukehotel08@gmail.com. A range of reasonably cosy rooms above the hubbub of Netaji Subhash Marg on the east side of Old Delhi, and handy for the Red Fort and Jama Masjid. ❸–❹

Maidens 7 Sham Nath Marg, Civil Lines; metro Civil Lines ⓣ011/2397 5464, ⓦwww.maidenshotel.com. A nice bit of understated luxury in a lovely old colonial mansion dating back to Company days; quiet and relaxing with comfortable period rooms, big bathrooms and leafy gardens as well as a swimming pool and a good restaurant. Doubles from US$269. ❾

New City Palace 726 Jama Masjid Motor Market ⓣ011/2327 9548, ⓔnewcitypalace@hotmail.com. Though it doesn't quite live up to its billing of "a home for palatial comfort", this budget hotel is clean and well situated, directly behind the Jama Masjid (reserve ahead if you want a room with a view). Showers are hot and the best rooms have a/c, though not all the cheaper ones have outside windows. 24hr checkout. ❷–❸

New India 172 Katra Bariyan ⓣ011/2395 5117, ⓔsubhashkathuria@hotmail.com. Friendly and quite pleasingly rustic hotel with rooms around a bright upper-floor courtyard, mostly non-attached, though one or two have their own bathrooms, and the ones at the front share a veranda overlooking the street. 24hr checkout. ❷

South Delhi

Most of the accommodation **south of Connaught Place** lies firmly in the luxury category, although there are a few guesthouses in Sunder Nagar, the odd mid-range hotel tucked away in a residential area and a modern youth hostel near the exclusive diplomatic enclave in Chanakyapuri. The hotels listed below appear on the New Delhi **map** on p.104.

Ambassador Sujan Singh Park, off Subramaniam Bharti Marg ⓣ011/2463 2600, ⓦwww.tajhotels.com. Low-key but well-run and classy, this is a friendly place with comfortable-sized rooms and huge bathrooms, plus a couple of good restaurants and free use of the pool and health club at the other Taj Group hotel, *Taj Mahal*. Doubles start from US$304. ❾

The Claridges 12 Aurangzeb Rd ⓣ011/3955 5000, ⓦwww.claridges.com. One of Delhi's oldest and finest establishments, oozing elegant 1930s style from its facade to its rooms and even its bathrooms. Facilities include four restaurants, a vodka bar and a swimming pool. Doubles start at US$455. ❾

La Sagrita 14 Sunder Nagar ⓣ011/2435 9541, ⓦwww.lasagrita.com. Tucked away down a quiet side street in an exclusive colony, opposite a small park and next door to the Grenadian high commission, this small guesthouse might just suit if you want to escape the din of central Delhi. The rooms are cosy, carpeted, attached and tastefully done out, and there's a little garden out front to relax in. ❼

Maurya Sardar Patel Marg, Chanakyapuri ⓣ011/2611 2233, ⓦwww.itcwelcomgroup.in. An extremely plush hotel on the edge of Chanakyapuri, opposite the Ridge forest, with an imposing range of luxury rooms and some of the best dining in Delhi (see p.122). It regularly hosts visiting heads of state, with Bill Clinton among those who have stayed here. Full-price room rates start at Rs19,311, but promotional rates are often available. ❾

Youth Hostel 5 Nyaya Marg, off Kautilya Marg, Chanakyapuri ⓣ011/2611 6285, ⓦwww.yhaindia.org. Away from the bustling city centre, this ultra-modern and ecofriendly grey concrete building, with dorms (a/c Rs350; non-a/c Rs150) and a/c or non-a/c singles and doubles, is the showpiece-cum-administration centre of the Indian YHA. You need to be an HI member to stay here (maximum stay seven days) but you can join on the spot (Rs250). Rates include breakfast. ❷–❹

Majnu Ka Tilla

If you want to avoid Delhi's hustle and bustle, or have a change from Indian culture and cuisine, the Tibetan colony at **Majnu Ka Tilla**, a couple of kilometres north of Old Delhi, offers excellent-value budget hotels with immaculately kept rooms, much nicer than what you'd get for the same price in Paharganj. It's a relatively quiet district with Tibetan food, internet facilities and money changers close by, but it isn't very convenient for central Delhi (Connaught Place is Rs80 away by auto, Vidhan Sabha metro Rs20 by rickshaw). Book ahead, as hotels are often full here. There's only one main drag in Majnu ka Tilla, so everything's pretty easy to find.

Lhasa House 16 New Camp, just east of the main street ⓣ011/2393 9777 or 9888, ⓔlhasahouse@rediffmail.com. The rooms are a little bit smaller and simpler than at *Wongdhen House* next door, but all are attached, with TV and fan. The cheapest rooms are on the top floor. ❶–❷

White House 44 New Camp ⓣ011/2381 3644, ⓔwhitehouse02@yahoo.com. On the Tibetan colony's main street (such as it is), 100m north of the other two hotels mentioned here; the rooms are quite large, attached, with TV, and certainly well kept, but the mattresses are a bit on the hard side. ❷

Wongdhen House 15-A New Camp, just east of the main drag, next to *Lhasa House* ⓣ011/6415 5330, ⓔwongdhenhouse@hotmail.com. Friendly guesthouse with a choice of rooms, some attached and some overlooking the Yamuna River. There's also a good restaurant (Tibetan food, or breakfast items) and a terrace with a great river view. ❷–❹

The City

Delhi is both daunting and alluring, a sprawling metropolis with a stunning backdrop of ancient architecture. Once you've found your feet and got over the initial impact of the commotion, noise, pollution and sheer scale of the place, the city's geography slowly slips into focus. Monuments in assorted states of repair are dotted around the city, especially in **Old Delhi** and in southern enclaves such as Hauz Khas. The British-built modern city centres on Connaught Place, the heart of **New Delhi** (though actually on its northern edge), from which it's easy – by taxi, bus, auto-rickshaw or metro – to visit pretty much anywhere else in town.

New Delhi

The modern area of **NEW DELHI**, with its wide tree-lined avenues and solid colonial architecture, has been the seat of central government since 1931. At its hub, the royal mall, **Rajpath**, runs from the palatial **Rashtrapati Bhavan**, in the west, to the **India Gate** war memorial in the east. Its wide grassy margins are a popular meeting place for families, picnickers and courting couples. The

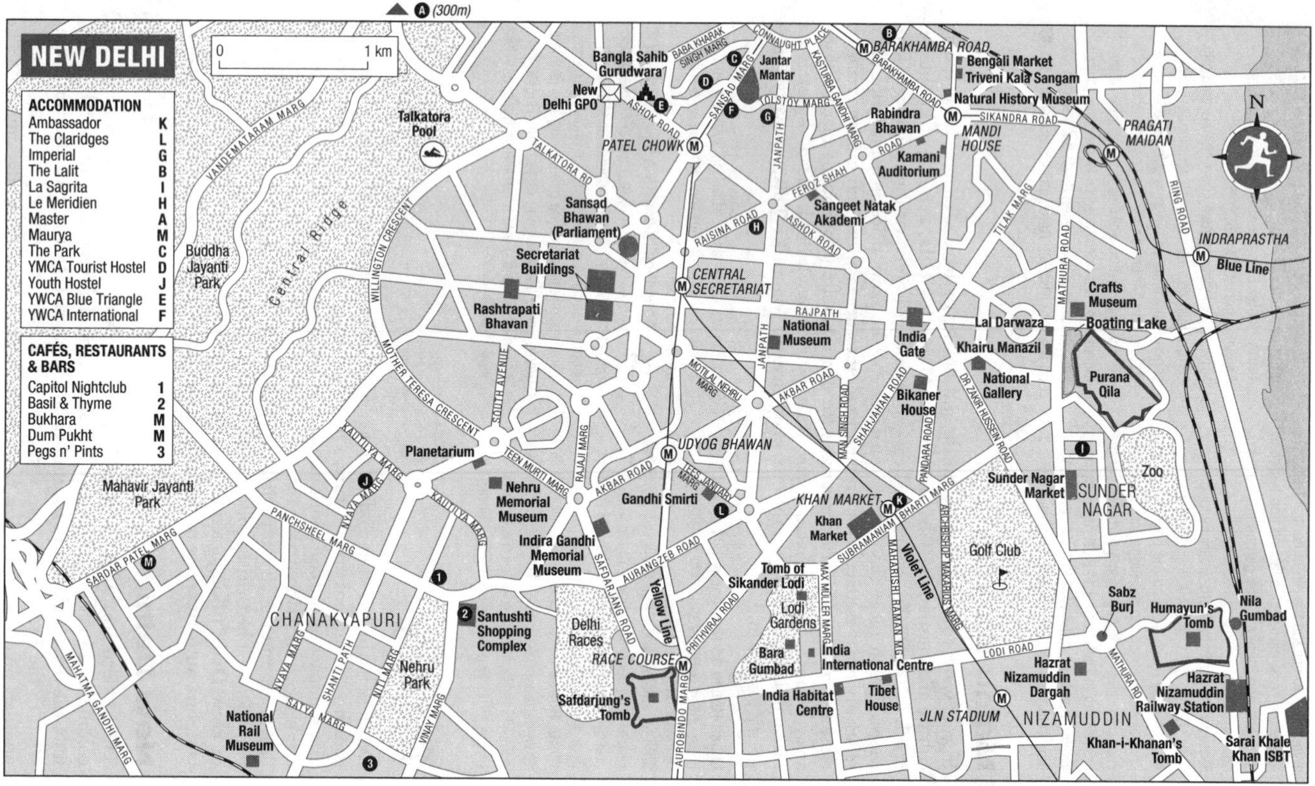
NEW DELHI
ACCOMMODATION
Ambassador K
The Claridges L
Imperial G
The Lalit B
La Sagrita I
Le Meridien H
Master A
Maurya M
The Park C
YMCA Tourist Hostel D
Youth Hostel J
YWCA Blue Triangle E
YWCA International F
CAFÉS, RESTAURANTS & BARS
Capitol Nightclub 1
Basil & Thyme 2
Bukhara M
Dum Pukht M
Pegs n' Pints 3
A (300m)
0
1 km
N
Central Ridge
Buddha Jayanti Park
Talkatora Pool
Mahavir Jayanti Park
Bangla Sahib Gurudwara
New Delhi GPO
Jantar Mantar
Patel Chowk
Sansad Bhawan (Parliament)
Secretariat Buildings
Rashtrapati Bhavan
Central Secretariat
National Museum
India Gate
Rabindra Bhawan
Kamani Auditorium
Sangeet Natak Akademi
Mandi House
Bengali Market
Triveni Kala Sangam
Natural History Museum
Pragati Maidan
Indraprastha
Blue Line
Crafts Museum
Boating Lake
Lal Darwaza
Khairu Manazil
National Gallery
Bikaner House
Purana Qila
Zoo
Sunder Nagar Market
Sunder Nagar
Golf Club
Khan Market
Violet Line
Udyog Bhawan
Gandhi Smirti
Planetarium
Nehru Memorial Museum
Indira Gandhi Memorial Museum
Tomb of Sikander Lodi
Lodi Gardens
Bara Gumbad
India International Centre
India Habitat Centre
Tibet House
Yellow Line
Delhi Races
Race Course
Safdarjung's Tomb
Santushti Shopping Complex
Chanakyapuri
Nehru Park
National Rail Museum
Sabz Burj
Humayun's Tomb
Nila Gumbad
Hazrat Nizamuddin Dargah
Hazrat Nizamuddin Railway Station
JLN Stadium
Nizamuddin
Khan-i-Khanan's Tomb
Sarai Khale Khan ISBT
Barakhamba Road
Connaught Place
Baba Kharak Singh Marg
Sansad Marg
Ashok Road
Tolstoy Marg
Kasturba Gandhi Marg
Janpath
Sikandra Road
Ring Road
Feroz Shah Road
Raisina Road
Talkatora Rd
Tilak Marg
Mathura Road
Rajpath
Willington Crescent
Vandemataram Marg
Mother Teresa Crescent
South Avenue
Motilal Nehru Marg
Akbar Road
Man Singh Road
Shahjahan Road
Pandara Road
Dr Zakir Hussein Road
Teen Murti Marg
Rajaji Marg
Tees January Marg
Subramaniam Bharti Marg
Archbishop Makarios Marg
Maharishi Raman Mg
Max Muller Marg
Aurangzeb Road
Safdarjang Road
Prithviraj Road
Aurobindo Marg
Lodi Road
Kautilya Marg
Nyaya Marg
Panchsheel Marg
Sardar Patel Marg
Mahatma Gandhi Marg
Shanti Path
Niti Marg
Satya Marg
Vinay Marg

National Museum is located just south of the central intersection. At the north edge of the new capital lies the thriving business centre, **Connaught Place**, where neon advertisements for restaurants, bars and banks adorn the flat roofs and colonnaded verandas of the white buildings that circle its central park.

Rashtrapati Bhavan and Rajpath

After George V, king of England and emperor of British India, decreed in 1911 that Delhi should replace Calcutta as the capital of India, the English architect **Edwin Lutyens** was commissioned to plan the new governmental centre. **Rashtrapati Bhavan**, the official residence of the president of India, is one of the largest and most grandiose of the Raj constructions, built by Lutyens and Sir Herbert Baker between 1921 and 1929. Despite its classical columns, Mughal-style domes and chhatris and Indian filigree work, the whole building is unmistakably British in character. Its majestic proportions are best appreciated from India Gate to the east – though with increasing pollution, the view is often clouded by a smoggy haze. The apartments inside are strictly private, but the **gardens** at the west side are open to the public for two weeks each February (free). Modelled on Mughal pleasure parks, with a typically ordered square pattern of quadrants dissected by waterways and refreshed by fountains, Lutyens' gardens extend beyond the normal confines to include tennis courts, butterfly enclosures, vegetable and fruit patches and a swimming pool.

Vijay Chowk, immediately in front of Rashtrapati Bhavan, leads into the wide, straight **Rajpath**, flanked with gardens and fountains that are floodlit at night, and the scene of annual **Republic Day** celebrations (Jan 26). Rajpath runs east to **India Gate**. Designed by Lutyens in 1921, the high arch, reminiscent of the Arc de Triomphe in Paris, commemorates ninety thousand Indian soldiers killed fighting for the British in World War I, and bears the names of more than three thousand British and Indian soldiers who died on the Northwest frontier and in the Afghan War of 1919. The extra memorial beneath the arch honours the lives lost in the Indo-Pakistan War of 1971.

Connaught Place and around

New Delhi's commercial hub, **Connaught Place** (known as "CP"), with its classical colonnades, is radically different from the bazaars of Old Delhi, which it superseded. Named after a minor British royal of the day, it takes the form of a circle, divided by eight radial roads and three ring roads into blocks lettered A–N. The term Connaught Place originally referred to the inner circle (now renamed Rajiv Chowk after Rajiv Gandhi), the outer one being Connaught Circus (now Indira Chowk, after Rajiv's mum). CP is crammed with restaurants, bars, shops, cinemas, banks and airline offices (there's a good online index at Ⓦwww.connaughtplacemall.com). For a **map** of Connaught Place, see p.98.

Jantar Mantar

South of Connaught Place on Sansad Marg, the **Jantar Mantar** (daily sunrise–sunset; Rs100 [Rs5]) was built in 1725, the first of five open-air observatories designed by the ruler of Jaipur, Jai Singh II, and precursor to his larger one in Jaipur (see p.146). Huge red and white slanting stone structures looming over palm trees and neat flowerbeds were used to calculate time, solar and lunar calendars and astrological movements with an admirable degree of accuracy.

Two tourist-friendly temples

Southwest of Connaught Place, on Ashok Road by the New Delhi General Post Office (GPO), the vast white marble structure of **Bangla Sahib Gurudwara** is

Delhi's biggest Sikh temple, topped by a huge, golden, onion-shaped dome which is visible from some distance. The temple commemorates a 1664 visit to Delhi by the eighth Sikh guru, Hare Krishan, and welcomes visitors; deposit shoes at the information centre, where you can also enlist the services of a free guide. Remember to cover your head and dress conservatively. Live devotional music (vocals, harmonium and tabla) is relayed throughout the complex, and everybody is invited to share a simple meal of dhal and chapattis, served three times daily.

Lakshmi Narayan Mandir (daily 4am–1.30pm & 2.30–9pm; deposit cameras, shoes and mobile phones at the entrance), northwest of the GPO and directly west of Connaught Place on Mandir Marg, is a modern Hindu temple which also welcomes tourists. With its white, cream and red brick domes, it was commissioned by a wealthy merchant family, the Birlas (hence its alternative name, Birla Mandir). The main shrine is dedicated to Lakshmi, goddess of wealth (on the right), and her consort Narayana, aka Vishnu, the preserver of life (on the left, holding a conch). At the back is a tiny ornate chamber decorated with coloured stones and mirrors and dedicated to Krishna, one of Vishnu's earthly incarnations. Devotional music is played throughout, and quotes from Hindu scriptures adorn the walls, many translated into English.

Paharganj

North of Connaught Place and directly west of New Delhi railway station, **Paharganj**, centred around Main Bazaar, provides the first experience of the Subcontinent for many budget travellers. Packed with cheap hotels, restaurants, cafés and *dhabas*, and with a busy fruit and vegetable market halfway along, it's also a paradise for shoestring shoppers seeking psychedelic clothing, joss sticks, bags and oils of patchouli or sandalwood. For a **map** of Paharganj and neighbouring Ram Nagar, see p.100.

There is also a less-visible underside to life in Paharganj, in the shape of the **street children**. Most are runaways who've left difficult homes, often hundreds of kilometres away, and the majority sleep on the streets and inhale solvents to numb their pain. The Salaam Baalak Trust (Ⓦwww.salaambaalaktrust.com), a local NGO working to help them, organizes **walking tours** of Paharganj conducted by former street children. Tours last two hours, usually start at 10am and cost Rs200. For bookings, contact Ⓣ0/9873 130383 or Ⓔsbttour@yahoo.com. Proceeds go towards providing shelter, education and healthcare for the area's street children.

National Museum

The **National Museum** (Tues–Sun 10am–5pm; Rs300 [Rs10]; cameras Rs300 [Rs20]; Ⓦwww.nationalmuseumindia.gov.in), just south of Rajpath at 11 Janpath, provides a good overview of Indian culture and history. The foreigners' entry fee includes a free audio tour (Rs150 in English for Indian citizens), but you need to leave a passport, driving licence, credit card or Rs2000 (or US$40/£40/€40) as a deposit, and the exhibits it covers are rather random. At a trot, you can see the museum in a couple of hours, but to get the best out of your visit you should set aside at least half a day.

The most important exhibits are on the ground floor, kicking off in **room 4** with the Harappan civilization. The Gandhara sculptures in **room 6** betray a very obvious Greco-Roman influence. **Room 9** has some very fine bronzes, most especially those of the Chola period (from south India in the ninth to the thirteenth century), and a fifteenth-century statue of Devi from Vijanaraya in south India, by the left-hand wall. Among the late medieval sculptures in **room 10** is a fearsome, vampire-like, late chola *dvarapala* (a guardian figure built to flank the doorway to a shrine), also from south India, and a couple of performing musicians from Mysore. **Room 12** is devoted to the Mughals, and in particular their miniature paintings. Look out also for two paintings depicting a subject you wouldn't expect – the nativity of Jesus. It's worth popping upstairs to the **textiles**, and the **musical instruments** collection on the second floor is outstanding. The **Central Asian antiquities** collection includes a large number of paintings, documents, ceramics and textiles from Eastern Turkestan (Xinjiang) and the Silk Route, dating from between the third and twelfth centuries. On your way out, take a look at the massive twelve-tiered temple chariot from Tamil Nadu, an extremely impressive piece of woodwork in a glass shelter just by the southern entrance gate.

Memorial museums

The **Nehru Memorial Museum** (Tues–Sun 9am–5.30pm; free; Ⓦwww.nehrumemorial.com) on Teen Murti Marg was home to India's first prime minister, Jawaharlal Nehru, and is now preserved in his memory. One of Nehru's passions was astronomy, and there's a **planetarium** (Rs2; 40min astronomy shows in English Tues–Sun 11.30am & 3pm, Rs15; Ⓦnehruplanetarium.org) in the grounds of the house.

Nehru's daughter, Indira Gandhi, despite her excesses during the 1975–77 Emergency (see p.1063), is still remembered by many with respect and affection. The **Indira Gandhi Memorial Museum** (Tues–Sun 9.30am–4.45pm; free), 1 Safdarjang Rd, was the house where she was assassinated by her Sikh bodyguards in 1984; her bloodstained sari, chemically preserved, is on display, and there's a section devoted to her son Rajiv, including the clothes he was wearing when Sri Lankan Tamil separatists assassinated him in 1991.

Still more tragic than the deaths of Rajiv and Indira Gandhi was the 1948 assassination of the nation's founder, Mahatma Gandhi, who shared their surname but was not related. The **Gandhi Smriti** (Tues–Sun 10am–5pm; free), 5 Tees January Marg, is the house where the Mahatma lived his last days. He had come to Delhi to quell the sectarian rioting that accompanied Partition, but Hindu sectarian extremists hated him for protecting Muslims, and on 30 January 1948, one of them shot him dead. Visitors can view an exhibition about his life, and follow in his last footsteps to the spot where he died.

National Gallery of Modern Art

Once the residence of the Maharaja of Jaipur, the extensive **National Gallery** (Tues–Sun 10am–5pm; Rs150 [Rs10]; Ⓦngmaindia.gov.in) housed in Jaipur House near India Gate, is a rich showcase of Indian contemporary art. The permanent displays, focusing on post-1930s work, exhibit many of India's most important works of modern art, including pieces by the "Bengali Renaissance" artists Abanendranath Tagore and Nandalal Bose, the great poet and artist, Rabindranath Tagore, and Jamini Roy, whose work, reminiscent of Modigliani, reflects the influence of Indian folk art. Also on show are the romantic paintings and etchings of Thomas Daniell and his nephew William, British artists of the Bombay or Company School, which combined Indian delicacy with Western realism. The ground-floor galleries are used for temporary exhibitions.

Crafts Museum

Immediately north of Purana Qila (see p.113) on Bhairon Marg, the **Crafts Museum** (Tues–Sun 10am–5pm; Rs150 [Rs10]) is a dynamic exhibition of the rural arts and crafts of India, divided into three sections. The **exhibition galleries** show a range of textiles, carvings, ceramics, painting and metalwork from across India, while the **village complex** displays an assortment of traditional homes from different parts of the country. The **craft demonstrations** do feature a few artisans actually at work, but mostly they are more like shops selling crafts typical of different Indian regions. There's also a library and a fixed-price museum **shop**.

Old Delhi (Shahjahanabad)

Though it's not in fact the oldest part of Delhi, the seventeenth-century city of **Shahjahanabad**, built for the Mughal emperor Shah Jahan, is known as **OLD DELHI**. Construction began on the city in 1638, and within eleven years it was substantially complete, surrounded by over 8km of ramparts pierced by fourteen main gates. It boasted a beautiful main thoroughfare, **Chandni Chowk**, an imposing citadel, the **Red Fort** (Lal Qila), and an impressive congregational mosque, the **Jama Masjid**. Today much of the wall has crumbled, and of the fourteen gates only four remain, but it's still a fascinating area, crammed with interesting nooks and crannies, though you'll need stamina, patience, time and probably a fair few chai stops along the way to endure the crowds and traffic. Old Delhi is served by metro stations at Chandni Chowk (actually nearer Old Delhi train station), Chawri Bazaar, and the Ajmeri Gate side of New Delhi railway station (the metro stop's name of "New Delhi" is in this instance misleading).

The Red Fort (Lal Qila)

The largest of Old Delhi's monuments is Lal Qila, known in English as the **Red Fort** (Tues–Sun sunrise–sunset, museums 10am–5pm; Rs250 [Rs10]) because of the red sandstone from which it was built. It was commissioned by Shah Jahan to be his residence and modelled on the fort at Agra. Work started in 1638, and the emperor moved in ten years later. The fort contains all the trappings you'd expect at the centre of Mughal government: halls of public and private audience, domed and arched marble palaces, plush private apartments, a mosque, and elaborately designed gardens. The ramparts, which stretch for over 2km, are interrupted by two gates – **Lahori Gate** to the west, through which you enter, and Delhi Gate to the south. Shah Jahan's son, Aurangzeb, added barbicans to both gates. In those days, the Yamuna River ran along the eastern wall, feeding both the moat and a "stream of paradise" which ran through every pavilion. As the Mughal Empire declined, the fort fell into disrepair. It was attacked and plundered by the Persian emperor Nadir Shah in 1739, and by the British in 1857. Nevertheless, it remains an impressive testimony to Mughal grandeur. Keep your ticket stub as you will have to show it several times (for example, to enter the museums).

The main entrance to the fort from Lahori Gate opens onto **Chatta Chowk**, a covered street flanked with arched cells that used to house Delhi's most talented jewellers, carpet-makers, goldsmiths and silk-weavers, but is now given over to souvenir sellers. At the end, a path to the left leads to the **Museum of the Struggle for Independence**, depicting resistance to British rule.

Sound-and-light shows

Each night except Monday, a **sound-and-light show** takes place in the **Red Fort**: the palaces are dramatically lit, and a historical commentary blares from crackly loudspeakers. The show starts after sunset and lasts an hour (in English Feb–April & Sept–Oct 8.30pm, May–Aug 9pm, Nov–Jan 7.30pm; weekdays Rs60, weekends and public holidays Rs80; ⓣ011/2327 4580). The mosquitoes are ferocious, so bring repellent. Heavy monsoon rains may affect summer shows.

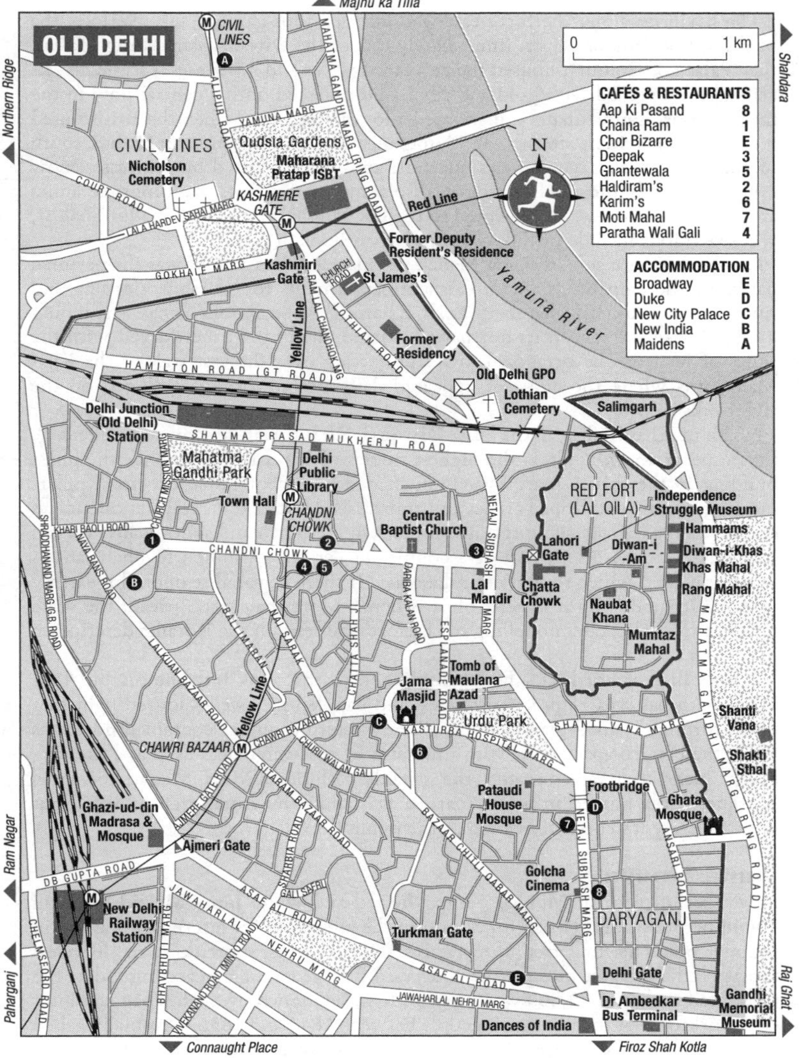

The **Naubhat Khana** ("Musicians' Gallery") marked the entrance into the royal quarters. Beyond it, a path leads ahead through wide lawns to the **Diwan-i-Am**, or Hall of Public Audience, where the emperor used to meet commoners and hold court. In those days it was strewn with silk carpets and partitioned with hanging tapestries. Its centrepiece is a marble dais on which sat the emperor's throne, surrounded by twelve panels inlaid with precious stones, mostly depicting birds and flowers. The most famous of them, in the middle at the top (and not easy to see), shows the mythological Greek Orpheus with his lute. The panels were made by a Florentine jeweller and imported from Italy, but the surrounding inlay work was done locally.

The pavilions along the fort's east wall face spacious gardens and overlook the banks of the Yamuna River. Immediately east of the Diwan-i-Am, **Rang Mahal**, the "Palace of Colour", housed the emperor's wives and mistresses. Originally, its ceiling was overlaid with gold and silver and reflected onto a central pool in the marble floor. Unfortunately, it suffered a lot of vandalism when the British used it as an Officers' Mess after the 1857 uprising. The similar **Mumtaz Mahal**, south of the main *zenana*, or women's quarters, and probably used by princesses, now houses an **Archeological Museum**, displaying manuscripts, paintings, ceramics and textiles, with a section devoted to the last Mughal emperor, Bahadur Shah II, whose exhibits include his silk robes and silver hookah pipe.

On the northern side of Rang Mahal, the marble **Khas Mahal** was the personal palace of the emperor, split into separate apartments for worship, sleeping and sitting. The southern chamber, **Tosh Khana** ("Robe Room"), has a stunning marble filigree screen on its north wall, surmounted by a panel carved with the scales of justice. The octagonal tower projecting over the east wall of the Khas Mahal was where the emperor appeared daily before throngs gathered on the riverbanks below.

North of Khas Mahal, in the large **Diwan-i-Khas** ("Hall of Private Audience"), the emperor would address the highest nobles of his court. Today it's the finest building in the fort, a marble pavilion shaded by a roof raised on stolid pillars meeting in ornate scalloped arches and embellished with exquisitely delicate inlays of flowers made from semiprecious stones. On the north and south walls you can still make out the inscription of a couplet in Persian attributed to Shah Jahan's prime minister, which roughly translates as: "If there be paradise upon this earthly sphere / It is here, oh it is here, oh it is here". More than just a paean, the verse refers to the deliberate modelling of the fort's gardens on the Koranic description of heaven.

A little further north are the **hammams**, or baths, sunk into the marble floor inlaid with patterns of precious stones, and dappled in jewel-coloured light that filters through stained-glass windows. The western chamber contained hot baths while the eastern apartment, with fountains of rosewater, was used as a dressing room. Next to the hammams, the sweetly fashioned **Moti Masjid**, or Pearl Mosque, triple-domed in white marble, was added by Aurangzeb in 1659, but unfortunately it's currently closed to the public.

Jama Masjid

A wonderful piece of Mughal pomp, the red-and-white **Jama Masjid** (8am till 30min before sunset; closed for 30min in the afternoon for afternoon prayers; in summer opens at 7am; free; cameras Rs200; no shorts, short skirts or sleeveless tops) is India's largest mosque. Its courtyard is large enough to accommodate the prostrated bodies of 25,000 worshippers. It was designed by Shah Jahan and built by a workforce of five thousand people between 1644 and 1656. Originally called Masjid-i-Jahanuma ("mosque commanding a view of the world"), this grand structure stands on Bho Jhala, one of Shahjahanabad's two hills, and looks east to the sprawling Red Fort, and down on the seething streets of Old Delhi. Broad, red-sandstone staircases lead to gateways on the east, north and southern sides, where worshippers and visitors alike must remove their shoes (the custodian will guard them for you for a small tip).

Once inside the courtyard, your eyes will be drawn to the three bulbous marble domes crowning the **main prayer hall** on the west side (facing Mecca), fronted by a series of high cusped arches, and sheltering the *mihrab*, the central niche in the west wall indicating the direction of prayer. The pool in the centre is used for ritual ablutions. At each corner of the square yard a slender minaret crowned with a marble dome rises to the sky, and it's worth climbing the **tower** (Rs100; women must be accompanied by a man) south of the main sanctuary for a view over Delhi. In the northeast corner a white shrine protects a collection of Muhammad's relics, including his sandals, a hair from his beard, and his "footprint" miraculously embedded in a marble slab.

Chandni Chowk

Old Delhi's main thoroughfare, **Chandni Chowk** was once a sublime canal lined with trees and some of the most opulent bazaars in the whole of Asia. The British paved over the canal after 1857. In 2007, the courts ordered a daytime (8am–8pm) ban on cycle rickshaws along the street, and they were replaced by a fleet of green minibuses (fare Rs5), but the ban has been challenged and may not last. In any event, the best way to take it in is on foot. Along it, look out for numbered "heritage buildings" signposted at intervals, with placards outside explaining their historical importance, especially during the 1857 uprising.

At Chandni Chowk's eastern end, opposite the Red Fort, the **Lal Mandir** Jain temple (daily 5.30–11.30am & 6–9.30pm) is not as ornate as the Jain temples in Rajasthan (see p.225 & p.230), but it does boast detailed carvings, and gilded paintwork in the antechambers surrounding the main shrine. Remove your shoes and leave any leather articles at the kiosk before entering. The attached **bird hospital** (daily 7am–9pm; free but donations appreciated) puts into practice the Jain principle that all life is sacred by rescuing injured birds, with each species having its own ward; the sparrow ward is largely occupied by victims of ceiling fans, with which these poor critters frequently collide.

Raj Ghat

When Shah Jahan established his city in 1638, its eastern edges bordered the Yamuna River, and a line of *ghats*, or steps leading to the water, was installed along the riverbanks. *Ghats* have been used in India for centuries, for mundane things like washing clothes and bathing, but also for worship and funeral cremation. **Raj Ghat** (daily: April–Sept 5am–7.30pm; Oct–March 5.30am–7pm; free), east of Delhi Gate – really more a park than a *ghat* – is the place where Mahatma Gandhi was cremated, on the day after his assassination in 1948. The Mahatma's *samadhi* (cremation memorial), a low black plinth inscribed with his reputed last words, "Hai Ram" ("Oh God"), receives a steady stream of visitors, and he is remembered through prayers here every Friday evening at 5pm, and on the anniversaries of his birth and death (Oct 2 & Jan 30). Opposite Raj Ghat's southwest corner, the small **Gandhi Memorial Museum** (daily except Mon 9.30am–5.30pm; free) houses some of Gandhi's photographs and writings, and at weekends you can watch a one-hour film on his political and personal life (English Sat 4pm; Hindi Sun 4pm).

North of Raj Ghat, memorials also mark the places where Jawaharlal Nehru (at Shanti Vana), his daughter Indira Gandhi (at Shakti Sthal), and his grandson Rajiv Gandhi (at Vir Bhumi) were cremated.

Firoz Shah Kotla

Supposedly, Firoz Shah, sultan of Delhi from 1351 to 1358, had a whole fifth city of Delhi built – Firozabad, founded in 1354. Today few traces survive of what was in any case probably never more than a suburb of the main city, but what does remain is the fortified palace of **Firoz Shah Kotla** (Tues–Sun sunrise–sunset; Rs100 [Rs5]), now a crumbling ruin with ornamental gardens, 1500m south of Delhi Gate. Its most incongruous and yet distinctive element is the third-century BC polished sandstone **Ashokan pillar**, carried down the Yamuna River by raft from Ambala. For a reasonable view of the column, you'll need to climb to the top of the building, entering the compound through a gate on the west side, then mounting a stairway in the northeast corner. From the top you also get a view of the neighbouring mosque and *baoli* (step-well), as well as the lawns which make the site such a pleasant place to visit.

North of the Red Fort

Netaji Subhash Marg leads north from the Red Fort and under a railway bridge to Old Delhi GPO. Just before the post office, on the east side of the road, **Lothian Cemetery**, the burial ground for officers of the East India Company from 1808 until just after the 1857 uprising, had become very run-down, but was being renovated at last check. In the middle of the road in front of the post office, the remains of the East India Company's **Magazine** or arsenal is now used mainly as an unofficial public toilet, so watch your step if you cross the street to explore it. Another part of the magazine, with a memorial plaque, stands on a second traffic island just to the north.

Continuing north along Lothian Road, you'll pass another remnant of Company days on your right in the form of the old **Residency**, now the Archeology Department of Guru Gobind Singh Indraprastha University. A couple of hundred metres further is the rather fine cream-and-white baroque facade of **St James's Church** (daily 8.30am–1pm & 2–5pm, or whenever you can find the caretaker), commissioned in 1836 by **James Skinner**, the son of a Scottish Company-wallah and a Rajput princess. Because of his mixed ancestry, and the increasing racism of the British regime, Skinner was refused a commission in the Company's army, but set up his own irregular cavalry unit (Skinner's Horse, also called the Yellow Boys after their uniform) and made himself pretty much indispensable to the Company in northern India. Though he was continually snubbed over pay and rank, his astounding victories over the forces of the Maharajah of Jaipur and the great Sikh leader Maharajah Ranjit Singh eventually forced the Company to begrudgingly grant him the rank of Lieutenant Colonel and absorb his cavalrymen into its ranks. Skinner died in 1842 and is buried just in front of the altar.

The double-arched **Kashmiri Gate**, on the west side of Lothian Road just 300m north of the church, was where the Mughal court would leave Delhi every summer bound for the cool valley of Kashmir. To its north is Maharana Pratap ISBT, beyond which, across the busy Lala Hardev Sahai Marg, the peaceful **Qudsia Gardens** are a fading remnant of the magnificent pleasure parks commissioned in the mid-eighteenth century by Queen Qudsia, favourite mistress of Muhammad Shah, and mother of Ahmed Shah. Just west of the gardens, on Qudsia Road, is Delhi's oldest burial ground, **Nicholson Cemetery**, named after Brigadier General John Nicholson, who was shot down while leading the British attack to regain Delhi from the 1857 insurgents.

South Delhi

Most of the early settlements of Delhi, including its first city at Qila Rai Pithora (around the Qutb Minar), are to be found not in "Old Delhi" but in **South Delhi**, the area south of Lutyens' carefully planned boulevards, where the rapid expansion of suburban Delhi has swallowed up what was previously countryside. Whole villages have been embedded within it, and the area is littered with monuments from the past. Meanwhile, as the centre becomes more and more congested, South Delhi's housing enclaves and colonies are increasingly home to the newest shopping centres and the most happening locales.

Purana Qila

The majestic fortress of **Purana Qila** (daily sunrise–sunset; Rs100 [Rs5]), whose crumbling ramparts dominate busy Mathura Road, east of India Gate, is thought to stand on the site of Indraprastha, the Pandava city of Mahabharata fame. Considered the sixth city of Delhi, it was begun by Humayun, the second Mughal emperor, as Din-Panah, and renamed Shergarh by Sher Shah Suri, who displaced him in 1540 and oversaw most of the construction. Purana Qila is served by **buses** #453, #454, #457 and #458 from New Delhi railway station gate 2 (Ajmeri Gate side) – ask for the zoo, which is the same stop.

Most of the inside of the fortress is taken up by pleasant lawns and gardens, but two important buildings survive. Of them, the **Qila-i-Kuhna Masjid** is one of Sher Shah's finest monuments. Constructed in 1541 in the Afghan style, it has five elegant arches, embellished with white and black marble to complement the red sandstone. The geometric patterns and carved Arabic calligraphy around the main doorway all represent a more sophisticated degree of decorative artwork than on anything seen before in Delhi. Previous decorative carving on buildings was in plaster, but here it's in stone, a more serious affair as it's obviously much harder to work.

The Purana Qila's other main building, the **Sher Mandal**, is a red-sandstone octagonal observatory and library built for Sher Shah. It was here in 1556 that the emperor Humayun died. He stumbled down its treacherously steep steps while hurrying to answer the muezzin's call to prayer, just a year after he had defeated Sher Shah's son Sikander Suri and regained power.

Humayun's Tomb

Close to the medieval Muslim centre of Nizamuddin and 2km from Purana Qila, **Humayun's Tomb** (daily sunrise–sunset; Rs250 [Rs10]) stands at the crossroads of the Lodi and Mathura roads, 500m from Hazrat Nizamuddin railway station (one stop from New Delhi Station on the suburban line), and easily accessible by bus (#181 and #414 from Chelmsford Road by New Delhi station; #893, #894 and #966 from Kasturba Gandhi Marg by Connaught Place), or by pre-paid auto from Connaught Place (Rs60). Late afternoon is the best time to photograph it. Delhi's first Mughal mausoleum, it was constructed to house the remains of the second Mughal emperor, Humayun, and was built under the watchful eye of Haji Begum, his senior widow and mother of Akbar, who camped here for the duration, and is now buried alongside her husband. The grounds were later used to inter several prominent Mughals, and served as a refuge for the last emperor, Bahadur Shah II, before his capture by the British in 1857.

The tomb's sombre, Persian-style elegance marks this as one of Delhi's finest historic sites. Constructed of red sandstone, inlaid with black and white marble, on a commanding podium looking towards the Yamuna River, it stands in the centre of the formal *charbagh*, or quartered garden. The octagonal structure is crowned with a double dome that soars to a height of 38m. Though it was the very first Mughal garden tomb – to be followed by Akbar's at Sikandra (see p.257) and of course the Taj Mahal at Agra (see p.250), for which it can be seen as a prototype – Humayun's mausoleum has antecedents in Delhi in the form of Ghiyas-ud-Din Tughluq's tomb at Tughluqabad (see p.117), and that of Sikandar Lodi in Lodi Gardens (see p.115). From the second of those it adopted its octagonal shape and the high central arch that was to be such a typical feature of Mughal architecture – you'll see it at the Taj, and in Delhi's Jama Masjid (see p.110), for example.

Within the grounds southeast of the main mausoleum, another impressive square mausoleum, with a double dome and two graves bearing Koranic inscriptions, is that of Humayun's barber, a man considered important because he was trusted with holding a razor to the emperor's throat. Nearby but outside the compound (so you'll have to walk right round for a closer look) stands the **Nila Gumbad** ("blue dome"), an octagonal tomb with a dome of blue tiles, supposedly built by one of Akbar's nobles to honour a faithful servant, and which may possibly predate Humayun's Tomb. On your way round to the Nila Gumbad (depending on your route), you pass the **tomb of Khan-i-Khanan** (daily sunrise–sunset; Rs100 [Rs5]), a Mughal general who died in 1626; unfortunately, the tomb looks rather ragged as the facing was all stripped for use in Safdarjang's tomb, and the garden that surrounded it has mostly gone. The blue-domed structure in the middle of the road junction in front of the entrance to Humayun's tomb is a seventeenth-century tomb called **Sabz Burj** – the tiles on its dome are not original, but the result of a recent restoration.

Nizamuddin

Just across the busy Mathura Road from Humayun's Tomb, and now engulfed by a busy road network and plush suburbs, the self-contained *mahalla* (village) of **Nizamuddin**, with its lack of traffic, ancient mosques and tombs and slow pace of life, is so different from the surrounding city that to enter it is like passing through a time warp. At its heart, surrounded by a tangle of narrow alleyways lined with shops and market stalls, lies one of Sufism's greatest shrines, the **Hazrat Nizamuddin Dargah**, which draws a constant stream of devotees from far and wide.

The marble *dargah* is the tomb of Sheikh Nizam-ud-Din Aulia (1236–1325), fourth saint of the Chishtiya Sufi order founded by Khwaja Muin-ud-din Chishti of Ajmer (see p.177), and was built the year the sheikh died, but has been through several renovations, and the present mausoleum dates from 1562. Lattice screens and arches in the inner sanctum surround the actual tomb (closed to women), which is surrounded by a marble rail and a canopy of mother-of-pearl. Sheikh Nizam-ud-Din's disciple, the poet and chronicler **Amir Khusrau** – considered to be the first Urdu poet and the founder of *khyal*, the most common form of north Indian classical music – lies in a contrasting red-sandstone tomb in front of his master's mausoleum.

Religious song and music play an important role among the Chishtiyas, as among several Sufi orders, and *qawwals* (bards) gather to sing in the evenings (especially on Thurs and feast days). Comprising a chorus led by solo singing accompanied by clapping and usually a harmonium combined with a *dholak* (double-membraned barrel drum) and tabla (paired hand-drums), the hypnotic rhythm of their **qawwali music** is designed to lull its audience into a state of *mast* (spiritual intoxication), which is believed to bring the devotee closer to God.

The oldest building in the area, the red-sandstone mosque of **Jamat Khana Masjid**, looms over the main *dargah* on its western side. It was commissioned in 1325 by Khizr Khan, the son of the Khalji sultan Ala-ud-Din. Enclosed by marble lattice screens next to Amir Khusrau's mausoleum, the tomb of **Princess Jahanara**, Shah Jahan's favourite daughter, is topped by a hollow filled with grass in compliance with her wish to have nothing but grass covering her grave. Just east of the *dargah* compound, the elegant 64-pillared white marble **Chausath Khamba** was built as a mausoleum for the family of a Mughal politician who had been governor of Gujarat, and the building, with its low, wide form and elegant marble screens, bears the unmistakable evidence of a Gujarati influence. The compound containing the Chausath is usually locked, but the caretaker should be on hand somewhere nearby to open it up if you want to take a closer look.

Lodi Gardens

Two kilometres west of Nizamuddin along Lodi Road, the leafy, pleasant **Lodi Gardens** (daily 5am–8pm; free) form part of a belt of fifteenth- and sixteenth-century monuments that now stand incongruously amid golf greens, large bungalows and elite estates. The park is especially full in the early mornings and early evenings, when fitness enthusiasts come for brisk walks or to jog through the manicured gardens against a backdrop of much-graffitied medieval monuments; it's also a popular lovers' hangout. The gardens, a Rs40 auto-ride from Connaught Place, also contain the **National Bonsai Park**, which has a fine selection of diminutive trees. The best time to come is at sunset, when the light is soft and the tombs are all lit up.

Near the centre of the gardens, the imposing **Bara Gumbad** ("large dome") is a square, late fifteenth-century tomb capped by the eponymous dome, its monotonous exterior relieved by grey and black stones and its interior adorned with painted stuccowork. **Shish Gumbad** ("glazed dome"), a similar tomb 50m north, still bears a few traces of the blue tiles liberally used to form friezes below the cornice and above the entrance. Inside, plasterwork is inscribed with ornate Koranic inscriptions.

The octagonal **tomb of Muhammad Shah** (ruled 1434–45) of the Sayyid dynasty stands 300m southwest of Bara Gumbad, surrounded by verandas and pierced by arches and sloping buttresses. Enclosed within high walls and a square garden, 300m north of Bara Gumbad, the **tomb of Sikandar Lodi** (ruled 1489–1517) repeats the octagonal theme, with a central chamber encircled by a veranda. **Athpula** ("eight piers"), a sixteenth-century ornamental bridge, lies east, in the northwest corner of the park.

Safdarjang's Tomb

The tomb of **Safdarjang** (daily dawn to dusk; Rs100 [Rs5]), the Mughal viceroy of Avadh under Muhammad Shah (1719–48), stands at the junction of Lodi Road and Aurobindo Marg, 5km southwest of Connaught Place; from Ajmeri Gate or Connaught Place (Kasturba Gandhi Marg), or from Connaught Place by pre-paid auto-rickshaw (Rs50). Constructed between 1753 and 1774, the double-storeyed mausoleum, built of red and buff sandstone and relieved by marble, rises on a dramatic platform overlooking the adjacent airport of the Delhi Flying Club. It was the very last of India's great Mughal garden tombs, dating from the period after Nadir Shah's sacking of the city, by which time the empire was reduced to a fraction of its former size and most of the capital's grander buildings lay in ruins. Emblematic of the decadence and degeneracy that characterized the twilight of the Mughal era, the mausoleum sports an elongated, tapered dome and absurdly ornate interior filled with swirling plasterwork. In *City of Djinns*, William Dalrymple aptly describes its quirky design as "blowzy Mughal rococo" typifying an age "not so much decaying into impoverished anonymity as one whoring and drinking itself into extinction".

National Rail Museum

The cream of India's royal coaches and oldest engines are on permanent display at the **National Rail Museum** (Tues–Sun: April–Sept 9.30am–1pm & 1.30–7.30pm; Oct–March 9.30am–1pm & 1.30–5.30pm; Rs10, video Rs100) in the embassy enclave of Chanakyapuri, southwest of Connaught Place; take bus #620 from Shivaji Stadium terminal by Connaught Place, or a pre-paid auto (Rs60). Some 27 locomotives and seventeen carriages – including the ornate 1886 gold-painted saloon car of the Maharaja of Baroda (Rs50 to go inside), the teak carriage of the Maharaja of Mysore, trimmed in gold and ivory, and the cabin used by the Prince of Wales in 1876 – are kept in the grounds. A steam-hauled miniature "Joy Train" does a circuit of the grounds (Rs10) whenever it has enough passengers.

The covered section of the museum houses models of famous engines and coaches, displays of old tickets, and even the skull of an elephant hit by a train near Bombay in 1894. The pride of the collection, however, is a model of India's very first train, a steam engine which made its inaugural journey of 21 miles from Bombay to Thane in 1853.

Hauz Khas

Set amid parks and woodland 4km south of Safdarjang's Tomb, the wealthy suburban development of **Hauz Khas** is typical of South Delhi in being a thoroughly modern area dotted with remnants of antiquity. The modern part takes the form of Hauz Khas village, a shopping area packed with chic boutiques and smart restaurants. There's also a very pleasant deer park and a rose garden, but of most interest to visitors, apart from the upmarket shopping possibilities (see pp.124–126), are the ruins of a fourteenth-century reservoir at the western end of the village.

Sultan Ala-ud-Din Khalji had the reservoir (or "tank") built in 1304 to supply water to his citadel at Siri, Delhi's "second city", and it was known after him as **Hauz-i-Alai**. Half a century later, it was expanded by Firoz Shah, who added a two-storey seminary and a mosque at its northern end. Among the anonymous tombs scattered throughout the area is that of Firoz Shah himself, directly overlooking the southern corner of the tank. Its high walls, lofty dome, and doorway spanned by a lintel with a stone railing outside are fine examples of Hindu Indian traditions effectively blended with Islamic architecture.

Siri itself was located a couple of kilometres east of Hauz Khas, and the remains of its ramparts can be seen from Khel Gaon Marg. Much of the site has been given over to parkland, which makes it pleasant enough to visit, but part of it has been subsumed by a village built to house athletes competing in the 1982 Asian Games.

Baha'i Temple

Often compared visually to the Sydney Opera House, Delhi's **Baha'i Temple** (Mon–Sat: April–Sept 9am–7pm; Oct–March 9.30am–5.30pm; you may be asked to wait briefly outside during services, which are on the hour 9am–noon & 3–5pm) is an iconic piece of modern architecture that dominates the surrounding suburban sprawl. Twenty-seven spectacular giant white petals of marble in the shape of an unfolding lotus spring from nine pools and walkways, to symbolize the nine unifying spiritual paths of the Baha'i faith; each petal alcove contains an extract from the Baha'i holy scriptures. Set amid well-maintained gardens, the temple is at its most impressive at sunset. It'll cost you Rs80 to get here by pre-paid auto from Connaught Place, or you can take bus #440 from New Delhi Station (gate 1) or Connaught Place (Scindia House) to the Outer Ring Road by Kalkaji bus depot, a short walk from the temple. Kalkaji Mandir metro (violet line) will also be within walking distance when it opens (at the end of 2010 or shortly thereafter).

Ashoka's Rock Edict

Northwest of the Baha'i Temple, just off Raja Dhirsain Marg, **Ashoka's Rock Edict** is a ten-line epigraph inscribed in ancient Brahmi script on a smooth, sloping rock. The rock, now protected by a shelter in its own little park, was used as a slide by neighbourhood kids until 1966, when local residents noticed the ancient inscription, which was promulgated by the Mauryan emperor Ashoka the Great in the third century BC, and shows there must have been an important settlement nearby. It states that the emperor's exertions in the cause of dharma (righteousness) had brought the people closer to the gods, and that through their efforts this attainment could be increased even further.

Tughluqabad

Fifteen kilometres southeast of Connaught Place on the Mehrauli–Badarpur Road (the entrance is a kilometre east of the junction with Guru Ravidas Marg), a rocky escarpment holds the crumbling 6.5km-long battlements of the third city of Delhi, **Tughluqabad** (daily sunrise–sunset; Rs100 [Rs5]), built during the short reign of Ghiyas-ud-din Tughluq (1320–24). After the king's death the city was deserted, probably due to the lack of a clean water source nearby. The most interesting area is the high-walled **citadel** in the south-western part of the site, though only a long underground passage, the ruins of several halls and a tower now remain. The grid pattern of some of the city streets to the north is still traceable. The palace area is to the west of the entrance, and the former bazaar to the east.

The southernmost of Tughlaqabad's thirteen gates still looks down on a causeway, breached by the modern road, which rises above the flood plain, to link the fortress with **Ghiyas-ud-Din Tughluq's tomb** (same hours and ticket as Tughlaqabad). The tomb is entered through a massive red-sandstone gateway leading into a courtyard surrounded by cloisters in the defensive walls. In the middle, surrounded by a well-kept lawn, stands the distinctive mausoleum, its sloping sandstone walls topped by a marble dome, and in its small way a precursor to the fine series of garden tombs built by the Mughals, which began here in Delhi with that of Humayun (see p.113). Inside the mausoleum are the graves of Ghiyas-ud-Din, his wife and their son Muhammad Shah II. Ghiyas-ud-Din's chief minister Jafar Khan is buried in the eastern bastion, and interred in the cloister nearby is the sultan's favourite dog.

The later fortress of **Adilabad** (free entry), built by Muhammad Shah II in much the same style as his father's citadel, and now in ruins, stands on a hillock to the southeast.

Tughluqabad is served by buses #34, #525 and #717 along the Mehrauli–Badarpur Road from Lado Sarai near the Qutb Minar, and by #430 from Kalkaji near the Baha'i Temple. From Connaught Place, the easiest way to get here is by pre-paid auto-rickshaw (Rs115). Tughluqabad metro station (violet line), scheduled to open at the end of 2010, will be around 1km east of the site.

Qutb Minar Complex

Above the foundations of Lal Kot, the "first city of Delhi" founded in the eleventh century by the Tomar Rajputs, stand the first monuments of Muslim India, known as the **Qutb Minar Complex** (daily sunrise–sunset; Rs250 [Rs10]). You'll find it 13km south of Connaught Place off Aurobindo Marg, easy to reach by bus #505 from Connaught Place (Scindia House), or by pre-paid auto from Connaught Place (Rs85). Qutab Minar metro station is 500m south of the site; Saket station is actually nearer. One of Delhi's most famous landmarks, the fluted red-sandstone tower of the **Qutb Minar** tapers upwards from the ruins, covered with intricate carvings and deeply inscribed verses from the Koran, to a height of just over 72m. In times past it was considered one of the "Wonders of the East", second only to the Taj Mahal; but historian John Keay was perhaps more representative of the modern eye when he claimed that the tower had "an unfortunate hint of the factory chimney and the brick kiln; a wisp of white smoke trailing from its summit would not seem out of place".

Work on the Qutb Minar started in 1202; it was Qutb-ud-Din Aibak's victory tower, celebrating the advent of the Muslim dominance of Delhi (and much of the Subcontinent) that was to endure until 1857. For Qutb-ud-Din, who died four years after gaining power, it marked the eastern extremity of the Islamic faith, casting the shadow of God over east and west. It was also a minaret, from which the muezzin called the faithful to prayer. Only the first storey has been ascribed to Qutb-ud-din's own short reign; the other four were built under his successor Iltutmish, and the top was restored in 1369 under Firoz Shah, using marble to face the red sandstone.

The Quwwat-ul-Islam mosque

Adjacent to the tower lie the ruins of India's first mosque, **Quwwat-ul-Islam** ("the Might of Islam"), commissioned by Qutb-ud-Din and built using the remains of 27 Hindu and Jain temples with the help of Hindu artisans whose influence can be seen in the detail of the masonry and the indigenous corbelled arches. Steps lead to an impressive courtyard flanked by cloisters and supported by pillars unmistakably taken from a Hindu temple and adapted to accord with strict Islamic law forbidding iconic worship – all the faces of the decorative figures carved into the columns have been removed. Especially fine ornamental arches, rising as high as 16m, remain of what was once the prayer hall. Beautifully carved sandstone screens, combining Koranic calligraphy with the Indian lotus, form a facade immediately to the west of the mosque, facing Mecca. The thirteenth-century Delhi sultan Iltutmish and his successors had the building extended, enlarging the prayer hall and the cloisters and introducing geometric designs, calligraphy, glazed tiles set in brick, and squinches (arches set diagonally to a square to support a dome).

The Khalji sultan Ala-ud-Din had the mosque extended to the north, and aimed to build a tower even taller than the Qutb Minar, but his **Alai Minar** never made it beyond the first storey, which still stands, and is regarded as a monument to the folly of vain ambition. Ala-ud-Din also commissioned the **Alai Darwaza**, an elegant mausoleum-like gateway with stone lattice screens, to the south of the Qutb Minar.

In complete contrast to the mainly Islamic surroundings, an **Iron Pillar** (7.2m) stands in the precincts of Qutb-ud-Din's original mosque, bearing fourth-century Sanskrit inscriptions of the Gupta period attributing it to the memory of King Chandragupta II (375–415 AD). Once topped with an image of the Hindu bird god, Garuda, the extraordinarily pure but rust-free pillar has puzzled metallurgists. Its rust resistance is apparently due to its containing as much as one percent phosphorous, which has acted as a chemical catalyst to create a protective layer of an unusual compound called misawite around the metal. The pillar was evidently transplanted here by the Tomars, but it's not known where from.

Archeological Park

The area south of the Qutb Minar Complex, rich with remains from all sorts of historical periods, has been turned into an **Archeological Park** (daily sunrise–sunset; free). Here, within a very pleasant stroll of each other, and of Qutab Minar metro station, you'll find: the tomb of Ghiyas-ud-Din Balban, one of the Slave Dynasty sultans (reigned 1265–87), believed to be the first building in India constructed with true arches; the beautiful 1528 mosque and tomb of the poet Jamali Kamali (you may need to find the caretaker to open up the tomb for you); and the octagonal Mughal tomb of Muhammad Quli Khan, one of Akbar's courtiers, which was occupied in the early nineteenth century by Sir Thomas Metcalfe, the East India Company's resident at the Mughal court, who rather bizarrely converted it into a country house. Metcalfe made his mark on the area in other ways too, restoring a Lodi-period dovecote and constructing "follies" – mock-ancient pavilions, a typical feature of English country estates of the time, except that Metcalfe's were Indian in style. The park extends over more than a hundred hectares and contains over eighty monuments, including tombs, mosques, gateways and *baolis*, dating from every century between the thirteenth and the twentieth.

Akshardham Temple

Across Nizamuddin Bridge on the east side of the Yamuna River (metro blue line or Rs70 by pre-paid auto from Connaught Place), the opulent **Akshardham Temple** (Tues–Sun: April–Sept 10am–7pm, Oct–March 9am–6pm; free; Ⓦwww.akshardham.com) was erected in 2005 by the Gujarat-based Shri Swaminarayan sect. The temple is a stunning piece of art, embellished with wonderful carvings made using the same tools and techniques as in ancient times. Cameras, mobile phones, mirrors and any electronic equipment, including USB keys, are prohibited and should be deposited at the cloakroom outside. Visitors may not enter wearing shorts or skirts above the knee. The **main shrine** is surrounded by a pink sandstone relief (you must walk round it clockwise) whose theme is elephants; wild, domesticated or in legend. Inside, the centrepiece and main object of devotion is a 3m-high gold statue of the sect's founder, Bhagwan Shri Swaminarayan, attended by four disciples. Behind it are paintings depicting scenes from his life, and also some personal objects such as his sandals and even some of his hair and nail clippings. The four subsidiary shrines are devoted to conventional Hindu gods.

Eating

Most restaurants close around 11pm, but those with bars usually stay open until midnight. If you're looking for a **late-night** meal, you have a number of choices: eat in one of the restaurants in a top hotel, or the 24-hour coffee shops in *Le Meridien*, the *Park* or *The Claridges*; try a snack in Paharganj's round-the-clock rooftop cafés; or head to Pandara Road market (open till 1.30am). Old Delhi railway station also has a couple of 24-hour places, and the refreshment hall just down the corridor from the foreigners' booking office in New Delhi station is also open round the clock.

Connaught Place

Connaught Place ("CP") is dominated by upmarket restaurants and Western-style fast-food places, with a few cheap and cheerful restaurants hidden away if you know where to look. The **Bengali Market**, on Tansen Marg, off Barakhamba Road, is a good place for sweets and snacks. The restaurants and cafés listed below are marked on the Connaught Place **map** on p.98.

Anand Connaught Lane, three doors from *Sunny Guest House*. Good, cheap eats including great biriyanis, with non-veg dishes at around Rs93 a throw (thali Rs94 veg, Rs114 non-veg).

Barista N-16 Connaught Place. Popular coffee bar, the first of what is now a nationwide chain that claims to do the best espresso in India, plus cakes and muffins to accompany. Rival chain *Café Coffee Day* has numerous CP outlets (almost one in every block).

Bikanervala 1st floor, Rajiv Gandhi Bhawan, between the two state emporium buildings, Baba Kharak Singh Marg. Sparkling canteen-style restaurant serving snacks, meals (thalis Rs125–140), sweets and *namkeens*.

Fire *Park Hotel*, 15 Sansad Marg ⓣ011/2374 3000 ext 1827. Scintillating if expensive modern restaurant whose contemporary Indian cuisine bears a strong hint of European influence. The menu is seasonal, with lighter dishes in summer, fierier ones in winter. Main non-veg dinner dishes are Rs775–1150, but at lunchtime there's a set meal (Rs1200 veg, Rs1500 non-veg). Booking advisable.

India Coffee House 2nd floor, Mohan Singh Place Shopping Complex, Baba Kharak Singh Marg. Down-at-heel canteen with a large roof terrace, part of a mainly south Indian co-op chain, serving filter and espresso coffee, snacks and basic meals (thalis Rs40) to an eclectic cross-section of downtown New Delhi's daytime population.

Kake Da Hotel 74 Municipal Market, Outer Ring, Connaught Place. A small, cramped diner (the term "hotel" does not imply accommodation) that's been here so long it's become a Delhi institution, known for unpretentious but reliably good Punjabi curries, mostly non-veg, such as butter chicken or sag meat (palak mutton), at around Rs100 a plate. Takeaway available.

Kwality 7 Regal Building, Sansad Marg. Originally set up to serve American GIs during World War II, this is one of CP's better mid-market choices (non-veg mains Rs225–325), quite elegantly decorated with lots of mirrors and chandeliers (though the odd mouse has been spotted. Good choices include chicken tikka with green peas, and mutton *shahi kurma*.

Parikrama Kasturba Gandhi Marg ⓣ011/2372 1616. Novel and expensive Indian (mainly tandoori) and Chinese cuisine in a revolving restaurant affording superb views over Delhi; a single rotation takes ninety minutes. Main dishes cost Rs220–650. Specialities include *murg pasandey parikrama* (chicken breast stuffed with minced chicken and nuts in a cashew-nut sauce) and *murg tikka parikrama* (chicken tikka in a spicy cashewnut marinade). Booking advisable.

Q'BA E-42/3 Connaught Place. Cool and stylish upmarket bar-restaurant on two floors and two terraces, with views over CP, though its "world cuisine" actually boils down to Indian, Italian and Thai, with pizza, pasta, green and red curry, and specialities such as *Q'BA raan* (char-grilled leg of lamb with herbs) and *sarsun wali machi tikka* (tandoori fish pieces in a mustard marinade). Main courses go for Rs350–700.

Sagar Ratna K-15 Connaught Place. The CP branch of the renowned Defence Colony restaurant (see p.122), great for *vadas*, *dosas* or a south Indian veg thali (Rs130). Main dishes Rs80–120.

Saravana Bhavan P-15 Connaught Place and 46 Janpath. Excellent low-priced south Indian snacks and meals, including thalis (Rs117) and quick lunches (Rs80), as well as the usual dosas, *iddlis* and *uttapams*. The mini tiffin (Rs80) has a taste of everything.

Spice Route *Hotel Imperial*, Janpath. This beautifully decorated restaurant, rarified and expensive, if perhaps a little overpriced (non-veg main dishes Rs650–775, seafood Rs1150–1850), specializes in spicy Southeast Asian and Keralan cuisine. If you want to eat well in the CP vicinity, this is one of your best bets.

Veda H-27 Connaught Place ⓣ011/4151 3535. CP's swankiest restaurant, heavy on the "ambience" (all smoochy red and black decor with low lights), which is what you pay for here, though the food isn't at all bad (main dishes such as Peshawari kebabs and malai fish tikka at Rs400–800; a tandoori platter for Rs355 veg, Rs755 non-veg).

Zen B-25 Connaught Place. Excellent Chinese meals (as well as a few Thai and Japanese dishes) served in a relaxed and traditional style, plus Western snacks (3–7pm), and a broad selection of wines, spirits and beers. Most non-veg main dishes are Rs285–300 (prawns Rs400–600).

Paharganj and Ram Nagar

With so much good food on offer in Delhi, it's a shame to dine in **Paharganj**, even if that's where your hotel is. Most of the restaurants on the Main Bazaar are geared to unadventurous foreign tastebuds, offering poor imitations of Western, Israeli, Japanese, and even Thai dishes, or sloppy, insipid versions of Indian curries for foreigners who can't handle chilli. Most serve breakfasts of toast, porridge, muesli and omelettes, though they'll do you a *paratha* as well. Eating options in **Ram Nagar** are more indigenous. If you decide to eat in any of the *dhabas* opposite New Delhi Station, especially those with waiters outside trying to hustle you in, and unless you can read the price list in Hindi, always ask the price of a dish before ordering, or you're likely to be overcharged. The restaurants listed below are marked on the Paharganj **map** on p.100.

Club India 4797 Main Bazaar. First-floor and rooftop restaurant with the best views over central Paharganj, lively music and the usual travellers' breakfast options, plus Israeli, Japanese, Tibetan and even tandoori dishes. Non-veg main courses go for Rs60–150, thalis and meal combos Rs100–175.

Darbar Restaurant and **Bikaner Sweets Corner** 9002 Multani Dhanda Chowk, just off Desh Bandhu Gupta Rd ⓣ011/2351 6666. Upstairs, it's a no-nonsense moderately priced veg restaurant, serving tasty thalis (Rs50–106) and Punjabi veg curries (Rs70–105); it also has a take-away service and delivers orders over Rs100 within a kilometre radius. Downstairs, it's a wonderful sweets emporium, with all sorts of multicoloured Bengali and Rajasthani confections, plus *namkeens* and savouries.

Diamond Café 5069 Main Bazaar. Backpacker restaurant with a good if typical menu (main dishes Rs70–150 non-veg), including a choice of set breakfasts (Continental, Indian, American, Israeli; Rs60–80), fruit salads, pancakes and also some Indian dishes. *Kholsa Cafe*, down the street at no. 5024, is very similar, but slightly cheaper.

Golden Café 1 Nehru Bazaar, Ramdwara Rd, opposite Sri Mahavir Mandir. Cheap and cheerful café popular with Korean and Japanese travellers, serving Chinese, Korean and European food with main dishes at Rs60–135.

Malhotra Laksmi Narain Rd. One of the better restaurants in Paharganj, offering passable tandoori and Mughlai dishes at reasonable prices (Rs130–225 for non-veg dishes). There's a basement and an a/c upstairs section, plus a veg south Indian branch two doors down.

Metropolis 1634 Main Bazaar. Cosy a/c ground-floor restaurant in the hotel of same name (downstairs or on the roof terrace). Paharganj's priciest venue serves full breakfasts, reasonable curries and tandoori specials, plus Western dishes, beer, spirits, cocktails and non-alcoholic "mocktails". Main dishes are Rs125–200 veg, Rs250–350 non-veg.

Ritu Raj Bhojnalya Arakashan Rd, below *Delhi Continental Hotel*. Cheap, popular *dhaba* serving excellent Indian breakfasts, simple veg curries, and south Indian snacks (Rs20–50). A great place for *chana* rice or *iddli sambar*.

Sonu Chat House 5046 Main Bazaar. Popular cheap diner serving noodles, soup, samosas, curries, and even masala dosa to the backpacker crowd. Set breakfasts Rs60–80, non-veg main dishes Rs65–120.

Sonu South Indian Restaurant 8849/2 Multani Dhanda Chowk, off Desh Bandhu Gupta Rd, Ram Nagar. Basic south Indian grub (masala dosa, *iddlis*, *vadas* and the like) at low prices (Rs35–65, or Rs60–80 for a thali).

Tadka 4986 Ramdwara Rd (Nehru Bazaar) ⓣ011/3291 5216. The best dining in Paharganj: a clean, bright, modern little restaurant serving low-priced Indian veg dishes (mains Rs65–75, thalis Rs85–100). They'll deliver to any address within 2km.

Old Delhi

Old Delhi's crowded streets contain numerous simple food-halls that serve surprisingly good, and invariably fiery, Indian dishes for as little as Rs20. Upmarket eating is thin on the ground, but some of the mid-range restaurants serve food every bit as good as the posh eateries of South Delhi, and the sweets and snacks in Old Delhi are the best in town. The restaurants listed below are marked on the Old Delhi **map** on p.109.

Aap ki Pasand 15 Netaji Subhash Marg ⓦwww.aapkipasandtea.com. You can get a chai on any street corner, but for a superior cuppa, head to this refined tea room, where Rs50 will buy you a bone china cup of first- or second-flush Darjeeling, Assam or Nilgiri; you can buy it all by the packet as well.

Chaina Ram 6499 Fatehpuri Chowk, next to Fatehpuri Mosque. Established in Karachi in 1901, and forced to relocate in 1947, this little shop is well known for its Sindhi-style sweets; the delicately aromatic Karachi halwa, with almonds and pistachios, is the best in town.

Chor Bizarre *Hotel Broadway*, 4/15 Asaf Ali Rd. A wide selection of excellent Indian cuisine including specialities from around the country, but above all from Kashmir. Eccentric, delightful decor featuring a four-poster bed, sewing table and a servery made from a 1927 vintage Fiat. Non-veg main dishes go for Rs325–495. The speciality is a Kashmiri sampler (*tarami*).

Deepak Chandni Chowk. A *dhaba* in the bazaar opposite the Jain temple, serving inexpensive south Indian snacks (*iddli sambar*, dosas and *uttapams* at Rs22–65) and thalis (Rs38–40).

Ghantewala 1862-A Chandni Chowk. Established in 1790, this famous confectioner supplied sweets to the last Mughal emperors; its *ladoo* was already renowned in the nineteenth century and the cashew fancies are out of this world, but their speciality is a nutty, butterscotch-like sweet called *sohan halwa*.

Haldiram's 1454 Chandni Chowk. Very clean, low-priced snack-bar and takeaway with sweets and samosas downstairs, drinks and snacks (Rs36–50) upstairs, including excellent *puris*, lassis, lime sodas, kulfis and thalis (Rs140). If you've never tried one, check the *raj kachori* (Rs46), a crunchy pastry shell enclosing a tangy chickpea curry with yoghurt.

Karim's Gali Kababian. A perennial Delhi favourite, located in a passage down a side street, opposite the south gate of the Jama Masjid, consisting of four eating halls (same kitchen) offering the best meat dishes in the old city, at moderate prices, with delicious fresh kebabs, hot breads and great Mughlai curries. Full dishes cost Rs110–385, but half-dishes are also available.

Moti Mahal 3704 Netaji Subhash Marg. Renowned for its tandoori chicken, this medium-priced restaurant is another local favourite – one of the first Punjabi restaurants in town – with both indoor seating and a large open-air courtyard. Main dishes go for Rs160–265, or Rs270 for the speciality, *murg musallam* (chicken with kidney, egg and mincemeat).

Paranthe Wali Gali Off Chandni Chowk, opposite the Central Bank. Head down this alleyway by Kanwarji Raj Kumar Sweet Shop (itself pretty good), and you'll be rewarded with *parathas* filled with anything from *paneer* and *gobi* to *mutter* and *mooli*, all cooked to order and served with a small selection of curries for Rs30–45. There are three *paratha*-wallahs in the alley, all good, but the most renowned is the first one, *Pandit Babu Ram*.

South Delhi

The enclaves and villages spread across the vast area of **South Delhi** offer countless eating options, and most of its upmarket shopping zones (Hauz Khas, Defence Colony, Ansal Plaza, and the like) contain several good restaurants. **Dilli Haat**, the tourist market in Safdarjang, has 25 food stalls offering dishes from nearly every state in India. **Pandara Road Market**'s restaurants and snack bars, just south of India Gate, stay open until 1.30am. Unless otherwise stated, the restaurants listed here are marked on the Delhi **map** on pp.90–91.

Basil & Thyme Santushti Shopping Complex. See New Delhi map, p.104. Bistro-style Mediterranean eating with dishes like shitake crepes, asparagus and arugula risotto, and desserts including seasonal fruit cheesecake or tiramisu; mains cost Rs355–525. The 6pm closing time however, means it's lunch not supper, unless you want to make that tea. Closed Sun.

Bukhara *Maurya Hotel*, Sardar Patel Marg, Chanakyapuri ⓣ011/2611 2233. See New Delhi map, p.104. Delhi's top restaurant, specializing in succulently tender tandoori kebabs (Rs1550), with a menu that's short but very sweet, and a kitchen separated from the eating area by a glass partition, so you can watch the chefs at work. Bill Clinton is among the celebs who flock here. The *Maurya* also has another fine restaurant, *Dum Pukht* (evenings only), which specializes in the *dum* (slow-cooked casserole) cuisine of Avadh (eastern Uttar Pradesh), with à la carte dining or a choice of set menus (Rs2400–3000).

Flavors C-52 Defence Colony. Run by an Indian–Italian couple, this is one of Delhi's very best Italian restaurants, where you'll find excellent risotto, great pasta and pizzas and wonderful tiramisu. Main dishes cost Rs335–500.

Park Balluchi Deer Park, Hauz Khas ⓣ011/2685 9369, ⓦwww.parkballuchi.com. Kebabs and Baluchistan-region dishes (veg Rs205–295, non-veg Rs360–450) amid pleasant sylvan surroundings. The speciality is a *murg potli* kebab, served on a flaming sword.

Punjabi by Nature Priya Cinema Complex, Basant Lok, Vasant Vihar ⓣ011/4151 6666. It's quite a haul from the centre (Rs120 by pre-paid auto from CP), but this restaurant has made a big name for itself among Delhi foodies with its fabulous Punjabi and north Indian cuisine – expensive, but worth it (most main dishes Rs425–575). The Amritsari fish tikka is succulent, the tandoori prawns wonderful, but for something really special, try the *raan-e-Punjab* (leg of lamb, Rs725). There's a more easily accessible branch on the third floor of City Square Mall, Raja Garden (ⓣ011/4222 5656 or 5757), by Rajaouri Garden metro.

Sagar 18 Defence Colony Market. Delicious, inexpensive south Indian vegetarian food, with *vadas*, *iddlis*, *ravas* and dosas (Rs60–85), plus great thalis (Rs130). They've also opened a north Indian restaurant a few doors down at no. 24, and they have branches all over town, but the original is still the best.

Swagath 14 Defence Colony Market. A non-veg off-shoot of *Sagar*, a few doors away. There are Indian and Chinese meat dishes on the menu, but ignore them and go for the Mangalore-style seafood – the *Swagath* special (chilli and tamarind), *gassi* (coconut sauce) and *sawantwadi* (green masala) dishes are all great (Rs295–305 with pomfret or Rs335–605 for prawn versions).

Nightlife and entertainment

With an ever-increasing number of pubs and clubs, Delhi's **nightlife** scene is in full swing. During the week, lounge and dance bars are your best bet, but come the weekend the **clubs** really take off. Most, if not all, of the ones popular with Delhi's young jet-set are in the luxury hotels, and many don't allow "stag entry" (men unaccompanied by women), which makes them a whole lot more comfortable for women, but is tough luck if you're male and alone; the big exception is *Elevate* – *the* spot in Delhi for serious clubbers. Cover charges are Rs500–2000 per couple depending on the club and the night. India Gate and Rajpath attract nightly **people's parties** where large crowds mill about, snacking and eating ice cream; these are not advisable for women on their own, as you're likely to get hassled.

For **drinking**, the five-star hotels all have plush and expensive bars, and many of the better ones have dance floors. Lounge bars with laid-back music have become very popular of late, and there are some good ones scattered about the southern suburbs. The drinking age in Delhi is 25.

Bars

Blues N-17 Connaught Place. See map, p.98. Snazzy bar and restaurant, offering an eclectic range of loud music (Thurs is rock night). The bar staff are all pros at mixing extravagant cocktails. Happy hour is 4–8pm, after which there's a Rs300 minimum food order, and lone males aren't allowed in.

Cibo *Janpath Hotel*, Janpath. See Connaught Place map, p.98. An Indian version of Mediterranean ambience, including an outside dining area decorated with gilded statues and Italian food, and through the tiled doorway, a bar surrounded by gilt fireplaces. It all just manages to be chic rather than kitsch, though it works well as either.

Gem 1050 Main Bazar, Paharganj. See map, p.100. Not a place to seek out over other options in town, but handy if you're in Paharganj and don't want to venture too far afield for a beer, though women won't be comfortable drinking here without a male escort. For a classier drink in the area, try the *Metropolis Hotel* (see p.121).

Lizard Lounge E-5, 1st Floor, South Extension II. See Delhi map, p.91. Lounge music (what else?) and hookah pipes (21 flavours) at this well-established, but still trendy lounge bar, with Mediterranean and Middle Eastern food.

My Bar 5136 Main Bazar, Paharganj. See map, p.100. A decent bar that also serves food, but it's the cheap beer (Rs84) that you come for.

Pegs n' Pints Forte Grand Complex, Chanakya Lane (behind Akbar Bhawan), Chanakyapuri ⓣ011/2687 8320. See Delhi map, p.104. Scruffy, inexpensive bar with music (mainly hip-hop) and an impressive wine list, but mostly of note for its Tuesday gay nights.

Rodeo A-12 Connaught Place. See map, p.98. Saloon-style bar with Wild West waiters, swinging-saddle bar stools, pitchers of beer, tequila slammers, and Mexican-style bar snacks (tacos, enchiladas, fajitas, quesadillas).

Splash Minto Rd (Viveknand Marg), just north of the rail bridge. See Connaught Place map, p.98. Quite a civilized bar with food and reasonably priced beer, a stone's throw from Connaught Place.

Clubs

Elevate 6th floor, Center Stage Mall, Sector 18, Noida ⓣ0120/436 4611, ⓦwww.elevateindia.com. See Delhi map, p.90. Across the river, and indeed just across the state line in UP, this is the biggest and most kicking club in town, modelled on London's *Fabric*, with three floors (dance floor, chill-out and VIP), a roof terrace and Indian and international DJs playing bhangra, filmi, hip-hop, trance or techno, depending on the night (techno and trance on Fri). Wed–Sat till 3.30am.

Capitol *Ashok Hotel*, 50-B Chanakyapuri ⓣ011/2687 9802. See map, p.104. Upmarket club playing unashamedly commercial filmi and pop music. Open Wed & Thur till 2am, Fri & Sat till 4am.

Dance and drama

Dances of India Parsi Anjuman Hall, Bahadur Shah Zafar Marg, near Delhi Gate ⓣ011/2623 4689. See Old Delhi map, p.109. Excellent classical, folk and tribal dance featuring six to seven items every night from different parts of India, usually including Bharatnatyam, Kathakali, Bhawai and the graceful dance of the north-eastern state of Manipur. Daily 6.45pm.
India Habitat Centre Lodi Rd ⓣ011/2468 2001 to 5, ⓦwww.indiahabitat.org. See New Delhi map, p.104. Popular venue for dance, music and theatre as well as talks and exhibitions.
Kamani Auditorium 1 Copernicus Marg ⓣ011/4350 3351 or 2, ⓦwww.kamaniauditorium.org. See New Delhi map, p.104. Bharatnatyam and other dance performances.
Sangeet Natak Akademi Rabindra Bhavan, 35 Firoz Shah Rd ⓣ011/2338 7246 to 8, ⓦwww.sangeetnatak.com. See New Delhi map, p.104. Delhi's premier performing arts institution.
Triveni Kala Sangam 205 Tansen Marg, just south of the Bengali Market ⓣ011/2371 8833. See New Delhi map, p.104. Dance shows, and art exhibitions.

Cinemas

Bollywood movies are shown at **cinemas** such as the Regal (ⓣ011/2336 1583) in Connaught Place, the Imperial in Rajguru Marg, Paharganj (ⓣ011/2252 8253), or the Shiela (ⓣ011/2367 2100) on Desh Bandhu Gupta Road, near New Delhi railway station. Tickets cost Rs25–80. CP's Odeon (ⓣ011/4151 7899) and Plaza (ⓣ011/4151 3787) cinemas are plusher and nowadays more popular. In addition, some of the cultural centres listed above occasionally run international film festivals. If you want to see Hindi films with English subtitles, your best bet is to buy them on DVD.

Sports and outdoor activities

The recreational activity most likely to appeal to visitors in the pre-monsoon months has to be a dip in one of Delhi's **swimming pools**. Unfortunately most public pools require you to take out membership; aside from Siri Sports Complex (listed below), try Talkatora Pool, Park Road (ⓣ011/2309 4832; see New Delhi map, p.104). Luxury hotels usually restrict their pools to residents, but may allow outsiders to join their health clubs; the *Ashok Hotel*, 50-B Chanakyapuri (ⓣ011/2611 0101; same location as *Capitol* on the New Delhi map, p.104) usually allows non-guests to use its pool (Rs400).

Delhi Races Kamal Ataturk Rd ⓣ011/2379 2869. Regular horse racing Tues from 1.30pm, sometimes other days too. Men usually Rs50, women Rs20. Mobile phones not allowed inside (you can deposit them at the entrance).
Delhi Riding Club Safdarjang Rd, behind Safdarjang's Tomb ⓣ011/2301 1891. Rides for adults at 7.30am, 8.30am and 9.30am, and for children at 2.45pm, 3.45pm and 4.45pm; open to the public by prior arrangement through the Club Secretary.
Indian Mountaineering Foundation 6 Benito Juárez Marg ⓣ011/2411 1211, ⓦwww.indmount.org. Official organization governing mountaineering and permits throughout India, with a library and an outdoor climbing wall. Some equipment can be rented here, and you can get information on local crags and climbing groups.
Siri Fort Sports Complex Siri Fort ⓣ011/2649 7482, ⓦwww.dda.org.in. An Olympic-sized swimming pool, a toddlers' pool, plus tennis, squash and badminton courts are among the facilities here, the most central of the city's fourteen sports complexes. Out-of-towners can use it for Rs100 [Rs40] a day.

Shopping

Although the traditional places to **shop** in Delhi are around **Connaught Place** (particularly the underground Palika Bazaar) and **Chandni Chowk**, a number of suburbs created by the rapid growth of the city are emerging as fashionable shopping districts. To check prices and quality for crafts, you can't do better than the **state emporiums** on Baba Kharak Singh Marg.

Unlike the markets of Old Delhi, most shops in New Delhi take credit cards; beware of touts trying to sweet-talk you into visiting supposed "government shops" which pay them a commission. In all bazaars and street markets, the rule is to **haggle**.

Art, antiques, crafts and jewellery

For crafts and jewellery, the **government emporiums** on Baba Kharak Singh Marg should be your first stop, especially if you want to check prices. **Paharganj** and Janpath's **Tibetan market** are good for trinkets such as cheap jewellery, decorated boxes and sandalwood carvings. For upmarket art, antiques (remember that export of anything over a hundred years old requires a permit) and jewellery, there's **Sunder Nagar Market** (see map, p.104).

Central Cottage Industries Emporium Jawahar Vyapar Bhawan, Janpath, opposite *Imperial Hotel* ⓣ011/2332 0439, ⓦwww.cottageemporium.in. Popular and convenient multistorey government-run complex, with handicrafts, carpets, leather and reproduction miniatures at fixed (if fractionally high) rates. Jewellery ranges from tribal silver anklets to costume pieces and precious stones.

Cottage of Arts and Jewels 50 Hauz Khas Village ⓣ011/2696 7418. Interesting, eccentric mix of jewellery, curios and papier-mâché crafts. The best of the collection, including miniatures and precious stones, is not on display: ask to see it.

Neemrana Shop 22-B Khan Market ⓣ011/2462 0262. Run by the renowned hotel group of the same name, the shop has a chic clientele and offers a range of clothes and a small collection of antiques and *objets d'art*.

Plutus 10 Hauz Khas Village ⓣ011/2653 6898, ⓦwww.plutusexports.com. An attractively presented shop selling replica antiques, bronze statues and an assorted collection of silver and gold jewellery. Ethnic Silver, two doors down at 9A, has a nice selection of jewellery and silverware.

Books

Connaught Place has many good general **bookshops**, including Amrit (N-21), Galgotia & Sons (B-17), New Book Depot (B-18) and Rajiv Book House (30 Palika Bazaar). **Secondhand bookstalls** include Jacksons at 5106 Paharganj Main Bazaar, opposite *Vishal* hotel, as well as an unnamed stall around the corner by Imperial cinema on Rajguru Marg, and Anil Book Corner by the Plaza Cinema on Connaught Place; on Sundays there's also Daryaganj Market by Delhi Gate in Old Delhi.

Fabrics and clothes

Delhi's **fabric** and **clothes** shops sell anything from high-quality silks, homespun cottons, saris, Kashmiri shawls and traditional *kurta* pyjamas to multicoloured tie-dyed T-shirts and other hippy gear. For T-shirts and tie-dyed clothing, try **Paharganj** or the **Tibetan Market**. For bargain Western-style trousers, skirts and shirts, the export-surplus market at **Sarojini Nagar** (see Delhi map, p.91) is very good. Roadside stalls behind the Tibetan Market off Janpath sell lavishly embroidered and mirrored spreads from Rajasthan and Gujarat, but silks and fine cotton are best bought in **government emporiums** on Baba Kharak Singh Marg.

Anokhi 5 & 6 Santushti Shopping Complex ⓣ011/2688 3076, ⓦwww.anokhi.com. Soft cotton and raw silk clothes and soft furnishings; particularly renowned for hand-block printed cottons combining traditional and contemporary designs. Also at 32 Khan Market and 16 N-Block Market.

Fabindia 5, 7 & 14, N-Block Market, Greater Kailash ⓣ011/4669 3724, ⓦwww.fabindia.com. Spread over several shops in the market, with a range from furnishings and interiors to chic cotton clothing for men, women and children and wearable block-printed cottons, sourced from villages across India; also sells organic spices, jams and pickles, and has branches around town including Khan Market (central hall, above nos.20 & 21) and B-28 & N-5 Connaught Place.

Handloom House 3rd floor, Rajiv Gandhi Bhawan, between the two state emporium buildings, Baba Kharak Singh Marg ⓣ011/2334 1984. Government outlet with roll after roll of fine hand-woven cotton and silk textiles, plus cotton and linen shirts and silk saris.

Harsiba 5 Rajiv Gandhi Bhawan, between the two state emporium buildings, Baba Kharak Singh Marg ⓣ011/3948 9374. Lovely clothes, accessories and furnishings made by self-employed women, mostly working at home, and sold through their own cooperatively run outlet.

Khadi Gramodyog Bhawan 24 Regal Building, corner of Sansad Marg and Connaught Place ⓣ011/2336 0902, ⓦwww.kvic.org.in. Government-run and a great place to pick up hardy, lightweight travelling clothes. Reasonably priced, ready-made traditional Indian garments include *salwar kameez*, woollen waistcoats, pyjamas, shawls and caps, plus rugs, cloth by the metre, tea, incense, cards and tablecloths.

People Tree 8 Regal Building, Sansad Marg, Connaught Place ⓣ011/2334 0699, ⓦwww.peopletreeonline.com. An interesting selection of alternative designs, with an emphasis on T-shirts, ethnic chic and jewellery.

Shaw Brothers D-47 Ground Floor, Defence Colony ⓣ011/2469 0364, ⓦwww.shaw-brothers.com. Upmarket purveyors of shawls, rugs, pashminas and silks. Also at 8 Palika Bazar, Connaught Place ⓣ011/2332 9080.

Vedi Tailors M-60 Connaught Place ⓣ011/2341 6901. Originally established in Rangoon in 1926, this gents' tailor can run you up a made-to-measure suit for anything from Rs8000 to Rs30,000, depending on fabric and cut. They usually take a week, but for a little extra they can do it in 24 hours. S.L. Kapur at G-7 is an equally reputable firm offering a similar service.

Music and musical instruments

Lahore Music House Netaji Subhash Marg, Old Delhi (next-door to *Moti Mahal* restaurant) ⓣ011/2327 1305, ⓦwww.lmhindia.com. Long-established north Indian musical instrument makers with a reputation for quality.

Rikhi Ram G-8, Outer Circle, Connaught Place ⓣ011/2332 7685, ⓦwww.rikhiram.com. Once sitar makers to the likes of renowned musician Ravi Shankar, and still maintaining an exclusive air, with prices to match. Check out the display of their own unique instrumental inventions.

Shielma 11 & 27 Palika Bazar, Connaught Place ⓣ011/2332 2900. CDs of classical, folk and film music, plus DVDs of Hindi (and English) movies.

Miscellaneous

Indian Art Collection 1 Hauz Khas Village. Old Bollywood film posters are the speciality here, mostly in the Rs1000–5000 range. You can buy them framed, but it's generally easier to have them rolled up and slipped into in a protective tube. Indian Popular Art, a few doors away at no.5, also sells film posters.

Jain Super Store 172 Palika Bazaar, Connaught Place ⓣ011/2332 1031, ⓦwww.jainperfumers.com. Essential oils, natural perfumes and their own in-house fragrances, as well as joss sticks, scented candles and aroma diffusers.

Mother Earth (Industree) 8 Rajiv Gandhi Bhawan, between the two state emporium buildings, Baba Kharak Singh Marg ⓦwww.industreecrafts.com. A light, bright shop with equally light, bright designs, including mats, blinds, boxes and bags made of natural fibres such as jute, reeds and rattan, crafted by small producers mostly working from home and sold by a fair-trade NGO.

Nath Stationers (The Card Shop) B-38 Connaught Place. A small shop with a big selection of greeting cards featuring Indian artwork and designs.

Listings

Airlines Air Canada, 803, 8th floor, Ansal Bhawan, 16 Kasturba Gandhi Marg ⓣ011/4152 8181; Air France, c/o KLM; Air India, 2nd floor, Tower 1, Jeevan Bharati Building, 124 Connaught Circus at Sansad Marg ⓣ011/2373 1225; Asiana Airlines, 2 Ansal Bhawan, ground floor, 16 Kasturba Gandhi Marg ⓣ011/2331 5631; British Airways, DLF Plaza Tower, DLF Qutab Enclave, Gurgaon, Haryana ⓣ95124/412 0747 from Delhi, 0124/412 0747 outside Delhi, or 1800/102 3592; Cathay Pacific, 413 Ashoka Estate Building, Barakhamba Rd ⓣ011/4354 4777 or 1800/209 1616; China Airlines, c/o Ascent Air, upper ground floor, Kanchenchunga Building, 18 Barakhamba Rd ⓣ011/2332 7131; Continental, 2nd floor, Tower C, Cyber Green, DLF Phase 3, Gurgaon, Haryana ⓣ95124/431 5500 from Delhi, 0124/431 5500 from outside Delhi; Delta, c/o Interglobe Enterprises, Thapar House, 124 Janpath ⓣ011/4351 3140 or 41; Emirates, 7th floor, DLF Centre, Sansad Marg ⓣ011/6631 4444; Gulf Air, 201 Ansal Bhawan, 16 Kasturba Gandhi Marg ⓣ011/4352 1482; Indian Airlines, c/o Air India; IndiGo, Level 1, Tower C, Global Business Park, Mehrauli–Guragon Rd, Gurgaon ⓣ1800/180 3838 or 0124/435 2500; Jet Airways, N-40 Connaught Place ⓣ011/4132 3247; JetLite, IGI Airport ⓣ011/2567 5879 (domestic) or 2565 3609 (international); Kenya Airways, Ground Floor, Ambadeep Building, 14 Kasturba Gandhi Marg ⓣ011/2376 6248; Kingfisher, N-42 Connaught Place ⓣ1800/180 0101; KLM, airport terminal 2 ⓣ011/2335 7747; Kuwait Airways, 4 Ansal Bhawan, ground floor, 16 Kasturba Gandhi Marg ⓣ011/2335 4373; Lufthansa, 56 Janpath ⓣ011/2372 4200; Malaysia Airlines, 16th floor, Dr Gopaldas Bhawan, 28 Barakhamba Rd ⓣ011/4151 2121; Nepal Airlines, 44 Janpath ⓣ011/2332 1164; Qatar Airways, ground floor, Dr Gopaldas Bhawan, 28 Barakhamba Rd ⓣ011/4363 6000; Royal Jordanian, G-56 Connaught Place ⓣ011/2332 7418; SAA, Thapar House, 124 Janpath ⓣ011/4351 3131; Singapore Airlines, Unit 514 A & B, Time Tower, MG Road, Gurgaon, Haryana ⓣ0124/431 0999; SpiceJet, 319 Udyog Vihar, Phase IV, Gurgaon ⓣ1800/180 3333; Thai, *Hotel Intercontinental Eros*, American Plaza, Nehru Place ⓣ011/4149 7777; United, Corporate Park, Block 2B, DLF City, DLF Phase III, Gurgaon, Haryana ⓣ95124/235 8201 from Delhi, 0124/235 8201 from outside Delhi; Virgin Atlantic, 8th floor, DLF Centre, Sansad Marg ⓣ011/4130 3030 or 1800/102 3000.

Banks and exchange Almost every block on Connaught Place has ATMs that take Visa or MasterCard, as do metro stations, and there are several along Chandni Chowk and Asaf Ali Rd in Old Delhi. There's an HFDC bank ATM opposite the *Metropolis Hotel* on Paharganj Main Bazaar, and a couple more just up Rajguru Marg beneath the *Roxy Hotel*. You can change money at the DTTDC office, N-36 Connaught Place, and at numerous other authorized exchange offices in Connaught Place and Paharganj. All major hotels have exchange facilities; the *Ajanta*, near the *Grand Godwin* on Arakashan Rd in Ram Nagar has a 24hr bureau. Thomas Cook is upstairs at C-33 Connaught Place (ⓣ011/6627 1971; Mon–Fri 9.30am–6pm, Sat 10am–5.30pm), with branches at CP post office and the *Hotel Janpath*. American Express is represented by Standard Chartered Bank at A-1 Connaught Place (ⓣ011/4365 4027; Mon–Fri 9am–6pm, Sat 9am–4pm).

Car rental Avis, D-4 Shubam Gardens, near Hari Bhawan, Ram Mandir Marg, Vasant Kunj ⓣ011/6568 0664 or 0627, ⓔcrsdelhi@avis.co.in; Budget, *Lemon Tree Hotel*, East Delhi Mall, Kaushambi, Ghazaibad ⓣ0120/442 3202; Europcar, Suite 105, 1st floor, Indra Prakash Building, 21 Barakhamba Rd ⓣ011/4166 7760, ⓔreservation.del@europcar.co.in; Hertz, c/o Carzonrent, Khasra no.78, Dagar Farm House (opposite BP petrol pump), Bijwasan ⓣ011/4184 1212, ⓔreserve@carzonrent.com (also in Dwarka, near airport & Dwarka Sector 12 metro station, at F-3 Building 1, Malik Plaza, Plot no.2, pocket 6, Sector 12, Dwarka ⓣ011/4553 5501/2, ⓔdwarka@carzonrent.com).

Embassies, consulates & high commissions Call ahead for opening hours before you visit. Australia, 1/50-G Shanti Path, Chanakyapuri ⓣ011/4139 9900; Bangladesh, EP-39, D Radha Krishan Marg, Chanakyapuri ⓣ011/2412 1389; Bhutan, Chandragupta Marg, Chanakyapuri ⓣ011/2688 9230; Burma, 3/50-F Nyaya Marg, Chanakyapuri ⓣ011/2467 8822; Canada, 7/8 Shanti Path, Chanakyapuri ⓣ011/4178 2000; China, 50-D Shanti Path, Chanakyapuri ⓣ011/2611 2345 (entrance for visa applications in Nyaya Marg); Denmark, 11 Aurangzeb Rd ⓣ011/4209 0700; Indonesia, 50-A Kautilya Marg, Chanakyapuri ⓣ011/2611 8642 to 5; Iran, 5 Barakhamba Rd ⓣ011/2332 9600 to 02; Ireland, 230 Jor Bagh-3 (near Safdarjang's Tomb) ⓣ011/2462 6733; Malaysia, 50-M Satya Marg, Chanakyapuri ⓣ011/2611 1291 to 3; Maldives, B-2 Anand Niketan ⓣ011/4143 5701; Nepal, Barakhamba Rd by Mandi House Chowk, southeast of Connaught Place ⓣ011/2332 7361;

Netherlands, 6/50-F Shanti Path, Chanakyapuri ⓣ011/2419 7600; New Zealand, 50-N Nyaya Marg, Chanakyapuri ⓣ011/2688 3170; Norway, 50-C Shanti Path, Chanakyapuri ⓣ011/4177 9200; Pakistan, 2/50-G Shanti Path, Chanakyapuri ⓣ011/2467 6004; Singapore, E-6 Chandragupta Marg, Chanakyapuri ⓣ011/4600 0800; South Africa, B-18 Vasant Marg, Vasant Vihar, ⓣ011/2614 9411; Sri Lanka, 27 Kautilya Marg, Chanakyapuri ⓣ011/2301 0201 to 3; Sweden, 4–5 Nyaya Marg, Chanakyapuri ⓣ011/2419 7100; Thailand, 56-N Nyaya Marg, Chanakyapuri ⓣ011/2611 8103 or 4; UK, Shanti Path, Chanakyapuri ⓣ011/2687 2161; US, Shanti Path, Chanakyapuri ⓣ011/2419 8000.

Hospitals All India Institute of Medical Sciences (AIIMS), Ansari Nagar, Aurobindo Marg (ⓣ011/2658 8500), has a 24hr emergency service, as does Lok Nayak Jai Prakash Hospital, Jawaharlal Nehru Marg, Old Delhi (ⓣ011/2323 6000), near Delhi Gate. Dr Ram Manohar Lohia Hospital, Baba Kharak Singh Marg (ⓣ011/2334 8200, ⓦrmlh.nic.in), is another government hospital. Private clinics include East West Medical Centre, B-28 Greater Kailash Part I (ⓣ011/2924 3701 to 3, ⓦwww.eastwestrescue.com) and Indraprastha Apollo Hospital, Sarita Vihar, Delhi–Mathura Rd (ⓣ011/2692 5801, ⓦwww.apollohospdelhi.com). The US embassy maintains a list of hospitals and doctors on its website at ⓦnewdelhi.usembassy.gov/medical_information2.html.

Internet Reliable places include: Sunrise N-9/II Connaught Place (Rs35/hr); Shivam, 651 Tooti Chowk, just off Main Bazaar, Paharganj (Rs20/hr); Kesri, 5111 Main Bazaar, Paharganj (near *Kholsa Café*; Rs20/hr).

Left luggage Rs10–15/day at the railway stations. Most hotels in Paharganj offer a left-luggage service.

Money transfers Western Union agents include several post offices, most conveniently Old Delhi and New Delhi GPOs, but if having money sent to a post office, be sure to specify the name correctly, as with poste restante (see below). WU agents also include the Punjab and Sind Bank, M-14 Connaught Place, and Bank of Baroda at B-3 and M-9. MoneyGram's agents can be found in branches of Thomas Cook (such as at C-33 Connaught Place), and branches of the Central Bank of India, including 1763 Chuna Mandi near Paharganj, and 70 Janpath near Connaught Place.

Motorcycles The Karol Bagh area has many good bike shops selling new or secondhand Enfields. Reliable dealers include Inder Motors, 1744-A/55 basement, Hardhyan Singh Nalwala St, Abdul Aziz Rd (ⓣ011/2875 0869, ⓦwww.lallisingh.com), two blocks east of Ajmal Khan Rd, turning right at the *chowki*, then the third alley on the left; closed Mon. Also worth trying is Ess Aar Motors, 1-E/13 Jhandewalan Extension, between Karol Bagh and Paharganj (ⓣ011/2367 8836).

Opticians Lawrence & Mayo, 76 Janpath; R.K. Oberoi, H-14 Connaught Place.

Pharmacies Nearly every market has at least one pharmacy. Apollo, G-8 Connaught Place and at New Delhi Station (*Ginger Hotel*) is open 24hr.

Photographic services Kinsey Brothers, 2-A Connaught Place (under *India Today*); Delhi Photo Company, 78 Janpath.

Police ⓣ100 (national number). Delhi has a dedicated squad of tourist police based at the airport, main stations and major tourist sights and hotel areas, whose aim is specifically to help tourists in trouble. If you need to involve the police, your hotel reception or the Government of India tourist office will direct you to the appropriate station.

Postal services Poste restante (Mon–Sat 9am–5pm) is available at the GPO (Gole PO) on the roundabout at the intersection of Baba Kharak Singh Marg and Ashoka Rd (sale of stamps Mon–Sat 9am–8pm). You must show your passport to claim mail or check the register for parcels. Have mail for this post office addressed to "Poste Restante, New Delhi GPO, Gole Dakhana, Delhi 110001", as letters sent to "Poste Restante, Delhi" will go to Old Delhi GPO, north of the railway line on Lothian Rd (but if you want mail to be held there, specify "Old Delhi GPO, Lothian Rd, Delhi 110006" just to be sure). There is a branch office at A-6 Connaught Place (Mon–Sat 10am–5.45pm).

State tourist offices Andaman and Nicobar Islands, 12 Chanakyapuri ⓣ011/2687 1443, ⓦtourism.andaman.nic.in; Andhra Pradesh, P Bhawan, 1 Ashoka Rd ⓣ011/2338 1293, ⓦwww.aptourism.in; Arunachal Pradesh, Arunchal House, opposite Chanakya Cinema, Bir Tikendrajit Marg, Chanakyapuri ⓣ011/2611 7728, ⓦwww.arunachaltourism.com; Assam, State Emporia Complex, B-1 Baba Kharak Singh Marg ⓣ011/2334 5897, ⓦwww.assamtourism.org; Bihar, Room 6, *Hotel Janpath*, Janpath ⓣ011/2336 8371, ⓦbstdc.bih.nic.in; Chandigarh, 21-B Telegraph Lane, Harish Chandra Mathur Lane, off Kasturba Gandhi Marg behind Max Muller Bhawan ⓣ011/2335 3359, ⓦwww.citcochandigarh.com; Chhattisgarh, 3rd floor, Chanakya Bhawan (opposite Chanakya Cinema), Malcha Marg, Chanakyapuri ⓣ011/2611 6823, ⓦwww.chhattisgarhtourism.net; Daman and Diu, Daman and Diu Bhawan, Plot 16, Tenzing Norgay Marg, State Guest House Area, Chanakyapuri ⓣ011/2467 7391 or 2, ⓦwww.damandiutourism.com; Goa, Goa Sadan, 18 Amrita Shergil Marg, near

Khan Market ⓣ011/2462 9968, ⓦwww.goa-tourism.com; Gujarat, A-6 State Emporia Building, Baba Kharak Singh Marg ⓣ011/2374 4015, ⓦwww.gujarattourism.com; Haryana, Chanderlok Building, 36 Janpath ⓣ011/2332 4910 or 11, ⓦharyanatourism.gov.in; Himachal Pradesh, Chanderlok Building, 36 Janpath ⓣ011/2332 5320, ⓦwww.hptdc.nic.in; Jammu & Kashmir, Rooms 14 & 15, *Hotel Janpath*, Janpath ⓣ011/2374 4938 or 48, ⓦwww.jktourism.org; Jharkhand, Room 2, *Hotel Janpath*, Janpath ⓣ011/2336 5545, ⓦwww.jharkhandtourism.in; Karnataka, C-4 State Emporia Building, Baba Kharak Singh Marg ⓣ011/2336 3863, ⓦwww.karnatakatourism.org; Kerala, Travancore House, Kasturba Gandhi Marg, near Bharatiya Vidya Bhawan ⓣ011/2338 2067, ⓦwww.keralatourism.org; Lakshadweep, F-301 Curzon Road Hostel, Kasturba Gandhi Marg ⓣ011/2338 6807, ⓦlakshadweeptourism.nic.in; Madhya Pradesh, Room 12, *Hotel Janpath*, Janpath ⓣ011/2336 6528, ⓦwww.mptourism.com; Maharashtra, Room 10, *Hotel Janpath*, Janpath ⓣ011/2336 6940, ⓦwww.maharashtratourism.gov.in; Manipur, C-7 State Emporia Building, Baba Kharak Singh Marg ⓣ011/2374 6359, ⓦmanipur.nic.in/tourism.htm; Meghalaya, Meghalaya House, 9 Aurangzeb Rd ⓣ011/2301 4417, ⓦmegtourism.gov.in; Mizoram, Mizoram Bhawan, Circular Rd, Chanakyapuri ⓣ011/2301 5951, ⓦmizotourism.nic.in; Nagaland, Government of Nagaland, 29 Aurangzeb Rd ⓣ011/2301 5638, ⓦwww.tourismnagaland.com; Orissa, B-4 State Emporia Building, Baba Kharak Singh Marg ⓣ011/2336 4580, ⓦwww.orissa-tourism.com; Puducherry, 3 Sardar Patel Marg, Chanakyapuri ⓣ011/2611 1302, ⓦtourism.pondicherry.gov.in; Punjab, Room 11, *Hotel Janpath*, Janpath ⓣ011/2334 3055, ⓦpunjabgovt.nic.in/tourism/tour1.htm; Rajasthan, Bikaner House, Pandara Rd, near India Gate ⓣ011/2338 3837, ⓦwww.rajasthantourismindia.com; Sikkim, New Sikkim House, 14 Panchsheel Marg, Chanakyapuri ⓣ011/2611 5346, ⓦsikkimtournet.com; Tamil Nadu, C-1 State Emporia Building, Baba Kharak Singh Marg ⓣ011/2374 5427, ⓦwww.tamilnadutourism.org; Tripura, Tripura Bhavan, Kautilya Marg, Chanakyapuri ⓣ011/2301 5157, ⓦwww.tripuratourism.in; Uttarakhand, Room 1, *Hotel Janpath*, Janpath, GMVN (Garhwal) ⓣ011/2335 0481, ⓦwww.gmvnl.com, KMVN (Kumaon) ⓣ011/2371 2246, ⓦwww.kmvn.gov.in; Uttar Pradesh, Chandralok Building, 36 Janpath ⓣ011/2332 2251, ⓦwww.up-tourism.com; West Bengal, A-2 State Emporia Building, Baba Kharak Singh Marg ⓣ011/2374 2840, ⓦwww.westbengaltourism.gov.in.

Telephones Way2Talk, 1126 Main Bazaar, Paharganj, has low-cost international VoIP calls (Rs7/min to the UK, North America, Australia and New Zealand), and the first ten seconds are free.

Visa extensions and exit formalities The first place to go if you need to extend your visa is the Ministry of Home Affairs, Foreigners' Division, Jaisalmer House, 26 Man Singh Rd (Mon–Fri 10am–noon). If your total stay will exceed six months, you will also need to go to the Foreigner's Regional Registration Office (FRRO), East Block 8, Level 2, Sector 1, Ramakrishna Puram (Mon–Fri 9.30am–1.30pm & 2–4pm; ⓣ011/2671 1443). Forms can be downloaded from ⓦwww.immigrationindia.nic.in. If you've been in India more than 120 days, before leaving you'll need to fill in a tax clearance certificate, obtainable from the Foreign Section, Income Tax Office, Central Revenue Building, Indraprastha Estate (Mon–Fri 10am–1pm & 2–5pm; ⓣ011/2337 9171 ext 1650); have foreign exchange certificates and ATM receipts to hand.

Moving on from Delhi

Delhi has good international and domestic **travel connections**; it seldom takes more than a day to arrange an onward journey. Scores of **travel agents** (see p.130) sell bus and air tickets, while many hotels (budget or otherwise) will book private buses for you. There's an ever-expanding network of internal flights, but it's still best to book as far ahead as possible; at peak times such as Diwali, demand is very high.

If leaving India for a country that requires a **visa** (including Pakistan, Nepal and Bangladesh), make sure you have obtained the necessary documentation from the relevant embassy (see pp.127–128); call in advance to check opening hours, specific requirements (such as how many photos you'll need), and the likely waiting period.

Travel agents and tour operators

The Rajasthan Tourism Development Corporation, Bikaner House, Pandara Road (ⓣ011/2338 3837 or 6069), organizes **package tours** including wildlife tours and trips on the *Palace on Wheels* and *Heritage on Wheels* trains. The Delhi Tourism and Transport Development Corporation, N-36, Bombay Life Building, Middle Circle, Connaught Place (ⓣ011/5152 3073), offers day-trips to Agra (Rs950) and three-day "Golden Triangle" excursions to Agra, Ajmer, Bharatpur and Jaipur (Rs4200). For competitively priced car tours around Rajasthan try *Hotel Namaskar*, Paharganj (ⓣ011/2358 2233, ⓔnamaskarhotel@yahoo.com). The India Tourism Development Corporation's commercial arm, Ashok Travels, *Janpath Hotel*, Janpath (ⓣ011/2334 9062, ⓔtravel@attindiatourism.com), sells excursions and air tickets.

For **ticketing**, recommended operators specializing in international and domestic flights include: HRG Sita, F-12 Connaught Place (ⓣ011/2462 2152) and Travel Corporation of India, 5th floor, New Delhi House, 27 Barakhamba Road (ⓣ011/2341 6082 to 5, ⓦwww.tcindia.com). Aa Bee Travel, in the lobby of *Hare Rama Guest House* (ⓣ011/2356 2171 or 2117, ⓔaabee@mail.com) at T-298 off Main Bazaar, Paharganj, is a reliable firm for competitively priced air and private bus tickets. The Student Travel Information Centre, G-55 Connaught Place (ⓣ011/4620 6600, ⓦwww.statravel.co.in), issues or renews ISIC cards.

Don't book flights or excursions through any agency that you're directed to by a street tout, and that goes double for any agency spuriously trying to pass itself off as a tourist information office.

By air

Indira Gandhi International Airport (ⓦwww.newdelhiairport.in; automated information line for international flights ⓣ011/2560 2999, domestic flights ⓣ011/2566 2275) is 20km southwest of the city centre. Most tourists on night-flights book a **taxi** to the airport in advance (around Rs250; 30–60min) through their hotel. By **auto-rickshaw** it's around Rs150 (Rs115 pre-paid from CP). Otherwise, there's a bus service every 30min from Maharana Pratap ISBT via New Delhi station gate 2 (Ajmer Gate side) and Connaught Place (Scindia House), costing Rs50.

Domestic flights to almost every other airport in India leave from Terminal 1, **international flights** from Terminal 2. If you don't already have a ticket for a **flight** out of India, you'll have little trouble finding one, except between December and March when it may be difficult at short notice. While you can buy tickets directly from the airlines (addresses on p.127), it can save time and leg-work to book through an **agency** (see above). Some airlines require you to **reconfirm** your flight between a week and 72 hours before leaving.

By train

New Delhi railway station has regular departures to all corners of India, and a very efficient **booking office** (Mon–Sat 8am–8pm, Sun 8am–2pm) for foreign tourists, on the first floor (above ground) of the main departure building. Staff will give you advice on the fastest trains, and you should have little difficulty finding a seat or berth: **women** travelling alone in second class may prefer to ask for a berth in the ladies' carriage. Foreigners must show passports, and may possibly be asked to pay in foreign currency or show exchange certificates. Ignore roadside advice to book train tickets elsewhere, and don't try buying one at the reservations building down the road – you'll be faced with a confusion of queues and crowds. Also, ignore claims that the tourist booking office has moved or is closed (see p.94 for more on scam merchants).

Many southbound trains leave from New Delhi, but all trains to Rajasthan, except those to Bharatpur, Kota and Sawai Madhopur, leave from either **Old Delhi** or **Sarai Rohilla** stations. Quite a few trains to south and central India leave from **Hazrat Nizamuddin** station, so check carefully when you buy your ticket. Bookings for all trains can be made at New Delhi station.

For recommended trains from Delhi, see box below.

By bus

Buses are of most use for travelling to mountainous areas of neighbouring states that aren't served by trains, but they may also be faster than trains on shorter routes. On longer routes there's usually a choice between the ramshackle state-run

Recommended trains from Delhi

The trains below are recommended as the fastest and/or most convenient for specific cities. Daily unless marked.

Destination	Name	No.	From	Departs	Total time
Agra	*Shatabdi Express**	#2002	ND	6.15am	2hr (except Fri)
	Taj Express	#2180	HN	7.15am	2hr 52min
	Mangala Express	#2618	HN	9.20am	3hr
	Kerala Express	#2626	ND	11.30am	2hr 50min
Ahmedabad	*Ashram Express*	#2916	OD	3.36pm	16hr 04min
	*Rajdhani Express**	#2958	ND	7.55pm	14hr 10min
Ajmer	*Shatabdi Express**	#2015	ND	6.05am	6hr 55min (except Wed)
	Ahmedabad Mail	#9106	OD	10.35pm	8hr 53min
Chandigarh	*Shatabdi Express**	#2011	ND	7.40am	3hr 25min
	Paschim Express	#2925	ND	11.15am	4hr 37min
	*Shatabdi Express**	#2005	ND	5.25pm	3hr 12min
Chennai	*Tamil Nadu Express*	#2622	ND	10.30pm	32hr 40min
	GT Express	#2616	HN	6.40pm	35hr 35min
Haridwar	*Shatabdi Express**	#2017	ND	6.50am	4hr 35min
	Haridwar Mail	#9105	OD	5.50am	6hr 25min
Jaipur	*Shatabdi Express**	#2015	ND	6.05am	4hr 40min
	*Rajdhani Express**	#2958	ND	7.55pm	4hr 45min
	Ashram Express	#2916	OD	3.05pm	5hr 20min
Jhansi	*Shatabdi Express**	#2002	ND	6.15am	4hr 33min
Kolkata	*Kolkata Rajdhani**	#2302 /2306	ND	5pm	16hr 55min (Fri 19hr 40mi)
	*Sealdah Rajdhani**	#2314	ND	4.35pm	17hr 40min
	Howrah–Poorva Express	#2304	ND	4.25pm	24hr 25min (W, Th, Sa, Su)
	Kalka Mail	#2312	OD	7.30am	24hr 30min
Mumbai	*Rajdhani Express**	#2952	ND	4.30pm	16hr 05min
Udaipur	*Mewar Express*	#2963	HN	7.05pm	12hr 15min
Varanasi	*Varanasi Special*	#0458	OD	6.15pm	12hr 15min
	Shiv Ganga Express	#2560	ND	6.45pm	11hr 45min
Vasco da Gama	*Goa Express*	#2780	HN	3pm	39hr 25min

OD Old Delhi   ND New Delhi   HN Hazrat Nizamuddin   SR Sarai Rohilla

*a/c only

buses and more comfortable private buses, which some see as potentially more dangerous, as they travel faster and often overnight.

The majority of **state-run buses** depart from the **Maharana Pratap ISBT** (Ⓣ011/2386 8836; see Old Delhi map, p.109) by Kashmiri Gate metro and Rs60 from Connaught Place by auto. Be sure to arrive up to an hour before departure to allow time to find the correct counter (there are thirty or so) and book your ticket. Ask for the numbers of both platform and licence plate to ensure you board the right bus.

Services for Uttarakhand hill stations like Nainital, Almora and Ramnagar (for Corbett National Park) leave from **Anand Vihar ISBT** in East Delhi (Ⓣ011/2215 2431; bus #73 or #85, metro, or Rs75 by pre-paid auto from Connaught Place). Buses to Agra, and some to Ajmer and Jaipur leave from the **Sarai Kale Khan ISBT** (Ⓣ011/2435 8343; see New Delhi map, p.104) east of Hazrat Nizamuddin Station. However, for Jaipur, Udaipur, Jodhpur and Ajmer, the **Rajasthan Roadways terminal** at Bikaner House, India Gate (Ⓣ011/2338 3469; see New Delhi map, p.104), has by far the best service, with a range that includes comfortable deluxe buses.

Private **deluxe buses** usually depart from near the Ramakrishna Mission at the end of Main Bazaar, Paharganj, but some pick up passengers at hotels. Popular destinations include Kullu, Manali and Dharamsala, which are not accessible by train, as well as Pushkar and the Uttarakhand (Uttaranchal) hill stations. You can book tickets a day or two in advance at the agencies in Paharganj or Connaught Place.

The only **international service** is to Lahore in Pakistan, leaving from Dr Ambedkar Terminal on Jawaharlal Nehru Marg near Delhi Gate daily except Sunday at 6am (Ⓣ011/2331 8180, Ⓦwww.dtc.nic.in/lahorebus.htm).

2

Rajasthan

* **Keoladeo National Park, Bharatpur** Flocks of rare birds – and bird-watchers – travel from across Asia and Europe each winter to visit this remarkable wetland sanctuary. See p.170

* **Ranthambore National Park** One of the easiest places in the world to see tigers in the wild, thanks to its large and exhibitionist population of big cats. See p.171

* **Savitri Temple, Pushkar** For optimum views of the famous lake and whitewashed holy town, climb to the hilltop Savitri Temple at sunset. See p.183

* **Meherangarh Fort, Jodhpur** Spectacular hilltop citadel, with maximum-impact views of the blue city below. See p.190

* **Camel trekking** There's no better way to experience the Thar Desert than by riding a camel through it. See p.196

* **Jaisalmer Fort** One of India's most beautiful forts, its massive, honey-coloured bastions enclosing a labyrinth of narrow streets dotted with sandstone havelis and temples. See p.201

* **Udaipur** Rajasthan's – if not India's – most romantic city: a fairy-tale ensemble of lakes, floating palaces and sumptuous Rajput architecture ringed by dramatic green hills. See p.214

▲ Camel trekking, Thar Desert

The state of **RAJASTHAN** emerged after Partition from a mosaic of twenty-two feudal kingdoms, known in the British era as Rajputana, "Land of Kings". Running northeast from Mount Abu, near the border with Gujarat, to within a stone's throw of the ruins of ancient Delhi, its backbone is formed by the bare brown hills of the Aravalli Range, which divide the fertile Dhundar basin from the shifting sands of the mighty Thar Desert, one of the driest places on earth.

Rajasthan's extravagant **palaces**, **forts** and finely carved **temples** comprise one of the country's richest crop of architectural monuments. But these exotic buildings are not the only legacy of the region's prosperous and militaristic history. Rajasthan's strong adherence to tradition is precisely what makes it a compelling place to travel. Swaggering moustaches, heavy silver anklets, bulky red, yellow or orange turbans, pleated veils and mirror-inlaid saris may be part of the complex language of **caste**, but to most outsiders they epitomize India at its most exotic.

Colour also distinguishes Rajasthan's most important tourist cities. **Jaipur**, the vibrant state capital, is known as the "Pink City" thanks to the reddish paint applied to its ornate facades and palaces. **Jodhpur**, the "Blue City", is centred on a labyrinthine old walled town, whose sky-blue mass of cubic houses is overlooked by India's most imposing hilltop fort. Further west, the magical desert city of **Jaisalmer**, built from local sandstone, is termed the "Golden City". In the far south of the state, **Udaipur** hasn't gained a colour tag yet, but it could be called the "White City": coated in decaying limewash, its waterside palaces and havelis are framed by a distant vista of sawtooth hills.

The route stringing together these four cities has become one of the most heavily trodden tourist trails in India. But it's easy to escape into more remote areas. Northwest of Jaipur, the desert region of **Shekhawati** is dotted with atmospheric market towns and innumerable richly painted havelis, while the desert city of **Bikaner** is also well worth a stopover for its fine fort, havelis and the unique "rat temple" at nearby Deshnok. The same is true of **Bundi**, in the far south of the state, with its magnificent, muralled fort, as well as the superb fort at **Chittaurgarh** nearby, not to mention the engaging hill station and remarkable Jain temples of **Mount Abu**.

Another attraction is Rajasthan's wonderful **wildlife sanctuaries**. Of these, the popular tiger-sanctuary at **Ranthambore** is deservedly the most popular, while the **Keoladeo National Park** at **Bharatpur**, on the eastern border of Rajasthan near Agra, is unmatched in South Asia for its incredible avian population, offering a welcome respite from the frenetic cities that inevitably dominate most visitors' itineraries.

Visiting Rajasthan

Rajasthan's **climate** reaches the extremes common to desert regions, with temperatures topping 45°C during the hottest months of May and June. The monsoon breaks over central and eastern Rajasthan in July, continuing, in theory at least, through until September, although in recent years rainfall has become increasingly unpredictable and sporadic. The fierce summer heat lingers until mid-September or October, when night temperatures drop considerably. The best time to visit is between November and February, when daytime temperatures rarely exceed 30°C; in midwinter, you'll need a shawl or thick jumper if you're outdoors at night.

Getting around the state is rarely problematic, though there's no avoiding some tedious long hauls. **Trains** connect all major cities and many smaller towns, while the state-run **bus** company, RSTDC, and various **private operators** have regular services between cities.

Festivals and fairs in Rajasthan

Rajasthan's vibrant local costumes are at their most dazzling during the state's **festivals**. For dates of specific events, ask at tourist offices; most festivals fall on days determined by the lunar calendar.

Desert Festival (Feb). Two-day event in Jaisalmer. See p.204 for details.

Elephant Festival (March). Parades of brightly painted elephants march through the streets of Jaipur, concluding with an extraordinary elephant-versus-*mahout* tug of war.

Mewar Festival (March & April). The ranas of Udaipur celebrate Holi with traditional dances, the lighting of a sacred fire, and music by the city's famous bagpipe orchestra.

Gangaur (April). Women pray for their husbands, and unmarried girls wish for good ones. At its best in Jaisalmer and Mount Abu.

Nagaur Cattle Fair (late Jan/early Feb). Thousands of farmers and around seventy thousand steers, cows and bullocks descend on Nagaur, south of Bikaner.

Pushkar Camel Fair (Nov). The world's largest livestock market and Rajasthan's most colourful festival. See p.185.

Rani Sati Mela (Aug). Vast crowds gather in Jhunjhunu for a day of prayers and dances in memory of a merchant's widow who committed sati in 1595.

Tilwara Cattle Fair (held over a fortnight in March or April). One of Rajasthan's biggest livestock markets, held at Tilwara, 93km southwest of Jodhpur.

Urs Mela (Oct). India's largest Islamic festival, held in Ajmer. See p.177.

Some history

The turbulent history of Rajasthan only really begins in the sixth and seventh centuries AD, with the emergence of warrior clans such as the Sisodias, Chauhans, Kachchwahas and Rathores – the **Rajputs** ("sons of princes"). Never exceeding eight percent of the population, they were to rule the separate states of **Rajputana** for centuries. Their code of honour set them apart from the rest of society – as did the myth that they descended from the sun and moon.

The Rajput codes of chivalry that lay behind endless clashes between clans and family feuds found their most savage expression in battles with Muslims. **Muhammad of Ghor** was the first to march his troops through Rajasthan, eventually gaining a foothold that enabled him to establish the **Sultanate** in Delhi. During the 350 years that followed, much of central, eastern and western India came under the control of the sultans, but, despite all their efforts, Rajput resistance prevented them from ever taking over Rajputana.

Ghor's successors were pushed out of Delhi in 1483 by the Mughal Babur, whose grandson **Akbar** came to power in 1556. Aware of the futility of using force against the Rajputs, Akbar chose instead to negotiate in friendship, and married Rani Jodha Bai, a princess from the Kachchwaha family of Amber. As a result, Rajputs entered the Mughal courts, and the influence of Mughal ideas on art and architecture remains evident in palaces, mosques, pleasure gardens and temples throughout the state.

When the Mughal empire began to decline after the accession of Aurangzeb in 1658, so too did the power of the Rajputs. Aurangzeb sided with a new force, the **Marathas**, who plundered Rajput lands and extorted huge sums of protection money. The Rajputs eventually turned for help to the Marathas' chief rivals, the **British**, and signed formal treaties as to mutual allies and enemies. Despite growing British power, the Rajputs were never denied their royal status, and relations remained largely amicable.

The International boundaries on this map are neither purported to be correct nor authentic by Survey of India directives. Publisher.
PAKISTAN
Kali Bangan
Indira Gandhi Canal
Thar Desert (Great Indian Desert)
Bikaner
Gajner
Deshnok
Kolayat
Nokha
NH-15
Kishangarh
Bhuttewala
Ramgarh
Lodurva
Phalodi
R A J
Jaisalmer
Sam
Khuhri
Pokaran
Osian
Dechhu
Mandor
Jodhpur
Shiv
Balotra
Barmer
Luni
Pali
Marwar
Sanderav
Jalor
Ranakpur
Sirohi
KUMBALGARH SANCTUARY
Sanchor
Nagda
Mt Abu
Abu Rd
Udaipur
Rann of Kutch
Palanpur
Rishdeo
GUJARAT
Dungarpur
Himatnagar
Little Rann of Kutch
Ahmedabad
Bhuj
RAJASTHAN
Mumbai

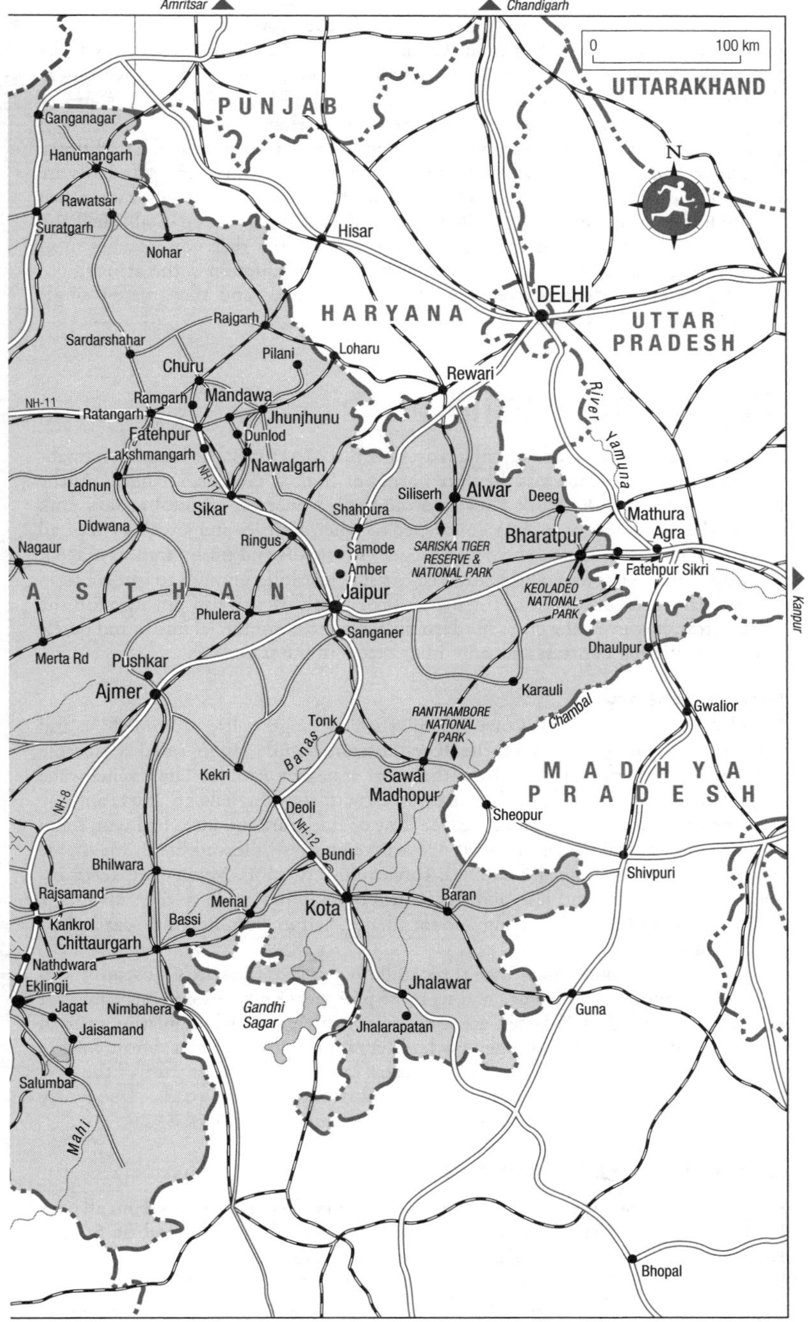

Amritsar
Chandigarh
0
100 km
UTTARAKHAND
PUNJAB
N
Ganganagar
Hanumangarh
Rawatsar
Suratgarh
Nohar
Hisar
HARYANA
DELHI
UTTAR PRADESH
Rajgarh
Sardarshahar
Pilani
Loharu
Churu
Rewari
Ramgarh
Mandawa
NH-11
Ratangarh
Jhunjhunu
Fatehpur
Dunlod
Lakshmangarh
Nawalgarh
River Yamuna
Ladnun
Sikar
Siliserh
Alwar
Deeg
Shahpura
Mathura
Didwana
Agra
Ringus
Samode
Bharatpur
Nagaur
Amber
SARISKA TIGER RESERVE & NATIONAL PARK
Fatehpur Sikri
RAJASTHAN
Jaipur
KEOLADEO NATIONAL PARK
Kanpur
Phulera
Sanganer
Dhaulpur
Merta Rd
Pushkar
Ajmer
Karauli
Chambal
Gwalior
RANTHAMBORE NATIONAL PARK
Tonk
Banas
MADHYA PRADESH
Kekri
Sawai Madhopur
NH-8
Deoli
Sheopur
NH-12
Bundi
Bhilwara
Shivpuri
Rajsamand
Menal
Kota
Baran
Kankrol
Bassi
Chittaurgarh
Nathdwara
Eklingji
Jhalawar
Jagat
Nimbahera
Gandhi Sagar
Guna
Jaisamand
Jhalarapatan
Salumbar
Mahi
Bhopal

The nationwide clamour for Independence in the years up to 1947 eventually proved stronger in Rajasthan than Rajput loyalty; when British rule ended, the Rajputs were left out on a limb. With persuasion from the new Indian government they agreed one by one to join the Indian Union, and in 1949 the 22 states of Rajputana finally merged to form the state of **Rajasthan**.

Modern Rajasthan remains among the poorest and most staunchly traditional regions of India, although attempts to raise educational and living standards are gradually bearing fruit. Since 1991 Rajasthan has tripled its literacy rate, a feat unmatched by any other state, while several universities have been established and new industries have benefited from an electricity supply that now reaches most villages. Irrigation schemes have also improved crop production in this arid region, although ongoing **drought** remains an acute problem, and the greatest single threat to Rajasthan's future prosperity.

Jaipur and around

A flamboyant showcase of Rajasthani architecture, **JAIPUR** has long been established on tourist itineraries as the third corner of India's "Golden Triangle". At the heart of Jaipur lies the **Pink City**, the old walled quarter, whose **bazaars** rank among the most vibrant in Asia, renowned for their textiles and jewellery. For all its colour, however, Jaipur's heavy traffic, dense crowds and pushy traders make it a taxing place to explore, and many visitors stay just long enough to catch a train to more laid-back destinations further west or south. If you can put up with the urban stress, however, the city's modern outlook and commercial hustle and bustle offer a stimulating contrast to many other places in the state.

Some history

Established in 1727, Jaipur is one of Rajasthan's youngest cities, founded by (and named after) **Jai Singh II** of the **Kachchwaha** family, who ruled a sizeable portion of northern Rajasthan from their fort at nearby Amber. The Kachchwaha Rajputs had been the first to ally themselves with the Mughals, in 1561, and, by the time of Jai Singh's accession, the free flow of trade, art and ideas had won them great prosperity. Jai Singh's fruitful 43-year reign was followed by an inevitable battle for succession, and the state was thrown into turmoil. Much of its territory was lost to Marathas and Jats, and the British quickly moved in to take advantage of Rajput infighting. Following Independence, Jaipur became **state capital** of Rajasthan in 1956.

Today, with a population of over three million, Jaipur is the state's most advanced commercial and business centre and its most prosperous city – some estimates put it amongst the world's 25 fastest growing cities, with an annual population growth of over 3.5 percent, and gleaming new high-rises springing up on an almost weekly basis. Evidence of Jaipur's severe growing pains can be seen in older parts of the city, however, with creaking infrastructure and traffic-choked roads, frequently approaching gridlock during the morning and evening rush hours.

Arrival and information

Jaipur's **railway station** lies 1.5km west of the Pink City; state buses from all over Rajasthan and further afield pull in at the **Inter-state Bus Terminal** on Station Road. Buses arriving from Delhi or Agra skirt the southern side of the city, stopping briefly at Narain Singh Circle, where rickshaw-wallahs frequently board the bus and, with the connivance of the bus driver, announce that it's the end of the line ("bus going to yard") – a ploy to get you aboard their rickshaws and into a hotel that pays them commission. The city's modern Sanganer **airport** is 15km south of the centre. There are airport buses into town; alternatively, a rickshaw will cost around Rs200, a taxi Rs330–400.

The **RTDC** has tourist information offices on Platform 1 of the railway station (daily 7am–10pm; ⓣ0141/231 5714); on MI Road opposite the GPO (daily 8am–8pm; ⓣ0141/237 5466); and on platform 3 at the state bus terminal (daily 9.30am–5pm). **RTDC tours** (see below) can be booked through any of these offices. There's an **India Tourism** office at the *Khasa Kothi* hotel (Mon–Fri 9am–6pm, Sat 9am–1.30pm; ⓣ0141/237 2200), with a good range of leaflets and countrywide information. The monthly *Jaipur City Guide* (Rs40), available at some hotels, bookshops and newspaper stalls, has **listings** of all the latest events in the city.

City transport and tours

Jaipur is very spread out, and although it's possible to explore the Pink City on foot (despite the crowds), you may need some form of transport to get you there from your hotel. It's best to avoid the morning and evening rush hours, especially within the Pink City. **Auto-rickshaws** are available all over the city, as are **cycle rickshaws**, though these can take forever to get anywhere in the heavy traffic. **Prepaid auto-rickshaws** can be booked at the kiosks (open 24hr) in front of the railway station and in front of the bus station. Rates for these are much cheaper than you're likely to get on the street (Rs380/Rs212 for a full/half day's hire, for example, or just Rs84 for a one-way ride to Amber). **Cars with driver** can be rented through most hotels or through any RTDC office, usually costing around Rs900–1000 per day.

One very inexpensive, albeit very rushed, way to see Jaipur's main attractions is on one of the two **guided tours** run by the RTDC (5hr half-day tour, Rs150; 9hr full-day tour, Rs200; entrance fees not included), which cram in most of the major city sights. They also run a "Pink City by Night" tour (6.30–10.30pm; Rs250), which includes dinner at Nahargarh Fort. Tours depart from (and can be booked through) any of the RTDC offices listed above or through the RTDC *Hotel Gangaur* on MI Road.

Accommodation

Jaipur has a wide range of **accommodation**, mostly found west of the city centre, along (or close to) MI Road and in the upmarket suburb of Bani Park. It's a good idea to **book ahead**, particularly around the Elephant Festival (first half of March). Note that almost all the places listed below offer **free pick-up** from the bus or train station, and all have **internet** access (and often **wi-fi** as well).

Budget

Atithi Guest House 1 Park House Scheme, just off MI Rd ⓣ0141/237 8679, ⓔatithijaipur@hotmail.com. Long-established guesthouse and still one of the nicer budget places in town, with pleasant modern tiled rooms (air-cooled and a/c) and an attractive rooftop terrace. A smart new in-house Indian veg restaurant and coffee shop should have opened by the time you read this. ❸–❹

Jaipur Inn Shiv Marg, Bani Park ⓣ0141/220 1121, ⓦwww.jaipurinn.com. Reliable, pleasantly old-fashioned budget option, with comfortable and well-equipped rooms with TV and (optional) a/c, plus nightly buffets on the breezy rooftop. ❹, a/c ❺

Kailash Johari Bazaar ⓣ0141/257 7372. One of the few budget hotels in the Pink City itself. Rooms are a bit shabby and pokey, but perfectly comfortable (although avoid the noisy rooms directly overlooking Johari Bazaar) while the brilliant central location can't be beaten. ❸

Karni Niwas C-5 Motilal Atal Rd (behind *Hotel Neelam*) ⓣ0141/236 5433, ⓦwww.hotelkarniniwas.com. Long-running budget

Moving on from Jaipur

Jaipur is Rajasthan's main **transport hub**, with frequent bus and train services to all major destinations around the state, as well as nationwide air connections. **Sanganer Airport** (see Arrival and information p.139) has several flights daily to Mumbai, and is used by Air-India Express (IX), Air India Regional (CD), GoAir (G8), Indian Airlines (IC), IndiGo (6E), Jet Airways (9W), Kingfisher (IT) and SpiceJet (SG). There are currently flights to: Ahmedabad (6E, SG); Bengaluru (Bangalore; G8, 6E, IT, SG); Chandigarh (IT); Chennai (6E, SG); Delhi (IX, CD, IC, 9W, IT); Goa (SG); Guwahati (6E); Hyderabad (6E, SG); Indore (G8); Jammu and Srinagar (IT); Kolkata (Calcutta; IX, 6E, SG); Mumbai (IC, G8, 6E, 9W, SG, IT); Udaipur (IX, 9W, IT). A rickshaw to the airport should cost around Rs200; a taxi, Rs350–400.

Short journeys to destinations like Bharatpur, Ajmer (for Pushkar) and towns in Shekhawati are usually best made by bus; one exception is Sawai Madhopur, which is most easily reached by train.

RSRTC government buses leave from the Inter-state Bus Terminal (also known as "Sindhi Camp") on Station Road, with frequent, direct services to pretty much every major town in Rajasthan and beyond. For longer journeys, faster but less frequent deluxe Gold Line ("Volvo") and Silver Line government services guarantee seats (enquiries on ⓣ0141/220 4445, bookings up to 24hr in advance on ⓣ0141/220 5790). For other services it's easier to just turn up at the bus stand and head for the relevant booking office – destinations are listed outside each cabin. The deluxe services have their own separate booking hatch on platform 3 (open 24hr). There's an RTDC bus for **Pushkar** daily at 1pm; otherwise catch one of the regular buses for Ajmer and change there, or take a private bus (see below).

Private bus services also serve a wide range of destinations, often in comfortable modern coaches, although they may cram too many passengers on board and make unscheduled stops during the journey to tout for custom. You can book tickets for these at the string of agents on Station Road. A reliable company for direct buses to **Pushkar** is Jai Ambay Travels (daily 7.30am–9am; ⓣ0141/220 5177), on Station Road near the junction with MI Road, whose comfortable deluxe coaches leave at 9.30am; you can buy tickets just prior to departure, but it's a good idea to get them in advance (you can also book by phone). They also sell tickets for private buses to Agra (hourly; 5hr 30min), Ajmer (6 daily; 2hr 30min), Bharatpur (hourly; 4hr 30min), Bikaner (5 daily; 6hr), Bundi (2 daily; 4hr), Chittaurgarh (1 daily; 6hr), Jaisalmer (1 nightly; 12hr), Jodhpur (3 daily, including 10.30pm sleeper; 6–7hr), Kota (2 daily; 5hr), Nawalgarh (hourly; 3hr) and Udaipur (2 nightly; 9hr).

Bookings for **trains** should be made at least a day in advance at the computerized reservations hall just outside the main station (Mon–Sat 8am–8pm, Sun 8am–2pm; ⓣ0141/220 1401); go to the special "Foreign Tourist and Freedom Fighter" counter.

stalwart, with comfortable air-cooled and a/c rooms (either in the old-fashioned main building or the more modern extension) and pleasant communal seating on outside balconies overlooking a small garden. ❸–❹

Krishna Palace E-26 Durga Marg, Bani Park ⓣ0141/220 1395, ⓦwww.krishnapalace.com. Set in a rather grand, haveli-style building, this friendly, family-run budget option offers a range of bright and comfortable air-cooled and a/c rooms, all newly renovated and decorated with traditional Rajasthani touches. ❸, a/c ❺

Pearl Palace Hari Kishan Somani Marg, Hathroi Fort ⓣ0141/237 3700, ⓦwww.hotelpearlpalace.com. One of the best guesthouses in Rajasthan, with a selection of spotless and excellent-value modern air-cooled and a/c rooms (a few with shared bathroom) attractively decorated with local arts and crafts. The well-drilled staff can take care of all your needs, and facilities include 24hr money exchange, internet access and travel ticketing, plus an excellent rooftop restaurant (see p.149). Advance bookings recommended. ❷–❹

Recommended trains from Jaipur

Destination	Name	No.	Departs	Arrives
Abu Road	*Aravali Express*	9708	(daily) 8.45am	5.10pm
Agra	*Gwalior Express*	2987	(daily) 6.10am	10.55am
	Sealdah Express	2988	(daily except Thurs) 2.50pm	7.30pm
	Marudhar Express	4864/ 4854/ 4866	(daily) 3.40/ 3.50pm	9pm
Ajmer	*Shatabdi Express*	2015	(daily except Wed) 10.55pm	1am
	Aravali Express	9708	(daily) 8.45am	11am
Alwar	*Jammu Tawi Express*	2413	(daily) 4.35pm	6.56pm
	Shatabdi Express	2016	(daily except Wed) 5.45pm	7.26pm
Bikaner	*Bikaner Intercity*	2468	(daily) 3.50pm	10.45pm
	Hanumangarh Special	0234	(daily) 9.05pm	4.55am
Chittaurgarh	*Udaipur Express*	2965	(daily) 10.28pm	3.50am
Delhi	*Jaisalmer Express*	4060	(daily) 5am	11.05am
	Shatabdi Express	2016	(daily except Wed) 5.50pm	10.40pm
Jaisalmer	*Jaisalmer Express*	4059	(daily) 11.57pm	11.30am
Jodhpur	*Marudhar Express*	4853/ 4863/ 4865	(daily) 11.50am	5.30pm
	Ranthambore Express	2465	(daily) 5.05pm	10.30pm
	Jaisalmer Express	4059	(daily) 11.57pm	5am
Kota	*Intercity Express*	2466	(daily) 10.55am	2.45pm
	Mumbai Superfast	2956	(daily) 2.10pm	5.25pm
Sawai Madhopur (for Ranthambore National Park)	*Intercity Express*	2466	(daily) 10.55am	1.15pm
	Mumbai Superfast	2956	(daily) 2.10pm	4pm
Udaipur	*Udaipur Express*	2965	(daily) 10.28pm	6.10am
Varanasi	*Marudhar Express*	4854/ 4864/ 4866	(daily) 3.40pm	8.35/ 9.30/ 10.30am

Pearl Palace Heritage 54 Gopal Bari, Lane no.2, Ajmer Rd ⓣ0141/237 5242, ⓦwww.pearlpalaceheritage.com. Attractive new sister-hotel to the excellent *Pearl Palace*, with a slightly more upmarket heritage theme – each of the spacious a/c rooms is individually themed (Jaisalmer, Colonial, Shekhawati, etc), complete with traditional wooden doors, assorted artworks and artefacts, and a superb sequence of stone carvings adorning the first-floor corridors – a miniature museum in itself. Given the quality, room rates are a steal. ❹–❺

Sunder Palace Sanjay Marg, Hathroi Fort, Ajmer Rd ⓣ0141/236 0878, ⓦwww.sunderpalace.com. One of the city's standout budget options, with spotless, attractively decorated modern rooms (air-cooled or a/c) at very competitive prices. There's a choice of garden and rooftop restaurants (see p.149), while the two friendly brothers who run the place can also take care of money exchange, travel arrangements and anything else you're likely to think of. Advance bookings recommended. ❷–❹

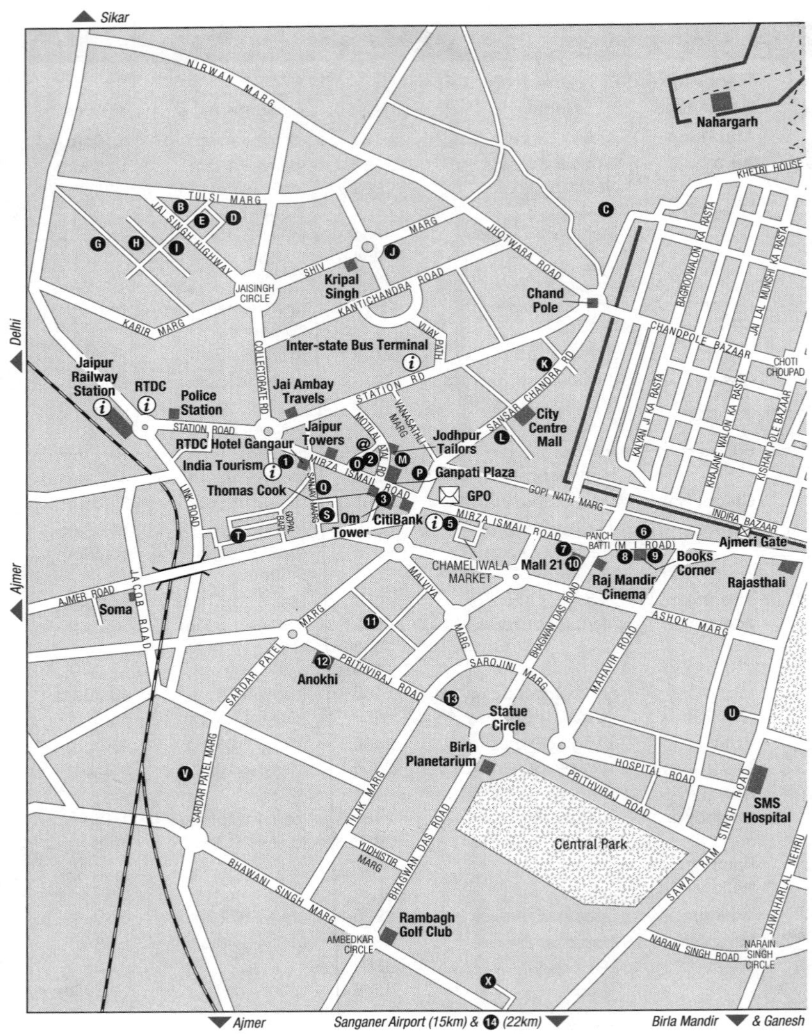

Mid-range

Arya Niwas Sansar Chandra Rd ⓣ 0141/237 2456, ⓦ www.aryaniwas.com. Dependable old hotel arranged around a couple of intimate courtyards, with a lovely expanse of lawn and spacious veranda out front. Rooms (most of which have been recently renovated) are comfy and nicely furnished; all come with a/c, apart from a few air-cooled singles. Popular with tour groups. ❺

Bissau Palace Khetri House Rd ⓣ 0141/230 4371, ⓦ www.bissaupalace.com. Tucked away in a down-at-heel part of town, this attractive heritage hotel is less flash than others in Jaipur but has bags of old-world atmosphere, especially the time-warped antique library and Sheesh Mahal; also has a decent-sized pool and Ayurveda room. Discounts in summer. ❺–❻

Diggi Palace SMS Hospital Rd ⓣ 0141/237 3091, ⓦ www.hoteldiggipalace.com. One of the city's most appealing heritage hotels, occupying a characterful old haveli set amid huge gardens in a conveniently central location. Rooms are a mixed bunch, and the air-cooled budget rooms are rather drab. It's worth splashing out on

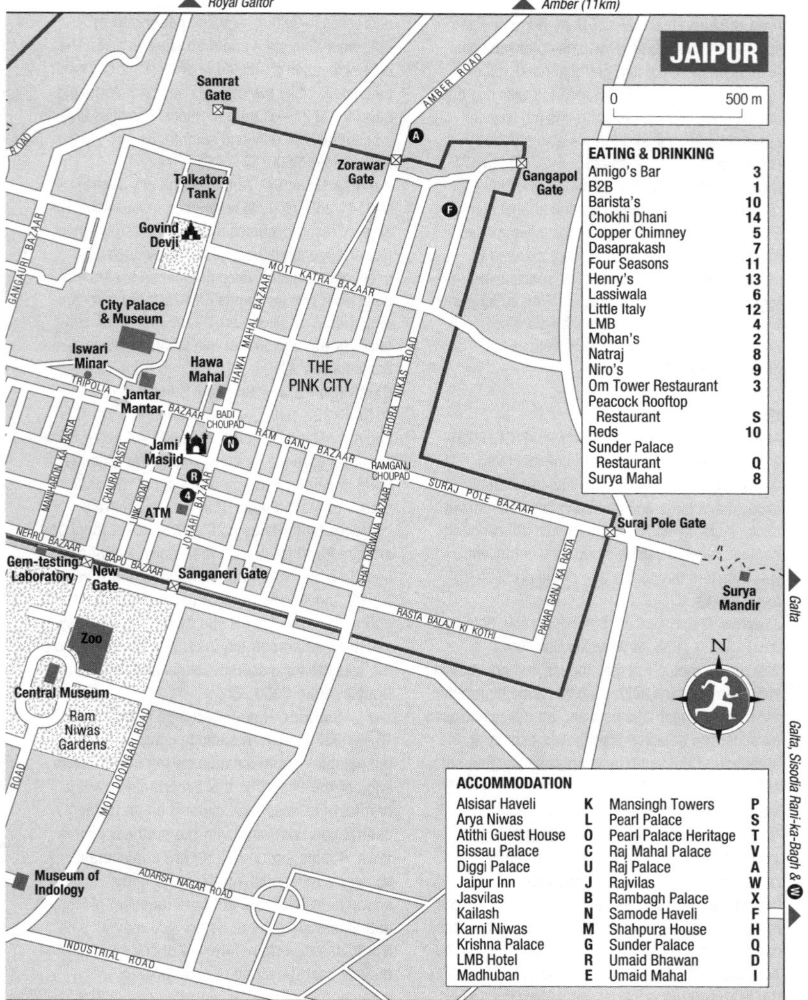

one of the more expensive traditional-style rooms in the main building, or (nicer still) one of the stylish modern "Premium" rooms in the new annexe. 5–8

LMB Hotel Johari Bazaar ⓣ0141/256 5844, ⓦwww.hotellmb.com. Passable mid-range hotel next door to the well-known *LMB* restaurant and right in the thick of the Pink City action. The cheaper "Executive" rooms are neat and comfortable; the more expensive "Royal Deluxe" rooms have nothing to recommend them excepting some spectacularly tasteless furniture. Avoid the noisy rooms overlooking Johari Bazaar. 6–7

Madhuban D-237 Behari Marg, Bani Park ⓣ0141/220 0033, ⓦwww.madhuban.net. Less imposing than the city's other heritage hotels – it's more of an overgrown suburban villa than a genuine palace – though also better-value than most, with attractively furnished rooms (though some of the cheaper ones are a bit small) and plenty of quaint Rajasthani decorative touches, plus a pleasant garden and small pool round the back. 5–6

Umaid Bhawan D1-2A Off Bank Rd, Bani Park ⓣ0141/220 6426, ⓦwww.umaidbhawan.com. Flamboyantly decorated heritage hotel, full of eye-catching murals, old wooden furnishings and other Rajasthani artefacts. Rooms (all a/c) are spacious and cool, and there's also a pool. Discounts in summer. ❺–❻

Umaid Mahal C-20/B-2 Bihari Marg, Bani Park ⓣ0141/220 1952, ⓦwww.umaidmahal.com. Extravagantly decorated heritage-style modern hotel, with virtually every surface covered in colourful traditional murals. The spacious a/c rooms are attractively furnished with antique-style wooden furniture, and there's also a nice basement pool and bar. Check website for discounts. ❺–❻

Expensive

Alsisar Haveli Sansar Chandra Rd ⓣ0141/236 8290, ⓦwww.alsisar.com. An unexpectedly upmarket haven in a ramshackle part of town, occupying a large and immaculately modernized century-old haveli. It's not the most atmospheric heritage hotel in Jaipur, though it's comfy and well-run, and the pool is one of the prettiest in town. ❼–❽

Jasvilas C-9, Sawai Jai Singh Highway, Bani Park ⓣ0141/220 4638, ⓦwww.jasvilas.com. Welcoming family-run guesthouse in a gracious old suburban mansion, with spacious and comfortable a/c rooms, a neat little pool and attractive enclosed gardens. The adjacent *Meghniwas*, occupying the other half of the same building, is similar, but not quite as nice. ❼–❽

Mansingh Towers Sansar Chandra Rd ⓣ0141/237 8771, ⓦwww.mansinghhotels.com. Modern hotel occupying an attractive red-sandstone building with graceful Rajput decorative touches, offering cosy (if characterless) rooms and a conveniently central location. Guests can use the pool, health club and spa at the *Hotel Mansingh* next door. Prices from around $215. ❾

Raj Mahal Palace Sardar Patel Marg ⓣ0141/510 5666, ⓦwww.royalfamilyjaipur.com. This former palace of Jai Singh's favourite maharani has plenty of rather dog-eared period charm, with a grand old banqueting hall, wood-panelled library and spacious lawns, plus a medium-size pool, although the large, old-fashioned rooms (all a/c) are rather gloomy and somewhat past their best. ❽

Raj Palace Zorawar Gate, Amer Rd ⓣ0141/263 4077, ⓦwww.rajpalace.com. One of the smartest addresses in Jaipur, regularly patronized by Bollywood film stars and Arab sheikhs alike. The central location on the edge of the Pink City can't be beaten, while the setting – in a wonderful old haveli of 1727 – is pure romance. Facilities include a beautiful little pool and sumptuous spa. Rooms from around $500. ❾

Rajvilas Goner Rd, 7km from the city centre ⓣ0141/268 0101, ⓦwww.oberoihotels.com. This dreamy resort occupies a superb fake Rajasthani fort-style complex beautifully landscaped with pools and pavilions. Accommodation is either in delectable creamy rooms (US$750) or luxury a/c tents (US$870). There are all the mod cons and facilities you'd expect at this price, including a beautiful spa. ❾

Rambagh Palace Bhawani Singh Marg ⓣ0141/221 1919, ⓦwww.tajhotels.com. This opulent palace complex, set amid 47 acres of beautiful gardens, is indisputably the grandest hotel in Jaipur, and one of the most romantic places to stay in India. Rooms are superbly equipped, with Rajasthani artworks, reproduction antique furniture and all mod-cons. Facilities include a clutch of fine restaurants and bars (see p.149), indoor and outdoor pools (guests only) and a Jiva spa. Even if you can't afford to stay, call in for afternoon tea (Rs1200 for two). Check the website for discounts, especially in summer. Doubles from $950. ❾

Samode Haveli Gangapole ⓣ0141/263 2370, ⓦwww.samode.com. In an unbeatably central location on the northeastern edge of the Pink City, this superb old haveli is brimful of atmosphere, centred on an idyllic central courtyard and with the prettiest pool in town. Rooms (around $320) are a mishmash: some are functional, modern and fairly characterless; others are pure museum pieces; and others are a bit of both – you may as well ask to see several before you check in, since they all cost the same. A good deal in summer (May–Sept), when rates can fall by forty percent. ❾

Shahpura House Devi Marg, Bani Park ⓣ0141/220 3392, ⓦwww.shahpurahouse.com. Characterful but affordable heritage hotel, superbly decorated throughout with lavish murals and Rajasthani architectural touches. Rooms all come with a/c, minibar and bathtub, and are attractively furnished with old wooden furniture; there's also a small pool. ❼–❽

The city

Jaipur's attractions fall into three distinct areas. At the heart of the urban sprawl, the historic **Pink City** is where you'll find the fine City Palace, along with myriad bazaars stuffed with enticing Rajasthani handicrafts. The much leafier and less hectic area **south of the Pink City** is home to the Ram Niwas Gardens and Central Museum, while the city's **outskirts** are dotted with a string of intriguing relics of royal rule, most notably Nahargarh Fort, the cenotaphs at Royal Gaitor, and the temples (and monkeys) of Galta.

The Pink City

At the heart of Jaipur lies Jai Singh's original city, popularly known as the **Pink City**, enclosed by walls and imposing gateways. One of the Pink City's most striking features is its regular **grid-plan**, with wide, straight streets, broadening to spacious squares (*choupads*) at major intersections – a design created in accordance with the *Vastu Shastra*, a series of ancient Hindu architectural treatises. The city's other striking feature is its uniform **pink colour**, intended to camouflage the poor-quality materials from which its buildings were originally constructed. A **heritage walk** audioguide (2.5km; around 2hr; Rs110), covering some of the most interesting sights in the Pink City, is available from the Hawa Mahal.

City Palace

At the heart of the Pink City stands the magnificent **City Palace** (daily 9.30am–5.45pm, last entry 5pm; Rs300 including audioguide[Rs40]; video Rs200; same ticket also valid for Jaigarh Fort at Amber if used within 24hr). To reach the palace entrance, go through the small archway on the north side of Tripolia Bazaar just west of the junction with Chaura Rasta and follow the road as it veers round to the right, past the Jantar Mantar (see p.146). The entrance is past here, on your left.

The palace was originally built by Jai Singh in the 1720s and has lost none of its original pomp and splendour. The royal family still occupies part of the palace, advancing in procession on formal occasions through the grand **Tripolia Gate** on the south side of the palace. Less exalted visitors enter through a modest gate on the eastern side of the palace that leads into the first of the palace's two main courtyards, centred on the elegant **Mubarak Mahal**. Built as a reception hall in 1899, the building now holds the museum's **textile collection**, housing some of the elaborately woven and brocaded fabrics that formerly graced the royal wardrobe. On the north side of the courtyard, the **Armoury** is probably the finest such collection in Rajasthan, a vast array of blood-curdling but often beautifully decorated weapons.

Past the Mubarak Mahal, an ornate gateway flanked by pair of fine stone elephants leads into the palace's second main courtyard, painted deep salmon pink. In its centre the raised **Diwan-i-Khas** (Hall of Private Audience), an open-sided pavilion where important decisions of state were taken by the maharaja and his advisers. The hall contains two silver urns, or *gangajalis*, listed in the *Guinness Book of World Records* as the largest crafted silver objects in the world, each more than 1.5m high with a capacity of 8182 litres. When Madho Singh II went to London to attend the coronation of King Edward VII in 1901, he was so reluctant to trust the water in the West that he had these urns filled with Ganges water and took them along with him.

On the left (west) side of the courtyard, a small corridor leads through to the **Pritam Niwas Chowk**, or "Peacock Courtyard", adorned with four superbly painted doorways representing the four seasons. This courtyard also gives the best view of the soaring yellow **Chandra Mahal**, the residence of the royal family (closed to the public), its heavily balconied seven-storey facade rising to a slope-shouldered summit. When the maharaja is in residence his flag is flown from the topmost pavilion.

On the opposite (east) side of the Diwan-i-Khas courtyard, beneath a large clocktower, sits the ornate **Sabha Niwas**, the Hall of Public Audience (or **Diwan-i-Am**), bare except for a pair of thrones in the middle and portraits of various former maharajas around the walls. Beyond here is the small **Diwan-i-Am courtyard**, with a collection of old carriages tucked into one end.

Jantar Mantar

Immediately south of the City Palace lies the remarkable **Jantar Mantar** (daily 9am–5pm, last entry 4.30pm; Rs100 [Rs20]; audioguide Rs150), a large grassy enclosure containing eighteen huge stone astronomical measuring devices constructed between 1728 and 1734 at the behest of Jai Singh, who invented many of them himself, their strange, abstract shapes lending the whole place the look of a weird futuristic sculpture park. The Jantar Mantar is one of five identically named observatories created by the star-crazed Jai Singh across North India (including the well-known example in Delhi – see p.105), though his motivation was astrological rather than astronomical.

It's a good idea to pay (Rs150) for the services of a **guide** to explain the workings of the observatory, which was able to identify the position and movement of stars and planets, tell the time and even predict the intensity of the monsoon. Probably the most impressive of the observatory's constructions is the 27-metre-high sundial, the **Samrat Yantra**, which can calculate the time to within two seconds. A more original device, the **Jaiprakash Yantra**, consists of two hemispheres laid in the ground, each composed of six curving marble slabs with a suspended ring in the centre, whose shadow marks the day, time and zodiac symbol – vital for calculating auspicious days for marriage.

Hawa Mahal

Jaipur's most instantly recognizable landmark, the **Hawa Mahal**, or "Palace of Winds" (daily 9am–5pm, last entrance 4.30pm; Rs50 [Rs10]; audioguide Rs110; guided tours Rs100), stands to the east of the City Palace – best appreciated from the outside during the early morning, when it glows orange-pink in the rays of the rising sun. Built in 1799 to enable the women of the court to watch street processions while remaining in purdah, its five-storey facade, decked out with hundreds of finely screened windows and balconies, makes the building seem far larger than it really is; in fact, it's little more than a facade. To get inside the palace itself you need to walk for five minutes around the rear of the building, following the lane that runs north from Tripolia Bazaar. Once inside, you can climb up the back of the facade to the screened niches from which the ladies of the court would once have looked down, and which still offer superb views over the mayhem of Jaipur below.

The rest of the Pink City

North of the City Palace is the **Govind Devji**, the family temple of the maharajas of Jaipur. The temple is dedicated to Krishna in his character of Govinda, and the principal shrine houses an image of Govinda brought from Vrindavan (near Agra) in 1735 that is considered to be the guardian deity of the rulers of Jaipur.

Just west of the City Palace, the slender **Iswari Minar Swarg Suli**, or **Isar Lat** (Heaven-piercing Minaret; daily 9am–4.30pm; Rs10 [Rs5]), was built by Jai Singh II's son and successor, Iswari Singh to celebrate a minor victory over a combined Maratha–Rajput force in 1747. Its summit offers the definitive view of the Pink

City, with fascinating glimpses into the tangled labyrinth of alleyways which honeycomb the city in the spaces between the major roads. To reach the minaret, go through the archway off Tripolia Bazaar which leads to the City Palace, but then head round to the left, away from the palace, and you'll see the minaret ahead of you.

South of the Pink City

Immediately south of the Pink City, the road leading out from New Gate is flanked by the lush **Ram Niwas Gardens**, named after their creator, Maharaja Ram Singh (1835–1880). The centrepiece is the florid **Albert Hall** of 1867, designed in a whimsical mix of Venetian and Mughal styles (Italian below, Indian on top) and housing the city's recently renovated **Central Museum** (daily except Mon 9am–5.30pm [last entrance 5pm]; Rs100 [Rs15]; audioguide Rs110). The bulk of the collection focuses on regional and Indian themes, including fine displays of Jaipur pottery, Hindu statuary and Mughal and Rajasthani miniature paintings, supported by an eclectic array of artefacts from around the globe – everything from Egyptian antiquities to decorative tiles from Stoke-on-Trent, with forays into Japan, Burma and Persia.

Further south, off Jawaharlal Nehru Road, the **Museum of Indology** (daily 8am–4pm; Rs20 including guided tour, plus tip) holds assorted curiosities collected by the late Acharya Vyakul stuffed into a rambling suburban house. Exhibits include oddities such as a map of India painted on a grain of rice, letters written on a hair and a glass bed, along with enormous quantities of junk, all heaped up together in great mouldering piles.

Outlying sights

The rocky hills that overlook Jaipur to the north and east are home to a string of spectacularly situated forts and temples, all accessible via steep paths climbing up from the city (or, for the less energetic, via longer roads around the back of the hills).

Nahargarh

Teetering on the edge of the hills north of Jaipur is the dramtic **Nahargarh**, or "Tiger Fort" (open 24hr; free), built by Jai Singh II in 1734 and offering superb views of Jaipur, best enjoyed towards dusk. The fort's imposing walls sprawl for the best part of a kilometre along the ridgetop, although the only significant surviving structures within are the **palace apartments** (daily 9.30pm–5.30pm; Rs30 [Rs10]), built inside the old fort by Madho Singh II between 1883 and 1892 as a love nest in which he kept his most treasured concubines away from the disapproving eyes of his courtiers and four official wives.

Vehicles can only get to the fort along a road that branches off Amber Road, a fifteen-kilometre journey from Jaipur. It's simpler to **walk** to the fort along the steep path that climbs up from the north side of the city centre, a stiff fifteen- to twenty-minute walk, although the path is a bit tricky to find, so you might want to take a rickshaw to the bottom. It's best to avoid going up too late in the day or returning after dark – the fort is popular with delinquent teenagers and other unsavoury types, and the atmosphere can be a tad seedy at the best of times. There are a couple of **cafés** in the palace complex.

Royal Gaitor

On the northern edge of the city centre, the walled funerary complex of **Royal Gaitor** (daily 9am–4.30pm; free, camera Rs10, video Rs20) contains the stately marble mausoleums (chhatris) of Jaipur's ruling family. The compound consists of two main courtyards, each crammed full of imposing memorials. The first (and more modern) courtyard is dominated by the grandiose twentieth-century cenotaph of **Madho Singh II** (d. 1922), a ruler of famously gargantuan appetites, whose four wives and fifty-odd concubines bore him "around 125" children. The second, older, courtyard is dominated by the elaborate tomb of **Jai Singh II** (d. 1743), the founder of Jaipur and the first ruler to be interred at Gaitor. Further memorials to Ram Singh II (d. 1880), Madho Singh I (d. 1768), Pratap Singh (d. 1803) and Jagat Singh (d. 1819) lie close by.

On the ridgetop above Gaitor (reachable via a steep path) lies the **Ganesh Mandir**, the second of the city's two major Ganesh temples – a huge building instantly recognizable from the huge swastika painted on its side.

Galta "Monkey Palace"

Nestling in a steep-sided valley 3km east of Jaipur, **Galta** (daily sunrise–sunset; free, camera Rs50, video Rs150) comprises a picturesque collection of 250-year-old temples squeezed into a narrow rocky ravine. Galta owes its sacred status in large part to a freshwater spring that seeps constantly through the rocks in the otherwise dry valley, keeping two **tanks** full. These putrid-smelling ponds are now the domain of over five thousand macaque monkeys, which have earned Galta its nickname of the "Monkey Palace". For many tourists the sight of the splashing monkeys outstrips the attraction of the temples themselves, though the assorted shrines, dedicated variously to Krishna, Rama and Hanuman, are attractively atmospheric. It's also worth walking up to the spectacularly situated **Surya Mandir**, perched above the tanks on the ridgetop overlooking Jaipur and commanding dramatic views of the city below.

To reach Galta **by vehicle** you'll need to drive 10km or so along the road past the small royal pleasure palace and gardens of **Sisodia Rani-ka-Bagh** (daily 8am–5pm; Rs10, or Rs20 5–8pm) around the hills behind Jaipur, passing through beautiful countryside – remarkably quiet and unspoilt given its proximity to the city. You can also **walk** to Galta, following the path beyond Suraj Pole gate on the eastern edge of the Pink City and climbing steeply up to the Surya Mandir on the crest of the hill above the main temple complex – a stiff twenty-minute walk.

Eating

Jaipur has Rajasthan's best selection of quality **restaurants**, both veg and non-veg, albeit at higher-than-average prices.

Barista's Bhagwan Das Rd, opposite the Raj Mandir cinema. Jaipur branch of the popular India-wide chain of coffee houses, serving up good, freshly ground espresso, cappuccino and latte.

Chokhi Dhani 22km south of Jaipur on the Tonk Rd ⓣ0141/277 0554. This Rajasthani theme-park-cum-restaurant attracts droves of well-heeled Jaipuris, especially at weekends, when the whole place gets wildly busy. The Rs300 entrance fee includes an evening meal plus access to a wide range of attractions (though tips are expected at many) – elephant, camel and bullock-cart rides, folk dances, puppet shows, magicians and chapatti-making demonstrations, to name just a few. When you've done with the entertainment, head off to the mud-walled restaurant where you'll be sat on the floor and served an authentically original (albeit very salty) Rajasthani village thali quite unlike anything you'll find in the restaurants of Jaipur, with lots of rustic rural delicacies like cornflour chapattis, *gatta* and unusual curried vegetables. It's all a bit hokey, but fun. An auto-rickshaw charges Rs300–350 for the round trip. Open Mon–Sat 6–11pm & Sun from 11am.

Copper Chimney MI Rd. Plush glass-fronted restaurant with a good range of north Indian standards (albeit sometimes a bit heavy on the oil and spices), plus local specialities like *laal maans* (special Rajasthani desert-style mutton) and *gatta*, and a few Chinese and continental dishes. Mains Rs85–205. Licensed.

Dasaprakash MI Rd. This unpretentious a/c restaurant serves up a tasty range of classic south Indian veg fare – *iddlis*, *vadas*, *uttapams*, *upuma*, thalis, and no less than seventeen types of dosa – plus a selection of sweet-toothed ice-cream sundaes in various colourful combinations. Mains Rs90–150.

Four Seasons Bhagat Singh Marg. Generally reckoned the best Indian veg restaurant in town, with top-notch dosas and *uttapams* along with a big choice of delicious north Indian curries, plus some Chinese. You may have to queue, especially later on in the evening when the place fills with locals. No alcohol.

Lassiwala 312 MI Rd. A Jaipur institution for its sublime lassis, served in old-style terracotta mugs. Its popularity has sparked a small lassi-wallah-war, with two impostors setting up shop to the right (as you face it) of the original – check for the correct street number. Closes early afternoon.

Little Italy KK Square Mall, Prithviraj Rd. Svelte modern restaurant serving up passable – if not particularly authentic – pizza, pasta, risotto and a few Italian-style meat dishes, plus (for culinary reasons which remain unclear) assorted Mexican snacks. Also has a decent selection of Indian wines. Mains from around Rs300.

LMB Johari Bazaar. The only real restaurant in the Pink City, although the food (mains from around Rs120) is disappointingly pedestrian, compensating for a lack of flavour with incendiary amounts of chili. Alternatively, stick to the sweet counter outside, which dishes up a famous *paneer ghewar* (honeycomb cake soaked in treacle) and piping hot *tikkis* in spicy mango sauce.

Mohan's Motilal Atal Rd, opposite *Hotel Neelam.* Cosy and unpretentious little veg restaurant, popular with locals thanks to its well-prepared and excellent-value food, with virtually everything under Rs50. There's not much room, so you might end up sharing a table.

Natraj MI Rd. Long-established pure-veg restaurant offering a big range of north Indian standards, plus thalis, dosas and superb sweets piled up at the counter by the door. Mains Rs70–175.

Niro's MI Rd. Some of the best non-veg food in Jaipur, with Rajasthani specialities such as *sula* (lamb), *lal maans* (mutton) and *gatta* along with a big choice of tandoori dishes and other meat and veg curries, plus Western and Chinese. Mains Rs155–300. Licensed.

Om Tower Restaurant Om Tower, MI Rd. Rajasthan's first revolving restaurant, on the 14th floor of the landmark Om Tower. The head-spinning views are the main attraction; the north Indian food (veg only) is acceptable but rather expensive (mains Rs150–350). No alcohol.

Peacock Rooftop Restaurant *Pearl Palace* hotel, Hari Kishan Somani Marg, Hathroi Fort. The city's most appealing rooftop restaurant, with quirky original décor featuring cute metal chairs and a striking peacock canopy – particularly pretty after dark. There's a big menu of veg and non-veg Indian options, all well prepared, with flavoursome sauces, crisp breads and cold beers, plus Chinese, pizzas and the usual Western snacks. Mains Rs60–260.

Rambagh Palace Bhawani Singh Marg ⓣ0141/221 1919, ⓦwww.tajhotels.com. Jaipur's most opulent hotel serves up a pair of memorable dining options. Choose between *Swarna Mahal*, offering Indian fine-dining in a superbly over-the-top neoclassical-style dining room, or the slightly less ostentatious *Rajput Room* multi-cuisine restaurant (Indian, Continental and Chinese). Mains at both start at around Rs850. Reservations strongly recommended.

Reds 5th floor, Mall 21. Mains Rs225–595. Stylish modern restaurant-bar, with red and black sofas and fine views of the Raj Mandir cinema opposite. There's a good range of mainly North Indian food (veg and non-veg), or just come for a drink.

Sunder Palace *Sunder Palace* hotel, Sanjay Marg, Hathroi Fort, Ajmer Rd. Breezy, flower-filled rooftop restaurant at a popular guest house, specializing in tasty, pure-veg Indian cooking at bargain prices. Mains Rs50–85. Licensed.

Surya Mahal MI Road. Neat little modern veg restaurant specializing in South Indian food, with tasty dosas, *uttapam, iddlis, vadas* and thalis. There's also a good range of north Indian veg curries and a few Rajasthani specialities like *kadi pakora* and *gatta masala*, plus pasta, pizza and Chinese. Mains Rs70–175.

Drinking and entertainment

For **drinks**, *Amigo's Bar*, on the ninth floor of the Om Tower on MI Road, has fine city views, a reasonable drinks list (including a few cocktails) and passable TexMex snacks, while the nearby *Reds* bar-restaurant (see above), offers more upmarket décor and food, plus a fine view of the adjacent Raj Mandir cinema. *Henry's* in the *Hotel Park Prime* on Prithviraj Road is the city's most appealing English-style pub, complete with oak bar and sporting memorabilia; alternatively, the same hotel also has a fine rooftop bar with a small pool and city views – particularly attractive after dark. For a truly memorable tipple, head to the

Rambagh Palace, where you can choose between the swanky, colonial-style *Polo* bar or the more laid-back *Steam* lounge-bar (evenings only; closed Tues), built inside the carriages of an old steam train.

If you go to the **cinema** just once while you're in India, it should be at the Raj Mandir on Bhagwan Das Road just off MI Road, which boasts a stunning Art Deco lobby and 1500-seat auditorium. Most movies have four daily showings (usually at 12.30pm, 3.30pm, 6.30pm and 9.30pm), and there's always a long queue, so get your tickets (Rs60/80) an hour or so before the show starts.

Shopping

If you come across an Indian **handicraft** object or garment abroad, chances are it will have been bought in Jaipur. As a regular tourist, you'll find it harder to hunt out the best merchandise, but as a source of souvenirs, perhaps only Delhi can surpass it.

In keeping with Maharaja Jai Singh's original city divisions, different streets are reserved for purveyors of different goods. **Bapu Bazaar**, on the south side of the Pink City, is the best place for clothes and textiles, including Jaipur's famous **block-print** work and *bandhani* **tie-dye**. On the opposite side of town, along Amber Road just beyond Zorawar Gate, rows of emporiums are stacked with gorgeous patchwork wall-hangings and **embroidery**; these places do a steady trade with bus parties of wealthy tourists, so be prepared to haggle hard.

For old-style Persian-influenced vases, along with tiles, plates and candle-holders, visit the outlets of the city's renowned **blue potteries** along Amber Road or the workshop of the late Kripal Singh (see opposite). For **bookshops**, see "Listings" opposite.

Anokhi 2nd Floor, KK Square Mall, Prithviraj Rd, ⓦwww.anokhi.com. This is the place to buy high-quality "ethnic" Indian evening wear, *salwar kameez* and shirts. They also do lovely bedspreads, quilts, tablecloths and cushion covers. Daily 9.30am–8pm.

Jodhpur Tailors Motilal Atal Rd (behind *Hotel Neelam*). One of the best tailors in town, patronized by the maharaja himself. Hand-stitched suits run from around Rs7500, or you could just pick up a shirt (from Rs700), trousers (Rs1200) or jodhpurs (Rs1400). Mon–Sat 10.30am–9.30pm, Sun 2–6pm.

Jewellery and gemstones in Jaipur

The two best places for silver jewellery are **Johari Bazaar**, the broad street running north of Sanganeri Gate in the Pink City, and **Chameliwala Market**, just off MI Road in the tangle of alleyways behind the *Copper Chimney* restaurant. The latter also has the city's best selection of gems, though it's also a hard place to shop in peace, thanks to a particularly slippery breed of scam merchant, known locally as *lapkars*. These young men – usually smartly dressed and speaking excellent English – will regale you with beguiling tales about how you can buy gems in Jaipur and sell them back home for a massive profit. This is nonsense, of course, but by the time you realize this you'll be thousands of miles away with a handful of worthless cut-glass "gems" wondering where the all mysterious entries on your credit-card bill came from. If you're paying for gemstones or jewellery with a credit card in Jaipur, don't let it out of your sight, and never agree to leave a docket as security.

There's a government-sponsored **gem-testing laboratory** (Mon–Fri & every first and third Sat of month 10am–4pm) at the Gem and Jewellery Export Promotion Council, 2nd floor, Rajasthan Chamber Bhavan, M Rd near Ajmeri Gate, where you can have gemstones tested for authenticity. The cost is Rs605 per stone, with reports delivered the following working day (or Rs935 per stone for a same-day report if you deliver the stone before 2pm).

Kripal Kumbh Shiv Marg, near the *Jaipur Inn.* The former workshop-cum-home of Jaipur's most famous ceramist, the late Kripal Singh, full of attractive and affordable examples of the city's traditional blue-and-white pottery. They also claim to be the only workshop in Jaipur producing entirely lead-free pottery that can safely be used with hot food (as well as featuring colours such as red and orange which are impossible with lead glazes). Daily 10am–7pm.

Rajasthali MI Rd, just south of Ajmer Gate. This large, government-run emporium (Mon–Sat 11am–7.30pm) is a good place to get a feeling for the range of handicrafts available and to gauge approximate costs – although you'll probably find similar items at cheaper prices in the Pink City bazaars.

Soma 5 Jacob Rd ⓦwww.somashop.com. Similar range of clothes (ladieswear only) and fabrics to Anokhi, though at slightly cheaper prices. Mon–Sat 10am–8pm, Sun 10am–6pm.

Listings

Airlines Jaipur Towers on MI Rd is home to dozens of airline agents, not all of them particularly reliable. The best place to head for is Travel-Care (open 24hr; ⓣ0141/237 1832, ⓦwww.travelcare india.com), on the ground floor around the right-hand side of the building, who act as agents for virtually every domestic airline and most major international operators, including Air India, BA, Air France, KLM, Lufthansa, Thai Airways, Singapore Airlines and Gulf Air.

Banks and exchange There are plentiful ATMs around town, especially along MI Rd. There are many private exchange places in Jaipur offering more or less the same rates as the banks; these include two branches of Thomas Cook on MI Rd (both Mon–Sat 9.30am–5.30pm), one on the ground floor of Jaipur Towers, the other opposite Ganpati Plaza, where you can also get cash advances on Visa and MasterCard. Many of the guesthouses and hotels listed on pp.139–144 can change money (though rates can be poor); the *Pearl Palace Hotel* has 24hr money-changing facilities.

Bookshops Bookwise, in Mall 21, opposite the Raj Mandir cinema, has an excellent selection of English-language fiction and India-related titles. Close by on MI Rd, Books Corner (a couple of doors west of *Niro's* restaurant) has a passable selection of India-related titles crammed into a poky little shop.

Hospitals For emergencies, the government-run SMS Hospital (ⓣ0141/256 0291), on Sawai Ram Singh Rd, is best; treatment is usually free for foreigners. The best private hospital is the Santokba Durlabhji Memorial Hospital (SDMH), Bhawani Singh Marg ⓣ0141/256 6251.

Internet access All the guesthouses and hotels listed on pp.139–144 have internet access (and an increasing number also have wi-fi). If you can't get online where you're staying (or at another guest-house), the iWay internet café (daily 9am–11pm; Rs30/hr), opposite the *Atithi Guest House*, is one of the few reliable alternatives.

Meditation The Dhamma Thali Vipassana Centre (ⓣ0141/268 0220, ⓦwww.dhamma.org), located in beautiful countryside on the road to Galta, is one of fifty centres across the world set up to promote the practice of Vipassana meditation. Courses (3–45 days; see website for schedule and details) are free, but a donation is expected.

Photography Sentosa Colour Lab (Mon–Sat 10am–8pm), Ganpati Plaza (on the side facing MI Rd), and Goyal Colour Lab, next to *Lassiwalla* on MI Rd, both offer good digital and print services.

Police stations The main police post is on Station Rd opposite the railway station ⓣ0141/220 6324.

Post and couriers For poste restante, go to the GPO on MI Rd (Mon–Sat 10am–6pm). Parcels and registered mail are kept at the sorting office behind the main desks; packages are cotton-wrapped and sewn at the concession (Mon–Sat 10am–4pm) by the main entrance. It's preferable to bring your own box. If you're sending a parcel, take it to the customs office on the first floor to have it checked before wrapping and posting; this will speed up delivery by about ten days. The city's DHL office is at G-8, C Scheme, Vinobha Marg ⓣ0141/236 1159; they also have a desk inside Standard Chartered Bank on the south side of MI Rd just west of Panch Batti, while the owner of the *Pearl Palace Hotel* is also a registered DHL agent.

Swimming pools The nicest hotel pool currently open to non-guests is at the *Alsisar Haveli* (a pricey Rs200/hr); cheaper options include the pools at the following hotels: *Shahpura House* (free if you take a meal at the hotel), *Umaid Bhawan* (Rs150/3hr), *Madhuban* (Rs100), and *Raj Mahal* (Rs170).

Travel agents It's usually easiest to arrange something through your hotel or guesthouse. Alter-natively, try the reputable Rajasthan Travel Service, on the ground floor of Ganpati Plaza on MI Rd (ⓣ0141/238 9408, ⓦwww.rajasthantravelservice .com) or Travel-Care (see "Airlines", above).

Yoga Rajasthan Swasth Yog Parishad, New Police Academy Rd (ⓣ0141/239 7330); the Rajasthan Yoga Centre, 2km north of Bani Park in Shastri Nagar; and Madhavanand Ashram (ⓣ0141/220 0317), also in Bani Park.

Around Jaipur

Forts, palaces, temples and assorted ruins from a thousand years of Kachchwaha history adorn the hills and valleys near Jaipur. The superb palace at **Amber** provides the most obvious destination for a day-trip, easily combined with a visit to the impressive fort of **Jaigarh**.

Amber

On the crest of a rocky hill 11km north of Jaipur, **AMBER** (or Amer) was the capital of the leading **Kachchwaha** Rajput clan from 1037 until 1727, when Jai Singh established his new city at Jaipur. Amber's palace buildings are less impressive than those at Jaipur, but the natural setting – perched high on a narrow rocky ridge above the surrounding countryside and fortified by natural hills and high ramparts – is unforgettably dramatic.

Buses to Amber leave from outside Jaipur's Hawa Mahal (every 5–10min; 20–30min), stopping on the main road below the palace; alternatively, an auto will cost around Rs250 return, including a couple of hours' waiting time. Arrive early in the day if you want to avoid the big coach parties. There's a small **tourist office** (daily 8am–4pm) at the bottom of the path up to the palace; it's a pleasant fifteen-minute uphill walk from here to the palace. Alternatively you could hire a jeep (they hang out along the main road and around the tourist office and charge Rs200 for the return trip, including 1hr waiting time) or waddle up on an elephant (Rs570 for 1–2 people).

The palace complex

The path from the village leads up to Suraj Pole (Sun Gate) and the large **Jaleb Chowk** courtyard at the entrance to the main **palace complex** (daily 8am–6pm; Rs150 [Rs25], audioguide Rs150), where you'll find the ticket office and assorted official guides (Rs200). On the left-hand side of the courtyard is the **Shri Sila Devi temple** (closed noon to 4pm), dedicated to Sila, an aspect of Kali. The statue within is one of the most revered in Jaipur, framed by an unusual arch formed from stylized carvings of banana leaves.

Next to the Shri Sila Devi temple, a steep flight of steps leads up to **Singh Pole** (Lion Gate), the entrance to the main palace. The architectural style is distinctly Rajput, though it's clear from the mirrored mosaics covering the walls that Mughal ideas also crept in. Singh Pole leads into the first of the palace's three main courtyards, on the far side of which stands the **Diwan-i-Am** (Hall of Public Audience), constructed in 1639. This open-sided pavilion is notably similar in its overall conception to contemporary Mughal audience halls in Delhi and Agra, even if the architectural details are essentially Rajput.

Diagonally opposite, the exquisitely painted **Ganesh Pole** leads into a second courtyard, its right-hand side filled with a miniature fountain-studded garden, behind which lie the rooms of the **Sukh Mahal**, set into the side of the courtyard. The marble rooms here were cooled by water channelled through small conduits carved into the walls, an early and ingenious system of air-conditioning – the central room has a particularly finely carved example.

On the opposite side of the courtyard, the dazzling **Sheesh Mahal** houses what were the private chambers of the maharaja and his queen, its walls and ceilings decorated with intricate mosaics fashioned out of shards of mirror and coloured glass. On the far side of the courtyard beyond the Sheesh Mahal, a narrow stairwell leads up to the small **Jas Mandir**, decorated with similar mosaics and guarded from the sun by delicate marble screens.

From the rear of the Sheesh Mahal courtyard, a narrow corridor leads into a further expansive courtyard at the heart of the **Palace of Man Singh I**, the oldest part of the palace complex. The buildings here are plain and austere compared to later structures, though they would originally have been richly decorated and furnished. The pillared *baradari* in the centre of the courtyard was once a meeting area for the maharanis, shrouded from men's eyes by flowing curtains.

Jaigarh

Perched high on the hills behind Amber Palace, the rugged **Jaigarh** fort (daily 9am–5pm; Rs75 [Rs25]) offers incredible vistas over the hills and plains below. The fort was built in 1600, though as the Kachchwahas were on friendly terms with the Mughals, it saw few battles. At the centre of the fort, a small **museum** has the usual old maps and photographs, plus a good selection of cannons dating back to 1588. None of them, however, can hold a candle to the immense **Jaivana** cannon, the largest in Asia, which sits in solitary splendour at the highest point of the fort, five minutes' walk beyond the museum. Needing one hundred kilos of gunpowder for a single shot, the Jaivana could purportedly hurl a cannonball 35km – though its true military value was never accurately gauged since it was never fired in battle.

Most people walk to Jaigarh from Amber Palace, a steep fifteen- to twenty-minute climb. The path to the fort goes from just below the entrance to the palace, branching off from near the top of the zigzagging road (the one used by elephants; not the pedestrian path). By car or jeep, you'll need to follow the much longer road that leads to both Jaigarh and Nahargarh; jeeps can be hired in Amber village for the return trip to the fort (Rs400, including 2hr waiting time).

Amber town

Below the palace, the atmospheric but little-visited **Amber town** is full of remnants of Kachchwaha rule. One of the most striking local landmarks is the unusual **Jagat Shiromani Temple**, built by Man Singh after the death in battle of his son and would-have-been successor, a large and florid structure, its shrine topped by an enormous *shikhara* and fronted by an unusually large, two-storey *mandapa* with a curved roof inspired by those on Mughal pavilions.

The town is also home to an excellent **Anokhi Museum of Hand Printing** (Tues–Sat 10.30am–5pm, Sun 11am–4.30pm; closed May to mid-July; Rs30, camera Rs50, video Rs150; Ⓦwww.anokhimuseum.com) at Kheri Gate, a ten-minute walk from the fort. Housed in an attractive old haveli, the museum has an interesting collection of hand block-printed textiles and garments, along with live demonstrations of printing and carving by resident craftsmen.

Samode

Hidden among the Aravalli Hills 42km northwest of Jaipur, **SAMODE** is notable for its impeccably restored eighteenth-century **palace**, now an award-winning heritage hotel, the *Samode Palace* (Ⓣ01423/240014, Ⓦwww.samode.com; from around US$300; rates drop by 30 percent May–Sept; ⑨), with uncompromisingly romantic rooms covered with murals and filled with antiques. Non-guests have to shell out a hefty Rs500 (redeemable against food and drink inside) to visit. Some three hundred steps lead up from the palace to a hilltop **fort**, with panoramic views.

Sanganer

SANGANER, 16km south of Jaipur, is the busiest centre for handmade **textiles** in the region, and the best place to watch traditional block printers in action. There are a couple of large factories here, but most of the printing is done as a cottage industry in family homes. The town itself has ruined palaces and a handful of elegant Jain **temples**, including the Shri Digamber temple near Tripolia Gate. Government **buses** and minibuses to Sanganer from Jaipur run from Chand Pol via Ajmer Road (every 15min), or you can catch government bus #201 from Ajmeri Gate.

North of Jaipur: Shekhawati

North of Jaipur, the land becomes increasingly arid and inhospitable, with farms and fields gradually giving way to wind-blown expanses of undulating semi-desert dotted with endless *khejri* trees and isolated houses enclosed in stockades of thorn. Although now something of a backwater, this region, known as **Shekhawati**, once lay on an important caravan route connecting Delhi and Sind (now in Pakistan) with the Gujarati coast, before the rise of Bombay and Calcutta diverted the trans-Thar trade south and eastwards. Having grown rich on trade and taxes, Shekhawati's Marwari merchants and landowning thakurs spent their fortunes competing with one another to build the grand, ostentatiously decorated **havelis** which still line the streets of the region's dusty little towns – an incredible concentration of mansions, palaces and cenotaphs plastered inside and out with elaborate and colourful **murals**. Considering the wealth of traditional art here, and the region's proximity to Jaipur, however, most of Shekhawati still feels surprisingly far off the tourist trail.

Getting around is best done by road. Regular local buses, always overcrowded, connect Shekhawati's main towns, while jeeps also shuttle between towns and villages, picking up as many passengers as they can cram in. Railway services are hopelessly slow, unreliable and inconvenient.

Nawalgarh

At the centre of Shekhawati, surrounded by desert and *khejri* scrub, the lively little market town of **NAWALGARH** makes – along with nearby Mandawa – the most convenient and congenial base for exploring Shekhawati, with a bumper crop of painted havelis and a picturesque bazaar, along with a decent range of accommodation.

Arrival and information

Nawalgarh's **bus** and **jeep** stand is 1.5km west of town, around Rs50–70 by auto-rickshaw to the town's various hotels and guesthouses. For trips around the region, you can either jump on and off cheap, cramped village-to-village **jeeps** or rent a vehicle through *Apani Dhani* (see opposite) or the *Ramesh Jangid Tourist Pension* (see opposite). The owners of these two guesthouses also run socially responsible **tours** of Shekhawati including jeep tours of nearby towns and other places of interest (Rs1500–2000); walking tours of Nawalgarh (Rs350/person); and tours by camel cart (Rs1200/day). Alternatively, Babloo Sharma at the Moraka Haveli (Ⓣ9828 191232; beware of imitators in the streets outside) can also arrange car and walking tours at similar prices, plus horseriding excursions (Rs600/hr). The *Roop Niwas Kothi* hotel offers horseriding (Rs600/hr) jaunts on its stable of pure-bred Marwari steeds, as well as short camel rides (Rs500/hr) and

Visiting Shekhawati's havelis

A number of Shekhawati's havelis, particularly in Nawalgarh, have now been restored and opened as museums. Most, however, remain in a state of picturesque dilapidation and are still occupied by local families, while others have been abandoned, and are now empty apart from a solitary **chowkidar** (caretaker-cum-guard). Visitors are welcome to look around inside some havelis in return for a small tip (Rs20–30 is sufficient), while others remain closed to outsiders. If in doubt just stick your head in the front door and ask, but remember that you're effectively entering someone's private home, so never go inside without permission.

Moving on from Nawalgarh

RSRTC buses leave the main bus stand for **Jaipur** every 15min (3hr 30min), and there's also a deluxe service at 8am; some private buses also serve Jaipur, though these drop passengers 5km outside the centre of Jaipur so are best avoided. Other services include **Jhunjhunu** (every 15–30min; 1hr), **Fatehpur** (1–2 hourly; 1hr 15min) and **Bikaner** (hourly; 3hr 30min). There are a few direct morning buses to **Delhi** (8hr); otherwise change at Jhunjhunu, from where there are hourly services. Buses to **Dundlod** and **Mandawa** (every 30min; 20min & 45min respectively) leave from the bus stand just past Baori Gate on the north edge of town. Local destinations are also served by **shared jeep**, which leave when full.

The **railway station** is a further kilometre beyond the bus station. The line between Nawalgarh and **Delhi** is currently being converted from metre gauge to broad gauge and there are no through trains; it's much easier to take the bus. There are several trains to **Jaipur**, but again the bus is faster and more reliable.

more extended horse and camel safaris – see Ⓦ www.royalridingholidays.com for full details. **Cycles** can be rented at *Apani Dhani* and the *Ramesh Jangid Tourist Pension* (Rs50/day).

Accommodation and eating

Nawalgarh has a surprisingly good selection of **places to stay**, while several places also do good organic vegetarian home-cooking.

Apani Dhani Northwest edge of town Ⓣ01594/222239, Ⓦwww.apanidhani.com. Occupying a fetching cluster of mud-walled Rajasthani village-style huts, this pretty little eco-resort offers an a perfect example of sustainable local tourism – a proportion of profits goes to support environmental and educational projects, and local artisans earn some income through involvement in the resort's stimulating programme of craft and cultural activities. Rooms (especially those in the slightly more expensive superior category) have plenty of rustic charm, and there's excellent organic food, served up in the bougainvillea-strewn garden, as well as activities including tie-dye and cookery classes, plus tours (see below). Book ahead. ❹

Ramesh Jangid Tourist Pension On the western edge of town, just north of Maur Hospital Ⓣ01594/224060, Ⓦwww.touristpension.com. Homely guesthouse offering simple but spotless and good-value rooms in a sociable Brahmin family home; the more expensive rooms have solar-heated water and beautiful murals. There's also excellent pure-veg food, internet access, jeep tours, plus tie-dye, cooking and Hindi classes. ❷–❸

Roop Niwas Kothi 1km east of the town centre Ⓣ01594/222008, Ⓦwww.roopniwaskothi.com. Popular with passing coach parties, this rambling Raj-era mansion has a certain faded elegance, old-fashioned rooms and plenty of period charm at a fairly modest price. ❼

Roopvilas Palace 1km east of the town centre, next to *Roop Niwas Kothi* hotel Ⓣ01594/224321, Ⓦwww.roopvilas.com. Gracious heritage hotel, set in a nineteenth-century royal palace and modern outbuildings scattered around spacious and beautifully maintained grounds. Accommodation is in a mix of rooms and suites, plus three luxury a/c tents, while facilities include a swimming pool and Ayurvedic massage centre. ❼, tents ❽

Shekhawati Guest House 1km east of the town centre, 200m south of the *Roop Niwas Kothi* Ⓣ01594/224658, Ⓦwww.shekhawatiguesthouse.com. Run by charming owner Kalpana Singh, this friendly family guesthouse offers accommodation either in neat and clean, if rather dark, air-cooled rooms in the main house or in slightly more expensive garden cottages (with fan). Fresh organic produce is used in the excellent food (veg and non-veg), and guests also get free cookery lessons, while tours can be arranged. ❸, cottages ❹

Thikana (also known locally as *Vishnu Basotia's*) 100m west of the Bhagton ki Haveli Ⓣ9414 082 791, Ⓦwww.heritagethikana.com. Friendly family-run hotel in an unbeatably central location, with nicely furnished rooms and lovely views from the upstairs terrace – though the slightly chintzy pink modern building doesn't really live up to its billing as a so-called "heritage" hotel. ❹

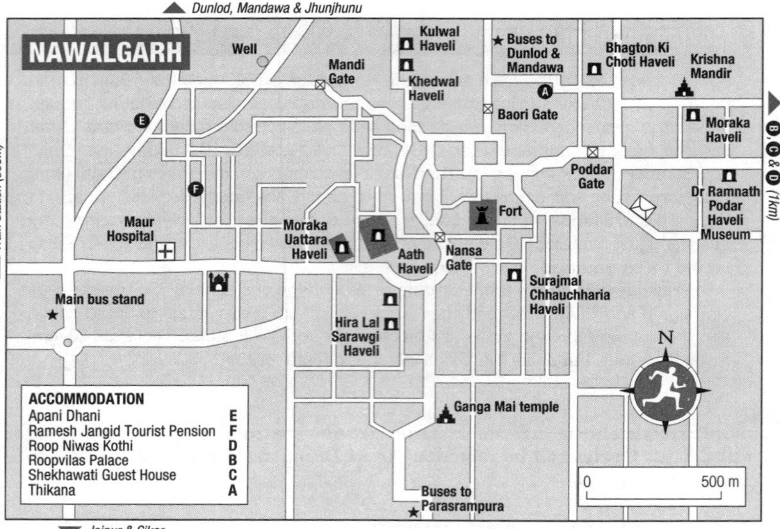

The Town

The logical place to start a tour of Nawalgarh is on the east side of town at the magnificent Anandi Lal Poddar Haveli, which now houses the **Dr Ramnath A. Poddar Haveli Museum** (daily 8am–7pm; Rs100 [Rs75], camera Rs30, video Rs50; Ⓦwww.poddarhavelimuseum.org). Built in 1920, this is one of the few havelis in Shekhawati to have been restored to its original glory, and boasts the most vivid murals in town, including steam trains, soldiers drilling with rifles, and a clever 3D-like panel of a bull's head that transmogrifies into that of an elephant as you move from left to right. There's also a mildly diverting series of **exhibits** showcasing aspects of Rajasthani life.

A short walk to the north lies the fine **Moraka Haveli** (daily 8am–7pm; Rs50, Indian residents free), decorated with murals of Shiva, Parvati, Krishna and Jesus, plus a *baithak* complete with a fine old hand-pulled fan (*punkah*). Directly opposite the Moraka Haveli lies the eye-catching **Krishna Mandir**, dating from the mid-eighteenth century, a florid mass of delicate chhatris.

About 200m east of the Moraka Haveli, the unrestored, 150-year-old **Bhagton ki Choti Haveli** (no set hours; Rs40) has an unusually varied selection of murals including a European-style angel and Queen Victoria (over the arches by the right of the main door). On the left, a *trompe-l'oeil* picture shows seven women in the shape of an elephant, while other pictures show Europeans riding bicycles, along with a steamboat and a train.

The fort and eastern havelis

At the heart of the town, the **fort** (Bala Qila) has more or less vanished under a clutch of modern buildings huddled around a central courtyard which now hosts the town's colourful vegetable market. The dilapidated building on the far left-hand side of the courtyard (by the Bank of Baroda) boasts a magnificent, eerily echoing **Sheesh Mahal**, covered in mirrorwork, which once served as the dressing room of the maharani of Nawalgarh, its ceiling decorated with pictorial maps of Nawalgarh and Jaipur. You'll have to pay Rs10–20 baksheesh to see the room; if no one's around, ask at the sweet factory on the opposite side of the courtyard.

Heading west through the Nansa Gate (signed, confusingly, as the "Rambilas Podar Memorial Gate") and following the road around brings you to the so-called **Aath Haveli** ("Eight Havelis", built by eight brothers, although only six were actually completed), a complex of heavily decorated mansions featuring murals in a range of styles depicting the usual mishmash of subjects both ancient and modern. The newly restored **Moraka Uattara Haveli**, opposite (daily 8am–6pm; Rs50) also has a richly painted exterior and *mardana* (men's) courtyard, with elephants and horses framed in a mass of florid decoration. Close by stands the **Hira Lal Sarawgi Haveli**, its facade adorned with three large cars, plus an elaborate bridge.

Further havelis dot the streets south and southeast of the Nansa Gate, one of the quietest and most atmospheric parts of town. These include the **Surajmal Chhauchharia Haveli**, whose murals include two small pictures of Europeans floating past in a hot-air balloon. The painter took some playful licence as to the mechanics involved, with the passengers keeping their balloons aloft by blowing into them through small pipes.

Dundlod and Parasrampura

The most obvious target for a day-trip from Nawalgarh is **DUNDLOD**, 7km north and the site of an old fort and some large havelis. The musty old **fort** (Rs20) is worth a quick visit for its fine old Diwan-i-Khana, filled with antique European furniture. The fort also houses the *Dundlod Fort* (Ⓣ01594/252519 or 0141/211275, Ⓦwww.dundlod.com; ❻); rooms are a bit shabby and overpriced, though it's a good place to organize local horseriding tours (3–12 days). The **village** itself harbours several interesting havelis, including the meticulously restored **Seth Arjun Das Goenka Haveli** of 1870 (daily 8am–7pm; Rs40), its interior covered in a profusion of finely detailed frescoes on assorted religious themes. Close by lies the delicate chhatri of Ram Dutt Goenka of 1888, with vibrant friezes lining its dome.

More painted buildings are dotted around the serene hamlet of **PARASRAMPURA**, 20km southeast of Nawalgarh. Buses run every thirty minutes or so. Monuments include the **Gopinath temple**, built in 1742, whose murals depict the torments of hell alongside images of the famous local Rajput ruler, Sardul Singh, with his five sons. Some of the paintings are unfinished, as the artists were diverted to decorate the chhatri of **Rajul Singh**, who died that same year. The large dome of this exquisite memorial contains a flourish of lively murals, once again including images of hell, and of Sardul Singh with his sons. Parasrampura's modest **fort** is on the west bank of the dry riverbed.

Jhunjhunu

Spreading in a mass of brick and concrete from the base of a rocky hill, **JHUNJHUNU** is a busy and fairly unprepossessing town, though it preserves an interesting old central bazaar and a fine collection of painted havelis. Jhunjhunu is usually visited as a day-trip from nearby Nawalgarh or Mandawa, though it has a few good accommodation options if you want to stay.

Arrival and information

The government bus stand is just south of the town centre. Jhunjhunu is quite spread out, and walking around can be tiring, but many of the streets of the old town are too narrow for cars; **rickshaws** operate as taxis, picking up as many passengers as they can. Laxmi Jangid, the owner; Jamuna Resort (see p.158), offers full-day **tours** around Shekhawati by car or jeep for Rs2000, as well as shorter camel tours (2hr; Rs600/person).

Moving on from Jhunjhunu

Buses run from the government stand in the south of town to Nawalgarh (every 30min; 1hr) and towns throughout Shekhawati, as well as to Bikaner (hourly; 5hr 30min), Jaipur (every 30min; 4hr–4hr 30min) and Delhi (hourly; 7hr 30min). Buses to Mandawa (every 30min; 45min–1hr) also stop by Mandawa Circle near the *RTDC Tourist Bungalow*. **Train** services are currently in a state of flux due to the conversion of the line to Delhi from metre gauge to broad gauge – wherever you're heading, buses tend to be faster and more reliable.

Accommodation and eating

The following are the best of Jhunjhunu's limited supply of **accommodation** options. There are no good restaurants in town, and you'll almost certainly end up **eating** where you're staying.

Fresco Palace Paramveer Path, off Station Rd ⓣ01592/395233, ⓦwww.frescopalace.com. Pleasant modern hotel (although there aren't many frescoes in evidence), with comfortable, slightly chintzy rooms (all a/c) and a relaxing garden restaurant. The *Shekhawati Heritage* hotel next door is cheaper but less appealling. ❻

Jamuna Resort Delhi–Sikar Rd ⓣ01592/232871, ⓦwww.shivshekhawati.com. This attractive village-style resort on the eastern edge of town comprises a cluster of thatch-roofed cottages (all a/c) set amid extensive grounds complete with pool (non-guests Rs50) and garden restaurant. The more expensive rooms are exquisitely decorated with mirrorwork and traditional murals. They also run courses in Indian cooking and art, plus free yoga classes. Also a good place to arrange tours. ❹–❻

Sangam Paramveer Path, opposite the government bus stand ⓣ01592/232544. Basic cheapie with large, bare, slightly shabby rooms – make sure you get one away from the noisy main road. ❷–❸

Shiv Shekhawati Khemi Shakti Rd, near Muni Ashram ⓣ01592/232651 or 512695, ⓦwww.shivshekhawati.com. Well-maintained modern hotel with large, clean rooms (all a/c), restaurant and internet access. ❷–❹

The Town

Hidden away in the alleyways behind the main bazaar is Jhunjhunu's most striking building, the magnificent **Khetri Mahal** of 1760 (entrance Rs20), a superb, open-sided sandstone palace with cusped Islamic-style arches which wouldn't look out of place amid the great Indo-Islamic monuments of Fatehpur Sikri. The whole edifice seems incongruously grand amid the modest streets of central Jhunjhunu, but now stands empty. A covered ramp, wide enough for horses, winds up to the roof, from where there are sweeping views over the town and across to the massive ramparts of the sturdy **Badalgarh Fort** (currently closed to the public) on a nearby hilltop.

Stretching east of the Khetri Mahal is Jhunjhunu's main bazaar, centred around **Futala Market**, a fascinating, and hopelessly confusing, tangle of narrow streets crammed with dozens of tiny, charmingly old-fashioned shops. On the northern edge of the bazaar, facing each other across the small square of Chabutra Chowk, lie the two so-called **Modi havelis**, boasting the usual range of murals – the one on the eastern side of the chowk is the most impressive, entered via a grand, three-metre-high ramp.

Jhunjhunu's finest havelis are spread out along **Nehru Bazaar**, immediately east of the main bazaar. Heading east, you'll first reach the striking **Kaniram Narsinghdas Tibrewala Haveli** of 1883, perched on a platform above the surrounding vegetable stalls and sporting a fine selection of paintings inside (the entrance is around the back). Further east down Nehru Bazaar, entered via an impressive ramp up from street level, the **Mohanlal Ishwardas Modi Haveli** has a good selection of entertainingly naive portraits. Unusual oval miniatures of various Indian bigwigs frame the entrance to the zenana (women's) courtyard, while in the zenana itself a long frieze of miniature portraits runs around the top of the arches showing assorted European and Indian personages sporting a range of flouncy costumes, silly hats and magnificent moustaches. Immediately north of here, the striking little **Bihari temple** features some of the oldest murals in Shekhawati, painted in 1776 in black and brown vegetable pigments, including a dramatic depiction inside the central dome of Hanuman's monkey army taking on the forces of the many-headed demon king Ravana.

Outlying sights

West of the Khetri Mahal at the foot of the craggy Nehara Pahar lies the **Dargah of Kamaruddin Shah**, an atmospheric complex comprising a mosque and madrasa arranged around a pretty courtyard (still retaining some of its original murals), with the ornate *dargah* (tomb) of the Sufi saint Kamaruddin Shah in the centre.

North of the town centre lies the **Mertani Baori**, one of the region's most impressive step-wells, while further east is the extraordinary **Rani Sati Mandir**, dedicated to a merchant's wife who commited sati in 1595. The shrine is reputedly the richest temple in the country after Tirupati in Andhra Pradesh (although similar claims are made for the Nathdwara temple – see p.224), receiving hundreds of thousands of pilgrims each year and millions of rupees in donations, its immense popularity bearing witness to the enduring awe with which satis are regarded in the state.

Mandawa

Rising from a flat, featureless landscape roughly midway between Jhunjhunu and Fatehpur, **MANDAWA** was founded by the Shekhawats in 1755 and is now the most tourist-oriented place in Shekhawati, although the handicraft shops, touts and guides detract very little from the town's profusion of beautifully dilapidated mansions.

Arrival and information

Buses from Jhunjhunu, Nawalgarh, Jaipur and Bikaner arrive at Sonthaliya Gate in the east of town. From Fatehpur, most buses pull in at a stand in the centre, just off the main bazaar. **Jeeps** ply the same routes. The town is so small that both bus

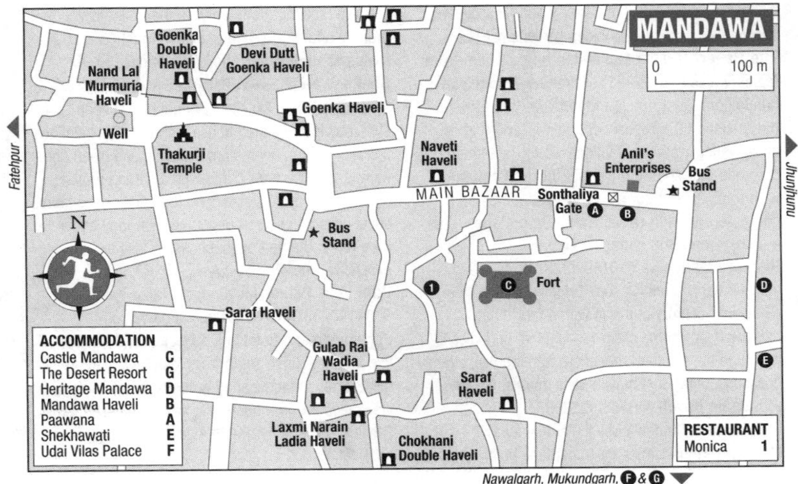

Moving on from Mandawa

Regular **buses** run from Sonthaliya Gate to Jhunjhunu (every 30min; 1hr) and Nawalgarh (every 30min; 45min). Services to Fatehpur (every 30min; 1hr), leave from the stand in the centre of town, just off the main bazaar. There are also a number of services (mostly in the morning) from Sonthaliya Gate to Jaipur (4hr) and Bikaner (3hr 30min).

stands are within walking distance of most hotels. **Internet** access is generally available at all hotels; if not there are various places along the main bazaar – try Anil's Enterprises (Rs50/hr; open 24hr), opposite the *Mandawa Haveli* hotel; they also **change cash and** travellers' cheques.

Walking tours of Mandawa's havelis can be arranged through your hotel, or at Classic Shekhawati Tours (ⓣ01592/223144, ⓔclassicshekhamnd@yahoo.co.in), by the entrance to the fort (Rs250–350 for a 2–3hr walk). Most guesthouses and hotels can also arrange trips out into the surrounding desert either by jeep or on horseback, camel-back or in camel-drawn carts. Prices for all these activities vary wildly, but are usually cheapest if booked through the *Hotel Shekhawati* (see below). Classic Shekhawati Tours also arranges more upmarket day and overnight **camel safaris**, though you'll need to book five days in advance.

Accommodation and eating

Mandawa has a good spread of **hotels** in all price ranges. You'll probably **eat** at your hotel or guesthouse. If you want to venture out, head for the *Monica* rooftop restaurant (follow the signs from the entrance road to the fort), which dishes up probably the best food in town, with well-prepared veg and non-veg north Indian standards (mains Rs90–250) backed up with cold beer and friendly but discreet service.

Castle Mandawa ⓣ01592/223124, ⓦwww.castlemandawa.com. Mandawa's fanciest accommodation, set in the old town fort, with an atmospheric mishmash of buildings around a sand-filled courtyard. All rooms are different, so look at several before you decide, since standards of comfort and decor vary considerably – and prices are relatively high for what you get. Amenities include a spa, gym, pool (guests only) and spacious gardens. ❼–❽

The Desert Resort Mukandgarh Rd, 1.5km from Mandawa ⓣ01592/223151, ⓦwww.mandawahotels.com. Just outside Mandawa, this attractively rustic little resort occupies a tangle of mud-walled traditional village-style Rajasthani cottages in a soothingly peaceful rural setting, with a mixture of comfy rooms and nicely decorated (though rather dark) a/c cottages, plus a pool. Rooms ❼, cottages ❽

Heritage Mandawa ⓣ01592/223742, ⓦwww.hotelheritagemandawa.com. Brightly painted, late nineteenth-century mansion with a mixed bag of rooms (all a/c), some cosily furnished in period style (although the standard rooms are rather poky), others boasting vibrant Shekhawati-style murals. ❺–❼

Mandawa Haveli ⓣ01592/223088, ⓦhttp://hotelmandawa.free.fr. Far and away Mandawa's most atmospheric heritage hotel, occupying a superb old haveli with original murals. Rooms (all a/c) and, especially, suites, have bags of period character, and there's also a nice rooftop restaurant. Rates discounted in summer by 20–40 percent. ❻–❼

Paawana ⓣ01592/223663, ⓦwww.hotelpaawana.com. Recently opened hotel in a neat modern building (done up with the obligatory murals) and offering attractively furnished a/c rooms at surprisingly affordable prices. ❸–❹

Shekhawati ⓣ9314 698079, ⓦwww.hotelshekhawati.com. Excellent budget option in an eye-catchingly painted house (although the paintings are all modern). Rooms are spacious and clean (the more expensive ones come with a/c and pretty murals), and there's also good food and cheap tours. Local drivers in search of commission may try to take you to the nearby (but considerably more expensive) *Heritage Mandawa*. ❶–❸, a/c ❹–❺

Udai Vilas Palace Mukundgarh Road ⓣ9414023378,ⓦwww.uvpmandawa.com. Upmarket resort hotel in a peaceful rural location five minutes' drive south from Mandawa, set amid three acres of landscaped grounds with fine desert views and accommodation in smart modern rooms. Facilities include a Keralan Ayurvedic spa, gym and pool. ❼

The Town

Tours usually begin with the **Naveti Haveli** (now the State Bank of Bikaner & Jaipur), on the main bazaar. Duck through the metal gate to the right of the bank (no charge) for a look at Mandawa's most entertaining murals, including well-preserved images of a bird-man attempting to take flight, the Wright Brothers' aeroplane, a man using a telephone and a strongman pulling a car.

A ten-minute walk west from here brings you to an interesting cluster of buildings centred around the **Nand Lal Murmuria Haveli**. The murals here are relatively modern, dating from the 1930s and executed in a decidedly flowery and sentimental style, perhaps influenced by contemporary European magazines, with images of various Venetian scenes, George V, Nehru riding a horse and the legendary Maratha warrior Shivaji. Next door, the sun-faded **Goenka Double Haveli** (not to be confused with either of the other Goenka havelis nearby) is one of the largest and grandest in Mandawa, with two separate entrances and striking elephants and horses on the facade. The **Thakurji temple** opposite has a rather odd mural showing soldiers being fired from the mouths of cannon, a favoured British method of executing mutinous sepoys during the 1857 uprising.

South of the main bazaar, the **Gulab Rai Wadia Haveli** is one of the finest in town. The south-facing exterior wall is particularly interesting, with unusually racy (albeit modestly small) murals depicting, amongst other things, a Kama Sutra–like scene in a railway carriage. The interior of the haveli is entered via a grand ramp, with Belgian-glass mirrorwork over the finely carved door leading into the zenana (women's) courtyard.

Immediately south of here lies the almost equally fine **Laxmi Narain Ladia Haveli**. The zenana courtyard boasts naive paintings of a plane and a steamship, along with a cannon being pulled by horses and a tiger attacking a centaur. Some 100m further south, the unusually large **Chokhani Double Haveli** (Rs20) consists of two separate wings built for two brothers; look for the miserable British soldiers and chillum-smoking sadhu facing one another in the recess at the centre of the facade.

Fatehpur

Lying just off NH-11, **FATEHPUR** is the closest town in Shekhawati to Bikaner, 116km west, and a convenient place to stop if you're taking the northern route across the Thar. The town itself is fairly run-down, but it does have several elaborately painted mansions. The most celebrated is the **Nadine Le Prince Haveli** (daily 8am–7pm; Rs100), an 1802 mansion restored to its original splendour by its current owner Nadine Le Prince, a French artist who purchased the haveli in 1998. Some local aficionados complain about the manner in which the haveli has been restored – with large-scale repainting of murals, rather than the simple cleaning and preservation of existing art – but the overall effect is undeniably impressive, and the haveli as a whole is one of the few in Shekhawati where you get a real sense of how these lavish mansions would originally have looked.

Close to the Nadine Le Prince Haveli, the imposing **Jagannath Singania Haveli** (closed to visitors) towers over the main road north. Most of the exterior paintings have faded; the best are on the western facade of the small building around the back, including Krishna and Radha framed by elephants and some heavily bewhiskered Europeans toting guns. South from here, the **Geori Shankar Haveli** (next to an unusually fine bangle stall) is the polar opposite of the Nadine Le Prince Haveli, dilapidated but hugely atmospheric, and still inhabited by a number of impoverished local families.

Practicalities

Fatehpur has two **bus stands**, near each other in the centre of town on the main Sikar–Churu (north–south) road. Buses from the government Roadways stand, furthest south, serve Jaipur (every 30min; 3hr 30min), Ramgarh (hourly; 30min), Bikaner (14 daily; 3hr 30min–4hr) and Delhi (5 daily; 6hr). Private buses run from the stand further north along the bazaar to Mandawa (every 30min; 45min), Jhunjhunu (every 30min; 1hr), Mahansar (4 daily; 45min) and Ramgarh (hourly; 30min). Arriving in Fatehpur, note that many buses drop passengers off at the NH-11 intersection, about 1km south of town.

Just off NH-11, the modern RTDC *Hotel Haveli* (ⓣ01571/230293; ❹–❺) is the town's only plausible hotel, though its large and light rooms (some with a/c) don't quite compensate for the dodgy plumbing and general air of neglect.

Mahansar, Ramgarh and Lakshmangarh

Some of the most outstanding murals and Hindu monuments in the region are scattered across three small towns in the far north and west of Shekhawati: **Mahansar**, **Ramgarh** and **Lakshmangarh**. Only Mahansar has any accommodation, but you can reach the other two on day-trips from Fatehpur, Mandawa or Nawalgarh, either with your own vehicle, or (much more slowly) on inter-village jeeps and occasional buses.

Mahansar

The relative inaccessibility of **MAHANSAR**, marooned amid a sea of scrub and drifting sand north of Mandawa, has ensured that its monuments remain among the least visited in the region, making the village a peaceful place to hole up for a day or two. There are two main reasons to come here. The first is to **stay** at the quirky *Narayan Niwas Castle* (ⓣ01595/264322, ⓦwww.mehansarcastle.com; ❹–❺). Managed by Mahansar's royal family in their crumbling 1768 abode, it contains fourteen rooms of varying standards, including two memorably appointed heritage rooms (#1 and #5) and some cheaper, but still deeply atmospheric standard doubles (albeit stronger on period charm than creature comforts).

The second reason is to visit the stunning **Sona ki Dukan Haveli** ("Gold Shop Haveli"; Rs100; no set hours; ask around the shops for the key) in the middle of the village. The paintings in the entrance hall are the finest in Shekhawati, with murals depicting the exploits of Rama, the incarnations of Vishnu, and the life of Krishna, all painted in superb detail and picked out in lavish gold leaf (hence the haveli's name). While you're here, it's also worth having a look at the nearby **Raghunath Mandir**, covered in colourful floral murals and offering good views over town from its chattri-fringed rooftop.

Ramgarh and Lakshmangarh

RAMGARH, 20km north of Fatehpur, was founded in 1791 and developed as something of a status symbol by disaffected members of the wealthy Poddar merchant family, who made every effort for the town to outshine nearby Churu, which they left following a dispute with the local thakur over taxes. They succeeded in their aim: Ramgarh is one of the most beautiful – but also one of the least-visited – towns in Shekhawati, with the usual fine havelis along with an exceptional array of religious architecture as well.

Starting from the bus stand on the west side of town, follow either of the two roads east into the town centre. After about five minutes' walk you'll reach the **Poddar family havelis**, a superb cluster of ornate mansions decorated with scenes from local folk stories and a frequently repeated motif, comprising three fishes joined at the mouth, which is unique to Ramgarh. Just beyond here lies the town's main square, surrounded by the disintegrating remains of further lavishly painted havelis. Turn left here and head through the Churu Gate, beyond which the road is lined with a dense cluster of extraordinarily ornate temples and memorial chhatris erected by various members of the Poddar clan, their rooftops capped with a fantastical array of domes and arcades. If you have a guide (it's virtually impossible to find otherwise) it's also worth searching out the nearby **Shanicharji Mandir**, a diminutive temple dedicated to Saturn and decorated with sparkling mirrorwork.

The small town of **LAKSHMANGARH**, 20km south of Fatehpur, is another archetypal, but seldom visited, Shekhawati destination, its neat grid of streets (a layout inspired by that of Jaipur's Pink City) dotted with dozens of ornate havelis in various stages of picturesque decay. The town is dominated by its dramatic nineteenth-century **fort**, which crowns a rocky outcrop on the west side of town; it's now closed to the public, though you can walk up the steep track to the entrance to enjoy the fine views over town. Looking down from here you can also see the extensive **Char Chowk Haveli** (Four-Courtyard Haveli), off to the left, the finest in town and one of the largest in Shekhawati.

East of Jaipur

The area **east of Jaipur**, interspersed with the forested slopes of the Aravalli Hills, holds an inviting mixture of historic towns and wildlife sanctuaries. To the northeast is the fortified town of **Alwar**, jumping-off point for the **Sariska Tiger Reserve and National Park**. Further east are the former princely capitals of **Deeg** and **Bharatpur**, and India's finest bird sanctuary, **Keoladeo National Park**. The wildlife sanctuary at **Ranthambore**, in idyllic scenery southeast of Jaipur, offers the best chance in India of spotting wild tigers.

Alwar

Roughly 140km northeast from Jaipur towards Delhi, the large, bustling town of **ALWAR** sprawls across a valley beneath one of eastern Rajasthan's larger and more impressive **forts**, whose massive ramparts straggle impressively along craggy ridges above. The town is mostly visited as a jumping-off point for Sariska National Park, though it has a number of interesting attractions in its own right, including a fine city palace and a string of colourful bazaars.

Arrival and information

Alwar's **bus stand** is right in the middle of town while the **railway station** is around 1.5km east of the centre; you'll find plenty of cycle rickshaws, but

Moving on from Alwar

There are **bus** services to Bharatpur via Deeg (every 15min; 4hr), Sariska (every 30min; 1hr–1hr 30min), Delhi (every 30min; 5hr) and Jaipur (hourly; 4hr). **Trains** run to and from Delhi, Jaipur, Jodhpur, Ajmer and Ahmedabad (but not Bharatpur). For Jaipur, the best service is the *Ajmer Shatabdi* (#2015; daily except Wed; dep. 8.44am, arr. 10.45am); for Delhi, the *Jaisalmer–Delhi Express* (#4060; daily; dep. 7.19am, arr. 11.05am) and the *Ajmer Shatabdi* (#2016; daily except Wed; dep. 7.33pm, arr. 10.40pm) are two of the faster services.

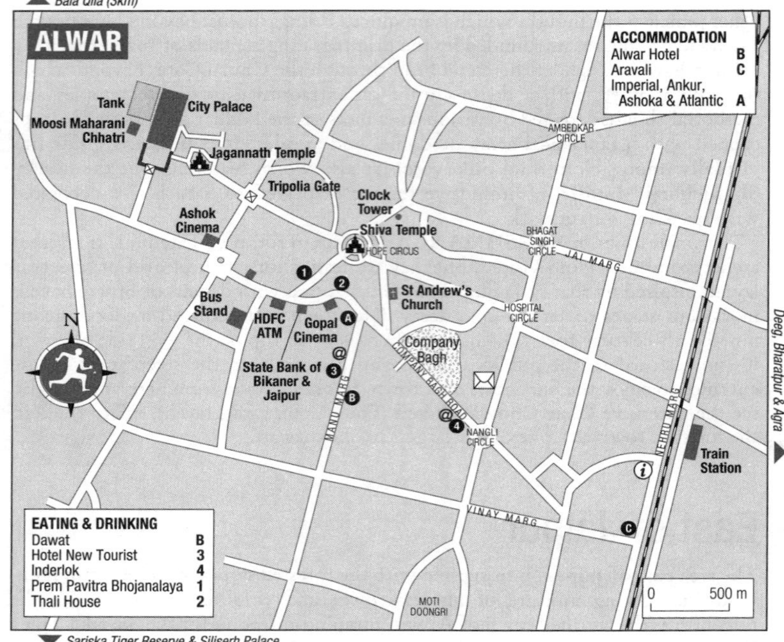

surprisingly few autos (try the railway station). The **tourist office** (Mon–Fri 10am–5pm; ☎0144/234 7348) is just south of the station. You can **change currency** and travellers' cheques at the State Bank of Bikaner & Jaipur, in the centre of town, which also has an **ATM** that accepts foreign Visa and MasterCards; if this isn't working, there's an HDFC ATM nearby. For **internet** access, try the well-equipped Cyberlink (daily 8am–8pm; Rs20/hr) on the south side of Company Bagh, or Manish Cyber on Manu Marg (daily 8.30am–10pm; Rs20/hr).

Accommodation

Alwar

Alwar Hotel 26 Manu Marg ☎0144/270 0012, ⓦwww.alwarhotel.com. This trim little mid-range hotel is easily the nicest place to stay in Alwar itself, with smart and spacious a/c rooms set around a neat garden. The in-house *Dawat* restaurant (see opposite) is another major bonus. ❺

Ankur, **Ashoka**, **Atlantic** and **Imperial** hotels. Clustered together on the corner of Manu Marg, a 5min walk from the bus station, this group of four adjacent and more or less indistinguishable hotels offers a range of simple but cheap, tolerably clean and reasonably comfortable fan and a/c rooms, and there are always plenty of vacancies. ❷–❹

Aravali Just south of the railway station on Nehru Marg ☎0144/233 2883. The town's only plausible budget alternative to the *Ankur* group of hotels. It's definitely seen better days, and the wide variety of rooms (fan, air-cooled and a/c) are all rather run-down, though reasonably clean. There's also a bar, internet access, and a pool (guests only) in summer. ❸–❻

Around Alwar

Hill Fort Kesroli 12km east of Alwar ☎01468/289352, ⓦwww.neemranahotels.com. India's oldest heritage hotel, occupying a rugged old fifteenth-century fort impeccably restored and centred on a lush inner courtyard filled with plants and birds. Rooms are pleasantly rustic and have great views over Kesroli village and the surrounding countryside. ❻–❼

Neemrana Fort-Palace Neemrana (just north of the Delhi–Jaipur NH-8 Highway, close to the state border, around 75km from Alwar, 120km from Delhi and 140km from Jaipur) ⓣ01494/246006, ⓦwww.neemranahotels.com. One of Rajasthan's longest-running heritage hotels, offering a wide range of rooms in Rajasthani and colonial style inside the vast and wonderfully crusty old Neemrana Fort (1464) – a labyrinthine maze of courtyards and corridors. ❼–❾

The Town

Alwar's principal attraction is its rambling and atmospheric **City Palace**, or Vinai Vilas Mahal, a sprawling complex of ornate but now slightly dilapidated buildings, covered in crumbling ochre plaster and studded with endless canopied balconies. Most of the palace's innumerable rooms are now put to more mundane use as government offices, while the courtyard in front provides open-air office space for dozens of typists, lined up behind clanking old antique metal machines, and lawyers, who prosecute their business under the trees. The palace's time-warped **museum** (Tues–Sun 10am–5pm; Rs10 [Rs5]), on the top floor of the palace, has extensive collections of weapons and miniatures paintings, alongside a medley of objects belonging to former maharajas ranging from musical instruments to stuffed animals. Steps at the left-hand end of the main facade lead up to a large **tank**, flanked by symmetrical *ghats*, pavilions and a terrace on which stands the delicate **Moosi Maharani Chhatri**, built in memory of Bhaktawar Singh's mistress, who immolated herself on his funeral pyre.

Perched high above Alwar is **Bala Qila** fort, whose well-preserved walls climb dramatically up and down the thickly wooded hillsides that rise above the town. There's not much actually to see inside the fort – besides a temple and a few old cannons – but it's a pleasant walk up from town, with fine views and fresh hill breezes. It takes about two hours to make the return trip on foot up to the fort's outermost gate, or about twice that to reach the topmost point of the fortifications. If you don't want to walk, you'll have to arrange for a taxi through your hotel or the tourist office – the road up is far too steep for a cycle rickshaw to tackle.

Eating and drinking

Alwar is famous throughout Rajasthan for its cavity-causing **milk cakes** (*palang torh*), which you can buy at the stalls around Hope Circus. Note that none of the following places serves alcohol. If you want a **drink** the gloomy mosquito-plagued garden at the *Hotel New Tourist* on Manu Marg is about as good as it gets.

Dawat *Hotel Alwar*, Manu Marg. Reliable little a/c restaurant serving up a good range of veg and non-veg north and south Indian food, plus better-than-average Chinese. Mains Rs40–140.

Inderlok Company Bagh Rd, near Nangli Circle. Comfortable a/c veg restaurant, popular with locals, serving up good north and south Indian standards along with a few Chinese dishes. Mains Rs80–125.

Prem Pavitra Bhojanalya This cosy little restaurant dishes up the best food in town, with a very short, very cheap menu of basic north Indian standards (all mains under Rs50). The entrance is easily missed: go up the road roughly opposite the State Bank of Jaipur & Bikaner, past the Bharat Petroleum petrol station. It's on the left about 50m up.

Thali House Simple little a/c café serving up a short but passable range of south Indian dishes (plus a few Chinese offerings). Mains Rs35–65.

Sariska Tiger Reserve and around

Alwar is the access point for **Sariska Tiger Reserve and National Park**, a former maharaja's hunting ground managed since 1979 by Project Tiger. Accustomed to being overshadowed by the more famous Ranthambore, Sariska was suddenly thrust into the headlines in 2005 when it was discovered that its tiger population, estimated at around 28 in 2003, had all but vanished due to poaching – one of India's biggest-ever conservation scandals. Tigers were reintroduced to Sariska in 2008, with the arrival of one male and two females from Ranthambore, with two more planned to follow in the near future.

One silver lining from the whole affair is that the number of visitors to the sanctuary has dwindled significantly, and for birders and wildlife enthusiasts put off by the crowds and hassle of Ranthambore, Sariska's relative serenity comes as a welcome relief. The 881-square-kilometre sanctuary is home to abundant **wildlife** including *sambar*, *chital*, wild boar, nilgai and other antelopes, jackals, mongooses, monkeys, peacocks, porcupines, and numerous birds. The park is also dotted with a number of evocative ruins and other man-made structures, including the old **Kankwari Fort**, and a **Hanuman temple** deep within the park that gets surprisingly lively on Saturdays and Tuesdays, when visitors to the temple are allowed into the park for free.

Practicalities

Sariska is **open** daily from October to June (Oct–Feb 7am–3.30pm; March–June 6am–4pm); note that the **park is closed** from July to September. The park lies 35km southwest of Alwar on the main Alwar–Jaipur road; **buses** between the two (every 30min; 1hr journey from Alwar) will stop, on request, at the *Sariska Palace* hotel, a five-minute walk from the park. Alternatively, you may be able to arrange a **taxi through a hotel at Alwar** (around Rs1000), which also gives you time to visit Siliserh (see below) on the way back.

Entrance to the park costs Rs200 per person [Rs25] plus Rs125 per vehicle, Rs200 for a compulsory guide, and Rs200 for a video camera. **Jeeps** can be hired at the entrance and cost Rs900 for a three-hour drive around the park; Rs1400 for the longer (4–5hr) ride to Kankwari Fort; or Rs2700 for a full day. You can also take your own vehicle into the park, but you'll be restricted to metalled roads.

Accommodation

There are several **places to stay** close to the reserve, although all are seriously overpriced.

Alwar Bagh 20km from Sariska (and 16km from Alwar) on the Sariska–Alwar highway ⓣ0294/241 2081, ⓦwww.alwarbagh.com. Large and comfortable a/c rooms in a sequence of attractive lemon-yellow buildings arranged around spacious gardens, plus a fine pool. Much better value than the various places closer to the park. ❻

RTDC Hotel Tiger Den ⓣ0144/284 1342. Attractive, if rather overpriced, option conveniently situated right next to the park entrance, with spacious, old-fashioned fan and a/c rooms, plus a nice garden, though service can be lackadaisical. ❺–❻

Sariska Palace A couple of minutes' drive down the main road from the park entrance ⓣ011/4651 5651, ⓦwww.thesariskapalace.in. This former maharaja's residence has plenty of atmosphere, though rooms in the main building are surprisingly shabby given the price, while those in the various modern annexes scattered around the grounds are poky and boring. There's also a pool, and large swathes of manicured lawns to loll around on. ❽

Sariska Tiger Heaven Off the main road 5km before the park entrance on the Jaipur side (signposted as "Sariska Tiger Haven") ⓣ9114 652248. In a very peaceful rural setting, arranged around attractive gardens with pool, although the cottages are surprisingly shabby given the hefty price tag, and the restaurant is nothing but a concrete bunker. ❽

Siliserh Palace

Fifteen kilometres south of Alwar, **Siliserh Palace** is easily visited en route to or from Sariska if you've got your own vehicle (there's no public transport here). Maharaja Vijay Singh had the palace built in 1845 to win over a beautiful commoner, a certain Sheela, who agreed to marriage on the condition that she live within sight of her family's modest home. The whitewashed palace itself is fairly humdrum, but the Shangri-La setting, on the edge of a ten-square-kilometre lake ringed by jungle-clad hills, is idyllic. The palace now houses the disappointingly shabby RTDC *Lake Palace Hotel* (Ⓣ0144/288 6322; ❺–❻). It's a nice spot to while away an afternoon, even so, and you can also rent out paddle-boats and motorboats if you want to get out onto the water.

Deeg

Some 30km northwest of Bharatpur, the dusty little market town of **DEEG** is the unlikely home of one of eastern Rajasthan's most lavish **palaces** (daily except Fri 9.30am–5.30pm; Rs100 [Rs5]), a fascinating blend of Mughal and Hindu architectural styles constructed by the local Jat overlords in the mid-eighteenth century. The extensive complex comprises a large number of finely carved buildings scattered around extensive *charbagh*-style gardens dotted with thirty-odd water jets – though sadly, the water channels are dry and the fountains are only switched on during local festivals.

Entering the palace, the first and largest of the various *bhawans*, the **Gopal Bhawan** (closed Fri), lies immediately ahead, a spacious and plushly furnished hall which originally served as Surajmal's summer residence. Behind it lies the first of the palace's two large tanks, the **Gopal Sagar**. On the opposite side of the gardens lies the ornate **Kesav Bhawan**, or "Monsoon Palace", a richly carved open-sided pavilion surrounded by a deep water channel dotted with hundreds of tiny fountains. This unusual structure was designed to recreate the cool ambience of the rainy season, with water released from rooftop pipes to imitate a shower of monsoon rain, while metal balls were agitated by further streams of pressurized water to simulate the sound of thunder. Immediately behind here is the second of the palace's **tanks**, its stepped *ghats* usually covered in washing laid out by local housewives, while beyond rise the enormous walls of the town's huge fort.

Deeg is served by **bus** from Alwar (every 15min; 3hr) and Bharatpur (every 15min; 1hr). The town is easily visited as a day-trip from Bharatpur, or en route between Bharatpur and Alwar. There's nowhere to stay.

Bharatpur and Keoladeo National Park

The walled town of **BHARATPUR** is just a stone's throw from the border with Uttar Pradesh and a mere 18km from the magnificent abandoned city of Fatehpur Sikri. The town itself has an interesting mix of bazaars, palaces and temples, but the real reason to come here is to visit India's most famous bird sanctuary, the **Keoladeo National Park**, on the town's southern edge, one of India's, if not the world's, top ornithological destinations.

Arrival and information

Bharatpur's **bus stand** is in the west of town. If you're arriving from Fatehpur Sikri you'll save yourself time (and a rickshaw fare) by getting off the bus at the crossroads on the southeast side of town near the park gates and guesthouses – look out for the prominent Rajasthan government tourist office right on the crossroads, or the large RTDC *Hotel Saras* opposite. The **railway station** is a couple of kilometres northwest of the town centre, a Rs40–50 ride from Keoladeo National Park and the nearby guesthouses.

The town's **tourist office** (Mon–Sat 9.30am–6pm; Ⓣ05644/222542, Ⓦwww.bharatpur.nic.in) is at the crossroads near the park entrance where Fatehpur Sikri

Moving on from Bharatpur

Buses run from the main bus stand to Jaipur (every 30min; 4hr), Delhi (every 30min–1hr; 5hr), Agra (hourly; 1hr 30min–2hr) and Fatehpur Sikri (every 30min–1hr; 30–45min). Bharatpur's railway station lies on the main Delhi–Mumbai line. There are three or four **trains** daily to Agra Fort, including the *Howrah Superfast* (#2308; daily; dep. 5.10am, arr. 6.35am) and *Sealdah Express* (#2988; daily except Wed; dep. 5.35pm, arr. 7.30pm); seven services to Sawai Madhopur, the best being the Golden *Temple Mail* (#2904; daily; dep. 10.41am, arr. 1.14pm) and *Kota Jan Shatabdi* (#2060; daily; dep. 3.43pm, arr. 6pm), which both continue to Kota (arriving at 2.25pm & 7.40pm respectively), and four services to Jaipur, the best of which is the *Marudhar Express* (#4853/4863/4865; dep. 7.13am, arr. 11.30am).

buses pull in. Nearby, on New Civil Lines, *The Perch* and the *Royal Guest House Forex* (both open till around 10/11pm) offer **internet** access (Rs30/hr) and also change cash and travellers' cheques and can arrange taxis; *The Perch* also gives cash advances on credit cards.

Accommodation and eating

All the town's best **hotels** and **guesthouses** are located near the entrance to Keoladeo National Park, some 3km south of the town centre itself. Bharatpur's reputation as a tourist-friendly oasis has made it an attractive base for day-trippers to Agra and the Taj Mahal – a day-trip by taxi to Agra and back should cost about Rs1000. There are no independent restaurants in Bharatpur – most people **eat** where they're staying.

Budget

Evergreen ⓣ05644/225917. One of the cheapest options in Bharatpur, with simple but clean rooms with fan and private bathroom (though hot water comes in a bucket in some rooms). ❶

Falcon ⓣ05644/223815, ⓔfalconguest_house@hotmail.com. Attractive modern guesthouse with a selection of comfortable fan, air-cooled and a/c rooms, plus a small garden restaurant with good food. Internet access available. ❷–❹

Jungle Lodge ⓣ05644/225622, ⓦwww.junglelodge.dk. Run by a knowledgeable naturalist, this friendly place has a range of clean and spacious modern rooms (fan, air-cooled and a/c) overlooking a tranquil flower-filled garden. The pleasant little terrace restaurant and evening fires (in winter) give the place a pleasantly sociable feel, and there are bikes and binoculars for rent, plus internet access. ❶–❷

Kiran ⓣ05644/223845, ⓦwww.kiranguesthouse.com. Run by an extremely friendly and helpful pair of brothers, this place offers a range of clean and comfortable fan, air-cooled and a/c rooms at rock-bottom prices. There's free pick-up and drop-off from bus and train stations, plus binoculars for rent (Rs50). ❶–❸

Mid-range to expensive

The Bagh Agra Rd, 1km past *Laxmi Vilas Palace* ⓣ05644/228333, ⓦwww.thebagh.com. This idyllic upmarket hotel occupies a cluster of pink, low-rise buildings scattered around *charbagh*-style gardens which are home to over fifty species of bird. Rooms are cool, spacious and attractively furnished, and there's also also a spa and large pool. Prices from US$180. ❾

Bahratpur Ashok (formerly the *Bharatpur Forest Lodge*) 1km inside park ⓣ05644/222760. In a pleasantly sylvan setting inside the park (note that you'll have to pay one day's park entrance fee for every night you stay here), this very sleepy hotel has spacious and comfortable old-fashioned rooms with balconies overlooking the sanctuary, a pleasant garden out the back and a passable restaurant. Relatively expensive, but the setting is pretty much unbeatable. ❼

Birders' Inn ⓣ05644/227346, ⓦwww.birdersinn.com. The most inviting place in town, usually full of serious bird-watchers who gather nightly to compare checklists in the inviting thatch-roofed restaurant. Rooms (all a/c) are large, smart, and excellent value. Internet access available. ❺

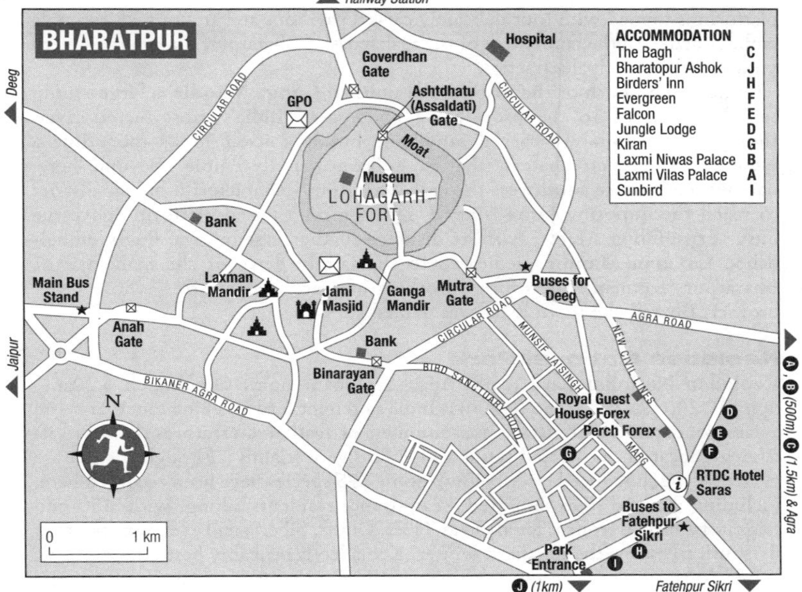

Laxmi Niwas Palace Agra Rd ☎05644/223522, Ⓦwww.laxminiwas.com. Swanky new hotel in traditional Rajasthani style right next to the *Laxmi Vilas Palace* – a bit more comfortable than its older neighbour, though not nearly as atmospheric. ❽

Laxmi Vilas Palace Agra Rd ☎05644/223523, Ⓦwww.laxmivilas.com. Former royal palace, set amid extensive grounds east of town. It's all a trifle kitsch, but undeniably romantic, with reasonably priced a/c rooms complete with four-poster beds and other regal decorative touches. ❽

Sunbird ☎05644/225701, Ⓦwww.hotelsunbird.com. Attractive mid-range hotel, and a decent alternative if you can't get into the adjacent *Birders' Inn*, with a range of modern and very comfortably furnished fan and a/c rooms, plus a few traditional Rajasthani-style cottages in the spacious garden. ❺

The Town

Bharatpur was founded by the Jat king Surajmal, who constructed the virtually impregnable **Lohagarh** (Iron Fort) at the heart of town in 1732; time and modern development have had little effect on its magnificent eleven-kilometre-long bastions and immense moat. You're most likely to enter the fort from the south, though it's worth having a look at the impressive **Ashtdhatu** (or Eight-Metal) **Gate**, named on account of the number of different types of metal that apparently went into the making of its extremely solid-looking doors.

The fort is home to no less than three large royal palaces in various stages of dereliction, all built by the Jats between 1730 and 1850. The best preserved is the large orange **Kamra Khas Mahal**, on the west side of the fort, which now serves as the town's mildly diverting **museum** (daily except Fri 10am–4.30pm; Rs3, camera Rs10, video Rs20), home to a large collection of finely carved sculptures and a superb little marble hammam (baths), plus the usual ragtag collection of miniature paintings, weaponry and other regal memorabilia.

Turn left as you exit the museum and follow the narrow road up around the edge of the palace to reach the lofty **Jawahar Burj** next door. This small, elevated platform is topped with four delicately carved pavilions and an unusual iron pole embellished with the family tree of the maharajas of Bharatpur, though the superb views are the principal attraction.

Immediately south of the fort lies the unusual **Ganga Mandir**, a large Hindu temple dedicated to the proprietary goddess of India's most sacred river, though the elaborately carved sandstone building itself looks more like a Neoclassical French chateau than a Subcontinental temple. Beyond here, narrow roads snake southwest through Bharatpur's characterful bazaar district to reach the imposing **Jama Masjid**, set high on a raised platform above the busy surrounding streets. A short distance further east lies the finely embellished **Laxman Mandir**, dedicated to the family deity of the maharajas of Bharatpur, Laxman, one of the brothers of Lord Rama, after whose other brother, Bharat, the town itself was named.

Keoladeo National Park

Keoladeo National Park (daily April–Sept 6am–6pm; Oct–March 6.30am–5pm; Rs200 [Rs25], video Rs200) is India's premier birdwatching sanctuary – an avian wonderland that attracts vast numbers of feathered creatures thanks to its strategic location, protected status and extensive wetlands (although the last are currently much reduced – see below). Some 375 species have been recorded here, including around two hundred year-round residents along with 150-odd migratory species from as far afield as Tibet, China, Siberia and even Europe, who fly south to escape the northern winter. Keoladeo is probably best known for its stupendous array of **aquatic birds**, which descend en masse on the park's wetlands following the dramatic arrival of the monsoon in July. These include the majestic saras crane and a staggering two thousand painted storks, as well as snake-necked darters, spoonbills, pink flamingos, white ibis and grey pelicans. There are also various **mammals** in the park, including wild boar, mongoose, *chital*, nilgai and *sambar*.

The **best time to visit** is following the monsoon (roughly Oct–March), when the weather is dry but the lakes are still full and the migratory birds in residence (although mists in December and January can hinder serious birdwatching). Unfortunately, the **drought** suffered by Rajasthan in the past decade has taken a massive toll on Keoladeo. Diminished rains over recent years have left the park's lakes at a fraction of their customary size, with a huge consequent reduction in the number of aquatic birds in residence. A plan to artificially irrigate the park may have improved the situation by the time you read this, but don't hold your breath. For the time being, even a waterless Keoladeo is still a richly rewarding place to visit.

Park practicalities

The park entrance is around 4km south of Bharatpur railway station; free **maps** are available here. A single road passes through the park, while numerous small paths cut around lakes and across marshes and provide excellent cover for birdwatching. You can hire a **guide** at the gate (Rs100/hr for up to five people), who will probably have binoculars for you to borrow. The best way to get around is by **bike**, available at the main entrance (Rs25; note that outside bikes aren't currently allowed into the park), or by cycle rickshaw (Rs70/hr) – drivers are trained by the park authorities and very clued up. During the winter, gondola-style **boats** (Rs25/person, minimum four people) offer short rides across the wetlands, assuming there's enough water. The *Bharatpur Ashok Hotel* (see p.168) at the north end of the park is a reliable place to get a drink or something **to eat**.

Ranthambore National Park

No Indian nature reserve can guarantee a tiger sighting, but at **RANTHAMBORE NATIONAL PARK** the odds are probably better than anywhere else: the park itself is relatively small, and the resident tigers are famously unperturbed by humans, hunting in broad daylight and rarely shying from cameras or jeep-loads of tourists. Combine the big cats' bravado with the park's proximity to the Delhi–Agra–Jaipur "Golden Triangle", and you'll understand why Ranthambore attracts the number of visitors it does.

Arrival and information

Ranthambore National Park is reached via the small town of **Sawai Madhopur**, which is served by **trains** on the main Mumbai–Delhi line, and is thus easily accessible from Bharatpur, Agra, Jaipur, Delhi and Kota. The **station** is right in the middle of town, close to the **bus stand**. The helpful **tourist office** (Mon–Sat 10am–5pm; ⓣ07462/220808) in the station hands out free **maps** of the town. There are **exchange** facilities at many hotels and in the State Bank of Bikaner & Jaipur in Sawai Madhopur. A couple of places along the main road just before you reach the *Ankur Hotel* offer **internet** access including the reasonably reliable Tiger Track shop (Rs50/hr).

Accommodation and eating

Most of the area's numerous **hotels** and **guesthouses** are strung out along the 14km road between Sawai Madhopur and the national park; some of the better places are featured on ⓦwww.hotelsranthambhore.com. Accommodation **prices** in Ranthambore are significantly above average, and genuine budget accommodation is almost non-existent (hoteliers claim that they only really see six months' business every year – and therefore have to charge double prices). For cheap **food**, the garden restaurant at the *Tiger Safari* hotel is the best place in town. If you want to push the boat out, head for *Sawai Madhopur Lodge* (which does lunch and dinner buffets for Rs550/650 respectively) or the lovely *Vanyavilas* (dinner from around Rs1500).

Moving on from Ranthambore

There are virtually no **rickshaws** in Ranthambore, so you'll have to arrange transport to the bus or railway station through your hotel when you come to leave.

Sawai Madhopur straddles the main Delhi–Mumbai railway line and is well served by **trains**. There are daily services for Jaipur (6.45am, 10.10am, 10.45am & 2.40pm; 2hr 10min–2hr 45min), Bharatpur (7.10am & 12.35pm; 2hr 10min–2hr 30min), Jodhpur (2.40pm; 8hr), Kota (1.08pm, 1.30pm, 4.10pm, 6.05pm & 7.40pm; 1hr 20min–1hr 30min), Delhi (6.33am, 7.10am, 12.35am & 1.08am; 4hr 30min–6hr), and Mumbai (1.08pm, 4.10pm, 8.37pm & 10.05pm; 16–17hr). For Bundi, it's easiest to take a train to Kota and then catch a bus, or catch a direct bus all the way (see below).

Ongoing improvements to the previously awful roads around Ranthambore are gradually making **bus** travel a quicker and more comfortable option, although taking the train is still preferable for most destinations. Services run to Jaipur (6 daily; 4–5hr), Bundi (3 daily; 4–5hr), and Ajmer (1 daily; 8hr). Buses depart from one of the two bus stands close to one another in the middle of Sawai Madhopur; check with the person who's taking you that you're at the right stand.

Budget to mid-range

Aditiya Resort Ranthambore Rd, 3km north of town ⓣ9414 728468. The cheapest option in Ranthambore, with just six simple but clean modern rooms (including a couple of very cheap ones with shared bath, plus a couple with a/c) in a small family house. ❶–❹

Ankur Resort Ranthambore Rd, 2km from town ⓣ07462/220792, ⓦwww.hotelankurresort.com. A wide array of accommodation, ranging from uninspiring budget rooms with fan in the bare and institutional main building up to smarter and much more cheerful a/c "cottages" in the gardens behind (though some are decidedly overpriced). There's also a small pool (non-guests Rs150) and a passable restaurant. ❸–❻

Anurag Resort Ranthambore Rd, 2.5 km from town ⓣ07462/220751, ⓦwww.anuragresort.com. Sprawling pink resort set around expansive, rambling gardens. Rooms (all air-cooled) are uninspiring but modern and spacious, and there are also some slightly more expensive a/c cottages set around the gardens at the back, plus the biggest pool in town (non-guests Rs200/hr) and a Kerala Ayurvedic massage centre and gym. Fifty percent discounts April–Sept. ❺

Hammir Wildlife Resort Ranthambore Rd, 7km from town ⓣ9414 446566, ⓦwww.nivalink.com/hammir. Popular with Indian tourists, this is one of the more sensibly priced places in town (though the rooms are much better value than the garden cottages). Facilities include a pool (non-guests Rs100) and money exchange. ❺–❻

Raj Palace Resort Ranthambore Rd, 2km from town ⓣ07462/224793, ⓦwww.rajpalaceranthambhore.com. One of the best-value places in Ranthambore, with spacious and clean modern a/c rooms in the main building and some slightly more homely a/c "cottages" around the gardens at the back, plus a pool (non-guests Rs200/hr). ❸–❹

Tiger Safari Ranthambore Rd, 2.5 km from town ⓣ07462/221137, ⓦwww.tigersafariresort.com. The best of Ranthambore's cheaper hotels, with helpful service and comfortably furnished rooms (almost all with a/c) plus spacious cottages around the rear garden. There's also internet access, a pool (free to non-guests), free pick-up/drop-off from the station, and a pleasant garden restaurant. ❹–❺

Expensive

Aman-i-Khás ⓣ07462/252052, ⓦwww.amanresorts.com. Situated in a very quiet rural setting, this place rivals *Vanyavilas* (see below) for tasteful opulence (and even outdoes it for wallet-crunching expense, with rates at around $950/day). Accommodation is in ten superb, cavernous luxury tents, and there's also a traditional step-well for swimming and a spa tent. Closed May to Sept. ❾

Khem Villas ⓣ07462/252099, ⓦwww.khemvillas.com. Delightful little eco-resort on the far side of the park entrance set amid ten acres of carefully nurtured wilderness that is home to abundant birdlife and other fauna. Accommodation is in a mix of rooms, luxury tents or stylish little cottages, and there's also home-grown organic vegetarian food and an interesting range of excursions. From around $200 full board. ❾

Nahargarh 2km south of park entrance, Khilchipur Village, Ranthambore Rd ⓣ07462/252281, ⓦwww.alsisar.com. Superbly theatrical-looking hotel, built in the style of an old-fashioned Rajput palace and looking every inch the regal retreat. Rooms are sumptuously decorated in traditional style and there's also a large pool. ❽–❾

RTDC Castle Jhoomar Baori On a hillside 7km out of town ⓣ07462/220495, ⓦwww.hotelsranthambhore.com. Former royal hunting lodge on a lofty hilltop site inside the park, with superb views from the roof terrace and large, and atmospheric – albeit slightly shabby – a/c rooms. ❼

Sawai Madhopur Lodge Ranthambore Rd, 1.5km from town ⓣ07462/220541, ⓦwww.tajhotels.com. Occupying an atmospheric 1930s hunting lodge, this luxury heritage hotel has bags of charm, with pleasantly leafy grounds and accommodation in beautifully appointed colonial-style rooms (from around $350 – it's worth paying a little extra for one of the more stylish luxury rooms), plus a pool (non-guests Rs400) and attractive restaurant. Rooms from around $330 (full board only). ❾

Vanyavilas Ranthambore Rd, about 7km from town ⓣ07462/223999, ⓦwww.oberoihotels.com. Superbly stylish (and expensive) jungle resort centred around a lavishly decorated building in the style of a royal hunting palace, with accommodation scattered around the rustic grounds in beautifully equipped wooden-floored a/c tents. Rooms from around US$850. ❾

The park

Ranthambore National Park (ⓦwww.ranthamborenationalpark.com) is one of India's most popular, with more than eighty thousand visitors a year, and can get ridiculously busy throughout the cool winter months, especially around Diwali and New Year. The summer months from April to June are a lot quieter, but obviously very hot. There are currently around 35 adult tigers in the park, plus healthy populations of *chital*, nilgai, jackals, leopards, jungle cats and a wide array of birds. The original core section of the national park has recently been extended with the addition of three new **buffer zones**, designed to provide space for the park's ever-expanding number of tigers. You're also allowed to get out of your vehicle and walk in these areas (which you're not allowed to do in the main park), although in general they're not so good for tiger-spotting.

Note that the core section of **Ranthambore is closed** annually from 1 July to 30 September with the exception of the three buffer zones, which remain open year round. The **best time to visit** is during the dry season (Oct–March), when the lack of water entices the larger animals out to the lakeside. During and immediately after the monsoons they're more likely to remain in the forest. More information can be gleaned from Project Tiger's excellent booklet, *The Ultimate Ranthambore Guide* (Rs250), on sale in local souvenir shops.

Visiting the park

Rules about **visiting Ranthambore** seem to change every couple of years, so don't be surprised if the following information has become obsolete by the time you arrive. At present, the number of vehicles allowed into the park is strictly controlled, with a maximum of around fifteen six-seater **jeeps** (also known as "Gypsys") and 25 **Canters** (open-top buses seating twenty people) being allowed in during each morning and afternoon session. Obviously, most visitors prefer the much smaller and quieter jeeps, although demand usually outstrips supply, and a lot of people find themselves having to make do with a place on a Canter instead. It's worth emphasizing that your chances of seeing a tiger are the same whether you're in a Canter or a jeep – travelling by jeep may feel more like a "real" safari, but tours run daily every morning and afternoon, and last around three hours. Departure times vary slightly depending on sunrise, leaving between 6.30am and 7am and between 2.30pm and 3pm. Dress in layers: early mornings can be surprisingly cold.

Seats officially cost Rs555 in a Canter and Rs600 in a jeep (or Rs370/430 for Indian residents; all prices include the park entrance fee); video cameras Rs200. If you want to book your own seat, the best option is to **reserve online** at Ⓦwww.rajasthanwildlife.in. The alternative is to battle the chaotic, feral and occasionally violent crowds of local touts at the **Ranthambhore Tiger Reserve Tourist Centre** (daily 5.30–6.30am & 12.30–1.30pm) near *Tiger Safari* hotel, about 7km along Ranthambore Road, where you can buy tickets for tours on the day, though you'll be lucky to bag a seat in a jeep.

A much easier option is to book a seat in a jeep or Canter through your hotel – in fact it's a good idea to book your safari at the same time you book your room (or even before). You'll pay a surcharge for this, which can be anything from Rs50/100 for a seat in a Canter/jeep booked through a cheaper hotel up to Rs2000 for a place in a jeep booked through a top-end establishment. In practice, seats in a Canter usually go for around Rs600, while prices for seats in jeeps fluctuate wildly according to demand, anything from Rs700 to Rs1200 or more. You shouldn't have any problems getting a seat in a Canter if you book the day before (except possibly on Fri and Sun between 1 Oct and 15 April, when five to eight Canters are block-booked by the *Palace on Wheels and Royal Rajasthan on Wheels*). If you want to go in a jeep it's best to book ahead, although you might get lucky, especially from around April through to June, when visitor numbers fall significantly. Your chances drop considerably closer to Diwali, New Year and around any other public holiday.

Ranthambore Fort

It's well worth setting aside some time from the tigers to visit the dramatic **Ranthambore Fort** (daily 6am–6pm; free), set atop a rocky crag near the entrance to the national park. The fort was founded in 944 by the Chauhan Rajputs and, following the decisive defeat of Prithviraj III by Muhammad of Ghor in 1192, became a key strategic focus in Rajput resistance to the expanding power of the Delhi Sultanate.

A few kilometres along the road into the park, a twisting flight of two hundred eroded stone steps leads up through gateways and crumbling fortifications to reach the fort, enclosed by some 7km of walls and bastions which snake around the ridgetop, offering fine views over the surrounding countryside. The numerous remains within the fort include a mosque, a large tank, assorted chhatris and several temples – the one dedicated to Ganesh is particularly revered, and people from all over the country write to the elephant-headed god's shrine here to invite him to their weddings.

The easiest way to **visit the fort** is to go on a tour; these can be arranged through the *Tiger Safari* hotel (Rs600/jeep), or just ask at your hotel to see if they can arrange a jeep. Note that you don't have to pay the park entry fee if you're just going to the fort.

Ajmer

The Nag Pahar ("Snake Mountain"), a steeply shelving spur of the Aravallis west of Jaipur, forms an appropriately epic backdrop for **AJMER**, home of the great Sufi saint **Khwaja Muin-ud-din Chishti**, who founded the Chishtiya Sufi order. His tomb, the **Dargah Khwaja Sahib**, remains one of the most important Islamic shrines in the world. The streams of pilgrims and dervishes (it is believed that seven visits here are the equivalent of one to Mecca), especially pick up during Muharram (Muslim New Year) and Eid, and for the saint's anniversary day, or **Urs Mela** (see box, p.177).

For Hindu pilgrims and foreign travellers, Ajmer is important primarily as a jumping-off place for **Pushkar**, a twenty-minute bus ride away, and most stay only for as long as it takes to catch a bus out, but as a day-trip from Pushkar it's a highly worthwhile excursion, and as a stronghold of Islam, Ajmer is unique in Hindu-dominated Rajasthan.

History

A fort was first established at Ajmer in the tenth century by local Rajput chieftain Ajay Pal Chauhan, whose clan, the Chauhans, went on to become the dominant power in eastern Rajasthan until they were beaten in 1193 by Muhammad of Ghor (see p.1155). The Delhi sultans allowed the Chauhans to carry on ruling as their tributaries, but in 1365, with Delhi on the wane as a regional power, Ajmer fell to the kingdom of Mewar (Udaipur).

During the sixteenth century, the city became the object of rivalry between Mewar and the neighbouring kingdom of Marwar (Jodhpur). The Marwaris took it in 1532, but the presence of Khwaja Muin-ud-Din Chishti's *dargah* made Ajmer an important prize for the Muslim Mughals, and Akbar's forces marched in only 27 years later.

The Mughals held onto Ajmer for over two centuries, but as their empire began to fragment, the neighbouring Rajput kingdoms once again started giving the city covetous looks. It was eventually taken in 1770 by the Marathas, who subsequently

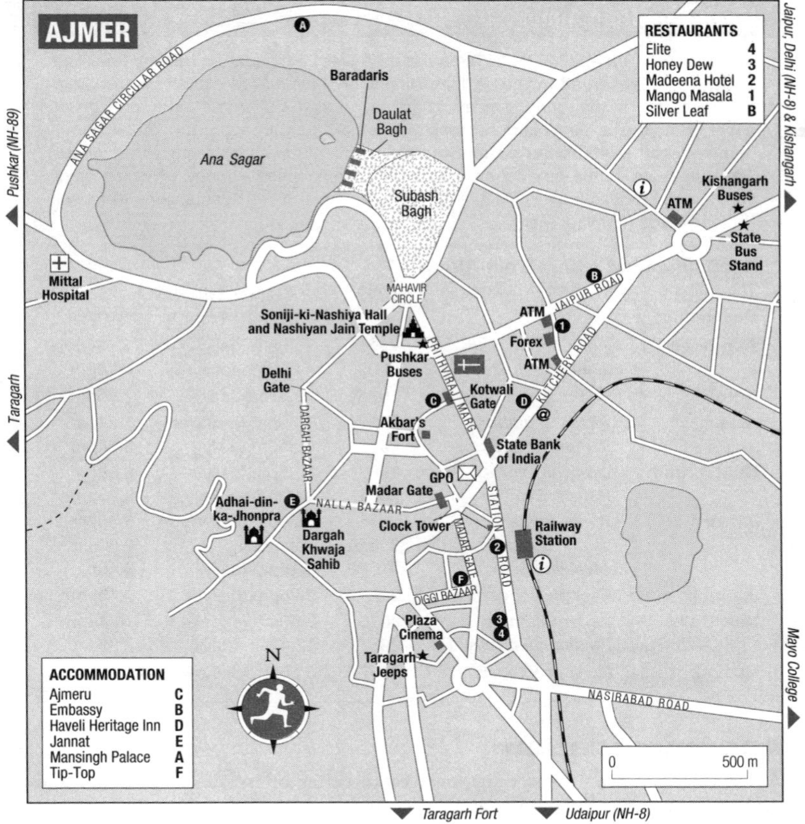

sold the city to the East India Company for fifty thousand rupees in 1818. Thus, while most of Hindu-dominated Rajasthan retained internal independence during the Raj, Ajmer was a little Muslim enclave of directly-ruled British territory, only reunited with Jodhpur and Udaipur, its former overlords, when it became part of Rajasthan in 1956.

Arrival and information

Ajmer's **railway station** is slap-bang in the centre of town. The **State Bus Stand** lies some 2km to the northeast on the Jaipur Road – an auto-rickshaw from here into town costs around Rs40. If you're heading straight on to **Pushkar**, buses depart from the bus stand every 15min or so until around 9pm. The majority of travellers visit Ajmer **on a day-trip from Pushkar**, but note that buses to and from Pushkar no longer travel through the centre of Ajmer en route to the bus stand, so you'll have to traipse into town from the bus stand, and then back out again at the end of your visit.

The RTDC runs **tourist offices** near the state bus stand next to the RTDC *Hotel Khadim* (Mon–Sat 10am–5pm; ⓣ0145/262 7426) and at the railway station (daily 9am–5pm; no phone – it's just inside the station's smaller, southern entrance).

Moving on from Ajmer

Ajmer station (☎0145/243 2535) is on the main Delhi–Ahmedabad **railway line**. The computerized **reservations** hall is on the first floor of the railway station's south wing; get there early in the morning to avoid queues or shell out a little extra for a travel agent. State buses – including services to **Pushkar** (roughly every 15min until about 9pm) – depart from the **State Bus Stand** (☎0145/242 9398) on Jaipur Road, about 2km northeast of the city centre. Seats on private buses – many of which have connecting services from Pushkar – can be reserved at travel agents along Kutchery Road towards Prithviraj Marg.

Recommended trains from Ajmer

The trains below are recommended as the fastest and/or most convenient.

Destination	Name	No.	Departs	Arrives
Abu Road	*Ahmedabad Mail*	9106	7.40am (daily)	12.37pm
	Aravali Express	9708	11.10am (daily)	5.10pm
Agra	*Sealdah Express*	2988	12.35am (daily)	7.30pm
Alwar	*Ajmer Shatabdi*	2016	3.50pm (exc Wed)	7.31pm
	Jammu Tawi Express	2413	1.55pm (daily)	6.54pm
Chittaurgarh	*Udaipur Express*	2992	3.55pm (daily)	6.55pm
	Ratlam Express	9654	1.20pm (daily)	5.05pm
Jaipur	*Ajmer Shatabdi*	2016	3.50pm (exc Wed)	5.45pm
	Jaipur Special	9655A	7am (daily)	9.30am
	Aravali Express	9707	4.15pm (daily)	6.40pm
Jodhpur	Fast passenger train	2JA	2.25pm (daily)	7.45pm
New Delhi	*Ajmer Shatabdi*	2016	3.50pm (exc Wed)	10.40pm
	Rajdhani Express	2957	12.42am (daily)	7.25am
Udaipur	*Udaipur Express*	2992	3.55pm (daily)	9.20pm

Accommodation

Ajmer's **hotels** aren't great value and you're better off staying in Pushkar and visiting from there. Accommodation also tends to get chock-full during the Urs Mela (see opposite). Note that many cheaper hotels tend to operate a 24-hour checkout system.

Ajmeru Off Prithviraj Marg, just inside Kotwali Gate ☎0145/243 1103, Ⓦwww.hotelajmeru.com. This comfortable modern hotel is one of the best-value places to stay in town, with bright, clean and well-kept fan, air-cooled and a/c rooms. 24hr checkout. ❸–❹

Embassy Jaipur Rd ☎0145/242 5519, Ⓦwww.hotelembassyajmer.com. Comfortable modern three-star. All rooms come with a/c, TV and minibar, and there's also the good in-house *Silver Leaf* restaurant (see p.179). ❺

Haveli Heritage Inn Kutchery Rd, Phul Nawas ☎0145/262 1607, Ⓦwww.haveliheritageinn.com. In an old house from the 1870s that was once used as the state HQ of the Congress Party – Nehru and Gandhi both stayed here. It actually sounds grander than it is, but if you think of this as a *pension* rather than a haveli, you'll get the right idea – the big attractions are the peaceful atmosphere and the delightful family that runs it. Rooms (air-cooled and a/c) are bright, spacious and attractively furnished, and there's great home-cooking too. ❸–❺

Jannat Dargah Bazaar, near Nizam Gate ☎0145/243 2494, Ⓦwww.ajmerhoteljannat.com. A stone's throw from the Dargah Khwaja Sahib, and the best hotel in the area, it fills up quickly on Thurs and Fri, but usually has space the rest of the week. There's a range of rooms, all modern and clean, some a/c, plus a good restaurant and friendly service. 24hr checkout. ❹–❺

Tip-Top Cinema Rd, off Diggi Bazaar ☎0145/510 0241. Best of the hotels around the station, and good value by Ajmer standards, with comfortable a/c or non-a/c attached rooms. 24hr checkout. ❷–❹

The Town

Although Ajmer's dusty modern roads are choked with traffic, the narrow lanes of the bazaars around the **Dargah Khwaja Sahib** retain an almost medieval character, with lines of rose-petal stalls and shops selling prayer mats, beads and lengths of gold-edged green silk offerings. Finely arched Mughal gateways still stand at the main entrances to the **old city**, whose skyscape of mosque minarets and domes is overlooked from on high by the crumbling **Taragarh** – for centuries India's most strategically important fortress.

Dargah Khwaja Sahib

Housing the tomb of the revered Sufi saint, Khwaja Muin-ud-Din Chishti, the **Dargah Khwaja Sahib**, or Dargah Sharif (daily 5am to midnight; Ⓦwww.wdargahajmer.com), is the most important Muslim shrine in India, attracting thousands of pilgrims daily. Founded in the thirteenth century, the *dargah* contains structures financed by many Muslim rulers, particularly the three great Mughals – Shah Jahan, Jahangir and, especially, Akbar, who came to the *dargah* to pray for a male heir and rewarded it with a new mosque when his wish was granted.

You enter the complex through the lofty **Nizam Gate**, donated by the Nizam of Hyderabad in 1911. Once inside, you may be accosted by stern-looking young men claiming they are "official guides". In fact, they are *khadims*, hereditary priests who lead pilgrims through rituals in the *dargah* in exchange for donations. Their services are not compulsory, whatever they may say.

Beyond the Nizam Gate lies the smaller **Shajahani Gate**, commissioned by Shah Jahan. Carry on through this to reach a courtyard, from where steps lead up on the

Khwaja Muin-ud-Din Chishti and the Urs Mela

Born in Afghanistan in 1156, **Khwaja Muin-ud-Din Chishti**, India's most revered Muslim saint, began his religious career at the age of thirteen, when he distributed his inheritance among the poor and adopted the simple life of an itinerant Sufi *fakir* (the equivalent of the Hindu sadhu). On his travels, he soaked up the teachings of the great Central Asian Sufis, whose emphasis on mysticism, ecstatic states and pure devotion as a path to God were revolutionizing Islam during this period. Khwaja Sahib and his disciples settled in Ajmer at the beginning of the thirteenth century. Withdrawing into a life of meditation and fasting, he preached a message of renunciation, affirming that personal experience of God was attainable to anyone who relinquished their ties to the world. More radically, he also insisted on the fundamental **unity of all religions**: mosques and temples, he asserted, were merely material manifestations of a single divinity. Khwaja Sahib thus became one of the first religious figures to bridge the gap between India's two great faiths. After he died at the age of 97, his followers lauded the Bhagavad Gita as a sacred text, and even encouraged Hindu devotees to pray using names of God familiar to them, equating Ram with "Rahman", the Merciful Aspect of Allah – a spirit of acceptance which explains why **Khwaja Sahib's** shrine in Ajmer continues to be loved by adherents of all faiths.

The anniversary of Khwaja Sahib's death is celebrated with the **Urs Mela**, one of Rajasthan's most important religious festivals, held on the sixth day of the Islamic month of Rajab (approximately 7 June 2011, 27 May 2012 and 16 May 2013). Pilgrims flock to the town to honour the saint with *qawwali* (Sufi devotional) chanting, while *kheer* (rice pudding) is cooked in huge vats at the *dargah* and distributed to visitors. At night religious gatherings called *mehfils* are held. It isn't really an affair for non-religious tourists, but the city does take on a festive air, with devotees from across the Subcontinent and beyond converging on Ajmer for the week leading up to it.

right to the **Akbari Masjid (Akbar's Mosque)**, built by a grateful Akbar following the birth of his son Salim, the future emperor Jahangir.

Just past the Shajahani Gate is a third gateway, the imposing, blue-and-green **Buland Darwaza**. After passing through it, you'll see, resting on raised platforms on either side, two immense cauldrons, known as **degs**, into which pilgrims throw money to be shared among the poor. The larger of the two, on the right, was donated by Akbar in 1567; the other was a gift from Jahangir upon his accession in 1605.

Beyond the *khanas* is an inner courtyard where the Tomb of Khwaja Sahib lies inside the **Mazar Sharif**, a domed mausoleum made of marble. Nightly recitations of *qawwali* are held in the courtyard here (from an hour or so before sunset until 9pm), an exuberant form of religious singing accompanied by harmonium and drums which aims to lull the participants into a trance-like state called *mast*. The **tomb** inside (closed daily 3–4pm, except Thurs when it's shut 2.30–3.30pm) is surrounded by silver railings and surmounted by a large gilt dome. Devotees file past carrying brilliant *chadars*, gilt-brocaded silk covers for the saint's grave, on beds of rose petals in flat, round head-baskets. Visitors are blessed, lightly brushed with peacock feathers and given the chance to touch the cloth covering the tomb in return for a suitable offering.

Subsidiary shrines in the inner courtyard include one belonging to a daughter of Shah Jahan, plus a handful of generals and governors, and some Afghani companions of the saint. The delicately carved marble mosque behind the saint's tomb, the **Jama Masjid** or Shahjahani Masjid, was commissioned by Shah Jahan in 1628 and took nine years to build. Despite its grand scale, the emperor deliberately had it built without a dome so as not to upstage the saint's mausoleum next door.

Other Islamic monuments

Often overlooked by visitors, the **Adhai-din-ka-Jhonpra**, or "two-and-a-half-day hut", is the oldest surviving monument in the city, and one of the finest examples of medieval architecture in Rajasthan. Originally built in 660 AD as a Jain temple, and converted in 1153 into a Hindu college, it was destroyed forty years later by the invading Afghan chieftain Muhammad of Ghor, who later had it renovated as a mosque. Tradition holds that its name derives from the speed with which it was constructed, but in fact the reconstruction took fifteen years, using materials plundered from Hindu and Jain temples; the name actually refers to a *fakirs'* festival which used to be held here in the eighteenth century, a *jhonpra* (hut) being the abode of a *fakir* (Sufi mendicant). Defaced Hindu motifs are still clearly discernible on the pillars and ceilings, but the mosque's most beautiful feature are the bands of Koranic calligraphy that decorate its seven-arched facade.

A more recent Islamic relic is the small but attractive **Akbar's Fort** (Tues–Sun 9.45am–5pm; Rs10 [Rs5]), which encloses a rectangular pavilion made of golden sandstone that was used by Akbar and his son Jahangir; it was here in 1616 that Jahangir received Sir Thomas Roe, the first British ambassador to be granted an official audience, after four years of trailing between the emperor's encampments. Today, the old palace houses a small **museum**, displaying mainly Hindu and Jain statues.

Laid out in the twelfth century, the artificial lake northwest of Ajmer known as **Ana Sagar** is worth a visit to see the line of exquisite white-marble pavilions called **baradaris**, or summer shelters, erected by Shah Jahan on the lake's eastern shore. Modelled on the Diwan-i-Am in Delhi's Red Fort, four of the five pavilions remain beautifully preserved, standing in the shade of trees and ornamental gardens laid out by Jahangir – particularly beautiful an hour or so before sunset.

Taragarh Fort

Three kilometres to the south, and just visible on the ridge high above the city, **Taragarh** (the Star Fort) was for two thousand years the most important strategic objective for invading armies in northwest India. Any ruler who successfully breached its walls, rising from a ring of forbidding escarpments, effectively controlled the region's trade. The fort is now badly ruined but is still visited in large numbers by pilgrims, who come to pay their respects at what must be one of the few shrines in the world devoted to a tax inspector. The **Dargah of Miran Sayeed Hussein Khangsawar** honours Muhammad of Ghor's chief revenue collector, slain in the Rajput attack of 1202 when, following one of the fort's rare defeats, the entire Muslim population of the fort was put to the sword.

The best way of getting to Taragarh is to take a ninety-minute **hike** along the ancient paved pathway from Ajmer, with superb **views** across the plains and neighbouring hills. To pick up the trailhead, follow the lane behind the Dargah Khwaja Sahib, past the Adhai-din-ka-Jhonpra and on towards the saddle in the ridge visible to the south. Alternatively, you can take an auto (around Rs200 return) or one of the **jeeps** (Rs50) that leave from behind the Plaza Cinema on Diggi Chowk, west of the train station; ask for the "Ta-ra-garh jeeps", pronouncing all the syllables clearly, or you may end up at the main Khwaja Sahib Dargah. To return to Ajmer you can either walk back or catch a jeep from the lot on the northeast side of the village, near the Dargah.

Other attractions

While most of Rajasthan consisted of princely states, Ajmer was under British rule, and relics of the colonial period can be found scattered across the city, among them the **Jubilee clock tower** opposite the railway station and the **King Edward Memorial Hall** a little to the west. The famous **Mayo College**, originally built as a school for princes and now a leading educational institution, is known in society circles as the "Eton of the East".

Perhaps the most bizarre sight in Ajmer is the mirrored **Soniji-ki-Nashiya** hall adjoining the **Nashiyan Jain temple**, or "Red Temple" (daily 8.30am–5.30pm; Rs20). Commissioned in the 1820s by an Ajmeri diamond magnate, the hall contains a huge diorama-style display commemorating the life of Rishabha (or Adinath), the first Jain *tirthankara*. The glowing tableau (containing a tonne of gold) features a huge procession of soldiers and elephants carrying the infant *tirthankara* from Ayodhya to Mount Sumeru to be blessed, while musicians and deities fly overhead. Admission to the main temple alongside is restricted to Jains.

Eating

Note that none of the following serves alcohol; if you want a **drink** you'll have to find a local bottle shop or try room service in your hotel.

Elite Station Rd. Reliable veg restaurant serving moderately priced curries and thalis (Rs50–90), plus a sprinkling of vegetarian Chinese, Continental and south Indian options. You can eat either inside in the white-tablecloth dining room or outside at a table in the garden. The *Honey Dew* restaurant, a few doors to the north, is very similar.

Madeena Hotel Station Rd. Muslim establishment serving very tasty non-veg Mughlai curries, mostly involving "mutton" (ie goat), in the form of korma, mughlai, *keema*, masala or biriyani, in full or half portions (Rs40–80) with freshly baked tandoori breads. There are also chicken, egg and veg options.

Mango Masala Sardar Patel Marg. Popular, studenty establishment serving pizzas, snacks, veg burgers, salads, shakes, mocktails and ice-cream sodas, as well as veg set-meals and thalis, and lots of *paneer* curries. Mains Rs60–145.

Silver Leaf *Embassy Hotel*, Jaipur Rd. Sedate veg restaurant, with a big selection of curries (most around Rs70–120), plus Chinese and Continental dishes, snacks and breakfasts.

Listings

Banks and exchange There are State Bank of India ATMs opposite the GPO on Prithviraj Marg and near the tourist office, a Bank of Baroda ATM between the *Elite* and *Honey Dew* restaurants, and ICICI and HDFC ATMs at either end of Sardar Patel Marg (the road which *Mango Masala* restaurant is on). If you need a forex bureau, UAE Money Exchange at 10 Sardar Patel Marg (Mon–Sat 9am–1.30pm & 2–7pm) changes cash and travellers' cheques.

Internet access Satguru has branches at 61 Kutchery Rd (daily 9am–10pm; Rs20/hr) and near *Haveli Heritage Inn*, and at 10 Sardar Patel Marg (daily 11am–9pm; Rs20/hr).

Left luggage There's a left-luggage office (open 24hr) directly opposite the tourist information office in the railway station.

Pushkar

According to legend, **PUSHKAR**, 15km northwest of Ajmer, came into existence when Lord Brahma, the Creator, dropped a lotus flower (*pushpa*) to earth from his hand (*kar*). At the three spots where the petals landed, water magically appeared in the midst of the desert to form three small blue lakes, and it was on the banks of the largest of these that Brahma subsequently convened a gathering of some 900,000 celestial beings – the entire Hindu pantheon. Surrounded by white-washed temples and bathing *ghats*, the lake is today revered as one of India's most sacred sites: Pushkaraj Maharaj, literally "Pushkar King of Kings". During the auspicious full-moon phase of October/November (the anniversary of the gods' mass meeting, or *yagya*), its waters are believed to cleanse the soul of all impurities, drawing pilgrims from all over the country. Alongside this annual religious festival, Rajasthani villagers also buy and sell livestock at what has become the largest **camel market** (*unt mela*) in the world, when more than 150,000 dealers, tourists and traders fill the dunes to the west of the lake.

Arrival and information

Pushkar does not have a railway station, and most long-distance journeys to and from Pushkar, even by bus, have to be made via Ajmer. The **Ajmer Bus Stand**, in the east of town, is served by local buses from Ajmer. Services from destinations further afield, such as Delhi, Jaipur, Jodhpur and Bikaner (most of which also stop en route at Ajmer), arrive in the north of town at **Marwar Bus Stand**. There are

Moving on from Pushkar

Buses to Ajmer (every 15min; 30min) leave from the **Ajmer Bus Stand**. Government and private intercity **buses** leave from the **Marwar Bus Stand** (☎0145/242 9398) for **Bikaner** (9 daily; 6hr 30min), **Bundi** (2 daily; 5hr), **Delhi** (5 daily, including 3 overnight sleeper services; 10–11hr), **Jaipur** (8 daily; 3hr 30min), **Jodhpur** (1 daily plus 1 nightly; 5hr) and **Jaisalmer** (2 nightly; 9hr). For Udaipur, change at Ajmer. Further destinations are served from Ajmer (see p.176), and connecting services are available, but it's not unknown for people who have bought tickets at agencies in Pushkar to find their seats double-booked when they try boarding in Ajmer. If possible, it's best to make bookings for bus journeys from Ajmer in Ajmer itself. Services to Delhi in particular are often reserved days ahead.

For recommended **trains from Ajmer**, see p.176. EKTA Travels acts as Indian Railways' agent in Pushkar and can arrange tickets for train journeys out of any station in India for a Rs40 charge, and also handles bus and plane tickets. They have offices at both the Marwar (☎0145/277 2131) and Ajmer bus stands (☎0145/277 2888).

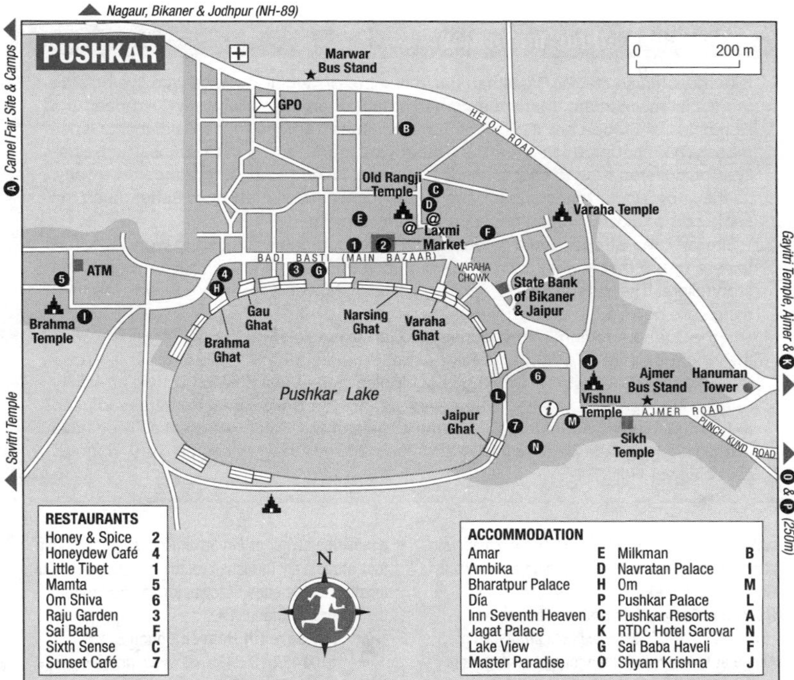

very few cycle rickshaws in Pushkar, and no auto-rickshaws, so you'll probably have to walk to your hotel. Pushkar's **tourist office** (daily 10am–5pm; 24hr during camel fair; ⓣ0145/277 2040) is located inside the main gate of the RTDC *Hotel Sarovar*.

Accommodation

Note that prices rise dramatically during the **camel fair**, with increases of anything from two to five times the normal rate.

Budget

Amar Holika Chowk (back entrance on Main Bazaar) ⓣ0145/277 2809, ⓔamar-hotel@yahoo.com.in. Very central place set around a large and peaceful garden, though rooms (all attached with fan, air-cooler or a/c) are disappointingly shabby. ❶–❹

Ambika Opposite Old Rangji Temple ⓣ0145/277 3154. Right in the thick of the action, with simple but cheap and clean whitewashed rooms, all attached, some with views over the street below – colourful, if a bit noisy. Good value during the Camel Fair. ❶

Bharatpur Palace Main Bazaar ⓣ0145/277 2320, ⓔbharatpurpalace_pushkar@yahoo.co.in. A bit basic and overpriced for what you get, but the location's wonderful, right on the lake, with views across the *ghats* from some rooms. A couple of rooms have a/c; cheaper ones have shared bathroom. ❶–❹

Lake View Main Bazaar ⓣ0145/277 2106, ⓦwww.lakeviewpushkar.com. Simple rooms (some with shared bath; more expensive ones with a/c) – a bit pricey for what you get, compensated for by great views over the lake from the terrace and rooftop restaurant (although the food's no great shakes). ❶–❹

Milkman Maili Mohalla ⓣ0145/277 3452. Intimate and sociable little family-run place hidden away in the backstreets with a range of cosy,

Rajasthan's ethnic minorities

Like most Indian states, Rajasthan has a number of "tribal" peoples who live outside the social mainstream. Many are nomadic, and often called "Gypsies" – indeed the Romanies of Europe are thought to have originated among these Rajasthani Gypsy tribes. The most prominent are the **Kalbeliyas**, found largely in Pushkar. The Kalbeliyas discovered how to charm snakes, and they used to sing and dance for royalty, as they now do for tourists, but living on the margins of society, they suffer much the same sort of discrimination as their brethren in Europe.

Similarly, the **Bhopas** are a green-eyed tribe of nomads who used to work as entertainers to the maharajas, and to this day they make a living as itinerant poets and storytellers. They are asked to perform particularly where someone is sick, as their songs are believed to aid recovery.

In the Jodhpur region, many tourists take an excursion into the countryside to visit the **Bishnoi** (see p.194), a religious rather than strictly ethnic group, whose tree-hugging beliefs chime with those of hippies in the West. Living in close proximity to them, though with a very different lifestyle, are the **Bhils**, great hunters who used to hire themselves out as soldiers in the armies of the Rajput kingdoms. They have their own language and religion, and their dances have become very popular, especially at Holi.

well-kept rooms (fan, air-cooled or a/c; some with shared bath) and a nice rooftop café and terrace. Good value. ❶–❸

Navratan Palace Near Brahma Temple ⓣ0145/277 2145, ⓦwww.pushkarhotel.com. Aimed at Indian rather than foreign visitors, this modern place has fresh, spotless rooms (some a/c), well-kept gardens and one of the best pools in town (non-guests Rs50). Great value. ❷–❸

Om Ajmer Rd ⓣ0145/277 2672, ⓦwww.hotelompushkar.co.cc. Pleasantly tranquil hotel with a wide variety of very competitively priced fan, air-cooled and a/c rooms (all attached), a relaxing garden for lounging and a nice little pool. Good value during the fair. ❶–❸

Sai Baba Haveli Off Varaha Chowk ⓣ0145/510 5161, ⓔlola_singh_modiano@hotmail.com. Run by a French–Indian couple, this place offers a range of fan rooms with attached bathroom in an attractive old house set around a pleasant garden patio. There's also a good restaurant (see p.184). ❷–❸

Shyam Krishna Guest House Main Bazaar near Vishnu temple ⓣ0145/277 2461. Attractively tranquil guesthouse with a variety of rooms (some with shared bathroom) set around a garden in a lovely old blue-washed former temple compound. Excellent value, especially during the camel fair. ❶–❷

Mid-range to expensive

Día Next to *Masters Paradise Resort*, Panch Kund Road ⓣ0145/277 2585, ⓦwww.inn-seventh-heaven.com. Low-key new guesthouse recently opened by owner of *Inn Seventh Heaven*, with just four attractively furnished rooms in a very peaceful location on the edge of town, around 500m from the Ajmer Bus Stand. ❺

Inn Seventh Heaven Chhoti Basti ⓣ0145/510 5455, ⓦwww.inn-seventh-heaven.com. Beautiful hotel in a fine old haveli, mixing traditional and contemporary styles to memorable effect, with vine-draped balconies around a spacious interior courtyard and a range of beautifully furnished rooms. Excellent value. ❷–❺

Jagat Palace Ajmer Rd ⓣ0145/277 2953, ⓦwww.hotelpushkarpalace.com. Well-run luxury hotel in a slightly inconvenient location on the outskirts of town. The impressive buildings incorporate masonry plundered from an old fort, decorated with elaborate wall paintings and period fittings. Sweeping views, a huge pool, steam bath, Jacuzzi and walled garden add to the allure. ❼

Master Paradise Punch Kund Rd ⓣ0145/277 3933, ⓦwww.masterparadise.com. Spotless, well-kept three-star in a peaceful setting just outside town, with lovely gardens, a pool, steam bath and Jacuzzi. ❺–❻

Pushkar Palace ⓣ0145/277 3001, ⓦwww.hotelpushkarpalace.com. Attractive hotel occupying a characterful old maharaja's palace in a plum position overlooking the lake. The whole place has lots of charm, with period-style rooms (most with lake views) and a pretty courtyard garden, though rates are a bit steep – and exorbitant during the Camel Fair. Rooms from ❽

Pushkar Resorts Motisar Rd, Ganehara ⓣ011/2649 4531, ⓦwww.sewara.com. Modern resort, inconveniently situated 5km out of town in the desert, with 40 swish a/c cottages in pristine gardens and a kidney-shaped pool. Their restaurant is the only one hereabouts with a non-veg menu, and an alcohol licence. Booking recommended. ❻–❼

RTDC Hotel Sarovar ⓣ0145/277 2040, ⓦhttp://rtdc.in/sarover.htm. State-run hotel, a bit institutional but boasting a nice lakeside setting, a nice garden and pool, and spacious, pleasantly old-fashioned rooms (air-cooled or a/c; the cheapest ones have shared bath). ❸–❺

The Town

There are more than five hundred **temples** in and around Pushkar, although some, like the splendid **Vishnu Temple**, are out of bounds to non-Hindus. Pushkar's most important shrine, the **Brahma Temple**, houses a four-headed image of Brahma in its main sanctuary, and is one of the few temples in India devoted to him. Raised on a stepped platform in the centre of a courtyard, the inevitably crowded chamber is surrounded on three sides by smaller subsidiary shrines topped with flat roofs providing views across the desert to **Savitri Temple** on the summit of a nearby hill. The one-hour climb to the top of that hill is rewarded by matchless vistas over the town, surrounded on all sides by desert, and is best done before dawn, to reach the summit for sunrise, though it's also a great spot to watch the sun set. The temple itself is modern, but the image of Savitri is supposed to date back to the seventh century. **Gayitri Temple** (Pap Mochini Mandir), set on a hill east of the town, also offers great views, especially at sunrise.

The lake and ghats

Everything in Pushkar revolves around the **lake**, although this was almost largely waterless at the time of writing, having been drained for cleaning in 2009; all being well it will have refilled naturally during the 2010 monsoon, assuming there's sufficient rain. The lake is ringed by five hundred beautiful whitewashed

Brahma, Savitri and Gayitri

Although **Brahma**, the Creator, is one of the trinity of top Hindu gods, along with Vishnu (the Preserver) and Shiva (the Destroyer), his importance has dwindled since Vedic times and he has nothing like the following of the other two. The story behind his temple here in Pushkar serves to explain why this is so, and also reveals the significance of the temples here named after Brahma's wives, **Savitri** and **Gayitri**.

The story goes that Lord Brahma was to marry Savitri, a river goddess, at a sacrificial ritual called a *yagna*, which had to be performed at a specific, astrologically auspicious moment. But Savitri, busy dressing for the ceremony, failed to show up on time. Without a wife, the Creator could not perform the *yagna* at the right moment, so he had to find another consort quickly. The only unmarried woman available was a shepherdess of the untouchable Gujar caste named Gayitri, whom the gods hastily purified by passing her through the mouth of a cow (*gaya* means "cow", and *tri*, "passed through"). When Savitri finally arrived, she was furious that Brahma had married someone else and cursed him, saying that henceforth he would be worshipped only at Pushkar. She also proclaimed that the Gujar caste would gain liberation after death only if their ashes were scattered on Pushkar lake – a belief which has persisted to this day. After casting her curses, disgruntled Savitri flew off to the highest hill above the town. To placate her, it was agreed that she should have her temple on that hilltop, while Gayitri occupied the lower hill on the opposite, eastern side of the lake, and that Savitri would always be worshipped before Gayitri, which is exactly how pilgrims do it, visiting Savitri's temple first, and Gayitri's temple afterwards.

temples, connected to the water by 52 *ghats* – one for each of Rajasthan's maharajas, who built separate guesthouses in which to stay during their visits here. Primary among the *ghats* is **Gau Ghat**, sometimes called Main Ghat, from which ashes of Mahatma Gandhi, Jawaharlal Nehru and Shri Lal Bahadur Shastri were sprinkled into the lake. **Brahma Ghat** marks the spot where Brahma himself is said to have worshipped, while at the large **Varaha Ghat**, just off the market square, Vishnu is believed to have appeared in the form of Varaha (a boar), the third of his nine earthly incarnations. At all the *ghats* visitors should remove their shoes at a reverential distance from the lake and refrain from smoking and taking photos.

Indian and Western tourists alike are urged by local Brahmin priests to worship at the lake; that is, to make **Pushkar Puja**. This involves the repetition of prayers while scattering rose petals into the lake, and then being asked for a donation. On completion of the puja, a red thread taken from a temple is tied around your wrist. Labelled the "Pushkar passport" by locals, this simple token means that you'll no longer attract pushy Pushkar priests and can wander unhindered onto the *ghats*. Indians usually give a sum of Rs21 or Rs31; Rs51 or, at most, Rs101 should suffice for a foreign tourist. A favourite trick of (usually phoney) priests is to ask how much you want to pay, then say a blessing for assorted members of your family, and demand the amount you stated times the number of family members blessed; don't be bullied by such cheap tricks into giving any more than you agreed.

Eating

As Pushkar is sacred to Lord Brahma, all food within city limits is strictly veg: meat, eggs and alcohol are banned. Pushkar's sweet speciality is **malpua**, which is basically a chapatti fried in syrup, sold at sweetshops around town, and on Halwai Gali, the street directly opposite Gau Ghat.

Honey & Spice Laxmi Market Main Bazaar. A bit more imaginative than your average Pushkar backpacker café, with a short but sweet menu of tasty vegetarian wholefood dishes (Rs40–75), plus juices, lassis and speciality teas. Good for breakfast. Closes 7pm.

Honeydew Café Main Bazaar near *Bharatpur Palace* hotel. A hole-in-the-wall place that's been a hippy hang-out since the days of the overland trail. It still knocks out a decent breakfast, especially if you like filter coffee, and its pasta dishes (Rs40–70) aren't bad either.

Little Tibet *Payal Guest House*, Main Bazaar. Attractive garden restaurant set beneath the overhanging boughs of an enormous tree, serving up decent Tibetan and Indian food alongside the usual medley of faux Italian, Israeli and Mexican tourist fodder accompanied by the inevitable chill-out soundtrack – and even sleepier service. Mains Rs50–170.

Mamta Near Brahma Temple. This is where a lot of Pushkar's Indian visitors come to eat, not surprisingly as it serves up the best veg curries (Rs60) in town. What's available depends on what vegetables are in season, but there's always a good selection.

Om Shiva On the lane heading down to *Pushkar Palace* from Main Bazaar. The best of Pushkar's various all-you-can-eat buffet deals – superb value considering the Rs70 price tag. Avoid copycats with similar names.

Raju Garden Main Bazaar. Above-average Indian, Chinese and Western food in a lovely lakeside setting, dishing up good veg shepherd's pie and baked potatoes, plus a decent range of veg curries. Mains Rs40–80.

Sai Baba Haveli Off Varaha Chowk. The usual Indian veg curries (Rs50–80) plus great pasta and the best pizza (Rs60–110) in Pushkar (the tandoor doubles as a pizza oven). You can sit out front or, more atmospherically, in the garden. There's gypsy dancing on Saturdays at 8pm, when there's an excellent Rs150 buffet.

The Sixth Sense On the top floor of the *Inn Seventh Heaven*, this stylish café-restaurant offers a welcome alternative to Pushkar's grungy backpacker cafes, with a small but carefully chosen range of Indian and Italian food using fresh seasonal ingredients, plus snacks, fresh juices and breakfasts. Mains Rs40–120.

Sunset Café East side of the lake. The perfect place to enjoy Pushkar's legendary lakeside sunsets, with great views (though the outside seats fill up quickly towards dusk) and an impressive selection of juices, lassis, shakes, plus the usual range of Italian, Mexican, Tibetan and Chinese food. Mains Rs50–120.

Listings

Banks and exchange There's a useful State Bank of Bikaner & Jaipur ATM near the Brahma Temple. Alternatively, you can change cash or travellers' cheques quickly at any of the dozens of forex offices in the Main Bazaar. Two reliable places are the Thomas Cook office (Mon–Sat 9.30am–6.30pm) opposite the *Shyam Krishna* guesthouse, and Mantri Forex, on the main bazaar a few doors east of Laxmi Market, near the *Honey & Spice* cafe (daily 9am–8pm), which is also open Sun. Both also give cash advances on Visa and MasterCard.
Bicycle rental Malakar Bicycle Shop, by the Ajmer Bus Stand (the unsigned pink shop next to EKTA Travels), has basic bikes for Rs25/24hr.

Camel safaris A number of places arrange short camel rides and safaris (including overnight trips) in the desert around Pushkar – try EKTA Travels (see p.180), who run trips for around Rs130/hr.
Dance The Colleena Shakhti Dance Center (Ⓦwww.colleenashakti.com) in the old Rangji Temple runs Intensive courses in Odissi dance, plus drop-in sessions covering a range of styles.
Hospital Government Hospital, opposite the GPO near Marwar Bus Stand Ⓣ0145/277 2029.
Internet access Numerous small places around town charge around Rs30/hr. Try the well-equipped New Cyber Space, along the road near the Old Rangji Temple, or KK Internet opposite.

Kartika Purnima and Pushkar camel fair

Hindus visit Pushkar year-round to take a dip in the redemptory waters of the lake, but there's one particular day when bathing here is believed to relieve devotees of all their sins. That day is the full moon (*purnima*) of the **Kartika** month (usually Nov). During the five days leading up to and including the full moon, Pushkar hosts thousands of celebrating devotees, following prescribed rituals on the lakeside and in the Brahma Temple.

At the same time, a huge, week-long **camel fair** is held west of the town, with hordes of herders from all over Rajasthan gathering to parade, race and trade over forty thousand animals. With the harvest safely in the bag and the surplus livestock sold, the villagers, for this brief week or so, have a little money to spend enjoying themselves, which creates a lighthearted atmosphere that's generally absent from most other Rajasthani livestock fairs, backed up with entertainments including camel races, moustache competitions and a popular funfair, complete with an eye-catching sequence of enormous big wheels.

The popularity of Pushkar's fair has – inevitably – had an effect on the event, with camera-toting package tourists now bumping elbows with the event's traditional pilgrims and camel traders. But while the commercialism can be off-putting, the festive environment and coming together of cultures does produce some spontaneous mirth: in 2004, the second prize in the moustache contest was won by a Mancunian.

Practicalities

It's best to get here for the **first two or three days** to see the *mela* in full swing; by the final few days of the festival most of the buying and selling has been done and the bulk of the herders have packed up and gone home. The **day before the festival** officially starts is also good – pretty much all the traders and livestock have arrived, but there are relatively few tourists around.

It's best to **book a room** as far ahead as possible, though if you arrive early in the day – and with a bit of hunting – securing accommodation shouldn't be a problem. If you get stuck, the RTDC runs several tented compounds close to the fairgrounds, offering dormitory beds (Rs400), deluxe tents (❾), or huts (❹) complete with private bathrooms – ask at the tourist office or check Ⓦwww.rajasthantourism.gov.in. Additional luxury camping is offered by *Royal Camp* (reservations c/o WelcomHeritage Ⓣ0291/257 2321, Ⓦwww.welcomheritagehotels.com; Rs16,500+20 percent) and *Royal Desert Camp* (reservations c/o *Pushkar Palace* or *Jagat Palace* hotels; Rs10,000). The **dates** of the next camel fairs are: 13–21 Nov 2010, 2–10 Nov 2011, 20–28 Nov 2012 and 9–17 Nov 2013.

Laundry Chhotu, just off Varaha Chowk (daily 7am–8.30pm). Bring clothes early for same-day service.
Motorcycle rental There are a number of places just east of the Ajmer Bus Stand renting out scooters and motorbikes for around Rs100–200/day.
Police Next to the GPO ⓣ0145/277 2046.
Post office In the north of town near the Marwar Bus Stand (Mon–Sat 9am–5pm).
Shopping Though it isn't a craft centre as such, Pushkar is a good place to pick up touristy souvenirs, with its shops conveniently strung out along the Main Bazaar. As well as lots of hippy-type clothes, T-shirts and silver jewellery, not to mention ceramic chillums (Pushkar's rival those of Hampi and Pondicherry in the south), you'll find lac bangles, Rajasthani textiles, incense, essential oils and – always handy for a paint fight – Holi dyes. For new and used books, there's a slew of shops on the Main Bazaar just south of Varaha Chowk.
Swimming pools The *Navratan Palace Hotel* charges non-guests Rs50 to use theirs, or you can use the smaller pool at the *Om* hotel if you take a meal or drink.
Yoga and meditation Experienced teacher Yogesh Yogi runs intensive yoga and meditation courses (3–30 days) at the tranquil Pushkar Yoga Garden (ⓣ9828 279835, ⓦwww.pushkaryoga.org), on Vamdev road opposite the Ajmer Bus Stand, behind the Sikh *gurudwara*.

Jodhpur and around

On the eastern fringe of the Thar Desert, **JODHPUR**, dubbed "the Blue City" after the colour-wash of its old town houses, huddles below the mighty **Meherangarh Fort**, the most spectacular citadel in Rajasthan. Jodhpur was once the most important town of Marwar, the largest princely state in Rajputana, and now has a population of around a million. Most people stay just long enough to visit the fort, though there's plenty to justify a longer visit. Getting lost in the blue maze of the old city you'll stumble across Muslim tie-dyers, puppet-makers and traditional spice markets, while Jodhpur's famed cubic roofscape, best viewed at sunset, is a photographer's dream.

Some history

The **kingdom of Marwar** came into existence in 1381 when Rao Chanda, chief of the **Rathore** Rajput clan, seized the fort of Mandor (see p.193) from its former rulers, the Parihars. In 1459, the Rathore chief **Rao Jodha** moved from the exposed site at Mandor to a massive steep-sided escarpment, naming his new capital Jodhpur, after himself. His high barricaded fort proved virtually impregnable, and the city soon amassed great wealth from trade. The Mughals were keen to take over Jodhpur, and **Akbar** got his hands on the city in 1561, but he eventuallly allowed Marwar to keep its internal independence so long as the Rathore maharajas allied themselves to him.

In the eighteenth century, Marwar, Mewar (Udaipur) and Jaipur sealed a triple alliance to retain their independence against the Mughals, though the three states were as often at each other's throats as they were allied together. At the end of the century, maharaja **Man Singh** found himself under pressure from the expanding

Jodhpurs

The city of Jodhpur gives its name to a type of **trouser** – baggy around the thigh but narrow around the calf – designed for **horseback riding**. They were invented for his own personal use by Sir Pratap Singh, brother of Maharaja Jaswant Singh II, in 1887, and his custom-made riding trousers caught on big-time among Britain's aristocracy, who were soon flocking to Savile Row to get their own pairs made.

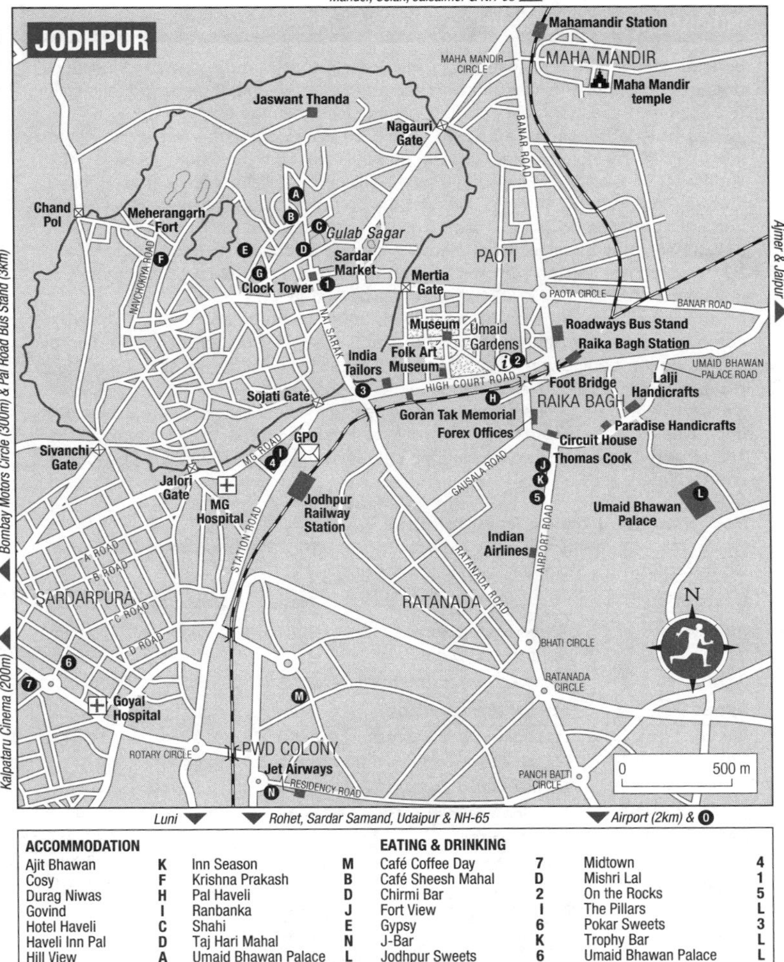

ACCOMMODATION				EATING & DRINKING			
Ajit Bhawan	K	Inn Season	M	Café Coffee Day	7	Midtown	4
Cosy	F	Krishna Prakash	B	Café Sheesh Mahal	D	Mishri Lal	1
Durag Niwas	H	Pal Haveli	D	Chirmi Bar	2	On the Rocks	5
Govind	I	Ranbanka	J	Fort View	I	The Pillars	L
Hotel Haveli	C	Shahi	E	Gypsy	6	Pokar Sweets	3
Haveli Inn Pal	D	Taj Hari Mahal	N	J-Bar	K	Trophy Bar	L
Hill View	A	Umaid Bhawan Palace	L	Jodhpur Sweets	6	Umaid Bhawan Palace	L
Indrashan	O	Yogi's	G	Marwar	N		

Maratha empire to his south, so in 1818 he turned for help to a new power, the **British**. Under the terms of his deal with them – not unlike Marwar's old arrangement with the Mughals – the kingdom retained its internal independence, but had to pay the East India Company an annual tribute equivalent to the one previously enforced by the Marathas.

The last but one maharaja before Independence, **Umaid Singh**, is commemorated by the immense Umaid Bhawan Palace. In 1930 he agreed in principle with the British to incorporate Marwar into an independent India. Despite the loss of official status, his descendants retain much of their wealth, alongside a great deal of influence and genuine respect in Jodhpur.

Moving on from Jodhpur

Jodhpur stands at the nexus of Rajasthan's main **tourist routes**, with connections northeast to Jaipur, Pushkar and Delhi, south to Udaipur and Ahmedabad, and west to Jaisalmer. Buses for most destinations are faster than the train.

Most **private buses** leave from the stand on Pal Road, 4km west of the centre (about Rs40 by auto); a few private buses leave from Kalpataru Cinema, 4km southwest of town (Rs30 by auto). Private buses for Jaisalmer leave from Bombay Motors Circle, nearby. You can book **tickets** on private buses at most travel agents and a lot of hotels (for a Rs50 fee). **Government buses** leave from the Roadways (Raika Bagh) Bus Stand just east of town – turn up an hour or so before departure to buy a ticket. For timetable information, it's best to ask your hotel or guesthouse to ring on your behalf (Ⓣ0291/254 4686 or 0291/254 4989).

The **railway station** is on Station Road, 300m south of Sojati Gate. There's a computerized **reservations office** (Mon–Sat 8am–8pm, Sun 8am–2pm), just north of the station behind the GPO. *Govind Hotel* allows customers at its *Fort View* restaurant (see p.192) to leave baggage free of charge and use toilet facilities while waiting for a train. Recommended services are listed below; there's also the once-weekly *Thar Express* to Karachi in **Pakistan** (Sat at 11.30pm; 24hr). The **airport** (see Arrival and information below) has flights to Delhi, Jaipur, Mumbai and Udaipur.

Recommended trains from Jodhpur

All the following trains run daily. Note that there are no direct trains to **Udaipur** or **Chittaurgarh** – it's much easier to catch the bus.

Destination	Name	No.	Departs	Arrives
Abu Road	*Ahmedabad Express*	9224	5.50am	10.40am
	Ranakpur Express	4707	3.00pm	7.55pm
Agra	*Howrah Superfast*	2308	8pm	6.35am
Ajmer	Fast passenger train	1JA	7am	12.35pm
Alwar	*Jaisalmer–Delhi Express*	4060	10.30pm	7.50am
Bikaner	*Ranakpur Express*	4708	10.05am	4pm
	Barmer-Kalka Express	4888	10.45am	4.40pm
	Howrah Express	2307	midnight	8.15am
Delhi	*Mandor Express*	2462	7.30pm	6.25am
	Jaisalmer–Delhi Express	4060	10.30pm	11.05am
Jaipur	*Jaipur Intercity Express*	2466	5.55am	10.45am
	Marudhar Express	4854/ 4864/ 4866	9.30am	3.20pm
Jaisalmer	*Delhi–Jaisalmer Express*	4059	5.20am	11.30pm
	Jaisalmer Express	4810	11pm	5am
Sawai Madhopur	*Intercity Express*	2466	5.55am	1.15pm
	Bhopal passenger train	492	7.30am	8.25pm

Arrival and information

Jodhpur's main **railway station** is pretty central, just south of the old city on Station Road. The state (Roadways) **bus stand** is east of the old city. **Private buses from Jaisalmer** drop you by Bombay Motors Circle at the western end of Sardarpura, 4km southwest of town, Rs50 by auto. **Other private buses** deposit you nearby at Kalpataru Cinema. From the **airport**, 4km south, a pre-paid auto-rickshaw into town costs Rs100, taxis Rs250–300. The **tourist office** (Mon–Fri

9.30am–6pm; ⓣ0291/254 5083) is next to the RTDC *Goomar Hotel* on High Court Road. **Online**, ⓦjodhpur.nic.in and ⓦwww.maharajajodhpur.com both have lots of interesting background information on the city.

Accommodation

Jodhpur has plenty of good accommodation in all brackets, although **commission rackets** are a real problem, meaning that some auto-wallahs will do all they can to avoid taking you to any hotel that doesn't pay them commission. Most guesthouses offer **free pick-ups**; alternatively, take an auto to a point nearby and then walk.

Budget

Cosy Bhram Puri, Chuna ki Choki, Navchokiya ⓣ0291/261 2066, ⓦwww.cosyguesthouse.com. Friendly little guesthouse in a pretty blue-washed building buried deep in the maze of lanes in the west of the old city (call for free pick-up; it's tricky to find otherwise). Rooms (fan, air-cooled and a/c; a few with shared bathroom) are simple but neat and cosy, and there are killer views of the fort from the rooftop terrace. ❶–❹

Durag Niwas 1 Old Public Park, Raika Bagh ⓣ0291/251 2385, ⓦwww.durag-niwas.com. Very friendly and well-run little place with cosy air-cooled and a/c rooms set around a peaceful courtyard, Also runs various programmes helping disadvantaged local women (half the guests are usually long-stay volunteers). Gay and lesbian friendly. ❶–❹

Govind Station Rd ⓣ0291/262 2758, ⓦwww.govind-hotel.com. A longstanding travellers' favourite, with bright, spotless rooms (some with a/c; all air-cooled in summer), a clean dorm (Rs110), excellent rooftop restaurant (see p.192) with wi-fi and friendly, professional management. There's also an in-house cybercafe and travel agents (see p.193), and it's conveniently close to the station if you're arriving late or leaving early. ❷–❹

Hill View Old City, on the road up to the fort (about 200m beyond *Krishna Prakash* hotel – see below). Sociable guesthouse run by hotelier turned local Congress politician Zafran and family. Rooms (all attached) are basic but very cheap, and there are fine views over town. ❶–❷

Hotel Haveli Old City (exit the northern gateway of Sardar Market, turn left then first right, then right again past the *Ganpati* guesthouse) ⓣ0291/261 4615, ⓦwww.hotelhaveli.net. One of the oldest and tallest havelis in the Sardar Bazaar area, with a wide range of accommodation from simple, inexpensive fan rooms to much fancier a/c rooms with window seats and traditional decor. Great views from the obligatory rooftop restaurant. ❷–❺

Yogi's Old City (about 50m down the road in front of the *Krishna Prakash* Hotel) ⓣ0291/264 3436, ⓦwww.yogiguesthouse.com. The best of the innumerable guesthouses just north of Sardar Bazaar, with lovely blue decor, clean, comfy rooms (most with a/c) and excellent fort views from the rooftop restaurant. ❶–❹

Mid-range

Haveli Inn Pal Near Gulab Sagar Lake (exit the north gate of Sardar Market, turn right and first left) ⓣ0291/261 2519, ⓦwww.haveliinnpal.com. Appealing mid-range option right in the heart of the old city, with large, well-appointed a/c rooms (some with fort or lake views) in an eighteenth-century haveli. ❺–❻

Indrashan 593 High Court Colony, 3km south of town ⓣ0291/244 0665, ⓦwww.rajputana discovery.com. Eight thoroughly comfortable rooms in an authentic homestay, with sumptuous cooking classes that draw amateur chefs from around the world. Non-guests are welcome for dinner if they call ahead (Rs425). ❺

Inn Season PWD Rd ⓣ0291/261 6400, ⓦwww .innseason.in. Stylish boutique hotel whose Art Deco rooms and (especially) suites pay homage to the owner's love affair with vintage cars. One drawback: it's noisy during wedding season (approx Oct–March) due to the wedding ground next door. Book ahead. ❺–❻

Krishna Prakash Nayabas (exit the northern gateway of Sardar Market, turn left then first right and continue straight ahead; it's on your left after about 150m) ⓣ9829 241547, ⓦwww.kpheritage.com. Heritage hotel in an old haveli right below the fort walls. The building itself isn't that exciting, but rooms (all with a/c) are nicely furnished with antique bric-à-brac and rates are surprisingly inexpensive, although the pool is horrible. ❹–❺

Pal Haveli Near Gulab Sagar Lake ⓣ0291/329 3328, ⓦwww.palhaveli.com. Atmospheric heritage hotel in the heart of the old city with attractively furnished rooms and plenty of period character.

Standard ("Royal Heritage") rooms are reasonably affordable, though the "Historical" rooms are only slightly nicer, and twice the price. ❼–❾

Shahi Gandhi St, City Police district, off Katla Bazaar opposite Narsingh Temple ⓣ0291/262 3802, ⓦwww.shahiguesthouse.com. Welcoming family guesthouse occupying a quirky 350-year-old haveli buried deep in the warren of lanes beneath the fort's southwest wall – and with superb views of it from the roof. The six rooms (with optional a/c) are brimful of character, decorated with a medley of quaint murals and assorted curios. Call for free pick-up (it's difficult to find otherwise). ❹–❺

Expensive

Ajit Bhawan Airport Rd ⓣ0291/251 1410, ⓦwww.ajitbhawan.com. Despite the Flintstones-like theme-park design, this self-contained resort – built to resemble a *dhani* village – gets rave reviews for its try-hard attitude and relaxing environment. Accommodation is in cute little round chalets or more conventional rooms, and there's a quaint waterfall-fed pool, thatch-roofed outdoor restaurant and spa. From around $210. ❾

Bal Samand Lake Palace 8km north of Jodhpur ⓣ0291/257 2321, ⓦwww.welcomheritagehotels.com. Among the most attractive heritage hotels in the state, converted from the maharaja's lakeside summer palace, with ten beautiful "Palace Suites" in the main building – all huge, airy and exquisitely furnished. From around $380. ❾

Jhalamand Garh Jhalamand, 7km south of Jodhpur ⓣ0291/272 0481, ⓦwww.heritagehotelsindia.com. Just outside Jodhpur, in the elegant, late eighteenth-century palace of the thakurs of the village of Jhalamand. The meals feature traditional Rajput cuisine, while dance performances by a Kalbeliya Gypsy troupe are held around an outdoor fire every night. ❽

Ranbanka Airport Rd ⓣ0291/251 2800, ⓦranbankahotels.com. In the other half of the palace occupied by *Ajit Bhawan*, this is more authentic in some ways (the rooms are actually inside the palace), but generally less appealling, with uninspiring rooms and flakey service – though the expansive gardens and good-sized pool (non-guests Rs700) are a major plus. ❽

Taj Hari Mahal 5 Residency Rd, 1km south of town ⓣ0291/243 9700, ⓦwww.tajhotels.com. All the luxury you'd expect from a five-star Taj hotel, with swanky traditional-style decor, two good restaurants (including *Marwar*, see p.192), a spa and good-sized pool, and spacious and attractively furnished rooms (from around US$300). ❾

Umaid Bhawan Palace ⓣ0291/251 0101, ⓦwww.tajhotels.com. The Maharaja of Jodhpur's princely pile (also see opposite) ranks among the world's grandest hotels, with celebrity guests and lashings of trendy Art Deco. But being king or queen for a day can be a solitary experience – some find the oversized suites, stately salons and dark, marbled passageways a bit foreboding. Rooms start at around US$950. ❾

The City

Most views of Jodhpur are dominated by the dramatic **Meherangarh Fort**, looming massively above the city from atop its huge sandstone plinth. Below it, the houses of the walled **old city** huddle like a Cubist painting, most of them decorated in the blue wash that gives the city its distinctive colour. Blue originally denoted a high-caste Brahmin residence, resulting from the addition of indigo to lime-based whitewash, which was thought to protect buildings from insects, and to keep them cool in summer. Over time the colour caught on – there's now even a blue-wash mosque on the road from the Jalori Gate, west of the fort.

The bazaars of the old city, with different areas assigned to different trades, radiate out from the 1910 **Sardar Market** with its tall **clock tower**, a distinctive local landmark marking the centre of town. Most of the ramparts on the south side of the old city have been dismantled, leaving **Jalori Gate** and **Sojati Gate** looking rather forlorn as gates without a wall.

Meherangarh Fort

For size, strength and sheer physical presence, few sights in India can rival Jodhpur's mighty **Meherangarh Fort**, a great mass of impregnable masonry whose soaring, windowless walls appear to have grown directly out of the enormous rock outcrop on which it stands (daily 9am–5.30pm; Rs300 entry includes audio tour if you leave ID, credit card or deposit; students Rs250 [Rs30];

video Rs200; elevator Rs20; guide Rs150; Ⓦwww.mehrangarh.org). The walk up to the fort from the old city is pretty steep, but you can reach the entrance by taxi or auto along the road from Nagauri Gate. The outstanding audio tour takes about two hours to complete.

You enter the fort through **Jai Pol** (or Jey Pol), the first of the fort's seven defensive gates. The sixth of the seven gates, **Loha Pol**, has a sharp right-angle turn and sharper iron spikes to hinder the ascent of charging enemy elephants. On the wall just inside it you can see the handprints of Maharaja Man Singh's widows, placed there in 1843 as they left the palace to commit sati on his funeral pyre – the last mass sati by wives of a Marwari maharaja.

Beyond the final gate, the **Suraj Pol**, lies the **Coronation Courtyard** (Shangar Chowk), where maharajas are crowned on a special marble throne. Looking up from the courtyard, you can see the fantastic *jali* (lattice) work that almost entirely covers the surrounding sandstone walls. The adjoining apartments now serve as a **museum** showcasing solid silver *howdahs* (elephant seats), palanquins and assorted armaments including Akbar's own sword. Upstairs are some fine **miniature paintings** of the Marwari school.

The most elaborate of the royal apartments, the magnificent 1724 **Phool Mahal** (Flower Palace), with its jewel-like stained-glass windows and gold filigree ceiling, was used as a venue for dancing, music and poetry recitals. The nearby **Takhat Vilas** was created by nineteenth-century Maharaja Takhat Singh, its ceiling hung with huge Christmas tree balls. In the **Jhanki Mahal**, or Queen's Palace, there's a colourful array of cradles of former rulers. The **Moti Mahal** (Pearl Palace) was used for councils of state. The five alcoves in the wall opposite the entrance are in fact concealed balconies where the maharaja's wives could listen in secretly on the proceedings.

Beyond the Moti Mahal is the **Zenana**, or women's quarters. From here, you descend to the **Temple of Chamunda**, the city's oldest temple, dedicated to Jodhpur's patron goddess, an incarnation of Durga.

Jaswant Thanda

Some 500m north of the fort, and connected to it by road, **Jaswant Thanda** (daily 9am–5pm; Rs20, camera Rs25, video Rs50) is a pillared marble memorial to the popular ruler Jaswant Singh II (1878–95), who purged Jodhpur of bandits, initiated irrigation systems and boosted the economy. The cenotaphs of members of the royal family who have died since Jaswant are close to his memorial; those who preceded him are commemorated by chhatris at Mandor (see p.193). In the morning, this southwest-facing spot is an excellent place from which to photograph the fort.

Umaid Bhawan Palace

Dominating the city's southeast horizon is the **Umaid Bhawan Palace**, a colossal Indo-Saracenic heap commissioned by Maharaja Umaid Singh in 1929 as a famine relief project, keeping three thousand labourers gainfully employed for sixteen years at a total cost of over nine million rupees. The furniture and fittings for its 374 rooms were originally ordered from Maples in London during World War II, but were sunk by a U-boat en route to India. The maharaja was thus forced to turn to Stephen Norblin, a wartime Polish refugee, who gave the palace its fabulous Art Deco interiors.

The present incumbent, Maharaja Gaj Singh, occupies only one-third of the palace; the rest is given over to a luxury **hotel** (see opposite) and a rather dull **museum** (daily 9am–5.30pm; Rs50, [Rs15]), containing assorted European crockery and glassware, plus a mildly entertaining gallery of clocks and barometers, some in the form of railway locomotives, lighthouses and windmills. Far more interesting (and expensive) is the palace itself, its Art Deco furniture and fittings nearly all original, enlivened with lashings of typically Rajasthani gilt and sweeping staircases. To see them, non-guests will need to spend a minimum of Rs3000 at the hotel's bar or one of its restaurants (see opposite). It's also a good idea to reserve in advance.

Umaid Gardens

On High Court Road, the **Umaid Gardens** are home to the city's depressing **zoo** (daily except Tues 8.30am–5.30pm; Rs50, camera Rs10, video Rs40), whose animals are housed in enclosures scattered around the park, and the **Sardar Government Museum** (Tues–Sun 10am–4.30pm; Rs10 [Rs5]), exhibiting the usual collection of skinned, stuffed, decapitated and pickled animals, along with a few other Rajasthani artefacts. Just outside the gardens, the Rajasthan Sangeet Natak Akademi runs a **Folk Art Museum** (Mon–Sat 11am–5pm; free) with a slightly moth-eaten collection of Rajasthani musical instruments and puppets.

Eating and drinking

Jodhpur's **restaurants** cater for all tastes and all budgets. Local **specialities** include *mirchi bada*, a big chilli covered in wheatgerm and potato and then deep-fried like a pakora. The most memorable place for a **drink** is the *Trophy Bar* at the *Umaid Bhawan Palace* (see p.190) – if you can afford the Rs3000 minimum charge; alternatively, the beautiful *J-Bar* at the *Ajit Bhawan* hotel, has comfy chairs, cool decor and assorted tipples at a fraction of the price. Other options include the uninspiring but quiet *Chirmi Bar* at the RTDC *Hotel Goomar*, next to the tourist office, which also has a pleasant garden, or the rather grungy, male-dominated bars around the *Midtown* restaurant on Station Road.

Fort View *Govind Hotel*, Station Rd. A cut above the usual tourist places, with good, reasonably priced veg curries and thalis (Rs45–120), local specialities such as *makhania* lassi and excellent *gulab jamun* (not the Bengali sweet, but a savoury Rajasthani dish made with *mawa*), plus good breakfast options, including real coffee. Also has wi-fi coverage, and you can hang out here while waiting for a bus or train (baggage storage facilities are available). Licensed.

Gypsy C Rd, Sardarpura. Downstairs it's a run-of-the-mill diner selling Indian snacks and ice cream. Upstairs it's a comfortable restaurant serving one thing only: an unlimited and delicious veg thali (Rs125) which they keep refilling for as long as you carry on eating.

Jodhpur Sweets C Rd, Sardarpura, next to *Gypsy*. The best sweet shop in town, and an excellent place to try *makhan wada*, *mawa kachori*, or any other Rajasthani or Bengali sweets.

Marwar At the *Taj Hari Mahal* hotel ⓣ0291/243 9700. Pricey, but the best place in town to sample traditional Marwari cuisine, such as Jodhpuri *mas* (a spicy mutton dish) or *gatta di subzi* (its veg equivalent). Mains Rs210–400.

Midtown On a side road off Station Rd opposite the station. Bright, clean and friendly pure-veg restaurant with a delicious range of curries, south Indian dishes, Gujarati and Rajasthani thalis and other Rajasthani specialities, as well as some pizza and Chinese. Mains Rs70–150. Licensed.

Mishri Lal In the eastern arch of the south gate to Sardar Market. The most famous purveyor of *makhania* lassi, made with cream, saffron and cardamom, very rich and thick, but those with delicate stomachs should take note that they use crushed ice made from tap water.

On the Rocks Next to *Ajit Bhawan* hotel, Airport Rd ⓣ0291/230 2701. Upmarket garden restaurant specializing in kebabs and tandoori cuisine. Though the service is slow, and the buffet no great shakes, it's fun and festive at night. The lunch crowd is mostly tour groups. Mains Rs70–120 veg, Rs120–300 non-veg.

Pokar Sweets Corner of Nai Sarak with High Court Rd. Known for their *makhan wada* (wheatflour, semolina and sugar, fried in ghee), and their *mirchi bada*'s pretty hot too. This is also a good place to try *doodh feni* (wheat strands in hot milk).

Cafe Sheesh Mahal Sardar Bazaar (exit the northern gate of Sardar Bazaar and turn right; it's ahead of you on the corner just before the entrance to the *Pal Haveli* hotel). Surprisingly smart little a/c coffee shop offering a good range of real coffees and speciality teas, along with snacks, sandwiches and light meals, plus entertaining bird's-eye views of the street below.
Umaid Bhawan Palace ⊤0291/251 0101, ⓦwww.tajhotels.com. The opulent *Umaid Bhawan Palace* boasts various eating and drinking possibilities, though whatever you do you'll have to stump up a Rs3000 minimum charge, payable on entry (and advance reservations for the restaurants are also strongly recommended) – although this at least gives you the chance to wander around the hotel's opulent Art Deco interior. *The Pillars* veranda café has sweeping views over the palace gardens and light snacks during the day, and is also a good place for a sundowner; alternatively, for a drink head to the sumptuous *Trophy Bar*. Full meals (with fixed menus for around Rs4000) are available at the *Risala* multi-cuisine restaurant, set in a lavish, olde-worlde European-style dining room, and at *The Pillars* during the evening.

Listings

Airlines Indian Airlines, East Patel Nagar, Airport Rd ⊤0291/251 0758; Jet Airways, Osho Apartments, Residency Rd ⊤0291/510 3333.
Banks and exchange There are ATMs at 151 & 157 Nai Sarak; on MG Rd 100m east of Sojati Gate; on the little street off MG Rd opposite Sojati Gate; on Station Rd near *Govind Hotel*; and next to the tourist office. Forex offices can be found north of the clock tower in Sardar Market and on Hanwant Vihar just north of Circuit House (there's also a Thomas Cook on Airport Rd).
Bookshops Sarvodaya Bookstall, opposite Raj Ranchodji Temple on the same side-road off Station Rd as *Midtown* restaurant; and Krishna Book Depot, upstairs at Krishna Art and Export in Sardar Market, just east of the north gate.
Festival Jodhpur's annual two-day Marwar Festival, held at the full moon of the Hindu month of Ashvina (Oct 21–22, 2010; Oct 10–11, 2011; Oct 28–29, 2012; Oct 17–18, 2013; Oct 7–8, 2014) is a showcase of performing arts, mainly music and dance.
Hospital The best private hospital is the Goyal on Residency Rd in the Sindhi Colony, 2km south of town (⊤0291/243 2144).
Internet access Internet (usually Rs30–40 an hour) is widely available. Handy places include *Govind Hotel*'s internet office on Station Rd (daily 24hr; Rs40/hr) and Sify i-Way (daily 9am–11pm; Rs40/hr), opposite the north gate of Sardar Market.
Motorcycle rental Jodhpur Travels, Station Rd (a few doors south of the *Govind Hotel*) has motorbikes and mopeds for rent for Rs300–1000/day.
Police ⊤0291/265 0777. There's a police tourist assistance booth by the clock tower in Sardar Market.
Post office The GPO is opposite the *Govind Hotel* on Station Road. Stamps can be bought in the section through the right-hand entrance (Mon–Sat 9am–5pm, Sun 11am–4pm). For poste restante and parcel packing head through the left-hand entrance (Mon–Fri 9am–1pm & 2–3pm, Sat 9am–1pm).
Shopping Jodhpur's first-rate antique reproductions – everything from chests of drawers to sculptures of Jain *tirthankaras* – attract dealers from around the world. There's a line of shops selling them along Umaid Bhawan Palace Road east of the Circuit House (Lalji Handicrafts and Paradise Handicrafts are particularly good). Other good buys in town include textiles, and Jodhpur riding britches (try India Tailors on High Court Rd, 75m east of the junction with Nai Sarak). For bookshops, see Listings, above.
Swimming pool Non-guests can use the lovely pool at the *Ajit Bhawan* hotel (see p.190) for Rs500.
Travel agents Staff at the *Govind* hotel (see p.189) can book train, bus and plane tickets for a modest service charge (Rs40–50), and can also arrange car hire for Rs1200–1700/day.

Mandor

Some 9km north of Jodhpur lies the sleepy village of **MANDOR**, former capital of the state of Marwar and home to a superb sequence of **royal cenotaphs** erected in memory of the kingdom's former rulers. Mandor served as the capital of the Parihar Rajputs from the sixth century until 1381, when they were ousted by Rathore Rao Chauhan, and although the capital was moved to Jodhpur in 1459, the Marwari rulers continued to have their memorial cenotaphs (*dewals*) erected here. Temple-like in their sombre dark red sandstone, the cenotaphs grew in size and grandeur as the Rathore kingdom prospered (the canopy-like chhatris next to them are for lesser royals). The largest is Ajit Singh's, built in 1724. His six queens, along with assorted mistresses, concubines, maids and entertainers – 84 women in all – committed sati on his funeral pyre.

At the end of the gardens, on the far side of the chhatris, you'll find the octagonal **Ek Thamba Mahal** (Single Pillared Palace), a three-storey pagoda-like affair built at the beginning of the eighteenth century for royal ladies to watch public events without breaking their purdah. Behind it is a small **museum** (daily except Fri 10am–4pm; Rs5), home to a few dull sculptures and paintings. Much more interesting are the extensive remains of **Mandor Fort**, citadel of the Parihar and Rathore Rajputs when Mandor was their capital, reached via a flight of steps behind the museum.

Mandore can be reached on **minibuses** #1, #5 and #7 from Sojati Gate. If you'd like to **stay** in Mandor, try the pleasantly sylvan little *Mandore Guest House*, close to the gardens on Dadawari Lane (Ⓣ0291/254 5210, Ⓦwww.mandore.com; ❺). It's actually more of a miniature resort than a guesthouse, with accommodation in a mix of air-cooled and a/c rooms and (rather dark) round huts set in a tree-studded garden.

The Bishnoi villages

Jodhpur's surroundings can be explored on organized "**village safaris**", which take small groups of tourists out into rural Rajasthan, usually stopping at four or five **Bishnoi villages** where you can taste traditional food, drink opium tea and watch crafts such as spinning and carpet-making. You'll also probably spot nilgai (bluebull) antelopes and gazelles.

The Bishnois – a religious sect rather than an ethnic group in the usual sense – are among the world's earliest tree-huggers. Their origins go back to a drought in the year 1485. Observing that this was caused largely by deforestation, a guru by the name of Jambeshwar Bhagavan formulated 29 rules for living in harmony with nature and the environment – his followers are called Bishnoi after the Marwari word for twenty-nine. As well as enforcing strict vegetarianism, Jambeshwar's rules forbid the killing of animals or felling of live trees. In particular, Bishnoi hold the **khejri** tree sacred. In 1730, at the village of **Khejadali**, workers sent by the maharaja of Marwar to make lime for the construction of a palace started felling *khejri* trees to burn the local limestone. A woman by the name of Amrita Devi put her arms around a tree and declared that if they wanted to cut it down, they would have to cut her head off first. The leader of the working party ordered her decapitation, upon which her three daughters followed her example, and were similarly beheaded. Bishnoi people from the whole of the surrounding region then converged on the site to defend the trees – 363 of them gave their lives doing so. When news reached the maharaja, he ordered the felling to cease and banned cutting down trees and hunting animals in Bishnoi territory. Today, a small temple marks the place where all this happened, while in its grounds, 363 *khejri* trees commemorate the martyrs.

Although it is possible to go to Khejadali by bus, you'll be hard put to find a villager who speaks English, and it's a lot better to go with a tour group, which will also visit other villages. Most tours stop at Khejadali for lunch. This is usually followed by an **opium ceremony** in which opium is dissolved in water in a specially designed wooden vessel, and poured through a strainer into a second receptacle. The process is repeated twice more, and the resulting tea is drunk from the palm of a hand. Strictly speaking, it's illegal, but blind eyes are turned to this kind of traditional opium use, though in fact opium addiction is something of a social problem in rural Rajasthan.

Good and inexpensive **tours** of the Bishnoi villages are run by several guesthouses in Jodhpur including *Govind Hotel*, *Durag Niwas* and *Yogi's Guest House*. Rates start at around Rs600 per person in a couple (cheaper in larger groups).

Osian

Rajasthan's largest group of early Jain and Hindu temples lies on the outskirts of the small town of **OSIAN (or Osiyan)**, 64km north of Jodhpur. The temples date from the eighth to the twelfth centuries when Osian was a regional trading centre. The town's ruler and population apparently converted to Jainism in the eleventh century, and the town is still an important Jain pilgrimage centre.

The town centre is dominated by the imposing twelfth-century **Sachiya Mata Temple**, overlooking the whole of Osian from its elevated hilltop position. At the very top of the complex, the main shrine to Sachiya (an incarnation of Durga) is unusually decorated with multicoloured mirrorwork and topped by a cluster of finely carved *shikharas*.

A five-minute walk from the Sachiya Mata Temple lies Osian's most beautiful monument, the **Mahavira Jain Temple** (Rs5, Rs40 camera, Rs100 video; no leather items permitted, and women should not enter during menstruation). Built in the eighth century, renovated in the tenth, and restored quite recently, the temple's beautifully carved central shrine is fronted by twenty elegant pillars and surrounded by shrines to further *tirthankaras*. A trio of smaller temples lies nearby, including a pair of Surya temples and the unusual **Peeplaj Temple**, surrounded by gargoyle-like projecting elephants, along with a massive Pratihara-period (eighth and ninth centuries) step-well.

Just south of the bus stop lies Osian's oldest collection of temples, centred on the **Vishnu and Harihara temples**, also built in the Pratihara period. The nine temples in this group retain a considerable amount of decorative carving, particularly in the surrounding friezes.

Government **buses** from Jodhpur (every 30min–1hr; 1hr 30min) drop you at the stand on the main road just south of town. Most people **stay** at the basic but welcoming *Priest Bhanu Sarma Guesthouse* (Ⓣ9414 440479; ❷) opposite the Mahavira temple, run by the (Hindu) priest who looks after the (Jain) temple, who can also provide information and arrange camel safaris and tours of local Bishnoi villages. More upmarket accommodation can be found at the luxury *Camel Camp Osian* (reservations c/o the *India Safari Club* in Jodhpur on Ⓣ0291/243 7023, Ⓦwww.camelcamposian.com; ❾, from around $260), with carpeted tents and a pool. **Camel treks** around Osian can also be arranged through the *Govind* and *Cosy* guesthouses in Jodhpur; rates start at around Rs1000 per person per day (minimum two people).

Legend of the Thar

Legend ascribes the **creation of the Thar** to Rama, hero of the Ramayana. In it, Rama, an earthly incarnation of the god Vishnu, has to rescue his wife Sita from the clutches of the demon Ravana, who is holding her on the island of Sri Lanka. To cross to the island, Rama loads his bow with a magical arrow that will dry up the ocean, but the sea god Sagara begs him not to shoot, offering him free passage instead. Well, says Rama, my bow is now drawn and must be shot, where shall I aim it? There is a sea to the north, replies Sagara, where evil-doers drink my water and hurt me; shoot your arrow there, and you'll be doing me a favour. So Rama takes aim and shoots, drying up the sea that Sagara has described, and creating the desert of Marwar ("Land of the Dead"). By Rama's special boon, this new land, though desert, is blessed, full of sweet herbs and fit for grazing cattle.

In fact, the legend would seem to be based on some degree of truth, for the fossil record shows that back in the Jurassic period (206–144 million years ago), the Thar was indeed covered by sea. Indeed, you may notice that slabs of sandstone often bear tell-tale ripple marks showing that they once formed part of the seabed.

Jaisalmer

In the remote westernmost corner of Rajasthan, **JAISALMER** is the quintessential desert town, its golden, sand-coloured ramparts rising out of the arid Thar like a scene from the *Arabian Nights*. Rampant commercialism may have dampened the romantic vision somewhat, but even with all the touts and tour buses, the town deservedly remains one of India's most popular destinations. Villagers dressed in voluminous red and orange turbans still outnumber foreigners in the bazaar, while the exquisite sandstone architecture of the "Golden City" is quite unlike anything else in India.

Camel safaris from Jaisalmer

Few visitors who make it as far as Jaisalmer pass up the opportunity to go on a **camel trek**, which provides an irresistibly romantic chance to cross the barren sands and sleep under one of the starriest skies in the world. Sandstorms, sore backsides and camel farts aside, the safaris are usually great fun. Treks normally last from one to four days, with **prices** varying from Rs600 to Rs1500 per night. The highlight is spending a night under the desert stars, and most travellers find that an overnight trip, departing around 3pm one day and returning the next at noon, is sufficient. Unfortunately, the price you pay is not an adequate gauge of the quality of services you get, and it pays to shop around and ask other travellers for recommendations. We've listed a few dependable operators below, though the list is far from exhaustive. Make sure you'll be provided with your own camel, an adequate supply of blankets (it can get very cold at night), food cooked with mineral water, and a campfire. You should also make sure that your operator is committed to either burning or removing all rubbish (including plastic bottles).

The traditional Jaisalmer camel safari used to head west out of town to Amar Sagar, Bada Bagh, Lodurva, Sam and Kuldera (see pp.205–206). Some operators still cover these areas, although encroaching development and crowds of other tourists (around Sam especially) mean that there is very little sense of the real desert hereabouts. The better operators are constantly seeking out new and unspoilt areas to trek through – this usually means an initial drive out of Jaisalmer of around 50–60km, though it's worth it to avoid the crowds. Longer seven- to ten-day treks to Pokaran, Barmer and Bikaner can also be arranged, though these shouldn't be attempted lightly.

Finally, don't book anything until you get to Jaisalmer. Touts trawl trains and buses from Jodhpur, but they usually represent dodgy outfits. Some offer absurdly cheap rooms if you agree to book a camel trek with them. Guesthouse notice-boards are filled with sorry stories by tourists who accepted. As a rule of thumb, any firm that has to tout for business – and that includes hotels – is worth avoiding.

Recommended operators

Celebrating its 25th birthday in 2011, **Adventure Travel** (ⓣ9414 149176, ⓦwww.adventurecamels.com), just south of the First Fort Gate, gets rave reviews for seeking out remote locations and providing fringe amenities, like real mattresses and sheets, at low prices. Slightly cheaper, but equally dependable, is **Sahara Travels** in Gopa Chowk (ⓣ02992/252609, ⓦwww.mrdesertemeritus.com), run by the instantly identifiable "Mr. Desert," a former truck driver turned Rajasthani model and movie star. "Don't make a booking until you see the face," is his motto. Of the **hotels** that organize camel safaris, *Shahi Palace* has a deservedly good reputation and virtually guarantees you won't see another tourist, while the friendly *Renuka* offers reliable tours at some of the lowest rates in town.

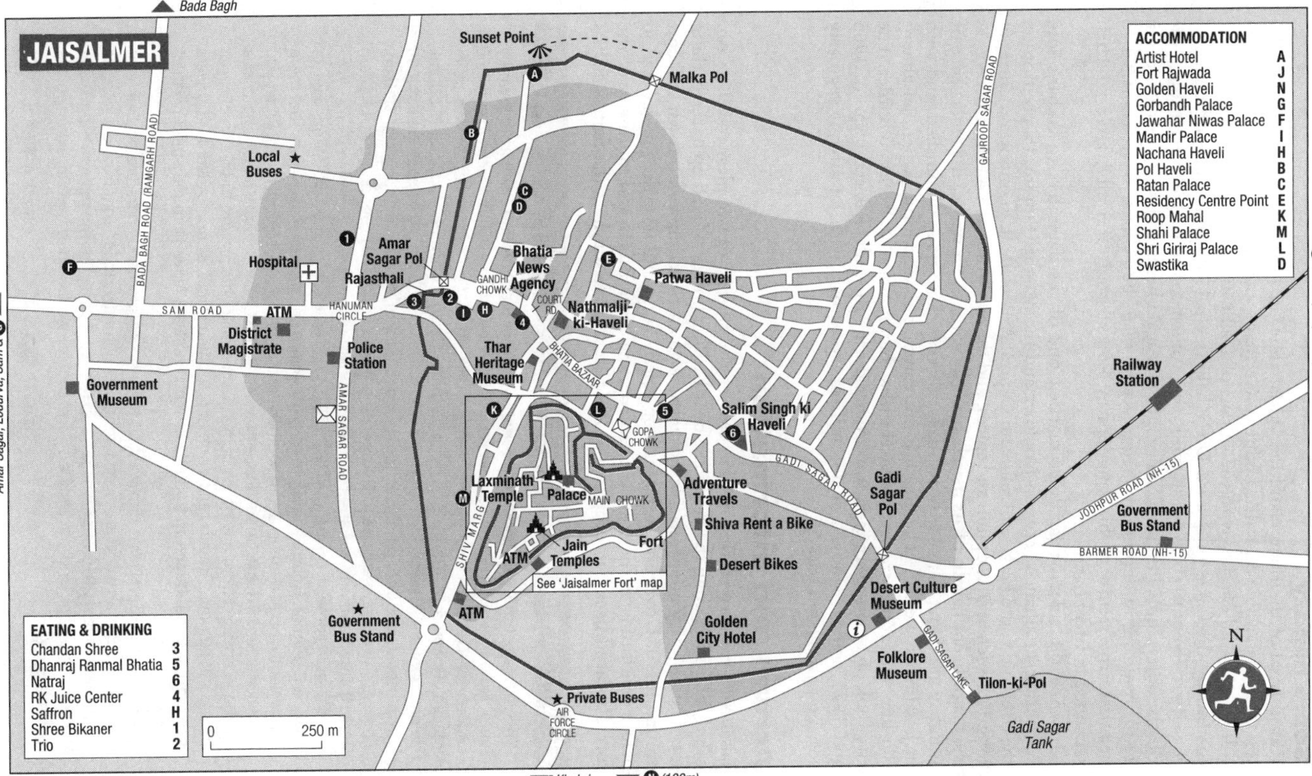
JAISALMER
Bada Bagh
Sunset Point
Malka Pol
Local Buses
Hospital
Amar Sagar Pol
Rajasthali
Bhatia News Agency
GANDHI CHOWK
COURT RD
Nathmalji-ki-Haveli
Patwa Haveli
BADA BAGH ROAD (RAMGARH ROAD)
SAM ROAD
HANUMAN CIRCLE
ATM
District Magistrate
Police Station
Thar Heritage Museum
BHATIA BAZAAR
Government Museum
AMAR SAGAR ROAD
GAJROOP SAGAR ROAD
Salim Singh ki Haveli
GOPA CHOWK
Laxminath Temple
Palace
MAIN CHOWK
SHIV MARG
Jain Temples
Fort
See 'Jaisalmer Fort' map
Adventure Travels
Shiva Rent a Bike
Desert Bikes
GADI SAGAR ROAD
Gadi Sagar Pol
Railway Station
JODHPUR ROAD (NH-15)
Government Bus Stand
BARMER ROAD (NH-15)
Desert Culture Museum
Golden City Hotel
Folklore Museum
GADI SAGAR LAKE
Tilon-ki-Pol
Gadi Sagar Tank
Private Buses
AIR FORCE CIRCLE
Khuhri
N (100m)
J & Jodhpur (NH-15)
Barmer (NH-15)
Amar Sagar, Lodurva, Sam & G
N
0 250 m
ACCOMMODATION
Artist Hotel A
Fort Rajwada J
Golden Haveli N
Gorbandh Palace G
Jawahar Niwas Palace F
Mandir Palace I
Nachana Haveli H
Pol Haveli B
Ratan Palace C
Residency Centre Point E
Roop Mahal K
Shahi Palace M
Shri Giriraj Palace L
Swastika D
EATING & DRINKING
Chandan Shree 3
Dhanraj Ranmal Bhatia 5
Natraj 6
RK Juice Center 4
Saffron H
Shree Bikaner 1
Trio 2

Some history

Rawal Jaisal of the Bhati clan founded Jaisalmer in 1156 as a replacement for his less easily defensible capital at Lodurva. Constant wars with Jodhpur and Bikaner followed, as did conflict with the sultans of Delhi. In 1298, a seven-year siege of the fort by the forces of Ala-ud-Din Khalji (see p.1156) ended when the men of the city rode out to their deaths while the women committed *johar* – although the Bhatis soon resumed their rule. The city was again besieged by Sultanate forces in 1326, resulting in another desperate act of *johar*, but Gharsi Bhati managed to negotiate the return of his kingdom as a vassal state of Delhi, after which it remained in Bhati hands.

In 1570 the ruler of Jaisalmer married one of his daughters to Akbar's son, cementing an alliance between Jaisalmer and the Mughal Empire. Its position on the overland route between Delhi and Central Asia made it an important entrepôt for goods such as silk, opium and spices, and the city grew rich on the proceeds, as the magnificent havelis of its merchants bear witness. However, the emergence of Bombay and Surat as major ports meant that overland trade diminished, and with it Jaisalmer's wealth. The death-blow came with Partition, when Jaisalmer's life-line trade route was severed by the new, highly sensitive Pakistani border. The city took on renewed strategic importance during the Indo-Pakistani wars of 1965 and 1971, and it is now a major **military outpost**, with jet aircraft regularly roaring past the ramparts.

Arrival and information

Jaisalmer's **railway station** is 2km east of the city; reservationless travellers can calmly enquire among the sandwich-board-toting hoteliers lined up in the parking lot. The majority offer free rides; otherwise an auto-rickshaw into town will cost around Rs30. **Government buses** stop briefly at a stand near the railway station before continuing to the more convenient new **State Bus Stand** southwest of the fort. **Private buses** will drop you at Air Force Circle south of the fort. RTDC's

Moving on from Jaisalmer

The **railway station** is east of town on the Jodhpur road, around Rs40 from town by auto. Note that **night trains** can get very cold – close to freezing in winter. The #4060 **Jaisalmer–Delhi** *Express*, which departs daily at 4.45pm, stops at, among other places, Pokaran (6.10pm), Phalodi (7.22pm), Osian (8.27pm), Jodhpur (9.50pm), Jaipur (4.50am), Alwar (7.17am) and Old Delhi (11.05am). The overnight #4809 **Jaisalmer-Jodhpur** *Express* departs daily at 11.15pm, arriving in Jodhpur at 5.10am. There are two daily services to **Bikaner**: the #4703 and #4701, departing at 11.20am and 10.45pm and arriving at 4.50pm and 3.55am respectively.

Most **government buses** (☎02992/251541) **depart** from the bus stand east of town on Barmer Road, although early-morning departures leave from the more conveniently located stand at the southern end of Amar Sagar Road; check when you buy your ticket. **Private buses** leave from Air Force Circle. **Tickets** for private buses can be purchased from any of the numerous travel agents around town – try Swagat Travels or Hanuman Travels, just north of Hanuman Circle, or from Adventure Travels (see p.196). **Local buses** to Lodurva, Khuhri and Sam leave from the stand north of Hanuman Circle.

Jaisalmer's **airport** lies 14km west of town on Khuri Road. There are no flights at present, though a new passenger terminal is currently under construction, due for completion in late 2010 after which it's expected that flights will resume – probably to Delhi via Jaipur, and possibly also to Mumbai via Udaipur, though exact details remain vague.

tourist office (Mon–Sat 10am–5pm; ⓣ02992/252406), southeast of town near Gadi Sagar Pol, is of little use, and its "recommended" operators pay for the privilege. **Online**, it's worth having a look at ⓦwww.jaisalmer.org.uk and ⓦjaisalmer.nic.in.

Accommodation

Jaisalmer has plenty of places to stay in all categories, and fierce competition keeps prices low. The basic choice is between staying in one of the old places within the wonderfully atmospheric fort itself (but read the "Jaisalmer in Jeopardy" box on p.200 first) or in one of the newer places outside (many of which are built in traditional sandstone and come with superb fort views). Most places offer free pick-up from the bus or railway stations, and the majority also have internet access. Almost all accommodation offers **camel treks**, which vary in standard and price, and some managers even at reputable hotels can be uncomfortably pushy if you don't arrange a safari through them.

In the fort

The hotels listed below are shown on the Jaisalmer Fort map on p.202.

Desert ⓣ02992/250602, ⓦwww.deserthotel.com. Friendly little budget place with cheaper rooms downstairs (including a couple of bargain singles with shared bathroom), and brighter rooms upstairs, some with fort views. ❶–❷

Desert Haveli ⓣ02992/251555, ⓔdesertguest house@hotmail.com. Simple guesthouse offering variously sized rooms with bare stone walls and attached bathroom at rock-bottom prices. ❶

Moti Palace ⓣ02992/254693, ⓔkailash_bissa @yahoo.co.uk. Friendly budget option, with a range of good-value rooms (all attached, and air-cooled in summer) and unbeatable views over the main gate. ❶–❹

Paradise ⓣ02992/252674, ⓦwww.paradiseon fort.com. Atmospheric old haveli with a leafy courtyard and a wide selection of rooms, ranging from cheap downstairs rooms with common baths to prettily decorated upstairs rooms with a/c. ❶–❺

Suraj ⓣ02992/251623, ⓦwww.hotelsuraj jaisalmer.webs.com. This superbly atmospheric haveli of 1526 is one of the nicest places to stay in the fort (though rates are relatively pricey), with simple but characterful old fan rooms and a privileged rooftop view of the Jain temples. ❹–❺

Surja ⓣ9414 761394, ⓦwww.surjahotel.com. A range of basic attached fan rooms (the more expensive ones with fine views) and a relaxing rooftop terrace with one of the best panoramas in town. ❶–❸

In town

Unless otherwise stated, the hotels listed below are shown on the Jaisalmer map, p.197.

Artist Hotel Manganyar colony ⓣ02992/252082, ⓦwww.artisthotel.info. Run by an Austrian expat as a co-op for members of the Manganyar (minstrel musician) caste, who play here most evenings. The rather rustic rooms (fan or air-cooled), with bare stone walls, are comfortable enough, if a bit gloomy, and there's a nice rooftop restaurant with good food and a real pizza oven. ❷–❸

Golden Haveli Bera Rd ⓣ02992/250821, ⓦwww.goldenhaveli.com. Stylish new hotel occupying a modern sandstone haveli in a peaceful location on the southern edge of town. Rooms (all a/c) are unusually spacious and attractively furnished, and there's also a pleasant rooftop restaurant overlooking the desert. Good value at current rates. ❺

Mandir Palace Gandhi Chowk ⓣ02992/252788, ⓦwww.mandirpalace.com. Occupying part of the exquisite Mandir Palace (see p.203), with pleasantly spacious rooms sporting discreet heritage touches, attractive public areas (including the fine old Durbar Hall, now housing a miniature museum) and a pool (non-guests Rs350). ❽

Nachana Haveli Gandhi Chowk ⓣ02992/251910, ⓦwww.nachanahaveli.com. This venerable old haveli is one of the best choices in its class. The atmospheric ground-floor rooms (all a/c) are virtually windowless but have stone walls and are attractively decorated with antique fittings; the suites upstairs are brighter. There's also the good *Saffron* rooftop restaurant (see p.204). ❻

Pol Haveli Near Geeta Ashram, Dedansar Rd ⓣ02992/250131, ⓦwww.hotelpolhaveli.com. Attractive new guest house in a stylish little sandstone building. Rooms (fan or a/c) are neat and comfortable (although larger ones are

Jaisalmer in jeopardy

Erected on a base of soft bantonite clay, sand and sandstone, the foundations of **Jaisalmer Fort** are rapidly eroding due to huge increases in water consumption, mainly related to tourism. At the height of the season, around 120 litres per head are pumped into the area – and due to problems with the drainage system, a large proportion of this water seeps back into the soil beneath the fort, weakening its foundations. The results have been disastrous. In 1998 six people died when an exterior wall gave way, and five more bastions fell in 2000 and 2001. Jaisalmer is now listed among the World Monument Fund's 100 Most Endangered Sites.

An international campaign, **Jaisalmer in Jeopardy** (JiJ; ⓦwww.jaisalmer-in-jeopardy.org), has been set up to facilitate repairs throughout the fort, including assistance with upgrading underground sewerage – the scheme relies largely on donations; see the website for details if you'd like to help. Despite the work so far carried out, however, some authorities think the best way to save the fort would be to evacuate its two thousand inhabitants and start repairs to the drainage system from scratch, an expensive and time-consuming venture much opposed by the guesthouse owners inside whose earnings depend on tourism.

Given all this, some people (and guidebooks) suggest that travellers **should avoid staying in the fort** in order to relieve pressure on its crumbling foundations. Unfortunately, this also has a serious side-effect in that it deprives many local hoteliers – some of whom have been in the fort for decades, and who are in no way responsible for Jaisalmer's current plight – of a living. We have therefore continued to list certain guesthouses within the fort. All are long-established, low-impact, and occupy original and largely unmodified buildings. On the other hand, we haven't listed any of the fort's modern, custom-built hotels. Remember, too, that if you do stay in the fort, you can do your bit by minimizing your water usage as much as possible.

slightly lacking in furniture), and there's a lovely rooftop terrace for idle lounging and fort-gazing. ❶–❺

Ratan Palace Off Gandhi Chowk ⓣ02992/252757, ⓔhotelrenuka@rediffmail.com. One of the best cheapies in this part of town, with a friendly owner and hassle-free accommodation in old-fashioned but spotless rooms (the cheapest with shared bathrooms; the more expensive with a/c). They run good camel treks (see p.196) and have further, slightly larger and more expensive rooms (Rs350–750) in the *Renuka* guest house just down the street. ❶–❸

Residency Centre Point Khumbara Para ⓣ9414 76 0421, ⓔresidency_guesthouse@yahoo.com. Small, family-run guesthouse in the backstreets near Patwa Haveli and Nathamal ki Haveli. Rooms (a couple with a/c) are comfortable and good value, and there are nice town views from the rooftop. Advance booking recommended. ❷–❸

Roop Mahal Off Shiv Marg ⓣ02992/251700, ⓔhotelroopmahal@yahoo.com. Comfortable new guesthouse in a good central location, with bright, inexpensive modern rooms (some with fort views and cheap a/c), helpful staff and a pleasant rooftop restaurant. There's also wi-fi, parking space and free use of an Enfield motorbike. ❶–❸

Shahi Palace Off Shiv Marg ⓣ02992/255920, ⓦwww.shahipalacehotel.com. See also Fort map on p.202. Outstanding little hotel tucked away just south of the fort in a stylish modern sandstone building with stunning fort views from the rooftop terrace restaurant and immaculate rooms. The only caveat is that the cheaper rooms are a bit small – it's well worth coughing up for one of the superb larger a/c rooms. The same family also run the slightly cheaper *Oasis Haveli* and *Star Haveli next door*. ❷–❺

Shri Giriraj Palace Near Gopa Chowk ⓣ02992/252268. Simple, friendly local hotel with some of the cheapest rooms in town, including ultra-cheap shared bath doubles, plus budget attached and a/c rooms – great value at current prices. ❶–❷

Swastika Off Gandhi Chowk ⓣ02992/252152, ⓔswastikahotel@yahoo.com. Old-fashioned guest-house offering simple but comfy fan and a/c rooms (a couple with shared bathroom) at bargain prices, although planned renovations may bump rates up slightly. ❶–❸

Out of town

Fort Rajwada Off Jodhpur Rd, 3.5km east of town ⓣ02992/253233, ⓦwww.fortrajwada.com. One of the best of the new resort hotels on the outskirts of town, with five-star facilities (pool, bar, good restaurant and grand coffee shop), and 25 percent discounts April–Sept. ❽

Gorbandh Palace Sam Rd, 2km west of town ⓣ02992/253801, ⓦwww.eternalmewar.in. Another upmarket, resort-style hotel just outside town. Not the most atmospheric lodgings in Jaisalmer, but well-run and very comfortable, and with facilities including a smart restaurant and bar, pool and Ayurvedic spa. ❽

Jawahar Niwas Palace 1 Bada Bagh Rd ⓣ02992/252208 or 288. Late nineteenth-century royal guesthouse with turreted sandstone exterior, large and graceful rooms, and a good pool (Rs250 for non-guests). ❼–❽

The Town

Getting lost in the narrow winding streets of Jaisalmer is both easy and enjoyable, though the town is so small that it never takes long to find a familiar landmark.

Jaisalmer Fort

Every part of Jaisalmer Fort is made of soft yellow Jurassic sandstone. Outside, the thick **walls**, punctuated with barrel-sided bastions, drop almost 100m to the town below, while inside narrow winding streets are flanked with carved golden facades. Two thousand people still live within its walls; seventy percent of them are Brahmins and the rest, living primarily on the east side, are predominantly Rajput. A paved road punctuated by four huge gateways winds up to the fort's **main chowk** (square) – large round stones lie atop the ramparts above the entrance, waiting to be pushed down on the heads of any approaching enemy. The main chowk was the scene of the three terrible acts of *johar* during the fourteenth and fifteenth centuries, when the women of the royal palace, which overlooks the chowk, had a huge fire built, and jumped from the palace walls into it.

Palace of the Maharawal

The chowk is dominated by the **Palace of the Maharawal**, open to the public as the **Fort Palace Museum** (Oct–March daily 9am–6pm, April–Sept daily 8am–6pm; Rs250 including audioguide, students Rs200 [Rs30], video Rs150). The palace's balconied, five-storey facade displays some of the finest masonry in Jaisalmer, while the ornate marble throne to the left of the palace entrance is where the monarch (known in Jaisalmer as the maharawal rather than the maharaja) would have addressed his troops. Inside, the museum offers an intriguing snapshot of the life of Jaisalmer's potentates through the ages, with artefacts ranging from a fancy silver coronation throne to more homely items, such as the bed and thali dish of a nineteenth-century ruler. There's also an interesting array of other exhibits – from fifteenth-century sculptures (including an unusual bearded Rama) through to local stamps and banknotes, while the rooftop terrace gives unrivalled views over the city and the surrounding countryside.

Hindu and Jain temples

The fort has a number of Hindu temples, including the venerable **Laxminath Temple** of 1494, dedicated to Laxmi. None, however, is as impressive as the complex of seven **Jain temples** (daily 8am–noon; Rs30, camera Rs70, video Rs120, mobile-phone camera Rs30). The temples, connected by small corridors and stairways, were built between the twelfth and fifteenth centuries with yellow and white marble shrines and exquisite sculpted motifs covering the walls, ceilings and pillars. Two of the seven temples are open between 8am and noon; the other

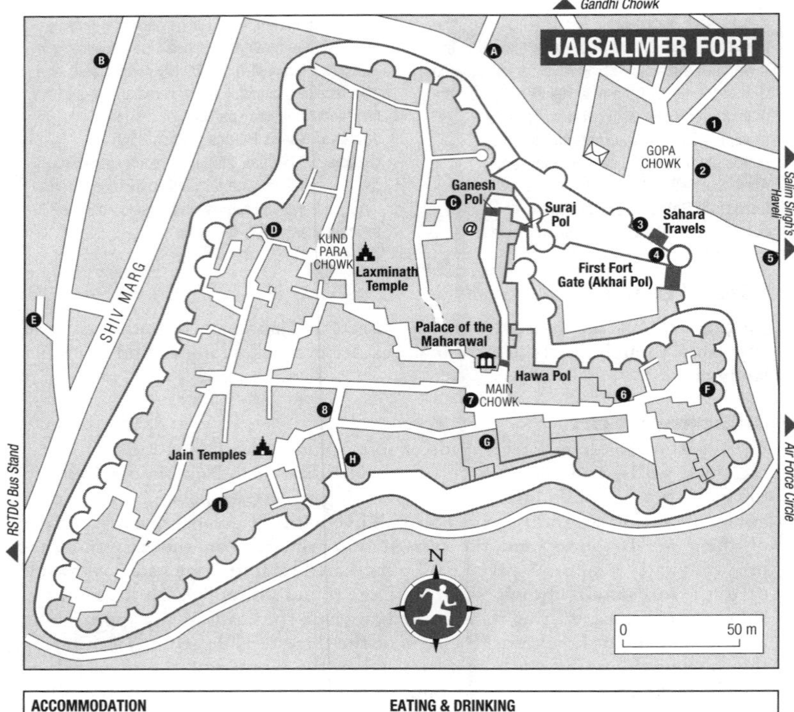

ACCOMMODATION				EATING & DRINKING			
Desert	D	Shahi Palace	E	8 July	7	Krishna's Boulangerie	8
Desert Haveli	H	Shri Giriraj Palace	A	Bhang Shop	3	Little Italy	4
Moti Palace	C	Suraj	I	Dhanraj Ranmal Bhatia	1	Little Tibet	6
Paradise	G	Surja	F	Joshi's German Bakery	2	Monica	5
Roop Mahal	B						

five only open from 11am to noon, when the whole place gets overrun with coach parties, so it's best to visit before 11am to see the first two temples, then come back later to see the rest.

The havelis

The streets of Jaisalmer are flanked with numerous pale honey-coloured facades, covered with latticework and floral designs, but the city's real showpieces are its **havelis**, commissioned by wealthy merchants during the eighteenth and nineteenth centuries.

Just north of Bhatia Bazaar (take the small road between the Ajanta Photo Studio and Dev Handicrafts), the **Nathmalji-ki-Haveli** was built in 1885 for Jaisalmer's prime minister by two brother stonemasons, one of whom built the left half, the other the right, as a result of which the two sides are subtly different. It's guarded by two elephants, and the first-floor bay window above the main doorway is surmounted by a frieze of little figures including elephants, horses, a steam train and a horse-drawn carriage.

The larger and even more finely decorated **Patwa Haveli**, or Patwon-ki-Haveli (daily 8am–6.30pm; Rs20) lies a couple of blocks north of here down a street to the right, its exterior a positive riot of exuberantly carved *jharokhas* (protruding balconies). The haveli was constructed in the first half of the nineteenth century by the Patwa merchants – five brothers from a Jain family who were bankers and traders in brocade and opium. There are actually five separate suites within the haveli. Two are closed to visitors. Two, preserved in their original condition, are open as **government museums** (daily 10am–5pm; Rs50 combined ticket [Rs10]). One, the **Kothari Patwa Haveli Museum** (daily 10am–5pm; Rs120 [Rs40], camera Rs30) has been done up as a museum with various traditional artefacts on display and replica mirrorwork on the walls, giving you some idea of how the haveli would originally have looked. As well as visiting the interior of the Patwa Haveli, it's worth taking a little stroll down the street whose entrance it bridges, to check out the stonework on four impressive neighbouring havelis.

The third of Jaisalmer's famous trio of havelis, the **Salim Singh ki Haveli** (daily summer 8am–7pm; winter 8am–6pm; Rs20, camera Rs20), lies on the east side of town and is immediately recognizable by the lavishly carved overhanging rooftop balcony that gives the whole building a strangely top-heavy appearance. Its upper floor, enclosed by an overhanging balcony, is best seen from the roof of *Natraj Restaurant*.

In addition to these havelis, parts of the **Mandir Palace**, now partly converted into a heritage hotel (see p.199), can be visited (daily 10am–5pm; Rs20), though its most striking feature, the elegant **Badal Vilas tower**, is best seen from the west, just outside Amar Sagar Pol.

Gadi Sagar Tank and museums

South of town through an imposing triple gateway lies **Gadi Sagar Tank**, once Jaisalmer's sole water supply, flanked with sandstone *ghats* and temples – a peaceful spot, staring out into the desert; you can rent boats here for a spin on the water. The nearby **Folklore Museum** (daily 8am–6pm; Rs20, camera Rs20) has displays of folk art, textiles and paraphernalia relating to the consumption of opium, while there are further local curiosities, including musical instruments, fossils and rare manuscripts, at the **Desert Culture Museum** (daily 10am–5pm; Rs20), just up the road next to the tourist office.

Back in the centre of town, the modest little **Thar Heritage Museum** (daily 9am–9pm; Rs40) showcases the personal collection of local historian L.N. Khatri, who may be on hand to explain some of the stories and customs behind the quirky array of local artefacts on display, ranging from bits of fossilized tree and old chillums through to camel regalia and antique musical instruments.

Eating and drinking

Jaisalmer's tourist **restaurants**, usually rooftop affairs with fort views, offer the usual mix of tourist and Indian fare; most also serve beer. Alternatively, for a drink, the *Nachana Haveli* on Gandhi Chowk should have opened a bar in its former stables by the time you read this. Unless otherwise indicated, all the following are shown on the Jaisalmer map on p.197.

Restaurants

8 July Main Chowk, in the fort. See Fort map, opposite. Recommended for its privileged terrace view of the fort's bustling main chowk and palace rather than for its food, though it has a good selection of smoothies, lassis, juices and snacks, along with Indian, Italian, Chinese and Mexican mains (Rs70–95). Good spot for breakfast.

Chandan Shree Restaurant Just west of Amar Sagar Pol. Popular local diner for inexpensive veg curries (Rs25–90) and thalis (Rs60–140), as well as Rajasthani specialities such as *govind gatta* and *ker sangri*.

Little Italy Just inside first Fort gate. See Fort map, opposite. Italian restaurant with great pasta dishes (Rs120–180), served in heaped portions at reasonable prices (the pizzas make a stab at authenticity, but don't really cut it) and a superb terrace directly opposite the main ramparts – beautiful at night.

Little Tibet In the Fort. See Fort map, p.202. Run by a team of young Tibetans, this travellers' café serves up all the usual Indian and Chinese choices, plus pasta, Mexican, and a good range of Tibetan specialities. Also a good venue for breakfast. Mains Rs60–95.

Monica Near the first Fort gate. See Fort map, p.202. Moderately priced Rajasthani and tandoori dishes, along with delicious veg and non-veg Rajasthani thalis (Rs145/210). Mains Rs65–145.

Natraj Opposite the Salim Singh ki Haveli. Friendly rooftop non-veg restaurant, popular for its excellent, gently spiced Mughlai chicken, *malai kofta* and other Indian dishes (mains Rs85–190). Licensed.

Saffron *Nachana Haveli*, Gandhi Chowk ⓣ02992/251910. Slightly upmarket restaurant with fine tandoori and Mughlai food, plus Indian veg, Italian and Chinese options (mains Rs60–170) and live music nightly.

Shree Bikaner Restaurant North of Hanuman Circle. No-frills pure-veg restaurant serving up Punjabi veg curries (Rs45–100), a choice of Rajasthani, Gujarati and Bengali thalis (Rs80–125), and a wonderful *dal bati churma* (a traditional Rajasthani dish consisting of baked wheatflour balls served with dhal and sweet *churma* sauce; Rs125), which they'll keep refilling till you've had enough.

Trio Gandhi Chowk ⓣ02992/252733. Slightly upscale choice known for its sumptuous tandoori and Mughlai meat dishes (mains Rs145–280), alongside some Rajasthani specialities and a reasonable veg selection. Book early for the best tables overlooking the Mandir Palace and Fort.

Drinks and snacks

Bhang shop Gopa Chowk. See Fort map, p.202. If you like bhang (and be warned that it doesn't agree with everybody – see p.75), this is one of the best places in the country to get it, with a whole menu of bhang-laced drinks and sweets, and a choice of different strengths.

Dhanraj Ranmal Bhatia Court Rd. Wonderful, moist milk-based sweets (*ladoo*, *barfi* and the like), plus great samosas and *mirchi badas*, and you can even watch them being made, as they do it all out front.

Joshi's German Bakery Gopa Chowk. See Fort map, p.202. Scrumptious range of fresh cakes, croissants and cookies, especially in the morning. Too bad the coffee's instant.

Krishna's Boulangerie In the Fort, near the Jain temples. See Fort map p.202. A handy place to stop for a breather in the Fort, with decent coffee and light snacks, plus pizza and pasta. A good breakfast option too.

RK Juice Center Bhatia Bazaar. Wonderful freshly pressed juices using whatever fruits are available on the day (usually including some or all of orange, pomegranate, pineapple, banana, carrot and ginger). They promise not to add ice or tap water (though they do use it to rinse out the juice extractor).

Listings

Banks and exchange There's are ATMs just inside Amar Sagar Pol, one directly opposite the gate on the outside, one by the District Magistrate's office on Sam Road, and a couple just outside the southern edge of the fort. There's a cluster of exchange bureaux in Gandhi Chowk, while the reliable Adventure Travels (see p.196) also change cash and travellers' cheques.

Bicycle rental Narayan Cycles, in the street directly opposite *Nachana Haveli* hotel (100m up on the left, just where the street starts to bend); Rs5/hr.

Bookshops Bhatia News agency on Court Rd, just beyond Gandhi Chowk, plus numerous stalls in the Fort.

Doctor Dr S.K. Dube (ⓣ02992/251560) speaks good English; Rs500 per consultation.

Festival Jaisalmer's Desert Festival is held over three days at the full moon in the lunar month of Magha (Feb 16–18, 2011; Feb 5–7, 2012; Feb 23–25, 2013). Unlike many of the region's other festivals, this is not a livestock fair, but a festival of performing arts, and generally a fun occasion, with folk dancing, turban-tying competitions, camel racing and craft bazaars. Main events are held at Dedansar Polo Ground. Hotels tend to get full at this time, but they don't generally increase their prices. There's usually a programme of events posted at ⓦjaisalmer.nic.in.

Hospital The government hospital is on Sam Rd, west of Hanuman Circle (ⓣ02992/252495), but a better bet is the small, private Maheshwari Hospital off Sam Rd opposite the court and District Magistrate's office (ⓣ02992/250024).

Internet access Internet is widely available but mostly slow. The *Chai Bar*, inside the Fort just beyond Ganesh Gate, has the best machines (Rs50/hr including a drink). Joshi Cyber Café (Rs30/hr), in *Joshi's German Bakery* nearby, is slower but cheaper.
Motorbike rental There are a couple of places south of Gopa Chowk including Desert Bikes (☎94141 50033) and Shiva Rent a Bike (☎9462 094620), with bikes and scooters for Rs300–400/day.
Police Just south of Hanuman Circle on Amar Sagar Rd (☎02992/252233). A new Tourist Protection Police office on Sam Road should have opened by the time you read this.
Post office The main post office, with poste restante, is on Amar Sagar Rd 200m south of Hanuman Circle (Mon–Sat 9am–3.30pm); there's a smaller office opposite the Fort wall behind Gopa Chowk (Mon–Sat 10am–5pm).
Shopping Jaisalmer is one of the best places in India to shop for souvenirs. Prices are comparatively high and the salesmen push hard, but the choice of goods is excellent – virtually the whole Fort has now been turned into an enormous souvenir bazaar, while there are dozens of further places along Bhatia Bazaar. Jaisalmer is a particularly good place to pick up textiles, fabrics and leatherwork (including camel leather bags and shoes), as well as cheap hippy-style clothes. Rajasthali, the official Rajasthan state crafts emporium outside Amar Sagar Pol, is rather dry and unattractively arranged, and not always the very best quality, but handy for checking prices as they're fixed and marked.
Swimming pool Non-guests can use the pools at the *Mandir Palace* hotel (Rs350) and the small pool at the *Golden City* hotel (Rs100) on the south side of town. Alternatively, try the pools at *Fort Rajwada*, *Gorbandh Palace* and *Jawahar Niwas Palace* hotels, out of town; these usually cost around Rs250–300.
Travel agents Adventure Travels (see p.196) can arrange bus, train and plane tickets for a modest commission, and can also sort out hotel bookings.

Around Jaisalmer

The desert around Jaisalmer harbours some unexpected monuments, dating from the era when the area lay on busy caravan routes. Infrequent buses negotiate the dusty roads, or you can rent a jeep through your hotel.

Bada Bagh, Amar Sagar and Lodurva

Six kilometres north of Jaisalmer, in the fertile area of **Bada Bagh**, a cluster of **cenotaphs** (daily sunrise to sunset; Rs50 [Rs20], camera Rs20, video Rs50) built in memory of Jaisalmer's rulers stands incongruously on a hill amid a cluster of modern wind turbines. The green oasis below is where most of the area's fruit and vegetables used to be grown.

Seven kilometres northwest of Jaisalmer is **AMAR SAGAR**, a small and peaceful town set around a large artificial lake (empty during the dry season) where you'll find the eighteenth-century Amar Singh Palace and three Jain temples (Rs10 entry, Rs50 camera), including the Adeshwar Nath Temple, commissioned in 1928 by a member of the same family who put up the Patwa Haveli in Jaisalmer.

A further 10km northwest of Amar Sagar, **LODURVA** was the capital of the Bhati Rajputs from the eighth century until the twelfth, when it was sacked by Muhammad of Ghor, after which the Bhatis moved their capital to Jaisalmer. Only a few **Jain temples**, rebuilt in the seventeenth century, remain. The main temple (daily 7am–8pm; Rs30 [free], camera Rs70, video Rs120), dedicated to Parshvanath, features an ornately carved eight-metre *toran* (arch), just inside the entrance to the main temple compound, perhaps the most exquisite in Rajasthan, plus a finely carved exterior.

There are three or four daily **buses** to Lodurva, but taking a **rickshaw** or **taxi** is a more leisurely option (Rs250/400 respectively for the round-trip including stops at Amar Sagar and Bada Bagh) – or you could **cycle**.

Kuldara, Sam and Khuhri

South of the Sam road, around 25km west of Jaisalmer, the ghost village of **Kuldara** (daily sunrise–sunset; Rs50, vehicles Rs100) was one of 84 villages abandoned, for unknown reasons, simultaneously one night in 1825 by the Paliwal Brahmin community, which had settled here in the thirteenth century. The Paliwals' sense of industry and order is attested by their homes, each with its living quarters, guest room, kitchen and stables, and parking space for a camel. You can take an atmospheric stroll through them to the temple at the heart of the village.

The huge, rolling sand dunes 40km west of Jaisalmer are known as **SAM**, though strictly this is the name of a small village further west. Unfortunately, the once pristine desert here has now vanished beneath endless tented camps, as around five thousand tourists descend daily to watch sunset and make merry in the desert. If you've come to the Thar in search of vast crowds, psychotic camel touts and endless piles of windblown plastic, then you'll be in seventh heaven. If not, the entire area is best given a wide berth. You can overnight here in one of the numerous tented camps, but we wouldn't recommend it.

A rather nicer place to watch the sun set over the dunes is the village of **KHUHRI**, 42km south of Jaisalmer. Many camel safaris either start here or pass through – most time their arrival so that tourists can see flamboyantly dressed local women arriving with large jugs on their heads to fill up with water at caste-specific wells. The village also has a certain charm – many of its homes are still made of mud and thatch rather than concrete, their exterior surfaces beautifully decorated with ornate white murals. Unfortunately, tourist development has already eroded much of Khuhri's traditional character. Virtually every building now seems to have been converted into a guesthouse, while ugly new concrete buildings and endless signboards are beginning to mushroom on every available space, accompanied by the usual tide of discarded plastic and other rubbish.

Khuhri can be reached by four daily **buses** (10.30am, 1.30pm, 3pm & 5.30pm) from the local bus stand in Jaisalmer, or by jeep (Rs500 for the round-trip from Jaisalmer) or taxi (Rs250 round-trip). Despite the profusion of guesthouses in the village (and upmarket tented camps around it), prices tend to be steep. If you want **to stay**, you probably can't do better than very simple but extremely peaceful *Badal House* (no phone; ❷ including full board). which is much more like staying with a local family, and a good place to chill out for a few days and get a feel of village life. They can also arrange camel safaris.

Pokaran

Some 110km east of Jaisalmer at the road and rail junctions between Jodhpur, Bikaner and the west is the quiet and little-visited town of **POKARAN**. Pokaran became the centre of international attention in May 1998 when three massive **nuclear explosions** were detonated 200m beneath the sands of the Thar Desert, 20km northwest of the town, announcing India's arrival as one of the world's fully-fledged atomic powers.

Despite its unwelcome moment of international fame, Pokaran remains something of an outpost, but does offer excellent **accommodation** at its sixteenth-century **fort** (Ⓣ02994/222274, Ⓦwww.fortpokaran.com; ❼–❽), a wonderful old sandstone building that feels more authentic for having only been partly restored. The only other accommodation is the RTDC *Motel* at the road junction on the edge of town (Ⓣ02994/222275; ❹).

Phalodi and Keechen

The main highway and railway line wind in tandem east from Jaisalmer across the desert, separating at the small junction settlement of **PHALODI**, almost exactly

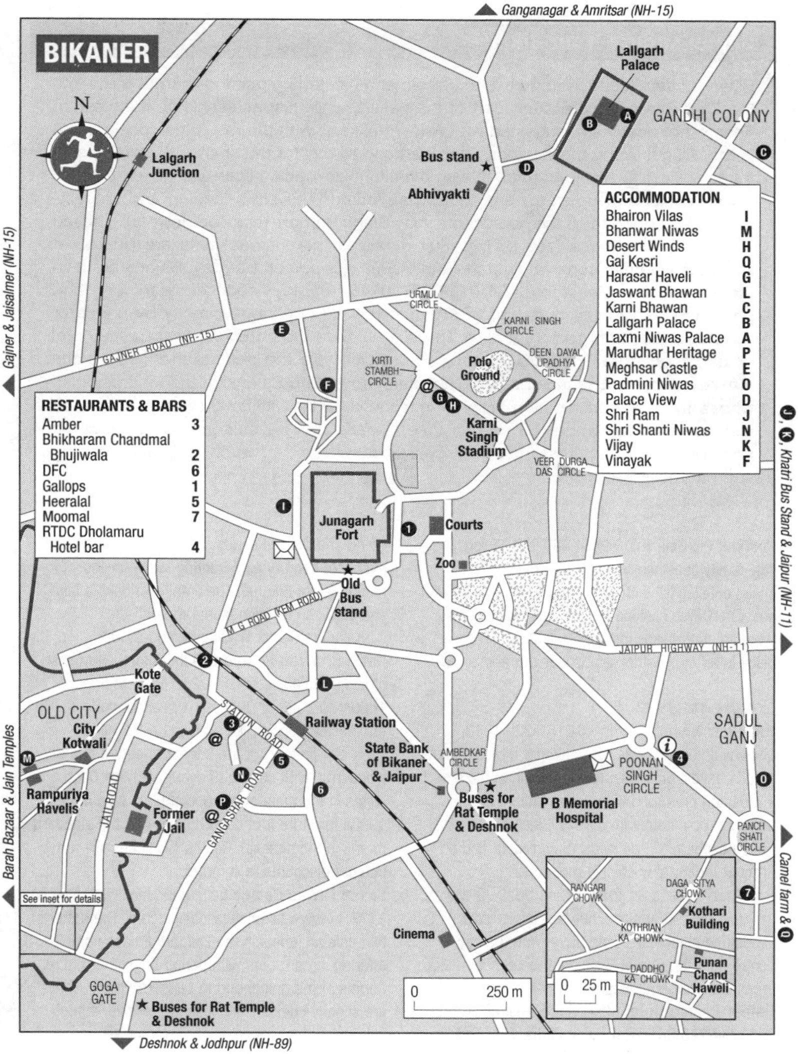

BIKANER

RESTAURANTS & BARS

Amber	3
Bhikharam Chandmal Bhujiwala	2
DFC	6
Gallops	1
Heeralal	5
Moomal	7
RTDC Dholamaru Hotel bar	4

ACCOMMODATION

Bhairon Vilas	I
Bhanwar Niwas	M
Desert Winds	H
Gaj Kesri	Q
Harasar Haveli	G
Jaswant Bhawan	L
Karni Bhawan	C
Lallgarh Palace	B
Laxmi Niwas Palace	A
Marudhar Heritage	P
Meghsar Castle	E
Padmini Niwas	O
Palace View	D
Shri Ram	J
Shri Shanti Niwas	N
Vijay	K
Vinayak	F

pleasantly old-fashioned rooms (some a/c), a homely little dining room and views of Lallgarh Palace. ❹

Shri Ram Sadul Ganj, 1.5 km east of the city centre ⓣ0151/252 2651, ⓦwww.hotelshriram.com. Friendly suburban hotel. The more expensive rooms are spacious and very comfortably furnished, though the cheaper ones are a bit cramped. There are also five-bed dorms (Rs200). ❸–❺

Shri Shanti Niwas Gangashahar Rd ⓣ0151/252 4231. The cleanest of the ultra-cheapies near the station, although they might be reluctant to accept non-Indians. The various rooms include some very inexpensive singles (Rs80) with shared bath. Doubles are all attached. 24hr checkout. ❶–❸

Vijay Opposite Sophia School, 5km east of centre along the Jaipur Highway ⓣ0151/223 1244, ⓦwww.camelman.com. Sociable family guesthouse with spacious and very comfortable rooms (some with optional a/c) at bargain prices. There's also camping space, plus a nice garden and free bicycles. ❷–❹

Camel safaris from Bikaner

Bikaner offers a good alternative to Jaisalmer as a starting point for **camel treks** into the Thar Desert. This eastern part of the desert, while just as scenic as the western Thar, is not nearly as congested with fellow trekkers, with the result that local people in the villages along the route don't wait around all day for the chance to sell Pepsi to tourists. Wildlife is also abundant, with plentiful blackbuck, nilgai, and desert foxes.

Your choices of **operator** are somewhat limited. The city's leading and longest-established operator is the personable Vijay Singh Rathore (aka "Camel Man"), based at *Vijay Guest House* (see p.209). Full details of his various treks are posted at ⓦwww.camelman.com; rates start from Rs900 per person per day. Safaris are also offered by *Vino Guesthouse* (ⓣ0151/227 0445, ⓦwww.vinodesertsafari.com) and promoted by various touts hanging around the old city (book directly by phone or email to avoid commission) and by Thar Camel Safari, c/o the *Meghsar Castle* hotel or direct on ⓣ9351 206093. Another possibility are the safaris arranged by the *Vinayak Guest House* (see below). These are led by Jitu Solanki, a trained zoologist, whose trips offer fascinating insights into the desert's wildlife and enivronment, as well as visits to remote Bishnoi villages. Safaris can be customized to focus on particular areas of interest, including specialized wildlife, birdwatching, snake-spotting and photographic tours.

Vinayak Old Ginani ⓣ0/9414 430 948. Welcoming little family guesthouse offering simple but very cheap doubles (all with bathroom, though not all with hot water). Free cooking lessons are available and there are motorbikes for hire (Rs.200/day). A good place to arrange camel safaris (see box above). ❶

Expensive

Bhanwar Niwas Old City ⓣ0151/220 1043, ⓦwww.bhanwarniwas.com. Bikaner's most ostentatious haveli, built for a textile tycoon in the late 1920s and crammed with kitsch fittings and furniture, complete with a 1927 Buick in the lobby, an atmospheric *fin de siècle* dining room and an array of memorably chintzy rooms. ❽

Gaj Kesri Bypass Rd ⓣ0151/240 0372, ⓦww.gajkesri.com. Grandiose, heritage-style red sandstone palace, a 15min drive from the city centre near the Camel Farm, with beautiful public areas and well-equipped rooms. ❽

Gajner Palace Hotel 32km southwest of Bikaner ⓣ01534/275 061, ⓦwww.hrhindia.com. This grand affair in red sandstone was built in the early twentieth century as a hunting lodge for the maharajas of Bikaner. The hotel overlooks a lake, and staff can arrange jaunts through the surrounding Gajner Wildlife Sanctuary. ❽

Karni Bhawan Palace Gandhi Colony, 1km east of Lallgarh Palace ⓣ0151/252 4701 to 5, or 1800/180 2933 or 2944, ⓦwww.hrhindia.com. On the outside it looks like an oversized English suburban house, but the interior is period and wonderful, with superb (if overpriced) Art Deco suites in the main building, complete with original 1930s furniture (but don't bother with the standard rooms in the annexe). Rooms ❼, suites ❽; forty percent discounts in summer.

Laxmi Niwas Palace Lallgarh Palace ⓣ0151/220 2777, ⓦwww.laxminiwaspalace.com. The better of two palatial hotels in the Lallgarh Palace complex, offering large rooms with period English furniture. Rooms at the neighbouring *Lallgarh Palace Hotel* are slightly cheaper and less impressive, though still boast plenty of colonial character. ❽

The City

Bikaner's main sight is the impressive **Junagarh Fort**, but it's also worth making time for a wander through the **old city**, with its rich array of quirky, early twentieth-century havelis.

Junagarh Fort

Built at ground level and defended only by high walls and a wide moat, **Junagarh Fort** (daily 10am–5.30pm (last entry 4.30pm); Rs150, students Rs100 [Rs20]; camera Rs30, video Rs100; or combined ticket including entrance, camera and audioguide Rs250) isn't as immediately imposing as the mighty hill forts elsewhere in Rajasthan, though its richly decorated interiors are as magnificent as any in the state. The fort was built between 1587 and 1593, and progressively enlarged and embellished by later rulers. The entrance price includes a **compulsory guided tour**, though it's easy enough to break away from the tour and make your own way around.

Entering the fort, look out for handprints set in stone near the second gate, **Daulat Pol**, which bear witness to the satis of various royal women. From here a passageway climbs up to the small Vikram Vilas courtyard, beyond which you'll find the main courtyard. Opening onto the main courtyard is the **Karan Mahal**, built in the seventeenth century to commemorate a victory over the Mughal emperor Aurangzeb and adorned with gold-leaf painting and an old *punkah* (fan). Next to here in the **Rai Niwas** are Maharaja Gai Singh's ivory slippers, one of Akbar's swords, and a representation of the Pisces zodiac sign which looks remarkably like a dinosaur in a headscarf.

Past here is the **Anup Mahal** (Diwan-i-Khas), the grandest room in the palace, with stunning red and gold filigree decorative painting and a red satin throne framed by an arc of glass and mirrors. The carpet was made by inmates of Bikaner jail – a manufacturing tradition that has only recently ceased. After such a hectic display of opulence, the **Badal Mahal** ("cloud palace"), built in the mid-nineteenth century for Maharaja Sardar Singh (1851–72) is pleasantly understated. Upstairs, a room exhibits beds of nails, sword blades and spear heads used by sadhus to demonstrate their immunity to pain, while across the terrace in the finely painted **Gaj Mandar** is the maharaja's chaste single bed and the maharani's more accommodating double.

The next part of the palace, the twentieth-century **Ganga Niwas**, created by Maharaja Ganga Singh (1887–1943), can be reached either via a long and labyrinthine passageway from the Gaj Mandar or, more directly, from the Vikram Vilas courtyard (see above). This section of the palace is centred on the cavernous **Diwan-i-Am**, dominated by a World War I de Havil and biplane, a present from the British to Bikaner's state forces. Next door is the early-twentieth-century office of Ganga Singh, followed by several further rooms stuffed full of guns and swords.

Also in the fort complex, the **Prachina Museum** (daily 9am–6pm; Rs50 [Rs10], camera Rs20, video Rs70; Ⓦwww.prachina-museum.com) houses a pretty collection of objects (glassware, crockery, cutlery and walking sticks) demonstrating the growing influence of Europe on Rajasthani style in the early twentieth century. A whole circa-1900 salon has been recreated, and there's also an interesting collection of Rajasthani textiles and clothing.

The old city

Bikaner's labyrinthine **old city** is notable for its profusion of unusual **havelis** whose idiosyncratic architecture demonstrates an unlikely fusion of indigenous sandstone carving with Art Nouveau and red-brick municipal Britain. The city is confusing to navigate, so accept getting lost as part of the experience.

Entering the old city through Kote Gate, bear left (south) down Jail Road. After 300m, turn right just past the florid pink gateway to a Hindu temple to reach the City Kotwali (the old city's central police station). Follow the road past here to reach the three striking **Rampuriya Havelis**, commissioned in the 1920s by three brothers from a Jain trading family and faced with reliefs of a mixture of personages, including Maharaja Ganga Singh, Britain's George V and Queen Mary, and Krishna and Radha.

Turn left just before the third Rampuriya Haveli, walking past the boarded-up 1918 **Golchha Haveli**, and continue roughly straight ahead, following the road as it makes two dog-legs to the right, to emerge after 100m onto a street full of ironmongers. Turn right here and continue for 300m to reach the small square called **Rangari Chowk**, centred on a neat white Hindu temple. Walk along the right-hand side of the temple and straight ahead is the small, triangular square called **Kothrion ka Chowk**, lined by handsome havelis. Follow the road as it swings round to the left, past the **Kothari Building** (on your right), with five wonderfully extravagant Art Nouveau balconies, to reach the small **Daga Sitya Chowk**. A house on the left still has fading murals of steam trains, while Diamond House, on the right, gets wider as it goes up, each storey overhanging the one below it. Retrace your steps back to just before Kothrion ka Chowk, then turn left to reach the **Punan Chand Haveli** boasting an amazingly carved floral facade. Turn round again and head back towards Kothrion ka Chowk, then take the first left to reach the large **Daddho ka Chowk**, surrounded by fine havelis.

Cross the square, to where the street ends at a T-junction, then turn right and continue for around 400m to reach **Barah Bazaar**, centred on a large pillar painted in the colours of the Indian flag. Follow the street round to the left and you'll eventually reach the **Bhandreshwar (Bhandasar) Temple**, unusual among Jain temples in being covered in a rich, almost gaudy, array of paintings. Porcelain tiles imported from Victorian England decorate the main altar, and steps lead up the unusually large tower, where you get a great view over the old city.

Immediately to the rear on the edge of the high city wall lies the large Hindu **Laxminath Temple**, commissioned in the early sixteenth century by Lunkaran Singh, the third ruler of Bikaner. In a small park just beyond (follow the road between the Laxminath and Bhandreshwar temples) is a second Jain temple, the **Sandeshwar (Neminath) Temple** of 1536, also profusely but more sobrely painted in dark greens and reds. A large model behind the temple shows the huge Jain religious complex at Palitana in Gujarat.

Lallgarh Palace and Shri Sadul Museum

The sturdy red-sandstone **Lallgarh Palace** in the north of the town is home to the royal family of Bikaner, although parts have now been converted into a pair of hotels. It was built during the reign of Ganga Singh, who lived here from 1902, and the sheer scale and profusion of the exterior decoration is impressive, even if it lacks the romantic allure of older Rajasthani palaces. The **Shri Sadul Museum** (Mon–Sat 10am–5pm; Rs40 [Rs20], camera Rs50, video Rs100) houses an enormous and surprisingly engrossing collection of old photographs showing various viceregal visits, pictures of Ganga Singh at the signing of the Versailles Treaty and royal processions.

The camel farm

What claims to be Asia's largest camel-breeding farm, the **National Research Centre on Camels** (daily 3–6pm; Rs20 [Rs10], camera Rs20; camel ride Rs20, guided tour Rs100) lies out in the desert 10km south of Bikaner (around Rs120 round-trip by auto including waiting time). Bikaner is renowned for its famously sturdy beasts – the camel corps was a much-feared component of the imperial battle formation – but the growing proliferation of motor vehicles has severely reduced the camel's traditional role as the staple means of rural transport. It's best to take a guided tour of the farm; aim to be here at 3.30–4pm, when you'll be wowed by the sight of three hundred stampeding dromedaries arriving from the desert for their daily chow. A new **museum** was under construction at the time of writing. There's also a kiosk selling camel milk and milk-based products such as lassis and kulfi.

Eating and drinking

Restaurants are thin on the ground in Bikaner and most visitors eat at their hotels. For a **drink**, try the bar of the RTDC *Dholamaru Hotel* at Pooran Singh Circle or the more expensive bar at the *Lallgarh Palace* hotel. Bikaner is famous for **sweets** such as *kaju katli*, made with cashew nuts, and *tirangi*, a three-coloured confection made with cashews, almonds and pistachios.

Amber Station Rd. Simple but clean local restaurant popular with Westerners, with a long menu of Indian veg standards along with a few snacks. Most mains Rs50–70.

Bhikharam Chandmal Bhujiawala Just off Station Rd on the road to Kote Gate (the English sign is very small and easy to miss). Top *mithai* shop, known for its excellent Bengali and Rajasthani sweets, though it also has a good range of savoury snacks.

DFC (Dwarika Food Cuisine) Station Rd, by Silver Square mall. Clean and pleasant restaurant offering a big list of veg mains (most Rs60–80), thalis (Rs60–110) and even train tiffins (Rs90) to take with you on a rail journey.

Gallops Court Rd. Pleasant but seriously overpriced restaurant opposite the fort that has grown fat on the easy pickings of passing coach parties. The food's not bad, however, with a range of North Indian veg and non-veg standards, plus a few local specialities, served in big portions. Usually full of tour groups at lunchtime, though quieter and nicer in the evenings. Mains Rs175–450. Licensed.

Heeralal Opposite the train station. Clean and spacious veg restaurant serving up north and south Indian cuisine, including a good Rajasthani thali (Rs125) and other local specialities. Mains Rs100–140.

Moomal Panch Shati Circle. Popular with well-heeled locals, this white-linen restaurant serves sumptuous south Indian veg food – the cashew and cherry Moomal Special alone is worth the trip. Mains around Rs100–180.

Listings

Banks and exchange There are ATMs directly opposite the station, and another one 100m south; on Station Rd almost opposite the road from Kote Gate; and between RTDC *Hotel Dhola Maru* and Panch Shati Circle. Thomas Cook (Mon–Sat 9am–6pm), inside the entrance to the fort, changes cash and travellers' cheques.

Bicycle rental Available for Rs4/hr from a couple of shacks just south of the main post office, opposite the southwest corner of the fort.

Festival Bikaner's colourful camel fair (Jan 18–19, 2011; Jan 8–9, 2012; Jan 26–27, 2013) has the usual camel races and camel hairstyle competitions, plus dancing and firework displays. Most of the action takes place at the polo ground north of town near *Harasar Haveli* hotel. Advance accommodation booking recommended.

Hospital PB Memorial Hospital by Ambedkar Circle ⓣ0151/222 6334.

Internet access Internet is widely available for around Rs30-40/hr but generally slow. There are lots of places around Kirti Stambh Circus; alternatively, try New Horizons behind the *Amber Restaurant* on Station Rd or Cyber World (just Rs10/hr), immediately south of the *Marudhar Heritage* hotel.

Police Station Rd ⓣ0151/252 2225.

Post office Just west of the fort (Mon–Fri 10am–3pm, Sat 10am–1pm).

Shopping Bikaner is famous for its skilled lacquerwork and handicrafts, and for its hand-woven woollen *pattu* (a kind of shawl-cum-blanket). The best place to buy the latter is the Abhivyakti handicrafts shop (closed Sun afternoon) on Ganganar Road, near the bus stand, whose manager can also arrange visits to villages to see how the textiles are woven by local women's co-ops. Vichitra Arts, at *Bhairon Vilas*, sells vintage royal garb and miniature paintings.

Swimming pool The *Padmini Niwas Hotel* allows non-guests to use theirs for Rs100.

Deshnok and the temple of rats

The **Karni Mata Temple** (daily 6am–10pm; free; Rs20 camera, Rs50 video; ⓦwww.karnimata.com) in **DESHNOK**, 30km south of Bikaner, is one of India's more bizarre attractions. Step inside the Italian-marble arched doorway and everywhere you'll see free-roaming rats, known as *kabas*, which devotees believe are

The Deshnok Devi

Members of the Charan caste of musicians believe that incarnations of the goddess Durga periodically appear among them, one of whom was **Karni Mata**, born at a village near Phalodi in 1387, who went on to perform miracles such as water divination and bringing the dead back to life, eventually becoming the region's most powerful cult leader. According to legend, one of Karni Mata's followers came to her because her son was grievously ill, but by the time they got to him, he had died. Karni Mata went to Yama, the god of the underworld, to ask for him back, but Yama refused. Knowing that of all the creatures upon the earth, only rats were outside Yama's dominion, Karni Mata decreed that all Charans would henceforth be reincarnated as rats, thus escaping Yama's power. It is these sacred rats (*kabas*) that inhabit the Deshnok temple.

reincarnated souls saved from the wrath of Yama, the god of death. The innermost shrine, made of rough stone and logs cut from sacred *jal* trees, houses the yellow-marble image of Karniji (see box above). This in turn is encased by a much grander marble building. Pilgrims bring offerings for the rats to eat inside the main shrine, and it's considered auspicious to eat the leftovers after they've been nibbled by the *kabas*. Some pilgrims spend hours searching for a glimpse of the temple's venerated white rat, while it's also considered fortunate for a rat to run over your feet (stand still for a while – preferably next to some food), but whatever you do don't step on one, or you'll have to donate a gold model of a rat to placate the deity. Shoes have to be removed at the gate, leaving you to wander among the rat droppings barefoot or in your socks.

Buses for Deshnok from Bikaner leave roughly every fifteen minutes (journey time 45min) from the main bus stand, stopping on the east side of Ambedkar Circle near PB Memorial Hospital, and just south of Goga Gate Circle, near the southeast corner of the old city. There are also **trains** (1hr journey) at 9.45am and 10.45am, with return services from Deshnok at 2.54pm and 3.25pm.

Udaipur

Spreading around the shores of the idyllic Lake Pichola and backdropped by a majestic ring of craggy green hills, **UDAIPUR** seems to encapsulate India at its most quintessentially romantic, with its intricate sequence of ornately turreted and balconied palaces, whitewashed havelis and bathing *ghats* clustered around the waters of the lake – or, in the case of the *Lake Palace* hotel and Jag Mandir, floating magically upon them. Not that the city is quite perfect. Insensitive lakeside development, appalling traffic and vast hordes of tourists mean that the city is far from unspoilt or undiscovered. Even so, Udaipur remains a richly rewarding place to visit, and although it's possible to take in most of the sights in a few days, many people spend at least a week exploring the city and the various attractions scattered about the surrounding countryside.

Some history

Udaipur is a relatively young city by Indian standards, having been established in the mid-sixteenth century by Udai Singh II of the **Sisodia** family, rulers of the state of **Mewar**, which covered much of present-day southern Rajasthan. The Sisodias are traditionally considered the foremost of all the Rajput royal dynasties. The present Sisodia maharana is the seventy-sixth in the unbroken line of Mewar

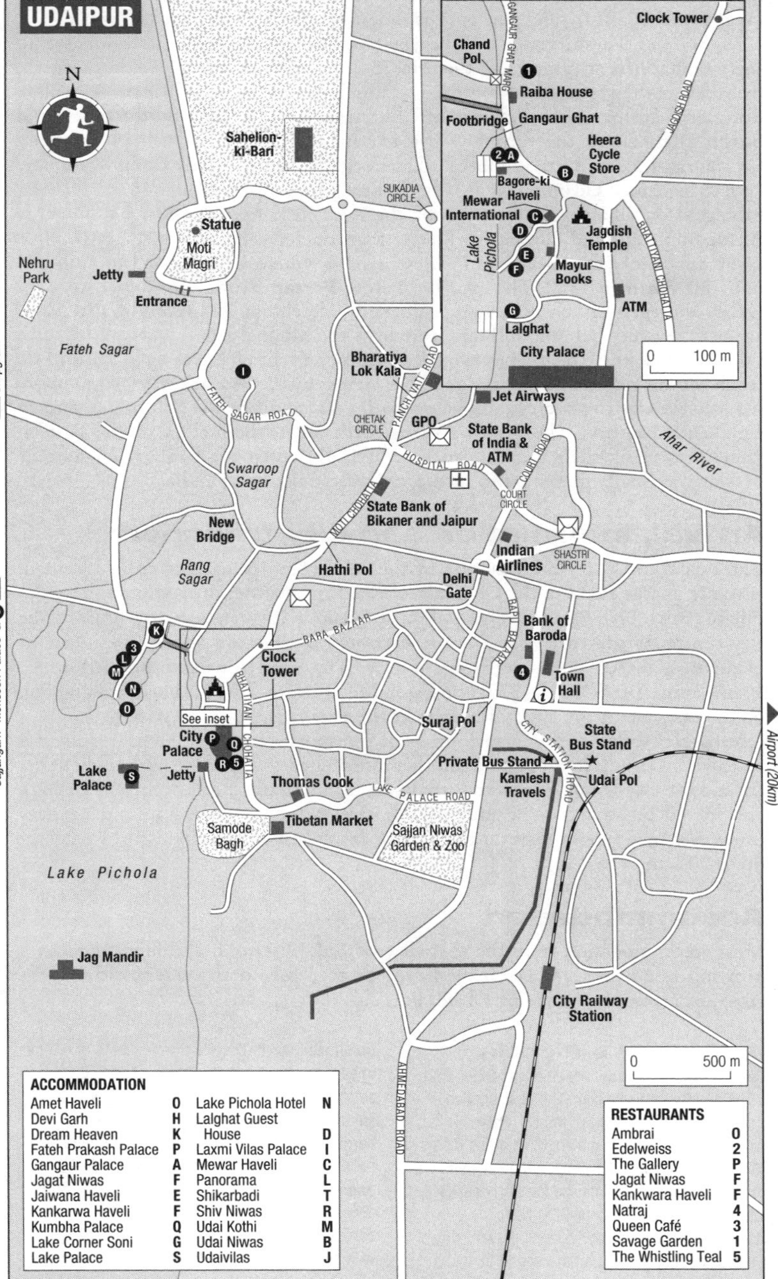
UDAIPUR
N
H (25km), Eklingji & Mount Abu
Shilpgram
Sajjangarh "Monsoon Palace" & J
Airport (20km)
T & Ahmedabad
Sahelion-ki-Bari
Sukadia Circle
Statue
Moti Magri
Nehru Park
Jetty
Entrance
Fateh Sagar
Fateh Sagar Road
Bharatiya Lok Kala
Panch Vati Road
Chetak Circle
GPO
Jet Airways
State Bank of India & ATM
Hospital Road
Court Road
Court Circle
Ahar River
Swaroop Sagar
New Bridge
Rang Sagar
Moti Chohatta
State Bank of Bikaner and Jaipur
Hathi Pol
Indian Airlines
Shastri Circle
Delhi Gate
Bara Bazaar
Bapu Bazaar
Bank of Baroda
Town Hall
Clock Tower
Bhattiyani Chohatta
See inset
Suraj Pol
City Palace
Lake Palace
Jetty
City Station Road
State Bus Stand
Private Bus Stand
Kamlesh Travels
Udai Pol
Thomas Cook
Lake Palace Road
Samode Bagh
Tibetan Market
Sajjan Niwas Garden & Zoo
Lake Pichola
Jag Mandir
City Railway Station
Ahmedabad Road
0 500 m
Clock Tower
Chand Pol
Gangaur Ghat Marg
Raiba House
Footbridge
Gangaur Ghat
Jagdish Road
Heera Cycle Store
Bagore-ki Haveli
Mewar International
Jagdish Temple
Lake Pichola
Mayur Books
Bhattiyani Chohatta
ATM
Lalghat
City Palace
0 100 m
ACCOMMODATION
Amet Haveli O
Devi Garh H
Dream Heaven K
Fateh Prakash Palace P
Gangaur Palace A
Jagat Niwas F
Jaiwana Haveli E
Kankarwa Haveli F
Kumbha Palace Q
Lake Corner Soni G
Lake Palace S
Lake Pichola Hotel N
Lalghat Guest House D
Laxmi Vilas Palace I
Mewar Haveli C
Panorama L
Shikarbadi T
Shiv Niwas R
Udai Kothi M
Udai Niwas B
Udaivilas J
RESTAURANTS
Ambrai O
Edelweiss 2
The Gallery P
Jagat Niwas F
Kankwara Haveli F
Natraj 4
Queen Café 3
Savage Garden 1
The Whistling Teal 5

suzerains, which makes the Mewar household the longest lasting of all royal families of Rajasthan, and perhaps the oldest surviving dynasty in the world.

The state of Mewar was established by Guhil in 568 AD. His successors set up their capital first at Nagda and then, in 734, at the mighty fort of Chittaurgarh, from where they established control over much of present-day southern Rajasthan (for a brief history of the Sisodias at Chittaurgarh, see p.233). By the time **Udai Singh II** inherited the throne of Mewar in 1537, however, it was clear that Chittaurgarh's days were numbered. Udai began looking for a location for a new city, to be named Udaipur, eventually choosing a swampy site beside Lake Pichola, protected on all sides by outcrops of the Aravalli range. The Mughal emperor Akbar duly captured Chittaurgarh after a protracted seige in 1568, but by then Udai was firmly established in his new capital, where he remained unmolested until his death in 1572. His son, the heroic **Pratap Singh**, continued to defy Akbar and spent much of his reign doggedly defending his kingdom's freedom against the overwhelming military muscle of the Mughal army.

Following Akbar's death, peace finally ensued, and the city prospered until 1736, when Mewar suffered the first of repeated attacks by the **Marathas**, who gradually reduced the city to poverty until being finally driven off by the British in the early eighteenth century. The Sisodias thenceforth allied themselves to the British, while preserving their independence until 1947, when the famous old state of Mewar was finally merged into the newly created nation of India.

Arrival, information and city transport

The **bus stand** is on the east side of the centre; pre-paid autos from the main entrance charge Rs32 to the City Palace area. Private buses drop you on the other side of Town Hall Road. **Trains** pull in at Udaipur City Station, southeast of the city centre. **Flights** arrive at **Dabok Airport** (ⓣ0294/265 5453), 20km east of Udaipur, a Rs300 taxi ride from the city. The main **tourist office** (Mon–Sat 10am–5pm; ⓣ0294/241 1535) is in Fateh Memorial on Airport Road at Suraj Pol, on the east side of the city, with desks at the airport and railway station.

Auto-rickshaws are the usual means of transport; there are no cycle rickshaws in town. Renting a **bicycle** is another possibility (see p.223), although traffic around the city is bad. **Tours** to Ranakpur, Kumbalgarh, Nathdwara and Eklingji are offered by some of the innumerable **travel agents** dotted around the city centre (see p.224), as well as car rental with driver (usually around Rs1200/day for up to 300km).

Accommodation

Most accommodation is on the **east side of Lake Pichola**, although there are a growing number of places on the far more peaceful **northwestern side** of the lake, just across the bridge by Chand Pol.

East of Lake Pichola

Fateh Prakash Palace City Palace ⓣ0294/252 8016, ⓦwww.hrhindia.com. The best location in the city, right in the heart of the City Palace complex, with prices to match. Most of the rooms ($365) have superb lake views, although some are rather small and characterless for the price. ❾

Gangaur Palace Gangaur Ghat Marg ⓣ0294/242 2303, ⓦwww.ashokahaveli.com. Popular budget hotel in an atmospheric traditional haveli. There's a wide range of rooms of varying standards (fan and a/c), including some with lake views, though prices for the smarter rooms can be a bit steep – try bargaining. Facilities include in-house palmist, painting lessons and German bakery. ❷–❺

Jagat Niwas 23–25 Lalghat ⓣ0294/242 2860, ⓦwww.jagatniwaspalace.com. Beautifully restored seventeenth-century haveli right on the lakeside, with pleasant a/c rooms (some with lake views)

Moving on from Udaipur

Flights from **Dabok Airport** (see Arrival and information opposite) serve Delhi, Jaipur, Jodhpur and Mumbai. **Government buses** leave from the main RSTRC bus stand at Udai Pol. **Private buses** depart from across Town Hall Road, and are a better option for longer and (especially) overnight journeys – most night buses are sleepers, and there are nightly a/c sleeper services to Mumbai, Delhi and Jaipur. It's easiest to book **tickets** for private buses through one of the many travel agents in town (usually for a modest surcharge of around Rs20). If you want to book your own ticket you'll need to make a reservation with one of the bus-company offices around Udai Pol – try the reliable Kamlesh Travels (☎0294/248 5823). **Local buses** to destinations such as Nagda, Eklingji, Nathdwara and Kankroli leave regularly from the RSTRC bus stand.

Train services from Udaipur are surprisingly limited; those listed below are the best of a bad bunch. Note that there are no direct services to Jaipur or Jodhpur (change at Kota), or Mumbai (change at Ahmedabad). You can save a trip to the station by booking tickets through travel agents in town (see Listings p.224) for a surcharge of around Rs50–75, which is about what you'd pay for a rickshaw to the station and back.

Recommended trains from Udaipur

Destination	Name	No.	Departs	Arrives
Ahmedabad	*Ahmedabad Fast Passenger*	431	9.35am daily	9.05pm
	Ahmedabad Express	9943	7.45pm daily	4.25am
Ajmer	*Ajmer Express*	2991	6.15am daily	11.40am
Bundi	*Mewar Express*	2964	6.15pm daily	10.46pm
Chittaurgarh	*Mewar Express*	2964	6.15pm daily	8.30pm
Delhi (HN)	*Mewar Express*	2964	6.15pm daily	6.30am
Kota	*Mewar Express*	2964	6.15pm daily	11.40pm
Sawai Madhopur	*Mewar Express*	2964	6.15pm daily	1.06am

and a good restaurant (see p.222), though not as peaceful or as good value as the nearby *Kankarwa* and *Jaiwana* havelis. ❺–❼

Jaiwana Haveli 14 Lalghat ☎0294/241 1103, ⓦwww.jaiwanahaveli.com. Good-value lakeside haveli accommodation with a range of spotless modern rooms; some have a/c, and the more expensive ones have fine lake views, as does the good rooftop restaurant. ❺

Kankarwa Haveli 26 Lalghat ☎0294/241 1457, ⓦwww.indianheritagehotels.com. Romantically restored haveli right on the waterfront. Not quite as pristine as the nearby *Jagat Niwas*, but more atmospheric and much better value, with colourful, antiquey rooms (all a/c; some with superb lake views). There's also excellent veg food (see p.222). ❺–❻

Kumbha Palace 104 Bhatiyani Chohatta ☎0294/242 2702, ⓦwww.indianheritagehotels.com. Friendly, Dutch-owned guesthouse hidden under the east walls of City Palace and backed by a bougainvillea-filled garden. Rooms (a few with a/c) are simple but bright and clean, and the whole place is refreshingly peaceful. ❷–❹

Lake Corner Soni Paying Guest House Lalghat ☎0294/252 5712. This simple little guesthouse, run by a charming elderly couple, offers some of the cheapest lodgings in Udaipur. Rooms (some with shared bathroom) are basic but clean and peaceful, and there are fine lake views from the rooftop terrace and some rooms. ❶

Lake Palace Lake Pichola ☎0294/252 8800, ⓦwww.tajhotels.com. One of India's most famous and romantic hotels, sailing in magnificent isolation on its own island amid the serene waters of Lake Pichola. Accommodation is in a selection of rooms and suites, which range from the merely luxurious to the opulently theatrical, while facilities include a spa, pool, butler service and limousine rental. The full rate for a standard room is Rs5115, but check the website for discounts. ❺

Lalghat Guest House Lalghat ☎0294/252 5301, ⓔlalghat@hotmail.com. One of the oldest guesthouses in Udaipur, and still going strong thanks to its superb lakeside position and cheapish rates. There's a mix of rooms (all attached, some a/c, and some with lakeside views), plus a nicer-than-average ten-person dorm (Rs100). ❶–❹

Mewar Haveli 34–35 Lalghat ⓣ0294/252 1140, ⓦwww.mewarhaveli.com. Spotless and well-run modern mid-range hotel in a very central location. Rooms (some with a/c and lake views) are chintzy but comfortable, and there are further lake views from the attractive rooftop restaurant. ❹–❺

Shiv Niwas City Palace ⓣ0294/252 8016, ⓦwww.hrhindia.com. This upmarket heritage hotel trades on its superb location inside the City Palace complex, with grand public areas, a dreamy pool (non-guests Rs300) and a brand-new spa. The viewless standard ("palace") rooms are disappointingly small and ordinary given the Rs12,960 price tag; suites (from $585) are far more memorable, with genuine old-world atmosphere and marvellous lake views. 20 percent discounts in summer. ❾

Udai Niwas Gangaur Ghat Marg ⓣ0294/241 4303, ⓦwww.hoteludainiwas.com. Bright modern high-rise hotel with a range of smart rooms in various price categories (the more expensive ones with a/c), although road noise and the periodic outbursts of massively amplified music from the nearby Jagdish Temple mean that it's not particularly peaceful. ❷–❺

Northwestern side of Lake Pichola

Amet Haveli Chand Pol ⓣ0294/243 4009, ⓔamethaveli@sify.com. This fine old white haveli is one of the best lakefront properties in town. All rooms are beautifully decorated with traditional touches and come with a/c, TV and fine lake views, though you might want to spend a little bit extra to get one of the superb suites, with big windows right over the water. Also home to the excellent *Ambrai* restaurant (see p.222). ❼

Dream Heaven Chand Pol ⓣ0294/243 1038, ⓔdeep_rg@yahoo.co.uk. Deservedly popular (book ahead) with a good range of clean, cheap and competitively priced rooms; some have superb lake views, as does the rooftop restaurant. ❶–❹

Lake Pichola Hotel Chand Pol ⓣ0294/243 1197, ⓦwww.lakepicholahotel.com. This long-established hotel won't win any design awards but the lakeside location and City Palace views are just about perfect, and prices quite reasonable. Don't bother with the viewless standard rooms, though. All rooms with a/c and TV. ❻

Panorama Chand Pol ⓣ0294/243 1027, ⓔkrishna2311@rediffmail.com. Excellent budget hotel, efficiently run and with cheap, cosy and excellent-value rooms (some with slight lake views; a few with a/c). There's also a nice rooftop restaurant with superb lake views and better-than-average food. Book ahead. ❶–❹

Udai Kothi Chand Pol ⓣ0294/243 2810, ⓦwww.udaikothi.com. Smart and spotless modern hotel in traditional style, with lots of flowery murals and chintz architectural touches. Rooms all come with TV, a/c and plenty of slightly twee furnishings; there's also a pool (non-guests Rs300) and a lovely garden. ❼–❾

Outside the city centre

Laxmi Vilas Palace Off Fateh Sagar Rd ⓣ0294/252 9711, ⓦwww.thelalit.com. Luxury hotel occupying a nineteenth-century hilltop guesthouse above Fateh Sagar Lake. It's strong on creature comforts, with well-equipped rooms and a huge pool, although less atmospheric than the similarly priced hotels in the City Palace. Double rooms from $470. ❾

Udaivilas ⓣ0294/243 3300, ⓦwww.oberoihotels.com. Udaipur's most opulent hotel, occupying a sprawling palace, embellished with acres of marble and a novel "moated pool" which flows around the outside of the main building. Suites come with their own infinity swimming pools and private butler, and the spa is pure indulgence. Doubles start at $878 in high season. ❾

Around Udaipur

Devi Garh Delwara Village, 25km north of Udaipur ⓣ02953/289211, ⓦwww.deviresorts.com. Hidden away in the Aravalli Hills a 40min drive north of Udaipur, this luxury hotel occupies the magnificent seventeenth-century Devi Garh palace, mixing traditional Rajasthani palace opulence with contemporary style to memorable effect. Facilities include a superb spa and a spectacular pool. Suites only, starting at $607 in high season. ❾

Shikarbadi Goverdhan Vilas, 5km south of Udaipur on the NH-8 ⓣ0294/258 3201, ⓦwww.hrhindia.com. Former royal hunting lodge with its own pool, lake, deer park and stud farm – less ostentatious (and significantly cheaper) than the palaces in town. Suites in the old 1930s block have more character than the newer a/c rooms. Rooms $145, suites $170. ❽

The City

The original settlement of Udaipur grew up around the grand **City Palace**, on the east shore of **Lake Pichola** and bounded to the north by the **old city**'s maze of tightly winding streets. North of here stretches the second of Udaipur's two major lakes, **Fateh Sagar**.

Lake Pichola

Udaipur's idyllic **Lake Pichola** provides the city's most memorable views, a beautiful frame for the City Palace buildings, havelis, *ghat*s, temple towers and other structures which crowd its eastern side – best seen from a boat trip around the lake (see below). The lake's two **island palaces** are among Udaipur's most famous features. **Jag Niwas**, now the *Lake Palace* hotel, was built in amalgamated Rajput–Mughal style as a summer palace during the reign of Jagat Singh (1628–52), after whom it was named. Unfortunately, as a security measure following the 2008 gun attacks in Mumbai, non-guests can no longer visit the hotel. The **Jag Mandir** palace, on the island to the south, is arranged around a large garden guarded by stone elephants. The main building here is the **Gol Mahal**, which has detailed stone inlay work within its domed roof and houses a small exhibition on the history of the island. The young Shah Jahan once stayed here and was apparently so impressed by the building that he used it as one of the models for his own Taj Mahal, though it's difficult to see the resemblance.

Boat rides around the lake depart from the jetty towards the south end of the City Palace complex, offering unforgettable views of the various palaces. Choose between a quick thirty-minute circuit of the lake (Rs200) or the same trip with an additional stop at the Jag Mandir (Rs300). Both tours depart hourly on the hour from 10am to 6pm. To make the most of them, sit on the side of the boat facing the palace (they usually run anticlockwise around the lake). You can also hire your own boat (seating up to seven people) here for Rs3000. Alternatively, on the waterfront betweeen the *Jaiwana* and *Kankarwa* havelis, you can rent pedalos (two-seater Rs125/30min) or motorboats (from Rs700/30min), or take a sunset jaunt around the lake (Rs200/person).

City Palace museum

Udaipur's fascinating **City Palace** stands moulded in soft yellow stone on the northeast side of Lake Pichola, its thick windowless base crowned with ornate turrets and cupolas. The largest royal complex in Rajasthan, it is made up of eleven different *mahals* (palaces) constructed by successive rulers over a period of three hundred years. Part of the palace is now a **museum** (daily 9.30am–4.30pm; Rs50, camera Rs200, video Rs200, audioguide Rs250, guides Rs150 for up to five people). Narrow low-roofed passages connect the different *mahals* and courtyards, creating a confusing, labyrinthine layout designed to prevent surprise intrusion by armed enemies – fortunately visitors are directed around a clearly signed one-way circuit, so your chances of getting lost are limited.

The entrance to the museum is on the far side of the **Moti Chowk** courtyard (look out for the large portable tiger trap in the middle of the courtyard), past the

> Note that to reach certain parts of the City Palace, including the *Fateh Prakash Palace* and *Shiv Niwas* hotels, the Durbar Hall, Crystal Gallery and the jetty for boats around Lake Pichola and over to the *Lake Palace* hotel, you'll have to fork out Rs25 for a **general entrance ticket** to the City Palace complex. You don't have to buy this ticket if you're just visiting the City Palace Museum or the courtyard outside, or if you're actually staying at any of the three hotels.

palace's small **armoury**. Go in, past propitious statues of Ganesh and Lakshmi, and head upstairs to reach the first of the palace's myriad courtyards, the **Rajya Angan**. A room off to one side is devoted to the exploits of Pratap Singh, one of Udaipur's most famous military leaders. From here, steps lead up to pleasantly sylvan **Badi Mahal** (Garden Palace; also known as Amar Vilas after its creator, Amar Singh II, reigned 1695–1755), its main courtyard embellished with finely carved pillars and a marble pool and dotted with trees which flourish despite being built some 30m above ground level.

From the Badi Mahal, twisting steps lead down to the **Dilkushal Mahal**, whose rooms house a superb selection of paintings depicting festive events in the life of the Udaipur court and portraits of the maharanas, as well as the superb **Kanch ki Burj**, a tiny little chamber walled with red zigzag mirrors. Immediately past here, the courtyard of the **Madan Vilas** (built by Bhim Singh, reigned 1778–1828) offers fine lake and city views; the lakeside wall is decorated with quaint inlaid mirrorwork pictures.

Stairs lead down to the **Moti Mahal** (Pearl Palace), another oddly futuristic-looking little mirrored chamber, its walls entirely covered in plain mirrors, the only colour supplied by its stained-glass windows. Steps lead around the top of the Mor Chowk courtyard (see below) to the **Pitam Niwas** (built by Jagat Singh II, reigned 1734–1790) and down to the small **Surya Choupad**, dominated by a striking image showing a kingly-looking Rajput face enclosed by a huge golden halo – a reference to the belief that the rulers of the house of Mewar are descended from the sun.

Next to here, the wall of the fine **Mor Chowk** courtyard is embellished with one of the palace's most flamboyant artworks, a trio of superb mosaic peacocks (*mor*), commissioned by Sajjan Singh in 1874, each made from around five thousand pieces of glass and coloured stone. On the other side of the courtyard is the opulent little **Manek Mahal** (Ruby Palace), its walls mirrored in rich reds and greens.

From here a long corridor winds past the kitsch apartments of queen mother Shri Gulabkunwar (1928–73) and through the **Zenana Mahal** (Women's Palace), whose long sequence of rooms now houses a huge array of paintings depicting royal fun and frolics in Mewar. Continue onwards to emerge, finally, into the last and largest of the palace's courtyards, **Lakshmi Chowk**, the centrepiece of the Zenana Mahal. The exit is at the far end.

The rest of the City Palace complex

The small **Government Museum** (daily 10am–4.30pm; Rs10; closed for refurbishment at last check), opposite the entrance to the City Palace Museum, is mainly of interest for its impressive sculpture gallery of pieces from Kumbalgarh, including some outstanding works in black marble. More interesting in many ways – and certainly far more atmospheric – is the vast **Durbar Hall** in the Fateh Prakash Palace (the building immediately behind the main City Palace building which now houses the *Fateh Prakash Palace* hotel). This huge, wonderfully time-warped Edwardian-era ballroom was built to host state banquets, royal functions and the like, and remains full of period character, complete with huge chandeliers, creaky old furniture and fusty portraits. You can have afternoon tea here as part of a visit to *The Gallery* café (see p.222). In a gallery overlooking the hall is the eccentric **Crystal Gallery** (daily 9am–6.30pm; Rs525), housing an array of fine British crystal ordered by Sajjan Singh in the 1880s and featuring outlandishly kitsch items including crystal chairs, tables and lamps – there's even a crystal hookah and a crystal bed. The extortionate entrance charge is a bit of a turn-off, though it does include a free audioguide and also gets you a drink at *The Gallery* café.

Jagdish Temple

Just north of the City Palace, **Jagdish Temple** is one of Udaipur's most popular and vibrant shrines. Built in 1652 and dedicated to Lord Jagannath, an aspect of Vishnu, its outer walls and towering *shikhara* are heavily carved with figures of Vishnu, scenes from the life of Krishna and dancing *apsaras* (nymphs). The circular *mandapa* leads to the sanctuary where a black stone image of Jagannath sits shrouded in flowers, while a small raised shrine in front of the temple protects a bronze Garuda. Subsidiary shrines to Shiva, Ganesh, Surya and Durga stand at each corner of the main temple.

Bagore-ki-Haveli

North of Jagdish Temple, a lane leads to Gangaur Ghat and the **Bagore-ki-Haveli**, a 138-room lakeside haveli of 1751. A section of the building has been converted into a worthwhile **museum** (daily 10am–5pm; Rs25, camera Rs10, video Rs50), arranged on two floors around one of the rambling haveli's several courtyards. The upper floor has several immaculately restored rooms with original furnishings and artworks, plus some fine murals. The lower floor has rooms full of women's clothes, musical instruments, kitchen equipment and – the undisputed highlight – what is claimed to be the world's largest turban. Traditional **music and dance** shows (Rs60, camera Rs50, video Rs50) are staged here nightly at 7pm.

Bharatiya Lok Kala

Just north of Chetak Circle in the new city, the hoary old **Bharatiya Lok Kala** museum (daily 9am–6pm; Rs35 [Rs20], camera Rs10, video Rs50) is home to a mildly interesting collection of exhibits covering the folk traditions of Rajasthan and India, with dusty displays of colourful masks, puppets and musical instruments. Short, amusing **puppet shows** (tip expected) are staged throughout the day on demand (the performers will probably hunt you down and drag you into the theatre shortly after your arrival), while there's an hour-long show, with music, dancing and more puppets, daily at 6pm (Rs50 [Rs30], camera Rs10, video Rs50).

Sahelion-ki-Bari

Northeast of Moti Magri, **Sahelion-ki-Bari** (daily 8am–7pm; Rs5), the "garden of the maids of honour", was laid out by Sangram Singh (1710–34) as a summer retreat for the diversion and entertainment of the ladies of the royal household – though the fountains weren't installed until the reign of Fateh Singh (1884–1930). The gardens are centred on a peaceful courtyard enclosing a large pool and surrounded by attractive formal walled gardens, at the back of which four elephant statues surround Udaipur's most striking fountain – a fanciful tiered creation which looks a bit like a huge, multi-coloured cake stand.

Shilpgram

Some 5km west of town, the popular rural arts and crafts centre of **Shilpgram** (daily 11am–7pm; Rs30, camera Rs25, video Rs50) was set up to promote the traditional architecture, music and crafts of the tribal people of western India, with displays dedicated to the diverse lifestyles and customs of the region's rural population. Around thirty replica houses and huts in traditional style are arranged in a village-like compound, with examples of buildings from various states. Musicians, puppeteers and dancers – hijras (eunuchs) among them – hang out around the houses and strike up on the approach of visitors (tip expected), while you may also see people weaving, potting and embroidering as they would in their original homes – though most of the actual handicrafts on sale are fifth-rate, if that. Despite its honourable intentions, many tourists find the atmosphere contrived and resent the hustling by musicians and their ilk. Even so, it's well worth a visit if only for the scenic journey out along the road around Fateh Sagar Lake, best done by bicycle. Alternatively, the return journey by auto-rickshaw costs around Rs150 including waiting time.

Sajjangarh

High on a hill 5km west of the city, the so-called "Monsoon Palace", **Sajjangarh**, was begun in 1883 by Maharana Sajjan Singh to serve as a summer retreat, complete with a nine-storey observatory from which the royal family proposed to watch the monsoon clouds travelling across the countryside below. Unfortunately, the maharana's untimely death the following year put paid to the planned observatory, and although the palace itself was finished by Singh's successor, Maharana Fateh Singh, it was found to be impossible to pump water up to it, and the whole place was abandoned shortly afterwards. The large though rather plain building is now a somewhat melancholy sight, but the views over Udaipur, more than 300m below, are unrivalled. The journey up to the palace takes a good fifteen minutes by rickshaw or taxi (around Rs300 for the round-trip); the climb is too steep to tackle comfortably by bicycle, though some people try. The palace is located inside the **Sajjangarh Wildlife Sanctuary** (Rs80 [Rs10], plus Rs25 for an auto-rickshaw or Rs65 for car). It's open daily from 8am, with last entry at 5.30pm, although you can come down after sunset.

Eating, drinking and entertainment

Bagore-ki-Haveli (see p.221) has nightly **dance** performances, while Shilpgram (see p.221) often hosts out-of-town performers. Hour-long displays of traditional Rajasthani **folk dances** are staged at the Meera Kala Mandir, Meera Bhawan, Sector 11, on the Ahmedabad Road (Mon–Sat 7pm; Rs60; ⓣ0294/258 3176); call ahead for tickets. Many of Udaipur's tourist cafés screen the James Bond movie *Octopussy*, with its manic boat and auto-rickshaw chases round the city's landmarks, every evening at 7pm.

Restaurants and cafés

Ambrai *Amet Haveli*, Chand Pole. In a superlative setting facing the City Palace, this is one of the few lakeside restaurants where the cooking lives up to its location. The menu features an extensive selection of north Indian veg and non-veg dishes (including top-notch tandooris), as well as a few Chinese and European offerings. Or just come for a sundowner and watch the sun set over the lake. Non-veg mains Rs165–210.

Edelweiss 71 Gangaur Ghat Marg, next to *Gangaur Palace*. Excellent hole-in-the-wall bakery and pastry shop that receives a steady stream of customers thanks to its tasty home-baked apple pie, chocolate cake and fresh ground coffee.

The Gallery City Palace. Buried away in the innards of the *Fateh Prakash Palace* hotel (just finding it is half the fun), this is Udaipur's most memorable spot for a classic English-style high tea (daily 3–6pm), served either on a sunny terrace overlooking the lake or in the grandiose Durbar Hall (see p.220). Cream teas cost Rs325, or just come for a tea or coffee.

Jagat Niwas 23–25 Lalghat. Popular restaurant in the hotel of the same name, serving up well-prepared north Indian standards (non-veg mains Rs170–235), with nice views over the lake from its comfy window seats and discreet live sitar music.

Kankarwa Haveli 26 Lalghat. The low-key rooftop restaurant at this excellent hotel offers a welcome alternative to your average tourist menu, with a choice of three thalis (Rs200–450) featuring authentic and delicious home-cooked dishes like sweet aubergine and pumpkin curries. Cold beer and panoramic lake views complete the ambience.

Natraj New Bapu Bazaar (behind Town Hall Road's Ashok Cinema). Udaipur's top thali joint for over twenty years, but well off the tourist trail and fiendishly hard to find (from Suraj Pol gate, head north up Bapu Bazaar, turn right after 30m, then left, and it's 20m up on your right). Easily the best cheap meal in town – just Rs60 for unlimited portions of veg curries, soups, dhal, curd and chapattis.

Queen Café Chand Pol. This homely and unpretentious little café offers a refreshing alternative to Udaipur's mainstream tourist restaurants, with an authentic taste of home-style vegetarian Indian cooking including coconut-flavoured banana, mango and pumpkin curries – all at giveaway prices, with most mains at Rs55–60.

Savage Garden Chand Pol. Stylish restaurant set in an old haveli given a funky modern makeover, with loads of blue and white paint and minimalist decor. Food is Middle Eastern and European, with slight gourmet pretensions, and the menu is short but well chosen. Pasta Rs150–180, mains Rs160–550.

The Whistling Teal *Raj Palace* hotel, 103 Bhattiyani Chohatta. Attractive, tented garden restaurant serving well-prepared north Indian and Rajasthani veg and non-veg dishes from around Rs125 veg, Rs225 non-veg – pricier than average, but worth it. There are also hookah pipes with fruit-flavoured tobacco (Rs250), plus good coffee.

Listings

Airlines Indian Airlines, Sahelion-ki-Bari Rd ⓣ0294/241 0999; Jet Airways, airport ⓣ0294/265 6288; Kingfisher Airlines, Chetak Circle ⓣ0294/510 2468.

Banks and exchange There are ATMs all over the new city, plus a particularly handy 24hr machine on the street leading to the City Palace. Lots of places around Jagdish Temple offer forex. Mewar International (daily 9am–11pm), on Lalghat, changes cash and all brands of travellers' cheques, as well as giving cash advances on Visa and MasterCard. Thomas Cook on Lake Palace Rd (Mon–Sat 9am–6pm) changes cash and travellers' cheques.

Bicycle and motorbike rental Heera Cycle Store at 86 Gangaur Ghat Marg near Jagdish Temple (ⓣ0294/513 0625; daily 7.30am–9pm), rents out basic bicycles for Rs50/day, and mountain bikes for Rs100/day. They also have mopeds (Rs200/day), Vespas (Rs350/day) and Enfields (Rs450/day); you'll need to bring your passport and leave a hard-currency deposit.

Bookshops Mewar International, on Lalghat behind the Jagdish Temple, has new and second-hand books. Mayur Book Paradise, on another branch of the same alley, is particularly good for secondhand titles, and OK, a few doors away, isn't bad either. All three sometimes buy or exchange used books.

Cooking lessons Available at numerous places around town. Good options include the *Panorama Guest House* (see p.218; Rs500 for 3hr classes) or, more expensive, the homely little *Queen Café* (see above; Rs900 for 3hr).

Horseriding Various places around town offer horseriding expeditions into the surrounding countryside. The reputable *Hotel Kumbha Palace* (see p.217; ⓦwww.krishnaranch.da.ru) runs half- and full-day excursions (Rs950/Rs1800), as well as longer trips. Princess Trails (ⓣ0294/309 6909, ⓦwww.princesstrails.com) specializes in more extended, 4- to 8-day safaris on thoroughbred Mewari mounts.

Hospital Aravalli Hospital (private), 332 Ambamata Rd ⓣ0294/243 0222.

Internet access Dozens of places around Lalghat and Gangaur Ghat (going rate currently Rs30/hr). Try Mewar International, on Lalghat near the Jagdish Temple, or the cybercafé on the ground floor of *Udai Niwas* hotel.

Music The enthusiastic Rajesh Prajapat at the Prem Musical Instrument shop (ⓣ0294/243 0599), opposite the *Gangaur Palace* hotel, offers sitar and tabla lessons (Rs350 for 90min) and can also arrange flute lessons with his brother, or musical appreciation classes if you just want to learn more about Indian music.

Painting lessons Lessons in traditional Indian painting are offered by many places around town; the *Gangaur Palace* guesthouse is a reliable option (Rs100/hr).

Palm readings The resident palmist at the *Gangaur Palace* guesthouse charges Rs300 for a 20min reading.

Photography Mewar International, on Lalghat behind the Jagdish Temple, burn CDs and DVDs, sell memory cards and have equipment to download photos from most types of digital cameras; they also offer back-up and photo recovery from defective memory cards.

Post office Parcels are best sent from the GPO at Chetak Circle (Mon–Sat 10am–4pm).

Shopping Udaipur is one of Rajasthan's top shopping destinations, with an eclectic array of local artisanal specialities along with other crafts from across the state. The city's particular speciality is miniature painting, with numerous shops selling traditional Mewari-style works on paper and silk. Many places also do a good line in leather- and cloth-bound stationery using handmade paper. Udaipur is well known for its silver jewellery – Jagdish St, Bara Bazaar and Moti Chohatta, around the clock tower, are home to lots of shops. For bookshops, see p.223.

Travel agents Virtually every shop and guesthouse around the Jagdish Temple seems to offer bus and rail ticketing. Reliable agents include Mewar International, on Lalghat behind the Jagdish Temple; Gangaur Tour 'n' Travels, close by on Gangaur Ghat Marg; and the travel agency inside the *Udai Niwas* hotel.

Volunteer work The Animal Aid Society, Badi Village, across from T.B. Hospital, Main Rd ⓣ0294 2513359; ⓦwww.animalaidunlimited.com, run by a friendly American expat couple, maintains a pet hospital where volunteers and visitors are encouraged and no special skills are required – just a willingness to work with animals, usually including street dogs, cows, donkeys, cats and monkeys.

Yoga Ashtanga Yoga Ashram (aka "Raiba House"), Chand Pol (ⓣ0294/252 4872). Daily 90min hatha yoga classes for all standards at 8.30am. Free, but donations appreciated – proceeds go to a local animal charity. Individual lessons also available.

Around Udaipur

North of the city are the historic temples of **Nagda**, **Eklingji**, **Nathdwara** and **Kankroli**, while to the northwest, en route to Jodhpur, lie the superb Jain temples of **Ranakpur** and the rambling fort at **Kumbalgarh**. Renting a car or motorcycle saves time, though local buses serve both routes.

Nagda and Eklingji

Dating back to 626 AD, the ragged remnants of the ancient capital of Mewar, **NAGDA**, stand next to a lake 20km northeast of Udaipur. Buses from Udaipur travelling north along the main road to Eklingji set passengers down at the turn-off for Nagda, next to a small bicycle shop (bike rental Rs5/hr). Nagda itself is a further 5km away down this side-road. Most of the buildings here were either destroyed by the Mughals or submerged by the lake, which has expanded naturally over the centuries. All that survives is a fine pair of tenth-century Vaishnavite temples known as **Saas-Bahu** – literally "mother-in-law" and "daughter-in-law". The more impressive mother-in-law temple has lost its *shikhara* (tower) but preserves a wealth of carving inside, while within the *mandapa*, a marriage area is marked by four ornate pillars, bearing images of the gods Brahma, Vishnu, Shiva and Surya to which couples are supposed to pay homage.

Returning to the main road, you can continue to **EKLINGJI** via the road or along a path that leads behind the old protective walls and downhill. Ask for directions at the bike shop. The god **Eklingji**, a manifestation of Shiva, has been the protective deity of the rulers of Mewar ever since the eighth century, when Bappa Rawal was bestowed with the title *darwan* (servant) of Eklingji by his guru. To this day, the maharana of Udaipur still visits the 108-temple complex every Monday evening (the day traditionally celebrated all over India as being sacred to Shiva) and the whole place is usually lively with local pilgrims seeking his blessings. The milky-white marble main temple (daily 10.30am–1.30pm & 5–7.30pm) is crowned by an elaborate two-storey *mandapa* guarded by stone elephants; inside, a four-faced black marble lingam marks the precise spot where Bappa Rawal received his accolade. Frequent **buses** leave for Eklingji from Udaipur's main bus stand, dropping passengers off close to the temple.

Nathdwara

The temple dedicated to Krishna – known also as **Nath**, the favourite avatar (incarnation) of Vishnu – at **NATHDWARA**, "Gateway to God", is one of the richest temples in India, and gets incredibly crowded during major religious festivals. It dates from the seventeenth century when a chariot laden with an image of Krishna – being carried from Mathura to Udaipur to save it from destruction by Aurangzeb – became stuck in the mud here. Its bearers interpreted the event as a divine sign, establishing the new **Shri Nathji Temple** where it had stopped.

The temple lies about 1km south of the town's bus stop, surrounded by a fascinating tangle of narrow streets where stalls display incense, perfumes and small Krishna statues. The temple opens for worship eight times daily, when the image is woken, dressed, washed, fed and put to bed. Don't miss the radiant *pichwai* paintings in the main sanctuary, made of hand-spun cloth and coloured with strong vegetable pigments. You could also ask a guide to show you the "footsteps of Krishna", a process that requires rubbing rose petals on the marble floor. Nathdwara is on NH-8, and sees a constant flow of buses en route north and south.

Ranakpur

Some 90km north of Udaipur, the spectacular **Jain temples** at **RANAKPUR** boast marblework on a par with that of the more famous Dilwara shrines at Mount Abu (see p.230). The temples are hidden away in a beautiful wooded valley, deep in the Aravalli Hills, that was originally gifted to the Jain community in the fifteenth century by Rana Kumbha, the Hindu ruler of Mewar.

Arrival and information

Ranakpur is a bumpy **bus** ride from Udaipur (6 daily; 3hr), or from Jodhpur (6 daily; 4–5hr) via the market town of Falna (the nearest railway station) on the NH-14; there are also two daily buses to Abu Road (5–6hr). Buses stop right outside the Jain temples, which are 2–4km from the hotels; if you're lucky, you might find an auto or jeep at the bus stop – if not you'll have to ring your hotel and ask to be picked up, or (worst-case scenario) walk.

Ranakpur can also be visited as a day-trip from Udaipur, either on its own or in combination with nearby Kumbalgarh; count on around Rs1200 for the round trip by **car**. If you're intending to visit Kumbalgarh as well, though, think about **trekking** between the two sites, a beautiful hike through an unspoilt section of the Aravalli Hills. As Kumbalgarh is on the top of the range, it's much easier to hike from there down to Ranakpur (for more on this route see p.226), but guides may be arranged at the hotels listed below for the six-hour uphill climb in the other direction.

Accommodation and eating

You can stay with the Jain pilgrims at the temple complex for a Rs10 donation, but don't expect anything more than a mattress on a cold, cement floor. Other **accommodation** in Ranakpur is relatively expensive. There are no restaurants outside the hotels and guesthouses, and virtually everyone **eats** where they are staying.

Aranyawas 11km from Ranakpur on the Kumbalgarh road ⓣ02956/239029, ⓦwww.aranyawas.com. Small jungle lodge with rustically elegant rooms and cottages overlooking a watering hole sometimes frequented by leopards – an ideal place to recharge your batteries in complete isolation. Breakfast included. ❼

Fateh Bagh 4km south of the temples ⓣ02934/286186, ⓦwww.hrhindia.com. Ranakpur's best accommodation, a 200-year-old palace transported piece by piece for 50km, and rebuilt here. Rooms are comfy and characterful, and facilities include a pool, spa and Ayurveda centre. Rooms from $148. ❽

Maharani Bagh Orchard 3.5km south of the temples ⓣ02934/285105, ⓦwww.jodhanaheritage.com. Pleasantly low-key resort, with attractively furnished rooms (all a/c) in red-brick cottages around rambling gardens. There's also a pool. ❽

Ranakpur Hill Resort 3km south of the temples ⓣ02934/286411, ⓦwww.ranakpurhillresort.com. Chintzy pink little resort with a range of rooms (air-cooled and a/c) of varying standards, and some less appealing tents (available Oct–March only; ❻). Also has a decent-size pool and a small Ayurveda centre, and can arrange half-day horse safaris. Rooms ❺–❻

Shivika Lake Hotel 2km south of the temples ⓣ02934/285078 or ⓣ9929 918419, ⓦwww.shivikalakehotel.com. The only real budget option in Ranakpur, although the cheaper rooms are disappointingly basic given the price; the more expensive rooms (some with a/c) are relatively better value. Local treks (Rs350pp) and jeep safaris (Rs650pp) can be arranged here. ❸–❹

The temples

The **main temple** (noon–5pm; free, camera or mobile with camera Rs50, video Rs100) was built in 1439 according to a strict system of measurement based on the number 72 (the age at which the founder of Jainism, Mahavira, achieved nirvana). The entire temple sits on a pedestal measuring 72 yards square and is held up by 1440 (72 x 20) individually carved pillars. Inside, there are 72 elaborately carved shrines, some octagonal in shape, along with the main deity (a 72-inch-tall image of the four-faced Adinath, the first *tirthankara*) encased in the central sanctum. The carving on the walls, columns and the domed ceilings is superb. Friezes depicting the life of the *tirthankara* are etched into the walls, while musicians and dancers have been modelled out of brackets between the pillars and the ceiling.

Three smaller temples nestle among the trees in the enclosure in front of the main temple. The most impressive is the **Parshwanath Temple**, around 100m from the main temple, with a small but finely carved shrine, while a further 100m walk brings you to the simpler **Neminath Temple**. Close by (a short walk across the car park) is a contemporary Hindu temple dedicated to **Surya**.

Kumbalgarh

The remote hilltop fort of **KUMBALGARH** (daily 8am–5.30pm; Rs100 [Rs5]), 80km north of Udaipur, is the most formidable of the 32 constructed or restored by Rana Kumbha of Chittaurgarh in the fifteenth century. Protected by a series of monumental walls and bastions, it was only successfully besieged once, when a confederacy led by Akbar poisoned the water supply. Aside from the fort itself, Kumbalgarh is worth a visit to experience the idyllic Aravalli countryside, dotted with tribal villages, and magnificent views.

The most memorable panorama of all is from the pinnacle of the rather plain **palace** building, crowning the summit of the fort, with striking bird's-eye views over the numerous Jain and Hindu **temples** clustered around the main gate and scattered over the hills below. The oldest are thought to date from the second century; the **tombs** of the great Rana Kumbha himself (murdered by his eldest son) and his grandson Prithviraj (poisoned by his brother-in-law) stand to the east. Some 36km of crenellated ramparts wind around the rim of the hilltop, and it's possible to walk around them in two comfortable days, sleeping rough midway around. You won't need a guide, but be sure to take food and water.

Lining the deep valley that plunges west from the fort down to the plains, the **Kumbalgarh Wildlife Sanctuary** comprises a dense area of woodland that offers a refuge for wolves and leopards. With a local guide, you can trek through it to Ranakpur, a rewarding and easy hike of between four and five hours (the alternative is a long journey on an infrequent country bus). Entry **permits** (Rs80 [Rs10], camera Rs200) are obtainable from the District Forest Officer at **Kelwara**, 7km down the road, though local guides – contactable through the hotels listed opposite, or at local shops, or at the café just inside the fort gates – can obtain permits for you, and will charge around Rs600–1000 to do the walk with you, or Rs1500 including entry fees to go round in a jeep.

Practicalities

Kumbalgarh and Ranakpur can easily be visited as a (longish) day-trip from Udaipur (around Rs1200 for the round-trip by taxi for up to four people). Otherwise, take a shared jeep from Chetak Circle to **Kelwara**, 7km down the road, from where you should be able to pick up a jeep or rickshaw to Kumbalgarh. There's no budget **accommodation** in Kumbalgarh, but 1km below the fort there's the *Aodhi* (Ⓣ02954/242341, Ⓦwww.eternalmewar.in; ❽), a peaceful and welcoming heritage hotel with stylishly furnished rooms, a big pool and jeep safaris to local villages (2hr, Rs1550); and the *Kumbhal Castle* (Ⓣ02954/242171, Ⓦwww.thekumbhalcastle.com; ❺–❻), a pleasant modern hotel with spacious rooms and a pool, where you can also arrange jeep and car hire. 5km down the Kelwara road *Club Mahindra Fort Kumbalgarh* (Ⓣ02954/242171, Ⓦwww.the kumbhalcastle.com; ❽) is a modern upmarket hotel, recently renovated, with superb views from its pool and garden terrace.

Mount Abu

Rajasthan's only bona-fide hill station, **MOUNT ABU** (1220m) is a major Indian resort, popular above all with honeymooners who flock here during the winter wedding season (Nov to March) and with visiting holiday-makers from nearby Gujarat. Mount Abu's hokey commercialism is aimed squarely at these local vacationers rather than foreign tourists, but the sight of lovestruck honeymooners shyly holding hands and jolly parties of Gujarati tourists on the loose lends the whole place a charmingly idiosyncratic holiday atmosphere quite unlike anywhere else in Rajasthan – and the fresh air is exhilarating after the heat of the desert plains. The town also occupies an important place in Rajput history, being the site of the famous *yagna agnikund* fire ceremony, conducted in the eighth century AD, from which all Rajputs claim mythological descent.

Note that during the peak months of April to June, and at almost any major festival time (especially Diwali in Nov) the town's population of thirty thousand mushrooms, room rates skyrocket, and peace and quiet are at a premium.

Arrival and information

Mount Abu is accessible only by road. The nearest railhead is at **Abu Road**, from where buses make the 45-minute ascent up to Mount Abu itself. Entering Mount Abu, you have to pay a Rs10 fee (plus Rs10 for a car or jeep).

The **tourist office** (Mon–Sat 10am–1.30pm & 2–5pm) is opposite the main bus stand; there's also information online at Ⓦwww.mountabu.com. To **change travellers' cheques** the best bet is the Union Bank of India, hidden away in the bazaar near the **post office**. The State Bank of India has an **ATM** in front of the tourist office, and there are two more between there and the polo ground. For **internet** access, the Yani-Ya Cyber Zone, just south of the post office, or the Shree Krishna Cybercafe in the lane just behind it, charge Rs30/hr. *Shri Ganesh* guest-house runs jeep **tours** (Rs400 for the vehicle for a half-day trip) out to places like Achalgarh and Guru Shikar.

Accommodation

The steady stream of pilgrims and honeymoon couples ensures that Mount Abu has plenty of **hotels**, lots of them offering luxuries for newlyweds in special "couple rooms". Check-out time in most places is a chippy 9am. Prices rocket in

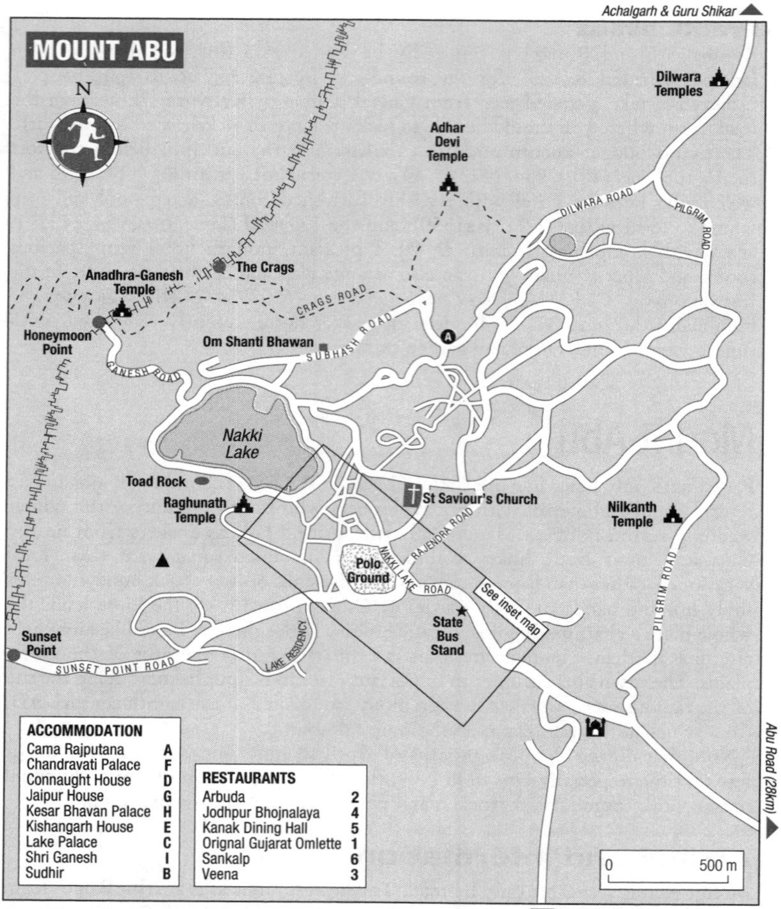

Achalgarh & Guru Shikar

MOUNT ABU

N

Dilwara Temples
Adhar Devi Temple
Dilwara Road
Pilgrim Road
The Crags
Anadhra-Ganesh Temple
Crags Road
Subhash Road
Honeymoon Point
Om Shanti Bhawan
Ganesh Road
Nakki Lake
Toad Rock
Raghunath Temple
St Saviour's Church
Rajendra Road
Nilkanth Temple
Polo Ground
Nakki Lake Road
See inset map
State Bus Stand
Sunset Point
Sunset Point Road
Lake Residency
Abu Road (28km)
0 500 m
Gaumukh Temple

ACCOMMODATION	
Cama Rajputana	A
Chandravati Palace	F
Connaught House	D
Jaipur House	G
Kesar Bhavan Palace	H
Kishangarh House	E
Lake Palace	C
Shri Ganesh	I
Sudhir	B

RESTAURANTS	
Arbuda	2
Jodhpur Bhojnalaya	4
Kanak Dining Hall	5
Orignal Gujarat Omlette	1
Sankalp	6
Veena	3

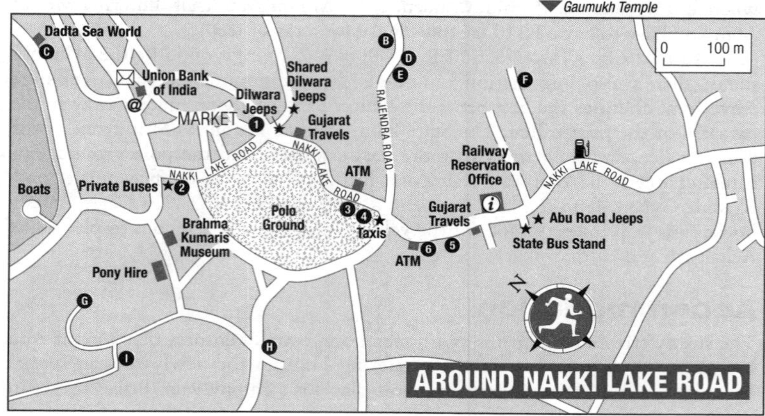

Moving on from Mount Abu

Government buses run from the State Bus Stand on Nakki Lake Road. **Private buses** are run by a string of operators along Nakki Lake Road west of the State Bus Stand (Gujarat Travels is a reliable option). There are currently private services to Ajmer (1 nightly; 7hr), Ahmedabad (3 daily; 6hr), Jaipur (1 nightly; 11hr), Jodhpur (1 daily; 6hr) and Udaipur (3 daily; 5hr).

There's a computerized **train booking office** (daily 8am–2pm) upstairs at the tourist office. Buses leave Mount Abu for **Abu Road**, the nearest railhead, every hour until 9pm; jeeps leave when full (from next to the bus stand), and taxis can be hired at the corner by the *Jodhpur Bhojnalaya* restaurant for Rs300.

Recommended trains from Abu Road

The trains below are recommended as the fastest and/or most convenient daily services.

Destination	Name	No.	Departs	Arrives
Ahmedabad	*Ahmedabad Express*	9224	11am (daily)	3.30pm
	Ahmedabad Mail	9106	12.47pm (daily)	6.40pm
Ajmer	*Aravali Express*	9707	10.10am (daily)	4.05pm
	Haridwar Mail	9105	2.15pm (daily)	8.20pm
Delhi	*Rajdhani Express*	2957	8.33pm (daily)	7.25am
	Ashram Express	2915	9.13pm (daily)	10.10am
Jaipur	*Aravali Express*	9707	10.10am (daily)	6.40pm
	Haridwar Mail	9105	2.15pm (daily)	10.40pm
Jodhpur	*Jammu Tawi Express*	9223	3.20pm (daily)	8pm
Mumbai	*Aravali Express*	9708	5.20pm (daily)	6.45am
	Surya Nagri Express	2479	11.07pm (daily)	11.45am

high season (April–June & Nov–Dec), reaching their peak during Diwali. The price codes given below are for high season.

Cama Rajputana Adhar Devi Rd ⓣ02974/238205, ⓦwww.camahotelsindia.com. Attractive resort-style place occupying a neatly refurbished colonial building in sprawling grounds. Rooms (all a/c) are cool and spacious, while the extensive facilities include a gym, massage centre and a big pool (guests only). Popular with tour groups. Double rooms from $400. ❾

Chandravati Palace 9 Janta Colony ⓣ02974/238219. Excellent and very good-value little guesthouse on a quiet side-road. The small, bright modern rooms are impeccably maintained and have good-sized balconies and hill views. ❶

Connaught House Rajendra Rd ⓣ02974/238560, ⓦwww.jodhanaheritage.com. Mount Abu's most memorable accommodation option, occupying a time-warped colonial-era retreat set in a flower-filled garden with sweeping views. Rooms (all a/c) in the old house are beautifully preserved, with period furniture and decor; those in the modern block on the hill above are much less atmospheric. ❼

Jaipur House South of the lake ⓣ02974/235176, ⓦwww.royalfamilyjaipur.com. A fine old summer palace perched on a hilltop above town, with some of the town's best accommodation in tastefully decorated suites with wooden furnishings – although the "deluxe" rooms, in an ugly modern block halfway down the drive, are dull and overpriced. ❻

Kesar Bhavan Palace Sunset Rd ⓣ02974/238647, ⓦwww.kesarpalace.com. Functional modern hotel rather than the promised "palace", though rooms (some with a/c) are pleasantly spacious and sunny, with views over the treetops from large individual verandas. The rooms in the new annexe (same price) are darker and less appealing. ❻–❼

Kishangarh House Rajendra Rd ⓣ02974/238092, ⓦwww.royalkishangarh.com. Not as memorable as the neighbouring *Connaught House*, but still offering a modest helping of colonial-era charm. Accommodation is in neatly furnished rooms (mostly a/c) in the old building itself, or in cheaper but fairly characterless "cottage" rooms in a new block outside. ❻–❼

Lake Palace Nakki Lake Rd ⓣ02974/237154, ⓦwww.savshantihotels.com. One of the town's best mid-range options, in a scenic position facing Nakki Lake, with good service and a range of well-maintained modern rooms (all a/c, the more expensive ones with lake view and balcony). ❺–❻

Shri Ganesh Southwest of the polo ground, near Sophia High School ⓣ02974/237292, ⓔlalit_ganesh@yahoo.co.in. Easily the best budget hotel in town, and the only one geared towards foreign backpackers. There are plenty of simple, clean rooms (some attached, some with very hard beds) plus dorm beds (Rs60–100/person), plus Indian cooking lessons (Rs200), guided walks, jeep tours (see p.227), reliable internet access, and free pick-up from bus stand. ❶–❷

Sudhir Opposite *Connaught House*, Rajendra Rd ⓣ02974/235120, ⓔhotelsudhir@gmail.com. Functional modern hotel with bright and spacious rooms: choose between the rather bare "semi-deluxe" and the significantly nicer "deluxe" categories. ❻–❼

The town and around

At the centre of town, **Nakki Lake** is popular in the late afternoon for pony and pedalo rides. Of several panoramic viewpoints on the fringes of town above the plains, **Sunset Point** is the favourite – though the hordes of holiday-makers and hawkers also make it one of the noisiest and least romantic. **Honeymoon Point**, also known as Ganesh Point (after the adjacent temple), and **Anadhra Point** offer breathtaking views over the plain at any time of day, and tend to be more peaceful. 4pm is a good time to visit, but don't try to take clifftop paths between Sunset and Honeymoon points, as tourists have been mugged here.

The **Brahma Kumaris Museum** (daily 8am–8pm; free), between the polo ground and the lake, is devoted to the spiritual ideals of the Brahma Kumaris ("children of Brahma"), whose headquarters are situated nearby. The Brahma Kumaris preach that all religions reach for the same goal, but label it differently. Once through the "Gateway to Paradise," you'll be greeted by freakish, life-sized mannequins including blue monsters wielding long knives. Each personifies greed, sex-lust and other vestiges of the so-called "iron age" that temple leaders promise deliverance from. If it all sounds somewhat cultish you'll understand why many locals try to keep foreigners from entering into the sect's clutches.

Dilwara temples

The **Dilwara temples** (daily noon–6pm; free, but donation requested; no photography, usual Jain temple restrictions apply), 3km northeast of Mount Abu,

Hiking in Mount Abu

Down in Mount Abu's market area, you gain little sense of the wonderfully wild **landscape** enfolding the town, but head for a few minutes up one of the many trails threading around the sides of the plateau, and it's easy to see why the area has inspired sages, saints and pilgrims for centuries. Unfortunately **hiking alone** is not recommended, as there have been robberies and even murders of unaccompanied visitors, and police will turn back anyone spotted heading out alone. There's also a chance of running into bears and leopards – bears, in particular, can be dangerous if surprised, or when with young.

Two good local **guides** are Lalit Kanojia at the *Shri Ganesh* hotel, who leads 5hr treks every morning (Rs100/person); and Mahendra Dan, better known as "Charles" (ⓦwww.mount-abu-treks.blogspot.com), who runs a range of half-day (from Rs380) and full-day (from Rs610) walking tours focusing on village life, wildlife spotting and local Ayurvedic plants, as well as overnight camping expeditions. He can be contacted via the *Lake Palace* hotel or on ⓣ9414 154854, or emailed on ⓔmahendradan@yahoomail.co.in.

are some of the most beautiful Jain shrines in India. All five are made purely from marble, and the carving is breathtakingly intricate. Entrance to the temples is by guided tour only – you'll have to wait until sufficient people have arrived to make up a group – though once inside it's easy enough to break away and look around on your own.

The oldest temple, the **Vimala Vasahi**, named after the Gujarati minister who funded its construction in 1031, is dedicated to Adinath, the first *tirthankara*. Although the exterior is simple – as, indeed, are the exteriors of all the temples here – inside not one wall, column or ceiling is unadorned, a prodigious feat of artistry which took almost two thousand labourers and sculptors fourteen years to complete. There are forty-eight intricately carved pillars inside, eight of them supporting a domed ceiling arranged in eleven concentric circles alive with dancers, musicians, elephants and horses, while a sequence of 57 subsidiary shrines run around the edge of the enclosure. In front of the entrance to the temple the so-called "Elephant Cell" (added after the construction of the temple itself in 1147) contains ten impressively large stone pachyderms. A more modest pair of painted elephants, along with an unusual carving showing stacked-up tiers of *tirthankaras*, flanks the entrance to the diminutive **Mahaveerswami Temple**, built in 1582, which sits by the entrance to the Vimala Vasahi.

The **Luna Vasahi Temple**, second of Dilwara's two great temples, was built in 1231, and is dedicated to Neminath, the 22nd *tirthankara*. It follows a similar plan to the Vimala Vasahi, with a central shrine fronted by a minutely carved dome and surrounded by a long sequence of shrines (a mere 48 this time). The carvings, however, are even more precise and detailed, especially so in the magnificently intricate dome covering the entrance hall.

The remaining two temples, both fifteenth-century, are less spectacular. The **Bhimasah Pittalhar Temple** houses a huge gilded image of the first *tirthankara*, Adinath, installed in 1468, which measures over eight feet high and weighs in at around 4.5 tons. The large three-storey **Khartar Vasahi Temple** (near the entrance to the temples) was built in 1458 and is consecrated to Parshvanath. The temple is topped by a high grey stone tower and boasts some intricate carving in places, though overall it's only a pale shadow of the earlier temples

To **get to Dilwara**, you can charter a jeep (Rs50 one way or Rs150 return) from the junction at the north end of the polo ground, or take a place in a shared one (Rs5) from just up the street. The hour-long walk up there is also pleasant, though many prefer to save their energy for the downhill walk back into town.

Hindu temples

On the north side of town, en route to the Dilwara temples, a flight of more than four hundred steps climbs up to the **Adhar Devi Temple** (dedicated to Durga). The small main shrine is cut into the rocky hilltop and entered by clambering under a very low overhang. There are fine views from the terrace above, where there's another tiny shrine cut out of solid rock. The milk-coloured water of the **Doodh Baori** well at the foot of the steps is considered to be a source of pure milk (*doodh*) for gods and sages.

A further 8km northeast (not served by public transport, so you'd need to hire a jeep or a taxi), the temple complex at **ACHALGARH** is dominated by the **Achaleshwar Mahadeo Temple**, believed to have been created when Lord Shiva placed his toe on the spot to still an earthquake. Its sanctuary holds a yoni with a hole in it that is said to reach into the netherworld. Nearby, the **Jamadagni Ashram** is site of the *yagna agnikund*, where the sage Vashishtha presided over the fire ritual that produced the four Rajput clans (the Parmars, Parihars, Solankis and Chauhans).

The lesser visited, but more dramatically situated, **Gaumukh Temple** lies 7km south of the market area and is also not served by public transport, so you'll have to hire a jeep or taxi. Standing at the head of a steep flight of 750 steps, the small pool inside the shrine – which continues to flow even during times of drought – is believed to hold water from the sacred Sarawati Ganga River. Pilgrims come here to perform puja, to invoke the blessings of India's two greatest *rishis* (sages), Vashishtha and Vishwamitra, who are thought to have meditated and debated here.

The last important Hindu pilgrimage site on Mount Abu is the Atri Rishi Temple at **Guru Shikar**, 15km northeast of town, which at 1772m above sea level marks the highest point in Rajasthan. You can enjoy superb panoramic vistas either from the temple itself, or from the drinks stall at the bottom of the steps leading up to it. There's no public transport there, however, so you'll have to hire a jeep (around Rs400).

Eating and drinking

Mount Abu's predominantly middle-class Gujarati visitors are typically hard to please when it comes to food, so standards are exceptionally high and prices low. Meat is fairly rare in Mount Abu; if you get carniverous cravings, there are a couple of non-veg Punjabi restaurants in the bazaar.

Arbuda Nakki Lake Rd. Perennially popular spot with a huge veggie menu ranging from pizza, burgers and sandwiches through to Chinese and Indian (mains Rs50–80), as well as good fresh juices. Lightning-fast, friendly service and a popular, airy terrace.

Orignal [*sic*] **Gujarat Omlette** [*sic*] Nakki Lake Rd. If you need an eggy snack, omelette sandwiches are Rs30 a go at this little shack opposite the northern tip of the Polo Ground.

Jodhpur Bhojnalaya Nakki Lake Rd. The best place in town for authentic Rajasthani veg food, heavy on ghee and spices. It's famous for its definitive *dhal bati churma* (a traditional Rajasthani dish consisting of baked wheatflour balls served with dhal and sweet *churma*, Rs90), and also has the usual big list of Indian veg dishes.

Kanak Dining Hall Nakki Lake Rd. Friendly place offering the best Gujarati thalis in town – a superb array of subtly spiced veg delicacies for a very modest Rs90 per head. Come hungry – portions are literally limitless. They also have a Punjabi thali (Rs100) and a range of veg dishes.

Sankalp Nakki Lake Rd. Branch of a south Indian chain offering the usual fare (*iddlis*, dosas, *uttapams* and the like) in comfortable, modern surrounds, with specialities such as veg pulao (Rs80) or tomato *masala uthappa* (Rs100), or if you really want to go to town, a four-foot-long dosa (Rs500).

Veena Nakki Lake Rd. Open-air seating next to the main road. Brightly lit and can be kind of tacky when it's got the latest *filmi* hits blaring out, but the fast food is second to none and they have a welcome open fire on the terrace most evenings. Try a tangy *pao bhaji* (Rs50–70) or melt-in-the-mouth dosas (Rs50–85).

Chittaurgarh, Kota and Bundi

The belt of hilly land east of Udaipur is the most fertile in Rajasthan, watered by several perennial rivers and guarded by a sequence of imposing forts perched atop the craggy ridges that crisscross the region. Heading east, the first major settlement is the historic town of **Chittaurgarh**, capital of the kingdom of Mewar before Udaipur and site of one of Rajasthan's most spectacular and historic forts. Further east, the tranquil town of **Bundi** boasts another atmospheric fort and picturesque old bazaars and havelis, while an hour away by bus, **Kota** is home to another impressive palace.

A prime crop in this area for centuries has been **opium**. Although grown for the pharmaceutical industry according to strict government quotas, the legal

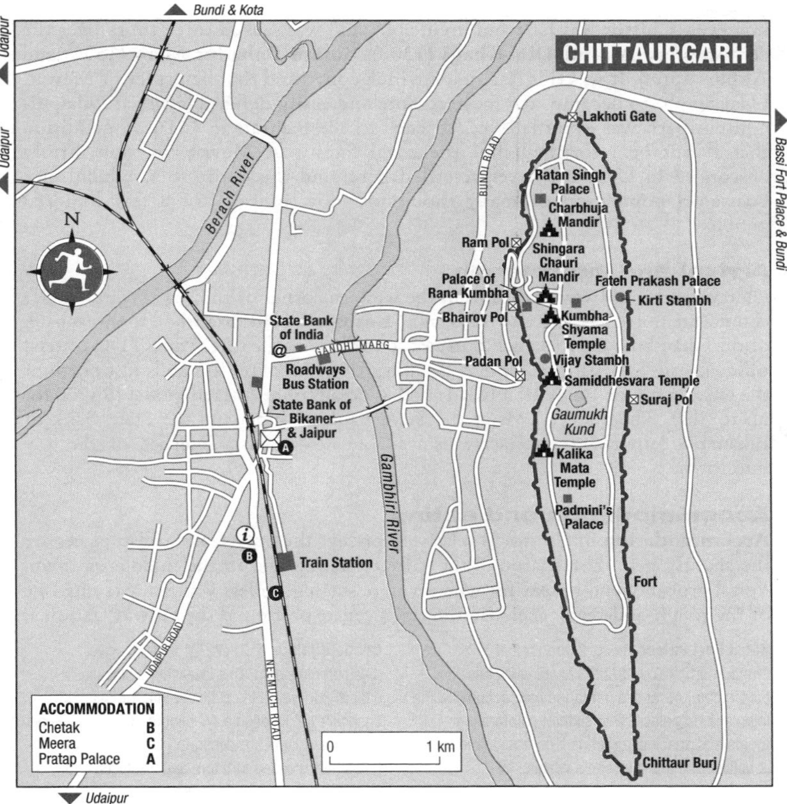

cultivation masks a much larger illicit production overseen by Mumbai drug barons. An estimated one in five men in the area is addicted.

Chittaurgarh

Of all the former Rajput capitals, **CHITTAURGARH** (or Chittor), 115km northeast of Udaipur, was the strongest bastion of Hindu resistance against the Muslim invaders. No less than three mass suicides (*johars*) were committed over the centuries by the female inhabitants of its **fort**, and an air of desolation still hangs over the honey-coloured old citadel. As a symbol of Rajput chivalry and militarism only Jodhpur's Meherangarh Fort compares.

Some visitors squeeze a tour of Chittaurgarh into a day-trip, or en route between Bundi and Udaipur, but it's well worth stopping overnight to give yourself time to explore the fort properly.

Some history

The origins of Chittor Fort are obscure, but probably date back to the seventh century. It was seized by **Bappa Rawal**, founder of the Mewar dynasty, in 734, and remained the Mewar capital for the next 834 years, bar a couple of brief interruptions. Despite its commanding position and formidable appearance, however, Chittor was far from invincible, and was sacked three times over the centuries, by **Ala-ud-Din-Khalji** (1303), **Sultan Bahadur Shah** (1535) and **Akbar** (1568). It was this last attack which convinced the then ruler of Mewar, Udai Singh, to decamp to a more remote and easily defensible site at Udaipur. Chittaurgarh was eventually ceded back to the Rajputs in 1616 on condition that it not be refortified, but the royal family of Mewar, by now firmly ensconced in Udaipur, never resettled here, and the entire fort, which once boasted a population of many thousands, now houses just a few hundred people.

Arrival and information

Chittaurgarh's **railway station** is in the western corner of the city. From here it's about 2km north to the **Roadways** (aka "**Kothwali**") **Bus Stand** on the west bank of the Ghambiri, and a further 2km east to the base of the fort. The RTDC **tourist office** (Mon–Sat 10am–1.30pm & 2–5pm; ⓣ01472/241089) stands just north of the railway station on Station Road and has details of registered guides (Rs230 for up to 4hr). There are **ATMs** at the State Bank of India and the State Bank of Bikaner & Jaipur. **Internet** access is available at Megavista Internet, on the way into town.

Accommodation and eating

Accommodation in Chittor is relatively pricey; the only really cheap places are the slightly grim hotels around the railway station and in the middle of town. You'll probably end up **eating** where you're staying, unless you fancy trying one of the rough-and-ready *dhabas* in the town centre or around the railway station.

Bassi Fort Palace Bassi, 24km east of Chittaurgarh ⓣ01472/225321, ⓦwww.bassifortpalace.com. Attractive heritage hotel, occupying the town's florid palace, with sixteen comfortable rooms and spacious grounds where a sacred tree is believed to grant all one's wishes. ❻

Castle Bijaipur ⓣ01472/240099, ⓦwww.bijaipurhotels.com. This lovely hotel occupies a superb 350-year-old castle set in a tranquil and unspoilt rural location a 45-minute (32km) drive east of Chittor. Rooms are decorated with traditional Rajasthani wooden furniture and artefacts, and

Moving on from Chittaurgarh

There are **buses** to Ajmer (7 daily; 5hr), Udaipur (roughly hourly; 2hr 30min) and Kota (2 daily; 4hr 30min), but no direct buses to Bundi – to get there (and usually to Kota), take a bus to Bhilwara, and another one from there.

Recommended trains from Chittaurgarh

The trains below are recommended as the fastest and/or most convenient for specific cities.

Destination	Name	No.	Departs (daily)	Arrives
Ajmer	*Udaipur–Ajmer Express*	2991	8.42am	11.40pm
	Ratlam–Ajmer Express	9653	10.10am	1.55pm
Bundi	*City Link Express*	9019A	2.55pm	5.10pm
	Mewar Express	2964	8.50pm	10.46pm
Delhi (HN)	*Mewar Express*	2964	8.50pm	6.30am
Jaipur	*Gwalior Superfast*	2966	12.35am	6am
Kota	*Nimach–Kota Express*	9019A	2.55pm	6.05pm
Udaipur	*Mewar Express*	2963	5.05am	7.20am
	Ajmer–Udaipur Express	2992	7.15pm	9.20pm

there's a pool, Ayurvedic massages, daily group yoga and meditation sessions (and individual tuition on request), plus cycle, jeep and horse safaris to nearby villages. Day-trips to Chittor can be arranged for Rs700. They also have tented accommodation (❼) a few kilometres away in an even more remote rural location at Pangarh Lake. Breakfast included. ❼–❾

Chetak Neemuch Rd, immediately outside the railway station ☎01472/245192. Passable budget option, with spotless modern rooms (though avoid the noisy ones next to the main road) and a busy little restaurant downstairs. ❸–❹

Meera Neemuch Rd ☎01472/240266. The best budget option in town, with a wide selection of fan and a/c rooms, a dorm (Rs150) and some very quirkily decorated suites; facilities include an inexpensive restaurant and a good bar. ❷–❹

Pratap Palace Opposite the GPO on Shri Gurukul Rd ☎01472/240099, Ⓦwww.bijaipurhotels.com. Functional mid-range hotel, a bit shabby in places, but with an attractive garden and good food. The smarter deluxe rooms are the nicest in town (though rather expensive); the cheaper rooms are relatively unappealing and overpriced. They can also arrange countryside tours starting from *Castle Bijaipur* (see opposite). ❹–❼

The fort

The entire fort is 5km long and 1km wide, and you could easily spend a whole day up here nosing around the myriad remains, although most visitors content themselves with a few hours. **Tours** of the fort are most easily made by auto-rickshaw (Rs200 for around 3hr); alternatively, take a rickshaw to the entrance and explore on foot, or (perhaps best) rent a **bike** from the shop on the road leading west from the crossroads outside the station. It's a long, steep climb up to the fort, but most of the roads on the plateau itself are flat.

The ascent to the fort (daily 7am–6pm; foreign visitors Rs100 [Rs5]; plus Rs5 per rickshaw), protected by massive bastions, begins at **Padan Pol** in the east of town and winds upwards through a further six gateways. The houses of the few people who still inhabit the fort are huddled together near the final gate, Rama Pol, where you buy your ticket.

Entering the fort, you first reach the slowly deteriorating fifteenth-century **Palace of Rana Kumbha** (reigned 1433–68), built by the ruler who presided over the period of Mewar's greatest prosperity. The main palace building still stands five storeys high, though it's difficult now to make much sense of the confusing tangle of partially ruined walls and towers. Opposite the palace stands the intricately carved fifteenth-century **Shingara Chauri Mandir**, a small but lavishly adorned Jain temple dedicated to Shantinath, the sixteenth *tirthankara*. Nearby, the modern **Fateh Prakash Palace**, a large, plain edifice built for the maharana of Udaipur in the 1920s, is home to a small **archeological museum** (daily except Fri 10am–5pm; Rs10), containing a fine array of Jain and Hindu carvings recovered from various places around the fort.

A couple of hundred metres further on lies the imposing **Kumbha Shyama Temple**, constructed by (and named after) Rana Kumbha. A black statue of Garuda stands in its own pavilion in front of the shrine, while an image of Varaha, the boar incarnation of Vishnu, occupies a niche at the rear. A second shrine stands close by within the small walled enclosure, dedicated to **Meerabai**, a Jodhpur princess and poet famed for her devotion to Krishna.

The Vijay Stambh and beyond

The main road within the fort continues south to its focal point, **Vijay Stambh**, the soaring "tower of victory" erected by Rana Kumbha to commemorate his 1440 victory over the Muslim sultan Mehmud Khilji of Malwa. This magnificent sand-coloured tower, whose nine storeys rise 36m, took a decade to build; its walls are lavishly carved with mythological scenes and images from all Indian religions, including Arabic inscriptions in praise of Allah. You can climb the dark narrow stairs to the very summit for free.

The area around the Vijay Stambh is littered with an impressive number of further remains, including a pair of monumental gateways and a number of florid temples, including the superbly decorated **Samiddhesvara Temple**, whose shrine houses an image of the *trimurti*, a composite, three-headed image of Shiva, Brahma and Vishnu. A path leads from here down to the **Gaumukh Kund**, a large reservoir fed by an underground stream that trickles through carved mouths (*mukh*) of cows (*gau*) and commands superb views across the plains.

Buildings further south include the **Kalika Mata Temple**, and **Padmini's Palace**, its rather plain buildings enclosing a series of attractive little walled gardens leading to a tower overlooking the small lake. The road continues south to the point once used for hurling traitors to their deaths, then returns north along the eastern ridge to **Suraj Pol** gate, with spectacular vistas across a patchwork of farmland. Several temples line the route, but the most impressive monument is **Kirti Stambh**. The inspiration for the tower of victory, this smaller "tower of fame" was built by Digambaras as a monument to the first *tirthankara* Adinath, whose unclad image appears throughout its six storeys.

Bundi

The walled town of **BUNDI**, 37km north of Kota, lies in the north of the former Hadaoti state, shielded by jagged outcrops of the Vindhya Range. The site was the capital of the Hadachauhans, but although settled in 1241, 25 years before Kota, Bundi never amounted to more than a modest market centre, and remains relatively untouched by modern development. The palace alone justifies a visit thanks to its superb collection of **murals**, while the well-preserved **old town**, crammed with crumbling havelis, makes this one of southern Rajasthan's most appealing destinations – a fact recognized by the ever-increasing numbers of foreign tourists who are now visiting the place.

Arrival and information

Buses arrive in the southeast part of town near the post office, from where it's around Rs30 by auto-rickshaw to the palace and guesthouses; the railway station is around 5km south of town (Rs50 or so by auto-rickshaw). Bundi's **tourist office** (Mon–Fri 9.30am–6pm; ⓣ0747/244 3697) is south of town near the Circuit House. You can **change money** at Pandey Forex, about 100m south of the palace, and at the *Kasera Heritage* guesthouse; there are also several ATMs

Moving on from Bundi

Heading south, there are regular buses to **Kota** (every 30min; 45min–1hr), and two evening trains: 39019A Kota Express (departs 5.12pm, arrives 6.05pm) and #1771 *Haldighati Passenger* (departs 5.50pm, arrives 7.30pm). The same trains run the other way to **Chittaurgarh** in the morning at 7.15am (#1772 *Haldighati Passenger*, arriving 10.35am) and 9.38am (#9020A *Dehra Dun Express*, arriving 12.05pm). No buses run direct to Chittaurgarh, but there are plenty to Bhilwara, and from there to Chittor. There are four buses daily to Udaipur (7–8hr), but the only train is the #2963 *Mewar Express*, which currently passes through Bundi at 2.02am nightly, arriving in Udaipur at 7.20am.

Heading north, there are buses to **Sawai Madhopur** (for Ranthambore National Park; 4 daily; 4hr 30min); alternatively, take a bus to Kota and a train from there (see p.240 for details). Buses are the best way of reaching **Ajmer** (every 20min; 4hr), **Jaipur** (every 20min; 5hr) and **Jodhpur** (5 daily; 10hr).

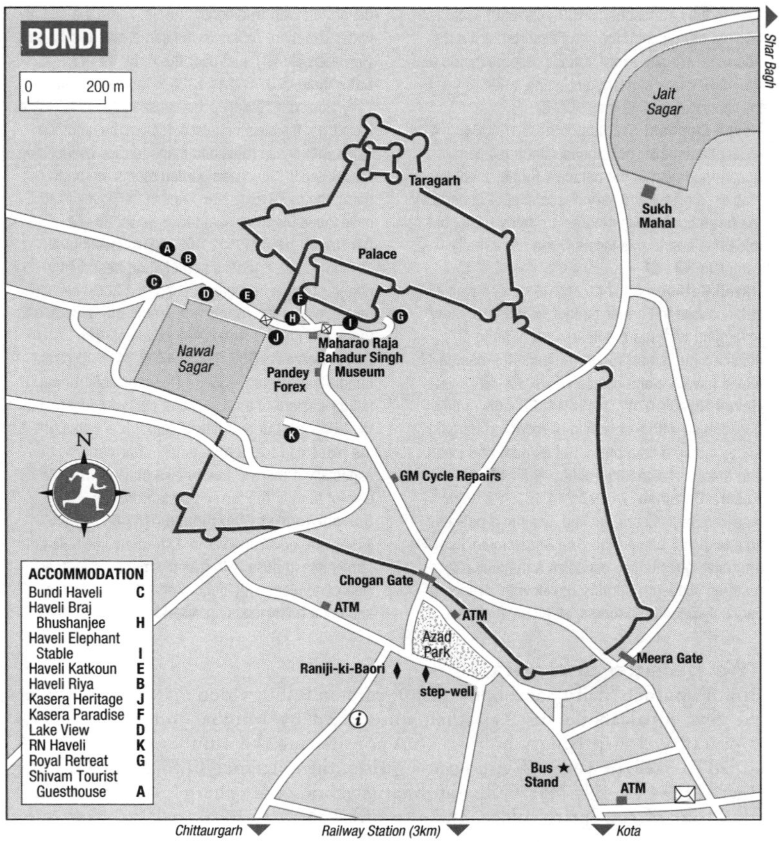

in the southern end of town. Dozens of places offer **internet** access for around Rs40 per hour, while lots of places also rent out **motorbikes** (around Rs250/day), and a few also have **bicycles** (around Rs30/day; try GM Cycle Repairs in the bazaar).

If you're in the area around mid-November try to arrive for the annual **Bundi Festival**, a celebration of Hadaoti heritage with a very local, country-fair feel.

Accommodation and eating

Much of Bundi's **accommodation** is in old havelis, with a wide range of standards and prices. Most people **eat** where they're staying. To eat out, the *Bundi Haveli* (see below) has a good rooftop restaurant (non-veg mains Rs175–260) and real coffee in a stylishly laid-back setting, while the terrace at the *Royal Retreat* (see p.238) has fine town views and is a great spot for a sundowner.

Bundi Haveli ⓣ0747/244 6716, ⓦwww.bundihotel.com. Traditional old haveli given a stylish contemporary makeover, with beautifully furnished rooms (most with a/c), a good restaurant and facilities including internet access and money exchange. Excellent value at current rates. ❹–❺

Haveli Braj Bhushanjee ⓣ0747/244 2322, ⓦwww.kiplingsbundi.com.

Wonderfully atmospheric 150-year-old haveli, with original murals, antiques and assorted artworks adorning virtually every surface. Rooms (some with a/c and TV) are similarly engaging, and immaculately maintained. ❹–❼

Haveli Elephant Stables ⓣ9928 154064, ⓔelephantstable_guesthouse@hotmail.com. Accommodation in the palace's former elephant stables, a pretty and very peaceful spot underneath the fort's huge walls. Rooms are fairly basic, but at this price and in this location you can't really complain. ❶–❷

Haveli Katkoun ⓣ0747/244 4311, ⓦhavelikatkoun.free.fr. Former budget guesthouse, now revamped with marble floors and a range of spacious and smart modern rooms, the best of which have a/c and palace views. ❸–❺

Haveli Riya ⓣ0747/244 4211. Friendly family guesthouse with a selection of rooms at bargain prices, some a little basic, but all neat and clean, and there's a nice little rooftop café. ❶–❷

Kasera Paradise ⓣ0747/244 4679, ⓦwww.kaseraparadise.com. Tucked away in a peaceful little lane just behind the *Braj Bhushanjee*, this attractive guesthouse occupies a meticulously restored sixteenth-century haveli with a range of variously priced a/c rooms, all nicely furnished and decorated with traditional murals. There's a slightly wider variety of rooms in the same owner's *Kasera Heritage* (❷–❻), just over the road. ❷–❺

Lake View ⓣ0747/244 2326, ⓔlakeviewbundi_@yahoo.com. Scruffy guesthouse in an old lakeside haveli, not the cleanest place in town, but compensates with cheap rates and a fine terrace overlooking Nawal Sagar. The cheap garden rooms are pretty basic; the more expensive ones in the haveli itself have faded old murals and lake views. ❶–❷

RN Haveli ⓣ0747/512 0098, ⓔrnhavelibundi@yahoo.co.in. Friendly, homely and deservedly popular female-run guesthouse in a 200-year-old haveli, where the rooms are simple but decent, and the home-cooked meals are excellent. ❶

Royal Retreat ⓣ0747/244 4426, ⓔroyalretreatbundi@yahoo.com. Just four comfortable rooms (all air-cooled) in a superb and peaceful location in the lower part of the palace complex – although the place can feel a mite lonely after dark, especially if there's no one else staying. There's decent food in the terrace restaurant. ❸–❹

Shivam Tourist Guesthouse ⓣ0747/244 7892, ⓔshivam_pg@yahoo.com. Extremely sociable little family guesthouse with friendly management, six clean and pleasantly decorated attached rooms, and good home-cooking. ❶–❹

The palace and fort

Bundi's **palace** (daily 8am–6pm; Rs60; camera Rs50, video Rs100) was one of the few royal abodes in Rajasthan untouched by Mughal influence, and its appearance is surprisingly homogenous considering the number of times it was added to over the years. If you want a **guide**, the extremely informative Keshav Bhati (ⓣ9414 394241, ⓔbharat_bhati@yahoo.com) charges around Rs250 for a tour of the entire palace, and also offers visits to local rock-painting sites and of Kota.

A short steep path winds up to the main gateway, **Hathi Pol**, surmounted by elephant carvings, beyond which lies the palace's principal courtyard. On the right-hand side, steps lead up to the **Ratan Doulat**, the early seventeenth-century Diwan-i-Am, or Hall of Public Audience, an open terrace with a simple marble throne overlooking the courtyard below.

At the far end of the Ratan Daulat, further steps lead up to the **Chhatra Mahal**. Go through the open-sided turquoise-painted pavilion on the southern side of the courtyard and the room beyond to reach a superb little **antechamber** (or "dressing room"), every surface covered in finely detailed murals from the 1780s embellished with gold and silver leaf. The opposite side of the courtyard is flanked by a pavilion with columns supported on the backs of quaint black trumpeting elephants, at the back of which you'll find a well-preserved old squat toilet, offering the best view from any public convenience in Rajasthan.

From the Chhatra Mahal courtyard, a narrow flight of steps leads up to an even smaller courtyard flanked by the superbly decorated **Phool Mahal** (built in 1607, though the murals date from the 1860s), whose murals include a vast procession featuring regiments of soldiers in European dress and a complete camel corps. From here, further narrow steps ascend to the **Badal Mahal**

(Cloud Palace), home to what are often regarded as the finest paintings in the whole of southern Rajasthan. A vividly coloured ring of Krishnas and Radhas dance around the highest part of the vaulted dome, flanked by murals showing Krishna being driven to his wedding by Ganesh, and Rama returning from Sri Lanka to Ayodhya.

There are further outstanding murals in the **Chittra Sala** (sunrise–sunset; free), just above the palace. At the rear left-hand corner of the garden inside, steps lead up to a small courtyard embellished with an outstanding sequence of murals painted in an unusual muted palette of turquoises, blues and blacks, the majority devoted to magical depictions of scenes from the life of Krishna.

A steep twenty-minute climb above the Chittra Sala, the monkey-infested **Taragarh** fort offers even more spectacular views over Bundi, its palace and the surrounding countryside.

The rest of the town

Right in the centre of town, the recently opened **Maharao Raja Bahadur Singh Museum** (daily: April–Sept 9am–1pm & 2–6pm, Oct–March 9am–1pm & 2–5pm; Rs50, camera Rs50) houses a skull-crackingly tedious collection of self-congratulatory portraits of assorted maharajas of Bundi, plus a gallery of stuffed tigers and other dumb animals massacred in the name of sport by notables ranging from Lord Mountbatten to Haile Selassie. Save your cash.

On the south side of town is the much more rewarding **Raniji-ki-Baori** (no set hours), one of Rajasthan's most spectacular step-wells. Built in 1699, the well is reached by a flight of steps punctuated by platforms and pillars embellished with sinuous S-shaped brackets and elephant capitals. As you descend, look for the beautifully carved panels showing the ten avatars of Lord Vishnu, which line the side walls.

Northeast of the town on the southern shore of Jait Sagar tank is the pretty but now rather neglected **Sukh Mahal** – Rao Raja Vishnu Singh's summer palace – where Rudyard Kipling (who stayed here for a few months at the invitation of the raja) wrote parts of *Kim* and the *Jungle Book*. The building itself is closed to visitors but it's a pleasant spot, and you can walk for a short distance along the lakeshore on either side of the palace. Some 1.5km further along the side of the lake, **Shar Bagh** encloses sixty crumbling royal cenotaphs. If the door is locked, ask for the key at the *chowkidar*'s hut on your left just after the gateway over the main road some 100m north of the cenotaphs. Count on around Rs80 return by auto from town to Sukh Mahal, or Rs120 to Shar Bagh.

Kota

KOTA, 230km south of Jaipur on a fertile plain fed by Rajasthan's largest river, the Chambal, is one of the state's dirtier and less appealing cities. With a population nudging 700,000, it is one of Rajasthan's major commercial and industrial hubs, with hydro, atomic and thermal power stations lining the banks of the Chambal, alongside Asia's largest fertilizer plant, whose enormous chimneys provide a not-very-scenic backdrop to many views of the town. Kota is worth a visit if only for its city palace, which houses one of the better museums in Rajasthan, while the old town has a commercial hustle and bustle which makes a nice contrast to somnolent Bundi, just down the road.

Arrival and information

Kota's **railway station** is in the north of town, a few kilometres from the central **bus stand** on Bundi Road. The **tourist office** (Mon–Fri 9am–5pm;

Moving on from Kota

Buses leave regularly from the stand near Nayapura Circle to Bundi (every 30min; 45min–1hr), Ajmer (every 30min; 6hr), Chittor (5 daily; 4hr 30min), Jaipur (every 30min; 6hr) and Udaipur (7 daily; 6hr). Kota also has good **train** connections.

Recommended trains from Kota

Destination	Name	No.	Departs	Arrives
Agra (Agra Fort)	*Avadh Express*	9037	2.50pm (Mon, Wed, Thu & Sat)	9.50pm
	Haldighati Passenger	1771	9pm (daily)	6am
Bundi	*Dehra Dun Express*	9020A	9.05am (daily)	9.36am
Chittaurgarh	*Dehra Dun Express*	9020A	9.05am (daily)	12.05pm
Delhi (Hazrat Nizamuddin)	*Kota Jan Shatabdi*	2059	6am (daily)	12.30pm
	Golden Temple Mail	2903	11.20am (daily)	6.30pm
	Mewar Express	2964	11.55pm (daily)	6.30am
Jaipur	*Dayodaya Express*	2181	8.15am (daily)	12.30pm
	Jaipur Express	2955	8.50am (daily)	12.55pm
	Ranthambore Express	2465	12.40pm (daily)	4.45pm
Mumbai (Central)	*Jaipur–Mumbai SF*	2956	5.35pm (daily)	7.50am
Sawai Madhopur (for Ranthambore National Park)	*Dayodaya Express*	2181	8.15am (daily)	9.50am
	Golden Temple Mail	2903	11.20am (daily)	12.30pm
	Ranthambore Express	2465	12.40pm (daily)	2.25pm
	Dehra Dun Express	9019	7.40pm (daily)	9.20pm

Ⓣ0744/232 7695) is in the RTDC *Chambal Hotel*, just north of the Kishor Sagar. The best place for changing **travellers' cheques** is the inconveniently located State Bank of Bikaner & Jaipur in the south of town. There are several **ATMs** scattered around the road intersection by the *Navrang* hotel.

Accommodation and eating

Kota's **hotels** cater mainly for passing business travellers; if you can't afford to stay in one of the places below, it's better to base yourself in Bundi. For **eating**, the modern *Venue* pure-veg restaurant, attached to the *Navrang* hotel, has a good selection of north Indian veg mains (mains Rs50–80) plus dosas, pizzas and Chinese dishes.

Brijraj Bhawan Civil Lines Ⓣ0744/245 0529, Ⓦwww.indianheritagehotels.com. An idyllic retreat in the heart of noisy Kota, occupying a fine old colonial mansion set in a peaceful spot overlooking the river. Rooms are pure Victorian period pieces, all scrupulously maintained and very comfortable. ❼

Navrang Station Rd Ⓣ0744/232 3294. The nicest cheap hotel in town, with a mix of simple air-cooled and more attractively furnished a/c rooms, all with TV. The adjacent *Phul Plaza* is reasonable too, but not quite so appealing. ❸–❹

Sukhdham Kothi Civil Lines Ⓣ0744/232 0081, Ⓦwww.sukhdhamkothi.com. Marvellously atmospheric guesthouse located in a hundred-year-old stone mansion set amid extensive gardens. Comfy and atmospheric rooms with old wooden furniture and assorted nineteenth-century bric-à-brac. ❻

Umed Bhawan Palace Station Rd, Khelri Phatak Ⓣ0744/232 5262, Ⓦwww.welcomheritagehotels.com. Occupying a huge and rather ugly former royal residence, this fancy hotel offers upmarket comforts (and a fair bit of chintz) at a reasonable price. ❼

The Town

Kota is a surprisingly large and sprawling city, and you'll need a rickshaw to cover the sights below, especially if arriving at the railway station, on the far northern side of town. Arriving at the bus station, it's a long but feasible walk through the bustling main bazaar to the City Palace.

The City Palace

On the southern side of the town centre, around 2km from the bus station, lies the **City Palace**, a well-preserved cluster of blue and pink royal residences; construction on them began in 1625 and continued sporadically until the early years of the twentieth century. The palace now houses the excellent **Maharao Madho Singh Museum** (daily except official holidays 10am–4.30pm; combined entrance to museum and palace Rs100 [Rs10]; camera Rs50, video Rs100). The first room is filled with a selection of luxury items belonging to the maharaja, while diagonally across the courtyard lies the dazzling **Raj Mahal**, built by Rao Madho Singh (ruled 1625–49), richly decorated with paintings and mirrorwork, which served as the ruler's public audience hall. From the Raj Mahal, a corridor leads into a further sequence of rooms housing a well-stocked armoury and a small art gallery, and a depressing wildlife gallery, filled with the mothy remains of various leopards and tigers.

Exit the museum then follow the steps up past the Raj Mahal to reach a series of finely painted palace buildings. Three storeys up is the **Barah Mahal**, one of whose rooms is richly decorated with dozens of square miniatures placed together on the wall like tiles and depicting a range of religious and contemporary scenes, from Krishna lifting Mount Goverdhan to exotic-looking European ladies and gentlemen.

The rest of the city

Kishore Sagar, an artificial lake built in 1346, gives some visual relief from the city's grim industrial backdrop; the red-and-white palace in its centre, **Jag Mandir**, was commissioned by Prince Dher Deh of Bundi in 1346. On the northern edge of the lake the dusty **Government Museum** (daily 10am–5pm; Rs10) serves as the dispiriting home for an excellent collection of local stone carvings (signs in Hindi only, if at all).

On the edge of the river a few kilometres south of the fort, crocodiles and gharial sometimes sun themselves in a shallow pond in the **Chambal Gardens** (Rs5); boats from here offer brief jaunts (Rs30) on the crocodile-infested River Chambal.

3

Uttar Pradesh

* **Taj Mahal** The world's most beautiful building, marking the zenith of Mughal architecture, never fails to impress. See p.250
* **Akbar's mausoleum, Sikandra** The great Mughal's tomb looks just as it does in old miniatures, with tame monkeys and deer wandering in its ornamental gardens. See p.257
* **Fatehpur Sikri** An awesomely grand, deserted palace complex, straddling an arid ridge near the Rajasthani border. See p.260
* **Kalinjar Fort** Remote fortifications in Uttar Pradesh's dusty badlands, far from the tourist trail. See p.280
* **Varanasi** Take a boat on the Ganges before dawn to watch the sun rise over India's most ancient and sacred city. See p.281
* **Sarnath** Evocative ruins on the site where the Buddha gave his first sermon. See p.295

▲ Ghat and boats at dawn in Varanasi

UTTAR PRADESH, or "the Northern State" – formerly the United Provinces, but always **UP** – is the heartland of Hinduism and Hindi, dominating the nation in culture, religion, language and politics. A vast, steamy plain of the Ganges, its history is very much the history of India, and its temples and monuments – Buddhist, Hindu and Muslim – are among the most impressive in the country.

Western UP, which adjoins Delhi, has always been close to India's centre of power. Its main city, **Agra**, once the Mughal capital, is home to the Taj Mahal, and a short hop from the abandoned Mughal city of Fatehpur Sikri. **Central UP** constituted the **Kingdom of Avadh**, the last centre of independent Muslim rule in northern India until the British unceremoniously took it over, fuelling the resentment that led to the 1857 uprising, in which its capital **Lucknow** (now UP's state capital), played such a celebrated role.

Bundelkhand – the area north of the craggy Vindhya Mountains, which stretch across northeastern Madhya Pradesh – was part of a ninth-century kingdom

carved out by the Chandella Rajputs. The same kingdom included Khajuraho in Madhya Pradesh (see p.374), for which **Jhansi** – another centre of resistance in 1857 – is a convenient jumping-off point.

In **eastern UP** lies Hinduism's holiest city, the *tirtha* (crossing-place) of **Varanasi**, where it's believed death transports the soul to final liberation. Sacred since antiquity, it was frequented by Mahavira, the founder of Jainism, and also by Buddha, who preached his first sermon in nearby **Sarnath**.

Although UP was once a thriving centre of Islamic jurisprudence and culture, many Muslims departed during the years after Independence, and the Muslim population now comprises just sixteen percent. As the heart of what is known as the "cow belt" (equivalent to America's "bible belt"), UP has been plagued by caste politics and was for some years dominated by the Hindu sectarian BJP. It acquired an unfortunate reputation as the focus of bitter communal tensions, most notoriously in the wake of the 1992 destruction of the Babri Masjid mosque in **Ayodhya** (east of Lucknow, near Faizabad), which sparked off sectarian riots across India. In recent years, state politics has been dominated by two largely local left-wing parties, the socialist Samajwadi Party (SP) and the mainly low-caste Bahujan Samaj Party (BSP).

With an efficient if basic state bus system and an excellent railway network, **travelling around** the state is generally straightforward (except in Bundelkhand in the south). The major tourist cities, Agra and Varanasi, have been coping with visitors and pilgrims for centuries, and today have good transport connections and all the facilities a traveller might need. **UP Tourism** (Ⓦ www.up-tourism.com) has offices in most major towns.

Agra

The splendour of **AGRA** – India's capital under the Mughals – remains undiminished, from the massive fort to the magnificent **Taj Mahal**. Along with Delhi, 204km northwest, and Jaipur in Rajasthan, Agra is the third apex of the "Golden Triangle", India's most popular tourist itinerary. It fully merits that status; the Taj effortlessly transcends all the frippery and commercialism that surrounds it, and continues to have a fresh and immediate impact on all who see it. That said, Agra city itself can be an intense experience, even for seasoned India hands. The traffic pollution is appalling (some mornings you can barely see the sun through the fog of fumes), and as a tourist you'll have to contend with crowds at the major monuments, high admission fees and some of Asia's most persistent touts, commission merchants and rickshaw-wallahs. Don't, however, let this put you off. Although it's possible to see Agra on a day-trip from Delhi, the Taj alone deserves so much more – a fleeting visit would miss the subtleties of its many moods, as the light changes from sunrise to sunset – while the city's other sights and Fatehpur Sikri can easily fill several days.

Some history

Little is known of the pre-Muslim history of Agra, but a 1080 AD account describes a robust fort here, with a flourishing city strategically placed at the crossroads between the north and the centre of India. Agra remained a minor administrative centre until 1504, when the Delhi Sultan, **Sikandar Lodi**, moved his capital here to keep a check on the warring factions of his empire. The ruins of his city can still be seen on the Yamuna River's east bank. After defeating the last Lodi sultan, Ibrahim Lodi, at Panipat in 1526, **Babur**, the founder of the Mughal

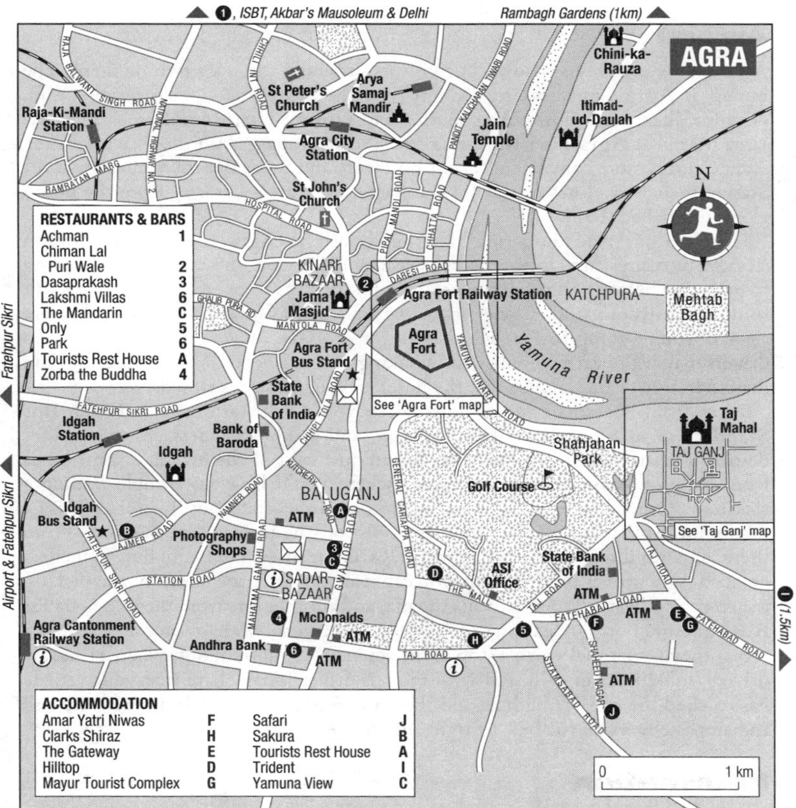

empire, sent ahead his son **Humayun** to capture Agra. In gratitude for their benevolent treatment at his hands, the family of the Raja of Gwalior rewarded the Mughal with jewellery and precious stones – among them the legendary **Koh-i-noor Diamond**, now among Britain's crown jewels.

Agra saw its heyday under Humayun's son, **Akbar the Great** (1556–1605), when Agra Fort was built, and it remained the empire's capital for over a century. Even when **Shah Jahan**, Jahangir's son and successor, built a new city in Delhi – Shahjahanabad, now known as Old Delhi – his heart remained in Agra. He pulled down many of the earlier red-sandstone structures in the fort, replacing them with his trademark – exquisite marble buildings. The empire flourished under his successor Aurangzeb (1658–1707), although his intolerance towards non-Muslims stirred up a hornets' nest. Agra was occupied successively by the Jats, the Marathas, and eventually the British.

After the 1857 uprising, the city lost the headquarters of the government of the Northwestern Provinces and the High Court to Allahabad and went into a period of decline. Its Mughal treasures have ensured its survival, and today the city is once again prospering, as an industrial and commercial centre as well as a tourist destination.

Arrival

Agra has six **railway stations**, but visitors generally use only two of them. The busiest is **Agra Cantonment** ("Cantt"), in the southwest, which serves Delhi, Gwalior, Jhansi and most points south. Trains from Rajasthan pull in close to the Jama Masjid at **Agra Fort station** (a few also stop at Agra Cantt – see opposite). Agra Cantt is more convenient for the hotels around Sadar Bazaar, while Agra Fort Station is slightly closer to the Taj Ganj area; both are a fair way from the hotels along Fatehabad Road.

There's a pre-paid auto-rickshaw/taxi booth at Agra Cantonment Station (Rs52/85 to anywhere in town); drivers may collar you on your way out, trying to grab you before you reach the pre-paid booth so as to overcharge you or work some commission scam. Cycle rickshaws wait in the forecourt outside, but are slow if you're going to Fatehabad Road or Taj Ganj. Cycle rickshaw and auto drivers may try to earn commission by taking you to a hotel of their choosing, and may therefore claim (falsely) that the hotel of your choice is closed.

Buses from Rajasthan and some services from Delhi terminate at **Idgah Bus Stand** close to Agra Cantonment Station, and a few local services from other destinations arrive at **Agra Fort Bus Stand**, just west of the fort, and some buses from Delhi stop outside the fort gate, where you'll have no trouble finding a rickshaw. Other bus services arrive at the new Inter-state Bus Terminal (ISBT), 12km north of town at Transport Nagar, just off the Delhi–Agra highway. From there, an auto into town will cost some Rs70, but if you're really determined to get into Agra proper on the cheap, you can walk down to the highway and pick up a shared auto (Rs5–7) to Baghwan Cinema, and another one from there to Gwalior Road or Agra Fort bus station (Rs10). One **scam** to be aware of on buses to Idgah is that they sometimes make a stop in the suburbs, about 6km out, where rickshaw drivers (sometimes in collusion with the bus drivers) may claim that your vehicle has reached the end of the line, and that you need to disembark; if there are still Indian passengers on the bus, sit tight till you get to Idgah.

Information

Agra has two **tourist offices**, India Tourism at 191 The Mall (Mon–Fri 9am–5pm, Sat 9am–2pm; ⓣ0562/222 6368), and UP Tourism at 64 Taj Road (Mon–Sat 10am–5pm; ⓣ0562/222 6378); there is also an information booth (24hr; ⓣ0562/242 1204) at Cantonment Station. UP Tourism runs a whistlestop **tour** (daily except Friday) of Agra aimed mainly at day-trippers from Delhi. The tour leaves the India Tourism office at around 9.45am, and Agra Cantonment Railway station at around 10.20am, coinciding with the *Taj Express* from Delhi, which arrives at 10.07am. The full-day tour (Rs1700 including all entrance and guide fees) whisks you at breakneck speed around the Taj, Agra Fort and Fatehpur Sikri, ending at around 6pm in time for the *Taj Express* back to Delhi at 6.55pm; you can also join the tour just for the afternoon visit to Fatehpur Sikri (Rs550). Tours can be booked either through the UP Tourism or India Tourism offices.

City transport

Agra is very spread out and its sights too widely separated to explore on foot, so wherever you're staying you'll end up spending a fair amount of time in rickshaws or taxis. Getting from one part of the city to another can prove surprisingly time-consuming, and crossing from one side of the Yamuna River to the other is particularly tedious, given the condition of the city centre's two over-used and under-maintained bridges.

Moving on from Agra

Kheria airport, 7km southwest of town (☎0562/240 0569), has seasonal Kingfisher flights to Delhi, but given the time needed to check in and travel between airports and city centres, it's just as fast, and a lot cheaper and easier, to go by train.

By train

Train tickets, especially to the capital, should be booked well in advance at either Agra Cantonment or Agra Fort stations; both have computerized booking offices and separate tourist counters. Trains for Delhi leave from Cantonment Station, the fastest, most comfortable and most expensive being the *Shatabdi Express* #2001 to New Delhi (8.30pm except Fri; 2hr). The *Taj Express* #2279 to Hazrat Nizamuddin (6.55pm daily; 3hr 05min) is an alternative option. In the other direction, the *Shatabdi Express* #2002 (8.17am except Fri) travels to Gwalior (1hr 20min) and on to Jhansi (2hr 30min). From Jhansi you can get a bus to Khajuraho, but you can also get there direct three times a week on the *Sampark Kranti Express* #2448, leaving Agra Cantonment at 12.25am on Tuesday (Mon night), Friday (Thurs night) and Sunday (Sat night), to arrive in Khajuraho fresh and early at 7.50am. A convenient but relatively slow early-morning service to New Delhi is the *Intercity Express* #4211 (6am; 4hr 15min); the fastest midday train is the *Kerala Express* #2625 (10.28am; 3hr 12min). Jaipur trains from Agra include the 5.40pm #2965 *Gwalior–Udaipur Super Express* from Cantonment (arrives 10.13pm) and the 6.15am #4853/4863/4865 *Marudhar Express* from Agra Fort (arrives 11.30am). The *Marudhar Express* will also get you to Jodhpur (arrives 5.30pm), or you can travel overnight on the #2307 *Howrah–Jodhpur Express* at 7.35pm, which arrives at 6.30am next morning; some carriages split off at Merta Road, destination Bikaner (arrive 8.15am). For Kolkata, the *Ajmer–Sealdah Express* #2988 leaves Agra Fort at 7.52pm, pulling into Sealdah at 3.45pm next day. To Lucknow, the 10pm #9037/9039 *Avadh Express* from Agra Fort, though not the fastest service, runs daily overnight, arriving at 6.25am next morning. The best train for Varanasi is the nightly #4854/4864/4866 *Marudhar Express* (9.20pm from Agra Fort, arriving 8.35am Wed, Sat & Mon, but later on other days). For Goa, the #2780 *Goa Express* leaves Agra Cantonment at 5.50pm, pulling in at Vasco 36hr 40min later (at 6.30am); the two night departures for Chennai (the #2616 GT *Express* at 9.52pm and the #2622 *Tamil Nadu Express* at 1.10am) are faster, the #2622 taking only 30hr.

By bus

Travelling by bus along the main highways, especially to the capital on the Grand Trunk road and to Jaipur on NH-11, is considerably more hair-raising than travelling the same routes by train. Accidents, most of them head-on collisions with other buses or trucks, are disconcertingly frequent.

Agra has three bus stands, but Agra Fort Bus Stand is now used for local services only. Idgah Bus Stand, near Cantonment station in the southwest of town, has services to Fatehpur Sikri (every 30min; 1hr–1hr 30min), Delhi (every 10min; 5–6hr), Madhya Pradesh and Rajasthan. For Rajasthani destinations beyond Jaipur, take a bus to Jaipur (every 30 mins; 5–6hr) and pick up a connecting service (an exception is Ajmer, which has four daily direct services, taking 10hr). Deluxe and a/c services for Jaipur leave from the forecourt of *Hotel Shakpura*, next to the bus stand. The 12hr ride to Khajuraho (leaving at 5am) is a bit gruelling – it's better to take the train, or failing that, take a train to Jhansi (3hr) and pick up a bus there (5hr).

The ISBT in Transport Nagar has services to UP destinations such as Lucknow (hourly; 9hr 30min) and Varanasi (2 daily; 14hr), as well as to Haridwar (3 daily; 10hr), Rishikesh (3 daily; 12hr) and Dehra Dun (5 daily; 13hr).

Hotels and travel agents can book seats on private buses to Delhi, Gwalior, Khajuraho, Lucknow and Nainital.

Cycle rickshaws are good for short trips and provide a livelihood for some of the city's poorest inhabitants, as well as being cleaner and greener than autos, but are slow for long journeys, and rickshaw drivers are the biggest source of hassle in Agra – attempt to walk anywhere, and they will be constantly on your case, though walking on the right-hand side of the street makes it harder for them to follow you.

Auto-rickshaws are faster and fares, including waiting time, are very reasonable if you haggle: sample fares from Taj Ganj are Rs40–50 to Sadar Bazaar, Rs50–70 to Agra Cantt Station, and Rs30–40 to the fort. **Taxis** are handy for longer trips to Sikandra or Fatehpur Sikri; agree a fare before you set off. There are taxi ranks at the stations, or your hotel should be able to arrange a vehicle. There's also a cheap and environmentally friendly **electric bus** (Rs5) which shuttles back and forth between the fort and the west gate of the Taj Mahal, though you could easily spend twenty or thirty minutes waiting for it to arrive.

On rickshaws and taxis, haggle hard. Agra sees so many "fresh" tourists that drivers almost always quote significantly inflated prices to start with (the best policy, if a rickshaw driver names a silly price, is simply to walk away – they'll usually chase after you and offer a more realistic fare). Also, note that the main agenda for many rickshaw- and taxi-drivers is to get you into shops that pay them **commission**, added to your bill of course; if they offer you a ride for an absurdly low price, this is what their aim is.

Many locals get around by **bicycle**, but for foreigners unused to the anarchic traffic and treacherous road surfaces, travel on two wheels can be stressful and potentially dangerous. You're better off hiring a cycle rickshaw and getting someone else to do the pedalling for you.

Motorized vehicles are excluded from a small area around the Taj, supposedly to protect it from pollution. This makes the roads beside the Taj quite peaceful, but a taxi or auto will have to drop you short of your hotel if it's within the exclusion zone.

Accommodation

Taj Ganj, the jumble of narrow lanes immediately south of the Taj, is where most budget travellers end up in Agra. With their unrivalled rooftop views, laid-back cafés and low room rates, the little guesthouses here can be great places to stay, though some are quite basic. There are more modern and upmarket lodgings along **Fatehabad Road**, southwest of Taj Ganj, while the leafier **Cantonment** area and the adjacent **Sadar Bazaar** have places to suit every budget, as well as offering a convenient location more or less at the centre of the city. The Taj Ganj hotels and guesthouses listed below are marked on the Taj Ganj map opposite; all other accommodation appears on the Agra map on p.245.

Taj Ganj

Amarvilas East Gate ⓣ0562/223 1515, ⓦwww.oberoihotels.com. Easily the loveliest (and most expensive) hotel in Agra, virtually a work of art in its own right, constructed in a serene blend of Mughal and Moorish styles around a gorgeous *charbagh*-style courtyard water garden – particularly magical by night. Most rooms have Taj views (prices start at $709). Facilities include a large pool, idyllic terraced gardens, two smart restaurants and a very chichi bar. ❾

Kamal Chowk Kagzi ⓣ0562/233 0126, ⓔhotelkamal@hotmail.com. Right in the thick of the Taj Ganj action, with well-maintained rooms (but no hot showers in the cheapest ones) and a great view from the rooftop restaurant. ❷–❹

Shah Jahan Chowk Kagzi ⓣ0562/320 0240, shahjahan_hotel@hotmail.com. Looks grotty at first glance, but the rooms are fresh, clean and good value, and even the cheapest have hot showers. There's a rooftop restaurant, and internet access downstairs. ❷–❹

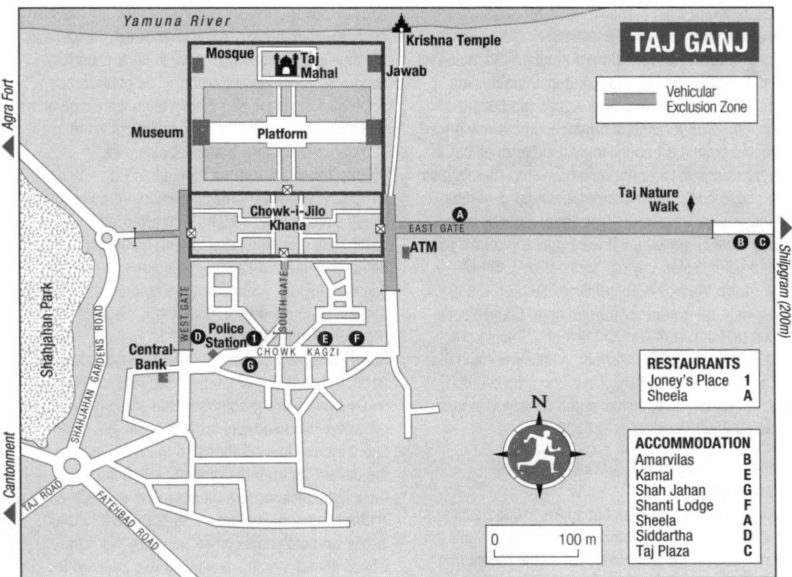

Shanti Lodge Chowk Kagzi ⓣ0562/233 1973, ⓔshantilodge2000@yahoo.co.in. Deservedly popular backpacker lodge with superb Taj views from the rooftop restaurant, a mixed bag of rooms, including some of the cheapest in town (but those in the annexe are newer and larger), and good deals for single occupancy. 1–3

Sheela East Gate ⓣ0562/233 1973, ⓦwww.hotelsheelaagra.com. Clean and spacious rooms ranged around a lovely little garden, with fan, air-cooled and a/c options, friendly staff and a good restaurant, but the cheapest rooms aren't such great value, with hot water in buckets only. 2–4

Sidhartha West Gate ⓣ0562/233 0901, ⓦwww.hotelsidhartha.com. Bigger and better rooms than the other Taj Ganj budget joints, set around a restaurant in a leafy courtyard that includes fragments of Mughal-era walls, but cheapest rooms lack hot running water. 2–4

Taj Plaza East Gate ⓣ0562/223 2515, ⓦwww.hoteltajplaza.com. A slightly more upmarket alternative to the nearby Taj Ganj guesthouses, this small modern hotel has a range of clean, bright air-cooled and a/c rooms with cable TV; the more expensive ones are well overpriced but have good Taj views. 4–7

Cantonment and Sadar Bazaar

Clarks Shiraz 54 Taj Rd ⓣ0562/222 6121, ⓦwww.hotelclarksshiraz.com. Sprawling five-star in a pleasant cantonment setting with small but cosy rooms, the more expensive of which have distant Taj views. Facilities include three restaurants, two bars, a swimming pool and a health club. Rooms start at Rs6300, with the most expensive in the $140 range. 8–9

Hilltop 21 The Mall ⓣ0562/222 6836, ⓔhotelhilltopagra@yahoo.com. Set in pleasant grounds with peacocks and parrots, this place is a little bit ramshackle, and the cheaper rooms are on the small side, but the smarter ones are better value. If you're utterly strapped for cash, there are also some ultra-basic cell-like singles with shared bath for just Rs120, and you can camp for Rs150. *Rough Guide* readers are promised a discount. 3–4

Sakura Near Idgah Bus Station ⓣ0562/242 0169, ⓦwww.hotelsakuraagra.com. Well-run and good-value guesthouse on the west side of town. Rooms (all with air-coolers) are large, bright, spacious and nicely furnished, and the helpful owner is a mine of local information. The only drawback is the location: handy for Idgah bus and

Cantonment train stations, but a bit of a hike from everywhere else. ❷–❹

Tourists Rest House Kutchery Rd, Baluganj ⓣ0562/246 3961, ⓔdontworrychicken curry@hotmail.com. One of Agra's top budget options, with a range of bright, competitively priced rooms around a tranquil leafy courtyard; all but the very cheapest have hot running water. There's also a phone booth, wi-fi internet, back-up generator and free pick-up from bus or train stations with a day's notice (rickshaw drivers may try to take you to a commission-paying "soundalike"). ❶–❸

Yamuna View 6-B The Mall ⓣ0562/246 2989, ⓦwww.hotelyamunaviewagra.com. Conveniently central but run-of-the-mill five-star. Rooms are rather plush, though showing a little wear and tear. Facilities include a pool, a bar and a couple of smart restaurants, including the snazzy *Mandarin* (see p.259). Doubles from $105. ❾

Fatehabad Road and around

Amar Yatri Niwas Fatehabad Rd ⓣ0562/223 3030, ⓦwww.amaryatriniwas.com. Good-value mid-range hotel with well-maintained rooms (the cheaper ones small but still very comfortable) and a multi-cuisine restaurant. ❺–❻

The Gateway Fatehabad Rd ⓣ0562/660 2000, ⓦwww.tajhotels.com/gateway. This boxy little place doesn't look like much from the outside, but has lots of style within. Rooms (some with distant Taj views) are amongst the most attractive in Agra, cheerfully decorated in orange and white, while public areas are pleasantly plush and there's the usual range of five-star amenities including a pool. Doubles from $209 at the rack rate, but usually less. ❾

Mayur Tourist Complex Fatehabad Rd ⓣ0562/233 2302, ⓔmayur268@rediffmail.com. Dinky pagoda-like cottages with attached bathrooms around a large garden (generally peaceful, but often used for weddings Nov–Jan). Facilities include a multi-cuisine restaurant, dingy bar and swimming pool. Camping is also possible (Rs600/person). ❺–❻

Safari Shaheed Nagar, Shamsabad Rd ⓣ0562/248 0106, ⓔhotelsafari@hotmail.com. Friendly and relaxed hotel on the southern side of town. Rooms (fan, air-cooled and a/c) are rather old, but clean and very well looked after, and there are views of the distant Taj from the rooftop café. Good value, though the location is a bit out of the way. ❷–❸

Trident Tajnagri, Fatehabad Rd ⓣ0562/233 2400, ⓦwww.tridenthotels.com. A peaceful five-star, whose cheerful rooms (including two adapted for wheelchair users) are in low-lying buildings around a spacious garden with a large pool and multi-cuisine restaurant. The rack rate for doubles starts at $221. ❾

The City

Agra is huge and disorienting. There's no real "centre", but rather a series of self-contained bazaar districts embedded within the formless urban sprawl, which stretches over an area of well over twenty square kilometres. Most of the city's major Mughal monuments are lined up along the banks of the **Yamuna River**, which bounds the city's eastern edge, including the Taj Mahal. Clustered around the Taj, the tangled little streets of **Taj Ganj** are home to most of the city's cheap accommodation and backpacker cafés. A couple of kilometres to the west, on the far side of the leafy **Cantonment** area, lies **Sadar Bazaar**, linked to Taj Ganj by **Fatehabad Road**, where you'll find many of the city's smarter places to stay, as well as numerous restaurants and crafts emporia. Northwest of Taj Ganj lies **Agra Fort** and, beyond, the third of the city's main commercial districts, **Kinari Bazaar**, centred on the massive Jama Masjid.

The monuments in Agra date from the later phase of Mughal rule and the reigns of Akbar, Jahangir and Shah Jahan – exemplifying the ever-increasing extravagance which, by Shah Jahan's time, had already begun to strain the imperial coffers and sow the seeds of political and military decline.

The Taj Mahal

Described by Bengali poet Rabindranath Tagore as "a teardrop on the face of eternity", the **Taj Mahal** (daily 6am–7pm, closed Fri; Rs750 [Rs20]) is undoubtedly the zenith of Mughal architecture. Volumes have been written on its perfection, and its image adorns countless glossy brochures and guidebooks; nonetheless, the reality never fails to overwhelm all who see it, and few words can do it justice.

The magic of the monument is strangely undiminished by the crowds of tourists who visit, as small and insignificant as ants in the face of the immense mausoleum. That said, the Taj is at its most alluring in the relative quiet of early morning, shrouded in mist and bathed with a soft red glow. As its vast marble surfaces fall into shadow or reflect the sun, its colour changes, from soft grey and yellow to pearly cream and dazzling white. This play of light is an important decorative device, symbolically implying the presence of Allah, who is never represented in physical form.

Overlooking the Yamuna River, the Taj Mahal stands at the northern end of a vast walled garden. Though its layout follows a distinctly Islamic theme, representing Paradise, it is above all a monument to romantic love. **Shah Jahan** built the Taj to enshrine the body of his favourite wife, Arjumand Bann Begum, better known by her official palace title, **Mumtaz Mahal** ("Chosen One of the Palace"), who died shortly after giving birth to her fourteenth child in 1631 – the number of children she bore the emperor is itself a tribute to her hold on him, given the number of other wives and concubines which the emperor would have been able to call on. The emperor was devastated by her death, and set out to create an unsurpassed monument to her memory – its name, "Taj Mahal", is simply a shortened, informal version of Mumtaz Mahal's palace title. Construction by a workforce of some twenty thouand men from all over Asia commenced in 1632 and took over twenty years, not being completed until 1653. Marble was brought from Makrana, near Ajmer in Rajasthan, and semi-precious stones for decoration – onyx, amethyst, lapis lazuli, turquoise, jade, crystal, coral and mother-of-pearl – were carried to Agra from Persia, Russia, Afghanistan, Tibet, China and the Indian Ocean. Eventually, Shah Jahan's pious and intolerant son Aurangzeb seized power, and the former emperor was interned in Agra Fort, where as legend would have it he lived out his final years gazing wistfully at the Taj Mahal. When he died in January 1666, his body was carried across the river to lie alongside his beloved wife in his peerless tomb.

The complex

The south, east and west **entrances** all lead into the **Chowk-i-Jilo Khana** forecourt. The main entrance into the complex, an arched gateway topped with delicate domes and adorned with Koranic verses and inlaid floral designs, stands at the northern edge of Chowk-i-Jilo Khana, directly aligned with the Taj, but shielding it from the view of those who wait outside.

Once through the gateway, you'll see the Taj itself at the end of the huge **charbagh** (literally "four gardens"), a garden dissected into four quadrants by waterways (usually dry), evoking the Koranic description of Paradise, where rivers flow with water, milk, wine and honey. Introduced by Babur from Central Asia, *charbaghs* remained fashionable throughout the Mughal era. Unlike other Mughal mausoleums such as Akbar's (see p.257) and Humayun's (see p.113), the Taj isn't at the centre of the *charbagh*, but at the northern end, presumably to exploit its riverside setting.

The Taj's **museum**, in the enclosure's western wall (in theory daily except Fri 8am–5pm, although it sometimes shuts for no apparent reason; Rs5), features exquisite miniature paintings, two marble pillars believed to have come from the fort and portraits of Mughal rulers including Shah Jahan and Mumtaz Mahal, as well as architectural drawings of the Taj and examples of *pietra dura* stone inlay work.

Steps lead from the far end of the gardens up to the high square marble platform on which the **mausoleum** itself sits, each corner marked by a tall, tapering minaret. To the west of the tomb is a domed red-sandstone **mosque** and to the east

The Taj Mahal: a monument under threat

Despite the seemingly impregnable sense of serenity and other-worldliness which clings to the Taj, in reality, India's most famous building faces serious threats from traffic and industrial pollution, and from the millions of tourists who visit it each year. Marble is all but impervious to the onslaught of wind and rain that erodes softer sandstone, but it has no natural defence against the sulphur dioxide that lingers in a dusty haze and shrouds the monument; sometimes the smog is so dense that the tomb cannot be seen from the fort. Sulphur dioxide mixes with atmospheric moisture and settles as sulphuric acid on the surface of the tomb, making the smooth white marble yellow and flaky, and forming a subtle fungus that experts have named "marble cancer".

The main sources of pollution are the continuous flow of vehicles along the national highways that skirt the city, and the seventeen hundred factories in and around Agra – chemical effluents belched out from their chimneys are well beyond recommended safety limits. Despite laws demanding the installation of pollution-control devices, the imposition of a ban on all petrol- and diesel-fuelled traffic within 500m of the Taj Mahal, and an exclusion zone banning new industrial plants from an area of 10,400 square kilometres around the complex, pollutants in the atmosphere have continued to rise (many blame the diesel generators of nearby hotels), and new factories have been set up illegally.

Cleaning work on the Taj Mahal rectifies the problem to some extent, but the chemicals used will themselves eventually affect the marble – attendants already shine their torches on "repaired" sections of marble to demonstrate how they've lost their translucency. The government has responded by setting up a pollution monitoring station to check on levels of N_2O and SO_2 in the atmosphere, but in 2007 a parliamentary committee reported that, aside from the threat from these acidic gases, particulate matter in the air was slowly turning the Taj yellow; the report recommended treatment with a non-corrosive clay pack – something like a building-sized face-pack – to remove particle deposits from the marble.

From time to time scare reports surface to the effect that the Taj's four minarets are listing and in danger of keeling over. Luckily. this proves to be a false alarm: the minarets were deliberately constructed leaning slightly outwards in order to counteract an optical illusion which would have made them appear to lean inwards when seen from ground level if they were actually exactly vertical. Despite their lean, they are quite stable.

a replica **jawab**, put there to complete the architectural symmetry of the complex – it cannot be used as a mosque as it faces away from Mecca.

The Taj itself is essentially square in shape, with pointed arches cut into its sides and topped with a huge central dome which rises for over 55m, its height accentuated by a crowning brass spire almost 17m high. On approach, the tomb looms ever larger and grander, but not until you are close do you appreciate both its sheer size and the extraordinarily fine detail of relief carving, highlighted by floral patterns of precious stones. Arabic verses praising the glory of Paradise fringe the archways, proportioned exactly so that each letter appears to be the same size when viewed from the ground.

The south face of the tomb is the main entrance to the **interior**: a high octagonal chamber whose weirdly echoing interior is flushed with pale light. A marble screen, decorated with precious stones and cut so finely that it seems almost translucent, protects the cenotaph of Mumtaz Mahal in the centre, perfectly aligned with the doorway and the distant gateway into the Chowk-i-Jilo Khana, and that of Shah Jahan crammed in next to it – the only object which breaks the perfect symmetry of the entire complex. The inlay work on the marble tombs is the finest in Agra, and no pains were spared in perfecting it – some of the petals and leaves are made of up to sixty separate stone fragments. Ninety-nine names of Allah adorn the top of Mumtaz's tomb, and set into Shah Jahan's is a pen box, the hallmark of a male ruler. These cenotaphs, in accordance with Mughal tradition, are only representations of the real coffins, which lie in the same positions in a crypt below.

Taj Mahal viewing practicalities

A day ticket to see India's most famous monument costs foreign visitors Rs750 (Rs250 to the Archeological Survey of India, Rs500 in local tax), but few regard the expense as money wasted once they are inside. To appreciate the famous play of light on the building, you'd have to stick around from dawn until dusk (ticket valid all day, but only for one entrance). Ticket queues are longest at the west gate, shortest at the south gate, and at the east gate the ticket office has been shifted half a kilometre down the road to the Shilpgram crafts village. You are not allowed to enter with food (and none is available inside), nor with a mobile phone or a travel guidebook (not even this one) – these can be deposited at lockers near the entrances. Foreigners are given a free bottle of water and a pair of shoe covers on entry. The Taj entrance ticket also entitles you to tax-free entry at a few other sites if used on the same day, giving you Rs50 off the admission fee at Agra Fort, and Rs10 off at Sikandra, Itimad-ud-Daulah and Fatehpur Sikri.

It's possible to see the Taj by moonlight on the night of the full moon itself and on the two days before and after. Only four hundred visitors are admitted per night (in batches of fifty between 8pm and midnight, but not Fridays or during Ramadan). Tickets (Rs750 [Rs510]) have to be purchased a day in advance from the ASI office, 22 The Mall (Mon–Sat 10am–6pm; ⓣ0562/222 7261). If a viewing is cancelled, you'll get a refund.

You can **see the Taj for free** by climbing onto a Taj Ganj hotel rooftop, or heading down the eastern side of the compound to a small Krishna temple by the river, where you can see the Taj, and also take a little boat ride (Rs100 to Rs1000, depending on the size of your camera) to see it from the river. Better still, head across the Yamuna River to **Mehtab Bagh**. From the opposite bank of the river the view is breathtaking, especially at dawn. You cross the river on the road bridge north of Agra Fort, and turn right when you reach the far bank, following the metalled road until it enters the village of Katchpura; here, it becomes a rough track that eventually emerges at a small Dalit shrine on the riverside, directly opposite the Taj and next to the entrance of the Mehtab Garden (daily sunrise–sunset; Rs100 [Rs5]). You can see the Taj from the garden's floodlit walkways, and from outside the gardens on the riverbank. Unfortunately, you can no longer access the gardens by boat from across the river by the Taj itself.

Agra Fort

The high red-sandstone ramparts of **Agra Fort** (sunrise–sunset; Rs300 [Rs20], Rs50 discount for foreigners on production of a Taj ticket for the same day) dominate a bend in the Yamuna River 2km northwest of the Taj Mahal. Akbar laid the foundations of this majestic citadel, built between 1565 and 1573 in the form of a half moon, on the remains of earlier Rajput fortifications. The structure developed as the seat and stronghold of the Mughal Empire for successive generations: Akbar commissioned the walls and gates, his grandson, Shah Jahan, had most of the principal buildings erected, and Aurangzeb, the last great emperor, was responsible for the ramparts.

The curved sandstone bastions reach a height of over twenty metres and stretch for around two and a half kilometres, punctuated by a sequence of massive gates, (although only the **Amar Singh Pol** is currently open to visitors). The original

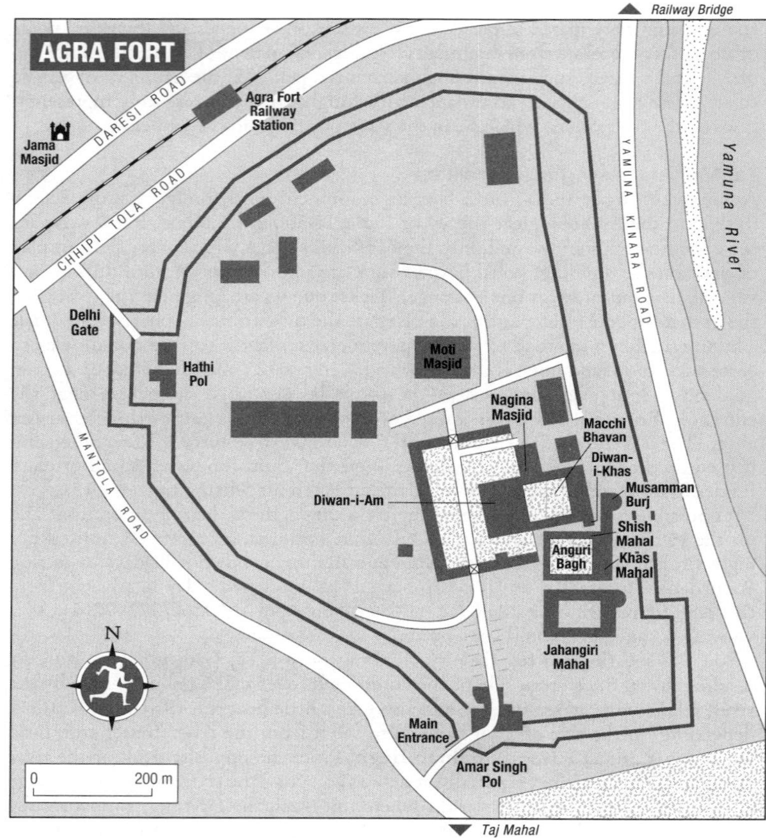

and grandest entrance, however, was through the western side, via the **Delhi Gate** and **Hathi Pol** or "Elephant Gate", now flanked by two red-sandstone towers faced in marble, but once guarded by colossal stone elephants with riders which were destroyed by Aurangzeb in 1668. Access to much of the fort is restricted, and only those parts open to the public are described below.

There's nowhere to buy drinks inside the fort, and exploring the complex can be thirsty work, so unless you're happy to take your chances at the public drinking taps, it's a good idea to take water in with you.

Diwan-i-Am and the great courtyard

Entrance to the fort is through the **Amar Singh Pol**, actually three separate gates placed close together and at right angles to one another to disorientate any potential attackers and to deprive them of the space in which to use battering weapons against the fortifications. From here a ramp climbs gently uphill flanked by high walls (another defensive measure), through a second gate to the spacious courtyard, with tree-studded lawns, which surrounds the graceful **Diwan-i-Am** ("Hall of Public Audience"). Open on three sides, the pillared hall, which replaced an earlier wooden structure, was commissioned by Shah Jahan in 1628. The elegance of the setting would have been enhanced by the addition of brocade, carpets and satin canopies for audiences with the emperor.

The ornate throne alcove – built to house a gem-encrusted Peacock Throne, which was eventually moved to Delhi, only to be looted from there by Nadir Shah and finishing up in Tehran – is inlaid in marble decorated with flowers and foliage in bas-relief, and connects to the royal chambers within. In front of the alcove, the **Baithak**, a small marble table, is where ministers would have sat to deliver petitions and receive commands. This is also where trials would have been conducted, and justice speedily implemented.

The area to the north of the Diwan-i-Am courtyard is, sadly, closed to visitors, though you can make out the delicate white marble domes and chattris of the striking, if rather clumsily proportioned, **Moti Masjid** ("Pearl Mosque") rising beyond the courtyard walls, best seen from the Diwan-i-Am itself. Directly in front of the Diwan-i-Am an incongruously Gothic Christian tomb marks the **grave of John Russell Colvin**, lieutenant governor of the Northwestern Provinces, who died here during the 1857 uprising, when Agra's British population barricaded themselves inside the fort.

The royal pavilions

Heading through the small door to the left of the throne alcove in the Diwan-i-Am and climbing the stairs beyond brings you out onto the upper level of the **Macchi Bhavan** (Fish Palace), a large but relatively plain two-storey structure overlooking a spacious, grassy courtyard. This was once strewn with fountains and flowerbeds, interspersed with tanks and water channels stocked with fish on which the emperor and his courtiers would practise their angling skills, though the Maharaja of Bharatpur subsequently removed some of its marble fixtures to his palace in Deeg, and William Bentinck (governor general from 1828 to 1835) auctioned off much of the palace's original mosaics and fretwork.

On the north side of the courtyard (to the left as you enter) a small door leads to the exquisite little **Nagina Masjid** (Gem Mosque), made entirely of marble. Capped with three domes and approached from a marble-paved courtyard, it was commissioned by Shah Jahan for the ladies of the *zenana* (harem). At the rear on the right, a small balcony with beautifully carved lattice screens offers a discreet viewpoint from where ladies of the harem were able to inspect luxury goods – silks, jewellery and brocade – laid out for sale by merchants in the courtyard below, without themselves being seen.

The raised terrace on the far side of the Macchi Bhavan is adorned by two **thrones**, one black slate, the other white marble. The white one was used by Shah Jahan, the black one by the future emperor Jahangir to watch elephant fights in the eastern enclosure. It now serves, somewhat less gloriously, as a favoured perch for couples posing for photos against the backdrop of the distant Taj.

To your right (as you face the river), a high terrace overlooking the Yamuna is topped with a sequence of lavish royal apartments designed to catch the cool breezes blowing across the waters below. The first is the delicate **Diwan-i-Khas** (Hall of Private Audience), erected in 1635, where the emperor would have received kings, dignitaries and ambassadors, and is one of the most finely decorated buildings in the fort, with paired marble pillars and peacock arches inlaid with lapis lazuli and jasper.

A passageway behind it leads to the tiny **Mina Masjid**, a plain white marble mosque built for Shah Jahan and traditionally said to have been used by him during his imprisonment here. Beyond, the passageway leads to a two-storeyed pavilion known as the **Musamman Burj**, famous as the spot where he is said to have caught his last glimpse of the Taj Mahal before he died, and the most elaborately decorated structure in the fort. Its lattice-screen balustrade is dotted with ornamental niches and with exquisite *pietra dura* inlay covering almost every surface. In front of the tower a courtyard, paved with marble octagons, centres on a **pachisi board** where the emperor, following his father's example at Fatehpur Sikri (see p.263), played *pachisi* (a form of ludo) using dancing girls as pieces.

Past the Musamman Burj, another large courtyard, the **Anguri Bagh** (Grape Garden), is a miniature *charbagh*, its east side flanked by the marble building known as **Khas Mahal** (Private Palace), possibly a drawing room or the emperor's sleeping chamber. The palace is flanked by two so-called **Golden Pavilions**, their curved roofs covered with gilded copper tiles in a style inspired by the thatched roofs of Bengali village huts. In front of the Khas Mahal, steps descend into the northeast corner of the Anguri Bagh and the **Shish Mahal** (Glass Palace), where royal women bathed in the soft lamplight reflected from the mirror-work mosaics that covered the walls and ceiling; unfortunately the building is currently locked, so you can only peek in through the windows.

The Jahangiri Mahal

South of the Khas Mahal lies the huge **Jahangiri Mahal** (Jahangir's Palace), although the name is misleading since it was actually built for Jahangir's father, Akbar, and probably served not as a royal palace, but as a harem. Compared to the classic Mughal designs of the surrounding buildings, this robust sandstone structure has quite a few Hindu elements mixed up with traditional Mughal and Islamic motifs.

From the central courtyard, a gateway leads out through the main gateway into the palace, whose impressive facade shows a characteristic mix of Mughal and Indian motifs, with Islamic pointed arches and inlaid mosaics combined with Hindu-style overhanging eaves supported by heavily carved brackets. Immediately in front of the palace sits **Jahangir's Hauz** (Jahangir's Cistern), a giant bowl with steps inside and out, made in 1611 from a single block of porphyry and inscribed in Persian. Filled with rosewater, it would have been used by the emperor as a bathtub, whilst it's also believed that the emperor took it with him on his travels around the empire – though it seems difficult to credit this, given the bath's size and weight.

Jama Masjid and the bazaars

Opposite the fort, and overlooking Agra Fort railway station is the city's principal mosque, the soaring red-sandstone **Jama Masjid** (Friday Mosque). Built in 1648 it was originally connected directly to the fort's principal entrance, the Delhi Gate, by a large courtyard, but the British ran a railway line between the two, leaving the mosque stranded in no-man's land on the far side of the tracks.

Standing on a high plinth above the chaotic streets of the surrounding bazaar (of which it affords fine views), the mosque is crowned by three large sandstone domes covered in distinctive zigzagging bands of marble. Five huge arches lead into the main prayer hall, topped by a prettily inlaid band of sandstone decorated in abstract floral patterns, while inside the mihrab is surrounded by delicate flourishes of Koranic script, inlaid in black, a design mirrored in the principal archway.

The space around the base of the mosque is now filled with the crowded – but refreshingly hassle-free – streets of **Kinari Bazaar**, a fascinating warren crammed full with shops and stalls, though the numbers of people, scooters, cycle rickshaws and cows pushing their way through the streets make exploring it a slow and tiring business. Opposite the northeast corner of the complex, look out for the **petha-wallahs**, purveyors of Agra's most famous sweet (see p.258).

Itimad-ud-daulah

On the east bank of the Yamuna River some 3km north of Agra Fort, the beautiful **Itimad-ud-daulah** (pronounced "Atma Dolla"; daily sunrise–sunset; Rs110 [Rs10]), is the tomb of Mirza Ghiyas Beg, *wazir* (chief minister) and father-in-law of Emperor Jahangir, who gave him the title of Itimad-ud-daulah, or "Pillar of the State". The tomb is popularly known among Agra's rickshaw-wallahs as the "**Baby Taj**", and though it's much smaller and less successfully proportioned than its more famous relative, it does foreshadow the Taj in being the first building in Mughal Agra to be faced entirely in marble, with lavish use of *pietra dura* inlay to decorate its translucent exterior walls.

The tomb sits at the centre of a *charbagh* garden, though here entered from the eastern (rather than the usual southern) side, presumably to highlight its setting against the backdrop of the Yamuna River – another element of its design which anticipates that of the Taj. The building's undersized rooftop pavilion replaces the usual dome, and has four stocky minarets stuck onto each corner. However, these imperfections seem unimportant given the superbly intricate **inlay work** which covers virtually the entire tomb – an incredible profusion of floral and geometrical patterning in muted reds, oranges, browns and greys that give it the appearance of an enormous, slightly hallucinogenic experiment in medieval op-art. Elegant inlaid designs showing characteristic Persian motifs including wine vases, trees and honeysuckles adorn the arches of the four entrances, and the walls inside are covered in rather eroded and clumsily restored paintings of further vases, flowers and cypresses.

Chini-ka-Rauza and Rambagh

Around 1km north of Itimad-ud-daulah is the **Chini-ka-Rauza**, built between 1628 and 1639 as the mausoleum of Afzal Khan, a Persian poet from Shiraz who was one of Shah Jahan's ministers. As befits his origins, Afzal Khan's tomb is of purely Persian design, the only such building in Agra.

A kilometre or so north of the Chini-ka-Rauza, amidst the dusty sprawl of northern Agra, the **Rambagh** gardens (daily sunrise–sunset; Rs110 [Rs10]) are one of the very few surviving physical remains in India from the reign of the Mughal dynasty's founder Babur, though there's little left to see here now. The gardens were originally laid out in 1526 following the Persian *charbagh* plan, which would subsequently prove the prototype for all later Mughal gardens in the Subcontinent.

Akbar's mausoleum: Sikandra

Given the Mughal tradition of magnificent tombs, it is no surprise that the mausoleum of the most distinguished Mughal ruler was one of the most ambitious structures of its time. **Akbar's mausoleum** (daily sunrise–sunset; Rs110 [Rs10]) borders the side of the main highway to Mathura at **SIKANDRA**, 10km northwest of Agra. Rickshaws charge at least Rs120 for the round trip, or you could hop on a Mathura-bound bus from Agra Fort Bus Stand.

The complex is entered via its huge **Buland Darwaza** (Great Gate), surmounted by four tapering marble minarets, and overlaid with marble and coloured tiles in repetitive geometrical patterns, bearing the Koranic inscription "These are the gardens of Eden, enter them and live forever". Through the gateway, extensive, park-like **gardens** are divided by fine raised sandstone walkways into the four equal quadrants of the typical Mughal *charbagh* design. Langur monkeys may be seen along the path, while deer roam through the tall grasses, just as they do in the Mughal miniature paintings dating from the era when the tomb was constructed, lending the whole place a magically peaceful and rural atmosphere.

The **mausoleum** itself sits in the middle of the gardens, at the centre of the *charbagh* and directly in front of Buland Darwaza. The entire structure is one of the strangest in Mughal Agra, its huge square base topped not by the usual dome but by a three-storey open-sided sandstone construction crowned with a solid-looking marble pavilion. The mishmash design may be attributable to Jahangir, who ordered changes in the mausoleum's design halfway through its construction, Akbar himself having neglected to leave finished plans for his mausoleum. By the standards of India's other Mughal buildings, it's architecturally a failure, but not without a certain whimsical charm, and much of the inlay work around the lower storey is exquisite.

A high marble gateway in the mausoleum's southern facade frames an elaborate lattice screen shielding a small vestibule painted with rich sea-blue frescoes and Koranic verses. From here a ramp leads down into a large, echoing and absolutely plain subterranean **crypt**, lit by a single skylight, in the centre of which stands Akbar's grave, decorated with the pen-box motif, the symbol of a male ruler, which can also be seen on Shah Jahan's tomb in the Taj Mahal.

Off the road on the opposite side, a kilometre north of Sikandra, lies the altogether more modest **Mariam's tomb** (daily sunrise–sunset; Rs100 [Rs5]), the mausoleum of Akbar's wife and Jahangir's mother Mariam Zamani.

Eating

In culinary terms, Agra is famous as the home of **Mughlai cooking**. Imitated in Indian curry houses throughout the world, the city's traditional Persian-influenced cuisine is renowned for its rich cream- and curd-based sauces, accompanied by naan and tandoori breads roasted in earthen ovens, pulao rice dishes and milky sweets such as *kheer*. Mughlai specialities can be sampled in many of the town's better restaurants, the majority of which can be found in **Sadar Bazaar** and along **Fatehabad Road**. There are also innumerable scruffy little travellers' cafés around **Taj Ganj**, though standards of hygiene are often suspect and the food is generally uninspiring, with slow service the norm. Taj Ganj's saving grace is the **rooftop cafés**, many with fine Taj views, which cap most of its buildings – the best views are from the *Kamal* and *Shanti Lodge* guesthouses – though of course you can't see anything after dark, except on or around full-moon days.

Local **specialities** of Agra are *petha* (crystallized pumpkin) – the best is the Panchi brand, available at various outlets all over Agra, particularly in the row of *petha* shops in Kinari Bazaar along the northeast side of the Jama Masjid (past *Chimman Lal Puri Wale*). Look out too for *ghazak*, a rock-hard candy with nuts, and *dalmoth*, a crunchy mix made with black lentils.

Agra's restaurants – including even apparently reputable establishments – are not immune to the epidemic of **credit-card fraud** (see p.260). It's best not to pay by credit card except in the city's five-star establishments, or, if you do, to supervise the operation carefully. Other than *Sheela* and *Joney's Place*, which are shown on the Taj Ganj map (p.249), all the places listed below are marked on the Agra map, p.245.

Achman Agra–Delhi Highway (NH-2), Dayal Bagh, 5km out of town near Baghwan Cinema. Highly rated among Agra-wallahs in the know, famous for its *navratan* korma (a mildly spiced mix of nuts, dried fruit and *paneer*), *malai* kofta and chickpea masala, as well as wonderful stuffed naans. Well off the tourist trail in the north of the city, but ideally placed for dinner on your way home from Sikandra (to which it's about halfway), and reachable by shared auto from Agra Fort bus station or Gwalior Road. Mains Rs95–145.

Chimman Lal Puri Wale Opposite northeast wall of Jama Masjid. An Agra institution for five generations, this much-loved little café-restaurant looks a touch grubby from the outside, but serves delicious *puri*-thalis, with two veg dishes and a sweet – all for Rs30. Ideal pit-stop after visiting the Jama Masjid.

Dasaprakash Meher Theatre Complex, 1 Gwalior Rd, close to the *Tourists Rest House*. Offshoot of the famous Chennai restaurant, serving a limited menu of top-notch South Indian food and an extensive ice-cream menu – the "hot fudge bonanza split" wins by a nose. Most mains Rs80–150, thalis Rs100–210.

Joney's Place Chowk Kagzi, Taj Ganj. Oldest and best of the Taj Ganj travellers' cafés, going since 1978, and open from 5am in case you need breakfast ahead of a dawn visit to the Taj. The Indian breakfast (*puris*, chickpea curry, *jalebi* and chai) is pretty good, or there's spaghetti, macaroni, veg or non-veg curries, even (on occasion) hummus and a version of falafel. Main dishes Rs30–70.

Lakshmi Villas 50-A Sadar Bazaar. Unpretentious but deservedly popular South Indian café in the middle of Sadar Bazaar offering the usual menu of *iddlis,* dosas and *uttapams*, plus a couple of thalis – a good, and much cheaper, alternative to *Dasaprakash*, with most dishes at a bargain Rs55–80, thali Rs88.

The Mandarin *Yamuna View Hotel*. One of the best non-Indian restaurants in town, this rather snazzy-looking Chinese offers a possibly welcome change from Mughlai curries and masala dosas. The large (though rather expensive) menu features a good selection of delicately prepared dishes like stir-fried vegetables in almond sauce and chicken in honey chilli, with the emphasis on light ingredients and subtle flavours. Non-veg mains Rs330–400 (seafood Rs400–575).

Only Corner of The Mall and Taj Rd. One of Agra's most popular North Indian restaurants, usually packed with local families and tourist groups and known for its well-prepared tandoori and Mughlai creations, though there's also a wide selection of more mainstream North Indian meat and veg standards, plus a few Chinese and continental offerings. There's seating in an indoor a/c dining room or in the pleasant courtyard. Non-veg mains Rs140–295.

Park Restaurant Taj Rd, Sadar Bazaar. A long-established favourite with both locals and tourists, this simple a/c restaurant dishes up an excellent range of classic Mughlai chicken dishes, along with more mainstream tandooris and meat and veg curries accompanied by superb naan breads, plus a modest selection of continental and Chinese favourites. Most mains Rs90–185; the house speciality is a *banno* kebab, made of chicken pieces in spicy cashew paste (Rs200).

Sheela East Gate, Taj Ganj. The most dependable and pleasant place to eat near the Taj, with outside seating in the shady garden or inside the narrow café. The menu features a good choice of simple Indian dishes, as well as drinks and snacks, and the fruit lassis are more of a yogurty dessert than a drink. Non-veg mains Rs90–250.

Tourists Rest House Kutchery Rd, Baluganj. Atmospheric, candle-lit garden restaurant serving a modest selection of breakfasts and Indian veg dishes to a clientele of foreign backpackers. Try the tasty vegetable kofta, rounded off with banana custard. Mains Rs35–80.

Zorba the Buddha E-19 Shopping Arcade, Sadar Bazaar. Aimed unashamedly at foreign tourists, though you'll find Indian people eating here too, this prettily decorated little place promises no chilli unless you ask for it, and offers, along with Indian veg dishes, odd specialities such as a Hawaiian spree (vegetables and pineapple in pineapple sauce) or a fiesta (vegetables in tomato and cashew sauce), but generally tasty and well presented, at Rs90–150 a throw, with a Rs350 (plus VAT) set meal. Closed in June.

Shopping

Agra is renowned for its **marble** tabletops, vases and trays, inlaid with semi-precious stones in ornate floral designs, in imitation of those found in the Taj Mahal. It is also an excellent place to buy **leather**: Agra's shoe industry supplies all India, and its tanneries export bags, briefcases and jackets. **Carpets** and **dhurries** are manufactured here too, and traditional embroidery continues to thrive. *Zari* and *zardozi* are brightly coloured, the latter building up three-dimensional patterns with fantastic motifs; *chikan* uses more delicate overlay techniques.

There are several large emporiums such as the official-sounding Cottage Industries Exposition on the Fatehabad Road, which is well presented but outrageously expensive; it is one of the places you're likely to be taken to by a commission-seeking driver. Shops in the big hotels may be pricey, but their quality and service are usually more reliable. State emporiums round the Taj include UP's

Gangotri, which has fixed prices. Close to the East Gate, Shilpgram is an extensive crafts village with arts and handicrafts from all over India, and occasional live music and dance performances.

Shopping or browsing around The Mall, MG Road, Munro Road, Kinari Bazaar, Sadar Bazaar and the Taj Complex is fun, but you need to know what you're buying and be prepared to haggle; you should also be wary of ordering anything to be sent overseas. It's advisable never to let your credit card out of your sight, even for the transaction to be authorized, and you should make sure that all documentation is filled in correctly and fully so as not to allow unauthorized later additions; a large number of serious cases of **credit-card fraud** have been reported in Agra. A list of stores against whom complaints have been lodged is maintained by the local police department. Remember that if you arrive at any shop in a **rickshaw** or **taxi**, the prices of anything you buy will be inflated to cover the driver's commission. If you're planning on buying, ask to be dropped off nearby, and then walk to the shop.

Listings

Airlines Indian Airlines, *Clarks Shiraz* hotel ⓣ0562/222 6821; Jet, *Clarks Shiraz* hotel ⓣ0562/222 6527.
Banks and exchange There are two ATMs at Cantonment railway station, and a few dotted around the city (marked on the maps on p.245 & p.249). The State Bank of India is just south of Taj Rd in the Cantonment (Amex travellers' cheques not accepted); Allahabad Bank is in the *Clarks Shiraz* hotel. There are several private exchange offices in Taj Ganj, and in the Tourist Complex Area around *Amar Yatri Niwas* and *Mansingh Palace* hotels (Varun Forex, opposite *Amar Yatri Niwas* on Fatehabad Rd, for example).
Hospitals Clean and dependable private hospitals with English-speaking doctors: SR Hospital, Namner Cross Roads ⓣ0562/242 1362; GG Nursing Home, 106/2 Sanjay Place ⓣ0562/285 3952; Pushpanjali, Delhi Gate ⓣ0562/252 7566 to 8. The District Hospital, MG Rd, Chipitola ⓣ0562/236 3043 gives free treatment, and may be preferable for minor injuries. Avoid backstreet clinics, even if recommended by your hotel manager, and in particular, if you fall ill with what appears to be food poisoning, do not go to a clinic or doctor suggested by someone in the restaurant concerned.
Internet There's plenty of internet access available around town, particularly in Taj Ganj; rates virtually everywhere are Rs30/hr. Many hotels and guesthouses have their own internet connections.
Photography Numerous places on MG Rd, a block north of The Mall, can download and burn digital images to disc or make prints, as can Moonlight Studio (corner of West Gate and Chowk Kagzi) in Taj Ganj.
Police There are police stations on Chowk Kagzi in Taj Ganj (ⓣ0562/233 1015) and on Mahatma Gandhi Rd in Sadar Bazaar, slightly south of the intersection with Fatehpur Sikri Rd (ⓣ0562/222 6561). Agra now has a dedicated tourist police force, specifically to protect tourists from crime; they can be contacted through UP Tourism or on ⓣ9454 402764.
Post The Head Post Office is on The Mall, near India Tourism.
Swimming The pools at most of Agra's hotels are usually reserved for the use of hotel guests only, though a few places admit outsiders on payment of a fee. These currently include the *Yamuna View* (Rs350) and *Clarks Shiraz* (Rs500), and (both near *Amar Yatri Niwas) the Amar* (Rs300) and *Mansingh Palace* (Rs400).

Fatehpur Sikri

The ghost city of **FATEHPUR SIKRI**, former imperial capital of the great Mughal emperor **Akbar**, straddles the crest of a rocky ridge 40km southwest of Agra. The city was built here between 1569 and 1585 as a result of the emperor's enthusiasm for the local Muslim divine **Sheikh Salim Chishti** (see p.264), though the move away from Agra may also have had something to do with Akbar's weariness of the crowds and his desire to create a new capital that was an

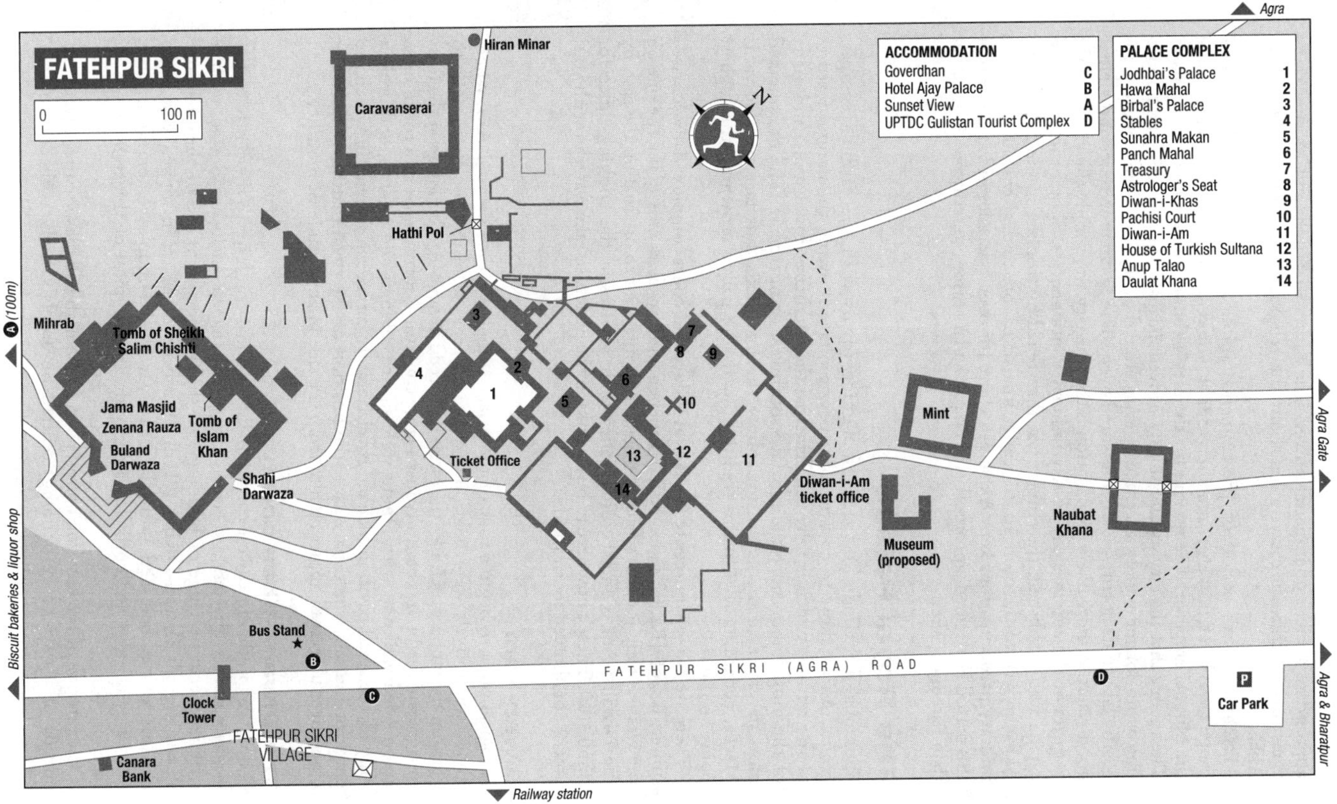

FATEHPUR SIKRI

0 100 m

ACCOMMODATION

Goverdhan	C
Hotel Ajay Palace	B
Sunset View	A
UPTDC Gulistan Tourist Complex	D

PALACE COMPLEX

Jodhbai's Palace	1
Hawa Mahal	2
Birbal's Palace	3
Stables	4
Sunahra Makan	5
Panch Mahal	6
Treasury	7
Astrologer's Seat	8
Diwan-i-Khas	9
Pachisi Court	10
Diwan-i-Am	11
House of Turkish Sultana	12
Anup Talao	13
Daulat Khana	14

Agra
Hiran Minar
Caravanserai
Hathi Pol
Mihrab
Tomb of Sheikh Salim Chishti
Jama Masjid
Zenana Rauza
Tomb of Islam Khan
Buland Darwaza
Shahi Darwaza
Ticket Office
Diwan-i-Am ticket office
Mint
Museum (proposed)
Naubat Khana
Agra Gate
Agra & Bharatpur
Car Park
FATEHPUR SIKRI (AGRA) ROAD
Bus Stand
Clock Tower
FATEHPUR SIKRI VILLAGE
Canara Bank
Railway station
Biscuit bakeries & liquor shop
A (100m)

appropriate symbol of imperial power. The fusion of Hindu and Muslim traditions in its architecture says a lot about the religious and cultural tolerance of Akbar's reign.

Fatehpur Sikri's period of pre-eminence amongst the cities of the Mughal Empire was brief, however, and after 1585 it would never again serve as the seat of the Mughal emperor. The reasons for the **city's abandonment** remain enigmatic. The theory that the city's water supply proved incapable of sustaining its population is no longer widely accepted – even after the city had been deserted, the nearby lake to its northwest still measured over 20km in circumference and yielded good water. A more likely explanation is that the city was simply the victim of the vagaries of the empire's day-to-day military contingencies. Shortly after the new capital was established, the empire was threatened by troubles in the Punjab, and Akbar moved to the more strategically situated Lahore to deal with them. These military preoccupations kept Akbar at Lahore for over a decade, and at the end of this period he decided, apparently for no particular reason, to return to Agra rather than Fatehpur Sikri.

The Royal Palace

Shunning the Hindu tradition of aligning towns with the cardinal compass points, Akbar chose to construct his new capital following the natural features of the terrain, which is why the principal thoroughfare, town walls, and many of the most important buildings face southwest or northeast. The mosque and most private apartments do not follow the main axis, but face west towards Mecca, according to Muslim tradition, with the palace crowning the highest point on the ridge.

There are two **entrances** to the **Royal Palace** and court complex (daily sunrise–sunset; Rs260 [Rs20], video Rs25). Independent travellers mostly use the one on the west side, by Jodhbai's Palace; organized tours tend to use that on the east, by the Diwan-i-Am. Official **guides** offer their services at the booking office for Rs50–100. There's nowhere to buy drinks in the palace, so take water in with you; you're not allowed to eat inside.

Diwan-i-Am

A logical place to begin a tour of the palace complex is the **Diwan-i-Am**, where important festivals were held, and where citizens could exercise their right to petition the emperor. Unlike the ornate pillared Diwan-i-Am buildings at the forts in Agra and Delhi, it is basically just a large courtyard, surrounded by a continuous colonnaded walkway with Hindu-style square columns and capitals, and broken only by the small pavilion, flanked by elaborately carved *jali* screens, in which the emperor himself would have sat – the position of the royal platform forced the emperor's subjects to approach him from the side in an attitude of humility.

The Diwan-i-Khas courtyard

A doorway in the northwest corner of the Diwan-i-Am leads to the centre of the *mardana* (men's quarters), a large, irregularly shaped enclosure dotted with a strikingly eclectic range of buildings. At the far (northern) end of the enclosure stands the tall **Diwan-i-Khas** ("Hall of Private Audience"), topped with four chhatris and embellished with the heavily carved Hindu-style brackets, large overhanging eaves and corbelled arches which are typical of the architecture of Fatehpur Sikri.

The interior of the building consists of a single high hall (despite the appearance outside of a two-storey building) centred on an elaborately corbelled column known as the **Throne Pillar**, supporting a large circular platform from which four balustraded bridges radiate outwards. Seated upon this throne, the emperor held discussions with representatives of diverse religions, aiming to synthesize India's religions into one. The pillar symbolizes this project by incorporating motifs drawn from Hinduism, Buddhism, Islam and Christianity.

Next to the Diwan-i-Khas lies the three-roomed **Treasury**, its brackets embellished by mythical sea creatures, guardians of the treasures of the deep; it's also known as Ankh Michauli, meaning hide and seek, which it's said was played here – in fact both names are probably just fanciful inventions, and the building most likely served as a multi-purpose pavilion which could be used for a variety of functions, as could most buildings in Mughal palaces. Attached to it is the so-called **Astrologer's Seat**, a small pavilion embellished with elaborate Jain carvings.

In the middle of the courtyard, separating the Diwan-i-Khas from the buildings on the opposite (south) side of the complex is the **Pachisi Court**, a giant board used to play *pachisi* (similar to ludo). Akbar is said to have been a fanatical player, using slave girls dressed in colourful costumes as live pieces. Abu'l Fazl, the court chronicler, related that at "times more than two hundred persons participated, and no one was allowed to go home until he had played sixteen rounds. This could take up to three months. If one of the players lost his patience and became restless, he was made to drink a cupful of wine. Seen superficially, this appears to be just a game. But His Majesty pursues higher objectives. He weighs up the talents of his people and teaches them to be affable."

House of the Turkish Sultana

Diagonally opposite the *pachisi* board, the **House of the Turkish Sultana** (or Anup Talao Pavilion) gained its name from the popular belief that it was the residence of one of Akbar's favourite wives, the Sultana Ruqayya Begum – though this seems unlikely given its location in the centre of the men's quarters. The name was probably made up by nineteenth-century guides to titillate early tourists, and the building is more likely to have served as a simple pleasure pavilion. Its superbly carved stone walls are covered with a profusion of floral and geometrical designs, plus some partially vandalized animal carvings.

South of here is the **Anup Talao** (Peerless Pool), a pretty little ornamental pond divided by four walkways connected to a small "island" in the middle – a layout reminiscent of the raised walkways inside the Diwan-i-Khas.

The Daulat Khana and Panch Mahal

Facing the Turkish Sultana's house from the other side of the Anup Talao are Akbar's former private sleeping and living quarters, the **Daulat Khana** ("Abode of Fortune"). The room on the ground floor with alcoves in its walls was the emperor's library, where he would be read to (he himself was illiterate) from a collection of fifty thousand manuscripts he allegedly took everywhere with him. Behind the library is the imperial sleeping chamber, the **Khwabgah** ("House of Dreams"), with an enormous raised bed in its centre.

One of Fatehpur Sikri's most famous structures, the **Panch Mahal** or "Five-Storeyed Palace", looms northwest of here, marking the beginning of the **zenana** (women's quarters) which make up the entire western side of the palace complex. The palace tapers to a final single kiosk and is supported by 176 columns of varying designs; the ground floor contains 84 pillars – an auspicious number in Hindu astrology. The open spaces between the pillars were originally covered with latticed screens, so that ladies of the *zenana* could observe goings-on in the courtyard of the *mardana* below without themselves being seen.

The women's quarters

Directly behind the Panch Mahal, a courtyard garden was reserved for the *zenana* (harem). The adjoining **Sunahra Makan** (Golden House), also known as Mariam's House, is variously thought to have been the home of the emperor's mother or of Akbar's wife Mariam. It is enlivened by the faded remains of paintings on its walls (whose now vanished golden paint gave the pavilion its name), by the lines of verse penned by Abu'l Fazl, inscribed around the ceiling in blue bands, and by the quaint little carvings tucked into the brackets supporting the roof, including several elephants and a tiny carving of Rama attended by Hanuman (on the north side of the building, facing the *zenana* courtyard garden).

Solemnly presiding over the whole complex is the main harem, known as **Jodhbai's Palace**. The residence of several of the emperor's senior wives, this striking building is the grandest and largest in the entire city, and looks decidedly Hindu even in the eclectic context of Fatehpur Sikri, having been modelled after Rajput palaces such as those at Gwalior and Orchha.

On the north side of the palace, the **Hawa Mahal** ("Palace of the Winds"), a small screened tower with a delicately carved chamber, was designed to catch the evening breeze, while a raised covered walkway, lined with five large chhatris, leads from here to a (now vanished) lake.

Northwest of Jodhbai's Palace lies a third women's palace, known as **Birbal's Palace** – though this is another misnomer, as Birbal, Akbar's favourite courtier, was a man and would have been most unwelcome in the middle of the *zenana*. It's more likely to have been the residence of two of Akbar's senior wives.

Jama Masjid

At the southwestern corner of the palace complex, with the village of Fatehpur Sikri nestling at its base, stands the **Jama Masjid** (daily dawn to dusk) or Dargah Mosque, one of the finest in the whole of India. Unfortunately, the mosque is rife with self-appointed "guides" (around Rs20 for a tour) who make it all but impossible to enjoy the place in peace. The mosque was apparently completed in 1571, before work on the palace commenced, showing the religious significance which Akbar accorded the entire site. This was due to its connections with the Sufi saint Sheikh Salim Chishti, who is buried here, and who played a crucial role in the founding of Fatehpur Sikri by prophesying the birth of a son to the emperor: when one of Akbar's wives Rani Jodhabai, a Hindu Rajput princess from Amber, became pregnant she was sent here until the birth of her son Salim, who later became the emperor Jahangir. Fatehpur Sikri was constructed in the saint's honour.

The neck-cricking **Buland Darwaza** (Great Gate), a spectacular entrance scaled by an impressive flight of steps, was added around 1576 to commemorate Akbar's military campaign in Gujarat. Flanked by domed kiosks, the archway of the simple sandstone memorial is inscribed with a message from the Koran: "Said Jesus Son of Mary (peace be on him): The world is but a bridge – pass over without building houses on it. He who hopes for an hour hopes for eternity; the world is an hour – spend it in prayer for the rest is unseen." The numerous horseshoes nailed to the doors here date from the beginning of the twentieth century – an odd instance of British folk superstition in this very Islamic place.

The gate leads into a vast cloistered courtyard, far larger than any previous mosque in India. The **prayer hall**, on the west (left) side, is the focus of the mosque, punctuated by an enormous gateway. More eye-catching is the exquisite **Tomb of Sheikh Salim Chishti**, directly ahead as you enter the courtyard. Much of this was originally crafted in red sandstone and only later faced in marble: the beautiful lattice screens – another design feature probably imported from Gujarat,

Akbar's harem

Although remembered primarily for his liberal approach to religion, Akbar was typically Mughal in his attitudes to women, whom he collected in much the same way as a philatelist amasses stamps. At its height of splendour, the **royal harem** at Fatehpur Sikri held around five thousand women, guarded by a legion of eunuchs. Its doors were closed to outsiders, but rumours permeated the sandstone walls and several notable travellers were smuggled inside the Great Mughals' seraglios, leaving for posterity often lurid accounts of the emperors' private lives.

The size of Akbar's harem grew in direct proportion to his empire. With each new conquest, he would be gifted by the defeated rulers and nobles their most beautiful daughters, who, together with their maidservants, would be installed in the luxurious royal **zenana**. In all, the emperor is thought to have kept three hundred wives; their ranks were swollen by a constant flow of concubines (*kaniz*), dancing girls (*kanchni*) and female slaves (*bandis*), or "silver bodied damsels with musky tresses" as one chronicler described them, purchased from markets across Asia. Screened from public view by ornately pierced stone *jali* windows were women from the four corners of the Mughal empire, as well as Afghans, Turks, Iranians, Arabs, Tibetans, Russians and Abyssinians, and even one Portuguese, sent as presents or tribute.

The **eunuchs** who presided over them came from similarly diverse backgrounds. While some were hermaphrodites, others had been forcibly castrated, either as punishment following defeat on the battlefield, or after having been donated by their fathers as payment of backdated revenue – an all too common custom at the time.

Akbar is said to have consumed prodigious quantities of Persian wine, *araq* (a spirit distilled from sugar cane), bhang and opium. The lavish dance recitals held in the harem, as well as sexual liaisons conducted on the top pavilion of the Panch Mahal and in the *zenana* itself, would have been fuelled by these substances. Over time, Akbar's hedonistic ways incurred the disapproval of his highest clerics – the *Ulema*. The Koran expressly limits the number of wives a man may take to four, but one verse also admits a lower form of marriage, known as *muta*, more like an informal pact, which could be entered into with non-Muslims. Akbar's abuse of this long-lapsed law was heavily criticized by his Sunni head priest during their religious disquisitions.

What life must actually have been like for the women who lived in Akbar's harem one can only imagine, but it is known that alcoholism and drug addiction were widespread, and that some also risked their lives to conduct illicit affairs with male lovers, smuggled in disguised as physicians or under heavy Muslim veils.

In fact, the notion that the harem was a gilded prison whose inmates whiled their lifetimes away in idle vanity and dalliance is something of a myth. Many women in the *zenana* were immensely rich in their own right, and wielded enormous influence on the court. Jahangir's wife, Nur Jahan, virtually ran the empire from behind the screen of purdah during the last five years of her husband's ailing reign, while her mother-in-law owned a ship that traded between Surat and the Red Sea, a tradition continued by Shah Jahan's daughter, who grew immensely wealthy through her business enterprises.

Partly as a result of the money and power at the women's disposal, jealousies in the harem were also rife, and the work of maintaining order and calm among the thousands of foster mothers, aunties, the emperor's relatives and all his wives, minor wives, paramours, musicians, dancers, amazons and slaves, was a major preoccupation. As Akbar's court chronicler wryly observed, "The government of the kingdom is but an amusement compared with such a task, for it is within the (harem) that intrigue is enthroned."

though it would later become a staple of Mughal architecture – are unusually intricate, with striking serpentine exterior brackets supporting the eaves.

Practicalities

Buses leave either from the crowded bus stand in the centre of the village or from the bus stop on the bypass near Agra Gate, about 1.5km from town (about Rs10 by tonga from the village) – it's usually quickest to pick up a bus from Agra Gate, especially if you're heading to Jaipur (every 30min; 4hr). Services from the bus stand itself go to Agra's Idgah Bus Stand (every 30min; 1hr–1hr 30min) and to Bharatpur (hourly; 30–45min). There are shared jeeps from the village to Agra (Rs25), but they depart very full, the driving isn't marvellous and they frequently have accidents. There are four daily **trains** from Fatehpur Sikri to Agra, overnight services to Lucknow and to Kota, Bundi and Chittaurgarh, and even a direct (though not conveniently timed) train to Mumbai; the station also has a computer reservation office.

Transport around the village takes the form of tongas and auto-rickshaws, but for most people it's just as easy to walk. Canara Bank has an **ATM**, and the *Hotel Goverdhan* will change cash dollars, pounds or euros.

Accommodation and eating

You'll probably **eat** where you stay. If you want to go out, try the *Goverdhan* or the *Ajay Palace* hotel. Fatehpur Sikri's delicious biscuits are not to be missed – you can savour them hot out of the oven each evening at the bakeries on the lane leading up from the bazaar to the Jama Masjid.

Ajay Palace Agra Rd ⓣ05613/282950. Simple hotel in the village, with small, plain rooms, but very clean (though hot water comes in buckets), and there's a nice little rooftop terrace. ❶

Goverdhan Buland Gate Rd, just east of the bus stand ⓣ05613/282643, ⓦwww.hotelfatehpursikriviews.com. A wide range of well-kept rooms arranged around a neat lawn, as well as good food (made with filtered or mineral water) and a friendly and helpful proprietor. ❶–❹

UPTDC Gulistan Tourist Complex Agra Rd, 1km east of the village ⓣ05613/282490. A low-rise, modern building in red sandstone, which looks rather like an academic institution, and has decent if functional rooms, plus a restaurant, a pool room and a small bar. ❸–❹

Sunset View 100m west of the Jama Masjid ⓣ05613/283129. Backpacker guesthouse offering neat, clean if basic rooms, and superb views over the Jama Masjid and the countryside beyond. ❶

Jhansi

Despite its seventeenth-century fort, the rail- and road-junction town of **JHANSI**, in an anomalous promontory of UP that thrusts south into Madhya Pradesh, is not very exciting. Most visitors stop only long enough to catch a connecting bus to **Khajuraho**, 175km southeast in Madhya Pradesh. Like Avadh (see p.243), Jhansi was an independent state until the British summarily annexed it in 1854, and was consequently a major centre of support for the 1857 uprising, under the leadership of **Rani Lakshmibai**, its last ruler's widow, and the uprising's great heroine.

Arrival and information

Trains pull in at the station on the west side of town, near the Civil Lines area. There are UP and MP **tourist information** kiosks on platform 1; UP (Mon–Sat 10am–5pm, but closed on the second Saturday of the month, and often closed for breaks as it has a staff of only one) gives town plans, while MP (daily 9am–5pm; ⓣ0510/244 2622) has information about getting to Khajuraho. In town, the **UP Tourist Office** at the *Hotel Veerangana* on Shivpuri Road (Mon–Sat 10am–5pm;

Moving on from Jhansi

Jhansi is the most convenient main railway station for Khajuraho and Orchha. Buses to Khajuraho go from the **bus stand** 3km east – private buses (5 daily; 4hr 30min; Rs98) are faster and more comfortable than the state buses (5 daily; 5hr 30min; Rs90). In addition to the thrice-weekly #2448 *Sampark Kranti Express* from Delhi, which departs Jhansi at the ungodly hour of 3.30am (Mon, Wed and Sat) to arrive at Khajuraho at 7.50am, there's also the local Khajuraho Link Passenger Train #229, which leaves Jhansi at 7.20am daily, reaching Khajuraho at 12.10pm. Shared **tempos** for **Orchha** (45min; Rs10) wait alongside the bus stand, or you can take an auto (Rs225 pre-paid from Jhansi railway station). **Car rental** is available through the larger hotels, as well as the helpful Baghel Travels (Ⓣ0510/244 1255), opposite Damru Cinema, off Elite Cross, the busy intersection in the middle of town.

Ⓣ0510/244 1267) provides information on Bundelkhand and the route to Khajuraho. There's a pre-paid auto booth in front of the station, where you'll pay Rs40 to the fort (Rs175 for a round trip plus waiting time), Rs45 to the bus stand. There are two **ATMs** next to Damru Cinema, and there's a State Bank of India 200m east on Jhokan Bagh Road.

Accommodation and eating

With Orchha just down the road, few people **stay** in Jhansi. Options if you do want to stay include: the *Jhansi* on Shastri Marg, opposite the GPO (Ⓣ0510/247 0360, Ⓔjhansihotel@sancharnet.in; ❹), a former haunt of British burra sahibs, with a well-stocked and atmospheric colonial bar and restaurant, and a small garden; or the more modern and functional *Shrinath Palace* on Station Road in the Civil Lines district, between the station and Damru Cinema (Ⓣ0510/244 5555; ❹–❺), where all the rooms have a/c and TV, but only the deluxe rooms have windows. Most Jhansi **hotels** operate 24-hour checkout.

For a cheap alternative to hotel **restaurants**, try the *Railway Refreshment Rooms* in the station, which serve freshly cooked thalis (Rs22 veg, Rs27 non-veg) and budget breakfasts. Otherwise, there's a row of places on Shastri Marg including *Let's Eat*, a bright, new air-conditioned restaurant serving snacks and meals, largely chicken (butter, handi or green masala, among other variations; non-veg mains Rs140–160). The *Nav Bharat*, 200m up the street, has veg or non-veg thalis, dosas, curries, burgers and sizzlers (non-veg mains Rs80–110; closed Tues). Next door, Sharma Sweets is a good spot for a bit of *mithai* confectionery – the nutty dry fruit *ladoo* is wonderful.

The Town

Like many former British cities, Jhansi is divided into two distinct areas: the wide tree-lined avenues, leafy gardens and bungalows of the **Cantonment** and **Civil Lines** to the west, and the clutter of narrow lanes, minarets and *shikharas* of the **old town** to the east. Dominating it all from a bare brown craggy hill, **Jhansi Fort** (daily sunrise–sunset; Rs100 [Rs5], video camera Rs25), built in 1613 by Bir Singh Joo Deo, raja of Orchha, is worth visiting primarily for the **views** from its ramparts – to the old town on one side, and the Cantonment on the other. Rani Lakshmibai is supposed to have leapt over the west wall on horseback to escape the British, though she must have had a very athletic horse to do so. Inside the fort are a couple of unremarkable temples, plus an old cistern and the ruins of a palace. The fort also has a nightly **sound and light show** (in English April–Oct 7.30pm, Nov–March 6.30pm; Rs250 [Rs20]).

Two minutes' walk from the roundabout below the fort, the **Rani Lakshmi Mahal** (daily sunrise–sunset; Rs100 [Rs5], no photography allowed) is a small stately home in "Bundela style" (lots of ornate balconies and domed roofs), built as a palace for the *rani*. The home was the scene of a brutal massacre in 1858, when British troops bayoneted all its occupants (they murdered some five thousand people in all after recapturing Jhansi from the insurgents). These days, the building is a memorial and archeological museum, with unlabelled fragments of antique stone sculpture littered around its attractive interior courtyard.

The grounds of a Cantonment seminary between the station and the GPO hold one of the most important Catholic pilgrimage sites in India, **St Jude's Shrine**. A bone belonging to Jude the Apostle, patron saint of hopeless causes, is said to be buried in the foundations of the sombre grey and white cathedral. On his feast day, October 28, thousands come to plead their causes.

Lucknow

UP's state capital **LUCKNOW** is best remembered for the ordeal of its British residents during a five-month **siege** of the Residency in 1857. Less remembered are the atrocities perpetrated by the British when they recaptured the city. Lucknow saw the last days of Muslim rule in India, and the summary British deposition in 1856 of Wajid Ali Shah, the last nawab of **Avadh**, was one of the main causes of the 1857 uprising.

Avadh (Oudh, as the British spelt it) broke away from the Mughal Empire in the mid-eighteenth century after its nawab, Safdarjang, was thrown out of office in Delhi for being a Shi'ite, but as the Mughal Empire declined, Avadh became the centre of Muslim power. Under the decadent later nawabs, the arts flourished. Lucknow, the Avadhi capital, became a magnet for artisans. Courtesans became poets, singers and dancers, and under the last nawab the amorous musical form called *thumri* emerged here (see p.1182). The city was also an important repository of Shi'a culture and Islamic jurisprudence, its Farangi Mahal law school attracting students from China and Central Asia.

The patronage of the Shi'a nawabs also produced new expressions of the faith, notably in the annual **Muharram** processions. Held in memory of the martyrdom of Muhammad's grandson Hussain (the second Shi'ite Imam) at Karbala in Iraq, these developed into elaborate affairs with **tazia**, ornate paper reproductions of Hussein's Karbala shrine, being carried through the streets. During the rest of the year the *tazia* images are kept in Imambara (houses of the Imam); these range from humble rooms in poor Shi'a households to the **Great Imambara** built by Asaf-ud-daula in 1784.

Extraordinary sandstone monuments, now engulfed by modern Lucknow, still testify to the euphoric atmosphere of this unique culture. European-inspired edifices, too, are prominent on the skyline, often embellished with flying buttresses, turrets, cupolas and floral patterns, but the brick and mortar with which they were constructed means that they are not ageing as well as the earlier stone buildings, and old Lucknow is, literally, crumbling away.

Arrival and information

From **Amausi airport**, 16km south on the Kanpur Road, a taxi to the centre of Lucknow costs around Rs500. Lucknow's busy **railway station** (with a computerized reservations office), located at Charbagh, 4km southwest of the central hub

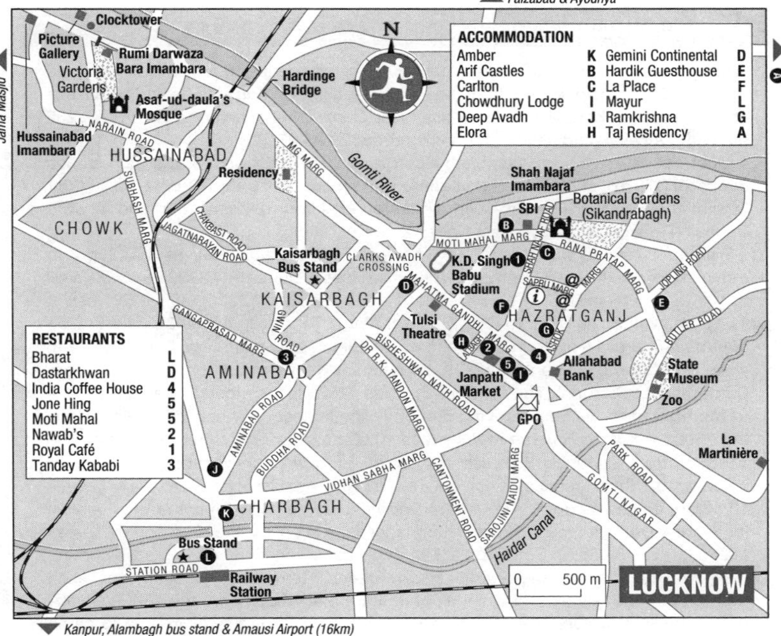

of Hazratganj (Rs45 by pre-paid auto), is a remarkable building, with prominent chhatris above the entrance arcade and a roof inspired by chess pieces. Most intercity **buses** pull in at **Alambagh Bus Stand**, 3km southwest of the station, Rs50 from Hazratganj by auto, or Rs5–8 on shared Vikrams from Charbagh or Ashoka Marg. A few buses arrive at the more central **Kaiserbagh Bus Stand**, just Rs30 by cycle rickshaw from Hazratganj.

The **UP Tourism office** is at *Hotel Gomti*, 6 Sapru Marg (Mon–Sat 9am–7pm; ⓣ0522/261 2659). There are plenty of **ATMs** around town (at the station and the bus stand, and on MG Rd and Shah Najaf Rd); otherwise, there's Allahabad Bank on Park Road in Hazratganj and the State Bank of India on Moti Mahal Marg. For **internet** connections, try Meeting Point, on Sapru Marg near the junction with Ashok Marg, or UP Business Centre opposite (both Rs20/hr). February's **Lucknow Festival** (details from UP Tourism) is an opportunity to sample the city's vibrant traditions of music and dance.

City transport

Multi-seater **tempos** have more or less taken over from city buses, plying regular routes such as from Charbagh to the GPO. **Cars** can be rented from *Hotel Clarks Avadh*, 8 MG Marg at Clarks Avadh Crossing (ⓣ0522/261 6500), and UP Tours at the *Hotel Gomti* (see above; ⓣ0522/261 2659). Comprehensive daily **city tours** (Rs550 including entry fees), which must be booked in advance through UP Tours, and only run if they have three or more takers, leave the *Hotel Gomti* at 9.30am and return at 2.30pm. You can also be picked up from the station (at 9.00am) and from various other hotels. The price includes guide and entrance fees.

Moving on from Lucknow

Amausi **airport** is around Rs500 by taxi from the city centre, but Rs210 by pre-paid taxi or Rs95 by pre-paid auto from the railway station. **Airlines** include: Indian Airlines and Air India, 9 Rani Laxmi Bai Marg (near *Gemini Continental* hotel) ⓣ0522/262 0927; Jet Airways and JetLite, 6 Park Rd ⓣ0522/223 9612.

Most **buses** leave from Alambagh Bus Stand, 3km southwest of the train station (around Rs70 by auto from Hazratganj), but services to Dehra Dun (2 daily, 10hr 30min) and Haridwar (2 daily; 10hr), some to Gorakhpur (2 hourly; 8hr) and most to Sonauli (7 daily; 12hr) leave from Kaiserbagh Bus Stand.

Trains to **Delhi** include the #2003 *Shatabdi Express*, which leaves at 3.35pm to arrive in New Delhi at 10.05pm. Overnight services include the #2229 *Lucknow Mail* at 10.10pm, which reaches New Delhi at 7.10am, and the #2225 *Kaifiyat Express* at 11.15pm, which pulls in to Old Delhi at 7am. To **Agra**, the #4863/4865/4853 *Marudhar Express* leaves daily at half past midnight, arriving in Agra Fort at 5.55am, while the *Lucknow Express* #2179 departs Lucknow at 3.45pm to reach Agra Cantonment at 9.30pm. The *Pushpak Express* #2533 is the most convenient service to **Mumbai** (daily 7.45pm, arriving 6.40pm). The fastest daily service to **Kolkata** is the #3006 *Amritsar–Howrah Mail* (leaves 10.50am, arriving 7.20am next day). The #4236 *Bareilly–Varanasi Express* leaves at 11.15pm for **Varanasi**, arriving at 6.50am; daytime services include the #3006 *Amritsar–Howrah Mail* (leaves 10.50am, arrives 4.45pm). The #3009 *Doon Express* at 6.35pm is the best service for **Dehra Dun** (arrives 7.10am). Ramnagar is served by the *Dheradun Express* #4265 (arrives 6.05am). Both stop at Haridwar, but inconveniently, in the wee hours. Also to Uttarakhand, the #3019 *Bagh Express* leaves at 12.30am to reach Kathgodam, the railhead for Nainital, at 9.30am. For **Khajuraho**, the #5009 *Chitrakoot Express* at 5.30pm gets in to Satna at a bleary 4.15am, well in time to catch an onward bus.

For **Nepal**, daily overnight trains to Gorakhpur – where you can get a bus to the Sonauli border, and then buses to Kathmandu and Pokhara on the other side – include the #5708 *Amritsar–Katihar Express* (12.55am, arriving 5.50am), and the #1015 *Kushinagar Express* (1.55am, arriving 7.25am). There are also buses direct to Sonauli, but it's a gruelling twelve-hour journey.

Agents for air, rail and bus tickets include Thomas Cook, 13-A Jopling Rd (ⓣ0522/400 2181), and UP Tours, *Hotel Gomti*, 6 Sapru Marg (ⓣ0522/261 2659).

If you're heading for Uttarakhand, Lucknow has offices of both **GMVN**, at 4-7-RF Khushnuma Complex, Bahadur Marg (ⓣ0522/220 7844), and **KMVN**, 3rd floor, Sarang Menor, Shah Nzaf Road, behind *Hotel Gomti* (ⓣ0522/261 5866), who organize tours of, and accommodation in, **Garhwal** and **Kumaon** respectively.

Accommodation

There's a concentration of budget hotels around Subhaj Marg, north of the station, with more upmarket places mainly within easy each of Hazratganj in the centre of town.

Amber Subhash Marg, Naka Hindola ⓣ0522/268 3201, ⓔamberhotel@yahoo.com. Good value near the station: a range of spacious rooms at different prices, some air-cooled, some with a/c. 24hr checkout. ❷–❹

Arif Castles 4 Rana Pratap Marg ⓣ0522/409 8777, ⓔarifcastles@hotmail.com. Quite well-appointed in marble, brass and light blue, this "business class hotel", as it calls itself, has cool rooms, a/c, cable TV and an Avadhi cuisine restaurant. Rates include breakfast. ❻–❽

Carlton Shah Najaf Rd ⓣ0522/222 4021. Fabled Lucknow address, a *fin-de-siècle* Euro–Avadhi edifice with big rooms, ancient plumbing and musty hunting trophies. Currently closed for total refurbishment, and should eventually emerge spanking new. ❾

Chowdhury Lodge 3 Vidhan Sabha Marg ⓣ0522/227 3135. Grimy, *paan*-stained city-centre cheapie down an alley by a filling station. The attached doubles (hot water in buckets) aren't really as cheap as they ought to be, but it's very central, and there are non-attached singles for only Rs150. ❶–❹
Deep Avadh Aminabad Rd, Naka Hindola ⓣ0522/268 4381 to 7, ⓔdeepavadh@sify.com. Good a/c rooms in various sizes with 24hr room service, as well as two restaurants, bar and travel desk, in an interesting part of town close to the station and on the edge of bustling Aminabad. 24hr checkout. ❺–❼
Elora 3 Lalbagh ⓣ0522/221 1307. Friendly, popular place with a good range of clean rooms, including some with a/c. Facilities include cable TV in all rooms, 24hr room service and a multi-cuisine restaurant. ❸–❺
Gemini Continental 10 Rani Laximbai Marg ⓣ0522/401 1111, ⓦwww.geminicontinental.com. Snazzy, upscale hotel in the centre of town. Spacious, modern rooms with great views, minibar, cable TV and a/c, and 24hr room service. Doubles start at $140, including buffet breakfast. ❽–❾
Hardik Guest House 16 Rana Pratap Marg, by the junction with Jopling Rd ⓣ0522/220 9497. Clean and comfortable family-run guesthouse with friendly, helpful staff and good home-cooking. ❺–❼
La Place 6 Shah Najaf Rd, Hazratganj ⓣ0522/400 4040, ⓦwww.sarovarhotels.com. Small but smart modern business hotel crackling with brisk efficiency. Facilities include wi-fi, a business centre and executive offices, but no pool. ❾
Mayur Subhash Marg, at Station Rd, Charbagh (above *Bharat Restaurant*) ⓣ0522/245 1824. Unattractive cheaper rooms, but those at the other end of the range are much better value. Opposite the train station so handy for early morning get-aways and late-night arrivals. 24hr checkout. ❶–❹
Ramkrishna Ashok Marg ⓣ0522/223 0499. Best-value cheapie in the Hazratganj vicinity, but very often full, as is its similar neighbour the *New Ram Krishna* (ⓣ0522/262 4225). ❷
Taj Residency Vipin Khand, Gomti Nagar ⓣ0522/239 3939, ⓦwww.tajhotels.com. Built in Avadhi style, this is easily Lucknow's most elegant and comfortable hotel, with a swimming pool and a range of restaurants, but inconveniently situated 3km out of town. Doubles from $198. ❾

The Town

Most of Lucknow's monuments are spread along or near the southern bank of the Gomti River, which is sluggish and weed-covered except at monsoon time, when its waters swell enough to accommodate hordes of local fishermen's dugout boats. Close to the main central bridge lies the modern commercial centre of **Hazratganj**. Between here and Charbagh, the old city sector of **Aminabad** holds a maze of busy streets and fascinating markets.

Hussainabad

In the west of the city, in the vicinity of Hardinge Bridge around "old" Lucknow, lie several crumbling relics of the nawabs of Avadh. Chief among them is the Great or **Bara Imambara** (daily sunrise–sunset, closed during Muharram; Rs300 [Rs25], ticket includes Hussainabad Imambara and Picture Gallery), which boasts one of the largest vaulted halls in the world – 50m long and 15m high. Flat on top, slightly arched inside, and built by Asaf-ud-daula in 1784 without the aid of a single iron or wooden beam, the roof was constructed using a technique known as *kara dena*, in which bricks are broken and angled to form an interlocking section and then covered with concrete – here several metres thick. The arcaded structure is approached through what must have been an extravagant gate, now pockmarked and on the verge of collapse. Two successive courtyards lead from the gates to the unusually festive-looking Imambara itself. Steps lead up to a labyrinth of chambers known as *bhulbhulaiya* – the "maze". Adjacent to the Bara Imambara and overlooking it is **Asaf-ud-daula's Mosque**, set upon a two-tiered arcaded plinth with two lofty minarets. Closed to non-Muslims, it can be readily viewed from the Victoria Gardens that adjoin it to the west (daily except Fri dawn to dusk; free).

Straddling the main road west of the main gates, the colossal **Rumi Darwaza** is an ornamental victory arch modelled on one of the gates to Asia Minor in Istanbul (known to the Islamic world in Byzantine times as "Rumi"). Now decaying, it sports elaborate floral patterns and a few extraordinary trumpets; steps lead up to open chambers that command a general prospect of the monuments of Hussainabad.

A short distance further west, the lavish **Hussainabad Imambara** (same hours and ticket as Bara Imambara) is also known as the Chhota (small) Imambara, or the Palace of Lights, thanks to its fairy-tale appearance when decorated and illuminated for special occasions. The raised bathing pool in front of it, which is approached via a spacious courtyard, adds to the overall atmosphere. A central gilded dome dominates the whole ensemble, busy with minarets, small domes and arches and even a crude miniature Taj Mahal. Built in 1837 by Muhammad Ali Shah, partly to provide famine relief through employment, the Imambara houses a silver-faced throne, plus the tombs of important Avadhi personalities. The dummy gate opposite the main entrance was used by ceremonial musicians, while the unfinished watchtower is known as the Satkhanda or "Seven Storeys", even though only four were ever constructed. West of the Imambara, and surrounded by ruins, are the two soaring minarets and three domes of the **Jama Masjid** (no admission to non-Muslims), completed after the death of Muhammad Ali Shah.

Beyond the Hussainabad Tank, east of the Hussainabad Imambara, is the isolated 67-metre-high **Hussainabad Clocktower**, an ambitious Gothic affair completed in 1887 which carries the largest clock in India. Close to this bizarre monolith lies **Taluqdar's Hall**, built by Muhammad Ali Shah to house the offices of the Hussainabad Trust and the dusty **Picture Gallery**, also known as the **Muhammad Ali Shah Art Gallery** (same hours and ticket as Bara Imambara). Arranged chronologically, the portraits of nawabs graphically demonstrate the decline of their civilization, as the figures become progressively portlier. In a famous image, the androgynous-looking last nawab, Wajid Ali Shah (1847–56), is shown in a daringly low-cut top that reveals his left nipple.

The Residency

The blasted **Residency** (daily sunrise–sunset; Rs100 [Rs5], video cameras Rs25) rests in peace amid landscaped gardens southeast of Hardinge Bridge – a battle-scarred ruin left exactly as it stood when the siege was finally relieved by Sir Colin Campbell on November 17, 1857 (see box opposite). Its cannonball-shattered tower became a shrine to the tenacity of the British in India, and continued to be maintained as such even after Independence.

During the siege, every building in the complex was utilized for the hard-fought defence of the compound. The **Treasury**, on the right through the **Baillie Guard Gate**, served as an arsenal, while the sumptuous **Banqueting Hall**, immediately west, was a makeshift hospital, and the extensive single-storey **Dr Fayrer's House**, just south, housed women and children. Most of the original structures, such as **Begum Kothi**, were left standing to impede direct fire from the enemy. On the lawn outside Begum Kothi, a large cross honours the astute Sir Henry Lawrence, responsible for building its defences, who died shortly after hostilities began.

The pockmarked Residency itself holds a small **museum** (daily 9am–5pm). On the ground floor, the **Model Room**, the only one with its roof intact, houses a large model of the defences and of the Residency and a small but excellent collection of images, including etchings showing wall breaches blocked up with billiard tables and a soldier blacking up in preparation for a dash across enemy lines.

The Lucknow Residency siege

The insurgent sepoys who entered Lucknow on June 30, 1857, found the city rife with resentment against the recent British takeover of the kingdom of Avadh. The tiny and isolated **British garrison**, under the command of Sir Henry Lawrence, took refuge in the **Residency**, which became the focus of a fierce struggle.

Less than a third of the three thousand British residents and loyal Indians who crammed into the Residency survived the four-and-a-half-month siege. So unhygienic were their living conditions that those who failed to succumb to gangrenous and tetanus-infected wounds often fell victim to cholera and scurvy. While a barrage of heavy artillery was maintained by both sides, the insurgents attempted to tunnel under the defences and lay mines, but among the British were former tin-miners in the 32nd (Cornish) Regiment, who were far more adept at such things, and were able to follow the sounds of enemy chipping, defuse mines, and even blow up several sepoy-controlled buildings on the peripheries of the complex.

Morale remained high among the 1400 **noncombatants**, who included fifty schoolboys from La Martinière (see below), and class distinctions were upheld throughout. While the wives of European soldiers and non-commissioned officers, children and servants took refuge in the *tikhana* (cellar), the "ladies" of the Residency occupied the higher and airier chambers, until the unfortunate loss of one Miss Palmer's leg on July 1 persuaded them of the gravity of their predicament. Sir Henry Lawrence was fatally wounded the next day. The wealthier officers managed to maintain their own private hoard of supplies, living in much their usual style. Matters improved when, after three months, Brigadier-General Sir Henry Havelock arrived with reinforcements, and the normal round of visits and invitations to supper was resumed despite the inconvenient shortage of good food and wine. Not until November 17 was the siege finally broken by a force of Sikhs and Highlanders under Sir Colin Campbell. Their offers of tea, however, were turned down by the Residency women; they were used to taking it with milk, which the soldiers could not supply.

Hazratganj

Along the river, opposite the *Carlton Hotel* on Rana Pratap Marg, squats the huge dome of the **Shah Najaf Imambara** (daily except Fri sunrise–sunset; donations), named after the tomb of Ali in Iraq and at its best when adorned with lights during the holy month of Muharram. Its musty interior holds some incredibly garish chandeliers used in processions, several *tazia*, and the silver-faced tomb of the decadent and profligate Ghazi-ud-Din-Haidar (ruled 1814–27), buried with three of his queens.

The Imambara was commandeered as a sepoy stronghold in 1857, and the crucial battle that enabled the British to relieve the Residency was fought in the adjacent pleasure gardens of **Sikandrabagh** on November 16. It took one and a half hours of bombardment by Sir Colin Campbell's soldiers to breach the defences of the two thousand sepoys; then the Sikhs and 93rd Highlanders poured through. There was no escape for the terrified sepoys, some of whom are said to have believed the bloodstained, red-faced, kilted Scots to be the ghosts of the murdered European women of Kanpur. Driven against the north wall, they were either bayoneted or shot, and the dead and dying piled shoulder-high. Tranquil once again, Sikandrabagh is now home to the National Botanical Research Institute and the beautiful **Botanical Gardens** (Mon–Fri: April–Sept 5–8am, Oct–March 6–8.30am; Rs1), with manicured lawns, conservatories, nurseries and herb, rose and bougainvillea gardens.

Towards the east of Lucknow, an extraordinary chateau-like building has become almost a symbol of the city – **La Martinière** remains to this day an exclusive boys' school in the finest colonial tradition. It was built as a country retreat by Major-General Claude Martin, a French soldier-adventurer taken prisoner by the British in Puducherry. The enigmatic Martin later joined the East India Company, made his fortune in indigo, and served both the British and the nawabs of Avadh. The building is an outrageous but intriguing amalgam, crowned by flying walkways; Greco-Roman figures on the parapets give it a busy silhouette, gigantic heraldic lions gaze across the grounds, and a large bronze cannon graces the front. Martin himself is buried in the basement. During the siege, La Martinière was occupied by rebels, while its boys were evacuated to the Residency.

Close to the centre of Hazratganj, its grounds dotted with derelict Avadhi monuments, Lucknow's small **zoo** also serves as an amusement park with a miniature train to view the animals (Tues–Sun 8am–5pm; Rs20 Tues–Sat, Rs25 Sun and public holidays). Head through the large zoo gardens to reach the **State Museum** (Tues–Sun 10.30am–4pm; Rs100 [Rs5], camera Rs20), with its delicate, speckled-red-sandstone sculpture from the Mathura school of the Kushana and Gupta periods (first to sixth centuries AD). Besides sculpture from Gandhara, Mahoba, Nalanda and Sravasti, it boasts a gallery of terracotta artefacts and even an Egyptian mummy. Musical instruments, paintings and costumes provide atmosphere in the Avadh gallery, while the natural history section is a taxidermist's dream.

Eating

The rich traditional **Lucknavi cuisine** – featuring Mughlai dishes as well as the local *dum pukht* (steam casserole) style, sometimes known as *handi* after the pot it's cooked in – is available from food stalls throughout the city, in places such as Shami Avadh Bazaar, near the K.D. Singh Babu Stadium, the Chowk, Aminabad and behind the Tulsi Theatre in Hazratganj. The bazaars are also the place to get Lucknow's popular breakfast speciality *paya-khulcha*, a spicy mutton soup served with hot breads.

Bharat Subhash Marg, at Station Rd, Charbagh. Cheap *dhaba* opposite the station serving good dosas and curries (veg Rs30–80, non-veg Rs60–170).

Dastarkhwan China Gate. One of a number of open-air diners in this little street by UP Press Club, with non-veg Mughlai dishes including kebabs, kormas and biriyanis. Main dishes Rs45–130.

Indian Coffee House Ashok Marg. Once a hotbed of Lucknow's political intelligentsia, nicknamed the "maternity ward" for the ideas it gave birth to, now reborn as a bright, new café serving excellent filter coffee plus cakes, shakes, snacks and South Indian or Chinese food (mains Rs35–80).

Jone Hing MG Marg, Hazratganj. Chinese restaurant serving the usual sweet and sour, chop suey and chow mein, plus specialities such as ginger chicken and Manchurian fish. Main dishes are Rs100–130 for meat, Rs135 for fish.

Moti Mahal MG Marg, Hazratganj. The sweet shop at the front has some great milky confections, including sugar-free ones; the family restaurant upstairs serves excellent veg curries (Rs65–120), including three types of *dum aloo* (Lucknavi, Banarsi or Kashmiri).

Nawab's In *Capoor's* hotel, MG Marg, Hazratganj. A refined restaurant, with live *qawwali* music in the evening (except Tues). Top dishes include *murg nawabi*, a mild, creamy dish of chicken in cashew butter, or there's a great mushroom tikka masala. Non-veg main dishes are Rs140–290.

Royal Café Shah Najaf Rd. Lively place that's popular amongst Lucknavi families. Mughlai non-veg main dishes go for Rs130–205, *handi dum* biriyanis at Rs130–170. There's another branch by *Capoor's* hotel on MG Marg.

Tanday Kababi Naaz Cinema Rd, just off Aminabad main chowk. For an authentic Avadhi gastronomic experience, head to this popular and inexpensive place (the best in a street of them), where the tandoori chicken, and mutton or even beef kebabs are prepared out front and served up within. Main dishes Rs30–75.

Shopping

Chikan is a long-standing Lucknavi tradition of embroidery, in which designs are built up to form delicate floral patterns along edges on saris and on necklines and collars of *kurtas*. Workshops can be found around the Chowk, the market area of old Lucknow, and shops and showrooms in Hazratganj (especially Janpath Market), Nazirabad and Aminabad. The fixed prices at **Gangotri**, the UP government emporium on MG Marg in Hazratganj (a block west of Lalbagh), are more expensive than those in the markets, but the quality is assured and you don't have to haggle.

Lucknow is also renowned for its **ittar** (or *attar*), concentrated perfume sold in small vials – an acquired (and expensive) taste. Small balls of cotton wool are daubed with the scent and placed neatly within the top folds of the ear; musicians believe that the aroma heightens their senses. Popular *ittar* include *ambar* from amber, *khus* from a flowering plant and rose-derived *ghulab*. A well-established dealer is Sugandhco at D-4 Janpath Market (on the south side of the market).

Allahabad and around

The administrative and industrial city of **ALLAHABAD**, 135km west of Varanasi and 227km southeast of Lucknow, is also known as **Prayag** ("confluence"): the point where the Yamuna and Ganges rivers meet the mythical Saraswati River (see p.278). Sacred to Hindus, the **Sangam** (which also means "confluence"), east of the city, is one of the great pilgrimage destinations of India. Allahabad comes alive during its *melas* (fairs) – the annual **Magh Mela** (Jan/Feb), and the colossal **Maha Kumbh Mela**, held every twelve years (2013 and 2025 are the next ones).

Allahabad is a pleasant city to visit, with vast open riverside scenery and good amenities, but is without major temples or monuments. At the junction of the fertile Doab, the "two-river" valley between the Yamuna and the Ganges, it did however possess a crucial strategic significance; its massive **fort**, built by the emperor Akbar in 1583, is still used by the military. Another Mughal, Jahangir's son Khusrau, was murdered here by his brother Shah Jahan, who went on to become emperor. Allahabad was briefly the centre of power after the 1857 uprising, when the British moved the headquarters of their Northwestern Provinces here from Agra; the formal transfer of power from the East India Company to the Crown took place here the following year.

Bundelkhand

The harshness of the terrain in the **Bundelkhand** region, south of Lucknow along the Madhya Pradesh border, and the all but unbearable heat in the summer, make it the most difficult, if intriguing, part of the state to control, and even today, its labyrinthine hills and valleys are home to infamous bands of outlaw **dacoits**. Many of these have become folk-heroes among local villagers, who shelter them from the almost equally brutal police force. The most celebrated in recent years was **Phoolan Devi**, the "Bandit Queen", from a village near Behmai who was kidnapped by a dacoit gang, became the leader's lover, and took over from him after he was killed. She eventually surrendered to the police, was released in 1994, and even became an MP for the socialist Samajwadi Party before being assassinated in 2001.

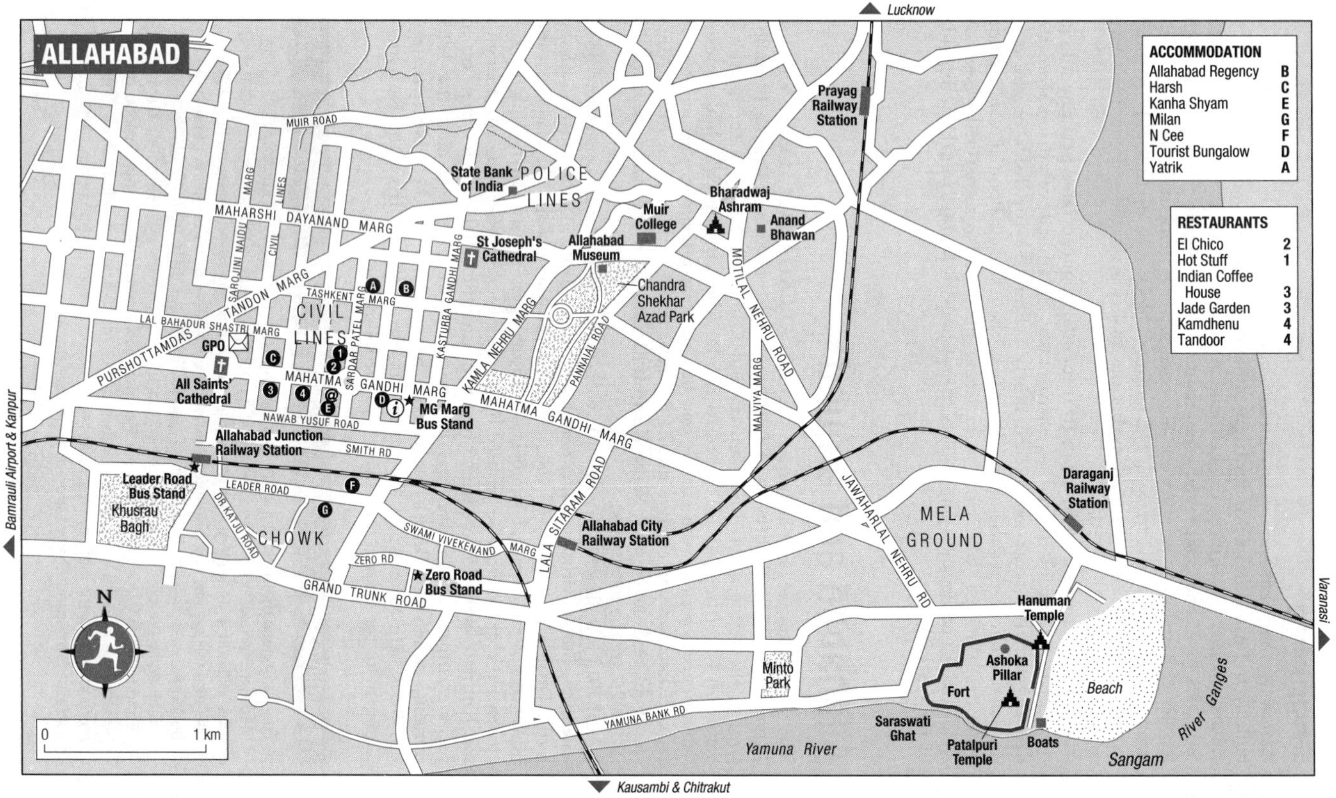

ALLAHABAD

ACCOMMODATION

Allahabad Regency	B
Harsh	C
Kanha Shyam	E
Milan	G
N Cee	F
Tourist Bungalow	D
Yatrik	A

RESTAURANTS

El Chico	2
Hot Stuff	1
Indian Coffee House	3
Jade Garden	3
Kamdhenu	4
Tandoor	4

Lucknow
Prayag Railway Station
MUIR ROAD
State Bank of India
POLICE LINES
Bharadwaj Ashram
Anand Bhawan
Muir College
Allahabad Museum
Chandra Shekhar Azad Park
MAHARSHI DAYANAND MARG
SAROJINI NAIDU MARG
CIVIL LINES
St Joseph's Cathedral
KASTURBA GANDHI MARG
TASHKENT MARG
TANDON MARG
CIVIL LINES
LAL BAHADUR SHASTRI MARG
PURSHOTTAMDAS TANDON MARG
SARDAR PATEL MARG
KAMLA NEHRU MARG
PANNAIAL ROAD
MOTILAL NEHRU ROAD
MALVIYA MARG
GPO
All Saints' Cathedral
MAHATMA GANDHI MARG
MG Marg Bus Stand
NAWAB YUSUF ROAD
Allahabad Junction Railway Station
SMITH RD
Leader Road Bus Stand
LEADER ROAD
Khusrau Bagh
DR KATJU ROAD
CHOWK
SWAMI VIVEKENAND MARG
LALA SITARAM ROAD
Allahabad City Railway Station
JAWAHARLAL NEHRU RD
MELA GROUND
Daraganj Railway Station
ZERO RD
Zero Road Bus Stand
GRAND TRUNK ROAD
Bamrauli Airport & Kanpur
Varanasi
Hanuman Temple
Ashoka Pillar
Fort
Beach
Minto Park
YAMUNA BANK RD
Saraswati Ghat
Patalpuri Temple
Boats
River Ganges
Yamuna River
Sangam
Kausambi & Chitrakut
N
0 1 km

Arrival and information

Allahabad has four **railway stations**, but express trains use **Allahabad Junction**. Most hotels are nearby; be sure to use the right exit for the area where you plan to stay.

Leader Road Bus Stand, used by buses from western destinations such as Agra, Lucknow, Kausambi and Delhi, is just outside Allahabad Junction station's south gates on the city side. **Zero Road Bus Stand**, serving Mahoba, Satna and Chitrakut to the south (with connections for Khajuraho) is 1km southeast. Buses from all over and especially points east, including Varanasi, arrive at the larger **MG Marg Bus Stand**, next to the *Tourist Bungalow*. Bamrauli **airport**, 18km west on the road to Kanpur, has flights to Delhi with Indian Airlines, whose office is at the airport (Ⓣ0532/258 1370).

Taxis are widely available around Allahabad Junction Station, but cycle- and auto-rickshaws are the most common modes of transport; a trip to the Sangam from the Civil Lines crossing costs around Rs35 (hang on to your vehicle for the return journey). **Car rental** through general travel agencies such as Varuna in Tulsiani Plaze, next to *Harsh* hotel on MG Marg (Ⓣ0532/242 7287, Ⓔvarunatravels@hotmail.com), costs in the region of Rs650 per day, plus mileage.

The **tourist information office** at the *Tourist Bungalow*, 35 MG Marg, Civil Lines (Mon–Sat 10am–5pm, but closed on the second Saturday of the month; Ⓣ0532/260 1873), is very helpful and is particularly informative during the *melas*. Allahabad's **post office** (known as the GPO or HPO) is at Sarojini Naidu Marg, near All Saints' Cathedral in the Civil Lines. There are several **ATMs** along MG Marg, and there's a State Bank of India inconveniently located at Kutchery Road, Police Lines. Several places in Maya Bazaar, next to *Tandoor* restaurant, and Angelica's Cyber Point opposite *Hotel Sangam* down an alley off MG Marg, have **internet** connections for Rs15–20 per hour.

Accommodation

Allahabad Regency 16 Tashkent Marg Ⓣ0532/261 1110, Ⓦwww.hotelallahabadregency.com. Nineteenth-century colonial bungalow with comfortable a/c rooms, a decent garden restaurant, a sauna, jacuzzi, swimming pool and well-equipped gym. ❼

Harsh 118/116 MG Marg Ⓣ0532/242 7897. Shabby colonial bungalow offering budget accommodation. Huge rooms with attached bathrooms; those at the front have small fireplaces and open onto the lawn. Under renovation at last check, so should be spruced up by the time you read this. ❷

Ilawart Tourist Bungalow 35 MG Marg Ⓣ0532/260 7440, Ⓔrahiilawart@up-tourism.com. The new block, around a central well, overlooks the bus stand, so choose your room carefully to avoid noise. The older block is quieter, but showing its age. As well as rooms, there's a dorm (Rs125), a restaurant with haphazard service but good food, and a popular bar. Run by UP Tourism. ❹–❺

Kanha Shyam Strachey Rd, Civil Lines Ⓣ0532/256 0123 to 32, Ⓦwww.hotelkanhashyam.com. Classy four-star with quite stately rooms done out in burgundy and dark wood There's a bar, a 24hr coffee shop, a rooftop restaurant and a pool. ❷–❹

Milan 46 Leader Rd Ⓣ0532/240 3776 or 7, Ⓦwww.milanhotels.in. A cut above the other hotels in the area south of the station, and not a bad mid-market choice. The cheaper rooms are a bit shabby, and the mattresses a little hard, but there are better a/c rooms. ❸–❹

N Cee 108 Leader Rd Ⓣ0532/240 1166. Popular budget hotel south of the railway line in the busy bazaar area. Rooms are small, but it's cheap and friendly (and often full), with 24hr checkout. ❶–❷

Yatrik 33 Sardar Patel Marg Ⓣ0532/226 0921 to 6, Ⓦwww.hotelyatrik.com. Best of the upmarket places, with more character than its rival the *Kanha Shyam*. Popular, well run and with a beautiful garden graced with elegant palms, and a pool (April–Sept). 24hr check-out. ❻–❼

The Town

Central Allahabad is split in two by the railway line, with the chaotic and congested **Old City** or **Chowk** south of Allahabad Junction station, and the grid of the **Civil Lines** (the residential quarter of the Raj military town) to the north.

The Kumbh Mela

Hindus traditionally regard river confluences (**sangams**) as auspicious places, and none more so than the one at Allahabad, where the Yamuna and Ganges rivers meet the River of Enlightenment, the mythical subterranean Saraswati. According to legend, Vishnu was carrying a *kumbha* (pot) of *amrita* (nectar), when a scuffle broke out between the gods, and four drops were spilled. They fell to earth at the four *tirthas* of Prayag, Haridwar, Nasik and Ujjain. The event is commemorated every three years by the **Kumbh Mela**, held at each *tirtha* in turn; the Allahabad Sangam is known as Tirtharaja, the "King of *tirthas*", and its *mela*, the **Maha Kumbh Mela** or "Great" Kumbh Mela, is the greatest and holiest of all.

The largest religious fair in India, Maha Kumbh Mela was attended by an astonishing **seventeen million** pilgrims in 2001 (the next is in 2013, then 2025). The vast flood plains and riverbanks adjacent to the confluence were overrun by tents, organized in almost military fashion by the government, the local authorities and the police. The *mela* is especially renowned for the presence of an extraordinary array of religious ascetics – sadhus and *mahants* – enticed from remote hideaways in forests, mountains and caves. Once astrologers have determined the propitious bathing time or *kumbhayog*, the first to hit the water are legions of Naga Sadhus or Naga Babas, who cover their naked bodies with ash and wear their hair in dreadlocks. The sadhus, who see themselves as guardians of the faith, approach the confluence at the appointed time with all the pomp and bravado of a charging army.

Although the Kumbh Mela is only triennial, and not always in Allahabad, there is a smaller annual bathing festival, the Magh Mela, held here every year in the month of Magha (Jan–Feb).

A kilometre north of Allahabad Junction railway station, the yellow-and-red sandstone bulk of the Gothic **All Saints' Cathedral** dominates the surrounding avenues. Designed by Sir William Emerson, architect of Kolkata's Victoria Memorial, the cathedral retains much of its stained glass, and an impressive altar of inlaid marble. Plaques provide interesting glimpses of Allahabad in the days of the Raj, while flying buttresses and snarling gargoyles on the exterior add to the effect of an English county town – though the impression is subverted by the palm trees in the garden. Sunday services continue to attract large congregations, as do Masses at the flamboyant **St Joseph's Roman Catholic Cathedral**, a short distance northeast.

On the edge of the pleasant **Chandra Shekhar Azad Park**, the grounds of the **Allahabad Museum** (Tues–Sun 10.30am–4.45pm, closed the Sun following the 2nd Sat of the month; Rs100 [Rs5]) are dotted with pieces of ancient sculpture. Inside, you'll find early terracotta artefacts, eighth-century sculptures from the Buddhist site of Kausambi, and a striking twelfth-century image from Khajuraho of Shiva and Parvati. A copious collection of modern Indian art includes work by Haldar, Sajit Khastgir and Rathin Mitra, as well as Jamini Roy, who was inspired by folk art. European paintings concentrate on spiritual themes, with bright, naive canvases by the Russian artist Nicholas Roerich, and pieces by the Tibetologist Lama Angarika Govinda. A natural history section features stuffed animals and birds, while photographs and documents cover the Independence struggle.

North of the museum rise the nineteenth-century sandstone buildings of **Allahabad University**, and the Gothic **Muir College**, built in 1870. A 61m-high tower accompanies domes clad with blue and white glazed tiles (some of which are missing), and a quadrangle with tall and elegant arches. Just beyond the college, in beautiful grounds roughly 1km northeast of the museum, is **Anand Bhawan**

(Tues–Sun 9.30am–5pm; ground floor free, first floor Rs8; no tickets sold 12.45–1.30pm). This ornate Victorian building, crowned by a chhatri and with Indo-Saracenic effects finished in grey-and-white trim, was the boyhood home of the first prime minister of an independent India, **Jawaharlal Nehru**. It's now maintained as a museum, allowing visitors to peer through plate glass into the opulent interior and see how the first family lived. More diverting than Nehru's spoons and trousers is the colonial court document of his trial for making salt. Nehru's daughter Indira Gandhi was born here, and Mahatma Gandhi (no relation) stayed when he visited the city. In the grounds, as at the Nehru Memorial Museum in Delhi, is a **planetarium**, which puts on five hour-long shows per day (11am, noon, 2pm, 3pm, 4pm; Rs20, all in Hindi with a 30min lecture prior to the show).

A short way south of Allahabad Junction railway station, a lofty gateway leads to the attractive walled gardens of **Khusrau Bagh**, where the remains of Jahangir's tragic son Khusrau rest in a simple sandstone mausoleum, completed in 1622. Khusrau made an unsuccessful bid for power that ended in death at the hands of his brother Shah Jahan, and is buried far from the centre of Mughal power. His mother's two-storeyed mausoleum is a short way west, beyond a tomb reputed to be that of his sister. Once Jahangir's pleasure garden, today much of Khusrau Bagh has been made into an orchard, famous for its guavas, and a rose nursery, but parts are unkempt and overgrown.

The river frontage

Most of Allahabad's river frontage is along the Yamuna, where women perform *arati* or evening worship at **Saraswati Ghat** by floating *diya* downstream. Immediately to the west, in **Minto Park**, a memorial marks the spot where, in 1858, the British Raj was born, as India officially passed from the East India Company to the Crown.

East of Saraswati Ghat, close to the sangam, Akbar's **Fort** is best appreciated from boats on the river (see below). Much of it is still occupied by the military, and public access is restricted to the leafy corner around the **Patalpuri Temple**, approached through any of the fort's three massive gates. Much of the superstructure is neglected; the **zenana** with its columned hall does survive, but can only be viewed with prior permission. At the main gate, a poorly restored polished stone **Ashoka Pillar** is inscribed with the emperor's edicts and dated to 242 BC.

Where the fort's eastern battlements meet the river, a muddy *ghat* is busy with boatmen jostling for custom from pilgrims heading to the sangam. Inland along

The sangam

Around 7km from the centre of the Civil Lines, overlooked by the eastern ramparts of the fort, wide flood plains and muddy banks protrude towards the sacred **sangam**. At the point at which the brown Ganges meets the greenish Yamuna, *pandas* (priests) perch on small platforms to perform puja and assist the devout in their ritual ablutions in the shallow waters. Beaches and *ghats* here are littered with the shorn hair of pilgrims who come to offer *pind* for their deceased parents, and women sit around selling cone-shaped pyramids of bright red and orange *tilak* powder.

Boats to the sangam, used by pilgrims and tourists alike, can be rented at the *ghat* immediately east of the fort, for the recommended government rate of Rs30 per head. However, most pilgrims pay around Rs60 and you can be charged as much as Rs150. Official prices for a whole boat are Rs150 but can soar to more than Rs500 during the *melas*. On the way to the sangam, high-pressure aquatic salesmen loom up on the placid waters selling offerings such as coconuts for pilgrims to discard at the confluence. Once abandoned, the offerings are fished up and sold on to other pilgrims.

the base of the fort, with the flood plain of the sangam to the right, a road leads past rows of stalls catering to pilgrims to the brightly painted **Hanuman Temple**. Unusually, the large sunken image of the monkey god inside is reclining rather than standing erect; during the annual floods the waters rise to touch his feet before once again receding.

Eating

Most of the better **cafés** and **restaurants** are in the Civil Lines area. In the early evening, the snack stalls along MG Marg ply their specialities.

El Chico 24 MG Marg. One of the city's best, a smart place with good Indian, Chinese and Western cuisine, including grills, sizzlers, Szechuan-style pork or baked fish in cheese sauce. Non-veg mains Rs185–300.

Hot Stuff 21 Sardar Patel Marg. Popular hang-out for Allahabad's young and trendy, offering burgers, shakes, Chinese food and ice cream. Main dishes Rs50–130.

Indian Coffee House MG Marg, set back from the road. Allahabad branch of the South Indian co-op, serving great filter coffee and basic cheap snacks (nothing over Rs35) with no frills or pretensions.

Jade Garden 123–127 MG Marg. Small garden restaurant offering Chinese food of the chop suey, chow mein and sweet-and-sour variety, plus veg and non-veg Indian dishes (mains Rs90–175).

Kamdhenu 37 MG Marg, in the beautiful nineteenth-century Palace Theatre building. Famous Allahabad sweetshop whose specialities include milk cake with almonds, and less cloyingly sweet fig and nut confections.

Tandoor 33 MG Marg. Upmarket non-veg restaurant and one of the best places in the city for Indian food, serving all the tandoori classics including chicken or fish tikka, kebabs and Mughlai curries. Non-veg mains Rs85–195.

Around Allahabad

Just 63km south of Allahabad, on the banks of the Yamuna, are the extensive ruins of **Kausambi**, a major Buddhist centre where Buddha himself once preached. The city flourished between the eighth century BC and the sixth century AD; archeological evidence suggests even earlier habitation. According to legend, it was founded by descendants of the Pandavas, after floods destroyed their city of Hastinapur. Mud ramparts (originally faced with brick) tower over the fields, running along an irregular 6km perimeter, and sections remain of a defensive moat. Within the complex, excavations have revealed a paved road, brick houses, wells, tanks and drains, a monastery with cloisters and a large *stupa*, and the ruins of a palace in the southeast corner. The only standing feature is a damaged sandstone column ascribed to **Ashoka** – a second column, moved by the Mughals, now graces the gates of the fort at Allahabad. If you have your own vehicle or hire a taxi (around Rs1000), Kausambi is a straightforward day-trip from Allahabad. Otherwise, there are buses from Leader Road stand (Rs50).

Allahabad also makes a good base from which to venture into the remoter parts of **Bundelkhand** (see p.243) to the south. The sprawling pilgrimage town of **CHITRAKUT (also called Sitapur)** is 128km southwest, and easily accessible by both train and bus. It's also a good place to catch onward transport to Kalinjar and Khajuraho. Together with its twin town of **Karbi**, 8km east (where there are train connections to Allahabad, Kolkata and Delhi), Chitrakut is a major Vaishnavite pilgrimage centre. Most of its religious and leisure activity revolves around the charming central **Ramghat**, where boats with electric-blue mattresses and pillows create a pretty picture against a backdrop of ashrams and *ghats* to either side of the narrow, slow-moving river.

About 88km southwest of Chitrakut, the abandoned star-shaped fortress of **KALINJAR** looks down on the Gangetic valley from the final escarpments of the craggy Vindhya hills, above the town of the same name. Much of the fort has been reclaimed by dry shrubby forest, populated by monkeys; once-grand avenues are now rocky footpaths that wind through the few crumbling yet ornately carved buildings that remain. Kalinjar has no tourist facilities to speak of – most of those who do come are either on day-trips from Chitrakut or Allahabad, or stay in Banda, which is on major train and bus routes and is connected to Kalinjar by local buses. Steep steps lead straight up for 3km from Kalinjar village to the fort's main gate, **Alam Darwaza**, but the southern **Panna Gate** has rock carvings depicting seven deer (like the fort's seven gates, these represent the then-known planets). Beneath **Bara Darwaza**, the "Large Gate", in the artificial cave of Sita Sej, a stone couch dating from the fourth century holds some of Kalinjar's earliest inscriptions. The fort's colossal rambling **battlements** provide sweeping views of the Gangetic plain to the north and the Vindhya hills to the south.

Varanasi

Older than history, older than tradition, older even than legend, and looks twice as old as all of them put together.

Mark Twain

The great Hindu city of **VARANASI**, also known as **Banaras** or **Benares**, stretches along the River Ganges, its waterfront dominated by long flights of stone *ghats* where thousands of pilgrims and residents come for their daily ritual ablutions. Known to the devout as **Kashi**, the Luminous – the City of Light, founded by Shiva – Varanasi is one of the oldest living cities in the world. It has maintained its religious life since the sixth century BC in one continuous tradition, in part by remaining outside the mainstream of political activity and historical development of the Subcontinent, and stands at the centre of the Hindu universe, the focus of a religious geography that reaches from the Himalayan cave of Amarnath in Kashmir to India's southern tip at Kanniyakumari, Puri to the east, and Dwarka to the west. Located next to a ford on an ancient trade route, Varanasi is among the holiest of all *tirthas* – "crossing places", that allow the devotee access to the divine and enable gods and goddesses to come down to earth. It has attracted pilgrims, seekers, *sannyasins* and students of the *Vedas* throughout its history, including sages such as Buddha, Mahavira (founder of the Jain faith) and the great Hindu reformer Shankara.

Anyone who dies in Varanasi attains instant *moksha*, or enlightenment. Widows and the elderly come here to live out their final days, finding shelter in temples, assisted by alms from the faithful. Western visitors since the Middle Ages have marvelled at the strangeness of this most alien of Indian cities: the tight mesh of alleys, the religious accoutrements, the host of deities – and the proximity of death.

Arrival and information

A pre-paid taxi from **Babatpur airport**, 22km northwest of the city, costs Rs450. Autos charge Rs250 for the same journey.

Varanasi is served by two main railway stations: **Varanasi Cantonment** in the town itself, and **Mughal Sarai**, 17km east of town. Cantonment is the most conveniently located station, with pre-paid auto and taxi booths, but depending on where you are travelling from, you may find yourself using the Mughal Sarai line. There are retiring rooms at Mughal Sarai station and local buses and taxis run regularly into Varanasi. Most **buses** terminate a couple of hundred metres east of the railway station along the main Grand Trunk Road and at the **Roadways Bus Stand**. Buses from Nepal are met by the rickshaw mafia – see p.284.

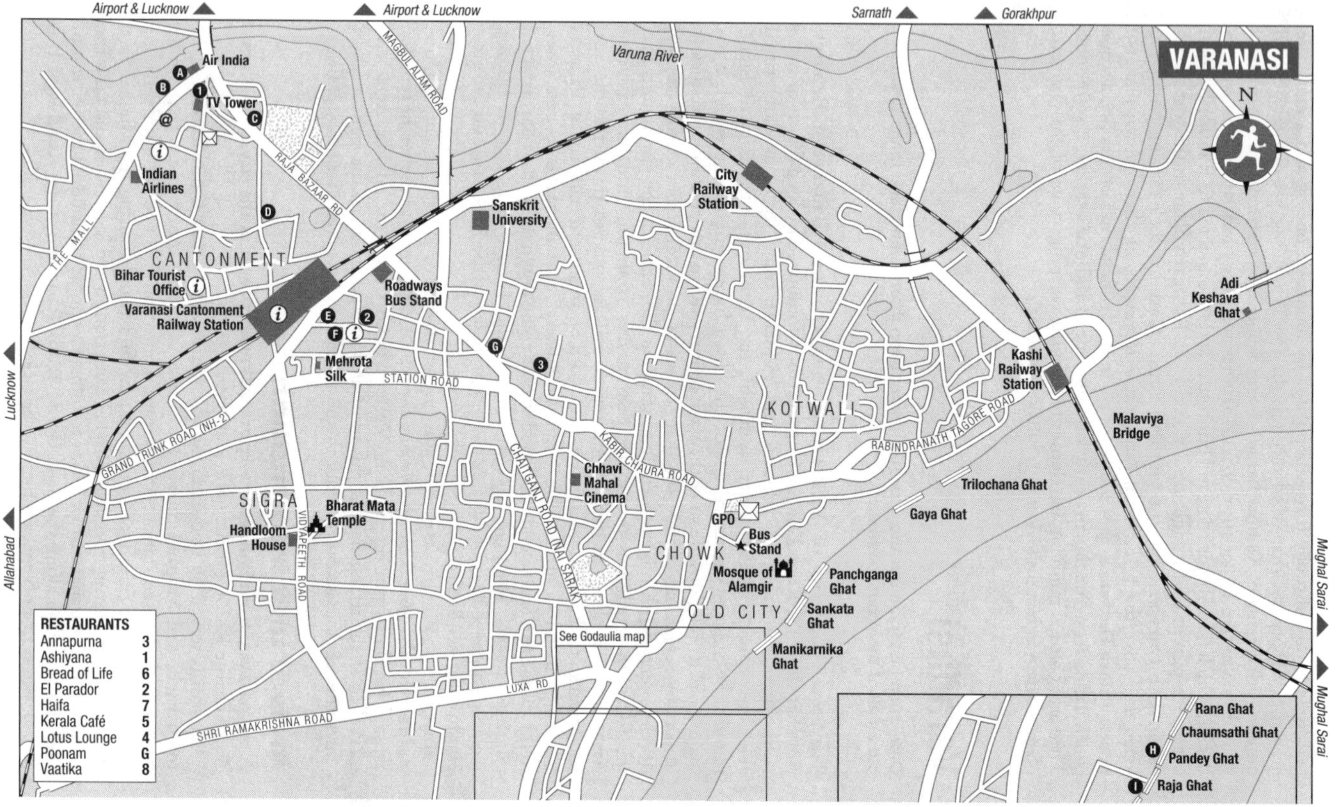

VARANASI

N

Airport & Lucknow
Airport & Lucknow
Sarnath
Gorakhpur
Lucknow
Allahabad
Mughal Sarai
Mughal Sarai

Varuna River
Air India
TV Tower
Indian Airlines
MAGBUL ALAM ROAD
RAJA BAZAAR RD
THE MALL
CANTONMENT
Bihar Tourist Office
Varanasi Cantonment Railway Station
Roadways Bus Stand
Sanskrit University
City Railway Station
Mehrota Silk
STATION ROAD
GRAND TRUNK ROAD (NH-2)
SIGRA
Bharat Mata Temple
Handloom House
VIDYAPEETH ROAD
CHAITGANJ ROAD (NAI SARAK)
Chhavi Mahal Cinema
KABIR CHAURA ROAD
KOTWALI
RABINDRANATH TAGORE ROAD
Kashi Railway Station
Malaviya Bridge
Adi Keshava Ghat
Trilochana Ghat
Gaya Ghat
GPO
Bus Stand
CHOWK
Mosque of Alamgir
Panchganga Ghat
Sankata Ghat
Manikarnika Ghat
OLD CITY
See Godaulia map
LUXA RD
SHRI RAMAKRISHNA ROAD
Rana Ghat
Chaumsathi Ghat
Pandey Ghat
Raja Ghat

RESTAURANTS	
Annapurna	3
Ashiyana	1
Bread of Life	6
El Parador	2
Haifa	7
Kerala Café	5
Lotus Lounge	4
Poonam	G
Vaatika	8

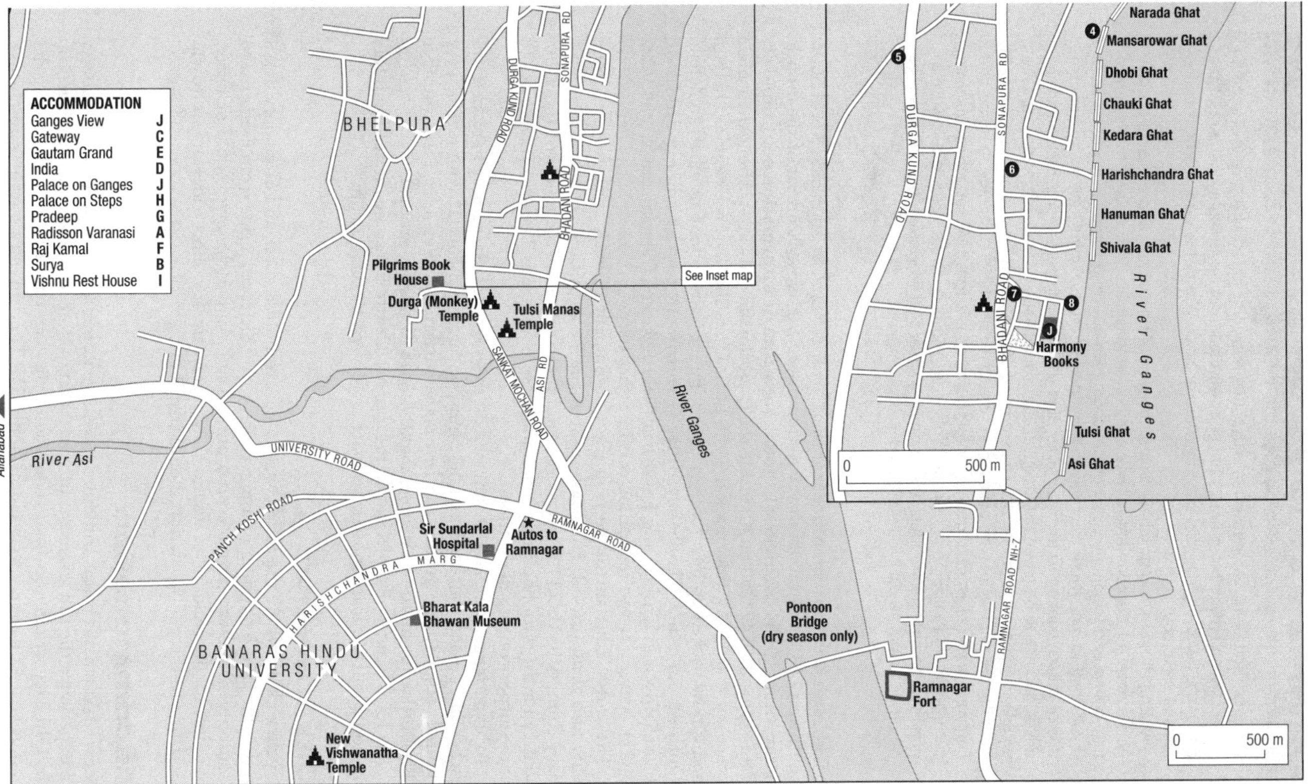
ACCOMMODATION
Ganges View J
Gateway C
Gautam Grand E
India D
Palace on Ganges J
Palace on Steps H
Pradeep G
Radisson Varanasi A
Raj Kamal F
Surya B
Vishnu Rest House I
BHELPURA
Durga Kund Road
Sonapura Rd
Bhadani Road
See Inset map
Pilgrims Book House
Durga (Monkey) Temple
Tulsi Manas Temple
Sankat Mochan Road
Asi Rd
River Ganges
Allahabad
River Asi
University Road
Panch Koshi Road
Sir Sundarlal Hospital
Autos to Ramnagar
Ramnagar Road
Harishchandra Marg
Bharat Kala Bhawan Museum
BANARAS HINDU UNIVERSITY
New Vishwanatha Temple
Pontoon Bridge (dry season only)
Ramnagar Fort
Ramnagar Road NH-7
0 500 m
Narada Ghat
Mansarowar Ghat
Dhobi Ghat
Chauki Ghat
Kedara Ghat
Harishchandra Ghat
Hanuman Ghat
Shivala Ghat
Harmony Books
Tulsi Ghat
Asi Ghat
River Ganges
0 500 m

Tout dodging

Like Agra and Delhi, Varanasi is rife with **touts**, and you'll have to be careful of scams, especially on arrival. Most hotels pay a **commission** of up to eighty percent of the room rate (for every day you stay) to whoever takes you to the door – a cost that is passed on to you.

All English-speaking rickshaw drivers are part of this racket, and avoiding it takes persistence. At Cantonment railway station, first visit the very helpful tourist office (see below) and telephone your hotel of choice. They'll send someone to pick you up. If you want to make your own way to the hotels of the old town, walk away from the bus or railway station to the main road, find a non-English-speaking cycle rickshaw driver, and ask to be taken to Godaulia, 3km southeast – a Rs30 ride. Rickshaws are unable to penetrate the maze of lanes around Vishwanatha Temple and are banned from the central part of Godaulia. Again, you can call a hotel from here to come and find you – if you attempt to get to a hotel yourself, touts may try to attach themselves and claim a commission on arrival. When trying to find hotels in the old town that don't pay commission to touts, it's common to hear that they have "burned down" or "flooded"; touts also try to remove signs directing people to them.

The main **UP Tourism office** is at their *Tourist Bungalow*, on Parade Kothi 500m southwest of Cantonment railway station (Mon–Sat, closed 2nd Sat of the month, 10am–5pm; ⓣ0542/220 6638), though their **tourist information counter** (daily 7am–7pm; ⓣ0542/250 6670) inside the Cantonment railway station is their main office for giving out information – the boss, Uma Shankar, is extremely helpful and is now backed up by a force of tourist police (same phone number) to defend tourists from crime. The shabby **Bihar Government tourist office** at 3rd Floor, Hans Sarowar, Englishis Lane, Jawaharlal Nehru Market, Cantonment (ⓣ0542/222 3821), is useful if you're heading east into that state.

The **India Tourism office** is in the Cantonment district, away from the Old City and *ghats*, just off The Mall on Stranger Road (Mon–Fri 9am–5.30pm, Sat 9am–2pm; ⓣ0542/250 1784). It gives out information on the whole of India, but staff can assist with booking accommodation in Varanasi. They maintain a booth at the airport during flight times.

To experience the *ghats* at sunrise, or the peace of Sarnath, you're best off eschewing guided tours and making your own arrangements. If your time is very limited, official tour **guides** can be organized through the India Tourism office (Rs600/day for up to five people, slightly more for bigger groups).

The local branch of the National Informatics Centre has some interesting information about Varanasi on their **website** at ⓦwww.varanasi.nic.in.

City transport

Cycle rickshaws are the easiest way to get around Varanasi, and often defy death and traffic jams by cycling up the wrong side of the road; a ride from Godaulia to Cantonment railway station costs around Rs30. Auto-rickshaws should be faster, but due to the volume of traffic they rarely are for short rides across town. Godaulia to the railway station should cost Rs50.

Accommodation

Most of Varanasi's better and more expensive hotels lie on its peripheries, though to experience the full ambience of the city, stay close to the *ghats* and the lanes of the **Old City**, where top-floor rooms, with views and more light, are generally the best. If you want to stay with a local family, UP Tourism run a **paying guesthouse**

Moving on from Varanasi

To get to the **airport** through the gridlock (Rs400 by pre-paid taxi from Cantonment station, or Rs200 by auto – Rs50–100 more from town if you don't pre-pay), allow at least ninety minutes from the Old City.

From the Roadways Bus Stand on GT Road (Ⓣ0542/220 3476), UPSRTC run hourly **buses** 5.30am–8.30pm to the **Nepal** border at Sonauli (hourly; 10hr) via Gorakhpur (7hr), and there are good and regular buses for Allahabad (every 30min; 3hr), making road a better option than rail for that destination. For **Bihar**, bus services are now few and far between (with none at all to Patna), and road conditions not great, so rail is your best bet.

Varanasi Cantonment station has a foreign tourists' reservations office (Mon–Sat 8am–8pm, Sun 8am–2pm). Many trains on the main east–west Delhi–Kolkata line bypass Varanasi but stop at Mughal Sarai, around 45 minutes away by road or rail. The fastest train to Agra and Jaipur, for example, is the daily #2307 *Howrah–Jodhpur Express*, which leaves Mughal Sarai at 9.55am, arriving at Agra Fort at 7.15pm, Jaipur at midnight, and Jodhpur at 6.30am the next morning, but there's also a thrice-weekly overnight service from Varanasi itself, the #4853/4863/4865 *Marudhar Express* (departing 5.20–6.15pm, depending on the day, arriving Agra Fort 5.55am, Jaipur 11.30am, Jodhpur 5.30pm). For Delhi, though a couple of *Rajdhani* express trains pass through Mughal Sarai around 1am, the most convenient trains leave from Varanasi, including the #2559 *Shiv Ganga Express* (leaves 7.15pm, arrives New Delhi 7.40am). The best daytime service, the #2875 *Neelachal Express* (leaves 7.38am, arrives New Delhi 9.40pm) runs Tuesday, Friday and Sunday only. To Kolkata, convenient overnight services include the #3006 *Howrah Mail*, leaving Varanasi at 5pm, for a chirpy 7.20am arrival at Howrah; you can get a faster service from Mughal Sarai (the 1.55am #2302 *Rajdhani* takes only eight hours on most days), but it isn't worth the extra effort. The *Mahanagri Express* #1094 is the fastest train to Mumbai (departs 11.30am, arriving Mumbai CST 2.15pm next day).

The most convenient train to **Patna** is the 2.35pm *Secunderabad–Patna Express* #2791, which reaches Patna at 7.10pm. For an earlier arrival, the 8am *Magadh Express* #2402 from Mughal Sarai gets in at 11.30am. To **Gaya** the *Doon Express* #3010 leaves Varanasi at 4.25pm and arrives at 9.17pm.

To **Uttarakhand**, the #3009 *Doon Express* (10.35am arriving Dehra Dun 7.10am next day) is the best option for Dehra Dun, but a section of the #4265 *Dehra Dun Express* (departs 8.30am) also serves Ramnagar (arrives 6.05am next day). For Khajuraho, take a train to Satna (the 4-weekly #1062 *Lokmanyatilak Express* does it overnight, departing Mon, Wed, Fri & Sun 11.20pm, arriving at 6.45am; the fastest daily daytime service is the #2168 *Dadar Superfast Express* at 10.25am, arriving at 3.50pm), where you can pick up a bus for the three-hour journey.

scheme – ask at their station office. Places listed below under the Godaulia heading appear on the Godaulia map (p.289); all others appear on the main Varanasi map (pp.282–283).

Godaulia

Alka D-3/23 Mir Ghat Ⓣ0542/239 8445, Ⓦwww.hotelalkavns.com. Often booked up by tour groups, but a good mid-market riverside choice, with a big variety of well-maintained quality rooms, plus a terrace and a pleasant little lawn overlooking the river. ❷–❺

Ganga Fuji D-7/21 Sakarkand Gali Ⓣ0542/232 7333, Ⓦwww.gangafujihome.com. Well-run family guesthouse near the Golden Temple, with a range of tastefully decorated rooms, scrupulously clean (though it's down a rather dirty alley), some with a/c, clean bathrooms and hot showers. ❷–❺

Ganpati D-3/24 Mir Ghat Ⓣ0542/239 0059, Ⓦwww.ganpatiguesthouse.com. Rooms here overlook the Ganges or are arranged around a courtyard, and there's a restaurant and a sociable balcony overlooking the river. The 10am checkout time is a bit inconvenient. ❷–❺

Golden Lodge D-8/35 Kalika Gali, near Shanishvara ⓣ0542/239 8788, ⓔgoldenvaranasi@gmail.com. Friendly staff, a range of attached rooms (plus some non-attached singles), and a decent restaurant, but make sure the price they quote includes tax and service or they may try to add those to your bill when you leave. ❶–❹

Shanti Guest House Ck 8/129 Garwasi Tola, near Manikarnika Ghat ⓣ0542/239 2568, ⓔvaranasishanti@yahoo.com. An old favourite – though in need of a lick of paint – tucked away near the burning *ghats*. Large building with loads of (generally) clean rooms with attached bathrooms, as well as dorm beds (Rs50). Excellent views from the lively rooftop restaurant. ❶–❹

Sri Venkateswar D-5/64 Dashaswamedh Rd ⓣ0542/239 2357, ⓔvenlodge@yahoo.com. Simple but clean and close to the *ghats* and to Vishwanatha Temple, capturing the ambience of the Old City. Large rooms, nice courtyard, friendly staff, 24hr checkout and no intoxicants allowed. ❷–❸

Yogi Lodge D-8/29 Kalika Gali ⓣ0542/239 2588, ⓔyogilodge@yahoo.com. An old budget-traveller favourite in the heart of the Old City that's been going for years; very well run, with a safe for valuables. Spotless restaurant, clean rooms and dorms (Rs65). ❶

South of Godaulia, near the river

Ganges View Asi Ghat ⓣ0542/231 3218, ⓦwww.hotelgangesview.com. A great veranda looking out onto the river, a lobby full of good books, a pleasant ambience and an interesting landlord mean this popular place is often booked up. The rooms are small but tastefully and stylishly decorated. You pay a premium to stay on the upper floor, with better views. ❻–❼

Palace on Ganges B-1/158 Asi Ghat ⓣ0542/231 5050, ⓦwww.palaceonganges.com. The only luxury hotel on the Ganges, with 22 individually decorated rooms representing the states of India – Gujarati is particularly colourful. Facilities include central a/c, TV, minibar, tour desk and rooftop restaurant. ❼

Palace on Steps D-21/11 Rana Ghat ⓣ0542/245 0970, ⓔpalaceonsteps@gmail.com. Originally two hotels (separated by a big banyan tree), now combined to make one, with rooms ranging from budget to a/c, but all immaculate, though you pay a premium if you want one with views over the *ghats* (which you get from the hotel's terrace anyway). ❷–❼

Vishnu Rest House D-24/17 Pandey Ghat ⓣ0542/245 0206. One of the nicest of the riverside lodges, with rooms, dorms (Rs60) and a lovely patio and café overlooking the Ganges; popular and often booked up. Best approached via the *ghats*, south of Dashaswamedh. ❶–❹

Cantonment and around

Gateway Nadesar Palace Grounds, Raja Bazaar Rd, ⓣ0542/250 3001 to 19, ⓦwww.thegatewayhotels.com. The poshest gaff in town, set among vast grounds (explore them by buggy, or on a birdwatching walk), with stately rooms, fine dining, a pool and fitness centre, and also yoga classes. Double rooms start at Rs9450, or take a deluxe suite for $315. ❾

Gautam Grand Parade Kothi ⓣ0542/220 8288, ⓦwww.hotelgautamgrand.com. Good-value modern hotel near the station; the rooms (some a/c) are not huge, but they're reasonably well-kept, each with a balcony. There's also 24hr room service, a dorm for those on a budget (Rs100), and the staff are eager to please. ❸–❹

India 59 Patel Nagar ⓣ0542/250 7593, ⓦwww.hotelindiavns.com. A three-star hotel that makes a pretty good attempt at being stylish. The rooms are quite smart and modern (cool white with pinewood – even the laminated floor doesn't look too naff) with attached bathrooms and a/c; and a health and fitness centre, a rooftop bar and four restaurants, including the excellent *Palm Springs*. ❻

Hotel Pradeep Kabir Chaura Rd, Jagatganj ⓣ0542/220 7231 or 2, ⓦwww.hotelpradeep.com. Comfortable, quite smart and popular with tour groups; away from, but within striking distance of, the *ghats*. Good restaurant (see p.294). ❺–❻

Radisson Varanasi The Mall ⓣ0542/250 1515 or 1800/1800 333, ⓦwww.radisson.com/varanasi.in. One of Varanasi's best-value luxury places, with classy and well-appointed rooms, stylish but not huge, plus a swimming pool, two restaurants, a bar and a coffee shop. Rates (doubles from $163) include a huge buffet breakfast. ❾

Raj Kamal Parade Kothi ⓣ0542/220 8844. Budget option near the railway station, very near the UPTDC's *Tourist Bungalow*. Useful for early and late train departures, but often full. ❷

Surya S-20/51, A5 The Mall ⓣ0542/250 8465 or 6, ⓦwww.hotelsuryavns.com. Well-run, comfortable and relaxing hotel arranged around a small lawn that doubles up as an alfresco restaurant. Rooms are small but well-kept, with modern bathrooms, and many have balconies. Facilities include internet, tour desk, foreign exchange, a pool (Rs200 for non-guests) and a decent restaurant. You can also camp (Rs100/person). ❹–❺

What's in a name?

The **Yogi Lodge** (near Vishwanatha Temple), **Vishnu Rest House** (overlooking the river) and **Shanti Guest House** (near Manikarnika Ghat), three of the Old City's oldest and best-run guesthouses, face dubious competition from lookalike hotels copying their names and paying rickshaw-wallahs to divert customers. Four other bogus Vishnu lodges have sprung up – the *Old Vishnu Lodge*, the *Vishnu Guest House*, the *Real Vishnu Guest House* and the *New Vishnu Guest House*. And several more "Shanti" lodges and "Yogi" lodges are playing the same name game. Legally, the con merchants are safe, as no one owns the copyright to such universal Indian words as "Yogi", "Vishnu" and "Shanti", but tourists should beware: no hotel that pays commission to touts or tries to trick you like this is going to be honest in other ways either.

The ghats

The great riverbanks at Varanasi, built high with eighteenth- and nineteenth-century pavilions and palaces, temples and terraces, are lined by stone steps – the **ghats** – which stretch along the whole waterfront, changing dramatically in appearance with the seasonal fluctuations of the river level. Each of the hundred *ghats*, big and small, is marked by a lingam, and occupies its own special place in the religious geography of the city. Some have crumbled over the years while others continue to thrive, visited by early-morning bathers, brahmin priests offering puja, and people practising meditation and yoga. Hindus regard the Ganges as *amrita*, the elixir of life, which brings purity to the living and salvation to the dead, but in reality the river is scummy with effluent, so don't be tempted to join the bathers; never mind the chemicals and human body parts, it's the level of heavy metals, dumped by factories upstream, that are the real cause for concern. Whether Ganga water still has the power to absolve sin if sterilized is a contentious point among the faithful; current thinking has it that boiling is acceptable but chemical treatment ruins it.

For centuries, pilgrims have traced the perimeter of the city by a ritual circumambulation, paying homage to shrines on the way. Among the most popular routes is the **Panchatirthi Yatra**, which takes in the *pancha* (five) *tirthi* (crossings) of Asi, Dash, Manikarnaka, Panchganga, and finally Adi Kesh. To gain merit or appease the gods, the devotee, accompanied by a *panda* (priest), recites a *sankalpa* (statement of intent) and performs a ritual at each stage of the journey. For the casual visitor, however, the easiest way to see the *ghats* is to follow a south–north sequence either by boat or on foot.

Asi Ghat to Kedara Ghat

At the clay-banked **Asi Ghat**, where the River Asi runs into the Ganges, pilgrims bathe prior to worshipping at a huge lingam under a peepal tree. A small marble temple just off the *ghat* houses another lingam called **Asisangameshvara**, the "Lord of the Confluence of the Asi". Traditionally, pilgrims continued from these to **Lolarka Kund**, the "Trembling Sun", a rectangular tank 15m below ground level, approached by steep steps, but it's now almost abandoned – except during the Lolarka Mela fair (Aug/Sept), when thousands come to propitiate the gods and pray for the birth of a son. It is actually one of Varanasi's earliest sites, and was attracting bathers in the days of Buddha. Equated with the twelve *adityas* or divisions of the sun, it is one of only two remaining sites in Varanasi that are linked with the origins of Hinduism, when worship of the sun god Surya predominated over that of the modern deities Shiva and Vishnu.

Boat trips on the Ganges

All along the *ghats*, and especially at the main ones such as Dashaswamedh, the prices of **boat** (*bajra*) **rental** are highly inflated, with local boatmen under pressure from touts to fleece tourists and pilgrims. There's a police counter at the top of Dashaswamedh, but the lack of government tourist assistance means that renting a boat to catch the dawn can be a bit of a free-for-all, and haggling is essential. There is an official rate, determined by UP Tourism, of Rs50 per hour for a small (one- to four-person) boat, Rs75 for a larger (five- to ten-person) one, but you won't find a boatman who'll agree to it.

Much of the adjacent **Tulsi Ghat** – originally Lolarka *ghat*, but renamed in honour of the poet Tulsi Das, who lived nearby in the sixteenth century – has crumbled. **Hanuman Ghat**, to its north, is believed by many to be the birthplace of the fifteenth-century Vaishnavite saint, Vallabha, who was instrumental in reviving the worship of Krishna (Vishnu's human incarnation in the Mahabharata). As well as a new South Indian temple, the *ghat* also has a striking image of **Ruru**, the dog, one of the eight forms of **Bhairava**, a ferocious and early form of Shiva.

The next set of steps northwards is **Harishchandra Ghat**, named after a legendary king who gave up his entire kingdom in a fit of self-abnegation. One of Varanasi's two **burning ghats** (*ghats* used for cremation, that is, the other being Manikarnika Ghat), it is easily recognizable from the smoke of its funeral pyres.

Further north still, **Kedara Ghat** is connected mythologically to Kedarnath, Shiva's home in the Himalayas. Pilgrims on the Panchatirthi Yatra don't visit it, but it's always busy and becomes a hive of activity in the sacred month of Shravana (July/Aug), at the height of the monsoon. Above its steps, a red-and-white-striped temple houses the **Kedareshvara lingam**, made of black rock shot through with a vein of white.

Chauki Ghat to Chaumsathi Ghat

Northwards along the river, **Chauki Ghat** is distinguished by an enormous tree that shelters small stone shrines to the *nagas*, water-snake deities, while at the unmistakable **Dhobi** ("Laundrymen's") **Ghat**, clothes are still rhythmically pulverized in pursuit of purity. Past smaller *ghats* such as **Mansarowar**, named after the holy lake in Tibet, and **Narada**, honouring the divine musician and sage, lies **Chaumsathi Ghat**, where impressive stone steps lead up to the small temple of the **Chaumsathi** (64) **Yoginis**. Images of Kali and Durga in its inner sanctum represent a stage in the emergence of the great goddess as a single representation of a number of female divinities. Overlooking the *ghats* here is Peshwa Amrit Rao's majestic sandstone haveli (mansion), built in 1807 and currently used for religious ceremonies and occasionally as an auditorium for concerts.

Dashaswamedh Ghat

Dashaswamedh Ghat is Varanasi's most popular and accessible bathing *ghat*, with rows of *pandas* sitting on wooden platforms under bamboo umbrellas, masseurs plying their trade and boatmen jostling for custom. It's the second and busiest of the five *tirthas* on the Panchatirthi Yatra. Its **Brahmeshvara** lingam is supposed to have been planted by the god Brahma. South of here, a flat-roofed building houses the shrine of **Shitala**, which is likewise extremely popular, even in the rainy season when devotees have to wade to the temple or take a boat.

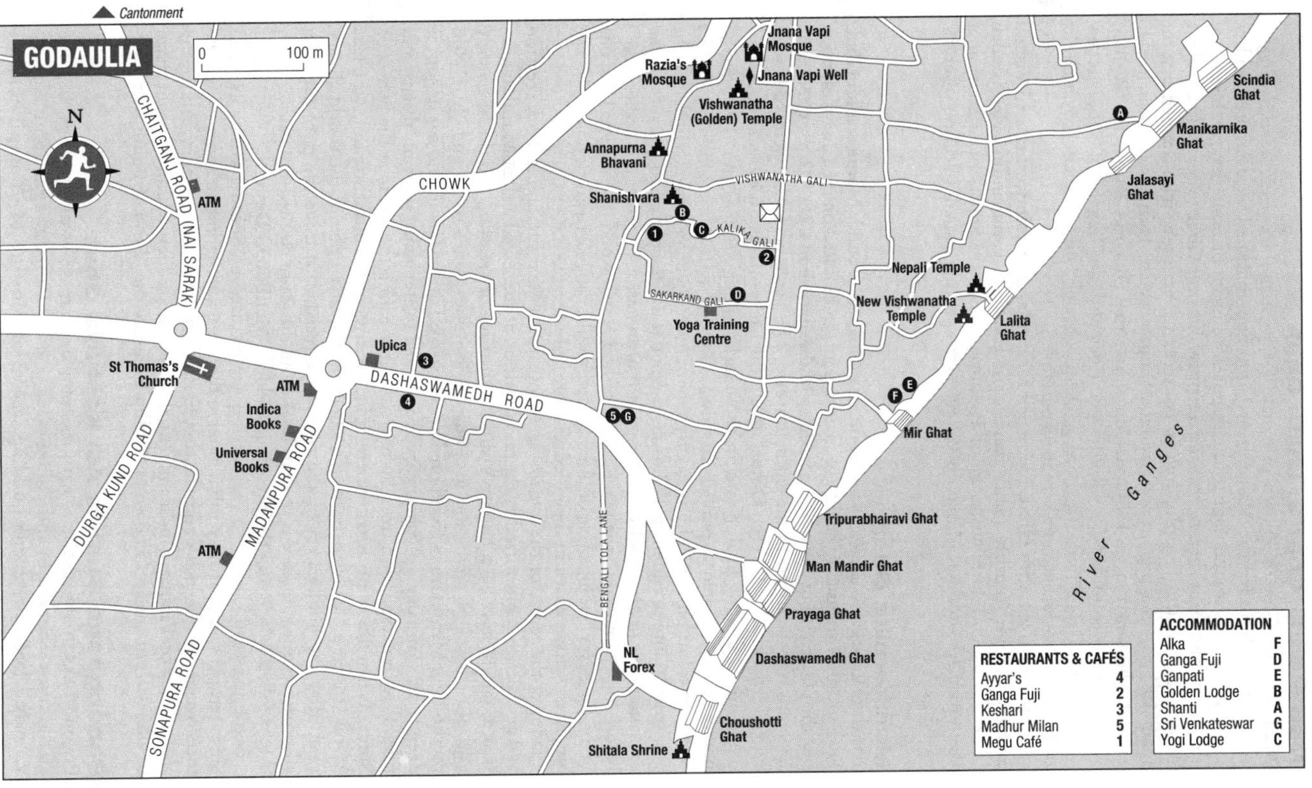

RESTAURANTS & CAFÉS	
Ayyar's	4
Ganga Fuji	2
Keshari	3
Madhur Milan	5
Megu Café	1

ACCOMMODATION	
Alka	F
Ganga Fuji	D
Ganpati	E
Golden Lodge	B
Shanti	A
Sri Venkateswar	G
Yogi Lodge	C

Man Mandir Ghat to Lalita Ghat

Man Mandir Ghat is known primarily for its magnificent eighteenth-century observatory, built for the Maharaja of Jaipur and equipped with ornate window casings. Pilgrims pay homage to the important lingam of Someshvara, the lord of the moon, alongside, before crossing **Tripurabhairavi Ghat** to **Mir Ghat** and the **New Vishwanatha Temple**, built by conservative brahmins who claimed that the main Vishwanatha lingam was rendered impure when Harijans (Untouchables) entered the sanctum in 1956. At Mir Ghat, the **Dharma Kupa**, the Well of Dharma, is surrounded by subsidiary shrines and the lingam of **Dharmesha**, where it is said that Yama, the Lord of Death, obtained his jurisdiction over all the dead of the world – except here in Varanasi.

To the north is **Lalita Ghat**, renowned for its **Ganga Keshava** shrine to Vishnu and the **Nepali Temple** (daily 5am–8pm; Rs10), a Kathmandu-style wooden structure which houses an image of **Pashupateshvara** – Shiva's manifestation at Pashupatinath, in the Kathmandu Valley – and sporting a small selection of erotic carvings.

Manikarnika Ghat

North of Lalita lies Varanasi's pre-eminent cremation ground, **Manikarnika Ghat**. Such grounds are usually held to be inauspicious, and located on the fringes of cities, but the entire city of Shiva is regarded as **Mahashamshana**, the "Great Cremation Ground", for the corpse of the entire universe. The *ghat* is perpetually crowded with funeral parties, as well as the **Doms**, its Untouchable guardians, busy and preoccupied with facilitating final release for those lucky enough to pass away here. Seeing bodies being cremated so publicly has always exerted a great fascination for visitors to the city, but photography is strictly taboo; even having a camera visible may be construed as intent, and provoke hostility. Wood touts descend on tourists at the *ghat* explaining the finer metaphysical points of transmutation ("cremation is education") before subtly shifting to the practicalities of how much wood is needed to burn one body, the never-ending cycle of inflation and would you like to give a donation. The amounts written down in their "ledgers" are unbelievable.

Lying at the centre of the five *tirthas*, Manikarnika Ghat symbolizes both creation and destruction, epitomized by the juxtaposition of the sacred well of **Manikarnika Kund**, said to have been dug by Vishnu at the time of creation, and the hot, sandy ash-infused soil of cremation grounds where time comes to an end. In Hindu mythology, Manikarnika Kund predates the arrival of the Ganga and has its source deep in the Himalayas. Vishnu carved the *kund* (water tank) with his discus, and filled it with perspiration from his exertions in creating the world at the behest of Shiva. When Shiva quivered with delight, his earring fell into this pool, which as Manikarnika – "Jewelled Earring" – became the first *tirtha* in the world. Every year, after the floodwaters of the river have receded to leave the pool caked in alluvial deposits, the *kund* is re-dug. Its surroundings are cleaned and painted with bright folk art depicting the presiding goddess, **Manikarni Devi**.

Bordering Manikarnika to the north is the picturesque **Scindia Ghat**, its tilted Shiva temple lying partially submerged in the river, after falling in as a result of the sheer weight of the *ghat*'s construction in the mid-nineteenth century. Above the *ghat*, several of Varanasi's most influential shrines are hidden within the tight maze of alleyways of the area known as **Siddha Kshetra** (the "Field of Fulfilment").

Panchganga Ghat to Adi Keshava Ghat

Beyond Lakshmanbala Ghat, with its commanding views of the river, lies one of the most dramatic – and contentious – *ghats*, **Panchganga**, dominated by Varanasi's largest riverside building, the great **Mosque of Alamgir**, known locally as Beni Madhav-ka-Darera. With its minarets now much shortened, the mosque stands on the ruins of the **Bindu Madhava**, a Vishnu temple that extended from Panchganga to Rama Ghat before it was destroyed by Aurangzeb and replaced with the mosque. Panchganga also bears testimony to more favourable Hindu–Muslim relations, being the site of the initiation of the medieval saint of the Sufi-Sant tradition, Kabir, the son of a humble Muslim weaver who is venerated by Hindus and Muslims alike. Along the riverfront lies a curious array of three-sided cells, submerged during the rainy season, some with lingams, others with images of Vishnu, and some empty and used for meditation or yoga. Above **Trilochana Ghat**, further north, is the holy ancient lingam of the three (*tri*)-eyed (*lochana*) Shiva. Beyond it, the river bypasses some of Varanasi's oldest precincts, now predominantly Muslim in character; the *ghats* themselves gradually become less impressive and are usually of the *kaccha* (clay-banked) variety. At **Adi Keshava Ghat** (the "Original Vishnu"), on the outskirts of the city, the Varuna River flows into the Ganga. Unapproachable during the rainy season, when it is completely submerged, the *ghat* marks the place where Vishnu supposedly landed as an emissary of Shiva, and stands on the original site of the city before it spread southwards; around Adi Keshava are a number of Ganesha shrines.

The Old City

At the heart of Varanasi, between Dashaswamedh Ghat and Godaulia to the south and west and Manikarnika Ghat on the river to the north, lies the maze of ramshackle alleys that comprise the **Old City**, or Vishwanatha Khanda. The whole area buzzes with the activity of pilgrims, *pandas* and stalls selling offerings to the faithful, and there are lingams and shrines tucked into every corner. If you get lost just head for the river.

Approached through labyrinthine alleys and the **Vishwanatha Gali** (or Lane), the temple complex of **Vishwanatha** or Visheshwara, the "Lord of All", is popularly known as the **Golden Temple**, due to the gold plating on its massive spire. Hidden behind a wall, the opulent complex is closed to non-Hindus, who have to make do with glimpses from adjacent buildings. Vishwanatha's history has been fraught. Sacked by successive Muslim rulers, it was repeatedly rebuilt and destroyed; in 1785, Queen Ahilyabai Holkar of Indore built the temple that stands today. Its simple white domes tower over the **Jnana Vapi** ("Wisdom Well"), immediately north, housed in an open-arcaded hall built in 1828, where Shiva cooled his lingam after the construction of Vishwanatha. Adjacent to the temple, guarded by armed police to protect it from Hindu fanatics, stands the **Jnana Vapi Mosque**, also known as the Great Mosque of Aurangzeb. Close by, the temple of **Annapurna Bhavani** is dedicated to Shakti, the divine female energy. Manifest in many forms, including the awesome Kali and Durga with their weapons and gruesome garlands of skulls, she's seen here as the provider of sustenance and carries a cooking pot. Nearby is a stunning image, faced in silver against a black surround, of **Shani** or Saturn. Slightly north, across the main road, the thirteenth-century **Razia's Mosque** stands atop the ruins of a still earlier Vishwanatha temple that was destroyed under the Sultanate.

Bharat Mata

About 3km northwest of Godaulia, outside the Old City, the modern temple of **Bharat Mata** ("Mother India"), inaugurated by Mahatma Gandhi, is unusual in that it has a huge relief map in marble of the whole of the Indian Subcontinent and the Tibetan plateau, with mountains, rivers and the holy *tirthas* all clearly visible. Pilgrims circumambulate the map before viewing it in its entirety from the second floor. The temple can be reached by rickshaw from Godaulia for around Rs30.

South of the Old City

The nineteenth-century **Durga Temple** – stained red with ochre, and popularly known as the Monkey Temple, thanks to its aggressive and irritable monkeys – stands in a walled enclosure 4km south of Godaulia, not far from Asi Ghat. It is devoted to Durga, the terrifying aspect of Shiva's consort, Parvati, and the embodiment of **Shakti** (divine female energy), and was built in a typical North Indian style, with an ornate *shikhara* in five segments, symbolizing the elements. The best views of the temple are from across Durga *kund*, the adjoining tank. A forked stake in the courtyard is used during some festivals to behead sacrificial goats. Non-Hindus are admitted to the courtyard, but not the inner sanctum.

Access to the neighbouring **Tulsi Manas Temple**, on the other hand, is unrestricted (daily 5am–noon & 3.30–9pm). Built in 1964 of white-streaked marble, its walls are inscribed with verses by Goswami Tulsidas, the poet and author of the Ramcharitmanas, the Hindi equivalent of the great Sanskrit epic Ramayana.

A little further south, the **Bharat Kala Bhawan** museum (Mon–Sat: May & June 7.30am–1pm; July–April 10.30am–4.30pm; Rs100 [Rs10], camera Rs50) has a fabulous collection of miniature paintings, sculpture, contemporary art and bronzes. A gallery dedicated to the city of Varanasi, with a stunning nineteenth-century map, has a display of the recent Raj Ghat excavations and old etchings of the city. Along with Buddhist and Hindu sculpture and Mughal glass, further galleries are devoted to foreign artists who found inspiration in India, such as Nicholas Roerich and Alice Boner; the Bengali renaissance painter Jamini Roy, so influenced by folk art, is also well represented.

Bharat Kala Bhawan forms part of Banaras Hindu University (BHU), the campus of which also holds the **New Vishwanatha Temple** (daily 4am–noon & 1–9pm), distinguished by its lofty white-marble spire. The temple was the brainchild of Pandit Malaviya, founder of the university and a great believer in an egalitarian and casteless Hindu revival, and was built by the Birlas, a wealthy Marwari industrial family. Although supposedly modelled on the original temple destroyed by Aurangzeb, the building displays characteristics of the new wave of temple architecture, amalgamating influences from various parts of India with a garish interior. Outside the gates a small market with teashops, flower-sellers and other vendors caters for the continuous flow of visitors.

Ramnagar Fort

South of Asi Ghat, on the opposite side of the river, the residence of the Maharaja of Varanasi, **Ramnagar Fort** looks down upon the Ganges. The best views of the fortifications – especially impressive in late afternoon – are to be had from the rickety pontoon bridge that crosses the river to the fort on the south bank, which is reached by a road heading south from the BHU area. During the monsoon the bridge is dismantled and replaced by a ferry, still preferable to taking the long main road that crosses the main Malaviya Bridge to the north before heading down the eastern bank of the river. The fort can also be reached by chartering a boat from Dashaswamedh Ghat.

Inside, the fort bears testimony to the wealth of the maharaja and his continuing influence. A dusty and poorly kept **museum** (daily 10am–5pm; Rs15) provides glimpses of a decadent past: horse-drawn carriages, old motor cars, palanquins, ornate gilded and silver *howdahs* (elephant seats), hookahs, costumes and old silk in a sorry state are all part of the collection, along with an armoury, some minute ivory carvings, an astronomical clock and hunting trophies. Some visitors have reported having tea with the affable maharaja after chance encounters.

Varanasi is renowned for its **Ram Lila**, held during Dussehra (Oct), during which episodes from the Ramayana are re-enacted throughout the city and the maharaja sponsors three weeks of elaborate celebrations. Across the courtyard, a section is devoted to the Ram Lila procession and festivities.

Eating

Most of the Old City **cafés** are vegetarian, and alcohol is not tolerated, but the Cantonment is less constrained, and some hotels have bars. After an early morning boat trip, try the traditional snack of *kachori*, savoury deep-fried pastry bread sold in the Old City next to the *ghats* – but avoid the chai stalls here as the cups are washed in the river.

Stomach disorders are common in Varanasi, so stick to bottled or treated water and be careful when choosing where you eat. Among hotel restaurants, *Vishnu Rest House* on Pandey Ghat does excellent thalis and the *Yogi Lodge* must have the cleanest kitchen in the Old City, dishing out non-spicy curries and travellers' favourites. Places listed below under the Godaulia heading appear on the Godaulia map (p.289); all others appear on the main Varanasi map (pp.282–283).

Godaulia

Ayyar's Dashaswamedh Rd. Small, inexpensive café at the back of a shopping arcade, serving South Indian food (Rs16–32), including great masala dosas, excellent filter coffee and delicious milk drinks.

Ganga Fuji D5/8 Kalika Gali, Dashaswamedh. Pleasant little restaurant near Vishwanatha, with a friendly host who guides diners through the multi-cuisine menu (main dishes Rs50–100 veg, Rs80–200 non-veg) – North Indian dishes are particularly good. Live classical music every evening from 7.30pm.

Keshari D-14/8, Teri Neem, off Dashaswamedh Rd. The menu lists a huge variety of veg curries at Rs40–100, "all items available", they say. The *paneer* tomato and the mushroom masala are its specialities, but every dish is delicious.

Madhur Milan Dashaswamedh Rd, just past Vishwanatha Lane. Cheap and very popular café, great for dosas, sweets, *kachoris* and samosas (watch them being fried out front, and grab them while they're piping hot). Main dishes Rs28–72, thalis Rs40–110.

Megu Café D-8/1 Kalika Gali. Down the alley leading to the *Golden Lodge* and *Yogi Lodge*, this small place run by a Japanese–Indian couple (shoes off at the door), serves a short menu of Japanese treats including veg sushi rolls, veg tempura and ginger chicken (main dishes Rs75–85). Closed Sundays.

The rest of the town

Annapurna J-12/16A Ramkatora Ⓣ0542/220 0151, Ⓦwww.sriannapurna.com. Gleaming multi-cuisine restaurant serving continental, subcontinental and Chinese veg food (main dishes Rs85–140, thalis Rs120–140, mini-meals Rs85–110); also does home delivery, and even delivers thalis at two hours' notice to any train passing through Varanasi (give train name and number, plus coach and seat number).

Ashiyana Major Singh Place, Lt Rohan Marg, Cantonment. Chinese and Indian meals, snacks and drinks served in an a/c lounge or on a rather noisy lawn, with non-veg mains at Rs75–150.

Bread of Life B3/322 Sonapura Rd. Bakery providing brown bread, cinnamon rolls, muffins and confectionery, with a small, clean restaurant serving Western food such as tuna burgers and crème caramel. Main dishes Rs70–120; profits go to charity, but service is slow.

El Parador Maldahia Rd. Remarkable restaurant round the corner from the *Tourist Bungalow*, serving outstanding Mexican, Italian, Greek and French cuisine in a bistro atmosphere. All the pasta is home-made, main dishes Rs175–350.

Haifa 1/108 Asi Rd. Laidback place serving approximations of Middle Eastern dishes – including hummus, fresh-baked pittas and falafel – as well as the more usual Indian fare, in a congenial atmosphere. Main dishes Rs60–110, breakfasts Rs60–90. The "Middle Eastern thali" (a selection of mezze with pitta) is a great deal at Rs80.

Kerala Café Durga Kund Rd, Bhelpura Thana. A very popular South Indian restaurant with good snacks (dosas, *vadas*, *uttapams* and the like, at Rs16–32) and lemon rice, tamarind rice, sambar rice or curd rice (Rs40).

Lotus Lounge 14/21 Mansarowar Ghat. Not a lounge at all, but a bright and breezy terrace restaurant overlooking the *ghats*, and serving an eclectic mix of international cuisine from chicken satay to Thai red curry to moussaka, plus pastas and salads, with main dishes at Rs75–180.

Poonam *Hotel Pradeep*, Kabir Chaura Rd, Jagatganj. Good, moderately priced (Rs200–235 for non-veg mains), Mughlai food served in a comfortable air-conditioned environment.

Vaatika Asi Ghat. A leafy terrace right on the *ghat*, serving good pizza (Rs70–120) and pasta (Rs60–100), plus freshly made juices and salads (all vegetables sterilized in permanganate, all water boiled and filtered).

Shopping

With hustlers and rickshaw drivers keen to drag tourists into stores offering commission, **shopping in Varanasi** can be a nightmare – but it's worth seeking out the city's rich silk-weaving and brasswork. The best **areas to browse** are the Thatheri Bazaar (for brass), or Jnana Vapi and the Vishwanatha Gali in Godaulia with its Temple Bazaar (for silk brocade and jewellery). State-run emporiums such as UP Handlooms in Lahurabir (B-21 Rathyatra Crossing) and Nichi Bagh (39/6 near City Post Office), and Handloom House in Sigra (D64/132K) – offer fixed prices and assured quality. **Open Hand Café and Shop** (Ⓦwww.openhandonline.com), B1/128-3 Dumraun Bagh, Colony Asi, near *Haifa* restaurant and *Tiwari Lodge*, is a community-run project selling bed linen, clothes, bags, cards, and it doubles up as a café, so you can enjoy filter coffee and chocolate cake while you shop.

Sales pitches tend to become most aggressive when it comes to **silk**, and you need to be wary of the hard sell. Qazi Sadullahpura, near the Chhavi Mahal Cinema, lies at the heart of a fascinating Muslim neighbourhood devoted to the production of silk. Mehrotra Silk, 21/72 Englishia Lane, off Station Road near the railway station (Ⓣ0542/220 0189, Ⓦwww.mehotrasilk.in) is highly recommended, and will happily run you up a shirt and deliver it to your hotel, as well as selling ready-made scarves, shawls and bedsheets; they also have a branch at K4/8A Lalghat, and offer free hotel or station pick-ups for customers (rickshaw-wallahs are liable to take you to commission-paying imitators). Upica, the government-run emporium, has outlets at Godaulia and opposite the *Gateway* hotel, and Paraslakshmi Exports, D-61/16, Sidhgiribagh (Ⓣ0542/241 1496), offers a wide range of silk fabrics as well as scarves, shawls and bedspreads at fixed prices, and also free pick-ups for customers.

Listings

Airlines Air India, 52 Yadunath Marg, Cantonment Ⓣ0542/250 2547; Indian Airlines, c/o Air India; Jet Airways and JetLite, 1st floor, Krishnayatan Building S-20/56 Kennedy Rd, off The Mall, Cantonment Ⓣ0542/250 6444.

Banks and exchange There are plenty of ATMs in town, including on the Godaulia roundabout. Several of the cheap hotels, as well as the upmarket ones, will change money, as well as NL Forex on Dashaswamedh Rd and in the street opposite *Gateway* hotel. The State Bank of India by *Hotel Surya* in the Cantonment (Mon–Fri 10am–4pm, Sat 10am–1pm) also changes cash and travellers' cheques.

Bookshops Indica Books, D40/18 Madanpura Rd, Godaulia (with a parcel mailing service); Universal Book Company, D40/60 Madanpura Rd; Pilgrims Book House, B27/98-A-8, Nawabganj Road, Durga Kund Ⓦwww.pilgrimsbooks.com; Harmony, B1/158 Asi Ghat.

Car rental Rental at around Rs2000–3000/day for a car with driver from UPTDC (Ⓣ0542/220 5845).

Hospitals Sir Sunderlal Hospital, Benares Hindu University (Ⓣ0542/230 7565); Shiv Prasad Gupta Hospital (government-run), Kabir Chaura (Ⓣ0542/221 4720 to 3); Marwari Hospital, Godaulia (Ⓣ0542/239 2611); Ram Krishna Mission Hospital, Luxa (Ⓣ0542/245 1727).

Internet Internet cafés aimed at travellers cluster around Kachauri Lane and Bengali Tola Lane in the Godaulia area, mostly charging Rs20/hr. In the Cantonment, they usually cost Rs30/hr, but Cyber Café on Parade Kothi (50m towards the station from *Gautam Grand* Hotel) charges Rs15/hr.
Motorcycles Mechanics and workshops specializing in Enfields are clustered in the Jagatganj area, near the Sanskrit University; ask around for a secondhand bike.
Music The International Music Ashram, D33/81 Kalishpura in the Old City (Ⓣ0542/245 2302, Ⓔkeshvaraonayak@hotmail.com), is an excellent place to get a few lessons in tabla, sitar and theory.
Pharmacies Singh Medical pharmacy near Prakash Cinema, Lahurabir (a couple of kilometres north of Godaulia), opens late; every hospital has a neighbouring 24hr pharmacy.
Post The main post office in the Old City is on Kabir Chaura Rd near Kotwalii police station at the top end of the Chowk district. The one in the Cantonment is off Raja Bazaar Rd near the big TV mast at its top end. Branch offices are located in *Clarks* hotel, on the Mall in the Cantonment, on Dashaswamedh Rd near the river, and on Sakarkand Gali near *Ganga Fuji* restaurant.
Travel agencies General travel agencies include the friendly Nova International on Shubhash Nagar, near Parade Kothi Ⓣ0542/220 8361, and Thomas Cook, Sridas Foundation Building, 4 The Mall (next to *Radisson* hotel) Ⓣ0542/250 0589, Ⓦwww.thomascook.in.
Yoga There is a yoga institute at the Benares Hindu University, but the Yoga Training Cente (D5/15 Shakarkand Lane, near Mir Ghat Ⓣ9919 857895, Ⓦwww.yogatrainingcentre.com) in Godaulia is more central; alternatively try Yogi Rakesh Pandeep, B-4/35 Hanuman Ghat (Ⓣ9415 817882).

Sarnath

Ten kilometres north of Varanasi, the ruins and temples at **SARNATH** are a Buddhist pilgrimage centre, and also popular with day-trippers from Varanasi. It was here, around 530 BC, just five weeks after he had found enlightenment, that Buddha gave his first ever sermon. According to Buddhist belief, this set in motion the Dharmachakra ("Wheel of Law"), a new cycle of rebirths and reincarnations leading eventually to ultimate enlightenment for everybody. During the rainy season, when Buddha and his followers sought respite from their round of itinerant teaching, they would retire to Sarnath. Also known as **Rishipatana**, the place of the *rishis*, or **Mrigadaya**, the deer park, Sarnath's name derives from Saranganatha, the Lord of the Deer.

Over the centuries, the settlement flourished as a centre of Buddhist (particularly Hinayana) art and teaching. Seventh-century Chinese pilgrim Xuan Zhang recounted seeing thirty monasteries, supporting some three thousand monks, and a life-sized brass statue of the Buddha turning the Wheel of Law, but Indian Buddhism floundered under the impact of Muslim invasions and the rise of Hinduism. Sarnath's expanding Buddhist settlement eventually dissolved in the wake of this religious and political metamorphosis. Except for the Dhamekh *Stupa*, much of the site lay in ruins for almost a millennium, prey to vandalism and pilfering, until 1834, when Alexander Cunningham, head of the Archeological Survey, excavated the site. Today it is once more an important Buddhist centre, and its avenues house missions from all over the Buddhist world.

The main site and the Dhamekh Stupa

Dominated by the huge bulk of the Dhamekh Stupa, the extensive archeological excavations of the main site of Sarnath are maintained within an immaculate park (daily sunrise–sunset; Rs100 [Rs5], video camera Rs25). Entering from the southwest, the pillaged remains of the **Dharmarajika Stupa** lie immediately to the north: within its core the *stupa* holds a green marble casket containing relics of Buddha (Ashoka gathered these up from seven original locations and redistributed

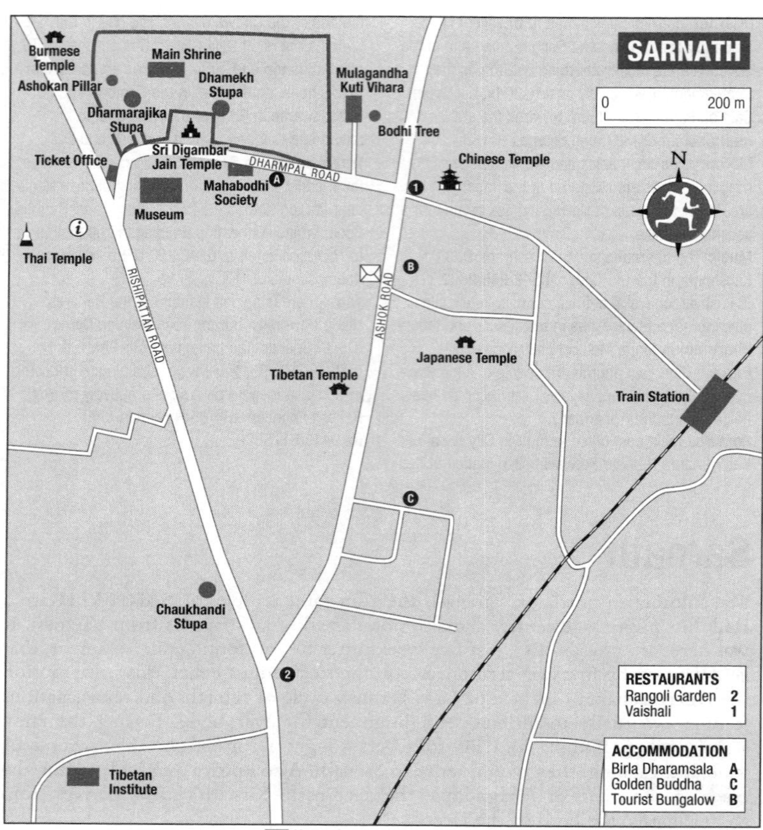

among numerous *stupas* nationwide including this one) and precious objects, including decayed pearls and gold leaf. Commemorating the spot where the Buddha delivered his first sermon, Dharmarajika is attributed to the reign of Ashoka in the third century BC, but was extended a further six times.

Adjacent to Dharmarajika Stupa are the ruins of the **main shrine**, where Ashoka is said to have meditated. To the west stands the lower portion of an **Ashoka Pillar** – minus its famous capital, now housed in the museum. The ruins of four monasteries, dating from the third to the twelfth centuries, are also contained within the compound; all bear the same hallmark of a central courtyard surrounded by monastic cells.

The most impressive of the site's remains is the **Dhamekh Stupa**, also known as the **Dharma Chakra Stupa**, which stakes a competing claim as the exact spot of Buddha's first sermon. The *stupa* is composed of a cylindrical tower rising 33.5m from a stone drum, ornamented with bas-relief foliage and geometric patterns; the eight-arched niches halfway up may once have held statues of the Buddha.

In its own enclosure outside the park, so accessible for free, the **Sri Digamber Jain Temple**, or Shreyanshnath Temple, is believed to mark the birthplace of Shreyanshnath, the eleventh Jain *tirthankara*. Built in 1824, the interior houses a large image of the saint, as well as attractive frescoes depicting the life of Mahavira, contemporary of Buddha and founder of the Jain religion.

The museum

Opposite the gates to the main site, the **museum** (ticket office across the street; daily 8am–5pm; Rs5; leave cameras and mobiles in lockers at the entrance) is designed to look like a *vihara*. Its small but renowned collection of Buddhist and brahmanist antiquities consists mostly of sculpture made from Chunar sandstone. The most famous exhibit is the **lion capital**, removed here from the Ashoka column on the main site. Constructed by Ashoka (273–232 BC), the great Mauryan king and convert to the *dharma*, it has become the emblem of modern India: four alert and beautifully sculpted lions guard the four cardinal points, atop a circular platform. Belonging to the first and second centuries AD are two impressive life-size standing *bodhisattvas* – one has a stone parasol with fine ornamentation and emblems of the faith. Among the large number of fifth-century figures is one of **Buddha**, cross-legged and with his hands in the *mudra* gesture. Perfectly poised, with his eyes downcast in deep meditation and a halo forming an exquisite nimbus behind his head, the Buddha is seated above six figures, possibly representing his companions, with the Wheel of Law in the middle to signify his first sermon. Later sculptures, dating from the tenth to twelfth centuries, include an exceptionally delicate image of the deity **Avalokiteshvara** with a lotus, and another of **Lokeshvara** holding a bowl.

Chaukhandi Stupa, Mulagandha Kuti Vihara and the modern sites

The dilapidated brick remains of the **Chaukhandi Stupa**, 1km south of the main site along Ashoka Marg, date from the Gupta period (300–700 AD), and are said to mark the spot where Buddha was reunited with the Panchavargiya Bikshus, his five ascetic companions who had previously deserted him. The *stupa*, standing atop a terraced rectangular plinth, is capped by an incongruous octagonal Mughal tower, which was built by Akbar in 1589 AD to commemorate his father's visit to the site.

Northeast of the Dhamekh Stupa, the lofty church-like **Mulagandha Kuti Vihara** monastery (no set hours; free entry) was built in 1931 with donations from the international Buddhist community. Run by the Mahabodhi Society, it drew devotees from all over the world to witness its consecration, and has become one of Sarnath's greatest attractions for pilgrims and tourists alike. The entrance foyer is dominated by a huge bell – a gift from Japan – and the interior houses a gilded reproduction of the museum's famous image of the Buddha, surrounded by fresco-covered walls depicting scenes from his life.

A little way east, shielded by a small enclosure, Sarnath's **bodhi tree** is an offshoot of the tree at Bodhgaya in Bihar, under which Buddha attained enlightenment. Sangamitra, Emperor Ashoka's daughter, took a branch from the original tree in 288 BC and planted it in Anuradhapura, in Sri Lanka, where its offshoots have been nurtured through the ages.

Buddhist communities from other parts of the world are well represented in Sarnath. In addition to the long-established **Mahabodhi Society** (Ⓣ0542/259 5955), the **Central Institute of Higher Tibetan Studies** (Ⓣ0542/258 5242, Ⓦwww.smith.edu/cihts), just out of Sarnath toward Varanasi, offers degree courses in Tibetan philosophy and the ancient language of Pali. Close to the post office is the traditional-style **Tibetan Temple** with frescoes and a good collection of *thangkas* (Tibetan Buddhist paintings): its central image is a colossal Shakyamuni, or "Buddha Calling the Earth to Witness" (his enlightenment). Two hundred metres to the east of the main gates is the **Chinese Temple**, while to the northwest, the **Burmese Temple** houses a white marble image of the Buddha flanked by two disciples. Behind the *Tourist Bungalow* is the **Japanese Temple**, run by the Mrigdayavana Mahavihara Society.

Practicalities

Sarnath-bound blue **buses** depart regularly from outside Varanasi Cantonment railway station and cost Rs10, but can get crowded. A pre-paid auto-rickshaw from Varanasi Cantonment station will cost Rs80; shared autos (Rs20/person) also sometimes run. Once you are in Sarnath, the sites are easy, and pleasant, to visit on foot.

Opposite the post office, southeast of the park, the UPTDC-run *Tourist Bungalow* (Ⓣ0542/259 5965, Ⓔrahimrigdava@up-tourism.com; ❸–❹) has reasonable **rooms** and a **dorm** (Rs150). Some of the monasteries, such as the pleasant *Burmese Vihara*, northwest of the main site, have basic rooms where visitors can stay for a donation. Right in front of the Mahabodhi Society gates, the *Birla Dharamsala* (❶) is a central option with very basic facilities. Further out of town, a ten-minute walk south from the Japanese temple, *Hotel Golden Buddha* (Ⓣ0542/236 9695, Ⓦwww.goldenbuddhahotel.com; ❹) is the most comfortable option in the area, with some very chic rooms and a decent restaurant serving good home-cooking. **Restaurants** include *Vaishali*, upstairs at the junction near the Chinese Temple, which has South Indian snacks, veg and non-veg curries, Chinese dishes and even pancakes (non-veg mains Rs70–140). *Rangoli Garden Restaurant*, just past Chukhandi Stupa, at the crossroad on the way from Varanasi, is popular for north and south Indian food (non-veg mains Rs100–185) and has an outdoor sitting area.

Gorakhpur

Some 230km north of Varanasi, **GORAKHPUR** rose to prominence as a waystation on a pilgrims' route linking Kushinagar (the place of Buddha's enlightenment) and **Lumbini** (his birthplace, across the border in Nepal), and is now known primarily as a gateway to Nepal. It was named after the Shaivite yogi **Gorakhnath**, and holds a large ashram and temple dedicated to him. Tourists and pilgrims tend to hurry through, their departure hastened by the town's infamous flies and mosquitoes; if you do get stranded, there's a bustling bazaar, adequate amenities and a few passable hotels.

Arrival and information

Gorakhpur has three **bus** stands: the Railway Bus Stand, near the station (150m up Station Rd, which is opposite the station, marked by a statue of Maharana Pratap Singh on horseback), for services from the Nepalese border at **Sonauli** and **Kushinagar**; the Kacheri Bus Stand, 1km southwest of the station, for buses from Allahabad, Lucknow and Varanasi; and **Pedleyganj**, 2km southeast of the station, used by some Varanasi services.

Daily **trains** from Gorakhpur include the #2555 *Gorakdam Express* at 4.35pm for **Lucknow** (arrives 9.45pm) and **New Delhi** (arrives 5.55am), and the #5018 *Gorakhpur–Lokmanyatilak Express* at 5.30am for **Mumbai** (arrives at Kalyan 5.30pm next day) via Varanasi (arrives 11.05am); other trains to **Varanasi** (6hr) include the overnight #549 *Gorakhpur–Manduadih* passenger train (it has sleepers), which leaves at 11.15pm, arriving 6.15am. Station facilities include pleasant retiring rooms, a basic restaurant and a tourist information booth (theoretically Mon–Sat 9am–5pm, but usually closed).

The **airport** (currently served only by JetLite to Delhi) is 7km east of Gorakhpur towards Kushinagar. Taxis charge Rs150 into town.

Cycle rickshaws are the main means of **transport** around town, with few hotels more than 2km from the station. Beware of ticket touts and poor service from the travel agents opposite the station. There are **ATMs** in Golghar (1km southwest of the station) and directly outside the station; the State Bank of India on Bank Road will change travellers' cheques. The **GPO** is in Golghar.

Practicalities

Gorakhpur **hotels** range from dingy flophouses near the station to mid-range places in Golghar (1km southwest) and Niyamachak (1.5km west). There are retiring rooms at the railway station which are good value, with or without a/c or dorms (Rs75); recommended if you need to catch an early train (❶–❷). For **eating**, there's a row of cheap *dhabas* opposite the station. Elsewhere, the best restaurants are in the more expensive hotels or the multi-cuisine *Bobis* in Golghar (mains Rs75–125 veg, Rs80–140 non-veg). All the following hotels have 24hr checkout.

Accommodation

Bobina Nepal Rd, Niyamachak ⓣ0551/233 6663, ⓦwww.hotelbobina.com. Decent mid-range choice, with a/c rooms, slightly worn, a decent restaurant and bar and even a pool. ❹–❺

Clarks Inn Grand Park Rd, near Golghar ⓣ0551/220 5015, ⓦwww.clarksinngrand.in. Gorakhpur's most upmarket option, an unexciting but reliable business hotel with large rooms, a fitness centre and a pool. ❽

President Golghar ⓣ0551/233 7654, ⓦwww.hotelpresident.net.in. A range of presentable a/c rooms at this prominent mid-range hotel, which even has a presidential suite. The *Marina*, in the same yard (ⓣ0551/233 7630) is grubbier and rather down-at-heel, but has very cheap single rooms (Rs150–250). ❹–❺

Standard Station Rd, by the statue of Maharana Pratap Singh ⓣ0551/220 1439. Cleanest of the cheap hotels opposite the station. Rooms are attached, but hot water comes in a bucket (Rs8). ❷

Getting to Nepal

Gorakhpur is a convenient jumping-off point for western **Nepal**, offering access to Pokhara and even Kathmandu. Direct buses to or from Kathmandu and Pokhara are not a good deal – it's much better to get a bus to Sonauli, cross over, and pick up onward transport connections on the other side.

Buses for Sonauli (3hr) depart from Gorakhpur's Railway Bus Stand between 4.30am and 9pm: deluxe buses leave from in front of the railway station. Take one of the earliest if you want to get a connecting bus to **Pokhara** or **Kathmandu** (both 10hr) in daylight, to enjoy the views; night buses also ply the routes. Private buses leave Sonauli almost hourly in the mornings, between 5am and 11am. The most popular bus service for Kathmandu actually operates from **Bhairawa**, 4km away in Nepal; the booking office is near Bhairawa's *Yeti Hotel.* Local jeeps cover the 24km from Bhairawa to Lumbini (Nepal), the birthplace of the Buddha.

If you want to **break your journey**, UPTDC's *Hotel Niranjana* (ⓣ05522/238201; [Rs300 (up to Rs650)]) in Sonauli, 1km short of the border, has air-cooled rooms and a dorm (Rs100). There's more choice over the border in Nepal; and in Bhairawa, 4km up the road from the border, the *Yeti* and the *Himalayan Inn are* popular.

Nepalese visas (valid for one month) are available at the border for US$30. There is a State Bank of India on the Indian side of the border; moneychangers across the border will also cash travellers' cheques. Indian Rs500 and Rs1000 notes are **illegal** in Nepal; yours may be "confiscated", and you can even be arrested for having them on you.

Kushinagar

Set against a pastoral landscape 53km east of Gorakhpur, the small village of **KUSHINAGAR** is revered as the site of Buddha's death and cremation, and final liberation (**Mahaparinirvana**) from the cycles of death and rebirth. During his lifetime, **Kushinara**, as it was then called, was a small kingdom of the Mallas, surrounded by forest. It remained forgotten until the late nineteenth century, when archeologists rediscovered the site and began excavations based on the writings of the seventh-century Chinese pilgrims.

Set in a leafy park in the heart of Kushinagar, the **Mahaparinirvana Temple** (or **Nirvana Stupa**), dated to the reign of Kumaragupta I (413–455 AD), was extensively rebuilt by Burmese Buddhists in 1927. The large gilded **reclining Buddha** inside the shrine was reconstructed from the remains of an earlier Malla image. At the road crossing immediately southwest, the **Matha Kuwar** shrine holds a tenth-century Buddha made of blue schist rock, also covered in gilt, and usually locked up (you can look in through the windows), though the caretaker may offer to open it up for you if he's around. Just round the corner, there's a "Bauddha Museum" (Tue–Sat and most Sun 10.30am–4.30pm; free), housing a so-so collection of ancient Buddhist sculpture, not all original; the most interesting exhibits are the small pieces in a case of antiquities unearthed locally. The crumbling bricks of the **Ramabhar Stupa**, about 1.5km southeast of the main site (around Rs50 for the round trip by rickshaw), are thought to be the original **Mukutabandhana Stupa**, erected to mark the spot where Buddha was cremated.

Today Kushinagar is rediscovering its roots as a centre of international Buddhism, and is home to several monasteries sponsored by Buddhists from Tibet, Burma, Thailand, Sri Lanka and Japan. The strikingly simple **Japanese Temple** consists of a single circular chamber housing a great golden image of Buddha, softly lit through small, stained-glass windows. In stark contrast, the recently constructed **Thai Monastery** is a large complex of lavish, traditionally styled temples and shrines.

Practicalities

Regular **buses** link Kushinagar with **Gorakhpur** (2hr). **UP Tourism** maintains an office (Mon–Sat 10am–5pm) at *Pathik Niwas* hotel. Both India Tourism and UP Tourism run comprehensive tours of the whole "Buddhist Circuit" of Uttar Pradesh, which can be booked in Kushinagar, or at UP Tourism in Delhi (see p.129). There's a moneychanger next to *Yama Café*, and you can also change money at the *Lotus Nikko* hotel.

Most of the temples offer **accommodation** for visiting pilgrims in return for a donation (in the region of Rs200/person). Of these, the Linh Son (Chinese) Temple (ⓣ9936 132062; ❷) has clean, spacious doubles with attached baths and hot water; the *Shree Birla* opposite (ⓣ05564/273090; ❷) is more basic. The relatively expensive state-run tourist bungalow, *Pathik Niwas* (ⓣ05564/273046, ⓔrahipathikniwas@up-tourism.com; ❸–❺), has air-conditioned rooms, luxury cottages called "American Huts" and a restaurant. *Lotus Nikko* (ⓣ05564/273025, ⓦwww.lotusnikkohotels.com; ❽), next to the Japanese Temple, is a three-star with air-conditioned rooms and moneychanging facilities, but it is sometimes booked up by tour groups.

Restaurants are scarce, but the pleasant and clean *Yama Café* next to Linh Son Temple, has a small menu of home-cooked Indian, Tibetan and Chinese food (main dishes Rs25–55) – the vegetable or chicken-noodle soup is particularly recommended. It opens at 8am for breakfast but closes around 8pm. Food stalls at the Kasia crossing also provide inexpensive snacks. Ask at the *Yama Café* about their 13km hike to surrounding villages and holy sites (8am–4pm; Rs750/person including breakfast and lunch; minimum five people).

4

Uttarakhand

* **Char Dham** The pilgrim circuit around the four holy sites of Garhwal reveals a cross-section of the Indian Himalayas' most superb scenery. See p.303

* **Haridwar** This holy city on the Ganges is one of the four sites of the Kumbh Mela and a great place for witnessing Hindu practice at any time. See p.313

* **Rishikesh** This busy pilgrimage place on the banks of the turquoise Ganges is a renowned yoga and meditation centre. See p.315

* **Gangotri** Hole up at the source of the Ganges, high in the mountains, where sadhus offer accommodation for spiritual retreats. See p.323

* **Valley of the Flowers** A hidden valley, only discovered in 1931 by Europeans, whose lush meadows are a botanist's dream: hike here after the monsoons. See p.329

* **Curzon Trail** A ten-day trail over the Kuari Pass, offering stunning views of the Great Himalayan Watershed. See p.330

* **Corbett Tiger Reserve** Established in the 1930s, India's most famous nature reserve is renowned for its population of tigers.See p.334

▲ Sadhu practising yoga, Rishikesh

Northeast of Delhi, bordering Nepal and Tibet, the mountains of the Garhwal and Kumaon regions rise from the fertile sub-Himalayan plains. Together they form the state of **UTTARAKHAND**, which was shorn free from lowland Uttar Pradesh in 2000 after years of agitation, and changed its name from Uttaranchal in 2007. The region has its own distinct languages and cultures, and successive deep river valleys shelter fascinating micro-civilizations, where Hinduism meets animism and Buddhist influence is never too far away. Although not as high as the giants of Nepal, further east, or as the Karakoram, the snow peaks here rank among the most beautiful mountains of the inner Himalayas, forming an almost continuous chain that culminates in **Nanda Devi**, the highest mountain in India at 7816m.

Garhwal is the more visited region, busy with pilgrims who flock to its holy spots. At **Haridwar**, the Ganges thunders out from the foothills on its long journey to the sea. The nearby ashram town of **Rishikesh** is familiar from one of the classic East-meets-West images of the 1960s; it was where the Beatles came to stay with the Maharishi. From here pilgrims set off for the high temples known as the Char Dham – **Badrinath**, **Kedarnath**, **Yamunotri** and **Gangotri**, the source of the Ganges. Earthier pursuits are on offer at **Mussoorie**, a British hill station that's now a popular Indian resort. The lesser-visited **Kumaon** region is more unspoilt, and boasts pleasant small towns famed for mountain views and hill walks, such as **Kausani** and **Ranikhet**, as well as its own Victorian hill station, **Nainital**, whose promenade throngs with refugees from the heat of the plains. Further down, the forests at **Corbett Tiger Reserve** offer the chance to go tiger-spotting from the back of an elephant. Both districts abound in classic **treks**, many leading through the *bugyals* – summer pastures, where rivers are born and paths meet.

Facilities are good in the big towns of the foothills, but not upcountry, so if you're aiming to ascend, you should make the most of foreign exchange services, internet cafés and satellite TV before you set out. In the mountains, roads are good – maintained by the army, which has a large presence up here thanks to the proximity of the Tibetan border – but **getting around** is not always easy as the monsoon (Aug–Sept) causes landslides and avalanches which block the roads; similar troubles occur during the winter snow season (Dec–Feb). There are buses, but, especially high up, most locals get around by shared jeep, with many vehicles crammed to bursting. Compared to the plains, there's little caste strife (most mountain people are high-caste rajput or brahmin) and you'll see few beggars other than religious mendicants. A few words of Hindi are certainly handy as the mountain people usually speak little English. **Uttarakhand Tourism** (Ⓦgov.ua.nic.in) plays second fiddle to the two regional tourism organizations, **GMVN** in Garhwal (see p.303) and **KMVN** in Kumaon (see p.331).

Some history

The first known inhabitants of Garhwal and Kumaon were the **Kuninda** in the second century BC, who seem to have had a close affinity with contemporaneous Indo-Greek civilization. Essentially a central Himalayan tribal people practising an early form of Shaivism, they traded in salt with Tibet. A second-century Ashokan edict at Kalsi in western Garhwal shows that Buddhism made some inroads in the region, but Garhwal and Kumaon remained Brahmanical. The Kuninda eventually succumbed to the **Guptas** around the fourth century AD, who, despite controlling much of the north Indian plains, failed to make a lasting impact in the hills. Between the seventh and the fourteenth centuries, the Shaivite **Katyuri** dominated lands of varying extent from the Katyur-Baijnath valley in Kumaon, where their stone temples still stand. Under them **Jageshwar** was a major pilgrimage centre, and Brahmanical culture flourished. Eastern Kumaon prospered under the

Chandras, from the thirteenth to the fifteenth century, when learning and art took on new forms and the Garhwal school of painting was developed. Later on, the westward expansion of the Gurkha empire was brought to an end by British annexation in the nineteenth century.

Following Independence, Garhwal and Kumaon became part of Uttar Pradesh, but failure by the administration in Lucknow to develop the region led to increasingly violent calls for a **separate state**. Things came to a head in October 1994 when a peaceful protest march to Delhi was violently disrupted in Mussoorie by the UP police. The separatist cause was taken up by the sympathetic high-caste BJP when they came to power in March 1998 and the new state was created in November 2000.

The process of creating this new state was somewhat acrimonious; there are deep cultural **differences** between Garhwal and Kumaon, and both regions wanted the capital to sit in their patch (Dehra Dun, a city in Garhwal, was eventually chosen, which upset the Kumaonis considerably). Meanwhile in Haridwar – culturally a part of the plains – farmers took to the streets to demand things remain as they were. Currently, the new administration faces serious environmental problems. **Deforestation** is causing the loss of arable land in the hills, and glaciers are retreating at an alarming rate as a result of global warming, causing water shortages lower down. Yet while officialdom founders, scattered mountain villages – inspired by self-reliance crusader Dr Anil Joshi and his **Himalayan Environmental Studies and Conservation Organization** (HESCO) – are taking sustainable development into their own hands, working to meld local resources and modern technology.

Garhwal

As the sacred land that holds the sources of the mighty Ganges and Yamuna rivers, **GARHWAL** has been the heartland of Hindu identity since the ninth century when, in the wake of the decline of Buddhism in northern India, the reformer Shankara incorporated many of the mountains' ancient shrines into the fold of Hinduism. He founded the four main **yatra** (pilgrimage) temples, deep within the Himalayas, known as the **Char Dham** – **Badrinath**, **Kedarnath**, and the less-visited pair of **Gangotri** and **Yamunotri**. Each year, between May and November, once the snows have melted, streams of pilgrims penetrate high into the mountains, passing by way of **Rishikesh**, the land of yogis and ashrams.

For more than a millennium, the *yatris* (pilgrims) came on foot. However, the annual event has been transformed in the last few years; roads blasted by the military through the mountains during the war against China in the early 1960s are now the lifelines for a new form of motorized *yatra*. Eastern Garhwal in particular is getting rich, and the fabric of hill society is changing rapidly – visitors hoping to experience the old Garhwal should spend at least part of their time well away from the principal *yatra* routes. In addition to their spiritual significance, the hills are now becoming established as a centre for **adventure sports**, offering all levels of trekking, whitewater rafting, paragliding, skiing and climbing.

Garhwal is a challenging place to **travel** around, with extremely long and often nerve-wracking bus and jeep rides being the order of the day. However, you are rewarded with spectacular views of snowy peaks offset by gaudily painted Garhwali villages in deep valleys. All of the tourist bungalows are operated by Garhwal Mandal Vikas Nigam – **GMVN** (Ⓦwww.gmvnl.com). Most are concentrated along the pilgrimage routes, although their network has been expanding. Standards vary widely, but most bungalows offer a range of rooms and dorms to

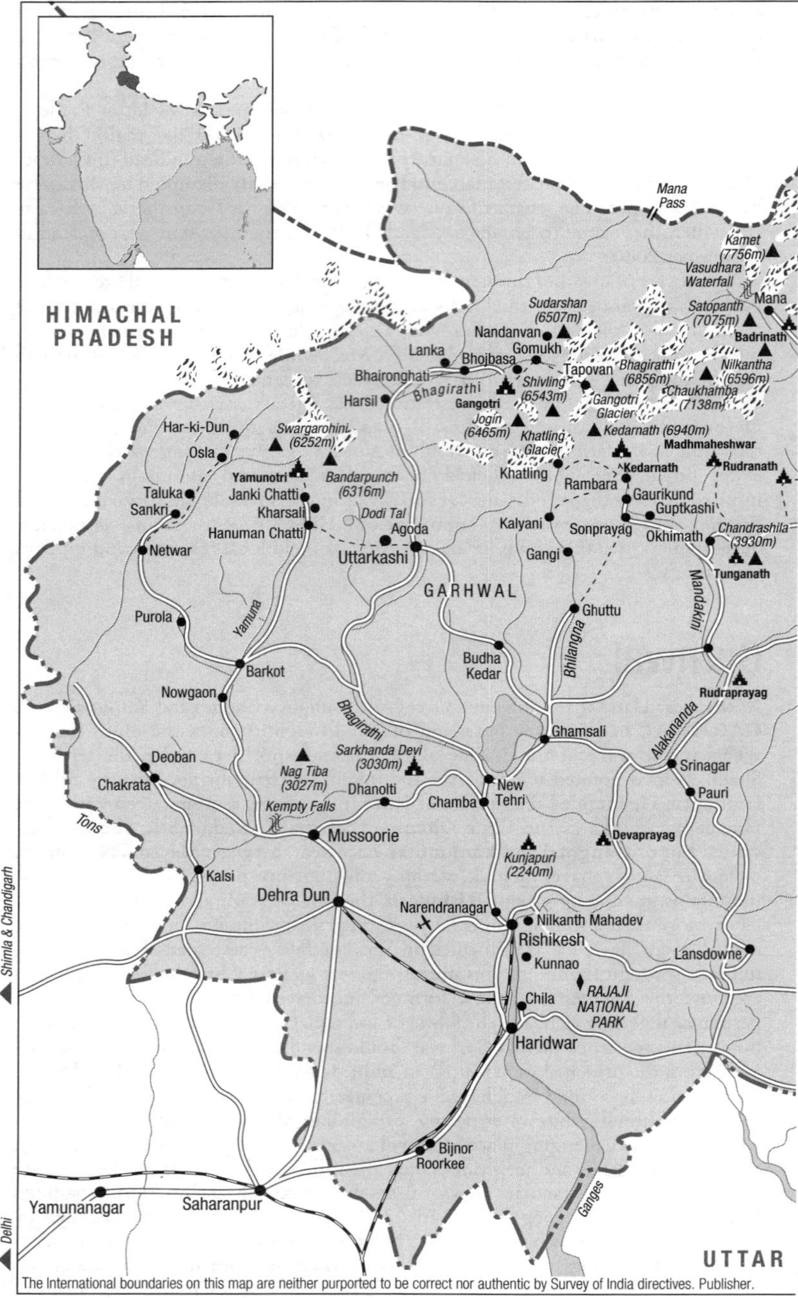

The International boundaries on this map are neither purported to be correct nor authentic by Survey of India directives. Publisher.

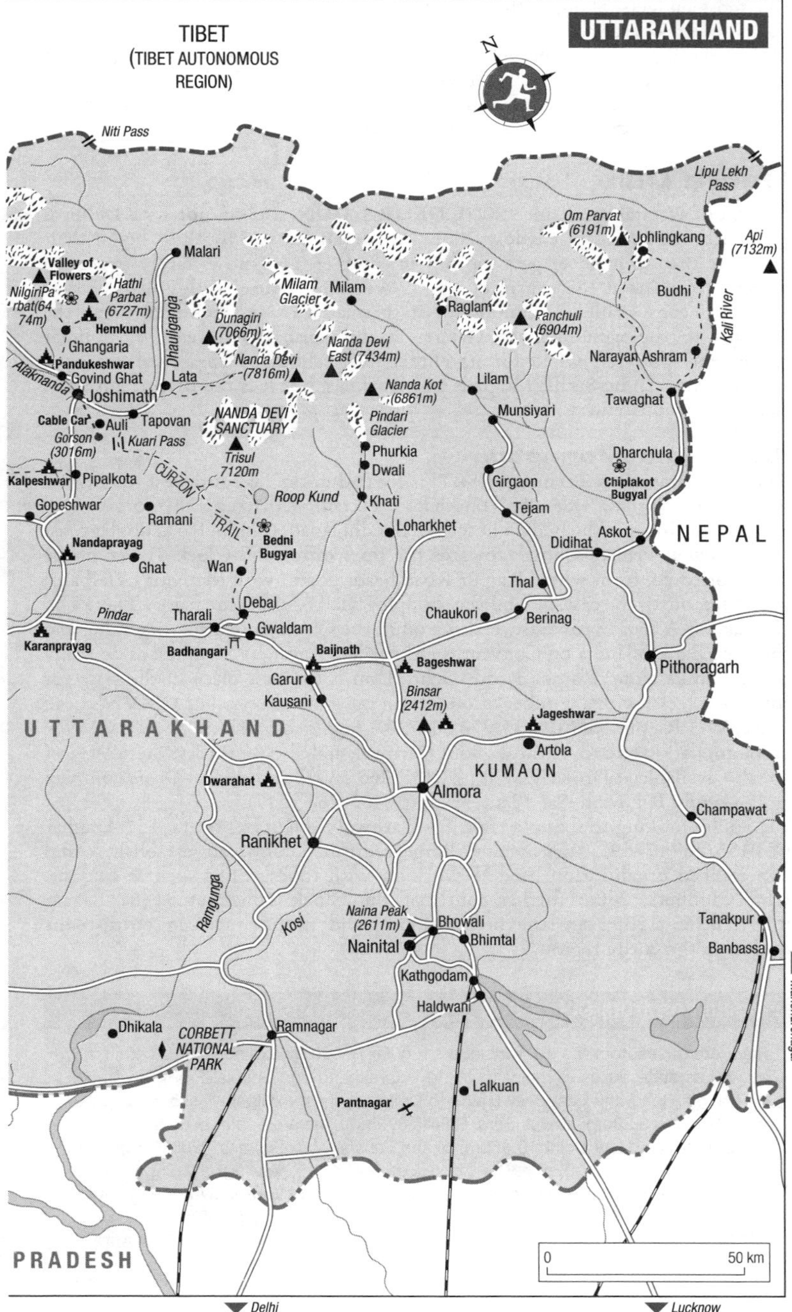

4 UTTARAKHAND

suit most budgets, along with a restaurant. GMVN also organizes Char Dham **tours** (often overpriced and inefficient), and offers expensive **car rental**. The GMVN headquarters are in Dehra Dun (see below), although you will get more help from their office in Delhi (☎011/2335 0481). The GMVN Trekking and Mountaineering Division, based in Rishikesh (see p.317), is the office to contact for adventure-sports packages such as skiing and trekking.

Dehra Dun

Capital of Uttarakhand since 2000, **DEHRA DUN**, 255km north of Delhi, is pleasantly located at just below 700m, as the Himalayan foothills begin their dramatic rise, so it never gets too hot in summer, and snows rarely appear in winter. It stands at the centre of the 120km-long **Doon Valley** (*dun* or *doon* literally means "valley"), famous for its basmati rice and hemmed in by the Yamuna to the west and the Ganges at Rishikesh to the east. A popular retirement spot, renowned for its elite public schools, Dehra Dun has been occupied in turn by Sikhs, Mughals and Gurkhas, but it is the British influence that is most apparent.

Arrival and information

The **Inter-state Bus Terminal** (ISBT) is located in the far southwest of town, a Rs60 auto-rickshaw ride (Rs6 on shared Vikram #5) from the more central **railway station** and the budget hotels on Gandhi Road. Gandhi Road doglegs east then north at Princes Chowk towards the **post office** and Clock Tower in the centre of town, from where Rajpur Road heads north, with the Astley Hall area branching off to the east, behind the shopping mall of the same name. There's no shortage of ATMs in town (several surround the Clock Tower for example), and the State Bank of India on Convent Road changes travellers' cheques, as do many of the **banks** along Rajpur Road. Dehra Dun is the best place in the state for **internet** access, with a number of outlets on the main streets. The **GMVN**'s head office, 74/1 Rajpur Rd (☎0135/274 6817, Ⓔgmvn@sacharnet.in), books GMVN accommodation and tours throughout Garhwal, and also rents cars; these services are also available at Drona Travels (☎0135/265 3309) in the *Hotel Drona* complex at 45 Gandhi Rd (Mon–Sat 10am–5pm; ☎0135/265 3217).

If you're looking to fix up a **trek**, try Garhwal Adventure Tours, 151 Araghar (☎0135/267 7769, Ⓔgarhwaltrekking@rediffmail.com), an established and experienced organization used to working with tour groups such as Exodus. Cliff Climbers, 200m further south of the Clock Tower at 51–61 Bazaar (☎0135/265 1235), are the best trekking and mountaineering **equipment** dealers in the entire region.

Moving on from Dehra Dun

Frequent buses from the ISBT include a regular Rs200 deluxe service to Delhi (7hr), as well as state buses to major towns in Uttarakhand and Shimla. From the station off Gandhi Road, the best daily **trains** to **Delhi** are the overnight *Mussoorie Express* #4042 (leaves 9.20pm, arrives Sarai Rohilla 8.35am), the a/c *Shatabdi Express* #2018 at 5pm (arrives New Delhi 10.45pm) or the *Janshatabdi Express* #2056 at 5.10am (arrives New Delhi 11.15am). The *Doon Express* #3010, leaving at 8.25pm, is the most convenient service to **Lucknow** (arrives 8.20am) and **Varanasi** (arrives 4.10pm), and continues to **Kolkata** (arrives 7am on second morning). The *Ujjaiyani Express* #4310, on Tuesdays and Wednesdays only, leaves at 6am and reaches **Agra** at 4.55pm.

Accommodation

Dehra Dun has a good selection of mid-range **hotels**, many of them strung along Rajpur Road as it heads north to Mussoorie. What little budget accommodation there is can be found between the railway station and the Clock Tower – or in the old-fashioned railway retiring rooms.

Ashrey 10 Tyagi Rd ⓣ0135/262 3388. In a quiet, but still central spot, 3min walk south of Princes Chowk; the private lawn in front complements the spotless, spacious and well-furnished new rooms. Good value. ❹–❺

Great Value 74-C Rajpur Rd, 2.5km north of the Clock Tower ⓣ0135/274 4086, ⓦwww.greatvaluehotel.com. Large, well-run chain hotel with good facilities including a nice garden, bar and in-room wi-fi internet connections (Rs120/hr). ❻–❽

Madhuban 97 Rajpur Rd ⓣ0135/274 0066, ⓔhotelmadhuban@bsnl.in. A large, imposing upmarket hotel with a popular restaurant, bar, steam room and gym, considered the best in town, with the presidential suite costing a princely Rs10,000, though the *Comfotel Inn* annexe has cheaper rooms. ❽–❾

Moti Mahal 7 Rajpur Rd ⓣ0135/265 1277, ⓔhotelmotimahal@rocketmail.com. A bright, modern hotel where smoked-glass double-glazing in the immaculate a/c rooms keeps the noise and fumes out. ❺

Victoria 70 Gandhi Rd ⓣ0135/262 3486. Basic lodge near the railway station, established in 1936, far from deluxe (hot water comes in buckets), but it has a certain ramshackle charm and is the best of the real cheapies. ❶

White House 15/7 Subhash Rd (aka Lytton Rd) ⓣ0135/265 2765. Atmospheric old Art Deco Raj residence near Astley Hall, with huge verandas, lofty ceilings, sturdy furniture (rather hard beds) and moody plumbing. A peaceful retreat from the centre of Dehra Dun, yet only a few minutes' walk away. ❷

The town and around

Driven by Dehra Dun's status as state capital, increasing local investment has resulted in a mini-boom – and accompanying noise and traffic problems – within the city centre. Most of Dehra Dun's bustling markets lie near the tall Victorian **Clock Tower**, or around Gandhi Road and Rajpur Road. Four kilometres north is the vast leafy colony occupied by the **Survey of India**, founded in 1767. Its greatest achievement was to determine the height of Mount Everest and name it after the surveyor general, Sir George Everest. While the Survey's shop is poor, Natraj **bookshop** at 17 Rajpur Rd is one of the best in the country for wildlife books.

Crossing the rainy-season riverbed of Bindal Rao, Kaulagarh Road progresses northwest past Dehra Dun's top private school, the **Doon School**, to the expansive grounds of the chateau-like **Forest Research Institute** (Mon–Fri 9.30am–5pm; Rs15), devoted to the preservation of India's much-threatened woodlands. There's a large and interesting **museum** here holding wood samples, insects, furniture, pickled animal embryos and the like. The **Botanical Survey of India**, in the next building, is only of interest to the specialist.

Somewhat further afield, **Rajpur**, 12km to the north, past the Survey of India and accessible by shared Vikrams, has a sizeable Tibetan community. Its striking *gompa* – the **Shakya Centre** – decorated with ornate frescoes, stands next to a centre of Tibetan medicine next door. There's another *gompa* on the main road around 5km towards Mussoorie.

Eating

Dehra Dun has several commendable mid-priced **eating places** and a bunch of adequate cheaper cafés around Gandhi Road. Posh espresso cafés include *Barista* next to *Kumar Veg*, and *Coffee Day* opposite the *Madhuban* hotel. *Kumar Sweets* by the Clock Tower is the town's favourite *mithai* centre.

Black Pepper 3 Astley Hall, Rajpur Rd. Grotto-style decor appeals to both families and bright young things. Wide range of Indian, Chinese and good continental, such as steak sizzlers and chicken stroganoff for Rs150–200.

Countdown Fast Food Subhash Rd, behind Astley Hall. Options include pizzas and burgers as well as Indian and Chinese dishes, including pork. Portions are huge, for Rs60–90.

Kumar Foods 15B Rajpur Rd. Excellent veg and non-veg cooking at reasonable prices (mains Rs100–150), and comfortable surroundings. There's a pure veg branch 40m further north.

Moti Mahal 7 Rajpur Rd. In the all a/c hotel of the same name, this is the place for a spot of posh nosh, especially chicken and *paneer*; non-veg dishes (Rs150–250) include chicken karahi, chicken muglai, and that great Anglo-Bangladeshi contribution to Indian cuisine, chicken tikka masala.

Tirupati 27-B Rajpur Rd. Clean and friendly multi-cuisine restaurant, particularly strong on south Indian dishes. A north Indian thali will set you back Rs115, or for Rs90 you can try a south Indian combination featuring dosa, *iddli* and *vada*.

Yeti 55-A Rajpur Rd. Interesting Chinese and Thai menus, including spicy Szechuan cuisine. Main dishes (non-veg) are Rs75–150, or Rs120–250 for seafood.

Mussoorie

Spreading for 15km along a high serrated ridge, **MUSSOORIE** is the closest hill station to Delhi, just 278km north of the capital and 34km north of Dehra Dun, from where it is visible on a clear day. At an altitude of 2000m, it gives travellers from the plains their first glimpse of the snow-covered Himalayan **peaks** of western Garhwal, as well as dramatic views of the Dehra Dun valley below.

These days, Mussoorie is a very popular weekend retreat for middle-class Indians up from the plains. Most foreign visitors come to Mussoorie to **study** Hindi at the excellent Landour Language School, but the town is also a useful base camp for **treks** into the western interior of Garhwal. Dominated by the long Bandarpunch Massif (6316m), with Swargarohini (6252m) in the west and the Gangotri group in the east, Mussoorie's mountain panorama may not be as dramatic as some other hill stations, but it forms a pleasant backdrop to the busy holiday town.

Arrival and information

As Mussoorie's 2km-long **Mall** is closed to motor vehicles during the tourist season, its two ends – the **Library** area at the west end, and the **Kulri** area in the east – serve as **transport hubs**. Cycle rickshaws operate mostly towards the flat Library end, while porters will carry luggage to hotels for Rs50 at most. Buses (Rs30) and shared taxis (about Rs100) from Dehra Dun, the plains and the rest of Garhwal arrive either at the **Library Bus Stand** at Gandhi Chowk, or the **Kulri** Bus Stand (which is also called the **Masonic Lodge Bus Stand**). At the smaller **Tehri Bus Stand**, east of Landour 2.5km from the Mall, buses pull in from Chamba (where you have to change buses if travelling between Mussoorie and Uttarkashi). Shared taxis and cars to various destinations are available at the bus stands.

Facilities along the Mall include the **tourist bureau** (Mon–Sat 10am–5pm; ⓣ0135/263 2863) next to the cable car, where you can get a small booklet of local information; a **post office** at the Kulri end, and a **GMVN transport office** (Mon–Sat 10am–5pm; ⓣ0135/263 1281) next to the Library Bus Stand, which runs tours of the town and further afield. The State Bank of India and Apex Bank both change money and have **ATMs**, of which there are two more along the Mall. **Internet** access is available at Visual Knot near *Green* restaurant and just round the corner at Banares Cyber Café (both Rs15/hr). Trek Himalaya, on the steep street opposite the cable car (ⓣ0135/263 0491, ⓦwww.trekhimalaya.com), can put together trekking packages, while Kulwant Travels (ⓣ0135/263 2717) at Kulri Bus Stand are approved tour and **car rental** operators, and the taxi office opposite

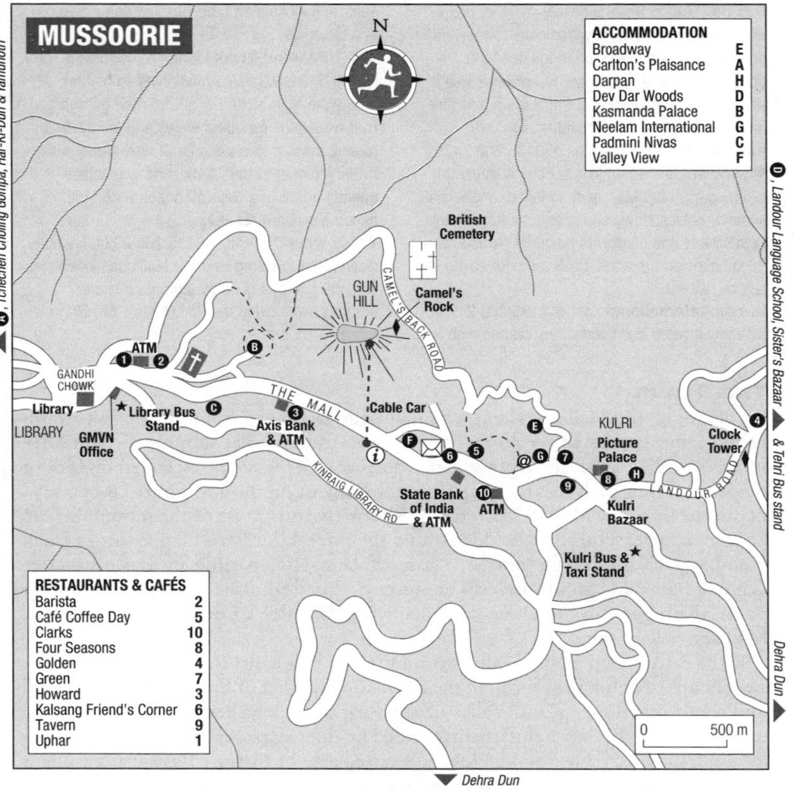

has services to destinations including Dehra Dun (Rs400), Delhi (Rs4000), Gangotri and Yamunotri (both Rs5000).

Accommodation

Mussoorie's **hotel** rates fluctuate between three rather vague **seasons**; low (Jan–March & July–Sept, reflected below), shoulder or mid-season (Christmas, April and the "Bengali season" of Oct & Nov), and peak (May–early July), when prices quadruple and a dingy room can cost over Rs1000. The town suffers from occasional **water shortages**, which may affect some of the cheaper hotels. Check-out time in Mussoorie is 10am.

Broadway Camel's Back Rd ⓣ0135/263 2243. Rambling old guesthouse perching on the edge of Kulri Bazaar with charming, bright window boxes, lovely views and a friendly atmosphere. A good bet for budget travellers, indeed the only budget hotel in season. ❶–❷

Carlton's Plaisance Happy Valley Rd, 1.5km from town ⓣ0135/263 2800, ⓦwww.nivalink.com/carltonsplaisance. Atmospheric Raj-era house plus a more modern annexe, both stuffed full of period memorabilia. Edmund Hillary stayed here and loved it, and George Everest's house is just up the road. Lovely gardens and an ideal base for gentle rambles away from the town. Book two weeks ahead in season. ❼–❽

Darpan Landour Rd, near Picture Palace, Kulri ⓣ0135/263 2483. Reasonable and clean, with hot showers, mountain views from some rooms, and a good Gujarati veg restaurant. ❷

Dev Dar Woods Sister's Bazaar ⓣ0135/263 2644, ⓔanilprakash56@yahoo.com. Craggy old hotel on a secluded site, often full due to its proximity to the language school, so book well in advance – you may even get picked up from the bus stop. Rates include breakfast. ❸

Kasmanda Palace The Mall ⓣ0135/263 2424, ⓦwww.welcomheritagehotels.com. A short, stiff climb up from the Mall leads to this ex-maharaja's summer palace, now opened as a heritage hotel. Comfortable and quiet with beautiful gardens and rhino heads on the walls. Book a month ahead in season. ❼–❽

Neelam International Kulri ⓣ0135/263 2195. Centrally located and good value, even in high season; it looks a bit tatty, but the rooms are cosy and clean. ❷

Padmini Nivas Library ⓣ0135/263 1093, ⓦwww.hotelpadmininivas.com. Just below the Mall, with a beautiful rose garden and fruit trees plus excellent views and lovely, fresh rooms, most with a veranda. It was founded by a British colonel in the 1840s, and was subsequently home to a Gujarati queen (Padmini), hence the name. ❺–❼

Valley View The Mall ⓣ0135/263 2324. Friendly, clean place towering over the Mall and close to all amenities, with a good restaurant and sunny terraces overlooking the Doon Valley. ❷–❹

The Town

Surprisingly, the Mall and the town's main hub face away from the snows towards Dehra Dun; the distant peaks can best be seen from the flat summit of **Gun Hill**, which rises like a volcano from central Mussoorie. This can be ascended on foot or pony on a bridle path that forks up from the Mall, or on the 400-metre "Ropeway" **cable car** from the Mall (Rs55 return). Alternative prospects of the mountains can be seen on a peaceful stroll or ride around the three-kilometre-long **Camel's Back Road**, which girdles the northern base of Gun Hill, passing by the distinctive Camel's Rock and an old **British cemetery** (closed to visitors). Another vantage point, the highest in the immediate vicinity, is **Childer's Lodge**, 5km east of the Mall above Landour.

At the eastern end of the Mall, beyond the bustling Kulri Bazaar, the road winds steeply upwards for 5km through the fascinating market of **Landour**, where you'll find shops overflowing with relics of the Raj, silver jewellery and books. At the top of Landour Bazaar, a square surrounded by cafés attracts both travellers and the local intelligentsia. Nearby, the lovely forested area of **Sister's Bazaar** is excellent for walks, especially to the **Haunted House**, a deserted Raj-era mansion, and around the famous **Landour Language School** (ⓣ0135/263 1487, ⓦwww.landourlanguageschool.com; open mid-Feb to mid-Dec).

Away from the noise and bustle, close to Convent Hill and 3km west of the Library, the Tibetan settlement of **Happy Valley** holds a large school, a shop selling hand-knitted sweaters and the small but beautiful **Tchechen Choling** *gompa* overlooking the Doon Valley and surrounded by gardens. It makes an enjoyable walk from the Mall along wooded roads, but you can also catch a taxi (around Rs120 return).

Eating

Cafés and **restaurants**, mostly strung along the Mall, serve everything from hotdogs to Chinese specialities; in addition to those recommended below, there are good restaurants in many of the hotels. Espresso chains *Barista* and *Café Coffee Day* both have branches in town. Prakash's Store, in Sister's Bazaar, is a wonderful place to shop if you're in the neighbourhood, with home-made breads, jams, peanut butter, cheddar cheese and even Marmite.

Clarks The Mall, Kulri. Multi-cuisine restaurant that manages to maintain a period atmosphere of sorts. Non-veg Indian and Chinese menus. Main dishes Rs90–150.

Four Seasons The Mall. Not as much fun as the *Tavern* across the street, but locals claim its mostly Indian menu is the best in town. Free delivery to your hotel. Non-veg mains Rs100–200.

Har-ki-Dun Valley trek

A relatively undemanding but superb trek **from Mussoorie** takes three days (plus one on the bus) to reach the sparsely populated "Valley of the Gods", **HAR-KI-DUN**, in the **Fateh Parvat** region of northwestern Garhwal. The valley trails are open from mid-April until mid-November, but the mountain passes only from mid-June to mid-September. All the trails on the trek are clear, and villagers will happily point you in the right direction. Recommended maps of the trail and region include those published by Leomann – sheet 8 covers Garhwal – and the Ground Survey of India map of the area available from any major Uttarakhand tourist office. In the valley itself, if not higher in the mountains, accommodation is widely available, and food can usually be bought. This area is being developed as a national park, so there are **fees** to be paid if you pass the forest checkpoint at Netwar: Rs350 in total for the first three days, plus Rs175 for each extra day, and a daily camping fee of Rs50–100.

The rivers and streams of Har-ki-Dun drain the glaciers and snowfields of the peaks of **Swargarohini** (the "Ascent to Heaven"; 6252m) and **Bandarpunch** (the "Monkey's Tail"; 6316m). Local people trace their lineage back to the Mahabharata, claiming descent from Duryodhana and his brothers. Like the Pandavas of the epic, they practise a form of polyandry and follow intriguing religious customs, including witchcraft. Worship at Taluka's Duryodhana temple, for example, consists of throwing shoes at the idol; at Pakola, the image has its back to the congregation. Their distinctive alpine buildings have beautifully carved wooden doors and windows, with the mortar construction punctuated by wooden slats.

The trek to Har-ki-Dun

Starting out from Mussoorie on **Day 1**, catch a Yamunotri bus (1 daily; 10am) at the Library Bus Stand and change at Nowgaon (9km short of Barkot, from where a road climbs to Hanuman Chatti) and take a bus or jeep from there to **Purola** and (changing vehicles at Purola if necessary) on to Netwar – a total of 148km. Set amid a patchwork of wheat and rice terraces in Netwar is a **PWD** bungalow with rooms; you can also obtain permission here or at the PWD office in Purola to stay at the forest bungalows further on. Simple cafés can be found around the bus stand.

Early the next morning – **Day 2** – take the bus to the roadhead at **Sankri**, which also has a bungalow. From here a road passable by jeep leads 12km through deodar and sycamore woods to **Taluka** (1900m), where there is another bungalow serving simple food. On **Day 3**, the trail descends to follow the River Tons through beautiful forests. Although you can get tea at the hamlet of Gangar, no food is available until you've walked the full 11km to **Osla** (2259m). The forest bungalow, GMVN hotel and *dhaba* stalls are all on the main trail in an area known as Seema, below Osla; from here on you have to carry your food, so stock up. A steep climb of 14km from Osla on **Day 4** finally brings you to the campground at **Har-ki-Dun** (3560m) – an excellent base from which to explore the *bugyals* (high alpine meadows) below the Swargarohini to the east, and the Jaundhar Glacier (3910m) at the head of the valley.

Golden Landour Bazaar. A popular if unremarkable local place next to the Clock Tower, serving Tibetan, Chinese and Indian dishes, and breakfasts. Mains Rs40–70 veg, Rs80–100 non-veg.

Green The Mall, Kulri. Justifiably popular veg (but licensed) restaurant serving Indian and Chinese food and snacks; in season, you may have to queue. Main dishes Rs80–100.

Howard The Mall. Rickety-looking revolving restaurant (non-veg mains Rs65–180) offering all-round views. Pastry and coffee shop on ground floor.

Kalsang Friend's Corner The Mall, by the post office. Hearty Tibetan fare (including *momos*, *thukpas* and pork dishes) as well as Chinese, Indian and the odd Thai dish, all tasty, with non-veg mains at Rs55–130.

Tavern The Mall. Hip place near the Picture Palace, offering pricey Western, Thai, Chinese and Indian dishes, such as chilli prawns. There's a small bar and live music most nights. Billiards hall and internet café upstairs. Non-veg main dishes are Rs150–400.

Uphar Gandhi Chowk. Clean, friendly north and south Indian veg food joint with an ice-cream bar. One of the best in the Library area. Main dishes Rs30–80.

Haridwar

At **Haridwar** – the Gates (*dwar*) of God (*Hari*) – 214km northeast of Delhi, the **River Ganges** emerges from its final rapids past the Shivalik Hills to start the long slow journey across northern India to the Bay of Bengal. Stretching for roughly 3km along a narrow strip of land between the craggy wooded hills to the west and the river to the east, Haridwar is especially revered by Hindus, for whom the **Har-ki-Pairi** *ghat* (literally the "Footstep of God") marks the exact spot where the river leaves the mountains. As a road and rail junction, Haridwar links the Gangetic plains with the mountains of Uttarakhand and their holy pilgrimage (*yatra*) network. Along with Nasik (see p.631), Ujjain (see p.400) and Allahabad (see p.275), Haridwar is one of the four holy *tirthas* or "crossings" that serve as the focus of the massive **Kumbh Mela** festival (see p.278). Every twelve years (next due in 2022), thousands of pilgrims come to bathe at a preordained moment in the turbulent waters of the channelled river around Har-ki-Pairi.

Arrival and information

Haridwar's **railway station** and **Station Bus Stand** face each other across the town's main thoroughfare, just southwest of the centre. **Tourist information** is available at a booth inside the station, from the more helpful **GMVN tourist office** (Ⓣ01334/224240) near Lalita Rao Bridge on Upper Road, or from the **state tourism office** at *Rahi Motel* on Railway Road by the bus stand (Ⓣ01334/265304); all open Monday to Saturday 10am to 5pm. Konark Tourist Service on Jassa Ram Road (Ⓣ01334/227210, Ⓦwww.konarktravels.com) offers **tours** of the state by bus or car.

There's a **post office** on Upper Road. The most central ATM is the State Bank of India's on Railway Road, where you can also change cash. Canara Bank on Railway Road also changes travellers' cheques and cash, and has an ATM. Upper Street has two more ATMs and an LPK Forex, with an attached **internet office**.

Moving on from Haridwar

Major **trains** passing through Haridwar include the overnight *Mussoorie Express* #4042, which leaves town at 11.10pm, reaching **Delhi** (Sarai Rohilla) at 8.35am. The a/c *Janshatabdi Express* #2056, which leaves at 6.20am, gets to New Delhi at 11.15am. For **Agra**, the *Kalingautkal Express* #8478 leaves daily at 6am, arriving at 3.50pm. The *Doon Express* #3010, leaving at 10.15pm, is the most convenient service to **Lucknow** (arrives 8.20am), **Varanasi** (arrives 4.10pm) and **Kolkata** (arrives 7am second morning). Local trains on the branch line to **Rishikesh** aren't that useful in view of the excellent and more frequent road connections.

The **Station Bus Stand** has services to Delhi every 30min (6hr) and Rishikesh (30min) from 4am till 11pm, and to Dehra Dun (1hr 15min) from 5am till 7.30pm. Shared Vikrams to Rishikesh from next to *Shivalik* restaurant provide a cramped alternative for much the same price. The **Taxi Association** near the railway station sets prices slightly higher than those quoted elsewhere, charging Rs2500 for a taxi to Delhi, Rs450 to Rishikesh, Rs310 to Chila. Travellers heading into the mountains should go to Rishikesh to pick up onward transport.

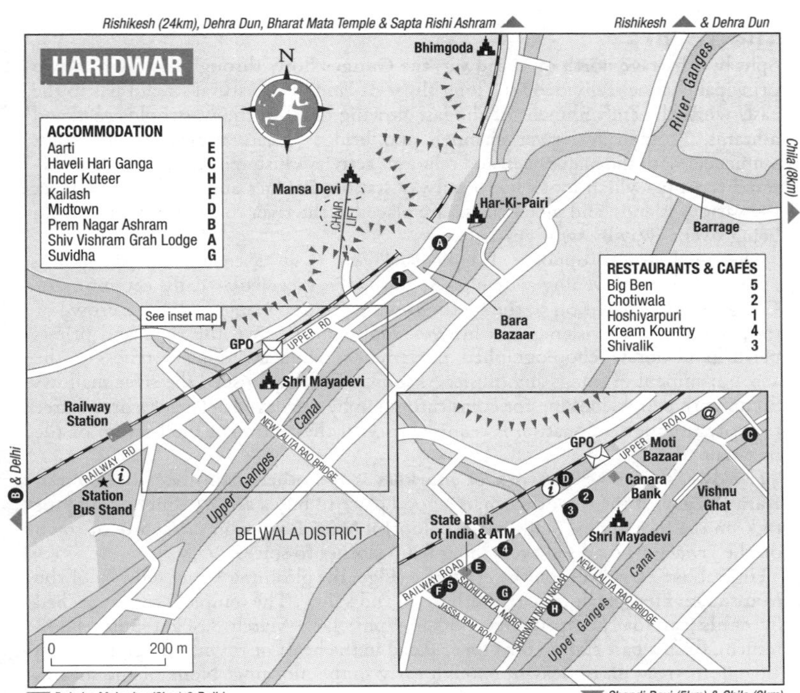

Accommodation

Haridwar has **accommodation** to suit most budgets, but none of it is very good value compared to Rishikesh, 24km north (see p.315). The rates below are subject to change with seasonal discounts and hard bargaining.

Aarti Railway Rd ⓣ01334/226365, ⓦwww.hardwarhotels.com. A bit grimy, but convenient for the railway station and bus stand, with good discounts off-season. The priciest rooms have a/c. ❸–❹

Haveli Hari Ganga 21 Ramghat ⓣ01334/265207, ⓦwww.havelihariganga.com. A beautiful haveli set up by two merchant brothers in 1917, now converted into a beautiful heritage hotel. Superior rooms cost $132 for foreigners. ❽

Inder Kuteer Guest House Sharwan Nath Nagar ⓣ01334/226336. Near the river, with small rooms and hard beds, a terrace, great rooftop views, a friendly vibe and hot water in buckets (though geysers are promised in the near future). Best value in this price range. ❶–❸

Kailash Railway Rd ⓣ01334/227789. Central hotel near the railway station, with a range of rooms, all either air-cooled or a/c. Up to fifty percent discounts off-season. ❸–❹

Midtown In an alley off Upper Rd, opposite *Chotiwallah* restaurant ⓣ01334/227507, ⓔhotelmidtown@gmail.com. Haridwar's best-value mid-range hotel, with clean rooms and friendly staff. Rooms at the front have balconies but the a/c ones are pricey. ❹–❼

Prem Nagar Ashram Jawalapur Rd, 2km west of the station ⓣ01334/226345, ⓦwww.manavdharam.org. Very calm and peaceful, if rather removed from town (Rs5 by shared Vikram). The staff are charming and the rooms clean and cheap. ❶

Shiv Vishram Grah Lodge Upper Rd, near Har-ki-Pairi ⓣ01334/227618. The budget rooms are air-cooled and pretty spacious; the deluxe ones have TVs and balconies overlooking the central parking area; dorm Rs100. The location is bang in the heart of town. ❸

Suvidha Sharwan Nath Nagar, behind Chitra Talkies cinema ⓣ01334/227023. Comfortable, plush place with a pleasant location near the river, away from the bustle of the bazaars and main roads. A/c and non-a/c rooms – make sure yours has a geyser. ❹–❺

The Town

Split by a barrage north of Haridwar, the **Ganges** flows through the town in two principal channels, divided by a long sliver of land. The natural stream lies to the east, while the embankment of the fast-flowing canal to the west holds *ghats* and ashrams. Promenades, river channels and bridges create a pleasant riverfront ambience, with the major *ghats* and religious activity clustered around the **Har-ki-Pairi temple**, which looks like a railway station. Bridges and walkways connect the various islands, and metal chains are placed in the river to protect bathers from being swept away by swift currents.

The clock tower opposite Har-ki-Pairi *ghat* is an excellent vantage point, especially during evening worship. At dusk, the spectacular daily ceremony of **Ganga Aarti** – devotion to the life-bestowing goddess Ganga – draws a crowd of thousands onto the islands and bridges. Lights float down the river and priests perform elaborate choreographed movements while swinging torches to the accompaniment of gongs and music. As soon as they've finished the river shallows fill up with people looking for coins thrown in by the devout. The *ghat* area is free to visit, although a donation is required to visit the section at the bottom of the first staircase.

Haridwar's teeming network of **markets** is the other main focus of interest. **Bara Bazaar**, at the top of town, is a good place to buy a *danda* (bamboo staff) for treks in the mountains. Stalls in the colourful **Moti Bazaar** in the centre of town on the Jawalapur road sell everything from clothes to spices.

High above Haridwar, on the crest of a ridge, the gleaming white *shikhara* of the **Mansa Devi** temple dominates both town and valley. The temple is easily reached by **cable car** (daily: April–Oct 7.30am–7pm; Dec–March 8.30am–5pm; Rs48 return), from a base station off Upper Road in the heart of town, though the steep 1.5-kilometre walk is pleasant enough early in the morning. None of the shrines and temples up top holds any great architectural interest, but you do get excellent views along the river.

The modern, seven-storeyed **Bharat Mata** temple – 5km north of Haridwar and reachable in shared Vikrams from next to *Shivalik* restaurant for Rs10 – is dedicated to "Mother India". Each of its various floors – connected by lifts – is dedicated to a celestial or political theme, and populated by lifelike images of heroes, heroines and Hindu deities.

Eating

As a holy city, Haridwar is strictly **vegetarian** and booze-free.

Big Ben Railway Rd. Hotel restaurant with a good range of veg curries (Rs65–100), set meals (Rs125–150), breakfasts (Rs100–140) and a few Chinese and Continental dishes including cheese steak or veg steak (they mean "cutlets").

Chotiwala Upper Rd. Established in 1937, this comfortable, dimly lit place is still one of the best around, offering good Indian food (main dishes Rs45–85) as well as breakfast (tea, coffee, toast and the like, but no omelettes of course), and some south Indian and Chinese dishes.

Hoshiyarpuri Upper Rd. Busy and friendly *dhaba*-like restaurant close to Har-ki-Pairi. Delicious Indian (especially Punjabi) and Chinese mains (Rs25–80), and great *kheer* (creamed rice pudding).

Kream Kountry Railway Rd. Bright new canteen serving Indian snacks from Rs8, pizza from Rs45 and kulfi for Rs15.

Shivalik Railway Rd. A small hotel restaurant whose chef prides himself on his small selection of Chinese dishes (try the chop suey). Tasty south Indian snacks, including dosas, are also on offer. Mains are Rs50–100, breakfasts and thalis both Rs80–120.

Rajaji National Park and around

Around 830 square kilometres of the Himalayan foothills immediately east of Haridwar are taken up by **RAJAJI NATIONAL PARK** (Rs350 [Rs40] for three days, Rs150 [Rs25] each additional day, plus Rs100–500 per vehicle, Rs100 for a camera; Ⓦ www.rajajinationalpark.in), which belongs to the same forest belt as Corbett Tiger Reserve, 180km east. Although not geared up to tourism to the same extent as Corbett, the park is absolutely beautiful, with a similar range of **wildlife** – most notably elephants, but also antelope, leopard and even a rare species of anteater – although no tigers. The **Van Gujjars**, a nomadic tribe whose summer homes lie within the park, have long been engaged in a land-rights dispute with the forestry department over designation of the forest for wildlife use, but a July 2007 state high court ruling upheld a petition allowing those already resident within the park to remain under the terms of the federal government's 2006 Forest Rights Act.

There are eight **entry gates** into the national park, including **Kunnao** close to Rishikesh and the main gates at **Chila** (see below), 9km east of Haridwar by road and across the Ganges. **Accommodation** is available at ten forest rest houses within the park and is bookable through the Rajaji National Park Office, 5/1 Ansari Marg, Dehra Dun (Ⓣ 0135/262 1669). However, visitors don't have to go into the core area to experience the jungles – it's possible to venture in from Chila or Rishikesh, or from the road between the two, which runs parallel to the canal marking the boundary of the huge fringe forest.

Chila

To get to **CHILA** from Haridwar, catch one of the Rishikesh-bound buses which leave hourly 7am to 2pm from the GMOU office by the bus stand, take a taxi (about Rs300–350 one way, or Rs500–600 for the round trip), or even **walk** (Chila is visible from Haridwar, and taking a short cut from Har-ki-Pairi via the riverbeds and a bridge makes it a journey of just 4km east). The town itself is neither attractive nor interesting, located right beside the Ganges barrage and its massive electricity pylons. However, it makes a good base for explorations of the park, and **Chila Beach** – occasionally used by large river turtles – lies within walking distance through the woods, 1km north along the Ganges. **Elephant rides** from here cost around Rs300 per head for two hours; to arrange one, just ask the trainers who tout for business.

Accommodation is available at the large GMVN *Chila Tourist Bungalow* (Ⓣ 01382/266678; ❹–❺), which has a dorm (Rs190), deluxe and a/c rooms, huts and grassy camping facilities. Rooms here can also be reserved through the Haridwar GMVN office.

Rishikesh and around

RISHIKESH, 238km northeast of Delhi and 24km north of Haridwar, lies at the point where the wooded mountains of Garhwal rise abruptly from the low valley floor and the Ganges crashes onto the plains. The centre for all manner of New Age and Hindu activity, its many ashrams – some ascetic, some opulent – continue to draw devotees and followers of all sorts of weird and wonderful gurus, with the large **Shivananda Ashram** in particular renowned as a yoga centre. Rishikesh is also emerging as an **adventure-sports** hub, with rafting, trekking and mountaineering all on offer.

> The **telephone code** for Rishikesh is Ⓣ 0135 unless you're dialling from within a 75km radius, in which case the Ⓣ 0135 code changes to Ⓣ 95135.

Rishikesh has one or two ancient shrines, but its main role has always been as a way-station for *sannyasin*, yogis and travellers heading for the high Himalayas. The arrival of the Beatles, who came here to meet the Maharishi in 1968, was one of the first manifestations of the lucrative expansion of the *yatra* pilgrimage circuit; these days it's easy to see why Ringo thought it was "just like Butlin's". By far the best times to visit are in winter and spring, when the mountain temples are shut by the snows – without the *yatra* razzmatazz, you get a sense of the tranquillity that was the original appeal of the place. At other times, a walk upriver leads easily away from the bustle to secluded spots among giant rocks ideally suited for yoga, meditation or an invigorating dip in the cold water (but not a swim: fast currents make that too dangerous).

Confusingly, the name Rishikesh is applied to a loose association of five distinct areas, encompassing not only the town but also hamlets and settlements on both sides of the river: **Rishikesh** itself, the commercial and communications hub; sprawling suburban **Muni-ki-Reti**; **Shivananda Nagar**, just north; the assorted ashrams around **Swarg Ashram** on the east bank; and the riverbank temples of **Lakshmanjhula**, a little further north.

Arrival

The **Main Bus Stand**, used by Haridwar and Dehra Dun government buses, as well as services from Delhi, is on Bengali Road, close to the centre; buses for the Garhwal hills use the **Yatra Bus Stand**, also known as the **Tehri Bus Stand**, off the Dehra Dun Road. Rishikesh is at the end of a small branch **railway** line from Haridwar, served by six trains daily.

Local transport connecting the main areas includes cycle and auto-rickshaws and shared Vikrams; the fare from Rishikesh to Lakshmanjhula is Rs30 (Rs6 shared

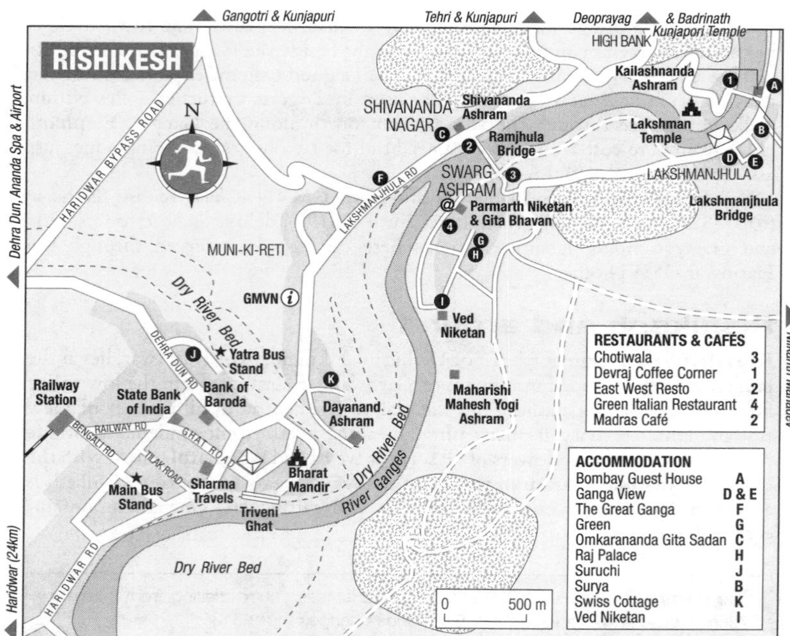

Moving on from Rishikesh

All **trains** from Rishikesh go to Haridwar (though it's easier by bus or Vikram), and the 7am #372 passenger train even continues to Delhi, but it's very slow, so it's better to pick up a faster service in Haridwar.

Buses to lowland destinations such as Dehra Dun (1hr 30min) and Delhi (6hr 30min). leave from the main bus stand on Bengali Road. During the April-to-October pilgrimage season, when the **Char Dham** temples are open in the Garhwal hills, direct buses connect Rishikesh's Yatra Bus Stand with **Badrinath** (297km), **Kedarnath** (210km, via Gaurikund), **Gangotri** (250km) and **Yamunotri** (280km, via Hanuman Chatti). Book at least a day in advance. Buses start to leave around 4am and only the early ones complete the journey in a day; the roads are treacherous and tedious, so you might prefer to break up the journey.

Every morning, from around 5am, a fleet of **press jeeps** heads up into the mountains to deliver the day's newspapers, and they also act as share-taxis, leaving from Haridwar Road in front of Nagar Palika Parashad (just south of Tilak Rd). Advance bookings for at least some of them can be made at Sharma Travels (aka Kaushik Telecom), 86 Haridwar Road, by *Akash Ganga Hotel* (Ⓣ0135/243 0364). They cost more than the bus (Rs300 to Joshimath, for example), but are a lot faster, and they may agree to pick you up at your hotel if you book in advance and are staying on the west side of the river.

GMVN in Muni-ki-Reti (see below) organizes **package tours** (a four-day trip to Badrinath, including bus, food and lodging, costs around Rs5000), as well as expensive car rental.

ride). There are also shared Vikrams to Haridwar. Rishikesh, like many of the hill towns, is increasingly turning to seasonal tourism, and a negative impact of this has been the dramatic rise of unregulated tour and **travel operators** with no insurance cover for their drivers and cars, or for you. Ask for recommended travel agents at your hotel or at the tourist office. Reliable agencies for renting **cars** and **taxis** include Ajay Travels, at the *Hotel Neelkanth*, Haridwar Road (Ⓣ0135/243 0644), and Mahayama Travels, Urvasi Complex, Dehra Dun Road (Ⓣ0135/243 2968).

Information

The **Uttarakhand Tourist Office** and **GMVN Yatra Office** on Haridwar Bypass Road can provide local information, though GMVN in practice restrict themselves to selling their own tours or to booking accommodation in their tourist lodges. Their **Mountaineering and Trekking** division on Lakshmanjhula Road, Muni-ki-Reti (Ⓣ0135/243 0799), however, rents basic equipment, arranges guides, and can also organize ski trips to Auli. Most of the established river camps on the Ganges above Rishikesh operate from the end of September to mid-December, and from mid-February until late April. **Rafting excursions** vary in length from half-day runs to extended camping–rafting expeditions; expect to pay around Rs800 per head for a half-day raft trip, or Rs4500 for three days all-in. Unfortunately, cowboy operators abound, so beware; a reliable local firm is Red Chilli on Lakshmanjhula Road in High Bank (Ⓣ0135/243 4021, Ⓦwww.redchilliadventure.com).

Banks in town include the Bank of Baroda, 70 Dehra Dun Rd, and Apex Bank very near by, both with ATMs. There are other ATMs on Haridwar Road at the corner of Ghat Road, on Lakshmanjhula Road by the GMVN trekking office, and on the east bank near Ramjhula Bridge. A number of travel agents in Lakshmanjhula will change cash and travellers' cheques. The main post office is on Ghat Road, with branch offices in Lakshmanjhula, and near both sides of Ramjhula

Bridge. **Internet** cafés abound; one of the best is Blue Hill Travel and Cyber Café (Rs20/hr) in the Swarg Ashram area near Parmarth Niketan; their travel agency, however, has a bad reputation.

Accommodation

Rishikesh town has plenty of hotels but it's noisy and polluted; the only reason to stay here is to be near the bus station and amenities. New Agers tend to stay around **Swarg Ashram** and the east bank of the river, away from the noise and near the ashrams, while backpackers head for the cheap little guesthouses of **Lakshmanjhula**.

Bombay Guest House Lakshmanjhula ⓣ0135/325 0038. Basic accommodation with shared baths off a leafy courtyard, handy for exploring the unspoilt upper reaches of this stretch of the river, and popular with hippy travellers. ❶

Ganga View Lakshmanjhula ⓣ0135/244 0320. A good-value choice among the many, generally similar, small budget hotels in the area – this one has nice fresh rooms (all with attached bathrooms and hot water), and it's off the main drag, so reasonably quiet. New second location 50m downstream. ❶

The Great Ganga Lakshmanjhula Rd, Shivananda Nagar ⓣ0135/244 2243, ⓦwww.thegreatganga.com. It's worth braving the steep and very grotty pathway to reach this comfortable upmarket hotel whose fresh rooms have river-facing balconies and lovely views; there's also a good restaurant. If you really want to push the boat out, go for a suite (Rs7550). ❻

Green Swarg Ashram ⓣ0135/243 1242. Popular little travellers' hotel tucked behind Gita Bhavan Ashram. All rooms have attached bathrooms, most with running hot water, there's a roof terrace and a restaurant which serves under-spiced Indian and Italian food. The sister-hotel *Green View* behind is a slightly more upmarket option and also recommended. ❶–❹

Omkarananda Gita Sadan Lakshmanjhula Rd, Shivananda Nagar ⓣ0135/243 6346, ⓔomkara@vsnl.com. Run by the ashram of the same name, this lovely guesthouse has a relaxed atmosphere, plain but spacious and immaculately clean rooms, great views over the river, and even a four-person family suite, but you'll need to book ahead. ❹

Raj Palace Swarg Ashram behind Parmarth Niketan ⓣ0135/244 0079. Well-managed hotel popular with yoga students due to its location near the ashrams and large, sunny yoga room. Rooftop café. Discounts up to fifty percent off-season. ❶–❹

Suruchi Yatra Bus Stand ⓣ0135/243 2602. Friendly but rather dingy hotel whose main attraction is that it's convenient for early Char Dham buses. ❶–❷

Surya Lakshmanjhula Rd ⓣ0135/243 3211, ⓔhotelsurya@hotmail.com. Clean and marble-floored double rooms, the best (and priciest) being at the front with river views, though the darker back rooms are quieter. There's also a rooftop restaurant. ❶–❷

Swiss Cottage Chandra Bhaga ⓣ0135/243 5012, ⓔshivgangamylove@rediff.mail.com. Near the bridge and down unnamed lanes towards the river is Rishikesh's first guesthouse, founded in 1961 by Swami Brahmananda, disciple of Swami Shivananda's. It's a small but peaceful haven with a motley assortment of rooms. Popular with long-term visitors and good value, so often booked up. ❶–❷

Ved Niketan Swarg Ashram ⓣ0135/243 0279. Enormous orange ashram on the east bank of the river, with cheap accommodation that is very popular with budget travellers. ❶

The Town

Most of the pilgrims who pass through Rishikesh on their way to the Himalayan shrines of the Char Dham pause for a dip and puja at what is left of the large sandy expanse of **Triveni Ghat**, close to the centre of town. The river here looks especially spectacular during *arati* (evening worship), when *diya* lights float on the water. Nearby, at **Bharat Mandir**, Rishikesh's oldest temple, a black stone image of Vishnu is supposed to have been consecrated by the great ninth-century Hindu revivalist Shankara; the event is commemorated during Basant Panchami, to mark the first day of spring.

The dense-knit complex of cafés, shops and ashrams collectively known as **Swarg Ashram**, opposite Shivananda Ashram, backs on to forest-covered hills where caves are still inhabited by sadhus. The river can be crossed at this point either on the Ramjhula footbridge, or on **ferries**, which operate between 8am and 7pm according to demand (Rs5 oneway, Rs8 return). Swarg Ashram itself, popularly referred to as Kale Kumbli Wale, was founded in honour of Swami Vishudhanand, who came here in 1884 and habitually wore a black (*kala*) blanket (*kumble*). The most conspicuous of the other ashram-temples is **Parmarth Niketan**, whose large courtyard is crammed with brightly clad gods and goddesses. **Gita Bhavan**, next door, runs an Ayurvedic dispensary up the street (Tues–Sun 10am–noon; first three days of medicine free), where they also sell books and *khadi* handloom cloth.

Around 2km north of Swarg Ashram, a path skirts the east bank of the river and beautiful sandy beaches sheltered by large boulders, en route to **Lakshmanjhula**. A footbridge spans the river here as it negotiates its final rocky course out of the mountains. It's the most appealing part of Rishikesh, featuring the enormous, gaudy **Kailashnanda Ashram**. The attractive landscape and turquoise river are best appreciated from the *Devraj Coffee Corner* on the west side where travellers spend days watching daredevil monkeys cavorting on the bridge and pouncing on unsuspecting passers-by.

Eating

Rishikesh has plenty of worthy **restaurants** and *dhabas*, many with pleasant river views and tourist-orientated menus. Expect only vegetarian food in this holy town.

Chotiwala Swarg Ashram. Two neighbouring establishments with the same name vie for custom and constantly attempt to outdo each other. The one closest to the river has slightly better service and a congenial roof terrace. Both places are large, busy and open at 7am for breakfast; the extensive menus (main dishes Rs40–100) include ice cream, sweets and cold drinks.

Devraj Coffee Corner Lakshmanjhula, just above the bridge on the town side of the river. Enjoy cinnamon rolls, muesli fruit curd and superb cakes, or dine on pizzas, veg sizzlers, curries, veggie-burgers, or even the odd attempt at a Mexican dish, as you watch the Ganges and the pilgrims flow past. Most dishes are in the Rs50–100 range.

East West Resto Directly opposite ferry quay, Ramjhula. Tiny, cheap café serving up strong coffee and healthy, tasty lunches such as brown basmati rice with veg (main dishes Rs45–100).

Green Italian Restaurant Swarg Ashram. Pizzas and pastas head the list of treats at this offshoot of the *Green Hotel*'s in-house Italian eatery. There's a choice of spaghetti or penne with a range of veg sauces, or cannelloni with a choice of three veg fillings (Rs80–100), plus a range of set breakfasts (Rs40–90).

Madras Café Directly opposite ferry quay, Ramjhula. Busy, welcoming restaurant, with great filter coffee, and reasonably priced south Indian food (main dishes Rs40–90, thali Rs60). The "Himalayan Health Pullao" (Rs75) is made with vegetable sprouts and ayurvedic herbs.

Around Rishikesh: local treks

Although a road has now been blasted through the forest to the small Shiva shrine in the hamlet of **Nilkanth Mahadev** (Nilkantha), east of Rishikesh, it's still possible to walk there along the older and shorter pilgrim path. This beautiful forest track rises through the forests behind Swarg Ashram, passes Mahesh Yogi's ashram, and eventually crosses a spur before descending to Nilkantha. There's a chance you may encounter wildlife along the way; keep a safe distance from wild elephants. Nilkantha itself is changing, as an ever-growing number of pilgrims travel along the new road that has cut a swathe through the forests.

You can also follow the river along the motorable track north of Lakshmanjhula, passing several good beaches before arriving at the beautiful ashram of **Phool Chatti** (5km), which lies on a bend in the river and has giant boulders and excellent swimming.

Ashrams, yoga and meditation

Due to an ongoing dispute with the government, Maharishi Mahesh Yogi's beautifully situated ashram, home to the Beatles in 1968, stands empty on a high forested bluff above the river. Although there are no classes here, it's a wonderfully atmospheric place to wander around – but don't come alone, as there have been reports of muggings. Yoga Niketan Ashram should also be avoided as there have been incidents of theft and worse; indeed, complaints about theft and harassment in ashrams are surprisingly common. However, a number of reputable ashrams in Rishikesh welcome students of yoga, offering courses of varying duration – from one day to several months – and cost.

Ananda Spa ⓣ01378/227500, ⓦwww.anandaspa.com. Not an ashram but an internationally renowned luxury resort on the outskirts of Rishikesh, offering yoga, spa and Ayurvedic-based beauty treatments. Rooms, suites and villas from $530 to $1855 per night.

Parmarth Niketan Ashram ⓣ0135/244 0077, ⓦwww.parmarth.com. Runs regular yoga classes and, in association with Uttarakhand Tourism, sponsors a yoga week in late Feb/early March. There are a range of courses to choose from, with accommodation at a variety of hotels throughout Rishikesh.

Phool Chatti Ashram ⓣ0135/698 1303, ⓦwww.phoolchattiyoga.com Peaceful ashram with lush gardens away from the noise, 5km north of Lakshmanjula. Specialises in week-long courses in hatha and astanga yoga.

Shivananda Ashram ⓣ0135/243 0040, ⓦwww.divinelifesociety.org. Large institution, with branches all over the world, run by the Divine Life Society and founded by the remarkable Swami Shivananda (who passed into what is referred to as *maha samadhi*, final liberation, in 1963). It has a well-stocked library, a forest retreat and a charitable hospital. Sessions in meditation and yoga, plus other activities, are always going on. To arrange a long-term stay, contact the Secretary two months in advance by following the website link.

Ved Niketan Ashram ⓣ0135/243 0279. Across the river south of Swarg Ashram. Month-long courses run by the charismatic Swamiji Dharmananda, introducing students to all aspects of yoga. Hatha yoga classes held every morning (8–9.30am) and evening (4–5.30pm).

Another hike leads high above Lakshmanjhula for 10km to the small white Shakti temple of **Kunjapuri**, at the sharp point of an almost perfectly conical hill with stupendous views of the Himalayas to the north and towards Haridwar to the south. Try to catch the sunrise from the top, before the haze seeps into the atmosphere. A less strenuous alternative is to take the bus to Hindola Khal on the road to Tehri and walk the remaining 3km to the temple. Bring a guide or partner in any of these areas as incidents of **robbery** along the trails have been reported.

The trek to Yamunotri

Cradled in a deep cleft in the lap of Bandarpunch, and thus denied mountain vistas, the temple of **Yamunotri** (3291m), 223km northeast of Rishikesh, marks the source of the Yamuna, India's second holiest river after the Ganges. The least dramatic but most beautiful of the four *dhams* (temples) of Garhwal, it's also the least spoiled and commercial. **Access** (mid-April to early Nov only; exact dates vary annually) has become easier following road improvements; from the roadhead at Janki Chatti it's a mere 5km along a trail that follows the turbulent ice-blue river as it runs below rocky crags, with snowy peaks in the distance. The walk can also be combined with the **Dodi Tal trek** linking nearby Hanuman Chatti to Uttarkashi (see box, p.722).

Janki Chatti and around

The enchanting little village of **JANKI CHATTI** marks the end of a motorable road connected by bus with Dehra Dun, Mussoorie and Rishikesh. Some routes require a change at **BARKOT**, a four-hour bus ride (Rs100) beyond Mussoorie, which has a GMVN *Tourist Bungalow* (Ⓣ01375/224236; ❷–❹) but very little to eat. Jeeps and buses (Rs40) travel another two and a half hours to reach the small riverside hamlet of **HANUMAN CHATTI**, which has an excellent GMVN *Tourist Bungalow* (Ⓣ01375/233371; ❸–❹) with river-facing rooms and a comfortable dorm (Rs190). Crossing a bridge at the edge of town, a brand-new road weaves into the mountains for 9km until it reaches Janki Chatti, home to a GMVN *Tourist Rest House* (Ⓣ01375/235639; ❹, dorms Rs150–200), and a travellers' lodge (❹). The *Ganga Yamuna* (Ⓣ01375/233301; ❷) and the *Arvind Ashram* (❶) are alternatives, both along the main trail, and there are a number of decent **restaurants** offering thalis, cold drinks and snacks. While you're in Janki Chatti, it's worth making the one-kilometre detour across the river to the traditional Garhwali village of **KHARSALI**, home to the *pandas* (pilgrim priests) of Yamunotri. Among the drystone buildings with their beautifully carved wooden beams stands a unique three-storey Shiva temple – dedicated to Someshwar, lord of the mythical intoxicant Soma. If travelling on to Gangotri (an eleven-hour journey), it is best to take the first bus (at 5.30am) if you want to be sure of arriving the same day, though the second bus (at 7am) should also reach Gangotri that evening; buses usually leave from Hanuman Chatti, but may serve Janki Chatti too.

Yamunotri

A short way beyond Janki Chatti, the trail becomes much steeper but increasingly dramatic and beautiful as it passes through rocky forested crags to **YAMUNOTRI**. Sited near the river, around three piping-hot sulphur springs, Yamunotri's temple is new and architecturally uninteresting; it has to be completely rebuilt every few years due to the impact of heavy winter snows and monsoon rains. Its main shrine – actually part of the top spring, worshipped as the source of the river – holds a small silver image of the goddess Yamuna, bedecked with garlands. The daughter of Surya, the sun, and Sangya, consciousness, Yamuna is the twin sister of Yama, the lord of death; all who bathe in her waters are spared a painful end, while food cooked in the water is considered to be *prasad* (divine offering). Most pilgrims also bathe in the **hot spring** (free); both male and female pools have been built. If you choose to **stay** in Yamunotri, there's a simple dormitory (Rs200) at the GMVN *Tourist Bungalow* near the temple. The best of the few *dharamshalas* is the *Ramananda Ashram* (❶), commanding good views from the hill above the temple, and owned by the head priest. Simple **food** arrangements can be made through the ashrams and the bungalow.

Technically, the source of the Yamuna is the glacial lake of **Saptarishi Kund**. This is reached via a hard twelve-kilometre trek, which heads straight up the mountain alongside the river until finally easing towards the base of Kalinda Parbat. Both this trek and the route over the challenging Yamunotri Pass to Har-ki-Dun (see p.311) necessitate at least one day's acclimatization, adequate clothing, supplies and a guide.

Uttarkashi

The largest town in the interior of Garhwal, **UTTARKASHI** made the news when it was hit by an earthquake in 1991, but this was neither the first nor the last disaster to hit it. It suffered severe floods in 1978, and in 2003 a massive landslide wiped out several hotels on the main road, as well as the tourist office and the bus stand. Miraculously nobody was hurt, but it left a large gap in the

The Dodi Tal trek

The relatively short **Dodi Tal trek**, which links the Gangotri and Yamunotri regions without straying into high glacial terrain, is one of Garhwal's all-time classics. It's not a difficult hike, but local villagers are keen to offer their services as porters or guides, and you should definitely avail yourself of their help if you want to wander off the beaten track and visit the villages. Carry as much of your own food as possible, and also your own tent. The best maps for this trek are the Ground Survey map of Garhwal, and Leomann map (sheet 7 in the India Series), both available from major Uttarakhand Tourism offices.

The trek is described below from east to west, starting from **Uttarkashi** on the way to Gangotri, and ending at **Hanuman Chatti**, 14km south of Yamunotri.

On **DAY ONE**, catch one of the three daily buses or an hourly jeep from Uttarkashi to **Kalyani** (1829m) via Gangotri (the first is at 7am; 1hr). From Kalyani, it's a gentle 7km climb through fields and woodland to **Agoda** (2286m), where the *Tourist Bungalow* at the far end of the village is currently in a state of disrepair, so you will have to put up a tent for the night.

On **DAY TWO**, the trail from Agoda climbs beside a river and then zigzags steadily upwards through lush pine and spruce forests, with a couple of chai shops en route. After 14km and a final undulation, it arrives at **Dodi Tal** (3024m), a lake set against a backdrop of thickly forested hills. Near the basic forest bungalow in the clearing are chai shops and areas for camping.

Some trekkers consider the full 18km from Dodi Tal to Shima on **DAY THREE** too long and arduous, and prefer to split it into two days. Follow the well-marked path along (and often across) the stream that feeds Dodi Tal, which can get steep and entail scrambling; continue straight ahead, ignoring tracks that cross the trail, until you emerge above the treeline. After a further 1.5km the trail heads left to a small pass then zigzags up scree to **Darwa Pass** (4130m), about halfway to Shima. This is the highest point of the trek, providing superb panoramas of the Srikanta Range. If you're ready to rest here, a leftward path beyond the top leads to camping and water. The main route goes down to a valley and then climbs sharply again. It takes about four more hours to reach **Shima**, where you rejoin the treeline. There's basic hut accommodation, but bring your own food.

The beautiful twelve-kilometre trail down from Shima on **DAY FOUR** kicks off with a steep 1.5km scramble alongside a stream, then eases past forest and *bugyal*, where shepherds have their huts. A well-defined rocky path drops steadily through two villages and zigzags down to the Hanuman Ganga River. It emerges at **Hanuman Chatti** (see p.321) from where buses run via Barkot to Uttarkashi, Mussoorie and other points in Garhwal. The Dodi Tal trek can easily be tied in with hikes in the **Har-ki-Dun** and **Yamunotri** areas; see also p.320.

middle of town, which has not been rebuilt, though the hillside has been secured against further landslides.

The town occupies the flat and fertile valley floor of the Bhagirathi; most pilgrims and tourists stop here to break the long journey between Rishikesh, 148km south, and Gangotri, 100km northeast. Uttarkashi's busy and well-stocked **market** is ideal for picking up supplies before high-altitude treks, and the town is also a good place to contact experienced **mountain guides** – mostly graduates of its highly esteemed Nehru Institute of Mountaineering (Ⓣ01374/222123, Ⓦwww.nimindia.org). The going rates stand at around Rs250 per porter and Rs400–500 for a guide. Specialist operators include Mount Support, BD Nautial Bhawan, Bhatwari Road (Ⓣ01374/222419, Ⓔmountsupport@rediffmail.com), on the main road, who also have equipment for rent and porters for hire.

Practicalities

All **buses** to and from Uttarkashi – which has regular services to both Gangotri (until 2pm) and Rishikesh between May and November – park up by the main road in the centre of town (for Mussoorie, take a Rishikesh-bound bus and change at Chamba). **Taxis** can be picked up in the market area; a seat in a shared jeep to Gangotri costs around Rs120 per person. There is an **ATM** two doors from the *Bandhari* hotel, and **internet** access is available around town at a pricey Rs60 per hour.

On the main road, the *Bandhari* (ⓣ01374/222203; ❷–❸) has a range of double **rooms**, some with hot water and TV. Their annexe (ⓣ01374/222384; ❷–❹), 300m up the road on the left, is newer, cleaner and brighter, with balconies overlooking the road. In the lanes by the market you'll find the simple but well-kept *Amba* (ⓣ01374/222150; ❶), and the GMVN *Tourist Bungalow* (ⓣ01374/222271; ❸–❺), with spacious rooms and a dorm (Rs190), set around a small lawn. By far the best accommodation and food is just over 2km north at the delightful *Monal Tourist Home* (ⓣ01374/222270, ⓦwww.monaluttarkashi.com; ❷–❹). The friendly owner, a graduate of the Nehru Institute of Mountaineering, will pick you up from the bus stand if you phone in advance, and is more than happy to provide information (and company) if you're interested in trekking in the region. In town, the best place to **eat** is the restaurant of the *Bandhari* hotel, which serves breakfast items and basic veg curries at Rs40–70 a go.

Gangotri and around

Set amid tall deodar and pine forests at the head of the Bhagirathi gorge, 248km north of Rishikesh at 3140m, **Gangotri** is the most remote of the four *dhams* (pilgrimage sites) of Garhwal, and is **closed from early November till mid-April**. Although the wide Alaknanda, which flows past Badrinath, has in some ways a better claim to be considered the main channel of the Ganges, Gangotri is for Hindus the spiritual source of the great river, while its physical source is the ice cave of **Gomukh** on the Gangotri Glacier, 14km further up the valley. From here, the **River Bhagirathi** begins its tempestuous descent through a series of mighty gorges, carving great channels and cauldrons in the rock and foaming in white-water pools.

From Uttarkashi, frequent buses, taxis and jeeps head up to Gangotri. A shared jeep (Rs120; 3hr 30min) is the most enjoyable way of making the journey; buses stop frequently and can take more than five hours to make the trip. Ten kilometres beyond the uninspiring village of **Harsil**, the road crosses the deep Bhagirathi gorge at **Lanka**, on a dramatic bridge said to be among the highest in the world. This is an army area, so don't take any photographs. At the hamlet of **Bhaironghati**, 3km further on and 11km short of Gangotri, the Rudragaira emerges from its own gorge to meet the Bhagirathi. A small temple stands in towering deodar forests, and there are a few teashops as well as a barely used GMVN *Tourist Bungalow* (❸–❹).

Gangotri

Although most of the nearby snow peaks are obscured by the desolate craggy mountains looming immediately above **GANGOTRI**, the town itself is redolent of the atmosphere of the high Himalayas, populated by a mixed cast of Hindu pilgrims and foreign trekkers. Its unassuming **temple**, overlooking the river just beyond a small market on the left bank, was built early in the eighteenth century by the Gurkha general Amar Singh Thapa. Capped with a gilded roof, consisting of a squat *shikhara* surrounded by four smaller replicas,

Gangotri ashrams

Although most of the so-called "ashrams" in Gangotri are in reality boarding houses, a few sadhus offer rooms on a donation basis for visitors looking for a quiet retreat. The simple, atmospheric **Kailash Ashram**, overlooking the confluence of the Kedar Ganga and the Bhagirathi, is run (along with a small Ayurvedic clinic) by the affable Bhim Yogi, who welcomes guests for medium- and long-term stays. Nearby, **Nani Mata's Ashram** belongs to an Australian *mataji* (female sadhu), who has lived in Gangotri for many years and is held in high esteem.

it commemorates the legend that the goddess Ganga was enticed to earth by acts of penance performed by King Bhagirath, who wanted her to revitalize the ashes of his people. Inside the temple is a silver image of the goddess, while a slab of stone adjacent to the temple is venerated as **Bhagirath Shila**, the spot where the king meditated. Steps lead down to the main riverside *ghat*, where the devout bathe in the freezing waters of the river to cleanse their bodies and souls of sin.

Across the river, a loose development of ashrams and guesthouses dwarfed by great rocky outcrops and huge trees leads down to **Dev Ghat**, overlooking the confluence with the Kedar Ganga. Not far beyond, at the impressive waterfall-fed pool of **Gaurikund**, the twenty-kilometre-long gorge starts to get into its stride. Beautiful forest paths lead through the dark deodar woods and past a bridge along the edge of the gorge to a flimsy rope-bridge, commanding great views of the ferocious torrent below.

GMVN's *Tourist Bungalow* (☎013772/22221; ❸–❺), over the footbridge from the bus stand, offers rooms and a reasonably cheap dorm (Rs190). Next to the main cantilever bridge, the large and popular *Ganga Niketan* (☎013772/22219; ❷) has a café and shop overlooking the river, while the *Himalayan Sadan* (☎094129/23149; ❶), along the riverside opposite the temple, offers basic, friendly accommodation with fantastic views up the valley to the snow peaks. A number of *dhabas* and cafés on both sides of the river serve thalis, good breakfasts and much-needed, warming chai. For pilgrims heading toward Gomukh, the market area also marks the last chance to buy gloves and woolly hats.

Gomukh and Gangotri Glacier

A flight of steps alongside the temple at Gangotri leads up to join a large pony path that rises gently, providing gorgeous mountain vistas, towards the **Gangotri Glacier**, long regarded as one of the most beautiful and accessible glaciers in the inner Himalayas. Sadly, it is retreating hundreds of metres per year, and today only 150 tourists are allowed on the trek each day, and permits must be obtained in advance at the Divisional Forest Office in Uttarkashi. Two kilometres into the trek, the forest **checkpoint** confiscates any potential plastic rubbish you may be carrying in your rucksack.

Approaching the oasis of **Chirbasa**, 7km out of Gangotri, the skyline is dominated by magnificent buttresses and glass-like walls, culminating in the sharp pinnacles of Bhagirathi 3 (6454m) and Bhagirathi 1 (6856m). The path then climbs above the treeline, continuing along the widening valley to enter a high mountain desert. Just beyond Chirbasa, the trail across a cliff face has badly deteriorated and gusts of wind can send small rocks cascading down onto the narrow path, so great care is called for. Soon after crossing a stream, the path rounds a shoulder to offer a glimpse of the glacier's snout near **Gomukh** ("the cow's mouth"), the ever-present Bhagirathi peaks and the huge expanse of the Gangotri Glacier – 23km long, and up to 4km wide – sweeping like a gigantic highway through the heart of the mountains. Visitors must keep 500m back from the mouth of the glacier.

Down below on the flat valley bottom, 5km from Chirbasa, is the cold grey hamlet of **Bhojbasa**, cowering in the shadow of the beautiful **Shivling Peak** (6543m), where most visitors spend the night before heading on to Gomukh and beyond. If you're planning on trekking any further than Gomukh, this is a good point at which to stop and acclimatize. The GMVN *Tourist Bungalow* here (no phone) provides a **dorm** (Rs300) but no private rooms. Guests huddle in the evening in the small, friendly café, which is the place to arrange a mountain guide if you plan to cross the glaciers. Accommodation is also available at *Lal Baba's Ashram* (no phone; ❷), which offers only sheets and the odd floor mattress – though food is included in the price. There is a good **campground** down by the river if you have your own tent.

If you've stayed in Bhojbasa, it really is worth braving the cold to walk to Gomukh for **sunrise**. A good track continues from Bhojbasa for 5km to Gomukh, where the river emerges with great force from a cavern in the glacier. The ice is in a constant state of flux, so the huge greyish-blue snout of the glacier continually changes appearance as chunks of ice tumble into the gushing water. Be careful of standing above or below the cave; many pilgrims have been crushed to death by falling ice while attempting to collect water.

The route to Kedarnath

It's hard to imagine a more dramatic setting for a temple than **Kedarnath**, 223km northeast of Rishikesh, close to the source of the Mandakini at 3583m above sea level, and overlooked by tumbling glaciers and huge buttresses of ice, snow and rock. Kedarnath, the third of the sacred Char Dham sites, is the most important shrine in the Himalayas and as one of India's twelve *jyotrilinga* – lingams of light – attracts hordes of Hindu pilgrims (*yatri*) in the summer months, but is **closed from early November to early April**. The area makes a refreshing change from the rocky and desolate valleys of west Garhwal, with lush hanging gorges, immaculately terraced hillsides and abundant apple orchards. Kedarnath is also a good base for short treks to the beautiful lakes of Vasuki Tal and Gandhi Sarovar.

Gaurikund

GAURIKUND, a friendly and bustling small town perched above the roadhead for Sonprayag, marks the starting point of the trek up to the **temple of Kedarnath**, although there are plans to extend the road as far as Rambara.

Direct **buses** run to Gaurikund all the way from Rishikesh, but most visitors arrive on local buses and taxis from the larger bus terminal at **Guptkashi**, 29km lower down. This receives services from **Rudraprayag**, 109km south on the busy main Rishikesh–Joshimath–Badrinath route, and **Gopeshwar**, 138km southeast.

Inexpensive *dharamshalas* and **hotels** in Gaurikund itself include the *Vijay Tourist Lodge* (Ⓣ01364/269242; ❶), which is on the main bazaar road and has clean if basic rooms. Opposite, the *Annapurna* (Ⓣ01364/269209; ❷) has large carpeted doubles with sunny balconies and dorms. The squat GMVN *Tourist Bungalow* (Ⓣ01364/269202; ❸–❺) has pricier but cosy doubles, a dorm (Rs200) and a **restaurant** offering soup and salad.

The trail from Gaurikund

So popular is Kedarnath on the *yatra* trail that the path up from Gaurikund is being slowly stripped of its vegetation, which is used for fuel and to feed the ponies that carry wealthier pilgrims. You can hire a horse for the trip for Rs300 – a bargain compared to the Rs2500 that some pilgrims pay to be hauled up by a four-man team of *doli*-wallahs.

The large pony track that climbs from Gaurikund is dotted with chai shops and traveres the hillside through the disappearing forests to the village of **Rambara**, 7km up and halfway to Kedarnath. With its many cafés and rest houses (and open sewers), Rambara signals the end of the treeline and the start of the alpine zone. Several conspicuous short-cuts scar the hillside as the track rises steeply to **Garur Chatti**, then levels off roughly 1km short of Kedarnath. Suddenly, rounding a corner, you come face to face with the incredible south face of the peak of Kedarnath (6940m) at the end of the valley, with the temple town dwarfed beneath it in the distance.

Kedarnath: town and treks

KEDARNATH is not a very attractive town – in fact it's almost unbearable at the height of the pilgrimage season (May, June & Sept). It's a grey place, whose central thoroughfare stretches 500m between the temple and the bridge, lined with resthouses and *dharamshalas*, pilgrim shops and administrative offices. However, the sheer power of its location tends to sweep away any negative impressions, and it's always possible to escape to explore the incredible high-altitude scenery.

At the head of the town, the imposing **temple** is constructed along simple lines in stone, with a large *mandapa* (fore-chamber) housing an impressive stone image of Shiva's bull, Nandi. Within the inner sanctum, open to all, *pandas* (pilgrim priests) sit around a rock considered to be Shiva's upraised bottom, left here as he plunged head-first into the ground. Mendicant sadhus congregate in the elevated courtyard in front of the temple.

A solid path from near the main bridge, before the town, crosses the Mandakini to the left of the valley, and ends 4km away at the **glacier**. At its edge, the **Chorabari Tal** lake is now known as **Gandhi Sarovar**, as some of the Mahatma's ashes were scattered here. Close by, around 800m before the lake, is the source of the Mandakini; it emerges from a hole in the moraine on extremely suspect ground, which should not be approached. You could also cross the river by the small bridge behind the temple, and scramble up the rough boulder-strewn moraine to meet the main track.

East of town, a well-marked path rises diagonally along the hillside to the prayer flags that mark a small shrine of the wrathful emanation of Shiva – **Bhairava**. The cliff known as **Bhairava Jhamp** is said to be somewhere nearby; until the British banned the practice in the nineteenth century, fanatical pilgrims used to leap to their deaths from it in the hope of gaining instant liberation.

Practicalities

Kedarnath's GMVN *Tourist Bungalow* (Ⓣ01364/263218; ❸–❺), located close to the centre of town, offers large, anonymous double **rooms** and a dorm (Rs200). Alternatives include the clean, comfortable *Bharat Seva Ashram* (Ⓣ01364/27213; ❷), a large red building beyond the temple on the left, and the pleasantly located bungalow of *Modi Bhavan* (no phone; ❷), behind and above the temple near the monument, which has large rooms and kitchenettes.

Food in the cafés along Kedarnath's main street is simple but expensive, as all supplies have to be brought up from the valley on horseback. The one most familiar with the needs of the western palate is *Kedar Mishthan Bhandar*, which can rustle up passable salads and potato dishes. The canteen run by the temple committee, *Shri Badrinath Kedarnath Mandi Samiti*, behind the temple, serves curries and *aloo paratha*.

Joshimath

The scattered administrative town of **JOSHIMATH** clings to the side of a deep valley 250km northeast of Rishikesh, with tantalizing glimpses of the snow-capped peaks high above and the prospect, far below, of the road disappearing into a sunless canyon at Vishnu Prayag, the confluence with the Dhauli Ganga. Few of the thousands of pilgrims who pass through en route to Badrinath linger, but Joshimath has close links with **Shankara**, the ninth-century reformer, who attained enlightenment here beneath a mulberry tree, before going on to establish **Jyotiramath**, one of the four centres of Hinduism (*dhams*) at the four cardinal points. The town itself consists of a long drawn-out **upper bazaar**, and, around 1km from the main square on the Badrinath road, a **lower bazaar** that holds the colourful Narsingh, Navadurga, Vasudev and Gauri Shankar **temples**.

Practicalities

Most **buses** and **jeeps** up to Joshimath stop in the upper bazaar. For **trekking** and skiing advice, head for Eskimo Adventure Company (ⓣ01389/222864, ⓔaeskimoadventures@rediffmail.com), opposite *Hotel Sriram*, which is run by two graduates of the Nehru Institute of Mountaineering who can organize treks, rock climbing, skiing and river rafting, as well as provide permits, guides and equipment. They also have **internet** access, as does KCE Uniyal Infotech (both Rs50/hr), further along Upper Bazaar by the Badrinath jeep stand. There is a **tourist office** (ⓣ01389/222181; Mon–Fri and usually Sat 10am–5pm) by the new GMVN block; you can also get information here about the **ski centre** 15km away at Auli.

Rooms at the grim GMVN *Tourist Rest House* (ⓣ01389/222118; ❸–❺), up a short lane at the north end of the upper bazaar, include a dorm (Rs200); a café serves simple meals. The new block, up above the old (accessed by the lane opposite the GMOU office), is much better but still not great value (ⓣ01389/222226; ❹, dorm Rs200). Next to the old GMVN block the *Hotel Sriram* (ⓣ01389/222332; ❷) has better-value rooms; the deluxe include a TV and hot water geyser while standard rooms have a hot bucket. South of the centre, *Dronagiri* (ⓣ01389/222254; ❹–❺) is the most comfortable hotel in town, with good views, a clean restaurant and satellite TV. **Food** options in Joshimath are not exciting: the restaurants at the *Dronagiri* and *Sriram* are the best; of the *dhabas* the busy *Marwari* on the main square has good special thalis (Rs60), while the *New Star*, on Upper Bazaar near the GMVNs and *Sriram*, opens early for breakfast.

Badrinath

BADRINATH, "Lord of the Berries", just 40km from the Tibetan border, is the most popular of Garhwal's four main pilgrimage temples, and one of Hinduism's holiest sites. It was founded by Shankara in the ninth century, not far from the source of the Alaknanda, the main tributary of the holy Ganges. Although the temple boasts a dazzling setting, deep in a valley beneath the sharp snowy pyramid of Nilkantha (6558m), the town that has grown up around it is grubby and unattractive. All motorized transport from Joshimath is obliged to move in **convoys**; a gate system controls traffic in each direction, in two equal 24-kilometre stages – the first between Joshimath and Pandukeshwar, the second between Pandukeshwar and Badrinath. Several convoys leave Joshimath each day, the first at 6.30am and the last at 4.30pm. At night the road is closed, and Badrinath itself remains closed from mid-November to early April.

Badrinath is still presided over by a Nambudiri brahmin from Kerala – the Rawal, who also acts as the head priest for Kedarnath. According to myth, the two temples were once close enough together for the priest to worship at both on the same day. The **temple** itself, also known as **Badri Narayan**, is dedicated to Vishnu, who is said to have done penance in the mythical Badrivan ("Forest of Berries") that once covered the mountains of Uttarakhand. Unusually, it is made of wood; the entire facade is repainted each May, once the snow has receded and the temple opens for the season. From a distance, its bright colours, which contrast strikingly with the concrete buildings, snowy peaks and deep blue skies, resemble a Tibetan *gompa*; there's some debate as to whether the temple was formerly a Buddhist shrine. Inside, where photography is strictly taboo, the black stone image of **Badri Vishal** is seated like a *bodhisattva* in the lotus position (some Hindus regard Buddha as an incarnation of Vishnu). *Pandas* (pilgrim priests) sit around the cloisters carrying on the business of worship and a booth enables visitors to pay in advance for *darshan* (devotional rituals) chosen from a long menu.

This site, on the west bank of the turbulent Alaknanda, may well have been selected because of the sulphurous **Tapt Kund** hot springs on the embankment right beneath the temple, which are used for ritual bathing. Immediately south of the temple, the old **village** of Badrinath is still there, its traditional stone buildings and a small market seeming like relics from a bygone age. The main road north of Badrinath heads into increasingly border-sensitive territory, but visitors can normally take local buses and taxis 4km on to the end of the road where the intriguing Bhotia village of **Mana** nestles – check the current situation before setting out. It's also possible to walk to Mana along a clear footpath by the road. The village itself consists of a warren of small lanes and buildings piled virtually on top of each other; the local Bhotia people, Buddhists of Tibetan origin who formerly traded across the high Mana Pass, now tend livestock and ponies and sell yak meat and brightly coloured, handmade carpets. Past the village and over a natural rock bridge, a path leads up the true left bank of the river towards the mountain of Satopanth (7075m), to the base of the impressive high **waterfall** of **Vasudhara**, considered to be the source of the Alaknanda. Walking time is just an hour and a half and, unusually, there are no chai stalls en route.

Practicalities

Badrinath is awash with rough, flea-bitten budget **hotels** strung along the main road. A better choice is the GMVN *Devlok* (Ⓣ01381/22212; ⑤–⑥), behind the post office, with pleasant rooms, a restaurant and excellent local advice. There are two other GMVN establishments near the bus stand: *Yatri Niwas* (Ⓣ01381/222338) has five hundred dorm beds (Rs100), while the *Tourist Rest House* has cosy and carpeted doubles (no phone; ③–④). *Hotel Narayan Palace* (Ⓣ01381/22380; ⑤–⑥) isn't bad, but the worn carpets and lack of heating don't quite merit the price. The poshest hotel in town is the plush new *Sarovar Portico* (Ⓣ01381/222267, Ⓦwww.sarovarhotels.com; ⑦–⑧). The most atmospheric area for **cafés** and chai shops is the old section close to the temple, but the more commercial east bank holds a few more upmarket neon-lit restaurants, such as *Laxmi* and *Saket*, along with numerous bogstandard *dhabas*.

Traffic back down to Joshimath, including the regular local **buses**, moves in the same convoy system as on the way up, the last one departing at 3.30pm. Long-distance buses run direct to Rishikesh with an overnight halt en route, and to Gaurikund near Kedarnath (14hr), bookable at the bus-stand office above the town.

Hemkund and the Valley of the Flowers

Starting from the hamlet of **Govind Ghat**, 28km south of Badrinath on the road to Joshimath (local buses will stop on request), an important pilgrim trail winds for 21 steep kilometres up to the snow-melt lake of **Hemkund** (4329m). In the Sikh holy book, the *Guru Granth Sahib*, Govind Singh recalled meditating at a lake surrounded by seven high mountains; only in the twentieth century was Hemkund discovered to be that lake. A large *gurudwara* (Sikh temple) and a small shrine to Lakshmana, the brother of Rama of Ramayana fame, now stand alongside. However, to protect the deodar forests along the trail, visitors can no longer spend the night here.

Instead, the overgrown village of **Ghangaria**, 6km below Hemkund, serves as a base for day-hikes. It has several chai shops, a small tourist information centre, *gurudwaras* and some basic lodges. Apart from the GMVN *Tourist Bungalow* (mid-April to early Nov; ❹–❺, dorm Rs250), the best bet is *Hotel Prya* (ⓣ01389/222595; ❷), which also has a good restaurant. Govind Ghat also has a large *gurudwara*, run on a donations system.

An alternative trail forks left from Ghangaria, climbing 5km to the mountain *bugyals* of the Bhyundar valley – the **Valley of the Flowers**. Starting at an altitude of 3352m, the valley was discovered in 1931 by the visionary mountaineer Frank Smythe, who named it for its multitude of rare and beautiful plants and flowers. The meadows are at their best towards the end of the monsoons, in early September; they too have suffered at the hands (or rather feet) of large numbers of visitors, so camping is not allowed here either. As a result, it is not possible to explore the ten-kilometre valley in its entirety in the space of a day's hike from Ghangaria. At the entrance of the valley, foreigners must pay Rs350 for a three-day **permit**.

Nanda Devi National Park

East of Joshimath the majestic twin peaks of **Nanda Devi** – at 7816m, the highest mountain that is completely in India – dominate a large area of north-eastern Garhwal and Kumaon. The eponymous goddess is the most important deity for all who live in her shadow, a fertility symbol also said to represent Durga, the invincible form of Shakti. Surrounded by an apparently impenetrable ring of mountains, the fastness of Nanda Devi was long considered inviolable; when mountaineers Eric Shipton and Bill Tilman finally traced a way through, along the difficult **Rishi Gorge**, in 1934, it was seen as a defilement of sacred ground. A string of catastrophes followed, and in 1976 an attempt on the mountain by father and daughter team Willi and Nanda Devi Unsoeld ended in tragedy when Nanda Devi died below the summit after which she was named.

The beautiful wilderness around the mountain now forms the **Nanda Devi Sanctuary**. This is the core zone of the 5860-square-kilometre **Nanda Devi National Park**, which was declared a UNESCO Biosphere Reserve in October 2004. Access into the core zone has been prohibited since 1982 for environmental reasons, and trekking in the National Park is restricted to a limited number of visitors between May and October on a single route from the roadhead village of Lata to Dharansi Pass, which has fabulous views over to the twin peaks of Nanda Devi. The nine-day trek can be arranged through the GMVN **Mountaineering and Trekking** division in Rishikesh (ⓣ0135/243 0799), and costs around Rs25,000 per person all-in, in groups of three to five only. Further information on getting permits can be obtained from the Forestry Office in Joshimath (up two lots of steps to the left of the *Dronagiri* hotel, and then right).

Kumaon

The Shaivite temples of **Kumaon** do not attract the same fervour as their equivalents in Garhwal, so there is far less tourist traffic, villages are largely unspoilt and trekking routes unlittered. To the east, Kumaon's border with Nepal follows the Kali valley to its watershed with Tibet; threading through it is the holy trail (closed to foreigners) to the ultimate pilgrimage site, Mount Kailash in Tibet, the

Kuari Pass and the Curzon Trail

The long route over **KUARI PASS** (4268m) in northeastern Garhwal provides some stunning mountain views. It is known as the **Curzon Trail** after a British Viceroy who trekked along parts of it, though officially it was renamed the **Nehru Trail** after Independence. Traversing the high ranges without entering the permanent snowline, the ten-day trail starts on the border with Kumaon at Gwaldam above the River Pindar and ends around 150km north, at the hot springs of Tapovan in the Dhauli Ganga Valley near Joshimath. There are numerous alternative paths and shorter trails to approach the pass, including one of around 24km from Auli. The whole route, and connected hikes, is mapped out on the Leomann map of Kumaon–Garhwal (sheet 8 in the India Series). The best time to go is from May to June and mid-September to November.

An ideal expedition for those not equipped to tackle glacial terrain, the trail over Kuari Pass follows alpine meadows and crosses several major streams, skirting the outer western edge of the Nanda Devi National Park. Along the way you'll get excellent views of Trisul (7120m), the trident, Nanda Ghunti (6309m), and the elusive tooth-like Changabang (6864m), while to the far north on the border with Tibet rises the unmistakable pyramid of Kamet (7756m).

Camping equipment is needed, especially on the pass. Guides can be negotiated in Gwaldam, on the main road between Karnaprayag and Almora, or at several points along the route. You can either take local transport from Gwaldam, which has a range of accommodation, or trek down through beautiful pine forests and cross the River Pindar to **Debal** 8km away, where there is a forest resthouse and a tourist lodge. Motorized transport is available from Debal to **Bagrigadh**, just below the beautiful hamlet of Lohajung, which has a pleasant tourist lodge. Also here is the shrine of *lohajung* – a rusted iron bell suspended from a cypress tree and rung to announce your arrival to the *devta* or local spirit.

Following the River Wan for 10km from Debal, the trail arrives at the large village of **Wan**, where there's a choice of accommodation, including a GMVN *Tourist Bungalow* (dorm Rs90) and a forest resthouse. The small village of **Sutol** is 14km from Wan, along a trail following pleasant cypress and deodar forests. From Sutol to **Ramani**, a gentle 10km trail passes through several villages. A steep trail rises for 4km through dense forest from Ramni to the pass of **Sem Kharak** before descending for a further 9km to the small village of **Jhenjhenipati**, from where a rough track continues to the village of Panna 12km away, passing the beautiful **Gauna Lake**. From Panna a relentlessly steep trail rises for 12km to **Kuari Pass** (4298m) on the high divide between the lesser and the greater Himalayas, with rewarding views of Nanda Devi and Trisul.

Using Kuari Pass as a base, a climb to the peak of **Pangerchuli** (5183m), 12km up and down, is thoroughly recommended – the views from the summit reveal almost the entire route, including breathtaking mountain vistas. Although snow may be encountered on the climb, it is not a technical peak and no special equipment is necessary, save a good stick. From Kuari, a gruelling, knee-grinding 22-kilometre descent brings you straight down to the small village of **Tapovan**, overlooking the Dhauli Ganga, which has a hot-spring-fed tank. From here, local buses run 11km to Joshimath. An alternative descent from Kuari Pass is the picturesque and less abrupt 24km route through forest to the ski centre of **Auli** via Chitrakantha.

abode of Shiva and his consort Parvati. Kumaon Mandal Vikas Nigam, or **KMVN** (Ⓦ www.kmvn.gov.in), are in charge of tourism in Kumaon, providing a similarly patchy range of services to GMVN in Garhwal. Note too that Kumaon's **electricity** supply can be capricious, with frequent power cuts, and that, ATMs apart, the only banks that **change cash** are in Nainital, though you can change travellers' cheques in Ranikhet and Almora.

Nainital

The dramatic, peanut-shaped crater lake of Nainital (*tal* means lake), set in a mountain hollow at an altitude of 1938m, 277km north of Delhi, gives its name to the largest town in Kumaon. Discovered for Europeans in 1841 by Mr Barron, a wealthy sugar merchant, **NAINITAL** swiftly became a popular escape from the summer heat of the lowlands, and continues to be one of India's main hill stations. Throughout the year, and especially between March and July, hordes of tourists and honeymooners pack the **Mall**, the promenade that links **Mallital** (head of the lake), the older colonial part of Nainital at the north end, with **Tallital** (foot of the lake).

Nainital's position within striking range of the inner Himalayas – the peaks are visible from vantage points above town – makes it a good base for exploring Kumaon. When the town's commercialism gets a bit much, it's always possible to escape into the beautiful surrounding country, to lakes such as **Sat Tal**, where the foothills begin their sudden drop towards the plains to the south, or to the forested ridges around **Kilbury**.

Arrival and information

Most jeeps and buses arrive in Tallital; a rickshaw from here up the lakeside Mall to Mallital, where most of the hotels are, costs Rs8. Buses from Ramnagar mostly arrive at a stand in Sukhatal, north of town, from where Mallital is a Rs50 taxi ride, or a longish but downhill walk.

The **KMVN** representative, Parvat Tours, on the Mall in Tallital (Ⓣ 05942/235656), organizes tours and car rental, and books accommodation at KMVN lodges. Cars can also be rented from agencies along the Mall, such as Hina Tours (Ⓣ 05942/235860). There's an **Uttarakhand Tourism office** on the Mall near Mallital (Mon–Sat 10am–5pm; Ⓣ 05942/235337), but you'll find better information online at Ⓦ www.nainitaltourism.com. For more advice on **trekking** and **mountaineering**, call in at Nainital Mountaineering Club, CRST Inter College Building, opposite *City Heart* hotel (Ⓣ 05942/235119).

Moving on from Nainital

Most **buses** leave from Tallital Bus Stand. For several Kumaon destinations, such as Ranikhet (3hr) and Almora (3hr), you'll need to get a bus (every half-hour from 7am to 6pm) or shared jeep to Bhowali to pick up onward transport there. Buses to Ramnagar (3hr) mostly leave from a stand in Sukhatal, north of Mallital, but two morning services leave from Tallital.

The **Railway Reservation Office** (Mon–Sat 9am–noon & 2–5pm, Sun 9am–2pm; Ⓣ 05942/231010) is by the Tallital Bus Stand. The nearest railhead is at Kathgodam, served by buses from Tallital (every half-hour; 5am–7pm). Among **trains** from Kathgodam, the Raniket Express #5014 at 8.40pm goes to **Delhi** Sarai Rohilla (arrives 5.30am), the Dehra Dun Express #4119 at 7.45pm to **Haridwar** (arrives 2.40am) and **Dehra Dun** (arrives 4.20am) and the Kathgodam–Howrah Express #3020 at 9.55pm to **Lucknow** (arrives 5.55am), **Gorakpur** (arrives 12.35pm) and **Kolkata** (arrives Howrah 12.40pm on the third day).

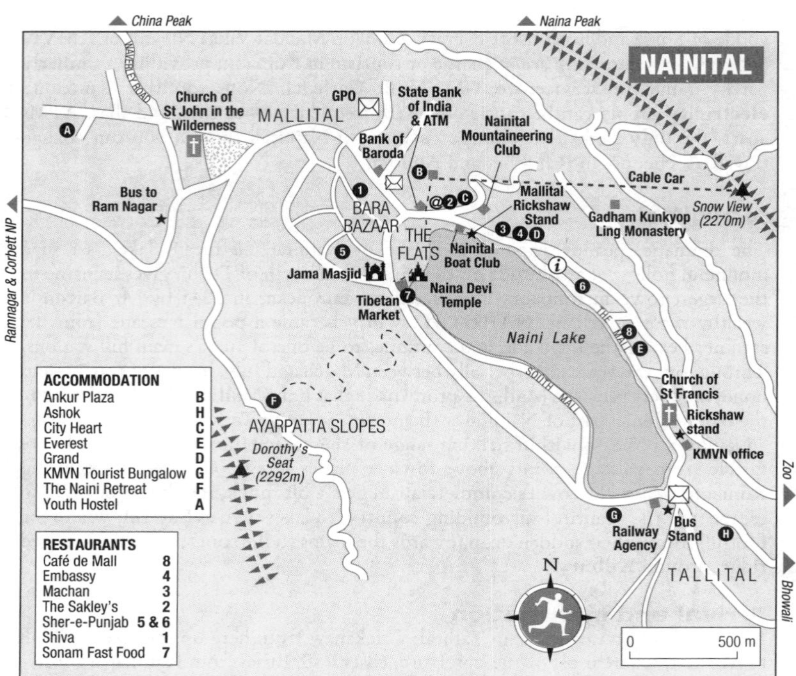

There are a handful of **ATMs** along the Mall and in Mallital. The State Bank of India and the Bank of Baroda change cash and travellers' cheques, and it's a good idea to do that here if you are moving on into the mountains, as no banks further north will change cash. The best place for **internet access** is Cyberia, by the path to the ropeway (Rs30/hr).

Accommodation

As a holiday town, Nainital is full of **hotels**, but budget accommodation is hard to come by in season. **Rates** are highest between March and July, peaking between mid-April and mid-June. The off-season prices indicated below come down substantially, however. On the whole, rooms are cheaper in Tallital than in Mallital.

Ankur Plaza Mallital, by the ropeway station ⓣ05942/235448, ⓦwww.hotelankurplaza.com. High prices in season, but friendly management and good bargains off-season, when this is among the best budget options. Rooms are cosy, and plastic flowers show attention to detail if not great taste. ❸

Ashok Tallital ⓣ05942/235721, ⓔashoknainital@yahoo.co.in. Barely 100m from the bus stand, this functional old-style hotel offers a range of compact rooms, fine for a short stay. ❷–❹

City Heart Mallital rickshaw stand ⓣ05942/235228, ⓦwww.cityhearthotel.netfirms.com. Expensive in high season but reasonable otherwise, and has some of the best lake views in town, especially from the upper rooms and rooftop restaurant. The manager is a wildlife photographer and bass guitarist in a hard rock band. ❸–❺

Everest The Mall ⓣ05942/235453. One of the grander places towards the Tallital end of the lake, with a striking ochre exterior and classy wood-carved decor within. Rooms all have comfortable period furnishings. ❹–❼

Grand The Mall ⓣ05942/235406, ⓕ05942/237057. One of Nainital's oldest establishments, where time seems to stand still. A good location and plenty of period atmosphere in the large, high-ceilinged rooms, some of which are showing their age a bit. Closed Nov–March. 6–7

KMVN Tourist Bungalow Tallital ☎05942/235570. Lodge with a welcoming reception area, functional rooms and a cheap dorm (Rs150) in a quiet part of Tallital, but not far from the bus stand. 5–7

The Naini Retreat Ayarpatta Slopes ☎05942/235105, www.leisurehotels.in. Beautifully situated high above the lake, with extensive and immaculate grounds and a great terrace for barbecues. A lake-facing room costs Rs9000. 8–9

Youth Hostel Mallital ☎05942/236353. Fifty dorm beds (Rs50 for YHA members, otherwise Rs80) in a charming, secluded spot wi th a lovely garden 1.5km above Mallital; likely to be either deserted or jammed with schoolkids. Friendly staff and excellent value – but no generator.

The Town

Most of the activity in Nainital takes place along the 1.5-kilometre-long **Mall**, a promenade of restaurants, hotels and souvenir shops. A favourite pastime for day-trippers is to **rent a boat** on **the lake** by the boat club on the northeast corner; rates start at Rs100 per hour, but can shoot up to Rs200 in summer. The boat club stands on the large plain known as the **Flats**, the result of a huge landslide in 1880, which buried the Victoria Hotel along with 150 people. The Flats now hosts sporting events and a **Tibetan Market**. Overlooking the town is Nainital's excellent **High Altitude Zoo** (Tues–Sun 10am–4.30pm; Rs25, camera Rs25), a steep 1.5km climb from the southern end of the Mall, and home to all sorts of exotic creatures such as Siberian tigers, Tibetan wolves, leopards and Himalayan black bears. It's well managed, with detailed explanations in English and a tiny Shiva temple tucked away at the top.

A ropeway (daily: summer 7am–7pm; winter 10am–5pm) climbs from near the *Mayur* restaurant on the Mall to **Snow View** (2270m); the Rs100 return ticket covers a one-hour stay at the top. Otherwise it's a two-kilometre hike along a choice of steep trails, which can also be undertaken on ponies for Rs200. At the top, which gets overcrowded in season, you'll find a promenade, cafés and a viewpoint; views of the snow peaks are most likely early in the morning. Trails lead on for five kilometres to **Naina Peak** (2611m), one of the best vantage points around, and to the isolated **China Peak** (pronounced "Cheena"), the craggy rise to the west. About halfway up to Snow View, conspicuous thanks to its abundant prayer flags, lies the small Tibetan *gompa* (temple) of **Gadhan Kunkyop Ling**, which has recently been rebuilt in traditional *gompa* style. Three kilometres out of town along the Almora Road, **Hanuman Garh**, a temple teeming with monkeys and young priests monkeying around, is a popular place to watch the sunset.

Eating

Nainital has plenty of places to **eat**, with restaurants and fast-food options along the Mall geared to tourists and everyday *dhabas* (which serve cheap and tasty fish curry) in the bazaars at either end.

Café de Mall The Mall. A restaurant rather than a café, though it does offer coffee of a sort (instant), and has an open eating area overlooking the lake. There are south Indian snacks, pizzas and sizzlers, and thalis (Rs100–150). Non-veg mains go from Rs135.

Embassy The Mall, Mallital. One of Nainital's better restaurants, with a wood-panelled interior. Strongest on tandoori, Chinese and Tibetan dishes, as well as pizzas (Rs75–115) and sizzlers (Rs160–240).

Machan The Mall. Just west of the *Embassy*, boasting "Bronze Age chic" decor and good service, this is a well-run upstairs restaurant that's good for people-watching on the promenade below as well as for excellent Indian cuisine and some Chinese dishes (non-veg mains Rs85–290).

The Sakley's The Mall, Mallital. Quite posh if pricey international cuisine (main dishes Rs175–375) including seafood dishes such as steamed fish delight and fierce (spicy) dragon prawns. Alternatively, pop in for a tea and a pastry – very civilized.

Sher-e-Punjab The Mall. Good non-veg Indian food (Rs80–275) including chicken sagwala, karahi, *handi* and, of course, butter chicken. A second, bigger branch, near Bara Bazaar is just as good, and popular with locals.

Shiva Bara Bazaar, Mallital. Cheap, good and popular *dhaba* with tasty *paneer* and mushroom dishes among other veg options (Rs40–90). The next-door clone is equally good.

Sonam Fast Food Tibetan Market, Mallital. Small café up an alley in the market selling veg *momos* (steamed dumplings), noodles and *thukpa* (soup), all at around Rs30–40, but without much in the way of seating.

Corbett Tiger Reserve

Based at **Ramnagar**, 250km northeast of Delhi and 63km southwest of Nainital, **Corbett Tiger Reserve** (Ⓦ www.corbettnationalpark.com) is one of India's premier wildlife reserves. Established in 1936 by Jim Corbett (among others) as the Hailey National Park, India's first, and later renamed in his honour, it is one of Himalayan India's last expanses of wilderness. Almost the entire 1288-square-kilometre park, spread over the foothills of Kumaon, is sheltered by a buffer zone of mixed deciduous and giant *sal* forests, which provide impenetrable cover for wildlife. Most of the core area of 520 square kilometres at its heart remains out of bounds, and safaris on foot are only permissible in the fringe forests.

Corbett is most famous for its big cats, and in particular the **tiger** – this was the first designated Project Tiger Reserve, in 1973 – but its 110 or so tigers are extremely elusive. Sightings are very far from guaranteed, and should be regarded as an unlikely bonus. Nonetheless, although there have been problems elsewhere with the project, and with the very survival of the tiger in India in serious jeopardy (see Contexts, p.1178), Corbett does at least seem to be prioritizing the needs of tigers over those of other wildlife and of tourists. Still, **poaching** is not unheard of, though it's Corbett's **elephants** that face the most serious threat. The best place to see them is around the picturesque Dhikala camp near the reservoir; spring is the best time, when the water level drops and the animals have more space to roam. The reservoir also shelters populations of **gharial**, a long-snouted, fish-eating crocodile, and **maggar**, a large marsh crocodile, as well as other reptiles.

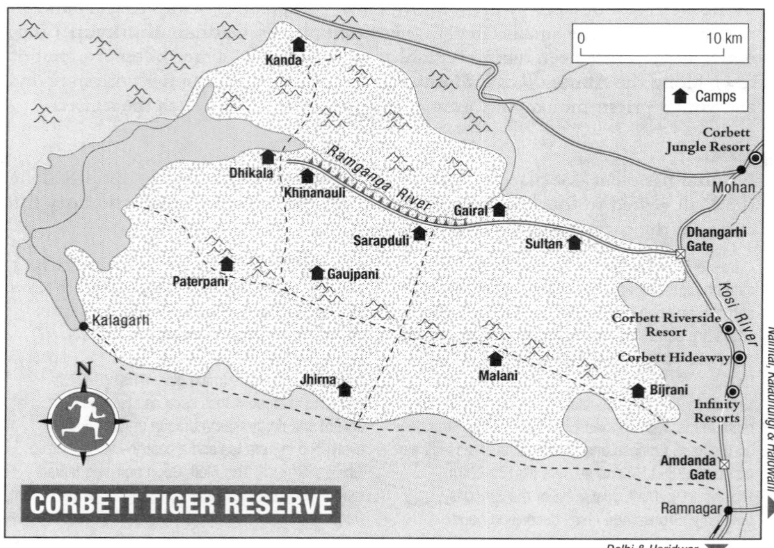

Organizing entry into Corbett Tiger Reserve

Safaris in Corbett Tiger Reserve take place in the morning (around 6.30–9.30am) and afternoon (around 1.30–5.30pm). Half-day or one-day safaris from Ramnagar to the fringes of the park (around Jhirna or Bijrani) are possible, but if you want to visit the heart of the park, around Dhikala (the best place for wildlife viewing), you will have to book **accommodation**. This should be done at least thirty days in advance (twenty days for Indian nationals) in peak season, via the **Ramnagar reception centre** (daily 6–8am & 10am–4pm; Ⓣ&Ⓕ05947/251489), where you also obtain your entry permit (Rs450 [Rs50] for three days and two nights plus Rs200 [Rs30] for each additional day) and pay vehicle and driver entry fees and guide fees. A tariff sheet at the centre lists all the prices.

Jeeps, the most convenient way to travel to and around the reserve, can only be rented at Ramnagar. Reckon on Rs1500 per day for up to five people. Girish at *Govind* restaurant (Ⓣ05947/251615) is one person who can arrange this; other operators can be found outside the bus stand – shop around and be clear about what you're getting for your money (fuel, driver's accommodation and a specific number of 3hr safaris should all be included). A petrol 4WD, such as a Maruti Gypsy, is best as it is quiet and built for the terrain. All jeep safaris must be accompanied by a **guide** (another Rs150/day) – who may or may not be able to identify wildlife and speak English, and is allotted to your jeep by a rota system. If you require a guide with specific knowledge (eg for birding), fax the Field Director one month in advance with your request (Ⓕ05947/251489).

Note that Corbett (apart from the area around Jhirna) is only **open** between 15 October and 15 June, and the zone around Dhikala from 15 November to 15 June. Between June and October the monsoons flood the riverbanks and cut the fragile road links. One way to avoid all the restrictions and bureaucracy is by going on safari instead to a forest area outside the park such as Sitabani – again Girish at the *Govind* can arrange this – this would also allow you to choose your own guide. For more on the park, see Ⓦwww.corbettnationalpark.com.

Jackal are common, and wild boar often run through the camps in the evenings. The grasslands around Dhikala are home to deer species such as the spotted **chital**, hog and barking **deer** and the larger **sambar**, while rhesus and common langur, the two main classes of Indian **monkey**, are both abundant, and happy to provide in-camp entertainment. Bird life ranges from water birds such as the pied kingfisher to **birds of prey**, including the crested serpent eagle, Pallas's fishing eagle and Himalayan greyheaded fishing eagle.

The closest of the various **gates** into the park, 1km from central Ramnagar, is Amdanda on the road to **Bijrani camp**, 11km away, a base for day-trips. **Dhangarhi Gate**, 18km along the highway north to Ranikhet, provides access to the northern and northwestern portions of the park along the Ramganga river valley, and to the main camp of **Dhikala**.

Ramnagar

Situated in the rich farm-belt of the *terai*, on the southeastern fringes of the great forests, the busy market town of **RAMNAGAR** is the administrative hub for **Corbett Tiger Reserve**. **Permits** and **accommodation reservations** (see box above) are issued at the **reception centre**, about 100m north of the bus stand on the other side of the road. There's little to do around Ramnagar itself except go **fishing**. At Lohachaur, 15km north along the River Kosi, good anglers are in with a chance of landing the legendary mahseer, a redoubtable battling river carp.

Moving on

There are buses every 30min to **Delhi (8hr)**, nine a day to **Haridwar (5hr)** and **Dehra Dun (6hr 30min)**, and four direct to **Nainital (3hr)**. From the **railway station** (1km south of town beyond the *Corbett Kingdom* hotel), the *Corbett Park Link Express* #5014A leaves at 9.45pm for **Delhi** Sarai Rohilla (arrives 5.30am). For faster trains and connections to other parts change at Moradabad (7 daily; 2hr).

Although most tourists head straight to Dhikala in the park as soon as they arrive, Ramnagar does have some **accommodation**. The KMVN *Tourist Lodge* (ⓣ05947/251225; ④–⑤), next to the Corbett Tiger Reserve reception, is as institutional as usual, with a dorm (Rs150) as well as spartan doubles. Around 100m south of the bus stand, the modest *Anand* (ⓣ05947/254385; ①) is the best cheapie, offering clean rooms, all with bathrooms and TV. The immaculate *Corbett Kingdom*, 300m further south along the main road (ⓣ05947/251601, ⓦwww.corbettkingdom.com; ⑦), is the best hotel in town. Opposite the *Anand*, *Govind* is a good non-veg **restaurant** but strongest on veg dishes such as stuffed tomato or peppers (mains Rs65–200). *Green Valley*, 200m south of *Govind*, offers fine open-air eating (main dishes Rs60–180). There are a couple of **ATMs** and several internet cafés (Rs40/hr) on the main road south of the bus stand.

Dhikala

Beautifully situated overlooking the Ramganga reservoir and the forested hills beyond, Corbett's main camp, **DHIKALA**, lies 49km northwest of Ramnagar. As you can only stray beyond the confines of the camp on elephant-back or in a car or jeep, the whole place has something of the air of a military encampment. **Accommodation**, all bookable via the Corbett Tiger Reserve reception in Ramnagar, ranges from the 24 rather uncomfortable bunk beds in the *Log Huts* (Rs200) to slightly better bungalows and cabins (④–⑥) that sleep two. Indian and Western **food** is available in the KMVN-run *Parvat* restaurant, which also has a reading room and outdoor area where you can watch films on wildlife (in Hindi). Food of a similar quality is served at lower prices and minus the eight percent sales tax at a *dhaba* at the other end of the camp.

It's normally possible to see plenty of animals and birds from the Dhikala **watchtower**, which is a 1km wander down the path near the restaurant (turn left where the path meets a junction); bring binoculars, remain quiet and don't wear bright colours or perfume. Chital, sambar and various other deer species find refuge in the savannah grasslands known as the *chaur*, behind the camp to the south, and tigers are occasionally drawn in looking for prey. Two-hour **elephant rides from the camp** (Rs250/person) explore this sea of grass, rarely penetrating far into the deep jungles beyond; try to convince your *mahout* (elephant driver) to venture in, as they can be quite magical.

On the way to Dhikala from the Dhangarhi gate, the road passes through magnificent forest – if you have your own transport, stop at the **High Bank** vantage point, and try to spot crocodiles or even elephants on the river below. You can stop for a night en route at the *Sultan* (⑤), *Gairal* (⑤–⑥) and *Sarapduli* (⑥) forest resthouses, all surrounded by deep forest and bookable through the Reserve reception centre.

Resort accommodation around Corbett

A number of self-contained **resorts** have sprung up on the fringes of Corbett, providing a higher standard of accommodation than in Dhikala or Ramnagar – at

Jim Corbett (1875–1955)

Hunter of man-eating tigers, photographer, conservationist and author, **Jim Corbett** was born in Nainital of English and Irish parentage. A childhood spent around the Corbett winter home of Kaladhungi (halfway between Nainital and Ramnagar) brought young Jim into close communion with nature and to an instinctive understanding of jungle ways. After working on the railways, he joined the Indian army in 1917 at the age of forty, rising to the rank of Lieutenant-Colonel and seeing action in Flanders at the head of the 70th Kumaon Company.

Known locally as "Carpet Sahib", a mispronunciation of his name, Jim Corbett was called upon time and time again to rid the hills of Kumaon of **man-eating tigers** and leopards. Normally shy of human contact, such animals become man-eaters when infirmity brought upon by old age or wounds renders them unable to hunt their usual prey. Many of those killed by Corbett were found to have suppurating wounds caused by porcupine quills embedded deep in their paws; tigers always seem to fall for the porcupine's simple defensive trick of walking backwards in line with its lethal quills.

One of Corbett's most memorable exploits was the killing of the **Champawat tiger**, which was responsible for a documented 436 human deaths, and was bold enough to steal its victims from the midst of human habitation. By the mid-1930s, though, Corbett had become dismayed with the increasing number of hunters in the Himalayas and the resultant decline in wildlife, and diverted his energies into conservation, swapping his gun for a movie camera and spending months capturing tigers on film. His adventures are described in books such as *My India*, *Jungle Lore* and *Man-Eaters of Kumaon*; Martin Booth's *Carpet Sahib* is an excellent biography of a remarkable man. Unhappy in post-Independence India, Jim Corbett retired to East Africa, where he continued his conservation efforts until his death at the age of eighty.

a price – as well as guides for expeditions in the neighbouring forests, which can be as rich in wildlife as the park, without the restrictions.

Corbett Hideaway Garija, Ramnagar ⓣ05947/284132 or 011/4652 0000, ⓦwww.corbetthideaway.com. Luxurious terracotta-coloured huts with all mod cons, dotted around a pleasant orchard on a bluff overlooking the river and pretending to be rustic without success. Safaris and the usual tours arranged. 8–9

Corbett Jungle Resort Kumeria Reserve Forest, Mohan ⓣ05947/287820, ⓦwww.corbettjungleresort.com. Wood-panelled stone cottages in a leafy mango orchard above the Kosi, 29km from Ramnagar on the road north to Ranikhet, 9km beyond the Dhangarhi gate. Elephant rides into the forest and safaris into the park itself; food is included in the rates, and there are good off-season discounts. 7–8

Corbett Riverside Resort Garija, Ramnagar ⓣ05947/284125, ⓦwww.corbettriverside.com. A picturesque setting, 10km north of Ramnagar looking across the River Kosi to forest-covered cliffs. Riverfront suites (around Rs10,000) have a veranda directly above the river beach. 8–9

Infinity Resorts Garija, Ramnagar ⓣ05947/251279, ⓦwww.infinityresorts.com. Corbett's most ostentatious resort overlooks the Kosi and the forested hills beyond, with large comfortable rooms ($220–280), a library, a well-stocked bar and a swimming pool. Activities include nature trails with the resort's own naturalists, jungle rides, fishing, trekking and films. 9

Ranikhet

The small and deliberately undeveloped hill station of **RANIKHET**, 50km west of Almora, is essentially an army cantonment, the home of the Kumaon Rifles. New construction is confined to the **Sadar Bazaar** area, while the rest of the town above it, climbing up towards the crest of the hill, retains atmospheric leafy pine woods. Beautiful forest trails abound, including short cuts from the bazaar to the Mall; leopards still roam some of the more remote areas within the town boundaries, despite efforts by army officers to prove their hunting skills.

Ranikhet's Mall – something of a misnomer, as it's a quiet road with few buildings apart from officers' messes – starts just above the town and continues for 3km along the wooded crest of the ridge. Above the Narsingh Stadium Parade Ground, at the very start of the Mall, the **KRC Shawl and Tweed Factory** (summer Mon–Sat 9am–7pm, Sun 10am–5pm; winter Mon–Sat 10am–6pm, Sun 10am–5pm), in an old church equipped with looms and wheels, offers the opportunity to watch the weavers in action, a fascinating display of concentration, dexterity and counting. The herringbone and houndstooth tweeds are sold in the shop next door. For a taste of Indian military life, men and women can join the **Ranikhet Club** (ⓣ05966/220611; Rs50/day), 1km up the Mall, which has a rather fine bar, restaurant and billiards room, and features men with grand moustaches calling each other chaps.

Arrival and information

Buses from all over Kumaon, including the railhead at Kathgodam, 84km away, arrive at the bazaar, at either of two bus stops. The KMOU stand, on the Haldwani road, is the base for buses to Haldwani (7 daily; 4hr), via Bhowali and Kathgodam (the nearest railhead). There is only one direct bus a day to Nainital, but you can change at Bhowali; frequent shared jeeps also ply this route. The Roadways (Almora) bus stand, 500m on, is used by regular bus and shared jeep services to Almora (2hr). The **taxi rank** is just above the KMOU Bus Stand. The **rail reservation office** (Mon–Sat 9am–noon & 2–5pm) is just above the Almora bus stand. The main **post office** is on the Mall, not far beyond the Ranikhet Club. There's a trio of **ATMs** in town, and the State Bank of India will change travellers' cheques (Mon–Fri 10am–4pm), but not cash.

Accommodation and eating

If you're just passing through Ranikhet, **hotels** in the busy bazaar are sufficient, while the Mall is better for an extended stay. Most places offer big discounts (thirty to fifty percent) off-season. **Eating** choices are pretty limited; the best food is found in the better hotels, but there are a few simple cafés and *dhabas* in the market area.

Chevron Rosemount 1km off the Mall (sharp left just after *Hotel Meghdoot* if coming from town) ⓣ05966/221391, ⓦwww.chevronhotels.com. A beautifully restored 1897 colonial mansion, deep in the woods, all pine and teak with lovely rooms, a restaurant, and gardens complete with tennis, croquet, badminton and snow views from the lawn. There's also a four-person cottage. ❻–❽

KMVN Tourist Bungalow 500m off the Mall (uphill left just after *Hotel Meghdoot* if coming from town) ⓣ05966/220893. A reasonably well-kept complex of bungalows and a cheap dorm (Rs150) in a beautiful wooded spot. ❹

Meghdoot The Mall, 1.5km from town ⓣ05966/220475, ⓔhotelmeghdoot@yahoo.com. Comfortable suites set back from balconies full of potted plants and flowers, with running hot water, parking and room service, plus a good mid-price restaurant that serves up a range of tasty biriyani, pulao and other non-veg dishes (mostly Rs50–100). ❸–❺

Norton's Off the Mall (right just after *Hotel Meghdoot* if coming from town) ⓣ05966/220377. Eccentric, family-run hotel established in 1880, homely but slightly run-down, with a friendly manager who still remembers the Raj, and a choice of rooms, suites or cottages. ❷–❹

Rajdeep Bazaar ⓣ05966/220017, ⓦwww.hotelrajdeep.com. The best budget hotel in the bazaar area and nearly always busy. A bit noisy, but clean, with long verandas facing the snow peaks. ❷–❹

Almora and around

ALMORA, 67km north of Nainital and set at a pleasant altitude of 1646m, was founded by the Chand dynasty in 1560, and occupied successively by the Gurkhas and the British. It remains a major market town, considered the cultural capital of the region, and has attracted an eclectic assortment of visitors over the years, including Swami Vivekananda, Timothy Leary and the Tibetologist author of *The Way of the White Clouds*, Lama Angarika Govinda.

Arrival and information

Access to much of the centre, including the market area, is restricted to pedestrians. Most **buses** arrive and depart from the **bus stand** in the middle of Almora's main street, the Mall, which has a **taxi stand** close by. Bus tickets for Dehra Dun, Haridwar and Delhi are sold from an office 50m east of the bus stand, down some steps by Deewan's Sweets, though nearby Lion Tours (ⓣ05962/232922) sometimes runs a luxury bus to Delhi. There's a computerized **railway reservation centre** (Mon–Sat 9am–noon & 2–5pm) at the KMVN *Holiday Home* hotel, up the Mall 1km west of the centre.

Uttarakhand Tourism maintains a **tourist office** next to the *Savoy Hotel* (Mon–Sat 10am–5pm; ⓣ05962/230180). The best places to find out about taxi excursions, **treks** and other activities or to hire equipment and guides are Discover Himalaya (ⓣ05962/231470, ⓔdiscoverhimalaya@indiatimes.com) and High Adventure (ⓣ05962/232277), both on the Mall by *Hotel Kailas*.

There are four ATMs along the Mall; otherwise, the State Bank of India (Mon–Fri 10am–1pm) will change travellers' cheques (preferably Amex), but not cash – Nainital is the nearest town for that. A lot of places along the Mall offer **internet** access – the going rate is around Rs20, but all close around 8pm.

Accommodation

Accommodation in Almora itself is largely centred along the Mall. However, there's a thriving long-term travellers' scene around Kasar Devi (nicknamed "hippyland" by some locals; Rs20 by shared jeep from the Bharat filling station just west of *Hotel Shikhar*), where you can ask at the chai shops about rooms to rent. The prices below shoot up in high season.

Bansal Lala Bazaar ⓣ05962/230864. At the top of the steep lane opposite *Hotel Shikhar*. Spotless, simple rooms with en-suite bath (free hot bucket water), fantastic rooftop views and very friendly management, who'll deliver their renowned lassis and good food to your room. The top room is the best. Fixed price year round. ❷

Deodar Holiday-Inn The Mall, 750m west of the bus stand ⓣ05962/231295. Time seems to have forgotten this friendly place, home to Swami Vivekananda and his disciple Nivedita between 1890 and 1898. The rooms are simple – the pricier ones have geysers and a TV – and there's a lovely sunny terrace and tranquil patio with a log fire at night. Fixed prices year round. ❷–❹

Kailas The Mall, above the GPO ⓣ05962/230624, ⓔjawaharlalshah@india.com. They aren't kidding when they call this ramshackle heap "a hotel like no other". People either view it as (almost literally) a dump or as a charming old place inspired by Nek Chand's rock garden in Chandigarh (see p.526). It's run by aged and charming Mr Shah, who'll happily regale guests with fascinating tales of times gone by. ❶–❷

Konark The Mall, just east of the bus stand ⓣ05962/231217. The rooms are simple, but clean and good value, especially with off-season discounts. The bigger rooms upstairs have geysers, with hot water in a bucket for the cheaper downstairs rooms. ❸

Savoy Police Line, above and east of the GPO ⓣ05962/230329. A quiet place, away from the noise of the Mall but still central, and with pleasant gardens, a veranda and good restaurant. Spacious, dim rooms – geysers upstairs, hot water in buckets downstairs. ❸–❹

Shikhar The Mall ⓣ05962/230253, 150m northeast of the bus stand ⓦwww.hotelshikhar.in.

Don't be put off by the expensive-looking exterior. There's a wide range of rooms, some at very reasonable prices, most with balconies. The welcoming, cavernous restaurant serves good breakfasts, and there's an internet café. Fixed prices year round, and a generator. ❶–❻

The Town

Although most of Almora's official business is conducted along the **Mall**, the **market area**, immediately above and parallel to it along the crest of the saddle, holds much more of interest. Exploring its well-stocked bazaars, knitted together with lanes flanked by beautifully carved wooden facades, at times you feel as though you're drifting into the distant past. Among items you might want to buy are *khadi* (home-spun) cotton textiles and ready-mades from the Khadi Bhawan just west of the Boshi Sen clock tower, scarfs and shawls from Panchachuli on the Mall near *Hotel Shikhar*, and local woollens from Kumaon Woollens, further west by *Hotel Himsagar*. However, the great local tradition is the manufacture of **tamta**, beaten copper pots plated with silver, which are sold in the busy Lala Bazaar and the Chowk area at the northeast end of the market.

Towards the top of town, beyond Chowk, a compound holds a group of Chand-period stone **temples**. The main one, a squat single-storey structure, is dedicated to **Nanda Devi**, the goddess embodied in the region's highest mountain. More typical of Kumaoni temple architecture are two larger Shaivite painted stone temples, capped with umbrella-like wooden roofs covering their stone *amalaka* (circular crowns). During September a large fair is held here in honour of Nanda Devi.

Eating

Cafés and **restaurants** are strung along the Mall, especially around the bazaar area; locally grown and prepared Kumaon rice and black dhal are particularly delicious. Hotels such as the *Savoy* can produce a feast of Kumaoni dishes, if given plenty of advance notice.

Chatpat Chicken Corner The Mall, 300m west of the bus stand. Plain and simple, brightly-lit place serving tasty roast chicken for under Rs100.

City Heart The Mall, by the Gandhi statue. Reasonable attempts at pizza, south Indian, Tibetan and Chinese dishes (Rs30–80), but as snacks rather than meals.

Glory The Mall, near *Shikhar Hotel*. Multi-cuisine café/restaurant, strong on north Indian cooking (veg dishes Rs40–70, non-veg Rs70–120), and also good for breakfast.

New Dolma Kasa Devi, 5km west of the town. A café run by Tibetans that shows the locals how it's done. Located at a beauty spot with a view of the Himalayas. *Momos*, *thukpa* rice and chow mein at Rs30–60 a throw, with breakfasts too, and rooms upstairs (Rs300) in case you want to stay.

New Soni The Mall, near the bus stand. Excellent, Sikh-run *dhaba*: famed for its chicken (full Rs140, half Rs70) and mutton (Rs80) dishes; it can get crowded.

Binsar and Jageshwar

Both **Binsar** and **Jageshwar** are in easy reach of Almora and can be visited as a day-trip (around Rs500 return for a taxi), though it's well worth overnighting at both places as they are lovely spots. **BINSAR**, known locally as Jhandi Dhar ("hill top"), 34km north of Almora, rises in isolation to a commanding 2412m. A steep road leads 11km up from the main Almora–Bageshwar highway to a KMVN tourist complex near the top of the hill (Ⓣ05962/280176; ❹–❺), offering bland but comfortable **accommodation**. This was the summer capital of Kumaon's kings, the Chandras, but today little remains in the area except the bulbous stone Shiva temple of **Bineshwar** 3km below the summit. Most visitors come to see the 300-kilometre panorama of Himalayan peaks along the northern horizon, including, from west to east, Kedarnath, Chaukhamba,

Trisul, Nandaghunti, Nanda Devi, Nandakot and Panchuli. Closer at hand, you can enjoy quiet forest walks through oak and rhododendron woods. Recently designated a nature reserve, Binsar is rich in alpine flora, ferns, hanging moss and wild flowers.

JAGESHWAR, 34km northeast of Almora, is the very heart of Kumaon, a place where language and customs seem to have resisted change. An idyllic small river meanders through dark pines for 3km off the main road from **Artola** (accessible by bus from Almora), stumbling onto a complex of 124 ancient shrines and temples which cluster at the base of venerable deodar trees. Jageshwar village retains much of its traditional charm, with stone-paved lanes and beautifully carved wooden doors and windows painted in green, turquoise and other striking colours. **Accommodation** can be found either in the large, comfortable KMVN *Tourist Bungalow* (☎05962/263028; ❹–❺), which also has a dorm (Rs150), or up the hill at *Tara Guesthouse* (☎05962/263068; ❶); there is also a handful of simple **dhabas**. Good local **walks** include the steep 3km ascent through beautiful pine forests to the hamlet and stone temples of **Vriddha** or **Briddh Jageshwar** (Old Jageshwar), with an extensive panorama from the mountains of Garhwal to the massifs of western Nepal. A trail from here leads 12km along an undulating ridge to Binsar (see opposite); the trail finally emerges from the woods near the stone temple of **Bineshwar**.

Kausani and around

Spreading from east to west along a narrow pine-covered ridge, 52km northwest of Almora, the village of **KAUSANI** has become a popular resort thanks to its spectacular Himalayan panorama. It's a simple day-trip from Almora, though as the peaks – Nanda Choti, Trisul, Nanda Devi and Panchol – are at their best at dawn and dusk, it's worth staying overnight. The tourist scene is growing and a number of new hotels and restaurants have sprung up in recent years to cater for the very seasonal demand. There are several **ashrams**, including one that once housed Mahatma Gandhi, who walked here in 1929, thirty years before the road came through. There are numerous possibilities for short **day-hikes** in the woods and valleys around Kausani, as well as longer excursions to the important pilgrimage sites of **Baijnath** and **Bageshwar**. Kausani is connected by **bus and shared jeep** to Almora.

Practicalities

Hill Queen Café near Snow View Point above town offers **internet** access (Rs30/hr), and telescopes for admiring the peaks and the stars. The *Ashoka* **restaurant** nearby serves inexpensive multi-cuisine dishes (Rs40–70) including local Kumaoni specialities and great *kheer*; the *Uttarkhand Tourist Lodge* has a wonderful terrace and imported goodies like olive oil and parmesan (main dishes Rs60–140). The State Bank of India has an **ATM**.

Accommodation

The prices below are for the **low season**, but can double during high season (April 15–June 15 & Oct 1–Nov 15). Rooms with views are much more expensive than those without.

Anashakti Ashram Snow View Rd, looking down on the Mall ☎05962/258028. Guests prepared to observe house rules, such as attending compulsory prayers and not smoking, are welcome to stay at Gandhi's pleasant but spartan former ashram. Even if you don't stay it's worth visiting the main prayer hall which doubles as a Gandhi museum (daily 8am–6pm). Good views, but no generator. ❶

Himalaya Mount View 1km north of town downhill towards Baijnath ☎05962/258080. Very quiet and rather pleasant, with chunky but elegant wooden furnishings and tile floors. Little English is spoken. ❸–❺

Hotel Uttarakhand Up the steps that head north from the bus stand ⓣ05962/258012. Foreigner-friendly place that can offer good hiking advice and makes a great place to hang out. Clean doubles and a great terrace with Himalayan views; the second-storey rooms with satellite TV and flush bidet toilets are the best value. ❸–❺

Krishna Mountview ⓣ05962/258008, ⓦwww.kumaonindia.com. Huge place next to the *Anashakti Ashram*, with lovely gardens, comfortable rooms, a gym and an expensive restaurant. Friendly management, and good views of the snows. ❻–❽

Baijnath and Bageshwar

BAIJNATH lies 20km northwest of Kausani. The road, served by buses and shared jeeps, drops down to a broad valley and to eleventh-century stone temples, standing at a bend in a beautiful river. This was once an important town of the Katyurs, who ruled much of Garhwal and Kumaon; now it's more like a park. Unusually, the main temple is devoted to Parvati, the consort of Shiva, rather than Shiva himself; its 1.5m image of the goddess is one of the few in the complex to have withstood the ravages of time. The only **amenities** are KMVN's modern *Tourist Rest House* (ⓣ05963/250101; ❹–❺) – which has large en-suite rooms, a dorm (Rs100), garden and great views of Trishul – and a couple of simple cafés.

BAGESHWAR, nestled in a steamy valley 90km north of Almora, is one of Kumaon's most important pilgrimage towns. The lush Gomti River valley around is lovely, the market is a good place to stock up on provisions, and it's used by hikers as the base for the trek to Pindari. Most foreigners stay in the rooms or dorm (Rs100) at the large, ugly KMVN *Tourist Bungalow* (ⓣ05963/220034; ❷–❸), 2km south of the bus station across a bridge; there are basic *dharamshalas* and *dhabas* around the temple.

5

Madhya Pradesh and Chhattisgarh

* **Sanchi** A finely restored Buddhist *stupa* complex, complete with intricately carved gateways. See p.353

* **Pachmarhi** Central India's only hill station, where you can trek to the top of a sacred Shiva peak, hunt out prehistoric rock art or simply relax in the cool air. See p.360

* **Orchha** Madhya Pradesh at its most exotic: crumbling riverside tombs and ornate Rajput palaces amid lush, tranquil countryside. See p.370

* **Khajuraho** Temples swathed in erotic sculpture, lost for centuries in thick jungle but now beautifully restored. See p.374

* **Kanha and Bandhavgarh national parks** Archetypal Kipling country, teeming with wildlife, notably tigers. See p.388 & p.391

* **Mandu** A medieval fort on a plateau where the emperor got down to serious pleasure-seeking in his vast harem, theatre, steam baths and pavilions. See p.396

▲ Devi Jagadambi temple, Khajuraho

Hot, dusty **MADHYA PRADESH** is a vast landlocked expanse of scrub-covered hills, sun-parched plains and one third of India's forests. Stretching from beyond the headwaters of the mighty **Narmada River** to the fringes of the Western Ghats, it's a transitional zone between the Gangetic lowlands in the north and the high, dry **Deccan plateau** to the south.

Despite its diverse array of exceptional attractions, ranging from ancient **temples** and hilltop **forts** to some of India's best **tiger reserves**, Madhya Pradesh receives only a fraction of the tourist traffic that pours between Delhi, Agra, Varanasi and the south. For those who make the effort, this gem of a state is both culturally rewarding and largely hassle-free.

In the centre of Madhya Pradesh, the state capital **Bhopal**, though synonymous with industrial disaster (see p.351), has a vibrant Muslim heritage and some interesting museums. Nearby is **Sanchi**, one of India's most significant Buddhist sites. The hill station of **Pachmarhi**, meanwhile, has echoes of the Raj, numerous hiking routes and the little-visited Satpura National Park.

In the north of the state, the city of **Gwalior** has a stunning hilltop fort and is within striking distance of **Datia's** Rajput palace, the Scindia family's mausoleums at **Shivpuri**, and **Orchha**, the atmospheric ruined capital of the Bundella rajas. Further east is the state's biggest attraction, the cluster of magnificent sandstone temples at **Khajuraho**, renowned for their intricate erotic carvings.

Nondescript **Jabalpur** is the biggest city in eastern Madhya Pradesh, which has few historic sites but does boast the **Kanha**, **Bandhavgarh** and **Pench** reserves, among the last strongholds for many endangered species, notably the **tiger.** Alongside **Orchha** and **Khajuraho**, these parks are the only places in Madhya Pradesh you're likely to meet more than a handful of tourists.

Western Madhya Pradesh is home to **Indore**, a modern city of industry. Though of little interest in itself, Indore is a good base for exploring **Mandu**, the romantic former capital of the Malwa sultans, the Hindu pilgrimage centres of **Omkareshwar** and **Maheshwar**, and the holy city of **Ujjain**, one of the sites of the Kumbh Mela.

Some history

Any exploration of central India will be illuminated if you have a grasp of its long and turbulent history. Most of the marauding armies that have swept across the Subcontinent over the last two millennia passed through this corridor, leaving in their wake a bumper crop of monuments.

The very first traces of settlement in Madhya Pradesh are the 10,000-year-old paintings on the lonely hilltop of Bhimbetka, near Bhopal. Aboriginal rock art was

Chhattisgarh

In November 2000, sixteen districts seceded from Madhya Pradesh to form the state of **Chhattisgarh**, which has rich mineral resources but is badly affected by violent **Naxalite** (Maoist rebel groups) activities. As such, it receives a mere trickle of foreign visitors. While there are few stand-out attractions, the state has fascinating tribal groups, particularly in the **Bastar** region, which also boasts beautiful landscapes. However, before travelling anywhere south of the capital, **Raipur**, you must obtain up-to-date information about the **state of security** around your intended destination. **Violent conflict** between Naxalite guerrillas and state-sponsored militias continues to blight parts of southern Chhattisgarh, with some remote areas more or less permanently controlled by the rebels. Transport facilities are also patchy outside of the main cities, leaving travellers with little alternative but to hire a car. For more information, visit the Chhattisgarh Tourism Board's website: ⓦwww.chhattisgarhtourism.net.

still being created here during the Mauryan emperor Ashoka's evangelical dissemination of Buddhism, in the second century BC. Nearby Sanchi is this era's most impressive relics.

By the end of the first millennium AD, central India was divided into several kingdoms. The Paramaras, whose ruler Raja Bhoj founded Bhopal, controlled the southern and central area, known as Malwa, while the Chandellas, responsible for some of the Subcontinent's most exquisite temples – most notably at Khajuraho – held sway in the north.

Muslim influence started to grow in the thirteenth century, and by the mid-sixteenth century the whole region was under Mughal rule, which left its mark on the architecture and culture of Mandu, Gwalior and Bhopal, in particular. The Marathas briefly took control, before the arrival of the British in the seventeenth century. Under the **British**, the middle of India was known as the "Central Provinces", and administered jointly from Nagpur (now in Maharashtra), and the summer capital **Pachmarhi**.

Madhya Pradesh, or **MP**, only came into being after Independence, when the Central Provinces were amalgamated with a number of smaller princedoms. Since then, the over ninety-percent-Hindu state, with a substantial rural and tribal population, has remained far more stable than neighbouring Uttar Pradesh and Bihar. Major civil unrest between Hindus and Muslims was virtually unheard of until the Bhopal riots of 1992–93, sparked off by events in Ayodhya, Uttar Pradesh. Now Hindu-Muslim relations in MP are relatively cordial again, the state has turned to focus on the latest enemy – recurring **drought** across the poverty-stricken plains and the social and environmental consequences of the damming of the Narmada River. The state remains one of India's poorest, despite flourishing automotive, cement and soybean industries. Attracting more tourists is seen by the state government as one way of boosting Madhya Pradesh's economic prospects.

Visiting Madhya Pradesh

Getting around Madhya Pradesh without your own vehicle normally involves a lot of bone-shaking bus journeys, usually under the auspices of MPSRTC, the state road transport authority. For longer distances, **trains** are the best bet. The Central Railway, the main line between Mumbai and Kolkata, scythes straight through the middle of the state, forking at **Itarsi** junction. One branch veers north towards Bhopal, Jhansi, Gwalior and Agra, while the other continues northeast to Varanasi and eastern India via Jabalpur. In the far west, at Indore and the holy city of **Ujjain**, you can pick up the Western Railway, which heads up through eastern Rajasthan to Bharatpur and Delhi.

The **best time to visit** Madhya Pradesh is during the relatively cool winter months (Nov–Feb). In April, May and June, daytime temperatures frequently exceed 40°C, but if you can stand the heat, this is the best time to catch glimpses of tigers in the national parks. The increasingly meagre rains finally sweep in from the southeast in late June or early July.

Madhya Pradesh Tourism (commonly known as MP Tourism) has **hotels**, **lodges** and the odd **hostel** scattered throughout the state, of variable standards but often in excellent locations; book them at any MP Tourism office (Ⓦwww.mptourism.com).

Bhopal

With around a million and a half inhabitants, **BHOPAL**, Madhya Pradesh's capital, sprawls out from the eastern shores of a huge artificial lake, its packed old city surrounded by modern concrete suburbs and green hills. The nineteenth-century **mosques** emphasise its enduring Muslim legacy, while the hectic **bazaars** of the walled old city are worth a visit. Elsewhere, a couple of good archeological **museums** house hoards of ancient sculpture and the lakeside **Bharat Bhavan** ranks among India's premier centres for performing and visual arts. The **Museum of Man** on the city's outskirts is the country's most comprehensive exhibition of *adivasi* houses, culture and technology. Despite all this, Bhopal will always be known for the 1984 **gas disaster**, which continues to cast a long shadow over the city and its people.

Some history

Bhopal's name is said to derive from the eleventh-century **Raja Bhoj**, who was instructed by his court gurus to atone for the murder of his mother by linking up the nine rivers flowing through his kingdom. A dam, or *pal*, was built across one of them, and the ruler established a new capital around the two resultant lakes – **Bhojapal**. By the end of the seventeenth century, **Dost Mohammed Khan**, an erstwhile general of Aurangzeb, had occupied the now-deserted site to carve out

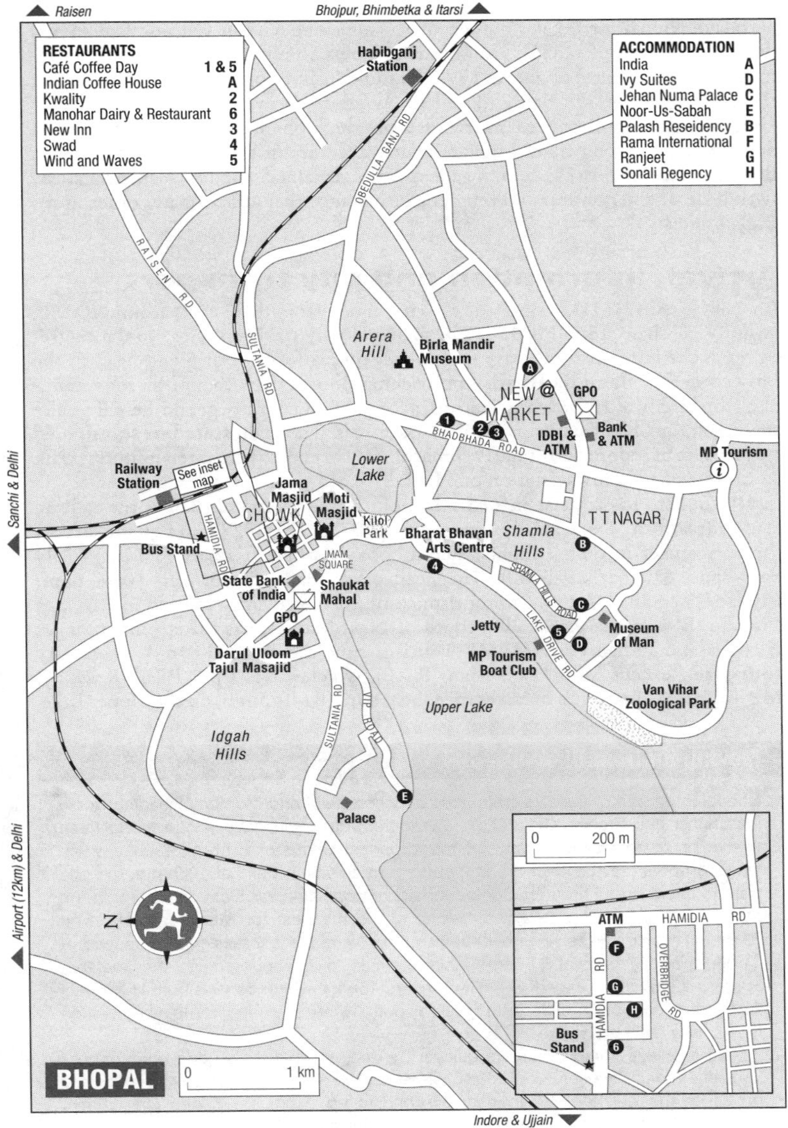

his own kingdom from the chaos left in the wake of the Mughal Empire. The Muslim dynasty he established became one of central India's leading royal families. Under the Raj, its members were among the select few to merit the accolade of a nineteen-gun salute from the British. In the nineteenth century, Bhopal was presided over largely by female rulers, who revamped the city with noble civic works, including the three sandstone **mosques** that still dominate the skyline.

Today, Bhopal carries the burden of the appalling Union Carbide factory gas disaster of 1984 (see p.351), with residents quick to remind you of their continuing legal and medical plight. In 1992, Hindu-Muslim rioting broke out following the destruction of the Babri Masjid in Ayodhya. However, the many tales of Hindus sheltering their Muslim friends from the mobs at this time and vice versa demonstrate the long tradition of religious tolerance in the city. In recent years, Bhopal – and Madhya Pradesh in general – has remained true to its lenient nature, with little of the political and religious intolerance that afflicts many other north Indian states.

Arrival, information and city transport

Bhopal's **airport** is 12km north of the city: a taxi from there costs around Rs250, an auto-rickshaw around Rs150. The main **railway station** is close to the centre: to reach the hotel district, leave by the exit on platforms 4 or 5 and head to the busy corner of **Hamidia Road**. Approaching Bhopal from the south, most trains also stop briefly at **Habibganj Station**, a long way out – only get off here if you're staying in the Shamla Hills or New Market areas. The main **state bus stand**, used by buses from Indore, Jabalpur, Pachmarhi, Sanchi and Ujjain, is ten minutes' walk southwest of the railway station on Hamidia Road.

MP Tourism has **tourist information** offices in the arrivals hall at the railway station (platform 1 exit; daily 8am–8pm; ⓣ0755/274 6827), and at the airport (opens to meet incoming flights), and a booking office at *Palash Residency* (daily 8am-8pm; ⓣ0755/329 5040). The head office (daily except Sun 10am–6pm; ⓣ0755/277 8383, ⓦwww.mptourism.com), inconveniently located in Paryatan Bhawan, Bhadbhada Road, 2km south of New Market, has ticket offices for Jet Airways and Indian Airlines. MP Tourism runs the **Bhopal-On-Wheels city tour** (daily except Mon 11am–3pm; Rs60), which leaves from *Palash Residency*. MP Tourism's Boat Club operates speedboat trips (Rs40/5min) on the Upper Lake.

Moving on from Bhopal

Bhopal is on one of the two **train** lines between Delhi and Mumbai. Heading **north** via Jhansi (for Orchha/Khajuraho), Gwalior or Agra, you have a choice between twelve or so regular services and the superfast *Shatabdi Express* #2001, which leaves Bhopal (daily except Fri) at 2.40pm and arrives in Delhi at 10.30pm; the one train to avoid on this route is the super-slow *Dadar-Amritsar Express* #1057. In the other direction, the 5pm *Punjab Mail* #2138 is the best for **Mumbai** (daily; 14hr 35min). The nightly service to **Jabalpur**, the *Narmada Express* #8233, leaves at 11.35pm and gets in at 6.30am. Other services to Jabalpur include the *Shatabdi Express* #2061 (daily except Sun 5.40pm; 5hr 15min), which departs from Habibganj Station and calls at **Itarsi Junction**, 92km south, where you can pick up a connection for Kolkata and Varanasi.

Most journeys from Bhopal are quicker by train, but the city's good **bus** connections are especially useful for **Indore**, which can be reached either on frequent state buses or the quicker MP Tourism air-conditioned express services (4hr 30min; departing from *Palash Residency*); **for Ujjain**, get off at Dewas and pick up a local bus for the remaining 37km. Buses leave for **Sanchi** every 30 minutes (1hr 30min) from the state bus stand. There are seven daily buses to **Pachmarhi** (6hr 30min–7hr 30min) from the Hamidia Road bus station; the most convenient depart at 8.15am and 10.15am.

Jet Airways and Indian Airlines operate daily **flights** to Delhi, Mumbai, Hyderabad and Indore; see p.353 for contact details.

Most of Bhopal's principal places of interest are so far apart that the best way of **getting around** is by **auto-rickshaws**. Taxis can be found outside all of the top hotels, or arranged through MP Tourism. There's also a pre-paid taxi and auto-rickshaw booth outside the station on Hamidia Road.

Accommodation

If you're not bothered by traffic noise and fumes, **Hamidia Road**, Bhopal's busy main thoroughfare, is the most convenient **place to stay**. Shoestring options are thin on the ground and even the dingiest dives will slap a ten percent "luxury" tax onto your bill (and often a service charge too). Most of Bhopal's top hotels are close to Upper Lake in the Shamla Hills area, a fifteen-minute ride from the railway station.

Hotel India New Market ⓣ0755/255 4594. Smoothly run by the Indian Coffee House cooperative, this has clean and comfortable mid-range rooms with attached bathrooms, TV and phone. It's very popular, so book in advance. ❹–❺

Ivy Suites A. Nadir Colony, Shamla Hills ⓣ0755/423 5508, ⓦwww.ivysuites.com. Tucked away in an upmarket housing estate, this wonderfully relaxed guesthouse has ten spacious rooms, each thoughtfully furnished with paintings, books and plants; those upstairs have ivy-filled balconies overlooking the Upper Lake. ❻–❼

Jehan Numa Palace 157 Shamla Hills Rd ⓣ0755/266 1100, ⓦwww.hoteljehanumapalace.com. Bhopal's top hotel is a palazzo-style building set around a central courtyard covered by bougainvillea-clad walkways. The luxurious rooms are all of a high standard (Rs4300–7500), though the cheaper ones are a bit tight, and there are three fabulous restaurants (around Rs650/person for dinner). ❼–❾

Noor-Us-Sabah Palace Grounds, VIP Rd ⓣ0755/522 3333, ⓦwww.noorussabahpalace.com. The "Light of Dawn" is an impeccably renovated 1920s' nawab's palace, perched on a hill overlooking the Upper Lake. Opulent rooms (Rs4700–7200) come with elegant mirrors, regal red furniture and private balconies, and there's a pool and fine restaurant. ❽–❾

Palash Residency T T Nagar Rd, near New Market ⓣ0755/255 3006, ⓔpalash@mptourism.com. An uncharacteristically stylish MP Tourism hotel with chic rooms – featuring tea/coffee-making facilities and baskets of toiletries – a small garden, restaurant and bar. Rates include breakfast. Bookings are advised. ❻

Rama International Hamidia Rd ⓣ0755/274 0542. Set back from the main road, and very popular with Indian tourists, this relatively peaceful, rambling hotel has simple, clean rooms with either fans or a/c. ❸–❹

Ranjeet Hamidia Rd ⓣ0755/274 0500, ⓔranjeethotels@sancharnet.in. The green marble lobby gives off a subterranean feel, but the rooms are bright enough and come with complimentary breakfast. Those at the front are very noisy, so ask for one at the back. 24hr checkout. ❸–❹

Sonali Regency Just off Hamidia Rd ⓣ0755/274 0880, ⓔsonali@mantrafreenet.com. Quieter than the other hotels in the area, and although some rooms are boxy and the beds are a bit hard, they all boast marble floors or carpets, TV and clean private bathrooms. Nice touches like free newspapers, internet access, 24hr checkout and good service make it the choice over similarly-priced competition. ❸–❹

The City

Bhopal has two separate centres. Spread over the hills to the south of the lakes, the partially pedestrianised **New Market** area is a mix of shopping arcades, internet cafés, ice-cream parlours, cinemas and modern office blocks. Once you've squeezed through the strip of land that divides the Upper and (smaller) Lower lakes, sweeping avenues, civic buildings and gardens give way to the more heavily congested **old city**. This area includes the **Jama Masjid** and the bazaar, centred on **Chowk**, a dense grid of streets between the **Moti Masjid** and Hamidia Road. The art **galleries** and **museums** are on side-roads off New Market, or along the hilly southern edge of the Upper Lake.

Chowk

Bhopal's lively **bazaar** (Tues–Sat) provides a welcome splash of colour after the dismal, traffic-filled streets around the railway station. Famous for *zarda*, *purdah*, *garda* and *namarda* (tobacco, veils, dust and eunuchs), it retains a strong Muslim ambience, with overhanging balconies intricately carved with Islamic geometric designs. Each of the narrow streets radiating from the central square specializes in a different type of merchandise, including Chanderi silk saris, bass drums and clarinets, tussar silk, silver jewellery and Bhopal's famous beaded purses. At the heart of the market loom the rich red-sandstone walls and stumpy minarets of the **Jama Masjid**, built in 1837 by Kudsia Begum.

Imam Square to the Tajul Masajid

Southwest of Chowk, **Imam Square** was once the epicentre of royal Bhopal. Nowadays, it's little more than a glorified traffic island, only worth stopping at to admire the **Moti Masjid** on its eastern edge. The "Pearl Mosque", erected in 1860 by Sikander Begum, Kudsia's daughter, is a diminutive and much less imposing version of Shah Jahan's Jama Masjid in Old Delhi, notable more for its slender, gold-topped minarets and sandstone cupolas than its size.

Lining the opposite, northern side of the square near the ceremonial archway is a more eccentric nineteenth-century pile. A fusion of Italian, Gothic and Islamic influences, the **Shaukat Mahal** palace was originally designed by a French architect. Unfortunately, both it and the elegant **Sadar Manzil** ("Hall of Public Audience") are now government offices and closed to visitors.

Leaving Imam Square by the archway to the west, a five-minute walk brings you to Bhopal's most impressive monument. With its matching pair of colossal pink minarets soaring high above the city skyline, the **Darul Uloom Tajul Masajid** (daily except Fri and during Id-ul-Fitr) lives up to the epithet of "mother of all mosques", as denoted by the extra "a" in its name. Whether it also deserves to be dubbed the biggest in India, as locals claim, is less certain. Work on the building commenced under Sultan Jehan Begum (1868–1901), the eighth ruler of Bhopal. After the death of her domineering husband, the widow queen embarked on a spending spree that left the city with a postal system, new schools and a railway, but which all but impoverished the state – and the Tajul Masajid was never actually completed.

The Birla Mandir museum

To the east of Lower Lake, the **Birla Mandir** collection (daily except Mon 10.30am–5.30pm; Rs100 [Rs10]) includes some of the finest stone sculpture in Madhya Pradesh, informatively displayed with explanatory panels in English in the main galleries. The museum is in a detached mansion beside Birla Mandir, the garish modern Hindu Lakshmi Narayan temple that stands high on Arera Hill overlooking the Lower Lake. Aside from the museum itself, the **temple gardens**, which overlook the city, are a fine place to watch the sunset.

The exhibition is divided between Vishnu, the mother goddesses and Shiva. The **Vishnu** section contains some interesting representations of the god's diverse and frequently bizarre reincarnations, while in the **Devi** gallery next door, a cadaverous Chamunda (the goddess Durga in her most terrifying aspect) stands incongruously amid a row of voluptuous maidens and fertility figures. The **Shiva** room, by contrast, is altogether more subdued. Finally, have a look at the replicas of the 3500-year-old **Harappan** artefacts encased under the stairs.

Bharat Bhavan Arts Centre

Bharat Bhavan (Tues–Sun: Feb–Oct 2–8pm; Nov–Jan 1–7pm; Rs10, free on Fri; Rs20–50 for plays and performances) was set up in 1982 as part of a wider

The Bhopal gas tragedy

At 12.05am on December 3, 1984, a lethal cloud of methyl isocyanate (MIC), a toxic chemical used in the manufacture of pesticides, exploded at the huge, US-owned **Union Carbide** plant on the northern edge of Bhopal.

Highly reactive, MIC must be kept under constant pressure at a temperature of 0°C – yet cost-conscious officials had reduced the pressure to save some $70 a day. When water entered tank E-610 through badly maintained and leaking valves to contaminate the MIC, a massive reaction was triggered. Wind dispersed the gas throughout the densely populated residential districts and slums. There was neither a warning siren nor adequate emergency procedures in place, leaving the thick cloud of gas to blind and suffocate its victims. The leak killed 1600 instantly (according to official figures) and between 7000 and 10,000 in the aftermath, but the figure now totals well over 23,000 in the years since the incident. More than 500,000 people were exposed to the gas, of whom about one-fifth have been left with chronic and incurable health problems, often passed on to children born since the tragedy. The water in the community pumps of the affected residential areas remains contaminated with dangerous toxic chemicals that seeped out from the now-deserted factory. Campaigners say the factory still contains thousands of tonnes of toxic waste.

Though the incidence of TB, cancers, infertility and cataracts in the affected area remains way above the national average, the factory officials initially said the effect of MIC was akin to that of tear gas, causing only temporary health problems. They accepted moral responsibility for the accident, but blamed the Indian government for inadequate safety standards when it came to the issue of compensation. Only in 1989 did Union Carbide agree to pay an average of Rs25,000 to each adult victim – a paltry sum that didn't even cover loans for the medical bills in the first five years, let alone compensate for the loss of life and livelihoods, and other consequences of the disaster. In 2001, the Bhopal Memorial Hospital and Research Centre opened to treat patients.

Despite both US and Indian former bosses being charged with serious offences – including manslaughter – the government and factory authorities had been keen to sweep the whole episode under the carpet. It took until June 2010 for some measure of justice to be dispensed, when a Bhopal court gave seven former factory employees two-year prison sentences for causing "death by negligence". The court also fined the former Indian unit of Union Carbide Rs500,000. NGOs and local campaigners dismissed the ruling as completely inadequate. Warren Anderson, the former CEO of Union Carbide in the US, has yet to face justice; in 2002, a Bhopal court directed India's Central Bureau of Investigation to pursue his extradition, but the US authorities have so far refused to extradite him. (Anderson fled India after the court there granted him bail.)

After much lobbying, the government in 2005 launched a legal case to recoup money from Dow Chemical, which bought Union Carbide in 2001 but denies ongoing liability. To date, little progress has been made but people in Bhopal continue to stage regular protests and rallies.

If you're interested in learning more about the disaster or **volunteering** your services, contact the Sambhavna Trust at Bafna Colony, Berasia Road, Bhopal ⓣ0755/273 0914, ⓦwww.bhopal.org. *Five Past Midnight in Bhopal* by Dominique Lapierre and Javier Moro, and the 2007 Booker Prize–nominated *Animal's People* by Indra Sinha are both highly recommended further reading.

government project to promote visual and performing arts in Indian state capitals. The initiative fizzled out after Prime Minister Indira Gandhi's death, but Bharat Bhavan has since become provincial India's pre-eminent arts centre.

Inside Goan architect Charles Correa's campus of concrete domes and dour brickwork are temporary exhibitions as well as a large split-level **permanent collection** of modern Indian painting and sculpture. Rather incongruously placed amid the latter, look out for an eighteenth-century gilt-framed landscape by the Daniells – the uncle-nephew duo employed as a part of the Company School of Painting during the Raj. Bharat Bhavan has a gallery devoted exclusively to **adivasi art**, in search of which talent scouts spent months roaming remote regions. Among their more famous discoveries was the Gond painter **Jangarh Singh Shyam**. Many of his works are on display here, along with a colourful assemblage of masks, terracottas, woodcarvings and ritual paraphernalia.

The Museum of Man

The story of India's indigenous minorities – the *adivasi*, literally "original inhabitants" – is all too familiar. Dispossessed of their land by large-scale development projects or exploitative moneylenders, the "tribals" have seen a gradual erosion of their traditional culture. The **Museum of Man** (Tues–Sun: March–Aug 11am–6.30pm; Sept–Feb 10am–5.30pm; Rs10, plus Rs10 for a vehicle and Rs50 for video), or the Rashtriya Manav Sangrahalaya, is an enlightened attempt to redress the balance.

Overlooking New Market on one side and the majestic sweep of Upper Lake on the other, the two-hundred-acre hilltop site includes a reconstructed Keralan coastal village, and a winding, mythological trail where each tribal group from the state has contributed their own interpretation of the creation. A large exhibition hall draws on all the daily and ritual elements in the *adivasi* lifestyle, and dotted amongst the forest scrub are botanical trails, a research centre and a permanent open-air display of traditional *adivasi* buildings.

Before tackling the exhibition, have a quick look at the **introductory gallery** in the small building opposite the main entrance. From here, a flight of steps leads underneath a thatched gateway up to the top of the hill, where the seventeen or so dwelling complexes are scattered. Of particular note are the multicoloured paintings of horses adorning the walls of the Rathwa huts and the famous Worli wedding paintings of northern Maharashtra.

The only way to **get to the museum** without your own vehicle is by auto-rickshaw; it's best to negotiate a flat rate for the round trip, including at least an hour's waiting time (around Rs150).

Van Vihar Zoological Park

A trip to the **Van Vihar Zoological Park** (daily: March–Sept 8am–5.30pm; Oct–Feb 6.30am–5.30pm; Rs200 [Rs15]; camera Rs40, video Rs300; for transport around the park, an auto-rickshaw is Rs150 plus Rs20 entrance fee for the driver, bicycle Rs10) ties in nicely with a visit to the Museum of Man next door – keep the same auto-rickshaw for the whole trip. The stars of the park are two regal **white tigers**, but there are also gharial, leopards, Himalayan bears and tigers. You can get a longer look at the 207 species of birds by taking a boat from the jetty half a kilometre northeast of the park gate (9am to sunset; pedal boats Rs30/30min).

Eating

Restaurants in Bhopal's larger hotels serve uniform multi-cuisine menus; the cafés opposite the bus stand do thalis and *subzi*, rice and dhal for next to nothing. For breakfast, try local favourites *poha* (a steamed rice cake) and *katchoris* (a fried, lentil-stuffed snack). There are branches of *Café Coffee Day* on Bhadbada Road and Lake View Drive.

Indian Coffee House *Hotel India*, New Market. Aside from a couple of vintage coffee posters, the dining hall is nondescript, but the filter coffee (Rs10), south Indian breakfast options (Rs30–50), main meals (Rs50–145) and service from white-suited waiters are all excellent.

Kwality New Market. Popular branch of the national chain, with outdoor seating, a busy canteen area and a more sedate a/c dining room. There is a vast array of veg snacks like *pani puri*, pizzas, Chinese and Indian main meals (Rs48–100).

Manohar Dairy & Restaurant Hamidia Rd. Bustling fast-food-style joint where yellow-shirted waiters dish up a steady stream of *katchoris*, veg burgers, pizzas and ice-cream sundaes (Rs22–85). There's also an attached sweet shop.

New Inn Bhadbhada Rd, New Market. Behind the glass frontage – incongruously decorated with a dragon motif – is a garish mix of yellow and orange walls and brown leather seats. Thankfully the keenly-priced food (particularly the *sheesh* kebabs and mutton cutlets) is much better judged. Mains Rs23–90.

Swad Bharat Bhavan Arts Centre. A refreshingly mixed crowd of students, artists and visitors gather here for economically-priced samosas, pakoras and mini meals (Rs5–35), The terrace is a great place to watch the sunset (bring mosquito repellent).

Wind and Waves Lake Drive Rd. While the MP Tourism menu (Indian, Chinese and a few continental dishes) holds few surprises, the setting – conveniently close to the museums and boat club, and overlooking the Upper Lake – is appealing, and there's a bar upstairs. Mains Rs75–195.

Listings

Airlines Air India/Indian Airlines, Airlines House, Bhadbhada Rd, TT Nagar ☎0755/277 0480; Jet Airways, Ranjit Towers, MP Nagar Rd ☎0755/276 0371.

Banks and exchange Only the main banks in New Market and the top hotels offer foreign exchange. ATMs are common: the State Bank of India is by the GPO; IDBI bank is opposite and there's one in the petrol station on Hamidia Rd.

Bookstores Variety Book House at the top of Bhadbhada Rd in New Market, and Book's World opposite.

Hospital Hamidia Hospital (☎0755/254 0222) is on Sultania Rd, between Imam Square and the Darul Uloom Tajul Masajid. The small, private Hajela Hospital (☎0755/277 3392) on Sultania Rd, in Geetanjali, is excellent.

Internet Try the unnamed internet café near *Hotel Ranjeet* (Rs20/hr) or Hub, opposite the State Bank of India in New Market (Rs10/hr).

Post office The Head Post Office is just off Bhadbhada Rd, in New Market; there's also a GPO on Sultania Rd near the Darul Uloom Tajul Masajid.

Shopping Chowk (bazaar Mon–Sat) is the best place for silk and silver. The New Market area has some bigger stores, including the state-run fixed-price Mrignayani, which sells handicrafts, *salwar kameez*, batiks, dokra metalwork, *khadi* clothes, bedspreads and saris; there's also a branch on Hamidia Rd. Close to the New Market branch, the government-run Tribes India sells adivasi goods at fixed prices.

Around Bhopal

A wealth of impressive ancient monuments lie within a couple of hours' journey from Bhopal. To the northeast, the third-century BC *stupas* at **Sanchi** are an easy day-trip. Its peaceful setting also makes an ideal base for visits to more *stupas* at **Satdhara** or **Udaigiri**'s rock-cut caves and the nearby Column of Heliodorus at **Besnagar**. South towards Hoshangabad and the Narmada Valley, the prehistoric cave paintings at **Bhimbetka** can be visited in a day by bus.

Sanchi

From a distance, the smooth-sided hemispherical object that appears on a hillock overlooking the main train line at **SANCHI**, 46km northeast of Bhopal, has the surreal air of an upturned satellite dish. In fact, the giant stone mound stands as testimony to a much older means of communing with the cosmos. Quite apart from being India's finest Buddhist monument, the **Great Stupa** is one of the earliest religious structures in the Subcontinent. It presides over a complex of

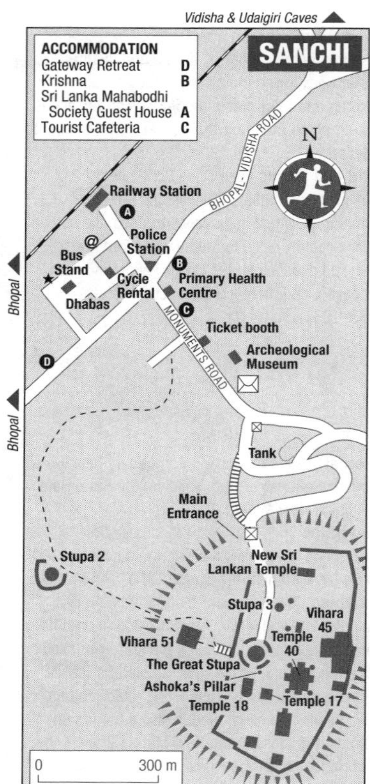

ruined temples and monasteries that collectively provide a rich and unbroken record of the development of Buddhist art and architecture from the faith's first emergence in central India during the third century BC, until it was eventually squeezed out by the resurgence of Brahmanism during the medieval era.

Some history

Unlike other famous Buddhist centres in eastern India and Nepal, Sanchi has no known connection with Buddha himself. It first became a place of pilgrimage when the Mauryan emperor **Ashoka**, who married a woman from nearby Besnagar (see p.359), erected a polished stone pillar and brick-and-mortar *stupa* here midway through the third century BC. The complex was enlarged by successive dynasties, but after the eclipse of Buddhism, Sanchi lay deserted and overgrown until its rediscovery in 1818 by General Taylor of the Bengal Cavalry. In the following years a swarm of heavy-handed treasure hunters invaded the site, yet the explorer Sir Alexander Cunningham was the only one to find anything more than rubble; in 1851, he unearthed two soapstone relic boxes, containing bone fragments and bearing the names of two of Buddha's most noted followers, Sariputra and Maha-Mogalanasa. Historians equated the discovery with "finding the graves of Saints Peter and Paul". The find transformed Sanchi, for centuries neglected, into a Buddhist place of pilgrimage once again. (The caskets themselves are displayed once a year, in late November, in the Sri Lankan temple).

By the 1880s, amateur archeologists had left the ruins in a sorry state. Deep gouges gaped from the sides of *stupas* 1 and 2, a couple of ceremonial gateways had completely collapsed and much of the masonry was plundered by local villagers. **Restoration work** made little impact until 1912, when the jungle was hacked away, the main *stupas* and temples rebuilt, lawns and trees planted and a museum erected to house what sculpture had not been shipped off to Delhi or London.

Arrival and information

There are four daily trains from Bhopal to Sanchi, starting at 8am (40min); on the slower return leg the first train also leaves at 8am. The nearest mainline station is **Vidisha**, 10km northeast and connected by plenty of local buses; there are daily trains from here to Mumbai and Delhi. **Buses** from Bhopal to Sanchi (1hr 30min) depart every half-hour from the Hamidia Road bus stand. To catch a bus back to Bhopal, wait opposite the *Gateway Retreat* (see opposite) and flag one down. A

Stupas

The hemispherical mounds known as **stupas** have been central to Buddhist worship since the sixth century BC, when Buddha himself modelled the first prototype. Asked by one of his disciples for a symbol to help disseminate his teachings after his death, Buddha took his begging bowl, teaching staff and a length of cloth – his only worldly possessions – and arranged them into the form of a *stupa*, using the cloth as a base, the upturned bowl as the dome and the stick as the projecting finial, or spire.

Originally, *stupas* were simple burial mounds, but as the religion spread, the basic components multiplied and became imbued with **symbolic significance**. The main dome, or **anda** – representing the "divine axis" linking heaven and earth – grew larger, while the wooden railings, or **vedikas**, surrounding it were replaced by massive stone ones. A raised ambulatory terrace, or **medhi**, was added to the vertical sides of the drum, along with two flights of stairs and four ceremonial entrances, carefully aligned with the cardinal points. Finally, crowning the tip of the *stupa*, the single spike evolved into a three-tiered umbrella, or **chhattra**, standing for the Three Jewels of Buddhism: the Buddha, the Law and the community of monks.

The *chhattra*, usually enclosed within a low square stone railing, or **harmika**, formed the topmost point of the axis, directly above the reliquary in the heart of the *stupa*. Ranging from bits of bone wrapped in cloth to fine caskets of precious metals, crystal and carved stone, the reliquaries were the "seeds" and their protective mounds the "egg". Excavations of the 84,000 *stupas* scattered around the Subcontinent have shown that the solid interiors were also sometimes built as elaborate **mandalas** – symbolic patterns that exerted a beneficial influence over the *stupa* and those who walked around it. The ritual of circumambulation, or **pradhakshina**, which enabled the worshipper to tap into cosmic energy and be transported from the mundane to the divine realms, was always carried out in a clockwise direction from the east, imitating the sun's passage across the heavens.

Of the half-dozen or so giant *stupa* sites dotted around ancient India, only **Sanchi** still survives. To see one being used, however, you have to head southwards to Sri Lanka, northwards to the Himalayas and the Tibetan plateau, or across the Bay of Bengal to Southeast Asia, where, as **dagobas**, **chortens** and **chedis**, *stupas* are still revered as repositories of sacred energy.

handful of wooden stalls surround the bus stand, constituting Sanchi's tiny bazaar, where there's also an **internet** booth (Rs40/hr). Staff at the *Gateway Retreat* can provide local **information**. You can rent **bicycles** for around Rs40 per day from the bazaar. **Power cuts** occur frequently, so bring a torch.

Practicalities

For inexpensive **accommodation** try the *Sri Lanka Mahabodhi Society Guest House* (Ⓣ07482/266699; ❶–❸) – primarily aimed at visiting Buddhists, though tourists are very welcome – which has spartan rooms with shared facilities facing a shady garden and more comfortable attached rooms. The friendly family-run *Krishna* (Ⓣ07482/266610; ❷) above the Jaiswal chemist shop on the Bhopal–Vidisha Road, has the best set-up for travellers, with clean tiled rooms (the best are at the back), squat or sit-down toilets and a roof terrace facing the *stupas*. Pancakes, sandwiches, noodles and Indian main meals (Rs30–80) are also available. MP Tourism's *Gateway Retreat*, also on the Bhopal–Vidisha Road, (Ⓣ07482/266723; ❺), is Sanchi's smartest option, with slightly overpriced white-washed attached rooms in neatly-tended grounds. There's also a computerised train-reservation office and a meditation centre. It's often busy, so book ahead. MP Tourism's *Tourist Cafeteria* has two plain attached quads

(☎07482/266743; ❸), and serves unimaginative but well-executed **food**, including tandoori chicken, Chinese and fish and chips from Rs50–150, in a pleasant garden. *Gateway Retreat* has the same menu but is a better spot for an evening meal, particularly as it has Sanchi's only **bar**. The *dhabas* and stalls by the bus stand serve inexpensive thalis. Try the local speciality, sweet coconut *nariyal* samosas.

The site

Floating serenely above a vast expanse of open plains, Sanchi's ruins have preserved the tranquillity that attracted the original occupants. Most visitors find a couple of hours sufficient to explore the site, though you could easily spend several days poring over the four exquisite gateways, or **toranas**, surrounding the Great Stupa. Paved walkways and steps lead around the hilltop enclosure (daily 8am–6pm; Rs250 [Rs10], video Rs25, car Rs10), dotted with interpretative panels and shady trees.

Once you've bought an entrance **ticket** from the roadside booth outside the museum, head up the winding path on the right for ten minutes to the main entrance. From here, the central walkway runs alongside the new Sri Lankan Buddhist temple, before leading to the Great Stupa.

The Great Stupa

Stupa 1, the **Great Stupa**, stands at the western edge of the plateau and is surrounded by some of the richest and best-preserved ancient sculpture you're likely to see in situ. Fragments of the original construction, a much smaller version built in the third century BC by Ashoka, lie entombed beneath the thick outer shell of lime plaster added a century later. The **Shungas** were responsible for the raised processional balcony, and the two graceful staircases that curve gently around the sides of the drum from the paved walkway at ground level, as well as the aerial-like *chhattra* and its square enclosure which crown the top of the mound. Four elaborate gateways were added by the **Satavahanas** in the first century BC, followed by the four serene meditating **Buddhas** that greet you as you pass through the main entrances. Carved out of local sandstone, these were installed during the Gupta era, around 450 AD, by which time figurative depictions of Buddha had become acceptable (elsewhere in Sanchi, Buddha is represented by an empty throne, a wheel, a pair of footprints and even a parasol).

As you move gradually closer to the *stupa*, the extraordinary wealth of sculpture adorning the **toranas** slips slowly into focus. Every conceivable space on the eight-metre upright posts and three curving cross-bars teems with delicate figures of humans, demigods and goddesses, birds, beasts and propitious symbols. In between are purely decorative panels and illustrations of heaven intended to inspire worshippers to lead meritorious lives on earth. Start with the *torana* on the south side, which is the oldest, and, as is the custom at Buddhist monuments, proceed in a clockwise direction around the *stupa*.

Southern torana

Opening directly onto the ceremonial staircase, the **southern torana** was the Great Stupa's principal entrance, borne out by the proximity of the stump of Ashoka's original stone pillar. Over the years, some of the panels with the best sculpture have dropped off the gateway (and are now housed in the site museum), but those that remain on the three crossbeams are still in reasonable condition. A carved frieze on the middle architrave shows Ashoka visiting a *stupa* in a traditional show of veneration. On the reverse side the scene switches to one of the Buddha's previous incarnations, the **Chhaddanta Jataka**, where the *bodhisattva* adopts the guise of an elephant who, in extreme selflessness, helps an ivory hunter saw off his own (six) tusks.

Western torana

The **western torana** collapsed during the nineteenth century, but has been skilfully restored and has some of Sanchi's liveliest sculpture. In the top right panel, a troupe of monkeys scurries across a bridge over the Ganges, made by the *bodhisattva*, their leader, from his own body to help them escape a gang of soldiers. According to the **Mahakapi Jataka** (a traditional Buddhist tale), the troops were dispatched by the local king to capture a coveted mango tree from which the monkeys had been feeding. You can also just about make out the final scene, where the repentant monarch gets a stern ticking-off from the *bodhisattva* under a *peepal* tree.

One of the most frequently represented episodes from the life of Buddha features on the first two panels of the left-hand post facing the *stupa*. In the **Temptation of Mara**, Buddha, who has vowed to remain under the *bodhi* tree until he attains enlightenment, heroically ignores the attempts of the evil demon Mara to distract him with violent threats and her seductive daughters.

Northern torana

Crowned with a fragmented Wheel of the Law and two tridents symbolizing the Buddhist trinity, the **northern torana** is the most elaborate and best preserved of the four gateways. Scenes crammed onto its two vertical posts include Buddha performing an aerial promenade and a monkey presenting him with a bowl of honey. Straddling the two pillars, a bas-relief on both faces of the lowest crossbeam depicts the **Vessantara Jataka** (another traditional Buddhist tale), telling of a *bodhisattva*-prince banished by his father for giving away a magical rain-making elephant. A better view of the inner, south-facing side of the plaque can be had from the balcony of the *stupa*'s raised terrace. Note the little tableau on the far right showing the royal family trudging through the jungle.

Eastern torana

Leaning languorously into space from the right capital of the **eastern torana** is Sanchi's most celebrated piece of sculpture, the sensuous **salabhanjika**, or wood-nymph. The full-breasted fertility goddess is one of several such figures that once blessed worshippers as they entered the Great Stupa. Most of the others are now in museums in Los Angeles and London.

Panels on the inner face of the pillar below the *salabhanjika* depict scenes from the life of the Buddha, including his conception when the *bodhisattva* entered the body of his mother, Maya, in the form of a white elephant. The front face of the middle architrave picks up the tale some years later, when the young Buddha, represented by a riderless horse, makes his **great departure** from the palace where he grew up to begin the life of a wandering ascetic. The reverse side shows the fully enlightened Buddha, symbolized by an empty throne.

Elsewhere around the enclosure

Of the dozens of other numbered ruins around the 400-metre enclosure, only a handful are of more than passing interest. The smaller, plainer but immaculately restored **Stupa 3**, immediately northeast of Stupa 1, is upstaged by its slightly older cousin in every way but one. In 1851, a pair of priceless reliquaries was discovered deep in the middle of the mound. The caskets were found to contain relics belonging to two of Buddha's closest disciples. In one, fragments of bone were encased with beads made from pearls, crystal, amethyst, lapis lazuli and gypsum, while on the lid, the initial of the saint they are thought to have belonged to, Sariputra, was painted in ink. Once in London's British Museum, both are now in the new Buddhist temple outside the *stupa* enclosure and are brought out for public view for one day in late November.

From Stupa 3, pick your way through the clutter of pillars, small *stupas* and exposed temple floors nearby to the large complex of interconnecting raised terraces at the far **eastern edge** of the site. The most intact monastery of the bunch, **Vihara 45**, dates from the ninth and tenth centuries and has the usual layout of cells ranged around a central courtyard. Originally, a colossal, richly decorated sanctuary tower soared high above the complex, but this collapsed, leaving the inner sanctum exposed. The river goddesses Ganga and Yamuna number among the skilfully sculpted figures flanking the entrance to the shrine itself. Inside, Buddha still reigns supreme.

The enclosure's tenth-century eastern **boundary wall** is the best place from which to enjoy Sanchi's serene **views**. To the northeast, a huge, sheer-sided rock rises from the midst of Vidisha, near the site of the ancient city that sponsored the monasteries here (traces of the **pilgrimage** trail between Besnagar and Sanchi can still be seen crossing the hillside below). South from the hill, a wide expanse of well-watered wheat-fields stretches off towards the angular sandstone ridges of the Raisen escarpment.

The southern area

The **southern area** of the enclosure harbours some of Sanchi's most interesting temples. Pieces of burnt wood dug from the foundations of **Temple 40** prove that the present apsidal-ended *chaitya* was built on top of an earlier structure contemporary with the Mauryan Stupa 1. **Temple 17** is a fine example of early Gupta architecture and the precursor of the classical Hindu design developed later in Orissa and Khajuraho.

Before leaving the enclosure, hunt out the stump of **Ashoka's Pillar** on the right of Stupa 1's southern *torana*. The Mauryan emperor erected columns like this all over the empire to mark sacred sites and pilgrims' trails. Its finely polished shaft was originally crowned with the magnificent lion capital now housed in the site museum. The inscription etched around its base is in the Brahmi script, recording Ashoka's edicts in Pali, the early Buddhist language and forerunner of Sanskrit.

The western slope

A flight of steps beside Stupa 1 leads down the **western slope** of Sanchi hill to the village, passing two notable monuments. The bottom portions of the thick stone walls of **Vihara 51** have been carefully restored to show its floorplan of 22 cells around a paved central courtyard. Further down, the second-century BC **Stupa 2** stands on an artificial ledge, well below the main enclosure – probably because its relics were less important than those of *stupas* 1 and 3. The ornamental railings and gateways around it are certainly no match for those up the hill, although the carvings of lotus medallions and mythical beasts that decorate them are worth close scrutiny. The straps dangling from some of the horse-riders' saddles are believed to mark the first appearance in India of stirrups.

The archeological museum

Sanchi's small **archeological museum** (daily except Fri 10am–5pm; Rs5), to the left of the road up to the hilltop, houses a modest collection of artefacts, mostly fragments of sculpture, jewellery, pottery, weapons and tools. Its **main hall** contains the most impressive pieces, including the famous Ashokan lion-capital (see opposite) and two damaged *salabhanjikas* from the gateways of *Stupa* 1. Also of note are the distinctive Mathuran red-sandstone Buddhas.

Satdhara

Perched on the edge of a dramatic ravine amid rolling hills 30km north of Bhopal, the rarely visited **SATDHARA** ("seven streams") is well worth the detour for *stupa* enthusiasts, though you'll need your own vehicle to get here. There are 34 **stupas** dating from the Mauryan period in the third century BC, and fourteen monasteries, three of which have substantial foundations still visible. Several *stupas* and two of the **monasteries** have been reconstructed using original methods and materials, and others are under renovation.

Stupa 1, standing 13m high and with a *medhi* (broad circumambulatory path) around the base, is the most impressive of the *stupas*. Immediately behind it is the imposing three-metre-tall foundation platform of **Monastery 1**, while to the right are two circular **mills**, where oxen still push a great stone around a rut to crush the lime, sand and stone rubble for cement – the technique used by the original architects.

Vidisha and around

The main reason to call in at the bustling market town of **VIDISHA**, a 56-kilometre train or bus ride from Bhopal, and also served by buses from nearby Sanchi, is to hop on a *tonga* to the archeological sites at **Udaigiri** and **Besnagar**. If you're not pushed for time, there's a small **museum** (daily except Mon 10am–5pm; Rs50 [Rs5], camera Rs50), behind the railway station in the east of town. The majority of its pieces, such as Kubera Yaksha, the three-metre, pot-bellied male fertility figure in the hallway, are second-century Hindu artefacts unearthed at Besnagar.

Udaigiri

A modest collection of ruined temples and fifth-century rock-cut caves stand just 6km west of Vidisha at **UDAIGIRI**. The caves, many decorated by Hindu and Jain mendicants, lie scattered around a long, thin outcrop of sandstone surrounded by wheat fields. To get here, take a *tonga* from Vidisha bus stand (around Rs50 return trip); alternatively it's an easy **cycle** from Vidisha (rental bikes are available at shops near Vidisha bazaar) or a more strenuous one from Sanchi (1–2hr).

Heading out from Vidisha, a left turn just after crossing the Betwa River leads along a gently undulating tree-lined avenue for 2–3km. As it approaches the hillside, the road takes a sharp left turn towards the village. Stop here, at the base of the near-vertical rock face, to climb a steep flight of steps to **Cave 19**, which has worn reliefs of gods and demons around the doorways, and a **Jain cave temple** on the northern edge of the ridge. Ask the *chowkidar* to unlock the doors for you.

The site's pièce de résistance, a four-metre image of the boar-headed hero Varaha, stands carved into **Cave 5**. Vishnu adopted this guise to rescue the earth-goddess, Prithvi, from the churning primordial ocean. Varaha's left foot rests on a Naga king wearing a hood of thirteen cobra heads, while the river goddesses Ganga and Yamuna hold water vessels on either side. In the background you can see Brahma and Agni, the Vedic fire-god. The scene is seen as an allegory of the emperor Chandra Gupta II's conquest of northern India.

Besnagar

The ruins of ancient **BESNAGAR**, known locally as **Khambaba**, are in a tiny village down the main road from Vidisha, 5km after the Udaigiri turn-off. During the Mauryan and Shunga empires, between the third and first centuries BC, a thriving provincial capital overlooked the confluence of the Beas and Betwa rivers. The emperor Ashoka himself was once governor here and even married a local banker's daughter. Now, a few mounds and some scattered pieces of masonry are all that remain. Yet one small monument makes the short detour worthwhile. The sixteen-sided stone pillar in an enclosed courtyard, known as the **Column of Heliodorus**, was erected in 113 BC by a Bactrian-Greek envoy from Taxila, the capital city of Gandhara (now the northwest frontier region of Pakistan), who converted to the local Vaishnavite cult during his long diplomatic posting here. The shaft, dedicated to Krishna's father Vasudeva, was originally crowned with a statue of Vishnu's vehicle Garuda.

Bhimbetka

Shortly after NH-12 peels away from the main Bhopal–Hoshangabad road, 45km southeast of Bhopal, a long line of boulders appears high on a scrub-covered ridge to the west. The hollows, overhangs and crevices eroded over the millennia from the crags of this malleable sandstone outcrop harbour one of the world's largest collections of **prehistoric rock art**. Discovered in 1957, **BHIMBETKA** (sunrise to sunset; Rs10 [Rs2]) makes a fascinating day-trip. Regular **buses** (1hr) run from Bhopal's Hamidia Road bus stand to the town of Obaidullaganj, 7km away from Bhimbetka, from where you can take an auto-rickshaw (around Rs50) to the site. MP Tourism's *Highway Treat* (Ⓣ07480/281558, Ⓔbhimbetka@mptourism.com; ❹) has a trio of bland attached **rooms** and a restaurant; it's on the main road, at the turning for Bhimbetka.

Around half the thousand **shelters** so far catalogued along the ten-kilometre hilltop contain rock paintings, dating from three different periods. The oldest (around 10,000 years old) are green outline drawings of human figures and large red images of animals. The second, more prolific phase accounts for the bulk of Bhimbetka's rock art, and were created in the "Stone Age" – between 8000 and 5000 BC. These friezes depict dynamic hunting scenes full of rampaging animals, initiation ceremonies, burials, masked dances, sports, wars, pregnant women and a drinking party. Bhimbetka's third and final spate of cave painting took place during the early historic period; the stylized, geometric figures bear a strong resemblance to the art still produced by the region's *adivasi* groups.

From the car park at the top of the hill, a paved pathway winds through the jumble of rocks containing the most striking and accessible of Bhimbetka's art. The *chowkidars* will show you around for a bit of baksheesh. Look out for the Paleolithic images in green, the wonderful "X-ray" animals filled in with cross-hatching and complex geometric designs, and the recurrent image of a bull chasing a human figure and a crab – believed to represent a struggle between the totemic heroes of three different tribes.

Pachmarhi

Among the last tracts of central India mapped by the British, the **Mahadeo Hills** weren't explored until 1857, when Captain J. Forsyth and his party of Bengal Lancers stumbled upon an idyllic saucer-shaped plateau at the heart of the range, strewn with huge boulders and crisscrossed by streams. Five years later a road was cut from the railhead at **Piparia**, and by the end of the century **PACHMARHI** had become the summer capital of the entire Central Provinces, complete with a military sanatorium, churches, clubhouses, racecourse and polo pitch.

Sacred spaces and pilgrimage places

For most Indians, the presence of the divine is a daily fact of life. There's scarcely a street in the Subcontinent that doesn't boast its own shrine or temple, while innumerable natural features are also considered sacred, from village trees to entire mountains and rivers. According to some accounts, the country boasts almost two thousand major temples and other places of spiritual significance, stretching from remote Himalayan caves and mountains to the sprawling Dravidian temple complexes of Tamil Nadu.

Pilgrims on their way to the source of the Ganges ▲

Bathing at the Varanasi *ghats* ▼

On the road to the gods

The Indian tradition of **pilgrimage** dates back to at least the time of the Mahabharata, and remains a popular occupation today among all sections of Indian society. Pilgrims range from wandering Hindu sadhus and Jain monks who spend their lives walking barefoot across the country from shrine to shrine, begging for sustenance en route, to the more thoroughly modern variety, who tear between temples in specially chartered video buses, combining the high-speed accrual of religious merit with sightseeing and shopping.

Crossing points to the divine

Hindus describe sacred places using the Sanskrit word *tirtha*, literally meaning a river crossing, but also understood to signify a spiritual crossing point where earth and heaven meet, where the gods descend to earth, and where humans may transcend *samsara* (see p.1168) and rise towards the gods. The act of pilgrimage is called *tirtha-yatra* – visiting *tirthas* in order to encounter the divine, experience *darshan* (see p.1172) and accumulate spiritual merit, either for its own sake or in pursuit of a particular goal – anything from praying for the birth of a son to asking for good exam results. Near the end of their lives, many Hindus make one final pilgrimage to **Varanasi**, following the belief that all those who die there will gain instant liberation (*moksha*) from the endless cycle of rebirth.

Pilgrimage traditions are also particularly strong among **Jains**. Jain monks and nuns can often be seen walking between important shrines such as Shatrunjaya and

Sravanabelagola and the Jain temples of Rajasthan. **Buddhists** visit the four places more closely associated with Buddha: Bodhgaya, Sarnath, Kushinagar and Lumbini (just over the border in Nepal). For **Muslims**, the ultimate pilgrimage is the *Haj* to Mecca. Failing that, seven trips to the shrine of Khwaja Muin-ud-din Chishti in Ajmer are considered equivalent.

India's sacred geography

India's religious sites are grouped into a variety of different categories, most covering local areas or, occasionally, the entire country. At the apex of the spiritual hierarchy lie the **Seven Sacred Cities**, or *Sapta Puri* (Ayodhya, Mathura, Haridwar, Varanasi, Kanchipuram, Ujjain and Dwarka), which are believed to confer *moksha* on anyone who dies within them, and the **Four Abodes**, or *Char Dham* (Rameshwaram, Puri, Dwarka and Badrinath), at the far compass points of the country; don't confuse the latter with the *Char Dham* linking Badrinath, Kedarnath, Gangotri and Yamunotri in Uttarakhand.

Each of the major deities (except Brahma) also has their own pilgrimage circuit and religious sites. **Shiva** is represented by no less than three major groups of temples: twelve *jyotir linga* temples, five *bhuti linga* temples and 68 *svayambhu linga* temples. There are extensive temple circuits devoted to Mahadevi and Vishnu, plus more localized south Indian shrines dedicated to Murugan and those associated with the planets (the *Nava Graha Sthalas*). Finally, there are natural places of spiritual significance, such as the four sites of the **Kumbh Mela** (Allahabad, Haridwar, Ujjain and Nasik).

▲ Monks reading holy scripture, Bodhgaya

▼ A sadhu offering prayers, Ujjain

▼ Kumbh Mela, Haridwar

Jagannath temple, Puri ▲

Temples at Shatrunjaya ▼

Ramanathaswamy temple, Rameshwaram ▼

Ten famous pilgrimage places

▸▸ **Varanasi** The most famous pilgrimage site in India, sacred to Shiva, and the place where many Indians come to die and be cremated. See p.281.

▸▸ **Haridwar** Literally the door (*dwar*) of God (*Hari*). The place where the Ganges leaves the Himalayas for the plains, and one of the four locations of the Kumbh Mela. See p.312.

▸▸ **Allahabad** The meeting point of the Ganges and the Yamuna, India's two holiest rivers, and home to the Maha Kumbh Mela, the world's largest religious festival. See p.275.

▸▸ **Shatrunjaya** The holiest of all Jain pilgrimage sites, with more than nine hundred temples clustered atop a fragment of mountain on which the first Jain *tirthankara*, Adinath, gained enlightenment. See p.581.

▸▸ **Puri** The eastern of the four *Char Dham*, and home to the great temple of Lord Jagannath, in whose honour the vast Rath Yatra is held. See p.887.

▸▸ **Tirupati** Sacred to Vishnu, this dramatic Andhran hilltop shrine complex is said to attract more pilgrims than either Rome or Mecca. See p.918.

▸▸ **Sabarimala** This remote Keralan shrine to Sri Ayappa is said to be the second most popular pilgrimage site in the world. See p.1055.

▸▸ **Tiruvanamalai** One of the twelve *bhuti linga* temples, sacred to Shiva, and the site of his famous manifestation as a lingam of fire. See p.971.

▸▸ **Srirangam** The largest temple complex in India and the most important of the country's 108 principal Vishnu shrines, housing a revered image of the god reclining on the coils of the snake Adisesha. See p.995.

▸▸ **Rameshwaram** One of the finest temples in the south, and one of the most famous of the twelve *jyotir linga* temples, sacred to Shiva. See p.1104.

Aside from the faded Raj atmosphere and myriad walks and **hikes**, the main incentive to travel up here is the chance to scramble around the surrounding forest in search of **prehistoric rock art** or visit **Satpura National Park,** home to a handful of (elusive) tigers and leopards. Popular during the summer with Indian tourists, Pachmarhi remains sleepy for the rest of the year. In winter, things liven up during the annual **Shivratri Mela** (Feb/March), when hundreds of thousands of pilgrims pour through en route to the top of nearby Chauragarh Mountain.

The best **time to visit** Pachmarhi is between October and March, when the cool, clear mountain air makes a refreshing change from the heat and dust at lower elevations. It's best to avoid long holiday weekends, when the popular spots attract big crowds.

Arrival and information

Buses connect Pachmarhi with Bhopal (7 daily; 6hr 30min–7hr 30min); the 6.30pm and 8pm services carry on to Indore (12-13hr). There are also a couple of daily services to Chindwara (4–5hr) en route to Nagpur. At the time of writing, MP Tourism was planning to restart its daily "luxury" air-conditioned bus service from Bhopal. **Piparia**, 52km northeast and one hour away by frequent buses, is the nearest railhead. It is on the Mumbai–Howrah (via Allahabad, Varanasi and Itarsi) line. If you're coming from Bhopal, you need to get off at **Itarsi Junction** and catch a bus (3hr) or train (several daily; 1–2hr) to Piparia. The last bus for Pachmarhi leaves Piparia at 7.30pm but shared taxi-jeeps (Rs40) run till late. MP Tourism's *Tourist Motel* (ⓣ07576/222299, ⓔpipariya@mptourism.com; ❹) behind the station is the only decent **place to stay**.

The main MP Tourism **information** office (Mon–Sat 10am–6pm; ⓣ07578/252100) is next to *Hotel Amaltas* near the military training area, Tehsil, on the far side of a lotus-filled lake, a five-minute jeep or auto-rickshaw ride south of the bus station. There's also a small information booth at the bus station (Mon–Fri 10am–5pm; ⓣ07578/252029). Any of the eight MP Tourism hotels can organise **jeep hire** (Rs1000–1500/day). **Shared jeeps** do the rounds of Pachmarhi's main sights; a seat costs Rs100–200 per day. Shops in the bazaar have a few **bikes** for rent (around Rs50/day); take a chain and padlock and hide the bike in the bushes while you are trekking to stop them being pinched. The State Bank of India has an **ATM** on the main road, but no foreign exchange facilities. Bagri **Internet** Centre (Rs40/hr) is opposite *Khalsa Restaurant*, but the connection is erratic.

Accommodation

Accommodation in Pachmarhi is in short supply during the *melas*, over Christmas and New Year, and May to June, when you should book in advance. Outside these times, you should be able to negotiate a good discount almost everywhere. The budget accommodation lies in the bazaar, but most of the MP Tourism hotels are near Tehsil.

Amaltas Near Tehsil ⓣ07578/252098, ⓔamaltas@mptourism.com. MP Tourism hotel in an old British-built building with a collection of simple a/c deluxe rooms with the odd flash of character such as a curved wall or marble fireplace (room no. 5 is particularly good). The standard rooms, in a separate annexe, are not as appealing. ❺

Evelyn's Own In Tehsil, near *Golf View* ⓣ07578/252056, ⓔevelynsown@gmail.com. A colonial-era bungalow with homely rooms (they vary in quality, so ask to see a few), lush garden, small pool and tennis court. But the real draw is the owner, former army colonel Bunny Rao and wife Pramila, who are a mine of information. ❺–❼

Golf View Tehsil, overlooking the golf course ⓣ07578/252115, ⓦwww.welcomheritagehotels.com. Pachmarhi's priciest hotel has classy attached rooms with 1920s-style furniture, fireplaces, high ceilings and modern features like tea/coffee-makers and whirlpool baths. Outside you find manicured lawns, mango trees and, unexpectedly, a running track. ❽

Hotel Highlands Main Road, about 600m before the bus stand ⓣ07578/252099, ⓔhighland@mptourism.com. MP Tourism's most affordable option has attached rooms with TV and either fans or a/c in whitewashed cottages with green corrugated iron roofs; although comfortable they could do with a lick of paint. ❹

Rock-End Manor Near Tehsil ⓣ07578/252079, ⓔrem@mptourism.com. MP Tourism's well-restored British bungalow is a long-established favourite of visiting VIPs for its pukka rooms (they feel more like suites) and stately atmosphere. Easy chairs on the veranda offer views over the hills and the flower garden. Rates include full board. ❽

Saket Patel Marg, in the heart of the bazaar, 5min from the bus stand ⓣ07578/252165, ⓔhotelsaket2003@yahoo.com. A friendly hotel offering clean rooms with TV, attached bathroom (some with squat toilets) and luminous stars on the ceilings; the more expensive ones are bigger and have tubs, a/c and small balconies. Hot water is only available 7am–9am. ❷–❸

The town and hikes

Pachmarhi **town**, more than 1000m above sea level, is clean, green and relaxed, despite the presence of a large military cantonment in its midst. It has retained a distinctly colonial ambience enhanced by the elegant British bungalows and church spires that nose incongruously above the tropical tree line. In the evenings families stroll and picnic in the parklands, while army bands and scout troops march around the *maidans*.

The web of forest tracks and pilgrim trails that thread their way around Pachmarhi's widely dispersed archeological and religious sites make for excellent **walking**. Few of the paths are marked in English, so if you plan to attempt any routes more ambitious than those outlined below, consider employing a local **guide**. A reliable agency is the Satpura Adventure Club (ⓣ07578/252165), run by Vinay Sahu from *Hotel Saket*, which can organise guides (Rs150–200/day). The guides are young tribal men with expert local knowledge of the area, and the fees go directly to them and their villages, though they may not speak English. The agency also offers parasailing (Rs350), and can organise rock climbing and overnight stays in nearby villages. Kamal Dhoot from *Hotel Kachnar* (ⓣ07578/252547) is another good source of trekking information. Guides (Rs350/day) are also available from Bison Lodge (see below) Most of the longer hikes go through Satpura National Park, and so require a **permit** (see below).

Satpura National Park

The 524-square-kilometre **Satpura National Park**, around 3km southwest of town and dominated by the rugged Mahadeo Hills, is worth a visit to see the Indian bison, barking deer, sambar, jackals and wild dogs, although you'll be lucky to see any of the handful of tigers and leopards. Permits are available from the Forestry Commission office (Mon–Sat 10am–6pm) at Bison Lodge, a five-minute walk south of *Hotel Amaltas*. **Trekking permits** (Rs500 [Rs100]; guide Rs150; video camera Rs350) and **safari permits** (Rs2000 [Rs500] for a vehicle seating eight, Rs1500 [Rs250] for a vehicle seating five; walking safari Rs200 [Rs20]; guide Rs150; video camera Rs350) are each valid for one day. The office's small **museum** (daily except Mon 9am–1pm & 3–7pm) provides a good introduction to the park's flora and fauna. If you want to get the most out of Satpura, and have a bit of money to spare, *Forsyth Lodge* (ⓣ07575/21306, ⓦwww.forsythlodge.com;US$255) is a wonderful place to stay. Set in 44 acres of jungle near the village of Sarangpur, opposite the Madai entrance to the park, it has twelve beautiful cottages (Rs12,000/person) and a pool. Rates include full board, jeep and elephant safaris.

Pachmarhi Hill and the Jata Shankar cave

The following are two popular short excursions that do not require either a guide or a permit. The first is a fifteen-minute climb from the whitewashed Muslim shrine in the Babu Lines area of town (1km southwest of the bus stand) to the top of **Pachmarhi Hill**. From here you have a fine panoramic view over the town on one side and the thickly forested valley of **Jambu Dwip** on the other. The craggy cliffs lining the north side of the uninhabited gorge below are riddled with hidden rock-shelters and caves.

The second is a thirty-minute walk following a well-beaten track from the bus stand, twisting north from the main bazaar into the hillside through a narrow steep-sided canyon to **Jata Shankar**, a sacred cave that's a prominent point in the Shivratri *yatra*. En route, in a small cluster of prehistoric rock-shelters just off the path, look out for **Harper's cave**, named for its naturally formed seated figure of a man playing a harp. Beyond it, at the head of a dark chasm, the Jata Shankar cave itself lurks at the foot of a long flight of stone steps. The grotto's name, which literally means "Shiva's hairstyle", derives from the rock formation around a natural lingam on the cave floor, supposed to resemble the god's matted dreadlocks.

Pandav Caves, Fairy Pool and Big Falls

A two- to three-hour walk around the eastern fringes of the plateau strings together a small cluster of interesting sights. First head up to the **Pandav Caves** (40min), which occupy a knobbly sandstone hillock just east of the road between the ATC cantonment (an army training centre) and the petrol pump. Hindu mythology tells these five (*panch*) simple cells (*marhi*) sheltered the Pandava brothers of Mahabharata fame during their thirteen-year exile. Yet archeologists maintain a group of Buddhist monks excavated the bare stone chambers and pillared verandas around the first century BC.

Rejoin the road in front of the caves and head around the back of the hill to the melancholy **British cemetery**. Beyond that, the road becomes a dirt track leading to a small car park. If you plan to head on to Fairy Pool or Big Falls, you will need to buy a permit first (see opposite). From the car park, take the footpath down the hill through the woods for about twenty minutes till the trail flattens out, and turn right at a fork to descend to **Apsara Vihar**, or "Fairy Pool" – a popular bathing and picnic spot at the foot of a small waterfall. A five-minute scramble over the boulders downstream takes you to the 150m-high **Rajat Prapat**, or "Big Falls". If you walk back to the fork and continue along the trail, a five-minute walk brings you to a railing facing the 105m-high falls. Beyond this point you will need a guide to find the two-kilometre trail down to the deep, cold pool at the bottom.

Chauragarh

The 23-kilometre climb to the sacred summit of **Chauragarh Mountain** (no permit required), on the south rim of the plateau, follows the main *yatra* trail used by pilgrims during the Shivratri *mela*. The first 8km can be covered by bike. From the bazaar, head south across the lake towards the crossroads in front of *Hotel Amaltas*, then take the road to **Mahadeo cave**, passing a vantage point above the narrow **Handi Kho** ravine, just before the road makes its first sharp descent at the turn-off for **Priyadarshini**, or "Forsyth's Point".

The **footpath** proper begins at the very bottom of the valley, after the road has plunged down a sequence of hairpin bends. Before setting off, make a brief diversion up the *khud* behind the modern **temple** to the Mahadeo cave, where pilgrims take a purifying dip in the cool springwater. From here, a strenuous two-hour climb follows an ancient trail to the top of the mountain, which is crammed with tens of thousands of worshippers and sadhus during the Shivratri festival. At the summit, where a temple houses the all-powerful Chauragarh lingam, a thicket of orange tridents surrounds a bright blue statue of Shiva. The views are suitably sublime.

Eating

The inexpensive *dhabas* along the main road serve generous and inexpensive thalis, although hygiene is not always a priority.

Chatora's *Misty Meadows Resort*, bottom end of bazaar, off the main road. A huge TV screen (usually showing cricket) dominates this veg restaurant, whose menu features a selection of north Indian curries (Rs40–85) and thalis (opt for the Rs150 "VIP" version, if you're hungry).

Khalsa *Hotel Khalsa*, bottom end of bazaar, off the main road. Sikh-run place with predictably good veg and non-veg Punjabi food (including a tasty Peshwari naan), plus a decent attempt at a Gujarati thali. The bizarre dining room features fake tree-trunk roof supports and fairy lights. Mains Rs38–150.

Rock-End Manor *Rock-End Manor* hotel ⓣ07578/252079. All the MP Tourism properties have restaurants serving the solid but hardly earth-shattering north Indian and Chinese menu, but the Raj-era charm here elevates it over the others – given the surroundings, fish and chips (Rs175) seems the most appropriate choice. Book a table in advance during the peak season.

South Indian Coffee House Main Rd, just before the bus stand. This simple establishment is a good spot for a south Indian breakfast (though it only serves instant coffee) or a more substantial veg meal (mains Rs35–60) later on; try the Hyderabadi biriyani.

Gwalior

Straddling the main Delhi-Mumbai train line, **GWALIOR** is northern Madhya Pradesh's largest city and boasts one of India's most magnificent hilltop forts. The sandstone citadel, with its temples and palaces, peers down from the edge of a sheer-sided plateau above a haze of petrol fumes and busy streets. The city's other unmissable attraction is the extraordinarily flamboyant **Jai Vilas Palace**, owned by the local ruling family, the **Scindias**. Their personalities and influence are everywhere, from the **chhatris** (cenotaphs) north of Jayaji Chowk to the excellent **Sarod Ghar** classical music museum. Despite its proximity to Agra, 119km north, Gwalior sees few foreign tourists and its drab modern centre lacks the charm of its nearby Rajasthani counterparts. Nevertheless, it is a worthwhile place to pause for a day, particularly around late November or early December, when the old **Mughal tombs** host one of India's premier classical music events, the **Tansen Festival**.

Some history

An inscription unearthed in a now-defunct sun temple proves Gwalior was first occupied in the sixth century BC by Hun invaders from the north. Local legend, however, attributes the founding of the fort to the Kuchwaha prince **Suraj Sen**, said to have been cured of leprosy during the tenth century by the hermit **Gwalipa** after whom the city is named. The Kuchwahas' successors, the Parihars, were brutally overthrown in 1232 by **Iltutmish**.

A third Rajput dynasty, the **Tomars**, retook Gwalior in 1398, ushering in the city's "golden age". Under **Man Singh**, who ascended to the Tomar *gadi* (throne) in 1486, the hilltop gained the magnificent palaces and fortifications that were to earn it the epithet "the pearl in the necklace of the castles of Hind". Skirmishes with neighbouring powers dogged the Rajputs' rule until 1517, when the **Lodis** from Delhi besieged the fort for a second time and Man

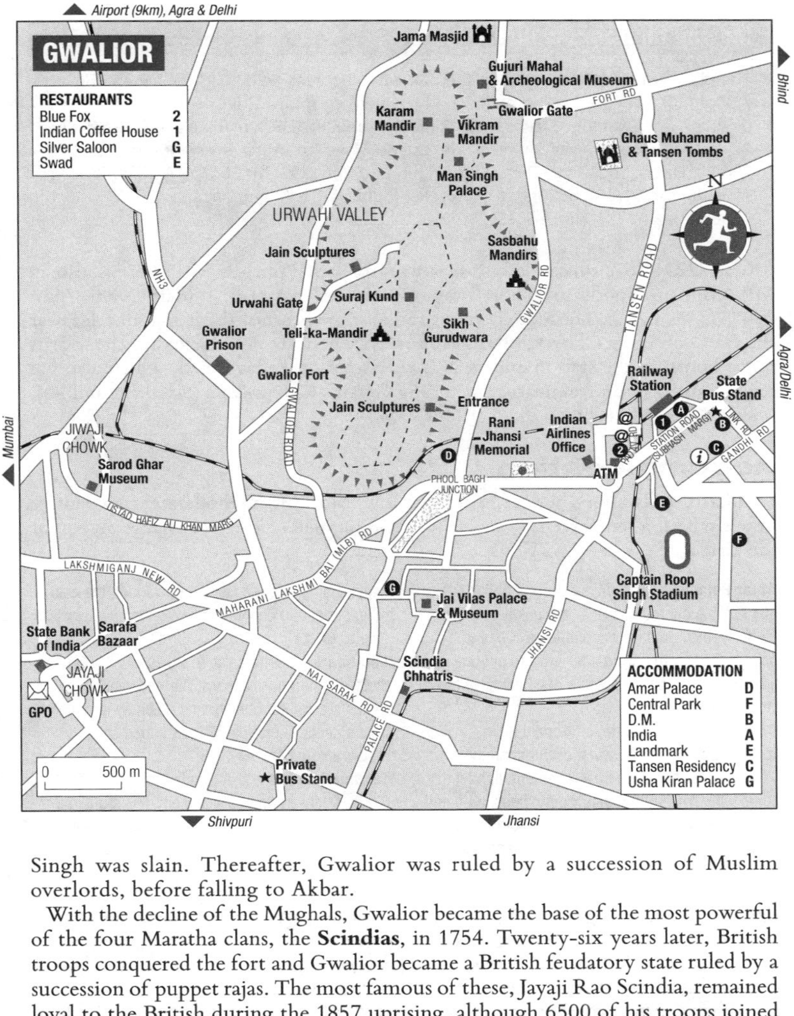

GWALIOR

RESTAURANTS
Blue Fox 2
Indian Coffee House 1
Silver Saloon G
Swad E

ACCOMMODATION
Amar Palace D
Central Park F
D.M. B
India A
Landmark E
Tansen Residency C
Usha Kiran Palace G

Singh was slain. Thereafter, Gwalior was ruled by a succession of Muslim overlords, before falling to Akbar.

With the decline of the Mughals, Gwalior became the base of the most powerful of the four Maratha clans, the **Scindias**, in 1754. Twenty-six years later, British troops conquered the fort and Gwalior became a British feudatory state ruled by a succession of puppet rajas. The most famous of these, Jayaji Rao Scindia, remained loyal to the British during the 1857 uprising, although 6500 of his troops joined the opposing forces led by Tantia Tope and **Rani Lakshmi Bai** of Jhansi (see p.266). Both rebel leaders were killed in the ensuing battle, and the maharaja quickly resumed his role as host of some of the grandest viceregal dinners, royal visits and tiger hunts ever witnessed by the Raj. The Scindias remained influential after Independence, and still live in Gwalior.

Arrival and information

Gwalior's **railway station** lies in the east of the city, just around the corner from the **state bus stand**. The **private bus stand** is inconveniently situated on the southwestern edge of town. The airport is 9km north of the city. MP Tourism's **information** office at *Tansen Residency* on Gandhi Road (daily 10am–6pm;

Moving on from Gwalior

The quickest **train** for **Delhi** is the *Shatabdi Express* #2001 (daily except Fri at 7.05pm; 3hr 25min), calling at **Agra** (1hr 25min) en route. Travelling in the opposite direction, the *Shatabdi Express* #2002 (daily except Fri 9.39am) travels to **Bhopal** (4hr 26min) via **Jhansi** (1hr 9min). State **buses** travel to **Agra** every 30min (3hr–3hr 30min), **Datia** (1hr 30min–2hr), **Jhansi** (3hr) and **Shivpuri** (2hr 30min). Air India/Indian Airlines (ⓣ0751/237 6820) has six weekly **flights** to Delhi and Jabalpur.

ⓣ0751/223 4557) runs a daily **bus tour** (10.30am–7pm; Rs75). There is also an MP Tourism booth in the railway station on platform 1 (daily 9am–7pm; ⓣ0751/404 0777). The State Bank of India, at the heart of the bazaar district near the **GPO** on Jayaji Chowk, **changes money**. There are **ATMs** next to the tourist office booth in the station and near *Hotel Shelter* on Padav Road, which also has several **internet** centres nearby, including Gwala's Cyber Zone (Rs10/hr) and R.J. Cyber Zone (Rs20/hr).

Accommodation

Standards at Gwalior's budget **hotels** are low. Most of the moderate to expensive hotels whack a ten percent "luxury" tax and ten percent service charge on top of the tariff.

Amar Palace Phool Bagh Junction ⓣ0751/232 5843. While the rooms are a little pokey and can be noisy, they do have marble floors, TVs and phones. It's worth paying a bit extra to get one with a/c and a small balcony, some of which have fort views. ❸–❹

Central Park City Centre, off Gandhi Rd ⓣ0751/223 2440, ⓦwww.thecentralpark.net. Rooms at this business traveller-oriented hotel come with swish bathrooms, comfy beds, wi-fi and complimentary breakfast. Sadly, it's somewhat overpriced and the service is inconsistent. The restaurant, pastry shop and pool, however, help compensate. ❼

D.M. Near the state bus stand ⓣ0751/234 2083. Miniscule but clean and quiet rooms; the cheaper ones have squat toilets. The ancient TVs are locked inside cabinets, lest you were thinking of pinching one. Mosquitoes can be a problem, so put up a net. ❸–❹

India Station Rd ⓣ0751/234 1983. Popular no-frills lodge run by the Indian Coffee House chain. The rooms are clean but overlook the noisy main street and only the deluxe units have western toilets. ❷–❹

Landmark Manik Vilas ⓣ0751/401 1271, ⓦwww.hotellandmarkgwalior.com. The mid-range a/c rooms are comfortable, but let down by their dull brown decor. There's a 24-hour coffee shop, restaurant and bar. ❼

Tansen Residency 6-A Gandhi Rd ⓣ0751/234 0370, ⓔtansen@mptourism.com. MP Tourism's efficient hotel, in its own gardens near the station, has well-furnished but cramped rooms, plus a decent restaurant and bar. It's popular, so book in advance. ❺

Usha Kiran Palace Jayendraganj, Lakshar ⓣ0751/244 4000, ⓦwww.tajhotels.com. Romantic 120-year-old palace set in nine acres of landscaped gardens. Charming rooms (from US$202) have Indian-style divans, 1930s furniture and silk cushions. There's a pool and spa, and cookery and yoga classes are available. ❾

The fort

Gwalior's imposing **fort** (daily: dawn to dusk; Rs100 [Rs5], camera Rs20, video Rs25) sprawls over a 3km-long outcrop of sandstone to the north of the modern city. Its mighty turreted battlements encompass six palaces, three temples and several water tanks and cisterns, as well as a prestigious public school and a Sikh *gurudwara*.

Two routes wind up the hill. In the west, a driveable track just off Gwalior Road climbs the steep gorge of the **Urwahi valley** to the **Urwahi Gate**, passing a line of rock-cut Jain statues along the way. The other, more accessible **Gwalior Gate** is on the northeast corner of the cliff. Official **guides** (around Rs250/3hr) tout for trade at the Urwahi Gate and the cold drinks shop at the entrance to the palace complex. There's a nightly **sound-and-light** show in English and Hindi (April–Sept 8.30pm, Oct–March 7.30pm; 45min; Rs250 [Rs50]) at the Man Mandir.

The Gwalior Gate approach and museum

Just beyond the Gwalior Gate is the modest **Gujuri Mahal**, built by Man Singh to woo his favourite *rani*, Mrignayani, when she was still a peasant girl. The elegant sandstone palace now houses Gwalior's **archeological museum** (Tues–Sun 10am–5pm; Rs100 [Rs10]), where the large exhibition of sculpture, inscriptions and painting is well worth a look, even if the labels are woefully uninformative. Highlights include the twin Ashoka lion capitals from Vidisha in gallery two, and gallery nine's erotic bas-relief. Yet the most famous exhibit is the exquisitely carved **salabhanjika**, a small female figurine; noted for her sensuous curves and sublime facial expression, the statue is often dubbed "India's Mona Lisa".

The Man Singh Palace

Entered via the **Hathiya** ("elephant") **Paur** gateway, with its twin turrets and ornate blue tilework, the **Man Singh Palace** was declared "the noblest specimen of Hindu domestic architecture in northern India" by nineteenth-century explorer Sir Alexander Cunningham. Built between 1486 and 1517 by the Tomar ruler Man Singh, it's also known as the Chit Mandir ("painted palace") for the rich ceramic **mosaics** encrusting its facade. The best-preserved fragments of tilework, on its south side, can be seen from the bank left of the main Hathiya Paur gateway. Spread in luxurious bands of turquoise, emerald green and yellow across the ornate stonework are tigers, elephants, peacocks and crocodiles brandishing flowers.

By contrast, the **interior** of the four-storeyed palace is very plain. However, there are some fine pierced-stone *jali* screens, behind which the women of the palace would assemble to receive instruction from Gwalior's great music gurus. The circular chambers in the lower storeys were once dungeons.

The Teli-ka-Mandir and Suraj Kund

The 30m-tall **Teli-ka-Mandir**, on the south side of the plateau, is the fort's oldest surviving monument. Dating from the mid-eighth century, it consists of a huge rectangular sanctuary tower capped with an unusual vaulted-arch roof, whose *peepal*-leaf shape derives from the *chaitya* windows of much earlier rock-cut Buddhist caves. In the aftermath of the 1857 Indian uprising, the Vishnu temple was used by the British as a soda factory, and restoration work continues. At the head of the Urwahi ravine, just north of the Teli-ka-Mandir, the **Suraj Kund** is the 100m-long tank whose waters are supposed to have cured the tenth-century ruler Suraj Sen, later Suraj Pal, of leprosy.

The Sasbahu mandirs and Sikh gurudwara

The **Sasbahu**, or "mother-and-daughter-in-law", temples overlook the city from the eastern edge of the fort, near an unsightly TV mast. The larger one has a three-storey *mandapa* (assembly hall), supported by four intricate pillars, while the smaller one consists of an open-sided porch with a pyramidal roof. Both were erected late in the eleventh century and are dedicated to Vishnu.

The huge, gold-tipped, white-domed marble building to the south is a modern **Sikh gurudwara**, built to commemorate a Sikh hero who was imprisoned in the fort. Before entering, cover your arms, legs and head, remove your socks and shoes and wash your feet in the tank at the bottom of the steps.

The Jain sculptures

The sheer sandstone cliffs around the fort harbour some imposing rock-cut **Jain sculptures**. Carved between the seventh and fifteenth centuries, most of the large honey-coloured figures depict the 24 Jain teacher-saviours – the *tirthankaras*, or "Crossing Makers" – standing with their arms held stiffly at their sides, or sitting cross-legged, the palms of their hands upturned. Many lost their faces and genitalia when Mughal emperor Babur's iconoclastic army descended on the city in 1527.

The larger of the two main groups lines the southwestern approach to the fort, along the sides of the **Urwahi** ravine. The largest image, to the side of the road near Urwahi Gate, portrays Adinath, 19m tall, with decorative nipples, a head of tightly curled hair and drooping ears, standing on a lotus bloom beside several smaller statues. A little further from the fort, on the other side of the road, another company of *tirthankaras* enjoys a more dramatic situation, looking over a natural gorge. All have lost their faces, save a proud trio sheltered by a delicate canopy.

The third collection stands on the southeast corner of the plateau, overlooking the city from a narrow ledge. To get here, follow Gwalior Road north along the foot of the cliff from Phool Bagh junction, near the **Rani Jhansi memorial**, until you see a paved path winding up the hill from behind a row of houses on the left. Once again, the *tirthankaras*, which are numbered, occupy deep recesses hewn from the rock wall. One of the few not defaced by the Muslim invaders, no. 10, is still visited by Gwalior's small Jain community as a shrine.

The old town and south of the fort

A number of interesting Islamic monuments are tucked away down the narrow backstreets of Gwalior's predominantly Muslim **old town**, clustered around the north and northeast corners of the hill. The **Jama Masjid**, erected in 1661, stands close to the Gujuri Mahal, near the main entrance to the fort. The city's most famous Muslim building, however, is 1km further east. The sixteenth-century **Tomb of Ghaus Mohammed**, an Afghan prince who helped Babur take Gwalior fort, is a fine specimen of early Mughal architecture, and a popular local shrine. Elegant hexagonal pavilions stand at each of its four corners; in the centre, the large central dome retains a few remnants of its blue-glazed tiles. The tomb's walls are inlaid with exquisite pierced-stone *jali* screens.

The second and smaller of the tombs in the gardens is that of the famous Mughal singer-musician **Tansen**, one of the "Nine Jewels" of Emperor Akbar's court. Every year, performers and aficionados from all over India flock here for Gwalior's annual **music festival** (Nov/Dec). Local superstition holds that the leaves of the **tamarind tree** growing on the plinth nearby have a salutary effect on the singing voice, which is why its bottom branches have been stripped bare.

The Jai Vilas Palace

Due south of the fort, the **Jai Vilas Palace** (daily except Mon 10am–5.30pm; Rs250 [Rs30], Rs30 camera, Rs80 video) is one of India's most grandiose and eccentric nineteenth-century relics, although the lack of labelling and information make it an unsatisfactory experience. **Guides** charge about Rs50 per tour.

The palace was built in 1875 during the reign of Maharaja Jayaji Rao Scindia. He dispatched his friend Colonel Michael Filose on a grand tour of Europe to seek inspiration; Filose returned with a vast shipment of furniture, fabric, paintings, tapestries and cut glass, together with the blueprints for a building that borrowed heavily from Buckingham Palace, Versailles, Greek ruins and Italian-Baroque stately homes. The result is a shamelessly over-the-top blend of Doric, Tuscan and Corinthian architecture.

The Scindias, who still occupy part of the palace, have opened two wings to the public. The first wing, a **museum**, includes countless Mughal paintings, Persian rugs, gold and silver ornaments and antique furniture that had originally belonged to the estate of Louis XVI before the French Revolution.

A still more extravagant wing lies across the courtyard from the museum. The **durbar hall** was where the maharaja entertained important visitors. A sweeping Belgian glass staircase leads from the lobby upstairs to the gargantuan assembly hall, which has the world's biggest chandeliers. At over three and a half tonnes apiece, they could not be installed until the strength of the roof had been tested with eight elephants. The rug lining the floor of the hall, woven by inmates of Gwalior jail, took twelve years to complete and, at over 40m in length, is the largest handmade carpet in Asia.

Sarod Ghar museum

Tucked away in the west of the city (take an auto-rickshaw), the **Sarod Ghar** music museum (Tues–Sun 10am–1pm & 2–4pm; Ⓦwww.sarod.com) is on Ustad Hafiz Ali Khan Marg, Jiwaji Ganj. It occupies the beautiful ancestral home of the Bangash family, whose ancestors, originally Afghan horse-traders who settled in India, produced a dynasty of musical virtuosos, including **Ustad Hafiz Ali Khan** and his son **Ustad Amjad Ali Khan**. The museum traces Gwalior's rich musical legacy from Tansen, who performed in Mughal emperor Akbar's court, to the invention by Gulam Ali Khan Bangash of the **sarod**, whose ethereal tones accompany you as you progress through the galleries.

The Scindia chhatris

Two typically ostentatious Scindia family tombs stand a short rickshaw ride east of Jayaji Chowk. Inside a walled courtyard, the **chhatris** feature intricate stonework and ornately painted scenes of life inside the nineteenth-century Maratha royal court. Built in 1817 to commemorate Maharaja Jiyaji Rao Scindia, the larger of the pair is most remarkable for the intricate outside panelling of interwoven flowers. The second chhatri is a more compact and finely detailed version of the former. Constructed in 1843 for the newly departed Maharaja Janakaji Scindia, sculptures and carvings depict the hectic lifestyle of a king.

Eating

The **best places to eat** in Gwalior are in the smarter hotels. More basic and much cheaper *dhabas* are outside the railway station.

Blue Fox *Hotel Shelter*, Padav Rd. Grab one of the cosy booths and select one of the – surprisingly artfully presented – chicken or mutton kebabs: the *shashlik* is particularly good. If you want a guilt-free treat, try the hot chocolate (it's listed under "health drinks"). Mains Rs60–150.

Indian Coffee House Station Rd. Low-key place with white-turbaned waiters that consistently produces the goods: toast and filter coffee, south Indian dosas and more substantial meals (Rs35–140).

Silver Saloon *Usha Kiran Palace* hotel. If you can't afford to stay at the hotel, a visit to its exemplary restaurant is the next best thing. Gourmet Mughal, Marathi, Nepalese and international dishes (Rs350–750) are impeccably served in evocative surroundings. Afterwards, head to the hotel's *Bada Bar* for a drink and a game of billiards.

Swad *Hotel Landmark*. As well as tasty north and south Indian dishes, this is the place to come for comfort food like baked beans on toast, porridge and French toast (Rs80–200).

Datia

Constructed by Bir Singh Deo at the height of the Bundela's "golden age", the little-visited majestic palace at **DATIA**, 30km northwest of Jhansi, is one of India's finest Rajput buildings. On the main Delhi–Mumbai train line, Datia is generally visited as a day-trip from Jhansi, or Gwalior, 71km to the northwest. Buses run from both cities every thirty minutes and there are several daily trains. Coming from Shivpuri, 97km west, you'll have to change buses at Karera. *Tongas* and cycle rickshaws ferry passengers into town from the small **railway station**, 2km southwest. **Buses** pull in on the south side of the centre.

Presiding over a mass of white- and blue-washed brick houses from its seat atop a rock outcrop, the **Nrsing Dev Palace** (daily dawn to dusk) stands in the north of town. Half the fun of visiting the labyrinthine palace is trying to find a path from its pitch-black subterranean chambers, hewn out of the solid base of the hill for use during the hot season, to the *rani*'s airy apartment on the top floor. In between, a maze of cross-cutting corridors, flying walkways, walls encrusted with fragments of ceramic tiles, latticed screens and archways, hidden passages, pavilions and suites of apartments lead you in ever-decreasing circles until you eventually run out of staircases. The views from the upper storeys are breathtaking.

Shivpuri

Shivpuri, 112km south of Gwalior and the former summer capital of the Scindias, is worth a stop-off to see the **Madhav Rao Scindia Chhatri**, a white marble synthesis of Hindu and Islamic architectural styles with spires and pavilions (daily 8am–noon & 3–8pm; Rs40, camera Rs10, video Rs40). There are also several other lesser chhatris, and tranquil gardens, complete with Victorian lamps and ornamental balustrades. Nearby, the **Madhav National Park** (daily dawn–4.30pm; fee/vehicle Rs1500 [Rs400], camera Rs40, video Rs300, guide Rs150) has deer, leopards, sloth bears, crocodiles and blackbucks, as well as a Scindia-era hunting lodge and castle. MP Tourism's *Tourist Village* (ⓣ07492/223760, ⓔtvshivpuri@mptourism.com; ❺) has a pleasant, if overpriced, collection of air-conditioned **rooms**, a pool and a restaurant-bar. Staff can organize jeep hire. Shivpuri is linked to Gwalior by **train** (4hr), but the state **buses** (3hr) are quicker.

Orchha

An essential stop en route to or from Khajuraho, **ORCHHA** ("hidden place") certainly lives up to its name, residing amid a tangle of scrubby *dhak* forest 18km southeast of Jhansi. In spite of its tumbledown state, the fortified and now deserted medieval town remains an architectural gem, its guano-splashed temple *shikharas*, derelict palaces, havelis and weed-choked sandstone cenotaphs floating serenely above the banks of the River Betwa. Clustered around the foot of the exotic ruins, the sleepy village makes an excellent spot to unwind after the hassle of northern cities. However, it's now firmly established on the tour-group circuit, so try to spend a night or two here to see Orchha after the bus parties have moved off.

Some history

After being chased by several generations of Delhi sultans from various capitals around central India, the Bundela dynasty finally settled at the former Malwan fort of **Orchha** in the fifteenth century. Work on Orchha's magnificent fortifications, palaces and temples was started by Raja **Rudra Pratap**, and continued after he was killed in 1531 trying to wrestle a cow from the clutches of a tiger. Thereafter, the dynasty's fortunes depended on the goodwill of their mighty neighbours, the **Mughals**. After being defeated in battle by Akbar, the proud and pious **Madhukar Shah** nearly signed his clan's death warrant by showing up at the imperial court with a red *tilak* smeared on his forehead – a mark at that time banned by the emperor. Madhukar's bold gesture, however, earned Akbar's respect, and the two became friends – an alliance fostered in the following years by Orchha's most illustrious raja. During his 22-year rule, **Bir Singh Deo** erected 52 forts and palaces, including the citadel at Jhansi, the rambling Nrsing Dev at Datia and many of Orchha's finest buildings. In 1627, he was killed by bandits while returning from the Deccan with a camel train full of booty. Afterwards, relations with the Mughals rapidly deteriorated, and the Bundelas eventually fled Orchha for the comparative safety of **Tikamgarh**. Apart from the *Sheesh Mahal*, now a hotel, the magnificent monuments have lain virtually deserted ever since.

Arrival and information

Packed **tempos and buses** from Jhansi bus station run frequently to Orchha's main crossroads, 18km away; both take twenty to forty minutes, and cost Rs10 (plus Rs10 for luggage in a *tempo*). An **auto-rickshaw** from Jhansi costs Rs150–200, a taxi Rs350–400; both are more expensive at night. Coming from **Khajuraho**, you can ask to be dropped at the Orchha turning on the main road and pick up a *tempo* for the remaining 7km.

If you're heading in the other direction, **towards Khajuraho**, don't bank on being able to flag down one of the quicker private buses (8 daily; 4hr 30min–6hr) on the highway, as they're often full. Instead, get to Jhansi bus station, and get on before they depart. Three daily public buses (5–7hr) also make the journey. **Taxis** (Rs1800) cut the journey time to Khajuraho, and can be hired through the MP Tourism **information** office (daily 7am–10pm; Ⓣ07680/252624) at the *Sheesh Mahal*, which also organizes **river rafting** trips (Rs1200/90min; Rs3000/3hr, including lunch). You can change **travellers' cheques** at Canara Bank on the main square and there is a State Bank of India **ATM** on Tikamgarh Road, a few minutes south of the market. There are several **internet** centres; try Cyber Café (Rs30/hr) next to *Bhola* restaurant, which also offers Skype (Rs40/hr). AR Tours and Travel, Tikamgarh Road, rents **bikes** for around Rs50 per day.

Accommodation

Two grassroots organisations, Sarthak and Friends of Orchha (Ⓣ9993/385405, Ⓦwww.orchha.org), jointly offer **homestays** with local families (❸).

Amar Mahal Bypass Rd, 200m south of the market Ⓣ07680/252102, Ⓦwww.alsisar.com. A Mughal-themed hotel whose attached rooms, each with elegantly carved wooden beds and elaborately painted ceilings, are set around a series of peaceful, interlinked courtyards. There's a pool, restaurant and mini spa (treatments Rs500–2000). ❼

Betwa Retreat Off Tikamgarh Rd, 10mins south of the market Ⓣ07680/252618, Ⓔbetwa@mptourism.com. MP Tourism lodge with faded but tastefully decorated salmon-coloured cottages and comfy a/c tents, each with TV, fridge and marble bathroom, in a peaceful garden close to the river. There's a restaurant, bar and small pool. ❺

Bundelkhand Riverside Off Jhansi Rd, 600m north of the market Ⓣ07680/252612, Ⓦwww.bundelkhandriverside.com. Former hunting lodge of Orchha's last maharaja, dating back to 1895, with a blend of traditional Indian and British colonial architecture, spacious art-filled attached rooms (most with river views), a restaurant and pool. ❼

Ganpati Jhansi Rd ⓣ07680/252765, ⓦwww.hotelganpati.in. Welcoming, family-run hotel with a range of rooms set around a small garden, from which there are spectacular views of the old fortifications. All the rooms are immaculately clean and have attached bathrooms; the more expensive have a/c and some (notably no. 21) boast vistas of their own. ❷–❹

Sheesh Mahal Jehangir Mahal Rd, next to the Raj Mahal ⓣ07680/252624, ⓔsmorchha@mptourism.com. The local raja's former country bolthole in the heart of the fort is now an atmospheric hotel with eight charming (and very good value) a/c rooms and a personalised approach. If you can afford it, treat yourself to a romantic night in the Maharaja suite – perks include a vast marble bathtub and the ultimate loo with a view. Advance booking recommended. ❺–❽

Shri Mahant Guesthouse Overlooking the market ⓣ07680/252715. Backpacker stalwart in the heart of the action: rooms are a little claustrophobic, and the most basic have squat toilets, but for a few more rupees you get air-coolers, TV and western toilets. ❷–❹

Shri Mahant Hotel Lakshmi Narayan Temple Rd, 200m northwest of the market ⓣ07680/252341. Run by the same people as *Shri Mahant Guesthouse*, this relaxed place has huge pastel coloured rooms with spotless bathrooms (some with tubs) and balconies; you pay more for a/c and a TV. There are good views from the roof terrace. ❸–❹

The monuments

The best-preserved of Orchha's scattered **palaces**, **temples**, **tombs** and **gardens** (daily 8am–6pm; "day passport" for all monuments Rs250 [Rs10], Rs25 camera, Rs200 video) lie within comfortable walking distance of the village and can be seen – at breakneck speed – in a day; yet to get the most out of a trip you should plan on staying the night. English-speaking **guides** can be hired at the main gate for around Rs200 for a short tour of the fort, or near the main square for Rs350 for a half-day tour of Orchha. There's a nightly **sound and light** show (English show: March–October 7.30pm; November–February 6.30pm; 1hr; Rs250 [Rs75], children Rs150 [Rs40]).

The Raj Mahal and the Rai Praveen Mahal

The first building you come to across Orchha's medieval granite bridge is the well-preserved ruin of the royal palace, or **Raj Mahal** (unrestricted access). From the end of the bridge, bear left at the main entrance, and then right to reach the *Sheesh Mahal* hotel. Of the two rectangular courtyards inside, the second, formerly used by the Bundela *ranis*, is the most dramatic. Opulent royal quarters, raised balconies and interlocking walkways rise in symmetrical tiers on all four sides, crowned by domed pavilions and turrets; the apartments projecting into the quadrangle on the ground floor belonged to the most-favoured queens. As you wander around, look out for the fragments of mirror inlay and vibrant **painting** plastered over their walls and ceilings. Some of the friezes are in remarkable condition, depicting Vishnu's various outlandish incarnations, court and hunting scenes, and lively festivals.

Reached via a path that leads from the Raj Mahal around the northern side of the hill, the **Rai Praveen Mahal** is a small, double-storeyed brick apartment built by Raja Indramani for his concubine in the mid-1670s. The gifted poetess, musician and dancer, Rai Praveen, beguiled the Mughal emperor Akbar when she was sent to him as a gift, but was eventually returned to Orchha to live out her remaining days. Set amid the well-watered lawns of the **Anand Mahal gardens** (unrestricted access), it has a main assembly hall on the ground floor (used to host music and dance performances), a boudoir upstairs and cool underground apartments.

The Jahangir Mahal

Orchha's most admired palace, the **Jahangir Mahal** was built by Bir Singh Deo as a monumental welcome present for the Mughal emperor when he paid a state visit here in the seventeenth century. Jahangir had come to invest his old ally with the sword of Abdul Fazal – the emperor's erstwhile enemy whom Bir Singh had murdered some years earlier. Entered through an ornate ceremonial gateway, the main, east-facing facade is still encrusted with turquoise tiles. Two stone elephants flank the stairway, holding bells in their trunks to announce the arrival of the raja, and there are three storeys of elegant hanging balconies, terraces, apartments and onion domes piled around a central courtyard. This palace, however, has a much lighter feel, with countless windows and pierced stone screens looking out over the exotic Orchha skyline to the west, and a sea of treetops and ruined temples in the other direction.

The Sheesh Mahal

Built during the early eighteenth century, long after Orchha's demise, the **Sheesh Mahal** ("Palace of Mirrors") was originally intended as an exclusive country retreat for the local raja, Udait Singh. Following Independence, the property was inherited by the state government, who converted it into a hotel. The rather squat palace stands between the Raj Mahal and the Jahangir Mahal, at the far end of an open-sided courtyard. Covered in a coat of whitewash and stripped of most of its Persian rugs and antiques, the building retains only traces of its former splendour, though there are stunning views from its upper terraces and turrets. If they're not occupied, check out the palatial suites (rooms 1 and 2), which contain original bathroom fittings.

Saket Museum of Ramayana Correlogram

This small **gallery** (daily except Mon 10am–5pm), a couple of minutes' walk south of the Raj Mahal, has an intriguing collection of Hindu folk art from across India. Highlights include Mithila paintings (produced using paint made from cow's milk) from Bihar and colourful masks from Orissa and Uttar Pradesh.

Around the village

Dotted around the **village** below the hill are several other interesting monuments. The **Ram Raja Mandir** stands at the end of the small bazaar, in a cool marble-tiled courtyard. Local legend has it that Madhukar Shah constructed the building as a palace for his wife, Rani Ganesha, and it only became a temple after a Rama icon, which the queen had dutifully carried all the way from her home town of Ayodhya, could not be lifted from the spot where she first set it down; it remains there to this day, and the temple is a popular pilgrimage site.

With its huge pointed *shikharas* soaring high above the village, **Chatturbuj Mandir** is the temple originally built to house Rani Ganesha's icon. In cruciform shape, representing the four-armed Vishnu, with seven storeys and spacious courtyards ringed by arched balconies, it epitomizes the regal Bundelkhand style, inspired by the Mughals, with Rajput, Persian and European touches. It's unusual for a Hindu temple, with few carvings and a wealth of space – perhaps to accommodate followers of the **bhakti** cult (a form of worship involving large congregations of people rather than a small elite of priests). You can climb up the narrow staircases between storeys to the temple's roof, pierced by an ornate *shikhara* whose niches shelter nesting vultures.

On the other side of Ram Mandir, a path leads through the Mughal-style **Phool Bagh** ornamental garden to **Hardaul ka Baithak**, a grand pavilion where Bir Singh Deo's second son, Hardaul, ally of Jahangir and romantic paragon, once held court. Newlyweds come here to seek blessing from Hardaul, who, despite being poisoned by his jealous brother who accused him of intimacy with his sister-in-law, is thought to confer good luck. The tall towers rising above the gardens like disregarded bridge supports are *dastgirs* ("wind-catchers"), Persian-style cooling towers that provided air-conditioning for the neighbouring palace, Palkhi Mahal; they're thought to be the only ones of their kind surviving in India.

A solemn row of pale brown weed-choked domes and spires, the fourteen riverside **chhatris**, the cenotaphs of Bundelkhand's former rulers, are Orchha's most melancholy ruins. Just north of the chhatris, and across a bridge, is the **Orchha Nature Reserve** (dawn–dusk; Rs150), where you can take an idle wander or cycle along a peaceful nature trail in the company of monkeys and peacocks.

The Lakshmi Narayan Mandir

The solitary **Lakshmi Narayan temple** crowns a rocky hillock just under 1km west of Orchha village, at the end of a long, paved pathway. From the square directly behind the Ram Raja temple, a leisurely fifteen-minute stroll is rewarded with fine views, and excellent seventeenth- and nineteenth-century paintings. For a small tip, the *chowkidar* will lead you through the galleries inside the temple. Look out for the frieze depicting the battle of Jhansi, in which the *rani* appears in an upper room of the fort next to her horse, while musket-bearing British troops scuttle about below. Elsewhere, episodes from the much-loved Krishna story crop up alongside portraits of the Bundela rajas and their military and architectural achievements, while a side pillar bears a sketch of two very inebriated English soldiers.

Eating and drinking

The delicious local **speciality**, *kalakand* (milk cake), can be bought from the small stalls in the market.

Betwa Tarang On the approach to the Fort Bridge. The relatively pricey thin-crust pizzas and pastas (Rs95–240) are worth a try, even if the chef is at times a bit over-ambitious. There's also a separate menu with cheaper veg Indian dishes (Rs60–85).

Bhola On the approach to the Fort Bridge. Established restaurant with an eclectic menu that jumps from Korean, Dutch and Israeli dishes to veg Indian staples to traveller favourites like banana pancakes. The "Fresh Pomme Grenade Juice" isn't as lethal as it sounds. Main Rs15–60.

Blue Sky Jhansi Rd. Friendly rooftop restaurant where you can tuck into veg Indian, Chinese and Korean food (mains Rs50–80) and observe the street scene below or the fort in the distance.

Jharokha *Hotel Sheesh Mahal*. If you're not staying here, soak up the palace's evocative surroundings in the colonnaded dining hall, which has tasty veg and non veg food (mains Rs50–200; try the chicken in spinach sauce) and live music and dancing in the evenings.

Neeraj In the market. While this popular veg thali stall has moved to a new spot, the food is as good as ever and won't hurt your wallet (Rs20–50). Ideal for anyone tired of Orchha's ubiquitous international menus.

Ram Raja On the approach to the Fort Bridge. Cheerful little place with an extensive breakfast menu (served all day) that features hash browns, peanut butter on toast, filter coffee and as many kinds of eggs as you can think of. They also serve simple veg Indian meals and *momos* (Tibetan dumplings). Mains Rs20–60.

Khajuraho

The resplendent Hindu temples of **KHAJURAHO**, immaculately restored after almost a millennium of abandonment and neglect, and now a UNESCO world Heritage site are an essential stop on any itinerary of India's historic monuments. Famed for the delicate sensuality – and forthright **eroticism** – of their sculpture, they were built between the tenth and twelfth centuries AD as the greatest architectural achievement of the **Chandella** dynasty.

Waves of Afghan invaders soon hastened the decline of the Chandellas, however, who abandoned the temples shortly after they were built for more secure ground. The temples gradually fell out of use and by the sixteenth century had been swallowed by the surrounding jungle. It took "rediscovery" by the British in 1838 before these masterpieces were fully appreciated in India, let alone internationally. It is still not known exactly why the temples were built and there are a number of competing theories (see p.380), including a "how to" guide for Brahmin boys or to symbolise the wedding party of Shiva and Parvati.

Some 400km southeast of Agra and the same distance west of Varanasi, Khajuraho might look central on maps of the Subcontinent, but remains almost as **remote** from the Indian mainstream as it was when the temples were built – which is presumably what spared them the depredations of the marauders, invaders and zealots who devastated so many early Hindu sites. Nevertheless, a new train route now crosses this extended flood plain, making Khajuraho much easier to visit today.

The exquisite intricacy of the temples themselves – of which the most spectacular are **Kandariya Mahadeva**, **Vishvanatha** and **Lakshmana**, all in the conglomeration known as the **Western Group** – was made possible by the soft fawn-coloured sandstone used in their construction. Considering the propensity of such stone to crumble, they have withstood the ravages of time remarkably well. Much of the ornate **sculpture** adorning their walls is in such high relief as to be virtually three-dimensional, with strains of pink in the stone helping to imbue the figures with flesh-like tones. The incredible skill of the artisans is evident throughout, with friezes as little as 10cm wide crammed with naturalistic details of ornaments, jewellery, hairstyles and even manicured nails. To add to the beauty of the whole ensemble, the temples subtly change hue as the day progresses, passing from a warm pink at sunrise, to white at midday sun, and back to pink at sunset. Dramatic floodlights pick them out in the evening, and they glow white when the moon is out.

The sheer splendour of the temples rather overshadows **Khajuraho village**, which is crammed with hotels, restaurants and trinket shops. Still, if you stay a night or two, you'll discover a relaxed pace of life, especially in the evening when the local market and open-air restaurants create a very sociable atmosphere.

Arrival and information

The **airport** is 5km south of the main square of Khajuraho village; the new **railway** station is 2km further south; a taxi to either costs around Rs100. The **bus** stand, less than 1km southeast of the main square, is within walking distance of most hotels; alternatively a cycle rickshaw costs Rs10, an auto-rickshaw Rs15.

The **India Tourism office** is on the main square (Mon–Fri 9.30am–6pm; Ⓣ07686/272347, Ⓔgoito.khr@gmail.com). The **MP Tourism office**, in the Tourist Facilitation Centre (Mon–Sat 10am–5pm; closed 2nd and 4th Sat of the month; Ⓣ07686/274051), can book accommodation and car rental. **Money** can be changed at the State Bank of India on the main square (Mon–Fri 10.30am–4.30pm, Sat 10.30am–1.30pm); it has an **ATM** opposite Shiv Sagar lake, and there's a Union Bank ATM next to *Raja Café* (see p.384). There's a **post office** near the bus stand. **Internet access** is widely available at most hotels and along Jain Temples Road. Touts can be a pain, but the most common **hassle** for tourists is being approached by children who offer to take you to visit their school, hospital or village – a visit that ends with demands for money. There's a **Tourist Police** booth on Main Road, if you have any serious problems.

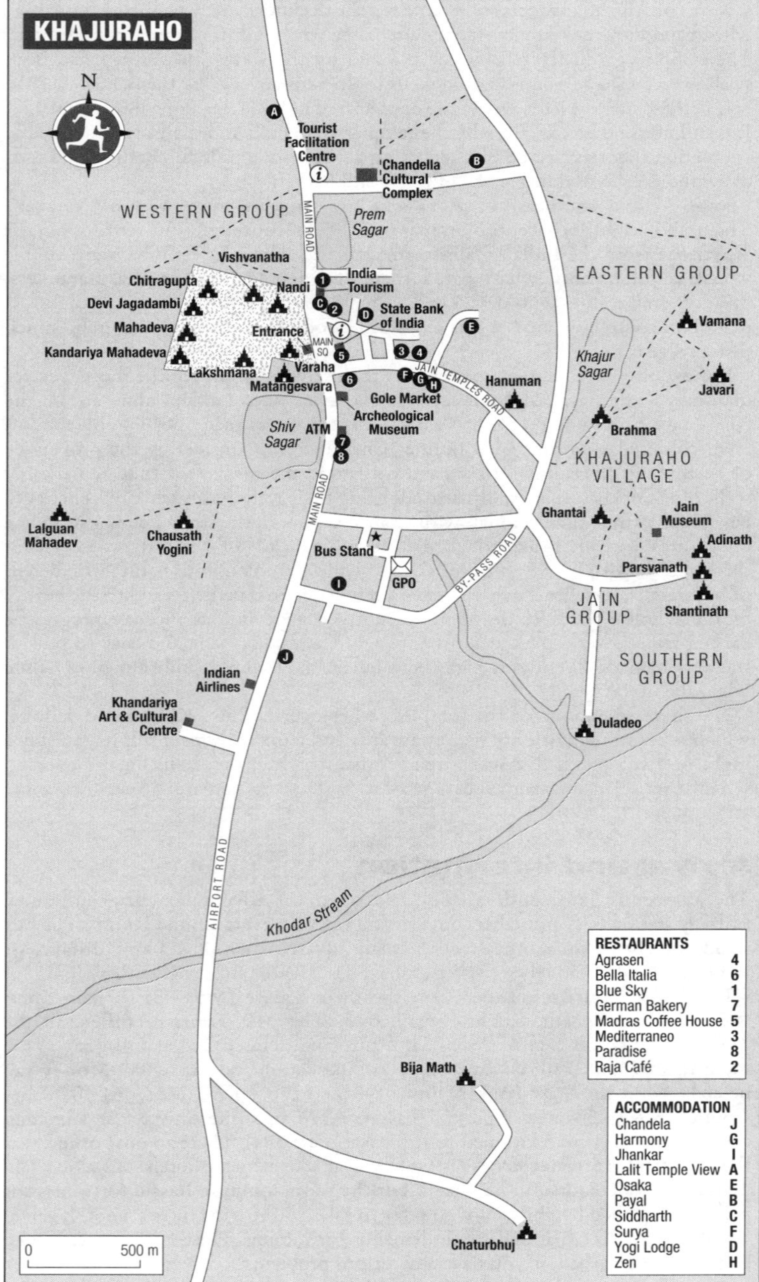
Rajnagar (5km) & Raneh Falls (20km)
KHAJURAHO
N
Tourist Facilitation Centre
Chandella Cultural Complex
WESTERN GROUP
MAIN ROAD
Prem Sagar
Vishvanatha
Chitragupta
Nandi
India Tourism
Devi Jagadambi
State Bank of India
Mahadeva
Entrance
MAIN SQ
Kandariya Mahadeva
Lakshmana
Varaha
Matangesvara
Gole Market
JAIN TEMPLES ROAD
Hanuman
Archeological Museum
Shiv Sagar
ATM
EASTERN GROUP
Vamana
Khajur Sagar
Javari
Brahma
KHAJURAHO VILLAGE
Ghantai
Jain Museum
Adinath
Parsvanath
Shantinath
Lalguan Mahadev
Chausath Yogini
Bus Stand
GPO
BY-PASS ROAD
JAIN GROUP
SOUTHERN GROUP
Indian Airlines
Khandariya Art & Cultural Centre
Duladeo
AIRPORT ROAD
Khodar Stream
Bija Math
Chaturbhuj
0
500 m
RESTAURANTS
Agrasen 4
Bella Italia 6
Blue Sky 1
German Bakery 7
Madras Coffee House 5
Mediterraneo 3
Paradise 8
Raja Café 2
ACCOMMODATION
Chandela J
Harmony G
Jhankar I
Lalit Temple View A
Osaka E
Payal B
Siddharth C
Surya F
Yogi Lodge D
Zen H
Airport (1km), Jhansi, Panna National Park & Railway Station (3km)

Moving on from Khajuraho

There are around eight daily private **buses** to **Jhansi** (4hr 30min–6hr), 174km west – the 8am departure is generally the quickest – as well as three slower public buses (5–7hr). There are regular services to **Gwalior** (7–9hr), daily buses to **Agra** (8hr) and **Bhopal** (12hr), and occasional ones to **Varanasi** (14hr).

The new **railway** station has made **Khajuraho** much more accessible. The *Khajuraho-Nizamuddin Link Express* #2447A (Mon, Wed & Sat; departs 6.15pm) travels to Jhansi (11.10pm) and Agra (2.20am) before terminating at Delhi's Nizamuddin station (5.25am). In the opposite direction, the *Nizamuddin-Khajuraho Link Express* #2448A (Tue, Fri & Sun; departs Nizamuddin 9.35pm), calls at Agra (00.20am), Jhansi 3.10am) and Khajuraho (7.50am). Tickets get booked quickly, so arrange your journey in advance. At the time of writing, there were also plans to introduce a service to **Varanasi** via Allahabad, 415km east.

Alternatively for **Varanasi**, catch one of the three daily **buses** to **Satna** (3hr 30min), 125km east, which is served by trains on the Mumbai–Varanasi–Kolkata network, as well as to **Gorakhpur**, from where buses head for the Nepal border. The daily *Kamayani Express* #1071 departs from Satna at 11.50am, arriving in Varanasi at 7.25pm. Another route to Varanasi is to take one of the regular daily buses north to Mahoba (3hr), from where the daily *Bundelkhand Express* #1107 departs at 01.08pm (9hr 42min). There are also several trains from Satna to **Jabalpur**; the most convenient is the daily *Howrah-Mumbai Mail* #2321 (departs 2.55pm; 3hr). There is a computerized **train booking office** at the bus stand (daily 9am–noon & 2–4pm), though there are plans to move it to the railway station.

Air India/Indian Airlines (ⓣ07686/274035; airport ⓣ07686/274036), Jet Airways (airport ⓣ07686/274407) and Kingfisher Airlines (ⓦwww.flykingfisher.com) each have (generally heavily booked) daily **flights** to Delhi (around Rs7500) via Varanasi (around Rs5500).

Village transport

Khajuraho is an overgrown cluster of tiny villages, and has no public **transport**, so visitors are dependent on various rentals. **Taxis** and **cars** are available at the main square, through *Raja Café* and most hotels. A taxi to Orchha costs Rs2200–2500, to Satna Rs1600–1800; ignore requests from drivers for extortionate "road tolls" and firmly agree a price first. **Cycle rickshaw** tours of all the temples cost Rs100. **Auto-rickshaws** charge Rs150 for a half-day of temple-spotting, or Rs250 for a full day. Many places rent **bikes** (Rs20–50/day), including Mohammad Bilal, on Jain Temples Road.

There are several recommended, highly experienced **guides** including: Ganga, owner of the *Harmony* hotel and a tantra expert; Mr D.S. Rajput, Mr Mama and Mr Chandel, all three of whom can be contacted through the *Raja Café*; Raghuvir Singh, who can be contacted at the Tour Aids office; and Anurag Sukla (ⓣ9425 143963). Guide rates are set by the government at Rs600 for one to five people for a half-day, Rs750 for a full day; there's a Rs225 surcharge for tours in languages other than Hindi and English for a half-day, Rs350 for a full day.

Accommodation

For travellers coming from elsewhere in Madhya Pradesh, Khajuraho's **touts** and commission system can be a shock. Avoid going into **hotels** with taxi or auto-rickshaw drivers and be firm about where you want to stay. The sheer number of hotels means competition is fierce, so standards are high in all price ranges and substantial **discounts** can be negotiated. The India Tourism office (see p.375) can organise **homestays** in nearby villages.

Chandela Airport Rd ⓣ07686/272355, ⓦwww.tajhotels.com. Sophisticated attached cottages in 11 acres of neatly tended gardens, with all the hallmarks of the Taj Group: mini-golf, tennis and croquet, fitness centre, pool (Rs300 for non-guests), coffee shop, bar and two restaurants. ❽

Harmony Jain Temples Rd ⓣ07686/274135, ⓦwww.hotelharmonyonline.com. The Mediterranean influence in the design lends an air of spaciousness to this long-established hotel, which has a range of budget and mid-range attached rooms – each airy, surgically clean and with a TV – and a bird-filled courtyard. The food's good too. ❸–❺

Jhankar By-Pass Rd ⓣ07686/274063, ⓔjhankar@mptourism.com. Away from the tourist and tout scrum near the Western Group, this well-kept, though dated, MP Tourism hotel is a big hit with Indian tourists. The clean a/c doubles are brightened up with paintings of the temples, and rates include breakfast. ❺

Lalit Temple View Main Rd ⓣ07686/272111, ⓦwww.thelalit.com. If money is no object, this is the place to stay. Sumptuous rooms (US$181–202) look out either towards the temples or the enticing pool and shaded groves of *mahua* trees. The spa treatments, however, are the real selling point and include Ayurvedic and Thai massage and reflexology. ❾

Osaka Off Jain Temples Rd ⓣ07686/272839, ⓔosaka4guest@ymail.com. A decent choice for those on a budget, this has a handful of large but faded rooms with tiled floors and private bathrooms. Rooms vary, so look at a few; some even come with ancient a/c units. Mosquitoes can be a problem here. ❶

Payal Across the fields northeast of the centre ⓣ07686/274064, ⓔpayal@mptourism.com. Also run by MP Tourism, this sleepy lodge has pleasant gardens and an inviting pool to cool off in. While the rooms, all with mini verandas and either fans or a/c, could do with a spruce up, they're certainly comfortable. ❺

Siddharth Opposite the western group temples ⓣ07686/274627, ⓔhotelsiddharth@rediffmail.com. The staff at this mid-range hotel are amiable, but the rooms feel a little tired. Still, the a/c deluxe double at the front has wonderful temple views and the rooftop restaurant produces some of the town's best Indian food. ❹–❺

Surya Jain Temples Rd ⓣ07686/274144, ⓦwww.hotelsuryakhajuraho.com. This popular and efficiently run hotel has clean and comfortable rooms, a lush garden, 24hr internet access, a book exchange, yoga and massage sessions and an alfresco eating area. ❸–❺

Yogi Lodge On a cul-de-sac between the row of shops behind *Raja Café* ⓣ07686/274158, ⓔyogi_sharm@yahoo.com. The shoestring rooms here are pretty clean and have attached bathrooms, though are still somewhat austere. But you can't argue with the price, particularly as it includes free yoga and meditation sessions. ❶

Zen Jain Temples Rd ⓣ07686/274228, ⓦwww.hotelzenkhajuraho.co.in. The Zen-influenced garden complete with lotus ponds and pet rabbit is the focal point of this lodge, which has reasonably priced attached rooms with TVs; the more expensive ones also have a/c. The on-site Italian restaurant serves great chocolate cake. ❸–❺

The Village

Facilities for visitors are concentrated in the uncluttered avenues of the small village of **Khajuraho**; the gates of the western group of temples open immediately onto its main square, which is surrounded by hotels, cafés and curio shops where you should brace yourself for some hard selling. If you aren't up to the haggling, head instead for the **Khandariya Art and Cultural Centre**, 1km south of the centre, an upmarket fixed-price emporium; in the same complex, there are evening performances of **dances** from across India (daily 7pm & 8pm; Rs350). There are also shows of traditional dances from the local area at the Tourist Facilitation Centre (daily 7pm & 8.30pm; Rs300). On the south side of the main square, the small **Archeological Museum** (daily except Fri 10am–5pm; Rs5) is principally noteworthy for a remarkable sculpture of a pot-bellied dancing Ganesh; at the time of writing there were plans to move it to a new site near *Lalit Temple View*. The **Adivart State Museum of Tribal and Folk Art** in the Chandella Cultural Complex (daily except Tues 10am–5pm; Rs50) has a small but interesting collection of paintings, sculptures and artwork by Madhya Pradesh's many tribal groups.

Khajuraho is a bustling epicentre during **Phalguna** (Feb/March), when the festival of **Maha Shivratri** draws pilgrims from all over the region to commemorate the marriage of Shiva and Parvati. It also hosts one of India's premier dance events, the **Khajuraho Festival of Dance**. Precise dates for the festival tend to be confirmed late, so check with the India Tourism authorities, and book early.

The western group

Stranded like a fleet of stone ships amid pristine lawns and flowerbeds fringed with bougainvillea, the **western group** of temples (daily sunrise to sunset; Rs250 [Rs10], camera Rs25) is Khajuraho's prime attraction. With the exception of Matangesvara, just outside the main complex, all are now virtually devoid of religious significance, and only spring back to life during Shivratri (see opposite). Visitors must remove their shoes before entering individual temples. An informative **audio tour** (Rs50 plus Rs500 deposit) is available from the temple booking office, and there's a nightly **sound-and-light** show (English show: March–Oct 7.30pm; Nov–Feb 6.30pm; 50min; Rs300 [Rs90]).

Varaha

Just inside the complex a small open *mandapa* pavilion, built between the tenth and eleventh centuries, houses a huge, highly polished sandstone image of **Vishnu** as the boar – **Varaha**. Carved in low relief on its body, 674 figures in neat rows represent the major gods and goddesses of the Hindu pantheon. Lord of the earth, water and heaven, the alert boar straddles Shesha the serpent, accompanied by what T.S. Burt (see p.380) conjectured must have been the most beautiful form of **Prithvi**, the earth goddess – all that remains are her feet, and a hand on the neck of the boar. Above the image the lotus ceiling stands out in relief.

Lakshmana

Beyond Varaha, adjacent to the Matangesvara temple across the boundary wall, the richly-carved **Lakshmana** temple, dating from around 950 AD, is the oldest of the western group. It stands on a high plinth covered with processional friezes of horses, elephants and camels, as well as soldiers, domestic scenes, musicians and dancers. Among explicit sexual images is a man sodomizing a horse, flanked by shocked female onlookers. The sheer energy of the work gives the whole temple an astounding sense of movement and vitality.

While the plinth depicts the human world, the temple itself, the *adhisthana*, brings one into contact with the celestial realm. Two tiers of carved panels decorate its exterior, with gods and goddesses attended by *apsaras*, "celestial nymphs", and figures in complicated sexual acts on the lower tier and in the recesses. Fine detail includes a magnificent dancing Ganesh on the south face, a master architect with his students on the east, and heavenly musicians and dancers.

Successive pyramidal roofs over the *mandapa* and the porch rise to a clustered tower made of identical superimposed elements. Small porches with sloping eaves project from the *mandapa* and passageway, with exquisite columns, each with eight figures, at each corner of the platform supported by superb brackets in the form of *apsaras*. The inner sanctum, the *garbha griha*, is reached through a door whose lintel shows Vishnu's consort **Lakshmi**, accompanied by **Brahma** and **Shiva**; a frieze depicts the **Navagraha**, the nine planets. Inside, the main image is of Vishnu as the triple-headed, four-armed Vaikuntha, attended by his incarnations as boar and man-lion.

Kandariya Mahadeva

Sharing a common platform with other temples in the western corner of the enclosure, the majestic **Kandariya Mahadeva** temple, built between 1025 and 1050 AD, is the largest and most imposing of the western group. A perfect consummation of the five-part design instigated in Lakshmana and Vishvanatha,

The erotic art of Khajuraho

Prurient eyes have been hypnotized by the unabashed **erotica** of Khajuraho ever since its "rediscovery" in February 1838. A young British officer of the Bengal Engineers, **T.S. Burt**, had deviated from his official itinerary when he came upon the ancient temples all but engulfed by jungle.

Frank representations of oral sex, masturbation and copulation with animals may have fitted into the mores of the tenth-century Chandellas, but, as Burt relates, were hardly calculated to meet with the approval of the upstanding officers of Queen Victoria:

I found...seven Hindoo temples, most beautifully and exquisitely carved as to workmanship, but the sculptor had at times allowed his subject to grow a little warmer than there was any absolute necessity for his doing; indeed some of the sculptures here were extremely indecent and offensive...The palki [palanquin] bearers, however, appeared to take great delight at those, to them, very agreeable novelties, which they took care to point out to all present.

Burt found the inscription on the steps of the Vishvanatha temple that enabled historians to attribute the site to the Chandellas, and to piece together their genealogy, but it was several years before Major-General Sir Alexander Cunningham produced detailed plans of Khajuraho, drawing the distinction between "western" and "eastern" groups. Cunningham thought all the sculptures "highly indecent, and most of them disgustingly obscene."

The erotic images remain the subject of a disproportionate amount of controversy and debate among academics and curious tourists alike. The task of explanation is made more difficult by the fact that even the Chandellas themselves barely mentioned the temples in their literature, and the very name "Khajuraho" may be misleading, simply taken from that of the nearby village.

Among attempts to account for the sexual content of the carvings have been suggestions of links with **Tantric** cults, which use sex as a pivotal part of worship. Some claim they were inspired by the **Kama Sutra**, and similarly intended to serve as a manual on love, while others argue the sculptures were designed to entertain the gods, diverting their wrath and thus protecting the temples against natural calamities. Alternatively, the geometric qualities of certain images have been put forward as evidence that each represents a *yantra*, a pictorial form of a mantra, for use in meditation.

The sixteen large panels depicting sexual union that appear along the northern and southern aspects of the three principal temples – Kandariya Mahadeva, Lakshmana and Vishvanatha – are mostly concerned with the junction of the male and the female elements of the temples, the *mandapa* and the *garbha griha* (the "womb"). They might therefore have been intended as a visual pun, elaborated by artistic licence.

A radical approach that ties history and architecture with living traditions has been proposed by Shobita Punja in her book *Divine Ecstasy*. Citing historic references to Khajuraho under the name of Shivpuri – the "City of Shiva" – she uses ancient Sanskrit texts to suggest that the dramatic temples and their celestial hordes represent the **marriage party of Shiva and Parvati**, taking place in a mythical landscape that stretches along the Vindhya hills to Kalinjar in the east. Thus Punja argues the lower panel on Vishvanatha's southern walls shows Shiva as a bridegroom accompanied by his faithful bull, Nandi, while the intertwined limbs of the panel above – the couple locked in *mithuna*, assisted by a maiden to either side – show the consummation, with the lustful Brahma a pot-bellied voyeur at their feet.

this Shiva temple represents the pinnacle of Chandellan art, its ornate roofs soaring dramatically to culminate 31m above the base in a *shikhara* consisting of 84 smaller replicas.

Kandariya Mahadeva is especially popular with visitors for the extraordinarily energetic and provocative erotica that ornaments its three tiers, covering almost every facet of the exterior. Admiring crowds can always be found in front of a particularly fine image of a couple locked in **mithuna** (sexual intercourse) with a maiden assisting on either side. One of Khajuraho's most familiar motifs, it seems to defy nature, with the male figure suspended upside down on his head; only when considered as if from above do the sinuous intertwined limbs begin to make sense.

An elaborate garland at the entrance to the temple, carved from a single stone, acts as a *torana*, the ritual gateway of a marriage procession. Both inside and out, lavish and intricate images of gods, goddesses, musicians and nymphs celebrate the occasion; within the sanctuary a dark passage leads to its central *shivalingam*. Niches along the exterior contain images of **Ganesh**, **Virabhadra** and the **Sapta Matrikas**, the Seven Mothers responsible for dressing the bridegroom, Shiva. Wrathful deities and fearsome protectors, the seven consist of Brahmi, a female counterpart of Shiva, seated on the swan of Brahma; a three-eyed Maheshvari on Shiva's bull Nandi; Kumari; Vaishnavi, seated on the bird Garuda; Varahi, the female form of Vishnu as the boar; Narasimhi, the female form of Vishnu as man-lion; and the terrifying Chamunda, the slayer of the *asuras* or "demons" Chanda and Munda, and the only one of the Sapta Matrikas who is not a female representation of a major male god.

Devi Jagadambi

North of Kandariya Mahadeva along the platform, the earlier **Devi Jagadambi** temple is a simpler structure, whose outer walls lack projecting balconies. Originally dedicated to Vishnu, its prominent *mandapa* is capped by a massive pyramidal roof. Three *bhandas* (belts) bind the *jangha* (body), adorned with exquisite and sensuous carvings; the erotica on the third is arguably Khajuraho's finest. Vishnu appears throughout the panels, all decorated with sinuous figures of nymphs, gods and goddesses, some in amorous embrace. Some consider the image in the temple sanctum to be a standing Parvati, others argue that it is the black goddess Kali, known here as Jagadambi.

Between Kandariya Mahadeva and Jagadambi, the remains of **Mahadeva** temple shelter a metre-high lion accompanied by a figure of indeterminate sex. Recurring throughout Khajuraho, the highly stylized lion motif, seen here rearing itself over a kneeling warrior with drawn sword, may have been an emblem of the Chandellas.

Chitragupta

Beyond the platform, and similar to its southern neighbour, Jagadambi, the heavily (and in places clumsily) restored **Chitragupta** temple is unusual in being dedicated to **Surya**, the sun god. Ornate depictions of hunting scenes, nymphs and dancing girls accompany processional friezes, while on the southern aspect a particularly vigorous ten-headed Vishnu embodies all his ten incarnations. Within the inner chamber, the fiery Surya rides a chariot driven by seven horses. The small and relatively insignificant temple in front of Chitragupta, also heavily restored and now known as **Parvati**, may originally have been a Vishnu temple, but holds an interesting image of the goddess Ganga riding on a crocodile.

Vishvanatha

Laid out along the same lines as Lakshmana, **Vishvanatha**, in the northeast corner of the enclosure – the third of the three main western group shrines – can be precisely dated to 1002 AD as the work of the ruler Dhangadeva. Unlike some other temples at Khajuraho, which may have changed their presiding deities, Vishvanatha is most definitely a Shiva temple, as confirmed by the open *mandapa* pavilion in front of the main temple, where a monolithic seated **Nandi** waits obediently. Large panels between the balconies once more show *mithuna*, with amorous couples embracing among the sensuous nymphs. Idealized representations of the female form include women in such poses as writing letters, playing music and cuddling babies. Decorative elephant motifs appear to the south of Vishvanatha, and lions guard its northern aspect.

Matangesvara

The simplicity of the **Matangesvara** temple, outside the complex gates, shows it to be one of Khajuraho's oldest structures, but although built early in the tenth century it remains in everyday use. Deep balconies project from the walls of its circular sanctuary, inside which a pillar-like *shivalingam* emerges from the pedestal yoni, the vulva – the recurring symbol of the union of Shiva. During the annual festival of Shivratri, the great wedding of Shiva and Parvati, the shrine becomes a hive of activity, drawing pilgrims for ceremonies that hark back to Khajuraho's distant past.

Chausath Yogini

Southwest of Shiv Sagar lie the remains of the curious temple of **Chausath Yogini** – the "Sixty-Four Yoginis". Dating from the ninth century, it consists of 35 small granite shrines clustered around a quadrangle; there were originally 64 shrines, with the presiding goddess's temple at the centre. Only fourteen other temples, all in northern India, are known to have been dedicated to these wrathful and bloodthirsty female attendants of the goddess Kali. Around 1km further west lie the ruins of Lalguan Mahadev, a small temple dedicated to Shiva.

The eastern group

The two separate networks of temples that make up Cunningham's **eastern group** (daily sunrise to sunset) are reached via the two forks of the road east of town. One is the tightly clustered **Jain group**, while slightly north there are a number of shrines and two larger temples, **Vamana** and **Javari**, both dating from the late eleventh century.

The temples to the north

On the north side of Jain Temples Road a more modern temple is home to a two-metre-high image of monkey god **Hanuman** that may predate all of Khajuraho's temples and shrines. As the road forks left along the eastern shore of the murky Khajur Sagar lake, at the edge of Khajuraho village, it passes the remains of a single-room temple erroneously referred to as the **Brahma** temple. It is in fact a shrine to Shiva, as demonstrated by its *chaturmukha* – "four-faced" – lingam. While the eastern and western faces carry benign expressions, and the north face bears the gentler aspect of Uma, the female manifestation of Shiva, the ferocious southern face is surrounded by images of death and destruction. Crowning the lingam is the rounded form of **Sadashiva**, Shiva the Infinite at the centre of the cosmos.

The dirt road continues to the small **Javari** temple. It may not have the exuberance seen elsewhere but nevertheless contains some fine sculpture, including nymphets in classic Khajuraho style.

The largest of the Khajuraho village temples, **Vamana**, stands alone in a field 200m further north. Erected slightly earlier than Javari, in a fully evolved

Chandella style, Vamana has a simple uncluttered *shikhara* that rises in bands covered with arch-like motifs. Figures including seductive celestial nymphs form two bands around the *jangha*, the body of the temple, while a superb doorway leads to the inner sanctum, which is dedicated to Vamana, an incarnation of Vishnu. On the way to the Jain Group, the road runs near what survives of a late tenth-century temple, known as **Ghantai** for its fine columns sporting bells (*ghantai*), garlands and other motifs.

The Jain group temples

The temple of **Parsvanath**, dominating the walled enclosure of the **Jain group**, is probably older than the main temples of Khajuraho, judging by its relatively simple ground plan. Its origins are a mystery; although officially classified as a Jain monument, it may have been a Hindu temple that was donated to the Jains, who settled here at a later date. Certainly, the animated sculpture of Khajuraho's other Hindu temples is well represented on the two horizontal bands around the walls, and the upper one is crowded with Hindu gods in intimate entanglements. Among Khajuraho's finest work, they include Brahma and his consort; a beautiful Vishnu; a rare image of the god of love, **Kama**, shown with his quiver of flower arrows embracing his consort **Rati**; and two graceful female figures. A narrow strip above the two main bands depicts celestial musicians playing cymbals, drums, stringed instruments and flutes. Inside, beyond an ornate hall, a black monolithic stone is dedicated to the Jain lord Parsvanath, inaugurated as recently as 1860 to replace an image of another *tirthankara*, Adinath.

Immediately north of Parsvanath, **Adinath**'s own temple, similar but smaller, has undergone drastic renovation. Three tiers of sculpture surround its original structure, of which only the sanctum, *shikhara* and vestibule survive; the incongruous *mandapa* is a much later addition. Inside the *garbha griha* stands the black image of the *tirthankara* Adinath himself. The huge 4.5m-high statue of the sixteenth *tirthankara*, **Shantinath**, in his newer temple, is the most important image in this working Jain complex. With its slender beehive *shikharas*, the temple attracts pilgrims from all over India, including naked sadhus.

Sculpture in the small circular **Jain Museum** (Mon–Sat 7am–6pm; Rs5), at the entrance to the Jain temples, includes stone carvings of all 24 *tirthankaras*.

The southern group

Khajuraho's **southern group** consists of three widely separated temples. The nearest to town, **Duladeo**, is down a dirt track south of the Jain Group, 1.5km from the main square. Built early in the twelfth century, Duladeo bears witness to the decline of temple architecture in the late Chandellan period, noticeable particularly in its sculpture, which lacks Khajuraho's hallmark fluidity. Nonetheless, its main hall contains some exquisite carving, and the angular rippled exterior of the main temple is unique to Khajuraho.

Across the Khodar stream and south along Airport Road, a small road leads left to the disproportionately tall, tapering **Chaturbhuj**. A forerunner to Duladeo, built around 1100 AD and bearing some resemblance to the Javari temple of the Eastern Group, Chaturbhuj is plainer than Duladeo and devoid of erotica. A remarkable image of Vishnu, however, graces its inner sanctum.

To reach the third temple, **Bija Math**, return to the cluster of houses before Chaturbhuj and take a right along the dirt track through the small village. The structure lay below a suspiciously large mound of mud until 1998, when an excavation discovered the delicately carved platform. Unfortunately, the temple itself has disintegrated into the debris of ornate sculpture lying strewn around the site.

Around Khajuraho

Around 20km northwest, the **Raneh Falls** (daily dawn–dusk; Rs150 [Rs15], guide Rs40) crash through a valley of black and pink basalt. Despite what you might be told, gharials (a reptile similar to a crocodile) are rarely seen here outside of the monsoon months, which is also when the falls are at their most spectacular. **Panna National Park** (Nov–June dawn–dusk; Rs2180 [Rs680]/jeep/safari, compulsory guide Rs150), 37km south of Khajuraho, had 24 tigers in 2006, according to official figures. In July 2009 the MP government admitted there were no longer any tigers left, blaming the shocking decline on poachers. At the time of writing, three tigers had been relocated here from other parks, but for those eager to spot any, Kanha, Bandhavgarh and Pench national parks are far better bets. Panna does, however, boast two hundred species of birds, as well as sloth bears, wolves and pythons.

Eating

Khajuraho has scores of **restaurants**, from simple and cheap rice and *sabzi* joints to sophisticated and expensive multi-cuisine and Italian places. At the top of the range, hotels like *Chandela* and *Lalit Temple View* offer fine dining for very reasonable prices. Many rooftop restaurants erroneously claim you can see the evening sound-and-light shows from their establishments – what you actually get are occasional flashes of light and muffled voices.

Agrasen Jain Temples Rd. This plant-filled roof restaurant produces the typical multi-cuisine menu (mains Rs40–120) with a bit more flair than normal: there's lots of choice for breakfast, economical thalis and set menus. The coconut lassi is a treat.

Bella Italia Jain Temples Rd. Now in a new location, with a climbing plant-covered terrace, this is a more economical alternative to *Mediterraneo* for thin crust pizzas, pastas and crepes (mains Rs125–215). In the early evening, hundreds of parrots congregate in the neighbouring trees to make an almighty racket, before settling down for the night around 8pm.

Blue Sky Main Rd. While it's a bit of a tourist trap, this rooftop restaurant offers a unique experience: a table in a (slightly precarious) treehouse – just ring the bell for service. Even if you don't have a head for heights, the thalis, Chinese and continental dishes aren't bad. The refreshing *jeevan rakshak ghol* (mineral water, lime juice, sugar and salt) is hard to beat on a hot day. Mains Rs80–150.

German Bakery Main Rd. A tiny shop-front, with a few plastic stools, a rickety table and tempting home-baked rolls, croissants, *pain au chocolat*, coconut cookies and cakes all for around Rs5–50, plus filter coffee. Those with more adventurous palates can try the Nepalese yak's milk cheese sandwiches.

Madras Coffee House Jain Temples Rd. This modest canteen, popular with locals and frugal travellers, is a great spot for an inexpensive south Indian breakfast of dosas, *vadas* and *uttapams* (Rs30–70).

Mediterraneo Jain Temples Rd ⓣ07686/272246. Authentic thin-crust pizzas from a wood-fired oven, handmade pasta, home-baked brown bread, crepes, a superb Dutch apple pie and unparalleled espressos and cappuccinos make this the top joint in town. Bookings advised. Mains Rs185–275.

Paradise Airport Rd. This roof terrace bar and restaurant overlooking Shiv Sagar lake is ideal for a sundowner with cocktails (Rs90–280), Kingfisher beer (Rs130) and Indian wine and "champagne" (Rs1200–1250 a bottle), as well as a menu of traveller classics such as banana pancakes.

Raja Café Main Square. A buzzing one-stop shop: as well as offering official guides, internet access and a bookstore, *Raja* also does a good line in continental dishes like rostis, goulash and southern fried chicken, as well as excellent Indian and Chinese options. Try the banana flambée for dessert, or settle for a cold beer. Mains Rs60–100.

Jabalpur and around

After running in tandem across an endless expanse of wheat fields and tribal villages, the main Kolkata to Mumbai road and train lines converge on eastern Madhya Pradesh's largest city. However, **JABALPUR**, 330km east of Bhopal, is only really worth visiting en route to the **Marble Rocks**, gouged by the Narmada River nearby, or to the national parks and tiger reserves, Kanha, Bandhavgarh and Pench, all half a day's journey away.

If you do have some time to kill, visit the **Rani Durgawati Museum** (daily except Mon 10am–5pm; Rs30 [Rs5], camera Rs20, video Rs50), about 2km west of the railway station, which houses a predictable assortment of ancient temple sculpture, bronze plates and seals recording regional dynastic histories, plus a better-than-expected display on the state's *adivasi* minorities. Three kilometres further west in the direction of the Marble Rocks (see p.387), the main highway skirts a large moraine of enormous granite boulders, on the top of which stand the ruins of the **Madan Mahal** – a fortress-cum-pleasure-palace built by the Gond ruler Madan Shah in 1116. Another kilometre west, you reach an impressive bridge spanning the Narmada River. Known locally as **Tilwara Ghat**, the handful of shrines near the water's edge below marks one of the sacred places where Mahatma Gandhi's ashes were scattered.

Arrival and information

The **railway station** is 2km east of the centre. An auto-rickshaw ride into town costs Rs20–30. The shambolic city **bus stand** is a short way south of the bazaar and west of Naudra Bridge, site of several cheaper hotels. The airport is 21km

Moving on from Jabalpur

Kanha National Park is most travellers' next stop after Jabalpur. Direct state **buses** leave three times daily (7am, 11am and noon, returning 6.30am, 8.30am and 12.30pm; 5–7hr) from the central bus stand for the main gate at Kisli; the first buses of the day are invariably the quickest. Buses to **Mandla**, halfway to the park, leave every half hour. **Bandhavgarh** is harder to reach: you need to catch a train (frequent; 1hr 30min) or bus (hourly; 2hr) to Murwara (also known as Katni), then travel down the Eastern Railway line to Umaria, where you can pick up a local bus to the park gate. At the time of writing, MP Tourism had plans to start regular air-conditioned buses to both Kanha and Bandhavgarh; check at the tourist office for the latest.

To get to **Khajuraho**, there are several daily **trains** to Satna (3hr), from where you can pick up direct state buses. **Varanasi** is on the main Mumbai–Kolkata line; aim for the *Varanasi Express* #2165 (Mon, Thurs and Fri; departs 9.20pm, arrives 7.05am), as the other services leave in the early hours or entail a long day journey. Daily trains from Jabalpur to Patna help travellers en route to **Nepal**. Of the five or six daily **express trains** to **Mumbai**, the *Howrah-Mumbai Mail* #2321 is the most convenient (daily; departs 6.05pm, arrives 11.25am). For **Delhi**, take the *Gondwana Express* #2411 (daily; departs 3.55pm, arrives Nizamuddin 7.20am) or the *Jabalpur-New Delhi Express* #2192 (daily; departs 5.45pm, arrives New Delhi 11.40am). For **Bhopal**, the *Vindhyachal Express* #1271 is a convenient train (daily; departs 9pm, arrives 9.25am). Pooja Travels (ⓣ0761/261 0118) is a reputable agency with **cars** (and drivers) for hire; a journey to Kanha costs around Rs2000.

Air India/Indian Airlines (airport ⓣ0761/290 4090) has six weekly **flights** to Delhi and Gwalior; Kingfisher Airlines (ⓦwww.flykingfisher.com) flies daily to Delhi. An auto-rickshaw to the airport costs around Rs300, a taxi Rs500-600.

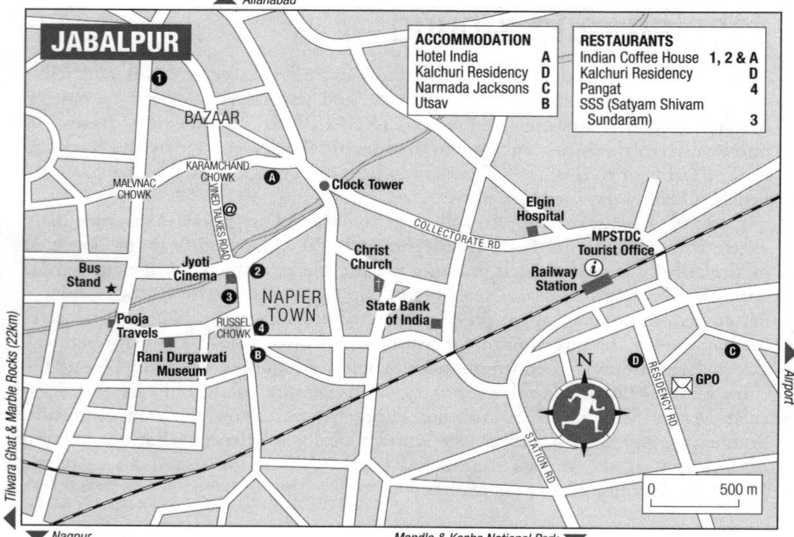

northwest of the railway station; taxis into town cost Rs500–600, auto-rickshaws Rs300. MP Tourism's **information office**, inside the main arrivals hall at the railway station (Mon–Sat 7am–7pm, Sun 7am–2pm; ⓣ0761/267 7690, ⓔjabalpur@mptourism.com), runs **boat cruises** on the Narmada River (Rs1500–Rs4000/person). The **post office** is a five-minute walk south of the railway station. If you need to **change money** (there are no exchange facilities in the reserves), you can change cash and travellers' cheques at the State Bank of India, around 1km west of the railway station, or at the *Rishi Regency* hotel opposite, which has a 24 hour exchange counter. **Cars** for day-trips around Jabalpur can be rented through the smarter hotels (around Rs1400/day). The Cyber Junction offers **internet** access (albeit in someone else's home) for Rs20/hr.

Accommodation

The majority of Jabalpur's accommodation options are within easy reach of the bus stand. Watch out for "luxury taxes" and "service charges" at the hotels.

Hotel India Near Karamchand Chowk ⓣ0761/248 0093, ⓔicwcsltdjbp@rediffmail.com. Owned by the cooperative society behind the *Indian Coffee House* chain – and run with the same quiet professionalism – this hotel has well-appointed, very clean attached rooms with TVs and phones; the more expensive ones have a/c. 24hr checkout. ❹

Kalchuri Residency Residency Rd ⓣ0761/267 8491, ⓔkalchuri@mptourism.com. MP Tourism's welcoming hotel, around the corner from the railway station, has care-worn but amply sized a/c rooms and an appealing restaurant and bar. ❺

Narmada Jacksons Civil Lines ⓣ0761/400 1122, ⓦwww.jacksons-hotel.net. Bijou 5-star heritage hotel with modern a/c attached rooms, as well as an inviting pool, Ayurvedic spa, sauna and steam room, and restaurant. ❼–❽

Utsav Russel Chowk ⓣ0761/401 7269, ⓦwww.hotelutsav.com. While *Utsav's* keenly-priced rooms are pretty grungy, their attached bathrooms, TVs and phones help to make them acceptable for a night. It's on the corner of a busy junction, so bring earplugs. 24hr checkout. ❷–❹

Eating

Outside of the better **hotels**, eating out options are limited in Jabalpur.

Indian Coffee House Bazaar district, opposite Jyoti Cinema and in *Hotel India*. The *Hotel India* branch has black and red seats, glass walls, and a (normally dry) water feature, as well as top Chinese and south and north Indian meals and snacks (Rs28–140), and filter coffee (Rs8). The two other branches aren't as smart, but the food and service are just as good.

Kalchuri *Kalchuri Residency* hotel. The usual MP Tourism menu – standard Indian and Chinese meat, fish and veg dishes (Rs50–150) – is unlikely to generate too much excitement, but this is a good place for a cold beer in the evening.

Pangat *Shikhar Palace* hotel, Russel Chowk. With orange walls and multicoloured cube-shaped lights, it's fortunate this a/c restaurant is dimly lit. The veg Indian and Chinese food, by contrast, is reassuringly straightforward (mains Rs45–90).

SSS (Satyam Shivam Sundaram) Near Jyoti Cinema, Naudra Bridge. This understated local pure-veg canteen is popular for its superior bottomless thalis, wide range of dhals and unbeatable prices (Rs28–50). The mushroom curry is particularly good.

The Marble Rocks

West of Jabalpur, the Narmada River suddenly narrows, plunges over a series of dramatic waterfalls, then squeezes through a seam of milky white marble before continuing on its westward course across the Deccan. The thirty-metre cliffs and globulous shapes worn by the water out of the rock may not exactly rank as one of the seven wonders of the natural world, but the **Marble Rocks**, known locally as Bheraghat, are a good place to while away an idle afternoon.

BHERAGHAT village itself, overlooking the gorge, is a sleepy little place, with few signs of activity beyond the ringing of chisels in the workshops of its many **marble-carvers**. Most pieces on display in the shop fronts are heavy-duty Hanumans, *shivalingams* and other deities, destined for sites around India.

From the main street, a flight of steps leads down to the river and the **ghats**, from where **rowing boats** (Rs21–31/head on a shared basis; Rs250–450 for the whole boat) ferry visitors up the gorge, although these don't run during the monsoon (July to mid-Oct). Avoid the boatmen who try and squeeze in twenty-five passengers. Once underway, the boatman begins his spiel, in Hindi, pointing out the more interesting **rock formations**. The most appreciative noises from the other passengers are not reserved for the "monkey's leap" (jumped over by Hanuman on his way to Lanka), but for the places used as Bollywood film locations. Look out for the enormous **bees' nests** dangling from the crevices in the rock. The formations are floodlit after dark.

Bheraghat is also something of a **religious site**. From the fork in the river, 107 stone steps lead up to the tenth-century **Mandapur temple**, a circular building known for the 64 beautifully carved Tantric goddesses, or Chausath Yogini, which stand in its enclosure. Beyond the temple, at the far end of the gorge, the Dhuandhar, or "Smoke Cascade" waterfall, is particularly dramatic after the monsoons.

Practicalities

Getting to Bheraghat from Jabalpur involves picking up an excruciatingly slow **tempo** (Rs15–20; 45min) from the bus stand next to the museum, an auto-rickshaw (around Rs350 return) or a taxi (around Rs650 return). If you want to **stay** the night, head for MP Tourism's pleasant *Motel Marble Rocks* (Ⓣ0761/283 0424, Ⓔmmr@mptourism.com; ④–⑤), a converted colonial bungalow just off the road out to the falls, complete with veranda, garden and easy chairs from which to enjoy the vistas. There's a small **restaurant**; service is friendly but glacially slow.

A cheaper alternative is the nearby *Hotel River View* (Ⓣ0761/290 5937, Ⓦwww.marblerock-hotelriverview.com; ❸–❹), whose smarter rooms and garden have good views of the gorge; sheets could be cleaner, however. There's also a decent vegetarian restaurant.

From Jabalpur to Kanha

From Jabalpur, the bone-shaking journey to Kanha takes you into some of eastern Madhya Pradesh's most isolated rural districts. When Captain J. Forsyth and his Bengal Lancers pushed through en route to the uncharted interior at the end of the nineteenth century, this landscape was a virtually unbroken tract of sal forest teeming with Indian bison, deer and tigers. Since then, the local Barga tribals have taken up the plough, and all but a few patches of forest clinging to the ridges of nearby hillsides have been logged, cleared for farmland or simply burned as firewood by the burgeoning populations of sharecroppers.

The only major town en route to Kanha is **MANDLA**, worth a brief pause to visit the sacred confluence of **Triveni Sangam**, at the bottom of town beyond the bazaar. If you're rushing through en route to Kanha, note that the last bus to the park departs at 4.15pm. Heading in the opposite direction, buses to Jabalpur leave every thirty minutes throughout the day. The State Bank of India exchanges cash only, and is the nearest place to Kanha with this facility.

Kanha National Park

Widely considered the greatest of India's wildlife reserves, **KANHA NATIONAL PARK** encompasses some 940 square kilometres of deciduous forest, savanna grassland, hills and gently meandering rivers – home to hundreds of species of birds and animals, including **tigers**. Despite the arduous overland haul to the park, few travellers are disappointed by its beauty, which is particularly striking at dawn. Tiger sightings are not guaranteed, but even a fleeting glimpse of one should be considered a great privilege. Moreover the wealth of other creatures and some of central India's most quintessentially Kiplingesque countryside make it a wonderful place to spend a few days.

Some history

Central portions of the Kanha Valley were designated a wildlife sanctuary in 1933. Previously, the whole area was one enormous viceregal hunting ground, its game the exclusive preserve of high-ranking British army officers and civil servants seeking trophies for their colonial bungalows. Not until the 1950s though, after a particularly voracious hunter bagged thirty tigers in a single shoot, did the government declare Kanha a bona fide national park. Kanha was one of the original participants in Indira Gandhi's **Project Tiger** (see p.1178), which helped numbers recover. The forest department claims there are around 78 tigers, but guides and naturalists say 35–40 is a more accurate estimate (for most of India's tiger reserves, halving the official figures will generally give you a more realistic idea). As part of a long-term project, the park has expanded to encompass a large protective buffer zone – a move not without its opponents among the local tribal community, who depend on the forest for food and firewood. Over the years, the authorities have had a hard time reconciling the needs of the villagers with the demands of conservation and tourism; but for the time being at least, an equitable balance seems to have been struck.

Yet serious challenges remain: in recent years **poaching** has become an issue again and traps have even been discovered in the park's "tourist zone" (the area visited on safaris). Illegal timber felling is also a problem, the buffer zone is increasingly being encroached upon and there is little effort to check the growth of new hotels. Visit the website of campaign organisation Travel Operators for Tigers (ⓦ www.toftigers.org) to find out about the role travellers can play in protecting India's tigers.

Arrival and information

The most straightforward way to **get to Kanha** is via Jabalpur, which is well connected by **rail** to most other parts of the country. If you're coming from **Orissa**, take a direct train to Katni on the main Mumbai–Kolkata line and change onto one of the many southbound services such as the *Howrah–Mumbai Mail* #2321 (daily 4.25pm; 1hr 30min) to Jabalpur, the park's nearest railhead. The nearest airports with scheduled domestic flights are at Jabalpur and Nagpur, 226km away. Daily **buses** leave Jabalpur for **Kisli** (via Mandla) at 7am, 11am and noon (5–7hr). All stop briefly at the barrier in **Khatia**, 4km down the road from Kisli. Buses back to Jabalpur leave Khatia at 6am, 8am and 1.30pm. There's also a daily bus to Nagpur (6hr 30min). A **taxi** to the park from Jabalpur should cost Rs1900–2500 one way.

Kanha is **open** (daily: winter 6.30am–noon & 3–5.45pm; summer 5–11am & 4–7pm; Rs2180 [Rs680]/vehicle with up to seven people/safari, compulsory guide Rs150/safari) from November 1 until the monsoon arrives at the end of June. During peak season (Nov–Feb), the nights and early mornings can get very **cold**, and there are frequent frosts, so bring warm clothing. The heat between March and June keeps visitor numbers down, but tiger sightings are more common then, when the cats are forced to come out to the waterholes and streams.

If you're not staying on a **Jungle Plan** package, which includes accommodation, food and safaris, you will have to hire an open-top jeep – or "gypsy" – (around Rs1500 for a morning safari and Rs1000 for an afternoon safari) to **get around the park**. These are available through most hotels, private operators in Khatia or at the main gates: try and get a group together and book at least a day in advance. Jeeps can comfortably sit four people (excluding guides/driver), although you can squeeze in eight at a push. Given the increasing popularity of Kanha – and Madhya Pradesh's other tiger reserves – vehicle restrictions may be introduced in the future. Walking inside the park is strictly forbidden due to the danger tigers pose.

Accommodation

MP Tourism has two **lodges** in **Kisli**, atmospherically situated inside the park proper, and one close to the **Mukki** gate. Private hotels outside the west gate, in and around the village of **Khatia**, range from walk-in budget lodges to five-star resorts, while those close to Mukki are high-end places; all should be booked several days in advance (and up to three months in the high season). However, at any hotel it's worth asking about discounts. The Khatia hotels are scattered along a six-kilometre stretch of road that sees very little traffic during the day, so make sure you are dropped off at the right place. To reach the Mukki hotels from Khatia, you will require your own transport. Avoid visiting during **Indian holidays** like Diwali and Holi, when hotels are packed.

Baghira Log Huts/Tourist Hostel Kisli ⓣ07649/277227, ⓔblh@mptourism.com. MP Tourism's lodge, in the core zone, has spacious a/c chalets with private bath (Rs3890–4590 per double full board; ❼–❽); nos. 1–8 overlook a meadow where animals come to graze. There's also a decent restaurant and bar. The nearby *Tourist Hostel* (ⓣ07649/277310, ⓔthk@mptourism.com), with 24 dorm beds (Rs690 full board), is a great budget choice. ❸

Kanha Safari Lodge Mukki ⓣ07636/290715, ⓔksl@mptourism.com. MP Tourism's tree-filled lodge on the quieter side of the park overlooks the river and has pristine a/c and fan rooms with blue-tiled bathrooms, kettles and (rather redundant) TVs in villa-style buildings (Rs2490–3190 per double full board), plus a restaurant and bar. ❻–❼

Kipling Camp 4km south of Khatia ⓣ07649/277218, ⓦwww.kiplingcamp.com. British-run camp in a secluded forest location offering five-star comfort, plus the company of Tara, the elephant made famous by Mark Shand's book (see p.1186). Beautiful cottages (Jungle Plan US$360 for two) have exposed wooden beams, cane chairs and private verandas, and there's a great photo-filled bar with a well-stocked library. ❾

Krishna Jungle Resort 4.5km south of Khatia ⓣ07649/277 207, ⓦwww.jungleresort.in. Established and rightly popular complex with colonial-style rooms (with tiger print chairs), pool, heavenly food and an enthusiastic manager (a wildlife expert). A small massage and spa centre was being set up at the time of writing. Room only, B&B and Jungle Plan packages available. ❼

Pugmark Resort Khatia ⓣ07649/277291 ⓔinfo@pugmarkresort.com. Cheerful turquoise and green rooms with either fans or a/c are set in overgrown gardens with a campfire at the centre. There's also an attractive restaurant, open to non-guests. It's a winding 10min walk from the main road; follow the signs. ❹–❺

Shergarh Mukki ⓣ9098 187346, ⓦwww.shergarh.com. Katie and Jehan Bhujwala run an intimate, environmentally and socially-responsible camp of luxury tents, each with a slick attached bathroom and private veranda. Outstanding service and thoughtful touches (like personal hot water bottles for chilly early morning safaris) create a wonderfully serene ambiance. The excellent chef makes use of organic produce from the camp's butterfly-filled gardens, while the small lake in the centre is home to kingfishers and cormorants. Jungle Plan US$223/person. ❾

Singinawa Mukki ⓣ07636/200031, ⓦwww.singinawa.in. Top-end lodge that combines an ecofriendly "plastic free" ethos with luxury: accommodation is in tasteful cottages (some are wheelchair accessible), 55 acres of wildlife-filled grounds, a lovely pool and the fascinating company of Nanda SJB Rana, a wildlife photographer and film-maker, and his wife Latika, a leading wildlife biologist. Jungle Plan US$634 for two. ❾

Van Vihar Khatia, 500m off the main road from Khatia Gate ⓣ07649/277241. This shoestring choice has a shocking pink colour-scheme and variable rooms that could be cleaner: the cheapest ones have squat toilets and are pretty scuzzy, but the more expensive ones are acceptable for the price. ❷–❹

The park

From the main gates, at **Kisli**, in the west, and **Mukki**, 35km away in the south, a complex network of driveable dirt tracks fans out across the park, taking in a good cross-section of its diverse terrain. Which animals you see from your open-top jeep largely depends on where your guide decides to take you. Kanha is perhaps best known for the broad sweeps of grassy rolling meadows, or **maidans**, along its river valleys, which support large concentrations of deer. The park has several different species, including the endangered "twelve-horned" **barasingha** (swamp deer), plucked from the verge of extinction in the 1960s. The ubiquitous **chital** (spotted deer – the staple diet of Kanha's tigers) congregates in especially large numbers during the rutting season in early July, when it's not uncommon to see several thousand at one time.

The **woodlands** carpeting the spurs of the Maikal Ridge that taper into the core zone from the south consist of *sal*, teak and moist deciduous forest oddly reminiscent of northern Europe. Troupes of langur monkeys crash through the canopy, while **gaur**, the world's largest wild cattle, forage through the fallen leaves; years of exposure to snap-happy humans seem to have left the awesome, hump-backed bulls impervious to camera flashes, but it's still wise to keep a safe distance. Higher up, you may catch sight of a **dhol** (wild dog) as well as porcupines, pythons, sloth bears, wild boar, mouse deer or the magnificent **sambar**. You might even spot a **leopard**, although these shy animals tend to steer well clear of vehicles. Kanha also supports an exotic and colourful array of **birds**, including Indian rollers, bee-eaters, golden orioles, paradise flycatchers, egrets, some outlandish **hornbills** and numerous kingfishers and birds of prey.

Kanha's **tigers**, though, are its biggest draw, and the jeep drivers and guides, who are well aware of this, scan the sandy tracks for pug marks and respond to the agitated alarm calls of nearby animals. Tigers are often spotted via an "elephant show" (Rs600 [Rs100]): when a tiger is spotted sleeping or sitting, visitors disembark from their jeeps to take a short elephant ride to see the big cat. Some, however, find the experience a little contrived. If you're intent on **seeing a tiger**, plan on spending three nights at the park and taking around five excursions; the cats are most often spotted lounging among camouflaging brakes of bamboo or in the tall elephant grass lining streams and waterholes.

Bandhavgarh National Park

Madhya Pradesh's second national park, **BANDHAVGARH**, tucked away in the hilly northeast of the state, has one of the highest relative densities of **tigers** of any of India's reserves and shelters some fascinating ruins. Although it's a long haul to Bandhavgarh from either Jabalpur (195km) or Khajuraho (237km), it's worth it – not only to track tigers but also, as all the accommodation is close to the park gates, to watch the array of birdlife from the comfort of your lodge.

Some history

Bandhavgarh, one of India's newer national parks, has a long history. Legend dates the construction of its hilltop **fort** to the time of the epic Ramayana (around 800 BC). Excavations of caves tunnelled into the rock below the fort have revealed inscriptions scratched into the sandstone in the first century BC, from which time Bandhavgarh served as a base for a string of dynasties, including the **Chandellas**, responsible for the Khajuraho temples. They ruled here until the **Bhagels** took over in the twelfth century, staking a claim to the region that is still held by their direct descendant, the Maharaja of Rewa. The dynasty shifted to Rewa in 1617, allowing Bandhavgarh to be slowly consumed by forest, bamboo and grasslands that provided prime hunting ground for the Rewa kings. The present maharaja ended his hunting days in 1968 when he donated the area to the state as parkland. In 1986, two more chunks of forest were added to the original core zone, giving the park a total area of 448 square kilometres.

Arrival and information

Without your own vehicle, **getting here** can be tricky. The easiest option by rail is to catch the daily overnight *Narmada Express* #8233 which goes through Indore (5pm), Bhopal (11.25pm) and Jabalpur (6.40am) to Umaria (10.42am), the nearest railhead, from where regular shared jeeps and taxis (Rs15/300) make the trip to Tala (1hr). Approaching from Khajuraho or Varanasi, make your way to **Satna** on the main train line and pick up a train straight to Umaria (there are currently no buses between Satna and Umaria). If you're coming from Delhi, the best train is the daily *Utkal Express* #8478, which leaves Delhi's Nizamuddin Station at 12.10pm, travels via Agra, Gwalior and Jhansi, and arrives in Umaria early the next day at 5.25am (going the other way, it leaves Umaria 8.46pm). Travelling by taxi from either Khajuraho or Jabalpur takes roughly five hours, and will cost upwards of Rs2500.

Bandhavgarh is **open** from November to end of June (dawn to dusk; Rs2180 [Rs680]/jeep/safari, compulsory guide Rs150/safari). For wildlife-spotting the **best time to visit** is during the hotter months between March and June, when thirsty tigers and their prey are forced out to the waterholes and the park's three perennial streams; the heat can be trying at this time, however. Visiting in the cooler months, when wildlife viewing is still good, is more comfortable.

Jeeps (Rs1000–1500/safari) can be booked at the park headquarters or through your hotel. For the serious wildlife enthusiast, there are a few very experienced **naturalists** in Tala, who can be contacted through your hotel. S.K. Tiwari of Skay's Camp (ⓣ07627/265309, ⓦwww.skayscamp.com) specializes in nature photography, and has an impressive knowledge of Indian flora and fauna.

Accommodation and eating

Most of Bandhavgarh's hotels, all of which are in and around **Tala**, cater for travellers on a higher budget, and offer Jungle Plan packages, which include accommodation, meals and two jeep safaris; there are a couple of mid-priced and budget lodges also. The only places to eat outside the hotels are the inexpensive *dhabas* on Tala's main road.

Bandhavgarh Jungle Lodge Close to the river ⓣ07627/265317, ⓦwww.welcomheritagehotels.com. Rustic (but eminently comfortable) mud walled huts with thatched roofs and brown and beige interiors, lush gardens and enthusiastic staff give this lodge plenty of character. Deer can often be seen at the nearby meadow. Jungle Plan US$439 for two. ❾

Tiger's Den Resort Umaria Rd ⓣ011/2704 9446, ⓦwww.tigerdenbandhavgarh.com. This efficient and friendly lodge has a cluster of large cottages with soothing decor and bathtubs in flower-filled gardens, plus an atmospheric wooden dining room. Jungle Plan US$319 for two. ❾

Tiger Trails 2.5km beyond Tala; book through Indian Adventures ⓣ022/2640 8742, ⓦwww.indianadventures.com. One of the best-value deals in Tala: cosy cottages have tiled roofs and exposed brickwork, while the alfresco dining room overlooks a little lake, which is great for birdwatching. Jungle Plan Rs5800 for two. ❻

Treehouse Hideaway Ketkiya Village ⓣ011/2588 9516, ⓦwww.treehousehideaway.com. Blending seamlessly into the surrounding jungle, these five stunning treehouses, made from local materials, are far removed from anything you may have played in as a child, combining top-end comforts with a sense of adventure. The camp has 21 acres of forest and even its own watering hole, which is sometimes visited by tigers. Jungle Plan US$425 for two. ❾

White Tiger Forest Lodge Umaria Rd, next to the barrier over the main road ⓣ07627/265366, ⓔwtfl@mptourism.com. MP Tourism's large complex has snug a/c and fan attached rooms (Rs2890–3890/double full board), linked by raised walkways, and a restaurant and bar. Rooms 17–21 are in bungalows with verandas overlooking the river, which attracts myriad birds and – very occasionally – tigers. ❻–❼

The park

Though there are flat grassy *maidans* in the south of the park, Bandhavgarh is predominantly rugged and hilly, with *sal* trees in the valleys, and mixed forest in the upper reaches, which shelter a diverse avian population. Bandhavgarh's headquarters and main gate are in the village of **Tala**, connected to Umaria, 32km southwest, by a road slicing through the park's narrow midriff.

On the whole, jeep safaris tend to stick to the core area where the chances of spotting a **tiger** (there are estimated to be around 35–45) are high. Deer species include gazelle, barking deer, *nilgai* (blueball) and *chital* (spotted deer). Sloth bears, porcupines, *sambar* and muntjac also hide away in the forest, while hyenas, foxes and jackals appear occasionally in the open country. If you're very fortunate, you may catch sight of an elusive leopard. Look out too for some very **exotic birds**, including red jungle fowl, white-naped woodpecker, painted spurfowl and long-billed vultures. Perhaps the most enjoyable way of viewing game is to take an **elephant ride** in the misty dawn.

The crumbling ramparts of the **fort** crown a hill in the centre of the park, 300m above the surrounding terrain. Its ramparts offer spectacular views and the best birdwatching in the park. Beneath the fort are a few modest temples, the rock-cut cells of monks and soldiers, and a massive stone Vishnu reclining on his cobra near a pool that dates from the tenth century. Tigers may be found in the area; they're more likely to stick to the lower levels, and there are no instances of people actually being harmed by tigers here or even suddenly coming across them – but the risks are real nonetheless.

Pench Tiger Reserve

Pench Tiger Reserve (Nov–July dawn to dusk; Rs2180 [Rs680]/jeep/safari, compulsory guide Rs150, elephant ride Rs600 [Rs100]) has around 20–25 tigers and sightings are relatively common. The 758-square-kilometre park, largely tropical deciduous forest, is also home to leopards, jackals, deer and 250 species of birds, and is far quieter than its more famous counterparts.

Daily buses link Jabalpur (192km; 4–5hr) and Nagpur (92km; 2hr 30min) with Khawasa, from where you can catch a shared jeep to Turia, 2km from the main gates and location of the hotels; alternatively, hire a taxi from either Jabalpur (Rs2500–3000) or Nagpur (around Rs2000).

In Turia, MP Tourism's *Kipling's Court* (Ⓣ07695/232830, Ⓔkcpench@mptourism.com; ❻–❼) offers no-nonsense lodgings in air-conditioned and fan **rooms**, plus ten great-value dorm places (Rs700). All rates include full board. *Pench Jungle Camp* (Ⓣ07695/232817, Ⓦwww.wildlife-camp-india.com; ❾), has luxury tents with wicker furniture and attached bathrooms, a handful of appealing cottages and some more traditional hotel rooms, plus a pool (Jungle Plan Rs15,000 for two).

Indore and around

The state's economic powerhouse and the biggest city in western Madhya Pradesh, **INDORE** is huge, modern and pretty dull. If you find yourself with time to kill en route to or from **Mandu**, 98km southwest, however, there are a couple of worthwhile sights. For centuries a stopover on the pilgrimage trails to Omkareshwar and Ujjain, Indore became the capital of Malhar Rao's **Holkar** dynasty in the eighteenth century. Later, Rao's daughter-in-law, **Ahilya Bai**, took over control of the state, which then stretched as far as the Ganges and the Punjab, and founded modern Indore. When she died in 1795, the state plunged into a series of bloody conflicts, which only ended in 1818 when the dynasty secured a small but rich dominion with Indore as the capital. The city expanded in the nineteenth century, fuelled by trade in cotton and opium, and the maverick Holkar maharajas remained in power until Independence. Since then it's become a major and affluent industrial hub.

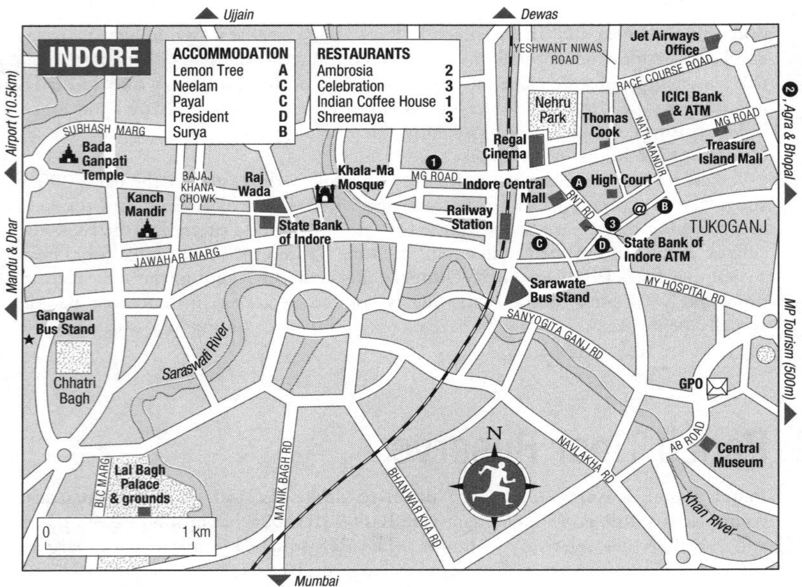

Arrival and information

The mainline railway station is in the middle of the city. The principal **bus stand**, Sarawate (☎0731/246 5688), is a short walk south from platform 1, beyond the overpass. Other buses use the Gangawal bus stand, 3km west towards the **airport**, which is 10km out of town. MP Tourism's **information** office (daily except Sun 10am–5.30pm; ☎0731/249 9566), inconveniently located on Agricultural College Rd in the east of the city, is only worth a visit if you want to take a **city tour** (daily 9am–6pm; Rs100) or catch an express air-conditioned bus to Bhopal (see below). The State Bank of Indore has a **foreign exchange** office opposite their main branch on Raj Wada, and has an ATM on RNT Road. ICICI Bank, 576 MG Rd, and Thomas Cook (Mon–Sat 9.30am–6pm; ☎0731/254 2525), Yeshwant Niwas Road, are efficient alternatives. Internet access (Rs10/hr) is available at Rimzim, in the Silver Mall, off RNT Road.

Accommodation

Most of Indore's **hotels** cater for business visitors and are scattered around the prosperous suburb of **Tukoganj**, 1km east of the railway station. Budget travellers should ignore the dire lodges opposite the bus stand, and head for the better-value low-cost hotels along **Chhoti Gwaltoli**, a lane just east of the railway station beneath the big Patel flyover. Most hotels levy a ten percent **luxury tax**.

Lemon Tree RNT Rd ☎0731/442 3232, Ⓦwww.lemontreehotels.com. With a bright yellow exterior, smart service and sleek attached rooms set around a vast atrium decorated with modern art, this is the pick of Indore's top-end hotels. There's a restaurant, café, sports bar and fitness centre, and the rooms have nice touches like kettles, ergonomic chairs and orthopaedic mattresses. 7–8

Neelam 33/2 Patel Bridge Corner ☎0731/246 6001, Ⓕ251 8774. Despite its location on a dingy alley, this friendly establishment is the best of the backpacker options. Lining a central courtyard, the compact rooms with tiny attached bathrooms (some have squat toilets) are clean and have TV, phones and tiled floors. 24hr checkout. The nearby *Hotel Payal* (☎0731/504 5151; 2) is a decent alternative. 2

Moving on from Indore

Two branches of the Western Railway connect Indore to cities in northern India. The fastest service to **Delhi**, the daily *Nizamuddin Express* #2415 (departs 4.20pm, arrives 5.40am) heads north via Ujjain, Kota and Bharatpur. The other branch, serviced by the daily *Malwa Express* #2919 (departs 12.25pm, arrives 5am next day), runs east to Bhopal, then north to Delhi on the Central Railway via Jhansi, Gwalior and Agra. For **Rajasthan**, the daily *Ranthambore Express* #2465 leaves at 6.20am, arriving in Jaipur at 4.45pm. The daily 5pm (13hr 30min) *Narmada Express* #8233 is the best train to **Jabalpur**.

There are a couple of direct daily **buses** to **Mandu** (3hr 30min–4hr) from Gangawal Bus Stand. Alternatively, take any of the frequent services to Dhar (2hr), which is connected to Mandu by buses every 30 minutes (1hr 30min–2hr). MP Tourism operates eight daily "luxury" buses to Bhopal (4hr 30mins; Rs220). **Taxis** for day-trips to Mandu, Omkareshwar or Maheshwar cost Rs1100–1400. President Travels at *Hotel President*, 163 RNT Rd (Ⓣ0731/253 3472) is a reliable **travel agent**.

There are daily **flights** to Delhi, Bhopal and Mumbai with Air India/Indian Airlines (Ⓣ0731/243 1595, airport Ⓣ0731/262 0758). Jet Airways (Ⓣ0731/262 0454) flies regularly to Mumbai, Ahmedabad and Nagpur. Kingfisher Airlines (Ⓦwww.flykingfisher.com) has flights to Mumbai, Delhi, Ahmedabad, Nagpur, Pune and Raipur. A taxi to the airport costs around Rs200, an auto-rickshaw around Rs100.

President 163 RNT Rd Ⓣ0731/252 8866, Ⓦwww.hotelpresidentindore.com. A pinkish building housing identikit – and a little soulless – a/c rooms, all with fridge and TV, a reputable in-house travel agent, rooftop café, and a motley library of potboilers in the lobby. ❻

Surya 5/5 Nath Mandir Rd Ⓣ0731/407 9111, Ⓦwww.suryaindore.com. While the rooms at this established mid-range hotel are starting to show their age, they're still comfortable, particularly those in the "executive" class. Service is good, and there's an excellent multi-cuisine restaurant and bar. ❺–❻

The City

Indore's sights lie west of the railway line, in and around the **bazaar**. Two broad thoroughfares, MG Road and Jawahar Marg, form the north and south boundaries of this cluttered and chaotic district, which is interrupted in the east by the confluence of the Saraswati and Khan rivers. The city's principal landmark is the eighteenth-century former Holkar palace of **Raj Wada**, which presides over a palm-fringed square in the heart of the city and boasts a seven-storey gateway. Most of the palace collapsed after a fire in 1984, and only the facade and a temple survive.

The Jain **Kanch Mandir** or "Mirror Temple" (daily 10am–5pm; no photography), deep in the bazaar district, is one of the city's more eccentric religious monuments; surprisingly, for a faith renowned for its austerity, the interior is decked with multicoloured glass **mosaics**. The Sarafa Bazaar, around the corner from the Mirror Temple, is good for **jewellery**. Also worth seeking out are shops on Bajaj Khana Chowk that specialize in traditional embroidered and beadwork costumes, and the atmospheric fruit and vegetable market on the riverbank beneath the lime-green **Khala-Ma mosque**.

The **Central Museum of Indore** (daily except Mon 10am–5pm; Rs30 [Rs10]) on AB Road houses Holkar-era swords, shields and armour, as well as terracotta, coins and paintings from throughout MP.

The Lal Bagh palace

On the banks of the River Khan, the **Lal Bagh Palace** (daily except Mon 10am–5pm; Rs100 [Rs5], camera Rs10) is an extravagant Neoclassical creation.

Given a limitless budget, its British designers produced a vast stately home dripping with Doric columns, gilt stucco, crystal chandeliers and replica Rococo furniture. The Lal Bagh's main entrance is via a pair of grandiose wrought-iron gates, modelled on those at Buckingham Palace. Inside, a vast array of family heirlooms is housed in the former durbar hall, banquet rooms and the ballroom. Check out the jewel-encrusted portrait of Tukoji Rao (1902–25) – the ruler responsible for completing the palace – in the billiards room. There's also a **planetarium** (Rs5).

Eating

Indore is known for **salty nibbles** called *namkeens*. The Treasure Island mall on MG Rd has *McDonalds*, *Pizza Hut* and *Baskin Robbins*, as well as a *Barista* coffee shop. There's a *Café Coffee Day* in the Indore Central mall on RNT Rd.

Ambrosia *Hotel Fortune Landmark*, Vijaynagar, 3km northeast of the city centre. The grand dining room has the air of a stately home, and the extensive Indian, Chinese and international menu (try the mutton *rogan josh*) is suitably lofty. Not quite the food of the gods, but still pretty good. Mains Rs100–300.

Celebration RNT Rd, in the annexe to the right of *Hotel Shreemaya*. A hygienic bakery and café renowned for its sweet goodies, including cavity-inducing black forest, pineapple and chocolate truffle cakes (Rs35–50/slice), as well as savoury snacks like *katchoris* (Rs12–20).

Indian Coffee House next to Rampura Building, off MG Rd. Waiters in turbans and cummerbunds serve quality veg south Indian breakfast items, north Indian meals and fine coffee (Rs10). A perfect place for a leisurely read of the newspaper. There's another branch in the Commissioner's Office compound off MG Rd. Mains Rs28–75.

Shreemaya *Hotel Shreemaya*, RNT Rd. Peach-coloured dining room with a curvy Art Deco-style ceiling, frosted glasswork and mouthwatering food: the vast chicken biriyani, *missi* roti and – if you have any space left – chocolate brownie and ice cream are not to be missed. Mains Rs90–200.

Mandu

Set against the rugged Vindhya hills, the medieval ghost-town of **MANDU**, 98km southwest of Indore, is one of central India's most atmospheric monuments. Visit at the height of the monsoons, when the rocky plateau and its steeply shelving sides are carpeted with green vegetation, and you'll understand why the Malwa sultans christened their capital **Shadiabad** – "City of Joy".

Even during the relentless heat of the dry season, the ruins are an exotic spectacle. Elegant Islamic palaces, mosques and mausoleums crumble beside large medieval reservoirs and precipitous ravines, while below, an endless vista of scorched plains and tiny villages stretches off to the horizon. Mandu can be visited as a day-trip from Indore, but you'll enjoy it more if you spend a couple of nights, giving you time not only to explore the ruins, but to witness the memorable sunsets over the Narmada Valley.

Some history

Archeological evidence suggests the remote hilltop was fortified around the sixth century AD, when it was known as Mandapa-Durga, or "Durga's hall of worship" – later corrupted to "Mandu". Four hundred years later, the site gained in strategic importance when the powerful **Paramaras** moved their capital from Ujjain to Dhar, 35km north. Yet the plateau's natural defences proved unable to withstand persistent attacks by the Muslim invaders and the fort eventually fell to the sultans of Delhi in 1305.

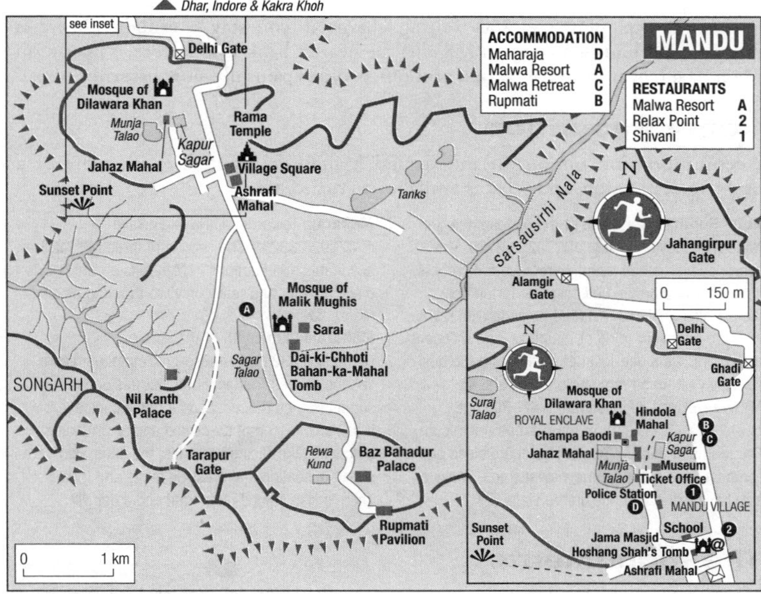

While the Sultanate was busy fending off the Mongols on their northern borders a century or so later, Malwa's Afghan governor, Dilawar Khan Ghuri, seized the chance to establish his own independent kingdom. He died after only four years on the throne, however, leaving his ambitious young son at the helm. During **Hoshang Shah**'s illustrious 27-year reign, Mandu was promoted from pleasure resort to royal capital, and acquired some of the finest Islamic monuments in Asia.

Mandu's golden age continued under the **Khaljis**, who took over from the Ghuri dynasty in 1436. Another building boom and several protracted wars later, Mandu settled down to a lengthy period of peace and prosperity under **Ghiyath Shah** (1469–1500). He amassed a harem of fifteen thousand courtesans, and a bodyguard of a thousand women, whom he accommodated in the appropriately lavish Jahaz Mahal. The sybaritic sultan was poisoned by his son shortly after his eightieth birthday. His successor, Nasir Shah, died ten years later, and Mandu, dogged by feuds and the threat of rebellion, became an easy target for the militaristic Sultan of Gujarat, who invaded in 1526. In the centuries that followed, control over the fort and its rapidly decaying monuments passed between a succession of independent rulers and the Mughals. By the time King James I's ambassador, **Sir Thomas Roe**, followed the mobile court of Emperor Jahangir here in 1617, most of the city lay in ruins, its mansions and tombs occupied by Bhil villagers whose descendents continue to scratch a living from the surrounding fields. Mandu today is a tranquil backwater that sees far fewer visitors than it deserves, save for the busloads of exuberant Indian day-trippers on weekends.

Arrival and information

Although there are a few direct private **buses** to Mandu from Indore (3hr 30min–4hr), it's often quicker to travel to Dhar and pick up the local service every 30 minutes (1hr 15min) from there. **Taxis** from Indore charge around Rs1250 for the round trip, plus a Rs250 waiting charge if you stay overnight. There is nowhere to **change money** in Mandu; the nearest bank is in Indore. Vinayak on Main Road, near the disorganised post office, offers painfully slow **internet** access.

Accommodation

Accommodation options in and around Mandu are limited, as it's more of a day-trip destination, and what is available isn't fantastic.

Hotel Rupmati North end of the plateau near the Nagar Panchayat barrier ⓣ07292/263270. The overpriced, attached rooms here have red carpets, pink walls and brown bed covers – fortunately there's also a TV and a shared veranda with ravine views to take your mind of the décor, and a decent restaurant. It's a one-kilometre hike from the bus stand, so ask to be dropped off en route. ❹

Malwa Retreat Just south of Hotel Rupmati ⓣ07292/263221, ⓔmretreatm@mptourism.com. The rooms at this MP Tourism hotel are clean and compact, with partial gorge views; some, however, also have water damage on the walls. ❺

Maharaja Towards the Royal Enclave ⓣ07292/263288. The second of three MP Tourism accommodation options in Mandu is a ramshackle piece of work and really only worth trying as a last resort. ❷

Maharaja 2km south of the square ⓣ07292/263235, ⓔmresortm@mptourism.com. Yet another MP Tourism hotel, but this one is by some distance the most comfortable choice in town. It has a collection of air-cooled and a/c cottages, both with lake-facing verandas; the latter also have separate seating and dressing areas and fridges. There's also a good restaurant and a bar. ❺

The monuments

Mandu's monuments derive from a unique school of Islamic architecture that flourished here, and at Dhar, between 1400 and 1516. The elegantly simple buildings are believed to have exerted a considerable influence on the Mughal architects responsible for the Taj Mahal. Mandu's platform, a 23-square-kilometre plateau, is separated from the body of hills to the north by the **Kakra Khoh** ("deep ravine"). A narrow causeway forms a natural bridge across the gorge, carrying the present road across and up via a series of subsidiary gates to the fort's modern entrance, beside the original, Delhi Gate.

If you don't have your own vehicle, the most pleasant way of getting around the fort and its widely dispersed monuments is by **bicycle** (Rs100/day from Malwa Resort, or half that from Ritik Bicycle Shop, near *Shivani* restaurant). Alternatively, rent an **auto-rickshaw** for a complete tour (around Rs200).

The Royal Enclave

Reached via the lane that leads west off the village square is **the Royal Enclave** (daily except Fri sunrise to sunset; Rs100 [Rs5], video Rs25). Just inside the entrance is a bookshop and a small **museum** (9am–5pm) with a modest collection of stone carvings and pottery fragments. The Royal Enclave is dominated by Ghiyath Shah's majestic **Jahaz Mahal**, or "Ship Palace". The name derives from its unusual shape and elevated situation on a narrow strip of land between two large water tanks. A rooftop terrace, crowned with four domed pavilions, overlooks **Munja Talao** lake to the west, and the square, stone-lined **Kapur Sagar** to the east. From the northern balcony, you also get a good view of the geometric sandstone bathing pools.

The next building along the lane is the **Hindola Mahal**, or "Swing Palace" – so-called because its distinctive sloping walls supposedly look as though they are swaying from side to side. The design was, in fact, purely functional, intended to buttress the graceful but heavy stone arches that support the ceiling inside. At the far end of the T-shaped assembly hall, a long stepped ramp allowed the sultan to reach the upper storey on elephant-back.

Sprawling over the northern shores of Munja Talao are the dilapidated remains of a second royal pleasure palace. The **Champa Baodi** boasts an ingeniously complex ventilation and water-supply system, which kept its dozens of subterranean chambers cool during the long Malwan summers. Immediately to the north stands the venerable **Mosque of Dilawara Khan**, dating from 1405. The chunks of Hindu temple used to build its main doorway and colonnaded hall are still very evident.

The **Hathi Pol**, or "Elephant Gate", with its pair of colossal, half-decapitated elephant guardians, was the main entrance to the Royal Enclave but is now closed. To reach the edge of the plateau and the grand **Delhi Gate** you will have to return to the bazaar and follow the road out of Mandu. Built around the same time as Dilawara Khan's mosque, this great bastion, towering over the cobbled road in five sculpted arches, is the most imposing of the twelve that stud the battlements along the fort's 45-kilometre perimeter.

The village group

Some of the fort's best-preserved buildings are clustered **around the village** (daily sunrise to sunset; Rs100 [Rs5], video Rs25). Work on the magnificent pink-sandstone mosque, the **Jama Masjid** on the west side of the main square, commenced during the reign of Hoshang Shah and took three generations to complete. Said to be modelled on the Great Mosque in Damascus, it rests on a huge raised plinth pierced by rows of tiny arched chambers – once used as cells for visiting clerics. Beyond the ornate *jali* screens and bands of blue-glazed tiles that decorate the main doorway, you emerge in the Great Courtyard, where a prayer hall at the far end is decorated with finely carved Koranic inscriptions.

Hoshang Shah's tomb (c.1440), behind the Jama Masjid, is this group's real highlight. It stands on a low plinth at the centre of a square-walled enclosure, and is crowned by a squat central dome and four small corner cupolas. Now streaked with mildew and mud washed down from the bats' nests inside its eaves, the tomb is made entirely from milky-white marble – the first of its kind in the Subcontinent. The interior is very plain, save the elaborate pierced-stone windows that illuminate Hoshang's sarcophagus.

The **Ashrafi Mahal**, or "Palace of Coins", was a theological college (madrasa) that the ruler Muhammad Shah later converted into a tomb.

Around Sagar Talao lake

Heading south from the village group en route to the Rewa Kund group, a further handful of monuments are scattered around the fields east of Sagar Talao lake. Dating from the early fifteenth century, the **Mosque of Malik Mughis** is the oldest of the bunch, once again constructed using ancient Hindu masonry; note the turquoise tiles and fine Islamic calligraphy over the main doorway. The high-walled building opposite was a *caravanserai*, where merchants and their camel trains would rest during long treks across the Subcontinent. A short way south, the octagonal tomb known as the **Dai-ki-Chhoti Bahan-ka-Mahal** looms above the surrounding fields from a raised plinth, still retaining large strips of the blue ceramic tiles that plastered most of Mandu's beautiful Afghan domes.

The Rewa Kund group

The road to the **Rewa Kund Group** (daily sunrise to sunset; Rs100 [Rs5], video Rs25) heads past herds of water buffalo grazing on the muddy foreshores of the lake, then winds its way gently through a couple of Bhil villages towards the far southern edge of the plateau; stately old baobabs line the roadside, like giant upturned root vegetables. The **Rewa Kund** itself, an old stone tank noted for its curative waters, lies 6km south of the main village. Water from it used to be pumped into the cistern in the nearby **Baz Bahadur Palace**. Bahadur, the last independent ruler of Malwa, retreated to Mandu to study music after being trounced in battle by Rani Durgavati. Legend has it that he fell in love with a Hindu singer named Rupmati, whom he enticed to his hilltop home with an exquisite palace. The couple eventually married, but did not live happily ever after. When Akbar heard of Rupmati's beauty, he dispatched an army to Mandu to capture her and the long-coveted fort. Bahadur managed to slip away, but his bride, left behind in the palace, poisoned herself rather than fall into the clutches of the attackers.

The romantic **Rupmati Pavilion**, built by Bahadur for his bride-to-be, rests on a ridge high above the Rewa Kund; beneath its lofty terrace, the plateau plunges a sheer 300m to the Narmada Valley. The view is breathtaking, especially at sunset or on a clear day.

Eating

The open-air canteen in the Royal Enclave is one of the most appealing **places to eat**, with a moderately priced menu limited to Indian veg dishes. *Shivani*, halfway between the square and the Nagar Panchayat barrier, has a broader range of north and south Indian dishes (Rs20–50), including a tasty Gujarati thali. *Relax Point* on the square offers chai, snacks and all-you-can-eat thalis. Avoid meat and *paneer*, as frequent power-cuts mean even places with refrigerators have problems keeping perishables fresh.

Ujjain

On the banks of the sacred Shirpa River, **UJJAIN**, 55km north of Indore, is one of India's seven holiest cities. Like Haridwar, Nasik and Prayag, it plays host every twelve years to the country's largest religious gathering, the **Kumbh Mela** (see p.278), which has in the past drawn an estimated thirty million pilgrims here to bathe. Outside festival times, Ujjain is great for people-watching, as pilgrims and locals alike go about their daily business. Around the main temples, you see modern Hinduism at its most kitsch, with all types of devotional paraphernalia, gaudy lighting and plastic flower garlands for sale. At the *ghats*, women flap wet saris dry, children splash in the water, and *pujaris* ply their trade beneath the rows of riverside shrines. A mini-Varanasi Ujjain is not, but the temples rising behind the *ghats* are majestic at dusk, and with the ringing of bells and incense drifting around, this atmospheric place can feel timeless.

Some history

Excavations north of Ujjain have yielded traces of settlement as far back as the eighth century BC. The ancient city was a major regional capital under the Mauryans (Ashok was once governor here), when it was known as **Avantika** and lay on the main trade route linking northern India with Mesopotamia and Egypt. According to Hindu mythology, Shiva later changed its name to **Ujjaiyini**, "He Who Conquers With Pride", to mark his victory over the demon king of Tripuri. Chandra Gupta II, renowned for his patronage of the arts, also ruled from here in the fourth and fifth centuries AD. Among the Nava Ratna, or "Nine Gems", of his court was the illustrious Sanskrit poet **Kalidasa**, whose much-loved narrative poem *Meghduta* ("Cloud Messenger") includes a lyrical evocation of the city. (**E.M. Forster** visited Ujjain in 1914, determined to get an idea of what it looked

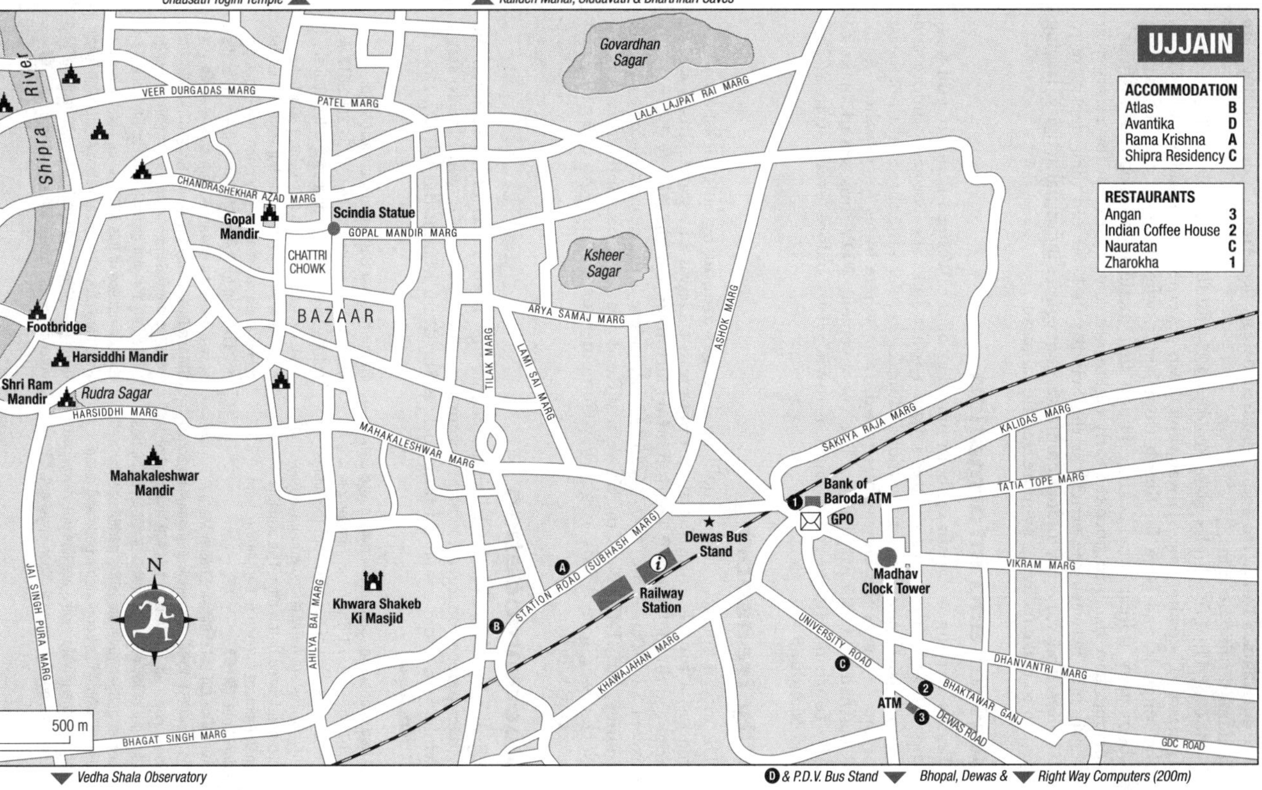
UJJAIN
ACCOMMODATION
Atlas B
Avantika D
Rama Krishna A
Shipra Residency C
RESTAURANTS
Angan 3
Indian Coffee House 2
Nauratan C
Zharokha 1
Chausath Yogini Temple
Kalideh Mahal, Siddavath & Bhartrihari Caves
Vedha Shala Observatory
D & P.D.V. Bus Stand
Bhopal, Dewas &
Right Way Computers (200m)
Govardhan Sagar
Ksheer Sagar
Shipra River
VEER DURGADAS MARG
PATEL MARG
LALA LAJPAT RAI MARG
CHANDRASHEKHAR AZAD MARG
Gopal Mandir
Scindia Statue
GOPAL MANDIR MARG
CHATTRI CHOWK
BAZAAR
ARYA SAMAJ MARG
ASHOK MARG
TILAK MARG
LAMI SAI MARG
Footbridge
Harsiddhi Mandir
Shri Ram Mandir
Rudra Sagar
Ram Ghat
HARSIDDHI MARG
MAHAKALESHWAR MARG
Mahakaleshwar Mandir
SAKHYA RAJA MARG
KALIDAS MARG
TATIA TOPE MARG
VIKRAM MARG
DHANVANTRI MARG
BHAKTAWAR GANJ
DEWAS ROAD
GDC ROAD
UNIVERSITY ROAD
KHAWAJAHAN MARG
STATION ROAD (SUBHASH MARG)
Bank of Baroda ATM
GPO
Dewas Bus Stand
Railway Station
Madhav Clock Tower
ATM
Khwara Shakeb Ki Masjid
AHILYA BAI MARG
JAI SINGH PURA MARG
BHAGAT SINGH MARG
N
0 500 m

like in Kalidasa's day. He soon admitted defeat, declaring: "Old buildings are buildings, ruins are ruins.")

Most of Ujjain's temples were razed in 1234 by Iltutmish, of the Delhi Slave Dynasty. Thereafter, the Malwan capital was governed by the sultans of Mandu, the Mughals, and **Raja Jai Singh** from Jaipur, who designed the Vedha Shala observatory (Ujjain straddles the Hindu first meridian of longitude). Ujjain's fortunes have declined since the early eighteenth century, except for a sixty-year renaissance between the arrival of the Scindias in 1750 and their departure to Gwalior. Today, nearby Indore dominates the region's industrial activity, leaving Ujjain to make its living by more traditional means.

Arrival and information

Trains arriving in Ujjain on both branches of the Western Railway pull in at the station in the town centre; Ujjain is on a link line between Indore and Bhopal, with regular intercity trains shunting between the three. Just northeast of the station is the **Dewas bus stand**, from where buses for Gwalior, Agra, Rajasthan and Bhopal depart. The inconvenient **PDV bus stand**, next to MP Tourism's *Avantika* 2km south of town, serves Indore (every 30 min; 2hr) and Mandu.

City transport

The city is spread out, so you'll need to **get around** by auto-rickshaw or by renting a **bicycle** from the shop opposite the Dewas bus stand. **Taxis** can be arranged through the MP Tourism **information** office in the railway station (daily except Sun 10am–5pm; ⓣ0734/256 1544). Indore is the nearest place to **change money**, but IDIBI Bank on University Road and State Bank of India, near the clock tower, have **ATMs**. Right Way Computers on Dewas Road offers **internet** access (Rs20/hr).

Accommodation

Ujjain's **hotels** are underwhelming, making the "luxury" tax of between ten and fifteen percent charged on most rooms even more galling. If you plan to stay a while, you could try an **ashram**, such as Shri Ram Mandir (no tel; ❶), close to Rudra Sagar.

Atlas Station Rd (Subhash Marg), Indore Gate ⓣ0734/256 0473. The hotel's hyperbole about "deluxe" is wide of the mark, but the rooms themselves are fairly priced and have reasonably clean, attached bathrooms. The amiable management is open to bargaining. 9am checkout. ❸–❹

Avantika Off Lal Bahadur Shastri Marg ⓣ0734/251 1398, ⓔavantika@mptourism.com. Also known as *Yatri Niwas*, this MP Tourism hotel, 2km out of town, has an institutional feel. The best bet for budget travellers is the partitioned dorm (Rs90), which has comfortable beds and clean sheets; the private rooms are fine but overpriced. There's a good restaurant. Noon checkout. ❹

Rama Krishna Station Rd (Subhash Marg), opposite the railway station ⓣ0734/255 3017. A notch above the other flophouses in the station area; the large but tired rooms have attached bathrooms with fairly reliable hot water. While the rooms themselves are pretty clean, the bedding is not. Look out for the "RK" sign on the roof, as it's easy to miss the entrance. 9am checkout. ❸

Shipra Residency University Rd ⓣ0734/255 1495, ⓔshirpa@mptourism.com. A tranquil, white-tiled courtyard with distinct Moorish influences is the centrepiece of this MP Tourism hotel, around which are charming a/c attached rooms with fancy quilts. Complimentary breakfast, restaurant, bar and noon checkout provide the icing on the cake. ❺

Places to eat are thin on the ground: the best option is *Cottage Garden*, an inconvenient 1km away from the fort, next to *Hotel Kumal* on the main road.

Omkareshwar

East of the main river crossing at Barwaha, the Narmada River dips southwards, sweeps north again to form a wide bend, and then forks around a two-kilometre-long wedge-shaped outcrop of sandstone. Seen from above, the island, cut by several deep ravines, bears an uncanny resemblance to the "Om" symbol. This, coupled with the presence on its sheer south-facing side of a revered *shivalingam*, has made **OMKARESHWAR**, 77km south of Indore, one of central India's most sacred Hindu sites. Since ancient times, pilgrims have flocked here for *darshan* and a holy dip in the river, but in recent years, the town's remoteness and loaded religious feel have made it a favourite with hard-core Western and Israeli dopeheads. Despite this, and the contentious Omkareshwar dam, the building of which led to the displacement of many thousands of people from nearby villages, the place manages to retain an authentic atmosphere among its temples, wayside shrines, bathing places and caves, which are strung together by an old paved pilgrims' trail.

From the bus stand at the bottom of the village on the mainland, Omkareshwar's only street runs 400m uphill to a ramshackle square, where you'll find most of the *dharamshala*s and chai shops, and a handful of stalls hawking lurid puja paraphernalia (including the excellent stylized **maps** taken home by pilgrims as souvenirs). To get to the island itself, cross the high concrete footbridge or take one of the flat-bottomed ferries that shuttle between the *ghat*s crouched at the foot of the river gorge.

The prominent white *shikhara* that soars above the **Shri Omkar Mandhata Mandir** is a relatively new addition to the dense cluster of buildings on the south side of the island. Below it, the ornate pillars in the assembly hall, or *mandapa*, are more representative of the shrine's great antiquity. Myths relating to the origins of the deity in the low-ceilinged sanctum date back to the second century BC. Another of India's twelve **jyotrilingams** ("lingams of light"), it is said by Hindus to have emerged spontaneously from the earth after a struggle between Brahma, Vishnu and Shiva.

Around the island

Traditionally, the *parikrama* (circular tour) of Omkareshwar begins at the *ghat*s below Shri Mandhata and proceeds clockwise **around the island**. The walk takes at least a couple of hours, so carry plenty of water.

The first section of the trail is a leisurely half-hour stroll from the footbridge to the pebble-strewn western tip of the island, where you'll find a small chai stall and a couple of insignificant shrines. The **Triveni Sangam**, or "Three-rivers Confluence", is an especially propitious bathing place where the Narmada River forks as it merges with the Kaveri River. From here, the path climbs above the fringe of fine white sand lining the northern shore until it reaches level ground. The ruins of the **Gaudi Somnath temple** stand in the middle of the plateau, surrounded by a sizeable collection of sculpture mounted on concrete plinths. The sanctuary houses a colossal *shivalingam*, attended by an equally huge Nandi bull. At this point, drop down a steep flight of steps to the village, or continue east towards the old fortified town that crowned the top of the island before it was ransacked by Muslims in the medieval era. Numerous chunks of temple sculpture lying discarded among the rubble include a couple of finely carved gods and goddesses, used for shade by families of langur monkeys.

After scaling the sides of a gully, the trail leads under the large ornamental archway of the **Surajkund Gate**, flanked by three-metre figures of Arjun and Bheema, two of the illustrious Pandava brothers. The tenth-century **Siddhesvara temple** stands five minutes' walk away to the south, on a patch of flat ground overlooking the river. Raised on a large plinth decorated with rampaging elephants, it has some fine *apsaras*, or celestial dancers, carved over its southern doorway.

Of the two possible routes back to the village, one takes you along the top of the plateau before dropping sharply down, via another ruined temple and the **maharaja's palace**, to the Shri Mandhata temple. The other follows a flight of steps to the riverbank, and then heads past a group of sadhus' caves to the main *ghats*.

Practicalities

Omkareshwar is connected by **bus** to Indore (3–4hr) and Maheshwar (2–3hr). Omkareshwar Road is the nearest railhead, but only slow passenger services stop here. Barwaha, on the north bank of the Narmada River, is the closest main-line railway station. There's a State Bank of Indore **ATM** and a small **post office** offering reliable poste restante on the main street.

Omkareshwar has a good range of **accommodation**. For those seeking the ascetic experience, the central *dharamshalas* in the mainland village are inexpensive (Rs50–100), and offer close-hand experience of pilgrim culture. On the down side, rooms tend to be windowless cells, with washing facilities limited to a standpipe in the yard and communal toilets. One of the best is *Jat Samaj*, facing the river, to the right of the bridge on the main square – look for the rooftop figure on horseback. Alternatively head to *Ahilya Bai*, tucked away behind the Vishnu temple off the road to Mamaleshwar temple and the *ghats*, or its neighbour, *Tirole Kunbi Patel*.

If you can't face a spell in a *dharamshala*, there are a few alternatives. The friendly *Ganesh Guest House* (Ⓣ07280/271370; ❶), near *Tirole Kunbi Patel*, has a cool traveller vibe, good views and a "foreign tourists only" policy, though very spartan rooms. *Hotel Geeta Shree* (Ⓣ07280/271560; ❸), near the main market area, has more comfortable rooms with attached baths and western toilets, though some lack external windows. The smartest option is MP Tourism's *Narmada Resort* (Ⓣ07280/271455, Ⓔomkareshwar@mptourism.com; ❹–❺), a couple of kilometres before the bus stand; it has plain, attached rooms with either air-conditioned or air coolers, and a better-than-average restaurant.

Long-stay visitors and pilgrims tend to opt for cooking their own **meals** using stoves provided by the *dharamshalas* or bought at minimal cost in the bazaar, where you can also get basic provisions. Alternatively, head to the *Ganesh Guest House's Third Eye* garden restaurant, whose veg menu (mains Rs50–120) features pizza, pasta, a sprinkling of Israeli and Indian dishes, pancakes, and some great Tibetan *momos* (steamed dumplings) and *thukpas* (soups).

6

Himachal Pradesh

* **The toy train** A rattly ride through stunning mountain scenery to the Raj-era hill station of Shimla. See p.414
* **Rewalsar** Buddhist pilgrimage site based around a sacred lake, with monasteries, temples, caves and hermitages. See p.427
* **Dharamsala** This relaxing hill station, home of the Dalai Lama, is an ever-popular place for rest, meditation retreats and trekking. See p.429
* **Dhauladhar trek** A fantastic five-day trek leading through Dhauladhar forest to the Indrahar Pass, visiting traditional villages. See p.436
* **Naggar** This quiet spot high up on the side of the Kullu Valley is a great place to relax and enjoy sweeping views. See p.449
* **Manali** Travellers en route to Ladakh chill out at this honeymoon capital, enjoying Himalayan panoramas from flower-filled gardens. See p.451
* **Spiti Valley** Tiny Tibetan villages and beautiful white *gompas* dot Spiti's astonishing, weathered landscape. See p.462
* **Manali–Leh Highway** The second-highest road in the world, passing through a vast wilderness. See p.467

▲ Prayer flags, Spiti Valley

Ruffled by the lower ridges of the Shivalik Range in the far south, cut through by the Pir Panjal and Dhauladhar ranges in the northwest, and dominated by the great Himalayas in the north and east, **HIMACHAL PRADESH** (HP) is India's most popular and easily accessible hill state. Sandwiched between the Punjab and Tibet, its lowland orchards, subtropical forests and maize fields peter out in the higher reaches where pines cling to the steep slopes of mountains whose inhospitable peaks soar in rocky crags and forbidding ice fields to heights of more than 6000m.

Together with deep gorges cut by rivers crashing down from the Himalayas, these mountains form natural boundaries between the state's separate districts. Each has its own architecture, from rock-cut shrines and *shikhara* temples to colonial mansions and Buddhist monasteries. Roads struggle against the vagaries of the climate to connect the larger settlements, which are way outnumbered by remote villages, many of which are home to semi-nomadic **Gaddi** and **Gujjar** shepherds.

An obvious way to approach the state is to head north from Delhi to the state capital, **Shimla**, beyond the lush and temperate valleys of **Sirmaur**. The former summer location of the British government, Shimla is a curious, appealing mix of grand homes, churches and chaotic bazaars, with breathtaking views. The main road **northeast** from Shimla tackles a pass just north of **Narkanda**, then follows the River Sutlej east to **Sarahan**, with its spectacular wooden temple, and enters the eastern district of **Kinnaur**, most of which is accessible only to those holding **Inner Line permits** (see below). Alpine and green in the west, Kinnaur becomes more austere and barren as it stretches east to the Tibetan plateau, its beauty enhanced by delicate timber houses, temples and fluttering prayer flags.

Another road from Shimla climbs slowly northwest to **Mandi**, a major staging post for the state. To the north is Himachal's most popular tourist spot, the **Kullu Valley**, an undulating mass of terraced fields, orchards and forests overlooked by snowy peaks. Its epicentre is the continuously expanding tourist town of **Manali** – long a favourite hangout of Western hippies – set in idyllic mountain scenery and offering trekking, whitewater rafting and relaxing hot springs in nearby

Restricted areas and Inner Line permits

Foreigners travelling between Sumdo in Spiti and Morang in Kinnaur – where the road passes within a few kilometres of Western Tibet – require **Inner Line permits**, valid for travel through the border districts. Officially you are required to travel in a group of four or more, but in practice that is never enforced – though in some places you may have to apply as part of a group.

Inner Line permits are valid for seven days and available from **Shimla**, **Manali**, **Kullu**, **Rampur**, **Kaza** and **Rekong Peo**. If travelling independently, you're best off applying at Rekong Peo (see p.423) in Kinnaur or **Kaza** (see p.464) in Spiti, where you can do the legwork yourself and obtain a permit in an hour or two, usually free. In Shimla, Manali, Kullu and Rampur officials normally insist that you can only apply as a group of four through a travel agent – who will charge a fee of Rs150 per person. It's a good idea to bring three photographs and photocopies of the relevant pages of your passport and visa with you, though in some places officials like to take these directly. Although you are unlikely to need them, make at least four photocopies of your permit should the local authorities demand to retain a copy at checkpoints along the way.

When travelling through restricted areas, you should never take photographs of military installations or sensitive sites like bridges. Stick to the main route and you should have no problems with officialdom.

Vashisht. The sacred site of **Manikaran** in the Parvati Valley also has hot sulphur-free springs.

Beyond the Rohtang Pass in the far north of Kullu district, the high-altitude desert valleys of **Lahaul and Spiti** stretch beneath massive snowcapped peaks and remote settlements with Tibetan *gompas* dotting the landscape. **Permits** are needed for travel through to Kinnaur, but **Ki**, **Kaza** and **Tabo** have unrestricted access, as does the road through Lahaul to Leh in Ladakh.

Visitors to the densely populated **Kangra Valley** west of Manali invariably make a beeline for **Dharamsala**, whose large community of Tibetan exiles includes the Dalai Lama himself. Trekking paths lead north from here across the treacherous passes of the Dhauladhar mountains into the **Chamba Valley**.

Finding guides and porters for **treks** is rarely difficult. The season runs from July to late November in the west, and to late October in the north and east. In **winter**, all but the far south of the state lies beneath a thick blanket of snow. The region north of Manali is accessible only from late June to early October when the roads are clear. Even in **summer**, when the days are hot and the sun strong, northern Himachal is beset with cold nights.

Some history

The earliest known inhabitants of the area now known as Himachal Pradesh were the **Dasas**, who entered the hills from the Gangetic plain between the third and second millennium BC. By 2000 BC the Dasas had been joined by the **Aryans**, and a number of tribal republics, known as *janapadas*, began to emerge in geographically separate regions, where they fostered separate cultural traditions. The terrain made it impossible for one ruler to hold sway over the whole region, though by 550 AD Hindu Rajput families had gained supremacy over the northwestern districts of Brahmour and Chamba, just two of the many princely states created between the sixth and sixteenth centuries. Of these, the most powerful was **Kangra**, where the Katoch Rajputs held off various attacks before finally falling to the Mughals in the sixteenth century.

During the medieval era, **Lahaul and Spiti** remained aloof, governed not by Rajputs, but by the Jos of Tibetan origin, who introduced Tibetan customs and architecture. After a period of submission to Ladakh, Lahaul and Spiti came under the rajas of **Kullu**, a central princely state that reached its apogee in the seventeenth century. Further south, the region around **Shimla** and **Sirmaur** was divided into over thirty independently governed *thakurais*. In the late seventeenth century, the newly empowered **Sikh** community, based at **Paonta Sahib** (Sirmaur), added to the threat already posed by the Mughals. By the eighteenth century, under **Maharaja Ranjit Singh**, the Sikhs had gained strongholds in much of western Himachal, and considerable power in both Kullu and Spiti.

Battling against Sikh expansion, Amar Singh Tapur, the leader of the **Gurkha** army, consolidated Nepalese dominion in the southern Shimla hill states. The *thakurai* chiefs turned to the **British** for help, and forced the last of the Gurkhas back into Nepal in 1815. Predictably, the British assumed power over the south, thus tempting the Sikhs to battle in the **Anglo-Sikh War**. With the signing of a treaty in 1846 the British annexed most of the south and west of the state, and in 1864 pronounced Shimla the summer government headquarters.

After Independence, the regions bordering present-day Punjab were integrated and named Himachal Pradesh ("Himalayan Provinces"). In 1956 HP was recognized as a Union Territory and ten years later the modern state was formed, with Shimla as its capital. Despite being a political unity, Himachal Pradesh is culturally very diverse. With more than ninety percent of the population living outside the main towns, and many areas remaining totally isolated during the long winter

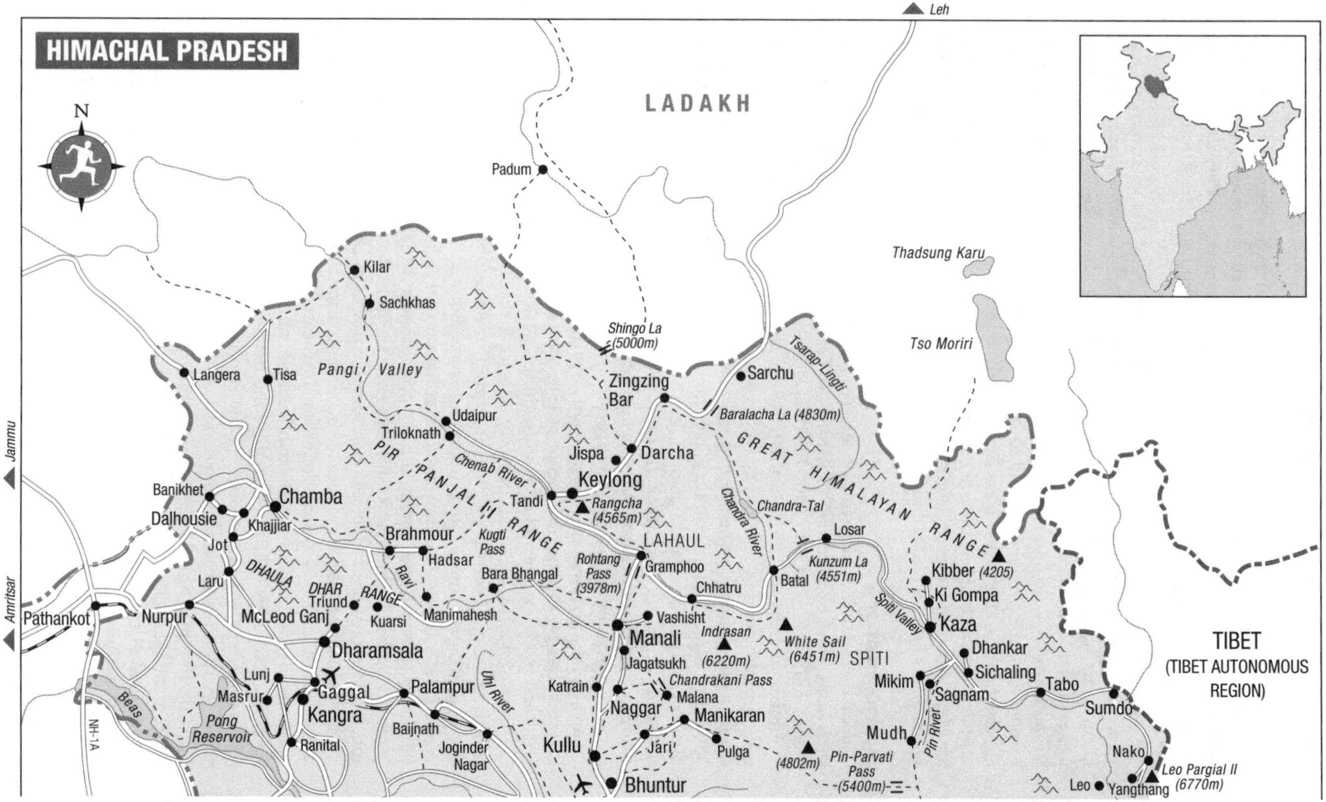

HIMACHAL PRADESH

N
LADAKH
Leh
Padum
Thadsung Karu
Tso Moriri
Shingo La (5000m)
Zingzing Bar
Sarchu
Tsarap-Lingti
Baralacha La (4830m)
GREAT HIMALAYAN RANGE
Kilar
Sachkhas
Pangi Valley
Langera
Tisa
Udaipur
Triloknath
PIR PANJAL RANGE
Chenab River
Jispa
Darcha
Keylong
Tandi
Rangcha (4565m)
Chandra River
Chandra-Tal
Losar
Kunzum La (4551m)
Batal
Kibber (4205)
Ki Gompa
Kaza
Spiti Valley
Dhankar
Sichaling
Tabo
Sumdo
Nako
Leo Pargial II (6770m)
Leo
Yangthang
TIBET
(TIBET AUTONOMOUS REGION)
Banikhet
Dalhousie
Chamba
Khajjiar
Jot
Brahmour
Hadsar
Kugti Pass
Rohtang Pass (3978m)
LAHAUL
Gramphoo
Chhatru
Laru
DHAULA DHAR RANGE
Triund
Ravi
Bara Bhangal
Manimahesh
Kuarsi
Pathankot
Nurpur
McLeod Ganj
Dharamsala
Vashisht
Manali
Indrasan (6220m)
White Sail (6451m)
SPITI
Mikim
Sagnam
Pin River
Mudh
Jagatsukh
Chandrakani Pass
Malana
Lunj
Masrur
Gaggal
Kangra
Palampur
Uhl River
Katrain
Naggar
Manikaran
Beas
Pong Reservoir
Ranital
Baijnath
Joginder Nagar
Kullu
Jari
Pulga
(4802m)
Pin-Parvati Pass (5400m)
Bhuntur
NH-1A
Jammu
Amritsar

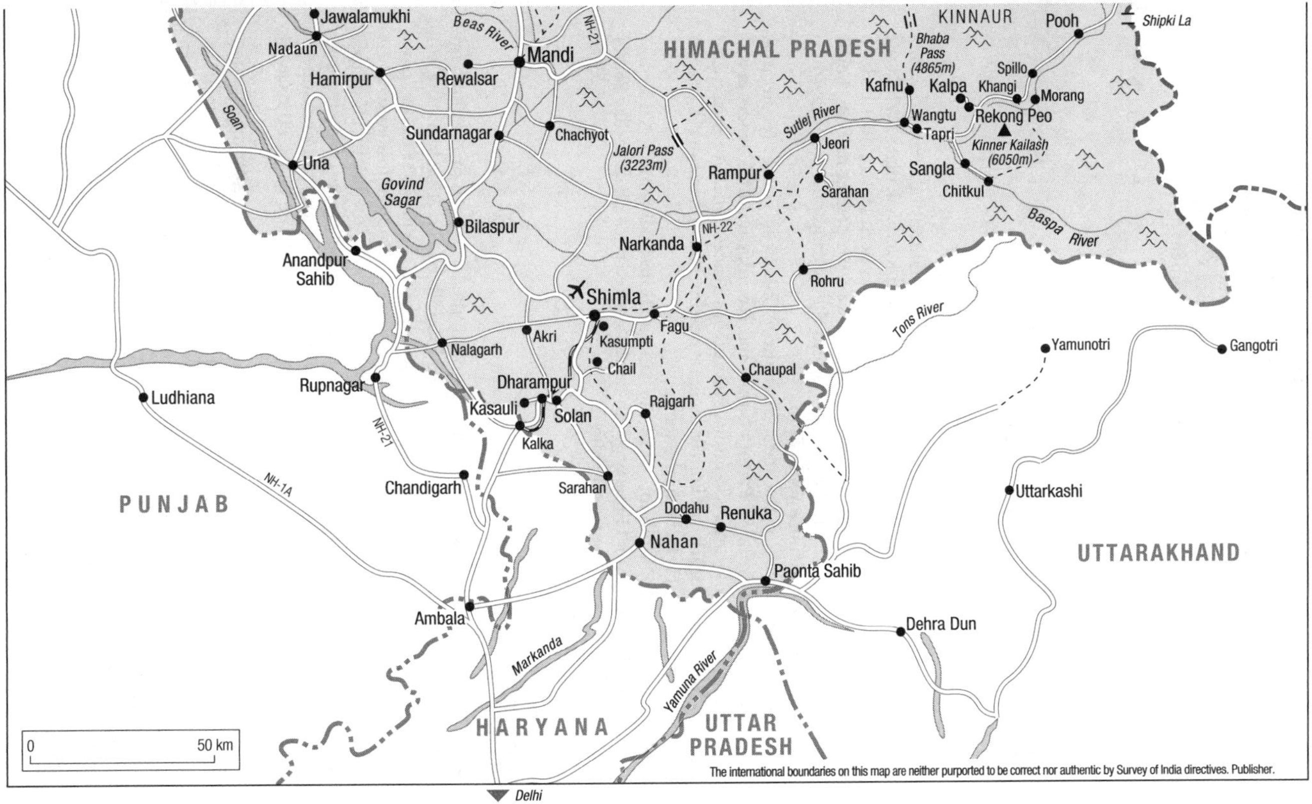

HIMACHAL PRADESH
KINNAUR
Shipki La
Pooh
Spillo
Khangi
Morang
Kalpa
Rekong Peo
Kafnu
Bhaba Pass (4865m)
Wangtu
Tapri
Kinner Kailash (6050m)
Sangla
Chitkul
Baspa River
Sutlej River
Jeori
Sarahan
Rampur
Rohru
Tons River
NH-22
Narkanda
Jalori Pass (3223m)
Chachyot
Jawalamukhi
Nadaun
Beas River
Mandi
NH-21
Hamirpur
Rewalsar
Sundarnagar
Soan
Una
Govind Sagar
Bilaspur
Anandpur Sahib
Shimla
Fagu
Kasumpti
Chail
Akri
Nalagarh
Chaupal
Rajgarh
Dharampur
Kasauli
Solan
Kalka
Rupnagar
NH-21
Ludhiana
NH-1A
Chandigarh
Sarahan
Dodahu
Renuka
Nahan
Paonta Sahib
Ambala
Markanda
Yamuna River
Dehra Dun
Yamunotri
Gangotri
Uttarkashi
UTTARAKHAND
PUNJAB
HARYANA
UTTAR PRADESH
0 50 km
Delhi

The international boundaries on this map are neither purported to be correct nor authentic by Survey of India directives. Publisher.

months, Himachal's separate districts maintain distinct customs, architecture, dress and agricultural methods. Though Hinduism dominates, there are substantial numbers of Sikhs, Muslims and Christians, and Lahaul, Spiti and Kinnaur have been home to Tibetan Buddhists since the tenth century. This may explain why the state is usually a **stronghold** for the more inclusive Congress Party, although recent years have seen the BJP control the state government.

Shimla and around

Shimla, Himachal's capital, is India's largest and most famous hill-station, where much of the action in Rudyard Kipling's colonial classic *Kim* took place. While the city is a favourite spot for Indian families and honeymooners, its size does little to win it popularity among Western tourists. It is however, a perfect halfway house between the plains and the Kullu Valley. It's also the starting post for forays into the remoter regions of Kinnaur and Spiti.

The southernmost area of the state, **Sirmaur**, is Himachal's most fertile area, with the major Sikh shrine in **Paonta Sahib** and **Renuka wildlife sanctuary** as noteworthy sights. Southeast of Shimla, **Kasauli** is a peaceful place to break your journey from Chandigarh in Punjab, whilst nearby **Nalagarh Fort** has been converted into the finest hotel in the state.

Northeast of Shimla, **Sarahan**, site of the famous **Bhimakali temple**, set against a backdrop of the majestic Himalayas, can be visited in a two- or three-day round trip from Shimla, or en route to Kinnaur.

Shimla

Whether you travel by road or rail from the south, the last stretch of the climb up to **SHIMLA** seems interminable. Deep in the foothills of the Himalayas, the hill station is approached via a sinuous route that winds from the plains at Kalka across nearly 100km of precipitous river valleys, pine forests, and mountainsides swathed in maize terraces and apple orchards. It's not hard to see why the British chose this inaccessible site as their summer capital. At an altitude of 2159m, the crescent-shaped ridge over which it spills is blessed with perennially cool air and superb **panoramas** across verdant country to the snowy peaks of the Great Himalayan range.

Named after its patron goddess, Shamla Devi (a manifestation of Kali), the tiny village that stood on this spot was "discovered" by a team of British surveyors in 1817. Glowing reports of its beauty and climate gradually filtered to the imperial capital, Calcutta, and within two decades the settlement had become the Subcontinent's most fashionable summer resort. The annual migration was finally rubber-stamped in 1864, when Shimla – by now an elegant town of mansions, churches and cricket pitches – was declared the Government of India's official hot-season HQ. With the completion of the **Kalka–Shimla Railway** in 1903, Shimla lay only two days by train from Delhi. Its growth continued after Independence, especially after becoming state capital of Himachal Pradesh in 1966.

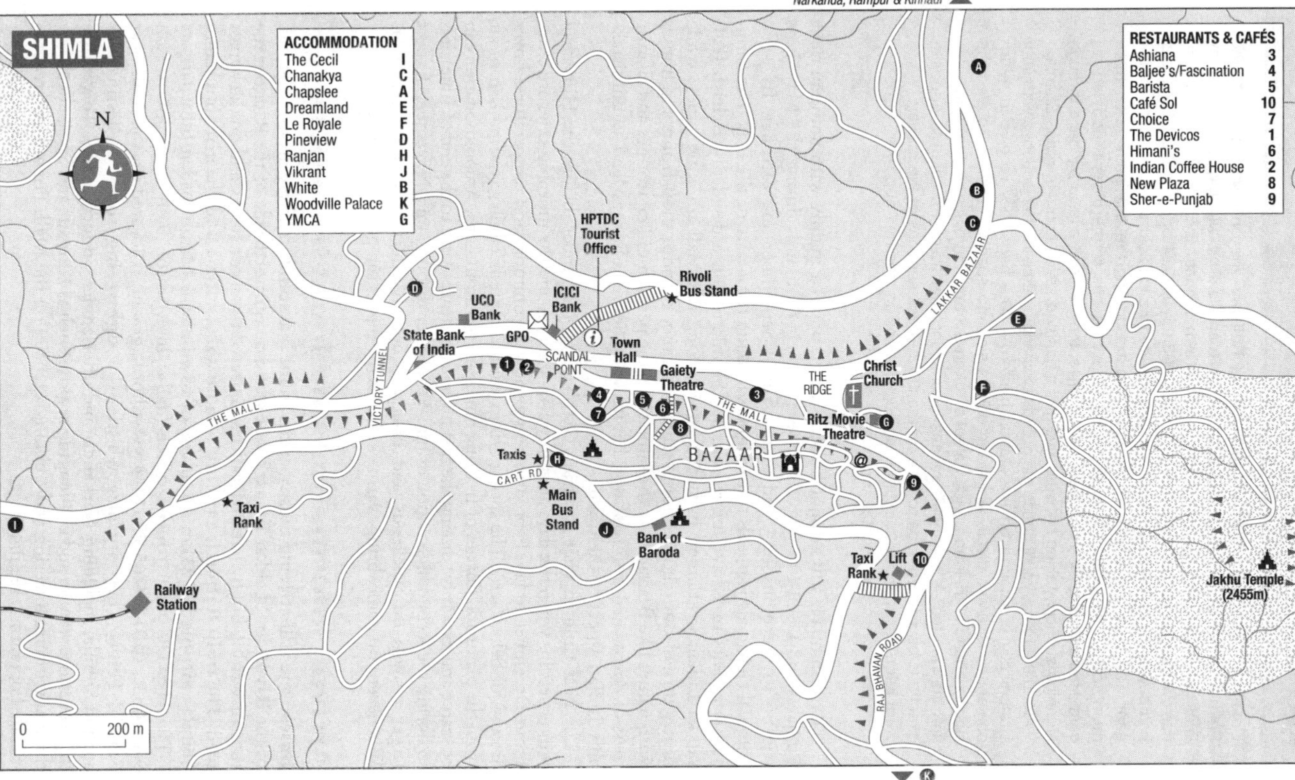
SHIMLA
N
ACCOMMODATION
The Cecil I
Chanakya C
Chapslee A
Dreamland E
Le Royale F
Pineview D
Ranjan H
Vikrant J
White B
Woodville Palace K
YMCA G
RESTAURANTS & CAFÉS
Ashiana 3
Baljee's/Fascination 4
Barista 5
Café Sol 10
Choice 7
The Devicos 1
Himani's 6
Indian Coffee House 2
New Plaza 8
Sher-e-Punjab 9
Narkanda, Rampur & Kinnaur
Kufri
Museum & Viceregal Lodge
Chandigarh, Delhi & Airport (21km)
HPTDC Tourist Office
Rivoli Bus Stand
ICICI Bank
UCO Bank
GPO
State Bank of India
Scandal Point
Town Hall
Gaiety Theatre
The Ridge
Christ Church
Ritz Movie Theatre
Lakkar Bazaar
The Mall
Victory Tunnel
Bazaar
Taxis
Cart Rd
Main Bus Stand
Bank of Baroda
Taxi Rank
Lift
Raj Bhavan Road
Railway Station
Jakhu Temple (2455m)
0
200 m

The Viceroy's toy train

Until the construction of the **Kalka–Shimla Railway**, the only way to get to the Shimla hill station was on the so-called **Cart Road** – a slow, winding trail trodden by lines of long-suffering porters and horse-drawn tongas. By the time the 96-km narrow-gauge line was completed in 1903, 103 tunnels, 24 bridges and 18 stations had been built between Shimla and the railhead at Kalka, 26km northeast of Chandigarh. These days, buses may be quicker, but a ride on the "toy train" is far more memorable – especially if you travel first-class, in one of the glass-windowed rail cars. Hauled along by a tiny diesel locomotive, they rattle at a leisurely pace through stunning scenery, taking between five and a half and seven hours to reach Shimla.

Along the route, you'll notice the guards exchanging little leather pouches with staff strategically positioned on the station platforms. The bags they receive in return contain small brass discs, which the drivers slot into special machines to alert the signals ahead of their approach. "**Neal's Token System**", in place since the line was first inaugurated, is a fail-safe means of ensuring that trains travelling in opposite directions never meet face to face on the single-track sections of the railway.

For information about train times and ticket booking, see box opposite.

Today, Shimla is still a major holiday resort, popular mainly with nouveau riche Punjabis and Delhi-ites who flock here in their thousands during the May–June run-up to the monsoons, and then again in September and October. Its jaded colonial charm also appeals to foreigners looking for a taste of the Raj. The *burra-* and *memsahibs* may have moved on, but Shimla retains a decidedly **British feel**: pukka Indian gentlemen in tweeds stroll along the Mall smoking pipes, while neatly turned-out schoolchildren scuttle past mock-Tudor shop-fronts and houses with names like Braeside. At the same time, the pesky monkey troupes and chaotic mass of corrugated iron rooftops that make up Shimla's **bazaar** lend an unmistakably Indian aspect to the town.

The **best time to visit** is during October and November, before the Himachali winter sets in, when the days are still warm and dry, and the morning skies are clear. From December to late February, heavy snow is common, and temperatures hover around, or below zero. The spring brings with it unpredictability: warm blasts of air from the plains and flurries of freezing rain from the mountains. Accommodation can be scarce and expensive during the first high season (mid-April to the end of June), less so during the second high season of mid-September through mid-November. Expect larger crowds on weekends and holidays, notably Christmas and New Year. Whenever you come, bring warm clothes as the nights can get surprisingly chilly.

Arrival, information and local transport

Buses were still arriving mostly at the **main bus stand**, halfway around the hill, or the **Rivoli** (or "Lakkar Bazaar") **bus stand** on the north side of the Ridge at the time of writing but by late 2010 all are expected to serve a new stand on the bypass road. The **train station** is a twenty-minute walk southwest of the main bus stand. Shimla's **airport** lies 21km southwest of town on the Mandi road at Jubarhati.

The HPTDC main **tourist office** (daily: high season 9am–8pm; low season 9am–6pm; ⓣ0177/265 2561, ⓦwww.hptdc.gov.in) is located on the Mall near Scandal Point. They organize whistle-stop **sightseeing tours** to destinations around Shimla, including Narkanda, and offer advice on local walks. To venture into the more remote and challenging regions such as Kinnaur and Spiti, check out the many mountaineering and trekking agencies on the Mall. For a list of recommended operators, see p.418.

Moving on from Shimla

The **toy train** leaves Shimla for **Kalka**, where you can change onto the main broad-gauge line for **Chandigarh** and **Delhi**. The 10.30am departure gets you into Kalka in good time to catch either the *Himalayan Queen* #4096 at 4.50pm or the faster *Shatabdi Express* #2012 at 5.45pm, both arriving in Delhi around 10pm. The other toy train services depart at 8.30am, 2.25pm, 4.15pm, 5.40pm and 6.15pm; they should take around 5hr each, though it's often longer. **Reservations** for onward journeys from Kalka can be made at Shimla Station (Ⓣ0177/265 2915, enquiries Ⓣ131). Alternatively, you can catch a bus to Chandigarh and continue to Delhi by train from there.

There are regular **buses** to Chandigarh (every 15min; 4hr), Delhi (hourly; 10hr), Mandi (8 daily; 5hr), Kullu (8 daily 7–8hr), Dharamsala (4 daily; 10hr), Manali (8 daily; 8–9hr), Rampur (hourly; 6hr), Sarahan (2 daily; 7–8hr) and Rekong Peo (6 daily; 9–10hr). Passengers for **Manali** or **Delhi** can choose between luxury a/c, deluxe non-a/c, or Himachal's standard bone-shaking state buses. Tickets for the former two should be booked a day in advance at travel agents on the Mall, while state bus tickets can be reserved at the ticket counter (Mon–Sat 10am–4.30pm) outside the HPTDC tourist office near Scandal Point or at the bus stand. For **Chandigarh**, services are so frequent there's no need to book.

Flights on small aircraft from Shimla to Delhi (1hr 15min) are operated once daily at noon by Kingfisher, whose prices vary wildly with demand. Tickets are available from various agents along The Mall.

Wherever you arrive in Shimla, you'll be mobbed by **porters**. Most of the town is pedestrianized, and seriously steep, so you may be glad of the extra help to carry your gear, but bear in mind that most porters double as touts and demand a commission which will increase the cost of your room.

Taxis are the best way to get to the pricier hotels on the outskirts. The main Vishal Himachal Taxi Union rank (Ⓣ0177/265 7645) is 1km east of the bus stand, at the bottom of the **lift** (Rs7 each way) that connects the east end of Cart Road with the Mall. The list of set fares they publish applies to high season; at other times, you should be able to negotiate discounts. Another, more central, taxi rank can be found just above the main bus stand on Cart Road.

Accommodation

Most travellers only spend a couple of nights in Shimla – just long enough to see the sights and to book an onward ticket. There's little to detain you any longer, and **accommodation** is costlier than average. In May and June prices soar and it's essential to book in advance. At other times, it may be possible to negotiate a discount of up to fifty percent.

The Cecil The Mall Ⓣ0177/280 4848, Ⓦwww.oberoihotels.com. Raj-era building, frequented by Rudyard Kipling among others, bought and revamped by the Oberoi group in 1939. It is now opulent but devoid of character, with little but the facade as a reminder of its past. Rooms from Rs14,000, suites a whopping Rs30,000. ⑨

Chanakya Lakkar Bazaar Ⓣ0177/265 4465. Cosy, clean and friendly. The cheaper rooms are small but good value, especially off-season when rates drop sharply. ③

Chapslee Lakkar Bazaar Ⓣ0177/280 2542, Ⓦwww.chapslee.com. Exclusive, beautiful old manor house set in its own grounds on the edge of town and stuffed with antiques. Five luxurious suites, one single room, plus a library, card room, tennis court and croquet lawn. Rs12,500–15,500 half-board. ⑨

Dreamland The Ridge, above the church Ⓣ0177/265 3005, Ⓦwww.hoteldreamlandshimla.com. Excellent value during the low season; all rooms are clean, with hot showers and Star TV.

Cheaper rooms have squat toilets, the pricier rooms fantastic views over to the Himalayas. Pleasant restaurant on the top floor and internet access. ②–④

Le Royale Jakhoo Rd ⓣ0177/265 1002, ⓔle_royale@hotmail.com. Great views in all directions from high above the Ridge and a variety of deluxe rooms, all with nice furnishings. ⑤–⑦

Pineview Mythe Estate, on the far side of the Victory tunnel ⓣ0177/265 8604, ⓔpineview shimla@gmail.com. A good location in an apple orchard facing north, with a wide choice of comfortable attached rooms. ④–⑤

Ranjan Just above the main bus stand ⓣ0177/265 2818. Originally built in 1907, this large white building is showing its age. The attached rooms are large and basic, with some original fittings and a sunny balcony. Good if you can't face the climb with your bags from the bus stand. ③

Vikrant Cart Rd, near the bus stand ⓣ0177/265 3602. Large hotel with clean doubles and some singles. The cheaper ones have a common bathroom with hot bucket water. There's also a dorm (Rs250). ④

White Lakkar Bazaar ⓣ0177/265 5276, ⓦwww .hotelwhiteshimla.com. Well-managed hotel with light rooms overlooking the Himalayas. Cleanliness can vary. The deluxe suite (Rs1700) is excellent. Fixed prices all year. ④

Woodville Palace Raj Bhavan Rd ⓣ0177/262 3919, ⓦwww.woodvillepalacehotel.com. Twenty mintues' walk south from Christ Church, this elegant 1930s mansion lies on the peaceful western side of town, with huge rooms, period furniture, lawns and a badminton court. Members of Shimla's former royal family still live upstairs. The showpiece Royal Suite goes for Rs11,000. ⑧–⑨

YMCA The Ridge. Take the steps to the left of the Ritz movie theatre ⓣ0177/265 0021, ⓔymcashimla@yahoo.co.in. Large rooms, including seven attached. In-house dining hall (breakfast is included) and sun-terrace, along with Star TV, snooker tables, weights, table tennis and internet café; low-season rates negotiable. ②–④

The Town

Although Shimla and its satellite districts sprawl over the flanks of five or more hills, the centre is fairly compact, on and immediately beneath a shoulder of high ground known as "**the Ridge**". Shimla's busy social scene revolves around the broad and breezy piazza that straddles the Ridge, overlooking rippling foothills with the jagged white peaks of the Pir Panjal and Great Himalayan ranges on the horizon. A true geographic divider, it is said all water that drains off the north side ends up in the Arabian Sea, while from the south side it ends up in the Bay of Bengal. During high season the Ridge is a hive of activity, with entertainment provided by brass bands, pony rides and a giant screen showing sporting events. The Victorian Gothic spire of **Christ Church** is Shimla's most prominent landmark. The **stained-glass windows**, the finest in British India, depict (from left to right) Faith, Hope, Charity, Fortitude, Patience and Humility. At the other end of the Ridge, **Scandal Point** is the focus of Shimla's famous mid-afternoon meet when crowds gather here to gossip.

From the Ridge, a tangle of roads and lanes tumbles down in stages, each layer connected to the next by stone steps. **The Mall**, the main pedestrian thoroughfare, curves around the south slope of the hill. Flanked by a long row of unmistakably British half-timbered buildings, Shimla's main shopping street was, until World War I, strictly out-of-bounds to all "natives" except royalty and rickshaw-pullers. These days, rickshaws, man-powered or otherwise, are banned and non-Indian faces are in the minority. The quintessentially colonial **Gaiety Theatre** was renovated in 2008 and puts on regular performances.

Walk down any of the narrow lanes leading off the Mall, and you're plunged into a warren of twisting backstreets. Shimla's **bazaar** is the hill station at its most vibrant – a maze of dishevelled shacks, brightly lit stalls and minarets, cascading in a clutter of corrugated iron to the edge of Cart Road. Apart from being a good place to shop for authentic souvenirs, this is also one of the few areas of town that feels Himalayan: multicoloured Kullu caps (*topis*) bob about in the crowd, alongside the odd Lahauli, Kinnauri or Tibetan face.

The hike to Jakhu Temple

The early-morning hike up to **Jakhu**, or "Monkey", **Temple** is something of a tradition in Shimla. The top of the hill (2455m) on which it stands offers a superb panorama of the Himalayas – particularly breathtaking before the cloud gathers later in the day. The relentlessly steep climb takes twenty to forty minutes – or you could arrange a horse. The path starts just left of Christ Church; during the season, all you need do is follow the crowds.

After the hard walk up, the temple itself, a red-and-yellow-brick affair crammed with fairy lights and tinsel, comes as something of an anticlimax. The shrine inside houses what are believed to be the footprints of **Hanuman**. Legend has it that the monkey god, adored by Hindus for his strength and fidelity, rested on Jakhu after collecting healing Himalayan herbs for Rama's injured brother, Lakshmana. Watch out for the troupes of mangy monkeys around the temple. Pampered by generations of pilgrims and tourists, they have become real pests; hang on to your bag and don't flash food.

The state museum

The HP state **museum** (Tues–Sun 10am–1pm & 2–5pm, closed 2nd Sat of month; Rs50 [Rs10], camera Rs50) is a 1.5km hike west from the centre, but well worth the effort. The ground floor of the elegant colonial mansion is given over largely to temple sculpture, and a gallery of magnificent **Pahari miniatures** – examples of the last great Hindu art form to flourish in northern India before the deadening impact of Western culture in the early nineteenth century. The Mughal-influenced Pahari or "Hill" school is renowned for subtle depictions of romantic love, inspired by scenes from Hindu epics. Among the museum's **paintings** are dozens of Mughal and Rajasthani miniatures and a couple of fine "Company" watercolours. Produced for souvenir-hunting colonials by the descendants of the Mughal and Pahari masters, the *fakirs*, itinerant sadhus and mendicants they depict could have leapt straight from the pages of Kipling. One room is devoted to Mahatma Gandhi, packed with photos of his time in Shimla and amusing cartoons of his political relationship with the British.

To get here, follow the Mall downhill past the post office, then take the right fork at the first intersection after the *Classic* hotel and left at the second, from where it is signposted.

The Viceregal Lodge and Prospect Hill

Shimla's single most impressive colonial monument, the old **Viceregal Lodge** (daily 9am–5pm; Rs50 [Rs20]; guided tours every 30min except 1–2pm), summer seat of British government until the 1940s and today home to the **Institute of Advanced Studies**, is a fifteen-minute walk west of the museum. The lodge is Shimla at its most British. The solid grey mansion, built in Elizabethan style with a lion and unicorn set above the entrance porch, surveys trimmed lawns fringed by pines and flowerbeds. Inside is just as ostentatious, though only sections of the ground floor are open to the public: a vast teak-panelled entrance hall, an impressive library (formerly the ballroom) and the guest room. The **conference room**, hung with photos of Nehru, Jinnah and Gandhi, was the scene of crucial talks in the run-up to Independence. On the stone terrace to the rear of the building, a plaque profiles and names the peaks visible in the distance.

The short hike up to **Prospect Hill** (2176m), a popular picnic spot, ties in nicely with a visit to the lodge. By cutting through the woods to the west of the mansion, you can drop down to a busy intersection known as **Boileauganj**, from where a tarmac path climbs steeply up to the small shrine of Kamana Devi, which affords fine views.

Eating

Few **restaurants** in Shimla retain any colonial ambience and standards are generally poor, with the emphasis on rich, spicy, meat-based menus for Indian tourists. Apart from the top hotels and listings below, various **fast-food** restaurants along The Mall offer south Indian, Chinese and Mughlai snacks, while its many **bakeries** and ice-cream parlours offer comfort for the sweet-toothed. For a really cheap and filling meal, try the fried potato patties (*tikki*) or chickpea curry and *puris* (*channa batura*) at one of the snack bars that line the steps opposite the Gaiety Theatre. Alternatively, the bazaar is good for cheap *dhabas*.

Ashiana The Ridge. HPTDC restaurant in a converted bandstand offering mainly non-veg Indian food, including tasty chicken *makhanwalla*, plus pizzas and a few Chinese dishes. Mains mostly Rs100–150.

Baljee's The Mall. A landmark on Shimla's culinary and social map, this hectic smart-set coffee house does a roaring trade in snacks, sweets and ice cream in the evenings, but serves no alcohol. The swish à la carte *Fascination* restaurant upstairs offers a good selection of Indian and Chinese dishes for around Rs120–200, as well as sausage, egg and chips for Rs80.

Barista The Mall. Western-style coffee bar, complete with excellent lattes, muffins, chocolate brownies and chirpy service, for a fraction of the price back home.

Café Sol The Mall, on the roof of *Combemere Hotel* below. Slick modern cafeteria-cum-restaurant, serving reasonable Italian and Thai dishes from Rs180–500, as well as standard Indian and good bakery items.

Choice Middle Bazaar, down steps from *Baljee's*. Tiny, no-nonsense Chinese restaurant with an exhaustive menu, serving delicious veg and non-veg dishes for Rs50–80.

The Devicos The Mall. Lively Western-style fast food joint with south Indian snacks, veggie-burgers, and shakes. Most items under Rs100. There's an additional restaurant downstairs and a plush bar upstairs.

Himani's 48 the Mall. The ground floor is taken up by a flashy videogame arcade, a lively (mostly male) bar on the first floor and a family-style restaurant, pool den and sundeck on the top floor. Menu includes tandoori chicken (full, Rs190) and south Indian dishes.

Indian Coffee House The Mall. Atmospheric, faded café with colonial ambience, offering the usual *Coffee House* package of veg snacks and attentive waiter service to the predominantly male clientele.

New Plaza 60/1 Middle Bazaar, down the steps beside *Himani's*. Popular family restaurant. Good-value food including tasty meat sizzlers for Rs130.

Sher-e-Punjab Upper Bazaar. The best of the *dhabas* just below the Mall. Hearty portions of spicy beans, chickpeas and dhal at Rs40–60.

Listings

Airlines Indian Airlines, Kingfisher and Jagson Airlines, c/o Ambassador Travels, The Mall ⓣ0177/265 8014.

Banks and exchange ATMs of Citibank, UCO Bank and ICICI are among half a dozen along the Mall. Only the SBI will cash travellers' cheques, although cash can be exchanged at other banks and agents. Visa encashments can be made at the Bank of Baroda on Cart Rd.

Bookshops Maria Brothers, a pricey antiquarian bookshop on the Mall, sells old maps and etchings as well as a limited selection of new books. Asia Bookhouse and Minerva, also on the Mall, both stock paperbacks.

Hospitals Indira Gandhi Medical College Hospital ⓣ0177/280 4251; Deen Dayal Hospital, near the ISBT ⓣ0177/265 4071.

Internet access There are several places dotted along the Mall, charging Rs20/hr. The *Dreamland* hotel has facilities too.

Permits Inner Line permits (see p.408) are issued at the Additional District Magistrate's office (Mon–Sat 10am–5pm, closed 2nd Sat of the month; ⓣ0177/265 7005) on the first floor of the modern courthouse, one street below the Mall, opposite Sheel SJ Jewellers.

Pharmacies Indu Medical, the Mall (9am–8pm).

Post The GPO (Mon–Sat 10am–6pm), with its poste restante counter, is near Scandal Point on the Mall.

Travel agents Reliable operators include Band Box, 9 the Mall, near Scandal Point (ⓣ0177/265 8157, ⓔbboxhy@satyam.net.in), which specializes in tailor-made itineraries, and Great Himalayan Travels (ⓣ0177/265 8934, ⓦwww.ghtravels.com). The *YMCA* (ⓣ0177/280 4085) also organizes treks and safaris, as does Silver Dreams (ⓣ0177/280 6897, ⓦwww.blueskiestrekking.com) at the *Dreamland*.

South of Shimla

On the border with Uttarakhand, the town of **PAONTA SAHIB**, where pastel-yellow houses are packed tightly into the cobbled streets, holds an important shrine dedicated to **Guru Gobind Singh**, the tenth Sikh guru, who lived here in the late 1680s. Paonta Sahib provides good bus connections for travel between Shimla and points such as Mussoorie, Dehra Dun, Haridwar and Rishikesh. Should you decide to stay, the HPTDC *Hotel Yamuna* (ⓣ01704/222341; ❸–❻), on the banks of the River Yamuna, has pleasant rooms, a restaurant and bar.

Though it sees few Western tourists, the small, slow-paced town of **KASAULI**, cradled by pine forests 77km southwest of Shimla, and with a touch of Raj architecture, makes a good stop-off on the way to or from Delhi. Criss-crossed by spindly cobbled streets, spreading along low ridges carpeted with forests and flower-filled meadows, Kasauli offers an abundance of gentle short strolls, such as the one to nearby Sanawar. The nearest railway station is Dharampur on the Kalka–Shimla line, from where buses travel the 11km up to Kasauli; there are also direct buses from Shimla. From Kasauli, an easy and scenic 12km trek leads through forests to **Kalka**, railhead for the **toy train** to Shimla. Aside from the cheaper lodges, of which the best is *Gian* (ⓣ01792/272244; ❷–❸) on Post Office Road, most of Kasauli's **hotels** have high-ceilinged rooms with fireplaces, carpets and balconies, in true Raj style. A good option on the Lower Mall is the reliable state-run HPTDC *Ros Common* (ⓣ01792/272005; ❻–❼). Apart from the larger hotels, **food** options are limited to standard *dhabas*.

If you can afford it, the eighteenth-century **Nalagarh Fort** (ⓣ01795/223179, ⓔfortresort@satyam.net.in; ❽), converted into probably the finest **hotel** in Himachal Pradesh, is an excellent place to break the journey between Delhi and Kullu. It lies 60km from Chandigarh, 12km off the main Chandigarh–Mandi road. Accommodation is in beautifully maintained suites, each with period furniture. An atmospheric lounge bar overlooks terraced grounds with a tennis court, croquet lawn and swimming pool, and an Ayurvedic clinic offers massage. Book in advance.

Northeast of Shimla

A three-hour (65km) bus ride northeast of Shimla, the scruffy hill town of **NARKANDA** (2725m) makes a reasonable resting point on the bumpy, six-hour journey to Sarahan. This former staging post on the Hindustan–Tibet caravan route acts as the roadhead and main market town for the area's widely dispersed apple and potato growers. There are some good rambles through the cedar forests that surround the town, and great **views** of the Himalayas. **Hatu Peak** (3143m), crowned by a lonely hilltop **Durga temple**, 7km east of town, looks out over the River Sutlej winding far below, and a string of white-tipped mountains to the north and east.

Accommodation options include HPTDC's quietly situated *Hotel Hatu* (ⓣ01782/242430; ❹–❺), with large well-appointed rooms, great views from the lawns and a restaurant, and *Mahamaya Palace* (ⓣ01782/242448; ❸) which has reasonable attached rooms and a **restaurant**. Otherwise, the *New Himalayan Dhaba* opposite serves up simple but tasty veg food.

Rampur

Once over the pass at Narkanda, the highway winds steadily down the Sutlej Valley towards **RAMPUR**, a major transport hub 132km northeast of Shimla. Formerly the capital of the princely state of Bhushar, the town today is a gritty and cheerless cluster of concrete houses hemmed in by a forbidding wall of rock. Across the main road from the bus stand, a small Buddhist **gompa** houses a huge metal prayer wheel and a rock reputedly bearing ten million minute inscriptions of the mantra "Om Mane Padme Hum".

Rampur has **bus** connections to Rekong Peo and onward all the way to Kaza in Spiti. **Inner Line permits** for Kinnaur can be obtained from the Sub-Divisional Magistrate's office opposite the fire station on the main road, but it's easier in Rekong Peo (see p.423). Down the steps from the bus stand, the *Amar Jyoti* (ⓣ01782/233185; ❶) and slightly plusher *Bhagwati* (ⓣ01782/233117; ❶–❸) are adequate but top of the range is the HPTDC *Bushehar Regency* (ⓣ01782/234103; ❹–❺), on the Shimla-facing edge of town. For **food**, the *Bhagwati* has the best restaurant; *Café Sutluj*, 200m west of town, makes up for its lack of atmosphere with air-conditioning, a bar and a great terrace overlooking the river.

Sarahan

Secluded **SARAHAN**, erstwhile summer capital of the Bhushar rajas, sits astride a 2000-metre ledge above the River Sutlej, near the Shimla–Kinnaur border. Set against a spectacular backdrop, the village harbours one of the northwestern Himalayas' most exotic spectacles – the **Bhimakali temple**. With its two multi-tiered sanctuary towers, elegantly sloping slate-tiled roofs and gleaming golden spires, it is the most majestic early timber temple in the Sutlej Valley – an area renowned for housing holy shrines on raised wooden platforms. Although most of the structure dates from the early twentieth century, parts are thought to be more than eight hundred years old.

A pair of elaborately decorated metal doors lead into a large courtyard flanked by rest rooms and a small carved-stone **Shiva shrine**. After ascending to a second, smaller yard, you pass another golden door, also richly embossed with mythical scenes, beyond which the innermost enclosure holds the two **sanctuary towers**. The one on the right houses musical instruments, flags, paladins and ceremonial weapons, a selection of which is on show in the small "museum" in the corner of

Blood sacrifice in Sarahan

The **Bhimakali** deity, a local manifestation of the black-faced, bloodthirsty Hindu goddess Kali (Durga), has for centuries been associated with **human sacrifice**. Once every decade, until the disapproving British intervened in the 1800s, a man was killed here as an offering to the *devi*. Following a complex ceremony, his newly spilled blood was poured over the goddess's tongue for her to drink, after which his body was dumped in a deep well inside the temple compound. If no victim could be found, it is said that a voice would bellow from the depths of the pit, which is now sealed up.

The tradition of blood sacrifice continues in Sarahan to this day, albeit in less extreme form. During the annual **Astami** festival, two days before the culmination of **Dussehra**, a veritable menagerie of birds and beasts are put to the knife, including a water-buffalo calf, sheep, goat, fish, chicken, crab, and even a spider. The gory spectacle draws large crowds, and is a memorable alternative to the Dussehra procession in Kullu, which takes place at around the same time in mid-October.

the courtyard. Non-Hindus who want to climb to the top of the other, more modern tower (no photography) to view the highly polished gold-faced deity must don a saffron cap. Bhimakali herself is enshrined on the top floor, decked with garlands of flowers.

Practicalities

Buses from Shimla to Sangla and Rekong Peo pass through the small town of Jeori, from where several buses a day and taxis climb the 17km to Sarahan. There's also a direct bus service from Rampur. Keen walkers might fancy ambling along the well-worn mule track to Sarahan from Jeori. There's a fair choice of **accommodation** for such a small place. HPTDC's *Hotel Srikhand* (Ⓣ01782/274234; ❹–❺; dorm Rs100) is a concrete monster, but has a delightful garden and a restaurant serving good veg meals on a relaxing terrace. For more atmosphere, the *Temple Guest House* (Ⓣ01782/274248; ❶–❷), inside the Bhimakali courtyard, has a range of pleasant rooms and a basement dorm (Rs75). The slightly faded *Hotel Trehan's* (Ⓣ01782/274205, Ⓔhotel-trehan47@rediffmail.com; ❷–❸) offers spacious attached rooms with TV. When the temple kitchens aren't dishing up their usual cheap and delicious meals, try one of the several Tibetan *dhabas* around the square outside, such as *Dev Bhumi*.

Kinnaur

Before 1992, the remote backwater of **KINNAUR**, a rugged buffer zone between the Shimla foothills and the wild western extremity of Chinese-occupied Tibet, was strictly off-limits to tourists. Although visitors are now allowed to travel through the **"Restricted Area"**, and on to Spiti, Lahaul and the Kullu Valley, permits are still required (see p.408). Other areas of Kinnaur, notably the **Baspa Valley** and the sacred **Kinner-Kailash** massif visible from the mountain village of **Kalpa**, are completely open.

Straddling the mighty River Sutlej, which rises on the southern slopes of Mount Kailash, Kinnaur has for centuries been a major trans-Himalayan corridor. Merchants travelling between China and the Punjabi plains passed through on the **Hindustan–Tibet caravan route**, stretches of which are still used by villagers and trekkers. The bulk of the traffic that lumbers east towards the frontier, however, uses the newer NH-22, which veers north into Spiti just short of the ascent to Shipki La pass, on the Chinese border, which remains closed.

In the well-watered, mainly Hindu west of the region, the scenery ranges from subtropical to almost alpine: wood-and-slate villages, surrounded by maize terraces and orchards, nestle beneath pine forests and vast blue-grey mountain peaks. Further east, largely beyond the reach of the monsoons, it grows more austere, and glaciers loom on all sides. **Buddhism** arrived in Kinnaur with the tenth-century kings of Guge, who ruled what is now southwestern Tibet. When **Rinchen Zangpo** (958–1055), the "Great Translator" credited with the "Second Spreading" of the faith in Guge, passed through here, he left behind several monasteries and a devotion to a pure form of the Buddhist faith that has endured here for nearly one thousand years. In the sixteenth century, after Guge had fragmented

Trekking in Kinnaur

Unfrequented mountain trails criss-cross Kinnaur, offering **treks** ranging from gentle hikes to challenging climbs over high-altitude passes. The routes along the **Sutlej Valley**, punctuated with government resthouses and villages, are feasible without the aid of ponies, but away from the main road you need to be completely self-sufficient. **Porters** can usually be hired in Rampur, Rekong Peo and the Baspa Valley except in early autumn (Sept/Oct), when they're busy with the apple harvest.

The Kinner-Kailash circuit

The five- to seven-day *parikrama* (circumambulation) of the majestic Kinner-Kailash massif, a sacred pilgrimage trail, makes a spectacular trek for which you won't need an Inner Line permit. The circuit starts at the village of **MORANG**, on the left bank of the Sutlej, served by buses from Tapri or Rekong Peo. A track, passable by jeep, runs southeast from here to **Thangi**, the trailhead, and continues through Rahtak, over the **Charang La** pass (5266m) to **Chitkul** in the Baspa Valley. The trail then follows the river down to the beautiful village of **Sangla**, from where a couple of worthwhile day-hikes can be made – to **Kamru fort** behind the village, or the steep ascent to the **Shivaling La** pass, from where there are superb views of Raldang (5499m), the southernmost peak on the Kinner-Kailash massif. The final stage passes through the lower Baspa Valley, via Shang and Brua to **Karcham**, which overlooks the NH-22 highway. The best time for the Kinner-Kailash *parikrama* is between July and October; August is the most popular month with local pilgrims.

Kafnu to Kaza, via the Pin Valley

This challenging route across the Great Himalayan range, via the Kalang Setal glacier and the Shakarof La pass, is a dramatic approach to Spiti and the **Pin Valley**, and no restrictions apply. The trail, which is very steep, snow-covered, and hard to follow in places, should definitely not be attempted without ponies, porters, adequate gear and a reliable **guide**. It starts in earnest at Kafnu village, now connected to Wangtu on the main road by a paved surface, continuing via Mulling, Phustirang (3750m), and over the **Bhaba Pass** (4865m), a gruelling slog through snowfields, before dropping down into the beautiful and isolated **Pin Valley**. You can then trek onwards or get a vehicle to **Kaza** (see p.464). More of this route may become paved, as the delayed Wangtu–Mudh road project painfully progresses.

Chitkul to Har-ki-Dun

This ten-day trek to **Garhwal** (see p.311) passes along the edge of the Inner Line and is subject to restrictions. Starting from **Chitkul** and crossing the River Baspa to Doaria, the route then climbs up a side valley to follow a lateral moraine up to the Zupika Gad and then a steep ascent – the final section of which is up a crevassed glacier – to the **Borsu Pass** (5300m). The other side of the pass is down a steep snow and boulder field requiring some scrambling; you arrive a few days later in the beautiful valley of **Har-ki-Dun** in Garhwal. A guide is essential.

The old Hindustan–Tibet road from Kalpa to the Rupa Valley

Another route to consider is the relatively easy five-day trek starting at **Kalpa** and following the old Hindustan–Tibet road through the remote hamlets of upper Kinnaur (permits needed), past Shi Asu to the Rupa Valley. The views along the route are superb and the villagers are extremely hospitable. The road, now crumbling in places, is also ideal for mountain biking.

into dozens of petty fiefdoms, the **Bhushar kings** took control of Kinnaur. They remained in power throughout the British Raj, when this was one of the battlegrounds of the espionage war played out between agents of the Chinese, Russian and British empires – the "Great Game" evocatively depicted in the novels of Rudyard Kipling.

Rekong Peo

East of Jeori, the road climbs high above the Sutlej into ever more remote territory, traversing sheer ravines on cable bridges, while tiny wooden villages, each with a pagoda-roofed temple, cling to the mountainsides. At **Wangtu** bridge, the trailhead for the Kinnaur–Pin Valley–Kaza trek (see box opposite), the highway switches to the north bank of the river beside the huge Karcham Dam hydro-electric project. Beyond the village of **Tapri**, a right fork leads to **Sangla** in the Baspa Valley, while the main highway continues to **REKONG PEO**, district headquarters of Kinnaur, 7km above the main road. Its batch of concrete houses and government buildings around a small *maidan* gives it the air of an upstart frontier settlement, only boasting a modestly interesting **bazaar**. The only reason to stop is to buy trekking supplies, pick up the trail to Kalpa, or obtain an Inner Line **permit** (see p.408) from the District Commissioner's office; this is actually arranged through the nearby Tourist Info Centre (Mon–Sat 10am–5pm; ⓣ01786/222857) in the open courtyard below the bazaar bus stop. They charge Rs150 but take your photo and make copies of your passport themselves.

Practicalities

Rekong Peo's **buses** are fairly frequent, considering its relative isolation. Buses drop off and pick up at the bend in the main bazaar before proceeding up the hill on the Kalpa road for 2km to the **main bus stand**. There are several daily services to Shimla, an early morning departure direct to Mandi, direct buses to Chandigarh, Delhi and nearby Sangla, two buses daily to Pooh and a morning departure for Kaza. More services can be picked up from the main road at the bottom of the valley, 6km below.

Accommodation in town is overpriced for what you get; the pink *Hotel Fairyland* (ⓣ01786/222477; ❷–❸), on the road behind the *Cafeteria Roof*, has modest but clean attached rooms and great views over the bazaar to Kinner Kailash. A reasonable fallback is *Hotel Mehfil* (ⓣ01786/223600; ❷), also above the main bazaar. About 1km up the road to the main bus stand is the new *Hotel City Heart* (ⓣ9418 018615; ❸–❹), which has immaculate, spacious doubles with bath; the pricier rooms have the best views. **Food** options in Peo itself are pretty much limited to the *Cafeteria Roof*, 100m east of the lower bus stand, which has sizzlers, pizza and a couple of Kinnauri dishes. Also on the bazaar the *Punjabi dhaba* serves up cheap mutton, chicken and veg. There is internet access at Network, 100m beyond the main bus stand. You can get cash from the SBI ATM in the bazaar.

Kalpa (Chini)

Almost 250km northeast of Shimla and 9km along a twisting road from Rekong Peo, **KALPA** can be reached by road, or on foot along various steep tracks. Its narrow atmospheric lanes and dramatic location astride a rocky bluff, high above the right bank of the Sutlej, make the hike worthwhile. The ancient Tibetan *gompa* here was founded by Rinchen Zangpo, and there is also a small Shiva temple. Facing the village, the magnificent **Kinner-Kailash** massif sweeps 4500m up from the valley floor. The mountain in the middle, Jorkaden (6473m), is the highest, followed by the sacred summit of Kinner-Kailash (6050m) to the north, and the needle point of Raldang (5499m) in the south. Up the valley you'll see remains of the Hindustan–Tibet caravan route.

Kalpa is a far more attractive place to stay than Rekong Peo, although finding **accommodation** can involve some walking. On the upper road, the *Kinner Villa* (ⓣ01786/226006, ⓔkinnervilla@rediffmail.com; ❹–❻) is the most tasteful place around, with sleek, refurbished rooms, spotless bathrooms and a grassy pitch out front. On the same road the HPTDC *Kinner Kailash Cottage* (ⓣ01786/226159; ❺–❻) contains a range of doubles and larger chalets, as well as a seasonal campsite, while the smart new *Rakpa Regency* (ⓣ01786/245285; ❸–❺) is set in pleasant grounds and the front rooms have balconies with splendid views. In Kalpa itself, the *Blue Lotus Guest House* (ⓣ01786/226001; ❷–❹), a concrete block 100m beyond the lower bus stand, has rooms priced according to their view. The **restaurant** here and at *Hotel Shivalik*, just above the village, offer the widest choice; otherwise there are just a few basic *dhabas*. Buses and taxis between Kalpa and Rekong Peo run every thirty minutes or so until 6pm; convenient connections include three daily buses to Shimla (6.30am, 11.30am & 2.30pm) and one to Sangla and Chitkul (8.30am).

The Baspa Valley

Hemmed in by the pinnacles of Kinner-Kailash to the north and the high peaks of the Garhwal range to the south, the seventy-kilometre **River Baspa** rises in the mountain wilderness along the Indo–Tibetan border to flow through what was until recently one of Kinnaur's most beautiful and secluded areas. The lower reaches of the valley below Sangla are now dominated by a massive and ugly hydroelectric plant, but beyond Sangla the scenery remains unspoilt. Although the head of the valley is closed to tourists, there are still plenty of walking opportunities exploring side valleys.

The valley's largest settlement, **SANGLA**, is served by daily **buses** from Shimla, Rampur, Rekong Peo and Tapri, and makes an excellent base to visit nearby **Kamru** village, 25 minutes' walk above Sangla, with its warren of lanes and slate-roofed stone houses, and its wood-and-stone gable-roofed **fort**. Tibetan prayer flags flutter in the breeze and the inhabitants retain Buddhist funerary rites, although they are now mostly Hindu and no longer read Tibetan. The inner sanctum of the **temple** below the fort is off-limits to visitors unless a goat is paid for and sacrificed. In September and October Sangla fills up with Bengali holiday-makers, and hotel options are increasing every year; the best **places to stay** are mostly dotted around the road in. One good choice is the *Monal Regency* (ⓣ01786/242922; ❷–❹), 500m before town, which has pleasant rooms with a well-tended lawn out front. The next bend in the road leads up a short path to the friendly *Sangla Resorts* (ⓣ01786/242401; ❷), offering clean doubles, a dorm (Rs70) and a good restaurant. Just below the main road, the adjacent *Highland Guest House* (ⓣ01786/242285; ❶) and *Himalaya Home* (ⓣ01786/242256; ❶) both offer basic but clean rooms. **Eating** options are limited to hotel restaurants and several small cafés in the centre; *Sonam*, the middle of three adjacent places just above street level in the middle of the main bazaar, does fair Tibetan and Chinese. The bazaar also includes a Net Café and a snooker hall.

Two daily **buses** head further up the increasingly dramatic Baspa Valley to Chitkul, though they are unreliable and sometimes cancelled, in which case you'll need to hitch or hire a jeep (Rs500). Eight kilometres beyond Sangla, on the banks of the river, is the wonderful *Banjara Camp* (ⓣ01786/242536, ⓦwww.banjaracamps.com; ❼), with luxurious tents, attentive service and meals included. At quiet **RAKCHAM**, 14km and forty minutes by bus from Sangla, the *Rupin River View Guest House* (ⓣ01786/244225; ❷) – offering pleasant wood-panelled rooms with shared bath and hot water – can organize **porters** and **guides** for treks such as the tough three-day hike to Thangi on the Kinner-Kailash circuit.

On a rise with dramatic views of the opening valley, **CHITKUL**, 25km from Sangla, is as far up the valley as you can go – a gate and checkpoint at the far end of the village marks the start of the guarded Inner Line. The bright, friendly *Amar Guesthouse* (❶), a rickety wooden structure in the upper part of the village west of the fort, is extremely basic but cosier than the blue *Thakur Guesthouse* (ⓣ01786/244320; ❶–❸; dorm Rs75), down by the bus stand, which boasts some attached rooms, great views and can give trekking advice. The upstairs *Great Himalayan* restaurant, almost opposite *Thakur*, offers tasty food but service is very slow. Visible above the village, a trail winds steeply up to a huge saddle below the **Charang La pass** – the route of the Kinner-Kailash pilgrimage circuit (see p.422).

Upper Kinnaur

Inner Line permits are required beyond the dull hamlet of **Spillo** for **upper Kinnaur**, the remote region east of Kalpa. Several hours by jeep from Rekong Peo and within a day's hike of the frontier, the small town of **Pooh**, perched 4km above the main road, is the first main settlement you encounter. Evidence from inscriptions suggest that Pooh was, in the eleventh century, an important trading centre that fell under the influence of the Tibetan kingdom of Guge when the Great Translator, Rinchen Zangpo travelled through the area. The temple here is devoted to Sakyamuni, with wooden columns supporting a high ceiling and a circumambulatory path around the altar. The *Om Guest House* (ⓣ01785/232601; ❷–❹) has decent rooms, two dorms (Rs125) and a good restaurant.

Beyond Pooh, the road bends north, crossing the muddy Sutlej for the last time at **Khab**, where it meets the turquoise waters of River Spiti. To the northeast, Kinnaur's highest peak, **Leo Pargial II** (6770m), rises in a near-vertical 4000-metre wall which marks the border with Tibet and overlooks the old Indo–Tibet road at the **Shipki La pass** (5569m). The NH-22 continues north through the barren wastes of the Hanglang Valley, very similar to parts of Ladakh.

NAKO, the valley's largest village, nestling high above the river at 3640m around a small artificial **lake**, is now on the main Rekong Peo–Kaza road, which was redirected uphill to avoid the infamous **Malling Slide**. Unfortunately, the road still gets blocked during bad weather, as do many other points on the Kinnaur–Spiti circuit. In the northwest corner of the village, the eleventh-century complex of the **Nako Chokhor** (arrange entry through the Youth Club tent above the bus stand; Rs50) is attributed to Rinchen Zangpo; although it's in desperate need of restoration, its exquisite interior paintings are comparable to those of Alchi (see p.510). The finest building of all is the Serkhang or "Golden Hall", dedicated to the Tathagatas or Supreme Buddhas. There are some basic **accommodation** options: the best of the trio of lodges by the bus stand is the *Reo Purguil* (ⓣ01785/236339; ❷–❹), where all rooms have bathrooms and balconies, while the *Galaxy Guest House* (ⓣ01785/263617; ❶) has spartan attached rooms. Down by the lake, the *Lake View Guest House* (ⓣ01785/236041; ❷–❸) also has decent attached rooms. The best choice of **food** is at the *Reo Purguil*, although there are a couple of good Tibetan *dhabas* too. There is at least one daily **bus** and numerous **jeeps** leaving in each direction, for Kaza via Tabo and Rekong Peo.

Northwest Himachal

From Shimla the main road winds west and north to the riverside market town of **Mandi**, an important crossroads linking the Kullu Valley and the hills to **the northwest**. The rolling foothills on this side of the state are warmer and more accessible than Himachal's eastern reaches, though less dramatic and considerably lower. The area sees little tourism outside **Dharamsala**, the British hill station turned Tibetan settlement, home to the Dalai Lama. Dharamsala is an excellent base for treks over the soaring Dhauladhar range to the **Chamba Valley**, which harbours uniquely styled Hindu temples in **Brahmour** and **Chamba**. South of Chamba, the fading hill station of **Dalhousie** still has a certain ex-Raj charm, and is popular with Indian tourists who arrive in droves during the hot season.

Mandi to Dharamsala

The following section traces the River Beas and NH-21 as they weave from Mandi to Dharamsala, linking a string of quiet mountain towns and villages. While most visitors make the six-hour journey to Dharamsala in one go on one of the nine daily **buses**, those with more time can pause at sacred **Rewalsar**, just outside Mandi, or stop in the **Kangra Valley** at **Joginder Nagar** or **Baijnath** to pick up the narrow-gauge train that trundles through patchwork fields and light forest to **Kangra**, just an hour away from Dharamsala.

Mandi

The junction town of **MANDI**, 158km north of Shimla, straddles the River Beas, its riverside *ghats* dotted with stone temples where sadhus and pilgrims pray. Once a major trading post for Ladakhis heading south – *mandi* means market – the town still bustles with commercial activity, now centred on the attractive **Indira Market** and its sunken garden, in the centre of the town square. A collection of sixteenth-century Naggari-style temples sits above the town on **Tarna Hill**. On the summit is the main Kali temple, decorated with garish paintings of the fierce mother goddess draped in skulls and blood.

The frenetic **bus stand** is a short ride across the river on the east bank; its café does delicious veg food. There are departures every half-hour or so for Rewalsar, Kullu, Manali, Dharamsala and hourly for Shimla, with a possible change in Bilaspur, as well as longer-distance services. The town has plenty of **hotels**, most of them in the Indira Market area. The nicest place to stay is the ramshackle *Raj Mahal* (Ⓣ01905/222401; ❸), above the town square, a period-furnished palace set in spacious shady gardens, with a good restaurant and atmospheric gentlemen's bar. Also on the square is the *Shiva* (Ⓣ01905/224211; ❷), less atmospheric but cheaper, and the larger *Evening Plaza* (Ⓣ01905/225123, Ⓔmalhotralalji@hotmail.com; ❷–❹), which has a range of rooms, some with air-conditioning. The government-run *Café Shiraz*, at the edge of the main square, serves south Indian snacks and can book **bus tickets**. Indira Market is handy for fast-food joints, **internet cafés** and the computerized **railway ticketing office** on the north end. Apart from a couple of ATMs, both the Bank of Baroda and the Overseas India Bank can **change money** and cash travellers' cheques, but the most convenient exchange is at the *Evening Plaza*.

Rewalsar

If you've any interest in Buddhism it's worth taking a detour 24km southeast of Mandi to **REWALSAR**, where three Tibetan monasteries (Nyingma, Drikung Kagyu and Drukpa Kagyu) mark an important place of pilgrimage. There are also Sikh and Hindu temples here, all of which draw a steady stream of pilgrims and tourists. The devout complete a *chora* around the small sacred lake and along narrow lanes full of shrines and stalls selling Tibetan curios, before lounging beneath the prayer flags on the lake's grassy fringes.

It's believed that Padmasambhava left many footprints and handprints in rocks and caves up in the hills around the lake, and steep paths lead up from the lake to **caves** that are used today as isolated meditation retreats. Of the three monasteries around the lake, **Tso-Pema Ogyen Heruka Gompa**, below the tourist lodge, is the most venerated and atmospheric; check out the tree planted in 1957 by the Dalai Lama, who visited India that year to celebrate the 2500th anniversary of the Buddha's birth, two years before his exile from Tibet. Towering dramatically over the lake and visually dominating the Rewalsar setting is the large but much newer **Drukpa Kagyu Zigar Gompa**.

For **Hindus**, Rewalsar is regarded as the abode of the sage Lomas, for whose sake the lake was created with waters from the Ganga and Yamuna. Three small temples dedicated to Krishna, Lomas and Shiva, along with a Nandi bull statue and lakeside *ghats*, reflect Rewalsar's Hindu connections. On the west shore, the Sikh **gurudwara** attracts pilgrims retracing the steps of Guru Gobind Singh, who came here in 1702; this is one of the few sites associated with his life in Himachal. To the south a small **sanctuary** protects deer and Himalayan black bears.

The HPTDC *Tourist Inn* (Ⓣ01905/240252; ❶–❹), a short way back from the north shore, has comfortable rooms with hot showers, as well as a small dorm (Rs100) in the older block. Visitors who plan to stay for a while may well prefer the pleasant **monastery accommodation** at the *Nyingma Gompa* (Ⓣ01905/280226; ❶), or the more comfortable *Drukpa Kagyu Gompa* (Ⓣ01905/280210; ❶–❷). Local families are also keen to rent out rooms; ask at the *Zigar Tibetan Food Corner* restaurant. **Eating** is limited to several small but reasonable Tibetan restaurants near the lake, which serve *thukpa*, *momos* and noodles, and the *dhabas* along the main road serving north Indian food.

Joginder Nagar and Baijnath

JOGINDER NAGAR, 63km northwest of Mandi, is a nondescript village: little more than two streets flanked by wooden-fronted houses and a crowded bus stand. The main reason to stop here is that it is the eastern terminal of the Kangra Valley **train** (see box, p.428) to Kangra and Pathankot. The bus stand and railway station are 500m apart, and the smart HPTDC *Hotel Uhl* (Ⓣ01908/222002; ❹–❺) is at the eastern end of town; enquire here about paragliding at **Bir**, 15km west.

Around 30km northwest of Joginder Nagar, **BAIJNATH** is perhaps a better spot to pick up the toy train, as more services originate here and it gives you a chance to visit the **Baidyanath Shiva temple**, parts of which are intricately carved and supposed to date from 804 AD.

Kangra and around

Although most travellers bypass **KANGRA** on their way to Dharamsala, 18km further north, it's worth a brief detour. Buses from all over the Kangra Valley and further afield pull into the bus stand 1km north of the town centre, where there are frequent connections to Dharamsala. Kangra can also be reached from

The Kangra Valley Railway

India has five of the twenty or so vintage "toy trains" or narrow-gauge mountain railways in the world – three in the Himalayas and two of these in Himachal Pradesh. Most famous is the Kalka–Shimla line (see p.414), but the little-known 163-kilometre **Kangra Valley Railway** is also a magnificent engineering feat. Unlike the Kalka line, with its 103 tunnels and tortuous switchbacks, engineers of this route preferred bridges – 950 in all, many of which are still considered masterpieces – that give passengers uninterrupted views all the way from Pathankot to Joginder Nagar. Although slower than the equivalent road journey, the scenery is far more impressive, particularly the stretch between Kangra and Mangwal.

There are six trains daily from Pathankot, departing between 2.20am and 4.10pm; four terminate at Baijnath (6hr 30min–7hr), while two go all the way to Joginder Nagar (10hr). In the opposite direction there are departures from Joginder Nagar at 7.20am and 12.20pm, and four more from Baijnath between 4.15am and 5.35pm. All services pass through Kangra.

Pathankot (see p.527) and from Joginder Nagar by the daily **narrow-gauge railway** service (see box above).

Kangra's crumbling, overgrown **fort** (daily sunrise–sunset; Rs100 [Rs5]) was also damaged by an earthquake in 1905 and is now inhabited by screeching green parrots that flit through a few simple temples still tended by priests. High gates, some British-built, span a cobbled path to the deserted ramparts. To get here, head 3km south on the road to Jawalamukhi, then turn up the 1km access road just before the bridge.

Places to stay on the road between the bus stand and town include the simple *Hotel Preet* (Ⓣ01892/265260; ❶), which has its best rooms on the first floor alongside a cosy little terrace, and the cleaner *Hotel Yatrika* (Ⓣ01892/262258; ❷–❹) whose deluxe rooms have a/c. The noisy *Raj*, opposite the bus stand, is not worth staying in, but does have a good **restaurant** and bar.

Thirty-five kilometres southwest of Kangra, the tiny village of **MASRUR** is the only place in the Himalayas with **rock-cut Hindu temples** (daily sunrise–sunset; Rs100 [Rs5]) similar to those at Ellora in Maharashtra (see p.641). Though nowhere near as impressive, the fifteen temples, devoted to Ram, Lakshman and Sita were hewn from natural rock in the ninth and tenth centuries. You can get here by taking a **bus** towards Pir Bindu, getting off at the tiny village of Nagrota Suriyan, then walking 1.5km up to the temples.

A simple whitewashed temple in the otherwise nondescript town of **JAWALAMUKHI**, 35km south of Kangra, protects one of north India's most important Hindu shrines. The sanctuary, crowned with a squat golden spire, contains a natural blue gas flame emitted from the earth, revered as a manifestation of the goddess of fire, Jawalamukhi. Frequent **buses** (1hr) depart from Kangra and there are also direct services to Dharamsala, 53km north. The two best **hotels** are the plush HPTDC *Hotel Jwalaji* (Ⓣ01970/222280; ❹–❻) on the outskirts, and *Mata Vaishno Devi Hotel* (Ⓣ01970/222135; ❸–❹), 250m north of the bus stand, though a basic cell at the *Geeta Bhawan Ashram* (Ⓣ01970/222242; ❶) is much cheaper.

Dharamsala and McLeod Ganj

Home to the Dalai Lama and Tibetan government in exile, and starting point for some exhilarating treks into the high Himalayas, **DHARAMSALA**, or more correctly, its upper town **McLEOD GANJ**, is one of Himachal's most irresistible destinations. Spread across wooded ridges beneath the stark rock faces of the Dhauladhar Range, the town is divided into two distinct and separate sections, separated by 10km of perilously twisting road and almost a thousand metres in altitude. Originally a British hill station, **McLeod Ganj** has been transformed by the influx of **Tibetan refugees** fleeing Chinese oppression in their homeland. Tibetan influence here is subsequently very strong, their achievements including the construction of temples, schools, monasteries, nunneries, meditation centres

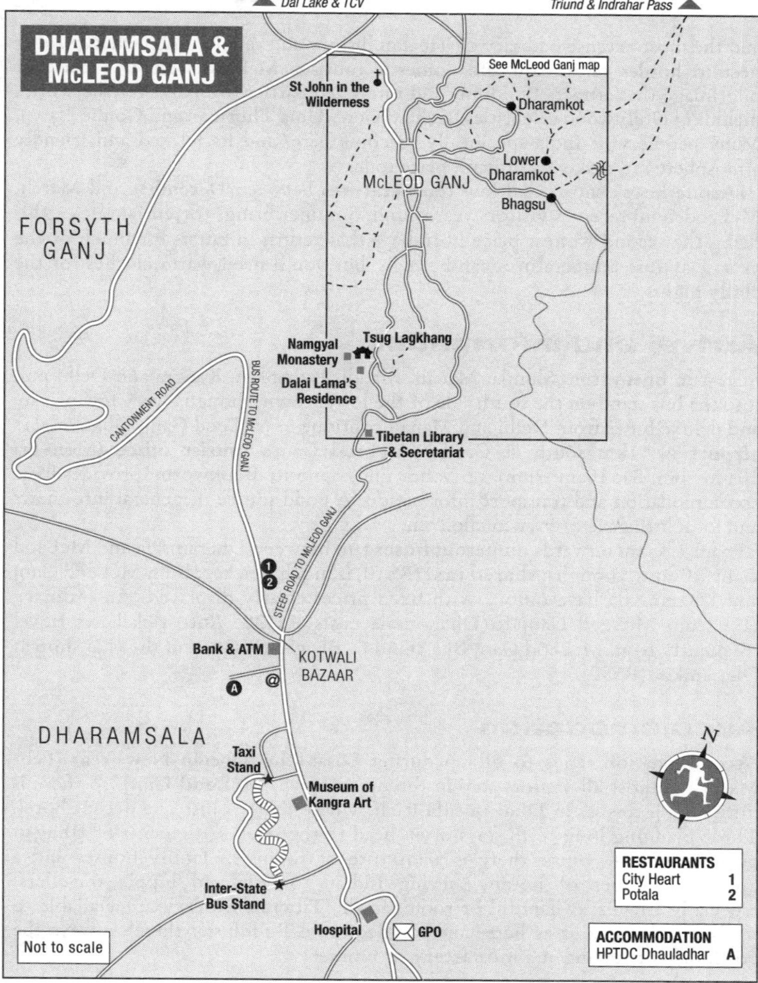

Moving on from Dharamsala

Kingfisher operates a daily **flight** to Delhi, with deals going from as little as Rs1200 one way, but flights are often cancelled in bad weather, so it's wise not to cut it fine with any international connections. HRTC run numerous **buses** to destinations in Himachal Pradesh and beyond from the main bus stand in the lower town, including buses every 30 minutes from Gaggal, for the airport. Three buses a day (6am, 8am & 8pm; 10hr) travel to **Manali**, and two run to **Delhi** (6pm & 7pm; 15–16hr) via Chandigarh, although more are put on according to demand. There are two daily government buses to **Dalhousie** (8am & noon; 6–7hr)) and four to **Shimla** (10hr). Many tourists prefer to book private "deluxe" buses through agents in McLeod Ganj (see "Listings", p.438), especially the new sleeper buses to Delhi (Rs700). Pathankot (every 30min; 3hr), is the nearest **railhead**.

and the most extensive library of Tibetan history and religion. As well as playing host to hordes of foreign and domestic tourists, McLeod Ganj is a place of pilgrimage that attracts Buddhists and interested parties from all over the world, including Hollywood celebrities Richard Gere, Uma Thurman and Goldie Hawn. Many people visit India specifically to come here, and its relaxed and friendly atmosphere can make it a difficult place to leave.

Despite heavy snows and low **temperatures** between December and March, McLeod Ganj receives visitors year round. Summer brings torrential rains – this being the second wettest place in India – that return in bursts for much of the year. Daytime temperatures can be high, but you'll need warm clothes for the chilly nights.

Arrival and information

State-run **buses** from Shimla, Manali, Mandi, Pathankot, Kangra and Delhi pull into the bus stand on the south side of the lower town, though a very few private and deluxe buses from Delhi and Manali continue to McLeod Ganj. Dharamsala's **airport** is 11km south at Gaggal. McLeod Ganj's **tourist office** (Mon–Fri 10am–5pm, Sat 10am–2pm), on South End, opposite Bookworm, provides basic accommodation and transport information. A good source of general info, news and local listings is Ⓦ www.mcllo.com.

From 7.45am onwards numerous **buses** run between Dharamsala and McLeod Ganj (40min), though a **shared taxi** (Rs10) is much quicker; both McLeod Ganj and Dharamsala have unions with fixed prices clearly displayed. An ordinary taxi from McLeod Ganj to Dharamsala costs Rs130. Auto-rickshaws travel frequently from McLeod Ganj Bus Stand to Bhagsu (Rs30) and the chai shop at Dharamkot (Rs50).

Accommodation

Accommodation tends to fill up during Losar, the Tibetan New Year (Feb/March). Almost all visitors stay in the upper town, **McLeod Ganj**, so there is little reason to stay in **Dharamsala** itself, where there is just one decent hotel. Those planning long-term stays often head to the small settlements of **Bhagsu** or **Dharamkot**, where there is a mixture of rooms in family houses and a growing number of hotels, serving Indian tourists and hippie travellers, especially Israelis. A handful of rooms in the **Tibetan Library** are available to students taking courses here, and for dedicated Buddhists, there's always the possibility of staying at a **monastery** or nunnery.

McLeod Ganj

Asian Plaza Main Chowk ⓣ01892/220655, ⓦwww.asianplazahotel.com. Snazzy new hotel with nicely decorated rooms and huge suites, right in the heart of town. Also has a rooftop restaurant that serves a standard range of Indian, Chinese and continental. ❺

Chonor House Near Thekchen Choeling Gompa, South End ⓣ01892/221006, ⓦwww.norbulingka.org. Part of the Norbulingka Institute for Tibetan Culture, with very well presented rooms decorated by artists, combining traditional Tibetan decor with modern comfort. There's also an excellent restaurant, with garden seating. All proceeds go to Norbulingka. ❻

Glenmoor Cottages above Mall Rd ⓣ01892/221010, ⓦwww.glenmoorcottages.com. Five luxurious cottages with impressive wood panelling and less expensive rooms in the main building, set in picturesque woodlands about 1km above the main bazaar. ❼–❽

Green Bhagsu Rd ⓣ01892/221200, ⓦwww.greenhotel.biz. Wide range of well-kept, comfortable rooms, with valley views, a good restaurant, and adjacent internet café. Deservedly popular. ❶–❷

Kunga's Bhagsu Rd ⓣ01892/221180, ⓔtenzin_dhonyo@yahoo.co.in. Clean and centrally located with a variety of rooms and a fantastic sun deck; larger rooms are spacious and light, with big balconies. The down-to-earth owner Tenzin caters to the needs of all guests and manages one of the best restaurants in town. ❶–❷

Ladies Venture Jogiwara Rd, past the *Chocolate Log* ⓣ01892/221559, ⓔshantiazad@yahoo.co.in. Well-appointed rooms of varying size in a welcoming Tibetan-run hotel. Quiet location, with a garden and a small café. Fixed price year round. Dorm beds Rs80. ❶–❷

Loseling Guest House Off Jogiwara Rd ⓣ01892/221087, ⓦwww.loselingmonastery.org. Simple monastery-owned lodge, plain and well maintained with good views from an open roof terrace. Upstairs rooms are best but usually fill up first; space in the 3-bed dorm is just Rs60. Fixed price year round. ❶

Om Near the bus stand ⓣ01892/221322, ⓔomhotel@hotmail.com. Simple, quiet and very friendly lodge on the western edge of town. A variety of rooms; the cheapest ones share squat toilet bathrooms and hot showers. The upper terrace and pleasant restaurant are popular spots for sunset. ❶

Paljor Gakyil TIPA Rd ⓣ01892/221443, ⓔngapal@yahoo.com. Immaculate lodge with plain or carpeted rooms, dorm beds (Rs50) and great views over McLeod Ganj. To get here, climb the steps between the *Seven Hills* and *Kalsang* guesthouses. ❶

Pema Thang South End ⓣ01892/221871, ⓦwww.pemathang.net. Friendly hotel, the best maintained on South End. Rooms all have heaters, hot showers and TV; you'll pay more for a good view. Popular with well-off Westerners interested in Buddhism. ❹

Surya McLeod South End ⓣ01892/221418, ⓦwww.suryamcleod.com. Big, brash, modern hotel, with some large glass-fronted rooms facing west over the plains, aimed mainly at businessmen and domestic tourists. ❻

Tibet Bhagsu Rd ⓣ01892/221587, ⓔhtdshala@sancharnet.in. Excellent hotel with the superb *Snow Lion* restaurant; the downstairs valley-facing rooms offer the best value. Popular and central. Fixed prices all year. ❸–❹

Zilnon Kagyeling Monastery Bhagsu Rd ⓣ01892/ 220581. Basic and extremely cheap single and double rooms with shared facilities in an active *gompa*. You'll find the monk in room 50. Great café. ❶

Bhagsu

Sky Pie Guest House Off the left turning as you approach temple ⓣ01892/220497, ⓔdenisraaz8@gmail.com. Friendly and lively place with standard budget rooms, some with shared bathrooms. ❶–❸

Trimurti Guest House Upper Bhagsu towards Dharamkot ⓣ01892/221364, ⓦwww.trimurtimusic.com. A few rooms in a quiet family place with a lawn and colourful shrine. The owner runs a small music school; see p.434. ❷–❸

Dharamkot

Dev Cottages Off the main road before the teashop ⓣ01892/221558. Smart and spacious new cottages, comfortably furnished with fine valley views. ❹–❺

New Blue Heaven Off the main road before the teashop ⓣ01892/221005, ⓔsandeep74gill@yahoo.co.in. Two-storey family house with sociable terrace and garden. All rooms are simple but attached. ❶–❷

Dharamsala

HPTDC Dhauladhar Off Kotwali Bazaar, near the bank ⓣ01892/224926, ⓔdharamshala@hptdc.in. Institutional-feeling place with spacious attached rooms with constant hot water and balconies giving superb views over the plains to the south. Plus a good mid-priced restaurant, bar, garden terrace and lawns. ❺–❻

Dharamsala

It's easy to see why most visitors bypass Dharamsala itself, a haphazard jumble of shops, offices and houses. The only place of interest is the **Museum of Kangra Art** (Tues–Sun 10am–5pm; Rs50), with a small collection of Kangra miniatures and some modern art. On foot, the quickest route up to McLeod Ganj is up a steep 3km track that starts from behind the vegetable market, passing the Tibetan Library and Secretariat.

McLeod Ganj

The ever-expanding settlement of **McLeod Ganj** extends along a pine-covered ridge with valley views below and the near vertical walls of the Dhauladhar range towering behind. Despite being named after David McLeod, the Lieutenant Governor of Punjab when the hill station was founded in 1848, little evidence of British occupation remains. Intersected by two narrow potholed roads, the focal point of McLeod Ganj is its Buddhist **temple**, ringed with spinning red and gold prayer wheels. Today, Indian residents are outnumbered by Tibetans, who bedeck their ramshackle buildings with fluttering prayer flags: McLeod Ganj is not simply a political haven for them, but also home to their spiritual leader, the Dalai Lama, and to the Tibetan government in exile.

It's easy to **find your way around** McLeod Ganj. At its northern end, the road up from the lower town arrives at a small square that serves as the bus stand. Roads radiating from here head south to the Dalai Lama's Residence and the **Library of Tibetan Works and Archives**, northeast to the village of Dharamkot, the Tushita Retreat Meditation Centre and to the Tibetan Children's Village next to Dal Lake, and east to the hamlet of Bhagsu.

The Dalai Lama's Residence and the Tibet Museum

The Dalai Lama settled temporarily in McLeod Ganj in 1960; five decades later he's still here, and his **Residence** on the south edge of town has become his permanent home in exile. His own quarters are modest, and most of the walled compound overhanging the valley is taken up by government offices. In front of the private enclosure, Dharamsala's main Buddhist temple, **Tsug Lakhang**,

Meeting His Holiness the Dalai Lama

The **Dalai Lama** is in great demand. Tibetans fleeing their homeland come to him for blessing and reassurance; monks and nuns from all over India and Nepal look to him for spiritual guidance; and an ever-increasing number of Westerners arrive in Dharamsala hoping for a moment of his attention. Twenty years ago it might have been possible for people to meet His Holiness on an individual basis; now casual visitors should count on attending a **public audience**, when he greets and shakes the hands of several hundred people. These are held every few weeks if His Holiness is in town, though there are no fixed dates or timings. Ask the Branch Security Office (above the Welfare Office on Bhagsu Road ⓣ01892/221560) when the next audience will be, but note that they themselves only know a couple of days in advance. You'll need to register here too; bring a passport and some passport photos, and expect to wait. If you're interested in attending His Holiness's **public teachings**, check ⓦwww.tibet.net for dates, locations and what to expect. **Private audiences** are granted to a select few, and can only be arranged by writing at least four months in advance. The Dalai Lama's secretary receives hundreds of such letters each day, and each case is reviewed on its merits.

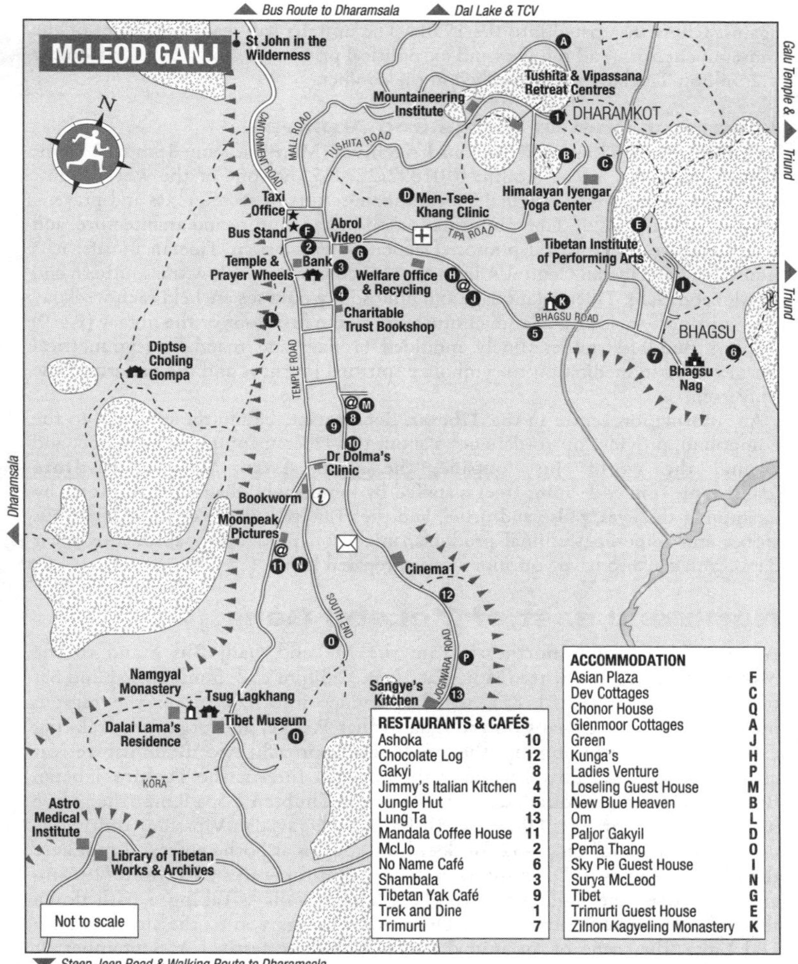

shelters images of Sakyamuni (the historical Buddha), Padmasambhava (who introduced Buddhism to Tibet) and Avalokitesvara (the *bodhisattva* of compassion) seated in meditation postures, surrounded by offerings from devotees. After paying homage to the Buddha inside, devotees complete a *kora*, a circumambulation of the temple complex (clockwise, starting at the trailhead below the monks' quarters), turning the numerous prayer wheels to send prayers out in all directions. Every afternoon monks from the nearby **Namgyal monastery** hold fierce but disciplined debates in the courtyard opposite the temple. The small *Namgyal Café* provides quality meals and snacks.

Next to the monastery, the **Tibet Museum** (Tues–Sun 9am–5pm; Rs5) displays in graphic detail the plight of the Tibetan people since China invaded Tibet in 1949. Using photographs and video clips, the self-guided tour describes how Tibetan freedom fighters, backed by the CIA, waged an impossible guerrilla war against China that lasted into the 1970s. The upstairs hall features profiles of the museum curators – all refugees and ex-political prisoners – and a memorial to the 1.2 million Tibetans who have died in the conflict.

Library of Tibetan Works and Archives

The **Library of Tibetan Works and Archives** (Mon–Sat 9am–1pm & 2–5pm; closed 2nd & 4th Sat of month; ⓣ01892/222467) has one of the world's most extensive collections of original Tibetan manuscripts of sacred texts and prayers, books on all aspects of Tibet, information on Indian culture and architecture, and a rich archive of historical photos. Decorated with bright Tibetan motifs, it is housed in the Tibetan Central Administration compound, below the southern end of McLeod Ganj. Tibetan language and philosophy **courses** are held each weekday (see "Listings", p.437), and a small **museum** on the first floor of the library (Rs10) displays Buddhist statues, finely moulded bronzes and mandalas (symmetrical images, used in meditation to symbolize spiritual journeys and the pattern of the universe).

An information centre in the **Tibetan Secretariat**, beside the entrance to the compound, provides up-to-date news about the Tibetan community in Tibet and around the world. Just outside, the small **Astro Medical Institute** (daily 9am–1pm & 2–5pm; free) is staffed by monks who diagnose symptoms by examining the eyes, pulse and urine, and prescribe pills made of herbs, precious stones and sometimes animal products, mixed on particularly auspicious lunar dates. You can also have your horoscope prepared here.

North and east of McLeod Ganj

A minor road winds northeast from the McLeod Ganj Bus Stand to the **Mountaineering Institute** (Mon–Sat 10am–1.30pm & 2–5pm; closed 2nd Sat of month; ⓣ01892/221787), which provides information on the region, including books and maps on the Dhauladhar Range, and organizes trekking expeditions. Continuing up the road you approach two Buddhist retreat centres, both beautifully situated in the midst of forests: the **Tushita** Tibetan Buddhist Centre was founded in 1972 by Lama Thubten Zopa Rinpoche, while just around the corner is **Dhamma Sikhara**, a Theravadan Vipassana centre (see under "Meditation" on p.437 for details of courses at both centres). From here the road continues to Dharamkot, starting point for walks to **Triund** (2975m) and treks over the high passes to the Chamba Valley. Taking a path down through the wooded slopes from Dharamkot brings you to the small, murky **Dal Lake**, the scene of an animal fair and Shaivite festival in September. It stands behind the **Tibetan Children's Village** (TCV), a huge complex providing education and training in traditional handicrafts for around two thousand students, many of whom are orphans or have been brought to safety by parents who have returned to Tibet.

Bhagsu Road heads east from McLeod Ganj's main square, skirting the hillside for 2km before reaching the village of **Bhagsu** with its ancient Shiva temple. The last few years have seen big changes here, with the construction of several hotels catering primarily for the domestic tourist market. However it's still a pleasant enough place, with a few cafés near the temple complex. Beyond the temple a path meanders up the boulder-strewn slopes of a small stream up to a **waterfall**. If you're interested in studying tabla, contact Ashoka at the *Trimurti Guest House* (see p.431); he runs the **Trimurti International Music School** from his home. Note: there have been several **attacks** on women walking between Bhagsu and McLeod Ganj in the past few years. Don't walk it alone.

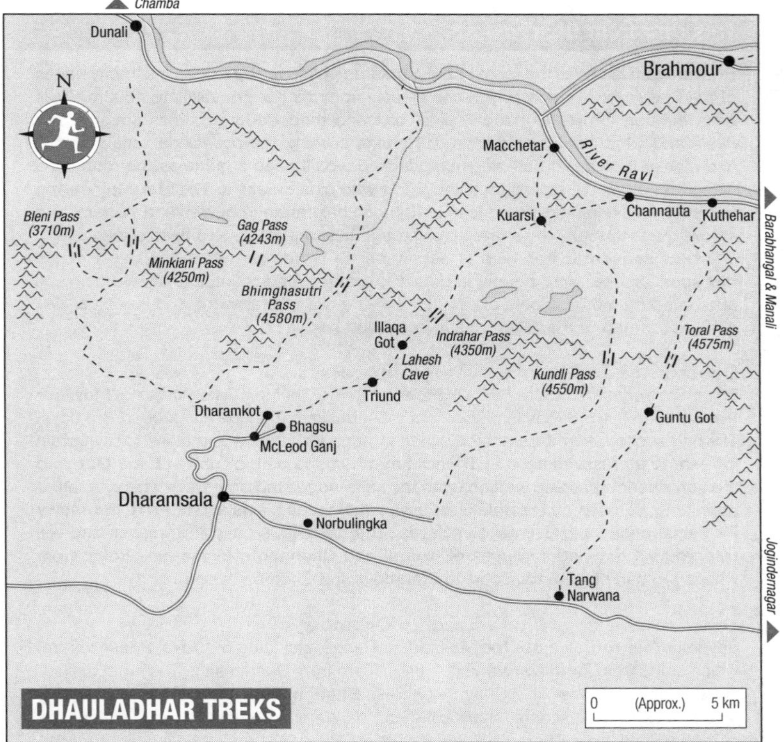

Tibetan Institute of Performing Arts

The **Tibetan Institute of Performing Arts** was founded in 1959 to preserve the Tibetan identity in exile. Around 150 people live on its campus, in the forests above McLeod Ganj overlooking Bhagsu, including artists, teachers, musicians and administrators. The TIPA troupe perform traditional *lhamo* operas, which derive from ancient masked dance dramas, and have played a morale-building role at Tibetan refugee camps throughout India, while also sharing Tibet's cultural heritage with international audiences. Visit its office for information on upcoming events and tours (Mon–Sat 9am–noon & 1–5pm, closed 2nd & 4th Sat of month; ⓣ01892/221478, ⓦwww.tibetanarts.org).

South of McLeod Ganj: the Norbulingka Institute

Eight kilometres (30min) from Dharamsala, near the village of Sidpur, the **Norbulingka Institute** (Mon–Sat 8am–5pm; ⓣ01892/246402, ⓦwww.norbulingka.org) is dedicated to preserving literary and artistic Tibetan culture. The complex of Tibetan-style buildings, built in 1985, is set amidst peaceful Japanese gardens, and centres on the two-storey **Deden Tsuglakhang temple**, which houses 1173 images of the Buddha and frescoes of the fourteen Dalai Lamas in the upper gallery. The gilded copper statue of Sakyamuni in the hall

Trekking from Dharamsala

Dharamsala is one of the most popular starting points for **treks** over the rocky ridges of the Dhauladhar Range, which rise steeply from the Kangra Valley to 4600m. Trails pass through forests of deodar, pine, oak and rhododendron, cross streams and rivers and wind along vertiginous cliff tracks passing the occasional lake waterfall and glacier. Unless you are very experienced, you'll need a guide as the routes are steep and memorial stones testify to those who didn't make it. The **Mountaineering Institute** on Dharamkot Road (see p.434) can help arrange guides and porters, and stocks maps. Despite the availability of rough huts and caves, it's best to take a tent. The best **season** to trek here is September to November, when the worst of the monsoon is over and before it gets too cold. Winter climbing should only be attempted by mountaineers experienced in the use of crampons and ice axes. See p.435 for a **map** of the hiking routes described below.

Dharamsala to Chamba over Indrahar Pass

The most frequented route from Dharamsala to the Chamba Valley, over the **Indrahar Pass** (4350m), is arduous in places, but most trekkers manage it in around five days. The first section, from Dharamkot, winds through thick forest and steep rocky terrain for 9km to a grassy plateau at **Triund**. From here the path climbs to **Laqa Got**, and then on a seriously steep section up to the knife-edged Indrahar Pass where, weather permitting, you'll enjoy breathtaking views south to the plains and north to the snowy Pir Panjal peaks and Greater Himalayas. The descent is difficult in places and will take you via the Gaddi villages of **Kuarsi** and **Channauta** to the main road, from where you can pick up transport to Brahmour and Chamba by road.

Other routes from Dharamsala to Chamba

Several **other routes** cross the Dhauladhar Range, including the **Toral Pass** (4575m) which starts from **Tang Narwana** (1150m), 10km from Dharamsala. The most difficult route north is the five- or six-day trek across **Bhimghasutri Pass** (4580m), covering near-vertical rocky ascents, sharp cliffs and dangerous gorges. A much easier four- or five-day trek from Dharamsala crosses **Bleni Pass** (3710m) in the milder ranges to the northwest, weaving through alpine pastures and woods and crossing a few streams, before terminating at **Dunali**, on the Chamba road.

downstairs is the largest of its kind outside Tibet. Elsewhere in the complex, the **Losel Doll Museum** shows colourful dioramas packed with traditionally clothed dolls. If you'd like to **stay**, the *Norling Guest House* (☎01892/246406; ❻–❼) in the gardens is clean and well decorated; even if you don't stop over it's worth a look for its upstairs gallery of fifty drawings that chronicle the life of the fourteenth Dalai Lama.

Eating

McLeod Ganj is one of those places where sitting, chatting and philosophizing in **restaurants** is the favoured activity. Tibetan dishes such as *thukpa* and *momos* are prominent, along with Chinese egg noodles, chow mein and stir-fry. Fresh-baked Tibetan bread and cakes are widely available, and you'll also come across omelettes, chips, toast, veggie-burgers and plenty of Israeli dishes. If you fancy making some Tibetan food, *Sangye's Kitchen* near the Post Office on Jogiwara Road holds **cooking lessons** (Sun–Fri 11am–1pm & 5–7pm; Rs150). In **Dharamsala**, there's no shortage of snack stalls, but less choice of cuisine: your best bet for Indian and Western dishes is the *City Heart* hotel, while *Potala* is a small but clean Tibetan café with a simple menu. In **Dharamkot**, *Trek and Dine*, a ten-minute walk uphill from the chai stall at the junction, is a good place to grab a bite with pizza and pies. In **Bhagsu**, the great-value *Trimurti*, next to the temple (not in the guesthouse of the same name), is an excellent Indian veg café with a rooftop terrace. Halfway up towards the waterfall the *No Name* café serves basic snacks.

Ashoka Jogiwara Rd. Huge portions of fine and, if required, spicy Indian food are served in two indoor rooms and on a plain roof terrace for Rs100–200. Try the *karai* chicken.

Chocolate Log Jogiwara Rd. Delicious cakes, pies and truffles plus savouries such as spinach pizza. Eat inside or laze on deck chairs in a pleasant garden. Most items Rs50–100. Closed Tues.

Gakyi Jogiwara Rd. Humble and homely, with great Tibetan and Western veg dishes, plus the town's best fruit muesli and Tibetan bread. All items under Rs100.

Jimmy's Italian Kitchen Jogiwara Rd. Snug café decorated with classic film posters. Good salads, baked potatoes, lattes and home-made desserts; dinners mainly Rs100–150. A brand-new upstairs branch 30m towards the temple has live music on Wed and Sat.

Jungle Hut Bhagsu Rd. This bamboo structure perched on the top of a hillside building offers the best views in the area. Food ranges from western breakfasts to standard Indian and Chinese mains for around Rs100.

Lung Ta Jogiwara Rd. Japanese vegetarian place with a constantly changing menu that usually includes miso soup, sushi, tempura vegetables and tofu steak; main courses around Rs100. Profits go to assisting former Tibetan political prisoners. The Korean restaurant next door, *Dokebi Nara*, offers hotpot dishes in a cozy atmosphere.

Mandala Coffee House Temple Rd. Great hang-out place offering comfort food like cakes (Rs30–50) and proper coffee. Also has wi-fi.

McLlo Central Square. Massive neon-lit monstrosity overlooking the bus stop. Large selection of good Western food (from Rs100), an official *Baskin-Robbins* ice-cream parlour and a second-floor drinking den which is pleasant early evening but can get very rowdy later on.

Shambala Jogiwara Rd. One of the best venues in Dharamsala for Tibetan and Chinese food, veg and non-veg; also fish specials for around Rs100.

Tibetan Yak Cafe Jogiwara Rd. Tiny, simple restaurant, popular with locals, serving good Tibetan food for Rs40–60.

Listings

Banks and exchange The Punjab National Bank (Mon–Fri 10am–2pm, Sat 10am–noon) in McLeod Ganj near the bus stand will change travellers' cheques and cash, as will the upper branch of State Bank of India in Dharamsala. Both also have ATMs. There are several authorized exchange agencies in McLeod Ganj, such as Thomas Cook and LKP Forex on Temple Rd, who provide cash advances on credit and debit cards.

Bookshops The Tibetan Bookshop and Information Office is a good place to browse for books on Tibetan Buddhism, as is the Charitable Trust Shop, both on Jogiwara Rd in McLeod Ganj's main bazaar. Bookworm, opposite the tourist office, South End, is small but has a very good selection, especially on Buddhism, and also stocks second-hand books.

Cinema Cinemaa1 and Abrol Video, both on Jogiwara Rd, show Hollywood flicks, often with a Tibetan or Indian theme.

Courses Numerous courses are available in McLeod Ganj, including *dharma* teachings, Tibetan language, Hindi, ancient Thai massage, yoga, tabla, karate, Xi Gung, Tai Chi, Reiki, and Indian vegetarian and Tibetan cookery. Free classes on *dharma* are given in translation by Buddhist monks from 11am until noon most weekdays at the Library of Tibetan Works and Archives. Philosophy courses and three-month Tibetan language courses (beginning March, June & Sept) are also run from the library (contact the Secretary for Tibetan Studies ⓣ01892/222467).

Hospitals The Tibetan Delek Hospital (ⓣ01892/222053), above the Astro Medical Institute, is one of the best hospitals in the state and has Western doctors on call.

Internet access McLeod Ganj has a multitude of internet cafés, either attached to hotels such as the *Green* or in separate establishments, mainly on Bhagsu Rd or Jogiwara Rd. Most charge Rs20/hr.

Meditation Tibetan Buddhist meditation courses are held at the Tushita Meditation Centre in Dharamkot (office Mon–Sat 9.30–11.30am & 1–4.30pm; ⓣ01892/221866, ⓦwww.tushita.info). Courses range from short retreats of eight to ten days to an intensive three-month summer purification retreat (Vajrasattva). Accommodation is available in simple rooms and dorms and there's also an excellent library. Book well in advance.

The Vipassana Centre, next door, follows teachings more akin to Theravada Buddhism. They run ten-day silent retreats and daily sittings (register in person Mon–Sat 4–5pm or contact ⓣ01892/221309, ⓦwww.sikhara.dhamma.org).

Post office McLeod Ganj's post office, on Jogiwara Rd, has a poste restante counter that holds letters for up to one month. Letters not addressed to McLeod Ganj, Upper Dharamsala, end up in the GPO in the lower town.

Shopping Stalls and little shops along the main streets stock Tibetan trinkets, inexpensive warm clothing, incense, prayer bells, rugs and books. The large handicrafts shop on Jogiwara Rd sells *thangkas* of all sizes, along with prayer flags, and you can have a *bakku* (a Tibetan women's dress) stitched here for around Rs600 plus the cost of the cloth. The Green Shop, Bhagsu Rd, sells recycled painted cards, hand-painted T-shirts, books on the environment and filtered boiled water for Rs5.

Teaching The Yong Ling School, Jogiwara Rd on the left past the post office, welcomes volunteer teachers. An excellent resource for jobs is Volunteer Tibet (ⓦwww.volunteertibet.org), whose office is opposite the school.

Tibetan settlement For enquiries about the Tibetan settlement, call in either at the Welfare Office on Bhagsu Rd in McLeod Ganj or directly at the Reception Centre below the post office, where donations of clothes, books, blankets and pens for new Tibetan arrivals are always gratefully accepted. Another good place for information is the Tibetan Bookshop and Information Office on Jogiwara Rd.

Travel agents Himachal Travels, Jogiwara Rd (ⓣ01892/221428), books local and private buses, trains from Pathankot and domestic flights, and confirms or alters international flights. You can also rent taxis for journeys within Himachal Pradesh or beyond, and enquire about treks. Ways Tours & Travels, Temple Rd (ⓣ01892/221910), is a well-organized agency that handles international flights, organizes tailor-made itineraries around India and changes money. Yeti Trekking, on the road to the Mountaineering Institute (ⓣ01892/221032), offers treks and has plenty of equipment for rent.

Yoga The Himalayan Iyengar Yoga Centre (ⓦwww.hiyogacentre.com) in Dharamkot runs five-day courses in hatha yoga, starting every Thurs.

Dalhousie and around

The quiet, relaxed hill station of **Dalhousie** spreads over five low-level hills at the western edge of the Dhauladhar Range. While the town itself, mostly modern hotels interspersed with Raj-era buildings and low-roofed stalls, is unremarkable, the pine-covered slopes around it are intersected with paths and tracks ideal for short undemanding walks.

From Dalhousie the road east zigzags through forests to **Khajjiar**, a popular local day out, before descending through terraced mountain slopes to **Chamba**, perched above the rushing River Ravi. It's a slow and relaxed place with some fascinating temples and a small art museum. **Brahmour**, three hours further east by bus and the final settlement on the road into the mountains, holds more Hindu temples – both towns make good bases for **treks** into the remote **Pangi Valley**.

Dalhousie

DALHOUSIE owes its name to Lord Dalhousie, Governor General of Punjab (1849–56), who was attracted by the cool climate to establish a sanatorium here for the many British, who, like himself, suffered ill health. Early in the twentieth century, it was a popular alternative to crowded, expensive Shimla, but thereafter declined. Today Dalhousie is a favourite summer retreat for holidaying Punjabis, but receives only a handful of Western tourists, few of whom stay longer than a day or two. A small population of Tibetans has lived here since the Chinese invasion of Tibet in 1959.

The town is spread over a series of hills with winding roads connecting the two focal points, the chowks. **Gandhi Chowk**, with its restaurants and post office, is the busiest section. From here the Mall and Garam Sarak dip and curve

2km to **Subhash Chowk**, at the top end of the largely Muslim Sadar Bazaar. North of here, the bus stand and information office mark the main road out of town.

Practicalities

Dalhousie is usually approached by **bus** from Pathankot in the Punjab, 80km southwest, or Chamba, 47km east; the journey through the Himalayan foothills from Dharamsala (6hr) and Shimla (18hr) is made via Nurpur. Transport to Chamba (2hr 15min) usually goes via Banikhet, though four buses also travel via Khajjiar. The **tourist information office** (Mon–Sat 10am–5pm; ⓣ01899/242136), 50m from the bus stand, provides transport information. A steep path leads up from the bus stand to the Mall; if you don't fancy the walk, local Maruti taxis (Rs50) ply the route. The State Bank of India at the bus stand has foreign **exchange** facilities and an ATM. Eva's Cyber Café, in the Tibetan Lhasa market above the bus stand, has internet facilities.

Numerous **hotels** cater for Dalhousie's hot-season hordes and most offer substantial **discounts** in the off-season. The *Silverton*, above the Circuit House on the Mall (ⓣ01899/240674, ⓦwww.heritagehotels.com/silverton; ❹–❼), is an old-world manor house with large rooms and immaculate lawns set within private woodlands. *Aroma-N-Claires* (ⓣ01899/242199, ⓕ242639; ❹–❺), a rambling 1930s building south of Subhash Chowk on Court Road, is atmospheric, cluttered and eccentric, with a library and leafy patios. Half a kilometre along a footpath, from Subhash Chowk, *Hotel Crags* on Garam Sarak Road (ⓣ01899/242124; ❷–❹) is a quiet and exceptionally friendly hotel with a large terrace, tasty food and great views down to the plains. The basic **youth hostel** (ⓣ01899/242189, ⓔyh_dalhousie@rediffmail.com; ❶), five minutes' walk behind the *dhabas* from the bus stand, has dorm beds (Rs60) and doubles. Apart from the hotel restaurants and scattered *dhabas*, **places to eat** include *Food Junction* at the bus stand, *Kwality's* at Gandhi Chowk, and *Moti Mahal* and *Sher-e-Punjab* at Subhash Chowk.

Khajjiar

Heading east towards Chamba, the road descends through deodar forests to the meadow of **Khajjiar** where the small twelfth-century temple of **Khajjinag** looks down over a vast rolling green with a small lake cupped in the centre. Khajjiar is a popular day-trip from Dalhousie for Indian tourists who come to take pony rides. If you want to stay, the *Shining Star Resort* (ⓣ01899/236336, ⓦwww.shiningstarkhajjiar.com; ❺) is a plush hotel with a decent restaurant and fine views. The road past Khajjiar dips across denuded and terraced hillsides down towards Chamba. Prince Travels at the bus stand in Dalhousie runs a tourist **bus** to Khajjiar and Chamba, departing at 10am and returning to Dalhousie at 6.30pm; alternatively, four Chamba-bound buses travel via Khajjiar every day.

Chamba

Shielded on all sides by high mountains, **CHAMBA** was ruled for an entire millennium by kings descended from Raja Sahil Varma, who founded it in 920 AD and named it after his daughter Champavati. Unlike Himachal states further south, it was never formally under Mughal rule and its distinct Hindu culture remained intact until the first roads were built to Dalhousie in 1870. When the state of Himachal Pradesh was formed in 1948, Chamba became the capital. Today, only a handful of visitors make it out here, passing through before or after trekking, or stopping off to see the unique **temples**.

Chamba festivals

Chamba's annual four-day **Suhi Mata Festival**, in early April, commemorates Rani Sunena, the wife of the tenth-century Raja Sahil Verma. A curious legend relates that when water from a nearby stream failed to flow through a channel supposed to divert it to the town, local brahmins advised Raja Verma that either his son or his wife would have to sacrifice themselves. The queen obliged; she was buried alive at the head of the channel, and the water flowed freely. Only women and children participate in the festival, dancing on the *chaugan* before processing with an image of Champavati (Rani Sunena's daughter who gave her name to the town) and banners of the clan's solar emblem to the Suhi Mata temple in the hills behind the town.

Minjar, a week of singing and dancing at the start of August to celebrate the growth of maize, is also peculiar to Chamba. Its climax comes on the last day, when a rowdy procession of locals, Gaddis and Gujjars, dressed in traditional costumes, leaves the palace and snakes down to the riverbank, where bunches of maize are thrown into the water. Before Independence, locals had the custom of pushing a male buffalo into the river; its drowning was an auspicious sign but if the beast managed to swim to the opposite bank bad fortune was expected for the coming year.

The *chaugan*, a large green used for sports, evening strolls and festive celebrations, marks the centre of town, overlooked by the **Rang Mahal** palace, now a government building. At the south end of the *chaugan*, the **Bhuri Singh museum** (Tues–Sun 10am–5pm; free) holds a reasonable display of local arts and crafts. Its eighteenth- and nineteenth-century **Kangra miniature paintings**, depicting court life, amorous meetings and men and women smoking elaborate hookahs, are much bolder than their Mughal-influenced Rajasthani equivalents. The museum's best feature is its small cache of **rumals**. Made by women since the tenth century, *rumals* are like embroidered paintings, depicting scenes from popular myth. Today only a few women continue this tradition, but a weaving centre in the old palace is attempting to revitalize the art.

The temples

The intimate complex of **Lakshmi Narayan temples**, behind Dogra Bazaar west of the *chaugan*, is of a style found only in Chamba and Brahmour. Three of its six earth-brown temples are dedicated to Vishnu and three to Shiva, all with profusely carved outer walls and curious curved *shikharas*, topped with overhanging wooden canopies and gold pinnacles added in 1678 in defiance of Aurangzeb's order to destroy all Hindu temples in the hill states. Niches in the walls contain images of deities, but many stand empty, some statues lost in the earthquake of 1905 and others looted more recently.

Entering the compound, you're confronted by the largest and oldest temple, built in the tenth century and enshrining a marble idol of Lakshmi Narayan. The buxom maidens flanking the entrance to the sanctuary, each holding a water vessel, represent the goddesses Ganga and Yamuna, while inside a frieze depicts scenes from the Mahabharata and Ramayana. Temples dedicated to Shiva fill the third courtyard. In the inner sanctuary, you'll see sturdy brass images of Shiva, Parvati and Nandi, inlaid with silver and copper brought from mines nearby. Outside the temple complex, **coppersmiths** manufacture curved ceremonial trumpets and brass hookahs.

Of Chamba's other temples, the most intriguing is the tenth-century **Chamunda Devi temple** high above the town in the north, a steep half-hour climb up steps that begin near the bus stand. Decorated with hundreds of heavy brass bells and

Treks around Chamba and Brahmour

The most popular treks from Chamba lead south over the **Dhauladhar** via the Minkiani or Indrahar pass to Dharamsala. **Equipment** can be rented and porters and **guides** hired in Chamba and Brahmour. Mani Mahesh Travels in Chamba (Ⓣ01899/222507) organizes and equips treks.

Treks in the Pangi Valley to Lahaul

Few trekkers make it to the spectacular, all but inaccessible **Pangi Valley**, between the soaring Greater Himalayan Range in the north and the Outer Himalayan Range in the south. Several peaks within it have never been climbed, and onward paths lead to Kashmir, Lahaul and Zanskar. The trek to Lahaul takes nine or ten days from **Traila** (90km north of Chamba) via Satraundhi (3500m) over the Sach Pass to Killar, Sach Khas, and finishing in Purthi from where you can take a bus via Tindi to **Udaipur**. Buses run from here to Keylong, capital of Lahaul, for connections northwards to Leh or south over the Rohtang Pass and down to Manali.

Treks from Brahmour

Trekking routes lead north from **Brahmour** (2130m) over the Pir Panjal range across passes that are covered with snow for most of the year. The challenging six- to seven-day trek over **Kalichho Pass** (4990m), "The Abode of Kali", ends in the village of **Triloknath**, whose ancient temple to three-faced Shiva is sacred to both Hindus and Buddhists. Buses run from here to Udaipur, and on to Keylong and Manali.

Another demanding five- to six-day route crosses the **Kugti Pass** (5040m). From **Hadsar**, an hour by bus from Brahmour, the path follows the River Budhil for 12km to **Kugti**, then up to **Kuddi Got**, a vast flower-filled meadow (4000m). The next stage, over the pass, requires crampons and ice axes for an incredibly taxing six-hour climb. Having enjoyed views of the towering peaks of Lahaul and Zanskar from the summit, you plummet once again to the head of a glacier at **Khardu**, continuing down to Raape, 7km from **Shansha**, which is linked to Udaipur and Keylong by road.

Finally, a delightful three-day trek to the sacred lake of **Manimahesh** (4183m) starts from and returns to Hadsar. The awesome Manimahesh Kailash massif, with its permanent glaciers and ice fields, overlooks the lake.

protecting a fearsome image of the bloodthirsty goddess Chamunda, the temple is built entirely of wood, and commands an excellent view up the Ravi gorge. Back in town, south of the *chaugan* near the post office, the small, lavishly carved eleventh-century **Harirai temple** contains a smooth brass image of Vaikuntha, the triple-headed aspect of Vishnu.

Practicalities

Buses arrive at the cramped bus stand in the north of town, close to several **lodges**, the best of which is the slightly shabby *Chamunda View* (Ⓣ01899/224067; ❶), below the bus stand. The HPTDC *Hotel Iravati* (Ⓣ01899/222671; ❹–❺) on the nearest corner of the *chaugan*, has comfortable, carpeted attached rooms; their cheaper annexe, *Champak* (Ⓣ01899/222774; ❷), has reasonable doubles and a dorm (Rs100). The best hotel in town is the modern *City Heart* (Ⓣ01899/225930, Ⓦwww.hotelcityheartchamba.com; ❺–❻), above the far end of the *chaugan*.

The best **food** can be found at the *Khaatir* in the *City Heart*, though the *Rishi* in Dogra Bazaar and *Park View* on Museum Road are decent alternatives. Try the local speciality, *madhra*, a rich, oily and slightly bitter mix of beans and curd. The uninspiring **tourist office** (Mon–Sat 10am–5pm; Ⓣ01899/224002) is part of the *Iravati* complex. **Internet** access is available at Mani Mahesh Travels. The Punjab

National Bank on Hospital Road cannot change **money** but will cash American Express travellers' cheques.

From Chamba, there is one **bus** a day for Dharamsala (9.30pm; 8–9hr), and two for Shimla (4am & 5pm; 15–16hr). There are buses every half-hour to **Banikhet** and hourly to **Pathankot**, and a daily departure to **Amritsar** (11pm; 8hr).

Brahmour

BRAHMOUR is a one-horse town of slate-roofed houses, apple trees and small maize fields, shadowed on all sides by high snowy peaks. The **temples**, whose curved *shikharas* dominate the large, neatly paved central square, are more dramatic and better preserved than their rivals at Chamba. The sanctuaries are unlocked only for puja in the mornings and evenings, permitting a glimpse of bold bronze images of Ganesh, Shiva and Parvati, unchanged since their installation in the seventh and eighth centuries when Brahmour was capital of the surrounding mountainous region.

Except during the September *yatra* or pilgrimage when everywhere is booked up, you can find **rooms** at a handful of guesthouses. Best choices are *Divya Cottage* (Ⓣ01090/275033; ❷) – probably the best in Brahmour – and *Shanti Guesthouse* (Ⓣ01090/225018; ❶) nearby. There isn't much choice of **food**; the *Chourasi* restaurant is a notch above the handful of stalls lining the main road between the bus stand and the square. The efficient Mountaineering Institute has details of local **treks**, reliable guides and porters, and equipment for rent.

The Kullu Valley

The majestic **KULLU VALLEY** is cradled by the Pir Panjal to the north, the Parvati Range to the east, and the Barabhangal Range to the west. This is Himachal at its most idyllic, with roaring rivers, pretty mountain villages, orchards and terraced fields, thick pine forests and snow-flecked ridges.

Known in the ancient Hindu scriptures as **Kulanthapitha**, or "End of the Habitable World", the Kullu Valley extends 80km north from the mouth of the perilously steep and narrow **Larji Gorge**, near Mandi, to the foot of the **Rohtang Pass** – gateway to Lahaul and Ladakh. For centuries, it formed one of the major trade corridors between Central Asia and the Gangetic plains, and local rulers, based first at **Jagatsukh** and later at **Naggar** and Sultanpur (now **Kullu**), were able to rake off handsome profits from the through traffic. This trade monopoly, however, also made it a prime target for invasion, and in the eighteenth and early nineteenth centuries the Kullu rajas were forced to repulse attacks by both the Raja of Kangra and the Sikhs, before seeing their lands annexed by the British in 1847. Over the following years, colonial families crossed the Jalori Pass from Shimla, making the most of the valley's alpine climate to grow the **apples** that, along with **cannabis** cultivation, today form the mainstay of the rural economy. The first road, built in 1927 to export the fruit, spelled the end of the peace and isolation, prompting many settlers to pack up and leave long before Independence. The population expanded again in the 1950s and 1960s with an influx of **Tibetan refugees**.

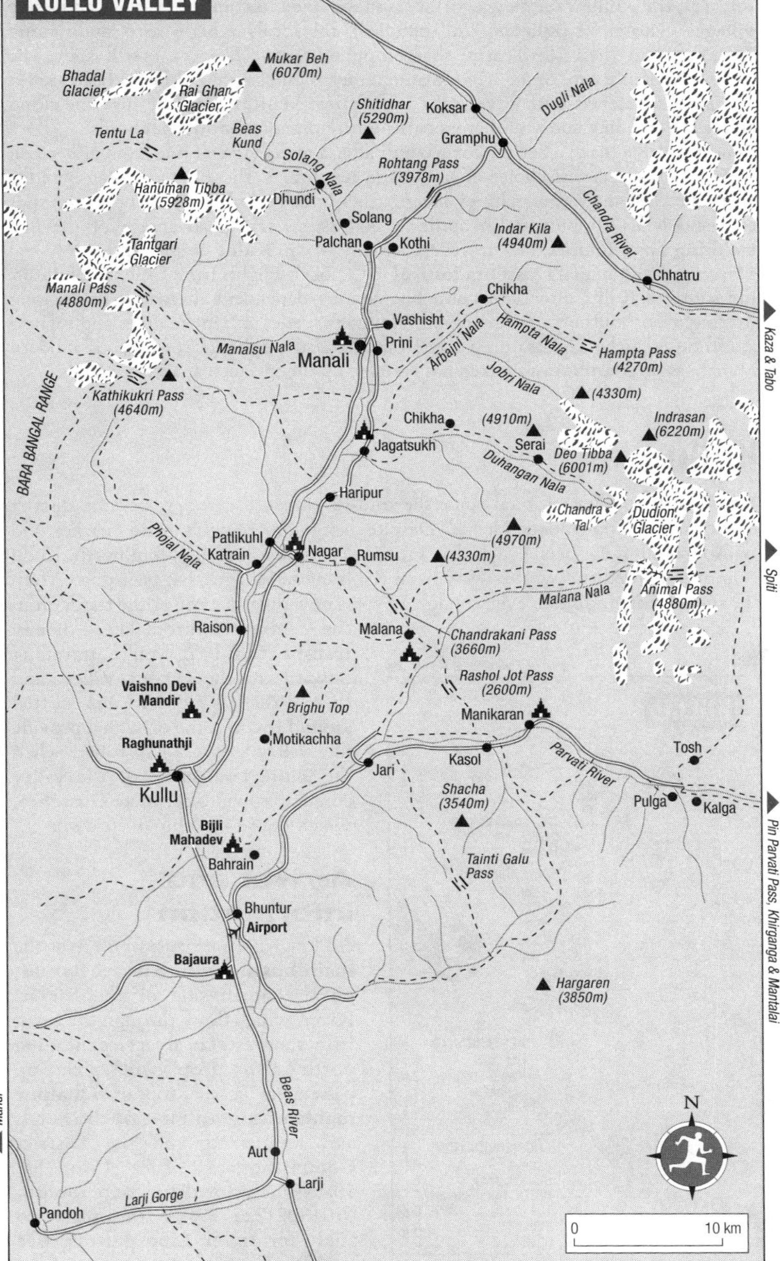
KULLU VALLEY
Leh & Lahaul
Mukar Beh (6070m)
Bhadal Glacier
Rai Ghan Glacier
Shitidhar (5290m)
Koksar
Dugli Nala
Tentu La
Beas Kund
Gramphu
Solang Nala
Rohtang Pass (3978m)
Hanuman Tibba (5928m)
Dhundi
Chandra River
Solang
Indar Kila (4940m)
Tantgari Glacier
Palchan
Kothi
Chhatru
Manali Pass (4880m)
Chikha
Vashisht
Hampta Nala
Prini
Arbajni Nala
Hampta Pass (4270m)
Manalsu Nala
Manali
Jobri Nala
Kathikukri Pass (4640m)
(4330m)
BARA BANGAL RANGE
Chikha
(4910m)
Indrasan (6220m)
Serai
Jagatsukh
Deo Tibba (6001m)
Duhangan Nala
Haripur
Chandra Tal
Dudion Glacier
Phojal Nala
Patlikuhl
(4970m)
Katrain
Nagar
Rumsu
(4330m)
Animal Pass (4880m)
Malana Nala
Raison
Malana
Chandrakani Pass (3660m)
Rashol Jot Pass (2600m)
Vaishno Devi Mandir
Brighu Top
Manikaran
Motikachha
Tosh
Raghunathji
Kasol
Parvati River
Jari
Kullu
Shacha (3540m)
Pulga
Kalga
Bijli Mahadev
Bahrain
Tainti Galu Pass
Bhuntur
Airport
Bajaura
Hargaren (3850m)
Mandi
Beas River
N
Aut
Larji
Larji Gorge
Pandoh
0
10 km
Banjar
Kaza & Tabo
Spiti
Pin Parvati Pass, Khirganga & Mantalai

In spite of the changes wrought by roads, immigration and, more recently, mass tourism, the Kullu Valley's way of life is maintained in countless timber and stone villages. Known as **paharis** ("hill people"), the locals – high-caste landowning Thakurs, and their (low-caste) sharecropping tenant farmers – still sport the distinctive Kullu cap, or *topi*. The women, meanwhile, wear colourful headscarves and *puttoos* fastened with silver pins and chains. Venture into the lush meadows above the tree line and you'll cross paths with nomadic **Gaddi** shepherds.

Most tourists make a beeline for **Manali** after a gruelling bus ride from either Leh or Delhi. With its vast choice of hotels and restaurants, there is something here for everyone. Still an evergreen hippy hangout, it's India's number-one honeymoon spot too, and is also popular with outdoors enthusiasts taking advantage of the fine **trekking** opportunities. Few travellers actually stay in **Kullu town** and the only real attraction is the annual **Dussehra festival** in October. Flights from Delhi to Bhuntur, just south of Kullu, offer a welcome but weather-dependent alternative to the long overnight bus journeys. To the north, **Naggar**'s castle, ancient temples and relaxed guesthouses make a pleasant change from the claustrophobic concrete of modern Manali, as do **Manikaran**'s sacred hot springs, up the spectacular **Parvati Valley**.

Kullu

KULLU, the valley's capital since the mid-seventeenth century, became district headquarters after Independence. Despite being the region's main market and transport hub it has been eclipsed as a tourist centre by Manali, 40km north. Kullu is noisy, polluted and worlds away from the tranquil villages that peer down from the surrounding hillsides, even though a bypass now diverts some of the traffic from the centre. Kullu makes a handy **transport hub** if you're travelling onwards to the Parvati Valley, and there are several **temples** dotted around town, some of which provide fine valley views. In October, when the entire population of the valley comes to town to celebrate **Dussehra**, the city takes on a life of its own.

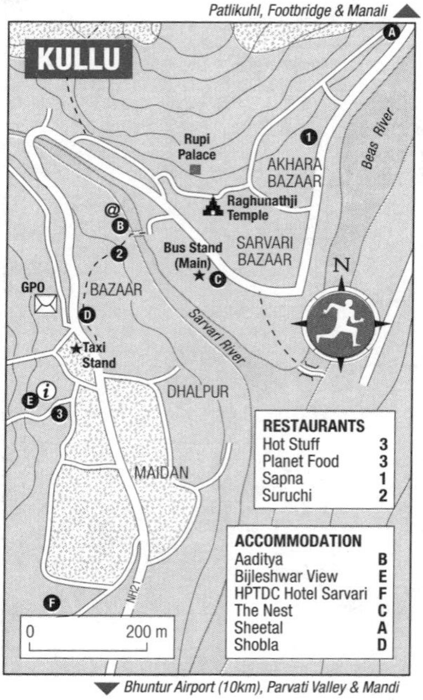

Arrival and information

All long-distance **buses** pull in at the **main bus stand** in **Sarvari Bazaar**, on the north side of the Sarvari River, which flows through the town from the west. Local services heading north also drop and pick up passengers at the top of **Dhalpur maidan**, close to most of the hotels and restaurants and the District Commissioner's office (Mon–Sat 10am–5pm, closed 2nd Sat of month; ⓣ01902/222727) – the place to apply for **Inner Line permits** (see p.408). HPTDC's **tourist office**

Moving on from Kullu

If you're travelling on to **Naggar**, catch one of the frequent Manali-bound buses that run north along the main road, on the west side of the valley, and jump off at **Patlikuhl**, where you can pick up a shared taxi or local bus for the remaining 6km. Roughly hourly buses also run direct to **Manali** via Naggar, a slower, but far more scenic route.

(daily 10am–6pm, until 8pm April–June; ⓣ01902/222349), on the west side of Dhalpur *maidan*, can book tickets on HPTDC's deluxe buses to Delhi, Shimla and Chandigarh. **Flights** to Kullu from Delhi and Shimla arrive in **Bhuntur**, thirty minutes south of Kullu by bus. Taxis to the airport (Rs200) should be booked in the union office (ⓣ01902/222322) on the main road close to the tourist office. Indian Airlines, Kingfisher and MDLR are all handled by Ambassador Travels (ⓣ01902/225286), in the LAC Building opposite the Dhalpur *maidan*. The most convenient **internet** café is next to the *Aaditya*.

Accommodation and eating

Kullu has a reasonable choice of **accommodation**. The rates quoted below are for low season; prices can double during high season and even quadruple for Dussehra. Apart from hotel **restaurants**, the best places to eat are at *Planet Food* and *Hot Stuff*, two similarly priced mixed-menu joints close to the tourist office. *Sapna*, an inexpensive sweetshop in Akhara Bazaar, also offers south Indian dishes, as does *Suruchi*, on the town side of the footbridge.

Aaditya Lower Dhalpur ⓣ01902/224263. Centrally located 200m from the bus stand, with attached rooms; the basic rooftop double is cheapest and has good views. ❷–❹

Bijleshwar View Behind the tourist office ⓣ01902/222677, ⓔvimalsharma27@yahoomail.com. Quiet, clean, central and friendly; large attached rooms with fireplaces, and cheaper bungalow accommodation. ❷–❸

HPTDC Hotel Sarvari South of the *maidan* and up a small lane ⓣ01902/222471. Quiet location with a wide range of rooms in old and new blocks. Good views down the valley, Ayurvedic massage, and a restaurant and bar. Dorm Rs100. ❹–❻

The Nest Next to the main bus stand ⓣ01902/222685, ⓔhotelnest@rediffmail.com. The best option near the bus stand, with clean, very good value doubles. The cheapest ground-floor rooms have bucket hot water; two of the pricier second-floor rooms have attached bathrooms with tubs. Fixed rates all year. ❶–❷

Sheetal Akhara Bazaar ⓣ01902/224548. Pleasant little guesthouse with rooms overlooking the river. Excellent value. ❷

Shobla Dhalpur ⓣ01902/222800. Kullu's top hotel, which has recently had a major revamp. Large rooms, a good mixed-cuisine restaurant and a relaxing lawn. ❹–❼

The temples

Kullu's most famous temple, the **Raghunathji Mandir** is home to a sacred statue of Lord Raghunathji, a manifestation of Rama, brought to Kullu by Raja Jagat Singh in the mid-seventeenth century. The raja had been advised by his priests to install the sacred icon here and crown it king in his place, and to this day the Kullu rajas consider themselves mere viceroys of Raghunathji, the most powerful *devta* in the valley and the focus of the Dussehra procession. The temple is tucked away behind the Kullu raja's **Rupi Palace** above the bus station. Half an hour's walk further up, the paved trail leads beyond the village of Sultanpur to a high ridge, with excellent views over the Beas River to the snow peaks in the east. **Vaishno Devi Mandir**, a small cave-temple that houses an image of the goddess Kali (Durga), is a stiff 3km further on.

Dussehra in the Valley of the Gods

In the Kullu region, often dubbed the **"Valley of the Gods"**, the village deity reigns supreme. No one knows how many *devtas* and *devis* inhabit the hills south of the Rohtang Pass, but nearly every hamlet has one. The part each one plays in village life depends on his or her particular **powers**; some heal, others protect the "parish" borders from evil spirits, summon the rains, or ensure the success of the harvest. Nearly all, however, communicate with their devotees by means of **oracles**. When called upon to perform, the village shaman, or **gaur** – drawn from the lower castes – strips to the waist and enters a trance in which the *devta* uses his voice to speak to the congregation. The deity, carried out of the temple on a ceremonial palanquin, or *rath*, rocks back and forth on the shoulders of its bearers as the *gaur* speaks. His words are always heeded, and his decisions final; the *devta*-oracle decides the propitious dates for marriages, and for sowing crops, and arbitrates disputes.

Dussehra

The single most important outing for any village deity is **Dussehra**, which takes place in the town of **Kullu** every October after the monsoons. Although the week-long festival ostensibly celebrates Rama's victory over the demon-king of Lanka, Ravana, it is also an opportunity for the *devtas* to reaffirm their position in the grand pecking order that prevails among them – a rigid hierarchy in which the Kullu raja's own tutelary deity Rama, alias **Raghunathji**, is king.

On the tenth day of the new, or "white" moon in October, between 150 and 200 *devtas* make their way to Kullu to pay homage to Raghunathji. As befits a region that holds its elderly women in high esteem, the procession proper cannot begin until **Hadimba**, the grandmother of the royal family's chief god, arrives from the Dunghri temple in Manali. Like her underlings, she is borne on an elaborately carved wooden *rath* swathed in glittering silk and garlands, and surmounted by a richly embroidered parasol, or chhatri. Raghunathji leads the great **procession** in his six-wheeled *rath*. Hauled from the Rupi palace by two hundred honoured devotees, the palanquin lurches to a halt in the middle of Kullu's *maidan*, to be circumambulated by the raja, his family, and retinue of priests. Thereafter, the festival's more secular aspect comes to the fore. **Folk dancers** perform for the vast crowds, and the *maidan* is taken over by market stalls, sweet-sellers, snake charmers, astrologers, sadhus and tawdry circus acts. The revelries finally draw to a close six days later on the full moon, when the customary **blood sacrifices** of a young buffalo, a goat, a cock, a fish and a crab are made to the god.

Kullu's Dussehra, now a major tourist attraction, has become increasingly staged and commercialized. Book accommodation in advance, and be prepared for a crush if you want to get anywhere near the *devtas*.

Another important temple, the **Bijli Mahadev Mandir**, stands 8km southeast of town, atop the bluff that overlooks the sacred confluence of the Beas and Parvati rivers. Although it's closer to Bhuntur than Kullu, you have to approach the temple via the Akhara Bazaar–Tapu suspension bridge and a well-worn track south along the left bank of the Beas. Bijli Mahadev is renowned for its extraordinary **lingam**. Bolts of lightning, conducted into the inner sanctum by means of the twenty-metre, trident-tipped pole, are said to periodically shatter the icon, which later, with the help of invocations from the resident *pujari*, magically reconstitutes itself. From the temple there are superb panoramic views of the Parvati and Kullu valleys and Himachal's highest peaks. You can **stay** in the temple resthouse (donations welcome), a simple affair with a single cold tap and no toilets, and walk down into the Parvati Valley the next day.

The Parvati Valley

Hemmed in by giant-pinnacled mountain peaks, the **Parvati Valley**, which twists west from the glaciers and snowfields on the Spiti border to meet the Beas at Bhuntur, is the Kullu Valley's longest tributary. It's a picturesque place, with quiet hamlets perching precariously on its sides amid lush terraces and old pine forests. Though the landscape around **Jari** has been scarred by the ugly **Malana hydro project**, there is strong local pressure to at least camouflage the site. Visitors to the valley are an incongruous mix – a combination of Western hippies (especially Israelis) and van-loads of Sikh pilgrims bound for the *gurudwara* at **Manikaran**, 32km northeast of the Beas–Parvati confluence. Crouched at the foot of a gloomy ravine, this ancient religious site, sacred to Hindus as well as Sikhs, is famous for the **hot springs** that bubble out of its stony river banks.

To make the most of Parvati's stunning scenery you'll have to **hike**. Two popular trails thread their way up the valley: one heads north from the fascinating hill village of **Malana** (see box, p.457), over the Chandrakhani Pass to Naggar; the other follows the River Parvati east to another sacred hot spring and sadhu hang-out, **Khirganga**. The trail continues from Khirganga to **Mantalai** with its Shiva shrine and over the awesome 5400m Pin–Parvati pass into **Spiti**. This serious snowfield is riddled with crevasses and takes several hours to cross. A guide is absolutely essential (see box below).

Jari, Mateura and Kasol

Spilling over the main road and down the south side of the Parvati Valley, **JARI**, 15km from Bhuntur, looks across to the precipitous Malana *nala* in the north, and to the snow-flecked needles of the Baranagh Range on the eastern horizon. Like many of its lookalike cousins, the tatty settlement supports a small transient population of stoned Westerners, attracted by the top-quality *charas*. For basic **accommodation**, the *Dharma Guest House* (Ⓣ01902/276059; ❶), just above the bus stand, and the cleaner *Om Shiva* (Ⓣ01902/276202; ❶–❷), on the left-hand side as you enter the village, are simple and welcoming. The best place to eat is *Deepak* restaurant at the bus stand. Those wanting a shortcut to **Malana**

Parvati disappearances

For over a decade the Parvati Valley has seen the mysterious **disappearance** of at least twenty travellers. Most were travelling alone, although one incident in August 2000 involved three campers who were brutally attacked in their tent, thrown into the gorge and left for dead – one survived. Most of the vanished have never been found, including the Israeli who went missing in the most recently publicized case in July 2009. Several theories have been put forward to explain these disappearances, from drug-related accidents on the treacherous mountain trails, to attacks by bears or wolves or foul play by the numerous cannabis cultivators in the region; some even claim that the disappeared may have joined secret cults deep in the mountains. Most likely, however, they were victims of bandit attacks, motivated solely by money, with the wild waters of the River Parvati conveniently placed for disposing of bodies. Individual travellers should **take heed** and only use recognized guides on treks across the mountains. Don't attempt solo treks – even along the relatively simple trail over the Chandrakhani Pass between Naggar and Malana and the straightforward trek to the hot springs at Khirganga. There are many trekking agencies in Kullu and Manali who can put you in touch with a reputable guide.

(see box, p.457), can hire a vehicle up to the Malana hydro project roadhead, from where the village is a mere 4km trek.

Just ten minutes' walk up the hill from the bus stand is the unspoilt village of **MATEURA**, which has spectacular views over the Parvati Range and is home to the small but important Kali Anagha temple. The *Village Guest House* (Ⓣ01902/276070; ❷) is a traditional wooden-balconied house, whose immaculate rooms have satellite TV; set in a wonderful garden, it's popular year-round. The roof terrace of the nearby *Rooftop Restaurant & Guest House* (Ⓣ01902/275434; ❶) overlooks the village.

Beyond Jari, the road winds down towards the rushing grey-green Parvati, which it meets at **KASOL**, a pleasant village straddling a mountain stream and surrounded by forest. A mere 4.5km from Manikaran and a nice walk along a wooded road, Kasol has grown in popularity, and now has a large resident population of *charas*-smoking travellers, mostly Israelis – earning it the nickname of "little Israel" from the locals. A trickle of trekkers also plod through on their way to or from the pass of Rashol Jot (2440m), a hard day's climb up the north side of the valley which provides an alternative approach to Malana and the Chandrakhani route to the Kullu Valley. You can **change money** here at Swagtam Tourism, who will also give cash advances against credit cards for a three percent fee. **Accommodation** ranges from basic rooms in village houses and simple lodges to more organised hotels such as *Deep Forest* (Ⓣ01902/273048; ❷), up the hill just beyond the bridge, or the plusher *Hotel Sandhya Kasol* (Ⓣ01902/273745; ❸–❺), 300m beyond the village, with comfortable rooms and discounts up to seventy percent in the off-season. The best value is offered by the two-storey *Alpine Guest House* (Ⓣ01902/273710, Ⓦwww.alpineguesthouse.net; ❷–❸), with spacious rooms set in wooded grounds by the river. Kasol's **travellers' cafés** are cheap and plentiful. The *Moondance Restaurant and Bakery* has an excellent location near the bridge; it faces the pleasant *Sasi Palace* on the opposite bank. Back on the Bhuntur side of the village *Little Italy* dishes up spaghetti and other western staples on a popular terrace. Sadhus and Western hippies pass *charas* round at the *Tushar Tea Stall*.

Manikaran and around

A short distance beyond Kasol, clouds of steam billowing from the rocky riverbank herald the Parvati Valley's chief attraction. Hindu mythology identifies **MANIKARAN** as the place where the serpent king Shesha stole Parvati's earrings, or *manikara*, while she and her husband Shiva were bathing in the river. When interrogated, the snake flew into a rage and snorted the earrings out of his nose. Ever since, boiling water has poured out of the ground. The site is also venerated by Sikhs, who have erected a massive concrete *gurudwara* over the springs.

Boxed in at the bottom of a vast, sheer-sided chasm, Manikaran is a damp, dark and claustrophobic place where you're unlikely to want to spend more than a night. Most of the action revolves around the springs themselves, reached via the lane that leads through the village from the footbridge. On the way, check out the finely carved pale-grey stone **Rama temple** just beyond the main square, and the pans of rice and dhal cooking in the steaming pools on the pavements. Down at the riverside **Shiva shrine**, semi-naked **sadhus** sit in the scalding waters smoking chillums. Sikh pilgrims, meanwhile, make their way to the atmospheric **gurudwara** nearby, where they take a purifying dip in the underground pool, sweat in the hot cave and then congregate upstairs to listen to musical recitations from the Sikhs' holy book, the Guru Granth Sahib. If you visit, keep your arms, legs and head covered; tobacco is prohibited inside the complex.

Practicalities

Buses leave Bhuntur at least hourly for Manikaran (1hr 30min). The last bus back to Kullu, via Bhuntur, leaves around 6pm. You can also hire Maruti-van **taxis**. Except during May and June, when Manikaran fills up with Punjabi visitors, **accommodation** is plentiful and inexpensive. Most hotels have a steaming indoor hot tub but the abundance of moisture has left many of them feeling rather damp and dirty. *Hotel Shivalik* (Ⓣ01902/273817; ❷–❹), on the main road at the turn-off to the bus stand, has large rooms, TV and balconies with river views. Just before the bus stand itself, the *Country Charm* (Ⓣ01902/273703; ❸) is a rather dowdy place catering mainly for domestic tourists, with kitsch rooms and a hot pool. Crossing the footbridge brings you to a clutch of cheap guesthouses and overcrowded temple dorms. Best of these is the *Fateh Guest House* (Ⓣ01902/273767; ❶), whose rooms all have hot showers and TVs. At the far end of the bazaar the *Sharma Guest House* (Ⓣ01902/273742; ❶) is the better of the two near the *gurudwara* but only has shared bathrooms. Manikaran is **strictly veg**, when it comes to food. The best **restaurant** is the *Holy Palace*, on the main lane between the Rama Temple and the *gurudwara*. In the corner of the bus stand, the *Veerda Janta* is a good *dhaba* for spicy local cuisine, while *Sharma Sweets*, by the Rama Temple, is the spot for chai and snacks.

Naggar

Stacked up the lush, terraced lower slopes of the valley as they sweep towards the tree line from the left bank of the Beas, **NAGGAR**, 6km from the main road junction at Patlikuhl, is the most scenic and accessible of the hill villages between Kullu and Manali. Clustered around an old **castle**, this was the regional capital before the local rajas decamped to Kullu in the mid-1800s. A century or so later, European settlers began to move in. Seduced by the village's ancient **temples**, peaceful setting and unhurried pace, visitors often find themselves lingering in Naggar – a far less hippified village than those further north – longer than they intended. Numerous tracks wind up the mountain to more remote settlements, providing a choice of enjoyable **hikes**.

Arrival and information

Naggar is equidistant (21km) from Kullu and Manali and connected to both by regular **buses**. The direct services that ply the road on the eastern side of the valley are slower (1hr 30min from Manali or Kullu), but more scenic and straightforward than the more frequent services along the main highway on the opposite, west side. The latter drop at **Patlikuhl** (6km from Naggar), from where taxis, auto-rickshaws and hourly buses cross the Beas to climb up to Naggar. If you arrive in daylight and are not weighed down with bags, you can also walk from Patlikuhl on the old mule track – a hike of at least an hour.

Naggar village proper, its sights and accommodation lie a way above the small bazaar on the main road where the buses pull in. If you have your own vehicle, you can drive all the way up to the Roerich Gallery at the top of the village. If you are thinking of **trekking** around Naggar, you are advised to use guides, especially if crossing the **Chandrakhani Pass** to Malana (see p.457). Himalayan Mountain Treks at *Poonam Mountain Lodge* (see p.450) have equipment, will arrange porters and guides, and can fix up jeep trips to Lahaul and Spiti. Local guides are also easy to find, though make sure they are reputable.

Accommodation

Alliance Guest House Halfway between the village and the Roerich Gallery ⓣ01902/248263, ⓔvoyagealliance@yahoo.co.in. Popular guesthouse with simple, clean rooms, a self-catering flat (Rs1500), a small lending library and a warm family atmosphere. ❶–❸

Chanderlok Guest House In adjoining Chanalti village below Naggar ⓣ01902/248213. Simple guesthouse with attached rooms in a quiet location. Korean restaurant also on premises. ❶–❷

HPTDC Hotel Castle ⓣ01902/248316. Atmospheric castle with well-furnished attached doubles, some offering superb views from spacious wooden balconies, plus dorm beds (Rs100). Book in advance at any HPTDC tourist office to secure one of the more expensive rooms in the west wing. ❺–❼

Karbo Shin Guesthouse Ghourdor village ⓣ01902/248342, ⓔawhitecloud46@hotmail.com. Dutch-owned guesthouse with four rooms, a shared bathroom with hot shower, excellent food and superb views. They can also arrange local and long-distance treks. To get here follow the forest road from Naggar to Bijli Mahadev Mandir temple; the guesthouse is down the path signed off the road (10–15min). ❶

Poonam Mountain Lodge Below the castle ⓣ01902/248248, ⓦwww.poonammountain.in. Cosy doubles, three with fireplaces for winter stays, internet access, a lovely outside seating area and a good veg restaurant serving local specialities such as red rice. Extremely welcoming and knowledgable owner too. ❶–❷

Sheetal Hotel ⓣ01902/248250, ⓔsheetal_hotel_naggar@yahoo.com. An alternative to the nearby *Castle*, offering better-value rooms of similar standard, with balconies, a roof-top restaurant and substantially reduced rates off-season. Also runs some nearby cottages. ❷–❹

The Town

Naggar is a very pleasant place, often sadly overlooked by travellers making a beeline for Manali. The relaxed atmosphere, refreshing elevation, stunning views and a variety of interesting sites combine to make it an excellent spot to while away a few days.

The castle

Since it was erected by Raja Sidh Singh (c.1700), Naggar's central **castle**, astride a sheer-sided bluff, has served as palace, colonial mansion, courthouse and school. It is now a hotel, but nonresidents can wander in for Rs15 to admire the views from its balconies. Built in the traditional "earthquake-proof" *pahari* style (layers of stone bonded together with cedar logs), the castle has a central courtyard, a small shrine and a shop selling local handicrafts downstairs. The **Jagti Patt temple**'s amorphous deity, a triangular slab of rock strewn with rose petals and rupee notes, is said to have been borne here from its home on the summit of Deo Tibba by a swarm of wild honeybees – the valley's *devtas* in disguise.

The Nicholas Roerich Gallery

Perched on the upper outskirts of the village, the **Nicholas Roerich Gallery** (Tues–Sun: May–Aug 10am–1pm & 1.30–6pm; Sept–March 10am–1pm & 1.30–5pm; Rs30, camera Rs25, video Rs60; ⓦwww.roerichtrust.org) houses an exhibition of paintings and photographs dedicated to the memory of its former occupier, the Russian artist, writer, philosopher, archeologist, explorer and mystic. Around the turn of the beginning of the twentieth century, Roerich's atmospheric landscape paintings and esoteric philosophies – an arcane blend of Eastern mysticism and *fin-de-siècle* humanist-idealism – inspired a cult-like following in France and the United States. Financed by donations from devotees, Roerich was able to indulge his obsession with Himalayan travel, eventually retiring in Naggar in 1929 and dying here eighteen years later.

A path winds further up above the road through the forest for around 100m to **Urusvati-Himalayan Folk Art Museum** (same ticket). Founded by Roerich's wife in 1928, the museum features a collection of local folk art, costumes, more of Roerich's paintings, several paintings by his Russian followers, and a gallery of Russian folk art.

The temples

The largest and most distinctive of Naggar's ancient Hindu **temples** and shrines, the wooden pagoda-style **Tripuri Sundri** stands in a small enclosure at the top of the village, just below the road to the Roerich Gallery. Like the Dunghri temple in Manali, it is crowned with a three-tiered roof, whose top storey is circular. Its *devta* is the focus of an annual *mela* (mid-May) in which deities from local villages are brought in procession to pay their respects.

Ten minutes' walk further up the hill – follow the stone steps that lead right from the road – brings you to a clearing where the old stone **Murlidhar** (Krishna) **Mandir** looks down on Naggar, with superb views up the valley to the snow peaks around Solan and the Rohtang Pass. Built on the ruins of the ancient town of Thawa, the shrine, set in a large courtyard, is strictly off-limits to non-Hindus.

Finally, on your way to or from the bus stand at the bottom of the village, look out for the finely carved stone *shikharas* of the **Gaurishankar Mandir**. Set in its own paved courtyard below the castle, this Shiva temple, among the oldest of its kind in the valley, houses a living lingam, so slip off your shoes before approaching it.

Eating

The *Ragini Hotel Rooftop* **restaurant**, beside the *Sheetal Guest House*, serves good food, including grilled trout, which is also available at the *Zenith Café*, just before the Roerich Gallery. It is aptly named given its splendid views and also does Tibetan food. Back in the village *La Purezza* serves excellent Italian cuisine and rainbow trout specials in a downstairs room and more pleasant roof terrace.

Manali and around

Himachal's main tourist resort, **MANALI**, stands at the head of the Kullu Valley, 108km north of Mandi. Despite lying at the heart of the region's highest mountain range, it remains easily accessible by road from the plains; after one hour on a plane and a short hop by road, or sixteen hours on a bus from Delhi, you could be staring from your hotel veranda across apple orchards and thick pine forests to the snowfields of Solang Nala, which shine a tantalizing stone's throw away to the north. Manali has become increasingly popular with domestic tourists (five million annually), giving rise to an eclectic mix of honeymooners, holiday-makers, hippies, trekkers and traders.

The Manali that lured travellers in the 1970s has certainly changed, although the majestic mountain scenery, thermal springs and quality *charas* can still be enjoyed. **Old Manali** retains some of its atmosphere, and the village of **Vashisht** across the valley, with its increasing choice of guesthouses and cafés, has become a popular place to chill out. For those preferring to venture into the mountains, Manali makes an ideal **trekking** base for short hikes and serious expeditions, and countless agencies can help put a package together for you. The relaxing hotels in Manali's cleaner, greener outskirts, and dozens of sociable cafés and restaurants ranged around a well-stocked **bazaar**, provide a welcome relief from the rigours of the mountain trails. For more on treks around Manali and the Kullu Valley, see box, pp.456–457.

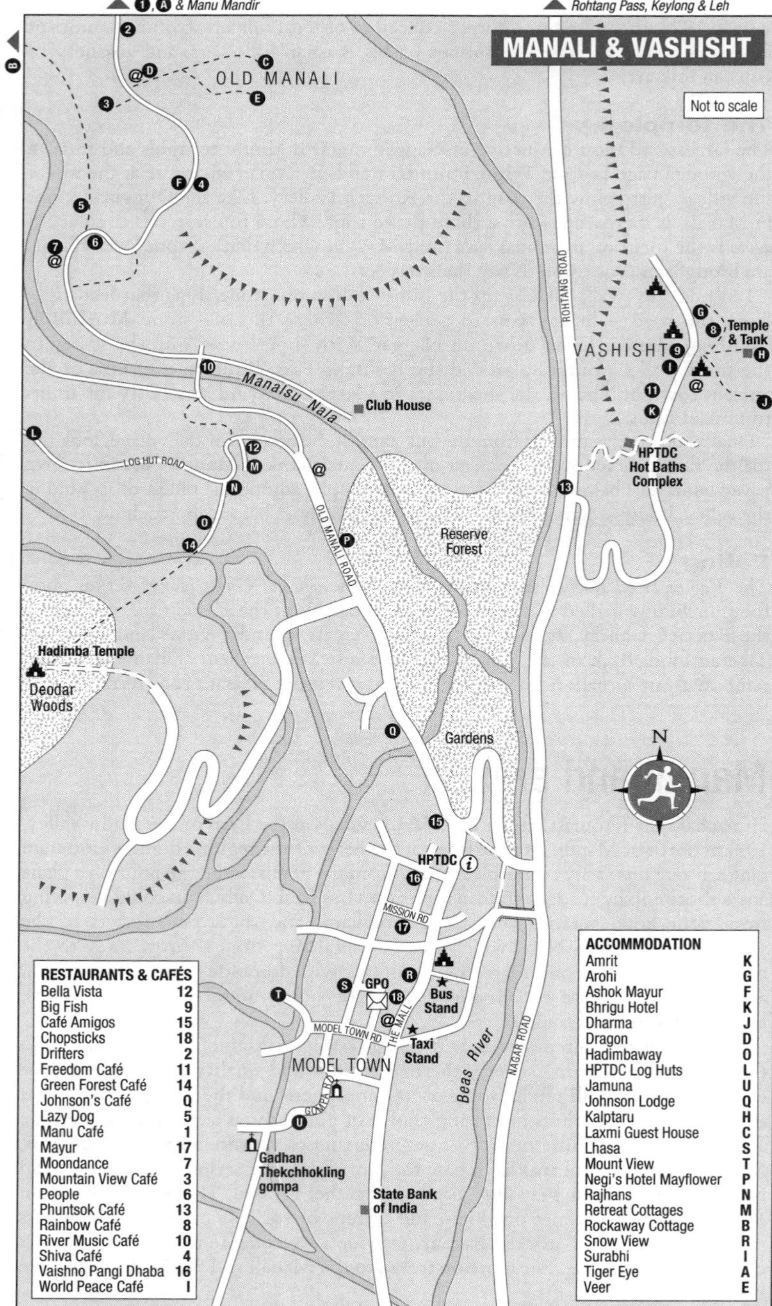
MANALI & VASHISHT
Not to scale
1, A & Manu Mandir
Rohtang Pass, Keylong & Leh
B
OLD MANALI
VASHISHT
Temple & Tank
ROHTANG ROAD
Manalsu Nala
Club House
LOG HUT ROAD
OLD MANALI ROAD
HPTDC Hot Baths Complex
Reserve Forest
Hadimba Temple
Deodar Woods
Gardens
HPTDC
MISSION RD
GPO
Bus Stand
Taxi Stand
MODEL TOWN RD
THE MALL
MODEL TOWN
GOMPA RD
Beas River
NAGAR ROAD
Gadhan Thekchhokling gompa
State Bank of India
Kullu
Aleo, Nagar, Jagatsukh & Mountaineering Institute
RESTAURANTS & CAFÉS
Bella Vista 12
Big Fish 9
Café Amigos 15
Chopsticks 18
Drifters 2
Freedom Café 11
Green Forest Café 14
Johnson's Café Q
Lazy Dog 5
Manu Café 1
Mayur 17
Moondance 7
Mountain View Café 3
People 6
Phuntsok Café 13
Rainbow Café 8
River Music Café 10
Shiva Café 4
Vaishno Pangi Dhaba 16
World Peace Café I
ACCOMMODATION
Amrit K
Arohi G
Ashok Mayur F
Bhrigu Hotel K
Dharma J
Dragon D
Hadimbaway O
HPTDC Log Huts L
Jamuna U
Johnson Lodge Q
Kalptaru H
Laxmi Guest House C
Lhasa S
Mount View T
Negi's Hotel Mayflower P
Rajhans N
Retreat Cottages M
Rockaway Cottage B
Snow View R
Surabhi I
Tiger Eye A
Veer E

Arrival and information

Coming from Delhi, most private buses pull into the bus stand 100m south of the State Bank of India at the bottom of town; government buses pull in to Manali's **bus stand** in the middle of the Mall, a short walk from the friendly **tourist office** (daily: 8am–8pm high season; 10am–1.30pm & 2–5pm rest of year; ⓣ01902/252175). You can make reservations for the town's state-run hotels at the HPTDC office (ⓣ01902/253531), two doors down. Manali's **Taxi Operators' Union kiosk** (ⓣ01902/252450) lies just up from the tourist office; the taxis have fixed rates which are negotiable off-season. If you need to **change money**, the State Bank of India is on the main road 250m south of the Mall and there are also two SBI and one UCO Bank ATMs on the Mall. A handful of authorized private exchange agencies open longer hours but offer lower rates. The main **post office**, off Model Town Road, has a reliable poste restante counter (Mon–Sat 9am–1pm & 1.30–5pm); broadband **internet** facilities are available at several places on the Mall and more in Old Manali. Although most people apply for **Inner Line permits** either in Kaza (see p.464), or if travelling south–north, in Rekong Peo (see p.423), if you want to get one in Manali, you must do so through a registered travel agent (see p.455 for recommendations). Take along three photos, and a photocopy of your passport and visa details.

Moving on from Manali

Manali is well connected by **bus** to other Himachali towns and major cities on the plains. HPSRTC run luxury, deluxe and ordinary buses, all of which can be booked at the bus stand. During the summer, demand invariably outstrips supply, particularly for the faster services, so book as far in advance as possible. The numerous travel agents dotted around town also sell tickets for **private** "deluxe" services to **Delhi** (8 daily; 16–17hr), **Shimla** (8 daily; 8–9hr) and **Dharamsala** (3 daily; 10hr). Consider breaking your journey in Mandi (for Rewalsar; every 30min; 4hr) or using the **Kangra Valley Railway** to reach Dharamsala or Pathankot from where you can pick up **trains** for **Amritsar**, **Delhi** and **Rajasthan**. Buses also cross the Rohtang La to **Kaza** (2 daily; 11–12hr), capital of Spiti, from where you can continue all the way round via Kinnaur to Shimla, although **permits** are required to travel beyond Sumdo. Harisons Travels (ⓣ01902/253519), Monal Himalayan Travels (ⓣ01902/254215), Swagtam (ⓣ01902/253990) and Valleycon (ⓣ01902/253776), at the bus stand and at *Mayur* restaurant, all sell tickets.

Transport to Leh

Eight daily **buses** travel over the **Rohtang Pass** to **Keylong**, capital of Lahaul, but it can be difficult to book onward transport from Keylong to Leh as buses nearly always arrive full, so try to reserve a seat in advance. Most travellers, therefore, still cover the 485km to Leh by direct bus – an arduous but unforgettable two-day trip, involving a night halt under canvas en route. HPTDC's "super-deluxe" bus, bookable through their Mall office, runs on alternate days and costs Rs1800, which includes accommodation and two meals at the tent colony in Keylong. Otherwise, choice is limited to the beaten-up buses operated by HPSRTC and their J&K equivalents, which cost under Rs600. It is quite easy to book single places in **jeeps** and Maruti Gypsy **taxis** to **Leh** from Manali – prices start from Rs1200, though front seats cost a bit more and all prices rise in the early summer high season. This is the fastest way, as most vehicles try to cover it in 17–19hr after a 2am start but that means you do miss the scenery at the beginning and end of the ride. There are also frequent complaints of the drivers, who often lack sleep, taking unnecessary risks on the sharp bends and long sections of unpaved road. For more on the Manali–Leh highway, see p.467.

Accommodation

There are three main accommodation areas in Manali. Most longer-stay budget places are clustered in **Old Manali**, where rough-and-ready family-run guesthouses, joined by a handful of less appealing modern hotels, nestle amid the orchards. A *charas*-induced torpor hangs over many of them, but the peace and quiet and views from their flower gardens make the 2km hike (or Rs40 auto-rickshaw ride) from New Manali worthwhile. Most of Manali's classic hotels with gardens and character are dotted around the **northern and western outskirts**, midway between Old Manali and the Mall. In town, tucked away behind the Mall, is a cluster of identikit concrete hotels known as **Model Town**.

Tariffs rocket in Manali during **high season** (April–June & Sept–Oct). At other times, a fifty percent reduction on the advertised rates for more expensive hotels is standard. The few hotels that stay open in **winter** cater mainly for skiing parties. All prices listed below are for low season.

Old Manali

Ashok Mayur ⓣ01902/252868, ⓔmanurishi72@yahoo.com. Small, basic (verging on dingy) and friendly guesthouse opposite *Shiva* café, with balconies warmed by the morning sun. ❶–❷

Dragon ⓣ01902/252790, ⓦwww.dragontreks.com. Newer hotel with brash exterior but comfortable, spacious attached rooms with hot water and balconies. The top floor has some great wooden-floored duplexes for Rs800–1500. Useful internet café and travel centre. ❷

Laxmi Guest House ⓣ01902/253569. Small, friendly place with rickety wooden rooms and shared bathrooms, which stay cheap in high season. Uninterrupted valley views and a small garden are the best features. ❶

Rockway Cottage 500m along the track starting just past the *Mahalsu Café* ⓣ01902/253428. Pleasant rooms, some with wood heaters, in an idyllic setting. Good food in the garden café, set above the river. Well worth the effort, but bring a torch. ❶

Tiger Eye Tucked into lanes at top of village but signposted ⓣ01902/252718, ⓔtigereyeindia@yahoo.com. Peaceful, newly built family guesthouse run by friendly Indian–Dutch couple. Immaculate rooms and balconies with great views. Well worth the little extra. ❶–❷

Veer ⓣ01902/252410, ⓔsesramthakur@hotmail.com. Simple place with fine views down the valley from a lovely leafy garden and communal eating area. Some attached bathrooms and some rooms with a/c and TV. ❶–❷

Northern and western outskirts

Hadimbaway Log Huts Area ⓣ01902/251552, ⓦwww.hotelhadimbaway.com. Best value of the several places in this quiet little enclave near the Hadimba Temple. Unusually, the upstairs rooms are cheaper. ❷

HPTDC Log Huts Overlooking Manalsu Nala ⓣ01902/253225, ⓔmanali@hptdc.in. Comfortable but overpriced timber holiday cottages tucked away in the woods, with one or two double bedrooms, kitchens and most comforts including Star TV. ❽

Johnson Lodge Old Manali Rd ⓣ01902/251523, ⓦwww.johnsonslodge.com. Three-star comfort in an old colonial building. Spacious and neat wooden-floored rooms overlook the garden; the carpeted downstairs rooms are cheaper, with wood-burning heaters for winter. ❻

Negi's Hotel Mayflower Old Manali Rd ⓣ01902/252104, ⓦwww.mayflowermanali.com. One of Manali's most agreeable hotels. The large rooms are new, but feel traditional with wood panelling and views over the pine forests. Balconies out front catch the afternoon sun. Fixed rates year round. ❻

Rajhans Off Old Manali Rd ⓣ01902/252209, ⓔhotelrajhans@gmail.com. Stylish new four-storey brick building with valley views from the more luxurious higher rooms; all attached with TV. ❸–❻

Retreat Cottages Log Hut Rd ⓣ01902/252042, ⓔtibetemporium@hotmail.com. Immaculate, huge self-catering two- and three-bedroom (Rs7000) suites with baths in a tastefully designed building. Recommended for groups of 6–8. Meals can also be ordered. ❼–❾

Model Town

Jamuna Gompa Rd ⓣ01902/252506. Old-style hotel but the rooms are clean and spacious enough and about as cheap as it gets in Model Town. ❶

Tours and adventure sports around Manali

Weather and road conditions permitting, HPTDC run daily bus **tours** to the **Rohtang Pass** (10am–5pm; Rs250) and day-trips to **Manikaran** in the Parvati Valley (9am–6.30pm; Rs275). Tickets can be bought in advance from their transport counter.

Considering the fierce white-water that thrashes down the Kullu Valley during the spring melt, Manali's **rafting** scene is surprisingly low-key. Raft trips down the River Beas are offered between the end of May and early July, when water levels are highest, beginning at Piridi (above Bhuntur) around 15km downstream at Jhiri. The price (around Rs1200) should include meals, lifejackets, helmets, and return travel; check exactly what you're paying for, as some unscrupulous operators expect you to make your own way back after the trip.

Skiing in the Solang Valley is popular from January to April – but the slope isn't much bigger than a cricket pitch. A new ski centre in conjunction with the Finnish government is being planned for the Rohtang Pass. The valley is also a popular spot for **paragliding**, **kitesurfing** (both Rs600–2500) and **helicopter rides** (Rs1750/person). One of the best ways to explore Kullu is by **mountain biking**, which is possible from mid-June to mid-October. The best local guide is Raju Sharma (Ⓣ9816 056934, Ⓦwww.magicmountainadventures.com), who can arrange bike hire (Rs300/day for a European bike, Rs500 with Raju as guide), and suggest routes around Manali as well as expeditions up to Leh. Popular routes include the descent from Rohtang, the forest trail to the Bijli Mahadev Temple and the back road to Naggar.

If you're planning a trekking or rafting trip, shop around to compare prices and packages; many agencies are fly-by-night operators who make their money from mark-ups on long-distance bus tickets to Delhi, Chandigarh and Leh. Long-established, **reputable agents** include the very experienced Rup Negi at Himalayan Adventurers (Ⓣ01902/253050, Ⓦhimalayanadventurersindia.com), opposite the tourist office, and Himanshu Sharma at Himalayan Journeys (Ⓣ01902/252365, Ⓦwww.himalayanjourneysindia.com), next to *Café Amigos*. They can organize trekking, rock climbing, rafting and ski packages at Solang. The most reliable agent in Old Manali is Tiger Eye Adventure (Ⓣ01902/252718). A number of agents also operate **jeep safaris** to remote regions such as Spiti.

Lhasa Just off Model Town Rd Ⓣ01902/252134. One of the friendlier and better-value places in the area. Slightly faded decoration and furnishings but all rooms have bathrooms and TV. ❷

Mount View Far end of Model Town Rd Ⓣ01902/252465. Pleasant ivy-clad building in a quieter area with decent-sized doubles and a rooftop terrace with splendid views. ❶

Snow View The Mall Ⓣ01902/253084, Ⓦwww.hotelsnowviewmanali.com. Large, functional hotel with comfortable decent-sized rooms. ❹

The Town

Manali's main street, **the Mall**, quite unlike its namesake in Shimla, is a noisy scene of constant activity, fronted by the bus stand, several shopping markets, travel agents, and a line of hotels and restaurants. It's a great place to watch the world go by – locals in traditional caps, Tibetan women in immaculate rainbow-striped pinafores, Nepali porters, Buddhist monks, the odd party of Zanskaris swathed in fusty woollen *gonchas*, souvenir-hunting Indian tourists and a curious mix of Westerners.

Manali's days as an authentic *pahari* bazaar ended when the mule trains were superseded by Tata trucks, but it's still great for souvenir **shopping**. Woollen goods are the town's real forte, particularly the brilliantly patterned **shawls** for

Treks around Manali and the Kullu Valley

The Kullu Valley's spectacular alpine scenery makes it perfect for **trekking**. Trails are long and steep, but more than repay the effort with superb views, varied flora and the chance to visit remote hill stations. Within striking distance of several major trailheads, **Manali** is the most popular place to begin and end treks. While **package deals** (around Rs2000/person for three days with a group of four) offered by the town's many agencies can save time and energy, it is relatively easy to organize your own trip with maps and advice from the tourist office and the Mountaineering Institute at the bottom end of town. Porters and horsemen can be sought out in the square behind the main street. Always take a reliable **guide**, especially on less-frequented routes, as you cannot rely solely on **maps**. Some trekkers have reported difficulties when descending from the Bara Bangal Pass, as maps don't do the terrain justice.

The optimum trekking **season** is right after the monsoons (mid-Sept to late Oct), when skies are clear and pass-crossings easier. From June to August, you run the risk of sudden, potentially fatal snow, or view-obscuring cloud and rain.

Manali to Beas Kund

The relatively easy trek to Beas Kund, a glacial lake at the head of Solang *nala*, is the region's most popular short hike. Encircled by 5000m-plus peaks, the well-used campground beside the lake, accessible in two days from Manali, makes a good base for side-trips up to the surrounding ridges and passes.

From **Palchan**, a village 30 minutes north of Manali by bus, follow the jeep track up the valley to **Solang**, site of a small ski station, resthouse and the Mountaineering Institute's log huts. The next two hours take you through pine forests and grassy meadows to the campground at **Dhundi** (2743m). A more strenuous walk of 5–6 hours the next day leads to **Beas Kund**. The hike up to the **Tentu La** Pass (4996m) and back from here can be done in a day, as can the descent to Manali via Solang.

Manali to Lahaul, via the Hampta Pass

The three-day trek from the Kullu Valley over the Hampta Pass to Lahaul, the old caravan route to Spiti, is a classic. Rising to 4330m, it is high by Kullu standards; do not undertake it without allowing good time to acclimatize. **Day one**, from the trailhead at **Jagatsukh** or Hampta (both villages near Manali) to the campground above **Sethen**, is an easy hike (4–5hr) up the verdant, forested sides of the valley. **Day two** (5hr) brings you to **Chikha**, a high Gaddi pasture below the pass; stay put for a day or so if you're feeling the effects of altitude. The ascent (700m) on **day three** to the **Hampta Pass** (4330m) is gruelling, but the views from the top – of Indrasan and Deo Tibba to the south, and the moonscape of Lahaul to the north – are sublime recompense. It takes six to seven hours of relentless rock-hopping and stream-crossing to reach **Chhatru**, on the floor of the Chandra Valley. From here, you can turn east towards Koksar and the **Rohtang Pass**, or west past the world's largest glacier, **Bara Shigri**, to **Batal**, the trailhead for the Chandratal–Baralacha trek (see p.463).

which Kullu Valley is famous. Genuine pure-wool handloom shawls with embroidered borders start at around Rs500, but those made from finest pashmina cost several thousand rupees. Shop around and check out the fixed-price factory shops to get an idea of what's available: the government-sponsored Bhutico on the Mall opposite the tourist office, the Bodh Shawl factory shop just off the Mall south of the bus stand and The Great Hadimba Shop & Factory next to the Manu Temple in Old Manali are recommended; the NSC (New Shopping Centre) market near the bus stand also has a good selection.

Elsewhere around the bazaar, innumerable stalls are stacked with handwoven goods and pillbox Kullu **topis**. Those with gaudy multicoloured up-turned flaps

Naggar to Malana via the Chandrakhani Pass and onwards

The trek to Jari in the Parvati Valley from Naggar, 21km south of Manali, is quintessential Kullu Valley trekking with superb scenery and fascinating villages. The round trip can be completed in three days, but you may be tempted to linger in **Malana** and explore the surrounding countryside. A **guide** is essential for several reasons: the first stage of the trek involves crossing a maze of grazing trails; Malana is culturally sensitive and requires some familiarity with local customs; and a number of people have **disappeared** in the Parvati Valley in recent years in suspicious circumstances (see p.447). The descent to the Parvati Valley is too steep for pack ponies, but porters are available in Naggar through the guesthouses, including Himalayan Mountain Treks at *Poonam Mountain Lodge* (see p.450).

The trail leads through the village of Rumsu and then winds through wonderful old-growth forests to a pasture just above the tree line, which makes ideal camping ground. From here, a climb of 4km takes you to the **Chandrakhani Pass** (3660m), with fine views west over the top of the Kullu Valley to the peaks surrounding Solang *nala* and north to the Ghalpo mountains of Lahaul. Some prefer to reach the base of the pass on the first day and then camp below the final ascent.

The inhabitants of **MALANA**, a steep 7km descent from the pass, are known for their frostiness and staunch traditions. Plans by regional developers to extend a paved road here are vehemently opposed by the insular locals. Although notions of **caste pollution** are not as strictly adhered to as they once were, you should observe a few basic "**rules**" in Malana: approach the village quietly and respectfully; stick to paths at all times; keep away from the temple; and above all, don't touch anybody or anything, especially children or houses. If you do commit a cultural blunder, you'll be expected to make amends: usually in the form of a Rs1000 payment for a sacrificial offering of a young sheep or goat to the village deity, **Jamlu**, one of the most powerful Kullu Valley gods. His **temple**, open to high-caste Hindus only, is decorated with lively folk carvings, among them images of soldiers – the villagers claim to be the area's sole remaining descendants of Alexander the Great's army. Popular **places to stay** include the *Renuka Guesthouse* (❶), which has hot water, and the *Himalaya Guesthouse* (❶), run by the former village headman. The owner of *Santu Ram's* (❶) is an authority on local trails. All the guesthouses offer simple meals. The official camping ground lies 100m beyond the village spring.

The **final stage** of the trek takes you down the sheer limestone sides of Malana *nala* to the floor of the Parvati Valley – a precipitous 12km drop that is partially covered by a switchback road. From the hamlet of **Rashol**, you have a choice of three onward routes: either head east up the right bank of the river to **Manikaran** (see p.448); follow the trail southwest to the sacred **Bijli Mahadev Mandir**; or climb the remaining 3km up to the road at **Jari**, from where regular buses leave for Bhuntur, Kullu and Manali.

and gold piping are indigenous to the valley, but you can also pick up the plain-green velvet-fronted variety favoured by Kinnauris. Manali's other specialities are **Tibetan curios** such as prayer wheels, amulets, *dorjees* (thunderbolts), masks, antiques are genuine, but it takes an expert eye to spot a fake. The same applies to silver **jewellery** inlaid with turquoise and coral, which can nonetheless be attractive and relatively inexpensive.

The Hadimba Temple

Resting on a wide stone platform fifteen minutes' walk northwest of the bazaar, the **Hadimba Temple** is Manali's oldest shrine and the seat of Hadimba (or

"Hirma Devi"), wife of Bhima. Considered to be an incarnation of Kali, Hadimba is worshipped in times of adversity, and also plays a key role in the Dussehra festival (see p.446). Hadimba is supposed to have given the kingdom of Kullu to the forefathers of the rajas of Kullu, and in veneration and affection the family to this day refer to her as "grandmother". The massive triple-tiered wooden pagoda crowned by crimson pennants and a brass ball and trident (Shiva's *trishul*), dates from 1553, and is a replica of earlier ones that burned down in successive forest fires. The facade writhes with wonderful woodcarvings of elephants, crocodiles and folk deities. Entered by a door surmounted by wild ibex horns, the gloomy **shrine** is dominated by several large boulders, one of which shelters the stone on which goats and buffalo are sacrificed during important rituals. The hollow in its middle, believed to be Vishnu's footprint, channels the blood to Hadimba's mouth.

Soft-drinks stands, curio stalls and yak rides cater for visitors while the presiding deity looks on. The nearby **Kullu Cultural Museum** (Rs10) displays detailed models of the valley's temples.

Old Manali

Old Manali, the village from which the modern town takes its name, lies 2km north of the Mall, on the far side of the Manalsu Nala. Built in the old *pahari* style, most of the houses of Old Manali have heavy stone roofs and wooden balconies hung with bushels of drying herbs and tobacco. Unlike its crowded, concrete offspring, the settlement retains an unhurried and traditional feel – out of season. In summer, travellers on throaty Enfields roar through its lanes, guesthouses blare trance music and the cafés are thick with chillum smoke. In the wake of the tourists come the Kashmiris, Rajasthani tailors and other opportunists, eager to make good business before returning to Goa in the autumn.

To get here, head north up Old Manali Road, bear right at the fork in the road, and keep going until you reach the iron bridge across the river. A bit of leg work will bring you to the village proper, clustered on top of a steeply shelving ledge of level ground above the *nala*. It is also known as **Manaligarh** after its ancient citadel – now a ruined fort surrounded by a patchwork of maize terraces and deep-green orchards. At the centre of the village is an unusual, brash new temple dedicated to **Manu**, who laid the foundations of Hindu law that continues to today, as well as *varna* or "colour" – the basis of the caste system. Inscribed stones dating from the Middle Ages embedded into the concrete paving reveal the site's antiquity. Although Manali itself is considered safe, women should be wary of walking along the lane from town to Old Manali after dark; it has been the scene of several attempted **rapes** over the last decade.

The gompas

Manali harbours the highest concentration of **Tibetan refugees** in the Kullu Valley, hence the prayer flags fluttering over the approach roads into town, and the presence, on its southern edge, of two **gompas**.

Capped with polished golden finials, the distinctive yellow corrugated-iron pagoda roof of the **Gadhan Thekchhokling Gompa** is an exotic splash of colour amid the ramshackle huts of the Tibetan quarter. Built in 1969, the monastery is maintained by donations from the local community and through the sale of **carpets** handwoven in the temple workshop. When they are not looking after the **shop**, the young lamas huddle in the courtyard to play *cholo* – a Tibetan dice game involving much shouting and slamming of wooden *tsampa* bowls on leather pads. Beside the main entrance, a roll of honour recounts the names of Tibetans killed during the violent political demonstrations that wracked China in the late 1980s.

The smaller and more modern of the two *gompas* stands nearer the bazaar, in a garden that in late summer blazes with sunflowers. Its main shrine, lit by dozens of bare electric bulbs and filled with fragrant Tibetan incense, houses a colossal gold-faced Buddha, best viewed from the small room on the first floor.

Eating and drinking

Manali's wide range of **restaurants** reflects the town's melting-pot credentials: Tibetan *thukpa* joints stand cheek-by-jowl with south Indian coffee houses, Gujarati thali bars and Nepalese-run German pastry shops. Whatever their ostensible speciality, though, most offer mixed menus that include Chinese and Western dishes alongside standard north Indian favourites and many do traveller-friendly **breakfasts** of eggs, porridge, pancakes, toast and jam. Competition and a preponderance of domestic tourists and foreign backpackers keep prices reasonable so, unless indicated, most places charge in the Rs60–120 range for main courses. For rock-bottom budget food, head for one of the *dhabas* opposite the bus stand. Stock up on energy-rich **trekking food** at the local produce stores and bakeries in the bazaar. The state-sponsored co-op, near the temple on the Mall, sells sacks of nuts, dried fruit and pots of pure honey at fixed prices. One legendary spot, 5km away in Jagatsukh (Rs60 by auto-rickshaw), is the laid-back Brit-run *Alchemy Bar*, serving health-conscious Western food among creature comforts such as sofas, films, world music and a pool table.

The Mall and around

Bella Vista Log Hut Rd. Just across the bridge from Old Manali, this snazzy place serves the best Italian dishes in the area for around Rs200.

Café Amigos The Mall. Wooden tables, colourful pottery, chilled-out music and a fantastic range of cakes and brownies, as well as main meals.

Chopsticks The Mall. Very popular Tibetan-run restaurant with a pleasant atmosphere and varied menu. Try the filter coffee and the great muesli, fruit and curd.

Green Forest Café Off Log Hut Rd. Small local restaurant, serving the best *momos* in Manali for only Rs40–60.

Johnson's Café Part of *Johnson Lodge*. A great café, with garden seating and an inviting menu including beer, fresh trout and crème caramel. Some items top Rs200 but they're worth it.

Mayur Mission Rd, just off the Mall. Exciting and extensive Indian menu featuring dishes from all over the Subcontinent – try the excellent *jalfrezi*. Candles, serviettes and classical Indian music create a pleasant vibe.

Vaishno Pangi Dhaba Just off The Mall. One of the best cheap joints, serving dosas and other North and South Indian snacks from only around Rs40.

Old Manali

Drifters A hip new hotel restaurant with low tables and cushions downstairs, plus an outdoor terrace. Does grilled trout with the trimmings for Rs250, as well as more modest Indian, Chinese and Western dishes.

Lazy Dog Popular Korean restaurant overlooking the river, beautifully decorated and fine for hanging out, if you like loud Western music. Try the tasty *Kadimba* rice plate (Rs180).

Manu Café A local house with a small upstairs café, which despite the usual travellers' menu is best for local food. Most veg items Rs50 or less.

Moondance Popular garden café and meeting place above the river with a varied menu that includes Mexican and Italian dishes.

Mountain View Café Set away from most of the guesthouses, with extensive views of the surrounding mountains. Simple yet varied menu; open 24hr in season or when there's sufficient demand.

People Small Russian-run corner joint where you are given paper and crayons to draw with. Dishes like *sirniki* and *droniki* make a change, plus they do the best Western breakfasts around.

River Music Café Hang-out place by the bridge with tables on the terrace or floor-cushion seating under shelter. Usual menu and a good sound-system.

Shiva Café Sociable, laid-back balcony, an open fire most evenings, and Chinese, Indian and pasta dishes make this popular among budget travellers.

Vashisht

Famous for its sweeping valley views and sulphurous hot-water springs, the ever-expanding village of **VASHISHT**, 3km north of Manali, is an amorphous jumble of traditional timber houses and modern concrete cubes, divided by paved courtyards and narrow muddy lanes. It is the epicentre of the local budget travellers' scene, with a good choice of guesthouses and cafés. The tranquil and traditional atmosphere is only interrupted by the occasional rave that takes place in the woods, or if the weather is poor, in one or two obliging hotels.

You can get to Vashisht from Manali by road, or along the footpath from the main highway that passes the **HPTDC hot baths complex** – which has been closed for several years now due to a dispute between the villagers and the Himachal government. In the meantime, the only place for a **hot soak** is in the bathing pools of Vashisht's ancient temple (free), which is far more atmospheric anyway. Divided into separate sections for men and women, they attract a decidedly mixed crowd of Hindu pilgrims, Western hippies, semi-naked sadhus and groups of local kids.

Vashisht boasts two old stone **temples**, opposite each other above the main square and dedicated to the local patron saint Vashishta, guru of Raghunathji. The smaller of the two opens onto a partially covered courtyard and is adorned with elaborate woodcarvings. Those lining the interior of the shrine, blackened by years of oil-lamp and *dhoop* smoke, are worth checking out.

If you're up for more than just leaning back with a chillum, the **Himalayan Extreme Centre** (ⓣ9816 174164, ⓦwww.himalayan-extreme-center.com), on the road into the village, organizes days out snowboarding, kite-surfing and rock climbing.

Accommodation

Vashisht is packed with budget **guesthouses**, many of them old wooden buildings with broad verandas and uninterrupted vistas up the valley. If you don't mind primitive plumbing, grungy beds and dope smoke, the only time you'll not be spoilt for choice is during high season (May–June & Sept–Oct), when even floor-space can be at a premium. On the outskirts, a couple of larger **hotels** offer good-value, comfortable rooms. The places below are marked on the Manali & Vashisht map on p.452.

Amrit Tucked up behind the temples ⓣ01902/254209. A turquoise wooden house with basic facilities, including common bathrooms with bucket hot water. Grubby but atmospheric with rickety balconies affording fine views. ❶

Arohi Just up from the *Bhrigu* ⓣ01902/254421, ⓦwww.arohiecoadventures.com. Immaculate rooms with cable TV, intercom and balconies overlooking the river. The ex-army owner speaks excellent English and gives up to fifty percent discounts off-season. ❷–❹

Bhrigu Hotel On the main road into the village ⓣ01902/253414. Large hotel whose west-facing rooms all have attached bathrooms and superb views from their spacious balconies. ❷–❸

Dharma Five minute walk up the lane behind the temples ⓣ01902/252354. Complete with new wing, most rooms have fantastic views, as does the marble terrace with a swing and loungers. There's even a tiny swimming pool, filled by the hot springs. ❷–❸

Kalptaru Overlooking the temple tanks ⓣ01902/253443. You can't get any closer to the baths – with great-value rooms, all attached, with hot bucket water. Small garden and veranda from which to watch the world go by. ❶

Surabhi Halfway up the main road ⓣ01902/252796, ⓦwww.surabhihotel.com. The airy, smart new rooms upstairs all have views of the valley. The cheaper ground-floor rooms are colder and darker. ❷–❹

Eating

A backpackers' paradise, Vashisht has numerous **cafés** serving the typical fried rice, noodles, omelettes, pancakes and lassis, all at standard rates. In addition, bakeries provide wholemeal bread, apple pies and a variety of sticky things. Most of the cafés are hang-out places and several have open-air terraces with views, but there is little to choose between them.

Big Fish On the main road, opposite the temples. Upstairs restaurant serving trout for around Rs200 and other travellers' favourites.
Freedom Café On the main road past *Bhrigu Hotel*. Floor seating and a grassy deck with good views; food is Mexican, Tibetan and Italian.
Phuntsok Café By the river, on the lower road. Outdoor café serving delicious and wholesome home-cooked Tibetan food. One of Vashisht's best.
Rainbow Café Near *Kalptaru* hotel. Traveller-friendly offerings such as pancakes, pasta and spring rolls, with terrace views of the temple tanks.
World Peace Café On the main road, above the *Surabhi* hotel. The food is a fairly standard Indian/Western mix but there's Turkish coffee, as well as movies, board games and frequent live gigs. There's a roof terrace too.

Lahaul and Spiti

Few places on earth can mark so dramatic a change in landscape as the **Rohtang Pass**. To one side, the lush green head of the Kullu Valley; to the other, an awesome vista of bare, chocolate-coloured mountains, hanging glaciers and snowfields that shine in the dazzlingly crisp light, with just flecks of flora deep in the valley to soften the stark image. The district of **Lahaul and Spiti**, Himachal's largest, is named after its two subdivisions, which are, in spite of their numerous geographical and cultural similarities, distinct and separate regions.

Lahaul

Lahaul, sometimes referred to as the Chandra-Bhaga Valley, is the region that divides the Great Himalayas and Pir Panjal ranges. Its principal river, the Chandra, rises deep in the barren wastes below the **Baralacha Pass**, and flows south, then west towards its confluence with the River Bhaga near Tandi. Here, the two rivers become the Chenab, and crash north out of Himachal to Kishtwar in Kashmir. Being closer to what rains the monsoon brings across the Rohtang pass from the south, Lahaul's **climate** is notably less arid than Ladakh and Zanskar to the north and as a consequence, the key highway passes of Rhotang La and Baralacha La are much more prone to early snow than the higher examples further north. So it is that between late October and late March, heavy snows close the passes, and seal off the region. Even so, its inhabitants, a mixture of Buddhists and Hindus, enjoy one of the highest per capita incomes in the Subcontinent. Using glacial water channelled through ancient irrigation ducts, Lahauli farmers manage to coax a bumper crop of **seed potatoes** from their painstakingly fashioned terraces. The region is also the sole supplier of **hops** to India's breweries, and harvests prodigious quantities of wild herbs, used to make perfume and medicine. Much of the profit generated by these cash crops is spent on lavish jewellery, especially seed-pearl necklaces and coral and turquoise-inlaid silver plaques, worn by the women over ankle-length burgundy or fawn woollen dresses. Lahaul's traditional costume and Buddhism are a legacy of the Tibetan influence that has permeated the region from the east.

State **buses** run from Manali up the Chandra and Bhaga valleys to **Keylong** and **Darcha** from whenever the Rohtang Pass is cleared, usually in late June, until it snows up again in late October. You can also travel through Lahaul on Leh-bound buses if there are free seats. If coming down from Ladakh and heading east for Spiti rather than Manali, jeeps and, incredibly, state buses leave the tarmac at tiny **Grampoo** for the spectacular but rough 80km track over the snowy, 4550-metre Kunzum La and down the far side to **Losar** (see p.464) at the head of the Spiti valley.

Keylong

Lahaul's largest settlement and the district headquarters, **KEYLONG**, 114km north of Manali, is the last significant settlement on the long road journey to Ladakh. Although of little interest itself, the town lies amid superb scenery, within a day's climb of three Buddhist **gompas**. A couple of **stores** in the busy market sell trekking supplies if you are heading off to Zanskar.

Lahauli Buddhists consider it auspicious to make a clockwise circumambulation – known as the **Rangcha Parikarma** – of the sacred **Rangcha Mountain** (4565m), which overlooks the confluence of the Bhaga and Chandra rivers. A well-worn trail that makes a long and arduous day-hike from Keylong, the route is highly scenic, and takes in the large **Khardung gompa** along the way. A rough motorable road leads to Khardung *gompa* (10km), but closer to Keylong and on the same side of the valley are two quiet and picturesque *gompas* high up the mountain-side, **Shasher Gompa** (3km) and **Gungshal Gompa** (5km).

Practicalities

Keylong is connected by regular state **buses** to Manali, and (in summer) by private buses to all points north along the main highway. Note that onward **transport to Leh** can be difficult to arrange in high season (July & Aug), as most buses are full by the time they get there. Travellers frequently find themselves having to hitch a lift on one of the trucks that stop at the *dhabas* on the roadside above the village. There are eight buses daily to Manali, the first one leaving at 5.30am and the last at 1.30pm.

Keylong's **hotels** can be found along the main road above the town and strung out along the Mall that runs through the bazaar below the main highway. Aside of the grubby lodges by the bus stand, the *Tashi Deleg* (ⓣ01900/222450; ❷–❹) on the Mall has a range of clean and comfortable attached rooms with hot showers. The *Gyespa*, also on the Mall (ⓣ01900/222207; ❷), has attached rooms with hot showers, a dorm (Rs50), and a small *chorten* in the garden. Back up on the main road, 1km towards Darcha, the HPTDC *Chander Bhaga* (ⓣ01900/222393; ❺–❼, dorm Rs150) is comfortable but bland and typically overpriced. Below it, on a path between the main road and the bus stand, the *Nordaling* (ⓣ01900/222294; ❸) has bright rooms with bathrooms and TV. All these hotels have inspiring views of Khardung Gompa. Apart from the *dhabas* such as *Friends*, the best **eating** is at the abovementioned hotels.

The **post office** is on the main road a little way beyond the bus stand. There are no internet or official foreign **currency facilities** here, but *Tashi Deleg* will change money for a poor rate.

Spiti

From its headwaters below the **Kunzum La** pass, the River Spiti runs 130km southeast to within the flick of a yak's tail of the border with Tibet, where it meets the Sutlej. The valley itself, surrounded by huge peaks with an average altitude of

Trekking in Lahaul and Spiti

Although parts of the old trade routes to Ladakh and Tibet are now sealed with tarmac, most of this remote and spectacular region is still only accessible on foot. Its trails, though well frequented in high season, are long, hard and high, so you must be self-sufficient and have a guide. Pack-horses and provisions are most readily available in **Manali**, or in **Keylong** and **Darcha** (Lahaul) and **Kaza** (Spiti) if you can afford to wait a few days. A good rope for river crossings will be useful on many of the routes, particularly in summer when the water levels are at their highest.

The **best time** to trek is July to early September, when brilliant blue skies make this an ideal alternative to the monsoon-prone Kullu Valley. By late September, the risk of snowfall deters many visitors from the longer expeditions. Whenever you leave, allow enough time to acclimatize to the **altitude** before attempting any big passes: AMS (Acute Mountain Sickness) claims victims here every season (see Basics, p.37).

Lahaul: Darcha to Padum via the Shingo La Pass

The most popular trek is from **Darcha** over the **Shingo La** pass (5000m) to **Padum** in Zanskar. The trail passes through **Kargyak**, the highest village in Zanskar, and follows the Kargyak Valley down to its confluence with the Tsarap at **Purne**. There is a small café, shop, and camping ground here and it's a good base for the side trip to **Phuktal gompa**, one of the most spectacular sights in Zanskar. During the high season (July & Aug), a string of chai stall–tent camps spring up at intervals along the well-worn trail through the Tsarap Valley to Padum, meaning that you can manage without a guide or ponies from here on. Do not bank on finding food and shelter here at the start or end of the season.

Lahaul: Batal to Baralacha Pass

Lahaul's other popular trekking route follows the River Chandra north to its source at the **Baralacha Pass** (4920m) and makes a good extension to the Hampta Pass hike described on p.456. Alternatively, catch a Kaza bus from Manali to the trailhead at **Batal** (3960m) below the **Kunzum La** (4551m). The beautiful milky-blue **Chandratal** ("Moon") **Lake** is a relentless ascent of 7hr from Batal, with stunning views south across the world's longest glacier, **Bara Shigri**, and the forbidding north face of the **White Sail** massif (6451m). The next campground is at **Tokping Yongma** torrent. **Tokpo Yongma**, several hours further up, is the second of the two big side-torrents and is much easier to ford early in the morning; from here it is a steady climb up to the **Baralacha Pass**. You can then continue to Zanskar via the Phirtse La, or pick up transport (prearranged if possible) down to Keylong and Manali or onwards to Leh.

Spiti: Kaza via the Pin Valley to Manikaran or Wangtu

One of the best treks in **Spiti** is up the **Pin Valley**. The track alongside the River Pin, which passes a string of traditional settlements and monasteries, is now motorable as far as Mudh, around 40km south of Kaza. Over the next few years it is expected to be paved right through to Wangtu, but for now it forks beyond Mudh into two walking paths; the northern path over the Pin–Parvati Pass (5400m) to **Manikaran** in the Parvati Valley (see p.448), and the southern one to Wangtu in **Kinnaur** via the Bhaba Pass (4865m). The last section to Wangtu itself has also fallen to the roadbuilders, so you might decide just to hitch a ride.

4500m, is one of the highest and most remote inhabited places on earth – a desolate, barren tract scattered with tiny mud-and-timber hamlets and lonely lamaseries. Until 1992, Spiti in its entirety lay off-limits to foreign tourists. Now, only its far southeastern corner falls within the **Inner Line** – which leaves upper Spiti, including the district headquarters **Kaza**, freely accessible from the northwest via Lahaul. If you are really keen to complete the loop through the restricted area to or from Kinnaur (see p.421), you will need a **permit** (see p.408). The last main stop before reaching the restricted zone is the famed **Tabo** *gompa*, which harbours some of the oldest and most exquisite Buddhist art in the world.

In summer, once the **Rohtang La** and **Kunzum La** (4550m) are clear of snow, two buses leave Manali for Spiti every morning. It is also possible to hire **jeeps** from Manali (through HPTDC or any other travel agency) and to trek in from the Kullu Valley or south from the Baralacha La. From Grampoo it's a rough, 80km track to Losar but with the gorge, waterfalls, snowy peaks and not least, the white-knuckle ascent over Kunzum La, it's also a mind-boggling entry into the Spiti. Soon after crossing Kunzum La the track reaches the sprawling village of **LOSAR**, (4113m) where a police checkpoint sits alongside a couple of basic guesthouses: the *Sam Song* (❶–❷) and the notably rougher *Serchu* (❶). From this point the track becomes a road for the last section to Kaza.

Kaza and around

KAZA, the subdivisional headquarters of **Spiti**, lies 76km southeast of the Kunzum Pass, and 201km from Manali. Overlooking the north bank of the River Spiti, it's Spiti's least picturesque town, but as the region's main market and roadhead it's a good base from which to head off on two- or three-day treks to monasteries and remote villages such as Kibber. Rates for porters and ponymen are comparable to those in Kullu. It is also possible to trek to Dhankar (32km) and on to Tabo (43km). Those planning to continue on to Kinnaur can pick up a free **Inner Line permit** from the Additional Deputy Commissioner's office in the new town. You will need two passport-sized photos and copies of the relevant pages in your passport, as well as a police stamp, obtainable from the police station down the hill from the DC office towards the river. Spiti Holiday Adventure (Ⓣ01906/222711, Ⓦwww.spitiholidayadventure.com) is the most reliable travel agent and also does currency exchange, while Ecosphere (Ⓣ01906/222652, Ⓦwww.spitiecosphere.com) has info about trekking, wildlife and conducts eco-projects such as water refills. There is one erratic internet place in the square.

Accommodation and eating

The thirty or so mostly simple **places to stay** are roughly equally spread between the new and old quarters, which are divided by a (usually dry) creek. Most visitors **eat** in the **hotel restaurants** or in the growing number of tourist cafés, mostly in the old town, such as *Sachen Kunga Nyingpo*, which does good Tibetan and other cuisines and the predictable *German Bakery*, both in the village square. The oddly named *Hesty Testy* is the best place for hearty home-style cooking, while the first floor *Mahabudha* offers reasonable Indian and Chinese.

Moving on from Kaza

Two daily **buses** depart for Tabo (2hr) at 9am and 2pm, the morning departure continuing all the way to Rekong Peo in Kinnaur. A lone bus leaves for Mudh in the Pin Valley at 4.30pm (2hr 30min), returning the next morning. The only daily bus to Kibber departs at 5.30pm, returning the next morning at 8am. Double-check the bus times for these destinations, as they change frequently. Hiring a **jeep** in Spiti – where the roads are dangerous and public transport unreliable – is a good idea. You can pick them up near the bus stand; expect to pay Rs1800 return for the Pin Valley, Rs1500 for Tabo or Rs720 for Kibber via Ki. The road beyond Sumdo, where the Inner Line starts, has been upgraded but the area is prone to **landslides** so it's still wise to check road conditions.

Banjara Retreat Towards the river, new Kaza, ⓣ01906/222236. One of the better places, with twelve comfortable double rooms and a good restaurant. ❸

Khangasar Hotel Old Kaza ⓣ01906/222276. This simple lodge has large, pleasant attached rooms, all with TV. ❷

Phuntsok Palbar Near the creek, new Kaza ⓣ01906/222360. Offers the best value in town, with spotless rooms and hot bucket showers; it also has a warm sitting room, sunny yard and free luggage storage. ❶

Sakya's Abode Main road, new Kaza ⓣ01906/222254, ⓔsakya_abode@yahoo.com. This attractive place offers smartish rooms and a cheap dorm (Rs100). ❸

Zangchuk Guest House Near the creek, Old Kaza ⓣ01906/222510. The rooms and facilities are very basic but there are excellent views from its peaceful terrace. ❶

Ki Gompa

Set against a backdrop of snow-flecked mountains and clinging to the steep sides of a windswept conical hillock, **Ki Gompa** is a picture-book example of Tibetan architecture and one of Himachal's most exotic spectacles. Founded in the sixteenth century, Ki is the largest **monastery** in the Spiti Valley, supporting a thriving community of lamas whose Rinpoche, Lo Chien Tulkhu from Shalkar near Sumdo, is said to be the current incarnation of the "Great Translator" Rinchen Zangpo. His glass-fronted quarters crown the top of the complex, reached via stone steps that wind between the lamas' houses below. A labyrinth of dark passages and wooden staircases connects the prayer and assembly halls, home to collections of old *thangkas*, weapons, musical instruments, manuscripts and devotional images (no photography). Many of the rooms have seen extensive renovation since an earthquake struck in 1975; a new prayer hall, dedicated by the Dalai Lama, was also added in 2000. During the new moon towards late June or early July, Ki plays host to a large **festival** celebrating the "burning of the demon" when *chaam* dances are followed by a procession that winds its way down to the ritual ground below the monastery where a large butter sculpture is set on fire.

Ki village lies 12km northwest of Kaza on the road to Kibber, and Ki Gompa is a steep 1km walk up from the town. The most scenic approach is to take the 5.30pm bus from Kaza to Kibber; get off at Ki village and walk the last section to appreciate the full effect of the *gompa*'s dramatic southern aspect. Alternatively, the 8am bus from Kibber detours to the monastery on its way down to Kaza. **Accommodation** in Ki is scant. You can stay at monastery for Rs300 (including food, ⓣ9418 626613) or try the welcoming *Tashi Khangsar Guesthouse* (ⓣ01906/226277; ❶), located after the first bend in the road and marked with a small green sign.

Kibber

KIBBER (4205m) is amongst the highest settlements in the world with a drivable road and electricity. Jeep tracks, satellite dishes and the odd tin-roofed government building aside, its smattering of a hundred or so old Spitian houses is truly picturesque. Surrounded in summer by lush green barley fields, Kibber also stands at the head of a trail that picks its way north across the mountains, via the high glaciated **Parang La** pass (5600m) to Ladakh. Before the construction of roads into the Spiti Valley, locals used to lead ponies and yaks this way to trade in Leh bazaar. Some Manali-based trekking companies (see p.455) offer a seventeen-day trek from here to the lake of **Tso Moriri** in Ladakh (see p.503) and on to Leh.

Taking the 5.30pm **bus** from Kaza to Kibber (1hr) means you have to spend the night. Alternatively you could hire a **jeep**, hitch with a tour group, or forego transport altogether and walk the 16km of trails, although the outbound trip is nearly all uphill. Kibber's fabulous location makes for a great overnight stop, and it's easy to end up staying longer than you planned in one of the congenial **guesthouses**, all very simple with hot bucket shared baths. Opposite the school at the start of the village the *Norling* (☎01906/200091; ❶–❷) is slightly better than the adjoining *Rainbow* (☎01906/200316; ❶) and has a better restaurant. Further into the village itself, the quaint *Serkong* (☎01906/200156; ❶) has common bathrooms but a nice roof terrace.

Dhankar and the Pin Valley

Nearly a third of the way between Kaza and Tabo, near the meeting of the Pin and Spiti rivers, a rough road veers off to the east for 8.5km to the village of **DHANKAR** (3890m). The **Dhankar Gompa** on the uppermost peak behind the village is famed for its brilliant murals, probably painted in the seventeenth century, depicting the life of the Buddha. Although some of the work has been vandalized, the scenes depicting the Buddha's birth, rebirth and life in Kapilavastu and his rejection of worldly ways are spectacular. The *gompa* also affords superb views down to the confluence of the main River Spiti and the Pin tributary. Dhankar is not on a bus route so you will have to arrange your own transport (a taxi from **Sichaling** on the main road is Rs160) or walk – the shortcut starts from the storm shelter by the main road under the *gompa* 3km before Sichaling. Visitors are welcome to **stay** at the monastery for a donation but bring your own sheets – Dhankar's bedbugs are merciless. Alternatively, the *Tenzin* homestay (☎9459 270036; ❷ including food), above the monastery near the Old Fort, provides a tad more comfort.

The Pin Valley

Thirty minutes east of Kaza a bridge at Attargu crosses the Spiti and begins a sixteen-kilometre run up the **Pin Valley** to **GULLING**, above which stands the important Nyingma *gompa* of Gungri, believed to date back to the eighth or ninth century. There's a simple hotel here, the *Himalaya* (❶), a couple of cafés serving *thukpa* and *momos*, and a camping ground. Tiny **Mikim** lies 3km beyond Gulling at the confluence of the Pin and Parahio rivers; the slightly larger settlement of **SAGNAM** across the river has a few basic places to stay including a *PWD Resthouse* (❶), the *Norzang Guesthouse* (❶) and the *Shambala Guesthouse* (☎01906/224221; ❶).

Beyond Sagnam the road deteriorates rapidly, but vehicles can push ahead another 14km to **MUDH**, an enchanting hamlet with a tiny nunnery that peers over a breathtaking valley, the end of which is flanked by the pyramid-shaped Tordang Mountain. There are several **guesthouses** for the increasing number of trekkers passing through, though conditions remain pretty rough and none currently have private bathrooms. The *Dawa* (❶) is the nicest, and offers a huge dorm (Rs50); food is served in the main house and a new wing under construction promises attached rooms. Also recommended are the friendly *Himalayan Pin Parvati Guest House* (❶) and *Tara Guest House* (☎9418 441453; ❶). Check times for the one crowded and frequently delayed daily **bus** between Kaza and Mudh.

Tabo

One of the main reasons to brave the rough roads of Spiti is to get to **Tabo Gompa**, 43km east of Kaza. The mud and timber boxes that nestle on the steep north bank of the Spiti may look drab, but the multi-hued murals and stucco sculpture they contain are some of the world's richest and most important ancient Buddhist art treasures – the link between the cave paintings of Ajanta (see p.648) and the more exuberant Tantric art that flourished in Tibet five centuries or so later. According to an inscription in its main assembly hall, the monastery was established in 996 AD, when **Rinchen Zangpo** was disseminating *dharma* across the northwestern Himalayas. In addition to the 158 Sanskrit Buddhist texts he personally transcribed, the "Great Translator" brought with him a retinue of

Kashmiri artisans to decorate the temples. The only surviving examples of their exceptional work are here at Tabo, at Alchi in Ladakh, and Toling and Tsaparang *gompas* in Chinese-occupied western Tibet.

Enclosed within a mud-brick wall, Tabo's **Chogskhar**, or "sacred enclave", contains eight temples and 24 *chortens* (*stupas*). The largest and oldest structure in the group, the **Sug La-khang**, stands opposite the main entrance. Erected at the end of the tenth century, the "Hall of the Enlightened Gods" was conceived in the form of a three-dimensional *mandala*, whose structure and elaborately decorated interior functions as a mystical model of the universe complete with deities. There are three distinct bands of detail – the lower-level paintings depict episodes in the life of the Buddha and his previous incarnations; above are stucco gods and goddesses; and the top of the hall is covered with meditating Buddhas and *bodhisattvas*. Bring a torch to see the full detail of the murals.

The other temples date from the fifteenth and eighteenth centuries. Their contents illustrate the development of Buddhist iconography from its early Indian origins to the Chinese-influenced opulence of medieval Tibetan Tantricism that still, in a more lurid form, predominates in modern *gompas*. The new *gompa*, inaugurated by the Dalai Lama in 1983, houses nearly fifty lamas and a handful of *chomos* (nuns), some of whom receive training in traditional painting techniques under a *geshe*, or teacher from eastern Tibet. Visitors are welcome to attend daily 6.30am puja. It's also worth exploring the caves across the main road, one of which houses more paintings, but you need to be let in by the *gompa* caretaker.

Practicalities

There are a number of **accommodation** options in Tabo. The atmospheric *Millennium Monastic Guest House*, outside the main monastery gates (Ⓣ01906/223333; ❶), has simple rooms, some attached, and a dorm (Rs50). Behind the monastery near the river, the welcoming *Tashi Khangsar Hotel* (Ⓣ01906/233346; ❷) has bland but good-value attached rooms and a pleasant garden, while the *Panma Guest House* (Ⓣ9459 270055; ❶–❸) and *Maitreya Guest House* (Ⓣ9418 981957; ❶–❷) are also both fine. The *Millennium Monastery* restaurant and the *Zion Café* at the *Panma*, offer basic Tibetan and Indian **food**. *Café Kunzon Top* does good breakfasts in its flowery courtyard and claims to have the "highest cappuccino in the world". Two **buses** per day travel to Kaza, the 4am departure going all the way to Manali. In the opposite direction, a bus passes through at around 11am on its way from Kaza to Rekong Peo in Kinnaur.

The Manali–Leh Highway

Since it opened to foreign tourists in 1989, the famous **Manali–Leh Highway** has replaced the old Srinagar–Kargil route as the most popular approach to Ladakh. In summer, a stream of vehicles set off from the Kullu Valley to travel along the second-highest road in the world, which reaches a dizzying altitude of 5328m at Tanglang La. Its surface varies wildly from fairly smooth asphalt through potholes of differing depths to dirt tracks sliced by glacial streams, traversing a starkly beautiful lunar wilderness. Depending on road conditions and type of vehicle, the 485-kilometre journey can take anything from seventeen to thirty hours' actual driving. Bus drivers invariably stop for a short and chilly night in one of the spartan **tent camps** along the route. These, however, are few and far between after September 15, when the highway officially closes; in practice, all this means is that the Indian government won't airlift you out if you get trapped in snow. Yet some companies run regardless

Cycling the Manali–Leh Highway

Touring cylists revere the Manali–Leh highway as one of the most challenging road rides in the world and each summer up to three hundred intrepid two-wheelers set off to attempt the nearly 500km route. While the **gradients** are rarely unrideable, the two-day ascents, rough tracks over the **passes** and, most crucially, the **altitude** demand respect and some preparation.

Hauling a fully laden bike up 50km climbs to well over 5000m may sound daunting, but the exhilaration can be rewarding – especially if you're set up to camp rather than relying on the noisy, dirty parachute camps. You'll need wind- and waterproof clothing, a warm fleece, sunglasses and headwear, plus a good supply of high-energy snacks like the blocks of peanut brittle found in the bazaars. A water filter increases your autonomy too as you'll drink at least three litres a day. Check your bike has a suitably low gearing for crawling up the passes (most MTBs will), and that you have near-new brake pads for the long descents that follow, as well as a secure baggage system. As for clothing, choose quick-drying items that will wick away sweat before it brings on exposure on a chilly pass.

Most riders set off from Manali (1900m) and take eight to ten days to get to Leh (3500m). However, starting in Leh gives you a chance to acclimatize before you set off, involves less climbing but no less drama. Whichever direction you take, don't fret too much about you or your bike packing up halfway, as you'll always be able to hitch a lift. If riding alone is not for you, see p.455 for **mountain-bike tour operators** in Manali. For more information, see ⓦwww.himalayabybike.com.

of this until the passes become blocked by snowfall in late October. For more details on **transport** between Manali and Leh, see p.453 and p.491.

Manali to Keylong

Once out of **Manali**, the road begins its long ascent of the **Rohtang Pass** (3978m) and, annoyingly, often gets clogged only an hour or so up, when trucks get bogged down in wet weather; it's not uncommon to have an unscheduled wait of up to four hours when this happens. Buses pull in for breakfast (or brunch) 17km before the pass at a row of makeshift *dhabas* at Marhi (3360m). Though not all that high by Himalayan standards, the pass itself is one of the most treacherous in the region and every year locals and tourists alike are caught unawares by sudden weather changes – hence Rohtang's name, which literally means "piles of dead bodies". The road descends from Rohtang to the floor of the **Chandra Valley**, finally reaching the river at **Koksar**, little more than a scruffy collection of chai stalls with a **checkpoint** where you have to enter passport details in a ledger – one of several such stops on the road to Leh. The next few hours are among the most memorable on the entire trip. Bus seats on the left are best, as the road runs across the northern slopes of the valley through the first Buddhist settlements, hemmed in by towering peaks and hanging glaciers towards **Keylong** (see p.462). The HPTDC super-deluxe and some other buses break the journey here, leaving the bulk of the journey to the second day (the opposite obviously applies if travelling to Manali from Leh).

Keylong to Sarchu

Beyond Keylong, the Bhaga Valley broadens, but its bare sides support very few villages. At **Darcha**, a lonely cluster of dry-stone huts and dingy tent camps, plus another checkpost, the landscape is still fairly green. All buses stop here for passengers to grab a hot bowl of Tibetan *thukpa* from a wayside *dhaba*. There's little else to do in Darcha, though the Shingo La trailhead – the main trekking route north to Zanskar (see p.463) – is on the outskirts. If you are not on one of the through Manali–Leh buses, you're better off stopping at **JISPA** 7km south, a pleasant little village with ample camping along the river as well as the pricey *Hotel Jispa* (☎01900/233203; ⑤), which also has dorm beds for Rs200.

From Darcha, the newly-surfaced road climbs steadily northeast to the **Baralacha La** pass (4950m). On the other side, some buses stop for the night at **SARCHU**, where HPTDC's *Tent Camp* (③), a rather ordinary affair, serves steaming plates of rice, dhal and veg, as do a handful of similarly priced *dhabas* nearby. There are several more expensive camps dotted along the road charging up to Rs800 per person including food. Note that Sarchu Serai is 2500m higher than Manali, and travellers coming straight from Manali might suffer from the higher altitude here.

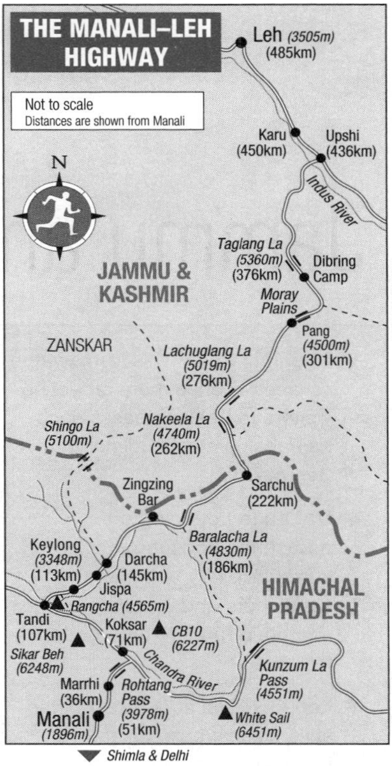

Sarchu to Taglang La

Sarchu packs up for the season from September 15. Northbound buses that haven't overnighted in Keylong thereafter press on over **Lachuglang La** (5019m), the second-highest pass on the highway, to the tent camp at **PANG** (4500m), which stays open longer. Unfortunately, this means that the drive through one of the most dramatic stretches of the route, through an incredible canyon, is in darkness. North of Pang, the road heads up to the fourth and final pass, the **Taglang La**, the highest point on the Manali–Leh Highway at a literally breathtaking 5328m. Drivers pull in for a quick spin of the prayer wheels and a brief photo session alongside the altitude sign and small shrine. If the weather's clear enough, you can gaze north beyond the multicoloured tangle of prayer flags across Ladakh to the Karakoram Range, just visible on the horizon.

Taglang La to Leh

Thirty kilometres beyond the pass is **Rumtse**, the first Ladakhi village. There are two basic guesthouse/*dhabas* (①) here, located opposite a store selling unperishable snacks. Just down the road the next village of **Gya** has a health clinic (with oxygen) and just back below the tree line, **Lato** has a particularly nice campsite in season, as well as a basic hotel (①). At **Upshi**, the road reaches the dramatic Indus Valley, tracing the **Indus River** past slender poplars, sprawling army camps and ancient monasteries. Traffic builds as you approach **Choglamsar**, then climb the final dusty kilometres to **Leh** (see p.489) – past the world's highest golf course – through the modern outskirts to the haberdashers, canny traders and wrinkled apricot-sellers of Leh's Main Bazaar.

Jammu and Kashmir

* **Kashmir Valley** This lush swathe of green is once more attracting visitors to trekking bases such as Pahalgam and Gulmarg. **See p.478**
* **Dal Lake** Lounging on a Kashmiri houseboat, surrounded by waterlilies, kingfishers and a stunning mountain range – unforgettable. **See p.482**
* **Leh** Medieval streets, a Tibetan-style palace, bazaars and looming snowy peaks. **See p.489**
* **Tikse** Along with Lamayuru and Hemis, the Indian Himalayas' most impressive monastery complex. **See p.499**
* **Tso Moriri** This exquisite high-altitude lake inhabited by nomadic herders features snow-fringed desert mountains and rare migratory birds. **See p.503**
* **Nubra Valley** Sand dunes, Bactrian camels and views of the mighty Karakorams await across the world's highest drivable road. **See p.503**
* **Alchi** Wonderful painted murals and stucco images are hidden behind the simple exterior of this ancient monastery. **See p.510**
* **Zanskar** Walled in by the Himalayas, during the winter this isolated valley can only be reached by following the frozen river route. **See p.515**

▲ Paddling on Dal Lake, Srinagar

India's northernmost and sixth-largest state, **Jammu and Kashmir** (usually shortened to J&K), is one of its most mountainous and staggeringly beautiful. It also encapsulates the cultural and religious diversity of the Subcontinent by falling into three distinct regions. The southwestern end of its thick bracket-shaped expanse is the Hindu-majority area around the winter capital of **Jammu**. Directly to the north across the first range of the Himalayas is the almost exclusively Muslim **Kashmir**, as infamous for its ongoing political woes (see box, pp.476–477) as it is renowned for its enchanting beauty. Finally, to the northeast, hugging the disputed borders with both Pakistan and China, the remote and rugged region of **Ladakh**, which occupies nearly seventy percent of the state according to its de facto borders, is populated mostly by adherents of Tibetan Buddhism.

Jammu is the state's largest city and the traditional stepping-stone into the region, though it merits a stopover in its own right for its admirable collection of temples. Most foreigners, however, head immediately for the summer capital of **Srinagar**, lynchpin of the famed Kashmir Valley, which also offers the green hills and meadows of **Gulmarg** and **Pahalgam**. Unless you fly direct to the enchanting capital of Ladakh, **Leh**, the decision of **when to visit Ladakh** is largely made for you: the passes into the region are only open between late June and late October, when the sun is at its strongest and the weather, at least during the day, pleasantly warm. From November onwards, temperatures drop fast, often plummeting to minus 40°C between December and February, when the only way in and out of Zanskar is along the frozen surface of the river. Leh is surrounded by numerous villages dominated by venerable monasteries such as **Tikse** and **Hemis** or, further west, **Lamayuru**. The latter provides a good stopover en route to **Kargil**, halfway along the Srinagar–Leh road and the jumping-off point for the isolated **Zanskar Valley**. Other sparsely populated but exquisite areas worth the bumpy detours involved in reaching them from Leh include the icy lakes of **Pangong Tso** and **Tso Moriri**, as well as the almost surreal **Nubra Valley**, with its sand dunes and wandering camels.

Some history

The region that comprises the current state of J&K has been a cultural, religious and political crossroads for millennia. There is archaeological evidence that the area around Jammu, whose name appears in the Mahabharata, was part of the **Harappan** civilization, based in the Indus Valley, one of the oldest in the world. Remains of other powerful kingdoms, such as those of the **Mauryas** and **Guptas**, have also been found near the city, although the foundation of Jammu itself is credited to the **Raja Jambu Lochan** in the late fourteenth century. It later fell under the control of the **Sikhs** but after their defeat by the British in 1846 it became part of the Hindu **Dogra dynasty** in the mid-nineteenth century. Indeed the majority of its people still identify themselves as Dogras and speak the Dogri dialect.

Kashmir, meanwhile, had become an important centre of Buddhism and, subsequently, Hinduism during the first half of the first millennium AD and these faiths coexisted side by side regardless of the region's rulers for the best part of a thousand years. In 1349, **Shah Mir** became the first Muslim ruler of Kashmir and it continued to be controlled by followers of Islam from **Mughals** to **Afghans** until it was taken over by the Sikhs and followed the same historical path as Jammu from the 1840s until Independence. Its problems since 1948 are chronicled in greater detail in the box on pp.476–477 but under the guidance of its youngest ever Chief Minister, **Omar Abdullah**, who was elected in January 2009, there is increased confidence among Kashmiris that the future may see more positive developments.

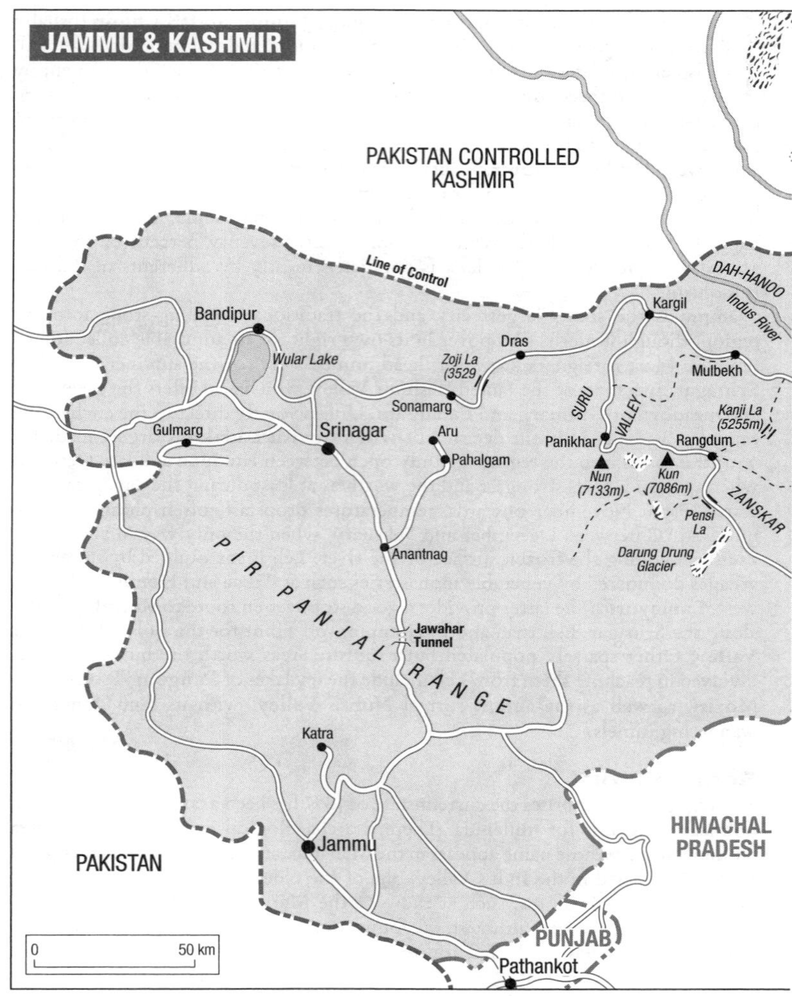

The first inhabitants of Ladakh are thought to have been a mixture of nomadic herdsmen from the Tibetan plateau and a small contingent of early Buddhist refugees from northern India called the Mons, joined in the fourth or fifth century by the Indo-Aryan **Dards**, who introduced irrigation and settled agriculture. The first independent kingdom in the region was established in the ninth century by the maverick nobleman Nyima Gon, at around the same time as **Buddhism** was first disseminated by the wandering sage-apostles such as Padmasambhava (alias Guru Rinpoche). This was followed by the **Second Spreading**, among whose key proselytizers was the "Great Translator" **Rinchen Zangpo**.

Around the fourteenth century, Ladakh passed through a dark age before being reunified by **Tashi Namgyal** (ruled 1555–70), who established a new capital and palace at Leh. This power eventually succumbed to the mightier Mughals, when

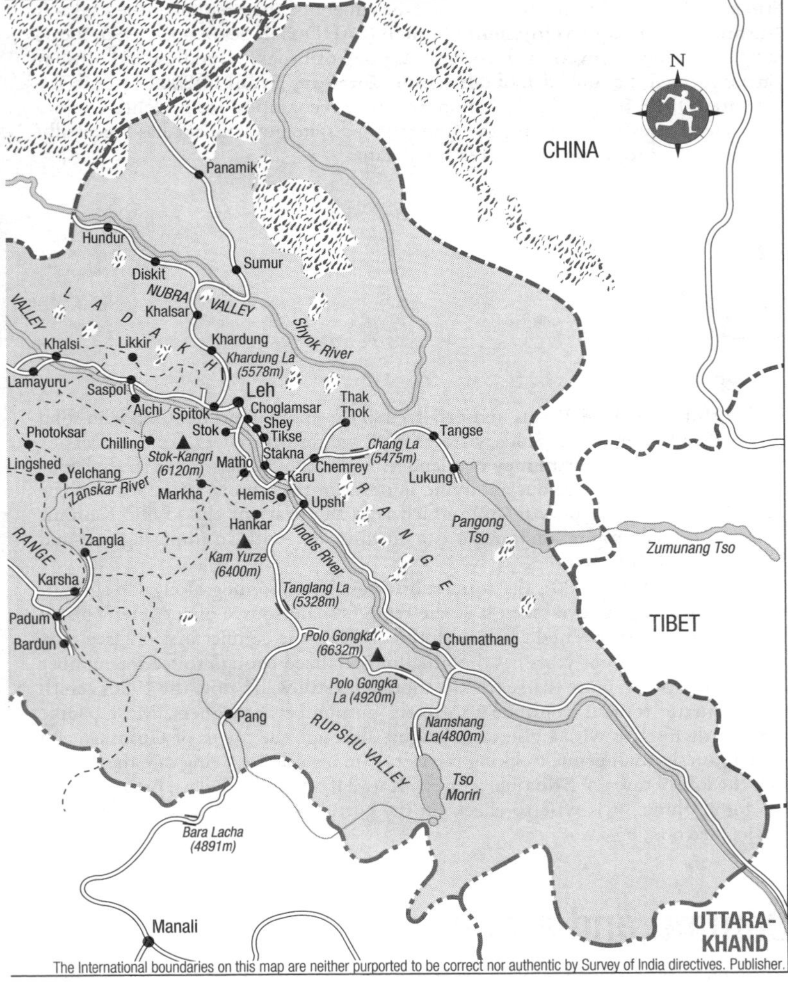

Aurangzeb demanded more tribute, ordered the construction of a mosque in Leh and forced the Ladakhi king to convert to Islam. Trade links with Tibet resumed in the eighteenth century, but Ladakh never regained its former status. Plagued by feuds and assassinations, the kingdom teetered into terminal decline, and was an easy target for the **Dogra** general Zorawar Singh, who annexed it for the Maharaja of Kashmir in 1834.

Ladakh became a part of J&K in independent India in 1948, following the first of the three Indo-Pak wars fought in the region. Tensions over the disputed line of control still flare up sporadically (see box, pp.476–477). When you consider the proximity of China, another old foe who annexed a large chunk of Ladakh in 1962, it's easy to see why this is India's most sensitive border zone. There is also a degree of internal friction. Long dissatisfied with the state government based in

Srinagar, the Ladakhis finally saw the establishment of their region as the **Ladakh Autonomous Hill Development Council** (LAHDC) in September 1995, localizing – in theory – government control. A group of Ladakhi Buddhist and Muslim parties formed the unified **Ladakh Union Territory Front** in 2002 to push for separation from J&K and gain Union Territory recognition from Delhi. Despite local success in state elections, the Congress-led state government has repeatedly blocked moves to set up Union Territory status.

Kashmir

Long before **KASHMIR** was immortalized in the eponymous Led Zeppelin song it had already achieved legendary status with western travellers, from officers of the British Raj to the first hippy overlanders in the 1960s. No stint in the Subcontinent was complete without an idyllic sojourn on the famous houseboats of the capital **Srinagar** (see box, p.482), which is at the heart of the idyllic Kashmir Valley. The state capital of **Jammu** is a bustling city with an imposing fort and liberal sprinkling of temples.

By the end of the 1980s, the **tourist business** was booming alongside agriculture, and had in fact overtaken it as the region's main source of income. This all came to an almost overnight halt with the onset of the conflict in 1989 (see box, p.476). Only in recent years has the situation stabilized enough to see the number of visitors swell to more than a trickle, though it's still well below the 1980s zenith and domestic tourists continue to greatly outnumber foreigners. Most people content themselves with a visit to **Srinagar**, although the towns of **Gulmarg** and **Pahalgam**, both in prime trekking territory, are regarded as being safe these days, as is the lovely town of **Sonamarg** on the Kargil road. Nevertheless, before setting off for Kashmir, it is wise to check on the current security situation; for more advice, see box, p.479.

Jammu and around

Known as "the city of temples" because of the many shrines that dot the town, **JAMMU** is more attractive than its reputation suggests and worthy of at least a full day en route to Kashmir, for which it is the railhead (at least until the line to Srinagar is complete). The main place of worship in town is the revered **Ragunath** temple, although it is surpassed in importance by **Vaishno Devi**, near Katra, some 60km north. The city also boasts the impressive **Bahu Fort**, which crowns a hill overlooking the River Tawi and the splendid **Baja-u-Bahu** gardens. The town's principal museum is the mildly absorbing **Amar Mahal**, which showcases period art.

Arrival and information

Trains from all over India, including those on the country's longest route, the weekly three-day marathon from Kanyakumari, pull into the station 4km south

Moving on from Jammu

Numerous **buses** to Srinagar (11–12hr; Rs250) depart between 5am and 8am from the main bus stand. There are also services to Pathankot, Amritsar, Delhi and other destinations; the only way of leaving any later is in one of the shared **jeeps** (9–10hr; Rs450). JKTDC buses depart from near the tourist office on Vir Marg aka Residency Road (see below). Returning to Delhi by train, catch the *Jammu All Express* #2414 (daily: dep. 6.15pm, arr. Delhi 4.15am). Jammu's airport (Ⓣ0191/243 7843) is 8km southwest of the city and has several daily **flights** to Delhi and Srinagar with Air India and Jet.

of the centre. There are at least seven daily trains from Delhi, of which the fastest is the *All Jat Express* #2413 (daily: departs 10.35pm, arrives 8am). City buses go frequently to the centre of the old town, just north of the river, where the main **bus stand** is. The helpful **Tourist Reception Centre** (Ⓣ0191/254 4527; Ⓦwww.jktourism.org), is on Vir Marg, which starts around ten minutes' walk north of the bus stand, opposite the Ragunath temple. It hands out quite a good map of the state and its two largest cities. The most convenient ATM is the HFDC bank at the bus stand, while the J&K Bank on Shalimar Road can **exchange** cash and travellers' cheques.

Accommodation

Finding a room is rarely a problem in Jammu, though there is little choice in the middle to upper end of the market. Most of the budget places are to be found on Gumat Bazaar or around the bus stand.

Diamond Gumat Bazaar Ⓣ0191/257 7792. Plenty of adequate rooms of varying sizes. Sees the most western visitors but not the best in terms of value. ❶–❷

Nagima Gumat Bazaar Ⓣ0191/256 6008. Very clean Sikh-run establishment, containing only ten rooms, some a/c. ❸–❹

Savera Opposite Ragunath temple Ⓣ0191/254 9936. Budget place that is much better value than most of the bus stand and Gumat Bazaar hotels, with larger rooms. ❶–❸

Tourist Reception Centre Dak Bungalow Vir Marg Ⓣ0191/257 9554. Several fairly characterless government blocks, offering a range of rooms, some a/c, and the odd suite. ❷–❺

Vivek Just south of bus stand Ⓣ0191/254 7545. Centrally air-conditioned hotel with comfortable rooms and a snazzy lobby, though the restaurant's not great. ❺

The town

If you only have time to visit one of Jammu's many temples, it should be the buzzing **Ragunath** (daily 6–11.30am & 6–9.30pm), about ten minutes' walk through the commercial lanes east of the bus stand. Once you've got through the tight security, you enter a large courtyard surrounded by multiple *shikharas* and two gardens. Within lies an inner courtyard, housing the main shrine of Lord Ragunath, an incarnation of Vishnu, and his two consorts, watched over by an orange-robed statue of Hanuman nearby.

The other main attraction is **Bahu Fort** (daily 9am–9pm; free), which stands proudly on a high bluff above the south bank of the River Tawi, around 3km southeast of the centre. The solid, squat battlements of the fort enclose some beautifully manicured lawns, although the principal draw for Hindus is the small **Mata Kali temple** within the complex. Next to the fort, the odd fish-shaped metal **Aquarium Awareness Centre** (daily 9am–9pm; Rs20) contains a mildly

The Kashmir conflict

The Himalayan state of **Kashmir** is the main reason why India and Pakistan have remained bitter enemies for most of the sixty-plus years since Independence. The region's troubles date from Partition, when the ruling Hindu maharaja Hari Singh opted to join India rather than Pakistan (see p.1162), and the geopolitical tug-of-war over the state has soured relations between the two countries ever since, at least until the last few years.

The conflict in Kashmir has taken two forms: firstly, a **military confrontation** between the Pakistani and Indian armies along the de facto border – on three occasions leading to fully fledged war (in 1947, 1965 and 1999); and, secondly, a violent **insurgency-cum-civil war** since 1989, during which both Kashmiri and foreign Muslim fighters have launched various attacks against Indian military and civilian targets inside Kashmir itself, leading to equally bloody reprisals by Indian security forces – a conflict which has now cost an estimated seventy thousand lives.

The roots of the problem

Following the cessation of hostilities in 1948, a UN resolution demanded a plebiscite should take place whereby the Kashmiri people would decide their own future. This India has resolutely refused to hold. The Ceasefire Line, or so-called **Line of Control**, became the effective border between India and Pakistan; the third of Kashmir held by Pakistan is referred to by those who support independence from India as **Azad (Free) Kashmir**. India lost a further slice of Kashmiri territory to the Chinese during the 1962 conflict (see p.1162) before a resumption of hostilities with Pakistan during the **Second Indo-Pakistan War** of 1965 (see p.1162). Again, Kashmir was the focus of attention, though at the end of the war both sides returned to their original positions. The **Simla Agreement** of 1972 committed both sides to renounce force in their dealings with one another, and to respect the Line of Control and the de facto border between their two states.

Insurgency and civil war

Simmering Kashmiri discontent with Indian rule and Delhi's political interference in the region, which had been due to gain virtual autonomy in return for joining India, began to transform into **armed resistance** around 1989 – the arrival of mujahideen in the Kashmir Valley after the end of the war with Russia in Afghanistan is often blamed for the sudden surge of militancy. The key incident, however, was the unprovoked massacre, in 1990, of around one hundred unarmed protesters, by Indian security forces on **Gawakadal Bridge** in the capital, Srinagar. By the following year, violence and human-rights abuses had become endemic, both in the Kashmir Valley itself and further south around Jammu. **Curfews** became routine, and thousands of suspected militants were detained without trial amid innumerable accusations of torture, the systematic rape of Kashmiri women by Indian troops, disappearances of countless boys and men, and summary executions. The conflict continued to ebb and flow throughout the 1990s, with regular

diverting assortment of fish. Descending in attractive tiers below the fort, the impressive **Baja-u-Bahu Gardens** (daily summer 8am–10pm, winter 9am–9pm; Rs10) contain a series of well-tended flower gardens and decorative pools, which act as swimming baths for the local monkeys.

A couple of kilometres northeast of the bus stand on the Srinagar Road, the **Amar Mahal Museum** (daily 9am–12.50pm & 2–5.50pm, closes at 4pm in winter; Rs45 [Rs10]), housed in a converted palace, is basically an art gallery with some regal memorabilia. The portraits and miniatures date mostly from the early twentieth century.

atrocities on both sides, while the region's once-thriving tourist industry was dealt a fatal blow when the extremist Al-Faran Muslim group kidnapped five tourists trekking near Pahalgam in 1995; one was beheaded, and the others were never found. At the end of the decade, the crisis brought India and Pakistan to the verge of yet another all-out war. With both countries now fully fledged **nuclear states**, Kashmir has become one of the world's most dangerous geopolitical flashpoints.

In May 1999, at least eight hundred Pakistani-backed mujahideen crept across the Line of Control overlooking the Srinagar–Leh road near **Kargil** and began to occupy Indian territory. India moved thousands of troops and heavy artillery into the area, and swiftly followed up with an aerial bombardment. In the event the conflict was contained, and by July 1999 the Indian army had retaken all the ground previously lost to the militants. All-out war was only narrowly averted again in early 2003 after intense diplomatic pressure was brought to bear on both sides by US emissary **Colin Powell**. Within Kashmir, long-established organizations like the Jammu and Kashmir Liberation Front and the All Party Hurriyat Conference, which had traditionally adopted a secular and nationalist stance, were being increasingly eclipsed by militantly Islamic and pro-Pakistani groups such as Lashkar-e-Toiba and Jaish-e-Mohammad.

The road to peace?

The first signs of genuine rapprochement came in May 2003, when Indian prime minister Vajpayee made a **declaration of peace**, announcing that hundreds of Pakistanis detained in Indian prisons since the Kargil war would be released. Pakistani prime minister Mir Zafarullah Khan Jamali responded by announcing that Pakistan would ease trade restrictions and improve travel and sporting links. In 2004 and 2005 the Indian and Pakistani governments also held their first-ever talks with Kashmiri separatists from the Hurriyat Conference, establishing a peaceful "Road Map" for progress in the region. A further round of Indo-Pak talks following the appointment of Manmohan Singh as India's new prime minister resulted in further small but encouraging signs of progress, symbolized by the inauguration, in April 2005, of a fortnightly **bus service** between Srinagar and Muzaffarabad in Pakistani-controlled Kashmir. Further détente was signalled in the aftermath of the devastating **earthquake** in Pakistani Kashmir in October 2005, which killed around 73,000 people in Pakistan and a further 1400 in Indian Kashmir, when the Line of Control was opened to speed up relief operations.

Various **long-term solutions** to the whole Kashmir issue are currently being mooted. These have ranged from India suggesting that the Line of Control might be converted into a permanent border to Pakistan possibly even being prepared to give up all claims to Kashmir if India allowed it some form of self-government. Kashmir's future looks brighter now than it has for decades, although there is the perpetual risk that a single violent incident could trigger a new phase of conflict.

Eating and drinking

Though it's no gourmet's paradise, Jammu has plenty of cheap snack joints and vegetarian *vaishno dhabas*. Hotel restaurants are the best choice for meat and more comfortable surroundings.

Falak KC Residency, Vir Marg. This odd revolving restaurant on top of the hotel has good Indian and international cuisine. Mains mostly over Rs200.

JKTDC Café Baja-u-Bahu Gardens. At the lower end of the gardens, this simple café is a nice spot to enjoy a cup of tea or simple snack such as a samosa.

Mehfil *Hotel Samrat*, Gumat Bazaar. Reasonable veg and non-veg Indian and Chinese dishes are available at this low-key hotel restaurant for around Rs100.

Mughal Darbar Vir Marg. One of the best places to get a foretaste of Kashmiri cuisine, including its famous richly spiced mutton dishes (Rs120–160).

Regal Opposite Ragunath temple. Busy restaurant that feeds the hungry crowd of pilgrims tasty veg food.

Around Jammu

Although most foreigners head straight towards the Kashmir Valley, there are a couple of places you might consider stopping near the road to Srinagar, which is predictably punctuated by army signs spouting militaristic slogans – "the power behind the punch" is a common one. Around 30km north of Jammu a road branches off to the small town of **Katra**, which is the base for the 12km hike to **Vaishno Devi** temple. One of the region's most important pilgrimage centres, the cave shrine is entered via an ankle-deep stream, whose chilly waters you must brave in order to get *darshan* of the image of the goddess, a triple incarnation of the female *shakti*. Katra itself is pleasant enough, connected by frequent buses and jeeps with Jammu and offers basic accommodation. One of the best places is the JKTDC *Tourist Bungalow* (Ⓣ0191/254 9065; ❷–❹).

A further 70km along, just as the pines start to take over from the deciduous forest, the main road passes by **Patnitop**, an alpine-style resort, popular with lowland Indians for its views, fresh air and relative accessibility.

The Kashmir Valley

There could hardly be a greater contrast than that between the hot and dusty plains around Jammu and the cool green belt of the **Kashmir Valley**. Apart from the geographical divide, separated as they are by a rise in altitude of over 1000m, there are huge cultural and religious differences. While the whole area around Jammu is predominantly Hindu, the Kashmir Valley and its capital, **Srinagar**, are distinctly Muslim, hence the notorious sectarian problems (see box, pp.476–477). The initial impression of the Vale of Kashmir, whether you approach it via the Jawahar Tunnel which cuts through the mountains from Jammu in the south or via the Zoji La pass from Kargil to the west, remains one of a lush rural paradise guarded by the grandeur of the surrounding peaks, the mighty **Pir Pinjal** range snow-capped except in the very height of summer. Vivid green fields of corn and wheat form a patchwork quilt with fruit orchards and groves of nut trees, principally walnut and almond. These are most often lined with towering poplars and willows, hence the preponderance, on the approach to the capital, of shops selling high quality cricket bats. Heavy industry has yet to appear in the valley.

When to visit

Although the climate is not as harsh as neighbouring Ladakh and the road up from Jammu is kept open by the army, the winter months see some seriously sub-zero temperatures and heaps of **snow**. If you do come between November and March, you will need some very warm clothing – locals wear a thick woollen cloak called a *pheran*. By contrast, as much of the Kashmir Valley, including Srinagar itself, is well under 2000 metres in altitude, **high summer** can be surprisingly hot, sometimes topping 35°C. Therefore, the late spring or early autumn is the **best time** to come, especially if you intend to do any trekking. The former sees the

Security concerns and scams in Kashmir

Although the situation in Kashmir is calmer than it has been for twenty years, it is still essential to check the current situation with reputable media sources before travelling – Ⓦwww.kashmirtimes.com is a good local resource. No tourists have been directly targeted since 1995 (see box, p.477) but if trouble is flaring up, then you will have to endure a very heavy **military presence** and may even run the risk of getting literally caught in the crossfire or an act of **terrorism**. You should not necessarily be put off by government advisories, however, as these tend to be extremely cautious and Kashmir has remained on the list of no-go areas even when at its most peaceful.

Once in Jammu and the Kashmir Valley, **security** is taken very seriously and the vast majority of tourist sites, such as temples, mosques, museums and forts, are heavily guarded. You are usually prohibited from taking bags or electronic items inside; tokens are given when you check them but if you are not comfortable about leaving possessions like cameras or mobile phones in the cloakroom, then it is better to lock them in your hotel. Both Jammu and Srinagar **airports** have extra high security and passengers are often not allowed into the terminal until a certain time before departure, usually two hours but occasionally less. Sometimes no hand luggage is allowed on board, so it is best to check in advance.

The other potential pitfall to be aware of is the variety of **scams** perpetrated on unsuspecting tourists by unscrupulous Kashmiris, especially in Delhi's Paharganj area or Jammu. It is best to take any advice about safety in Kashmir (or the lack of it) from people who approach you with a pinch of salt. Some make out you will be in danger without a guide and then try to sell a tour costing hundreds, if not thousands of dollars. These people should be avoided at all costs, as should agents trying to sell you rooms on houseboats. At best you will be overcharged for investing sight unseen and in the worst case you will be seriously ripped off. For more advice on houseboats see the box on p.482.

meadows carpeted in an abundance of flowers, while the latter offers warm golden days, chillier nights and the first signs of the foliage changing hue.

Srinagar

Steeped in tradition and set in one of the most dramatic locations in India, with majestic mountains pressing in on three sides, **SRINAGAR** is the summer administrative capital of J&K. All too often associated with strife in recent times, this city of almost a million inhabitants is most famous with tourists for the **houseboats** that line the fringes of **Dal Lake** and **Nageen Lake**, as well as the central section of the **Jhelum River**, a tributary of the Indus. The town has some other splendid attractions, which in recent years have once again been open to visitors after long periods of being off-limits. Chief among these are two of the most venerated mosques, **Jami Masjid**, deep in the heart of the atmospheric **Old City**, and the lakeside **Hazratbal**. Another important Islamic place of worship is the Sufi shrine of **Makhdoom Sahib**, halfway up to the inaccessible fort.

Srinagar, like the rest of Kashmir, is predominantly Muslim, even more so since the advent of serious trouble in 1990, when almost all the Hindu Pandits were driven out – though this region was known for centuries for its religious tolerance, where adherents of all the major eastern faiths lived side by side. The most important Hindu temple is the **Shankaracharya Mandir**, atop a hill overlooking Dal Lake.

Of the city's secular sights, options include the engaging **Sri Pratap Singh Museum** and the Mughal pleasure gardens that surround the lake, such as **Shalimar Bagh** and **Nishat Bagh**.

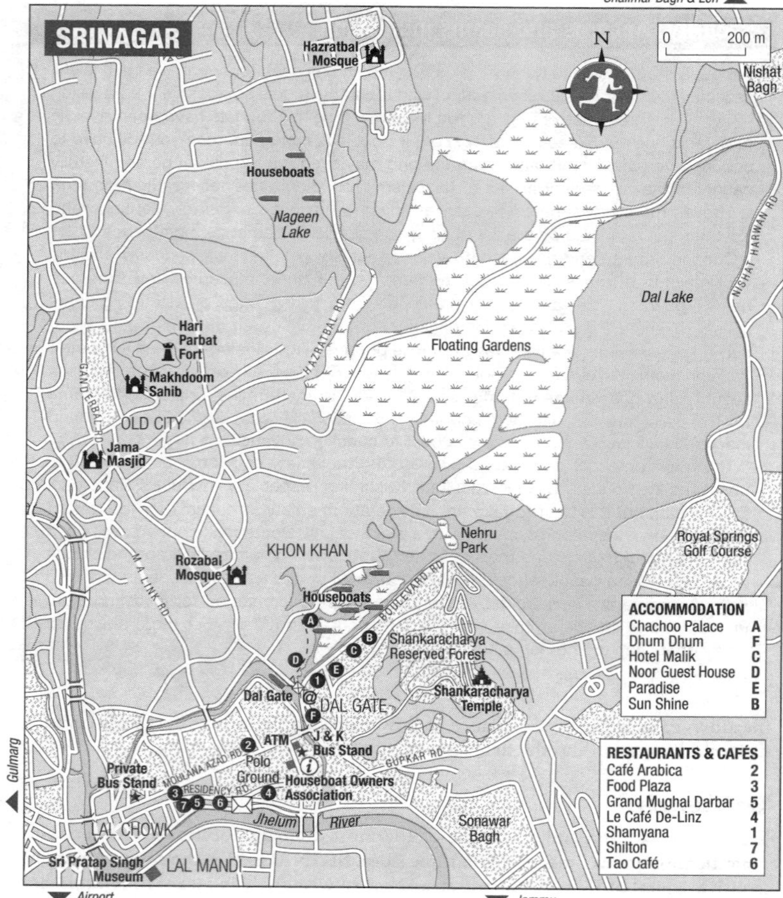

Arrival and information

Srinagar's **airport** (Ⓣ0194/243 0334) lies 14km south of the city centre. Taxis into town cost a whopping Rs400; auto-rickshaws around half that. Until the rail link with Jammu and the rest of the country is completed (supposedly by 2012), the only other way to reach Srinagar is by **bus** or **jeep**. Government buses and jeeps pull in on Residency Road, a few minutes' walk south of Dal Gate, while the private bus stand is around a kilometre further west.

The **Tourist Reception Centre** (Ⓣ0194/245 2691, Ⓦwww.jktourism.org) is right beside the government bus stand on Residency Road and claims to be open 24 hours. It's not all that much help beyond giving out a useful map and a few glossy brochures. Beware of the **touts** who hang around here and other arrival points to besiege tourists with offers of houseboats, guided tours and "cheap" carpets.

Most other useful facilities are also on or just off Residency Road, which doglegs to the west, including the main **post office** and a couple of **ATMs**. You can also

Moving on from Srinagar

Jet Airways and Air India operate **flights** to Delhi (8–10 daily; 1hr 25min–2hr 25min), some via Jammu. AI runs a weekly flight to Lehi (Wed; 1hr).

There are frequent **buses** to Jammu (10 daily; 11–12hr), Kargil (6–8 daily; 10–11hr) and Leh (4–6 daily; 2 days). **Jeeps** ply the same routes, operating more flexible hours and costing at least half as much again but getting you there much quicker.

do foreign exchange at branches of the J&K Bank on MA Road or the Boulevard. There are a number of **internet** outlets, such as Skybiz on the town side of Dal Gate or Nida Tours & Travel (Ⓣ0194/250 1684, Ⓔnidatours@yahoo.com), along the lakeside path on the far side of it. The latter is principally a **travel agent**, which can book tickets and arrange treks or give useful advice on them, as can Kashmir Valley Travels, also near Dal Gate (Ⓣ0194/210 7527). For more on trekking see the box on p.485.

Accommodation

The first thing most people think about when considering where to stay in Kashmir is **houseboats** (see box, p.482) and there are certainly plenty to choose from. There are, however, also numerous reasonable **hotels** on dry land. Note that since many houseboats will only do a full-board deal, the prices below are for room only unless otherwise indicated; discounts can be bargained for at most times and even in high season if business is slack.

Hotels

Chachoo Palace New Rd, Khon Khan, Dal Lake Ⓣ9906 523796. This quaint wooden hotel with a lakeside lawn has the charm of a houseboat with easier access. The comfortable attached rooms have TV and the friendly proprietors can also provide food. ❶

Dhum Dhum Front Line Dal Gate Ⓣ0194/245 0779. This backpackers' favourite is convenient for transport and the town but rather noisy. Rooms are passable. ❷

Hotel Malik Boulevard Dal Lake Ⓣ0194/247 3672, Ⓔmas_inc786@yahoo.com. A standard square block beside the lake, with decent, well-furnished but somewhat overpriced rooms. ❻

Noor Guest House Abi-Buchara, Dal Lake Ⓣ0194/245 0872. Nice and colourful place with a great front lounge and delightful garden. Good value. ❷–❸

Paradise Boulevard Dal Lake Ⓣ0194/250 0663, Ⓦwww.hotelparadisesgr.org. Several blocks of rather classy rooms that vary in size. Set just off the lakefront, thus cheaper than its mid-range competitors. ❺

Sun Shine Boulevard Dal Lake Ⓣ0194/247 2469, Ⓦwww.hotelsunshinesgr.com. Painted a suitably bright yellow, this modern hotel is among the best in this range. The smart rooms are more expensive with a lake view. There's a coffeeshop on the roof. ❻–❼

Houseboats

Bendemeer Khon Khan Dal Lake Ⓣ0194/247 5418. Accessible from the road, this beautifully carved deluxe class boat provides expert service and excellent value. ❺

Dunhill Khon Khan Dal Lake Ⓣ9622 946264. Also accessible from the road, you won't find a boat much cheaper than this simple two-room affair, run by a mother and daughter. Two meals cost an extra Rs400/day. ❶

Kashmir View Dal Lake Ⓣ9906 722897. The dining room, where meals are ordered a la carte, is particularly attractive. Rooms in the attached pontoon hotel cost Rs300. Free self-paddle *dunghy*, a wooden, canoe-type boat. ❹

Lakeview East side of Nageen Lake Ⓣ9906 532015. Actually a group of eight jointly run houseboats – reception is in a nearby house. Well kept and good value. ❹

Mughal Sheraton Dal Lake Ⓣ9906 864924, Ⓔmughalsheraton@yahoo.co.in. This is the biggest of four sister boats, with spacious and luxurious rooms. Three daily meals for two cost Rs1000 extra. ❻

New Bulbul Dal Lake Ⓣ9906 476085. A small boat in a pleasantly open setting and with a homely feel. Good value, especially if you take the full board option. ❸

Royal Pleasure Nageen Lake Ⓣ0194/242 4675, Ⓔroyaljeweller@rediffmail.com. A rarity in being a

The lullaby of lapping lakes

Few experiences are as romantic as lounging on an exquisitely carved **houseboat**, watching kingfishers diving for their dinner between the floating lilies or gazing at the moon reflected on the darkened waters. These floating hotels of one to four rooms have existed for generations and many originated at the peak of the British Raj, when Victorian families would spend the entire hot season here. They originally chose boats to get round laws that forbade them from owning land.

Srinagar has no fewer than 1200 **houseboats** lining the shores of the **two main lakes**, Dal and Nageen, and the banks of the Jhelum River. And that's just the official ones. Consequently, it can seem like a bewildering business to know where to start looking. The golden rule is to fend off **touts** in town (or further afield) who try to get you to commit yourself with all sorts of promises. Some establishments are also infamous for poor service and rip-offs – anybody connected with the name Baktoo, in particular, should be given a wide berth.

One approach is to organise your stay through the **Houseboat Owners Association** (Ⓣ0194/245 0326, Ⓦwww.houseboatowners.org), whose office is opposite the Tourist Reception Centre on Residency Road. They produce a clear price list of the different categories of boat from Deluxe Class (Rs4500 for a double with full board) down to D Class (Rs1100 for the same). They will also help you negotiate moderate discounts on these prices at slack times such as late summer and off-season.

Undoubtedly the best way to find a houseboat, however, is to hole up in a town hotel for the first night and then hire a **shikara**, a colourful flat-bottomed water taxi that is steered with a heart-shaped paddle, to embark on a scouting mission. This way you can stop and look at a number of boats to compare prices, amenities and location. Once you've chosen your vessel, be sure to agree exactly what is included in the price, such as the number of meals, drinks or whether a daily *shikara* ride to the shore is part of the deal. It is also wise to make it clear if you do not want to be pestered by floating salesmen and that there should be no deterioration in service if you do turn them away. Note that some houseboats on the far side of Dal Gate and most on Nageen are accessible by road or footpath. Those on Nageen are generally a little cheaper. It is also worth noting that there is a potential threat to the very existence of houseboats after a 2009 government mandate that they should install expensive sewage treatment units in order to prevent further water pollution.

new construction but intricately carved in traditional style. Very friendly and the owners also run treks. Two meals included. ❹

Sea Palace Dal Lake Ⓣ9906 722914. A small group of boats of varying sizes. One unusual feature is that some have baths. Two daily meals cost Rs500 per couple. ❹

Veena Palace Dal Lake Ⓣ9797 056134, Ⓔfindous123@yahoo.co.in. Set amidst a water lily pond, this friendly place offers extremely good value. Meals for two cost Rs500 daily for veg, Rs600 for non-veg. ❶

The lakes and gardens

Srinagar would be a major draw on the strength of its Himalayan scenery alone but it is the city's serene lakes and grand gardens that make it irresistable. There are actually several large bodies of water dividing the urban sprawl into its constituent neighbourhoods but by far the largest is **Dal Lake**, with a surface area of approximately twenty-one square kilometres. The lake is usually as flat as a mirror and incredibly photogenic, with the surrounding peaks reflected in the greenish blue waters. Apart from the houseboats that cover its southern end, nearest the town centre, the lake is famous for its **floating gardens**, as well as the **floating flower and vegetable market**, best visited in the early morning. The nearby island of **Nehru Park** has pontoons for swimming (Rs50/hr) and even water-skiing facilities (Rs600 including lesson). The best way to tour the lake is on a *shikara*, (see box opposite). Depending on your bargaining skills, these cost around Rs100 per hour to hire.

The perimeter of Dal Lake is punctuated by lavishly ornamental gardens, a legacy of the seventeenth-century Mughal period. These collections of fountains, terraced lawns and flowerbeds reach their zenith in **Nishat Bagh** (daily 6am–7pm; Rs5), halfway along the eastern shore, and **Shalimar Bagh**, set a little way back from the northeastern corner. Towards the northern end of the western shore stands **Hazratbal mosque**, whose huge white marble dome towers above its spacious courtyard. It is considered to be Kashmir's holiest shrine, as its plain but vast interior houses a single hair of the prophet Mohammed, purportedly brought from Medina centuries ago. The scene of heavy fighting during the worst of the insurgency, it is once more a tranquil spot that welcomes outsiders along with the constant stream of worshippers.

Tucked between the spit of land behind Hazratbal and the Old City, much smaller **Nageen Lake** does not have any particular sights but is more peaceful for that very reason and quite a popular choice for houseboaters.

The Old City

The typical Kashmiri architectural style of wooden buildings with carved balustrades and ornate frames on windows and doors, which can be seen in the older parts around Dal Gate, becomes ubiquitous as you enter the maze of streets that constitute the **Old City**. Strictly off-limits until a few years ago, this fascinating area is once again safe to visit. A taxi from Dal Gate costs Rs250, an auto around Rs120. The focal point of the area is **Jama Masjid**, Srinagar's largest mosque. Built of sturdy stone and brick with the distinctive pagoda-style wooden minarets unique to Kashmir, it was erected between 1398 and 1402 by Sikander But-Shikoh but has been destroyed by fire and rebuilt several times, most recently in 1961. A couple of kilometres to the southeast, the small square mosque of **Rozabal**, with its simple octagonal dome, is purported to enshrine the tomb of Jesus by those who subscribe to the theory – the subject of Holger Kersten's *Jesus Lived In India*– that Christ actually lived to a ripe old age and died here in Kashmir.

Another lively place of worship, the Sufi shrine of **Makhdoom Sahib**, is located on the northern edge of the Old City, halfway up towards Hari Parbat Fort on the hill of the same name. Whereas the fort is occupied by the army and thus entry prohibited, the shrine is open, but only to men. Good views across Nageen Lake and further afield can be enjoyed by all from the nearby steps.

The rest of the city

The bustling centre of Srinagar, which revolves around the two main thoroughfares of Residency Road and MA Road, is not particularly appealing, although the bazaar area of **Lal Chowk** at the western end of these streets holds more interest. As so many Kashmiri merchants have decamped to other parts of India, however, you will be disappointed if you expect to find any better deals on souvenirs such as pashmina shawls or carpets than you would elsewhere and caution should be exercised when contemplating such purchases.

The outstanding **Sri Pratap Singh Museum** (Tues–Sun 10am–4pm; Rs50 [Rs10]; Ⓦwww.spsmuseum.org) is in Lal Mandi, south across the Jhelum River from Lal Chowk. The former maharaja's palace houses a huge collection that includes archeological findings such as terracotta tiles and Buddhist tablets, decorative arts from enamelware to papier mâché, textiles, manuscripts and miniature paintings.

The city's main Hindu temple, **Shankaracharya Mandir**, occupies the crest of the eponymous hill about a half-our hike south of the Boulevard. The temple itself is nothing special architecturally speaking and security is predictably tight, but the views across the city and lakes to the mountains beyond are quite breathtaking.

Eating and drinking

The **local cuisine** of Kashmir is known as *wazwan* and is heavily meat-based, its signature dish being *roghan josh*, richly spiced mutton in a tomato sauce. Dishes often include **saffron**, as the costly spice is grown locally and therefore less expensive than elsewhere. Kashmiris are also famed for their green *kahwa* tea, drunk sweet and milkless but usually spiced with cardamom or almond. The alternative beverage, a salty black tea known as *noon*, is a more acquired taste. **Alcohol** is once more available in several places, another sign of Srinagar being less in the grip of militancy. Most independent restaurants are on Residency Road.

Café Arabica *Hotel Broadway*, Moulana Azad Rd. The trendiest spot in town, serving coffee and snacks to a mainly young crowd. There is also a bar in the hotel.

Food Plaza Residency Rd. Bright and breezy joint, specializing in seafood such as lake fish and prawns. Chinese and Kashmiri dishes, such as kebabs, are also available. Mains range from Rs80–160.

Grand Mughal Darbar Residency Rd. Mostly tandoori and *wazwan* dishes, with some fish. There is a bakery as well. Items cost Rs50–130.

Le Café De-Linz Residency Rd. Housed in a unique but rather dingy round building, this restaurant offers a wide Indian menu and some Chinese food, with most items under Rs100.

Shamyana Boulevard, Dal Lake. This pleasant lakeside garden restaurant offers Indian, Chinese, continental and even some Mexican cuisine in the evening, plus a daytime bakery. Main courses between Rs150–250.

Shilton Residency Rd. As well as the standard Indian and Chinese menu, you can get reasonable steaks and local specialities in this popular establishment for around Rs80–150.

Tao Café Residency Rd. Srinagar's most atmospheric restaurant, where you can dine in the lovely rose garden. There is a wide choice of favourites from India, China and Tibet for Rs100–200.

Gulmarg

Some 56km west of Srinagar and at an elevation of around 2700m, **GULMARG**, whose name means "flower meadow", is a pleasant escape from the city but is rather more geared towards domestic tourists and can get very crowded. It is also rather spread out, with no discernible centre. The meadow itself is a kilometre wide and over three long, allowing ample room for picnics, pony rides and even one of the world's highest golf courses. The surrounding pine slopes can be ascended for a distant view of 8126m **Nanga Parbat** to the north, in Pakistan-controlled Baltistan. The more sedentary can ascend one of these slopes on a gondola for Rs300–800, depending how high up you go. In winter, the gondola comes into its primary usage as the means to get to the top of Gulmarg's **skiing** slopes, which are underused but highly recommended for the quality of powdery snow. Equipment ($7–20) and ski intsructors ($38) can be hired through what purports to be the world's smallest ski shop, Kashmir Alpine (Ⓣ0195/425 4638, Ⓦwww.kashmiralpine.com). The same operation also runs trekking expeditions during the warmer months. Another recommended operation is the British-run Mountain Tracks (Ⓦski-gulmarg.co.uk).

Practicalities

Aside of the erratic bus service, the best way to get to Gulmarg from Srinagar is by shared **jeep** (Rs60) or you can hire a vehicle for a day-trip for Rs1300.

Trekking in Kashmir

Despite being prime trekking territory, the security concerns of recent decades mean that relatively few foreigners take to the hills. The once booming industry is slowly picking up, however, and there have been no unpleasant incidents involving foreign tourists since 1995 (see box, p.477). Given the tricky terrain and the delicate political situation, however, it is not recommended to set off without at least a **local guide**. Trekking agencies in Srinagar (see p.481) and some hotels mentioned in the text can provide fully organized treks with ponies, porters and all the requisite equipment.

Pahalgam is still the main base for treks, which vary in length and level of difficulty from the two-day round trips within the Lidder Valley to the week-long hike to Panikhar in Ladakh's Suru Valley (see p.514). You can also do some good walking from **Sonamarg**, the last main town in Kashmir before the Zoji La pass. Conditions for trekking are pretty hot and uncomfortable in high summer and the shoulder seasons of late spring and early autumn are the optimum time to trek; the best **map** is Sheet 1 in Leomann's India Himalaya series. For more general advice about trekking, see Basics, p.64.

Amarnath trek

Kashmir's most trodden route becomes crowded during the July/August full moon with thousands of pilgrims, who flock to see the natural ice lingam in the **Amarnath cave**, at an altitude of 3962m. The trek from Pahalgam usually takes four days and includes overnight stays at Chandanwari (2900m), Sheshnag (3720m) and Panchtarni (3933m). The final stage involves crossing the Mahagunas pass. After visiting the cave, you can either return the same way or make the more direct descent to Baltal, 8km east of Sonamarg on the Srinagar–Leh road.

Kolahoi glacier trek

The five-day trek from Pahalgam to the impressive but receding **Kolahoi glacier** (3400m) can be shortened by a day if you take a jeep to the first overnight stop at picturesque Aru (2414m). The next day the ascent is via alpine meadows and streams to Lidderwat (3049m), before a gentler stage to Satlanjan (3150m), which allows you to preserve energy for the steep climb to the glacier and back to Lidderwat on the following day. You can then walk back down to Aru or Pahalgam itself on the fifth day.

Sonamarg to Wangat trek

This popular route takes you through a beautiful stretch of the mountains via a number of delightful **high altitude lakes**, where fishing is permitted with a permit (available through agents in Srinagar). The first staging post at Nichnai (3620m) affords views of the Thajiwas glacier before the second day's walking undulates to Kishanar (3819m). On the third day you cross over the 4191m Bazkal Gali pass and descend past Gadsar Lake to overnight at Dubta Pani (3280m). Next day's walking takes in the seven tiered lakes of Satsar en route to the region's largest body of water, Gangabal Lake (3507m) for a final night's camping before the descent to Wangat, where there are buses and jeeps to Srinagar.

Accommodation is far flung and on the pricey side, one of the more moderate places being the chalet-style *Gulmarg Sahara* (Ⓣ0195/425 4505, Ⓦwww.hotelgulmargsahara.com; ❺), beside the meadow. Further up in price and altitude, near the gondola, the flashier *Hilltop* (Ⓣ0195/425 4477, Ⓦwww.hilltophotelgulmarg.com; ❽) offers lavishly furnished rooms and suites. Apart from the hotel restaurants, the only other **places to eat** are roadside *dhabas* between the bus stand and the gondola.

Pahalgam

Kashmir's number one trekking base (see box, p.485), **PAHALGAM** enjoys a stunning location around 100km east of Srinagar in the deep-cut Lidder Valley, whose pine-crested ridges ascend sharply from each bank of the chilly, fast-flowing river. The town, whose altitude is 2139m, is mostly located on the slightly flatter east bank and the lower surrounding slopes. Main Market, the central thoroughfare of the modern town, runs parallel to the river and contains most of the facilities, while the more pleasant **old village** lies 1.5km north, beyond Pushwan Park with its fancy flowerbeds and topiary. There are no specific sights to visit but eager pony men tout rides at fixed government rates (Rs200/hr) to various local beauty spots.

Practicalities

Again, the bus service from the capital to Pahalgam is rather unreliable but it is easy to get a **bus** or shared jeep (Rs60) to Anantnag (known locally as Islamabad) and another from there. The **Tourist Reception Centre** on the main market (Ⓣ01936/243224) claims to be open 24 hours in season. There are plenty of **places to stay**, which only fill up on major holidays. The town's premier hotel, occupying vast grounds between Main Market and the river, is the luxurious *Pahalgam Hotel* (Ⓣ01936/243252, Ⓦwww.pahalgamhotel.com; ❾). The spacious rooms in its alpine-style blocks cost over Rs7000 ($160) in high season. A smart mid-range option, further south on Main Market, is the *Paradise* (Ⓣ01936/243368; ❺), while the best budget deals are to be found in the old village. Foremost of these is the riverside *Beach Resort* (Ⓣ9797 292332, Ⓔmehrajganai2001@gmail.com; ❶–❹), which has comfortable rooms of varying sizes and whose welcoming owners also run treks. Best of the hotel **restaurants** is *The Trout Beat* at the *Pahalgam Hotel*, which expertly prepares the eponymous fish and other non-veg fare. Simpler places on Main Market include *Purnima Gujrati*, which does dosas and other veg snacks, and *Dana Pani*, great for filling Punjabi veg meals.

Sonamarg

The third rural location in Kashmir that has started to see a return of foreign travellers is **SONAMARG**, 84km northeast of Srinagar. Perched beside the River Sindh and surrounded by forests of pine, fir, beech and sycamore, with towering peaks all around, it is a scenic place to break the journey to Kargil or Leh. This is also the place with the best display of spring and early summer flowers. A further attraction is that the **Thajiwas glacier** is only 4km away and so makes one of the easiest treks. The only downside is that its location on the vital Srinagar–Leh road means there is a fairly constant and noticeable military presence.

Practicalities

The advantage of Sonamarg being right on the main route to Ladakh is that there are plenty of **buses** from Srinagar, especially in the morning. Most vehicles heading further east are liable to be full up, however. There is also a reasonable choice of **accommodation** on or around the main road – try the sturdy brick *Glacier Heights* (Ⓣ0194/241 9224; ❹) or reliable JKTDC *Tourist Huts* (Ⓣ0194/241 7208; ❷–❺). Apart from the J&K *Tourist Café*, the *Lolabi* **restaurant** does a standard menu of Indian and Chinese dishes.

Ladakh

The culturally and administratively separate region of **LADAKH** (La-Dags – "land of high mountain passes"), variously described as "Little Tibet" or "the last Shangri-La", is one of the last enclaves of Mahayana **Buddhism**, which has been the principal religion for nearly a thousand years, now brutally suppressed by the Chinese in its native Tibet. Except near the transition zone into Kashmir the outward symbols of Buddhism are everywhere: strings of multicoloured prayer flags flutter from the rooftops of houses, while bright prayer wheels and white-washed *chortens* (the regional equivalent of *stupas*; see p.493) guard the entrances to even the tiniest settlements. More mysterious still are Ladakh's medieval **monasteries**. Perched on rocky hilltops and clinging to sheer cliffs, **gompas** are both repositories of ancient wisdom and living centres of worship. Their gloomy prayer halls and ornate shrines harbour remarkable art treasures: giant brass Buddhas, *thangkas*, libraries of antique Tibetan manuscripts, weird musical instruments and painted walls that writhe with fierce Tantric divinities. This is India's most remote and sparsely populated region, a high-altitude **desert** cradled by the Karakoram and Great Himalaya ranges and criss-crossed by myriad razor-sharp peaks and ridges.

The highest concentration of monasteries is in the **Indus Valley** near **Leh**, the region's capital. Surrounded by sublime landscapes and crammed with hotels,

Restricted areas and permits

Parts of Ladakh are still inaccessible to the casual tourist, but with the easing of tensions along the border between India and China, much of this incredible land, once hidden behind the political veil of the "Inner Line", has now been opened up. Three areas in particular are now firm favourites with travellers: the **Nubra Valley** bordering the Karakoram Range to the north of Leh; the area around **Pangong Tso**, the lake to the east of Leh; and the region of **Rupshu** with the lake of **Tso Moriri**, to the southeast of Leh. Both Indian and foreign visitors need **permits** to visit these areas. In theory, these are only issued to groups of at least four people accompanied by a guide, and only through a local tour operator. However, in practice travel agents are generally happy to issue permits to solo individuals travelling independently, though you'll have three imaginary friends (usually people applying at the same time) listed on the permit to bump up the numbers. As long as your name and passport number are on the permit, the checkpoints are quite relaxed about how many of you there are.

Permits are issued by the **District Magistrate's Office** in **Leh** but the office now only deals through Leh's many **tour operators** (see p.497), who charge a **fee** – usually around Rs50–100 per head. As some of the areas in question (such as Pangong Tso) are served by infrequent public transport, you may well find yourself using a tour operator anyway, in which case they will include your permit in the package. You will need two photocopies of the relevant pages of your passport and visa. Provided you apply in the morning, permits are usually issued on the same day. Once you have your permit, usually only valid for a maximum period of seven days, make at least five copies before setting off, as checkpoints often like to keep a copy when you report in. They may also occasionally spot-check to see the original copy. If you go on an organised trip, however, the driver takes care of all this and you may never even handle your permit.

guesthouses and restaurants, this atmospheric little town, a staging post on the old Silk Route, is most visitors' point of arrival and an ideal base for side trips. North of Leh, across the highest drivable pass in the world – **Khardung La**, lies the valley of **Nubra**, where sand dunes carpet the valley floor in stark contrast to the towering crags of the Karakoram Range. It is also possible to visit the great wilderness around the lake of **Tso Moriri** in **Rupshu**, southeast of Leh, and to glimpse Tibet from the shores of **Pangong Tso** in the far east of Ladakh. For these areas you will, however, need a permit (see p.487). West of Leh, beyond the windswept **Fatu La** and **Namika La** passes, Buddhist prayer flags peter out as you approach the predominantly Muslim district of **Kargil**. Ladakh's second largest town, at the mouth of the breathtakingly beautiful **Suru Valley**, marks the halfway stage of the journey to or from Srinagar, and is the jumping-off point for **Zanskar**, the vast wilderness in the far south of the state that forms the border with Lahaul in Himachal Pradesh.

Far beyond the reach of the monsoons, Ladakh receives little snow, especially in the valleys, and even less rain (just four inches per year). Only the most frugal methods enable its inhabitants to **farm** the thin sandy soil, frozen solid for eight months of the year and scorched for the other four. In recent years, **global warming** has meant drier winters with even less snow; the consequent loss of snow-melt has put pressure on traditional farming and irrigation, resulting in a real fear of drought. Two main "highways" connect Ladakh with the rest of India: the legendary Srinagar–Leh road and the route up from **Manali** (see p.487), almost 500km south. These two, plus the rough road from Kargil to Padum in Zanskar,

Festivals in Ladakh

Most of Ladakh's Buddhist **festivals**, in which masked **chaam** dance dramas are performed by lamas in monastery courtyards, take place in January and February, when roads into the region are snowbound. This works out well for the locals, for whom the festivals relieve the tedium of the relentless winter, but it means that few outsiders get to experience some of the northern Himalayas' most vibrant and fascinating spectacles. Recently, however, a few of the larger *gompas* around Leh have followed the example of **Hemis**, and switched their annual festivals to the **summer** to attract tourists. The tourist office in Leh produces a listings booklet called *Ladakh*, giving dates for forthcoming years.

Gompas that hold their *chaams* (dance festivals) in winter or spring include **Matho** (mid-Feb to mid-March), **Spitok** (mid-Jan), **Tikse** (late Oct to mid-Nov) and **Diskit** (mid-Feb to early March) in Nubra. Other important festivals in Ladakh include **Losar** (the Tibetan/Ladakhi New Year), which falls any time between mid-December and early January.

Summer festivals

Hemis Tsechu: July 10–11, 2011; June 29–30, 2012; June 18–19, 2013. See p.501.

Karsha Gustor, Zanskar: July 27–28, 2011; July 15–16, 2012; July 6–7, 2013. See p.517.

Thak Thok Tsechu Aug 8–9, 2011; July 28–29, 2012; July 18–19, 2013. See p.502.

Sani Nasjal, Zanskar: Aug 12–13, 2011; Aug 1–2, 2012; July 21–21, 2013.

Phyang Tsedup July 28–29, 2011; July 16–17, 2012; July 6–7, 2013. See p.507.

Festival of Ladakh Sept 1–15. This popular J&K Tourism-sponsored two-week event, held principally in Leh, is designed to extend the tourist season, featuring archery contests, polo matches, Bactrian camels from Nubra and traditional Ladakhi dance accompanied by some tedious speeches.

also link the majority of Ladakh's larger settlements with the capital. **Bus services** along the main Indus Valley highway are frequent and reliable, but grow less so the further away you get from Leh. To reach off-track side-valleys and villages within a single day, it is much easier to splash out on a jeep **taxi** – either a Gypsy or a Tata Sumo – available in Kargil and Leh. The alternative, and more traditional way to get around the region, of course, is by **trekking**.

Leh

As you approach **LEH** for the first time, via the sloping sweep of dust and pebbles that divide it from the floor of the Indus Valley, you'll have little difficulty imagining how the old trans-Himalayan traders must have felt as they plodded in on the caravan routes from Yarkhand and Tibet: a mixture of relief at having crossed the mountains in one piece, and anticipation of a relaxing spell in one of central Asia's most scenic towns. Spilling out of a side valley that tapers north towards eroded snow-capped peaks and looks south towards the majestic **Stok-Kangri massif** (6120m), the Ladakhi capital sprawls from the foot of a ruined Tibetan-style palace – a maze of mud brick and concrete flanked on one side by cream-coloured desert and on the other by a swathe of lush, irrigated farmland.

Leh only became regional capital in the seventeenth century, when Sengge Namgyal shifted his court here from Shey, 15km southeast, to be closer to the head of the Khardung La–Karakoram corridor into China. The move paid off: within a generation the town had blossomed into one of the busiest markets on the Silk Road. Leh's prosperity, managed mainly by the Sunni **Muslim** merchants whose descendants live in its labyrinthine old quarter, came to an abrupt end with the closure of the Chinese border in the 1950s. Only after the Indo-Pak wars of 1965 and 1971, when India rediscovered the hitherto forgotten capital's strategic value, did its fortunes begin to look up. Today, khaki-clad *jawans* (soldiers) and their families from the nearby military and air force bases are the mainstay of the local economy in winter, when **foreign visitors**, to whom the region was opened up in 1974, are few and far between. Leh has more than doubled in size since the advent of tourism and is a far cry from the sleepy Himalayan town of the early 1970s. Many of the provision stores and old-style outfitters on the main street have been squeezed out by Kashmiri handicraft shops, internet cafés, art emporiums and Tibetan restaurants.

The abiding impression of Leh, however, remains that of a lively yet laid-back place to unwind after a long bus journey. Attractions in and around the town itself include the former **palace** and **Namgyal Tsemo gompa**, perched amid strings of prayer flags above the narrow dusty streets of the **old quarter**. A short walk north across the fields, the small monastery at **Sankar** harbours accomplished modern Tantric murals and a thousand-headed Avalokitesvara deity. Leh is also a good base

Altitude sickness

As Leh is 3505m above sea level, some travellers, and especially those who arrive by plane from Delhi, experience mild **altitude sickness**. The best way to avoid the symptoms – persistent headaches, dizziness, insomnia, nausea, loss of appetite or shortness of breath – is to rest for at least 48 hours on arrival. Drink 3–4 litres of water a day, avoid alcohol, and don't exert yourself. For more information, see p.37.

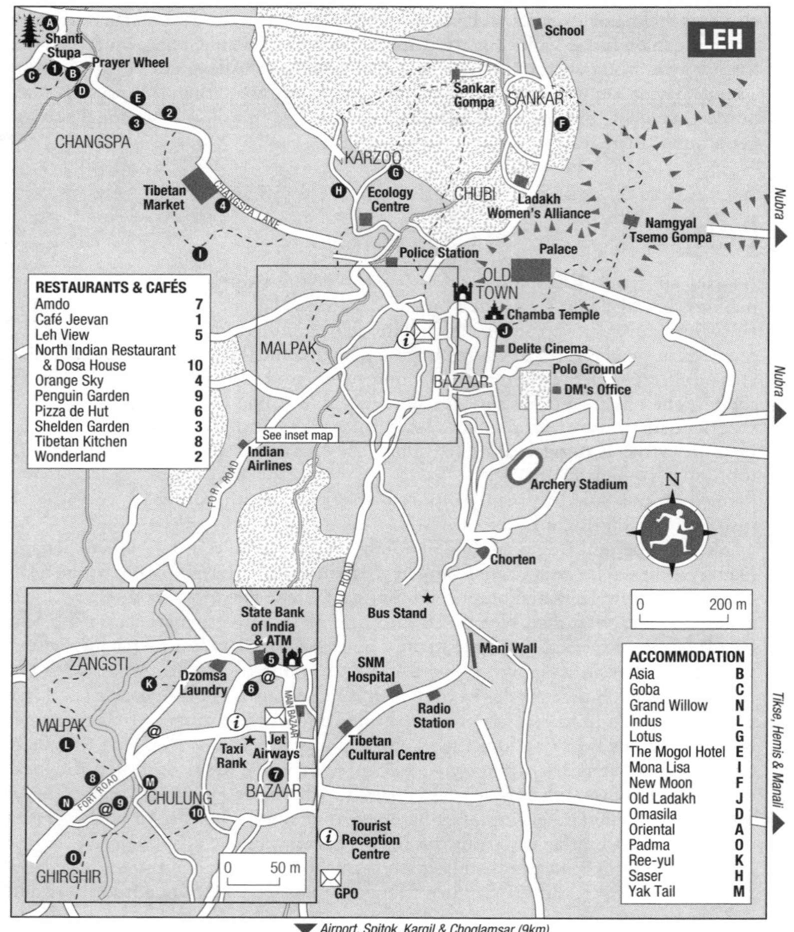

for longer **day-trips** out into the Indus Valley. Among the string of picturesque villages and *gompas* within reach by bus are **Shey**, site of a derelict seventeenth-century palace, and the spectacular **Tikse gompa**.

Arrival, information and local transport

A taxi from Leh **airport**, 5km southwest of town on the main Srinagar highway, will set you back a fixed fare of Rs150 to the bazaar or Rs165 to Changspa, where many of the hotels are located. State and private **buses** pull into the dusty town bus stand, fifteen minutes' walk or a Rs50 taxi ride south of the bazaar and many of the hotels. Manali buses terminate on Fort Road, near the *Hotel Dreamland*.

The main J&K **tourist reception centre** (Mon–Sat 10am–4pm; ⓣ01982/252094, ⓦwww.jktourism.org), 3km from the bazaar on the airport

Moving on from Leh

During the summer, weather permitting, Air India, Jet Airways and Kingfisher all operate daily **flights** to **Delhi** (1hr 30min). AI also flies to **Jammu** (Fri & Sun; 1hr) and **Srinagar** (Wed). The rest of the year, flights are less frequent and reliable. Tickets can be booked and confirmed at the Air India/Tushita Travels office on Fort Road (daily 10am–5pm; ⓣ01982/252076). The Jet office is located in the main bazaar (Mon–Sat 10am–5pm, Sun 10am–3pm; ⓣ01982/250999, ⓦwww.jetairways.com), not far down from the mosque. As usual, Kingfisher tickets must be obtained through a travel agent. One-way summer ticket prices to Delhi range from around Rs5000 with Kingfisher to over Rs10,000 with all carriers at peak times.

The overland route to **Manali** in Himachal Pradesh (see p.451) is officially open until September 15, when HPTDC **bus** services stop, although some private buses continue to ply the route through to early October, as do 4WD Gypsies and Sumos. A full account of the 485km route, starting at Manali, is given on pp.467–469. Tickets for **HPTDC**'s alternate-days "super-deluxe" bus (Rs1800 including an overnight stop and meal in Keylong) can be booked at their upstairs office on Fort Road (daily 10am–8pm; ⓣ9697 376404). Under half the price are the ramshackle **state transport** corporation buses run by HPSRTC and J&KSRTC, bookable the day before departure at the town bus stand. Several agencies along Fort Road sell tickets for **private buses** to Manali for around Rs900–1000. They will also help arrange a Sumo or Gypsy **4WD taxi** to Manali for Rs1200–1800 per person. This is by far the most comfortable option and, if you don't mind leaving at 2am, they usually get to Manali that evening. The downside of this is that you will miss some of the spectacular scenery by travelling in the dark and the drivers are often accused of reckless driving.

J&KSRTC buses (2 days; Rs560–700) to **Srinagar** run from mid-June to late October, stopping overnight at Kargil before grinding up the bleak Zoji La pass (3540m) and descending steeply into the fabled Vale of Kashmir.

road, is too far out of town and hardly worth visiting. The **tourist information centre** on Fort Road in the bazaar (most of year 10am–4pm; ⓣ01982/253462) is a bit more helpful.

The **taxi** rank (daily 6am–7pm; ⓣ01982/253039) is almost directly opposite the tourist information centre. Each driver carries a list of fixed fares to just about everywhere you might want to visit in Ladakh, taking into account waiting time and night halt charges. These rates apply to peak season; reductions of up to forty percent can be had at other times. Prices are high as the season is so short – expect to pay around Rs80 to Changspa, Rs650 return to Tikse, Rs1300 to Hemis and Rs5200 to Pangong Lake, with an additional Rs1000 for a night's stay.

Accommodation

Leh is glutted with **accommodation**, much of it refreshingly neat, clean and excellent value, mainly due to strict regulation. Most of the town's **cheap guesthouses** are immaculately whitewashed traditional houses, set in the leafy outskirts, especially in the areas of **Changspa** to the west and **Karzoo** to the north. Simple double rooms with common baths go from around Rs150, even in high season, and from Rs300 for attached. For a little more, you can often find a sunny en-suite "glass room" with a view all to yourself.

Rooms in Leh's increasing number of **mid-range and upmarket hotels** come with attached bathrooms and piped hot water. The prices below are for high season; off-season, prices can be slashed by as much as sixty percent. For homestays outside Leh, see "Listings" on p.497.

Asia Changspa Lane ⓣ01982/253403, ⓔladakhasia@yahoo.co.in. Large riverside guesthouse with a spanking new block. Sociable roof terrace-cum-café, as well as yoga, meditation, reiki and pranic healing. ❷–❹
Goba Down path off Changspa Lane ⓣ01982/253670. Well-maintained traditional house with a pleasant garden and views of Shanti Stupa. Rooms are immaculate, and those in the new block have attached bathrooms. ❶–❷
Grand Willow Fort Rd ⓣ01982/251835, ⓦwww.hotelgrandwillow.net. Blessed with beautifully ornate wooden balconies and mountain views, the hotel's spacious rooms have cable TV and colourful soft furnishings. ❼
Indus Malpak, off Fort Rd ⓣ01982/252502, ⓔmasters_adv@yahoo.co.in. Cheap singles and a few doubles, all with attached bathrooms and solar-heated water. Central, pleasant, with a family atmosphere and open in winter. ❶–❸
Lotus Upper Karzoo ⓣ01982/250265, ⓔri_wangtrek@gmail.com. The laid-back staff and leafy location make this a relaxing and welcoming option, although the rooms are better at other places. It's done in a traditional style and the more expensive rooms have mountain views. ❼
The Mogol Hotel Changspa Lane ⓣ01982/253439, ⓦwww.hotelmogol.com. Smart new place with welcoming staff and large, nicely furnished rooms, half of them with TV. ❼
Mona Lisa Down path off Changspa Lane ⓣ01982/252456, ⓔriggs_pisces@yahoo.co.in. Run by monks who lovingly tend the vegetable garden. Simple attached and non-attached rooms. Breakfast available. ❶–❸
New Moon Sankar Rd, Chubi ⓣ01982/250296, ⓔangchok@india.com. New place built in traditional style with spacious rooms and a good location below Namgyal Tsemo Gompa. ❹
Old Ladakh Old town ⓣ01982/252951, ⓔold_ladakh@rediff.com. Ladakh's first-ever guesthouse is homely and central, and offers a choice of rooms: the kitsch "deluxe" one (pink pillows and Tibetan rugs) is a real winner. Cross-check any trekking prices they quote though. *Tak*, across the lane, handles overflow. ❶–❸
Omasila Changspa Lane ⓣ01982/252119, ⓦwww.hotelomasila.com. Friendly, accommodating 35-room hotel, including five suites and six centrally heated rooms. The large terrace offers sweeping views of the mountains and the lovely dining room serves excellent dishes featuring vegetables grown in the garden outside. Open year round. ❼
Oriental Below the Shanti Stupa, Changspa ⓣ01982/253153, ⓦwww.oriental-ladakh.com. Congenial, extremely popular guesthouse with spotless rooms (many now with attached bath), free filtered water, an internet café, superb views, nourishing home-cooked meals and a genuinely warm welcome, even in winter. Booking advisable in summer. ❶–❹
Padma Ghirghir, off Fort Rd ⓣ01982/252630, ⓦwww.padmaladakh.net. There are two parts to this hotel: a traditional old building with immaculate rooms with shared baths, a beautiful kitchen, a garden and mountain views; and a modern annexe with comfortable doubles and attached baths and a rooftop restaurant. ❸–❻
Ree-yul Zangsti, on lane off Fort Rd ⓣ01982/252911, ⓔlimbijal@rediffmail.com. Tucked in a quiet corner of the centre, boasting a lovely courtyard and exquisitely carved woodwork, this convivial place has clean rooms, all attached, some with TV. ❶–❷
Saser Karzoo, up the path from the Ecology Centre ⓣ01982/250162, ⓔnamy_z@yahoo.com. Modern hotel that successfully embraces elements of traditional architecture, with a pleasant garden courtyard and comfortable rooms with baths – a bargain off-season. ❷–❸
Yak Tail Fort Rd ⓣ01982/252118. Large, central hotel with thirty-odd high-standard rooms, all with cable TV, arranged around a courtyard. ❸–❻

The Town

With the mighty hulk of the **palace** looming to the north, it's virtually impossible to lose your bearings in Leh. The broad **main bazaar** runs north to south through the heart of town, dividing the labyrinthine **old town** and nearby polo ground from the greener and more spacious residential districts of **Karzoo** and **Suki** to the west. **Fort Road**, the other principal thoroughfare, turns west off the main street and then winds downhill past the taxi rank and a host of hotels, restaurants and shops, towards the Air India office on the southern outskirts.

The bazaar and old town

After settling into a hotel or guesthouse, most visitors spend their first day in Leh soaking up the atmosphere of the **bazaar**. Eighty or so years ago, this bustling tree-lined boulevard was the busiest market between Yarkhand and Kashmir. Merchants from Srinagar and the Punjab would gather to barter for pashmina wool brought down by nomadic herdsmen from western Tibet, or for raw silk hauled across the Karakorams on Bactrian camels. These days, though the street is awash with kitsch curio shops and handicraft emporiums, it retains a distinctly Central Asian feel. Even if you're not shopping for trekking supplies, check out the surviving **provision stores** along the street, where bright pink, turquoise, and wine-red silk cummerbunds hang in the windows.

When you've had enough of the bazaar, head past the new green-and-white-painted **Jama Masjid** at the top of the street, and follow one of the lanes that lead into the **old town**. Apart from the odd electric cable and concrete path, nothing much has changed here since the warren of flat-roofed houses, crumbling *chortens* and *mani* walls (see box below) was laid down in the late sixteenth century – least of all the plumbing. One place definitely worth a visit, however, is the **Chamba temple**. It's not easy to find on your own; when you get to the second row of shops on the left beyond the big arch ask for the key-keeper (*gonyer*), who will show you the way. Hemmed in by dilapidated medieval mansions, the one-roomed shrine houses a colossal image of Maitreya, the Buddha to come, and some wonderful old wall paintings.

The palace

Lording it over the old town from the top of a craggy granite ridge is the derelict **palace** (daily sunrise to sunset; Rs100 [Rs5]) of the sixteenth-century ruler Sengge Namgyal. A scaled-down version of the Potala in Lhasa, it is a textbook example of medieval Tibetan architecture, with gigantic sloping buttressed walls

Chortens and mani walls

Among the more visible expressions of Buddhism in Ladakh are the chess-pawn-shaped **chortens** at the entrance to villages and monasteries. These are the Tibetan equivalent of the Indian *stupa* (see p.355) – large hemispherical burial mounds-cum-devotional objects, prominent in Buddhist ritual since the third century BC. Made of mud and stone (now also concrete), many *chortens* were erected as acts of piety by Ladakhi nobles, and like their southern cousins, they are imbued with mystical powers and **symbolic significance**: the tall tapering spire, normally divided into thirteen sections, represents the soul's progression towards nirvana, while the sun cradled by the crescent moon at the top stands for the unity of opposites, and the oneness of existence and the universe. Some contain sacred manuscripts that, like the *chortens*, wither and decay in time, illustrating the central Buddhist doctrine of impermanence. Those enshrined in monasteries, however, generally made of solid silver and encrusted with semiprecious stones, contain the ashes or relics of revered *rinpoches* (incarnate lamas). Always pass a *chorten* in a clockwise direction: the ritual of circumambulation mimics the passage of the planets through the heavens and is believed to ward off evil spirits. Look out for the giant, brightly painted specimen between the bus station and Leh bazaar.

A short way downhill from the big *chorten*, near the radio station, stands an even more monumental symbol of devotion. The 500-metre **mani wall**, erected by King Deldan Namgyal in 1635, is one of several at important religious sites around Ladakh. Ranging from a couple of metres to over a kilometre in length, the walls are made of hundreds of thousands of stones, each inscribed with prayers or sacred mantras – usually the invocation *Om Mani Padme Hum*: "Hail to the Jewel in the Lotus". It goes without saying that such stones should never be removed and visitors should resist the urge to climb onto the walls to have photographs taken.

and projecting wooden balconies that tower nine storeys above the surrounding houses. Since the Ladakhi royal family left in the 1940s, damage inflicted by nineteenth-century Kashmiri cannons has caused large chunks of it to collapse. Take a torch, and watch where you walk: in spite of restoration work, holes gape in the floors and dark staircases.

Namgyal Tsemo Gompa

Once you are acclimatized to the altitude, the stiff early-morning hike up to **Namgyal Tsemo Gompa** (daily 7–9am & 5–8pm), the monastery perched precariously on the shaly crag above Leh palace, is a great way to start the day. Two trails lead up to "the Peak of Victory", whose twin peaks are connected by giant strings of multicoloured prayer flags; the first and most popular path zigzags across its south side from the palace road, while a second scales the more gentle northern slope via the village of Chubi, the route followed by the lama from Sankar *gompa* (see below) who tends to the shrine each morning and evening. Alternatively, you could drive here along the dirt track that turns left off the main Khardung La highway, 2km north of the bus stand.

Approaching the *gompa* from the south, the first building you come to is the red-painted **Maitreya temple**. Thought to date from the fourteenth century, the shrine houses a giant Buddha statue flanked by *bodhisattvas*. However, its wall paintings are modern and of less interest than those in the **Gon-khang** (temple of protector deities) up the hill.

The Shanti Stupa

A relatively new addition to the rocky skyline around Leh is the toothpaste-white **Shanti Stupa** above Changspa village, nearly 3km west of the bazaar by road. Inaugurated in 1983 by the Dalai Lama, the "Peace Pagoda", whose sides are decorated with gilt panels depicting episodes from the life of the Buddha, is one of several such monuments erected around India by a "Peace Sect" of Japanese Buddhists. It can be reached by car, or on foot via a steep flight of more than five hundred steps, which winds up from the end of Changspa Lane via the café just below the *stupa*. Its broad terrace makes an excellent spot to watch the sunrise, and is popular with early morning *yogis*.

Sankar Gompa

Nestled amid the shimmering poplar coppices and terraced fields of barley that extend up the valley behind Leh, **Sankar Gompa**, 2km north of the town centre, is among the most accessible monasteries in central Ladakh – hence its restricted visiting hours for tourists (daily 7am–6pm; Rs30). You can get here either by car or on foot: turn left at the *Antelope Guesthouse* and then right onto the concrete path that runs alongside the stream. Sankar appears after about fifteen minutes' walk, surrounded by sun-bleached *chortens* and a high mud wall. You can also work your way through the fields behind the burgeoning tourist area of Karzoo.

The monastery, a small under-*gompa* of Spitok, is staffed by twenty monks, and is the official residence of the **Kushok Bakula**, Ladakh's head of the Gelug-pa sect. Above the **Du-khang** (main prayer hall) stands the *gompa*'s principal deity, Tara, in her triumphant, one-thousand-armed form as Dukkar, or "Lady of the White Parasol", presiding over a light, airy shrine room whose walls are adorned with a Tibetan calendar and tableaux depicting "dos and don'ts" for monks – some of which are very arcane indeed. Another flight of steps leads to the *gompa* **library** and, eventually, a roof terrace with fine views towards the north side of Namgyal Tsemo hill and the valley to the south.

Environmental issues and voluntary organizations

Damage to the **environment** has become an issue of paramount importance in Ladakh. Although plastic bags are officially banned in Leh, as they clog up the vital river systems that the state so depends on, shopkeepers continue to use them. Plastic mineral-water bottles are a particular headache; you are advised to bring your own filtration system (see p.33) with you, or refill your plastic water bottles at guesthouses with filtered water or at Leh's **Dzomsa Laundry**, near the main bazaar. As well as providing safe water and delicious local juices, such as seabuckthorn, this establishment provides a vital service in ecologically sound washing, using biodegradable detergent and water at a safe distance from habitation. It also serves as a co-op for rural, semiliterate people.

With limited resources at their disposal, a handful of **voluntary organizations** battle to protect Ladakh's delicate environment and ancient culture. These include LEDeG (the Ladakh Ecological Development Group) – a local nongovernmental organization that aims to counter the negative impact of Western-style "development" by fostering economic independence and respect for traditional culture. Its headquarters are five minutes' walk north of the main bazaar at the **Ecology Centre** (Mon–Sat 10am–4.30pm; ⓣ01982/253221, ⓦwww.ledeg.org), which has a small **library** and a **handicraft shop**, selling locally made clothes, *thangkas*, T-shirts, books and postcards.

Helena Norberg-Hodge, the Swedish-born founder of LEDeG, is also behind the International Society for Ecology and Culture (**ISEC**) website (ⓦwww.isec.org.uk), devoted to promoting sustainable ways of living in both "developing" and "developed" countries. ISEC employs **volunteers** in Ladakh on the **Farm Project** to help local farmers maintain traditional farming methods. Closely aligned to the Farm Project, the co-operative Women's Alliance of Ladakh (**WAL**), based in Chubi, north of central Leh (Mon–Sat 10am–5pm; ⓣ01982/250293, ⓔwomenallianceleh@yahoo.com), works to reinforce traditional Ladakhi culture. One of their more noticeable achievements was to ban plastic bags from Leh in 1998; the alliance now boasts more than five thousand members in one hundred villages. The best time to visit them is during one of their **fêtes**, where you can sample local produce, pick up handicrafts and catch exhibitions of colourful traditional costume and folk dance performances. They also show **films**, including Norberg-Hodge's *Ancient Futures: Learning From Ladakh* at 3pm, which gives an insightful account of Ladakhi culture and the sweeping changes of the past thirty or so years; it is also available in book form. At 11am there is a revolving programme of films and afterwards lunch is available for Rs45. Occasionally, when she's in town in July or August, Norberg-Hodge speaks at the centre.

Another group is **LEHO** (Ladakh Environment and Health Organization), which places its emphasis on the proper utilization of land and water resources and the management of livestock on a sustainable basis. Their office and showroom is on the first floor of the Himalaya Complex, beneath the *Amdo* restaurant, on Main Bazaar (Mon–Sat 10am–5pm; ⓣ01982/253691, ⓔsultanaleho@yahoo.com).

For tips on **trekking** sensitively, see p.508.

Eating and drinking

As Leh's thriving restaurant and café scene has been cornered by the refugee community, **Tibetan food** has a high profile alongside tourist-oriented Chinese and European dishes. **Beer** is widely available in most of Leh's tourist restaurants while **chang**, a local barley brew, is harder to come by.

Amdo Main Bazaar. Popular Tibetan restaurant, with freshly prepared food that is generally excellent but can take up to an hour to appear; main courses Rs50–80. There's a second *Amdo* across the street, which catches the morning sun and serves hearty *tsampa* porridge.

Café Jeevan Changspa Lane. Modern pure-veg Sikh-run restaurant featuring a variety of cuisines in the Rs60–100 range. Lovely decor both downstairs and in the partially enclosed roof terrace.

Leh View Main Bazaar. The best 360-degree view in town from the roof terrace is offset by painfully slow service, making this a better bet for a drink than a meal.

North Indian Restaurant & Dosa House South of Fort Rd. Cuisine from both ends of the Subcontinent plus a few western dishes. Best *masala dosas* in town, for Rs40.

Orange Sky Changspa Lane. French-run courtyard restaurant with mountain views and a canopied chill-out zone. Quality European dishes such as lasagne cost in excess of Rs200.

Penguin Garden Old Rd, just off Fort Rd. A great place for a beer, *German Bakery* snacks or a meal (around Rs80–150) in a leafy garden location.

Pizza de Hut Main Bazaar, almost opposite SBI. Good for breakfast or for a beer in the evenings, with a great rooftop location in the centre of town. The mixed menu includes wood-fired pizzas and tandoor dishes (Rs100–150). Better than adjacent *La Terrasse*.

Shelden Garden Changspa Lane. Specializes in succulent barbecued meat and fish for around Rs150, served in a pleasant landscaped courtyard or in a tent where a nightly DVD is shown.

Tibetan Kitchen Down alley off Fort Rd. Considered by many, locals and visitors alike, to be the best Tibetan food in town. Great mutton *thukpas* for Rs70, *momos* a bit pricey at Rs120.

Wonderland Changspa Lane. Excellent rooftop joint with a cushioned chill-out corner and unusually attentive service. Good selection of Indian, Chinese, Tibetan and Continental mains for Rs80–120.

Shopping

Between June and September, Leh is swamped by almost as many transient Tibetan and Kashmiri **traders** as souvenir-hungry tourists. Most of the merchandise hawked in their temporary boutiques and stalls comes from outside the region: papier-mâché bowls, shawls and carpets from Srinagar, jewellery and miniature paintings from Jaipur, and "Himalayan" handicrafts, including *thangkas*, churned out in Nepal and by Tibetan refugees in Old Delhi. Prices tend to be high, so haggle hard, and don't be conned into shelling out for cleverly faked "antiques". Much of the "silver" on sale is in fact cheap white metal.

Tibetan and Ladakhi **curios** account for the bulk of the goods on sale in Leh's emporia, though most of these are run by Kashmiris. The Ladakh Art Palace off the main bazaar, one of the very few locally run souvenir stores, is a good place to browse. If money is no object, you could splash out on a **perak**, a long Ladakhi headdress, encrusted with turquoise, which costs upwards of Rs5000. **Turquoise** is sold by the *tolah* (there are eighty *tolahs* to a kilogram), and quality and age determine the price. You'll find vendors sitting on the main road; otherwise try the locally owned Potala – an atmospheric old-world shop well worth a rummage – down Nowshara Lane, off the main road close to the Jama Masjid. Next door, Himalayan Art is also locally owned, with an extensive selection of curios, ranging from stones to *thangkas*.

For **authentic Ladakhi souvenirs**, try the outfitters and provision stores dotted along the main bazaar. Worth browsing is Konchok Lobzang's shop, a few doors north of the Lehling bookshop, which makes its own Ladakhi-style handicrafts, including wonderfully carved tables and *thangkas*. The lanes running off the bazaar towards old town are home to hole-in-the-wall seamstress shops that can produce custom-fit **local clothing**, including the dapper stovepipe hats (*tibi*), hand-dyed *gonchas*, raw silk cummerbunds, tie-dyed rope-soled shoes (*pabbu*) and Bhutanese cross-button shirts. Yak wool shawls go for around Rs750–950. Try the Lonpo Shop up the lane across from *Amdo* restaurant, or around the corner to the right at the Namgail Dorje and Tsereng Yangskit shops. The handicraft shops at the organisations mentioned in the box on p.495 are other sources of quality traditional clothing, including hand-knitted woollen jumpers, shawls, hats and socks.

Most of the wool gathered in Ladakh lands up in the Kashmir Valley for milling and weaving, and few of the **pashmina shawls** on offer in the shops along Fort Road are genuine.

Of the **bookshops** in Leh, Ladakh Bookshop, on the first floor below the *Leh View* restaurant in the Main Bazaar, and Book Lovers Retreat on Changspa Lane both have a fine selection of literature, reference and souvenir books. Secondhand paperbacks are sold or part-exchanged at Parkash Stationers opposite the vegetable market. Fairdeal Stationers near the Jami Masjid, Main Bazaar Square, is good for **newspapers**.

Listings

Banks and exchange The J&K Bank, 1st Floor, Himalaya Shopping Complex, Main Bazaar and the State Bank of India on the main market square have exchange facilities. Both these, plus the Punjab National Bank have ATMs. Private licensed operators include many hotels and travel agents around Fort Road and along Changspa Lane.

Bike rental Mountain bikes can be rented from Luna Ladakh Travel, Zangsti Rd (50m from Dzomsa Laundry), for Rs250/day.

Homestays Homestays can be arranged in remote villages, which offer a dinner, bed and breakfast for Rs400/person (Rs600/couple), with ten percent of the proceeds going towards village development programmes. The scheme is currently running in the areas between Likkir and Temisgang, and Stok and Chilling. For more information contact Snow Leopard Trails (Ⓣ01982/252188) in the *Hotel Kanglhachhen* complex off Fort Road.

Hospital Leh's overstretched, poorly equipped SNM Hospital (Ⓣ01982/252014) is 1km south of the centre on the main road. For urgent medical treatment, contact a doctor through any upmarket hotel. PT Alamdar Chemist & Clinic (Ⓣ01982/252587), off the lower end of the Bazaar, has a good English-speaking morning surgery from 9am.

Internet access Now that most places have a satellite connection, broadband internet cafés have popped up all over the main bazaar, Fort Road and Changspa Lane. The standard charge is Rs1.50/min.

Laundry Dzomsa Laundry (see box, p.495).

Libraries The Ecology Centre's excellent library (Mon–Sat 10am–4pm) keeps books on everything from agriculture to Zen Buddhism, as well as periodicals, magazines and files of articles on Ladakh and development issues. Students of Buddhism should check out the collection of books at the Chokhang Vihara Monastery, across from the State Bank of India, or the Tibetan Cultural Centre in the south of town.

Massage Indian Vedyashala on Changspa Lane (Ⓣ9906999502) offers a range of Ayurvedic massages for around Rs500–1000.

Meditation, yoga and alternative therapy In high season small classes are run by the Mahabodhi Society in Changspa which specializes in Vipassana Ⓣ01982/253689; their extensive complex in Devachan (Ⓣ01982/244155, Ⓦwww.mahabodhi-ladakh.org) towards Choglamsar, 3km south of Leh, includes a meditation centre with courses ranging from three to seven days. The *Asia Guesthouse*, Changspa Lane, houses a German-run Vajrayana Meditation and Healing Arts Centre. Numerous posters and flyers advertise classes and sessions in yoga, reiki, shiatsu and other alternative therapies.

Motorbikes Although several places now hire motorcycles, with the going rate starting around Rs600/day for an Enfield, you should check the bikes carefully. By far the most reliable of the agencies is Enntrax Tours (Ⓣ01982/250603), a few doors down from the *Khangri Hotel*; mopeds here are Rs400/24hr.

Pharmacy Het Ram Vinay Kumar at the top of the main bazaar sells a range of allopathic pills and potions, as well as batteries and tampons. For Tibetan medicine, two *amchis* at the LSTM Amchi Clinic, Changspa Lane (daily: July–Sept 8am–8pm; Oct–June 10am–4pm), speak English and charge Rs50 for a consultation using traditional diagnostic techniques.

Police Ⓣ01982/252018 or 252200. Ⓣ100 for the operator.

Post The post office is in the main bazaar (Mon–Sat 10am–1pm & 2–5pm). For parcels, go to the GPO (Mon–Sat 10am–4.30pm), out of town on Airport Rd, whose unreliable poste restante counter is tucked around the back. You can also receive letters through the Tourist Information Centre on Fort Rd.

Tour operators Reliable agents recommended for trekking and jeep safaris include: Yama Adventures,

Changspa Lane (ⓣ01982/250833, ⓦwww.yamatreks.com); Mountain Trails, 2 Hemis Complex, Zangsti Rd (ⓣ01982/254855); Footprints, Fort Rd (ⓣ01982/251799, ⓦwww.footprintsindia.com); and Dreamland Trek & Tours, Fort Rd (ⓣ01982/250784, ⓦwww.dreamladakh.com).

Alternatively, smaller agencies such as Oriental Travels, at the *Oriental Guest House* in Changspa (ⓣ01982/253153), offer a more personalized service. Some agents also offer rafting on the River Indus (see p.506).

Southeast of Leh

Southeast of Leh, the Indus Valley broadens to form a fertile river basin. Among the spectacular Buddhist monuments lining the edges of the flat valley floor are **Shey**, site of a ruined palace and giant brass Buddha, and the stunning monastery of **Tikse**. Both overlook the main highway and are thus served by regular buses.

With the exception of **Stok Palace**, home of the Ladakhi queen, sights on the opposite (south) side of the Indus, linked to the main road by a relatively unfrequented and partly surfaced road, are harder to reach by public transport. South of Stok, **Matho** *gompa* is more famous for its winter oracle festivals than its art treasures, but is well worth a visit, if only for the superb views from its roof terrace. Further south still, continue to **Hemis**, Ladakh's wealthiest monastery and the venue for one of the region's few summer religious festivals. To side-step your fellow tourists without spending a night away from Leh, head up the austerely beautiful tributary valley back on the opposite side of the river from Hemis to the *gompas* of **Chemrey** and **Thak Thok**, the latter built around a fabled meditation cave.

East of Thak Thok, the road crosses the Chang La and then veers east to the high mountain lake of **Pangong Tso**, most of which lies in Tibet. Far more relaxing and inviting is the vast wilderness of **Rupshu** with trekking possibilities around the shores of **Tso Moriri**, in the deep south. Permits are required for these three areas; for full details see the box on p.487.

Shey

SHEY, 15km southeast of Leh and once the capital of Ladakh, is now all but deserted, the royal family having been forced to abandon it by the Dogras midway through the nineteenth century. Only a semi-derelict palace, a small *gompa* and a profusion of *chortens* remain, clustered around a bleached spur of rock that juts into the fertile floor of the Indus Valley. The ruins overlook the main highway, and can be reached on the frequent minibuses between Leh Bus Stand and Tikse. Alternatively, you could walk to Shey from Tikse monastery along a winding path that passes through one of Ladakh's biggest *chorten* fields with hundreds of whitewashed shrines of varying sizes scattered across the surreal desert landscape.

The **palace**, a smaller and more dilapidated version of the one in Leh, sits astride the ridge, below an ancient fort. Crowned by a golden *chorten* spire, its pride and joy is the colossal metal Shakyamuni Buddha housed in its ruined split-level temple (daily 6–9am; Rs30). Installed in 1633, the twelve-metre icon allegedly contains a hoard of precious stones, mandalas and powerful charms. Entering from a painted antechamber, you come face to face with the Buddha's huge feet, soles pointing upwards. Upstairs, a balcony surrounding the statue's torso surveys the massive Buddha in better light. Preserved for centuries by thick soot from votary butter lamps, the gold-tinted murals coating the walls are among the finest in the valley.

Easily missed as you whizz past on the road is Shey's most ancient monument. The **rock carving** of the five Tathagata or "Thus gone" Buddhas, distinguished by their respective vehicles (*vahanas*) and hand positions (*mudras*), appears on a smooth slab of stone on the edge of the highway; it was probably carved soon after the eighth century, before the "Second Spreading" (see p.472). The large central figure with hands held in the gesture of preaching (turning the wheel of *dharma*), is the Buddha Resplendant, Vairocana, whose image is central in many of the Alchi murals (see p.510).

Practicalities

Rooms are available at the *Besthang Hotel*, a converted traditional Ladakhi house (Ⓣ01982/252792; ❷) with attached rooms, a pleasant garden and simple home cooking, located a few minutes' walk down the lane behind the roadside *Shilkhar Restaurant,* the only eating option in Shey, serving a varied menu of Indian and western food. Buses pass in both directions every thirty minutes to one hour (Leh, 30min) until around 6pm.

Tikse

Ladakh's most photographed and architecturally impressive *gompa* is at **TIKSE**, 19km southeast of Leh. Founded in the fifteenth century, its whitewashed *chortens* and cubic monks' quarters rise in ranks up the sides of a craggy bluff, crowned by an imposing ochre- and red-painted temple complex whose gleaming golden finials are visible for miles in every direction.

Tikse's reincarnation as a major tourist attraction has brought it mixed blessings: its constant stream of summer visitors spoils the peace and quiet necessary for meditation, but the income generated has enabled the monks to invest in major refurbishments, among them the **Maitreya temple** immediately above the main courtyard. Inaugurated in 1980 by the Dalai Lama, the shrine is built around a gigantic fourteen-metre gold-faced Buddha-to-come, seated not on a throne as is normally the case, but in the lotus position. The bright murals on the wall behind, painted by monks from Lingshet *gompa* in Zanskar, depict scenes from Maitreya's life.

For most foreign visitors, however, the highlight of a trip to Tikse is the view from its lofty **roof terrace**. A patchwork of barley fields stretches across the floor of the valley, fringed by rippling snow-flecked desert mountains and a string of monasteries, palaces, and Ladakhi villages. To enjoy this impressive panorama accompanied by primeval groans from the *gompa*'s gargantuan Tibetan trumpets – played on the rooftop at the 7am puja – you'll have to stay overnight or arrange an early jeep from Leh.

Practicalities

An asphalted road cuts up the empty west side of the hill from the main highway to the monastery's small car park. If you arrive by **minibus** from Leh (every 30min, from the town bus stand), pick your way across the wasteground below the *gompa* and follow the footpath up through its lower buildings to the main entrance, where monks issue tickets (Rs30). The last bus back to Leh leaves at 6pm. You can **stay** in the rooms behind the monastery's restaurant (Ⓣ01982/267005; ❷); they are spacious and clean but only have shared facilities. Down by the road, *Chamba Hotel* (April–Sept; Ⓣ01982/267005; ❺) offers decent attached rooms at rather inflated rates but there is a good garden **restaurant** serving a varied menu from Tibetan food to pancakes, as well as a Rs250 buffet.

Stok

Just beyond the Tibetan refugee camp at **Choglamsar**, at the head of a huge moraine, the elegant four-storey **Stok Palace** stands in the shadow of an intrusive TV mast, overlooking barley terraces studded with whitewashed farmhouses. Built early in the nineteenth century by the last ruler of independent Ladakh, it has been the official residence of the Ladakhi royal family since they were ousted from Leh and Shey two hundred years ago.

The present Gyalmo or "queen", Deskit Angmo, a former member of parliament, still lives here during the summer, and has converted one wing of her 77-roomed palace into a small **museum** (daily 8am–6pm; Rs30). The fascinating collection comprises some of the royal family's most precious heirlooms, including exquisite sixteenth-century **thangkas** illuminated with paint made from crushed rubies, emeralds and sapphires. The *pièces de résistance*, however, are the Gyalmo's **peraks**. Still worn on important occasions, the ancient headdresses, thought to have originated in Tibet, are encrusted with slabs of flawless turquoise, polished coral, lapis lazuli and nuggets of pure gold. **Stok gompa** (dawn–dusk; Rs30), twenty minutes' walk up the valley, boasts a collection of dance-drama masks and some lurid modern murals painted by lamas from Lingshet *gompa* in Zanskar, the artists responsible for the Maitreya statue in Tikse (see p.499).

Practicalities

Buses leave Leh for Stok (40min) at 8am, 2pm and 4pm. The last bus returning to Leh leaves at 5pm; if you miss it or are tempted to **stay**, try the *Hotel Highland* (Ⓣ01982/242005, Ⓔtangdul@yahoo.co.in; ❼), a palatial two-storey house with fine views from its well-furnished attached rooms. About 2km down the road towards Leh is the imposing *Hotel Skittsal* (Ⓣ01982/242049, Ⓦskittsal.com; ❷–❺), with panoramic views over the Indus Valley. Both of these close in early September, unlike the small and basic *Kalden Guest House* (Ⓣ01982/242057; ❶) at the foot of the palace.

Matho

MATHO, 27km south of Leh, straddles a spur at the mouth of an idyllic side-valley that runs deep into the heart of the Stok-Kangri massif. Though no less interesting or scenically situated than its neighbours, it sees comparatively few visitors. The *gompa* is the only representative in Ladakh of the **Sakyapa** sect, which held political power in thirteenth-century Tibet. As it's relatively isolated from the main highway, **buses** aren't all that frequent: services leave Leh daily at 7.30am, 2pm and 4.30pm, returning at 7.30am, 4pm and 4.30pm. By car, Matho also makes an ideal halfway halt on the journey along the little-used left-bank road between Stok and Hemis.

Despite its collection of 400-year-old *thangkas*, the monastery is best known for its **oracle festival**, Matho Nagran, held on the twenty-fifth and twenty-sixth day of the second Tibetan month (Feb/March). Two oracles, known as *rongzan*, are elected by lot every three years from among the sixty or so resident lamas. During the run-up to the big days, the pair fast and meditate in readiness for the moment when they are possessed by the spirit of the deity. Watched by crowds of rapt onlookers, they then perform all manner of death-defying stunts that include leaping blindfold around the *gompa*'s precipitous parapets while slurping kettle-fulls of *chang*, and slashing themselves with razor-sharp sabres without drawing blood. The events are rounded off with colourful *chaam* dances in the monastery courtyard, and a question-and-answer session in which the *rongzan*, still under the influence of the deity, make prophecies about the coming year.

You can admire the costumes and masks worn by the monks during the festivals in Matho's small **museum**, tucked away behind the Du-khang. Men are also permitted to visit the eerie **Gon-khang** on the roof, where the oracles' weapons and ritual garments are stored. The floor of the tiny temple lies under a deep layer of barley brought as harvest offerings by local villagers.

Hemis

Thanks to its famous festival – one of the few held in summer, when the passes are open – **HEMIS**, 45km southeast of Leh, is visited in greater numbers than any other *gompa* in Ladakh. Every year in mid-July (see p.488 for dates), hundreds of foreigners join the huge crowds of locals, dressed in their finest traditional garb, which flock to watch the colourful two-day pageant. However, at other times, the rambling and atmospheric seventeenth-century **monastery** (daily 8am–6pm; Rs30) can be disappointingly quiet. Although it's one of the region's foremost religious institutions, only a skeleton staff of monks and novices are resident off-season.

The main entrance opens onto the large rectangular courtyard where the festival **chaam dances** are performed. Accompanied by cymbal crashes, drum rolls and periodic blasts from the temple trumpets, the culmination of the event on the second day is a frenzied dismemberment of a dummy, symbolizing the destruction of the human ego, and thus the triumph of Buddhism over ignorance and evil. Once every twelve years, the Hemis festival also hosts the ritual unrolling of a giant *thangka*. The *gompa*'s prize possession, which covers the entire facade of the building, it was embroidered by women whose hands are now revered as holy relics. Decorated with pearls and precious stones, it was last displayed in 2004. There is a **museum** (8am–6pm; Rs100 [Rs50]) in the corner of the courtyard but the modest collection of *thangkas*, masks and musical instruments barely justifies the inflated fee.

Practicalities

By car, Hemis is an easy day-trip from Leh. By **bus**, services are only frequent during the festival; at other times a single morning service leaves Leh at 9.30am and returns at noon, but there are ten daily shared minibuses, the last of which returns at 6pm. Another bus leaves Leh at 4pm but stays the night at Hemis, returning the next morning at 7am. An overnight stay means you can attend the 7am puja, and there is now more choice in the basic **accommodation** available, all with shared bathrooms. You can camp for free below nearby Chomoling village or for Rs100 at the *Hemis Restaurant* (Ⓣ01982/249072; ❶), which also has a couple of tatty rooms below the *gompa*, run by young *carrom*-playing monks. The newer *Hemis Spiritual Retreat* (Ⓣ01982/249011; ❶) has slightly better rooms and also serves **food** in its garden. Both the *Hemis Restaurant* and the *Parachute Restaurant* in Chomoling serve simple meals; the latter is cheaper, has a selection of pancakes and is a useful stop-off for trekkers heading for the Markha Valley.

Chemrey

Clinging like a swallow's nest to the sides of a shaly conical hill, the magnificent *gompa* of **CHEMREY** (Rs50, including museum) sees very few visitors because of its location – tucked up the side valley that runs from Karu, below Hemis, to the Chang La pass into Pangong. If you don't have your own vehicle, you'll have to be prepared to do some walking to get here. It takes around fifty minutes to follow the dirt track down to the river and up to the monastery after the Leh–Thak Thok bus drops you off beside the main road.

Founded in 1664 as a memorial to King Sengge Namgyal, the monastery is staffed by a dwindling community of around twenty Drugpa monks and their young novices. Its main **Du-khang**, off the courtyard on the lower level, boasts a fine silver *chorten* and a set of ancient Tibetan texts whose title pages are illuminated with gold and silver calligraphy. Upstairs in the revamped **Guru-La-khang** sits a giant brass statue of Padmasambhava. The new museum on the top floor houses statues, *thangkas*, scrolls and utensils.

Thak Thok

A few kilometres up the valley from Chemrey above the village of **Sakti**, **THAK THOK** (pronounced *Tak-Tak* and meaning "rock roof") *gompa* shelters a cave in which the apostle Padmasambhava is said to have meditated during his epic eighth-century journey to Tibet. Blackened over the years by sticky butter-lamp and incense smoke, the mysterious grotto is now somewhat upstaged by the monastery's more modern wings nearby. As well as some spectacular twentieth-century wall paintings, the **Urgyan Photan Du-khang** harbours a collection of multicoloured yak-butter candle-sculptures made by the head lama. For a glimpse of state-of-the-art Buddhist iconography, head to the top of Thak Thok village, where a shiny new temple houses a row of huge gleaming Buddhas, decked out in silk robes and surrounded by garish modern murals.

Apart from during the annual **festivals** (see p.488), the village of Sakti is a tranquil place, blessed with serene views south over the snowy mountains behind Hemis. Accommodation is available in the J&K *Tourist Bungalow* (❷) on the road directly below the *gompa*. There are also plenty of ideal camping spots beside the river, although as ever you should seek permission before putting up a tent on someone's field. Four minibuses a day leave Leh for Sakti (8am, 8.30am, 2.30pm and 3.30pm); the last one back to Leh departs at 3.30pm.

Pangong Tso

Pangong Tso, 154km southeast of Leh, is one of the largest saltwater lakes in Asia, a long narrow strip of water stretching from Ladakh east into Tibet. Only a quarter of the 134-kilometre-long lake is in India, and the army, who experienced bitter losses along its shores in the war against China in 1962, jealously guard their side of the frontier. Until the mid-1990s, it was off-limits to visitors, and tourists still need a permit to come here (see box, p.487). The lake, at an altitude of 4267m, with the dramatic glacier-clad Pangong Range to its south and the Changchenmo Range reflected in its deep blue-green waters to the north, measures 8km across at its widest point and provides a tantalizing view of Tibet in the distance, although the bitter winds blowing over the brackish water make it one of the coldest places in Ladakh. The only public **bus** from Leh (Sun 6am) drops off visitors at the village of **Spangmik** before continuing to the restricted border area; it returns around 7am on Monday. There is basic **accommodation** and food at Spangmik, such as the *Diskit Guest House* (no phone; ❶) and a hugely overpriced tent camp. A better deal is back where the road meets the lake at *Padma* (Ⓣ9419 819078, Ⓔtonybuddhist@yahoo.co.in; ❺); meals are included with your room or tent. Most tourists come here on an organized two-day **jeep safari** from Leh (from Rs6100 for up to five people). To add further interest to the trip, take in the monasteries of Chemrey and Thak Thok en route.

Tso Moriri

Famous for the large herds of *kiang*, or wild ass, which graze on its shores, the lake of **Tso Moriri**, 210km southeast of Leh, lies in the sparsely populated region of **Rupshu**. You need a permit to travel here (see box, p.487).

Nestling in a wide valley flanked by some of the highest peaks in Ladakh – **Lungser Kangri** (6666m) and **Chanmser Kangri** (6622m) – the 20km-long lake is home to flocks of migratory *nangpa* or bar-headed geese, as well as occasional herds of pashmina goats and camps of nomadic herders. Located on the shores of the lake at an altitude of 4595m, **Korzok** – the only large village in the area – is a friendly place with a small *gompa*. To help protect the fragile ecosystem against the influx of tourists, a new directive stipulates that no habitation can be built within 700m of the shoreline. Visitors should bring their own food supplies and make sure they take all their rubbish away.

The open spaces around Tso Moriri make for some pleasant **trekking**, including the relatively easy – if you are acclimatized – three-day, 40km circuit of the lake. Another route gaining popularity is the trail from Rumtse near Upshi via Tso Kar to Tso Moriri. Some trekking operators in Manali and Leh can arrange more ambitious routes such as the ancient trade route linking **Spiti** to Tso Moriri and Leh via Kibber. Treks start from around $45 per person per day in a group of four, which usually includes transport, food and tents.

Practicalities

From Leh, three **buses** depart for Tso Moriri on the 10th, 20th and 30th of each month at 6am, returning the following day. Most tourists visit on a **jeep safari**, which start at around Rs7700 for a two-day trip. These usually follow a circular itinerary through Upshi and Mahe Bridge, winding up at Korzok. From there they then continue on towards the Manali–Leh Highway, passing the lake of Tso Kar and Thukse village along the way. **Accommodation** is in local homestays and in Korzok, at the Delhi-run and fairly grotty and overpriced *Lake View* (❺), just below the bus stand. Similarly overpriced is the tent colony, where a bed costs a whopping Rs1000.

North of Leh: Nubra Valley

Until 1994, the lands north of Leh were off-limits to tourists and had been unexplored by outsiders since the nineteenth century. Now, the breathtaking **Nubra Valley**, unfolding beyond the world's highest stretch of drivable road as it crosses the **Khardung La** (5602m), can be visited with a seven-day **permit** (see p.487), which gives you enough time to explore the stark terrain and trek out to one or two *gompas*. The valley's mountain backbone looks east to the Nubra River and west to the Shyok River, which meet amid silver-grey sand dunes and boulder fields. To the north and east, the mighty Karakoram Range marks the Indian border with China and Pakistan. In the valley it's relatively mild, though **dust storms** are common, whipping up sand and light debris in choking clouds above the broad riverbeds.

Before the region passed into the administrative hands of Leh, Nubra's ancient kings ruled from a palace in **Charasa**, topping an isolated hillock opposite Sumur, home to the valley's principal monastery. Further up the Nubra River, the hot springs of **Panamik**, once welcomed by footsore traders, are blissfully refreshing after all day on a bumpy bus. By the neighbouring Shyok River, **Diskit**, surveyed by a hillside *gompa*, lies just 7km from **Hundur**, known for its peculiar high-altitude double-humped Bactrian camels.

Getting around the Nubra Valley

Buses leave Leh for Panamik via Sumur (Tues & Thurs 6am; 7–8hr) and Hunder via Diskit (Tues, Thurs & Sat 6am; 6–7hr). The buses return to Leh the next day and you should book your return journey on arrival. Alternatively, **jeeps** for a maximum of five people can be rented from Leh taxi rank or any tour operator (see p.497). A complete three-day itinerary, including a visit to Diskit and Panamik, costs in the region of Rs6800 for the jeep plus driver. Once in the valley, **hitching** on military or road-builders' trucks is an option, though it's inadvisable for lone travellers. The few **taxis** at Diskit charge from around Rs1000 for a day's exploration of the valley, with trips to Sumur and Panamik adding up. **Buses** between Diskit and Panamik travel daily, leaving Panamik at 7am and returning at 4pm.

The route north to Nubra, a steep and rough road that forces painful groans from buses and trucks, keeps Leh in sight for three hours before crossing the Khardung La, and ploughing down more gently towards the distant Karakoram Range. Due to its strategic importance as the military road to the battlefields of the Siachen Glacier, the road to Nubra is kept open all year round but conditions can be treacherous at any time.

Sumur

Beyond the confluence of the Shyok and Nubra rivers, **SUMUR**, a sleepy oasis spread over a large area, is home to the valley's most influential monastery, **Samstem Ling gompa**, a pleasant forty-minute walk behind the village. Built in 1841, the *gompa* accommodates just under a hundred Gelug-pa monks of all ages. To catch the morning or evening pujas, you'll have to **stay** in Sumur. Most of the guesthouses are on the sand lane that leads off from the bus stop at the prayer wheel. Closest to the main road is the *AO Guesthouse* (ⓣ01980/223506; ❶–❷), which has basic doubles including six with attached baths, a garden, vegetarian café and camping (Rs50); two newer alternatives, 500m further down the lane, are *K-Sar Guest House* (ⓣ01980/223574; ❷), where all the spruce rooms are attached and you can camp for Rs300 in their spacious tents or Rs100 in your own, and *Saser Guest House* (ⓣ01980/223584; ❶–❷), which has shared and attached rooms and allows camping for Rs100. The smartest option in the area is the spacious new bamboo cottages of *Silk Route Cottages* (ⓣ9990 094107, ⓦwww.hotelmogol.com; ❻), nicely situated at the top of the village.

Panamik

A one-hour bus journey (22km) up the valley from Sumur, **PANAMIK** (aka Pinchimik), a dusty hamlet overlooked by the pin-point summit of Charouk Dongchen, marks the most northerly point in India accessible to tourists. A kilometre past the underwhelming **hot springs**, beyond the stone walls that line the pitted road, is the village proper. Splitting into wide rivulets at this point, the sapphire Nubra seems shallow and tame, but it's not – heed local advice not to ford it as there have been several reported accidents involving travellers.

A dot on the mountainside across the river, **Ensa gompa** is the main attraction. The walking route, three hours each way, passes through the village and crosses a bridge beyond the vast boulder field 3km upstream, then joins a wide jeep track above the river for several kilometres. Though the *gompa* is usually locked, the views from rows of crumbling *chortens* nearby make the climb worthwhile. If one of the few semi-resident monks is there, however, you'll be shown inside to see the old wall paintings in the temples, and the footprint of Tsong-kha-pa, allegedly imprinted at this spot when he journeyed from Tibet to India in the fourteenth century.

The *Hot Spring Guesthouse* (❷) just beyond the hot springs themselves, and the unsigned *Bangka Guesthouse* (❷), 600m further along, comprise Panamik's unexciting **accommodation** options.

Diskit and Hundur

DISKIT feels rather dull on first impressions, but it does possess an appealing old town, whose low, balconied houses lie below the main road before the diversion to the centre. Buses stop on Diskit's main road by the prayer wheel where the road descends through the old quarter to the bazaar, and then again on the new road to the bazaar, before continuing to Hundur. For the guesthouses, get off at the first bus stop. The main road climbs on past the newly constructed 30m statue of the seated Buddha up the hillside above the town to Diskit's picturesque **gompa**, built in 1420. If you're on foot, follow the long *mani* wall, which continues on the other side of the road, and trace the path that winds upwards from its end to the monastery – a steep walk of around thirty minutes. The *gompa*'s steps climb past the monks' quarters to the first of a group of temples (Rs30). Local legend has it that a Mongol demon, a sworn enemy of Buddhism, was slain nearby, but his lifeless body kept returning to the *gompa*. What are reputed to be his wrinkled head and hand are now clasped by a pot-bellied protector deity in the spooky **Gon-khang**.

The diminutive **Lachung temple**, higher up, is the oldest here. Soot-soiled murals face a huge Tsong-kha-pa statue, topped with a Gelug-pa yellow hat. In the heart of the *gompa*, the **Du-khang**'s remarkable mural, filling a raised cupola above the hall, depicts Tibet's Tashilhunpo *gompa*, where the Panchen Lama is receiving a long stream of visitors approaching on camels, horses and carts. Finally, the **Kangyu Lang** (bookroom) and **Tsangyu Lang** temples act as storerooms for hundreds of Mongolian and Tibetan texts.

HUNDUR, a tiny village in a wooded valley beyond some impressive sand dunes, 7km north, is as far as one is allowed to go along this part of the Nubra Valley. The main monastery lies just below the main road, near the bridge and the end of the route. Further down and across the brook is a creaky, cobweb-filled old manor that once belonged to the local Zimskhang royal family, and is now occasionally unlocked by a key-keeper at the *Goba Guesthouse*. The village is renowned for its herd of Bactrian camels (a vestige of its days on the old trans-Karakoram trade route), which you will invariably encounter if you walk out onto the dunes. **Camel rides** start around Rs150 for a short lope across the sand.

Accommodation and eating

There are plenty of cosy **guesthouses** to choose from in Diskit, while the accommodation scene in Hundur is even more laid-back. The establishments listed invariably provide at least basic food. The one worthwhile independent **restaurant** is the *Sangam View*, in the centre of Diskit.

Goba 400m down from the roadside *gompa*, Hundur ☎01980/221083. This friendly hangout is a quaint, low-key affair with a sunny yard and hundreds of flowers. ❶–❸

Hotel Sangam Near the village centre, Diskit ☎01980/220404. The newest and smartest place in the area. Its spacious attached and non-attached rooms are great value. ❶–❸

Olthang Close to the main road prayer wheel, Diskit ☎01980/220025. Offers a range of attached rooms and camping for Rs300; home-grown vegetables from the picturesque garden are served for dinner in the dining hall (around Rs50), which doubles as a bar in the evenings. ❷–❹

Semba On the road from Diskit, Hundur ☎01980/221348. Small guesthouse with just three rooms with shared bathrooms and the village bar. ❶

Snow Leopard Signposted off the main road at the back of the village, Hundur ☎01980/221097. Set in a beautiful vegetable garden, this secluded guesthouse has great views and offers some rooms with bath. ❶–❹

Sunrise Diskit ☎01980/220011. Along a *mani* wall to the right of the road down from the prayer wheel. This simple place offers cheap beds, shared bathrooms and a pleasant garden. ❶

Thachung Diskit ☎01980/220 002. Along a lane beyond the village's second prayer wheel. Boasts beautiful sunny glass rooms and clean bathrooms. ❷

West of Leh

Of the many *gompas* accessible by road **west of Leh**, only **Spitok**, piled on a hilltop at the end of the airport runway, and **Phyang**, which presides over one of Ladakh's most picturesque villages, can be comfortably visited on day-trips from the capital. The rest, including **Likkir** and the temple complex at **Alchi**, with its wonderfully preserved eleventh-century murals, are usually seen en route to or from **Kargil**. The 231km journey, which takes in a couple of high passes and some mind-blowing scenery, can be completed in a single eight-hour haul, slightly less by jeep. To do this stretch of road justice, however, you should spend at least a few days making short forays up the side valleys of the Indus, where idyllic settlements and *gompas* nestle amid barley fields and mountains.

One of the great landmarks punctuating the former caravan route is the monastery of **Lamayuru**. Reached via a nail-biting sequence of hairpin bends as the highway climbs out of the Indus Valley to begin its meandering ascent of **Fotu La**, it lies within walking distance of some extraordinary lunar-like rock formations, at the start of the main trekking route south to Padum in Zanskar. Further west still, beyond the dramatic **Namika La** pass, **Mulbekh** is the last Buddhist village on the highway. From here on, *gompas* and *gonchas* give way to onion-domed mosques and flowing *salwar kameez*.

There is, on average, an accident a day on the narrow, high and twisting Leh–Kargil road. Tata trucks are the most prone to toppling off the tarmac, and it can take hours for the rescue vehicles from Leh and Kargil to arrive and then clear the

Rafting and kayaking on the River Indus

While water levels are high, between the end of June and late August, Leh's more entrepreneurial travel agents operate **rafting** trips on the River Indus. The routes are tame in comparison with Nepal's, but floating downstream in a twelve-seater rubber inflatable is a hugely enjoyable way to experience the valley's most rugged and beautiful landscape. Two different stretches of the river are used: from **Spitok** to the Indus–Zanskar confluence at **Nimmu** (3hr), and from Nimmu to the ancient temple complex at **Alchi** (2hr 30min). Experienced rafters may also want to try the more challenging route between Alchi and Khalsi, which takes in the kilometre-long series of rapids at **Nurla**. The annual multi-day expedition down the River Zanskar to the Indus is by far the most rewarding as it also includes the spectacular road approach to Padum.

Several adventure-tour operators in Leh offer whitewater rafting or kayaking on the Indus. **Tickets** should be booked at least a day in advance. One of the best operators is Splash Adventure Tours, Changspa Lane (☎01982/251042, Ⓦwww.kayakindia.com); **prices** start from around Rs1400 for one-day trips. Make sure when you book that the price includes transport to and from the river, rental of life jackets and helmets, and meals, and that there is a waterproof strongbox for valuables.

road. In summer, **transport** along the highway is straightforward as ramshackle state and private buses ply the route; getting to more remote spots, however, can be hard. Some travellers resort to paying for a ride on one of the countless Tata trucks that lumber past, or hitch with an army convoy, but getting a group together to rent a **jeep** from tour operators in Leh (p.497), while expensive, will be safer, save time and give more access to the side valleys.

Spitok

SPITOK gompa, rising incongruously from the end of the airport runway, makes a good half-day foray from Leh, 10km up the north side of the Indus Valley. Either take a taxi (around Rs100) or any of the **buses** heading west along the main Srinagar highway. The fifteenth-century **monastery**, which tumbles down the sides of a steep knoll to a tight cluster of farmhouses and well-watered fields, is altogether more picturesque. Approached by road from the north, or from the south along a footpath that winds through Spitok village, its spacious rooftops command superb views. The main complex is of less interest than the **Palden Lumo** chapel, perched on a ridge above. Although visiting soldiers from the nearby Indian army barracks consider the deity inside the temple to be Kali Mata, the key-keeper will assure visitors that what many consider to be the black-faced and bloodthirsty Hindu goddess of death and destruction is actually **Yidam Dorje Jigjet**. Coloured electric lights illuminate the cobwebbed chamber of veiled guardian deities whose ferocious faces are only revealed once a year. If you have a torch, check out the 600-year-old paintings on the back wall, partially hidden by eerie *chaam* masks used during the winter festival season.

Phyang

A mere 17km west of Leh, **PHYANG gompa** looms large at the head of a secluded side-valley that tapers north into the Ladakh Range from the Srinagar highway. Eight daily **buses** serve the *gompa* from Leh; if you miss your return bus, just walk down the paved access road to the main highway (30min) and flag down a vehicle bound for Leh.

The *gompa* itself houses a fifty-strong community of lamas, but few antique murals of note, most having recently been painted over with brighter colours. Its only treasures are a small collection of fourteenth-century Kashmiri bronzes in the modern Guru-Padmasambhava temple and the light and airy **Du-khang**'s three silver *chortens*, one of which is decorated with a seven-eyed **dzi stone**. The gem, considered to be highly auspicious, was brought to Phyang from Tibet by the monastery's former head lama, whose ashes the *chorten* encases. Tucked away around the side, the shrine in the *gompa*'s gloomily atmospheric **Gon-khang** (Rs30) houses a ferocious veiled protector deity and an amazing collection of weapons and armour plundered during the Mongol invasions of the fourteenth century. Also dangling from the cobweb-covered rafters are several sets of yak horns, believed to be 900-year-old relics of the Bon cult.

Phyang's annual **festival**, Phyang Tsedup, held in summer (between mid-July and early Aug; see p.488) to coincide with the tourist season, is the second largest in Ladakh after Hemis (see p.501). Celebrated with the usual masked *chaam* dances, the event is marked with a ritual exposition of a giant ten-metre brocaded silk *thangka*.

Likkir

Five kilometres to the north of the main Leh–Srinagar highway, shortly before the village of Saspol, the large and wealthy *gompa* of **LIKKIR**, home to around one

Trekking in Ladakh and Zanskar

The ancient footpaths that crisscross **Ladakh** and **Zanskar** provide some of the most inspiring **trekking** in the Himalayas. Threading together remote Buddhist villages and monasteries, cut off in winter behind high passes whose rocky tops bristle with prayer flags, nearly all are long, hard and high – but never dull. Whether you make all the necessary preparations yourself, or pay an agency to do it for you, **Leh** (see p.489) is the best place to plan a trek; the **best time** to trek is from June to September.

Trekking **independently** is straightforward if you have a copy of *Trekking in Ladakh* (see below), don't mind haggling and are happy to organize the logistics yourself. To find ponies and guides, head for the Tibetan refugee camp at Choglamsar, 3km south of Leh. Count on paying around Rs300 per horse and Rs200 per donkey each day – two people trekking through the Markha Valley for example would pay around $30 each for the entire week. By contrast, a **package trek** sold by a trekking agent in Leh will cost around $50 per day, and more if your group is less than four people.

You can **rent equipment**, including high-quality tents, sleeping bags, sleeping mats and duck-down jackets, either through your chosen agency or at places like **Frontier Adventure Company**, across from the taxi stand on Fort Road (☎01982/253011), or Spiritual Trek, Changspa Lane (☎01982/251701, ©spiritualtrek@yahoo.com). Both also act as trek operators, supplying guides, porters, transport and food. Expect to pay around Rs100–150 a day for a tent, Rs80–100 for a sleeping bag and Rs40–50 for a gas stove; if you're intending to climb Stok-Kangri you may need to dish out Rs50 for an ice axe. Independent trekkers might consider buying Indian equipment in the bazaar, which could be resold.

Minimize your impact in culturally and ecologically sensitive areas by being as **self-reliant** as possible, especially with food and fuel. Buying provisions along the way puts an unnecessary burden on the villages' subsistence-oriented economies, and encourages strings of unsightly "tea shops" (often run by outsiders) to sprout along the trails. Always burn kerosene, never wood – a scarce and valuable resource. Refuse should be packed up, not disposed of along the route, no matter how far from the nearest town you are, and plastics retained for recycling at the Ecology Centre in Leh. Always bury your faeces and burn your toilet paper afterwards. Finally, do not defecate in the dry-stone huts along the trails; local shepherds use them for shelter during snow storms. For more details about environmental issues in Ladakh, see p.495.

An excellent **book** covering everything you need to know to undertake an expedition in the region is Trailblazer's *Trekking in Ladakh* by Charlie Loram, on sale in bookshops in Leh. For information about trekking to **Zanskar** from the south, see "Trekking in Lahaul and Spiti" (p.463).

The Markha Valley

The beautiful **Markha Valley** runs parallel with the Indus on the far southern side of the snowy Stok-Kangri massif, visible from Leh. Passing through cultivated valley

hundred monks, is renowned for its new 23-metre-high yellow statue of the Buddha-to-come which towers serenely above the terraced fields. A pleasant break from the bustle of Leh, the village of Likkir offers a small but adequate choice of accommodation that, along with the sheer tranquillity of the surroundings, tempts many travellers to linger a few days.

The *gompa*, 3km up the valley from the village, was extensively renovated in the eighteenth century and today shows little sign of the antiquity related to the site. It overlooks the starting point for the popular two-day hike to Temisgang via Rhizong, which provides a comparatively gentle introduction to trekking in Ladakh.

floors, undulating high-altitude grassland and snow-prone passes, the winding trail along it enables trekkers to experience life in a roadless region without having to hike for weeks into the wilderness – as a result, it has become the most frequented route in Ladakh. Do not attempt this trek without adequate wet- and cold-weather gear: snow flurries sweep across the higher reaches of the Markha Valley even in August.

The circuit takes six to eight days to complete, and is usually followed anticlockwise, starting from the village of **Spitok** (see p.507), 10km south of Leh. A more dramatic approach via **Stok** (see p.500) affords matchless views over the Indus Valley to the Ladakh and Karakoram ranges, but involves a sharp ascent of **Stok La** (4848m) on only the second day; don't try it unless you are already well acclimatized to the altitude.

Likkir to Temisgang

A drivable road along the old caravan route through the hills between **Likkir** and **Temisgang** makes a leisurely two-day hike, which takes in three major monasteries (Likkir, Rhizong and Temisgang) and a string of idyllic villages. It's a great introduction to trekking in Ladakh, the perfect acclimatizer if you plan to attempt any longer and more demanding routes. Ponies and guides for the trip may be arranged on spec at either Likkir or Temisgang villages, both of which have small guesthouses and are connected by daily buses to Leh.

Lamayuru to Alchi

Albeit short by Ladakhi standards, the five-day trek from **Lamayuru** to **Alchi** is one of the toughest in the region, winding across high passes and a tangle of isolated valleys past a couple of ancient *gompas*, and offering superb panoramic views of the wilderness south of the Indus Valley. It's very hard to follow in places, so don't attempt it without an experienced guide, ponies and enough provisions to tide you over if you lose your way.

Padum to Lamayuru

The trek across the rugged Zanskar Range from **Padum** to **Lamayuru** on the Srinagar–Leh highway, usually completed in ten to twelve days, is a hugely popular but very demanding long-distance route, not to be attempted as a first-time trek nor without adequate preparation, ponies and a guide.

Stok Kangri

Visible from most of Leh, **Stok-Kangri** (6120m) is reputed to be the easiest peak above 6000m in the world. Several agents in Leh advertise five-day **climbing expeditions** via the village of Stok with a non-technical final climb for around $45 per head per day for a group of four. If you've got *Trekking in Ladakh* in your rucksack, it's straightforward to walk up it independently, though you'll need to carry enough food for three or four days.

The direct **minibus** from Leh (4pm; 3hr) goes past the village and makes the 3km haul up the valley to the *gompa*, returning to Leh at 7am the next morning. Otherwise, take any west-bound vehicle, get dropped off at the turning from the main Leh–Kargil highway and walk the short but treeless 1km road to the village, where you can hire a taxi for the *gompa*. Simple **rooms** are available at the *gompa* itself and next door at the monastic school; both ask for a donation. The pleasant *Gaph-Chow* (Ⓣ01982/252748; ❷) in the lower village has simple, comfortable rooms with attached baths, camping space in the lovely vegetable garden, internet, a garden café and traditional Ladakhi kitchen. The other option is the friendly

Norboo Spon (❸ full board), easily spotted from the road to the monastery; the owner offers woodcarving and *thangka*-painting lessons to his guests. He can also give good trekking advice – aided by the scale model of the Likkir–Temisgang trek in his garden.

Alchi

Driving past on the nearby Srinagar–Leh highway, you'd never guess that the spectacular sweep of wine-coloured scree 3km across the Indus from **Saspol** conceals one of the most significant historical sites in Asia. Yet the low pagoda-roofed *Chos-khor*, or "religious enclave", at **ALCHI**, 70km west of Leh, harbours an extraordinary wealth of ancient wall paintings and wood sculpture, miraculously preserved for more than nine centuries inside five tiny mud-walled temples. The site's earliest murals are regarded as the finest surviving examples of a style that flourished in Kashmir during the "Second Spreading". Barely a handful of the monasteries founded during this era escaped the Muslim depredations of the fourteenth century; Alchi is the most impressive of them all, the least remote and the only one you don't need a special permit to visit.

Legend tells that Rinchen Zangpo, the "Great Translator" (see p.472), stuck his walking stick in the ground here en route to Chilling and upon his return found it had become a poplar, an auspicious sign that made him build a temple on the spot. One tree near the entrance to the *Chos-khor*, denoted with a signboard, is symbolic of this event. The *Chos-khor* itself consists of five separate temples, various residential buildings and a scattering of large *chortens*, surrounded by a mud-and-stone wall. It is best to concentrate on the two oldest buildings, the **Du-khang** and the **Sumtsek**, both in the middle of the enclosure. Entrance **tickets** (Rs30) are issued by a caretaker lama from nearby Likkir *gompa*, who will happily unlock the doors to these but isn't keen to open the three less important shrines.

The Du-khang

An inscription records that Alchi's oldest structure, the **Du-khang**, was erected late in the eleventh century. Its centrepiece is an image of Vairocana, the "Buddha Resplendent", flanked by the four main Buddha manifestations that appear all over Alchi's temple walls, always presented in their associated colours: Akshobya ("Unshakeable"; blue), Ratnasambhava ("Jewel Born"; yellow), Amitabha ("Boundless Radiance"; red) and Amoghasiddhi ("Unfailing Success"; green). The other walls are decorated with six elaborate mandalas, interspersed with intricate friezes.

The Sumtsek

Standing to the left of the Du-khang, the **Sumtsek** marks the highwater mark of early medieval Indian-Buddhist art. Its woodcarvings and paintings, dominated by rich reds and blues, are almost as fresh and vibrant today as they were nine hundred years ago when the squat triple-storey structure was built. The heart of the shrine is a colossal statue of **Maitreya**, the Buddha-to-come, his head shielded from sight high in the second storey. Accompanying him are two equally grand **bodhisattvas**, their heads peering serenely down through gaps in the ceiling. Each of these stucco statues wears a figure-clinging *dhoti*, adorned with different, meticulously detailed motifs. Avalokitesvara, the *bodhisattva* of compassion (to the left), has pilgrimage sites, court vignettes, palaces and pre-Muslim style *stupas* on his robe, while that of Maitreya is decorated with episodes from the life of Gautama Buddha. The robe of Manjushri, destroyer of falsehood, to the right, shows the 84 masters of Tantra, the *mahasiddhas*, adopting complex yogic poses in a maze of bold square patterns.

Among the exquisite **murals**, some repaired in the sixteenth century, is the famous six-armed green goddess Prajnaparamita, the "Perfection of Wisdom". Amazingly, this, and the multitude of other images that plaster the interior of the Sumtsek, resolve, when viewed from the centre of the shrine, into a harmonious whole.

Practicalities

An alternative to hiring a taxi from Leh is to catch the 8am or 4pm private **bus**, which takes three hours to cover the 70km and returns at 3.45pm or 7am the next day. Otherwise you can board any Kargil-bound vehicle, get off at the metal truss bridge west of **Saspol** and walk across the river and up the remaining 6km.

Of the growing selection of **guesthouses** in Alchi, the *Lotsava* (Ⓣ01982/227129; ❶–❷), down below the group-oriented *Alchi Resort* as you approach the taxi stand, is pleasant and simple with good views; with a little warning, the owner will serve filling breakfasts and evening meals in the small garden. On both sides of the lane that leads to the *gompa*, the *Zimskhang* (Ⓣ01982/227086, Ⓔzimskhang@yahoo.com; ❷–❺) has two identities: to the right a modern hotel, and to the left a cheaper guesthouse with a pleasant garden. More upmarket is the purpose-built *Samdupling* (Ⓣ01982/221704; ❸), 100m above the taxi stand, approached by following the stream behind the adequate *gompa*-owned *Hotel Potala* (Ⓣ9419 178747, Ⓔangchok1@rediffmail.com; ❸). The only **restaurant**, apart from a couple of cheap *dhabas* near the taxi stand, is the *Golden Oriole German Bakery* just above the *gompa*, which does a standard mixture of Western and Indian dishes. If you've a real appetite, you might try the quality veg buffet at the *Zimskhang*.

Lamayuru

If one sight could be said to sum up Ladakh, it would have to be **LAMAYURU gompa**, 130km west of Leh. Hemmed in by a moonscape of scree-covered mountains, the whitewashed medieval monastery towers above a scruffy cluster of tumbledown mud-brick houses from the top of a near-vertical, weirdly eroded cliff. A major landmark on the old silk route, the *gompa* numbers among the 108 (a spiritually significant number) founded by the Rinchen Zangpo in the tenth and eleventh centuries. However, its craggy seat, believed to have sheltered Milarepa during his religious odyssey across the Himalayas, was probably sacred long before the advent of Buddhism, when local people followed the shamanistic Bon cult. Just thirty lamas of the Brigungpa branch of the Kagyu school are now left, as opposed to the four hundred that lived here a century or so ago. Nor does Lamayuru harbour much in the way of art treasures. The main reason visitors make a stop on this section of the Srinagar–Leh road is to photograph the *gompa* from the valley floor, or to pick up the trail to the Prikiti La pass – gateway to Zanskar – that begins here.

The steep footpath from the highway above town brings you out near the main entrance to the monastery, where you should be able to find the lama responsible for issuing entrance tickets (Rs30) and unlocking the door to the **Du-khang**. Lamayuru's newly renovated prayer-hall houses little of note other than a **cave** where Naropa, Milarepa's teacher, is said to have meditated, and a collection of colourful yak-butter sculptures. If you're lucky, you'll be shown through the tangle of narrow lanes below the *gompa* to a tiny **chapel**, whose badly damaged murals of mandalas and the Tathagata Buddhas date from the same period as those at Alchi (see opposite).

Practicalities

Lamayuru lies too far from either Leh or Kargil, 107km west, to be visited in a day-trip, so unless you call in en route with a jeep, you'll have to spend the night here. The daily Leh–Kargil and Kargil–Leh **buses** both depart around 5.30am from their respective towns of origin and pass through Lamayuru between 9am and 10am, stopping near the central chai stalls. Some private buses also pass through up to early afternoon. **Trekkers** in search of reliable guides and ponies could ask at the *Dragon Guest House* (see below) or try arranging them in advance through their office in Leh (Ⓣ01982/253164). Dominating the village skyline by the *gompa* entrance, the four-storey *Niranjana Hotel* (Ⓣ01982/224555; ❸) has twenty concrete **rooms** with good views of the surrounding valleys; the shared bathrooms have hot running water. Alternatively, the welcoming, family-run *Dragon Guest House* (Ⓣ01982/224510, Ⓕ252414; ❶–❸) has a range of rooms, including one coveted glass room, and a pleasant garden restaurant, which is the best place to **eat** in Lamayuru. The *Siachen Guesthouse* (Ⓣ01982/224538; ❶), on the opposite side of the footpath into the village, is a decent fallback. All accommodation prices double during the **festival** (late June/early July).

Mulbekh

West of Lamayuru, the main road crawls to the top of **Fotu La** (4091m), the highest pass between Leh and Srinagar, then ascends **Namika** ("Sky-Pillar") **La** (3760m), so called because of the jagged pinnacle of rock that looms above it to the south. Once across the windswept ridge, it drops through a dramatic landscape of disintegrating desert cliffs and pebbly ravines to the wayside village of **MULBEKH** – the last sizeable Buddhist settlement along the road before the Muslim Purki settlements around Kargil. The village is scattered around the banks of the River Wakha, lined with poplars and orchards of walnut and apricot trees and would be a sleepy hamlet were it not for the endless convoys of trucks and tourist buses that thunder through while the passes are open. Those visitors who stop at all tend only to stay long enough to grab a chai at a roadside *dhaba* and to have a quick look at the seven-metre-high **Maitreya** ("Chamba" in Tibetan) **statue** carved from the face of a gigantic boulder nearby. The precise origins of the shapely four-armed Buddha-to-be are not known, but an ancient inscription on its side records that it was carved between the seventh and eighth centuries, well before Buddhism was fully established in Tibet. The single-chambered *gompa* (Rs10), in front of the statue and decorated with particularly beautiful murals, is dedicated to the thousand-armed Chenrazig (Avalokitesvara).

Accommodation in Mulbekh itself is limited to shabby rooms above basic restaurants such as the *Paradise* (Ⓣ01985/270010; ❶) and the *Tsomo Riri* (Ⓣ01985/270013; ❶) on the main road opposite the Chamba statue; serving *thukpa*, dhal, rice, *momos* and butter tea during the day, they later turn into cheap drinking dens. More comfort and attached rooms can be found 1km west along the main road at *Maitreya Guest House* (Ⓣ01985/270035; ❸).

Kargil

Though it is surrounded by awesome scenery, most travellers don't spend more than a few hours in **KARGIL**, capital of the area dubbed "Little Baltistan", which rises in a clutter of corrugated-iron rooftops from the confluence of the Suru and Drass rivers. As a halfway point between Leh and Srinagar, its grubby hotels fill up at night-time with weary bus passengers, who then get up at 4am and career off under cover of darkness. Although the town has expanded several kilometres along and above the riverside, the central area around the main bazaar, which loops round into a northerly orientation, is very compact and walkable.

Moving on from Kargil

Buses for Mulbekh leave at 3pm, 3.30pm and 4pm every day. In the mornings you may be able to catch a shared Matador minibus. The government service to Padum in Zanskar is very patchy at best, with no fixed schedule, and is often full when it does come through from Leh. If you're not alone and don't mind hitching, you could catch a bus to Panikhar (every 1–2 hours until 2pm) and wait by the checkpost there. **Hiring a taxi** is much less hassle; the one-way fare to Padum is around Rs9000 (Rs1800/person). For **Leh**, several buses depart daily between 4am and 5am (Rs200), but the quick and easy option is to book a seat the day before in a Tata Sumo (Rs500–600), which also tend to depart early in the day.

Arrival and information

State buses arriving in Kargil from Leh, Srinagar and Padum pull in by the river, 150m below the middle of the bazaar, while private buses, minibuses and jeeps share a larger compound further south, just below the bazaar.

The unreliable J&K **tourism reception centre** (Mon–Sat 10am–4pm; ⓣ01985/232721) is on the east side of town, on the river side of the **taxi stand**. The only exchange facility is State Bank of India's **ATM** in the bazaar. Kargil has several **internet** places (Rs80/hr), the best being the one near the *Hotel Tourist Marjina*.

Accommodation

The Kashmir crisis, which reduced tourist traffic to a trickle, squeezed half of Kargil's **hotels** out of business, and perhaps surprisingly, it's the more salubrious ones that survived. Consequently, budget options are very limited and room tariffs soar in July and August when most travellers pass through; the rates below reflect this, but discounts are usually available at other times.

Crown Near state bus stop. Rambling old budget hotel that's seen better days but still attracts backpackers. Some rooms come with attached bathrooms and there's a dirt-cheap dorm (Rs50). Running water on request. ❶

Greenland Just off the lane heading towards the state bus stop ⓣ01985/232324. The old block is dire, with grubby rooms, while the new one is better but overpriced. OK as a last resort. ❸–❺

J&K Tourist Bungalow unit no.1 A 5min walk uphill from the crossroads above the bus stand ⓣ01985/232328. Clean rooms, clean sheets and peaceful atmosphere, with a small dining room. By far the best budget deal in town but needs to be booked in advance through any J&K office. *Unit no.2* in the tourist office complex is shabbier but has river views. ❶

Siachen On a lane down to taxi stand ⓣ01985/233055, ⓔhotel_siachen_kargil@rediffmail.com. One of the best downtown hotels, large and comfortable with attached rooms, a few cheaper options on the first floor, and a good restaurant. ❻

Hotel Tourist Marjina On the lane heading towards the state bus stop ⓣ01985/232578. A notch above rock-bottom, with reasonable rooms (all with bath), divided into two blocks; those on the upper floor are more spacious. ❷

The Town

While Kargil has no attractions, it is an atmospheric place to pass a day or more while waiting for a bus to Zanskar (see box above). Woolly-hatted and bearded old men and slick youngsters stroll the streets past old-fashioned wholesalers with their sacks of grains, spices and tins of ghee, Tibetans selling Panasonic electricals and butchers displaying severed goats' heads on dusty bookshelves. The town feels more Pakistani than Indian, and the faces (nearly all male) and food derive from Kashmir and Central Asia. Western women should keep their arms and legs covered; those walking around alone will probably encounter both giggling teenage boys and curious elderly Kargili gentlemen.

The majority of Kargil's eighty thousand inhabitants, known as Purki, are strict **Muslims**. Unlike their Sunni cousins in Kashmir, however, the locals here are orthodox **Shias**, which not only explains the ubiquitous Ayatollah photographs, but also the conspicuous absence of women from the bazaar. You might even spot the odd black turban of an Agha, one of Kargil's spiritual leaders, who still go on pilgrimage to holy sites in Iran and have outlawed male–female social practices such as dancing. Descendants of settlers and Muslim merchants from Kashmir and Yarkhand, Purkis speak a dialect called **Purig** – a mixture of Ladakhi and Balti. Indeed, had it not been for the daring Indian reconquest of the region during the 1948 Indo-Pak War, Kargil would today be part of Baltistan, the region across the Ceasefire Line which it closely resembles. Indeed, Kargil is so close to the Ceasefire Line and Pakistani positions that it served as the logistics centre in the 1999 war (see p.477) and was repeatedly targeted by Pakistani artillery. Aside from the odd building destroyed, however, much of the town escaped unscathed as the army bases and airport lie on the outskirts of town. Since further conflict in the summer of 2002 the dust has settled markedly and, as dialogue continues between India and Pakistan on Kashmir, tourist numbers have been steadily increasing.

Eating

Besides upmarket hotels like the *Siachen*, finding somewhere to **eat** in Kargil is a toss-up between the small tourist-oriented joints and local *dhabas* that are dotted on and around the main bazaar. Most restaurants are closed for **breakfast**, but the street food can be delicious – chai, chapattis and omelettes, with hot Kashmiri bread slathered with butter. Spicy shish kebabs go for just Rs10 later in the day.

Karan Singh Punjabi Janata South end of Main Bazaar. One of the town's better *dhabas*: spicy Indian sauces spooned onto groaning platefuls of rice. Eat well for around Rs50.

Las Vegas On the lane from the taxi stand to Main Bazaar. One of the more salubrious places, serving mainly non-veg Indian, Kashmiri and Chinese fare for around Rs80–100.

Rubby South end of Main Bazaar. Popular restaurant serving local specialities including *yakhani* (meat boiled in yoghurt) and *gustaba* (meat balls), both of which can be daunting if you're not adjusted to Central Asian cuisine. Most items well under Rs50.

Tibetan Food Restaurant Main Bazaar. All the favourites like *momo* and *thukpa*, dished up for around Rs40–60. Very authentic atmosphere in this attractive upstairs dining room.

Zojila Bakery Main Bazaar. A good place to stop for a morning tea, or to pick up bread and cookies. One of the few places for a sit-down brekky.

The Suru Valley

Dividing two of the world's most formidable mountain ranges, the **Suru Valley** winds south from Kargil to the desolate Pensi La – the main entry point for Zanskar. The first leg, usually undertaken in the pre-dawn darkness by bus, leads through the broad lower reaches of the Suru Valley, strewn with Muslim villages clustered around metal mosque domes. As you progress southwards, the pristine white ice-fields and twin pinnacles of **Nun-Kun** (7077m) nose over the horizon. Apart from a brief disappearance behind the steep sides of the valley at **Panikhar**, this awesome massif dominates the landscape all the way to Zanskar.

Shortly beyond Panikhar, the Suru veers east around the base of Nun-Kun, passing within a stone's throw of the magnificent **Parkachik Gangri** glacier. Having wound across a seemingly endless boulder field, closed in on both sides by sheer mountain walls, the road then emerges at a marshy open plain surrounded by snow peaks and mountainsides of near-vertical strata. **Juldo**, a tiny settlement whose fodder-stacked rooftops are strung with fluttering prayer flags, marks the beginning of Buddhist **Suru**.

The climb to the pass from **Rangdum gompa**, across the flat river basin from Juldo, is absolutely breathtaking. One glistening 6000-metre peak after another appears atop a series of side valleys, many lined with gigantic folds of rock and ice. The real high point, though, is reserved for the dizzying descent from **Pensi La** (4401m), as the road's switchbacks swing over the colossal S-shaped **Darung Drung Glacier**, whose milky-green meltwaters drain southeast into the Stod Valley, visible below.

Panikhar

Although by no means the largest settlement in the Suru Valley, **PANIKHAR**, three hours' bus ride south of Kargil, is a good place to break the long journey to Padum. Before the Kashmir troubles, it was a minor trekking centre, at the start of the Lonvilad Gali–Pahalgum trail. These days, despite the improving situation, it sees far fewer tourists, even in high season.

The main reason to stop is to hike to nearby **Parkachik La**, for panoramic views of the glacier-gouged north face of the mighty **Nun-Kun massif**. The **trail** up to the pass begins on the far side of the Suru, crossed via a suspension bridge thirty minutes south of the village. It may look straightforward from Panikhar, but the four-hour round-trip climb to the ridge gets very tough indeed towards the top, especially for those not used to the altitude. However, even seasoned trekkers gasp in awe at the sight that greets them when they finally arrive at the cairns. Capped with a plume of cloud and with snow streaming from its huge pyramidal peak, Nun sails 3500m above the valley floor, draped with heavily crevassed hanging glaciers and flanked by its sisters, multi-pinnacled Kun and saddle-topped Barmal.

There are only two **places to stay** in Panikhar. The *Kayoul* (Ⓣ9469 192810, Ⓔsaki_muna@yahoo.com; ❶), directly opposite the bus stand, has a few very basic rooms. For marginally more comfort, try the modest J&K *Tourist Bungalow* (Ⓣ01985/259137; ❶), 100m further down the road on the left, which serves simple veg meals, the only food available in the village. If you're looking for a lift to Padum, walk the five kilometres back down to the checkpost on the main road and try your luck there, the earlier the better.

Zanskar

Walled in by the Great Himalayan Divide, **ZANSKAR**, literally "Land of White Copper", has for decades exerted the allure of Shangri-La on visitors to Ladakh. The region's staggering remoteness, extreme climate and distance from the major Himalayan trade routes has meant that the successive winds of change that have blown through the Indus Valley to the north had little impact here. The annual influx of trekkers and a drivable road have certainly quickened the pace of development, but away from the main settlement of Padum, the Zanskaris' way of life has altered little since the sage Padmasambhava passed through in the eighth century.

The nucleus of the region is a Y-shaped glacial valley system drained by three main rivers: the **Stot** (or Doda) and the **Tsarap** (or Lingit) join and flow north as the **Zanskar**. Lying to the leeward side of the Himalayan watershed, the valley sees a lot more snow than central Ladakh. Even the lowest passes remain blocked for seven or eight months of the year, while midwinter temperatures can drop to a bone-numbing minus 40°C. Fourteen thousand or so tenacious souls subsist in this bleak and treeless terrain – among the coldest inhabited places on the planet – muffled up for half the year inside their smoke-filled whitewashed crofts, with a winter's-worth of fodder piled on the roof.

Until the end of the 1970s, anything the resourceful Zanskaris could not produce for themselves (including timber for building) had to be transported into the region over 4000- to 5000-metre passes, or, in midwinter, carried along the frozen surface of the Zanskar from its confluence with the Indus at Nimmu – a ten- to twelve-day round trip that's still the quickest route to the Srinagar–Leh road from Padum. Finally, in 1980, a drivable dirt track was blasted down the Suru and over Pensi La into the Stot valley. Landslides and freak blizzards permitting (Pensi La can be snowbound even in August), the bumpy journey from Kargil to Padum can now be completed in as little as ten hours.

Most visitors come to Zanskar to **trek**. Numerous trails wind their way north from Padum to central Ladakh, west to Kishtwar and south to neighbouring Lahaul – all long, hard hikes (see box, p.463). Only a handful of Zanskar's widely scattered *gompas* and settlements lie within striking distance of the road. The rest are hidden away in remote valleys, reached after days or weeks of walking. Improved communications may yet turn out to be a mixed blessing for Zanskar. While the road undoubtedly brought a degree of prosperity to Padum, it has also forced significant changes upon the rest of the valley – most noticeably a sharp increase in tourist traffic – whose long-term impact on the region's fragile ecology and **traditional culture** has yet to be fully realized. Increased tourism has, in fact, done little to benefit the locals financially, with agencies in Leh, Manali, Srinagar and even Delhi pocketing the money paid by trekking groups. Zanskaris, weary of seeing their region come second to Kargil, have been campaigning for years for a sub-hill council status with more control over **development**. Buddhist concerns have also been heightened in the face of state government mismanagement and occasional communal tensions with their Muslim neighbours. There has been some outside aid emerging – one excellent initiative is the Dutch-based Stichting Zanskar Scholen foundation (Ⓦwww.zanskarscholen.com), which equips some of the impoverished state and monastery schools.

Padum

After a memorable trek or bus ride, **PADUM**, 240km to the south of Kargil, comes as a bit of an anticlimax. Instead of the picturesque Zanskari village you might expect, the region's administrative headquarters and principal roadhead turns out to be a desultory collection of typical concrete cubes, oily truck parks and tin-roofed government buildings. The settlement's only real appeal lies in its superb location. Nestled at the southernmost tip of a broad, fertile river basin, Padum presides over a flat patchwork of farmland enclosed on three sides by colossal walls of scree and snow-capped mountains.

Arrival and information

If you manage to find a **bus** to Padum, it's best to get off by most of the guest-houses, on the main road just south of the J&K **Tourist Office** (Mon–Sat 10am–4pm; Ⓣ01983/245017), which is good for general advice, though it doesn't rent out trekking gear. Due to the short season and the limited tourist trade, renting a taxi in Padum (through the Padum Taxi Union office) is expensive: a trip to Karsha and back costs at least Rs1200. As yet, there is nowhere in Padum to change money, although you can mail letters from the **post office** next door to the tourist centre. There are two internet **cafés** but unsurprisingly connections are erratic and slow.

Accommodation

Accommodation options in Padum are continually improving.

Chamling Kailash North end of main bazaar ⓣ9469 457379, ⓔlobel@sancharnet.in. The best budget option, with comfortable attached rooms, decorated in Buddhist style and set around a courtyard. ❷–❸

Hotel Ibex Main bazaar ⓣ01983/245012. Good standard lodge, also arranged around a pleasant courtyard. ❸

J&K Tourist Complex North end of main bazaar ⓣ01983/245017. Institutional but comfortable government lodge with well-maintained attached doubles, as well as dorm beds and tent sites (both Rs50). ❶

Marq 200m west of main bazaar ⓣ01983/245021, ⓦwww.zanskarmarqinn.com. The smartest place in town, with bright spacious attached rooms, all of which enjoy splendid views. ❹

Mont Blanc South end of main bazaar ⓣ01983/245183. Friendly French-run place with simple rooms and Rs50 tent pitches. ❷–❸

Local treks

Straddling a nexus of several long-distance trails, Padum is an important **trekking hub** and the only place in Zanskar where tourism has thus far made much of an impression. During the short summer season, you'll see almost as many weather-beaten Westerners wandering around its sandy lanes as locals – a mixture of indigenous Buddhists and Sunni Muslims. Even so, facilities are still limited to a small tourist office and a small but growing number of shops, restaurants and guesthouses. Nor is there much to see while you're waiting for your blisters to heal. The only noteworthy sight within easy walking distance is a small **Tagrimo gompa** fifteen minutes' walk to the west.

Basic **trekking supplies** are sold at the hole-in-the-wall stores along the bazaar. Prices are much higher than elsewhere, so it pays to bring your own provisions with you from Kargil. Most trekkers arrange **ponies** through the tourist office or guesthouse owners, or you could try Zanskar Trek (ⓣ01983/245053), who also supply guides (Rs500–1000/day). Expect to pay Rs300 per pony per day, depending on the time of year (ponies transport grain during the harvest, so they're more expensive in early September). If you have trouble finding a horse-wallah in Padum, ask at a neighbouring village, such as Pipiting, a thirty-minute walk north across the fields from Padum, where many of them live.

Eating

Finding **food** in Padum only tends to be a problem towards the end of the trekking season; by mid-October, stocks of imported goods (virtually everything except barley flour and yak butter) are low, and even a fresh egg can be a cause for celebration. Apart from the guesthouse restaurants, two of the best seasonal joints for Tibetan and Chinese food are the *Lhasa* and *Gyaskit*, while *Shahi Darbar UP Restaurent* (sic) is a good cheap Indian *dhaba*.

Around Padum

Public transport around the Zanskar Valley is erratic, although one public bus travels from Padum to Zangla on Wednesday and Friday, leaving in the morning and returning the same afternoon. Otherwise you will have to shell out for the vastly inflated fares demanded by Padum's taxi union. Determined trekkers can alternatively set out on foot; the hike across the fields to **KARSHA gompa**, Zanskar's largest Gelug-pa monastery, is the most rewarding objective.

This cluster of whitewashed mud cubes clinging to the rocky lower slopes of the mountain north of Padum dates from the tenth to the fourteenth century. Of the prayer halls, the recently renovated Du-khang and Gon-khang at the top of the complex are the most impressive, while the small Chukshok-jal, set apart from the *gompa* below a ruined fort on the far side of a gully, contains Karsha's oldest wall paintings, contemporaneous with those at Alchi (see p.510).

The quickest way to get to Karsha on foot is to head north from Padum to the cable bridge across the Stot, immediately below the monastery. Set off early in the morning; the violent icy storms that blow in from the south across the Great Himalayan Range around mid-afternoon make the ninety-minute hike across the exposed river basin something of an endurance test. Karsha is a far more pleasant place to stay than Padum and some villagers rent **rooms** to tourists. Try the wonderful glass room belonging to Thuktan Thardot in Sharling Ward just below the *gompa* (❶) or the basic *Lobzang Guest House* (❶).

Karsha can also be reached by road, via the bridge at **Tungri**, 8km northwest of Padum. En route, you pass another large *gompa*, **SANI**, lauded as the oldest in Zanskar, and the only one built on the valley floor. Local legend attributes its foundation to the itinerant Padmasambhava (Guru Rinpoche) in the eighth century. Set apart from the temples a little to the north is a two-metre-high Maitreya figure, carved out of local stone sometime between the eighth and tenth centuries.

8

Haryana and Punjab

* **Rock Garden, Chandigarh** This bizarre and seemingly haphazard sculpture garden, assembled from rubbish by a local eccentric, offers curious contrast to the ordered city that surrounds it. **See p.526**

* **The Golden Temple, Amritsar** One of the great sights – and sounds – of India; *kirtan* (devotional songs) are performed throughout the day and into the night. **See p.531**

* **Border ceremony, Wagha** Shorter and more colourful than a cricket match, the border ceremony is a highly charged event, especially on Sundays, when hundreds of people gather. **See p.535**

▲ Devotees at the Golden Temple, Amritsar

The prosperous states of **HARYANA** and **PUNJAB** occupy the fertile river plain northwest of Delhi. Crossed by the five major tributaries of the **Indus River**, the former British-administered region of Punjab ("Five Rivers") was split down the middle at Independence. Indian Muslims fled west into Pakistan, Sikhs and Hindus east, in an exodus accompanied by horrific massacres. In 1966, Indira Gandhi, in response to Sikh pressure, made the Punjab Hills into Himachal Pradesh and divided the plains into the predominantly Sikh Punjab, and the 96-percent Hindu Haryana, both governed from the newly built capital of **Chandigarh**.

There is little of tourist interest in the two states other than the Golden Temple in Amritsar and the wacky Rock Garden of Chandigarh, but the region, India's breadbasket, is very important to the nation's **economy**. Its farmers produce nearly a quarter of India's wheat and one-third of its milk and dairy foods, while Ludhiana churns out ninety percent of the country's woollen goods. Helped by remittance cheques from millions of expatriates in the UK, US and Canada, the state's per capita income is almost double the national average.

Crossing Haryana and Punjab, you're bound to travel at some stage along part of the longest, oldest and most famous highway in India – the NH-1, alias the **Grand Trunk Road**, stretching 2000km from Peshawar, near the rugged Afghan–Pakistan frontier, to Kolkata on the River Hooghly. The first recorded mention of this trade corridor dates from the fourth century BC, when it was known as the Uttar Path (the "North Way").

Some history

Punjab's first urban settlement, dating back to 3000 BC and now known as the **Harappan** Civilization, was invaded by the Aryans around 1700 BC. Among the Sanskrit scriptures set down in the ensuing **Vedic** age was the **Mahabharata**, whose epic battles drew on real-life encounters between the ancient kings of Punjab at Karnal, 118km north of Delhi. Conquered by the Mauryans in the third century BC, it saw plenty more action as various invading Mughal armies passed through on their way from the Khyber Pass to Delhi – including Babur, who routed Ibrahim Lodi at Panipat in 1526.

Meanwhile, further north, **Sikhism** was beginning to establish itself under the tutelage of Guru Nanak (1469–1539). Based on the notion of a single Formless God, the guru's vision of a casteless egalitarian society found favour with both Hindus and Muslims, in spite of Mughal emperor Aurangzeb's attempts to stamp it out. Suppression actually strengthened the Sikh faith in the long run, inspiring the militaristic and confrontational tenth guru **Gobind Singh** to introduce the Five Ks, part of a rigorous new orthodoxy called the **Khalsa**, or "Community of the Pure" (see p.1157).

Having survived repeated seventeenth-century Afghan invasions, the Sikh nation emerged to fill the power vacuum left by the collapse of the Mughals. Only in the 1840s, after two bloody wars with the British, was the Khalsa army finally defeated. Thereafter, the Sikhs played a vital role in the Raj, helping to quash the Mutiny of 1857. The relationship only soured after the **Jallianwalla Bagh massacre** of 1919 (see p.534), which also ensured that the Punjab's puppet leaders (who hailed the general responsible as a hero) were discredited, leaving the way open for the rise of radicalism.

After Independence and Partition, things calmed down enough to allow the new state to grow wealthy on its prodigious agricultural output. As it did, militant Sikhs began to press for the creation of the separate Punjabi-speaking state they called Khalistan. A compromise of sorts was reached in 1966, when the Hindu district of Haryana and the Sikh-majority Punjab were nominally divided.

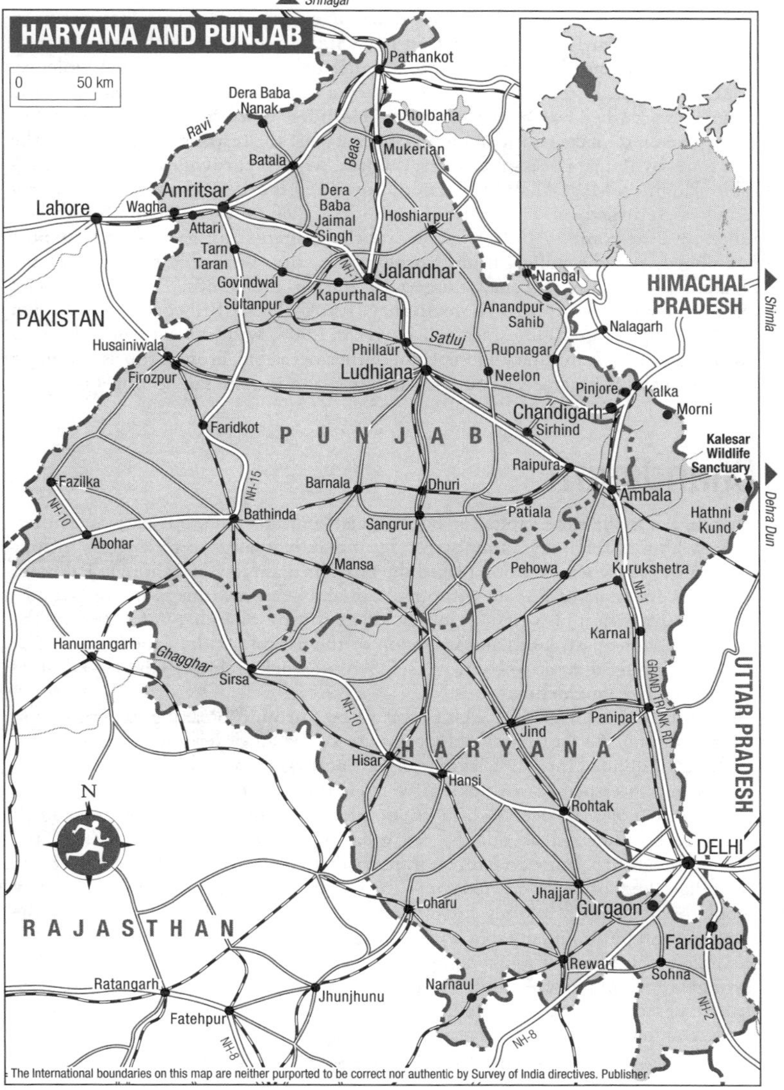

However, the move did not silence the separatists, and in 1977 Indira Gandhi's Congress was trounced in state elections by a coalition that included the Sikh religious party, the **Akali Dal**.

A more sinister element entered the volatile equation with the emergence of an ultra-radical separatist movement led by **Sant Jarnail Singh Bhindranwale**. Covertly supported by the national government (who saw the group as a way to defeat the Akali Dal), Bhindranwale and his band waged a ruthless campaign of sectarian terror in the Punjab which came to a head in 1984, when they occupied Amritsar's Golden Temple; **Operation Blue Star**, Indira Gandhi's brutal response, (see p.1163), plunged the Punjab into another ugly bout of communal violence. Four years later, history repeated itself when a less threatening occupation of the temple was crushed by **Operation Black Thunder**. Since then, the Punjab police have gone on to make considerable advances against the terrorists – helped, for the first time, by Punjabi peasant farmers, the **Jats**, who had grown tired of the inexorable slaughter. Most Akali Dal factions boycotted the 1992 elections, which saw Congress returned on a 22 percent turnout. Chief minister **Beant Singh** was killed by a car bomb in 1995, but this was the militants' last gasp. Public support had ebbed, and the police, using strong-arm tactics, were able to wipe out the paramilitary groups that had burgeoned during the 1980s. Subsequent state elections have seen a **return to normality**. An Akali Dal/BJP coalition – thrown out by Congress in 2002 – regained power in 2007, with voter turnout back to normal and no paramilitary violence on either occasion. From a tourist point of view, Punjab has regained its political stability, and is quite safe to travel in.

Chandigarh

Chandigarh is the state capital of both Punjab and Haryana, but part of neither, being a Union Territory administered by India's federal government. Its history begins in 1947, when Partition placed the Punjab's main city of Lahore in Pakistan, leaving India's state of Punjab without a capital. Nehru saw this as an opportunity to realize his vision of a city "symbolic of the future of India, unfettered by the traditions of the past, [and] an expression of the nation's faith in the future". The job of designing it went to controversial Swiss-French architect Charles-Edouard Jeanneret, alias **Le Corbusier**.

Begun in 1952, **CHANDIGARH** was to be a ground-breaking experiment in town planning. Le Corbusier's blueprints were for an orderly grid of sweeping boulevards, divided into 29 neat blocks, or **Sectors**, each measuring 800 by 1200 metres, and interspersed with extensive stretches of green. The resulting city has been a source of controversy since its completion in the 1960s. Some applaud Le Corbusier's brainchild as one of the great architectural achievements of the twentieth century, but detractors complain that the design is self-indulgent and un-Indian. Le Corbusier created a city for fast-flowing traffic at a time when few people owned cars, while his cubic concrete buildings are like ovens during the summer – all but uninhabitable without expensive air-conditioning. The city has expanded from the first phase comprising sectors 1 to 30 (there is no Sector 13), through a second phase – sectors 31 to 47 – and is now into the third phase with (half-size) sectors 48 to 61. Satellite towns emulating Chandigarh's grid plan and sterile concrete architecture have also sprung up on either side, with Panchkula in Haryana and Mohali in Punjab easing the pressure on a city left with nowhere else to grow.

Despite Chandigarh's shortcomings, its inhabitants are proud of their capital, which is cleaner, greener and more affluent than other Indian cities of comparable size, and boasts a rock garden said to be India's second most visited tourist site after the Taj Mahal.

Arrival and information

The **Inter-state Bus Terminus** (**ISBT**) is on the south edge of the main commercial and shopping district, Sector 17, but services from Punjab or Himachal

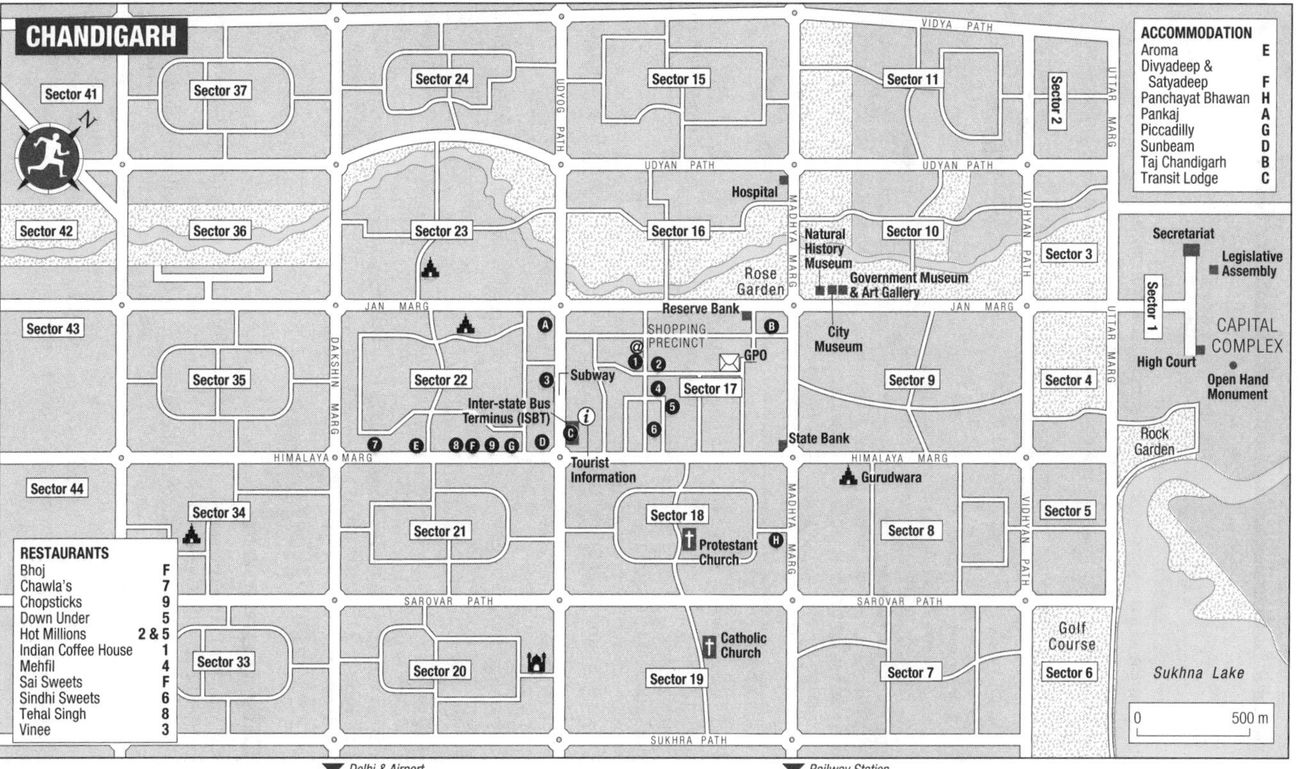
CHANDIGARH
ACCOMMODATION
Aroma E
Divyadeep & Satyadeep F
Panchayat Bhawan H
Pankaj A
Piccadilly G
Sunbeam D
Taj Chandigarh B
Transit Lodge C
RESTAURANTS
Bhoj F
Chawla's 7
Chopsticks 9
Down Under 5
Hot Millions 2 & 5
Indian Coffee House 1
Mehfil 4
Sai Sweets F
Sindhi Sweets 6
Tehal Singh 8
Vinee 3
Manali
Sector 43 Bus Stand
Delhi & Airport
Railway Station
Sector 1
Sector 2
Sector 3
Sector 4
Sector 5
Sector 6
Sector 7
Sector 8
Sector 9
Sector 10
Sector 11
Sector 15
Sector 16
Sector 17
Sector 18
Sector 19
Sector 20
Sector 21
Sector 22
Sector 23
Sector 24
Sector 33
Sector 34
Sector 35
Sector 36
Sector 37
Sector 41
Sector 42
Sector 43
Sector 44
VIDYA PATH
UTTAR MARG
UDYAN PATH
UDYOG PATH
VIDHYAN PATH
MADHYA MARG
JAN MARG
DAKSHIN MARG
HIMALAYA MARG
SAROVAR PATH
SUKHRA PATH
Secretariat
Legislative Assembly
CAPITAL COMPLEX
High Court
Open Hand Monument
Rock Garden
Sukhna Lake
Golf Course
Hospital
Natural History Museum
Government Museum & Art Gallery
City Museum
Rose Garden
Reserve Bank
SHOPPING PRECINCT
GPO
Subway
Inter-state Bus Terminus (ISBT)
Tourist Information
State Bank
Gurudwara
Protestant Church
Catholic Church
0 500 m

Moving on from Chandigarh

There are direct **trains** to Delhi (7 daily; 3hr 17min–5hr 15min), Jodhpur (1 daily; 17hr 35min), Mumbai (1 daily; 27hr 55min) and Kolkata (1 daily; 30hr 20min). The superfast a/c *Shatabdi Express* runs to New Delhi railway station (#2006 & #2012 departing at 6.53am & 6.20pm). Second-class tickets cost Rs435, four times the bus price, but the journey is far more comfortable and almost twice as fast. Other useful daily trains include the #4096 *Himalayan Queen* (dep. 5.32pm, arr. New Delhi 10.30pm) and the #4887 *Kalka–Jodhpur Express* (dep. 10.25pm, arr. Jodhpur 4pm next day).

Most travellers leave town by **bus** from the ISBT in Sector 17. Tickets can be pre-booked at the counters on the ground floor, or just pay on the bus. Daytime departures to Punjab and Himachal Pradesh leave from bus station no. 2 in Sector 43, connected to the ISBT by city bus #18.

The **airport** is 11km south of town (Rs100 by auto from the ISBT, Rs250 by taxi); destinations include Delhi, Mumbai and Goa.

Chandigarh is an important transport hub for **Shimla**, most swiftly reached by bus from Sector 43 (every 10min; 4hr–4hr 30min). You can also get there on the slower but more congenial Viceroys' "Toy Train" (see p.414) from **Kalka** 26km to the northeast, and connected to Chandigarh by trains and frequent buses. The scenic 75-kilometre journey from Kalka to Shimla takes around 5hr (dep. 4am, 5.15am, 6am & 12.10pm). See p.415 for Shimla–Kalka times.

Pradesh may leave you at Sector 43 bus stand, connected to the ISBT by local bus #18. Chandigarh's **airport** is 11km south of the city centre, its **railway station** 8km southeast. Both have pre-paid auto-rickshaw counters with fixed rates, as does the ISBT (the booth is at its western corner, but is sometimes closed for no apparent reason). A pre-paid auto to the ISBT costs around Rs100 from the airport (a taxi is around Rs250), or Rs55 from the railway station; an auto from the ISBT to the Rock Garden is around Rs40. There's a rail reservation centre at the ISBT (Mon–Sat 8am–2pm & 2.15–8pm, Sun 8am–2pm).

The **tourist office** at the ISBT (daily 9.30am–5.30pm; ⓣ0172/270 0054, ⓦchandigarhtourism.gov.in) is helpful and friendly, and the place to get a permit to visit the Capital Complex (see p.526). Their tour and travel wing, CITCO (Chandigarh Industry and Tourism Development Corporation; ⓣ0172/270 7267, ⓦcitcochandigarh.com), is in the same office. Himachal Pradesh's office (Mon–Sat 10am–6pm; ⓣ0172/270 3839), next door to the tourist office, is useful for booking HP Tourist Development Corporation tours and buses to HP destinations such as Manali and Shimla. Punjab Tourism has an office at 3 Sector 38-A (ⓣ0172/269 9140); Haryana Tourism's office is at 17–19 Sector 17-B (ⓣ0172/270 2955).

City transport

Chandigarh is too spread out to explore on foot, but cycle and auto-**rickshaws** cruise the streets. Cycle rickshaws are cheaper, but the drivers find the long haul up to the north end of town or to the railway station tough going, so allow plenty of time. The main **taxi** stand (ⓣ0172/270 4621; 24hr) is next to the ISBT's pre-paid auto-rickshaw booth. CITCO at the ISBT can also arrange half- or full-day excursions in and around town, and also offers **half-day tours** (Rs50) in an open-top tourist bus, visiting the museum and art gallery and the Rock Garden; if there are twenty or more takers, they also offer a full-day tour (Rs75) taking in the Capital Complex as well.

Accommodation

Chandigarh's sky-high property prices make its **accommodation** expensive, especially at the bottom end where choice is very limited.

Aroma Himalaya Marg, Sector 22-C ⓣ0172/270 0047 or 8, ⓦwww.hotelaroma.com. A vintage Austin guards the doorway of this attractive-looking hotel, which has a range of bars and restaurants. The rooms themselves are disappointing though, with laminated floors and scuffed walls, but it's a reasonable fall-back if the *Sunbeam*'s full. Breakfast included. ❻

Divyadeep Himalaya Marg, 1090–1 Sector 22-B ⓣ0172/270 1169. Pleasant budget hotel run by Sai Baba devotees. The rooms are decent enough, with a/c and hot running water, and there's a large rooftop area, though liquor is banned. If it's full, try the neighbouring (and identically priced) *Satyadeep*, 1102–03 Sector 22-B (ⓣ0172/270 3103), run by the same management. ❹

Panchayat Bhawan Madhya Marg, Sector 18 ⓣ0172/270 0791 or 2, ⓔpbhutchd@yahoo.co.in. The cheapest place to stay in town, hostel-like but well-kept, with large, clean rooms, some of them with a/c. ❶–❸

Pankaj Udyog Path, Sector 22-A ⓣ0172/270 9891, ⓦchandigarh-hotelpankaj.com. Squeaky-clean a/c rooms and fancy showers but of the "regular" rooms, only those on the top floor have outside windows; bigger and better "deluxe" and "super deluxe" rooms all have windows and a seating area. ❹–❻

Hotel Piccadily Himalaya Marg, Sector 22-B ⓣ0172/270 7571 or 2, ⓦwww.thepiccadily.com. Rather plush establishment with thickly carpeted corridors and rooms, central a/c, classy restaurant, bar and coffee shop. Breakfast included. ❼–❾

Sunbeam Udyog Path, Sector 22-B ⓣ0172/270 8100 to 07, ⓦwww.hotelsunbeam.com. Upmarket hotel opposite the ISBT with swish marble lobby and comfortable rooms, though the decorative brickwork in front of the windows makes them a bit dark. ❻

Taj Chandigarh Block 9, Sector 17-A ⓣ0172/661 3000, ⓦwww.tajhotels.com. Chandigarh's poshest option by a long chalk, in a well-designed building whose minimalist modern decor in cool, light colours makes it something like an elegant, beautiful version of one of Le Corbusier's concrete boxes. Doubles start at $233.❾

Transit Lodge ISBT, Sector 17 ⓣ0172/464 4485. Cheap and cheerful, slap bang in the middle of the bus station, and institutional but clean with attached rooms and hot water; also has dorm accommodation (Rs200). Rates include breakfast and dinner. ❸

The City

Chandigarh's numbered **sectors** are further subdivided into lettered blocks, making route-finding relatively easy. Le Corbusier saw the city plan as a living organism, with the imposing **Capital Complex** to the north as a "head", the shopping precinct, **Sector 17**, a "heart", the green open spaces as "lungs", and the crosscutting network of roads, separated into eight different grades for use by various types of vehicles (in theory only), a "circulatory system".

The museums

Situated in the green belt known as the Leisure Valley, Chandigarh's museums, located in Sector 10, form part of a cultural complex that includes the neighbouring Rose Garden and open-air theatre, where free concerts are occasionally staged. A Rs10 ticket covers the three museums, with a Rs5 camera charge for each. The **Government Museum & Art Gallery** (Tues–Sun 10am–4.30pm) houses a sizeable and informatively displayed collection of textiles, Harappan artefacts, miniature paintings and contemporary Indian art, including five original Roerichs and a couple of A.N. Tagore's atmospheric watercolours. The ancient sculptures are the compelling exhibits, notably the Gandhara Buddhas with their delicately carved "wet-look" *lunghis* and distinctly Hellenic features – a legacy of Alexander the Great's conquests.

station and then 300m south of Railway Road on Dhangu Road (Ⓣ0186/222 5061, Ⓦwww.venicehotelindia.com; ❹–❺), is Pathankot's top business hotel, but lacks atmosphere.

Himachal Pradesh Tourism has a downbeat but friendly office at the railway station (in principle Aug–March Mon–Sat 10am–6pm, April–July daily 7am–8pm, but often closed for no apparent reason; Ⓣ0186/222 0316). The slow passenger **trains** to Jogindernagar (daily 2.40am & 9.50pm; 8hr 35min–9hr 50min; plus four trains to Baijnath only) wind through the scenic Kangra Valley and make a pleasant alternative to the busy road to both Dharamsala (change at Kangra) and the Kullu Valley (bus from Joginder Nagar). Pathankot's **bus station**, on Railway Road, 300m west of the rail station, has services to Amritsar (every 10min; 3hr), Chandigarh (44 daily; 6hr), Dharamsala (15 daily; 4hr), Jammu (every 15–30min; 3hr), Manali (8 daily; 12hr) and Shimla (6 daily; 12 hr).

Amritsar

The Sikhs' holy city of **AMRITSAR** is the largest city in Punjab: noisy, dirty and hopelessly congested. Its one saving grace is the fabled **Golden Temple**, whose domes soar above the teeming streets. Amritsar is also an important staging-post for those crossing the Indo–Pakistan frontier at Wagha, 29km west (see box, p.530).

Some history

Amritsar was founded in 1577 by **Ram Das**, the fourth Sikh guru, beside a bathing pool famed for its healing powers. The land around the tank was granted in perpetuity by the Mughal emperor Akbar to the Sikhs. When merchants moved in to take advantage of the strategic location on the Silk Route, Amritsar expanded rapidly, gaining a grand new temple under Ram Das's son and heir, **Guru Arjan Dev**. Sacked by Afghans in 1761, the shrine was rebuilt by the Sikhs' greatest secular leader, **Maharaja Ranjit Singh**, who also donated the gold used in its construction.

Amritsar's **twentieth-century** history has been blighted by a series of appalling **massacres**. The first occurred in 1919, when thousands of unarmed civilian demonstrators were gunned down without warning by British troops in **Jallianwalla Bagh** (see p.534) – an atrocity that inspired Gandhi's Non-Co-operation Movement. Following the collapse of the Raj, Amritsar experienced some of the worst communal blood-letting ever seen on the Subcontinent. The Golden Temple, however, remained unaffected by the volatile politics of post-Independence Punjab until the 1980s, when as part of a protracted and bloody campaign for the setting up of a Sikh homeland, heavily armed fundamentalists under the preacher-warrior Sant Jarnail Singh **Bhindranwale** occupied the Akal Takht, a building in the Golden Temple complex that has traditionally been the seat of Sikh religious authority. The siege was brought to an end in early June 1984, when Prime Minister Indira Gandhi ordered an inept paramilitary attack on the temple, code-named **Operation Blue Star**. Bhindranwale was killed along with two hundred soldiers and two thousand others, including pilgrims trapped inside.

Widely regarded as an unmitigated disaster, Blue Star led directly to the assassination of Indira Gandhi by her Sikh bodyguards just four months later, and provoked the worst riots in the city since Partition. Nevertheless, the Congress government seemed to learn little from its mistakes. In 1987, Indira

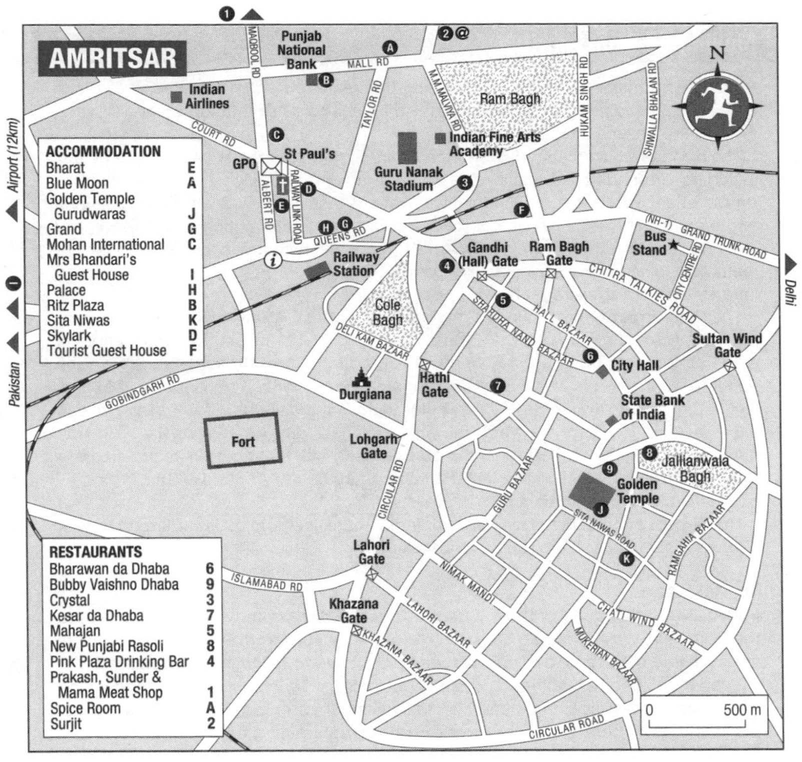

Gandhi's son, Rajiv Gandhi, reneged on an important accord with the Sikhs' main religious party, the Akali Dal, thereby strengthening the hand of the separatists, who retaliated by occupying the temple for a second time. This time, the army responded with greater restraint, leaving **Operation Black Thunder** to the Punjab police. Neither as well provisioned nor as well motivated as Bhindranwale's martyrs, the fundamentalists eventually surrendered.

Arrival, information and city transport

Amritsar's **airport** is 12km northwest of the city; taxis (around Rs300) and auto-rickshaws (Rs150) run to the town centre. The **railway station** is conveniently located in the centre of town, north of the old city. The large, new **bus stand** is off Grand Trunk Road (NH-1) on the eastern edge of the city centre. PTDC's **tourist office** (Mon–Sat 9am–5pm; ⊕0183/240 2452), at the western exit from the railway station on Queens Road, is friendly and helpful, and the *Grand Hotel* is also usually helpful with information.

You may find Amritsar too large and labyrinthine to negotiate on foot; if you're crossing town or are in a hurry, flag down an **auto-rickshaw**. Otherwise, stick to **cycle rickshaws**, which are the best way to get around the narrow, packed streets of the old quarter.

Moving on from Amritsar

Amritsar is a major hub for traffic heading northeast to Kashmir, southeast towards Delhi and Chandigarh (the main jumping-off place for Shimla and central HP), and west to the Pakistani border at Wagha.

The **bus stand** is on Grand Trunk Road (NH-1), north of the old city. Private buses, including air-conditioned services, leave from around the railway station or outside on the street, just north of Gandhi (Hall) Gate. Agencies outside Gandhi (Hall) Gate and on Queens Road operate deluxe and a/c buses to **Delhi** (8hr) and **Chandigarh** (4–5hr). For **Pathankot** (every 10min; 3hr) and other connections to HP, you are restricted to state transport buses. Delhi, 475km away, is a long and tiring road journey – most travellers prefer to go by train.

The best **trains** for Delhi are the daily superfast all-air-conditioned chaircar *Amritsar–New Delhi Shatabdis* – the #2014 (dep. 5.10am, arr. 11.15am) and the #2030/2032 (dep. 5pm, arr. 11.05pm). If you prefer to travel overnight, there's the #2904 *Golden Temple Mail* (dep. 9.25pm, arr. 6.55am), which continues to Mumbai (arr. 5.40am the following day). Other trains include the daily #3050 *Amritsar–Howrah Express* (dep. 6.15pm) via Varanasi (arr. 7pm next day) to Kolkata (arr. Howrah 3.45pm the day after that), and the twice-weekly #9782 *Amritsar–Jaipur Express* (Tues & Thurs 6pm), which is a little bit faster than the #9772 (Wed & Sun 2.30pm) – both arrive in Jaipur at 8.20am.

The **airport** (for flights to Delhi with Air India, Kingfisher and Jet) is 12km northwest of town (Rs300 by taxi, Rs150 by auto-rickshaw).

To Pakistan

For **Pakistan**, take one of the frequent buses to **Attari**, from where it's just 2km to the border at **Wagha** (see p.535), or hire a taxi or auto from Amritsar. Rickshaws are available between Attari and Wagha. You'll have to cross into Pakistan by foot – it can take up to two hours to complete formalities. Tourists just wishing to watch the bizarre border spectacle can rent taxis (Rs400) or auto-rickshaws (Rs200) for the round trip. There is a **cross-border train** to Lahore in the Pakistani part of the Punjab, but its operation depends on the political situation, and at present it may only be boarded in Delhi, not in Amritsar.

Accommodation

Amritsar's numerous **hotels** are spread out all over the city. While mid-range and upmarket accommodation is plentiful, budget options are limited; one solution is to stay in one of the Golden Temple's *niwas* (see box opposite).

Bharat Off Railway Link Rd ⓣ0183/222 7536, ⓔbharat_hotel@yahoo.com. Decent enough and handy for the station, offering a range of rooms of varying size, all with attached bathrooms (the best ones with hot showers; bucket hot water in the cheapest). Ignore demands for spurious extra "taxes" when you check out. ❷–❸

Blue Moon Mall Rd ⓣ0183/222 0759, ⓔhotelbluemoon@gmail.com. Friendly, helpful place, much better value than its more expensive competitors. There's a decent restaurant (see p.535) open to nonresidents. ❺–❻

Grand Queens Rd, opposite the railway station ⓣ0183/256 2977, ⓦwww.hotelgrand.in. Neat, clean, convenient and central with rooms around a pleasant garden courtyard, though windows all face inward. There's an adjacent bar decorated with Hollywood movie posters. The friendly manager can organize a shared taxi to Wagha for the border ceremony. ❺–❻

Mohan International Albert Rd ⓣ0183/222 7801, ⓦwww.mohaninternationalhotel.com. One of Amritsar's top hotels but overpriced, though it does have a/c, room service, a 24hr coffee shop and a pool. Popular in season (Nov–March) for Punjabi wedding receptions which are colourful but noisy. Rates include breakfast. ❼–❽

Mrs Bhandari's Guest House 10 Cantonment ⓣ0183/222 8509, ⓦbhandari_guesthouse.tripod.com. Wonderful old-fashioned rooms with wood fires and bathtubs in a colonial home with lawns, gardens and a small swimming pool. "British-style" three-course meals are available but pricey. You can camp in the grounds for Rs170/person. Popular with those taking overland package tours, it's become an Amritsar institution. ❺

Palace Opposite the railway station, Queens Rd ⓣ0183/256 5111. This place has seen better days, but it's conveniently located and reasonably priced. Rooms are attached, with piped hot water in the pricier ones and bucket hot water in the cheaper ones. ❶–❷

Ritz Plaza 45 Mall Rd ⓣ0183/256 2836, ⓦwww.ritzhotel.in. Low-key but reasonably classy establishment, though it gets mixed reviews, with central a/c, good-sized rooms and a relaxed atmosphere, surrounded by lawns; facilities include a pool, lounge bar, 24hr coffee shop and international restaurant. Wheelchair friendly with an adapted room. ❽

Sita Niwas 61 Sita Niwas Rd ⓣ0183/254 3092, ⓕ254 1898. A good-value and popular budget option near *Guru Ram Das Niwas* and the Golden Temple, with a wide range of rooms, most attached, though the very cheapest ones lack hot water. ❷

Skylark 79 Railway Link Rd ⓣ0183/265 2053. One of the better hotels on this street opposite the station; the rooms, if slightly shabby, are huge, with comfortable beds and hot water round the clock (except during power cuts). ❷–❹

Tourist Guest House Hide Market, near Bhandari Bridge, Grand Trunk Rd ⓣ0183/255 3830, ⓔbubblesgoolry@yahoo.com. Popular with budget travellers since hippy trail days, offering a variety of rooms. The cheapest are rather dingy with shared bathrooms; attached ones with hot water are quite nice and still not pricey. Ignore commission-hungry rickshaw-wallahs telling you it's full. ❶–❷

The City

The Golden Temple stands in the heart of the **old town**, itself a maze of narrow lanes and bazaars. Eighteen fortified **gateways** punctuate the aptly named **Circular Road**, of which only Lohgarh Gate (to the north) is original. Skirting the edge of the old quarter, the railway line forms a sharp divide between the bazaar and the more spacious British-built side of the city. Further north, long straight tree-lined streets eventually peter out into leafy residential suburbs. The neat military barracks of the **cantonment** form the northwestern limits of the city.

The Golden Temple

Even visitors without a religious bone in their bodies cannot fail to be moved by Amritsar's resplendent **Golden Temple**, spiritual centre of the Sikh faith and open to all. Built by **Guru Arjan Dev** in the late sixteenth century, the richly gilded **Harmandir** rises from the middle of an artificial rectangular lake, connected to the surrounding white-marble complex by a narrow causeway. Every Sikh tries to

Staying at the Golden Temple Complex

Undoubtedly the most authentic places to stay in Amritsar are the five **Niwas** or pilgrim hostels run by the Golden Temple management committee. Intended for Sikh pilgrims, these charitable institutions also open their doors to foreign tourists. Charges are nominal but stays are limited to a maximum of three nights.

The first building as you approach on the east side of the temple,is the *Guru Arjan Dev Niwas*, which has the check-in counter for all the *niwas* and simple, spacious rooms. The most comfortable of the five, is the new, excellent-value *Guru Hargobind Niwas*. The *Sri Guru Nanak Niwas* was where Bhindranwale and his men holed up prior to the Golden Temple siege in 1984.

Apart from the inevitable dawn chorus of throat-clearing, the downside of staying at these *niwas* is that facilities can be basic (*charpoy* beds and communal wash-basins in the central courtyard are the norm) and **security** can be a problem. It is advisable to book in advance as rooms and beds are almost always at a premium.

Golden rules

Visitors of all nationalities and religions are allowed into the Golden Temple provided they respect a few basic **rules**, enforced by patrolling guards. Firstly, tobacco, alcohol and drugs of any kind are forbidden. Before entering, you should also leave your shoes at the free cloakrooms, cover your head (cotton scarves are available outside the main entrance – or wear your Kullu hat) and wash your feet in the pool below the steps. **Photography** is permitted around the pool, but not inside any of the shrines.

make at least one pilgrimage here during their lifetime to listen to the sublime music (*shabad kirtan*), readings from the Adi Granth and also to bathe in the purifying waters of the temple tank – the **Amrit Sarovar** or "Pool of Immortality-Giving Nectar".

The best time to visit is early morning, to catch the first rays of sunlight gleaming on the bulbous golden domes and reflecting in the waters of the Amrit Sarovar. Sunset and evenings are an excellent time to tune in to the beautiful music performed in the Harmandir. The helpful information office (daily 7am–8pm) to the right of the main entrance organizes **guided tours**, provides details on temple accommodation and has books and leaflets about the temple and Sikh faith.

The Parikrama

The principal north entrance to the temple, the **Darshini Deori**, leads under a Victorian **clocktower** to a flight of steps, from where you catch your first glimpse of the Harmandir, floating serenely above the glassy surface of the Amrit Sarovar. Dropping down as a reminder of the humility necessary to approach God, the steps end at the polished marble **Parikrama** that surrounds the tank, its smooth white stones set with the names of those who contributed to the temple's construction.

The shrines on the north edge of the enclosure are known as the **68 Holy Places**. Arjan Dev, the fifth guru, told his followers that a visit to these was equivalent to a pilgrimage around all 68 of India's most sacred Hindu sites. Several have been converted into a **Gallery of Martyrs**, in which paintings of glorious but gory episodes from Sikh history are displayed.

Four glass-fronted booths punctuate the Parikrama. Seated in each is a priest, or **granthi**, intoning verses from the Adi Granth (Sikh scriptures). The continuous readings are performed in shifts; passing pilgrims touch the steps in front of the booths with their heads and leave offerings of money.

At the east end of the Parikrama, the two truncated **Ramgarhia Minars** – brick watchtowers whose tops were blasted off during Operation Blue Star – overlook the Guru-ka-Langar (see below) and the main bathing **ghats**. Hang around here long enough and you'll see a fair cross-section of modern Sikh society parade past: families of Jat farmers, NRIs (Non-Resident Indians) on holiday from Britain and North America and the odd group of fierce-looking warriors carrying lances, sabres and long curved daggers. Distinguished by their deep-blue knee-length robes and saffron turbans, the ultra-orthodox **nihangs** (literally "crocodiles") are devotees of the militaristic tenth guru, Gobind Singh.

The Guru-ka-Langar

For Sikhs, no pilgrimage to the Golden Temple is considered complete without a visit to the **Guru-ka-Langar**. The giant communal canteen, which overlooks the eastern entrance to the temple complex, provides **free food** to all comers. Sharing meals with strangers reinforces one of the central tenets of the Sikh faith, the

principle of equality, instigated by the third guru, **Amar Das**, in the sixteenth century to break down caste barriers.

Some ten thousand chapatti and black dhal dinners are dished up here each day in an operation of typical Sikh efficiency, which you can witness for yourself by joining the queues that form outside the hall (open 24hr). The meal begins after grace has been sung by a volunteer, or *sevak*, and continues until everyone has eaten their fill. By the time the tin trays have been collected up and the floors swept for the next sitting, another crowd of pilgrims has gathered at the gates, and the cycle starts again. Although the meals are paid for out of the temple's coffers, most visitors leave a small donation in the boxes in the yard outside.

The Akal Takht

Directly opposite the ceremonial entrance to the Harmandir, the **Akal Takht** is the second most sacred shrine in the Golden Temple complex. A symbol of God's authority on earth, it was built by Guru Hargobind in the seventeenth century and came to house the Shiromani Gurudwara Parbandhak Committee, the religious and political governing body of the Sikh faith founded in 1925.

During the 1984 siege, **Bhindranwale** and his army used this golden-domed building as their headquarters, fortifying it with sandbags and machine-gun posts. When Indian paratroopers tried to storm the shrine, they were mown down in their hundreds while crossing the courtyard in front of it: the reason why the army ultimately resorted to much heavier-handed tactics to end the siege. Positioned at the opposite end of the Amrit Sarovar, tanks pumped a salvo of high-explosive squash-head shells into the delicate facade, reducing it to rubble within seconds. The destruction of the Akal Takht offended Sikh sensibilities more than any other aspect of the operation. The shrine has been largely rebuilt and now looks almost the same as it did before June 6, 1984. Decorated with elaborate inlay, its ground floor is where the Adi Granth is brought each evening from the Harmandir, borne in a gold and silver palanquin.

The Jubi Tree

The gnarled old **Jubi Tree** in the northwest corner of the compound was planted around 450 years ago by the Golden Temple's first high priest, or Babba Buddhaya, and is believed to have special powers. Women wanting a son hang strips of cloth from its branches, while marriage deals are traditionally struck in its shade for good luck – a practice the modern temple administration frowns upon.

The Harmandir

Likened by one guru to "a ship crossing the ocean of ignorance", the triple-storey **Harmandir**, or "Golden Temple of God" was built by Arjan Dev to house the Adi Granth, which he compiled from teachings of all the Sikh gurus; it is the focus of the Sikh faith. The temple has four doors indicating it is open to people of all faiths and all four caste divisions of Hindu society. The large dome and roof, covered with 100kg of gold leaf, is shaped like an inverted lotus, symbolizing the Sikhs' concern for temporal as well as spiritual matters.

The long causeway, or **Guru's Bridge**, which joins the Harmandir to the west side of the Amrit Sarovar, is approached via an ornate archway, the **Darshani Deorh.** As you approach the sanctum check out the amazing Mughal-style inlay work and floral gilt above the doors and windows.

The **interior** of the temple – decorated with yet more gold and silver, adorned with ivory mosaics and intricately carved wood panels – is dominated by the enormous **Adi Granth**, which rests on a sumptuous throne beneath a jewel-encrusted silk canopy. Before his death in 1708, Guru Gobind Singh, who revised the Adi

The Jallianwalla Bagh massacre

Only 100m northeast of the Golden Temple, a narrow lane leads between two tall buildings to **Jallianwalla Bagh** memorial park (daily: summer 6am–9pm; winter 7am–8pm), site of one of the bloodiest atrocities committed by the British Raj.

In 1919, a series of one-day strikes, or *hartals*, was staged in Amritsar in protest against the recent **Rowlatt Act**, which enabled the British to imprison without trial any Indian suspected of sedition. When the peaceful demonstrations escalated into sporadic looting, the lieutenant governor of Punjab declared martial law and called for reinforcements from Jalandhar. A platoon of infantry arrived soon after, led by **General R.E.H. Dyer**.

Despite a ban on public meetings, a mass demonstration was called by Mahatma Gandhi for April 13, the Sikh holiday of Baisakhi. The venue was a stretch of waste ground in the heart of the city, hemmed in by high brick walls and with only a couple of alleys for access. An estimated twenty thousand people gathered in Jallianwalla Bagh for the meeting. However, before any speakers could address the crowd, Dyer and his 150 troops, stationed on a patch of high ground in front of the main exit, opened fire without warning. By the time they had finished firing, ten to fifteen minutes later, hundreds of unarmed demonstrators lay dead and dying, many of them shot in the back while clambering over the walls. Others perished after diving for cover into the well that still stands in the middle of the *bagh*.

No one knows exactly how many people were killed. Official estimates put the death toll at 379, with 1200 injured, although the final figure may well have been several times higher; Indian sources quote a figure of two thousand dead. Hushed up for over six months in Britain, the Jallianwalla Bagh massacre caused an international outcry when the story finally broke. It also proved seminal in the Independence struggle, prompting Gandhi to initiate the widespread civil disobedience campaign that played such a significant part in ridding India of its colonial overlords.

Moving first-hand accounts of the horrific events of April 13, 1919, and contemporary pictures and newspaper reports are displayed in Jallianwalla Bagh's small **martyrs gallery**. The **well**, complete with chilling bullet holes, has been turned into a memorial to the victims.

Granth, declared that he was to be the last living guru, and that the tome would take over after him – hence its full title, the Guru Granth Sahib. *Granthis* intone continuous readings from the text as the worshippers file past, accompanied by singers and musicians – all relayed by loudspeakers around the complex. Known as Shri Akhand Path, a single continuous reading of the Guru Granth Sahib is carried out in three-hour shifts and takes around 48 hours to complete.

Eating

For cheaper food, try the simple vegetarian **dhabas** around the Golden Temple and bus stand, which serve cheap and tasty *puris* and *chana* dhal. Local specialities include **Amritsari fish** (fillets of river fish – sole is the best, but *singara* is cheaper – fried in a spicy batter), as well as *dal pinni* and *matthi*, sweets made from lentils that are sold at places such as *Mahajan* on Hall Bazaar.

Bharawan da Dhaba Near the City Hall. One of the best *dhabas* in Amritsar, though it's now grown into a full-sized restaurant, serving simple and inexpensive but good veg curries (Rs40–85).

Bubby Vaishno Dhaba 201 Gantagar Market (opposite the Golden Temple main entrance). A handy place for veg curries (Rs40–80), thalis (Rs50–80) and breakfast options such as *parathas* or *puris*, plus a few south Indian dishes for good measure.

Crystal Crystal Chowk. One of the city's most popular restaurants, with Indian, Chinese and Western dishes (non-veg mains Rs200–240) served in comfortable surroundings, or from "fast-food" outlets on the street.

Kesar da Dhaba Passian Chowk, between Golden Temple and Durgiana Temple. A limited menu of basic veg curries (Rs30–80) in an establishment that's been going since 1916, but is well hidden away in the back streets (you'll need to ask for directions, or get a rickshaw to bring you).

New Punjabi Rasoli By Jallianwalla Bagh. Indian veg dishes, plus some Chinese and continental, at reasonable prices (Rs65–100). Most of the Indian dishes involve *paneer* (the *paneer* tomato is good), but there's also a delicious mushroom tikka masala.

Pink Plaza Drinking Bar 1 Pink Plaza Market, outside Gandhi (Hall) Gate. A grubby and insalubrious-looking *dhaba*, but they cook all the food out front. The Amritsari fish (Rs250/kg) is succulent and the tandoori chicken's pretty good too (Rs60/portion). Despite the name, you have to buy your booze at the liquor store opposite, and bring it here to drink.

Prakash Meat Shop, **Sunder Meat Shop** and **Mama Meat Shop** Maqbool Rd, 500m north of Mall Rd. This trio of locally renowned *dhabas* are an Amritsar institution, frying up spicy mutton tikka or (for the brave) brain curry, on *tawas* (griddles) out front, at Rs100 a throw.

Spice Room *Blue Moon Hotel*, Mall Rd. Mainly Chinese dishes, with the accent on spicy, plus some Indian and Western options. Main dishes go for Rs195–295.

Surjit GT 3–4 Nehru Plaza, Lawrence Rd. Excellent Punjabi dishes at this bright new restaurant (formerly a *dhaba* across the street), including cream chicken, butter chicken and Amritsari fish, with non-veg mains at Rs150–300.

Listings

Airlines Air India, *MK International Hotel*, Ranjit Ave ⓣ0183/250 8122 or 33; Indian Airlines, 39-A Court Rd ⓣ0183/221 3392 or 3; Jet, airport ⓣ0183/250 8003.

Banks and exchange There are ATMs across town, including five in the train station forecourt, one at the bus station and several around Jallianwalla Bagh. There's a clutch of forex bureaux opposite the train station on Railway Link Rd, many of which will change Pakistani rupees.

Hospitals The best in the city are Kakkar Hospital, Green Avenue ⓣ0183/250 6015, and Munilal Chopra Hospital, 361 Mall Rd ⓣ0183/222 2072.

Internet A couple of places in Nehru Plaza, Lawrence Rd, including Cyber World at GF 55 (Rs20/hr).

Left luggage Baggage can be left for short periods at the Golden Temple's *gurudwaras*, or at the railway station or bus stand cloakroom.

Shopping Tablas (hand-drums), harmonia and other musical instruments are available at the shops outside the Golden Temple, where you can also buy cheap cassettes and CDs of the beautiful *kirtan* played in the shrine itself. Other possible souvenirs include a pair of traditional *Arabian Nights*-style Punjabi leather slippers, sold at stalls east of the temple's main entrance.

Swimming pools The *Mohan International* and *Ritz Plaza* hotels allow nonresidents discretionary use of their pools (Rs110–300).

Bedlam at the border

Every evening as sunset approaches, the **India-Pakistan border** closes for the night with a spectacular and somewhat Monty Pythonesque show. It takes place at a remote little place 27km west of Amritsar called **Wagha** (the nearest town, 2km away, is Attari), connected by frequent minibuses to Amritsar. Hundreds, if not thousands, of Indians make their way westwards to Wagha (and Pakistanis eastwards) to watch the popular tourist attraction from specially erected stands.

Indian guards sporting outrageous moustaches and outlandish hats perform synchronized speed marching along a 100-metre walkway to the border gate where they turn and stomp back. Raucous cheering, clapping and much blowing of horns accompanies the spectacle. Guards on the Pakistan side then emulate their neighbours' efforts to much the same sort of cacophony on the other side of the gate. The guards strut their military catwalk several times and then vanish into the guardhouse. Flags are simultaneously lowered, the gates slammed shut and the crowds on either side rush forward for a massive and congenial photo session. On both sides, more empathy than ever occurs on a cricket pitch permeates the air; photos are taken with the stone-faced guards and then everyone heads home – back to business as usual.

9

Gujarat

* **Ahmedabad** Superb Indo-Islamic architecture, bustling bazaars and Mahatma Gandhi's Sabarmati Ashram. **See p.542**

* **Sun temple, Modhera** A beautiful eleventh-century temple, set in peaceful gardens: the finest example of Solanki architecture. **See p.552**

* **Kutch** Distinct from the rest of Gujarat; traditional embroidery, costume and culture still thrive in this harsh and remote landscape. **See p.554**

* **Dwarka** India's westernmost holy town, this important pilgrimage centre was famed in legend as Krishna's capital. **See p.565**

* **Gir National Park** This reserve is the last remaining habitat of the rare Asiatic lion. **See p.573**

* **Diu** West India's most congenial beach venue, this relaxed island has a Portuguese flavour in its colonial architecture. **See p.574**

* **Palitana temples** Shatrunjaya Hill bristles with sumptuously carved marble shrines and stunning views. **See p.581**

* **Champaner** A Solanki fortress and Jain temples are among the attractions around this ancient Muslim city. **See p.585**

▲ Embroidery workers, Kutch

Heated in the north by the blistering deserts of Pakistan and Rajasthan, and cooled in the south by the gentle ocean breeze of the Arabian Sea, **GUJARAT** forms India's westernmost bulkhead. The diversity of its topography – forested hilly tracts and fertile plains in the east, vast tidal marshland and desert plains in the Rann of Kutch in the west, with a rocky shoreline jutting into its heartland – is challenged only by the multiplicity of its politics and culture. Home to significant populations of Hindus, Jains, Muslims and Christians, as well as tribal and nomadic groups, the state boasts a patchwork of religious shrines and areas steeped in Hindu lore. Gujarat is the homeland of **Mahatma Gandhi**, who was born in Porbandar and worked for many years in Ahmedabad. Having long lived by his credo of self-dependence, Gujaratis are consistently at or near the top of the chart in terms of India's economic output, and have also fanned around the world to settle abroad. The region's **prosperity** dates as far back as the third millennium BC, when the Harappans started trading shell jewellery and textiles, with the latter Jain-dominated industry remaining an important source of income to the state. India's most industrialized state, Gujarat also boasts some of the Subcontinent's biggest oil refineries; thriving cement, chemicals and pharmaceutical manufacturing units; and a lucrative ship-breaking yard at Alang. Kandla is one of west India's **largest ports**, while much of the country's diamond cutting and polishing takes place in Surat, Ahmedabad and Bhavnagar. Rural poverty remains a serious problem, however, and health and education developments have not kept pace with economic growth.

Gandhi's primary mission – to instigate political change through nonviolent means – has not always been adhered to in Gujarat, and Muslim-Hindu tensions have boiled over to violence on a cyclical basis. In 2002, the state suffered India's worst **communal rioting** since Partition, with around two thousand people killed. The fighting came on the heels of the devastating January 2001 **earthquake**, centred in Kutch. These events added to the woes of a state already beleaguered by severe **water shortages** and **drought**.

Nevertheless, Gujarat has plenty to offer those who take time to detour from its more famous northerly neighbour Rajasthan, and it's free of the hassle tourists often encounter there. The lure of important **temple cities**, **forts** and **palaces** is balanced by the chance to search out unique **crafts** made in communities whose way of life remains scarcely affected by global trends. Gujarat's **architectural diversity** reflects the influences of its many different rulers – Buddhist Mauryans, Hindu rajas and Muslim emperors.

Ahmedabad, state capital until 1970 and the obvious place to begin a tour, harbours the first mosques built in the curious **Indo-Islamic** style, richly carved temples and step-wells dating from the eleventh century. Just north is the ancient capital of **Patan** and the Solanki sun temple at **Modhera**, while south is the Harappan site, **Lothal**. In the northwest, the largely barren region of **Kutch** was largely bypassed by Gujarat's foreign invaders, and consequently preserves a village culture where crafts long forgotten elsewhere are still practised.

The Kathiawar Peninsula, or **Saurashtra**, is Gujarat's heartland, scattered with temples, mosques and palaces that bear testimony to centuries of rule by Buddhists, Hindus and Muslims. Highlights include superb Jain temples on the hills of **Shatrunjaya**, near Bhavnagar, and **Mount Girnar**, close to Junagadh. The temple at **Somnath** is said to have witnessed the dawn of time, and that at **Dwarka** is built on the site of Krishna's ancient capital. At **Junagadh**, rocks bearing 2000-year-old Ashokan inscriptions stand a stone's throw from flamboyant mausoleums and Victorian Gothic-style palaces. There's plenty of scope for spotting **wildlife**, too, in particular the lions in **Gir National Park**, blackbucks at **Velavadar National Park**, and the Indian wild ass in the **Little Rann Sanctuary**. Separated from the

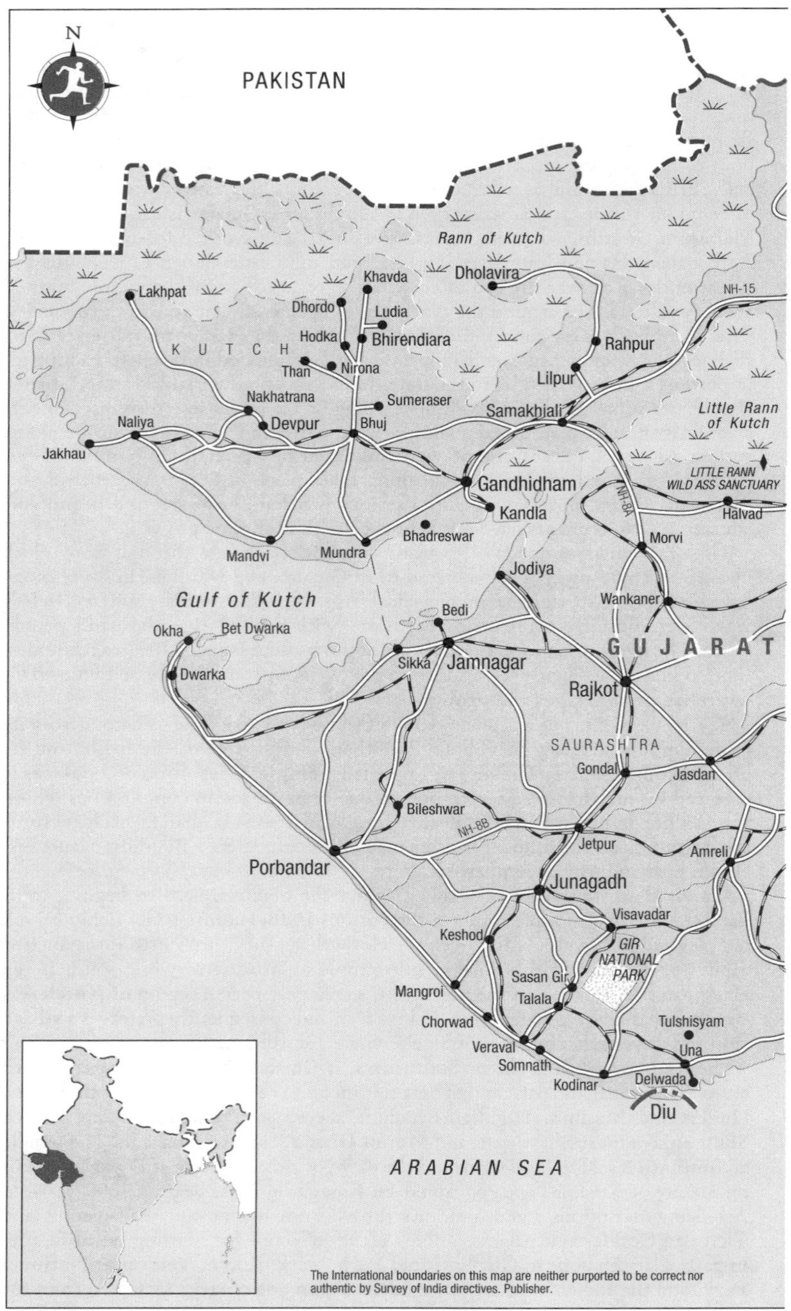
N
PAKISTAN
Rann of Kutch
Dholavira
Khavda
Lakhpat
Dhordo
Ludia
Hodka
Bhirendiara
K U T C H
Than
Nirona
Rahpur
Lilpur
Nakhatrana
Sumeraser
Samakhiali
NH-15
Little Rann of Kutch
Naliya
Devpur
Bhuj
Jakhau
Gandhidham
LITTLE RANN WILD ASS SANCTUARY
Kandla
NH-8A
Halvad
Bhadreswar
Morvi
Mandvi
Mundra
Jodiya
Gulf of Kutch
Wankaner
Bedi
Okha
Bet Dwarka
G U J A R A T
Sikka
Jamnagar
Dwarka
Rajkot
SAURASHTRA
Gondal
Jasdan
Bileshwar
NH-8B
Jetpur
Amreli
Porbandar
Junagadh
Visavadar
Keshod
GIR NATIONAL PARK
Sasan Gir
Mangroi
Talala
Tulshisyam
Chorwad
Veraval
Una
Somnath
Delwada
Kodinar
Diu
ARABIAN SEA
The International boundaries on this map are neither purported to be correct nor authentic by Survey of India directives. Publisher.

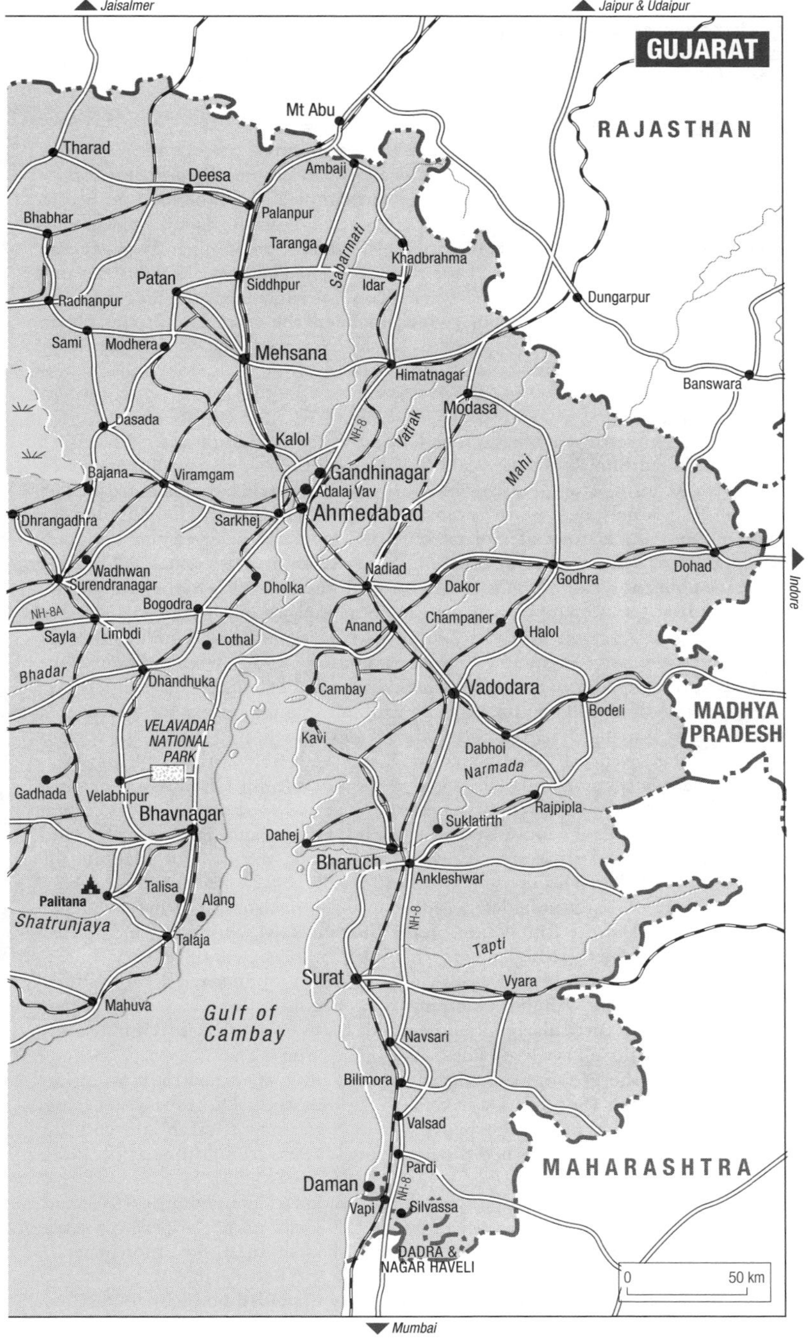

Jaisalmer
Jaipur & Udaipur
GUJARAT
RAJASTHAN
Mt Abu
Tharad
Ambaji
Deesa
Palanpur
Bhabhar
Taranga
Sabarmati
Khadbrahma
Patan
Siddhpur
Idar
Dungarpur
Radhanpur
Sami
Modhera
Mehsana
Himatnagar
Banswara
Modasa
Dasada
Vatrak
NH-8
Kalol
Mahi
Bajana
Viramgam
Gandhinagar
Adalaj Vav
Dhrangadhra
Sarkhej
Ahmedabad
Wadhwan
Surendranagar
Dholka
Nadiad
Dakor
Godhra
Dohad
Indore
NH-8A
Bogodra
Anand
Champaner
Sayla
Limbdi
Lothal
Halol
Bhadar
Dhandhuka
Cambay
Vadodara
Bodeli
VELAVADAR NATIONAL PARK
Kavi
MADHYA PRADESH
Dabhoi
Narmada
Gadhada
Velabhipur
Rajpipla
Bhavnagar
Suklatirth
Dahej
Bharuch
Ankleshwar
Talisa
Palitana
Alang
Shatrunjaya
NH-8
Talaja
Tapti
Surat
Vyara
Mahuva
Gulf of Cambay
Navsari
Bilimora
Valsad
Pardi
MAHARASHTRA
Daman
NH-8
Vapi
Silvassa
DADRA & NAGAR HAVELI
0
50 km
Mumbai

south coast by a thin sliver of the Arabian Sea, the island of **Diu**, a Union Territory and not officially part of the state, is fringed with beaches, palm groves and white-washed Portuguese churches.

Visiting Gujarat

Thanks to its well-surfaced roads and extensive train links, **travel** within the state presents few problems, though communication barriers require a little effort to overcome (few timetables are in English, for example). You'll be hard pushed to find a luxury **hotel** outside the big cities, but several local maharajas and nawabs have turned their homes into heritage hotels. **Food** is predominantly vegetarian with the region's thalis renowned for their size and sweetness. Gujarat is a **dry state**, but tourists can get free one-week alcohol permits from the bigger hotels. (Avoid illicitly produced alcohol, which claimed the lives of 136 people in Ahmedabad in July 2009.) Alcohol is legally served in the Union Territory enclaves of Daman and Diu.

Some history

The first known settlers in what is now Gujarat were the **Harappans**, who arrived from Sindh and Punjab around 2500 BC. Despite their craftsmanship and trade links with Africans, Arabs, Persians and Europeans, the civilization fell into decline in 1900 BC, largely because of severe flooding. From 1500 to 500 BC, little is known about the history of Gujarat but it is popularly believed the **Yadavas**, Krishna's clan, held sway over much of the state, with their capital at Dwarka. Gujarat's political history begins in earnest with the powerful **Mauryan** empire, established by Chandragupta with its capital at Junagadh and reaching its peak under Ashoka. After his death in 226 BC, Mauryan power dwindled; the last significant ruler was Samprati, Ashoka's grandson, a Jain who built fabulous temples at tirthas (pilgrimage sites) such as Girnar and Palitana.

During the first millennium AD, control of the region passed between a succession of warring dynasties and nomadic tribes, including the **Gurjars**, from whom the state eventually derived its name, and the Kathi warriors of Saurashtra. Gujarat eventually came under the sway of the **Solanki** (or **Chalukyan**) dynasty in the eleventh and twelfth centuries, a golden period in the state's architectural history as the rulers commissioned splendid Hindu and Jain **temples** and **step-wells**. Many of these structures suffered during the raids of Mahmud of Ghazni in 1027, but Muslim rule was not actually established until the Khalji conquest in 1299. Eight years later, Muzaffar Shah's declaration of independence from Delhi marked the foundation of the **Sultanate of Gujarat**, which lasted until its conquest by the Mughal emperor Akbar in the sixteenth century. In this period Muslim, Jain and Hindu styles were melded to produce remarkable **Indo-Islamic** mosques and tombs. Contrary to impressions encouraged by recent sectarian violence, particularly in Ahmedabad, Islam never eclipsed Hinduism or Jainism, and the three have lived side by side for centuries.

In the 1500s, the **Portuguese**, already settled in Goa, turned their attention to Gujarat. Having captured Daman in 1531, they took Diu four years later, building forts and typically European towns. Fending off Arab and Muslim attacks, the Portuguese governed the ports until they were subsumed into India in the 1960s.

The **British East India Company** set up its headquarters in Surat in 1613, and soon established their first factory, sowing the seeds of a prospering textile industry. When British sovereignty was established in 1818, governor-generals signed treaties with about two hundred princely and petty states of Saurashtra. Under British rule the introduction of machinery upgraded textile manufacture,

Godhra and Gujarat's communal violence

When the BJP shocked India with its landslide victory in the December 2002 election, analysts needed only to point to a single word to find an answer for the victory – **Godhra**. The town was an anonymous railway depot until February 27, 2002, when a Muslim mob set fire to railway cars filled with Hindu pilgrims returning from the controversial temple at Ayodhya, killing 59.

The incident sparked huge **riots** across Gujarat. Muslim neighbourhoods burned while sword- and stick-wielding Hindus rampaged, looted and raped. In many cases police forces allegedly stood by and watched. Officially, more than one thousand people died in the weeks following the Godhra incident, although human rights organizations estimate the real figure at more than two thousand, the vast majority Muslims, while thousands more moved to refugee camps, too frightened to go back to their own homes.

The violence was politicized after Congress accused the government of not doing enough to ensure the safety of Muslim citizens. Gujarat's BJP chief minister **Narendra Modi** earned the moniker "Muslim killer" for his passive attitude as the violence continued, and his lack of support for the survivors. Just days after NGO Human Rights Watch reported Gujarat state officials "were directly involved in the killings of hundreds of Muslims since February 27 and are now engineering a massive **cover-up** of the state's role in the violence", parliament attempted to censure the BJP government. Following a sixteen-hour debate Prime Minister Atal Bihari Vajpayee apologized for not having "tried harder" to end the riots and announced a $31 million rehabilitation package.

With the state elections approaching, Modi intensified his *Hindutva* rhetoric and campaign "to prevent" another Godhra, in a blatant attempt to haul in as many Hindu votes as possible amid a climate of ethnic tension. Yet it wasn't until the December 12 election that his cult status among ordinary Gujaratis was at last verified by his surprising landslide win.

The 2004 national elections, however, saw a turnaround, ushering in a Congress-led government. Though BJP retained the majority in Gujarat, the elections were closely contested. Following protests that the violence had been government-supported and that the authorities were biased, the Supreme Court ruled the cases of the violence-affected families be moved to courts in other states for their safety and ordered investigations into the riots. As yet, none of the investigations have been able to come to any firm conclusion regarding the train-burning at Godhra.

In October 2007, in the run-up to the state elections, respected magazine *Tehelka* published secretly-filmed footage of senior Gujarati Hindu politicians, mainly from the BJP, describing in graphic detail how they took part in and helped to orchestrate the riots. The report alleged Modi allowed the violence to continue unabated, ordered the police to side with Hindu rioters and sheltered the perpetrators from justice. Thus far no attempt has been made to investigate the claims at a judicial or political level, and Modi was resoundingly re-elected in December 2007. He was subsequently talked about as a possible candidate for Prime Minister, but at the time of writing his star appeared to be on the wane.

For a powerful account of the post-Godhra violence, read Dionne Bunsha's *Scarred: Experiments With Violence In Gujarat*.

which brought substantial wealth to the region but put many manual labourers out of business. Their cause was valiantly fought by Gujarat-born **Mahatma Gandhi** (see box, p.567). After Partition, Gujarat received an influx of Hindus from Sind and witnessed terrible sectarian fighting as Muslims fled to their new homeland.

In 1960, after the Marathi and Gujarati **language riots** (demonstrators sought the redrawing of state boundaries according to language, as had happened in the south), Bombay state was split and Gujarat created. The Portuguese enclaves were forcibly annexed by the Indian government in 1961. After Independence Gujarat was generally a staunch Congress stronghold, until the fundamentalists of the BJP took control in 1991. The communal violence of 2002 reopened an old chapter of history by pitting Muslim and Hindu neighbours against one another (see box, p.541). Nine years on, the communal tensions continue to cast a long shadow, with neighbourhoods often divided along religious lines and Muslims marginalized and discriminated against.

Ahmedabad

A tangled mass of factories, mosques, temples and skyscrapers, Gujarat's commercial hub, **AHMEDABAD** (or Amdavad), sprawls along the banks of the River Sabarmati, 90km from its mouth in the Bay of Cambay. The state's largest city, with a population of around five million, is appallingly polluted, renowned for its dreadful congestion and repeated outbreaks of communal violence. However, the mix of medieval and modern makes it a compelling place to explore.

A wander through the bazaars and pols (residential areas) of the bustling **old city** is rewarding, but Ahmedabad is also packed with diverse architectural styles, with over fifty **mosques** and **tombs**, plus Hindu and Jain **temples** and grand **step-wells** (*vavs*). The **Calico Museum of Textiles** is one of the world's finest, while Gandhi's **Sabarmati Ashram** is an essential stop for anyone with an interest in the Mahatma.

Particularly in the old city, it's advisable to cover your mouth and nose with a handkerchief to reduce inhalation of **carbon monoxide**. In 2002, a controversial **canal project** diverted water from the River Narmada into the Sabarmati, which previously had virtually dried up outside the monsoon. This has given the city a cooler feel, but Ahmedabad has a long way to go before it can breathe easily.

In mid-January the city plays host to the world's largest **kite festival**.

Some history

When **Ahmed Shah** inherited the Sultanate of Gujarat in 1411, he moved his capital from Patan to Asawal, a small settlement on the east bank of the Sabarmati, modestly renaming it after himself. The city quickly grew as artisans and traders were invited to settle, and its splendid mosques, intended to assert Muslim supremacy, heralded the new **Indo-Islamic** style of architecture.

In 1572, Ahmedabad became part of the Mughal Empire and was regarded as India's most handsome city. It profited from a flourishing **textiles trade**, but two devastating famines coupled with political instability led the city into **decline**. It wasn't until 1817, when the newly-arrived British lowered taxes, that the merchants returned. Trade in opium grew and the introduction of modern machinery re-established Ahmedabad as a textile exporter. In the run-up to Independence, while **Mahatma Gandhi** was revitalizing small-scale textile production, the "Manchester of the East" became an important seat of political power and a hotbed for religious tension. In recent years, **communal rioting** – in particular a series of ugly clashes between Hindus and Muslims – has darkened Ahmedabad's reputation.

Arrival, information and city transport

Ahmedabad's **international airport** (☎079/286 9266) is linked to the city, 10km south, by pre-paid taxi (Rs230–300), auto-rickshaw (around Rs150) and

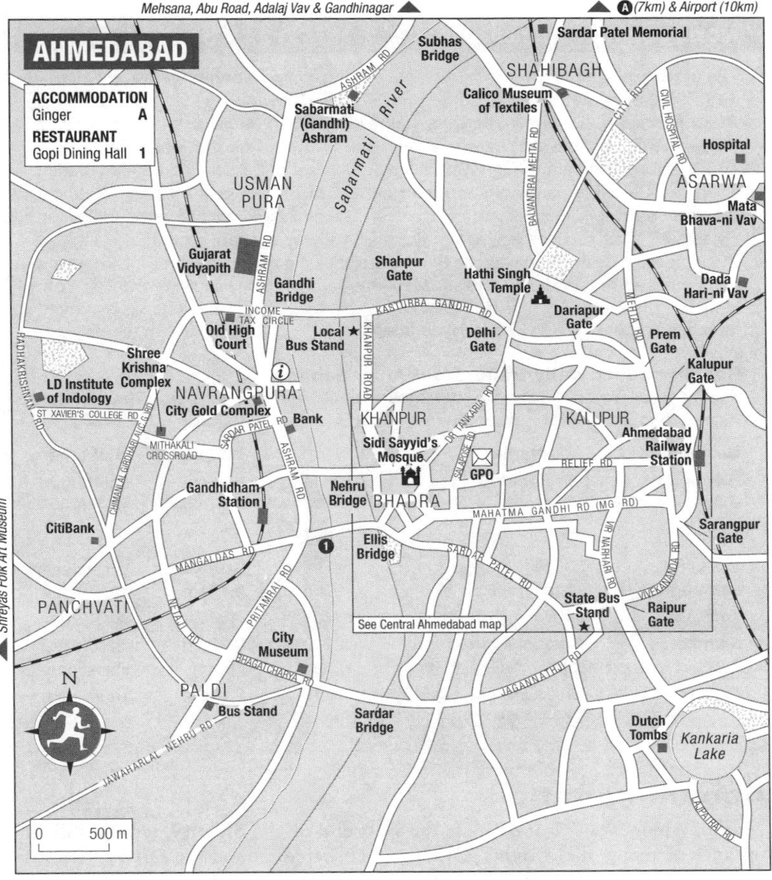

bus #105, which terminates at **Lal Darwaja**, the local bus station in the west of the old city. Long-distance buses arrive at the **state bus stand** in the southeast of the old city, while **Ahmedabad railway station** is to the east. Some trains also arrive at the **Gandhidham Station** in the west of the city. In October 2009, a **Bus Rapid Transit System** was introduced, which despite some early teething problems should make travelling around the city quicker and more comfortable. **Taxis** and **auto-rickshaws** are abundant. Although most of the attractions are on the east bank of the Sabarmati, the helpful **tourist office** is across the river in HK House, just off Ashram Road, 1km north of Nehru Bridge (Mon–Sat 10.30am–1.30pm & 2–6pm, closed 2nd & 4th Sat of month; ⓣ079/2658 9172, ⓦwww.gujarattourism.com); the attached **travel service** can book airline tickets and arrange tours. The Municipal Transport Service runs **city bus tours** (9am–1pm & 1.30–5.30pm; Rs75; ⓣ079/2550 7739) from the Lal Darwaja bus stand. *House of MG* runs a **heritage night walk** (daily at 10pm; 1hr; Rs50), taking in some of the city's oldest areas, and self-guided **audio tours** (daily 8am–5pm; Rs100).

Moving on from Ahmedabad

The **state bus stand** serves local destinations including **Gandhinagar** (every 15min; 1hr), **Dholka** (for Lothal, every 30min; 1hr 30min), **Mehsana** (every 10min; 2hr), and **Dhrangadhra** (every 30min; 3hr), as well as Rajasthan, Maharashtra and Madhya Pradesh. Frequent private buses to **Bhavnagar** (4–5hr), **Rajkot** (5–6hr), **Bhuj** (8–9hr) and **Mumbai** (14hr) are run by agencies in Paldi, west of Sardar Bridge. Ahmedabad is on the Delhi–Mumbai **train** line, and serves as the jumping-off point for most destinations within Gujarat, as well as for Mount Abu, Jodhpur and Udaipur in Rajasthan. Most services leave from the main **railway station**, though Gandhigram Station serves destinations across Saurashtra, including Delwada (for Diu). There are computerized **reservation centres** (Mon–Sat 8am–8pm & Sun 8am–2pm) at both stations. There are daily **flights** to Bangalore, Chennai, Delhi, Goa, Indore, Jaipur and Mumbai, and weekly services to Hyderabad.

Recommended daily trains from Ahmedabad

The services listed below are the most convenient and/or fastest trains from Ahmedabad. All run daily except the *Shatabdi Express* #2010 (daily except Sun).

Destination	Name	No.	Departs	Total time
Bhavnagar	*Bhavnagar Express*	#2971	5.45am	5hr 45min
Bhuj	*Nagari Express*	#9115	00.10am	7hr 10min
Delhi	*Rajdhani Express*	#2957	5.25pm	14hr
Dwarka	*Saurashtra Mail*	#9005	5.15am	9hr 53min
Jamnagar	*Saurashtra Mail*	#9005	5.15am	7hr 10min
Jodhpur	*Ranakpur Express*	#4708	00.25am	9hr 15min
Mumbai	*Shatabdi Express*	#2010	2.30pm	7hr 5min
	Gujarat Mail	#2902	10pm	8hr 45min
Porbandar	*Saurashtra Express*	#9215	8.05pm	10hr 5min
Udaipur	*Udaipur City Express*	#9944	11pm	9hr 5min

Accommodation

Most of Ahmedabad's **hotels** are in the **west end of the old city**, within walking distance of many of the sights. Others are clustered around the **railway station** and in the classy **Khanpur** area, with a few others in the **north** of the city. Unless otherwise specified, all the below are on the map on opposite.

Lal Darwaja

Cadillac Advance Cinema Rd, near Sidi Sayyid's Mosque ⓣ079/2550 7558. Just about the best shoestring option with welcoming staff, but very austere rooms: the paint's peeling, the beds are hard and the toilets - private or shared - are squat. There's also a crowded men-only dorm (Rs100). ❷

Good Night Dr Tankaria Rd, opposite Sidi Sayyid's Mosque ⓣ079/2550 7181, ⓔhotelforyou2002@yahoo.com. Neat and tidy rooms with private white-tiled bathrooms, TVs and a choice of either a/c or fans. The a/c triples are particularly good value. ❹

House of MG Dr Tankaria Rd, opposite Sidi Sayyid's Mosque ⓣ079/2550 6946, ⓦwww.houseofmg.com. This 1920s heritage hotel has spacious, individually decorated rooms (from $130), most with four-poster beds. Courtyards have period furniture, old photos line the walls, and there are playful touches, like popcorn makers in the suites ($235-275). Two excellent restaurants and an indoor pool complete the package. ❽–❾

Serena Dr Tankaria Rd, near Sidi Sayyid's Mosque ⓣ079/2551 0136. Beyond the unprepossessing exterior are reasonable attached "klassic", "empress" and "senate" rooms; the more expensive have a/c and extra space. A decent fall-back, if *Volga* and *Good Night* are full. ❹

Volga Just off Relief Rd, opposite Electricity Houses ⓣ079/2550 9497, ⓕ2550 9636. Friendly service is matched by spotless pastel-shaded attached rooms, each with TV, phone and 24hr

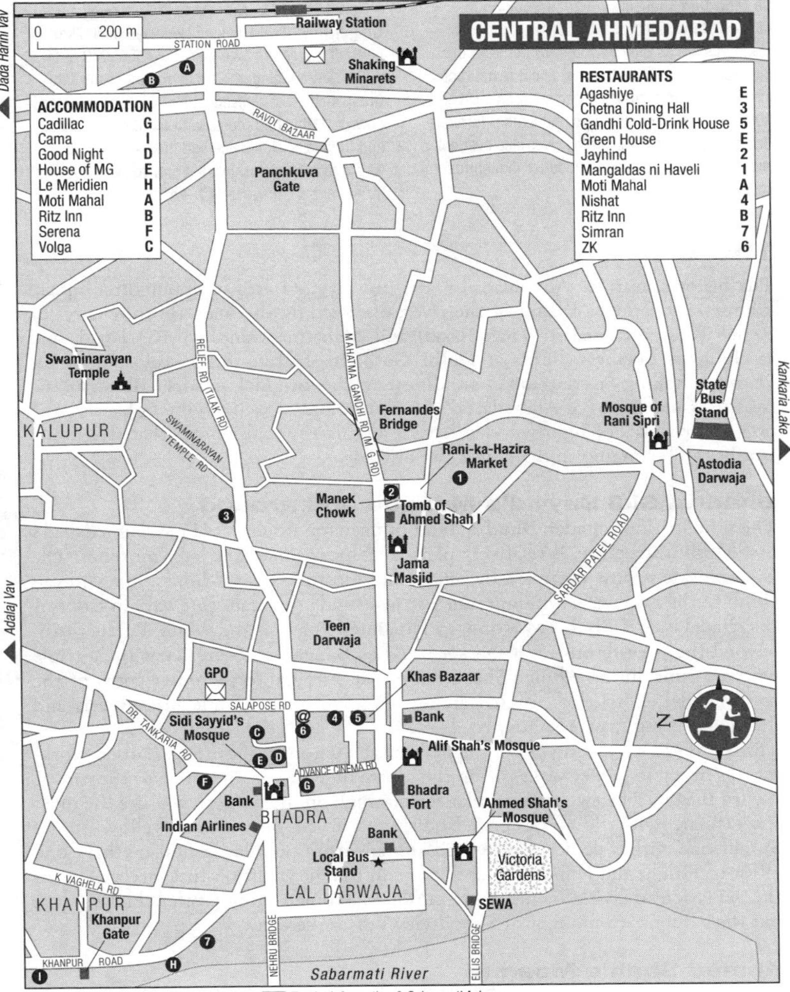

checkout; the more expensive have a/c, but some of the cheaper ones only have internal windows. As quiet as it gets in Lal Darwaja. ❹–❺

Around the railway station

Moti Mahal Station Rd, Kapasia Bazaar ⓣ079/212 1881, ⓕ213 6132. Very well-kept, clean hotel offering identikit rooms with attached bathrooms and TVs. ❹

Ritz Inn Station Rd, Kapasia Bazaar ⓣ079/2212 3842. A recommended three-star with Art Deco flourishes and smart service. The charming rooms have black and white bathrooms, TVs and writing desks. ❻–❼

Khanpur district

Cama Khanpur Rd ⓣ079/2550 1234, ⓦwww.camahotelsindia.com. The large rooms (from $150), the more expensive ones featuring tubs and carpets, overlooking the Sabarmati are let down by slightly dated decor. However, the manicured garden, curvy pool, top restaurant and 24hr coffee shop are ample compensation. 9am checkout. ❾

Le Meridien Khanpur Rd ⓣ079/2550 5505, ⓦwww.starwoodhotels.com. Service and standards are as high as you'd expect from this international chain, with an excellent restaurant, indoor pool and gym. The attached rooms ($150–300) have wood-effect floors and leather furniture. Unfortunately those facing the river also overlook a slum, which provides some food for thought during your stay. ❾

Northern Ahmedabad

Ginger Drive-In Rd, behind Himalaya Mall, 7km north of the centre (see map, p.543) ⓣ079/6666 3333, ⓦwww.gingerhotels.com. Part of the Tata Group's chain of stylised hotels, *Ginger* has pared down a/c attached rooms with tea/coffee makers and fridges, slick service and modern touches like wi-fi and "self check-in". It's only really convenient for the airport, however. ❻–❼

The City

The historic heart of Ahmedabad is the **old city**, an area of about three square kilometres on the east bank of the river, dissected by the main thoroughfares of Relief Road (also called Tilak Road) and Mahatma Gandhi (MG) Road, and reaching its northern limits at **Delhi Gate**. It's best to start exploring in Lal Darwaja, taking in the squat buildings of the original citadel, **Bhadra**, the **mosques** and tombs of Ahmedabad's Muslim rulers, as well as vibrant bazaars and pols – labyrinths of high wooden havelis and narrow cul-de-sacs that still house families all belonging to the same caste or trade.

Bhadra, Sidi Sayyid's Mosque and around

The solid fortified citadel, **Bhadra**, built of deep red stone in 1411 as Ahmedabad's first Muslim structure, is relatively plain in comparison to the later mosques. The palace inside is now occupied by offices and most of it is off-limits, but you can climb to the roof via a winding staircase just inside the main gateway. In front of the citadel is **Alif Shah's Mosque**, gaily painted in green and white. Further east, beyond the odoriferous meat market in **Khas Bazaar**, is **Teen Darwaja**, a triple gateway built during Ahmed Shah's reign that once led to the outer court of the royal citadel. A trio of pointed arches engraved with Islamic inscriptions and detailed carving spans the busy road below.

Sidi Sayyid's Mosque (1573), famed for the ten magnificent *jali* (lattice-work) screens lining its upper walls, sits in the centre of a busy traffic circle to the east of Nehru Bridge. The two semicircular screens high on the western wall are the most spectacular, with floral designs exquisitely carved out of the yellow stone. Stonework within depicts heroes and animals from popular Hindu myths – one effect of Hindu and Jain craftsmanship on an Islamic tradition that rarely allowed the depiction of living beings in its mosques. Women cannot enter this mosque, but the gardens around it afford good views of the screens.

Ahmed Shah's Mosque

West of Bhadra, not far from Victoria Gardens, **Ahmed Shah**'s small and attractively simple **mosque** was the private place of worship for the royal household. Sections of an old Hindu temple, perhaps dating back to 1250 AD, were used in its construction – hence the incongruous Sanskrit inscriptions on some of the pillars in the sanctuary. The *zenana* (women's chamber) is hidden behind pierced stone screens above the sanctuary in the northeast corner.

Jama Masjid

A short walk from Teen Darwaja along MG Road leads to the spectacular **Jama Masjid**. Completed in 1424, it stands today in its entirety, except for two minarets destroyed by an earthquake in 1957. Always bustling, the mosque is busiest on Fridays, when thousands converge to worship. The 260 elegant pillars supporting the roof of the domed prayer hall (*qibla*) are covered with unmistakably Hindu carvings, while close to the sanctuary's principal arch a large black slab is said to be the base of a Jain idol inverted and buried as a sign of Muslim supremacy.

Manek Chowk

East of Jama Masjid, the jewellery and textiles market **Manek Chowk** is filled with craftsmen working in narrow alleys amid newly dyed and tailored cloth. Immediately outside the east entrance of the mosque, the square **Tomb of Ahmed Shah I**, who died in 1442, stands surrounded by pillared verandas. Women are not permitted to enter the central chamber, site of his grave, and those of his son and grandson. Further into the market area is the mausoleum of Ahmed Shah's queens, **Rani-ka-Hazira**, surrounded by the dyers' colourful stalls. Its plan is identical to Shah's own tomb, with pillared verandas clearly inspired by Hindu architectural tastes.

Swaminarayan Temple

Heading north from Rani-ka-Hazira along Temple Road, a narrow street of fabric shops, and crossing Relief Road brings you to the **Swaminarayan Temple**. A delicate contrast to the many hard-stone mosques in the city, both the temple and the houses in the courtyard surrounding it are of finely carved wood, with elaborate and intricate patterns typical of the havelis of north and west Gujarat. The temple's main sanctuary is given over to Vishnu and his consort Lakshmi.

Mosque and Tomb of Rani Sipri

Near Astodia Darwaja in the south of the city, the small, elegant **mosque of Rani Sipri** was built in 1514 at the queen's orders. Her grave lies in front, sheltered by a pillared mausoleum. The stylish mosque shows more Hindu influence than any other in Ahmedabad: its pillared sanctuary has an open facade to the east and fine tracery work on the west wall.

Shaking minarets

South of the railway station, opposite Sarangpur Darwaja, **Sidi Bashir's minars** are all that remain of this mosque, which was named after one of Ahmed Shah's favourite slaves. More than 21m high, these are the best existing example of the "**shaking minarets**" – built on a foundation of flexible sandstone, probably to protect them from earthquake damage – once a common sight on Ahmedabad's skyline.

Dada Hari-ni Vav and Mata Bhava-ni Vav

Northern Gujarat abounds with remarkable **step-wells** – deep, with elaborately carved walls and broad flights of covered steps leading to a shaft – but **Dada Hari-ni Vav**, in the northeast of the city just outside the old boundaries, is among the finest. An auto-rickshaw from Lal Darwaja costs around Rs60. While it's a Muslim construction, built in 1500, the craftsmen were Hindu, and their influence is clear in the lavish and sensuous carvings on the walls and pillars. Visit around 11am when the sculpted floral patterns and shapely figurines inside are bathed in sunlight. **Bai Harir**'s lofty mosque and lattice-walled tomb stand west of the well. A couple of hundred metres north, the neglected **Mata Bhava-ni Vav** was probably constructed in the eleventh century, before Ahmedabad was founded. It's profoundly Hindu in character, and dedicated to Bhava-ni, an aspect of Shiva's consort Parvati.

Hathi Singh Temple

The Svetambara **Hathi Singh Temple** (daily 10am–noon & 4–7.30pm), north of Delhi Gate, is easily distinguished by its high carved column. Built entirely of white marble embossed with smooth carvings of dancers, musicians, animals and flowers, this serene temple is dedicated to Dharamnath, the fifteenth *tirthankara*, or "ford-maker", one of twenty-four great teachers sanctified by the Jains.

Calico Museum of Textiles

Nobody should leave Ahmedabad without taking a tour of the **Calico Museum of Textiles** (Ⓣ079/2786 8172, Ⓦwww.calicomuseum.com), in the Sarabhai Foundation, 3km north of Delhi Gate opposite Shahibagh Underbridge (bus #101 or #105; an auto-rickshaw costs Rs50); it's simply India's finest collection of textiles, clothes, furniture and crafts. Highlights of the **morning tour** (daily except Wed 10.30am–12.30pm) include exquisite pieces made for the British and Portuguese, while from India's royal households there's an embroidered tent and Shah Jahan's robes. There are *patola* saris from Patan (see p.553) and extravagant *zari* work that gilds saris in heavy gold stitching and can bring their weight to almost nine kilos. Other galleries are dedicated to embroideries, *bandhani* tie-and-dye, textiles made for overseas trade and woollen shawls from Kashmir and Chamba. The **afternoon tour** (daily except Wed 2.45–4.45pm) includes the galleries of *pichwais* and other temple paintings and decorations, including Jain statues housed in a replica haveli temple and centuries-old manuscripts and mandalas painted on palm leaves. Arrive early, as tours fill up quickly and you can't look round on your own.

City Museum

Just west of Sardar Bridge in the modern Sanskar Kendra on Bhagatcharya Road, the **City Museum** (Tues–Sun 10am–6pm) is worth a visit, covering subjects such as the history of the city, urban growth, sociological development and the activities of Gandhi and the freedom movement. There is a **Kite Museum** (same hours) in the basement.

SEWA

Almost ninety percent of women who work in India are self-employed. Outside the protection of labour laws and the minimum wage, they are subject to exploitation, often at the hands of unscrupulous banks and private lenders. Ahmedabad, however, has maintained a tradition of self-help since the days of Gandhi, achieving global recognition as the base of the ground-breaking **Self-Employed Women's Association, SEWA** (Ⓣ079/2550 6444, Ⓦwww.sewa.org). Founded in the early 1970s, SEWA provides legal advice, training, support and childcare, and runs its own co-operative bank.

Following a major slump in the textile industry in 1984, SEWA set up training centres in weaving, sewing, dyeing and printing, and provided efficient machinery. This helped to re-establish many women in the textile labour force, and provided an outlet for their products. In 1987, a SEWA protest against *sati* (widow burning) and a campaign to have verbal divorce and polygamy banned in Gujarat resulted in a change in the law. SEWA also strongly opposes the sex determination tests that lead to female foeticide, particularly widespread in Gujarat. With almost a million members nationwide, more than half of them in Gujarat, the organisation is now involved with projects throughout India and overseas.

It has two **craft shops** (Mon–Sat 10am–6.30pm): one on the east side of Ellis Bridge, in the organization's reception centre, another on CG Road at the Banascraft Chandan Complex.

Sabarmati (Gandhi) Ashram

At the northern end of Ashram Road, the **Sabarmati Ashram** (daily 8.30am–6.30pm; ⓣ079/2755 7277, ⓦwww.gandhiashram.org.in) is where the Mahatma lived from 1917 until 1930, holding meetings with weavers and Harijans as he helped them find security and re-establish the manual textile industry in Ahmedabad. In keeping with the man's uncluttered lifestyle, the collection of his personal property is modest but poignant – wooden shoes, white seamless clothes and a pair of round spectacles. The ashram itself is no longer operating, but many people come here simply to sit and meditate. Regular evening **sound-and-light shows** are also held.

Other museums

The informative **Shreyas Folk Art Museum**, way out to the west near the city limits (Fri–Tues 10.30am–1.30pm & 2–5.30pm; Rs90 [Rs10]; photography prohibited; bus #34/2 or 34/3 from Lal Darwaja), displays the traditional work of Gujarat's many tribes. Also illuminating is the **Tribal Museum** (daily except Mon 11am–5pm) in Gujarat Vidyapith, north of Income Tax Circle on Ashram Road, detailing the various peoples of the state and their customs. The N.C. Mehta Gallery in the LD Institute of Indology in the west of town (Tues–Sun: May & June 8.30am–5.30pm; July–April 10.30am–5.30pm) has a superb collection of miniature paintings from all over India; an Indology Museum in the same complex has Jain sculpture and manuscripts.

Eating

Ahmedabad's most popular **restaurants** are clustered around Relief Road, Salapose Road and Badhra; for **snacks**, there are good stalls at Khas Bazaar. If you are making only a brief stop in Gujarat, make sure you sample the state's delicious thali.

Agashiye *House of MG*. One of the state's best restaurants, with a roof terrace, cushions to sit on and an open kitchen: prices are steep (lunch Rs325–425; dinner Rs345–495), but the mouthwatering Gujarati thalis (and sometimes international dishes) are as good as it gets. A series of recipe books is on sale, and cookery classes are in the pipeline.

Chetna Dining Hall Relief Rd. Don't be put off by the gloomy entrance, inside is a busy veg place with excellent, inexpensive south Indian dosas, *vadas* and *uttapams* (Rs21–40).

Gandhi Cold-Drink House Khas Bazaar. Hole-in-the-wall place with plastic chairs out front and a range of refreshing milk and ice-cream concoctions (around Rs15), including an Indonesian-style "Royal Faluda", unique to Ahmedabad, and a butterscotch lassi.

Gopi Dining Hall Pritamrai Rd (see map, p.543) ⓣ079/657 6388. Welcoming veg place on the west side of Ellis Bridge, offering Gujarati and Kathiawadi thalis at unbeatable prices (Rs65–85). It's very popular, so reserve or wait in line.

Green House *House of MG*. Cheaper than *Agashiye* (mains around Rs125), and almost as appealing: sit on wooden benches under an ivy-covered pavilion and tuck into snacks, light meals and sorbets, frozen yogurts and ice creams (try the saffron or star anise flavours).

Jayhind Manek Chowk. One of the best places to sample Ahmedabad's famous sweets, *Jayhind* has been producing wonderful dry-fruit halwa and *kaju pista roll* (Rs5–30) since 1948.

Mangaldas ni Haveli Lakha Patel ni Pol. Run by *House of MG*, this rooftop café, craft museum and shop is in a wonderfully-restored 200-year-old wooden haveli; a veg thali costs Rs125. Open daily 6.30pm–11pm. It's difficult to find, so ask for directions at *House of MG* or take an auto-rickshaw.

Moti Mahal *Moti Mahal* hotel. This non-veg restaurant and sweet centre is renowned for its great biriyanis (Rs30–80) and a refreshing salted lassi flavoured with cumin.

Nishat Khas Bazaar. With its huge flashing neon sign, *Nishat* is hard to miss, which is fortunate, as its non-veg thali – with chicken tikka, mutton curry and biriyani – is a firm favourite. There's a hectic downstairs dining room and a calmer, slightly more expensive, a/c area above. Mains Rs50–100.

Ritz Inn *Ritz Inn* hotel. A peaceful hotel restaurant with stained-glass windows, chandeliers and delectable veg Indian and Chinese dishes (Rs65–90).

Simran Khanpur Rd. An a/c restaurant handy for those staying at the big hotels nearby: good choices include *tawa jhinga* (prawn curry), mutton kebabs, *shahi raan* (tandoori leg of lamb) and fish curries (Rs60–180).

ZK Relief Rd. A dimly lit restaurant with a pink-and-maroon colour scheme and an ancient fish tank. Trawling through the exhaustive menu – well over 200 dishes – certainly builds up an appetite: the tandoori items (Rs70–90) are particularly good.

Listings

Airlines, Domestic Indian Airlines, between Sidi Sayyid's Mosque and Nehru Bridge ☎079/2658 5622; Jet Airways, Ashram Rd opposite Gujarat Vidyapith ☎079/2754 3304; Kingfisher Airlines, airport ☎1800/233 3131.

Airlines, International Air India, between Sidi Sayyid's Mosque and Nehru Bridge ☎079/2658 5622; Air France, Madhuban House near Ellis Bridge ☎079/2754 0451; British Airways, Centre Point Building, Panchwati Circle, CG Rd ☎079/2643 1188; Cathay Pacific, Ratnanabh Complex, opposite Gujarat Vidyapith ☎079/2754 5421; Singapore Airlines, SP Nagar Rd ☎079/3001 2828.

Banks and exchange Change US dollars, sterling and travellers' cheques at the Bank of India in Khas Bazaar, the Central Bank of India opposite Sidi Sayyid's Mosque and the State Bank of India opposite Lal Darwaja bus station (all Mon–Fri 11am–3pm, Sat 11am–1pm). Thomas Cook is at 208 Sakar III, off Ashram Rd near the old High Court. CITIBank has a branch on CG Rd at B/201 Fairdeal House, near Swastik Four Rd. ATMs are very common.

Bookshops Crossword in the Shree Krishna Complex, near the Mithakali crossroad; People's Book House on Relief Rd, 200m east of Salapose Rd; and Art Book Centre, just off Mangaldas Rd, 350m east of Ellis Bridge.

Cinemas City Gold Cinema (☎079/2658 7782), near the tourist office on Ashram Rd screens English and Hindi films.

Hospitals VS General, Ellis Bridge (☎079/2657 7621), is a large government hospital; for traditional treatments, try Akhandanand Ayurvedic, Akhandanand Rd (☎079/2550 7796).

Internet access Relief Cyber Café, opposite the Relief Rd cinema, and Wizard Online, 50m down an alley, just north of Income Tax Circle, on the west side of Ashram Rd. Both Rs15/hr.

Photography One Hour Photo, Ashram Rd, northwest corner of Income Tax Circle.

Post office Salapose Rd (Mon–Sat 10am–8pm, Sun 10am–4pm).

Around Ahmedabad

The most obvious day-trips from Ahmedabad are north to **Adalaj**, with its impressive step-well, and beyond to **Gandhinagar**, with its extraordinary Swaminarayan religious complex. South of town, the lake, pavilions and mausoleums of **Sarkhej** make a pleasant break from the crowded city, while further south is the ancient Harappan site at **Lothal**.

Adalaj Vav

One of Gujarat's most spectacular step-wells, **Adalaj Vav** (daily 8am–6pm), stands in neat gardens 1km from a bus stop on the route between Ahmedabad, 19km away, and Gandhinagar. The monument, built in 1498 and now out of use, is best seen around midday, when sunlight penetrates to the bottom of the five-storey octagonal well shaft. Steps lead down to the cool depths through a series of platforms raised on pillars. Alive with exquisite sculptures, the walls, pillars, cornices and niches portray erotica, dancing maidens, musicians and animals.

Gandhinagar

The second state capital after Chandigarh to be built from scratch since Independence, uninspiring **GANDHINAGAR** is laid out in thirty residential sectors in an ordered style influenced by **Le Corbusier**. There's little to warrant spending much time here, save the headquarters of the Swaminarayan sect, **Akshardham**. This Hindu revivalist movement promotes Vedic ideals pronounced by Lord Swaminarayan (1781–1830).

Swaminarayan Complex

The Akshardham may advocate simplicity and poverty, but the colossal **Swaminarayan complex** on J Road, Sector 20 (daily except Mon 9.30am–6.30pm) is hugely extravagant. Built of six thousand tonnes of pink sandstone, it houses the gold-leaf-coated statues of Swaminarayan and two other prominent gurus. The rest of the complex is a surreal **theme park**, with a Hall of Holy Relics containing possessions of Swaminarayan and a state-of-the-art audiovisual show. On September 24, 2002, 33 people were killed and 72 injured at Akshardham by Pakistani suicide terrorists. Links were quickly made between the attack and the post-Godhra rioting. Today, the only evidence of the **massacre** is a few scattered bullet holes and the security presence at the entrance.

Practicalities

Regular **buses** run between Gandhinagar and Ahmedabad (45min), but there's only one train a day in each direction (1hr) and the station is inconveniently out in Sector 14. The budget and mid-range **hotels** aren't up to much, but if you want a bit of pampering, try the *Cambay Spa and Golf Resort* (Ⓣ079/2328 9000, Ⓦwww.thecambay.com; ❽) in sector 25, which has minimalist attached rooms, an excellent spa and a nine-hole golf course.

Sarkhej

Just under 10km southwest of Ahmedabad (bus #31 from Lal Darwaja), **Sarkhej** holds a complex of beautiful monuments arranged around an artificial **lake**. On the southwest side of the lake, the square **tomb** of the revered saint Sheikh Ahmed Khattu, the spiritual mentor of Ahmed Shah, who died in 1445, is Gujarat's largest mausoleum. It was constructed by Ahmed Shah's successor, Mohammed Shah, in 1446. The later Sultan Mohammed Beghada (died 1511) added palaces, a harem, a vast lake and, eventually, his own tomb as well. Sarkhej became a retreat of Gujarati sultans and remains a charming place.

Lothal

The largest excavated **Harappan** (or Indus Valley; see box, p.552) site is at **Lothal** (daily dawn to dusk), close to the mouth of the River Sabarmati, 100km south of Ahmedabad, and an easy journey by bus (change at Dholka) or train (3hr). Foundations, platforms, crumbling walls and paved floors are all that remain of the prosperous sea-trading community that dwelt here between 2400 and 1900 BC, when a flood all but destroyed the settlement. A walk around the **central mound** reveals the old roads that ran past ministers' houses and through the acropolis. The lower town comprised a bazaar, workshops and residential quarters. Evidence has been found here of an even older culture, perhaps dating from the fourth millennium BC, known as the **Red Ware Culture**. You can see remains from this period and from the Indus Valley Civilization in the illuminating **museum** (daily except Fri 10am–5pm; Rs2).

Northern Gujarat

North of Gandhinagar, the district of Mehsana was the Solankis' seat of government between the eleventh and thirteenth centuries. Some remains of their old capital – including the extraordinary **Rani-ki-Vav** step-well – still stand at **Anhilawada Patan**, just outside the modern city of Patan, home to Gujarat's last remaining *patola* weavers. From the city of **Mehsana**, at the province's centre, it's easy to get to the ancient sun temple at **Modhera**. A Jain temple in the hills at **Taranga** can be reached from Mehsana or Ahmedabad.

Mehsana

The crowded city of **MEHSANA**, 100km north of Ahmedabad, is home to one of Asia's largest dairy industries. The only building of any interest is the old **Rajmahal** palace, but the city makes a useful overnight halt if you are exploring northern Gujarat. About 3km from the station on the Ahmedabad–Palanpur highway, the *Savera Guesthouse* (ⓣ02762/256710; ❸–❹) is the best **accommodation** option, with fairly clean, spacious doubles and some a/c rooms. If you're coming from Modhera you'll arrive on the other side of town; ask a rickshaw driver to take you to the "highway". Across the road is the pure veg *Navjivan* **restaurant**. The **budget lodges** in town are some of Gujarat's worst – the *A-One Guesthouse* (ⓣ02762/51394; ❶) near the station is the least bad. There are three **banks** nearby. **Trains** link Mehsana to Ahmedabad (2–3hr), Abu Road (2hr 10min–3hr), Ajmer (6hr 30min–7hr), Jodhpur (7hr 30min) and Patan (2hr). **Buses** tend to be faster and serve cities in Rajasthan and Gujarat, including Bhuj.

Modhera

If you visit only one town in northern Gujarat, make it **MODHERA**, where the eleventh-century **Sun Temple** (daily 8am–6pm; Rs200 [Rs5]) is the state's best example of Solanki temple architecture. Almost a thousand years old, the temple has survived earthquakes and Muslim iconoclasm; apart from a missing *shikhara* and slightly worn carvings, it remains largely intact. The Solanki kings were probably influenced by Jain traditions; deities and their vehicles, animals,

The Indus Valley Civilization

Before the Mauryan Empire took hold in the fourth century BC, India's greatest empire was the **Indus Valley Civilization**. Sophisticated settlements dating back to 2500 BC were first discovered in 1924 on the banks of the River Indus in present-day Sind (in Pakistan), at **Mohenjo Daro**. Further excavations in 1946 in Punjab revealed the city of **Harappa**, from the same era. In its prime, this great society spread from the present borders of Iran and Afghanistan to Kashmir, Delhi and southern Gujarat. It lasted until 1900 BC, when it was destroyed by heavy floods.

A prosperous and literate society, importing raw materials from regions as far west as Egypt and trading ornaments, jewellery and cotton, it also had a remarkable, centrally controlled **political system**. Each town was almost identical, with complex drainage systems. **Lothal**, close to the Gulf of Cambay in southern Gujarat, was a major port. Although much about this complex society remains unknown, similarities exist between the Indus Valley Civilization and present-day India. For example, like Hindus, there was a strong custom of worshipping a mother goddess, and there is evidence of phallic worship, still popular among Shaivites.

voluptuous maidens and complex friezes adorn the sandy brown walls and pillars. Within the *mandapa*, or pillared entrance hall, twelve *adityas* set into niches in the wall portray the transformations of the sun in each month of the year. Closely associated with the sun, *adityas* are the sons of Aditi, the goddess of infinity and eternity. Modhera's sun temple is positioned so that at the equinoxes the rising sun strikes the images in the sanctuary, which at other times languishes in a dim half-light.

Modhera is linked by road to Mehsana (40min) and Ahmedabad (2–3hr). If you are coming from Ahmedabad by **bus** and want to save time, ask to get out at Mehsana highway and you can intercept the hourly Modhera buses at the junction without going all the way into town. The return fare for a **taxi** from Mehsana is around Rs350. There are also buses from Modhera to Patan. Although there's nowhere to **stay** in Modhera, the *Toran Cafeteria* in the temple grounds sells **snacks**. There's a **dance festival** in January.

Patan and Anhilawada Patan

PATAN, roughly 40km northwest of Mehsana, has few monuments, but in the **Salvivad** area of town you can watch the complex weaving of silk *patola* saris, once the preferred garment of queens and aristocrats, and an important export of Gujarat, now made by just one extended family. Each sari, sold for Rs50–75,000, takes from four to six months to produce. Frequent buses run between Mehsana and Patan (1hr 15min). The big-city bustle of Patan is a far cry from the old Gujarati capital at **ANHILAWADA PATAN**, 2km northwest, which served several Rajput dynasties between the eighth and the twelfth centuries, before being annexed by the Mughals. It fell into decline when Ahmed Shah moved the capital to Ahmedabad in 1411. Little remains now except traces of fortifications scattered in the surrounding fields, and the stunning **Rani-ki-Vav** (daily 8am–6pm; Rs100 [Rs5]), Gujarat's greatest **step-well**. It was built for the Solanki queen Udaimati in 1050 and extensively restored during the 1980s, recreating as perfectly as possible the original extravagant carving. Near the well are the remains of the **Sahastraling Talav**, the "thousand-lingam tank" built at the turn of the twelfth century, but razed during Mughal raids. This is part of the same **complex** (daily 8am–6pm) that includes a modest open-air **museum**. An auto-rickshaw out to Rani-ki-Vav costs Rs30–40 from the town centre, where, near the Kohinoor Cinema, *Hotel Neerav* (ⓣ02766/222127; ❹) has decent **rooms** with attached bathrooms; some also have a/c.

The Jain temple at Taranga

Well off the tourist trail, the **hilltop temple complex** at **TARANGA**, 60km or so northeast of Mehsana is nonetheless easily accessible by bus from Ahmedabad (3hr 30min) and Mehsana (1hr 30min); buses drop you off at Timba, from where you catch a shared jeep (Rs5) for the remaining 8km to Taranga.

Built during the Solanki period, the striking shrines are better preserved than more famous sites such as Mount Abu, Girnar and Shatrunjaya. Pilgrims, monks and nuns gather year-round to take blessings and pray. The **main temple**, built of durable sandstone, is dedicated to Ajitanath, the second of twenty-four *tirthankaras*. There is little in the way of tourist facilities here, although you can get an inexpensive lunch at a *dharamshala*.

Kutch

Bounded on the north and east by marshy flats and on the south and west by the Gulf of Kutch and the Arabian Sea, the province of **KUTCH** (also Kuchchh or Kachchha) is a place apart. All but isolated from neighbouring Saurashtra and Sind, the largely arid landscape is shot through with the colours of the heavily embroidered local dress. Kutchi legends can be traced in sculptural motifs, and its strong folk tradition is still represented in popular craft, clothing and jewellery designs. Few tourists make it here, but those who do are invariably enchanted. You can easily head out from the central city of **Bhuj** – which was devastated by the 2001 earthquake – to villages, ancient fortresses, medieval ports and isolated monasteries. The treeless marshes to the north and east, the Great and Little **Ranns of Kutch**, can flood completely during a heavy monsoon, effectively transforming the region into an island. Home to the rare wild ass, the Ranns are also the only region in India where flamingos breed successfully. The southern district of **Aiyar Patti** supports crops of cotton, castor-oil plants, sunflowers, wheat and groundnuts. Northern Kutch, or **Banni**, by contrast, is semi-desert with dry shifting sands and arid grasslands.

Kutchi pastoral groups

Kutch has the most significant population of **pastoral communities** in Gujarat. Each tribe can be identified from its costume, and gains income from farming or crafts such as weaving, painting, woodcarving and dyeing. Traditionally, each concentrated on different crafts, although the distinctions today are less clear-cut.

The **Rabari,** the largest group, rear cattle, buffalo and camels, sell ghee, weave, and are known for their fine **embroidery**. Most of the men sport a white turban, and wear white cotton trousers tight at the ankle and in baggy pleats above the knee, a white jacket (*khediyun*), and a blanket thrown over one shoulder. Rabari women dress in black pleated jackets or open-backed blouses, full black skirts and tie-dyed head cloths, and always wear heavy silver jewellery and ivory bangles around the upper arms. Child marriages are customary among the Rabari. In **Bhujodi**, near Bhuj, the Rabari weave camel wool into blankets and shawls.

The **Bharvad** tribes infiltrated Gujarat from Vrindavan, close to Mathura in Uttar Pradesh. The men are distinguishable by the peacock, parrot and flower motifs sewn into their *khediyun*, and the women by their bright backless shirts, *kapadun*, rarely covered by veils. Mass marriages take place among the Bharvad every few years.

The wandering **Ahir** cattle-breeders came to Gujarat from Sind, and settled as farmers. Baggy trousers and *khediyun* are worn by the men, together with a white loosely wound headcloth; the women dress like the Rabaris, with additional heavy silver nose-rings. The children's bright *topis*, or skull-caps, are like those common in Pakistan. Today the Ahirs are prospering as entrepreneurs.

The **Charans**, long-established bards of Gujarat, encompass in their clans the Maldharis, who raise prize cattle, and the leather-workers known as Meghavals. They claim descent from a celestial union between Charan and a maiden created by Parvati. The women are often worshipped by other tribes, as their connection with Parvati links them closely to the mother goddess, Ashpura, who is popular in Kutch.

Said to have migrated from Pakistan, the **Jats** are an Islamic pastoral group. The men can be identified by their black dress, while young Jat girls have dainty plaits curving round the sides of their faces, and wear heavy nose-rings.

Some history

Remains from the third millennium BC in eastern Kutch suggest migrating Indus Valley communities crossed the Ranns from Mohenjo Daro in modern Pakistan to Lothal in eastern Gujarat. Despite being so cut off, Kutch felt the effect of the Buddhist Mauryan empire, later coming under the control of Greek Bactrians, the Western Satraps and the powerful Guptas. The Arab invasion of Sind in 720 AD pushed refugees into Kutch's western regions, and tribes from Rajputana and Gujarat crossed its eastern borders. Later in the eighth century the region fell under the sway of the Gujarati capital Anhilawada (now Patan), and by the tenth century the Samma Rajputs, later known as the Jadejas, had infiltrated Kutch from the west and established themselves as rulers. Their line continued until Kutch was absorbed into the Indian Union in 1948, though the region has retained its customs, laws and a thriving maritime tradition, built originally on trade with Malabar, Mocha, Muscat and the African coast.

Bhuj

In the heart of Kutch, the narrow streets and old bazaars of the walled town of **BHUJ** retain a medieval flavour unlike any other Gujarati city, although much of it was reduced to rubble in the **earthquake** of January 2001 (which killed around twenty thousand people and destroyed 1.2 million homes in the region). The section immediately behind the famed **Aina Mahal** ("Palace of Mirrors") suffered the most damage and is still being redeveloped. Since the earthquake, however, Bhuj has got a new airport, railway line and university, while the region's road infrastructure has been greatly improved. The multi-million-dollar reconstruction has created new jobs, and new businesses have moved to the region. Locals are generally positive about the changes, although the process has not been smooth: reconstruction was slow to start; there were persistent concerns about how aid money was being spent; and the prices of staple goods have risen. Reconstruction has almost finished, however, and the city finally seems to have emerged from the tragedy.

Bhuj was established as the capital of Kutch in the mid-sixteenth century by Rao Khengarji, a Jadeja Rajput. The one interruption before 1948 in his family's continuous rule was a brief period of early nineteenth-century British domination. When the governance of the state was handed back to Maharao Desal in 1834, the import of slaves from Africa was banned and Africans were given homes in the north of the city. With the establishment of Gandhidham city and the port of Kandla southeast of the capital, the economic centre of gravity shifted from Bhuj, leaving it to carry on its traditions little affected by the modernizations of the twentieth century.

Arrival and information

The railway station is 1.5km north of the Aina Mahal and the bus stand is on ST Station Road on the southern edge of the old city. The airport is 5km north of the centre. Bhuj has no official tourist office, so head to the tourist desk at Aina Mahal (daily except Sat 9am–noon & 3–6pm; ⓣ02832/291702, ⓔpkumar_94@yahoo.com), manned by the friendly and well-informed Pramod Jethi, who also organizes heritage walks (3hr; Rs500).

Hotel Gangaram and *City Guest House* can organise **motorbike** hire (Rs350–400/day), though many are in a poor state of repair. Santosh Cycle Centre, near the bus station, rents **bicycles** (Rs25–50/day). The State Bank of India on Hospital Road **changes cash** and travellers' cheques, as does ICICI across the street. There are numerous **ATMs**. Western Cyber Café, near the new vegetable market, offers **internet** access (Rs20/hr). The Crossword **bookshop** is close to the bus station.

Moving on from Bhuj

The best **train** services to **Ahmedabad** are the *Nagari Express* #9116 (daily; departs 10pm, arrives 5.05am) or the *Hazrat Express* #4312 (Mon, Thurs, Sat & Sun; departs 11.05am, arrives 6.50pm). Several daily trains travel to Gandhidham, but it's easier to take the bus. There are state **buses** to Ahmedabad (8–9hr), Rajkot (6–7hr) and Jamnagar (8hr), as well as Mandvi and Mundra. Less frequent buses serve villages in northern Kutch. Private bus operators are strung along Station Road: Ashapura Travels (ⓣ02832/252491), opposite the bus stand, has a daily bus to Barmer (Rajasthan), which continues to Jaisalmer every other day, as well as a bus to Ajmer (for Pushkar); Patel Tours and Travels (ⓣ02832/657781), 100m west of the station, has two sleeper buses to Ahmedabad. Jay Somnath (ⓣ02832/221919), opposite *Green Rock* restaurant, has buses to Rajkot. Jet Airways (ⓣ02832/253671, ⓦwww.jetairways.com) and Kingfisher (ⓦwww.flykingfisher.com) each have a daily **flight** to Mumbai.

Bhuj is one of the cheapest places in western India to pick up **handicrafts** and there are shops all over town, especially at Shroff Bazaar and Vaniyawad near the old railway station around 1km north of town. For socially-responsible items, *Hotel Ilark* has a Kala Raksha (see p.560) outlet and *Hotel Prince* sells products from Kutch Mahila Vikas Sangathan, an organisation that ensures artisans are fairly rewarded for their work.

Accommodation

City Guest House Langa St, just off Shroff Bazar, ⓣ02832/221067. If rupees are tight, head here for no frills but clean rooms – some with attached bathrooms – set around a small courtyard. 24hr checkout. ❶–❷

Gangaram Behind the Aina Mahal in the old city ⓣ02832/222948, ⓔhotelgangaram@yahoo.com. Run by the obliging Rajesh Jethi, a mine of information, this travellers' stalwart has comfortable rooms with private bathrooms and TV. There's also internet access, a good restaurant and a roof terrace. ❸–❹

Garha Safari Lodge 14km north of Bhuj overlooking the Gorudra Reservoir ⓣ079/657 9672, ⓔgbglad1@sancharnet.in. A good option for those with their own transport, this camp has white concrete huts resembling traditional *bhungas* (mud-brick and straw homes) and a restaurant that often features live music. ❼

Ilark Station Rd ⓣ02832/258999, ⓦwww.hotelilark.com. A modern red-and-black-glass exterior shields the most chick rooms in town: all have laminate floors, large beds and big TVs. There are also two smart restaurants, and – incongruously – a tree in the lobby. ❻–❽

Oasis New Station Rd ⓣ02832/254303. Although it looks similar to *Ilark* from the outside, *Oasis* is a more modest prospect. Still, the good-value attached rooms have TVs, kettles and either fans or a/c, though some lack much natural light. ❹–❻

Prince Station Rd ⓣ02832/220370, ⓔprincad1@sancharnet.in. Long-established mid-range choice, with large, if slightly dated, attached rooms, welcoming staff, a foreign exchange counter and two fine restaurants. ❹–❻

The Town

Bhuj is overlooked from the east by the old, crumbling fort on Bhujia Hill, closed to the public as it lies in a military area, while the vast **Hamirsar Tank**, with a small park on an island in its centre, stands on its western edge. The remnants of the **old city** form an intricate maze of streets and alleyways leading to the **palace complex**, guarded by sturdy walls and high heavy gates, enclosing the Aina and Prag mahals. Built in the eighteenth century during the reign of Maharao Lakho, and later turned into a museum showcasing the opulence of the royal dynasty, the **Aina Mahal** suffered much damage in the 2001 earthquake. Fortunately, despite its roof collapsing, the famed **Hall of Mirrors** (daily except Sat 9am–noon & 3–6pm; Rs10, camera Rs30, video camera Rs100) remained largely intact; the interior has now been fully restored, but work is ongoing on the exterior. The chief architect of the palace, Ram Singh Malam, was an Indian seafarer who studied in Europe for seventeen years after being rescued from a shipwreck by Dutch sailors off the coast of Africa. His masterpiece was the tiled pleasure-chamber at the heart of the palace where the maharaja, soothed by an ingenious system of fountains, used to compose poetry and listen to music. Royal heirlooms on display include a couple of original Hogarths and a portrait of Catherine the Great.

The nearby **Prag Mahal**, built in the 1860s and combining Mughal, British, Kutchi and Italian architectural styles, also suffered damage during the quake, and visitors are currently only allowed inside the main hall (Mon–Sat 9am–noon & 3–6pm; Rs12, camera Rs30, video Rs100). The palace was one of the locations used in the hit film *Lagaan*.

On the southwest corner of Hamirsar Tank, the **Sharad Bagh Palace** (daily except Fri 9am–noon & 3–6pm; Rs10, camera Rs20, video Rs100) was built in 1867 as the retreat of the last maharao. Its small porticoed buildings are delicately proportioned and include a plush drawing room, decked with hunting trophies, photographs and old clocks, and a dining room containing Maharao Madansinjhi's coffin. The palace's most appealing feature, however, is its well-tended garden. The worthwhile **Kachchh Museum** (daily except Wed and second and fourth Sat of month 10am–1pm & 2.30pm–5.30pm; Rs50 [Rs2]) at the southeast corner of Hamirsar Tank has topographical, historical and cultural exhibits on the region, including interesting finds from Dholavira and Kutchi textiles and crafts.

Just south of Hamirsar Tank and west of College Road, a path leads to the 250-year-old bone-dry **Ramkund Tank**, made of hard grey stone and shaded by trees. Decorated with skilfully crafted images of Kali, Vishnu, Nag and Ganesh, the tank also has small niches in the walls where oil lamps would glitter in the dusk as devotees prayed at the evening puja. Nearby is a set of sixteenth-century *sati* stones.

Bhuj's private **Folk Museum**, on Mandvi Road 100m west of the Collectors' Office (daily except Mon 10.30am–1.15pm & 2–5pm; Rs50 [Rs10], camera Rs50), contains fine examples of Kutchi pottery, embroidery, games and wall hangings.

Eating

Station Road is the place to pick up the local **snack**, *dhabeli* (spiced lentils and peanuts in a bun). *Hotel Prince* has a wine shop and can provide **alcohol permits**.

Anando Foods Near the Kachchh Museum. Hygienic fast-food joint with inexpensive south Indian snacks, Chinese noodles, soups and fried rice, and ice cream. Mains Rs30–70.

Green Hotel Just off Shroff Bazar. Low-key veg joint, popular with locals for its filling thalis (from Rs55), dosas, Punjabi dishes and selection of so-so pizzas, sandwiches and burgers. Mains Rs30–70.

Green Rock ST Rd. Smart a/c restaurant with photos of Bollywood and cricket stars on the walls and a veg menu of north and south Indian, Chinese and western dishes. Mains Rs65–100. Thalis Rs110.

Jesal and Toral *Hotel Prince*. If you're feeling homesick you can find fish fingers and beans on toast at *Jesal*, as well as some interesting north Indian fish dishes, plus veg and non-veg Indian and Chinese staples (mains Rs90–200). *Toral*, meanwhile, offers a lavish all-you-can-eat thali (Rs140).

Nilam Station Rd. Courteous staff serve up excellent veg Indian and Chinese – the sweetcorn and green pepper masala is recommended – plus inexpensive breakfasts (though only from 11am). Mains Rs60–90.

Vijay Shroff Bazar. Quintessential Indian teashop, where local men gather to drink small cups of sweet tea and discuss the issues of the day.

Around Bhuj

Bhuj is a useful base for visiting the **outlying craft villages**. Exploring the area by **taxi** or **motorcycle** (see p.555 for rental details) gives you the most freedom.

Kutchi handicrafts

Kutch is known for its distinctive traditional crafts, particularly its **embroidery**, practised by pastoral groups like Hindu Rabaris and Ahirs, and Muslim Jats and Muthwas, as well as migrants from Sind including the Sodha Rajputs and Meghwal Harijans. Traditionally, each community has its own stitches and patterns, though these distinctions are becoming less apparent as time goes on.

The northern villages of Dhordo, Khavda and Hodko are home to the few remaining communities of **leather embroiderers**, who stitch flower, peacock and fish motifs onto bags, fans, horse belts, wallets, cushion covers and mirror frames. Dhordo is also known for its **woodcarving**, while Khavda is one of the last villages to continue the printing method known as **ajrakh**. Cloth is dyed with natural pigments in a lengthy process similar to batik, but instead of wax, a mixture of lime and gum is used to resist the dye in certain parts of the cloth when new colours are added. Women in Khavda also paint **terracotta pots**.

Rogan painting is practised by only a few artisans at Nirona in northern Kutch. A complex process turns hand-pounded castor oil into coloured dyes that are used to decorate cushion covers, bedspreads and curtains with simple geometric patterns. Craftsmen also make melodic **bells** (once used for communication among shepherds) coated in intricate designs of copper and brass. Silver jewellery is common, featuring in most traditional Kutchi costumes, but Kutchi **silver engraving**, traditionally practised in Bhuj, is a dwindling art form. The anklets, earrings, nose-rings, bangles and necklaces are similar to those seen in Rajasthan; many of them are made by the Ahir and Rabari communities who live in both areas. The main centres for silver are Anjar, Bhuj, Mandvi and Mundra.

Kutchi clothes are distinctive not only for their fine embroidery but also their bold designs. The most common form of **cloth** printing is **bandhani**, or tie-dye, practised in most villages, but concentrated in Mandvi and Anjar. One craft unique to the area is *mushroo*-weaving (*ilacha*). The yarn used is silk, carefully dyed before it is woven in a basic striped pattern, with a complex design woven over the top in such fine detail that it seems to be embroidered.

There are also slow and infrequent public **buses** from Bhuj to Nirona (6 daily), Dhordo (2 daily) and Khavda (3 daily). For advice on where to visit, talk to Pramod Jethi (see p.555), who has written a couple of useful guidebooks on Kutch (Rs100), available in English and French, and runs tours to the craft villages (Rs1300 by car; Rs100 by auto-rickshaw).

Permits are required for many of the outlying villages, and are available from the District Superintendent of Police's Office, a five-minute walk southeast of the Hamirsar Tank (daily except Sun; 11am–2pm & 3–6pm); the permits are free, and the process takes about fifteen minutes; take photocopies of your passport and visa, as well as the originals.

Mandvi and Mundra

The compact town of **MANDVI**, on the west bank of a wide tidal estuary 60km southwest of Bhuj, faces the Arabian Sea to the south and supports a dwindling *dhow*-building industry. Merchants, seamen and later the British settled in this once-flourishing port; though few remained long, they left behind grand European-style mansions.

Mandvi today has a leisurely feel, with cluttered shops and **markets** stocked with *bandhani* and silver. The estuary is blocked on the south side by shifting sands, forming a long, uncrowded **beach** good for swimming. Beside the estuary you can see the **dhows** being hand-built: around fifty men spend two years building each ship, the largest of which cost upwards of $500,000 and are bought by wealthy Gulf Arabs.

Mandvi's little-visited **Vijay Vilas Palace** (daily 9am–1pm & 3pm–6pm; Rs35, camera Rs50, video Rs200), 8km west of town (turn left after 4km), is a sandy-white domed building in almost 700 acres of land, built as a summer retreat by Kutch's maharao in the 1940s, and now often used as a film set. Inside, European furniture fills the high-ceilinged carpeted rooms, hunting trophies deck the walls and a grand stairway leads to the ladies' quarters on the first floor. The palace estate has a private beach (Rs50) with a royal pavilion. **Buses** every 30min (1hr 30min–2hr) and slightly quicker crammed shared taxis (around Rs35) run between Bhuj and Mandvi.

In recent years **MUNDRA**, 44km east of Mandvi, has grown into India's largest privately owned port. Although it has few sights of its own, it is still a good place to pick up local crafts in the markets. Mundra is best visited on a day trip from Mandvi (hourly buses; 1hr 30min) or Bhuj (hourly buses; 1hr 30min).

Accommodation and eating

On the waterfront, in a former hospital near Bridge Gate, the *Rukmavati Guest House* (Ⓣ02834/223558, Ⓔhotelrukmavati@gmail.com; ❹) is a great budget option: all **rooms** have private bathroom and TV, but it's worth paying the extra Rs25 or so for a balcony. There's a small library, and the owner has loads of local information. Also on the waterfront, near the bus station, *Hotel Sea View* (Ⓣ02834/224481, ❹) has twee attached rooms; although they don't have "sea views", those at the front look straight out onto the *dhow*-builders. On a private stretch of the Vijay Vilas Palace's beach, *The Beach at Mandvi Palace* (Ⓣ02834/295725, Ⓦwww.mandvibeac.com; ❽), has ten luxury a/c tents, each with private bathroom and veranda, and an excellent restaurant. It's just a shame the tents are a bit too close together. Other than *The Beach*, the best bet for **food** is *Zorba the Buddha* on KT Shah Road, west of the bus stand behind an old town gate, which produces top veg thalis.

Southeast of Bhuj

The 50km journey southeast from Bhuj to **KANDLA**, one of the busiest ports on India's west coast, takes you past dry scrubland. In the small village of **Bhujodi**, about 7km out of Bhuj, artisans weave thick shawls and blankets on pit looms dug into the floors of squat mud houses. You can buy their products from the small shop run by the Bhujodi Handweaving Co-op Society. Further along on this road are the villages of **Paddhar**, known for Rabari embroidery, and **Dhaneti**, a centre for Ahir embroidery. **Dhamadka** is still an important centre for Ajrakh block-printing, though after the earthquake many artisans were moved to a new village, **Ajrakhpur**, around 10km east of Bhuj on the main highway.

The first main town beyond Bhuj, **ANJAR**, was the capital of Kutch until 1548. It was badly affected by the earthquake; recovery here was much slower than in Bhuj, with serious disruption to traditional craftsmaking – Ahir embroidery, *bandhani*, batik and nutcrackers. Things have improved in recent years, however, and a market where you can buy crafts is now held again once or twice a week.

North and west of Bhuj

North of Bhuj are the craft centres of **HODKA**, **DHORDO** and **KHAVDA**, where clusters of grass-roofed mud huts are decorated with traditional clay and whitewash patterns. Around **LUDIA**, a Rabari village, there's a fairly commercial attitude towards tourists, so expect insistent sales pitches. Embroidery and patchwork centres include **BHIRENDIARA**, where some houses feature beautiful mud-work (*liponkan*) interiors, and **SUMERASER SHEIKH**, where

NGO **Kala Raksha** (Ⓣ02808/277238, Ⓦwww.kala-raksha.org) maintains an archive of antique textiles, a handicraft workshop, a museum and a fixed-price shop. Most of Kala Raksha's participants are women from marginalized communities, and this is a great place to learn about local embroidery, tie-dying, patchwork and inlay techniques. Call ahead if you want a tour. Kala Raksha's work is vital as the future of many of the craft centres is in doubt: the post-earthquake reconstruction created many largely unskilled labouring jobs, which have attracted lots of craft workers with higher wages.

In the village of **Hodka**, 50km north of Bhuj, the *Shaam-e-Sarhad Village Resort* (Ⓣ02832/654124, Ⓦwww.hodka.in; full-board; ❻–❼) is a sustainable tourism project run by the local Halepotra people. Open October to March, "Sunset at the Border", as the name means, offers accommodation in circular mud huts or luxury tents, craft workshops, birdwatching excursions and trips to local villages. You need a permit to visit (see p.558).

To the north of Hodka are the semi-arid **Banni Grasslands**, home to a vast array of birds, including flamingos, pelicans, cranes, painted storks and hornbills. Ecologist Jugal Tiwari (Ⓣ02835/200025, Ⓦwww.cedobirding.com) organizes informative birdwatching trips in the area.

In the village of **DEVPUR**, 40km west of Bhuj, is *Darbargadh Devpur*, a sandstone fort built in 1905 in the traditional Kutchi (or Roha) style and now a charming homestay (Ⓣ02835/283065, Ⓦhttp://sites.google.com/site/devpurhomestay; ❻).

Than and Dhinodar

The monastery at **THAN**, 60km northwest of Bhuj, is home to a Tantric order of Hindu sadhus known as Kanphata ("split-ear") after the heavy agate rings they traditionally wear in their ears. This whitewashed complex at the foot of the hill encloses a handful of medieval temples, tombs and domed dwellings. Hardy travellers can spend the night in its *dharamshala* for a small donation. From Than, you can walk up a rocky ravine via an ancient pilgrims' trail to the mountaintop behind, where **Dhinodar** is the site of a small painted temple, home to a Kanphata yogi, Hiranath Baba, and his acolytes. Allow three hours for the round trip from Than and take ample water supplies.

Dholavira

In the far north of Kutch, 250km from Bhuj, on an island surrounded by snow-white salt flats, the tiny village of **DHOLAVIRA** is strewn around the remnants of a once-thriving city which, six thousand or more years ago, maintained trade links with Persia and the Euphrates Delta. Yet this so-called "Indus Valley" or "Harappan" archeological centre (daily 9am–dusk; no video cameras) attracts barely a trickle of visitors. Archeological digs started here in the 1970s after a local farmer ploughed up a small terracotta seal. Soon, the existence of a major planned city with monumental structures, palace complex and extraordinary water management system was revealed. It's best to travel here by taxi, as the only **bus** from Bhuj (2pm; around 7hr) doesn't arrive until late in the evening; on the return leg, the bus departs at 5am. Simple **rooms** in cottages are on offer at the state-run *Toran Tourist Complex* (Ⓣ02837/277395; ❷), which also has a **cafeteria**.

Little Rann Wild Ass Sanctuary

Spanning 4850 square kilometres, the **Little Rann Wild Ass Sanctuary**, a vast salt-encrusted desert plain that becomes inundated during the rains (July–Sept), is home to an abundance of wildlife, including the endangered Indian **wild ass**. Usually seen in loosely knit herds, this handsome chestnut-brown-and-white member of the horse family is capable of running very fast. The sanctuary is also home to wolves, foxes, jackals, jungle and desert cats, nilgai and blackbuck antelopes and the chinkara gazelle. Large flocks of flamingo, pelicans and winter-visiting cranes can be seen at Bajana Lake; October to March is the time to see the migratory birds.

The sanctuary headquarters is at Dhrangadhra in Saurashtra, but most tourist facilities are at **Dasada**, a six-hour bus-ride east from Bhuj and 33km from Viramgam (on the Bhuj–Ahmedabad train line). From Dasada (or any of the resorts below) you can rent a jeep (around Rs1500/day) and guide to take a tour of the sanctuary. Entrance fees (Rs1050 [Rs250] per vehicle seating up to six, camera Rs100) are paid at the entrance to the sanctuary near **Bajana** village, thirty minutes' drive from Dasada. All the **accommodation** options in the area can arrange to pick you up from the bus station. *Rann Riders* (Ⓣ02757/280257, Ⓦwww.rannriders.com; ❽), 2km from Dasada, has thirteen comfortable a/c *kooba* mud huts with tiled or grass roofs, a restaurant, pool and several inviting hammocks. Its all-in package (Rs2900/person) includes full board and two jeep safaris. Another 12km on towards the sanctuary gates, *Camp Zainabad* (AKA "Desert Coursers"; Ⓣ0257/241333, Ⓦwww.desertcoursers.net; ❽) is in a similar vein, only slightly cheaper, with all-in packages from Rs2500 per person. However, the best option is wildlife photographer Devjibhai Dhamecha's excellent *Eco Tour Camp* (Ⓣ02754/280560, Ⓦwww.littlerann.com; ❺), in Jogad village, close to Sumera lake, which has traditional thatched-roof huts for Rs2000 per couple full board.

Saurashtra

SAURASHTRA, or the **Kathiawar Peninsula**, forms the bulk of Gujarat state, a large knob of land spreading south from the hills and marshes of the north out to the Arabian Sea, cut into by the Gulf of Cambay to the east and the Gulf of Kutch to the west. This is Gujarat at its most diverse, populated by cattle-rearing tribes and industrialists, with Hindu, Jain, Buddhist and Muslim architecture, modern urban centres and traditional bazaars. Saurashtra boasts India's finest Jain temple city at **Shatrunjaya** near **Palitana**, Krishna temples at **Dwarka** and **Somnath,** and Ashoka's Buddhist capital, **Junagadh**. Lions can still be found in **Gir National Park**, while northeast of Bhavnagar, India's largest herd of blackbuck lives in **Velavadar National Park**. Gandhi's birthplace is honoured in **Porbandar** and his former family home in **Rajkot** has been turned into a museum. For sun, sea and beer, head to the formerly Portuguese island of **Diu**, just off the south coast.

Rajkot

Founded in the sixteenth century, **RAJKOT** was ruled by the Jadeja Rajputs until merging with the Union of Saurashtra after Independence, since when it has become a successful industrial centre with a large middle class. Best known for its association with **Mahatma Gandhi**, there is little to attract tourists save a museum and Gandhi's family home. Rajkot is, however, a good base for trips to nearby princely towns.

Arrival and information

Three main roads radiate from the busy road junction at Sanganwa Chowk in the centre of Rajkot: **Dhebar Road** heads south, past the state bus stand, 100m away; **Lakhajiraj Road** goes east, through the old city; and **Jawahar Road** runs north, past Alfred High School (Gandhi's former school, and now officially named

Moving on from Rajkot

There are regular state **buses** to Jamnagar (2hr), Junagadh (2hr–2hr 30min), Porbandar (5hr) and Veraval (5hr). Eagle Travels on Ring Road, opposite the Adani Hyper Market (ⓣ0281/554444) has more comfortable **a/c buses** to Ahmedabad, Vadodara and Mumbai. Jay Somnath (ⓣ0281/243 3315) on Gondal Road, 50m south of the Telegraph Office, has buses to Bhuj (5–6hr). Jet Airways (near *Lord's Banquet* ⓣ0281/247 9623) has a daily **flight** to Mumbai.

Mahatma Gandhi High School, though most people still use its old name) and Jubilee Gardens towards **Rajkot Junction Station**, 2km northeast (get off here rather than at City Station if arriving by train), and the airport 4km northwest.

Rajkot's rather redundant **tourist office** (Mon–Sat 10.30am–1.30pm & 2–6pm, closed 2nd and 4th Sat of month; ⓣ0281/223 4507) is off Jawahar Road, north of Sanganwa Chowk behind the **State Bank of Saurashtra**; look for the blue **ATM** sign as the bank's name is in Gujarati. The **post office** is on Sadar Road, off Jawahar Road opposite Jubilee Gardens. For **internet** access, try Buzz Cyber Café (Rs15/hr), opposite *Lord's Banquet*.

Accommodation

The cheapest **hotels** near the bus stand leave much to be desired, so it's worth spending a bit more to escape the noise and dirt of the city.

Bhabha Hotel Panchnath Rd, off Jawahar Rd just south of Alfred High School ⓣ0281/222 0861, ⓕ222 1384. A reasonable budget option with small singles, doubles, triples and quads; all have TV and private bathroom, but the more expensive rooms also come with tubs and a/c. 24hr checkout. ❷–❹

Galaxy Jawahar Rd, 100m north of Sanganwa Chowk ⓣ0281/222 2905. A refurbishment has brightened up this hotel (and pushed up prices): sizeable a/c attached rooms in creams and browns have TV, but the bathrooms could be better. It's on the third floor of a shopping complex, and accessed via a creaking lift. ❹–❺

Imperial Palace Hotel Dr Yagnik Rd ⓣ0281/248 0000, ⓦwww.theimperialpalace.biz. Rajkot's classiest hotel attracts visiting cricketers and Bollywood stars with sophisticated rooms, pool, fitness suite and excellent restaurant. Rates include breakfast. Unusually for Gujarat, it's also wheelchair-accessible. ❼

Jyoti Kanak Rd, 200m north of the bus stand ⓣ0281/222 5472. The best of the scruffy and poky lodges in the area, *Jyoti* is bearable for a night, thanks largely to its welcoming manager. ❶–❷

Kavery Kanak Rd ⓣ0281/223 9331, ⓦwww.hotelkavery.com. This mid-range business hotel has spacious attached rooms. with pale wood fittings. Perks include free airport pick-up and wi-fi. ❻

Silver Palace Gondal Rd ⓣ0281/248 0008. With the same management as the *Imperial Palace*, and recently renovated, this is a professional hotel with small but perfectly formed attached rooms. There are nice touches like kettles and "keep fit in your room" leaflets. ❻

The Town

Rajkot's most appealing area is the **old city**, where you'll see plenty of typical Gujarati wooden-fronted houses with intricately carved shutters and stained-glass windows. The Gandhis moved here from Porbandar in 1881. Tucked away in the narrow streets on Ghitaka Road, off Lakhajiraj Road about 300m east of Sanganwa Chowk (the turning is marked by an easy-to-miss blue signpost) the family house **Kaba Gandhi no Delo** (Mon–Sat 9am–noon & 3–5.30pm) has a small display of artefacts and photographs. In a nineteenth-century building in Jubilee Bagh, the **Watson Museum** (daily except Sun and 2nd & 4th Sat of month, 9am–6pm; Rs50 [Rs2]) is named after Colonel Watson, British Political Agent from 1886 to 1893, and displays relics from 2000 BC to the nineteenth century, including finds from Indus Valley sites, medieval statues and manuscripts.

Eating

Look out for the **Kathiawadi version** of the Gujarati thali, spiced with ginger and garlic. Rajkot is also known for milk **sweets** like *thabdi halwas* and the saffron-flavoured *kesar pedas*.

Adingo Limda Chowk, next to *Hotel Harmony*. Sleek eatery decked out with red tables and chairs and dishing up breakfast, fast food, Indian and Chinese fare; the *paneer* tikka stands out (Rs45–100).

Bukhara *Hotel Kavery*, Kanak Rd. Smart restaurant serving a Gujarati thali at lunchtimes and, for dinner, top-notch north and south Indian, Chinese, Mexican and Italian dishes (mains Rs50–150).

Grand Regency *Hotel Grand Regency*, Debar Rd. Recommended multi-cuisine hotel restaurant; the glass-walled kitchen is an attraction in itself, as diners get to see Indian breads like naan being prepared on the spot. Mains Rs75–150.

Lord's Banquet Kasturba Rd. Where locals go for a treat, this efficient a/c place serves superior north Indian food (Rs80–150). You can specify the spiciness of your dish and even the crispiness of your roti. Run by the same management, *Temptations*, in the neighbouring building, has snacks, fast food and ice cream.

Around Rajkot

The princes of Rajkot district left a rich legacy of elaborate **residences** whose architectural styles range from the delicate detail of the seventeenth century to bold Art Deco. Most buses between Rajkot and Ahmedabad stop at **SAYLA**, 87km east of Rajkot, where a colonial bungalow has been converted into the *Old Bell Guest House* (Ⓣ02755/280017, Ⓔsaylaheritage@rediffmail.com; ❻–❼) with large a/c rooms and a fine restaurant. The relaxing grounds are home to a giant chessboard and an aged tennis court. At Sayla, you can see a range of handicrafts, including beadwork and weaving; it is also a good base if you want to visit nearby Wadhwan, known for its *bandhani* tie-dye and brassware.

The flamboyant Ranjit Vilas Palace (call ahead to visit; Ⓣ02828/220000) at **WANKANER**, 39km northeast of Rajkot, is still home to the family who once ruled the old state of the same name. Built between 1899 and 1914, the building can be seen from far across the flat Saurashtran plains. Its fancy arched facade shows a frenzy of Mughal, Italianate, Moorish and Victorian Gothic styles with stained-glass windows, domed towers and chandeliers. You can stay in Art Deco splendour at the family's nearby summer home, the *Royal Oasis* (Ⓣ02828/220000, Ⓕ220002; full board ❽), which has sumptuous rooms and an indoor pool.

GONDAL, 39km south of Rajkot and served by buses every 30min (1hr), is a centre for beadwork embroidery, handloom weaving, silverware, handmade brass boxes and Ayurvedic medicine. Good places for shopping include the market on Darbargadh Road and the Udyog Bharati emporium near the palace. The former royal family have converted the guest wing of their Huzoor Palace into the *Orchard Palace Hotel* (Ⓣ02825/224550, Ⓔhghgroup@yahoo.com; full board ❼–❽). Facing onto groves of fruit trees, it has large high-ceilinged rooms, four-posters and period furniture.

Jamnagar

Close to the northwest coast of Saurashtra, the busy, noisy city of **JAMNAGAR** has some fabulous architectural surprises. Founded in the sixteenth century, the walled city was built to the east of Ranmal Lake, centred on the circular Lakhota Fort. **K.S. Ranjitsinhji**, who played cricket for England alongside W.G. Grace, ruled Jamnagar at the start of the twentieth century, replacing run-down buildings with attractive constructions that remain as testimony to his prosperous and efficient rule. The city is renowned for excellent *bandhani* (tie-dye), sold in the markets near the Darbargadh.

Moving on from Jamnagar

There are frequent **state buses** to Rajkot (2hr), Junagadh (4hr), Porbandar (4hr) and Dwarka (3–4hr). **Private buses** leave from Pancheshwar Tower near Teen Batti: Patel Tours & Travels (ⓣ0288/255 2419) has services to Ahmedabad and Bhuj. For air tickets and other travel queries, try Savetime Travel (ⓣ0288/255 3137) on Bedi Gate Road. The **airport** is 8km west of the bus stand: Indian Airlines (Bhid Bhanjan Rd ⓣ0288/255 0211) has a daily **flight** to Mumbai.

Arrival and information

From the **state bus station**, it's a 2km walk or rickshaw ride west, past Ranmal Lake, to **Bedi Gate** and the **New Super Market**, the unofficial centre of town. Coming from Rajkot, your bus will pass through town before arriving at the bus station, so ask to be dropped off at Bedi Gate; if travelling to Rajkot, flag down a bus outside *Hotel President*. From the **main railway station**, it's a six-kilometre ride southeast into town, past **Teen Batti**, an important square; most trains also stop at the smaller **Gandhinagar railway station**, 2km from the centre. Thomas Cook, opposite the town hall, **changes cash** and travellers' cheques. For **internet** access, try Venus (Rs20/hr) opposite the Teen Batti **post office**.

Accommodation

Acceptable **accommodation** in Jamnagar is limited. The inexpensive places in and around New Super Market are largely substandard.

Aram Nand Niwas, Pandit Nehru Marg ⓣ0288/255 1701, ⓦwww.hotelaram.com. Palatial white building – once the home of a scion of the state's ruling family – with blue awnings, giving it something of the feel of a British seaside hotel. Its large a/c rooms, nostalgic for the days of the Raj and filled with European antiques, have a faded charm. ❺

Ashiana Third Floor, New Super Market ⓣ0288/255 9110. The rooms are spacious for a downtown budget hotel and come with TV and bathroom – choose from carpeted a/c rooms or grubbier ordinary ones. ❷–❹

Gayatri Guest House Summer Club Rd ⓣ0288/256 4727. A 5min walk south of the bus stand, on the second floor across from Rathi Hospital; decent doubles, some with a/c and TV, good-value singles and 24hr checkout. ❸–❹

President Teen Batti ⓣ0288/255 7491, ⓦwww.hotelpresident.in. A well-managed hotel, home to plain rooms with private balconies and TVs, a currency exchange and a good restaurant. Staff can organize birdwatching and sailing trips and visits to the local marine park. Free airport transfers. ❸–❺

Punit Pandit Nehru Marg, just northwest of Teen Batti ⓣ0288/255 9275, ⓕ255 0561. A popular place with a small but pleasant roof terrace and airy turquoise-coloured rooms, which come with carpets and slightly dated decor. ❸–❹

The City

The most remarkable of Ranjitsinhji's constructions is **Willingdon Crescent**, the swooping arches of its curved facade overlooking the wide streets of Chelmsford Market and the old palace, the **Darbargadh**. In the heart of town, just off Ranjit Road southwest of Bedi Gate, stands the late nineteenth-century **Ratan Bai Mosque**. This grand domed prayer-hall, its sandalwood doors inlaid with mother-of-pearl, is the unlikely neighbour to a magnificent pair of **Jain temples**, both decorated with extraordinary **murals**. The most spectacular of the two, **Shantinath Mandir**, is a maze of brightly coloured columns. The outer side of the large dome over **Adinath Mandir** is inlaid with gold and coloured mosaic and both temples have cupolas enriched with a design of mirrors above the entrance porch. The temples form the hub of **Chandni Bazaar**, an almost circular market area enlivened by carved wooden doors, mosaics and balconies.

Stretching west towards the bus stand, Ranmal Lake and **Lakhota Palace** (daily except Wed and 2nd & 4th Sat of month, 10.30am–2pm & 2.30–5.30pm; Rs50 [Rs2]) were part of an employment-generating measure during a spell of drought in Jamnagar state during the 1750s. The palace is connected to solid land in both directions by a causeway but only accessible from the north side. On entering you'll pass a guardroom containing muskets, swords and powder flasks; the **museum** on the upper floor holds a mediocre display of paintings, sculpture, folk art and coins. South of the lake stands the solid **Bhujia Fort**, one of the few casualties of the earthquake in Jamnagar and closed ever since. To its northwest, on the edge of the old city, the **Bala Hanuman Temple** has been the scene of round-the-clock nonstop chanting ("Shree Ram, Jay Ram, Jay Jay Ram") since 1964, a feat cited in the *Guinness Book of Records*. Jamnagar's **Ayurvedic University** (Ⓣ0288/277 0103, Ⓦwww.ayurveduniversity.com), 1km northwest of Teen Batti, runs a vast array of courses, and offers massage, yoga and mud-therapy sessions.

Eating

7 Seas *Hotel President*. Continuing the hotel's vaguely nautical theme with a porthole-like door and maritime paintings, *7 Seas* serves up some of Jamnagar's best non-veg food (Rs60–140): the roast mutton curry stands out and the pineapple lassi's not to be missed.

Fresh Point Near the Town Hall. An unassuming joint with a strong local following, serving Punjabi and other north Indian dishes (Rs30–70).

Kalpana Teen Batti. The decor may be ancient, but the tempting veg snacks – burgers, dosas, milkshakes and ice cream (Rs20–50) – certainly hit the spot.

Madras Teen Batti. A cramped dining room, with separate slightly more spacious a/c area; great Punjabi, south Indian, Jain and Chinese dishes, including a mean veg *jalfrezi* (Rs30–80).

Dwarka

In the far west of the peninsula, fertile wheat, groundnut and cotton fields emerge in vivid contrast to the arid expanses further inland. According to Hindu legend, Krishna fled Mathura to this coastal region, declaring **DWARKA** his capital. A labyrinth of narrow winding streets cluttered with temples, the town resonates today with the bustle of eager saffron-clad pilgrims and the clatter of celebratory drums. Dwarka really comes to life during the major Hindu **festivals**; the most fervent are the Shivratri Mela (Feb/March) and Janmashtami (Aug/Sept).

The elaborately carved tower of the sixteenth-century **Dwarkadish Temple** (daily 7am–12.30pm & 5–9.30pm) looms 50m above the town. Non-Hindus can enter the shrine only on signing a form declaring respect for religion.

When Krishna came to Dwarka with the Yadava clan, he eloped with Princess Rukmini. One kilometre east of town, the small twelfth-century **Rukmini Temple** is, if anything, more architecturally impressive than the Dwarkadish temple, with carvings of elephants, flowers, dancers and Shiva in several of his aspects covering every wall. For great sea and town **views**, climb to the top of the **lighthouse** (daily 5pm–6.30pm; Rs10).

Practicalities

Trains arrive at the station north of town. The **bus stand** on the Okha road has regular services to Jamnagar (3–4hr), Porbandar (3hr), Junagadh (5–6hr) and Veraval (6hr). Dwarka Darshan (Ⓣ02892/234093) in the vegetable market runs **tours** (8am & 2pm; Rs50) to the underground *jyotrilingam* at the Nageshwar Temple, 16km from Dwarka. **Internet** access is available at Shreeji Cybercafé (Rs40/hr) opposite *Hotel Uttam*. **Accommodation** is good value: *Gurupreena* (Ⓣ02892/235512; ❸–❹), just off the approach road leading from the highway to the bus stand, has clean, comfortable rooms; the more expensive ones come with a/c. The modern *Hotel Rajdhani* on Hospital Road (Ⓣ02892/234070; ❹), just off the main road between the bus stand and the temple, has simple rooms with TV and choice of a/c or fans. *Meera*, on the approach road, serves inexpensive veg **thalis**.

Porbandar

Once an international port and princely state capital, **PORBANDAR**, between Veraval and Dwarka, is famed as Mahatma Gandhi's birthplace. The city is also linked with the legends of **Krishna** – in ancient times the settlement was called Sudampuri, after one of Krishna's comrades. Today, shrouded in a dim haze of excretions from the cement and chemical factories on its outskirts, Porbandar is pretty grimy, despite the flow of remittances from its many emigrants overseas.

Arrival and information

Porbandar's main street, **Mahatma Gandhi (MG) Road**, runs from a fountain at its eastern end – northeast of which is the **railway station** – to a triple gateway at its western end, near Gandhi's house. In the middle, at the **main square**, it is bisected by Arya Sumaj Road, which runs northwards across Jubilee Bridge, and southwards to the **GPO**. Just east is the **state bus stand** (connected to MG Road by ST Road) and, to its south, the main beach. **Banks** along MG Road change foreign currency and travellers' cheques. Beneath the *Indraprasth Hotel*, Shiny the Cyber Hut offers **internet** access (Rs30/hr).

Accommodation

Indraprasth Off ST Rd Ⓣ0286/224 2681, Ⓦwww.hotelindraprasth.biz. One of several decent, but uninspiring mid-range choices in Porbandar. It has straightforward rooms in warm colours with TV and private bathrooms; a/c costs extra. ❷–❹

Moon Palace MG Rd, 100m east of the main square Ⓣ0286/224 1172, Ⓔhmppbr@hotmail.com. While the rooms – all with attached baths and TVs – feel a bit sombre, they're clean, comfortable and good value. ❷–❹

Natraj MG Rd, close to *Moon Palace* Ⓣ0286/221 5658, Ⓦwww.hotelnatrajp.com. Porbandar's best hotel is a notch above the competition, with surprisingly cool, minimalist rooms – at bargain prices – plus a fine restaurant and a currency exchange. ❸–❺

Silver Palace Silver Complex, just off MG Rd Ⓣ0286/225 2591. *Silver Palace* is another good choice, with spick-and span-rooms (all with TVs, fridges and various superfluous pieces of furniture, such as padded stools and mini tables). Some have lurid decor, so ask to see a few. ❸–❹

The Town

The town harbours little of note, except **Gandhi's birthplace** (daily 7.30am–7.30pm; free but guides expect a donation), in the west of town. The place is empty, though some of the walls in the reading and prayer rooms on the upper floors bear faded traces of paintings. The Kirti Mandir, a memorial to the

Moving on from Porbander

Thankys Tours and Travels (Ⓣ0286/224 4344), on MG Road near Dreamland Cinema, can book taxis, domestic flights and tickets on the daily *Saurashtra Express* #9216 **train**, which departs at 8.30pm, arriving in Ahmedabad at 6am and Mumbai at 7.15pm. Eagle Travels (Ⓣ0281/221 2089) runs regular **buses** to Rajkot (5hr), Ahmedabad (10hr) and Junagadh (3hr); there are also slower state buses. Jet Airways has five weekly **flights** to Mumbai; the airport is 5km from town.

Mahatma Gandhi – India's great soul

Gujarat's most famous son **Mohandas Karamchand Gandhi** was born on October 2, 1869, in Porbandar. Although merchants by caste – Gandhi means grocer – both his grandfather and father rose to positions of political influence. Young Mohandas was shy and sickly, only an average scholar, but from early on questioned the codes of power around him and even flouted accepted Hindu practice: he once ate meat for a year believing it would give him the physical edge the British appeared to possess. As a teenager, he began to develop an interest in spirituality, particularly the Jain principle of **ahimsa** (nonviolence).

Gandhi moved to London to study law at 19, outwardly adopting the appearance and manners of an English gentleman, but also keeping to his mother's wish that he resist meat, alcohol and women. Avidly reading the Bible alongside the *Bhagavad Gita*, he started to view different religions as a collective source of truth from which everyone could draw spiritual inheritance.

After a brief spell back in India, Gandhi left again to practise law in South Africa, where the plight of fellow Indians – coupled with his own indignation at being ejected from a first-class rail carriage – fuelled his campaigns for racial equality. His public profile grew and he gained crucial victories for minorities against the practices of indentured labour. During this time he also opted to transcend material possessions, dressing in the handspun *dhoti* and shawl of a peasant, and took a vow of celibacy. This turn to ascetic purity he characterized as *satyagraha*, which derived from Sanskrit ideas of "truth" and "firmness", and would become the touchstone of **passive resistance**. Returning to India with his messianic reputation well established – the poet Tagore named him **"Mahatma"** (Great Soul) – Gandhi travelled the country campaigning for **swaraj** (home rule). He also worked tirelessly for the rights of women and untouchables, whom he called **Harijans** (children of God), and founded an ashram at Sabarmati outside Ahmedabad where these principles were upheld. Gandhi stepped up his activities in the wake of the brutal massacre of protesters at Amritsar, leading a series of self-sufficiency drives during the 1920s, which culminated in the great **salt march** from Ahmedabad to Dandi in 1930. This month-long 386-kilometre journey led a swelling band of followers to the coast, where salt was made in defiance of the British monopoly on production. It drew worldwide attention: although Gandhi was promptly imprisoned, British resolve was seen to have weakened and on release he was invited to a round-table meeting in London to discuss home rule. The struggle continued for several years and Gandhi served more time in jail – his wife Kasturba dying by his side in 1944.

As the nationalist movement gained strength, Gandhi grew more concerned about the state of Hindu–Muslim relations. He responded to outbreaks of **communal violence** by subjecting his own body to self-purification and suffering through fasting. When Britain finally guaranteed independence in 1947, it seemed Gandhi's dream of a united and free India was possible after all. But **Partition** left him with a deep sense of failure. Once more he fasted in Calcutta in a bid to stem the violence as large numbers of Hindus and Muslims flowed between the new countries. Gandhi's commitment to the fair treatment of Muslim Indians and his intention to visit and endorse Pakistan as a neighbour enraged many Hindu fundamentalists. He survived an attempt on his life on January 20, 1948, only to be shot dead from close range by a lone Hindu gunman in Delhi ten days later. Prime Minister Nehru announced the loss on national radio: "Friends and comrades, the light has gone out of our lives and there is darkness everywhere."

Mahatma and his wife erected in the 1950s, has photographs and artefacts from his life. The former Maharaja's palaces can be seen near the Chowpatty Seaface. **Huzoor Palace** is occupied by the family when they visit from their present home in London, while the **Daria Rajmahal Palace** near the lighthouse is now a college. **Grishmabhawan**, near the bus stand, is an impressive arched pavilion, built for the eighteenth-century poet Maharaja Sartanji. Porbandar's lake is a designated bird sanctuary, but you can actually see more **flamingos** – along with *dhow*-builders – at the creeks along the coast than here. Over a thousand **whale sharks** visit the coast each year close to Porbandar and Veraval: the Wildlife Trust of India (Ⓣ011/2632 6025, Ⓦwww.wti.org.in) can help organize dives (though you will need your own equipment) or trips on research boats.

Eating

Although Porbandar is known in Gujarat for its **seafood**, you'll have a job finding it. Outside the main hotels, there's an uninspiring choice of **restaurants**.

Moon Palace *Moon Palace* hotel. Popular restaurant serving Gujarati thalis (Rs50–85), Punjabi dishes and western snacks. It also opens early for breakfast.

National MG Rd. This unassuming Muslim-run place serves delicious (but small) meat and veg meals (Rs30–90) to a steady stream of contented customers.

Natraj *Natraj* hotel. Run with the same style and quiet efficiency as the hotel, *Natraj* has a modern dining room and varied menu of Indian, Chinese and even decent pizzas and pasta dishes – the latter a real rarity for Gujarat (Rs40–120).

Swagat MG Rd, 250m east of the main square. A relaxed, softly-lit place that offers good quality, reasonably-priced Punjabi and south Indian veg dishes (Rs30–85). It can get very busy at weekends.

Junagadh and around

The small town of **JUNAGADH** (or Junagarh), around 160km from Diu (via Veraval) is an intriguing place, with a skyline broken by domes and minarets. Its lively bazaars, Buddhist monuments, Hindu temples, mosques, Victorian Gothic-style archways and faded mansions – plus the magnificent Jain temples on **Mount Girnar** – make Junagadh an exciting city to explore.

From the fourth century BC to the death of Ashoka (*c*.232 BC), Junagadh was the capital of Gujarat under the Buddhist Mauryas. The brief reigns of the Kshatrapas and the Guptas came to an end when the town passed into the hands of the Hindu Chudasanas, who in turn soon lost out to Muslim invaders. Muslim sovereignty lasted until Independence when, although the leaders planned to unite Junagadh with Pakistan, local pressure ensured that it became part of the Indian Union. Because of the sanctity of Mount Girnar, 4km away, the **Shivratri Mela** (Feb/March) assumes particular importance in Junagadh, when thousands of saffron-clad sadhus come to camp around the town. Fireworks, processions, chanting, chillum-smoking and demonstrations of body-torturing ascetic practices continue for nine days and nights. Meanwhile, every November up to a million

Moving on from Junagadh

Trains to Rajkot, Ahmedabad and the south coast call at Junagadh. For Ahmedabad, the daily *Veraval-Ahmedabad Express* #9120 departs 8.40am (7hr 15min), calling at Rajkot at 11.09am. There are also daily services to Veraval, Sasan Gir and Delwada (for Diu); for the latter two destinations, buses are quicker, but less comfortable. **Buses** from the long-distance bus stand, just west of Chittakhana Chowk, serve destinations around the state, including hourly services to Una, for **Diu** (the 7am goes direct to Diu; 6hr). There are also hourly buses for **Ahmedabad** (7–8hr), **Jamnagar** (5hr), **Porbandar** (3hr), **Rajkot** (2hr 30min) and **Veraval** (2hr), and services to **Sasan Gir** every 30min (2hr). Mahasagar Travels (Ⓣ0285/262 6085) near the railway station sells tickets for private buses, notably to Mumbai (24hr); it has another office at Kalwa Chowk (Ⓣ0285/262 1913).

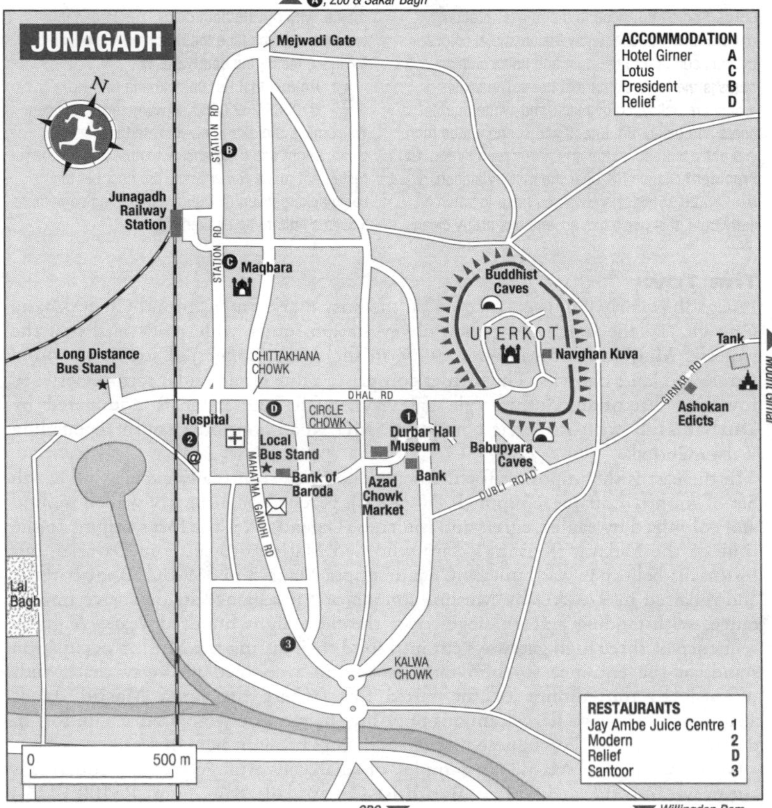

people take part in the **Parikrama**, a five-day 36km walk around the base of Mount Girnar and the surrounding hills. Tourists arriving in Junagadh at these times should book rooms well in advance.

Arrival and information

Arriving in Junagadh by bus or train, you're within walking distance of nearly all the hotels. Staff at *Relief Hotel* provide the best **information** on the town's sites and Gir National Park. The **GPO** is 2km south of town; there's also a smaller branch next to the local bus stand. The State Bank of India opposite the Durbar Hall Museum **changes** dollars and sterling; to exchange travellers' cheques, head for the Bank of Baroda, near the local bus stand; it also has an **ATM**. Try XS Cyber Café, near the bus station, for **internet** access (Rs15/hr).

Accommodation

Travellers, particularly women, should avoid the **hotels** in the Kalwa Chowk area.

Hotel Girner Outside town, 2km north of the bus station ⓣ0285/2621201. Run (without much enthusiasm) by Gujarat Tourism, *Girner* has reasonable rooms with attached bathroom; some also have balconies and a/c. An auto-rickshaw from the bus station should cost Rs15–20. ❸–❹

Lotus Station Rd, close to the railway station ⓣ0285/265 8500, ⓦwww.thelotushotel.com. A tranquil contrast to the dust and noise outside, *Lotus* is the town's smartest hotel. The swish rooms are enlivened by black-and-white marble floors and beige furniture. If you spend a little more you get a bathtub, kettle and flat-screen TV too. ❺

President Station Rd, near the railway station ⓣ0285/262 5661. Handy if you have to catch an early train, this place has acceptable, pretty clean rooms, with private bathrooms. The larger, more expensive rooms face the noisy main road, so opt for those facing the courtyard. ❹

Relief Dhal Rd, Chittakhana Chowk ⓣ0285/262 0280, ⓦwww.reliefhotel.com. Welcoming and extremely knowledgeable staff, clean, bright and inexpensive rooms, and a superior restaurant make *Relief* easily the best bet for backpackers, even though the plumbing sometimes leaves a little to be desired. ❸

The Town

Junagadh is fairly compact, focused on the busy market area around **Chittakhana Chowk**. To the north, near the railway station, quiet wide roads lead past the majestic **Maqbara monuments**, while in the south, congested streets surround Circle and Janta chowks. The former comprises a fine semicircular terrace between towering Victorian Gothic-style gateways, while the latter is dominated by **Durbar Hall** with its modest museum. MG Road continues south to bustling Kalwa Chowk.

In the east is the imposing fortified citadel of **Uperkot** (daily except 2nd & 4th Sat of month 7.30am–6.30pm; Rs50 [Rs2]), perched on a thickly walled mound and colonized by eagles, egrets and squirrels. Legend dates the fort's origins to the time of the Yadavas (Krishna's clan) who fled Mathura to settle in Dwarka, but historians believe it was built by Chandragupta Maurya in 319 BC. Rediscovered and repaired in 976 AD by Muslim conquerors, it regained its defensive importance, withstanding sixteen sieges over the next eight hundred years. A grand sequence of three high gateways cut into solid rock during the Muslim occupation stands at the entrance to the citadel, spanning a cobbled walkway that winds upwards to the summit of the raised fort, where the **Jama Masjid** stands abandoned. The two fierce cannons opposite the mosque were used at Diu fort in defence against the Portuguese in 1530 and were brought here in 1538.

North of the Jama Masjid is a complex of small cells arranged around courtyards cut down into the rock. These **Buddhist Caves** (daily 8am–6pm; Rs100 [Rs5]) were built in the third or fourth century AD – worn traces of figurines and foliage can still be made out on the columns in the lower level. Nearby, more than 170 steps descend to the **Adi Chadi Vav** (well), believed to date from the fifteenth century. The more impressive eleventh-century **Navghan Kuva**, in the southeast of the citadel, consists of a superb staircase that winds around the well shaft to the dimly-lit water level over 52m below.

Below the southern wall of the fort, the **Babupyara Caves** (Rs100 [Rs5]), hewn from the rock between 200 BC and 200 AD, were used by Buddhists until the time of Ashoka, and then by Jains. A little to the north of Uparkot, the slightly later, plainer **Khapra Kodia Caves** remain in good condition, intersected with staircases, colonnades and passages.

West of the main entrance to Uparkot, in Janta Chowk, the **Durbar Hall Museum** (daily except Wed & 2nd & 4th Sat of each month, 9am–12.15pm & 3–6pm; Rs50 [Rs5]) takes up part of the former palace of the nawabs. Silver chairs in the great hall stand in regal splendour around a large carpet, valuable silver clocks encase scruffy stuffed birds and huge coloured chandeliers hang from the ceiling.

Junagadh's chief Muslim monuments are the boldly decorated **maqbara** – unlike any other in Gujarat – on MG Road opposite the High Courts. Built for Muslim rulers in the nineteenth century, these squat and square mausolea are crowned with a multitude of bulbous domes. The most opulent tomb is the 1892 sepulchre of Mahabat Khan I, but more outstanding is that of Vizir Sahib Baka-ud-din Bhar, completed four years later and flanked on each corner by tall minarets hugged with spiral staircases.

Ashokan edicts

Two kilometres east of town on the road to Girnar, a rock engraved with the Buddhist **edicts of Ashoka** (daily 8am–1pm & 2–6pm; Rs100 [Rs5]), Junagadh's most famous monarch, remains where it was placed in the third century BC, its impact somewhat marred by a modern shelter and concrete platform. Written in the Prakrit dialect, the worn verses etched into the granite encourage the practice of *dharma* and equality and beseech different religious sects to live in harmony and repent the evils of war. Situated on the route taken by pilgrims to the sacred hill of Girnar, Ashoka's edicts had a lasting influence: even as late as the seventh century AD there were about three thousand Buddhists in Junagadh, and over fifty convents. Sanskrit inscriptions on the same rock were added during the reigns of King Rudraman (150 AD) and Skandagupta (455 AD).

Mount Girnar

At more than 1100m, **Mount Girnar** (an auto-rickshaw costs Rs60), a steep-sided extinct volcano 4km east of Junagadh, is a major pilgrimage centre for Jains and Hindus, and has been considered sacred since before the third century BC. It's best to start the ascent (at least two hours) well before 7am. The path of five thousand irregular steps climbs through eucalyptus forests before zigzagging across the sheer rock face; there are chai stalls along the way.

On a plateau below the summit, the picturesque huddle of Jain temples has been slightly renovated since its erection between 1128 and 1500. Neminath, the 22nd *tirthankara* who is said to have died on Mount Girnar after seven hundred years of meditation and asceticism, is depicted as a black figure sitting in the lotus position holding a conch in the marble **Neminath temple**, the first on the left as you enter the "temple city". It's well worth making the effort to climb the final two thousand steps to the summit of Mount Girnar; the views on the way are breathtaking. At the top, a temple dedicated to the Hindu goddess **Amba Mata** attracts both Hindu and Jain pilgrims. Steps lead down from this temple and then up again along a narrow ridge towards **Gorakhnath Peak**, where a small shrine covers what are supposedly the footprints of the pilgrim Gorakhnath, and further to a third peak where the imprints of Neminath's feet are sheltered by a small canopy. At the most distant point of the ridge, a shrine dedicated to the fierce Hindu goddess **Kalika**, the eternal aspect of Durga, is a haunt for near-naked **Aghora ascetics** who express their absolute renunciation of the world by ritually enacting their own funerals.

Eating

Dhal Road has many Gujarati thali restaurants and non-veg *dhabas*.

Jay Ambe Juice Centre Diwan Chowk. The place to come for fresh fruit juices, milkshakes and ice cream: don't miss the drinks made from Junagadh's famous *kesar* (saffron) mangos (around Rs25).

Modern Opposite the hospital. An a/c dining hall serving bottomless spicy-sweet thalis (Rs80). Tourists are unusual here, however, so you may have an audience while you eat.

Relief *Relief Hotel*. A smart restaurant with a tempting array of Mughul and tandoori meat and fish dishes – try the *murg malai* kebab – as well as vegetarian options (mains Rs55–95).

Santoor North of Kalwa Chowk on MG Rd. Delicious, reasonably priced south Indian and Punjabi dishes (Rs20–60), plus juices from locally-grown fruits, and milkshakes.

Veraval and Somnath

Midway between Porbandar and Diu, the fishing port of **Veraval** is the jumping-off point for trips to **Somnath**, 5km east, whose temple is one of the twelve *jyotrilingams* of Shiva. Its shrines to Vishnu and connection with Krishna – said to have lived here with the Yadavas during the time of the Mahabharata – make it equally important for Vaishnavites.

Veraval practicalities

Veraval's **bus stand** (Ⓣ02876/221666) is a ten-minute walk west of town. The town is well connected to Junagadh, Porbandar and Dwarka; local buses also run to Diu, but the service is slow and the roads are rough. Services to Sasan Gir (every 2hr; 1hr) start at 8am. Buses to Somnath (every 15–30min) terminate a few hundred metres east of the Shiva temple. **Trains** from Junagadh (2hr), Rajkot (4hr 30min) and Ahmedabad (12hr) pull in at the station (Ⓣ02876/220444) just over 1km north of town. For long journeys by train from Veraval it's quicker to change at Rajkot. The most convenient train for Sasan Gir (2hr) departs at 9.40am.

Veraval has a wider choice of **accommodation** than Somnath, although the smell and dirt may be enough to dissuade you from staying. *Hotel Kaveri* in Akar Complex on ST Road (Ⓣ02876/220842, Ⓦwww.hotelkaveri.in; ❹–❺) is the town's best, with clean, bright and well-appointed a/c and non-a/c rooms with TV and attached bathrooms. *Hotel Park*, 1.5km outside town on the approach road from Junagadh (Ⓣ02876/242703) feels tired, but the a/c rooms are okay, and there's a big pool. An auto-rickshaw from town should cost Rs30. *Hotel Utsav*, opposite the bus stand (Ⓣ02876/22306; ❷–❹), is grubby but just about habitable for those on a tight budget.

The comfortable a/c *Sagar* **restaurant**, near the clock tower, provides a varied veg menu of Indian and Chinese dishes. If you're hankering after fish, try the restaurant at the *Hotel Park*.

Somnath

SOMNATH consists of only a few streets and a bus stand – even its famed sea-facing **temple** (daily 6am–9.30pm; photography prohibited) is little to look at, despite its many-layered history. Legend has it the site, formerly known as **Prabhas Patan**, was dedicated to Soma, the juice of a plant used in rituals and greatly praised for its enlightening powers (and hallucinogenic effects) in the Rig Veda. The temple of Somnath itself is believed to have appeared first in gold, at the behest of the sun god, next in silver, created by the moon god, a third time in wood at the command of Krishna and, finally, in stone, built by Bhim, the strongest of the five Pandava brothers from the Mahabharata epic. The earliest definite record, however, dates the temple to the tenth century when it became rich from devotees' donations. Unfortunately, such wealth came to the attention of the brutal iconoclast Mahmud of Ghazni who destroyed the shrine and carried its treasure off to Afghanistan. The next seven centuries saw a cycle of rebuilding and sacking, though the temple lay in ruins for over two hundred years after a final sacking by Aurangzeb before the most recent reconstruction began in 1950. Very little of the original structure remains and, although planned in the style of the Solanki period, the temple is built from unattractive modern stone. The main pujas are held at 7am, noon and 7pm. An **architectural museum** (daily except Wed and 2nd & 4th Sat of month, 8.30am–12.15pm & 2.30–6pm) north of the temple, contains statues, lintels, sections of roof pillars, friezes and *toranas* from the tenth to twelfth centuries.

Somnath's **museum** (daily except Wed and 2nd & 4th Sat of month, 10.30am–5.30pm; Rs50 [Rs5]), across from the bus stand, is loaded up with seaworthy artefacts. Tongas and rickshaws gather outside the bus station, ready to take pilgrims to **temple sites east of Somnath**. Most important of these is **Triveni Tirth**, at the confluence of the Hiran, Saraswati and Kapil rivers as they flow into the sea. Before reaching the confluence, the road passes the ancient **Surya Mandir**, probably built during the Solanki period and now cramped by a newer temple and concrete houses built almost against its walls.

Practicalities

Somnath's best place to **stay** is *Shivam* (Ⓣ02876/233086; ❷–❹), on a side street near the temple, where you'll find clean and comfortable rooms, some with a/c. Slightly cheaper prices push *Mayuram* (Ⓣ02876/231286; ❷–❸), southeast of the bus stand, with a Gujarati sign, into second place, ahead of *Nandi* (Ⓣ02786/231839; ❷–❹) near the architectural museum. The temple trust dishes up good-value veg **thalis**.

Gir National Park

The **Asiatic lion** which, thanks to hunting, forest-clearance and poaching, has been extinct in the rest of India since the 1880s, survives in the wild in just 1150 square kilometres of the gently undulating Gir Forest. **Gir National Park** (mid-Oct or Nov to mid-June daily 7–11am & 3–5.30pm), accessed via **Sasan Gir**, 60km southeast of Junagadh and 45km northeast of Veraval, holds around 350 lions in its 260 square kilometres. They share the land with Maldhari cattle-breeders: many families have been relocated outside the sanctuary, but those who remain are paid compensation by the government for the inevitable loss of buffalo to marauding lions. Gir also shelters around two hundred **panthers**. In 2008, it emerged that some tourists had been paying to watch lions devour tethered cattle in cruel – and illegal – "*baitwalla* shows"; if anyone approaches you about one of these shows, inform the park's management team.

There is a well-presented **orientation centre** (daily 9am–6pm) to the right as you enter the walled-in park headquarters; close by is a **crocodile breeding**

The Asiatic lion

The rare **Asiatic lion** (*panthera leo persica*) is paler and shaggier than its more common African cousin, with longer tail tassles, more prominent elbow tufts and a larger belly fold. Probably introduced to India from Persia, the lions were widespread in the Indo-Gangetic plains at the time of the Buddha. In 300 BC Kautilya, the minister of Chandragupta Maurya, offered them protection by declaring certain areas *abharaya aranyas*, "forests free from fear". Later, in his rock-inscribed edicts, **Ashoka** admonished those who hunted the majestic animals.

The lion was favourite game for India's nineteenth-century rulers and by 1913, not long after it had been declared a protected species by the Nawab of Junagadh, its population was reduced to twenty. Since then, Gir Forest has been recognized as a sanctuary (1969), and a national park (1975), and their number has swelled to around 360. However, they remain under serious threat from poachers, while illegal timber-felling in the forest is still common. Three major roads and a railway line bisect the park, which also has four temples that attract over eighty thousand pilgrims each year; all this produces noise, pollution and littering. Moreover, when lions stray from the sanctuary – an increasingly common occurrence – there have been attacks on humans and livestock. Plans, meanwhile, to create another reserve outside Gujarat – to reduce the risk of the cats being wiped out by a particularly contagious disease or infection – continue to be resisted (for political rather than conservation reasons) by the state government. For more info, see Ⓦwww.asiatic-lion.org.

centre (daily 9am–6pm). Across the road from the orientation centre, **permits** can be obtained at the **park information** centre (daily: mid Oct–mid Feb 6.30–10.30am & 3–5pm; mid Feb–mid June 6.30am–1pm & 4–5.30pm). Entry for a vehicle seating up to six people is $40 [Rs400] during the week; at weekends and during festivals prices rise by twenty-five and thirty-three percent respectively. There's a mandatory **guide fee** of Rs50 per vehicle, and each person has to pay a sum of Rs250 [Rs50] as **camera** fee. You'll need to hire a **jeep**, available at the orientation centre (Rs700/2hr 30min–3hr trip). Even though some of the fees are priced in dollars, you have to pay in rupees. Though sightings are far from certain, the lions seem not to be disturbed by jeeps. Summer is the best time to spot them.

For a guaranteed sighting, head for **Dewaliya** (daily except Wed 8–11am & 3–5pm; $20 [Rs75]), a partially fenced-off area of the park known as the Gir Interpretation Zone. Jeeps (Rs200 return) leave regularly from Sasan Gir; once in the centre, you get a surprisingly good impression of the lions "in the wild" here – they still have to hunt their food even if the deer have limited space to escape.

Practicalities

Buses and **trains** connect Sasan Gir to Junagadh (1hr 30min–2hr 30min) and Veraval (1–2hr). From Diu, head to Una and then catch a bus (2hr 15min). Sasan Gir itself is a litter-strewn street of chai stalls, touts and ugly concrete blocks. One of the better inexpensive **hotels** is *Umang* (Ⓣ02877/285728; ❹–❻), close to the Forest Department's mediocre and wildly overpriced *Sinh Sadan Forest Lodge*, with bright but spartan rooms, some with a/c, plus a dorm (Rs300). At the sanctuary's Bambaphor Gate, the *Gir Birding Lodge* (Ⓣ079/2630 2019, Ⓔgirbirdinglodge@gmail.com; full-board ❽) has rooms in a main building and in cottages, with wood fittings and four-posters. There's a friendly naturalist-guide who takes guests for birdwatching walks, and a fine restaurant. Around 4km from Sasan Gir, just off the main road from Junagadh is *Anil Farmhouse* (Ⓣ02877/285590, Ⓦwww.giranilfarmhouse.com; ❹–❻) with lovely gardens. Its good-value rooms have checked floors, cane furniture and hot water, and there are also some cheaper tents. A pool is being built and the restaurant is excellent. South of the park in Talala is *Amidhara Resort* (Ⓣ02877/285950, Ⓦwww.amidhararesorts.com; full-board ❽), which has plain but comfortable attached rooms, a pool and a restaurant.

High-season (Dec) hotel **prices** can drop by up to seventy percent in the low season (June/July).

Diu

Set off the southern tip of Saurashtra, the island of **DIU**, less than 12km long and just 3km wide, was under Portuguese control until 1961. Today, governed along with Daman as a Union Territory from Delhi, it has a relaxed atmosphere quite different from anywhere in Gujarat. While its beaches are not as idyllic as Goa's, most visitors stay longer than intended, idling in cafés, cycling around the island or strolling along the cliffs. The leisurely pace is also due in part to the lack of alcohol restrictions.

Diu Town in the east is the focus: a maze of alleys lined with distinctive Portuguese buildings form the hub of the **old town**, while the **fort** stands on the easternmost tip of the island, staring defiantly out at the Gulf of Cambay. Along the northern coast, the island's main road runs past salt pans that give way to mud flats sheltering flocks of water birds, including flamingos that stop to feed in early spring. The route skirting the south coast passes rocky cliffs and beaches, the most popular of which is **Nagoa Beach**, before reaching the tiny fishing village of **Vanakbara** in the very west of the island.

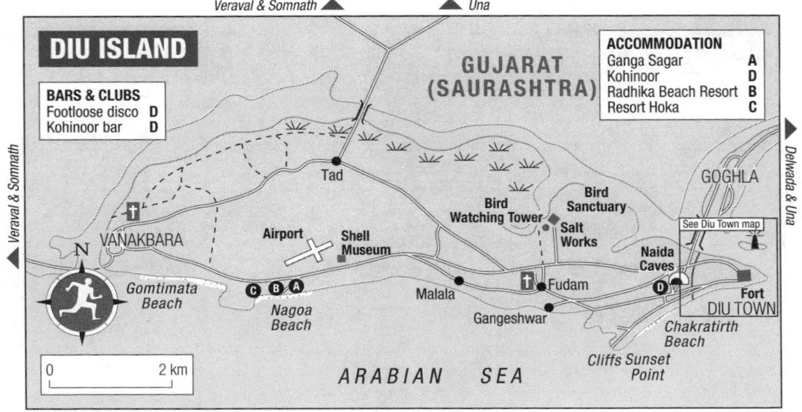

Some history

The earliest records of Diu date from 1298, when it was controlled by the Chudasana dynasty. Soon after it fell into the hands of invading Muslims and by 1349 was ruled by Mohammed bin Tughluq who successfully boosted the shipbuilding industry. Diu prospered as a harbour and in 1510 came under the government of the Ottoman Malik Ayaz, who repelled besieging **Portuguese** forces in 1520 and 1521. Aware of Diu's strategic position for trade with Arabia and the Persian Gulf, and having already gained a toehold in Daman, the Portuguese did not relent. Under **Nuno da Cunha**, they once more tried, but failed, to take the island in 1531. However, in 1535 Sultan Bahadur of Gujarat, who had agreed to sign a peace accord, was murdered and the Portuguese took control, immediately building the fort and a strong town wall. While local traders and merchants continued to thrive, many resented paying taxes to the Portuguese. In defiance, local seamen made a series of unsuccessful raids on Portuguese ships. Mughal and Arab attacks were resisted, too, but the Portuguese were finally forced out in 1961 by the Indian government, which, after a swift bombing campaign, declared Diu part of India.

Arrival

The usual point of entry to Diu is via **Goghla**, the small fishing village on the mainland that forms the northern edge of Diu territory. The hotels here are nothing special and most people head straight on to the island across the bridge that links it to the northwestern edge of Diu Town. If arriving directly from points west, you may come across the other bridge in the centre of the island. **Buses** pull in to the stand by the bridge, from where it's a ten-minute walk into town.

Moving on from Diu

There are state **bus** services to Porbandar, Rajkot, Jamnagar, Junagadh, Vadodara and Veraval; for Palitana, take a bus to Bhavnagar and change at Talaja. Private tour operators operate more comfortable buses to Ahmedabad and Mumbai. Far better transport connections are found on the mainland, at **Una** bus stand and **Delwada** railway station, both connected to Diu by auto-rickshaws and buses running every 30min. Jet Airways (airport ⓣ02875/253542) operates five weekly **flights** to Mumbai, via Porbandar.

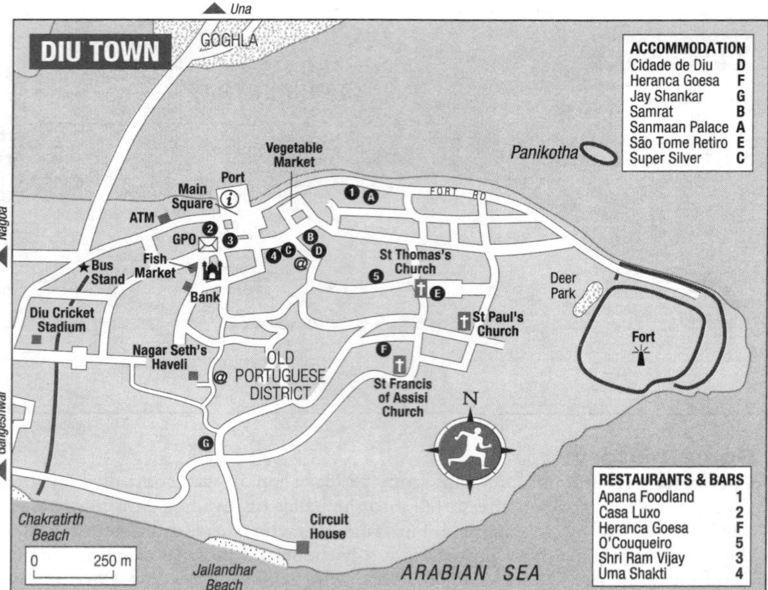

Information

Diu's **tourist office** (Mon–Sat 10am–1pm & 2–6pm; ⓣ02875/252653, ⓦwww.damandiutourism.com) in the port opposite the main square, offers maps and bus/train timetables but little else. The **GPO** is on the west side of the main square, upstairs, and the State Bank of India, near the square, will **exchange money**; Diu's only ATM is 250m east of the bus stand, though there are plans to open up another one. Super Surfing (Rs30/hr), below *Hotel Super Silver*, is one of several **internet** cafés, as is the useful A–Z Tourist Centre (Rs30/hr) in the Old Portuguese District, which can also organize car hire and **moped rental** (Rs150–170/day), plus train, bus and flight **tickets**. Many places rent out **bikes** (Rs20–30/day), and auto-rickshaws are widely available. Diu-by-Night **boat cruises** (daily in high season; Rs150; 1hr) leave from the jetty at 7pm.

Accommodation

The price codes below represent high-season **tariffs**; during festival periods, particularly Diwali and Holi, expect to pay even more, while in the off-season prices can come down by as much as seventy percent. Some people, especially women, may also be put off at festival times by the rowdy atmosphere.

Diu Town

Cidade de Diu Off Collectorate Rd ⓣ02875/254595, ⓦwww.cidadedediu.com. A pink, white and purple wedding cake of a building, illuminated by flashing neon lights at night. Thankfully the rooms are more tasteful: while the cheaper options are a bit worn, the more expensive ones are comfortable and come with balcony, TV and phone. ❺–❻

Heranca Goesa Close to Diu Museum ⓣ02875/253851. A handful of rooms in a very friendly Goan family home: all are immaculate and have attached bathrooms – though some also have shockingly pink decor. Those at the top of the house are the best, and there's great food on offer too. ❶–❷

Jay Shankar Jallandhar Beach ⓣ02875/252424. Remains a popular travellers' haunt for its low prices and location close to the beaches, but the rooms are beginning to show signs of wear and tear. ❶–❷

Samrat Collectorate Rd ⓣ02875/252354, ⓔsamrat_diu@yahoo.com.in. If you don't mind the clashing colour schemes, the rooms here, each with TV, a/c and private bathroom; some also have balconies, are a fine choice, particularly as the manager is open to bargaining. ❸–❺

Sanmaan Palace Fort Rd ⓣ02875/253031. This refurbished colonial mansion has an evocative exterior, which sadly does not quite translate to the rooms. Those at the front are airy and come with TV and a/c or fan, though the bathrooms are tiny. Avoid the "cottages" at the back: they're actually Portakabins. ❹–❺

São Tome Retiro St Thomas's Church ⓣ02875/253137. A classic place to soak up the chilled Diu vibe, with a handful of simple rooms in an atmospheric, old Portuguese church. If it's full, you can sleep on the roof (Rs100), and the D'Souza family, who run the place, throw legendary all-you-can-eat BBQs (Rs150) every other evening, September to April, open to non-guests. ❶–❸

Super Silver Super Silver Complex ⓣ02875/252020, ⓔsupersilverdiu@yahoo.com. Excellent-value rooms, all with attached bathrooms and TVs, and a warm welcome, make *Super Silver* a popular choice with foreign travellers. You can pay extra for a/c and more space, and there's a lovely roof terrace. ❶–❸

The rest of the island

Ganga Sagar Nagoa Beach ⓣ02875/252249. While it may be a bit of a dive, *Ganga Sagar* has economical tiled rooms and a great location right on the beach. ❸–❹

Kohinoor Near Fudum ⓣ02875/252209, ⓦwww.hotelkohinoordiu.com. This resort has a vaguely Mediterranean feel, with comfortable attached rooms, pool, restaurant, pastry shop, bar and the *Footloose* disco. ❻

Radhika Beach Resort Nagoa Beach ⓣ02875/252553, ⓦwww.radhikaresort.com. One of Diu's most upmarket options, with large, attractive attached rooms with fridges, TVs and tubs, that look out either onto the pool or the neatly-tended gardens. The restaurant/bar serves great seafood, including tandoori pomfret. ❻–❼

Resort Hoka Behind Nagoa Beach ⓣ02875/253036, ⓦwww.resorthoka.com. Pleasant hotel with enticing rooms, hammocks hanging in the communal areas, groves of palm trees, a small pool and a restaurant offering delicious fish dishes. ❺–❻

Diu Town

Little **Diu Town** is protected by the fort in the east and a wall in the west. **Nagar Seth's Haveli**, one of the grandest of the town's distinctive Portuguese mansions, is on Makata Road, hidden in the web of narrow streets that wind through the residential Old Portuguese District. Fishermen make daily trips from the north coast in wooden boats; their catch is sold in the market near the mosque.

Although the Christian population is dwindling along with the old language, a few **churches** built by the former European inhabitants are still used. Portuguese Mass is celebrated beneath the high ceilings and painted arches of **St Paul's**, though the church of **St Thomas**, to the northwest, is now a museum (daily 8am–9pm) and guesthouse (see above), and that of **St Francis of Assisi**, to the south, is partly occupied by the local hospital.

Diu's serene **fort** (daily 8am–6pm) stands robust, resisting the battering of the sea on three sides and sheltering birds, jackals and the town jail. Its wide moat and coastal position enabled the fort to withstand attack by land and sea, but there are obvious scars from the Indian government's air strikes in 1961 – notice the hole above the altar of the church in the southwest corner. Now abandoned almost completely to nature, and littered with centuries-old cannonballs, it commands excellent views out to sea and over the island. Just offshore, the curious, ship-shaped **Panikotha Fort** – connected to the mainland by tunnel, according to lore – is off-limits, but if it's calm, you can hire a boat (around Rs60) from the dock for a closer look.

Around the island

Cliffs and rocky pools make up much of the southern coast of the island, giving way to the occasional sandy stretch. South of Diu Town is the idyllic **Jallandhar**

Beach; the larger **Chakratirth Beach**, overlooked by a high mound, is a little to the west, just outside the city walls. In many ways this is the most attractive beach and usually deserted, making it the best option for an undisturbed swim, especially for female travellers. At its western end, **Sunset Point** provides the regular spectacle of a golden disc sinking into the waves. The longest and only developed beach is at **Nagoa**, 7km west of town, where there are several hotels, but sunbathers, particularly women, are more likely to get hassled here. Buses leave Diu Town for Nagoa, but times change frequently so check with the tourist office. With a vehicle, the invariably deserted **Gomtimata Beach**, between Nagoa and Vanakbara, lies within reach.

Not far out of town, a turning off the Nagoa Road leads to **FUDAM**, an attractive village of Portuguese houses washed in pale yellow and sky grey where a church has been converted into a medical clinic. Further along the main road, on the right just before the airport, the **Shell Museum** (daily 9am–6pm; Rs10) is the personal collection – 42 years in the making – of Captain Fulbari, who spent a lifetime on the ocean picking up shells wherever he weighed anchor.

Eating and drinking

Sadly, the main vestige of Portuguese influence on the dining scene in Diu is the availability of **alcohol**. *Casa Luxo*, which has been caught in a 1960s' time-warp, and the *Hotel Kohinoor's* more modern **bar** are decent drinking spots. Expect to pay Rs40–50 for a Kingfisher. *Hotel Kohinoor* also has Diu's only nightclub, *Footloose*. If you spot any seafood you fancy in the market, most restaurants will be happy to cook it for you.

Apana Foodland *Apana Hotel*, Fort Rd. A busy garden terrace, overlooking the sea, with popular all-day options: the tandoori chicken, shark tikka and grilled lobster stand out (mains Rs45–250).

Heranca Goesa Close to Diu Museum ☎02875/253851. An intimate eatery in a family home, and one of the only places to sample Portuguese and Goan food in Diu: the seafood's excellent and don't miss the delicious *bebinca* pudding if it's on. You can just walk in for breakfast, but book for dinner. Closed lunchtimes. Mains Rs150–200.

O'Couqueiro Lane behind Cidade de Diu. A family-run garden restaurant with hanging lanterns and palm trees, serving home-made muesli and yogurt, pasta dishes made with imported Italian olive oil and parmesan, some of the best fish and chips in town, and a handful of Portuguese options (mains Rs70–170). There's a selection of books and magazines to read, and international chillout music on the sound system.

Shri Ram Vijay Just off the main square. A wonderful slice of small-town Americana transported to Diu Town, this tiny parlour has home-made ice cream (Rs15–25/scoop), sundaes, banana splits, cream sodas and milkshakes.

Uma Shakti Behind the market. A good place for a breakfast of cornflakes, toast or pancakes, or a more substantial Indian or Chinese meal later on. The breezy roof terrace, with views over Diu Town, is good for a sundowner. Mains Rs50–120.

Bhavnagar

The port of **BHAVNAGAR**, founded in 1723 by the Gohil Rajput Bhavsinghji, whose ancestors came to Gujarat from Marwar (Rajasthan) in the thirteenth century, is an important trading centre whose principal export is cotton. With few sights of its own, Bhavnagar does, however, boast a fascinating bazaar in the old city, and is an obvious place to stay for a night before heading southwest to the Jain temples of Palitana. For Gujarati industrialists, it serves as the jumping-off point for the massive, controversial and currently booming ship-breaking yard at **Alang**. The yard, where twenty thousand labourers work, has been off-limits to foreigners since Greenpeace red-flagged it for environmental damage, toxic spills and

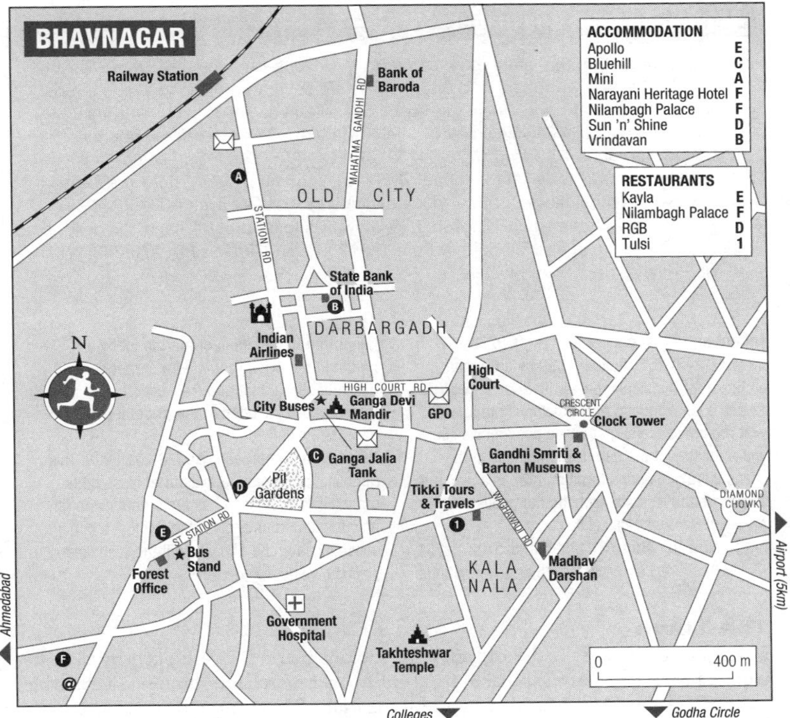

hazardous work. Bhavnagar has produced a string of artists and writers, notably poet **Jhaverchand Meghani**. Locals also claim to speak the most grammatically correct form of Gujarati.

Arrival and information

Arriving by **train**, the way into town is straight ahead along Station Road. From the state **bus stand**, turn right up ST Station Road for the town centre. The **airport** is 5km southeast of town. The State Bank of Saurashtra and the Bank of India have **exchange** facilities; they're on Amba Chowk near *Hotel Vrindavan*. The **GPO** is next to the High Court on High Court Road, with branches just off Station Road a block south of the station, and opposite the southeastern corner of Ganga Jalia Tank. **Internet** access is available at *Cyber Café*, close to *Nimabagh Palace* (Rs10/hr).

Accommodation

Apollo ST Station Rd, opposite the bus stand ⓣ0278/251 5655. The cheaper rooms in this mothballed hotel are shabby, but those with a/c are reasonable; all come with TVs, private bathrooms and complimentary breakfast. ❹

Bluehill Opposite Pil Gardens ⓣ0278/242 6951, ⓔhotelbluehill@yahoo.com. Rooms are spacious and come with a/c, TVs, fridges and cute separate seating areas. The more expensive ones also have views of the stork-filled Pil Gardens. ❹–❺

Mini Station Rd ⓣ0278/251 2915. Welcoming but super-basic hotel with pink decor, and rooms with private bathrooms and TVs in real need of a freshen-up. Worth trying if *Vrindavan* is full. ❷

Moving on from Bhavnagar

Services run from the state **bus** stand to Ahmedabad, Mumbai, Bhuj, Rajkot, Junagadh, Veraval, Vadodara and Surat. There are several services to Diu; the most convenient one is at noon. There are buses to Palitana (every 30min; 1hr 15min) but only a couple of daily services direct to Velavadar (1hr). **Private buses**, operated by firms such as Tanna Travels (ⓣ0278/2425218) at Crescent Circle and any of those on Waghawadi Road, serve Ahmedabad (4hr) and Vadodara (5hr). There are several **trains** too, but most leave or arrive in the early hours. Jet Airways (ⓣ0278/243 3371, ⓦwww.jetairways.com) and Kingfisher (ⓦwww.flykingfisher.com) each **fly** daily to Mumbai; tickets can also be bought from Tikki Tours and Travels (ⓣ0278/243 1477) in the Prithvi Complex in Kalanala.

Nilambagh Palace ST Station Rd ⓣ0278/242 4241, ⓕ242 8072. Built in 1859 by a German architect for the local crown prince, *Nilambagh Palace* is Bhavnagar's most luxurious hotel, with vast rooms, peaceful gardens, a pool, tennis courts, and remnants of the European influence in the chandeliers and period furniture (❼). In a separate annexe, is the less atmospheric but good-value *Narayani Heritage Hotel* (❺).

Sun 'n' Shine ST Station Rd ⓣ0278/251 6131, ⓕ251 6130. The high expectations generated by the elegant marble lobby are matched by swish rooms with carpets and bathtubs. Breakfast and free airport transfers are included in the price. It even has wi-fi. ❺

Vrindavan Darbargadh ⓣ0278/251 8928. This rambling, and from the exterior at least, quite dramatic-looking hotel has tired rooms with tiny private bathrooms and TV that are just a notch above those at the *Mini*. It's not the friendliest place however. ❷

The Town

The focus of interest is the **old city**, its vibrant markets overlooked by delicate wooden balconies and the pillared fronts of former merchants' houses. The marble temple, **Ganga Devi Mandir**, by the Ganga Jalia Tank in the town centre has a large dome and intricate latticework on its walls, while the **Takhteshwar Temple**, raised on a hill in the south of town, affords a good view over to the Gulf of Cambay in the east. Southeast of the town centre, on the road to Diamond Chowk, the **Gandhi Smriti Museum** (Mon–Sat 9am–1pm & 2–6pm, closed 2nd and 4th Sat of the month) exhibits old sepia photos of the Mahatma, who studied here at the Shamaldas Arts College & Sir PP Science Institute. The **Barton Museum** downstairs (Mon–Sat 9am–1pm & 2–6pm, closed 2nd and 4th Sat of the month; Rs50 [Rs2]) haphazardly shows off Buddhist, Jain and Hindu statues, medieval bronzes and Harappan terracotta. Bhavnagar also has a number of impressive buildings – including the government hospital – commissioned by the maharajas from prominent architects like Sir William Emerson.

Eating

Look out for **local specialities** like *ganthias* and *farsans* (both salty snacks) and sweet *pedas*.

Kayla *Apollo* hotel. A modern shiny orange dining area with glass partitions between the tables and an interesting selection of north Indian, Punjabi and Chinese meals (Rs50–100).

Nilambagh Palace *Nilambagh Palace* hotel. Superb and keenly priced chicken, mutton, fish and prawn dishes (Rs60–200). The real draw, however, is the atmosphere in the stately dining room and on the veranda, where the bustle of the city seems a world away.

RGB *Sun 'n' Shine* hotel. Excellent veg Gujarati, Jain and Chinese food – the rich *paneer* dishes are particularly good – as well as ice-cream sundaes. Staff are professional and happy to adjust spicing levels to suit personal tastes. Mains Rs70–110.

Tulsi Kalanala Chowk. Appealing veg Chinese and Indian food, including a comforting *chana masala*, and less appealing muzak are on offer at quiet, relaxed *Tulsi*. Steer clear of the handful of western dishes, however, especially the pineapple and vegetable macaroni. Mains Rs50–75.

Velavadar Blackbuck National Park

Outside the tiny village of **Velavadar**, 65km north of Bhavnagar, the 34-square-kilometre **Blackbuck National Park** (mid-Oct to mid-June) has the highest concentration of this Indian antelope anywhere in the country. Prior to Independence their number stood at eight thousand, but habitat loss and hunting cut this figure down to two hundred by 1966; they now number around three thousand four hundred. The park is also home to the endangered Indian wolf, nilgai antelopes, jackal foxes, jungle cats and Indian foxes. Birdwatchers can spot rare species like the Stoicka's bushchat and harrier hawks. Poor rainfall in recent years has forced many of the latter to roost elsewhere, however, with numbers falling from 2515 in 2002 to 979 in 2009. There are no jeeps available for hire on site, but a **taxi** costs around Rs1000 for a day-trip from Bhavnagar. If you arrive by **bus** (2 daily from Bhavnagar; 1hr), it is possible to walk to one of the watch-towers near the entrance and get a good view, but it's not the same.

Entry to the park is Rs250 [Rs10], plus Rs250 [Rs20] per vehicle and Rs250 [Rs5] for a camera. On top of this you are required to take a **guide** (Rs250 [Rs30]/4hr), though few speak English. **Accommodation** is decidedly limited; there are only four basic rooms (❸–❹) in the park itself, which can be booked through Bhavnagar's Forest Office (Mon–Fri 11am–6pm; ⓣ0278/242 6425), in the Bahumaliya Multi-Storey Building, Annexe F/10, just west of the bus stand. Alternatively contact the park directly (ⓣ0278/288 0342). Meals are available, and reservations are necessary.

Shatrunjaya and Palitana

For many visitors, the highlight of a trip to Saurashtra is a climb up the holy hill of **Shatrunjaya** (daily 6.30am–7.45pm, camera Rs40), India's principal Jain pilgrimage site, just outside the dull town of **PALITANA**, 50km southwest of Bhavnagar. More than nine hundred temples crown this hill, said to be a chunk of the mighty Himalayas from where the Jains' first *tirthankara*, Adinath, and his chief disciple gained enlightenment. While records show that the hill was a *tirtha* as far back as the fifth century, the existing temples date only from the sixteenth century, anything earlier having been lost in the Muslim raids of the 1500s and 1600s.

Climbing the wide steps up Shatrunjaya takes one to two hours, though, as with all hilltop pilgrimage centres, *dholis* (seats on poles held by four bearers) are available for those who can't make it under their own steam. The views as you ascend are magnificent, and you should allow at least two more hours to see even a fraction of the temples.

The individual *tuks* (temple enclosures) are named after the merchants who funded them. Together they create a formidable city, laid over the two summits and fortified by thick walls. Each *tuk* comprises courtyards chequered in black-and-white marble and several temples whose walls are exquisitely and profusely carved with saints, birds, animals, buxom maidens, musicians and dancers. Many are two or even three storeys high, with balconies crowned by perfectly proportioned pavilions. The largest temple, dedicated to Adinath, in the Khartaravasi *tuk* on the northern ridge is usually full of masked Svetambara nuns and monks, dressed in white and carrying white fly-whisks. The southern ridge and the spectacular Adishvara temple in its western corner are reached by taking the right-hand fork at the top of the path. On a clear day the view from the summit takes in the Gulf of Cambay to the south, Bhavnagar to the north and Mount Girnar to the west.

The **museum** (daily 11am–3pm & 4–6pm; Rs6), 400m before the start of the steps at the bottom of the hill, displays a collection of Jain artefacts, labelled in Gujarati but well worth seeing.

A path leads along the ridge and down into the valley of Adipur, 13km away; it's open for one day only, during the festival of **Suth Tera** (Feb/March), when up to fifty thousand pilgrims come to Shatrunjaya for this unique display of devotion.

Practicalities

Buses to Palitana depart from Bhavnagar (hourly; 1hr–1hr 30min), Junagadh (2 daily; 6hr) and Una (1 daily; 5hr). Auto-rickshaws (Rs30–40) and tongas run from Palitana to the foot of Shatrunjaya (10min).

There is no **accommodation** on Shatrunjaya, so you'll have to stay in Palitana, either at one of many Jain *dharamshalas* in the old part of town (all of which observe strict vegetarianism) or in one of the hotels on the bus stand side of town. *Hotel Sumeru* (Ⓣ02848/252327; ❷–❹), on Station Road between the bus stand and the railway station, has acceptable if scruffy rooms, some with a/c, dorm beds (Rs90) and a 9am checkout; its **restaurant** serves thalis and surprisingly decent pasta. *Hotel Shavrak* (Ⓣ02848/252428; ❸–❹), opposite the bus stand, has adequate, fairly clean rooms and 24hr checkout; there is also a men-only dorm (Rs100; 9am checkout). *Vijay Vilas Palace Hotel* (Ⓣ02848/282371; ❼) at Adpur, 4km from the bus station, is a good alternative for those who have their own vehicle (alternatively an auto-rickshaw costs around Rs50). This converted 1906 European-style palace guesthouse has rooms with four-posters, old dressers and other early twentieth-century paraphernalia.

For **food** outside the hotels, head for the narrow alley next to *Hotel Shavrak*, where the basic, busy and very cheap *Jagruti Restaurant* serves excellent Gujarati meals and snacks.

Southeastern Gujarat

The seldom-visited **southeastern** corner of Gujarat, sandwiched between Maharashtra and the Arabian Sea, harbours few attractions to entice you off the road or railway line to or from Mumbai. There's little to recommend **Vadodara** (Baroda), former capital of the Gaekwad rajas, other than its proximity to the old Muslim town of **Champaner** and the ruined forts and exotic Jain and Hindu temples that encrust **Pavagadh Hill**. Further south, dairy pastures gradually give way to a swampy, malaria-infested coastal strip of banana plantations and shimmering saltpans cut by silty, sinuous rivers. The area's largest city is modern, industrial **Surat**. The only place of real interest in the far south of the state is the former Portuguese territory of **Daman**, although it's nowhere near as appealing as Goa or Diu.

The west coast's main **transport** arteries, the NH-8 and Western Railway, run in tandem between Mumbai and Ahmedabad. The train is always more comfortable, especially between Ahmedabad and Vadodara, where the undivided highway is one of the most nail-bitingly terrifying roads in India.

Vadodara (Baroda)

The area between Ahmedabad and **VADODARA** (or Baroda) is primarily agricultural, but Vadodara itself is a congested industrial city with few

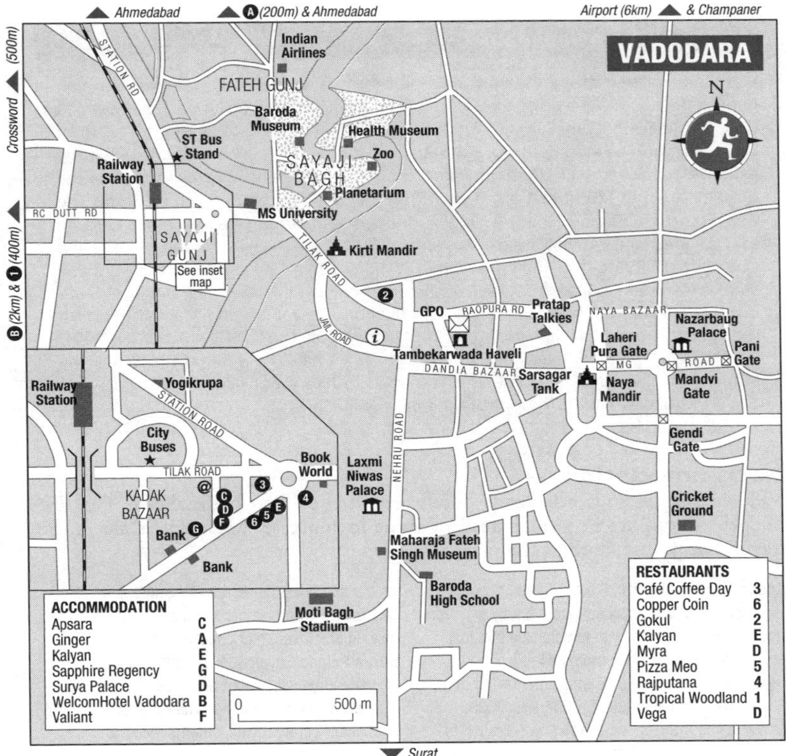

attractions. However, its old core retains some interest, with beautiful havelis and traditional bazaars, and the 100,000-strong student population at MS University gives it a youthful feel. **Vadodara** is the most convenient place to stay for a trip to the ruined city of **Champaner**. If you are here at the time of the **Navratri** festival (late Sept/early Oct), you can join the throngs watching thousands of colourfully dressed women, men and children dancing into the small hours.

Arrival and information

The **railway station** and **bus stand** are close together in the west of town, within easy walking distance of most of the hotels. The airport is 6km northeast (around Rs50 by auto-rickshaw). **Gujarat Tourism** (Mon–Sat 10.30am–6pm, closed 2nd & 4th Sat of month; ⓣ0265/242 7489) is a couple of kilometres from the station at C-Block, Ground floor, Narmada Bhavan, Jail Road. Cash and **travellers' cheques** can be changed at the Bank of Baroda in Sayaji Gunj behind Kadak Bazaar, the Bank of South India opposite or the State Bank of India on RC Dutt (Racecourse) Road close to *WelcomHotel Vadodara*. The Trade Wings agency behind *Hotel Amity* in Sayaji Gunj also has an efficient exchange service. The **GPO** is off Raopura Road in the centre of town. Crossword at Annapurna Society in Alkapuri, in the west of the city, is an excellent **bookshop**, alternatively try Book World in Sayaji Gunj. For **internet** access, try New Speedy Cyber Café (Rs15/hr), opposite the *Apsara* hotel.

Moving on from Vadodara

Vadodara **railway station's** crowded ticket reservation office is upstairs; you can bypass the hassle for a small fee if you buy your ticket from Yogikrupa Travel Service opposite (daily 8.30am–8.30pm; ⓣ0265/279 4977). All trains travelling on the main Delhi–Mumbai line stop here. For **Ahmedabad**, try the *Shatabdi Express* #2009 (daily except Sun; departs 11.20am, arrives 1.10pm). The *Shatabdi Express* #2010 is the quickest train to **Mumbai** (daily except Sun; departs 4.17pm, arrives 9.35pm). The **bus stand** on Station Road, a little north, has regular services to other Gujarati towns, including Ahmedabad (frequent; 2hr 30min), Rajkot (hourly; 8hr) and Champaner (hourly; 1hr 30min). Mumbai (14hr) is served by regular buses, but few start at Vadodara, so they may be full when they arrive – the train is far better. **Private bus** companies with frequent services to Mumbai, Rajasthan and Madhya Pradesh line Station Road. Jet Airways (opposite *WelcomHotel Vadodara*; ⓣ0265/234 3441) and Indian Airlines (Fateh Gunj; ⓣ0265/279 4747) have daily **flights** to Delhi; the former also flies daily to Mumbai. If you need to hire a **car and driver**, try Sweta Travels (ⓣ0265/278 6917), opposite the railway station. .

Accommodation

Vadodara's numerous mid-range hotels are often full, so book ahead. The few budget options are in serious need of some loving care. Most hotels are in the **Sayaji Gunj**, just south of the railway station.

Apsara Sayaji Gunj ⓣ0265/222 5399. Probably the best of the shoestring options – hardly a ringing endorsement – with ramshackle but (just about) habitable attached rooms. ❶–❷

Ginger Fatehgunj Camp Rd, 1km north of the railway station ⓣ0265/663 3333, ⓦwww.gingerhotels.com. Vadodara's branch of the uber-modern hotel chain boasts minimalist attached rooms, friendly staff, and perks like filtered water dispensers on each floor and wi-fi access. There's also a buffet restaurant and a branch of *Café Coffee Day*. Good online deals. ❻

Kalyan Sayaji Gunj ⓣ0265/236 2211, ⓦwww.kalyanhotel.com. This super-clean, efficient hotel has slick, well-furnished rooms. There's free internet access, 24hr checkout and staff will book train or flight tickets. ❹–❺

Sapphire Regency Sayaji Gunj ⓣ0265/236 1130, ⓦwww.sapphireregency.com. Brand-new business-oriented hotel, with sparkling attached rooms that boast flat-screen TVs, stylish bathrooms, white leather seats and wi-fi. Rates include breakfast. 24hr checkout. ❺–❻

Surya Palace Sayaji Gunj ⓣ0265/222 6000, ⓦwww.suryapalace.com. The pick of the Sayaji Gunj accommodation options has slightly dated but undeniably comfy rooms, smart service, an in-house travel agent, complimentary buffet breakfast and free airport pick-up/drop-off. ❺–❻

WelcomHotel Vadodara RC Dutt (Racecourse) Rd ⓣ0265/233 0033, ⓦwww.itcwelcomgroup.in. Vadodara's only five-star has swanky attached rooms (from Rs8000) with king-size beds, plus a quality restaurant specialising in "North West Frontier" cuisine, an outdoor pool and gym. Good online deals. ❾

Valiant 7th floor, BBC Tower, Sayaji Gunj ⓣ0265/236 3480, ⓕ236 2502. Accessed via an aged private lift, *Valiant* is another good, if slightly impersonal, mid-range hotel; rooms have clean attached bathrooms and TVs. 24hr checkout. ❹

The City

Vadodara's chief attractions are in **Sayaji Bagh**, a large green park with museums, planetarium, zoo and a vintage toy train; the main entrance is on Tilak Road. The large Indo-Saracenic **Baroda Museum** (daily 10.30am–5pm; Rs10), reached from University Road, holds art and textiles from all over the world, Gujarati archeological remains and Mughal miniatures.

From Sayaji Bagh, Tilak Road continues east across the river past **Kirti Mandir** (the mausoleum of Vadodara's rulers) towards the old city, the centre of which is MG Road, bounded at its western end by **Laheri Pura Gate** and **Naya Mandir** (literally "New Temple"), a fine Indo-Saracenic building, now a law court. There's another gate (Pani Gate) at the eastern end of MG Road, near the late nineteenth-century **Nazarbaug Palace** and, halfway between the two, the four-way **Mandvi Gate**, originally Mughal but much altered since.

To the west of MG Road is an artificial lake, the **Sarsagar Tank** (check out Pratap Talkies, an over-the-top Art Deco theatre at the northeastern corner), surrounded by glorious painted havelis and with a huge modern statue of Shiva in the middle. Other buildings worth a look include **Laxmi Niwas Palace** in the south of town, the most extravagant of Vadodara's palaces. If you wish to tour the palace's impressive Durbar Hall, armoury and palm-filled mosaic courtyards (Tues–Sun 10.30am–4pm; Rs100 [Rs25]), head to the **Maharaja Fateh Singh Museum** (daily 10.30am–5.30pm; Rs100 [Rs25]) in the palace grounds; the museum itself holds a modest selection of Indian, Japanese, Chinese and European art.

Eating

Café Coffee Day Opposite the Sardar Patel statue. Vadodara's branch of the reliable national chain draws a youthful crowd for pukka lattes, cappuccinos and ice-coffee concoctions (Rs45–80). There are also branches in the Crossword bookshop and *Hotel Ginger.*

Copper Coin World Trade Centre, Sayaji Gunj. An a/c restaurant with faded charm, a fish tank and fine non-veg options, including a wonderful butter chicken (Rs80–140).

Gokul Koti Char Rasta. Small snack-bar serving excellent south Indian dishes, Punjabi and Gujarati thalis, and ice cream at low, low prices (Rs25–60).

Kalyan Sayaji Gunj. Lively fast-food-style joint with multicoloured stools where students come to chat and tuck into anything from enchiladas to fondue, as well as Indian and Chinese snacks (Rs30–90).

Myra and Vega *Surya Palace* hotel. Two superior restaurants under one roof: head to the former for a hearty Gujarati thali (Rs110–175); the latter offers well-prepared curries and Chinese dishes (Rs80–150).

Pizza Meo Sayaji Gunj. Like the ambitious Renaissance-style painted ceiling, this Italian's veg pizzas and pastas (Rs105–185) are good efforts, if not entirely authentic.

Rajputana Sayaji Gunj. Tasty north Indian and Chinese dishes – as well as some dubious hybrids, such as "Paneer Manchurian" – served up in eccentric surroundings; the restaurant is kitted out with hanging chains, bells, dolls and fake wood beams. Mains Rs85–120.

Tropical Woodland 139 Windsor Plaza. One of the city's top restaurants, with excellent south Indian food, including no less than 17 different types of dosas, main meals and milkshakes: try the *chikoo* flavour (Rs70–150).

Pavagadh and Champaner

The hill of Pavagadh, 45km northeast of Vadodara, rises 820m above the plains, overlooking the almost forgotten Muslim city – and World Heritage Site – of **CHAMPANER** (daily 10am–6pm; Rs100 [Rs5]). The massive city walls with inscribed gateways still stand, encompassing several houses, exquisite mosques and Muslim funerary monuments, all imbued with a strange, time-warped atmosphere, as well as newer Jain *dharamshalas*. The largest mosque, the exuberant **Jama Masjid**, is east of the walls. Towering *minars* stand either side of the main entrance, and the prayer halls are dissected by almost two hundred pillars supporting a splendid carved roof raised in a series of domes. Your entrance ticket is also valid for the **Shahr-ki Matchi temple**, inside the city wall near the bus stand.

For **Pavagadh**, take a bus from Champaner, or walk up the path that ascends through battered gates and past the old walls of the Chauhan Rajput fortress to a mid-point where you can get snacks, souvenirs and chai. You can take the cable car to the top (Rs87 return), or follow a path on foot. On top of the hill a number of Jain temples sit below a Hindu temple dedicated to Mataji, which also has a shrine to the Muslim saint Sadan Shah on its roof.

While the view is Pavagadh's top draw, the most interesting part of the area is the ruined **fort**, opposite the main bus stand. In 1297 the Chauhan Rajputs made Pavagadh their stronghold, and fended off three attacks by the Muslims before eventually losing to Mohammed Begada in 1484. All the women and children committed *johar* (ritual suicide by self-immolation) and the men who survived the battle were slain when they refused to embrace Islam. After his conquest, Begada set to work on Champaner, which took 23 years to build. The town was the political capital of Gujarat until the death of Bahadur Shah in 1536, when the courts moved to Ahmedabad and Champaner fell into decline.

Buses from Vadodara leave hourly (via Halol; 1hr 30min) for Champaner. There are also several daily services to and from Ahmedabad. Halfway up Pavagadh, the slightly lacklustre *Hotel Champaner* (ⓣ02676/245641; ❷–❸) has a dorm (Rs75) and adequate **rooms** with magnificent views over the vast plains of south Gujarat, as well as a **restaurant** that serves decent veg thalis. However, the *Jambughoda Palace* (ⓣ02676/241258, ⓦwww.jambughoda.com; ❺–❻), 25km outside Champaner, is a much swisher option. The rooms are filled with personal touches, and the home-cooked meals make use of organic produce grown in the gardens. The family pile of the former Maharaja of Jambughoda, the palace overlooks the Jambughoda Wildlife Sanctuary, a haven for birds.

Surat

Packed around a tight bend in the River Tapti, sprawling **SURAT** is one of India's fastest growing industrial centres, but of real interest only to colonial-history buffs, who come to see what few vestiges remain of the East India Company's first foothold on the Subcontinent. In 1994, there was an outbreak of the **plague** here, which proved a wake-up call – Surat has since become one of India's cleanest cities.

Surat's two main sights can be seen in an hour if you take an auto-rickshaw. Start at **Chowk**, a busy intersection at the foot of Nehru Bridge, where the **castle** is the city's oldest surviving monument. Erected in 1540 by the Sultan of Gujarat, it was occupied by the Mughals and British, but now houses government offices. Fifteen minutes northeast, beside Kataragama Road, beyond the fortified gateway of the same name, are the domed mausolea of the weed-choked **English cemetery**. Its most impressive sepulchre is that of General Oxinden, who defeated the Marathas.

Practicalities

Surat has good **train and bus** connections; both stations are on the eastern edge of the city centre. Private buses off-load you about 50m from the railway station. An auto-rickshaw ride into the centre costs Rs30–40. The **tourist office** (Mon–Sat 10.30am–6pm, closed 2nd & 4th Sat of month; ⓣ0261/347 6586) is on Athugar St in Nanpura, as is the State Bank of India. Finding a **room** can be hard on weekdays, so book ahead. To the right of Sufi Baug, the street opposite the entrance to the station, *Embassy* (ⓣ0261/744 3170, ⓦwww.embassyhotelsurat.com; ❺) is a stylish mid-range **hotel**: rooms come with carpets, bathtubs and TV. Budget travellers should head to the busy *Omkar* (ⓣ0261/741 9329; ❷), eighth floor, Omkar Chambers, Sufi Baug, which has unfussy rooms with views over the city. Most of the big hotels have quality **restaurants**; try *Copper Chimney* at *Lords Park Inn* on the Ring Road.

Daman

Ask any Gujarati what they associate with **DAMAN** and they'll say "liquor". As a Union Territory, independent of the dry state that surrounds it, Daman has liberal licensing laws, making it a target at weekends for busloads of Gujarati men who drink themselves senseless. The rest of the time Daman is quieter, but generally disappointing, with a rather forlorn feel and a couple of uninspiring beaches. It does, however, offer excellent **seafood** and some well-preserved **Portuguese churches, houses** and **forts**.

Straddling the mouth of the **Damanganga River**, which rises in the Sahyadri Range on the Deccan plateau, Daman made an obvious target for the Portuguese, who took it in 1531 from the Sultan of Gujarat's Ethiopian governor, Siddu Bapita. The governor of Goa, Dom Constantino de Bragança, cajoled the Sultan into ceding the territory 28 years later, after which it became the hub of the Portuguese trans-Arabian Sea trade with East Africa. The town's economic decline was precipitated by the British occupation of Sind in the 1830s, which strangled its **opium** business. Colonial rule, however, survived until 1961 when Nehru lost patience with Portuguese refusal to negotiate a peaceful handover and sent in the troops.

Today Daman is administered from New Delhi as a Union Territory, along with the nearby ex-Portuguese colonies of Diu, Dadra and Nagar Haveli. The local

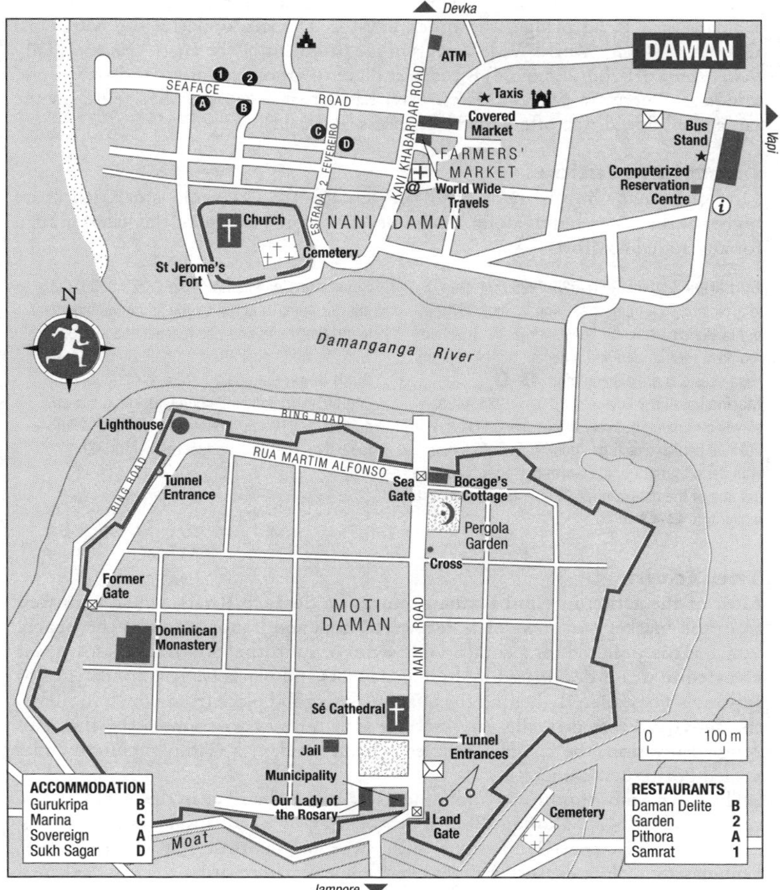

tourist office tries to promote the area as a mini-Goa, but while its coastline may look idyllic in the brochures, it is in fact grubby and subject to massive tides.

The town of Daman is made up of two separate districts. On the north side of the Damanganga River is **Nani** ("Little") **Daman**, where you'll find most of the hotels, restaurants, bars and markets; **Moti** ("Great") **Daman**, the old Portuguese quarter, lies to the south, its Baroque churches and Latinate mansions encircled by imposing stone battlements.

Arrival and information

The nearest **railhead** to Daman is 12km east at **Vapi**, one of the most polluted places in the world. **Shared taxis** (Rs15) will drop you on Daman's Seaface Road, close to most of the hotels. Just beyond the flyover is Vapi's state **bus station**, with buses every 30 minutes to Daman, or you can take an auto-rickshaw (Rs70). **Leaving Daman**, there are no direct buses to anywhere further than Vapi. You can reserve **train tickets** at the computerized reservation centre (daily except Wed 9.30am–1.30pm & 4–9pm), opposite the **tourist office** (Mon–Fri 9.30am–1.30pm & 2–6pm; ⓣ0260/225 5104, ⓦwww.damandiutourism.com), which is just south of the bus stand. There are two **post offices**: one north of the Damanganga Road bridge, the other in Moti Daman, opposite the Municipal Council building. World Wide Travels in the basement of the *Hotel Maharaja* (daily 9am–9pm; ⓣ0260/225 5734) is the best place to **change money and travellers' cheques**. There are two **ATMs** on Kavi Khabardar Road. Further south on the same road, Speed Age offers **internet** access (Rs20/hr).

Accommodation

Most of Daman's **hotels** are on or just off Seaface Road in Nani Daman. Prices are higher at the resort hotels along Devka Beach – more because of the location than for any added comfort.

Gurukripa Seaface Rd ⓣ0260/225 504. This long-established hotel is starting to show its age, but is still well-run and boasts large a/c attached rooms, a roof garden and a decent bar-restaurant. Yoga sessions are also on offer. ❹–❺

Marina Estrada 2 Fevereiro ⓣ0260/225 4420. A slowly crumbling but very atmospheric Portuguese-colonial house, which has good-value a/c rooms with period furniture; it's worth paying a bit extra to get one of the deluxe ones. The restaurant is worth a look too. ❸–❹

Sovereign Seaface Rd ⓣ0260/225 0236. Close to the *Gurukripa*, and run by the same management team, *Sovereign* also has respectable a/c rooms with TVs and small attached bathrooms. ❹–❺

Sukh Sagar Estrada 2 Fevereiro ⓣ0260/225 5089. This friendly little hotel, tucked away on a quiet street, has no-nonsense basic but clean rooms, as well as a budget restaurant. ❸

The Town

Most of the action in **Nani Daman** centres on **Seaface Road**, which runs west from the market past rows of hotels, seedy bars and liquor stores to the **beach**, which is too polluted for a comfortable swim or sunbathe. South across town, the **riverfront** area is dominated by fishing trawlers and markets. The ramparts of **St Jerome's Fort**, directly behind the quay, make a good place from which to survey the activity. Erected in the early seventeenth century to counter the threat of Mughal invasion, the citadel encircles a small maidan, a Catholic church and a walled Portuguese cemetery.

The town's most impressive monuments lie across the river in the leafy colonial compound of **Moti Daman**, 2km south of Seaface Road. Inside its hefty walls, elegant double-storeyed mansions with sweeping staircases, wooden shutters, verandas and colour-washed facades overlook leafy courtyards.

Moti Daman's highlights are its **churches**, among the oldest and best-preserved Christian monuments in Asia. Grandest of all is the **cathedral** (Church of Bom Jesus) on the main square. Built in 1603, its gigantic gabled Baroque facade opens onto a lofty vaulted hall. On the opposite side of the square, the **Church of Our Lady of the Rosary** is crammed with ornate woodwork.

Main Road links Moti Daman's two **gates**, installed in the 1580s following a Mughal invasion. A small cottage next to the northern ("sea") gate was once the home of the eighteenth-century Portuguese poet Bocage, while atop the bastion facing the southern ("land") gate is the cell where prisoners condemned to death in Portuguese times spent their final days.

Eating and drinking

Most of the **"bar-restaurants"** along Seaface Road are restaurants in name only and best avoided.

Garden Seaface Rd. A terrace restaurant-bar serving reasonably priced tandoori pomfret and lobster, as well as Goan meat and veg specialities (Rs40–200).

Daman Delite *Gurukripa* hotel. The place to come for a slap-up meal: choose from an extensive seafood menu – the rich fish curry is a highlight – and finish with a nip of potent Goan *feni* (coconut spirit). Mains Rs70–250.

Samrat Seaface Rd. Roadside restaurant specializing in eat-till-you-burst Gujarati thalis, which come with *namkeens* (salty titbits), a couple of different dhals and mouthwatering veg dishes (Rs40–70). No alcohol.

Pithora *Sovereign* hotel. Veg south Indian snacks, thalis and Chinese dishes, plus cold beer, served indoors or alfresco on a breezy balcony done up like a Gujarati village (mains Rs40–100).

10

Mumbai

* **The Gateway of India** Mumbai's defining landmark, and a favourite spot for an evening stroll. **See p.604**

* **Chhatrapati Shivaji Museum** A fine collection of priceless Indian art, from ancient temple sculpture to Mughal armour. **See p.606**

* **Maidans (parks)** Where Mumbai's citizens escape the hustle and bustle to play cricket, eat lunch and hang out. **See p.607**

* **CS (Victoria) Terminus** A fantastically eccentric pile, perhaps the greatest railway station ever built by the British. **See p.610**

* **Haji Ali's Tomb** Mingle with the crowds of Muslim worshippers who flock to the island tomb of Sufi mystic Haji Ali to listen to *qawwali* music on Thursday evenings. **See p.612**

* **Elephanta Island** Catch a boat across Mumbai harbour to see one of ancient India's most wonderful rock-cut Shiva temples. **See p.614**

* **Bollywood blockbusters** Check out the latest Hindi mega-movie in one of the city centre's gigantic Art-Deco cinemas. **See p.620**

▲ The Gateway of India by night

Ever since the opening of the Suez Canal in 1869, the principal gateway to the Indian Subcontinent has been **MUMBAI (Bombay)**, the city Aldous Huxley famously described as "the most appalling…of either hemisphere". Travellers tend to regard time spent here as a rite of passage to be survived rather than savoured. But as the powerhouse of Indian business, industry and trade, and the source of its most seductive media images, the Maharashtrian capital can be a compelling place to kill time. Whether or not you find the experience enjoyable, however, will depend largely on how well you handle the heat, humidity, hassle, traffic fumes and relentless crowds of India's most dynamic, Westernized city.

First impressions of Mumbai tend to be dominated by its chronic **shortage of space**. Crammed onto a narrow spit of land that curls from the swamp-ridden coast into the Arabian Sea, the city is technically an island, connected to the mainland by bridges and narrow causeways. In less than five hundred years, it has metamorphosed from an aboriginal fishing settlement into a megalopolis of over sixteen million people – one of the biggest urban sprawls on the planet. Being swept along broad boulevards by endless streams of commuters, or jostled by coolies and hand-cart pullers in the teeming bazaars, you'll continually feel as if Mumbai is about to burst at the seams.

The roots of the population problem and attendant poverty lie, paradoxically, in the city's enduring ability to create **wealth**. Mumbai alone generates one third of India's tax income, its port handles half the country's foreign trade, and its movie industry is the biggest in the world. Symbols of prosperity are everywhere: from the phalanx of office blocks clustered on Nariman Point, Maharashtra's Manhattan, to the expensively dressed teenagers posing in Colaba's trendiest nightspots.

The flip side to the success story is the city's much-chronicled **poverty**. Each day, an estimated five hundred economic refugees pour into Mumbai from the Maharashtrian hinterland. Some find jobs and secure accommodation; many more end up living on the already overcrowded streets, or amid the squalor of some of Asia's largest slums, reduced to rag-picking and begging from cars at traffic lights.

However, while it would definitely be misleading to downplay its difficulties, Mumbai is far from the ordeal some travellers make it out to be. Once you've overcome the major hurdle of finding somewhere to stay, you may begin to enjoy its frenzied pace and crowded, cosmopolitan feel.

Mumbai or Bombay?

In 1996 Bombay was renamed **Mumbai**, as part of a wider policy instigated by the right-wing Maharashtrian nationalist Shiv Sena Municipality to replace names of any places, roads and features in the city that had connotations of the Raj. The Shiv Sena asserted that the British term "Bombay" derived from the Marathi title of a local deity, the mouthless "Maha-amba-aiee" (Mumba Devi for short; see p.610). In fact, historians are unanimously agreed that the Portuguese, who dubbed the harbour "Bom Bahia" ("Good Bay") when they first came across it, were responsible for christening the site and that the later British moniker had nothing to do with the aboriginal Hindu earth goddess.

The name change was widely unpopular when it was first imposed, especially among the upper and middle classes, and non-Maharashtrian immigrant communities, who doggedly stuck to Bombay. Some fifteen years on, however, "Mumbai" seems to have definitively taken root with the dotcom generation and even outgrown the narrow agenda of its nationalist originators – just as "Bombay" outlived the Raj.

Some history

Mumbai originally consisted of seven **islands**, inhabited by small Koli fishing communities. In 1534, Sultan Bahadur of Ahmedabad ceded the land to the **Portuguese**, who subsequently handed it on to the English in 1661 as part of the Portuguese Infanta Catherine of Braganza's dowry during her marriage to Charles II. Bombay's safe harbour and strategic commercial position attracted the interest of the **East India Company**, based at nearby Surat, and in 1668 a deal was struck whereby they leased Bombay from Charles for a pittance.

Life for the English was not easy, however: "fluxes" (dysentery), "Chinese death" (cholera) and other diseases culled many of the first settlers, prompting the colony's chaplain to declare that "two monsoons are the age of a man". Nevertheless, the city established itself as the capital of the flourishing East India Company, attracting a diverse mix of settlers including Goans, Gujarati traders, Muslim weavers and the business-minded Zoroastrian Parsis. The cotton crisis in America following the Civil War fuelled the great Bombay **cotton boom** and established the city as a major industrial and commercial centre, while the opening of the Suez Canal in 1869 and the construction of enormous docks further improved Bombay's access to European markets ushering in an age of mercantile self-confidence embodied by the grandiloquent colonial-Gothic buildings constructed during the governership of **Sir Bartle Frere** (1862–67).

As the most prosperous city in the nation, Bombay was at the forefront of the **Independence** struggle; Mahatma Gandhi used a house here, now a museum, to co-ordinate the struggle through three decades. Fittingly, the first British colony took pleasure in waving the final goodbye to the Raj, when the last contingent of British troops passed through the Gateway of India in February 1948. Since Independence, Mumbai has prospered as India's commercial capital and the population has grown tenfold, to more than sixteen million, although the modern city has also been plagued by a deadly mixture of **communal infighting** and outside **terrorist attacks**.

Tensions due to the increasing numbers of immigrants from other parts of the country, and the resultant overcrowding, has fuelled the rise of the extreme right-wing Maharashtrian party, the **Shiv Sena**, founded in 1966 by Bal Thackery, a self-confessed admirer of Hitler. Thousands of Muslim Mumbaikars were murdered by Hindu mobs following the destruction of the Babri Masjid in Ayodhya in 1992–93, while in March 1993, ten massive retaliatory **bomb blasts** killed 260 people. The involvement of Muslim godfather Dawood Ibrahim and the Pakistani secret service was suspected, and both Ibrahim and the Pakistanis have been linked with subsequent atrocities. These include the bomb blasts in August 2003, which killed 107 tourists next to the **Gateway of India;** the subsequent explosions in July 2006, when coordinated bomb blasts simultaneously blew apart seven packed commuter trains across the city; and, most dramatically, the horrific attacks of **November 26, 2008** (see box opposite), during which a group of rampaging gunmen ran amok across the city, killing 172 people.

Despite these setbacks, Mumbai has prospered like nowhere else in India as a result of the country's ongoing **economic liberalization**. Following decades of stagnation, the textiles industry has been supplanted by rapidly growing IT, finance, healthcare and back-office support sectors. Whole suburbs have sprung up to accommodate the affluent new middle-class workforce, with shiny shopping malls and car showrooms to relieve them of their income. Even so, corruption in politics and business has drained away investment from socially deprived areas. Luxury apartments in Bandra may change hands for half a

The 2008 Mumbai attacks: 26/11

Despite all the previous terrorist outrages against Mumbai (see opposite), none succeeded in capturing the world's attention in the same way as the attacks which rocked the city in November 2008, during which a group of Pakistani gunmen embarked on a three-day orgy of murder and destruction at a string of high-profile locations across the city – India's own 9/11, and a chilling display of Islamic militancy at its most deadly.

The ten attackers, all men in their early twenties, travelled by boat from Karachi (hijacking an Indian fishing trawler and killing its crew en route) before coming ashore at Cuffe Parade on the evening of 26 November. Two of the attackers headed to **CST station**, where they opened fire in the main hall, killing 58 people before fleeing the scene, after which they continued to run amok across the city, machine-gunning seven Indian policemen and attempting to massacre patients and staff at nearby Cama Hospital before being intercepted by security forces. Two others headed to **Leopold's** café and began firing into the crowd, murdering ten people before escaping. Two more seized control of the Jewish centre at **Nariman House**, holding its six inhabitants hostage – all were subsequently killed, apparently after having been tortured. Two bombs were also left in taxis which later exploded, killing a further five people.

The main focus of the attacks, however, were two of the city's most prestigious hotels, the **Oberoi Trident** and the **Taj Mahal Palace and Tower**. At both, gunmen entered, firing randomly at guests in the hotels' public areas, before retreating upstairs, where they began setting off explosives and taking large numbers of guests hostage. The sight of smoke pouring out of the central dome of the old wing of the Taj became an almost permanent fixture on TV screens around the world, as Indian commandos began the hazardous task of flushing the terrorists out of the hotels and freeing their hostages, fighting floor by floor to clear the buildings – a job which took three days in the case of the Taj.

By the end of the attacks, some 172 people were dead, including 28 foreigners from sixteen different countries ranging from Mexico to Mauritius as well as 17 Indian policemen and commandos (including Mumbai's own Anti-Terrorism Chief, Hemant Karkare). Given the chosen targets, including two landmark luxury hotels, a Jewish centre and a café heavily patronized by westerners, suspicions inevitably pointed towards the various militant Islamist operations based in Pakistan. The Pakistani government initially denied that any of its citizens had been involved in the attacks, attempting to place the blame on jihadi organizations in Bangladesh and Indian criminals. Despite Pakistani denials, however, it soon emerged that all ten gunmen were in fact Pakistanis, all of whom had been trained by **Lashkar-e-Taiba**, one of the leading Pakistan-based militant organizations, originally founded to fight the Indian presence in Kashmir and subsequently connected with a string of high-profile attacks in other parts of India. Interrogations of the one surviving terrorist, Ajmal Kasab, revealed that the gunmen had been hand-picked during Lashkar-e-Taiba training camps in Pakistan, given advanced training in weapons and explosives and sent into "battle" fuelled by a heady mix of LSD and cocaine. Kasab also stated that the gunmen had hoped to kill five thousand people, an aim in which they mercifully failed. In November 2009, Pakistani authorities belatedly arrested seven men in connection with the attacks, though the Indian government continues to insist that those self-same authorities have not done enough to bring those responsible – the leaders of Lashkar-e-Taiba in particular – to justice.

million dollars or more, but an estimated seven to eight million people (just under fifty percent of Mumbai's population) live in slums with no toilets, on just six percent of the land.

Arrival and information

Unless you arrive in Mumbai by train at **Chhatrapati Shivaji Terminus** (formerly Victoria Terminus), be prepared for a long slog into the centre. The international and domestic **airports** are way north of the city, and ninety minutes or more by road from the main hotel areas, while from **Mumbai Central** railway or **bus station**, you face a laborious trip across town.

By air

Mumbai's busy **international airport**, **Chhatrapati Shivaji** (30km north; Ⓦwww.csia.in), is divided into two terminals, one for Air India flights (terminal 2C) and the other for foreign airlines (terminal 2B). All of the domestic airlines also have offices outside the main entrance. The arrivals concourse houses a 24-hour State Bank of India exchange facility and ATM, India Tourism and MTDC tourist information counters, car rental kiosks, while a handy 24-hour **left luggage** "cloakroom" is located in the car park nearby. There's also an **Indian Railways booking office** (terminal 2B; daily 8am–1pm & 2–8pm) – very useful if you know your next destination, since it could save you a long wait at the reservation offices downtown. If you're on one of the few flights to land in the afternoon or early evening – by which time most hotels tend to be full – it can be worth paying on the spot for a room at the **accommodation booking desk** in the arrivals hall. All of the domestic airlines have offices outside the main entrance.

While many of the more upmarket hotels, particularly those near the airport, send out **courtesy coaches** to pick up their guests, most people make use of the **pre-paid taxi** desk in the arrivals hall. Fares are slightly higher than the normal meter rate, but at least you can be sure you'll be taken by the most direct route and it might save you having to haggle. Fares are Rs355 (or Rs455 a/c) to Colaba, Rs165 (or Rs210 a/c) to Juhu. Taxi-wallahs sometimes try to persuade you to stay at a different hotel from the one you ask for. Don't agree to this; their commission will be added onto the price of your room. Alternatively, if you want to book a car with driver for your arrival, try RNK Travels (Ⓣ022/2437 1112, Ⓦwww.rnk.com).

Internal flights land at Mumbai's **domestic airport** (26km to the north of downtown and 2km west of the international airport); technically this is part of Chhatrapati Shivaji international airport, though it's still widely referred to by its old name, "Santa Cruz". Terminal 1A handles Air India, Indian Airlines and Kingfisher flights, while all other carriers use Terminal 1B. Note that if you're taking a flight departing from the newly opened Terminal 1C, you'll still have to check in at the existing counters in either of the older terminals. If you're transferring directly from here to an international flight take the free "fly-bus" that

In transit

If you're only passing through Mumbai between flights and need to sit out half the night, it's worth knowing that the *Leela Kempinski* and *Royal Meridien* five-stars are both a short, complimentary transfer bus ride from the international terminal at CST. Their air-conditioned restaurants, coffee shops and bars make much more comfortable places to kill time than the departure lounge at the grungy airport – and their toilets are in a different league. The **retiring rooms** at the domestic airport are an option worth considering if you'd like to get some shut-eye between planes – though they're rarely available at short notice. Check at the information desks in either the international or domestic terminals.

shuttles every fifteen minutes between the two; look for the transfer counter in your transit lounge."

India Tourism and the MTDC both have 24-hour **information counters** in the arrivals hall, and there's a foreign exchange counter and accommodation desk tucked away near the first-floor exit. The official "Pre-Paid" taxi counter on the arrivals concourse charges around Rs400 to Colaba. Don't be tempted by the cheaper fares offered by touts outside, and avoid **auto-rickshaws** altogether, as they're not allowed downtown and will leave you at the mercy of unscrupulous taxi drivers on the edge of vile-smelling Mahim Creek, the southernmost limit of their permitted area.

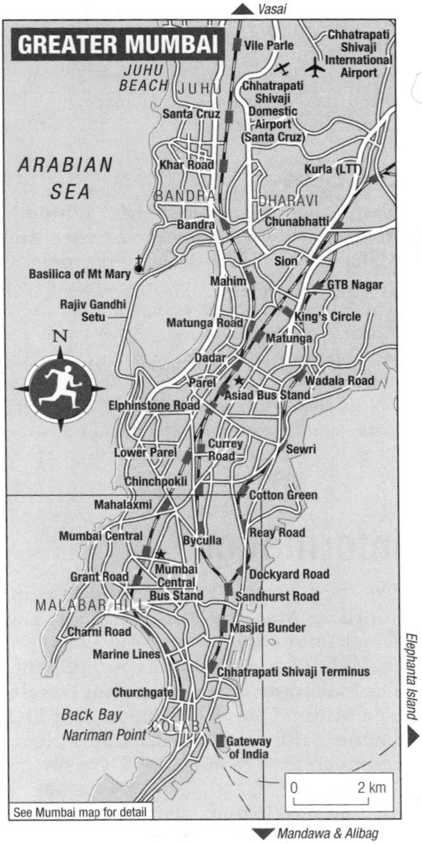

By train

Trains to Mumbai from most central, southern and eastern regions arrive at **Chhatrapati Shivaji Terminus** or **CST** (formerly **Victoria Terminus**, or **VT**), the main railway station at the end of the Central Railway line. From here it's a ten- or fifteen-minute ride to Colaba; taxis queue at the busy rank outside the south exit, opposite the new reservation hall.

Mumbai Central, the terminus for Western Railway trains from northern India, is a half-hour ride from Colaba; take a taxi from the forecourt, or flag one down on the main road – it should cost around Rs200–250.

Some trains from South India arrive at more obscure stations. If you find yourself at **Dadar**, way up in the industrial suburbs, and don't want to shell out on a taxi, cross the Tilak Marg road bridge onto the Western Railway and catch a suburban train into town (remembering to purchase a ticket at the hatch on platform 1 beforehand). **Kurla** station, where a few trains from Bengaluru (Bangalore) and Kerala pull in, is even further out, just south of the domestic

Malaria warning

Due to the massive slum encampments and bodies of stagnant water around the **airports**, both the international and domestic terminals are major **malaria** black spots. Clouds of mosquitoes await your arrival in the car park, so don't forget to smother yourself with strong insect repellent before leaving the terminal.

airport; taking a suburban train for Churchgate is the only reasonable alternative to a taxi. From either, it's worth asking at the station when you arrive if there is another long-distance train going to Churchgate or CST (Victoria Terminus) shortly after – far better than trying to cram into either a suburban train or bus.

By bus

Nearly all interstate **buses** arrive at **Mumbai Central Bus Stand**, a stone's throw from the railway station of the same name. Government services use the main **Maharashtra State Road Transport Corporation (MSRTC)** stand itself; private ones operate from the roadside next to Mumbai Central railway station, two minutes' walk west on the opposite side of busy Dr AN Marg (Lamington Road). To get downtown, either catch a suburban train from Mumbai Central's local platform, over the footbridge from the mainline, or jump in a cab at the rank in front of the station.

Note that while most MSRTC buses terminate at Mumbai Central, those from **Pune** (and surrounding areas) end up at the **ASIAD** bus stand, a glorified parking lot near the **Dadar** railway station (see p.595).

Information

The best source of **information** in Mumbai is the excellent **India Tourism** (Mon–Fri 9am–6pm, Sat 9am–2pm; ⓣ022/2207 4333 or 4334, ⓔindiatourism@mtnl.net.in) at 123 M Karve Rd, opposite Churchgate Station's east exit, with exceptionally helpful staff and lots of free maps and brochures. The **Maharashtra State Tourism Development Corporation (MTDC) office** is on Madam Cama Road opposite the LIC Building at Nariman Point (Mon–Sat 9.30am–5.30pm; ⓣ022/2284 5678, ⓦwww.maharashtratourism.gov.in); staff here can reserve rooms in MTDC resorts, and also sell tickets for city sightseeing tours (see p.598).

For detailed **listings**, the most complete source is Mumbai's *Time Out* (ⓦwww.timeoutmumbai.net). Alternatively, check out the "Metro" page in the *Indian Express* or the "Bombay Times" section of the *Times of India*. All are available from street vendors around Colaba and downtown.

City transport and tours

Gridlock is the norm during peak hours, and you should brace yourself for long waits at junctions if you take to the roads by taxi, bus or auto. Local **trains** get there faster, but can be a real endurance test even outside rush hours.

Trains

Mumbai's local **trains** carry an estimated 6.1 million commuters each day between downtown and the sprawling suburbs in the north – half the entire passenger capacity of Indian Railways (see box opposite). One line begins at CST (VT), running up the east side of the city; the other leaves Churchgate, travelling via Mumbai Central, Dadar to Santa Cruz and beyond. Services depart every few minutes from 5am until midnight, stopping at dozens of small stations. Carriages remain packed solid virtually the whole time, with passengers dangling precariously

A "Super-dense" Crush

The suburban rail network in Mumbai is officially the busiest on the planet. No other line carries as many passengers, nor crams them into such confined spaces. At peak times, as many as 4700 people may be jammed into a nine-carriage train designed to carry 1700, resulting in what the rail company, in typically jaunty Mumbai style, refers to as "Super-Dense Crush Load" of 14–16 standing passengers per square metre. Not all of these actually occupy floor space, of course: ten percent will be dangling precariously out of the doors.

The busiest stretch, a sixty-kilometre segment between Churchgate terminus and Virar in north Mumbai, transports nearly 900 million people each year, the highest of any rail network in the world. **Fatalities** are all too frequent: on average, 3500 die on the rail network annually, from falling out of the doors, crossing the tracks or because they're hit by overhead cables while riding on the roof.

out of open doors to escape the crush, so start to make your way to the exit at least three stops before your destination. Peak hours (approximately 8.30–10am & 4–7pm) are the worst of all. Women are marginally better off in the "ladies carriages"; look for the crowd of colourful saris and *salwar kameezes* grouped at the end of the platform.

Buses

BEST (Ⓣ022/2285 6262, Ⓦwww.bestundertaking.com) operates a **bus** network of labyrinthine complexity, covering every part of the city. You can check routes and bus numbers on their website; recognizing bus numbers in the street, however, can be more problematic, as numerals are written in Marathi (although in English on the sides). Aim, wherever possible, for the "Limited" ("Ltd") services, which stop less frequently, and avoid rush hours at all costs. Tickets are bought from the conductor on the bus.

Taxis and car rental

With rickshaws banished to the suburbs, Mumbai's ubiquitous black-and-yellow **taxis** are the quickest and most convenient way to nip around the city centre. In theory, all should have meters and a current "tariff card" (to convert the amount shown on the meter to the correct fare); in practice, particularly at night or early in the morning, many drivers refuse to use them. If this happens, either flag down another or haggle out a fare. As a rule of thumb, expect to be charged Rs10 per kilometre after the minimum fare of around Rs20, plus a small sum for heavy luggage (Rs5–10/article). The latest addition to Mumbai's hectic roads is the **Cool Cab** (Ⓣ022/2216 4466; Ⓦwww.citycoolcab.in), blue taxis with a/c and tinted windows; rates are around forty percent higher than in a normal cab.

Cars with drivers can be rented per eight-hour day (Rs1200–1500 for a non-a/c Ambassador, upwards of Rs1500 for more luxurious a/c cars) through any good travel agent (see p.624).

Boats

Ferryboats regularly chug out of Mumbai harbour, connecting the city with the far shore and some of the larger islands in between. The most popular with visitors is the **Elephanta Island** launch (see p.614), which departs from the Gateway of India (see p.604), as do frequent boats to **Mandawa Jetty**, for Alibag, the transport hub for the rarely used **coastal route south** (see p.627).

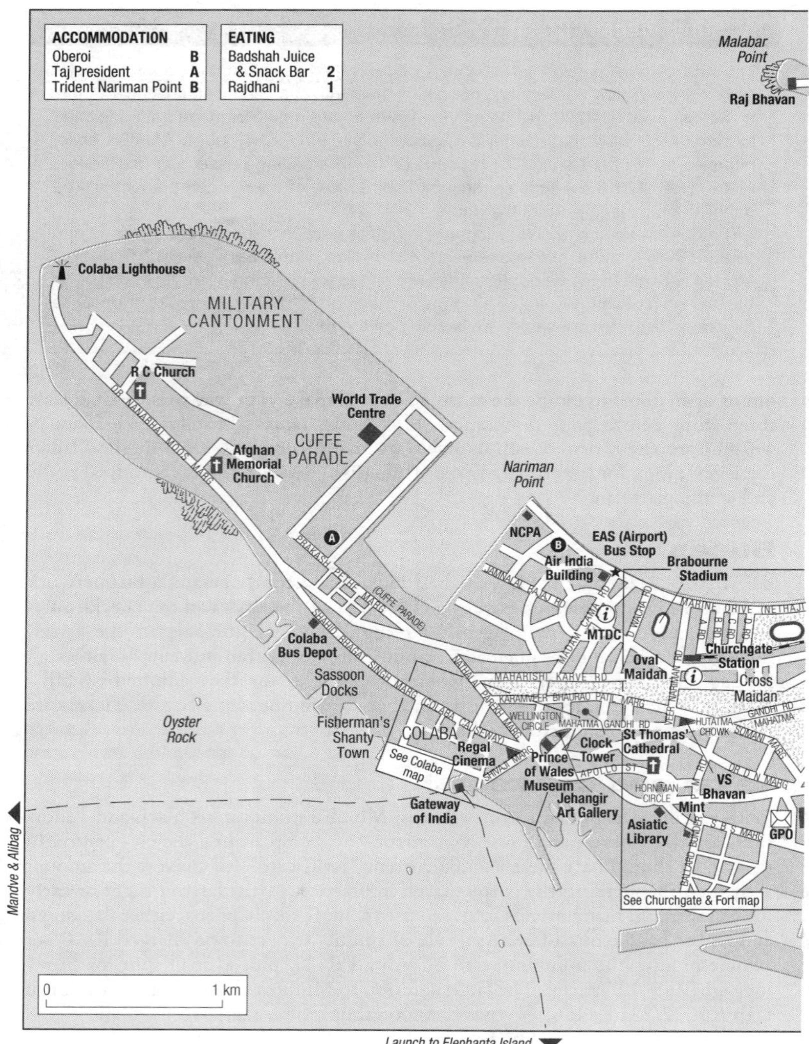

Tours

A number of operators around the Gateway of India offer whistlestop **one-day city tours** by bus (around Rs150, not including admission charges) – an inexpensive but usually very rushed way to cram Mumbai's tourist highlights into a single day. The MTDC run one-hour **after-dark tours** on an open-top bus (weekends 7pm & 8.15pm; upper deck Rs120, lower deck Rs150) of Mumbai's illuminated landmarks. Tours are bookable at the MTDC kiosk near the Gateway, which is also where they leave from.

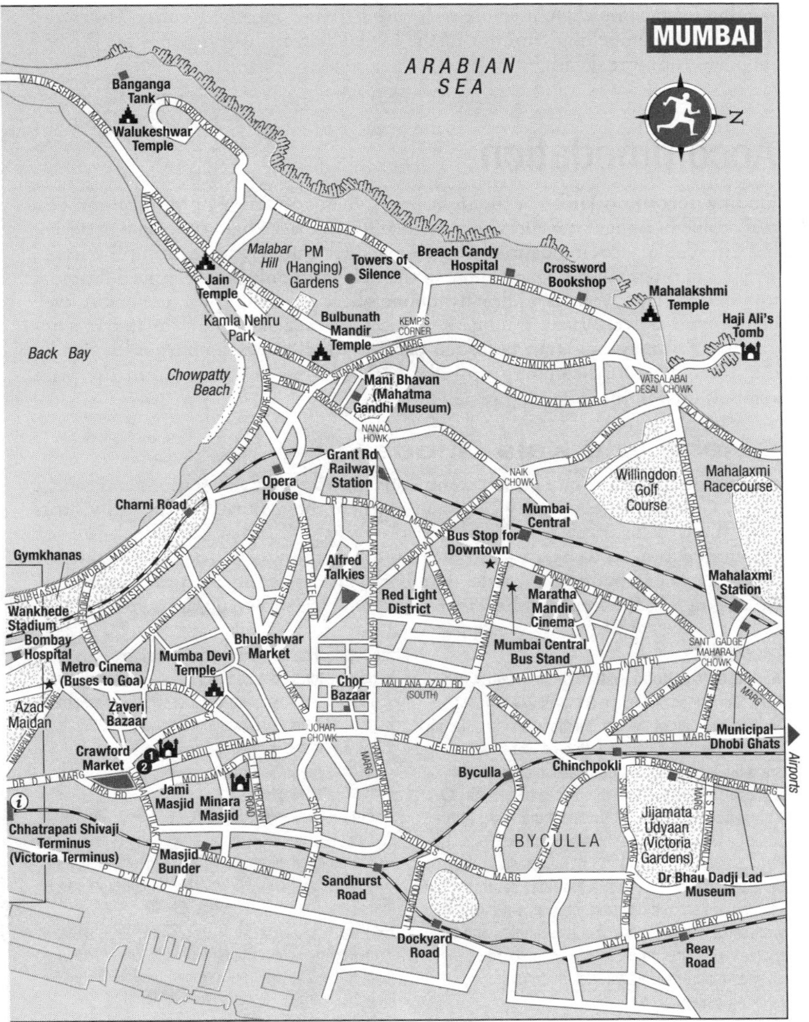

A more leisurely alternative, focusing mainly on period buildings and colonial history, is to go on one of the excellent guided walks organized by architects Abha Bahl and Brinda Gaitonde of **The Bombay Heritage Walks** (Ⓦ www.bombayheritagewalks.com). The two-hour walks (Rs1500 for up to three people; Rs500 per additional person) are offered mainly at weekends, though weekday evening walks can sometimes be arranged depending on availability. Advance bookings essential on Ⓣ 022/2369 0992 or Ⓔ info@bombayheritagewalks.com. Another possibility is **Mumbai Magic** (Ⓦ www.mumbaimagic.com), who offer a range of interesting walking and driving tours delving into various aspects of the city ranging from colonial architecture to Jewish heritage. Finally, **Reality Tours and Travels** run compelling trips out to the huge Dharavi shantytown – see the box on p.613 for more details.

Accommodation

Finding **accommodation** at the right price when you arrive in Mumbai can be a real problem. Budget travellers, in particular, can expect a hard time finding decent but affordable accommodation. The best budget places tend to fill up by noon, which can often mean a long trudge in the heat with only an overpriced fleapit at the end of it, so you should really phone ahead as soon as (or preferably well before) you arrive. Prices in upmarket places are especially high for India; state-imposed "**luxury tax**" (currently ten percent), and "**service charges**" levied by the hotel itself further bump up bills; both add-ons are included in the price symbols used in the following reviews.

Colaba and Kala Ghoda

A short ride from the city's main commercial districts, railway stations and tourist office, **Colaba** makes a handy base, and is where the majority of foreign visitors head first. The streets around the Gateway of India are chock-full of accommodation, and the area also offers more in the way of food and entertainment than neighbouring districts. The hotels below are marked on the map of Colaba on p.605, except for the *Taj President*, which is shown on the map on p.598.

Budget

Aga Bheg's & Hotel Kishan Ground, 2nd & 3rd floor, Shirin Manzil, Walton Rd ⓣ022/2284 2227. Muslim-run pair of budget guesthouses on different floors of the same building. Rooms (some with a/c) are a bit shabby, although a passable fallback if you can't get into any of the places below. ❹–❺

Lawrence 3rd floor, 33 Sri Sai Baba Marg (Rope Walk Lane), off K Dubash Marg, behind *TGI's* ⓣ022/2284 3618 or 6633 6107. Close to the Jehangir Art Gallery, this is arguably south Mumbai's best rock-bottom choice, with five well-scrubbed doubles (plus two singles and two triples) with fans, and not-so-clean shared shower-toilets; breakfast included. Advance booking essential. ❸

Red Shield Red Shield House, 30 Boram Behram (Mereweather) Rd, near the *Taj* ⓣ022/2284 1824, ⓔredshield@vsnl.net. Ultra-basic bunk beds (Rs225) in cramped, stuffy dorms (lockers available), or larger good-value doubles (some with shared bath, some with a/c). Rates include breakfast and lunch, served in a sociable canteen. Maximum one-week stay. ❹

Sea Shore 4th floor, 1-49 Kamal Mansion, Arthur Bunder Rd ⓣ022/2287 4237. Among the best budget deals in Colaba. The sea-facing rooms with windows are much nicer than the airless cells on the other side. Friendly management and free, safe baggage store. Common baths only. There are also slightly cheaper wooden-partitioned rooms (shared bath only) at the less salubrious *India* (ⓣ022/2283 3769; ❸) in the same building. ❸–❹

Mid-range

Ascot 38 Garden Rd ⓣ022/6638 5566, ⓦwww.ascothotel.com. One of the oldest and most comfortable small hotels in Mumbai, updated with contemporary glass-and-marble designer interiors and spacious modern rooms. ❽–❾

Bentley's 17 Oliver Rd ⓣ022/2284 1474, ⓦwww.bentleyshotel.com. Dependable old Parsi-owned favourite in five different colonial tenements, all on leafy backstreets. Rooms (with optional a/c for Rs300 extra) are quiet, secure and spacious, if a little worn, though the overall shabbiness isn't compensated for by the rates, which are higher than you'd expect for the level of comfort. ❻

Godwin Jasmine Building, 41 Garden Rd ⓣ022/2287 2050, ⓦwww.mumbainet.com/hotels/godwin. Top-class three-star with large, international-standard rooms and great views from upper floors (ask for #804, #805 or #806). ❽

Moti International 10 Best Marg ⓣ022/2202 1654, ⓔhotelmotiinternational@yahoo.co.in. Quiet and friendly hotel in a characterful old colonial building. Rooms are cosy and clean, and all come with a/c, fridge and TV. Good value. ❻

Sea Palace Kerawalla Chambers, 26 PJ Ramchandani Marg (Apollo Bunder) ⓣ022/2284 1828, ⓦwww.seapalacehotel.net. Comfortable, well-maintained hotel at the quiet end of the harbour front. All rooms are a/c but sea views cost extra. Breakfast and light meals are served on a sunny terrace at the front. ❼–❽

Strand PJ Ramchandani Marg (Apollo Bunder) ⓣ022/2288 2222, ⓦwww.hotelstrand.com. Deservedly popular mid-scale option on the seafront that's nicely situated and efficiently run. Rooms are old-fashioned but comfortable, with fine harbour views from the more expensive ones. *Hotel Harbour View* (ⓣ022/2282 1089, ⓦwww.viewhotelsinc.com; ❼), on the top two floors of the same building, is very similar. ❼

YWCA 18 Madam Cama Rd ⓣ022/2202 5053, ⓔywcaic@mtnl.net.in. Relaxing, secure and quiet hostel (open to men as well as women) with spotless attached rooms. Rates include breakfast and a generous buffet dinner – a bargain for south Mumbai. Advance booking (by money draft) obligatory. ❻–❼

Luxury

Fariyas 25, off Arthur Bunder Rd ⓣ022/6141 6141, ⓦwww.fariyas.com. Compact luxury hotel with five-star trimmings (including pool and health club), plus great views from more expensive rooms. Doubles from around $240. ❾

Gordon House 5 Battery St ⓣ022/2289 4400, ⓦwww.ghhotel.com. Chic designer boutique place behind the Regal cinema. Each floor is differently themed: "Scandinavian" (the easiest to live with), "Mediterranean" and "Country". Doubles from around $360; discounts at weekends. ❾

Taj Mahal Palace & Tower PJ Ramchandani Marg ⓣ022/6665 3366, ⓦwww.tajhotels.com. Perhaps India's most famous hotel and the haunt of Mumbai's *beau monde*, with 546 luxury rooms, shopping arcades, a huge outdoor pool and a big spread of bars and restaurants. The hotel was at the centre of the terrorist attacks of November 2008, during which the upper floors of the Palace wing were set ablaze by a series of bombs detonated by the terrorists within. The Tower wing reopened within a month of the attacks; the Palace wing was still being rebuilt at the time of writing but should have reopened by the time you read this. Prices start from around $250 in the Tower; considerably more in the Palace. ❾

Taj President 90 Cuffe Parade ⓣ022/6665 0808, ⓦwww.tajhotels.com. (see map, p.598). Modern, business-oriented five-star occupying a seventeen-floor skyscraper just south of Colaba. A much more competitively priced option than its sister concern, the *Taj Mahal Palace & Tower*, though lacking old-world style and atmosphere. There is a large outdoor pool and an adjacent multi-gym and steam room. Rates start at around $400. ❾

Marine Drive

At the western edge of the downtown area, swanky **Marine Drive** (officially Netaji Subhash Chandra Marg) is lined with a string of four- and five-star hotels taking advantage of the panoramic views over Back Bay and the easy access to the city's commercial heart. The hotels below are marked on the Churchgate and Fort map on p.609, apart from *Trident Nariman Point* (formerly *Hilton Towers*) and the *Oberoi*, which are marked on p.598.

Ambassador VN Rd ⓣ022/2204 1131, ⓦwww.ambassadorindia.com. Recently renovated four-star with smart (albeit bland) modern rooms and a choice location close to sea and cafes. The revolving *Pearl of the Orient* restaurant (see p.617) is another bonus. Doubles from around $260. ❾

Astoria Jamshedji Tata ⓣ022/6654 1234, ⓦwww.astoriamumbai.com. Smart business hotel in refurbished 1930s Art-Deco building near the Eros cinema. The rooms are nowhere near as ritzy as the lobby but offer good value this close to the centre. ❽–❾

Bentley 3rd floor, Krishna Mahal, Marine Drive ⓣ022/2281 5244. Not to be confused with *Bentley's* in Colaba (see opposite), this small, friendly guesthouse is across town on the corner of D Rd/Marine Drive, near the cricket stadium. The marble-lined a/c rooms are clean and comfortable for the price, though most share shower-toilets. Rates (from Rs1650) include breakfast. ❺

Chateau Windsor 5th floor, 86 Veer Nariman Rd ⓣ022/6622 4455, ⓦwww.chateauwindsor.com. Impeccably neat and central, with unfailingly polite staff and a selection of attractively renovated modern rooms. Very popular, so reserve well in advance. ❼–❽

Intercontinental 135 Marine Drive ⓣ022/3987 9999, ⓦwww.mumbai.intercontinental.com. This ultra-chic boutique hotel is currently one of India's most stylish modern addresses. The rooms have huge sea-facing windows and state-of-the-art gadgets (including 42-inch plasma screens and DVD players), while the rooftop pool, bars and restaurants (including the *Dome* – see p.619) rank among Mumbai's most fashionable. Rack rates from around $475, though online rates can be almost half this. ❾

Marine Plaza 29 Marine Drive ⓣ022/2285 1212, ⓦwww.hotelmarineplaza.com. Ritzy but small luxury hotel on the seafront, with the usual five-star facilities and a (pseudo) Art-Deco atrium lobby topped by a glass-bottomed rooftop pool. Rooms from around $560. ❾

Oberoi Nariman Point ⓣ022/2232 5757, ⓦwww.oberoihotels.com. One of the focal points of the November 2008 terrorist attacks, the *Oberoi* reopened in April 2010. Enjoying a prime spot overlooking Back Bay, the hotel is traditionally the first choice of business travellers to the city – lacking the heritage character of the *Taj Mahal Palace & Tower*, but with fine views from its soaring tower and an atmosphere of glittering opulence throughout. ❾

Sea Green/Sea Green South 145 Marine Drive ⓣ022/6633 6525, ⓦwww.seagreenhotel.com & 145-A Marine Drive ⓣ022/6633 6535, ⓦwww.seagreensouth.com. Jointly owned and enduringly popular pair of seafront hotels. Décor is old-fashioned going on shabby, and rates are quite high, although the sweeping bay views from front-facing rooms partly compensate. ❼

Trident Nariman Point (formerly the *Hilton Towers*) Nariman Point ⓣ022/6632 4343, ⓦwww.tridenthotels.com. Sitting next to the *Oberoi* (see above) on Nariman Point, the *Trident* suffered slight damage during the 2008 attacks but reopened shortly afterwards. Currently the city's premier business hotel, with full five-star facilities and trimmings, including a gigantic lobby and sea views from its pool. Doubles from around $250. ❾

Around Chhatrapati Shivaji (Victoria) Terminus

The area immediately around **CST** (VT) station and the nearby GPO, though fairly central, has little to recommend it, although there are a couple of decent mid-range and a few more upmarket options. CST (VT) itself also has upmarket **retiring rooms** (❺), although these can't be booked in advance, so you'll have to take pot luck. The following are all marked on the Churchgate and Fort map on p.609.

City Palace 121 City Terrace ⓣ022/2261 5515, ⓦwww.hotelcitypalace.net. Large and popular hotel bang opposite the station. Economy rooms are tiny and windowless (almost like in a capsule hotel), but have a/c and are perfectly clean. Deluxe rooms higher up the building are larger and have bird's-eye views. ❺–❻

Grand 17 Shri SR Marg, Ballard Estate ⓣ022/6658 0506, ⓦwww.grandhotelbombay.com. Characterful old British-era three-star out near the old docks, nicely refurbished and with well-equipped rooms at competitive rates. ❼–❽

Oasis 276 Shahid Bhagat Singh Marg ⓣ022/3022 7886, ⓦwww.hoteloasisindia.in. Very well placed for CST station, and the best-value budget option in this area: rooms (all attached; some a/c) have good beds, clean linen and TVs. It's worth splashing out on a top-floor "deluxe" room as they offer better views. ❺

Residency 26 Rustom Sidhwa Marg, off DN Rd ⓣ022/2262 5525, ⓦwww.residencyhotel.com. Great little mid-range hotel, close to the best shopping areas. Its variously priced rooms (all with safe and wi-fi) offer unbeatable value, especially the no-frills "standard" options, though you'll have to book at least a couple of weeks ahead to get one. ❻

Juhu and around the airports

Hotels in the congested area around the international **airport** cater predominantly for transit passengers and business executives. If you can face the thirty-minute drive across town and afford the first-world room tariffs, head for the beachside suburb of **Juhu**, one of the city's most upmarket addresses. Nearly all the hotels below have courtesy buses to and from the terminal building, or at worst can arrange for a car and driver to meet you.

Hyatt Regency Airport Rd, Andheri (East) ⓣ022/6696 1234, ⓦwww.mumbai.regency.hyatt.com. Ancient Hindu precepts on architecture and design were incorporated into this ultra-luxurious five-star, right next to the airport. The results are impressive, and a notch more stylish than the competition, with floor-to-ceiling windows, rain showers and dark marble floors. From around $200. ❾

ISKCON Guesthouse Juhu Church Rd, Juhu ⓣ022/2620 6860, ⓦwww.iskconmumbai.com (follow the "Guest House" link on left-hand menu). Idiosyncratic hotel run by the International Society for Krishna Consciousness. Rooms (some with a/c) are very large for the price, though certain restrictions apply (no alcohol, meat or caffeine may be consumed on the premises). Forty days' advance booking recommended. ❻

JW Marriott Juhu Tara Rd, Juhu ⓣ022/6693 3000, ⓦwww.marriott.com. Palatial five-star complex with five opulent restaurants, three pools (one of them filled with treated salt water), a top-notch spa and blocks of luxury rooms looking through landscaped grounds to the beach. From around $300. ❾

Lotus Suites Andheri Kurla Rd, International Airport Zone, Andheri (East) ⓣ022/2827 0707, ⓦwww.lotussuites.com. An "Eco-Four-Star at Three-Star prices" is how this environment-friendly hotel describes itself, designed using energy-saving materials and with "green" trimmings such jute slippers and recycling bins in the rooms. A very comfortable option for under $150 if you book online. ❽

Midland Jawaharlal Nehru Rd, Santa Cruz (East) ⓣ022/2611 0414, ⓦwww.hotelmidland.com. Dependable two-star with well-furnished twin-bedded rooms. Rates (from Rs4400) include courtesy bus and breakfast. ❼

Orchid 70-C Nehru Rd, Vile Parle (East) ⓣ022/2616 4040, ⓦwww.orchidhotel.com. Award-winning "Eco-Five-Star", built with organic or recycled materials and using low-toxin paints. Every effort is made to minimize waste of natural resources, with a water-recycling plant and "zero garbage" policy. Rooms from around ❽

The City

Nowhere reinforces your sense of having arrived in Mumbai quite as emphatically as the **Gateway of India**, the city's defining landmark. Only a five-minute walk north, the **Prince of Wales Museum** should be next on your list of sightseeing priorities, as much for its flamboyantly eclectic architecture as for the art treasures inside. The museum provides a foretaste of what lies in store just up the road, where the cream of Bartle Frere's Bombay – the **University** and **High Court** – line up with the open maidans on one side, and the boulevards of **Fort** on the other. But for the fullest sense of why the city's founding fathers declared it Urbs Prima in Indis, you should press further north still to visit the **Chhatrapati Shivaji Terminus (CST)**, the high-water mark of India's Raj architecture.

Beyond CST lie the crowded bazaars and Muslim neighbourhoods of **central Mumbai**, at their liveliest and most colourful around **Crawford Market** and **Mohammed Ali Road**. Possibilities for an escape from the crowds include an evening stroll along **Marine Drive**, bounding the western edge of downtown, or a boat trip out to **Elephanta**, a rock-cut cave on an island in Mumbai harbour containing a wealth of ancient art.

Colaba

At the end of the seventeenth century, **Colaba** was little more than the last in a straggling line of rocky islands extending to the lighthouse that stood on Mumbai's southernmost point. Today, the original outlines of the promontory (whose name derives from the Koli fishermen who first lived here) have been submerged under a mass of dilapidated colonial tenements, hotels, bars, restaurants and handicraft emporia. If you never venture beyond the district, you'll get a very distorted picture of Mumbai; even though it's the main tourist enclave and a trendy hang-out for the city's rich young things, Colaba has retained the sleazy feel of the port it used to be.

The Gateway of India and the Taj hotel

Commemorating the visit of King George V and Queen Mary in 1911, India's own honey-coloured Arc de Triomphe was built in 1924 by George Wittet, the architect responsible for many of the city's grandest constructions. Blending indigenous Gujarati motifs with high Victorian pomp, it was originally envisaged as a ceremonial disembarkation point for passengers alighting from the P&O steamers, although nowadays the only boats bobbing about at the bottom of its stone staircase are the launches that ferry tourists across the harbour to Elephanta Island (see p.614).

Directly behind the Gateway, the older hotel in the **Taj Mahal Palace & Tower** complex (see p.601) stands as a monument to local pride in the face of colonial oppression. Its patron, the Parsi industrialist J. N. Tata, is said to have built the old *Taj* as an act of revenge after he was refused entry to what was then the best hotel in town, the "whites only" *Watson's*. The ban proved to be its undoing. *Watson's* disappeared long ago, but the *Taj* still presides imperiously over the seafront, the preserve of Mumbai's air-kissing jet set. Lesser mortals are allowed in to experience the tea lounge, shopping arcades and vast air-conditioned lobby – there's also a fabulously luxurious loo off the corridor to the left of the main desk.

Colaba Causeway and Sassoon Docks

Reclaimed in the late nineteenth century from the sea, the district's main thoroughfare, **Colaba Causeway** (as this stretch of Shahid Bhagat Singh Marg is known), leads south towards the military cantonment. Few tourists stray much further down it than the claustrophobic hawker zone at the top of the street, but it's well worth doing so, if only to see the neighbourhood's earthy **fresh produce market**, a couple of blocks south of the Strand cinema. From here, return to the main road and turn left to reach the gates of Mumbai's wholesale seafood market, **Sassoon Docks**. The quaysides are at their liveliest immediately before and after sunrise, when coolies haul the night's catch in crates of crushed ice over gangplanks, while Koli women cluster around the auctioneers. The stench, as overpowering as the noise, comes mostly from bundles of one of the city's traditional exports, **Bombay duck** (see box below). Note that **photography** is strictly forbidden as the docks are adjacent to a sensitive navy area.

Hop on any bus heading south down Colaba Causeway (#3, #11, #47, #103, #123 or #125) through the cantonment to reach the **Afghan Memorial Church of St John the Baptist**, built in 1847–54 as a memorial to the British victims of the First Afghan War. With its tall steeple and tower, the pale yellow church wouldn't look out of place in Worcester or Suffolk.

Kala Ghoda and around

Immediately north of Colaba, **Kala Ghoda** ("Black Horse") district is named after the large equestrian statue of King Edward VII that formerly stood on the

Bombay duck

Its name suggests some kind of fowl curry, but **Bombay duck** is actually a fish – to be precise, the marine lizard fish (*Harpalon nehereus*), known in the local dialect of Marathi as *bummalo*. How this long, ribbon-like sea creature acquired its English name no one is exactly sure, but the most plausible theory holds that the Raj-era culinary term derives from the Hindustani for mail train, *dak*. The nasty odour of the dried fish is said to have reminded the British of the less salubrious carriages of the Calcutta–Bombay *dak* when it pulled into VT after three days and nights on the rails, its wooden carriages covered in the stinking mould that flourished in the monsoonal humidity.

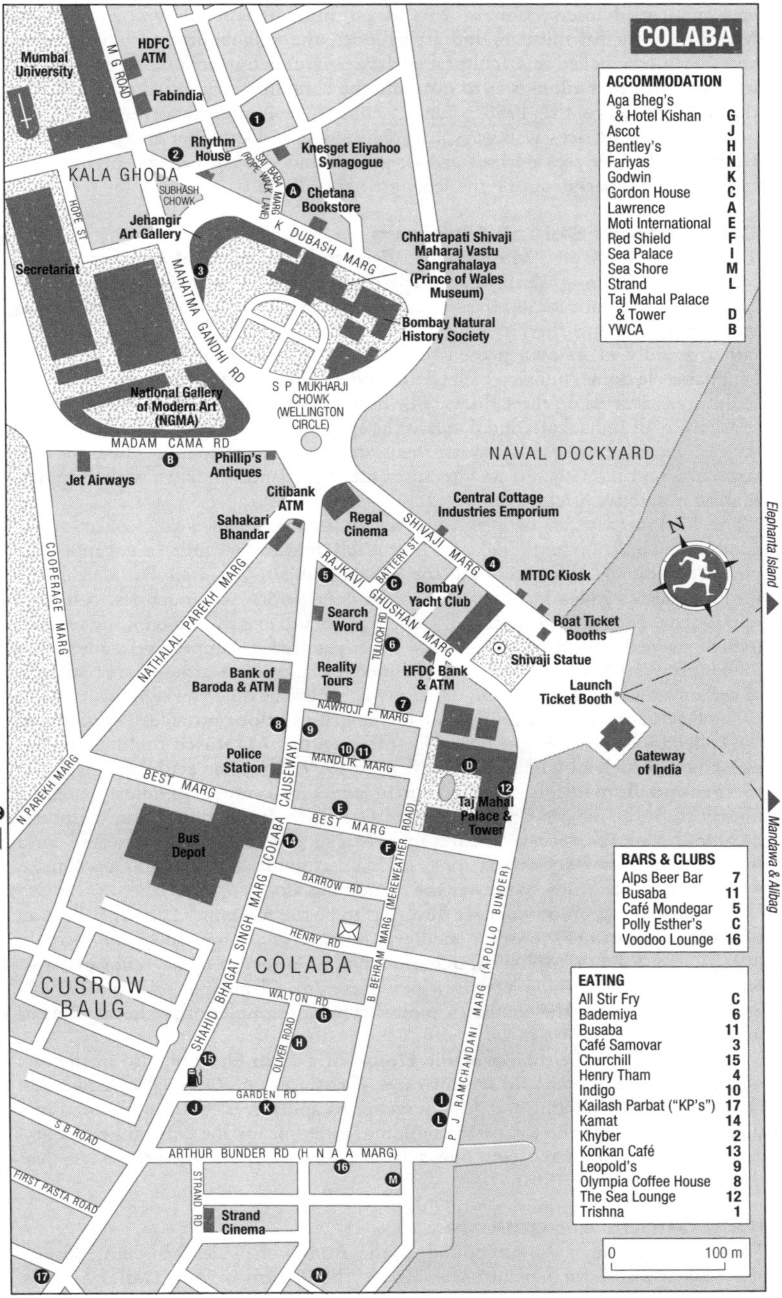

COLABA

ACCOMMODATION

Aga Bheg's & Hotel Kishan	G
Ascot	J
Bentley's	H
Fariyas	N
Godwin	K
Gordon House	C
Lawrence	A
Moti International	E
Red Shield	F
Sea Palace	I
Sea Shore	M
Strand	L
Taj Mahal Palace & Tower	D
YWCA	B

BARS & CLUBS

Alps Beer Bar	7
Busaba	11
Café Mondegar	5
Polly Esther's	C
Voodoo Lounge	16

EATING

All Stir Fry	C
Bademiya	6
Busaba	11
Café Samovar	3
Churchill	15
Henry Tham	4
Indigo	10
Kailash Parbat ("KP's")	17
Kamat	14
Khyber	2
Konkan Café	13
Leopold's	9
Olympia Coffee House	8
The Sea Lounge	12
Trishna	1

Mumbai University
HDFC ATM
M G ROAD
Fabindia
Rhythm House
KALA GHODA
SAI BABA MARG (ROPE WALK LANE)
Knesget Eliyahoo Synagogue
Chetana Bookstore
SUBHASH CHOWK
HOPE ST
Jehangir Art Gallery
K DUBASH MARG
Chhatrapati Shivaji Maharaj Vastu Sangrahalaya (Prince of Wales Museum)
Secretariat
MAHATMA GANDHI RD
Bombay Natural History Society
S P MUKHARJI CHOWK (WELLINGTON CIRCLE)
National Gallery of Modern Art (NGMA)
MADAM CAMA RD
Phillip's Antiques
Jet Airways
NAVAL DOCKYARD
Citibank ATM
Central Cottage Industries Emporium
Sahakari Bhandar
Regal Cinema
SHIVAJI MARG
BATTERY ST
COOPERAGE MARG
NATHALAL PAREKH MARG
RAJKAVI GHUSHAN MARG
Bombay Yacht Club
MTDC Kiosk
Search Word
TULLOCH RD
Boat Ticket Booths
Shivaji Statue
Bank of Baroda & ATM
Reality Tours
HFDC Bank & ATM
Launch Ticket Booth
NAWROJI F MARG
Elephanta Island
Police Station
MANDLIK MARG
Gateway of India
BEST MARG
N PAREKH MARG
Taj Mahal Palace & Tower
COLABA CAUSEWAY
Bus Depot
MEREWEATHER ROAD
BARROW RD
HENRY RD
SHAHID BHAGAT SINGH MARG
COLABA
B BEHRAM MARG
APOLLO BUNDER
CUSROW BAUG
WALTON RD
P J RAMCHANDANI MARG
OLIVER ROAD
GARDEN RD
S B ROAD
ARTHUR BUNDER RD (H N A A MARG)
FIRST PASTA ROAD
STRAND RD
Strand Cinema

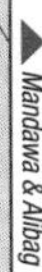

0 100 m

crescent-shaped intersection of MG Road and Subhash Chowk. Flanked by Mumbai's principal museum and art galleries, the neighbourhood has in recent years been relaunched as a "cultural enclave" – as much in an attempt to preserve its many historic buildings as to promote the contemporary visual arts that have thrived here since the 1950s. Fancy stainless-steel interpretative panels now punctuate the district's walkways, and on Sundays in December and January, the **Kala Ghoda Fair** sees portrait artists, potters and *mehendi* painters plying their trade in the car park fronting the Jehangir Art Gallery.

Chhatrapati Shivaji Museum

The **Prince of Wales Museum of Western India**, or **Chhatrapati Shivaji Maharaj Vastu Sangrahalaya** as it was renamed by the Shiv Sena (daily except Tues 10.15am–6pm; Rs300 [Rs25], camera Rs200, video Rs1000 – no tripods or flash), ranks among the city's most distinctive Raj-era constructions. It stands rather grandly in its own gardens off MG Road, crowned by a massive white Mughal-style dome, under which one of India's finest collections of paintings and sculpture is arrayed on three floors. The building was designed by George Wittet, of Gateway of India fame, and stands as the epitome of the hybrid **Indo-Saracenic** style – regarded in its day as an "educated" interpretation of fifteenth- and sixteenth-century Gujarati architecture, mixing Islamic touches with typically English municipal brickwork.

The foreigners' ticket price includes an **audio tour**, which you collect at the admissions kiosk inside, though you'll probably find it does little to enhance your visit. The heat and humidity inside the building can also be a trial. For a break, the institutional tea-coffee kiosk in the ground-floor garden is a much less congenial option than the *Café Samovar* outside (see p.616), but to exit the museum and re-enter (which you're entitled to do) you'll have to get your ticket stamped in the admissions lobby first. A number of galleries were closed for renovation at the time of writing, so certain exhibits might have moved around a bit by the time you read this.

The **Key Gallery** in the central hall of the **ground floor** provides a snapshot of the collection's treasures, including the fifth-century AD stucco Buddhist figures unearthed by archeologist Henry Cousens in 1909. The main **sculpture room** on the **ground floor** displays other fourth- and fifth-century Buddhist artefacts, mostly from the former Greek colony of Gandhara. Important Hindu sculptures include a seventh-century Chalukyan bas-relief depicting Brahma seated on a lotus, and a sensuously carved torso of Mahisasuramardini, the goddess Durga, with tripod raised ready to skewer the demon buffalo.

The main attraction on the **first floor** has to be the museum's famous collection of **Indian painting**. More fine medieval miniatures are housed in the recently inaugurated **Karl & Meherbai Khandalavala Gallery**, on the renovated east wing of this floor, along with priceless pieces of Ghandaran sculpture, Chola bronzes and some of the country's finest surviving examples of medieval Gujarati woodcarving.

Indian **coins** are the subject of the **House of Laxmi Gallery**, also in the east wing, while the **second floor** showcases a vast array of Oriental ceramics and glassware. Finally, among the grizzly **weapons** and pieces of armour stored in a small side-gallery at the top of the building, look out for the cuirass, helmet and jade dagger which the museum only recently discovered belonged to no less than the Mughal emperor Akbar.

Kala Ghoda art galleries

Technically in the same compound as the Prince of Wales Museum, though approached from further up MG Road, the **Jehangir Art Gallery** (daily

11am–7pm; free) is Mumbai's longest-established venue for contemporary art, with five small halls specializing in twentieth-century arts and crafts from around the world. You never know what you're going to find – most exhibitions last only a week and exhibits are often for sale.

On the opposite side of MG Road, facing the museum and Mukharji Chowk, stands the larger **National Gallery of Modern Art** (NGMA; Tues–Sun 11am–6pm; Rs150 [Rs10]; Ⓦwww.ngmaindia.gov.in), showcasing a mix of permanent and temporary exhibitions on three storeys and charting the development of modern Indian art from its beginnings in the 1950s to the present day. The installations, in particular, tend to be a lot more adventurous than those you'll find in the Jehangir across the road.

Around Oval Maidan

Northeast of Kala Ghoda stretches the breezy green **Oval Maidan**, where impromptu cricket matches are held almost every day. Some of the city's finest Victorian piles flank the eastern side of the Maidan, offering a good taste of what travel writer Robert Byron described as the city's "architectural Sodom" (adding, "Indian, Swiss chalet, French chateau, Giotto's tower, Siena cathedral & St Peter's are to be found altogether in almost every building"). Just north of here lies the characteristically ostentatious **High Court**, described in 1903 by Indian civil servant G.W. Forrest as "a massive pile whose main features have been brought from Venice, but all the beauty has vanished in transshipment".

Across AS D'Mello Road from the High Court are two major buildings belonging to **Mumbai University** (established 1857), which were designed in England by Sir Gilbert Scott, architect of the Gothic extravaganza that is London's St Pancras railway station. Funded by the Parsi philanthropist Cowasjee "Readymoney" Jehangir, the **Convocation Hall** greatly resembles a church. The **library** is topped by the 79.2-metre-high **Rajabhai Clock Tower**, which is said to have been modelled on Giotto's campanile in Florence and which formerly chimed tunes such as *Rule Britannia* and *Home Sweet Home*.

Fort

East of Oval Maidan stretches **Fort** district, site of Mumbai's original British settlement and first fort – hence the name. This is still the commercial hub of the southern city and a great area for aimless wandering, with plenty of old-fashioned cafés, department stores and street stalls crammed in between the stately Victorian piles.

At the heart of the district lies the spacious **Horniman Circle**, conceived in 1860 as the centrepiece of a newly-planned Bombay by the then Municipal Commissioner, Charles Forjett, on the site of Bombay's "Green". Later, the space served as a cotton market and parade ground. Flanking the east side of the circle, the impressive **Town Hall** on Shahid Bhagat Singh Marg was among the few buildings in Mumbai that pleased Aldous Huxley: "(Among) so many architectural cads and pretentious bounders," he wrote in 1948, "it is almost the only gentleman." The Doric edifice, dating from 1833, was originally built to house the vast collection of the **Asiatic Society Library**, still open to the general public (Mon–Sat 10am–7pm). Save for the addition of electricity, little has changed here since the institution was founded. Inside reading rooms, lined with wrought-iron loggias and teak bookcases, scholars pore over mouldering tomes dating from the Raj. Among the ten thousand rare and valuable manuscripts stored here is a fourteenth-century first edition of Dante's *Divine Comedy*, said to be worth around US$3 million, which the Society famously refused to sell to Mussolini. Visitors are welcome but should sign in at the Head Librarian's desk on the ground floor.

Dabawallahs

Mumbai's size and inconvenient shape create all kind of hassles for its working population – not least having to stew for over four hours each day in slow municipal transport. One thing the daily tidal wave of commuters does not have to worry about, however, is where to find an inexpensive and wholesome home-cooked lunch. In a city with a wallah for everything, it will find them. The members of the **Nutan Mumbai Tiffin Box Suppliers Charity Trust (NMTSCT)**, known colloquially, and with no little affection, as "**dabawallahs**", see to that. Every day, around 4500 to 5000 *dabawallahs* deliver freshly cooked meals from 175,000 to 200,000 suburban kitchens to offices in the downtown area. Each lunch is prepared early in the morning by a devoted wife or mother while her husband or son is enduring the crush on the train. She arranges the rice, dhal, *subzi*, curd and *parathas* into cylindrical aluminium trays, stacks them on top of one another and clips them together with a neat little handle.

This **tiffin box**, not unlike a slim paint tin, is the lynchpin of the whole operation. When the runner calls to collect it in the morning, he uses a special colour code on the lid to tell him where the lunch has to go. At the end of his round, he carries all the boxes to the nearest railway station and hands them over to other *dabawallahs* for the trip into town. Between leaving the wife and reaching its final destination, the tiffin box will pass through at least half a dozen different pairs of hands, carried on heads, shoulder-poles, bicycle handlebars and in the brightly decorated handcarts that plough with such insouciance through the midday traffic. Tins are rarely, if ever, lost – a fact recently reinforced by the American business magazine, **Forbes**, which awarded Mumbai's *dabawallahs* a 6-Sigma performance rating, the score reserved for companies that attain a 99.9 percentage of correctness. This means that only one tiffin box in 6 million goes astray, in efficiency terms putting the illiterate *dabawallahs* on a par with bluechip firms such as Motorola.

To catch them in action, head for **CST (VT)** or **Churchgate** stations around late morning, when the tiffin boxes arrive in the city centre. The event is accompanied by a chorus of "*lafka! lafka!*" – "hurry! hurry!" – as the *dabawallahs*, recognizable in their white Nehru caps and baggy pyjama trousers, rush to make their lunch-hour deadlines. Nearly all come from the same small village near Pune and are related to one another. They collect around Rs350–400 from each customer, or Rs5000–6000 per month in total – not a bad income by Indian standards. One of the reasons the system survives in the face of competition from trendy fast-food outlets is that *daba* lunches still work out a good deal cheaper, saving precious rupees for the middle-income workers who use the system.

Business leaders who have taken more than a passing interest in the *dabawallah* phenomenon include Sir Richard Branson: the Virgin tycoon spent a day accompanying a tiffin carrier on his round. If you'd like to do the same, contact the NMTSCT via its website, ⓦwww.mydabbawala.com, and look for the link to their "Day With a Dabbawala" scheme.

Just west of Horniman Circle lies small, simple **St Thomas' Cathedral** (daily 7am–6pm), reckoned to be the oldest British building in Mumbai, blending classical and Gothic styles. After the death of its founding father, Governor Aungier, the project was abandoned; the walls stood 5m high for forty-odd years until enthusiasm was rekindled in the second decade of the eighteenth century. It was finally opened on Christmas Day, 1718, complete with the essential "cannon-ball-proof roof". In those days, the seating was divided into useful sections for those who should know their place, including one for "Inferior Women". The whitewashed and polished brass-and-wood interior looks much the same at it did in the eighteenth century. Lining the walls are memorial tablets to British parishioners, many of whom died young, either from disease or in battle.

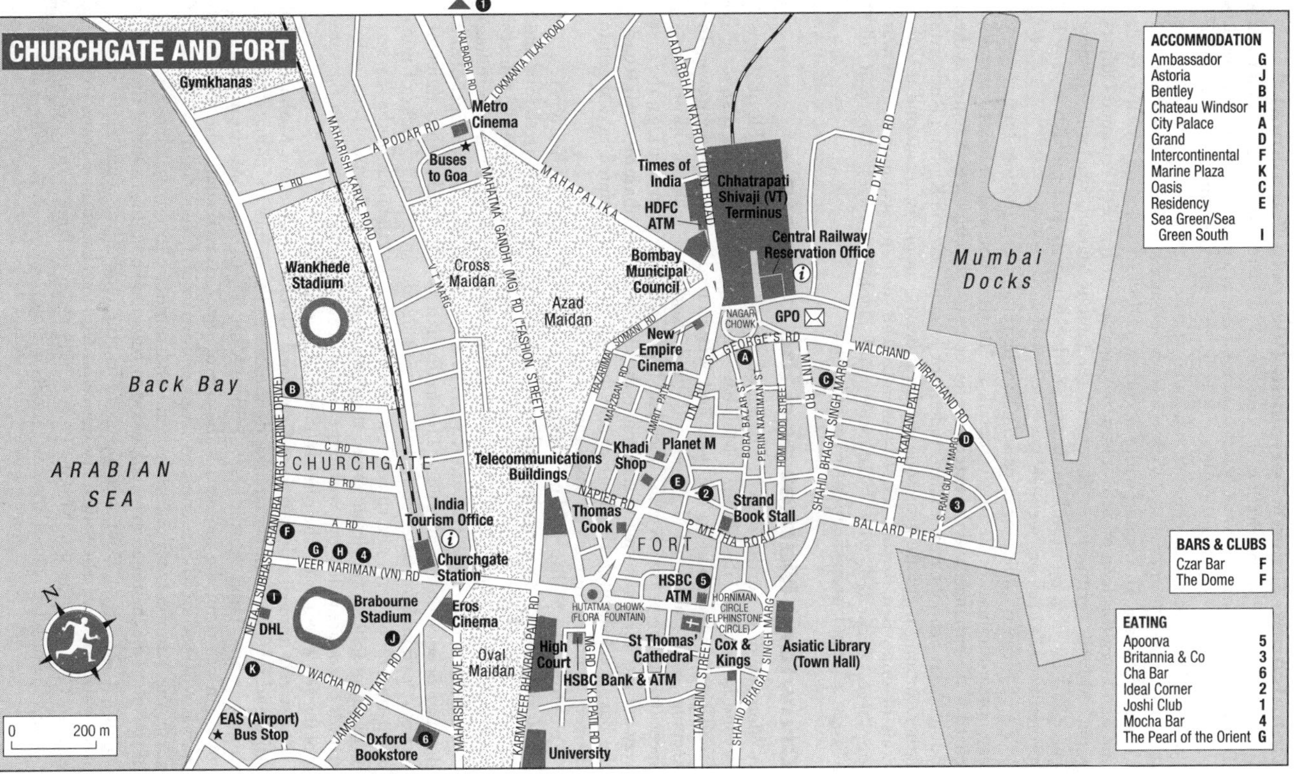
CHURCHGATE AND FORT
ACCOMMODATION
Ambassador G
Astoria J
Bentley B
Chateau Windsor H
City Palace A
Grand D
Intercontinental F
Marine Plaza K
Oasis C
Residency E
Sea Green/Sea Green South I
BARS & CLUBS
Czar Bar F
The Dome F
EATING
Apoorva 5
Britannia & Co 3
Cha Bar 6
Ideal Corner 2
Joshi Club 1
Mocha Bar 4
The Pearl of the Orient G
Gymkhanas
Metro Cinema
Buses to Goa
KALBADEVI RD
LOKMANTA TILAK ROAD
A PODAR RD
F RD
MAHARISHI KARVE ROAD
MAHATMA GANDHI (MG) RD ("FASHION STREET")
MAHAPALIKA
Times of India
HDFC ATM
DADARBHAI NAVROJI (DN) ROAD
Chhatrapati Shivaji (VT) Terminus
Central Railway Reservation Office
P. D'MELLO RD
Mumbai Docks
Wankhede Stadium
Cross Maidan
V T MARG
Azad Maidan
Bombay Municipal Council
NAGAR CHOWK
GPO
New Empire Cinema
SOMANI RD
HAZARIMAL
ST GEORGE'S RD
WALCHAND HIRACHAND RD
MARZBAN RD
AMRIT PATH
DN RD
BORA BAZAR ST
PERIN NARIMAN ST
HOMI MODI STREET
MINT RD
SHAHID BHAGAT SINGH MARG
R KAMANI PATH
S. RAM GULAM MARG
Back Bay
D RD
C RD
B RD
A RD
CHURCHGATE
ARABIAN SEA
Telecommunications Buildings
Khadi Shop
Planet M
NAPIER RD
Thomas Cook
Strand Book Stall
P METHA ROAD
BALLARD PIER
FORT
India Tourism Office
Churchgate Station
VEER NARIMAN (VN) RD
NETAJI SUBHASH CHANDRA MARG (MARINE DRIVE)
HSBC ATM
HUTATMA CHOWK (FLORA FOUNTAIN)
HORNIMAN CIRCLE (ELPHINSTONE CIRCLE)
Brabourne Stadium
Eros Cinema
DHL
Oval Maidan
MAHARSHI KARVE RD
KARMAVEER BHAVRAO PATIL RD
High Court
MG RD
K B PATIL RD
St Thomas' Cathedral
HSBC Bank & ATM
Cox & Kings
TAMARIND STREET
Asiatic Library (Town Hall)
D WACHA RD
JAMSHEDJI TATA RD
EAS (Airport) Bus Stop
Oxford Bookstore
University
0 200 m
N

Chhatrapati Shivaji Terminus (Victoria Terminus)

Inspired by St Pancras Station in London, F.W. Stevens designed **Victoria Terminus**, the most barmy of Mumbai's buildings, as a paean to "progress". Built in 1887 as the largest British edifice in India, it's an extraordinary amalgam of domes, spires, Corinthian columns and minarets that was succinctly defined by the journalist James Cameron as "Victorian-Gothic-Saracenic-Italianate-Oriental-St Pancras-Baroque". In keeping with the current re-Indianization of the city's roads and buildings, this icon of British imperial architecture has been renamed **Chhatrapati Shivaji Terminus**, in honour of the famous Maratha warlord. The new name is a bit of a mouthful, however, and locals mostly still refer to it as **VT** (pronounced "vitee" or "wee-tee").

Few of the two million or so passengers who fill almost a thousand trains every day notice the mass of decorative detail. A "British" lion and Indian tiger stand guard at the entrance, and the exterior is festooned with sculptures executed at the Bombay Art School by the Indian students of John Lockwood Kipling, Rudyard's father. Among them are grotesque mythical beasts, monkeys, plants and medallions of important personages. To minimize the sun's impact, stained glass was employed, decorated with locomotives and elephant images. Above it all, "Progress" stands atop the massive central dome.

Crawford Market and the bazaars

A kilometre or so north of CST (VT) station, lining the anarchic jumble of streets beyond Lokmanya Tilak Road, is Mumbai's bustling **central bazaar district** – a fascinating counterpoint to the wide and Westernized streets of downtown. In keeping with traditional divisions of guild, caste and religion, most streets specialize in one or two types of merchandise. If you lose your bearings, the best way out is to ask someone to wave you in the direction of **Mohammed Ali Road**, the busy road through the heart of the district (now surmounted by a gigantic flyover), from where you can hail a cab.

Crawford (aka Mahatma Phule) **Market**, ten minutes' walk north of CST, is an old British-style covered market dealing in just about every kind of fresh food and domestic animal imaginable. Before venturing inside, stop to admire the **friezes** wrapped around its exterior – a Victorian vision of sturdy-limbed peasants toiling in the fields designed by Rudyard Kipling's father, Lockwood, as principal of the Bombay School of Art in 1865. The **main hall** is still divided into different sections: pyramids of polished fruit and vegetables down one aisle, sacks of nuts or oil-tins full of herbs and spices down another. Around the back of the market, in the atmospheric wholesale wing, the pace of life is more hectic. Here, noisy crowds of coolies mill about with large reed-baskets held high in the air (if they are looking for work) or on their heads (if they've found some).

The streets immediately **north of Crawford Market** and west of **Mohammed Ali Road** form one vast bazaar area, dominated by the domes and minarets of the chintzy white **Jama Masjid**, or "Friday Mosque" (*c.*1800). **Memon Street**, cutting north from the mosque, is the site of the **Zaveri Bazaar**, the jewellery market where Mumbaikars come to shop for dowries and wedding attire. Further north, the **Mumba Devi temple**'s cream-and-turquoise tower rises above a maze of twisting lanes hemmed in by tall, wooden-balconied buildings. One of the most important centres of Devi worship in India, the temple was built early in the nineteenth century, when the deity was relocated from her former home to make way for CST (VT) station. Mumba Devi's other claim to fame is that her name is perhaps the original root of the city's modern name.

Marine Drive and Chowpatty Beach

Netaji Subhash Chandra Marg, better known as **Marine Drive**, is Mumbai's seaside prom, an eight-lane highway with a wide pavement built in the 1920s on reclaimed land. The whole three-kilometre stretch – still often referred to by Mumbaikars as the "Queen's Necklace" after the row of lights which illuminates its spectacular curve at night – is a favourite place for a stroll; the promenade next to the sea has uninterrupted views virtually the whole way along, while the peeling, mildewed Art-Deco apartment blocks on the land side remain some of the most desirable addresses in the city.

Chowpatty Beach, at the top of Marine Drive, is a Mumbai institution. On evenings and weekends, Mumbaikars gather here in large numbers – not to swim (the sea is foul) but to wander, sit on the sand, munch *kulif* and *bhelpuri*, get their ears cleaned and gaze across the bay while the kids ride a pony or a rusty Ferris wheel. Once a year in September the **Ganesh Chathurthi** festival draws gigantic crowds as idols, both huge and small, of the elephant-headed god Ganesh are immersed in the sea.

A ten-minute walk north from the middle of Chowpatty Beach along Pandita Ramabai Marg, **Mani Bhavan**, at 19 Laburnum Rd (daily 9.30am–6pm; free, with optional donation), was Gandhi's Bombay base between 1917 and 1934. Set in a leafy upper-middle-class road, the house has now been converted into a permanent memorial to the Mahatma. The lovingly maintained polished-wood interior is crammed with historic photos and artefacts – the most disarming of which is a friendly letter to Hitler suggesting world peace. Laburnum Road is a few streets along from the Bharatiya Vidya Bhavan music venue on KM Munshi Marg – if coming by taxi ask for the nearby Gamdevi Police Station.

Malabar Hill

Its shirt-tails swathed in greenery and brow bristling with gigantic skyscrapers, the promontory enfolding Chowpatty Beach at the north end of Back Bay has been south Mumbai's most desirable neighbourhood almost since the city was founded. The British were quick to see the potential of its salubrious breezes and sweeping sea views, constructing bungalows at the tip of what was then a separate island – the grandest of them the Government House, originally erected in the 1820s and now the seat of the serving Governor of Maharashtra, **Raj Bhavan**.

Although none of Malabar's landmarks can be classed as unmissable, its Hindu shrines and surviving colonial-era residences form an interesting counterpoint to the modernity towering on all sides. Bal Gangadhar Kher Marg (formerly Ridge Road) is the district's main artery. You can follow it from Mumbai's principal

The Towers of Silence

High on Malabar Hill, screened from prying eyes by a high wall and dense curtain of vegetation (and strictly closed to visitors), stand the seven **Towers of Silence**, where the city's dwindling Zoroastrian community (better known as Parsis) dispose of their dead. Pollution of the four sacred elements (air, water, earth and, holiest of all, fire) contradicts the most fundamental precepts of the 2500-year-old Parsi faith, first imported to India when Zoroastrians fled from Sassanid Persia to escape Arab persecution in the seventh century. So instead of being buried or cremated, the bodies are laid out on top of open-topped, cylindrical towers, called *dokhmas*, for their bones to be cleaned by **vultures** and the weather. The remains are then placed in an ossuary at the centre of the tower.

Jain Temple (see map, p.599), with its mirror-encrusted interior dedicated to Adinath, all the way to the tip of the headland, where the famous **Walkeshwar Temple** stands as the city's oldest Hindu shrine surviving *in situ*. According to the Ramayana, Rama fashioned a lingam out of sand to worship Shiva here, which over the centuries became one of the Konkan's most important pilgrimage centres. Today's temple, erected in 1715 after the original had been destroyed by the Portuguese, is of less note than the **Banganga Tank** below it – a rectangular lake lined by stone *ghats* and numerous crumbling shrines.

Central Mumbai: Mahalakshmi to Byculla

The centre of Mumbai, beyond Malabar Hill, is mostly made up of working-class neighbourhoods: a huge mosaic of dilapidated tenements, markets and industrial eyesores left over from the Victorian cotton boom. For relief from the urban cauldron, residents travel west to the seashore to worship at the **Mahalakshmi Temple** (if they're Hindus) or the island **tomb of Haji Ali** (if they're Muslims). Both make great excursions from south Mumbai, and can be combined with a foray across town to the recently revamped **Dr Bhau Dadji Lad Museum** in Byculla, calling en route at the **Mahalakshmi dhobi ghats** – one of the city's more offbeat sights.

Buses #83, #124 or #132 will take you from Colaba to Haji Ali, within a stone's throw of the Mahalakshmi Temple. Buses #124 and #153 continued from here to the *dhobi ghat*s, or alternatively catch the train to nearby Mahalakshmi Station direct from south Mumbai.

Mahalakshmi Temple and Haji Ali's Tomb

Mahalakshmi Temple, just off Bhulabhai Desai Road, is approached via an alley lined with stalls selling spectacular floral offerings and devotional pictures. Gifts for Mumbai's favourite *devi*, **Lakshmi**, goddess of beauty and prosperity – the city's most sought-after attributes – pile so high that the temple *pujari*s run a money-spinning sideline reselling them. While you're here, find out what your future holds by joining the huddle of devotees pressing rupees onto the rear wall of the shrine room. If your coin sticks, you'll be rich.

Occupying a small islet in the bay just north of the Mahalakshmi is the mausoleum of the Muslim saint, Afghan mystic **Haji Ali Bukhari**. The tomb is connected to the mainland by a narrow concrete **causeway**, only passable at low tide. When not immersed in water, its entire length is lined with beggars supplicating passers-by and chanting verses from the Koran. The site is a great place to head for on Thursday and Friday evenings, when large crowds gather around the headland to watch the sunset and listen to live **qawwali** music. Non-Muslims are welcome, but you'll need to keep well covered up (a headscarf should be worn by women). The entire complex was undergoing major **renovations** at the time of writing, but should have finished by the time you read this.

The traditional way to round off a trip to the mausoleum is to take a glass or two of fresh fruit juice at the legendary **Haji Ali Juice Centre**, just to the right of the entrance to the causeway. Customers either cram into the tiny dining hall or else order from their cars.

Mahalakshmi dhobi ghats

On the face of it, the idea of going out of your way to ogle Mumbai's dirty washing sounds like a very perverse pastime. If you're passing, however, the **municipal dhobi ghats**, near Mahalakshmi suburban railway station, are a sufficiently memorable spectacle to break a trip across town to see. Washing from all

Dharavi: the £700 million slum

Flying into Mumbai airport, your plane's undercarriage will almost skim the corrugated-iron rooftops of the vast shantytown spread across the middle of one of **India's largest slums**. Sprawling over 550 acres, **Dharavi**'s maze of dilapidated shacks and narrow, stinking alleyways is home to more than a million people. An average of 15,000 of them share a single toilet. Infectious diseases such as dysentery, malaria and hepatitis are rife; and there aren't any hospitals.

Despite the poverty, Dharavi has been described by the UK's *Observer* newspaper as "one of the most inspiring economic models in Asia": hidden amid the warren of ramshackle huts and squalid open sewers are an estimated fifteen thousand single-room factories, employing around a quarter of a million people and turning over a staggering £700 million (US$1 billion) annually. The majority of small businesses in Dharavi are based on **waste recycling** of one kind or another. Slum residents young and old scavenge materials from across the city and haul them back in huge bundles to be reprocessed. Aluminium cans are smelted down, soap scraps salvaged from schools and hotels are reduced in huge vats, leather reworked, disused oil drums restored and discarded plastic reshaped and remoulded. An estimated ten thousand workers are employed in the plastics sector alone. Ranging from Rs3000–15,000 per month, wages are well above the national average, and though Dharavi may not have any health centres, it does hold a couple of banks, and even ATMs.

As India's largest and most iconic slum, Dharavi has also found an unlikely niche in the history of Indian and international **cinema**. The district provided many of the settings for Mira Nair's seminal portrait of the city, *Salaam Bombay!*, and has also featured in numerous other Bollywood and Tamil flicks from the 1970s onwards. Dharavi's defining moment of celluloid fame, however, came in 2009 with Danny Boyle's multiple Oscar-winning **Slumdog Millionaire**. The slum provided many of the film's locations, as well as several of its leading child actors – although controversy subsequently dogged their involvement in the project, with one British tabloid making (unsubstantiated) claims that nine-year-old *Slumdog* actress Rubina Ali had been offered for sale by her father to an undercover reporter for £200,000 following the film's global success.

Despite its burgeoning international fame, however, Dharavi's future remains uncertain. The entire district is living in the shadow of a proposed $40billion **redevelopment project** which aims to bulldoze the entire slum. In return for agreeing to eviction, Dharavi's residents will be entitled to 225 square feet of apartment space per family in new multi-storey tower blocks. Schools, roads, hospitals and other amenities have also been promised. Opposition to the scheme among Dharavites has been all but unanimous, however, with slum dwellers insisting any future development should focus not on erecting a swanky new suburb but on improving existing conditions. Despite these protests, and extended bureaucratic delays, a new masterplan for the project was approved in early 2010 amidst rumours that private investors had already begun buying up thousands of shanty properties in the expectation of imminent redevelopment. Exactly when and how this will happen, however, remains unclear.

You can visit Dharavi yourself by joining one of the **"Slum Tours"** run by Reality Tours and Travels out of Colaba. Tickets for these engaging guided trips cost Rs400 (including transport), or you can also opt for a longer and more comfortable version with an a/c car for Rs800. For more details, contact Krishna Pujari on ⓣ022/2283 3872, or ⓣ9820 822253, check out ⓦwww.realitytoursandtravel.com, or just drop in to their booking office (Mon–Fri 10.15am–8.35pm, Sat 10.15am–3.45pm) off Colaba Causeway (SBS Marg), in Akber House on Nawroji Fardonji Marg, opposite the *Laxmi Vilas Hotel* (see map, p.605 – enter Akber House via the passageway through S. S. S. Corner next to the *New Apollo Restaurant*; the office is on the first floor, reached via the Unique Business Service Centre).

Colaba and Kala Ghoda

Except where noted, all the following are shown on the map on p.605.

All Stir Fry *Gordon House Hotel.* Cool modern restaurant specializing in build-your-own wok meals using a selection of fresh veg, meat, fish, noodles and sauces, flash-cooked in front of you. The satay and dim sum are particularly good. Rs420 for unlimited servings.

Bademiya Behind the *Taj Mahal Palace & Tower* on Tulloch Rd. Legendary Colaba kebab-wallah serving delicious flame-grilled chicken, mutton and fish steaks, as well as veg alternatives, wrapped in paper-thin, piping hot rotis, from benches on the sidewalk. Rich families from uptown drive here on weekends, eating on their car bonnets, but there are also little tables and chairs if you don't fancy a take-away.

Busaba 4 Mandlik Marg ⓣ022/2204 3779. Sophisticated bar-restaurant specializing in Far-Eastern cuisine – Thai, Korean, Burmese, Vietnamese and Tibetan staples, with exotic salads (green mango and glass noodle). One of *the* places to be seen (if you can't quite afford to eat at *Indigo* next door). Mains Rs350–550.

Café Samovar Jehangir Art Gallery, MG Rd ⓣ022/2284 8000. Very pleasant, peaceful semi-alfresco café opening onto the museum gardens, with plenty of à la carte choices (prawn curry, roti kebabs and fresh salads and dhansak). They also serve delicious chilled guava juice and beer. Daily except Sun 11am–7.30pm.

Churchill 103 Colaba Causeway. Tiny Parsi diner, with a bewildering choice of dishes, including salads, pastas and burgers, mostly meat-based and served in mild sauces alongside a blob of mash and boiled veg – ideal if you've had your fill of spicy food. No alcohol. Main Rs210–275.

Henry Tham Dhanraj Mahal, CST Road, Apollo Bunder, Colaba ⓣ022/2202 3186, ⓦwww.henrytham.com. Within spitting distance of the Gateway of India, this swanky restaurant serves up excellent contemporary-style Chinese food, including good dim sum and lunchtime set menus.

Indigo 4 Mandlik Marg ⓣ022/6636 8999, ⓦwww.foodindigo.com. One of the city's most fashionable restaurants, for once deserving the hype, and specializing in superb international and modern European cooking with an Indian twist (Kerala oysters with saffron ravioli, for example). Mains from around RS600. Reservations essential.

Kailash Parbat ("KP's") 1 Pasta Lane, near the Strand cinema. Uninspiring on the outside, but the breakfast *aloo parathas*, pure veg nibbles, hot snacks and sweets (across the road) are worth the walk. A Colaba institution – try their famous *makai-ka* (corn) rotis.

Kamat Colaba Causeway. Friendly little eatery serving unquestionably the best south Indian breakfasts in the area, as well as the usual range of southern snacks (*iddli, vada, sambar*), delicious spring dosas and (limited) thalis for Rs60–150. The best option in the area for budget travellers with big appetites.

Khyber Opposite Jehangir Art Gallery ⓣ022/2267 3227. Opulent Arabian Nights interior and uncompromisingly rich "Northwest Frontier" cuisine. The chicken tikka is legendary, and their tandoori dishes and kebab platter are superb too. Mains Rs240–425.

Konkan Café *Taj President Hotel*, Cuffe Parade (see map, p.598) ⓣ022/6665 0808. Just the place to push the boat out: a sophisticated five-star hotel restaurant serving fine regional cuisine from coastal Maharashtra, Goa, Karnataka and Kerala. You can choose from their thali platters (Rs845–1045) or go à la carte: butter-pepper-garlic crab is to die for. Quite simply some of the most mouthwatering South Indian food you'll ever eat.

Leopold's Colaba Causeway. A Mumbai institution for decades, *Leopold's* is the number-one hangout for India-weary Western travellers, who continue to cram onto its small tables for bland, overpriced Indian, Continental and Chinese tourist fare – despite (or perhaps because of) the fact that the café was one of the leading targets of the 2008 terror attacks (staff will show you the bullet holes in the walls, now discreetly hidden behind pictures). Expect to queue. Mains Rs150–300; beer Rs200.

Olympia Coffee House Colaba Causeway. *Fin-de-siècle* Irani café with marble tabletops, wooden wall panels, fancy mirrors and a mezzanine floor for women. Waiters in Peshwari caps and *salwar kameezes* serve melt-in-the-mouth kebabs and delicious curd-based dips. It gets packed out at breakfast time for cholesterol-packed mutton masala fry, which regulars wash down with bright orange chai. A quintessential (and inexpensive) Bombay experience. Mains Rs60–100.

The Sea Lounge *Taj Mahal Palace & Tower.* Gorgeously atmospheric 1930s-style lounge café on the first floor of the *Taj,* with fine Gateway and harbour views – good for coffee and cake (from around Rs600) or a sumptuous breakfast (Rs1000). Daily 7am–midnight.

Trishna 7 Sai Baba Marg (Ropewalk Lane), Kala Ghoda ⓣ022/2261 4991. Visiting dignitaries and local celebs, from the President of Greece to

Bollywood stars, have eaten in this dimly lit Mangalorean. There are wonderful fish dishes in every sauce going, including the signature butter-pepper-garlic crab (around Rs700–800) and superb pomfret stuffed with green masala (Rs490), plus cheaper north Indian standards (from Rs200). Very small, so book in advance.

Churchgate and Fort

All the following are shown on the map on p.609.

Apoorva SA Brelvi Rd ⓣ022/2287 0335. Popular Mangalorean, hidden up a side street off Horniman Circle (look for the tree trunk wrapped with fairy lights). The cooking's completely authentic and the seafood – simmered in spicy coconut-based gravies – comes fresh off the boat each day. Try their definitive Bombay duck, *surmai* (kingfish) in coconut gravy or sublime prawn *gassi*, served with perfect *sanna* and *appams*. Mains Rs100–475. Licensed.

Britannia & Co Shri SR Marg, Ballard Estate. Quirky little Parsi restaurant, famous as much for its quaint period atmosphere as its wholesome Irani food. Most people come for the sublime "berry pulao" (chicken, mutton or vegetable), made with deliciously tart dried berries imported from Tehran (Rs200, but portions are gigantic). For afters, there's the house "caramel custard". One of the city's unmissable eating experiences. Open 11.30am–3.30pm.

Cha Bar Oxford Bookstore, 3 Dinsha Wacha Rd, Churchgate. Chic a/c café at the back of downtown's top bookshop serving an exhaustive range of single-estate speciality teas, from Kashmiri *kawa* to Ladhaki butter tea, plus coffees, sandwiches, wraps and cakes.

Ideal Corner 12 F/G Hornby View, Gunbow St ⓣ022/2262 1930. Another Parsi café with a cult following, dishing up delicious home-made specialities like *kchchidi* prawn, lamb dhansak, chicken *farcha* and legendary *lagan* custard. Most mains Rs50–75. Mon–Sat 9am–4.30pm.

Mocha Bar VN Rd. Chilled terrace café where swarms of south Mumbai bratpackers pose over speciality coffees, tapas, panini, wraps and crepes (or puff on hookah pipes in the smoking area at the back). Very much the zeitgeist.

The Pearl of the Orient *Ambassador Hotel*, Veer Nariman Rd ⓣ022/229 1131. Revolving Oriental restaurant in this faded four-star hotel. The cooking's nothing special (and expensive at around Rs1000 for three courses), but the views over the city are extraordinary.

Crawford Market and the central bazaars

The following three places are shown on the map on p.609.

Badshah Juice and Snack Bar Opposite Crawford Market, Lokmanya Tilak Rd. Mumbai's most acclaimed *falooda* joint also serves delicious kulfi, ice creams and dozens of freshly squeezed fruit juices. The ideal place to round off a trip to the market, though expect to have to queue for a table.

Joshi Club 31-A Narottamwadi, Kalbadevi Rd ⓣ022/2205 8089. Also known as *The Friends Union Joshi Club*, this eccentric thali canteen serves what many aficionados regard as the most genuine and tasty Gujarati–Marwari meals in the city, on unpromising Formica tables against a backdrop of grubby walls. Rs95 buys you unlimited portions of four vegetable dishes, dhal and up to four different kinds of bread, with all the trimmings (and banana custard). Finding it requires some effort: walk or catch a cab to the bottom of Kalbadevi Rd (opposite the Metro cinema; see map, p.609); head north across Vardhaman Chowk, and continue up Kalbadevi Rd for 5min until you see a signboard on your right for "Bhojanalaya", below a first-floor window.

Rajdhani Sheikh Memon St. Outstanding, eat-till-you-burst Gujarati thalis. Very cramped and more expensive than usual (Rs250, or Rs299 for the "Special" Sun lunch), but they don't stint on quality. Closed Sun evenings. It's on the road leading to the Jama Masjid (approaching from Crawford Market cross the road by the entrance and turn right past the Lokmanya Tilak Marg Police Booth).

Bars and nightlife

Mumbaikars have an unusually easy-going attitude to alcohol; popping into a **bar** for a beer is very much accepted (for men at least), even at lunchtime. Colaba Causeway is the focus of the travellers' social scene but if you want to sample the pulse of the city's nightlife, venture up to Bandra and Juhu.

Despite a 1.30am curfew introduced in 2005 (only clubs within hotels are allowed to carry on later), Mumbai's **nightclub** scene remains the most full-on in India. Tiny, skin-tight outfits that show off razor-sharp abs and pumped-up pecs are very much the order of the day, especially in venues frequented by Bollywood's movers and shakers – and the pretty young things desperate to break into the industry. Dominated by *filmi* pop mixes, the music is far from cutting edge by the standards of London or New York, but no one seems to mind. Dancefloors get as rammed as a suburban commuter train and the cover charges are astronomical. Door policies and dress codes tend to be strict ("no ballcaps, no shorts, no sandals"), and, in theory, most clubs have a "couples-only" policy – they charge per couple on the door (with a portion of the entrance cost redeemable at the bar). In practice, if you're in a mixed group or don't appear sleazy you shouldn't have any problems. At the five-star hotels, entry can be restricted to hotel guests and members.

Bars

Alps Beer Bar Nawroji Marg, Colaba, behind *Taj Mahal Palace & Tower* (see map, p.605). Slightly down-at-heel but quiet alternative to the queues and crowds of nearby *Leopold's* and *Café Mondegar*, with the cheapest beer in Colaba plus a bit of food including curries, steaks and sizzlers.

Aurus Nichani House, Juhu Tara Rd, Juhu ⓣ022/6710 6666, ⓦwww.dishhospitality.com. Sexy beachside hang-out, boasting a funky bar-restaurant inside and a relaxing terrace overlooking Juhu Beach, backed up with good international fusion cuisine and a wide-ranging wine and cocktail list. Boasts its fair share of Bombabes and celebs, though the entry policy is usually less snooty than other places hereabouts.

Busaba 4 Mandlik Marg, Colaba (see map, p.605). Downstairs from the swanky *Busaba* restaurant (see p.616), this chic, dimly lit bar serves up a good selection of Australian, South African and New World wines, plus single malts, cool cocktails and a decent range of international beers.

Café Mondegar Colaba Causeway (see map, p.605). Draught and bottled beer (imported and Indian) and deliciously fruity cocktails are served in this small café-bar. The atmosphere is very relaxed, the music tends towards cheesy rock classics and the clientele is a mix of Westerners and local students; murals by a famous Goan cartoonist give the place a cheerful ambience. There's also a big menu of average Indian, Chinese and Continental food. Expect to queue to get in.

Czar Bar *Hotel InterContinental*, 135 Marine Drive (see map, p.609). Trendy vodka bar with chic, minimalist decor, clever lighting and over forty brands on offer (from Rs400), plus a full range of other drinks and cocktails. Music is lounge until around 11pm, then picks up. Quiet on weekday

Performing arts in Mumbai

Mumbai is a major centre for traditional **performing arts**, attracting the finest **Indian classical musicians** and **dancers** from all over the country. Frequent concerts and recitals are staged at venues such as Bharatiya Vidya Bhavan, KM Munshi Marg (ⓣ022/2363 0224), the headquarters of the international cultural (Hindu) organization, and the National Centre for the Performing Arts, Nariman Point (NCPA; ⓦwww.ncpamumbai.com).

For more contemporary **live music**, the leading venue is Blue Frog, in North Mumbai at D/2 Mathuradas Mills Compound, NM Joshi Marg, Lower Parel (ⓣ022/4033 2300, ⓦwww.bluefrog.co.in), opened in late 2007 and recently named by the UK's *Independent* newspaper as one of the world's top live music venues. Performances are staged inside a huge old warehouse in Mumbai's former mill district, showcasing leading Indian and international live music acts and DJs – anything from rock to hip-hop.

For **theatre**, head out to the Prithvi Theatre (ⓣ022/2614 9546, ⓦwww.prithvitheatre.org) on Juhu Church Road, a small but lively venue focusing mainly on Hindi-language theatre, along with some English productions.

nights, but popular on weekends. Daily 5.30pm–1.30am.

The Dome *Hotel InterContinental*, 135 Marine Drive (see map, p.609). This cool rooftop bar is easily south Mumbai's most alluring spot for a sundowner. Plush white sofas and candle-lit tables surround the eponymous domed rotunda and a very sexy raised pool, while the views over Back Bay make even the sky-high drink prices feel worth it. Daily 5.30pm–1.30am.

Henry Tham Dhanraj Mahal, CST Road, Apollo Bunder, Colaba (see map, p.605). Downstairs from the excellent Chinese restaurant (see p.616), this small but kicking bar is currently the preferred haunt of south Mumbai's beautiful people, boasting excellent cocktails and one of the city's best House soundtracks.

Indigo 4 Mandlik Rd, Colaba (see map, p.605). Attached to the fashionable *Indigo* restaurant (see p.616), this is the coolest hang-out in Colaba, with funky, stripped-bare décor, frequented by young media types and would-be wine buffs.

Olive 4 Union Park Rd, Pali Hill (between Juhu and Bandra). Nowhere pulls in Bollywood's A-list like *Olive*. If you want to rub shoulders with Hrithik, Abhishek and Aishwarya, Preity and Shilpa, this is your best bet, though dress to kill – and come armed with a flexible wallet. Although basically just a pretext to crowd-watch, the food is fine gourmet Mediterranean.

Vie Lounge 102 Juhu Tara Rd, Juhu ⓣ022/2660 3003, ⓦwww.vie.co.in. Chilled-out Ibiza-style beach bar overlooking Juhu Beach, with resident and visiting DJs and a brilliant cocktail list, plus a decent selection of seafood and Cajun cuisine.

Wink *Taj President*, 90 Cuffe Parade ⓣ022/6665 0808, ⓦwww.tajhotels.com (see map, p.598). Classy Asian-style lounge bar, with one of the city's best drinks lists, including a superb selection of speciality cocktails. A good place for a quiet drink early on, though the DJ gradually ramps up the volume as the evening progresses, with full-on club beats by the end of the night.

Zenzi 183 Waterfield Rd, Bandra West ⓣ022/5643 0670, ⓦwww.zenzi-india.com. Chic Dutch-owned bar-restaurant, decorated in contemporary Asian Balinese-cum-Thai style, with a choice of restaurant (dishing up classy pan-Asian cuisine), bar, posy DJ lounge and a breezy open-air terrace upstairs. Usually quiet before 11pm, but often gets rammed with glamorous locals later on.

Nightclubs

Enigma *JW Marriott Hotel*, Juhu Tara Rd. This is what Hindi film stars and hip young Indian millionaires do for kicks: the sexiest outfits, latest Bolly-bhangra mixes, most gorgeous decor and stiffest entrance cost (from Rs800–Rs2500 per couple depending on the night).

Polly Esther's *Gordon House Hotel*, Battery St, Colaba (see map, p.605). Retro club with brightly coloured Seventies/Eighties decor and waiters wearing ludicrous fluoro-coloured Afro wigs. Live music, hiphop, Bollywood and retro on different night. Rs900–1200 per couple. Open Wed–Sun.

Squeeze 5th Rd, Khar. Bandra's funkiest nightspot is aptly named: it's packed seven nights a week, and bursting at the seams on weekends, when the music's less dominated by Hindi pop than elsewhere. Admission around Rs1500 per couple.

Voodoo Lounge Arthur Bunder Rd, Colaba (see map, p.605). This cavernous, but delightfully louche, little dive off Colaba Causeway plays host to Mumbai's one and only gay club, from 9pm on Sat (it's dead and depressing the rest of the week). The atmosphere's restrained by Western standards, but welcoming and sociable for both gay and straight men and women, though most of the punters do come to cruise. Admission Rs300/head.

Shopping

Mumbai is a great place to shop, whether for last-minute souvenirs or essentials for the long journeys ahead. Locally produced **textiles** and export-surplus clothing are among the best buys, as are **handicrafts** from far-flung corners of the country. With the exception of the swish arcades in the five-star hotels, prices compare surprisingly well with other Indian cities. In the larger shops, rates are fixed and **credit cards** are often accepted; elsewhere, particularly dealing with street vendors, it pays to haggle. Uptown, the **central bazaars** – see p.610 – are better for spectating than serious shopping. The **Zaveri** (goldsmiths') **Bazaar** opposite Crawford Market is the place to head for new gold and silver **jewellery**. **Tea** lovers

Bollywood

The home of the Hindi blockbuster, the "all-India film", is Mumbai, famously known as **Bollywood**. Visitors to the city should have ample opportunity to sample the delights of a Hindi movie, traditional or otherwise. To make an educated choice, buy *Time Out Mumbai* magazine, which contains extensive **listings** and reviews. Alternatively, look for the biggest, brightest hoarding, and join the queue. Seats in a comfortable air-conditioned cinema cost Rs120–200, or less if you sit in the stalls (not advisable for women).

Of the two hundred or so **cinemas**, only a dozen or so regularly screen **English-language** films. The most central and convenient are the gloriously Art-Deco halls dating from the twilight of the Raj: the Regal in Colaba; the Eros opposite Churchgate station, and the Metro at Dhobi Talao junction – the latter was recently converted into a state-of-the-art multiplex. Down on Nariman Point, near Express Towers, the Inox (ⓦwww.inoxmovies.com) is another big multi-screen venue, built only a few years ago in retro Mumbai-Art-Deco style.

For more on Bollywood, see the "*Bollywood and beyond*" colour section.

should head to the Central Cottage Industries Emporium (see opposite), which sells a decent range of Assam, Nilgiri and (especially) Darjeeling black and green teas.

Antiques

The **Chor Bazaar** area, and Mutton Street in particular, is the centre of Mumbai's **antiques trade**. Another good, if much more expensive, place is **Phillip's** famous antique shop, opposite the Regal cinema in Colaba. Brass, bronze and wood Hindu sculpture, silver jewellery, old prints and aquatints form the mainstay of its collection. In the basement of the **Jehangir Art Gallery**, the upmarket **Natesan's Antiqarts** offers a tempting selection of antique (and reproduction) sculpture, furniture, paintings and bronzes.

Clothes

Mumbai produces the bulk of India's **clothes**, mostly the lightweight, light-coloured "shirtings and suitings" favoured by droves of uniformly attired office-wallahs. For cheap Western clothing, you can't beat "**Fashion Street**", a long row of stalls strung out along MG Road between Cross and Azad Maidans west of CST, specializing in reject and export-surplus goods ditched by big manufacturers, and selling off T-shirts, jeans, summer dresses and sweatshirts. Better-quality cotton clothes (often stylish designer-label rip-offs) are available in shops along **Colaba Causeway** and **Mandlik Marg** (behind the *Taj Mahal Palace & Tower*). It's also worth checking out the local branch of the nationwide Fabindia chain on MG Road in Kala Ghoda, which has an excellent and very affordable selection of stylish modern Indian-style shirts, *kurta*s, *shalwar kameeze*s and so on.

If you're looking for **traditional Indian clothes**, look no further than the Khadi shop (signed "Mumbai Khadi Gramodyog Sangh") at 286 Dr DN Marg, near the Thomas Cook office. As Whiteaway & Laidlaw, this rambling Victorian department store used to kit out all the newly arrived *burra-sahib*s with pith helmets, khaki shorts and quinine tablets. These days, its old wooden counters and shirt and sock drawers stock dozens of different hand-spun cottons and silks, sold by the metre or made up as vests, *kurta*s or block-printed *salwar kameeze*s. Other items include the ubiquitous white Nehru caps, *dhoti*s, Madras-check *lunghi*s and fine brocaded silk saris.

Handicrafts

Regionally produced **handicrafts** are marketed in assorted state-run emporia at the World Trade Centre, down on Cuffe Parade, and along Sir PM Road, Fort. The quality is consistently high – as are the prices, if you miss out on the periodic holiday discounts. The same goes for the **Central Cottage Industries Emporium**, 34 Shivaji Marg, near the Gateway of India in Colaba, whose size, central location and big range of inlaid furniture, wood- and metalwork, miniature paintings, jewellery, toys, clothing and textiles make it the single best all-round place to hunt for souvenirs. **Mereweather Road** (now officially B Behram Marg), directly behind the *Taj Mahal Palace & Tower*, is awash with Kashmiri handicraft stores stocking overpriced papier-mâché pots and bowls, silver jewellery, woollen shawls and rugs. Avoid them if you find it hard to shrug off aggressive sales pitches.

Perfume is essentially a Muslim preserve in Mumbai. Down at the south end of Colaba Causeway, around Arthur Bunder Road, shops with mirrored walls and shelves are stacked with cut-glass carafes full of syrupy, fragrant essential oils. **Incense** is hawked in sticks, cones and slabs of sticky *dhoop* on the pavement nearby (check that the boxes haven't already been opened and their contents sold off piecemeal). For bulk buying, the hand-rolled, cottage-made bundles of incense sold downstairs in the Khadi shop on Dr DN Marg (see opposite) are a better deal; it also has a handicraft department upstairs where you can pick up block-printed bedspreads, wooden toys, sandalwood statues and inlaid furniture.

Bookshops

Mumbai has a good range of English-language **bookshops** and bookstalls.

Crossword Bookstore Mohammed Bhai Mansion, Huges Rd, Kemp's Corner, a 10min walk north of Chowpatty Beach ⓣ022/2384 2001. Mumbai's largest retailer, in smart new a/c premises, complete with its own coffee bar.

Nalanda Ground floor, *Taj Mahal Palace & Tower*. An exhaustive range of coffee-table tomes and paperback literature, though at top prices.

Oxford Bookstore Apeejay House, 3 Dinsha Vacha Rd, Churchgate. Not quite as large as Crossword, but almost, and much more easily accessible if you're staying downtown or in Colaba. It also has a very cool a/c café, the *Cha Bar* (see p.617).

Search Word Shahid Bhagat Singh Marg (Colaba Causeway). The best bookshop in Colaba, with shelves full of guides and a great range of Indian fiction – at discounts only rivalled by the Strand Book Stall in Fort.

Strand Book Stall Next door to the Canara Bank, off PM Rd, Fort. The best-value bookshop in the city centre, with a big selection of discounted Penguins and Indian literature.

Music

The most famous of Mumbai's many **musical instrument shops** are near the Moti cinema along Sadar V Patel Road, in the central bazaar district. Haribhai Vishwanath, Ram Singh and RS Mayeka are all government-approved retailers, stocking sitars, *sarods*, tablas and flutes. For guaranteed top quality, however, it's advisable to make the trek north to Bhargava's Musik, at 4/5 Imperial Plaza, 30th Rd in Bandra, which numbers among its clients some of India's top classical performers.

For **cassettes and CDs** a good first stop is Rhythm House, on Subhash Chowk opposite the Jehangir Art Gallery. This is a veritable Aladdin's cave of classical, devotional and popular music from all over India, with a reasonable selection of Western rock, pop and jazz, as well as DVDs of classic and contemporary Hindi movies. A ten-minute walk further north along Dr DN Road in Fort, Planet M also has a good stock of music CDs and DVDs.

Sports

In common with most Indians, Mumbaikars are crazy about **cricket**. Few other spectactor sports get much of a look-in, although the **horse racing** at Mahalakshmi draws large crowds on Derby days. Previews of all forthcoming events are posted on the back pages of the *Times of India*, and in *Time Out Mumbai*.

Cricket

Cricket provides almost as much of a distraction as movies in the Maharashtrian capital, and you'll see games in progress everywhere, from impromptu sunset knockabouts on Chowpatty Beach to more formal club matches in full whites at the gymkhanas lined up along Marine Drive. In south Mumbai, **Oval Maidan** is the place to watch local talent in action, set against a wonderfully apt backdrop of imperial-era buildings. Something of a pecking order applies here: the further from the path cutting across the centre of the park you go, the better the wickets and the classier the games become.

Pitches like these are where Mumbai's favourite son, **Sachin Tendulkar**, cut his cricketing teeth. The world's most prolific batsman in both test and one-day cricket still lives in the city and plays regularly for its league-winning club side at the **Brabourne Stadium**, off Marine Drive. A kilometre or so further north, 45,000-capacity **Wankhede Stadium** is where major test matches are hosted, amid an atmosphere as intense, raucous and intimidating for visiting teams as any in India.

The Indian cricket season runs from October through February. Tickets for big games are almost as hard to come by as seats on commuter trains, but foreign visitors can sometimes gain preferential access to quotas through the Mumbai Cricket Association's offices on the first floor of Wankhede.

Horse racing and horseriding

The **Mahalakshmi Racecourse**, near the Mahalakshmi Temple just north of Malabar Hill, is the home of the **Royal Western India Turf Club** – a throwback

Laughter yoga

On the principle that laughter is the best medicine, Mumbai doctor Madan Kataria and his wife Madhuri – aka "the Giggling Gurus" – have created a new kind of therapy: *hasya* (laughter) yoga. There are now over three hundred **Laughter Clubs** in India and many more worldwide; around 50,000 people join the Laughter Day celebrations in Mumbai on the first Sunday of May each year, with tens of thousands more participating worldwide.

Fifteen-minute sessions start with adherents doing yogic breathing whilst chanting "Ho ho ha ha", which develops into spontaneous "hearty laughter" (raising both hands in the air with the head tilting backwards), "milkshake laughter" (everyone laughs while making a gesture as if they are drinking milkshake), and "swinging laughter" (standing in a circle saying "aaee-oo-eee-uuu") before the rather fearsome "lion laughter" (extruding the tongue fully with eyes wide open and hands stretched out like claws, and laughing from the tummy). The session then winds up with holding hands and the chanting of slogans ("We are the laughter club member [sic]...Y...E...S!").

Laughter Clubs take place between 6am and 7am at various venues around the city, including Colaba Woods in Cuffe Parade and Juhu Beach. For the full story, go to ⓦwww.laughteryoga.org.

to British times that still serves as a prime stomping ground for the city's upper classes. Race meets are held twice weekly, on Wednesdays and Saturdays between November and March, and big days such as the 2000 Guineas and Derby attract crowds of 25,000. Entrance to the public ground is by ticket on the day. Seats for the colonial-era stand, with its posh lawns and exclusive *Gallops Restaurant* are, alas, allocated to members only. Race cards are posted in the sports section of the *Times of India* and at Ⓦwww.rwitc.com.

On non-race days, the Mahalakshmi ground doubles as a riding track. Temporary membership of the **Amateur Riding Club of Mumbai**, another bastion of elite Mumbai, entitles you to use the club's thoroughbreds for classes. Full details on how to do this, along with previews of forthcoming club **polo** matches, are posted at Ⓦwww.arcmumbai.com.

Listings

Airlines, domestic Air India, Air India Building, Nariman Point Ⓣ1800/227722; Air India Express, Air India Building, Nariman Point Ⓣ022/2279 6330; GoAir Ⓣ1800 222111; Indian, Air India Building, Nariman Point Ⓣ1800 /180 1407; IndiGo Airlines, Ⓣ099/1038 3838 or 1800 180 3838; Jet Airways, B1, Amarchand Mansion, Ground Floor, Madam Cama Road, Colaba Ⓣ022/3989 3333; Jet Lite Ⓣ1800 223020; Kingfisher 241/242, Ground Floor, Nirmal Building, Nariman Point Ⓣ022/6649 9393; SpiceJet Ⓣ1800 180 3333.

Airlines, international See p.28 for airlines' website addresses. Air France, 201/B Sarjan Plaza, 2nd floor, 100 Dr. Annie Besant Road, Worli Ⓣ1800 110055; Air India, Air India Building, Nariman Point Ⓣ022/2548 9999 or 1800 227722; British Airways Ⓣ08925/77470; Cathay Pacific, 2 Brady Gladys Plaza (2nd Floor), 1/447 Senapati Bapat Marg, Lower Parel Ⓣ022/6657 2222; Emirates, 3 Mittal Chambers, Ground Floor 228, Nariman Point Ⓣ022/4097 4097; Gulf Air, Maker Chambers V, Ground Floor, Nariman Point Ⓣ1800 221122; Jet Airways, B1, Amarchand Mansion, Ground Floor, Madam Cama Road, Colaba Ⓣ022/3989 3333; KLM, 201/B, Sarjan Plaza, 100 Annie Besant Road, Worli Ⓣ0124/272 0273; Kuwait Airways, 902N Nariman Bhavan, 9th Floor, Nariman Point Ⓣ022 66555655; Lufthansa, Express Towers, 4th Floor, Nariman Point Ⓣ022/6630 1940; Qantas, 4th Floor, Rear Wing, Sunteck Centre, 37-40 Subhash Road, Vile Parle (East) Ⓣ022/2200 7440; Qatar Airways, Bajaj Bhavan, Nariman Point Ⓣ022/4456 6000; Singapore Airlines, *Taj Mahal Palace & Tower*, Apollo Bunder, Colaba Ⓣ022/2202 2747; South African Airways, Podar House, 10 Marine Drive Ⓣ022/2284 2237; Thai Airways, Mittal Tower A Wing, Ground floor 2A, Nariman Point Ⓣ022/6637 3737.

Airport enquiries Chhatrapati Shivaji international airport Ⓣ022/2681 3000, Ⓦwww.csia.in; Chhatrapati Shivaji (Santa Cruz) domestic airport Ⓣ022/2626 4000; Ⓦwww.csia.in.

Ambulance Ⓣ101 for general emergencies; but you're nearly always better off taking a taxi. See also Hospitals, p.624.

Banks and currency exchange The most convenient place to change money when you arrive in Mumbai is at the State Bank of India's 24hr counter in Chhatrapati Shivaji international airport. Rates here are standard but you may have to pay for an encashment certificate – you may need to produce this if you intend to buy tourist-quota train tickets or an Indrail pass at the special counters in Churchgate or CST (VT) stations. There are dozens of ATMs dotted around the city – see the various maps in the guide for precise locations. All the major state banks downtown change foreign currency (Mon–Fri 10.30am–2.30pm, Sat 10.30am–12.30pm); some (eg the Bank of Baroda) also handle credit cards and cash advances. Thomas Cook's big Dr DN Marg branch (Mon–Sat 9.30am–7pm; Ⓣ022/6160 3333), between the Khadi shop and Hutatma Chowk, can also arrange money transfers from overseas.

Consulates and high commissions Note that most of India's neighbouring states, including Bangladesh, Bhutan, Burma, Nepal and Pakistan, only have embassies in New Delhi and/or Kolkata (Calcutta). All of the following are open Mon–Fri only: Australia, 16th Floor, 36 Maker Chamber 6, Nariman Point (Ⓣ022/6669 2000, Ⓦwww.utsavaustralia.in); Canada, 41/42, 4th Floor Maker Chambers VI, Nariman Point (Ⓣ022/2287 6027); Republic of Ireland, Kamanwalla Chambers, 2nd

Floor, Sir PM Rd, Fort (☎022/6635 5635); South Africa, Gandhi Mansion, 20 Altamount Rd (☎022/2389 3725); United Kingdom, Naman Chambers, C/32 G Block, Bandra Kurla Complex, Bandra (East) (☎022/6650 2222, Ⓦukinindia.fco.gov.uk); USA, Lincoln House, 78 Bhulabhai Desai Rd (☎022/2363 3611, Ⓦmumbai.usconsulate.gov).

Hospitals The best hospital in the centre is the private Bombay Hospital, New Marine Lines (☎022/2206 7676, Ⓦwww.bombayhospital.com), just north of the government tourist office on M Karve Rd. Breach Candy Hospital (☎022/2367 1888, Ⓦwww.breachcandyhospital.org) on Bhulabhai Desai Rd, near the swimming pool, is also recommended by foreign embassies.

Internet access There are surprisingly few places to get online in Mumbai. A couple of cramped 24hr places (Rs40/hr) can be found in Colaba on Nawroji F Marg. If you have your own computer wi-fi access is available at many of the city's more upmarket hotels and at local branches of the Barista coffee shop chain (there's a branch next to the Regal Cinema in Colaba).

Left luggage There's a left-luggage office at CST (VT) Station (Rs12/day). Anything left here, even rucksacks, must be securely fastened with a padlock and can be left for a maximum of one month.

Libraries Asiatic Society (see p.607), Shahid Bhagat Singh Marg, Horniman Circle, Ballard Estate (Mon–Sat 10.30am–7pm); British Council (for British newspapers and magazines), A Wing, 1st floor, Mittal Tower, Nariman Point (Tues–Sat 10am–6pm); Bombay Natural History Society, Hornbill House, next to the Chhatrapati Shivaji Museum (Ⓦwww.bnhs.org; Mon–Fri 9.30am–5.30pm), has an international reputation for the study of wildlife in India. Visitors may obtain temporary membership, which allows them access to the library, natural history collection, occasional talks and the opportunity to join organized walks and field trips.

Pharmacies Regal Pharmacy, opposite *Gordon House Hotel* in Colaba (see p.601), is open 24hr.

Police The main police station in Colaba (☎022/2285 6817) is on the west side of Colaba Causeway, near the crossroads with Best Marg.

Postal services The GPO (Mon–Sat 9am–8pm, Sun 9am–4pm) is around the corner from CST (VT) Station, off Nagar Chowk. The parcel office (10am–4.30pm) is behind the main building on the first floor. Packing-wallahs hang around on the pavement outside. DHL (☎022/2850 5050) has eleven offices in Mumbai, the most convenient being the 24hr one under the *Sea Green Hotel* at the bottom of Marine Drive.

Travel agents The following travel agents are recommended for booking domestic and international flights, and long-distance private buses where specified: Cox and Kings India, 16 Bank St, Fort ☎1800 221235, Ⓦwww.coxandkings.co.in; Sita World, 11th Floor, Bajaj Bhavan, Nariman Point; Thomas Cook, 324 Dr DN Rd, Fort ☎022/6160 3333, Ⓦwww.thomascook.co.in.

Moving on from Mumbai

Most visitors aim to escape Mumbai as soon as possible, and the city is equipped with "superfast" services to make **onward travel** speedy and painless (by Indian standards). All the major international and domestic **airlines** have offices downtown, the **railway** networks operate special tourist counters in the main reservation halls, and dozens of **travel agents** and road transport companies are eager to help you on your way by **bus**.

By air

Mumbai is the main hub of the Indian domestic air network, with departures from Chhatrapati Shivaji domestic airport (aka Santa Cruz; Ⓦwww.csia.in) to just about every city of consequence in the country. Availability on popular routes should never be taken for granted – check with the airlines as soon as you arrive. **Tickets** can be bought directly from airline offices (see p.623), via the internet, or through any reputable travel agent. Make sure you leave plenty of time to get to the airport – the taxi ride up from Colaba can easily take ninety minutes or more if traffic is bad.

Bollywood and beyond

Film is massive in India. The country produces more movies than anywhere else in the world (around 1200 every year), while the fact that many Indian households still lack television ensures a huge and devoted cinema-going public. Although the traditional image of Indian film as a melodramatic medley of outlandishly choreographed musical sequences, badly dubbed songs, hamfisted overacting and wet saris persists, modern Indian movies have largely overturned these cinematic stereotypes, with acting, scripts and production values which are often on par with anything made in the West.

Publicity poster for *My Name is Khan* ▲

Dances sit below a Bollywood poster, Mumbai ▼

Bollywood dancers on set ▼

Made in Mumbai

Although sometimes used to refer to all Indian-made movies, strictly speaking the name **Bollywood** refers only to Hindi-language films made in Mumbai, whose studios churn out around nine hundred films every year. There are numerous other regional schools of cinema throughout India, most importantly the huge Tamil-language movie industry based in Chennai (so-called "Kollywood"; see p.949). But only Bollywood films attract nationwide – and, indeed, increasingly global – audiences. In the UK, for instance, successful Bollywood hits regularly gross more than £2m at the box office, while Bollywood films have an estimated global audience of 3.6 billion, compared to Hollywood's 2.5 billion.

Music and masalas

Bollywood films traditionally follow the so-called **masala** format (named after the Hindi word for a spice mixture), typically featuring an eclectic blend of romantic entanglements, rip-roaring action sequences and light-hearted comedy, with stock characters like corrupt politicians, scheming villains and star-crossed lovers. **Music** also plays a vital role in most Bollywood films, with numerous songs (or *filmi*; see p.1183) and elaborate dance sequences – indeed, many films live or die by the quality of their musical set pieces.

The traditional Bollywood masala formula has changed significantly in recent years, however, often moving far closer to the mainstream Hollywood model. The all-singing, all-dancing flicks of yesteryear are steadily giving way to more adventurous and challenging films depicting emerging new classes within

Indian society, such as Westernized urban youngsters and Indians living overseas, along with an increasingly liberal portrayal of sexual relations – even if the famous taboo against showing on-screen kissing is still widely observed.

Who's who in Bollywood

Bollywood's A-list film stars enjoy an almost god-like status in India – only the country's top cricketers come close to matching their exalted mass appeal. Images of the biggest celebrities seem to be everywhere: in newspapers and magazines, on streetside posters and cinema hoardings, and in innumerable raunchy music videos and cheesy TV commercials.

At the top of the heap are the white-bearded Amitabh Bachchan, Bollywood's *éminence grise*, and his rival Shahrukh Khan, the smouldering hero of countless romantic blockbusters. Other leading male stars include tough-guy Sanjay Dutt and younger hearthrobs like Aamir Khan, John Abraham, Hrithik Roshan and Bollywood bad-boy Salman Khan. Not surprisingly in such an image-obsessed industry, female stars tend to be younger and have a shorter shelf-life than their male counterparts, although contemporary starlets like Katrina Kaif, Kareena Kapoor and Preity Zinta are tackling increasingly demanding and unglamorous roles in an attempt to prove themselves as serious actresses. Even so, it's their off-screen doings and romantic dalliances which continue to command the most attention and fill the gossip columns, as do appearances of India's biggest celebrity couple, star actor Abhishek Bachchan (son of the legendary Amitabh) and his wife Aishwarya Rai, herself a leading Bollywood actress and a former Miss World.

▲ Bollywood legend Amitabh Bachchan

▼ Actress Aishwarya Rai

Scene from *Lagaan* ▲

Mother India poster ▼

Scene from *Salaam Bombay!* ▼

Bollywood classics

▸▸ **Devdas** (1955). Vintage Bollywood tale of tragic love, starring the great Dilip Kumar as doomed lover Devdas.

▸▸ **Dil Chahta Hai** ("The Heart Desires", 2001). Stylish and genre-breaking movie depicting the lives and loves of India's new and well-heeled urban elite.

▸▸ **Dilwale Dulhania Le Jayenge** ("The Brave-hearted will take the Bride", 1995). One of the biggest Bollywood hits ever, this classic chick-flick is an engaging London-based romantic comedy – one of the first Bollywood movies to be set overseas.

▸▸ **Lagaan** ("Land Tax", 2001). Emotive Raj-era drama in which a group of poor villagers attempt to beat the local British at cricket in exchange for a remission in punitive taxes.

▸▸ **Mother India** (1957). Classic rural epic highlighting the troubles and travails of an Indian mother living in an impoverished village at the mercy of an usurious money-lender and her own bandit son.

▸▸ **Mr India** (1987) Quirky action-movie featuring the battles between Mr India (Anil Kapoor) and megalomaniac arch-villain Mogambo.

▸▸ **Mughal-e-Azam** (1960). A spectacular historical epic that took nine years to make and remains unrivalled in its lavish depiction of love and intrigue at the court of Mughal emperor Akbar.

▸▸ **Munna Bhai M.B.B.S.** ("Brother Munna M.B.B.S.", 2003). Light-hearted comedy starring lovable bad-guy Sanjay Dutt as the amiably roguish Mumbai gangster Munna Bhai. The sequel, Lage Raho Munna Bhai (2006), was another massive hit.

▸▸ **Salaam Bombay!** (1988). Internationally acclaimed feature chronicling the lives of children living hand-to-mouth on the streets of Mumbai.

▸▸ **Sholay** ("Embers", 1975). Regarded as the greatest Bollywood film ever, this action-packed tale of warring outlaws stars the legendary Amitabh Bachchan.

Getting to Goa

Easily the best-value way to travel the 500km from Mumbai to Goa is by **plane** – prices often compare favourably with the cost of the same journey via the Konkan Railway, which has two departures daily. Whatever your budget, think twice before attempting the hellish overnight **bus** journey.

By air

Around fifteen flights leave daily from Mumbai's domestic airport for Goa's Dabolim airport (code GOI). Flights are currently operated by Jet Airways, JetLite, Kingfisher, IndiGo, SpiceJet, Go Air, Indian Airlines and Air India (for websites, see p.28) One-way fares start from around Rs2000; check ⓦwww.expedia.co.in and ⓦwww.travelocity.co.in for latest deals, or the websites of the airlines themselves (see p.28) for special offers and promotions.

Demand for seats can be fierce around Diwali and Christmas/New Year, when you're unlikely to get a ticket at short notice. At other times, one or other of the carriers should be able to offer a seat on the day you wish to travel – though perhaps not at the lowest fares. If you didn't pre-book when you purchased your international ticket, check availability with the airlines as soon as you arrive; tickets can be bought directly from their airport ticket desks, their downtown offices, if they have one (see p.623), through any reputable travel agent in Mumbai (bearing in mind that an agent may charge you the dollar fare at a poorer rate of exchange than that offered by the airline company), by phone or direct via the internet (though note that some low-cost airlines refuse payments by credit or debit cards not registered in India).

By train

The **Konkan Railway** line runs daily express trains from Mumbai to Goa. However, these services are not always available at short notice from the booking halls at CST and Churchgate and you may want to **book tickets online** (see p.42) before you leave home. Don't, whatever you do, be tempted to travel "unreserved" class on any Konkan service, as the journey as far as Ratnagiri (roughly midway) is overwhelmingly crushed. There are a number of convenient services – see the box on p.626 for details.

By bus

The Mumbai–Goa bus journey ranks among the very worst in India. Don't believe travel agents who assure you it takes thirteen hours. Depending on the type of bus you get, appalling road surfaces along the sinuous coastal route make sixteen to eighteen hours a more realistic estimate.

Fares start at around Rs250 for a push-back seat on a beaten-up Kadamba (Goan government) or MSRTC coach. Tickets for these services are in great demand in season with domestic tourists, so book in advance at Mumbai Central. Quite a few **private overnight buses** (around a dozen daily) also run to Goa, costing from around Rs250 for no-frills buses up to Rs1000 for swisher a/c Volvo coaches with berths (which bizarrely you may have to share). Tickets should be booked at least a day in advance through a reputable travel agent (see opposite), or direct through the bus company. The largest operator for Goa is Paulo Travels (ⓦwww.paulotravels.com); tickets can be booked by phone on ⓣ0832/663 7777 or online.

By train

The quickest and most convenient place for foreign nationals to make reservations is at the efficient tourist counter (#14) on the first floor of the **Western Railway's booking hall**, next door to the Government of India tourist office in **Churchgate** (Mon–Fri 8am–8pm, Sat 8am–2pm; ⓣ022/2209 7577). This counter, at the far end of the booking hall, has access to special "tourist quotas" (available three months in advance, but not online, so you'll have to come in person), or, failing that, to a special Emergency Quota. If the quota is "closed" or already used up, you will have to join the regular queue. As elsewhere in the country, periods before major national holidays (notably **Diwali**, when half of India is on the move) should be avoided at all costs. But if you do find yourself having to travel when there don't seem to be any tickets left, bear in mind you can pay extra for a special Tatkal seat (see p.42) – an option well worth

Recommended trains from Mumbai

Destination	Name	No.	From	Departs	Journey time
Agra	*Punjab Mail*	#2137	CST	Daily 7.40pm	22hr 10min
Ahmedabad	*Shatabdi Express*	#2009	MC	Daily except Sun 6.25pm	6hr 45min
Aurangabad	*Tapovan Express*	#7617	CST	Daily 6.10am	7hr 5min
Bengaluru (Bangalore)	*Udyan Express*	#6529	CST	Daily 8.05am	24hr 50min
Bhopal	*Punjab Mail*	#2137	CST	Daily 7.40pm	14hr
Chennai	*Chennai Express*	#1041	CST	Daily 2pm	26hr 45min
Delhi	*Rajdhani Express*	#2951	MC	Daily 4.40pm	15hr 50min
Goa (Margao)	*Konkan–Kanya Express*	#0111	CST	Daily 11.05pm	11hr 45min
	Jan Shatabdi	#2051	CST	Daily 5.10am	9hr
	Karwar Express	#2133	CST	Daily 10.15pm	8hr 45min
Hyderabad	*Hussain-sagar Express*	#2701	CST	Daily 9.50pm	14hr 20min
Jaipur	*Mumbai–Jaipur Express*	#2955	MC	Daily 6.50pm	18hr 5min
Jodhpur	*Ranakpur Express*	#4708	Bandra	Daily 3pm	18hr 40min
Kochi (Cochin)	*Netravati Express*	#6345	LTT (Kurla)	Daily 11.40am	26hr 25min
Kolhapur	*Sahyadri Express*	#1023	CST	Daily 5.50pm	12hr 10min
Kolkata (Calcutta/ Howrah)	*Gitanjali Express*	#2859	CST	Daily 6am	30hr 30min
Lonavala	*Udyan Express*	#6529	CST	Daily 8.05am	2hr 30min
Pune	*Udyan Express*	#6529	CST	Daily 8.05am	3hr 35min
Thiruva-nanthapuram	*Netravati Express*	#6345 (Kurla)	LTT	Daily 11.40am	31hr
Varanasi	*Muzaffarpur Express/ Darbhanga Express*	#1061/ #1065	LTT (Kurla)	Daily 1pm	25hr 5min

0considering, for example, if you want to get to Goa on the oversubscribed Konkan Railway route.

Mumbai's other "Tourist Ticketing Facility" is on the first floor (counter #52) of the air-conditioned **Central Railway Reservation Office** at **CST** (VT; Mon–Sat 8am–8pm, Sun 8am–2pm; ⓣ022/2262 2859). The office is on the right of the main station entrance (as you go in), just off the concourse where taxis pull up. Indrail passes can also be bought here. In theory you may be required to produce a foreign currency encashment certificate or ATM slip to buy tickets here, though it's unlikely to be asked for.

Tickets for seats on the **Konkan Railway** can be booked at either Churchgate or CST booking halls; for more information on getting to Goa by rail, see box opposite. Just to complicate matters, some **Central Railway** trains to **South India** – notably those running via the Konkan Railway to **Kerala** – do not depart from CST at all, but from **Kurla Station** (aka Lokmanya Tilak Terminus, or **LTT**), up near the airports. Others leave from **Dadar**, also way north of the centre. Getting to either on public transport can be a major struggle, though many long-distance trains from CST (VT) or Churchgate stop there and aren't as crowded.

By bus

The main departure point for long-distance **government buses** leaving Mumbai is the frenetic **Central Bus Stand** on J Boman Behram Marg, opposite Mumbai Central railway station. States with bus company **counters** (daily 8am–8pm) here include Maharashtra, Karnataka and Goa. Few of their services compare favourably with train travel on the same routes. Reliable timetable information can be difficult to obtain, reservations are not available on standard buses, and most long-haul journeys are gruelling overnighters. Among the exceptions are the deluxe buses run by MSRTC to Pune and Kolhapur; the small extra cost buys you more leg-room, fewer stops and the option of advance booking. The only problem is that most leave from the ASIAD bus stand in Dadar, or the new MSRTC stand in Thane, thirty and sixty minutes respectively by road or rail north of Mumbai Central.

Private buses cover most of the same routes. They tend to be faster, more comfortable and easier to book in advance – though again, long distance services invariably depart at night. Tickets are sold from a row of booths on busy Dr Anadao Nair Marg, just outside Mumbai Central railway station, on the opposite side of the main (north–south) road from the Central Bus Stand (see map, p.599). Note that fares on services to popular tourist destinations such as Goa and Mahabaleshwar increase by as much as 75 percent during peak season.

By boat

Three companies – PNP, Maldar Catamarans and Ajanta – operate boat services from the Gateway of India to **Mandawa jetty**, on the far side of Mumbai harbour, from where buses shuttle to nearby **Alibag**, transport hub for the route southwards down the Konkan coast. Ranging from comfortable air-conditioned catamarans (Rs110) to bog-standard launches (Rs65), the ferries leave roughly every hour; tickets should be purchased in advance from the PNP, Ajanta or Maldar company booths, on the north side of Shivaji Marg, near the MTDC information counter.

11

Maharashtra

* **Nasik** Pilgrimage centre and capital of India's nascent wine trade, Nasik is a fascinating contradiction of ancient and modern. See p.631

* **Ellora caves** Breathtaking Hindu, Buddhist and Jain caves carved from solid volcanic rock. See p.641

* **Ajanta caves** Hidden in a remote horseshoe-shaped ravine, Ajanta's murals are the finest storehouse of art to have survived from any ancient civilization. See p.648

* **Gandhi ashram, Sevagram** Learn about the great man's life and beliefs at the last ashram he lived in. See p.657

* **Miniature train to Matheran** Fantastic views across the Western Ghats are revealed during the two-hour ride to this quintessentially British hill-station. See p.660

* **Pune** Known as the "Oxford of the East", this sophisticated city is home to an absorbing old town, a riveting museum and some fine places to eat. See p.665

▲ The Kailash Temple, Ellora caves

Vast and rugged, the modern state of **MAHARASHTRA** is the third largest in India and the second most visited by foreign tourists. As soon as you leave the seething endless concrete housing projects, petrochemical works and swamplands of its seething port capital, **Mumbai**, you enter a different world with a different history.

Undoubtedly, Maharashtra's greatest treasures are its extraordinary **cave temples** and **monasteries**. The finest of all are found near **Aurangabad**, renamed after the Mughal emperor Aurangzeb and home to the **Bibi-ka-Maqbara**, dedicated to his wife. The busy commercial city is the obvious base for visits to the Buddhist caves at **Ajanta**, with their fabulous and still-vibrant murals, and the monolithic temples of **Ellora**, where the astonishing Hindu **Kailash temple** was carved in its entirety from one single rock.

Despite Maharashtra's early importance as a centre of Buddhism, the Hindu faith is very much at the core of the life in the state, accounting for eighty percent of the population. Balancing modern industry alongside ancient associations with the Ramayana, the main pilgrimage centre has always been **Nasik**, a handy place to break journeys en route to Aurangabad. As one of the four locations of the Kumbh Mela, the city is always a hive of devotional activity, and lies close to one of India's most sacred Shiva shrines, reached by a steep hike from the village of **Trimbak**. East of Aurangabad, Maharashtra extends for a further 500km across the Deccan to the geographical centre of the Subcontinent. In the state's far northeastern corner, the city of **Nagpur** is the focus of an area largely populated by several different tribal groups, and lies close to **Sevagram**, where Mahatma Gandhi set up his headquarters during the struggle for Independence.

Away from the cities, one of the most characteristic features of the landscape is a plenitude of **forts**, constructed to defend the important trade routes of this western borderland between north and south India. Rising abruptly a short distance inland from the sea, the Sahyadri Hills – part of the larger **Western Ghats** range – form a series of huge steps that march up from the narrow coastal strip to the edge of the **Deccan** plateau. These flat-topped hills could easily be converted into forts where small forces could withstand protracted sieges by large armies. Modern visitors can scale such windswept fortified heights at **Pratapgadh** and, most dramatically, **Daulatabad**.

During the nineteenth century, the mountains found another use. When the summer proved too much for the British in Bombay, they sought refuge in nearby **hill stations**, the most popular of which, **Mahabaleshwar**, now caters for droves of domestic tourists. **Matheran**, 108km east of Mumbai and 800m higher, has a special attraction: a rickety miniature train that twists up the hill on a sinuous track. South of Matheran, a further series of magnificent rock-cut caves clustered around another resort town, **Lonavala**, provides the main incentive to break the journey to the modern, cosmopolitan city of **Pune**, famous for its **Osho** resort founded by the New Age guru Bhagwan Rajneesh, but most appealing for its atmospheric old town and burgeoning eating and drinking scene that's fast rivalling Mumbai.

To the west, Maharashtra occupies 500km of the **Konkan coast** on the Arabian Sea, from Gujarat to Goa. The little-explored palm-fringed coast winds back and forth with countless inlets, ridges and valleys, studded with forts; highlights including **Murud-Janjira**, whose extraordinary fortress was the only one never conquered by the Mughals, and **Ganpatipule**, the region's chief pilgrimage centre, where you can walk on miles of virtually deserted, palm-fringed beaches. By the time you reach **Kolhapur**, the main town in the far south of the state, famous for its temple and Raj-era Maharaja's palace, Mumbai feels a world away.

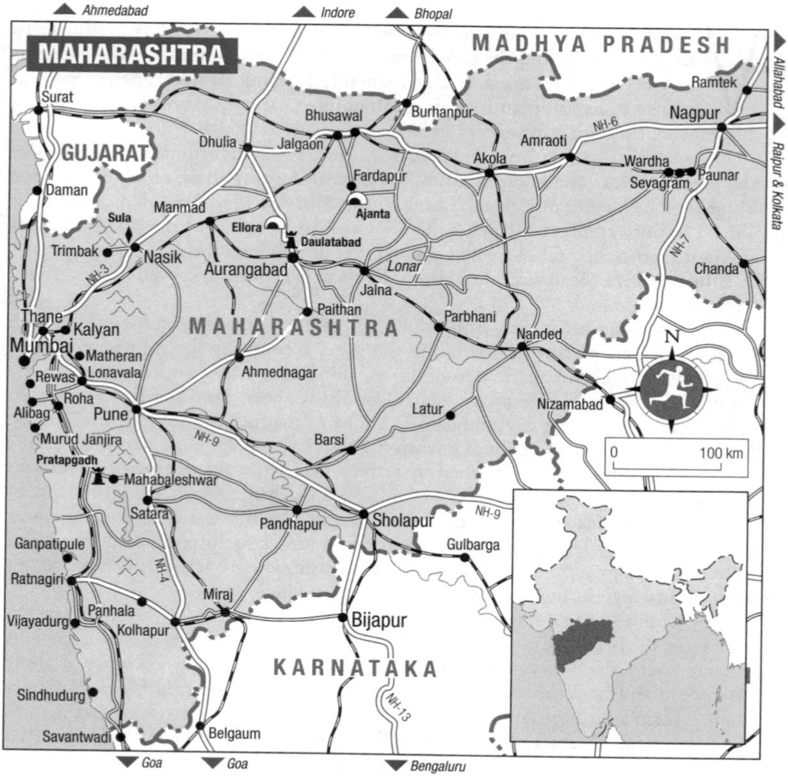

The Maharashtra Tourism Development Corporation (**MTDC**) runs a number of hotels across the state, often occupying superb locations – though standards are variable – and can also organize stays in local B&Bs. The most useful of their resorts are listed in this chapter and can be booked either at MTDC offices or at Ⓦ www.maharashtratourism.gov.in.

Some history

Maharashtra enters recorded history in the second century BC, with the construction of its first Buddhist caves. These lay, and still lie, in peaceful places of great natural beauty, but could never have been created without the wealth generated by the nearby caravan trade routes between north and south India.

The region's first Hindu rulers – based in Badami, Karnataka – appeared during the sixth century, and Buddhism was almost entirely supplanted by the twelfth century. Hinduism, in the form of the simple faith of Ramdas, the "Servant of Rama", provided the philosophical underpinning behind the campaigns of the Maharashtra's greatest warrior, **Shivaji** (1627–80), who remains a potent symbol for Maharashtrans, celebrated in prominently positioned equestrian statues across the state. The fiercely independent Maratha chieftain united local forces to place insurmountable obstacles in the way of any prospective invader; so effective were their guerrilla tactics that he could even take on the mighty Mughals, who by 1633 had got as far as capturing Daulatabad. By the time he died, in 1680, he had managed to unite the Marathas into a stable and secure state, funded by the plunder gleaned through guerrilla raids as far afield as Andhra Pradesh. In response, Mughal Emperor **Aurangzeb** moved his court and capital south to the Deccan, first to Bijapur (1686) and then Golconda (1687), but still failed to subdue Shivaji's dynasty. Yet by the end of the eighteenth century the power of both had weakened and the British were able to take full control.

Maharashtra claims a crucial role in the development of a nationalist consciousness. An organization known as the Indian National Union, originally convened in Pune, held a conference in Bombay in 1885, which was thereafter known as the **Indian National Congress**. This loose congregation of key local figures from around the country was to change the face of Indian politics. At first, its aim was limited to establishing a national platform to raise the status of Indians, and it remained loyal to the British. In the long term, of course, it was instrumental in the achievement of Independence 62 years later, with many of the Congress's factional leaders over the years hailing from Maharashtra.

With Independence, the Bombay Presidency, to which most of Maharashtra belonged, became known as Bombay State. Maharashtra as such was created in 1960 from the state's Marathi-speaking regions. Its manufacturing industries, centred on Mumbai and to a lesser extent cities such as Nagpur, Nasik, Aurangabad, Sholapur and Kolhapur, now account for fifteen percent of the nation's output. Textiles have long been important – the Deccan soils supplied the world with cotton in the nineteenth century after its main source was interrupted by the American Civil War – but this is now also one of the premier high-tech industry regions, especially along the Mumbai–Pune corridor. Still, the majority of Maharashtra's population of well over one hundred million are still engaged in agriculture: main crops include sugar cane, cotton, turmeric, peanuts, sunflowers, tobacco, pulses, wine grapes, fruit and vegetables.

Nasik and around

Lying at the head of the main pass through the Western Ghats, the fast-developing city of **NASIK** (also known as Nashik) makes an interesting stopover en route to or from Mumbai, 187km southwest. The city is one of the four sites of the world's largest religious gathering, the **Kumbh Mela** (see p.278), due to be hosted next in Nasik in 2015. Even outside festival times, the *ghat*-lined banks of the **River**

India's wine capital

With its temperate winters, rich soil and gently undulating landscape, Nasik's arid and dusty hinterland has over the past decade proved itself to be – incongruously enough – ideal for growing wine grapes, and the city has now firmly established itself at the centre of India's fast-expanding wine industry. The best established producer, enthusiastically supported by Mumbai's urban sophisticates, is **Sula Vineyards**, 14km west of Nasik, which runs forty-five minute tours of its winery (hourly 11.30am–5.30pm; Rs150; ⓣ0253/223 0575, ⓦsulawines.com), a slick and professional operation that wouldn't look out of place in California's Napa Valley. Tours conclude with a generous tasting of half a dozen varieties – all eminently drinkable – on the congenial *Tasting Terrace* (open till 10pm, Fri & Sat till 11pm), which looks out over acres of neat rows of vines towards the scenic Gangapur tank. If you fancy making a night of it, you can **stay** nearby at Sula's luxurious three-bedroom villa, *Beyond* (Rs18,000–22,000/night); some cheaper, new rooms (8) should also be ready by the time you read this.

Godavari are always animated. According to the Ramayana, Nasik was where Rama (Vishnu in human form), his brother Lakshmana and wife Sita lived during their exile from Ayodhya, and the arch-demon Ravana carried off Sita from here in an aerial chariot to his kingdom, Lanka, in the far south. The scene of such episodes forms the core of the busy pilgrimage circuit – a lively enclave packed with religious specialists, beggars, sadhus and street vendors touting puja paraphernalia. However, Nasik has a surprising dearth of historical buildings – even the famous temples beside the river only date from the **Maratha era** of the eighteenth century. Its only real monuments are the rock-cut caves at nearby **Pandav Lena**. Excavated at the peak of Buddhist achievement on the Deccan, these two-thousand-year-old cells hark back to the days when, as capital of the powerful **Satavahana** dynasty, Nasik dominated the all-important trade routes linking the Ganges plains with the ports to the west.

From Nasik, you can make an interesting day-trip to the highly auspicious village of **Trimbak**, from which a steep climb takes you to **Brahmagiri**, the source of the Godavari. Somewhat in contrast to its religious importance, Nasik is also the centre of Maharashtra's burgeoning **wine region** (see below).

Arrival and information

There are three principal bus stands. Buses from Mumbai pull in at the **Mahamarga Bus Stand**, ten minutes by rickshaw from the city centre, while Aurangabad and Pune buses terminate at the central **New City Bus Stand**. The **Old City Bus Stand** is around 500m north along the Old Agra Road (also known as Swami Vivekanand Road), and is primarily useful for buses to Trimbak; it's an easy walk from either stand to several cheap hotels and restaurants. Nasik Road **railway station**, the nearest railhead, lies 8km southeast of the centre; local buses regularly ply the route into town, and there is no shortage of shared taxis and auto-rickshaws (Rs100).

The helpful MTDC **tourist office** (Mon–Sat 10am–5.30pm; ⓣ0253/257 0059) is at T1, Golf Club, Old Agra Road, and easiest reached by cutting across the park opposite the New City Bus Stand. The State Bank of India, in between the two city bus stands on Old Agra Road, has an ATM and will **change money**. **Internet** access is available at Matrix (Rs20/hr), down an alley beside the *Suruchi* restaurant and at Bits 'n' Bytes (Rs15/hr), around the corner from the *Panchavati* hotel complex.

Moving on from Nasik

The most convenient **train** services from Nasik Road on to **Aurangabad** (3hr 15min–4hr) are the #7617 *Tapovan Express*, which leaves at 9.50am, and #2071 *Jan Shatabdi Express* (leaves 5.10pm). Back in the other direction, there are plenty of services to **Mumbai** (3hr 30min–4hr), the most useful being the #2110 *Panchavati Express* (departs 7am), and again the #2072 *Jan Shatabdi Express* (leaves 8.55am). If you don't book your onward train ticket on arrival, head for the **city booking office** (Mon–Sat 8am–8pm, Sun 8am–2pm), near HDFC House around 1km west of the city bus stands. Other directly accessible destinations from Nasik include Agra (3–5 daily; 17–21hr); Bhopal (6–12 daily; 9hr–11hr 30min); Delhi (3–4 daily; 20hr 30min–25hr); Jabalpur (9–12 daily; 11hr 30min–15hr); Jalgaon (frequent; 2hr 45min–4hr); and Nagpur (6–8 daily; 9hr 30min–11hr 30min).

MSRTC **buses** leave every one to two hours for Aurangabad (4hr–4hr 30min), hourly for Mumbai (4hr) and every 30min for Pune (4–5hr); private services also operate on these routes. There's also a daily **flight** to Mumbai with Kingfisher from Nasik's Gandhinagar airport, around 5km southeast of town en route to the railway station.

Accommodation

Most of Nasik's **hotels**, stretching along the Mumbai–Agra road en route to Pandav Lena, are pitched at business travellers, though there are a few more budget-friendly exceptions around the Old City Bus Stand chowk.

Gateway 7km southwest on Mumbai–Agra Rd ⓣ0253/660 4499, ⓦwww.thegatewayhotels.com. Set behind beautifully landscaped grounds, with a gleaming marble lobby designed in mock-Maratha style, this is the plushest place to stay in the area. Rack rates from around $170. ❾

Padma Sharanpur Rd, directly opposite the Old City Bus Stand ⓣ0253/257 6837. Safe and clean, with a restaurant and permit room. All rooms have attached bathrooms and hot water (6–9am). ❷–❸

Panchavati 430 Chandak Vadi ⓣ0253/257 2291, ⓦwww.panchavatihotels.com. Set mercifully off noisy MG Road a fifteen-minute walk from the New City Bus Stand, this four-part complex has rooms to suit most pockets, all of them scrupulously clean, attached and good value for money, though overall it's a little worn and institutional. At the bottom of the range is the budget *Panchavati Guest House* (ⓣ0253/257 8771; ❸), followed by the midscale, on-the-ball *Panchavati Yatri* (ⓣ0253/257 2290; ❺), the slightly swisher *Hotel Panchavati* (ⓣ0253/257 5771; ❺) and, at the top of the range, the *Panchavati Millionaire* (ⓣ0253/231 2318; ❻), where forking out a few hundred extra rupees will secure you a suite.

Rajmahal Sharanpur Rd ⓣ0253/258 0501, ⓦhotelrajmahalnashik.com. Bright, comfortable, modern rooms (ask for one away from the main road) in a smart new block opposite the Old City Bus Stand, with a pure-veg restaurant next door. Very good value. ❹

The City

Down on the riverbank, over 1km east of the bus stand, the **Ram Kund**, always buzzing with a carnival atmosphere, is the reason most people come to Nasik, although it can look more like an overcrowded municipal swimming pool than one of India's most ancient sacred places. Among the Ram Kund's more arcane attributes is its capacity to dissolve bones – whence the epithet of **Astivilaya Tirth** or "Bone Immersion Tank".

Follow the narrow street opposite Ram Kund up the hill to arrive at the city's second most important sacred area, the square around the **Kala Ram Mandir**, or "Black Rama Temple". Among the well-known episodes from the Ramayana to occur here was the event that led to Sita's abduction, when Lakshmana sliced off the nose of Ravana's sister after she had tried to seduce Rama by taking the form of a voluptuous princess. Sita's cave, or **Gumpha**, a tiny grotto known in the Ramayana as Parnakuti ("Smallest Hut"), is just off the square.

The Kala Ram temple itself, at the bottom of the square, houses unusual jet-black deities of Rama, Sita and Lakshmana; these are very popular with visiting pilgrims, as access is free from all caste restrictions. The best time to visit is around sunset, after evening puja, when a crowd, mostly of women, gathers in the courtyard to listen to a traditional storyteller recount tales from the Ramayana and other epics.

A steep fifteen-minute climb up one of the precipitous conical hills that overlook the Mumbai–Agra Road, 8km southwest of Nasik, is **Pandav Lena** (sunrise to sunset; Rs100 [Rs5]), a small group of 24 rock-cut caves famous for their well-preserved Pali inscriptions and fine ancient stone sculpture. Cave 18, the only *chaitya* hall, is one of the earliest, dating from the first century BC, and is notable for its striking facade, while Cave 3, the largest *vihara*, boasts some superb exterior stonework. The most straightforward way of getting to Pandav Lena without your own vehicle is by auto-rickshaw (around Rs100 each way), although the numerous local buses that pass nearby are not too packed most of the time.

Eating and drinking

Nasik's best-value meals are to be had in its traditional "keep it coming" thali **restaurants**, where for less than the price of a beer you can enjoy carefully prepared and tasty vegetable, pulse and lentil dishes, often including such regional specialities as *bajra* (wholemeal rotis) and *bakri* (hot oatmeal biscuits). The city's religious associations tend to mean that meat and alcohol are less easily available than elsewhere in Maharashtra, but most of the larger hotels have **bars** and restaurants with permits.

Annapurna MG Rd. The service may be unsmiling, but the south Indian and Punjabi veg dishes at this keenly priced stalwart are as good as they come. Dosas are a speciality; try the perfectly spiced and super-filling *Mysore paneer masala* dosa (Rs55).

Pangat Thali *Panchavati Yatri* hotel. Bustling Gujarati thali canteen where the industrious turbaned waiters will refill your tray with fresh, wholesome pure-veg morsels faster than you can chow them down. Unlimited thalis Rs90.

Suruchi Under *Basera Hotel*, Shivaji Rd. Cheap, clean, no-nonsense south Indian fast-food café close to the Old City Bus Stand that also serves inexpensive Udipi snacks and cold drinks. Full of crowds of office workers at lunch.

Talk of the Town Suyojit Chambers, Trimbak Rd, next to the New City Bus Stand. A rare upmarket option in central Nasik with a choice of fancy dining halls, from the family-friendly to the smoky and masculine. The north Indian non-veg (mains Rs130–230) can be variable but the long list of beers and spirits compensates.

Trimbak

Crouched in the shadow of the Western Ghats, 28km west of Nasik, the village of **TRIMBAK** – literally "Three-Eyed", another name for Lord Shiva, in Marathi – marks the spot where one of the four infamous drops of immortality-giving *amrit* nectar fell to earth from the *kumbh* vessel during the struggle between Vishnu's vehicle Garuda and the Demons – the mythological origin of the Kumbh Mela (see p.278). Numbering among India's most sacred centres for Shiva worship (it houses one of the twelve must sacred Shiva temples, known as *jyotirlingas*), the **Trimbakeshwar Mandir** temple, in the centre of the village, is unfortunately closed to non-Hindus. Its impressive eighteenth-century *shikhara* (tower), however, can be glimpsed from the backstreets nearby.

Trimbak is also near the source of one of India's longest and most sacred rivers, the **Godavari**; the spring can be reached via an ancient pilgrim-trail that cuts through a cleft in an awesome, guano-splashed cliff face. The round trip to **Brahmagiri**, the source of the Godavari, takes between two and three hours. It's a strenuous walk, particularly in the heat, so make sure you take adequate water. From the trailhead at the edge of the village, the way is paved and stepped as far as the first level outcrop, where there are some welcome chai stalls and a small hamlet. Beyond that, either turn left after the last group of huts and follow the dirt trail through the woods to the foot of the **rock-cut steps** (20min), or continue straight on to the three **shrines** clinging to the base of the cliff above. The first is dedicated to the goddess Ganga, the second – a

Going doolally

In the days of the Raj, soldiers who cracked under the stresses and strains of military life in British India were packed off to recuperate at a psychiatric hospital in the small Maharashtran cantonment town of **Deolali**, near Nasik. Its name became synonymous with madness and nervous breakdown; hence the English idiom "to go doolally".

cave containing 108 lingams – to Shankar (Shiva), and the third to the sage Gautama Rishi, whose hermitage this once was.

The steps climb 550m above Trimbak to the remains of **Anjeri Fort** – a site that was, over the years, attacked by the armies of both Shah Jahan and Aurangzeb before it fell into the hands of Shaha-ji Raj, father of the legendary rebel-leader Shivaji. The **source** itself is another twenty minutes further on, across **Brahmagiri Hill**, in the otherwise unremarkable Gaumukh ("Mouth of the Cow") temple. From its rather unimpressive origins, this paltry trickle flows for nearly 1000km east across the entire Deccan to the Bay of Bengal.

Trimbak makes an easy day-trip from Nasik. **Buses** leave every 30min from the Old City Bus Stand (45min). To return, you can catch a bus (until around 8pm) or one of the shared **taxis** that wait outside Trimbak Bus Stand; there's no difference in price as long as the car is full.

Aurangabad and beyond

On first impressions, it's easy to see why many travellers regard **AURANGABAD** as little more than a convenient, though largely uninteresting, place in which to kill time on the way to **Ellora** and **Ajanta**. Yet given a little effort, this city of over a million inhabitants can compensate for its architectural shortcomings. Scattered around its ragged fringes, the remains of fortifications, gateways, domes and minarets – including those of the most ambitious Mughal tomb garden in western India, the **Bibi-ka-Maqbara** – bear witness to an illustrious imperial past; the small but fascinating crop of **rock-cut Buddhist caves**, huddled along the flanks of the flat-topped, sandy yellow hills to the north, are remnants of even more ancient occupation.

The city was founded in the early seventeenth century by **Malik Ambar**, an ex-Abyssinian slave and prime minister of the independent Muslim kingdom of the Nizam Shahis; many of the **mosques** and palaces he erected still endure, albeit in ruins. Aurangabad really rose to prominence, however, towards the end of the seventeenth century, when **Aurangzeb** decamped here from Delhi. At his behest, the impressive city walls and gates were raised in 1682 to withstand the persistent Maratha attacks that bedevilled his later years. Following his death in 1707, the city was renamed in his honour as it changed hands once again. The new rulers, the **Nizams of Hyderabad**, staved off the Marathas for the greater part of 250 years, until the city finally merged with Maharashtra in 1956.

Modern Aurangabad is one of India's fastest growing commercial and industrial centres, specializing in car, soft drink and beer production. It's a decidedly upbeat place, boasting plenty of restaurants, bars and interesting shops in the old city. Easy day-trips from Aurangabad include the dramatic fort of **Daulatabad**, and, just a little further along the Ellora road, the tomb of Emperor Aurangzeb at the Muslim village of **Khuldabad**.

Arrival and information

Aurangabad's sparkling new **airport** terminal lies 10km east of the city. Metered **taxis** are on hand for the trip into town (around Rs150 to Station Rd East or West), though smarter places tend to offer pick-up. The mainline **railway station** stands on the southwest edge of the city centre, within easy reach of most of the cheaper hotels, and a 2.5km (Rs30) ride south down Station Road West from the **Central Bus Stand** – the hectic arrival point for most bus services.

Moving on from Aurangabad

All the state transport corporation (MSRTC) buses leave from the Central Bus Stand. Buses depart every 30min for **Ellora** (40min; via Daulatabad and Khuldabad), and every 30min to 1hr for **Jalgaon** (4hr), via Fardapur (for **Ajanta**; 3hr). There are frequent services to **Pune** (5hr) and **Nasik** (4hr 30min), including a few luxury a/c Volvo buses. Half a dozen nightly services leave for **Mumbai** (8–10hr), including a good-value nightly "luxury" bus. Other MSRTC destinations include Ahmedabad (2 nightly; 15hr); Bijapur (2 daily; 12hr); Indore (1 daily; 11hr 30min); and Nagpur (9 daily; 12hr). If you feel like a little more comfort, there are numerous private companies running a/c buses to most of the larger destinations; you can save yourself a lot of hassle by heading straight to the calm and efficient **Manmandir Travels** on Adalat Road (☎0240/236 5748), who operate night-time luxury services to destinations including Mumbai (Borivali), Goa, Indore, Nagpur, Hyderabad and Ahmedabad out of their own private terminus – a far cry from the usual bedlam.

As Aurangabad is not on the main line, **trains** to and from the city are fairly limited. Of the four daily services to **Mumbai** (6hr 45min–8hr), all of which stop at **Nasik Road** (3–4hr), the most convenient is the heavily booked *Devgiri Express* #7058, which departs daily at 11.25pm and arrives in CST (VT) at 7.10am, though it's often subject to lengthy delays. Otherwise, the #7618 *Jan Shatabdi Express*, leaving Aurangabad daily at 6am and arriving at CST at 12.45pm, and the #2072 *Tapovan Express*, leaving at 2.35pm and arriving in CST at 10.05pm, are usually more dependable alternatives. **Hyderabad**/Secunderabad is served by four to eight trains daily (10hr–15hr 30min), most convenient of which is the #7063 *Ajanta Express*, leaving at 10.40pm. There's a single daily train to Delhi, but **Jalgaon**, the nearest mainline station, 166km north, is served by far more services to many more destinations.

There are twice-daily **flights** with Jet Airways (☎0240/244 1392), and daily services with Air India (☎0240/248 5421) and Kingfisher Airlines to **Mumbai** from Aurangabad's Chikal Thana airport, the Air India flight continuing to **Delhi**. JetLite (☎0240/248 7076) runs a direct daily service to Delhi. The offices of Air India and Jet Airways are both on Jalna Road, en route to the airport; JetLite and Kingfisher maintain counters at the airport.

A counter at the airport (open at flight arrival times) provides arrival information, while more detailed enquiries are fielded at the Tourist Reception Centre in the MTDC *Holiday Resort* complex on Station Road East, where helpful offices of both **India Tourism** (Mon–Fri 8.30am–6pm, Sat 8.30am–1.30pm; ☎0240/233 1217) and **MTDC** (Mon–Fri plus the first and third Sat of the month 10am–5.45pm; ☎0240/233 1513) are housed on the first floor; Chandrashekar Jaiswal is a mine of information at the latter.

An efficient **foreign exchange** service is provided at Trade Wings (daily 9am–7pm) on Dr Ambedkhar Road, while there's an ICICI Bank **ATM**, as well as a couple of **internet** cafés (around Rs40/hr), opposite the MTDC *Holiday Resort*.

City transport and tours

Aurangabad's sights lie too far apart to take in on foot. The city is, however, buzzing with **auto-rickshaws**; longer sightseeing trips work out much cheaper if you settle on a fare in advance (from around Rs400/day). Taxis can be hailed in the street or found at the railway station and **cars with drivers** can be hired through travel agents such as the efficient Classic Travel (☎0240/233 7788,

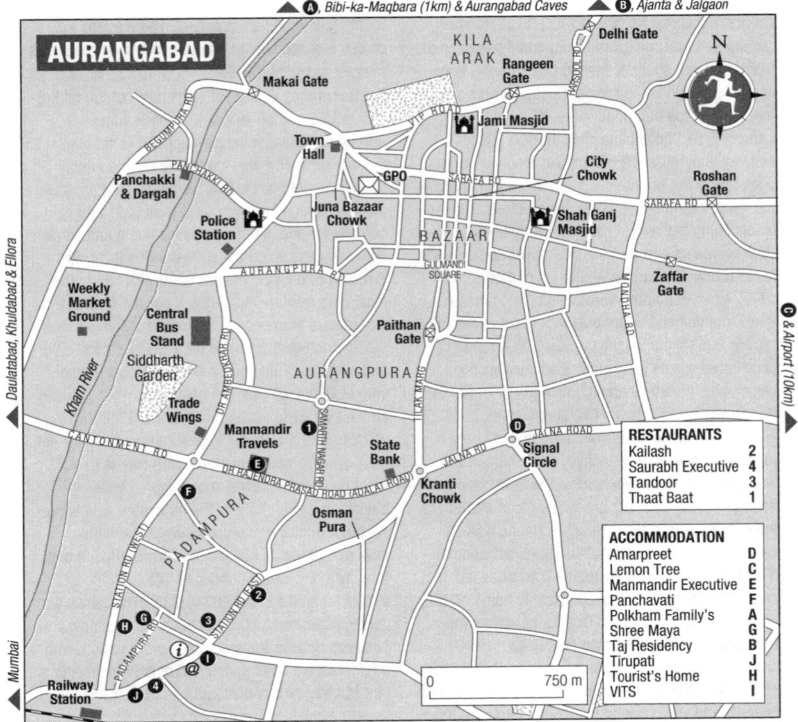

ⓔcontact@classicservices.in), on the ground floor of the Tourist Reception Centre in the MTDC *Holiday Resort* complex. For an eight-hour day, expect to pay Rs800–1000, depending on the size and comfort of the car. Trips beyond the city environs will usually be charged per kilometre (Rs10/km is standard), and there's an additional overnight charge of around Rs350.

Various companies run daily guided **tours** of Aurangabad and the surrounding area, all operating to the same itineraries and departure times, and all generally rushed. **Ellora and City** tours usually include the Bibi-ka-Maqbara, Panchakki, Daulatabad Fort, Aurangzeb's tomb at Khuldabad and the Ellora caves (though not the Aurangabad ones). **Ajanta** tours go to the caves only, but it's a long round trip to make in a day – if you want to spend more time at the site, stay at Fardapur (see p.650) or travel on to Jalgaon (see p.654). Classic Travel (see opposite) runs the best of the tours (Ellora and City Rs230, Ajanta Rs350), using smaller vehicles with a greater level of comfort.

Accommodation

Aurangabad's proximity to some of India's most important monuments, together with its new "boom-city" status, ensures a profusion of **hotels**. On the whole, standards tend to be high and prices very reasonable, particularly in the budget places, which cluster near the railway station. For local **B&Bs**, including a very comfortable, modern farmstay 18km southwest of town (Rs5500), contact MTDC. All hotels have 24-hour checkout unless otherwise stated.

Amarpreet Jalna Rd ⓣ0240/621 1133, ⓦwww.amarpreethotel.com. Smart mid-scale place, on a main road just south of the old city, offering large, comfortably furnished rooms. Quality non-veg restaurant, plus bar. Good value. ❼

Lemon Tree Chikalthana ⓣ0240/660 3030, ⓦwww.lemontreehotels.com. Set around a large pool, this is the brightest, cheeriest – and certainly the most fragrant – of the upper-bracket business hotels lining the airport road. The unfussy *Citrus Café* serves up some of the city's best non-veg. ❽

Manmandir Executive Adalat Rd ⓣ0240/236 5777, ⓦwww.manmandirmotels.com. Immaculately maintained budget business hotel above the private bus terminus (see p.536), with a range of good-sized rooms (non-a/c is particularly good value), plus a very clean a/c dorm (Rs150). ❹–❻

Panchavati Off Station Rd West ⓣ0240/232 8755, ⓦwww.hotelpanchavati.com. A couple of dozen neat, clean rooms (all attached; some a/c) on the western edge of the city centre. The best choice in its price range, and staff are very welcoming. ❸–❹

Polkam Family's Nipat Niranjan Nagar, New Pahadsingpura ⓣ0240/240 0916. Aurangabad's nicest B&B: three homely rooms (two attached) in a charming and peaceful Muslim family home on the edge of town between the Bibi-ka-Maqbara and the caves. Book direct or via MTDC. ❹

Shree Maya Bharuka Complex, Padampura Rd, off Station Rd West ⓣ0240/233 3093. Friendly and very popular place with large, cleanish rooms (some a/c; all attached). There's also a chilled and sociable restaurant with good food, plus internet terminal. ❷–❸

Taj Residency Ajanta Rd, 4km north of the centre ⓣ0240/661 3737, ⓦwww.tajhotels.com. Aurangabad's most luxurious option is set in a domed, gleaming-white wedding cake confection. Rooms (printed tariffs from around $160) are tastefully finished in dark wood, all with bath tubs and balcony/terrace, and facilities include a spa, large pool and croquet on the palm-fringed lawn. ❾

Tirupati Station Rd East ⓣ0240/233 3814. The most clued-up and colourful, if not the cheapest, of a parade of snazzy new "executive lodgings" (both a/c and non-a/c) opposite the railway station. The better rooms, kitted out in pastel colours, come with LCD TVs. ❹–❺

Tourist's Home Station Rd West ⓣ0240/233 7212 or ⓣ9326 262611. Best of the cheapies, set on a quiet, rambling campus, with rooms to suit most pockets. Smartest rooms (some with balconies and a/c) are in the renovated new wing, set back from the main road, while the high-ceilinged old wing has simple dorms (Rs150) and the city's cheapest doubles. ❷–❹

VITS Station Rd East ⓣ0240/235 0701, ⓦwww.vitshotelaurangabad.com. This ambitious new business hotel is the smartest central option, with an impressive atrial space and plush rooms with a hint of style, plus a pool and wi-fi. Big discounts usually available. Breakfast included. ❽

The City

The old city, laid out on a grid by Malik Amber in the early seventeenth century, still forms the core of Aurangabad's large **bazaar** area. It's best approached via **Gulmandi Square** to the south, along any of several streets lined with colourful shops and stalls. Sections of Aurangzeb's city wall survive, though more impressive is the network of city **gates**, some of which have been restored to something approaching their former glory.

On the left bank of the Kham River, on Panchakki Road, is an unusual watermill known as the **Panchakki** (daily 6.15am–9.15pm; Rs20 [Rs5], free on Fri). Water pumped underground from a reservoir in the hills 6km away drives a small grindstone, once used to mill flour, and collects in an attractive fish-filled tank, shaded by a large banyan tree. The Panchakki forms part of the **Dargah** of Baba Shah Muzaffar, a religious compound built by Aurangzeb as a memorial to his spiritual mentor, a Chishti mystic. The complex makes a lively place to wander around in the early evening with lots of chai shops, *mehendi* (henna hand-painting) artists and souvenir shops.

The Bibi-ka-Maqbara

Although the most impressive Islamic monument in the whole of Maharashtra, Aurangabad's Mughal tomb-garden, the **Bibi-ka-Maqbara** (daily sunrise–10pm; Rs100 [Rs5]), has always suffered from comparison with the Taj Mahal, built forty years earlier, of which it's an obvious imitation. Completed in 1678, the mausoleum was dedicated by **Prince Azam Shah** to the memory of his mother **Begum Rabi'a Daurani**, Aurangzeb's wife. Lack of resources dogged the 25-year project, and the end result fell far short of expectations. Looking at the mausoleum from beyond the ornamental gardens and redundant fountains in front of it, the truncated minarets and ungainly entrance arch make the Bibi-ka-Maqbara appear ill-proportioned compared with the elegant height and symmetry of the Taj, an impression not enhanced by the abrupt discontinuation of marble after the first 2m – allegedly a cost-saving measure.

An enormous brass-inlaid **door** – decorated with Persian calligraphy naming the maker, the year of its installation and chief architect – gives access to the archetypal *charbagh* garden complex. Of the two entrances to the mausoleum itself, one leads to the inner balcony while the second drops through another beautiful door to the **vault** (visitors may no longer climb the minarets). Inside, an exquisite octagonal **lattice-screen** of white marble surrounds the raised plinth supporting Rabi'a Daurani's grave. Like her husband's in nearby Khuldabad, it is "open" as a sign of humility. The unmarked grave beside it is said to be that of the empress's nurse.

The caves

Carved out of a steep-sided spur of the Sahyadri range overlooking the Bibi-ka-Maqbara, Aurangabad's own **caves** (sunrise–sunset; Rs100 [Rs5]), around 3.5km from the city centre, bear no comparison to those in nearby Ellora and Ajanta, but their fine **sculpture** makes a worthwhile introduction to rock-cut architecture. In addition, the infrequently visited site is peaceful and pleasant in itself, with commanding views over the city and surrounding countryside.

The caves, all Buddhist, consist of two groups, eastern and western (a third group is inaccessible), around 500m apart. The majority were excavated between the fourth and eighth centuries, under the patronage of two successive dynasties: the **Vakatkas**, who ruled the western Deccan from Nasik, and the **Chalukyas**, a powerful Mysore family who emerged during the sixth century. All except the much earlier Cave 4, which is a *chaitya* hall, are of the *vihara* (monastery) type, belonging to the Mahayana school of Buddhism. **Cave 3** is the most impressive of the western group, with vivid friezes adorning the pillars in the main chamber. In the eastern group, Cave 6 has some finely carved *bodhisattvas*, but it's the superb sculpture in **Cave 7** that provides the real highlight, including a couple of zaftig representations of Tara and, to the left of the Buddha in the sanctuary, a celebrated frieze showing a dancer in classic pose accompanied by six female musicians.

The most practical way of **getting to the caves** is by auto-rickshaw; a round-trip encompassing the Bibi-ka-Maqbara and caves should cost around Rs200.

Eating and drinking

Aurangabad is chock-full of places to eat, with most restaurants serving either strictly vegetarian **Gujarati** food or meat-oriented north Indian Muslim dishes. As elsewhere in the state, non-veg places tend to be synonymous with dim lights, drawn curtains and a male clientele – exceptions are noted below – while the veg restaurants attract families. **Drinking** is an exclusively male preserve, usually carried out in the many specially segregated bars (aka "permit rooms"), with the exception of the larger, more tourist-oriented hotels and restaurants.

Kailash *Nandavan Hotel*, Station Rd East. Well turned out but good-value pure-veg café, popular with local workers, featuring the usual mix of tasty south Indian and Punjabi specialities. Mains Rs50–60.

Saurabh Executive Station Rd East, opposite MTDC office. Beyond the unassuming, narrow-fronted facade, this salubrious new business-oriented joint dishes up some of Aurangabad's finest non-veg. Highlights include the

Tashtari platter, a mouthwatering array of tandoori bites (Rs175), and some sinfully rich Mughlai mains (try the *murgh makhani*); there are also some western dishes for the homesick. Mains from Rs80.

Tandoor Shyam Chambers, Station Rd East. Dominated by an imposing bust of Egyptian pharaoh Tutankhamun, this welcoming traveller's favourite is one of the city's best-established non-veg restaurants. Tandoori chicken and mutton kebabs are the house specialities, while for monster appetites there's the full-on "sizzling tandoori platter" (Rs495 and copious enough for two). Mains Rs90–250.

Thaat Baat Beneath *Embassy Hotel*, near Vivekanand College, Samarth Nagar Rd. There's a festive air at this fun, family-friendly thali place, where armies of smartly dressed young waiters breezily ladle out dollops of tasty pure-veg against a backdrop of Rajasthani puppets, paintings and handicrafts. Arrive hungry. Unlimited thalis Rs110.

Daulatabad

Dominating the horizon 13km northwest of Aurangabad, the awesome hilltop citadel of **DAULATABAD** crowns a massive conical volcanic outcrop whose sides have been shaped into a sheer sixty-metre wall of granite. Not least for the panoramic **views** from the top of the hill, Daulatabad makes a rewarding pause en route to or from the caves at Ellora, 17km northwest.

It was the eleventh-century **Yadavas** who were responsible for scraping away the jagged lower slopes of the mount – originally known as **Deogiri**, "Hill of the Gods" – to form its vertical-cliff base, as well as the fifteen-metre-deep moat that encircles the upper portion of the citadel. Muslim occupation of Deogiri began in earnest with the arrival in 1327 of sultan Ghiyas-ud-Din **Tughluq**, who decreed that his entire court should decamp here from Delhi, an epic 1100-kilometre march that cost thousands of lives, and ultimately proved futile – within seventeen years, drought and famine had forced the beleaguered ruler to return to Delhi. Thereafter, the fortress fell to a succession of different regimes, including Shah Jahan's **Mughals** in 1633, before it was finally taken by the **Marathas** midway through the eighteenth century.

The fortress

Beyond the formidable sets of outer defences which enclose a series of high-walled courtyards at the foot of the hill, Daulatabad's labyrinthine **fortress** (daily 6am–6pm; Rs100 [Rs5]) unfolds around the enormous **Chand Minar**, or "Victory Tower", erected in 1435. The Persian blue-and-turquoise tiles that once plastered it in complex geometric patterns have disappeared, but it remains an impressive spectacle, rising from the ruins of the city that once sprawled from its base. The **Jama Masjid**, back along the main path, is Daulatabad's oldest Islamic monument. Built in 1318, the well-preserved mosque comprises 106 pillars plundered from the Hindu and Jain temples which previously stood on the site. It now functions as a Bharatmata temple, much to the chagrin of local Muslims. Adjoining the mosque, the large stone-lined "Elephant" **tank** was once a central component in the fort's extensive water-supply system. Two giant terracotta pipes channelled water from the hills into Deogiri's legendary fruit and vegetable gardens.

From the Chand Minar, the main walkway continues through another set of bastions and fortified walls before emerging close to the **Chini Mahal**, or "Chinese Palace". The impressive **Mendha Tope** ("Ram-headed Cannon"), inscribed in Persian, rests on a squat stone tower just above. From here onwards, a sequence of macabre traps lay in wait for the unwary intruder. First, a moat infested with man-eating crocodiles (now spanned by an iron bridge) had to be crossed to reach the main citadel. Next the attackers would have had to clamber through a maze of claustrophobic, zigzagging passageways, the last of which was closed with an iron cover that could be heated to generate toxic gases.

From the final tunnel, it's a fairly steep ten-minute climb up a broad flight of steps to the **Baradari**, an attractive octagonal pavilion used by Shah Jahan during his visits to Daulatabad. The **views** from the flat roof of the building are superb, but an even more impressive panorama is to be had from the **look-out post** perched on the summit of the hill, marked with another grand cannon.

Practicalities

Although Daulatabad features on the guided **tours** of Ellora from Aurangabad (see p.637), you'll have more time to enjoy it by travelling here on one of the shuttle **buses** every 30min between Aurangabad and the caves. From Daulatabad, it is easy to catch another bus or shared taxi on to Khuldabad and Ellora; the stop is directly opposite the main entrance to the fort. If you're not on a tour, try to arrive early as the place is often overrun with schoolchildren, and bring a torch as some of the passages in the fort are pitch-black and hopelessly confusing – one reason why you might also consider hiring a guide (Rs600).

Khuldabad

Nestled on a saddle of high ground, 22km from Aurangabad and just 4km from Ellora, **KHULDABAD**, also known as **Rauza**, is an old walled town famous for a wonderful crop of onion-domed **tombs**. Among the Muslim notables deemed worthy of a patch of earth in this most hallowed of burial grounds ("Khuldabad" means "Heavenly Abode") were the emperor Aurangzeb himself, who raised the town's granite battlements and seven fortified gateways, a couple of nizams, and a fair few of the town's Chishti founding fathers.

The last of the great Mughals' tomb lies inside a whitewashed **dargah** (sunrise–10pm; donation), midway between the North and South gates. The grave itself is a humble affair decorated only by the fresh flower petals scattered by visitors, open to the elements instead of sealed in stone. The devout emperor insisted that it be paid for not out of the royal coffers, but with the money he raised in the last years of life by selling his own hand-quilted white skullcaps. Aurangzeb chose this as his final resting place primarily because of the presence, next door, of **Sayeed Zain-ud-Din**'s tomb, which occupies a quadrangle separating Aurangzeb's grave from those of his wife and second son, Azam Shah. Locked away behind a small door in the mausoleum is Khuldabad's most jealously guarded relic, the **Robe of the Prophet**, revealed to the public once a year on the twelfth day of the Islamic month of Rabi-ul-Awwal, when the tomb attracts worshippers from all over India. Directly opposite Zain-ud-din's tomb is the **Dargah of Sayeed Burhan-ud-Din** (same hours), a Chishti missionary buried here in 1334. The shrine is said to contain hairs from the Prophet's beard which magically increase in number when they are counted each year.

MSRTC **buses** running every 30min between Aurangabad and Ellora stop at Khuldabad's small bus stand, a ten-minute walk from the tombs. Bring plenty of small change as you'll be expected to be liberal with tips.

Ellora

Palaces will decay, bridges will fall, and the noblest structures must give way to the corroding tooth of time; whilst the caverned temples of Ellora shall rear their indestructible and hoary heads in stern loneliness, the glory of past ages, and the admiration of ages yet to come.

Captain Seely, *The Wonders of Ellora*

Admission to the caves

Admission to the Ellora caves (Wed–Mon dawn to dusk) costs Rs250 for foreigners, or Rs10 for Indians. The complex is **closed on Tuesdays**.

Maharashtra's most visited ancient monument, the **ELLORA** caves, 29km northwest of Aurangabad, may not enjoy as grand a setting as their older cousins at Ajanta, but the amazing wealth of **sculpture** they contain more than compensates, and this is an unmissable stop if you're heading to or from Mumbai, 400km southwest. In all, 34 Buddhist, Hindu and Jain caves – some excavated simultaneously, in competition – line the foot of the two-kilometre-long Chamadiri escarpment as it tumbles down to meet the open plains. The site's principal attraction, the colossal **Kailash temple**, rears from a huge, sheer-edged cavity cut from the hillside – a vast lump of solid basalt fashioned into a spectacular complex of colonnaded halls, galleries and shrines.

Some history

The original reason why this apparently remote spot became the focus of so much religious and artistic activity was the busy **caravan route** that passed through here on its way between the prosperous cities to the north and the ports of the west coast. Profits from the lucrative trade fuelled a five-hundred-year spate of excavation, beginning midway through the sixth century AD at around the same time that Ajanta, 100km northeast, was abandoned. This was the twilight of the **Buddhist** era in central India; by the end of the seventh century, **Hinduism** had begun to reassert itself. The Brahmanical resurgence gathered momentum over the next three hundred years under the patronage of the Chalukya and Rashtrakuta kings – the two powerful dynasties responsible for the bulk of the work carried out at Ellora, including the eighth-century Kailash temple. A third and final flourish of activity on the site took place towards the end of the first millennium AD, after the local rulers had switched allegiance from Shaivism to the **Jain** faith. A small cluster of more subdued caves to the north of the main group stand as reminders of this age.

Unlike the isolated site of Ajanta, Ellora did not escape the iconoclasm that accompanied the arrival of the **Muslims** in the thirteenth century. The worst excesses were committed during the reign of Aurangzeb who ordered the demolition of the site's "heathen idols". Although Ellora still bears the scars from this time, most of its best pieces of sculpture have remained remarkably well preserved, sheltered from centuries of monsoon downpours by the hard basalt hillside.

Ellora practicalities

Most visitors use Aurangabad as a base for day-trips to the caves, **getting to Ellora** either via the MSRTC buses every 30min or on a guided **tour** (see p.637). These tours are very rushed, however; if you prefer to take in the caves at a more leisurely pace and climb Daulatabad Hill, either spend the night at Ellora or leave Aurangabad early in the morning. Official multilingual **guides** are on hand to take you on a tour of the most interesting caves (groups of up to five people Rs600–750). Travelling back to Aurangabad, it's often quickest to jump in a shared taxi as they ply the route more frequently than buses.

Ellora's best **place to stay**, right opposite the caves, is the peaceful *Hotel Kailas* (ⓣ02437/244543, ⓦwww.hotelkailas.com; ❹–❻), a small campus of well-maintained chalets with private sitouts, and a fewer cheaper rooms closer to the

Rock-cut caves of the northwestern Deccan

The **rock-cut caves** scattered across the volcanic hills of the northwestern Deccan rank among the most extraordinary religious monuments in Asia. Ranging from tiny monastic cells to elaborately carved temples, they are remarkable for having been hewn by hand from solid rock. Their third-century BC origins seem to have been as temporary shelters for Buddhist monks when heavy monsoon rains brought their travels to a halt. Modelled on earlier wooden structures, most were sponsored by **merchants**, for whom the casteless new faith offered an attractive alternative to the old, discriminatory social order. Gradually, encouraged by the example of the Mauryan emperor Ashoka, the local ruling dynasties also began to embrace Buddhism. Under their patronage, during the second century BC, the first large-scale monastery caves were created at **Karla**, **Bhaja** and **Ajanta**.

Around this time, the austere **Hinayana** ("Lesser Vehicle") school of Buddhism predominated in India. Caves cut in this era were mostly simple worship halls, or **chaityas** – long, rectangular apsed chambers with barrel-vaulted roofs and two narrow colonnaded aisles curving gently around the back of a monolithic **stupa**. Symbols of the Buddha's Enlightenment, these hemispherical burial mounds provided the principal focus for worship and meditation, circumambulated by the monks during their communal rituals.

By the fourth century AD, the Hinayana school was losing ground to the more exuberant **Mahayana** ("Greater Vehicle") school. Its emphasis on an ever-enlarging pantheon of **bodhisattvas** (merciful saints who postponed their accession to nirvana to help mankind towards Enlightenment) was accompanied by a transformation in architectural styles. *Chaityas* were superseded by lavish monastery halls, or **viharas**, in which the monks both lived and worshipped, and the once-prohibited image of the Buddha became far more prominent. Occupying the circumambulatory recess at the end of the hall, where the *stupa* formerly stood, the colossal **icon** acquired the 32 characteristics, or **lakshanas** (including long dangling ear-lobes, cranial protuberance, short curls, robe and halo) by which the Buddha was distinguished from lesser divinities. The peak of Mahayanan art came towards the end of the Buddhist age. Drawing on the rich catalogue of themes and images contained in ancient scriptures such as the **Jatakas** (legends relating to the Buddha's previous incarnations), Ajanta's exquisite wall **painting** may, in part, have been designed to rekindle enthusiasm for the faith, which was, by this point, already starting to wane in the region.

Attempts to compete with the resurgence of **Hinduism**, from the sixth century onwards, eventually led to the evolution of another, more esoteric religious movement. The **Vajrayana**, or "Thunderbolt" sect stressed the female creative principle, **shakti**, with arcane rituals combining spells and magic formulas. Ultimately, however, such modifications were to prove powerless against the growing allure of Brahmanism.

The ensuing shift in royal and popular patronage is best exemplified by **Ellora** where, during the eighth century, many old *viharas* were converted into temples, their shrines housing polished *shivalinga* instead of *stupas* and Buddhas. Hindu cave architecture, with its dramatic mythological **sculpture**, culminated in the tenth century with the magnificent **Kailash temple**, a giant replica of the freestanding structures that had already begun to replace rock-cut caves. It was Hinduism that bore the brunt of the iconoclastic medieval descent of Islam on the Deccan, Buddhism having long since fled to the comparative safety of the Himalayas, where it still flourishes.

road, plus a decent restaurant. Moderately priced veg and non-veg **food** is available inside the complex at the MTDC restaurant (9am–5pm), which also serves beer, though you'll eat better at *Kailas*'s slightly pricier restaurant and from the roadside *dhabas* opposite the bus stand.

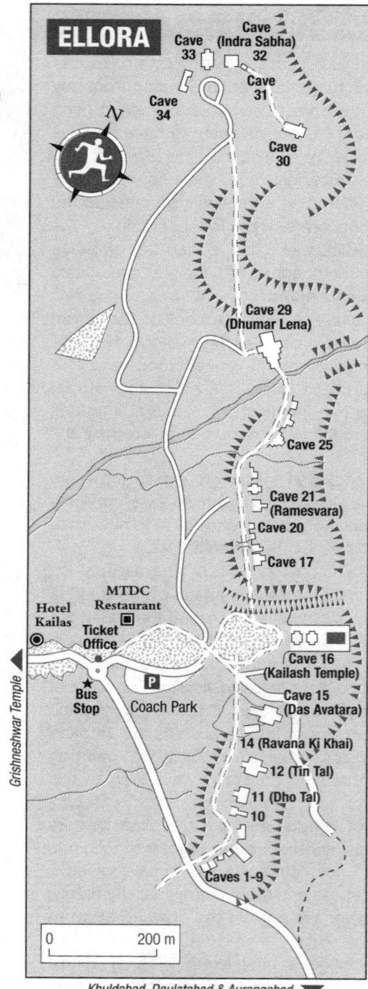

The caves

All the **caves** are numbered, following a roughly chronological plan. Numbers 1 to 12, at the south end of the site, are the oldest, from the Vajrayana Buddhist era (500–750 AD). The Hindu caves, 13 to 29, overlap with the later Buddhist ones and date from between 600 and 870 AD. Further north, the Jain caves – 30 to 34 – were excavated from 800 AD until the late eleventh century. Because of the sloping hillside, most of the cave entrances are set back from the level ground behind open courtyards and large colonnaded verandas or porches.

A new **visitor centre** is set to open at the caves in 2012, and promises to provide an excellent introduction to cave art. To see the oldest caves first, turn right opposite Cave 16, the vast Kailash temple, and follow the main pathway down to Cave 1. From here, work your way gradually northwards again, avoiding the temptation to look around Cave 16, which is best saved until late afternoon when the bus parties have all left and the long shadows cast by the setting sun bring its extraordinary stonework to life.

The Buddhist group

The **Buddhist caves** line the sides of a gentle recess in the Chamadiri escarpment. All except Cave 10 are *viharas*, or monastery halls, which the monks would originally have used for study, solitary meditation and communal worship, as well as the mundane business of eating and sleeping. As you progress through them, the chambers grow steadily more impressive in scale and tone. Scholars attribute this to the rise of Hinduism and the need to compete for patronage with the more overtly awe-inspiring Shaivite cave-temples being excavated so close at hand.

Caves 1 to 9

Cave 2 is the first cave of interest, a large central chamber supported by twelve massive, square-based pillars while the aisles are lined with seated Buddhas. The doorway into the shrine room is flanked by two giant, bejewelled *dvarpalas*, or guardian figures: an unusually muscular Padmapani, the *bodhisattva* of compassion, on the left, and an opulent Maitreya, the "Buddha-to-come", on the right. Both are accompanied by their consorts. Inside the sanctum itself, a stately Buddha is seated on a lion throne, looking stronger and more determined than his serene forerunners in Ajanta. **Caves 3 and 4** lack the artifice of Cave 2, though the latter retains some fine capital work. **Cave 5** is the largest single-storeyed *vihara* in Ellora. Its enormous 36-metre-long rectangular assembly hall is thought to have been used by the monks as a refectory, and has two rows of benches carved from the stone floor.

Caves 6–9 were excavated at roughly the same time in the seventh century, and are reached via a single door and stairwell cut into the rock. On the walls of the antechamber at the far end of the central hall in **Cave 6** are two of Ellora's most famous and finely executed figures: Tara, the buxom female consort of the *bodhisattva* Avalokitesvara, stands to the left; on the opposite side, the Buddhist goddess of learning, Mahamayuri, is depicted with her emblem, the peacock, while a diligent student sets a good example at his desk below. From Cave 6, a short flight of steps leads up to diminutive **Cave 9**, with a fine frieze decorating the facade.

Caves 10, 11 and 12

Excavated in the early eighth century, **Cave 10** is one of the last and most magnificent of the Deccan's rock-cut *chaitya* halls. Steps lead from the left of its large veranda to an upper balcony, where a trefoil doorway flanked by flying threesomes, heavenly nymphs and a frieze of playful dwarfs leads to an interior balcony. Inside the long apsidal hall (which you may need to ask to be unlocked), the rib-vaulting effect on the ceiling imitates the beams that would have appeared in earlier freestanding wooden structures. A slender Buddha sits enthroned in front of a votive *stupa*, the hall's devotional centrepiece.

In spite of the rediscovery in 1876 of its hitherto hidden basement, **Cave 11** continues to be known as the **Dho Tal**, or "Two Floors" cave. Its top storey is a long columned assembly hall housing a Buddha shrine and, on its rear wall, images of Durga and Ganesh, the elephant-headed son of Shiva – evidence that the cave was converted into a Hindu temple after being abandoned by the Buddhists. **Cave 12** next door – the **Tin Tal**, or "three floors" – is another triple-storeyed *vihara*, approached via a large open courtyard. Again, the main highlights are on the uppermost level. The shrine room at the end of the hall, whose walls are lined with five large *bodhisattvas*, is flanked on both sides by seven Buddhas – one for each of the Master's previous incarnations.

The Hindu group

Ellora's seventeen **Hindu caves** are grouped around the middle of the escarpment, to either side of the majestic Kailash temple. Excavated at the start of the Brahmanical revival in the Deccan during a time of relative stability, the cave-temples throb with a vitality absent from their restrained Buddhist predecessors. In place of benign-faced Buddhas, huge **bas-reliefs** line the walls, writhing with dynamic scenes from the Hindu scriptures. Most are connected with **Shiva**, the god of destruction and regeneration (and the presiding deity in all of the Hindu caves on the site), although you'll also come across numerous images of Vishnu (the Preserver) and his various incarnations.

The same tableaux crop up time and again, a repetition that gave Ellora's craftsmen ample opportunity to refine their technique over the years leading up to their greatest achievement, the **Kailash temple** (Cave 16). Covered separately (see p.646), the temple is the highlight of any visit to Ellora, but you'll appreciate its beautiful sculpture all the more if you visit the earlier Hindu caves first. Numbers 14 and 15, immediately south, are the best of the bunch if you're pushed for time.

Cave 14

Dating from the start of the seventh century AD, and among the last of the early excavations, **Cave 14** was a Buddhist *vihara* converted into a temple by the Hindus. The entrance to the bare sanctum is guarded by two impressive river goddesses, Ganga and Yamuna, while lining the ambulatory wall behind and to the right, seven heavy-breasted fertility goddesses, the **Sapta Matrikas**, dandle chubby babies on their laps. Shiva's elephant-headed son, Ganesh, sits to their right beside two cadaverous apparitions, Kala and Kali, the goddesses of death. Superb **friezes** adorn the cave's long side-walls.

Cave 15

Like its neighbour, the two-storeyed **Cave 15**, reached via a long flight of steps, began life as a Buddhist *vihara* but was hijacked by the Hindus and became a Shiva shrine. Behind the Natya Mandapa ("Hall of Dance") in the centre of the courtyard, make for the upper level of the main structure to find some of Ellora's most magnificent sculpture. The cave's name, **Das Avatara,** is derived from the sequence of panels along the right wall, which show five of **Vishnu**'s ten incarnations (*avatars*).

A carved panel in a recess to the right of the antechamber shows Shiva emerging from a lingam. Brahma and Vishnu stand before the apparition in humility and supplication – symbolizing the supremacy of Shaivism in the region at the time the conversion work was carried out. Finally, halfway down the left wall of the chamber as you're facing the shrine, the cave's most elegant piece of sculpture shows Shiva, as Nataraja, poised in a classical dance pose.

Caves 17 to 29

Only three of the Hindu caves strung along the hillside north of the Kailash temple are really worth exploring in depth. **Cave 21** – the **Ramesvara** – was excavated late in the sixth century. Thought to be the oldest Hindu cave at Ellora, it harbours some well-executed sculpture, including a fine pair of river goddesses on either side of the veranda, two wonderful door guardians and some sensuous loving couples, or *mithunas*, dotted around the walls of the balcony. **Cave 25**, further along, contains a striking image on the exterior ceiling of the main shrine of the sun-god **Surya** speeding in his chariot towards the dawn.

From here, the path picks its way past two more excavations, then drops steeply across the face of a sheer cliff to the bottom of a small river gorge. Once under the seasonal **waterfall**, the trail climbs the other side of the gully to emerge beside **Cave 29**, the huge **Dhumar Lena**. Dating from the late sixth century, the cave boasts an unusual cross-shaped floor plan similar to the Elephanta cave in Mumbai harbour. Pairs of rampant lions guard its three staircases while, inside, the walls are covered with huge **friezes**. On the right-hand side of the (southern) entrance, a dice-playing scene shows Shiva teasing Parvati by holding her arm back as she prepares to throw. Left of the exit, Shiva skewers the Andhaka demon, while in the opposite wall panel he foils the many-armed Ravana's attempts to shake him and Parvati off the top of Mount Kailash; look for the cheeky dwarf baring his bum to taunt the evil demon.

The Kailash temple (Cave 16)

Cave 16, the colossal **Kailash temple**, is Ellora's masterpiece. Here, the term "cave" is not only a gross understatement but a complete misnomer. For although the temple was, like the other excavations, hewn from solid rock, it bears a striking resemblance to earlier freestanding structures in south India. The monolith is believed to have been the brainchild of the Rashtrakuta ruler **Krishna I** (756–773).

One hundred years and four generations of kings, architects and craftsmen elapsed, however, before the project was completed. Climb up the track leading along the lip of the compound's north-facing cliff to the ledge overlooking the squat main tower, and you'll see why.

The sheer scale is staggering. Work began by digging three deep trenches into the top of the hill using pickaxes and lengths of wood which, soaked with water and stuffed into narrow cracks, expanded to crumble the basalt. Once a huge chunk of raw rock had been exposed in this way, the royal sculptors set to work. In all, around a quarter of a million tonnes of chippings and debris were cut from the hillside, with no room for improvisation or error. The temple was conceived as a giant replica of Shiva and Parvati's Himalayan abode, the pyramidal **Mount Kailash**. Today, all but a few fragments of the thick coat of white-lime plaster that gave the temple the appearance of a snowy mountain have flaked off, to expose elaborately carved surfaces of grey-brown stone beneath. Around the rear of the tower, these have been bleached and blurred by centuries of erosion, as if the giant sculpture is slowly melting in the fierce Deccan heat.

The temple

The main **entrance** to the temple is through a tall stone screen, intended to mark the transition from the profane to the sacred realms. After passing between two guardian river goddesses, Ganga and Yamuna, you enter a narrow passage that opens onto the main forecourt, opposite a panel showing **Lakshmi**, the goddess of wealth, being lustrated by a pair of elephants. Custom requires pilgrims to circumambulate clockwise around Mount Kailash, so descend the steps to your left and head across the front of the courtyard towards the near corner.

From the top of the concrete steps in the corner, all three principal sections of the complex are visible: first, the shrine above the entrance housing Shiva's vehicle, **Nandi**, the bull; next, the intricate recessed walls of the main assembly hall, or **mandapa**, which still bear traces of the coloured plaster that originally coated the whole edifice; and finally, the sanctuary itself, surmounted by the stumpy, 29-metre, pyramidal tower, or **shikhara** (best viewed from above). These three components rest on an appropriately huge raised platform, borne by dozens of lotus-gathering elephants. As well as symbolizing Shiva's sacred mountain, the temple also represented a giant **chariot**. The transepts protruding from the side of the main hall are its wheels, the Nandi shrine its yoke, and the two life-sized, trunkless elephants in the front of the courtyard (disfigured by Muslim raiders) are the beasts of burden.

Most of the main highlights of the temple itself are confined to its sidewalls, which are plastered with vibrant **sculpture**. Lining the staircase that leads up to the north side of the *mandapa*, a long, lively narrative panel depicts scenes from the Mahabharata, and below this the life of **Krishna**. Continuing clockwise, the majority of the panels around the lower sections around the temple are devoted to **Shiva**. On the south side of the *mandapa*, in an alcove carved out of the most prominent projection, you'll find the finest piece of sculpture in the compound. It shows Shiva and Parvati being disturbed by the multi-headed **Ravana**, who has been incarcerated inside the sacred mountain and is now shaking the walls of his prison with his many arms. Shiva is about to assert his supremacy by calming the earthquake with a prod of his toe. Parvati, meanwhile, nonchalantly reclines on her elbow as one of her handmaidens flees in panic.

From here, head up the steps at the southwest corner of the courtyard to the **Hall of Sacrifices**, with its striking frieze of the seven mother goddesses, the Sapta Matrikas, and their ghoulish companions Kala and Kali (shown astride a heap of corpses). The sixteen-columned assembly hall is shrouded in a gloomy half-light designed to focus worshippers on the presence of the deity within. Using a portable arc light, the *chowkidar* will illuminate fragments of painting on the ceiling, where Shiva, as **Nataraja**, performs the dance of death.

The Jain group

Ellora's small cluster of four **Jain caves** is north of the main group, just a five-minute walk north along the path from Cave 29 or, alternatively, reachable from the Kailash temple via a curving asphalt road.

Excavated in the late ninth and tenth centuries, after the Hindu phase had petered out, the Jain caves are Ellora's swansong, featuring some fine decorative carving and a few exquisite paintings. Of principal interest is **Cave 32**, the **Indra Sabha** ("Indra's Assembly Hall"), a miniature version of the Kailash temple. The lower of its two levels is plain and incomplete, but the upper storey, guarded by huge *yaksha* and *yakshi* figures facing each other across the veranda, is crammed with elaborate stonework, notably the ornate pillars and the two *tirthankaras* guarding the entrance to the central shrine. The naked figure of Gomatesvara, on the right, is fulfilling a vow of silence in the forest. He is so deeply immersed in meditation that creepers have grown up his legs, and animals, snakes and scorpions crawl around his feet.

The Grishneshwar Mandir

Rising above the small village west of the caves, the cream-coloured *shikhara* of the eighteenth-century **Grishneshwar Mandir** pinpoints the location of one of India's oldest and most sacred deities. The lingam enshrined inside the temple's cavernous inner sanctum is one of the twelve "self-born" **jyotirlingas** ("linga of light"), thought to date back to the second century BC. Non-Hindus are allowed to join the queue for *darshan*, but men have to remove their shirts before entering the shrine itself.

Ajanta

Hewn from the near-vertical sides of a horseshoe-shaped ravine, the caves at **AJANTA** occupy a site worthy of the spectacular ancient art they contain. Less than two centuries ago, this remote spot was known only to local tribespeople; the shadowy entrances to its abandoned stone chambers lay buried deep under a thick blanket of creepers and jungle. The chance arrival in 1819 of a small detachment of East India Company troops, however, brought the caves' obscurity to an abrupt end. Led to the top of the precipitous bluff that overlooks the gorge by a young "half-wild" scout, the tiger-hunters spied what has now been identified as the facade of Cave 10 protruding through the foliage.

The British soldiers had made one of the most sensational archeological finds of all time. Further exploration revealed a total of 28 colonnaded caves chiselled out of the chocolate-brown and grey basalt cliffs lining the River Waghora. More remarkable still were the immaculately preserved **paintings** writhing over their interior surfaces. For, in addition to the rows of stone Buddhas and other **sculpture** enshrined within them, Ajanta's excavations are adorned with a swirling profusion of murals, depicting everything from battlefields to sailing ships, city streets and teeming animal-filled forests to snow-capped mountains. Even if you aren't wholly familiar with the narratives they portray, it's easy to see why these paintings are regarded as the finest surviving gallery of art from any of the world's ancient civilizations.

Admission to the Ajanta Caves

Admission to the Ajanta Caves (Tues–Sun 9am–5.30pm) costs Rs250 for foreigners, and Rs10 for Indians. Tickets are sold at the booth at the main entrance, a 4km bus ride from the Ajanta T-junction (see below). The complex is **closed on Mondays**.

In spite of its comparative remoteness, Ajanta receives an extraordinary number of visitors. If you want to enjoy the site in anything close to its original serenity, avoid coming on a weekend or public holiday – it takes a fertile imagination indeed to picture Buddhist monks filing softly around the rough stone steps when hundreds of riotous schoolkids and throngs of tourists are clambering over them. Among measures to minimize the impact of the hundreds of visitors who daily trudge through is a ban on **flash photography** – though the introduction of low-impact lighting has aided close viewing – and strict limits on the numbers allowed into the most interesting caves at any given time. Another significant move to reduce the ecological impact on the area has been the creation of the Ajanta T-junction (see below). The best **seasons to visit** are either during the monsoon, when the river is swollen and the gorge reverberates with the sound of the waterfalls, or during the cooler winter months between October and March. At other times, the relentless Deccan sun beating down on the south-facing rock can make a trip around Ajanta a real endurance test. Whenever you go, take a hat, some sunglasses, a good torch and plenty of drinking water.

Some history

Located close enough to the major trans-Deccan trade routes to ensure a steady supply of alms, yet far enough from civilization to preserve the peace and tranquillity necessary for meditation and prayer, Ajanta was an ideal location for the region's itinerant Buddhist monks to found their first permanent monasteries. Donative inscriptions indicate that its earliest cave excavations took place in the second century BC.

In its heyday, Ajanta sheltered more than two hundred monks, as well as a sizeable community of painters, sculptors and labourers employed in excavating and decorating the cells and sanctuaries. Sometime in the seventh century, however, the site was abandoned – whether because of the growing popularity of nearby Ellora, or the threat posed by the resurgence of Hinduism, no one knows. By the eighth century, the complex lay deserted and forgotten, overlooked even by the Muslim iconoclasts who wrought such damage to the area's other sacred sites during the medieval era.

Arrival and information

The only way of **getting to Ajanta**, unless you have your own transport, is by **bus**. All vehicles (including taxis) must terminate at **Ajanta T-junction**, 4km from the caves on the main Aurangabad–Jalgaon road, where you'll find a tourist complex with snack joints, toilets and hawker stalls; a new visitor centre is set to open here in 2012. It costs Rs7 to enter the complex; once inside, supposedly ecofriendly green buses regularly ply the route to and from the caves (non-a/c Rs7, a/c Rs12). All **MSRTC buses** between **Aurangabad**, 108km southwest, and the nearest railhead at **Jalgaon**, 58km north, stop at the T-junction on request. Provided you catch an early enough service up here, it's possible to see the caves, grab a bite to eat, and then head off again in either direction. You could alternatively do the round trip from Aurangabad on one of the rushed **tours** (see p.637), though Jalgaon makes a better base.

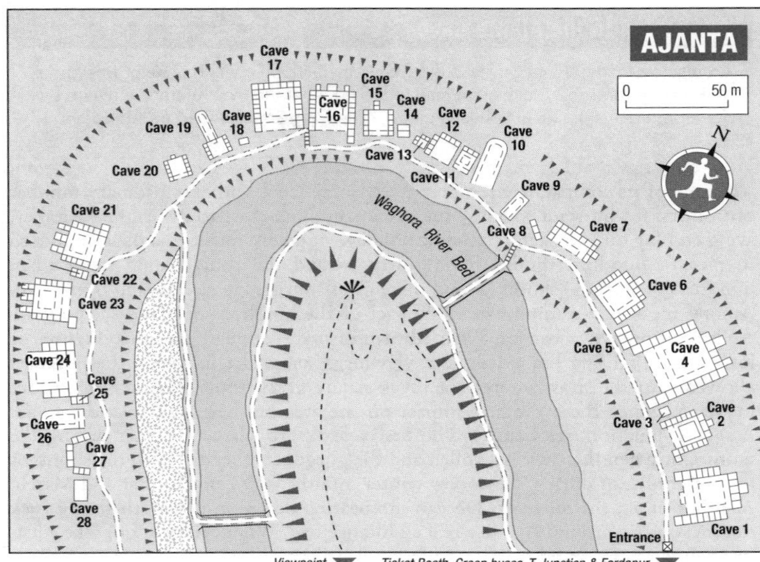

Accommodation and eating

Since the first bus from the T-junction to the caves doesn't leave till 9am, there's little advantage in staying locally, though there is some decent **accommodation**. The closest option, set in attractive gardens a short wander from the tourist complex and Ajanta bus stop, is MTDC's comfortable *T-Junction Guest House* (ⓣ02438/244230; ❺), with spacious, split-level rooms and private sitouts; the main drawback is that apart from the nearby snack stalls there's nowhere to eat. MTDC also offers cheaper chalet-style accommodation and a dorm (Rs150) in its *Holiday Resort* (same phone number; ❸–❹), 1.5km from the T-junction in the village of **Fardapur**, but the best budget alternative is the welcoming *Padmapani Park* (ⓣ02438/244280, ⓔpadmapanipark@yahoo.co.in; ❸–❹), with simple but clean attached rooms in a colourful block 1km further along the Jalgaon road at the edge of the village; phone ahead from the bus stand and they'll pick you up on arrival.

For **food**, at Ajanta itself you're limited to the uninspiring MTDC restaurant just outside the entrance to the caves, which serves veg and non-veg Punjabi dishes and thalis (until 6pm). The equally moribund MTDC dining hall at Fardapur (open to non-residents) serves an identical menu – unless you want beer, you're much better to make for the *Padmapani Park*'s popular and cheerful pure-veg restaurant. Alternatively, several typical Maharashtran roadside *dhabas* line the main highway between the two, including the *Hotel Ajanta*, which rustles up delicious chicken, fish and mutton masala with hot rotis freshly baked over a *shigdi* (charcoal) brazier.

The caves

An obvious path leads up from the admissions kiosk to the grand **Mahayana** *viharas*; if you'd prefer to see the caves in chronological order, however, start with the smaller **Hinayana** group of *chaitya* halls at the bottom of the river bend (caves 12, 10 & 9), then work your way back up, via Cave 17. For help getting up the steps, sedan-chair bearers (around Rs400), or *dhooli*-wallahs, stand in front of the stalls below, while porters (Rs100) are on hand to carry bags. Official **guides** make two-hour tours (Rs600) which can be arranged through the ticket office; most deliver an interesting spiel but you may well feel like taking in the sights again afterwards at a more leisurely pace.

Cave 1

There's always a queue for **Cave 1**, which contains some of the finest and stylistically most evolved paintings on the site. By the time work on it began, late in the fifth century, *viharas* served not only to shelter and feed the monks, but also as places of worship in their own right. In common with most Mahayana *viharas*, the extraordinary murals lining the walls and ceilings depict episodes from the *Jatakas*, tales of the birth and former lives of the Buddha.

Left of the doorway into the main shrine stands another masterpiece. **Padmapani**, the lotus-holding form of Avalokitesvara, is surrounded by an entourage of smaller attendants, divine musicians, lovers, monkeys and a peacock. His heavy almond eyes and languid hip-shot *tribhanga* (or "three-bend") pose exudes a distant and sublime calm. Opposite, flanking the right side of the doorway, is his counterpart, **Vajrapani**, the thunderbolt holder. Between them, these two *bodhisattvas* represent the dual aspects of Mahayana Buddhism: compassion and knowledge.

The real focal point of Cave 1, however, is the large sculpted Buddha seated in the shrine room – the finest such figure in Ajanta. Using portable electric spotlights, guides love to demonstrate how the expression on the Buddha's exquisitely carved face changes according to where the light is held.

On the way out, you should be able to spot this cave's other famous trompe-l'oeil, crowning one of the pillars (on the fourth pillar on the left as you face the exit): the figures of four apparently separate stags which, on closer inspection, all share the same head.

Cave 2

Cave 2 is another impressive Mahayana *vihara*, dating from the sixth century. Here, the ceiling is decorated with complex floral patterns, including lotus and medallion motifs. Sculpted friezes in the small subsidiary shrine to the right of the main chapel centre on a well-endowed fertility goddess, **Hariti**, the infamous child-eating ogress, and Kubera, the god of wealth. The side walls teem with lively **paintings** of the Jatakas and other mythological episodes. A mural on the left veranda shows the birth of the Buddha, emerging from under his mother's arm, and his conception when a white elephant appeared to her in a dream (bottom left).

Caves 3 to 9

Caves 3 is inaccessible but unfinished **Cave 4**, the largest *vihara* in the complex, is worth a quick look for its 28 pillars and huge Buddha. It's also worth popping into **Cave 6**, a double-storeyed *vihara* with a finely carved doorjamb and lintel around the entrance to its shrine room. Cave 8 is always closed; it contains the generator for the lights.

Cave 9, which dates from the first century BC, is the first *chaitya* you come to along the walkway. Resting in the half-light shed by a characteristic *peepal*-leaf-shaped window in the sculpted facade, the hemispherical **stupa**, with its inverted pyramidal reliquary, forms the devotional centrepiece of the fourteen-metre-long hall. The fragments of painting that remain, including the procession scene on the left wall, are mostly superimpositions over the top of earlier snake-deities – *nagarajas*.

Cave 10

Though, like Cave 9, marred by the unsightly wire meshing used to keep out bats, the facade of **Cave 10**, a second-century BC *chaitya* hall – the oldest of its kind in the ravine – is still a grand sight. The cave's main highlights, however, are far smaller and more subdued. Along the left wall, you may be able to pick out the fading traces of painting (now encased in glass) that depict a scene in which a raja and his retinue approach a group of dancers and musicians surrounding a garlanded *bodhi* tree – a symbol of the Buddha (the Hinayanas preferred not to depict him figuratively); it's believed to be the earliest surviving Buddhist mural in India. Elsewhere on the walls is graffiti scrawled by the British soldiers who rediscovered the caves in 1819.

The apsidal-ended hall itself, divided by three rows of painted octagonal pillars, is dominated by a huge monolithic **stupa** at its far end. If there's no one else around, try out the *chaitya*'s amazing acoustics.

Caves 16 and 17

The next cave of interest, **Cave 16**, is another spectacular fifth-century *vihara*, with the famous painting known as the **Dying Princess** near the front of its left wall. The "princess" was actually a queen named **Sundari**, and she isn't dying, but fainting after hearing the news that her husband, King Nanda (Buddha's cousin), is about to renounce his throne to take up monastic orders. The opposite walls show events from Buddha's early life as **Siddhartha**.

Cave 17, dating from between the mid-fifth and early sixth centuries, boasts the best-preserved and most varied paintings in Ajanta. While you wait to enter, have a look at the frescoes on the **veranda**. Above the door, eight seated Buddhas, including Maitreya, the Buddha-to-come, look down. To the left, an amorous princely couple share a last glass of wine before giving their worldly wealth away to the poor. The wall that forms the far left side of the veranda features fragments of an elaborate "Wheel of Life". Inside the cave, the murals are, once more, dominated by the illustrations of the Jatakas, particularly those in which the Buddha takes the form of an animal to illustrate certain virtues. This is also where you'll find the exquisite and much-celebrated portrait of a sultry, dark-skinned princess admiring herself in a mirror while her handmaidens and a female dwarf

Cave painting techniques

The basic **painting techniques** used by the artists of Ajanta to create the caves' lustrous kaleidoscopes of colour changed little over the eight centuries the site was in use, from 200 BC to 650 AD. First, the rough-stone surfaces were primed with a thick coating of paste made from clay, cow-dung, animal hair and vegetable fibre. Next, a finer layer of smooth white lime was applied. Before this was dry, the artists quickly sketched the outlines of their pictures using red cinnabar, which they then filled in with an undercoat of terre-verte. The **pigments**, all derived from natural water-soluble substances (kaolin chalk for white, lamp soot for black, glauconite for green, ochre for yellow and imported lapis lazuli for blue), were thickened with glue and added only after the undercoat was completely dry. Thus the Ajanta paintings are not, strictly speaking, frescoes (always executed on damp surfaces), but **tempera**. Finally, once dry, the murals were painstakingly polished with a smooth stone to bring out their natural sheen. The artists' only sources of **light** were oil-lamps and sunshine reflected into the caves by metal mirrors and pools of water (the external courtyards were flooded expressly for this purpose), a constraint that makes their extraordinary mastery of line, perspective and shading – which endow Ajanta's paintings with their characteristic other-worldly light – all the more remarkable.

look on. The *chowkidars* will demonstrate how, when illuminated from the side, her iridescent eyes and jewellery glow like pearls against the brooding, dark background.

Cave 19

Excavated during the mid-fifth century, when the age of Mahayana Buddhism was in full swing, **Cave 19** is indisputably Ajanta's most magnificent *chaitya* hall, its **facade** teeming with elaborate sculpture. Inside, the faded frescoes are of less note than the sculpture around the tops of the pillars. The standing Buddha at the far end, another Mahayana innovation, is even more remarkable. Notice the development from the stumpier *stupas* enshrined within the early *chaityas* (caves 9 & 10) to this more elongated version. Its umbrellas, supported by angels and a vase of divine nectar, reach right up to the vaulted roof.

Caves 21 to 26

Caves 21 to 26 date from the seventh century, a couple of hundred years after the others, and form a separate group at the far end of the cliff. Apart from the unfinished **Cave 24**, whose roughly hacked trenches and pillars give an idea of how the original excavation was carried out here, the only one worth a close look is **Cave 26**. Envisaged on a similarly grand scale to Cave 19, this impressive *chaitya* hall was never completed. Nevertheless, the sculpture is among the most vivid and sensuous at Ajanta. On the left wall as you enter the cave, the colossal image of **Parinirvarna** (Siddhartha reclining on his deathbed) is the essence of tranquillity. Note the weeping mourners below, and the flying angels and musicians above, preparing to greet the sage as he drifts into nirvana. Two panels down, and in dramatic contrast, the **Temptation of Mara** frieze depicts Buddha ensconced under a *peepal* tree as seven tantalizing sisters try to seduce him. Their father, the satanic Mara, watches from astride an elephant in the top left corner. The ruse to lead the Buddha astray fails, of course, eventually (bottom right) forcing the evil adversary and his daughters to retreat.

The viewpoint

The climb to the **viewpoint** from where the British hunting party first spotted the Ajanta Caves is well worth the effort – the panorama over the Waghora gorge and its surrounding walls of bare, flat-topped mountains is spectacular. From the far side of the iron footbridge beneath Cave 8, steps lead up the opposite side of the ravine to a small tin-roofed shelter, where the full majesty of the sheer-sided gorge becomes clear. From here it's a stiff twenty-minute climb straight ahead to the clearly visible viewpoint at the ridge of the hill.

Lonar

Few visitors reach the crater at **LONAR** but those who do find this **meteorite-formed lake** an amazing and tranquil place. Referred to as "Taratirth" in a Hindu legend that correctly claimed it was created by a shooting star, the gigantic hole in the ground was formed about fifty thousand years ago when a lump of space rock survived its fiery descent through the atmosphere to bury itself here. As the only such crater formed in basalt rock in the world, the site is not just a geological curiosity but also highly valuable to scientists – NASA has made extensive studies due to its apparent similarity to some lunar and Martian landscapes – though many of the lake's mysteries, such as the extreme alkalinity of its thick, sulphurous water, continue to baffle.

Numerous steep paths lead down to the lake from the rim, the principal one starting around 500m from the MTDC *Holiday Resort* and emerging in the basin near a twelfth-century temple dedicated to Shiva. A complete circuit of the lake, surrounded by forest and home to a rich array of birdlife, takes around three hours. En route you will discover numerous other seemingly lost Shaivite shrines, while huddling along a ravine etched into the crater's northeastern slope – an alternative path back up – is a fascinating cluster of temples, fed by a spring, or *dhar*, supposedly originating from the Ganges. Before leaving, it's well worth searching out the tenth-century Chalukyan **Daitya Sudana** temple in Lonar village, its walls inside and out crawling with a profusion of exquisite carvings of mythological scenes.

Practicalities

The easiest way to get to Lonar is by **taxi** from Aurangabad, which costs Rs1800–2500 for a day-trip, depending on the car and your negotiating skills. There are two morning **buses** direct from Aurangabad (4hr), with the last bus back around 4pm; services stop in the centre of Lonar village, around 2km from the lake. For more on the crater, it's worth hiring a local **guide**; Gajanan Kharat (Ⓣ07260/221428) is recommended. The only **accommodation**, right opposite the crater, is at the comfortable if rather ghostly MTDC *Holiday Resort* (Ⓣ07260/221602; ❹), built for a tourist rush that never came. Its restaurant has a superbly sited terrace from which to survey the lake.

Jalgaon

Straddling an important junction on the Central and Western Railway networks, as well as the main trans-Deccan trunk road, NH-6, **JALGAON** is a prosperous market town for the region's cotton and banana growers, and a key jumping-off point for travellers heading to or from the Ajanta Caves, 58km south. Even though the town holds nothing of interest, you may find yourself obliged to hole up here to be well placed for a morning departure.

Practicalities

The busy MSRTC **bus stand** is 1.5km across town (Rs15 in a rickshaw) from the **railway station**. For **internet** try the Om Internet Café (Rs20/hr), on the first floor of the Golani Market shopping centre, just beyond the roundabout at the top of Station Road.

By far the best **place to stay** in Jalgaon – in fact one of the best budget hotels in India – is the welcoming and very spruce *Plaza Hotel* (Ⓣ0257/222 7354, Ⓔhotelplaza_jal@yahoo.com; ❸–❹), two minutes from the railway station on the left side of Station Road, with a range of harmoniously designed singles and doubles, each spotlessly white, excellent value and sporting immaculate tiled bathrooms; there's also an air-conditioned dorm (Rs150) and a crisp suite (Rs900), and they'll provide tea in your room if you're leaving early in the morning. If the *Plaza*'s full, fallbacks include the dark but reasonably clean *Kewal* (Ⓣ0257/222 3949; ❹), also on Station Road, or the mid-range *Royal Palace* (Ⓣ0257/223 3888; ❺), 3km back beyond the bus stand, though the grand aspirations of its towering atrium aren't quite matched in the comfortable, bland rooms.

There's no better place to **eat** than the unfussy but congenial *Hotel Arya*, a ten-minute walk from the railway station (turn left at the top of Station Road and left again at the clock tower), which gets packed out at lunchtime for its freshly made and hearty north Indian veg specialities. En route you'll pass the cavernous

Moving on from Jalgaon

The fastest **buses** to **Ajanta** (1hr) are the services every 30min to Aurangabad (4hr), 160km south, all of which stop at the Ajanta T-junction. MSRTC also run daytime services to Mumbai (1 daily; 11hr), Nagpur (2 daily; 10hr) and Pune (5 daily; 9–10hr), but preferable are the numerous **private night buses** running on these, and other, routes. These can be booked through any of the travel agents that line up along Station Road; currently the most comfortable ride to Pune is with Shree Durga Travels (ⓣ0257/222 8124), while for other major destinations, including Mumbai, Indore and Ahmedabad, Uncle Travels (ⓣ0257/224 1294) is best.

Jalgaon is well served by mainline **trains** between Delhi, Kolkata and Mumbai, and convenient for most cities to the north on the Central Railway. Express services also pass through en route to join the Southeastern Railway: there are at least nine daily trains to **Nagpur** (7–9hr), via Wardha Junction (for Sevagram; 5hr 30min–6hr 30min), most convenient of which is the #2139 *Sewagram Express*, leaving Jalgaon at 10pm and arriving at Nagpur Junction at 6.10am. Services to **Mumbai** (7–8hr 45min) are frequent. Jalgaon also serves Agra (4–5 daily; 14hr–17hr 30min); Bengaluru (1 daily; 24hr); Bhopal (7 daily; 7hr–8hr 45min); Chennai (1 daily; 23hr); Delhi (4 daily; 18hr–21hr 45min); Gwalior (4–5 daily; 12hr–15hr 30min); Pune (4 daily; 8hr 30min–10hr 15min); and Varanasi (10–12 daily; 18hr 30min–28hr).

Arya Niwas, run by the same people and one of the town's best pure-veg thali joints. For non-veg and a **drink**, head for the respectable if smoky *Bombay Hotel*, next to the railway station, though get there early unless you want to share the evening with a posse of boozed-up sales reps.

Nagpur and around

Capital of the "land of oranges", **NAGPUR** is the focus of government attempts to develop industry in the remote northeastern corner of Maharashtra – most foreigners in the city are here for business rather than aesthetic purposes. The trickle of visitors who do stop here tend to do so en route to Madhya Pradesh, or the Gandhian ashrams at **Sevagram** and **Paunar**, a two-hour journey southwest. The other worthwhile excursion is the ninety-minute bus ride northeast to the hilltop temple complex at **Ramtek**.

In the city itself, the most prominent landmark is the **Sitabuldi Fort**, standing on a saddle between two low hills above the railway station, though it's closed to the public. North and west of the fort, the pleasantly green **Civil Lines** district holds some grand Raj-era buildings, dating from the time when this was the capital of the vast Central Provinces region.

Arrival and information

Nagpur's busy central mainline **railway station** is a Rs20 auto-rickshaw ride from the main hotel district along Central Avenue. MSRTC **buses** pull in at the state bus stand, 2km southeast of the railway station. The **airport** is around 8km southwest of the centre; auto-rickshaws shouldn't cost more than Rs150. The MTDC **tourist office** (daily 10am–6pm; ⓣ0712/253 3325) is 2.5km west of the centre on West High Court Road in Civil Lines, but is only useful for booking accommodation. At the helpful MP Tourism office, on the fourth floor of the Lokmat Building, Wardha Road (Mon–Fri 11am–5pm, plus first & last Sat of the

Moving on from Nagpur

Geographically at the virtual centre of India, Nagpur is handily placed for connections all across the country – though a long way from anywhere. The fastest **train** service to **Mumbai** (6–8 daily) is the #2290 *Nagpur Mumbai Duronto*, which leaves at 8.25pm (Mon, Wed & Fri only) and arrives at CST (VT) at 7.55am; all other services take at least two hours longer. The majority of services to **Wardha** (for Sevagram; 11–13 daily; 1–2hr) also stop at **Jalgaon** (9 daily; 6hr 30min–7hr 45min). Other destinations from Nagpur include: Bhopal (8–17 daily; 5hr 30min–9hr); Chennai (3–6 daily; 14hr 45min–23hr 30min); Delhi (10–13 daily; 13hr 30min–21hr 45min); Hyderabad (2–5 daily; 8hr 15min–11hr 15min); Indore (1–2 daily; 10hr 30min–12hr); Jabalpur (2–5 daily; 8hr 15min–10hr); Kolkata (5–8 daily; 17hr 30min–22hr 45min); Nasik (5–7 daily; 9hr 30min–11hr); and Pune (2–3 daily; 15–18hr).

In addition to services to Ramtek and Wardha, state **buses** leave the MSRTC bus stand bound for Aurangabad (6 daily; 12hr); Indore (1 daily; 11–12hr); Jabalpur (3 daily; 7–8hr); Jalgaon (2 daily; 9hr); and Pune (4 daily; 16hr).

Air India currently operates **flights** two or three times a day from Nagpur to **Mumbai**; the same route is served daily by GoAir, IndiGo and Jet Airways and Kingfisher, and less frequently by JetLite. There are also daily (or more frequent) flights to **Delhi** with Air India, GoAir and IndiGo; **Kolkata** on Air India and IndiGo; and **Bengaluru** with Kingfisher and Air India, the latter continuing to **Chennai**. In addition, IndiGo fly twice daily to **Pune**, and Kingfisher flies once a day to both **Goa** (via Indore and Pune) and **Hyderabad**.

month; ⓣ0712/244 2378), you can book accommodation for Pench Tiger Reserve (see p.393), Pachmarhi (see p.360) and for Kanha National Park (see p.388). **Banks** that deal in foreign exchange include the State Bank of India on Kingsway, near the railway station.

Accommodation

There's a cluster of reasonable budget **hotels** along Central Avenue, around 1km east of the railway station. The most salubrious – and with a good restaurant – is the welcoming *Skylark* at no. 119 (ⓣ0712/272 4654; ❹–❺), where the best of the rooms (with a/c) are large and clean, though the cheapest are a tad grubby and marred by traffic noise. The least seedy of the cheaper alternatives is the *Blue Moon* (ⓣ0712/272 6061; ❹–❺), a five-minute walk back to the west, though the poky bathrooms could do with a scrub. Of Nagpur's numerous upper-bracket, business-oriented hotels, the *Tuli International* (ⓣ0712/665 3555, ⓦwww.tuligroup.com; ❽), 1km northwest of the railway station in the quiet Sadar district, has the most charm; its chandeliered lobby, carpeted corridors and chintzy decor give it an endearingly old-fashioned feel.

Eating and drinking

For **food**, *Shivraj*, a few doors down from the *Blue Moon* hotel, does tasty and cheap south Indian snacks and thalis, while good-quality veg and non-veg (mains Rs125–250) is served up to the accompaniment of live *ghazals* at *The Grill*, the comfy, if smoky, male-dominated dining room and bar at the *Skylark*. Right in the centre of town, off the lethal Jhowsi Rani Chowk in Sitabuldi, the swish, first-floor ★ *Naivedhyam* is something of a Nagpur institution, dishing up delicious veg food (mains Rs90–175) to a background of Hindi-Hawaiian music.

Ramtek

The picturesque cluster of whitewashed hilltop temples and shrines at **RAMTEK**, 40km northeast of Nagpur on the main Jabalpur road (NH-7), is one of those alluring apparitions you spy from afar on long journeys through central India. According to the Ramayana, this craggy, scrub-strewn outcrop was the spot where Rama, Sita and Lakshmana paused on their way back from Lanka. Although few traces of these ancient times have survived, the site's old paved pilgrim trails, sacred lake, tumbledown shrines and fine views across the endless plains more than live up to its distant promise.

Buses from Nagpur stop a few kilometres short of **Ram Mandir** (the temple complex) in Ramtek town, from whose fringes a flight of stone steps climbs steeply up the side of Ramtek hill. Built in 1740, the temple stands on the site of an earlier fifth-century structure, of which only three small sandstone shrines remain. Just beneath the temple complex stands the circular **Kalidas Smarak** (daily 8.30am–8pm; Rs5), a modern memorial to the great Sanskrit poet, Kalidasa. The pavilion's interior walls are decorated with painted panels depicting scenes from his life and works.

Another of Ramtek's sacred sites is **Ambala Lake**, a holy bathing tank which lies 1.5km along a pilgrims' trail at the bottom of the gully, enfolded by a spur of parched brown hills. Its main attractions are the temples and *ghat*s clinging to its muddy banks. More energetic visitors may wish to combine a look with a *parikrama*, or circular **tour** of the tank, taking in the semi-derelict cenotaphs and weed-choked shrines scattered along the more tranquil north and western shores. A rickshaw (around Rs40) will get you back to the main bus stand.

Practicalities

Direct **buses** to Ramtek leave Nagpur (MSRTC stand) every thirty minutes. If you don't feel like hiking up to the temple, **auto-rickshaws** will whisk you up from the town bus stand via Ambala Lake for around Rs100. Though the food's pretty so-so, the *Rajkamal Resort* (Ⓣ07114/202761; ❹–❺), a few hundred metres along the hill from the temple complex, has a picturesquely sited open-air **restaurant**, as well as some pricey but acceptable rooms.

Sevagram

SEVAGRAM, Gandhi's model "Village of Service", is set deep in the serene Maharashtran countryside, 9km from the railroad town of **WARDHA**. The Mahatma moved here from his former ashram in Gujarat during the monsoon of 1936, on the invitation of his friend Seth Jamnalal Bajaj. Right at the centre of the Subcontinent, within easy reach of the Central Railway, it made an ideal headquarters for the national, non-violent *Satyagraha* movement, combining seclusion with the easy access to other parts of the country Gandhi needed in order to carry out his political activities.

These days, the small settlement is a cross between a museum and living centre for the promulgation of Gandhian philosophies. Interested visitors are welcome to spend a couple of days here, helping in the fields, attending discussions and prayer meetings (daily 5.45am & 6pm; bring mosquito repellent for the latter), and learning the dying art of hand-spinning. The older ashramites, or **sadhaks**, are veritable founts of wisdom when it comes to the words of their guru, Gandhiji.

Once past the absorbing **visitors' centre** (daily except Tues 10am–6pm), with its photos and documents recounting Gandhi's life, the real focal-point of the ashram is the sublimely peaceful main compound (daily 6am–6pm), entered a few hundred metres along the road. These modest rustic **huts** – among them the Mahatma's main residence – have been preserved exactly the way they were when the great man and his disciples lived here in the last years of the Independence struggle. A small *khadi* shop sells hand-loomed cloth and other products made on site.

Practicalities

Local **buses** run every 30min from Wardha, 77km southwest of Nagpur and on the mainline railway (see box, p.655), to the crossroads outside the Kasturba Gandhi Hospital, from where it's a 1km walk to the ashram. An **auto-rickshaw** from the bus stand to Sevagram and Paunar (see below) and back shouldn't cost more than Rs200. There are frequent "express" buses to Wardha from Nagpur's MSRTC bus stand (2hr).

If you decide to remain and learn something of Gandhi and the philosophy of non-violence, you can **stay** in the basic but spotless *Rustam Bhavan Guest House* (❶) or *Bajaj Bhavan* dorm (Rs60) in the main compound (Ⓣ07152/284753), though you'll be expected to do a couple of hours' communal work a day. There's slightly scruffier accommodation in thatch-roofed brick huts in the ashram's own *Yatri Niwas* (Ⓣ9822 797520; rooms ❶; dorms Rs40), opposite the principal compound. Simple, cheap and super-healthy Maharashtran **thalis** and snacks are available at the *Organic Nutrition Centre*, next to the visitor centre.

Paunar

Vinoba Bhave's ashram at **PAUNAR**, just 3km from Sevagram. has an altogether more dynamic feel than its more famous cousin at Sevagram. Bhave (1895–1982), a close friend and disciple of Gandhi, best remembered for his successful Bhoodan, or **land gift**, campaign to persuade wealthy landowners to hand over farmland to the poor, founded the ashram in 1938 to develop the concept of **swarajya**, or "self-sufficiency". Consequently, organic gardening, milk production, spinning and weaving have an even higher profile here than the regular meditation, prayer and yoga sessions. Another difference between this institution and the one up the road is that the *sadhak*s here are almost all female.

In the ashram's living quarters, Bhave's old **room** is kept as a shrine. Stone steps lead down from the upper level to a small terrace looking out over the **ghats**, where two small memorials mark the spots where a handful of Gandhi's, and later Bhave's, ashes were scattered onto the river. Every year, on January 30, the *ghat*s are inundated with half a million people who come here to mark the anniversary of Gandhi's death.

Paunar can be reached by **bus** from either Nagpur or Wardha by hopping off at the old stone bridge near the ashram. Alternatively, you can **walk** the 3km from Sevagram. The path, a cart track that runs over the hill opposite the hospital cross-roads, comes out in the roadside village 1km west of the Paunar ashram. As with Sevagram, it is possible to **stay** in one of the visitors' rooms or dorms (Ⓣ07152/288388; ❶), though call in advance to check there's space. **Meals**, made from organic, home-grown produce, are available on request.

South of Mumbai: The Konkan Coast

Despite the recent appearance of a string of upscale resorts pitched at wealthy urbanites, the coast stretching south from Mumbai, known as the **Konkan**, remains relatively unspoilt. Empty beaches, backed by casuarina and areca trees and coconut plantations, regularly slip in and out of view, framed by the distant Ghats, while little fortified towns preserve a distinct coastal culture, with its own dialect of Marathi and fiery cuisine. The number of rivers and estuaries slicing the coast meant that for years this little-explored area was difficult to navigate, but the Konkan railway, which winds inland between Mumbai and Kerala via Goa, now renders it more easily accessible.

Murud-Janjira

The first interesting place to break the journey south is the small port of **MURUD-JANJIRA**, 165km south of Mumbai. A traditional trade centre that once belonged to a dynasty of former Abyssinian slaves known as the Siddis, it still features plenty of attractive wood-built houses, some brightly painted and fronted by pillared verandas. The gently shelving beach is wide and safe for swimming, though you'll find the sea more inviting further south.

Just offshore some 5km south stands the imposing sixteenth-century **Janjira Fort**, one of the few the Marathas failed to penetrate, and now a picture of majestic dereliction. Local *hodka* boats (20min; Rs20) sail to the fortress – a serene trip – from the Rajpuri jetty, a Rs50 rickshaw ride from Murud, though since they seat twenty and only leave when full at quiet times you may have to charter the boat yourself (Rs400). Once there you're given an hour so to explore the formidable battlements, though the interior lies mostly in ruins.

Back in Murud, the 1661 Kasa Fort sits in the open sea 2km off the beach but cannot be visited, nor can the impressive nineteenth-century palace of the last nawab, which dominates the northern end of the bay. Fine views of the coast and surrounding countryside can be had, however, from the hilltop **Dattatreya Temple**, sporting an Islamic-style tower but dedicated to the triple-headed deity comprising Brahma, Vishnu and Shiva.

Arrival and information

The nearest railhead to Murud is Roha, a two-hour bus ride away, which is why most travellers still reach the town by jumping on one of the roughly hourly hydrofoil catamarans or regular ferries (1hr) from the Gateway of India in Mumbai to **Mandawa**, on the southern side of Mumbai harbour (see p.627). Buses meet the boats and shuttle passengers straight to Alibag (45min), from where you can catch regular government buses to Murud (2hr). Most direct bus services from Mumbai Central take six hours; there are also two faster ASIAD buses (4hr 30min) which must be booked in advance. **Buses** stop along Murud's main street, Durbar Road, parallel to the coast, where you'll find the tiny **post office** and, south of the central chowk, a handful of basic restaurants. You can access the **internet** at Fahim Internet Café (Rs35/hr), 200m east of the chowk. Bring enough **cash** to cover your stay – at the time of writing there was no ATM in the village nor would the sole bank exchange foreign currency.

Accommodation and eating

The best of the **accommodation** is lined up along Durbar Road. Slap on the sands, the *Golden Swan Resort* (Ⓣ02144/274078, Ⓦwww.goldenswan.com; ❼–❽) sits on the edge of town 1km north of the chowk and is the most comfortable option, with smart air-conditioned chalets plus more basic non-air-conditioned rooms in the colonial *Beach House* a few doors down, as well as bike rental and a restaurant serving local Malvani cuisine. Around 500m south, *Mirage Holiday Homes* (Ⓣ9423 377004; ❹–❺) occupies an attractive period building, with high-ceilinged rooms and more character than the competition, though it lacks direct access to the beach. Just south of the chowk, *V.M. Dandekar's* (Ⓣ9221 260260; ❹) is a simple family homestay right on a narrow strip of beach and provides home-cooked meals; look for the "Rooms available here" sign.

There is no shortage of regular, clean and inexpensive local **eating options** south of the chowk, none better than *Patil's*, a thali specialist set in a shady garden a few paces inland off Durbar Road and justly celebrated for its dry-fry fish.

Ganpatipule

Some 215km south of Murud-Janjira lies **GANPATIPULE**, a tiny village centred on a modern **Ganapati temple**. Approached via a long covered walkway, the temple is built around a Ganapati *omnar*, a naturally formed – though hardly accurate – image of the elephant god, which attracts thousands of Indian pilgrims each year. Much more impressive is Ganpatipule's spectacular white-sand **beach**, which extends for several kilometres either side of the village. The sea is generally safe for swimming, though you should exercise caution between June and October.

The obvious **place to stay** is the MTDC *Resort* (Ⓣ02357/235248, ❺–❼), set around neat lawns right at the heart of the village, with a range of reasonable rooms, some with breezy balconies, occupying a row of attractive two-storey villas a stone's throw from the sea; their Konkani huts, in a shaded beachside compound a ten-minute walk north, are disappointingly poorly maintained. A cheaper alternative, five minutes' walk from the beach back along the approach road, is the *Shreesagar* (Ⓣ02357/235145, Ⓔhotel_shreesagar@hotmail.com; ❹–❺), with decent, reasonably clean doubles and a pure-veg garden restaurant. For **food**, MTDC's popular *Tarang* restaurant is one of their better concerns, serving up fresh Malvani cuisine and cold beer.

To get to Ganpatipule, either make your way to **Ratnagiri** (on the Konkan railway and well connected by state and private buses) and take a local bus (every 30min–1hr; 1hr 30min) the last 32km, or catch one of the direct MSRTC services from Mumbai, Pune or Kolhapur. Buses usually stop outside the MTDC resort, though at festival times you may be dropped along the main road at the edge of the village, a 1.5km walk or rickshaw ride from the beach.

Matheran

The quirky, Raj-era hill station of **MATHERAN**, 108km east of Mumbai, is set on a narrow north–south ridge at an altitude of 800m in the Sahyadri range. From evocatively named viewpoints, at the edge of sheer cliffs that plunge into deep ravines, you can see way across the hazy plains – on a good day, so they say, as far as Mumbai. The town itself, shrouded in thick mist for much of the year, has, for the moment, one unique attribute: cars, buses, motorbikes and auto-rickshaws are prohibited. That, added to the journey up, on a **miniature train** that chugs its way through spectacular scenery to the crest of the hill, gives the town an agreeably quaint, time-warped feel.

Matheran (literally "mother forest") has been a popular retreat from the heat of Mumbai since the nineteenth century. These days, few foreign visitors venture up here, and those that do only hang around for a couple of days, to kill time before a flight or to sample the charms of Matheran's colonial-era hotels. The tourist season lasts from mid-September to mid-June (at other times it's raining or misty), and is at its most hectic around Diwali and Christmas, in April and May, and over virtually any weekend. There's really nothing up here to do but relax, explore the woods on foot or horseback and enjoy the fresh air and views.

As the crow flies, Matheran is only 6.5km from Neral on the plain below, but the train climbs up on 21km of track with no less than 281 curves, said to be among the sharpest on any railway in the world. Sadly, the steam engines that once handled the demanding haul puffed their last in 1980, to be replaced by cast-off diesels from Darjeeling, Shimla and Ooty. The train ride is a treat, especially if you get a window seat, but be prepared for a squash unless you upgrade to first class.

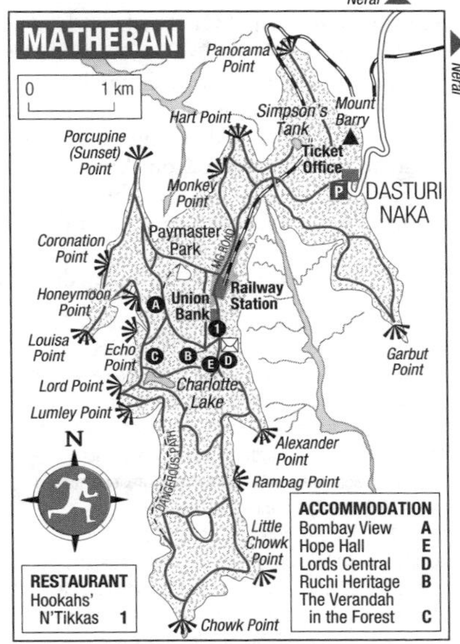

Arrival and information

To reach Matheran by **rail**, you must first get to **Neral Junction**, served by frequent overground metro trains from Mumbai's CST and Dadar (1hr 30min–2hr 15min), terminating at Karjat. Only two daily fast services stop at Neral: the #1007 *Deccan Express* (departs 7.10am) and the #1029 *Koyna Express* (departs 8.45am), both of which should get there around 45 minutes quicker than the metro. Travelling in the opposite direction from **Pune** (3hr), the #1024 *Sahyadri Express* (departs 7am) is the only fast train that pauses at Neral, though plenty do stop at Karjat, from where you can backtrack on suburban services.

From mid-October to mid-June, four narrow-gauge trains each day chug up from Neral to **Matheran** (1hr 40min–2hr), departing at 7.30am, 8.50am, 10.15am and 5.05pm, with an additional weekend service at 12.15pm. During the monsoon services are dependent on the weather and best not relied on. All trains are timed to tie in with incoming mainline expresses, so don't worry about missing a connection if the one you're on is delayed – the toy train should wait – but it's worth booking a day in advance at weekends in order to guarantee a seat. Matheran railway **station** is in the centre of the hill station on MG Road, which runs roughly north–south.

All **motor transport**, including shared taxis and minibuses from Neral (Rs50/person, Rs250/car), parks at the taxi stand next to the MTDC *Resort* at Dasturi Naka, 2km from Matheran. From here you can walk with a porter (Rs100–120), be led by rather fragile-looking horse (Rs150–180), or take a hand-pulled rickshaw (Rs250–300). If you're happy to carry your own bags, follow the rail tracks, which cut straight to the middle of Matheran, rather than the more convoluted dirt road. However you arrive, you must pay a **toll** (Rs25) to enter the town, valid for your entire stay.

Neither of Matheran's banks offers **foreign exchange**, though the ATM at the Union Bank, just south of the station, accepts foreign cards.

Accommodation and eating

Matheran has plenty of **hotels**, though few could be termed cheap – particularly at weekends, when rates almost double (and you should book ahead), or during peak periods when they become uniformly astronomical; the price codes quoted below reflect standard midweek rates outside peak times. Most are close to the railway station on MG Road, with pricier, more family-oriented places on the road behind it, Kasturba Bhavan. Note that 10am or 11am checkouts are standard, and that many places close down during the rainy off-season. Single male travellers should brace themselves for a long room-hunt as the town's hoteliers almost universally refuse beds to unaccompanied males ("stags"). The reason: so many come to the hill station from Mumbai to kill themselves. This applies in particular to places at the lower end of the scale.

Virtually all the hotels provide **full** or **half-board** at reasonable rates, but if you want to eat out, or are on a tight budget, try one of the numerous thali joints around the station or tasty kebab and tikka dishes at *Hookahs'N'Tikkas*, also on MG Road.

Bombay View Southwest of Paymaster Park, 1.5km from the station ⓣ02148/230453, ⓦwww.bombayviewhotelmatheran.com. Housed in a huge converted colonial-era mansion and annexe, this establishment is a notch pricier than the more basic places down by the station, but well worth the extra. Most of its rooms are spacious, with sitouts and forest or garden views, and the staff are helpful. ❸–❹

Hope Hall MG Rd, opposite *Lord's Central* ⓣ02148/230253. Decent-sized, clean, attached rooms – the better ones with high ceilings and a shared veranda – scattered across a secluded yard with badminton and table tennis, at the quiet end of town. During the week it's one of the best bargains in Matheran, but poor value at weekends when rates quadruple. ❷–❹

Lords Central MG Rd ⓣ02148/230228, ⓦwww.matheran.com. Though worn at the edges – its wonky verandas, poinsettias, hard beds and stodgy (but tasty) set meals give it the feel of a 1930s boarding house – eccentric, Raj-era *Lord's* is one of Matheran's best-loved institutions, thanks in no small part to its irreverent, anecdote-loving Parsi owners. It also boasts spectacular views from its poolside garden. Full board only (from Rs1600–2300/person/night; 30 percent discounts for stays of 2 nights or more). ❼–❽

Ruchi Heritage MG Rd ⓣ02148/230072. Though its gauche facade is a car crash of architectural bad taste, complete with plaster giant Corinthian columns, mini-grand staircase and pair of toothy lions, this ersatz heritage hotel houses decent-sized, modern, clean rooms, painted in shades of lilac and peach – as a fallback you could do much worse. ❹

The Verandah in the Forest 2km southwest of station ⓣ02148/230296, ⓦwww.neemranahotels.com. Set in woods a short way above Charlotte Lake, this sumptuously restored nineteenth-century bungalow is reason enough to come to Matheran. Apart from the evocative period decor and furnishings, its greatest asset is a huge west-facing veranda smothered in foliage – one of the most perfect spots in India for lunch (if pre-booked) or afternoon tea and biscuits (though if you eat here beware of the pilfering monkeys). Rates are reasonable and fairly constant throughout the year; open year-round. ❼–❾

The points and forest walks

Matheran occupies a long, narrow, semicircular plateau, bounded for most of its extent by sheer cliffs. These taper at regular intervals into outcrops, or **points**, revealing through the tree canopy wonderful panoramas of distant hills and plains. Few visitors manage more than half a dozen in a single outing, but in midwinter when temperatures are pleasantly cool, it's possible to tick off the majority in a long day's trek.

For a quick taster, head south from the main bazaar past *Lord's Central Hotel* on Matheran's eastern flank to Alexander Point, pressing on beyond it to Chowk Point – the most southerly of the mountain's spurs. This shouldn't take more than a couple of hours there and back. Another enjoyable route on an old cart track winds around the western rim, past a series of gorgeous British-era bungalows to Louisa, Coronation and Sunset (or Porcupine) points, the last – as its name implies – regarded as the choicest place to see the sun go down.

Accurate topographical maps of the mountain and its many paths are all but impossible to come by, although there's a wonderful old British one proudly on display in the dining room of *Lord's Central Hotel*, which walkers are welcome to consult.

Lonavala and around

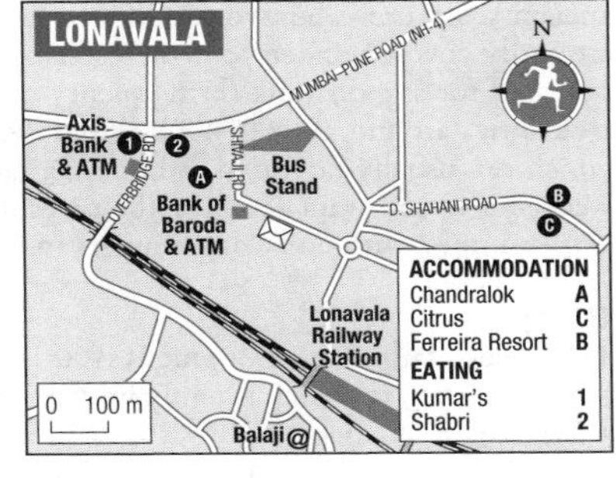

Just thirty years ago, the town of **LONAVALA** (also spelt Lonavla), 110km southeast of Mumbai and 62km northwest of Pune, was a quiet retreat in the Sahyadri hills. Since then, the place has mushroomed to cope with hordes of weekenders and second-home owners from the state capital, and is now only of interest as a base for the magnificent **Buddhist caves** of **Karla** and **Bhaja**, some of which date from the Satavahana period (second century BC).

Arrival and information

Lonavala's central **bus stand** is just off the old Mumbai–Pune Road, but the train is infinitely preferable. Lonavala is on the main railway line between Mumbai (3hr) and Pune (1hr), and most express trains stop here. The **railway station** is on the south side of town, a ten-minute walk from the bus stand area; take the path right at the end of platform one to get there. Several of the banks around town have **ATMs**, and there's a small **internet** café, Balaji's, on the road running south from the railway station (9am–10pm; Rs20/hr).

Accommodation

With a few exceptions, Lonavala's limited **accommodation** offers poor value, mainly because demand well outstrips supply for much of the year. Rates drop between October and March, and you can expect a twenty to thirty percent reduction on weekdays. But this isn't somewhere you're likely to want to unpack your bags.

Chandralok Close to the bus stand on Shivaji Rd ⓣ02114/272294. Set back from the market street, this well-run mid-range place has good-sized, well-aired, modern a/c and non-a/c rooms, plus a quality thali restaurant at ground level. ❺–❻

Citrus D Shahani Rd, a 5min rickshaw ride from the bus or railway station ⓣ02114/279531, ⓦwww.citrushotels.com. Slick new Mumbai-style business hotel somewhat incongruously tucked into a sleepy backstreet. Designer-tinged rooms occupy fashionably lemon-fragranced blocks overlooking an Astroturf-covered courtyard filled with white-cushioned sofas – a curiosity perhaps, but rates and facilities compare favourably with Lonavala's other offerings. ❼

Ferreira Resort Opposite *Citrus Hotel*, D Shahani Rd ⓣ02114/272689, ⓔiris19@rediffmail.com. Pleasantly old-fashioned place located down a quiet suburban street. Rooms are all attached, peaceful and clean, and have little balconies opening on to the street or a leafy rear plot. ❺

MTDC Karla Resort 7km east of Lonavala, 1.5km west of Karla Junction ⓣ02114/282230. Occupying a large, leafy compound a few hundred metres off the Mumbai–Pune Highway, this tranquil place has a range of good-value rooms and suites in chalets and cottages, plus paddle-boats for rent on the river behind. Checkout 9am. ❹–❺

Karla and Bhaja caves

The Buddhist cave sites of **Karla** and **Bhaja** comprise some of the finest rock-cut architecture in the northwest of the Deccan region. Though not on nearly such an impressive scale as Ajanta and Ellora, they harbour some beautifully preserved ancient sculpture. The two sites lie some 6km apart, to the east of Lonavala, and are easily covered under your own steam by bus and/or train in a day, if you are prepared for a good walk (bring plenty of water), though you can rent an **auto-rickshaw** (around Rs300–400) or **car** (Rs600 for 4hr) for the tour, either of which can usually be found at Lonavala railway station. It's a good idea to avoid weekends if you want to enjoy the caves in peace and quiet; Karla, in particular, gets swamped with noisy day-trippers to its Hindu shrine.

Bhaja

The **caves** (daily 9am–5.30pm; Rs100 [Rs5]) at **BHAJA** lie 2km from Malavli railway station, to which roughly hourly passenger trains run from Lonavala (9km west). To reach them, follow the road south of the station until it peters out (1.5km), from where it's a steep ten-minute climb up to the caves.

The excavations are among the oldest in India, dating from the late second to early first century BC, during the earliest, Hinayana, phase of Buddhism. You enter the complex opposite Bhaja's apsidal **chaitya** hall, which contains a *stupa* but no figures. Its 27 plain bevelled pillars lean inwards, mimicking the style of wooden buildings, and sockets in the stone of the exterior arch reveal that it once contained a wooden gate or facade. Most of the other caves consist of simple halls – *viharas* – with adjoining cells that contain plain shelf-like beds; many are fronted by rough verandas. Further south, past a mysterious dense cluster of fourteen **stupas**, the veranda of the **last cave**, a *vihara*, is decorated with superb carvings, which scholars have identified as the figures of the Hindu gods, Surya and Indra.

Karla

KARLA (also Karli) is 3km north of **Karla Caves Junction** on the Mumbai–Pune Road and 11km from Lonavala. Take any bus or shared taxi to the junction (from where it's a Rs30–40 rickshaw ride), or there are three morning **buses** (9am, 10am & 11.30am) that head for the caves directly from Lonavala, with the last bus returning from Karla at 5pm.

The rock-cut Buddhist **chaitya** hall at Karla (daily 9am–5pm; Rs100 [Rs5]), reached by steep steps that climb 110m, is the largest and best preserved in India, dating from the first century AD. Though partially obstructed by a modern Hindu

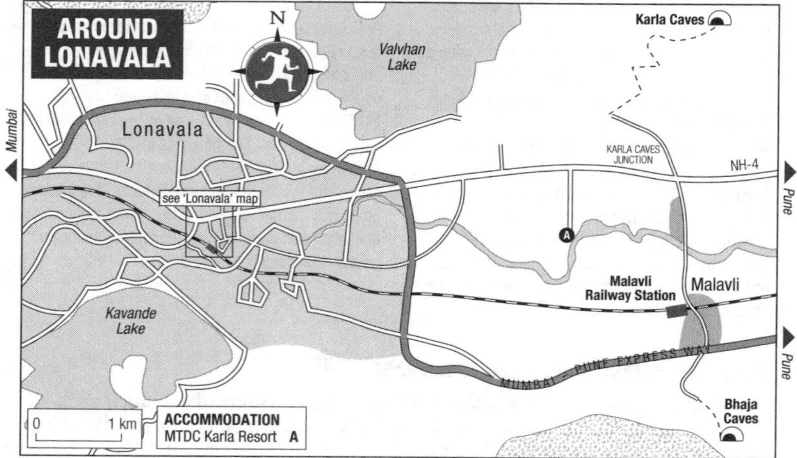

temple housing a shrine to Ekviri, the enormous fourteen-metre-high facade of the hall, topped by a horseshoe-shaped window, is still an impressive sight. To the left of the entrance stands a *simhas stambha*, a tall column capped with four lions, while in the porch of the cave, dividing its three doorways, are panels of figures in six couples, presumed to have been the wealthy patrons of the hall. With their expressive faces and sensuous bodies, it's hard to believe these figures were carved around two thousand years ago. Two rows of octagonal columns with pot-shaped bases divide the interior into three, forming a wide central aisle and, on the outside, a hall that allowed devotees to circumambulate the monolithic *stupa* at the back. Above each pillar's fluted capital kneel a pair of finely carved elephants, each mounted by two riders, one with arms draped over the other's shoulders. Amazingly, some of the timber rafters supporting the arched roof appear to date from the time when the hall was in use.

Eating and drinking

Lonavala holds a bewildering number of shops selling the local sweet speciality, **chikki** – a moreish amalgam of nuts, seeds or coconut set in rock-solid jaggery. Many of the town's hotels like to lay on full board, but you'll eat fresher food in places along the main street, which cater more for the brisk through-trade. The pick of the bunch is *Kumar*'s, a big, bustling place that gets packed out on weekends for its great Mughlai and tandoori specialities: try the delicious *murg handi (*Mughlai-style boneless chicken) mopped up with hot naan bread. *Shabri*, beneath the *Ramkrishna Hotel*, is the well-heeled Mumbaikars' other favourite, serving a wide range of north and south Indian dishes in a large, busy ground-floor dining hall, and its street-side terrace is a popular spot for breakfast. Both places serve cold beer.

Pune

At an altitude of 598m, the prosperous city of **PUNE** (occasionally still anglicized as Poona), Maharashtra's second largest, lies close to the Western Ghat mountains (known here as the Sahyadri Hills), on the edge of the Deccan plains as they stretch away to the east. Capital of the Marathas' sovereign state in the sixteenth century until its rulers were deposed by the Brahmin Peshwa family, Pune was – thanks to its cool, dry climate – chosen by the British in 1820 as an alternative headquarters for the Bombay Presidency. Since colonial days, Pune has continued to develop as a major industrial city and now ranks along with Hyderabad, Bengaluru and Chennai as one of southern India's fastest growing business centres. Signs of the new prosperity abound, from huge hoardings advertising multistorey executive apartment blocks and gated estates, to cappuccino bars, air-conditioned malls and hip clothing stores.

The full-on traffic and ultra-Westernized city centre may come as a shock if all you know about Pune is its connection with India's famously laidback, New Age guru, Bhagwan Rajneesh, or **Osho** (1931–90). The spiritual teacher founded his ashram in the leafy suburb of Koregaon Park in 1974 and, although its activities nowadays generate a lot less publicity than they did during Rajneesh's lifetime, the centre continues to attract followers from all over the world. It was at least partly due to Osho's enduring popularity with foreigners that the nearby *German Bakery*, Koregaon Park's erstwhile hippie hangout, was targeted for a Mumbai-style **terrorist attack** in February 2010, which left seventeen dead and around sixty injured – a huge shock for this normally peaceful little enclave. Pune's other main claim to spiritual fame is the presence on its outskirts of *yogarcharya* **BKS Iyengar**'s illustrious yoga centre – a far more sober and serious institution than the Osho ashram (see p.671).

Arrival and information

From Pune's Lohagaon **airport**, 10km northeast of the centre, pre-paid coaches ("city drop" Rs150) and taxis (non-a/c Rs250, a/c Rs350) take between fifteen and thirty minutes to reach the centre, depending on the traffic. The main **railway station** is in the centre of town, south of the river. See the "Moving on" box below for details of Pune's **bus** stands.

The **MTDC Tourist Office** (Mon–Fri plus the first and third Sat of the month 10am–5.45pm; ☎020/2612 6867) is inside "I" block of Central Building (enter between Ambedkar Chowk and Sadhu Vaswani Circle). They also have an **information counter** (allegedly the same times) opposite the railway station's first-class booking office. For changing currency or **travellers' cheques**, Thomas Cook is at 13 Thacker House, just off General Thimmaya Road (☎020/2634 6171). The very efficient **GPO** is on Sadhu Vasavani (Connaught) Road. Manneys Booksellers, next to *The Place* (see p.672) on Moledina Road, and Crossword, on the first floor of Sohrab Hall (close to the *Hotel Shree Panchratna*), are the best central **bookshops**. You can access the **internet** in many places, including a 24-hour cybercafé on the first floor of the railway station (Rs30/hr). If you're up

Moving on from Pune

Pune's prominence as a business capital means that it's well connected to towns and cities in southern India. However, demand for seats on planes, trains and buses far exceeds supply and you'd do well to book onward transport as soon as possible.

By train

Pune is one of the last stops for around twenty long-distance **trains** to and from Mumbai, so rail services are excellent – despite many of them departing in the early morning; some terminate at Dadar or (worse still) Kurla, so always check first. Reservations for all trains should be made as far in advance as possible at the **Reservation Centre** next to the main station (Mon–Sat 8am–8pm, Sun 8am–2pm).

Trains leave for: Bengaluru (2–3 daily; 19hr 50min–23hr 35min); Chennai (3 daily; 19hr 35min–25hr 25min); Delhi (3–5 daily; 20hr–27hr 25min); Ernakulam (for Kochi; 1–2 daily; 33hr); Hyderabad/Secunderabad (3–6 daily; 8hr 30min–14hr 15min); Jalgaon (4–5 daily; 8–9hr); Kolhapur (5–6 daily; 6hr 50min–10hr 15min); Lonavala (20–25 daily; 50min–1hr 20min); Mumbai (20–23 daily; 3hr 5min–4hr 55min); and Nagpur (2–3 daily; 15hr 45min–18hr). The following services are recommended as the fastest and/or most convenient:

Destination	Name	No.	Frequency	Departs	Journey time
Bengaluru	*Udyan Express*	#6529	Daily	11.45pm	21hr 5min
Chennai	*Chennai Express*	#2163	Daily	12.10am	19hr 35min
Delhi	*Jhelum Express*	#1077	Daily	5.20pm	27hr 25min
Goa	*Goa Express*	#2780	Daily	4.40pm	14hr
Hyderabad/ Secunderabad	*Konark Express*	#1019	Daily	7.05pm	12hr 45min
Kolhapur	*Sahyadri Express*	#1023	Daily	10.05pm	8hr
Mumbai CST	*Deccan Queen*	#2124	Daily	7.15am	3hr 10min

in Koregaon Park, Zorba Net Surfing, on the ground floor of the *Hotel Surya Villa*, and Arihant Communication, opposite the top of Lane 5 on North Main Road, are the best options; both cost Rs20/hr.

Accommodation

Upmarket **hotels** are springing up all over Pune, but there's a chronic shortage of budget and mid-range places, which explains why prices are high for what you get and vacancies like gold dust: advance booking is all but essential. For information on staying at Osho, see p.670.

Grand Near Dr Ambedkar statue at the top of MG Rd ⓣ020/2636 0728, ⓔgrandhotelpune@gmail.com. A colourful paint job has revitalized the colonial-era *Grand*, set behind a dimly lit beer garden, following a period in the doldrums. The dirt-cheap, bathroom-less, wood-partitioned singles off reception (Rs300) aren't conducive to much sleep, but the refurbished high-ceilinged doubles in the rear annexe are fine for a night or two. ❹

Le Meridien RBM Rd, just northwest of the railway station ⓣ020/6641 1111, ⓦwww.starwoodhotels.com. Though no longer the biggest hotel in Pune, this vast cathedral of marble still feels like its most

By bus

There are three main bus stands: the **City Bus Stand**, next to the railway station, is split into two sections, one serving Pune itself (with signs and timetables only in Marathi), the other for destinations south and west, including Goa (4 daily; 11hr), Mahabaleshwar (hourly; 3hr 30min–4hr) and Kolhapur (hourly; 5–6hr). ASIAD buses to Mumbai (via Lonavala) also leave here every fifteen minutes, between 5.30am and 11.30pm (3hr 15min). **Swargate Bus Stand**, about 5km south, close to Nehru Stadium, services Karnataka and some of the same destinations as City, while the stand next to **Shivaji Nagar** railway station, 3km west of the centre, runs buses every half hour to points north, such as Aurangabad (4hr 30min) and Nasik (3–4hr). To establish which station you require for your destination, ask at the enquiries hatch of the City Bus Stand or at the MTDC counter at the railway station.

By taxi

For Mumbai, 24-hour **taxis** leave from agencies at the taxi stand in front of Pune railway station, charging Rs290 per passenger – but they'll only get you as far as Dadar. Pricier a/c "cool cabs" operate from the same place (Rs355/passenger).

By air

Pune's airport is a major hub. There's a daily service to **Goa** with Kingfisher, leaving at 12.25pm. IndiGo, Kingfisher and SpiceJet each fly two or three times a day to **Delhi**; Air India, Jet Airways and JetLite also offer a daily flight. **Bengaluru** is served once or twice a day by Kingfisher and Jet Airways, daily by IndiGo and SpiceJet and six times weekly by Air India; Jet Airways, Kingfisher and Air India (not Sat) also cover **Hyderabad**. Kingfisher offers a twice-daily flight to **Chennai**, also served daily by IndiGo, SpiceJet, Paramount Airways (except Sat) and Jet Airways (via Bengaluru). Jet Airways flies twice a day to **Mumbai**, one service continuing to Indore, the other to **Kolkata**; **Indore** is directly served by Kingfisher, who also fly to Raipur and Nagpur via Hyderabad. Finally, IndiGo is the only airline offering direct flights to **Nagpur** (1–2 daily) and **Ahmedabad** (daily except Sat).

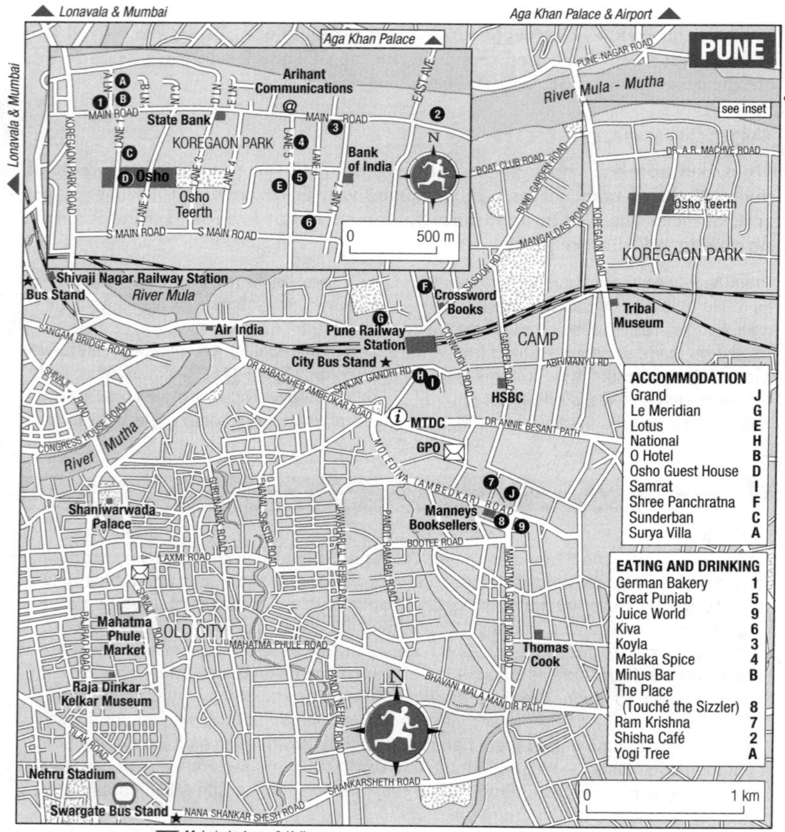

opulent and luxurious. Large, plush yet airy rooms come with thick honey-coloured carpets and huge beds, and the rooftop bar (complete with two-tiered pool) is the city centre's most heavenly space for an evening drink. Printed rates start at around US$400. ❾

Lotus Plot No. 356, Lane No.5, Koregaon Park ☎020/2613 9701, Ⓦwww.hotelsuryavilla.com. Housed in an unassuming salmon-pink block in tranquil, leafy surroundings, the *Surya Villa*'s renovated sister hotel is Koregaon's Park's best-value hideaway. Bright, spotless, modern rooms are blessed with big windows, comfy beds and cosy balconies, and there's free wi-fi. A basic breakfast (included) is served to the rooms, and it's handy for the area's best restaurants. ❻

National 14 Sassoon Rd, opposite the railway station ☎020/2612 5054. Huge, high-ceilinged, cleanish rooms in a rambling, sparse and somewhat dilapidated colonial mansion occupying a surprisingly peaceful plot set back from the main road. The smaller, quieter, cheaper rooms in the courtyard annexe have private sitouts. ❹

O Hotel North Main Rd ☎020/4001 1000, Ⓦwww.ohotelsindia.com. Goa chic comes to Pune: outside, a forbidding sandstone-coloured tower block; inside, an exuberant designer playground of bold textures, colours and shapes. Rooms are suitably Zen-like, blending simple lines and stylish details with warm, muted tones and natural materials, and facilities include a gorgeous spa open to the skies and spectacular rooftop pool and bar. Rack rates from around US$280. ❾

Samrat 17 Wilson Garden, opposite the railway station ☎020/2613 7964, Ⓔthesamrathotel@vsnl.com. Smart, centrally a/c tower block, with large, spotless rooms in galleries opening onto a central atrium. It's tucked away down a hidden backstreet close to the railway station, but easy to find and offers superb value by Pune standards. Wi-fi-enabled; buffet breakfast included. 6–7

Shree Panchratna 7 Tadiwala Rd ⓣ020/2605 9999, ⓦwww.hotelshreepanchratna.in. Plain but well-maintained and efficient business hotel close to the railway station, down a quiet side-street. The rooms are all a/c, fresh and simply furnished, with wi-fi-enabled desks and some have balconies. 7

Sunderban 19 Koregaon Park ⓣ020/2612 4949, ⓦwww.tghotels.com. Fine Art Deco mansion, set behind an immaculate expanse of lawn right next to Osho. Rooms in the main house, furnished in swathes of leather and acres of teak and mahogany, are better value than those in the flash modern garden block (around US$180), though there are big discounts April–Sept and breakfast is included. 7–9

Surya Villa 294/1 Koregaon Park ⓣ020/2612 4501, ⓦwww.hotelsuryavilla.com. Good-sized if somewhat spartan rooms spread over four floors in a suburban block close to Osho. It's hugely popular, mainly with long-staying foreign ashram-ites. 5–6

The City

Pune's centre is bordered to the north by the **River Mula** and to the west by the **River Mutha** – the two join in the northwest to form the Mutha-Mula, at Sangam Bridge. The principal shopping area, and the greatest concentration of restaurants and hotels, is in the streets south of the railway station, particularly Connaught and, further south, **MG Road**. The old Peshwa part of town, by far the most interesting to explore, is towards the west between the fortified **Shaniwarwada Palace** and fascinating **Raja Dinkar Kelkar Museum**; old wooden *wada*s – palatial city homes – survive on these narrow, busy streets, and the Victorian, circular **Mahatma Phule Market** is always a hive of activity.

Raja Dinkar Kelkar Museum

Dinkar Gangadhar Kelkar (1896–1990), aside from being a celebrated Marathi poet published under the name Adnyatwasi, spent much of his life travelling and collecting arts and crafts from all over the country. In 1975, he donated his collection to the Maharashtran government for the creation of a museum dedicated to the memory of his son, Raja, who had died at the age of 12. Housed in a huge old-town mansion, the **Raja Dinkar Kelkar Museum** (daily 9.30am–6pm; Rs200 [Rs50]) at 1378 Shukrawar Peth is a wonderful potpourri in which beauty and interest is found in both artistic and everyday objects, though the sheer scale of the collection – 21,000 pieces strong – means that only a fraction can be shown at any one time. Paraphernalia associated with paan, the Indian passion, includes containers in every conceivable design: some mimic people, animals or fish, others are egg-shaped and in delicate filigree. Also on show are musical instruments, superb Marathi and Gujarati textiles and costumes, domestic shrines, puppets, ivory games and a model of Shaniwarwada Palace, while curiosities include a suit of fish-scale armour, a collection of intricate noodle-makers and an entire cabinet full of "erotic nut cutters".

Shaniwarwada Palace

In the centre of the oldest part of town 1km north of the Kelkar Museum, only the imposing high walls of the **Shaniwarwada Palace** (daily 8am–6pm; Rs100 [Rs5]) survived a huge conflagration in 1828. The chief residence of the Peshwas from 1732 until it was captured by the British in 1817, the building has little to excite interest today, though there's a **sound-and-light** show in English (daily except Tues 8pm; Rs25). The entrance is through the Delhi gate on the north side, one of five set into the perimeter wall, whose huge teak doors come complete with nasty elephant-proof spikes. The interior of the palace is now grassed over, the seven-storey building entirely absent.

Aga Khan Palace and Gandhi Memorial

In 1942, Mahatma Gandhi, his wife Kasturba and other key figures of the freedom movement were interned at the grand **Aga Khan Palace** (daily 9am–5.30pm; Rs100 [Rs5]), which is set in quiet leafy gardens across the river, 5km northeast of the centre (buses #157, #158 & #163). The Aga Khan donated the palace to the state in 1969, and it is now a small **Gandhi museum**, typical of many all over India, with captioned photos and simple rooms unchanged since they were occupied by the freedom fighters. A memorial behind the house commemorates Kasturba, who died during their imprisonment.

Tribal Museum

The Tribal Research and Training Institute, which runs the **Tribal Museum** on Koregaon Road (daily 10.30am–5.30pm; Rs10 [Rs5]; Ⓦtrti.mah.nic.in), 1.5km east of the railway station, is dedicated to the protection and documentation of Maharashtra's forty-plus tribal groups, who number around ten million. The museum's photos, artefacts and outdoor dioramas serve as an excellent introduction to this little-known world, but the highlights are the wonderful collections of dance masks and Worli paintings. Talk to the museum curator if you're interested in guided (but culturally sensitive) **tours** to tribal areas.

Osho International Meditation Resort

Pune is the headquarters of the infamous **Osho International Meditation Resort**, 17 Koregaon Park Rd (Ⓣ020/2401 9999, Ⓦwww.osho.com), 2km northeast of the railway station. Set amid forty acres of landscaped gardens and woodland, the ashram of the now-deceased New Age guru, Shri Bagwan Rajneesh (aka "Osho"; see box opposite), comprises a dreamy playground of cafés, marble walkways, swimming pools, spas, tennis courts and clinics, with a shop selling Osho's enormous list of books, DVDs and CDs. Courses at its Multiversity, mostly one to three days in duration (around $100/day), are offered in a variety of therapies and meditation techniques, alongside more offbeat workshops with titles such as "Disappear into the Painting", "Squeeze the Juice of Life" and "Doing Dying Differently".

This ecofriendly bubble follows a strict door policy, with security beefed up following the revelation of visits to Osho by 26/11 conspirator David Headley – guided tours had at the time of writing been indefinitely cancelled, and in the wake of Pune's own attack in 2010 were unlikely to resume. If you're interested in taking a course, you must take your passport to the Welcome Center (9am–12.30pm & 2–3.30pm), where you'll have to take an on-the-spot HIV test in order to register – the induction, HIV test and initial day-pass package costs Rs1550 for foreigners, after which it's Rs700 per day. You'll also need two robes (maroon for daywear, white for evenings), on sale at the ashram's "mini-mall". If you want to actually stay inside the resort, the smart *Osho Guest House* (Ⓣ020/6601 9900; ⑧) offers stylish, minimalist, Zen rooms – though be warned that the accommodation is situated above the main auditorium, which, as the ashram likes to put it, "can make the 6am Dynamic Meditation hard to resist".

The beautiful gardens laid out to the east of the main Osho complex, known as **Osho Teerth**, are open to the public (daily 6–9am & 3–6pm; admission free; no photography), and make a serene place for a stroll, with babbling streams, stands of giant bamboo, mature trees and Zen sculpture artfully placed amid the greenery.

Eating and drinking

Pune's affluent young things have money to burn these days, and new, innovative places to eat and drink open up every month to relieve them of their info-tech

Osho

It is over forty years since followers began to congregate around **Bhagwan Rajneesh**, the self-proclaimed New Age guru better known to his tens of thousands of acolytes worldwide as simply **Osho**. Underpinned by a philosophical mishmash of Buddhism, Sufism, sexual liberationism, Tantric practices, Zen, yoga, hypnosis, Tibetan pulsing, disco and unabashed materialism, the first Rajneesh ashram was founded in Pune in 1974. It rapidly attracted droves of Westerners, and some Indians, who adopted new Sanskrit names and a uniform of orange or maroon cottons and a bead necklace (*mala*) with an attached photo of the enlightened guru, in classic style, sporting long greying hair and beard.

Few early adherents denied that much of the attraction lay in Rajneesh's novel approach to fulfilment. His dismissal of Christianity ("Crosstianity") as a miserably oppressive obsession with guilt struck a chord with many, as did the espousal of liberation through sex. Rajneesh assured his devotees that material comfort was not to be shunned. Within a few years, satellite ashrams were popping up throughout Western Europe, and by 1980 an estimated 200,000 devotees had liberated themselves in six hundred meditation centres across eighty countries.

To protect itself from pollution, nuclear war and the AIDS virus, the organization poured money into a utopian project, **Rajneeshpuram**, on 64,000 acres of agricultural land in Oregon, US. It was at this point that the tabloids and TV documentary teams really got interested in Rajneesh, now a multimillionaire. Infiltrators leaked stories of strange goings-on at Rajneeshpuram and before long its high-powered female executives became subject to police interest. Charges of tax evasion, drugs, fraud, arson and a conspiracy to poison several people in a neighbouring town to sway the vote in local elections provoked further sensation. Although he claimed to know nothing of this, Rajneesh pleaded guilty to breaches of US immigration laws and was deported in 1985. Following protracted attempts to resettle in 21 different countries, the Valium-addicted Rajneesh returned home to Pune, where he died in 1990, aged 59.

The ashram went through a period of internal squabbles and financial trouble in the 1990s. At his death, Rajneesh appointed an inner circle to manage the group, though several departed and the Osho "brand" – which sells around four million books each year, supplemented by CDs, DVDs, paintings and photos – is now controlled from Zurich and New York. The Pune ashram wasn't seeing enough of this to meet its costs and consequently has had to relaunch and re-style itself, changing both its name (from Osho Commune International to **Osho International Meditation Resort**) and the pattern of life inside its walls; whereas in its heyday an average stay was three to six months, today people typically stay no more than two weeks and few followers live on site.

salaries, the largest concentration of them up at the eastern end of Koregaon Park. Booking is advisable at the smarter places at weekends.

Cafés and restaurants

German Bakery 291 Koregaon Park. The tragic scene of the 2010 terrorist attack, this hugely popular branch of this chain of faded hippy cafés was poised to reopen with a new look at the time of writing, though was slated to retain part of its shack-like charm. Light, healthy meals and heavy pastries and cakes are provided to a mixed clientele of well-heeled locals and maroon-robed Osho-ites.

Great Punjab 5 Jewel Tower, Lane 5, Koregaon Park ☎020/2614 5060. One of Koregaon Park's most popular north Indians, offering generous kebabs, grills and tandoori dishes – and a long list of cocktails and spirits – in smart if subdued surroundings. Dedicated carnivores should sample the *karela kebab*, a mountain of succulent tandoori chicken stuffed with a robust mix of minced meat and herbs. Mains Rs240–390.

Juice World 2436/B East Street Camp. Freshly squeezed fruit juices (Rs25–80) and shakes (try the fabulous dried fruit and *badam*) are the mainstay of this buzzy, studenty haunt just east of the top of MG Rd. They also serve piping-hot snacks such as *aloo paratha* and, throughout the afternoon and evening, tangy Bombay-style *pao bhaji,* which bubbles away on a huge counter griddle.

Koyla Mira Nagar Corner, North Main Rd, Koregaon Park. Pune's most extravagantly decorated restaurant, featuring twinkling, mirror-inlaid Arabian Nights murals. The waiters sport long Muslim djellabas and fez caps, and serve sumptuous, complicated Hyderabadi cuisine. Count on Rs750–900 for three courses.

Malaka Spice Lane 5, Koregaon Park ⓣ020/2615 6293. Longstanding Southeast Asian specialist, dishing up reasonably authentic stir-fries, curries and noodle dishes (Rs195–260) in arty surroundings. It's relaxed at lunchtime and intimate in the evening when the candlelit covered veranda and garden terrace twinkle alluringly with fairy lights.

The Place (Touché the Sizzler) 7 Moledina Rd. Succulent sizzlers (veg, fish, pork or beef) and tender, juicy steaks are the house specialities of this popular Parsi-run old timer in the city centre. Mains Rs220–375.

Ram Krishna 6 Moledina Rd. Top-notch north and south Indian veg food, including some fantastic Punjabi tandooris, dished up in a high-ceilinged dining hall with black-tie service, but at restrained prices (most mains Rs65–110).

Yogi Tree *Hotel Surya Villa*, 294/1 Koregaon Park. This is the favourite hangout of health-conscious Osho-ites, serving pure, hygienic juices, grilled sandwiches, tofu steaks (Rs165) and delicious koftas (Rs130–160), in addition to a very popular stir-fried pak choi (Rs165). And their desserts are great too.

Bars

Kiva Serenebay, Lane 6, Koregaon Park. A ten-foot totem pole looming by the entrance introduces the ethnic theme of this hip hangout for Pune's young and beautiful. Inside, aboriginal paintings and tribal masks, liberal use of rattan and coir and a cool-blue underlit bar provide the backdrop, and loud Western pop the soundtrack, for pan-Asian nibbles and the city's best-mixed cocktails (Rs160–320). Daily 7–11.30pm.

Minus Bar *O Hotel*, Koregaon Park. Soaring high over the cityscape, the *O*'s lantern-lit rooftop bar is Pune's dreamiest spot for a sundowner. Sink into a low-slung white-cushioned sofa, Kutchi-patchwork beanbag or dabble your feet in one of the gently lapping shallow pools as you muse over the enterprising list of cocktails (mostly Rs325–375) and soak up the views.

Shisha Café ABC Farms, Koregaon Park ⓣ020/6520 0390. One of the city's most congenial watering holes: a cavernous gastro-bar awash with greenery and capped with a huge thatched roof hung with Persian carpets. Kebabs and Iranian food dominate the menu, but the walls are lined with posters of jazz greats and the music's Cuban and Bebop. They also serve beer and spirits, and hookahs with strawberry-flavoured tobacco. Live jazz most Thurs evenings.

Mahabaleshwar and around

The former capital of the Bombay Presidency, **MAHABALESHWAR**, 250km southeast of Mumbai and rivalling Matheran as the most visited hill-resort in Maharashtra, is easily reached from Pune, 120km northeast. The highest point in the Western Ghats (1372m), it is subject to extraordinarily extreme **weather** conditions. The start of June brings heavy mists and a dramatic drop in temperature, followed by a deluge of biblical proportions: up to 7m of rain can fall in the hundred days up to the end of September. As a result, tourists tend only to come here between October and early June; during April and May, at the height of summer, the place is packed. There is a Rs20 per head entry fee for visitors, collected at toll booths at each end of town.

For most foreign visitors, Mahabaleshwar's prime appeal is its location mid-way between Mumbai and Goa, but it holds enough good **hiking trails** to keep walkers here for a few days, with tracks through the woods to waterfalls and assorted vantage points overlooking the peaks and plains. One enjoyable route – along which you may well not see another soul – is the three-kilometre forested walk along the **Tiger Path** bridleway to **Mumbai Point**, which starts around 1km southwest of the bus stand opposite the *Hotel Sathar,* just south of the Christian cemetery. The sunset panoramas from here can be breathtaking. If there's a group of you, you could rent a **boat** out on the **Venna Lake** (Rs300–400/hr; seating 6–8), 2.5km north of town, though it's not as peaceful a pastime as you might think. Otherwise, the main activity in town is to amble up and down the animated pedestrianized **main bazaar** (Dr Sabne Road) – which with its chip shops, amusement arcades and popcorn stands bears a passing resemblance to an English seaside resort – and graze on the locally grown **strawberries** and other fruits for which the town is famous.

Arrival and information

The central **State Bus Stand** is at the northwest end of the bazaar. There are six daily MSRTC buses from Mumbai, the best option being the semi-luxury bus which departs from the Mumbai Central Bus Stand at 6am (7hr). Auto-rickshaws are banned in Mahabaleshwar but **taxis** line up at the west end of the bazaar, charging a flat fare of Rs40 for short hops in and around town. **Bikes** can be hired from a stall at the *Dreamland* hotel (Rs150/day). There are a couple of unreliable **internet** joints in the bazaar, and plenty of **ATMs**.

Accommodation

As in many hill stations, despite an abundance of **hotels**, at busy times prices in Mahabaleshwar are well above average. Room rates are a moveable feast, particularly at the lower end of the scale, but fall roughly into three categories: peak months are April and especially May, when as at Diwali, Christmas and New Year, tariffs at the cheaper places double or even treble and the place is well worth avoiding. Prices quoted below are for off-season, which broadly covers most of the rest of the year, bar long weekends ("mid-season"). The cheapest places to stay are on the Main Bazaar and the road parallel to it, Murray Peth, where with a little haggling, you can pick up rooms for under Rs400 when business is slack. Note that some places close during the monsoon.

Blue Star 114 Dr Sabne Rd ⓣ02168/260678. Offers as competitive off-peak deals as you'll find for a basic attached room in the centre of town, but with correspondingly low standards. ❷

Deluxe Dr Sabne Rd ⓣ02168/260095. Above a fabrics shop, this is one of the better budget deals in town, with small but clean and comfortable a/c or non-a/c rooms. ❹

Dina 1km northeast of the bus stand ⓣ02168/260246, ⓦwww.themumbaimall.com/hoteldina. Mahabaleshwar's most atmospheric heritage hotel, occupying a hundred-year-old bungalow and annexe set in beautifully tended flower gardens high above Venna Lake. Best are the spacious rooms in the main house, which feature four-poster beds and fine views from the partitioned veranda. Full-board only: Rs1800–3000/person/day. ❼

Dreamland Below the State Bus Stand ⓣ02168/260228, ⓦwww.hoteldreamland.com. Large, established resort hotel in extensive gardens. Rooms range from simple chalets ("cottages") to a/c apartments with stupendous views. The poolside garden café serves decent coffee and the restaurant fine Indian, Continental, Mexican and Chinese cooking. ❻–❽

Mann Palace Valley View Rd, off Murray Peth Rd, 1km southeast of the bus stand ⓣ02168/261778.

Moving on from Mahabaleshwar

The only MSRTC bus service to Panaji in **Goa** departs at 9am (12hr), but numerous agents along the bazaar offer private night buses. There are also services to Kolhapur (5 daily; 5hr 30min), Pune (every 30min–1hr; 3hr 30min) and Ratnagiri (1 daily; 6hr).

Large, clean rooms in a helpful and well-run place in a rather down-at-heel neighbourhood a short hoof from the main bazaar. Good value midweek, and big discounts for longer stays. ❺

MTDC Holiday Resort 2km southwest of the centre ⓣ02168/260318. Huge campus with a wide range of accommodation, all with sitouts, ranging from austere but good-value economy rooms, through classic high-ceilinged standard rooms to spruce modern cottages sleeping four, in a peaceful location ten minutes' walk from Mumbai Point. ❸–❻

Valley View Resort Valley View Rd, off Murray Peth Rd ⓣ02168/260066, ⓦwww.valleyview-resort.com. Most congenial of Mahabaleshwar's upscale modern options: an 80-room campus close to the centre, set in a garden plot and boasting spectacular views. Facilities include a smart pure-veg restaurant (no alcohol) and large, heated indoor pool. ❻–❼

Eating and drinking

You'll **eat** well in Mahabaleshwar. Alongside the hotels, *Aman Restaurant* at the eastern end of the main bazaar is the best in town, dishing up juicy seekh kebabs and tikkas, tasty curries and enormous biryanis (Rs60–100). *Tinklers-The Taste Bud*, a few doors further along, does good south Indian and other snacks. To avoid permit-room shame, or for something a bit different, make for the idiosyncratic *Grapevine* at the western end of Masjid Road (parallel with the main bazaar), where a decent list of **wines**, beers and spirits complements a delightfully eclectic (if expensive) menu ranging from Parsi home-cooking to fish and chips and pasta with home-made pesto, all to a soundtrack of mid-1980s power ballad covers.

Pratapgadh

An hour's bus ride away from Mahabaleshwar, the seventeenth-century **fort** of **PRATAPGADH** (daily dawn to dusk; free) stretches the full length of a high ridge affording superb views over the surrounding mountains. Reached by a flight of five hundred steps, it is famously associated with the Maratha chieftain, **Shivaji**, who lured the Mughal general Afzal Khan here from Bijapur to discuss a possible truce. Neither, it would seem, intended to keep to the condition that they should come unarmed. Khan attempted to knife Shivaji, who responded by killing him with the gruesome *wagnakh*, a set of metal claws worn on the hand. Modern visitors can see Afzal Khan's tomb, a memorial to Shivaji, and views of the surrounding hills.

Taxis charge Rs560 for the return trip to Pratapgadh. State buses also do the journey each day, leaving the bus stand at 9am and returning at 12.30pm.

Kolhapur

KOLHAPUR, on the banks of the River Panchaganga 225km south of Pune, is thought to have been an important centre of the Tantric cult associated with Shakti worship since ancient times. The town probably grew around the sacred site of the present-day **Mahalakshmi temple**, still central to the life of the city, although there are said to be up to 250 other shrines in the area. With a population of more than half a million, Kolhapur has become a major industrial centre, but has retained enough Maharashtran character to make it worthy of a stopover.

Arrival and information

The **railway station** is 400m west from the **bus stand** on Station Road, near the centre of town. The helpful **MTDC tourist office** (Mon–Fri plus 1st and 3rd Sat of the month 10am–5pm; ⓣ0231/269 2935) is a fifteen-minute walk north on

Moving on from Kolhapur

By **train**, the #1012 *Mahalaxmi Express* (departs 8.30pm) and #1030 *Koyna Express* (7.55am) and #1024 *Sahyadri Express* (10.50pm) all leave daily for Mumbai (11–13hr), via Pune (7–8hr). Heading south, the #6590 *Rani Chennamma Express* (departs 2.05pm) is the only daily service to Bengaluru (17hr 30min). Heading north by **bus**, there are buses to Pune every 30min (5–6hr) and at least two daily buses to Mahabaleshwar (5hr 30min). Services to Goa leave roughly hourly in the morning, though they thin out after 1pm. Kingfisher **flies** daily to Mumbai from Kolhapur **airport**, 8km southeast of the town centre.

Assembly Road (ask locally for the Collector's Office). There are plenty of banks with **ATMs** lining Station and Assembly roads, and places to access the **internet** between the railway and bus stations include SkyNet (Rs15/hr).

Accommodation and eating

There's no shortage of decent, good-value **accommodation** in Kolhapur, much of it within easy reach of the bus stand along Station Road. Kolhapur is legendary across Maharashtra for the fieriness of its **cuisine**. Apart from the hotels – of which the *Woodland*'s *Sunderban* restaurant is the standout – there's decent north and south Indian veg at the bustling *Subraya* at the top of Station Square.

Hotels

Maharaja Station Rd ⓣ0231/265 0829. Basic lodge directly opposite the bus stand, with dozens of good-value, no frills, clean rooms and a veg restaurant. ❸

Shalini Palace On the outskirts of town, overlooking Rankala Lake ⓣ0231/263 0401, ⓔhotelshalini palace@rediffmail.com. The maharaja's former summer residence may have lost some of its grandeur but remains the most atmospheric place to stay. Furnishings are disappointingly modern throughout, though the enormous suites (Rs5000–6000) retain a few delightful period details. Even if you don't stay, it's worth considering a trip for a meal in the former Durbar Hall and a lakeside stroll in the extensive verdant grounds. ❻–❼

Tourist Station Rd ⓣ0231/265 0421, ⓦwww.hoteltourist.co.in. The best value of a row of welcoming mid-range hotels a few minutes' walk east of the bus stand. Rooms are unfussy but large and well maintained; ask for one away from the traffic. Veg and non-veg restaurants; breakfast included. ❹–❺

Vrindavan Deluxe Station Rd ⓣ0231/266 4343. Newer, business-oriented alternative to the *Tourist*, offering very clean tiled rooms and a pure-veg restaurant in a smart metallic-grey block. ❹–❺

Woodland 204 E Ward, Tarabai Park ⓣ0231/265 0941, ⓦwww.hotelwoodland.net. Good-value, welcoming upper-bracket option in a peaceful suburb 2km north of the stations. Spacious, light and comfortable a/c rooms have free modem facility, and there's a terrific non-veg garden/veranda restaurant plus bar. Buffet breakfast included. ❺–❻

The City

The **Mahalakshmi temple**, whose cream-painted sanctuary towers embellish the centre of Kolhapur's old city, is thought to have been founded in the seventh century, though what you see today dates from the early eighteenth century. The devout queue around the block from the complex's east gate for *darshan* at the image of the goddess Mahalakshmi, beneath the largest of five domed towers; you're welcome to join in. Presiding over the square just up the road from the Mahalakshmi temple, the **Rajwada**, or Old Palace, is still occupied by members of the former ruling Chhatrapati family, though its entrance hall is usually busy with worshippers to its Bhawani temple – you can access it by passing under the pillared porch that extends out into the town square.

Kolhapur is famous as a centre for traditional wrestling, or *kushti*. On leaving the palace gates, turn right and head through the low doorway in front of you, from where a path picks its way past a couple of derelict buildings to the *motibaug*, or **wrestling pit**. Come here between 6am and 9am or 4pm and 6pm (except Sat), and you can watch the wrestlers training. The main season is between June and September but you may see them active at other times. Matches take place at the **Khasbag Maidan** wrestling stadium nearby.

The maharaja's **New Palace**, 2km north of the centre, was built in 1884, following a fire at the Rajwada. Designed by Major Mant, founding father of the Indo-Saracenic school of so much British colonial architecture, it fuses Jain and Hindu influences with local touches from the Rajwada while remaining indomitably Victorian, with a prominent clock tower. The present maharaja lives on the first floor, while the ground floor houses the **Shahaji Chhatrapati Museum** (daily 9.30am–6pm; Rs30 [Rs13]), a dozen or so rooms crammed with fascinating memorabilia that demonstrates above all else the Chhatrapati family's extraordinary history of bloodlust: among the maharaja's collection of portraits, costumes, embroidery, riding paraphernalia and old Raj-era photos is an astonishing array of swords, rifles and torture equipment, a gruesome display cabinet of a huntsman's homeware – fans fashioned from tails, an elephant's-foot occasional table – and, in the final room, a scandalous *Who's Who* of stuffed endangered species, including half the current tiger population of India. Rather less macabre is the spectacular church-like Durbar Hall, with its superb carvings and mosaic floor.

12

Goa

* **Old Goa** The belfries and Baroque church facades looming over the trees on the banks of the Mandovi are all that remains of this once splendid colonial city. **See p.688**

* **Beach shacks** Tuck into a fresh kingfish, tandoori pomfret or lobster, washed down with a *feni* cocktail or an ice-cold Kingfisher beer. **See p.694, p.699, p.708, p.715** & **p.724**

* **Night Market, Arpora** Cooler and less frenetic than the flea market, with better-quality goods on sale and heaps more atmosphere. **See p.700**

* **Flea market, Anjuna** Goa's famous tourist bazaar is the place to pick up the latest party gear, shop for souvenirs, and watch the crowds go by. **See p.703**

* **Liquid Sky, Aswem** The hippest place to experience the distinctive sound of Goa trance music, at a remote hilltop café with panoramic sea views. **See p.712**

* **Arambol** An alternative resort with exquisite beaches and some of Asia's best budget restaurants. **See p.712**

* **Palacio do Deão** An extravagant, painstakingly restored colonial-era mansion in south Goa, with lunch served on a leafy garden terrace. **See p.720**

* **Sunset stroll, Palolem** Tropical sunsets don't come much more romantic than at this idyllic palm-fringed cove in the hilly deep south. **See p.727**

▲ Palolem Beach

The former Portuguese enclave of **GOA**, midway down India's southwest coast, has been a holiday destination since colonial times, when British troops and officials used to travel here from across the country for a spot of "R&R". Back then, the three Bs – bars, brothels and booze – were the big attractions. Now it's the glorious, golden, palm-fringed beaches spread along the state's 105km-coastline that pull in the tourists – around two million of them each winter. Cheap air travel to Goa's airport, Dabolim, from the rest of India has spawned a dramatic rise in the number of domestic visitors holidaying here in recent years. Plane loads of free-spending Russians have also begun to dominate a charter market formerly the preserve of working-class Brits and Scandinavians. As a result, Goa in peak season is a far cry from the laid-back image portrayed by the Indian media, yet in spite of the increasing chaos of its resorts, you can, if you're prepared to travel a bit further, still find relatively quiet corners in which to recuperate from the travails of life on the road.

Serving as the linchpin for a vast **trade network for over 450 years**, Goa was Portugal's first toe-hold in Asia. However, when the Portuguese empire began to flounder in the seventeenth century, so too did the fortunes of its capital. Cut off from the rest of India by a wall of mountains and hundreds of miles of un-navigable alluvial plain, it remained aloof from the wider Subcontinent until 1961, when the exasperated Prime Minister, Jawaharlal Nehru, finally gave up trying to negotiate with the Portuguese dictator Salazar and sent in the army.

It was shortly after the "Liberation" (or "Occupation" as some Goans still regard it), that the first **hippy travellers** came to the region on the old overland

Getting around and away from Goa

White Maruti van **taxis** are how most foreign visitors travel around Goa. Fares are often posted at ranks, but they tend only apply to peak season; at other times you should settle on the sum in advance.

A cheaper alternative is to rent either a **bicycle** (gearless, Indian-made cycles are on offer in all the resorts for around Rs100–150/day) or, for longer trips, a **motorbike**. Buzzing around Goa's tropical backroads on a scooter or motorcycle gives a great sense of freedom, but be warned that it can be perilous. Make sure, therefore, that the lights and brakes are in good shape, and be especially vigilant at night.

Officially, you need an **international driver's licence** to rent and ride anything, but in practice a standard licence will suffice if you're stopped and asked to produce your papers by the local police. All rented motorcycles should carry special **yellow-and-black licence plates**; make sure yours does, to avoid harassment by Goa's notoriously corrupt traffic cops.

Helmets are also compulsory these days while riding on the highways, but not on backroads. **Rates** for motorbikes vary according to season, duration of rental and vehicle; most owners also insist on a deposit and/or passport as security. The cheapest bike, a scooter-style Honda Activa 100cc, which has automatic gears, costs around Rs200 per day. Other options include the perennially stylish Enfield Bullet 350cc, although these are heavy, unwieldy and – at upwards of Rs350 per day – the most expensive bike to rent.

Fuel is sold at service stations around the state (known locally as "petrol pumps"). In smaller settlements, including the resorts, it's sold in mineral-water bottles at general stores or through backstreet suppliers – but you should avoid these as some bulk out their petrol with low-grade kerosene or industrial solvent, which makes engines misfire and smoke badly.

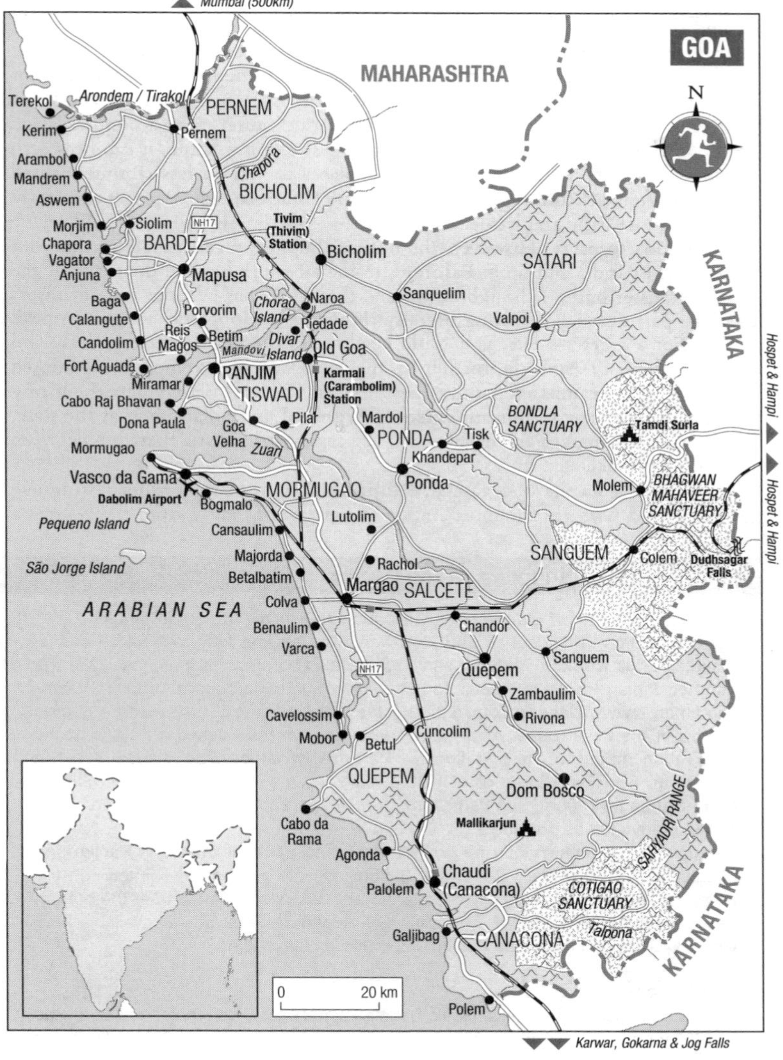

trail. They found a way of life little changed in centuries: back then Portuguese was still very much the lingua franca of the well-educated elite, and the coastal settlements were mere fishing and coconut cultivation villages. Relieved to have found somewhere culturally undemanding to party, the "freaks" got stoned, watched the mesmeric sunsets over the Arabian Sea and danced like lunatics on full-moon nights.

Since then, the state has been at pains to shake off its reputation as a druggy drop-out zone, and its beaches have grown in popularity year on year. Around two dozen stretches of soft white sand indent the region's coast, from spectacular 25-kilometre sweeps to secluded palm-backed coves. The level of development behind them varies a great deal; while some are lined by swanky Western-style resorts, the most sophisticated structures on others are palm-leaf shacks.

Which beach you opt for when you arrive largely depends on what sort of holiday you have in mind. More developed resorts such as **Calangute** and **Baga** in the north, and **Colva** and **Benaulim** in the south, offer more accommodation than elsewhere. Even if you're looking for a less touristy scene, it can be worth heading for these centres first, as finding places to stay in less commercialised corners is often difficult. **Anjuna**, **Vagator** and **Chapora**, where places to stay are generally more basic and harder to come by, are the beaches to aim for if you've come to Goa to party. However, the bulk of budget travellers taking time out from tours of India end up in **Palolem**, in the far south beyond the reach of the charter transfer buses – though be warned that it too has become a major resort over the past decade, attracting literally thousands of long-stay visitors in peak season. For a quieter scene, you could head for **Patnem**, just over the headland from **Palolem**, or **Agonda**, further up the coast, where development is limited to a string of hut camps and family guest houses. The only place where the **hippy scene** endures to any significant extent is **Arambol**, in the far north of the state, where you can dip in to any number of yoga styles and holistic therapies between spells on the beach.

Some 10km from the state capital, **Panjim**, the ruins of the former Portuguese capital at **Old Goa** are foremost among the attractions away from the coast – a

Moving on from Goa

The price of seats on **planes from Goa** fluctuates wildly at certain times of year, but peaks around Christmas and New Year. The easiest way to book is online. Tickets for all **Konkan Railway** services are also most easily purchased via the internet: Indian Railways reservation site, ⓦwww.irctc.co.in, is a lot less streamlined than ⓦwww.cleartrip.com, although the latter charges a Rs100 service charge on top of the ticket price. Alternatively, you can join the queues at KRC's hectic reservation office on the first floor of Panjim's Kadamba Bus Stand (Mon–Sat 8am–8pm, Sun 8am–2pm), or at KRC's main reservation hall in Margao Station (Mon–Sat 8am–4.30pm, Sun 8am–2pm; ⓣ0834/271 2780). Make your reservations as far in advance as possible.

Kadamba **bus tickets** can be bought in advance at their offices in Panjim and Mapusa bus stands (daily 9–11am & 2–5pm); private companies sell through the many travel agents immediately outside the bus stand in Panjim, and at the bottom of the square in Mapusa. **Information** on all departures and fares is available from Goa Tourism's counter inside Panjim's Bus Stand (see p.683).

To Mumbai

A couple of dozen flights leave Goa's Dabolim airport daily, with fares from as low as Rs1000 (or even less) if you book well in advance with one of the no-frills airlines – or as much as Rs30,000 on New Year's Eve. Try SpiceJet, IndiGo, Go Air, JetLite or Kingfisher Airlines (for websites, see p.28). Flying with Air India or Jet Airways will set you back more – typically around US$100 each way.

Four to five services run daily on the **Konkan Railway**, the most convenient being the overnight Konkan *Kanya Express* (#0112), which departs from Margao (see p.718) at 6pm (or Karmali, near Old Goa, 11km west of Panjim, at 6.30pm), arriving at Mumbai CST (still commonly known as Victoria Terminus, or VT) at 5.50am the following day. The other fast train from Goa to CST is the *Mandovi Express* (#0104), departing Margao at 10.10am (or Karmali, at 10.37am) and arriving at 9.45pm the same evening.

sprawl of Catholic cathedrals, convents and churches that draw crowds of Christian pilgrims from all over India. Another popular day excursion is to Anjuna's Wednesday **flea market**, a sociable place to shop for souvenirs and dance wear. Further inland, the thickly wooded countryside around **Ponda** harbours numerous temples, where you can experience Goa's peculiar brand of Hindu architecture. The district of Salcete, and its main market town, **Margao**, is also littered with Portuguese mansions, churches and seminaries. Finally, wildlife enthusiasts may be tempted into the interior to visit the nature reserve at **Cotigao** in the far south.

The **best time to come** to Goa is during the dry, relatively cool winter months between late-November and mid-March. At other times, either the sun is too hot for comfort, or the humidity, clouds and rain make life miserable. During peak season, from mid-December to the end of January, the weather is perfect, with temperatures rarely nudging above 32°C. Finding a room or a house to rent at that time, however – particularly over Christmas and New Year when tariffs double, or triple – can be a real hassle.

Some history

Goa's sheer inaccessibility by land has always kept it out of the mainstream of Indian history; on the other hand, its control of the seas and the lucrative spice trade made it a much-coveted prize for rival colonial powers. Until a century

Finally, a fleet of **night buses** also covers the 500km from Goa to Mumbai – a terrible 14- to 18-hour journey to be avoided at all costs. Paulo Travels is the top firm running the route, with a range of different services, from no-frills buses for Rs350 to swisher a/c Volvo coaches with berths costing Rs700. For tickets, contact their office just outside the Kadamba Bus Stand, Panjim (Ⓣ0832/222 3736, Ⓦwww.paulotravels.com). In south Goa, the firm's main outlet is at the *Hotel Nanutel*, opposite *Club Harmonia*, in Margao (Ⓣ0834/272 1516). Information on all departures and fares is available online.

To Hampi

The most stress-free and economical way to reach Hospet from Goa is the four-times-weekly **train** service from **Margao**. The *Vasco–Howrah Express* (#8048) departs every Tuesday, Thursday, Friday and Sunday at 8.15am, arriving just over six hours later. **Fares** range from Rs200 for a seat in an ultra-basic, crowded second-class compartment to Rs675 for second-class a/c – the most comfy option. **Tickets** can be bought on the day at either point of departure. Arrive at Margao by at least 7.30am, as the "queues" are invariably more like rugby scrums.

The **bus** journey covering the same route is no cheaper than the train (sleeper class) and is far more gruelling. Two or three clapped-out government services leave Panjim's Kadamba stand (platform #9) each morning for Hospet, the last one at 10.30am. Brace yourself for a long, hard slog; all being well, it should take nine or ten hours, but delays and breakdowns are frustratingly frequent.

To Gokarna, Jog Falls, Mangalore and southern Karnataka

From Goa, the fastest and most convenient way to travel down the coast to Gokarna is via the **Konkan Railway**. At 2.25pm, the *Madgaon–Mangalore Passenger* (KR1 DN) leaves Margao, passing through Chaudi at 3.05pm en route to Gokarna Road, the town's railhead, where it arrives at 4.20pm. As this is classed as a passenger service, you don't have to buy tickets in advance; just turn up at the station 30min before the departure time and pay at the regular ticket counter.

before the arrival of the Portuguese, Goa had belonged for over a thousand years to the kingdom of **Kadamba**. They, in turn, were overthrown by the Karnatakan Vijayanagars, the Muslim Bahmanis, and Yusuf Adil Shah of Bijapur, but the capture of the fort at Panjim by **Afonso de Albuquerque** in 1510 signalled the start of a Portuguese occupation that was to last 451 years.

As Goa expanded, its splendid capital (now Old Goa) came to hold a larger population than Paris or London. Though Ismail Adil Shah laid siege for ten months in 1570, and the Marathas under Shivaji and later chiefs came nail-bitingly close to seizing the region, the greatest threat was from other European maritime nations, principally Holland and France. Meanwhile, conversions to **Christianity**, started by the Franciscans, gathered pace when St Francis Xavier founded the **Jesuit** mission in 1542. With the advent of the **Inquisition** soon afterwards, laws were introduced censoring literature and banning any faith other than Catholicism. Hindu temples were destroyed, and converted Hindus adopted Portuguese names, such as Da Silva, Correa and De Sousa, which remain common in the region. Thereafter, the colony, whose trade monopoly had been broken by its European rivals, went into gradual decline, hastened by the unhealthy, disease-ridden environment of its capital.

Despite certain liberalization, such as the restoration of Hindus' right to worship and the final banishment of the dreaded Inquisition in 1820, the nineteenth century saw widespread civil unrest. During the British Raj many Goans moved to Bombay, and elsewhere in British India, to find work.

The success of the post-Independence Goan struggle for freedom owed as much to the efforts of the Indian government, which cut off diplomatic ties with Portugal, as to the work of freedom fighters such as **Menezes Braganza** and **Dr Cunha**. After a "liberation march" in 1955 resulted in a number of deaths, the state was blockaded. Trade with Bombay ceased, and the railway was cut off, so Goa set out to forge international links, particularly with Pakistan and Sri Lanka: that led to the building of Dabolim airport, and a determination to improve local agricultural output. In 1961, Prime Minister Jawaharlal Nehru finally sent in the armed forces. Mounted in defiance of a United Nations resolution, "**Operation Vijay**" met only token resistance, and the Indian army overran Goa in two days. Thereafter, Goa (along with Portugal's other two enclaves, Daman and Diu) became part of India as a self-governing **Union Territory**, with minimum interference from Delhi.

Since Independence, Goa has continued to prosper, bolstered by iron-ore exports and a booming tourist industry. Dominated by issues of statehood, the status of Konkani and the ever-rising levels of immigration, its political life has been dogged by chronic **instability**, with frequent changes of government and chief ministers, interrupted by occasional periods of **President's Rule**, when the state had to be governed directly from New Delhi.

At the start of the twenty-first century, renewed fears over the pace of change on the coastal strip have started to dominate the news. A sudden influx of wealthy **Russians** and Indian **property developers** from Delhi and Mumbai has provoked a backlash from successive ruling coalitions, with a state-sponsored land grab of expatriate property. Hundreds of resident Europeans have had their assets confiscated, and fled. A series of high-profile attacks on and by foreigners – notably the murder in 2008 of British teenager Scarlett Keeling – has done little to improve the state's image abroad. Meanwhile, as ever-improving infrastructural links with the rest of India render Goa's borders more porous, the survival of the region as a culturally distinct entity continues to hang in the balance.

Panjim and central Goa

Stacked around the sides of a lush terraced hillside at the mouth of the River Mandovi, **PANJIM** (also known by its Marathi name, **Panaji** – "land that does not flood") was for centuries little more than a minor landing stage and customs house, protected by a hilltop fort and surrounded by stagnant swampland. It only became state capital in 1843, after the port at Old Goa had silted up and its rulers and impoverished inhabitants had fled the plague.

Today, the town ranks among the least congested and hectic of any Indian capital. Sights are thin on the ground, but the backstreets of the old quarter, **Fontainhas**, have retained a faded Portuguese atmosphere, with colour-washed houses and Catholic churches.

The area **around Panjim** attracts far fewer visitors than the coastal resorts, yet its paddy fields and wooded valleys harbour several attractions worth a day or two's break from the beach. **Old Goa** is just a bus ride away. Further inland, the forested lower slopes of the Western Ghats, cut through by the main Panjim–Bengaluru (Bangalore) highway, shelter the impressive **Dudhsagar falls**, reachable only by four-wheel-drive jeep.

Arrival, information and local transport

European charter planes and domestic flights arrive at **Dabolim airport** (Ⓣ0832/254 0788), 29km south of Panjim on the outskirts of Vasco da Gama, Goa's second city. Pre-paid taxis into town (45min; Rs550), booked at the counter in the forecourt, can be shared by up to four people.

There's no **train** station in town itself; the nearest one, on the Konkan Railway, is at **Karmali** (11km east of Panjim at Old Goa). State buses to central Panjim await arrivals.

Long-distance and local **buses** pull into Panjim's busy Kadamba Bus Stand, 1km east of the centre in the district of Pato. Ten minutes' walk, across Ourem Creek to Fontainhas, brings you to several budget hotels. For the more modern west end of town, jump into an auto-rickshaw at the rank outside the station concourse (Rs30–50).

GTDC's **information** counter, inside the concourse at the main Kadamba Bus Stand (daily 9.30am–1pm & 2–5pm; Ⓣ0832/222 5620, Ⓦwww.goa-tourism.com) is useful for checking train and bus timings, but little else. The more reliable **India Tourism office** is across town on Church Square (Mon–Fri 9.30am–6pm, Sat 9.30am–1pm; Ⓣ0832/222 3412, Ⓦwww.incredibleindia.org).

Auto-rickshaws are the most convenient way of **getting around** Panjim; flag one down at the roadside or head for one of the ranks around the city. If you're not weighed down with luggage, motorcycle taxis – unique in India, and known throughout Goa as "pilots" – offer a cheaper and faster alternative.

Accommodation

The majority of Goa's Indian visitors prefer to stay in Panjim rather than the coastal resorts, which explains the huge number of **hotels** and **lodges** crammed into the town centre, especially its noisy, more modern west end. Foreigners spending the night here instead of on the coast, on the other hand, tend to do so primarily to sample the atmosphere of the old quarter, Fontainhas. Finding a room is only a problem during the festival of St Francis (Nov 24–Dec 3), Dussehra (Sept/Oct) and during peak season (mid-Dec to mid-Jan); the codes below apply to October through March, excluding the above periods, when prices can double or triple. Note that **checkout times** vary wildly.

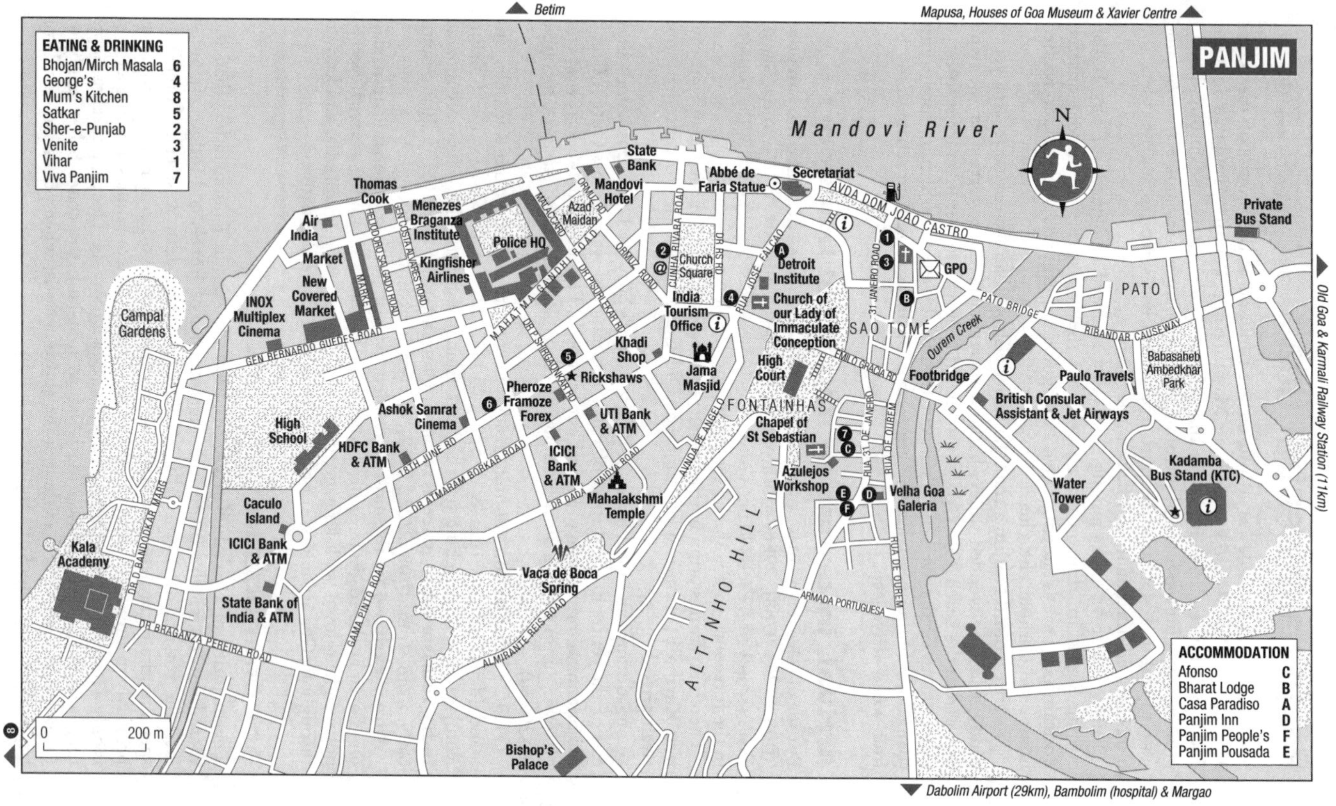

Betim
Mapusa, Houses of Goa Museum & Xavier Centre
Old Goa & Karmali Railway Station (11km)
Dabolim Airport (29km), Bambolim (hospital) & Margao
PANJIM
EATING & DRINKING
Bhojan/Mirch Masala 6
George's 4
Mum's Kitchen 8
Satkar 5
Sher-e-Punjab 2
Venite 3
Vihar 1
Viva Panjim 7
ACCOMMODATION
Afonso C
Bharat Lodge B
Casa Paradiso A
Panjim Inn D
Panjim People's F
Panjim Pousada E
Mandovi River
N
Private Bus Stand
State Bank
Abbé de Faria Statue
Secretariat
AVDA DOM JOAO CASTRO
Thomas Cook
Mandovi Hotel
Azad Maidan
Air India
Menezes Braganza Institute
Police HQ
Market
Kingfisher Airlines
New Covered Market
INOX Multiplex Cinema
Campal Gardens
Church Square
India Tourism Office
Detroit Institute
Church of our Lady of Immaculate Conception
GPO
PATO
PATO BRIDGE
RIBANDAR CAUSEWAY
Babasaheb Ambedkhar Park
SAO TOMÉ
Ourem Creek
Footbridge
Paulo Travels
British Consular Assistant & Jet Airways
Khadi Shop
Jama Masjid
High Court
Rickshaws
FONTAINHAS
Pheroze Framoze Forex
Ashok Samrat Cinema
UTI Bank & ATM
Chapel of St Sebastian
High School
HDFC Bank & ATM
ICICI Bank & ATM
Azulejos Workshop
Velha Goa Galeria
Water Tower
Kadamba Bus Stand (KTC)
Mahalakshmi Temple
Caculo Island
ICICI Bank & ATM
Kala Academy
Vaca de Boca Spring
ALTINHO HILL
State Bank of India & ATM
Bishop's Palace
MALACCARD
ORMUZ RD
ORMUZ ROAD
CUNHA RIVARA ROAD
DR RS RD
RUA JOSE FALCAO
31 JANEIRO ROAD
EMILO GRACIA RD
RUA 31 DE JANEIRO
RUA DE OUREM
ARMADA PORTUGUESA
MAHATMA GANDHI ROAD
DR PISURLEKAR RD
DR P SHIRGAONKAR RD
HELIODORO SALGADO ROAD
GEN COSTA ALVARES ROAD
MARKET
GEN BERNARDO GUEDES ROAD
18TH JUNE RD
DR ATMARAM BORKAR ROAD
VAIDYA ROAD
DR DADA
AVNDA PE ANGELO
GAMA PINTO ROAD
ALMIRANTE REIS ROAD
DR D BANDODKAR MARG
DR BRAGANZA PEREIRA ROAD
0 200 m
8

Afonso St Sebastian Chapel Square, Fontainhas ⓣ0832/222 2359 or ⓣ9764 300165. This refurbished colonial-era house in a picturesque backstreet is a safe bet if you can't quite afford the *Panjim Inn* down the road. Spotless attached rooms, friendly owners and rooftop terrace with views and cool ceramic mosaic floors – though someone's gone overboard with the textured wall paint recently. Single occupancy available. ❺

Bharat Lodge Sao Tome Rd, near GPO ⓣ0832/222 4862. Good value budget guesthouse, located at the heart of the old quarter in a terracotta-washed,150-year-old building that's retained many of its original features, but which has been extensively modernized internally. The rooms are large for the price, have quiet fans and good-sized bathrooms: ask for 106 or 102 if they're vacant. ❹

Casa Paradiso Ghanekar Building, Rua Jose Falcao ⓣ0832/222 6291,ⓦcasaparadisogoa.com. This guest house is the only mid-range place outside Fontainhas worth considering. The location, on a busy thoroughfare close to the secretariat and Church Square, is none too inspiring, and there's no outside sitting space, but it is central and the rooms themselves are spotless, with a/c and shiny ceramic floors. ❺

Panjim Inn/Panjim Pousada E-212, Rua 31 de Janeiro, Fontainhas ⓣ0832/243 5628, ⓦwww.panjiminn.com. Grand three-hundred-year-old townhouse, managed as a homely heritage hotel, with period furniture, sepia photos, balconies and a veranda where meals and drinks are served. Their adjacent three-storey wing overlooking the river is in the same style, but with better views, while the *Pousada* annexe over the road has two lovely rearside rooms sharing a wooden balcony, itself surveying a secret courtyard. ❻

Panjim People's Rua 31 de Janeiro, Fontainhas ⓣ0832/222 1122, ⓦwww.panjiminn.com. Sister concern of the *Panjim Inn*, in a former high school opposite the original house (see above). It's more upmarket than their other two buildings, with new a/c units and large TVs in the rooms, themselves all huge, and fitted with antique rosewood furniture, gilded pelmets and lace curtains. Tariffs mid-season start at around Rs8000 ($175) per night. ❾

The Town

The leafy rectangular park opposite the India Government tourist office, known as **Church Square** or the **Municipal Gardens**, forms the heart of Panjim. Presiding over its southeast side is the town's most distinctive landmark, the whitewashed Baroque facade of the **Church of Our Lady of the Immaculate Conception**. At the head of a crisscrossing laterite walkway, the church was built in 1541 for the benefit of sailors arriving here from Lisbon. The weary mariners would stagger up from the quay to give thanks for their safe passage before proceeding to the capital at Old Goa – the original home of the enormous bell that hangs from its central gable.

Running north from the church, Rua José Falcao brings you to the riverside, where Panjim's main street, Avenida Dom Joao Castro, holds the town's oldest surviving building. With its sloping tiled roofs, carved-stone coats of arms and wooden verandas, the stalwart **Secretariat** looks typically colonial. Yet it was originally the summer palace of Goa's sixteenth-century Muslim ruler, the Adil Shah. Later, the Portuguese converted it into a temporary resthouse for the territory's governors (who used to overnight here en route to and from Lisbon) and then a residence for the viceroy. Today, it houses municipal offices.

A hundred metres east, a peculiar statue of a man holding his hands over the body of an entranced reclining woman represents **Abbé de Faria** (1755–1819), a Goan priest who emigrated to France to become one of the world's first professional hypnotists.

Just behind the esplanade, 500m west of the Abbé de Faria statue, stands another grand vestige of the colonial era, the **Menezes Braganza Institute**. Now the town's Central Library (Mon–Fri 9.30am–1.15pm & 2–5.30pm), this Neoclassical building was erected as part of the civic makeover initiated by the Marquis de Pombal and Dom Manuel de Portugal e Castro in the early nineteenth century. Its entrance lobby on Malacca Road is lined with panels of blue-and-yellow-painted ceramic tiles, known as **azulejos**, depicting scenes from Luis Vaz de Camões' epic poem, *Os Lusíades*.

Fontainhas

Panjim's oldest and most interesting district, **Fontainhas**, comprises a dozen or so blocks of Neoclassical houses rising up the sides of leafy Altinho Hill on the eastern edge of town, near the bus stand. Many have retained their traditional coat of ochre, pale yellow, green or blue – a legacy of the Portuguese insistence that every Goan building (except churches, which had to be white) should be colour-washed after the monsoons. While some have been restored, most remain in a state of charismatic decay.

The **Chapel of St Sebastian** stands at the centre of Fontainhas, at the head of a small square where the Portuguese-speaking locals hold a lively annual street *festa* to celebrate their patron saint's day in mid-November. The eerie crucifix inside the chapel, brought here in 1812, formerly hung in the Palace of the Inquisition in Old Goa. Unusually, Christ's eyes are open – allegedly to inspire fear in those being interrogated by the Inquisitors.

Just off the bottom of the square is a small workshop where you can watch traditional Goan *azulejos* being made. The main sales room, **Velha Goa Galeria** is a couple of blocks away, next door to the *Panjim Inn*.

Eating and drinking

Catering for the droves of tourists who come here from other Indian states, as well as fussy, more price-conscious locals, Panjim is packed with good **places to eat**. Most are connected to a hotel, but there are also plenty of other independently run establishments offering quality food for far less than you pay in the coastal resorts. If you're unsure about which regional cooking style to go for, head for *The Fidalgo*

Goan food and drink

Not unnaturally, after 451 years of colonization, Goan **cooking** has absorbed a strong Portuguese influence – palm vinegar (unknown elsewhere in India), copious amounts of coconut, tangy *kokum* and fierce local chillies also play their part. Goa is the home of the famous **vindaloo** (from the Portuguese *vinho d'alho*, literally "garlic wine"), originally an extra-hot and sour pork curry, but now made with a variety of meat and fish. Other **pork** specialities include *chouriço* red sausages, *sorpotel*, a hot curry made from pickled pig's liver and heart, *leitao*, suckling pig and *balchao*, pork in a rich brown sauce. Delicious alternatives include mutton *xacuti*, made with a sauce of lemon juice, peanuts, coconut, chillies and spices. The choice of **seafood**, often cooked in fragrant masalas, is excellent – clams, mussels, crab, lobster, giant prawns – while **fish**, depending on the type, is either cooked in wet curries, grilled, or baked in tandoori clay ovens. *Sanna*, like the south Indian *iddli*, is a steamed cake of fermented rice flour, but here made with palm toddy. Sweet tooths will adore *bebinca*, a rich, delicious solid egg custard with coconut.

As for **drinks**, locally produced wine, spirits and beer are cheaper than anywhere in the country, thanks to lower rates of tax. The most famous and widespread **beer** is Kingfisher, which tastes less of glycerine preservative than it does elsewhere in India, but you'll also come across pricier Fosters, brewed in Mumbai and nothing like the original. Goan **port**, a sweeter, inferior version of its Portuguese namesake, is ubiquitous, served chilled in large wine glasses with a slice of lemon. Local **spirits** – whiskies, brandies, rums, gins and vodkas – come in a variety of brand names for less than Rs30–50 a shot, but, at half the price, local speciality **feni**, made from distilled cashew or from the sap of coconut palms, offers strong competition. Cashew *feni* is usually drunk after the first distillation, but you can also find it double-distilled, flavoured with ginger or cumin to produce a smooth liqueur.

Food Enclave, in the *Hotel Fidalgo* on 18th June Road, which hosts six different outlets, from Goan to Gujarati.

Bhojan/Mirch Masala *Hotel Fidalgo*, 18th June Rd. Authentic, pure-veg Gujarati thali joint, in the a/c restaurant complex of a popular upscale hotel. You won't eat finer Indian vegetarian cuisine anywhere in Goa. Rs140 for the works: five or six different vegetables, dhals, *papad*, rice and various traditional breads, plus fragrant milk sweets for desert. For equally superb non-veg, north Indian food (kebabs, curries, tandoori and the like) head next door to *Mirch Masala*.

George's Emilio Gracia Rd. This is a great little Goan-Catholic café serving proper local food at local prices, on cramped tables near the Immaculate Conception church. Grab a seat under a fan and tuck into calamari chilli fry, prawn-curry-rice, millet-fried fish fillets or one of the good-value seafood thalis. Most mains around Rs100.

Mum's Kitchen Dr D Bandodkar (DB) Marg (Panjim–Miramar Rd) ⓣ9011 095557, ⓦwww.mumskitchengoa.com. Rony and Suzette Martins, the owners of this great Goan restaurant in the suburb of Miramar, 10min by auto from the centre of Panjim, collected old family recipes from mothers, grandmas and aunties across the state in an attempt to revive disappearing culinary traditions. The results are as authentic and flavour-packed as any you'll encounter in Goa. Most mains Rs250–300.

Satkar 18th June Rd. Popular south Indian snack and juice joint. There's a huge range of dishes, including Chinese and north Indian, but most people go for their fantastic masala dosas and piping hot, crunchy samosas – the best in town.

Sher-e-Punjab Above Hindu Pharmacy, Cunha Rivara Rd, Municipal Gardens (Church Square) ⓣ0832/242 5657. This north Indian restaurant, an old Panjim favourite which recently had a major facelift, occupies a funky, glass-sided dining hall overlooking the square. Steer clear of the Goan and Chinese menu – Mughlai is the thing here: chicken, mutton and *paneer* prepared in the tandoor or steeped in a rich, spicy, creamy sauces, which you scoop up with flaky naan breads. Mains only Rs150–210.

Venite Rua 31 de Janeiro. With its wooden floors and tiny, candle-lit balcony tables, this touristy place in the old Sao Tomé district is one of the most atmospheric places to eat in Panjim. Continental and Goan seafood dishes dominate their somewhat overpriced menu (mains Rs200–300), but the down-at-heel, old-world ambience is why most punters come here.

Vihar Around the corner from *Venite*, on Avda Dom Joao Castro. One of the best South Indian snack cafés in town, and more conveniently situated than its competitors if you're staying in Fontainhas. Try their tasty *rawa* masala dosas or cheese *uttapams*. The only drawback is the traffic noise, so avoid it during rush hours.

Viva Panjim 178 Rua 31 de Janeiro, behind Mary Immaculate High School, Fontainhas. Traditional Goan home cooking – *xacutis*, vindaloo, prawn *balchao*, *cafreal*, *amotik* and delicious freshly grilled fish – served by a charming local woman, Linda de Souza, in a pretty colonial-era backstreet. This place should be your first choice for dinner if you're staying in Fontainhas.

Listings

Airlines Indian Airlines/Air India, Dempo House, Dr D Bandodkar Marg ⓣ0832/242 8787 or 223 7826; Jet Airways/JetLite, Sesa Ghor, Patto Plaza, next to GTDC *Panjim Residency*, Pato ⓣ0832/243 8792; Kingfisher Airlines Shop G-4, 5–6 Glass Tower, Swami Vivekanand Road, Opposite Panjim Traffic Cell ⓣ1800/209 3030.

ATMs & Banks Nearly all the banks in town nowadays have ATMs, where you can make withdrawals using Visa or MasterCard; several are marked on the map on p.684. The most efficient places to change currency and travellers' cheques are: Thomas Cook, near the Air India/Indian Airlines office at 8 Alcon Chambers, Dr D Bandodkar (DB) Marg (Mon–Sat 9am–6pm, Oct–March also Sun 10am–5pm).

Bookshops The bookshops in the *Hotel Fidalgo* and the *Hotel Mandovi* on Ave Dom Jaoa Castro, overlooking the waterfront, stock English-language titles, but the best selection of Goa-related books is at the Broadway Book Centre on 18th June Rd, near the Caculo Island intersection. It sells a great range of old texts in facsimile editions and lots of architecture and photographic tomes in hardback at discounted prices.

British Consular Assistant The British High Commission of Mumbai has a Tourist Assistance Office Panjim – a useful contact for British nationals who've lost passports, get into trouble with the law or need help dealing with a death. It's over near the Kadamba bus stand at 13/14 Dempo Towers, Patto Plaza ⓣ0832/243 8734 or 243 8897,

Ⓕ0832/664 1297, Ⓦwww.ukinindia.com. Outside office opening hours (Mon–Fri 8am–1pm & 2.30–4pm), you should contact the main British High Commission in Delhi Ⓣ011/2419 2100, which in theory has a duty officer on call 24/7.
Cinema Panjim's swanky multiplex, the 1272-seater Inox, is in the northwest of town on the site of the old Goa Medical College, Dr D Bandodkar (DB) Marg (Ⓣ0832/242 0999, Ⓦwww.inoxmovies.com). It screens all the latest Hindi blockbusters, and some English-language Hollywood movies; see the local press or their websites for listings and booking details.
Hospital The state's main medical facility is the new Goa Medical College, aka GMC (Ⓣ0832/245 8700–07), 7km south on NH-17 at Bambolim, where there's also a 24hr pharmacy. Ambulances (Ⓣ102) are likely to get you there a lot less quickly than a standard taxi. Conditions are grim by Western standards. Less serious cases can receive attention at the Vintage Hospital, next to the fire brigade headquarters in Panjim's St Inez district (Ⓣ0832/564 4401–05).
Internet access Most hotels and guesthouses offer internet access to guests. Otherwise, Cozy Nook Travels, at No 6 Municipal Bldg, 18th June Rd, has a fast ADSL connection.
Music and dance Regular recitals of classical Indian music and dance are held at Panjim's school for the performing arts, the Kala Academy in Campal (Ⓦwww.kalaacademy.org), at the far west end of town on Dr D Bandodkar (DB) Marg. For details of forthcoming concerts, consult the listings pages of local newspapers.
Pharmacies Hindu Pharma, near the tourist office on Church Square (Ⓣ0832/222 3176), stocks a phenomenal range of Ayurvedic, homeopathic and allopathic medicines.

Old Goa

A one-time byword for splendour with a population of several hundred thousand, Goa's erstwhile former capital, **OLD GOA**, was virtually abandoned following malaria and cholera epidemics from the seventeenth century onwards. Today, despite its coveted UNESCO World Heritage Site status, you need considerable imagination to picture the once-great capital as it used to be. The maze of twisting streets, piazzas and ochre-washed villas has gone, and all that remains is a score of cream-painted churches and convents. Foremost among the surviving monuments is the tomb of **St Francis Xavier**, the legendary sixteenth-century missionary, whose remains are enshrined in the **Basilica of Bom Jesus**.

Just thirty minutes by road from the state capital, Old Goa is served by buses every fifteen minutes from Panjim's Kadamba Bus Stand; alternatively, hop into an auto-rickshaw (Rs120), or rent a taxi (Rs300–400). There is nowhere commendable to eat in Old Goa; for a snack or coffee, head a couple of kilometres back along the road to Panjim, where the lifestyle store **Casa de Goa**, housed in a beautifully converted, late sixteenth-century *palacio*, has an excellent **café**.

The Viceroy's Archway and the Church of St Cajetan

On arriving at the river landing stage to the north, seventeenth-century visitors passed through the **Viceroy's Archway** (1597), constructed to commemorate Vasco da Gama's arrival in India and built from the same porous red laterite as virtually all Old Goa's buildings. Above it a Bible-toting figure rests his foot on the cringing figure of a "native", while its granite facade, facing the river, holds a statue of Da Gama himself. A short way up the lane from the Gate, the distinctive domed **Church of St Cajetan** (1651) was modelled on St Peter's in Rome by monks from the Theatine Order. While it boasts a Corinthian exterior, non-European elements are also evident in the decoration, such as the cashew-nut designs in the carving of the pulpit. Hidden beneath the church is a crypt where the embalmed bodies of Portuguese governors were once kept in lead coffins before they were shipped back to Lisbon. Forgotten for over thirty years, the last batch (of three) was only removed in 1992 on the eve of the state visit to Goa by the then Portuguese president.

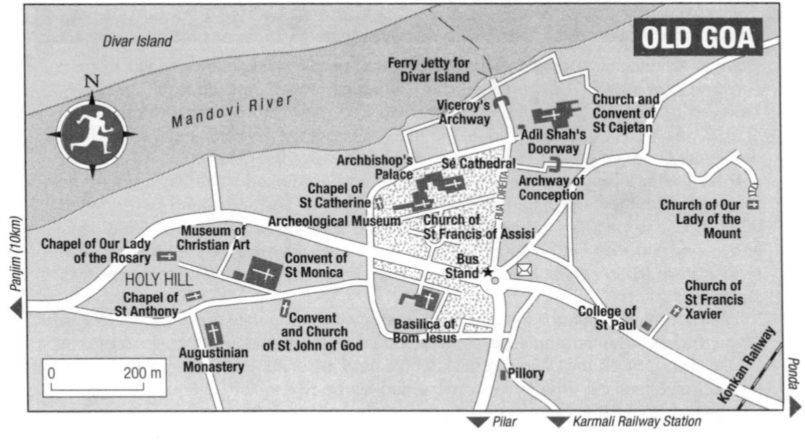

The Sé (St Catherine's Cathedral)

The Portuguese viceroy Redondo (1561–64) commissioned the **Sé**, or **St Catherine's Cathedral**, southwest of St Cajetan's, to be "a grandiose church worthy of the wealth, power and fame of the Portuguese who dominated the seas from the Atlantic to the Pacific". Today it stands larger than any church in Portugal, although it was beset by problems, not least a lack of funds and the motherland's temporary loss of independence to Spain. It took eighty years to build and was not consecrated until 1640.

On the Tuscan-style exterior, the one surviving tower houses the **Golden Bell**, cast in Cuncolim (south Goa) in the seventeenth century. During the Inquisition its tolling announced the start of the gruesome autos-da-fé that were held in the square outside, when suspected heretics were subjected to public torture and burned at the stake. The scale and opulence of the Corinthian-style interior is overwhelming; no fewer than fifteen altars are arranged around the walls, among them one featuring a **Miraculous Cross**, said to heal the sick. The staggeringly ornate, gilded main **altar** is surrounded by panels depicting episodes from the life of St Catherine of Alexandria (died 307 AD).

The Church of St Francis of Assisi and Archeological Museum

Southwest of the cathedral is the ruined **Palace of the Inquisition**, in operation up until 1774, while to the west stands the **Convent of St Francis of Assisi**, built by Franciscan monks in 1517 and restored in the mid-eighteenth century. Today, the core of its **Archeological Museum** (daily except Fri 10am–6pm; Rs5) is a gallery of **portraits** of Portuguese viceroys, painted by local artists under Italian supervision. Other exhibits include coins, domestic Christian wooden sculpture, and downstairs in the cloister, pre-Portuguese Hindu sculpture. Next door, the **Church of St Francis** (1521) features fine decorative frescoes, *hidalgos*' tombstones in the floor paving, and paintings on wood showing the life of St Francis of Assisi.

Basilica of Bom Jesus

Close to the Convent of St Francis, the 1605 church of **Bom Jesus**, "Good" or "Menino Jesus", is known principally for the **tomb of St Francis Xavier**. In 1946, it became the first church in India to be elevated to the status of Minor

St Francis Xavier

Francis Xavier, the "Apostle of the Indies", was born in 1506 in the old kingdom of Navarre, now part of Spain. When the Portuguese king, Dom Joao III (1521–57), received reports of corruption and dissolute behaviour among the Portuguese in Goa, it was Xavier, a recent graduate in theology from the University of Paris, whom the Jesuit Order selected to restore the moral climate of the colony.

Arriving after a year-long journey, the young priest embarked on a busy programme throughout southern India, founding numerous churches and converting an estimated thirty thousand people – primarily by performing such miracles as raising the dead and curing the sick with a touch of his beads. Subsequently he took his mission further afield to Sri Lanka, Malacca (Malaysia), China and Japan, where he was less successful.

When Xavier left Goa for the last time, it was with the ambition of evangelizing in China; however, he contracted dysentery aboard ship and died on the island of San Chuan (Sancian), off the Chinese coast, where he was buried. On hearing of his death, a group of Christians from Malacca exhumed his body – which, although the grave had been filled with lime to hasten its decomposition, they found to be in a perfect state of preservation. Reburied in Malacca, his body was later removed and taken to Old Goa, where it has remained ever since, enshrined in the **Basilica of Bom Jesus**.

However, St Francis's incorruptible corpse has never rested entirely in peace. Chunks of it have been removed over the years by **relic hunters** and curious clerics: in 1614, the right arm was dispatched to the pope in Rome (where it allegedly wrote its name on paper), a hand was sent to Japan, and parts of the intestines to Southeast Asia. One Portuguese woman, Dona Isabel de Caron, even bit off the little toe of the cadaver in 1534; apparently, so much blood spurted into her mouth, it left a trail to her house and she was discovered.

Every ten years, the saint's body is carried in a three-hour ceremony from the Basilica of Bom Jesus to the Sé cathedral, where visitors file past, touch and photograph it. During the 2004–05 "**exposition**", around 256,000 pilgrims flocked for *darshan* or ritual viewing of the corpse, these days a shrivelled and somewhat unsavoury spectacle.

Basilica. On the west, the three-storey Renaissance facade encompasses Corinthian, Doric, Ionic and Composite styles.

The interior is entered beneath the choir, supported by columns. On the northern wall, in the centre of the nave, is a cenotaph in gilded bronze to **Dom Jeronimo Mascarenhas**, the Captain of Cochin and benefactor of the church. The main altar, extravagantly decorated in gold, depicts the infant Jesus under the protection of St Ignatius Loyola (founder of the Jesuit Order); to each side are subsidiary altars to Our Lady of Hope and St Michael. In the southern transept, lavishly decorated with twisted gilded columns and floriate carvings, stands the **Chapel and Tomb of St Francis Xavier**. Constructed of marble and jasper in 1696, it was the gift of the Medici, Cosimo III, the Grand Duke of Tuscany; the middle tier contains panels detailing the saint's life. An ornate domed reliquary in silver contains his remains; for a week around his feast day, December 3, tens of thousands of pilgrims – Hindus as well as Christians – queue for *darshan* (ritual viewing) of the casket before attending open-air Mass in the square outside.

Holy Hill

A number of other important religious buildings and a museum stand opposite Bom Jesus on **Holy Hill**. The **Convent of St Monica**, constructed in 1627, was the only Goan convent at the time and the largest in Asia. It housed around a hundred nuns, the Daughters of St Monica, and also offered accommodation to women whose husbands were called away to other parts of the empire. As they had to remain away from the public gaze, the nuns attended mass in the choir loft of the adjacent chapel. A **Miraculous Cross** rises above the figure of St Monica at the altar.

Next door stands Goa's foremost **Museum of Christian Art** (daily 9.30am–5pm; Rs15). Exhibits include processional crosses, ivory ornaments, damask silk clerical robes and some finely sculpted wooden icons dating from the sixteenth and seventeenth centuries, among them an unusual statue of John the Baptist wearing a tiger-skin wrap (in the style of the Hindu god Shiva).

Nearby, the **Convent of St John of God**, built in 1685 by the Order of Hospitallers of St John of God to tend to the sick, was rebuilt in 1953. At the top of the hill, the **Chapel of Our Lady of the Rosary**, constructed in 1526 in the Manueline style (after the Portuguese king Manuel I, 1495–1521), features Ionic plasterwork with a double-storey portico, cylindrical turrets and a tower that commands fine views across the river from the terrace where Albuquerque surveyed the decisive battle of 1510. Its cruciform interior is unremarkable, except for the marble tomb of **Catarina a Piró**, believed to have been the first European woman to set foot in the colony. A commoner, she eloped here to escape the scandal surrounding her romance with Portuguese nobleman Garcia de Sá, who later rose to be governor of Goa. Under pressure from no less than Francis Xavier, Garcia eventually married her, but only *in articulo mortis* as she lay on her deathbed. Her finely carved tomb, set in the wall beside the high altar, incorporates a band of intricate Gujarati-style ornamentation, probably imported from the Portuguese trading post of Diu.

Dudhsagar waterfalls

Measuring a mighty 600m from head to foot, the famous **Dudhsagar waterfalls**, on the Goa–Karnataka border, are some of the highest in India, and a spectacular enough sight to entice a steady stream of visitors from the coast into the rugged Western Ghats. The Konkani name for the falls, which literally translated means "sea of milk", derives from clouds of foam kicked up at the bottom when the water levels are at their highest. Overlooking a steep, crescent-shaped head of a valley carpeted with pristine tropical forest, Dudhsagar is set amid impressive **scenery** that is only accessible on foot or by jeep.

The **best time to visit** is immediately after the monsoons, from October until mid-December, when water levels are highest, although the falls flow well into April. The only practicable way to get there and back is by four-wheel-drive **jeep** from **Colem** (reachable by train from Vasco, Margao and Chandor, or by taxi from the north-coast resorts for around Rs1750). The cost of the onward thirty- to forty-minute trip from Colem to the falls, which takes you across rough forest tracks and two or three river fords, is Rs1000–1250 per person; the drive ends with an enjoyable ten-minute hike. Just turn up in Colem and look for the "Controller of Jeeps" near the station. However, if you're travelling alone or in a couple, you may have to wait around until the vehicle fills up, or else fork out to cover the cost of hiring the whole jeep yourself.

North Goa

Development in North Goa is concentrated mainly behind the seven-kilometre strip of white sand that stretches from the foot of **Fort Aguada**, crowning the peninsula east of Panjim, to Baga creek in the north. Encompassing the resorts of **Candolim**, **Calangute** and **Baga**, this is Goa's prime charter belt and an area most independent travellers steer clear of.

Since the advent of mass tourism in the 1980s, the alternative "scene" has drifted progressively north away from the sunbed strip to **Anjuna** and **Vagator** – site of some of the region's loveliest beaches – and scruffier **Chapora**, a workaday fishing village. Further north still, **Arambol** has thus far escaped any large-scale development, despite the completion of the new road bridge across the Chapora River. What little extra traffic there is since the new road link tends to focus on the low-key resorts just south of Arambol, namely **Aswem** and **Mandrem**.

North Goa's market town, **Mapusa**, is this area's main jumping-off place, with bus connections to most resorts on the coast. If you're travelling here by train via the **Konkan Railway**, get off the train at **Tivim** (Thivim), 12k east of Mapusa, from where you'll have to jump in a bus or taxi for the remaining leg.

Mapusa

MAPUSA (pronounced "Mapsa") is the district headquarters of Bardez *taluka*. A dusty collection of dilapidated, mostly modern buildings ranged around a busy central square, the town is of little more than passing interest, although it does host a lively **market** on Friday mornings. Anjuna's market may be a better place to shop for souvenirs, but Mapusa's is much more authentic. Local specialities include strings of spicy Goan sausages (*chouriço*), bottles of toddy (fermented palm sap) and large green plantains from nearby Moira.

Practicalities

Tivim (Thivim), the nearest railway station to Mapusa, is 12km east in the neighbouring Bicholim district. Buses should be on hand to transport passengers into town, from where you can pick up local services to Calangute, Baga, Anjuna, Vagator, Chapora and Arambol. These leave from the **Kadamba Bus Stand**, five minutes' walk west of the main square, where all state-run services from Panjim also pull in. **Motorcycle taxis** hang around the square to whisk lightly laden shoppers and travellers to the coast for around Rs50–65. **Taxis** charge considerably more (around Rs150), but you can split the fare with up to five people.

The Konkan Railway's *Konkan Kanya Express* (#KR0111 arrives in Tivim at around 9.30am, leaving plenty of time to find **accommodation** in the coastal resorts west of Mapusa. Best of the **eating** options on or around the main square is the *Ruchira*, within the *Hotel Satyaheera* on the north side of the main square, which serves a standard multi-cuisine menu and cold beer. For quick, authentically Goan food, you won't do better than the recently revamped *FR Xavier* café over in the Municipal Market, which has been here since the Portuguese era.

Candolim and Fort Aguada

CANDOLIM is prime package tourist country, and not a resort that sees many backpackers but, with lots of pleasant places to stay tucked away down quiet back lanes, it can make a good first landfall if you've just arrived in Goa. The busy strip running through the middle of town holds a string of banks and handy shops where you can stock up with essentials before moving further afield, and there are some great places to eat and drink, frequented mostly by boozy, middle-aged Brits and young Russians.

The one sight worth seeking out in the area is **Fort Aguada**, crowning the rocky flattened headland to the south, at the end of the beach. Built in 1612 to protect the northern shores of the Mandovi estuary from Dutch and Maratha raiders, the bastion encloses several natural springs, the first source of drinking water available to ships arriving in Goa after the long sea voyage from Lisbon. The ruins of the fort can be reached by following the main drag south from Candolim as it bears left, past the turning for the *Fort Aguada Beach Resort*; keep going for 1km until you see a right turn, which runs uphill to a small car park. Nowadays, much of the site serves as a prison, and is therefore closed to visitors. It's worth a visit, though, for the panoramic views from the top of the hill where a four-storey Portuguese **lighthouse**, erected in 1864 and the oldest of its kind in Asia, looks down over the vast expanse of sea, sand and palm trees.

From the base of Fort Aguada on the northern flank of the headland, a rampart of red-brown laterite juts into the bay at the bottom of what's left of **Sinquerim Beach**, which was virtually wiped out by a series of particularly heavy monsoon storms in 2009. This was among the first places in Goa to be singled out for upmarket tourism. The Taj Group's *Fort Aguada* resort, among the most expensive hotels in India, lords it over the sands from the slopes below the battlements. Off-shore, the hulk of the **MV River Princess** lurches in the shallows, more than a decade after it ran aground in a monsoon gale. Several attempts have been made to refloat and tow the wreck away in one piece, but to no avail: the *River Princess* sinks deeper into the sand each year – a surreal spectacle so close to India's flagship tourist beach.

Lots of wonderful **old mansions** and typically Goan

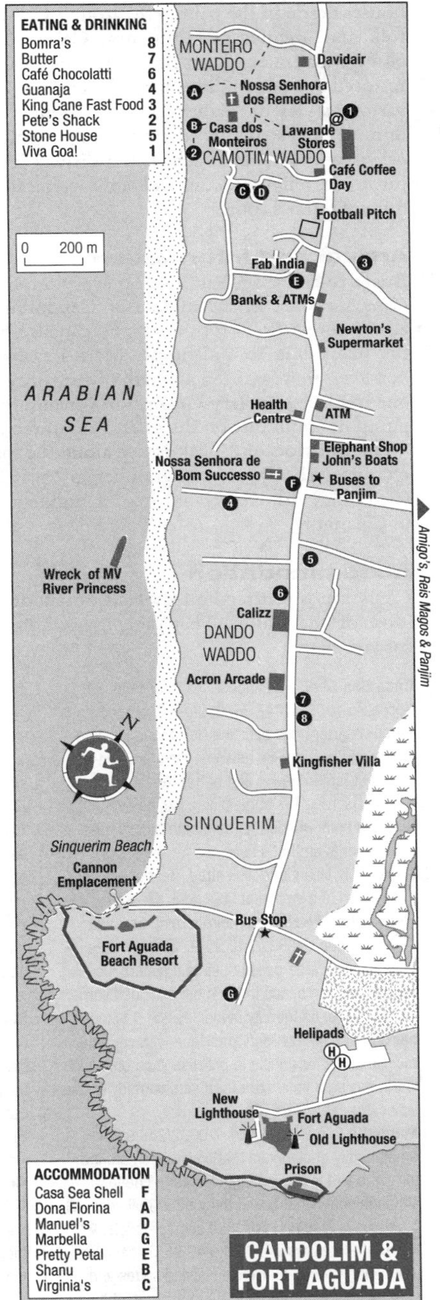

houses nestle in the palm trees around Candolim, some of the best of them in the folk and architectural museum, **Calizz** (daily 10am–7pm; admission Rs300; Ⓦwww.calizz.com), on the south side of the resort. Comprising five beautifully restored period buildings spread over a site of several acres, the complex showcases various styles of traditional Goan homes – both Christian and Hindu – from humble mud structures dating from pre-colonial times to a sumptuous Portuguese *palacio* with chapel attached. On display inside is an engaging array of antiques, furniture, religious icons and daily artefacts. The ticket price includes a forty-five-minute guided tour.

Arrival and information

Buses to and from Panjim stop every ten minutes or so at the stand opposite the *Casa Sea Shell*, in the middle of Candolim. A few head south here to the *Fort Aguada Beach Resort* terminus; you can also flag them down from anywhere along the main drag to Calangute. Maruti **taxis** are ubiquitous. During the season, however, there is often a dearth of **motorcycles for rent**, in which case search for one in Calangute (try *Gabriel's* in Calangute; see map, p.696). The nearest petrol pump lies 5km east on the main Panjim road, just beyond Nerul.

There are lots of ATMs dotted along the main drag (see map, p.693) and you can **change money** at any number of private exchange places dotted around Candolim, although their rates are unlikely to be as competitive as those on offer in Calangute.

Accommodation

Candolim is charter-holiday land, so **accommodation** tends to be expensive for most of the season. That said, if bookings are down you can find some great bargains here.

Casa Sea Shell Fort Aguada Rd, near Bom Successo ⓣ0832/247 9879. Old-established former charter hotel near the Nerul road junction where you've a choice between standard non-a/c rooms or larger, newer and better furnished ones with flat-screen TVs and air-con. Facing each other across a palm-shaded garden, both blocks offer accommodation that's spacious for the price, impeccably clean, and well aired. Best of all, you get the run of a well kept little pool. ❹–❺

Dona Florina Monteiro's road, Escrivao Waddo ⓣ0832/248 9051, Ⓦwww.donaflorina.co.in. Large guesthouse in a superb location, overlooking the beach in the most secluded corner of the village. Its friendly owner, Jessie D'Souza, has added a breezy rooftop terrace with ceramic mosaic floors for guests to practise yoga on. Well worth paying a little extra for if you want idyllic sea views. No car access. ❹

Manuel's Camotim Waddo ⓣ0832/248 9729. Small family guesthouse that's also been around for years and is welcoming, clean and cheap, although somewhat boxed in by other buildings. All rooms have fans and attached shower-toilets. ❸

Marbella Sinquerim ⓣ0832/247 9551, Ⓦwww.marbellagoa.com. Individually styled suites and spacious rooms (from Rs3000) in a beautiful house built to resemble a traditional Goan mansion. The decor, fittings and furniture are gorgeous, especially in the top-floor "Penthouse" (Rs5500), and the whole place is screened by a giant mango tree. Unashamedly romantic and well worth splashing out on. ❼–❽

Pretty Petal Camotim Waddo ⓣ0832/248 9184, Ⓦwww.prettypetalsgoa.com. Not as twee as it sounds: very large, modern rooms, all with fridges, quality mattresses, balconies, and relaxing, marble-floored communal areas overlooking lawns. Their top-floor apartment, with windows on four sides and a huge balcony, is the best choice, though more expensive. ❹–❺

Shanu Escrivao Waddo ⓣ0832/248 9899. Good-sized, well-furnished rooms with narrow balconies right on the dunes, some of them with uninterrupted views of the sea. Ask the hospitable owners for #120 (or failing that #118, #111, #110 or #107). Breakfast is served in your room. ❹

Virginia's Camotim Waddo ⓣ0832/6451069, 9923 640584. Another cheerful budget option, boasting better beds and furniture than the competition, as well as safe lockers in the attached rooms and relaxing bentwood chairs to lounge on. Try this place first – it's great value. ❸

Eating and drinking

Candolim's numerous beach **cafés** are a cut above your average seafood shacks, with pot plants, high-tech sound systems and prices to match. The further from the *Taj* complex you venture, the lower the prices become. As for **nightlife**, the only thing resembling a club in the resort is *Butter*, at 242 Souza Waddo on the south side of the village towards Sinquerim (look for the trademark giant saxophone on the roadside). Big-spending over-30s from Mumbai and Delhi flock in around Christmas and New Year to lap up the overpriced cocktails. Unless, like most of the clientele, you're on air-kissing terms with the owner, count on an Rs1000 admission charge.

Bomra's Souza Waddo, CHOGM (Fort Aguada) Rd ⓣ9822 149633 or 9822 106236. Understated, relaxed place, on a dimly-lit gravel terrace by the roadside. From the outside you'd never know this was one of Goa's gastronomic highlights, but the food – contemporary Burmese and Kachin cuisine – is superb. The menu's reassuringly short; try their spinach wraps in fragrant *tahini* sauce for starters, and the beef in peanut curry or snapper with lemongrass, tofu and noodles for main. They also do fantastic *mojitos* and, for dessert, delicious ginger crème brûlée.

Café Chocolatti Near Calizz. Goa's answer to Juliette Binoche's "Vianne Rocher" in the movie *Chocolat*, the British-raised owner of this delightful café in south Candolim, Nazneen, has conjured up a has conjured up a chocoholic heaven. Over a perfect cup of freshly ground coffee in the garden, you can indulge in gourmet Belgian-style truffles, tinged with chilli, mocca and orange, and crunchy almond-flavoured Italian biscuits.

Guanaja River Princess Lane. Step in to Savio's quirky wood cabin for a proper choco-fest featuring flavours you won't find anywhere else, many of them derived from local, typically Goan ingredients such as mango, chilli, sour kokum and coconut. They also bake crunchy fresh croissants, biscuits and savouries (though the coffee isn't up to much).

King Cane Fast Food Bosio Hospital Rd, near the football pitch and covered market. Terrific little Goan snack cart, on the roadside in the market area, run by husband and wife team Salvador and Maria Barretto. Everyone comes for the spicy beef chilly fry, served in a bap like a burger, but the *sorpotel* (a pungent mix of pork cuts, offal, blood, *toddi* vinegar and spices) is knockout. Maria cooks it over four days, simmering the stew for 10min each day to bring out the flavours.

Pete's Shack Sequeira Waddo. One beach shack that deserves singling out because it's always professional and serves great healthy salads (Rs85–225) with real olive oil, mozzarella and balsamic vinegar. All the veg is carefully washed in chlorinated water first, so the food is safe and fresh. The same applies to their seafood sizzler and tandoori main courses. For dessert, try the wonderful chocolate mousse or cooling mint lassis.

Stone House CHOGM (Fort Aguada) Rd. Blues-nut Chris D'Souza hosts this lively, low-lit bar-restaurant, spread in front of a gorgeous bare-laterite Goan house. Prime cuts of beef and kingfish served with scrumptious baked potatoes are their most popular dishes. Blues enthusiasts should come just for the CD collection. Most mains under Rs250.

Viva Goa! CHOGM (Fort Aguada) Rd. Succulent, no-nonsense Goan food fresh from the market – musselfry, barramundi (*chonok*), lemonfish (*modso*) and sharkfish steaks fried *rechado* style in chilli paste or in millet (*rawa*) – served on a roadside terrace. Tourists are welcome, but it's essentially local food at local prices.

Calangute

A 45-minute bus ride up the coast from Panjim, **CALANGUTE** was, in Portuguese times, where well-to-do Goans would come for their annual *mudança*, or change of air, in May and June, when the pre-monsoonal heat made life in the towns insufferable. It remains the state's busiest resort, but has changed beyond recognition since the days when straw-hatted musicians in the beachfront bandstand would regale smartly dressed strollers with Lisbon *fados* and Konkani *dulpods*. Mass package tourism, combined with a huge increase in the number of Indian visitors (for whom this is Goa's number-one beach resort), has placed an impossible burden on the

CALANGUTE & BAGA

EATING & DRINKING	
A Reverie	16
Baba Rhum	2
Casa Tito's	1
Fiesta	6
Florentine's	15
Infantaria Pastelaria	10
J&A's	3
Kamaki	9
Le Poisson Rouge	5
Lila Café	4
Lloyd's	17
Mambo's	7
Plantain Leaf	12
Souza Lobo	11
Sublime	14
Tito's	8
West End Club	13

ACCOMMODATION	
Alidia (Alírio & Lidia)	E
Andrade (Rita)	H
Angelina	G
Camizala	K
Cavala	B
CoCo Banana	J
Divine	A
Gabriel's	L
Indian Kitchen	I
Larissa	C
Villa Emmanuel	D
Villa Fatima	F

town's rudimentary infrastructure. Hemmed in by four-storey buildings and swarming with traffic, the market area, in particular, has taken on the aspect of a typical makeshift Indian town of precisely the kind that most travellers used to come to Goa to get away from. In short, this is somewhere to avoid, although most people pass through here at some stage, to change money or shop for supplies. The only other reason to endure the chaos is to eat: Calangute boasts some of the best **restaurants** in the whole state.

Arrival and information

Buses from Mapusa and Panjim pull in at the small bus stand-cum-market square in the centre of Calangute. Some continue to Baga, stopping at the crossroads behind the beach en route.

For **changing money**, Thomas Cook have a branch in the main market area (Mon–Sat 9.30am–6pm), where there's also an efficient ICICI Bank with 24hr ATM. Private currency changers on the same street include Wall Street Finances (Mon–Sat 9.30am–6pm), opposite the petrol pump and in the shopping complex on the beachfront, who exchange both cash and travellers' cheques at bank rates. At the Bank of Baroda (Mon–Fri 9.30am–2.15pm, Sat 9.30am–noon, Sun 9.30am–2pm), just north of the market on the Anjuna road, you can make encashments against Visa cards; commission is one percent of the amount changed, plus Rs125 for the authorization phone-call.

Accommodation

In spite of the encroaching mayhem, plenty of budget travellers return to Calangute year after year, staying in little family guesthouses in the fishing *waddo* where the pace of life remains remarkably unchanged.

Camizala 5-33B Maddo Waddo ⓣ9689 156449. A lovely, breezy haven amid the brouhaha of Calangute, with four rooms, common verandas and sea views. About as close to the beach as you can get, and the *waddo* is very quiet. Cheap considering the location. ❸

CoCo Banana 1195 Umta Waddo ⓣ0832/227 6478 or 227 9068, ⓦwww.cocobananagoa.com. Very comfortable, spacious chalets, all with bathrooms, fridges, mosquito nets, extra-long mattresses and verandas, around a central garden – but no a/c. Down the lane past *Meena Lobo's* restaurant, it's run by a very sorted Swiss–Goan couple, Walter and Marina Lobo, who have been here for nearly twenty years. ❺–❻

Gabriel's Gauro Waddo ⓣ0832/227 9486, ⓔgabrielsguesthouse@gmail.com. A congenial guesthouse very close to the beach, midway between Calangute and Candolim, run by a fantastic family who go out of their way to help guests. The rooms are large, with new a/c units, lockable steel cupboards and decent mattresses; the rear side ones have balconies looking across the *toddi* groves and dunes. ❹

Indian Kitchen Behind Our Lady of Piety Church ⓣ0832/227 7555. Jazzily decorated guesthouse with crazy mosaic tiling, brightly patterned walls and lanterns. The rooms, all attached, have fridges and music systems – and, amazingly for a budget hotel, there's a little pool to the rear. ❹

Eating and drinking

Ever since *Souza Lobo* opened on the beachfront to cater for Goan day-trippers in the 1930s, Calangute has been somewhere people come as much to eat as for a stroll on the beach, and even if you stay in resorts elsewhere you'll doubtless be tempted down here for a meal.

A Reverie Near *Goan Heritage Resort*, Gauro Waddo ⓣ9823 174927, 9326 114661. Unashamedly over-the-top gourmet place on the south side of Calangute, centred on a grand terracotta-tiled canopy. Both the gastronomic menu and ambience are about as extravagant as Goa gets, but the prices remain within reach of most budgets (around Rs1000 per head, plus drinks). Reservation recommended.

Florentine's 4km east of St Alex's Church at Saligao, next door to the Ayurvedic Natural Health Centre. It's well worth venturing inland to taste Florence D'Costa's legendary chicken *cafreal*, made to a jealously guarded family recipe that pulls in crowds of locals and tourists from across north Goa. The restaurant is a down-to-earth place, with prices to match, serving only chicken, some seafood and vegetarian snacks.

Infantaria Pastelaria Next to St John's Chapel, Baga road. Roadside terrace café run by *Souza Lobo's* that gets packed out for its stodgy croissants, freshly baked apple pie and traditional Goan sweets (such as *dodol* and home-made *bebinca*). Top of the savoury list, though, are the prawn and veg patties, which locals buy by the boxload.

Lloyd's South Calangute, near the turning for Kerkar Art Gallery. This inconspicuous little roadside joint, which stays open until 4am (or later), is where the local restaurateurs and Delhi expats chill out after hours. Sample the char-grilled steaks and spicy barbecued chicken, and you'll understand why. They also do knock-out Goan specialities – *chouriço* chilli fry, pork *sorpotel*, and eye-watering fiery shark *amotik* – rustled up fresh each day by the owner's mum. Cold beers and local prices.

Plantain Leaf Market area. The best *udipi* restaurant outside Panjim, if not all Goa, where waiters in matching shirts serve the usual range of delicious dosas and other spicy snacks in a clean, cool marble-lined canteen, with relentless background *filmi* music. Try their definitive *iddli-vada* breakfasts, delicious masala dosas or the cheap and filling set thalis.

Souza Lobo Beachfront. A Calangute institution, even though the food – served on gingham tablecloths by legions of fast-moving waiters – isn't always what it used to be. Stuffed crab, full baby kingfish and crepe Souza are the house specialities. Most main dishes Rs195–300.

Sublime, 1/9-A Grande Morod, Saligao, 5km inland from Calangute market, ⓣ9822 484051. Indian-American chef Salim (aka Chris) has earned a cult following for his focused, stylish menu, served by waiters in gold-trimmed *lunghis*. Popular mains include balsamic beefsteak on a feta gratin, and fish fillet pan-fried in crunchy macadamia nuts with sweet-potato and maple syrup mash. For starters, the ginger-battered squid is hard to top. Count on Rs600–800 for three courses, plus drinks. And reserve ahead.

Nightlife

Calangute's **nightlife** is surprisingly tame for a resort of its size. The only place to party worthy of note is **Club Westend** (2–3 times weekly 9pm–4.30pm;

Ⓣ0832/324 6727), at a hilltop site in the Mollem Bhat Valley, 4km inland at Sangolda. With a dance floor surrounded by jungle, rooftop pool and chillout areas, it's one of Goa's few bona-fide dance venues. Admission fees fluctuate around Rs500–600, the music is dominated by trance, and the clientele is mostly twenty-something Russians. Queues and crowds can be horrendous in peak season, but there's really nowhere else worth bothering with south of Vagator.

For a more serene evening out, check out Tuesdays at the **Kerkar Art Gallery**, in Gauro Waddo at the south end of Calangute (Ⓣ0832/227 6017, Ⓦwww.subodhkerkar.com), which hosts weekly **classical music and dance** recitals from 6.45 to 8.30pm, held in the candle-lit back garden. The little concerts, performed by students and teachers from Panjim's Kala Academy, are kept comfortably short for the benefit of Western visitors, and are preceded by a short introductory talk. Tickets, available in advance or at the door, cost Rs300.

Baga

BAGA, 10km west of Mapusa, is basically an extension of Calangute. The only difference between this far northern end of the beach and its more congested centre around Calangute is that the scenery here is marginally more varied and picturesque. Overlooked by a rocky headland draped in vegetation, a small tidal river flows into the sea at the top of the village, past a spur of soft white sand where ranks of brightly coloured fishing boats are moored.

Since the package boom, Baga has developed more rapidly than anywhere else in the state and today looks less like the Goan fishing village it still was in the early 1990s and more like a small-scale resort on the Spanish Costas, with a predominantly young, charter-tourist clientele to match. If you can steer clear of the lager louts, Baga boasts distinct advantages over its neighbours: a crop of excellent **restaurants** and a **nightlife** that's consistently more full-on than anywhere else in the state, if not all India.

Accommodation

Accommodation is harder to arrange in Baga than in Calangute, as most of the hotels have been carved up by the charter companies; even rooms in smaller guesthouses tend to be booked up well before the season gets under way. The majority of family-run places lie around the north end of the beach, where night-times have been a lot more peaceful since Goa's premier club, *Tito's*, acquired soundproofing.

Alidia (Alirio & Lidia) Baga Rd, Saunta Waddo Ⓣ0832/227 6835, Ⓔalidia@rediffmail.com. A compact resort hotel snuggled in the dunes, less than 1min walk from the beach. Offering three types of differently priced rooms, it's efficiently run, stylishly designed (with wooden floors and traditional shell windows in the newer block), and swathed in creepers and foliage. A gorgeous little curvi-form pool, meanwhile, makes it great value in this bracket. ❺–❻

Andrade (Rita) Just south of Tito's Lane, Saunta Waddo Ⓣ0832/227 9087. Clean, simply furnished rooms, some of them sea-facing, in a pair of modern blocks attached to a family house. The slightly pricier ones to the rear are nicer, though you don't get the views. Friendly management, and close to the liveliest stretch of beach. ❸–❹

Angelina Saunta Waddo Ⓣ0832/227 9145, Ⓔangelinabeachresort@rediffmail.com. Spacious, well-maintained rooms with large, gleaming tiled bathrooms and big balconies, in the thick of things off Tito's Lane. The best rooms are on the top storey of the newest of the three blocks. A/c available. Unbeatable value for money in this enclave. ❸–❹

Cavala Baga Rd Ⓣ0832/227 7587 or 227 6090, Ⓦwww.cavala.com. Modern hotel in tastefully traditional laterite, with a pool in a plot across the road surrounded by banana groves. The twin-bedded rooms have separate balconies front and back, the rear-side ones looking across open fields. Rooms range from simple non-a/c doubles to luxurious suites and are quiet despite the roadside location. ❺–❽

Divine Near *Nani's and Rani's* north of the river ⓣ0832/227 9546, ⓦwww.indivinehome.com. Run by a couple of hospitable animal-lovers, with rooms on the small side, if impeccably clean; some have attached shower-toilets, and there's a lovely upper terrace with sunbeds and shades, presided over by a menagerie of animal finials on the rooftops.

Larissa Saunta Waddo ⓣ9823 269242. You could probably spot this dayglow, tangerine-coloured block from space. Thankfully its rooms are set up in more restrained style. They're huge for the price, impeccably clean, modern, have fridges and big, fat mattresses. Surveying the village from atop a dune, they're also right behind the beach, only a short stagger from the shacks. ❹

Villa Emmanuel Calypso Hotel, Saunta Waddo ⓣ0832/227 5667 or 9923 653514. You can't stay any closer to the beach than this double-storey block, run by local family Manuel and Meena Fernandes. The beds are a bit basic for the price, but most rooms have uninterrupted sea views. ❹–❺

Villa Fatima Baga Rd ⓣ0832/227 7418, ⓦwww.villafatima.com. Old established backpackers' guesthouse boasting thirty-two attached rooms centred on a sociable garden terrace, with a nice big pool to the rear. Rates are reasonable, varying with room size. ❹

Eating

Nowhere else in the state offers such a good choice of quality **eating** as Baga. Restaurateurs – increasing numbers of them European expats or refugees from upper-class Mumbai – vie with each other to lay on the trendiest menus and most romantic, stylish gardens or terraces. It's all a very far cry indeed from the rough-and-ready beach-shack culture that held sway only seven or eight years ago.

Baba Rhum Arpora ⓣ98220 78759. This funky French bakery-patisserie hidden deep in the expat enclave of Arpora is a bit off the beaten track, but worth hunting out for its crumbly croissants, baguettes, pains au raisins, fruit salads, juices and perfect café au lait, served on heavy wood tables, with infectious World grooves playing in the background. To find it, turn left off the main Calangute–Anjuna road when you see their signboard. Closed Sun.

Fiesta Tito's Lane ⓣ0832/227 9894, ⓦwww.fiestagoa.com. Baga's most sumptuously decorated restaurant enjoys a perfect spot at the top of a long dune, with sea views from the veranda of a 1930s house. Giant paper lanterns and an old fishing boat filled with scatter cushions set the tone. The contemporary Mediterranean food is as delectable as the decor. Try their carpaccio of beef for starters, followed by lasagne, ravioli or the succulent wood-baked pizzas (Rs250). Most starters and mains Rs300–400. Reservations recommended.

J&A's Baga Creek ⓣ0832/227 5274 or ⓣ9823 139488, ⓦwww.italyingoa.com. Authentic Italian food (down to the imported Parmesan, sun-dried tomatoes and olive oil) served in the gorgeous candle-lit garden of an old fisherman's cottage. There's an innovative range of salads and antipasti, a choice of sumptuous pasta dishes, wood-fired pizzas and tender steaks (with rosemary potatoes) for mains, though their signature dish, seafood lasagne, is hard to beat. For dessert, go for the melt-in-the-mouth hot chocolate soufflé. Count on at least Rs1000 per head for three courses, plus drinks.

Le Poisson Rouge Baga Creek ⓣ0832/324 5800 or ⓣ9823 859276. The latest star addition to north Goa's gastronomic map, situated in a palm-shaded garden lit by pretty tea lights. Gregory Bazire, a second-generation chef from Normandy, adds a splash of Gallic panache to local ingredients and the results are *magnifique*. Try the golden-fried Chapora calamari, served with basil hummus and a green coulis, followed by fragrant pomfret filet in anis-butter sauce, or asparagus risotto. Most mains around Rs500. Advance reservation recommended.

Lila Café Baga Creek. Laid-back bakery-cum-snack-bar, run by a German couple who've been here for decades. Their healthy home-made breads and cakes are great, and there's an adventurous lunch menu featuring spinach à la crème, aubergine pâté and smoked water-buffalo ham. Open 8am–8pm.

Nightlife

That Baga's **nightlife** has become legendary in India is largely attributable to one club, *Tito's*. Lured by TV images of skimpy dancewear and a thumping sound-and-light system, hundreds of people descend on its long narrow terrace each night to drink, shuffle about and watch the action, the majority of them men from other

Saturday night bazaars

One of the few genuinely positive improvements to the north Goa resort strip over the past decade has been the **Saturday Night Bazaar**, held on a plot inland at Arpora, midway between Baga and Anjuna. Originally the brainchild of an expat German called Ingo, it's run with great efficiency and a sense of fun that's palpably lacking these days from the Anjuna Flea Market. The balmy evening temperatures and pretty lights are also a lot more conducive to relaxed browsing than the broiling heat of mid-afternoon on Anjuna beach.

Although far more commercial than its predecessor in Anjuna, many old Goa hands regard this as far truer to the original spirit of the flea market. A significant proportion of the stalls are taken up by foreigners selling their own stuff, from reproduction Indian pop art to antique photos, the latest trance party wear, hand-polished coconut shell art and techno DJ demos. There's also a mouthwatering array of ethnic food concessions to choose from and a stage featuring live music from around 7pm until midnight, when the market winds up. Admission is free.

A **competitor** in much the same mould – **Mackie's** – has opened nearby, closer to Baga by the riverside. Spurned by the expatriate designers and stallholders, this one is not quite as lively as its rival, though in recent years has made an effort to close the gap, with better live acts and more foreign stallholders.

states who've come to Goa as an escape from the moral confines of life at home. For Western women, in particular, this can sometimes make for an uncomfortably loaded atmosphere, although since a facelift (and a hike in door charges), *Tito's* seems to have put the era of Kingfisher-fuelled brawls behind it. New theme-bars and clubs are also popping up each year, offering increasingly sophisticated alternatives.

For anyone who's been travelling around the rest of the country, Baga by night – complete with all the garishness of a Saturday in British clubland – can come as an unpleasant shock. For more on the area's nightlife, see the accounts of Calangute (p.697) and Anjuna (p.704).

Bars and clubs

Casa Tito's Arpora, opposite Ingo's Night Market. Chic Italian gastro-lounge bar in an old Portuguese-era house, with traditional furniture, family memorabilia, resident DJs, cocktails and gourmet food. Perfect post-Ingo's chillout spot.

Kamaki Tito's Lane, Saunta Waddo. Big-screen sports and a state-of-the-art karaoke machine account for the appeal of this a/c, Brit-dominated bar just up the lane from *Tito's*. Rs200 cover charge sometimes applies.

Mambo's Tito's Lane, Saunta Waddo. Large, semi-open-air pub with wooden decor and a big circular bar that gets packed out most nights in season with a lively, mixed crowd. Once again, karaoke is the big draw, though drinks cost well above average, and they slap on a Rs400 cover charge after 11pm, or when there's live entertainment. "Ladies Night", on Wed, means free entry and free drinks for women.

Tito's Tito's Lane, Saunta Waddo Ⓦ www.titosgoa.com. Occasional cabarets, fashion shows and guest DJs feature throughout the season at India's most famous nightclub. Music policy is lounge grooves till 11pm, and hip-hop, house, salsa and trance thereafter. See the noticeboard for retro and other theme nights. Admission prices are Rs700 for men, which includes free drinks, and free for women (who also get free drinks). At Christmas, prices can soar to Rs1500 or more depending on the attraction. Open 8pm–late Nov–Dec, and until 11pm out of season. Tues and Sat are busiest.

Anjuna

ANJUNA, the next sizeable village up the coast from Baga, was, until a few years back, the last bastion of alternative chic in Goa – where the state's legendary full-moon parties were staged each season, and where the Beautiful Set would rent pretty red-tiled houses for six months at a time, make trance mixes and groovy dance clothes, paint the palm trees fluoro colours and spend months lazing on the beach. A small contingent of fashionably attired, middle-aged hippies still turn up, but thanks to a combination of the Y2K music ban (see p.705) and overwhelming growth in popularity of the flea market, Anjuna has seriously fallen out of fashion. Even the young Israeli hellraisers who inundated the village during the late 1990s – and were largely responsible for the government's crackdown on parties – have stopped coming.

As a consequence, the scattered settlement of old Portuguese houses and whitewashed churches, nestled behind a long golden sandy beach, nowadays resembles the place it was before the party scene snowballed. There are, however, two downsides to staying here. One is an enduringly druggy atmosphere. Levels of substance abuse, both among visitors and locals, remain exceptional, and the village suffers more than its fair share of dodgy characters. Just how seedy the scene revolving around Anjuna's shacks has grown became apparent in February 2008, after a British teenager, 15-year-old Scarlett Keeling, was raped and murdered.

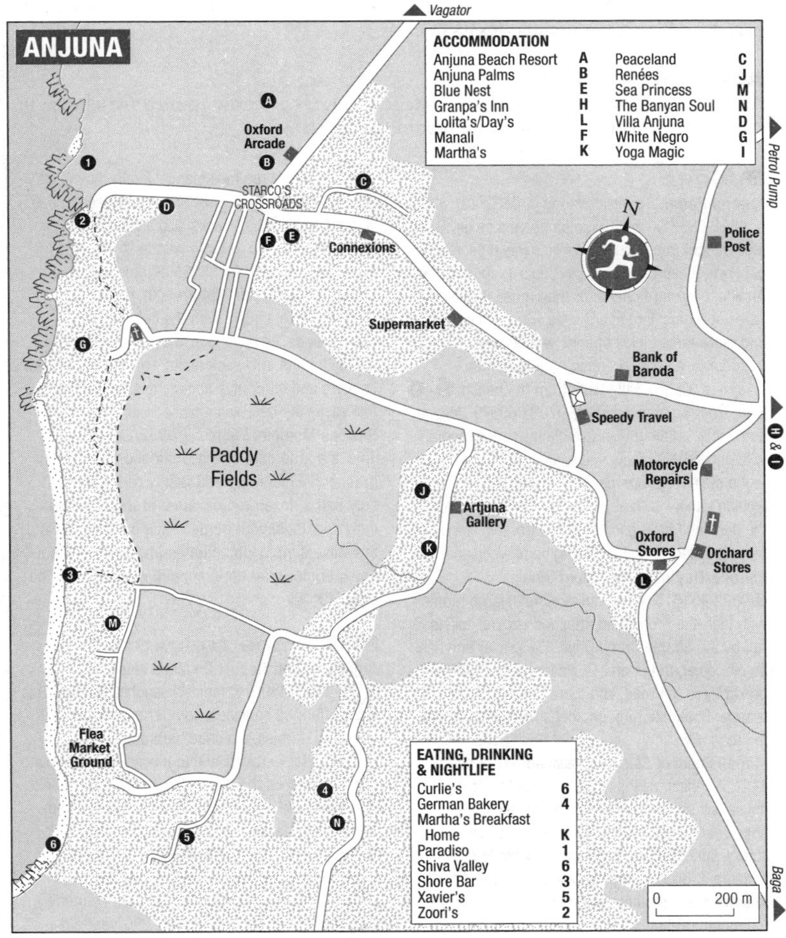

The other negative thing about the village – at least, if you're staying here – is the famous **flea market**. Every Wednesday, the beach and coconut groves at the south end of the beach get swamped with tourists and sellers from other resorts, forcing most of the resident tourist population north to neighbouring Vagator for the day.

Arrival and information

Buses from Mapusa and Panjim drop passengers at various points along the tarmac road across the top of the village, which turns north towards Chapora at the main *Starco's* crossroads. If you're looking for a room on spec, get off here as it's close to most of the guesthouses. The crossroads has a couple of small **stores**, a **motorcycle taxi** rank, and functions as a de facto village square and **bus stand**.

The *Manali* guesthouse (see below) and Oxford Stores **change money** (at poor rates). The Bank of Baroda on the Mapusa road will make encashments against Visa cards, but doesn't do foreign exchange. The **post office**, on the Mapusa road near the bank, has an efficient poste restante counter. The *Manali* guesthouse also offers broadband **internet access** (Rs40/hr).

Accommodation

After years of **accommodation** shortages, visitors are now spoiled for choice in Anjuna, especially those on more flexible budgets.

Budget

Anjuna Palms De Mello Waddo ⓣ0832/227 3268 or 9822 686817, ⓦwww.anjunapalms.co.uk. This little budget guesthouse, tucked away behind an old Portuguese-era house next door to the Oxford Arcade, has more character than most. It offers two types of rooms: larger, a/c ones with high ceilings; and more ramshackle options with shared bathrooms. All of them open on to a garden courtyard. Only a 5min walk from the beach. ❷–❸

Blue Nest Soronto Waddo ⓣ9763 063379. Jospah and Cecilia's little row of five old fashioned rooms, with pitched-tiled roofs and wood rafters, are close to the main road through the village, but you wouldn't know it. Neatly painted, they're large for the price and have good thick mattresses, as well as nice little tiled verandas looking on to woodland. ❸

Lolita's/Day's Behind Oxford Stores ⓣ9822 461615. A handful of simple, large rooms with high-tiled roofs and attached shower-toilets, run by the affable Darryl Days. The pricier one has an air cooler, fridge and TV. Peaceful, despite its proximity to the road, and there's a relaxing roof terrace. Bookable through Joel's Mini Store across the road. ❹

Manali South of *Starco's* crossroads ⓣ0832/227 4421. Anjuna's most popular all-round budget guest-house has simple rooms (shared toilets) opening onto a yard, fans, safe deposit, money-changing, library, internet connection and sociable terrace-restaurant. Good value, so book in advance. ❷–❸

Martha's 907 Montero Waddo ⓣ0832/227 4194, ⓔmpd8650@hotmail.com. Eleven immaculate attached rooms run by a friendly family. Amenities include kitchen space, fans and running solar-heated water. Two pleasant houses also available. ❹

Peaceland Soronto Waddo ⓣ0832/227 3700 or 9822 685255. Simple attached rooms in two blocks (Rs400–500), run by a charming local couple with the help of a pair of friendly dogs. All have high, clay-tiled roofs, mosquito nets, rucksack racks, hammocks, clothes hangers and other nice homely touches that make this easily the best-value place in its class. ❸

Renées Monteiro Waddo ⓣ0832/227 3405. This is a little gem of a guesthouse. Swathed in greenery, welcoming and family run, it holds only half a dozen rooms, most of them surprisingly spacious, with garden-facing balconies. A few have simple kitchenettes and fridges. It's a notch pricier than the competition, but worth the extra. ❹–❺

Mid-range to luxury

Anjuna Beach Resort De Mello Waddo ⓣ0832/227 4499, ⓔfabjoe@sancharnet.com. This place offers 32 spacious, comfortable rooms with balconies, fridges, attached bathrooms and solar-heated water in two concrete blocks ranged around a pool. Those on the upper floors are best. There's also a block of apartments for long stayers; both are very good value, though the complex is showing signs of age. ❺–❻

Granpa's Inn Gaun Waddo ⓣ0832/227 3270, ⓦwww.granpasinn.com. Formerly known as *Bougainvillea*, a lovely 200-year-old house set in half an acre of lush gardens, with a kidney-shaped pool and shady breakfast terrace. They offer three categories of rooms: non-a/c standards; suites in the main house; and poolside. Yoga on site and there's a billiards table. Very popular, so book well ahead. ❻–❼

Sea Princess House #649 Goenkar Waddo, Dando ⓣ9890 449090. Simple guesthouse in a prime position in the middle of the beach, near the *Shore Bar*. The rooms are spacious, and all have bathrooms with dependable plumbing, but aren't as well maintained as they might be and suffer from the invasion of mosquitoes. Its main selling point is the location, right on the dunes. ❺

The Banyan Soul Temp ⓣ9820 707283, ⓦwww.thebanyansoul.com. Leafy, designer chic on the quiet, southeastern fringes of the village, near the German Bakery. Shaded by an old banyan tree, the rooms are attractively decorated – though small for the price – and each has a private outdoor sitting area that's well screened from the neighbours. Some readers find this place a bit overpriced and boxed in; others love its tucked-away feel. ❻–❼

Villa Anjuna Near Anjuna beachfront ⓣ0832/227 3443, ⓦwww.anjunavilla.com. Modern, efficient resort hotel close to the beach, on the main road through the village. Amenities include a fair-sized pool and Jacuzzi. Popular with clubbers, as it's a short amble from *Paradiso* (so sometimes a little noisy at night). ❻–❼

White Negro 719 Praia de St Anthony, south of the village, near St Anthony's Chapel ⓣ0832/227 3326, ⓔdsouzawhitenegro@rediffmail.com. A row of twelve spotless back-to-back chalets catching the sea breeze, all with attached bathrooms, tiled floors, safe lockers and mosquito nets. Quiet, efficient and good value. ❺

Yoga Magic ⓣ0832/652 3796 or ⓣ9370 565717, ⓦwww.yogamagic.net. Innovative "Canvas Ecotel", offering low-impact luxury on the edge of Anjuna in Rajasthani hunting tents. The structures are all decorated with block-printed cotton, furnished with cushions, silk drapes, coir carpets and solar halogen lights, and colour-themed to correspond with the Yogic chakras. Loos are of the biodegradable, non-smelly compost kind. Open mid-Nov to May. ❼

The beach and flea market

The north end of Anjuna **beach**, just below where the buses pull in, is no great shakes by Goan standards, with a dodgy undertow and lots of even dodgier Kashmiris selling hash, as well as parties of whisky-filled daytrippers in constant attendance. The vibe is much nicer at the far, southern end, where a pretty and more sheltered cove accommodates a mostly twenty-something tourist crowd. A constant trance soundtrack thumps from the shacks behind it, cranking up to proper parties after dark, when **Curlies** and neighbouring **Shiva Valley** take turns to max their sound systems, hosting international DJs through the season. Chai ladies and food stall holders sit in wait on the sands, just like for the raves of old, but the party grinds to a halt at 10pm sharp.

The biggest crowds gather on Wednesdays, after Anjuna's **flea market**, held in the coconut plantation behind the southern end of the beach, just north of *Curlie's*. Along with the Saturday Night Market at Arpora (see p.700), this is *the* place to indulge in a spot of souvenir shopping. Two decades ago, the weekly event was the exclusive preserve of backpackers and the area's seasonal residents, who gathered here to smoke chillums and to buy and sell party clothes and jewellery. These days, however, everything is more organized and mainstream. Pitches are rented out by the metre, drugs are banned and the approach roads to the village are choked all day with a/c buses and Maruti taxis ferrying in tourists from resorts further down the coast. Even the beggars have to pay *baksheesh* to be here.

Each region of India is represented in the stalls. At one end, ever-diminishing ranks of Westerners congregate around racks of fluoro party gear and designer beachwear, while in the heart of the site, Tibetan jewellery sellers preside over orderly rows of turquoise bracelets and Himalayan curios. Most distinctive of all are the Lamani women from Karnataka, decked from head to toe in traditional tribal garb and selling elaborately woven multicoloured cloth, which they fashion into everything from jackets to money belts. Elsewhere, you'll come across dazzling Rajasthani mirrorwork and block-printed bedspreads, Gujarati appliqué,

Orissan palm-leaf manuscripts, pyramids of colourful spices and incense, sequined shoes and Ayurvedic cures for every conceivable ailment.

What you end up paying for this exotic merchandise largely depends on your ability to **haggle**. Prices are sky-high by Indian standards. Be persistent, though, and cautious, and you can usually pick things up for a reasonable rate, except from the Westerner designers, who are not so fond of haggling.

Even if you're not spending, the flea market is a great place just to sit and watch the world go by. Mingling with the suntanned masses are bands of strolling musicians, mendicant sadhus and fortune-telling bulls. And if you happen to miss the show, rest assured that the whole cast reassembles every Saturday at Baga/Arpora's **night markets** (see p.700).

Eating and drinking

Responding to the tastes of its alternative visitors, Anjuna boasts a good crop of quality **cafés** and **restaurants**, many of which serve healthy vegetarian dishes and juices. If you're hankering for a taste of home, call in at **Orchard Stores** on the northern side of the village, which serves the expatriate community with a vast range of pricey imported delights.

German Bakery South Anjuna, on the road to *Nirvana Hermitage* Ⓦ www.german-bakery.org. The one and only, original outlet of this much copied wholefood café-restaurant, hidden away in a tree-shaded garden on the south side of the village, is Goa's ultimate travellers' hangout. Under old trees strung with Tibetan prayer flags and Pipli lanterns, you can order from an ever-evolving menu featuring such rarities as buckwheat porridge, cambucha tea and wheat grass. For the less health conscious there's a full mains menu of Italian, Indian, Tibetan and seafood, and of course the bakery's famous cakes and coffee. Live music, dance and circus cabarets are frequent in season, and the place is wi-fi enabled.

Martha's Breakfast Home *Martha's* guesthouse, 907 Montero Waddo. Secluded, very friendly breakfast garden serving fresh Indian coffee, crepes, healthy juices, apple and cinnamon porridge, fruit salads with curd and – the house speciality – melt-in-the-mouth waffles with proper maple syrup.

Shore Bar Above the beach, mid-way down. Fantastic selection of food from amazing toasted *paneer* salads to traditional Goan fish dishes. There's also a good smattering of fusion such as calamari wraps. Great vibe, especially at sunset – though the music's full-on.

Xavier's South Anjuna. Nestled in the palm forest just inland from the Flea Market ground, *Xavier's* has formed the hub of the south Anjuna alternative scene for decades, and is still going strong. Most people come for the seafood, kebabs, tikkas and tandoori dishes, but they also serve tasty Chinese and Italian, organic salads and delicious home-made pickles. Look for the sign on the left off the market lane.

Zoori's North end of the beach, next to Paradiso. Chilled Israeli-run café-restaurant occupying a perfect spot on the clifftops – one of the most beautiful places in Goa for sunset, though the views outstrip the food. Open 10am–midnight.

Nightlife

Anjuna's far from the rave venue it used to be, but at least one big **party** is still held in the area around the Christmas–New Year full-moon period. For the rest of the season, techno heads have to make do with the rather shabby, mainstream **Paradiso**, overlooking the far north end of Anjuna beach. Part owned by the government, this place epitomizes the new, more above-board face of Goa Trance. Presiding over a dance space surrounded by spacey statues of Hindu gods and Tantric symbols, visiting DJs spin trance for a mainly Indian and Russian crowd. *Paradiso* keeps to a sporadic timetable, but should be open most nights from around 10pm until dawn; admission charges are Rs300–700, depending on the night.

At the opposite end of Anjuna, **Curlie's** and **Shiva Valley** (see p.703) form the focus of a mini rave scene, with large, mixed crowds of both Indian and Western tourists gathering from sunset until 10pm. Some kind of "arrangement" has

The dark side of the moon

Lots of visitors come to Goa expecting to be able to party on the beach every night, and are dismayed when the only places to dance turn out to be **mainstream clubs** they probably wouldn't look twice at back home. But the truth is that the full-on, elbows-in-the-air beach party of old, when tens of thousands of people would space out to huge techno sound systems under fluoro-painted palm trees, is well and truly a thing of the past in Goa – thanks largely to the stern attitude of the local government.

Goa's coastal villages saw their first big parties back in the 1960s with the influx of **hippies** to Calangute and Baga. Much to the amazement of the locals, the preferred pastime of these wannabe sadhus was to cavort naked on the sands together on full-moon nights, amid a haze of chillum smoke and loud rock music. The villagers took little notice of these bizarre gatherings at first, but with each season the scene became better established, and by the late 1970s the **Christmas and New Year parties**, in particular, had become huge events, attracting travellers from all over the country.

In the late 1980s, the local party scene received a dramatic shot in the arm with the coming of Acid House and techno. Ecstasy became the preferred dance drug as the rock and dub-reggae scene gave way to rave culture, with ever-greater numbers of young clubbers pouring in for the season on charter flights. Goa soon spawned its own distinctive brand of psychedelic music, known as **Goa Trance**, cultivated by artists such as Goa Gill, Juno Reactor and Hallucinogen.

The **golden era** for Goa's party scene, and Goa Trance, was in the early 1990s, when big raves were held two or three times a week in beautiful locations around Anjuna and Vagator. For a few years the authorities turned a blind eye to them. Then, quite suddenly, the plug was pulled: during the run up to the Y2K celebrations a **ban on amplified-music** was imposed between 10pm and 7am. A decade on, the curfew is still in place and the rave scene has virtually disappeared, limited to a couple of established, above-board clubs – notably the *Nine Bar* and *Hilltop* in Vagator (see p.708) and *Paradiso* and *Curlie's* in Anjuna (see p.703 & p.704). The occasional party does from time to time escape the notice of the local police (notably up in **Aswem**, at or around *Liquid Sky*; see p.712) but don't come to Goa expecting Ko Pha Ngan or Ibiza-on-the-Arabian Sea.

clearly been made with the local police here: chillums and joints are smoked openly in and around the cafés, but arrests are commonplace along the paths and lanes behind. Be warned that rumours are rife of cops, or fake cops, extorting bribes and sexual favours from tourists caught in possession of illegal drugs. The death of 15-year-old Scarlett Keeling, whose body was found after she'd been raped and murdered in the dunes in 2008, showed just how dangerous the village's druggy underbelly can be.

Yoga in Anjuna

The **Brahmani Centre** (Ⓦwww.brahmaniyoga.com, Ⓣ9370 568639) offers drop-in Ashtanga yoga classes by expert teachers at their studio in the garden of *Granpa's Inn* (see p.702); all levels of ability are catered for. If you're looking for a fully fledged retreat or course, you won't do better than the **Purple Valley** centre, ten minutes' ride away in Assagao (Ⓦwww.yogagoa.com), which has accommodation for up to forty guests and what must be one of the loveliest yoga *shalas* (practice areas) in India. Their top-drawer teachers include Manju Jois and Sharath Rangaswamy, the eldest son and grandson of the illustrious Ashtanga guru, Shri K.Pattabhi Jois.

Vagator

Barely a couple of kilometres of clifftops and parched grassland separate Anjuna from the southern fringes of **VAGATOR**. Spread around a tangle of winding back lanes, this is a more chilled, undeveloped resort that appeals, in the main, to Israeli and southern European beach bums who come back year after year.

With the red ramparts of Chapora fort looming above it, Vagator's broad sandy **beach** – known as "**Big Vagator**" – is undeniably beautiful. However, a peaceful swim or lie on the sand is out of the question here as it's a prime stop for bus parties of domestic tourists. A much better option, though one that still sees more than its fair share of day-trippers, is the next beach south. Backed by a steep wall of crumbling palm-fringed laterite, **Ozran** (or "Little") **Vagator beach** is actually a string of three contiguous coves. To reach them you have to walk from where the buses park above Big Vagator, or drive to the end of the lane running off the main Chapora–Anjuna road (towards the *Nine Bar*), from where footpaths drop sharply down to a wide stretch of level white sand (look for the mopeds and bikes parked at the top of the cliff). Long dominated by Italian tourists, the southernmost – dubbed "**Spaghetti Beach**" – is the prettiest, with a string of well established shacks, at the end of which a face carved out of the rocks, staring serenely skywards, is the most prominent landmark. Relentless racquetball, trance sound systems and a particularly sizeable herd of stray cows are the other defining features.

Arrival and information

Buses from Panjim and Mapusa, 9km east, pull in every fifteen minutes or so at the crossroads on the far northeastern edge of Vagator, near where the main road peels away towards Chapora. From here, it's a one-kilometre walk over the hill and down the other side to the beach. *Bethany Inn*, on the north side of the village, has a **foreign exchange** licence (for cash and travellers' cheques), and an efficient **travel agency** in the office on the ground floor.

Accommodation

Accommodation in Vagator is composed of a couple of pricey resort hotels, family-run budget guesthouses and dozens of small private properties rented out for long periods. **Water** is in very short supply here, and you'll be doing the villagers a favour if you use it frugally at all times. Tariffs typically double here between Christmas and New Year.

Bethany Inn Just south of the main road ⓣ0832/227 3731, ⓦwww.bethanyinn.com. Eleven immaculate, self-contained rooms with minibar fridges, balconies and attached bathrooms (Rs800); plus four additional a/c options in a new block, with big flat-screen TVs, larger balconies and more spacious tiled bathrooms (Rs1800). ❹–❺

Boon's Ark Near *Bethany Inn* ⓣ9822 175620, ⓦboonsark.com. Honest, clean, family-run place offering modern rooms with excellent beds, stone shelves, fridges and pleasant little verandas opening on a well-tended courtyard garden. Owners Peter and Jessie Mungu also offer room service, money changing and bikes to rent. ❹

Dolrina Vagator Beach Rd ⓣ0832/227 3382, ⓣ9822 980447. Nestled under a lush canopy of trees near the beach, Vagator's largest budget guesthouse is run by a friendly local couple and features attached or shared bathrooms, a couple of larger family rooms, sociable garden café, individual safe deposits and roof space. Single occupancy rates, and breakfast is served in their atmospheric rear garden. ❷–❸

Jackie's Daynite Beach Rd ⓣ0832/227 4330, ⓣ9822 133789. The best all-round budget place in the village, perfectly placed within easy reach of both the *Nine Bar* and *Hilltop*. Jackie De Souza has been running a café and shop here for more than 30 years, and recently added rooms behind. They're clean and great value, though often booked up so reserve in advance. ❸–❹

Jolly Jolly Lester Vagator Beach Rd ⓣ0832/227 3620, ⓣ9822 488536, ⓦwww.hoteljollygoa.com.

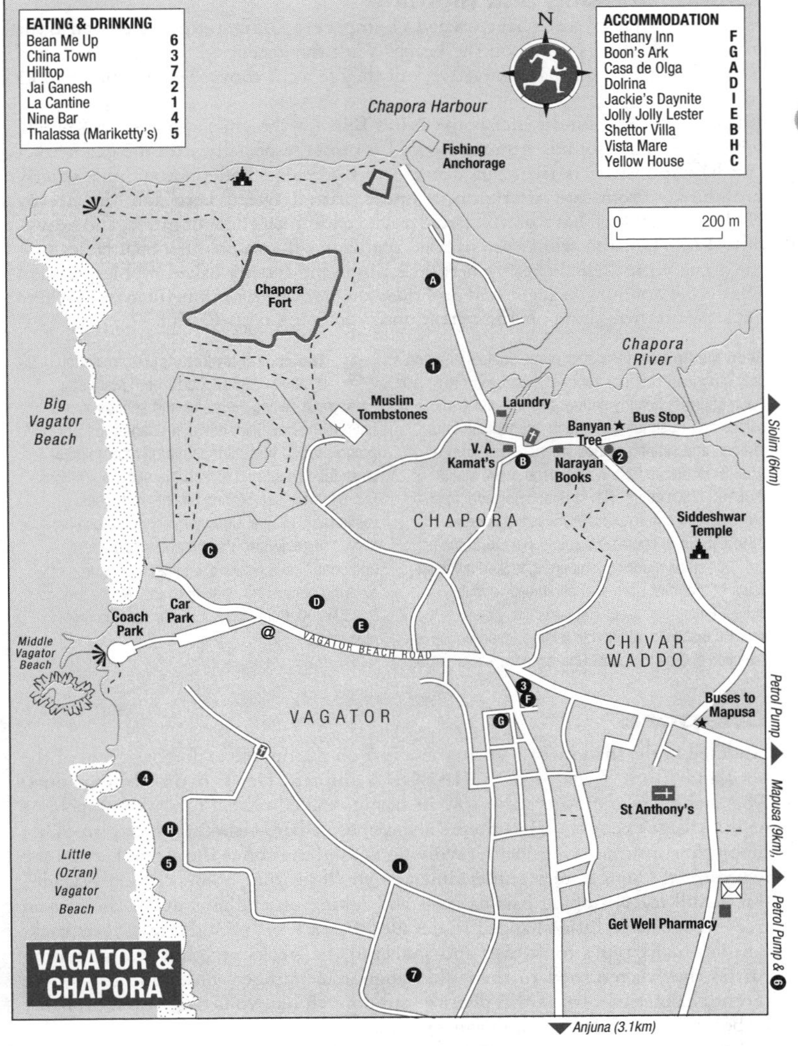

Eleven agreeable doubles with tiled bathrooms, lockers and fresh towels provided, set in shady woodland and a garden lovingly protected by owners Lazarus and Remy from marauding monkeys. Small restaurant on site; single occupancy is possible. ❹

Vista Mare Ozran clifftop ☎9822 120980. Lovely big rooms behind a (quiet-ish) restaurant on the clifftop, boasting kingsize beds, spacious attached bathrooms, marble-topped tables and huge verandas. A top location and good value. ❺

Yellow House Big Vagator ☎9822 125869. Henriquita Moniz and son Jubert recently renovated this guesthouse behind Big Vagator beach, which now looks better than ever after more than 20 years in business. It's peaceful and secluded, despite the proximity of the surf, and the rooms are neat and pleasantly furnished, though not all have outside sitting space. ❹

Eating, drinking and nightlife

Vagator's travellers' scene has spawned a bumper crop of **restaurants**, as well as the usual rash of shacks down on the beach. With the exception of *Bean Me Up* and *Thalassa*, none are all that innovative, but they're a cut above the dives in Chapora bazaar.

The place for a sundowner is the **Nine Bar**, on the cliffs above Ozran beach, where big trance sounds attract a crowd for sunset, especially after the flea market (Weds). Admission is free, but drink prices are high and photography strictly prohibited. From late afternoon, punters drift between here and the nearby **Hilltop** bar, which has a pretty, circular dancefloor in a coconut grove, and heavy-duty PA. The palm trunks are painted regulation fluoro colours, chai ladies ring the arena with their flickering kerosene lamps and freshly baked nibbles, foreign DJs do the honours on stage, and on Friday nights there's a colourful market where expat Westerners show off their creations. Admission costs Rs150.

Bean Me Up Near the petrol pump. India's one and only American-run tofu joint – the last word in Goan gourmet healthy eating. Design-your-own salads and fresh juices, or tuck into various tofu, tempeh and seitan combos steeped in creamy sauces, or pizzas from a real wood oven. Mains (Rs8100–250) come with steamed spinach, fresh brown bread and hygienically washed greens.

China Town Chapora crossroads, next to *Bethany Inn*. This small roadside restaurant, tucked away just south of the main drag, is a perennially popular budget eating place, serving particularly tasty seafood dishes in addition to a large Chinese selection and all the usual Goa-style travellers' grub.

Thalassa (Mariketty's) Ozran clifftop ⓣ9850 033537. Corfu-born Mariketty started out selling *souvlakis* and kebabs from a hole-in-the-wall joint down in Chapora bazaar, and progressed to this clifftop taverna after middle-class foodies started joining the queues. *Thalassa* is now firmly established as one of the best restaurants in Goa. Unpretentious and hospitable, it serves honest, flavoursome and scrupulously authentic Greek cooking, against a backdrop of swaying palms and rippling ocean. Mains around Rs250–300. Count on Rs650 for three courses, plus drinks.

Chapora

Huddled in the shadow of a Portuguese fort on the opposite, northern side of the headland from Vagator is **CHAPORA**, north Goa's main fishing port. The anchorage and boatyard below its brown-walled citadel forms the backbone of the village's economy, but there's always been a hard-drinking, heavy-smoking hippy tourist scene alongside it, revolving around the coffee shops and bars on the main street. Come here at sunset time and you'll see the "boom shankar brigade" out in full force, sipping banana lassis and toking on chillums under the banyan tree – a spectacle little changed in decades. For a brief period a few years back, Russian mafia types took over and squeezed the freaks out, but like migrating turtles they've returned to their old hangout in numbers undiminished by the recent changes in Goa. If this doesn't sound much like your bag, you'll probably be best off sticking to neighbouring Vagator.

Chapora's chief landmark is its venerable old **fort**, most easily reached from the Vagator side of the hill. At low tide, you can also walk around the bottom of the headland, via the anchorage and the secluded coves beyond it to Big Vagator, then head up the hill from there. The red-laterite bastion, crowning the rocky bluff, was built by the Portuguese in 1617 on the site of an earlier Muslim structure (thus the village's name – from Shahpura, "town of the Shah"). Deserted in the nineteenth century, it lies in ruins today, although the **views** up and down the coast from the weed-infested ramparts are still superb. Also worth a visit is the village's busy little **fishing anchorage**, where you can buy delicious calamari fresh off the boats most evenings.

Practicalities

By far the most (in fact, the only) congenial place to stay in Chapora is the *Casa de Olga* (☎0832/227 4355, 9822/157145; ❸), an immaculate, red-and-white-painted little guesthouse near the fishing anchorage. It's run with great efficiency and enthusiasm by a young couple called Edmund and Elifa. Their nicest rooms are the five in a new block to the rear, which are all attached and have good-sized balconies. Cheaper and more basic is *Shettor Villa* (☎0832/227 3766, 9822 158154; ❷), off the west side of the main street. Half a dozen of its rooms, ranged around a sheltered backyard, come with fans and attached bathrooms; the other eighteen share shower-toilets. Both places appear on our map on p.707.

Out on the road to the fishing anchorage, *La Cantine* is justifiably the most popular place in Chapora to eat these days. Run by an expat chef called Max, it serves healthy, home-cooked food – chickpea and pumpkin soup, beetroot tartare, pasta al forno and zucchini quiche – in a basic roadside shack. Otherwise, take your pick from the crop of inexpensive little cafés and restaurants lining the main street. *Jai Ganesh Café*, just up from the banyan tree, is the focal point of the tourist scene, where Chapora's resident Westerners watch the world go by over fresh-fruit juices and milkshakes. All of the above appear on the map on p.707.

Morjim

Viewed from Chapora fort, **MORJIM** appears as a dramatic expanse of empty sand sweeping north from a surf-lashed spit at the river mouth. Due to its relative isolation, the Hindu–Christian village behind the beach was where Goa's first **Russian tourists** made a beeline for back in the early noughties. Nowadays dubbed 'Mojimograd' by other foreign visitors, it's since become a resolutely Russian-only enclave, with hotels, guesthouses and rental villas controlled, if not owned outright, by Moscow mafiosi. A lot of sensational stories have appeared in the Indian media in recent years, reporting on the upscale prostitution and drug rackets run out of here. Although such reports do have a basis in truth, the majority of young sunseekers you see fizzing around Morjim on scooters are just regular, law-abiding holiday-makers. That said, the atmosphere in the guest-houses and restaurants can feel less than friendly, and most Western travellers find the experience of staying in Morjim a disconcerting one – not to mention eye-wateringly expensive – preferring to continue north to the more culturally mixed resorts of Aswem and Mandrem.

Morjim **beach** itself is dramatic and well worth at least a walk, especially in the early morning, when you'll see teams of fishermen hauling giant handnets from the surf. The spit at its southern end, opposite Chapora fort, is also a great birding hotspot: neither the local avian population – nor indeed the villagers who empty their bowels into the surf each morning – seem in the least deterred by the bizarre fitness routines practised by the Russians before breakfast.

Practicalities

Half a dozen **buses** per day skirt Morjim en route to Panjim, the first at 7am; heading the other way, you can pick up a direct bus from Panjim at 5pm, and there are frequent services from Mapusa via Siolim. They'll drop you on the main road, five minutes' walk from the beachfront area at **Vithaldas Waddo**.

Because of the unwelcoming Russian vibe, the hotels and guesthouses immediately behind the beach, in the dunes and along the beachfront road, are best avoided. There are, however, a couple of really nice options on the edges of Morjim. Facing the riverbank on the village's south side, *Jardin d'Ulysse* (☎9822 581928, ulyssemorjim@gmail.com; ❹) is a charming Goan-French-run place comprising five "cottages" with tiled roofs, ochre-washed floors and kitchenettes.

The turtle wind

When a strong and steady on-shore breeze blows through the night in early November at Morjim, the locals call it a **turtle wind** because such weather normally heralds the arrival of Goa's rarest migrant visitors: **Olive Ridley marine turtles** (*Lepidochelys olivacea*).

For as long as anyone can remember, the spoon-shaped spit of soft white sand at **Temb**, the southern end of Morjim beach, has been the nesting ground of these beautiful sea reptiles. Each winter, a succession of females emerge from the surf during the night and, using their distinctive flippers, crawl to the edge of the dunes to lay their annual clutch of 105–115 eggs. Just over two months later, the fresh hatchlings clamber out and crawl blinking over their siblings to begin the perilous trek back to the water, guided into the sea by moonlight.

Little more is known about how these enigmatic creatures spend the rest of their long lives (turtles frequently live for over a century), but it is thought that the females return to the beaches where they were born to lay their own eggs. Some have been shown to travel as far as 4500 kilometres to do this.

Once a thriving species, with huge populations spread across the Pacific, Atlantic and Indian oceans, the Olive Ridley is nowadays **endangered**. Aside from a wealth of traditional predators (such as crows, ospreys, gulls and buzzards, who pick off the hatchlings during their dash for the sea), the newborns and their parents are vulnerable to a host of threats from humans. In Morjim, as in most of Asia, the eggs are traditionally considered a delicacy and local villagers collect them to sell in Mapusa market. Many (perhaps as many as 35,000 worldwide) are killed accidentally by fishermen each year, caught up in fine shrimp nets or attracted by squid bait used to catch tuna. Floating litter, which the hapless turtles mistake for jellyfish, has also taken its toll over the past two decades, as have tar balls from oil spills, which coat the animals' digestive tracts and hamper the absorption of food. The growth of tourism poses an additional danger: electric lights behind the beaches throw the hatchlings off course as they scuttle towards the sea, and sand compressed by sunbathers' trampling feet damages nests, preventing the babies from digging their way out at the crucial time.

In a bid to revive numbers, locals are employed by the Goa Forest Department to watch out for the females' arrival in November and to guard the nests after the eggs have been laid until they hatch. You'll see them camped under palm-leaf shades on the beach, with the nests fenced in and marked by red and green signs.

So far, the government-led conservation attempt has not proved all that effective. After an initial leap in hatchling figures, recent results have been mixed, which the Forest Department ascribes to an increase in tourist activity.

Watching the nesting turtles is an unforgettable experience, although one requiring a certain amount of dedication, or luck. No one knows for sure when an Olive Ridley female will turn up, but with a strong turtle wind blowing at the right time, the chances are good. Much more predictable are the appearances of the hatchlings, who emerge exactly 54 days after their mothers laid the eggs. If you ask one of the wardens looking after the nests, they can tell you when this will be.

Down in the front garden, a small restaurant whips up an eclectic menu of steaks, scrumptious lasagne, Tibetan *momos* and salads for mostly French and British travellers.

Aswem

You could hardly call **ASWEM**, the next settlement north of Morjim, a village, let alone a resort. Enforcement of the Coastal Protection Zone (CPZ) planning law by the local council has managed to hold at bay repeated attempts by developers to build behind the beach here, with the result that permanent structures are few and far between. However, the past few seasons have seen a belt of temporary hut camps and shacks spring up in the coconut *mand* backing the sand, and the place has started to feel quite crowded in December and January.

It's a much more wholesome scene than that holding sway around the headland to the south, though. Clean-living thirty- and forty-something couples from northern Europe are the main demographic, increasing numbers of them with toddlers in tow, along with a sprinkling of old Goa hands who have outgrown, or given up on, Anjuna and Morjim.

Aside from the recent Russian invasion, the main catalyst for this sudden upsurge in Aswem's popularity was the arrival a few years back of an incongruously chi-chi beach restaurant, *La Plage*, set up by a trio of French restaurateurs from Baga.

Arrival and information

Sporadic **buses** from Panjim and Mapusa cover the quiet stretch of road running parallel to the beach inland, from where a five-minute walk across the paddy fields brings you to the shacks and hut camps attached to them. The places listed below were the only ones we came across offering distinctive accommodation, and/or reasonable value for money; the rest of the camps were either too cramped for comfort, or absurdly overpriced, or both. Tourist facilities are thin on the ground in Aswem. Nearly everyone who stays rents a scooter from somewhere else to get to and around the area. The nearest internet access and shops are in Morjim, half an hour's plod south.

Accommodation

Leela Cottages Near *La Plage* ⓣ9823 400055, ⓦwww.goaleela.com. Swish designer huts (all a/c) of various sizes and prices, grouped in a gated property under the palms only a stone's throw from the beach, but far enough away from the restaurants to remain peaceful and quiet (and free from cooking smells). The interiors are furnished with antiques collected from all over India. ❼–❽

Yab Yum ⓣ0832/ 224 7712, ⓦwww.yabyumresorts.com. A campus of beautiful domed structures made from palm thatch, mango wood and laterite, with curvy moulded concrete floors and walls, painted pale purple. Large and attractively furnished inside, the rooms have beds on platforms and comfy mattresses, glitter balls, paper lanterns and muslin drapes – though such alt-chic comes at quite a high price (Rs4800 per double or Rs5500 for suites). ❺

Yoga Gypsies ⓣ0832/645 3077, ⓣ9326 130115. This spot, in the coconut plantation under the Ajoba temple just north of *La Plage*, is arguably the finest nook on the coast hereabouts. The place holds five octagonal cottages, made from dark mango wood. They're large, well spaced, have wrap-around verandas, and are naturally cross-ventilated, with quality beds and simple, relaxing décor. There's also yoga space and a great lounge area. ❼

Eating

Change Your Mind Just north of *La Plage*. Quality food – notably north Indian specialities – which won't dent your wallet. Also worth a visit is nearby *Pink Orange*, whose fusion menu fills their beach terrace each evening.

La Plage Aswem beach ⓣ9850 258543. Against a diaphanous backdrop of floaty white muslin and swaying palm trees, *La Plage* does a brisk trade in cool Gallic-Mediterranean snacks and drinks (chilled asparagus soup, mint lassis, Moroccan salads, fresh strawberries and cream), served by Nepali waiters in black *lunghis*. Their menu also features delicious chargrilled seafood and barbequed main courses; and don't miss the divine bloody mary with a coriander and mustard seed twist.

The Place *Liquid Sky* (see p.712), on the hilltop above Aswem beach. *The Place* takes itself a bit more seriously than most restaurants in the area, with chefs in proper hats toiling over hot grills in an open-sided kitchen. Bulgarian, Russian and Siberian specialities dominate a menu heavy on pork and veal, though there are plenty of veggie alternatives, and the baked fish in garlic butter and white wine with parsnips is consistently good. Most mains around Rs250.

Nightlife & entertainment

La Plage is not the only Goa-chic outfit to have set up shop in Aswem. It's also the current home of the **Liquid Sky Collective**, an innovative electro party outfit pioneered by Belgian DJ Axailes (Ⓦwww.myspace.com/axailes). With its beautiful "Lookout" dancefloor, sound-proofed interior space for post-10pm grooves, and great music, the venue has established itself as the coolest in Goa. Keep your ear to the ground for their period boat parties down the Mandovi, co-organized with the Arambol Experience (Ⓦwww.myspace.com/arambolexperience). Back down on the beach, *Shanti* also has a nice dancey vibe, with sets by international DJs.

Mandrem

From the far side of the creek bounding the edge of Aswem, a magnificent, and largely empty beach stretches north towards Arambol – the last undeveloped stretch of the north Goan coast. Whether or not **MANDREM** can continue to hold out against the rising tide of tourism remains to be seen, but for the time being, nature still has the upper hand here. Olive Ridley marine turtles nest on the quietest patches, and you're more than likely to catch a glimpse of one of the white-bellied fish eagles that live in the casuarina trees – their last stronghold in the north of Goa.

Most of the village's accommodation is tucked away inland at **Junasa Waddo**, where a handful of small guesthouses and hotels cater to a mixed, peace-and-quiet-loving crowd. A couple of small grocery stores, internet cafés and travel agents are on hand to provide essential services. But you'll have to rent a scooter, or walk for half an hour, to reach **Madlamaz-Mandrem**, the village's market hub, straddling the main road inland. Slap in the middle of it, **Parsekar Stores** holds an unrivalled stock of tourist-oriented food and drink – including muesli, olive oil, miso, Nilgiri cheese and natural cosmetics.

Accommodation

Dunes Ⓣ0832/224 7219 or 224 7071, Ⓦwww.dunesgoa.com. Huge "holiday village" of twin-bedded, yellow-painted leaf huts. They're a notch too close together for comfort and are brightly lit, so spoiling the aspect of the beach at night, but this is an efficiently run outfit that fills up in peak season. Pricier attached rooms available. ❸–❺

Mandala Ⓣ9657 898021, Ⓦwww.themandalagoa.com. Exquisitely painted murals adorn the buildings at *Mandala*, a "back-to-nature boutique resort" just upriver from the Ashiyana Retreat Centre, where the theme is celebration of the natural world through art. You can opt to stay in the main house with all mod cons, or take one of the two-tier "touses" – designer tents with patios and lake views. It's close to the beach, but there's no direct road access. ❼

Villa River Cat Ⓣ0822/224 7928 or Ⓣ9890 157060, Ⓦwww.villarivercat.com. Quirky riverside hotel, screened from the beach by the dunes, with distinctive hippy-influenced decor and furniture. The sixteen rooms are all individually designed: mosaics, shells, devotional sculpture and hammocks set the tone. Some have balconies, and there's a great sunset roof terrace and rear garden for lounging in. Host Rinoo Seghal is an animal lover, so brace yourself for a menagerie of cats and dogs. Artists and musicians receive a ten percent discount. ❺–❼

Arambol

ARAMBOL, 32km northwest of Mapusa, is by far the most populous village in the far north, and the area's main tourist hub. Traditionally a refuge for a hard-core hippy fringe, the village nowadays attracts a lively and eclectic mix of travellers, the majority of whom stick around for the season, living in rented rooms, hut camps and small houses scattered behind the magnificent white-sand beach. Hedonistic, well-heeled young Russians way outnumber the older, more alternative, spiritually-inclined types from northern Europe who have long formed Arambol's mainstay. But the two groups rub along harmoniously enough, and the overall vibe here is inclusive and positive, with plenty of live music to enjoy in the evenings, lots of relaxed places to eat and drink, and more opportunities to learn new yoga poses and reshuffle your chakras than you could get through in several lifetimes, let alone a winter. Moreover, beach life is generally laidback too – except on weekends, when day-tripping drinkers descend en masse in SUVs from nearby Maharashtra.

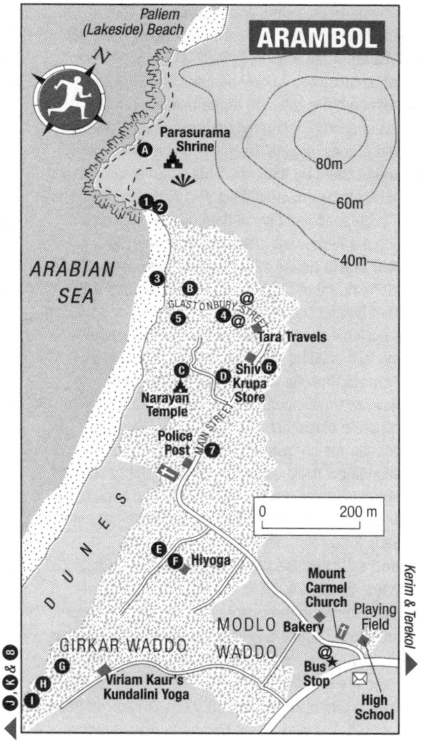

ARAMBOL

ACCOMMODATION		EATING & DRINKING	
Arun Huts	D	Double Dutch	7
Atman	J	Eyes of Buddha	1
Ave Maria	E	Fellini's	5
Famafa	B	Lamuella	6
God's Gift	H	Loeki's	4
Ivon's	G	Relax Inn	3
Om Ganesh Cottages	A	Rice Bowl	2
Piya	F	Sole e Luna	8
Silver Sands	C	Surf Club	K
Surf Club	K		
Villa Pedro	I		

Arrival and information

Taxis charge Rs1200 for the run from Dabolim airport to Arambol, and Rs350 for the thirty-minute trip from the nearest railhead at Tivim (Thivim). **Buses** to and from Panjim (via Mapusa) pull into the village every thirty minutes until noon, and every ninety minutes thereafter, at the small bus stop on the main road. A faster private **minibus** service from Panjim arrives daily opposite the chai stalls at the beach end of the village.

The **post office** is on the east side of the village, beyond the big church. There are no ATMs, but several places **change money** and do **cash advances** on debit and credit cards: try Delight, on the east side of the main road, and Tara Travel, directly opposite, where you can also reconfirm and book air tickets.

Accommodation

The cost of **accommodation** in Arambol has risen sharply over the past few seasons, reflecting the village's popularity with free-spending young Russians, but it's still nearly all pitched at budget travellers: no-frills, Goan-run guesthouses and expat-inspired hippy-chic predominate here rather than mainstream hotels.

Arun Huts Near Narayan Temple ⓣ9850 096468, ⓦarunhuts.arambolbeach.info. We loved this quirkly little hut camp, run by local beautician, Mrs Mala Singh, in the thick of Arambol village. Only 60m from the sea, it comprises two rows of neatly painted wood huts, fitted with decent mattresses, attached shower toilets and fans. The whole earth-floored compound is smothered in banana trees, palms and flowers, and very atmospheric, especially in the evening. Good value. ❸

Atman Girkar Waddo ⓣ9881 311643, ⓦwww.atmangoa.com. Lovely bamboo and wood tree huts on the south side of the beach, prettily thatched and decorated with coco mats, colourful sari drapes, original fractal-fluoro wall hangings, and bolsters on their spacious sitout areas. Smiling Italian-Indian owners, Michaela and Sunil, also run a yoga space and small boutique, as well as a popular restaurant (see 'Eating' below). ❺

Ave Maria House #22, Modlo Waddo ⓣ0832/224 2974. Arambol's largest guesthouse offers well kept budget rooms, with or without bathrooms, and a sociable rooftop restaurant in a three-storey modern building. ❷

Famafa Khalcha Waddo ⓣ0832/229 2516, ⓦwww.travelingoa.com/famafa. Large, anodyne concrete place just off "Glastonbury Street"; popular mainly with Israeli backpackers, and correspondingly rowdy, but very close to the beach and great value for money. They don't take bookings and instead operate a 9am checkout so get here early for a room. ❷–❸

God's Gift House #411, Girkar Waddo ⓣ0832/224 2391, ⓣ9923/427570. Variously priced, good-sized rooms in three-storey purple blocks; some have living space and kitchenettes. Not as good as *Ivon's* (the balconies are mostly tiny), but their rates are low. ❹

Ivon's Girkar Waddo ⓣ0832/224 2672 or ⓣ9822 127398. The pick of the budget bunch: immaculately clean, tiled rooms, all with attached bathroom and fronted by good-sized tiled balconies opening onto the dunes or a well-groomed family compound. ❸

Om Ganesh Cottages In the cove between the village and Lakeside beach; book at the Om Ganesh stores on the main drag ⓣ0832/229 7614. Nicest of the "cottages" stacked up the cliffside just south of Lakeside beach. The sea views from their verandas are superb, but some may find the Israeli chillum scene in the nearby cafés a turn-off. Rates vary wildly according to demand, and advance booking (with a deposit) is all but essential by mid-season. ❺

Piya Modlo Waddo ⓣ0832/224 2661. Well run little budget guesthouse – the best fallback if nearby *Ave Maria* is full. Rock-bottom prices, and cheap roof huts for only Rs100. ❶–❷

Silver Sands 4-S Tara Ankush ⓣ0832 224 2648, ⓣ9923 667448. Huge, immaculately clean rooms with terracotta-tiled roofs and shining ceramic floors, overlooking the Narayan temple. The best ones are on the first storey of the newest block; cheaper budget options with shared bathrooms occupy the ground floor. Close to the beach and well maintained by resident owners, the Lavu family. ❷–❸

Surf Club Girkar Waddo ⓣ9850 554006, ⓔcontactus@surfclubgoa.com. Brit couple Phil and Maggie offer some of the nicest mid-scale rooms in north Goa, at a prime location on the far south side of Arambol beach. With high ceilings and comfy beds, they're well aired and light, and have lots of those homely touches (seagrass mats, shell lanterns and floaty white curtains). Ask for one on the upper floor – worth the extra for their fine sea views and breezes. Don't come here expecting peace and quiet in the evenings, though, as one of Arambol's most popular live music venues occupies the ground floor. ❹–❺

Villa Pedro Girkar Waddo ⓣ0832/224 2989. Slightly scruffy but welcoming ten-room guesthouse, a stone's throw from the surf. It possesses plenty of local atmosphere, with pigs and kids running around, and crows hopping around the balconies, and its west-facing rooms look over a little chapel towards the beach. A pleasant and dependable budget choice. ❷

The village and beaches

Arambol's main drag is a winding road lined cheek-by-jowl with clothes and bedspread stalls, travel agents, internet cafés and souvenir shops selling tourist knick-knacks. Dubbed "Glastonbury Street" by the village's festival-savvy Brit population, it bends downhill to the **main beach** – dotted with wooden outriggers and one of the most picturesque in south India. The best view of it is to be had from the crucifix and small **Parasurama shrine** on the hilltop to the north (see map, p.713 for route of the path), which is an especially serene spot at sunset. After dark, when the hoola-hoopers, fire jugglers and *bhajan* singers have turned homewards, the candles and fairy lights of the shacks illuminate the beachfront to magical effect.

Bathing is safe here during the daytime, but less inspiring than around the headland at **Paliem** or **"Lakeside" beach**, reached by following the track through a series of rocky-bottomed coves, emerging at a broad strip of soft white sand hemmed in by cliffs. Behind it, a small **freshwater lake** extends along the bottom of the valley into the jungle, lined with sulphurous mud, which, when smeared over the body, dries to form a surreal, butter-coloured shell.

Keep following the path around the back of the lake and you'll soon come to Paliem's famous **banyan tree**, a monster specimen with giant runners extending more than fifty metres – long a popular chillum-smoking spot. Keen walkers can continue over the cliffs immediately north – Arambol's prime parascending venue – to reach the generally quiet **Kerim beach**.

Eating and drinking

Thanks to its annually replenished pool of expatriate gastronomic talent, Arambol harbours a handful of unexpectedly good **restaurants** – not that you'd ever guess from their generally lacklustre exteriors. The village's alternative, western-European contingent cares more about flavours than fancy decor, and prices reflect this. Russians with money to splurge, meanwhile, tend to gravitate towards the fancier seafood joints spread along the beachfront, where the day's catch is displayed on cold trays for selection, then grilled alfresco in front of you. Prices can be eye-popping, so get a quote before you order. If you're on a rock-bottom budget stick to the "rice-plate" *dhabas* at the bottom of the village: *Sai Deep* has a devoted following, and serves copious fruit salads as well as thalis, and a good travellers' breakfast menu of pancakes, eggs and curd.

Double Dutch Main St, halfway down on the right (look for the yellow signboard). Spread under a palm canopy in the thick of the village, this laid-back café is the hub of alternative Arambol. Renowned for its melt-in-the-mouth apple pie, it also does a tempting range of home-baked buttery biscuits, cakes, healthy salads and sumptuous main meals (from Rs175), including fresh buffalo steaks and the perennially popular "mixed stuff" (stuffed mushrooms and capsicums with sesame pesto).

Eyes of Buddha North end of beach. Perennially popular travellers' hangout, occupying a perfect spot overlooking the main beach. It's renowned above all for its mountainous fruit-salad and curd breakfasts, and lunchtime salads, but they also do a great north Indian menu after sunset: try the succulent *paneer* and chicken kebabs with hot naan bread.

Fellini's "Glastonbury Street". Italian-run place serving delicious wood-fired pizzas (Rs100–175), and authentic pasta or gnocchi with a choice of over twenty sauces. It gets horrendously busy in season, so be here early if you want snappy service.

Lamuella Main St. Funky little roadside café, serving healthy breakfasts, toasties, hummus plates and filling salads during the daytime, as well as energizing juice combos and herb teas. After sunset you can order from an eclectic dinner menu featuring chocolate fondant-ice cream for dessert. Most mains around Rs250.

Relax Inn North end of beach. Top-quality seafood straight off the boats and unbelievably authentic pasta (you get even more expat Italians in here than at *Fellini's*). Try the *vongole* (clam) sauce. Inexpensive, but expect a wait as they cook to order.

Rice Bowl North end of beach. This place serves the best Chinese in Arambol, with a perfect view of the beach to match, and a pool table (Rs100/hr). Any of their tasty noodle dishes are safe bets, as are the Japanese and Tibetan specialities. Most mains Rs150–200.

Sole e Luna South end of beach. Real Italian home cooking – pasta-pesto, pizzas and cheesy bakes – served in Arambol's most colourful and funkily decorated shack, on low or high tables, with plenty of hammocks and coco-mat chill-out space. This place also makes a pleasant beach base during the day as it's quite a plod from the main strip further north.

Surf Club South end of beach. Most people come here for the music, but the *Surf Club* does some great food too. Try the knockout Tahitian raw tuna, Thai-style spiced cashew and chickpea croquets or the yummy honeybee chicken breast in cream sauce. Most mains around Rs200.

Nightlife

Evenings in Arambol tend to revolve around the café-restaurants and whichever bar is hosting **live music**. Jam sessions and live bands are hosted by *Loeki's*, just up from the beachfront, on Sunday and Thursday evenings. Standards vary with whoever happens to blow in, but there have been some memorable impromptu gigs held here over the past few seasons. Further down the beach, the *Surf Club* also hosts bands and occasional DJs in their bar-restaurant.

Outdoor activities and holistic therapies

Posters pinned to palm trees and café noticeboards around Arambol advertise an amazing array of **activities**, from kite surfing to reiki. Good places to get a fix on what's happening are the noticeboard at *Lamuella* and *Double Dutch's* "Bullshit Info" corner, which displays email addresses and meeting details for just about everyone who does anything – including their own popular *dokra* **bronze casting** workshops, held annually each January.

For the adventurous, there's **paragliding** from the clifftops above Lakeside beach, run by a couple of German and British outfits who've been here for the best part of a decade, alternating between Goa and Manali. The cost of the flight includes all the equipment you'll need and full instruction. For more information, go to Arambol Hammocks, close to the *Rice Bowl* restaurant at the north end of the beach (see map, p.713).

Each season, an army of holistic therapists also offer their services and run courses in Arambol. Iyengar **yoga** teacher **Sharat** (Ⓦwww.hiyogacentre.com) holds five-day classes in his studio in Modlo Waddo. Prospective students should sign up at the centre from 1–3pm; to find it, head for the *Priya* guesthouse (see map, p.713) and follow the 'HIYC' signs from there. **Viriam Kaur**'s Kundalini yoga classes, held amid the leafy retreat of a rooftop garden in Girkar Waddo (see map, p.713), have attracted a strong following over the past few years. Check out her website (Ⓦwww.organickarma.co.uk) for dates and contact details.

Terekol

The tiny enclave of **TEREKOL**, the northernmost tip of Goa, is reached via a clapped-out car ferry (every 30min; 5min) from the hamlet of Querim, 42km from Panjim. If the tide is out and the water levels are too low for the ferry to run, you can either backtrack 5km, where there's another one, or arrange for the boatman at the jetty to run you across (for a negotiable fee).

Set against the backdrop of a filthy iron-ore complex, the old **fort** that dominates the estuary from the north – an ochre-painted building with turreted ramparts that wouldn't look out of place in coastal Portugal – was built by the Marathas at the start of the eighteenth century, but taken soon after by the Portuguese. These days, it serves as a low-key luxury Heritage Hotel, *The Fort Tiracol* (Ⓣ0832/227 6793 or 02366/227631, Ⓦwww.nilaya.com/tiracol.htm; ⑨). The seven rooms are all decorated in traditional ochre and white, with black-oxide floors, black-tiled drench showers and rustic wood and wrought-iron furniture; tariffs start at a hefty $250 per night. Non-residents are welcome to visit the restaurant and stylish lounge bar, where you can eat authentic Goan cooking while enjoying what must rank among the finest seascapes in southern India.

South Goa

Goa's south coast is fringed by some of the region's finest **beaches**, backed by a lush band of coconut plantations and green hills scattered with attractive villages. An ideal first base if you've just arrived in the region is **Benaulim**, 6km west of Goa's second city, **Margao**. The most traveller-friendly resort in the area, Benaulim stands slap in the middle of a spectacular 25-kilometre stretch of pure white sand.

Although increasingly carved up by Mumbai time-share companies, low-cost accommodation here is plentiful and of a consistently high standard. Nearby Colva, by contrast, has degenerated over the past decade into an insalubrious charter resort. Frequented by huge numbers of day-trippers, and boasting few discernible charms, it's best avoided.

With the gradual spread of package tourism down the coast, **Palolem**, a couple of hours south of Margao along the main highway, has emerged as the budget travellers' preferred resort, despite its relative inaccessibility. Set against a backdrop of forest-cloaked hills, its beach is spectacular, although the number of visitors can feel overwhelming in high season. For a quieter scene, try **Agonda**, just up the coast, or **Patnem**, immediately south of Palolem. Among the possible day-trips inland, a pair of elegant Portuguese-era mansions at **Chandor** and **Quepem** are your best options; and in the far south, the **Cotigao Wildlife Sanctuary** affords a rare glimpse of unspoilt forest and its fauna.

Margao

The capital of prosperous Salcete *taluka*, **MARGAO** – referred to in railway timetables and on some maps by its official government title, **Madgaon** – is Goa's second city, and if you're arriving in Goa on the Konkan Railway, you'll almost certainly have to pause here to pick up onward transport by road. The town, surrounded by fertile rice paddy and plantain groves, has always been an important agricultural market, and was once a major religious centre, with dozens of wealthy temples and *dharamshala*s – however, most of these were destroyed when the Portuguese absorbed the area into their **Novas Conquistas** ("New Conquests") during the seventeenth century. Today, Catholic churches still outnumber Hindu shrines, but Margao has retained a cosmopolitan feel due to a huge influx of migrant labour from neighbouring Karnataka and Maharashtra.

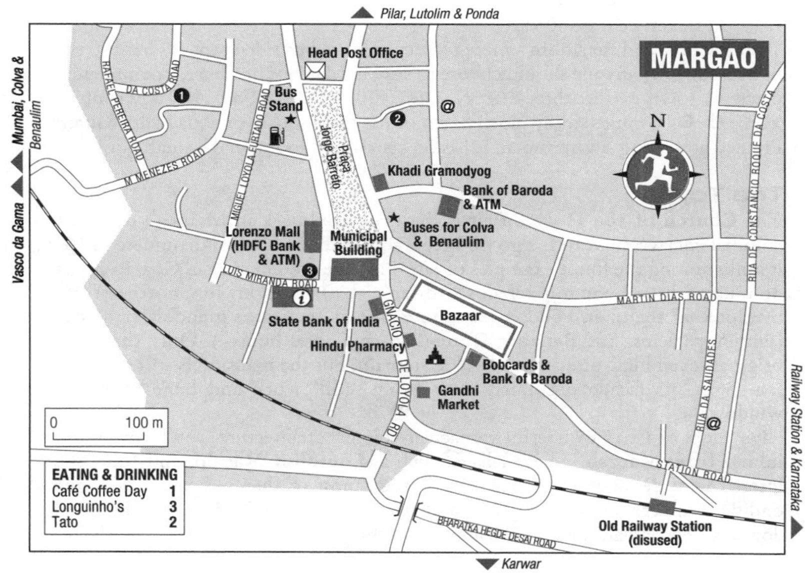

Arrival, information and accommodation

Margao's huge **railway station** lies 3km south of the centre, its reservation office (Mon–Sat 8am–4.30pm, Sun 8am–2pm; ⓣ0832/271 2940) divided between the ground and first floors. Tickets for trains to Mumbai are in short supply, so make your reservation as far in advance as possible. If you're catching the train to Hospet (en route to Hampi; four weekly) get here early to avoid long queues. Several principal trains stop in Margao at unsociable times of night, but there's a 24-hour information counter (ⓣ0832/271 2790) and a round-the-clock pre-paid auto-rickshaw and taxi stand outside the exit.

Local private buses to Colva and Benaulim leave from in front of the *Kamat Hotel*, on the east side of Margao's main square. Arriving on long-distance government services you can get off either here or at the main **Kadamba Bus Stand**, 3km further north, on the outskirts of town. The latter is the departure point for interstate services to Mangalore, via Chaudi and Gokarna, and for services to Panjim and north Goa. Paulo Travel's deluxe coach to and from Hampi works from a lot next to the *Nanutel Hotel*, 1km or so south of the Kadamba Bus Stand on Padre Miranda Road.

GTDC's **information office** (Mon–Fri 9.30am–5.30pm; ⓣ0832/222 5528), which sells tourist maps and keeps useful lists of current train and bus times, is inside the lobby of the GTDC *Margao Residency*, on the southwest corner of the main square. There are plenty of ATMs dotted around the town centre: try HFDC, in the Lorenzo Mall, on the west side of Praça Jorge Barreto just up from *Longuinho's*, or the Bank of Baroda on the opposite side of the square. Bobcards office in the market sub-branch of the Bank of Baroda, on Station Road, does Visa encashments.

The GPO is at the top of the central municipal gardens. For visitors in need of medical attention, Margao's two main **hospitals** are the Hospicio (ⓣ0832/270 5664 or 270 5754), Rua De Miranda, and the Apollo Victor Hospital, in the suburb of Malbhat (ⓣ0832/272 8888 or 272 6272). Margao also boasts south Goa's principal **cinema**, the Osia Multiplex (ⓣ0832/270 1717), out in the north of town near the Kadamba Bus Stand. It screens Hollywood as well as Bollywood releases; tickets cost Rs80–120.

With Colva and Benaulim a mere twenty-minute bus ride away, it's hard to think of a reason why anyone should choose to **stay** in Margao: however, a commendable place in town is the three-star *Nanutel* (ⓣ0832/270 0900, ⓦwww.nanuindia.com; ❺–❻), a multi-storey block north of the main square on Rua Padre Miranda. Pitched at visiting businessmen, it has 55 central a/c rooms and a small pool.

The Town

The **Church of the Holy Spirit** is the main landmark in Margoa's dishevelled colonial enclave, next to **Largo de Igreja** square. Built by the Portuguese in 1675, it ranks among the finest examples of late-Baroque architecture in Goa, its interior dominated by a huge gilt reredos dedicated to the Virgin. Just northeast of it, overlooking the main Ponda road, stands one of the state's grandest eighteenth-century palacios, **Sat Banzam Ghor** ("Seven Gables house"). Only three of its original seven high-pitched roof gables remain, but the mansion is still an impressive sight, its facade decorated with fancy scroll work and huge oyster-shell windows.

For more of Goa's wonderful vernacular colonial architecture, you'll have to head **inland from Margao**, where villages such as **Loutolim**, **Racaim** and **Rachol** are littered with decaying old Portuguese houses, most of them empty – the region's traditional inheritance laws ensure that old family homes tend to be owned by literally dozens of descendants, none of whom are willing or can afford to maintain them.

Another reason to come here is to shop at the town's **market**, whose hub is a labyrinthine covered area. Also worth checking is the little government-run **Khadi Gramodyog** shop, on the main square, which sells the usual range of hand-spun cottons and raw silk by the metre, as well as ready-made traditional Indian garments.

Eating and drinking

After a browse around the bazaar, most visitors make a beeline for *Longuinho's*, the long-established hang-out of Margao's English-speaking middle classes. If you are on a tight budget, try one of the south Indian–style pure-veg cafés along Station Road.

Café Coffee Day Shop 18/19 Vasanth Arcade, near Popular High School. Goa's answer to *Starbucks* has a super-cool a/c branch tucked away off the Municipal Gardens square, popular with local college kids. Aside from a perfect latte, it serves spicy savouries (such as mini-pizzas and salad wraps) and, most memorably, a very sinful "sizzling brownie" (Rs85), which will have chocoholics begging for loyalty cards.

Longuinho's Luis Miranda Rd. Relaxing, old-fashioned café serving a selection of meat, fish and veg mains, freshly baked savoury snacks, cakes and drinks. The food isn't up to much these days, and the 1950s Goan atmosphere has been marred by the arrival of satellite TV, but it's a pleasant enough place to catch your breath over a beer.

Tato Tucked away up an alley off the east side of Praça Jorge Barreto. The town's brightest and best south Indian café serves the usual range of hot snacks (including especially good samosas at breakfast time, and masala dosas from midday on). A bit cramped downstairs, but well worth the effort to find. For a proper meal, climb the stairs to their cool a/c floor, where you can order wonderful thalis (for Rs45) and a range of north Indian dishes, as well as all the *udipi* nibbles dished up on the ground floor.

Chandor and Quepem

Thirteen kilometres east of Margao across Salcete district's fertile rice fields lies sleepy **CHANDOR** village, a scattering of tumbledown villas and farmhouses ranged along shady tree-lined lanes. The main reason to venture out here is the splendid **Braganza-Perreira/Menezes-Braganza house** (daily except holidays, no set hours; ⓣ0832/278 4227 or 9822 160009; recommended donation Rs100/ per person), regarded as the grandest of Goa's colonial mansions. Dominating the dusty village square, the house, built in the 1500s by the wealthy Braganza family for their two sons, has a huge double-storey facade, with 28 windows flanking its entrance. Braganza de Perreira, the great-grandfather of the present owner, was the last knight of the king of Portugal; more recently, Menezes Braganza (1879–1938), a journalist and freedom fighter, was one of the few Goan aristocrats actively to oppose Portuguese rule. Forced to flee Chandor in 1950, the family returned in 1962 to find their house, amazingly, untouched. The airy tiled interiors of both wings contain a veritable feast of **antiques**.

The house is divided into two separate wings, owned by different branches of the old family. Both are open to the public, though there are no set hours as such – just turn up between 10am and noon or 3 and 6pm, go through the main entrance, up the stairs and knock at either of the doors. You'll be expected to leave a donation of at least Rs100. Furniture enthusiasts and lovers of rare Chinese porcelain, in particular, will find plenty to drool over in the Menezes-Braganza wing (to the right as you face the building). Next door in the **Braganza-Perreira** portion, an ornate oratory enshrines St Francis Xavier's diamond-encrusted toenail, retrieved from a local bank vault. The house's most famous feature, however, is its ostentatiously grand ballroom, or **Great Salon**, where a pair of matching high-backed chairs, presented to the Braganza-Perreiras by King Dom Luís of Portugal, occupy pride of place.

Another superb colonial-era palacio stands at **QUEPEM**, half an hour's drive southeast of Margao on the fringes of the state's iron-ore belt. In 1787, a high-ranking member of the Portuguese clergy, **Father José Paulo de Almeida**, built a country house in the town. Known as the **Palacio do Deão** (Ⓦwww.palaciododeao.com) it grew to become one of the most grandiloquent in the colony, later served as a retreat for the colony's Viceroys. The palacio was recently restored to its former glory by a Goan couple who scoured libraries in Lisbon for original plans of the building. What you see today is thus a faithful approximation of how the house would have looked in José Paulo's day. The engaging guided **tour** (daily, except Fri 10am–6pm; Ⓣ0832/266 4029; free) lasts around half an hour, winding up on the lovely rear terrace overlooking the river where, by prior arrangement, you can enjoy a copious Indo-Portuguese lunch (Rs450) – an experience not be missed.

Colva

A hot-season retreat for Margao's moneyed middle classes since long before Independence, **COLVA** is the oldest and largest – but least appealing – of south Goa's resorts. Its outlying *waddos* are pleasant enough, dotted with colonial-style villas and ramshackle fishing huts, but the beachfront is dismal: a lacklustre collection of concrete hotels, souvenir stalls and fly-blown snack bars strewn around a bleak central roundabout. The atmosphere is not improved by heaps of rubbish dumped in a rank-smelling ditch that runs behind the beach, nor by the stench of drying fish wafting from the nearby village. Benaulim, only a five-minute drive further south, has a far better choice of accommodation and range of facilities, and is altogether more salubrious.

Benaulim

The predominantly Catholic fishing village of **BENAULIM** lies in the dead centre of Colva beach, scattered around the coconut groves and paddy fields, 7km west of Margao. Two decades ago, the settlement had barely made it onto the backpackers' map. Nowadays, though, affluent holiday-makers from Metropolitan India come here in droves, staying in the huge resort and time-share complexes mushrooming on the outskirts, while long-staying, heavy-drinking Brit pensioners and thirty-something European couples taking time out of trips around the Subcontinent make up the bulk of the foreign contingent.

Benaulim's rising popularity has certainly dented the village's old-world charm, but time your visit well (avoiding Diwali and the Christmas peak season), and it is still hard to beat as a place to unwind. The seafood is superb, accommodation and motorbikes cheaper than anywhere else in the state, and the beach breathtaking, particularly around sunset, when its brilliant white sand and churning surf reflect the changing colours to magical effect.

Shelving away almost to Cabo da Rama on the horizon, the beach is also lined with Goa's largest, and most colourfully decorated, fleet of **wooden outriggers**, and these provide welcome shade during the heat of the day. Hawkers, itinerant masseurs and fruit wallahs appear at annoyingly short intervals, but you can usually escape them by renting a bike and pedalling south on the hard tidal sand.

Conventional sights are thin on the ground along this stretch of coast, though one exception stands out on the eastern fringes of Benaulim: a splendid new ethnographic museum, **Goa Chitra** (Tues–Sun 9.15am–6pm, last tour 5.15pm; Ⓣ0832/657 0877, Ⓦwww.goachitra.com; Rs300), which looks likely to establish itself as one of Goa's foremost cultural attractions. Set against a backdrop of a working organic farm, the exhibition comprises a vast array of antique agricultural tools and artefacts, ranging from giant cooking pots and ecclesiastical robes to

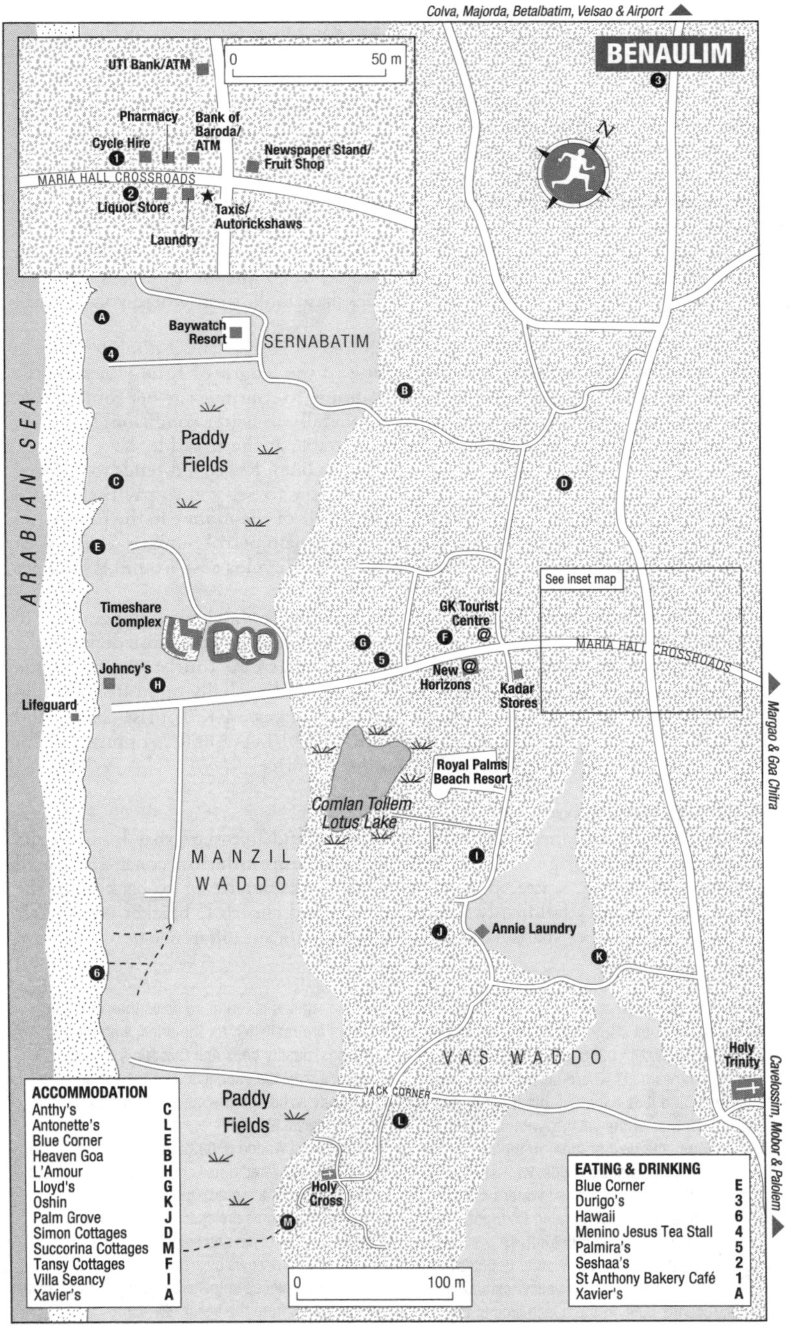

BENAULIM

Colva, Majorda, Betalbatim, Velsao & Airport

UTI Bank/ATM
Pharmacy
Bank of Baroda/ ATM
Cycle Hire
Newspaper Stand/ Fruit Shop
MARIA HALL CROSSROADS
Liquor Store
Taxis/ Autorickshaws
Laundry
0 50 m

ARABIAN SEA
Baywatch Resort
SERNABATIM
Paddy Fields
Timeshare Complex
Johncy's
Lifeguard
GK Tourist Centre
New Horizons
Kadar Stores
See inset map
MARIA HALL CROSSROADS
Margao & Goa Chitra
Royal Palms Beach Resort
Comlan Tollem Lotus Lake
MANZIL WADDO
Annie Laundry
VAS WADDO
Holy Trinity
JACK CORNER
Paddy Fields
Holy Cross
Cavelossim, Mobor & Palolem
0 100 m

ACCOMMODATION

Anthy's	C
Antonette's	L
Blue Corner	E
Heaven Goa	B
L'Amour	H
Lloyd's	G
Oshin	K
Palm Grove	J
Simon Cottages	D
Succorina Cottages	M
Tansy Cottages	F
Villa Seancy	I
Xavier's	A

EATING & DRINKING

Blue Corner	E
Durigo's	3
Hawaii	6
Menino Jesus Tea Stall	4
Palmira's	5
Seshaa's	2
St Anthony Bakery Café	1
Xavier's	A

tubas and sugarcane presses. The idea is to promote appreciation of the region's traditional agrarian lifestyle – a world of traditional knowledge and skills fast disappearing today. To get to Goa Chitra by bike or motorcycle, head east from Maria Hall crossroads towards Margao, and take the first turning on your left at a fork after 1.5km. When you reach the T-junction ahead, turn sharply right; the museum lies another 500m on your right.

Arrival and information

Buses from Margao and Colva roll through Benaulim every fifteen minutes or so, dropping passengers at the Maria Hall crossroads. Ranged around this busy junction are two well-stocked general stores, a couple of café-bars, a bank, pharmacy, laundry and the taxi and auto-rickshaw rank, from where you can pick up **transport** to the beach, 1.5km west.

Signs offering **motorbikes** for rent are dotted along the lane leading to the sea: rates are standard, descending in proportion to the length of time you keep the vehicle. Worth bearing in mind if you're planning to continue further south is that motorbikes are much cheaper to rent (and generally in better condition) here than in Palolem. **Petrol** is sold by the litre from a table at the roadside, two minutes' walk south down the road leading to *Royal Palms Beach Resort*, but tends to be laced with solvent and smokes badly. Local boys will try to get you to pay them to fill your bike up in Margao, but invariably pocket half of the money in the process, so if you've a valid licence do it yourself (Margao's main petrol pump is on the west side of the Praça Jorge Barreto – see map, p.717). **Bicycles** cost around Rs100 per day to rent.

For **changing money**, the Bank of Baroda on Maria Hall has a (temperamental) ATM; the UTI one around the corner on the main road is a bit more dependable. Currency and travellers' cheques may be changed at GK Tourist Centre, at the crossroads in the village centre, and New Horizons, diagonally opposite. It's often worth comparing rates at the two. For **internet access**, GK Tourist Centre and New Horizons have broadband connections (Rs40/hr). Annie's, opposite Palm Grove, offers an inexpensive same-day **laundry** service.

Accommodation

Aside from the unsightly time-share complexes and five-stars that loom in the fields around the village, most of Benaulim's **accommodation** consists of small budget guesthouses, scattered around the lanes a kilometre or so back from the beach. The majority fall firmly into the "cheap and cheerful" bracket – clean but featureless annexes of spartan rooms; the only significant difference between them is their location.

Inexpensive

Antonette's Jack Corner, House #1695 Vas Waddo ⓣ0832/277 0358 or ⓣ9922 312984. Next to a crossroads where all the local fishermen and lads hang out, but in an otherwise peaceful corner of the village, with simple but clean rooms, the best of them to the rear of the building looking over the fields. Well-stocked fridges with beers and bottled water on the upstairs landing. Owner Geraldo Rodrigues is exceptionally friendly and helpful. ❶

Lloyd's 1554/A Vas Waddo ⓣ0832/277 1492. With its garish yellow exterior, this place, recently built on the beach side of the village, stands out in more ways than one. The rooms are really big for the price, with high ceilings, quality beds and fans, plus neat mozzie screens over the windows. And they offer variously sized apartments upstairs (❺) for longer stays. ❸

Oshin Mazil Waddo ⓣ0832/277 0069, ⓔinaciooshin@rediffmail.com. Large complex set well back from the road. Opening on to leafy terraces, its rooms are spacious and clean, with attached bathrooms and balconies; those on the top floor afford views over the treetops. A notch above most places in this area, and good value, but quite a walk from the beach. ❸–❹

Simon Cottages Ambeaxir Sernabatim ⓣ0832/277 0581. Perennially among the best budget deals in Benaulim, in a quiet spot at the unspoilt north side of the village and with huge rooms on three storeys, all with shower-toilets and verandas, opening onto a sandy courtyard. ❷

Succorina Cottages 1711/A Vas Waddo ⓣ0832/277 0365. Small but immaculate rooms in a jazzily decorated, pink house, 1km south of the crossroads in the fishing village, offering glimpses of the sea across the fields from large first-floor sitouts. A perfect place to get away from the tourist scene, and a 5min walk from the quietest stretch of beach. Telephone bookings accepted by hosts Sebby and Succorina. ❷

Mid-range and expensive

Anthy's Sernabatim ⓣ0832/277 1680, ⓔanthysguesthouse@rediffmail.com. Nicely furnished rooms right on the sea, with tiny bathrooms and breezy verandas – though you pay through the nose for the location. ❺

Blue Corner Sernabatim. Popular hut camp on the beach, run by an enthusiastic young crew led by hospitable owner, Raj. Large palm-leaf structures with fans, mosquito nets, attached shower-toilets and plywood sitouts. Quiet and secure, and the bar-restaurant is one of the most happening places on the beach in the evenings. ❹

Heaven Goa 1 Ambeaxir Sernabatim, ⓣ0832/275 8442, ⓣ9890 698202, ⓦwww.heavengoa.in. Run by a welcoming Swiss-Keralan couple, Karin & Sunil, this new-ish block of a dozen or so rooms occupies a plum spot, 10min back from the sea beside a lily pond alive with frogs, egrets and water buffalo. The rooms are spacious and well set up (with wood shelves, mosquito nets, shiny tiled floors and balconies overlooking the water). Expert Ayurvedic massages are offered; and they bake fresh pizzas in a wood oven, too. Excellent value for money in this bracket. ❹

L'Amour Beach Rd ⓣ0832/277 0404, ⓦwww.lamourbeachresort.com. Benaulim's oldest hotel comprises a comfortable thirty-room cottage complex; its chalets (some a/c) are spacious and cool, with ceramic tiled floors and little verandas opening on to a central garden. Reasonable rates, but avoid the rooms on the first floor of the main block, which get horribly hot. ❸–❺

Palm Grove Tamdi-Mati, 149 Vas Waddo ⓣ0832/277 0059, ⓦwww.palmgrovegoa.com. Secluded hotel surrounded by beautiful gardens, offering three classes of mostly a/c rooms, the newest block very luxurious indeed. A bike ride back from the beachfront, but very pleasant, and the management is helpful. ❺–❻

Tansy Cottages Beach Rd ⓣ0832/277 0574, ⓔtansycottages@yahoo.in. Not a great location and the shocking green paintwork is hard to live with, but the rooms here are some of the nicest lower-midrange options in Benaulim: they're a generous size, with tiled floors and new attached bathrooms. ❹

Villa Seancy Vas Waddo ⓣ0832/227 0496 or 9822 108453. This is a sound choice if you want to extend your stay. Hostess Percy Rodrigues offers half a dozen modern apartments, equipped with kitchenettes, large bedrooms and balconies, close to the centre of the village – the nicest of them on the upper floors. Bargain rates, too. ❹

Xavier's Sernabatim ⓣ0832/277 1489, ⓔjovek@sanchar.net. Well-maintained, large rooms ranged around a lovely garden, virtually on the beach but within walking distance of the village centre. All rooms have private terraces and low-slung cane chairs to lounge on, and the local owners, who have been here for decades, are genuinely hospitable. A peaceful, well-managed and perfectly situated option. ❺

Eating and drinking

Benaulim's proximity to Margao market, along with the presence of a large Christian fishing community, means its **restaurants** serve some of the tastiest, competitively priced seafood in Goa. The largest and busiest shacks flank the beachfront area, where *Johncy's* catches most of the passing custom. However, you'll find better food at lower prices at places further along the beach, which seem to change chefs annually; the only way to find out which ones offer the best value for money is to wander past and see who has the most customers. An enduring favourite is *Domnick's*, whose garrulous owner hosts bonfire parties one night per week (traditionally on Thurs), featuring a live band; prices here are on the high side. *Pedro's* on the beachfront is marginally better value and also puts on gigs, mostly on Saturday nights.

Blue Corner Sernabatim. Great little beachside joint specializing in seafood and authentic Chinese. House favourites include "fish tomato eggdrop soup", scrumptious "dragon potatoes" and, best of all, their "super special steak". Also featured on their eclectic menu are tasty Italian dishes, sizzlers and, for homesick veggies, a pretty good cauliflower cheese. Most mains Rs150–250.

Durigo's Sernabatim, 2km north of Maria Hall crossroads on the outskirts of Colva. This is the locals' favourite place to eat, serving traditional Goan seafood of a kind you rarely find in the shacks: try their tasty mussels, lemonfish (*modso*) or barramundi (*chonok*), marinated in spicy, sour *rechead* sauce and pan-fried in millet. Some may find the atmosphere a bit rough and ready (though the service is unfailingly polite), in which case follow the example of the village's middle classes and order a takeout.

Hawaii South end of beach. Nadia and Vinod from Himachal Pradesh have run this welcoming little shack for a nearly a decade, and can claim one of the most loyal clienteles in the village, most of whom come for the Italian dishes, prepared with home-made pasta, fresh herbs, olive oil and proper cheese. The prawn lasagne and moussaka also get the thumbs up, and they do a zingy, fresh-mint *mojito*. During the day, extra large backgammon sets and a dedicated kids' play area are additional attractions. Mains Rs120–160.

Menino Jesus Tea Stall Sernabatim. If you've ever wondered what beach shacks were like 30 years ago, check this place out. It's where the local rickshaw drivers refuel on spicy fish-curry-rice plates, piping hot slices of millet-fried mackerel and *pao bhaji* for only Rs50. Rough and ready, but the food's delicious, and the sea view perfect.

Palmira's Beach Rd ⓣ0832/277 1309. Benaulim's best breakfasts: wonderfully creamy and fresh set curd, copious fruit salads with coconut, real espresso coffee, warm local bread (*bajri*) and the morning paper. For a light lunch, try their delicious prawn toast or tomato or ginger-carrot soups.

Seshaa's/St Anthony Bakery Café Maria Hall crossroads. A local institution, *Sesha's* is a gloomy and rather cramped lads' café that's great for pukka Goan *channa bhaji* and, best of all, deliciously flaky veg or beef patties. On the opposite side of the road, *St Anthony Bakery Café* is equally popular (especially in the mornings) serving the same local grub, but is less male-dominated – and its patties come straight out of the ovens.

Xavier's Sernabatim. Host Jovek's mum, Maria, does most of the masala preparation and cooking for this breezy beachside restaurant, so the Goan dishes – prawn vindaloo, fish *caldin* and a knock-out *chouriço* chilli-fry are top notch. Less spicy alternatives include a particularly tasty lemon rice. Facing one of the most tranquil stretches of the beach, the terrace is most atmospheric at night, with the waves crashing in only a few feet away.

Agonda

AGONDA, 10km northwest of Chaudi, comes as a pleasant surprise after the chaos reigning elsewhere in Goa. Accommodation in this predominantly Catholic fishing village is in small-scale, family-run guesthouses and hut camps, the restaurant scene is relatively unsophisticated, and the clientele easygoing and health-conscious. Granted, you don't get a dreamy brake of palm trees as a backdrop, but since the Boxing Day Tsunami the beach seems to have lost its menacing undertow and the sand is as clean as any in the state. Moreover, the surrounding hills and forest are exquisite.

The smart money says Agonda could all too soon go the way of Palolem (several large hut-camp owners have recently purchased leases on land here in anticipation of a mass exodus) but for the time being the village deserves to be high on the hit list of anyone seeking somewhere quiet and wholesome, with enough amenities for a relaxing holiday, but still plenty of local atmosphere.

Arrival and information

Four **buses** run daily between Agonda and the nearest market town, Chaudi (departing Chaudi 8.30am, 9.00am, 3.30pm & 4.30pm), and two run all the way to and from Margao (departing Agonda 6.15am & 2.30pm). Most services stop at the junction on the main Palolem road, 1km east (you can usually find a rickshaw for the trip into the village), but a couple go as far as the church in the centre of

Agonda, which stands near the middle of the beach. From here, a surfaced lane extends left (south), leading to most of the pukka-built hotels and guesthouses. In the other direction, a second tarmac lane heads north, soon degenerating into a dirt track which runs behind an unbroken row of hut camps to a small footbridge over the river, at the far end of the beach.

True Value Travel Agency, a couple of hundred metres north of the church, and Shri Kaushik (opposite the bakery, also just north of the church) provide **cash withdrawals** on credit and debit cards, as well as train, bus and flight **ticketing**, and broadband **internet** access. The nearest **ATMs** are in Chaudi, 10km south.

Accommodation

Tariffs are on a par with those of Palolem and Patnem, though dropping dramatically if the season is slack. Few places accept advance bookings so you'll probably have to plod around to find somewhere that suits, or else phone ahead from the comfort of a café table (though note that mobile coverage tends to be patchy hereabouts).

Bioveda Doval Kazan ⓣ9422 388982, ⓦwww.bioveda.in. Luxurious huts with attached bathrooms opening on to the beach. A thirty-second skip from the surf and roofed with paddy thatch, they're attractively set up, cool and comfortable, and equipped with quality beds, split-cane blinds and lots of other homely touches. The welcoming British-Keralan owners also run an excellent little Ayurveda centre on site where you can enjoy authentic massages by qualified staff. ❺

Chattai Doval Kazan ⓣ9423 812287, ⓦwww.chattai.co.in. One of Agonda's more stylish options, comprising a dozen or so well-spaced huts that wouldn't look out of place in an Amazon rainforest. They're right on the beach behind a little bar area, and roomier than most, with pitched jute roofs, well-aired bathrooms, quality mattresses and mozzie nets. ❺

Chris-Joana Near the Church ⓣ0832/264 7306 or ⓣ9421/155814, ⓔbelu_miranda5@yahoo.in. Smart new house on the roadside just south of St Anne's Church. Its bargain-priced rooms are clean, light and airy, and have decent beds. Go for one on the rear side, overlooking the rooftops and creek to coconut plantations; the front ones get warm in the afternoons. ❸

Dersy's South end of the beach, on the roadside ⓣ0832/264 7503. Very clean and cosy rooms, with tiled floors and good-sized bathrooms. Those on the first floor (front side) have a common sea-facing veranda that catches the breezes; you can lie in bed and hear the waves crashing only 100m away. They also run a couple of rows of (rather overpriced) beach huts on the opposite side of the lane. ❷

Jardim A Mar Doval Kazan ⓣ9420 820470, ⓦwww.jardim-a-mar.com. Professionally run "palm-tree-garden resort", offering budget rooms and pricier beachside huts, nicely decorated with Rajasthani quilts and blockprint throws, grouped around a sandy plot only a stone's throw from the surf. Partly German-owned, it has a slicker feel than most of the competition. ❺

Mahnamahnas Vall Waddo ⓣ9421 152158, ⓦwww.agondabeach.com. Great value, double-storey plywood huts with proper tiled roofs, and big bathrooms on the ground floor, plus hammocks strung on large balconies boasting uninterrupted sea views. The camp is German-owned and accepts advance bookings online. ❹

Maria Paulo Just north of *Dersy's* towards the church ⓣ0832/264 7606, ⓦwww.mariapauloagonda.com. This modern pink building on the roadside – look for the "Welcome Aboard" life ring – is a bigger and slightly more anonymous guest-house than the others in the village, which some might prefer. Six large, cool marble-floored rooms, all with quality beds and mozzie nets; the pricier ones have generous verandas. ❸–❹

Palm Beach Lifestyle Resort Behind *Dersy's* ⓣ0832/264 7783 or ⓣ9422 450380, ⓦwww.palmbeachgoa.com. Simple but very pleasant, terracotta-coloured chalets, ranged over terraces under a coconut plantation. They all have attractive wood floors, comfy mattresses and sea views from raised decks. Far better value than comparable places on the beach. ❹

Eating and drinking

Agonda's restaurants are as much hangouts as places to eat. Most are furnished with relaxing cane chairs, pretty lanterns and lounge areas with bolsters, and are on or near the beach – the excellent *Greek Place* being the notable exception.

Arabian Nights Near *Jardim A Mar. Arabian Nights* hosts a popular BBQ each evening with fresh grilled seafood and tasty steaks (from Rs250), rounded off with a slice of their famous banoffee pie.
Cuba Set well away from the village houses, this beachside café runs a late bar that serves as Agonda's unofficial party place.
Dunhill's Goyam & Goyam South of the church. Same owners as *Dropadi* in Palolem (see p.728) and *Goyam* in Patnem (see p.730), and the same great service, with wide selection of fabulous north Indian food and fresh fish. Most mains around Rs150.
Greek Place Opposite St Anne's Church. Proper Greek café on a secluded roadside terrace in the centre of Agonda, where you can order scrumptious *souvlaki* (Rs100–140) and proper *horiatiki* salads with real feta (Rs180) to a background of rembetiko music. Owners Kosmas and Maria make this a friendly, fun, and very Hellenic little hangout.
Jardim A Mar Doval Kazan. A café-restaurant that ticks all the boxes: it's slap on the sand, well shaded (under palms and a Ladakhi parachute), with comfy cane chairs, hammocks and silk cushions scattered on lounge mats. And it's a great breakfast spot, churning out fresh fruit juices, proper coffee, grilled baguettes and, the house speciality, rice pudding, as well as a popular all-day menu.
Madhus North side of beach. For years, the best tandoori outfit on the beach: great for fresh local fish and Indian dishes alike. It's inexpensive and always busy, so get here early. Most mains only Rs100.

Palolem

Nowhere else in peninsular India conforms so closely to the archetypal image of a paradise beach as **PALOLEM**, 35km south of Margao. Lined with a swaying curtain of coconut palms, the bay forms a perfect curve of golden sand, arcing north from a giant pile of boulders to a spur of the Sahyadri Hills, which tapers into the sea draped in thick forest. Palolem, however, has become something of a paradise lost over the past decade. It's now Goa's most popular resort, deluged from late-November by legions of long-staying tourists, and bus loads of day-trippers from Karnataka and beyond. Visitor numbers become positively overwhelming in peak season, when literally thousands of people spill across a beach backed by an unbroken line of shacks and Thai-style huts camps.

Basically, Palolem in full swing is the kind of place you'll either love at first sight, or want to get away from as quickly as possible. If you're in the latter category, try smaller, less frequented **Patnem** beach, a short walk south around the headland, where the shack scene is more subdued and the sands marginally emptier.

Arrival

Regular buses to Palolem from Margao stop at the end of the lane leading from the main street to the beachfront. Frequent **buses** also run between Margao and Karwar (in Karnataka) via the nearby market town of **Chaudi** (every 30min; 2hr), 2km southeast across the rice fields. The last bus from Palolem to Chaudi/Margao leaves at around 4.30pm; check with the locals for the precise times, as these change seasonally. Chaudi is also the nearest railhead to Palolem; the station lies a short way north of the main bazaar. Rickshaws charge Rs75–100, taxis Rs150–200 for the ride to the beach.

Accommodation

The local municipality's strict enforcement of a rule banning new concrete construction in Palolem (it went so far as to bulldoze without warning the entire resort a few years back) has ensured that most of the village's accommodation consists of simple palm-leaf **huts** or "tree houses". Apart from the more snazzily set up places listed below, there's very little difference between the camps: check in to the first that takes your fancy and reconnoitre the rest of the beach at leisure when you've found your feet.

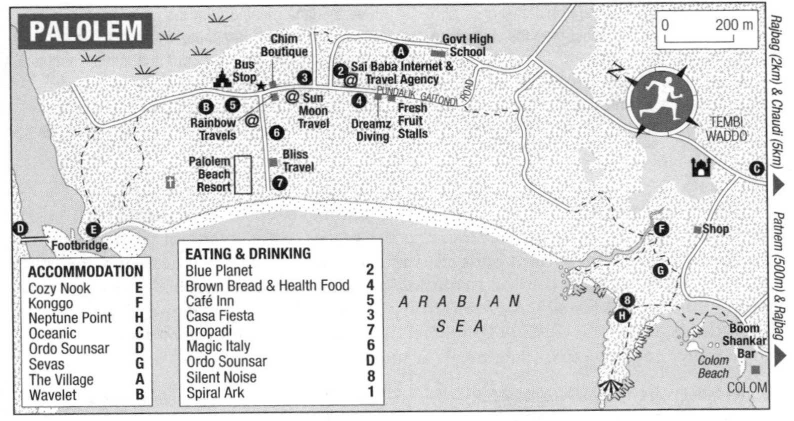

Cozy Nook North end of the beach, near the island ⓣ0832/264 3550, ⓦwww.cozynookgoa.com. One of the most attractive setups in the village, comprising 25 bamboo huts (sharing seven toilets, but with good mattresses, mosquito nets, safe lockers and fans) opening onto the lagoon on one side and the beach on the other – an unbeatable spot, which explains the higher than average tariffs. 6

Konggo Ourem ⓣ9422 059217 or 9764 267511. Run by the welcoming Claire and Dominic Pinko, *Konggo* has the most interesting huts currently on offer in Palolem, ingeniously constructed around cliffs and rocks in a beautiful tropical garden alive with birds and butterflies, just behind the far south end of the beach. The larger ones (Rs1500) are huge, with long, deep decks, and plenty of room to do yoga and even cook your own meals in, while the bathrooms have proper plumbing. And they're good value given the prime location. 4–5

Neptune Point South Palolem ⓣ9822 584968 or 9764 686555, ⓦwww.neptunepoint.com. *Neptune* occupies the sweet spot atop the boulder headland dividing Palolem and Patnem, and its huts, stacked up the hillside under giant coconut palms, make the most of the stupendous views. They're basic by today's standards, but comfortable enough, and having the sea on three sides is a unique selling point. The only downside is the *Silent Noise* disco and movie evenings (see p.728), held on the premises twice weekly, which bring in big crowds. 4–5

Oceanic Tembi Waddo ⓣ0832/264 3059, ⓦwww.hotel-oceanic.com. Ten minutes' walk inland from the beach (and also reachable via the backroad to Chaudi), *Oceanic* is owned and managed by a resident British couple, its marble-floored rooms stylishly designed, fresh, cool and relaxing, with large mosquito nets, blockprinted bedspreads and bedside lamps. There's also a pool on a forested patio behind, and a quality restaurant. 7

Ordo Sounsar Far northern end of Palolem beach, on the far side of the creek (look for the rickety footbridge to the right as you head for the island) ⓣ9822 488769 or 9422 639497, ⓦwww.ordosounsar.com. Run by a hospitable brother and sister team, Serafin and Shelly, this is Palolem's most idyllic hut camp, tucked away on the tranquil side of the river, which you get to via a rickety wooden footbridge. The huts themselves are a generous size and comfortable, with great sitouts to lounge on and funky thatched roofs; and there's an excellent restaurant. 4–5

Sevas Far southern end of the beach, on the hill dividing Palolem from Colom ⓣ0832/264 3977 or ⓣ9422 065437, ⓦwww.sevaspalolemgoa.com. Beautiful "ethnic" *cabañas* sporting traditional rice-straw roofs, mud-and-dung floors, hygienic squat-style loos and bucket baths. They also offer massages and yoga classes, and there's a pleasant restaurant serving very good thalis for Rs125–150. 3–4

The Village House #196, near Government High School ⓣ0832/264 5767, ⓣ9960 487627, ⓦwww.villageguesthousegoa.com. This British-run boutique guest house, on the fringes of Palolem ten minutes' walk from the beach, is the most comfortable and stylish place to stay in the area. Furnished with four-posters and vibrant silk bed covers, its wi-fi enabled, a/c rooms are large – and the designer bathrooms palatial. A shady rear garden serves as a common breakfast area, and you can take your drinks out onto the veranda in the evenings. ❼

Wavelet Palolem village ⓣ0832/264 3451, ⓦwww.waveletbeachresort.com. Ceramic-tiled rooms in a modern three-storey block, situated near the lane running from the main junction in the village to the far north end of the beach. Not exactly the kind of architecture that enhances the village's natural feel, but it's an out-of-the-way spot and some may consider the comfort and security a good trade-off. It's also good value. ❸

Eating

Palolem's **restaurants** reflect the cosmopolitan make-up of its visitors. Each year, a fresh batch of innovative, ever more stylish places opens, many of them managed by expats. For those on tight budgets, there also are a couple of cheap and cheerful local **tea shops** along the road running parallel with the beach – the *Sai Kripa* serves filling breakfasts of *pao bhaji*, fluffy bread rolls, omelettes and chai for next to nothing, while the *Calcutta Restaurant* dishes up piping hot *paratha*s and chapattis in the morning, and rice-plate meals at lunchtime.

Blue Planet Just off Pundalik Gaitondi Rd ⓦwww.blueplanet-café.com. Organic, veggie-vegan place located a stone's throw from the main drag, turning out healthy, balanced and tasty meals to Palolem's health-conscious contingent. Their spinach lasagne, served with baby corn, dry tomato, stir fry and green salad, is the house favourite; and they do a great selection of juices, herbal teas and non-dairy milks.

Brown Bread & Health Food Pundalik Gaintondi Rd. Not exactly the funkiest name on the strip, but the breakfasts served in this clean, friendly café are copious and delicious. The croissants come straight out of the oven, and their pineapple pancakes pull in hungry souls from far and wide.

Café Inn Pundalik Gaitondi Rd. By far the best coffee in Palolem, made with a proper Italian coffee machine by an Israeli duo. They get packed out for breakfast, and have a small but eclectic menu of meals. The best reason to come here, though, is the legendary coffee slush. Open daily 10am–11pm.

Casa Fiesta Pundalik Gaitondi Rd. Popular place on the main drag, offering an eclectic menu of world cuisine: hummus, Greek salad, wood-baked pizzas, Mexican specialities and fish *pollichatu*; mains (mostly under Rs200) come with delicious roast potatoes.

Dropadi Beachfront. This place enjoys both a top location and Palolem's best Indian chef, who specializes in rich, creamy Mughlai dishes and tandoori fish. Go for the superb *murg makhini* or crab masala with spinach. Most main courses are in the range Rs150–400.

Magic Italy Beach Rd. On the busy approach to the seafront, this is South Goa's number one Italian restaurant, serving home-made ravioli and tagliatelle, along with scrumptious wood-fired pizzas (Rs150–250).

Ordo Sounsar Far northern end of Palolem beach (for directions see "Accommodation"). With most places using previously frozen fish instead of fresh these days, this laid-back restaurant, on a terrace in a hut camp of the same name, is something special. Seasonal Goan seafood and vegetarian dishes are their specialities: pomfret stuffed with green chilli; papaya curry in coconut juice; green-pea *xacuti*; prawn *balchao*; shark *ambotik*; white cabbage in lime dressing – all made with the choicest and freshest ingredients. Count on Rs300–400 for two courses.

Spiral Ark Agonda Rd. Delightful fair-trade deli and terrace café serving fresh, wholesome juices, salads, soups, home-made breads, cakes and organic thalis on the terrace of an old Portuguese-era house. It's a 10min ride from the beach area, but worth the effort, and you can browse their gorgeous shop afterwards.

Drinking and nightlife

As with everywhere else in Goa, the ubiquitous 10pm amplified music ban is strictly observed in Palolem, although one crew has found a way of circumventing the rule. Hosted by *Neptune's Point* at the far south end of the bay, the **Silent Noise** collective stages weekly **headphone parties** on Saturday nights (9pm–4am; Rs400), where the music is broadcast digitally to individual headsets instead of through PAs. You've a choice of different house, electro and big beats mixes on three separate channels, synced with live AV screens, lights and lasers, and of course there's a dreamy view through the palm trees of India's most beautiful beach. For details of forthcoming programmes, and sample mixes, go to Ⓦwww.silentnoise.in.

In addition, the same site (featured on our map, p.727) screens movies on Wednesdays, which you can watch while enjoying a *mojito* from *Neptune Point*'s bar. For a full-on pub experience, try *Cuba* on the main street, which has a full-size pool table, big-screen TV showing live football matches and a great range of cocktails. A handful of bar-restaurants stage popular open-mic and music performances, among them *Laguna Vista* in Colom, where you can enjoy live Indo-French Fusion on Friday nights. Other than that, lounging in beachside cafés takes up most visitors' evenings.

Listings

Doctor Dr Sandheep, at the private Dhavalikar Hospital (Ⓣ0832 264 3147), 2km out of Palolem at Devabag on the road to Agonda, just before *Spiral Ark*.
Driving Dreamz Diving, in *Sea Shells Guest House*, Pundalik Gaitondi Rd (Ⓣ9326/113466, Ⓦwww.dreamzdiving.com), offer guided dives to sites in much clearer waters than you get around Palolem.
Foreign exchange Several agents in Palolem are licensed to change money; LKP Forex in the *Palolem Beach Resort* (see map, p.727) offers competitive rates. Sai Baba International, Sun Moon Travel and Rainbow Travels on the main street all do cash advances against Visa and MasterCards. The nearest ATM (for Visa and MasterCard withdrawals) is in Chaudi.
Internet cafés Bliss Travel, on the left near the main entrance to the beach; Rs40/hr for the village's fastest broadband lines. Go armed with an extra layer – the a/c's fierce.
Pharmacy Palolem's main pharmacy is 1km out of the village on the Chaudi road, to your right just after the Agonda turning. It's closed on Sundays, but out of hours you can call at the pharmacist's house immediately behind the shop.
Sailing Goa Sailing (Ⓣ9850 458865, Ⓦwww.goasailing.com) has three 15-foot Prindle Catamarans for hire – by the hour (Rs1250), half day (Rs3000) or full day (Rs4000) – ideal for exploring remote beaches in the area.
Telephones Bliss Travel (see "Internet" above) is one of the few surviving IST/STD places in Palolem with a reliable connection.
Trekking Goa Jungle Adventures (Ⓦgoajungle.free.fr) runs guided treks to natural swimming sites from Rs1500–1800/half day, including all equipment.

South of Palolem: Colom, Patnem and Rajbag

Once across the creek and boulder-covered spur bounding the south end of Palolem beach, you arrive at **COLOM**, a largely Hindu fishing village scattered around a series of rocky coves. Dozens of long-stay rooms, leaf huts and houses are tucked away under the palm groves and on the picturesque headland running seawards. This is the best place in the village to start an accommodation hunt – the lads will know of any vacant places; but be warned that most of the rooms here are very basic indeed.

A string of hut camps and shacks line the next beach south, **PATNEM**. The beach, curving for roughly a kilometre to a steep bluff, is broad, with little shade, and shelves quite steeply at certain phases of the tide, though the undertow rarely gets dangerously strong. On the headland dividing Patnem from Colom, the **Harmonic Healing & Eco Retreat Centre** (Ⓣ9822 512814, Ⓦwww.harmonicingoa.com) is the place to come if you need to sort out your body and soul. Wrapped in greenery with panoramic views of the beach, the centre hosts daily yoga, Pilates and Thai massage classes, as well as lessons in Bollywood dance and classical Indian singing (Rs250 for drop-ins).

At low tide, you can walk around the bottom of the steep-sided headland dividing Patnem from neighbouring **RAJBAG**, another kilometre-long sweep of white sand. Sadly, its remote feel has been entirely submerged by the massive five-star recently erected on the land behind it – much to the annoyance of the locals, who campaigned for four years to stop the project.

It's possible to press on even further **south from Rajbag**, by crossing the Talpona River via a hand-paddled ferry, which usually has to be summoned from the far bank (fix a return price in advance). Once across, a short walk brings you to **Talpona Beach**, backed by low dunes and a line of straggly palms. From here, you can cross the headland at the end of the beach to reach **Galjibag**, a remote white-sand bay that's a protected nesting site for Olive Ridley marine **turtles**. A strong undertow means swimming isn't safe here.

Accommodation

A more relaxed scene holds sway around the headland from Palolem. Accommodation prices are comparable, but it's generally easier to find a vacancy, while the vibe is a lot more chilled on the beach.

Boom Shankar Colom ⓣ0832 264 4035. Simply furnished, but clean attached rooms on the southern edge of the village, with lots of lounging space and fine views across the cove. They can also help you find longer-term rentals in houses nearby. ❷–❸

Goyam Patnem ⓣ9822/685138 or 9890 877844; ⓦwww.goyam.net. Luxury, double-storeyed wooden bungalows painted pretty pastel colours. Partly screened by casuarina trees, each is smartly furnished and fitted with bathrooms, mosquito nets and swings on sea-facing balconies; those at the front are the village's number-one des reses. ❼

Home Patnem ⓣ0832/264 3916, ⓦwww.homeispatnem.com. A chic little Swiss-British-run guest-house, comprising an annexe of attached rooms under Mangalorean tiles, pleasantly decked out with textiles, coconut mats, lampshades and other touches to justify their hefty tariffs. ❺–❻

Papaya's Patnem ⓣ9923 079447, ⓦwww.papayasgoa.com. A delightfully green oasis, where water is recycled to keep the plants in their prime. The eco-huts have breezy little sitouts, shaggy palm-frond fringes made from locally-sourced materials, and the power comes from solar panels. ❺–❻

Parvati Patnem ⓣ9822 189913, ⓦwww.parvatihuts.in. A cut above your average hut camp, offering spacious, circular bamboo huts, each with a good-sized bathroom, western-style toilet and shower, safe locker and mozzie net. The best value in this category, it's set in a leafy garden smothered in hibiscus plants – and has a more chilled vibe than most of the neighbours. ❹–❺

Namaste Patnem ⓣ9850 477189. Among the string of budget traveller camps in Patnem is a dependable, lively budget option, run by the amiable Satay. Rates range from Rs700–1500 depending on size and comfort of the bamboo hut, time of year and how far back you are from the sand; all have individual shower-toilets. ❹–❺

Tree Shanti Colom ⓣ0832/264 4460, 9923 795290. A small family guesthouse, run by a feisty couple of sisters, Gita and Sarita Komarpunt. They have five comfortable, red-tiled cottages and four spacious rooms (all with big bathrooms), set in a leafy garden swathed in forest. It's a fun place to stay, with a friendly atmosphere that's a world away from Palolem's hut camps. ❻–❼

Eating

It's a safe bet you'll spend a few hours each day in one or other of the cafés in Colom or behind Patnem beach, among which the following stand out.

Bocado de Cardinales Colom. This little place tucked under the palms rustles up heavenly tapas, great fish dishes and more-ish cocktails – but watch your alcohol intake as there is a very tempting clothes and textile boutique on the premises too.

Boom Shankar Colom. *Boom Shankar* does a great range of food – including its perennially popular fresh mozzarella and tomato salads – and, with a rear terrace overlooking the bay and gorgeous views, is the perfect place for a sundowner.

Bora Dista Café Harmonic Healing Centre. Up on the rocks overlooking the beach, this laid-back café boasts the most extensive views of any hereabouts, and serves up healthy foods as well as a few treats, though it's open only until 4.30pm.

Goyam North end of the beach. This swanky beachside restaurant, an off-shoot of the popular

Dropadi in Palolem, does superb seafood prepared in rich north-Indian style: crab *makhini* and tandoori sea bass (Rs350–400) are their signature dishes.

Home Middle of the beach. Patnem's nicest beach café, serving mezes, freshly baked bread, Swiss röstis, fresh salads (from around Rs150), proper Lavazza espresso and wonderful desserts (banoffee pie, warm apple tart with fresh cream, chocolate and walnut cake). It's a particularly pleasant option for breakfast, with Chopin playing over the sound system and sparrows chirping in the palms.

UTI (United Tastes of India) Set back from the beachfront. South Indian dosas and *iddlis*, complete with *chatni* and spicy *samber*, are UTI's speciality, but they also rustle up big portions of traditional north Indian fare, including tasty *palak paneer* and veg *makanwalla*, which hungry punters shovel in with fluffy naan breads and chapattis.

Cotigao Wildlife Sanctuary

The **Cotigao Wildlife Sanctuary**, 10km southeast of Chaudi, was established in 1969 to protect a remote and vulnerable area of forest lining the Goa–Karnataka border. Best visited between October and March, Cotigao is a peaceful and scenic park that makes a pleasant day-trip from Palolem, 12km northwest. Encompassing 86 square kilometres of mixed deciduous woodland, the reserve is certain to inspire tree lovers, but less likely to yield many wildlife sightings: its tigers and leopards were hunted out long ago, while the gazelles, sloth bears, porcupines, panthers and hyenas that allegedly lurk in the woods rarely appear. You do, however, stand a good chance of spotting at least two species of monkey, a couple of wild boar and the odd gaur (the primeval-looking Indian bison), as well as plenty of exotic birdlife. Any of the buses running south on the NH-17 to Karwar via Chaudi will drop you within 2km of the gates. However, to explore the inner reaches of the sanctuary, you really need your own transport. The wardens at the reserve's small **Interpretative Centre** at the gates, where you have to pay your entry fees (Rs5, plus Rs100 for a car, Rs50 for a motorbike; Rs50 for a camera permit) will show you how to get to a 25-metre-high treetop watchtower, overlooking a **waterhole** that attracts a handful of animals around dawn and dusk. You can also stay here at a rather unprepossessing little room (Rs250/night), in the compound behind the main reserve gates. Food and drink may be available by prior arrangement, and there's a shop at the nearest village, 2km inside the park.

13

Kolkata & West Bengal

* **Victoria Memorial** This monument to the British Empire in Kolkata is a dizzying blend of Mughal and Italian architecture. See p.750
* **Eden Gardens** Enjoy the chaos and spectacle of a match at Kolkata's famous cricket ground. See p.752
* **Sundarbans** Float through the endless mangrove forests, home to a profusion of wildlife, including the majestic Bengal tiger. See p.764
* **Shantiniketan** This tranquil university town exudes the spirit of its founder, the poet and philosopher Rabindranath Tagore. See p.769
* **Toy Train** This steam-driven Victorian railway makes a leisurely journey from the steamy plains to the tea gardens that carpet the steep hillsides around Darjeeling. See p.774
* **Darjeeling** A charming hill-station with spectacular views and famously fine tea. See p.776
* **Singalila Trek** This Darjeeling trek features unforgettable mountain vistas, especially beautiful in April and May, when the rhododendrons are in bloom. See p.784
* **Kalimpong** The horticultural capital of the northeast, with quiet walks, orchid nurseries and colourful markets. See p.786

▲ Harvesting tea in the Darjeeling Hills

Unique among Indian states in stretching all the way from the Himalayas to the sea, **WEST BENGAL** is nonetheless explored in depth by few travellers. That may have something to do with the exaggerated reputation of its capital, **KOLKATA (CALCUTTA)**, a sophisticated and friendly city that belies its popular image as poverty-stricken and chaotic. The rest of Bengal holds an extraordinary assortment of landscapes and cultures, ranging from the dramatic hill-station of **Darjeeling**, within sight of the highest mountains in the world, to the vast mangrove swamps of the **Sundarbans**, prowled by man-eating Royal Bengal tigers. The narrow central band of the state is cut across by the huge River Ganges as it pours from Bihar into Bangladesh where the **Farrakha Barrage** controls the movement of south-flowing channels such as the River Hooghly, the lifeline of Kolkata.

At the height of British rule, in the nineteenth and early twentieth centuries, Bengal flourished both culturally and materially, nurturing a uniquely creative blend of West and East. The **Bengali Renaissance** produced thinkers, writers and artists such as Bankim Chandra Chatterjee and **Rabindranath Tagore**, whose collective influence still permeates Bengali society a century later.

Not all of Bengal is Bengali; the current Nepalese-led separatist movement for the creation of an autonomous "Gurkhaland" in the Darjeeling area has focused on sharp differences in culture. Here, the Hindu Nepalese migration eastward from the nineteenth century onwards has largely displaced the indigenous tribal groups of the north but Lamaist Tibetan Buddhism continues to flourish. In the southwest, on the other hand, tribal groups such as the Santhals and the Mundas still maintain a presence, and itinerant Baul **musicians** epitomize the region's traditions of song and dance, most often heard around Tagore's university at **Shantiniketan**; Tagore's own musical form, Rabindra Sangeet, is a popular amalgam of influences including folk and classical. Other historical specialities of Bengal include its ornate **terracotta temples**, as seen at Bishnupur, and its **silk** production, concentrated around **Murshidabad**, the state's last independent capital.

Bengal's own brand of Hinduism emphasizes the **mother goddess**, who appears in such guises as the fearsome Kali and Durga, the benign Saraswati, goddess of learning, and Lakshmi, the goddess of wealth. The most mysterious of all is Tara, an echo of medieval links with Buddhism; her temple at **Tarapith** is perhaps the greatest centre of Tantrism in the entire country.

Some history

Although Bengal was part of the Mauryan empire during the third century BC, it first came to prominence in its own right under the Guptas in the fourth century AD. So dependent was it on trade with the Mediterranean that the fall of Rome caused a sharp decline, only reversed with the rise of the Pala dynasty in the eighth century.

After a short-lived period of rule by the highly cultured Senas, based at **Gaur**, Bengal was brought under Muslim rule at the end of the twelfth century by the first Sultan of Delhi, Qutb-ud-din-Aibak. Sher Shah Suri, who briefly usurped power from the Mughals in the mid-sixteenth century, developed the infrastructure and built the Grand Trunk Road, running all the way to the Northwest Province on the borders of his native Afghanistan. Akbar reconquered the territory in 1574, before the advent of the Europeans in the eighteenth century.

The Portuguese, who were the first to set up a trading community beside the Hooghly, were soon joined by the British, Dutch, French and many others. Rivalry between them eventually resulted in the ascendancy of the **British**, with the only serious indigenous resistance coming from the tutelary kingdom of **Murshidabad**, led by the young Siraj-ud-Daula. His attack on the fledgling

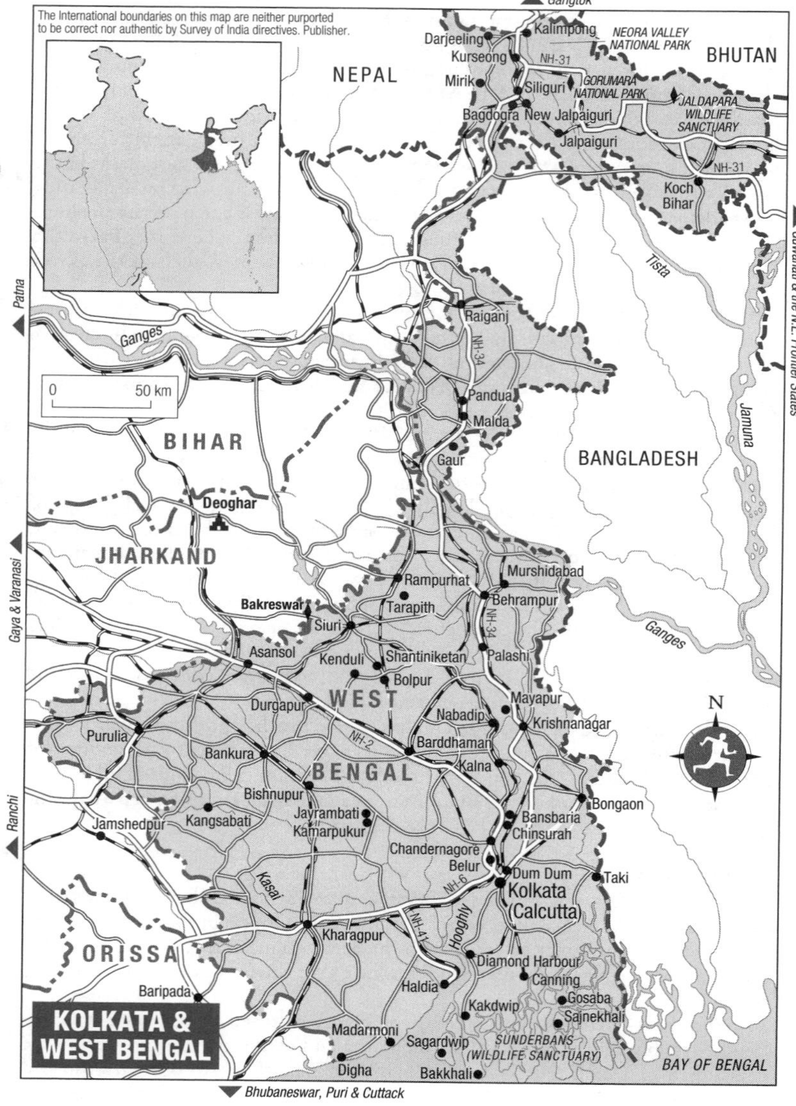

British community of Calcutta in 1756 culminated in the infamous **Black Hole** incident (see p.751), when British prisoners suffocated to death. Vengeance, in the form of a British army from Madras under **Robert Clive**, arrived a year later. The defeat of Siraj-ud-Daula at the **Battle of Plassey** paved the way for British domination of the entire Subcontinent. Bengal became the linchpin of the British East India Company and its lucrative trading empire, until the company handed over control to the Crown in 1858.

Maoist insurgency

A word of warning: the western extremities bordering on Jharkhand and Orissa in parts of the districts of Purulia, West Midnapur and Bankura are currently embroiled in a Maoist insurgency supported by tribals and fuelled by poverty. There is little governance from either the centre or the state and battles involving security forces are frequently reported.

Up to 1905, Bengal encompassed Orissa and Bihar; it was then split down the middle by Lord Curzon, leaving East Bengal and Assam on one side and Orissa, Bihar and West Bengal on the other. The move aroused bitter resentment, and the rift it created between Hindus and Muslims was a direct cause of the second Partition, in 1947, when East Bengal became East Pakistan. During the war with Pakistan in the early 1970s that resulted in the creation of an independent **Bangladesh**, up to ten million refugees fled into West Bengal. Shorn of its provinces, and with the capital moved from Calcutta to Delhi in 1911, the story of West Bengal in the twentieth century was largely a chronicle of decline.

The state's political life has been dominated by a protracted – and sometimes violent – struggle between the **Congress** and the major left-wing parties: the Marxist Communist Party of India, or **CPI(M)**, and the Marxist-Leninist **Naxalites** (Communist Party of India (ML)). In the 1960s and 1970s, the latter launched an abortive but bloody attempt at revolution. Bolstered by a strong rural base, the CPI(M) eventually emerged victorious under the enigmatic Jyoti Basu (d.2010), weathering the collapse of world communism. The CPI(M) has seen its grip on the state crumble in recent years, especially at the peripheries, where more and more ethnic groups are calling for autonomy from Bengal. In Kolkata – booming with expatriate wealth and a surge in business confidence – the political turmoil now seems a world away.

Kolkata (Calcutta) and around

One of the four great urban centres of India, **KOLKATA (CALCUTTA)** is, to its proud citizens, the equal of any city in the country in charm, variety and interest. As the showpiece capital of the British Raj, it was the greatest colonial city of the Orient, and descendants of the fortune-seekers who flocked from across the globe to participate in its eighteenth- and nineteenth-century trading boom remain conspicuous in its cosmopolitan blend of communities. Despite this, there has been a recent rise in Bengali nationalism, which has resulted in the renaming of Calcutta as Kolkata (the Bengali pronunciation and official new name), which has yet to be universally embraced – leading English-language paper *The Telegraph* continues to use Calcutta.

Since Indian Independence, mass migrations of dispossessed refugees caused by twentieth-century upheavals within the Subcontinent have tested the city's infrastructure to the limit. The resultant suffering – and the work of Mother Teresa in drawing attention to its most helpless victims – has given Kolkata a reputation for **poverty** that its residents consider ill-founded. They argue that the city's problems – the continuing influx of refugees notwithstanding – are no longer as acute as those of Mumbai or other cities across the world. In fact, though Kolkata's mighty Victorian buildings lie peeling and decaying, and its central avenues are choked by traffic, the city exudes a warmth and buoyancy that leaves few visitors unmoved. Kolkata is expanding rapidly, with shopping arcades, restaurants and satellite towns springing up all around the city. The downside of all this development, however, is some of the worst air pollution in the world, while the increase in traffic has seen the roads become some of the most dangerous in India.

In terms of the city's cultural life, Kolkata's Bengalis exude a pride in their artistic heritage and like to see themselves as the **intelligentsia** of India. The city is home to a multitude of **galleries** and huge Indian classical music festivals, with a thriving Bengali-language **theatre** scene and a tradition of **cinema** brought world renown by Satyajit Ray.

Though Marxists may rule from the chief bastion of imperialism (the **Writers' Building**, which has changed little over the decades), visitors still experience Kolkata first and foremost as a colonial city. Grand edifices in a profusion of styles include the imposing **Victoria Memorial** and the gothic **St Paul's Cathedral**, while the collection at the eclectic **Indian Museum**, one of the largest museums

The festivals of Kolkata

Most of Kolkata's Hindu festivals are devoted to forms of the mother goddess, **Shakti**. Kolkata's own deity, the black goddess **Kali**, is an emanation of **Durga**, the consort of Shiva. Kali is most commonly depicted with four arms, standing on the prostrate Shiva after killing the demon Raktviya, her tongue protruding in horror; other forms include the terrifying Chinemasta (torn head), where Kali holds her own severed head and drinks her own blood. The two-week **Durga Puja** (Sept/Oct) is Kolkata's most lavish festival. A symbol of victory, **Durga** is shown with ten arms slaying the demon Mahisasura, who assumed the shape of a buffalo and threatened the gods. Durga sits on, or is accompanied by, a lion.

In preparation for the festivals, artisans in the Kumartuli area (see p.753) sculpt voluptuous women from straw, papier-mâché, clay and *pith* (banana-tree marrow). Clothed and decorated, these lavish images of the goddesses are then carried in noisy procession to elaborate marquees called *pandal*s. Supported by donations from businesses and local residents, with popular music blaring through loudspeakers, *pandal*s block off small streets for days. After the puja, the images are taken to the river for immersion, a colourful scene that's best viewed via one of the boat cruises offered by the West Bengal tourist office (see p.743); they also offer bus tours that take in the *pandal*s.

The major festivals

Jaidev Mela (early Jan) Commemorating Joydeb, the revered author of the *Gita Govinda*, and held in the village of Kendubilwa, also known as Kenduli, near Shantiniketan; the place to hear Baul minstrels in their element.

Ganga Sagar Mela (mid-Jan) During the winter solstice of Makar Sankranti, hundreds of thousands of Hindu pilgrims and sadhus travel through Kolkata from all over India for a three-day festival at Sagardwip, 150km south where the Ganges meets the sea.

in Asia, ranges from natural history to art and archeology. Among numerous venerable Raj institutions to have survived are the racecourse, the reverence for cricket and several exclusive gentlemen's clubs.

Kolkata's **climate** is at its best during its short winter (Nov–Feb), when the daily maximum temperature hovers around 27°C, and the markets are filled with vegetables and flowers. Before the monsoons, the heat hangs unbearably heavily; the arrival of the rains in late June brings relief, but usually also floods that turn the streets into a quagmire. After a brief period of post-monsoon high temperatures, October and November are quite pleasant; this is the time of the city's biggest festival, **Durga Puja**.

Some history

By the time the remarkable **Job Charnock** established the headquarters of the **East India Company** at **Sutanuti** on the east bank of the Hooghly in 1690, the riverside was already dotted with trading communities from European countries. A few years later, Sutanuti was amalgamated with two other villages to form the town of **Calcutta**, whose name probably originated from *kalikutir*, the house or temple of Kali (a reference to the **Kalighat** shrine). With trading success came ambitious plans for development; in 1715 a delegation to the Mughal court in Delhi negotiated trading rights, creating a territory on both banks of the Hooghly of around 15km long. Later, it became entangled in the web of local power politics, with consequences both unforeseen (as with the Black Hole; see p.751) and greatly desired, as when the Battle of Plassey in 1758 made the British masters of Bengal. Recognized by Parliament in London in 1773, the company's trading

Dover Lane Music Festival (Jan/Feb) A week-long festival in south Kolkata, attracting many of the country's best musicians.

Saraswati Puja (Jan/Feb) Popular and important festival to the goddess of learning staged throughout Bengal.

Chinese New Year (Jan/Feb) Celebrated with a week-long festival of dragon dances, firecrackers and fine food, concentrated around Chinatown and the suburb of Tangra.

Muharram (dates determined by the lunar calendar; see ⓦwww.when-is.com) Shi'ite Muslims mark the anniversary of the martyrdom of Hussein by severe penance including processions during which they flagellate themselves.

Durga Puja (Sept/Oct) At the onset of winter, Durga Puja (known elsewhere as Dussehra) is the Bengali equivalent of Christmas. It climaxes on Mahadashami, the tenth day, when images are immersed in the river.

Lakshmi Puja (Oct/Nov) Held five days after Mahadashami on the full moon, to honour the goddess of wealth.

Id ul Fitr (dates determined by the lunar calendar; see ⓦwww.when-is.com) Celebrating the end of the fasting month of Ramadan and heralded by the new moon, the festival is a time of joyousness when people don new clothes and sample wonderful food at the restaurants and stalls around Park Circus.

Diwali and Kali Puja (Oct/Nov) Two weeks after Lakshmi Puja, Kali Puja is held on a moonless night when goats are sacrificed, and coincides with Diwali, the festival of light.

Christmas (Dec 25) Park Street and New Market are adorned with fairy lights and the odd Christmas tree. Plum pudding is sold, and Midnight Mass is well attended.

Poush Mela (late Dec) Held in Shantiniketan around Christmas, the *mela* attracts Bauls, the wandering minstrels who attract large audiences.

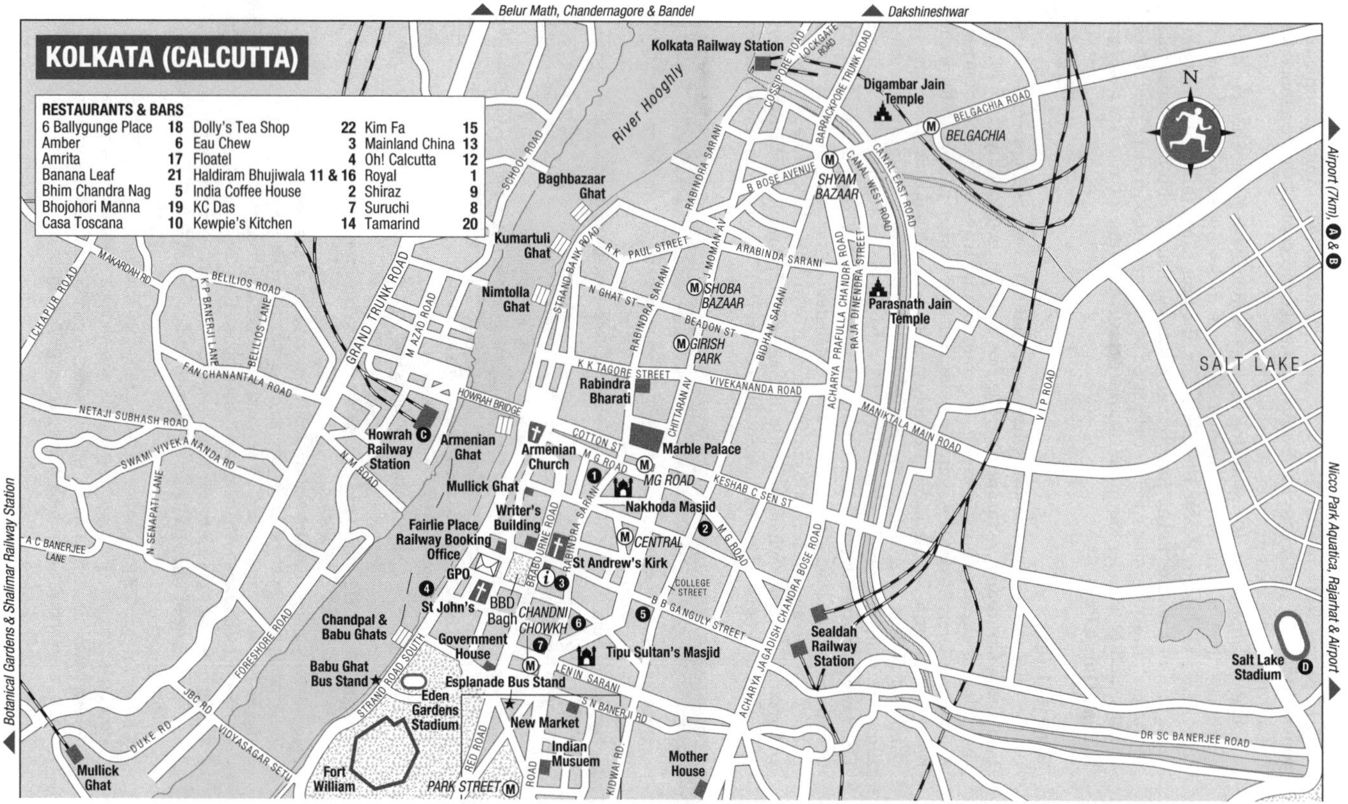

KOLKATA (CALCUTTA)

RESTAURANTS & BARS

6 Ballygunge Place	18	Dolly's Tea Shop	22	Kim Fa	15
Amber	6	Eau Chew	3	Mainland China	13
Amrita	17	Floatel	4	Oh! Calcutta	12
Banana Leaf	21	Haldiram Bhujiwala	11 & 16	Royal	1
Bhim Chandra Nag	5	India Coffee House	2	Shiraz	9
Bhojohori Manna	19	KC Das	7	Suruchi	8
Casa Toscana	10	Kewpie's Kitchen	14	Tamarind	20

Belur Math, Chandernagore & Bandel
Dakshineshwar
Airport (7km), A & B
Nicco Park Aquatica, Rajarhat & Airport
Botanical Gardens & Shalimar Railway Station
N
Kolkata Railway Station
Digambar Jain Temple
Parasnath Jain Temple
River Hooghly
Baghbazaar Ghat
Kumartuli Ghat
Nimtolla Ghat
Howrah Railway Station
Armenian Ghat
Armenian Church
Mullick Ghat
Writer's Building
Fairlie Place Railway Booking Office
GPO
St John's
BBD Bagh
Chandpal & Babu Ghats
Babu Ghat Bus Stand
Government House
Eden Gardens Stadium
Esplanade Bus Stand
Fort William
New Market
Indian Musuem
Mother House
Rabindra Bharati
Marble Palace
Nakhoda Masjid
St Andrew's Kirk
Tipu Sultan's Masjid
Sealdah Railway Station
Salt Lake Stadium
SALT LAKE
BELGACHIA
SHYAM BAZAAR
SHOBA BAZAAR
GIRISH PARK
MG ROAD
CENTRAL
CHANDNI CHOWKH
PARK STREET
COSSIPORE ROAD
LOCKGATE ROAD
BARRACKPORE TRUNK ROAD
BELGACHIA ROAD
CANAL WEST ROAD
CANAL EAST ROAD
SCHOOL ROAD
B BOSE AVENUE
RABINDRA SARANI
R K PAUL STREET
J MOMAN AV
ARABINDA SARANI
ACHARYA PRAFULLA CHANDRA ROAD
RAJA DINENDRA STREET
STRAND BANK ROAD
N GHAT ST
BEADON ST
BIDHAN SARANI
K K TAGORE STREET
VIVEKANANDA ROAD
CHITTARAN AV
MANIKTALA MAIN ROAD
V I P ROAD
COTTON ST
HOWRAH BRIDGE
M G ROAD
KESHAB C SEN ST
BRABOURNE ROAD
COLLEGE STREET
B B GANGULY STREET
ACHARYA JAGADISH CHANDRA BOSE ROAD
LENIN SARANI
S N BANERJI RD
DR SC BANERJEE ROAD
STRAND ROAD SOUTH
RED ROAD
KIDWAI RD.
GRAND TRUNK ROAD
M AZAD ROAD
N M ROAD
ICHAPUR ROAD
MAKARDAH RD
BELILIOS ROAD
K P BANERJI LANE
BELILIOS LANE
FAN CHANANTALA ROAD
NETAJI SUBHASH ROAD
SWAMI VIVEKANANDA RD
N SENAPATI LANE
A C BANERJEE LANE
FORESHORE ROAD
JBC RD
DUKE RD
VIDYASAGAR SETU
Mullick Ghat

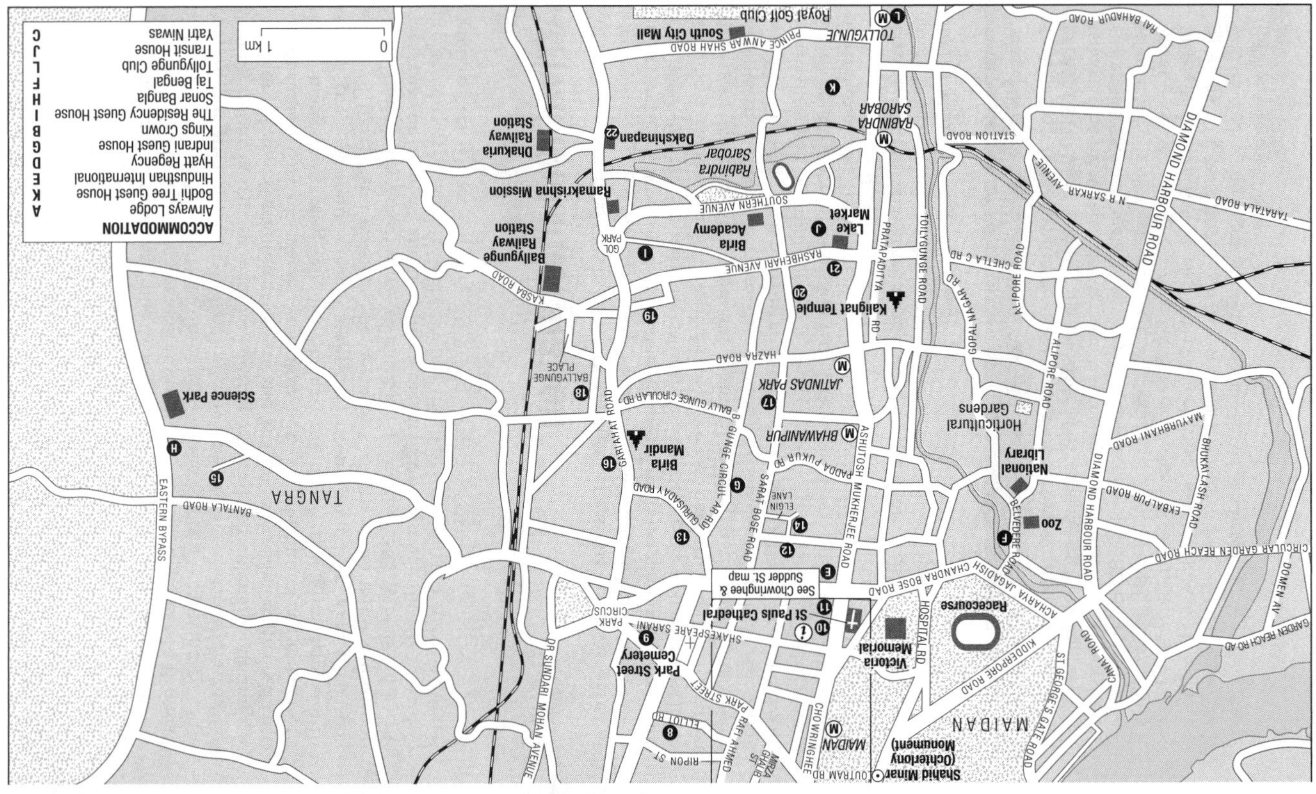
ACCOMMODATION
Airways Lodge A
Bodhi Tree Guest House K
Hindusthan International E
Hyatt Regency D
Indrani Guest House G
Kings Crown B
The Residency Guest House I
Sonar Bangla H
Taj Bengal F
Tollygunge Club L
Transit House J
Yatri Niwas C
0 1 km
TANGRA
Science Park
EASTERN BYPASS
BANTALA ROAD
KASBA ROAD
Ballygunge Railway Station
Ramakrishna Mission
Dhakuria Railway Station
Dakshinapan
Rabindra Sarobar
RABINDRA SAROBAR
GOL PARK
SOUTHERN AVENUE
Birla Academy
Lake Market
RASHBEHARI AVENUE
Kaliighat Temple
PRATAPADITYA RD
TOLLYGUNGE ROAD
TOLLYGUNJE
Royal Golf Club
South City Mall
PRINCE ANWAR SHAH ROAD
STATION ROAD
N R SARKAR AVENUE
TARATALA ROAD
DIAMOND HARBOUR ROAD
RAI BAHADUR ROAD
CHETLA C RD
ALIPORE ROAD
GOPAL NAGAR RD
HAZRA ROAD
JATINDAS PARK
BALLYGUNGE PLACE
BALLY GUNGE CIRCULAR RD
GARIAHAT ROAD
Birla Mandir
GURUSADAY ROAD
B. GUNGE CIRCUL AR RD
BHAWANIPUR
PADDA PUKUR RD
ELGIN LANE
SARAT BOSE ROAD
ASHUTOSH MUKHERJEE ROAD
Horticultural Gardens
National Library
Zoo
BELVEDERE ROAD
MAYURBHANI ROAD
BHUKAILASH ROAD
EKBALPUR ROAD
CIRCULAR GARDEN REACH ROAD
DOMEN AV
GARDEN REACH ROAD
CANAL ROAD
ST GEORGE'S GATE ROAD
KIDDERPORE ROAD
MAIDAN
Racecourse
ACHARYA JAGADISH CHANDRA BOSE ROAD
HOSPITAL RD
Victoria Memorial
Shahid Minar (Ochterlony Monument)
OUTRAM RD
MAIDAN
CHOWRINGHEE
MIRZA GHALIB ST
RAFI AHMED
PARK STREET
ELLIOT RD
RIPON ST
St Pauls Cathedral
See Chowringhee & Sudder St. map
SHAKESPEARE SARANI
PARK CIRCUS
Park Street Cemetery
DR SUNDARI MOHAN AVENUE
Botanical Gardens

monopoly led it to shift the capital of Bengal here from Murshidabad, and Calcutta became a clearing house for a vast range of commerce, including the lucrative export of opium to China.

At first, the East India Company brought young bachelors out from Britain to work as clerks or "writers" and accommodated them in the **Writers' Building**. Many took Indian wives, giving rise to the new Eurasian community known as the **Anglo-Indians**. Merchants and adventurers – among them Parsis, Baghdadi Jews, Afghans and Indians from other parts of the country – contributed to the melting pot after the East India Company's monopoly was withdrawn. The ensuing boom lasted for decades, during which such splendid buildings as the Court House, Government House and St Paul's Cathedral earned Calcutta the sobriquet "City of Palaces". In reality, however, the humid and uncomfortable climate, putrefying salt marshes and the hovels that grew haphazardly around the metropolis created unhygienic conditions that were a constant source of misery and disease. The death of Calcutta as an international port finally came with the opening of the Suez Canal in 1869, which led to the emergence of Bombay, and the end of the city's opium trade. In 1911, the days of glory drew to a definitive close when the imperial capital of India was transferred to New Delhi.

Arrival and information

Kolkata's **airport** (☎033/2511 8787), 20km north of the city centre, is served by international flights. Officially **Netaji Subhash Bose International Airport**, it is still universally known by its old name of **Dum Dum**. Undergoing a long, slow facelift, the dreary international terminal has 24-hour money-changing facilities including a Thomas Cook, as well as a pre-paid taxi booth and an India Tourism information counter. The domestic terminal, 500m to the south, has more amenities, including an accommodation booking counter and a railway reservation desk. The airport also has **retiring rooms** (Rs700 a/c, Rs225 non-a/c and a dorm) booked through the airport manager's office at either international (there is a left-luggage counter opposite) or domestic terminals. A pre-paid **taxi** to the central Sudder Street area costs around Rs260. An alternative is to take a taxi (around Rs70) or the shuttle bus to the Dum Dum Metro station (5km), and then the **Metro** (see p.743) into town; Sudder Street is a short walk from Park Street station. Bear in mind that you can't take large items (bikes, sports equipment etc) onto the Metro system.

What's in a name?

Though most of the old British **street names** were officially changed years ago, habits die hard and some of the original names continue to be widely used in tandem. The most important of these is Chowringhee or Jawaharlal Nehru Road (still called Chowringhee). Other name changes to note are BBD Bagh (still often referred to by its old name of Dalhousie Square or simply "Dalhousie"), Mirza Ghalib Street (Free School St), Dr Mohammed Ishaque Road (Kyd St), Muzaffar Ahmed Street (Ripon St), Rafi Ahmed Kidwai Street (Wellesley St), Ho Chi Minh Sarani (Harrington St), AJC Bose Road (Lower Circular Rd), Shakespeare Sarani (Theatre Rd), Rabindranath Tagore Street (Camac St), Lenin Sarani (Dharamtala) and Rabindra Sarani (Chitpore Rd).

Moving on

By plane

Kolkata has excellent domestic flights but its international connections are limited with direct flights to Bangkok, Singapore, Myanmar, Bangladesh, Kathmandu and Bhutan; Air India, Jet Airways, Emirates and Lufthansa fly, with changes, to Europe. For contact details of airlines, see "Listings", p.762. Check *Graphiti*, *The Telegraph*'s weekly supplement, for current flight (and train) information.

By train

Centralized information on train connections is available on ⓣ033/2230 3545/54 and 033/2230 3535. Making reservations to leave Kolkata by train is easy, with computerized booking offices (Mon–Sat 10am–1pm & 1.30–5pm, Sun & hols 10am–2pm) at the four main railway stations and throughout the city: Eastern and South Eastern Railways, Alexandra Court, 61 Chowringhee Rd, Rabindra Sadan; Computerized Booking Office, 3 Koilaghat St; New Koilaghat, 14 Strand Rd. You can also book online (see p.42) or through an agent. The tourist office on the first floor of the Eastern Railways office, in the northwest corner of BBD Bagh at 6 Fairlie Place books tourist quota train tickets (same hours; ⓣ033/2222 4206). You'll need to bring proof of encashment (an exchange or ATM receipt) to reserve a berth if paying in rupees. Reservations up to sixty days in advance can be made for most trains. For general reservation enquiries call ⓣ033/2230 3496, 1331 or 135.

By bus

For those willing to brave the 560km overnight journey to Siliguri – handy for Darjeeling and Sikkim – the best bus is the Royal Cruiser service (6.30pm; 12hr; Rs900 a/c) departing from the **Esplanade Bus Stand**. Other services leaving from Esplanade include Behrampur (for Murshidabad), Bishnupur, Malda and Rampurhat (for Tarapith). Several buses from here head to Basanti and the Sundarbans (especially early morning) and for points south to Diamond Harbour and beyond. Frequent buses for Bhubaneswar and Puri in Orissa leave the **Babu Ghat Bus Stand**, where Orissa Roadways (ⓣ9433 143428) and West Bengal State Transport (ⓣ033/241 6388) have booths.

To Bangladesh

Kolkata is the main gateway to Bangladesh from India. The **Bangladesh Consulate** is at 9 Circus Ave (Mon–Fri 9am–5pm; ⓣ033/2247 5208 ext 207 for visa section). Visas must be obtained in advance and will be issued on the same day if you submit your passport before 10am. You can reach Bangladesh by train or road and there are several **flights** daily from Kolkata to Dhaka. Departing Kolkata Station, the *Moitri Express* (Wed, Sat 7.10am; tickets from Foreign Tourist Bureau, Fairlie Place [see above]) is the only **direct train** to Dhaka and you need a visa to book. One direct **bus** runs from Salt Lake International Karunamoyee terminal (ⓣ033/2359 8448), a Rs140 taxi ride from the centre, to Dhaka (Mon–Sat 6.30am; 12hr; Rs1000); you will need to show your visa to book. Several travel agents around Sudder and Marquis streets sell tickets for private buses to Dhaka, which depart from the Esplanade stand, but involve changes at the border.

To the Andaman Islands

Flights with Air India and Jet Lite leave daily for Port Blair. To go by **ship** (there are three to four sailings a month), you'll need to book through the Shipping Corporation of India, 13 Strand Rd (ⓣ033/2248 2354); the journey takes three to five days, so bring plenty to read and food to supplement the dull meals. Free thirty-day **permits** are granted on arrival.

Kolkata has three main **railway stations** and a fourth is under development. Numerous trains are being re-routed so double check from which station your train will be leaving. Unfortunately, none of the stations are linked to the Metro system. **Howrah** – the point of arrival for most major trains from the south and west – stands on the far bank of the Hooghly a couple of kilometres west of the centre. To reach the central downtown area, traffic has to negotiate **Howrah Bridge** – the definitive introduction to the chaos of the city. Avoid the touts and **taxis** outside the station building, and head straight for the **pre-paid taxi** booth, from where the fare to central Sudder Street and the Park Street areas is Rs65–100. **Minibuses** and buses also operate from Howrah to destinations all over the city, but tend to be very crowded. A good alternative is to follow the signs from the station gate and take a **ferry** (Rs 4) across the Hooghly to Babu Ghat or the adjacent Chandpal Ghat, close to BBD Bagh, and pick up a metered taxi or bus from there.

Gleaming **Kolkata Station** (or Terminus, also known as **Chitpur Station**) lies 1km from Shyambazar Metro station from where it is a convenient seven stops south to Park Street (for Sudder St hotels). There isn't a pre-paid booth but auto-rickshaws to Shyambazar are available and there is a taxi rank. **Shalimar**, the city's newest station, is under construction 5km to the south of Howrah with just a handful of trains so far; the station is to be the main hub for Southern Railways.

Recommended trains from Kolkata

Destination	Name	No.	From	Departs	Total time
Allahabad	*Kalka Mail*	#2311	Howrah	7.40pm	13hr 20min
Bhubaneswar	*Falaknuma Express*	#2703	Howrah	7.40pm	6hr 20min
Bolpur	*Shantiniketan Express*	#2337	Howrah	10.10pm	2hr 15min
Chennai	*Coromandel Express*	#2841	Howrah	2.50pm	26hr 30min
Delhi	*Rajdhani Express**	#2301/05	Howrah	4.55pm	17hr 20min
	*Rajdhani Express**	#2313	Sealdah	4.50pm	18hr 5min
Gaya	*Jammu Express*	#2307	Howrah	11.30pm	6hr 45min
	Mumbai Mail	#2321	Howrah	10pm	7hr 25min
Guwahati	*Saraighat Express*	#2345	Howrah	13.50pm	17hr 40min
Mumbai	*Mumbai Mail*	#2321	Howrah	10pm	31hr 20min
New Jalpaiguri	*Darjeeling Mail*	#2343	Sealdah	10.05pm	9hr 55min
(for Siliguri**)	*Kanchenjunga Express*	#5657	Sealdah	6.35am	11hr 35min
Patna	*Lal Qila Express*	#3111	Kolkata	8.15pm	10hr 15min
	Danapur Express	#2351	Howrah	8.35pm	11hr 30min
Puri	*Puri Express*	#2837	Howrah	10.35pm	8hr 45min
Raxaul (for Birganj in Nepal)	*Mithila Express*	#3021	Howrah	3.45pm	16hr 40min
Varanasi	*Amritsar Mail*	#3005	Howrah	7.10pm	14hr 5min

Due to the recent opening of Kolkata and Shalimar stations, some trains may have switched stations since the time of writing.

*A/c only

**Connect here for Darjeeling, Kalimpong and Gangtok; always check planned change in schedule to connect with the Toy Train.

Sealdah Station, with its own **pre-paid taxi** booth in the car park, is on the eastern edge of the centre. Once the main terminus for trains from the north, Sealdah is gradually being downgraded to a local station. Long-distance **buses** from the south terminate at **Babu Ghat Bus Stand**, not far from Fort William on the east bank, while most others, such as those from Darjeeling, arrive at **Esplanade Bus Stand**, less than 500m north of Sudder Street.

Information and tours

The **India Tourism office**, off the central Chowringhee Road at 4 Shakespeare Sarani (Mon–Fri 9am–6pm, Sat 9am–1pm; Ⓣ033/2282 5813 or 2282 7731, Ⓔindtour6100@dataone.in), is your best bet for information on Kolkata, West Bengal and destinations further afield, and can assist with itineraries and booking tours. The **Government of West Bengal Tourist Bureau**, near the Writers' Building at 3/2 BBD Bagh East (Mon–Sat 10.30am–4.30pm; Ⓣ033/4401 2048 Ⓦwww.westbengaltourism.gov.in), arranges tours of Kolkata and package trips around West Bengal. They also issue **permits** and book tours and accommodation in the Sundarbans (Mon–Fri only). **Tourist information counters** at both the domestic and international terminals of the airport and Howrah and Sealdah stations offer similar services.

English-language **newspapers** such as the *Telegraph*, *Hindusthan Standard* and *Statesman* remain the primary source for information on what's on, but the monthly *Cal Calling* (Rs45) is excellent for listings and general information on the city. A booklet found free in more expensive hotels, *Explocity Kolkata* (Ⓦkolkata.explocity.com) is also useful.

Numerous private operators offer tours of the city. **Help Tourism's** walking tours (4–5hr; from Rs600) (Ⓣ033/2455 0917, Ⓦwww.helptourism.com) provide a great insight into the historic heart of the city. **Calcutta Walks** (Ⓣ9830 184 030; from Rs1250; Ⓦwww.traveleastindia.com) is very well organized, but expensive. They also do river cruises as do **Vivada Cruises** (Ⓣ033/2463 1990; Ⓦwww.vivadacruises.com). If you want to devise your own walking itineraries, the essential companion is *A Jaywalker's Guide to Calcutta* by Soumitra Das, available at bookshops such as Oxford.

City transport

The **Metro**, India's first and Kolkata's pride and joy, provides a fast, clean and efficient way to get around. The **river** is also used for transport, with the *ghats* near Eden Gardens at the hub of a **ferry** system. You can beat the traffic by jumping on one of the frequent ferries from Chandpal Ghat to Howrah Station (Rs4), though they're crowded at rush hour. While using public transport, be wary of **pickpockets**, especially on crowded buses.

The Metro

Kolkata's Russian-designed **Metro**, inaugurated in 1984 and now ageing, is still every bit as good as its inhabitants proudly claim, with trains operating punctually every few minutes. Services run from 7am to 9.45pm Monday to Saturday and 3pm to 9.45pm on Sundays. Tickets are cheap, starting at Rs4, and you can travel the entire length of the line from Dum Dum near the airport to Kavi Nazrul Islam (Garia) in the south for just Rs8. An east-west line is planned. For more information, visit Ⓦwww.kolmetro.com.

Buses and trams

Kolkata supports a vast and complicated **bus** network (for route information, check Ⓦwww.calcuttaweb.com), in operation each day roughly between 5am and 11pm, and subject to overcrowding and pickpocketing. Useful **bus routes** include: **#8** from Howrah via Esplanade to Gariahat; **#S17** from Chetla near Kalighat via Esplanade to Dakshineshwar; and **#5** and **#6**, which both travel via Howrah and the Esplanade–Chowringhee area, and stop at the Indian Museum at the head of Sudder Street. The **#C6** travels via Chowringhee, passing the top of Park Street before crossing the Vidyasagar Setu (the second bridge over the Hooghly) to the Botanical Gardens; in the other direction (north), it goes to College Street. Buses with an "S" prefix denote special express buses charging marginally more. Of the six Executive (Green Line) bus routes, the **#GL1** runs from Esplanade to the airport. The air-conditioned **Whiteliners** travel between Tollygunge (via Gariahat) and the airport.

In addition, private brown-and-yellow **minibuses** travel at inordinate speeds on ad-hoc routes; their destinations are usually painted boldly in Bengali and English on their sides. They tend not to pull over to the kerb to stop, making getting on and off hazardous and causing numerous accidents.

Kolkata's cumbersome trams (Ⓦwww.calcuttatramways.com), barely changed save for a lick of paint since they started operating in 1873, have been phased down, but certain routes linger on and a "new" model has been introduced with high glass windows. Female travellers may well be glad of the rush-hour women-only coaches. Routes include, amongst others, #29, BBD Bagh to Tollygunge via the Maidan, Hazra Mor and Kalighat; and #1, Esplanade to College Street.

Taxis

Taxis in Kolkata – painted black and yellow – are extremely good value, especially on long journeys such as to and from the airport (around Rs250 for a twenty-kilometre ride), but a few drivers can be unwilling to take you on short journeys or to areas they don't like the sound of. There's a night-time surcharge between 10pm and 6am of 25 percent. Up to two pieces of luggage are free, but there's an additional charge for further pieces and for placing bags in the boot. Most cabs have working **meters** and tend to use them in conjunction with the **conversion charts** they are obliged to carry. The latest conversion charts are published in *Cal Calling*. **Pre-paid taxis** are available at some railway stations and the airport.

Several **private taxi firms**, with vehicles at the airport and railway stations as well as the major hotels, provide more safety and luxury with air conditioning and printed receipts, including **Kolkata Cabs** (Ⓣ4433 3222), **Mega Cab** (Ⓣ4141 4141) and **Blue Arrow** (Ⓣ13658 or Ⓣ9239 244416).

Rickshaws

Despite efforts to ban them, Kolkata still has **human-drawn rickshaws**, though they're only available in the central areas of the city, especially around New Market where some pullers supplement their meagre income by acting as touts and pimps. Rickshaws come into their own during the monsoons, when the streets get flooded to hip height and the rickshaw-men can extract healthy amounts of money for their pains. Most of the rickshaw-pullers are Bihari pavement-dwellers, who live short and very hard lives. Haggle for a realistic price but feel free to give a handful of baksheesh too.

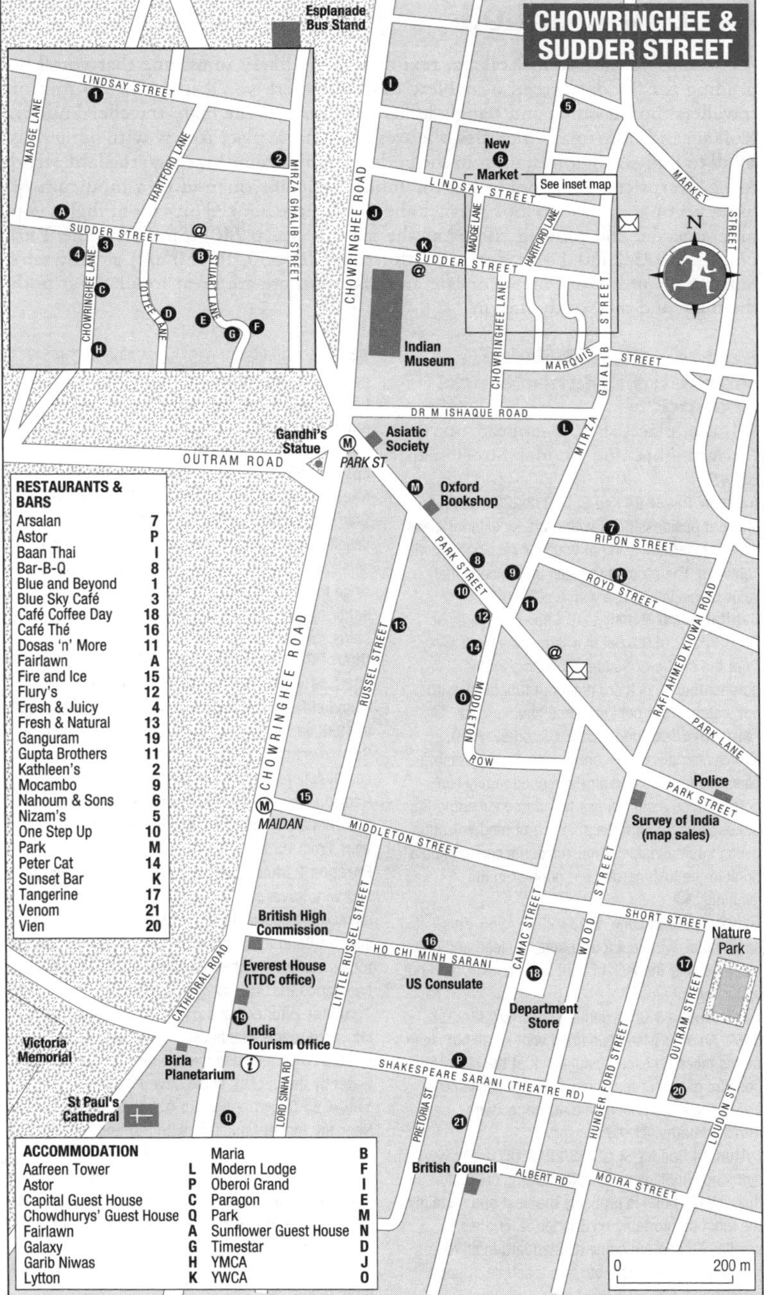

CHOWRINGHEE & SUDDER STREET
Esplanade Bus Stand
New Market
See inset map
Indian Museum
Asiatic Society
Gandhi's Statue
PARK ST
Oxford Bookshop
MAIDAN
British High Commission
Everest House (ITDC office)
US Consulate
Department Store
India Tourism Office
Victoria Memorial
Birla Planetarium
St Paul's Cathedral
British Council
Police
Survey of India (map sales)
Nature Park
Park Street Cemetery
LINDSAY STREET
SUDDER STREET
MADGE LANE
HARTFORD LANE
MIRZA GHALIB STREET
CHOWRINGHEE LANE
TOTTEE LANE
STUART LANE
CHOWRINGHEE ROAD
MARQUIS STREET
DR M ISHAQUE ROAD
OUTRAM ROAD
PARK STREET
RIPON STREET
ROYD STREET
MARKET STREET
RAFI AHMED KIDWAI ROAD
PARK LANE
RUSSEL STREET
MIDDLETON ROW
MIDDLETON STREET
LITTLE RUSSEL STREET
HO CHI MINH SARANI
CAMAC STREET
WOOD STREET
SHORT STREET
CATHEDRAL ROAD
LORD SINHA RD
SHAKESPEARE SARANI (THEATRE RD)
PRETORIA ST
HUNGERFORD STREET
OUTRAM STREET
LOUDON ST
ALBERT RD
MOIRA STREET
0
200 m
RESTAURANTS & BARS
Arsalan 7
Astor P
Baan Thai I
Bar-B-Q 8
Blue and Beyond 1
Blue Sky Café 3
Café Coffee Day 18
Café Thé 16
Dosas 'n' More 11
Fairlawn A
Fire and Ice 15
Flury's 12
Fresh & Juicy 4
Fresh & Natural 13
Ganguram 19
Gupta Brothers 11
Kathleen's 2
Mocambo 9
Nahoum & Sons 6
Nizam's 5
One Step Up 10
Park M
Peter Cat 14
Sunset Bar K
Tangerine 17
Venom 21
Vien 20
ACCOMMODATION
Aafreen Tower L
Astor P
Capital Guest House C
Chowdhurys' Guest House Q
Fairlawn A
Galaxy G
Garib Niwas H
Lytton K
Maria B
Modern Lodge F
Oberoi Grand I
Paragon E
Park M
Sunflower Guest House N
Timestar D
YMCA J
YWCA O

Accommodation

As soon as you arrive in Kolkata, taxi drivers are likely to assume that you'll be heading for Sudder Street, near New Market, where you'll find a heady mix of travellers, businessmen and Bangladeshis in transit. As the main travellers' hub in Kolkata and close to all amenities, the area is a sociable place to stay with numerous small to mid-sized hotels, most in the budget or mid-range brackets; the latter tend to be overpriced and poor value for money, and if you're after a modicum of luxury, you may have to look further afield. If you're booked on a night flight, you may consider the retiring rooms at the airport (see p.740). Similarly, the *Yatri Niwas* (ⓣ033/2660 1742; dorm Rs100; rooms Rs350, Rs550 a/c) at Howrah's South Station is convenient for late arrivals and there are great foodhalls at both the main and the South Station.

Sudder Street, New Market, Esplanade and around

All the places below appear on the Chowringhee and Sudder Street map, p.745.

Aafreen Tower 9A Kyd St ⓣ033/2229 3280. An efficient business hotel with a quirky exterior glass lift, the external casing of which is resplendent with cobwebs. The rooms are clean and exceptional value, especially those with a/c. ❸–❹

Capital Guest House 11-B Chowringhee Lane ⓣ033/2252 0598. Set in a large courtyard away from the bustle of Sudder St, rooms in this purpose-built block are plain but functional with hot water by the bucket; some have a/c. ❷–❹

Fairlawn 13-A Sudder St ⓣ033/2252 1510, ⓦwww.fairlawnhotel.com. Chock-full of memorabilia, this famous and old-fashioned family-run hotel exudes a charmingly faded and eccentric Raj atmosphere, though the absence of modernization doesn't suit all tastes. Non-residents can sample a drink in the lush garden bar popular in the evenings. ❻

Galaxy 3 Stuart Lane ⓣ033/2252 4565. This small hotel, with just four rooms, is clean and good value despite the lack of light and position, with hot water but no a/c. ❷

Garib Niwas 9 Chowringhee Lane ⓣ033/2217 5452. An otherwise plain hotel with small but clean rooms hides an exceptional block at the rear. The upstairs rooms of the annexe are spotless and vividly themed in deep blue or red; all with attached baths. ❸–❺

Lytton 14 Sudder St ⓣ033/2249 1872, ⓦwww.lyttonhotelindia.com. Despite lacking character, this reliable hotel is probably the best and certainly the most comfortable on Sudder St. Fridges, satellite TV and a/c come as standard in all rooms and facilities include a bar and a couple of good restaurants. ❽

Maria 5/1 Sudder St ⓣ033/2252 0860. The good-sized budget rooms – some with attached baths – in this old high-ceilinged, faded building are often booked up; there is also a dorm (Rs80), a reliable internet café and a pleasant terrace upstairs. ❷

Modern Lodge 1 Stuart Lane ⓣ033/2242 5960. Cramped place, with a relaxing roof terrace; despite the surly – sometimes downright rude – service, it's been popular with budget travellers since the 1960s, with a lot of history; there are better rooms upstairs and some with attached baths. ❷

Oberoi Grand 15 Chowringhee Rd ⓣ033/2249 2323, ⓦwww.oberoihotels.com. The white Victorian facade of this luxurious hotel, established in 1938, is very much part of the fabric of the city. Service is attentive, and the interior has been completely revamped in a modern-meets-traditional style; facilities include a swimming pool, and Thai and Indian restaurants; security is very tight. From US$400. ❾

Paragon 2 Stuart Lane ⓣ033/2252 2445. Popular and very traveller-friendly place, offering dark and dingy rooms downstairs, and better ones, though small, around the popular rooftop courtyard; some rooms come with attached baths and there are also two dorms (Rs110). ❷

Timestar 2 Tottee Lane ⓣ033/2252 8028.The fair-sized rooms in this peeling old villa, quietly located down a small drive, come with fans but hot water by the bucket; some have TV too. ❷

YMCA 25 Chowringhee Rd ⓣ033/2249 2192. Near the Indian Museum, with a grand but dilapidated wood-lined entrance, offering spacious, high-ceilinged rooms upstairs with morning tea and breakfast included in a safe environment; those with a/c are better value. Temporary membership (Rs50 a week) also allows access to a well-kept snooker table and table tennis. ❺

Park Street, Chowringhee and around

All the places below appear on the Chowringhee and Sudder Street map, p.745.

Astor 15 Shakespeare Sarani ⓣ033/2282 9950; ⓦwww.astorkolkata.com. Comfortable old garden hotel which has managed to retain some of the character of old Calcutta. The comfortable, modernized rooms all have satellite TV, fridge and a/c, and the hotel also has a nightclub and excellent restaurants (see p.757). ❽

Chowdhurys' Guest House 55 Chowringhee Rd ⓣ033/2282 1817. Popular with visiting businessmen and a few long-term residents, with old-fashioned rooms and high ceilings; close to the Maidan and quiet at night, yet not far from all amenities; the service can be slow but it's close to good restaurants. Best to book in advance. ❺–❻

Park 17 Park St ⓣ033/2249 9000, ⓦwww.theparkhotels.com. Modern five-star boutique hotel in a good location on a cosmopolitan street; amenities include swimming pool, health club, late checkout and good food at the three restaurants, including a popular nightclub and a bar with live music. Comfortable and stylish. From US$225. ❾

Sunflower Guest House 7 Royd St ⓣ033/2229 9401. A sizeable and well-maintained old building managed by one of the city's old *rajbari* families and serviced by a quaint lift; most of its spotless guestrooms – all with attached baths – are on the top three floors with the penthouse rooms providing good views; there's a spacious lobby and a small roof garden with food to order. ❹

YWCA 1 Middleton Row ⓣ033/2229 7033. Safe for women and especially good for longer stays, this clean, central hostel with plain but adequate rooms off Park St is built around a pleasant courtyard with a tennis court. Rates include breakfast. ❷–❹

South Kolkata

All the places listed below appear on the Kolkata map, p.739.

Bodhi Tree Guest House 48/44 Swiss Park ⓣ033/2424 6534, ⓦbodhitree-cal.spaces.live.com. A stunning little boutique guesthouse colourfully and artistically presented, across the tracks from the lakes and close to the Rabindra Saravar metro station; rooms are themed such as the adobe Yogacara cottage in the garden and are priced according to length of stay. ❺–❼

Hindusthan International 235/1 AJC Bose Rd ⓣ033/4001 8000, ⓦwww.hindusthan.com. Recently revamped, though plain and rather overpriced, this is a well-located business hotel with comfortable, conservatively decorated rooms. Facilities are good however, and include a travel desk, restaurants, nightclub, health club and an outdoor swimming pool. From US$270. ❾

Indrani Guest House 3-B Lovelock St ⓣ033/2486 6712. A comfortable family residence offering B&B and optional home-cooking in a residential part of the city off Ballygunge Circular Rd. There's a limited number of wonderful rooms so book well ahead; popular for longer stays. ❺

The Residency Guest House 50/1C Purna Das Rd ⓣ033/2466 9382. Spotless a/c rooms with tiled floors in a residential area just off Gol Park and within walking distance to the lakes and Gariahat. The custom-built guesthouse is welcoming and the complimentary breakfast is served in their swish sister establishment, the *Restaurant on the First Floor*, next door. ❺–❻

Tollygunge Club 120 Deshapran Sasmal Rd, at the southern end of the Metro line ⓣ033/2473 2316 ⓦwww.tollygungeclub.org. This exclusive club offers a choice of modern, characterless cottages or rooms. Rates include temporary membership allowing access to an eighteen-hole golf course, riding, swimming, tennis, squash facilities and Ayurvedic treatment. The outside *Wills Shamiana* bar is great for a sundowner and for watching scavenging jackals. Book well in advance ❼

Transit House 11-A Raja Basanta Roy Rd ⓣ033/2466 2700, ⓔtransit1@vsnl.net. Excellent, safe and comfortable guesthouse with good-sized rooms; away from the centre but in an interesting location close to markets and the lakes, and not far from the Metro. ❺

Elsewhere in the city

All the places listed below appear on the Kolkata map, pp.738–739.

Airways Lodge No. 2 Airport Gate, Kolkata airport ⓣ033/2512 7280. An inexpensive but welcoming place in the vicinity of the airport, with small, basic but clean rooms and a rooftop restaurant. Handy for early departures and late arrivals. ❷–❹

Hyatt Regency JA-1 Sector 3, Salt Lake City ⓣ033/2335 1234, reservations ⓣ1600 228001, ⓦwww.kolkata.regency.hyatt.com. Plush hotel with luxurious rooms on the Eastern Bypass, en route to the airport and handy for the city too. It's built to impress with capacious lobbies, restaurants, a palm-fringed swimming pool and all facilities. From US$260. ❾

Kings Crown Nazrul Islam Ave (VIP Rd), near the airport ⓣ033/2573 1712. On the Ultadunga road, with a good range of accommodation, from plain singles to comfortable a/c rooms, along with a decent restaurant and bar; very convenient for early or late flights. ❺–❻

Sonar Bangla Eastern Bypass ☎033/2345 4545, Ⓦwww.itcwelcomgroup.in. Busy hotel whose popularity rests on its convenient location between city and airport and its excellent range of restaurants, bars and nightclubs. All the comforts and services one would expect from a five-star, and a relaxed welcome. From US$215. ❾

Taj Bengal 24-B Belvedere Rd, Alipore ☎033/2223 3939, Ⓦwww.tajhotels.com. Opulent showpiece hotel, attempting to amalgamate Bengali features with the usual *Taj* grandeur. Excellent range of restaurants, including Chinese and Indian, and a pool and nightclub. From US$200. ❾

The City

Kolkata's crumbling, weather-beaten buildings and anarchic streets can create an intimidating first impression. With time and patience, though, this huge metropolis resolves itself into a fascinating conglomerate of styles and influences. The **River Hooghly**, spanned by the remarkable cantilever Howrah Bridge, is not all that prominent in the life of the city. Instead its heart is the green expanse of the **Maidan**, which attracts locals from all walks of life for recreation, sports, exhibitions and political rallies. At its southern end stands the white marble **Victoria Memorial**, and close by rise the tall Gothic spires of **St Paul's Cathedral**. Next to the busy **New Market** area looms the all-embracing **Indian Museum**. Further north, the district centred on BBD Bagh is filled with reminders of the heyday of the East India Company, dominated by the bulk of the **Writers' Building**, built in 1780 to replace the original structure which housed the clerks or "writers" of the East India Company; nearby stand **St Andrew's Kirk** and the pillared immensity of the **GPO**. A little further out, the **Armenian church** stands on the edge of the frenetic, labyrinthine markets of **Barabazaar**, while the renowned and influential temple of **Kalighat** is away to the south. Across the river, south of the marvellous **Howrah railway station**, lies the tranquillity of the **Botanical Gardens**.

The Maidan, New Market and Park Street

One of the largest city-centre parks in the world, the **Maidan** – literally "field" – stretches from the Esplanade in the north to the racecourse in the south, and is bordered by **Chowringhee Road** to the east and the Strand and river to the west. This vast open area stands in utter contrast to the chaotic streets of the surrounding city, and is big enough to swallow up several clubs, including the Calcutta Ladies Golf Club and the immaculate greens of the Calcutta Bowling Club. It was created when **Fort William**, now home to the military headquarters of the Eastern Command, was laid out near the river in 1758; Robert Clive cleared tracts of forest to give its guns a clear line of fire. Originally a haven for the elite, with a strict dress code, today ordinary citizens come to exercise each morning, while shepherds graze their flocks and riders canter along the old bridleways. In the late afternoons, the Maidan plays host to scores of impromptu cricket and football matches, as well as games of kabadi (see p.63).

Esplanade, New Market and Chowringhee

The 46-metre column of **Shahid Minar** (Martyrs' Memorial) towers over busy tram and bus terminals and market stalls at the northeast corner of the Maidan, known here as Esplanade. It was originally built in 1828 to commemorate David Ochterlony, who led the East India Company troops to victory in the Nepalese

Wars of 1814–16. On the east side of Esplanade, the once-elegant colonnaded front of **Chowringhee Road**, with its long line of colonial villas and palaces, is perpetually teeming with hawkers and shoppers. Following endless renovations and changes of management, only the Victorian **Grand Hotel**, its palm court inspired by the famous *Raffles* of Singapore, maintains a hint of colonialism.

Around the corner to the east, Chowringhee Road leads to the single-storey **New Market**, little changed inside since it opened in 1874 and with plenty of old-world charm. Beneath its Gothic red-brick clock tower, the market stocks a vast array of household goods, luggage, garments, textiles, jewellery, knick-knacks and books as well as meat, vegetables and fruit. **Chamba Lama** sells Tibetan curios, silver jewellery and bronzes. The **Symphony** store has a selection of classical and popular Indian music, while **Sujata's** is known for its silk, and **Nahoum & Sons** is a renowned Jewish bakery and confectioner with a diehard clientele for its rolls, pastries and cakes. Further up the corridor, condiment stalls offer dried fruit, miniature rounds of salty Bandel cheese (smoked and unsmoked) and *amshat*, blocks of dried mango; the produce, poultry, fish and meat market nearby is unmistakable by its aroma. Coolies, hoping for commission, eagerly offer assistance to any shopper who shows even a flicker of uncertainty.

Indian Museum

At the corner of Chowringhee and Sudder streets, the stately **Indian Museum** (Tues–Sun 10am–4.30pm; Rs150 [Rs10]) is the oldest and largest museum in India, founded in 1814. Visitors come in their thousands, many of them villagers who call it the *jadu ghar* or "house of magic". The main showpiece is a collection of **sculptures** obtained from sites all over India, which centres on a superb Mauryan polished-sandstone **lion capital** dating from the third century BC. One gallery houses the impressive remains of the second-century BC Buddhist **stupa from Bharhut** in Madhya Pradesh, partly reassembled to display the red-sandstone posts, capping stones, railings and gateways. Carvings depict human and animal figures, as well as scenes from the Jataka tales of the Buddha's many incarnations. There is also a huge collection of Buddhist schist sculptures, dating from the first to the third centuries, from the Gandhara region. You'll also see stone sculpture from **Khajuraho** and Pala bronzes, plus copper artefacts, Stone-Age tools and terracotta figures from other sites.

Along with an excellent exhibit of Tibetan *thangka*s, the museum holds Kalighat *pat* (see p.754) and paintings by the **Company School**, a group of mid-nineteenth-century Indian artists who emulated Western themes and techniques for European patrons. Finally, there's a spectacular array of fossils and stuffed animals, most of which look in dire need of a decent burial.

Park Street

Around the corner from the museum, the **Asiatic Society** at 1 Park St, established in 1784 by Orientalists including Sir William Jones, houses a huge collection of around 150,000 books and 60,000 manuscripts, some dating back to the seventh century. The society has a **reading room** open to the public (Mon–Fri 10am–8pm, Sat 10am–5pm; free) as well as a **gallery** of art and antiquities that holds paintings by Rubens and Reynolds, a large coin collection and one of Ashoka's stone edicts.

Around 2km east along Park Street from the Maidan, the disused **Park Street Cemetery** is one of the city's most haunting memorials to its imperial past. Inaugurated in 1767, it is the oldest in Kolkata, holding a wonderful concentration of pyramids, obelisks, pavilions, urns and headstones, under which many well-known figures from the Raj lie buried. The epitaphs make fascinating reading.

Victoria Memorial and the Calcutta Gallery

The dramatic white marble **Victoria Memorial** (Tues–Sun 10am–5pm, closed 2nd Sat of the month; Rs150 [Rs10], ⓦwww.victoriamemorial-cal.org), at the southern end of the Maidan, with its formal gardens and water courses, continues to be Kolkata's pride and joy (gardens daily 5.30am–7pm; Rs4). Other colonial monuments and statues throughout the city have been renamed or demolished, but the popularity of Queen Victoria seems to endure; attempts to change the name of the "VM" have come to nothing. This extraordinary hybrid building designed by Sir William Emerson, with Italianate statues over its entrances, Mughal domes in its corners, and elegant open colonnades along its sides, was conceived by Lord Curzon to commemorate the empire at its peak, though by the time it was completed in 1921, twenty years after Victoria's death, the capital of the Raj had shifted to Delhi. A sombre statue of Queen Victoria, flanked by two ornamental tanks, gazes out towards the Maidan from a pedestal lined with bronze panels and friezes. Faced with Makrana marble from Rajasthan, the building itself is capped by a dome bearing a revolving five-metre-tall bronze figure of Victory.

The main entrance, at the Maidan end, leads into a tall chamber beneath the dome. The 25 **galleries** inside still contain mementoes of British imperialism – statues and busts of Queen Mary, King George V and Queen Victoria; a huge canvas of the future Edward VII entering Jaipur in 1876; French guns captured at the Battle of Plassey in 1758; and the black marble throne of a nawab defeated by Robert Clive. Well worth seeing, the **Calcutta Gallery** provides a fascinating insight into the history and life of the Indians of the city and the Independence struggle through paintings, documents and old photographs. The evening **sound-and-light** show (March–June 7.45pm, Oct–Feb Tues–Sun 7.15pm; Rs20 [Rs10]) held in the grounds, concentrates on the same theme. After the gardens close, the Maidan in front of the gates, adorned with musical fountains, is transformed by crowds of people who come to enjoy the evening breeze, roadside snacks and pony and *ikka* (open carriage) rides.

St Paul's Cathedral and around

A little way from the Victoria Memorial, past the Birla Planetarium, stands the Gothic edifice of **St Paul's Cathedral** (daily 9am–noon & 3–6pm), erected by Major W.N. Forbes in 1847. Measuring 75m by 24m, its iron-trussed roof was then the longest span in existence. For improved ventilation, the lancet windows inside extend to plinth level, and tall fans hang from the ceiling. The most outstanding of the many well-preserved memorials and plaques to long-perished imperialists is the stained glass of the west window, designed by Sir Edward Burne-Jones in 1880 to honour Lord Mayo, assassinated in the Andaman Islands. The original steeple was destroyed in the 1897 earthquake; after a second earthquake in 1934 it was remodelled on the Bell Harry Tower at Canterbury Cathedral.

South of the cathedral, the **Academy of Fine Arts** (daily 3–8pm; Rs5) on Cathedral Road is a showcase for Bengali contemporary arts. As well as temporary exhibitions, it holds permanent displays of the work of artists such as Jamini Roy and Rabindranath Tagore (see p.768). A café and pleasant grounds enhance the ambience. **Rabindra Sadan**, the large auditorium nearby, features programmes of Indian classical music and next door, **Nandan**, designed by Satyajit Ray, is a lively film centre (see p.759).

Central Kolkata

The commercial and administrative hub of both Kolkata and West Bengal is **BBD Bagh**, which die-hard Kolkatans still insist on referring to as **Dalhousie Square**. The new official name, in a fine piece of official rhetoric, commemorates three

Galleries

Bengal has a lively tradition of contemporary art, and with increased prosperity and speculation in fine art, galleries showing a high standard of work are burgeoning throughout the city. Exhibitions are listed in *Cal Calling*; besides the Academy of Fine Arts and the Ashutosh Museum, the following are worth checking out.

Aakriti Art Gallery 1st floor, Orbit Enclave, 12/3A, Picasso Bithi, Hungerford St ⓣ033/2289 3027, ⓦwww.aakritiartgallery.com. A well-presented modern Indian art gallery with big name exhibitions and a shop (Mon–Sat noon–7pm; free).

Bengal Gallery Rabindranath Tagore Centre, 9A Ho Chi Minh Sarani ⓣ033/2287 2680, ⓦwww.tagorecentreiccr.org. Occasional art and craft exhibitions in this government-run, cultural establishment (Mon–Sat 10am–7pm; free).

Birla Academy of Art and Culture 108 Southern Ave ⓣ033/2466 2843, ⓦwww.birlaart.com. Ancient and modern art with regular exhibitions of contemporary Indian artists (Tues–Sun 4–7pm; Rs5).

CIMA (**Centre of International Modern Art**), 2nd Floor, Sunny Towers, 43 Ashutosh Chowdhury Ave ⓣ033/2474 8717, ⓦwww.cimaartindia.com. Prestigious Ballygunge gallery, displaying work by contemporary artists (Tues–Sun 2–8pm; free).

Galerie 88 28-B Shakespeare Sarani ⓣ033/2247 2274, ⓦwww.galerie88.in. Private gallery showing contemporary Indian paintings plus specialist exhibitions and some big names. Also stocks art supplies (Mon–Sat 10am–7pm; free).

revolutionaries hanged for trying to kill Lieutenant-Governor General Lord Dalhousie.

Built in 1868 on the site of the original Fort William – destroyed by Siraj-ud-Daula in 1756 – the **GPO** on the west side of the square hides the supposed site of the **Black Hole of Calcutta**. On a hot June night in 1756, 146 English prisoners were forced by Siraj-ud-Daula's guards into a tiny chamber with only the smallest of windows for ventilation; most had suffocated to death by the next morning. By all accounts, the guards were unaware of the tragedy unfolding and, on hearing the news, Siraj-ud-Daula was deeply repentant. A memorial to the victims that formerly stood in front of the Writers' Building was removed in 1940 to the grounds of St John's Church south of the GPO.

Beyond the headquarters of Eastern Railways on Netaji Subhash Road, you come to the heart of Kolkata's **commercial district**, clustered around the Calcutta Stock Exchange at the corner of Lyon's Range, which started out as a gathering of traders under a neem tree in the 1830s. The warren of buildings, erected along the same lines as the contemporary business districts of Shanghai, houses all sorts of old colonial trading companies including some still bearing Scottish names.

Of the eighteenth- and nineteenth-century British **churches** dotted around this district, the most interesting is **St John's** (daily 8am–5pm; Rs10), just south of the GPO. Erected in 1787, it houses memorials to British residents, along with an impressive painting of *The Last Supper* by Johann Zoffany, in which prominent Calcuttans are depicted as apostles. In the grounds, Kolkata's oldest graveyard holds the tomb of **Job Charnock**, the city's founding father, who earned eternal notoriety for marrying a Hindu girl he saved from the funeral pyre of her first husband; he is one of the few colonialists still cherished amongst Bengalis.

Dominating the area south of BBD Bagh, **Government House** (closed to the general public) overlooks the north end of the Maidan and the broad, ceremonial Red Road, which was once used as an airstrip. Until 1911, this was the residence of the British governor-generals and the viceroys of India; now the official home of the Governor of Bengal, it's known as **Raj Bhavan**. A short distance west, near the

Assembly House of West Bengal's Legislative Council, the colonnaded **Town Hall** houses **Kolkata Panorama** (Tues–Sun 11am–6pm; Rs15). The museum is dedicated to the popular history of the city and, with the help of a well-integrated multi-media presentation, emphasizes the freedom struggle. Visitors are guided through the display in groups. **Eden Gardens** sports complex, site of the world-famous **cricket** ground (officially known as the Ranji Stadium), sits opposite. Watching a test match here is an unforgettable experience as the 100,000-seat stadium resounds to the roar of the crowd and the sound of firecrackers thrown indiscriminately; to avoid the missiles sit in the covered sections. The pleasant palm-fringed **gardens** (daily dawn till dusk), with a lake and a **Burmese pagoda**, are free.

North Kolkata

The amorphous area of **north Kolkata**, long part of the "native" town rather than the European sectors, was where the city's prosperous nineteenth-century Bengali families created their little palaces, or *raj baris*, many now in advanced and fascinating states of decay.

North of BBD Bagh, the area known as **Barabazaar** has hosted a succession of trading communities; the Portuguese were here before Job Charnock landed at the fishing village that stood close by, and it later became home to Marwari and Gujarati merchants. The small hectic lanes south of MG Road are lined with shops and stalls selling everything from glass bangles to textiles. At the northwest corner of Barabazaar, near Howrah Bridge, is Kolkata's oldest church, the **Armenian Church of Our Lady of Nazareth** (Sun 9am–11pm). Founded in 1724 by Cavond, an Armenian from Persia, it was built on the site of an Armenian cemetery in which the oldest tombstone dates to 1630. The Armenian community was already highly influential at the courts of Bengal by the time the British arrived, and played an important role in the early history of the East India Company. Later they helped start the lucrative jute industry and still have a small community in the city.

East of Barabazaar on Rabindra Sarani (formerly Chitpore Rd), the huge red **Nakhoda Masjid**, whose two lofty minarets rise to 46m, is the great Jama Masjid (Friday mosque) of the city. Completed in 1942, it was modelled on Akbar's Tomb at Sikandra near Agra; its four floors can hold ten thousand worshippers. The traditional Muslim market that flourishes around the mosque sells religious items along with clothes, dried fruit and sweets such as *firni*, made of rice.

Until relatively recently, the chaotic jumble of streets to the south along Rabindra Sarani housed a thriving **Chinatown**, restaurants, opium dens and all. A handful of Chinese families continue to live around Chhatawala Gully, where a small early-morning street market (daily 6–7am) offers home-made pork sausages, noodles and jasmine tea. Kwai-Yun Li's *The Palm Leaf Fan and Other Stories* evocatively captures the spirit and tragedy of the Chinese community in Kolkata.

North of MG Road, on tiny Muktaram Babu Street off Chittaranjan Avenue, the ornate **Marble Palace** (closed Mon & Thurs 10am–4pm; free; no photography) holds a lavish collection of statues, European antiques, Ming vases, and paintings by Rubens and Gainsborough. To join one of the free guided tours of this extraordinary pile, get a pass from the tourist offices at BBD Bagh or Shakespeare Sarani (see p.743). To the north of Marble Palace, **Sonagachi**'s warren of lanes comprise Kolkata's largest red-light district.

On Dwarkanath Tagore Lane, a short walk northeast of the Marble Palace, the small campus of Rabindranath Tagore's liberal arts university, **Rabindra Bharati**, preserves the house where he was born and died as the **Rabindra Bharati Museum** (Tues–Sun 10am–4.30pm; Rs50 [Rs10], students Rs25 [Rs5]), or

Tagore House. A fine example of a nineteenth-century *raj bari*, the museum holds a large collection of Tagore's paintings. Nearby, in the Centenary Building just inside Calcutta University's College Street gateway, the **Ashutosh Museum of Indian Art** (Mon–Fri 11am–4.30pm; Rs10) is dedicated to the arts of Bengal, with a superb collection from eighth-century Pala-dynasty sculpture to nineteenth-century painted scrolls and contemporary art. Few come this way and you are more than likely to have the museum to yourself and a few officious staff. Further up, past a multitude of **College Street**'s famed book vendors, lies the frenetic **India Coffee House**, which maintains its reputation as a meeting place for the intelligentsia.

Of north Kolkata's two main Jain temples, **Parasnath**, 2km northeast of College Street at Manicktolla, is an extraordinary kitsch homage to the tenth *tirthankara*, Sitalnath, with neoclassical statues in a water garden and, inside, glitzy marble-work studded with silver and illuminated by a collection of ornate chandeliers. **Digambar temple** at Belgachia is relatively sedate.

The River Hooghly

Until silting rendered it impractical for large ships, the **River Hooghly**, a tributary of the Ganges, was responsible for making Calcutta a bustling port. The *ghats* lining the river's east bank serve as landings and places for ritual ablutions; unlike those at Varanasi, however, they have no mythological significance. Around 1.5km north of Howrah Bridge, **Nimtolla Ghat**, one of the city's main cremation grounds, is sealed off from public gaze. Further north, behind **Kumartuli Ghat**, a warren of lanes is home to a community of artisans who make the images of deities used for the major festivals. In the days leading up to the great pujas, especially that of Durga, Kumartuli is a fascinating hive of activity. As you walk north, you come next to **Baghbazaar Ghat**, where overloaded barges of straw arrive for the craftsmen of Kumartuli. Baghbazaar, the Garden Market, stands on the original site of **Sutanuti**, its grand but decaying mansions epitomizing the long-vanished lifestyle of the Bengali gentry, the *bhadra log* (lampooned by Kipling in *The Jungle Book*, whose monkey troupe he called the "bandar log").

South of Howrah Bridge, in its shadow, set behind the busy flower market of **Mullick Ghat**, the **Armenian Ghat** is most animated at the first light of dawn,

Howrah Bridge

One of Kolkata's most famous landmarks and officially Rabindra Setu, though few use this new name, **Howrah Bridge** (ⓦhowrahbridgekolkata.gov.in) is 97m high and 705m long, spanning the river in a single leap to make it the world's third-longest cantilever bridge. It was erected during World War II in 1943 to give Allied troops access to the Burmese front, replacing an earlier pontoon bridge that opened to let river traffic through. With its maze of girders, it was the first bridge to be built using rivets, and is still used by millions of commuters. Despite the removal of the tramlines, its eight lanes are still perpetually clogged with vehicles, and in the 1980s became so worn out that a man pushing his broken-down car is said to have fallen through a hole and disappeared. Don't let that put you off; the bridge has undergone major repairs in recent years, and joining the streams of pedestrians who walk across it each day is a memorable experience. **Vidyasagar Setu**, the second Hooghly bridge built 3km south to relieve the strain, was 22 years in the making. It's a vast toll bridge with spaghetti-junction-style approaches high enough to let ships pass below. Through sheer incompetence, the agency in charge of managing the tolls posted a loss of over $7 million in 2006; it has since been privatized.

when traditional gymnasts and wrestlers, devotees of Hanuman the monkey god, come to practise. As the Strand – separated from the river by the Circular Railway line – heads south, it passes several warehouses, **Millennium Park** and Fairlie Place and comes to another cluster of *ghats*. Frequent ferries (7.30am–8pm) from **Chandpal Ghat** provide an easy alternative to Howrah Bridge. **Babu Ghat**, identified by its crumbling colonnade, is used for early morning bathing, attended by *pujaris* (priests) and heavy-handed masseurs. Nearby, messy and busy Babu Ghat Bus Stand is one of Kolkata's main cross-country terminuses. Further south towards **Princep Ghat**, between Fort William and the river, the Strand comes into its own as a leafy promenade, pleasant during the early evening with a café, food stalls and boat rides from the small jetty near *Scoops* café (around Rs150/hr).

Botanical Gardens

The **Botanical Gardens** (daily 5.30am–5pm; Rs50 [Rs10]) at Shibpur lie 10km south of Howrah Station on the west bank of the Hooghly. Populated by countless bird species, the huge gardens are best seen in winter and spring, and early in the mornings, before the heat of the day sets in. Their most famous feature is the world's largest **banyan tree**, 24.5m high and an astonishing 420m in circumference. The Orchid House, the Herbarium and the Fern Houses are also worth seeing, and there's an attractive riverside promenade. Getting to the gardens involves a tedious road-trip from Esplanade on #C6 bus, the #T9 from Park Street or the #6 minibus from Dharamtala via Howrah. A taxi ride from the central Sudder Street area costs around Rs150 one way.

South Kolkata

South of the Maidan and Park Street, Kolkata spreads towards **suburbs** such as **Alipore** and Ballygunge, both within easy distance of the centre. The thoroughfare that starts life as Chowringhee proceeds south from Esplanade past **Kalighat** to **Tollygunge**, following the Metro line which terminates near the luxurious *Tollygunge Club* (see p.747), the mansion of an indigo merchant now surrounded by immaculate golfing fairways and bridle-paths. Northeast of Tollygunge, beyond a white-tiled mosque built in 1835 by descendants of Tipu Sultan (see p.1105), lies the parkland of Rabindra Sarobar, known locally as the Lakes, a popular spot for early evening walks.

Alipore

Around 3km southwest of Park Street, elegant triple-arched gates just south of the popular **Zoo** (daily except Tues 9am–5pm; Rs10) and Aquarium, lead to Belvedere, the former residence of the lieutenant-governor of Bengal and now

Kalighat paintings

Early in the nineteenth century, Kalighat was in its heyday, drawing pilgrims, merchants and artisans from all over the country. Among them were **scroll painters** from elsewhere in Bengal, who developed the distinctive style now known as **Kalighat pat**. Adapting Western techniques, using paper and water-based paints instead of tempera, they moved away from religious themes to depict contemporary subjects. By 1850, Kalighat *pat* had taken a dynamic new direction, satirizing the middle classes in much the same way as today's political cartoons. They serve as a witty record of the period, filled with images of everyday life, and can be found in galleries and museums around the world, and in the Indian Museum (see p.749) as well as the Birla Academy and Ashutosh Museum in Kolkata.

Mother Teresa

Beatified by Pope John Paul II on 19 October 2003, **Mother Teresa**, Kolkata's most famous citizen (1910–97), was born Agnes Gonxha Bojaxhiu to Albanian parents, and grew up in Skopje in the former Yugoslavia. Joining the Sisters of Loreto, an Irish order, she was sent as a teacher to Darjeeling, where she took her vows in May 1931 and became Teresa. In her work at St Mary's School in Kolkata, she became aware of the terrible poverty around her; in 1948, with permission from Rome, she changed her nun's habit for the simple blue-bordered white sari that became the uniform of the **Missionaries of Charity**.

The best known of their many homes and clinics is **Nirmal Hriday** at 251 Kalighat Rd, a hospice for destitutes. In the face of local resistance, Mother Teresa chose its site at Kalighat – Kolkata's most important centre of Hinduism – in the knowledge that many of the poor specifically come here to die, next to a holy *tirtha* or crossing-place. Mother Teresa's piety and single-minded devotion to the poor won her international acclaim, including the Nobel Peace Prize in 1979. Subsequently she also attracted a fair share of controversy with her fierce anti-abortion stance, giving rise to accusations of fundamentalist Catholicism. She was also accused of disregarding advances in medicine in favour of saving the souls of the dying and destitute. Censure, however, seems iniquitous in the light of her immense contribution to humanity.

If you're interested in the work of the Missionaries of Charity, they can be contacted at **Mother House**, near Sealdah Station at 54-A AJC Bose Rd (Ⓣ033/2249 7115, closed Thurs), where there is a small museum. Although they occasionally turn casual volunteers away, they run orientation workshops (a brief introduction to their work) on Mondays, Wednesdays and Fridays from 3pm to 5pm. Nearby Shishu Bhavan, 78 AJC Bose Rd, is an orphanage and a dispensary for children.

The appalling poverty highlighted by Mother Teresa has led to a number of NGO charities developing in the city. Established in 1979, **Calcutta Rescue** is a non-religious organization which, with the help of worldwide support groups, runs clinics, schools and a creche in Kolkata, as well as an outreach programme to help those in need further afield in West Bengal. For more information visit them online at Ⓦwww.calcuttarescue.org or call Ⓣ033/2217 5675.

serving as the **National Library** (Mon–Fri 9am–8pm, Sat–Sun 9.30am–6pm; free). The building was presented to Warren Hastings by Mir Jafar; its original simplicity was enhanced by double columns and the sweeping staircase leading to the Durbar Hall. When the capital shifted to Delhi, this library was left behind; today it houses a huge collection of books, periodicals and reference material, as well as rare documents in an air-conditioned chamber. Day membership to the Reading Room is available with ID and two photographs.

Kalighat

Some 5km south of Park Street along Ashutosh Mukherjee Road (an extension of Chowringhee Rd), Kolkata's most important temple, **Kalighat**, stands at the heart of a diverse and animated area, part residential, part bazaar. The destitute hoping for charity from pilgrims line the temple approaches and prostitutes linger on the thoroughfares and bridges offering their services in tragic, grimy circumstances. The typically Bengali temple itself, built in 1809 of brick and mortar but capturing the sweeping curves of a thatched roof, is dedicated to Kali, the black goddess and form of Shakti. According to legend, Shiva went into a frenzy after the death of his wife Sati, dancing with her dead body and making the whole world tremble. The gods made various attempts to stop him before Vishnu took his solar discus and chopped the disintegrating corpse into 51 bits. The spot where each piece fell became a *pitha*, or pilgrimage site, for worshippers of the female principal of divinity – Shakti. The shrine here marks the place where her little toe fell.

The temple is open all hours, and is always a hive of activity. Avaricious priests will try to whisk you downstairs to confront the dramatic monolithic image of the terrible goddess, with her huge eyes and bloody tongue. The courtyard beyond the main congregational hall is used for sacrificing goats on occasions such as Kali Puja; allegedly, humans were formerly sacrificed here to appease the fertility goddess. To the north of the compound, a lingam is worshipped by women praying for children, while shops all around cater for pilgrims. **Nirmal Hriday**, Mother Teresa's home for the destitute and dying, is on the northwest corner of the complex.

Eating

Although locals love to **dine out**, traditional Bengali cooking was, until recently, restricted to the home; however some excellent restaurants now offer the chance to taste this wonderful fish-based cuisine. The most popular option for dining out is Chinese food, spiced and cooked to local tastes: the city has a rich tradition including its own Chinatown at **Tangra** (closes early around 10pm) on the road to the airport. You'll also find several good south Indian restaurants, as well as rich Muslim cooking at places like *Shiraz*; the *kathi* roll, invented at *Nizam's*, is now part and parcel of Kolkata's cuisine. The coffee culture is growing with *Baristas* at Humayun Place and several *Café Coffee Day* outlets including one in Pantaloons department store on Camac Street; the *Cha Bar* at Oxford Bookshop and *Dolly's* (see p.758) are purveyors of fine tea. Numerous patisseries and confectioneries like Kookie Jar and Kathleen's work hard to keep abreast of demand. Fresh and Natural, with a branch on Russel Street, has some great ice-cream flavours including the fabulous custard apple.

Restaurants and cafés around **Sudder Street** cater for Western travellers staying in the local hotels, while roadside chai shops and snack vendors offer a tasty alternative. The busy environs around **New Market** include a Muslim quarter with several good restaurants, most with an emphasis on meat.

New Market and Sudder Street

All the places below appear on the Chowringhee and Sudder Street map, p.745.

Arsalan 119-A Ripon St ⓣ033/6569 9579. Large, new restaurant that serves a selection of Chinese and other food; you're best off sticking to its Mughlai cuisine – such as the kebabs and excellent biriyanis (around Rs300) – for which it is famous.

Baan Thai *Oberoi Grand* hotel, 15 Chowringhee Rd ⓣ033/2249 2323. Although expensive – Rs1600 per head and up – this in-hotel restaurant offers by far the best Thai cooking in town, with dishes like *poo krapaw* (stuffed crab) as well as standards such as red curry.

Blue and Beyond 9th floor, *Hotel Lindsay*, 8-A Lindsay St. This rooftop bar and restaurant provides an excellent vantage point over New Market and the surrounding city especially at dusk; there's good Indian and reasonable Chinese dishes such as sliced fish in chilli wine sauce, (Rs150) plus good-value breakfasts and buffets.

Blue Sky Café Sudder St. Budget travellers' haunt halfway down the strip on a corner, providing all the old favourites. Clean, well run, a/c and a popular meeting place. From Rs30.

Fresh & Juicy 2/7 Sudder St. Despite its fruity theme, this small café has a good and varied travellers' menu from breakfasts and "snakes" (snacks) to Chinese *haka*. Around Rs80 for a meal.

Nahoum & Sons F-20, New Market. Legendary Jewish bakery and confectioner selling delicious fruitcake, cashew macaroons, cheese straws, chicken patties and bagels with cream cheese. Selections start at around Rs40.

Nizam's 22–25 Hogg Market. The original restaurant here gave birth to the legendary *kathi* roll – a tasty sheesh kebab, rolled into a *paratha* of white flour. Today, its myth has all but died, but it's still worth a visit for a snacky meal around Rs60; try their egg roll.

Around Park Street

All the places below appear on the Chowringhee and Sudder Street map, p.745.

Astor 15 Shakespeare Sarani ☎033/2242 9950. This upmarket hotel houses a bar and several restaurants: the multi-cuisine *Serai*; the *Banyan Tree* serving Bengali food; and, best of all, the *Kebab-e-Que* in the garden, dishing up excellent tandoori meals – try the moti kebab (mushrooms and *paneer*). Expect to pay around Rs600 for a night out.

Bar-B-Q 43 Park St. An old and reliable favourite, offering Chinese and much-lauded tandoori cuisine in pleasant a/c surroundings with a bar downstairs; the special lunch menu includes Persian delicacies such as *chelo* kebabs on rice. Mains around Rs300.

Café Thé 9A Ho Chi Minh Sarani. A modern bistro in an exhibition centre with an extensive tea list including iced tea. An accompanying menu offers snacks, sandwiches, lasagne, Indian and Chinese. Best at lunch or early evening; expect to pay around Rs180.

Fire and Ice Kanak Building, 41 Chowringhee Rd ☎033/2288 4073. A trendy bistro and bar with free wi-fi serving authentic Italian cuisine including pizzas and *al fiumé* (fresh river prawns in olive oil); full meals around Rs700. Can get packed in the evenings.

Flury's 18 Park St, on the corner of Middleton Row. A Kolkata landmark, this legendary Swiss teashop and patisserie has been completely revamped, losing its laid-back atmosphere. Still worth visiting for breakfast or cakes, patties, home-made chocolates and Swiss pastries – try the rum balls.

Gupta Brothers 42-A Park Mansions, Mirza Ghalib St. Excellent, clean and cheap vegetarian snack bar and sweet counter with a good Rajasthani restaurant upstairs. Try the tandoori *bharwan aloo*. Next door, Dosas 'n' More, really don't do much more than dosas but these come in numerous permutations; from Rs35.

Mocambo 25-B Park St, around the corner on Mirza Ghalib St. A firm favourite for its good cooking and varied menu running from chicken Kiev (Rs200) to pizzas. Smart, yet relaxed.

Oh! Calcutta 4th Floor, The Forum, Elgin Rd. A chain restaurant offering chic dining with an emphasis on Bengali food – try their *dab chingri* (prawns in coconut); inventive menu in a relaxed atmosphere. Rs1200 with drinks.

One Step Up 18-A Park St. Bright bistro offering a range of options, from sandwiches and light meals to tandoori and pastries. Especially popular at lunch, but also good for an early evening drink. From Rs 80.

Park 17 Park St ☎033/2249 3121. This upmarket hotel has developed a reputation for some of the finest dining in town. *Zen*, a Terence Conran restaurant, serves dishes from Thailand, China, Japan and Indonesia; *Saffron* specializes in Indian cuisine; the 24hr *Atrium* coffee bar also provides a good food menu. Expect to pay from Rs600 for a night out.

Tangerine 2/1 Outram St ☎033/2281 5450. The first-floor windows take full advantage of this restaurant's position opposite a park. The mixed menu is full of surprises, from Singapore noodles to *meen moilly* (Keralan fish curry), and grilled lobster. From Rs300 for lunch.

Chandni Chowk and around

All the places listed below appear on the Kolkata map, p.738.

Amber 11 Waterloo St ☎033/2248 6520. A Kolkata landmark that refuses to fade away, serving celebrated Mughlai and tandoori cuisine with main dishes from Rs140. Plush and dimly lit, it covers three floors, with a bar downstairs.

Eau Chew P32 Mission Row Extension, Ganesh Chandra Ave ☎9830 141857. A legendary family-run restaurant and a remnant from the heyday of Chinatown, this unassuming place above a petrol station produces authentic Chinese food. The chimney stew, cooked slowly around a metal coal-burning container, is especially good, though you need to order in advance. From Rs120 for a meal.

India Coffee House 15 Bankim Chatterjee St (just off College St). Atmospheric, historic landmark café in the heart of the university area where students and intellectuals continue to meet. It's good for a snacky meal (from Rs40) and a chat and a break from trawling the bookshops of College St.

AJC Bose Road and around

All the places listed below appear on the Kolkata map, p.739.

Kewpie's Kitchen 2 Elgin Lane ☎033/2475 9880. Private home with a restaurant annexe, offering rich Bengali feasts fit for a *jamai babu* (son-in-law) first entering his wife's home – try their *lucci* (puris) and the fish

Sweetshops

Milk-based sweets such as the small and dry *sandesh* are a Bengali speciality. Though the white *rosogulla*, the brown (deep-fried) *pantua* and the distinctive black *kalojam*, all in syrup, are found elsewhere in north India, the best examples are made in Kolkata. Others worth trying are *lal doi* – a delicious red steamed yoghurt made with jaggery – or white *mishti doi*, yoghurt made with sugar. Sweetshops serve savoury snacks in the afternoons such as deep-fried pastry strips called *nimki* (literally "salty"); *shingara*, a delicate Bengali samosa; and *dalpuri*, *paratha*-like bread made with lentils.

Amrita 16-A Sarat Bose Rd. Excellent *mishti doi*.

Bhim Chandra Nag Surya Sen St, off College St. Best of several good sweetshops in the area.

Ganguram 46-C Chowringhee Rd. Once-legendary sweetshop near Victoria Memorial, with branches all over the city; try *mishti doi* and *sandesh*.

KC Das 11 Esplanade East and 57-A Ripon St. The city's most famous sweetshop; try their *rosogolla*.

Sen Mahasay 171-H Rashbehari Ave. Next to Gariahat Market, renowned for its *sandesh*; there are several other branches throughout the city.

Vien 34-B Shakespeare Sarani. Small, popular sweetshop, with excellent *sandesh* amongst other offerings.

and prawn preparations including *malai chingri* (prawns in cream) and *dab-er-chingri* (prawns in a green coconut). From Rs220; closed Mon.

Shiraz 56 Park St. One of the city's most legendary Mughlai restaurants renowned for its special mutton biriyani (Rs100), champ and *rumali* roti. Not much ambience, but good for lunch after a visit to nearby Park Street cemetery. Little choice for vegetarians.

Suruchi 89 Elliot Rd. Run by the All Bengal Women's Union (ⓦwww.abwu.org), a charity for rehabilitated prostitutes and their children, and a good place to taste Bengali home-cooking. Unpretentious atmosphere and reasonable prices; recommended for lunch despite its poor location; closed in the evenings and Sat and Sun; from Rs60.

South Kolkata

All the places listed below appear on the Kolkata map, p.739.

6 Ballygunge Place Ballygunge Place ⓣ033/2460 3922. One of a new breed of popular Bengali restaurants, with tasteful surroundings and a traditional homely ambience. Start with rice and *shuktoni* (bitter vegetables), follow with *bhetki paturi* (fish wrapped in banana leaf) and end with *mishti doi* (sweet yoghurt). From Rs300 for lunch.

Banana Leaf 73 Rashbehari Ave, Lake Market. Plain decor and a fast turnaround for this extremely popular restaurant that cooks up some of the best south Indian food in town. Try their dosas or lemon rice but an entire "meal" including cashewnut *uttapam* costs just Rs90.

Bhojohori Manna 18/1A Hindustan Rd ⓣ033/2466 3941. Popular chain serving Bengali food, with an emphasis on local cuisine but with a sprinkling of eclectic influences from other parts of the country, including tandoori – try the barbecued masala *bhekti*. Expect to queue; there's another (smaller) branch on nearby Ekdalia Rd. Uniquely, housewives of the area supply the cooking.

Dolly's Tea Shop Dakshinapan Shopping Centre, Dhakuria. A small but wonderful tea shop that lights up this cheerless concrete complex, with rattan furniture, a quiet ambience, a great selection of teas and snacks including sandwiches and cakes.

Tamarind 177 Sarat Bose Rd ⓣ033/6454 8011. Tasteful decor and a mixed menu that focuses on south India with a sprinkling of other regional cuisine. Stick to the south Indian selection including *pomfret masala* with *aapam (rice pancakes)*. Expect to pay around Rs600.

Elsewhere in the city

All the places listed below appear on the Kolkata map, pp.738–739.

Casa Toscana 56 Chowringhee Rd ⓣ033/4003 4358. Pleasant courtyard dining with an authentic Italian feel and an extensive menu. The creamy sauces are overdone and a bit heavy, the pizzas are filling, the minestrone passable but the seafood and spinach soup is excellent; the wine list is adequate. Expect to pay around Rs800.

Haldiram Bhujiwala 58 Chowringhee Rd. A snack bar, sweetshop and café all rolled into one, this self-service vegetarian chain offers good if predictable food, with everything from samosas, thalis (from Rs75) and dosas to ice cream. Other branches on Middleton Row and on Gariahat Rd in Ballygunge in a multi-floored supermarket.

Kim Fa 47 South Tangra Rd ⓣ033/2329 2895. One of Tangra's best Chinese restaurants – try the Thai soup, garlic prawns and chilli king prawns, which can be quite potent; from Rs120. If full, try *Lily's Kitchen* down the road.

Mainland China 3-A Gurusaday Rd ⓣ033/2287 2206. Chic Chinese restaurant with elegant service and excellent seafood; widely considered the city's finest, but perhaps a bit overdone, and for some, overcooked. Expect to pay around Rs800.

Royal Near Nakhoda Masjid, Rabindra Sarani. No trip to this area is complete without a visit to this legendary Muslim restaurant for a biriyani or a chicken or mutton *champ* (chop) (Rs60) cooked in aromatic spices and accompanied by *rumali* roti (thin "handkerchief" bread).

Drinking, nightlife and entertainment

The formerly tense, all-male atmosphere of Kolkata's **bars** is becoming a thing of the past, with designer-style places attracting a young, professional clientele. As well as the places below, the big hotels are a good option for a quiet drink; some of them also have discos. You'll sometimes hear Western live music at restaurants and bars, and Kolkata's spirited **arts scene** is known for its home-grown music – audiences here have a reputation as the most discerning in the country. The main concert season is winter to spring, with the huge week-long **Dover Lane Music Festival**, held in south Kolkata around the end of January and early February, attracting many of India's best musicians. Other popular venues for single- and multi-day festivals include Rabindra Sadan on the junction of AJC Bose Road and Cathedral Road, and Kala Bhavan on Theatre Road (Shakespeare Sarani). One of the country's leading North Indian classical music research institutes, **Sangeet Research Academy** in Tollygunge (ⓣ033/2471 3395, ⓦwww.itcsra.org) offers long-term courses in various music forms, and holds free Wednesday evening concerts.

Of the many nonreligious festivals each year, the **Ganga Utsav**, held over a few weeks around the end of January at Diamond Harbour, involves music, dance and theatrical events. **Rabindra Sadan** is Kolkata's theatre and concert hall district, with numerous venues. *Cal Calling* is a useful source for listings, as are local papers.

Cinemas showing English-language films several times each day can be found along Chowringhee near Esplanade and New Market. All are air-conditioned; some, like the Lighthouse on Humayan Place, are fine examples of Art Deco. Names to look for include Inox, a modern multiplex at the Forum on Elgin Road; Elite, SN Banerjee Road; and Chaplin, Chowringhee Place. **Nandan** (ⓣ033/2223 1210), behind Rabindra Sadan on AJC Bose Road, is the city's leading art-house cinema with a library, archives and three auditoria.

Bars and clubs

Bar-B-Q 43 Park St. Below the restaurant, this is one of the more stylish bars on the strip and the food is great (see map, p.745).

Blue and Beyond 9th floor, *Hotel Lindsay*, 8-A Lindsay St. The terrace is probably the best spot for a drink at dusk, with the bustle of New Market below yet out of earshot (see map, p.745).

Fairlawn 13-A Sudder St. The beer garden with its nooks and crannies amidst the vegetation makes a pleasant setting for an evening drink (see map, p.745).

Floatel 9/10 Kolkata Jetty, Strand Rd. The *Anchor Bar* at water level is a fine place to languish in a/c splendour and watch crowded ferries passing by. The bar restaurant upstairs with its expansive deck catches the river breeze but is sometimes booked for events (see map, p.738).

Park Hotel 17 Park St. This hotel is brimming with bars and discos. *Tantra* is still the liveliest nightclub in town starting at 7pm most days and 4pm on weekends; dimly lit yet lively *Someplace Else* features cover bands playing Western and Indian hits; the pool-side *Aqua* serves food and has DJs in the evening; and the cocktail bar *Roxy*, designed with a stunning mix of aluminium and brick, offers an ample wine list (see map, p.745).

Peter Cat 18-A Park St. Plush and pleasant, with a good reputation for its drink as well as its food, including the much-lauded *chelo* kebab (see map, p.745).

Sunset Bar *Lytton Hotel*, Sudder St. Friendly and relaxed bar, popular with travellers (see map, p.745).

Venom Fort Knox, 6 Camac St. All the rage in the evenings with a lounge bar as well as a dancefloor where the DJ pumps out a variety of music from bhangra to hip-hop (see map, p.745).

Shopping

Compared to Delhi, Kolkata has limited tourist shopping. However, there are many characterful **markets**, including the wide-ranging **New Market** (see p.749), as well as local institutions such as **Barabazaar** to the north (see p.752) and **Gariahat Market**, with its produce market best in the early mornings, in south Kolkata. Modern **shopping malls** – good for books, clothes, designer labels, leather and jewellery – are cropping up all over the city including Forum, 10/3 Elgin Rd; Emami Shoppers City at Lord Sinha Road; and South City Mall, which is very popular with several good restaurants, on Prince Anwar Shah Road in South Kolkata.

Typical Bengali handicrafts to look out for include **metal** *dokra* items from the Shantiniketan region northwest of the city: animal and bird objects are roughly cast by a lost-wax process to give them a wiry look. Long-necked, pointy-eared terracotta horses from Bankura, in all sizes, have become something of a cliché. *Kantha* **fabrics** display delicate line stitching in decorative patterns. Bengal boasts several good centres of cotton and **silk** weaving resulting in legendary **saris** such as the Baluchari style from Murshidabad.

Books

The month-long Kolkata Book Fair, held at the Milan Mela ground off the EM Bypass in January and February, is now among the biggest of its kind in the country, and provides a good opportunity to pick up books at a discount. The shops and the roadside stalls of **College Street** are well worth a browse, with an occasional rare gem turning up amidst stacks of science and computer study books.

Crossword 8 Elgin Rd. Large modern bookshop on two floors, with a good selection including novels, illustrated books and travel, plus a music section and a café.

Earthcare Books 10 Middleton St. At the back of a yard, a small and modest but focused bookshop that specializes in books on green issues, and publishes several titles too.

Starmark Emami Shoppers City, 3 Lord Sinha Rd. Modern and extensive bookshop carrying music and DVDs in a popular shopping complex.

Oxford Book & Stationery 17 Park St. An upmarket a/c bookshop with a small music section and the *Cha Bar* café upstairs. Nice ambience but the collection is fairly limited.

Seagull 31-A SP Mukherjee Rd ⓣ033/2476 5869, ⓦwww.seagullindia.com. Pleasant little bookshop owned by interesting and creative publishers; their resource centre, a block away, has a library and holds special exhibitions and events.

Emporia

Good selections of most handicrafts, including textiles and saris, can be found in various state **emporia**, many of which are located in the large **Dakhsinapan** shopping complex south of Dhakuria Bridge near Gol Park and the Lakes. Offering fixed (if slightly high) prices, these are the simplest places to start shopping.

Assam 8 Russel St. Part of Assam House, selling handicrafts and textiles from Assam including fabrics in *pat* and *moga*, two techniques of silk manufacturing.
Central Cottage Industries 7 Chowringhee Rd, Esplanade. Part of the national chain, with handicrafts, jewellery, silver, and fabrics from all over India, though the stock is a bit faded.
Kamala 1st floor, Rabindranath Tagore Centre, 9A Ho Chi Minh Sarani. A small but well-presented if pricey collection of traditional and fusion crafts from throughout India run by the Crafts Council of India.
Nagaland 13 Shakespeare Sarani. A fine assortment of Naga shawls, with red bands and white and blue stripes on black backgrounds. As with Scots tartan, certain patterns denote particular tribes.
Sasha 27 Mirza Ghalib St. This women's self-help group has a good collection of handicrafts and textiles including *kantha*.

Fabrics and clothing

Kolkata's dress sense tends to be conservative but a wide range of fabric is available and outlets can direct you toward a good (and very cheap) **tailor**; there are several around Mirza Ghalib Street and New Market. You can still get shoes made to order at one of the few remaining Chinese shoe shops around Chittaranjan Avenue.

Anokhi 2nd Floor, Forum, 10/3 Elgin Rd. Chic hand-printed cottons from this famous chain.
Balaram Saha 14/6 Gariahat Rd. Tangail, Baluchari and Kantha saris from Bengal.
Fabindia 234/3-A AJC Bose Rd. Good selection of hand-printed *kurta*s and *salwar kameez* as well as shirts, fabrics and furnishings from this trendy chain boutique; they use natural dyes which run, so wash cool and separate colours. Another branch is at 16 Hindusthan Park near Gariahat.
Ritu's 46A Rafi Ahmed Kidwai Rd. Chic boutique for *salwar kameez* from a designer who started her couture here before rising to international fame.

Musical instruments

Kolkata is renowned for its **sitar** and **sarod** makers – expect to pay upwards of Rs8000 for a decent instrument, much more for a premium one. Manoj Kumar Sardar & Bros, 8A Lalbazaar St, opposite Lalbazaar Police Station (Ⓣ033/2237 5835; Ⓦwww.monojkrsardar.com) makes good sitars and sarods to order and will ship them for you; they also have a small selection of off-the-shelf instruments. Shops around Sudder Street are strongest on Western instruments, but their traditional instruments are invariably of inferior quality and may be beyond tuning; Rabindra Sarani (Chitpore Rd) has a concentration of shops of varying quality, many catering to the wedding-band trade. Kolkata must produce more tabla players than any other city; tabla makers can be found next to Kalighat Bridge and at Keshab Sen Street off College Street.

Sports

Sport is enthusiastically followed in Kolkata, with **football** matches – especially those between the two leading clubs, Mohan Bagan and East Bengal – and **cricket** test matches drawing huge crowds. There are two major stadium complexes, **Ranji** at Eden Gardens and **Salt Lake** on the eastern edge of the city.

The **Maidan**, home to the Calcutta Bowling Club and the Ladies Golf Club, is a favourite venue for impromptu cricket and football matches, and the scene of regular race meetings in winter and spring run by the Calcutta Turf Club. Also in winter, army teams play **polo** on the grounds at the centre of the racecourse. The curious sport of **kabadi**, a fierce form of tag played by two teams on a pitch the size of a badminton court, can also be seen around the Maidan.

The *Hindusthan International Hotel*, 235-1 AJC Bose Rd (☎033/2247 2394), allows non-residents to use their **swimming pool** on a daily basis (Rs500). Across the road from the superbly equipped *Tollygunge Club*, where (with the right connections) you might get to use the pool and tennis courts, the elite Royal Calcutta Golf Club is the world's second-oldest golf club, after St Andrews in Scotland.

Listings

Airlines, domestic Air Deccan ☎9831 677008; Indian (Air India/Air India Express), 39 Chittaranjan Ave ☎1407 & ☎033/2211 0730 (24hr with a tourist counter), airport office enquiries ☎033/2511 9272, recorded flight enquiries: general ☎1400, arrival ☎1402, departure ☎1403; Indigo ☎9910 383838; Jet Airways, 18-D Park St ☎033/3984 0000, airport enquiries ☎033/2511 9894; Jet Lite ☎1800/223020; Kingfisher Airlines ☎1800/209 3030; Spicejet ☎1800/180 3333.

Airlines, international General airline/flight enquiries: ☎033/2511 8787 & 2511 9721; Air India (see Domestic: Indian); Bangladesh Biman, 55B Mirza Ghalib St ☎033/2227 6001; British Airways ☎9831 377470 & ☎033/2511 8424; Druk Air, 51 Tivoli Court, 1A Ballygunge Circular Rd ☎033/2280 5376; Emirates Airlines, Trinity Towers, 83 Topsia Rd (South) ☎1800/233 2030; GMG Airlines 20H, Park Street ☎033/3028 3030; Gulf Air, Chitrakoot Building, 230A AJC Bose Rd ☎033/2283 7996; KLM, Jeevan Deep, 1 Middleton St ☎033/2283 0151; Lufthansa,T2 8A Millennium City, IT Park, Salt Lake ☎4002 42000 or ☎033/2511 2266; Singapore Airlines, DN62, Unit 9A Millennium City, IT Park, Salt Lake ☎033/2367 5422; Thai Airways International, 8th floor, Crescent Tower, 229 AJC Bose Rd ☎033/2280 1630; United Airlines BD, Saberwal House, 55B Mirza Ghalib St ☎033/4001 7235.

Ambulance Call ☎102, or the Dhanwantary Clinic ☎033/2449 3734; St John's Ambulance Brigade ☎033/2248 5277; or Bellevue Clinic ☎033/2247 2321.

Banks and currency exchange Kolkata airport has a 24hr branch of the State Bank of India (SBI), as well as Thomas Cook at the international terminal. There are numerous private foreign exchange bureaux around Sudder St, New Market and in the vicinity of Park Street, some offering very competitive rates. Banks that offer foreign exchange around the centre include SBI, 38B Chowringhee Rd & 1 Strand Rd; Standard Chartered Bank, 41 Chowringhee Rd; Citibank, 43 Chowringhee Rd. Other currency exchange bureaux include Thomas Cook, Chitrakoot Building, 230 AJC Bose Rd (☎033/2247 5378), and American Express, 21 Old Court House St, near the West Bengal Tourist Office (☎033/2248 6283). The ATM machines at most banks (such as SBI and Axis, as well as HSBC at 3-A Shakespeare Sarani, HDFC at BBD Bagh East, and ICICI at 24-B Camac St) take MasterCard, Visa, Cirrus and Maestro.

Car rental Autoriders, 10-A Ho Chi Min Sarani ☎033/2282 3561; Avis, *Oberoi Grand* hotel, 15 Chowringhee Rd ☎033/2217 0147; Wentz ☎033/3293 4634 and at the airport ☎033/3958 7217.

Consulates Australia, 12th Floor, 10 Camac St ☎033/2282 2476; Bangladesh, 9 Circus Ave (Sheikh Mujib Sarani) ☎033/2290 5208; Canada, Duncan House, 31 Netaji Subhash Rd ☎033/2230 8515; Myanmar, 57K Ballygunge Circular Rd ☎033/2485 1658; Nepal, 1 National Library Ave, Alipore ☎033/2456 1224; Singapore, 8 AJC Bose Rd ☎033/2247 4990; South Africa, 225-D AJC Bose Rd ☎033/2247 0253; Sri Lanka, Nicco House, 2 Hare St ☎033/2281 5354; Thailand,18-B Mandeville Gardens ☎033/2440 7836; UK, 1A Ho Chi Minh Sarani ☎033/2288 5172; USA, 5/1 Ho Chi Minh Sarani ☎033/3984 2400.

Hospitals Cheap, government-run hospitals are notoriously mismanaged, and private medical care, if expensive by comparison, is infinitely superior. In case of serious illness, you are best advised to contact your consulate. Good private clinics include Belle Vue, 9 Loudon St ☎033/2287 2321; Ruby General, EM Bypass, Kasba ☎033/2442 0291; and Woodlands Nursing Home, 8/5 Alipore Rd ☎033/2456 7075-89.

Internet Net access (from Rs15 an hour) is easily available throughout the city. Of the many places around Sudder St, try *Hotel Maria* but by far the most pleasant is Gomukh, 7 Sudder St at the back of the courtyard with a gift shop and a new café next door – remove your shoes. Sify iWays are part of a dependable franchise with branches throughout the city including 57A and 59B Park St and at the New Empire Building, near New Market.

Libraries Asiatic Society Library, 1 Park St; British Council Library, 16 Camac St (a monthly rate which includes borrowing books, use of the reference section and discounted Internet use); National Library, 1 Belvedere Rd; Ramakrishna Mission Library, Gol Park; University of Kolkata library, College Square. Seagull Arts and Media Resource Centre, 36-CSP Mukherjee Rd, near the Bhowanipur police station, has a small but pleasant and well-organized a/c library.

Permits and visas The Foreigners' Registration Office is at 237-A AJC Bose Rd (ⓣ033/2247 3301).

Pharmacies Deys Medical Stores, 6 Lindsay St & 20-A Nelly Sengupta Sarani; Angel, 151 Park St (24hr); Dhanwantary Clinic, 65 Diamond Harbour Rd (24hr); Welmed, 4–1 Sambhunath Pandit St (24hr Mon & Tues).

Police ⓣ100. The central police station is on Lal Bazaar St, BBD Bagh ⓣ033/2241 3230. Others include Park St ⓣ033/2226 8321.

Postal services The GPO, on the west side of BBD Bagh, houses the poste restante and a philatelic department. If you're staying in the Sudder St area, the New Market Post Office, Mirza Ghalib St, is much more convenient. Sending parcels is easiest from the large and friendly post office on Park St, where enterprising individuals will handle the entire process for you for a negotiable fee. For a quicker service, DHL has several offices including 6 Kedia Villa, Marquis St ⓣ033/2217 1675.

River Cruises Hooghly, Sundarbans and Murshidabad cruises (Oct–April) are available through Vivada Cruises (ⓣ033/2463 1990; ⓦwww.vivadacruises.com) and the more luxurious Assam Bengal Navigation Company (ⓣ0361/260 2223; ⓦwww.assambengalnavigation.com).

State tourist offices The most useful of the many offices representing other states in Kolkata are those that cover the northeastern states (details of permit requirements can be found on pp.840–841), and the Andaman and Nicobar islands. Andaman and Nicobar, 2nd Floor, DP-7, Sector 5 ⓣ033/2356 7629; Arunachal Pradesh, Block CE, 109 Sector 1, Salt Lake ⓣ033/2321 3627; Assam, 8 Russel St ⓣ033/2229 5094; Manipur, 26 Rowland Rd ⓣ033/2475 8075; Meghalaya, 120 Shantipally, EM Bypass ⓣ033/2441 1932; Mizoram, 24 Old Ballygunge Rd ⓣ033/2461 5887; Nagaland, 11 Shakespeare Sarani ⓣ033/2282 5247; Orissa, 41 & 55 Lenin Sarani ⓣ033/2249 3653; Sikkim, 4/1 Middleton St ⓣ033/2281 5328; Tripura, 1 Pretoria St ⓣ033/2282 5703. Another useful tourist office is that of the Darjeeling Gurkha Hill Council, India Tourism, 4 Shakespeare Sarani ⓣ033/2282 1715.

Tour Operators Ethically minded Help Tourism (ⓣ033/2455 0917, ⓦwww.helptourism.com) offers a wide range of tours including the Sundarbans and wildlife in north Bengal. The flexible Kali Travel Home (ⓣ033/2248 7980, ⓦwww.traveleastindia.com) offers guided tours of Bengal, cooking classes and farm stays. Himalayan Footprints (ⓣ9830 033896) offers informative and flexible wildlife tours, nature treks and trips to the Sundarbans, Sikkim and Darjeeling.

Travel agents Thomas Cook, Chitrakoot Building, 2nd Floor, 230 AJC Bose Rd (ⓣ033/2247 5378), deals with inbound tours and international flights and foreign exchange. For domestic and international flights, there are numerous agents around Sudder St. Chocks-Off, 1 Cockburn Lane, off Royd St (ⓣ033/2246 8780, ⓔchocks@cal3.vsnl.net.in), is reliable and efficient for all flights. Warren Travels, 31 Chowringhee Rd (ⓣ033/22262 6612 & 13), is a well-established service dealing with international and domestic flights, hotel bookings, group tours and travel documents.

Around Kolkata

The Hindu temples of **Dakshineshwar** and **Belur Math**, and even the great Vaishnavite centres of **Nabadip** and **Mayapur** further north, can be taken in as day-trips on local trains from Kolkata's Sealdah and Howrah stations. Simple hotels are always available should you want to stay.

Dakshineshwar and Belur Math

At the edge of Kolkata, 20km north of Esplanade on the east bank of the river, the popular temple of **Dakshineshwar** stands in the shadow of Bally Bridge. Built in 1855, it was a product of the Bengali Renaissance, consecrated at a time when growing numbers of middle-class Hindus were questioning their faith. Typical Bengali motifs – a curved roof reminiscent of local village huts, nine chhatris and beehive cupolas – dominate the design. The mystic and influential religious philosopher **Ramakrishna** once officiated here, and his room, beside the main gate, now houses a collection of his personal effects. Not far from the main temple, **Yogoday Satsanga Math** is the headquarters of the Self-Realization Fellowship, founded in California in 1925 by the author of *Autobiography of a Yogi*, **Paramahansa Yogananda**.

Across the bridge from Dakshineshwar, 3km south along the west bank of the Hooghly, is the serene forty-acre riverfront campus of **Belur Math** (April–Sept 6–11am & 4–7pm; Oct–March 6.30–11am & 3.30–6pm; free; Ⓦ www.belurmath.org). Founded by a disciple of Ramakrishna, **Swami Vivekananda**, and completed (after his death) in 1938, the monastery houses temples and museums dedicated to the Mission. It incorporates elements from several world religions; the gate is inspired by early Buddhist sculpture, the windows by Islamic architecture, and the ground plan is based on the Christian cross. Local trains run from Sealdah to Bally Bridge adjacent to Dakshineshwar, and from Howrah to Belur Math.

Nabadip & Mayapur

Pilgrims come in thousands to the little town of **NABADIP** (or Nawadip), on the west bank of the Hooghly, around 100km north of Kolkata. Once the eleventh-century capital of Bengal under the Sen dynasty, Nabadip was also the home of Hindu sage **Sri Chaitanya** (1486–1533) and its temples are alive with his devotees singing *kirtan* (devotional song). A fifty-kilometre *padakrama*, or foot pilgrimage, links the various Vaishnava sites spread across nine islands. Nabadip may be a Vaishnava town, but its most atmospheric temple is the **Kali Bari** at Poramatolla, tucked into the folds of one of the most impressive banyan trees you are ever likely to see; a market huddles around it. Across the river from Boral Ghat (ferry Rs5), the Vaishnava centre of **MAYAPUR**, run by the Hare Krishna sect of ISKCON, draws huge crowds at weekends who throng to the labyrinthine temple and ornamental park.

Trains from Howrah run to Nabadip, 2.5km from the main Boral Ghat (Rs25 by cycle rickshaw). ISKCON's centre in Kolkata also organizes transport and books guesthouses and *dharamshalas* in the Mayapur complex (Ⓣ 033/2287 3757; Ⓦ mayapur.com ❶–❸).

South of Kolkata: the Sundarbans

South of Kolkata down to the coast, the Hooghly fringes one of the world's largest estuarine deltas, the **Sundarbans**, a 10,000-square-kilometre expanse of mangrove swamp and forested islets formed by silt swept down from the Himalayas. The region has been designated UNESCO world Heritage site and its abundant wildlife, includes saltwater crocodiles, Gangetic dolphins, otters and the world's largest population of **tigers**. Closer to the city, the former colonial port of **Diamond Harbour** on the east bank of the Hooghly is a popular weekend break and lies enroute to **Sagardwip**, a sacred island where the Ganges reaches the sea.

Sajnekhali and the Sundarbans Tiger Reserve

The cluster of mangrove-covered islands known as the **Sundarbans**, or "beautiful forest", lie in the Ganges Delta, stretching east from the mouth of the Hooghly to Bangladesh. They are home to the legendary **Royal Bengal tiger**, which has adapted remarkably well to this watery environment, swimming from island to island and covering distances of as much as 40km in one day. A half-million or so people find themselves sharing this delicate ecosystem with the mighty cats. All, regardless of their official religion, worship Banbibi, the goddess of the forest, and her Muslim consort Dakshin Rai, supreme ruler of the Sundarbans.

Practicalities

Foreigners require a permit (free) to visit the Sundarbans; if you're travelling to the area independently (tour companies will get them for you), get your permit in advance from the WB Tourist Centre in Kolkata (see p.743). You'll also need to book accommodation in the main camp of the **Sundarbans Tiger Reserve** (Rs15 to enter) at **SAJNEKHALI**, a small compound sealed off from the jungle by wire fencing. The *Sajnekhali Tourist Lodge* (Ⓣ03219/236560; ④) is a large, ramshackle forest lodge on stilts; rates include meals and there is a dorm (Rs220). The adjacent Project Tiger compound has a shrine to Banbibi, a watchtower and a mini-zoo where turtles and crocodiles are hatched. As tigers have been known to jump the fence, it's advised not to venture out after dark. Other Sundarbans watchtowers include Dobanki, where an aerial walkway skirts the top of the mangroves, and Netidhopani, which sits near the ruins of a four-hundred-year-old temple.

All **transport within the reserve** is by boat, which can be rented from the Boatman Association with the help of the lodge staff from Rs700 depending on your itinerary. You have to take along a Project Tiger guide (Rs300 [Rs250]) and pay an entry fee (Rs130) (video camera Rs300). The loud diesel motors scare wildlife away, but when they cut their engines the silence is awesome.

The best times to visit are winter and spring. As getting to the Sundarbans on your own is a laborious process, you might want to opt for an all-inclusive package tour booked through the West Bengal Tourist Centre (Ⓣ033/2248 5917; Sept–Mar). Two- and three-day packages with stays either on the boat or at the *Tourist Lodge* start from Rs2300. The cruises can get crowded and noisy reducing the likelihood of seeing any animals.

Tailor-made tours by private operators (from Rs14,000 for a 3-day itinerary) are more peaceful and leisurely: try Kali Travel Home (see p.763), or Neil Law of Himalayan Footprints (see p.813) who runs his own camp and boat. Help Tourism (see p.763) also have their own boat and resort, the *Sunderbans Jungle Camp* (⑧) on Bali Island at the edge of the reserve. The camp employs local villagers, some of whom are ex-poachers, in a unique rehabilitation project. The *Sunderban Tiger Camp* (Ⓣ033/3293 5749, Ⓦwww.sunderbantigercamp.com; ⑦) with a/c cottages near Gosaba is popular with WBTC tours from Kolkata. In season, Vivada Cruises (Ⓣ033/2463 1990; Ⓦwww.vivadacruises.com) offers luxury cruises to the Sundarbans. The Assam Bengal Navigation Company (Ⓣ0361/260 2223; Ⓦwww.assambengalnavigation.com) offers top-of-the-range cruises from US$195 per day. Alternatively you can arrange your own boat at Gosaba Ghat (Godkalai) (see p.766).

Getting to the Sundarbans using public transport is complicated, whether by train or bus and timing is crucial as the forest is closed to visitors entering after dusk. Suburban trains travel from Sealdah to Canning from where a ferry is available to Doc Ghat; take a shared auto-rickshaw to Basanti. Alternatively, take a bus from Kolkata's Babu Ghat to Basanti (6 daily; 3hr); aim for the one at 6.45am. From Basanti, take an auto to Gosaba Ghat (Godhkali), then ferry to Gosaba Bazaar from where you need to catch a cycle-van or negotiate an auto to Pakhirala (6km). Scheduled ferries cross the estuarine channel to Sajnekhali (7am & 6pm) or negotiate a country boat; boats are also available at Godkhali or Dayapur near Gosaba.

Along the Hooghly to the sea

The Hooghly reaches the Bay of Bengal at **DIAMOND HARBOUR**, 50km south of Kolkata. The harbour here was used by the East India Company, and a ruined fort is said to date back to Portuguese pirates. A two-week cultural festival, the **Ganga Utsav**, is held here towards the end of January – its theatre and dance performances are advertised in *Cal Calling* (see p.743). The trip down to Diamond Harbour from the city, by bus or train from Sealdah Station, is a popular day's excursion for Kolkatans who come to enjoy the river cruises, though it's also possible to stay at one of several hotels including the *Diamond Harbour Tourist Lodge* (❷–❹), with some a/c rooms; book through the tourist office (Ⓣ033/2248 8271). For a lot more luxury, the *Ffort* at nearby Raichak (Ⓣ033/2280 0043, Ⓦwww.ffort.com; ❽) offers an opulent taste of the Gangetic delta with a health spa, fine cuisine and extensive gardens.

Sagardwip, at the mouth of the Hooghly and accessible by ferry from Harwood Point near Diamond Harbour, is revered by Hindus as the point where the Ganges meets the sea. The confluence is venerated at the **Kapil Muni Temple**, on an island that bears the brunt of the savage Bay of Bengal cyclones and is gradually being submerged. On Makar Sankranti (mid-Jan), during the **Sagar Mela**, hundreds of thousands of pilgrims from all over India descend on the island, cramming into the water to bathe. A selection of small hotels, ashrams and *dharamshala*s offer basic accommodation, while the *Larika Sagar Vihar* (Ⓣ03210/240266; ❷–❸) provides more comfort. Direct buses from Kolkata's Babu Ghat travel to Harwood Point during the *mela*; the island can also be reached from Namkhana on the suburban railway network, from where the quiet casuarina-lined beach at Bakkhali is easily accessible. Once on Sagardwip, the temple is a further 32km from the ferry accessed by bus or taxi.

Central Bengal

A low-lying rural region where the pace of life is in stark contrast to that of Kolkata, **central Bengal** has a few sights to tempt tourists off the Kolkata–Darjeeling route. **Shantiniketan**, built on the site of Rabindranath Tagore's father's ashram, is a haven of peace, and a must for anyone interested in Bengali music, art and culture. The other highlights of the region include a cluster of exquisite terracotta temples in **Bishnupur**, the ruins of **Gaur**, the region's seventh-century capital, and the palaces of **Murshidabad**, capital of Bengal's last independent dynasty. With the Maoist insurgency along the borders of Jharkhand and Orissa, the southwestern districts of Bengal have become too dangerous to visit.

Bishnupur

BISHNUPUR, a sleepy backwater town 150km northwest of Kolkata, is a famous centre of Bengali learning, renowned above all for its exquisite **terracotta temples**. It was the capital of the Malla rajas, under whose patronage one of India's greatest schools of **music** developed. Largely beyond the sphere of Muslim influence in Bengal, Bishnupur's long tradition of temple-building had its roots in the basic form of the domestic hut. Translated into temple architecture, built of brick (as stone was rarely available) and faced with finely carved terracotta decoration often depicting scenes from the Ramayana, the temples combine striking simplicity of form with vibrant texture.

Several temples (daily 9am–5pm; all Rs100 [Rs5]) lie scattered in a wide area around Bishnupur. **Raas Mancha**, built in 1587 by Bir Hambir in a unique pyramidal style, is used to display the images of Krishna and Radha during the annual Raas festival. Nearby, the well-preserved **Shyamarai**, built in 1643, is a particularly fine example of terracotta art, while the smaller **Jorbangla** has fine detail. The unassuming tenth-century **Mrinmoyee temple** encloses the auspicious *nababriksha*, nine trees growing as one. To the north of town and dating from 1694, the **Madan Mohan**, with its domed central tower and scenes from the life of Krishna, is one of the largest.

Two express **trains** (#2883 & #2827) a day connect Bishnupur to Kolkata's Howrah Station. **Accommodation** in the centre includes the extensive *Tourist Lodge* (ⓣ03244/252013, reservations ⓣ033/2248 5168; ❷–❹), which also serves meals; otherwise, there's *Udayan Lodge*, College Rd (ⓣ03244/252278; ❸–❹), with a pretty garden. But the best place to stay is the rural idyll of Basudha, devoted to organic farming, conservation and research, in an adobe farmhouse 22km from Bishnupur, (ⓣ9434 062891 or book through Kali Travel Home ⓣ033/2248 7980, see p.763; ⓦwww.traveleastindia.com; ❷ see p.783).

Shantiniketan and around

Despite rapid growth and encroachment into the tribal Santhal habitat, the peaceful haven of **SHANTINIKETAN**, 136km northwest of Kolkata, remains a world away from the clamour and grime of the city. Founded by Nobel Laureate **Rabindranath Tagore** in 1921 on the site of his father's ashram, both the settlement and its liberal arts university **Vishwa Bharati** were designed to promote the best of Bengali culture. Towards the end of the Bengali Renaissance, Tagore's vision and immense talent inspired a whole way of life and art; the university and school still operate under this momentum.

Centred around the **Uttarayan** complex of buildings, designed by Tagore, the university is very much in harmony with its surroundings, despite its recent growth as Kolkatans have settled or built holiday homes nearby. Well-known graduates include Indira Gandhi and Satyajit Ray, and departments such as **Kala Bhavan** (art) and **Sangeet Bhavan** (music) still attract students from all over the world. The **Kala Bhavan Archive** (daily except Tues 10am–5pm; free, with

Rabindranath Tagore

The Bengali poet and literary giant **Rabindranath Tagore** (1861–1941) has inspired generations of artists, poets and musicians. He developed an early interest in theatre, and set his poems to music – now, as Rabindra Sangeet, one of the most popular musical traditions in Bengal. Introduced to England and the West by the painter William Rothenstein and the poet W.B. Yeats, Tagore had his collection of poems, *Gitanjali*, first published in translation in 1912, and the following year was awarded the Nobel Prize for Literature. Though he preferred to write in Bengali, and encouraged authors in other Indian languages, he was also a master of English prose. Not until he was in his 70s did his talent as an artist and painter emerge, developed from scribblings on the borders of his manuscripts. Tagore was an enormous inspiration to many, including his students, the illustrious painter Nandalal Bose, and later the film-maker Satyajit Ray, who based several of his films on the works of the master.

special permission from the head of department) houses twentieth-century Bengali sculpture and painting, including works by eminent artists such as Abanendranath and Gaganendranath Tagore, Nandalal Bose and Rabindranath Tagore himself, as well as a collection of Chinese and Japanese art. The **Vichitra Museum** (daily 10.30am–1pm & 2–4.30pm, Tues open am only, closed Wed; Rs5), also known as the Rabindra Bhavan Museum, captures the spirit of Tagore's life and work with a collection of his paintings, manuscripts and personal effects.

The renowned **Bauls**, Bengal's wandering minstrels who play a unique style of folk music, gather at the informal **shanibarer haat** (Sat market; 3–5pm) held under the trees by Shriniketan's canal. The large fair of **Poush Mela,** between December 22 and 25, attracts numerous Bauls each year.

Practicalities

Bolpur, 3km south of Shantiniketan, is the nearest railway station, on the main line between Kolkata and Darjeeling, served by several trains via Burddhaman (or Burdwan). The best train for Bolpur from Kolkata is the *Shantiniketan Express* #2337, which leaves Howrah at 10.10am and terminates at Bolpur at 12.25pm, departing for Howrah half an hour later. Baul singers occasionally busk in second-class carriages.

If you're heading on from Shantiniketan **to Darjeeling**, the best of the daily express trains is the *Darjeeling Mail* #2343, which stops late at night (00.34am) in Bolpur but arrives in New Jalpaiguri (NJP) at 8am the next morning. The best daytime train is the *Kanchenjunga Express* #5657, which departs at 9.40am and arrives at NJP at 6.20pm, which normally means a night's stay in Siliguri. **Reservations** are available from the Shantiniketan reservations counter (Mon–Sat 10am–3pm) near the post office where **quotas** from here are small. However, there's a computerized reservations counter at Bolpur Station which links you into the national network and offers more choice. The main **bus stand** is at Jamboni, 2km west towards Surul. Cycle rickshaws are the chief means of transport in the area, but the best way to experience Shantiniketan is to cycle – ask at your hotel or at one of the bicycle shops along the main road.

The Shantiniketan area holds a reasonable amount of **accommodation**, with several options along the noisy main Shantiniketan–Bolpur road, and more appealing places around the fringes of the campus. Though some of the better **restaurants** offer multi-cuisine menus, they tend to be strongest on local cuisine, especially fish. *Ghare Baire* at the Gitanjali Complex on Siuri Road is as smart as it gets in Shantiniketan, with upmarket Bengali cuisine, while at Ratanpalli, the delightful little garden café *Alcha* (daily, 7.30–10am & 4–8pm) combines a bookshop, a library (Rs200 refundable deposit), a gallery and a small but excellent boutique selling clothes and furnishings; it's also good for breakfasts. Outdoor cafés in Ratanpalli main market are popular student hangouts especially in the evenings.

Accommodation

Bolpur Lodge Bolpur ⓣ03463/252662. Large, long-established and welcoming lodge, set away from the bustle of the main road with a pleasant courtyard, large plain good-value rooms and a reasonable restaurant. ❷

Bonpulak Shyambati ⓣ03463/261193. Three pleasant, airy rooms in a friendly family home with a small, colourful garden on the edge of the campus; meals on request. ❸

Chhuti 241 Charu Palli, Jamboni ⓣ03463/252692, ⓦchhutiresort.com. Comfortable and well laid out cottages with an ethnic touch, some with a/c, and a restaurant. Still the most pleasant option around Shantiniketan; credit cards accepted with a 2 percent charge. ❹–❺

Hotel Shantiniketan Bhubandanga ⓣ03463/254434. Bright pink hotel with a pleasant garden and a quiet location down a lane; the cheaper rooms are better value but hot water comes by the bucket. ❸–❹

Shantiniketan Tourist Lodge Bolpur Tourist Lodge Rd ⓣ03463/252699. Large government-run place with some a/c rooms, good value cottages, a pleasant garden and a restaurant . ❸–❻

Tarapith

One of the most important centres of Tantric Hinduism, **TARAPITH** lies 50km north of Shantiniketan and is easily visited on a daytrip. The temple and the cremation ground, in a grove beside the river littered with shrines, are popular with Tantric sadhus, and it's not uncommon to witness rituals involving skulls and cremation ashes. The temple, in a perpetually busy courtyard, is dedicated to the mysterious and feared goddess Tara, who appears here with a silver face and large eyes. Of Tarapith's hotels, the *Bengal Lodge (ⓣ9775 164636; ❷–❹)* near the river and only 50m from the temple gates, captures the spirit of the place, and has good value rooms, some with a/c, and a popular restaurant; elsewhere the friendly *Sathi* (ⓣ03461/253287; ❷–❹) has large attached rooms, including some with a/c. The most luxurious is *Amantran* (ⓣ03461/253133; ❺–❻), 3km from the temple on the Rampurhat Road, which has airy rooms, a landscaped garden, a selection of small cottages, some a/c, and a good restaurant. One of several **trains**, the *Ganadevta Express* #3017 departs Howrah at 6.05am, passing through Bolpur Shantiniketan (8.52am) and arrives at **Rampurhat** railway station, 8km north of Tarapith, at 10.20am; the 4.45pm *Rampurhat Express* #2348 returns via Shantiniketan; buy tickets in advance as, towards the time of departure, the station and the footbridges become uncomfortably frenetic. Buses and shared auto-rickshaw taxis (Rs30) regularly ply between Tarapith and Rampurhat.

Kendubilwa

The town of **KENDUBILWA**, also known as **Kenduli**, on the bank of a wide shallow river 42km from Shantiniketan, is the birthplace of **Jaidev**, the author of *Gita Govinda*, and the spiritual home of the Bauls. Its small terracotta temple is engulfed each year in mid-January when the **Jaidev Mela** attracts streams of pilgrims, as well as a collection of yogis and sadhus who gather amongst the banyan trees to hear the Bauls perform through the night. Over the years the *mela* has grown to include a wide range of stalls and a funfair. During the *mela*, special buses leave regularly from Bolpur (2hr).

Murshidabad

Set 219km north of Kolkata in the brilliant green landscape of rural Bengal and close to the commercial town of **Behrampur**, **MURSHIDABAD** represents the grand and final expression of independent Bengal before the arrival of the British. Several eighteenth-century monuments along the banks of the Hooghly stand as melancholic reminders of its days as the last independent capital of Bengal. Established early in the eighteenth century by the **Nawab Murshid Quli Khan**, Murshidabad was soon eclipsed when the forces of Siraj-ud-Daula were defeated by Robert Clive at the Battle of Plassey in 1757, as a result of which the British came to dominate Bengal from the new city of Calcutta. Clive described Murshidabad as equal to London, with several palaces and seven hundred mosques; today most of its past glory lies in ruins, though it is still renowned for cottage industries, especially silk weaving.

Murshidabad's intriguing mixture of cultures is reflected in its architectural styles, which range from the Italianate **Hazarduari**, the nawab's palace, designed by General Duncan Macleod of the Bengal Engineers, to the **Katra Mosque**, built by Murshid Quli Khan in the style of the mosque at Mecca. The palace, with its mirrored banqueting hall, circular durbar room, armoury and library of fine manuscripts, is now a museum (daily except Fri 10am–4.30pm; Rs100 [Rs15]); some of the paintings are in dire need of restoration, but the portrait collection is excellent. A large oxbow lake, the **Moti Jheel** or **Pearl Lake**, guards the desolate ruins of Begum Ghaseti's palace, where Siraj-ud-Daula reigned before his defeat, and which was subsequently occupied for a while by Clive. To the south and across the river, **Khushbagh**, the **Garden of Delight**, holds the tombs of many of the nawabs, including Alivardi Khan and Siraj-ud-Daula.

Practicalities

Accommodation in Murshidabad is limited, but the friendly and welcoming *Hotel Manjusha* near Hazarduari (Ⓣ03482/270321; ❷–❹) offers rooms with balconies and a colourful flower garden right on the river. **Behrampur**, 12km away on the busy north–south highway and easily accessible by auto-rickshaw or bus, has more amenities. The *Samrat* (Ⓣ03482/251147; ❷–❺) is on the main highway 3km south of the centre at Panchanantatala, handy for the Murshidabad turn-off, and offers a wide range of accommodation, from plain doubles to carpeted a/c rooms, as well as an a/c restaurant-bar and a pleasant garden. A few **trains** run to Behrampur from Kolkata (Sealdah Station; 4–6hr), including the *Lalgola Passenger*, which also stops at Murshidabad; there is more choice from Azimganj, 20km and a Rs700 taxi-ride away. Frequent **buses** from Behrampur Station depart for Kolkata's Esplanade (5–6hr), as well as Malda (3hr 30min).

Malda and around

Famous for its mangos, the large, unattractive commercial town of **MALDA**, 340km north of Kolkata, makes a good base to explore the historic sites of **Gaur** and **Pandua**, both earlier capitals of Bengal. Malda is on the main line between Kolkata and north Bengal, served by several good **trains** such as the *Kanchenjunga Express* #5657/5658. There is a choice of **accommodation** and restaurants along Station Road, while on the main NH-34 highway, the *Purbanchal* (Ⓣ03512/266183; ❷–❹) offers more comfort, with some a/c rooms, one of the better restaurants in town and a dimly lit bar. Taxis to both Gaur and Pandua charge around Rs1500 for the day.

Gaur

Spread across a landscape of lush paddy fields, 16km south of Malda, **GAUR** was the seventh-century capital of King Sasanka, and then successively belonged to the Buddhist Palas and the Senas. The latter, the last Hindu kings of Bengal, were violently displaced by the Muslims at the start of the thirteenth century. The city was sacked in 1537 by Sher Shah Suri, and its remaining inhabitants wiped out by plague in 1575.

Gaur lay buried in silt for centuries, but excavations have revealed the extensive remains of a city that once boasted over a million inhabitants. Recent finds include a vast brick **palace** complete with waterways and a mint. A *ghat* with chains for anchoring barges suggests that the River Ganges may have once flowed past the palace. Elsewhere, Gaur's sites include various large tanks, such as 1.5km long **Sagar Dighi** from 1126, and the extensive embankments. **Dakhil Darwaza**, an impressive red-brick gateway built in 1425 during the Muslim period, leads into the **Fort**, in the southeast corner of which a colossal wall encloses the ruins of the old palace. Nearby are the **Qadam Rasul Mosque**, built in 1531 to contain the Prophet's footprint in stone, and the seventeenth-century tomb of Fateh Khan, one of Aurangzeb's generals, in Bengali-hut style. Other remains include the elegant **Tantipara Mosque**, with its finely detailed terracotta decoration, the Lattan or **Painted Mosque**, where traces remain of the enamelled bricks that gave it its name, and the massive **Bara Sona Masjid**, "Great Golden Mosque", northeast of the Fort.

Pandua

The splendid **Adina Masjid** at **PANDUA**, 18km north of Malda, built around 1370, was the largest mosque in the Subcontinent in its day. It now lies in ruins, but these still betray the origin of much of the building materials – carved basalt masonry from earlier Hindu temples was used to support 88 brick-built arches and 378 identical small domes, the design following that of the great eighth-century mosque of Damascus. Other monuments include the **Eklakhi mausoleum** – one of the first square brick tombs in Bengal, with a carved Ganesh on the doorway; and **Qutb Shahi Masjid**, or the Golden Mosque, built to honour saint Nur Qutb-ul-Alam whose ruined shrine is nearby.

North Bengal

NORTH BENGAL, where the Himalayas soar from the flat alluvial plains towards Nepal, Sikkim and Bhutan, holds some magnificent mountain panoramas, and also some of India's most attractive **hill stations**. Most visitors pass as quickly as possible through **Siliguri** en route to **Darjeeling**, **Kalimpong** and the small, mountainous state of Sikkim. If you've time on your hands, it's worth making a detour east of Siliguri to explore the sub-Himalayan **Dooars**, with its patchwork of tea gardens and forests that encompasses the **Jaldapara Wildlife Sanctuary**, home to the one-horned rhino, bison and wild boar.

The region has its fair share of political turmoil. The Gurkhaland movement, centred around Darjeeling, and the Kamtapuri Liberation Front, which purports to represent most of North Bengal south to Malda, have called for a complete break from the state of West Bengal. The strikes called by the Gurkha movement tend to paralyse the Darjeeling hills, including traffic on the very few roads in and out of the area. Tourist traffic is usually allowed to exit the district, but you may have to pay an exorbitant fee to the taxi driver. You should check the papers and with your hotel if travelling to the region; Ⓦwww.darjeelingtimes.com is also a useful source of information.

Siliguri and New Jalpaiguri

A major commercial hub and Bengal's second city, ever-expanding **SILIGURI** has a thriving tea-auction centre and serves as the gateway to Darjeeling, Kalimpong, Sikkim and Bhutan. Together with its main railway station, **NEW JALPAIGURI** – commonly referred to as NJP – and the airport at **Bagdogra**, it forms an unavoidable link between the rail and air connections to Kolkata and Delhi, and the roads up into the mountains. The border with Nepal at **Kakarbitta** nearby is open to tourists, though the bus journey from here to Kathmandu is an arduous one.

Most tourists pass straight through Siliguri, but travel connections may mean that you have to stop overnight. Besides teeming bazaars such as Bidhan Market,

Moving on from Siliguri

By air

Indian Airlines, Jet Airways, Kingfisher and the budget Air Deccan fly from **Bagdogra airport** to **Kolkata**, **Delhi** and **Guwahati**; Druk Air flies to Bangkok (Tue & Sat; Ⓦwww.drukair.com.bt) and also connects with Paro (Bhutan) (Wed & Sun). Direct flights from Bagdogra to Kathmandu are planned for the near future. For tickets, try Heat Flexi Holidays, 34 Bidyasagar Rd, Khalpara (Ⓣ0353/250 4631) or Travel & Rental, Sevoke More (Ⓣ0353/253 8749); Jet Airways has its own office in the *Hotel Vinayak*, Hill Cart Road (Ⓣ0353/243 1495).

Helicopter flights to **Gangtok** (daily 1.30pm; Rs2200) and **Pelling** (Mon only) leave from Bagdogra weather permitting, with a maximum baggage allowance of 10kg. The sole Siliguri agent is the Tourist Service Agency (TSA) in Pradhan Nagar, the lane opposite the bus terminal (Ⓣ0353/251 0872).

By rail

All major **trains**, most terminating or starting at Guwahati, use NJP Station, not Siliguri. Reservations can be made at NJP railway station or the **Central Railway Booking Office** (daily 8am–4pm), Bidhan Road, near Kanchenjunga Stadium in Siliguri. The best train to **Kolkata** is the *Darjeeling Mail* #2344, which terminates at Sealdah, while the most convenient for **Delhi** is the efficient *Rajdhani Express* #2423 (25hr 30min), which also passes through Patna with connections for Gaya and Bodhgaya; the *Rajdhani* #2435 (Mon & Fri) stops at Varanasi, while on other days take the *Rajdhani* #2423 and change at Mughal Sarai.

By bus

Overnight "luxury" **buses** to **Kolkata** (12hr), such as the Rocket Bus and Royal Cruiser, are cheaper than the train (Rs900 for a/c), and have the advantage of depositing you in Esplanade, near the central Sudder Street area. However, the roads are dire, so be prepared for a severe rattling. Standard buses run from Siliguri to Kolkata, **Patna** and **Guwahati**, although the train is far more comfortable. Frequent buses also travel to Chalsa and Madarihat, convenient for the wildlife sanctuaries.

there's little of interest to see save the impressive **Tashi Gomang Stupa** (daily 5am–noon & 1–5pm) in the small Tibetan enclave 2km or so from the centre on Sevoke Road.

Arrival and information

Bagdogra airport, 12km west of Siliguri, is served by flights from Delhi, Kolkata, Guwahati, Bhutan and Bangkok and soon Kathmandu; there's also a helicopter service from here to Gangtok in Sikkim (see box opposite). Taxis booked through the **pre-paid** counter run directly to Siliguri (Rs295), Darjeeling (Rs1185), Kalimpong (Rs1045) and Gangtok (Rs1505), though you can negotiate cheaper fares from the stand outside the gates with returning taxis. Siliguri does have its own railway station, used by the Toy Train, but the **New Jalpaiguri (NJP)** Station, 4km east, is the main rail junction in the region, with trains to and from Kolkata, Delhi and Assam. Cycle and auto-rickshaws (Rs45 and Rs90) ply the route between NJP and Siliguri, battling through the often-gridlocked market, while shared Vikrams (auto-taxis) charge Rs30 a seat; taxis charge up to Rs300. Use the pre-paid booth outside the main station for local and long-distance journeys in auto-rickshaws as well as taxis. Most buses arriving at Siliguri terminate at the **Tenzing Norgay Bus Terminal** on Hill Cart Road at Pradhan Nagar, close to most hotels and taxis to Darjeeling.

To Darjeeling and Kalimpong

The easiest way to get to **Darjeeling** is by **shared Jeep**. These depart from in front of NJP Station, and Sevoke More and Tenzing Norgay Bus Terminal in Siliguri, where Jeep transport syndicates have their own ticket booths and the prices are fixed. Taxis to Darjeeling depart when full, take 3–5 hours and cost Rs100 per seat. For a bit more comfort, take two seats up in front or a whole taxi (negotiate with returning taxis for reduced rates). Other options include the **Toy Train** (see p.774), or a bus from Tenzing Norgay Bus Terminal. Shared taxis to **Kalimpong** (Rs90) depart from Panitanki More across the bridge while buses to Kalimpong depart from around the Bus Terminal.

To Sikkim

Regular buses and shared Jeeps run to **Gangtok** (Rs120) from around the bus terminus in Pradhan Nagar. **Sikkim Nationalized Transport**, opposite the bus terminus (daily 6am–4pm; ☎0353/251 1496), runs bus services to **Gangtok** (departures 9.30am, 11.30am, 12.30pm & 1.30pm; Rs110), and other points in Sikkim. Get a Sikkim **permit** (see p.810) from Sikkim Tourism next door; shared Jeeps are also obtainable here; a reserved Jeep costs Rs1220.

To Kathmandu

To reach **Kathmandu** in Nepal, travel to **Panitanki**, the crossing (24hr) on the Indian side of the border, and use a cycle rickshaw (Rs30) to get to the Nepalese side at **Kakarbitta** (7am–7pm). Shared taxis (Rs70), regular buses from the terminal or outside it (from Rs20) and taxis (Rs600) travel to Panitanki, where you can pick up a **Nepalese visa** for US$30 in cash. The advantage of pausing in Kakarbitta is that it gives you a greater choice of onward **buses** to Kathmandu (17hrs). For a lot more luxury, take a **flight** from **Bhadrapur** (25km and a 45min taxi ride from Kakarbitta) to Kathmandu with Buddha Air or Yet Airlines. Flights can be booked through Siliguri agencies or at Kakarbitta itself.

The Government of West Bengal's **tourist office** (Mon–Fri 10.30am–4pm; ⓣ0353/251 1979), opposite the bus station on Pradhan Nagar, can book rooms in tourist lodges in places like Jaldapara Wildlife Sanctuary. There are also tourist office counters at NJP station and the airport. Siliguri's best private tour operator, Help Tourism, First Floor, Malati Bhavan, 143 Hill Cart Rd (ⓣ0353/253 5892, ⓦwww.helptourism.com), organizes wildlife tours, village home-stays, and treks and tours off the beaten track.

Opposite the bus stand in the same compound as Sikkim Nationalized Transport, **Sikkim Tourism** (Mon–Sat 10am–4pm; ⓣ0353/251 2646), provides information and **Sikkim permits** (see p.810). To **change money**, try the bureau at the *Delhi Hotel* across from the bus terminal on Hill Cart Road, or the State Bank of India, Mangaldeep Building, Hill Cart Road. There are several ATMs including one opposite the *Manila Hotel* on Hill Cart Road and around Sevoke More. The main **post office** is on Kacheri Road, with branches near the Central Railway Booking Office and the bus terminal.

Accommodation and eating

The best **restaurants** are located in hotels such as the *Vinayak* and *Saluja* along Hill Cart Road, both serving fine Chinese and Indian cuisine. There's also the excellent *Khana Khazana* café, at Pradhan Nagar opposite the bus terminal, which has everything from dosas to pizzas. For Bengali cuisine, try the basic but legendary *Kalpana Pice*, at Bidhan Market, or the *Kalpataru Pice Hotel*, Rani Tanki More, Sevoke Road, famous for fish. In terms of **accommodation**, note that some of the cheap

The Darjeeling Himalayan Railway: the Toy Train

Completed in 1881, the small-gauge (2ft or 610mm) **Darjeeling Himalayan Railway** was designed as an extension of the North Bengal State Railway, climbing from **New Jalpaiguri**, via **Siliguri**, for a tortuous 88km up to **Darjeeling**. Given World Heritage status by UNESCO in 1999, the **Toy Train** (as it's affectionately called) follows the Hill Cart Road, crossing it at regular intervals and even sharing it with traffic. The Toy Train is no longer an essential mode of transport, and has survived due to its unique historical importance and tourist appeal. Diesel engines now pull the coaches up the full route from Siliguri; if you're determined to experience the endearingly ancient blue steam engines, some over hundred years old, check the services starting at Kurseong.

Weather permitting, first-class coaches with large viewing windows provide magnificent views as the seven-hour journey from the plains progresses and the scenery gradually unfolds; second class can be fun but crowded. At its highest point at Jorebungalow near Ghoom (2438m), 7km short of Darjeeling, the dramatic panorama of the Kanchenjunga Range is suddenly revealed. Just beyond Ghoom, the train does a complete circle at the Batasia Loop – the most dramatic of the three loops encountered along the way; another method used to gain rapid height are the **reversing stations** where the track follows a "Z" shape.

Trains leave Siliguri at 9am and finally arrive in Darjeeling around 3pm (2nd class Rs42, 1st class Rs247). Some travellers find this claustrophobic and painfully slow ride a real test of endurance, especially after an overnight journey from Kolkata to Siliguri. An alternative is to take the steam train from Kurseong or take the short ride from Darjeeling to Ghoom, just 7km up the track (see box, p.786) from where you can visit a few monasteries and either walk, take a taxi, bus or the train back to Darjeeling.

For more **information** on the Toy Train, contact the Darjeeling Himalayan Railway Society (ⓦwww.dhrs.org), or, in India, the Director at Elysia Building, near Himali School, Kurseong 734203 (ⓣ0354/200 5734, ⓦwww.dhr.in).

hotels around the bus terminal – the *Delhi* and the *Shere-e-Punjab* in particular – have dubious reputations, especially in their treatment of women guests.

Apsara 18 Patel Rd, Pradhan Nagar ⓣ0353/251 4252. Down a lane parallel to the main road and opposite Tenzing Norgay Bus Terminal, this is a friendly budget hotel, handy for transport links and amenities and with basic, clean rooms, all with attached baths. ❷–❸

Holydon NJP Station Rd ⓣ0353/269 1335. Friendly and inexpensive hotel that's the closest decent place to the railway station, with some a/c rooms, a restaurant and a bar that can get busy in the evenings. ❷–❹

Manila Pradhan Nagar ⓣ0353/251 9342. Spotless modern hotel close to the taxi and bus stand, with attentive service, comfortable rooms, money exchange (with an ATM next door), and a good restaurant; if it's full, try the similar *Heritage* next door. ❸–❹

Marinas Naxalbari Rd, Bagdogra ⓣ0353/255 1371. A very pleasant garden hotel, handy both for the airport (with free transfers) as well as the Nepal border at Kakarbitta. The reasonably priced rooms all have attached baths, and there's a restaurant, a bar and *Glenary's* coffee shop. ❸–❻

Nirvana 18 Patel Rd, Pradhan Nagar ⓣ9832 014001. Right behind *Khana Khazana* restaurant, this conveniently located multi-storeyed block offers a bit more comfort than *Apsara* next door. The small carpeted rooms come with attached baths. ❸

Saluja Hill Cart Rd ⓣ0353/243 1684. Right in the city centre, with a wide range of rooms from budget ones sharing baths to comfortable doubles; the *Parivar* restaurant is excellent. For a bit more comfort, try the hotel's big sister *Saluja Residency* next door. ❷–❺

Sinclairs Pradhan Nagar ⓣ0353/251 7674, ⓦwww.sinclairshotels.com. Upmarket old hotel that remains popular for its convenient location on the road to Darjeeling. Comfortable, if a bit expensive with large refurbished rooms and complimentary breakfast, a good restaurant, a garden and a (summer only) swimming pool. ❼

Vinayak Hill Cart Rd ⓣ0353/243 1130. A reliable mid-range hotel conveniently located in the centre of town yet close to the taxi stands, with a choice of small but adequate rooms including some with a/c. The restaurant downstairs serves good Indian food. ❸–❻

Jaldapara and Gorumara

Apart from the Darjeeling hills, most of North Bengal is well off the beaten track, and few travellers make detours from the Darjeeling–Sikkim–Nepal route. Probably the best reason to do so is to visit one of a string of **wildlife sanctuaries** carpeting the **Dooars** along the southern approaches to the Himalayas. The largest of these, **Jaldapara Wildlife Sanctuary**, 124km from Siliguri, was established in 1943 to protect wildlife from the encroachment of tea cultivation. Set against a backdrop of forested foothills on the banks of the River Torsa, Jaldapara's 216 square kilometres hold large tracts of tall elephant grass, best explored by a dawn elephant ride (Rs300 [Rs200]). Fifty highly endangered one-horned rhinoceros, as well as wild elephants, sambar and hog deer reside in the sanctuary (Oct to May). A handful of buses and trains run from Siliguri to the town of **Madarihat**, 7km from the reserve and 1km from the sanctuary gates, from where taxis run to **Hollong** in the heart of the forest for around Rs150. **Accommodation** and **food** are available at the *Jaldapara Tourist Lodge* at Madarihat (ⓣ03563/262230; ❸–❺) or at the *Hollong Forest Lodge* (ⓣ03563/262228; ❺); both must be booked through the WB tourist offices in Siliguri, Darjeeling or Kolkata. Note that a Rs100 [Rs25] fee is payable at the entrance to the park.

More accessible, 80km to the east of Siliguri, the twin parks of **Gorumara National Park** and **Chapramari Wildlife Sanctuary** (Oct to May), shelter similar fauna. Access to the parks (Rs80 [Rs40]) is by Jeep, arranged at the entry point at **Lataguri**. **Accommodation** includes *Forest Rest Houses* (❸) booked through the Forest Officer (ⓣ03561/220017) and several alternatives such as the pleasant *Silver Ridge Resort* (☎9932 904028; ❸) close to the Lataguri gates. Buses travel regularly from the nearby town of Chalsa to Siliguri as well as to Lataguri; adjacent **New Mal Junction** has better train connections with Siliguri.

Darjeeling

Part Victorian holiday resort, part major tea-growing centre, **DARJEELING** (from *Dorje Ling*, "the place of the thunderbolt") straddles a ridge 2200m up in the Himalayas and almost 600km north of Kolkata. Over fifty years since the British departed, the town remains as popular as ever with holiday-makers from the plains, and promenades such as the Mall and the Chowrasta still burst with life. The greatest appeal for visitors has to be its stupendous mountain vistas – with Kanchenjunga (the third-highest mountain in the world) and a vast cohort of ice-capped peaks dominating the northern horizon. However, the infrastructure created under the Raj has been unable to cope with the ever-expanding population leading to acute shortages of water and electricity, and chaos on the hopelessly inadequate roads. Still, Darjeeling remains a colourful and lively, cosmopolitan place, with good shopping and dining, plenty of walks in the surrounding hills and attractions such as the Toy Train and colourful Buddhist monasteries. The best seasons to visit – and to attempt the magnificent trek to Sandakphu to see Everest – are after the monsoons and before winter (late Sept to late Nov), and spring (mid-Feb to May).

Until the nineteenth century, Darjeeling belonged to **Sikkim**. However in 1817, after a disastrous war with Nepal, Sikkim was forced to concede the right to use

Darjeeling tea

Although the original appeal of Darjeeling for the British was as a hill resort with easy access from the plains, inspired by their success in Assam they soon realized its potential for growing **tea**. Today, the Darjeeling tea industry continues to flourish, producing China Jat, China Hybrid and Hybrid Assam. A combination of factors, including altitude and sporadic rainfall, have resulted in a relatively small yield – only three percent of India's total – but the delicate black tea produced here is considered to be one of the finest in the world. It is also some of the most expensive with varieties fetching over Rs18,000 a kilo at auction.

Grades such as Flowery Orange Pekoe (FOP) or Broken Orange Pekoe (BOP) are determined by quality and length of leaf as it is withered, crushed, fermented and dried. To watch the process for yourself, call in at the **Happy Valley Tea Estate** (Tues–Sat 8am–noon & 1–4.30pm, Sun 8am–noon; free); it's a 30-minute-walk from town – follow the signs from the Hill Cart Road near the District Magistrate's office. As for **buying**, try the tea stores on the Chowrasta; The House of Tea on the Mall and Tea Cosy at the Rink Mall offer try-before-you-buy, with the latter's menu set clearly by the seasons (otherwise known as "flushes"). However, for the best price and an enthusiastic explanation of tea, explore the labyrinth of Chowk Bazaar to find Radhika & Son near the Laxmi Bhandar. Such vendors usually trade in unblended tea bought directly from tea gardens and are able to pick and choose according to quality. The typical cost of a kilo of good middle-grade tea is Rs600–700. You can get a taste of the opulence of a tea-manager's lifestyle by staying at *Glenburn*, off the Kalimpong road (☎033/2288 5630, Ⓦwww.glenburnteaestate.com; ❾ from US$180 all-inclusive including transport); for a less exclusive experience of life on a tea estate, try Makaibari's rustic **homestays** (☎9733 004577; Ⓦmakaibari.com ❹–❺) below Kurseong.

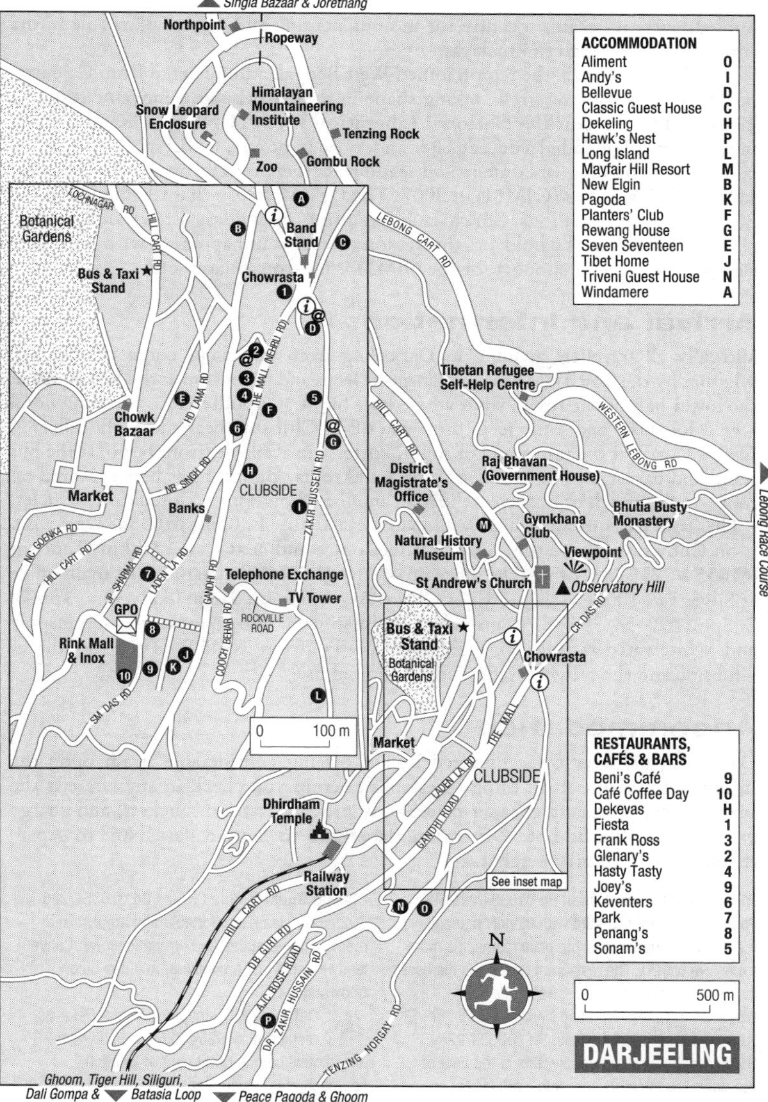

the site as a health sanatorium to the **British**, who had helped to broker a peace settlement. Darjeeling soon became the most popular of all hill resorts, especially after the Hill Cart Road was built in 1839 to link it with Siliguri. **Tea** arrived a few years later, and with it an influx of Nepalese labourers and the disappearance of the forests that previously carpeted the hillsides. The town's growing economic significance led Britain to force a treaty on the Sikkimese in 1861, thereby annexing Darjeeling and Kalimpong. In the early 1900s, Darjeeling's reputation grew as one of the most glamorous and far-flung outposts of the British Empire.

Subsequently it became a centre for mountaineering and played a key role in the conquest of the greater Himalayas.

After Independence, the region joined West Bengal, administered from Calcutta, but calls for autonomy grew, taking shape in the **Gurkhaland** movement of the 1980s, led by the **Gurkha National Liberation Front (GNLF)**. The subsequent violent campaign ended a decade later and, once in power, GNLF politicians grew complacent, fuelling discontent and leading to their overthrow by the **Gorkha Jana Mukti Morcha (GJMM)** in 2007. The GJMM victory has reinvigorated the push for an autonomous Gurkhaland, resulting in wildcat strikes designed to cripple West Bengal's hold on the region. Despite unhappiness with the West Bengal government, support for the GJMM is far from unanimous.

Arrival and information

Virtually all travellers arriving in Darjeeling from the plains come via Siliguri, whether by the Toy Train or road transport. Jeeps and buses stop at the **bus stand** in the lower half of the town, from where it's a bit of an uphill trek to the main hotel area. Most taxis and some Jeeps drop you off at **Clubside** near the **Mall** (officially Nehru Road), at the upper end of town. Porters are available (from Rs60) at the bus stand and bazaar, but be aware as some act as touts. Darjeeling is best explored on foot – in fact much of it, such as the Mall and the Chowrasta, is closed to all vehicles.

The **Tourist Bureau**, 1 The Mall (Mon–Fri 10am–4.30pm; ⓣ0354/225 5351), is on Chowrasta above the Indian Airlines office and next to the Sikkim Tourism (ⓣ0354/225 7248) office; the more pro-active **DGHC Tourism** has its main office at Silver Fir, 100m to the north of Chowrasta on Bhanu Sarani (daily 9am–1pm & 2–5pm; ⓣ0354/225 4879), providing useful information on tours, treks, transport and whitewater rafting on the River Teesta (from Rs450). Their booths at Clubside and the railway station are of limited use.

Accommodation

Darjeeling has over three hundred hotels, placing considerable strain upon the infrastructure. The main thing to establish before you check in anywhere is the **water** situation; many cheaper places only provide water in buckets, and charge extra if you like it hot. Off-season (late June to Sept & late Nov to April) **discounts** can be fifty percent.

Aliment 40 Dr Zakir Hussein Rd ⓣ0354/225 5068. Popular travellers' hang-out with friendly management and internet access, but plain rooms, the more expensive with TV. The restaurant upstairs is the best in this part of town with an eclectic mix from pancakes to Tibetan food and Nepalese thalis. ❷–❸

Andy's 102 Dr Zakir Hussein Rd ⓣ0354/225 3125. Run by a retired couple, this is the best of the ridge-top guesthouses: safe, with large, immaculate rooms and great views towards Kalimpong and Bhutan, but no restaurant. ❸

Bellevue The Mall ⓣ0354/225 4075. Above the tourist bureau, and dominating the Chowrasta, this once grand hotel, linked to Tibetan nobility, offers large, wood-panelled rooms with fireplaces. Service is low-key and meals need to be pre-arranged, but there are plenty of restaurants nearby. ❹–❺

Classic Guest House CR Das Rd ⓣ0354/225 7025. Five clean, comfortable and amply sized rooms with verandas and dramatic views. Conveniently located just a couple of minutes below Chowrasta. ❺

Dekeling 51 Gandhi Rd, above *Dekevas* restaurant ⓣ0354/225 4159, ⓦwww.elginhotels.com. A great central location approached up steep steps, with the luxury of running hot water – some rooms come with great views and the timbered ones upstairs are charming. The Tibetan owners are especially helpful and there is a welcoming log fire; good off-season discounts too. Their *Hawk's Nest* villa, a ten-minute walk, has four luxurious suites with fireplaces and good home cooking. ❹–❼

Long Island 11/A/2 Dr Zakir Hussein Rd ⓣ0354/225 2043. Tucked away on the other

Moving on from Darjeeling

By air

The nearest **airport** to Darjeeling is Bagdogra, 100km to the south (see p.773); allow plenty of time to get there by taxi. Tickets for Jet Airways and other airlines are available through Clubside Tours and Travels, JP Sharma Road (Ⓣ0354/225 4646), and Pineridge Travels, Nehru Rd, Chowrasta (Ⓣ0354/225 3912) which also handles Druk Air's flights to Bangkok. Both also handle flights from **Bhadrapur** in Nepal to **Kathmandu** (see p.773). Air India has its office on the Chowrasta (Ⓣ0354/225 4230).

By rail

The **Toy Train** (see p.774) leaves for **Siliguri** and **New Jalpaiguri** at 9.15am, weather and landslides permitting, but takes a leisurely seven to eight hours. **Railway reservations** (daily 8am–2pm) for selected **main-line trains** out of NJP can be made at Darjeeling's station a couple of days before departure. They have tourist quotas for trains to Delhi, Kolkata, Bengaluru (Bangalore), Cochin and Thiruvananthapuram. If stuck, try Gupta Tours & Travel, near the station at 5 Chachan Mansion (Ⓣ0354/225 4616), who can get tickets when quotas are "full" for a fee.

By road

A handful of **buses** and minibuses (from Rs50) run to **Siliguri** from the bus stand near Chowk Bazaar, while shared taxis and Jeeps charge Rs100. For overland bus travel to **Kathmandu**, head to the border town of **Kakarbitta** in Nepal to get a choice of coaches (see p.773). In the mornings, **Jeeps** run regularly to **Gangtok, Siliguri, Mirik, Kalimpong** and **Jorethang** (for West Sikkim; Rs100; foreigners need permits), and are by far the most efficient way to travel, especially if you pay for two front seats for yourself. Book in advance if you can at the Jeep stand (next to the bus stand); each route has its own syndicate, and some have two or three. Gangtok services (4hr 30min; Rs130) run frequently between 7am and 2pm.

Permits for Sikkim

Foreigners planning to head on to **Sikkim** will have to get a **permit**, a mere formality but one that does involve legwork. Travelling to Gangtok, you can get an initial fifteen-day permit instantly at the **Rangpo** border checkpoint (but not at the Naya Bazaar crossing for West Sikkim) and extend it once in Sikkim (see p.810). Getting a permit in Darjeeling allows you the option of travelling directly to West Sikkim on a hair-raising 27-kilometre road descending through tea plantations to Jorethang via Naya Bazaar. At the time of going to press, Sikkim Tourism's Chowrasta office was about to start issuing permits; otherwise pick up a form from the **District Magistrate's Office** (Mon–Fri 10am–4pm) on Hill Cart Road near Loreto Convent; take it to be stamped at the **Foreigners' Registration Office** (daily 10am–6pm) on Laden La Road, returning to the DM's office for the final stamp.

side of the ridge beyond the telecom tower, this is a friendly place with some of the best budget rooms on the ridge-top, most with shared baths and hot water by the bucket. The family-run *Kimchi* café serves genuine Korean food when ingredients are available, and there is a good trekking service. ❶–❸

Mayfair Hill Resort Below Government House, The Mall Ⓣ0354/225 6376, Ⓔdarjeeling@mayfairhotels.com. Once a maharaja's summer retreat, the rooms and garden cottages here offer ostentatious luxury. Facilities include restaurants, a bar and health spa; the gardens are immaculate, and the garden restaurant offers great views. The price includes breakfast and dinner. From US$190. ❾

New Elgin 32 HD Lama Rd Ⓣ0354/225 4114, Ⓦwww.elginhotels.com. Premier hotel, opulent and well maintained, with good facilities and an old-fashioned, formal atmosphere that captures the spirit of Darjeeling. Rates include all meals, and the tea service is the best in town. From US$135. ❾

Pagoda 1 Upper Beechwood Rd Ⓣ0354/225 3498. Keenly priced budget rooms, a fire in the lounge, free hot water by the bucket and a quiet, central location close to Laden La Rd and the post office. ❶–❷

Planters' Club The Mall ⓣ0354/225 4348. A local landmark (also known as the *Darjeeling Club*) with old-fashioned rooms, coal fires (Rs100), a billiard room, bar, restaurant and library. Residential guests must take temporary membership (Rs50); non-guests can use the facilities for Rs100. ❺–❻

Rewang House Dr Zakir Hussein Rd ⓣ9474 030016. Plain student rooms in a wonderful family home with running hot water and breakfast and dinner included in the price. The owner runs an educational charity and welcomes volunteers (see p.79). ❷

Seven Seventeen HD Lama Rd ⓣ0354/225 5099. Extensive, well-run hotel with airy rooms. Located just above the bazaar, so no mountain views. Exchange facilities and credit cards are accepted for undiscounted rooms; there is a cheaper annexe up the road. ❺–❻

Tibet Home Manjushree Centre, 12 Gandhi Rd ⓣ0354/225 2977. This non-profit cultural centre offers a range of rooms, from basic windowless doubles in the basement with shared baths to large, well-appointed rooms with attached baths and hot water. ❸–❹

Triveni Guest House 85/1 Dr Zakir Hussein Rd ⓣ9932 673511. Plain, roomier and a bit cheaper than the *Aliment* opposite but not as popular, with hot water by the bucket (Rs10) and a dorm (Rs80). Friendly, with a restaurant and nice views from the sun deck. ❶–❷

Windamere Observatory Hill ⓣ0354/225 4041, ⓦwww.windamerehotel.com. The most iconic and celebrated of Darjeeling's hotels has accommodated a pantheon of rich and famous guests in its old-world cottages decked out with Raj memorabilia; it also has a modern wing with comfortable suites but less character. Expensive, but well worth a visit for tea on the lawn or the occasional concert. From US$180. ❾

The Town

The heart of Victorian Darjeeling is the **Chowrasta**, an expansive traffic-free promenade resplendent with bandstand, high above the busy bazaar on Hill Cart Road. One of four main roads leading off it is the **Mall** (also called Nehru Road) which descends from Chowrasta to Clubside, the area below the prestigious **Planters' Club,** otherwise known as the **Darjeeling Club**. Established in 1868, this venerable institution was the centre of Darjeeling high society. Today, visitors are welcome to stay and sample the faded ambience and facilities such as the bar and snooker room, with temporary membership.

Taking the right fork of the Mall from the northern end of the Chowrasta, near the bandstand, brings you to the **viewpoint** from where you can survey the Kanchenjunga massif and almost the entire state of Sikkim. From near the *Windamere Hotel* steps, ascend the pine-covered hillside to the top of **Observatory Hill**, the original site of the Bhutia Busty monastery. Streaming with prayer flags, the shrine at the summit, dedicated to the wrathful Buddhist deity Mahakala, whom Hindus worship as Shiva, reflects a garish hybrid of styles. The picturesque **Bhutia Busty Monastery** was re-established one kilometre downhill from the Chowrasta approached by the steep CR Das Road. Another faded Raj-era institution, the **Gymkhana Club** (ⓣ0354/225 4342), stands near Observatory Hill. Casual visitors drop in to play billiards, tennis and even to roller-skate (Rs50 for day membership plus nominal game charges), or take advantage of the small library and bar.

Below the club, the small and little-visited **Natural History Museum** (daily except Thurs 10am–4.30pm; Rs5) holds a large collection of moths and butterflies, stuffed animals and birds, and a natural-habitat display complete with sound effects. Further away from Chowrasta, a steep drop down from Government House, lies the **Tibetan Refugee Self-Help Centre** (closed Sun). Founded in 1959, it houses seven hundred refugees, most of whom make carpets or Tibetan handicrafts. Tourists are welcome to watch the activities.

A kilometre further north towards the mountains and before the Gothic ramparts of **St Joseph's College**, Darjeeling's **Zoo** (daily except Thurs 8.30am–4pm; Rs100 [Rs30], combined with HMI ticket), is well maintained and worth a

Travel, tour, trek and adventure operators

Adventures Unlimited 142 Dr Zakir Hussein Rd ⓣ9933 070013 ⓦwww.adventuresunlimited.in. Gautam runs both motorbike and mountain-bike tours, as well as rental (motorbikes from Rs1200, mountain-bikes from Rs450/day) with a deposit; he also organizes kayaking on the Teesta.

Himalayan Travels 18 Gandhi Rd ⓣ0354/225 6956, or ⓣ9434 209847. An efficient organization run by the affable K.K. Gurung, and one of the first operators in town, offering tours and treks throughout Darjeeling, Sikkim and Bhutan.

Himalayan Mountaineering Institute ⓣ0354/225 4087 ⓦwww.himalayanmountaineeringinstitute.com (see below). Basic and advanced mountaineering courses centred around their Chaurikhang Base Camp at the foot of Rathong Glacier, Sikkim, last 28 days (US$650) and are run with military precision. The more rewarding advanced course requires previous mountaineering experience; to join either course, you must be aged between 17 and 40.

Pineridge Travels Nehru Road, Chowrasta ⓣ0354/225 3912. Specialists for domestic and international air tickets including flights to Kathmandu from Kakarbitta/Bhadrapur and to Bangkok.

Sandakphu Sikkim Tours & Trek *Hotel Long Island*, 11/A/2 Dr Zakir Hussein Rd ⓣ9434 467443 & 20 Chowrasta ⓣ9733 044986. A good local agency for the Sandakphu trek; owner Pritam puts some profits into the Child Welfare Society.

Tenzing Norgay Adventures DB Giri Rd ⓣ0354/225 3058 ⓦwww.tensing-norgay.com. An efficient, international organization run by Tenzing Norgay's celebrated son, Jamling: excellent for trekking and mountaineering.

Trek-Mate Singalila Arcade, Nehru Rd ⓣ0354/225 6611, or ⓣ9832 083241, ⓔchagpori@satyam.net.in. Tsewang Trogawa runs this very helpful agency arranging treks to Sandakphu and West Sikkim. It provides guides and porters and rents out sleeping bags, down jackets and day packs, and organizes day-treks as well as village homestays near Tukdah.

Xplore Himalaya *Hotel Seven Seas*, Clubside ⓣ9775 493432. With many years of experience in tourism, Micky is good at Sandakphu and Kalimpong treks and special interest tours.

visit. The zoo's Snow Leopard Breeding Centre (closed to the public), established in 1986, is the only place in the world to have successfully bred this endangered species, while Project Panda has produced several Red Pandas.

The **Himalayan Mountaineering Institute** (**HMI**) (see above), reached via the zoo and covered by the same ticket, is one of India's most important training centres for mountaineers. Its first director was **Sherpa Tenzing Norgay**, Sir Edmund Hillary's climbing partner on the first successful ascent of Everest, who lived and died in Darjeeling, and is buried in the Institute's grounds. In the heart of the leafy complex, the **HMI Museum** (daily except Thurs 9am–4.30pm; included in ticket price) is dedicated to the history of mountaineering, with equipment old and new, a relief map of the Himalayas, and a collection of costumes of hill people. The **Everest Museum** in the annexe recounts the history of ascents on the world's highest peak, from Mallory and Irvine's ill-fated 1924 expedition to Tenzing and Hillary's triumph in 1953 and the record-breaking 20-hour 24-minute climb by Kaji Sherpa in 1998.

Back in town, Lochnagar Road winds down from the bus stand in the bazaar to enter the **Botanical Gardens**, where pines, willows and maples cover the hillside and pleasant walks zigzag down to the slightly dilapidated central greenhouses, filled with ferns and orchids. One final prominent sight you're bound to notice is the multi-roofed **Dhirdham Temple**, below the railway station, built as a replica of the great Shiva temple of Pashupatinath on the outskirts of Kathmandu. Heading out of town on AJC Bose Road you come to the discreetly hidden **Nipponjan Myohoji Buddhist Temple** (daily 4.30am–7pm; prayers at 4.30am & 4.30pm), usually referred to as the Peace Pagoda, with great views over the valley to Kanchenjunga.

Eating and drinking

Darjeeling has plenty of choice for **eating out**, with the touristy places concentrated around the top of town; numerous cafés such as *Fiesta* on the Chowrasta, *Café Coffee Day* at Rink Plaza and *Frank Ross* on the Mall provide a wide choice and the tiny *Sonam's* on Dr Zakir Hussein Road is popular with travellers. *Beni's Café* opposite the Rink Plaza is renowned for its samosas. Hotels, such as the *Windamere* and *New Elgin*, have good multi-cuisine restaurants, and the latter has a superb tea service; budget hotels such as *Aliment* provide traveller-friendly meals.

Dekevas 51 Gandhi Rd. Popular with travellers and locals alike, this no-smoking restaurant with pleasant Tibetan decor offers the usual mixed menu, including a wide range of Tibetan dishes and a very good-value breakfast.

Glenary's The Mall. Darjeeling's most reputable eating place serves up tasty sizzlers and the best tandoori in town. There's also a great coffee shop and patisserie with an internet café; in the basement, *The Buzz* is an American-style bar with a pool table, which also serves burgers and pizzas.

Hasty Tasty The Mall. Offering Indian fast food, and very popular with Indian holiday-makers, this self-service place serves tasty cheese dosas and superb veg thalis. However the service is hardly hasty; *Frank Ross* nearby is quieter and faster with decent south Indian food.

Joey's Opposite Rink Plaza. A small and intimate pub, where everyone is made welcome – a popular rendezvous for visitors and locals alike. Not renowned for its food but rather its beer, ambience and chat.

Keventers Clubside. A landmark café serving toasted sandwiches, and fried breakfasts that include bacon and ham. The terrace above the crossroads is excellent for people-watching, even if the service is poor. A delicatessen downstairs sells cheese, ham and sausages.

Park 41 Laden La Rd. Widely considered Darjeeling's finest north Indian and tandoori cuisine, served in plush surroundings with a bar; reasonable Thai cooking as well; in season, the papaya salad is especially good.

Penang's Opposite the GPO, above Laden La Rd. As much a bar as a café, this cheap, grubby yet popular local haunt serves excellent *momos* and *thukpa* and their chilli chicken is legendary.

Listings

Banks and exchange There are several ATMs on Laden La Rd. The State Bank of India here also changes money and travellers' cheques; a short distance down the road, HDFC at Rink Mall offers foreign exchange. Licensed private foreign-exchange vendors offer an alternative but charge a bit more than the bank rate. Amongst these, the *Hotel Mohit* and *Hotel Seven Seventeen* are both on HD Lama Rd. Poddar's, 8 Laden La Rd near the GPO, is also good for cash advances on credit/debit cards.

Bookshops Oxford Books & Stationery, Chowrasta, has an excellent selection of novels and coffee-table books and will ship.

Car rental Darjeeling Transport Corporation, Laden La Rd (☎0354/225 2074), is one of the more established operators; numerous others are centred around Clubside.

Cinema Inox, Rink Mall (☎0354/225 7183). A modern new multiplex with three auditoria and the latest from Bollywood and Hollywood; can be loud so, depending on the film, take some cotton wool.

Hospital Try Planters' Hospital, Planter's Club, The Mall ☎0354/225 4327; Mariam Nursing Home, The Mall ☎0354/225 4327. The Tibetan Medical & Astro Institute, *Hotel Seven Seventeen*, 26 HD Lama Rd (☎0354/225 4735), is part of the Dalai Lama's medical organization, Men-Tsee-Khang, and has a clinic and a well-stocked dispensary. There is also a Women's Clinic

(Mon–Sat 1.30–5pm, Sun10am–1pm) under *Hotel Springburn*, 70 Gandhi Rd.
Internet access Of the numerous internet cafés, those at *Glenary's* and *Hotel Bellevue* (both Rs30/hr) are the most central and convenient. Broadband is slow so most do not allow Skype calls.
Pharmacies Frank Ross & Co, The Mall. There are several more pharmacies clustered around Sadar Hospital above the bus stand.
Post office The main post office (Mon–Fri 9am–5pm & Sat 9am–noon) is on Laden La Rd.
Shopping The best curio shops are around the Chowrasta including Habib Malik and Jolly Arts. For trekking gear try shops in the Singalila Market, The Mall and Rope, NB Singh Rd; for arts and crafts and especially carpets, head for Hayden Hall on Laden La Rd and the Tibetan Refugee Centre. Life & Leaf, The Mall, is a fair trade shop selling handicrafts and produce including tea.
Tibetan studies The Manjushree Centre of Tibetan Culture, 12 Gandhi Rd (ⓣ0354/225 6714, ⓦwww.manjushree-culture.org), founded in 1988 to preserve and promote Tibetan culture, offers both part-time Tibetan language classes (Mon–Sat 4–6pm) and more intensive three-, six- and nine-month courses and holds seminars, talks, video shows and exhibitions. The Chagpori Medical Institute at Takdah (en route to Teesta) runs excellent long courses in Tibetan medicine; ask at Manjushree.

Around Darjeeling

One really unmissable part of the Darjeeling experience is the early-morning mass exodus to **Tiger Hill** to watch the sunrise. This can easily be combined with a visit to the old monastery of **Ghoom**, and the huge monastery at **Sonada** on Hill Cart Road towards Siliguri.

Tiger Hill

Jeeps and taxis packed with tourists leave from Clubside in Darjeeling around 4am each morning, careering 12km through Ghoom to catch the sunrise at **TIGER HILL**. This incredible viewpoint (2585m) on the eastern extremity of

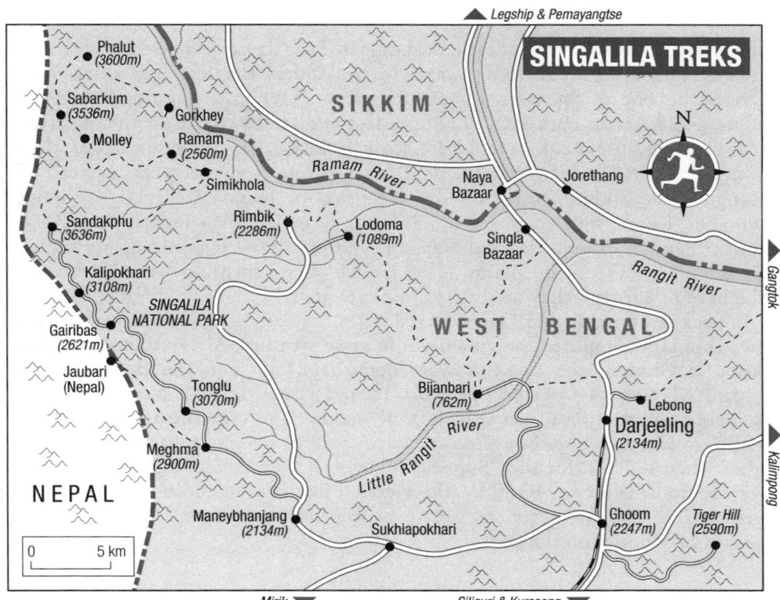

Singalila treks: the Maneybhanjang–Phalut trail

The single ridge of the **Singalila Range** rises near Darjeeling and extends all the way to the summit of Kanchenjunga. Unfortunately, although some longer trails have been opened in Sikkim (see pp.830–831), there is no provision yet to link them to the initial lower sections of the ridge to **Sandakphu** (3636m) and **Phalut** (3600m) in Darjeeling District.

Easily accessible from Darjeeling, the later stages of the Maneybhanjang–Phalut trail provide magnificent views of the higher ranges; lightweight expeditions are possible as there are trekking huts and simple food stalls along the way. Several organizations (see p.781) arrange porters, from Rs250 a day as well as **guides**, from Rs350 (around Rs700 for an English-speaking guide), as part of all-inclusive packages (from Rs1200 a day); amongst others, Trek-Mate in Darjeeling will **rent equipment** (sleeping bags Rs30 a day, plus Rs1500 deposit). The **best time** to trek is after the monsoon (Oct & Nov), and during spring (Feb–May). It gets hot at the end of April and into May, but this is an especially beautiful season, with the rhododendrons in bloom.

Maneybhanjang, a small town and roadhead 27km from Darjeeling, is the usual starting point for the route, with the finest views found along the **Sandakphu–Phalut** section of the trail while trekking north. The Forestry Department levy a fee (Rs150 [Rs100], cameras Rs50) to enter the **Singalila National Park**, and one has to take a guide. Local guides (Rs300–Rs500) and porters are cheaper, but there have been reports of unreliability due to drunkenness and lack of proper training – Darjeeling agencies are more professional. Foreigners are expected to register with the police at Maneybhanjang and border guards posted along the route are vigilant in checking papers. Taking an early taxi to Maneybhanjang from Darjeeling enables you to start the trek the same day, otherwise you can **stay** in the basic *Kanchenjunga* (➊) amongst others.

The normal route

DAY 1 Assuming you start from Maneybhanjang, the first day begins with a sharp climb to **Meghma**, then eases to the hut (➊) at **Tonglu** (3070m). One variation

the Singalila Range provides a 360-degree Himalayan panorama, with the steamy plains bordering Bangladesh to the south, the Singalila ridge with Everest beyond to the west, Kanchenjunga and Sikkim to the north, and the Bhutan and Assam Himalayas trailing into the distance to the northeast. From left to right, the **peaks** include: Lhotse (which actually looks larger than Everest); Everest itself; Makalu; then, after a long gap, the rocky summit of Kang on the Sikkim–Nepal divide; the prow of Jannu in Nepal; Rathong; tent-like Kabru south and north; Talung; Kanchenjunga main, central and south; Pandim; Simvo; horned Narsing; and the fluted pyramid of Siniolchu. As the sun rises from the plains, it lights each one in turn; not yet obscured by the haze of the day, they are bathed in pastel hues.

In peak season, up to 150 Jeeps leave Darjeeling daily, transporting more than two thousand people to the viewpoint in good weather. A Jeep tour with brief stops at Ghoom, the Gurkha War Memorial (Rs5) and the Batasia Loop, organized with one of the operators around Clubside, will cost Rs800 per vehicle or around Rs80 per seat, less off-season. The **viewing tower** at Tiger Hill provides a warmer but often crowded space to see the sunrise from behind glass: it costs Rs40 for the "Super Deluxe" top floor (including coffee), Rs30 for the floor below, or Rs20 for the viewing platform in addition to the Rs10 vehicle fee. The energetic can opt to walk back from Tiger Hill visiting the *gompas* of Ghoom on the way.

bypasses Tonglu to Tumling where there are lodges like the *Shikara* (❷), but most strong walkers should be able to press on to Gairibas, or to Kalipokhari where there are a couple of lodges including *Sherpa* (❷).

DAY 2 From Tonglu head on to **Kalipokhari** and **Bikhebhanjang**. The trail then rises steeply to **Sandakphu** (3636m), which has a trekkers' hut (❶), and lodges like the friendly *Sherpa Chalet* (❷).

DAY 3 The panorama opens out as you leave Sandakphu, and the trek follows the ridge to **Sabarkum**. There's no shelter or food here, but if you drop down to the right for thirty minutes to **Molley**, you'll find a trekkers' hut (❶).

DAY 4 Retrace your steps to Sabarkum and continue along the ridge to **Phalut** (3600m), where there is a trekkers' hut (❷). The panorama from here is particularly impressive.

DAY 5 Either retrace your steps to Sandakphu, or follow the trail from Phalut via **Gorkhey**, which has a trekkers' hut (❶) and the *Shanti Lodge* (❶–❸), or on to **Ramam** (2560m), home of the welcoming *Sherpa Hotel* (❶), and several other lodges. An alternative is to descend from Sabarkum to the pleasant riverside village of Sirikhola where accommodation is available at *Goparma Lodge* (❷)

DAY 6 The final day leads to **Rimbik** (2286m); check with locals before setting off as the route is confusing. In Rimbik there's the warm and cosy *Sherpa* (❷), where they'll help arrange bus tickets to Darjeeling; alternatives include the *Sherpa Tenzing* (❶) with shared baths, hot water by the bucket and good food. Rimbik is a roadhead served by buses and Jeeps (6–7am, noon–1pm) heading to Darjeeling, or you can set off by taxi or on foot to the idyllic *Karmi Farm* near Bijanbari (Email bookings only; ⓦwww.karmifarm.com, ⓔkarmifarm@yahoo.co.uk ❸), overlooking the Ramam river valley with vistas of West Sikkim. The farm makes an excellent base should you wish to do the trek in reverse.

Ghoom and other monasteries

Often obscured in cloud, **GHOOM** (2438m), with its charming little railway station and tiny bazaar on the edge of Jorebangla, holds several interesting monasteries. The most venerated of these is **Yiga Choling**, or the Old Ghoom Monastery, tucked off the main thoroughfare above the brash *Sterling Resort*. From Ghoom railway station, head back towards Darjeeling for 200m and turn left into the side road (signposted) and continue through the small market for 500m. Built in 1850 by Sharap Gyatso, a renowned astrologer, the monastery consists of a single chambered temple and a few residential buildings. Inside the prayer hall is a huge figure of Maitreya, the Buddha of the future – a statue of an exceptionally high standard of workmanship, with fine detail above and around the bronze face. Back on the main road, the **Shakya Choling** *gompa* has expanded in recent years, while **Samten Choling**, a small but colourful *gompa* on a bend in the main road to Darjeeling, is sometimes included on the Jeep tours to Tiger Hill.

Halfway between Ghoom and Darjeeling on the main road stands the imposing **Thupten Sanga Choling**, otherwise known as the **Dali Gompa**, inaugurated by the Dalai Lama in 1993. This is a very active **Drukpa Kagyu** *gompa* with two hundred monks, including several young lamas. The huge meditation hall is richly decorated with exquisite murals and ceiling mandalas.

South of Ghoom, down the Hill Cart Road towards Kurseong, the influential **Sonada Monastery** or **Samdrub Darjay Choling**, founded in the 1960s, was the

The Toy Train to Ghoom

Ghoom is the highest point on the **Toy Train** railway (see p.774), just 7km from Darjeeling. In season, two steam-driven tourist trains (Rs265 return trip) leave Darjeeling at 10.15am and 1.20pm to travel up to Ghoom, where they stop for just fifteen minutes, not enough time to view the monasteries, before returning to Darjeeling with another brief stop at Batasia Loop for views of the Himalayas. The regular 9.15am diesel service from Darjeeling to Siliguri via Ghoom is cheaper (Rs116 first class, Rs25 second class). You could use alternative transport back to Darjeeling or take the top road for a quiet walk back, with stupendous views along the way and a visit to the **Peace Pagoda** in the woods above the Dali Gompa.

seat of **Kalu Rinpoche** who developed a large American and French following. It has recently been extensively renovated to house Kalu Rinpoche's young *tulku* or reincarnation. Rooms (❶) are available for retreat and you can dine with the monks for a nominal fee.

Kalimpong and around

Though it may seem grubby at first, the quiet hill station of **KALIMPONG**, 50km east of Darjeeling, has much to offer, including a colourful market, an extraordinary profusion of orchids and other flowers, great views of Kanchenjunga, several monasteries and lots of potential for walks in the surrounding hills, which are still home to the tribal **Lepcha community**. Like Darjeeling, Kalimpong once belonged to Sikkim, and later to Bhutan. Unlike Darjeeling this was never a tea town or resort, but a trading centre on the vital route to Tibet – a location that rendered Kalimpong virtually out of bounds for tourists for a couple of decades after the Sino-Indian conflict of the early 1960s. Despite the large military presence, Kalimpong's recent history has been one of neglect, decaying infrastructure and water. A deep-rooted dissatisfaction has simmered for several years championed by the Gurkhaland movement (see p.778), but political uncertainties and wildcat strikes have not detracted from Kalimpong's charm. Its quiet leafy avenues offer a breath of fresh air after the razzmatazz of Darjeeling.

Arrival and information

Kalimpong, only accessible by **road**, is served by regular buses, taxis and Jeeps from Darjeeling, Siliguri and Gangtok. Most transport pulls in at the **Motor Stand** in the central market area.

Kalimpong's **DGHC tourist office**, Damber Chowkh (daily 9.30am–5pm; Ⓣ03552/257992), provides general information and arranges **whitewater rafting** on the Teesta (from Rs350). Amongst local **tour operators**, Gurudongma Tours and Treks (Ⓣ03552/255204, Ⓦwww.gurudongma.com) specializes in ornithological, culinary and trekking trips and has its own farmhouse (see p.789). The informative Holumba (Ⓣ03552/256936) organizes village tours and tailor-made itineraries including trips to the Neora Valley. Mondo Challenge, an educational charity that welcomes volunteers, also runs one- and two-day village treks (Ⓣ03552/260026; Ⓦwww.kalimpongvillagetour.wordpress.com). Not for the faint-hearted, the Swedish-run Himalayan Eagle has initiated paragliding tandem flights (Sept–June Ⓣ9635 156911) from near Deolo. Its sister operation, (Ⓦwww.himalayanbiketours.se) organizes motorbike tours of the region with payment in euros.

Moving on

You can pick up buses and Jeeps at the Motor Stand heading to Darjeeling (2hr 30min–4hr; Rs80), Siliguri (2hr 30min; Rs90) and Gangtok (3hr; Rs90); confusingly, each route has its own syndicate and ticket office. Other destinations include NJP, Lava, Kakarbitta, Pelling and Ghezing, but bear in mind that the last reliable transport links are mid-afternoon; Himalayan Travels (ⓣ9434 166498) on the corner is good for reserved taxis and the Motor Transport Syndicate (ⓣ9932 766064) runs services to Darjeeling (7am–3pm). Dynamic Solutions, Jopa Complex on Main Road (ⓣ03552/257874), is good for all air tickets; for **train tickets**, head to the railway agency on Rishi Road (daily 10am–4pm), although their quota for NJP is low.

ATMs next to the State Bank of India on the Main Road, ICICI next door, Axis on DS Gurung Rd above the Motor Stand, amongst others, accept credit and debit cards. On the Main Road near DGHC office, Soni Emporium and neighbouring Kaziratna Shakya **change cash and travellers' cheques**. The **post office** is near the town centre, above the bazaar area just behind the police station. There are a few **Internet** cafés; try Odyssey at Ma Supermarket, near the police station on the main road. Adarsh Nursinghome, SD Giri Rd (ⓣ03552/257743), is one of the best hospitals in town for emergencies.

Accommodation

Kalimpong's acute water shortages are likely to influence your choice of **accommodation** – few of the lower-range options have running water. Tenth Mile and the area around the Motor Stand hold most of the budget places.

Cloud 9 Ringkingpong Rd ⓣ03552/259554. Five spacious, airy and well-kept rooms with grand views across the distant town; above a restaurant and bar that's especially lively when the owner Binodh is around – guitar jams and Beatles covers. ❺

Crown Lodge Below the Motor Stand ⓣ03552/255846. Handy for early departures, this is a central and popular place with functional, clean rooms, hot running water and a good restaurant. ❷–❸

Deki Lodge Tirpai Rd ⓣ03552/255095. A 10min walk from the Motor Stand, this clean and very welcoming Tibetan-run hotel offers a wide choice, from budget rooms with hot water by the bucket to comfortable doubles with running hot water in the new wing at the rear; internet is available. ❷–❺

Gompus Damber Chowk ⓣ03552/2558181. This legendary hotel bang in the centre of town has been completely revamped into a smart business hotel with large rooms all with TV and modern plumbing, on three floors above a popular restaurant and bar. ❺

Himalayan Upper Cart Rd ⓣ03552/255248, ⓦwww.himalayanhotel.com. Historic family-run hotel full of Tibetan memorabilia, set amid exquisite, leafy gardens in an unspoilt spot above town; the modern cottages are luxurious but lack the ambience of the old house with its large wood-panelled rooms. ❻

Holumba Haven 8.5 Mile, near the Fire Station ⓣ03552/256936, ⓦwww.holumba.com. Beautifully presented cottages set in an orchid nursery complete with a menagerie of birds. Some cottages come with their own kitchens, or you can have home-cooked meals with the informative and extremely welcoming owners. ❹–❺

Sherpa Lodge Ongden Rd ⓣ9800 861462. Convenient central location with eight good budget rooms, three with attached bathrooms, and a lovely terrace for breakfast overlooking the playground. ❷

Silver Oaks Ringkingpong Rd ⓣ03552/255296, ⓦwww.elginhotels.com. One of the grandest addresses in town, with a central location, spacious, plush rooms with conservative decor, and a good restaurant; the garden is a pleasant setting for tea or drinks in the evenings. From Rs5400. ❽

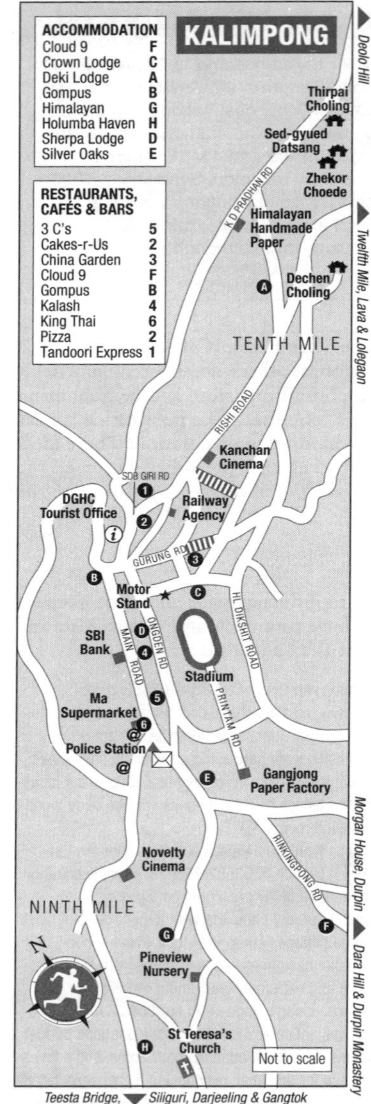

The Town

Kalimpong spreads along a curving ridge to either side of its main **market area**, known as **Tenth Mile.** Though there are few of the curio and tourist emporia so abundant in Darjeeling, there are plenty of places selling Buddhist handicrafts and religious paraphernalia, which attract wholesale buyers from all over India. Silk brocade, Tibetan incense, made-to-order monks' attire and silver bowls predominate. Of the tourist shops, both Kaziratna Shakya and Himalayan Handicrafts on Rishi Road have good selections and workshops; the wholesale shops are centred around RC Mintri Road. On Wednesdays and Saturdays, Tenth Mile gets very lively as villagers flock in from the surrounding areas for the principal weekly markets. The **Gangjong Paper** Factory (Mon–Sat 9am–4.30pm) welcomes visitors to their handmade paper workshop down steps off Printam Road; access to **Himalayan Handmade Paper**, on KD Pradhan Road near Thirpai, is easier and they also have a shop.

Rinkingpong Hill, also known as **Durpin Dara**, looms above Kalimpong to the southwest and, despite the army's presence, makes a pleasant 4km hike from the centre of town. At its highest point, **Zong Dog Palri Phodrang Gompa**, also known as Durpin ("telescope") Monastery, built in 1957 to house three copper statues brought from Tibet in the 1940s, was modelled on Guru Rinpoche's mythical "pure realm" palace and consecrated by the Dalai Lama. Despite the communication masts and the army campus next door, the *gompa*'s roof is a great place to take in the sunrise accompanied by the chanting of the monks below; you are welcome to sit in for the prayers.

The wooded roads leading up Rinkingpong Hill hide several interesting old manor houses, of which **Morgan House** was built for a British jute merchant but now serves as a tourist lodge, where tea on the lawn captures the atmosphere of the period; the views are stunning. Further up the hill and some 2km above town, **St Teresa's Church** was built in 1929 by a Swiss missionary and borrows heavily from vernacular Buddhist monastic architecture, mimicking a Bhutanese *gompa*.

There's beautiful carving inside and out; check out the doors, adorned with the eight sacred Buddhist symbols.

At the other end of town, half an hour's walk up Deolo Hill brings you to the **Thirpai Choling Gompa**, a breakaway Gelugpa monastery founded in 1892 and recently renovated, which hides the controversial image of Dorje Shugden, a deity proscribed by the Dalai Lama. Below and closer to town, the meditation halls of **Thongsa Gompa**, a small Bhutanese monastery founded in 1692, are covered with beautiful murals. The summit of **Deolo Hill** (1704m) is a popular picnic spot (daily 9am–6pm; Rs5) with a DGHC tourist lodge and restaurant, and a superb vista which ranges from the steamy Teesta Valley far below to the summit of Kanchenjunga, with the frontier ridge and the passes of Nathula and Jelepla into Tibet clearly visible.

Kalimpong is renowned for its **horticulture**, especially its orchids, cacti, amaryllis, palms and ferns. There are round fifty nurseries, such as Sri Ganesh Mani Pradhan at Twelfth Mile, Nurseryman's Haven (at *Holumba Haven* hotel; see p.787) and Pineview (Rs5) on Atisha Road, which specializes in exotic cacti. Although Kalimpong blossoms all year long, the best time to see orchids in bloom is between mid-April and mid-May, when the flower festival is usually held.

Eating and drinking

Kalimpong offers an eclectic mix of cuisines, from *momos* and *thukpa* to pizzas, coffee shops and vegetarian restaurants in the bazaar. The town's grand hotels such as *Silver Oaks* present fine dining and tea service on silver platters. There are several good bars too, like *Cloud 9*, to grab a beer and have a chat.

3C's Main Rd. A popular bistro with a snack bar, coffee shop and a patisserie counter; good for breakfast and for lunch, try their *rumali* roti and *paneer* tikka.

Cakes-r-us & Pizza SBG Rd, near DGHC tourist office. A pleasant patisserie with *Pizza* across the hall offering pizza and Indian food to eat in or take away.

China Garden Lall Gali, near Motor Stand. One of the few remnants of a once thriving Chinese community, this small and popular local restaurant offers authentic Chinese cooking at reasonable prices.

Gompus Damber Chowk. A famous and popular bar and restaurant in the centre of town with a wide menu but best known for *momos* and *thukpa*. A great place for a long, cold beer.

Kalash Main Rd. Signed in Hindi so you may need to ask. A vegetarian restaurant that offers good wholesome cooking at an incredible price with a thali for just Rs55.

King Thai Ma Supermarket, near the police station. A popular local bar and restaurant serving Indian and Chinese, rather than Thai. Local bands play here occasionally.

Tandoori Express SBG Rd, near DGHC tourist office. A small café and takeaway which does, as its name suggests, specialise in Indian food, but it also has a patisserie with patties and cakes.

Village tourism and homestays

Offering the chance to explore the rural landscape and experience local culture, organized **village tourism** is becoming increasingly popular. The main operators include Gurudongma and Holumba (see p.786) in Kalimpong, Help Tourism (see p.763) in Siliguri and Himalayan Footprints in Gangtok (see p.813). Gurudongma's *Farm House* (➑) is a tranquil and rustic but luxurious development on the beautiful **Samthar Plateau**, an 80km drive from Kalimpong. Other homestays include *Tinchuley Village House* (Ⓣ03542/262236; ➎), 28km from Kalimpong near Takdah, a tea and cardamom plantation on the edge of a forest. Across the border into Sikkim, the *Turuk Village House* (Ⓣ9434 022580; ➐–➑), 35km from Kalimpong, is a grand manor house set in an idyllic plantation that dates back to the late nineteenth century.

Around Kalimpong

Although the **Lepchas**, the original inhabitants of the area, have lost their traditional way of life in most parts of Darjeeling and Sikkim, their lifestyle has remained relatively untouched in the unspoilt forest-covered hills and deep river valleys to the south of Kalimpong. Lying on an old trade route to Bhutan, the small town of **Lava** (2184m), 35km from Kalimpong and accessible by shared Jeep, makes an ideal base for exploring the nature trails of **Neora Valley National Park**, a 880-hectare reserve stretching along a narrow river valley, with a huge variation in wildlife and abundant orchids and birds. Holumba in Kalimpong (see p.786) can arrange the necessary guides and permits as well as transport. Lava is also convenient for approaching the **Rachela Pass** (3152m) on the Sikkim–Bhutan border, which provides excellent views of the Chola Range including Chomalhari (7314m), the sacred mountain of Bhutan. There is plenty of basic **accommodation**, including huts at the *Forest Rest House* (❶), which should be booked through the Forest Department in Kalimpong, off Rinkingpong Road (Ⓣ03552/255780, Ⓦwww.wbfdc.com); the Forest Department also provides **permits** for visiting the Neora Valley. Buses and Jeeps link Kalimpong with Lava.

Pleasant **trails** lead west from Lava towards **Budhabare**, a market town in the Git River Valley which has a sprinkling of Lepcha, Gurkha and Bhutia villages. The track continues through forest to **Kafer**, where there's an old *Tourist Lodge* with large rooms (❸) and a dorm (Rs100). The sunrise from nearby **Lolegaon** is legendary and there is a Heritage Forest walk along a canopy trail. You can get here via a rough road from Kalimpong, but if you're fit, you could walk the trail that crosses the Relli River near the village of the same name and climbs directly to Kalimpong.

Bihar and Jharkhand

* **Sonepur Mela** This month-long festival and cattle fair is a spectacular gathering of pilgrims, sadhus and animals. See p.798

* **The Mahabodhi Temple** A cutting from the tree under which the Buddha attained enlightenment is the focal point of Bodhgaya's renowned temple. See p.802

* **Rajgir** A dusty Buddhist pilgrimage town filled with shrines and home to one of the region's most unusual hotels. See p.805

* **Nalanda** The site of a fifteen-hundred-year-old university, from the days when Buddhism dominated India, strewn with the remains of ancient *stupas* and monasteries. See p.805

▲ The Mahabodhi Temple, Bodhgaya

BIHAR occupies the flat eastern Ganges basin, south of Nepal, between Uttar Pradesh and West Bengal. To its south, **JHARKHAND**, occupying the hilly Chotanagpur plateau north of Orissa, was hewn out of Bihar in 2000, following agitation by its tribal majority. Both states are beset by poverty, lack of infrastructure, inter-caste violence, corruption and general lawlessness.

Although the ordinary visitor is usually unaffected by the banditry and guerrilla war, Buddhist pilgrims and tourists have on occasion been robbed and few travellers spend much time here, which is a shame, because the region is a fascinating mix of **religious history**. Check the **safety situation** with your foreign office and the local press (Ⓦwww.patnadaily.com and Ⓦwww.bihartimes.com are good sources of information) before travel; state and tourist authorities tend to downplay safety concerns. Avoid the region during local elections, when tensions run high, and riots and violent crime are not uncommon.

Patna and around

Patna, Bihar's capital, dates back to the sixth century BC, but shows few signs today of its former glory as the centre of the Magadhan and Mauryan empires. A sprawling metropolis hugging the south bank of the Ganges, Patna stretches for around 15km in a shape that has changed little since Ajatasatru (491–459 BC) shifted the Magadhan capital here from Rajgir.

The first Mauryan emperor, **Chandragupta**, established himself in what was then **Pataliputra** in 321 BC, and pushed the limits of his empire as far as the Indus; his grandson **Ashoka** (274–237 BC), one of India's greatest rulers, held sway over even greater domains. To facilitate Indo-Hellenic trade, the Mauryans built a Royal Highway from Pataliputra to Taxila, Pakistan, which later became the Grand Trunk Road. The city experienced two revivals, when the first Gupta emperor, **Chandra Gupta**, made it his capital early in the fourth century AD, and when it was rebuilt in the sixteenth century by Afghan ruler Sher Shah Suri.

Jharkhand

Carved out of Bihar in 2000 after years of agitation by its largely *adivasi* population, **JHARKHAND** yields almost forty percent of India's minerals, but suffers from extreme poverty, lawlessness and Naxalite (Maoist guerrilla) activity, and is rarely visited by tourists. Its main attraction is the beautiful *sal* forests of **Palamau National Park**, but sadly these have been damaged by years of drought and although it is part of Project Tiger (see p.1178), tiger sightings are now rare; you are more likely to see elephants, antelope, bison and wild boar. The park is open all year, but October to April is the best time to visit. Other forest reserves and parks pepper the state, including **Hazaribagh National Park** in the north, but bandits and Naxalites are active in these areas, and around **Parasnath temple**, so it's vital to check the **security situation** before venturing out, and you should avoid travelling at night anywhere in the state. If the situation is safe and you want to visit Palamau National Park, consider going on an excursion from **Ranchi**, the state capital, with Ashok Travels at the *Ranchi Ashok* (Ⓣ0651/248 0759) or Suhana Travels (Ⓣ0651/329 3808) on Station Road. The best **accommodation** in Ranchi is at the atmospheric Raj-style *BNR Hotel* on Station Road (Ⓣ0651/246 1481, Ⓔchanakyabnrranchi@hotmail.com; ❻). At Palamau you can stay in the state-run *Van Vihar* by the park entrance (Ⓣ06567/226513; ❷–❹; dorm Rs100).

Every March the city celebrates its illustrious history with several days of music, dancing and public events during the **Pataliputra Mahotsava** festival.

Arrival and information

All mainline **train** services arrive at Patna Junction station, in the west of the city. Patna's **airport** lies 5km to the west; a taxi from town costs Rs150–200, an auto-rickshaw around Rs100. The **New Bus Stand**, at Mithapur, is 2km south of Patna Junction (shared autos connect the two). North of Fraser Road and Gandhi Maidan, **Gandhi Maidan Bus Stand** is served by state buses.

The **Bihar State Tourism Development Corporation** is at *Kautilya Vihar Tourist Bungalow* (Mon–Sat 10.30am–5.30pm; ⓣ0612/222 5411, ⓦbstdc.bih.nic.in), with a

Lalu and the caste wars: politics in Bihar

Bihar – along with neighbouring Jharkhand – languishes at the bottom of almost every measure of development: from literacy rates to GDP. Roads are appalling, buses and trains are ancient, power cuts are common and even in Patna there are few streetlights. Author William Dalrymple has described Bihar as "the most ungovernable and anarchic state in India", even though it is blessed with ample coal and iron deposits and large tracts of arable land. The problem has been a disastrous combination of virulent intercaste conflict and criminal misgovernance.

Since Independence, Bihar has largely been ruled by a mafia of high-caste landowners, with the lower castes – who together with untouchables and tribal people make up over seventy percent of the state's population – marginalized to the point of persecution. All that seemed set to change in 1991 when a rabble-rouser from a lowly caste of buffalo milkers, **Lalu Prasad Yadav**, united the "backward castes", the Muslims and the untouchables under a banner of social justice, winning that year's state election by a landslide. In power, Lalu delighted with his common touch; he spontaneously unclogged traffic congestion in Patna by walking the streets with a megaphone and filled the grounds of his official residence with buffalo.

Unfortunately Lalu proved little better than his predecessors. His cabinet of caste brethren included men wanted for murder and kidnapping, and violence remained the main tool of political persuasion – as one hopeful election candidate said: "Without one hundred men with guns you cannot contest an election in Bihar." Much of the state degenerated into virtual civil war as the upper castes, lower castes, Maoist (Naxalite) guerrillas, police and private armies clashed violently.

Lalu's career seemed over in 1997, when he was imprisoned for a short spell for embezzling billions of rupees. He responded by getting his illiterate wife **Rabri Devi** proclaimed Chief Minister. Even though his RJD party was toppled in the 2005 state elections, Lalu went on to serve as Minister for Railways from 2004 to 2009, and remains a member of Parliament.

Meanwhile, at state level, things may have changed for the better. In 2005 a new coalition under Lalu's chief opponent Nitish Kumar took power, and with less obvious domination by organized crime, investors are starting to return. Whether this apparent improvement will last remains to be seen, but there does at least now seem to be a mood of cautious optimism.

booth at Patna Junction (daily 8am–8pm, but often closed; ⓣ0612/220 5755). **India Tourism** at Sudama Place, Kankar Bagh Road (Mon–Fri 9.30am–6pm; ⓣ0612/234 5776) can put you onto a guide. Thomas Cook and Bihar Tourism arrange tours and **car rental**, but many drivers won't go to isolated areas for fear of dacoits.

The State Bank of India, West Gandhi Maidan, handles **foreign exchange**; **ATMs** are dotted around town. The **GPO** is on Buddha Marg. For **internet access**, try Broadband Internet Café (Rs15/hr) on the second floor of the Jagat Trade Centre, Fraser Road, or the internet café at *Hotel Windsor* (Rs25/hr).

Patna has a higher **crime** rate than other Indian cities, and it's not a good idea to walk around on your own at night.

Accommodation

Akash Just off Fraser Rd (no working phone). One of Patna's better shoestring hotels, *Akash* has a motley collection of fairly clean, compact rooms; if it's busy try the *New Amar* next door. ❶

Chanakya Beer Chand Patel Path ⓣ0612/222 3141, ⓦwww.hotelchanakyapatna.in. This looming hotel has tastefully furnished beige- and apricot-coloured attached rooms. There's also a classy bar, a currency exchange and two top restaurants serving Indian and Chinese or Mughal and Afghan dishes. ❽

Garden Court Club Patna Super Market, Fraser Rd ⓣ0612/320 2279, ⓦwww.gardencourtclub.com.

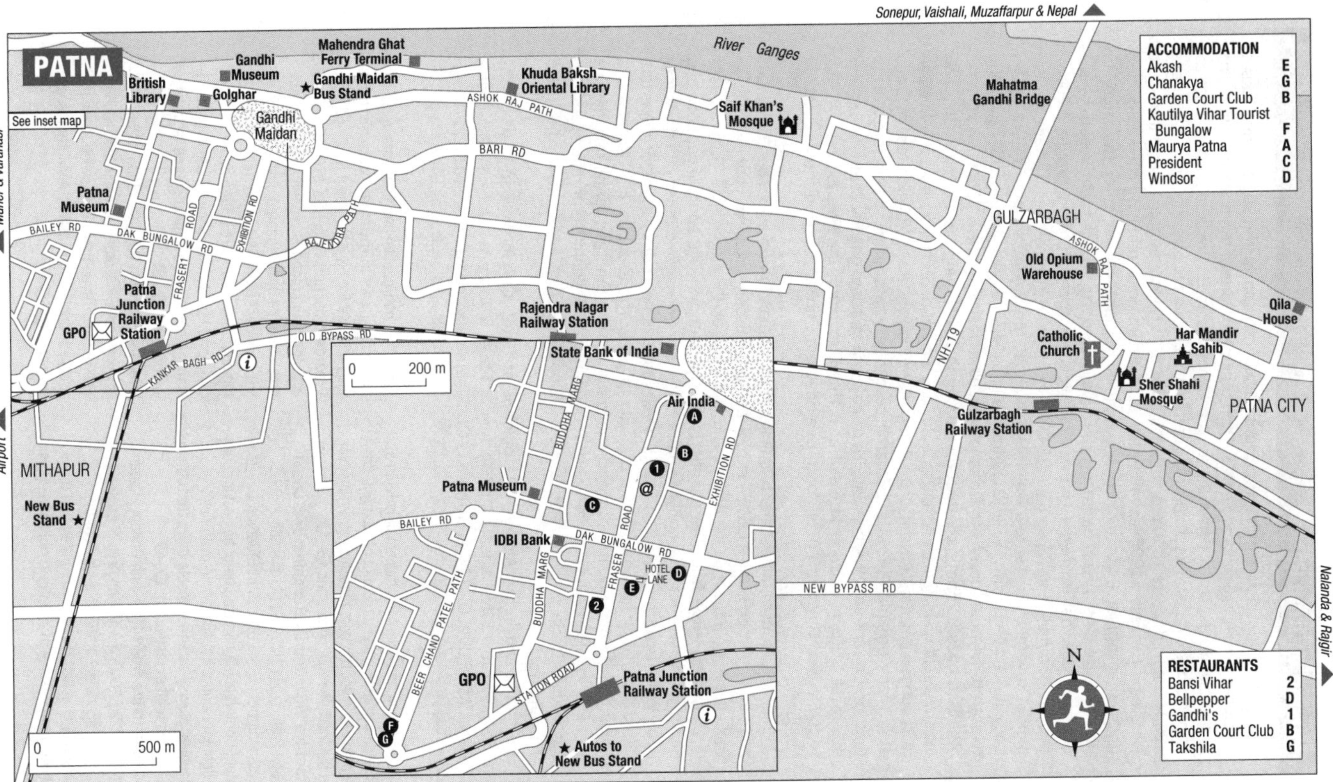
PATNA
See inset map
Sonepur, Vaishali, Muzaffarpur & Nepal
Muner & Varanasi
Airport
Nalanda & Rajgir
River Ganges
British Library
Golghar
Gandhi Museum
Mahendra Ghat Ferry Terminal
Gandhi Maidan Bus Stand
Gandhi Maidan
Khuda Baksh Oriental Library
Saif Khan's Mosque
Mahatma Gandhi Bridge
ASHOK RAJ PATH
BARI RD
RAJENDRA PATH
Patna Museum
BAILEY RD
DAK BUNGALOW RD
FRASER ROAD
EXHIBITION RD
Patna Junction Railway Station
GPO
OLD BYPASS RD
KANKAR BAGH RD
Rajendra Nagar Railway Station
GULZARBAGH
Old Opium Warehouse
Catholic Church
NH-19
Har Mandir Sahib
Sher Shahi Mosque
Qila House
PATNA CITY
Gulzarbagh Railway Station
NEW BYPASS RD
MITHAPUR
New Bus Stand
0 500 m
0 200 m
State Bank of India
Air India
BUDDHA MARG
IDBI Bank
HOTEL LANE
BEER CHAND PATEL PATH
STATION ROAD
Autos to New Bus Stand
N
ACCOMMODATION
Akash E
Chanakya G
Garden Court Club B
Kautilya Vihar Tourist Bungalow F
Maurya Patna A
President C
Windsor D
RESTAURANTS
Bansi Vihar 2
Bellpepper D
Gandhi's 1
Garden Court Club B
Takshila G

Moving on from Patna

Patna Junction is the most important railway station in the region, and has a foreigners' reservation window (No. 7) on the upper floor of the booking office. The best train to Kolkata (Howrah) is the *Janshatabdi Express* #2024 (Mon–Sat; departs 5.45am, arrives 1.25pm); overnight services include the *Vibhuti Express* #2334 (daily; departs 10.37pm, arrives 7.55am). For destinations beyond there, the *Northeast Express* #2506 leaves Patna at 10.20pm daily, reaching New Jalpaiguri (for Darjeeling) at 8.20am and Guwahati at 4.40pm. In the other direction, to Varanasi, the *Shramjeevi Express* #2391 (daily; departs 10.50am, arrives 3pm) is a good option. The *Rajdhani Express* #2309 (daily; departs 7.25pm, arrives 7.35am) and the *Sampark Kranti Express* #2393 (daily; departs 6pm, arrives 8.35am) are the pick of several trains to New Delhi. For Mumbai, the *Rajendra Nagar* #2142 leaves daily at 11.10am, arriving at 3.30pm the next day. Seven daily trains cover the two- to three-hour journey to Gaya, of which the fastest is the 6.15am *Janshatabdi* #2365 (arrives 8.25am), which continues on to Ranchi (arrives 1.55pm). Only one inconvenient weekly train links Patna directly with Puri, and no trains arrive in Gaya at a convenient time for the daily *Purshottam Express* #2802 (which leaves Gaya at 1.37pm, arriving in Puri at 5.20am), so either take a morning bus to Gaya for that, or, on Monday, Wednesday, Thursday or Saturday, get the *Intercity Express* #3243 at 5.30pm, arriving in Gaya at 8.15pm, to catch the *Puri Express* #2186, which leaves Gaya at 9.07pm on those days only, arriving in Puri the next day at 12.25pm.

Private travel companies offer bus tickets to Kathmandu with a voucher for the bus across the border, but it's just as easy – and often wiser – to make your own way to Raxaul (see p.799), cross the border, and find a bus on the Nepali side. Raxaul buses (4 daily; 8hr) leave from the chaotic New Bus Stand in Mithapur, except for one overnight service from Gandhi Maidan Bus Stand. Services to most other destinations leave from the New Bus Stand, where there is no enquiry office or departure board, and you'll have to depend on touts to guide you to a bus. For Nalanda and Rajgir (hourly; 4hr) you may have to change at Bihar Sharif, and for all destinations it's safer to stick to daytime services. The Bihar State Tourism Corporation runs two daily buses to Ranchi (8pm and 9pm) and Bodhgaya (7am and 2pm) from Kautilya Vihar Tourist Bungalow.

Air India and Indian Airlines' city office is at South Gandhi Maidan (ⓣ0612/222 2554). Reliable travel agents include Ashok Travel & Tours in the *Hotel Pataliputra Ashok* (ⓣ0612/250 4238) and Thomas Cook at the *Maurya Patna* (ⓣ0612/222 1699).

Accessed via an ancient lift, this small hotel in a shopping complex has a handful of neat and tidy rooms with TVs. The best reason to stay, however, is the lovely terrace restaurant. ❸–❺

Kautilya Vihar Tourist Bungalow Beer Chand Patel Path ⓣ0612/222 5411, ⓔbstdc@sancharnet.in. The Bihar State Tourism Development Corporation's rambling hotel has cavernous, brightly-coloured but somewhat overpriced doubles, as well as a reasonable dorm (Rs100) and a relaxed rooftop restaurant. ❸–❺

Maurya Patna Fraser Rd, South Gandhi Maidan ⓣ0612/220 3040, ⓦwww.maurya.com. Service can be impersonal at this five-star, but the luxurious attached rooms – decorated in a range of styles, from colonial to oriental – swimming pool (Rs490 for non-guests) and fine restaurants more than make up for it. The more expensive rooms in the range we list here are about $207. ❽–❾

President Just off Fraser Rd ⓣ0612/220 9203, ⓔhotelpresidentpatna@yahoo.com. Its decor may not have been updated since the 1970s, but *President* remains a good-value option. Although the rooms are a little stuffy, they're clean and boast multicoloured bedspreads. The management is also a good source of transport information. ❹–❺

Windsor Exhibition Rd ⓣ0612/220 3250, ⓦwww.hotelwindsorpatna.com. A reassuringly well-run mid-range hotel, with swish modern attached rooms and excellent restaurant (see opposite). ❺–❻

The City

Patna's most notable monument is the **Golghar**, also called "the round house", a huge colonial-era grain store built in 1786 to avoid a repetition of 1770's terrible famine; mercifully, it never needed to be used. Overlooking the river and Gandhi Maidan, its two sets of stairs spiralling up to the summit were designed so coolies could carry grain up one side, deliver their load through a hole at the top, and descend down the other. Sightseers now clamber up for views of the mighty river and the city. Within walking distance, the **Gandhi Museum** (daily except Sat 10am–5.30pm) is worth a quick visit for its pictures of the Mahatma's life.

The **Patna Museum** on Buddha Marg (Tues–Sun 10.30am–4.30pm; Rs250 [Rs10]), although faded and run-down, has an excellent collection of sculptures. Among its most famous exhibits is a polished sandstone female attendant, or *yakshi*, holding a fly-whisk, dating back to the third century BC. There are also Jain images from the Kushana period, a group of Buddhist *bodhisattvas* from Gandhara (in northwest Pakistan), some freakishly deformed stuffed animals and a gigantic fossilized tree thought to be 200 million years old. Don't bother paying the Rs500 [Rs100] extra to see the Buddha relic.

Founded in 1900, the **Khuda Bhaksh Oriental Library** (daily except Fri 9am–5pm), east of Gandhi Maidan, has a remarkable selection of books from across the Islamic world, including manuscripts rescued from the Moorish University in Cordoba, Spain, and a tiny Koran measuring just 25mm in width.

Har Mandir Sahib and beyond

In the most interesting area of Patna – the older part of town, 10km east of Gandhi Maidan – filthy congested lanes lead to **Har Mandir Sahib**, the second holiest of the four great Sikh shrines known as *takhts* (thrones). Set in an expansive courtyard off the main road, the dazzling white onion-domed marble temple is dedicated to Guru Gobind Singh, born in Patna in 1660. Visitors can explore the courtyard and even venture inside where devotional music is often playing. Remove your shoes and cover your head before entering. Shared auto-rickshaws cost around Rs10 from Gandhi Maidan.

A short way northeast, the private **Qila House** (or Jalan Museum; visits by appointment; ⓣ0612/264 2354) on Jalan Avenue holds a fine collection of art, including Chinese paintings and Mughal filigree work in jade and silver. Among the antiques are porcelain items that once belonged to Marie Antoinette, and Napoleon's four-poster bed. To the west, the East India Company's **Old Opium Warehouse** at **Gulzarbagh** is now home to a government printing press.

Midway between Har Mandir Sahib and Gandhi Maidan stands **Saif Khan's Mosque** or the "mosque of stone", built by Parwez Shah, son of the great Mughal emperor Jahangir.

Eating

There are several decent **restaurants** strung along Fraser Road, although most double as bars in the evening when the custom is all male. *Bansi Vihar* is a narrow, dimly-lit dining hall packed with locals, who come to sample tasty south Indian snacks, primarily dosas, of which there are twenty varieties (Rs32–75). Also on Fraser Road is *Gandhi's*, a polished and super-hygienic pure-veg restaurant (mains Rs65–130) that serves a rich *paneer* butter masala and seasonal hot *gulab jamun*. There are also a number of good hotel restaurants, including the *Bellpepper* at the *Hotel Windsor*, serving excellent tandoori dishes (non-veg mains Rs90–230), *Takshila* at the *Hotel Chanakya*, with a Mughlai and Afghan menu (non-veg mains Rs130–375), and the delightful fairy garden terrace restaurant at the *Garden Court*

Club (non-veg mains Rs80–160). Also keep an eye out for *littis* – baked balls of spiced chickpea dough – a Bihari speciality sold by street vendors.

Around Patna

Patna is a good base for exploring Nalanda, Rajgir and Vaishali (see below & p.80), but there are also places of interest closer at hand, notably the fabulous hilltop *dargah* at **Muner**, 27km west. The imposing but sadly neglected red sandstone shrine of Sufi saint Yahia Muneri, 1km west of Muner, was built in 1605. Every year, around February, a three-day *urs*, or festival, in the saint's honour attracts pilgrims from far and wide, with *qawwals* by Sufi musicians from Delhi and Ajmer. Muner is also known for its **sweets**, particularly lentil *ladoos*.

If you're in Bihar between early November and early December, don't miss the **Sonepur Mela**, staged 25km north of Patna across the huge Gandhi Bridge – Asia's longest river bridge – at the confluence of the Gandak and the Ganges. Cattle, elephants, camels, parakeets and other animals are brought for sale, pilgrims combine business with a dip in the Ganges, sadhus congregate, and festivities abound. The event is memorably described by Mark Shand in his quixotic *Travels on My Elephant* (see p.1186). The Bihar State Tourism Development Corporation in Patna (see p.793) organizes tours and maintains a tourist village at Sonepur during the *mela* (❶–❹).

Vaishali

Set amid paddy fields 55km north of Patna, the quiet village of **VAISHALI** was the site of the Buddha's last sermon. Named after King Visala, who is mentioned in the Ramayana, Vaishali is also believed by some historians to have been the first city-state in the world to practise a democratic, republican form of government. After leaving his family and renouncing the world, Prince Gautama studied here, but eventually rejected his master's teachings and found his own path to enlightenment. He returned to Vaishali three times and on his last visit announced his final liberation – *Mahaparinirvana* – and departure from the world, in around 483 BC. A hundred years later, the second Buddhist Council was held in Vaishali and two *stupas* erected.

A small but well-presented **archeological museum** (daily except Fri 10am–5pm; Rs2) provides a glimpse into the ancient Buddhist world. A short path next to the Coronation Tank (Abhishekh Pushkarni) leads off to the remains of the **stupa** where the ashes of the Buddha were reputedly found in a silver urn.

Two kilometres north among the ruins of **Kolhua**, the remarkably well-preserved **Ashokan Pillar** was erected by the Mauryan emperor (273–232 BC) to

Madhubani paintings

Jitwarpur, a village on the outskirts of the small town of **Madhubani**, in northern Bihar, is home to a vibrant tradition of folk art. Madhubani **paintings** by local women were originally decorations for the outside of village huts. The illustrations of mythological themes – including images of local deities as well as Hindu gods and goddesses – the paintings were eventually transferred onto handmade paper, often using bright primary colours to fill the strong black line drawings. **Fabrics** printed with Madhubani designs have become very chic; these days they tend to be professionally made elsewhere, and are sold in the expensive boutiques of India's major cities, although you can still pick them up cheaply in Madhubani itself.

Buses connect Patna to Madhubani (5hr 30min), where there are some basic hotels; rickshaws can take you on to Jitwarpur.

commemorate the site of Buddha's last sermon. Known locally as Bhimsen-ki-lathi (Bhimsen's Staff), the 18.3m-high pillar, made of polished red sandstone, is crowned by a lion sitting on an inverted lotus, which faces north towards Kushinagar, where Buddha died. Jains of the Svetambara sect, who believe that the last *tirthankara*, **Mahavira**, was born in Vaishali in 599 BC, have erected a **shrine** in the fields 1km east of Kolhua.

Travel agents in Patna can arrange **transport** to Vaishali or you can take a bus from Gandhi Maidan Bus Stand to Sonepur or Hajipur, and change there onto another bus or a shared taxi. There is no **accommodation** in Vaishali as such (most people take it in as a day-trip from Patna), but Hajipur has a handful of very simple hotels.

The road to Nepal

Some 55km north of Vaishali, **KESARIYA** (Kessaputta) has an impressive five-terraced eighth-century *stupa* said to have been built on top of one erected by the Buddha's Licchavi disciples after he announced he was about to attain nirvana and gave them his begging bowl as a souvenir. To get to Kesariya, take a bus (3hr) from Vaishali to **CHAKIA**, 20km away, then a taxi or rickshaw to the site.

In 1917, **MOTIHARI**, a poor and lawless town 298km north of Patna, was the site of one of Gandhi's first acts of civil disobedience – he refused bail after being arrested for protesting the plight of local farmers, who were being forced to grow indigo for the British textile industry. There's a small **museum** with photos and items such as Gandhi's walking stick and slippers. Motihari was also the birthplace of **George Orwell**, whose father worked here as a government opium agent. There are *dharamshalas* if you want to stay.

The border crossing for **Nepal** is at **RAXAUL**, a grubby, mosquito-infested town with limited amenities – you're better off staying over the border in Birganj. If you do have to spend the night, the functional *Kaveri* **hotel** on Main Road (Ⓣ06255/221148; ❶) is about the best Raxaul has to offer. There's a **café** along the main road by the cinema, serving the local dish of kebab and *muri* (puffed rice).

The border between Raxaul and the Nepalese town of **Birganj**, 5km away (Rs50 by auto-rickshaw), is open 24 hours for foreigners, but visas ($30 in cash, plus two passport photos; pay at border crossing) are only available from 5.30am–8pm. Early morning and night buses run from Birganj to Kathmandu (8–12hr) and Pokhara (10–12hr). Minibuses are quicker but cost slightly more – reserve a seat in advance if possible. The foreign exchange facility in Raxaul will only change Indian to Nepalese rupees, but Birganj has facilities for travellers' cheques and US dollars.

Gaya

GAYA, 100km south of Patna, is a transit point for visitors to **Bodhgaya**, 13km away. Gaya has no real tourist attractions but many Hindus come here to honour their parents a year after death by offering *pinda* – funeral cakes – at the massive **Vishnupad temple** (no entry to non-Hindus). Pilgrims also bathe at the riverside *ghats*. **Brahmajuni Hill**, 1km southeast of the Vishnupad temple, is said to be where Buddha preached his fire sermon.

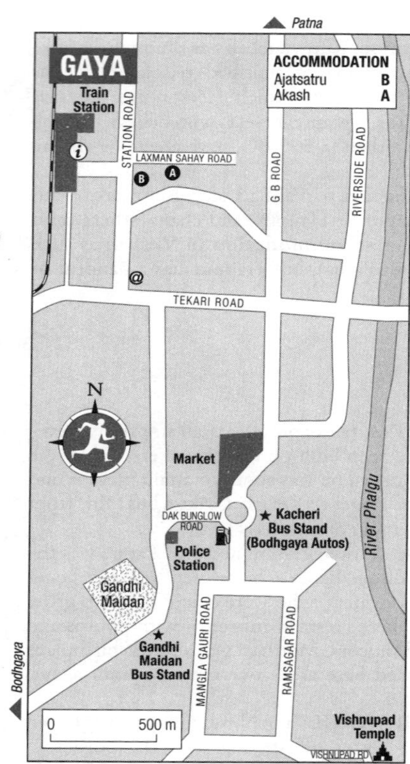

Practicalities

Most people arrive by **train**. Autorickshaws will take you to Bodghaya from the station (Rs90–100, though you may find a shared one), or you can take a cycle rickshaw to Kacheri Bus Stand and can continue to Bodhgaya by shared auto (Rs10). If you arrive after dark, stay overnight in Gaya as the route between the two can be unsafe. There is a rather useless **tourist office** in the railway station (Mon–Sat 8am–8pm but often closed; ⓣ0361/242 0155). I-Way and Vishal Cyber World on a narrow alley off Station Road have **internet** access (Rs25–35/hr; see which will offer the best rate).

Most of Gaya's **hotels** are on Station Road near the railway station. *Ajatsatru* (ⓣ0631/243 4584, ⓕ243 4202; ❷–❹) has grubby, basic rooms with squat toilets and cleaner, marginally more cheerful, but still overpriced, air-conditioned rooms. The downstairs restaurant, however, has good Indian and Chinese staples (non-veg mains Rs40–110). *Akash* (ⓣ0631/222 2205; ❶), close by on Laxman Sahay Road, is slightly better, offering simple rooms with squat toilets and hot water on request in a bucket (Rs10). If you have a train ticket, the **railway retiring rooms** are clean and some have air conditioning (Rs75–125) (❶–❸).

Bodhgaya

The world's most important Buddhist pilgrimage site, **BODHGAYA**, 13km south of Gaya, is wonderfully relaxed, with an array of monasteries, temples and retreats. Its focal point is the **Mahabodhi Temple**, where Buddha attained enlightenment.

The temple dates from the seventh century AD and flourished up to the sixteenth century, when it fell into the hands of Hindu priests, who professed to be baffled by its origins. In the early nineteenth century, British archeologists rediscovered its significance, and Bodhgaya has since been rejuvenated by overseas Buddhists, who have built monasteries, temples and shrines. From November to February, Bodhgaya is home to an animated community of exiled **Tibetans**, often including the Dalai Lama, as well as a stream of international Tibetophiles. Meditation courses (see p.803) attract others, while large monasteries from places like Darjeeling bring their followers to attend ceremonies and lectures. From mid-March to mid-October, the region becomes oppressively hot and Bodhgaya returns to its quiet ways.

The Mahabodhi Temple is also sacred to Hindus, who regard Buddha as an incarnation of Vishnu, and dominate the management committee, despite protests from the Buddhist world. The dispute is exacerbated by the contrasting forms of worship: Buddhists have a solitary inward approach; Hindus prefer spectacle and noisy ceremony.

Arrival and information

Gaya's international **airport** (ⓣ0631/221 0129) is around 12km west of Bodhgaya. There are **auto-rickshaws** to Bodhgaya from outside Gaya railway station (Rs90–100; less if you can find a shared one), and shared autos from Kacheri Bus Stand a couple of kilometres south (Rs10). An auto from the airport is Rs70–80. You'll need to travel back to Gaya for most onward services from Bodhgaya, although two direct daily buses (7am & 2pm) run from the Bihar State Tourism Corporation to Patna, and private buses to destinations including Ranchi, Raxaul, Varanasi and Siliguri leave from Kalchakra Maidan, especially in season.

The main **tourist office** in the Bihar State Tourism Corporation complex (Mon–Sat 10am–5pm; ⓣ0631/220 0672) is distinctly unenlightening but has a **computerized train reservation** booth next door. Middle Way Travels (ⓣ0631/220 0648, ⓔmiddleway_2006@yahoo.com), near the entrance to the temple, can arrange local tours and car rental, and book train, bus and flight tickets; beware of lookalike imitators. The Sri Lankan **Mahabodhi Society** (ⓣ0631/220 0742, ⓔmbsi_1891@yahoo.com), responsible for reviving Bodhgaya in the nineteenth century, maintains a small centre northwest of the Mahabodhi Temple and can offer advice on accommodation and **courses**.

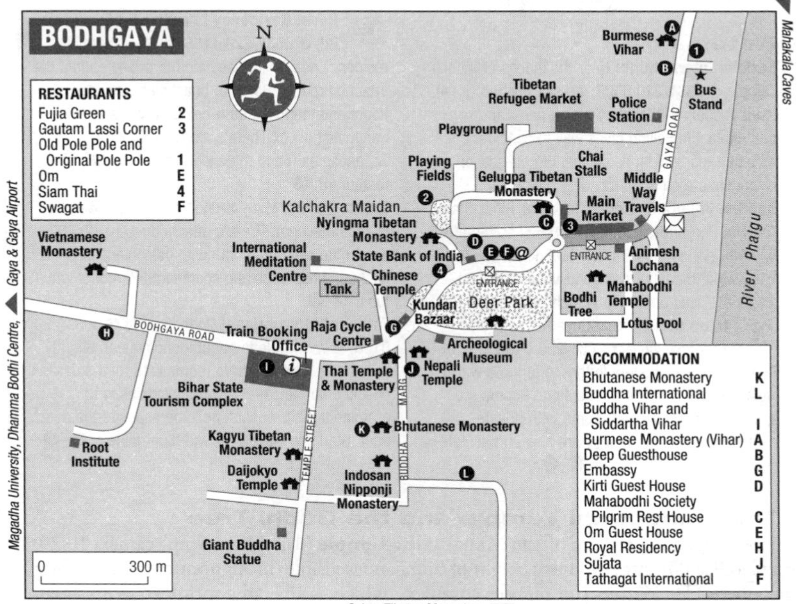

The State Bank of India (Mon–Fri 10.30am–4pm, Sat 10.30am–1.30pm) has **foreign exchange** and an **ATM** (there are others to its west along Bodhgaya Rd). NL Forex in Kundan Bazar, and Middle Way Travels (see p.801) also change cash and travellers' cheques, but compare rates and commissions before choosing where to change. Lotus Gems and Travel, close to *Hotel Tathagat International*, is among many places providing **internet** access (Rs30/hr). The Raja Cycle Centre, next door to the *Embassy Hotel*, is a good place to rent **bicycles**.

Accommodation

Outside the pilgrimage season (Nov–Feb) discounts of up to fifty percent are available in most hotels. Many **monastery guesthouses** welcome tourists, subject to the same rules as the pilgrims – in particular no smoking, alcohol or sex. The price codes below are based on recommended donations.

Monasteries

Bhutanese Monastery Buddha Marg ⓣ0631/220 0710. An old guesthouse, next to the monastery and full of character, with single and family rooms, some with private bathroom and hot water. ❶

Burmese Monastery (Vihar) Gaya Rd ⓣ0631/220 0721. Set in a pleasant garden, the rooms at this guesthouse are boxy but inexpensive. The absence of fans and the prevalence of biting insects will test your Buddhist indifference to personal comfort. ❶–❷

Mahabodhi Society Pilgrim Rest House (Sri Lankan Guest House) Bodhgaya Rd ⓣ0631/220 0742, ⓔmbsi_1891@yahoo.com. Very popular with pilgrims and often full, with a dorm (Rs50), a handful of private rooms and a modest veg canteen. ❶

Hotels

Buddha International Near the Indosan Nipponji Temple ⓣ0631/220 0506, ⓔask2pavitra@gmail.com. A cool marble lobby with a peculiar mini-stalactite ceiling gives way to spacious attached rooms with balconies. Big off-season discounts are on offer. ❺–❻

Buddha Vihar and **Siddartha Vihar** Bihar State Tourism Corporation complex ⓣ0631/220 0445. The former has three- to ten-bed dorms (Rs75–150), while the latter has good-value attached doubles. Prices don't rise in high season. ❸–❹

Deep Guesthouse Gaya Rd, near the *Burmese Vihar* ⓣ0631/220 0463. One of Bodhgaya's best budget lodges, offering a warm welcome and sociable atmosphere. Rooms are smallish but super-clean, some with private bathrooms, but shared ones are also immaculate, and there's 24hr hot water. ❶–❷

Embassy Bodhgaya Rd ⓣ0631/220 0799, ⓦwww.hotelembassybodhgaya.com. No-frills marble-floored rooms with gleaming bathrooms at this reliable mid-range hotel. ❹

Kirti Guest House Close to Kalchakra Maidan ⓣ0631/220 0744, ⓔkirtihouse744@yahoo.com. Serene guesthouse run by the Tibetan Monastery and accessed over a short bridge. The wood-panelled doubles with green carpets are a little overpriced, but the triples are great value. ❹–❺

Om Guest House Bodhgaya Rd ⓣ9934 057498. Not for the claustrophobic, and without the communal vibe of some other traveller places, *Om* nevertheless delivers spick-and-span rooms with attached bathrooms and primrose yellow walls. ❷–❹

Royal Residency Domuhan Rd (Bodhgaya Rd) ⓣ0631/220 1156, ⓦwww.theroyalresidency.net. An immaculate but pricey option: the attached rooms (Rs4950) boast sleek wooden floors and fittings, cream-coloured walls and minimalist decor. There's also a communal Japanese bath and the excellent *Amarapali* restaurant. ❽

Sujata Buddha Marg ⓣ0631/220 0481, ⓦwww.sujatahotel.com. The a/c attached rooms (Rs4620) are a little plain but come with balconies, gold-flecked bedspreads and sparkling bathrooms with tubs. ❼–❽

Tathagat International Bodhgaya Rd ⓣ0631/220 0106, ⓦwww.hoteltathagatbodhgaya.net. Slightly cramped but comfortable rooms with mini-sofas, checked curtains and private balconies in a prominent whitewashed building opposite the deer park. Staff can book train and flight tickets. ❺–❻

The Mahabodhi Temple and the Bodhi Tree

The elegant single spire of the **Mahabodhi Temple** (daily 4am–9pm; camera Rs20, video Rs500), rises to a lofty height of 55m, and is visible throughout the surrounding countryside. Within the temple complex, which is liberally sprinkled with small

Meditation courses in Bodhgaya

Especially during the winter high season, **meditation courses** are available in either of the two distinct traditions of Buddhism: Mahayana (the Great Vehicle), epitomized by the various forms of Tibetan Buddhism which spread across China and Japan; and Hinayana (or Theravada), as practised in Sri Lanka, Thailand and other parts of Southeast Asia. Check noticeboards in the various cafés, and ask at the *Root Institute* (see below) or the *Burmese Vihar*.

The **Root Institute for Wisdom Culture** (Ⓣ0631/220 0714, Ⓦwww.rootinstitute.com) is a real haven, a semi-monastic *dharma* centre 2km west of the main temple with pleasant gardens, a shrine room, library and accommodation. It organizes residential courses, focusing on the Mahayana tradition. There are drop-in meditation classes, one-day workshops and longer courses on Buddhism, yoga and meditation between October and March. A ten-day course, including fee, food and accommodation, typically costs from Rs7300 – book well in advance. The institute is always looking for volunteers (minimum three months) for general tasks and to help in its charitable school and polio, TB and mobile clinics.

The **Dhamma Bodhi International Meditation Centre** (Ⓣ0631/220 0437, Ⓦwww.bodhi.dhamma.org), a Vipassana centre, is a few kilometres out of town near Magadha University on Dobi Road, and holds regular courses throughout the year.

The **International Meditation Centre** (Ⓣ0631/220 0707), a couple of hundred metres behind the Chinese temple, also runs Vipassana courses for both beginners and advanced students; donations are accepted as there are no fixed fees.

Another centre of activity is the **Burmese Vihar**. Although not currently running meditation courses they have some useful information and are involved with voluntary social-work projects. **Insight Meditation** (Ⓦwww.bodhgayaretreats.org) runs seven- to ten-day Vipassana retreats with western teachers at the Thai Monastery.

stupas and shrines, the main brick temple stands in a hollow encircled by a stone railing dating from the second century BC. Shoes are tolerated within the grounds but not inside the temple: they can be left at the entrance. Guides also congregate at the entrance and charge around Rs100 per hour. Unlike most popular temples in India, this UNESCO World Heritage Site exudes an atmosphere of peace and tranquillity. Extensively renovated during the nineteenth century, it is supposed to be a replica of a seventh-century structure that in turn stood on the site of Ashoka's original third-century BC shrine. Inside the temple, a single chamber holds a large gilded image of the Buddha, while upstairs is a balcony and a small, plain meditation chamber.

At the rear of the temple to the west, the large **Bodhi Tree** grows out of an expansive base, attracting scholars and meditators, but it's only an off-shoot of the one under which the Buddha attained enlightenment – many legends surround the destruction of the original, but Ashoka, when he sent his daughter Sangamitra to Sri Lanka as an emissary of Buddhism, had sent a cutting with her. This had been planted at Anuradhapuram, and a cutting from that was later brought back to Bodhgaya and replanted. Pilgrims tie coloured thread to its branches and Tibetans accompany their rituals with long lines of butter lamps. A sandstone slab with carved sides next to the tree is believed to be the **Vajrasana**, or "thunder-seat", upon which Buddha sat facing east.

The small white **Animesh Lochana Temple** to the right of the compound entrance marks the spot where Buddha stood and gazed upon the Bodhi Tree in gratitude. Numerous ornate *stupa*s from the Pala period (seventh to twelfth centuries) are littered around the grounds and next to the temple compound to the south is a rectangular lotus pool where Buddha is believed to have bathed.

Temples and monasteries

Modern monasteries and temples around the Mahabodhi Temple open from around 7am until noon and between 2pm and 6pm. Some are very simple while others, like the **Thai Temple**, with its unmistakable roof, are elaborate confections. The **Gelugpa Tibetan Monastery**, or *gompa*, is within the Tibetan quarter northwest of the main shrine. The complex includes a central prayer hall, large prayer wheel and residential buildings. The bigger of the two other Tibetan monasteries further west belongs to the **Kagyu** sect; its spacious main prayer hall is decorated with beautiful modern murals, Buddha images and a large Dharma Chakra, or "Wheel of Law". The other two major Tibetan schools also have monastic representation here – there's a **Nyingma** *gompa* next to the Chinese temple and a small **Sakya** *gompa* close to *Hotel Buddha International*.

Next to the Kagyu Tibetan Monastery, the **Daijokyo Monastery** captures in concrete some elements of a traditional Japanese temple and belongs to the Nichiren sect. Opposite, the **Indosan Nipponji Temple** has an elegant and simple hut-like roof and a beautiful image of the Buddha inside its main hall. Next door, the exquisite **Bhutanese Monastery** features finely painted murals and ceiling mandalas. In a decorative garden at the end of the road, the imposing 25-metre Japanese-style **Giant Buddha Statue** was consecrated by the Dalai Lama in 1989.

Bodhgaya's **Archaeological Museum** (daily 8am–5pm; Rs5), west of the Mahabodhi Temple complex, has a collection of locally discovered sculptures and ninth-century bronzes of Hindu and Buddhist deities.

Eating

Bodhgaya has Bihar's widest range of places to eat, catering for visitors from all around the world. During November and February, Tibetan tent restaurants spring up throughout town – follow the crowds to find the best ones.

Fujia Green Kalchakra Maidan. An ever-popular Tibetan joint: a cross between a hut and a tent, with Christmas-style decorations and a vast array of *momos* (dumplings) and hearty noodle soups (Rs15–85).

Gautam Lassi Corner Opposite the Mahabodhi Temple entrance. A bustling low-key joint that does a brisk trade in refreshing lassis (try the pineapple flavour), freshly squeezed juices and instant coffee (Rs12–25).

Old Pole Pole and **Original Pole Pole** Opposite the *Burmese Vihar*. These neighbouring tent restaurants are locked in a dispute over which came first – either way they have similar traveller-oriented menus with big breakfasts, banana pancakes and cinnamon pastries (Rs20–70).

Om Bodhgaya Rd. Backpacker stalwart, serving dosas, chocolate chip cookies and apple pie (Rs20–85) as well as excellent-value thalis and set breakfasts (Rs50), with big portions and small prices.

Siam Thai Bodhgaya Rd. Appealing restaurant with reasonable Thai food. Try the red chicken curry or the jumbo prawns in yellow bean sauce (meat dishes Rs130–160, prawns Rs150–400). Thai food can be very hot, so ask them to go easy on the chilli if you prefer it mild.

Swagat *Hotel Tathagat International*. The dining room is a little dim but the menu has a tempting selection of veg and chicken burgers, north Indian dishes like *keema* mutton and decent stabs at continental mainstays such as chicken Kiev (non-veg mains Rs110–170).

Around Bodhgaya: Mahakala Caves

In remote, almost desert-like surroundings on the far side of the Falgu River, 18km northeast of Bodhgaya, sit the **Mahakala** (or Dungeshwari) **Caves**, where Buddha did the severe penance that resulted in the familiar image of him as a skeletal, emaciated figure. After years of extreme self-denial at Mahakala, he realized its futility and walked down to Bodhgaya, where he achieved nirvana. A short climb from the base of the impressive cliff leads to a Tibetan monastery and the small caves. A Buddhist shrine inside the main cave is run by Tibetans, although a Hindu priest has set up in competition.

Rajgir

Eighty kilometres northeast of Bodhgaya, the small market town of **RAJGIR** nestles in rocky hills that witnessed the meditations and teachings of both the Buddha and Mahavira, the founder of Jainism. The capital of the Magadha kingdom before Pataliputra (Patna), Rajgir was also where King Bimbisara converted to Buddhism. Rajgir is also considered a health resort because of its **hot springs**, which can get unpleasantly crowded.

A Japanese shrine at **Venuvana Vihara** marks the spot where a monastery was built for Buddha to live in, while at **Griddhakuta** (Vulture's Peak), on Ratnagiri Hill, 3km from the town centre, Buddha set in motion his second "Wheel of Law". The massive modern **Peace Pagoda**, built by the Japanese, dominates Ratnagiri Hill and can be reached by a rickety chairlift (daily 8.15am–1pm & 2–5pm, last ticket 4.30pm; Rs30). Griddhakuta is actually halfway down the hill, so you may prefer to wander down from here rather than climb back up to take the chair lift. Look out for the 26 Jain shrines on top of these hills, reached by a challenging trek attempted almost solely by Jain devotees. On an adjacent hill, in the **Saptaparni cave**, the first Buddhist council met to record the teachings of the Buddha after his death.

Practicalities

Rajgir is connected by **bus** to Gaya, Nalanda and sometimes Patna (for the latter you often have to change at Bihar Sharif, 25km away), and there are three daily **trains** from Patna, one of which actually starts in Delhi. You can also visit Rajgir as part of a long and tiring day-trip, including Nalanda and Pawapuri, from either Patna or Bodhgaya.

The town has several hotels, including the unique *Indo Hokke* (ⓣ06112/255 245, ⓦwww.theroyalresidency.net; ❾), 4km west of the bus stand, which fuses Japanese and Indian architectural influences. It has Japanese- and western-style rooms (Rs7313), a communal Japanese bath, and the outstanding *Lotus* restaurant (Indian and Chinese mains Rs75–120, Japanese dishes Rs150–400). Moving down the price scale, *Siddharth* (ⓣ06112/255616; ❹–❻), in Kund Market, a kilometre south of the bus stand, is a welcoming place with comfortable carpeted rooms with clean attached bathrooms. Run by the state tourist authority, *Gautam Vihar* (ⓣ06112/255273; ❷–❹), 300m from the bus station on the road to Nalanda, has spacious rooms with pleasant verandas, a decent dorm (Rs75) and a hit-and-miss garden restaurant. Outside of the hotels, *Green* **restaurant**, opposite the temple complex, offers reasonably priced Indian and Chinese food (non-veg mains Rs40–85) and a relaxed atmosphere on its terrace.

Nalanda and around

Founded in the fifth century AD by the Guptas, the great monastic **Buddhist university** of **NALANDA** attracted thousands of international students and teachers until it was sacked by the Afghan invader Bhaktiar Khilji in the twelfth century. Courses included philosophy, logic, theology, grammar, astronomy, mathematics and medicine. Education was provided free, supported by the revenue from surrounding villages and benefactors such as the eighth-century king of Sumatra.

Excavations have revealed nine levels of occupation on the site, dating back to the time of the Buddha and Mahavira in the sixth century BC. Most of it is now in ruins, but the orderliness and scale of what remains is staggering evidence of the strength of Buddhist civilization in its prime. The **site** (daily 9am–5.30pm or sunset if earlier; Rs100 [Rs5]) is strewn with the remains of *stupas*, temples and eleven monasteries, their thick walls impressively intact. Nalanda is now part of the modern Buddhist pilgrimage circuit, but even the casual tourist will appreciate taking the time to walk through the extensive site, or climb its massive 31-metre **stupa** for commanding views. Informative booklets available at the ticket booth render the numerous guides unnecessary. A small alfresco bar inside the grounds serves tea, coffee and soft drinks without the hassle of the touts and beggars at the entrance.

Nalanda Museum (daily except Fri 9am–5pm; Rs5) houses antiquities found here and at Rajgir, including Buddhist and Hindu bronzes and a number of undamaged statues of the Buddha. **Nava Nalanda Mahavihara**, the Pali postgraduate research institute, houses many rare Buddhist manuscripts, and is devoted to study and research in Pali literature and Buddhism.

Regular **buses** between Rajgir and Bihar Sharif (35km northeast, change here for Patna) stop at the turning to Nalanda, from where an assortment of transport, including shared tongas, is available for the remaining 2km to the gates of the site. The railway station, served by three daily trains each way between Rajgir and Patna, is 2km the other way. There are no hotels in Nalanda, but *Tourist Cafeteria* by the site entrance serves decent veg and non-veg food.

East of Nalanda

Eighteen kilometres east of Nalanda, at **PAWAPURI**, Mahavira, the founder of Jainism, is said to have attained enlightenment. He died and was cremated here around 500 BC, and the site is now a major draw for pilgrims, who come to visit the **Jalamandir**, a white marble temple in the centre of a lotus pond. Buses to Pawapuri run from Bihar Sharif.

A further 80km east of Pawapuri, at **MUNGER**, is the **Bihar School of Yoga** (ⓣ06344/222430, ⓦwww.yogamag.net). Led by Swami Niranjananda Saraswati, the ashram is the world's first accredited yoga university and runs popular four-month yoga courses (in English) from October to January, although short stays are also possible. Buses run from Bihar Sharif, or the ashram can help arrange transport. It has a sister school at Rikhia in Jharkhand.

15

Sikkim

* **Chaam** Catch this mysterious and colourful lama dance, held in most monasteries around the harvest festival of Losung (early December). See p.817, p.821, p.825 & p.827

* **Rumtek** One of Sikkim's most venerated monasteries, Rumtek is home to the Black Hat sect, and hosts a spectacular festival in February. See p.820

* **Maenam mountain** Take a day-trek through an ancient forest to the summit of the mountain – you may be lucky enough to spot red panda. See p.824

* **Varshey Rhododendron Sanctuary** Magnificent views and gentle trails through a botanical paradise. See p.826

* **Pemayangtse** A wonderful seventeenth-century monastery perched on a high ridge facing Darjeeling. See p.827

* **Dzongri and Singalila Trails** High-altitude treks through rhododendron forests, across high meadows and past remote lakes with breathtaking views of mighty Kanchenjunga. See p.830

* **Tashiding** An especially sacred monastic complex on a conical hill with marvellous views. See p.833

* **Yumthang** Walk through this spectacular rhododendron-filled valley with icy pinnacles towering overhead. See p.836

▲ Tibetan monks, Rumtek

The tiny and beautiful state of **SIKKIM** lies to the south of Tibet, sandwiched between Nepal to the west and Bhutan to the east. Measuring just 65km by 115km, its landscape ranges from sweltering deep valleys just 300m above sea level to lofty snow peaks such as Kanchenjunga (Kanchendzonga to the locals) which, at 8586m, is the third-highest mountain in the world. A small but growing network of tortuous roads penetrates this rugged and beautiful Himalayan wilderness.

For centuries Sikkim was an isolated, independent Buddhist kingdom, until war with China in the early 1960s led the Indian government to realize the area's strategic importance as a crucial corridor between Tibet and Bangladesh. As a result of its annexation by India in 1975, Sikkim has experienced dramatic changes. Now a fully-fledged Indian state, it is predominantly Hindu, with a population made up of 75 percent **Nepalese Gurungs**, and less than twenty percent **Lepchas**, its former rulers. Smaller proportions survive of **Bhutias**, of Tibetan stock, and **Limbus**, also possibly of Tibetan origin, who gave the state its name – *sukh-im*, "happy homeland". Nepali is now the lingua franca and the Nepalese are socially and politically the most dominant people in the state. However, the people of Sikkim continue to jealously guard their freedom and affluence and remain untouched by the Nepalese Gurkhas' autonomy movement in neighbouring Darjeeling who occasionally disrupt the only roads leading into the state. Although only Sikkimese can hold major shares in property and businesses, partnerships with Indian (non-Sikkimese) entrepreneurs and subsidies to indigenous Sikkimese industry have led to prosperity – fuelled by its special status within the union as well as the reopening of the lucrative trade route along its borders with **Tibet** at **Nathu La** – that's evident as soon as you cross the border from West Bengal.

Historically, culturally and spiritually, Sikkim's strongest links are with Tibet. The main draws for visitors are the state's off-the-beaten-track **trekking** and its many **monasteries**, over two hundred in all, mostly belonging to the ancient **Nyingmapa** sect. **Pemayangtse** in West Sikkim is the most historically significant, and houses an extraordinary wooden mandala depicting Guru Rinpoche's Heavenly Palace. **Tashiding**, a Nyingmapa monastery built in 1717, surrounded by prayer flags and *chortens* and looking across to snowcapped peaks, is considered Sikkim's holiest. **Rumtek** is the seat of the **Gyalwa Karmapa** – head of the **Karma Kagyu** lineage – and probably the wealthiest monastery in Sikkim. Besides monasteries and the staggering beauty of the land, many come to Sikkim to trek. The capital, **Gangtok**, a busy, colourful, bustling cosmopolitan town, perennially growing, is home to a bewildering array of trekking agents only too happy to take your money in dollars and to arrange the necessary permits.

River dams and roaming bears

Industrialization and the construction of **dams** and numerous **hydroelectric projects** on Sikkim's rivers has brought pressure on the state's diminishing indigenous population especially in Dzongu, the heartland of the Lepchas, threatening their lifestyle and heritage. Although the voice of their protest is now all but lost, the destruction of habitat and the extraordinary strain on the state's fragile road system is self-evident. For more information, visit ⓦwww.weepingsikkim.blogspot.com.

The loss of forest cover has also brought out **black bears** wandering into villages and towns, including the outskirts of Gangtok, foraging for food. Attacks are not uncommon and the State's only response seems to be to kill the unfortunate intruders rather than relocate them and protect their habitat.

Sikkim's gigantic mountain walls and steep wooded hillsides, drained by torrential rivers such as the **Teesta** and the **Rangit**, are a botanist's dream. The lower slopes abound in **orchids**, sprays of cardamom carpet the forest floor, and the land is rich with apple orchards, orange groves and terraced paddy fields (to the Tibetans, this was Denzong, "the land of rice"). At higher altitudes, monsoon mists cling to huge tracts of lichen-covered forests, where countless varieties of rhododendron carpet the hillsides and giant magnolia trees punctuate the deep verdant cover. Higher still, approaching the Tibetan plateau, larch and dwarf rhododendron give way to meadows abundant with gentians and potentilla. Sikkim's forests and wilderness areas are inhabited by a wealth of fauna, including extremely elusive snow leopards, tahr (wild goat on the Tibet plateau), *bharal* or blue sheep, black bear, flying squirrels and the symbol of Sikkim – the endangered **red panda**.

The **best time to visit** is between mid-March and June but especially March, April and May, when the rhododendrons and orchids bloom – although temperatures can be high at this time of year, especially in the valleys. Any earlier than that, and lingering winter snow can make high-altitude trekking arduous. During the monsoons, from the end of June until early September, rivers and some roads become impassable, though plants nurtured by the incessant rain erupt again into bloom towards the end of August. October (when orchids bloom once again) and November tend to have the clearest weather of all. The colourful harvest festival of **Losung** is in early December after which it can get bitterly cold (especially at high altitudes), with long periods of clear weather. The impact of global warming is proving tragic for Sikkim, with rapidly receding glaciers and unpredictable weather patterns resulting in excessive rain and the disruption of the state's fragile road systems.

Some history

No one knows quite when or how the **Lepchas** – or the Rong, as they call themselves – came to Sikkim, but their roots can be traced back to the animist

Permits and restrictions

Though foreigners need to obtain an **Inner Line Permit** (ILP) to visit Sikkim, getting one is a mere, if irritating, formality. Permits are available in India at the offices listed below and can also be obtained in advance along with your Indian visa, but agencies abroad charge exorbitant fees. In India Sikkim permits are **free**. Permits can be instantly acquired at the **Sikkim border** at Rangpo and there are plans also to make them available at Melli; go to the tourist office for an application form and then cross the road to have it registered by the police. If you're picking up your permit after arrival in India, you'll need two passport photographs, and photocopies of your passport and visa details.

Permits are date-specific and initially valid for fifteen days from entry (though at the time of writing this was being changed to an initial thirty days with an extension of a further thirty), normally renewable for a further fifteen days, and can be extended up to a maximum of sixty days. **Extensions** can be obtained at the Foreigners' Regional Registration Office, Kazi Road, Gangtok (☎03592/223041), and are also available through the superintendents of police at Mangan, Gyalshing and Namchi, the capitals of the three other districts. As well as Gangtok and its surroundings in East Sikkim, the general Sikkim permit (ILP) covers all of South Sikkim and most areas in the east and west of the state, apart from most high-altitude treks. Sensitive border areas, like Tsomgo Lake (also known as Changu or Tsangu) in East Sikkim, most of North Sikkim except for Mangan and its immediate vicinity, and all high-altitude treks including the Singalila Ridge and Dzongri, require the additional **Protected Area Permit** (PAP) (see box opposite); foreigners can only enter these areas in groups of at least two accompanied by representatives of approved travel agents who arrange the permits. Some areas, such as Nathu La on the border with Tibet in East Sikkim, and Gurudongma Lake in North Sikkim remain completely off-limits to foreigners.

Offices in India issuing permits

Airport immigration At the four main entry points: Delhi, Mumbai, Kolkata, Chennai.

Foreigners' Regional Registration Offices In Delhi, Mumbai, Kolkata and Chennai. Also in Darjeeling (see p.774 & p.779).

Sikkim House, 12–14 Panchsheel Marg, Chanakyapuri, New Delhi ☎011/2611 5346.

Sikkim Tourist Centre SNTC Bus Stand, Hill Cart Road, Siliguri ☎0354/251 2646.

Sikkim Tourist Information Centre Sikkim House, 4/1 Middleton St, Kolkata ☎033/2281 7905.

Trekking in Sikkim

Although the potential is huge, **high-altitude trekking** in Sikkim remains a restricted and expensive business. This is partly due to the stringent system of permits and the fact that foreigners have to pay for the services of Gangtok-based tour operators in US dollars.

Trekking **permits** (aka Protected Area Permits) for high-altitude treks are only available from the Sikkim Tourism offices in Gangtok (see p.815) and Delhi (see box opposite); trekking or tour operators in Gangtok (see p.813) make the necessary arrangements. Check papers before you set off, as the slightest error can lead to problems later on; check itineraries too as you don't want to be rushed, especially at altitude. Trekking parties consist of a minimum of two people; tour operators charge an official daily rate that ranges from $40 to $150 per head per day depending on group size and route.

The high-altitude treks most commonly offered by the operators are the **Dzongri–Goecha La** route (plus its variation starting from Uttarey) and the **Singalila Ridge**, both detailed on p.784 & pp.830–831. The exhilarating trek from **Lachen to Green Lake** is possible, but permission must be obtained from Delhi (most easily arranged through a Gangtok agent) at least three months in advance. At the moment, Dzongri still bears the brunt of the trekking industry in the state, and the pressure is beginning to tell severely on the environment. Softer, **low-level treks** such as the rhododendron trails around **Varshey** are a pleasant alternative (and only require local permits for protected forests), and there are numerous other rewarding possibilities throughout the state that you can do on your own. A word of **warning**: don't go trekking unaccompanied in forest areas due the threat of attack by **black bears** (see. p.808). The **Ecotourism and Conservation Society of Sikkim (ECOSS)** in Gangtok (Ⓣ03592/228211, Ⓦwww.sikkiminfo.net/ecoss) is an independent organization seeking to develop sustainable tourism while protecting natural resources, customs and the environment.

While most major peaks require special permits for **mountaineering** and permission from the Indian Mountaineering Foundation in Delhi (see p.65) with at least three months' notice, the Sikkim government, through the appropriate Gangtok trekking operator, hands out permits for Frey's Peak (5830m) near Chaurikhang on the Singalila Ridge; Thingchenkang (6010m) near Dzongri and Jopuno (5935m) in West Sikkim; and Lama Wangden (5868m) and Brumkhangse (5635m) in North Sikkim. On top of operational costs, fees starting at $350 (Rs15000 for Indians) are levied according to group size. Recommended Gangtok agents include Namgyal and Yak & Yeti (see p.813).

Nagas of the Indo-Burmese border. **Buddhism**, which arrived from Tibet in the thirteenth century, took its distinctive Sikkimese form four centuries later, when three Tibetan monks of the old Nyingmapa order, disenchanted with the rise of the reformist Gelugpas, migrated south and gathered at Yoksum in western Sikkim. Having consulted the oracle, they sent to Gangtok for a certain Phuntsog Namgyal, whom they crowned as the first **chogyal** or "righteous king" of Denzong in 1642. Both the secular and religious head of Sikkim, he was soon recognized by Tibet, and set about sweeping reforms. His domain was far larger than today's Sikkim, taking in Kalimpong and parts of western Bhutan.

Over the centuries, territory was lost to the Bhutanese, the Nepalese and the **British**. Sikkim originally ceded Darjeeling to the East India Company as a spa in 1817, but was forced to give up all claim to it in 1861 when the kingdom was declared a protectorate of the British. **Tibet**, which perceived Sikkim as a vassalage, objected and invaded in 1886, but a small British force sent in 1888 to Lhasa helped the British consolidate their hold. By importing workers from Nepal to work in the tea plantations of Sikkim, Darjeeling and Kalimpong, the British sought to diminish the strong Tibetan influence and helped alter the ethnic make-up of the region, with the new migrants soon outnumbering the indigenous population.

After Indian Independence, the reforming and intensely spiritual eleventh chogyal, **Tashi Namgyal**, strove hard until his death in 1962 to prevent the dissolution of his kingdom. Officially Sikkim was a protectorate of India, and the role of India became increasingly crucial, with the Chinese military build-up along the northern borders that culminated in an actual invasion early in the 1960s. His son **Palden Thondup**, the last chogyal, married as his second wife an American, Hope Cook, whose reforms as gyalmo (queen) did not prove popular and also came to irritate the Indian government. The embattled chogyal eventually succumbed to the demands of the Nepalese majority, and Sikkim was **annexed** by India in 1975 after a referendum with an overwhelming 97-percent majority. The chogyal remained as a figurehead until his death in 1981.

The state continues to be treated with care by the Indian government, partly through a lingering sense of unease amongst the disaffected Sikkimese minority and an increasingly complex ethnic patchwork but, more importantly, because Sikkim remains a bone of contention between India and China despite huge progress in cross-border diplomacy and trade. Today, the **Sikkim Democratic Front** forms the government of Sikkim; generous government subsidies and loans have helped to ensure that life remains generally contented, while extensive road-building is bringing benefits to remote communities despite the many landslides in recent years.

Gangtok

Capital of Sikkim, the overgrown and colourful hill-town of **GANGTOK** (1870m) occupies a rising ridge in the southeast of the state, on what used to be a busy trade route into Tibet. Today, rapid development means an ugly assortment of concrete multi-storey buildings is growing virtually unchecked, and the urban sprawl retains only a few traditional Sikkimese (688m) architectural elements. However, a short amble soon leads you away from the congested centre to bring you occasional glimpses of the snow-capped Himalayas, and on a good day you can see Kanchenjunga and the fluted pyramid of Siniolchu (6887m) poking above the surrounding hills. Though it lacks the colonial charm of nearby Darjeeling, Gangtok has a certain relaxed buzz with good food, bars and modern cafés alongside traditional markets where time seems to stand still.

While modern Gangtok epitomizes the recent changes in Sikkimese culture and politics, its Buddhist past is the root of its appeal for visitors, evident in the collection at the **Institute of Tibetology** and the charming **Enchey Monastery**, as well as the impressive **Rumtek Monastery**, 24km west of town. However, the **palace** on the wooded ridge above town, used by the chogyals between 1894 and 1975, is now out of bounds, part occupied by the government and a closed chapter in Sikkim's heritage. Sikkim's pride and joy, the **orchid**, is nurtured at several sites in and around Gangtok, and celebrated at the Flower Show Complex near **White Hall**, a colonial mansion on the ridge above town.

Arrival

Gangtok is not served directly by rail though a new line is being built to Melli; most travellers arrive by **jeep** from **Siliguri** in west Bengal (4hr 30min; see p.773), the current transport centre for the railhead at **New Jalpaiguri** (NJP) and for

Trekking and tour operators

All high-altitude treks in Sikkim have to be conducted in groups and arranged through the following **travel agents** or **tour operators**, all based in Gangtok, who will also secure the necessary permits. Prices vary a little between agents and according to route and group size: high-altitude treks cost $40–150 per person per day from established agencies, while low-altitude treks cost from $35. You can get lower rates, but ensure that quality is not compromised.

Adarsh Tours & Travels 17 Tse-ka Complex, Near Private Taxi Stand, NH-31A ⓣ03592/205053. A competitively priced and reliable operator, good for all transport, treks as well as motorbike tours.

Blue Sky Tours & Travels Tourism Building, MG Marg ⓣ9832 370680. Very helpful agency which specializes in jeep safaris, particularly in North Sikkim. Avoid their ski packages however.

Galaxy Tours & Treks, Metro Point, NH-31A ⓣ9832 014328. A new and ambitious agency run by Norgay from Lachung in North Sikkim, specialising in adventure travel and the ubiquitous jeep safari.

Himalayan Footprints Pineli Cottage, Upper Syari ⓣ9832 091078, ⓦwww.abouthimalayas.com. One of the few agencies run by a woman; they excel in nature tours and treks off the beaten track and village homestays, and run an extensive network throughout Northeast India.

Khangri Tours & Treks Tibet Road ⓣ03592/226050, ⓦwww.khangri.com. Owner Tsering Dorjee is an experienced trekking guide and a keen amateur botanist who can arrange cultural and monastic tours and treks throughout Sikkim, and who pioneered routes like the soft trek to Tosar Lake. Recommended.

Namgyal Treks & Tours Tibet Road ⓣ03592/203701 or ⓣ9434 033122, ⓦwww.namgyaltreks.net. Namgyal Sherpa is a highly capable and experienced high-altitude trek and expedition operator, recognized by both the Sikkim and Central Government tourist offices.

Sikkim Adventure 6th Mile, Tadong ⓣ03592/251250, ⓔsikkimorchid@hotmail.com. Sailesh Pradhan runs a plant nursery and is an extremely knowledgeable and enthusiastic botanist and specialist guide for trips focused around Sikkim's rich flora.

Sikkim Tours & Travels Church Road ⓣ03592/202188, ⓦwww.sikkimtours.com. Owner Lukendra is tremendously helpful and experienced, and specializes in nature tours and photography, birdwatching, homestays and treks.

Tashila Tours and Travels Below TNSS School Hall ⓣ03592/229842, ⓦwww.tashila.com. Experienced operator offering trekking, mountain-biking and kayaking and river-rafting expeditions, angling and monastery tours.

Yak & Yeti Zero Point, NH-31A ⓣ9233 522344, ⓦwww.yaknyeti.com. Experienced, reliable and well-equipped expedition specialists in mountaineering. Treks available too.

Bagdogra airport. Shared jeeps also run from **Darjeeling** and **Kalimpong**. A **helicopter** service, run in conjunction with Sikkim Tourism DC (ⓣ03592/203960), connects Bagdogra airport with Gangtok (Rs2200) but note that the baggage allowance is a mere 10kg though a larger helicopter is planned for the near future. An airport is being constructed at **Pakyong** (32km) southeast of Gangtok to take small passenger aircraft, and should be operational by 2011.

All **buses** run by **Sikkim Nationalized Transport (SNT)**, the state carrier, use the **SNT Bus Stand** on Paljor Stadium Road, but passengers may prefer to be dropped off earlier at Metro Point, MG Marg, which is more convenient for the tourist office and most hotels. Non-SNT buses stop at the **Private Bus Stand** just

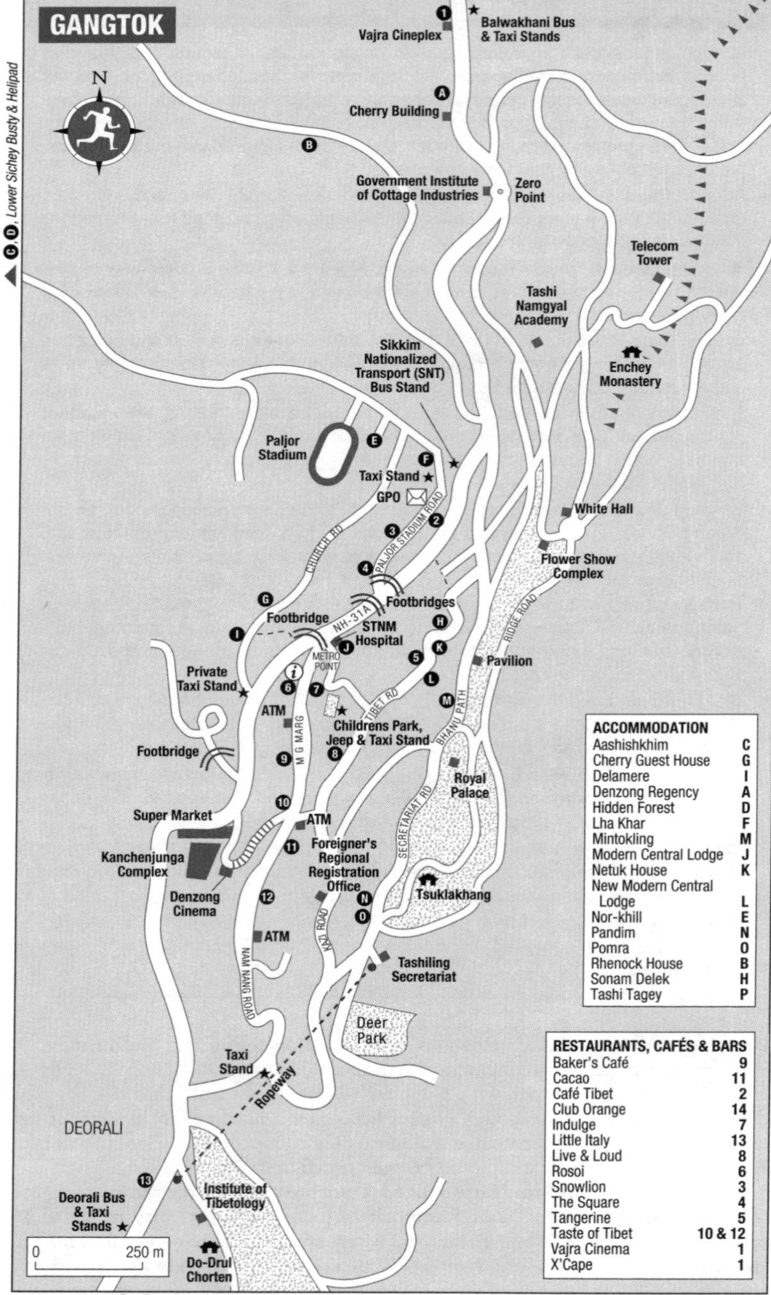

ACCOMMODATION	
Aashishkhim	C
Cherry Guest House	G
Delamere	I
Denzong Regency	A
Hidden Forest	D
Lha Khar	F
Mintokling	M
Modern Central Lodge	J
Netuk House	K
New Modern Central Lodge	L
Nor-khill	E
Pandim	N
Pomra	O
Rhenock House	B
Sonam Delek	H
Tashi Tagey	P

RESTAURANTS, CAFÉS & BARS	
Baker's Café	9
Cacao	11
Café Tibet	2
Club Orange	14
Indulge	7
Little Italy	13
Live & Loud	8
Rosoi	6
Snowlion	3
The Square	4
Tangerine	5
Taste of Tibet	10 & 12
Vajra Cinema	1
X'Cape	1

Moving on from Gangtok

The busiest route in and out of Sikkim is the road between Gangtok and Siliguri in West Bengal, site of the nearest airport (Bagdogra) and railway station (see p.773). Due to the Gurkha agitation in neighbouring Darjeeling District this route sees occasional closures, though the authorities endeavour to keep it open especially for emergency and tourist traffic.

Flights from Bagdogra can be booked either through Josse & Josse, MG Marg (℡03592/224682), agents for Jet Airways, or through Silk Route Tours and Travels, first floor, *Green Hotel*, MG Marg (℡03592/223354), who also sell tickets for the various airlines flying from Biratnagar (2hr from Siliguri) in eastern Nepal to Kathmandu. Sikkim Tourism Development Corporation, next to the tourist office (℡03592/203960) sells tickets for the **helicopter** flight (subject to weather conditions; daily 11am; Rs2200) to **Bagdogra** to connect with Indian Airlines and Jet flights. **Train reservations** from New Jalpaiguri can be made at the SNT complex on Paljor Stadium Road (Mon–Sat 8am–2pm, Sun 8–11am; ℡03592/222016), but the reservations quota for Gangtok is highly inadequate, so it's better to book in Siliguri.

With the deterioration in Sikkim's roads, shared **jeeps** are the most popular and efficient mode of transport. Jeeps to Siliguri (5–6hr; Rs120), New Jalpaiguri (NJP; Rs125), Kalimpong (3–4hr; Rs95) and Darjeeling (5–6hr; Rs125) leave from the Private Bus Stand on NH-31A below Deorali. Jeeps to other destinations within Sikkim, such as Gyalshing (4–5hr; Rs130), Pelling (5–6hr; Rs150) and Jorethang (3–4hr; Rs98) as well as to Rumtek (1hr; Rs30) leave from the Private Stand, NH-31A near Metro Point. Jeeps to North Sikkim depart from Balwakhani/Vajra. These services are timetabled and require **advance booking** (from the ticket booth at the taxi stand); all taxis and jeeps carry a rate chart. Those determined to suffer the **buses** can choose between SNT (Sikkim Nationalized Transport) or a number of private operators; services run to Kalimpong, Darjeeling and Siliguri in West Bengal and Jorethang in South Sikkim. See p.813 & below for details of bus stands in town.

off the National Highway (NH-31A) below Deorali, 2km south of the centre. Shared taxis and jeeps from Kalimpong, Darjeeling, Siliguri, NJP and Bagdogra also stop here; jeeps and taxis from East, West and South Sikkim terminate at the **Private Stand**, adjacent to the National Highway just below MG Marg and close to Metro Point; taxis and jeeps from North Sikkim terminate at **Balwakhani**, 1.5km north of the centre near the Vajra Cinema Hall.

With terminals at the Secretariat, Nam Nang and Deorali, the **ropeway** (daily 8am–6pm) provides a spectacular view of the southern city but is an expensive way to get around by local standards (Rs60 round trip, no one-way fare) and is not particularly useful for most accommodation. While it's scheduled to run every twelve minutes, in practice it waits to fill up before moving on. The numerous **shared local taxis** are the most common way of commuting along the main highway, with a ride from central Gangtok to Deorali costing around Rs8 per seat. After 9pm, taxis become scarce, but reserved taxis are available from stands near the SNT Bus Stand, the Private Bus Stand at Deorali, the supermarket, Children's Park between MG Marg and Tibet Road, and the Private Stand. All taxis carry a rate chart.

Information

Sikkim Tourism's **tourist information centre**, MG Marg (mid-March to early June & mid-Sept to Nov daily 9am–7pm; mid-June to mid-Sept & Dec–Feb Mon–Sat 10am–4pm; ℡03592/203960; Ⓦsikkimtournet.com), provides maps and will advise on arranging transport. This is also the place to extend your Sikkim permit from the initial fifteen days. Sikkim Tourism also sells tickets for their spectacular **helicopter flights** which operate on demand (from Rs7590 for a 15-minute flight or by charter for the entire aircraft at Rs1200/min) to West Sikkim, Yumthang, Gangtok and, the most breathtaking of them all, a ninety-minute Kanchenjunga trip up the Zemu Glacier. Note that cameras aren't allowed on most routes.

Accommodation

Gangtok's **hotels** are expensive in high season – broadly speaking April to June and September to November – but offer discounted rates at other times. Rooms with views are invariably more expensive. As the town spreads so does the choice of accommodation, with good hotels and excellent guesthouses springing up along the highway at Deorali and Tadong, and a growing number of alternatives away from the bustle but within striking distance of Gangtok.

Central Gangtok

Cherry Guest House Rai Cottage Complex, Church Rd ⓣ03592/205431 or ⓣ9932 351925. A short walk from MG Rd and the Bansilal taxi stand, this immaculate place set in a private courtyard offers a wide range of rooms, from plain to beautifully presented doubles opening onto large verandas with views. ❹–❻

Delamere Church Rd ⓣ03592/227646 or ⓣ9233 500158, ⓦwww.hoteldelamere.com. Central and modern, this lavish little hotel offers spotless, well-appointed rooms with tiled floors and good facilities that include a travel desk and a multi-cuisine restaurant but don't expect views; it's a short walk to the Metro Point. ❺–❻

Denzong Regency Cherry Banks ⓣ03592/201 565, ⓦwww.denzongregency.com. A pleasant location with quiet grounds away from the bustle of the bazaar but yet within easy walking distance, this brand-new hotel has a distinctive Sikkimese theme with large luxurious suite-like rooms, comfortable beds and a high level of service. ❽–❾

Lha Khar Opposite SNT Bus Stand, Paljor Stadium Rd ⓣ03592/225708. Clean but basic rooms with attached baths in a well-run modest guesthouse convenient for the SNT Bus Stand; its restaurant is simple but serves wholesome Sikkimese cooking with *thukpa* and *momos*. ❷–❸

Mintokling Bhanu Path (Tashiling Rd) ⓣ03592/228553, ⓦwww.mintokling.com. Run by an old Sikkimese family, with a lovely garden and a quiet location near the palace, high above the market yet in pleasant walking distance. Its twelve comfortable, airy rooms have good views over the valley to the mountains. ❺

Modern Central Lodge Metro Point ⓣ03592/221 081. Next to the bridge and suffering from traffic noise above this busy intersection; all doubles have attached baths while the better upper rooms are more expensive. There's a great terrace. Dorm Rs100. ❶–❸

Netuk House Tibet Rd ⓣ03592/226778, ⓔnetukhouse@gmail.com. A family home near the centre, with a comfortable hotel annexe: warm, atmospheric and beautifully presented, with Sikkimese decor and a pleasant roof terrace. The fully catered option is Rs4150 for a double. ❻

New Modern Central Lodge Tibet Rd ⓣ03592/201361. A bit run-down with indifferent service but still popular and geared towards backpackers, with a traveller-friendly restaurant and some rooms with attached baths and running hot water; dorms Rs100. ❶–❷

Nor-khill Paljor Stadium Rd ⓣ03592/225637, ⓦwww.elginhotels.com. Luxurious former royal guesthouse of the chogyal, this landmark hotel offers one of the finest address in town. Plush rooms in grand Sikkimese style, a good restaurant and cosy bar, but the location, overlooking the sports stadium, is poor; prices include all meals. ❾

Pandim Secretariat Rd ⓣ03592/227540. Welcoming and pleasant budget hotel with plain rooms (some on the dark side) and a superb location high above town – the rooftop restaurant has dramatic views and the Sikkimese cuisine is excellent. For more comfort try *Pomra* (❹–❺) next door ❸–❹

Sonam Delek Tibet Rd ⓣ03592/202566, ⓦwww.hotelsonamdelek.com. High above the bazaar, this reliable hotel has been tastefully refurbished offering a range of comfortable rooms most with views, a good restaurant and an expansive panorama from the terrace across the valley to the mountains. ❹–❻

Around Gangtok

Aashishkhim Indira Bypass, Helipad Rd, Lower Burtuk ⓣ03592/284500 or ⓣ9932 308551, ⓦwww.aashishkhim.com. A quiet spot, a beautiful lush garden, this is a family home with large comfortable if plain rooms and a relaxing living room, 2km away from the bustle of the centre. ❺

Hidden Forest Lower Sichey Busty ⓣ03592/205197, ⓦwww.hiddenforestretreat.com. A 2km taxi ride from the SNT bus terminus and Paljor Stadium brings you to this tranquil idyll, with organic food and sublimely comfortable cottages in a family-run nursery specializing in orchids and azaleas. Extremely good value. ❺

Rhenock House Jeewan Theeng Marg, Development Area ⓣ03592/204883 or ⓣ9832 096281. 1.5km north of Metro Point, a quiet, contemporary villa with comfortable clean rooms, good service, a restaurant and small bar and views across to Gangtok from the garden. ❻–❼

Tashi Tagey NH-31A, near State Bank of India, Tadong ⓣ03592/231631, ⓦwww.tashitagey.com. Small, welcoming Tibetan family-run hotel 4km from central Gangtok. Clean and homely, with a good licensed restaurant popular with locals and great for Tibetan home-cooking; there are more rooms in the annexe which also has a dorm for Rs250. It's a steep 15min walk up to Do-Drul *chorten*, and Gangtok is an easy Rs12 taxi ride away. ❹–❺

The Town

Though central Gangtok – which means "the hilltop" – is concentrated immediately below the palace, its unchecked urban sprawl begins almost as soon as the road rises from the valley floor at Ranipool, 11km southwest. Most of the town itself looks west; one explanation for the lack of development east of the ridge is that tradition dictates that houses face northwest, towards Kanchenjunga, Sikkim's guardian. Unlike Darjeeling, Gangtok is not renowned for its snow views but these are, nevertheless, available at different points including at **Tashi Viewpoint**, 5km to the north, best taken in at sunrise.

The town's best shopping areas are the **Main Market**, stretching for a kilometre along the pedestrianized MG Marg, and the local produce bazaar in the concrete **Kanchenjunga Shopping Complex**. Stalls sell dried fish, yak's cheese (*churpi*), and yeast for making the local beer, *tomba*. At the huge complex run by the **Government Institute of Cottage Industries**, on the National Highway north of the centre, visitors can watch rural Sikkimese create carpets, hand-loomed fabrics, *thangka* paintings and wooden objects, and buy their work at fixed prices. Curio shops on MG Marg and on Paljor Stadium Road sell turquoise and coral jewellery, plus religious objects such as silver ritual bowls and beads.

Right at the top of town just below a colossal telecom tower, 3km from the centre and reached by several roads (the most picturesque follow the west side of the ridge), **Enchey Monastery** is a small two-storey Nyingmapa *gompa*. It was built in the mid-nineteenth century on a site blessed by the Tantric master Druptob Karpo, who was renowned for his ability to fly. Visitors are welcome; the best time to go is between 7am and 8am, when the monastery is busy and the light is good. Surrounded by tall pines, and housing over a hundred monks, it's a real gem of a place. Built by the chogyal on traditional Tibetan lines, its beautifully painted porch holds murals of protective deities and the wheel of law, while the conch shells that grace the doors are auspicious Buddhist symbols. Enchey holds an annual *chaam*, or masked lama dance, during the Losung festival around early December according to the lunar calendar.

The walk down from Enchey leads to the **Flower Show Complex** (daily 10am–5pm; Rs10) at the northern end of Ridge Road near White Hall, where a large well-maintained greenhouse has a good collection of orchids and other Himalayan plants laid out around a set of water features. The complex, with a shop selling seeds, plants and bulbs, used to host the annual **International**

Flower Festival in March and April; it's sometimes staged at **Saramsa**, 14km from Gangtok near Ranipul. Although in theory guards deny entry to the **Royal Palace** to anyone without permission, visitors not carrying cameras are occasionally granted access to **Tsuklakhang**, the yellow-roofed royal chapel at its far end, to see its impressive murals, Buddhist images and vast collection of manuscripts. Here too there's a lama dance, known as *kagyat*, at the end of December, during which the main gates are open to the public; some years the *kagyat* takes place in Pemayangtse (see p.827) instead.

Beyond the chapel the road meanders down to the small **Deer Park** (daily 10am–4pm; free) and beyond to Deorali, 3km from the centre on the National Highway, where, set in wooded grounds, is the museum-cum-library of the **Namgyal Institute of Tibetology** (Mon–Sat 10am–4pm, closed 2nd Sat of each month; Rs10). Here you can see an impressive collection of books and rare manuscripts, as well as religious and art objects such as exquisite *thangkas* (scrolls) and a photography archive. You can also get here from the upper town via the new ropeway (see p.815).

A couple of hundred metres beyond the Institute on the brow of the hill, an imposing whitewashed *chorten* (see p.493), known as the **Do-Drul Chorten** – one of the most important in Sikkim – dominates a large, lively monastic seminary. The *chorten* is capped by a gilded tower, whose rising steps signify the thirteen steps to nirvana; the sun and moon symbol at the top stands for the union of opposites and the elements of ether and air surrounded by 108 prayer wheels. Behind the monastic complex, a prayer hall houses a large image of **Guru Rinpoche** (Padmasambhava) who brought Buddhism to Tibet at the request of King Trisong Detsen in the eighth century AD. He later travelled through Sikkim hiding precious manuscripts (*termas*) in caves, for discovery at a future date by *tertons*. Curiously, part of the head of the image projects into the ceiling protected by a raised section of roof; belief has it that the image is slowly growing.

Eating, drinking and nightlife

Some of the best food is served in the restaurants of hotels, and there are several fast-food places and patisseries in town, too. Most restaurants serve **alcohol**. "Foreign" liquor such as brandy and beer is cheap enough, but *tomba* (see box opposite) is usually found in less salubrious places where the mixture might be doctored to make it stronger; for a better-quality brew, try the more expensive hotels. Note that the Sikkimese have alcohol-free days during full moon. Of Gangtok's **cinemas,** *X'Cape*, at Vajra Cineplex, Balwakhani is state of the art while Denzong in Lall Market has been around for years – both show a mix of Indian and Hollywood films.

Baker's Café MG Marg. A modern patisserie a short walk from the tourist office, with a tempting selection of cakes and pizzas, as well as good filter coffee and a selection of fruit drinks. There's another outlet on the national highway near the Private Bus Stand.

Cacao MG Marg. A pleasant modern café and patisserie offering cakes, sandwiches, burgers, pizzas and great coffee, with a very well-placed terrace and tables overlooking the promenade, great for people-watching or just meeting up with friends.

Café Tibet NH-31A, past the hospital. Run by the *Hotel Tibet*, this lively café is popular with students, and serves pizzas and burgers, croissants, cakes and ice cream.

Club Orange *Orange Village Resort*, Ranipool, NH-31A. A large, well-stocked bar and disco with mezzanine floors, popular with a yuppyish set who drive down from Gangtok, especially at the weekends. Rs500 entrance.

Indulge Children's Park. This chic new upstairs hang-out is *the* place to be in the centre of town. Despite the mood lighting, Nirvana posters and bar-like atmosphere, the food is surprisingly good, from Indian and Chinese to local delicacies.

Little Italy Deorali, next to the petrol pump. Very popular, trendy upstairs bar-restaurant that serves

Flavours of Sikkim

Sikkimese food is a melange of Nepalese, Tibetan and Indian influences; rice is a staple and dhal is readily available, while **gyakho** is a traditional chimney stew served on special occasions. Sikkimese delicacies include **ningro** (fern rings), **shisnu** (nettle soup), **phing** (glass noodles), and **churpi** (yak cheese) cooked with chillies. Look out for **tomba,** a traditional drink consisting largely of fermented millet, with a few grains of rice for flavour, served in a wooden or bamboo mug and sipped through a bamboo straw. The mug is occasionally topped up with hot water; once it's been allowed to sit for a few minutes, you're left with a pleasant warm, milky beer best on a cold evening.

Italian food and is especially good for pizzas. Occasional live music.

Live & Loud Tibet Rd. A hip bar/restaurant with large sofas and live music, particularly at weekends when it gets packed for bands brought in from far and wide.

Rosoi MG Marg, next to the tourist information office. An old favourite in the heart of town, now reinvented as a good-value, multi-cuisine vegetarian restaurant best for Indian food; there's no bar, however.

Snowlion *Hotel Tibet*, Paljor Stadium Rd ☎03592/222523 or ☎223468. Still the best restaurant in Gangtok. The superb Tibetan and Indian food, with a selection of Sikkimese and Japanese dishes, is expensive by local standards (from around Rs700 a meal) but highly recommended.

The Square Paljor Stadium Rd, next to *Mount Jopuno*. Bright little café-bistro which offers a small but varied menu including good Thai, Continental and Nepalese cuisine. There's a bar, and great views.

Taste of Tibet *Hotel Bayul*, MG Marg. A café popular with locals for its good wholesome local cuisine, serving *momos*, *thukpa* and the ubiquitous chow mein all at reasonable prices. There is another branch a short distance south along MG Marg.

Tangerine *Chumbi Residency* hotel, Tibet Rd. Plush, elegant yet affordable restaurant serving Indian, Chinese and Sikkimese specialities, including the intriguing *churpi ningro* (cheese and fern). The adjacent lounge bar is good for a relaxing drink.

X'Cape Vajra Cineplex, Balwakhani. A popular local disco in the cinema complex and reasonably central, though of late it's seen some of its clientele drift away to new and chic venues. Wed–Sun 7pm–midnight; Rs400.

Listings

Banks and exchange Axis Bank has a choice of several ATMs accepting Visa, MasterCard and Maestro along MG Marg and elsewhere, including one next to Sikkim Tourism. State Bank of India (SBI) near the tourist office and Metro Point, changes most currencies and travellers' cheques; some tour operators also offer competitive rates. If you're travelling into the interior, note exchange facilities and ATMs are few and far between beyond here.

Internet Besides hotel access, Gangtok has several internet cafés (around Rs30/hr) including the Web Centre, NH-31A near *Café Tibet,* and New Light on Tibet Rd.

Medical and police The STN Memorial Hospital, on the junction of NH-31A and Paljor Stadium Rd, has a 24hr emergency wing and an ambulance service (☎03592/222944). For police, call ☎100.

Post Office The main branch is on Paljor Stadium Rd.

Around Gangtok

The most obvious destinations for day-trips from Gangtok are the great Buddhist monasteries of **Rumtek** to the southwest, and **Phodong** to the north. Closer to Gangtok, there are three popular viewing-points offering panoramas of the **Kanchenjunga Range**. The most accessible is **Ganesh Tok**, a short drive or a steep 1 hour 30 minute walk from the TV tower and Enchey Monastery. A small

Ganesh shrine and views of Gangtok and the mountains reward those that make the climb. Opposite the shrine lies the **Himalayan Zoological Park** (daily 9am–4pm; Rs10, car Rs25) with large open enclosures for the conservation of red pandas, snow leopards and other endangered species. **Hanuman Tok** (2300m), 7km out of town on the road to Tsomgo Lake, is the site of a Hanuman temple, and the cremation ground of the Royal Family, with *chortens* containing relics of the deceased. On the road to Phodong 6km out of Gangtok, **Tashi View Point** provides views of the eastern aspects of Kanchenjunga (whose tent-like appearance here is radically different from the way it looks from Darjeeling) and the snowy pyramid of Siniolchu (6887m), which the pioneering mountaineer Eric Shipton climbed and ranked among the most beautiful in the world.

Tsomgo Lake (pronounced "Changu"), 35km northeast of Gangtok and just 20km from the Tibetan border at **Nathu La**, is a scenic spot at an altitude of 3750m, popular with Indian visitors (foreigners and Indians need permits arranged through travel agents; see p.811) who flock here to sample the high-mountain environment and, hopefully, experience their first thrill of snow in the colder months. It's possible to visit the **Kyongnosla Alpine Sanctuary** (3350m) en route, where a profusion of wild flowers bloom between May and August and migratory birds stop over in winter on their annual journey from Siberia to India. Only Indians are allowed up to the trade post at **Serathang** and **Nathu La** (4130m), where they can gawk at bemused Chinese soldiers across the rope border marker.

Rumtek

Visible from Gangtok, and a 24-km trip southwest of the capital, the large *gompa* of **RUMTEK** is the main seat of the **Karma Kagyu** lineage – also known as the **Black Hat** sect – founded during the twelfth century by the first Gyalwa Karmapa, Dusun Khyenpa (1110–93). Dusun Khyenpa established the Tsurphu monastery in central Tibet near Lhasa, which became the headquarters of the Karma Kagyu for eight centuries until the Chinese invasion of Tibet in 1959. The sixteenth **Karmapa**, Rangjung Rigpe Dorje, fled Tibet for Sikkim, where he was invited to stay at the old Rumtek *gompa*. Within a couple of years, the Karmapa had begun the work of building a new monastery at Rumtek to become his new seat, on land donated by the Sikkimese king Chogyal Tashi Namgyal. One of the great Tibetan figures of the twentieth century, the sixteenth Karmapa was very influential in the spread of Tibetan Buddhism to the West, setting up over two hundred Karma Kagyu centres and raising funds for the rebuilding of Tsurphu. When he died in 1981, he left behind a wealthy monastery and a huge and lucrative international network, but one bitterly divided by an ugly squabble over his rightful successor. Two reincarnate Karmapas have now emerged as the main contenders to the throne – one blessed by the Dalai Lama and ensconced in Dharamsala, the other in nearby Kalimpong.

The new Rumtek, now heavily guarded against possible clashes between the feuding parties, is a large and lavish complex consisting of the main temple, golden *stupa*, and the Karma Shri Nalanda Institute, with a few smaller shrines and a guesthouse outside the monastery courtyard. Foreigners need to register passport details at the **checkpoint** off the bazaar. The **main temple** (daily 6am–5pm; Rs5; no photography allowed), with its ornate facade covered with intricate brightly painted wooden latticework, overlooks the expansive **courtyard**. Large red columns support the high roof of the **prayer hall**, where the walls are decorated with murals and *thangkas*. Visitors can attend daily rituals here, when lines of monks sit chanting. A chamber off the hall, used for Tantric rituals, is painted with gold against a black background and depicts wrathful protective deities. During

Losar, the Tibetan New Year (in Feb), the main courtyard stages a spectacular *chaam*, in which ceremonial **Black Hat dancers** spin to the sounds of horns, drums and clashing cymbals.

The **Karma Shri Nalanda Institute of Buddhist Studies**, behind the main temple, built in 1984 in traditional Tibetan style, is the most ornate of all the buildings of Rumtek. Monks spend a minimum of nine years studying here, followed by an optional three-year period of isolated meditation. The ashes of the sixteenth Karmapa are contained in a gilded four-metre-high *chorten* or *stupa*, studded with turquoise and coral, that sits in the **Golden Stupa** hall opposite the Institute. Behind the *stupa* is a central statue of Dorje Chang (Vajradhara) flanked by Tilopa, Naropa, Marpa and Milarepa, the four great Kagyu teachers. Statues of the previous sixteen Karmapas line the side walls.

Two kilometres beyond the new monastery and Rumtek village, a flower- and prayer flag-lined path leads to the simple **Old Rumtek Gompa**, the original monastery, founded in 1740 and recently renovated. The quiet setting, surrounded by empty outbuildings in traditional Sikkimese alpine style, with latticed wooden windows, is a world away from the charged atmosphere of the main complex. Behind the statues in the main prayer hall on the right side is a small shrine room dedicated to the Karma Kagyu protector Mahakala, an image so fierce that it is kept veiled.

The most rewarding route to Rumtek is via the impressive **Zum Gharwang** *gompa* of **Lingdum**, completed in 1998 and an easy 14km taxi ride (Rs30) from the centre of Gangtok. A haven of peace surrounded by deep woodland, the Lingdum is a grand example of modern monastic architecture, with an expansive terrace and courtyard. Inside, delicate and detailed murals depict the life of the Buddha.

Practicalities

If you don't arrange your own **transport**, the best way to get to Rumtek is by the shared jeeps that leave Gangtok from the Private Taxi Stand near Zero Point, when full (Rs30/head, Rs50 in the evenings). Similarly, jeeps returning to Gangtok do so on demand. In Rumtek itself, noodles and chai are available at the **teashops** clustered near the monastery gate and at the **bazaar**.

Accommodation

Rumtek has a limited choice of budget **accommodation**, but an increasing number of more upscale resorts offering a quiet alternative to crowded Gangtok.

Bamboo Resort Sajong, 1km before the monastery gates, ⓣ03592/252516 or ⓣ9232 513090, ⓦwww.bambooresort.com. A boutique hotel where Swiss chic meets formal Sikkimese style, set against a backdrop of forest with views towards Gangtok and Nathu La in the far distance. There's a herb garden, a herbal bath, library and a meditation room and mountain bikes are available to explore the countryside. Each bedroom has a unique colour scheme and breakfast and dinner are included in the price. ❼–❽

Sangay Near the monastery gates, ⓣ03592/252 238. Recently rebuilt into a contemporary concrete lodge where some of doubles come with attached baths. Local food – *momos* and *thukpa* – is available. ❷–❸

Sun-Gay ⓣ03592/252221. A welcoming guesthouse between the check-post and monastery gates, this is by far the best of the budget options, boasting large clean rooms, good home cooking, an expansive terrace and a garden guarded by a ferocious dog. ❷

Teen Taley Eco Garden Resort Lower Sajong ⓣ03592/252256, ⓦwww.sikkimresort.com. Around 2km from Rumtek and spread over six acres, this place is geared towards families with a small farm and guided walks, as well as mountain bikes for hire, pony riding and a pick-your-own organic vegetable garden. The mix of cottages, deluxe rooms and suites uses a blend of vernacular and modern architecture. ❻–❼

Zurmang Tara Hotel Lingdum ⓣ9933 008818. Run by Lingdum Monastery, with plain rooms and a restaurant, this is the only place to stay around here and is good for a quiet retreat. ❸–❹

Phodong and Labrang

The road to **Phodong**, 38km north of Gangtok on the Mangan road, another living monastery, but a far less ostentatious one, passes Kabi Lunchok, a pleasant wooded spot marking a historic treaty between the Lepchas and the Bhutias and some spectacular waterfalls. Lying on a spur of the hill 1km above the main road, Phodong commands superb views, and consists of a simple square main temple, several outhouses and residential quarters. Built in the early eighteenth century, this was Sikkim's pre-eminent Kagyu monastery until the growth of Rumtek in the 1960s. It too hosts colourful lama dances, similar to the *chaam* of Rumtek, each December. A rough road leads up a further 4km to another renovated old monastery – the unusual octagonal **Labrang**. A cluster of *chortens* between these two monasteries marks the ruins of **Tumlong**, Sikkim's capital city for most of the nineteenth century. The small bazaar of Phodong 3km on the main road has limited accommodation and cafés.

South Sikkim

Ignored by most travellers en route to higher trekking trails and the great *gompas* of West Sikkim, southern Sikkim nevertheless offers quiet charm, its lichen-covered forests draped with a stunning array of orchids and inhabited by rare and endangered animals. The region is dominated by the great, forested peak of **Maenam** – towering high above the town of **Ravangla** – a challenging day-trek and famous for its plants and flowers and for the tremendous view from its summit. Easier options such as the delightful jungle walk to the lesser heights of **Tendong** are just as rewarding, while high above the district capital **Namchi**, the gigantic statue and iconic symbol of modern Sikkim, **Samdruptse**, is clearly visible from as far away as Darjeeling.

Jorethang

The busy market town and crucial transport hub of **JORETHANG** lies in the very south of the state, just across the River Rangit from Singla Bazaar in West Bengal and a mere 30km north of Darjeeling, which is just visible high above the tea plantations. It is a useful supply stop, with a few decent budget **hotels** should you miss your connection and need to stay the night. The *Namgyal* (☎03595/276 852; ❸), next to the bridge and handy for the Darjeeling and SNT bus stands has good-value doubles with running hot water and a decent restaurant. *Walk-In* on Street No.2 serves good Indian and Chinese food, and also doubles as a popular bar. Jorethang is well connected by **bus** with the rest of Sikkim, and there is a direct service to Siliguri daily at 8am. Buses for Gangtok leave at 7.30am, for Pelling at 3pm, and Namchi at 8.30am. Shared **jeeps** make the extraordinarily steep 25-km journey to Darjeeling (2hr; Rs100), and go regularly to Legship (1hr; change here for Pelling, Ravangla, Yoksum and Tashiding) and to Namchi (1hr; Rs25); there are less frequent services to Gyalshing and Varshey. Jeeps travel regularly to Gangtok (4–5hr; Rs98) and Siliguri (4–5hr; Rs100). Few jeeps leave Jorethang after 1pm and the rule of thumb is to travel early.

Namchi and Samdruptse

Some 79km southeast of Gangtok and 24km to the northwest of Jorethang and pleasantly situated on a saddle at 1676m above sea level, busy **NAMCHI** is the administrative centre for South Sikkim, and is a popular magnet for domestic tourists due to the extraordinary statuary that is springing up around it. High above town, the gigantic 41m statue known as **Samdruptse** ("Guru Rinpoche"; daily 7am–5pm; Rs120 [Rs50]) sits on a ridge gazing south towards Darjeeling. Constructed by the government, the huge edifice has become one of South Sikkim's most popular attractions, its sheer size as much of an attraction as its spiritual significance. Inaugurated by the Dalai Lama in 2004, the statue cost Rs67,600,000 (around US$16 million) to build, and contains a meeting hall. Samdruptse lies 8km to the north of Namchi along the unfolding ridge; to get here, you'll either need to make the steep, gruelling climb past **Ngadak Monastery**, or take a jeep (Rs200) to the ornamental **Rock Garden** and then make a 3km climb up steps to the statue; taxis from Namchi's Central Park directly to the car park near the statue cost Rs250.

Not content with just one statue, the authorities have embarked upon yet another mammoth edifice, a 32m-high statue of the Hindu god Shiva towering on the top of **Solophok**, a hill high above Old Namchi, 5km to the south of town past the large Nyingmapa monastery of **Doling Gompa**. The more adventurous can opt for the trek up **Tendong Hill** (2623m) to a small monastery used by monks as a retreat. You can walk here from Samdruptse, but the trails are not clear and the best route is from the hamlet of **DAMTHANG**, 14km to the north of Namchi on the Ravangla road and accessible by shared taxi, from where it's a 6km trek along a pleasant brick-paved trail through dense, protected forest. **Beware** of **black bears** and take company. Tendong is especially revered by the Lepchas, who believe that the hill saved them from the great flood that once submerged the earth. On a clear day, the views from the summit stretch from the plains of Bengal to the high Himalayas, and in good weather it's worth camping at the top to catch the sunrise.

Namchi offers an increasing choice of **accommodation** near to the pedestrianized main square, Central Park, which has two magnificent trees including a pipal with an aquarium built around it. Some 200 metres down the Jorethang road, *Samdruptse* (Ⓣ03595/264708; ❷–❺) offers a large range of rooms, from grubby cubbyholes with shared facilities to more luxurious ones upstairs with attached baths; the bar and restaurant is one of the best in town, serving local, Indian and Chinese food. *Zimkhang* (Ⓣ03595/263625; ❸) on the square, has decent, clean budget rooms above a popular local bar and restaurant. *Kesang* (Ⓣ03595/263746; ❸–❺) near the pipal tree, has a handful of rooms renovated to a good standard above a first-floor bar and restaurant serving good mountain cuisine. There's an internet café below *Kesang,* and several ATMs in the vicinity of the square, including State Bank of India and Axis, take credit and debit cards (Visa and MasterCard). The town is well connected to all points in Sikkim as well as Siliguri, Kalimpong and Darjeeling; shared **jeeps** travel regularly (6am–2pm) to Gangtok (Rs90), Ravangla (Rs30), Gyalshing (Rs55) and to Jorethang (Rs25).

Ravangla and Maenam

Spread across a high saddle, 65km west of Gangtok and 52km east of Pelling, the sleepy market town of **RAVANGLA** (also known as Ravang and Rabang) makes for a convenient stopover, especially for those interested in trekking through one of the last remaining **rhododendron forests** in south-central Sikkim where the fabulous **Maenam Sanctuary** remains a botanist's dream, covering the flanks of the gigantic forested peak which looms over the town.

Moving on from Ravangla

Jeeps leave from the stand at the crossroads towards the southern end of the market, heading to **Gangtok** (Rs80) and **Namchi** (Rs40) via Damthang (Rs20), as well as Legship and Gyalshing. There are few direct taxis to Pelling (Rs80), so you'll need to change at Gyalshing; you can't be assured of regular transport much after midday. **Buses** travel to Gyalshing at around 11am and to Gangtok at around 9am and there are two to Namchi (9am & 1pm). The shortest route to Darjeeling is via Namchi, where you may have to change for a jeep or bus to Jorethang, and again there for Darjeeling.

Accommodation

There's a reasonable choice of **accommodation** on offer in and around Ravangla with plenty of choice along the Kewzing-Legship road.

10Zing Taxi Stand ⓣ03595/260705. The centrally located and friendly hotel at the main crossing offers small, plain rooms over a popular local restaurant and bar. ❷

Annexe at Mount Narsing Village Resort 3km along the Kewzing road ⓣ03595/260 558, ⓔyuksom@gmail.com. A quiet idyll, stunningly located, and a steep twenty-minute walk (or precarious jeep drive) up from the road to a plateau with open views. Comfortable chalets, built partly of local materials, are ringed around the main lodge where there's an open fire and a restaurant bedecked with lines of *tomba* vessels; the service is suitably low-key. ❹–❼

Reegyal Taxi Stand ⓣ03595/260221. Opposite *10Zing*, this hotel run by a Bengali is more comfortable and has a decent restaurant but hot water by the bucket. ❸–❹

Zumthang Kewzing Rd ⓣ03595/260870, ⓔzumthang@yahoo.com. On the outskirts of Ravangla, the delightful family offer a warm welcome and large, clean rooms, some with balconies; Karma can organize Buddhist retreats, voluntary work and homestays. ❸–❺

The town

Ravangla itself has a sizeable Tibetan settlement, with a handicrafts centre and shop at the **Kheunpheling Carpet Centre** in the refugee camp to the south. Steps north of the bazaar lead to a brand-new **Nyingmapa monastery** dedicated to Shakyamuni and Guru Rimpoche accompanied by stucco images of the wrathful protectors, alongside the old *gompa* within a recently landscaped garden graced by impressive dry-stone walls. This is the site of the annual three-day **Pang Lhabsol festival** in late August, which celebrates the worship of Kanchenjunga and draws thousands of Sikkimese to enjoy the traditional sports and **Pangtoed Chaam**, a festival of masked dances unique in that it is performed here, not by monks, but by *zigtempas* or lay people.

Maenem

The summit of **Maenam** (3235m), 10km from Ravangla bazaar, is home to a small chapel to Guru Rinpoche (Padma Sambhava) and boasts superlative views, weather permitting – the mountain's position on the watershed between the Teesta and the Rangit river systems means that overcast weather can veil the dramatic views of the horned summit of Narsing (5825m). Feasible as a day-trek, the stiff 1000-metre **ascent** of Maenam (2hr 30min–4hr) starts with steps rising from the bazaar up to the *gompa* before trailing off the road through the sanctuary where you may even be lucky enough to glimpse some wildlife, including the elusive red panda, black bear and a variety of birds. To catch the sunrise from the summit, take a good sleeping bag and food and water, as there is a dilapidated shelter in which to huddle from the elements, but little else. The route through the forest is confusing and you may want to take a local guide

Homestays

If you're interested in getting a taste of Sikkimese rural life, you might want to try a **homestay**, which provides some interesting insight into local communities and their customs. At the **Kewzing busti** (village), an idyllic spot surrounded by terraced fields just outside the sleepy market town of Kewzing, itself 8km east of Ravangla, Chewang Rinchen Bonpo's *Bon Farm House* (ⓣ9735 900165; ⓦwww.sikkimresorts.com, Rs1600 including food), has well-furnished wood-lined rooms with attached bathrooms and a common veranda; two new cottages are under construction. Chewang arranges nature walks and treks and is an expert on birds. The community itself represents an interesting mix of animist and Nyingmapa beliefs best seen in the small but very welcoming and rare pre-Buddhist, **Bon** *gompa* on the Ravangla road above Kewzing. Note that circumambulation is anti-clockwise.

Aside from Kewzing, there are also homestay options in **Yuksam** (contact Mr Pema Bhutia ⓣ9832 452527), **Pastenga** in eastern Sikkim (contact Mr Huna Rai ⓣ9832 033679) and **Dzongu** (contact Dr N.T. Lepcha ⓣ9434 179160). For more information visit ⓦsikkimtournet.com/WebForms/General/villagetourism.aspx

(Rs300), arranged through hotels in town or at the forest gate 1km above town where you pay an entry fee to the sanctuary (Rs25).

Nearby monasteries

Monasteries in the vicinity of Ravangla include the old and the new *gompas* at **Ralang**, 13km to the north, with shared jeeps (Rs30) travelling the route on demand. The old *gompa*, **Karma Rabtenling**, is linked to the ninth Karmapa and was founded in 1768. The new Ralang monastery, built in 1995 in much the same style as Rumtek, is one of the largest temple buildings in Sikkim. Usually held in December, the *chaam* (lama dance) which commemorates Losung (the end of the harvest) is a particularly colourful and local affair. The best place to stay around here is the idyllic and semi-rustic *Wildflower Retreat* (ⓣ9433 119535; ❺), a further 5km down the road at **Borong**; it's a good spot to unwind, enjoy the wonderful views of Narsing or walk to the hot springs (6km) by the Rangeet river. A challenging, **high-altitude trek** via the holy caves of **Lharingvigphuk** (3785m) ends at **Labdang** (31km), from where the occasional shared jeep travels the remaining 13km to **Tashiding** (see p.833). This is one of the few treks touching high altitude where you don't need a permit but a guide is recommended. For logistical support, try agencies such as Yuksom Tours & Treks (ⓣ03592/226822) of *Annexe at Mount Narsing Village Resort*, see opposite.

West Sikkim

This beautiful land, characterized by great tracts of virgin forest and deep river valleys, is home to ancient monasteries such as **Pemayangtse** and **Tashiding** and the attractive but rapidly developing town of **Pelling**. The old capital, **Yoksum**, lies at the start of the trail towards Dzongri and Kanchenjunga. In the far west, along the border with Nepal, the watershed of the Singalila Range rises along a single ridge, with giants such as Rathong and Kabru culminating in Kanchenjunga itself. Only two high-altitude trails are currently easily accessible but require **permits** (see p.811), and are expensive; however, several low-altitude treks with numerous variations provide ample opportunities to enjoy the wonderful profusion of orchids, rhododendron forests, waterfalls and terraced hillsides with

West Sikkim walks

The numerous trails crisscrossing the countryside of West Sikkim take you into the heart of the Singalila forests. Best visited between mid-April and mid-May, when the rhododendrons are in full bloom, the **Varshey Rhododendron Sanctuary** (aka Barsey or Varsey) covers 104 square kilometres, which range in altitude from 2840m to 4250m and are home to black bear, red panda and pheasant. Entry permits (Rs50 [Rs25]) for the sanctuary are available from forestry departments at **Hilley**, **Soreng**, **Uttarey** and **Gangtok**, and the most popular trail is the 8km round-trip from Hilley to **Varshey** (3030m), which offers majestic views. You can extend the walk to Uttarey (3–4 days with tented accommodation), from where you can either take transport to Jorethang and points en route, or continue on foot to the small town of **Dentam**. From Dentam, a river-valley trail leads to **Rinchenpong** (4–5hr), a good base for West Sikkim treks; another trail from Dentam leads east up the ridge to **Pelling** (4–5hr). There are numerous permutations and possibilities to trekking in this region including an extension, with prior arrangement with tour operators and the appropriate permits, into the long high-altitude **Singalila Ridge trek** to Dzongri and beyond (see pp.830–831).

Walk practicalities

Most Gangtok tour operators (see p.813) can arrange treks and tours of this part of West Sikkim or you can use local operators. Bases convenient to the sanctuary include the sylvan *Yangsum Farm* (ⓣ9733 085196, ⓦwww.yangsumfarm.com; ❽) below Rinchenpong, a working hill-farm with large, comfortable rooms furnished in local style, which can arrange forest walks and all-inclusive treks including transport, food, guides and tents. Closer to the sanctuary, *Gurash Kunj Lodge* (ⓣ9830 022469; ❺) at Varshey offers one double room and a dorm (Rs200); further choice is available at Soreng, Rinchenpong bazaar and Kaluk; all are connected by **jeep** services to Jorethang.

a backdrop of majestic vistas. If you're coming directly from Darjeeling via Jorethang for a high-altitude trek, arrange permits and itineraries in advance.

Gyalshing and Legship

The bustling market town of **GYALSHING** (pronounced and also known as Geyzing), 110km west of Gangtok, is the administrative centre and transport hub of western Sikkim, and a good place to stock up on provisions and extend **permits**, which you can do through the Superintendent of Police (Mon–Sat 10am–4pm) at **Tikjuk**, midway between Gyalshing and Pelling. There are a handful of **hotels** around the main square in the centre of Gyalshing should you miss connections, including some basic options and the more comfortable *Attri* (ⓣ03595/250602; ❸). A few yards from the market on the Tashigang road, *Denkhang* is one of the better restaurants in Gyalshing specializing in ocal cuisine.

Shared **jeeps** leave for Gangtok (4–5hr; Rs120) and Siliguri (Rs135; tickets in advance from the counter near the playground; ⓣ03595/250121); there are also regular services to Legship and Jorethang (2–3hr; change here for Darjeeling). Taxis and jeeps depart from the main square for Pelling (30min; Rs20) and other local destinations; most have left by midday, with the exception of those to Pelling which continue regularly until dark. If reserving a taxi, Omnis tend to be cheaper as they can travel up the steep short-cut to Pelling, which is closed to jeeps. An SNT **bus** to Gangtok leaves at 8am and to Siliguri at 8am via Jorethang where there are better connections and jeeps to Darjeeling.

The gateway to western Sikkim, **LEGSHIP** sits in the deep and recently dammed Rangit Valley, just under 100km west of Gangtok and 14km south of Gyalshing. It's an important regional road junction and one where you could find yourself with an hour or so to spare, but besides a temple across the river and grubby hot springs down the road, it's not an interesting destination. At the cross-roads, *Trishna* (Ⓣ03595/250887; ❸) has a few rooms and a restaurant. jeeps and buses connect Legship with Gangtok, Ravangla, Yoksum (via Tashiding) and Pelling, and there are also regular services to Gyalshing and Jorethang.

Pemayangtse

Perched at the end of a ridge with a grand panorama of the entire Parekh Chu watershed including the Kanchenjunga massif, the hallowed monastery of **PEMAYANGTSE**, 118km from Gangtok and a mere 2km from Pelling, is poised high above the River Rangit. It's a 9km journey along the main road from Gyalshing; or you can take a steep, 4km short-cut through the woods past a line of *chortens* and the otherwise uninteresting remains of Sikkim's second capital, **Rabdantse**, now made into a park.

Pemayangtse, the "Perfect Sublime Lotus", (daily 7am–5pm; Rs20 [Rs10]) founded in the seventeenth century by Lhatsun Chempo, one of the three lamas of Yoksum, and extended in 1705 by his reincarnation, is one of the most important *gompas* in Sikkim and belongs to the Nyingmapa sect. The views and the surrounding woods create an atmosphere of meditative solitude. Surrounded by outhouses featuring intricate woodwork on the beams, lattice windows and doors, the main *gompa* itself is plain in comparison. Built on three floors, it centres around a large hall which contains images of Guru Rinpoche and Lhatsun Chenpo (the latter was an enigmatic Tibetan lama who is the patron saint of Sikkim), and an exquisite display of *thangkas* and murals. On the top floor, a magnificent wooden sculpture carved and painted by Dungzin Rinpoche, a former abbot of Pemayangtse, depicts Sang Thok Palri, the celestial abode of Guru Rinpoche, rising above the realms of hell. The extraordinary detail includes demons, animals, birds, Buddhas and *bodhisattvas*, *chortens* and flying dragons, and took him just five years to complete. The two-day annual Guru Drogma *chaam* is held here during Losar, the New Year (Feb/March), and attracts visitors from all over Sikkim culminating with draping the monastery with a gigantic *thangka*.

In 1980, the **Denjong Padma Choeling Academy** was set up by the monastery to provide for destitute children and orphans; there are currently around three hudred children being housed, clothed, fed and educated here. Generous donations have enabled further building and projects including the yak and *dri* dairy project near Dzongri. Volunteer teachers are always welcome, for a minimum of two months, and have the opportunity to study meditation and Buddhism. For more information, contact Sonam Yongda at Pemayangste Gompa, West Sikkim 737 113 (Ⓣ03595/250760 or 250141) who also organizes occasional **meditation courses**.

Pelling and around

The quiet, relatively new yet rapidly swelling town of **PELLING**, situated 2085m above sea level only 2km beyond Pemayangtse, is most notable for its expansive views north towards the glaciers and peaks of Kanchenjunga. High above forest-covered hills, in an amphitheatre of cloud, snow and rock, the entire route from Yoksum over Dzongri La to the Rathong Glacier can be seen. Frenetic building activity hasn't detracted from Pelling's quiet charm, with numerous hotel terraces that allow you to gaze in awe at the world's third-highest peak, as well as easy

Moving on from Pelling

From the crossroads of Upper Pelling, shared **jeeps** travel regularly (6am–4pm) between Pelling and Gyalshing; there are also twice-daily services to Gangtok via Ravangla (7am & noon; Rs150), and one jeep daily for Siliguri (7am; Rs150); one **bus** (Rs120) leaves at the same time to Siliguri via Jorethang (pre-book at SNT, *Hotel Pelling*, Lower Pelling ⓣ03595/250707). The road from Pelling via Rimbi to Yoksum is poor so allow plenty of time; there are no scheduled services, but jeeps leave from Gyalshing and Legship for Tashiding and Yoksum. Father Travels runs a direct jeep service to Gangtok leaving at 12.30pm and direct jeeps to Darjeeling are also available through Simvo (Rs2000). Sikkim Tourism has announced a Mondays-only **helicopter** service to and from Bagdogra (see p.772) for Rs2200.

access to attractive walks in the hinterland. One noticeable element missing is a bazaar, though a few shops are now beginning to appear.

The **post office** is in Upper Pelling just above the crossroads; nearby, there's a State Bank of India **ATM**, but no official facilities for changing money. For trekking information consult the books at *Hotel Garuda*; other reliable trek and tour operators include Himalayan Heritage (ⓣ9733 076469), Upper Pelling; the Tourist Information Centre near the helipad (daily 10am–4pm) is good for general information, as is the excellent local website, ⓦwww.gopelling.com. There is also an **internet café** here during office hours (Rs30/hr); Paylink Cyberzone at Upper Pelling is an alternative.

Accommodation

Pelling's **hotels**, whose rates rise steeply in the high seasons (March–May & Sept–Nov) are spread along a 2km stretch of road between Upper, Middle and Lower Pelling, with Lower Pelling gearing itself more towards the domestic market and Upper Pelling offering the finest views.

Dubdi Near the helipad ⓣ03595/258349. This small hotel, located in a quiet corner above town and tucked beside the gates to the Norbu Ghang, is a lot less expensive than its neighbour, *Norbu Ghang*, with very comfortable, spacious and spotless rooms, some with great views. ❹–❺

The Elgin Mount Pandim Just below Pemayangtse monastery ⓣ03595/250756, ⓦwww.elginhotels.com. Darjeeling-style elegance has turned this old government hotel into the most luxurious address in western Sikkim. Every room has a view of the snowy peaks, the multi-cuisine restaurant is excellent and the quiet, unspoilt location makes this an excellent base from which to explore the area. ❾

Garuda At the crossroads ⓣ03595/258 319. A popular travellers' haunt with internet access and travel desk, this well-run family hotel offers a wide range of singles, doubles and dorms (Rs100) with a 40 percent off-season discount; useful comment books have the latest trekking information. The restaurant boasts good food including a Sikkimese set meal, beer and *tomba* (see p.819) in winter. ❶–❸

Kabur 200m before the crossroads ⓣ03595/258 504. A welcoming place with internet access and a helpful local trek-and-tour operation. The doubles are carpeted, with hot water and heaters in winter and there's an expansive rooftop terrace complete with sun loungers and great views. The restaurant that opens on to it offers a healthy range of meals, including Sikkimese cuisine. Very good value. ❷

Ladakh Upper Pelling ⓣ9733 210355. A rapidly dying breed in Pelling – a traditional, rustic Sikkimese house with six rooms and a dorm (Rs50) popular with drivers; the common bathrooms with squat toilets are outside; this is as basic as it gets but the location is good. ❶

Norbu Ghang Resort Near the helipad ⓣ03595/258272, ⓦwww.norbughangresort.com. Efficient upmarket hotel, with comfortable cottages spread around the manicured gardens; combining vernacular style with modern amenities, each has good views from verandas that take full advantage of the resort's position high above town. ❼

Phamrong Upper Pelling ⓣ03595/258218, ⓔmailphamrong@yahoo.com. At the crossroads, an old favourite with a wide range of comfortable, clean rooms and breakfast included, running hot water and attentive service; there's a pleasant restaurant serving Sikkimese, Indian and Chinese food, and great views from some of the more expensive rooms. Internet access is available. ❺

Around Pelling

A new road blasted up the steep ridge from near the helipad just above Pelling makes a good 4km walk to reach the small but highly venerated Nyingmapa monastery of **Sanga Choling**, one of the oldest *gompas* in Sikkim and another of Lhatsun Chenpo's creations. Gutted by fire, it was rebuilt in 1948 and houses some of the original clay statues including a stunning Samantha Bhadra. A giant statue of Chenrazee is being planned immediately above the *gompa* to draw tourists, which will probably wreck the solitude of the place. A trail past the *gompa* continues up the ridge through orchid-clad forest, past a giant hollow tree to the venerated rock of Thikchuyangtse, also known as Rani Dunga (9km).

A scenic low-altitude **trek** along roads and trails to Khecheopalri Lake, Tashiding and Yoksum starts in Pelling. Jeeps run from both Yoksum and Tashiding back to Legship, from where you can continue to Gyalshing and eventually back to Pelling. If you have less time on your hands, tour operators such as Simvo Tour and Travels (ⓣ03595/258549) in Upper Pelling and Father Jeep Service (ⓣ03595/258219) can arrange **day-trips** by jeep (around Rs2200 for 6–8 people). The hotel *Garuda* (see opposite) also has a good travel desk and can arrange local treks and tours and provide information.

Eating

Most **restaurants** are to be found in hotels, but traditional Sikkimese food is rather rarer than *dhal bhat* due to the strong Bengali presence. Upper Pelling has several cafés, some serving south Indian food while one of the best restaurant **bars** is *Taatopaani* at the *Hotel Chiminda* in Middle Pelling, where, along with a selection of drinks, mocktails and cocktails, the thali is good value (Rs125). Stock up at the Lotus Bakery near Pemayangtse where a small selection of croissants, breads and cakes go to support the children's charity. The best travellers' restaurants are in the hotels *Garuda* and *Kabur*. Pelling is a good place to sample a *tomba* (warm millet beer); it's best in Sikkimese-run hotels like *Phamrong* and *Garuda*.

Khecheopalri Lake

Surrounded by dense forests and hidden in a mountain bowl (2000m) 33km northwest of Pelling, **Khecheopalri Lake**, known as the "Wishing Lake", is sacred to the Lepchas. Legend has it that if a leaf drops onto the lake's surface, a guardian bird swoops down and picks it up, thereby maintaining the purity of the water. From the Pelling–Yoksum road, a turn-off diverts at "zero point" to Khecheopalri (11km), with only occasional jeeps travelling the route (landslides permitting) to the lake. If you want to trek from Pelling to Khecheopalri, there's a shortcut leading down to the river valley, steeply up to the Pelling–Yoksum road and then up to the lake (allow 5hr); you can continue the circuit to Yoksum (18km; 4–5hr), but arm yourself with provisions, information and a handy map from *Hotel Garuda* (see opposite) before setting off.

The Khecheopalri *gompa*, 2km from the lake on top of the ridge, provides good views of Mount Pandim (6691m), and several sacred caves are scattered through the hills. Guides for visiting these caves and for the trek to Yoksum can be arranged through the trekkers hut (ⓣ9733 076995; ❶), 300m before the village, one of the few places to stay at Khecheopalri – a friendly but very basic

West Sikkim high-altitude treks

Two **high-altitude treks** are currently allowed in Sikkim. The first, from **Yoksum** to **Dzongri**, in the shadow of Kanchenjunga, passes through huge tracts of forest and provides incredible mountain vistas; all-inclusive rates from a decent agency are around $50 per head per day. The second, the **Singalila Ridge**, explores the remote high pastures of the Singalila frontier range with breathtaking views of the massif; per-person daily rates are higher, at around $65. Trekkers for either of the two must have special **permits** (see p.811) and travel in groups of at least two organized by authorized agencies (see p.813). Check permits and arrangement for porterage, guides and food before you set off – all should be included in the cost; scrutinize itineraries too. Bring adequate clothing, boots and sleeping bags and a hat for warmth. The best time to do both treks is between October and mid-November, when the weather is clearest. For general advice on trekking equipment and health issues, see Basics, p.64.

The Dzongri Trail

Although Dzongri is the junction of several trails, the prescribed route onwards leads to **Goecha La** via Zemanthang and Samiti Lake. Well-marked and dotted with basic accommodation, the trail, also used by yak herders, is at its best in May when the rhododendrons bloom.

DAY 1 It takes approximately 6hr to climb the 16km from **Yoksum** (1780m) to **Tsokha** (3048m). The forested trail begins gently before arriving at the Parekh Chu above its confluence with the Rathong. The next 4.5km involve a knee-grinding ascent, entering the lichen zone and cloud forests, past the *Forest Rest House* at **Bakhim** (2684m) to the Tibetan yak herders' settlement of Tsokha where there are a couple of trekkers huts.

DAY 2 This day can be spent acclimatizing yourself to the altitude at Tsokha, perhaps with a short trek of around 5km towards Dzongri, to a watchtower for superb views of Kanchenjunga and Pandim.

DAY 3 The 11km section from **Tsokha** to **Dzongri** (4030m) takes at least 5hr, rising through beautiful pine and rhododendron forests to **Phedang Meadows** (3450m), before continuing to the hut at Dzongri.

DAY 4 Once again, it's worth staying around Dzongri for further acclimatization. This gives you the opportunity to climb Dzongri Hill above the hut, for early-morning and early-evening views of Kanchenjunga's craggy south summit and the black rocky tooth of Kabur, a holy mountain towering above Dzongri La (4400m), a pass that leads to the HMI base camp 12km away at Chaurikhang and the Rathong Glacier (a recommended variation).

option which serves simple meals. It also has some very useful information on the local area and a definitive list for bird-watchers. Tea stalls at the car park serve chai and simple meals.

Yoksum

The sleepy, spread-out hamlet of **YOKSUM** at the end of the road and at the entrance to the Rathong Chu gorge, 40km north of Pemayangtse, holds a special place in Sikkimese history. This was the spot where three lamas converged from different directions across the Himalayas to enthrone the first religious king of Sikkim, Chogyal Phuntsog Namgyal, in 1642. Named the "Great Religious King", he established Tibetan Buddhism in Sikkim. Lhatsun Chenpo is supposed to have buried offerings in Yoksum's **Norbugang Chorten**, a vast white stupa built with stones and earth from different parts of Sikkim, to be found in a nearby park (1km) which also houses the simple stone throne of the first chogyal. In front of the throne, a large footprint embedded

DAY 5 The 8km trek from **Dzongri** to **Thangsing** (3841m) takes around 4hr, descending against an incredible backdrop of peaks to a rhododendron forest, crossing a bridge and continuing through woods to the *Trekkers Hut* at **Thangsing** at the end of a glacial valley.

DAY 6 The 10km short, sharp shock up to **Samiti Lake** (4303m) takes around 3hr through alpine meadows traversing glacial moraine before arriving at the emerald-green **Samiti Lake** (local name Sungmoteng Tso). If you are still going strong, you could continue to **Zemanthang** (4453m) where there's a trekkers hut.

DAY 7 The climax of the trek, and also its most difficult section by far simply due to its high altitude. From **Samiti Lake**, the 14km round-trip climb takes around 4hr up to **Goecha La** and 2–3hr back down again. The trail follows glacial moraine to a dry lake at Zemanthang, before a final grinding rise following cairns and the occasional prayer flag to the narrow defile at Goeche La (5000m), where Kanchenjunga South is clearly visible on a clear day.

DAY 8 Most of the long 24km hike from **Samiti Lake** back to **Tsokha** is downhill and takes around 8hr, involving a short cut after the bridge to avoid Dzongri. There are several variations to this finish.

The Singalila Ridge

Itineraries for **Singalila Ridge** treks range between ten and nineteen days and though more expensive due to the area's remoteness, they prove exceptionally rewarding, with views from Everest to the huge Kanchenjunga massif ahead. It's best done from south to north facing the views as the trail rises towards the snows through remote alpine pastures and past hidden lakes. From the roadhead at **Uttarey** (1965m), 28km to the west of Pelling, or from **Soreng**, 30km to the west of Jorethang, the trek ascends to **Chewabhanjang** (3170m) on the Sikkim–Nepal frontier. Thereafter, the trail rarely descends below 3500m, high above the tree line; the highest point of the trail is the **Danfeybhir Tar**, a pass at 4400m. Several lakes such as **Lampokhari**, all considered holy, are encountered along the route, and here and there dwarf rhododendron forests bring a blaze of colour in season (April–May). The route dips down to **Gomathang** (3725m), a yak-herders' shelter on the banks of the Boktochu, then passes through a delightful forest of silver fir and rhododendron before arriving at the welcome sight of the bungalow at **Dzongri**. You could descend from here via Tsokha to Yoksum or continue to **Goecha La**, thus completing a grand and rewarding traverse.

in a rock belongs to one of the lamas. Disappointing today, **Kathok Lake**, a small scummy pond nearby at the top end of town, was also part of the original ceremony. High above Yoksum, prayer flags announce the site of the **Dubdi Monastery**, built in 1701 and one of the oldest monasteries in Sikkim. To get here, walk past the bazaar to the hospital at the top of the village. The road ends here and a path threads past water-wheels and a small river and rises through the forest to arrive at the *gompa* on an expansive shelf. It's best to enquire in the bazaar or the KCC office (see p.832) before you set out as it's often shut. Just above the bazaar, the small, new **Kathol Wodsal Ling** *gompa*, with its statue of Guru Rinpoche, adds some colour to the scene. There are several other shrines and *gompas*, some new, scattered around Yoksum.

The village's main role these days is as the start of the **Dzongri Trail**. Visitors are welcome in Yoksum itself, but unless you have a Dzongri Trek permit, you're not supposed to venture any further. The police are quite vigilant, so there's not much chance of a surreptitious high-mountain trek, but so long as you're not

Moving on from Yoksum

There are no buses to or from Yoksum itself, but jeeps start to depart at around 6.30am to **Gyalshing** (Rs70) via **Tashiding** (Rs40), **Pelling** (Rs60) and to **Gangtok** (Rs140) via Ravangla; you're unlikely to get shared transport after 1pm.

carrying a backpack they may allow a day-trip along the main trail to the Parekh Chu and its confluence with the Rathong Chu – a 28km round-trip. You won't see the high Himalayas, but you do pass through some beautiful forest scenery. Yaks – or rather *dzo*, a more manageable cross between yak and domestic cattle – travel this route carrying supplies for trekking parties and isolated communities.

Internet access is available at the Community Information Centre (Rs50/hr) above the bazaar. Besides hotel restaurants, the only other **places to eat** are cafés – such as *Guptas* and the friendly *Yak* – along the main drag, which serve snacks and basic meals.

Accommodation

Most options are around the small market area. The KCC (see box below) at the Visitors Information Centre, at the head of town (☎9832 452527) organizes several **home-stays** around the village.

Pemalingpa Cottage At the Tashi Gang gates, ☎9733 029569. The welcoming family here offer a taste of village life in a traditional home with basic wooden rooms and squat toilets outside. ❶

Pemathang ☎03595/241221. Approaching Yoksum's tiny market, this guesthouse has clean, airy rooms with attached bathrooms, and a small but picturesque garden; there is a trekking shop and agency next door. ❸

Tashi Gang ☎03593/241202. Just above the bazaar, the oldest of Yoksum's mid-range hotels is now being thoroughly and tastefully revamped; it also has a decent restaurant. ❺–❻

Wild Orchid ☎03595/241212. A rustic traditional house, centrally located, that offers basic budget rooms with shared bathrooms. ❶

Yangri Gang ☎03595/241217. Next door to *Pemathang*, this place has lately been completely rebuilt and offers doubles downstairs with attached toilets but shared showers; upstairs has more luxury but at a price. There's also a dorm for Rs60, a tour agency and a good restaurant. ❶–❹

Yuksam Residency Bazaar ☎03593/241277. This plush new hotel has a bit too much marble for a mountain village. It has a strong Buddhist theme with the more expensive rooms comfortably wood-lined. ❻–❼

Conservation and the Kanchenjunga National Park

Established in 1996 with the help of the Sikkim Biodiversity and Ecotourism Project, the **Khangchendzonga Conservation Committee** (**KCC**), a community-based NGO based in Yoksum, aims to promote ecological awareness to locals and visitors alike. The KCC's main concern is the impact of tourism on the fabric of the **Kanchenjunga National Park**, and their methods include planting trees, mobilizing local participation in the planning of ecotourism and organizing clean-up campaigns. Conservation has also been embraced by the Sikkim government, which has put in place a code of conduct, banning the use of wood for fuel in preference to kerosene; however, wood fires continue to be part and parcel of the Sikkim landscape. KCC initiatives include keeping trails clean, publishing leaflets to promote eco-awareness, training local workers including porters and guides in the ecotourism industry, and organizing self-help initiatives. For more information on the KCC, contact their coordinator Pema Chewang Bhutia at Visitors Information Centre, Gompa Road, Yoksum (☎03595/241 211 or ☎9832 452527, Ⓦwww.sikkimkcc.netfirms.com/kcc/). There is a **Biodiversity Centre** here and they also provide low-altitude **guides** for Rs300 a day.

Tashiding

Considered the holiest in Sikkim, the beautiful *gompa* of **Tashiding** occupies the point of a conical hill 19km southeast of Yoksum, high above the confluence of the Rangit and the Rathong. "The Devoted Central Glory" was built in 1717, after a rainbow was seen to connect the site to Kanchenjunga. While a new road has eaten its way through the forest to the monastery, the climb is still recommended – the well-marked path leaves the main road near an impressive *mani* wall (inscribed with the mantra *Om mani padme hum*: "Hail the jewel in the lotus" in silver paint) and leads steeply past rustic houses and fields and along a final flag-lined approach. The large complex consists of a motley collection of buildings, *chortens*, chapels and the unassuming main temple itself, which was recently rebuilt using some of the features and wooden beams of the original. At the far end of the temple complex, surrounded by numerous multi-coloured *mani* stones inscribed with a mantra, is an impressive array of *chortens* containing relics of Sikkim's chogyals and lamas. On the fifteenth day of the first month of the Tibetan New Year, devotees from all over Sikkim gather in Tashiding for the **Nyingmapa Bhumchu festival**, when they are blessed with the holy water from an ancient bowl said by legend never to dry up. Oracles consult the water's level to determine the future.

Practicalities

Around 2km below the *gompa*, Tashiding's tiny **Senik Bazaar** is situated near a saddle that separates the mountainside from the monastery hill. **Accommodation** here includes the friendly but very basic *Blue Bird* (no phone; ❶) with a restaurant serving simple food and the more spacious, slightly more expensive *Mount Siniolchu Guesthouse* (Ⓣ03595/243211; ❶) further up the hill which has simple doubles with shared baths; the *Dhakkar Tashiding Lodge* (Ⓣ03595/243249; ❶), between the market and the gates, is more comfortable, though it also has shared baths.

Leaving from the bottom of the bazaar's main street, one or two timetabled **jeeps** (7–9am) and a handful of unscheduled jeeps connect Tashiding to Yoksum (Rs30), Legship (Rs20), Gyalshing (Rs50) and one at noon to Gangtok (Rs130). The last regular shared jeeps depart at 9am. Trails through the forests and along stretches of the main road make trekking an alternative option to public transport; the route to Legship takes around two and a half hours.

North Sikkim

Access to much of spectacular **North Sikkim** is restricted: visitors are allowed in only with the necessary permits, and some areas along the borders remain completely out of bounds. A fragile road etches its way up the Teesta valley and splits at Chungthang with one branch bearing northwest to Lachung and beyond, while the other goes due north to Lachung, to the beautiful valley of Yumthang and eventually Zero Point on the high plateau. Groups armed with **Protected Area Permits** (see p.811) can go as far north as **Thangu past Lachung**, at the edge of the plateau; only Indians – similarly armed – can travel further on to the spectacular lake of Gurudongma, near the source of the Teesta on the Tibetan plateau. North of Mangan, foreigners are only allowed up in groups of two or more, and the **jeep safaris** are sold inclusive of transport and accommodation, with the choices in the hands of tour operators. In general, **permits** for North Sikkim (extendable through the Superintendent of Police in Mangan) are only good for five days and a further seven for trekking. Every year throughout the monsoon, landslides take out stretches of road, making travel even more tedious – at the height of the tourist season around five hundred jeeps battle their way up and down the tortuous and inadequate roads to and from Gangtok.

Mangan and around

The road north of Gangtok passes Phodong before reaching the town of **MANGAN**, the district capital of North Sikkim, high above the Teesta valley. This is the starting point for a few good **treks** including the **Tosar Lake** trail, a very rewarding and rarely-attempted eight-day mountain trek through forests of bamboo, silver fir and rhododendrons that culminates at the emerald-green Tosar Lake, cradled in a picturesque mountain hollow at an altitude of around 4500m; contact Khangri Treks & Tours of Gangtok (Ⓣ03592/226050) to arrange guides and permits.

A convenient stop on an arduous route to the north, Mangan itself has little interest other than its busy, little bazaar, a handful of hotels and the District Headquarters, 2km above town, a relatively easy place to get a permit if you haven't already picked one up in Gangtok. The limited choice of **food** and **accommodation** around the bazaar includes the *Mount View* (Ⓣ03592/234 473; ❸) with small rooms with attached baths and a decent restaurant and bar; and, across the road, the *Tamarind* (Ⓣ03592/234297; ❻–❽) is at the opposite end of the scale with marble lobbies, a good vegetarian restaurant, internet access and large spotless rooms with modern plumbing. It also accepts credit cards. Outside town, the drive down to picturesque **Namprikdang**, a popular angling spot on the Teesta, is hair-raising while 4km to the north, the village of **Singhik** provides spectacular views of the huge east face of Kanchenjunga, especially beautiful early in the morning. Singhik is a quiet place to chill out for a day or two, especially at the pleasant *Friendship Guest House* (Ⓣ03592/234 278; ❸), a cottage on the main road.

Few visit the permit-restricted but magnificent valley of **Dzongu** – the Lepcha homeland – that branches northwest from Mangan towards Kanchenjunga. At the heart of the valley, the ancient *gompa* of **Tholung** is home to ancient treasures of the chogyals; these are displayed every three years to the public with the next display due in January 2012. A few **homestay** options are available, arranged, along with permits (see p.811), through tour operators like Sikkim and Khangri in Gangtok (see p.813). A five-day trek starting at Lingza and passing through Tholung, Thizon and across Kyeshong La (3790m) explores the forests and meadows of this unspoilt region.

Lachung and around

A further 40km north of Mangan lies **CHUNGTHANG**, set in a deep valley that sees little sunlight, a grubby town with a destructive hydro-electric project at the confluence of the Teesta and Lachung rivers. The road forks here with the one to the right climbing rapidly to the group of small settlements of **LACHUNG**, the "big pass", a mere 15km west of Tibet. Across the river from the main cluster of settlement, **Lachung Monastery** is a two-storey Tibetan-style *gompa* belonging to the Nyingmapa sect worth visiting especially for its wonderful murals. The Bhotia people of Lachung and Lachen practise a unique social system known as *Dzumsa* – a sort of gathering of elders that controls everything from grazing rights to law and order. **Accommodation** here must be pre-booked along with all food and transport through tour operators such as Blue Sky, Galaxy and Khangri in Gangtok (see p.813);

options include the *Le Coxy*, a large comfortable timber lodge in the heart of the settlement while Tashi's welcoming *Season House*, (Ⓣ9434 449042, booked through Khangri in Gangtok, ❹) at Shingringten, 2km high above the village, provides dramatic views of the valley and has a range of rooms and a warm kitchen hearth. Overlooked by dramatic cliffs, the *Yarlam* (Ⓣ9434 330033, Ⓦwww.yarlamresort.com; ❽) offers a touch of ostentatious luxury in a brand-new development with large suite-like, heated rooms and vast lobbies; a heated outdoor swimming pool is in the works.

As the road north ascends past yak pastures, it enters the **Shingba Rhododendron Sanctuary** announcing the start of **Yumthang** (3645m), 25km north of Lachung, with spectacular rock and ice pinnacles towering to 6000m on either side. This beautiful tree-lined valley does not have accommodation but boasts somewhat neglected hot sulphur springs. A pleasant purpose-made **walking trail** leads 10km along the valley floor, back to the sanctuary gates – due to the high altitude and problems with acclimatization, descent rather than ascent is recommended. Past Yumthang, the road continues up the valley and emerges on the high plateau land at **Yumesamdong** or **Zero Point** (the end of the road), at an altitude of 4770m.

Lachen and around

The other road from Chungthang leads 26km to **LACHEN** and a further 36km to **THANGU**, tantalizingly close to the Tibetan plateau and as far as foreign tourists are allowed to go. This is the route to the sacred and spectacular **Gurudongma Lake**, considered blessed by Guru Rinpoche and the source of the River Teesta. A short day-hike (5km each way) from Thangu (no special trekking permit needed) leads to the picturesque **Chopta Valley** (4400m). There are several lodges around Lachen and Thangu, including the upmarket *Apple Orchard* (Ⓣ03592/204649 or Ⓣ9434 062514 ❽), one of finest lodges in North Sikkim, with striking parquet-floored rooms tastefully designed to incorporate vernacular architecture.

Several interesting **high-altitude treks** are now open to group tours in this isolated region, including the challenging **Lachen to Green Lake** (4850m) trek, which takes approximately nine days there and back, and offers great views of Mount Siniolchu (6887m) across the Zemu glacier and the gigantic east face of Kanchenjunga. You'll need to make your plans well in advance however, with red tape invariably proving a dampener; **trekking permits** for the north (see box, p.811) can be arranged through Sikkim Tourism in Delhi or through one of the Gangtok operators, taking a minimum of three months to process.

16

The Northeast

* **Kaziranga National Park, Assam** Spot the rare one-horned rhino on a dawn elephant ride. See p.847

* **Majuli Island, Assam** Fascinating Hindu monasteries on reputedly the world's largest river island. See p.849

* **Khasi Hills, Meghalaya** Explore impressive caves, dramatic waterfalls and intriguing root bridges in this picturesque area. See p.855

* **Tawang Monastery, Arunachal Pradesh** A spectacular Tibetan Buddhist monastery in one of the most remote locations imaginable. See p.859

* **Namdapha National Park, Arunachal Pradesh** A beautiful park in a stunning setting with prehistoric trees, pristine vegetation and some elusive big cats. See p.861

* **Kohima, Nagaland** Proud state capital, with a fascinating museum and poignant World War II memorial. See p.862

▲ One-horned rhino, Kaziranga National Park

The least explored and arguably most beautiful region of India, the **NORTHEAST** is connected to the rest of the country by a narrow stretch of land between Bhutan and Bangladesh, and was all but sealed off from the outside world until relatively recently. Arunachal Pradesh shares an extremely sensitive frontier with Chinese-occupied Tibet and, together with Nagaland, Manipur and Mizoram, a 1600km-border with Myanmar.

Insurgency has agitated the region since Independence, with tribal groups pushing for autonomy as well as fighting each other. A huge influx of Bangladeshis in the last decade and the displacement of many indigenous people has also created further tension. The situation has improved in recent years, though Tripura and Manipur remain unsafe for travel (see pp.867–868) and Restricted or Protected Area Permits are required for four of the seven states (see p.840). Tourists are not a target of violence, however, and an extraordinary diversity of peoples and spectacular landscapes make a visit well worth the effort. One of the world's wettest monsoon belts, the area also boasts an astounding array of flora and fauna, estimated at fifty percent of India's entire biodiversity.

Until the 1960s the region comprised just two states, the North East Frontier Agency, now Arunachal Pradesh, and Assam, but separatist pressures further divided it into seven states, dubbed "the seven sisters". **Assam** consists of the flat, low-lying Brahmaputra valley. Its capital, **Guwahati**, boasts two of India's most important ancient temples and is the gateway to the region, while an encounter with a one-horned rhino in the magnificent **Kaziranga National Park** is a highlight of any trip to the Northeast.

The other six states occupy the surrounding hills, and are quite distinct from the rest of India in landscape, climate and peoples. **Meghalaya** boasts beautiful lakes and is home to the wettest places on earth, Cherrapunjee and Mawsynram. Its capital, **Shillong**, retains some of the colonial atmosphere from its days as East India's summer capital. Majestic **Arunachal Pradesh**, one of India's most remote states, is inhabited by a fascinating range of peoples, many of Tibetan origin. In the state's northwestern corner lies the Buddhist monastery of **Tawang**, encircled by awesome mountains, while in the far northeast is the remote wilderness of **Namdapha National Park**. To the south, the lush mountains of **Nagaland** are home to fourteen distinctive tribal groups. **Mizoram**, in the Lushai hills, is predominantly Christian and has one of the highest literacy rates in India.

Travelling through the Northeast

Much of the region (particularly Nagaland) is easiest reached through tour operators (see p.841), but it is possible – and richly rewarding – for the adventurous to travel independently, though this demands considerable amounts of time, energy and perseverance. Be prepared for bureaucracy, language barriers, long drives on terrible roads, basic accommodation and (except in Assam) extremes in temperature. Consider hiring your own **jeep and driver**, at least for part of the trip, and using public Tata **Sumos**, jeeps that operate like shared taxis and are generally much quicker than buses. If travelling in winter, bring a sleeping bag and thermals, as much of the accommodation is not set up for cold weather. People rarely drive at night because of the threat of banditry, and, since the region shares the same time zone as the rest of India despite being so far east, the sun rises and sets early and a lot of places close by 6pm. Outside Guwahati, **money-changing** facilities are rare, so bring what cash you need with you. There are regular *bandh*s (strikes) throughout the region when shops, restaurants and public transport shut down – during a typical three-week trip you're likely to lose at least a couple of days to *bandhs*.

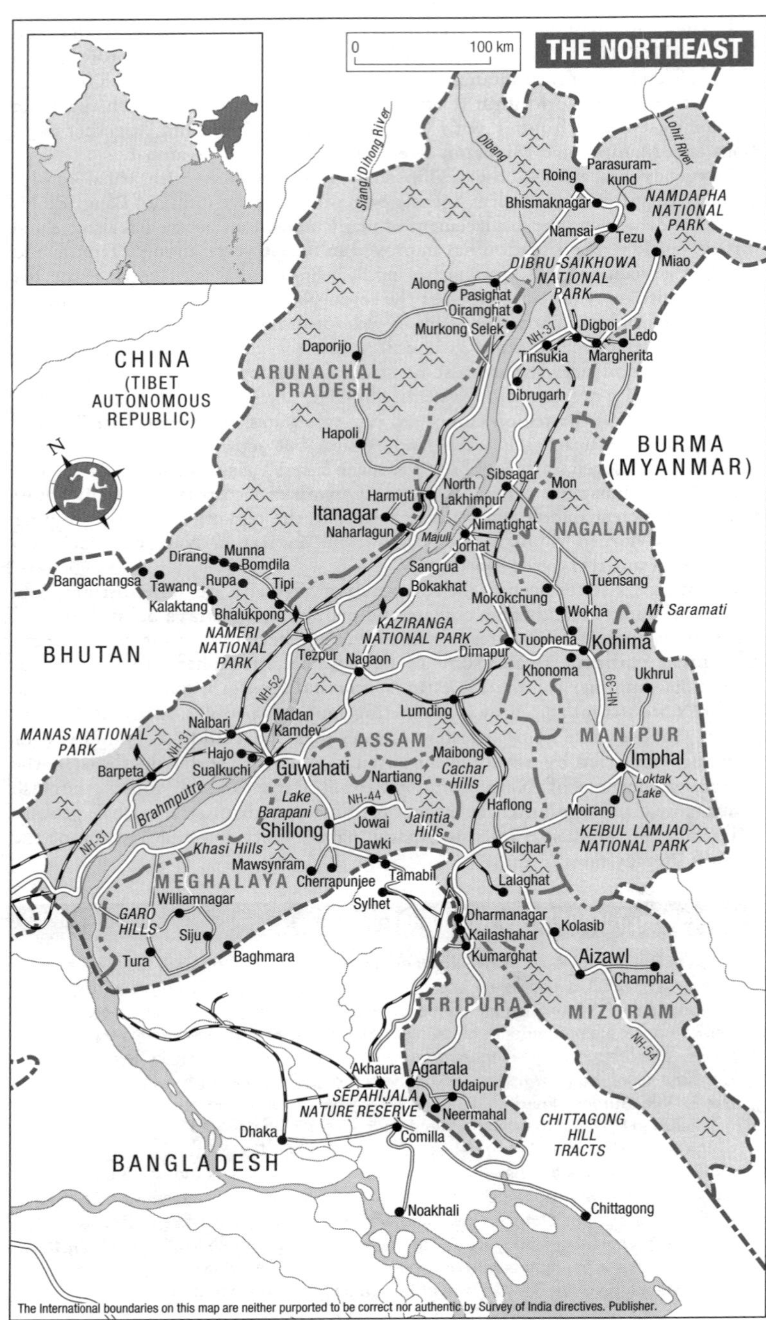
THE NORTHEAST
0
100 km
CHINA
(TIBET
AUTONOMOUS
REPUBLIC)
BURMA
(MYANMAR)
BHUTAN
BANGLADESH
ARUNACHAL
PRADESH
NAGALAND
ASSAM
MANIPUR
MEGHALAYA
TRIPURA
MIZORAM
NAMDAPHA
NATIONAL
PARK
DIBRU-SAIKHOWA
NATIONAL
PARK
KAZIRANGA
NATIONAL PARK
NAMERI
NATIONAL
PARK
MANAS NATIONAL
PARK
KEIBUL LAMJAO
NATIONAL PARK
SEPAHIJALA
NATURE RESERVE
CHITTAGONG
HILL
TRACTS
Siang/Dihong River
Dibang
Lohit River
Brahmputra
Roing
Parasuram-
kund
Bhismaknagar
Namsai
Tezu
Miao
Along
Pasighat
Oiramghat
Murkong Selek
Digboi
Ledo
Margherita
Tinsukia
Dibrugarh
Daporijo
Hapoli
Sibsagar
Mon
Harmuti
North
Lakhimpur
Itanagar
Naharlagun
Majuli
Nimatighat
Jorhat
Sangrua
Bokakhat
Mokokchung
Tuensang
Wokha
Mt Saramati
Kohima
Tuophena
Dimapur
Khonoma
Ukhrul
Dirang
Munna
Bomdila
Bangachangsa
Tawang
Rupa
Tipi
Kalaktang
Bhalukpong
Tezpur
Nagaon
Lumding
Madan
Kamdev
Nalbari
Hajo
Sualkuchi
Guwahati
Barpeta
Maibong
Cachar
Hills
Nartiang
Lake
Barapani
Jowai
Jaintia
Hills
Haflong
Shillong
Imphal
Loktak
Lake
Moirang
Khasi Hills
Mawsynram
Cherrapunjee
Dawki
Tamabil
Silchar
Lalaghat
Sylhet
Williamnagar
GARO
HILLS
Siju
Tura
Baghmara
Dharmanagar
Kailashahar
Kumarghat
Kolasib
Aizawl
Champhai
Akhaura
Agartala
Udaipur
Neermahal
Dhaka
Comilla
Noakhali
Chittagong
NH-37
NH-52
NH-31
NH-44
NH-39
NH-54
The International boundaries on this map are neither purported to be correct nor authentic by Survey of India directives. Publisher.

Manipur and **Tripura** were deemed unsafe for travel at the time of writing and the sections on the two states have not been updated for this edition (see p.867 & p.868). Although tourists are not a direct target, both states suffer from inter-tribal disputes, kidnapping, banditry, arson and killings. The people of Manipur are more closely related to the neighbouring Burmese population, while Tripura is bordered by Bangladesh on three sides having been cut off from the Bangladeshi plains during the 1947 Partition.

The best **time to visit** the Northeast is from November to April, although mountain areas can be extremely cold by December. It rains heavily from May to the end of September. In two weeks you could travel from West Bengal to Guwahati, Shillong and Kaziranga, while three weeks would be enough to cover the main sights of Assam and Meghalaya. A month would enable you to enjoy the two most beautiful and remote states, Arunachal Pradesh and Nagaland. To take in all the states together, including Mizoram, you'll need considerably longer.

Assam

ASSAM is dominated by the mighty **River Brahmaputra**, whose huge, lush valley is sandwiched between the Himalayan foothills to the north and the Meghalayan hills and plateau to the south. An attractive state, Assam is one of India's few **oil** regions, and produces around sixty percent of the nation's **tea**. However, the industry is not as profitable as it once was, and for the marginalized *adivasis* – tribal people from various indigenous groups, brought in from central India by the British to work as indentured labourers on the plantations – depressingly little has changed since colonial times.

The social divisions caused by this marginalization have been some of the major sources of **instability** in the state. The United Liberation Front of Asom (**ULFA**), a separatist group declared a terrorist organisation by the Indian government, began an armed struggle for independence in 1985, and in the early 1990s, Assamese nationalism sparked opposition from Bodos, Cachars and other ethnic minorities. However, though bombings, *bandhs* and in-fighting continue, the situation has improved and tourists are not targets.

Assam's busy capital, **Guwahati** has one of India's most important Kali temples, **Kamakhya**, and is a hub for the whole region. Within easy access of the city, the spectacular **Kaziranga National Park** is renowned for its one-horned **rhinos**. Further along the Brahmaputra lies the fascinating island of **Majuli**, home to unique Hindu monasteries. During your visit, keep an eye out for the *bhut jolokia*, the **world's hottest chilli**, which is native to the state.

Guwahati and around

The state capital **GUWAHATI** (or Gauhati) lies on the banks of the **Brahmaputra**, whose swollen sandy channel is so wide that the far shore is often invisible. It's a dirty and crowded city, but as it's the main gateway to the region you will probably need to stay here for at least a night or two. The busy downtown market area contrasts sharply with the rural riverside northeast of the centre, and the surrounding hills beyond. Guwahati's main attractions are the **Kamakhya, Navagraha** and **Umananda** temples, while northwest of the city are the silk village of **Sualkachi**, the pilgrimage site of **Hajo** and **Manas National Park**.

Access, permits and tour operators

Although the region is gradually opening up for tourism, **regulations** can change according to the current state of security, so check the latest information with the Indian Embassy before travelling. Currently **Assam**, **Meghalaya** and **Tripura** are completely free of restrictions. Foreigners require **Restricted** or **Protected Area Permits** to visit **Arunachal Pradesh**, **Nagaland, Mizoram** and **Manipur**; Indian nationals require Inner Line Permits for these four states. At the time of writing, the UK Foreign Office is advising against all travel to Tripura and Manipur. Arunachal Pradesh is the only state that charges for its permit (US$50), though Manipur demands a Rs1500 "royalty fee" when your permit is issued. Arunachal Pradesh permits are valid for 30 days; permits for the other states are valid for ten days, though it is sometimes possible to get an extension – ask on application or check with a tour operator in the region. Nagaland and Arunachal Pradesh permits start from a fixed date; Mizoram permits start when you enter the state.

Officially Nagaland and Mizoram require you to travel in a group of at least four. However, Nagaland may allow married couples to enter on their own, while in practice Mizoram tends to be more flexible (you can often obtain a permit even if you are travelling alone). Arunachal Pradesh officially requires you to be in a group of two, though individual travellers, applying through a travel agent, can obtain a permit by paying the full two-person US$100 fee. Make lots of photocopies of your permits, as you will have to leave copies behind at the border, with hotels and so on.

When you cross into Arunachal Pradesh or Mizoram, you may have to tell the border guards that the other – non-present or fictitious – people on your permit have been "delayed" and that you are meeting a local guide once you reach your destination, regardless of your actual intentions. Nagaland is far stricter, however, and you're unlikely to be allowed in on your own or without a guide; realistically you need to visit the state as part of an organized trip. If you are travelling with a tour operator in any of the states, expect to pay at least US$50 per person per day.

Independent travellers should have their permits endorsed at the **Foreigners' Registration Office** (or with the Superintendent of Police) in the state capitals. Permits are not date-stamped when you cross a **border**, so if your travels take you in and out of a state more than once, there may be some confusion as to whether you are allowed back in again. Passes are valid for the full period they are allocated for, no matter how many times you enter and exit a state, but in practice you may find yourself facing border guards demanding bribes. Stand your ground.

Obtaining permits

The easiest way of getting a **permit** for Mizoram, Nagaland and Arunachal Pradesh is by applying several weeks in advance through a tour operator. You'll have to pay an administration fee – and sometimes a few rupees to "ease" the permit's progress through the state bureaucracy – but they may be able to help put a group together. The alternative is to apply to the Foreigners' Division of the Ministry of Home Affairs, Lok Nayak Bhavan, Khan Market, New Delhi, or the Foreigners' Regional Registration

Arrival and information

The **railway station** is in the town centre, but the new **Inter State Bus Terminus (ISBT)** is inconveniently located on the NH-37, 9km to the east. The back of the station leads into hectic Paltan Bazaar, where most of the private bus companies are based. Guwahati's **airport** is 18km west of the centre.

Assam Tourism is on Station Road (daily except Sun and 2nd & 4th Sat of month: March–Oct 10am–5pm; Nov–Feb 10am–4.15pm; ⓣ0361/254 7102, ⓦwww.assamtourism.org); next door it has a commercial booth

Office, AJC Bose Road, Kolkata; however, the permits issued from these offices are often limited to certain areas within the states, which may not fit in with your travel plans. It is best to give yourself around a week to get the permits sorted. It's also possible to obtain permits from Indian embassies abroad – however, they all have to get permission from Delhi, so apply at least two months in advance.

To obtain **Inner Line Permits**, Indian citizens should apply with two passport photographs to representatives of the state governments concerned. Applications should only take a day to process, and can be extended for up to six months in the relevant state capital.

State Government representatives

Arunachal Pradesh Arunachal Bhawan, Kautilya Marg, Chanakyapuri, Delhi ⓣ011/2301 3915; Block CE-109, Sector 1, Salt Lake, Kolkata ⓣ033/2334 1243.

Manipur Manipur Bhawan, 2 Sardar Patel Marg, Chanakyapuri, Delhi ⓣ011/2687 3311; Manipur Bhawan, 26 Rowland Rd, Kolkata ⓣ033/2475 8075.

Mizoram Mizoram Bhawan, Circular Rd (behind the Sri Lankan Embassy), Chanakyapuri, Delhi ⓣ011/2301 0595; Mizoram House, 24 Old Ballygunge Rd, Kolkata ⓣ033/2475 7034.

Nagaland 29 Aurangzeb Rd, Delhi ⓣ011/2301 6411; Nagaland House, 12 Shakespeare Sarani, Kolkata ⓣ033/2242 5269.

Tour operators

Cultural Pursuits *Hotel Alpine Continental*, Shillong, Meghalaya ⓣ9436/303978, ⓦwww.culturalpursuits.com. Friendly, experienced and extremely well-informed Canadian operation arranging trips throughout the region, including tailor-made excursions for budget travellers.

Gurudongma Tours & Treks *Gurudongma Lodge*, Kalimpong, West Bengal ⓣ03552/255204, ⓦwww.gurudongma.com. Highly professional team arranging tours, trekking, mountain-biking, tribal and wildlife holidays in Assam, Meghalaya, Nagaland and Arunachal Pradesh, with particular expertise in birdwatching trips (ⓦwww.allindiabirding.com).

Jungle Travels India GNB Road, Silpukhuri, Guwahati, Assam ⓣ0361/266 0890, ⓦwww.jungletravelsindia.com. Guwahati-based agent organizing quality group and tailor-made tours, including luxury cruises.

Purvi Discovery Jalannagar, Dibrugarh, Assam ⓣ0373/230 1120, ⓦwww.purviweb.com. A tour operator with excellent guides, arranging personalized wildlife, fishing, golfing, horseriding, war memorial, tribal and tea tours around Dibrugarh and throughout the Northeast.

Travel The Unknown 52/1 Friends Rd, Croydon, London, UK ⓣ0845/053 0352, ⓦwww.traveltheunknown.com. A responsible and well-run UK-based company specializing in off-the-beaten-track destinations, with tours throughout the region, including to Tawang, Kaziranga and Cherrapunjee.

(ⓣ0361/213 0556) offering car rental, flight bookings, excursions to Kaziranga (two days, one night; Rs2850) and Manas (two days, one night; Rs3000), and a city tour (Rs300). The **India Tourism** office (Mon–Fri 9.30am–5pm; ⓣ0361/234 1603) is on Rehabari Road, Paltan Bazaar.

Accommodation

Guwahati has a good range of **places to stay** in all price categories, though it's advisable to book in advance.

Moving on from Guwahati

Public buses to destinations throughout the region including Dibrugarh (8–10 daily; 10hr), Jorhat (hourly; 7hr), Kaziranga (hourly; 5hr), Silchar (4–5 daily; 12hr), Siliguri (5–7 daily; 12hr) and Tezpur (1–2 hourly; 4–5hr) leave from the ISBT, but **private buses** are more comfortable, convenient and often quicker; most have ticket booths in Paltan Bazaar. Shared taxis and **Sumos** to Shillong (3hr 30min) and other destinations depart when full from the old bus stand, opposite *Hotel Tibet* in Paltan Bazaar.

Several **trains** link Guwahati to Delhi; the *Rajdhani Express* #2423 (Mon, Wed, Thurs, Fri & Sun at 7.05am; 27hr 5min) is the fastest. For Jorhat, the *Shatabdi Express* #2067 (daily except Sun at 6.30am; 6hr 40min) is the quickest train; it also calls at Lumding (2hr 52min) and Dimapur (4hr 15min). The *Kamrup Express* #5959 (daily at 4.30pm; 13hr 20min) travels to Dibrugarh. For Kolkata (Howrah), the *Kamrup Express* #5960 (daily at 7.45am; 22hr 20min) is a convenient option.

Lok-Priya Airport, 18km southwest of the city centre, has regular **flights** to Agartala, Aizawl, Bagdogra, Delhi, Dibrugarh, Dimapur, Imphal, Jorhat, Kolkata, Lilabari, Mumbai and Silchar. A taxi to the airport costs around Rs350 (45min); alternatively, shared minibuses (Rs100) leave when full from outside *Hotel Mahalaxmi*, next to *Hotel Nandan* on GS Road. There are Pawan Hans **helicopter** flights to Naharlagun (near Itanagar), Shillong, Tawang and Tura (ⓣ0361/241 6720).

For those with more time (and money), the Assam Bengal Navigation Company runs **cruises** on the Brahmaputra; book direct (ⓣ0361/260 2223, ⓦwww.assambengalnavigation.com), or through Jungle Travels India (see p.841).

Dynasty SS Rd, Fancy Bazaar ⓣ0361/251 6021, ⓦwww.hoteldynastyindia.com. Expectations are raised by the imposing palm-shaded entrance, water feature and opulent lobby, though not quite matched by the smart but overpriced attached rooms. There's a fine bar, excellent tandoori restaurant and a gym. ❻–❽

Ginger VIP Rd, behind the Tennis Association of Assam, 3km south of Bharalu River ⓣ0361/233 6333, ⓦwww.gingerhotels.com. Cool branch of the swish Tata Group chain, with great-value, minimalist attached rooms, wi-fi, gym and modish touches like "self check-in" the location is inconvenient though. ❺–❻

Kiranshree Portico Just off GS Rd, Paltan Bazaar ⓣ0361/273 5300, ⓦwww.kiranshreeportico.com. Very professional top-end hotel, with cool contemporary attached rooms featuring minibars, tea/coffee-making facilities, flatscreen TVs and swanky bathrooms, plus a gym, bar, coffee shop and accomplished restaurant. ❼–❽

Nandan GS Rd, Paltan Bazaar ⓣ0361/254 0855, ⓦwww.hotelnandan.com. This superior mid-range choice has sparkling attached rooms with wood-effect floors, wi-fi, efficient staff and a Mexican restaurant. ❻

Pragati Manor GS Rd, 1km south of Bharalu River ⓣ0361/234 1261, ⓦwww.pragatimanor.com. Although it's a bit of a trek from the centre, this is one of the city's best upmarket hotels. The shimmering gold exterior houses suave attached rooms with red lamps and tribal paintings. There's a good restaurant, 24hr coffee shop and bar. ❻–❼

Sagar MD Shah Rd, Paltan Bazaar ⓣ0361/273 7500, ⓦwww.hotelsagarguwahati.com. Perfect for anyone who hates clutter: the small, pared-down rooms have very clean bathrooms, flatscreen TVs, phones and little else. ❹–❺

Siroy Lily Solapara Rd, Paltan Bazaar ⓣ0361/260 8492, ⓦwww.hotelsiroylily.com. A solid but unspectacular choice, *Siroy Lily* has attached rooms – some a bit frayed around the edges – with TVs and desks. There's a good Manipuri restaurant and rates include breakfast. ❹–❺

Suudarban Guest House Just off ME Rd, Paltan Bazaar ⓣ0361/273 0722, ⓔkuljitbaruah_sgh@rediffmail.com. The pick of the backpacker lodges, *Suudarban* has good-value – generally pink – attached rooms with TVs, while the corridors are brightened up with houseplants, framed photos and religious posters. ❸–❹

Tibet AT Rd, Paltan Bazaar ⓣ9864023296, ⓔhoteltibet@redimail.com. The best of the budget lodges clustered around the old bus station, with cleanish, boxy rooms. It can be noisy, however, so bring earplugs. ❷–❸

Tourist Lodge Station Rd ⓣ0361/254 4475. Assam Tourism's green-and-white hotel has seen better days, but the attached rooms with TV and either fans or a/c are good value, so long as you don't mind the peeling paintwork. There's an inexpensive restaurant and bar. ❸–❹

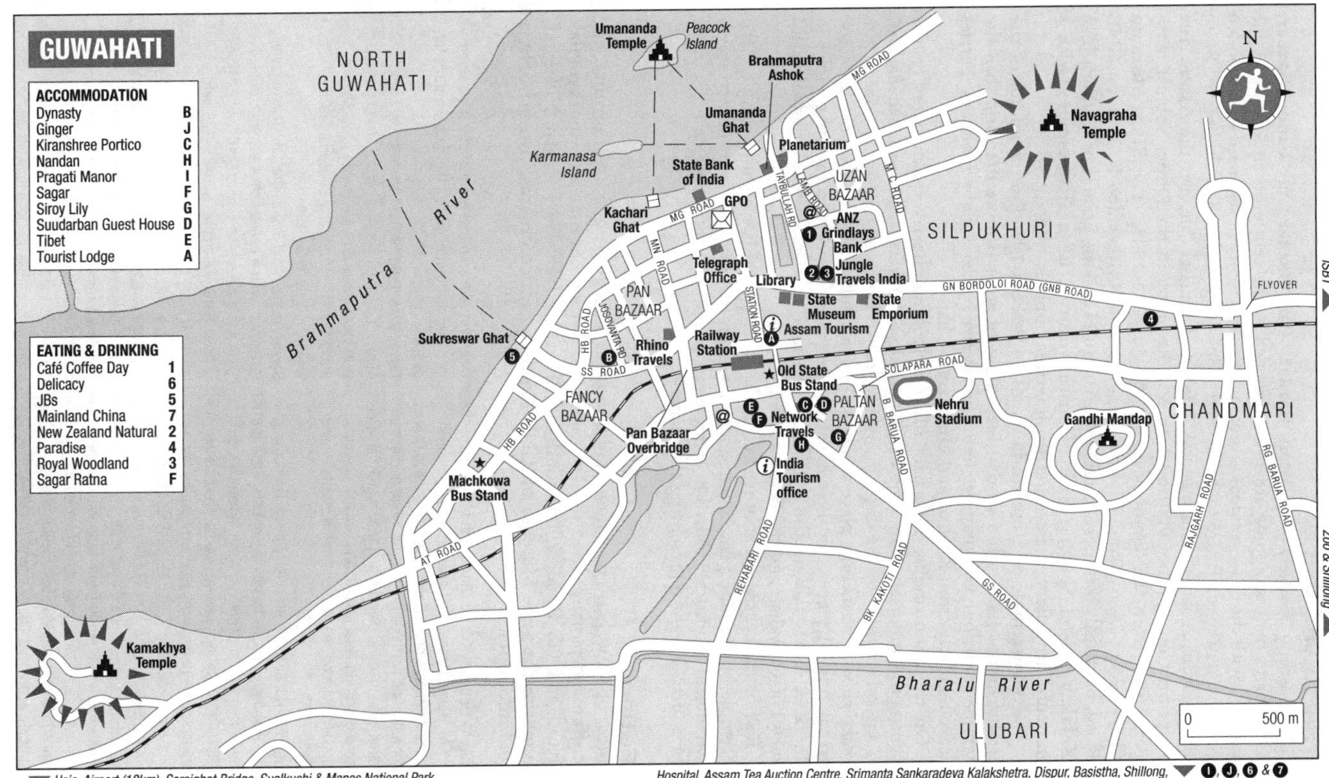
GUWAHATI
ACCOMMODATION
Dynasty B
Ginger J
Kiranshree Portico C
Nandan H
Pragati Manor I
Sagar F
Siroy Lily G
Suudarban Guest House D
Tibet E
Tourist Lodge A
EATING & DRINKING
Café Coffee Day 1
Delicacy 6
JBs 5
Mainland China 7
New Zealand Natural 2
Paradise 4
Royal Woodland 3
Sagar Ratna F
NORTH GUWAHATI
Brahmaputra River
Umananda Temple
Peacock Island
Karmanasa Island
Brahmaputra Ashok
Umananda Ghat
Planetarium
State Bank of India
Kachari Ghat
GPO
Telegraph Office
Library
ANZ Grindlays Bank
Jungle Travels India
State Museum
State Emporium
Assam Tourism
Railway Station
Old State Bus Stand
Rhino Travels
Network Travels
Pan Bazaar Overbridge
India Tourism office
Nehru Stadium
Gandhi Mandap
Navagraha Temple
Sukreswar Ghat
Machkowa Bus Stand
Kamakhya Temple
UZAN BAZAAR
SILPUKHURI
PAN BAZAAR
FANCY BAZAAR
PALTAN BAZAAR
CHANDMARI
ULUBARI
Bharalu River
MG ROAD
M C ROAD
TAYBULLAH RD
LAMB ROAD
MN ROAD
HB ROAD
JOSOVANTA RD
SS ROAD
STATION ROAD
GN BORDOLOI ROAD (GNB ROAD)
SOLAPARA ROAD
B BARUA ROAD
AT ROAD
REHABARI ROAD
BK KAKOTI ROAD
GS ROAD
RAJGARH ROAD
RG BARUA ROAD
FLYOVER
ISBT
Zoo & Shillong
0 500 m
N
Hajo, Airport (18km), Saraighat Bridge, Sualkuchi & Manas National Park
Hospital, Assam Tea Auction Centre, Srimanta Sankaradeva Kalakshetra, Dispur, Basistha, Shillong, 1, J, 6 & 7

The Town

The bustling markets of **Paltan Bazaar**, **Pan Bazaar** and **Fancy Bazaar**, Guwahati's main shopping areas, are bunched in the centre on either side of the railway, with the older residential areas north of the tracks. Assamese **silk**, wooden rhinos and other crafts are sold at several shops on GNB Road, including the **State Emporium**. Assam's main business is tea, and tourists can visit the **Assam Tea Auction Centre** (Tues 9.30am–1pm & 2.30–6pm), in the Dispur suburb, with permission from the Senior Manager (ⓣ0361/233 1845). The **State Museum** (daily except Mon 10am–4.15pm; Rs10, camera Rs10, video Rs250), on GNB Road, has tribal costumes and religious sculptures and the **Srimanta Sankaradeva Kalakshetra** on Shillong Road, Panjabari district, is an arts complex with a museum, art gallery, theatre and Vaishnavite temple.

The Shiva temple of **Umananda** stands on Peacock Island in the middle of the Brahmaputra. Its location atop a steep flight of steps is more dramatic than the temple itself, but you may get to see some rare golden langur monkeys. Ferries leave regularly from Kachari and Umananda Ghat.

On the commanding Nilachal Hill, overlooking the river 8km west of the centre, the important Kali temple of **Kamakhya**, with its beehive-shaped *shikhara*, is a good example of the distinctive Assamese style of architecture. As one of the *shakti pithas*, it marks the place where Sati's yoni (vulva) landed when her body fell to earth in 51 pieces, and is one of the three most important Tantric temples in India. A short walk up the hill brings you to a smaller temple with wonderful views of Guwahati and the Brahmaputra.

East of the centre, on another hill, is the atmospheric **Navagraha** temple – the "temple of the nine planets", an ancient seat of astrology and astronomy – with wonderful acoustics. Housed in a single red dome, the central lingam is encircled by a further eight representing the planets.

Eating

Most of Guwahati's mid-range and upmarket hotels have good **restaurants**. For **coffee** and pastries, head to *Café Coffee Day*, which has branches on Taybullah Road and GS Road, 200m south of Bharalu River. New Zealand Natural, opposite the State Museum on GNB Road, serves **ice creams**, frozen yoghurt and smoothies.

Delicacy GS Rd, 2km south of Bharalu River. Despite an unprepossessing location beneath an overpass, *Delicacy* is the place to come for authentic northeastern cuisine. Huge portions of duck, pigeon, pork, chicken and freshwater fish are served with unusual accompaniments like banana flowers, sesame seeds and bamboo shoots (mains Rs80–120).

JBs MG Rd, near the main ferry point. Overlooking the Brahmaputra, *JBs* has a pleasant first-floor a/c restaurant with superior veg north Indian dishes (Rs75–120): the rich *paneer makhani* and *paneer do-pyaza* are particularly good. Downstairs is a snack bar and bakery. There's another branch on GS Rd, just over 1km south of Bharalu River.

Mainland China Dona Planet mall, GS Rd, 700m south of Bharalu River. Guwahati's most fashionable restaurant wouldn't look out of place in downtown Mumbai. Exquisite and suitably expensive Chinese food (Rs90–470) – including *dim sum* and great seafood – served in classy surroundings. Try the date wontons for dessert.

Royal Woodland GNB Rd, close to the State Museum. Modest first-floor south Indian restaurant with inexpensive dosas – try the *rawa Mysore* masala dosa – *vada*s and *uttapam*s (Rs30–80), as well as a tasty Assamese thali.

Sagar Ratna *Hotel Sagar*. This first-floor a/c veg restaurant, with a peach colour scheme, frosted glass and enthusiastic serving staff, has 22 types of dosa, north Indian mains (Rs85–225) and a tempting array of ice-cream sundaes.

Paradise GNB Rd, 1km east of the State Museum. Unpretentious, low-lit joint with the menu printed on paper place mats, *Paradise* is a good place to sample a traditional Assamese thali (veg Rs90, non-veg Rs100). As well as nine savoury dishes, the thalis often feature *payash*, a sweet rice pudding. Beer (Rs100–130) is available.

Listings

Airlines Air India/Indian Airlines, GS Rd, Ganeshguri Charili, near Assam Assembly ⓣ0361/226 4420; Jet Airways, Taybullah Rd, near *Café Coffee Day* ⓣ0361/263 3252.
Banks and exchange ANZ Grindlays, GNB Rd, and the State Bank of India, MG Rd, change travellers' cheques and foreign currencies. Thomas Cook (ⓣ0361/222 9932) is on GS Rd, 3km south of Bharalu River. There are ATMs all over town.
Bookshops There are several bookshops in Pan Bazaar, notably Western Book Depot, Josovanta Rd, just off HB Rd; Vintage Bookshop on MN Rd; and Modern Book Depot on HB Rd, near MN Rd.
Hospital Down Town Hospital ⓣ0361/233 6906; Guwahati Medical College Hospital ⓣ0361/252 8417.
Internet access I-Way on Lamb Rd (Rs25/hr) and Pace Travels in Paltan Bazaar (Rs20/hr).
Pharmacy Life Pharmacy (8am–10.30pm), just south of B Barua Rd, near *Hotel Nandan*.
Police Emergencies ⓣ100; HB Rd ⓣ0361 /254 0138.
Post office ARB Rd, just round the corner from the State Bank of India.
Travel agents Rhino Travels, MN Rd, Pan Bazaar (ⓣ0361/254 0666), runs a range of tours, including safaris at Manas. Network Travels, Paltan Bazaar (ⓣ0361/260 5335, ⓦwww.networktravelsindia .net), can arrange tours, permits and air tickets; it's also one of the region's largest private bus operators. Jungle Travels India (see box, p.841) books flights, arranges permits and organizes tours.

Around Guwahati

Every home in the village of **SUALKUCHI**, 36km from Guwahati, produces golden *muga* **silk**, named after the rich amber colour of the *muga* cocoon, exclusive to Assam. The silk is cheaper than in Guwahati, and you can buy it direct from many villagers' homes. **HAJO**, 2km north, is a pilgrimage site for Hindus, Buddhists and Muslims, worth seeing for its mix of religious temples, including the Hindu **Hayagriba-Madhava Mandir**. Muslims believe visiting the **Poa Mecca Mosque** here four times is equivalent to a pilgrimage to Mecca.

MANAS NATIONAL PARK (Oct–March; Rs250 [Rs20], vehicle Rs200, camera Rs500 [Rs50]), 80km west of Guwahati on the border with Bhutan, has been on UNESCO's list of endangered World Heritage Sites since 1992. Troubled by insurgency, poachers and staff shortages, the park's population of large mammals sadly declined and sightings of tigers and elephants are now relatively rare. However, it is still worth a visit for its varied natural beauty, with water buffalo grazing on expansive stretches of sand and grass, and *sal* forests flanking the Manas River. Moreover, several rhinos have recently been relocated from Kaziranga, with others set to follow, and there are plans to expand the park and set up new hotels. In the meantime the *Mothunguri Forest Bungalow* overlooking the river has three atmospheric **rooms** (❸) – to book, contact the Field Director (ⓣ03666/260289). Otherwise try the more comfortable *Bansbari Lodge* (ⓣ0361/260 2223, ⓦwww.assambengalnavigation.com; ❺) just outside the park. You'll need to hire your own transport to get here – alternatively come on an organized tour.

Tezpur

TEZPUR, 174km northeast of Guwahati, is a busy little town on the north bank of the Brahmaputra. Literally meaning "full of blood", it's named after a mythical battle between Vishnu and Shiva. You may need to stay here en route to Arunachal Pradesh.

Chitralekha Udyan (daily 9am–8pm; Rs10), with its central lake (paddleboats Rs40/15min), is a good place to potter, especially in the early evening when the pathways are lit up with fairy lights. It is still known locally as Cole Park after its founder, the British deputy commissioner. The town's main market, **Chowk Bazaar**, is on MC Road; a little further north lies the ninth-century Shiva

Mahabhairav Temple. Along the river, 1km to the east, **Agnigarh Hill** (daily 8am–7.30pm; Rs10) commands great views, and is known as the place where Asura, king of the Ban dynasty, protected his beautiful daughter, Usha, from men who wanted to seduce her.

Arrival and information

Tezpur's **bus stand**, on Kabarkhana (KK) Road, is 500m north of the **tourist office** (daily except Sun and 2nd & 4th Sat of month 10am–5pm; ⓣ03712/221016), which is in the *Tourist Lodge* on KP Agarwalla Road. The **GPO** is on Head Post Office Road, parallel to the main road. No banks change foreign currency, but there are plenty of **ATMs**. Dhungana Cyber Café in the Anjana Complex, NB Road, 100m north of *Chinese Villa*, offers **internet** access (Rs20/hr). KK Road is lined with **Sumo** stands, with daily services to Bomdila (5–6hr), Dirang (7–8hr) and Tawang (14–18hr) in Arunachal Pradesh. There are **state buses** to Guwahati (1–2 hourly; 4–5hr), Jorhat (hourly; 4hr), Kaziranga (hourly; 2hr) and Itanagar (1–2 daily; 5hr). Tezpur **airport** serves Kolkata and Silchar.

Accommodation

Tezpur has numerous hotels, many of which are very good value.

Centre Point Main Rd, opposite the police station ⓣ03712/232359, ⓔhotelcentrepoint.tezpur@gmail.com. This business-traveller oriented hotel has good-value attached rooms that are functional rather than attractive. The halls, meanwhile, are brightened up with benches, plants and artwork. Service, however, is variable. ❸–❺

KF Mission Charali, 4km north of the bus station ⓣ03712/237825, ⓔskfood@gmail.com. *KF* is something of a surprise: immaculate, contemporary rooms with slick attached bathrooms, modern art, flat-screen TVs and tea/coffee-making facilities make this "boutique" hotel one of Assam's most stylish. It's also got a great restaurant. ❺–❻

Luit Off Ranu Singh Rd, 100m north of the bus station ⓣ03712/222083, ⓔhotel@rediffmail.com. The economy rooms in the "old wings" annexe of the venerable *Luit* are the best bet for backpackers. There are also more comfortable (and expensive) mid-range rooms with cane furniture, TVs and plenty of space. Old wings rooms ❷, mid-range rooms ❹–❺

Tourist Lodge KP Agarwalla Rd ⓣ03712/221016. Although it has seen better days, the *Tourist Lodge* is still an acceptable budget choice if the *Luit* is full. The simple rooms are quiet and pretty clean. ❷

Wild Mahseer 30km north of Tezpur ⓣ03714/234354, ⓦwww.oldassam.com. These four luxurious colonial-era bungalows are based on the Addabari Tea Estate. Prices include full board and activities: aside from enjoying the peace and quiet, guests can fish, cycle or hike. ❽

Eating and drinking

Tezpur has a handful of **restaurants**. *KF* has a cool modern feel and a quality menu, featuring veg and chicken burgers, pizzas, and Indian and Chinese favourites, including some tasty prawn curries (Rs90–165), plus an attached ice-cream parlour, cake shop and bar. *Chinese Villa*, on the second floor of the Baliram complex on the corner of NB and NC roads, 300m northeast of the bus station, has huge windows, stained-glass panels and red hanging lamps. Although there's a separate Indian menu, opt for the Chinese dishes (Rs70–130), such as barbecued lamb. Downstairs, *Veggie Foods* is an informal, wallet-friendly place serving dosas and thalis (Rs15–35).

Nameri National Park

A 35km journey north of Tezpur, accessible only by taxi, the 200-square-kilometre **NAMERI NATIONAL PARK** (Nov–March; Rs250 [Rs20]) flanks the River Bharali and is a lovely, quiet place for fishing, rafting, birdwatching or guided walks. There are more than three hundred species of bird, including the rare white-winged wood duck, fish eagles and hornbills. You may also see deer, but the park's tigers and elephants are rarely spotted. Guides, fishing, walking and rafting trips can be arranged via the atmospheric *Eco Camp* (ⓣ9435250052, ⓔnameriecocamp@gmail.com; ❺), 3km from the park, which has atmospheric tents protected by thatched roofs, with attached bathrooms, a dorm (Rs100, plus a compulsory Rs60 "membership") and a restaurant. Alternatively stay in Bhalukpong (see p.857), 10km from the park entrance. Gurudongma Tours & Treks (see p.841) and *Wild Grass* in Kaziranga (see p.848) arrange birdwatching tours to Nameri.

Kaziranga National Park

A World Heritage Site covering 430 square kilometres on the southern bank of the Brahmaputra, **KAZIRANGA NATIONAL PARK**, 217km east of Guwahati, occupies a vast valley floor against a backdrop of the Karbi Anglong hills. Its rivulets, shallow lakes and semi-evergreen forested highlands blend into marshes and flood plains covered with tall elephant grass. A visit here is exhilarating and you are likely to see elephants, deer and wild buffalos. The big draws, however, are the park's famous one-horned **rhinos** (officially there are around two thousand), which are best observed from the back of an elephant, first thing on a winter's morning, and its **tigers**, which are relatively elusive, despite a government report in 2010 that claimed Kaziranga has the highest density of tigers of any park in the world, with 32 big cats per 100 square kilometres. Jeeps take you deeper into the forest than elephants, but cannot get nearly as close to the rhinos and tigers. Driving through the park's landscape of open savanna grassland interspersed with dense jungle, is a wonderful experience. The abundant birdlife includes egrets, herons, storks, fish eagles, kingfishers and a grey pelican colony.

Kaziranga is open from November to early April. Avoid visiting on Sundays, when it gets busy with noisy groups of Indian tourists. During the monsoons (June–Sept), the Brahmaputra bursts its banks, flooding the low-lying grasslands and causing animals to move to higher ground within the park. It is important to **take care** when on safari; accidents are very rare, but occasionally occur, most recently in April 2009, when a Dutch tourist was trampled to death by a wild elephant.

Land encroachment and particularly **poaching** remain serious problems: at least 14 rhinos were killed in 2009. The understaffed park authorities appear unable to protect the animals whose horns fetch astronomical prices. Nevertheless, Kaziranga was named a tiger reserve in 2006 – as part of Project Tiger – which has resulted in extra funds, and in January 2010 army commandos were brought in to try to combat the poachers: whether this proves enough to make a real difference remains to be seen.

Kaziranga practicalities

There are hourly **buses** to Kaziranga from Tezpur (2hr), Jorhat (1hr 30min) and Guwahati (5hr), as well as less frequent services to Dibrugarh (5–7 daily; 6hr). State and private buses all stop at **Kohora**, the main gate, on the NH-37 (AT Road), with Network Travels serving as the pick-up and drop-off point. The nearest town is **BOKAKHAT**, 20km east. You pay the **entrance fees** (Rs250 [Rs20], vehicle Rs250, camera Rs500 [Rs50], video Rs1000 [Rs500], elephant ride Rs750 [Rs305]) in the tourist complex in Kohora. Jeeps can be hired (Rs600–1500) here, or you can get your hotel to arrange them. For **information**, visit the tourist office (03776/262423) in *Bonani* (see p.848).

Kaziranga has many **places to stay**. The four state-run lodges are in the tourist complex, which also has several **restaurants**, snack bars and a post office: *Aranya*

(Ⓣ03776/262429, Ⓕ262677; ❹) is the most comfortable, with clean but characterless attached rooms with balconies or verandas, a decent restaurant and bar; *Bonani* (Ⓣ03776/262423; ❹) has a vaguely colonial feel, large, worn rooms (some with a/c) and – unsettlingly – several animal skulls dotted around; *Bonoshree* (❷) has tatty but acceptable doubles; *Kunjaban* is the most basic, with several dorms (Rs50–100, plus Rs50 for bed linen) – ask for one of the three-bed rooms. *Bonoshree* and *Kunjaban* are booked through *Bonani*. Also in the tourist complex is the Network Travels-run *Jupuri Ghar* (Ⓣ9435 196377, Ⓔjupuri@gmail.com; ❺), which has attractive attached rooms in thatched-roof cottages with verandas and tasteful decor, welcoming staff and a good restaurant.

There are two good alternatives outside the complex. Set back from the NH-37 in quiet, peaceful gardens 1km from the park entrance, *Bon Habi Jungle Resort* (Ⓣ03776/262675, Ⓦwww.bonhabiresort.com; ❺) has large white- and terracotta-coloured cottages with easy chairs and private balconies, backing onto woodland. At the foot of the Karbi Hills, 4km east of Kohora and 1.5km off the road, the eco-friendly *Wild Grass* (Ⓣ03776/262085, Ⓦwww.oldassam.com; ❹–❺) offers cosy colonial-style attached rooms with wooden floors, a handful of cottages and lush gardens with two hundred types of plants. Both *Wild Grass* and *Bon Habi* can arrange visits to local Mising and Karbi villages.

Silchar

South Assam, divided from the north by the Cachar Hills, is the crossing point to Tripura, Mizoram and Manipur, with nondescript **SILCHAR** its main transport hub. The Cachar Hills are affected by militant activity, so it is worth checking the security situation before heading to Silchar. The **state bus stand** is near the Devdoot cinema; most **private bus** and **Sumo** companies also operate from here to Agartala (11hr), Aizawl (12hr), Guwahati (12hr) and Shillong (10hr). The road to Imphal is not recommended because of its poor condition and numerous army checkpoints. The **railway station** is 3km out of town, but services are limited. Silchar's **airport**, 13km away, has flights to Agatala, Guwahati, Imphal and Kolkata. If you need to **stay**, *Kanishka* (Ⓣ03842/246764; ❹) in Narsingtola has bright and breezy attached rooms.

Upper Assam

Around 310km northeast upriver from Guwahati, **Jorhat** has an airport and road connections to Kaziranga, Nagaland and northern Arunachal Pradesh. The unique Vaishnavite culture of **Majuli**, reputedly the world's largest river island, and **Sibsagar**, former capital of the Ahoms, are both close by. Further north, **Dibrugarh** is opening up as a gateway to northern Nagaland and eastern Arunachal Pradesh. There is good birdwatching at **Dibru-Saikhowa National Park**, while **Digboi** has an interesting oil museum and war memorial.

Jorhat

Well connected by railway, **JORHAT** is not in itself of great interest, but makes a good base for exploring Majuli, Kaziranga and Sibsagar. If you're here in February, check out the **Jorhat Gymkhana Club**'s (Ⓣ0376/231 1303) annual horseracing and polo event.

The **airport**, 5km from town, has weekly flights to Guwahati and Kolkata; Indian Airlines and Jet Airways have offices in *Hotel Paradise*, next to *Hotel Heritage*. The state **bus stand** is on AT Road, half a block north of the private companies' offices: there are hourly buses to Dibrugarh (4hr), Guwahati (7hr), Kaziranga (1hr 30min) and Tezpur (1hr 30min), as well as frequent services to Sibsagar

(1hr 30min) and several daily to Dimapur (5hr). The **railway station** is 3km southeast of here: the *Shatabdi Express* #2068 (daily except Sun at 1.55pm; 6hr 50min) travels to Guwahati.

The **tourist office** (daily except Sun and 2nd & 4th Sat of month 10am–5pm; ⓣ0376/232 1579) is in the *Tourist Lodge* on MG Road; to get there head east along AT Road from the bus stand and take the third road on your right. Nearby, Jorhat's modest **museum** (Tues–Sun 10am–4.30pm), in the Postgraduate Training College, has a mildly diverting collection of local crafts; there are plans to move it to a new purpose-built site nearby. The State Bank of India on AT Road, just east of the bus station, has an **ATM** and changes travellers' cheques. Computer Link Cyber Café, just off AT Road, 100m west of the bus stand, offers **internet** access (Rs20/hr).

The quiet *Tourist Lodge* (ⓣ0376/232 1579; ❸) has very clean **rooms** with tiled floors, balconies (but no views) and attached bathrooms. Mosquitoes can be a problem, but the beds come with nets. A better option is the attractive white-and-green *Hotel Heritage* (ⓣ0376/232 7393, ⓕ230 0008; ❸–❹), on Solicitor Road, next to the bus stand, with good-value airy rooms with marble floors, TVs, tiny but spotless bathrooms and an apricot colour-scheme. A 15km-drive south of Jorhat is the delightful *Thengal Manor* (ⓣ011/4603 5500, ⓦwww.welcomheritage hotels.com; ❼), the colonial-style former holiday home of the local Barooah family. It has an impressive white pillar facade and five rooms, all with stone fireplaces, four-poster beds and period furniture. Slightly cheaper is the *Burra Sahib's Bungalow* (booking details as above; ❼), a peaceful tea-planter's home on the Sangsua tea estate, 25km southwest of Jorhat, with a veranda and comfortable, spacious rooms. Guests can use the nearby golf course, play croquet, fish and take tea tours.

Jorhat's **eating** options are limited. *Heritage* has the pick of the Solicitor Road hotel restaurants – try the succulent chicken tikka butter masala or the roasted pomfret (Rs50–180). *Naffy* on AT Road, 100m west of the bus station, has a cheerful – or garish, depending on your point of view – orange-and-yellow colour-scheme, and a tasty, good-value Chinese and north Indian menu (Rs30–130).

Majuli

The most popular outing from Jorhat is to the World Heritage Site of **MAJULI**. It is often described as the largest inhabited river island in the world, but erosion in recent years has thrown that claim into doubt. Regardless of its precise status, Majuli is a fascinating place, largely because of its unique Vaishnavite *sattras* (Hindu monasteries), though it is also a haven for birdwatchers.

There are 22 *sattras* – institutions that contain elements of a temple, monastery, school and centre for the arts – on Majuli: each consists of a prayer hall (*namghar*) surrounded by living quarters for devotees, and *ghats* for bathing. In a day, you could visit **Natun Kamalabari**, and 1.5km away, **Uttar Kamalabari**. The monks will give you tea, and you can sometimes attend prayer meetings. Four kilometres further west at **Auniati**, another *sattra* keeps royal artefacts from the Ahom kingdom and has an interesting collection of Assamese handicrafts and jewellery. **Bengenati**, 4km east of Auniati, was built in the early seventeenth century, while **Shamaguri**, 6km beyond Bengenati, is renowned for its clay and bamboo masks. **Bongaori**, 8km beyond Shamaguri, and **Dakhinpat**, 5km further south, are also worth a visit.

Practicalities

Ferries for Majuli (10.30am & 3pm; 2hr 30min; Rs15) leave from **Nimatighat**, accessible by bus or taxi (around Rs300; 1hr) from Jorhat. As the ferry timings only give you an hour or so on the island, it is inadvisable to visit as a day-trip – you can hire your own boat for around Rs4500–5000 return (contact monk Dulal

Saikia (☎03775/273037 for details) but you'll get more out of the island if you stay overnight.

Distances are short and public transport around the island is limited to a handful of taxis and auto-rickshaws, and the occasional bus running to **Kamalabari** village (5–6 daily; 5km), and beyond to the island's "capital", **Garamur.** For those with plenty of time, the most relaxing way to explore is on foot or a bicycle hired from one of the lodges. The best **accommodation** is *La Maison de Ananda* (☎03775/274768; ❷), "The House of Joy". Built by a French couple, both architects, this lovely traditional cane and bamboo bungalow, raised on stilts, is set in peaceful gardens. The furnishings were made by local weavers, the kitchen produces local dishes like smoked pork, and guide – and poet – Danny Gam ensures everything runs smoothly. A shabby, but acceptable alternative is the *Natun Kamalabari Guesthouse* (☎03775/273302; ❷), with fairly clean but austere rooms.

There are two daily **ferries** (7.15am & 2pm; 2hr 30min) back to Nimatighat from Majuli. It is also possible to travel north from Majuli, with two daily ferries from Luhitghat, 3km north of Garamur; they arrive at Khabalughat on the north bank, from where there are **buses** to North Lakhimpur, and from there, buses on to Itanagar or Tezpur, and a **train** to Guwahati. Allow yourself plenty of time. There are tentative plans to increase the frequency of the ferry services and build a bridge linking Majuli with the mainland.

Sibsagar

The former capital of the Ahoms and one of Assam's oldest towns, **SIBSAGAR** lies 60km northeast of Jorhat. Its cluster of monuments from six centuries of Ahom rule remains significant to modern Assamese culture. A huge **tank**, constructed in 1734, lies at the heart of the complex, while rising from its southern shore, the massive 32m **Shivadol** is India's tallest Shiva temple, flanked by smaller temples dedicated to Durga and Vishnu. Nearly 4km west of the centre of town is the royal **Rang Ghar** pavilion and the ruins of the **Talatal Ghar** palace. Though best visited as a day-trip, there are a few **accommodation** options. Backpackers should head to *Kareng* on Temple Road (☎03772/222713; ❷–❸), which has acceptable, though spartan rooms. *Shiva Palace* (☎03772/225184, Ⓔhotel_shiva_palace@rediffmail.com; ❹–❺) on AT Road, 200m from the bus station, is easily Sibsagar's most comfortable hotel, with pristine, sparsely-furnished attached rooms (a/c or non a/c) and acres of marble. It also has the *Sky Chef* **restaurant**, with an extensive north Indian menu: highlights include the juicy kebabs and an outstanding poppy-seed *paratha* (Rs60–150). The attached *Fahrenheit* is a wonderfully retro 80s-style bar filled with chrome and black leather: grab a cocktail and pretend you're in a Duran Duran video.

Dibrugarh

The dusty town of **DIBRUGARH**, 443km north of Guwahati, is surrounded by nine golf courses and lies at the heart of tea-growing country. While there's little of interest in the town itself, Dibrugarh is a good place from which to explore eastern and northern Arunachal Pradesh and northern Nagaland – and, of course, to see how **tea** is produced. Purvi Discovery (see p.841) offers tours on its working tea estate.

Practicalities

Dibrugarh's **airport**, with flights to Guwahati, Kolkata and Lilabari, is 16km from town. The **state bus stand** is in Chowkidinghee in the town centre, with the **private bus stand** nearby at Phool Bagan; both have services to Digboi (6–8 daily; 4hr), Guwahati (8–10 daily; 10hr), Jorhat (hourly; 4hr) and Kaziranga (5–7 daily;

6hr). Around 1km south is the **railway station**, from where the *Kamrup Express* #5960 departs for Guwahati (daily at 6pm; 13hr 15min). **A car with driver** can be hired from Purvi Discovery (see p.841). There is a daily **ferry** to Oiramghat, near Pasighat (7–8hr; Rs67/passenger, from Rs2500 for a jeep), which leaves Dibrugarh at 9am (though times fluctuate, so check before you set off). Arrive at least an hour before departure to ensure a seat. The State Bank of India at Thanka Charali, the central commercial district, cashes **travellers' cheques**.

Places to stay include *Mona Lisa* on Mancotta Road (ⓣ0373/232 0416, ⓔpaneijonki@sancharnet.in; ❹), which has a pleasant courtyard, spacious rooms and a bar. Alternatively try one of the cool and airy rooms with TVs and phones at the reliable *Indsurya* on RKB Path (ⓣ0373/232 6322, ⓦwww.hotelindsurya.com; ❹–❺). The best option, however, is 5km from the railway station; set on a tea estate, the peaceful *Chang Bungalows* (book through Purvi Discovery; ❽) was built on stilts by British tea planters, to protect them from floods and wild animals. The 150-year-old bungalows have polished hardwood floors, elegant furniture and excellent service.

For **food**, *H20* on the first floor of Amrit Mansion on RNC Path is a trendy restaurant and bar serving Chinese, Thai, Indian and Assamese food (Rs50–120).

North of Dibrugarh

About 60km north of Dibrugarh, **DIBRU-SAIKHOWA NATIONAL PARK** is rich in birdlife and wild horses. Good rail services run to New Tinsukia Station, 10km from the park's southern entry point at **Guijan**. Information is available from the Range Officer here (ⓣ0374/233 7569). The park is reachable as a day-trip from Dibrugarh, or you can stay in the *Inspection Bungalow* at Guijan (ⓣ0374/233 7569; ❷) or the campsite (ⓣ0374/233 7666; ❶). Purvi Discovery (see p.841) has a simple bungalow in Guijan that is sometimes available for independent travellers.

DIGBOI, 20km northeast of the park, is a pleasant place to stop en route to Arunachal Pradesh, with an oil refinery established by the British in 1900, an oil museum, a World War II cemetery and a golf course. The *Oil India Guesthouse* has spacious attached rooms (ⓣ03751/64715; ❹).

Meghalaya

MEGHALAYA, one of India's smallest states, occupies the plateau and rolling hills between Assam and Bangladesh. Its people are predominantly Christian, belonging to three main ethnic groups, the Khasis, Jaintias and Garos. The state has a high literacy rate and teaching is in English. Much of Meghalaya ("the land of the rain-clouds") is covered with lush forests, rich in orchids. These "blue hills" bear the brunt of the Bay of Bengal's monsoon-laden winds and are among the wettest places on earth. Stupendous waterfalls can be seen near the capital, **Shillong**, but the most dramatic plummet from the plateau to the south, around **Cherrapunjee**.

Meghalaya's hills rise to almost 2000m, making for a pleasantly cool year-round climate. The **Jaintia Hills** offer good walking and caving, and the state is laced with historical sights such as **Nartiang** near **Jowai**, which has an impressive collection of monoliths.

On January 21, 1972, after an eighteen-year struggle for autonomy from Assam, Meghalaya became a full-fledged state. However, the HNLC, a rebel underground movement, still calls *bandhs* demanding independence from the rest of India.

Shillong

With its rolling hills of pine conifers and pineapple shrubs, **SHILLONG** was known to the British as "the Scotland of the East" – an impression first brought to mind by **Barapani** (or Umiam), the stunning loch-like reservoir on its fringes, and the sight of the local Khasi women wearing gingham and tartan shawls. At an altitude of around 1500m, Shillong became a popular hill-station for the British, who built it on the site of a thousand-year-old Khasi settlement and made it Assam's capital in 1874.

Sadly, the city has lost some of its charm, the surrounding hills have suffered severe deforestation and the influx of settlers from the plains has placed a strain on natural resources, especially water. Much of the original Victorian town, however, is still evident, and the large gardens around **Ward Lake** and the buildings surrounding it conjure up images of a colonial past. North of the polo ground is one of Asia's oldest golf courses, founded in 1898 by a group of British civil servants. **Rabindranath Tagore** wrote *Raktakarabi* in Shillong, and the city also features in his masterwork *Shesher Kobita*.

Arrival and information

Shillong (or Umroi) **airport** is 34km west of the city. Public **buses** pull into the Jail Road bus station in central Shillong. **Meghalaya Tourism** (daily 7am–6pm; ⓣ0364/222 6220, ⓦwww.meghalayatourism.org), on Jail Road, opposite the bus station, runs a good-value day-trip to Cherrapunjee (8am–4.30pm; from Rs200) and a city tour (8.30am–2.30pm; from Rs150). The India Tourism office is on GS Road (Mon–Fri 9.30am–5.30pm, Sat 9.30am–2pm; ⓣ0364/222 5632). KA Ibadasuk Books Agency just up the road stocks **books** and maps. The **GPO** is on Kacheri Road, as is the **State Bank of India**, which has foreign exchange facilities. There are many **ATMs**, but **internet** joints are thin on the ground – try *S.I.D.S Cyber*, on the first floor of the mall at the end of Police Bazaar Road (Rs20/hr).

The highly recommended Cultural Pursuits (see box, p.841) arranges homestays in Khasi villages, treks and tours, including a trip to the Garo Wangala and Khasi Nongkrem Dance religious festivals in October. It also runs the eco-friendly *MaplePine* lodge (ⓣ9436 303978, ⓔmp@culturalpursuits.com; ❷–❹) 25km south of Shillong near Mawphland Sacred Forest, which is great for hiking. Those interested in exploring the state's awesome **caves** can contact the Meghalaya Adventurers Association at the Mission Compound near the Synod Complex (ⓣ0364/254 5621).

Accommodation

Shillong has a wide range of **accommodation**, although staying on GS Road can be noisy.

Moving on from Shillong

Public **buses** depart from the bus stand on Jail Road, leaving hourly for Guwahati (4hr), although **Sumos** and shared taxis from Kacheri Road are quicker (3hrs 30min). Private bus firms have offices nearby and run services all over the Northeast. For Aizawl (1–2 daily; 18hr) you may prefer to travel to Silchar (2–3 daily; 10hr) and then continue by jeep. The border crossing to **Bangladesh** at Dawki, southeast of Cherrapunjee, is served by a couple of private buses (4–5hr) and a fleet of Sumos, which also run to Cheerapunjee (2hr) and Mawsynram (3hr), from Bara Bazaar. There are several weekly Indian Airlines **flights** to Jorhat and Kolkata from the airport, although weather conditions mean delays are common. Meghalaya Tourism runs buses to the airport (Rs100) on days when there are flights. There are also **helicopter** flights (ⓣ0364/222 3129 or book at the bus stand) to Guwahati and Tura.

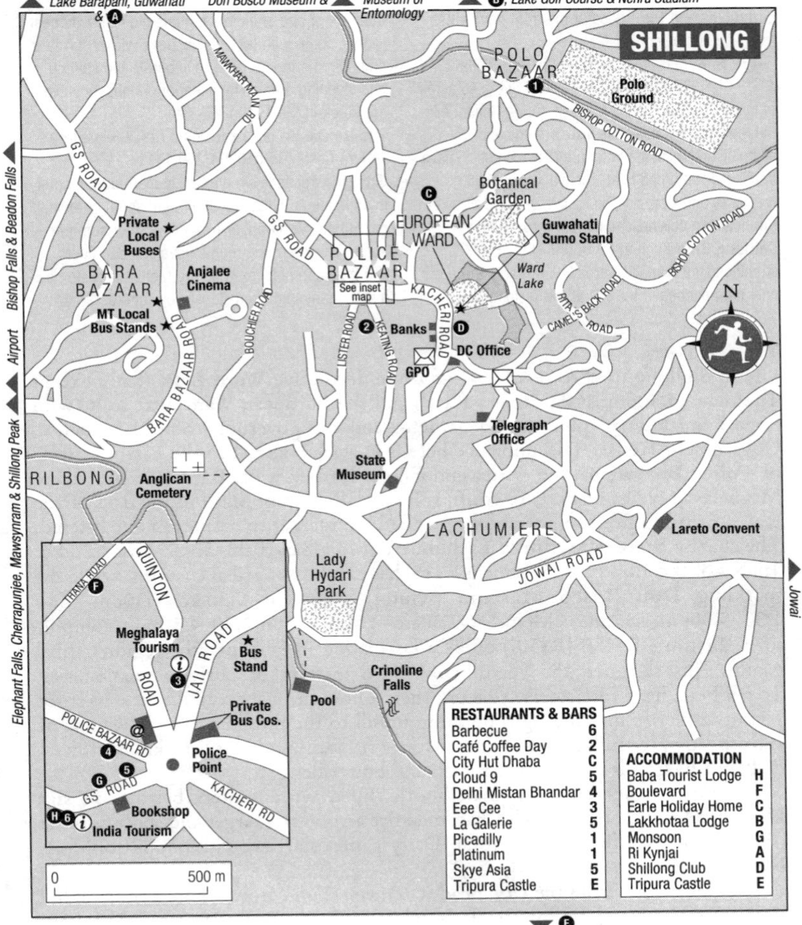

Baba Tourist Lodge GS Rd ⓣ0364/221 1285. A long-standing budget lodge with a motley collection of clean-enough attached rooms (mainly with squat toilets), with TVs and sloping roofs. Guests are obliged to eat one meal a day in the lodge's (decent) restaurant. ❷–❸

Boulevard Thana Rd ⓣ0364/222 9823, ⓕ222 9823. A very good mid-range hotel: even the cheapest rooms boast king-sized beds, clean bathrooms, TVs, high ceilings and minimalist decor. There's a veg restaurant, a bar, and rates include breakfast. ❺

Earle Holiday Home Oakland Rd ⓣ0364/222 8614. Recently renovated, *Earle* offers a range of clean but twee rooms (think lino floors and garish bed covers) in a traditional Meghalayan house or a more modern annexe; there's a distinct holiday camp feel. ❸–❺

Lakkhotaa Lodge Near the golf course ⓣ0364/259 0516, ⓦwww.lakkhotaalodge.com. A boutique hotel that blends Indian, US and Chinese influences. There are just nine rooms, each named after a different Native American tribe: "Cherokee", with a four-poster bed and a jacuzzi, stands out. It also has an excellent restaurant, open to non-guests who book ahead. ❼–❽

Monsoon GS Rd ⓣ0364/250 0084, ⓔhotel monsoon@hotmail.com. Distinctive little hotel filled with plant pots. The homely rooms are on the small side (and slightly overpriced) but have attached bathrooms and TVs. Those at the front have small (road-facing) balconies. ❹

Ri Kynjai 20km north of Shillong ⓣ9862 420300, ⓦwww.rikynjai.com. Set in 45 acres of forest in a spectacular location beside Umiam lake, the region's best hotel has luxury rooms and stunning cottages; the latter are raised on stilts, have traditional "upturned boat" roofs and come with fireplaces and jacuzzis. The restaurant specializes in Northeastern cuisine, and there's a spa. ❽

Shillong Club Kacheri Rd ⓣ0364/222 5497, ⓔshillongclubltdresi@hotmail.com. Sadly there are only faint echoes of the Raj at the residential quarters of one of India's famous old clubs. Its best rooms, some with lake views, have wicker furniture and shimmering curtains to separate the seating and sleeping areas. The cheaper options, however, are stuck in the 1970s. ❺–❻

Tripura Castle (also known as *Royal Heritage*) Tripura Castle Rd ⓣ0364/250 1111, ⓔrh_tripuracastle@rediffmail.com. Beautiful hotel in an inspiring hilltop location 3km south of town, next to the Maharaja of Tripura's former summer home. The charming rooms have wooden floors and brass fireplaces, while the Maharaja Suite has a mahogany bed once slept in by Tagore. ❻–❼

The Town

Life in Shillong used to revolve around the decorative **Ward Lake** (daily except Tues 8am–5.30pm; Rs5, camera Rs10) and the European Ward next to it, with large bungalows in pine-shaded gardens, and the governor's official residence, Government House. The ambience here is in stark contrast to the narrow streets of **Police Bazaar**, packed with vendors, or, further west, **Bara Bazaar**, where Meghalaya's oldest market, **Iewduh**, is held (daily except Sun): in the days of the Raj, a British officer on horseback patrolled the market to ensure no one littered. The shabby **State Museum** in Lachumiere (Mon–Sat 10am–5pm; closed 2nd & 4th Sat of the month; Rs5, camera Rs15) has exhibits on tribal customs, while the sparkling **Don Bosco Museum** (winter: Mon–Sat 9.30am–5.30pm, Sun 1.30–5.30pm; summer: Mon–Sat 9.30am–4.30pm, Sun 1.30–4.30pm; compulsory 1hr tours Rs150 [Rs50]) offers a fascinating insight into the region's tribal groups – just skirt over the woefully one-sided portrayal of Christian missionaries. To get here, head to *Hotel Polo Towers*, then follow the river round to the west for 1.5km until you find the signs pointing uphill to the museum. The **Museum of Entomology** (or Butterfly Museum; Mon–Fri 11am–4pm; Rs25), 2km northwest of Police Bazaar, is dedicated to moths and butterflies.

Shillong is peppered with small booths filled with punters betting on **siat khnam**, a local sport in which Khasi men fire arrows at a target and spectators bet on the final two digits of the total. Daily games start around 3.30pm opposite Nehru Stadium.

For some respite from the city, head to *Tripura Castle*, from where a short uphill walk takes you into pine-forested hills, while **Shillong Peak** (1965m), 10km west of town, also offers great views, as well as being home to the last four *ilex khasiana*, a high-altitude tree on the verge of extinction.

Eating and drinking

Police Bazaar and Jail Road have plenty of **snack bars**, including *Eee Cee*, a bakery that produces tasty – if not exactly authentic – pizzas. For a decent **cappuccino**, try *Café Coffee Day* on Keating Road. Shillong's small but flourishing local music scene has earned it the nickname "**rock city**". For performances look out for posters, or try one of the **bars**, such as *Cloud 9*, which adjoins *Skye Asia*, or *Platinum*, at *Hotel Polo Towers*, near the Polo Ground. *Hotel Polo Towers* also has a kitsch British-style pub, *Piccadilly*.

Barbecue GS Rd. Down a short flight of steps and beyond the fish tank is an authentic and very popular Chinese restaurant decked out with paper lamps and oriental trinkets. There are excellent chicken, pork and seafood dishes (Rs80–160), though some have off-putting names: "woolly chicken", for example, is tastier than it sounds.

City Hut Dhaba *Earle Holiday Home*. A cabin-like dining room with an extravagant water feature, *City Hut Dhaba* has a menu of more than 300 items (Rs55–140), including interesting dishes like spicy duck *chatpata*. Wrap up warm, as it can be decidedly chilly in the evenings.
Delhi Mistan Bhandar Police Bazaar Rd. A buzzing local joint with a classic range of Indian breakfasts, snacks and sweets (Rs5–40). There's no menu, and staff speak little English, so just point out what you want.
La Galerie and **Skye Asia** *Hotel Centre Point*, Police Bazaar. The former is a low-key canteen, ideal for a quick bite (Rs30–80); the latter, on the fifth floor, is far more refined, serving a Pan-Asian menu (mains Rs120–180) featuring well-executed Thai soups and *satays*, Korean barbecued chicken and Japanese *tepanyaki*.
Tripura Castle *Tripura Castle* hotel ⓣ0364/250 1111. Lovely setting for a leisurely meal: book ahead for dinner, and order the Khasi food in advance – dishes on offer include red rice with wild mushrooms (Rs120–300). Service, however, can be a bit sloppy.

Cherrapunjee and Mawsynram

CHERRAPUNJEE, 56km south of Shillong in the Khasi Hills, achieved fame as the wettest place on earth: the highest daily rainfall ever recorded fell here in 1876 – 104cm in 24 hours. Nearby **Mawsynram**, however, now gets slightly more water, with a staggering average annual rainfall of 1187cm. The area's numerous waterfalls are most impressive during the steamy monsoon season when awesome torrents plunge down to the Bangladeshi plains. However, in recent years the level of precipitation has decreased – most likely as a result of climate change – and **water shortages** have even been reported.

Cherrapunjee town is spread out over several kilometres. Every eight days a market is held here, with tribal jewellery and local orange-coloured honey on offer. The various nearby points of interest – the **Noh Kalikai waterfall, Bangladesh viewpoint**, and **Mawsmai village and cave** – are all within a few kilometres of Cherrapunjee, though in different directions. An easy way of seeing them all is to join Meghalaya Tourism's **day-trip** (see p.852). Alternatively, a taxi for the day costs Rs1200–1600.

There are several inexpensive lodges and restaurants in Cherrapunjee, but the best **accommodation** and food is to be found a short taxi ride (Rs250–300) away at the stunningly-located *Cherrapunjee Holiday Resort* (ⓣ9436115925, ⓦwww.cherrapunjee.com), perched on the edge of the East Khasi Hills with excellent views of the Bangladeshi plains below. There are six comfortable attached rooms (❺), a five-bed dorm (Rs450/ person) and several tents (Rs500/tent). From here you can explore some fascinating 150-year-old living root bridges, cool springs, waterfalls, caves and Khasi villages, or take caving, canyoning, angling or birdwatching trips. You can visit Cherrapunjee on a day-trek along the David Scott Trail from **Mawsphlang**, the site of an ancient sacred grove. Impulse Inc at the NGO Network in Shillong's Lachumiere (ⓣ0364/250 0587) can organize this.

The main attraction at **MAWSYNRAM**, 12km from Cherrapunjee, is the **Mawjinbuin cave**, where a stalagmite resembling a *shivalingam* is perpetually bathed by water dripping from a breast-shaped stalactite. There are no direct buses between Mawsynram and Cherrapunjee, so hire a taxi or join Meghalaya Tourism's day-trip.

Dawki

Ninety-six kilometres southeast from Shillong, **DAWKI** is the most important of the Meghalaya–Bangladesh border crossings and boasts excellent views. The equivalent border town in Bangladesh is **Tamabil**, two and a half hours from Sylhet. There's no Bangladesh visa office in Meghalaya, so you will need to acquire a visa beforehand; Kolkata has a consulate. If you are arriving at Dawki from Bangladesh, the last buses and Sumos to Shillong leave around 11am. Alternatively, a taxi costs Rs1300–1600.

Jowai and Nartiang

The market town of **JOWAI,** 64km northeast of Shillong in the **Jaintia Hills**, holds the Behdienkhlam dance festival every July. About 12km north of the town, at **NARTIANG**, are the remains of the Jaintia kings' summer palace and an impressive collection of monoliths and standing stones. A taxi costs about Rs400 from Jowai. There are caves throughout the area – Cultural Pursuits in Shillong can arrange visits and treks (see p.841). A couple of daily **buses** run from Shillong to Jowai (4hr), or you can take a taxi (2hr 30min).

Arunachal Pradesh

ARUNACHAL PRADESH, "the land of the dawn-lit mountains", is one of India's last unspoilt wildernesses. A wealth of fascinating cultures and peoples – plus a staggering five hundred species of orchid – are found in its glacial terrain, alpine meadows and subtropical rainforests.

The capital, **Itanagar**, is north of the Brahmaputra across from Jorhat. In the far west of the state, the road from **Bhalukpong** on the Assamese border to **Tawang** climbs steadily through rugged hills, streams and primeval forests, crossing the dramatic **Sela Pass** (4300m) midway. Along the route lie the Buddhist towns of **Bomdila**, **Rupa** and **Dirang**. In the far northeast, **Namdapha National Park** is home to clouded and snow leopards. Nearby **Parasuramkund** is one of India's most important and least accessible Hindu pilgrimage sites.

Despite its beauty, tourism has been discouraged because of the extremely sensitive border with Chinese-occupied Tibet in the north and Myanmar in the east. In 1962, the Chinese invaded Arunachal Pradesh, reaching Tezpur in Assam, a 300km incursion India has never forgotten. Since then, a strong military stance has been adopted in the area. All visitors require a **permit** (see box, p.840) to enter the state and most places are only accessible by jeep.

Between December and March, most of the state's hill towns are **bitterly cold** and accommodation is not geared up to cope – bring a winter sleeping bag, hot water bottle and torch, as **power cuts** are common.

Itanagar

Just under 400km northeast of Guwahati, **ITANAGAR**, the state's capital is of little interest, though as a transport hub you may need to spend a night here. Surrounded by densely-forested hills, the town itself is just a 4km stretch of road running between Zero Point, where the better hotels are located, and Ganga Market, the main bazaar, which has cheaper accommodation and the bus station.

The **Jawaharlal Nehru State Museum** (Sun–Thurs 9.30am–4pm; Rs75 [Rs10], camera Rs20), a ten-minute walk from Zero Point, showcases the festivals, dances, homes and lifestyles of local tribes. Its impressive ethnographic collection has wooden sculptures, musical instruments and esoteric objects like cane penis covers. The **Government Sales Emporium** above Zero Point sells interesting handicrafts. Ten kilometres from town, **Gyakar Sinyi** (Ganga Lake; Rs5, camera Rs10) and the lush surrounding jungle provide a taste of the state's magnificent scenery. You can get good views from the small **Tibetan Buddhist temple** on the way to the museum.

Arunachal Pradesh's tribal groups

Arunachal Pradesh is stunningly diverse, with 26 major tribal groups, each with its own culture, dialect, dress, social structure and traditions. Polygamy remains common among many of them, as does the religious blend of Hindu, Buddhist and animist beliefs. The main ethnic groups include Wanchos, Noctes, Tangsas, Singphos, Khamptis, Mishmis, Mijis, Galos, Padams, Miwongs, Membas, Tagins and Puroiks. However, within all the groups, tradition is slowly giving way to modern influences, particularly among the younger generation, who increasingly wear western clothes, watch Bollywood flicks and eat Chinese food.

Practicalities

The nearest **airport** is 67km away at **Lilabari**, near North Lakhimpur in Assam. **Helicopters** (Ⓣ0360/224 3262) to Guwahati, Hapoli (Ziro) and elsewhere depart from **Naharlagun**, 10km away. **Trains** from Guwahati run to Harmuti, 33km east in Assam. State and private **buses** connect Itanagar with Guwahati (10–11hr) and destinations throughout the state. **Sumos** are quicker; destinations include Along (10hr), Bomdila (7–8hr), Hapoli (5hr) and Pasighat (6–7hr). Agents around Ganga Market sell tickets. There's an intermittently open **tourist office** (Ⓣ 0360/221 4745, Ⓦwww.arunachaltourism.com) behind the Akash Deep complex in Ganga Market. Ocean Cyber Café, 300m downhill of Zero Point, offers **internet** access (Rs20/hr).

Itanagar has several decent **hotels**, including *Arun Subansiri*, just below Zero Point (Ⓣ0360/221 2806, Ⓕ229 0097; ❺–❻), which has a cool marble interior and vast rooms with reliable hot water and TVs. Nearby, the slightly cheaper *Moomsie* (Ⓣ0360/229 0971; ❹–❺) has pink- and peach-coloured rooms with TVs, cane furniture and clean attached bathrooms. The friendly *Blue Pine* on APST Road, Ganga Market (Ⓣ0360/221 1118; ❷–❹) has austere but acceptable rooms with TVs and shared or attached bathrooms (both have squat toilets), plus a dorm (Rs100).

The **restaurants** at *Arun Subansiri*, *Moomsie* and *Blue Pine* serve the usual mix of Indian and Chinese food (mains Rs40–140), plus a few interesting Northeastern dishes. Alternatively, try *Food Plaza*, near the entrance to the Akash Deep complex, which offers *momos* (dumplings), fried rice and noodles (Rs30–80).

West Arunachal

Bordered by Bhutan and Tibet, the isolated hills and valleys of western Arunachal climb to some of the remotest glaciers and peaks in the Himalayas. Most of the 6000m-plus mountains – except **Gori Chen** (6488m) and **Nyegi Kangsang** (7047m) – remain completely unknown. The solitary road serving the region runs from **Bhalukpong** on the Assamese border to **Tawang**, ending bone-shakingly high in the mountains at one of Asia's largest monasteries. On this spectacular journey you pass through the market town of **Bomdila**, home to three Tibetan monasteries, and **Dirang**, a fortress town a couple of hours up the valley. To the west of the Tawang road lies picturesque **Rupa**, with its colourful Tibetan monastery, **Chillipam**, whose Buddhist temple offers outstanding views, and the fascinating Buddhist settlements of **Tenzingang** and **Kalaktang.** Beyond Tawang, very close to the Tibetan border, stretches the lake district of **Bangachangsa**.

Bhalukpong

The **Kameng River** emerges from a deeply forested valley at **BHALUKPONG**. All public transport services from Tezpur, 56km away, to Bomdila stop here for border formalities. **Accommodation** options include the peaceful *Bhalukpong Tourist Lodge* (Ⓣ03872/234037; ❸–❹), just before the border, in Assam, which has large, clean cottages overlooking the river and surrounding hills. The lodge can arrange rafting and angling – the Kameng River is famed for its fighting *mahseer* fish. Alternatively, *Hotel Solu* (Ⓣ03782/234955; ❹), in upper Bhalukpong, 1km from the border gate, has bright and breezy attached rooms with TVs. From **Tipi**, 7km north of Bhalukpong, the narrow highway winds up through dense and beautiful mountain forests to Bomdila, 100km away.

Bomdila

BOMDILA is a friendly town set on a spur of the Thagla Ridge at 2530m, the dividing line between rainforests to the south and subalpine valleys to the north. There are a handful of **Tibetan Buddhist monasteries here**: the largest, a Gelugpa *gompa* high above town, was inaugurated by the Dalai Lama in 1997. The older *gompa* below houses a large blue Medicine Buddha statue. A few kilometres beyond Bomdila, the snow-covered peaks of Gori Chen (6488m) and Kangto (7042m) come into view.

Practicalities

The **tourist office** (Ⓣ03782/222049) is at the *Tourist Lodge*, while the professional Himalayan Holidays (Ⓣ03782/222017), on the main street, arranges **sightseeing trips** and treks, and provides **internet** access (Rs40/hr).

Most of Bomdila's budget **hotels** are also on the main street. *Passang* (Ⓣ03782/222627; ❶–❷) is the pick of the bunch, with simple, clean attached rooms. The *Tourist Lodge* (Ⓣ03782/222049; ❸), 1km uphill from the main street, near the stadium, is a step up in quality, with large but tatty rooms set around a central pond; the heaters are well worth the extra Rs100. The best place to stay, however, is the clean and welcoming *Doe Gu Khil* guesthouse (Ⓣ03782/223232; ❹) in the grounds of the main monastery.

Eating options include the cheerful *China Town*, on the main street, 100m south of Himalayan Holidays, which serves hearty bowls of noodles, soup and fried chicken and pork (Rs30–60). About 150m downhill is *Himalaya*, a tiny place that gives you the feeling you're eating in someone's home: it offers *thukpas* (thick noodle broths), *momos* (dumplings) and fried fish (Rs20–50).

There are just two **routes** out of Bomdila: onward and upward towards Tawang, and back down to Bhalukpong. State buses run from the bus station in the lower part of town to **Tezpur** (1–2 daily; 7–8hr); slightly faster **private buses** depart from outside Himalayan Holidays, though **Sumos** are the best way to travel: daily early morning services run via Rupa to Tezpur, and to Tawang; book tickets in advance.

Rupa and beyond

The picturesque settlement of **RUPA**, 17km below Bomdila, has an attractive Tibetan *gompa* and a colourful riverside *lhakang* (chapel) a little further up the valley. About 14km beyond Rupa, **Chillipam** has a peaceful monastery and an impressive new temple with astounding views. A further 40km takes you to the influential Tibetan refugee settlement of **Tenzingang.** The Gelugpa monastery here houses nearly four hundred lamas and is one of only two Tantric Gelugpa centres in India. Another 15km beyond Tenzingang lies the end-of-the-road settlement of **Kalaktang**, whose small *gompa* has some wacky sculptures.

Dirang and beyond

Ninety minutes beyond Bomdila, the ancient fortress town of **DIRANG** (1690m) stands over a narrow valley. Although most of Dirang's original **fort** lies in ruins, it's worth checking out, as is the 500-year-old *gompa* above the town. New Dirang is 5km further up the valley, with an interesting modern **monastery** (small donation requested) belonging to the Red Sect, the oldest Tibetan Buddhism sect. About 8km away, the **Sangti Valley** is the winter home of the black-necked crane and a popular place for birdwatching.

The best **place to stay** is the attractive *Pemaling* (ⓣ03780/242615, ⓦwww.welcomheritagehotels.com; ❻), halfway between Old Dirang and the new town, which has homely attached rooms with floral decor, and a restaurant with wonderful vistas; local treks and birdwatching can be arranged here. The adjacent *Tourist Lodge* (ⓣ03780/242157; ❹) is a cheaper alternative, with simple rooms, but equally good views.

The road from Dirang to **Tawang** (a 10–16hr drive) is truly spectacular, with alpine trees, waterfalls and lakes, grazing yaks and mellow villages with wooden houses. Signs along the way declare you have reached "rough and tough country", and you'll pass several army bases. En route is a war memorial dedicated to those who lost their lives during the 1962 Chinese invasion. A series of extraordinary switchbacks climbs up to the dramatic 4300m **Sela Pass**, where you can take tea in front of a *bakari* (wood-fired oven) at the tiny *Tenzing Restaurant*.

Thirteen kilometres on from Sela Pass, most buses and Sumos stop at the **Jaswant Singh Memorial**. Conflicting stories abound, but most claim this Indian soldier held off the invading Chinese army single-handedly for several days in 1962, before eventually being captured and killed.

Tawang

Some 180km beyond Bomdila, the great Buddhist monastery of **TAWANG**, the largest in India, dominates the land of the Monpas. Perched at around 3500m and looking out onto a semicircle of peaks, snow-capped for much of the year, Tawang town feels very much like the end-of-the-road place it is. It is cold here most of the time, so bring your thermals.

Tawang Monastery (daily dawn to dusk; camera Rs20, video Rs100), established in the seventeenth century when this area was part of Greater Tibet, was the birthplace of the sixth Dalai Lama. The colourful fortress-like complex, a couple of kilometres beyond the town, houses around five hundred monks and is renowned for its collection of manuscripts and *thangkas*. There is a small **museum** (Rs20) filled with Buddhist ornaments and relics, and a library. The main shrine room is richly decorated and has several statues, including a beautiful thousand-armed Chenrezig (or Avalokitesvara). If you're lucky the monks may invite you in for a cup of salted yak-butter tea. Much to the displeasure of the Chinese government, the present **Dalai Lama** – who passed through Tawang in 1959 after being forced out of Tibet – visited the monastery in late 2009.

Two *ani gompas* (nunneries) are visible from the main gate, clinging to the steep mountain slopes in the distance. They can be reached on foot in a couple of hours or by vehicle on a road that passes through a military camp and therefore requires a permit. A 5km ropeway connecting Tawang with the *ani gompas* was being constructed at the time of research.

Tawang is a friendly town, with **festivals** held throughout the year. The three-day Torgya celebration is staged every January to ward off evil spirits and natural disasters and the week-long Losar (Buddhist New Year) festival is held in February or early March, with more dancing and festivities.

Beyond Tawang, very close to the Tibetan border, is the lake district of **Bangachangsa**. Dotted with pristine high-altitude lakes, small *gompas* and caves associated with Guru Rinpoche, it is sacred to Tibetan Buddhists and Sikhs – Guru Nanak visited the region twice, hence the small Sikh *gurudwara*. There is no public transport but challenging treks can be arranged at *Hotel Pemaling* in Dirang or the tourist office in Bomdila.

Practicalities

Daily **Sumos** and **buses** run from Tawang to Bomdila, Dirang and Tezpur – book in advance from ticket agents near the bus stand. There are **helicopters** to Guwahati (daily except Sun; ⓣ0361/284 0300) from Lumla, 27km west. A one-way **taxi** trip to the monastery costs around Rs50 but it's worth asking the driver to wait as it can be difficult to find one for the return journey. The *Tourist Lodge* has a small **tourist office**, but Himalayan Holidays (ⓣ03794/223151), opposite *Hotel Gorichen*, is a better source of information. Manyul Cyber Café on the main market road offers **internet** access (Rs50/hr).

The best **hotel** is *Tawang Inn* (ⓣ03794/224096; ❹–❺), a pale pink building 400m southwest of the main market road with comfortable attached rooms; those on the top floor boast wonderful views. *Gorichen* (ⓣ03794/224151, ⓕ222327; ❹), on the main market road, is a good alternative, with large wood-panelled doubles, unreliable electric heaters and big beds. The ramshackle *Tourist Lodge* (ⓣ03794/222359, ⓕ 222567; ❶–❹), 300m uphill from the main market road, has a range of attached rooms that vary dramatically in quality, so look at a few. Near the bus terminus, *Shangri La* (ⓣ03794/222275; ❶–❷) certainly doesn't live up to its name, but is a reasonable choice for those on a real budget: the attached rooms are spartan but clean, though very cold in the winter.

Tawang Inn and *Gorichen* both have decent **restaurants**; alternatively *Dragon*, on the main market road, has a tinted-glass exterior and some of Tawang's best Chinese food (Rs40–70). Diagonally opposite, *Hotel Snowland* offers decent Chinese, Indian and Tibetan dishes (Rs20–50). Shops and restaurants tend to close around 6pm.

Central Arunachal

In central Arunachal, the town of **Hapoli** is of limited interest, but is surrounded by pine forests and some interesting **Apatani villages**. Beyond Hapoli, the settlements of **Along** and **Pasighat** offer good hiking and trekking opportunities.

Hapoli

The hill-station of **HAPOLI** (formerly Ziro), 1780m above sea level on the Apatani plateau, is 150km north of Itanagar. Although there is little to see in the town itself, the market area is lively. There are several villages dotted around the plateau – some within walking distance – where you can still see Apatani men with impressive facial tattoos and women with bamboo nose-plugs. **Old Ziro** is a scenic 7km walk from the town centre, or you can take one of the buses runing every half hour. **Accommodation** is available in Hapoli at *Hotel Blue Pine* (ⓣ03788/225223; ❷–❹), at Pai Gate, 2km from the town centre, which has simple rooms with shared or attached bathrooms, and a good **restaurant**. A more comfortable alternative is the clean and welcoming *Village Tourist Lodge* (ⓣ9436 223233; ❹). NGO Future Generations runs **homestays** (ⓣ03788/225808 or 03788/225809, ⓔarunachal@future.org; ❷–❸) in nearby Siiro village can put you in touch with **guides** and has a craft shop in Ngunu Ziro. **Sumo** services run to Along, Daporijo, Itanagar and Pasighat. Peak Tour and Travels (ⓣ03788/225221) can organize local tours.

Along and Pasighat

To the north and east, **ALONG** and **PASIGHAT**, the district headquarters of West and East Siang respectively, offer trekking and angling. Near Along, there are a number of Adi villages, while around Pasighat, Arunachal's oldest town, the population is primarily Mishmi. For **accommodation** in Along, *Hotel Holiday*

Cottage (☎03783/222463; ❷–❹) on Hospital Hill is a popular choice, with comfy doubles. In Pasighat, try the central *Oman Hotel* (☎0360/222 4464; ❷–❹), where the clean but basic rooms have attached bathrooms and buckets of hot water. The towns can be reached from Itanagar on the NH-52 (7hr to Along; 9hr to Pasighat), via **North Lakhimpur**. Sumos run from Itanagar and Hapoli, but having your own vehicle makes the journey a lot easier, quicker and more comfortable. A thirty-minute drive from Pasighat is **Oiramghat**, from where a daily ferry runs to Dibrugarh (see p.850).

Eastern Arunachal

In eastern Arunachal, the remote valleys of the **Dibang** and **Lohit** rivers, inhabited by the Mishmi, Singpho and Khampti tribes, descend from snow-covered passes through subtropical forests to the plains of the Brahmaputra. Highlights include Hindu pilgrimage centre **Parasuramkund**, **Bhismaknagar**'s twelfth-century fort, and the pristine **Namdapha National Park**.

Parasuramkund and Bhismaknagar

The sacred Hindu site of **PARASURAMKUND**, on the banks of the River Lohit, is mentioned in the Kalika Purana as the place where Parasuram washed away his act of matricide. Thousands of pilgrims make the arduous journey here on Makar Sankranti (mid-Jan), the most auspicious day of the year to take a dip as it's said to wash away all negative karma accumulated in this lifetime. The nearest town, **Tezu**, 20 km southwest, acts as the gateway to the site; stay at the no-frills *Osen* (☎03804/222776; ❷–❸).

At **BHISMAKNAGAR**, northwest of Tezu, are ruins of a twelfth-century hill fort, reputedly Arunachal's oldest archeological site, thought to have been built by the **Chutiyas**, a Mongolian tribe. The nearest significant town is **Roing**, about 25km away, where you can stay at the *Circuit House* (☎03803/222679; ❸), or, 3km outside town, the *Sally Lake Guest House* (☎03803/223061; ❸).

Namdapha National Park

The beautifully remote **NAMDAPHA NATIONAL PARK** (Oct–April; Rs50 [Rs10], jeep Rs100, ordinary camera Rs75, camera with a zoom lens Rs400, video Rs750) is unique for its massive range of altitudes (200–4500m). Close to the Myanmar border, Namdapha is home to tigers, leopards (clouded and snow), elephants, red pandas, deer and the endangered Hoolock gibbon, although you are unlikely to spot any big wildlife on a short visit. The journey here is long and uncomfortable, so it's advisable to visit with a tour operator: try Purvi Discovery, Gurudongma Tours & Treks or Jungle Travels India (see p.841).

The park headquarters are at **Miao** (☎03807/222249), where you can book **to stay** at the *Forest Rest House* (❸) in **Deban**, the main camp, which has wonderful views over the river valley: the two top rooms are the best. There are also rustic huts (❷) and a dilapidated dorm (Rs60). A better bet is the *Eco-Tourist Guest House* (☎9436 228763; ❹), run by a local NGO, which has four comfortable rooms. Simple **meals** are available at all the lodges. It's possible to take a guided elephant trek with overnight camping inside the park – contact the Field Director at Miao.

Buses to and from Miao pass through **Margherita**, 64km southwest, and **Tinsukia**, 40km further southwest in Assam, where rail services run to Guwahati. **Dibrugarh** is a further 47km beyond Tinsukia.

Nagaland

On the Myanmar border, south of Arunachal Pradesh and east of Assam, **NAGALAND** is physically and conceptually at the very edge of the Subcontinent. Home to the fiercely independent Nagas, its hills and valleys were only opened up to tourism in 2000. One of India's most beautiful states, it was once renowned for its head-hunters (see below) but is now ninety percent Christian.

When the British arrived in neighbouring Assam in the mid-nineteenth century, they initially left the Naga warrior tribes alone. But after continued Naga raids on Assamese villages, the British sought to push them back into the hills. The Angami warriors (a Naga tribe) defeated the British twice, but were finally overcome in 1879, and a truce was declared. The British later came to hold a certain authority here; the Nagas remained loyal during World War II and fought valiantly against the Japanese invaders. At the time of Independence, the Nagas found their land divided into two, with the larger area falling to Burma. Gandhi asked them to remain within India for ten years, promising them choice of destiny thereafter. His promise was never fulfilled, and more than sixty years on, the Nagas are still fighting for a homeland. Though a ceasefire is officially in place, violence continues – a bomb in 2004 killed seventy people in Dimapur, the largest attack in recent years.

A visit to a Naga village provides a fascinating insight into a rapidly disappearing way of life. Most tour operators will arrange trips here, but some Nagas are tired of having their homes on show. If you do visit, bring a gift and ensure your guide speaks the relevant dialect. You should also offer money for the village to the chief (or *angh*).

Traditional Angami villages surround the capital of **Kohima**, including **Khonoma**. From **Mon** you can see various Konyak villages such as **Shangnyu**. The Ao tribe inhabits **Mokokchung**, while **Tuensang** is home to six different tribes. The state's terrain is also ideal for trekking and mountain biking – Gurudongma Tours & Treks (see p.841) arranges trips. A good time to visit the state is during the **Hornbill Festival** (Ⓦ www.hornbillfestival.com), held in the first week in December, which showcases Naga art, dance, music and sport. You'll need a **permit** to enter Nagaland (see box, p.840).

Kohima

KOHIMA, Nagaland's capital, was built alongside the large Angami village of Kohima by the British in the nineteenth century. Traditional Naga villages –

The Nagas

Naga warriors have long been feared and respected, and head-hunting was practised within living memory. They are also skilful farmers, growing twenty different species of rice. They differentiate between the soul and the spirit, believing the soul resides in the nape of the neck, while the spirit, in the head, holds great power and brings good fortune. Heads of enemies and fallen comrades were once collected to add to those of the community's own ancestors. Some tribes tattooed their faces with swirling horns to mark success in **head-hunting**. The heads themselves were kept in the men's meeting house (*morung*) in each village, which was decorated with fantastic carvings of animals, elephant heads and tusks – you can still see examples in many villages. Although each tribe has its own dialect, a hybrid language drawn from various local languages and Assamese has developed into the common Naga tongue.

including **Khonoma**, 20km beyond Kohima, **Jakhema** and **Kigwema** – are just a short drive away.

Arrival and information

Most **private buses** from Imphal are through services to Dimapur and don't go into the town centre, so ask the driver to drop you off at the *Japfu* hotel. **State buses** drop you at the stand in the town centre. The **tourist office** (Mon–Fri 10am–4pm; ⓣ0370/224 3124, ⓦwww.tourismnagaland.com) is below the *Japfu*.

The Town

Spread loosely over the saddle of two large hills, Kohima forms a pass that played a strategic role during World War II. The Imphal–Dimapur highway – the route along which the Japanese hoped to reach the plains of India – crosses the saddle at the foot of the **World War II Cemetery**, designed by Edwin Lutyens, in a peaceful location overlooking the town. It stands tribute to the Allies who died during the three-month Battle of Kohima, which ended in June 1944 with a death toll of over ten thousand soldiers.

The **Cathedral**, on the way out of town towards the State Museum, contains India's largest wooden crucifix, while the fascinating **State Museum** (daily except Mon 10am–4pm; Rs5) in Bayavu Hill Colony, a twenty-minute walk from the centre, has an excellent collection of Naga jewellery, costumes, spears, corsets and crafts.

The large Angami settlement of **Kohima village** is set on a high hill overlooking modern Kohima. Only a few of the buildings still have the traditional pitched roofs and crossed "house-horns" on the gables, but its tightly knit labyrinth of lanes gives the village a definite Naga feel. Carved heads to signify family status, grain baskets in front of the houses, and troughs used to make rice beer are among the distinctive features.

Accommodation and eating

Kohima's showpiece **hotel** is the *Japfu* (ⓣ0370/224 0211, ⓔhoteljapfu@yahoo.co.in; ❺), at the top end of town, which has clean and spacious rooms with attached bathrooms, heaters, friendly staff and a decent restaurant. *Fira* (ⓣ0370/224 0940; ❸), nearby, has adequate, if dated, rooms and a restaurant. *Pine*, on Phool Bari (ⓣ0370/224 3129; ❸), has reasonable attached doubles. **Naga food** consists mainly of rice, boiled vegetables and lots of meat, cooked with ginger or chilli: try it at the *Bamboo Shoot* and *Sema* hotels. Most restaurants close around 6pm, though *Japfu*'s stays open later.

Khonoma and Tuophema

KHONOMA, 20km northwest of Kohima, is where the Angami warriors made their final stand against the British in 1879. Magnificent rice terraces surround the village, irrigated by a complex system of bamboo water pipes. Behind the village

Moving on from Kohima

From Kohima, roads lead west to the **railhead** and **airport** at **Dimapur**, north to Mokokchung and south to Imphal. From Mokokchung, the road continues to Jorhat in Assam. There are state and private **buses** in all directions; tickets for private buses can be bought from agents in the centre or on Phool Bari. State buses to Dimapur run every half-hour, and daily to Mokokchung and Imphal. Frequent **Sumos** to Dimapur depart from the taxi stand 200m up from the bus station.

lies the scenic Dzoukou valley, part of the Khonoma Nature Conservation and Tragopan Sanctuary, and graced with waterfalls and wonderful viewpoints. **Several public and private buses** travel from Kohima, and there's a single daily bus from Dimapur, but taxis are the best bet.

Forty-one kilometres north of Kohima on the way to Mokokchung, **TUOPHEMA** is a genuine Angami village; the adjoining **Tourist Village** was built by locals and has a small museum. Guided walks in the surrounding countryside can be arranged here. **Accommodation** is available in comfortable Naga huts with hot showers (Ⓣ0370/227 0786; ❹–❺). Regular **buses** run from Kohima (1hr 30min) and Dimapur (2hr), though hiring a taxi is preferable for day-trips.

Dimapur

Noisy and polluted **DIMAPUR**, 74km northwest of Kohima, functions primarily as a gateway to the state. On the riverside edge of town are the **Kachari ruins**, fertility symbols dating back to the Kachari kingdom. Nagaland's sole railhead, Dimapur has **trains** to Dibrugarh, Simaluguri (for Sibsagar) and Tinsukia in Assam. The best service for Guwahati is the *Shatabdi Express* #2068 (daily except Sun at 4.10pm; 4hr 35min). State and private **buses** run to Kohima (3hr) from the Nagaland bus stand, as do **Sumos** from the main drag outside. Private buses to Guwahati, Jorhat and Itanagar leave from the Assam bus stand in Golaghat Road across the railway tracks. Dimapur's **airport** is 6km out of town.

The best **accommodation** option is the *Saramati*, sister hotel to Kohima's *Japfu* (Ⓣ03862/234761, Ⓔhotelsaramati@yahoo.co.in; ❺), which also has a **restaurant**; the *Tourist Lodge* (Ⓣ03862/226355; ❸) near the Nagaland bus stand is cheaper, with clean if uninspiring rooms.

Mon and around

In the far northeast of Nagaland, 200km south of Dibrugarh in Assam, **MON** is the regional capital of the Konyak tribe. Its main attraction is as a base for visits to the surrounding villages. Look out for older Konyaks with elaborate facial tattoos and goat-horn earrings. Sennunger Imsong, based in Mokokchung (see below), is a reliable guide who can arrange day-trips.

Shangnyu is a typical village, a bumpy drive 23km from Mon, with a small museum housing an impressive wooden fertility sculpture. Outside is a huge log drum that the villagers used for festivals and to send messages across the hills. There's also a set of eerie tall stones on which the villagers once displayed hunted heads. The friendly *angh*'s home is packed with horns and animal skulls to indicate his status.

The *Mountain View* (Ⓣ03869/221730, Ⓔphejin@yahoo.com; ❹), on Mon's noisy main street, has large, clean **rooms**. **Buses** and **jeeps** to Mon run from Dibrugarh (at least 7hr) via Sibsagar in Assam, though trips are best undertaken with a tour operator. In late March or early April, the area celebrates its spring **festival**.

Mokokchung and around

A vibrant hill-town southwest of Mon and 160km (5hr by jeep) north of Kohima, **MOKOKCHUNG** is a good base for a visit to surrounding Ao villages, including **Longkhum**, 17km away, which has a small museum and a guesthouse. Day-trips – including to Tuensang – can be arranged by Sennunger Imsong, whose aunt Apokla Imsong rents out a pleasant double room with attached bathroom in *Tongpok Abode*, her home at Dilong Ward in Mokokchung (Ⓣ0369/222 7030, Ⓔimsong2003@rediffmail.com; ❸ full board).

TUENSANG, 115km southeast of Mokokchung, lies at the centre of a region inhabited by six different tribes – the Phom, Khiamniungan, Chang, Yimchunger and Sangtam. From here it's a two-day drive to **Thanamir,** and the start of a stunning two-day trek between tribal villages to **Mount Saramati**, Nagaland's highest peak (3826m), near the Burmese border. En route, there are basic places to stay at **Kiphere** – contact the Imsongs to arrange.

WOKHA, 80km south from Mokokchung, is a good place to stop on the NH-61 route to Kohima. Cultural and mountain-biking trips in the area are run by Gurungdoma Tours & Treks (see p.841).

Mizoram

Heading south from Assam into **MIZORAM**, "land of the highlanders", a winding mountain road takes you into forests and bamboo-covered hills. Mizoram is a gentle pastoral land, and the **Mizos** are a welcoming people who see very little tourism. Whitewashed churches dot the landscape, giving it more of a Central American feel than a state squashed between Myanmar and Bangladesh.

The Mizos, who migrated from the Chin Hills of Burma, were regularly raiding tea plantations in the Assam Valley right into the late nineteenth century; only in 1924 did the British finally manage to bring about some semblance of control. They opened up what was then the **Lushai Hills** to missionaries who converted much of the state to Christianity. **Aizawl**, the capital, is a large sprawling city built on impossibly steep slopes. In the heart of the state, traditional Mizo communities occupy the crests of a series of ridges, each village dominated by its chief's house and *zawlbuk*, or bachelors' dormitory. An egalitarian people, without sex or class distinctions, the Mizos remain proud of their age-old custom of *Tlawmgaihna*, a code of ethics that governs hospitality. They enjoy a 95 percent literacy rate, and many speak English and are culturally more influenced by the Christian West than by India. **Permits** required to enter (see box, pp.840–841).

Aizawl

One of India's remotest state capitals, **AIZAWL** (1250m) perches precariously on the steep slopes of a sharp ridge. Although the views are of hills rather than snowy mountains, it has something of the feel of a Himalayan hill-station. There are few monuments or temples, but the markets are interesting. Everything closes on Sunday, when everyone goes to church. Aizawl's rural surroundings are within easy reach by bus or on foot.

Zarkawt is the main downtown area, with **Bara Bazaar** (daily except Sun 6am–3pm) the city's main attraction: everything from Mizo music to bespoke shoes is on sale here. The **State Museum**, on MacDonald Hill (Mon–Fri 9am–5pm, Sat 9am–1pm; Rs5), has a small collection of traditional costumes. There are many vantage points offering great views – two of the best are **Chaltlang Hill**, high above Chandmari in the north, and the Theological College, perched above the dramatic cleft on the road into Aizawl.

The **Durtlang Hills** immediately north of Aizawl, and **Luangmual**, 7km west, provide pleasant **walking** country – both are easy day-trips. Buses leave for Luangmual from outside the Salvation Army Temple.

Arrival and information

The only recommended road out of Mizoram leads to **Silchar**, 180km north in Assam; **Sumos** (4–6hr) are the best way to travel, and there are several agents in

Bamboo, rats and revolution

Mizoram's two main species of bamboo flower every 48–50 years, attracting hordes of rats and boosting their fertility rate fourfold. The rats devour crops, leaving famine in their wake. The first time this happened, in 1959, the government was seriously unprepared, which led a council clerk, **Laldenga**, to found the **Mizo Famine Front** (MFF). Set up initially to combat famine, it transformed into the **Mizo National Front** (MNF), a guerrilla group fighting for secession. The government's heavy-handed response in 1967 – rounding up Mizos from their homes into guarded villages under curfew – boosted support for the MNF. Bangladeshi independence was a bitter blow to the MNF, however, which had relied on Pakistani support. Moderates on both sides eventually brought the MNF to the negotiating table, where statehood was granted in 1986 in return for an end to the insurgency. Mizoram is now the most peaceful of the "seven sisters." However, in 2007 the bamboo began to flower again, the rat population grew and crops were devastated. Although the state authorities were slightly better prepared this time, the national government was slow to react and many people suffered serious hardship.

Zarkawt. **Private bus** companies in Zarkawt also run services to Silchar. Sumos and state buses both travel to Shillong and Guwahati (both 14–18hr). Aizawl's **airport**, 35km west, has flights to Guwahati, Imphal and Kolkata. A taxi to the airport costs around Rs500. There's a **tourist office** in the Chandmari district (Mon–Fri 9am–5pm; ⓣ0389/231 2475). The State Bank of India, near First AR Ground, has an **ATM** and a **foreign exchange** counter.

Accommodation and eating

There's a good range of budget and mid-range **hotels**, but you'll struggle to find anything smarter. **Several** modest **restaurants** in Bara Bazaar serve traditional Mizo food, which tends to be quite mild. Aizawl's top restaurant is *David's Kitchen* at *David's Clover Hotel*, which serves Indian and Chinese dishes, including a succulent mutton *rogan josh*. *Blue Berry* in *Hotel Ritz* is a decent alternative, with a good range of fish and prawn dishes. Mains at both cost Rs75–265.

Ahimsa Zarkawt ⓣ0389/234 1133. One of Aizawl's better hotels, bang in the centre of town, with sizeable attached rooms, rooftop views and a decent restaurant. ❸–❹

Berawtlang Tourist Complex Zemabawk, 6km out of town ⓣ0389/235 2067. In a serene middle-of-nowhere location, these rustic cottages have wonderful views, and excellent food is served in the restaurant. ❷–❸

David's Clover Zarkawt ⓣ0389/230 5736. Solid mid-range hotel with comfortable attached rooms, each boasting a TV, fridge and wi-fi access. ❺

Ritz Bara Bazaar, near Machhunga Point ⓣ0389/231 0409, ⓦwww.ritzaizawl.com. A good option, popular with business travellers: staff are friendly, and there's a range of rooms, most with attached bathrooms and TVs, as well as a fine restaurant. ❸–❺

Manipur

MANIPUR, stretching along the border with Myanmar, centres on a vast lowland area watered by the lake system south of its capital **Imphal**. This almost forgotten region is home to the **Meithei**, who have created in isolation their own fascinating version of Hinduism. Manipur feels closer to Southeast Asia than India, and many locals speak neither English nor Hindi.

Although the area around Imphal is now all but devoid of trees, the outlying hills are still forested and shelter exotic birds and animals like the spotted

Safety in Manipur

Since Independence, Manipur has seen waves of violence as a result of self-rule campaigns and a brutal **conflict** between the Kukis and Nagas. Disturbances are still common, and there were almost four hundred militancy-related deaths in 2009. At the time of writing, the UK Foreign and Commonwealth Office advised against all travel to the state and all but essential travel to Imphal (only travel by air is recommended), and this section has not been updated for this edition. Carefully check the security situation before you decide to visit. For permit requirements, see pp.840–841.

linshang, Blyth's tragopan and even the clouded leopard, as well as numerous varieties of orchid. The unique natural habitat of **Loktak Lake** is home to the sangai deer.

Manipur's **history** can be traced back to the founding of Imphal in the first century AD. After long periods of independent and stable government, the state was incorporated into India at the end of the Indo-Burmese war in 1826, before coming under British rule in 1891. During World War II, much of Manipur was occupied by the Japanese, with 250,000 British and Indian troops trapped under siege in Imphal for three months. Thanks to a massive RAF air-lift from Agartala, they held out, and when Japanese troops received the order to end the Imphal campaign, it was in effect the end of the campaign to conquer India. Manipur became a fully-fledged Indian state in 1972.

Imphal and around

Circled by distant hills, Manipur's capital **IMPHAL** (785m) is somewhat lacking in dramatic monuments. The town centre is sandwiched between the stately avenue of Kanglapat and the somewhat stagnant River Nambu. The **Polo Ground** dominates the area; according to popular legend, the Manipuri game of *Sagol Kangjei* is the original form of the modern game of polo. In one corner, the **Shaheed Minar** memorial commemorates the Meithei revolt against British occupation in 1891, while just southeast is the **State Museum** (daily except Mon 10am–4.15pm; Rs2). At the heart of Imphal, along Kangchup Road, the fascinating daily **Khwairamband** market is run by more than three thousand Meithei women, making it the largest of its kind in Asia.

South of the old palace complex, the golden dome of **Shri Govindjee**, Manipur's pre-eminent Vaishnavite temple, can be seen amongst the palm trees. The beautifully maintained **British War Cemetery** is 500m north of the *Tourist Lodge*. **Langthabal**, on a small hillock 8km south of Imphal on the road to Myanmar, overlooking the University of Manipur, has remains of an old palace, together with a few temples and ceremonial houses. The **Khonghampat Orchidarium**, 12km north of Imphal on NH-39, displays more than a hundred varieties of orchid.

Practicalities

State **buses** arrive at the stand next to the Polo Ground and private buses at their individual offices, most of which are on MG Avenue, 200m north of Khwairamband Bazaar. The **state tourist office** (Mon–Sat 9.30am–5pm, Oct–March 4.30pm; closed 2nd Sat of month; ⓣ0385/222 0802) is at *Hotel Imphal*, north of the palace on the main Dimapur road. The **India Tourism** office is on Jail Road (Mon–Sat 9.30am–5.30pm; ⓣ0385/222 1131). Travellers can get permits endorsed at the **Foreigners' Registration Office** along from the **GPO**

Moving on from Imphal

Bus connections with Guwahati are good, and the 579km journey takes around twelve hours. Several private bus companies operate from MG Avenue near the State Bank of India, and also have stands on DM Road outside *Hotel Tampha*. The NH-39 links Imphal to Kohima in **Nagaland** and continues to Dimapur, the nearest railhead, 215km away. You will need a permit for Nagaland to travel this route. Buses to Dimapur (6hr) via Kohima leave daily at 6am. The 200km road journey to Silchar (14hr) is a bit of a nightmare; take one of the numerous weekly **flights** instead; the **airport**, 6km south of town, also has flights to Aizawl, Agatala, Delhi, Guwahati and Kolkata.

on Secretariat Road. The State Bank of India on MG Avenue has a **foreign exchange** service.

Imphal has a few decent **hotels** including *ITDC Imphal*, North AOC, Dimapur Road (ⓣ0385/222 0459; ❸–❹); *Anand Continental*, Khoyathong Road (ⓣ0385/222 3422; ❸–❹); *Nirmala*, MG Avenue (ⓣ0385/222 9014; ❸–❺); and *White Palace*, MG Avenue (ⓣ0385/222 05999; ❶–❸). The best **restaurant** is *Host* in the *Anand Continental*. There are no bars – Manipur is a **dry state**.

Loktak Lake

South of Imphal, Lotak Lake is home to a unique community of fishermen who live on large floating islands of matted vegetation, as do endangered sangai deer. Much of the lake is taken up by the **Keibul Lamjao National Park**. The *Tourist Bungalow* (ⓣ0385/222 0802; ❶) on **Sendra Island**, 48km from Imphal, has good views. On the western shore of Loktak, the small town of **MOIRANG**, 45km south of Imphal, is the traditional centre of Meithei culture, with a temple devoted to the pre-Hindu deity **Thangjing**. In April 1944, the Indian National Army under Netaji Subhas Chandra Bose planted its flag here, having fought alongside the Japanese against the British Indian Army for the cause of Independence. A **memorial** and **museum** commemorate the event.

Tripura

Surrounded by Bangladesh on three sides, the lush mountains and valleys of **TRIPURA** became part of India in 1949; since then, its fate has been entwined with that of Bengal. Partition and the subsequent creation of East Pakistan (now Bangladesh) in 1948, followed by war, famine and military regimes forced millions of Bangladeshis to flee into Tripura, where they now **significantly outnumber** the indigenous people, which has caused much resentment. Nevertheless, **Agartala**, the capital, is a relaxed city with a palace and a few temples, with

Safety in Tripura

Although Tripura is open to tourism, **insurgency** and **ethnic conflict** remain significant problems, particularly in the north. At the time of writing, travel to Tripura was deemed **unsafe**, and the UK Foreign and Commonwealth Office advised against all visits to the state. The information in this section has therefore not been updated for this edition, and it is essential to check the security situation before you travel.

Udaipur and the fairy-tale palace at **Neermahal** easily accessible. A handful of sanctuaries such as **Gumti**, **Rowa**, **Trishna** and **Sepahijala** protect the state's few remaining forests.

Agartala

AGARTALA, Tripura's capital, is a laid-back administrative centre. Its main attraction is the gleaming white **Ujjayanta Palace**, completed in 1901. Set amid formal gardens and artificial lakes, this huge building, now home to the State Legislative Assembly, covers around eight hundred acres. One of many temples nearby and open to the public, the **Jagannath Temple** with its orange tower rises from an octagonal plinth across the road.

Most of Agartala's amenities, bazaars, bus stands and administrative offices are concentrated in the centre, immediately south of the palace. Opposite the GPO, the **State Museum** (Mon–Sat 10am–5pm) displays ethnographic and archeological exhibits. The Tribal Cultural Research Institute and Museum (Mon–Sat 11am–1pm) at Supari Bagan lies well hidden in the backstreets of Krishna Nagar district, near the Jagannath Temple.

Practicalities

Arriving by bus, you'll probably be dropped off at one of the private company offices on LN Bari Road, or at the state bus stand at Krishna Nagar. The **tourist office** (Mon–Sat 10am–5pm, Sun 3–5pm; ⓣ0381/222 5930) is in a wing of the palace. There are several **ATMs**. Agartala has a good selection of **hotels**, including *Welcome Palace,* HGB Road (ⓣ0381/238 4940; ❺); *Ambar*, SD Barman Sarani (ⓣ0381/222 3587; ❷); and *Rajdhani*, BK Road (ⓣ0381/222 3387; ❷–❺). Choices for **eating** are more limited: try *Abhishek* on Durga Bari Road or *Ambar*, next to the hotel of the same name.

Around Agartala

The large **Kamala Sagar** lake, 27km south of Agartala, is overlooked by a small but important Kali temple. Its twelfth-century sandstone image of Mahishasuramardini, a form of Durga, has a *shivalingam* in front of it. Buses leave from Battala bus stand in Agartala to the lake (5 daily; 1hr). On the road to Udaipur, 35km south of Agartala, the **Sepahijala** nature reserve has a lake, zoo and botanical gardens, and is home to Hoolock gibbons and golden langurs. The beautiful *Abasarika Bungalow* (❶) offers comfortable rooms in jungle surroundings; book in

Moving on from Argatala

State buses leave from the corner of Hospital and LN Bari Roads for the gruelling stop-start convoy to Silchar, Shillong and Guwahati. **Private buses** depart from LN Bari Road, 100m east of the palace. Buses heading north from Agartala have to travel in thrice-daily army-escorted convoys from Teliamura to Kumarghat (the nearest railhead), leaving at 6am, 8am and 11.30am. Buses and Sumos to Udaipur (every 30min; 2hr) leave from the Battala bus stand at the western end of HGB Road. The **airport**, 12km north, has flights to Aizawl, Guwahati, Imphal, Kolkata and Silchar. Agartala is 2km from the **border with Bangladesh**. Rickshaws on the Bangladeshi side can take you to Akhaura Junction, 4km away, from where there are trains to Comilla, Sylhet and Dhaka (2hr 30min). The **Bangladeshi Embassy** (Mon–Thurs 8.30am–1pm & 2–4.30pm, Fri 8.30am–noon; ⓣ0381/222 4807), next to the *Brideway* hotel, issues visas on the spot. Two passport photos are needed and prices vary according to nationality.

advance at the Forestry Office (☎0381/222 2224) in Agartala, 2km up Airport Road on the left. All buses to Udaipur travel past the park gate.

Udaipur

The former Manikya capital of **UDAIPUR** retains an atmosphere of antiquity not found in Agartala. After staving off the Muslim rulers of Bengal, the Manikyas finally submitted to the Mughals, but continued to rule the kingdom until it was subsumed into British India. On the southwest bank of **Jagannath Dighi** tank stand the ruins of the **Jagannath** temple, while the seventeenth-century **Mughal Masjid** marks the furthest outpost of the Mughal Empire. **Tripura Sundari**, the most important temple in the area, is 5km outside Udaipur. This is one of the 51 *shakti pitha*s sacred to the Tantras, marking the spot where Sati's right leg is supposed to have fallen when Shiva was carrying her body from the funeral pyre. Most people visit Udaipur on a long day-trip from Agartala, but **accommodation** is available at the *Pantha Niwas Tourist Lodge* (❶–❷). There's also a small tourist office (☎0381/222432). **Buses** (every 30min; 2hr) and frequent **Sumos** run from Argatala.

Neermahal

The romantic water palace of **NEERMAHAL**, in the middle of **Rudrasagar Lake**, 55km south of Agartala, was built in 1930 as a summer residence for Maharaja Bir Bikram Kishore Manikya. Inspired by Mughal architecture, the palace (daily 9am–6pm) is rather derelict inside, but the exterior and gardens have been restored, and the sight of the domes and pavilions reflected in the lake is impressive. The lake is 1km from the town of **Melaghar**, which has bus services to Agartala (every 30min; 2hr) and Udaipur (every 30min; 30min). If you want **to stay**, try the *Sagarmahal Tourist Lodge* (☎0381/264418; ❸), which has a **restaurant**.

Orissa

* **Bhubaneswar** Hidden in the city's suburbs are around five hundred temples, with unique architecture and elaborate sculptures. See p.874

* **Udaigiri and Khandagiri** Orissa's premier historical sites, these two-thousand-year-old caves feature fascinating carvings and friezes. See p.882

* **Olive Ridley turtles** These endangered creatures journey to Gahirmatha beach for one night in February or March to lay their eggs – an unforgettable scene.See p.885

* **Puri** With one of India's holiest temples and a laid-back traveler scene, Puri is an essential stop-off for pilgrims and backpackers alike. See p.887

* **Rath Yatra** Pilgrims flock to Puri to celebrate Lord Jagannath during the frenetic midsummer "Car Festival". See p.891

* **Konark** An elegant thirteenth-century Hindu temple sitting astride a huge stone chariot. See p.896

▲ Sun temple, Konark

Despite being one of India's poorest states, **ORISSA** boasts a rich and distinctive cultural heritage. The coastal plains have the highest concentration of historical and religious monuments – Orissa's principal tourist attractions. **Puri**, site of the famous **Jagannath temple** and one of the world's most spectacular devotional processions, the Rath Yatra, combines the heady intensity of a Hindu pilgrimage centre with the hedonistic pleasures of the beach. Just a short hop off the main Kolkata–Chennai road and railway, Puri is a popular destination for backpackers. **Konark**, a short way up the coast, has the ruins of Orissa's most ambitious medieval temple, whose surfaces writhe with exquisitely preserved sculpture, including some eyebrow-raising erotica. The ancient rock-cut caves and ornate temples of **Bhubaneswar**, the state capital, hark back to an era when it ruled a kingdom stretching from the Ganges delta to the mouth of the River Godavari.

Away from the central "golden triangle" of sights, foreign travellers are few and far between, though you'll see plenty of Bengalis travelling throughout coastal Orissa. In the winter, the small islands dotted around **Chilika Lake**, a huge salt-water lagoon south of Bhubaneswar, is good for birdwatchers. Further north, in the **Bhitarkanika Sanctuary**, a remote stretch of beach is the nesting site for rare Olive Ridley **turtles.**

From the number of temples in Orissa, you'd be forgiven for thinking Brahmanical Hinduism was its sole religion. In fact, almost a quarter of the population are **adivasi**, or "tribal" (literally "first") people, thought to have descended from the area's pre-Aryan aboriginal inhabitants. In the more inaccessible corners of the state many of these groups have retained unique cultural traditions and languages. So-called "ethnic" tourism (see p.900) is the latest encroachment on the *adivasis*' way of life, following in the wake of dam builders, missionaries and "advancement programmes" initiated by the state government.

Getting around presents few practical problems if you stick to the more populated coastal areas. National Highway 5 and the Southeast Railway, which cut in tandem down the coastal plain via Bhubaneswar, are the main arteries of the region. A branch line also runs as far as Puri, connecting it by frequent, direct express **trains** to Delhi, Kolkata and Chennai. Elsewhere, **buses** are the best way to travel.

Some history

Other than scattered fragmentary remains of prehistoric settlement, Orissa's earliest archeological find dates from the fourth century BC. The fortified city of **Sisupalgarh**, near modern Bhubaneswar, was the capital of the **Kalinga** dynasty, about which little is known. In the third century BC, the ambitious Mauryan emperor **Ashoka** routed the Kalingan kingdom in a battle so bloody that the carnage was supposed to have inspired his legendary conversion to **Buddhism**. Rock edicts erected around the empire extol the virtues of the new faith, dharma, as well as the principles that Ashoka hoped to instil in his vanquished subjects. With the demise of the Mauryans, Kalinga enjoyed something of a resurgence. Under the imperialistic **Chedi** Jain dynasty, vast sums were spent expanding the capital and on carving elaborate monastery caves into the nearby hills of **Khandagiri** and **Udaigiri**. During the second century BC, however, the kingdom gradually splintered into warring factions and entered a kind of Dark Age. The influence of Buddhism waned, Jainism all but vanished, and **Brahmanism**, disseminated by the teachings of the Shaivite zealot Lakulisha, started to resurface as the dominant religion.

Orissa's golden age, during which the region's prosperous Hindu rulers created some of South Asia's most sophisticated art and architecture, peaked in the twelfth century under the **Eastern Gangas**. Fuelled by the gains from a thriving trade

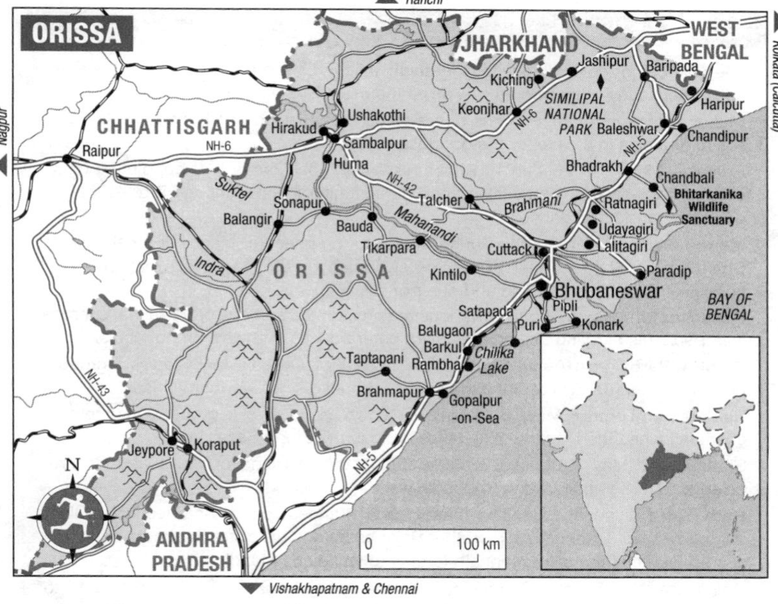

network (which extended as far east as Indonesia), the Ganga kings erected magnificent **temples** where Shiva worship and arcane tantric practices adopted by earlier Orissan rulers were replaced by new forms of devotion to Vishnu. The shrine of the most popular royal deity of all, Lord Jagannath, at Puri, was by now one of the four most hallowed religious centres in India.

In the fifteenth century, the **Afghans of Bengal** swept south to annex the region, with Man Singh's **Mughal** army hot on their heels in 1592. That even a few medieval Hindu monuments escaped the excesses of the ensuing iconoclasm is miraculous, and **non-Hindus** have never since been allowed to enter the most holy temples in Puri and Bhubaneswar. In 1751 the **Marathas** from western India ousted the Mughals as the dominant regional power. The East India Company, meanwhile, was also making inroads along the coast, and 28 years after Clive's victory at Plassey in 1765, Orissa finally came under **British rule**.

Since **Independence**, the state has sustained rapid **development**. Discoveries of coal, bauxite, iron ore and other minerals have stimulated considerable industrial growth and improvements to infrastructure. Despite such urban progress, however, Orissa remains a poor rural state (55 percent of children are malnourished, for example), heavily dependent on agriculture to provide for the basic needs of its 38 million inhabitants.

Events of recent years have damaged the state's reputation. Violent **Maoist** (or Naxalite) activity in rural areas has increased, drawing an often equally violent response from government forces. In 2008, there was a wave of attacks against the **Christian minority** by Hindu fundamentalists, who killed at least seventy people and forced tens of thousands from their homes. An ongoing campaign by environmental and human rights groups has been vociferous in its opposition to the multinational corporation **Vedanta**, which is pushing ahead with plans to develop a bauxite mine on Niyamgiri mountain in eastern Orissa, considered sacred by the local *adivasi* community.

Orissan festivals

The chances of coinciding with a **festival** while in Orissa are good, since the state celebrates many of its own as well as all the usual Hindu festivals.

Makar Mela (mid-Jan). Pilgrims descend on a tiny island in Chilika Lake to leave votive offerings in a cave for the goddess Kali.

Adivasis Mela (Jan 26–Feb 1). Bhubaneswar's "tribal" fair is a disappointing cross between New York's Coney Island and an agricultural show, though it does feature good live music and dance.

Magha Saptami (Jan & Feb). During the full-moon phase of Magha, a small pool at Chandrabhaga beach, near Konark, is swamped by thousands of worshippers in honour of Surya, the sun god and curer of skin ailments.

Panashankranti (early April). In various regions, on the first day of Vaisakha, saffron-clad penitents carrying peacock feathers enter trances and walk on hot coals.

Chaitra Parba (mid-April). Santals (the largest of Orissa's many *adivasi* groups) perform *Chhou* dances at Baripada in Mayurbhunj district, northern Orissa.

Ashokastami (April & May). Bhubaneswar's own Car Festival (a procession of temple chariots), when the Lingaraj deity takes a dip in the Bindu Sagar tank.

Sitalasasthi (May & June). Commemorating the marriage of Shiva and Parvati, celebrated in Sambalpur and Bhubaneswar.

Rath Yatra (June & July). The biggest and grandest of Orissa's festivals. Giant images of Lord Jagannath, his brother Balabhadra and his sister Subhadra make the sacred journey from the Jagannath temple to Gundicha Mandir in Puri.

Bali Yatra (Nov & Dec). Commemorates the voyages made by Orissan traders to Indonesia. Held at full moon on the banks of the River Mahanadi in Cuttack.

Konark Festival (early Dec). A festival of classical dance featuring Orissan and other regional dance forms in the Sun Temple at Konark.

Bhubaneswar

With its featureless 1950s architecture, **BHUBANESWAR** may initially strike you as surprisingly dull for a city with a population of well over half a million and a history of settlement stretching back more than two thousand years. However, the southern suburbs harbour the remnants of some of India's finest medieval **temples**, which are made all the more atmospheric by the animated religious life that continues to revolve around them, particularly at festival times.

Bhubaneswar first appears in history during the fourth century BC, as the capital of ancient **Kalinga**. It was here that Ashoka erected one of the Subcontinent's best-preserved rock edicts – still in place 5km south of **Dhauli**. Under the **Chedis**, ancient Kalinga gained control over the thriving mercantile trade in the region and became the northeast seaboard's most formidable power.

Bhubaneswar then declined, re-emerging as a regional force only in the fifth century AD, when it became an important Shaivite centre. Coupled with the formidable wealth of the **Sailodbhavas** two centuries later, the growing religious fervour fuelled an extraordinary spate of temple construction. Between the seventh and twelfth centuries some seven thousand shrines are believed to have been erected around the **Bindu Sagar** tank. Most were razed in the Muslim incursions of the medieval era, but enough survived for it to be possible in even a short visit to trace the evolution of Orissan architecture from its small, modest beginnings to the gigantic, self-confident proportions of the **Lingaraj** – the seat of Trimbhubaneshwara, or "Lord of Three Worlds", from which the modern

BHUBANESWAR

RESTAURANTS	
Bhuvanashree	5
Dalema	3
Dalma	1
Hare Krishna	4
Kanika	A
Lemon Tree	A
Rice Bowl	2
Tangerine 9	4

ACCOMMODATION			
Aristo Lodge	J	New Marrion	D
Bhagwat Niwas	K	Panthanivas	M
Ginger	B	Pushpak	L
Grand Central	I	Richi	H
Jajati	F	Swosti	G
Janpatha	E	Trident Bhubaneswar	C
Mayfair Lagoon	A		

city takes its name. A relative backwater until after Independence, Bhubaneswar was only declared the new state capital after nearby Cuttack reached bursting point in the 1950s.

Arrival, information and city transport

Taxis and auto-rickshaws (Rs100–130) cover the 2–3km journey to town from Biju Patnaik **airport**. Long-distance **buses** terminate at the inconveniently situated Baramunda bus stand, 5km out on the western edge of town, though not before making a whistle-stop tour of the centre. Ask to be dropped at **Station Square** (look for a statue of a horse in the middle of a large roundabout), close to most hotels.

The **OTDC tourist office** on Lewis Road, next to the *Panthanivas hotel* (daily except Sun & 2nd Sat of month 10am–5pm; ⓣ0674/243 1299,

Moving on from Bhubaneswar

Bhubaneswar lies on the main **Howrah–Chennai train** line. The fastest service to **Delhi** is the *Rajdhani Express* #2421 (Wed, Sat & Sun 11.30am; 23hr 5min). For **Puri**, take the *New Delhi Express* #2816 (Mon, Wed, Thurs & Sat 10.25am; 2hr) or the *Neelach Express* #2876 (Tues, Fri & Sun 3.10pm; 2hr). The fastest train to **Kolkata** is the *Jan Shatabdi Express* #2074 (daily except Sun 6.20am; 6hr 30min); the slower *Howrah Express* #2864 offers an overnight passage (daily 11pm; 7hr 10min). The *Coromandal Express* #2841 (daily 9.35pm; 19hr 40min) is the best bet for **Chennai**.

Public buses depart from Baramunda bus stand: there are services to Baleshwar (Balasore; 6–8 daily; 3hr 30min–5hr), Brahampur (Berhampur; 6–8 daily; 4hr) and Konark (hourly; 1hr 30min–2hr), as well as several daily buses to Kolkata (10–12hr). You can pick up buses to Puri, Pipli and Cuttack (all every 15min; 30min, 45min–1hr, 1hr 15min–2hr respectively) from Jayadev Nagar opposite the *Kalinga Ashok* hotel, and from near the railway station. **Minibuses** run to Puri as soon as they are full, but get extremely overloaded and go dangerously fast.

Daily **flights** serve destinations throughout India, including Bengaluru, Chennai, Delhi, Hyderabad, Kolkata and Mumbai.

Ⓦwww.visitorissa.org), and counters at the railway station (daily 24hr) and the airport (opens to meet incoming flights), can arrange hire cars (from Rs60/hr plus Rs7/km, minimum 5hr) and help with hotel bookings. The Lewis Road office also offers rather rushed **tours** of the city (daily except Mon 9am–5.30pm; Rs150, a/c vehicle Rs200), and Puri, Konark and Pipli (daily 9am–7pm; Rs180, a/c vehicle Rs250). The India Tourism office is behind the museum at B-21 BJB Nagar (Mon–Fri 10am–5pm; Ⓣ0674/243 2203).

Bhubaneswar is too spread out to explore on foot and is best seen by auto- or cycle **rickshaw**. Sights outside the city, such as Dhauli or the Udaigiri and Khandagiri caves, can be reached by local **buses** from the old city bus stand near Capital Market, by auto-rickshaw or on one of OTDC's **bus tours**.

Accommodation

While the better-class hotels are spread out all over the city, the inexpensive places are generally grouped around the **railway station** or near the busy **Kalpana Square** junction at the bottom of Cuttack Road, a five-minute auto-rickshaw ride away.

Aristo Lodge Kalpana Square Ⓣ0674/231 1093. If *Bhagwat Niwas* is full, shoestring travellers can try this ramshackle pale pink hotel: the staff are friendly, but the rooms – all with private facilities, some with fuzzy TV sets – are super-basic. ❶–❷

Bhagwat Niwas 9 Buddha Nagar Ⓣ0674/231 3708. Managed by an Aurobindo devotee, the hotel is safe and welcoming. There's a range of simple, clean rooms, some with balconies and a/c, as well as an in-house ISD booth for international calls and a good restaurant. ❶–❹

Ginger Jaidev Vihar, 4km from the railway station Ⓣ0674/230 3933, Ⓦwww.gingerhotels.com. The city's best mid-range hotel has ultra-modern, if somewhat bland, decor, and courteous and efficient staff. Rooms are large and surgically clean; each comes with a flat-screen TV and wi-fi access. Good online deals are available. ❺–❻

Grand Central Old Station Rd Ⓣ0674/231 3411, Ⓦwww.hotelgrandcentral.com. In a convenient, if unprepossessing, location, *Grand Central* has comfortable, though not particularly stylish, attached a/c rooms with TVs and wi-fi access; the more expensive also have tubs and minibars. The superb restaurant serves some of the best dosas you're likely to come across. Book online to get a 15 percent discount. ❺–❼

Jajati MG Marg, top end of Station Square Ⓣ0674/250 0352, Ⓔsahuramesh2003@hotmail.com. A popular hotel within striking distance of the railway station. Although a little frayed around the edges, the rooms (with either a/c or fans) are comfortable and good value. 24hr checkout. ❷–❹

Janapatha 29 Jan Path, 1km north of the railway station ⓣ0674/259 7147. An excellent value choice, *Janapatha* boasts cheerful staff, a travel agent, internet access and a good restaurant. The best rooms are at the front and overlook the Shri Ram Temple; all are large and comfortable. The free newspaper delivered each morning is a nice touch. ❷–❹

Mayfair Lagoon 8-B Jaydev Vihar, 4km from the railway station ⓣ0674/236 0101, ⓦwww.mayfairhotels.com. This luxury hotel is something of an oddity: sumptuous cottages (Rs9000) with dark-wood fittings and eye-wateringly expensive villas (Rs30,000) with four-poster beds and jacuzzis surround an ornamental lake; the attractive grounds, meanwhile, are filled with kitsch life-sized models of crocodiles, deer and sundry other beasts. ❾

New Marrion 6 Jan Path ⓣ0674/238 0850, ⓦwww.hotelnewmarrion.com. Upmarket hotel with slick attached rooms, a curvy pool, foreign exchange facilities and a travel agent. Each booking comes with a free bottle of wine and Rs1200 to spend in the hotel's two good restaurants. There's also a 24hr bar (open to non-residents). ❽

Panthanivas Lewis Rd ⓣ0674/243 2314, ⓦwww.visitorissa.org. An institutional OTDC-run hotel close to the museum and temples with dated but large and comfortable a/c rooms. There are a couple of good restaurants, breakfast is included in the rates and the 8am checkout is negotiable if they are not too busy. ❺

Pushpak 68 Buddha Nagar ⓣ0674/231 0185. Despite the rather dusty exterior, the friendly *Pushpak* is the pick of the Kalpana Square hotels. The attached rooms are large and clean, and have either fans or a/c; there are three decent restaurants and a bar. 24hr checkout and rates include breakfast. ❹

Richi Station Square ⓣ0674/253 4619, ⓕ539 418. Right next to the railway station, so not the quietest, but *Richi* is nevertheless an efficient and justifiably popular choice. All rooms are attached and have TV; the more expensive have a/c. Rates include breakfast. ❷–❹

Swosti 103 Jan Path ⓣ0674/253 4678, ⓦwww.swosti.com. The older and cheaper of the city's two *Swostis* is starting to show its age, but remains a reliable option. The slightly overpriced a/c attached rooms have tubs, minibars and thoughtful touches like hairdryers and kettles. There's also a good travel agency, a couple of restaurants and a bar. ❽

Trident Bhubaneswar Nayapalli, 4km from the railway station ⓣ0674/230 1010, ⓦwww.tridenthotels.com. The city's top hotel is exquisitely furnished with antique textiles, stone and metalwork. Facilities include an excellent restaurant, an efficient travel centre, foreign exchange, pool and even a running track. Immaculate doubles from Rs12,500. ❾

The temples

Of the five hundred or so **temples** that remain, only a handful are of interest to any but the most ardent temple-phile. They are quite spread out in the south of the city, but it's possible to see the highlights in a day by auto-rickshaw, which should cost around Rs250 for a tour of the main sites (including waiting time). The majority are active places of worship, so dress appropriately, remove your shoes (and any leather items) at the entrance and seek permission before taking photographs, particularly inside the buildings. The resident priest will expect a donation if he's shown you around, but don't believe the astronomical amounts recorded in the ledgers you'll be shown. Entry is free to all temples except Rajarani.

The central group

The compact **central group**, just off Lewis Road, includes some of Bhubaneswar's most celebrated temples. The best preserved and most beautiful early example, the lavishly decorated **Parasuramesvara Mandir**, stands in the shade of a large banyan tree. Dating from around 650 AD, the shrine's plain, rectangular assembly hall (*jagamohana*), simple stepped roof and squat beehive-shaped tower (*deul*) typify the style of the late seventh century. Besides the sheer quality of the building's exterior sculpture, Parasuramesvara is significant in marking the then-recent transition from Buddhism to Hinduism. Look out for panels depicting Lakulisha, the proselytizing Shaivite saint whose sect was largely responsible for the conversion of Orissa to Hinduism in the fifth century. More graphic assertions of Hindu supremacy mark corners of the *deul*, where rampant lions crouch or stand above elephants, symbols of the beleaguered Buddhist faith.

Erected in the mid-tenth century, the **Muktesvara Mandir** is often dubbed "the gem" of Orissan architecture for its compact size and exquisite sculptural detail. It stands in a separate walled courtyard, beside the small **Marichi Kund** tank (whose waters are believed to cure infertility). The temple was constructed two hundred years after the Parasuramesvara, and represents the new, more elaborate style that had evolved in Bhubaneswar. Its *jagamohana* sports the more distinctively Orissan pyramidal roof, while the *deul*, though similar in shape to earlier sanctuary towers,

Orissan temples

Orissan temples constitute one of the most distinctive regional styles of religious architecture in South Asia. They were built according to strict templates set down a thousand or more years ago in a body of canonical texts called the *Shilpa Shastras*. These specify not only every aspect of temple design, but also the overall symbolic significance of the building. Unlike Christian churches or Islamic mosques, Hindu shrines are not simply places of worship but objects of worship in themselves – recreations of the "Divine Cosmic Creator-Being" or the particular deity enshrined within them. For a Hindu, to move through a temple is akin to entering the very body of the god glimpsed at the moment of *darshan*, or ritual viewing, in the shrine room. In Orissa, this concept also finds expression in the technical terms used in the *Shastras* to designate the different parts of the structure: the foot (*pabhaga*), shin (*jangha*), torso (*gandi*), neck (*kantha*), head (*mastaka*) and so forth.

Most temples are made up of two main sections. The first and most impressive of these is the **deul**, or sanctuary tower. A soaring, curvilinear spire with a square base and rounded top, the *deul* symbolizes Meru, the sacred mountain at the centre of the universe. Its intricately ribbed sides, which in later buildings were divided into rectangular projections known as *raths*, usually house images of the accessory deities, while its top supports a lotus-shaped, spherical *amla* (a motif derived from an auspicious fruit used in Ayurvedic medicine as a purifying agent). Above that, the vessel of immortality, the *kalasha*, is crowned by the presiding deity's sacred weapon, a wheel (Vishnu's *chakra*) or trident (Shiva's *trishul*). The actual deity occupies a chamber inside the *deul*. Known in Oriya as the **garbha griha**, or inner sanctum, the shrine is shrouded in womb-like darkness, intended to focus the mind of the worshipper on the image of God.

The **jagamohana** ("world delighter"), which adjoins the sanctuary tower, is a porch with a pyramidal roof where the congregation gathers for readings of religious texts and other important ceremonies. Larger temples, such as the Lingaraj in Bhubaneswar and the Jagannath in Puri, also have structures that were tacked on to the main porch when music and dance were more commonly performed as part of temple rituals. Like the *jagamohana*, the roofs of the **nata mandir** (the dancing hall) and **bhoga-mandapa** (the hall of offerings) are pyramidal. The whole structure, along with any smaller subsidiary shrines (often earlier temples erected on the same site), is usually enclosed in a walled courtyard.

Over the centuries, Orissan temples became progressively grander and more elaborate. It's fascinating to chart this transformation as you move from the earlier buildings in Bhubaneswar to the acme of the region's architectural achievement, the stunning Sun Temple at **Konark**. Towers grow taller, roofs gain extra layers, and the **sculpture**, for which the temples are famous all over the world, attains a level of complexity and refinement unrivalled before or since.

places more emphasis on vertical rather than horizontal lines. Directly facing the main entrance, the ornamental **torana** (gateway), topped by two reclining female figures, is Muktesvara's masterpiece.

On the edge of Muktesvara's terrace, the unfinished **Siddhesvara** was erected at around the same time as the Lingaraj, but is far less imposing.

The eastern group

Although it was never completed, the twelfth-century **Rajarani Mandir** (daily sunrise to sunset; Rs100 [Rs5], video Rs25) ranks among the very finest of Bhubaneswar's later temples. From the far end of the well-watered gardens in which it stands, the profile of the *deul* dominates first impressions. The best of the sculpted figures for which Rajrani is famous surround the sides of the tower, roughly 3m off the ground, where the **dikpalas** ("guardians of the eight directions"), separated from one another by exquisite female *nayikas*, protect the main shrine.

Unlike most of its neighbours, the eleventh-century shrine within **Brahmesvara Mandir** still houses a living deity, as indicated by the saffron pennant flying from the top of the sanctuary. Here too *dikpalas* preside over the corners, with a fierce Chamunda on the western facade (shown astride a corpse and holding a trident and severed head), while curvaceous maidens admire themselves in mirrors or dally with their male consorts. An inscription, now lost, records that one Queen Kovalavati once made a donation of "many beautiful women" to this temple, recalling that **devadasis**, the dancers-cum-prostitutes who were to become a prominent feature of Orissan temple life in later years (see p.898), made an early appearance here. Non-Hindus are barred from the central shrine, whose majestic Nandi bull has testicles well polished by years of propitious rubbing from worshippers.

The Bindu Sagar group

The largest group of temples is clustered around the **Bindu Sagar** ("ocean drop tank"), 2km south of the city centre. This small artificial lake, mentioned in the *Puranas*, is said to contain nectar, wine and water drawn from the world's most sacred rivers. It's the main bathing place both for pilgrims visiting the city and for the Lingaraj deity, who is taken to the pavilion in the middle once every year during Bhubaneswar's annual **Car Festival** (Ashokastami) for his ritual purificatory dip. The hours around sunrise and sunset are the most evocative time for a stroll here, when the residents of the nearby *dharamshalas* file through the smoky lanes to pray at the *ghats*.

Lingaraj Mandir

Immediately south of the Bindu Sagar stands Orissa's most stylistically evolved temple. Built early in the eleventh century by the Ganga kings, one hundred years before the Jagannath temple at Puri, the mighty **Lingaraj Mandir** has remained a living shrine. For this reason, foreign visitors are not permitted inside, but there is a **viewing platform** overlooking the north wall of the complex, from where all four of the principal sections of the building are visible. The two nearest the entrance, the *bhoga-mandapa* (Hall of Offering) and the *nata mandir* (Hall of Dance, associated with the rise of the *devadasi* system – see p.898) are both later additions. Beautiful **sculpture** depicting the music and dance rituals that would once have taken place inside the temple adorns its walls.

The immense 45m *deul* is the literal and aesthetic high-point of the Lingaraj. The rampant lion projecting from the curved sides of the tower, and the downtrodden elephant beneath him, again symbolize the triumph of Hinduism over Buddhism. On the top, the typical Orissan motif of the flattened, ribbed sphere (*amla*) supported by gryphons, is crowned with Shiva's trident. As in the Brahmesvara temple, the long saffron pennant announces the living presence of the deity below.

The **shrine** inside is unusual. The powerful 2.5m-thick Svayambhu ("self-born") lingam that it contains, one of the twelve *jyotirlingas* in India, is known as "Hari-Hara" because it is considered half Shiva, half Vishnu – an extraordinary amalgam thought to have resulted from the ascendancy of Vaishnavism over Shaivism in the twelfth and thirteenth centuries. Unlike other lingams, which are bathed every day in a concoction prepared from hemlock, Svayambhu is offered a libation of rice, milk and *bhang* by the brahmins.

Vaital Deul Mandir

The **Vaital Deul** temple, one of the group's oldest buildings, is a real feast of Tantric art. The building was erected around 800 AD in a markedly different style from most of its contemporaries in Bhubaneswar, drawing heavily on earlier Buddhist influences. Among the panels of Hindu deities encrusting its outer walls, you can make out examples of some of India's earliest erotic sculpture.

Once past the four-faced lingam post at the main entrance (used for tethering sacrificial offerings), your eyes soon adjust to the darkness of the **interior**, whose grotesque images convey the macabre nature of the esoteric rites once performed here. Durga, in her most terrifying aspect as **Chamunda**, peers out of the half-light from behind the grille at the far end of the hall – her withered body, garlanded with skulls and flanked by an owl and a jackal, stands upon a rotting corpse. In front of her a man picks himself up from the floor, having filled his skull-cup with blood from the decapitated body nearby.

Around the town

The **Orissa State Museum**, at the top of Lewis Road (daily except Mon 10am–5pm; Rs50 [Rs5]), has a collection of "tribal" artefacts, manuscripts and archeological finds, including pre-twelfth-century Buddhist statues and reproductions of **chitra muriya**, the folk murals seen in village houses around Puri. The museum's real highlight, however, is its collection of antique **painting** and illuminated **palm-leaf manuscripts** (see p.894). Only New Delhi's National Museum holds finer examples of this traditional Orissan art form.

Close to the Baramunda bus stand on NH-5 is the anthropological **Museum of Man** (daily except Sun 10am–5pm), with exhibits on the distinctive cultures and art of the 62 different tribal groups spread throughout Orissa. Filling the gardens outside are somewhat idealized replicas of *adivasi* dwellings, decorated with more authentic-looking murals. The **library** reputedly holds copies of all the books and journals ever compiled on the *adivasi* groups of Orissa. Opposite the Museum of Man is Asia's largest **cactus collection** (daily 10am–5pm), home to more than a thousand species of cacti.

The **Orissa Modern Art Gallery** (Mon-Sat 11am–1.30pm & 4–8pm, Sun 4–8pm), 132 Forest Walk, in Surya Nagar, showcases the work of the state's best contemporary and most underprivileged artists. Original works are available to buy from Rs300 to more than Rs15,000.

Capital Market, in a residential area along Jan Path, is the place to buy typical Orissan handlooms, handicrafts and jewellery.

Eating

The few restaurants that specialize in traditional **Orissan cuisine**, or include some Orissan dishes on their menus, are well worth seeking out. Look out for *chenna poda* (cheesecake stuffed with almonds), *raswadi* (thickened milk with balls of curd) and *gajjar halwa* (a rich sweet made from grated carrots). For good **coffee**, try *Café Coffee Day*, which has branches at the *Ginger* and *New Marrion* hotels.

Bhuvanashree At the top of Station Square next to the *Jajati* hotel. Economical and hygienic veg restaurant with the usual south Indian options, a choice of thalis and decent coffee. Closed Tues. Mains Rs30–60.

Dalema Bhouma Nagar. Dark, low-key place offering authentic Orissan dishes like *macha bhaja* (fish curry), *chengudli tarkari* (prawn curry) and *dahi machho* (freshwater fish in a yoghurt sauce). Mains around Rs50.

Dalma Sachivalaya Marg. Named after the state's signature dish (potato, *brinjal* and other vegetables cooked in dhal), this modest eatery is the place to go for traditional regional cuisine. The fish curry is excellent, and there are some fine crab and prawn dishes. There's another branch in the Maruti Mall, Chandrasekharpur, 5km north of the centre. Mains from Rs70.

Hare Krishna Jan Path, just north of the junction with MG Marg. Waiters in dinner jackets rather than *dhotis* serve strictly ISKCON-style food (the Hare Krishna movement's cuisine, without garlic or onions): vegetarian and delicious. Mains Rs50–130.

Lemon Tree and **Kanika** *Mayfair Lagoon* hotel. The former serves top quality Thai, Chinese, Japanese and Indonesian cuisine amid decor that steers just the right side of Far Eastern pastiche; the latter specializes in traditional Orissan food. Expect to pay around Rs500 per head at *Lemon Tree*, Rs300 at *Kanika*.

Rice Bowl Shahid Nagar, 1.5km north of the railway station. This first-floor a/c restaurant, which gets packed out with local families on the weekends, produces above-average Chinese food, as well as some good fish and prawn curries. Mains Rs70–180.

Tangerine 9 Jan Path, just north of the junction with MG Marg. With well over 250 Indian and Chinese dishes (Rs70–250) on offer, the menu here can be a little overwhelming: if you're having trouble deciding, opt for one of the tasty kebabs or the tandoori pomfret.

Listings

Airlines Indian Airlines is on Raj Path, near New Market (☎0674/253 0544, airport ☎0674/253 5743). JetLite is on Jan Path (☎0674/253 5007, airport ☎0674/259 6180).

Banks and exchange The State Bank of India (Mon–Fri 10am–4pm, Sat 10am–2pm, closed 2nd Sat of month) on Raj Path changes foreign currencies, as does Thomas Cook (Mon–Fri 9am–5pm, Sat 10am–2pm, closed 2nd Sat of month), 130 Ashok Nagar, Jan Path. ATMs are numerous, notably around Kalpana Square and on Jan Path.

Bookshops Try the Modern Book Depot at the top of Station Square or, across the square, the Bookshop in Ashoka Market.

Dance Visits or lessons can be arranged through the Orissa Dance Academy, 64 Kharwal Nagar, Unit 3 (☎0674/234 0124). The Rabindra Mandap auditorium on Sachivalaya Marg (☎0674/241 7677), the Suchana Bhavan building, near the old bus stand (☎0674/253 0794), and the Utkal Sangeet Mahavidyalaya, Orissa's premier college of performing arts, on Sachivalaya Marg (☎0674/241 0234), all host regular music, dance and drama events.

Hospital The Capital Hospital and Homeopathic Clinic (☎0674/240 1983) is near the airport; for casualty, call ☎0674/240 0688. The Municipal Hospital, in Lingaraj Square, also has a casualty unit; call ☎0674/259 1237. There's an Ayurvedic hospital between the *Panthanivas* hotel and the Ramesvara temple (☎0674/243 2347). For a Red Cross ambulance, call ☎0674/240 2384.

Internet access There are plenty of internet cafés around Station Square, Cuttack Rd and Jan Path. Iway, next to the *Swosti* hotel, and beside the exhibition ground near the Shri Ram Temple, charges Rs35/hr for a fast connection. Reliance Web World in Shahid Nagar is also quick (Rs100/4hr).

Police station Raj Path, near the State Bank of India (☎0674/253 3732).

Post office On the corner of MG Marg and Sachivalaya Marg (Mon–Sat 9am–7pm).

Travel agents The *New Marrion*, *Swosti* and *Trident Bhubaneswar* hotels all have reliable in-house travel agents. Discover Tours (☎0674/243 0477, ⓦwww.orissadiscover.com), 463 Lewis Rd, is the most reliable agent for cultural, tribal and wildlife tours.

Around Bhubaneswar

A number of places around Bhubaneswar can be easily visited on a day-trip from the city. Fifteen minutes by auto-rickshaw out of the centre, the second-century BC caves at **Khandagiri** and **Udaigiri** offer a glimpse of the region's history prior to the rise of Hinduism. **Dhauli**, just off the main road to Puri, boasts an even older monument: a rock edict dating from the Mauryan era, commemorating the battle of c.260 BC that gave emperor Ashoka control of the eastern seaports, and thus enabled his missionaries to export the state religion across Asia. **Pipli**, 20km south, is famous for its appliqué work and colourful lampshades.

Udaigiri and Khandagiri caves

Six kilometres west of Bhubaneswar, a pair of low hills rises from the coastal plain. More than two thousand years ago, caves chiselled out of their malleable yellow sandstone were home to a community of **Jain monks**. Nowadays, they're clambered over by langur monkeys and occasional parties of tourists. Though by no means in the same league as the caves of the Deccan, **Udaigiri** and **Khandagiri** (daily 8am–5pm; Rs100 [Rs5], video Rs25) rank among Orissa's foremost historical monuments.

Inscriptions show that the **Chedi** dynasty, which ruled ancient Kalinga from the first century BC, was responsible for the bulk of the work. There are simple monk's cells, as well as royal chambers where the hallways, verandas and facades are encrusted with **sculpture** depicting court scenes, lavish processions, hunting expeditions, battles and dances. The later additions (from medieval times, when Jainism no longer enjoyed royal patronage in the region) are more austere, showing the twenty-four heroic Jain prophet-teachers, or *tirthankaras*.

From Bhubaneswar, the caves are approached via a road that follows the route of an ancient **pilgrimage path**. As you face the hills with the highway behind you, Khandagiri ("Broken Hill") is on your left and Udaigiri ("Sunrise Hill") is on your right.

Udaigiri

The **Udaigiri** caves occupy a fairly compact area around the south slope of the hill. **Cave 1** (Rani Gumpha or "Queen's Cave"), off the main pathway to the right, is the largest and most impressive of the group. A long frieze across the back wall shows rampaging elephants, panicking monkeys, sword fights and the abduction of a woman, perhaps illustrating episodes from the life of Kalinga's King Kharavela. **Caves 3** and **4** contain sculptures of a lion holding its prey and elephants with snakes wrapped around them, and pillars topped by pairs of peculiar winged animals. **Cave 9**, up the hill and around to the right, houses a damaged relief of figures worshipping a long-vanished Jain symbol. The crowned figure is thought to be the Chedi king, Vakradeva, whose donative inscription can still be made out near the roof. Inside the sleeping cells of all the caves, deep grooves in the stone wall at the back and in the floor were designed to carry rainwater down from the roof as an early air-conditioning system.

To reach **Cave 10**, return to the main steps and climb towards the top of the hill. Its popular name, "Ganesh Gumpha", is derived from the elephant-headed Ganesh carved on the rear wall of the cell on the right. From here, follow the path up to the ledge at the very top of Udaigiri hill for good views and the ruins of an old **chaitya hall**, probably the main place of worship for the Jain monks who lived below.

Below the ruins are **Cave 12**, shaped like the head of a tiger, and **Cave 14**, the Hathi Gumpha, known for the long **inscription** in ancient Magadhi carved onto its overhang. This relates in glowing terms the life history of King Kharavela, whose exploits brought in the fortune needed to finance the cave excavation.

Khandagiri

The caves on the opposite hill, **Khandagiri**, can be reached either by the long flight of steps leading from the road, or by cutting directly across from Hathi Gumpha via the steps that drop down from Cave 17. The latter route brings you out at **Caves 1** and **2**, known as Tatowa Gumpha ("Parrot Caves") for the carvings of birds on their doorway-arches. Cave 2, excavated in the first century BC, is the larger and more interesting. On the back wall of one of its cells, a few faint lines in red Brahmi script are thought to have been scrawled two thousand years ago by a monk practising his handwriting. The reliefs in **Cave 3**, the Ananta Gumpha ("Snake Cave"), contain the best of the sculpture on Khandagiri hill, albeit badly vandalized in places. **Caves 7** and **8**, left of the main steps, were former sleeping quarters, remodelled in the eleventh century as sanctuaries. Both house reliefs of *tirthankaras* on their walls as well as Hindu deities which had become part of the Jain pantheon by the time conversion work was done. From the nineteenth-century **Jain temple** at the top of the hill there are clear views across the sprawl of Bhubaneswar to the white dome of Dhauli.

Dhauli

The gleaming, white **Vishwa Shanti Stupa** on **Dhauli Hill**, 8km south of Bhubaneswar on the Pipli road, overlooks the spot where the Mauryan emperor **Ashoka** defeated the Kalingas in the decisive battle of 260 BC. Apart from bringing the prosperous Orissan kingdom to its knees, the victory also led the emperor, allegedly overcome by remorse at having slain 150,000 people, to renounce the path of violent conquest in favour of the spiritual path preached by Gautama Buddha. Built in 1972, the modern stupa, which eclipses its older predecessor nearby, is a memorial to this legendary change of heart, and the massive religious sea-change it precipitated.

After his conversion, Ashoka set about promulgating the maxims of his newly found faith in **rock edicts** installed at key sites around the empire. One such inscription, in ancient **Brahmi**, the ancestor of all non-Islamic Indian scripts, still stands on the roadside at the foot of Dhauli hill, etched in a rock featuring a beautifully carved figure of an elephant (symbolizing Buddhism). The Dhauli edict includes a mixture of rambling philosophical asides, discourses on animal rights and tips on how to treat your slaves. Particularly of note are the lines claiming the Buddhist doctrine of nonviolence was being recognized by "the kings of Egypt, Ptolemy and Antigonus and Magas", which proved for the first time the existence of a connection between the ancient civilizations of India and the West. The inscription diplomatically omits the account that crops up elsewhere describing how many Kalingas Ashoka put to the sword before he finally "saw the light".

Unless you're on a tour, **getting to Dhauli** involves a 2km walk. Get off the bus at Dhauli Chowk, the junction on the main Puri–Bhubaneswar road, and make your way along the avenue of cashew trees to the rock edict, from where the road begins its short climb up the hill.

Pipli

Fifteen minutes' drive or so beyond Dhauli, on the Puri road, splashes of bright colour in the shop fronts along the main street announce your arrival in **PIPLI**, Orissa's **appliqué** capital (see box, p.895). Much of what the artisans now produce is shoddy kitsch compared with the painstaking work traditionally undertaken for the Jagannath temple. Express enough interest and you'll be shown some of the better-quality pieces for which Pipli is justly famed. Bedspreads, wall-hangings and small chhatris (awnings normally hung above household and temple shrines) are the most authentic goods on offer. The shops do not open early; the best time to wander around is in the evening, when gas lamps and devotional music make the experience much more atmospheric.

Ratnagiri, Udayagiri and Lalitgiri

Nestled among picturesque verdant hills, 95km northeast of Bhubaneswar, are the remains of three Buddhist universities, **Ratnagiri**, **Udayagiri** and **Lalitgiri** (daily 8am–5pm; Rs100 [Rs5], video Rs25). The sites lie around 10km apart and are best reached in a day-trip from Bhubaneswar by hiring a car from the OTDC office. They are relatively inaccessible by public transport, which involves catching a bus north along NH-5 as far as **Chandikohl** (60km) and then taking an auto-rickshaw southeast along NH-5a towards the triangle of sites. The roundtrip from Chandikohl to the sites and back is around 60km. If you need to stay overnight, basic accommodation is available at the OTDC-run *Panthasala* (book ahead to give the warden notice that food is required; ⓣ0671/231 2225; ❷), a short way east of the Ratnagiri turn-off on the main road.

Ratnagiri

RATNAGIRI, the most impressive of the sites, lies 20km from the main road, on top of a hill overlooking the River Keluo. When Chinese chronicler Hiuen T'sang visited the university in 639 AD, it had already been a major Buddhist centre for at least two hundred years. In those days the sea reached much further inland, and would have been visible from this point – which may in part account for the choice of location. **Missionaries** were trained in such places before being sent away to China and Southeast Asia.

Two **monasteries** lie below the enormous stupa at the top of the hill. The larger and better preserved one, dating from the seventh century, has a paved courtyard surrounded by cells and a beautifully carved doorway made from local blue-green chlorite stone. The shrine inside houses a majestic Buddha. A **museum** (daily except Fri 10am–5pm; Rs2) houses the antiquities and architectural remains collected from the excavations at all three sites.

Udayagiri

Ten kilometres back towards the main road, **UDAYAGIRI** is the largest Buddhist complex in Orissa. Its main structure is a large stupa, better preserved than its counterpart at Ratnagiri. Of the two monasteries here, which flourished between the seventh and twelfth centuries, only one has been excavated. It features a large seated Buddha in its central shrine and an intricately carved entrance, along with an inscribed step-well. More rock-cut sculptures adorn the crest of the hill behind the monastery.

Lalitgiri

The turning for **LALITGIRI** is about 10km further along the main road towards Paradip. Most of the ruins of the four monasteries here are thought to date from around the ninth century, although inscriptions on an apsidal temple suggest that the site may have been occupied as early as the first century AD. Excavations in 1982 of the large stupa at the top of the hill revealed a gold casket containing a fragment of bone, believed to be a relic of the Buddha. The hill-top also provides grand panoramic views.

Northern Orissa

Cuttack, Orissa's second city, straddles the Mahanadi River. Devoid of attractions, it detains few travellers on the long journey to or from Kolkata. Once clear of Cuttack's polluted outskirts, however, you soon find yourself amid the flat paddy fields, palm groves and mud-walled villages of the **Mahanadi Delta**. Twisting through it is one of India's busiest transport arteries; the main railway line and NH-5 follow the path of the famous pilgrim trail, the **Jagannath Sadak**, which once led from Calcutta to Puri.

The area's biggest attraction is **Bhitarkanika Wildlife Sanctuary**, 130km northeast of Bhubaneswar, which has outstanding natural scenery, an abundance of fauna and flora and is visited by the endangered Olive Ridley turtles. Similipal National Park, close to the border with West Bengal, is similarly impressive, but is currently closed to visitors because of unrest (see p.886).

Bhitarkanika Wildlife Sanctuary

Covering 672 square kilometres overlying the Brahmani-Baitarani delta, the mangrove forests and wetlands of the **BHITARKANIKA WILDLIFE SANCTUARY** constitute one of the richest ecosystems of its type in India. As

Sea turtles

Every year around February or March, a strip of beach at the end of Orissa's central river delta witnesses one of the world's most extraordinary natural spectacles. Having swum right across the Pacific and Indian oceans, an average of around 200,000 female **Olive Ridley marine turtles** crawl onto the sand to nest. Almost as soon as the egg laying is complete, they're off again into the surf to begin the journey back to their mating grounds on the other side of the world.

No one knows quite why they travel such distances, but for local villagers the arrival of the giant turtles has traditionally been something of a boon. Turtle soup for breakfast, lunch and dinner...and extra cash from market sales. Over the years the annual slaughter began to turn into a green gold rush, and turtle numbers plummeted drastically until the Bhitarkanika Sanctuary on **Gahirmatha beach**, 130km northeast of Bhubaneswar, was set up in 1975 at the personal behest of Indira Gandhi. Weeks before the big three- or four-day invasion, coastguards monitor the shoreline and armed rangers aim to keep poachers at bay. For wildlife enthusiasts it's a field day.

In recent years, however, **environmental threats** have impacted on the turtles' habitat. Several hundred local families have begun to cultivate land within the sanctuary, water quality has been jeopardized by the growth of illegal prawn farms, and trawlers have been caught illegally fishing in the area without "turtle excluder devices". The turtles are further menaced by industrial pollution and the construction of a large seaport at Dhamra, 15km from Gahirmatha. Several conservation organizations, including Greenpeace and the WWF, are monitoring the area. To give a scale of the problem, in January 2010, the bodies of around one thousand dead turtles (according to official estimates) were found on the beach; although this is horrifyingly high, it was less than half of the figure for the previous year.

well as over two hundred species of birds, it's a refuge for saltwater crocodiles, monitor lizards, rhesus monkeys and a host of other reptiles and mammals, and incorporates the Olive Ridley turtle nesting beaches at Gahirmatha, Rushikulya and Devi. Bhitarkanika is open throughout the year, but the best time to visit is November to March, when most of the migratory birds that flock to the sanctuary are in situ, although the nesting season for the herons usually ends around the middle of November. If you're hoping to witness the arrival of Olive Ridley turtles, check first at the OTDC tourist office in Bhubaneswar (see p.875) to find out exactly when – or indeed if – they are expected. Other highlights include the crocodile conservation programme at Dangmar Island and the heronry at Bagagahana.

Practicalities

The hassle of reaching one of Bhitarkanika's entry points, obtaining permits (Rs1000 [Rs20]) and boat transport (up to Rs2500/day) and – if you're staying overnight in the sanctuary – accommodation, means it's much easier to take an **organized trip**: try Discover Tours in Bhubaneswar (ⓣ0674/243 0477, ⓦwww.orissadiscover.com) or Heritage Tours in Puri (ⓣ06752/223656, ⓦwww.heritagetoursorissa.com). Tours cost from around Rs1400 per person per day.

To minimise costs if you're doing it independently, it's possible to use the small port of **Chandbali**, reached by bus from Bhubaneswar (190km), or Bhadrak (the nearest railhead; 60km), as a base for day-trips into the sanctuary. There are several agents based around the jetty who can arrange permits and transport. If you want to obtain the permit yourself you'll need to contact the elusive Assistant Conservator of Forests, also based at the jetty (ⓣ06786/220372). Chandbali's best **accommodation** is at the OTDC-run *Ayanyanivas* (ⓣ06786/220397, ⓦwww.visitorissa.org; ❷–❹), near the jetty, which has a/c and fan doubles, a dorm (Rs150) and a reasonable restaurant. Alternatively, the *Swagat Lodge* (ⓣ06786/220225; ❶–❷) has small but habitable rooms. Within the sanctuary itself, accommodation is in dorms or basic rooms at one of the forest lodges at Dangmal, Ekakula, Gupti or Habalikathi (all ❸). You have to bring your own food and water, which the *chowkidar* will cook for you. Unless you use an agent, the only way to book this accommodation is in advance through the Divisional Forest Officer in the less than accessible outpost of Rajnagar (ⓣ06729/272460).

Similipal National Park

In March 2009, Maoist rebels launched an attack in Similipal National Park, the site of one of the first Project Tiger reserves and one of the last true wildernesses left in eastern India. Several buildings were blown up, forestry department vehicles were set on fire and a group of tourists staying at the park were robbed. The state authorities responded by announcing the **indefinite closure of the park**. Although the Indian government has launched a crackdown on rebel groups in Orissa (and several other states), reports suggest that Maoist activity in the area has increased. The park's closure, which resulted in most forestry department officials fleeing their posts, has put its animals – which include **tigers, leopards,** wild **elephants** and 231 species of **birds** – at serious risk. Alongside increased illegal tree-felling and hunting by local people, wildlife NGOs have warned that the actions of poachers are going virtually unchecked. The Orissa tourist authorities are tentatively optimistic that the park will reopen in the not too distant future (it was previously one of the state's top attractions), so it's worth checking out the latest information with the Bhubaneswar tourist office (see p.875). What state the park and its wildlife will be in by that time, however, is anyone's guess.

Puri

As the home of Lord Jagannath and his siblings, **PURI** ranks among Hindu India's most important sacred sites, visited by a vast number of pilgrims each year. The crowds peak during the monsoons for **Rath Yatra**, the famous "Car Festival", when millions pour in to watch three giant, multicoloured chariots being drawn up the main thoroughfare. At the centre of the maelstrom, the **Jagannath temple** soars above the town's medieval heart and colonial suburbs like some kind of misplaced space rocket. Non-Hindus aren't allowed inside its bustling precincts, but don't let this deter you; Puri's streets and beach remain the focus of intense devotional activity year round, while its bazaars are crammed with collectable religious souvenirs associated with Lord Jagannath.

Three distinct types of visitor come to Puri: middle-class Bengalis lured by the combined pleasures of puja and promenade; young Western and Japanese backpackers enjoying the low-key traveller scene; and thousands of pilgrims, mainly from rural eastern India, who flock in to pay their respects to Lord Jagannath. Over the years the three have staked out their respective ends of town and stuck to them. It all makes for a rather bizarre and intoxicating atmosphere, where you can be transported from the intensity of Hindu India to the sea and back to the relative calm of your hotel veranda at the turn of a bicycle wheel.

Some history

Until the seventh and eighth centuries, Puri was little more than a provincial outpost along the coastal trade route linking eastern India with the south. Then, thanks to its association with the Hindu reformer **Shankaracharya** (Shankara), the town began to feature on the religious map. Shankara made Puri one of his four *mathas*, or centres for the practice of a radically new, and more ascetic form of Hinduism. Holy men from across the whole Subcontinent came here to debate the new philosophies – a tradition carried on in the town's temple courtyards to this day. With the arrival of the **Gangas** at the beginning of the twelfth century, this religious and political importance was further consolidated. In 1135, Anantavarman Chodaganga founded the great temple in Puri, and dedicated it to **Purushottama**, one of the thousand names of Vishnu – an ambitious attempt to integrate the many feudal kingdoms recently conquered by the Gangas. Under the Gajapati dynasty in the fifteenth century Purushottama's name changed to **Jagannath** ("Lord of the Universe"). Henceforth **Vaishnavism** and the devotional worship of Krishna, an incarnation of Vishnu, was to hold sway as the predominant religious influence in the temple. Puri is nowadays one of the four most auspicious pilgrimage centres, or *dhams*, in India.

Western-style leisure **tourism**, centred on the town's long sandy beach, is a comparatively new phenomenon. The British were the first to spot Puri's potential as a resort. When they left, the Bengalis took over their bungalows, only to find themselves sharing the beach with an annual migration of young, chillum-smoking Westerners attracted to the town by its abundant hashish. Today, few vestiges of this era remain. Thanks to a concerted campaign by the municipality to clean up Puri's image, the "scene" has dwindled to little more than a handful of cafés, and is a far cry from the swinging hippy paradise some still arrive here hoping to find.

Arrival, information and city transport

Trains arriving at Puri's end-of-line **station**, in the north of town, are greeted by fired-up cycle rickshaw-wallahs sprinting alongside in the race to catch a foreigner. You'll encounter similar "rickshaw rage" at the main bus station and the Jagannath

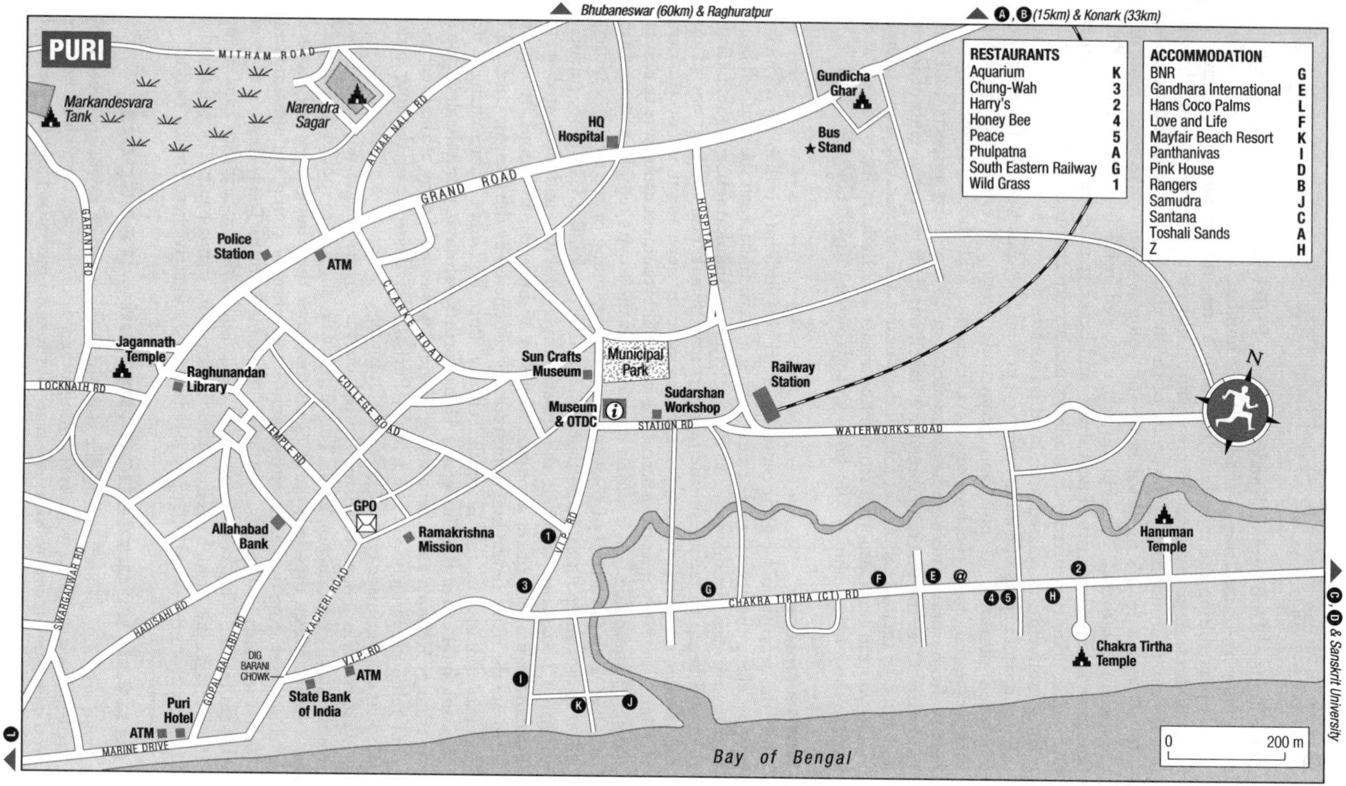

PURI

Bhubaneswar (60km) & Raghuratpur
A, B (15km) & Konark (33km)
C, D & Sanskrit University
L

RESTAURANTS	
Aquarium	K
Chung-Wah	3
Harry's	2
Honey Bee	4
Peace	5
Phulpatna	A
South Eastern Railway	G
Wild Grass	1

ACCOMMODATION	
BNR	G
Gandhara International	E
Hans Coco Palms	L
Love and Life	F
Mayfair Beach Resort	K
Panthanivas	I
Pink House	D
Rangers	B
Samudra	J
Santana	C
Toshali Sands	A
Z	H

Mitham Road
Markandesvara Tank
Narendra Sagar
Athar Nala Rd
Garanti Rd
Grand Road
HQ Hospital
Gundicha Ghar
Bus Stand
Hospital Road
Police Station
ATM
Clarke Road
Jagannath Temple
Raghunandan Library
Locknath Rd
Sun Crafts Museum
Municipal Park
Railway Station
Museum & OTDC
Sudarshan Workshop
Station Rd
Waterworks Road
College Road
Temple Rd
GPO
Ramakrishna Mission
Allahabad Bank
V.I.P. Rd
Kacheri Road
Swargadwar Rd
Hadisahi Rd
Gopal Ballabh Rd
Dig Barani Chowk
State Bank of India
Puri Hotel
Marine Drive
Chakra Tirtha (CT) Rd
Hanuman Temple
Chakra Tirtha Temple
N
0 200 m
Bay of Bengal

Moving on from Puri

Puri is joined to the main Kolkata–Chennai routes by a branch line of the busy South East **train** network and a good, well-surfaced road through Bhubaneswar, so it's well connected with most other major Indian cities. *The New Delhi Express* #2815 (Mon, Wed, Thurs & Sat 10.55am) calls at **Bhubaneswar** (1hr 40min), **Gaya** (for Bodhgaya; 14hr 10min), **Mughalsarai** (for Varanasi; 17hr 10min), and **Delhi** (29hr 5min). The slower *Neelachal Express* #2875 to Delhi (Tues, Fri & Sun, 33hr 45min) leaves Puri at the same time and calls at the same stations. A convenient train to **Kolkata** is the *Jagannath Express* #8410 (daily 11.50pm; 9hr 20min). For central Indian destinations such as Nagpur, take one of the Ahmedabad expresses (#2843 on Tues, Thurs, Fri & Sun, or #8405 on Wed). Getting to **Mumbai** involves changing at Bhubaneswar and a total journey time in excess of 40hr.

If you're heading for **South India**, it's also best to change at Bhubaneswar or Khurda Road, 44km from Puri, where you can pick up any of a number of daily trains to **Chennai** (20hr–21hr 20min), including the *Coromandel Express* #2841. Of the several weekly trains from Bhubaneswar to Thiruvananthapuram, the *Gurudev Express* #2660 (Wed 6.50am; 37hr 20min) is the quickest. Computerized reservations can be made at the station in Puri (Mon–Sat 8am–8pm, Sun 8am–2pm).

There are hourly buses to Bhubaneswar (1–2hr), although the frequent (until 5pm) **minibuses** are the easiest way to travel, between Puri and **Bhubaneswar**. Make sure the service is nonstop before you get on. The same applies to Konark minibuses (40min–1hr), which also leave when full from the main city bus stand in the northeast of town, near the Gundicha Ghar. **Jeeps** and buses also ply the same route. If you plan to head south by road along the Orissan coast, buses to **Satapada** on Chilika Lake leave every thirty minutes during the day from the main bus stand; some also go from outside the OTDC booking counter on Marine Drive.

temple, caused by competition for the commission offered by the hotels. The **bus stand** is further in the north of the city, a ten-minute rickshaw ride from the centre through the bumpy back-streets. The **OTDC tourist office** on Station Road (daily except Sun & 2nd Sat of the month 10am–5pm; ⓣ06752/222664) is friendly and helpful; the counter at the railway station (daily 24hr), by contrast, is a waste of time.

Puri is fairly spread out but flat, so **bicycles** (Rs25–30/day) are ideal for getting around and exploring the maze of streets around the Jagannath temple. There are several places to rent them on Chakra Tirtha (CT) Road, in the travellers' enclave between the *Gandhara International* and *Love and Life* – try Unique Tours opposite *Z* hotel. **Auto-rickshaws** are thin on the ground, though one or two are always hanging around the railway station and the hotels. **Mopeds** and **motorbikes** (Rs250–300/day) are rented out by a couple of travel agents and shops along CT Road for full or half-days and are useful for trips up the coast to Konark. The most reliable **travel agency** for ticket booking, flights and car/motorcycle/bike rental is Heritage Tours, based at the *Mayfair Beach Resort* (ⓣ06752/223656, ⓦwww.heritagetoursorissa.com).

Accommodation

Virtually all of Puri's **hotels** are on or near the beach, where a strict distinction is observed: those aimed at domestic tourists are lined up behind Marine Drive, the promenade on the west end of the beach, while budget-conscious Westerners are sandwiched further east around CT Road between the high-rise, upmarket resort hotels and the fishing village; this backpackers' enclave is known as **Pentakunta**. The less expensive hotels are quiet during the summer months, but the pricier accommodation tends to be booked solid well in advance of Rath Yatra. Checkout is 8am for most hotels, although off-season this rule is less rigidly enforced.

BNR (*South Eastern Railway Hotel*) CT Rd ⓣ06752/222063, ⓔbnr@hotmail.com. A must for Rajophiles, this faded hotel retains much of the old-world charm that once made it the premier bolt-hole for Calcutta's burra- and memsahibs, with the wide verandas still patrolled by turbaned bearers with big belts and bare feet. The attached rooms are worn, but undeniably evocative of times past. ❹–❺

Gandhara International CT Rd ⓣ06752/224117, ⓦwww.hotelgandhara.com. All the rooms here have hot water and TV, and most boast excellent views; there are also dorms (Rs75). There are two roof terraces and a restaurant serving authentic Japanese food, as well as internet access, a good travel agent, and free poste restante. Staff are welcoming, and the beach opposite is relatively salubrious. ❸–❺

Hans Coco Palms Marine Drive ⓣ06752/230038, ⓦwww.hanshotels.com. Modern complex in a superb setting some 2km west of the centre; all the rooms are a/c and overlook the sea. There's a pool, bar and restaurant, and the beach here is pleasant. ❽

Love and Life CT Rd ⓣ06752/224433, ⓔloveandlife@hotmail.com. Popular with Puri's many young Japanese visitors, this place has an easy-going atmosphere and a good restaurant. The clean attached rooms are either in the main block or in cottages in the garden. ❷–❹

Mayfair Beach Resort Off CT Rd ⓣ06752/227800, ⓦwww.mayfairhotels.com. This five-star resort has tastefully-decorated cottages and rooms surrounded by palm trees, a pool and an appealing stretch of beach out front. Facilities include a gym, massage centre, bar and seafood restaurant. ❽

Panthanivas Off CT Rd ⓣ06752/222562, ⓦwww.visitorissa.org. A good-value OTDC-run hotel, where some of the plain but spacious rooms catch cooling sea breezes; those in the older Raj-era building have more character. There's also a restaurant, bar and garden. ❹–❺

Pink House Off CT Rd ⓣ06752/222253. As the name suggests, this is a pinky-red pad, right on the beach at the edge of the fishing village, with rustic rooms (with either shared or private facilities), its very own travellers' scene and a restaurant. ❶

Rangers Puri-Konark Marine Drive ⓣ06752/211057, ⓔfreethinker.sanjay@gmail.com. Two cottages and a camping area (pitches; Rs200) secluded among trees adjacent to the beach, 15km from Puri and 20km from Konark. As close to a secluded beach paradise as you're likely to find around Puri, but inconvenient for actually visiting Puri or Konark. There's a restaurant, and bikes, kites, parasail and fishing equipment can be hired from the knowledgeable owner. ❷–❸

Samudra Off CT Rd ⓣ06752/222705 ⓕ06752/228654. This well-run hotel is one of the best mid-range options in Puri: the light and airy rooms have balconies facing the sea, while the restaurant serves excellent *puri bhaji* for breakfast. ❸–❺

Santana At the very end of CT Rd ⓣ06752/251491, ⓦwww.indiasantana.com. Small pleasant hotel with a good traveller set up (it's particularly popular with the Japanese). The economy rooms are narrow and sparsely-furnished, but the more expensive ones are larger and have a/c. All have bright mauve, green or purple walls and wonderfully clashing orange curtains. Rates include breakfast. ❷–❻

Toshali Sands Konark Rd ⓣ06752/250571, ⓦwww.toshalisands.com. A self-styled "ethnic village" 9km north of town, consisting of a/c cottages grouped around a garden and pool. Ideal for families, there's a good restaurant, gym and sauna. Rates include free pick-up from Puri railway station. ❼–❽

Z CT Rd ⓣ06752/222554, ⓦwww.zhotelindia.com. A Puri institution, the *Z* (pronounced "jed") is based in a mansion once owned by the Raja of Serampore. There is a range of appealing rooms – the cheaper ones share facilities, the more expensive options are attached – with sea views, a women-only dorm (Rs100), and plenty of communal areas, including a TV lounge, kitchen and a large garden. ❶–❸

The Jagannath temple

The mighty **Jagannath temple** in Puri is one of the four holy *dhams*, or "abodes of the divine", drawing pilgrims, or *yatris*, here to spend three auspicious days and nights near Lord Jagannath, the presiding deity. The present temple structure, modelled on the older Lingaraj temple in Bhubaneswar, was erected at the start of the twelfth century by the Ganga ruler Anantavarman Chodaganga.

Despite the temple's long-standing "caste no bar" rule, non-Hindu visitors are obliged to view proceedings from the flat roof of the **Raghunandan Library** (Mon–Sat 10am–noon & 4–6pm), directly opposite the main gate. One of the librarians will show you up the stairs to the vantage point overlooking the East Gate. You should make a donation for this service – but don't believe the big sums written in the ledger.

From the rooftop a fine view encompasses the immense **deul**, at 65m by far the loftiest building in the entire region. Archeologists have removed the white plaster from the tower to expose elaborate **carving** similar to that on the Lingaraj. Crowning the very top, a long scarlet pennant and the eight-spoked wheel (*chakra*) of Vishnu announce the presence of Lord Jagannath within.

The Jagannath deities and Rath Yatra

Stand on any street corner in Orissa and you'll probably be able to spot at least one image of the black-faced **Jagannath deity**, with his brother **Balabhadra** and sister **Subhadra**; each figure is legless, with undersized arms and prominent eyes. The origins of this peculiar symbol are shrouded in **legend**. One version relates that the image of Lord Jagannath looks the way it does because it was never actually finished. King Indramena, a ruler of ancient Orissa, once found the god Vishnu in the form of a tree stump washed up on Puri beach. He carried the lump of wood to the temple and, following instructions from Brahma, called the court carpenter Visvakarma to carve out the image. Visvakarma agreed – on condition that no one set eyes on the deity until it was completed. The king, however, unable to contain his excitement, peeped into the workshop; Visvakarma, spotting him, downed tools and cast a spell on the deity so that no one else could finish it.

Rath Yatra

The Jagannath deities are also the chief focus of Puri's annual "Car Festival", the **Rath Yatra** – just one episode in a long cycle of rituals that begins in the full moon phase of the Oriya month of Djesto (June & July). In the first of these, the **Chandan Yatra**, special replicas of the three temple deities, are taken to the **Narendra Sagar** where for 21 consecutive days they are smeared with *chandan* (sandalwood paste) and rowed around in a ceremonial, swan-shaped boat. At the end of this period, in a ceremony known as **Snana Yatra**, the three go for a dip in the tank, after which they head off for fifteen days of secluded preparation for Rath Yatra.

The Car Festival proper takes place during the full moon of the following month, Asadho (July & Aug). Lord Jagannath and his brother and sister are placed in their chariots and dragged by 4200 honoured devotees through the assembled multitudes to their summer home, the **Gundicha Ghar** ("Garden House"), 1.5km away. If you can find a secure vantage point and escape the crush, it's an amazing sight. The immense chariots are draped with brightly coloured cloth and accompanied down Grand Road by elephants, the local raja (who sweeps the chariots as a gesture of humility and equality with all castes) and a cacophony of music and percussion. Each chariot has a different name and a different-coloured cover, and is built anew every year to rigid specifications laid down in the temple's ancient manuals. Balabhadra's *rath*, the green one, leads; Subhadra is next, in black; and lastly, in the thirteen-metre-tall chariot with eighteen wheels and a vivid red and yellow drape, sits Lord Jagannath himself. It takes eight hours or more to haul the *raths* to their resting place. After a nine-day holiday, the sequence is performed in reverse, and the three deities return to the temple to resume their normal lives.

Conventional wisdom has it that the procession commemorates Krishna's journey from Gokhul to Mathura; historians cite the similarity between the *raths* and temple towers to claim it's a hangover from the time when temples were made of wood. Whatever the reason for the Car Festival, its devotees take it very seriously indeed. Early travellers spoke of fanatics throwing themselves under the gigantic wheels as a short cut to eternal bliss (whence the English word "**Juggernaut**", meaning an "irresistible, destructive force"). Contemporary enthusiasts are marginally more restrained, but like most mass gatherings in India, the whole event teeters at times on the brink of complete mayhem.

The pyramidal roofs of the temples' adjoining halls, or *mandapas*, rise in steps towards the tower. The one nearest the sanctuary, the *jagamohana* (Assembly Hall), is part of the original building, but the other two, the smaller *nata mandir* (Dance Hall) and the *bhoga-mandapa* (Hall of Offerings) nearest the entrance, were added in the fifteenth and sixteenth centuries. These halls still see a lot of action during the day as worshippers file through for *darshan*, while late every night they become the venue for devotional music. Female and transvestite dancers (*maharis* and *gotipuas*) once performed episodes from Jayadev's *Gita Govinda*, the much-loved story of the life of Krishna, for the amusement of Lord Jagannath and his siblings. Nowadays, piped songs have replaced the traditional theatre.

Outside the main building, at the left end of the walled compound surrounding the temple, are the **kitchens**. The food prepared here, known as *mahaprashad*, and blessed by Lord Jagannath, is said to be so pure that even a morsel taken from the mouth of a dog and fed to a brahmin by a Harijan (an "untouchable") will cleanse the body of sin. Devotees mill around carrying pieces of broken pots full of dhal and rice; they can only offer food to the deity from an imperfect pot as Lord Jagannath is the only perfection in this world. Among the ten thousand or so daily recipients of the *mahaprashad* are the six thousand employees of the temple itself. These **servants** are divided into 96 hereditary and hierarchical orders known as *chhatisha niyoga*, and include the priests who minister to the needs of the deities (teeth cleaning, dressing, feeding, getting them ready for afternoon siesta, and so forth), as well as the teams of craftspeople who produce all the materials required for the daily round of rituals.

Around the temple

The crowded streets **around the Jagannath temple** buzz with activity – commercial as much as religious. **Grand Road**, Puri's broad main thoroughfare, is lined with a lively **bazaar**, many of its stalls specializing in *rudraksha malas* (Shaivite "rosaries" made of 108 beads), Ayurvedic cures and the ubiquitous images of Lord Jagannath. Look out too for the wonderful "religious maps" of Puri.

Leading south from the main square in the temple surrounds, **Swargadwar** ("Cremation") **Road** leads through a dingy bazaar to the main promenade. The cremation ground itself, situated well beyond the south corner of the beach, is among India's most auspicious mortuary sites, where inquisitive tourists are definitely not welcome.

A more enjoyable foray from the main square is the trip to the **sacred tanks** in the north of town (best attempted by bicycle). Follow the north wall of the Jagannath temple up to the little road junction in the far corner, then turn right and stick to the same narrow twisting backstreet for about a kilometre until you arrive at the **Markandesvara tank**. This large, steep-sided bathing place is said to have been the spot where Vishnu once resided in the form of a neem tree while his temple was buried deep under a sand dune. There's no sign of the tree, but the temples on the south side are worth a look, particularly the smaller of the group, which contains images of the Jagannath trio.

If you retrace your route from here back down the lane as far as the first road junction, then bear left and continue for another kilometre or so, you'll emerge at the **Narendra Sagar**, Puri's most holy tank. A small temple stands in the middle, joined to the *ghats* by a narrow footbridge. During the annual **Chandan Yatra**, a replica deity of Lord Jagannath, Madan Mohan, is brought here every day for his dip. The temple itself is plastered with vivid **murals** that you can photograph on payment of the set fee listed nearby. The list also advertises the range of services offered by the temple *pujaris*, including the unlikely sounding "throw of bone" and "throw of hair" – references to the tank's role as another of Puri's famous mortuary ritual sites.

Museums and the Sudarshan workshop

The **Sun Crafts Museum** (daily 6am–10pm) showcases the more commercial side of the Lord Jagannath phenomenon. Run by a Hare Krishna devotee, it houses an extensive collection of images of the deity and his siblings, in various forms. There is also a workshop where little wooden replicas are carved and painted, before being dispatched to ISKCON centres around the world. A more controversial image of Lord Jagannath is the one depicting him mounted on the centre of a Christian crucifix – some regard it as a symbolic demand for religious tolerance in light of recent hostility between Hindus and Christians in Orissa. You may have to ask discreetly to be shown it.

Puri's small **museum** (daily except Mon 10am–5pm), above the tourist office on Station Road, houses tacky reproductions of the Jagannath deities' ceremonial garb and models of the *raths* used in the Car Festival, but little else of note.

Further down the road towards the railway station, the **Sudarshan workshop** is one of the few traditional stone-carvers' yards left in Puri. The sculptors and their apprentices are more interested in pursuing their art than selling it to tourists, but gladly direct potential customers to the factory **shop** next door. Most of the pieces here are large religious icons carved out of khondalite – the multicoloured stone used in the Sun Temple at Konark.

The beach

If a peaceful swim and a spot of sunbathing are your top priorities, you may be disappointed with **Puri beach**; the stretch in front of the fishing village is a 3km-long open-air toilet and rubbish dump. For a more salubrious dip, press on beyond the Sanskrit University, 3km further east.

In the west end of town, along **Marine Parade**, the atmosphere is more akin to a British Victorian holiday resort. This stretch is very much the domain of the domestic tourist industry and the beach is much cleaner here. It's a pleasant place to stroll and becomes highly animated after sunset when the nightly souvenir market gets going.

Local fishermen patrol the beach as **lifeguards**; recognizable by their triangular straw hats and *dhotis*, they wade with their punters into the surf and literally hold their hands to keep them on their feet – the **undertow** claims victims every year, so weak swimmers should be careful. When not saving lives, the fishermen are busy at the CT Road end of the beach, engaged in the more traditional industries of mending nets and boats. The **fishing village** is one of the biggest in Orissa, with dozens of tiny sails tacking to and fro off the coast during the day. Once landed, the catch is taken in baskets to the **fish market** in the village.

Eating

Most of the **restaurants** and cafés along CT Road offer inexpensive thalis, and there's good **fresh fish** to be had, though better food can be found at the nearby resort hotels. An interesting alternative to restaurant fare is the sacred food, or *mahaprasad*, the creation of four hundred cooks in the Jagannath temple kitchens, available from stalls in the nearby Anand Bazaar.

Aquarium *Mayfair Beach Resort*. This a/c restaurant with an open-air veranda is Puri's best option for a sophisticated evening. There's a delicious and unusually adventurous menu of Chinese, Thai and Indian dishes, as well as a few Orissan specialities (which should be ordered in advance), with the focus firmly on seafood. Expect to pay Rs300–500 a head.

Chung-Wah *Hotel Lee Garden*, VIP Rd. Run by a Chinese family from Kolkata, *Chung-Wah* is the pick of Puri's Chinese restaurants, with authentic food (including a range of tempting fish dishes) and a quick turnover. Mains Rs50–150.

Harry's CT Rd. This pure-veg restaurant serves tasty Indian food (around Rs50) made without

Orissan art and artists

Few regions of India retain as rich a diversity of **traditional art forms** as Orissa. While a browse through the bazaars and emporia in Puri and Bhubaneswar provides a good idea of local styles and techniques, a trip out to the **villages** where the work is actually produced is a much more memorable way to shop. Different villages specialize in different crafts – a division that harks back to the origins of the caste system in Orissa. Patronage from the nobility and wealthy temples during medieval times allowed local artisans, or *shilpins*, to refine their skills over generations. As the market for arts and crafts expanded, notably with the rise of **Puri** as a pilgrimage centre, **guilds** were formed to control the handing down of specialist knowledge and separate communities established to carry out the work. Today, the demand for **souvenirs** has given many old art forms a new lease of life.

- **Stone sculpture** With modern temples increasingly being built out of reinforced concrete, life for Orissa's stone sculptors is getting tougher. To see them at work, head for Pathuria Sahi ("Stonecarvers' Lane") and the famous Sudarshan workshop in **Puri** (see p.893), where mastercraftsmen and apprentices still fashion Hindu deities and other votive objects according to specifications laid down in ancient manuals.
- **Painting** *Patta chitra*, classical Orissan painting, is closely connected with the Jagannath cult. Traditionally, artists were employed to decorate the inside of the temples in Puri and to paint the deities and chariots used in the Rath Yatra. Later, the same vibrant colour-schemes and motifs were transferred to lacquered cloth or palm leaves and sold as sacred souvenirs to visiting pilgrims. In the village of **Raghurajpur** near Puri, where the majority of the remaining artists, or *chitrakaras*, now live, men use paint made from the local mineral stones. Specialities include sets of *ganjiffa* – small round cards used to play a trick-taking game based on the struggle between Rama and the demon Ravana, as told in the Ramayana.
- **Palm-leaf manuscripts** Palm leaves, or *chitra pothi*, have been used as writing materials in Orissa for centuries. Using a sharp stylus called a *lohankantaka*, the

onions or garlic in the Hare-Krishna ISKCON tradition, and good fresh juices.

Honey Bee CT Rd. An a/c joint with good breakfast options, filter coffee, decent attempts at pizza and pasta dishes (Rs30–160) and a relaxed and friendly vibe.

Peace CT Rd. This traveller stalwart is a friendly place, with tables in the garden, serving all the usual fare (mains from Rs35) but specializing in seafood.

Phulpatna *Toshali Sands* hotel. The distinguishing feature of *Phulpatna*'s menu is the inclusion of recipes revived from Kalingan times. Regardless of their derivation, the dishes (Rs100–300) are delicious, and the tables by the large bay windows give a relaxing view of the gardens below.

South Eastern Railway *BNR* hotel. The so-so food (mains Rs70–200) takes distant second place to the idiosyncratic colonial charm here – there are checked tablecloths, silver butter-dishes and waiters in turbans. Non-residents should give a couple of hours' warning.

Wild Grass Corner of VIP Rd and College Rd, 2km from CT Rd. Popular with the locals, *Wild Grass* serves superb tandoori, seafood, vegetarian and Orissan dishes at very reasonable prices (Rs40–120), with tables in a beautiful leafy garden. Open for lunch and dinner.

Listings

Banks and exchange The State Bank of India (Mon–Fri 10am–4pm, Sat 10.30am–1pm) beyond the *Nilachal Ashok Hotel*, on VIP Rd, changes travellers' cheques and US$, Aus$ and £, and has an ATM. You can also change money at Allahabad Bank (Mon–Fri 10am–5pm, Sat 10am–1pm) on Temple Rd, 200m up from the GPO towards the temple, and Trade Wings above the *Travellers Inn* on CT Rd. There is an ICICI ATM near the Police Station on Grand Rd and an Andhra Bank ATM near *Puri Hotel*.

artist first scratches the text or design onto the surface of palm leaves, then applies a paste of turmeric, dried leaves, oil and charcoal. When the residue is rubbed off, the etching stands out more clearly. Palm-leaf flaps are often tied onto the structure so an innocent etching of an animal or deity can be lifted to reveal *Kama Sutra* action. The best places to see genuine antique palm-leaf books, however, are the National Museum in New Delhi or the State Museum in Bhubaneswar.

- **Textiles** Distinctive textiles woven on handlooms are produced throughout Orissa. Silk saris from **Brahmapur** and **Sambalpur** are the most famous, though **ikat**, which originally came to Orissa via the ancient trade links with Southeast Asia, is also typical. It is created using a tie-dye-like technique known as *bandha*, also employed by weavers from the village of **Nuapatna**, 70km from Bhubaneswar, who produce silk *ikats* covered in verses from the scriptures for use in the Jagannath temple.
- **Appliqué** The village of **Pipli** (see p.884) has the monopoly on appliqué, another craft rooted in the Jagannath cult. Geometric motifs and stylized birds, animals and flowers are cut from brightly coloured cloth and sewn onto black backgrounds. Pipli artists are responsible for the chariot covers used in the Rath Yatra as well as for the small canopies, or chhatris, suspended above the presiding deity in Orissan temples.
- **Metalwork** *Tarakashi* (literally "woven wire"), or silver filigree, is Orissa's best-known metalwork technique. Using lengths of wire made by drawing strips of silver alloy through small holes, the smiths create distinctive ornaments, jewellery and utensils for use in rituals and celebrations. The designs are thought to have come to India from Persia with the Mughals, though the existence of an identical art form in Indonesia, with whom the ancient Orissan kingdoms used to trade, suggests that the technique itself may be even older. *Tarakashi* is now only produced in any quantity in **Cuttack** and is becoming a dying art-form.

Bookshops Loknath Bookshop is next to *Raju's* restaurant on CT Rd.
Hospitals Puri's main "HQ" hospital (ⓣ06752/223742) is well outside the town centre on Grand Rd. Hotels such as the *Panthanivas*, or Heritage Tours at the *Mayfair* can help find a doctor in an emergency.
Internet access There are numerous places along CT and VIP Rds; try the *Gandhara* hotel or nearby Nanako.com (both Rs30/hr).
Police The main station is on Grand Rd, near the Jagannath temple. There is another branch at the Kacheri Rd, VIP Rd junction (ⓣ06952/222025).
Post office The GPO, with poste restante, is on Kacheri Rd.
Shopping and markets Utkalika and the other handloom emporiums, just up from the GPO on Temple Rd, stock a good range of local crafts at fixed prices. Antique India, next to the *Holiday House* on CT Rd is good for antiques and jewellery. Sudarshan on Station Rd, close to the tourist office, is the best place to buy traditional stone sculpture. For classical Orissan paintings visit the Patta Chitra Centre on Nabakalebar Rd. There's a lively evening market on the beach off Marine Drive, south of *Puri Hotel*.
Tours OTDC runs tour buses from in front of the *Panthanivas* to nearby attractions including Bhubaneswar and Konark (daily except Mon 6.30am–7pm; Rs170, a/c vehicle Rs300), and Chilika Lake (daily 6.30am–7.30pm; Rs130, a/c vehicle Rs200). Gandhara Travel, at the *Gandhara International Hotel*, does tours and ticketing and organizes trips to Konark during the dance festival. Heritage Tours (ⓣ06752/223656, ⓦwww.heritagetoursorissa.com), based at the *Mayfair Beach Resort*, is well-established and reliable, offering tribal, wildlife and archeology tours in Orissa. Grass Routes on CT Rd (ⓣ06752/220560, ⓦwww.grassroutesjourneys.com) arranges excellent tours of the area, including to Chilika Lake, and tribal tours.

Konark and around

Time runs like a horse with seven reins,
Thousand-eyed, unageing, possessing much seed. Him the poets mount; His wheels are all beings.

The *Atharva Veda*

If you see only one temple in Orissa, it should be **KONARK**, one of India's most visited ancient monuments. Standing imperiously in its compound of lawns and casuarina trees, 35km north of Puri, this majestic pile of oxidizing sandstone is considered to be the apogee of Orissan architecture and one of the finest religious buildings anywhere in the world.

The temple is all the more remarkable for having languished under a huge mound of sand since it fell into neglect around three hundred years ago. Not until the dune and heaps of collapsed masonry were cleared away from the sides, early in the twentieth century, did the full extent of its ambitious design become apparent. In 1924, the Earl of Ronaldshay described the newly revealed temple as "one of the most stupendous buildings in India which rears itself aloft, a pile of overwhelming grandeur even in its decay". A team of seven galloping horses and 24 exquisitely carved wheels found lining the flanks of a raised platform showed that the temple had been conceived in the form of a colossal chariot for the sun god **Surya**, its presiding deity. Equally sensational was the rediscovery among the ruins of some extraordinary **erotic sculpture**. Konark, like Khajuraho (see p.374), is plastered with loving couples locked in ingenious amatory postures drawn from the *Kama Sutra* – a feature that may well explain the comment made by one of Akbar's emissaries, Abul Fazl, in the sixteenth century: "Even those who are difficult to please," he enthused, "stand astonished at its sight."

Apart from the temple, a small **museum** and a fishing **beach**, Konark **village** has little going for it. Sundays and public holidays are particularly busy here: aim to stay until sunset after most of the tour groups have left, when the rich evening light works wonders on the natural colours in the khondalite sandstone.

Some history

Inscription plates attribute the founding of the temple to the thirteenth-century Ganga monarch **Narasimhadeva**, who may have built it to commemorate his military successes against the Muslim invaders. Local legend attributes its aura of power to the two very powerful magnets said to have been built into the tower, with the poles placed in such a way that the idol was suspended in mid-air.

The temple's 70m tower became a landmark for European mariners sailing off the shallow Orissan coast, who knew it as the "**Black Pagoda**", and the frequent incidence of shipping disasters along the coast was blamed on the effect of the aforesaid magnets on the tidal pattern. The tower also proved to be an obvious target for raids on the region. In the fifteenth century, Konark was sacked by the Yavana army, causing sufficient damage to allow the elements to get a foothold. As the sea receded, sand slowly engulfed the building and salty breezes set to work on the spongy khondalite, eroding the exposed surfaces and weakening the superstructure. By the end of the nineteenth century, the tower had disintegrated completely, and the porch lay buried up to its waist, prompting one art historian of the day to describe it as "an enormous mass of stones studded with a few peepal trees here and there".

Restoration only really began in earnest in 1901, when British archeologists set about unearthing the immaculately preserved hidden sections of the building and salvaging what they could from the rest of the rubble. Finally, trees were planted to shelter the compound from the corrosive winds, and a museum opened to house what sculpture was not shipped off to Delhi, Calcutta and London.

Arrival and information

The easiest way to get to Konark **from Puri**, 33km down the coast, is by bus or jeep. There are regular services in both directions and the journey only takes an hour or so, which makes it possible to do the round trip in a day – the last bus back to Puri leaves around 6.30pm. An auto-rickshaw will do the return journey, including waiting time, for about Rs350. Hourly buses **from Bhubaneswar** take two to four hours, though some involve a change at Pipli. Alternatively, you could join one of OTDC's tours that leave from the *Panthanivas* in Bhubaneswar (see p.876). The helpful OTDC **tourist office** in Konark is in the *Yatrinivas* hotel (daily except Sun & 2nd Sat of month 10am–5pm; ⓣ06758/236821).

The temple

The main entrance to the **temple** complex (daily 9am–6pm; Rs250 [Rs10]) on its eastern, sea-facing side brings you out directly in front of the **bhoga-mandapa**, or "hall of offerings". Ornate carvings of amorous couples, musicians and dancers decorating the sides of its platform and stocky pillars suggest that the now roofless pavilion, a later addition to the temple, must originally have been used for ritual dance performances.

To get a sense of the overall scale and design, stroll along the low wall that bounds the south side of the enclosure before you tackle the ruins proper. As a giant model of Surya's war chariot, the temple was intended both as an offering to the Vedic sun god and as a symbol for the passage of time itself – believed to lie in his control. The seven **horses** straining to haul the sun eastwards in the direction of the dawn (only one is still intact) represent the days of the week. The **wheels** ranged along the base stand for the twelve months, each with eight spokes detailed with pictures of the eight ideal stages of a woman's day.

With the once-lofty **sanctuary tower** now reduced to little more than a clutter of sandstone slabs tumbling from the western wing, the **porch**, or *jagamohana*, has become Konark's real centrepiece. Its impressive pyramidal roof, rising to a height of 38m, is divided into three tiers by rows of lifelike statues – mostly musicians and dancers serenading the sun god on his passage through the heavens. Though now blocked up, the huge cubic **interior** of the porch was a marvel of medieval architecture. The original builders ran into problems installing its heavy ornamental ceiling, and had to forge ten-metre iron beams as support – a considerable engineering feat for the time.

Marvellously elaborate **sculpture** embellishes the temple's exterior with a profusion of deities, animals, floral patterns, bejewelled couples, voluptuous maidens, mythical beasts and aquatic monsters. Some of Konark's most beautiful **erotica** is to be found in the niches halfway up the walls of the porch; look for the telltale pointed beards of sadhus, clearly making the most of a lapse in their vows of chastity. Many theories have been advanced over the years to explain the lascivious scenes here and elsewhere on the temple. The most convincing explanation is that the erotic art was meant as a kind of metaphor for the ecstatic bliss experienced by the soul when it fuses with the divine cosmos – a notion central to **Tantra** and the related worship of the female principle, **shakti**, which were prevalent throughout medieval Orissa.

Moving clockwise around the temple from the south side of the main staircase, you pass the intricately carved **wheels** and extraordinary **friezes** that run in narrow bands above and below them. These depict military processions (inspired by King Narasimhadeva's tussles with the Muslims) and hunting scenes, featuring literally thousands of rampaging elephants. In the top frieze along the south side

Odissi dance

Even visitors who don't normally enjoy classical dance cannot fail to be seduced by the elegance and poise of Orissa's own regional style, **Odissi**. Friezes in the Rani Gumpha at Udaigiri (see p.882) attest to the popularity of dance in the Orissan courts as far back as the second century BC. By the time the region's Hindu "golden age" was in full swing, it had become an integral part of religious ritual, with purpose-built dance halls, or *nata mandapas*, being added to existing temples and corps of dancing girls employed to perform in them. **Devadasis**, literally "wives of the god", were handed over by their parents at an early age and symbolically "married" to the deity. They were trained to read, sing and dance and, as one disapproving early nineteenth-century chronicler put it, to "make public traffic of their charms" with male visitors to the temple. Gradually, ritual intercourse (a legacy of the Tantric influence on medieval Hinduism) degenerated into pure prostitution, and dance, formerly an act of worship, grew to become little more than a form of commercial entertainment. By the colonial era, Odissi was all but lost.

Its resurgence followed the rediscovery in the 1950s of the **Abhinaya Chandrika**, a fifteenth-century manual on classical Orissan dance. Like Bharatanatyam, India's most popular dance style, Odissi has its own highly complex language of poses and steps. Based on the *tribhanga* "hip-shot" stance, movements of the body, hands and eyes convey specific emotions and enact episodes from well-known religious texts – most commonly the **Gita Govinda** (the Krishna story). Using the *Abhinaya* and temple sculpture, dancers and choreographers were able to reconstruct this grammar into a coherent form and within a decade Odissi was a thriving performance art once again. Today, ironically, dance lessons with a reputed guru have become *de rigueur* for the young daughters of Orissa's middle classes.

Unfortunately, catching a **live performance** is a matter of being in the right place at the right time. The only regular recitals take place in the Jagannath temple. If, however, you're not a Hindu, the annual **festival of dance** at Konark, in the first week of December, is your best chance of seeing Orissa's top performers. If you're keen to learn, a number of dance academies in Bhubaneswar run **courses** for beginners (see p.881).

of the platform, the appearance of a giraffe proves that trade with Africa took place during the thirteenth century.

Beyond the porch, a double staircase leads to a shrine containing a **statue of Surya**. Carved out of green chlorite stone, this serene image – one of three around the base of the ruined sanctuary tower – is considered one of Konark's masterpieces. The other two statues in the series are also worth a look, if only to compare their facial expressions which, following the progress of the sun around the temple, change from wakefulness in the morning (south) to heavy-eyed weariness at the end of the day (north). At the foot of the western wall there's an altar-like platform covered with carvings: the kneeling figure in its central panel is thought to be King Narasimhadeva.

In early December, the temple hosts one of India's premier **dance festivals**, drawing an impressive cast of both classical and folk dance groups from all over the country. For the exact dates and advance bookings, contact the OTDC tourist offices in Bhubaneswar.

The village and around

Some way outside the compound, near the *Yatrinivas* hotel (see opposite), the **archeological museum** (daily except Fri 10am–5pm; Rs5) has lost most of its best pieces to Delhi, but still has fragments of sculpture, much of it erotic.

Outside, a small shed in the northeast corner of the enclosure houses a stone architrave bearing images of **nine planet deities**, the Navagrahas, which originally sat above one of the temple's ornamental doorways and is now kept as a living shrine. **Chandrabhaga beach**, 3km south of the temple, is a quiet and clean alternative to Puri's dirty sands. Although far from ideal for swimming or sunbathing, it's nonetheless a pleasant place to wander in the evening and watch the fishing fleet.

Accommodation and eating

Few people stay in Konark, but the **accommodation** here is convenient if you want to enjoy the temple in peace after the day-trippers have left. Near the main entrance to the monuments, the uninspiring OTDC-run *Panthanivas* (ⓣ06758/236831, ⓦwww.visitorissa.org; ❸–❹) offers gloomy but clean rooms, some with a/c. Next door, and also run by OTDC, is the more cheerful *Yatrinivas* (ⓣ06758/236820, ⓦwww.visitorissa.org; ❺), which has comfortable attached rooms with a/c, coloured fountains in the gardens and a well-informed manager. The *Labanya Lodge* (ⓣ06758/236824; ❶–❷), just out of the village on the beach road, is the most backpacker-friendly place, with a small garden, internet access and bikes for hire. The rooms vary though, so look at a few.

For **food** you have a choice between the row of thali and tea stalls opposite the temple or a more substantial meal in one of the hotel restaurants. The *Panthanivas* and *Yatrinivas* serve the usual range of veg and rice dishes; the latter is generally packed out at lunchtime with tour parties, all tucking into Orissan thalis. The *Sun Temple Hotel* is the pick of the *dhabas*.

Southern Orissa

Along the stretch of coast between Puri and Andhra Pradesh there are a couple of scenic detours that may tempt you to break the long journey south. Three hours south of the capital, at the foot of a barren, sea-facing spur of the Eastern Ghats, is India's largest saltwater lake. **Chilika**'s main attractions are the one million or so migratory birds that nest here in winter. Seventy kilometres further on, **Gopalpur-on-Sea** is a decidedly low-key beach town. **Brahmapur** (formerly Berhampur), 16km inland, is southern Orissa's biggest market town, and the main transport hub for the sinuous route west through the hills to the spa station of **Taptapani** and "tribal districts" beyond.

Chilika Lake

Were it not for its glass-like surface, **CHILIKA LAKE**, Asia's largest lagoon, could easily be mistaken for the sea; from its mud-fringed foreshore you can barely make out the narrow strip of marshy islands and sand-flats that separate the 1100-square-kilometre expanse of brackish water from the Bay of Bengal. Come here between December and February, though, and you'll see a variety of **birds**, from flamingos, pelicans and painted storks to fish eagles, ospreys and kites, many of them migrants from Siberia, Iran and the Himalayas. Chilika is also one of the few places in India where the **Irrawaddy dolphin** can be spotted.

The best way to see the lake and the birdlife is via a boat trip. Unfortunately, tourists are currently banned from visiting Nalabana island, a designated bird sanctuary, which has dramatically reduced the chances of seeing the migratory birds at close quarters. The state authorities claim this is to protect the birds from the disruption caused by visitors, but the move has been criticized by local travel agencies and boat operators, who are hopeful the policy will be overturned. In the meantime, it's still possible to see the migratory birds by taking a boat cruise or by visiting some of Chilika's other islands, which offer decent birdwatching opportunities, though not as good as those on Nalabana.

By and large, the fishing villages and fabled island "kingdom" of **Parikud** on the eastern side of the lake are passed up in favour of the boat ride to the *devi* shrine on **Kalijai** island. Legend has it that a local girl once drowned here on the way to her wedding across the lake, and that her voice was subsequently heard calling from under the water. Believing the bride-to-be had become a goddess, local villagers inaugurated a shrine to her that over the years became associated with **Kali** (Shiva's consort Durga in her terrifying aspect). Each year at *makar sankranti*, after the harvest, pilgrims flock to the tiny island from all over Orissa and West Bengal to leave votive offerings in the sacred cave where the deity was enshrined.

Practicalities

SATAPADA, on the coastal side, 45km from Puri and linked by several daily buses, is the best place to stay on the lake; the surrounding waters offer the best chance of seeing dolphins, and it's also home of an informative **visitor centre** (daily 10am–5pm; Rs10). The OTDC-run *Yatrinivas* (Ⓣ06752/262077, Ⓦwww.visitorissa.org; ❷–❺) houses the **tourist office** (daily except Sun & 2nd Sat of month 10am–5pm) and provides the best **accommodation** in Satapada; some rooms have private balconies overlooking the well-tended gardens that run down to the lake, and the **restaurant** serves delicious thalis and fresh seafood. Rooms can be booked from Puri's tourist office.

"Tribal" tourism

Most of Orissa's **adivasi** groups live in the remote southwest of the state, and once over the pass above the hot springs of Taptapani (see p.902), the appearance of pots attached to sago palms and windowless mud huts with low thatched roofs indicates that you've arrived in the traditional land of the **Saoras**. Further west around the Koraput and Jeypore area live the **Dongria Kondh**, the **Koya** and the **Bondas**.

Officially, you're not allowed into the district without first obtaining a permit from the local police superintendent: concern about **Naxalites** hiding out in the forests along the Andhra Pradesh border, coupled with a marked reluctance to allow foreigners into tribal zones, make these notoriously difficult to obtain. This, alongside the minimal infrastructure, rudimentary accommodation and unreliable public transport around the region, means that if you're really keen to visit *adivasi* villages, the best way is to arrange a **tour** (from around Rs1000/person/day) through a specialist travel agent in Bhubaneswar or Puri, who will take care of all the arrangements. Grass Routes (Ⓣ09437/029698, Ⓦwww.grassroutesjourneys.com) in Puri is considered by some NGOs to be one of the more culturally aware operators. Discover Tours (Ⓣ0674/243 0477, Ⓦwww.orissadiscover.com) in Bhubaneswar has guides with many years' experience and similarly makes every effort not to intrude where outsiders are not welcome.

That said, *adivasi* villages see little or no share of the spoils of such tours, a situation they feel justifiably angry about, and you may receive a very frosty reception. Whichever way you look at it, turning up in an isolated and **culturally sensitive** place with a camera has got to be a pretty unsound way of "meeting" the locals, and a glance from a car is hardly likely to enlighten you on traditions that have existed for centuries.

The scenery surrounding **BARKUL** is less impressive than at Satapada, and you're further from most of the islands, but it does have the best **accommodation** around the lake; the OTDC-run *Panthanivas* (Ⓣ06756/222 0488, Ⓦwww.visitorissa.org; ❸–❺) offers spacious rooms in chalets, and a fine restaurant; especially recommended is the *chinguri charchari* (shrimp with fried vegetables). To get here, take a bus from Puri or Bhubaneswar towards Brahmapur and get off at Balugaon, where you can get an auto-rickshaw for the remaining 7km to Barkul. If you plan to visit between September and March, it's best to book ahead at the Bhubaneswar OTDC tourist office.

There's a cheap and accessible OTDC-run *Panthanivas* (Ⓣ06810/278346, Ⓦwww.visitorissa.org; ❸–❺, dorm Rs150) near the railway station at **RAMBHA**, 135km from Bhubaneswar; it's somewhat lacklustre, but well placed for walks around the more scenic southern corner of the lake and for boat rides to Parikud.

Tourists can take **trips** on OTDC motor launches (Rs100) or cheaper rowing boats from Barkul and Satapada; it costs around Rs450 an hour to hire a seven-seater motor launch. The manager at the Barkul *Panthanivas* can help with arrangements. Rowing boats also depart from Rambha. Alternatively, Gandhara Travel (see p.895) in Puri runs **day-trips** to Chilika.

Gopalpur-on-Sea

More than two thousand years ago, when the Kalingas were accruing wealth from the pearl and silk trade with Southeast Asia, **GOPALPUR-ON-SEA**, formerly the ancient port of Paloura, must have been a swinging place. Today, the only time you're likely to encounter much action is during festivals and holidays, when the village is temporarily inundated with Bengali holiday-makers. For the rest of the year, its desultory collection of seafront hotels stands idle, left to the odd backpacker and armies of industrious fishermen (*katias*) hauling in hand nets on Gopalpur's endless empty shoreline. Paradise it certainly isn't, but if you're looking for a spot along the coast to unwind and enjoy the warm sea breezes, this is as appealing a place as any. **Sunbathing** on the beach will quickly make you the centre of attention, but its uncrowded sands, punctuated by coconut groves, sleepy lagoons and tiny creeks, make a good setting for a rejuvenating walk.

Arrival and information

Getting here is easiest via the town of Brahmapur (Berhampur), which is served by regular Bhubaneswar-bound **trains** (2hr 30min–3hr 30min) and **buses** (6–8 daily; 4–5hr); there are also a few trains to Puri (4–5hr). Frequent minibuses and jeeps depart from the central bus stand for the 16km trip. You'll be dumped at the top of Gopalpur's main street, ten minutes' walk from the seafront and most of the hotels. Alternatively an auto-rickshaw straight to your hotel costs Rs150. **Tourist information** can be had from the OTDC-run *Panthanivas* (see p.902). There's an **ATM** close to *Rosalin* on the seafront.

Accommodation and eating

Standards are generally fairly low at Gopalpur's hotels, which, conversely, are also comparatively expensive: it's worth haggling – only during holiday and festival times are they likely to be full. As for **eating**, there's a surprising dearth of seafood, though some restaurateurs can be cajoled into cooking the odd pomfret or prawn curry, given sufficient warning. The modest *Naaz*, diagonally opposite *Rosalin*, serves up inexpensive meals.

Mermaid On the north side of the beach ⓣ0680/224 2050. Friendly place, popular with holidaying Calcuttans, with plain rooms and private sea-facing balconies. With advance notice, non-residents can enjoy delicious Bengali thalis. ❸–❹

Panthanivas By the temple ⓣ0680/224 3931, ⓦwww.visitorissa.org. This OTDC-run hotel has cottages suitable for families or small groups, simple attached rooms – none sea-facing – and a six-bed dorm (Rs150). There's an excellent chef, and rates include breakfast, but checkout is a miserly 8am. ❷–❺

Rosalin On the seafront ⓣ0680/224 2071. Chaotic family-run establishment with small decidedly no-frills rooms set around a garden, and a restaurant. Cheap and (fairly) cheerful. ❶–❷

Sea Side Breeze On the beach ⓣ0680/224 2075. The only hotel actually on the beach, *Sea Side Breeze* has large, clean rooms, many with sea views, a good-value restaurant serving tasty seafood if you order in advance, and welcoming staff. The manager can arrange trips on a fisherman's boat in the backwaters of nearby "Blue Bay". ❷–❸

Swosti Palm Resort Near the Lighthouse ⓣ0680/224 2453, ⓦwww.swosti.com. Gopalpur's most upmarket hotel has spacious though seriously overpriced a/c attached rooms (without sea views) and pleasant gardens. The restaurant is strong on Indian seafood, such as *chengudi malai* (prawns in coconut cream) and *macha tarkari* (fish curry). ❼

Taptapani

One possible foray from the coast, if you're tempted by the lure of the nearby hills, is the trip to the spa village of **TAPTAPANI**, nestled in the *ghats* 51km west of Brahmapur; hourly buses (1hr 15min–2hr) run between the two. Little more than a line of dingy snack stalls and mildewed bungalows deep in the forest, it's the kind of place to which government servants pray not to be posted. Pilgrims, however, come here in large numbers for the legendary **hot springs**, which are believed to cure infertility. The boiling sulphurous water bubbles out of a cleft in the mountainside and is piped into a small pool, where little rocks smeared with vermilion and hibiscus petals mark the presence of the living deities believed to reside in the water (it is prohibited to dip any part of the body in the pool).

You can enjoy the water in the privacy of your own **hotel**; it's pumped into capacious sunken bathtubs in some of the more expensive rooms at the atmospheric OTDC-run *Panthanivas* (ⓣ06816/255031, ⓦwww.visitorissa.org; ❹–❻), a short way down the hill from the springs. Despite the fine views, the wooden cottages, cabins and cute tree-house room are rarely full, which is just as well, as there's nowhere else to stay for miles around (book in advance just to be on the safe side). There's also a decent restaurant.

18

Andhra Pradesh

* **Hyderabad** A predominately Islamic city with a compelling combination of monuments, museums and bazaars. See p.905

* **Golconda Fort** Set in a lush landscape just west of Hyderabad, the Qutb Shahi dynasty's capital boasts a dramatic fort. See p.911

* **Warangal** Features two important Hindu monuments: a medieval fort and a thousand-pillared Shiva temple. See p.914

* **Amaravati** At this village on the banks of the Krishna river, fine carvings surround the remains of a great Buddhist stupa. See p.917

* **Tirumala Hill** The world's most visited pilgrimage centre, crowned by the Venkateshwara Vishnu temple. See p.919

* **Puttaparthy** Sai Baba's main ashram, at the heart of a thriving community, attracts pilgrims from all over the globe. See p.920

▲ Charminar, Hyderabad

Although **ANDHRA PRADESH** occupies a great swathe of eastern India, stretching more than 1200km along the coast from Orissa to Tamil Nadu and reaching far inland from the fertile deltas of the Godavari and Krishna rivers to the semi-arid Deccan Plateau, most foreign travellers simply pass through en route to its more attractive neighbours. This is understandable as places of interest are few and far between, but the sights Andhra Pradesh does have are absorbing enough to warrant at least a brief stop-off.

Now a major hi-tech hub, the capital, **Hyderabad**, is an atmospheric city with lively bazaars, the eclectic Salar Jung Museum and the mighty **Golconda Fort**. **Warangal**, 150km northeast, has Muslim and Hindu remains from the twelfth and thirteenth centuries, while the region's Buddhist legacy is preserved in museums at sites such as **Nagarjunakonda** and **Amaravati**. In the east, the city of **Vijayawada** has little to recommend it, though it is a convenient access-point for Amaravati. Similarly, in the northeast, the fast-growing city of **Visakhapatnam** is little more than a handy place to break up a long trip. By contrast, the temple town of **Tirupati** in the far southeast is a fascinating, impossibly crowded pilgrimage site. In the southwest, **Puttaparthy** attracts a more international pilgrim crowd, drawn here by the prospect of *darshan* from spiritual leader Sai Baba.

Although modern industries have grown up around the capital, and shipbuilding, iron and steel are important on the coast, most people in Andhra Pradesh remain poor. Away from the Godavari and Krishna deltas, where the soil is rich enough to grow rice and sugar cane, the land is in places impossible to cultivate, which has contributed to the desperate plight of many farmers (see opposite).

Some history

The earliest accounts of the region, from the third century BC, refer to a people known as the Andhras. The **Satavahana dynasty** (second century BC to second century AD), also known as the Andhras, came to control much of central and southern India from their second capital at Amaravati on the Krishna. They enjoyed extensive international trade and were great patrons of Buddhism. Subsequently, the Pallavas, the Chalukyas and the Cholas all held sway. By the thirteenth century, the Kakatiyas of Warangal were under constant threat from Muslim incursions, while later on, after the fall of their city at Hampi, the Hindu Vijayanagars transferred operations to Chandragiri near Tirupati.

The next significant development was in the mid-sixteenth century, with the rise of the Muslim **Qutb Shahi dynasty**. In 1687, the son of the Mughal emperor Aurangzeb seized Golconda. Five years after Aurangzeb died in 1707, Hyderabad's viceroy declared independence and established the Asaf Jahi dynasty of **nizams**. In return for allying with the British against Tipu Sultan of Mysore, the nizam dynasty was allowed to retain a certain degree of autonomy even after the British had come to dominate India.

During the Independence struggle, harmony between Hindus and Muslims in Andhra Pradesh disintegrated. **Partition** brought matters to a climax, as the nizam wanted to join other Muslims in the soon-to-be-created state of **Pakistan**. In 1949 the capital erupted in riots, the army was brought in and Hyderabad state was admitted to the Indian Union. Andhra Pradesh state was created in 1956 from Telugu-speaking regions (although Urdu is widely spoken in Hyderabad) that had previously formed part of the Madras Presidency on the east coast and the princely state of Hyderabad to the west. Today almost ninety percent of the population is Hindu, with Muslims largely concentrated in the capital.

In 1999, the pro-business Telugu Desam Party eventually wrestled the power long held by Congress, and over the following five years there was huge development around Hyderabad, most famously, **HITEC City**. However, rural

areas – where drought and economic crisis led to thousands of farmer suicides – were neglected. In 2004 Congress regained control of the state government, although they were also criticized for not doing enough to help farmers, and suicides have continued with alarming frequency (there were 23,279 between 1997 and 2008).

In December 2009, following a high-profile hunger strike, the Indian government surprisingly bowed to pressure from the Telangana Rashtra Samithi (TRS) party and announced plans to carve a new state, **Telangana**, out of northwestern Andhra Pradesh. Although welcomed by TRS supporters who claimed their region had long been neglected, the decision sparked widespread protests, strikes and political resignations. The Indian government subsequently set up a commission to examine the practicalities of the issue, and at the time of writing it was unclear when the controversial division would actually go ahead.

Hyderabad/Secunderabad

A melting pot of Muslim and Hindu cultures, the capital of Andhra Pradesh comprises the twin cities of **HYDERABAD** and **SECUNDERABAD**, with a combined population of around seven million. Secunderabad, of little interest, is the modern administrative city founded by the British, whereas Hyderabad, the old city, has teeming **bazaars**, **Muslim monuments** and the absorbing **Salar Jung**

Museum. Hyderabad declined after Independence, with tensions often close to the surface due to lack of funding. Nowadays, although the overcrowded old city still suffers from substandard amenities, the conurbation as a whole is booming. In recent years Hyderabad has overtaken Bengaluru to become India's foremost computer and **IT centre**.

Hyderabad was founded in 1591 by **Mohammed Quli Shah** (1562–1612), beside the River Musi, 8km east of Golconda, the fortress capital of the Golconda empire. Unusually, the new city was laid out on a grid system, with huge arches and stone buildings that included Hyderabad's most famous monument, the **Charminar**. At first it was a city without walls; these were only added in 1740 as defence against the Marathas. Legend has it that a secret tunnel linked the city with the spectacular **Golconda Fort,** 11km away.

For the three hundred years of Muslim reign, there was harmony between the predominantly Hindu population and the minority Muslims. Hyderabad was the most important focus of Muslim power in south India at this time; the princes' fabulous wealth derived primarily from the fine gems, particularly diamonds, mined in the Kistna Valley at Golconda. The famous **Koh-i-Noor** diamond was found here – the only time it was ever captured was by Mughal emperor Aurangzeb, when his son seized the Golconda Fort in 1687. It ended up, cut, in the British royal crown.

In late 2009, Hyderabad's status was thrown into question by the **Telangana** decision (see p.905): at the time of research it was unclear whether the city would be part of the new state, remain part of Andhra Pradesh or serve as a joint capital for both states.

Arrival and information

Hyderabad's old city straddles the River Musi; most places of interest lie south of the river, while the majority of the hotels are on the north side. Further north, separated from Hyderabad by the Hussain Sagar lake, is **Secunderabad**, where some long-distance trains terminate. If you do have to get off at Secunderabad, your ticket is valid for any connecting train to **Hyderabad (Nampally) railway station**. The two stations are also linked to each other – and other points in the city, such as Banjar Hills and HITEC City – by the overground **Hyderabad Metro** (or MMTS; tickets Rs3–10). The **long-distance bus stand** occupies an island in the River Musi, 3km southeast of Nampally railway station.

The modern and efficient Rajiv Gandhi International **Airport** is around 20km south of central Hyderabad. There are plans to connect the MMTS to the airport, but funding rows have stymied progress so far; at present, the airport is linked to the city by taxis (about Rs650) and AeroExpress shuttle buses every 30min (Rs150); heading to the airport, you can catch the latter from a booth beside the **AP Tourism office** (daily except Sun 10am–5pm; ⓣ040/2345 3110, ⓦwww.aptourism.in) on Secretariat Road, near the huge flyover. The **APTDC office** next door (daily 7am–8pm; ⓣ040/2345 3036, ⓦwww.tourisminap.com) and the other APTDC office, on Sardar Patel Road, Secunderabad (ⓣ040/2789 3100), exist principally to book their tours. The **India Tourism office** is on Liberty Road, Himayatnagar (Mon–Fri 9am–5pm; ⓣ040/2326 1360). A good source of local information is the monthly **magazine**, *Channel 6* (Rs20; ⓦwww.channel6magazine.com), available from most bookstalls.

Accommodation

The area in front of **Hyderabad (Nampally) railway station** has the cheapest accommodation, but you're unlikely to find anything acceptable for less than

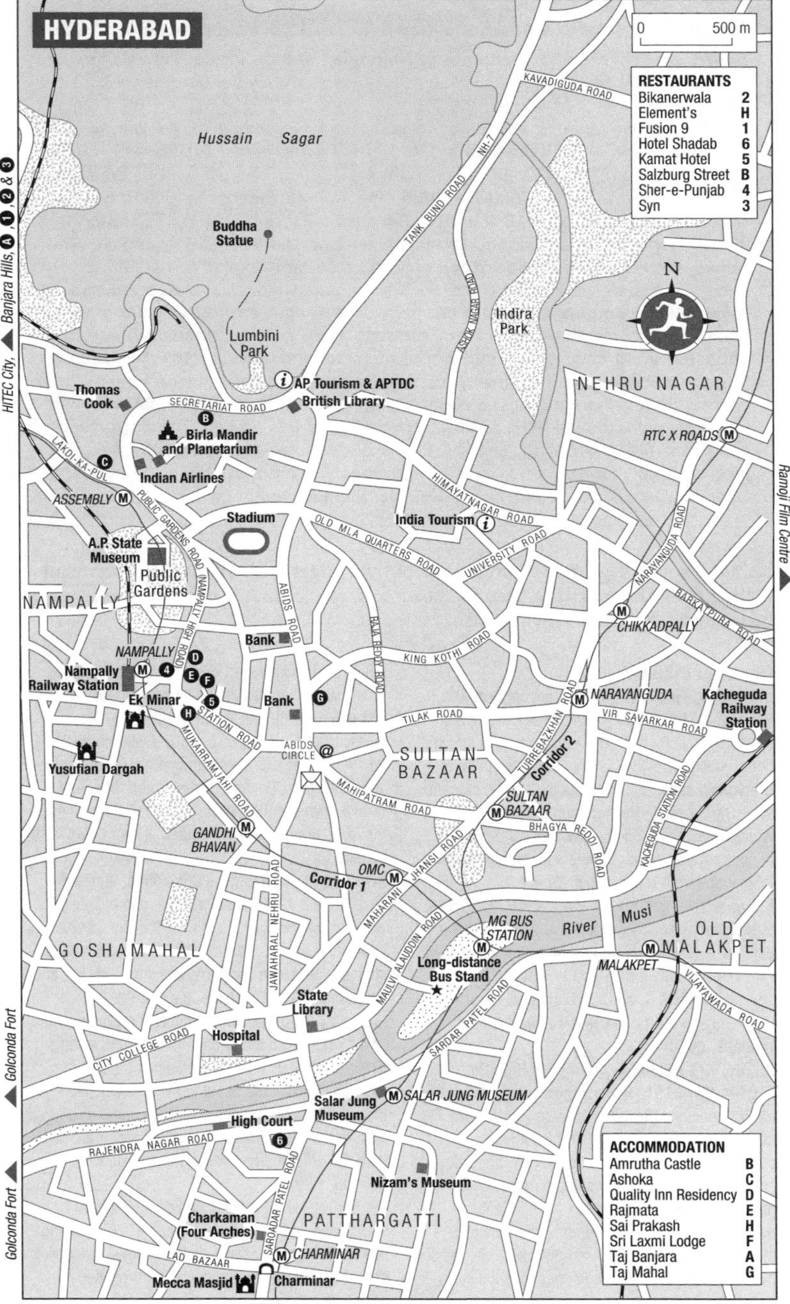
HYDERABAD
Secunderabad
0 500 m
RESTAURANTS
Bikanerwala 2
Element's H
Fusion 9 1
Hotel Shadab 6
Kamat Hotel 5
Salzburg Street B
Sher-e-Punjab 4
Syn 3
ACCOMMODATION
Amrutha Castle B
Ashoka C
Quality Inn Residency D
Rajmata E
Sai Prakash H
Sri Laxmi Lodge F
Taj Banjara A
Taj Mahal G
HITEC City, Banjara Hills, A, 1, 2 & 3
Ramoji Film Centre
Golconda Fort
Golconda Fort
Airport & Chowmahalla Palace
Hussain Sagar
Kavadiguda Road
NH-7
Tank Bund Road
Ashok Nagar Road
Indira Park
Buddha Statue
Lumbini Park
AP Tourism & APTDC
British Library
Secretariat Road
Thomas Cook
Birla Mandir and Planetarium
Indian Airlines
Lakdi-ka-pul
Assembly
Public Gardens Road
Stadium
A.P. State Museum
Public Gardens
Nampally
Nampally High Road
Nehru Nagar
RTC X Roads
Himayatnagar Road
India Tourism
Old MLA Quarters Road
University Road
Narayanguda Road
Barkatpura Road
Chikkadpally
Abids Road
Raja Reddy Road
King Kothi Road
Bank
Bank
Nampally Railway Station
Ek Minar
Station Road
Mukarramjahi Road
Yusufian Dargah
Abids Circle
Tilak Road
Sultan Bazaar
Narayanguda
Turrebazkhan Road
Vir Savarkar Road
Kacheguda Railway Station
Corridor 2
Mahipatram Road
Sultan Bazaar
Bhagya Reddi Road
Kacheguda Station Road
Gandhi Bhavan
Jawaharal Nehru Road
OMC
Corridor 1
Maharani Jhansi Road
Maulvi Alauddin Road
MG Bus Station
River Musi
Old Malakpet
Malakpet
Vijayawada Road
Goshamahal
Long-distance Bus Stand
State Library
Hospital
City College Road
Sardar Patel Road
Salar Jung Museum
Salar Jung Museum
High Court
Rajendra Nagar Road
Saroadar Patel Road
Nizam's Museum
Charkaman (Four Arches)
Patthargatti
Lad Bazaar
Charminar
Mecca Masjid
Charminar

Moving on from Hyderabad

Daily **train** services from **Hyderabad (Nampally) station** include: the *Charminar Express* #2760 to Chennai (6.30pm; 13hr 45min); the *Sabari Express* #7230 to Ernakulam (noon; 25hr 40min); the *Mumbai Express* #7032 (8.40pm; 16hr 25min); the *East Coast Express* #8646 to Kolkata (10am; 29hr 55min) via Vijayawada, Visakhapatnam and Bhubaneswar; and the *Rayasaleema Express* #7429 to Tirupati (5.25pm; 15hr 20min). Most northeast-bound services call at Warangal and Vijayawada. **From Secunderabad**, the *Konark Express* #1020 travels to Mumbai (11.45am; 16hr 10min). The Bangalore Express #2785 (7.05pm; 11hr 20min) departs from **Kacheguda** station, around 3km east of Nampally. The **railways reservations office** at Hyderabad (daily 8am–8pm) is to the left as you enter the station: counter #211 is for tourist reservations. The **Secunderabad reservation complex** is more than 400m to the right as you exit the station: counter 34 is for foreigners. From the long-distance bus stand, **regular bus services** run to destinations throughout the state and beyond, including Tirupati (8 daily; 12hr), Vijayawada (every 15min; 6hr) and Warangal (every 15min; 3hr). Various **"deluxe" private buses** depart for Bengaluru, Chennai, Mumbai and other major cities from outside Hyderabad (Nampally) railway station. The **airport** (see p.906) is fast becoming one of the busiest hubs in India, with frequent **international flights,** and excellent **domestic connections** to Bengaluru, Chennai, Delhi, Goa, Jaipur, Kochi, Kolkata, Mumbai and many other cities.

Rs300: avoid the grim little collection of five lodges with "Royal" in their name. A little over 1km north of Secunderabad railway station, several decent places can be found on **Sarojini Devi Road**.

Hyderabad

Amrutha Castle 5-9-16 Saifabad, opposite the Secretariat ⓣ040/6663 3888, ⓦwww.bestwesternamruthacastle.com. This extraordinarily kitsch hotel, which looks like a fairy castle, won't be to everyone's taste, but is undoubtedly a fun place to stay. The turreted attached rooms have faux wooden beams, fortified doors and paintings of famous royals. Although there's no moat, you can take a dip in the rooftop pool. ❼–❽

Ashoka 6-1-70 Lakdi-ka-Pul ⓣ040/2323 0105, ⓔhotelashoka222@yahoo.com. The monolithic exterior – grey concrete and blue tinted windows – doesn't exactly entice you in, but the clean and spacious attached rooms are good value; it's worth paying a bit extra to get one of the a/c versions. ❹

Quality Inn Residency Nampally High Rd ⓣ040/3061 6161, ⓦwww.theresidency-hyd.com. A business traveller-oriented hotel with comfy attached rooms set around a looming atrium. While the standard rooms are fine, the "classic" ones are pretty slick, particularly their plate glass desks. ❼–❽

Rajmata Nampally High Rd, opposite railway station ⓣ040/6666 5555, ⓕ6666 5876. Set back from the road, the popular *Rajmata* has a slightly overpriced collection of clean attached rooms: all have TVs and some also boast a/c. ❹–❺

Sai Prakash Station Rd ⓣ040/2461 1726, ⓦwww.hotelsaiprakash.com. The vast marble lobby gives way to keenly-priced attached rooms with flatscreen TVs and contemporary blue and brown flower motifs on the walls: the bathrooms, however, are decidedly cramped. It also offers wi-fi access. ❺

Sri Laxmi Lodge Gadwal Compound, Station Rd ⓣ040/5563 4200. Down a small lane opposite the *Sai Prakash*, *Sri Laxmi* is one of the city's better shoestring options. The rooms – if not always the sheets – are clean and have attached showers and squat toilets. A TV costs Rs50 extra. ❷

Taj Banjara Main Road No. 1, Banjara Hills, 4km from the centre ⓣ040/6666 9999, ⓦwww.tajhotels.com. In a pleasant lakeside location, with all the usual top-notch facilities including a pool, three classy restaurants and a 24hr coffee shop. Internet specials are often lower than the official rates, which hover around Rs8500. ❾

Taj Mahal 4-1-999 Abids Rd ⓣ040/6651 1122. This peeling white-and-pale-green 1920s building has a patio garden, spiral staircase and plenty of character. The rooms themselves are plainer, but

Guided tours

APTDC operates a number of good-value **guided tours**. The times quoted below are when tours set off from the Secunderabad office; the pick-up time in Hyderabad is 15–20 minutes later. There's a **city tour** (daily 7.45am–6.30pm; Rs270); a **Golconda Fort sound-and-light show tour** (daily 2–9pm; Rs200 including entry); and a **Ramoji Film City** (see p.912) tour (daily 7am–6pm; Rs500 including entry). For the latter, tours run by private agents in Nampally may be more convenient. The **Nagarjuna Sagar** tour (Sat & Sun 7am–9.30pm; Rs450, excluding entry) is a rushed but convenient way to reach this fascinating area (see p.915). The **Tirupati tours** are not worth considering as Tirupati is better reached from Chennai or elsewhere in south India. A **heritage walking tour** of Hyderabad (Sun & 2nd Sat of the month 7.30am–9am; Rs50; no advanced booking necessary) departs from Charminar (see below).

feature high ceilings, a/c, flatscreen TVs and fridges; those on the upper floor are better, though more expensive. ❺

Secunderabad

Baseraa Sarojini Devi Rd ⓣ040/2770 3200, ⓦwww.baseraa.com. The smartest hotel within walking distance (around 15min) of the station, *Baseraa* boasts modern attached rooms with a/c, TV, minibar and wi-fi access. ❻–❼

Ramakrishna St John's Rd ⓣ040/2783 4567, ⓕ2782 0933. With some a/c rooms, this comfy mid-range option, in a large concrete block opposite the railway reservation complex, is the best option in the immediate station area. ❹

The City

Hyderabad has three distinct sectors: **Hyderabad**, divided between the old city and newer areas towards HITEC City; **Secunderabad**, the modern city; and **Golconda**, the old fort. The two cities are basically one big sprawl, separated by a lake, **Hussain Sagar**. The most interesting area, south of the River Musi, holds the **bazaars**, the **Charminar** and the **Salar Jung Museum**. North of the river, the main shopping malls are found around **Abids Circle** and **Sultan Bazaar**, ten minutes' walk east of Nampally. Abids Circle is connected to MG Road, which runs north to join Tank Bund Road at Hussain Sagar and runs on to Secunderabad, while to the south it metamorphoses into Nehru Road. Four kilometres west of Hyderabad railway station lies the posh **Banjara Hills** district. Beyond here is the exclusive residential area of **Jubilee Hills**, while a further 6km brings you to **HITEC City**.

Salar Jung Museum

The unmissable **Salar Jung Museum** (daily except Fri 10am–5pm; Rs150 [Rs10]; no photography), on the south bank of the River Musi, houses part of the huge collection of Salar Jung, one of the nizam's prime ministers, and his ancestors. A well-travelled man of wealth, he bought whatever took his fancy from both East and West, from the sublime to, in some cases, the ridiculous. His extraordinary hoard includes Indian jade, miniatures, furniture, lacquer-work, Mughal opaque glassware, fabrics, bronzes, Buddhist and Hindu sculpture, manuscripts and weapons. The museum gets very crowded on weekends.

Charminar, Lad Bazaar, Mecca Masjid and Chowmahalla Palace

A maze of bazaars teeming with people, the old city has at its heart the **Charminar** (daily 9am–5.30pm; Rs100 [Rs5]), or Four Towers, a triumphal arch built at the centre of Mohammed Quli Shah's city in 1591 to commemorate an epidemic of the plague. It features four graceful 56m-high minarets, housing spiral staircases to the upper storeys. The (now defunct) mosque on the roof is the oldest in Hyderabad. The yellowish colour of the building is due to a special stucco made of marble powder, gram and egg yolk.

The Charminar marks the beginning of the fascinating **Lad Bazaar**, which leads to Mahboob Chowk, a market square featuring a mosque and Victorian clock tower. Lad Bazaar specializes in everything you could possibly need for a Hyderabadi marriage, including bangles, rosewater, herbs, spices and material. You'll also find silver filigree jewellery, antiques, *bidri*-ware, hookah paraphernalia and, in the markets near the Charminar, **pearls** – so beloved of the nizams that they ground them into powder to eat. Hyderabad is still the centre of India's pearl trade. The **Charkaman**, or Four Arches, north of the Charminar, were built in 1594; the western arch, **Daulat-Khan-e-Ali**, was at one time adorned with rich gold tapestries.

Southwest, behind the Charminar, the **Mecca Masjid** (daily 8am–noon & 3–8pm) was constructed in 1598 and can hold three thousand devotees, with room for up to ten thousand more in the courtyard. On the left of the courtyard are the tombs of the nizams. In May 2007, the mosque was rocked by a powerful bomb; the incident killed fourteen people. The perpetrators were never caught and since this and subsequent bombings, security has been very tight throughout the city.

The 150-year-old **Chowmahalla Palace** (daily except Fri 10am–5pm; Rs150 [Rs25]; camera Rs50), southwest of the Mecca Masjid, was used by the nizams to entertain royal visitors and official guests. Inspired by the Shah's palace in Tehran, it is actually a (partially-restored) complex of four palaces, a grand Durbar Hall, elegant courtyards and fountain-filled gardens.

North of the river

Just south of the railway station, the **Yusufian Dargah**, with its striking bulbous yellow dome, is the shrine of a seventeenth-century Sufi saint of the venerable Chishti order. About a kilometre north of the station, set in tranquil public gardens, the **State Museum** (daily except Fri and 2nd Sat of each month 10.30am–5pm; Rs10) displays a modest collection of bronzes, prehistoric tools, copper inscription plates and weapons.

The **Birla Venkateshwara Mandir** (daily 7am–noon & 2–8pm; no photography) on Kalapahad ("black mountain") Hill, north of the public gardens, is open to all. Constructed in 1976, the temple itself is not of great interest, but affords fine views. Nearby are two mildly diverting attractions: a **planetarium** (English: daily 11.30am, 4pm & 6pm, closed last Thurs of the month; Rs25) and a **science centre** (Sat–Thurs 10.30am–8pm, Fri till 3pm, closed last Tues of the month; Rs20), which has a lot of satellite hardware and photos, sensory perception machines and a small dinosaur display.

Hussain Sagar

Hussain Sagar, the large expanse of water separating Hyderabad from Secunderabad, lends a welcome air of tranquillity to the busy conurbation and the area is a popular place for a stroll, especially at sunset. In its centre stands a large stone statue of the **Buddha Purnima** ("Full Moon Buddha"), erected in 1992. Regular **boats** (Rs45 return) chug out to the statue from Lumbini Park, just off Secretariat Road. Two deluxe boats operated by APTDC offer hour-long **cruises** of the lake (11am–3pm & 6–8pm; Rs60–90). The park was the site of one of two bombs that exploded in August 2007, claiming 44 lives.

Golconda Fort and the tombs of the Qutb Shahi kings

Golconda, 122m above the plain and 11km west of old Hyderabad, was the capital of the seven Qutb Shahi kings from 1518 until the end of the sixteenth century, when the court moved to Hyderabad. Well preserved and set in thick green scrubland, it is one of India's most impressive forts, boasting 87 semicircular bastions and eight mighty gates, complete with gruesome elephant-proof spikes.

To get **to the fort**, bus #119 runs from Nampally, and #66G from Charminar. **For the tombs**, take #123 or #142S from Charminar. From Secunderabad the #5, #5S and #5C all go to Mehdipattanam, where you should hop onto #123. Or take an auto-rickshaw; agree a waiting fee in advance. Set aside a day to explore the fort, which covers an area of around four square kilometres.

Entering the **fort** (daily 9am–5pm; Rs100 [Rs5]) by the Balahisar Gate, you come into the Grand Portico, where guards clap their hands to show off the fort's acoustics. To the right is the **mortuary bath**, where the bodies of deceased nobles were ritually bathed prior to burial. If you follow the arrowed anticlockwise route, you pass the two-storey residence of ministers Akkana and Madanna before starting the stairway ascent to the Durbar Hall. Halfway along the steps, you arrive at a small, dark cell named after the court cashier **Ramdas**, who while incarcerated here produced the clumsy carvings and paintings that litter the gloomy room.

Nearing the top, you come across the small, pretty mosque of Ibrahim Qutb Shah; beyond here is an even tinier temple to Durga. The steps are crowned by the three-storey **Durbar Hall** of the Qutb Shahis, on platforms outside which the monarchs would sit and survey their domains.

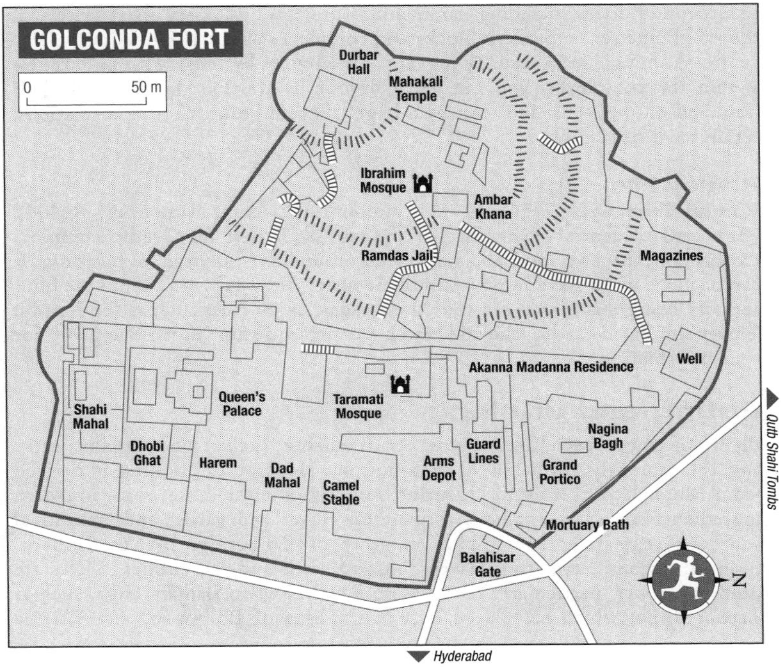

The ruins of the **queen's palace**, once elaborately decorated with multiple domes, stand in a courtyard centred on an original copper fountain that used to be filled with rosewater. You can still see traces of a "necklace" design on one of the arches, at the top of which a lotus bud sits below an opening flower with a cavity at its centre that once contained a diamond. At the entrance to the **palace** itself, four chambers provided protection from intruders. Passing through two rooms, the second of which is overgrown, you come to the **Shahi Mahal**, the royal bedroom. Originally it had a domed roof and niches on the walls that once sheltered candles or oil lamps. Golconda has a nightly **sound-and-light** show (English: March–Oct 7pm, Nov–Feb 6.30pm; 1hr; Rs50).

There are 82 **tombs** (daily except Fri 9.30am–4.30pm; Rs20) about 1km north of the fort's outer wall. Set in peaceful gardens, they commemorate commanders, relatives of the kings, dancers, singers and royal doctors, as well as all but two of the Qutb Shahi kings. Faded today, they were once brightly coloured in turquoise and green; each has an onion dome on a block, with a decorative arcade.

The western suburbs

Most of Hyderabad's new-found wealth is concentrated in the city's western suburbs. The nearest of these is **Banjara Hills**, around 4km from Nampally, which comprises spacious residences in quiet streets surrounding Main Road No. 1, a glitzy strip of trendy shops, restaurants and bars. The western appearance and dress, particularly of the young women here, is a sharp contrast to the niqabs and saris ubiquitous in the old city. Several kilometres further west you enter the even leafier and more upmarket district of **Jubilee Hills** which is largely residential.

The upturn in Hyderabad's fortunes was driven by its becoming a hi-tech hub in the late 1990s, earning it the nickname "Cyberabad", although it is also home to other industries including car manufacture. **HITEC City** itself is several square kilometres of modern blocks and complexes about 10km from the city centre. Although strict security prevents casual visits by those with no business within the complexes, you can get a flavour by touring the area, which is bordered on the south and west by a large lake and beautiful rock formations, reminiscent of Hampi.

Ramoji Film City

Ramoji Film City (RFC; Ⓦwww.ramojifilmcity.com; 9am–6pm; Rs400), 25km east of central Hyderabad, is the world's largest film studio complex. Covering nearly two thousand acres, with around five hundred set locations, it can produce up to sixty movies simultaneously. Although you cannot see films actually being made, you can tour the facades, enjoy rides such as the Ramoji Tower simulated earthquake and watch a dance and stunt show. See p.909 for tour information.

Eating and drinking

Plenty of places specialize in **Hyderabadi cuisine**, such as authentic biriyanis, and the famously chilli-hot Andhra cuisine. Hyderabadi cooking is derived from Mughal court cuisine, featuring sumptuous meat dishes with northern ingredients such as cinnamon, cardamom, cloves and garlic, and traditional southern vegetarian dishes with an array of flavourings like cassia buds, peanuts, coconut, tamarind leaves, mustard seeds and red chillies. There are numerous **bars**, particularly along Main Road No.1 in Banjara Hills, such as *Liquids Again*, which has played host to the likes of Bollywood star Katrina

Kaif. *Touch*, a futuristic club above a mall on Main Road No. 2, is another trendy hang-out. *Underdeck* at the *Taj Banjara* hotel (see p.908) has live music and dancing bartenders. For a decent **coffee**, try one of the many *Café Coffee Day* and *Barista* branches, such as those on Main Road No.1.

Hyderabad

Bikanerwala Main Rd No.1, Banjara Hills. At this bustling fast-food joint the focus is firmly on north Indian cuisine, with authentic *bhel puri*, *channa bhatura* and *aloo tikki* (Rs20–80) all on offer.
Element's *Hotel Sai Prakash*. The pricier of the hotel's two restaurants, with comfy armchairs and an accomplished Indian and Chinese menu featuring interesting dishes like shredded lamb with garlic sauce. The kebabs are good too, and there's chocolate soufflé for dessert. Mains Rs125–200. *Sukha Sagara* downstairs serves good veg meals.
Fusion 9 Main Rd No.1, Banjara Hills. Expensive (mains Rs350–475) but quality cuisine from regions as diverse as Mexico, Europe, the Middle East and Southeast Asia, served in a smart modern lounge. The same owners run the similarly good *F9 Diner* in Priyanka Plaza, Kondapur, near HITEC City.
Hotel Shadab Saroadar Patel Rd, Patthargatti. While there are some fine meat and fish tandoori items on the menu, the main reason to visit *Hotel Shadab* is its excellent mutton and chicken biriyanis (Rs125–180), some of the best in the city. You may have to queue for a table, but it's worth the wait.
Kamat Hotel Station Rd, opposite *Sai Prakash* hotel. At this conveniently located branch of the hygienic veggie chain, waiters in white shirts with red lapels serve up inexpensive veg dosas, *iddlis*, *vadas*, thalis and mains (Rs38–95).
Salzburg Street *Amrutha Castle* hotel. At the back of the lobby, overlooking a water feature, this restaurant has unusual, but well-executed, options like prawns cooked in a "Northwest Frontier" style and the Korean-Indian fusion *kimchi paneer*, as well as some more traditional Indian and Chinese dishes. Mains Rs120–200.
Sher-e-Punjab Corner of Nampally High Rd and station entrance. In a convenient, if not particularly appealing location, this popular basement restaurant offers tasty north Indian veg and non-veg food at low prices (Rs40–100).
Syn *Taj Deccan* hotel, Main Road No.1, Banjara Hills. This hip restaurant is the place to come for authentic Thai, Vietnamese and Japanese cuisine (mains from Rs200). It features a teppanyaki counter, and a slick bar that, alongside the usual range of alcoholic drinks, also serves "detox cocktails", if you've overindulged.

Secunderabad

Paradise-Persis MG Rd. This very popular multi-restaurant complex bashes out fine Hyderabadi cuisine. The biriyanis are recommended, but don't miss out on the succulent mutton kebabs. Mains Rs70–200.

Listings

Airlines, domestic Go Air, Babukhan Estate, Basheerbagh ☎040/2326 0037; Indian Airlines, opposite Assembly, Hill Fort Rd, Saifabad ☎040/2343 0334; IndiGo, 2nd floor, 5-9-86/1 Chapel Rd ☎040/2323 3590; Jet Airways, Hill Fort Rd, ☎040/3989 3333; Kingfisher Airlines, toll free ☎1800 180 0101; Paramount Airways, airport ☎040/4343 4444; SpiceJet, toll free ☎1800 180 3333.
Airlines, international Air India, 5-9-193 HACA Bhavan, opposite public garden, Saifabad ☎040/2425 5161; British Airways, Nijhawan Travel Services, 5-9-88/4 Ainulaman Fateh Maidan Rd ☎040/2324 1661; Emirates, Floor F, Reliance Classic Bldg 3 & 4, Main Rd No. 1, Banjara Hills ☎040/6623 4444; Lufthansa, 3-5-823 Shop #B1–B3, Hyderaguda ☎040/4433 1000; Qatar Airways, near Care Hospital, Banjara Hills ☎040/6660 5121.
Banks and exchange State Bank of Hyderabad, MG Rd, and Federal Bank, 1st floor, Orient Estate, MG Rd exchange foreign currency; both open Mon–Fri 10.30am–2.30pm, the latter also Sat 10.30am–12.30pm. Alternatively try Thomas Cook ☎040/2329 6521 at Nasir Arcade, Secretariat Rd or LKP Forex ☎040/2321 0094 on Public Gardens Rd, 10min walk north of Nampally Station; both open Mon–Sat 9.30am–6pm. ATMs are ubiquitous.
Bookshops AA Hussian & Co, 5-8-551 Arastu Trust Building, Abids Rd, Hyderabad; Higginbothams, 1 Lal Bahadur Stadium, Hyderabad; and Walden, 6-3-871 Snehalatha Complex, Greenlands Rd, Begumpet, Hyderabad.
Car rental Air Travels in Banjara Hills (☎040/2332 8561, ©airtravels@yahoo.com) and Classic Travels in Secunderabad (☎040/2775 5645).

Hospitals The government-run Gandhi Hospital is in Secunderabad ☎040/2770 2222; the private CDR Hospital is in Himayatnagar ☎040/2322 1221; and there's a Tropical Diseases Hospital in Nallakunta ☎040/2766 7843.
Internet access Some of the quickest connections are at Reliance Web World (Rs100/4hr), which has numerous branches, including on the second floor of a shopping mall near Abids Circle.
Library You must be a member or a British citizen to use the British Library, Secretariat Rd (Tues–Sat 11am–7pm; ☎040/2323 0774).
Pharmacies Apollo Pharmacy ☎040/2243 1734 and Health Pharmacy ☎040/2331 0618 both open 24hr.
Police ☎040/2323 0191. In an emergency call ☎100.
Souvenirs Lepakshi, the AP state government emporium at Gunfoundry on MG Rd, stocks a wide range of handicrafts. Utkalika (Government of Orissa handicrafts), between the Ravindra Bharati building and *Hotel Ashoka*, has a modest selection of silver filigree jewellery, handloom cloth, *ikat* tie-dye, Jagannath papier-mâché figures and buffalo bone carvings. Cheneta Bhavan is a modern shopping complex a little south of the railway station, stuffed with handloom cloth shops. For silks and saris, try Meena Bazar and Pochampally Silks & Sarees on Tilak Rd.
Travel agents Travel Club Forex ☎040/2323 4180, Nasir Arcade, Saifabad, close to Thomas Cook; and Kamat Travels in the *Hotel Sai Prakash* complex ☎040/2461 2096.

Around Hyderabad

As you head north from Hyderabad, the landscape becomes greener and hillier, sporadically punctuated by photogenic black-granite rock formations. There is little to detain visitors here except **Warangal**, which has a medieval fort and a Shiva temple. South of the capital, swathes of flat farmland stretch into the centre of the state, where the Nagarjuna Sagar Dam has created a major lake with the important Buddhist site of **Nagarjunakonda**, now an island in its waters.

Warangal

WARANGAL – "one stone" – 150km northeast of Hyderabad, was the Hindu capital of the Kakatiyan empire in the twelfth and thirteenth centuries. Like other Deccan cities, it changed hands many times between the Hindus and the Muslims – something reflected in its architecture and the remains you see today.

Warangal's **fort** (daily 9am–5pm; Rs100 [Rs5]), 4km south of the city, is famous for its two circles of fortifications: the outer made of earth with a moat, and the inner of stone. Four roads into the centre meet at the ruined Shiva temple of **Swayambhu** (1162). At its southern gateway, another Shiva temple, from the fourteenth century, is in much better shape; inside, the remains of an enormous lingam came originally from the Swayambhu shrine. Also inside the citadel is the **Shirab Khan**, or **Audience Hall**, an early eleventh-century building very similar to Mandu's Hindola Mahal (see p.398).

Some 6km north of town, just off the main road beside the slopes of Hanamkonda Hill, the largely basalt Chalukyan-style **"thousand-pillared" Shiva temple** (daily 6am–6pm) was constructed in 1163. A low-roofed building on several stepped stages, it features superb carvings and shrines to Vishnu, Shiva and Surya, the sun god. They lead off the *mandapa*, whose numerous finely carved columns give the temple its name. In front, a polished Nandi bull was carved out of a single stone. A Bhadrakali temple stands at the top of the hill.

Practicalities

If you make an early start, it's just about possible to visit Warangal as a day-trip from Hyderabad. Frequent buses and trains run to the city (roughly 3hr). Warangal's **bus** and **railway stations** are opposite each other in the centre. The easiest way to cover the site is to **rent a bike** from one of the stalls on Station Road (Rs5-10/hr). There's an **AP Tourism** office (Ⓣ0870/244 6606; daily except Sun 10am–5pm) opposite the Royal Engineering College. **Internet** facilities are available at Durga Xerox on Station Road, almost opposite the *Vijaya Lodge*. An auto-rickshaw to either the fort or the temple costs around Rs100, if you negotiate hard.

Accommodation is limited: basic lodges on Station Road include the *Vijaya Lodge* (Ⓣ0870/225 1222, Ⓕ244 6864; ❶–❷), which is close to the station and the best choice for those on a tight budget. A decent mid-range option even closer to the station on Station Road is *Hotel Surya* (Ⓣ0870/244 1834; ❸), with clean attached rooms and a good restaurant. Marginally smarter is *Hotel Ashoka* (Ⓣ0870/285491, Ⓦwww.hotelashoka.in; ❹), just beyond the thousand-pillared temple on Main Road, Hanamkonda, which has carpeted a/c rooms with TV and fridge. There are a few **eating places on** Station Road, including the modest *Bharati Mess*, which offers help-yourself meals. *Kadambari*, in *Hotel Ashoka*, provides well-prepared, though unadventurous, Indian and Chinese standards; there's also an attached **bar**.

Nagarjunakonda

NAGARJUNAKONDA, or "Nagarjuna's Hill", 166km south of Hyderabad and 175km west of Vijayawada, is all that remains of the vast area, rich in archeological sites, that was submerged when the huge Nagarjuna Sagar Dam was built across the River Krishna in 1960. Ancient settlements in the valley were first discovered in 1926, and extensive excavations carried out between 1954 and 1960 uncovered more than one hundred sites dating from the early Stone Age to late medieval times. Nagarjunakonda was once the summit of a hill, where a fort towered 200m above the valley floor; now it is just a small oblong island near the middle of Nagarjuna Sagar lake. Several Buddhist monuments have been reconstructed, in an operation reminiscent of that at Abu Simbel in Egypt, and a **museum** exhibits the more remarkable ruins of the valley. **VIJAYAPURI**, the village on the shore of the lake, overlooks the colossal dam itself, which produces electricity for the whole region. Many nearby villages had to be relocated to higher ground when the valley was flooded.

The island and the museum

Boats arrive on the northeastern edge of **Nagarjunakonda island** (daily 9am–5pm) at what remains of one of the gates of the fort, built in the fourteenth century and renovated by the Vijayanagar kings in the mid-sixteenth century. Low, damaged, stone walls skirting the island mark the edge of the fort, and you can see ground-level remains of the Hindu temples that served its inhabitants. Well-kept gardens lie between the jetty and the museum, beyond which nine Buddhist monuments from various sites in the valley have been rebuilt. West of the jetty, there's a reconstructed third-century AD bathing *ghat*.

The **maha-chaitya**, or stupa, constructed at the command of King Chamtula's sister in the third century AD, is the area's earliest Buddhist structure. It was raised over relics of the Buddha – said to include a tooth – and has been reassembled in the southwest of the island. Nearby, a towering **Buddha statue** stands beside a ground plan of a monastery that enshrines a smaller stupa. Close by are other **stupas**; the brick walls of the *svastika chaitya* have been arranged in the shape of swastikas, common emblems in early Buddhist iconography.

The **museum** (daily except Fri 10.30am–5pm; Rs100 [Rs5]) houses stone friezes decorated with scenes from the Buddha's life, and statues of the Buddha in various postures. Earlier artefacts include metal axe-heads and knives (dating from the first millennium BC). Later exhibits include inscribed pillars from Ikshvaku times. Medieval sculptures include a thirteenth-century *tirthankara* (Jain saint) and a seventeenth-century Ganesh.

Practicalities

APTDC tours from Hyderabad to Nagarjunakonda at weekends (see p.909) are rushed: if you want to spend more time in the area you can take a bus from Hyderabad (4hr; all the regular Macherla services stop at Vijayapuri) or Vijayawada (6hr; a direct service runs daily at 11am and frequent services leave from Guntur). The **AP Tourism** office (daily except Sun 10am–5pm; ⓣ08680/277364) is near the bus stand. Tickets for **boats** to the island (daily 9am & 1.30pm; 45min; Rs75) go on sale 25 minutes before departure. Each boat leaves the island ninety minutes after it arrives, which allows enough time to see the museum and walk briskly round the monuments, but if you want to soak up the atmosphere, take the morning boat and return in the afternoon.

Accommodation at Vijayapuri is limited and there are two distinct settlements 6km apart on either side of the dam. For easy access to the sites it's better to stay near the jetty on the right bank of the dam; ask the bus driver to leave you at the launch station. The drab-looking concrete *Nagarjuna Motel Complex* (ⓣ08642/278188; ❷–❸) has adequate rooms, some with a/c. APTDC runs the more comfortable all-a/c *Vijay Vihar* (ⓣ08680/277362; ❹–❺) on the near side of the dam as you approach the lake from Hyderabad.

Eastern and northern Andhra Pradesh

One of India's least visited areas, **eastern Andhra Pradesh** is sandwiched between the Bay of Bengal in the east and the red soil and high peaks of the Eastern Ghats in the north. Its one architectural attraction is the ancient Buddhist site of **Amaravati**, near the city of **Vijayawada**, whose sprinkling of historic temples is far overshadowed by impersonal, modern buildings. For anyone with a strong desire to explore, however, pockets of natural beauty along the coast and in the hills of eastern Andhra Pradesh can offer rich rewards. At the northern tip of the state, the nondescript city of **Visakhapatnam** is a useful place to break up a journey to northern India.

Vijayawada and around

Almost 450km north of Chennai, a third of the way to Kolkata, **VIJAYAWADA** is a bustling commercial centre on the banks of the Krishna delta, 90km from the coast. This mundane city, alleviated by a mountain backdrop of bare granite outcrops and some urban greenery, is seldom visited by tourists, but is an obvious stop-off point for visits to nearby **Amaravati.** The **Kanaka Durga** (also known as Vijaya) **temple** on Indrakila Hill in the east, dedicated to the city's patron goddess of riches, power and benevolence, is the most interesting of Vijayawada's handful of temples. Across the river, roughly 3km out of town, is an ancient, unmodified cave temple at **Undavalli**, a tiny rural village reachable on any Guntur-bound bus, or the local #13 service.

Practicalities

Vijayawada's **railway station**, on the main Chennai–Kolkata line, is in the centre of town: the daily *Janmabhoomi Express* #2805 (11.50am; 6hr 35min) is a convenient service to Hyderabad. Regular buses to Amaravati (hourly; 1hr 30m–2hr), Hyderabad (every 15min; 6hr) and Visakhapatnam (hourly; 6–9hr) depart from the Pandit Nehru **bus stand** 1.5km further west, on the other side of the Ryes Canal. There's a **tourist office** (daily except Sun 10am–5pm; ⓣ0866/252 3966) at the railway station, and APTDC has an office in the town centre at the *Hotel Ilapuram* complex, Gandhi Nagar (same times; ⓣ0866/257 0255). You can **change money** at Zen Global Finance, 40-6-27 Krishna Nagar in Labbipet, or use one of the **ATMs** on Atchutaramaiah Street, which links the railway station to Elluru Road. Reliance Web World in Surya Tower on Elluru Road provides **internet** access (Rs100/4hrs).

Vijayawada has a reasonable selection of **hotels**, most within 1km of the railway station and bus stand. *Monika Lodge* (ⓣ0866/257 1334; ❷), just off Elluru Road about 300m northeast of the bus stand, is one of the cheapest but a bit dingy. Two better-value places, both on Atchutaramaiah Street, are the *Hotel Narayana Swamy* (ⓣ0866/257 1221; ❸) and the *Hotel Sri Ram* (ⓣ0866/257 9377; ❸); they have spotless rooms, some with air conditioner and TV. The best bet, however, is *Raj Towers* (ⓣ0866/257 1311, ⓕ556 1714; ❹) on Elluru Road, a tall modern block with solid air conditioned rooms and a decent **restaurant**. Moving further up the scale, the reliable *Hotel Swarna Palace* (ⓣ0866/257 7222; ❺–❻), where Atchutaramaiah Street meets Elluru Road, has more comfortable, though slightly overpriced, air conditioned rooms. Its fourth-floor *Palace Heights* restaurant serves hearty portions of Indian, Chinese and continental food, and there's a **bar**. There are innumerable inexpensive "meals" joints around town.

Amaravati

A small town on the banks of the Krishna, 33km from Vijayawada, **AMARAVATI** is the site of a Buddhist settlement (daily except Fri 10am–5pm; Rs100 [Rs5]), formerly known as Chintapalli, where a stupa larger than those at Sanchi (see p.356) was erected over relics of the Buddha in the third century BC, during the reign of Ashoka. The stupa no longer stands, but its size is evident from the mound that formed its base. There was a gateway at each of the cardinal points, one of which has been reconstructed, and the meticulously carved details show themes from the Buddha's life. A Kalachakra initiation programme was conducted by the Dalai Lama here in January 2006 to commemorate 2550 years since the Buddha's birth.

Exhibits at the small but fascinating **museum** (same hours; Rs2) range in date from the third century BC to the twelfth century AD and include Buddha statues with lotus symbols on the feet, tightly curled hair and long ear lobes – all traditional indications of an enlightened teacher.

Practicalities

Buses run hourly from Vijayawada to Amaravati (1hr 30min–2hr) and more frequently from Guntur (every 15min; 45min–1hr), a dull market town in between. The excavated site and museum are under 1km from the bus stand. If you want to stay a night, try the APTDC-run *Amaravati Hotel* (ⓣ08645/255332; ❸), which has reasonable air conditioned rooms with private facilities, and a five-bed dorm (Rs100). Apart from an APTDC canteen, there are **food stalls** on the main street.

Visakhapatnam

Andhra Pradesh's second largest city, 650km east of Hyderabad and 350km north of Vijayawada, **VISAKHAPATNAM** (commonly known as Vizag) is a busy port and home to major ship-building, oil refining and steel industries. Apart from a few decent beaches and some interesting temples, there is little to detain tourists. However, the city is a useful place to break up a long journey north or south.

Practicalities

Visakhapatnam's **railway station**, on the main Chennai–Kolkata line, is close to the port. Regular **buses** for Vijayawada (6–9hr) and Hyderabad (11–14hr) leave from the bus stand, which is south of the city centre. **ATMs** are numerous. There are several good **hotels** on Beach Road, including the popular *YMCA* (Ⓣ0891/275 5826; ❸), which has a few economical attached rooms and a dorm (Rs150); the APTDC-run *Haritha Hotel* (Ⓣ0891/256 2333; ❹–❺), which has comfortable mid-range a/c rooms; and the top-end Taj Hotels-run *Gateway* (Ⓣ0891/662 3670, Ⓦwww.thegatewayhotels.com; ❼–❽), which has recently-renovated sea-facing attached rooms and an excellent Chinese **restaurant**. There are many other less expensive restaurants strung along Beach Road.

Southern Andhra Pradesh

The further south you travel from the fertile lands watered by the great Krishna and Godavari rivers, the less hospitable the terrain becomes, especially in the rocky southwest of the state. For Hindus, the main attraction in southern Andhra Pradesh is the **Venkateshvara temple**, outside **Tirupati**, India's most popular Vishnu shrine, where several thousand pilgrims come each day to receive *darshan*. **Puttaparthy**, home of spiritual leader Sai Baba, is the only other place in the region to attract significant numbers of visitors. Both Tirupati and Puttaparthy are closer to Chennai in Tamil Nadu and Bengaluru in Karnataka than to other points in Andhra Pradesh.

Tirupati and Tirumala Hill

Set in a stunning position, surrounded by wooded hills capped by a ring of vertical red rocks, the **Shri Venkateshvara temple** at Tirumala, 170km northwest of Chennai, is said to be one of the richest and the most popular place of pilgrimage in the world, drawing more devotees than Rome or Mecca. With its many shrines and *dharamshalas*, the whole area around Tirumala Hill, an enervating drive 700m up in the Venkata hills, provides a fascinating insight into contemporary Hinduism practised on a large scale. The hill is 11km as the crow flies from its service town of **TIRUPATI**, but double that by road.

A five-minute walk from the railway station, the one temple in Tirupati itself that's definitely worth a look is **Govindarajaswamy**, whose modern grey *gopura* is clearly visible from many points in town. The inner sanctum is open to

Moving on from Tirupati

Frequent express bus services run to Chennai (every 15–30min; 3hr 30min–4hr), but the train (2hr 30min–4hr) is more comfortable and generally quicker. There are hourly buses to both Kanchipuram (5hr), three of which continue to Mahabalipuram (7hr), and Bengaluru (7hr). A special section at the back of the bus stand has services every few minutes to **Tirumala** and the Venkateshvara temple; you can also access the hill via a local bus stop outside the railway station. There are daily **flights** to Hyderabad, Delhi and Visakhapatnam from the airport, 14km outside town.

non-Hindus and contains a splendid large black reclining Vishnu. In its own compound by the side entrance stands the fine little Venkateshvara Museum of Temple Arts (daily 8am–8pm; Rs5). The temple's impressive bathing tank lies 200m to the east.

Between Tirupati and Tirumala Hill, the **Tiruchanur Padmavati temple** is another popular pilgrimage halt. A gold *vimana* tower with lions at each corner surmounts the sanctuary, which contains a black stone image of goddess Lakshmi with one silver eye. A Rs40 ticket allows you to jump the queue to enter the sanctuary.

Arrival and information

The best way of **getting to Tirupati** is by train from Chennai; the trip can just about be done in a day if you get the *Chennai Express* #2164 (6.50am; 2hr 30min). From Hyderabad it's a long haul by bus (8–10 daily, 11–15hr) or train (4–6 daily). The **train station** is right in the town centre; the **bus stand** is around 500m east. The **AP Tourism** office (daily 7am–9pm; ⓣ0877/225 5385) is on the second floor of the Sri Devi Complex, Tilak Road. For **internet** access, try Reliance Web World (Rs100/4hrs) also on Tilak Road, 200m beyond the tourist office. There is a cluster of **ATMs** outside the Railway Reservation Centre, diagonally opposite the station.

Tirumala Hill, the Venkateshvara temple and Kapilateertham

The road trip up Tirumala Hill is a lot less terrifying now that there's a separate route down; the most devout, of course, climb the hill by foot. The steep **trail** starts at Alipuri, 4km from the centre of Tirupati; all the pilgrim buses pass through – look out for a large Garuda statue and the soaring *gopura* of the first temple. There are drinks stalls all along the route, which is covered for most of the way. The walk takes at least four hours, and an early start is recommended. When you get to the top, you will see barbers giving pilgrims tonsures as part of their devotions.

The **Venkateshvara temple** (aka Sri Vari) dedicated to **Vishnu** and started in the tenth century, has been renovated to provide facilities for the thousands of pilgrims who visit daily; a warren of passages wind their way around the complex towards the inner sanctum; weekends, public holidays and festivals are even busier. Unless your visit is intended to be particularly rigorous, you should buy a **special darshan ticket** (Rs50) as this can reduce the time it takes to get inside by quite a few hours; for an even quicker route in, go for a **seeghra darshan ticket** (Rs300). Both tickets can be purchased from the temple tourism office not far from the temple bus stand on Station Road: you have to sign a declaration of faith in Lord Venkateshvara, and take photocopies of your passport and visa, and the originals. Note that **no electronic devices** are allowed inside the temple.

At the entrance is a colonnade, lined with life-sized copper or stone statues of royal patrons. The *gopura* gateway leading to the inner courtyard is decorated with sheets of embossed silver; a gold *stambha* (flagstaff) stands outside the inner shrine next to a gold upturned lotus on a plinth. Outside, opposite the temple, is a small museum, the **Hall of Antiquities** (daily 8am–8pm). Your *darshan* tickets entitle you to enter the museum via shorter queues opposite the exit.

At the bottom of the hill, the **Sri Kapileswaraswami** temple at Kapilateertham is the only Tirumala temple devoted to Shiva.

Chandragiri Fort

In the sixteenth century, **Chandragiri**, 11km southwest of Tirupati, became the third capital of the Vijayanagars. It was here that the British negotiated the acquisition of the land to establish Fort St George, the earliest settlement at what is now Chennai. The original fort (daily except Fri10am–5pm; Rs100 [Rs5]), thought to date from around 1000 AD, was taken over by Haider Ali in 1782, followed by the British in 1792. A small **museum** is housed in the main building, the Indo-Saracenic Raja Mahal. Another building, the **Rani Mahal**, stands close by, while behind that is a hill with two freestanding boulders that was used as a place of public execution during Vijayanagar times. There's a nightly **sound-and-light** show (English: Nov–Feb 7.30pm; March–Oct 8pm; 45min; Rs30).

Accommodation and eating

Unless you're a pilgrim seeking accommodation in the *dharamshalas* near the temple, all the decent **places to stay** are in Tirupati. **Eating** is almost exclusively vegetarian, and there are many cheap "meals" places in town and on Tirumala Hill. Alternatively try the air conditioned restaurants at *Hotel Annapurna* and *Hotel Sindhuri Park*: the former serves south Indian snacks (including a carrot dosa), thalis (Rs85–110), Chinese rice and noodles and decent north Indian mains; the latter, slightly smarter but no more expensive, offers a good range of Indian *paneer* and veg dishes, as well as banana split for dessert.

Annapurna 349 G Car St, opposite the railway station ⓣ0877/225 0666. On a busy corner, this modern hotel has spacious, sparsely furnished attached rooms with tiled floors, TVs and either fans or a/c. ❹–❺

Apsara 213 TP Area ⓣ0877/557 8062. Almost opposite the bus station, this is a pretty standard shoestring place offering very basic but cleanish attached rooms of varying sizes. ❶

Bhimas Deluxe 34–38 G Car St, near the railway station ⓣ0877/222 5521. Despite an unappealing grey colour-scheme, the attached a/c rooms with TV here are a decent choice; 12hr "transit rooms" are available for two-thirds of the regular rate. ❺

Mayura 209 TP Area ⓣ0877/222 5925. The best of the lodges opposite the bus station, *Mayura* offers average mid-range rooms with clean bathrooms and TV. ❹–❺

Sindhuri Park Near the bus station, facing the bathing tank ⓣ0877/225 6430, ⓦwww.hotelsindhuri.com. The smartest place in the town centre, this all-a/c hotel has comfortable – if unremarkable – attached rooms with good views of the tank and temple. ❺–❻

Puttaparthy

Deep in the southwest of the state, amid the arid rocky hills bordering Karnataka, a thriving community has grown up around the once insignificant village of **PUTTAPARTHY**, birthplace of spiritual leader **Sai Baba**. Centring on **Prasanthi Nilayam** (Abode of Peace), the ashram where Sai Baba resides from July to March, the town has schools, a university, hospital and sports centre which offer up-to-date and free services to all. The ashram itself is a huge complex, with canteens, shops, a museum and library, and a vast assembly hall where Sai Baba gives *darshan* twice daily (7.45am & 3pm). Queues start more than an hour beforehand, and a lottery decides who gets to sit near the front. The museum (daily 10am–noon) contains detailed displays on the world's major faiths.

Practicalities

Buses from Bengaluru, Hyderabad, Tirupati and Chennai stop at the stand outside the ashram entrance. The **railway station**, named Sri Satya Sai Prasanti Nilayam, is 8km from town on the main north–south route, from which you should be able to get a shared auto-rickshaw to the ashram for around Rs10: the daily *Kacheguda Express* #7604 (7pm; 10hr) travels to Hyderabad. There are more services to and from **Dharmavaram**, 42km away, connected to Puttaparthy by regular buses. The small airport, 6km from the ashram, is currently closed. Exchange bureaus, **ATMs** and **internet** places dot Puttaparthy's main drag.

Shri Satya Sai Baba

Born on November 23, 1926, in Puttaparthy, **Satyanarayana Raju** is reported to have shown prodigious talents from an early age. His apparently supernatural abilities initially caused some concern to his family, who took him to Vedic doctors and eventually to be exorcised. Having been pronounced to be possessed by the divine rather than the diabolical, at the age of 14 he calmly announced he was the new incarnation of **Sai Baba**, a saint from Shirdi in Maharashtra who died eight years before Satya was born.

Gradually his fame spread, and a large following developed. In 1950 the **ashram** was inaugurated and a decade later Sai Baba was attracting international attention; today he has millions of devotees worldwide. Just 5ft tall, with a startling Hendrix-style Afro, his smiling, saffron-clad figure is seen on posters, photos and murals all over south India. Though his **miraculous powers** reportedly include the ability to materialize *vibhuti*, sacred ash, with curative properties, Sai Baba claims this to be an unimportant activity, emphasizing instead his message of **universal love**. In recent years a number of ex-followers have made serious accusations about coercion and even sexual abuse on the part of the guru himself, which have been vehemently denied. Whatever your feelings about the divinity of Sai Baba, the atmosphere around the ashram is undeniably peaceful. You can do some research on the guru at ⓦwww.saibabalinks.org.

Many visitors **stay** in the ashram accommodation, which is strictly segregated by sex, except for families. Costs are minimal, and although you can't book in advance, you can enquire about availability at the secretary's office (ⓣ08555/287583). Outside the ashram, many of the hotels are overpriced, but a good, cheap option is the friendly *Sai Ganesh Guest House* near the police station (ⓣ08555/287460; ❷). The *Sri Sai Sadan* at the far end of the main street (ⓣ08555/287507, ⓔsrisaisadan@yahoo.com; ❹–❺) is also decent value; all rooms have fridge, TV, phone and balcony with views of the countryside or the ashram, and there's a meditation room and rooftop **restaurant**. The *Sai Towers*, near the ashram entrance (ⓣ0855/287270, ⓦwww.saitowers.com; ❺–❻), charges a lot for its smallish fan and a/c rooms, but has a good veg **restaurant** downstairs. Delicious Tibetan *momos* (dumplings) and *thukpas* (thick noodle soups) are served at *Bamboo Nest* on Chitravathi Road and *Little Tibet Kitchen* just down from *Sai Towers*. The ashram also has a canteen open to non-residents.

19

The Andaman Islands

* **Wandoor** The white sandy beach and islets of the Mahatma Gandhi National Marine Park are the most popular day-trip destination from Port Blair, and a good appetizer for more remote parts. See p.933

* **Havelock Island** For the best diving and partying, head for Havelock, still laidback and friendly despite being the most developed of the Andamans. See p.935

* **Scuba diving** The Andamans' beautiful coral reefs teem with vivid underwater life. See p.936

* **North Andaman** The long haul by bus or boat from Port Blair is worthwhile for the backdrop of thick rainforest and the dazzling tropical beaches when you get there. See p.941

* **Little Andaman** As very few travellers make it to the archipelago's southernmost island, you may well have the stunning forest-fringed beaches to yourself. See p.942

▲ A fisherman casts his net among the mangroves on Havelock Island

Comprising India's most remote state, the **ANDAMAN ISLANDS** are situated over 1000km off the east coast in the middle of the Bay of Bengal, connected to the mainland by flights and ferries from Kolkata, Chennai and Vishakapatnam. Thickly covered by deep green tropical forest, the archipelago supports a profusion of wildlife, including some extremely rare species of bird, but the principal attraction for tourists lies in the beaches and the pristine reefs that ring most of the islands. Filled with colourful fish and kaleidoscopic corals, the crystal-clear waters of the Andaman Sea feature some of the world's richest and least spoilt marine reserves – perfect for **snorkelling** and **scuba diving**. Although parts of the archipelago still see few visitors, the Andamans are now firmly on the tourist circuit.

For administrative purposes, the Andamans are grouped with the **Nicobar Islands**, 200km further south, but these remain strictly off-limits to foreigners, as well as Indians with no direct business there. Approximately two hundred islands make up the Andaman group and nineteen the Nicobar. They are of varying size, the summits of a submarine mountain range stretching 755km from the Arakan Yoma chain in Burma to the fringes of Sumatra in the south. All but the most remote are populated in parts by **indigenous tribes** whose numbers have been slashed dramatically as a result of nineteenth-century European settlement and, more recently, rampant **deforestation**, now banned in theory at least.

Foreign tourists are only permitted to visit certain parts of the Andaman group. The point of arrival for boats and planes is the small but busy capital, **Port Blair** in **South Andaman**, which accounts for almost half the total population. Free thirty-day **permits** are granted on arrival by both sea and air and can be extended for fifteen days on production of a return ticket.

The most beautiful beaches and coral reefs are found on the outlying islands. These are not always easy to reach, as connections and transport can be erratic, frequently uncomfortable and severely limited. It's also worth pointing out that a surprising number of travellers fall sick in the Andamans. The dense tree cover, marshy swamps and high rainfall combine to provide the perfect breeding ground for mosquitoes, and **malaria** is endemic in even the most remote settlements. Sandflies are also ferocious in certain places and **tropical ulcer** infections from scratching the bites is a frequent hazard.

The **climate** remains tropical throughout the year, with temperatures ranging from 24°C to 35°C and humidity levels never below seventy percent. By far the best time to visit is between January and April. From mid-May to October, heavy rains flush the islands, often bringing violent cyclones that leave west-coast beaches strewn with fallen trees, while in November and December less severe rains arrive with the northeast monsoon. Despite being so far east, the islands run on Indian time, so the sun rises as early as 4.30am in summer and darkness falls soon after 5pm.

Some history

The earliest mention of the Andaman and Nicobar islands is found in **Ptolemy**'s geographical treatises of the second century AD. Other records from the Chinese Buddhist monk I'Tsing some five hundred years later and Arabian travellers who passed by in the ninth century depict the inhabitants as fierce and cannibalistic. It is unlikely, however, that the Andamanese were cannibals, as the most vivid reports of their ferocity were propagated by Malay pirates who held sway over the surrounding seas, and needed to keep looters well away from trade ships that passed between India, China and the Far East.

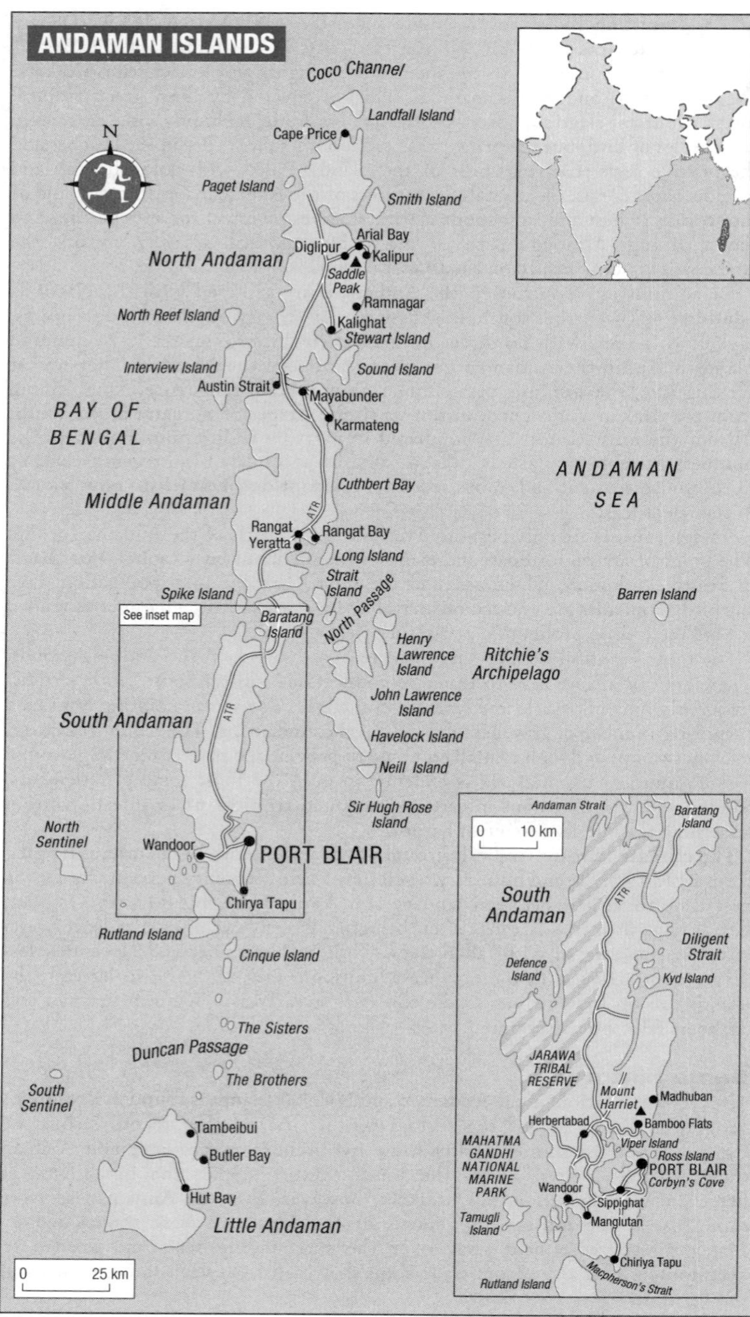
ANDAMAN ISLANDS
Coco Channel
Landfall Island
Cape Price
N
Paget Island
Smith Island
Arial Bay
Diglipur
Kalipur
North Andaman
Saddle Peak
Ramnagar
North Reef Island
Kalighat
Stewart Island
Interview Island
Sound Island
Austin Strait
Mayabunder
BAY OF BENGAL
Karmateng
ANDAMAN SEA
Cuthbert Bay
Middle Andaman
ATR
Rangat
Rangat Bay
Yeratta
Long Island
Strait Island
North Passage
Spike Island
Barren Island
See inset map
Baratang Island
Henry Lawrence Island
Ritchie's Archipelago
John Lawrence Island
South Andaman
ATR
Havelock Island
Neill Island
Sir Hugh Rose Island
North Sentinel
Wandoor
PORT BLAIR
Chirya Tapu
Rutland Island
Cinque Island
The Sisters
Duncan Passage
The Brothers
South Sentinel
Tambeibui
Butler Bay
Hut Bay
Little Andaman
0 25 km
Andaman Strait
Baratang Island
0 10 km
South Andaman
ATR
Diligent Strait
Defence Island
Kyd Island
JARAWA TRIBAL RESERVE
Mount Harriet
Madhuban
Herbertabad
Bamboo Flats
MAHATMA GANDHI NATIONAL MARINE PARK
Viper Island
Ross Island
PORT BLAIR
Corbyn's Cove
Wandoor
Sippighat
Tamugli Island
Manglutan
Chiriya Tapu
Rutland Island
Macpherson's Strait

Getting to the Andaman Islands

Port Blair on South Andaman is currently served by three **flights** daily from Chennai, operated by Kingfisher and Air India/Indian Airlines, who also fly once daily from Kolkata, as do JetLite. It's also possible to get to Port Blair by **ship**. Services from Chennai (see p.950) can be reasonably relied upon to leave in each direction once every week to ten days, while those from Kolkata (see p.741) sail roughly every two weeks; boats from Vishakapatnam are altogether more erratic, averaging once a month – call the Shipping Office on ☎0891/256 5597 for more information. Although cheaper than flying, sea crossings are long (3–5 days), uncomfortable and often delayed by bad conditions.

During the eighteenth and nineteenth centuries, **European missionaries** and trading companies turned their attention to the islands with a view to colonization. A string of unsuccessful attempts to convert the Nicobaris to Christianity was made by the French, Dutch and Danish, all of whom were forced to abandon their plans in the face of hideous diseases and a severe lack of food and water. Though the missionaries themselves seldom met with any hostility, several fleets of trading ships that tried to dock on the islands were captured, and their crews murdered, by Nicobari people.

In 1777, the British Lieutenant Archibald Blair chose the South Andaman harbour now known as **Port Blair** as the site for a **penal colony**, although it was not successfully established until 1858, when political activists who had fuelled the Mutiny in 1857 were made to clear land and build their own prison. Out of 773 prisoners, 292 died, escaped or were hanged in the first two months. Many also lost their lives in attacks by Andamanese tribes who objected to forest clearance but by 1864 the number of convicts had grown to three thousand. The prison continued to confine political prisoners until 1945 and still stands as Port Blair's prime "tourist attraction" (see p.930).

During World War II the islands were occupied by the **Japanese**, who tortured and murdered hundreds of indigenous islanders suspected of collaborating with the British, and bombed the homes of the Jarawa tribe. British forces moved back in 1945, and at last abolished the penal settlement. After **Partition**, refugees – mostly low-caste Hindus from Bengal – were given land in Port Blair and North Andaman, where the forest was clear-felled to make room for rice paddy, cocoa plantations and new industries. Since 1951, the population has increased more than ten-fold, further swollen by repatriated Tamils from Sri Lanka, thousands of Bihari labourers, ex-servicemen given land grants, economic migrants from poorer Indian states, and the legions of government employees packed off here on two-year "punishment postings". This replanted population greatly outnumbers the Andamans' indigenous people (see p.926), who currently comprise around half of one percent of the total.

With the timber-extraction cash cow now partially tethered, the hope is that **tourism** will replace tree-felling as the main source of revenue. However, the extra visitor numbers envisaged are certain to overtax an already inadequate infrastructure, aggravating seasonal water shortages and sewage disposal problems. Given India's track record with tourism development, it's hard to be optimistic. Delhi has already given the go-ahead for air services from Southeast Asia and eventually charter flights from Europe to land on the extended airport runway. If only a small percentage of the tourist traffic between Thailand and India is diverted through the Andamans, the impact on this culturally and ecologically fragile region could be catastrophic.

Native people of the Andaman and Nicobar islands

Quite where the **indigenous population** of the Andaman and Nicobar islands originally came from is a puzzle that has preoccupied anthropologists since Alfred Radcliffe-Brown conducted his famous field work among the Andamanese at the beginning of the twentieth century. Asian-looking groups such as the Shompen may have migrated here from the east and north when the islands were connected to Burma, or the sea was sufficiently shallow to allow transport by canoe, but this doesn't explain the origins of the black populations, whose appearance suggests African roots. The survival of the islands' first inhabitants has long been threatened by traders and colonizers, who introduced disease and destroyed their territories through widespread tree-felling. Thousands also died from addiction to the alcohol and opium which the Chinese, Japanese and British exchanged for valuable shells. Many have had their populations decimated, while others like the Nicobarese have assimilated to modern culture, often adopting Christianity. The indigenous inhabitants of the Andamans, divided into *eramtaga* (those living in the jungle) and *ar-yuato* (those living on the coast), traditionally subsisted as hunter-gatherers, living on fish, turtles, turtle eggs, pigs, fruit, honey and roots.

Although they comprised the largest group when the islands were first colonized, only around fifty **Great Andamanese** now survive. In the 1860s, the Rev Henry Corbyn set up a "home" for the tribe to learn English on Ross Island, insisting that they wear clothes and attend reading and writing classes. Five children and three adults from Corbyn's school were taken to Calcutta in 1864, where they were shown around the sights but treated more as curiosities themselves. Within three years, almost the entire population had died, victims of either introduced diseases or addiction. In recent years the surviving Great Andamanese were forcibly settled on Strait Island, north of South Andaman, as a "breeding centre", where they were forced to rely on the Indian authorities for food and shelter. Sadly, the last speaker of Bo, one of the oldest Andamanese languages, died in January 2010.

The **Jarawas**, who were shifted from their original homes when land was cleared to build Port Blair, currently number around 270 and live on the remote western coasts of Middle and South Andaman, hemmed in by the Andaman Trunk Road (ATR), which since the 1970s has cut them off from hunting grounds and freshwater supplies. During the 1980s and 1990s, encroachments on their land by loggers, road builders and settlers met with fierce resistance, and dozens, possibly hundreds, of people died in **skirmishes**, mostly on or near the ATR. Some more amicable **contact** between settlers and tribals was subsequently made through gift exchanges at each

South Andaman: Port Blair and around

South Andaman is the most heavily populated of the Andaman Islands – particularly around the capital, **Port Blair** – thanks in part to the drastic thinning of tree cover to make way for settlement. Foreign tourists can only visit its southern and east central reaches – including the beaches at **Corbyn's Cove** and **Chiriya Tapu**, the fine reefs on the western shores at **Wandoor**, 35km southwest of Port Blair, and the environs of **Madhuban** and **Mount Harriet**, on the east coast across the bay from the capital. With your own transport it's easy to find your way along the narrow bumpy roads that connect small villages, weaving through forests and coconut fields, and skirting the swamps and rocky outcrops that form the coastline.

Port Blair

A refreshingly leafy but ultimately characterless cluster of tin-roofed buildings tumbling towards the sea in the north, east and west, and petering out into fields full moon, although the initiative was later cancelled. These meetings nevertheless led to some Jarawas becoming curious about what "civilization" had to offer, and they started to hold their hands out for goodies to passing vehicles and even visiting Indian settlements near their territory. Despite the authorities trying to minimize contact, it is still a common sight to see Jarawas beaming up at your bus and some private vehicles ignore the rules and stop for photoshoots. The government has increased Jarawa land by 180 square kilometres, but lodged an ongoing appeal over a 2002 Indian Supreme Court order to close the ATR – a ruling made following protests by international pressure groups such as Survival International.

Relations with the **Onge**, who call themselves the **Gaubolambe**, have been relatively peaceful. Distinguished by their white-clay and ochre body paint, they continue to live in communal shelters and construct temporary thatched huts on Little Andaman. The remaining population of around one hundred retain their traditional way of life on two small reserves. Contact with outsiders is limited to an occasional trip into town to purchase liquor, and visits from rare parties of anthropologists. The reserves are strictly off-limits to foreigners, but you can learn about the Onge's traditional hunting practices, beliefs and rituals in Vishvajit Pandya's wonderful ethnography study, *Above the Forest*.

On the Nicobars, the most assimilated and numerous tribe, the **Nicobarese**, are of Mongoloid descent and number over twenty thousand. They live in villages, ruled by a headman, and have largely cordial relations with the Indian settlers. By contrast, only very limited contact is ever had with the isolated **Shompen** tribe of Great Nicobar, whose population of around 180 manage to lead a traditional hunting-and-gathering existence. The most elusive tribe of all, the **Sentinelese**, live on North Sentinel Island west of South Andaman. Following the first encounter with Indian settlers in 1967, some contact was made with them in 1990, after a team put together by the local administration left gifts on the beaches every month for two years, but subsequent visits have invariably ended in a hail of arrows. Since the early 1990s, the authorities have effectively given up trying to contact the Sentinelese, who are estimated to number anywhere between fifty and two hundred. Flying in or out of Port Blair, you pass above their island, ringed by a spectacular coral reef. It's reassuring to think that the people sitting at the bottom of the plumes of smoke drifting up from the forest canopy still manage to resist contact with the outside world.

For more information on the islands' original inhabitants, visit Survival International's website, ⓦwww.survival-international.org.

and forests in the south, **PORT BLAIR** merits only a short stay. There's little to see here – just the **Cellular Jail** and a few small **museums** – but as the point of arrival for the islands and the place with most facilities, it can't be avoided.

Arrival and information

Port Blair has two main jetties: **boats** from the mainland moor at **Haddo Jetty**, nearly 2km northwest of **Phoenix Jetty**, arrival point for inter-island ferries. The Director of Shipping Services at Phoenix Jetty has the latest information on boats and ferries, but you can also check details of forthcoming departures in the shipping-news column of the local newspaper, the *Daily Telegrams* (Rs2). Advice on booking ferry tickets appears in the box on p.930.

The smart, newly extended **Veer Savarkar airport** terminal is under 4km south of town at Lamba Line. **Taxis** and **auto-rickshaws** are on hand for short trips into town (Rs50), but if you've booked a room in any of the middle- or upper-range hotels or do so at the counter in the airport, you should find a shuttle bus waiting outside. Local **buses** also frequently ply the route to town

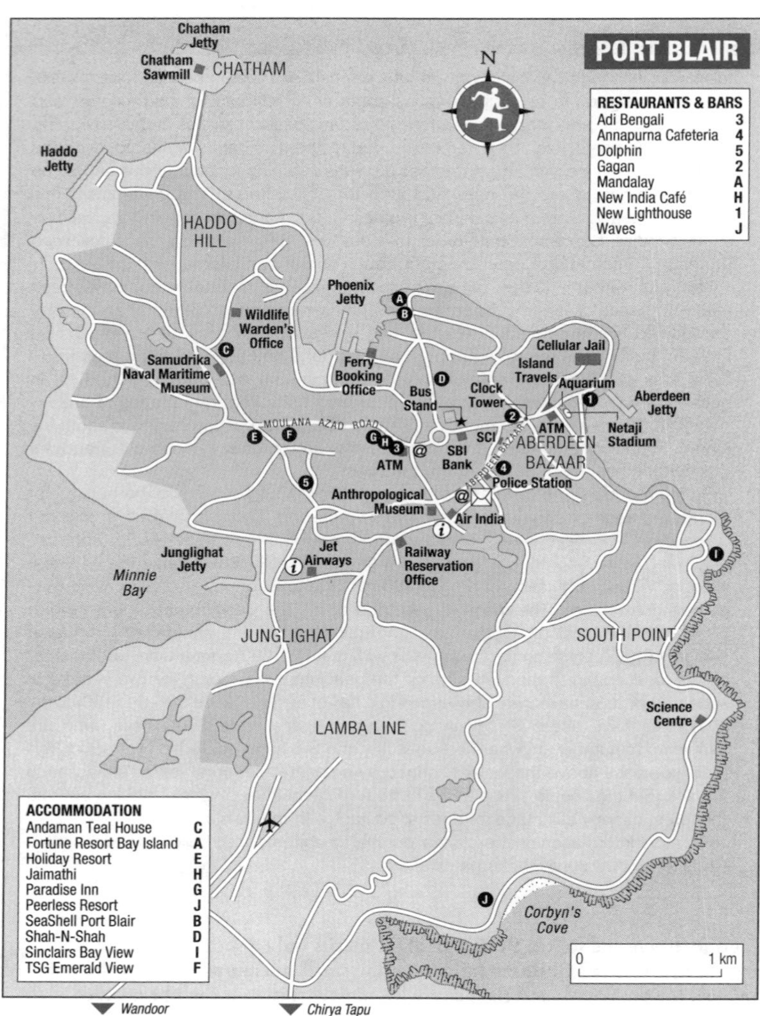

from outside the shop on the far side of the main road, barely 100m from the terminal building.

The counter at the airport (Ⓣ03192/232414) hands out a useful general brochure, but trying to get more than basic tour and hotel information from the main **A&N Directorate of Tourism office** (Mon–Fri 10am–5pm, Sat 10am–1pm; Ⓣ03192/232747, Ⓦwww.andaman.nic.in), situated in a modern building diagonally opposite Indian Airlines, can be frustrating. Further southwest on Junglighat Main Road, the **India Tourism office** (Mon–Fri 8.30am–5pm; Ⓣ03192/233006, Ⓦwww.incredibleindia.org) is not much better. If you intend to visit Interview Island (see p.941), you must first obtain a free permit from the **Chief Wildlife Warden**, whose office (Ⓣ03192/233270) is next to the zoo in Haddo.

Road names are not used much in Port Blair, with most establishments addressing themselves simply by their local area. The name of the busiest and most central area is **Aberdeen Bazaar**, where you'll find the Superintendent of Police (for permit extensions), the State Bank of India (Mon–Fri 9am–1pm, Sat 9–11am) and most other facilities. Some hotels will change travellers' cheques, but you'll get faster service and better rates at Island Travels (Mon–Sat 9am–6pm; ⓣ03192/233034), just up the road from the clock tower in Aberdeen Bazaar. The ICICI Bank has an **ATM** at the lower end of Moulana Azad Road, and there's a UTI Bank ATM near Netaji Stadium. **Internet** access is available at a number of locations around town, such as CyberNet, west of the bus stand, and Web World, next to the *Dolphin* restaurant.

Local transport and tours

Walking is tiring and time-consuming in hilly Port Blair, making transport preferable. **Taxis** gather opposite the bus stand in central Port Blair. They all have meters, but negotiating the price before leaving is the usual practice. Expect to pay at least Rs80 for a trip from the centre of town to Corbyn's Cove; **auto-rickshaws** try to charge just as much as taxis but a ride within town shouldn't cost more than Rs30.

Local **buses** run from the bus stand frequently to Wandoor and less so to Chiriya Tapu, so they can be used for day-trips. It's pleasant to rent a **motorbike** or **scooter** but there is currently no reliable outlet – try asking at the shops around Aberdeen Bazaar. If you do find one, there are petrol pumps on the crossroads west of the bus stand and on the road towards the airport. Petrol is hard to come by elsewhere.

The A&N Tourism town **tours** are a complete waste of time but their **harbour cruises** (daily 3–5pm; Rs75) are more worthwhile, departing from Phoenix Jetty for fleeting visits to the floating docks and **Viper Island**; there are also excursions to **Ross Island** (daily 8.30am, 10.30am, 12.30pm and 2pm; Rs75). They also run **day-trips** to **Mount Harriet** (8am; from Rs262) and **Wandoor/Mahatma Gandhi National Marine Park**; the bus tour to Wandoor (8am; Rs120) connects with the 10am boat to the islands of Red Skin and Jolly Buoy (see p.934).

Accommodation

Port Blair boasts a fair selection of places to stay and the abundance of options means availability is only an issue around Christmas and New Year, when prices are also hiked; they drop during the monsoon season.

Andaman Teal House Delanipur ⓣ03192/234060. High on the hill above Haddo Jetty, this A&N Tourism place offers great views, spacious and pleasant rooms, and is very good value, although it can be inconvenient without your own transport. Dorm beds Rs150. ❷–❹

Fortune Resort Bay Island Marine Hill ⓣ03192/234101, ⓦwww.fortuneparkhotels.com. Port Blair's swishest hotel is elegant and airy with polished dark wood. All rooms have carpets and balconies overlooking Phoenix Jetty. There's a quality restaurant, gardens and an open-air sea-water swimming pool. Prices for suites with full board reach $165. ❽

Holiday Resort Premnagar, a 15min walk from the centre ⓣ03192/230516, ⓔholidayresort88@hotmail.com. Much better value than most budget places that cost little less; all the rooms are clean and spacious, with TV. There's also a bar and computer room. ❸–❹

Jaimathi Moulana Azad Rd ⓣ03192/230836. The best real budget deal, offering large, fairly clean attached rooms, all with TV and communal balconies. Slightly cheaper than the *Jagannath* next door and more likely to have availability. ❶

Paradise Inn Moulana Azad Rd ⓣ03192/245772, ⓕ233479. Compact modern lodge, where all rooms have TV and phone. Great value and extra off-season discounts. ❸–❹

Peerless Resort Corbyn's Cove ⓣ03192/229263, ⓦwww.peerlesshotels.com. Lovely setting amid gardens of palms, jasmine and bougainvillea and opposite a white sandy beach, but the balconied a/c rooms and cottages are a bit tatty for the prices

Moving on from Port Blair

Port Blair is the departure point for all flights and ferry crossings to the **Indian mainland**; it is also the hub of the Andamans' inter-island bus and ferry network. Booking tickets (especially back to Chennai, Kolkata or Vishakapatnam) can be time-consuming, and many travellers are obliged to come back here well before their permit expires to make reservations, before heading off to more pleasant parts again.

To the mainland

If you're travelling back from the Andamans **by ship**, you can only book your return once on the islands, which invariably requires a trip back to Port Blair. Tickets for all three mainland ports (Chennai, Kolkata and Vishakapatnam) are now handled by the DSS (Ⓣ03192/245555) and go on sale a week in advance of departure at the allotted booths within the Computerized Reservation Centre (Mon–Fri 9am–1pm & 2–4pm and Sat 9am–noon) at Phoenix Jetty. The good news is that, at around Rs1550, the ship offers the cheapest route back. The downside is that schedules can be erratic, and accurate information about them difficult to obtain – keep calling the DSS. When they do go on sale, it's wise to be there to join the fray ahead of time. Make sure you get a ticket before your permit expires, as you will need to show it to get the fifteen-day extension.

Returning to the mainland **by plane** in just two hours instead of 72 is the easier option and most travellers have a return ticket from the mainland. If you have arrived by ship but want to fly back, book as early as possible. Flights at peak times like Diwali, Christmas and New Year through to February can be heavily subscribed. These periods also see prices sometimes reaching an incredible Rs20,000 one way; at other times they can be as low as Rs5000. The Air India/Indian Airlines office (Ⓣ03192/233108) is diagonally opposite the ANIIDCO office, while Jet Airways (Ⓣ03192/236922) is on the first floor at 189 Main Rd, Junglighat, next to the GITO office. Kingfisher can only be booked online or through travel agents such as Island Travels (see p.929).

they charge. There's a bar and mid-priced restaurant with an average evening buffet. ❼–❽

SeaShell Port Blair Marine Hill Ⓣ03192/242773, Ⓦwww.seashellportblair.com. Excellent new hotel, suited for business travellers and tourists alike. Spacious, beautifully furnished and decorated rooms with great showers and flat screen TVs. The more expensive rooms have balconies overlooking the sea. ❼–❽

Shah-N-Shah Mohanpura Ⓣ03192/233696. Conveniently located between the bus stand and Phoenix Jetty, this is basic but friendly and comfortable, with mostly attached rooms and a travel agent. Cheap single occupancy. ❷–❸

Sinclairs Bay View On the coast road to Corbyn's Cove Ⓣ03192/227824, Ⓦwww.sinclairshotels.com. Clifftop hotel offering spotless carpeted rooms with balconies, large bathrooms and dramatic views, as well as a missable bar and restaurant. ❽

TSG Emerald View 25 Moulana Azad Rd Ⓣ03192/246488, Ⓦwww.andamantsghotels.com. Smart mid-range place with a sparkling new lobby and spacious, colourfully furnished a/c rooms, boasting all mod cons. Also has a decent restaurant. ❺–❻

The Town

Port Blair's only firm reminder of its gloomy past, the sturdy brick **Cellular Jail** (Tues–Sun 9am–noon & 2–5pm; Rs10), overlooks the sea from a small rise in the northeast of town. Built between 1896 and 1905, its tiny solitary cells were quite different and far worse than the dormitories in other prison blocks erected earlier. Only three of the seven wings that originally radiated from the central tower now remain. Visitors can peer into the 3x3.5m cells and imagine the grim conditions in which the prisoners lived. Cells were dirty and ill-ventilated, drinking water was

Port Blair has an efficient computerized Southern Railways reservation office near the Secretariat (Mon–Sat 8.30am–1pm & 2–4pm) – useful for travellers intending to catch onward **trains** from their port of arrival on the mainland.

Inter-island services

Buses connect Port Blair with most all the major settlements on Middle and North Andaman via the Andaman Trunk Road. From the mildly chaotic bus-stand in the centre of town, there are two government services to each of **Rangat** (5.45am & 11.45am), **Mayabunder** (5am & 9.45am) and **Diglipur** (4am & 4.30am). Several private companies, including Lord Buddha Travels (just north of the bus stand) and Ananda (☎03192/233252), run deluxe or video coach services to the same destinations; these usually leave from outside the bus stand between 5–10am. Tickets are cheap at Rs100–250.

Most of the islands open to foreign tourists, including **Neill**, **Havelock**, **Middle**, **North** and **Little Andaman**, are also accessible by government-run **boats** from Phoenix Jetty. Details of sailings for the following two to three days are posted in the *Daily Telegrams* newspaper. During peak season you can expect two boats daily to Havelock, one or two daily to Neill, one daily to Little Andaman and four weekly to each of Rangat Bay, Long Island and Aerial Bay (for Diglipur). Boats can get cramped and uncomfortable, sometimes lacking shade outside and space inside; take adequate supplies of food and water, as minimal sustenance is sold onboard. More details of boat services to destinations outside the capital appear in the relevant accounts. The only way to guarantee a passage is to book tickets in advance at the Inter-Island booths in the Computerized Reservation Centre at Phoenix Jetty, though any unsold tickets are issued prior to departure on the quay. You can avoid these scrums by paying an agent, such as Island Travels, to get a ticket for you. **Fares** are very reasonable, even allowing for the two-tier pricing system for islanders and non-islanders: Havelock, for example costs Rs250–350. As of 2010, Havelock has a smart new private catamaran service, the *Makruzz* (daily 8.30am; Rs650; Ⓦwww.makruzz.com).

limited to two glasses per day, and the convicts were expected to wash in the rain as they worked clearing forests and building prison quarters. Food, brought from the mainland, was stored in vats where the rice and pulses became infested with worms; more than half the prison population died long before their twenty years' detention was up. Protests against conditions led to several hunger strikes, and frequent executions took place at the gallows that still stand in squat wooden shelters in the courtyards, in full view of the cells. The **sound-and-light show** (English version Mon, Wed & Fri 6.45pm; Rs20) outlines the history of the prison, and a small **museum** by the entrance gate (same hours as jail) exhibits lists of convicts, photographs and grim torture devices.

About 300m east of the jail near the Water Sports Complex, you can see murky tanks full of fish and coral from the islands' reefs at the **Aquarium** (Tues–Sun except 2nd Sat of each month 9am–1pm & 2–4.45pm; Rs10). Three kilometres out along the coast road towards Corbyn's Cove, Port Blair's newest attraction is the mildly diverting **Science Centre** (Tues–Sun 10am–5.30pm; Rs5), where you can choose to pay an extra Rs2 each to visit the main displays such as the Sky Observatory, Science Magic and other interactive exhibits.

On the south side of the centre, close to the Directorate of Tourism, the **Anthropological Museum** (Fri–Wed 9am–1pm & 1.30–4.30pm; Rs10, camera/mobile Rs20) has exhibits on the Andaman and Nicobar tribes, including weapons, tools and rare photographs of the region's indigenous people taken in the 1960s.

Among the most striking of these is a sequence featuring the Sentinelese, taken on April 26, 1967, when a party of Indian officials made the first contact with the tribe. After scaring the aborigines, the visitors marched into one of their hunting camps and made off with the bows, arrows and other artefacts now displayed in the museum.

Further northwest in Delanipur opposite ANIIDCO's *Teal House* hotel, the **Samudrika Naval Maritime Museum** (Tues–Sun 9am–5.30pm; Rs10) is an excellent primer if you're heading off to more remote islands, with a superlative shell collection and informative displays on various aspects of local marine biology. One of the exhibits features a cross-section of the different corals you can expect to see on the Andamans' reefs, followed by a rundown of the various threats these fragile organisms face, from mangrove depletion and parasitic starfish to clumsy snorkellers.

Eating and drinking

Between them, Port Blair's **restaurants** offer dishes from north and south India and a wide variety of seafood. **Alcohol** is becoming increasingly easy to come by, either in the upscale hotels or a smattering of less salubrious bars such as the one underneath the *Jaimathi* lodge (see p.929).

Adi Bengali Moulana Azad Rd. Clean new place serving tasty Bengali dishes such as *parsha* fish curry, a snip at Rs50. Also does chicken and a range of veg.

Annapurna Cafeteria Aberdeen Bazaar, towards the post office. Port Blair's best south Indian joint, serving a range of huge crispy dosas, plus north Indian and Chinese meals, delicious coffee, and wonderful *pongal* at breakfast. The lunchtime thalis are also great. Mains Rs30–80. Closed Sun.

Dolphin Marthoma Church Complex, Golgha. Pleasantly decorated with cane chairs and blinds, serving carefully prepared Indian and Chinese dishes, as well as some continental options and a few house specialities involving chicken and seafood (around Rs80–100).

Gagan Aberdeen Bazaar, opposite the clock tower. Simple canteen with a decent range of north and south Indian veg and non-veg dishes for around Rs40–80.

Mandalay *Fortune Resort*, Marine Hill. A la carte main courses (Rs200–300) or, when demand allows, a reasonable Rs400 dinner buffet can be enjoyed in the airy open restaurant with great bay views. Service can be a bit lax for its class. The adjacent *Nico Bar* is fine for a drink.

New India Café Moulana Azad Rd. In the basement of *Jaimathi* lodge, this cheap restaurant wins no prizes for decor but bashes out a wide menu of veg and meat dishes (Rs50–100). Expect to wait if you order anything that's not already prepared.

New Lighthouse Near Aberdeen Jetty. Popular place with outdoor seating, where you can catch the sea breeze while feasting on some of the cheapest lobster and other seafood (Rs150–250) in India.

Waves *Peerless Resort*, Corbyn's Cove. Slightly pricey but very congenial alfresco hotel restaurant under a shady palm grove, and one of the few places in town you can order a beer with your meal. Most dishes Rs120–200.

Around Port Blair

At some point, you're almost certain to find yourself killing time in Port Blair, waiting for boats to show up or tickets to go on sale. Rather than wasting days in town, it's worth exploring the **coast** of South Andaman which, although far more densely populated than other islands in the archipelago, holds a handful of easily accessible beauty spots and historic sites. Among the latter, the ruined colonial monuments on **Viper** and **Ross islands** can be reached on daily harbour cruises or regular ferries from the capital. For **beaches**, head southeast to **Corbyn's Cove**, or cross South Andaman to reach the more secluded **Chiriya Tapu**, both of which are easily accessible on day-trips if you rent a vehicle. By far the most rewarding way to spend a day out of town, however, is to catch the tourist boat from **Wandoor** to **Jolly Buoy** or **Red Skin islands** in the **Mahatma Gandhi National Marine Park** opposite, which boasts some of the Andamans' best snorkelling. The other area worth visiting is **Mount Harriet** and **Madhuban** on the central part of South Andaman, north across the bay from Port Blair.

Viper and Ross islands

First stop on the harbour cruise from Port Blair is generally **Viper Island** (entry Rs5), named not after the many snakes that doubtless inhabit its tangled tropical undergrowth, but a nineteenth-century merchant vessel that ran aground on it during the early years of the colony. Lying a short way off Haddo Wharf, it served as an isolation zone for the main prison, where escapees and other convicts were sent to be punished. Whipping posts and crumbling walls, reached from the jetty via a winding brick path, remain as relics of a torture area, while occupying the site's most prominent position are the original gallows.

No less eerie are the decaying colonial remains on **Ross Island** (entry Rs20), at the entrance to Port Blair harbour, where the British sited their first penal settlement in the Andamans. Originally cleared by convicts wearing iron fetters, Ross witnessed some of the most brutal excesses of British colonial history, and was the source of the prison's infamy as **Kalapani**, or Black Water. Of the many convicts transported here, distinguished by their branded foreheads, the majority perished from disease or torture before the clearance of the island was completed in 1860. Thereafter, it served briefly as the site of Rev Henry Corbyn's **Andaman Home** – a prison camp created with the intention of "civilizing" the local tribespeople – and then the headquarters of the revamped penal colony before the British were forced to evacuate by the Japanese entry into WWII. Little more than the hilltop **Anglican church**, with its weed-infested graveyard, has survived the onslaught of tropical creepers and vines. For boat tour details see p.929.

Corbyn's Cove and Chiriya Tapu

The best beach within easy reach of the capital lies 6km southeast at **Corbyn's Cove**, a small arc of smooth white sand backed by a swaying curtain of palms. There's a large hotel here (Peerless Resort; see p.929), but the water isn't particularly clear, and bear in mind that lying around scantily clothed may bring you considerable attention from crowds of local workers.

For more isolation, head 30km south to **Chiriya Tapu** ("Bird Island"), at the tip of South Andaman. The driveable track running beyond this small fishing village leads through thick jungle overhung with twisting creepers to a large bay, where swamps give way to shell-strewn beaches. Other than at lunchtime, when it often receives a deluge of bus parties, the beach offers plenty of peace and quiet, forest walks on the woodcutters' trails winding inland from it and easy access to an inshore reef. However, the water here is nowhere near as clear as at some spots in the archipelago. The village can be used to access **Cinque Island** (see p.942), a couple of hours further south.

Wandoor and the Mahatma Gandhi National Marine Park

Much the most popular excursion from Port Blair is to **WANDOOR**, 30km southwest. The long white **beach** here is littered with the dry, twisted trunks of trees torn up and flung down by annual cyclones. It's fringed not with palms but by dense forest teeming with birdlife. You should only snorkel here at high tide, as the coral is easily damaged when the waters are shallow. You can **stay** in the luxury cottages or rooms of the *Sea Princess Beach Resort* (☎03192/280002,

Ⓦwww.seaprincessbeachresortwandoor.com; ❻–❽), 500m back from the car park, or in the two ramshackle huts of the *Wandoor Paradise Resort* (Ⓣ9434 272135; ❷), right on the beach. Both places have **restaurants**, though the latter's is more of a drinking den.

Most people take a cruise around the fifteen islets comprising the **Mahatma Gandhi National Marine Park**, which boasts one of the richest coral reefs in the region. The downside is that entry into the park for foreigners now costs Rs500 [Rs50]. Boats depart at 10am (daily except Mon; Rs450) from Wandoor, which you can reach on A&N Tourism's **tour** (see p.929) or by local bus. From the jetty, the boats chug through broad creeks lined with dense mangrove swamps and pristine forest to either **Red Skin Island** or, more commonly, **Jolly Buoy**. The latter, an idyllic deserted island, boasts an immaculate shell-sand beach ringed by a bank of superb coral. The catch is that the boat only stops for around an hour, which isn't nearly enough time to explore the shore and reef. While snorkelling off the edges of the reef, beware of **strong currents**.

Mount Harriet and Madhuban

The richly forested slopes of **Mount Harriet** make for some decent exercise and can easily be done as a day-trip from Port Blair. You can take one of the passenger ferries (every 30min) from Chatham Jetty to **Bamboo Flats** or, if you want to have your own transport on the other side, one of the eight daily vehicle ferries from Phoenix Bay, which run between 5.30am and 8.30pm. From Bamboo Flats, it's a pleasant seven-kilometre stroll east along the coast and north up a path through trees hung with thick vines and creepers to the 365m summit, which affords fine views back across the bay. An intermittent bus service runs between Bamboo Flats and Hope Town, where the path starts, and saves you 3km. Alternatively, jeeps and taxis are available to take you all the way to the top, but they charge at least Rs400. There's a charge of Rs250 [Rs25] to enter Mount Harriet National Park, but the checkpost is on the road so you probably won't be asked if you take the path. It's 2.5km from the checkpost up to the resthouse and viewing tower at the summit. If you have strong legs, you can reach **Madhuban** on the coast northeast of the mountain by the sixteen-kilometre round route via Kala Patthar (Black Rock) and back via the coast. There is a decent beach at Madhuban and the area is still used for training logging **elephants**, so you stand a good chance of seeing them learning their trade.

Islands north of Port Blair

The majority of other **islands** your permit allows you to visit are north of Port Blair. It's surprising how many visitors make a beeline for the only two developed islands in the group, **Neill** and **Havelock**, both within easy reach of Port Blair. An enterprising minority then catch a ferry on to barely developed **Long Island**. To get further north, where tourism has also had very little impact so far, you can take a bus along the infamous **Andaman Trunk Road** (ATR) to ramshackle **Rangat** or **Mayabunder**, at the southern and northern ends of **Middle Andaman**, respectively, or direct to **Diglipur**, at the top of **North Andaman**. Alternatively, there are ferries to Rangat Bay and Arial Bay, the port of Diglipur. For connections between these islands and Port Blair see p.930; local transport is covered in the respective accounts.

Neill

Tiny, triangular-shaped **Neill** is the most southerly inhabited island of **Ritchie's Archipelago**, barely two hours northeast of Port Blair on a fast ferry. The source of much of the capital's fresh fruit and vegetables, its fertile centre, ringed by a curtain of stately tropical trees, comprises vivid patches of green paddy dotted with small farmsteads and banana plantations. The beaches are mediocre by the Andamans' standards, but worth a day or two en route to or from Havelock.

Neill boasts three **beaches**, all of them within easy cycling distance of the small bazaar just up the lane from the jetty; you can rent **bicycles** from one of several stallholders for Rs50 per day. The best place to swim is **Neill Kendra**, a gently curving bay of white sand on the north coast which straddles the jetty and is scattered with picturesque wooden fishing boats. This blends into **Lakshmangar**, which continues for nearly 3km west: to get here by road, head right at the *Hawabil Nest* (see below) and follow the road for around twenty minutes until it dwindles into a surfaced track, then turn right. Wrapped around the headland, the beach is a broad spur of white-shell sand, with shallow water offering good snorkelling but that makes entry into the water tough at any time other than high tide. Exposed to the open sea and thus prone to higher tides, **Sitapur** beach, 6km southeast, is also appealing and has the advantage of a sandy bottom extending into the sea. The ride there (by hourly bus or bicycle) across Neill's central paddy land is pleasant, but there are no facilities – at least until the new venture by the owners of *Wild Orchid* on Havelock (see p.938) opens.

Accommodation and eating

Neill only has five **places to stay**. Although many people stick to the **restaurants** at their beach huts, far and away the best place to eat is the delightful and welcoming *Gyan Garden*, 500m along the main road west opposite the football pitch, where fresh fish and home-grown veg dishes are a speciality. *Green Heaven*, 1.5km north of the bazaar, serves spicy Indian plus some Chinese and Western dishes in another garden setting. Of the few tiny *dhabas* in the bazaar, *Hotel Chand* serves up the tastiest, albeit somewhat oily, food.

A-N-D Beach Resort 250m east of the jetty, Neill Kendra ⓣ9474 238770. Tucked along the path behind the beach, this friendly place has some very cheap huts with common bathrooms and a few attached ones, as well as a decent restaurant. ❶–❷

Cocon Huts 600m west of the jetty, Neill Kendra ⓣ03192/282528, ⓔsrikudvt@yahoo.com. Choose between small huts with common facilities and roomier attached cottages. The bar at the back is the island's main boozer. ❶–❸

Hawabil Nest 200m inland from the jetty ⓣ03192/282630, ⓦwww.and.nic.in. A&N Tourism's hotel has a dozen a/c rooms with sitouts, ranged around a central courtyard, a couple of dorms (Rs150) and a standard restaurant; best booked in advance from Port Blair. ❹

Pearl Park Hotel Nearly 3km north of the jetty, Lakshmangar ⓣ03192/282510, ⓦwww.andamanpearlpark.com. Huts here vary in size but are all attached. There are also posher but overpriced a/c bungalows and traditional round, thatched Nicobari cottages. ❷–❺

Tango Beach Resort Nearly 2km north of the jetty, Lakshmangar ⓣ03192/282634, ⓔtangobeachresort@rediffmail.com. This friendly place right on the beach offers a range of accommodation from basic bamboo huts with shared bathrooms to some spacious concrete rooms. It also has the best resort restaurant. ❶–❹

Havelock

Havelock is the largest island in Ritchie's Archipelago, and the most intensively cultivated, settled – like many in the region – by Bengali refugees after Partition. Thanks to its regular ferry connections with the capital, it is also visited in greater numbers than anywhere else in the Andamans. In recent peak

Scuba diving in the Andaman Islands

The seas around the Andaman islands are some of the world's most unspoiled. Marine life is abundant, with an estimated 750 species of fish existing on one reef alone, and parrot, trigger and angel fish living alongside manta rays, reef sharks and loggerhead turtles. Many species of fish and coral are unique to the area, and fascinating ecosystems exist in ash beds and cooled lava based around the volcanic Barren Island. For a quick taste of marine life, you could start by **snorkelling**; most hotels can supply masks and snorkels, though some equipment is in dire need of replacement. The only way to get really close, and venture out into deeper waters, is to **scuba dive**.

The undisputed home of **diving** is Havelock, with seven centres up and running at the last count, but there's already one small operation on Neill as well. The premier dive centres are **Andaman Bubbles** (ⓣ03192/282140, ⓦwww.andamanbubbles.com), next to partners *Wild Orchid* on Beach #5, and **Barefoot Scuba Dive Resort** (ⓣ9566 063120, ⓦwww.barefootindia.com) on Beach #3; both offer excellent equipment, nitrox diving and mainly Western instructors. Andaman Bubbles should also be operating on Neill by the time you read this and Barefoot have plans for Long Island and South Andaman. Two other PADI-certified centres are **Dive India** (ⓣ0319 2214247, ⓦwww.diveindia.com), based at *Island Vinnie's* on Beach #5, and **Ocean Pearl** (ⓣ03192/282228, ⓦwww.dive-andaman.com, a relative newcomer up at Beach #2. The aforementioned centre on Neill is India Scuba Explorers (ⓣ9474 238646, ⓦwww.indiascubaexplorers.com) at Neill Kendra.

Prices are very similar at all the centres, with dives for those already certified running around Rs2000 for one tank, Rs3500 for two; more economical packages, often including accommodation and food, are available for multiple dives, while Discover Scuba introductory days go for Rs4000–5000. **Courses** cost about Rs18,000 for a basic four-day PADI open-water qualification, Rs13,500 for advanced or Rs45,000 to go all the way up to Divemaster, including all the tanks.

Underwater, it's not uncommon to come across schools of reef shark, which rarely turn hostile, but one thing to watch out for and avoid is the **black-and-white sea snake**. Though these seldom attack – and, since their fangs are at the back of their mouths, would find it difficult to get a grip on any human – their bite is twenty times deadlier than that of the cobra.

Increased tourism inevitably puts pressure on the delicate marine ecosystem, and poorly funded wildlife organizations can do little to prevent damage from insensitive visitors. Ensure your presence in the sea around the reefs does not harm the coral by observing the following **Green Coral Code** while diving or snorkelling:

- Never touch or walk on living coral, or it will die.
- Try to keep your feet away from reefs while wearing fins; the sudden sweep of water caused by a flipper kick can be enough to destroy coral.
- Always control the speed of your descent while diving; enormous damage can be caused by divers landing hard on a coral bed.
- Never break off pieces of coral from a reef, and remember that it is illegal to export dead coral from the islands, even fragments you may have found on a beach.

seasons, as many as five hundred tourists can be holed up here at one time, which has led to an explosion in accommodation and the opening of the first tourist shops.

Arrival, information and island transport

Havelock's **main jetty** is on the north side of the island, at the village known as **Beach #1**. After registering with the police as you disembark, it's best to make your own way to where you plan to stay, though if you've booked in advance, most places arrange a pick-up. There's a small and moderately helpful tourist office (daily 8am–5pm; ⓣ9474 222245) just outside the jetty gates and to the right the Seacology Centre (no fixed hours; ⓣ9476 029725, ⓦwww.wildandamans.com) has some interesting displays on the marine environment but is basically a front for selling Barefoot Adventures activities.

The only place to **change money** is the State Co-operative Bank (Mon–Fri 9am–1pm, Sat 9–11am), at the main bazaar, 2km inland of the main jetty, although there are now two ATMs en route. **Internet** access is available at the ticklishly named Anus Internet in the bazaar, the shop on the corner near *Dolphin Resort* (see below) and a number of the guesthouses; the going rate is Rs80 per hour for a dial-up connection, while the couple of places with satellite broadband charge an exorbitant Rs300.

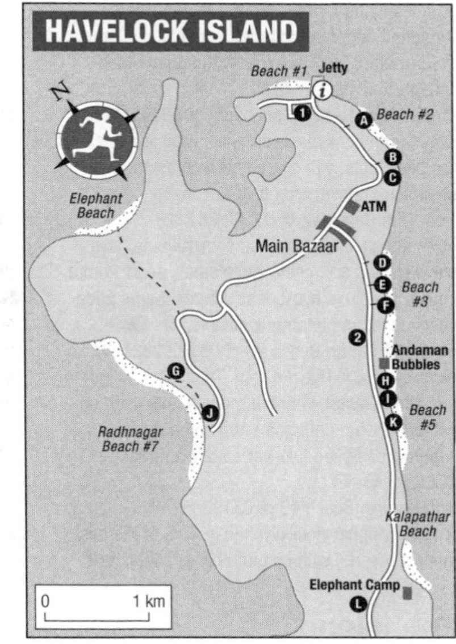

ACCOMMODATION	
Barefoot at Havelock	G
Barefoot Scuba Dive Resort	D
Dolphin Resort	I
Dreamland Resort	J
Eco Villa	B
Emerald Gecko	K
Holiday Inn	E
Island Vinnie's	F
Ocean Pearl	C
Pooja Paradise	L
SeaShell Havelock	A
Wild Orchid	H

RESTAURANTS	
Anju-coco	2
Barefoot Bar & Brasserie	1
Blackbeard's Bistro	K
Café del Mar	D
Full Moon Café	F
Nala's Kingdom	1
Red Snapper	H

Buses run hourly from 6.30am to **Radhnagar** (aka Beach #7), the last returning at 6pm, but only twice a day (6am & 1.30pm) down the east coast, where the bulk of the accommodation is located, to Kalapathar. Instead, you can take a Rs30–50 auto-rickshaw ride or rent a **scooter**, **motorbike** (around Rs250/day) or **cycle** (Rs50/day).

Accommodation

As the only fully developed tourist scene in the Andamans, Havelock now has well over thirty accommodation establishments to choose from, offering everything from the most basic unlockable **huts** to luxuriously furnished **cottages**. Price codes here indicate rates through most of the season. They can rise by fifty percent from mid-December to mid-January, and drop considerably between May and October.

Barefoot at Havelock Radhnagar ⓣ03192/220191, ⓦwww.barefoot-andaman.com. Havelock's most luxurious resort, with fan-cooled duplexes, "Nicobari" cottages, and a/c "Andaman" villas. Most of these, the excellent Italian-run restaurant and the new bar area are attractive timber and thatch structures. ❽–❾

Barefoot Scuba Dive Resort Beach #3 ⓣ03192/282343, ⓦwww.barefootindia.com. The home of Barefoot's dive centre offers a wide choice from small huts, through cabins and tents to smart bamboo duplexes with attached bathrooms. ❶–❼

Dolphin Resort Beach #5 ⓣ03192/282411, ⓦwww.and.nic.in. A&N Tourism's smartest resort is still lacking in atmosphere, though the detached concrete cottages are spacious and comfortable. More popular with Indians than foreign tourists. 4–6

Dreamland Resort Radhnagar T 03192/282120. Only 200m back along the main road, it comprises ten basic huts with shared bathrooms, the only cheapies at Havelock's best beach. 1

Eco Villa Beach #2 T 03192/282212, E andamanecovilla@yahoo.com. All huts have showers and are mostly quite small, apart from a couple of deluxe two-tier structures. Same price year-round, and internet available. 2–6

Emerald Gecko Beach #5 T 03192/282170, W www.emerald-gecko.com. The nicest budget to mid-range resort, with ten modest huts (with or without private bathroom) and half a dozen superbly designed two-tier cottages. Breakfast included. 3–6

Holiday Inn Beach #3 T 03192/282061, E holidayinnhavelock@yahoo.in. One of the best modest resorts, with comfortable attached huts and more spacious chalets. No relation to the US chain. 2–6

Island Vinnie's Beach #3 T 03192/282187, W www.islandvinnie.com. Spacious and beautifully constructed Rajasthani tents, some with attached bathrooms, as well as more humble huts and cabins. 2–5

Pooja Paradise Kalapathar T 9474 210549. The most remote place to stay on the island, with a mixture of simple huts and cement cottages. You'll definitely need your own transport to get here. 1–3

SeaShell Havelock Beach #2 T 03192/211830, W www.seashellhavelock.com. Arranged around a manicured lawn, the two dozen or so sturdy and spacious a/c chalets include all mod cons such as flat-screen TVs. 7

Wild Orchid Beach #5 T 03192/282472, W www.wildorchidandaman.com. Easily the best value higher-end resort, for its classy cottages (some with a/c), splendidly constructed timber restaurant and lounge, and all round laidback atmosphere. 7

The island

Havelock's hub of activity is not the jetty village, which just has a few stalls, a couple of dowdy lodges, the odd restaurant and the police station, but the **Main Bazaar**, which you come to if you follow the road straight ahead from the jetty for two kilometres, passing Beach #2 on the way. Here you'll find a greater variety of shops and places to eat, the only bank and the island's main junction. The right turn leads nine kilometres through paddy fields and other crops before dropping through some spectacular woodland to **Radhnagar** (Beach #7), a two-kilometre-long arc of perfect white sand, backed by stands of giant *mowhar* trees and often touted as the most beautiful in India. The water is a sublime turquoise colour and, although the coral is sparse, marine life here is diverse and plentiful, especially among the rocks around the corner from the main beach (accessible at low tide). The main drawback, which can make sunbathing uncomfortable, is a preponderance of pesky sandflies.

As the nesting site for a colony of Olive Ridley **turtles** (see p.885), Radhnagar is strictly protected by the Forest Department, whose wardens ensure tourists don't light fires or sleep on the beach. There's not much accommodation here but a clutch of *dhaba*s provides ample sustenance for day-trippers. A couple of kilometres before the road descends to Radhnagar, a path on the right leads over a hill and down through some scattered settlements to far wilder **Elephant Beach**, although the only trunks you are likely to spot are those of huge fallen trees. Snorkelling here is good, and coral reefs are accessible from the shore, but it can be tough to find the way unless somebody takes you; look out for the start of the path at a sharp bend in the road with a Forest Department noticeboard in a small clearing, and then keep asking the way whenever you see a local.

If you take the left turn through the busier strip of Main Bazaar, the road leads on past beaches #3 and #5, where most of the beach huts and resorts are located. As on Neill's north coast, these east-facing beaches, though exquisitely scenic, have fairly thin strips of golden-white sand, and when the sea recedes across the lumps of broken coral and rock lying offshore, swimming becomes all but impossible. After Beach #5 the road continues south for several kilometres before turning slightly inland and eventually petering out at **Kalapathar** beach. Here you can visit the Forest Department's elephant training camp, although the sight of the gentle giants being rather ferociously whacked with heavy sticks is hardly an edifying one. The entire southern half of Havelock consists of impenetrable forest.

Eating and drinking

Western travellers' favourites and bland curries are widely available at all the beach hut cafés, but if you want authentic (mainly Bengali) food, then it's better to head for a local restaurant in one of the settlements. **Beer** and basic spirits are sold at most travellers' haunts but are not cheap.

Anju-coco Beach #5. The best of the small crop of independent roadside restaurants. Serves filling Rs50 breakfasts, cheap fish'n'chips, Tibetan *momos* and some more adventurous dishes for Rs150.

Barefoot Bar & Brasserie Main jetty. Smart upper-storey wooden deck with film posters and expensive food such as bruschetta and canapes. Most mains around Rs300 and seafood sizzlers up to Rs800.

Blackbeard's Bistro *Emerald Gecko*, Beach #5. The lovely open dining area has a bar and furniture created from recycled timber, and offers rare dishes such as ceviche as well as fresh fish cooked in delicious and imaginative sauces for Rs150–250. There is also a stage for occasional live shows.

Café del Mar *Barefoot Scuba Dive Resort*, Beach #3. Convivial joint serving a mixture of Indian, Chinese, Western and seafood.

Full Moon Café *Island Vinnie's*, Beach #3. Wide menu, including some genuinely spicy Indian cuisine, as well as Western favourites and fresh seafood, mostly Rs100–150.

Nala's Kingdom Main jetty. The most salubrious place in the jetty area, serving Indian, Chinese and fish dishes for Rs50–100. Great thalis.

Red Snapper *Wild Orchid*, Beach #5. Excellent upmarket seafood, meat and veg menu, served in quality surroundings. Most dinners are in the Rs250–400 range. Regular recitals of traditional Bengali music.

Long Island

Just off the southeast coast of Middle Andaman, **Long Island** is gradually attracting a steadier trickle of travellers. Served by four boats per week from the capital and Rangat, plus two daily launches from Yeratta (9am & 4pm), it boasts a couple of excellent beaches, at **Marg Bay** and **Lalaji Bay**. Both are most easily approached by chartering a fisherman's dinghy from the jetty (around Rs500 each way), although Lalaji can be reached on foot by following the red arrows across the island and then turning left along the coast. You should not attempt this at high tide, and even when the sea is out it's quite an obstacle course of rocks and fallen trees.

The main settlement by the jetty has the island's only facilities, which amount to a handful of shops, a couple of basic *dhabas*, of which *Vasanti* is best for its Rs35 "meals", and the only two **places to stay**. Some people see if there is any availability at the Forest Office's guesthouse near the jetty (Ⓣ03192/278532; ❷) but most follow the blue arrows for fifteen minutes to *Blue Planet* (Ⓣ03192/278573; ❶–❹), which has around a dozen adjoining rooms of varying sizes, arranged compactly around the courtyard restaurant whose centrepiece is a giant *mowhar* tree. There's a jointly run campsite nearby and a decent stretch of beach only five minutes' walk away across the overgrown remains of the former plywood mill.

Middle Andaman

For most travellers, **Middle Andaman** is a charmless rite of passage to be endured en route to or from the north. The sinuous Andaman Trunk Road, hemmed in by walls of towering forest, winds through miles of jungle, crossing the strait that separates the island from its neighbour, Baratang, by means of rusting flat-bottomed ferry. The island's frontier feeling is heightened by the the knowledge that the impenetrable forests west of the ATR comprise the **Jarawa Tribal Reserve** (see p.926). Of its two main settlements, the more northerly **Mayabunder**, the port for alluring **Interview Island**, is slightly more appealing than characterless inland **Rangat** because of its pleasant setting by the sea, but neither town gives any reason to dally.

Rangat and around

At the southeast corner of Middle Andaman, **RANGAT** consists of a ramshackle sprawl around two rows of chai shops and general stores divided by the ATR. However, as a major staging-post on the journey north, it's impossible to avoid – just don't get stranded here if you can help it.

The four weekly **ferries** from Port Blair via Havelock and Long Island dock at **Rangat Bay**, 8km east; there are also two daily launches to Long Island from nearby **Yeratta**. In addition, Rangat is served by two daily government buses to Port Blair (6–7hr) as well as some private services, which pass through in the morning en route from further north.

The Andaman Public Works Department (APWD) *Rest House* (Ⓣ03192/274237; ❷–❹), pleasantly situated up a winding hill from the bazaar with views across the valley, is the best place to stay and eat, providing good, filling fish thalis. The newish *RK Lodge* (Ⓣ03192/274237; ❷), just off the main road, is a decent fall-back. The best places to eat are the *Hotel MK*, on the main road, which serves basic Indian and Chinese food; and the *Hotel Star*, on a nearby alley leading to the small market square, for Indian veg and non-veg.

An alternative base is 15km north at **Cuthbert Bay** (aka RRO), where you can stay at the characterless but comfortable A&N Tourism **hotel**, *Hawksbill Nest* (Ⓣ03192/279159; ❷–❹), which is invariably empty. If you have an early ferry out of Rangat Bay, it's better to stay down near the jetty at the friendly *Sea Shore Lodge* (Ⓣ03192/274464; ❷). Basic meals can be had from the motley conglomeration of stalls between the lodge and the jetty.

Mayabunder

Only 70km further north by road, **MAYABUNDER** is perched on a long promontory right at the top of the island and surrounded by mangrove swamps. Unfortunately, the bus journey from Rangat often exceeds three hours due to continual stops on the surprisingly populated route. Home to a large minority of former Burmese **Karen** tribal people who were originally brought here as cheap logging labour by the British, the village is more spread out and more appealing than Rangat. At the brow of the hill, before it descends to the jetty, a small hexagonal wooden structure houses the **Forest Museum** (Mon–Sat 8am–noon & 1–4pm; free), which holds a motley collection of turtle shells, snakes in formaldehyde, dead coral and a crocodile skull.

Next door to the museum, the APWD *Rest House* (Ⓣ03192/273211; ❷–❹) is large and very comfortable, with a pleasant garden and gazebo overlooking the sea, and a dining room serving good set meals. The only other reasonable **accommodation** nearby is back in the centre of the bazaar at the *Anmol Lodge* (Ⓣ03192/262695; ❶–❹), where some of the attached rooms have TV and a couple are a/c. Further afield at **Karmateng beach**, 14km southeast, there's another A&N Tourism hotel, the *Swiftlet Nest* (Ⓣ03192/273495; ❸–❹) but nothing else. Two buses are supposed to go there daily, failing which there are taxis or auto-rickshaws. Buses from Port Blair now continue over the new bridge to Diglipur on North Andaman at least twice a day. Heading towards the capital, there are a couple of private services, such as Lord Buddha Travels, as well as one government bus, all departing very early in the morning.

Interview Island

Mayabunder is the jumping-off place for **Interview Island**, a windswept nature sanctuary off the remote northwest coast of Middle Andaman – if you've come to the Andamans to watch **wildlife**, it should be top of your list. Large and mainly flat, it is completely uninhabited save for a handful of unfortunate forest wardens, coastguards and policemen, posted here to ward off poachers. Foreigners aren't permitted to spend the night on the island, and to do a day-trip you must first obtain permission from the Forest Museum in Mayabunder (see opposite). The only way to reach Interview is to charter a private fishing dinghy from Mayabunder jetty for around Rs3000–4000. Arrange one the day before and leave at first light. Ask your boatman to moor by the **beach** at the southern tip of the island, which has a perennial freshwater pool inside a low cave; legend has it that the well, a nesting site for white-bellied **swifts**, has no bottom. At the forest post, where you have to sign an entry ledger, ask the wardens about the movements of Interview's feral **elephants**, descendants of trained elephants deserted here by a Kolkata-based logging company after its timber operation failed in the 1950s. **Saltwater crocodiles** are found on the island's eastern coastline.

North Andaman

Shrouded in dense jungle, **North Andaman** is the least populated of the region's large islands, crossed by a single road linking its scattered Bengali settlements. Although parts have been seriously logged, the total absence of driveable roads into northern and western areas has ensured blanket protection for a vast stretch of convoluted coastline, running from Austin Strait in the southeast to the northern tip, Cape Price; it's reassuring to know at least one extensive wilderness survives in the Andamans. Despite the completion of the ATR's final section and the bridge from Middle Andaman, the main settlement of **Diglipur** and its nearby port of **Aerial Bay** continue to exist in relative seclusion.

Diglipur, Aerial Bay and around

Known in the British era as Port Cornwallis, **DIGLIPUR**, North Andaman's largest settlement, is another disappointing market where you're only likely to pause long enough to pick up a local bus further north to the coast. On the hill above the main road, the APWD *Rest House* (Ⓣ03192/272203; ❸–❹) offers the village's nicest **accommodation**, although the *Maa Yashoda Lodge* on the main street (Ⓣ03192/272258; ❷) is a cheaper alternative. Reasonable veg and non-veg food can be found at the central *Ganga Devi* **restaurant**, while *Ice Cube*, on the road north, serves Chinese and tandoori cuisine. Preferably, head 9km on to **AERIAL BAY**, where a smaller APWD *Rest House* (Ⓣ03192/271230; ❸–❹) stands on a hillock overlooking the settlement's tiny bazaar. The best place to while away time with a snack or beer while waiting for a boat is the Annu general store. From Aerial Bay, the **boat** that has made its way up from the capital returns direct to Port Blair overnight.

Better still, continue another 9km to **Kalipur**, served by several daily buses, where the ANIIDCO *Turtle Resort* (Ⓣ03192/272553; ❷–❹), occupies a perfect spot on a hilltop with superb views inland and to the sea. It's an unfeasibly large hotel for such a remote location, with spacious, clean rooms with fans and a restaurant. Their only competition is the bamboo huts of the *Pristine Jungle Resort* (Ⓣ03192/271793; ❶–❹), on the opposite side of the road below. Only five minutes' walk from the *Turtle* down the path by the sharp bend in the road there's an excellent deserted beach, backed by lush forest and covered in photogenic driftwood. Swimming is best at high tide because the water recedes across rocky mudpools.

Locals claim it's possible to walk from Kalipur to **Saddle Peak**, the highest mountain in the Andamans at 737m, which rises dramatically to the south, swathed in lush jungle. Permission to make the three- to four-hour climb must be obtained from the Range Officer at the forest checkpost near the start of the ascent, but don't attempt it without a guide and plenty of drinking water.

Many tourists find their way up here in order to explore the various **islands** dotted around the gulf north of Aerial Bay, particularly **Smith** and **Ross** (not to be confused with its namesake near Port Blair), whose white sandbars, coral reefs and flora are splendid. You can organise the requisite Rs500 permit and a boat (Rs500–700) for the return trip through the area guesthouses. At the time of writing, Smith was slated soon to be added to the list of places where you can overnight, as a luxury resort was being planned.

Other islands

The remaining islands open to foreign tourists in the Andaman group are all hard to get to and, with the exception of **Little Andaman**, where a vestigial population of Onge tribespeople (see p.927) have survived a massive influx of Indian Tamils and native Nicobar, uninhabited. Two hours' boat ride south of Chiriya Tapu on South Andaman, **Cinque Island** offers superlative diving.

Cinque Island

Cinque actually comprises two islets, joined by a spectacular sand isthmus with shallow water either side that covers it completely at high tide. The main incentive to come here is the superb diving and snorkelling around the reefs. However, heaps of dead coral on the beach attest to damage wreaked by the Indian navy during the construction of the swish "cottages" overlooking the beach. Rumour has it that these were built for the visit of a Thai VIP in 1996, but local government officials now use them as bolt holes from Port Blair.

Although there are no **ferries** to Cinque, it is possible to arrange dinghies for around Rs1000 per day from Chiriya Tapu village on the mainland (see p.933). Currently, overnight stays are prohibited.

Little Andaman

Little Andaman is the furthest point south in the archipelago that foreigners can travel to on their tourist permit. Most of the island has been set aside as a tribal reserve for the **Onge** and is thus off-limits. It was also the only island open to foreigners to sustain extensive damage in the 2004 **tsunami**, but although a number of buildings were destroyed, and sixty-four people died, Little Andaman has recovered well. Very few tourists ever make it down here, however. Daily boats from Port Blair arrive at **Hut Bay**, the faster ones making the voyage in under six hours. The main settlement, **INDIRA BAZAAR**, is two kilometres north. Of the few **places to stay** here, the best is the two-storey *Sealand Tourist Home* (Ⓣ03192/284306; ❶), whose splendid bayfront location is only marred by the fact that the architect inexplicably put all the windows facing the interior. Just a little further along, the *Vvet Guest House* (Ⓣ03192/284155; ❷) has simple rooms that cost a little more but are no better, although the small garden is pleasant enough to relax in. Basic **meals** are available at food-only hotels such as the *Snehu* and *AG Bengali*, while the *Kurinchi Parotta Stall* offers tasty savoury and sweet snacks. Bicycles can be rented for Rs50 per day from a stall between the two guest-houses, but are in very short supply.

Hut Bay curves gradually round in a majestic eight-kilometre sweep, and the quality of the sand and beauty of the adjacent jungle increase the further you go. The top stretch is named **Netaji Nagar** after the village on the island's only road, which runs behind it. There's the odd stall and one new resort, *Blue View* (Ⓣ9734 480842; ❶–❷), which has a few huts and a seafood restaurant. En route, you can detour a kilometre inland at the huge signpost about 2.5km north of Indira Bazaar to see the **White Surf Waterfalls** (daily dawn to dusk; Rs20). Made up of three 10- to 15m-high cascades, it's a relaxing spot; you can clamber into the right-hand fall for a soothing shower – yet crocodiles are said to inhabit the surrounding streams. Short elephant rides are available for Rs50 per person at the entrance to the falls. Over the headland at the top of Hut Bay, twelve or so kilometres from the jetty, lies the smaller but equally picturesque crescent of **Butler Bay**. There's not much to do here but swim, sunbathe or look around the slightly eerie remains of the government beach resort, which was swept away by the tsunami – that is unless you've brought your surfboard with you: Little Andaman has a cult reputation among surfers for having some of the best conditions anywhere in South Asia.

20

Tamil Nadu

* **Mamallapuram** Stone-carvers' workshops, a long sandy beach and a wonderful Pallava monuments have made this a top tourist attraction. See p.960

* **Puducherry** Former French colony that has retained the ambience of a Gallic seaside town: croissants, a promenade and gendarmes wearing *képis*. See p.973

* **Thanjavur** Home to some of the world's finest Chola bronzes, this town is dominated by the colossal tower of the Brihadishwara Temple. See p.986

* **Madurai** The love nest of Shiva and his consort Meenakshi, this busy city's major temple hosts a constant round of festivals. See p.996

* **Kanyakumari** The sacred meeting-point of the Bay of Bengal, Indian Ocean and Arabian Sea, at the southern tip of the Subcontinent. See p.1006

* **The Ghats** The spine of southern India, great for trekking through lush mountains and tea plantations from its refreshingly cool hill-stations. See p.1008

* **Mudumalai Wildlife Sanctuary** This densely forested park is becoming increasingly popular for its wild elephants and great accommodation. See p.1020

▲ Brihadishwara Temple, Thanjavur

When Indians refer to "the South", it's usually **TAMIL NADU** they're talking about. While Karnataka and Andhra Pradesh are essentially cultural transition zones buffering the Hindi-speaking north, and Kerala and Goa maintain their own distinctively idiosyncratic identities, the peninsula's massive Tamil-speaking state is India's Dravidian Hindu heartland. Traditionally protected by distance and the military might of the southern Deccan kingdoms, the region has, over the centuries, been less exposed to northern influences than its neighbours. As a result, the three powerful dynasties dominating the south – the Cholas, the Pallavas and the Pandyans – were able, over a period of more than a thousand years, to develop their own unique religious and political institutions, largely unmolested by marauding Muslims. The most visible legacy of this protracted cultural flowering is a crop of astounding **temples**, whose gigantic gateway towers, or *gopuras*, still soar above just about every town. It is the image of these colossal wedge-shaped pyramids, high above the canopy of dense palm forests, or against patchworks of vibrant green paddy fields, which Edward Lear described as "stupendous and beyond belief". Indeed, the garishly painted deities and mythological creatures sculpted onto the towers linger long in the memory of most travellers.

The great Tamil temples, however, are merely the largest landmarks in a vast network of **sacred sites** – shrines, bathing places, holy trees, rocks and rivers – interconnected by a web of ancient pilgrims' routes. Tamil Nadu harbours 274 of India's holiest Shiva temples, and 108 are dedicated to Vishnu. In addition, five shrines devoted to the five Vedic elements (Earth, Wind, Fire, Water and Ether) are to be found here, along with eight to the planets, as well as other places revered by Christians and Muslims. Scattered from the pale orange crags and forests of the Western Ghats, across the fertile deltas of the **Vaigai** and **Kaveri** rivers to the Coromandel coast on the Bay of Bengal, these sites were celebrated in the hymns of the Tamil saints, composed between one and two thousand years ago. Today, so little has changed that the same devotional songs are still widely sung and understood in the region and it remains one of the last places in the world where a classical culture has survived well into the present.

The Tamils' living connection with their ancient Dravidian past has given rise to a strong **nationalist movement**. With a few fleeting lapses, one or other of the pro-Dravidian parties has been in power here since the 1950s, spreading their anti-brahmin, anti-Hindi proletarian message to the masses principally through the medium of movies. Indeed, since Independence, the majority of Tamil Nadu's political leaders have been drawn from the state's prolific **cinema** industry.

Despite its seafront fort, grand mansions and excellence as a centre for the performing arts, the state capital **Chennai** is a hot, chaotic, noisy Indian metropolis that still carries faint echoes of the Raj. However, it is a good base for visiting **Kanchipuram**, a major pilgrimage and sari-weaving centre, filled with reminders of an illustrious past.

Much the best place to start a temple tour is nearby in **Mamallapuram**, a seaside village that – quite apart from some exquisite Pallava rock-cut architecture – boasts a long and lovely beach. Further down the coast lies the one-time French colony of **Puducherry**, now home to the famous Sri Aurobindo ashram; nearby, **Auroville** has carved a role as a popular New Age centre. The road south from Puducherry puts you back on the temple trail, leading to the tenth-century Chola kingdom and the extraordinary architecture of **Chidambaram**, **Gangaikondacholapuram**, **Kumbakonam** and **Darasuram**. For the best Chola bronzes, however, and a glimpse of the magnificent paintings that flourished under Maratha rajas in the eighteenth century, travellers should head for **Thanjavur**. Chola capital for four centuries, the city boasts almost a hundred temples and was the birthplace of Bharatanatyam dance, famous throughout Tamil Nadu.

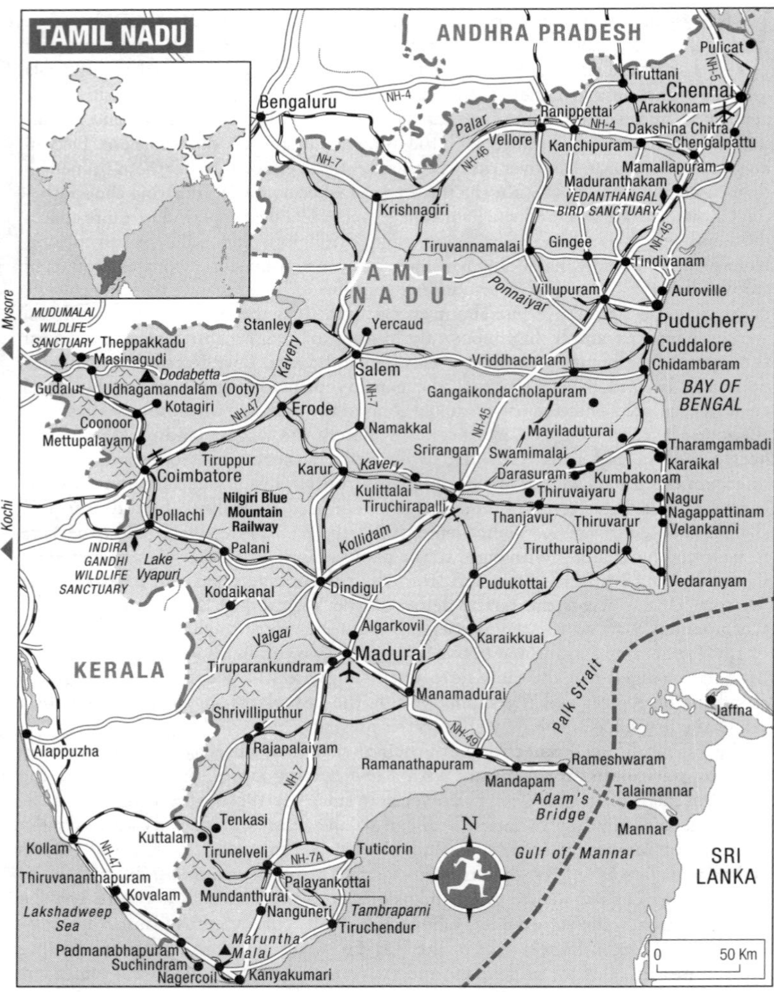

In the very centre of Tamil Nadu, **Tiruchirapalli**, a commercial town just northwest of Thanjavur, held some interest for the Cholas, but reached its heyday under later dynasties, when the temple complex in neighbouring **Srirangam** became one of south India's largest. Among its patrons were the Nayaks of **Madurai**, whose erstwhile capital further south, bustling with pilgrims, priests, peddlers, tailors and tourists, is an unforgettable destination. **Rameshwaram**, on the long spit of land reaching towards Sri Lanka, and **Kanyakumari** at India's southern tip are both important pilgrimage centres, and have the added attraction of welcome cool breezes and vistas over the sea.

While Tamil Nadu's temples are undeniably its major attraction, the hill-stations of **Kodaikanal** and **Udhagamandalam** (**Ooty**) in the west of the state are popular destinations on the well-beaten tourist trail between Kerala and Tamil Nadu. The verdant, cool hills offer mountain views and gentle trails through the forests and tea and coffee plantations. You can also spot wildlife in the teak forests of **Mudumalai Wildlife Sanctuary** and bamboo groves of **Indira Gandhi Wildlife Sanctuary**, situated in the Palani Hills.

Visiting Tamil Nadu

Temperatures in Tamil Nadu, which usually hover around 30°C, peak in May and June, when they often soar above 40°C away from the coast. The state is barely affected by the southwest monsoon that pounds much of India from June to September: it receives most of its **rain** between October and December, when the odd cyclone may well make an appearance. The cooler, rainy days, however, bring their own problems: large-scale flooding can disrupt road and rail links and imbue everything with an all-pervasive dampness.

Accommodation throughout the state is good and plentiful; all but the smallest towns and villages have something for every budget. Most hotels have their own dining halls that, together with local restaurants, usually serve sumptuous and unlimited thalis (known here simply as "meals"), tinged with tamarind and presented on banana leaves. **Indigenous dishes** are almost exclusively vegetarian; for north Indian or Western alternatives, head for the larger hotels or more upmarket city restaurants.

Some history

Since the fourth century BC, Tamil Nadu has been shaped by its majority **Dravidian** population, a people of uncertain origins and physically quite different from north Indians. The influence of the powerful *janapada*s, established in the north by the fourth and third centuries BC, extended as far south as the Deccan, but they made few incursions into **Dravidadesa** (Tamil country). Incorporating what is now Kerala and Tamil Nadu, it was ruled by three dynasties: the **Cheras**, who held sway over much of the Malabar coast (Kerala), the **Pandyas** in the far south, and the **Cholas**, whose realm stretched along the eastern Coromandel coast.

In the fourth century, the **Pallava** dynasty established a powerful kingdom centred in **Kanchipuram**. By the seventh century, the successors of the first Pallava king, Simhavishnu, were engaged in battles with the southern Pandyas and the forces of the Chalukyas, based further west in Karnataka. This was also an era of social development. **Brahmins** became the dominant community. The emergence of *bhakti*, devotional worship, placed temples firmly at the centre of religious life, and the inspirational *sangam* literature of saint-poets fostered a tradition of dance and music that has become Tamil Nadu's cultural hallmark.

In the tenth and eleventh centuries, the Cholas experienced a profound revival, ploughing their new wealth into the construction of splendid and imposing temples. Subsequently, the **Vijayanagars**, based in Hampi (Karnataka), resisted Muslim incursions from the north and spread to cover most of south India by the sixteenth century. This prompted a new phase of architectural development, including the introduction of colossal *gopura*s. In Madurai, the Vijayanagar governors, **Nayaks**, set up an independent kingdom whose impact spread as far as Tiruchirapalli.

Simultaneously, the south experienced its first significant wave of **European settlement**. First came the Portuguese, followed by the British, Dutch and French. The Western powers soon found themselves engaged in territorial disputes, most markedly between the French, based in **Pondicherry**, and the British, whose stronghold since 1640 had been Fort St George in **Madras**. It was the British who prevailed, confining the French to Pondicherry.

As well as occasional rebellions against colonial rule, Tamil Nadu also saw anti-brahmin protests, in particular in the 1920s and 1930s. **Independence** in 1947 signalled the need for state boundaries, and by 1956 the borders had been demarcated on a linguistic basis. Thus in 1965 Madras Presidency became **Tamil Nadu**.

Since Independence, Tamil Nadu's industrial sector has mushroomed. The state was a Congress stronghold until 1967, when the **DMK** (Dravida Munnetra Kazhagam), championing the lower castes and reasserting Tamil identity, won a landslide victory on a wave of anti-Hindi and anti-central government sentiment. Power has ping-ponged back and forth between the DMK and the breakaway party AIADMK ever since: this story is chronicled in the box opposite.

Chennai

In the northeastern corner of Tamil Nadu on the Bay of Bengal, **CHENNAI** (still commonly referred to by its former British name, **Madras**) is India's fourth largest city, with a population nudging seven and a half million. Hot, congested and noisy, it's the major transportation hub of the south and most travellers stay just long enough to book a ticket for somewhere else. The attractions of the city itself are sparse, though it does boast fine specimens of **Raj architecture**, pilgrimage sites connected with the apostle **Doubting Thomas**, superb **Chola bronzes** at its state museum, and plenty of **classical music** and **dance** performances.

As capital of Tamil Nadu, Chennai is, like Mumbai and Kolkata, a comparatively modern creation. It was founded by the **British East India Company** in 1639, on a 5-km strip of land between the Cooum and Adyar rivers, a few kilometres north of the ancient Tamil port of **Mylapore** and the Portuguese settlement of San Thomé; a fortified trading post, completed on St George's Day in 1640, was named **Fort St George**. Over the course of the next century and a half, as capital of the **Madras Presidency** which covered most of south India, the city expanded to include many surrounding villages. After losing it to the French in 1746, the British, with **Robert Clive** ("Clive of India") at their helm, re-established control three years later and continued to use it as their southern base, although Madras was surpassed in national importance by Calcutta.

The city's renaissance began after Independence, when it became the centre of the Tamil **movie industry**, and a hotbed of **Dravidian nationalism**. Renamed as Chennai in 1997, the metropolis has boomed since the Indian economy opened up to foreign investment in the early 1990s. The flip side of this rapid economic growth is that Chennai's infrastructure has been stretched to breaking point: poverty, oppressive heat and pollution are more likely to be your lasting impressions than the conspicuous affluence of the city's modern marble shopping malls.

Arrival

Chennai airport in Trisulam, 16km southwest of the city centre on NH-45, is comprehensively served by international and domestic flights; the two terminals are a minute's walk from each other. Out in the main concourse, you'll find a 24-hour post office, currency exchange facilities and a couple of snack bars. If open, the **Government of Tamil Nadu Tourist Information Centre** booth at the arrivals exit can book accommodation, while there's a computerized **ticket reservation** counter (Mon–Sat 8am–2pm & 2.15–8pm, Sun 8am–2pm) immediately outside the domestic terminal exit.

There are pre-paid **taxi** counters at both terminals. **Taxis** cost around Rs300 for the 35-minute ride to the main hotels or railway stations; from the main road,

Of movie stars and ministers

One notable difference between the Chennai movie industry and its counterpart in Mumbai is the influence of **politics** on Tamil films – an overlap that dates from the earliest days of regional cinema, when stories, stock themes and characters were derived from traditional folk ballads about low-caste heroes vanquishing high-caste villains. Already familiar to millions, such Robin Hood–style stereotypes were perfect propaganda vehicles for the nascent Tamil nationalist movement, the Dravida Munnetra Kazhagam, or **DMK**. It is no coincidence that the party's founding father, **C.N. Annadurai**, was a top screenplay and script writer. Like prominent Tamil Congress leaders and movie-makers of the 1930s and 1940s, he and his colleagues used the popular film genres of the time to convey their political ideas to the masses. From this politicization of the big screen were born the **fan clubs**, or *rasigar manrams*, that played such a key role in mobilizing support for the nationalist parties in elections.

The most influential fan club of all time was the one set up to support the superstar actor Marudur Gopalamenon Ramachandran, known to millions simply as "**MGR**". By carefully cultivating a political image to mirror the folk-hero roles he played in films, the maverick matinee idol generated fanatical grass-roots support in the state, especially among women, and rose to become chief minister in 1977. His eleven-year rule is still regarded by liberals as a dark age of chronic corruption, police brutality, political purges and rising organized crime. When he died in 1987, two million people attended his funeral and 31 grief-stricken devotees committed ritual suicide. Even today, MGR's statue, sporting trademark sunglasses and lamb's-wool hat, is revered at tens of thousands of wayside shrines across Tamil Nadu.

MGR's political protégée, and eventual successor, was a teenage screen starlet called **Jayalalitha**, a convent-educated brahmin's daughter whom he recruited to be both his leading lady and mistress, despite her being over 30 years younger. After 25 hit films together, Jayalalitha followed him into politics, becoming leader of the AIADMK, the party MGR set up after being expelled from the DMK in 1972. Larger than life in voluminous silver ponchos and heavy gold jewellery, the now portly Puratchi Thalavi ("Revolutionary Leader") has taken her personality cult to extremes brazen even by Indian standards. Jayalalitha's first spell as chief minister, however, was brought to an ignominious end at the 1996 elections, after allegations of fraud and corruption on an appropriately monumental scale. Despite being found guilty by the High Court, she nevertheless later ousted her arch-rival, **M. Karunanidhi**, leader of the DMK, wresting back power for two more spells as Chief Minister in 2001 and from 2002 to 2006. One of her first acts was to exact revenge on Karunanidhi, throwing him and one thousand of his supporters into prison on corruption charges. Predictably, he returned to trump his rival in the state elections of 2006 and the DMK also secured the lion's share of Tamil Nadu's seats in the national elections of March 2009.

rickshaws charge Rs150–200. A taxi to **Mamallapuram** costs in the region of Rs940. The quickest and cheapest way to get into town is by **suburban train** (see p.953) from **Trisulam** Station, 500m from the airport on the far side of the road, to Park, Egmore and North Beach stations, taking 30–40 minutes. If you want to leave Chennai straight away by bus, catch local bus #70 or #70a to the Moffussil Bus Stand (see p.950).

Arriving in Chennai by train, you come in at one of two long-distance railway stations, 1.5km apart on Periyar EVR High Road, towards the north of the city. **Egmore Station** is the arrival point for most trains from Tamil Nadu and Kerala. Most others pull in at **Central Station**, further east, on the edge of George Town. Both stations have left-luggage offices, while the latter also has pre-paid taxi and rickshaw booths.

Moving on from Chennai

All the major airlines, such as Jet Airways, Air India and Kingfisher and a number of the smaller operators, connect Chennai with multiple routes throughout India. In particular, there are over ten daily **flights** to Delhi, Mumbai, Bengaluru and Hyderabad. There are currently three flights a day to Port Blair.

Boats leave Chennai every week/ten days for **Port Blair**, capital of the **Andaman Islands**. However, getting a ticket can be a rigmarole: the first thing you'll need to do is contact the Directorate of Shipping on Rajaji Salai, George Town (☎044/2522 6873) to find out when the next sailing is and when tickets go on sale, usually during the week prior to departure. There are no ticket sales on the day of sailing. For more details, see the Andaman Islands chapter (p.925).

All long-distance **buses** leave from the **Moffussil Bus Stand** (see below, for local bus connections). The six platforms are each divided into thirty-odd bays, with frequent services to destinations throughout Tamil Nadu and the neighbouring states. The first stop beyond Chennai for many people is **Mamallapuram**, for which the fastest services are those marked "ECR" (East Coast Road; every 15–30min; less than 2hr). Myriad other state-run and private services run to the following: Bengaluru (every 15–30min; 8–11hr); Chengalpattu (every 5–10min; 1hr 30min–2hr); Chidambaram (20 daily; 5–7hr); Coimbatore (every 30min; 11–13hr); Kanchipuram (every 20min; 1hr 30min–2hr); Kanyakumari (10 daily; 16–18hr); Kodaikanal (1 daily; 14–15hr); Kumbakonam (every 30min; 7–8hr); Madurai (every 20–30min; 10hr); Mamallapuram (every 15–30min; 2–3hr); Puducherry (every 15–30min; 4–5hr); Rameshwaram (3 daily; 14hr); Thanjavur (20 daily; 8hr 30min); Thiruvananthapuram (6 daily; 20hr); Tiruchirapalli (every 15–30min; 8–9hr); Tirupati (every 30min–1hr; 4–5hr); Tiruvannamalai (every 20–30min; 4–5hr); Udhagamandalam (Ooty) (2 daily; 15hr).

Train services to most destinations in southern Tamil Nadu leave from **Egmore Station**, with the occasional service leaving from the suburban **Tambaram** Station. All other trains leave from **Chennai Central** where, left of the main building on the first floor of the Moore Market Complex, the efficient **tourist reservation counter** (Mon–Sat 8am–8pm, Sun 8am–2pm) sells tickets for trains from either station. The booking office at Egmore, up the stairs left of the main entrance (same hours), also handles bookings for both stations, but has no tourist counter. Main destinations are: Bengaluru (7 daily; 4hr 50min–8hr 30min); Chengalpattu (9–10 daily; 1hr–1hr 20min); Coimbatore (6 daily; 7hr 40min–8hr); Ernakulam, for Kochi (4 daily; 10hr 55min–14hr 15min); Hyderabad (2 daily; 13hr 50min–14hr 30min); Kanyakumari (1–2 daily;

Buses from all long-distance destinations arrive at the huge **Moffussil** Bus Stand, inconveniently situated in the suburb of Koyambedu, over 10km west of the centre. Moffussil is linked to other parts of Chennai by a host of city buses, which depart from the well-organized platforms outside the main terminal: buses #27, #15B, #15F and #17E go to the Egmore/Central area and Parry's Corner; bus #27B also goes on to Triplicane; while buses #70 and #70A link the bus stand to the airport. Note that most buses from Mamallapuram, Puducherry and other towns to the south of Chennai stop at Guindy suburban railway station; taking a train in from there saves time.

Information

The highly efficient and very helpful **India Tourism Office** at 154 Anna Salai (Mon–Fri 9am–6pm, Sat 9am–1pm; ☎044/2846 0285), has maps and leaflets, and can arrange accommodation. They also keep a list of approved **guides**. The **Tamil Nadu Tourism Development Corporation** (TTDC) is based in a smart complex

13hr 5min–16hr 55min); Kodaikanal Road (3–4 daily; 7hr 35min–8hr 30min); Kumbakonam (2 daily; 7hr 45min–8hr 30min); Madurai (6–8 daily; 7hr 45min–10hr 30min); Mettupalayam (1 daily; 9hr 15min); Mumbai (3 daily; 23hr–28hr 25min); Mysore (1–2 daily; 7hr–10hr 35min); Pune (3 daily; 19hr–24hr 15min); Thanjavur (1 daily; 7hr 45min); Thiruvananthapuram (2–3 daily; 15hr 40min–18hr 20min); Tiruchirapalli (9–10 daily; 5hr 10min–6hr 45min); Tirupati (3 daily; 3hr 5min–3hr 35min); Vijayawada (10–11 daily; 6hr 35min–8hr 30min).

Recommended trains from Chennai

Destination	Name	No.	From	Departs	Total time
Bengaluru	*Shatabdi Express*	#2007	Central	6am*	4hr 50min
	Bangalore Mail	#2657	Central	11.15pm	5hr 55min
Coimbatore	*Kovai Express*	#2675	Central	6.15am	7hr 30min
	Cheran Express	#2673	Central	10.10pm	8hr
Hyderabad	*Charminar Express*	#2759	Central	6.10pm	13hr 50min
Kanyakumari	*Kanyakumari Express*	#2633	Egmore	5.30pm	13hr 20min
Kochi/ Ernakulam	*Alleppey Express*	#6041	Central	9.15pm	11hr 45min
	Trivandrum Mail	#2623	Central	7.45pm	10hr 40min
Kodaikanal Road	*Pandian Express*	#2637	Egmore	9.45pm	7hr 50min
Madurai	*Vaigai Express*	#2635	Egmore	12.40pm	7hr 55min
Mettupalayam (for Ooty)	*Nilagiri Express*	#2671	Central	9pm	9hr 15min
Mumbai	*Mumbai Express*	#1042	Central	11.45am	26hr
	Dadar Express	#2164	Egmore	6.50am	23hr 50min
Mysore	*Shatabdi Express**	#2007	Central	6am	7hr
	Mysore Express	#6222	Central	9.30pm	10hr 30min
Thanjavur	*Rock Fort Express*	#6177	Egmore	10.30pm	7hr 50min
Thiruvananthapuram	*Trivandrum Mail*	#2623	Central	7.45pm	15hr 35min
Tirupati	*Sapthagiri Express*	#6057	Central	6.25am	3hr 5min

*Except Tues; a/c only

on Wallajah Road, near Anna Park in Triplicane (Mon–Sat 10am–5.30pm; ⓣ044/2538 3333), where you can also find the tourist offices of many other states including Kerala (ⓣ044/2536 9789). TTDC can book you tours or accommodation in their own hotels across the state.

The comprehensive quarterly directory *Madura Welcome Tamil Nadu* (Rs100) contains full transport, accommodation and tourist information details for Chennai and the rest of Tamil Nadu. For current cultural and entertainment listings, check out ⓦchennai.explocity.com or ⓦwww.chennaionline.com, which also has local news.

City transport

Chennai's sights and facilities are spread over such a wide area that it's impossible to get around without using some form of **public transport**. Most visitors jump in auto-rickshaws, but outside rush hours you can travel around comfortably by **bus** or suburban **train**.

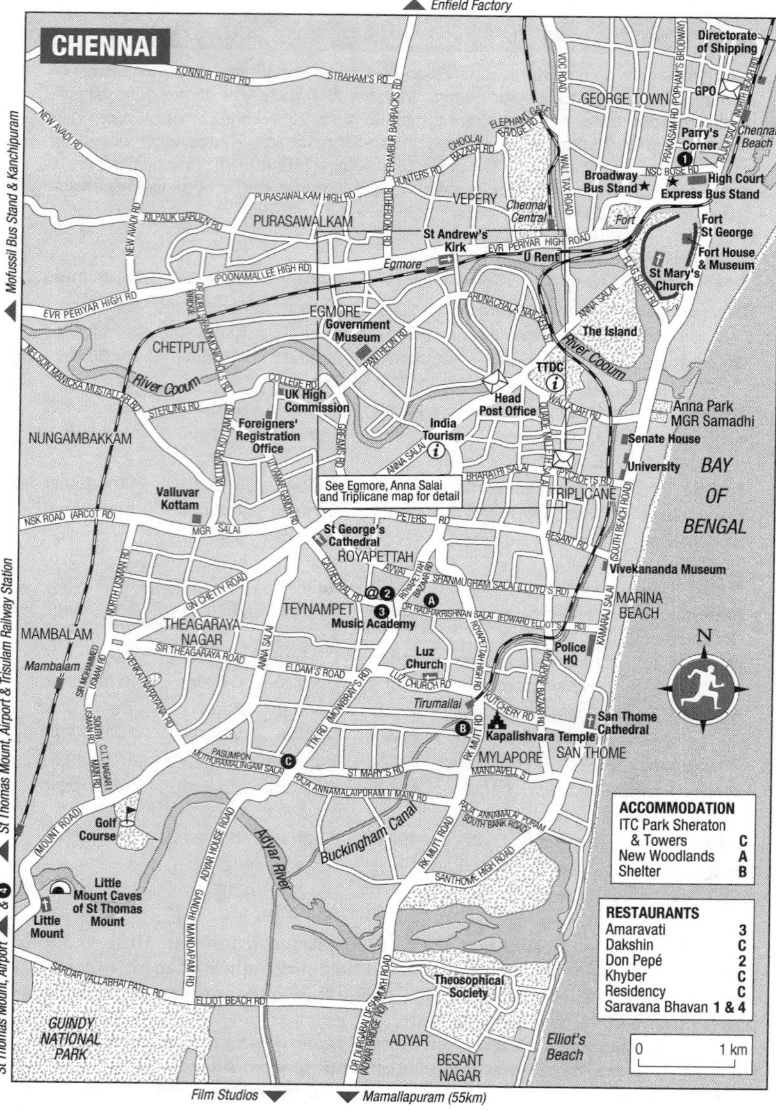

Buses

Most **local bus** routes radiate out from the amalgamated **Express** and **Broadway** bus stands, between Central train station and George Town. On Anna Salai and other major thoroughfares buses have dedicated stops, but on smaller streets you have to flag them down, or wait with the obvious crowd. Numbers of services to specific places of interest in the city are listed in the relevant accounts, while those to and from the Moffussil Bus Stand are listed in "Arrival", p.950.

Tours

One good way to get around the sights of Chennai is on a TTDC **bus tour**; bookings are taken at their office (see p.950). They're good value, albeit rushed, and the guides can be very helpful. The TTDC **half-day tour** (daily 8am–1pm or 1.30pm–6.30pm; Rs140 non-a/c, Rs200 with a/c) at their office on Periyar EVR High Road. It takes in Fort St George, the Government Museum (Birla Planetarium instead on Fri), the Snake Park, Kapalishvara Temple, Elliot's Beach and Marina Beach. TTDC also offer good-value **day-trips**, including visits to Mamallapuram, Kanchipuram and Puducherry, with meals included in the tariff; check at their office for the various itineraries and prices.

Trains

If you want to travel south from central Chennai to Guindy (Deer Park) or the airport, the easiest way to go is by **train**. Services run every fifteen minutes (on average) between 4.30am and 11pm, prices are minimal, and they only get overcrowded during rush hours (around 7–9am & 4–6pm). Buy a ticket before boarding.

City trains travel between: Beach (opposite the GPO), Fort, Park (for Central), Egmore, Nungambakkam, Kodambakkam, Mambalam (for T Nagar and silk shops), Saidapet (for Little Mount Church), Guindy, St Thomas Mount and Trisulam (for the airport).

Taxis, rickshaws and car rental

Chennai's yellow-top Ambassador **taxis** have meters but drivers often refuse to use them, so prepare yourself for some hard bargaining. At around Rs150 from Central Station to Triplicane, they're practically pricing themselves out of business. For this reason more reliable and economical **radio taxis** such as Bharati Call Taxi (ⓣ044/2814 2233) are becoming more popular.

Auto-rickshaw drivers in Chennai are notorious for demanding high fares from locals and tourists alike. A rickshaw from Triplicane to either of the bus stations, or Egmore and Central railway stations should cost no more than Rs50, but again meters are rarely employed. If you need to get to the airport or station early in the morning, book a rickshaw and negotiate the price the night before.

Car rental with driver is available at many of the city's upmarket hotels or through private agents such as Welcome Tours & Travels at 150 Anna Salai (ⓣ044/2846 0908, ⓦwww.allindiatours.com). An Ambassador car with driver costs Rs1200–1500 per day (or Rs1800–2000 for one with a/c) – rates may be negotiable.

Accommodation

Finding an inexpensive **place to stay** in Chennai can sometimes be a problem. With the 24-hour check-out system it's difficult to predict availability and some of the cheaper places don't take advance bookings. The good news is that standards in the cheapies are better than in other cities. Most of the mid-range and inexpensive hotels are around the railway station in **Egmore** and further east in **Triplicane**. The bulk of the top hotels are in the south of the city and several offer courtesy buses to and from the airport. Due to frequent shortages, visitors should use **water** as sparingly as possible.

Accommodation listed under the "Outside the centre" heading appears on the main Chennai **map** (opposite); all others are marked on the Egmore, Anna Salai and Triplicane map (p.954).

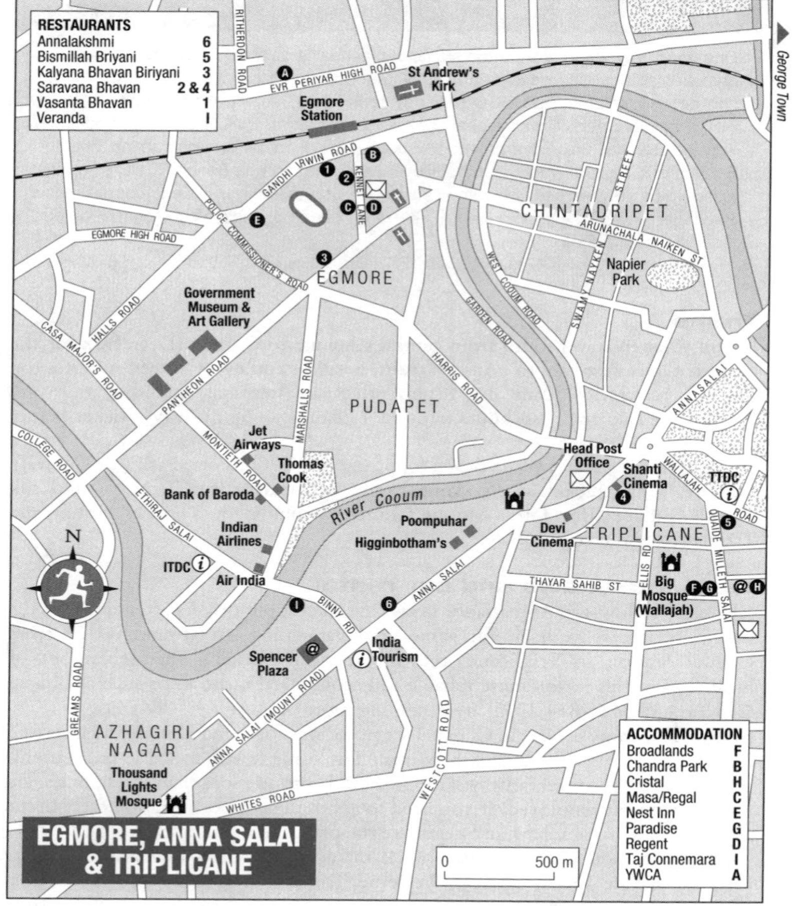

Egmore

Chandra Park 55 Gandhi Irwin Rd ⓣ044/2819 1177, ⓦwww.hotelchandrapark.com. Clean-cut business hotel with central a/c, foreign exchange, 24hr coffee shop, bar and rooftop restaurant. The spacious, light and well-furnished standard rooms are an especially good deal. ❹–❻

Masa 15/1 Kennet Lane ⓣ044/2819 3344, ⓕ2819 1261. Variously priced rooms with attached bathrooms and TVs in a cleanish, modern building, close to the station. Good value but no advance booking. The similar *Regal*, tacked onto the back, is marginally cheaper. ❷–❹

Nest Inn 55/31 Gandhi Irwin Rd ⓣ044/2819 2919, ⓦwww.hotelnestinn.co.in. Popular business hotel, now with central a/c. The rooms are small but comfortable and pleasantly decorated; there's also a multi-cuisine restaurant and bar. ❺–❻

Regent 11 Kennet Lane ⓣ044/2819 1801, ⓕ2819 1347. Quiet lodge set around a peaceful courtyard. The fair-sized non-a/c rooms are a bit shabby, though the bathrooms are spotless. ❸

YWCA 1086 Periyar EVR High Rd ⓣ044/2532 4234, ⓔywcamadras@sancharnet.in. Attractive hotel in quiet gardens behind Egmore Station, with spotless, spacious rooms, safe-deposit and a good restaurant. A highly recommended, safe and friendly place; book in advance. Rates include a buffet breakfast. ❹–❺

Anna Salai and Triplicane

Broadlands 18 Vallabha Agraham St, Triplicane ⓣ044/2854 5573, ⓔbroadlandshotel@yahoo.com. An old whitewashed house, with crumbling stucco and stained glass, ranged around a leafy courtyard, this is the kind of budget travellers' enclave you either love or loathe. There's a large roof terrace and clean rooms, a few with attached bathrooms, private balconies and views of the mosque. ❶–❷

Cristal 34 CNK Rd, Triplicane ⓣ044/2858 5605. In a modern building off Quaide Milleth Salai, this is a safe and friendly place run by a team of brothers. Rooms are tiled and clean, all with attached showers. TVs cost Rs25 extra. As cheap as it gets in Chennai. ❶

Paradise 17/1 Vallabha Agraham St, Triplicane ⓣ044/2859 4252, ⓔparadisegh@hotmail.com. Very friendly and a dependable choice, offering inexpensive rooms with attached bathroom, TV and a choice of Western or Indian loos. There's seating on a large roof terrace, and room service. Great value, especially for a/c. ❷–❹

Taj Connemara Binny Rd ⓣ044/5500 0000, ⓦwww.tajhotels.com. Dating from the Raj era, this whitewashed Art-Deco five-star near Anna Salai is a Chennai institution. The large "heritage" rooms feature Victorian decor, dressing rooms and verandas overlooking the pool. There is also a health club, 24hr coffee shop, two excellent restaurants (see p.959) and a bar. Rates start around $160. ❾

Outside the centre

ITC Park Sheraton & Towers 132 TTK Rd ⓣ044/2499 4101, ⓦwww.itcwelcomgroup.in. The last word in American-style executive luxury, somehow not too ostentatious despite the bow-tied valets. Three excellent restaurants, a 24hr coffee shop and other five-star facilities. The spacious rooms with plush furnishings make it an excellent choice for business travellers; rates start in excess of $300. ❾

New Woodlands 72–75 Dr Radhakrishnan Salai ⓣ044/2811 3111, ⓦwww.newwoodlands.com. Sprawling complex of clean, reasonably sized rooms and more spacious, self-contained apartments (called "cottages"), plus two restaurants and a swimming pool. Rooms ❺, cottages ❻–❼

Shelter 19–21 Venkatesa Agraharam St, Mylapore ⓣ044/2495 1919, ⓦwww.hotelshelter.com. A stone's throw from the Kapalishvara Temple, this sparklingly clean luxury hotel is better value than most upmarket places with good restaurants and a bar, although the rooms are a little kitsch. ❼

The City

Chennai divides into three main areas. The northern district, separated from the rest by the River Cooum, is the site of the first British outpost in India, **Fort St George**, and the commercial centre, **George Town**, which developed during British occupation. At the southern end of Rajaji Salai is **Parry's Corner**, George Town's principal landmark and a major bus stop – look for the tall grey building labelled Parry's.

Central Chennai is sandwiched between the Cooum and Adyar rivers, and crossed diagonally by the city's main thoroughfare, **Anna Salai**, the modern, commercial heart of the metropolis. To the east, this gives way to the atmospheric old Muslim quarters of **Triplicane** and a long straight **Marina** where fishermen mend nets and set small boats out to sea, and hordes of Indian tourists hitch up saris and trousers for a quick paddle. South of here, near the coast, **Mylapore**, inhabited in the 1500s by the Portuguese, boasts **Kapalishvara Temple** and **San Thomé Cathedral**, both tourist attractions and places of pilgrimage.

Fort St George and George Town

Quite unlike any other fort in India, **Fort St George** stands amid state offices facing the sea in the east of the city, just south of George Town on Kamaraj Salai. It looks more like a complex of well-maintained colonial mansions than a fort; indeed many of its buildings are used today as offices and are a hive of activity during the week.

The fort was the first structure of Madras town and the first territorial possession of the British in India. Construction began in 1640, but most of the original buildings were replaced later that century, after being damaged during French sieges. The most imposing structure is the eighteenth-century colonnaded **Fort House**, coated in deep slate-grey and white paint. Next door, in the more modestly proportioned **Exchange Building**, is the excellent **Fort Museum** (daily except Fri 10am–5pm; Rs100 [Rs5], video cameras Rs25). The collection within faithfully records the central events of the British occupation of Madras with portraits, regimental flags, weapons, East India Company coins, medals, stamps and thick woollen uniforms that make you wonder how the Raj survived as long as it did. The first floor is now an **art gallery**, where portraits of prim officials and their wives sit side by side with fine sketches of the British embarking at Chennai in aristocratic finery, attended by Indians in loincloths. Also on display are etchings by the famous artist **Thomas Daniells**, whose work largely defined British perceptions of India at the end of the eighteenth century.

South of the museum, past the State Legislature, stands the oldest surviving Anglican church in Asia, **St Mary's** (daily 9am–5pm), built in 1678 and partly renovated after the battle of 1759. Constructed with thick walls and a strong vaulted roof, the church served as a store and shelter in times of war. It's distinctly English in style, crammed with plaques and statues in memory of British soldiers, politicians and their wives. The grandest plaque, made of pure silver, was presented by Elihu Yale, former governor of Fort St George (1687–96) and founder of Yale University. A collection of photographs of visiting dignitaries, including Queen Elizabeth II, is on display in the entrance porch.

North of Fort St George, the former British trading centre of **George Town** (reached on bus #18 from Anna Salai) remains the focal area for banks, offices, shipping companies and street stalls. This confusing – if well-ordered – grid of streets harbours a fascinating medley of architecture: eighteenth- and nineteenth-century churches, Hindu and Jain temples and a scattering of mosques, interspersed with grand mansions. In the east, on Rajaji Salai, the **General Post Office** occupies a robust earth-red Indo-Saracenic building constructed in 1884. George Town's southern extent is marked by the bulbous white domes and sandstone towers of the **High Court**, and the even more opulent towers of the **Law College**, both showing strong Islamic influence.

Government Museum

The Chennai **Government Museum** (daily except Fri 9.30am–5pm; Rs250 [Rs15], camera Rs200, video camera Rs500) contains some remarkable archeological finds from south India and the Deccan, stone sculptures from major temples, and an unsurpassed collection of Chola bronzes. To get here, hop on bus #11H from Anna Salai for Pantheon Road, south of Egmore railway station.

Inside the deep-red, circular **main building**, built in 1851, the first gallery is devoted to archeology and geology; the highlights are the dismantled panels, railings and statues from the second-century AD *stupa* complex at **Amaravati** (see p.917). These sensuously carved marble reliefs of the Buddha's life are widely regarded as the finest achievements of early Indian art. To the left of here high, arcaded halls full of stuffed animals lead to the **ethnology gallery**, where models, clothes, weapons and photographs of expressionless faces in orderly lines illustrate local tribal societies, some long since wiped out. A fascinating display of wind and string **instruments**, drums and percussion includes the large predecessor of today's sitar and several very old tablas.

The museum's real treasure trove, however, is the modern wing, which contains the world's most complete and impressive selection of **Chola bronzes** (see p.990). Large statues of Shiva, Vishnu and Parvati stand in the centre, flanked by glass cases containing smaller figurines, including several sculptures of Shiva as **Nataraja**, the

Lord of the Dance, encircled by a ring of fire. One of the finest models is **Ardhanarishvara**, the androgynous form of Shiva (united with Shakti in transcendence of duality). Elsewhere, the magnificent Indo-Saracenic **art gallery** houses old British portraits of figures such as Clive and Hastings, plus Rajput and Mughal miniatures, and a small display of ivory carvings.

St Andrew's Kirk

Just northeast of Egmore Station, off Periyar EVR High Road, **St Andrew's Kirk**, consecrated in 1821, is a fine example of Georgian architecture. Modelled on London's St Martins-the-Fields, it's one of just three churches in India with a circular seating plan, laid out beneath a huge dome painted blue with gold stars and supported by a sweep of Corinthian columns. Marble plaques around the church give a fascinating insight into the kind of people who left Britain to work for the imperial and Christian cause. A staircase leads onto the flat roof, surrounding the dome, from where you can climb further up into the steeple past the massive bell to a tiny balcony affording excellent views of the city.

The Marina

One of the longest city beaches in the world, the **Marina** (Kamaraj Salai) stretches 5km from the harbour at the southeastern corner of George Town to near San Thome Cathedral. Going south, you'll pass the Indo-Saracenic **Presidency College** (1865–71), one of a number of stolid Victorian buildings that make up the **University**. Next door, the nineteenth-century Madras depot of the Tudor Ice Company has been converted into the interesting **Vivekananda Museum** (daily 10am–noon & 3–7pm, closed Wed; Rs2), which gives an excellent account of the life of the nineteenth-century saint, Swami Vivekananda.

Today the **beach** itself is a sociable stretch, peopled by idle paddlers, picnickers and pony-riders; every afternoon crowds gather around the beach market. However, its location just a little downstream from the port, which belches out waste and smelly fumes, combined with its function as the toilet for the fishing community detract somewhat from its natural beauty.

Mylapore

Long before Madras came into existence, **Mylapore**, south of the Marina (reached by buses #4, #5 or #21 from the LIC building on Anna Salai), was a major settlement; the Greek geographer Ptolemy mentioned it in the second century AD as a thriving port. During the Pallava period (fifth to ninth centuries) it was second only to Mamallapuram.

An important stop on the St Thomas pilgrimage trail, **San Thomé Cathedral** (daily 6am–8pm) marks the eastern boundary of Mylapore, lying close to the sea at the southern end of the Marina. Although the present neo-Gothic structure dates from 1896, it stands on the site of two earlier churches built over the tomb of St Thomas; his relics are kept inside, accessed by an underground passage from the museum at the rear of the courtyard.

The large **Kapalishvara temple** sits just under 1km west of the cathedral. Seventh-century Tamil poet-saints sang its praises, but the present structure, dedicated to Shiva, probably dates from the sixteenth century. The huge (40m) *gopura* towering above the main east entrance, plastered in stucco figures, was added in 1906. Surrounding an assortment of busy shrines, where priests offer blessings for devotees and non-Hindus alike, the courtyard features an old tree where a small shrine to Shiva's consort, Parvati, shows her in the form of a peahen (*mayil*) worshipping a lingam.

Little Mount Caves and St Thomas Mount

St Thomas is said to have sought refuge from persecution in the **Little Mount Caves**, 8km south of the city centre (bus #18A, #18B, or #52C from Anna Salai). Entrance to the caves is beside steps leading to a statue of Our Lady of Good Health. Inside, next to a small natural window in the rock, are impressions of what are believed to be St Thomas' handprints, created when he made his escape through this tiny opening. Behind the new circular church of Our Lady of Good Health is a natural **spring**. Tradition has it that this was created when Thomas struck the rock, so the crowds that came to hear him preach could quench their thirst; samples of its holy water are on sale.

It's said that St Thomas was speared to death while praying before a stone cross on **St Thomas Mount**, 11km south of the city centre – take a suburban train to Guindy railway station and walk from there. **Our Lady of Expectation Church** (1523), at the summit of the Mount, can be reached by 134 granite steps marked with the fourteen stations of the Cross, or by a road which curls its way to the top, where a huge old banyan tree provides shade.

The Theosophical Society headquarters

The **Theosophical Society** was established in New York in 1875 by American Civil War veteran Colonel Henry S. Olcott and the eccentric Russian aristocrat Madame Helena Petrovna Blavatsky, who claimed occult powers. Based on a fundamental belief in the equality and truth of all religions, the society in fact propagated a modern form of Hinduism, praising all things Indian and shunning Christian missionaries. Needless to say, its two founders were greeted enthusiastically when they transferred their operations to Madras in 1882, establishing their headquarters near Elliot's Beach in Adyar (buses #5, #5C or #23C from George Town/Anna Salai).

The society's buildings still stand today, sheltering several shrines and an excellent **library** (Mon–Sat 8.30–10am & 2–4pm) of books on religion and philosophy. The collection includes 800-year-old scroll pictures of the Buddha; rare Tibetan xylographs; exquisitely illuminated Korans; a giant copy of Martin Luther's *Biblia* printed in Nuremberg three hundred years ago; and a thumbnail-sized Bible in seven languages. Anybody is welcome to look around, but to gain full use of the library you have to register as a member.

The 270 acres of woodland and gardens surrounding the society's headquarters make a serene place to sit and restore the spirits. In the middle, a vast 400-year-old **banyan tree**, said to be the second-largest in the world, can provide shade for up to three thousand people at a time.

Eating

Chennai runs on inexpensive south Indian fast-food **restaurants** and "meals" (**thali**) joints, in particular the legendary *Saravana Bhavan* chain, which serves superb south Indian food for next to nothing. Mid-range options also abound. Unless otherwise stated, the restaurants listed below are marked on the Egmore, Anna Salai and Triplicane **map** on p.954.

Amaravati Corner of Cathedral and TTK roads (see Chennai map, p.952). One of four dependable options in this complex of regional speciality restaurants, south of the downtown area. This one does excellent Andhran food, including particularly tasty biriyanis, for Rs100–150.

Annalakshmi 804 Anna Salai. A charitable venture whose profits go to the community, run voluntarily by Sivananda devotees, where you can enjoy a leisurely and expensive (around Rs400/person) meal in beautiful surroundings. You choose one of several set menus, each with different Ayurvedic properties.

Bismillah Biriyani 1 Triplicane High Rd. Small *dhaba* serving tasty chicken in *tandoori*, kebab and *biriyani* form. The best of many such places on this road.

Dakshin/Khyber/Residency *ITC Park Sheraton & Towers*, 132 TTK Rd (see Chennai map, p.952) ⓣ044/2499 4101. Three excellent upmarket options in the one hotel: the *Residency* serves Indian, Western and Chinese, and the *Khyber* offers a meaty poolside barbecue, but best of all is the *Dakshin*, one of the country's top south Indian restaurants. It serves up a wide choice of unusual dishes, including seafood in marinated spices, Karnataka mutton biriyani and *appam* made on the spot. Live Carnatic music in the evenings. Book in advance and expect to pay around Rs600 for a meal with starter and drink.

Don Pepé 1st floor, above *Hot Breads*, Cathedral Rd (see Chennai map, p.952). Swish a/c Tex-Mex joint, serving a predictable menu of fajitas, enchiladas, tortillas and burritos, plus so-so pasta dishes (dubbed "Euro-Mex"). Main courses about Rs150. *Hot Breads* itself is a great bakery and coffee shop.

Kalyana Bhavan Biriyani 424 Pantheon Rd, Egmore. As the name suggests, this is a biriyani specialist, serving tasty plain, chicken and mutton versions (Rs35–70) on banana leaves, accompanied by aubergine sauce and a semolina sweet.

Saravana Bhavan Thanigai Murugan Rathinavel Hall, 77 Usman Rd, T Nagar (see both Chennai and Egmore, Anna Salai & Triplicane maps, p.952 & p.954). This famous south Indian fast-food chain is an institution among the Chennai middle class, with other branches opposite the bus stand in George Town, in Egmore and in the forecourt of the Shanti cinema (at the top of Anna Salai). Try their delicious *rawa iddlis*, or range of thalis rounded off with some freshly made *ladoo* or *barfi* from the sweets counter outside. Mains Rs30–80.

Vasanta Bhavan 20 Gandhi Irwin Rd. Easily the best "meals" joint among many around Egmore Station, with ranks of attentive waiters and delicious pure-veg food – just Rs35 for an unlimited thali. It's busy, spotlessly clean, and their coffee and sweets are delicious.

Veranda *Taj Connemara*, Binny Rd ⓣ044/5500 0000. The ideal venue for a posh Sun morning breakfast buffet, with crisp newspapers and fresh coffee served in silver pots. The blow-out lunchtime buffets (around Rs400) are also recommended, and à la carte Italian food is on offer in the evening. Reserve in advance.

Listings

Airlines, domestic Go Air ⓣ1800/222 111; IndiGo ⓣ1800/180 3838; Jet Airways ⓣ044/3987 2222; JetLite ⓣ1800/223 020; Kingfisher Airlines ⓣ044/4398 8400; Paramount Airways ⓣ044/4219 9999; SpiceJet ⓣ1800/180 3333.

Airlines, international Air India ⓣ044/2855 4488, airport ⓣ044/2256 0747; American Airlines ⓣ1800/200 1800; British Airways ⓣ1800/102 3592; Gulf Air ⓣ044/2815 6244; Lufthansa ⓣ1800/102 5838; Qatar Airways ⓣ044/4289 6000; Singapore Airlines ⓣ044/3254 7771; Sri Lankan Airlines ⓣ044/4392 1100; Thai Airways ⓣ044/4206 3311. Most offices are open Mon–Fri 10am–5pm, Sat 10am–1pm.

Banks and currency exchange Chennai has plenty of banks, though the major hotels offer exchange facilities to residents only. A conveniently central option is American Express, G-17, Spencer Plaza, 769 Anna Salai (Mon–Fri 9.30am–5.30pm, Sat 9.30am–2.30pm). Thomas Cook (Mon–Sat 9am–6pm) has offices at the Ceebros Centre, 45 Montieth Rd, Egmore, at the G-4 Eldorado Building, 112 Uttar Gandhi Salai, and also at the airport. For encashments on Visa cards, go to Bobcards, next door to the Bank of Baroda on Montieth Rd. There are now 24hr ATMs all over the city, including the airport and both major stations.

Consulates Australia, Raheja Towers, 177 Anna Salai ⓣ044/2860 1160; Canada, Khader Kawaz Khan Rd, Nungambakkam ⓣ044/2833 0888; New Zealand, 132 Cathedral Rd ⓣ044/2811 2472 ext 21; South Africa, 19 Rajaji Salai ⓣ044/2534 2141; Sri Lanka, 196 TTK Rd, Alwarpet ⓣ044/2498 7897; UK, 20 Anderson Rd, Nungambakkam ⓣ044/4219 2151; USA, 220 Anna Salai ⓣ044/2857 4000.

Hospitals Chennai's best-equipped private hospital is the Apollo, 21/22 Greams Rd ⓣ044/2829 3333. For an ambulance, try ⓣ044/102, but it's usually quicker to jump in a taxi.

Internet Access is widely available at internet cafés for around Rs20/hr, or for a bit more in hotel business centres.

Postal services Chennai's main post office is opposite Shanti theatre on Anna Salai (Mon–Sat 8am–8pm, Sun 10am–5pm). If you're using it for poste restante, make sure your correspondents mark the envelope "Head Post Office, Anna Salai". There are smaller branches in both Egmore and Triplicane.

Souvenirs Spencer Plaza on Anna Salai has an excellent selection of boutiques, clothes shops and small souvenir stalls. Across the road at 152 Anna Salai, the Indian Arts Emporium has a good selection of handicrafts, furniture and metalwork.

Travel agents Reliable agents include American Express Travels, 5th Floor, Phase 2, Spencer Plaza, 768–769 Anna Salai ⓣ044/2852 3592; Surya Travels, F-14 1st Floor, Spencer Plaza ⓣ044/2852 3937; Thomas Cook, Eldorado Building, 112 Nungambakkam High Rd ⓣ044/2827 5052; Welcome Tours and Travels, 150 Anna Salai ⓣ044/2846 0908.

The northeast

Fazed by the heat and air pollution of Chennai, most visitors escape as fast as they can, heading down the Coromandel coast to India's stone-carving capital, **Mamallapuram**, whose ancient monuments include the famous Shore Temple and a batch of extraordinary rock sculptures. En route, it's well worth jumping off the bus at **Dakshina Chitra**, a folk museum 30km south of Chennai, where traditional buildings from across south India have been beautifully reconstructed. Further inland, **Kanchipuram** is an important pilgrimage and silk-sari-weaving town from where you can loop southwest to **Tiruvannamalai**, a wonderfully atmospheric temple town clustered at the base of the sacred mountain, Arunachala. On the coast, you can breakfast on croissants and espresso coffee in the former French colony of **Puducherry**. A short way north, **Auroville**, the Utopian settlement founded by followers of the Sri Aurobindo Ghose's spiritual successor, The Mother, provides a New Age haven for soul-searching Westerners and an economy for the local population.

Both Mamallapuram and Puducherry are well connected to Chennai by fast bus services, running along the smooth East Coast Road. You can also get to Puducherry by train, but this usually involves a change at the junction town of **Villupuram**, from where services are slow and relatively infrequent.

Mamallapuram

Scattered around the base of a colossal mound of boulders is the small seaside town and UNESCO World Heritage Site of **MAMALLAPURAM** (aka Mahabalipuram), 58km south of Chennai. From dawn till dusk, the rhythms of chisels chipping granite resound down its sandy lanes – evidence of a stone-carving tradition that has endured since this was a major port of the Pallava dynasty, between the fifth and ninth centuries. It is only possible to speculate about the purpose of much of the boulder sculpture, but it appears that the friezes and shrines were not made for worship at all, but rather as a showcase for the talents of local artists. Due in no small part to the maritime activities of the Pallavas, their style of art and architecture had wide-ranging influence, spreading from south India as far north as Ellora, as well as to Southeast Asia.

Mamallapuram's monuments divide into four categories: open-air **bas-reliefs**, structured **temples**, man-made **caves** and **rathas** ("chariots" carved *in situ* from single boulders to resemble temples or the chariots used in temple processions). The famous bas-reliefs, **Arjuna's Penance** and the **Krishna Mandapa**, adorn massive rocks near the centre of the village, while the beautiful **Shore Temple,** one of India's most photographed monuments, presides over the beach. Sixteen man-made caves and monolithic structures, in different stages of completion, are scattered through the area, but the most complete of the nine *ratha*s are in a group, named after the five Pandava brothers of the Mahabharata.

Given the coexistence of so many stunning archeological remains with a long white-sand **beach**, it was inevitable this would become a major destination for Western travellers, with the inevitable presence of Kashmiri emporia, bus-loads of city dwellers at the weekends, massage-wallahs and hawkers on the beach, and a plethora of budget hotels and little fish restaurants.

The temples of Tamil Nadu

No Indian state is more dominated by its **temples** than Tamil Nadu, where temple architecture catalogues the tastes of successive dynasties and testifies to the centrality of religion in everyday life. Most temples are built in honour of Shiva, Vishnu and their consorts; all are characterized not only by their design and sculptures, but by constant activity: devotion, dancing, singing, pujas, festivals and feasts. Each is tended by brahmin priests, recognizable by their *dhoti*s (loincloths), a sacred thread draped over the right shoulder, and marks on the forehead. One to three horizontal (usually white) lines distinguish Shaivites; vertical lines (yellow or red), often converging into a near-V shape, are common among Vaishnavites.

Dravida, the temple architecture of Tamil Nadu, first took form in the Pallava port of **Mamallapuram**. A step-up from the cave retreats of Hindu and Jain ascetics, the earliest Pallava monuments were **mandapas**, shrines cut into rock faces and fronted by columns. The magnificent Arjuna's Penance **bas-relief** shows the fluid carving of the Pallavas at its most exquisite. This sculptural skill was transferred to freestanding temples, **rathas**, carved out of single rocks and incorporating the essential elements of Hindu temples: the dim inner sanctuary, the *garbhagriha*, capped with a modest tapering spire featuring repetitive architectural motifs. In turn, the Shore Temple was built with three shrines, topped by a **vimana** similar to the towering roofs of the *ratha*s; statues of Nandi, Shiva's bull, later to receive pride of place, surmount its low walls. In the finest structural Pallava temple, the Kailasanatha Temple at **Kanchipuram**, the sanctuary stands within a courtyard enclosed by high walls carved with images of Shiva, his consort and ghoulish mythical lions, *yali*s, the prototype for later styles.

Pallava themes were developed in Karnataka by the Chalukyas and Rashtrakutas, but it was the Shaivite **Cholas** who spearheaded Tamil Nadu's next architectural phase, in the tenth century. In **Thanjavur**, Rajaraja I created the Brihadeshvara Temple principally as a status symbol; its proportions far exceed any attempted by the Pallavas. Set within a vast walled courtyard, the sanctuary, fronted by a small *mandapa*, stands beneath a sculpted *vimana* that soars over 60m high. Most sculptures once again feature Shiva, but the *gopuras* each side of the eastern gateway to the courtyard were an innovation, as were the lions carved into the base of the sanctuary walls, and the pavilion erected over Nandi in front of the sanctuary. The second great Chola temple was built in **Gangaikondacholapuram** by Rajendra I. Instead of a mighty *vimana*, he brought new elements, adding subsidiary shrines and placing an extended *mandapa* in front of the central sanctuary, its pillars writhing with dancers and deities.

By the time of the thirteenth-century **Vijayanagar** kings, the temple was central to city life, the focus for civic meetings, education, dance and theatre. The Vijayanagars extended earlier structures, adding enclosing walls around a series of **prakaras**, or courtyards, and erecting freestanding *mandapas* for use as meeting halls, elephant stables, stages for music and dance, and ceremonial marriage halls (*kalyan mandapas*). Raised on superbly decorated columns, these *mandapas* became known as **thousand-pillared halls**. **Tanks** were added, doubling as water stores and washing areas, and used for festivals when deities were set afloat in boats.

Under the Vijayanagars, the *gopura*s were enlarged and set at the cardinal points over the high gateways to each *prakara*, to become the dominant feature. Rectangular in plan, and embellished with images of animals and local saints or rulers as well as deities, *gopura*s are periodically repainted in pinks, blues, whites and yellows, a sharp and joyous contrast to the earthy browns and greys of halls and sanctuaries beyond. **Madurai** is the place to check out Vijayanagar architecture. Its temples regularly come alive for festivals, in which Shiva and his "fish-eyed" consort are hauled through town on mighty wooden chariots. Outside Tiruchirapalli, the temple at **Srirangam** was extended by the Vijayanagar Nayaks to become south India's largest. Unlike that in Madurai, it incorporates earlier Chola foundations, but the ornamentation, with pillars formed into rearing horses, is superb.

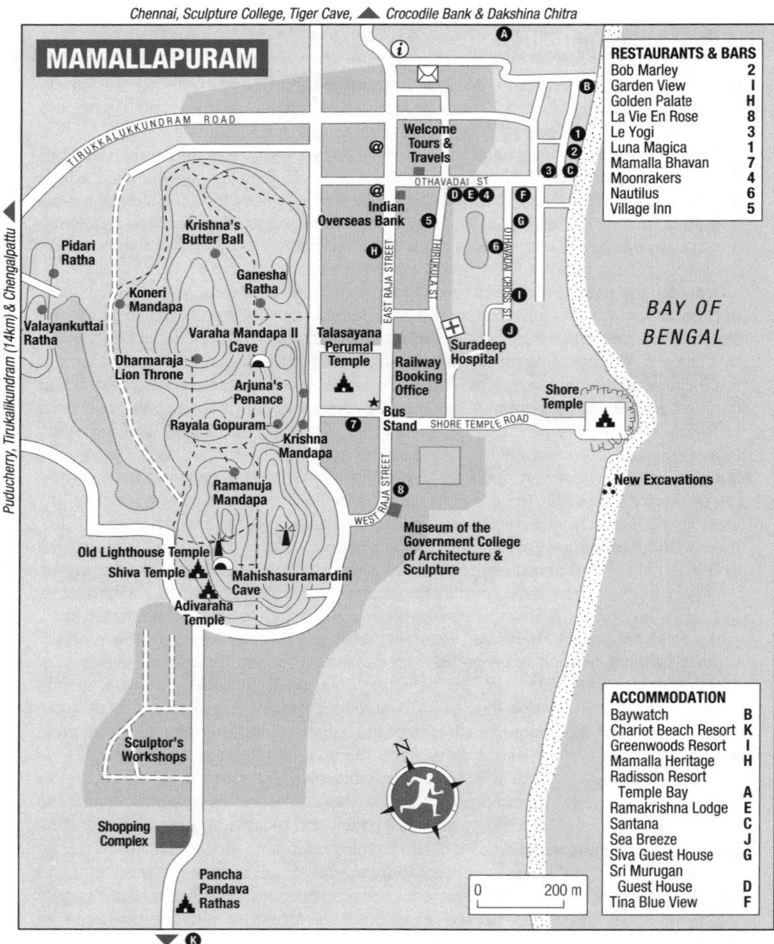

Arrival, information and getting around

Numerous daily **buses** ply to and from Chennai, Tiruvannamalai, Kanchipuram and Puducherry. The bus stand is in the centre of the village, though many express routes only stop on the highway, 1.5km from the centre.

The nearest **railway station**, at Chengalpattu (Chingleput), 29km northeast on the bus route to Kanchipuram, is on the main north–south line, but not really a convenient access point. **Taxis** to and from Chennai cost Rs1000–1200 or Rs800–900 to and from the airport. Mamallapuram suffers badly from aggressive touting by a small number of hotels; ignore the touts and walk briskly to your chosen destination.

The **Government of Tamil Nadu Tourist Office** (Mon–Fri 10am–5.45pm; ⓣ044/2744 2232) is one of the first buildings you see in the village, on your left as you arrive from Chennai. There are several official places to **change money** in the village: the Indian Overseas Bank and more efficient agencies such as LKP Forex (Mon–Sat 9.30am–7pm), both on East Raja Street.

Mamallapuram itself comprises little more than a few roads. By far the best way to get to the important sites is by **bicycle**, which you can rent from shops on East Raja Street or through your guesthouse for around Rs40 per day. **Scooters** and Enfield **motorcycles** are also available for Rs250–300 a day, from Poornima Travels, next to *Moonraker's* restaurant, or through guesthouses. Delhi-based Hi! Tours (Ⓣ044/2744 3260, Ⓦwww.hi-tours.com) have a slick operation for car hire, ticketing and other services at 125 East Raja Street, while a friendly local service is available from Travels Partners (Ⓣ9840 377033; Ⓔtravelspartners@gmail.com), on Othavadai Street. The going rate for **internet access** is Rs40 per hour, though beware of *Lakshmi Lodge*'s outrageous extra charge for using Skype; the outlet at *Ramakrishna Lodge* is a better bet. If you need **medical treatment**, the Suradeep Hospital on Thirukula Street (Ⓣ044/2744 2390) is highly recommended.

Accommodation

Except at the peak Christmas/New Year period, bargaining is the order of the day. All the cheap and mid-range places are within the village, and there are two upmarket resorts on the outskirts. All the places listed here are either on the beach or a short stroll from it.

Baywatch Fishermens Colony Ⓣ9840 297152, Ⓔhotelbaywatch@yahoo.co.in. Well-appointed guesthouse with smartly furnished rooms, the upstairs ones being more expensive. Just one building back from the beach and some sea views. ❶–❷

Chariot Beach Resort 69 Five Rathas Rd Ⓣ044/2498 6364, Ⓦwww.chariotbeachresorts.com. Brand-new resort with unobstructed sea views, arranged round a 57-metre swimming pool and only 5min walk from Five Rathas. Beautifully furnished, spacious rooms ($230), more luxurious cottages ($320) and sea-facing suites ($350). ❾

Greenwoods Resort Othavadai Cross St Ⓣ044/2744 3318, Ⓔgreenwoods_resort@yahoo.com. A very friendly family-run place, set in a lush garden that's lovingly tended by the ladies of the house. There's a choice of a/c or non-a/c rooms with bath, some with a private balcony. Extremely good value. ❶–❺

Radisson Resort Temple Bay 1km north of town, off Kovalam Rd Ⓣ044/2744 2251, Ⓦwww.grthotels.com. Great location on the beach, with views of the Shore Temple. Thatched beachside cottages have sea-facing balconies, and there are huge rooms in the main building. There's a swimming pool and restaurant on site. Rates start around $180. ❾

Mamalla Heritage 104 East Raja St Ⓣ044/2744 2060, Ⓦwww.hotelmamallaheritage.com. Efficient and modern hotel on the main drag through the village. Overlooking a courtyard, the comfortable and spotless a/c rooms have fridge and TV, and there are two very good restaurants on site (see p.956). ❺

Ramakrishna Lodge 8 Othavadai St Ⓣ044/2744 2331. Clean, well-maintained rooms in the heart of the tourist enclave, all with bathrooms and a few with a/c, set round a courtyard filled with pot plants; the newest rooms are on the top storey, and have sea views. There's a back-up generator, and they often have vacancies when everywhere else is full. ❶–❸

Santana Othavadai St Ⓣ9444 290832. Six sizeable and spotless first-floor rooms, of which the seafront one is a gem, sandwiched in between their popular ground-floor beachside restaurant and roof terrace. ❸–❹

Sea Breeze Othavadai Cross St Ⓣ044/2744 3035, Ⓔseabreezehotel@hotmail.com. The only bona fide beach resort within the village, featuring comfy and spacious a/c rooms (singles are particularly good value), a smart pool (open to non-residents for Rs200) and an Ayurveda centre. ❺–❽

Siva Guest House 2 Othavadai Cross St Ⓣ044/2744 3234, Ⓦwww.sivaguesthouse.com. Clean, tidy lodge with choice of a/c and non-a/c rooms. Good value. ❶–❹

Sri Murugan Guest House 42 Othavadai St Ⓣ044/2744 2552. Small and peaceful, with courteous service, clean rooms (some a/c) and a rooftop restaurant. One of the nicest options in the area and singles only Rs150. ❷–❹

Tina Blue View Othavadai St Ⓣ044/2744 2319. Established family guesthouse with simple turquoise and whitewashed rooms, all with attached bath and mosquito nets, and proceeds from the fine rooftop *Seagulls* restaurant go to an orphanage. ❶–❸

The Shore Temple

Visible for kilometres along the beach, the unforgettable silhouette of Mamallapuram's **Shore Temple** (daily sunrise to sunset; Rs250 [Rs10], includes Pancha Pandava *rathas* if visited on the same day) dates from the early eighth century and is considered to be the earliest stone-built temple in south India. Today, due to the combined forces of wind, salt and sand, much of the detailed carving has eroded, giving the whole temple a soft, rounded appearance.

The taller of the towers is raised above a cell that faces out to sea – don't be surprised to see mischievous monkeys crouching inside. Approached from the west through two low-walled enclosures lined with small Nandi (bull) figures, the temple comprises two lingam shrines (one facing east, the other west), and a third shrine between them housing an image of the reclining Vishnu. Recent excavations, revealing a tank containing a structured stone column thought to have been a lantern, and a large Varaha (boar incarnation of Vishnu) aligned with the Vishnu shrine, suggest that the area was sacred long before the Pallavas chose it as a temple site.

The Krishna Mandapa and Arjuna's Penance

A little to the west of the village centre, off Shore Temple Road, the enormous bas-relief known as the **Krishna Mandapa** shows Krishna raising Mount Govardhana aloft in one hand. The sculptor's original intention must have been for the rock above Krishna to represent the mountain, but the seventeenth-century Vijayanagar addition of a columned *mandapa*, or entrance hall, prevents a clear view of the carving. Krishna is also depicted seated milking a cow, and standing playing the flute. Other figures are *gopas* and *gopis*, the cowboys and girls of his pastoral youth. Lions (one with a human face) sit to the left, while above them is a bull.

Another bas-relief, **Arjuna's Penance** (also referred to as the "Descent of the Ganges") is a few metres north, opposite the modern Talasayana Perumal Temple. The surface of this rock erupts with detailed carving, most notably endearing and naturalistic renditions of animals. On the left-hand side, Arjuna, one of the Pandava brothers and a consummate archer, is shown standing on one leg. He is looking at the midday sun through a prism formed by his hands, meditating on Shiva, who is represented by a nearby statue fashioned by Arjuna himself. The Shiva Purana tells that Arjuna made the journey to a forest on the banks of the Ganges to do penance, in the hope that Shiva would part with his favourite weapon, the *pashupatashastra*, a magic staff or arrow. Shiva eventually materialized in the guise of Kirata, a wild forest-dweller, and picked a fight with Arjuna over a boar they both claimed to have shot. Arjuna only realized he was dealing with the deity after his attempts to drub the wild man proved futile; narrowly escaping death at the playful hand of Shiva, he was finally rewarded with the weapon. Not far away, mimicking Arjuna's devout pose, an emaciated (presumably ascetic) cat stands on hind legs, surrounded by mice. To the right of Arjuna, a natural cleft represents the **Ganges**, complete with *nagas* – water spirits in the form of cobras. You may well see sudden movements among the carved animals: lazing goats often join the permanent features.

Ganesha Ratha and Varaha cave

Just north of Arjuna's Penance a path leads west to a single monolith, the **Ganesha Ratha**. Its image of Ganesh dates from this century; some say it was installed at the instigation of England's King George V. The sculpture at one end, of a protecting demon with a tricorn headdress, is reminiscent of the Indus Valley civilization's 4000-year-old horned figure known as the "proto-Shiva".

Behind Arjuna's Penance, southwest of the Ganesha *ratha*, is the **Varaha Mandapa II Cave**, whose entrance hall has two pillars with horned lion-bases and a cell flanked by two *dvarpalas*, or guardians. One of four **panels** shows the boar-incarnation of Vishnu, who stands with one foot resting on the *naga* snake-king as he lifts a diminutive Prithvi – the earth – from the primordial ocean. Another is of Gajalakshmi, the goddess Lakshmi seated on a lotus being bathed by a pair of elephants. Trivikrama, the dwarf brahmin who becomes huge and bestrides the world in three steps to defeat the demon king Bali, is shown in another panel, and finally a four-armed Durga is depicted in another.

A little way north of Arjuna's Penance, precipitously balanced on the top of a ridge, is a massive, natural, almost spherical boulder called **Krishna's Butter Ball**. Picnickers and goats often rest in its perilous-looking shade.

The lighthouses and the Mahishasuramardini Cave

South of Arjuna's Penance at the highest point in an area of steep paths, unfinished temples, ruins, scampering monkeys and massive rocks, the **New Lighthouse** affords fine views east to the Shore Temple, and west across paddy fields and flat lands littered with rocks. Next to it, the **Olakanesvara** ("flame-eyed" Shiva), or **Old Lighthouse Temple**, used as a lighthouse until the early twentieth century, dates from the Rajasimha period (674–800 AD).

Nestling between the two lighthouses is the **Mahishasuramardini Cave**, whose central image portrays Shiva and Parvati with the child Murugan seated on Parvati's lap. Shiva's right foot rests on the back of the bull Nandi, and Parvati sits casually, leaning on her left hand. On the left wall, beyond an empty cell, a panel depicts Vishnu reclining on the serpent, his attitude of repose contrasted with the weapon-brandishing demons, Madhu and Kaithaba. Other figures seek Vishnu's permission to chase them. Opposite, an intricately carved panel shows the eight-armed goddess Durga as Mahishasuramardini, the "crusher" of the buffalo demon Mahishasura. The panel shows Durga riding a lion, in the midst of the struggle. Accompanied by dwarf *ganas*, she wields a bow and other weapons; Mahishasura, equipped with a club, can be seen to the right, in flight with fellow demons.

The tiny **Government College of Architecture and Sculpture Museum** (Mon–Sat 10am–5pm; Rs2, camera Rs10), on West Raja Street near the lighthouse, has a rather motley collection of unlabelled Pallava sculpture found in and around Mamallapuram.

Pancha Pandava Rathas (Five Rathas)

In a sandy compound 1.5km south of the village centre stands the stunning group of monoliths known as the **Pancha Pandava Rathas** (daily sunrise to sunset; Rs250 [Rs10] including the Shore Temple on the same day), the five chariots of the Pandavas. Dating from the period of Narasimhavarman I (c.630–670 AD), they consist of five separate freestanding sculptures that imitate structured temples plus some beautifully carved life-sized animals.

The "architecture" of the *rathas* reflects a variety of styles and stands almost as a model for much subsequent development in the southern style. Carving was always executed from top to bottom, enabling the artists to work on the upper parts with no fear of damaging anything below. Intriguingly, it's thought that the *rathas* were never used for worship.

The southernmost and tallest of the *rathas*, named after the eldest of the Pandavas, is the pyramidal **Dharmaraja**. Set on a square base, the upper part comprises a series of diminishing storeys, each with a row of pavilions. Four corner blocks, each with two panels and standing figures, are broken up by two pillars and pilasters supported by squatting lions. Figures on the panels include

Ardhanarishvara (Shiva and female consort in one figure), Brahma, the king Narasimhavarman I, and Harihara (Shiva and Vishnu combined). The central tier includes sculptures of Shiva Gangadhara and one of the earliest representations in Tamil Nadu of the dancing Shiva, Nataraja, who became all-important in the region. Alongside, the **Bhima** *ratha*, the largest of the group, is the least complete. Devoid of carved figures, the upper storeys, like in the Dharmaraja, feature false windows and repeated pavilion-shaped ornamentation.

The Arjuna and Draupadi *rathas* share a base. Behind the **Arjuna**, the most complete of the entire group and very similar to the Dharmaraja, stands a superb unfinished sculpture of Shiva's bull Nandi. **Draupadi** is unique in terms of rock-cut architecture, with a roof that appears to be based on a straw-thatched hut. There's an image of Durga inside, but the figure of her lion vehicle outside is aligned side-on and not facing the image, suggesting this was not a real temple. To the west, close to a life-sized carving of an elephant, stands the *ratha* named after the twin brothers **Nakula and Sahadeva**.

Eating and drinking

Mamallapuram is crammed with small restaurants, most of them specializing in **seafood** – tiger prawns, pomfret, tuna, shark and lobster – usually served marinated and grilled with chips and salad. Always establish in advance exactly how much your seafood will cost. As this is a traveller's hangout, there are also numerous places offering the usual array of pasta, pancakes, brown bread and bland Indian dishes. If you want to enjoy real Indian food, head to the *dhabas* by the bus stand and the stalls on the south side of the Shore Temple complex. **Beer** is widely available, but it's pricey (Rs100 or more).

Bob Marley 80m north of Othavadai St. Cheerful and lively beachfront place with a seated restaurant on the lower floor, serving fresh fish and good curries, and a chilled-out bar area above. Music varies from reggae to rock.

Garden View *Greenwoods Resort*, Othavadai Cross St. Friendly first-floor terrace restaurant which serves delicious sizzlers, seafood and curries – they'll actually make proper hot ones if you ask. There's a choice of views – the relaxed garden or busier street-life. Mains Rs50–100.

Golden Palate *Mamalla Heritage* hotel, 104 East Raja St. Blissfully cool café with a/c and tinted windows, serving the best veg food in the village – Rs70 meals at lunchtime, north Indian tandoori in the courtyard in the evenings – and wonderful ice-cream sundaes. The equally popular rooftop *Waves* restaurant does fish and seafood in the evening, too.

La Vie En Rose West Raja St. Pleasant garden location offering a Westerner-oriented menu including a few unusual salads, great spaghetti and chicken specialities for Rs80–120.

Le Yogi Othavadai St. Run by a French/Indian couple, this welcoming and relaxed place is a good spot to chill. Tasty pastas and salads can be washed down with good coffee and lassis. Most dishes Rs100–150.

Luna Magica 100m north of Othavadai St. Slap on the beach, with top-notch seafood, particularly tiger prawns and lobster, which are kept alive in a tank. The big specimens cost a hefty Rs600–800, but are as tasty as you'll find anywhere, served in a rich tomato, butter and garlic sauce. They also do passable sangria, made with sweet Chennai red wine, and cold beer, as well as plenty of less expensive dishes – including a good fish curry and sizzlers.

Mamalla Bhavan Shore Temple Rd, opposite the bus stand. Very popular pure-veg and "meals" joint that's invariably packed. Good for *iddli-wada* breakfasts, and evening dosas and other snacks. Unlimited lunchtime meals cost around Rs40.

Moonrakers Othavadai St. Cool jazz and blues sounds, great fresh seafood, chess sets and slick service ensure this place is filled year round with foreign tourists; the owners will try and entice you in every single time you pass by. A decent fish meal costs around Rs250

Nautilus Othavadai Cross St. High-quality but reasonably priced eatery, run by an amicable French chef. The menu features fine soups, meat, seafood and veg dishes, grilled or with an array of sauces, plus travellers' favourites, for Rs80–150.

Village Inn Thirukula St. This diminutive thatched eatery serves up seafood grilled on a charcoal fire, as well as a superb butter-fried chicken in a tomato-garlic sauce. Rs150–200 for meat or fish main courses.

Around Mamallapuram

The sandy hinterland and flat estuarine paddy fields around Mamallapuram harbour a handful of sights well worth making forays from the coast to see. A short way north along the main highway, the **Government College of Sculpture** and elaborately carved **Tiger Cave** can easily be reached by bicycle. To get to the **Crocodile Bank**, where rare reptiles from across south Asia are bred for release into the wild, or **Dakshina Chitra**, a museum devoted to south Indian architecture and crafts, you can take any coastal bus route between Mamallapuram and Chennai, or rent a moped for the day.

Government College of Sculpture and the Tiger Cave

A visit to the **Government College of Sculpture**, 2km north of Mamallapuram on the Kovalam (Covelong) Road (ⓣ044/2744 2261; hours vary; free), gives a fascinating insight into the processes of sculpture training. You can watch anything from preliminary drawing, with its strict rules regarding proportion and iconography, through to the execution of sculpture, both in wood and stone, in the classical Hindu tradition. Contact the college office to make an appointment.

A further 3km north along Kovalam Road from the college, set amid trees close to the sea, the extraordinary **Tiger Cave** (daily, sunrise to sunset; free) contains a shrine to Durga, approached by a flight of steps that passes two subsidiary cells. Following the line of an irregularly shaped rock, the cave is remarkable for its elaborate exterior, which features multiple lion-heads surrounding the entrance to the main cell. If you sit for long enough, the section on the left with seated figures in niches above two elephants begins to resemble an enormous owl.

Crocodile Bank

The **Crocodile Bank** (Tues–Sun 8am–6pm; Rs30, camera Rs10, video camera Rs75; ⓦwww.madrascrocodilebank.org) at Vadanemmeli, 14km north of town on the road to Chennai, was set up in 1976 by the American zoologist Romulus Whittaker, to protect and breed indigenous crocodiles. The Bank has been so successful (from fifteen crocs to five thousand in the first fifteen years) that its remit now extends to saving endangered species, such as turtles and lizards, from around the world.

Low-walled enclosures in its garden compound house hundreds of inscrutable crocodiles, soaking in ponds or sunning themselves on the banks. Breeds include the fish-eating, knobbly-nosed gharial, and the world's largest species, the saltwater *Crocodylus porosus*, which can grow to 8m in length. You can watch feeding time at about 4.30pm on Monday or Thursday or have your own brief feeding session any time for a fee of Rs20. The temptation to take photos is tempered by the sight of those hungry saurians clambering over each other to snap up the chopped flesh, within inches of the top of the wall.

Another important field of work is conducted with the collaboration of local Irula people, whose traditional expertise is with snakes. Cobras are brought to the bank for **venom collection**, to be used in the treatment of snakebites. Elsewhere, snakes are repeatedly "milked" until they die, but here at the bank only a limited amount is taken from each snake, enabling them to return to the wild. This section costs an extra Rs5.

Dakshina Chitra

Occupying a patch of sand dunes midway between Chennai and Mamallapuram, **Dakshina Chitra** (daily except Tues 10am–6pm; Rs200 [Rs75]; ⓦwww.dakshinachitra.net), literally "Vision of the South", is one of India's best-conceived folk museums, devoted to the rich architectural and artistic heritage of Kerala, Karnataka, Andhra Pradesh and Tamil Nadu. Set up by the Chennai Craft Foundation, the museum exposes visitors to many disappearing traditions of the region which you might otherwise not be aware of, from tribal fertility cults and *Ayyannar* field deities to pottery and leather shadow puppets.

A selection of traditional buildings from across peninsular India has been painstakingly reconstructed using original materials. Exhibitions attached to them convey the environmental and cultural diversity of the south, most graphically expressed in a wonderful textile collection featuring antique silk and cotton saris from various castes and regions. Snacks are available on site.

Kanchipuram

Ask any Tamil what **KANCHIPURAM** (aka "Kanchi") is famous for, and they'll probably say silk saris, shrines and saints – in that order. A dynastic capital throughout the medieval era, it remains one of the country's seven holiest cities, sacred to both Shaivites and Vaishnavites, and among the few surviving centres of goddess worship in the south. Year round, pilgrims pour through for a quick puja stop on the Tirupati tour circuit and, if they can afford it, a spot of shopping in the sari emporia. For non-Hindu visitors, however, Kanchipuram holds less appeal. Although the temples are undeniably impressive, the town itself is unremittingly hot, with only basic accommodation and amenities. Some people prefer to visit Kanchipuram as a **day-trip** from Chennai or Mamallapuram, both a two-hour bus ride away.

Established by the **Pallava** kings in the fourth century AD, Kanchipuram served as their **capital** for five hundred years, and continued to flourish throughout the Chola, Pandya and Vijayanagar eras. Under the Pallavas, it was an important scholastic forum, and a meeting point for Jain, Buddhist and Hindu cultures. Its **temples** dramatically reflect this enduring political prominence, spanning the years from the peak of Pallava construction to the seventeenth century, when the ornamentation of the *gopuras* and pillared halls was at its most elaborate (for more on Tamil Nadu's temples, see p.961). All can be easily reached by foot, bike or rickshaw, and shut daily between noon and 4pm. You might need to be a little firm to resist the attentions of pushy puja-wallahs, who try to con foreigners into overpriced ceremonies. If you've come for silk, head for the shops that line Gandhi and Thirukatchininambi roads.

Ekambareshvara Temple

On the north side of town, Kanchipuram's largest temple and most important Shiva shrine, the **Ekambareshvara Temple** (camera Rs10, video Rs20) – also known as Ekambaranatha – is easily identified by its colossal whitewashed *gopuras*, which rise to almost 60m. The main temple contains some Pallava work, but was mostly constructed in the sixteenth and seventeenth centuries, and stands within a vast walled enclosure beside some smaller shrines and a large fish-filled water tank.

The entrance is through a high-arched passageway beneath an elaborate *gopura* in the south wall which leads to an open courtyard and a majestic "thousand-pillared hall", or *kalyan mandapa*. This faces the tank in the north and the sanctuary in the west that protects the emblem of Shiva (here in his form as **Kameshvara**, Lord of Desire), *Prithvi lingam* (one of five lingams in Tamil Nadu that represent the elements, in this case *Prithvi,* the earth). Behind the sanctum, accessible from the covered hallway around it, an eerie bare hall lies beneath a

profusely carved *gopura*, and in the courtyard a venerable **mango tree** represents the tree under which Shiva and Kamakshi were married. This union is celebrated during a festival each April, when many couples are married in the *kalyan mandapa*.

Sankaramadam

Kanchipuram is the seat of a line of holy men bearing the title **acharya**, whose line dates back perhaps as far as 1300 BC to the saint Adi Sankaracharya. The 68th acharya, the highly revered Sri Chandrasekharendra Sarasvati Swami, died in January 1994 at the age of 101. Buried in the sitting position, as is the custom for great Hindu sages, his mortal remains are enshrined in a *samadhi* at the **Sankaramadam**, a *math* (monastery for Hindu renouncers) down the road from the Ekambareshvara Temple. Lined with old photographs from the life of the former swami, with young brahmin students chanting Sanskrit verses in the background, it's a typically Tamil blend of simple sanctity and garish modern glitz. The *math*'s two huge elephants are available to bestow blessings upon visiting pilgrims for a small fee.

Kailasanatha Temple

The **Kailasanatha Temple**, the oldest structure in Kanchipuram and the finest example of Pallava architecture in south India, is situated among several low-roofed houses just over 1km west of the town centre. Built by the Pallava king Rajasimha early in the eighth century, its intimate size and simple carving distinguish it from the town's later temples. Usually quieter than its neighbours, the shrine becomes the focus of vigorous celebrations during the **Mahashivratri**

festival each March. Like its contemporary, the Shore Temple at Mamallapuram, it is built of soft sandstone, but its sheltered position has spared it from wind and sand erosion, and it remains remarkably intact, despite some rather clumsy renovation work.

Kamakshi Amman Temple

Built during Pallava supremacy and modified in the fourteenth and seventeenth centuries, the **Kamakshi Amman Temple**, north of the bus stand, combines several styles, with an ancient central shrine, gates from the Vijayanagar period, and high, heavily sculpted, creamy *gopuras* set above the gateways.

This is one of India's three holiest shrines to Shakti, Shiva's cosmic energy depicted in female form, usually as his consort. The goddess Kamakshi, a local form of Parvati, shown with a sugar-cane bow and arrows of flowers, is honoured for having lured Shiva to Kanchipuram, where they were married, and thus having forged the connection between the local community and the god. In February or March, deities are wheeled to the temple in huge wooden "cars", decked with robed statues and swaying plantain leaves.

Practicalities

Kanchipuram is situated on the Vegavathi River 70km southwest of Chennai, and slightly less from Mamallapuram on the coast. **Buses** from Chennai, Mamallapuram and Chengalpattu stop at the stand in the town centre just off Kosa Street. The **railway station** in the northeast sees twelve daily passenger services from Chengalpattu (originating in Chennai, Arakkonam, Tirupathi and Puducherry) and two *Express* trains (the weekly Mumbai–Madurai and bi-weekly Mumbai–Nagercoil express).

As most of the main roads are wide and traffic rarely unmanageable, the best way to **get around** Kanchi is by **bicycle** – available for minimal rates (Rs3/hr) at stalls west and northeast of the bus stand. The town's vegetable markets, hotels, restaurants and bazaars are concentrated in the centre of town, near the bus stand.

There is an **ATM** on Gandhi Road, though the nearest official foreign exchange places are in Chennai and Mamallapuram. Fast **internet** connection is available at Net4U, at the town end of TK Road.

Accommodation and eating

There's no fancy **accommodation** in Kanchipuram, but plenty of good budget and lower mid-range places for a night or two. Best of the bunch is the *Baboo Surya*, 85 East Raja St (ⓣ044/2722 2556, ⓦwww.hotelbaboosoorya.com; ❸–❹), excellent value with immaculate attached rooms (❹), some with temple views, and its own restaurant. Another good option is *MM*, 65/66 Nellukkara St (ⓣ044/272 27250, ⓦmmhotels.com; ❸–❹), with clean, good-value rooms (❹). Opposite, at 20-B Nellukkara St, the simple but spotless *Raja's Lodge* (ⓣ044/2722 2603; ❶–❸) is the best real cheapie, with friendly staff and reasonable rooms (❷).

Moving on from Kanchipuram

Bus services run to Chennai (every 10min; 1hr 30min–2hr); Coimbatore (3 daily; 9–10hr); Madurai (4 daily; 10–12hr); Puducherry (10 daily; 3–4hr); Tiruchirapalli (3 daily; 7hr); Tiruvannamalai (every 30min–1hr; 3–4hr).

For train services see 'Practicalities', above.

Vedanthangal Bird Sanctuary

One of India's most spectacular bird sanctuaries lies roughly 1km east of the village of **Vedanthangal**, 30km from the east coast and 86km southwest of Chennai. The **sanctuary** is busiest with birdlife between December and February, when it's totally flooded. The rains of the northeast monsoon, sweeping through in October or November, bring local and migratory water birds including some that nest and settle here until the dry season (usually April), when they leave for wetter areas. Abundant trees on mounds above water level provide perfect nesting spots, alive by January with fledglings. Visitors can watch the avian action from a path at the water's edge, or from a watchtower (fitted out with strong binoculars). Try to come at sunset, when the birds return from feeding. Common Indian **species** to look out for are openbill storks, spoonbills, pelicans, black cormorants, and herons of several types. You may also see ibises, grey pelicans, migrant cuckoos, sandpipers, egrets (which paddle in the rice fields), and darting bee-eaters. **Getting to Vedanthangal** can present a few problems. The nearest town is Maduranthakam, 8km east, on NH-45 between Chengalpattu and Tindivanam, from where there are hourly buses to the sanctuary. Alternatively, direct services run every hour or two from Chengalpattu. Taxis make the journey from Maduranthakam for Rs.500 but cannot be booked from Vedanthangal. Entry to the sanctuary is Rs5 (camera–Rs 25, video recorders Rs100). To arrange accommodation, call the Forest Ranger (☎9444 266213) or Wildlife Warden in Chennai (☎044/2432 1471 or ☎9541 520006).

The most highly rated places to **eat** in town are the two branches of *Saravana Bhavan*, an offshoot of the famous Chennai chain of pure-veg restaurants, which offer superb Rs30 "meals" at lunchtime, and a long list of south Indian snacks the rest of the day. One is on Nellukkara Road near *Sri Kusal*, and the other, *Sai Saravana*, just off Gandhi Road.

Tiruvannamalai

Synonymous with the fifth Hindu element of fire, **TIRUVANNAMALAI**, 100km southwest of Kanchipuram, ranks, along with Madurai, Kanchipuram, Chidambaram and Trichy, as one of the five holiest towns in Tamil Nadu. Its name, meaning "Red Mountain", derives from the spectacular extinct volcano, **Arunachala**, which rises behind it, and which glows an unearthly crimson in the dawn light. This awesome natural backdrop, combined with the colossal **Arunachaleshvara Temple** in the centre of town, make Tiruvannamalai one of the region's most memorable destinations. Well off the tourist trail, it's a perfect place to get to grips with life in small-town Tamil Nadu, especially for those with an interest in Hinduism.

Mythology identifies Arunachala as the place where Shiva asserted his power over Brahma and Vishnu by manifesting himself as a lingam of fire, or **agni-lingam**. The event is commemorated each year at the rising of the full moon in November/ December, when a vast vat of two thousand litres of ghee and a 30m-wide wick is lit by priests on the summit of Arunachala. This symbolizes the fulfilment of Shiva's promise to reappear each year to vanquish the forces of darkness and ignorance with firelight.

The sacred Red Mountain is also associated with the famous twentieth-century saint, **Sri Ramana Maharishi**, who chose it as the site for his twenty-three-year meditation retreat. A crop of small ashrams have sprung up on the edge of town below Sri Ramana's Cave, some of them more authentic than others, and the ranks of white-cotton-clad foreigners floating between them have become a defining feature of Tiruvannamalai.

Arunachaleshvara Temple

Known to Hindus as the "Temple of the Eternal Sunrise", the enormous **Arunachaleshvara Temple**, built over a period of almost a thousand years, consists of three concentric courtyards whose gateways are topped by tapering *gopuras*, the largest of which cover the east and north gates. The best spot from which to view the precinct, a breathtaking spectacle against the sprawling plains and lumpy, granite Shevaroy Hills, is the path up to Sri Ramana Maharishi's meditation cave, Virupaksha (see below), on the lower slopes of Arunachala. To enter the temple, however, head for the huge eastern gateway, which leads through the thick outer wall carved with images of deities, local saints and teachers. In the basement of a raised hall to the right before entering the next courtyard is the Parthala lingam, where Sri Ramana Maharishi is said to have sat in a state of Supreme Awareness while ants devoured his flesh.

The caves and Sri Ramanashramam ashram

Opposite the western entrance of the temple complex, a path leads up a holy hill (15min) to the **Virupaksha Cave**, where the Maharishi stayed between 1899 and 1916. He personally built the bench outside and the hill-shaped lingam and platform inside, where all are welcome to meditate in peace. When this cave became too crowded, Ramana shifted to another, hidden away a few minutes further up the hill. He named this one, and the small house built onto it, **Skandasramam**, and lived there between 1916 and 1922. The inner cave here is also set aside for meditation, and the front patio affords splendid views across the temple, town and surrounding plains.

The caves can also be reached via the pilgrims' path winding uphill from the **Sri Ramanashramam ashram**, 2km south of the temple along the main road. This simple complex is where the sage lived after returning from his retreat on Arunachala, and where his body is today enshrined. The *samadhi* has become a popular place for Sri Ramana's devotees on pilgrimage, but interested visitors are welcome to stay in the dorms here (Ⓣ01475/237200 or Ⓣ9244 937292). There's also an excellent bookshop (daily 7.30–11am & 2.30–6.30pm) stocking a huge range of titles on the life and teachings of the guru, as well as quality postcards, calendars and religious images.

Practicalities

Tiruvannamalai is served by regular **buses** from Chennai, Puducherry and Trichy. Coming from the coast, it's easiest to make your way on one of the numerous buses from Tindivanam. The town **bus stand** is just over 1km north of the temple on the main road to Gingee. Half a kilometre east of there, the **railway station** is on the line between Tirupati and Madurai, with a daily service in each direction.

The Pradakshana

During the annual Kartiggai festival, Hindu pilgrims are supposed to perform an auspicious circumambulation of Arunachala, known as the **Pradakshana** (*pra* signifies the removal of all sins, *da* the fulfilment of desires, *kshi* freedom from the cycle of rebirth, and *na* spiritual liberation). Along the way, offerings are made at a string of shrines, tanks, temples, lingams, pillared meditation halls, sacred rocks, springs, trees, and caves related to the Tiruvannamalai legends. Although hectic during the festival, the paved path linking them all together is quiet for most of the year, and makes a wonderful day-hike, affording fine views of the town and its environs.

There is **internet** access at the Image Computer Centre, 52 Car St, and Sri Sai, 14-A Kadambarayam St.

For **food**, you've a choice of a dozen or so typical south Indian "meals" joints just off the bottom of Car Street. Delicious hot ghee chapattis are served here all afternoon, as well as all the usual rice specialities. The *Udipi Brindhavan* and the *Deepam* on Car Street opposite the temple's east entrance are typical *udipi* restaurants, serving, amongst other dishes, excellent *parotta*s for under Rs10. The latter also has an adjacent ice-cream and milkshake parlour. Of the hotels, the *Trisul* has a posh ground-floor restaurant which serves north Indian buffets for around Rs100, and tandoori in the evening, while the *Ramakrishna* does excellent lunchtime thalis and a range of north and south Indian food in the evenings.

Accommodation

Arunachala 5 Vada Sannathi St ⓣ04175/228300. Large, clean and comfortable hotel, right outside the main temple entrance. Not the quietest place to stay but certainly atmospheric. ❸–❹

NS Lodge 47 Thiruvoodal St ⓣ04175/225388. Facing the south entrance of Arunachaleshvara Temple. Clean attached rooms (some a/c) with cable TV; great temple view from the roof. ❷–❹

Park 26 Kosmadam St ⓣ04175/222471. Reliable budget option 2min walk northeast of the main temple. All rooms are non-a/c and basic but clean. There's a busy vegetarian canteen on the ground floor. ❶

Ramakrishna 34-F Polur Rd ⓣ04175/250005, ⓔinfo@hotelramakrishna.com. One of the best places in town, with large rooms with attached bath and a decent restaurant. It's a 5min walk north of the bus stand: follow Chinnakadai St north and take the left fork; the hotel is 200m along on the right. ❷–❹

SASA Lodge Chinnakadai St, almost opposite the bus stand ⓣ04175/252293 One of the best budget lodges, painted bright blue and white, with decent enough rooms, some of which are a/c. ❶–❸

Puducherry and Auroville

First impressions of **PUDUCHERRY** (**Pondicherry**, also often referred to simply as Pondy), the former capital of French India, can be unpromising. Instead of the leafy boulevards and *pétanque* pitches you might expect, its messy outer suburbs and bus stand are as cluttered and chaotic as any typical Tamil town. Closer to the seafront, however, the atmosphere grows tangibly more Gallic, as the bazaars give way to rows of houses whose shuttered windows and colourwashed facades wouldn't look out of place in Montpellier. For anyone familiar with the British colonial imprint, the town can induce culture shock to see richly ornamented Catholic churches, French road names and policemen in De Gaulle-style *képis*, and *boules* played in the dusty squares. Many of the seafront buildings were damaged by the 2004 tsunami, but Puducherry's tourist infrastructure remained intact.

Known to Greek and Roman geographers as "Poduke", Puducherry was an important staging post on the second-century maritime trade route between Rome and the Far East. When the Roman Empire declined, the Pallavas and Cholas took control and were followed by a succession of colonial powers, from the Portuguese in the sixteenth century to the French, Danes and British, who exchanged the enclave several times after the various battles and treaties of the Carnatic Wars in the early eighteenth century. Puducherry's heyday, however, dates from the arrival of the French governor Joseph **Dupleix**, who accepted the governorship in 1742 and immediately set about rebuilding a town decimated by its former British occupants. It was he who instituted the street plan of a central grid encircled by a broad oblong boulevard, bisected north to south by a canal dividing the "Ville Blanche", to the east, from the "Ville Noire", to the west.

Although relinquished by the French in 1954 – when the town became the headquarters of the **Union Territory of Pondicherry**, administering the three other former colonial enclaves scattered across south India – Puducherry's split personality still prevails. West of the canal stretches a bustling Indian market town, while to the east, towards the sea, the streets are emptier, cleaner and decidedly European. The seaside promenade, **Goubert Salai** (formerly Beach Road), has the forlorn look of an out-of-season French resort, complete with its own white Hôtel de Ville. Many visitors are grave Europeans in white Indian costume, busy about their spiritual quest. It was here that **Sri Aurobindo Ghose** (1872–1950), a leading figure in the freedom struggle in Bengal, was given shelter after it became unwise to live close to the British in Calcutta. His ashram attracts thousands of devotees from all around the world, most particularly from Bengal.

Ten kilometres north, the Utopian experiment-in-living **Auroville** was inspired by Aurobindo's disciple, the charismatic Mirra Alfassa, a Parisian painter, musician and mystic better known as "The Mother". Today this slightly surreal place is populated by numbers of expats and visited by long-stay Europeans eager to find inner peace.

Arrival, information and getting around

All buses pull into **New Bus Stand**, which lies on the west edge of town. From here, auto-rickshaws charge at least Rs50 into the old town, taxis double that, but you can jump in a *tempo* to central Ambour Salai for Rs5–10. Puducherry's **railway station** is in the south, five minutes' walk from the sea off Surbaiyah Salai.

The **Puducherry Tourism Development Corporation (PTDC)** office is at 40 Goubert Salai (daily 8.45am–5pm; ⓣ0413/233 9497, ⓦtourism.pondicherry.gov.in). The staff are extremely helpful, providing leaflets and a city map, and information about Auroville; they can also book you onto their **city tours** (half-day 1.30–5pm, non-a/c Rs100, a/c Rs150; full-day 9.45am–5pm, non-a/c Rs200, a/c Rs250) and help arrange **car rental**. There is a wealth of **ATMs**, and recommended places to **change money** include the State Bank of India on Surcouf Street and UCO Bank on Rue Mahe de Labourdonnais. The **GPO** is on Ranga Pillai Street (Mon–Sat 10am–7.30pm). **Internet access** is available throughout central Puducherry; several places, such as the iWay branch at 36 Nidarajapayar St, also offer Netphone facilities.

Puducherry is well served by auto-rickshaws, but for **getting around**, most tourists rent a **bicycle** from one of the many stalls dotted about town (Rs40/day, plus Rs200 refundable deposit). For trips further afield such as Auroville, you may want to rent a **moped** or **scooter**. Of the rental firms operating in town, both Sri Ganesh Cycle Store, 39 Mission St (ⓣ0413/222 2801), and Sri Sri Durga Pharameshwari Cycle Stores, 106-B Mission St (ⓣ0413/233 4101), have new models such as Honda Kinetics for Rs150 per day, plus a Rs500 deposit.

Accommodation

Puducherry's **basic lodges** are concentrated around the main market area, Ranga Pillai Street and Rue Nehru. Guesthouses belonging to the **Sri Aurobindo Ashram** offer fantastic value for money, but come with a lot of baggage apart from your own (regulations, curfews and overpowering "philosophy of life" notices) and are not overtly welcoming.

Moving on from Puducherry

There are numerous bus connections to: Bengaluru (4 daily; 10–12hr); Chennai (every 10–20min; 2hr 30min–3hr); Chidambaram (every 20min; 2hr); Coimbatore (10 daily; 9hr); Kanchipuram (10 daily; 3–4hr); Kanyakumari (hourly; 12–13hr); Madurai (hourly; 9–10hr); Mamallapuram (every 10–20min; 1hr 30min–2hr); Thanjavur (hourly; 5hr); Tiruchirapalli (every 30min; 5–6hr); Tiruvannamalai (every 20min; 2hr).

Amala Lodge 92 Ranga Pillai St ⓣ0413/233 8910. One of the best and most central cheapies. The rooms, some with common bathrooms, are a little poky but clean enough. ❶–❷

Aruna 3 Zamindar Garden, SV Patel Rd ⓣ0413/233 7756, ⓔarunahotel@yahoo.com. Set on a quiet side-street, the decent-value attached doubles here are of varying sizes. There is a/c and TV in some, and all have balconies. ❸–❹

French Guest House 38 Ambour Salai ⓣ0413/420 0853. Clean, spacious rooms, including some family suites, in a welcoming central hotel, better value than its larger competitors. All rooms have optional a/c. ❸–❹

Hotel de l'Orient 17 Rue Romain Rolland ⓣ0413/234 3067, ⓦwww.neemranahotels.com. A beautiful, UNESCO heritage-accorded French house with sixteen rooms, individually decorated with French antiques, tiled balconies and long shuttered windows overlooking a leafy courtyard restaurant. Wonderfully romantic. ❽

International Guest House 47 Gingee Salai ⓣ0413/233 6699, ⓔingh@vsnl.net. The largest Aurobindo establishment, with dozens of very large, clean rooms, some a/c. It's a good budget option but typically institutional, with a 10.30pm curfew. ❶–❹

Park Guest House Goubert Salai ⓣ0413/233 4412, ⓔparkgh@sriaurobindoashram.org.in. Another Sri Aurobindo Society pad, with strict rules (no alcohol or TVs) and a 10.30pm curfew. Rooms are spotless and very comfortable, with new mosquito nets and sitouts overlooking a well-watered garden and the sea. There's also bike rental, laundry and a restaurant. ❸

Soorya International 55 Ranga Pillai St ⓣ0413/233 6856, ⓔsooryainternational@hotelstamilnadu.com. Central hotel with very large, immaculate rooms. Recently further upgraded to include a/c in all rooms. Rates include breakfast. ❺–❼

Surya Swastika 11 ID Koil St ⓣ0413/234 3092, ⓔsuryaswastika@sify.com. Traditional Tamil guesthouse in a quiet corner of town, with nine basic rooms around a central courtyard that doubles as a pilgrims' canteen at lunchtime. Incredibly cheap, and cleaner than most of the bazaar lodges. ❶–❷

The Town

Puducherry's beachside promenade, **Goubert Salai**, is a favourite place for a stroll, though there's little to do other than watch the world go by. The Hôtel de Ville, today housing the Municipal Offices building, is still an impressive spectacle, and a 4m-tall Gandhi memorial, surrounded by ancient columns, dominates the northern end. Nearby, a French memorial commemorates French Indians who lost their lives in World War I.

Just north of the Hôtel de Ville, a couple of streets back from the promenade, is the leafy old French-provincial-style square now named **Government Place**. On the north side, the impressive, gleaming white **Raj Nivas**, official home to the present lieutenant-governor of Puducherry Territory, was built late in the eighteenth century for Joseph Francis Dupleix.

The **Pondicherry Government Museum** (Tues–Sun 10am–5pm; Rs2) is on Ranga Pillai Street, opposite Government Place. The archeological collection includes Neolithic and 2000-year-old remains from Arikamedu, a few Pallava (sixth- to eighth-century) and Buddhist (tenth-century) stone sculptures, bronzes, weapons and paintings. Alongside are a bizarre assembly of French salon furniture and bric-à-brac from local houses, including a velvet S-shaped "conversation seat".

The **Sri Aurobindo Ashram**, a few blocks north on Rue de la Marine (daily 8am–noon & 2–6pm; free; no children under 3; photography with permission; ⓦwww.sriaurobindosociety.org.in), is one of the best-known and wealthiest ashrams in India. Founded in 1926 by the Bengali philosopher-guru, Aurobindo Ghosh, and his chief disciple, personal manager and mouthpiece "The Mother", it serves as the headquarters of the Sri Aurobindo Society, or SAS. Today the SAS owns most of the valuable property and real estate in Puducherry, and wields what many consider to be a disproportionate influence over the town. The **samadhi**, or mausoleum, of Sri Aurobindo and "The Mother" is covered daily with flowers and usually surrounded by supplicating devotees with their hands and heads placed on the tomb. Inside the main building, an incongruous and very bourgeois-looking Western-style room, complete with three-piece suite and Persian carpet, is where "The Mother" and Sri Aurobindo chilled out. The adjacent bookshop sells a range of literature and tracts, while the building opposite hosts frequent cultural programmes.

In the southwest of town, near the railway station, you can hardly miss the huge cream-and-brown **Sacred Heart of Jesus**, one of Puducherry's finest Catholic churches, built by French missionaries in the 1700s. Nearby, the shady **Botanical Gardens**, established in 1826, offer many quiet paths to wander (daily 9.30am–6pm; free). The French planted nine hunderd species here, experimenting to see how they would do in Indian conditions; one mahogany tree, the *Khaya senegalensis*, has grown to a height of 25m. You can also see an extraordinary fossilized tree, found about 25km away in Tiravakarai. The aquarium inside the gardens (Rs5) is uninspiring.

Eating and drinking

If you've been on the road for a while and are hankering for healthy salads, fresh coffee, crusty bread, cakes and real pastry, you'll be spoilt for choice in Puducherry. **Beer** is available just about everywhere (except the SAS-owned establishments) and is half the regular Tamil Nadu price at around Rs50 a bottle.

Bombay Ananda Bhavan 199 Mission St. Good, quiet and very hygienic south Indian veg joint, serving particularly fine masala dosas for around Rs25.

Café Lune Rue Suffren, near the State Bank of India. A little place where old men gather to drink coffee and pass the time of day. The coffee is prepared with great pomp and style, and the ultra-cheap lunchtime plate of lemon rice and *vada* is superb.

Hot Breads 42 Ambour Salai. Crusty croissants, fresh baguettes, and delicious savoury pastry snacks, served in a squeaky-clean *boulangerie*-café full of French expats.

La Terrasse 5 Subbaiyah Salai. The most popular French restaurant in town amongst European backpackers, who hang out here to devour croissants and cappuccino alfresco. Excellent prawn dishes start at Rs90, pizzas go for Rs80–175, and there's also a range of Indian, Chinese and French food. Closed Wed.

Le Club 33 Rue Dumas. One of the best-known restaurants in town, its predominantly French menu features their famous coq au vin, steak au poivre, plenty of seafood options (all around Rs200) and a full wine list, plus cocktails (Rs150). There's also a bistro downstairs (closed Mon) that's great for Sunday brunch, and a decent Vietnamese and Southeast Asian restaurant in the same complex.

Le Rendezvous 30 Rue Suffren. Filling seafood sizzlers, fantastic pizza and tandoori brochettes are specialities of this popular expat-oriented restaurant. They also serve fresh croissants and espresso for breakfast. Dine indoors or up on the more romantic rooftop, where you can relax to eclectic sounds in the evenings. Most main dishes Rs120–250. Closed Tues.

Madame Santhé's Rue Romain Rolland. Attractively designed and atmospheric roof terrace serving a mixture of extremely tasty French, Indian and Chinese dishes for around Rs120–170. Their steak in mushroom sauce is a delight. More laidback and better value than the established quality restaurants.

Poudou Poudou 31 Rue Labourdonnais. One of the only Indian restaurants in the old part of town, with some seafood and continental cuisine. Most dishes under Rs100.

Qualithé 3 Rue Mahe de Labourdonnais. The rather dowdy ground floor of this rundown hotel on Government Place nonetheless remains a popular hangout for downing cheap and strong beers.

Satsanga 30 Rue Labourdonnais. Devised by the French *patron*, the menu in this converted colonial mansion is carefully prepared: organic salads with fresh herbs, tzatziki and garlic bread, sauté potatoes, tagliatelle alla carbonara and mouth-watering pizzas. Check their *plat du jour* for fresh fish dishes. Around Rs400 per head for three courses, with drinks.

Auroville

The most New Age place anywhere in India must surely be **AUROVILLE**, the planned "City of Dawn", 10km north of Puducherry, straddling the border of the Union Territory and Tamil Nadu. Founded in 1968, Auroville was inspired by "The Mother", the spiritual successor of Sri Aurobindo. Around 1700 people live in communes (two-thirds of them non-Indians), with such names as Fertile, Certitude, Sincerity, Revelation and Transformation, in what it is hoped will eventually be an ideal city for a population of fifty thousand. Architecturally experimental buildings, combining modern Western and traditional Indian elements, are set in a rural landscape of narrow lanes, deep red earth and lush greenery. Income is derived from agriculture, handicrafts, alternative technology, educational and development projects and Aurolec, a computer software company.

Considering how little there is to see here, Auroville attracts a disproportionately large number of day-trippers – much to the chagrin of its inhabitants, who rightly point out that you can only get a sense of what the settlement is all about if you stay a while. Interested visitors are welcomed as paying guests in most of the communes (see below), where you can work alongside permanent residents.

Begun in 1970, the space-age **Matri Mandir** – a gigantic, almost spherical hi-tech meditation centre at the heart of the site – was conceived as "a symbol of the Divine's answer to man's inspiration for perfection". Earth from 124 countries was symbolically placed in an urn, and is kept in a concrete cone in the amphitheatre adjacent to Matri Mandir, from where a speaker can address an audience of three thousand without amplification. The focal point of the interior of the Matri Mandir is a seventy-centimetre crystal ball symbolizing the neutral but divine qualities of light and space. See below for visiting arrangements.

Practicalities

Auroville lies 10km north of Puducherry, off the main Chennai road; you can also get here via the coastal highway, turning off at the village of Chinna Mudaliarchavadi. **Bus** services are frequent along both routes but as Auroville is spread over some fifty square kilometres it's best to come with your own transport. Alternatively, there's the PTDC half-day **tour** from Puducherry (see p.975).

In the middle of the site near the **Bharat Niwas**, which holds a permanent exhibition on the history and philosophy of the settlement, the **visitor centre** (daily 9am–5.30pm; Ⓣ0413/262 2239, Ⓦwww.auroville.org) is the place to get tickets for an exterior viewing of Matri Mandir (daily 10am–noon & Mon–Sat 2–4pm). Tickets are available from 9.45am–12.30pm and 1.45–4pm; before they are issued, you're shown a short video presentation about the village. To obtain "concentration entry" to Matri Mandir, whereby you can meditate on the crystal itself, you must book two days ahead (2–4pm). You can also pick up some inexpensive literature on Auroville in the adjacent bookshop and check the notice board for details of **activities** in which visitors may participate (these typically include yoga, reiki and Vipassana meditation, costing around Rs200/session). In addition, there are a couple of quality handicraft outlets and several pleasant little vegetarian cafés serving snacks, meals and cold drinks.

The information desk at the visitor centre is also the place to enquire about **paying guest accommodation** in Auroville's thirty or so communes. Officially there's no lower limit on the time you have to stay, but visitors are encouraged to stick around for at least a week, helping out on communal projects; tariffs are around Rs400–2500 per day, including meals. Alternatively, you can arrange to stay in one of the four a/c **guesthouses**, which have rooms for Rs2500. Beds here and in the communes are always in short supply, especially during the two peak periods of December to March and July to August, when it's advisable to book well in advance (ⓣ0413/262 2704, ⓔavguests@auroville.org.in). Otherwise, the best of the very limited options nearby is the *Satsanga Guest House* (ⓣ0413/222 5867, ⓔpierre_satsanga@yahoo.com; ❷–❹), only 500m from the beach, which has a choice of rooms with or without private bathrooms. For **food**, you won't do better than the excellent vegetarian "meals" served in Auroville itself.

Central Tamil Nadu: the Chola heartland

To be on the banks of the Cauvery listening to the strains of Carnatic music is to have a taste of eternal bliss

Tamil proverb

Continuing south of Puducherry along the Coromandel coast, you enter the flat landscape of the **Kaveri** (aka Cauvery) **Delta**, a watery world of canals, dams, dykes and rivulets that has been intensively farmed since ancient times. Only a hundred miles in diameter, it forms the verdant rice-bowl core of Tamil Nadu, crossed by more than thirty major rivers and countless streams. The largest of them, the **River Kaveri**, known in Tamil as Ponni, "The Lady of Gold" (a form of the Mother Goddess), is revered as a conduit of liquid *shakti*, the primordial female energy that nurtures the millions of farmers who live on her banks and tributaries. The landscape here is one endless swathe of green paddy fields, dotted with palm trees and little villages of thatched roofs and market stalls; it comes as a rude shock to land up in the hot and chaotic towns.

This mighty delta formed the very heartland of the **Chola** empire, which reached its apogee between the ninth and thirteenth centuries, an era often compared to classical Greece and Renaissance Italy both for its cultural richness and the sheer scale and profusion of its architectural creations. Much as the Cholas originally intended, every visitor is immediately in awe of their huge temples, not only at cities such as **Chidambaram**, **Kumbakonam** and **Thanjavur**, but also out in the countryside at places like **Gangaikondacholapuram**, where the magnificent temple is all that remains of a once-great city. Exploring the area for a few days will bring you into contact with the more delicate side of Chola artistic expression, such as the magnificent **bronzes** of Thanjavur.

Chidambaram

CHIDAMBARAM, 58km south of Puducherry, is so steeped in myth that its history is hard to unravel. As the site of the *tandava*, the cosmic dance of Shiva as **Nataraja**, King of the Dance, it's one of the holiest sites in south India, and a visit to its **Sabhanayaka Temple** affords a fascinating glimpse into ancient Tamil religious practice and belief. The legendary king **Hiranyavarman** is said to have made a pilgrimage here from Kashmir, seeking to rid himself of leprosy by bathing in the temple's Shivaganga tank. In thanks for a successful cure, he enlarged the temple. He also brought three thousand brahmins, of the Dikshitar caste, whose descendants, distinguishable by top-knots of hair at the front of their heads, are the ritual specialists of the temple to this day.

Few of the fifty *maths* (monasteries) that once stood here remain, but the temple itself is still a hive of activity and hosts numerous **festivals**. The two most important are ten-day affairs, building up to spectacular finales: on the ninth day of each, temple chariots process through the four Car streets in the **car festival**, while on the tenth there is an **abhishekham**, when the principal deities in the Raja Sabha (thousand-pillared hall) are anointed. For exact dates (one is in May/June, the other in Dec/Jan), contact any TTDC tourist office and plan well ahead, as they are very popular. Other local festivals include fire-walking and *kavadi* folk dance (dancing with decorated wooden frames on the head) at the Thillaiamman Kali (April/May) and Keelatheru Mariamman (July/Aug) temples.

The town also has a hectic market, and a large student population, based at Annamalai University to the east, a centre of Tamil studies.

Arrival and information

Chidambaram revolves around the Sabhanayaka Temple and the busy market area that surrounds it, along North, East, South and West Car streets. Buses from Chennai, Thanjavur, Mamallapuram and Madurai pull in at the **bus stand**, about 500m from the temple.

Staff at the TTDC **tourist office** (Mon–Fri 9.45am–5.45pm; ⓣ04144/238739), next to *Vandayar Gateway Inn* hotel on Railway Feeder Road, are charming and helpful, but only have a small pamphlet to give visitors. None of the **banks** in Chidambaram change money, although the *Saradharam* hotel, near the bus stand, will change cash and there is an ICICI Bank ATM in the forecourt, as well as a couple more on South Car Street. **Internet** is available at the *Saradharam*, as well as at I-Castle, by the east entrance to the temple.

Accommodation

To cope with the influx of tourists and pilgrims, Chidambaram abounds in budget **accommodation**, but few hotels even creep into the mid-range bracket.

Akshaya 17/18 East Car St ⓣ04144/220192, ⓔakshayhotel@hotmail.com. Pleasant, clean mid-range hotel, with a lawn backing right onto the temple wall. The rooms are a decent size with the non-a/c especially good value, and there are a couple of restaurants. ❷–❹

Mansoor Lodge 91 East Car St ⓣ04144/221072. A friendly and good-value cheapie, right opposite the temple. The freshly painted rooms have spotless tiled floors and clean bathrooms, and there are TVs in most. ❶

Raja Rajan 162 West Car St ⓣ04144/222690. Close to the west gate of the temple, the clean rooms here have tiled bathrooms and low tariffs; the a/c ones are good value. ❶–❸

Ritz 2 VGP St, near the bus stand ⓣ04144/223312, ⓕ221098. One of the better places in town, this comfortable hotel boasts a convenient location and big rooms (all with TV, and some with a/c), plus a good restaurant. ❷–❹

Sabanayagam 7 East Sannathi St, off East Car St ⓣ04144/220896. Despite a flashy exterior, this is a run-of-the-mill budget place, with clean rooms off dim corridors. Some are windowless, and there's a choice of a/c and non-a/c, and Western or Indian loos. Good veg restaurant downstairs. ❶–❸

Saradharam 19 Venugopal Pillai St, opposite the bus stand ⓣ04144/221336, ⓦhotelsaradharam.co.in. Large, clean and well-kept rooms (some with a/c and balconies, and non-a/c) in modern buildings, with three decent restaurants (including one non-veg), a small garden, bar, laundry and foreign exchange. ❸–❹

Moving on from Chidambaram

At the time of writing, the **railway station**, just over 1km southeast of the centre, was out of commission as the lines through Chidambaram were undergoing gauge conversion, but this should be completed by early 2011. There are bus services to: Chengalpattu (every 20–30min; 4hr 30min–5hr); Chennai (every 20–30min; 5–6hr); Coimbatore (6 daily; 7hr); Kanchipuram (hourly; 7–8hr); Kanyakumari (3 daily; 10hr); Kumbakonam (every 10min; 2hr 30min); Madurai (6 daily; 8hr); Puducherry (every 15–20min; 2hr); Thanjavur (every 15–20min; 4hr); Tiruchirapalli (every 30min; 5hr); Tiruvannamalai (hourly; 3hr 30min).

Sabhanayaka Nataraja Temple

For south India's Shaivites, the **Sabhanayaka Nataraja Temple** (daily 4am–noon & 4–10pm), where Shiva is enthroned as Lord of the Cosmic Dance (Nataraja), is the holiest of holies. Its huge *gopuras*, whose lights are used as landmarks by sailors far out to sea in the Bay of Bengal, soar above a fifty-five-acre complex, divided by four concentric walls. The oldest parts now standing were built under the Cholas, who adopted Nataraja as their chosen deity and crowned several kings here. If you have the time the best way to tackle the complex is to work slowly inwards from the third enclosure in clockwise circles.

Frequent **ceremonies** take place at the innermost sanctum, the most popular being at noon and 6pm, when a fire is lit, great gongs are struck and devotees rush forward to catch a last glimpse of the lingam before the doors are shut. On Friday nights before the temple closes, during a particularly elaborate puja, Nataraja is carried on a palanquin accompanied by music and attendants carrying flaming torches and tridents. At other times, you'll hear ancient devotional hymns from the *Tevaram*.

The western *gopura* is the most popular entrance, as well as being the most elaborately carved and probably the earliest (c.1150 AD). Turning north (left) from here, you come to the colonnaded **Shivaganga tank**, the site of seven natural springs. From the broken pillar at the tank's edge, all four *gopuras* are visible. In the northeast corner, the largest building in the complex, the **Raja Sabha** (fourteenth- to fifteenth-century) is also known as "the thousand-pillared hall"; tradition holds that there are only nine hundred and ninety-nine actual pillars, the thousandth being Shiva's leg. During festivals the deities Nataraja and Shivakamasundari are brought here and mounted on a dais for the anointing ceremony, *abhishekha*.

The importance of **dance** at Chidambaram is underlined by the reliefs of dancing figures inside the east *gopura*, demonstrating 108 *karanas* (a similar set is to be found in the west *gopura*). A *karana* is a specific point in a phase of movement prescribed by the extraordinarily comprehensive Sanskrit treatise on the performing arts, the *Natya Shastra* (c.200 BC–200 AD) – the basis of all classical dance, music and theatre in India. To get into the square **second enclosure**, head for its western entrance (just north of the west *gopura* in the third wall) which leads into a circumambulatory passageway. Once beyond this second wall it's easy to become disorientated, as the roofed inner enclosures see little light and are supported by a maze of colonnades. The atmosphere is immediately more charged, reaching its peak at the very centre.

The innermost **Govindaraja shrine** is dedicated to Vishnu – no surprise, as most Shiva temples have a Vishnu shrine inside them – though no Vaishnavite temple has a shrine for Shiva. The deity is attended by non-Dikshitar brahmins who, it is said, don't always get along with the Dikshitars. From outside the shrine, non-Hindus can see through to the most sacred part of the temple, the **Kanaka Sabha** and the **Chit Sabha**, adjoining raised structures, roofed with copper and gold plate and linked by a hallway. The latter houses bronze images of Nataraja and his consort Shivakamasundari; behind and to the left of Nataraja, a curtain, sacred to Shiva and strung with rows of leaves from the bilva tree, demarcates the most potent area of all. Within it lies the **Akashalingam**, known as the *rahasya*, or "secret", of Chidambaram: made of the most subtle of the elements, Ether (*akasha*) – from which Air, Fire, Water and Earth are born – the lingam is invisible – signifying the invisible presence of God in the human heart.

A crystal lingam, said to have emanated from the light of the crescent moon on Shiva's brow, and a small ruby Nataraja are worshipped in the Kanaka Sabha. They are ritually bathed in the flames of the priests' camphor fire or oil lamps six times a day. This inner area is where you're most likely to hear **oduvars**, hereditary singers from the middle, non-brahmin castes, intoning verses of ancient Tamil poetry. The songs with which they regale the deities at puja time, drawn from compilations such as the *Tevaram* or earlier *Sangam*, are believed to be more than a thousand years old.

Eating

There are plenty of basic, wholesome "meals" places on and around the Car streets – the *Sri Ganesa Bhavan*, on West Car Street, gets the locals' vote. East of the Sabhanayaka Temple, the *Sri Aishwarya*, by the clock tower near the bus stand, is a clean, modern south Indian and Chinese veg restaurant or, close by, there's the airy rooftop restaurant at the *RK Residency*, which serves non-veg food, both Indian and Chinese. Alternatively, the Middle Eastern *Dubai Restaurant* is a tiny hole-in-the-wall place on Venugopal Pillai (VGP) Street serving tasty kebabs, fish and other non-veg fare.

Gangaikondacholapuram

Devised as the centrepiece of a city built by the Chola king Rajendra I (1014–42) to celebrate his conquests, the magnificent **Brihadishwara Temple** (a replica of the Tanjore temple) stands in the tiny village of **GANGAIKONDA-CHOLAPURAM**, in Ariyalur District, 35km north of Kumbakonam. The tongue-twisting name means "the town of the Chola who took the Ganges". Under Rajendra I, the Chola empire did indeed stretch as far as the great river of the north, an unprecedented achievement for a southern dynasty. Aside from the temple and the rubble of Rajendra's palace, 2km east at Tamalikaimedu, nothing of the city remains. Nonetheless, this is among the most extraordinary archeological sites in south India, outshone only by Thanjavur, and the fact that it's devoid of visitors most of the time gives it a memorably forlorn feel.

Although it is marginally closer to Chidambaram, **bus** connections are better with Kumbakonam, running every fifteen minutes or so. The village is also served by some buses between Trichy and Chidambaram. Be sure not to get stuck here between noon and 4pm when the temple is closed. Facilities are minimal, with little more than a few cool-drinks stands. Parts of the interior are extremely dark, and a torch is useful.

Brihadishwara Temple

Dominating the village landscape, the **Brihadishwara Temple** (daily 6am–noon & 4–8pm; free) sits in a well-maintained grassy courtyard, flanked by a closed *mandapa* hallway. Over the sanctuary, to the right, a massive pyramidal tower (*vimana*) rises 55m in nine diminishing storeys. Though smaller than the one at Thanjavur, the tower's graceful curve gives it an impressive refinement.

Turning right (north) inside the courtyard, before you reach a small shrine to the goddess **Durga**, containing an image of Mahishasuramardini (the slaying of the buffalo demon), you come across a small well, guarded by a lion statue, known as Simha-kinaru and made from plastered brickwork. King Rajendra is said to have had Ganges water placed in the well to be used for the ritual anointing of the lingam in the main temple. The lion, representing Chola kingly power, bows to the huge Nandi respectfully seated before the eastern entrance of the temple, in line with the *shivalingam* contained within.

Directly in front of the eastern entrance to the temple stands a small altar for offerings. Two parallel flights of stairs ascend to the *mukhamandapa* or porch, which leads to the long pillared *mahamandapa* hallway, the entrance of which is flanked by a pair of large guardian deities. Immediately inside the temple a guide can show you the way to the tower, up steep steps. On either side of the temple doorway, sculptures of Shiva in his various benevolent (*anugraha*) manifestations include him blessing Vishnu, Devi, Ravana and the saint Chandesha. In the northeast corner, an unusual square stone block features carvings of the nine planets (*navagraha*). A number of **Chola bronzes** (see p.990) stand on the platform; the figure of Karttikeya, the war god, carrying a club and a shield, is thought to have had particular significance

The base of the main temple sanctuary is decorated with lions and scrollwork. Above this decoration, running from the southern to the northern entrance of the *ardhamandapa*, a series of sculpted figures in plastered niches portray different images of Shiva. The most famous is at the northern entrance, showing Shiva and Parvati garlanding the saint Chandesha, who here is sometimes identified as Rajendra I. For more on the temples of Tamil Nadu, see p.961.

Two minutes' walk northeast along the main road (turn right from the car park), the tiny **Archeological Museum** (daily except Fri 10am–1pm & 2–5.45pm; free) contains Chola odds and ends discovered locally. The finds include terracotta lamps, coins, weapons, tiles, bronze, bangle pieces, palm-leaf manuscripts and an old Chinese pot.

Kumbakonam

Sandwiched between the Kaveri (Cauvery) and Arasalar rivers is **KUMBAKONAM**, 74km southwest of Chidambaram and 38km northeast of Thanjavur. Hindus believe this to be the place where a water pot (*kumba*) of *amrita* – the ambrosial beverage of immortality – was washed up by a great deluge from atop sacred Mount Meru in the Himalayas. Shiva, who just happened to be passing through in the guise of a wild forest-dwelling hunter, for some reason fired an arrow at the pot, causing it to break. From the shards, he made the lingam that is now enshrined in **Kumbeswara Temple**, whose *gopuras* today tower over the town, along with those of some seventeen other major shrines. A former capital of the Cholas, who are said to have kept a high-security treasury here, Kumbakonam is the chief commercial centre for the Thanjavur region. The main bazaar, **TSR Big Street**, is especially renowned for its quality costume jewellery.

The main reason to stop in Kumbakonam is to admire the exquisite sculpture of the **Nageshwara Swami Shiva Temple**, which contains the most refined Chola stone carving still *in situ*. The town also lies within easy reach of the magnificent Darasuram and Gangaikondacholapuram temples, both spectacular ancient monuments that see very few visitors. Note that all temples in the area close between noon (or thereabouts) and 4pm. For a change, the village of Swamimalai, only a bike ride away, is the state's principal centre for traditional **bronze casting**.

Arrival and information

Kumbakonam's small **railway station**, in the southeast of town 2km from the main bazaar, is well served by trains both north and south, and has a left-luggage office (24hr) and decent **retiring rooms** (non-a/c Rs200, a/c Rs400). The hectic bus stand is in the southeast of town, just northwest of the railway station. All the timetables are in Tamil, but there's a 24-hour enquiry office with English-speaking staff. Buses leave for Gangaikondacholapuram, Puducherry and Thanjavur every five to ten minutes, many going via Darasuram. Frequent services run to Chennai, Trichy and several daily to Bengaluru. There are a few small **internet** places on TSR Big Street, where there is also an ICICI ATM machine, 100m east of the *Siva International* hotel.

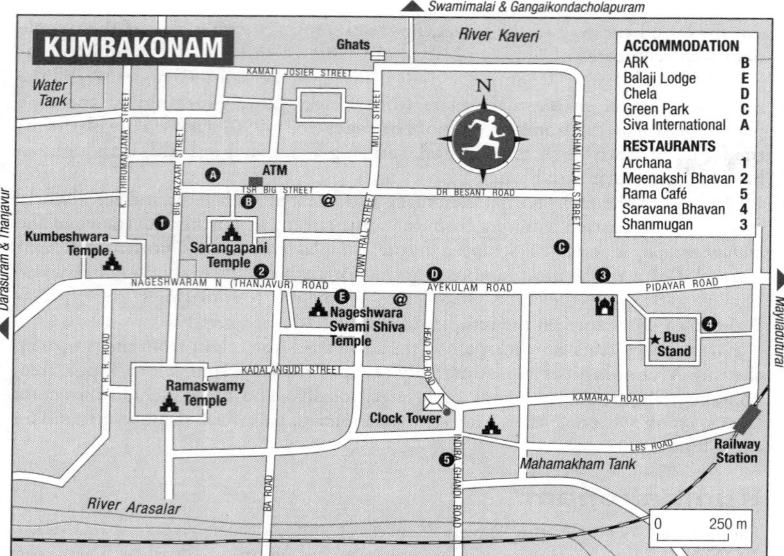

Accommodation

Kumbakonam is not a major tourist location, and has limited **accommodation**, with only one upper-range hotel, the *Sterling Swamimalai* (Ⓣ0435 2480044, ❽–❾), over 5km southeast of town on the outskirts of Swamimalai village (see p.986). The good news for budget travellers is that most of the inexpensive places are clean and well maintained.

ARK 21 TSR Big St Ⓣ0435/242 1234. Fifty large, clean rooms, on five floors, all with windows; TVs available on request. Bland, but comfortable enough, with an a/c bar serving snacks. ❹

Balaji Lodge 64 Nageshwaram N St Ⓣ0435/243 0546. Good-value budget lodge, offering clean rooms with attached bath and TV, though they are a little dark. ❶–❷

Chela 9 Ayekulam Rd Ⓣ0435/243 0336, Ⓦwww.hellokumbakonam.com/hotelchela. Large mid-range place, between the bus stand and centre, distinguished by its horrendous mock-classical facade. Soap, fresh towels and TVs are offered as standard. There are two restaurants (veg and non-veg) and a bar. ❸–❹

Green Park 10 Lakshmi Vilai St Ⓣ0435/240 3912, Ⓔhotelgreenpark@dataone.in. Excellent-value business-oriented hotel with spotless doubles, all with TV, some a/c. There's also a coffee shop and the *Peacock* non-veg restaurant. ❹–❺

Siva International 101/3 TSR Big St Ⓣ0435/242 4013, Ⓔhotelsiva@rediff.com. After the temple *gopuras*, this huge hotel complex is the tallest building in town. Their standard non-a/c is a bargain (ask for #301, which has great views on two sides) and all the spacious, airy doubles are decent value. You can climb onto the roof for incredible views of sunset and dawn behind the *gopuras*. ❷–❹

The Town

Surmounted by a multicoloured *gopura*, the east entrance of Kumbakonam's seventeenth-century **Kumbeswara Temple**, home of the famous lingam from which the town derived its name, is approached via a covered market selling a huge assortment of cooking pots, a local speciality, as well as the usual glass bangles and trinkets. At the gateway, you may meet the temple elephant, with a painted forehead and necklace of bells. Beyond the flagstaff, a *mandapa* houses a fine collection of silver *vahanas*, vehicles of the deities, used in festivals, and *pancha loham* (compound of five metals) figures of the 63 Nayanmar poet-saints.

The principal and largest of the Vishnu temples in Kumbakonam is the thirteenth-century **Sarangapani Temple**, entered through a ten-storey pyramidal *gopura* gate, more than 45m high. The **central shrine** dates from the late Chola period, with many later accretions. Its entrance, within the innermost court, is guarded by huge *dvarpalas*, identical to Vishnu whom they protect. Between them are carved stone *jali* screens, each different, and in front of them stands the sacred, square *homam* fireplace. During the day, rays of light from tiny ceiling windows penetrate the darkness around the sanctum, designed to resemble a chariot with reliefs of horses, elephants and wheels. A painted cupboard contains a mirror for Vishnu to see himself when he leaves the sanctum sanctorum.

The small **Nageshwara Swami Shiva Temple**, in the centre of town, is Kumbakonam's oldest, founded in 886 and completed a few years into the reign of Parantaka I (907–*c*.940). First impressions are unpromising, as much of the original building has been hemmed in by later Disney-coloured additions, but beyond the main courtyard, occupied by a large columned *mandapa*, a small *gopura*-topped gateway leads to an inner enclosure where the earliest Chola shrine stands. Framed in the main niches around its sanctum wall are a series of exquisite stone figures, regarded as the finest surviving pieces of **ancient sculpture** in south India. With their languid stance and mesmeric, half-smiling facial expressions, these modest-sized masterpieces far outshine the more monumental art of Thanjavur and Gangaikondacholapuram.

The most famous and revered of many sacred **water tanks** in Kumbakonam, the **Mahamakham** in the southeast of town is said to have filled with ambrosia (*amrit*) collected from the pot broken by Shiva. Every twelve years, when Jupiter passes the constellation of Leo, it is believed that water from the Ganges and eight other holy rivers flows into the tank, thus according it the status of *tirtha*, or sacred river crossing. At this auspicious time, as many as four million pilgrims come here for an absolving bathe; the last occasion was in early 2004.

Eating

There's nothing very exciting about **eating out** in Kumbakonam, and most visitors stick to their hotel restaurant.

Archana Big Bazaar St. Right in the thick of the market, and popular among shoppers for its good-value south Indian "meals" (Rs30) and great *uttapams*, although it can get hot and stuffy inside. Foreigners cause quite a stir here, but are made very welcome.

Meenakshi Bhavan Nageshwaram N St. Excellent, clean south Indian veg joint, which serves some rarer snacks like *adai*, a form of spicy rice cake. Great dosas for barely Rs20.

Rama Café Indira Gandhi Rd. Simple and wholesome veg "meals" (Rs20–40) and snacks restaurant, in a great setting by the Mahamakham tank.

Saravana Bhavan Just east of bus stand. South Indian veg restaurant serving *iddlis*, vegetable dishes, lunchtime thalis with chai and coffee, and early breakfasts. You can stuff yourself for under Rs50.

Shanmugan Pidayar Rd, opposite the mosque. One of the few places serving non-veg dishes, such as tasty chilli chicken and chicken fried rice (Rs60–90).

Darasuram and Swamimalai

The **Airavateshwara Temple**, built by King Rajaraja II (*c*.1146–73), stands in the village of **DARASURAM**, an easy 5km bus or bike ride (on the Thanjavur route) southwest of Kumbakonam. This superb, if little-visited, Chola monument ranks alongside those at Thanjavur and Gangaikondacholapuram; but while the others are grandiose, emphasizing heroism and conquest, this is far smaller, exquisite in proportion and detail and said to have been decorated with *nitya-vinoda*, "perpetual entertainment", in mind. Shiva is called Airavateshwara here because he was worshipped in this temple by Airavata, the white elephant belonging to the king of the gods, Indra.

Darasuram's finest pieces of sculpture are the Chola black-basalt images adorning wall niches in the *mandapa* and inner shrine. These include images of Nagaraja, the snake-king, with a hood of cobras, and Dakshinamurti, the "south-facing" Shiva as teacher, expounding under a banyan tree.

SWAMIMALAI, 8km west of Kumbakonam, is revered as one of the six sacred abodes of Lord Murugan, Shiva's son, whom Hindu mythology records became his father's religious teacher (*swami*) on a hill (*malai*) here. The site of this epic role-reversal now hosts one of the Tamils' holiest shrines, the **Swaminatha Temple**, crowning the hilltop of the centre of the village, but of more interest to non-Hindus are the **bronze-casters**' workshops dotted around the bazaar and the outlying hamlets.

Known as **sthapathis**, Swamimalai's casters still employ the "lost wax" process perfected by the Cholas to make the most sought-after temple idols in south India. Their finished products are displayed in numerous showrooms along the main street, from where they are exported worldwide, but it is more memorable to watch the *sthapathis* in action, fashioning the original figures from beeswax and breaking open the moulds to expose the mystical finished metalwork inside. For more on Tamil bronze casting, see p.990.

The nearby hamlet of **Thimmakkudy**, 2km back towards Kumbakonam, is the site of the area's grandest **hotel**, the *Sterling Swamimalai* (Ⓣ0435/242 0044, Ⓦwww.sterlingswamimalai.net; ❼), a beautifully restored nineteenth-century brahmins' mansion with all mod cons in its rooms. You can combine the two sights in an easy half-day trip from Kumbakonam. The route is flat enough to cycle, but keep your wits about you on the main Thanjavur highway. To reach Swamimalai from Darasuram, return to the main road from the temple and ask directions in the bazaar. Swamimalai is only 3km north, but travelling between the two involves several turnings, so expect to have to ask directions again. From Kumbakonam, the route is more straightforward; cross the Kaveri at the top of Town Hall Street (north of the centre), turn left and follow the main road west through a ribbon of villages.

Thanjavur

As one of the busiest commercial towns of the Kaveri Delta, **THANJAVUR** (aka "Tanjore"), 55km east of Tiruchirapalli and 35km southwest of Kumbakonam, is often overlooked by travellers. However, its history and treasures – among them the breathtaking **Brihadishwara Temple**, Tamil Nadu's most awesome Chola monument – give it a crucial significance to south Indian culture. The home of the world's finest Chola bronze collection, it holds enough of interest to keep you enthralled for at least a couple of days, and is the most obvious base for trips to nearby Gangaikondacholapuram, Darasuram and Swamimalai.

Thanjavur is roughly split in two by the east–west **Grand Anicut Canal**. The **old town**, north of the canal and once entirely enclosed by a fortified wall, was chosen, between the ninth and the end of the thirteenth century, as the capital of their extensive empire by all the Chola kings save one. None of their secular buildings survive, but you can still see as many as ninety temples, of which the Brihadishwara most eloquently epitomizes the power and patronage of Rajaraja I (985–1014), whose military campaigns spread Hinduism to the Maldives,

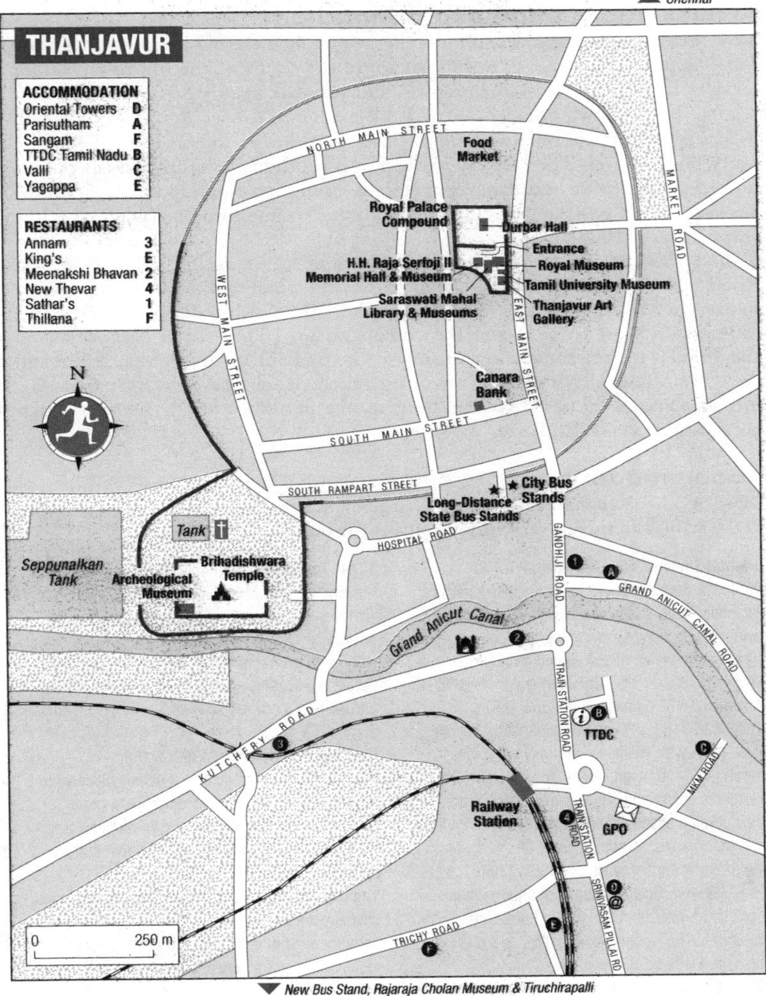

Sri Lanka and Java. Under the Cholas, as well as the later Nayaks and Marathas, literature, painting, sculpture, Carnatic classical music and Bharatanatyam dance all thrived here. Quite apart from its own intrinsic interest, the Nayak **royal palace compound** houses an important library and museums including a famous collection of bronzes.

Of major local **festivals**, the most lavish celebrations at the Brihadishwara Temple are associated with the birthday of King Rajaraja, in October. An eight-day celebration of **Carnatic classical music** is held each January at the Panchanateshwara Temple at **Thiruvaiyaru**, 13km away, to honour the great Carnatic composer-saint, Thyagaraja.

Arrival, information and orientation

Some **buses** from Chennai and Puducherry pull in at the old long-distance State Bus Stand, opposite the City Bus Stand, in the south of the old town. Other services from Madurai, Tiruchirapalli, and Kumbakonam stop at the New Bus Stand, 4km southwest of the centre. Rickshaws into town from here cost Rs50, or you can jump on one of the #74 buses that shuttle to and from the centre every few minutes. The **railway station**, just south of the centre, has a computerized system (Mon–Sat 8am–2pm & 2.15–8pm, Sun 8am–2pm & 3–5pm) for booking trains to Chennai, Tiruchirapalli and Rameshwaram (when the line reopens, see p.1005).

The **GPO** and most of the hotels and restaurants lie on or around **Gandhiji Road** (aka Train Station Rd), which crosses the canal and leads to the railway station in the south. The **TTDC tourist office** (Mon–Fri 10am–5.45pm; ⓣ04362/230984) is located in the compound of TTDC *Tamil Nadu* hotel on Gandhiji Road. You can **change money** at Canara Bank on South Main Street and there are a few ATMs around town, including one at the railway station. For **internet access**, head for Gemini Soft, on the first floor of the *Oriental Towers* hotel, Srinivasam Pillai Road.

Accommodation

Most of Thanjavur's **hotels** tend to charge higher rates than you'd pay elsewhere in the state, and there's very little choice at the bottom of the market.

Oriental Towers 2889 Srinivasam Pillai Rd ⓣ04362/230724, ⓦwww.hotelorientaltowers.com. Huge hotel-cum-shopping complex, with a small swimming pool and luxurious rooms. Good value for the price, with internet access and three restaurants serving the usual Indian/Chinese/Western fare. ❻–❽

Parisutham 55 Grand Anicut Canal Rd ⓣ04362/231801, ⓦwww.hotelparisutham.com. Plush hotel with spacious, centrally a/c rooms starting at $150, a large palm-fringed pool (residents only), multi-cuisine restaurant, craft shop, foreign exchange and a travel agent. Popular with tour groups, so book ahead. ❾

Sangam Trichy Rd ⓣ04362/239451, ⓦwww.hotelsangam.com. International four-star standards at this luxury hotel with comfortable a/c rooms (from $165), an excellent restaurant (see p.992), pool (Rs150 for non-residents) and beautiful Tanjore paintings – the one in the lobby is worth a trip here in itself. ❾

TTDC Tamil Nadu Gandhiji Rd, 10min from the bus and railway stations ⓣ04362/231325, ⓦttdconline.com. Once the raja's guesthouse, but now a typically dilapidated state-run hotel, with more character than modern alternatives. Large, comfortable carpeted rooms (some with a/c-Rs 1300) are set around a leafy enclosed garden. ❹–❺

Valli 2948 MKM Rd ⓣ04362/231580, ⓔarasu_tnj@rediffmail.com. Friendly place with super-clean rooms opening onto bright green corridors; there's a roof terrace and a popular restaurant on the ground floor. The best budget option in town. ❸–❹

Yagappa 1 Trichy Rd ⓣ04362/230421. Spacious, well-appointed rooms with sitouts and large, tiled bathrooms. Staff are friendly, there's a bar and restaurant, and the reception features intriguing picture-frames made from coffee roots. Good value. ❸–❹

Brihadishwara Temple

Thanjavur's skyline is dominated by the huge tower of the **Brihadishwara Temple** (daily 6am–8pm, ⓣ04362/274476), which for all its size and UNESCO World Heritage status lacks the grandiose excesses of later periods. The temple was constructed as much to reflect the power of its patron, King Rajaraja I, as to facilitate the worship of Shiva. Profuse **inscriptions** on the base of the main shrine provide incredibly detailed information about the organization of the temple, showing it to have been rich, both in financial terms and in ritual activity. No fewer than four hundred female dancers, **devadasis** (literally "slaves to the gods", married off to the deity), were employed, and each provided with a house. Other staff – another two hundred people – included dance teachers, musicians, tailors, potters, laundrymen, goldsmiths, carpenters, astrologers, accountants, and attendants for all manner of rituals and processions.

Entrance to the complex is on the east, through two **gopura** gateways some way apart. Although the outer one is the larger, both are of the same pattern: massive rectangular bases topped by pyramidal towers with carved figures and vaulted roofs. At the core of each is a monolithic sandstone lintel, said to have been brought from Tiruchirapalli, over 50km away. The outer facade of the inner *gopura* features mighty, fanged *dvarpala* door guardians, mirror images of each other, and thought to be the largest monolithic sculptures in any Indian temple.

Once inside, the gigantic **courtyard** gives plenty of space to appreciate the buildings. The **main temple**, constructed of granite, consists of a long pillared *mandapa* hallway, followed by the *ardhamandapa*, or "half-hall", which in turn leads to the inner sanctum, the *garbha griha*. Above the shrine, the pyramidal 61m *vimana* tower rises in thirteen diminishing storeys, the apex being exactly one-third of the size of the base. Such a design is quite different from later temples, in which the shrine towers become smaller as the *gopura* entranceways increasingly dominate – a desire to protect the sanctum sanctorum from the polluting gaze of outsiders. This *vimana* is an example of a "structured monolith", a stage removed from the earlier rock-cut architecture of the Pallavas, in which blocks of stone are assembled and then carved. As the stone that surmounts it is said to weigh eighty tonnes, there is considerable speculation as to how it got up there; the most popular theory is that the rock was hauled up a 6-km-long ramp. Others have suggested the use of a method comparable to the Sumer Ziggurat style of building, in which logs were placed in gaps in the masonry and the stone raised by leverage.

The black *shivalingam*, over 3.5m high, in the **inner sanctum** is called Adavallan, "the one who can dance well" – a reference to Shiva as Nataraja, the King of the Dance, who resides at Chidambaram and was the *ishtadevata*, chosen deity, of the king. The lingam is not always on view, but during puja ceremonies (8am, 11am, noon & 7.30pm), a curtain is pulled revealing the god to the devotees.

Outside, the walls of the courtyard are lined with **colonnaded passageways** – the one along the northern wall is said to be the longest in India. In the southwest corner of the courtyard, the small **Archeological Museum** (daily 9am–6pm; free) houses an interesting collection of sculpture, and where you can also buy the excellent ASI booklet, *Chola Temples*, which gives detailed accounts of Brihadishwara and the temples at Gangaikondacholapuram and Darasuram. For more on Tamil Nadu's temples, see p.961.

The Royal Palace Compound and around

The **Royal Palace Compound** (all sites daily 9am–6pm), where members of the erstwhile royal family still reside, is on East Main Street (a continuation of Gandhiji Road), 2km northeast of Brihadishwara Temple. Work on the palace began in the mid-sixteenth century under Sevappa Nayak, the founder of the Nayak kingdom of Thanjavur; additions were made by the Marathas from the end of the seventeenth century onwards. Dotted around the compound are several reminders of Thanjavur's past under these two dynasties, including an exhibition of oriental manuscripts and a superlative museum of **Chola bronzes**. Unfortunately, many of the palace buildings remain in a sorry state, despite various promises of funds for renovation.

Durbar Hall and its courtyard

Remodelled by Shaji II in 1684, the **Durbar Hall** (Rs50 [Rs10], camera Rs30, video Rs100), or hall of audience, houses a throne canopy decorated with the

Chola bronzes

Originally sacred temple objects, **Chola bronzes** are the only art form from Tamil Nadu to have penetrated the world art market. The most memorable bronze icons are the **Natarajas**, or dancing Shivas. The image of Shiva, standing on one leg, encircled by flames, with wild locks caught in mid-motion, has become almost as recognizably Indian as the Taj Mahal.

The principal icons of a temple are usually stationary and made of stone. Frequently, however, ceremonies require an image of the god to be led in procession outside the inner sanctum, and even through the streets. According to the canonical texts known as Agamas, these moving images should be made of metal. Indian bronzes are made by the **cire-perdue** (**"lost wax"**) process, known as *madhuchchishtavidhana* in Sanskrit. Three layers of clay mixed with burned grain husks, salt and ground cotton are applied to a figure crafted in beeswax, with a stem left protruding at each end. When that is heated, the wax melts and flows out, creating a hollow mould into which molten metal – a rich five-metal alloy (*panchaloha*) of copper, silver, gold, brass and lead – can be poured through the stems. After the metal has cooled, the clay shell is destroyed, and the stems filed off, leaving a unique completed figure, which the caster-artist, or *sthapathi*, remodels to remove blemishes and add delicate detail.

Knowledge of bronze-casting in India goes back at least as far as the Indus Valley Civilization (2500–1500 BC), and the famous "**Dancing Girl**" from Mohenjo Daro. The earliest produced in the south was made by the Andhras, whose techniques were continued by the Pallavas, the immediate antecedents of the Cholas. The few surviving **Pallava** bronzes show a sophisticated handling of the form; figures are characterized by broad shoulders, thick-set features and an overall simplicity that suggests all the detail was completed at the wax stage. The finest bronzes of all are from the **Chola** period, in the late ninth to the early eleventh century. As the Cholas were predominantly Shaivite, Nataraja, Shiva and his consort Parvati (frequently in a family group with son Skanda) and the 63 Nayanmar poet-saints are the most popular subjects. Chola bronzes display more detail than their predecessors. Human figures are invariably slim-waisted and elegant, with the male form robust and muscular and the female graceful and delicate.

The design, iconography and proportions of each figure are governed by the strict rules laid down in the **shilpa shastras**, which draw no real distinction between art, science and religion. Measurement always begins with the proportions of the artist's own hand and the image's resultant face-length as the basic unit. Then follows a scheme which is allied to the equally scientific rules applied to classical music, and specifically *tala* or rhythm. Human figures total eight face-lengths, eight being the most basic of rhythmic measures. Figures of deities are *nava-tala*, nine face-lengths.

Those bronzes produced by the few artists practising today invariably follow the Chola model; the chief centre is now **Swamimalai** (see p.986). Original Chola bronzes are kept in many Tamil temples, but as the interiors are often dark it's not always possible to see them properly. Important **public collections** include the Nayak Durbar Hall Art Museum at Thanjavur (see opposite), the Government Museum at Chennai (see p.956) and the National Museum, New Delhi (see p.106). Those interested in shopping for bronzes and other handicrafts should check out the Chola Art Galerie (☎04362/277355), a two-minute walk south of the palace entrance at 78/79 East Main St.

mirrored glass distinctive of Thanjavur. Although damaged, the ceiling and walls are elaborately painted. Five domes are striped red, green and yellow, and on the walls, friezes of leaf and pineapple designs and trumpeting angels in a night sky show European influence. The **courtyard** outside the Durbar Hall was the setting for one of the more poignant moments in Thanjavur's turbulent history when, in 1683, the last of the Nayak kings gave himself up to the king of Madurai. Its most imposing structure, the Sarja Madi or "seven-storey" bell tower, built by Serfoji II in 1800, is closed to the public due to its unsafe condition.

Saraswati Mahal Library museum

The **Saraswati Mahal Library** holds one of the most important oriental manuscript collections in India, used by scholars from all over the world. The library is closed to the general public, but a small **museum** (free) displays a bizarre array of books and pictures from the collection. Among the palm-leaf manuscripts is a calligrapher's *tour de force* in the form of a visual mantra, where each letter in the inscription "Shiva" comprises the god's name repeated in microscopically small handwriting. Most of the Maratha manuscripts, produced from the end of the seventeenth century, are on paper; they include a superbly illustrated edition of the Mahabharata. Sadists will be delighted to see the library managed to hang on to their copy of the explicitly illustrated **Punishments in China**, published in 1804. Next to it, full rein is given to the imagination of French artist **Charles Le Brun** (1619–90), in a series of pictures on the subject of physiognomy. Animals such as the horse, bullock, wolf, bear, rabbit and camel are drawn in painstaking care above a series of human faces which bear an uncanny, if unlikely, resemblance to them. You can buy postcards of this scientific study and exhibits from the other palace museums in the **shop** next door.

Thanjavur Art Gallery

A magnificent collection of **Chola bronzes** – the finest of them from the Tiruvengadu hoard, unearthed in the 1950s – fills the **Thanjavur Art Gallery** (Rs20 [Rs5], camera or video camera Rs30), a high-ceilinged audience hall with massive pillars, dating from 1600. The elegance of the figures and delicacy of detail are unsurpassed. A tenth-century statue of Kannappa Nayannar (#174), a hunter-devotee, shows minutiae right down to his embroidered clothing, fingernails and the fine lines on his fingers. The oldest bronze, four cases left of the main doorway (#58), shows Vinadhra Dakshinamurti ("south-facing Shiva") who, with a deer on one left hand, would have originally been playing the *vina* – the musical instrument has long since gone. However, the undisputed masterpiece of the collection shows Shiva as Lord of the Animals (#86), sensuously depicted in a skimpy loincloth, with a turban made of snakes. Next to him stands an equally stunning Parvati, his consort (#87), but the cream of the female figures, a seated, half-reclining Parvati (#97), is displayed on the opposite side of the hall.

Eating and drinking

For **food**, there's the usual crop of "meals" canteens dotted around town, but only a couple of non-veg places apart from the swish upmarket hotel restaurants.

Annam *Pandiyar Residency* hotel, 14 Kutchery Rd. Small, inexpensive and impeccably clean veg restaurant that's recommended for its cut-above-the-competition lunchtime thalis (Rs30), and evening south Indian snacks (especially the delicious cashew *uttapams*).

King's *Yagappa*, Trichy Rd. Seven kinds of beer are served in the usual dimly lit room, or on the "lawn" (read: "sandy back yard"), where decor includes stuffed lizards and plastic flowers in fish tanks. They also serve tasty chicken and pakora snacks for Rs40–60.

Meenakshi Bhavan Near corner of Gandhiji and Kutchery roads. Spotless veg restaurant serving excellent dosas and other, less common south Indian vegetarian snacks, such as *adai*. You can eat well for Rs20–40.

New Thevar Train Station Rd. Very clean place with an a/c hall, serving a wide range of veg and non-veg curries, as well as some noodle dishes for Rs40–80.

Sathar's Gandhiji Rd. This is the town's most popular non-veg restaurant, and serves a decent variety of chicken dishes. Seating for the predominantly male clientele is downstairs, or on a covered terrace. Dishes are Rs60–80.

Thillana *Sangam*, Trichy Rd. Swish multi-cuisine restaurant that's renowned for its superb lunchtime south Indian thalis (11am–3pm; Rs105). Evenings feature an extensive à la carte menu (their *chettinad* specialities are superb). Worth a splurge just for the live Carnatic music from 7.30–10pm featuring *vina*, flute or vocals with percussion. Count on Rs300–400 per head.

Tiruchirapalli (Trichy) and around

TIRUCHIRAPALLI – more commonly referred to as **Trichy** – stands in the plains between the Shevaroy and Palani hills, just under 100km north of Madurai. Dominated by the dramatic Rock Fort, it's a sprawling commercial centre with a modern feel; the town itself holds little attraction, but pilgrims flock through en route to the spectacular **Ranganathaswamy Temple** in **Srirangam**, 6km north.

The precise date of Trichy's foundation is uncertain, but though little early architecture remains, it is clear that between 200 and 1000 AD control of the city passed between the Pallavas and Pandyas. The Chola kings who gained supremacy in the eleventh century embarked upon ambitious building projects, reaching a zenith with the Ranganathaswamy Temple. In the twelfth century, the Cholas were ousted by the Vijayanagar kings of Hampi, who then stood up against Muslim invasions until 1565, when they succumbed to the might of the sultans of the Deccan. Less than fifty years later the Nayaks of Madurai came to power, constructing the fort and firmly establishing Trichy as a trading city. After almost a century of struggle against the French and British, who both sought lands in southeast Tamil Nadu, the town came under British control until it was declared part of Tamil Nadu state in 1947.

Arrival and information

Trichy's **airport** is 8km south of the centre. The journey into town, by taxi (Rs200) or bus (#7, #28, #59, #63 or #K1) takes less than half an hour. The main railway station, **Trichy Junction** – which has given its name to the southern district of town – is within easy reach of most hotels, restaurants and banks, as well as the two bus stands, **Central** and **State Express**, which are close to each other, though there are no fixed rules about where a particular bus will arrive or depart. The efficient local city service (#1) that leaves from the platform on Rockins

Moving on from Trichy

The airport (enquiries and bookings ⓣ0431/248 0233), has daily **flights** to and from Chennai, several weekly to Thiruvananthapuram and Kozhikode, as well as frequent services to Sri Lanka and the Gulf states. There are frequent **rail** links with the following: Bengaluru (1 daily; 8hr 55min); Chengalpattu (6–7 daily; 4hr–5hr 20min); Chennai (7–9 daily; 5hr 20min–7hr); Coimbatore (2 daily; 4hr 55min–5hr 10min); Kanyakumari (3 daily; 7hr 30min–9hr); Kochi (1 daily; 9hr 30min); Kodaikanal Road (2–4 daily; 1hr 50min–2hr 15min); Madurai (8–9 daily; 2hr 45min–3hr 30min); Thanjavur (2 daily; 1hr 10min–1hr 25min).

Of the two **bus** stands (see Arrival), **private buses** mainly use the Central stand: Chengalpattu (every 20–30min; 7–8hr); Chennai (every 20–30min; 8hr 30min–9hr 30min); Coimbatore (every 30min; 5hr); Kanchipuram (3 daily; 7hr); Kanyakumari (every 30min; 10–12hr); Kodaikanal (8–10 daily; 5hr); Madurai (every 30min; 4–5hr); Puducherry (every 30min; 5–6hr); Thanjavur (every 10min; 1hr–1hr 30min); Tiruvannamalai (5 daily; 6hr).

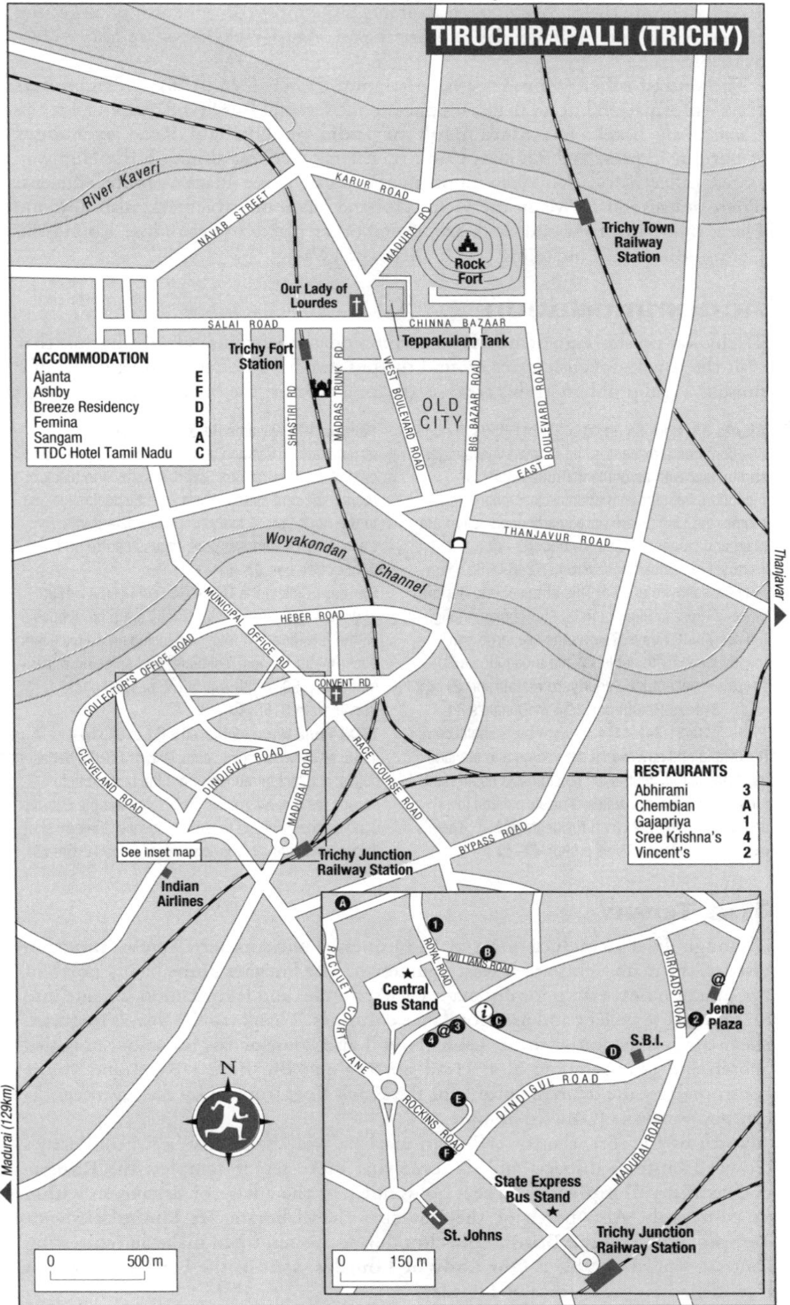
Sri Jambukeshwara Temple, Srirangam & Chennai (315km)
TIRUCHIRAPALLI (TRICHY)
River Kaveri
KARUR ROAD
NAVAB STREET
MADURA RD
Rock Fort
Trichy Town Railway Station
Our Lady of Lourdes
SALAI ROAD
CHINNA BAZAAR
Teppakulam Tank
Trichy Fort Station
SHASTIRI RD
MADRAS TRUNK RD
WEST BOULEVARD ROAD
OLD CITY
BIG BAZAAR ROAD
EAST BOULEVARD ROAD
ACCOMMODATION
Ajanta E
Ashby F
Breeze Residency D
Femina B
Sangam A
TTDC Hotel Tamil Nadu C
THANJAVUR ROAD
Woyakondan Channel
Thanjavur
MUNICIPAL OFFICE RD
HEBER ROAD
COLLECTOR'S OFFICE ROAD
CONVENT RD
CLEVELAND ROAD
DINDIGUL ROAD
MADURAI ROAD
RACE COURSE ROAD
RESTAURANTS
Abhirami 3
Chembian A
Gajapriya 1
Sree Krishna's 4
Vincent's 2
BYPASS ROAD
See inset map
Trichy Junction Railway Station
Indian Airlines
RACQUET COURT LANE
ROYAL ROAD
WILLIAMS ROAD
Central Bus Stand
BIROADS ROAD
Jenne Plaza
S.B.I.
DINDIGUL ROAD
ROCKINS ROAD
MADURAI ROAD
State Express Bus Stand
St. Johns
Trichy Junction Railway Station
N
Madurai (129km)
0 500 m
0 150 m
Airport (6km)

Road, opposite the *Shree Krishna* restaurant, is the most convenient way of getting to the Rock Fort, the temples and Srirangam. **Auto-rickshaws** are also widely available.

The **tourist office** (Mon–Fri 10am–5.45pm; ⓣ0431/246 0136), which proffers travel information but no maps, is opposite the Central Bus Stand, just outside the *Tamil Nadu* hotel. The **State Bank of India** on Dindigul Road **exchanges** American Express and Thomas Cook travellers' cheques, although the Highway Forex office (Mon–Sat 10am–6pm) in the plush Jenne Plaza is more efficient. There are several ATMs in the vicinity of the bus stands. Netpark, also in Jenne Plaza, offers **internet** and there are several other places to get online around the Central Bus Stand, including two branches of iWay.

Accommodation

Trichy has no shortage of **hotels** to accommodate the thousands of pilgrims that visit the town; dozens cluster around the bus stands and offer good value. Traffic noise is a real problem in this area, so ask for a room at the back.

Ajanta 6A, Rockins Rd ⓣ0431/241 5504. A huge, 85-room complex centred on its own Vijayanagar shrine, and with an opulent Tirupati deity in reception. Popular with middle-class pilgrims; rooms (the singles are particularly good value) are plain and clean. Towels provided. ❸–❹

Ashby 17-A Rockins Rd ⓣ0431/246 0652, ⓦwww.ashbyhotel.com. This atmospheric Raj-era place is most foreign tourists' first choice, though it's seen better days. The rooms are large and mostly clean, with cable TV and mosquito coils. There's a decent little courtyard restaurant. ❷–❹

Breeze Residency 3/14 McDonald's Rd ⓣ0431/241 4414, ⓦwww.breezehotel.com. Renovated and now with a new name and management, this large, central a/c hotel boasts comfortably furnished rooms and suites, a nicely painted foyer and a swimming pool (non-residents Rs100). There's also a fine restaurant (see p.996). ❻–❽

Femina 109 Williams Rd ⓣ0431/241 4501, ⓔfeminahotel@yahoo.com. Well-maintained place east of the Central Bus Stand. A sprawling block of rooms, a/c and suites, some with balconies looking to the Rock Fort, it features plush restaurants, travel services, shops, pool, fitness centre and a 24hr coffee bar. ❹–❻

Sangam Collector's Office Rd ⓣ0431/241 4700, ⓦwww.hotelsangam.com. Trichy's top hotel boasts all the facilities of a four-star, including an excellent pool (Rs100 for non-residents) and splendid restaurant (see p.996) with live music at weekends. Rooms from $165. ❾

TTDC Tamil Nadu McDonald's Rd ⓣ0431/241 4346, ⓦwww.ttdconline.com. One of TTDC's better hotels, and just far enough from the bus stand to escape the din. A/c rooms. Best value are the non-a/c doubles, though even these are dowdier than most of the competition; all a/c rooms have cable TV. ❷–❹

The Town

Although Trichy conducts most of its business in the southern **Trichy Junction** district, the main sights are at least 4km north. The **bazaars** immediately north of the Junction heave with locally made cigars, textiles and fake diamonds made into inexpensive jewellery and used for dance costumes. Thanks to the town's frequent, cheap air connection with Sri Lanka, you'll also come across boxes of smuggled Scotch and photographic film. Head north along Big Bazaar Road and you're confronted by the dramatic profile of the **Rock Fort**, topped by the seventeenth-century Vinayaka (Ganesh) Temple.

North of the fort, the River Kaveri marks a wide boundary between Trichy's crowded business districts and its somewhat more serene temples; the **Ranganathaswamy Temple** is so large it holds much of the village of Srirangam within its courtyards. Also north of the Kaveri is the elaborate **Sri Jambukeshwara Temple**, while several British **churches** dotted around town make an interesting contrast – most notable is **Our Lady of Lourdes**, west of the Rock Fort, which is modelled on the Basilica of Lourdes.

The Rock Fort

Trichy's **Rock Fort** (☎0431/270 4621; daily 6am–8pm; Rs2, camera Rs100, video camera Rs100) is best reached by bus (#1) from outside the railway station, or from Dindigul Road; rickshaws will try to charge you Rs50 or more for the five-minute ride.

The massive sand-coloured rock on which the fort rests towers to a height of more than 80m, its irregular sides smoothed by wind and rain. The Pallavas were the first to cut into it, but it was the Nayaks who grasped the site's potential as a fort, adding only a few walls and bastions as fortifications. From the entrance, off China Bazaar, a long flight of red-and-white painted steps cuts steeply uphill, past a series of Pallava and Pandya rock-cut temples (closed to non-Hindus), to the **Ganesh Temple** crowning the hilltop. The views from its terrace are spectacular, taking in the Ranganathaswamy and Jambukeshwara temples to the north, their *gopuras* rising from a sea of palm trees, and the cubic concrete sprawl of central Trichy to the south.

Sri Ranganathaswamy Temple

The **Sri Ranganathaswamy Temple** at **Srirangam**, 6km north of Trichy Junction, is among the most revered shrines to Vishnu in south India, and also one of the largest and liveliest. Enclosed by seven rectangular walled courtyards and covering more than sixty hectares, it stands on an island defined by a tributary of the River Kaveri. This location symbolizes the transcendence of Vishnu, housed in the sanctuary reclining on the coils of the snake Adisesha, who in legend formed an island for the god, resting on the primordial Ocean of Chaos.

Frequent **buses** from Trichy pull in and leave from outside the southern gate. A gateway topped with an immense and heavily carved *gopura*, completed in the late 1980s, leads to the outermost courtyard, the latest of seven built between the fifth and seventeenth centuries. Most of the present structure dates from the late fourteenth century, when the temple was renovated and enlarged after a disastrous sacking in 1313. The **outer three courtyards** form the hub of the temple community, housing ascetics, priests, musicians and souvenir shops.

At the fourth wall, the entrance to the temple proper, visitors remove footwear and can purchase camera and video camera tickets (Rs50/100) before passing through a high gateway, topped by a magnificent *gopura* and lined with small shrines to teachers, hymn-singers and sages. In earlier days, this **fourth** *prakara* would have formed the outermost limit of the temple, and was the closest members of the lowest castes could get to the sanctuary. It contains some of the finest and oldest buildings of the complex, including a temple to the goddess **Ranganayaki** in the northwest corner where devotees worship before approaching Vishnu's shrine. On the eastern side of the *prakara*, the heavily carved "thousand pillared" *kalyan mandapa*, or hall, was constructed in the late Chola period. The pillars of the outstanding **Sheshagiriraya Mandapa**, south of the *kalyan mandapa*, are decorated with rearing steeds and hunters, representing the triumph of good over evil.

To the right of the gateway into the fourth courtyard, a small **museum** (daily 9am–1pm & 2–6pm; Rs1) houses a modest collection of stone and bronze sculptures, and some delicate ivory plaques. For Rs10, you can climb to the roof of the fourth wall from beside the museum and take in the view over the temple rooftops and *gopuras*, which increase in size from the centre outwards. The central dome, crowning the holy sanctuary, is coated in gold and carved with images of Vishnu's incarnations, on each of its four sides.

Inside the gate to the **fifth courtyard** – the final section of the temple open to non-Hindus – is a pillared hall, the **Garuda Mandapa**, carved throughout in typical Nayak style. Maidens, courtly donors and Nayak rulers feature on the pillars that surround the central shrine to Garuda, the man-eagle vehicle of Vishnu.

For more on Tamil Nadu's temples, see p.961.

Eating

To **eat** well in Trichy, you won't have to stray far from the Central Bus Stand, where the town's most popular "meals" joints do a roaring trade all day long.

Abhirami 10 Rockins Rd, opposite Central Bus Stand. Trichy's best-known south Indian restaurant serves up unbeatable value lunchtime "meals" (Rs20), and the standard range of snacks the rest of the day. They also have a fast-food counter where you can get dosas and *uttapams* at any time.

Chembian *Hotel Sangam*, Collector's Office Rd. Excellent restaurant offering a range of delicious Indian dishes, as well as unusually good Western and Chinese cuisine, in an atmospheric, beautifully decorated dining hall. Main dishes around Rs200. Live Carnatic music at weekends.

Gajapriya Royal Rd, on the ground floor of the *Gajapriya* hotel. Non-veg north Indian and noodle dishes are specialities of this small but blissfully cool and clean a/c restaurant. A good place to chill out over coffee.

The Madras *Breeze Residency* 3/14 McDonald's Rd. Worth trying for the excellent-value diner buffet (Rs200), which features a range of mostly Indian and Chinese dishes, with some less common cuisine, such as Mexican, thrown into the mix.

Sree Krishna's 1 Rockins Rd, opposite the Central Bus Stand. Delicious and very filling American or south Indian "set breakfasts", unlimited banana-leaf thalis at lunchtime (Rs35) and south Indian specialities in the evenings – all served with a big smile.

Vincent's Dindigul Rd, next to the bakery. An "Oriental" theme restaurant, set back from the road in its own terrace garden, with mock pagodas, concrete bamboo and a multi-cuisine menu that includes tasty chicken tikka and other tandoori dishes. A bit shabby, but it's an escape from the hectic bus-stand area. No alcohol; evenings only.

Madurai

One of the oldest cities in South Asia, **MADURAI**, on the banks of the River Vaigai, has been an important centre of worship and commerce for as long as there has been civilization in south India – indeed, it has long been described as "the Athens of the East". Not surprisingly then, when the Greek ambassador Megasthenes came here in 302 BC, he wrote of its splendour, and described its queen, Pandai, as "a daughter of Herakles". Meanwhile, the Roman geographer Strabo complained at how the city's silk, pearls and spices were draining the imperial coffers of Rome. It was this lucrative trade that enabled the **Pandyan** dynasty to erect the mighty **Meenakshi-Sundareshwarar temple**. Although today surrounded by a sea of modern concrete cubes, the massive *gopuras* of this vast complex, writhing with multicoloured mythological figures and crowned by golden finials, remain the greatest man-made spectacle of the south. Any day of the week no fewer than 15,000 people pass through its gates, increasing to over 25,000 on Fridays (sacred to the goddess Meenakshi), while the temple's ritual life spills out into the streets in an almost ceaseless round of festivals and processions.

Some history

Although invariably interwoven with myth, the traceable history and fame of Madurai stretches back well over 2000 years. Numerous natural **caves** in local hills, and boulders often modified by the addition of simple rock-cut beds, were used both in prehistoric times and by ascetics such as the Ajivikas and Jains, who practised withdrawal and penance.

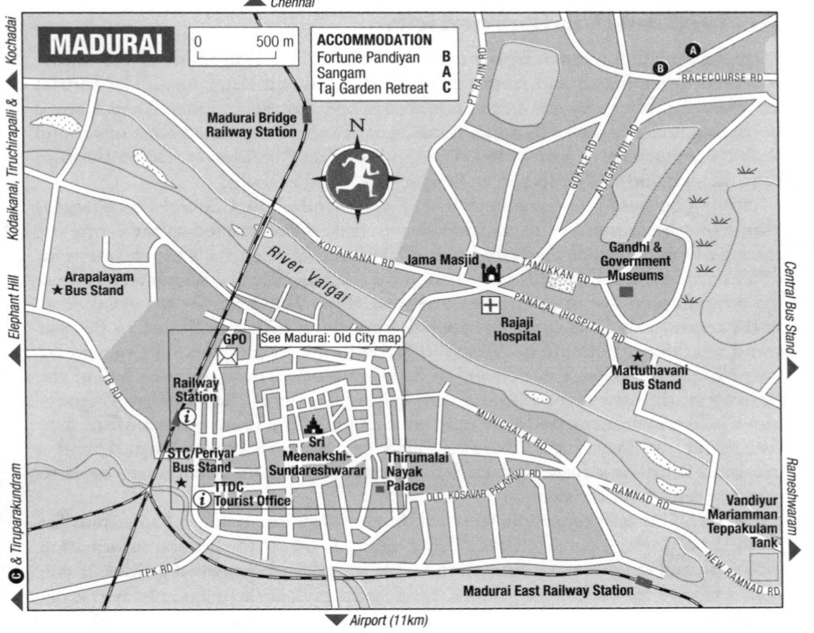

Madurai appears to have been capital of the Pandyan empire without interruption for at least a thousand years. It became a major commercial city, trading with Greece, Rome and China, and *yavanas* (a generic term for foreigners) were frequent visitors to Pandyan seaports. The Tamil epics describe them walking around town with their eyes and mouths wide open with amazement. Under the Pandya dynasty, Madurai also became an established seat of Tamil culture, credited with being the site of three **sangams**, "literary academies", said to have lasted 10,000 years and supported some eight thousand poets.

The Pandyas' capital fell in the tenth century, when the **Chola** king Parantaka took the city. In the thirteenth century, the Pandyas briefly regained power until the early 1300s, when the notorious **Malik Kafur**, the Delhi Sultanate's "favourite slave", made an unprovoked attack during a plunder-and-desecration tour of the south, and destroyed much of the city. Forewarned of the raid, the Pandya king, Sundara, fled with his immediate family and treasure, leaving his uncle and rival, Vikrama Pandya, to repel Kafur. Nevertheless, the latter returned to Delhi with booty said to consist of "six hundred and twelve elephants, ninety-six thousand *mans* of gold, several boxes of jewels and pearls and twenty thousand horses".

Shortly after this raid Madurai became an independent Sultanate; in 1364, it joined the Hindu **Vijayanagar** empire, ruled from Hampi and administered by governors, the **Nayaks**. In 1565, the Nayaks asserted their own independence. Under their supervision and patronage, Madurai enjoyed a renaissance, being rebuilt on the pattern of a lotus centring on the Meenakshi Temple. Part of the palace of the most illustrious of the Nayaks, **Thirumalai** (1623–55), survives today. The city remained under Nayak control until the mid-eighteenth century when the **British** gradually took over. A hundred years later the British de-fortified Madurai, filling its moat to create the four Veli streets that today mark the boundary of the old city.

Arrival and information

Madurai's small domestic **airport** (☎0452/269 0433), 12km south of the centre, is served by flights to and from Chennai, Mumbai and Bengaluru. The **tourist information** booth by the exit is not always open to meet flights. There's also a bookshop and a branch of Indian Bank here. **Taxis** charge fixed rates of around Rs200 for journeys to and within the city. City Bus #10A leaves frequently from near the exit and will drop you at Periyar Bus Stand in town.

Arriving by **bus**, you come in at one of two stands. The **Central Bus Stand** is 7km from the centre on the east side of the river: it's connected to the centre by, among others, the dedicated city buses #700 and #75. Central is the arrival point of all services except those from towns in the west and Kerala, which terminate at the **Arapalayam Bus Stand** in the northwest, about 2km from the railway station. In the centre, only local city buses operate from either **STC Bus Stand**, or **Periyar stand** next door. Both are on West Veli Street in the west of the old city, and are very close to the railway station and most accommodation. In the main hall of the **railway station** itself you'll find a very helpful branch of the **Tourism Department information centre** (daily 6.30am–8.30pm). The **reservations office** is to the left of the main hall. There's a small veg **canteen** on Platform 1, and a **pre-paid auto-rickshaw and taxi booth** outside the main entrance, open to coincide with train arrivals.

The **TTDC** tourist office, on West Veli Street (Mon–Fri 10am–5.45pm, plus Sat 10am–1pm during festivals; ☎0452/233 4757), is useful for general information and maps, and can provide information on **car rental and approved guides**. If you want a **taxi** to see the outlying sights, head to the rank at the main railway station, which abides by government set rates; a five-hour city tour will cost Rs1000.

Madurai's **GPO** is at the corner of West Veli and North Veli streets (Mon–Sat 8am–7.30pm, Sun & hols 9am–4.30pm; Speedpost 10am–7pm). **Internet access** is widely available: try Net Tower, next to the *Hotel International*, Friends, just round the corner at 13/8 Kaka Thoppu St, or the two branches of iWay on West Perumal Maistry Street; both offer Netphone connections.

Moving on from Madurai

There are regular **flights** to Chennai, with one Air India service daily going on to Mumbai and another with Paramount Airways flying on to Bengaluru; Jet and Air Deccan also operate to Chennai. To get to the airport, catch a taxi (around Rs200), or take city bus #10A from the Periyar Bus Stand. Air India's city office is at 7-A West Veli St, near the post office (☎0452/234 1234); Jet Airways, Air Deccan and Paramount Airways all have offices at the airport.

There are frequent bus services to the following, from the Central Bus Stand unless otherwise stated: Chengalpattu (every 20–30min; 9hr); Chennai (every 20–30min; 11hr); Chidambaram (6 daily; 8hr); Coimbatore (**Arapalayam stand**, every 30min; 5–6hr); Kanchipuram (4 daily; 10–12hr); Kanyakumari (every 30min; 6hr); Kochi/Ernakulam via Kottayam (**Arapalayam stand,** 9 daily; 10hr); Kodaikanal (**Arapalayam stand** hourly; 4hr); Kumbakonam (8 daily; 6hr–6hr 30min); Kumily, for Periyar Wildlife Sanctuary (**Arapalayam stand**, hourly; 5hr); Mysore (5 daily; 10hr); Puducherry (hourly; 9–10hr); Rameshwaram (every 30min–1hr; 4hr); Thanjavur (every 30min; 4–5hr); Thiruvananthapuram, Kerala (hourly; 7hr); Tiruchirapalli (every 30min; 4–5hr); Tirupati (4 daily; 15hr). There are no direct services from Madurai to Ooty; change in Coimbatore.

Madurai is on the main broad-gauge **train** line, and is well connected with most major towns and cities in south India, including the following: Bengaluru (1 daily; 10hr 30min); Chengalpattu (6–7 daily; 6hr 55min–9hr); Chennai (7–9 daily; 7hr

The best place to **change money** is Tradewings, almost opposite the post office at 168 North Veli St (Mon–Sat 9am–6.30pm). The State Bank of India is at 6 West Veli St, and there are several 24hr ATMs in town, including those at the Canara Bank on West Perumal Maistry Street and the UTI Bank on Station Road. **Bike rental** at low rates is available at SV, West Tower Street, near the west entrance to the temple, or the stall on West Veli Street, opposite the *Tamil Nadu* hotel.

Accommodation

Madurai has a wide range of **accommodation** to cater for the flocks of pilgrims and tourists, from rock-bottom lodges to good, clean mid-range places, with a cluster of hotels on **West Perumal Maistry Street**. Upmarket options lie a few kilometres out of the town centre, north of the Vaigai.

Unless otherwise stated, the hotels listed below are marked on the Old City map (p.1001).

Aarathy 9 Perumal Koil, West Mada St, off South Masi St ⓣ0452/233 1571, ⓕ233 6343. Great location overlooking the Kundalagar Temple, so often booked up. All rooms have TV, others have a/c and a balcony – some are better than others, so ask to see a range before checking in. There's an excellent a/c restaurant which extends out into the courtyard where the temple elephant is led through each morning and afternoon. ❷

Fortune Pandyan Racecourse Rd, north of the river (see Madurai map, p.997) ⓣ0452/4356789, ⓦwww.fortunepandiyanhotel.com. Smart, centrally a/c hotel with large comfortable rooms, all with TV and lavishly decorated with period-style furnishings. It's quiet and relaxed, being some way out of town, and there's a good restaurant, bar, exchange facilities and a travel agency. ❽–❾

International 46/80 West Perumal Maistry St ⓣ0452/4377463. Recently renovated lodge with lackadaisical service, but the rooms are decent and all have cable TV. ❷–❹

New College House 2 Town Hall Rd ⓣ0452/234 2971, ⓔinfo@newcollegehouse.com. This huge, maze-like place has more than 200 rooms, and one of the town's best "meals" canteens on the ground floor (see p.1004). The very cheapest rooms are grubby, but there are likely to be vacancies here when everywhere else is full. ❷–❹

55min–10hr 30min); Coimbatore (1–2 daily; 6hr 15min); Kanyakumari (6 daily; 4hr–5hr 50min); Kodaikanal Road (2–4 daily; 33–45min); Tiruchirapalli (7–8 daily; 2hr 15min–3hr 10min); Tirupati (3 weekly; 11hr 30min). For further **timetable** details, ask the Tourism Department Information Centre, to the right of the ticket counters. It's possible to reach the railhead for Kodaikanal by train, but the journey is much faster by express bus.

Recommended trains from Madurai

Destination	Name	No.	Departs	Total time
Bengaluru	*Tuticorin–Mysore Express*	#6731	8.05pm	10hr 35min
Chennai	*Vaigai Express*	#2636	6.45am	7hr 55min
	Pandiyan Express	#2638	8.45pm	9hr
Coimbatore (for Ooty)	*Madurai–Coimbatore Express*	#6716	10.50pm	6hr 10min
	Nagercoil-Coimbatore Fast Passenger	#383	12.40pm	6hr 05min
Nagercoil	*Chennai-Guruvayur Express*	#6127	4pm	5hr
Trichy	*Vaigai Express*	#2636	6.45am	2hr 20min

Padmam 1 Perumal Tank West St ⓣ0452/234 0702, ⓔhotelpadmam@hotmail.com. Clean, comfortable and modern hotel, centrally located and with a rooftop restaurant. The views from the front-side rooms, overlooking the ruined Perumal tank, are worth paying extra for. ❹–❺

Prem Nivas 102 West Perumal Maistry St ⓣ0452/234 2532, ⓔpremnivas@eth.net. From the outside this place looks a lot swankier than it is, but the spacious attached rooms make it among the best deals in the city; singles are especially good value. ❹

Rathna Residency 109 West Perumal Maistry St ⓣ0452/ 437444, ⓦwww.hotelrathnaresidency.com. Standard lower mid-range hotel with decent, clean a/c and non-a/c rooms (the latter are better value), plus two restaurants, one on the rooftop. ❹–❺

Sangam Alagar Koil Rd (see main Madurai map, p.997) ⓣ0452/253 7531, ⓦwww.hotelsangam.com. Situated in its own grounds on the northern outskirts of town, this plush, centrally a/c hotel has very comfortable rooms (from $165), 24hr room service, bar, currency exchange, swimming pool and pleasant gardens. ❾

Sree Devi 20 West Avani Moola St ⓣ0452/234 7431. Excellent-value, spotless non-a/c doubles right next to the temple mean this place is always filled with foreigners. For a romantic splurge, splash out on their "deluxe" a/c rooftop room, which has matchless views over the western *gopura*. No restaurant, but they will order in food and beer for you. ❶–❸

Supreme 110 West Perumal Maistry St ⓣ0452/234 3151, ⓦwww.supremehotels.com. A large, swish and central hotel, with a great rooftop restaurant, an a/c restaurant on the ground floor and a choice of comfortable a/c and non-a/c rooms in a seven-storey block; the more expensive have temple views. It's a little overpriced, but has good facilities including a 24hr forex desk, internet access and travel counter. Book in advance. ❹–❺

Taj Garden Retreat 40 TPK Rd, Pasumalai Hills (see main Madurai map, p.997) ⓣ0452/260 1020, ⓦwww.tajhotels.com. Madurai's most exclusive hotel, in a beautifully refurbished colonial house set within 25 acres of manicured gardens in the hills overlooking the city and temples, albeit 6km out. Of the three categories of room, the superior ones in the old colonial building are the most atmospheric, but the deluxe have the best views. Facilities include a gourmet restaurant, swimming pool, tennis court and bar. Rooms start at $ 160. ❾

TTDC Hotel Tamil Nadu I West Veli St ⓣ0452/233 7471, ⓦwww.ttdconline.com. Somewhat out on a limb, away from the atmosphere of the temples and the bazaar, but with spacious rooms overlooking a leafy courtyard. The cheapest rooms are especially good value. ❷–❹

The City

Although considerably enlarged and extended over the years, the overall layout of Madurai's **old city**, south of the River Vaigai, has remained largely unchanged since the first centuries AD, comprising a series of concentric squares centred on the massive **Meenakshi Temple**. Aligned with the cardinal points, the street plan forms a giant mandala, or magical diagram, whose sacred properties are believed to be activated during mass circumambulations of the central temple, always conducted in a clockwise direction.

North of the river, Madurai becomes markedly more mundane and irregular. You're only likely to cross the Vaigai to reach the city's more expensive hotels or the Gandhi Museum.

Sri Meenakshi-Sundareshwarar Temple

Enclosed by a roughly rectangular 6m-high wall, in the manner of a fortified palace, the **Sri Meenakshi-Sundareshwarar Temple** (daily 6am–12.30pm & 4–9.30pm; camera Rs30, no video cameras) is one of the largest temple complexes in India. Much of it was constructed during the Nayak period between the sixteenth and eighteenth centuries, but certain parts are very much older.

For the first-time visitor, confronted with a confusing maze of shrines, sculptures and colonnades, and unaware of the logic employed in their arrangement, it's very easy to get disorientated. Quite apart from the estimated 33,000 sculptures to arrest your attention, the life of the temple is absolutely absorbing, with the endless round of puja ceremonies, loud *nagaswaram* and *tavil* music, weddings, brahmin boys under

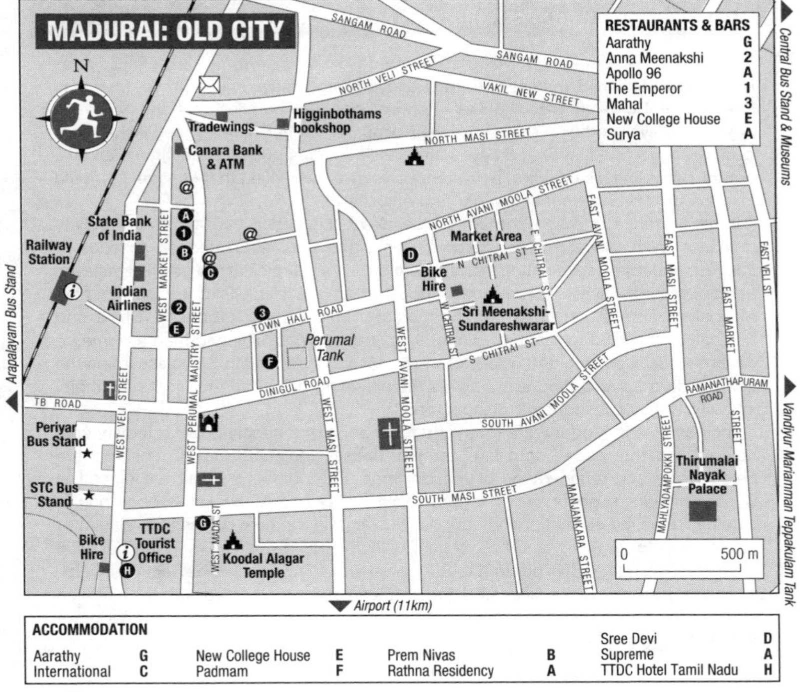

religious instruction in the Vedas, the prostrations of countless devotees, the glittering market stalls inside the east entrance or, best of all, a festival procession, something is always going on to make this one of the most compelling places in Tamil Nadu.

Approximately fifty priests live and work here; each wears a white *dhoti* tied between the legs; on top of this, around the waist, is a second, coloured cloth, usually of silk. Madurai takes the **gopura**, so prominent in other southern temples, to its ultimate extreme. The entire complex has no fewer than twelve such towers; set into the outer walls, the four largest reach a height of around 46m. Each is covered with a profusion of gaily painted stucco gods and demons. It is sometimes possible, for a small fee, to climb the tallest tower, to enjoy superb views over the town; enquire with the guards at one of the gateways.

The most popular **entrance** is on the east side, which leads directly to the Shiva shrine; there is another entrance nearby, through a towerless gate, which leads to the adjacent Meenakshi shrine deep inside. In the **Ashta Shakti Mandapa** ("Eight Goddesses Hallway"), a market sells puja offerings and souvenirs. Sculpted pillars illustrate different aspects of the goddess Shakti, and Shiva's sixty-four miracles at Madurai.

If you continue straight on from here, cross East Ati Street, and go through the seven-storey **Chitrai gopura**, you enter a passageway leading to the eastern end of the **Pottamarai Kulam** ("Golden Lotus Tank"), where Indra bathed before worshipping the *shivalingam*. From the east side of the tank you can see the glistening gold of the Meenakshi and Sundareshwarar *vimana* towers. Facing Meenakshi, just past the first entrance and in front of the sanctum sanctorum,

Meenakshi the goddess whose eyes are shaped like a fish

The goddess **Meenakshi** of Madurai emerged from the flames of a sacrificial fire as a three-year-old child, in answer to the Pandyan king Malayadvaja's prayer for a son. The king, not only surprised to see a female, was also horrified that she had three breasts. In every other respect, she was beautiful, as her name, Meenakshi ("fish-eyed"), suggests – fish-shaped eyes are classic images of desirability in Indian love poetry. Dispelling his concern, a mysterious voice told the king that Meenakshi would lose the third breast on meeting her future husband.

In the absence of a son, the adult Meenakshi succeeded her father as Pandyan monarch. With the aim of world domination, she then embarked on a series of successful battles, culminating in the defeat of Shiva's armies at the god's Himalayan abode, Mount Kailash. Shiva then appeared at the battlefield; on seeing him, Meenakshi immediately lost her third breast. Fulfilling the prophecy, Shiva and Meenakshi travelled to Madurai, where they were married. The two then assumed a dual role, firstly as king and queen of the Pandya kingdom, with Shiva assuming the title Sundara Pandya, and secondly as the presiding deities of the Madurai temple, into which they subsequently disappeared.

Their shrines in Madurai are today the focal point of a hugely popular fertility cult; centred on the gods' coupling, temple priests maintain that it ensures the preservation and regeneration of the Universe. Each night, the pair are placed in Sundareshwarar's bedchamber together, but not before Meenakshi's nose ring is carefully removed so that it won't cut her husband in the heat of passion. Fidelity is never taken for granted, and has to be ritually tested each year when the beautiful goddess Cellattamman is brought to Sundareshwarar "to have her powers renewed". After she is spurned, she flies into a fury that can only be placated with the sacrifice of a buffalo – one among the dozens of arcane ceremonies that make up Madurai's round of temple rituals.

stands Shiva's bull-vehicle, Nandi. At around 9pm, the moveable images of the god and goddess are carried to the **bed chamber**. Here the final puja ceremony of the day, the **lalipuja**, is performed, when for thirty minutes or so the priests sing lullabies (*lali*), before closing the temple for the night.

Sundareshwar and Meenakshi are brought every Friday (6–7pm) to the sixteenth-century **Oonjal Mandapa** further along, where they are placed on a swing (*oonjal*) and serenaded by members of a special caste, the Oduvars.

Walking back north, past the Meenakshi shrine, through a towered entrance, leads you to the area of the Sundareshwarar shrine. Just inside is the huge monolithic figure of Ganesh, **Mukkuruni Vinayaka**, believed to have been found during the excavation of the Mariamman Teppakulam tank. Chubby Ganesh is well-known for his love of sweets, and during his annual **Vinayaka Chaturthi festival** (Sept), a special *prasad* (gift offering of food) is concocted from ingredients including 300 kilos of rice, 10 kilos of sugar and 110 coconuts.

Causing a certain amount of fun, north of the flagstaffs are figures of Shiva and Kali in the throes of a dance competition. A stall nearby sells tiny **butter balls** from a bowl of water, which visitors throw at the god and goddess "to cool them down". If you leave through the gateway here, on the east, you'll find in the northeast corner the fifteenth-century **Ayirakkal Mandapa**, or thousand-pillared hall, now transformed into the temple's **Art Museum** (daily 10am–5.30pm; Rs5, camera Rs25). Throughout the hall, large sculptures of strange mythical creatures and cosmic deities rear out at you from the broad stone pillars, some of which have startlingly metallic-like musical tones when tapped.

For more on the temples of Tamil Nadu, see p.961.

Vandiyur Mariamman Teppakulam tank and the floating festival

At one time, the huge **Vandiyur Mariamman Teppakulam** tank in the southeast of town (bus #4 or #4A; 15min) was full with a constant supply of water, flowing via underground channels from the Vaigai. Nowadays, thanks to a number of accidents, it is only filled during the spectacular Teppam **floating festival** (Jan/Feb), when pilgrims take boats out to the goddess shrine in the centre. Before their marriage ceremony, Shiva and Meenakshi are brought in procession to the tank, where they are floated on a raft beautifully decorated with lights, which devotees pull by ropes three times, encircling the shrine. The boat trip is believed to be the overture to a seduction that reaches its passionate conclusion later that night in the temple. This traditionally makes the Teppam the most auspicious time of year for young couples to get married.

Thirumalai Nayak Palace

Roughly a quarter survives of the seventeenth-century **Thirumalai Nayak Palace** (☎0452/233 2945, daily 9am–1pm & 2–5pm; Rs50 [Rs10]; includes Palace Museum), 1.5km southeast of the Meenakshi Temple. Much of it was dismantled by Thirumalai's grandson, Chockkanatha Nayak, and used for a new palace at Tiruchirapalli; what remains today was renovated in 1858 by the governor of Madras, Lord Napier, and again in 1971 for the Tamil World Conference. The palace originally consisted of two residential sections, plus a theatre, private temple, harem, royal bandstand, armoury and gardens.

The Tourism Department arranges a nightly **Sound-and-Light Show** (in English 6.45–7.30pm; Rs10), which relates the story of the Tamil epic, Shilipaddikaram, and the history of the Nayaks, though the quality of the tape can be poor. In an adjoining hall, the **Palace Museum** (same hours as the palace) includes unlabelled Pandyan, Jain and Buddhist sculpture, terracottas and an eighteenth-century print showing the palace in a dilapidated state.

Tamukkam Palace: the Gandhi museum

Across the Vaigai, 5km northeast of the centre near the Central Telegraph Office (bus #1, #2, #11, #17 or #24; 20min), stands Tamukkam, the seventeenth-century multi-pillared and arched palace of Queen Rani Mangammal. Built to accommodate such regal entertainment as elephant fights, Tamukkam was taken over by the British, used as a courthouse and collector's office, and in 1955 became home to the Gandhi and Government museums. The **Gandhi Memorial Museum** (daily 10am–1pm & 2–5.30pm; free) charts the history of India since the landing of the first Europeans, viewed in terms of the freedom struggle. Generally the perspective is national, but where appropriate, reference is made to the role played by Tamils. Wholeheartedly critical of the British, it states its case clearly and simply, quoting the condemnation by Englishman John Sullivan of his fellow countrymen's insulting treatment of Indians. One chilling artefact, kept in a room painted black, is the bloodstained *dhoti* the Mahatma was wearing when he was assassinated. Next door to the museum, the **Gandhi Memorial Museum Library** (daily except Wed 10am–1pm & 2–5.30pm; free) houses a reference collection, open to all, of fifteen thousand books, periodicals, letters and microfilms of material by and about Gandhi.

Eating

When the afternoon heat gets too much, head for one of the **juice bars** dotted around the centre, where you can order freshly squeezed pomegranate, pineapple, carrot or orange juice for around Rs15 per glass. Madurai is hardly a drinking

Shopping and markets in Madurai

Old Madurai is crowded with **textile and tailors' shops**, particularly in West Veli, Avani Moola and Chitrai streets, and Town Hall Road. At the tailors' shops near the temple, locally produced textiles are generally good value, and tailors pride themselves on turning out faithful copies of favourite clothes in a matter of hours. Unfortunately, most of the **souvenir shops** in the vicinity of the temple employ touts who invite tourists to "come and enjoy temple view free of charge only looking". It's worth doing once as the views from the shops are impressive, but getting back down to street level without making a purchase at hugely inflated prices is quite a challenge.

South Avani Moola Street is packed with **jewellery**, particularly gold shops, and Madurai is also a great place to pick up south Indian **crafts**. Among the best outlets are All India Handicrafts Emporium, 39–41 Town Hall Rd; Co-optex, West Tower Street, and Pandiyan Co-op Supermarket, Palace Road, for handwoven textiles; and Surabhi, West Veli Street, for Keralan handicrafts. For souvenirs such as sandalwood, temple models, carved boxes and oil lamps head for Poompuhar, 12 West Veli St, or Tamilnad Gandhi Smarak Nidhi Khadi Gramodyog Bhavan, West Veli Street, opposite the railway station, which sells crafts, oil lamps, Meenakshi sculptures and *khadi* cloth and shirts.

town, but most pricier hotels have a bar, the most entertaining being *Apollo 96*, a sci-fi-themed extravaganza at the *Supreme Hotel* (see p.1000). All of the places below are marked on the Old City map (p.1001).

Aarathy *Aarathy Hotel*, 9 Perumalkoil, West Mada St. Tasty tiffin (dosas, *iddlis* and hot *wada sambar*), served on low tables in a hotel forecourt, where the temple elephant turns up twice daily. For more filling, surprisingly inexpensive and excellent lunch-time thalis (Rs40), step into their blissfully cool a/c restaurant.

Anna Meenakshi West Perumal Maistry St. Arguably the most hygienic and best-value food in the centre, this upmarket branch of *New College House*'s more traditional canteen (see opposite) serves top tiffin to a discerning, strictly vegetarian clientele. Absolutely delicious coconut or lemon "rice meals" and cheap banana-leaf thalis are served daily, and you can fill up for under Rs50.

The Emperor *Chentoor Hotel,* 106 West Perumal Maistry St. Not as stunning a view as at the *Surya,* but the multi-cuisine food is better and includes some non-veg dishes, such as delicious sizzlers. Rs80–150.

Mahal 21 Town Hall Rd. Nicely decorated street-level restaurant serving small but tasty portions of fish and chips, plus tandoori items and south Indian veg snacks for Rs40–80.

New College House *New College House* hotel, 2 Town Hall Rd. Huge meals-cum-tiffin hall in this old-style hotel. Lunchtime, when huge piles of Rs30 pure-veg food are served on banana leaves to long rows of locals, is a real deep-south experience; and the coffee's pure Coorg.

Surya *Supreme Hotel*, 110 West Perumal Maistry St. One of Madurai's most popular rooftop restaurants, with sweeping views of the city and temple. Although the pure-veg food is average and service a little lax, it's still a fine venue for a sundowner. Main courses Rs80–120.

Rameshwaram

The sacred island of **RAMESHWARAM**, 163km southeast of Madurai and less than 20km from Sri Lanka across the Gulf of Mannar is, along with Madurai, south India's most important pilgrimage site. Rameshwaram, being where the god Rama, an incarnation of Vishnu, worshipped Shiva in the Ramayana, draws followers of both Vishnu and Shiva. The **Ramalingeshwara Temple** complex, with its magnificent pillared walkways, is the most famous on the island, but there are several other small temples of interest, such as the **Gandhamadana Parvatam**, sheltering Rama's footprints, and the **Nambunayagi Amman Kali Temple**, frequented for its curative properties. **Danushkodi** ("Rama's Bow"), at the eastern end, is where Rama is said to have bathed. The boulders that pepper the sea between here and Sri Lanka, known as "Adam's Bridge"or "*Rama Sethu*"(Rama's bridge), were built by the monkey army so that they could cross over in their search for Rama's wife Sita after her abduction by Ravana, the demon king of Lanka. The town offers uncommercialized **beaches** (not India's most stunning) where foreigners can unwind or even do a spot of snorkelling.

Rameshwaram, whose streets radiate out from the vast block enclosing the Ramalingeshwara, is always crowded with day-trippers and ragged mendicants who camp outside the Ramalingeshwara and the **Ujainimahamariamman**, the small goddess shore temple. An important part of their pilgrimage is to bathe in the main temple's sacred tanks and in the sea; the narrow strip of beach is shared by groups of bathers, relaxing cows and mantra-reciting *swami*s sitting next to sand lingams. As well as fishing – prawns and lobsters for packaging and export to Japan – shells are a big source of income in the coastal villages.

Arrival and information

The NH-49, the main road from Madurai, connects Rameshwaram with Mandapam on the mainland via the impressive 2km-long Indira Gandhi Bridge. **Buses** from Madurai, Trichy, Thanjavur, Kanyakumari and Chennai pull in at the bus stand, 2km west of the centre. The railway station, 1km southwest of the centre, is the end of the line for trains from Chennai, Madurai and further afield, but services are currently suspended while the gauge is converted.

Yellow-and-green city bus #1 runs every ten minutes from the bus stand to the main temple; otherwise, **local transport** consists of unmetered cycle and auto-rickshaws. Jeeps are available for rent near the railway station, and bicycles from shops in the four Car streets around the temple.

The main TTDC **tourist office** at the bus stand (daily 10am–5.45pm; ⓣ04573/221371) gives out information about guides, accommodation and boat trips but opens rather erratically. TTDC also have a counter at the railway station (ⓣ04573/221373), opened to coincide with arriving trains. The **post office** is on Pamban Road, and there are a couple of **internet** places near the west entrance to the temple.

Accommodation

Apart from the TTDC complex, **accommodation** in Rameshwaram is restricted to basic lodges and very modest hotels, mostly in the Car streets around the temple. The temple authorities have a range of rooms for pilgrims; ask at the Devasthanam Office, East Car Street (ⓣ04573/221223).

Chola Lodge 25 North Car St ⓣ04573/221307. A basic but adequate lodge in the quietest of the Car streets. Most rooms are non-a/c, and some have TV. ❶–❸

Maharaja's 7 Middle St ⓣ04573/221271, ⓔhotelmaharajas@sancharnet.com. Located next to the temple's west gate, this place has clean and comfortable rooms with attached bathrooms and TV (some also have a/c), plus temple views from balconies. ❷–❹

Shriram Hotel Island Star 41-A South Car St ⓣ04573/224172, ⓕ239332. Fair-sized, clean hotel with pleasantly appointed a/c- and non-a/c rooms, most with sea views. The non-a/c ones are particularly good value, but the most expensive a/c rooms are a little overpriced. ❷–❹

TTDC Hotel Tamil Nadu Near the beach, 700m northeast of the main temple ⓣ04573/221277, ⓦwww.ttdconline.com. The best option in Rameshwaram, in a pleasant location and with a bar and restaurant. Comfortable, sea-facing rooms, some a/c Rs1050; the best ones are actually the cheaper ones in the new block, which have pleasant sitouts. ❸–❺

Venkatesh West Car St ☎04573/221296. Functional and modern three-storey hotel with clean, decent-sized rooms, most with TV and some with a/c. ❷–❹

Ramalingeshwara Temple

The core of the **Ramalingeshwara** (or Ramanathaswamy) **Temple** was built by the Cholas in the twelfth century to house two much-venerated **shiva-lingams** associated with the Ramayana. After rescuing his wife Sita from the clutches of Ravana, Rama was advised to atone for the killing of the demon king – a brahmin – by worshipping Shiva. Rama's monkey lieutenant, Hanuman, was despatched to the Himalayas to fetch a *shivalingam*, but when he failed to return by the appointed day, Sita fashioned a lingam from sand (the *Ramanathalingam*) so the ceremony could proceed. Hanuman eventually showed up with his lingam and in order to assuage the monkey's guilt Rama decreed that in future, of the two, Hanuman's should be worshipped first. The lingams are now housed in the inner section of the Ramalingeshwara, not usually open to non-Hindus. Much of what can be visited dates from the 1600s, when the temple received generous endowments from the Sethupathi rajas of Ramanathapuram.

Ramalingeshwara temple is enclosed by high walls which form a rectangle with huge pyramidal *gopura* entrances on each side. Each gateway leads to a spacious closed ambulatory, flanked to either side by continuous platforms with massive pillars set on their edges. These **corridors** are the most famous attribute of the temple, their extreme length – 205m, with 1212 pillars on the north and south sides – giving a remarkable impression of receding perspective. Before entering the inner sections of the temple, pilgrims are expected to bathe at each of the 22 temple **tirthas** (tanks) in the temple – hence the groups of dripping-wet pilgrims, most of them fully clothed, making their way from one tank to the next to be doused in a bucket of water by a temple attendant. Monday is Rama's auspicious day, when the Padilingam puja takes place. **Festivals** of particular importance at the temple include **Mahashivaratri** (ten days during Feb/March), **Brahmotsavam** (ten days during March/April) and **Thirukalyanam** (July/Aug), celebrating the marriage of Shiva to Parvati.

Eating

Abhirami Shore Rd, near the east entrance to the main temple. Reasonably clean south Indian veg joint en route to the seashore, with street views from the tables.

Ashoka Bhavan West Car St. Cheap south Indian vegetarian place, which also serves a variety of regional thalis.

Chola Hotel West Bazaar St. Food-only joint, not to be confused with lodge of same name; a good choice for carnivores, with biriyanis and other dishes including chicken, mutton, liver and "head curry". Rs50–80

Ganesh Mess Middle St. One of the better "meals" joints, serving lunchtime thalis as well as classic south Indian snacks throughout the day.

TTDC Hotel Tamil Nadu Near the beach. Gigantic, noisy, high-ceilinged glasshouse near the sea, serving good south Indian snacks and "meals", plus chicken and occasional fish dishes (Rs60–80). There is also a bar in the main hotel building.

Kanyakumari

At the southernmost extremity of India, **KANYAKUMARI** is almost as compelling for Hindus as Rameshwaram. It's significant not only for its association with a virgin goddess, Devi Kanyakumari, but also as the meeting point of the Bay of Bengal, Indian Ocean and Arabian Sea. Watching the sun rise and set from here is the big attraction, especially on full-moon day in April, when it's possible to see both the setting sun and rising moon on the same horizon. Although Kanyakumari is in the state of Tamil Nadu, most foreign visitors arrive on day-trips from Kerala. While the place is of enduring appeal to pilgrims and those who just want to see India's tip, some may find it bereft of atmosphere, its magic obliterated by ugly concrete buildings and hawkers. Kanyakumari was seriously affected by the 2004 tsunami, though the seafront and jetty have since been rebuilt.

Arrival and information

Trains from all over the Subcontinent (even Jammu – at 86hr the longest rail journey in India) stop at the **railway station** in the north of town, 2km from the seafront. The well-organized **Express Bus Stand**, near the lighthouse on the west side of town, is served by regular buses from Thiruvananthapuram, Madurai, Rameshwaram and Chennai. Taxis and auto-rickshaws provide **local transport**. The main **Tamil Nadu tourist office** is on Main Road (Mon–Fri 10am–5.30pm; ⓣ04652/246276); there's **internet** access further up Main Road, as well as just around the corner on Beach Road.

Accommodation

Lakshmi Tourist Home East Car St ⓣ04652/246333, ⓕ246627. Smart rooms, some sea-facing with a/c though the best views are from the non-a/c ones (especially room #408). There's also an excellent non-veg restaurant. ❷–❺

Maadhini East Car St ⓣ04652/246787, ⓕ246657. Large hotel right on the seafront above the fishing village, with fine sea views, comfortably furnished rooms, and one of the best restaurants in town (see p.1008). ❹–❺

Manickam Tourist Home North Car St ⓣ04652/246387. Spacious but simple and clean rooms, some with balconies and sea views, set in a building that faces the sunrise and the Vivekananda rock. Good value. ❷–❹

Samudra Sannathi St ⓣ04652/246162, ⓕ246627. Smart hotel near the temple entrance, with well-furnished deluxe rooms facing the sunrise. Facilities include satellite TV in rooms and a veg restaurant. ❸–❺

TTDC Hotel Tamil Nadu Seafront ⓣ04652/246257, ⓦwww.ttdconline.com. Cottages (some are a/c) and clean rooms (a/c on the first floor), most with sea views, as well as cheaper and very basic "mini" doubles at the back, and a dorm (Rs50). Good square meals are served in functional surroundings. ❸–❺

The Town

The seashore **Kumari Amman Temple** (daily 4.30–11.30am & 4–8pm) is dedicated to the virgin goddess **Devi Kanyakumari**, who may originally have been the local guardian deity of the shoreline, but was later absorbed into the figure of Devi, or Parvati, consort of Shiva. The image of Devi Kanyakumari inside the temple wears a diamond nose stud of such brilliance that it's said to be

Moving on from Kanyakumari

Between the town railway station and that of nearby Nagercoil, there are daily **trains** to the following destinations: Bengaluru (1 daily; 19hr 30min); Chennai (2–3 daily; 13hr 15min–15hr 25min); Coimbatore (2 daily; 11hr 55min); Kochi (2 daily; 6hr 15min–6hr 30min); Madurai (6 daily; 4hr 20min–5hr 15min); Mumbai (2 daily; 47hr 20min); Thiruvananthapuram (4 daily; 1hr 35min–2hr); Tiruchirapalli (5 daily; 7hr 15min–8hr 15min). **Bus** services include: Chennai (hourly; 16–18hr); Kovalam (10–12 daily; 2hr); Madurai (every 30min; 6hr); Puducherry (hourly; 12–13hr); Rameshwaram (3 daily; 10hr); Thiruvananthapuram (every 30min–1hr; 2hr 45min–3hr); Tiruchirapalli (every 30min; 10–12hr).

visible from the sea. Male visitors must be shirtless and wear a *dhoti* before entering the temple; non-Hindus are not allowed in the inner sanctum. It is especially auspicious for pilgrims to wash at the bathing *ghat* here.

Resembling a prewar British cinema, the **Gandhi Mandapam** (daily 7am–7pm), 300m northwest of the Kumari Amman Temple, was actually conceived as a modern imitation of an Orissan temple. It was designed so that the sun strikes the auspicious spot where the ashes of Mahatma Gandhi were laid, prior to their immersion in the sea, at noon on his birthday, October 2.

Possibly the original sacred focus of Kanyakumari are two **rocks**, about 60m apart, half-submerged in the sea 500m off the coast, which can be reached by the Poompuhar ferry service from the jetty on the east side of town (every 30min; daily 7am–4pm; Rs20). Known as the Pitru and Matru *tirthas*, they attracted the attention of the Hindu reformer Vivekananda (1862–1902), who swam out to the rocks in 1892 to meditate on the syncretistic teachings of his recently dead guru, Ramakrishna Paramahamsa. Incorporating elements of architecture from around the country, the 1970 **Vivekananda Memorial** (daily 8am–4pm; Rs50) houses a statue of the saint. The footprints of Devi Kanyakumari can also be seen here, at the spot where she performed her penance. The other rock features an imposing 40m-high statue of the ancient Tamil saint **Thiruvalluvar**.

For more on the life and teachings of Vivekananda, visit the **Wandering Monk Museum (Vivekananda Puram)**, just north of the tourist office on the main road (daily 8am–noon & 4–8pm; Rs2). A sequence of forty-one panels in English, Tamil and Hindi provide a meticulously detailed account of the *swami*'s odyssey around the Subcontinent at the end of the nineteenth century.

Eating

The *Archana* **restaurant**, at the *Maadhini Hotel* (see p.1007), has an extensive veg and non-veg multi-cuisine menu, served either inside a well-ventilated dining hall or alfresco in a courtyard (evenings only). They also have the town's widest selection of ice cream. *Saravana Bhavan*, north of the Kumari Amman Temple, on the main bazaar, is arguably the best of Kanyakumari's many "meals" restaurants, serving all the usual snacks in the morning and evening, and "meals" at lunchtime. Also look out for the excellent fried fish and chicken on sale for around Rs25 at small joints on and around Main Road, such as the *Sree Devi Tiffin Stall*. For a drink, the most salubrious of the **bars** around town is the seriously air-conditioned *Red Sun* on South Car Street.

The Ghats

Sixty or more million years ago, what we know today as peninsular India was a separate land-mass drifting northwest across the ocean towards central Asia. Current geological thinking has it that this mass must originally have broken off the African continent along a fault line that is today discernible as a north–south ridge of volcanic mountains, stretching 1400km down the west coast of India, known as the **Western Ghats**. The range rises to a height of around 2500m, making it India's second-highest mountain chain after the Himalayas.

Forming a natural barrier between the Tamil plains and coastal Kerala and Karnataka, the Ghats (literally "steps") soak up the bulk of the southwest monsoon, which drains east to the Bay of Bengal via the mighty Kaveri and Krishna river systems. The massive amount of rain that falls here between June and October (around 2.5m) allows for an incredible **biodiversity**. Nearly one-third of

Crafts to go

No country in the world produces such a tempting array of arts and crafts as India. Intensely colourful, delicately worked, exquisitely ornate and immensely varied, India's crafts have the added advantage of being amazingly inexpensive. Every part of the country has its specialities – textiles in Rajasthan, metalwork in Karnataka, carpets in Kashmir – but everywhere you'll see beautiful things that you'll find hard to resist buying. Whether it's sumptuous fabrics, intricate carvings or garish knick-knacks, India offers a feast of artistic creations that you'll want to gorge on.

Miniature painting ▲

Paintings

Most Tibetan **thangkas** (Buddhist religious paintings mounted on brocaded silk) are mass-produced (usually in Nepal) and modern, whatever the seller says, but even the cheapest boast the dense Buddhist symbolism inherent in the form. You'll find them mostly in the north, where there are Tibetan communities, and they come in quite an array of different styles.

Miniature paintings, on cotton, silk or paper, are a tradition in Rajasthan, where you'll find them on sale in almost every tourist centre in the state. Some of them are very fine and rather pricey but, at the other end of the scale, **leaf skeleton paintings**, originally from southern Kerala, are cheap as chips, and often sold in the form of greeting cards which you can post straight home.

Meenakari inlay ▼

Metalwork

Brass and **copperware** can be very finely worked into trays, plates, ashtrays, cups and bowls. In the north, particularly in Rajasthan, enamel inlay (*meenakari*) is common. **Bidri** work from Karnataka is made by inlaying a gunmetal alloy with fine designs in brass or silver, then blackening the gunmetal with sal ammoniac, to leave the inlay work shining. *Bidri* jewellery boxes, dishes and hookah pipes, among other things, are particularly good in Karnataka and Andhra Pradesh. In Orissa, filigree *tarakashi* is worth looking out for.

Especially in the south, brass statues of Hindu gods are still produced by the **lost-wax process**, in which a model is carved out of wax, surrounded in clay and fired. The wax melts to leave a terracotta mould from which the brass model is cast.

Carpets

Kashmiri rugs are among the best in the world, and given a little caution and scepticism, you can get yourself a bargain, though you can also get shafted if you're not careful. A pukka Kashmiri carpet should have a label on the back stating that it's made in Kashmir and what it's made of (wool, silk or "silk touch", which is wool with a little silk to give it a sheen). Choose your shop carefully, and remember that the best way of ensuring a carpet reaches home is to take it or post it yourself.

Dhurries (woven carpets or kilims), traditionally made of wool, are an older and less expensive art form. Uttar Pradesh is the main centre for these, but they are also made in Rajasthan, Gujarat, the Punjab and Andhra Pradesh. Tibetan rugs are available in areas with large Tibetan communities, such as Himachal Pradesh.

▲ Carpets and tapestries on display

▼ Traditional sandals for sale

Leatherware

Leatherware can be very cheap and well-made, though the leather doesn't normally come from cows, of course. Rajasthani camel-hide **mojadi slippers** are extremely comfortable, though **chappals** (slippers) – and particularly the distinctive **kolhapuri** variety from Maharashtra – will need to be broken in (dunking them in water for a minute or so should do the job); pointed **jootis**, popular around Delhi and the Punjab, also need some perseverance. Otherwise, buffalo-hide belts and bags can be very good value compared to similar items made of cowhide in the West; Chennai and Puducherry are good places to go looking. Upmarket shops offer a range of high-quality leather goods from handbags to briefcases at very reasonable prices.

Tailor at work ▲

Hand-painted silk umbrellas ▼

Clothing and textiles

India was known for its **textiles** long before colonization, and Gandhi in particular promoted self-sufficiency in textile production as a means of liberation from colonial exploitation. The kind of cloth he had in mind was the plain white homespun fabric called **khadi**, sold in government shops (Khadi Gramodyog) nationwide. Methods of dyeing and printing this and other cloth range from the tie-dyeing (*bandhani*) of Rajasthan to the block printing and screen printing of calico cotton (from Calicut – now Kozhikode – in Kerala), and of silk.

Saris are normally made of cotton for everyday use, although silk is used for special occasions. Although Varanasi silk is world famous, the best silk nowadays comes from the south of India: Kanchipuram and Madurai in Tamil Nadu, famous for their brightly coloured saris, and Mysore in Karnataka, where the silk shines with its own particularly scintillating sheen.

Rajasthan's heavy **mirror-embroidered** cloth is sumptuous and luxuriant, but it's far from being India's only fabulous decorated fabric. Bengal's wonderful **baluchari** silk brocade is decorated with scenes from Indian mythology. Alternatively,there's *ikat* and *batik* cloth from Orissa, Madhya Pradesh and Gujarat. **Block-printed bedsheets**, as well as being useful, make great wall-hangings, as do Punjabi *phulkari* (traditionally used on wedding sheets), and *lunghis* from the south (sheets as much as garments), but every region has its own fabrics and its own methods – the choice is endless. Popular **clothing** items with tourists are thick Tibetan sweaters from Darjeeling, and *salwar kameez*, the elegant women's pyjama suits, originally from the Punjab – Western women invariably find these easier to wear than a sari.

all of India's flowering plants can be found in the dense evergreen and mixed deciduous forests cloaking the Ghats, while the woodland undergrowth supports the Subcontinent's richest array of wildlife.

It was this abundance of game, and the cooler temperatures of the range's high valleys and grasslands, that first attracted the sun-sick British, who were quick to see the economic potential of the temperate climate, fecund soil and plentiful rainfall. As the forests were felled to make way for tea plantations, and the region's many tribal groups – among them the Todas – were forced deeper into the mountains, permanent **hill-stations** were established. Today, as in the days of the Raj, these continue to provide welcome escapes from the fierce summer heat for the middle-class Tamils, and foreign tourists, who can afford the break.

Much the best known of the hill-resorts – in fact better known, and more visited, than it deserves – is **Udhagamandalam** (formerly Ootacamund, and usually known just as "**Ooty**"), in the **Nilgiris** (from *nila-giri*, "blue mountains"). The ride up to Ooty on the **miniature railway** via Coonoor is fun, and the views breathtaking, but the town centre suffers from heavy traffic pollution and has little to offer. Further south and reached by a scenic switchback road, the other main hill station is **Kodaikanal**. The lovely walks around town provide views and fresh air in abundance, while the bustle of Indian tourists around the lake makes a pleasant change from life in the city.

The forest areas lining the state border harbour Tamil Nadu's principal **wildlife sanctuaries**, **Indira Gandhi** and **Mudumalai** which comprise part of the vast **Nilgiri Biosphere Reserve**, the country's most extensive tract of protected forest. Road building, illegal felling, hydroelectric projects and overgrazing have whittled away large parts of this huge wilderness area over the past two decades, but what's left still constitutes home to an array of wildlife. The main route between Mysore and the cities of the Tamil plains wriggles through the Nilgiris, and you may well find yourself pausing for a night or two along the way. Whichever direction you're travelling in, a stopover at the dull textile city of **Coimbatore** is hard to avoid.

Kodaikanal

Perched on top of the Palani range, around 120km northwest of Madurai, **KODAIKANAL**, also known as **Kodai**, owes its perennial popularity to its hilltop position which, at an altitude of more than 2000m, affords breathtaking views over the blue-green reaches of the Vaigai plain. Raj-era bungalows and flower-filled gardens add atmosphere, while short walks out of the centre lead to rocky outcrops, waterfalls and dense *shola* forest. With the more northerly wildlife sanctuaries and forest areas of the Ghats closed to visitors, Kodai's outstandingly scenic hinterland also offers south India's best **trekking** terrain.

After a while in the south Indian plains, a retreat to Kodai's cool heights is more than welcome. However, in the height of summer (April–July), when temperatures compete with those in the lowlands, it's not worth the trip – nor is it a good idea to come during the monsoon (Oct–Dec), when the town is shrouded in mists and drenched by heavy downpours. In late February and early March the nights are chilly; the **peak tourist season**, therefore, is from April to June, when prices soar.

Arrival and information

The **buses** from Madurai and Dindigul that climb the steep road up to Kodai pull in at the stand in the centre of town. There are two roads to Kodaikanal: the lesser-used route from Palani is by far the more spectacular approach, and during the

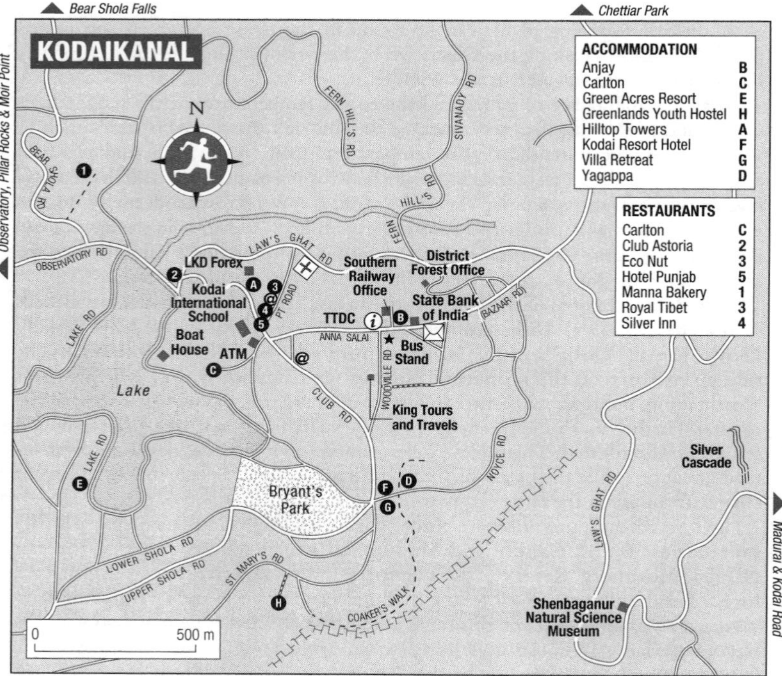

monsoon may be the only one open. Unless you're coming from as far as Chennai or Tiruchirapalli, the bus is much more convenient than the train: the nearest **railhead**, Kodai Road, is three hours away by bus.

The **tourist office** (Mon–Fri 10am–5.45pm; ⓣ04542/241675) on Anna Salai (Bazaar Road) can arrange **treks** (a 5hr trek with a guide costs Rs300 for groups of up to four); longer routes such as the three-day trek to Munnar in Kerala can also be negotiated; you'll pay around Rs1700 per day for groups of up to four, including basic accommodation. For **internet** access, try Q Internet on Club Road, or the slower Flashnet, next to the *Royal Tibet* restaurant on PT Road.

Taxis line Anna Salai in the centre of town, offering sightseeing at high fixed rates. Most tourists, however, prefer to amble around at their own pace. Kodaikanal is best explored on foot, or by **bicycle**, which you can rent from a stall on Anna Salai for Rs10 per hour or Rs75 per day from numerous stalls around the lake; it may be fun to freewheel downhill, but most journeys will involve a hefty uphill push too. If you need to **change money**, head for the State Bank of India or Canara Bank, both on Anna Salai; there is an SBI ATM near the *Carlton Hotel*.

Moving on from Kodaikanal

Tickets for onward rail journeys from Kodaikanal Road can be booked at the Southern Railway office, down a lane beside the *Anjay Hotel* (Mon–Sat 8am–noon & 2.30–5pm, Sun 8am–noon). Nearby King Tours and Travels on Woodville Road can reserve trains, buses and planes within south India.

Accommodation

Kodaikanal's inexpensive **lodges** are grouped at the lower end of Anna Salai. Always ask whether blankets and hot water are provided (the latter should be free, but you may be charged in budget places). **Mid-range hotels** are usually good value, especially if you get a room with a view, but they hike their prices drastically during high season (April–June).

Anjay Anna Salai ⓣ04542/241089, ⓕ242636. Simple budget lodge slap in the centre. Rooms are smarter than you'd expect from the outside (all have balconies, and the deluxe ones have views), but those at the front suffer some traffic noise. If they're full, check out the equally good-value *Jaya* behind. ❷

Carlton Off Lake Rd ⓣ04542/240056, ⓦwww.krahejahospitality.com. The most luxurious hotel in Kodaikanal, this is a spacious, tastefully renovated and well-maintained colonial house overlooking the lake, with a bar and comfortable lounge. Rooms in the house start around $150 and exude Raj-era charm; there are pricier cottages available within the grounds. All rates include meals. ❾

Green Acres Resort 11/213 Lake Rd ⓣ04542/242384, ⓦwww.greenacresresort.biz. Fancy resort in a great setting on a quiet corner of the lake, with rooms and suites (all attached and well furnished) of varying sizes dotted around carefully manicured grounds. ❺–❼

Greenlands Youth Hostel Coaker's Walk, off St Mary's Rd ⓣ04542/241099, ⓔgreenlandsyh@rediffmail.com. Attractive old stone house offering unrivalled views and sunsets from its deep verandas. The rooms are basic with wooden beds, open fireplaces (wood costs Rs50) and attached bathrooms, and there's a dorm (Rs150). Book ahead. ❺

Hilltop Towers Club Rd ⓣ04542/240413, ⓔhttowers@sancharnet.in. Very near the lake and school, with modern, comfortable rooms featuring arched doors. There's also a cosy and romantic honeymoon suite with a round bed. Good service in the three restaurants. ❺–❻

Kodai Resort Hotel Noyce Rd ⓣ04542/241301, ⓦwww.kodairesorthotel.com. Large complex of fifty incongruous-looking but very pleasant chalets situated at the top of the hill and offering good views of the town. There's a health club and rather dull restaurant on site. ❻–❼

Villa Retreat Coaker's Walk, off Club Rd ⓣ04542/240940, ⓦwww.villaretreat.com. Comfortable old stone house, with more character than most, in lovely gardens that afford superb views. Though a touch overpriced, all rooms have great views and attached hot-water bathrooms; some have fires. Wood and electric heaters are available upon request. ❺–❼

Yagappa Noyce Rd ⓣ04542/241235. The best budget deal in town, this small, clean lodge is set in old buildings ranged around a lawn-cum-courtyard and has good views. Rooms are modest but clean, and there's a great little bar with wicker chairs, and a tiny whitewashed restaurant serving veg "meals" and breakfasts. ❹

The Town

Kodai's focal point is its **lake**, sprawling like a giant amoeba over 60 acres just west of the town centre. This is a popular place for strolls or bike rides along the 5km path that fringes the water's edge, while pedal- or rowing boats can be rented on the eastern shore (Rs100–150 for 30min, plus Rs25 if you require an oarsman). Horseriding is also an option here – it costs Rs50 to be led along the lakeside for 500m, or Rs200 for an hour's ride. Shops, restaurants and hotels are concentrated in a rather congested area east of and downhill from the lake. The only monuments to Kodai's colonial past are the neat **British bungalows** that overlook the lake, and Law's Ghat Road on the eastern edge of town. The British first moved here in 1845, to be joined later by members of the American Mission, who set up schools for European children.

To the south is **Bryant's Park** (daily 8.30am–6.30pm, last entry 6pm; Rs5, camera Rs25, video camera Rs500), with tiered flowerbeds on a backdrop of pine, eucalyptus, rhododendron and wattle which stretches southwards to Shola Road, less than 1km from the point where the hill drops abruptly to the plains. A flower show is held here in May. A path, known as **Coaker's Walk** (Rs2, camera Rs5), skirts the hill, winding from the *Villa Retreat* to *Greenland's Youth Hostel* (10min), offering remarkable views that stretch as far as Madurai on a clear day.

One of Kodai's most popular natural attractions is the **Pillar Rocks**, 7km south of town, where a series of granite cliffs rise more than 100m above the hillside. To get here, follow the westbound Observatory Road from the northernmost point of the lake (a steep climb) until you come to a crossroads; the southbound road passes the gentle **Fairy Falls** on the way to Pillar Rocks. Some 2km west of the lake, the signposted **Bear Shola Falls** now sees barely a trickle of water but remains a popular picnic and photo-stop for local tourists.

Southeast of the town centre, about 3km down Law's Ghat Road (towards the plains), the **Shenbaganur Natural Science Museum** (Mon–Sat 9am–5pm; Rs5) has a very uninviting array of stuffed animals. However, the spectacular orchid house contains one of India's best collections, which can be viewed by appointment only (ask at the tourist office; see p.1010). Head 2km further along Law's Ghat Road to reach **Silver Cascade** waterfall, where the overflow from Kodai Lake has created a pleasant pool for bathing.

Chettiar Park, on the very northeast edge of town, around 3km from the lake at the end of a winding uphill road, flourishes with trees and flowers all year round, and every twelve years is flushed with a haze of pale-blue **Kurinji blossoms** (the next flowering will not be until 2018). These unusual flowers are associated with the god Murugan, the Tamil form of Karttikeya (Shiva's second son), and god of Kurinji, one of five ancient divisions of the Tamil country. A temple in his honour stands just outside the park.

Eating

If you choose not to eat in any of the **hotel restaurants**, head for the food stalls along **PT Road** just west of the bus stand. Menus include Indian, Chinese, Western and Tibetan dishes, and some cater specifically for vegetarians.

Carlton *Carlton Hotel*, off Lake Rd. Splash out on the evening veg and non-veg buffet spread (Rs330) at Kodai's top hotel, rounded off with a *chhota* peg of IMFL Scotch in the bar.

Club Astoria Lake Rd. Bright and breezy multi-cuisine restaurant with a large terrace overlooking the lake. Better to come for a snack or drink while enjoying the view than a main meal (around Rs150), though, as the food is fairly plain.

Eco Nut J's Heritage Complex, PT Rd. One of south India's few bona fide Western-style wholefood shops, and a great place to stock up on trekking supplies: muesli, home-made jams, breads, pickles and muffins, high-calorie "nutri-balls" and delicious cheeses from Auroville.

Hotel Punjab PT Rd. Top north Indian cuisine and reasonably priced tandoori specialities; try their great butter chicken and hot naan. Most main dishes are Rs80–120.

Manna Bakery Bear Shola Rd. Fried breakfasts, pizzas and home-baked brown bread and cakes served in an eccentric, self-consciously eco-friendly café-restaurant.

Royal Tibet PT Rd. The friendliest of three small Tibetan joints along this road, with dishes ranging from thick home-made bread to particularly tasty *momo*s and noodles, as well as some Indian and Chinese options, all for under Rs100.

Silver Inn PT Rd. Western favourites such as porridge, lasagne, mashed potato and apple crumble are all adequately cooked up at this hole-in-the-wall place. Most dinners around Rs100.

Indira Gandhi (Anamalai) Wildlife Sanctuary

Indira Gandhi (Anamalai) Wildlife Sanctuary is a 958-square-kilometre tract of forest on the southern reaches of the Cardamom Hills, 37km southwest of the busy junction town of **Pollachi**. Vegetation ranges from shola-grassland to dry deciduous to tropical evergreen, and the sanctuary is home to lion-tailed macaques (black-maned monkeys), *gaur*, *sambar*, spotted and barking deer, sloth bear, as well as leopards and tigers. Birds such as hornbills and frogmouths are also seen here. One of the highlights is taking a **trek** through the giant creaking stands of bamboo with a guide (7am–3pm; Rs70/person for 4hr treks with up to four people), and a Forestry Department minibus conducts **safari tours** on request (Rs675 for the van), and a forty-minute **elephant safari** (10am–4pm; Rs100/person) is also available. For reservations, contact the park reception office (see below).

Practicalities

Pollachi has good bus connections to Palani and Coimbatore. From the town there are only two buses a day (6am & 3pm; returning at 1pm & 6pm) up to the park's reception centre (Ⓣ04253/238360) at **Top Slip**. Hired cars/taxis, available at Pollachi, run via the official entrance at the **Sethumadai** checkpost from 6.30am–6pm daily. Private vehicles can drive into the park with prior permission from the Field Director. The Forestry Department runs six **resthouses**, ranging from the basic *Hornbill* (❶) to the luxurious *Pillar Top* (❼). Most are within easy walking distance of the reception centre and should be booked in advance through the Field Director, conservator's office at Pollachi (Ⓣ04259/225356). A canteen next to the reception centre serves very limited **meals** and drinks, while a nearby shop has equally scant provisions.

Coimbatore

Visitors tend only to use the busy industrial city of **COIMBATORE** as a stopover on the way to Ooty, 90km northwest. Once you've climbed up to your hotel rooftop to admire the blue, cloud-capped haze of the Nilgiris in the west, there's little to do here other than kill time wandering through the nuts-and-bolts bazaars, lined with lookalike textile showrooms, "General Traders" and shops selling motor parts.

Coimbatore has four main **bus stands**, three of which are fairly near each other in the northern part of town, a couple of kilometres north of the railway station. The Thiruvalluvar Bus Stand is the main state and interstate station; buses from Ooty, Coonoor and Mettupalayam use the Central Bus Stand, while the busy Town Bus Stand is sandwiched in between. The south of town holds the fourth bus stand, Ukkadam (which serves Palani, Pollachi, Madurai and towns in northern Kerala), as well as the **railway station**; for **Ooty**, join the daily #2671 *Nilgiri Express* at 5.15am, which will get you to **Mettupalayam** in time to join the Toy Train (see p.1019). Local buses ply the routes between bus and train stations. Coimbatore's **airport** is 12km northeast of town and served by buses to and from Town Bus Stand; a taxi will charge around Rs200.

Internet access and ATMs abound. For **eating**, your best bets are the bigger hotels (see p.1014) such as the *City Tower*, whose excellent rooftop restaurant,

Moving on from Coimbatore

Trains: Bengaluru (2–3 daily; 6hr 45min–9hr); Chennai (5–6 daily; 7hr 50min–8hr 55min); Ernakulam, for Kochi (7–8 daily; 4hr 20min–5hr 30min); Hyderabad (1 daily; 21hr 20min); Kanyakumari (2 daily; 11hr 45min); Madurai (1–2 daily; 6hr 15min–6hr 35min); Mettupalayam, for Ooty (1 daily; 1hr); Mumbai (2 daily; 31hr 15min–32hr 40min); Thiruvananthapuram (4–5 daily; 9hr 5min–10hr 25min); Tiruchirapalli (2 daily; 5hr 15min–5hr 45min).

Buses: Bengaluru (hourly; 8–9hr); Chennai (every 30min–1hr; 10–12hr); Kodaikanal (4 daily; 6hr); Madurai (every 30min; 5–6hr); Mysore (3 daily; 6hr); Udhagamandalam (Ooty) (every 15min; 3hr 30min–4hr); Palakaad (hourly; 2hr); Palani (hourly; 2hr 30min–3hr); Pollachi (every 30min; 1hr); Puducherry (10 daily; 9hr); Rameshwaram (2 daily; 14hr); Thrissur (hourly; 5hr); Tiruchirapalli (every 30min; 5hr).

Cloud 9, serves a top-notch multi-cuisine menu; mains are around Rs100. The *Malabar*, on the first floor of the *KK Residency*, is a less pricey option, popular for its quality non-veg Keralan cuisine. Carnivores will also enjoy the crispy fried chicken at *KR* opposite the railway station, which also has a good bakery, while the best place for south Indian veg food is the ultramodern *Gayathri Bhavan*, opposite the *Blue Star* hotel on Nehru Street.

Accommodation

Most of Coimbatore's **accommodation** is concentrated around the bus stands and railway station. The cheapest options line Nehru Street and Shastri Road, but avoid the rock-bottom places facing the bus stand itself, which are plagued with traffic noise from around 4am onwards.

Blue Star 369 Nehru St ⓣ0422/223 0635, ⓕ0422/223 3096. Impeccably clean rooms, some with balconies, quiet fans and bathrooms, in a modern multistorey building five minutes' walk from the bus stands. The best mid-priced place in this area. ❹

City Tower 56 Sivasamy Rd ⓣ0422/223 0681, ⓦwww.hotelcitytower.com. A smart, upscale hotel two minutes' walk south of the Central Bus Stand with modern interiors (featuring leatherette and vinyl); the "Executive" rooms are more spacious. ❻

KK Residency 7 Shastri Rd ⓣ0422/223 2433, ⓕ437 8111. Large tower-block hotel around the corner from the main bus stands, with very clean rooms and a couple of good restaurants. ❸–❹

New Vijaya Lodge 8/81 Geetha Hall Rd ⓣ0422/230 1794. Simple but adequate place with compact, clean rooms, very close to the railway station. ❹

TTDC Tamil Nadu 2 Dr Nanjappa Rd ⓣ0422/230 2176, ⓦwww.ttdconline.com. Opposite Central Bus Stand; convenient, clean, reliable and better than most in the chain, with a/c and non-a/c rooms. It's often fully booked, so phone ahead. ❹

Coonoor

At an altitude of 1858m, **COONOOR**, a scruffy bazaar and tea-planters' town on the Nilgiri Blue Mountain Railway (see p.1019 lies at the head of the Hulikal ravine, on the southeastern side of the Dodabetta mountains, 27km north of Mettupalayam and 19km south of Ooty. Thanks to its proximity to its more famous neighbour, Coonoor has avoided Ooty's overcommercialization, and can make a pleasant place for a short stop.

Coonoor loosely divides into two sections, with the bus stand (regular services to Mettupalayam, Coimbatore and elsewhere in the Nilgiris) and railway station (four trains daily to Ooty, and one daily service to Mettupalayam) in **Lower Coonoor**, where there's also a small but atmospheric hill market specializing in leaf tea and fragrant essential oils. In **Upper Coonoor**, there's a fine sprinkling of old Raj-era bungalows along narrow lanes edged with flower-filled hedgerows. At the top lies **Sim's Park**, a lush botanical garden on the slopes of a ravine with hundreds of rose varieties (daily 8am–6.30pm; Rs5).

Around the town, rolling hills and valleys carpeted with spongy green tea bushes and stands of eucalyptus and silver oak offer some of the most beautiful scenery in the Nilgiris, immortalized in many a Hindi-movie dance sequence. Cinema fans from across the south flock here to visit key locations from their favourite blockbusters, among them **Lamb's Nose** (5km) and **Dolphin's Nose** (9km), former British picnicking spots with paved pathways and dramatic views of the Mettupalayam plains. Buses run out here from Coonoor every two hours. It's a good idea to catch the first one at 7am, which gets you to Dolphin's Nose before the mist starts to build up, and walk the 9km back into town via Lamb's Rock – an enjoyable amble that takes you through tea estates and dense forest.

Visible from miles away as tiny orange or red dots amid the green vegetation, **tea-pickers** work the slopes around Coonoor, carrying wicker baskets of fresh leaves and bamboo rods that they use like rulers to ensure that each plant is evenly plucked. Once the leaves reach the factory, they're processed within a day, producing seven grades of tea. **Orange pekoe** is the best and most expensive; the seventh lowest grade, a dry dust of stalks and leaf swept up at the end of the process, will be sold on to make instant tea. To visit a tea or coffee plantation, contact UPASI (United Planters' Association of Southern India), "Glenview" House, Coonoor ⓣ0423/223 0270, ⓦwww.upasi.org.

Practicalities

When it comes to finding somewhere to **stay** or **eat**, there isn't much choice and it's not a good idea to leave it too late in the day to look for a room; you'll need an auto-rickshaw to find most of the hotels. The correct fare from the bus stand to Bedford Circle/*YWCA* is Rs30–40.

In the bazaar, the only commendable **restaurants** are *Hotel Tamizhamgam* (pronounced "Tamirangum"), on Mount Road near the bus stand, which is Coonoor's most popular vegetarian "meals"-cum-tiffin joint. For good-value non-veg north Indian tandoori and Chinese food, try the *Greenland* hotel, further up Mount Road, while at Bedford Circle, the *Dragon* serves up more authentic and tasty Chinese dishes.

The Travancore Bank, on Church Road in Upper Ooty, near Bedford Circle, **changes currency**, but not always travellers' cheques. Otherwise, the nearest place is the State Bank of India in Ooty (see p.1017).

Accommodation

La Barrier Inn Coonoor Club Rd ⓣ0423/223 2561. Comfortable mid-range option way up above the bazaar, with great views of surrounding hills. The rooms are spotless and very large, opening onto flower-filled balconies. ❹–❺

Sree Venkateshwara Lodge Cash Bazaar ⓣ0423/220 6309. The best option in Lower Coonoor, right by the railway station. Clean, average-sized attached rooms with TV. ❸

Taj Garden Retreat Church Rd, Upper Coonoor ⓣ0423/223 0021, ⓦwww.tajhotels.com. Luxurious but way overpriced, this colonial-era hotel has cottage accommodation, tea-garden lawns and spectacular views, plus a good range of sports and activities including freshwater fishing. The restaurant serves spectacular lunchtime buffets (around Rs300). Rooms from $150. ❾

Velan (aka Ritz) Ritz Rd, Bedford ⓣ0423/223 0784, ⓦwww.velanhotels.com. Recently refurbished mid-range hotel in a great location on the outskirts; it's very spacious with carpeted rooms, deep balconies and fine views.Much better value than the *Taj Garden Retreat*, but rather lacking in charm. ❺

Vivek Tourist Home Figure of Eight Rd, near Bedford Circle ⓣ0423/223 0658. Clean rooms (some with tiny balconies overlooking the tea terraces) in a rather starchy, institutional atmosphere. Just beware of the "monkey menace". ❸

YWCA Guest House Wyoming, near the hospital ⓣ0423/223 4426. A characterful Victorian-era house on a bluff overlooking town, with a flower garden, tea terraces and fine views from the verandas. There are five double rooms and two singles; superb home-cooked meals are available at very reasonable rates. No alcohol. ❹

Udhagamandalam

When John Sullivan, the British *burrasahib* credited with "discovering" **UDHAGAMANDALAM** – whose anglicized name, **Ootacamund**, is usually shortened to Ooty – first clambered into this corner of the Nilgiris through the Hulikal ravine in the early nineteenth century, the territory was the traditional homeland of the pastoralist **Toda** hill-tribe. Until then, the Todas had lived in almost total isolation from the cities of the surrounding plains and Deccan plateau lands. Sullivan quickly realized the agricultural potential of the area, acquired tracts of land for Rs1 per acre from the Todas, and set about planting flax, barley and hemp, as well

ACCOMMODATION

Co-operators Guest House	G
Fernhills Palace	F
Glyngarth Villa	A
Hills Palace	H
King's Cliff	B
Reflections Guest House	D
Sherlock	C
YWCA Anandagiri	E

RESTAURANTS

Chandan	2
Iranis	3
Preethi Palace	4
Shinkows	1
Willy's	5

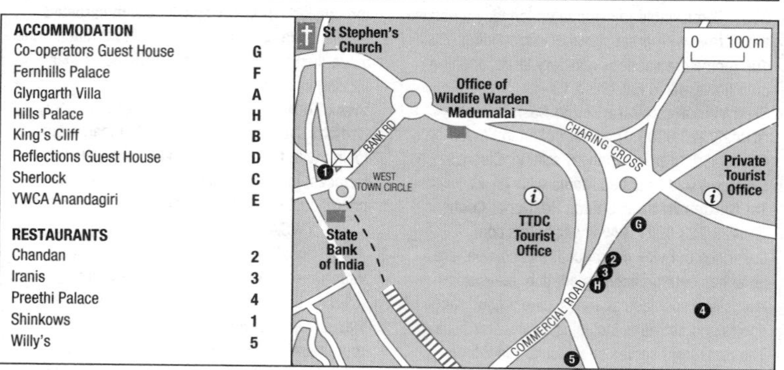

as potatoes, soft fruit and, most significantly of all, **tea**, which all flourished in the mild climate. Within twenty years, the former East India Company clerk had made a fortune. Needless to say, he was soon joined by other fortune-seekers, and a town was built, complete with artificial lake, churches and stone houses that wouldn't have looked out of place in Surrey or the Scottish Highlands. Soon, **Ooty** was the "Queen of Hill Stations" and had become the most popular hill-retreat in peninsular India.

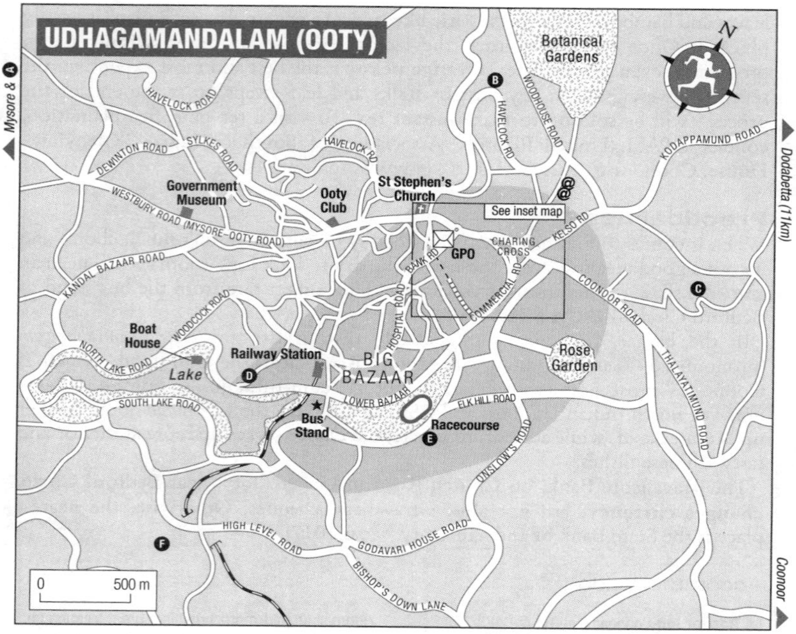

By a stroke of delicious irony, the Todas outlived the colonists whose cash crops originally displaced them – but only just. Having retreated with their buffalo into the surrounding hills and wooded valleys, they continue to preserve a more-or-less traditional way of life, albeit in greatly diminished numbers. Until the mid-1970s

"Snooty Ooty" continued to be "home" to the notoriously snobbish British inhabitants who chose to "stay on" after Independence. Since then, travellers have continued to be attracted by Ooty's cool climate and peaceful green hills, forest and grassland. However, if you come in the hope of finding quaint vestiges of the Raj, you're likely to be disappointed; what with indiscriminate **development** and a deluge of holiday-makers, they're few and far between.

The **best time to come** is between January and March, thereby avoiding the high-season crowds (April–June & Sept–Oct). In May, the summer festival brings huge numbers of people and a barrage of amplified noise, worlds away from the peaceful retreat envisaged by the *sahibs*.

Arrival, information and orientation

Most visitors arrive in Ooty either by bus from Mysore in Karnataka, or on the miniature **Nilgiri Blue Mountain Railway** from Coonoor and Mettupalayam. The **bus stand** and **railway station** are fairly close together, at the western end of the big bazaar and racecourse. **Local transport** consists of auto-rickshaws and taxis, which meet incoming trains and gather outside the bus stand and on Commercial Road around Charing Cross.

The **TTDC tourist office** (Mon–Sat 10am–5.45pm; ⓣ0423/244 3977) is at the TTDC *Hotel Tamil Nadu II*. You can book tours here, including a mammoth day-trip (daily 9.30am–7pm; Rs210) that includes Ooty, Pykara dam, falls and boathouse and Mudumalai Wildlife Sanctuary. There's also a less strenuous tour of just Ooty and Coonoor (daily 9.30am–5.30pm; Rs130), which goes to Sim's Park, the Botanical Gardens, the lake, Dodabetta Peak, Lamb's Rock and Dolphin's Nose. There's also a private **tourist information centre** (daily 10am–7pm; ⓣ9443 345258) in the clocktower building at Charing Cross that gives out leaflets and offers more reliable advice.

Ooty's **post office** is northwest of Charing Cross at West Town Circle, near St Stephen's Church. There are numerous **internet** outlets across town, including Cyber Link and Cyber Planet just north of Charing Cross. The only **bank** in Ooty that changes travellers' cheques and currency is the very pukka State Bank of India on West Town Circle, and there are now a number of ATMs dotted around town.

Moving on from Ooty

Ooty **railway station** has a booking office (6.30am–7pm), where you can buy tickets for the Nilgiri Blue Mountain Railway (see p.1019), and a reservation counter (daily 8am–12.30pm & 2.30–4.30pm) for booking onward services to most other destinations in the south. Four trains daily (9.15am, 12.15pm, 3pm & 6pm) pootle down the narrow-gauge line to Coonoor, but only one (3pm) continues down to Mettupalayam, which is on the main broad-gauge network. If you're heading to Chennai, the 3pm train should get you to Mettupayalam to connect with the daily #2672 *Nilgiri Express* (depart 7.45pm; 9hr 25min).

You can also book **buses** in advance at the bus stand, at the reservation office of state buses (daily 9am–12.30pm & 1.30–5.30pm) A combination of stop-start local and express "super-deluxe" state buses serve Bengaluru and Mysore (buses every 30min to both pass through Mudumalai), Kodaikanal, Thanjavur, Thiruvananthapuram and Kanyakumari, as well as Coonoor and Coimbatore nearer to hand. **Private buses** to Mysore, Bengaluru and Kodaikanal can be booked at hotels, or agents in Charing Cross; even when advertised as "super-deluxe", many turn out to be cramped minibuses.

Accommodation

Accommodation in Ooty is a lot more expensive than in many places in India; during April and May, the prices given below can rise by thirty to a hundred percent. It also gets very crowded, so you may have to hunt around to find what you want. The best by far are the grand old Raj-era places; otherwise, the choice is largely down to average hotels at above-average prices. In **winter** (Nov–Feb), when it can get pretty cold, most hotels provide extra blankets and buckets of hot water on request.

Co-operators Guest House Commercial Rd, Charing Cross T 0423/244 4046. An L-shaped Raj-era building with clean rooms whose yellow-and-turquoise balconies look down to a courtyard; slightly back from the main road, so it's relatively quiet. 4–5

Fernhills Palace off High Level Rd T 0423/2443910, W www.welcomheritagehotels.com. Luxury heritage hotel in what was the maharajah of Mysore's palace; the original exterior remains, but the interior has been tastefully renovated. All rooms ($120–300) are modern with attached bathrooms, and feature jacuzzis. *Regency Villas*, within the same grounds, is substantially cheaper. 9

Glyngarth Villa Golf Club Rd, 4.5km out of town on the Mysore Rd T 0423/ 244 5754, W www.glyngarthvilla.com. A 150-year-old colonial villa set in four acres of greenery. The five double rooms, comfortable and with wooden interiors, give the place a charming atmosphere, and there are great valley views. Rates include breakfast. 4–7

Hills Palace Commercial Rd, Charing Cross T 0423/244 6483, E hillspalace@sify.com. Modern place just below the main bazaar, but secluded, quiet and with spotlessly clean rooms. Great value in low season. 5–7

King's Cliff Havelock Rd T 0423/245 2888, W www.kingscliff-ooty.com. Imposing ancestral mansion with four grades of lavishly furnished rooms, each with a Shakespearian theme; great value. There's also a stylish dining room and lounge, with terrific food and a resident singer/guitarist. 7

Reflections Guest House North Lake Rd T 0423/244 3834, E reflectionsin@yahoo.co.in. Homely, relaxing guesthouse by the lake, 5min walk from the railway station, with rooms opening onto a small terrace. Easily the best budget option in Ooty, but it's small and fills up quickly, so book in advance. 4

Sherlock Tiger Hill Rd, 2.5km east of Charing Cross T 0423/244 1641, W www.littlearth.in/sherlock. Beautifully landscaped Victorian mansion with a Conan Doyle theme and stunning views from the grassy terrace. All rooms are tastefully furnished, and the deluxe ones have sitouts. Friendly service and quality food too. 6

YWCA Anandagiri Ettines Rd T 0423/244 2218. Charming 1920s building set in spacious grounds near the racecourse. Seven varieties of rooms and chalets are on offer, all immaculate, with bucket hot water and bathrooms, plus a dorm (Rs110). Excellent value and popular, so book ahead. 4

The Town

Ooty sprawls over a large area of winding roads and steep climbs. The obvious focal point is **Charing Cross**, a busy junction on dusty **Commercial Road**, the main, relatively flat, shopping street that runs south to the big bazaar and municipal vegetable market. Goods on sale range from fat plastic bags of cardamom and Orange pekoe tea to presentation packs of essential oils (among them natural mosquito-repelling citronella). A little way north of Charing Cross, the **Botanical Gardens** T 0423/244 2545 (daily 8.30am–6.30pm; Rs10, camera Rs30, video camera Rs500), laid out in 1847 by gardeners from London's Kew Gardens, consist of fifty acres of immaculate lawns, lily ponds and beds, with more than a thousand varieties of shrubs, flowers and trees. There's a refreshment stand in the park, and shops in the small Tibetan market sell ice creams and snacks.

Northwest of Charing Cross, the small Gothic-style **St Stephen's Church** was one of Ooty's first colonial structures, built in the 1820s on the site of a Toda temple; timber for its bowed teak roof was taken from Tipu Sultan's palace at Srirangapatnam and hauled up here by elephant. The area around the church gives some idea of what the hill-station must have looked like in the days of the Raj. To

The Nilgiri Blue Mountain Railway

The famous narrow-gauge **Nilgiri Blue Mountain Railway** climbs up from Mettupalayam on the plains, via Hillgrove (17km) and Coonoor (27km) to Udhagamandalam, a journey of 46km that passes through sixteen tunnels, eleven stations and nineteen bridges. It's a slow haul of four and a half hours or more – sometimes the train moves little faster than walking pace, and always takes at least twice as long as the bus – but the **views** are absolutely magnificent, especially along the steepest sections in the Hulikal ravine.

The line was built between 1890 and 1908, paid for by the tea-planters and other British inhabitants of the Nilgiris. It differs from India's two comparable narrow-gauge lines, to Darjeeling and Shimla, for its use of the so-called **Swiss rack system**, by means of which the tiny locomotives are able to climb gradients of up to 1 in 12.5. Special bars were set between the track rails to form a ladder, which cogs of teeth, connected to the train's driving wheels, engage like a zip mechanism. Because of this novel design, only the original locomotives can still run the steepest stretches of line, which is why the section between Mettupalayam and Coonoor has remained one of South Asia's last functioning **steam routes**. The chuffing and whistle screeches of the tiny train, echoing across the valleys as it pushes its blue-and-cream carriages up to Coonoor (where a diesel locomotive takes over) rank among the most romantic sounds of south India, conjuring up the determined gentility of the Raj era. Even if you don't count yourself as a trainspotter, a boneshaking ride on the Blue Mountain Railway should be a priority while traversing the Nilgiris between southern Karnataka and the Tamil plains.

See "Moving on from Ooty" box, p.1017 for timetable details for the line.

the right is the rambling and rather dilapidated **Spencer's store**, which opened in 1909 and sold everything a British home in the colonies could ever need; it's now a computer college. Over the next hill to the west, the snootiest of Ooty's institutions, the members-only **Club**, dates from 1830. Originally the house of Sir William Rumbold, it became a club in 1843 and expanded thereafter. Its one claim to fame is that the rules for snooker were first set down here. Further along Mysore Road, the modest **Government Museum** (daily except Fri & 2nd Sat of month 10am–5.30pm; free) houses a few paltry tribal objects, sculptures and crafts.

West of the railway station and racecourse (races mid-April to mid-June), the **lake**, constructed in the early 1800s, is one of Ooty's main tourist attractions, despite being heavily polluted with sewage. Boats are available for rent (daily 9am–6pm; paddle-boats Rs60–100, rowing boats Rs80–110, charter motor boats seating 8–15 people Rs250–450), and you can also go horseriding here for Rs150 per hour.

Eating

Many of the mid-range hotels serve up good south Indian food, but Ooty has yet to offer a gourmet **restaurant**. For an inexpensive *udipi* breakfast, head to one of the restaurants around Charing Cross for *iddli-dosa* and filter coffee.

Chandan *Nahar Hotel*, Commercial Rd, Charing Cross. Carefully prepared north Indian specialities (their *paneer kofta* is particularly good), and a small selection of tandoori vegetarian dishes, served inside a posh restaurant or on a lawnside terrace. They also do a full range of lassis and milkshakes. Main courses Rs60–100.

Iranis Commercial Rd. A gloomy old-style Persian joint run by Baha'ís. Uncompromisingly non-veg (the menu's heavy on mutton, liver and brains), but an atmospheric coffee stop, and a popular hang-out for both men and women. Most dishes Rs60–80.

Preethi Palace Ettines Rd. Excellent lunchtime thalis (north and south Indian) for Rs30–50, and a delicious range of pure-veg food served throughout the day.

Shinkows 42 Commissioners Rd. Good-value, authentic Chinese restaurant serving up decent-sized portions on the spicy and pricey side – main courses with meat cost Rs120–150.

Willy's KRC Arcade, Walsham Rd. First-floor café, with a modern, buzzy vibe that makes it popular with students, as well as tasty Western savouries and cakes, and range of gourmet coffees.

Mudumalai Wildlife Sanctuary

Set 1140m up in the Nilgiri Hills, the **MUDUMALAI WILDLIFE SANCTUARY**, ⓣ0423/252 6235, covers 322 square kilometres of deciduous forest, split by the main road from Ooty (64km to the southeast) to Mysore (97km to the northwest). Occupying the thickly wooded lower northern reaches of the hills, it boasts one of the largest populations of elephants in India, along with wild dogs, *gaur* (Indian bison), common and Nilgiri langur and bonnet macaques (monkeys), jackal, hyena and sloth bear, and even a few tigers and leopards. Of the wealth of local flora, the dazzling red flowers of the flame of the forest stand among the most noticeable. Now that the park is fully operational again, you can explore by vehicle or on foot. Generally speaking, the best time to visit is during and after monsoon.

The main focus of interest by the park entrance at **Theppakkadu** is the **Elephant Camp** show (daily 8–9.30am & 5.30–6.30pm; free), where you can watch the sanctuary's tame pachyderms being fed and bathed. This is also the starting point for the government **safari tour** (7–9am & 4–6pm; 40min; Rs35/erson, camera Rs25, video camera Rs150), which is the only way of accessing the official park limits. However you may well see more creatures if you take a private **Jeep tour** or **guided trek** into some of the parts of Mudumalai that are outside the state-controlled area. These can be arranged through any guesthouse or direct at Nature Safari in Masinagudi (ⓣ0423/252 6340, ⓔsaveelephasmaximus@yahoo.co.in).

Practicalities

The main route from Ooty to Mudumalai taken by most Mysore- and Bengaluru-bound buses takes 2.5 hours to reach **Theppakkadu**. The alternative route is a tortuous journey of very steep gradients and hairpin bends, which can only be attempted by smaller vehicles such as the Cheran transport minibuses. These take around one hour and end up at **Masinagudi**, which is closer to most of the area's growing **accommodation** options. Complete with eco-friendly swimming pool, the prime resort is *Jungle Retreat* (ⓣ0423/252 6469, ⓦwww .jungleretreat.com; ❼–❽) at Bokkapuram, 6km southwest of Masinagudi, with accommodation ranging from Rs525 beds in spacious dorms to a pair of elegant treehouses; Rs1200 covers three sumptuous buffet meals per day and unlimited tea and coffee. *Wild Haven* (ⓣ0423/252 6490, ⓔkarimjohn@hotmail.com; ❻) at Chadapatti, 6km south of Masinagudi, offers simple but spacious concrete rooms, set in open land with great mountain views. The only real budget places are the dowdy TTDC *Hotel Tamil Nadu* (ⓣ0423/252 6580, ⓦwww.ttdconline.com; ❷–❸) at Theppakkadu, and the spartan *St Xavier's Lodge* (ⓣ0423/252 6371; ❶) in Masinagudi, which also has a couple of basic "meals" restaurants.

21

Kerala

* **Temple festivals** Parades of extravagantly decorated elephants, backed by drummers and firework displays, form the focal point of Kerala's Hindu festivals. See p.1022

* **Ritual theatre** Elaborately costumed, arcane dance dramas, such as *kathakali* and *theyyem*, are an essential part of the Kerala experience. See p.1024 & p.1069

* **Varkala** Chill out in a cliff-top café, sunbathe on the beach or soak up the atmosphere around the town's busy temple tank. See p.1037

* **The backwaters** Explore the beautiful waterways of Kerala's densely populated coastal strip on a rice barge or punted canoe, following the narrow, overgrown canals right into the heart of the villages. See p.1046

* **The High Range** The tea plantations, pepper groves and grassy mountains around Munnar are the perfect antidote to the heat and humidity of the coast. See p.1052 & p.1058

* **Fort Cochin** Dutch, Portuguese, British and traditional Keralan townhouses line the backstreets of Malabar's old peninsular port. See the grandest of them from the inside by staying in a heritage hotel. See p.1064

▲ The backwaters

The state of **KERALA** stretches for 550km along India's southwest coast, divided between the densely forested mountains of the Western Ghats inland and a lush, humid coastal plain of rice paddy, lagoons, rivers and canals. Its intensely tropical landscape, fed by the highest rainfall in peninsular India, has intoxicated visitors since the ancient Sumerians and Greeks sailed in search of spices to the shore known as the **Malabar coast**. Equally, Kerala's arcane rituals and spectacular festivals – many of them little changed since the earliest era of Brahmanical Hinduism – have dazzled outsiders for thousands of years.

Travellers weary of India's daunting metropolises will find Kerala's cities smaller and more relaxed. The most popular is undoubtedly the great port of **Kochi** (Cochin), where the state's long history of peaceful foreign contact is evocatively evident in the atmospheric old quarters of Mattancherry and Fort Cochin. In Kerala's far south, the capital, **Thiruvananthapuram** (Trivandrum), is gateway to the nearby palm-fringed beaches of **Kovalam** and **Varkala**, and provides visitors with varied opportunities to sample Kerala's rich cultural and artistic life.

One of the nicest aspects of exploring Kerala, though, is the actual travelling – especially by **boat**, in the spellbinding Kuttanad region, around historic **Kollam** (Quilon) and **Alappuzha** (Alleppey). Cruisers and beautiful wooden barges known as *kettu vallam* ("tied boats") ply the **backwaters**, offering tourists a window on village life in India's most densely populated state. Furthermore, it's easy to escape the heat of the lowlands by heading for the **hills**, which rise to 2695m. Roads pass through landscapes dotted with churches and temples, tea, coffee, spice and rubber plantations, and natural forests, en route to wildlife reserves such as **Periyar**, where herds of mud-caked elephants roam freely.

Kerala is short on the historic monuments prevalent elsewhere in India, and most of its ancient temples are closed to non-Hindus. Following an unwritten law, few buildings in the region, whether houses or temples, are higher than the surrounding trees, which in urban areas often creates the illusion that you're surrounded by forest. Typical features of both domestic and temple architecture include long, sloping tiled and gabled roofs that minimize the excesses of rain and sunshine, and pillared verandas; the definitive examples are Thiruvananthapuram's **Puttan Malika Palace**, and **Padmanabhapuram Palace**, in neighbouring Tamil Nadu, but easily reached from the capital.

Huge amounts of money are lavished upon many, varied, and often all-night **festivals** usually associated with Kerala's temples. Fireworks rend the air, while processions of caparisoned elephants are accompanied by some of the loudest (and deftest) drum orchestras in the world. Thrissur's famous **Puram** festival (April/May) is the most astonishing, but smaller events take place throughout the state – often outdoors, with all welcome to attend. **Theatre** and **dance** also abound; not only the region's own female classical dance form, **mohiniyattam** ("dance of the enchantress"), but also the martial-art-influenced **kathakali** dance drama, which has for four centuries brought gods and demons from the Mahabharata and Ramayana to Keralan villages. Its two thousand-year-old predecessor, the Sanskrit drama **kudiyattam**, is still performed by a handful of artists, while localized rituals known as **theyyem**, where dancers wearing decorative masks and hats become "possessed" by temple deities, remain a potent ingredient of village life in the north. Few visitors witness these extraordinary all-night performances, but from December through March it is possible to spend weeks hopping between village festivals in northern Kerala, experiencing a way of life that has altered little in centuries.

A word of warning, however, for budget travellers. Kerala ranks among the most **expensive** regions of India. **Accommodation** is particularly pricey – and tends to be of a correspondingly high standard. Cheap places to stay are thin on the ground

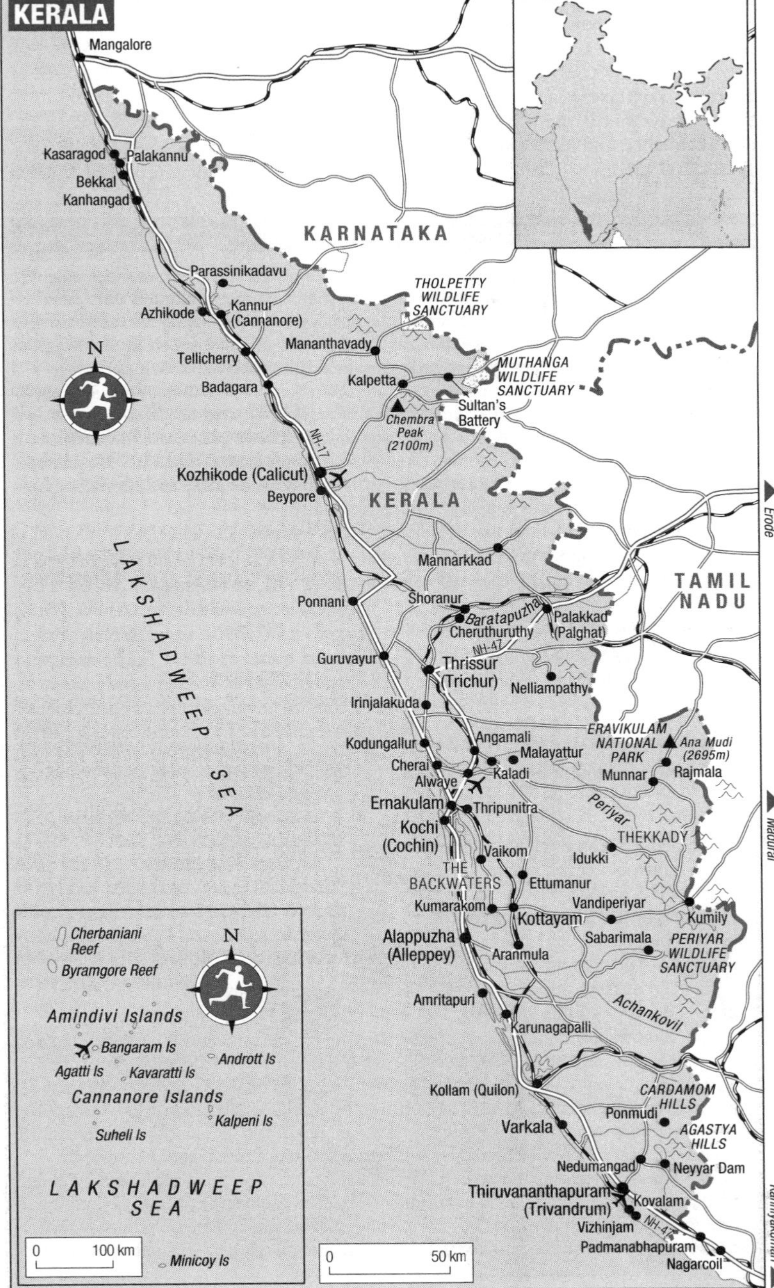
KERALA
Mangalore
Kasaragod
Palakannu
Bekkal
Kanhangad
KARNATAKA
Parassinikadavu
Azhikode
Kannur (Cannanore)
THOLPETTY WILDLIFE SANCTUARY
Mananthavady
Tellicherry
MUTHANGA WILDLIFE SANCTUARY
Kalpetta
Badagara
Sultan's Battery
Chembra Peak (2100m)
NH-17
Kozhikode (Calicut)
Beypore
KERALA
Erode
LAKSHADWEEP SEA
Mannarkkad
TAMIL NADU
Ponnani
Shoranur
Baratapuzha
Palakkad (Palghat)
Cheruthuruthy
NH-47
Guruvayur
Thrissur (Trichur)
Nelliampathy
Irinjalakuda
ERAVIKULAM NATIONAL PARK
Ana Mudi (2695m)
Angamali
Kodungallur
Malayattur
Cherai
Alwaye
Kaladi
Munnar
Rajmala
Ernakulam
Thripunitra
Periyar
Madurai
Kochi (Cochin)
THEKKADY
Idukki
Vaikom
THE BACKWATERS
Ettumanur
Kumarakom
Vandiperiyar
Kottayam
Kumily
Alappuzha (Alleppey)
Sabarimala
PERIYAR WILDLIFE SANCTUARY
Aranmula
Amritapuri
Achankovil
Karunagapalli
Kollam (Quilon)
CARDAMOM HILLS
Ponmudi
Varkala
AGASTYA HILLS
Nedumangad
Neyyar Dam
Thiruvananthapuram (Trivandrum)
Kovalam
Vizhinjam
NH-47
Kanniyakumari
Padmanabhapuram
Nagarcoil
0 50 km
Cherbaniani Reef
Byramgore Reef
Amindivi Islands
Bangaram Is
Andrott Is
Agatti Is
Kavaratti Is
Cannanore Islands
Kalpeni Is
Suheli Is
LAKSHADWEEP SEA
0 100 km
Minicoy Is
N
N

everywhere, but especially in the coastal resorts, hill stations and backwater areas, where it's not uncommon to pay upwards of Rs2000 for a room in a modest guesthouse in season.

Some history

Ancient Kerala is mentioned as the land of the **Cheras** in a third-century BC Ashokan edict, and in several even older Sanskrit texts, including the Mahabharata. Pliny and Ptolemy also testify to thriving trade between the ancient port of Muziris

Keralan ritual theatre

Among the most magical experiences a visitor to Kerala can have is to witness one of the innumerable ancient drama rituals that play such an important and unique role in the cultural life of the region. **Kathakali** is the best known; other less publicised forms, which clearly influenced its development, include the classical Sanskrit **kudiyattam**.

Many Keralan forms share broad characteristics. A prime aim of each performer is to transform the mundane to the world of gods and demons; his preparation is highly ritualized, involving other-worldly costume and mask-like make-up. In *kathakali* and *kudiyattam*, this preparation is a rigorously codified part of the classical tradition. One-off **performances** of various ritual types take place throughout the state, building up to fever pitch during April and May before pausing for the monsoon (June–Aug). Finding out about such events requires a little perseverance, but it's well worth the effort; enquire at tourist offices, or buy a Malayalam daily paper such as the *Malayalam Manorama* and ask someone to check the listings for temple festivals, where most of the action invariably takes place. Tourist *kathakali* is staged daily in **Kochi** (see p.1069) but to find authentic performances, contact **performing arts schools** such as Thiruvananthapuram's Margi (see p.1029) and Cheruthuruthy's Kerala Kalamandalam; *kudiyattam* artists work at both, as well as at Natana Kairali at Irinjalakuda (accessible from Thrissur, see p.1073).

Kathakali

Here is the tradition of the trance dancers, here is the absolute demand of the subjugation of body to spirit, here is the realization of the cosmic transformation of human into divine.

Mrinalini Sarabhai, classical dancer

The image of a **kathakali** actor in a magnificent costume with extraordinary make-up and a huge gold crown has become Kerala's trademark. Traditional performances, of which there are still many, usually take place on open ground outside a temple, beginning at 10pm and lasting until dawn, illuminated by the flickers of a large brass oil lamp centre-stage. Virtually nothing about *kathakali* is naturalistic, because it depicts the world of gods and demons; both the male and female roles are played by men.

Standing at the back of the stage, two musicians play driving rhythms, one on a bronze gong, the other on heavy bell-metal cymbals; they also sing the dialogue. Actors appear and disappear from behind a hand-held curtain and never utter a sound, save the odd strange cry. Learning the elaborate hand gestures, facial expressions and choreographed movements, as articulate and precise as any sign language, requires rigorous training which can begin at the age of eight and last ten years. At least two more drummers stand left of the stage; one plays the upright **chenda** with slender curved sticks, the other plays the *maddalam*, a horizontal barrel-shaped hand drum. When a female character is "speaking", the *chenda* is replaced by the hourglass-shaped *ettaka*, a "talking drum" on which melodies can be played. The drummers keep their eyes on the actors, whose every gesture is reinforced by their sound, from the gentlest embrace to the gory disembowelling of an enemy.

(now known as Kodungallur) and the Roman Empire. Little is known about the region's early rulers, whose dominion covered a large area, but whose capital, Vanji, has not so far been identified. At the start of the ninth century, King Kulashekhara Alvar – a poet-saint of the Vaishnavite *bhakti* movement known as the *alvars* – established his own dynasty. His son and successor, Rajashekharavarman, is thought to have been a saint of the parallel Shaivite movement, the *nayannars*. The great Keralan philosopher **Shankaracharya**, whose *advaitya* ("non-dualist") philosophy influenced the whole of Hindu India, was alive at this time.

Although it bears the unmistakable influences of *kudiyattam* and indigenous folk rituals, *kathakali*, literally "story-play", is thought to have crystallized into a distinct theatre form during the seventeenth century. The plays are based on three major sources: the **Hindu epics** the Mahabharata, Ramayana and the Bhagavata Purana. While the stories are ostensibly about god-heroes such as Rama and Krishna, the most popular characters are those that give the most scope to the actors – the villainous, fanged, red-and-black-faced *katti* ("knife") anti-heroes; these types, such as the kings Ravana and Duryodhana, are dominated by lust, greed, envy and violence. David Bolland's *Guide to Kathakali*, widely available in Kerala, gives invaluable scene-by-scene summaries of the most popular plays and explains in simple language a lot more besides.

When **attending a performance**, arrive early to get your bearings before it gets dark, even though the first play will not begin much before 10pm. (Quiet) members of the audience are welcome to visit the dressing room before and during the performance. The colour and design of the mask-like make-up, which specialist artists take several hours to apply, reveal the character's personality. The word *pacha* means both "green" and "pure"; a green-faced *pacha* character is thus a noble human or god. Red signifies *rajas*, passion and aggression, black denotes *tamas*, darkness and negativity, while white is *sattvik*, light and intellect. Once the make-up is completed, elaborate wide skirts are tied to the waist, and ornaments of silver and gold are added. Silver talons are fitted to the left hand. The transformation is complete with a final prayer and the donning of waist-length wig and crown. Visitors new to *kathakali* will almost undoubtedly get bored during such long programmes, parts of which are very slow indeed. If you're at a village performance, you may not always find accommodation, so you can't leave during the night. Be prepared to sit on the ground for hours, and bring some warm clothes. Half the fun is staying up all night to witness, just as the dawn light appears, the gruesome disembowelling of a villain or a demon *asura*.

Kudiyattam

Three families of the Chakyar caste and a few outsiders perform the Sanskrit drama **kudiyattam**, the oldest continually performed theatre-form in the world. Until recently it was only performed inside temples and then only in front of the uppermost castes. Visually it is very similar to its offspring, *kathakali*, but its atmosphere is infinitely more archaic. The actors, eloquent in sign language and symbolic movement, speak in the compelling intonation of the local brahmins' Vedic chant, unchanged since 1500 BC.

A single act of a *kudiyattam* play can require ten full nights; the entire play takes forty. A great actor, in full command of the subtleties of expression through gestures, can take half an hour to do such a simple thing as murder a demon, berate the audience, or simply describe a leaf fall to the ground. Unlike *kathakali*, *kudiyattam* includes comic characters and plays. The ubiquitous Vidushaka, narrator and clown, is something of a court jester, and traditionally has held the right to criticize openly the highest in the land without fear of retribution.

Eventually, the prosperity acquired by the Cheras through trade with China and the Arab world proved too much of an attraction for the neighbouring **Chola** empire, who embarked upon a hundred years of sporadic warfare with the Cheras at the end of the tenth century. Around 1100, the Cheras lost their capital at Mahodayapuram in the north, and shifted south to establish a new capital at Kollam (Quilon).

Direct trade with Europe commenced in 1498 with the arrival in the capital, Calicut, of a small Portuguese fleet under **Vasco da Gama** – the first expedition to reach the coast of India via the Cape of Good Hope and Arabian Sea. After an initial show of cordiality, relations between him and the local ruler, or zamorin, quickly degenerated, and da Gama's second voyage four years later was characterized by appalling massacres, kidnapping, mutilation and barefaced piracy. Nevertheless, a fortified trading post was soon established at Cochin from which the Portuguese, exploiting old enmities between the region's rulers, were able to dominate trade with the Middle East. This was gradually eroded away over the ensuing century by rival powers France and Holland, and in the early 1600s the Dutch East India Company entered the fray. An independent territory was subsequently carved out of the Malabar coast by Tipu Sultan of Mysore, but his defeat in 1792 left the British in control right up until Independence.

Kerala can claim some of the most startling **radical** credentials in India. In 1957 it was the first state in the world to democratically elect a communist government, and still regularly returns communist parties in elections (the present chief minister, V.S. Achuthanandan, is a communist party leader). Due to reforms made during the 1960s and 1970s, Kerala currently has the most equitable land distribution of any Indian state. Poverty appears far less acute than in other parts of the country, with life expectancy and per capita income well above the national averages. Kerala is also justly proud of its reputation for healthcare and education, with **literacy** rates that stand, officially at least, at 91 percent for men and 88 percent for women. Industrial development is negligible, however: potential investors from outside tend to fight shy of dealing with such a politicized workforce.

Thiruvananthapuram

Kerala's capital, **THIRUVANANTHAPURAM** (still widely known as **Trivandrum**), is set on seven low hills just a couple of kilometres inland from the Arabian Sea. Despite its administrative importance – demonstrated by wide roads, multistorey office blocks and gleaming white colonial buildings – it's an easygoing state capital by Indian standards, with enclaves of traditional red-tiled gabled houses breaking up the bustle of its modern concrete core, and a swathe of parkland spreading north of the centre. Although its principal sight, the **Sri Padmanabhaswamy temple**, is closed to non-Hindus, the city holds enough of interest to fill a day, including the splendid **Puttan Malika Palace**, one of the state's best museums and a typically Keralan bazaar, **Chalai**.

Arrival

Connected to most major Indian cities, as well as Sri Lanka, the Maldives and the Middle East, **Beemapalli airport** lies 6km southwest of town. The best way to get to the centre is on the state-of-the-art, a/c airport bus (Rs15), which runs from the arrivals concourse to the City bus stand in East Fort, and from there on to Kovalam (much to the chagrin of local taxi drivers). Auto-rickshaws can get you

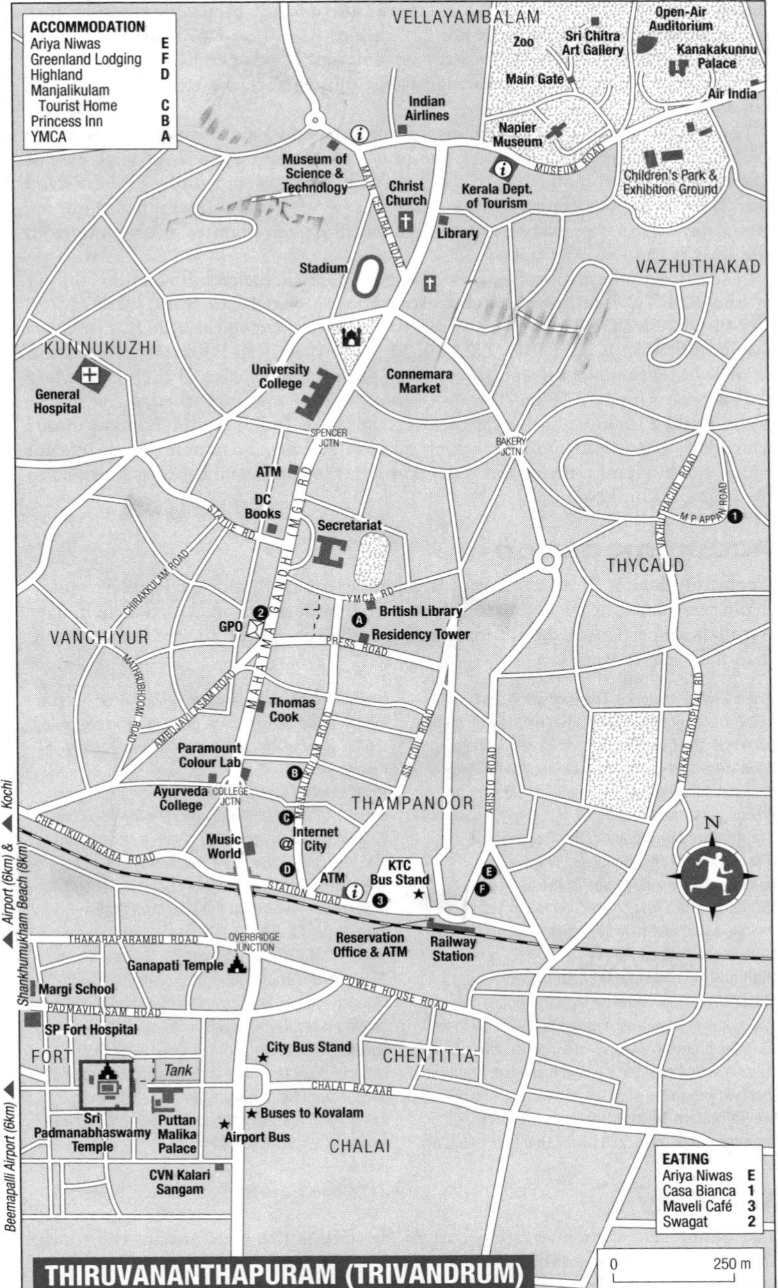

Kollam, Kochi & NH-47
ACCOMMODATION
Ariya Niwas E
Greenland Lodging F
Highland D
Manjalikulam Tourist Home C
Princess Inn B
YMCA A
VELLAYAMBALAM
Zoo
Sri Chitra Art Gallery
Open-Air Auditorium
Kanakakunnu Palace
Main Gate
Air India
Indian Airlines
Napier Museum
Museum of Science & Technology
MAIN CENTRAL ROAD
Christ Church
Kerala Dept. of Tourism
MUSEUM ROAD
Children's Park & Exhibition Ground
Library
Stadium
VAZHUTHAKAD
KUNNUKUZHI
University College
Connemara Market
General Hospital
SPENCER JCTN
BAKERY JCTN
ATM
DC Books
STATUE RD
MAHATMA GANDHI (MG) RD
Secretariat
VAZHUTHACAUD ROAD
M P APPAN ROAD
THYCAUD
CHIRAKKULAM ROAD
YMCA RD
British Library
Residency Tower
GPO
VANCHIYUR
PRESS ROAD
MATHRUBHOOMI ROAD
AMBUJAVILASAM ROAD
Thomas Cook
MANJALIKULAM ROAD
SS COIL ROAD
ARISTO ROAD
TAIKKAD HOSPITAL RD
Paramount Colour Lab
Ayurveda College
COLLEGE JCTN
THAMPANOOR
CHETTIKULANGARA ROAD
Internet City
Music World
N
ATM
KTC Bus Stand
STATION ROAD
Kochi
Airport (6km) & Shankhumukham Beach (8km)
THAKARAPARAMBU ROAD
OVERBRIDGE JUNCTION
Reservation Office & ATM
Railway Station
Ganapati Temple
Margi School
POWER HOUSE ROAD
PADMAVILASAM ROAD
SP Fort Hospital
City Bus Stand
FORT
Tank
CHENTITTA
CHALAI BAZAAR
Beemapalli Airport (6km)
Sri Padmanabhaswamy Temple
Puttan Malika Palace
Buses to Kovalam
Airport Bus
CHALAI
CVN Kalari Sangam
EATING
Ariya Niwas E
Casa Bianca 1
Maveli Café 3
Swagat 2
0 250 m
THIRUVANANTHAPURAM (TRIVANDRUM)
Kovalam & Kanyakumari

into the centre for around Rs100 and there's also a handy prepaid taxi service (pay before departure; Rs200 for the railway station, Rs400 for Kovalam's Lighthouse Beach). You'll find a Kerala Tourism information booth (in theory 24hr), ATM and Thomas Cook foreign exchange facility just before the exit of the arrivals concourse.

The long-distance KSRTC **Thampanoor bus stand** and **railway station** face each other across Station Road in the southeast of the city, a short walk east of Overbridge Junction on MG Road. There's a handy pre-paid auto-rickshaw stand directly outside the train station's main exit. **Local buses** (including those for Kovalam) depart from **City bus stand**, in East Fort, ten minutes' walk south from the KSRTC and railway stations.

In addition to the airport (see above), Kerala Tourism has an information counter at the KSRTC **Thampanoor bus stand** (Mon–Sat 10am–5pm; ⓣ0471/232 7224), while KTDC hosts a visitor reception centre next to the *KTDC Chaithram* hotel on Station Road (ⓣ0471/233 0031), where you can book accommodation in their hotel chain and tickets for various **guided tours**. Most of these, including the city tours (daily 7.30am–1pm & 1–7pm; Rs200), are too rushed, but if you're really pushed for time and want to reach the tip of India, try the **Kanyakumari** tour (daily 8am–9pm; Rs500), which takes in Padmanabhapuram Palace (except Mon), Suchindram temple, and Kanyakumari, the southernmost spot in India, in the state of Tamil Nadu.

Accommodation

Accommodation in all categories is a lot easier on the pocket in Thiruvananthapuram than at nearby Kovalam Beach. That said, this is one city where budget travellers, in particular, should consider spending a couple of hundred rupees more than they might usually.

Ariya Niwas Aristo Rd, Thampanoor ⓣ0471/233 0789. Large, spotless, well-aired rooms with comfy beds and great city views from its upper floors. Good value and just 2min walk from the railway station, with an excellent "meals" restaurant on the ground floor (see p.1030). ❹

Greenland Lodging Aristo Rd, Thampanoor ⓣ0471/232 8114. An efficient lodge with immaculate en-suite rooms (some a/c) for just Rs550. The best low-cost option in the vicinity of the bus stand and railway station – though you'll have to book ahead. ❸–❹

Highland Manjalikulam Rd, Thampanoor ⓣ0471/233 3200, ⓦwww.highland-hotels.com. The rooms in this lower mid-range option fail to live up to the promise of the six-storey concrete and tinted-glass facade, but it's well managed, just a short walk from the stations, and easy to find. ❸–❺

Manjalikulam Tourist Home Manjalikulam Rd, Thampanoor ⓣ0471/233 0776. Don't be fooled by the shining glass and marble ground floor – above lurks a basic budget place offering variously priced rooms, all of them clean and with good, comfy mattresses. ❸

Princess Inn Manjalikulam Rd, Thampanoor ⓣ0471/233 9150, ⓔprincess_inn@yahoo.com. Well-scrubbed, respectable cheapie close to the stations. One of the more welcoming and better-value small hotels in this busy enclave, though it's a bit more of a plod up the lane from Station Rd than some. ❷–❹

YMCA YMCA Rd, near the Secretariat ⓣ0471/233 0059, ⓔymcatvm@sancharnet.in. Neat, smartly furnished rooms at bargain rates for the levels of comfort. The "luxury" options (Rs500) are enormous and have high ceilings, quiet fans, TVs and spacious bathrooms. Singles from Rs290; some a/c. Amazing value, though you'll probably need to book at least two weeks in advance. ❸–❹

The City

The oldest and most interesting part of the city is the **Fort** area in the south, around the **Sri Padmanabhaswamy temple** and **Puttan Malika Palace**, with the traditional **Chalai bazaar** extending east. At the opposite, northern side of the centre, the **Sri Chitra Art Gallery** and **Napier Museum** showcase painting, crafts and sculpture in a leafy park. In addition, schools specializing in the martial art *kalarippayat* and the dance/theatre forms of *kathakali* and *kudiyattam* offer an insight into the Keralan obsession with physical training and skill.

Sri Padmanabhaswamy Temple

A Neoclassical gateway leads from the western end of Chalai Bazaar to the **Sri Padmanabhaswamy Temple**, which is still controlled by the Travancore royal family. Unusually for Kerala, it's built in the Dravidian style of Tamil Nadu, with a tall, seven-tiered *gopura* gateway and high fortress-like walls. Few foreigners get to see it (non-Hindus are not permitted inside) but the **deity** enshrined in the central sanctum – spectacularly large reclining Vishnu – is composed of 12,008 sacred stones, or *salagrams*, brought by elephant from the bed of the Gandhaki River in Nepal. The main approach road to Sri Padmanabhaswamy, where devotees bathe in a huge tank, is lined with stalls selling religious souvenirs. It's an atmospheric area for a stroll – particularly in the early morning.

Puttan Malika Palace

The **Puttan Malika Palace** (Tues–Sun 8.30am–12.30pm & 3–5.30pm; Rs20, camera Rs15) immediately southeast of the temple, became the seat of the Travancore rajas after they left Padmanabhapuram at the end of the nineteenth century. The cool chambers, with highly polished plaster floors and delicately carved wooden screens, house a crop of dusty royal heirlooms, including a solid crystal throne gifted by the Dutch. The real highlight, however, is the elegant Keralan architecture itself. Beneath sloping red-tiled roofs, hundreds of wooden pillars, carved into the forms of rampant horses (*puttan malika* translates as "horse palace"), prop up the eaves, and airy verandas project onto the surrounding lawns.

The royal family have always been keen patrons of the arts, and the open-air **Swathi Sangeetotsavam festival**, held in the grounds during the festival of Navaratri (Oct/Nov), continues the tradition. Performers sit on the palace's raised porch, flanked by the main facade, with the spectators seated on the lawn. For details, ask at the KTDC tourist office.

CVN Kalari Sangam and Chalai Bazaar

Around 500m southeast of the temple in East Fort, the red-brick **CVN Kalari Sangam** ranks among Kerala's top **kalarippayat** gymnasiums. It was founded in 1956 by C.V. Narayanan Nair, one of the legendary figures credited for the martial art's revival, and attracts students from across the world. From 6.30am to 8am (Mon–Sat) you can watch fighting exercises in the sunken *kalari* pit that forms the heart of the complex. Foreigners may join courses, arranged through the head teacher, or *gurukkal*, although prior experience of martial arts and/or dance is a prerequisite.

The main source of **textiles** in the city is **Chalai Bazaar**, the big market extending east from Fort district, jammed with little shops selling bolts of cloth, flowers, incense, spices, bell-metal lamps and fireworks.

The Margi Theatre School

Thiruvananthapuram has for centuries been a crucible for Keralan classical arts, and the **Margi Theatre School** (Ⓣ0471/247 8806, Ⓦwww.margitheatre.org), at the western corner of the Fort area, is one of the foremost colleges for **kathakali** dance drama and the more rarely performed **kudiyattam** theatre form (see p.1025). Most visitors venture out here to watch one of the authentic *kathakali* or *kudiyattam* performances staged once each month in its small **theatre**, details of which are posted on the school's website.

The Napier Museum, Zoo and Sri Chitra Art Gallery

A minute's walk east from the north end of MG Road, opposite Kerala Tourism's information office, brings you to the entrance to Thiruvananthapuram's **public gardens**. As well as serving as a welcome refuge from the noise of the city, the park holds the city's best museums. Give the dusty and uninformative Natural History Museum a miss and head instead for the more engaging **Napier Museum** (Tues–Sun 10am–5pm; Rs5). Built at the end of the nineteenth century, it was an early experiment in what became known as the "Indo-Saracenic" style, with tiled, gabled roofs, garish red-, black- and salmon-patterned brickwork, and a spectacular interior of stained-glass windows and loud turquoise, pink, red and yellow stripes. Highlights of the collection include fifteenth-century Keralan woodcarvings, minutely detailed ivory work, a carved temple chariot (*rath*), plus Chola and Vijayanagar bronzes.

You pass through the main ticket booth for the city's depressingly old-fashioned zoo to reach the **Sri Chitra Art Gallery** (Tues–Sun 10am–5pm; Rs50), which shows paintings from the Rajput, Mughal and Tanjore schools, along with pieces from China, Tibet and Japan. The meat of the collection, though, is made up of works by the celebrated artist **Raja Ravi Varma** (1848–1906), credited with introducing oil painting to India.

Eating

Freshly cooked dosas, *iddli-vada-sambar*, biriyanis and other traditional snacks are available at streetside cafés across town, including the perennially popular *Indian Coffee House* chain, which runs several branches in the city centre – most famously the circular *Maveli Café* next to the KSRTC bus stand in Thampanoor. For proper Kerala-style thali "meals" and Malabari specialities, stick to the places listed below and you'll be in for a treat.

Ariya Niwas *Ariya Niwas* hotel, Aristo Rd, Thampanoor. Top-class south Indian vegetarian thalis dished up on banana leaves in a scrupulously clean non-a/c dining room on the hotel's ground floor, or in the pricier a/c dining hall on the first storey. Hugely popular with everyone from office workers to company directors and their families, and deservedly so: there's really nowhere better to eat in the city.

Casa Bianca 96 MP Appan Rd. You couldn't make it up: a Swedish-run Italian restaurant in a middle-class district of Thiruvananthapuram – and a really fine one at that, serving scrumptious pizza, fresh pasta and crunchy house salads, as well as a range of Continental main courses, sandwiches and desserts. Well worth an auto ride across town.

Maveli Café Next to the bus station on Station Rd, Thampanoor. Part of the *Indian Coffee House* chain, this bizarre red-brick, spiral-shaped café (designed by the renowned expatriate British architect, Laurie Baker) is a Trivandrum institution. Inside, waiters in the trademark *ICH pugris* serve dosas, *vadas*, greasy omelettes, mountainous biriyanis and china cups of the usual (weak and sugary) filter coffee. An obligatory pit-stop, though a grubby one.

Swagat *Grand Central*, MG Rd. Fine Indian veg food served by bow-tied waiters in a blissfully cool a/c dining hall. Their Rs120 "Swagat Special" thali is one for monster appetites, and if you're in town on a Friday, don't miss their traditional banana-leaf Keralan *sadyas*.

Listings

Airlines Website addresses for the following carriers are listed on p.28. Air India, Museum Rd, Vellayambalam Circle ⓣ0471/231 0310 (airport ⓣ0471/250 0585); Gulf Air, Ground Floor, Saran Chambers, Vellayambalam ⓣ0471/272 8003 (airport ⓣ0471/250 1205); Jet Airways, 1st Floor, Akshaya Towers, Sasthamangalam Junction ⓣ0471/272 8864 (airport ⓣ0471/250 0710);

Kingfisher Airlines, Stargate Building, TC 9 / 888, Vellayambalam (☎1-800/209-3030); KLM/Northwest, c/o Spencer Travel Services, Spencer Junction, MG Rd ☎0471/246 3531; Paramount Airways (airport ☎9995/411 664 or ☎9995/400 002); Qatar Airways, Bela Vista, TC 30/1403, near SBT, Nalumukku, Pettah ☎0471/391 9091 (airport ☎0471/250 2548); SriLankan Airlines, 1st Floor, Spencer Building, Palayam, MG Rd ☎0471/247 1815 (airport ☎0471/250 1140).

Banks and exchange A string of big banks along MG Rd – including HDFC, SBI, UTI and ICICI – have ATMs and change travellers' cheques and currency; there are additional ATMs next to the KTDC Tourist Reception Centre opposite the railway station, and immediately outside the station exit, next to the reservations hall. Thomas Cook has a foreign exchange counter at the airport and at its travel agency on the ground floor of the Soundarya Building (near the big Raymond's tailoring store), MG Rd (Mon–Sat 9.30am–6pm).

Dentist Kamala Dental Speciality Hospital, Sri Mulam Club Junction, Vazhuthacaud (☎0471/233 8420, Ⓦwww.kamaladental.com).

Hospitals SP Fort Hospital (☎0471/245 0540), just down the road from the Margi School in West Fort, has a 24hr casualty and specialist orthopaedic unit; the private Cosmopolitan Hospital, in Pattom (☎0471/244 8182) is also recommended.

Internet access Internet City on Manhalikulam Rd charges Rs20/hr and is convenient if you're staying in Thampanoor. There's also a tiny, more cramped cybercafé to the rear of the *KTDC Hotel Chaithram*'s lobby, next to the bus stand (Rs30/hr).

Photography The efficient Paramount Colour Lab on Ayurveda College Junction, MG Rd, has state-of-the-art digital printers, sells memory cards and will load data onto discs.

Moving on from Thiruvananthapuram

Thiruvananthapuram's **Beemapalli airport**, 6km southwest of the city, offers international and domestic flights from a rapidly expanding list of carriers, several of whom have offices downtown (see opposite). As the roads to Beemapalli were recently upgraded, it's a comfortable enough journey by auto-rickshaw. There's also a modern, a/c bus service that you can pick up from the roadside opposite the City bus stand in East Fort. Buses to **Kovalam** leave every twenty to thirty minutes from the opposite side of the road, just south of the same bus stand. For anywhere else, you'll have to head for the grimy KSRTC **Thampanoor bus stand**. Services to **Varkala** leave from here at irregular intervals from 7.25am – many of them are nail-bitingly slow, winding through dozens of villages and taking up to 2hr 30min instead of the 90min by the

Recommended trains from Thiruvananthapuram

The following trains are recommended as the fastest and/or most convenient from Thiruvananthapuram.

Destination	Name	No.	Departs	Total time
Alappuzha	*Netravati Express**	#6346	daily 10am	2hr 50min
Bengaluru (Bangalore)	*Bangalore Express*	#6525	daily 12.55pm	6hr
Chennai	*Chennai Mail**	#2624	daily 2.30pm	16hr 30min
Ernakulam/Kochi	*Kerala Express*	#2625	daily 11.15am	4hr 15min
Kanyakumari	*Kanyakumari Express*	#6381	daily 10am	2hr 15min
Kollam	*Kerala Express*	#2625	daily 11.15am	1hr
Kozhikode	*Mangalore Express**	#6347	daily 8.45pm	10hr
Madurai	*Anantapuri Express*	#6124	daily 4.20pm	6hr 40min
Mangalore	*Mangalore Express*	#6347	daily 8.45pm	14hr 30min
Mumbai	*Netravati Express***	#6346	daily 10am	30hr 40min

*via Kollam, Varkala, Kottayam and Ernakulam
**via Kollam, Ernakulam, Thrissur, Kozhikode and Kannur

"super-fast" buses that follow the highway. Heading **north** up the coast (to Kollam, Alleppey, Ernakulam or Thrissur), aim for the 6am or 5.30pm "super-deluxe a/c" specials – **tickets** for these and all other long-distance routes may be bought in advance at the reservations hatch on the main bus stand concourse (daily 6am–10pm). The Tamil Nadu bus company, TNSRTC, has its own counter on the same concourse. Numerous private bus companies also run interstate services; many of the agents are on Aristo Road near the *Greenland Lodging*.

Kerala's capital is well connected **by train** with other towns and cities in the country, although getting seats at short notice on long-haul journeys can be a problem. Make **reservations** as far in advance as possible from the efficient computerized booking office at the station (Mon–Sat 8am–2pm & 2.15–8pm, Sun 8am–2pm), or online (see p.42).

Kovalam and around

You have to envy the travellers who first discovered **KOVALAM** back in the 1970s. Before the appearance of the crowds and sunbeds that nowadays spill over the resort's quartet of beaches, not to mention the warren of hotels, shops and restaurants crammed into the palm groves behind them, this must have been a heavenly location. Four decades of unplanned development, however, have wrought havoc on the famous headland and its golden sand bays. Virtually every conceivable patch of dry ground behind the most spectacular of them, **Lighthouse Beach**, has been buried under concrete, along with most of the area's Keralan character.

With charter flights from Europe suspended, Kovalam feels decidedly down on its luck these days, dependent on an unlikely mix of hedonistic British fifty-somethings and middle-aged German and Scandinavian ayurveda tourists – although it is hoped that the construction of an off-shore **artificial reef** may attract surfers and thus reverse the decline. The good news for budget backpackers is that the slump has sent room rates plummeting.

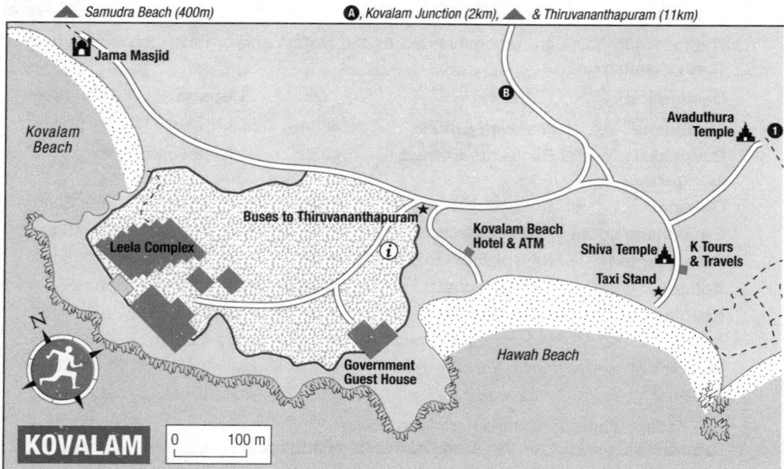

Arrival, information and transport

Buses from Thiruvananthapuram loop through the top of the village before coming to a halt outside the gates of the *Leela Kempinski*, on the promontory dividing Hawah and Kovalam beaches. If you don't intend to stay at this northern end of the resort, get down just past *Hotel Blue Sea* where the road bends – a lane branching to the left drops steeply downhill towards the top of Hawah Beach. The bus journey generally takes 30–45 minutes, but you can cover the 14km from Thiruvananthapuram more quickly by **auto-rickshaw** (Rs100–150) or **taxi** (Rs400–500).

Expect to be plagued by commission touts as you arrive; to avoid them, approach via the back paths. The friendly **tourist office** (daily 10am–5pm, closed Sun in low season; Ⓣ0471/248 0085, Ⓦwww.keralatourism.org), just inside the *Leela Kempinski* gates, close to where the buses pull in, stocks the usual range of glossy leaflets and can offer up-to-date advice about cultural events in the area.

Accommodation

Kovalam is chock-full of **accommodation** in all categories. Little of it could be considered great value by Indian standards, but since the demise of charter tourism in the resort, rates have taken a tumble, particularly mid-range, and you may be able to pick up some hefty last-minute discounts.

Amruthamgamaya (Amrutam) Panagodu, near Venganoor, 6km northeast Ⓣ0471/248 4600 or Ⓣ9048 813159, Ⓦwww.amruthamgamaya.com. A great option if you want to base yourself away from the busy coastal strip, but within striking distance of the beaches. It's essentially an ayurveda centre, but with comfortable accommodation in beautiful, large octagonal rooms overlooking a terraced garden. Veg meals are served on a high rooftop overlooking a sea of palm trees, and there's a gorgeous pool. Great value, but tricky to find: phone ahead for directions. ⑥

Blue Sea 100m before junction to Hawah Beach Ⓣ0471/248 1401 or Ⓣ9349 991992, Ⓦwww.hotelskerala.com/bluesea. Half-a-dozen quirky circular buildings in the rear garden of a grand double-fronted colonial-era mansion overlooking the main road above Hawah Beach. The rooms are spacious, cool and good value, with plenty of outside balcony space, and there's a pool. ⑤–⑥

Maharaju Palace 30m behind Lighthouse Beach Ⓣ0471/248 5320, Ⓦwww.maharajupalace.nl. This Dutch-owned guesthouse, a block in from the

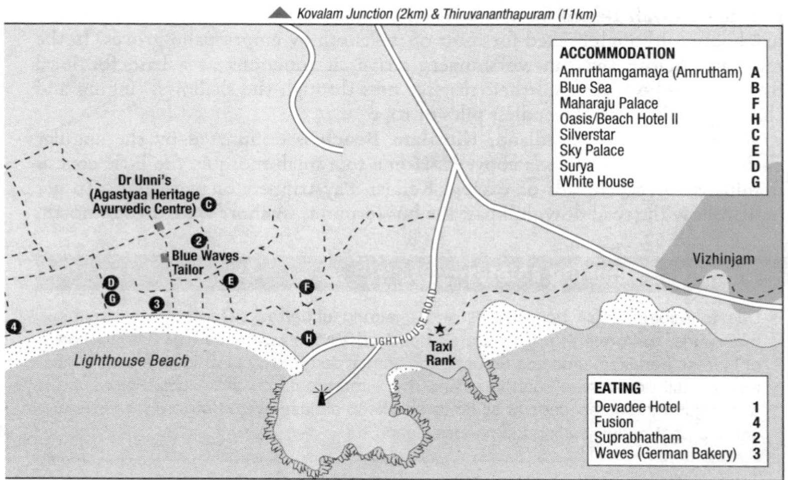

beach, offers boutique style at affordable rates. Occupying a modern house in a well-kept tropical garden, its marble-lined rooms are impeccably clean and decorated with Indian handicrafts and comfy cane chairs on the verandas. Breakfast is included in the price. ❺

Oasis/Beach Hotel II Lighthouse Beach ⓣ0471/248 6575, ⓦwww.thebeachhotel-kovalam.com. Stylish, German-run hotel at the quiet end of Lighthouse Beach. Its ten rooms (some a/c) all have big, sea-facing balconies, and are light, spacious and airy, with terracotta-tiled floors and block-printed cotton bedspreads Not to be confused with its sister concern, *Beach Hotel I*, below *Waves* restaurant, which isn't nearly as nice. ❻–❼

Silverstar Behind Lighthouse Beach ⓣ0471/248 2983 or ⓣ9895 673443, ⓦwww.silverstar-kovalam.com. Owned by a hospitable Swedish-Keralan couple, the *Silverstar* is hidden away in the palms a couple of hundred metres inland from the beach. Centred on a well-shaded, beaten-earth courtyard, the location is leafy and cool, and rooms are generous. Rates include breakfast, plus use of a small garden pool. ❺–❻

Sky Palace Lighthouse Beach ⓣ0471/248 7906 or ⓣ9745/841222. Basic but comfortable option two blocks back from the waterfront, just half a minute's walk from the beach. The very clean en-suite rooms, opening onto a sociable common veranda, are a good size, with gleaming floors and crisp white sheets. ❹

Surya Lighthouse Beach ⓣ0471/248 1012, ⓔkovsurya@yahoo.co.in. Professionally run budget travellers' guesthouse down a narrow lane from the seafront. It's secure and quiet, with pleasant rooms for the price (a/c and non-a/c); some of the verandas look straight onto adjacent buildings, but there's lots of space inside, with new beds and sound plumbing and electrics. If it's full, try the equally spruce *White House* (ⓣ0471/248 3388; ❹) next door. ❷–❸

The beaches

Kovalam consists of four distinct coves, each with markedly different characters. The largest and most developped, known for obvious reasons as **Lighthouse Beach**, is where most foreign tourists congregate. It takes about five minutes to walk from one end of the bay to the other, either along the sand or on the paved esplanade which fronts a long arc of hotels, guesthouses, handicraft shops and restaurants. A major sea-defences project was in full swing at the time of writing to create an **artificial reef** roughly 100m offshore (see p.1032). There's a red-and-white-striped **lighthouse** on the promontory at the southern end of the cove (daily 3–5pm; Rs25 [Rs10]; camera Rs20), when you can scale the 142 spiral steps and twelve ladder rungs to the observation platform.

Heading northwards from Lighthouse Beach, you round a small rocky headland to reach **Hawah Beach** (or **Eve's Beach**) – almost a mirror image of its busier neighbour, although backed for most of its length by empty palm groves. In the morning, before the sun-worshippers arrive, it functions as a base for local fishermen, who hand-haul their massive nets through the shallows, singing and chanting as they coil the endless piles of rope.

North of the next headland, **Kovalam Beach** is dominated by the angular chalets of the five-star *Leela* above it. Home to a small mosque, the little cove is dominated by coachloads of excited Keralan day-trippers on weekends. To get here, follow the road downhill past the bus terminus. A short walk further north,

Warning: swimming safety

Due to unpredictable rip currents and a strong undertow, especially during the monsoons, **swimming** from Kovalam's beaches is not always safe. The introduction of blue-shirted lifeguards has reduced the annual death toll, but at least a couple of tourists still drown here each year, and many more get into difficulties. Follow the warnings of the safety flags at all times and keep a close eye on children. There's a first-aid post midway along Lighthouse Beach.

Samudra Beach was until recently a European package tourist stronghold, though the large hotels clustered just beyond it, on the far side of a low, rocky headland, nowadays host mainly metropolitan Indian and Russian holiday-makers.

Eating, drinking and nightlife

Lighthouse Beach is lined with identikit cafés and restaurants specializing in **seafood**: you pick from displays of fresh fish, lobster, tiger prawns, crab and mussels. They are then weighed, grilled over a charcoal fire or cooked in a tandoor (traditional clay oven), and served with rice, salad or chips. Meals are **pricey** by Indian standards – typically around Rs300–500 per head for fish, and double that for lobster or prawns – and service is often painfully slow, but the food is generally very good and the ambience of the beachfront terraces convivial. For **breakfast** any number of cafés offer the usual brown bread, fruit salad and pancakes; you could also try a traditional Keralan breakfast at one of the local teashops near the bus stand. Freshly cooked, delicious Keralan rice-plate thali **"meals"** are served at the ramshackle *Devadee Hotel*, near the Avaduthura Devi temple behind Lighthouse beach, for only Rs40. It's a rough-and-ready place, and you'll have to squeeze onto narrow tables to eat, but the food is probably more hygienic than most of the stuff served on the beach.

Nightlife in Kovalam is sedate, revolving around the beachfront cafés. Beer and spirits are served in most places, albeit in discreet china teapots from under the table due to tight liquor restrictions.

Fusion Lighthouse Beach. Along with *Waves*, this is the funkiest place on Lighthouse Beach, with three innovative menus (Eastern, Western and fusion), served on a first-floor terrace overlooking the bay. Try the fish creole in orange vinaigrette with cumin potatoes, one of the Keralan seafood specialities, or home-made tagliatelle and chilli pesto. They also have a fine selection of drinks, and a hefty sound system playing Indo-Western music. Most mains Rs180.

Suprabhatham Near the *Silverstar*, next to a small Shiva temple. Simple, popular vegetarian café-restaurant in a well-shaded garden, where you can order inexpensive Indian breakfasts, fresh juices, lassis and shakes, as well as an extensive multi-cuisine menu: the "Bengali aubergine" and "chunky avocado salad" are popular specials. Staff tend to start downing stiff whisky-and-soda slammers around 10.30pm, after which the service and cooking degenerate rapidly.

Waves (German Bakery) Lighthouse Beach. This rooftop terrace, shaded by a high tiled canopy, functions as a laid-back café during the day, where you can order light meals, snacks, German cakes and delicious, freshly ground coffee. After sunset, its atmospheric designer lighting makes a great backdrop for more sophisticated cooking: the extravagantly outsized menus list Thai and Kerala seafood curries, lobster in vodka, fish steaks with sesame and coriander crust, or steamed prawns with lemon and chilli sauce. For dessert, go for the Malabar fruit flambée. Most mains Rs175–250.

Listings

Banks, exchange and ATMs There's an ATM in the *Kovalam Beach Hotel*, on the road leading up from the southern end of Hawah Beach; otherwise, the nearest are up at Kovalam Junction, 3km inland on the national highway (roughly Rs100 return in an auto-rickshaw), where both ICICI and Canara Bank have sub-branches. Pheroze Framroze, near the entrance to the *Leela* and bus stand, offers competitive rates for currency and travellers' cheques.

Internet access Countless places in the lanes behind Lighthouse Beach offer web browsing for Rs40/hr, though connection speeds are slow by Keralan standards.

Motorbike rental K Tours & Travel, behind Hawah Beach opposite the Shiva temple, offer Honda Kinetic 100cc scooters for Rs300–350/day. You'll need to leave your driver's licence or passport as security.

Ayurveda in Kerala

"Health tourism" is very much a buzz phrase in Kerala these days, and resorts such as Kovalam and Varkala are packed with places to de-stress and detox – the majority of them based on principles of **ayurveda medicine**. The Keralan approach to India's ancient holistic system of medicine has two distinct elements: first, the body is cleansed of toxins generated by imbalances in lifestyle and diet; secondly, its equilibrium is restored using herbal medicines, mainly in the form of plant oils applied using a range of different **massage** techniques. A practitioner's first prescription will often be a course of **panchakarma** treatment – a five-phase therapy during which harmful impurities are purged through induced vomiting, enemas, and the application of medicinal oils poured through the nasal cavity. Other less onerous components, tailored for the individual patient, may include: *dhara*, where the oils are blended with ghee or milk and poured on to the forehead; *pizhichi*, in which four masseurs apply different oils simultaneously; and, the weirdest looking of all, *sirovashti*, where the oils are poured into a tall, topless leather cap placed on the head. Alongside these, patients are prescribed special balancing foods, and given vigorous full-body massages each day.

Standards of both treatment and hygiene vary greatly between establishments, as do the prices. Woman travellers also sometimes complain of sexual harassment at the hands of opportunistic male masseurs; cross-gender massage is forbidden in ayurveda. Dodgy oils that can cause skin problems is another risk you might be exposed to at a backstreet clinic. Your best bet is to follow tips from fellow travellers and, if you're unsure, check the state of any treatment rooms in advance.

Tailors Dozens of little tailor shops are crammed in to the alleyways behind Lighthouse Beach. You can have light cotton clothes made to measure, or get them to copy your favourite garment from home, using a wide choice of coloured calico. Try Mr George of Blue Waves Tailoring (☎9388 676878), opposite *Seafood Corner* restaurant, who specializes in export-quality yoga clothing.

South of Kovalam

A tightly packed cluster of tiled fishermens' huts, **VIZHINJAM** (pronounced "Virinyam"), on the opposite (south) side of the headland from Lighthouse Beach, was once the capital of the Ay kings, the earliest dynasty in south Kerala. A number of simple small shrines survive from those times, and can be made the focus of a pleasant afternoon's stroll through coconut groves, best approached from the centre of the village rather than the coast road – brace yourself for the sharp contrast between hedonistic tourist resort and workaday fishing village.

Golden-sand beaches fringe the shore stretching **southwards from Vizhinjam**, interrupted only by the occasional rock outcrop and tidal estuary. This dramatic coastline, with its backdrop of thick coconut plantations, can appear peaceful compared with Kovalam, but it's actually one of the most densely populated corners of the state. Over the past decade, virtually every metre of land backing the prettiest stretches of coast has been bought up and built on. Even so, it's worth renting a scooter to explore the back lanes and more secluded beaches, where poor Christian fishing villages stand in surreal juxtaposition with luxury beach resorts and ayurveda spas. One of the most spectacular views hereabouts is from the top of the low headland at the north end of **Chowara** beach, 8km south of Kovalam, from which an endless stretch of sand sweeps to the horizon, scattered with hundreds of wooden boats.

Padmanabhapuram

Although now officially in Tamil Nadu, **PADMANABHAPURAM**, 63km southeast of Thiruvananthapuram, was the capital of Travancore between 1550 and 1750, and maintains its historic links with Kerala, from where it is still administered. For anyone with even a minor interest in local architecture, the small **Padmanabhapuram Palace** (Tues–Sun 9am–4.30pm; Rs50 [Rs20], cameras Rs20), is irresistible. With its exquisite wooden interiors, coconut-shell floors and antique furniture and murals, the building represents the high-water mark of regional building. Just **avoid weekends**, when the complex gets overrun with bus parties.

Frequent **buses** run to Padmanabhapuram along the main highway from Thiruvananthapuram and Kovalam. Hop on any service heading to Nagercoil or Kanyakumari and get off at **Thakkaly** (sometimes written Thuckalai).

Varkala

Devout Hindus have for hundreds, and possibly thousands, of years travelled to **VARKALA**, 54km north up the coast from Thiruvananthapuram, to immerse ashes of recently deceased relatives in the surf. Against a backdrop of superb, burnt-clay coloured cliffs, the ancient rituals are still performed daily on **Papanasam beach**, despite the presence just a stone's throw away of a fully fledged tourist resort, focused around the northern end of the bay.

The dramatic location, coupled with comparatively low-key development, makes Varkala a much more appealing place to spend a beach holiday than Kovalam. Tightly crammed along the rim of crumbling North Cliff, its row of restaurants and small hotels stare out across a vast sweep of ocean – a view that can seem almost transcendental after sunset, when a myriad tiny fishing boats light up their lanterns.

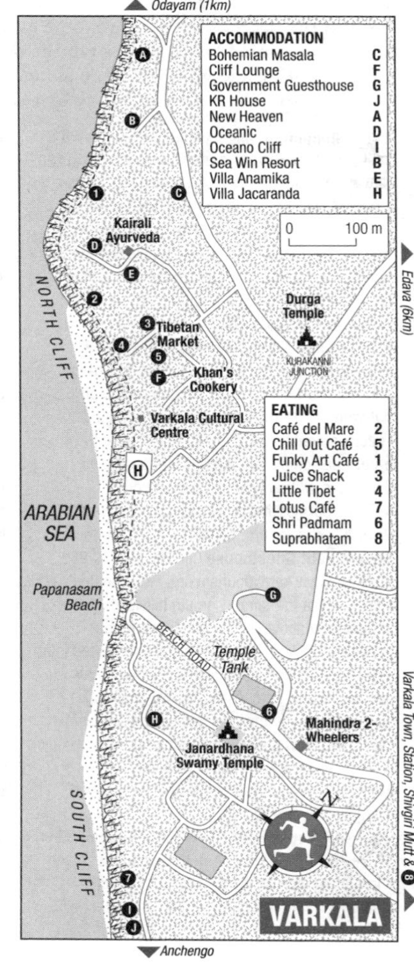

Arrival

Varkala beach lies 4km west of Varkala town, which is grouped around a busy market roundabout. The town's mainline railway station – Varkala-Sivagiri – is served by express and passenger **trains** from Thiruvananthapuram, Kollam and most other Keralan towns, and stands 500m north of this central junction. While some **buses** from Thiruvananthapuram's Thampanoor stand, and from Kollam to the north, continue on to within walking distance of the beach and clifftop area, most terminate in Varkala village, where you'll have to pick up an auto-rickshaw for the remaining five-minute ride (around Rs50–60) to the seashore.

If you can't get a direct bus to Varkala, take any "superfast" or "limited stop" bus running along the main NH-47 highway to **Kallamballam**, 15km east, from where slower local mini-bus services (Rs15), auto-rickshaws (Rs100–120) and taxis (Rs175–200) can take you to the beach.

Accommodation

Varkala offers a wide choice of **accommodation**. The hotels up on North Cliff are most people's first choice, with more inspiring views than those lining the road to the beach, but there are some even better options on quieter South Cliff if you don't mind being away from the thick of things. Auto-rickshaws from the railway station and village tank go as far as the helipad or round the back to North Cliff; South Cliff is also accessible by road.

Bohemian Masala Thiruvambadi, North Varkala ⓣ9287 215567 or ⓣ9567 441286, ⓦwww.thebohemianmasala.com. A chic hippie haven of 12 ethnic thatched huts moulded from mud, herbs and natural materials in a gorgeous garden. The interiors are a bit gloomy, but cool and beautifully styled using Indian handicrafts. Plus a funky earth-floored restaurant and in-house ayurveda massages. ❻

Cliff Lounge North Cliff ⓣ9895 633896, ⓦwww.clifflounge.com. The nicest mid-range place on North Cliff, set back behind the strip, but with uninterrupted sea views from its spacious double-bedded rooms. All have breezy balconies, and are pleasantly decorated with arty touches from your Keralan-German hosts, Sajeer and Elizabeth. Rs1000 extra for a/c. ❺–❻

Government Guesthouse Cliff Rd ⓣ0470/260 2227, ⓦwww.keralatourism.org. Five minutes' walk north of the temple, on the hillside immediately above the *Taj* hotel, this former maharaja's holiday palace has been converted into a guesthouse for visiting bigwigs, though it also opens its doors to tourists. The two enormous en-suite rooms in the original building are fantastic value. The others (all with large bathrooms) occupy a 1980s block and are much less inspiring – expect lots of creepy-crawlies and take a good mosquito net. ❶–❷

KR House South Cliff ⓣ0470/260 6400 or ⓣ9349 741998. A gem of a budget place – in a plum spot on South Cliff, with clean, modern, airy rooms, comfy mattresses, spotless bathrooms, and balconies overlooking a narrow garden running to the cliff edge, from where a flight of rock-cut steps drops steeply down to the beach. Away from the bustle of North Cliff, it's quiet, and run with great efficiency by the kindly Mr Ramchandran. ❷–❹

New Heaven North Cliff ⓣ0470/215 6388 or ⓣ9846 074818, ⓦwww.newheavenbeachresort.com. Neither new nor indeed heavenly, but well scrubbed, with decent-sized rooms and sea-facing common verandas, just a stone's throw from the shoreline. There's a popular yoga centre on the rooftop. ❹

Oceanic North Cliff ⓣ0470/302 1330 or ⓣ9846 096912, ⓔoceanicresidence@yahoo.co.in. Very pleasant rooms, with flowering climbers trailing from its balconies, close to the clifftop. Among the better-run, better-value budget options close to the strip. ❹

Oceano Cliff South Cliff ⓣ0470/309 4978, ⓦwww.oceanogate.com. Set on the highest stretch of secluded South Cliff, rooms here are light, cool, stylish and good value, with spectacular views from the sea-facing suites. You eat meals in little thatched gazebos on the cliff edge, from where steps lead to the beach via a plunge pool and spectacularly sited yoga platform. ❺–❻

Sea Win Resort Thiruvambadi, North Varkala ⓣ0470/260 1084 or ⓣ9747 902191. One of several swanky modern buildings to have sprung up at the end of the cliff on the back of Saudi riyals. The colour schemes are a bit off-beat, but the rooms are enormous, with quality beds, fridges, a spacious common veranda on one side and large private sitouts with cane furniture and sea views on the other. Very good value. ❺

Villa Anamika North Cliff ⓣ0470/260 0095, ⓦwww.villaanamika.com. A welcoming homestay, 200m from the cliff, run by Keralan artist Shobhana (aka "Chicku") and her German husband Frank. The five, variously priced rooms are light, airy, cool and attractive, with block-printed bedspreads and Shobhana's paintings. Guests get the run of a beautiful rear garden, and breakfasts feature home-made German bread and jams. ❺

Villa Jacaranda Temple Road West, South Cliff ⓣ0470/261 0296, ⓦwww.villa-jacaranda.biz. Bijou little guesthouse nestled amid the leafy lanes of the quiet South Cliff area, near the temple. Run by a refugee from the London rat race, it's small (with only four rooms) but perfectly formed, with relaxing sea blue and mauve colour schemes, cool wooden furniture, crisp white sheets, a fragrant garden and lily pond. Go for room 4 if it's vacant, which has expansive sea views from its own private terrace. ❽

The beaches and village

Known in Malayalam as Papa Nashini ("sin destroyer"), Varkala's beautiful white-sand **beach** has long been associated with ancestor worship. Devotees come here after praying at the ancient **Janardhana Swamy Temple**, reached by following the stepped path up the hill from the crossroads in the village centre, to bring the ashes of departed relatives for their "final rest". Non-Hindus are not permitted to enter the inner sanctum of the shrine, but you can peep over the perimeter walls from the encircling path – a pleasant stroll in the morning, when the temple elephant is led around the lanes on her exercise walk.

Backed by sheer red laterite cliffs, the coastline is imposingly scenic and the **beach** relatively relaxing – although its religious associations do ensure that attitudes to public nudity (especially female) are markedly less liberal than other coastal resorts in India. Western sun-worshippers are supposed to keep to the northern end of the beach (away from the main puja area reserved for the funerary rites) where they are serviced by a non-stop parade of local "hallo-pineapple-coconut?" vendors. Whistle-happy lifeguards ensure the safety of swimmers by enforcing the no-swim zones beyond the flags: the undercurrent is often strong, claiming lives every year. **Dolphins** are often seen swimming quite close to the coast, and, if you're lucky, you may be able to swim with them by arranging a ride with a fishing boat. Sea otters can also occasionally be spotted playing on the cliffs by the sea.

Few of Varkala's Hindu pilgrims make it as far as the **North Cliff area**, the focus of a well-established tourist scene. Bamboo and palm-thatch cafés, restaurants and souvenir shops jostle for space close to the edge of the mighty escarpments, which plunge vertically to the beach below in a dramatic arc. Several steep flights of steps cut into the rock provide shortcuts from the sand, and you can also get here via the gentler path that starts from the beachfront, or along the metalled road winding its way up from the village.

The **Varkala Cultural Centre** (ⓣ0470/608793), behind the *Sunrise* restaurant on North Clifftop, holds daily **kathakali** and **bharatanatyam** dance performances (make-up 5–6.45pm; performance 6.45–8.15pm; Rs150). Using live musicians instead of a recorded soundtrack, the show provides a pleasant and authentic enough introduction to the two types of dance, especially if you're not going to make it to Kochi (see p.1069). For anyone with a more serious interest in the classical arts, the centre also offers short courses on *kathakali* make-up and dance, *bharatanatyam*, devotional song (*bhajan*) and Carnatic percussion (*mridamgan*). In addition, the *Funky Arts Café* hosts free recitals of **Indian classical music**, with tabla, sitar and vocals, from 7.30pm most days. You can also take Indian **cookery** classes with local chef, Sajeer Khan, in a spruce little kitchen behind the *Chill Out Café* on North Cliff (Rs500 veg/Rs600 non-veg; ⓣ9895 633896).

Eating, drinking and nightlife

Varkala's clifftop **café-restaurants** specialize in locally caught seafood. (You'll also find plenty of Italian, Thai and Mexican items on offer – but they won't taste much like the real thing.) Prices are high, even by Keralan standards, and service painfully slow, but the superb location more than compensates. Although alcohol is available in just about all the clifftop places, due to Varkala's religious importance **beer** tends to be served in discreet teapots. Once the restaurants finish serving, **nightlife** is generally laid-back. After 10pm, a druggy scene takes over at cafés such as the *Funky Art* and nearby *Rock 'n' Roll*, and the *Chill Out Café* further down the clifftop, which all host low-key parties through the season, advertised by flyers.

Café del Mare North Cliff. The most professionally run place to eat on North Cliff, with an Italian coffee machine and polite, uniformed service. It offers the usual jack-of-all-trades menu, but they can actually cook everything on it. Made with imported cheeses, the Italian dishes are especially good (try the baked aubergine lasagne) and there are plenty of light bites and healthy salads. Most mains Rs200–300.

Chill Out Café North Cliff. Nicely set-up hippie hideaway, with lounge platforms and bolsters in a quiet palm garden just back from the cliff. An all-day café-restaurant, it comes alive after sunset, and has a lighter vibe than the *Funky Art*.

Juice Shack North Cliff. Fresh juices churned out by the larger-than-life, resplendently bearded Umesh and his team. They also do a range of healthy snacks, and host popular buffets (Rs250) on Weds & Sat (buy your ticket in advance).

Little Tibet North Cliff. Decorated with cheerful multi-coloured prayer flags and Buddhist *thangkas*, this large, bamboo and palm-thatch place, which catches the breezes at a prime cliff-edge location, whips up Mexican and Italian specialities, but most people come for the tasty Tibetan *momo* dumplings and *thukpa* soup (Rs100). Very friendly service and great views if you get a front-side table.

Lotus Café South Cliff. If you want to see what the North Cliff was like 15 or more years ago, head south to this German-run restaurant, which enjoys arguably the best position of any in Varkala. After a sundowner on the cliff edge, accompanied by a serene Indian classical soundtrack, you can order flavoursome Keralan and vegetarian north Indian dishes, or the day's specials from a good-value, three-course set menu (Rs400 per head); and there's delicious home-made ice cream for dessert.

Sri Padmam Temple Junction. This dingy-looking café on the temple crossroads serves freshly made, cheap and tasty south Indian veg food (including Rs35 "meals" at lunchtime). You can walk through the front dining room to a large rear terrace affording prime views of the tank – particularly atmospheric at breakfast time.

Suprabhatam Varkala village, 4km east of the beach. The cheapest and best pure-veg joint in Varkala, just off the main circle in a dining hall lined with coir mats. Their dosas and other fried snacks aren't great, but the lunchtime "unlimited" rice-plate "meals" (noon–3pm; Rs30), featuring the usual *thoran*, *avial*, dhal, *rasam*, buttermilk, curd, *papad* and red or white rice, pull in streams of locals and foreigners alike.

Listings

Banks and ATMs There are places to change money on North Cliff: City Tours and Travels, in front of the *Hilltop Beach Resort*, exchange currency and travellers' cheques, and offer advances on Visa cards for a small commission. The nearest ATMs are at the banks up in Varkala village, just off the crossroads.

Internet Centres in Varkala charge Rs40/hr for broadband surfing; connections are usually slow.

Motorcycles Mahindra2Wheelers (Mon–Sat 9.30am–5pm; ⓣ9846 701975), near Temple Junction; and Wheels of South India, a business of no fixed abode that works up in North Cliff (ⓣ9847 080412 or ⓣ9387 974698). The nearest petrol pump is up in Varkala town – 300m north of the main circle, on the left side of Station Road as you head towards the railway station.

Kollam (Quilon)

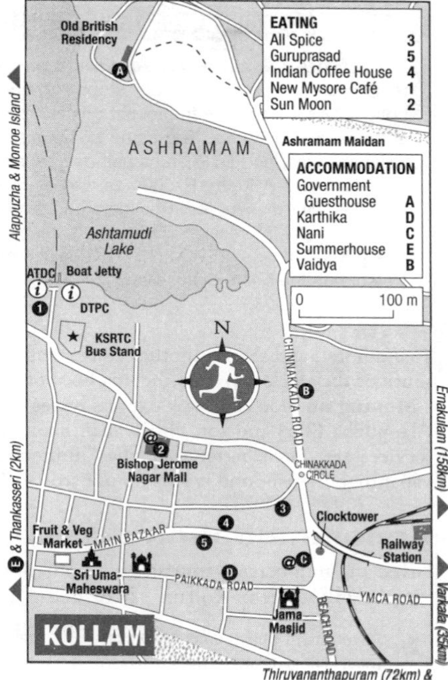

Sandwiched between the sea and Ashtamudi ("eight inlets") Lake, **KOLLAM** (pronounced "Koillam", and previously known as Quilon), was for centuries the focal point of the Malabar's spice trade. Phoenicians, Arabs, Greeks, Romans and Chinese all dispatched ships to the city, before the rise of Calicut and Cochin eclipsed the port. These days, it's a workaday market town and busy transport hub for the southern backwater region, with surprisingly few vestiges of its former prominence. Many travellers overnight here, however, en route to or from Alleppey on the excursion boats that leave each morning from its lakeside ferry jetty. To kill time in the evening, take a stroll through the town's traditional **bazaar**, with its old wooden houses and narrow backstreets lined by coir warehouses, rice stores and cashew traders. A short auto-rickshaw ride south, Kollam's **beach** provides a welcome escape if the heat and traffic of the centre get too much.

Of the few surviving colonial vestiges, the only one worth a detour is the former **British Residency**, a magnificent 250-year-old mansion on the shores of the lake, now used as a *Government Guesthouse* (see p.1042). Among the last monuments surviving in India from the earliest days of the Raj, it perfectly epitomizes the openness to indigenous influences that characterized the era, with typically Keralan gable roofs surmounting British pillared verandas. Much of the structure is falling apart, but you're welcome to visit: there are no set hours – just ask the manager if you can have a look around.

Arrival and information

Kollam's busy mainline **railway station** lies east of the clock-tower that marks the centre of town. Numerous daily trains run from Ernakulam and Thiruvananthapuram and beyond. The KSRTC **bus stand** is across town, near the boat jetty on Ashtamudi Lake. The **District Tourism Promotion Council** (DTPC) has a tourist office nearby (daily 9am–6pm; ⓣ0474/274 5625, ⓦwww.dtpckollam.com) at the **boat jetty** on Ashtamudi Lake, where you can book tickets for the daily tourist backwater cruises (see p.1042). The local **Alappuzha Tourism Development Council** office (ATDC; daily 7am–9pm; ⓣ0474/276 7440, ⓦwww.atdcalleppey.com), across the road, offers comparable services.

Exchange bureaux, ATMs and internet outlets can be found in the smart **Bishop Jerome Nagar shopping mall**, just south of the main road between the jetty and the clock-tower. The efficient ICICI bank also has a dependable ATM, next to the

Backwater cruises from Kollam

DTPC and ATDC run popular **cruises from Kollam to Alappuzha** (10.30am; 8hr; Rs300) on alternate days, with stops for lunch and tea. Tickets for both can be bought on the day from the tourist offices at the boat jetty on Ashtamudi Lake, and at some of the hotels. The same companies also offer exclusive overnight *kettu vallam* cruises, and DTPC runs half-day canal trips to nearby **Monroe Island** (daily 9am–1pm & 2–6.30pm; Rs500), as well as guided village tours taking in ayurveda factories, coir-makers, boat-builders and bird-nesting sites. You may find that you get a far better impression of backwater life by hopping between villages on the very cheap **local ferries**. DTPC and ATDC have timetables and route information; tickets are sold on the boats themselves.

Vaidya hotel; and there's another convenient, cheap internet place, Cyber.com, just south of the clock-tower on the first floor of Yeskay Towers, charging just Rs30/hr.

Moving on, you can book express **buses** (every 15min or so) for Kochi (3hr) via Alappuzha (2hr) and for Thiruvananthapuram (1hr 45min); as ever, the express services are much better than the "limited stop" buses. Note that most Thiruvananthapuram-bound **trains** do not stop in Varkala.

Accommodation

Given the numbers of tourists that pour through in season, **accommodation** is surprisingly scarce in Kollam – book ahead if you're arriving late.

Government Guesthouse Ashtamudi Lake, 2km northeast of town ⓣ0474/274 3620. Sleeping in this grand 250-year-old building, the former British Residency (see p.1041), feels like overnighting in a museum. Full of original furniture and fixtures, the rooms are gigantic for the price (go for an a/c one on the first floor if it's offered), but, as with most *Government Guesthouses*, you'll have to apply on spec as they rarely accept bookings – phone ahead to see if it's open, though (the place was closed for renovation at the time of writing). Breakfast and dinner available. ❶–❷

Karthika Off Main Rd, near the Jama Masjid mosque ⓣ0474/275 1831. Large, popular, central budget hotel offering a range of acceptably clean, plain rooms (some a/c) ranged around a courtyard that centres, rather unexpectedly, on three huge nude figures. ❷–❸

Nani Opposite the clock-tower ⓣ0474/275 1141, ⓦwww.hotelnani.com. Kollam's most stylish hotel, in a quirky, red-brick, Keralan-gabled tower block near the railway station. The beautifully furnished standard rooms (Rs1200 non-a/c; Rs1900 a/c) are the real bargain, though couples might appreciate the extra space in the "executive" room. ❺–❼

Summerhouse Thirumallawaram and Thankasseri ⓣ0474/279 4518 or ⓣ9895 662839, ⓔcontactsummerhouse@hotmail.com. Run by the amiable Mr Shashi, this trio of suburban homestays offers simple, characterful accommodation on the northwestern edge of town near, or next to, the sea. Best is "No.3", a cosy wood cabin with just three rooms (Rs600/day), opening onto a wonderful veranda enfolded by palm trees, slap on the sea wall. Also next to the waves, "No.1" is older and more spartan. "No.2", a former family house 5min walk from the shore in a leafy residential area, is large enough for a group and has its own garden. ❹

Vaidya Residency Rd, Chinnakkada ⓣ0474/274 8432, ⓦwww.hotelvaidyakollam.com. If you want somewhere comfortable to crash for a night, and aren't fussy about the view, give this business-oriented place on the north side of town a try. The characterless rooms have no balconies and zero outlook, but they're clean, and huge for the price. The standard ones (referred to as "deluxe") are the best value. ❺–❼

Eating

Most of Kollam's hotels and guesthouses provide meals, but if you'd prefer to eat out, try one of the following **restaurants** in the centre of town.

All Spice Off Chinakkada Circle. This determinedly Western, brightly lit fast-food joint, above a bakery, is where the town's middle classes come for family evenings out, and where foreign tourists come to get away from Indian food. The a/c certainly hits the spot, but the burgers, pizzas and fried chicken turn out to be less appealing than the north Indian and Chinese dishes (Rs125–175).

Guruprasad Main bazaar. Cramped and sweaty, but wonderfully old-school "meals" on the market's main street: blue-and-cream walls, framed ancestral photos and Hindu devotional art provide the typical backdrop for pukka pure-veg rice plates and *udipi*-style snacks.

Indian Coffee House Main bazaar. Typical *ICH* fare – limp dosas, oily biriyanis, toast, omelettes, pot-chai and filter coffee – served on regulation chipped china by waiters wearing pleated *pugris*, at the regulation rock-bottom rates. It's worth eating here for the dining hall alone – a real period piece.

New Mysore Café Boat jetty, opposite KSRTC bus stand. This is the most popular of the "meals" joints around the bus stand and boat jetty area, serving delicious "all-you-can-eat" rice plates for just Rs30 at lunchtime, then the usual *udipi* snacks through the rest of the day.

Sun Moon Top Floor, Bishop Jerome Nagar Mall ⓣ0474/301 3000. Kollam's best food – traditional Keralan *karimeen pollichathu* (white fish steamed in banana leaf) and masala-fried calamari, as well as Continental dishes and a big multi-cuisine buffet – served in a cool, a/c rooftop restaurant against a backdrop of carved stone temple brackets. Great panoramic views. Rs300 for three courses.

Alappuzha (Alleppey)

From the mid-nineteenth century, Alappuzha (or "Alleppey" as it was known in British times) served as the main port for the backwater region. Spices, coffee, tea, cashews, coir and other produce were shipped out from the inland waterways to the sea via its grid of canals and rail lines. Tourist literature loves to dub the town as "the Venice of the East", but in truth the comparison does few favours to Venice. Apart from a handful of colonial-era warehouses and mansions, and a derelict pier jutting into the sea from a sun-blasted **beach**, few monuments survive, while the old canals enclose a typically ramshackle Keralan market of bazaars and noisy traffic.

That said, Alappuzha makes a congenial place to while away an evening en route to or from the backwaters. Streams of visitors do just that during the winter season, for the town has become Kerala's pre-eminent **rice boat cruising** hub, with an estimated four hundred *kettu vallam* moored on the fringes of nearby Vembanad and Punnamada lakes. To cash in on the seasonal influx, the local tourist offices lay on excursion boats for day-trips, while in mid-December the sands lining the west end of town host a popular **beach festival**, during which cultural events and a procession of fifty caparisoned elephants are staged with the dilapidated pier as a backdrop.

Alappuzha's really big day, however, is the second Saturday of August, in the middle of the monsoon, when it serves as the venue for one of Kerala's major spectacles – the **Nehru Trophy snake boat race**. This event, first held in 1952, is based on the traditional Keralan enthusiasm for racing magnificently decorated longboats, their raised rears designed to resemble the hood of a cobra. Each boat carries 25 singers, and 100 to 130 enthusiastic oarsmen power the craft along, all rowing to the rhythmic *vanchipattu* ("song of the boatman"). There are a number of prize categories, including one for the women's race; sixteen boats compete for each prize in knockout rounds. Similar races can be seen at Aranmula and at Champakulam, 16km by ferry from Alappuzha. The ATDC office will be able to tell you the dates of these other events, which change every year.

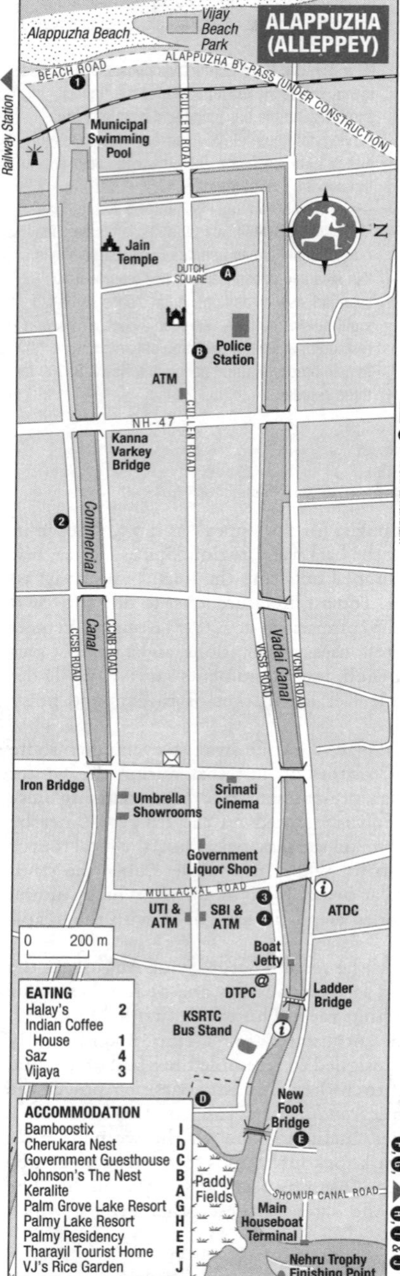

Arrival and information

The KSRTC **bus stand**, served by regular buses to and from Kollam, Kottayam, Thiruvananthapuram, Ernakulam and most other major Keralan towns, stands at the northeast edge of town. Close to its north exit, the main boat jetty on **Vadai Canal** is where the daily tourist ferry to and from Kollam, and local boat connections with Kottayam, arrive and depart. The **railway station**, on the main Thiruvananthapuram–Ernakulam line, lies 3km southwest across town, on the far side of Alappuzha's main waterway, **Commercial Canal**.

The town has several rival **tourist departments**, all of them eager to offer advice and book you onto their respective houseboat tours. The most conveniently situated – at the jetty itself on VCSB (Vadai Canal South Bank) Road – are the DTPC **tourist reception centre** (daily 9am–5pm; ⓣ0477/225 1796) and adjacent Kerala Tourism office (Mon–Sat 10am–5pm; ⓣ0477/226 0722, ⓦwww.keralatourism.org). On the opposite side of the canal on the corner of Mullackal and Vadai Canal North (VCNB) Road, ATDC's main information office (daily 8am–8pm; ⓣ0477/224346 or ask for "Shambhu" on ⓣ9895 010833, ⓦwww.atdcalleppey.com) is tucked away on the second floor of the Municipal Shopping Complex. Both ATDC and DTPC sell tickets for their ferries, backwater cruises and charter boats, and can help you fathom the intricacies of local ferry timetables. Though many of the houseboat booking agencies dotted around town call themselves "tourist information offices" – they're nothing of the kind; their sole purpose is to sell their cruises.

You can **change money** at the efficient UTI bank on Mullackal Road (Mon–Sat 9.30am–4.30pm). Both it and the State Bank of India opposite have reliable ATMs. **Internet** access is widely available for Rs30–40 per hour, with several outlets along the road facing the boat jetty; Mailbox, on VCSB Road, five minutes' walk west of Mullackal Road, boasts the town's fastest connection.

Accommodation

The choice of **places to stay** in the town centre is fairly uninspiring, but there are some great **homestay** possibilities if you're willing to travel to the outskirts and pay a little more, along with some good options a taxi-ride away, hidden in the surrounding **backwaters** and further up the coast.

Nearly everywhere, whatever its bracket, has some kind of tie-in with a houseboat operator: good-natured encouragement tends to be the order of the day rather than hard-sell tactics, but you may be able to negotiate a reduction on your tariff if you do end up booking a backwater trip. Whenever you come, and wherever you choose to stay, brace yourself for clouds of **mosquitoes**.

Bamboostix Thayyil Kayal, 2km northeast of town by boat ⓣ9995 821015 or 9995 821014, ⓦwww.istay.in. Australian-owned backpackers' lodge, only accessible by water. Set on a narrow strip of land facing Vembanad Lake, it consists of a row of bamboo and cement structures interconnected by metal walkways, with raised lounge platforms shaded by giant palm-thatch canopies. Accommodation is in 4- and 6-bed dorms (Rs550/650 per bed, or Rs1050/1150 full board). Phone ahead for their Rs50 launch transfer. ❸

Cherukara Nest 9/774 Cherukara Building ⓣ0477/225 1509 or ⓣ9947 059628. Nineteenth-century "heritage" home, on a quiet canal road just a short walk around the corner from the KSRTC bus stand. Breakfast is served in an old courtyard under a huge mango tree. Eco-friendly houseboat cruises are a sideline. ❹–❺

Government Guesthouse Next door to *KTDC Yatri Niwas*, NH-47 ⓣ0477/224 6504. Set up for the benefit of visiting officials, but they'll accommodate tourists if there are vacancies (though you'll probably have to call in person on the day). The rooms are plain and a touch institutional, but fantastic for the price (Rs250 non-a/c; Rs520 for much nicer a/c), with big, clean bathrooms. ❶–❸

Johnson's The Nest Lalbagh, Cullen Rd, 2km west of the centre ⓣ0477/224 5825 or ⓣ9961 466399, ⓦwww.johnsonskerala.com. Friendly, sociable homestay on a quiet suburban street, popular mainly with young backpackers. Its five themed en-suite rooms are large and most have funky little sitouts. Money exchange, laundry and meals available. ❷–❹

Keralite Vadakekalam House, north of Dutch Square ⓣ0477/224 3569 or ⓣ9847 073405, ⓔalice_thomas2150@hotmail.com. Opening onto a broad sand courtyard filled with pot plants, the heart of this delightful 100-year-old house is a high-ceilinged salon where hostess Alice Thomas serves traditional Syrian-Christian meals under the watchful eye of ancestral portraits. Comfortable antique beds furnish the rooms, which have lots of period atmosphere; some lack en-suite bathrooms – hence the bargain rates. No sign, so phone for entry. ❹

Palm Grove Lake Resort Punnamada Kayal, 3.5km north of boat jetty ⓣ0477/223 5004 or ⓣ9446 430434, ⓦwww.palmgrovelakeresort.com. Near where the canal meets Punnamada Lake, this relaxed resort overlooks the water – a perfect, tranquil spot from which to watch the snake boat races. Shaded by areca and coconut palms, its pretty cottages have gabled tile roofs, private outdoor showers and sitouts opening onto the garden. ❺–❻

Palmy Lake Resort Thathampally, 2km north of boat jetty ⓣ0477/223 5938 or ⓣ9447 667888, ⓦwww.palmyresort.com. Spacious, neatly painted red-tiled "cottages" (a/c and non-a/c), grouped behind a modern family home on the northeastern limits of town. Despite the name, it isn't actually on the lake, but offers exceptional value for money. You get loads of space for the price: all rooms have private pillared verandas opening onto a restful garden. Phone ahead for free pick-up. Internet available. ❹

Palmy Residency Off VCNB Rd, near main houseboat terminal ⓣ0477/223 5938 or ⓣ9447 667888, ⓦwww.palmyresort.com. Up a sidestreet 2mins' walk from Main Canal, this well-run guesthouse (an offshoot of the *Palmy Lake Resort*) is in a quiet neighbourhood. It has six rooms – the cheaper ones are great no-frills options, with mozzie nets and

Kuttanad: the backwaters of Kerala

One of the most memorable experiences for travellers in India is the opportunity to take a boat journey on the **backwaters of Kerala**. The area known as **Kuttanad** stretches for 75km from Kollam in the south to Kochi in the north, sandwiched between the sea and the hills. This bewildering labyrinth of shimmering waterways, composed of lakes, canals, rivers and rivulets, is lined with dense tropical greenery and preserves rural Keralan lifestyles that are completely hidden from the road.

The region's bucolic way of life has long fascinated visitors. And the ever entrepreneurial Keralans were quick to spot its potential as a visitor destination – particularly after it was discovered that foreigners and wealthy tourists from India's cities were prepared to pay vast sums in local terms to explore the area aboard converted **rice barges**, or *kettu vallam*. Since its inception two decades ago, the houseboat tour industry has grown exponentially in both size and sophistication, and has brought with it major environmental drawbacks as well as increased prosperity. You can, however, explore this extraordinary region in lower-impact ways, too.

Tourist cruises

The most popular excursion in the Kuttanad region is the full-day journey between **Kollam** and **Alappuzha**. All sorts of private hustlers offer their services, but the principal boats are run on alternate days by the ATDC and the DTPC (see p.1041). The double-decker boats leave from both Kollam and Alappuzha daily, departing at 10.30am (10am check-in); tickets (Rs300) can be bought in advance or on the day at the ATDC/DTPC counters, other agents and some hotels. Both companies make three stops during the eight-hour journey, including one for lunch, and another at the **Mata Amritanandamayi Math** at Amritapuri – ashram of Kerala's famous "hugging saint", Amma – around three hours north of Kollam. Although this is by far the main backwater route, many tourists find it too long, with crowded decks and intense sun. There's also something faintly embarrassing about being cooped up with a crowd of fellow tourists, madly photographing any signs of life on the water or canal banks, while gangs of kids scamper alongside the boat screaming "one pen, one pen". One alternative is to **charter** a four- or six-seater motorboat, which you can do through DTPC and ATDC for around Rs300/hr. Slower, more cumbersome double-decker country boats are also available for hire from Rs250 per hour.

Village tours and canoes

Quite apart from their significant environmental impact, most houseboats are too wide to squeeze into the narrower inlets connecting small villages. To reach these more idyllic, remote areas, therefore, you'll need to charter a punted **canoe**. The slower pace means less distance gets covered in an hour, but the experience of being so close to the water, and those who live on it, tends to be correspondingly more rewarding. You'll also find more formal "**village tours**" advertised across the Kuttanad area, tying together trips to watch coir makers, rice farmers and boat builders in action with the opportunity to dine in a traditional Keralan village setting.

Kettu vallam (houseboats)

Whoever dreamed up the idea of showing tourists around the backwaters in old rice barges, or **kettu vallam**, could never have imagined that, two decades on, six hundred or more of them would be chugging around Kuttanad waterways. These **houseboats**, made of dark, oiled jackwood with canopies of plaited palm thatch and coir, are big business, and almost every mid- and upmarket hotel, guesthouse and "heritage homestay" seems to have one. Nearly five hundred work out of Alappuzha alone, the flashiest fitted with a/c rooms, wide-screen plasma TVs on their teak sun decks, imported wine in their fridges and Jacuzzis that bubble away through the night. One grand juggernaut (called the *Vaikundan*, based near Amma's ashram in Kollam district) holds ten bedrooms and won't slip its lines for less than Rs100,000 ($2200). At the opposite end of the scale are rough-and-ready transport barges with gut-thumping diesel engines, cramped bedrooms and minimal washing facilities.

What you end up paying for your cruise will depend on the **size** and **quality** of the boat and its fittings; the number and standard of the **bedrooms**; and, crucially, the **time of year**. Rates double over Christmas and New Year, and halve off-season during the monsoons. In practice, Rs6000–15,000 is the usual bracket for a trip on a two-bedroom, a/c boat with a proper bathroom, including three meals, in early December or mid-January. The cruise should last a minimum of 22 hours, though don't expect to spend all of that on the move: running times are carefully calculated to spare gas. From sunset onwards you'll be moored at a riverbank, probably on the outskirts of the town where the trip started.

You'll save quite a lot of cash, and be doing the fragile ecosystem a big favour, by opting for a more environmentally friendly **punted** *kettu vallam*. This was how rice barges were traditionally propelled, and though it means you travel at a more leisurely pace, the experience is silent (great for wildlife-spotting) and altogether more relaxing.

Houseboat operators work out of **Kollam** and **Kumbakonam**, but most are in **Alappuzha**, where you'll find the lowest prices – but also the worst congestion on more scenic routes. Spend a day shopping around for a deal (your guesthouse or hotel-owner will be a good first port of call) and always check the boat over beforehand. It's also a good idea to get the deal fixed on paper before setting off, and to withhold a final payment until the end of the cruise in case of arguments.

Recommended operators include: **Lakes and Lagoons** (ⓣ0477/223 6181, ⓦwww.lakeslagoons.com); **River Goddess Houseboats** (UK ⓣ01726/844 867, India ⓣ9847 846441), ⓦwww.rivergoddesshouseboats.com); and **the Nest Houseboat** (ⓣ0477/2245825 or ⓣ9961 466399, ⓦwww.johnsonskerala.com).

Local ferries

Kettu vallam may offer the most comfortable way of cruising the backwaters, but you'll get a much more vivid experience of what life is actually like in the region by jumping on one of the local ferries that serve its towns and villages. Particularly recommended is the trip from **Alappuzha to Kottayam** (dep 7.30am, 9.35am, 11.30am & 5.15pm; 2hr 30min; Rs10), which winds across open lagoons and narrow canals, through coconut groves and islands. Arrive early to get a good place with uninterrupted views.

There are numerous other local routes that you can jump on and off, though working your way through the complexities of the timetables and Malayalam names can be difficult without the help of the tourist office. Good places to aim for from Alappuzha include Neerettupuram, Kidangara, and Chambakulam; all are served by regular daily ferries, but you may have to change boats once or twice along the way, killing time in local cafés and toddy shops (all of which adds to the fun, of course). Whatever service you opt for, take a **sun hat** and **plenty of water**.

Threats to the ecosystem

The **African moss** that often carpets the surface of the narrower waterways may look attractive, but it is a symptom of the many serious **ecological problems** currently affecting the region, whose population density ranges from between two and four times that of other coastal areas in southwest India. This has put growing pressure on land, hence a greater reliance on fertilizers, which eventually work their way into the water causing the build-up of moss. Illegal land reclamation, poses the single greatest threat to this fragile ecosystem. In a little over a century, the total area of water in Kuttanad has been reduced by two-thirds, while mangrove swamps and fish stocks have been decimated by pollution and the spread of towns and villages around the edges of the backwater region. Tourism adds to the problem, as the film of oil from motorized ferries and houseboats spreads through the waters, killing yet more fish, which has in turn led to a reduction of over fifty percent in the number of bird species found in the region.

attached bathrooms. Unbeatable value in the budget bracket. ❷

Tharayil Tourist Home Shornur Canal Rd, Thathampally ⓣ0477/223 3543 or ⓣ9447 505524, ⓦwww.tharayiltouristhome.com. In a 1990s building on the edge of town, this modest, family-run guesthouse soaks up most of the overspill from nearby *Sona* (see below). It has ten simple a/c and non-a/c rooms; they're spacious, brightly coloured, well ventilated and nicely furnished. If it's full, try *Sona* (ⓣ0477/223 5211, ⓦwww.sonahome.com; ❹–❺). ❸–❺

VJ's Rice Garden Pallathurthy, 6km southeast of Alappuzha ⓣ0477/270 2566 or ⓣ9446 118931, ⓦwww.ricegardenkerala.com. If you'd like to be marooned in the backwaters but can't afford any of the heritage homestays, give this quirky little guesthouse a try. Its rooms are basic, but occupy a dreamy location on a slither of riverbank backed by miles of rice fields. Access is by canoe. ❹

Eating

Aside from the **restaurants** listed below, most of Alappuzha's homestays and guesthouses provide meals for guests, usually delicious, home-cooked Keralan cooking that's tailored for sensitive Western palates.

Halay's CCSB Rd. Proper Keralan-Muslim restaurant that's been an Alleppey institution for generations. Much of its old-world character disappeared in a recent facelift, but the food's as delicious as ever. Nearly everyone comes for their blow-out chicken biriyanis (Rs100), which you eat with the legendary house date pickle. It's also good for spicy lamb curries (Rs60–70), hot *parottas* and Malabari-style *pathiri*.

Indian Coffee House Beach Rd. The usual smudged cotton uniforms and insipid *ICH* menu of *udipi* snacks and rice-based meals, but under a traditional pagoda-shaped shelter on the beachfront. The food may not be up to much, but the coffee is OK and the location pleasantly breezy in the afternoons.

Saz VCSB Rd, near Ladder Bridge. This no-frills non-veg place on Vadai Canal does a roaring trade at lunchtime with its fish-curry rice plate "meals" (Rs40), while in the evenings half the tourist population of Alappuzha pours in for the succulent flame-grilled barbecue and tandoori chicken, served at a brisk pace by waiters in black bow ties. They also have a full-on kebab counter outside, and offer a range of typical Kuttanadi "specials". It's a bit grubby, but hygienic enough and cheap, with most mains Rs100–150.

Vijaya VCSB Rd. Great little veg- and non-veg Keralan café serving tasty, freshly prepared thalis (Rs40) at lunchtime, and *udipi* snacks and biriyanis the rest of the day, served in neat white china bowls. It's cheap and popular, and much cleaner than the competition.

Moving on from Alappuzha

The filthy KSRTC **bus** stand, on the east side of town and a minute's walk from the boat jetty, is served by regular buses to most towns in the region. For Fort Cochin, catch any of the fast Ernakulam services along the main highway and get down at **Thoppumpady** (7km south), from where local buses run the rest of the way.

Recommended trains from Alappuzha

The following trains are recommended as the **fastest** and/or **most convenient** from Alappuzha.

Destination	Name	No.	Departs	Total time
Ernakulam/Kochi	*Jan Shatabdi Express*	#2076	daily 8.15am	1hr
	Alleppey–Chennai Express	#6042	daily 4.05pm	1hr 15min
Thiruvananthapuram	*Ernakulam–Trivandrum Express*	#6341	daily 7am	2hr 45min
	Jan Shatabdi Express	#2075	daily 6.20pm	2hr 35min

ATDC and DTPC tourist **boats** travel regularly to **Kollam** (see p.1046). From the jetty just outside the KSRTC bus stand, much cheaper local **ferries** travel to **Kottayam** (see below) and a constellation of satellite villages in the backwaters. Regular services run to Champakulam, where you pick up less frequent boats to Neerettupuram and Kidangara, and back to Alappuzha again. This round route ranks among Kuttanad's classic trips, but you'll need some help from one of the tourist offices to make sense of the timetables. Timetables are viewable online at the State Water Transport Department's website (Ⓦwww.swtd.gov.in).

As the backwaters prevent **trains** from continuing directly south beyond Alappuzha, only a few major daily services and a handful of passenger trains depart from the railway station, 3km southwest of the jetty. For points further north along the coast, take the *Jan Shatabdi Express* and change at Ernakulam, as the afternoon Alleppey–Cannanore Express (#6307), which runs as far as **Kozhikode** and **Kannur**, arrives at those destinations rather late at night. It is, however, a good bet if you want to get to Thrissur.

Kottayam and around

Some 76km southeast of Kochi and 37km northeast of Alappuzha, **KOTTAYAM** is a compact, busy Keralan town strategically located between the backwaters and the mountains of the Periyar Wildlife Sanctuary. For Keralans, it's synonymous with **money**, both old and new. The many **rubber plantations** around it, introduced by British missionaries in the 1820s, have for more than a century formed the bedrock of a booming local economy, most of it controlled by landed **Syrian Christians**.

The presence of two thirteenth-century churches on a hill 5km northwest of the centre (accessible by auto-rickshaw) attests to the area's deeply rooted Christian heritage. Two eighth-century Nestorian stone crosses with Palavi and Syriac inscriptions, on either side of the elaborately decorated altar of the **Valliapalli** ("big") church, are among the earliest solid traces of Christianity in India. The visitors' book contains entries from as far back as the 1890s, including one by the Ethiopian king, Haile Selassie, and a British viceroy. The apse of the nearby **Cheriapalli** ("small") church is covered with lively paintings, thought to have been executed by a Portuguese artist in the sixteenth century. If the doors are locked, ask for the key at the church office (9am–1pm & 2–5pm).

A twenty-minute bus ride west of Kottayam brings you to the shores of **Vembanad Lake**, where the **Kumarakom Bird Sanctuary** (daily dawn to dusk; Rs45), spread over a cluster of islands in the lagoon, forms the focus of a line of ultra-luxurious resorts on the water's edge. Between November and March, the wealthy metropolitan Indian tourists who holiday here are joined by flocks of migratory birds, though not in large enough numbers to entice non-specialists. Birds, or representations of them, also feature prominently in the area's most bizarre visitor attraction, the **Bay Island Driftwood Museum** (daily 10am–6pm; Rs50; Ⓦwww.bay-island-museum.com), just off the main road on the outskirts of Kumarakom village, in which lumps of driftwood collected by a former schoolteacher are exhibited in an idiosyncratic gallery.

Another possible day-trip from Kottayam is the magnificent Mahadeva (Shiva) temple at **ETTUMANUR**, 12km north on the road to Ernakulam, whose entrance porch holds some of Kerala's most celebrated medieval **wall paintings**. The most spectacular depicts Nataraja (Shiva) executing a cosmic *tandava* dance, trampling evil in the form of a demon underfoot. Foreigners can enter the temple for free, but you'll need to buy a camera ticket (Rs20; video Rs50) from the counter on the left of the main gateway.

Arrival and information

Kottayam's KSRTC **bus stand**, 500m south of the centre on TB Road (not to be confused with the private stand for local buses on MC Road), is an important stop on routes to and from major towns in South India. Four of the frequent buses to Kumily/Periyar (3–4hr) continue daily on to Madurai in Tamil Nadu (7hr), and there are regular services to Thiruvananthapuram, Kollam and Ernakulam. The **railway station**, 2km north of the centre, sees a constant flow of traffic between Thiruvananthapuram and points north, while **ferries** from Alappuzha and elsewhere dock at the weed-clogged jetty, 2km south of town. For details of backwater trips, see p.1046.

DTPC maintain a tiny **tourist office** at the jetty (daily 9am–5pm; ⓣ0481/256 0479). The best place to **change money** is the Canara Bank on KK Road, which also has one of several **ATMs** around the main square. **Internet** facilities are available at Intimacy (Rs30/hr), also on KK Road, just north of the KSRTC bus stand.

Accommodation and eating

Accommodation in Kottayam is limited for a town of its size. Those travellers that do pause here tend to do so in one of the resorts or homestays in the surrounding area, though there are a handful of places in town that are fine for a night.

For a delicious, freshly cooked pure-veg **thali** or *udipi* snack, head for *Anand* at the *Anand Lodge*, KK Road, just off the main square – the a/c family hall is the more relaxing of the two wings and meals only cost Rs10 more. The *Homestead*'s popular restaurant, *Meenachil*, provides quality non-veg Keralan food, such as Kuttanadi chicken curry, plus Punjabi-style tandoori, Chinese duck dishes and set Keralan "meals" (Rs50 veg, Rs60 non-veg).

Ambassador KK Rd ⓣ0481/256 3293. Solid, old-fashioned economy place on the northeast side of town that's worn around the edges but well scrubbed. A/c costs only Rs75 extra, but the air coolers are noisy. ❷–❹

Arcadia TB Rd ⓣ0481/256 9999, ⓦwww.arcadiahotels.net. The town's top hotel, occupying its tallest building – a towering, white, angular monster block just south of the centre. Its rooms look much nicer from the inside, however, and are very good value (especially the "standard doubles"); there's also a fantastic rooftop pool on the 14th floor, as well as a restaurant (*Déja Vu*) and bar (*Fahrenheit*). ❻–❼

Akkara Mariathuruthu ⓣ0481/251 6951, ⓦwww.akkara.in. Set on a bend in the Meenachil River, 5km northwest of Kottayam, this homestay is a model backwater B&B, offering an idyllic, typically Keralan setting, traditional architecture, comfortable rooms full of 1930s–50s period furniture, and wonderful Syrian-Christian cuisine. Access is by road or dugout canoe. ❼–❽

GK's Riverview Thekkakarayil, Kottaparambil, near Pulikkuttssery, 4km by water from Kumarakom ⓣ0481/259 7527 or ⓣ9447 197527, ⓦwww.gkhomestay-kumarakom.com. Award-winning homestay, buried deep in the watery wilds between Kottayam and Kumarakom. The accommodation comprises four comfortable guest rooms in a separate block behind a family home, overlooking paddy fields. Phone ahead from Kottayam to be picked up. ❻

Periyar and around

One of the largest national parks in India, the **Periyar Wildlife Sanctuary** occupies 777 square kilometres of the Cardamom Hills region of the Western Ghats. The majority of its visitors come in the hope of seeing **wild elephants** – or even a rare glimpse of a **tiger** – grazing the shores of the reservoir at the heart of the reserve. Safari boats daily ferry hundreds of day-trippers around this sprawling, labyrinthine lake, where sightings are most likely at the height of the dry season in

April. However, for the rest of the year, wildlife is less abundant than you might expect given Periyar's overwhelming popularity.

Just a few hours by road from the Keralan coastal cities, and Madurai in Tamil Nadu, it ranks among India's busiest reserves, attracting thousands of visitors over holiday periods. The park's ageing infrastructure, however, has struggled to cope with the recent upsurge in numbers. Just how overburdened facilities had become was horribly revealed in September 2009 when an excursion boat capsized on the lake, killing 45 tourists. Since the so-called **Thekkady disaster**, strict restrictions have been imposed, but the lake safari experience hasn't improved; most foreign visitors leave disappointed, not merely with the park, but also its heavily commercialized surroundings and apparent paucity of wildlife.

That said, if you're prepared to **trek** into the forest, Periyar can still be worth a stay. Elephant, *sambar*, Malabar giant squirrel, gaur, stripe-necked mongoose and wild boar are still commonly spotted in areas deeper into the park, where birdlife is also prolific. Another selling point is Periyar's much vaunted **eco-tourism** initiative. Instead of earning their livelihoods through poaching and illegal sandalwood extraction, local Manna people are these days employed by the Forest Department to protect vulnerable parts of the sanctuary. Schemes such as "Border Hiking", "Tiger Trail" and "Jungle Patrol" tours, in which visitors accompany tribal wardens on their duties, serve to promote community welfare and generate income for conservation work.

In addition, the area around Periyar holds plenty of engaging day-trip destinations, such as **spice plantations** and an **elephant camp**, as well as lots of scope for **trekking** in the surrounding hills and forest. It's also a lot cooler up here than down on the more humid coast, and many foreign visitors are glad of the break from the heat.

Kumily

As beds inside the sanctuary are in short supply, most visitors stay in nearby **KUMILY**, a typical High Range town, centred on a hectic roadside market, 1km or so north of the main park entrance (known as **Thekkady**). Hotels and Kashmiri handicrafts emporia have spread south from the bazaar to within a stone's throw of the park, and tourism now rivals the spice trade as the area's main source of income. That said, you'll still see plenty of little shops selling local herbs, essential oils and cooking spices, while in the busy **cardamom sorting yard** behind the *Spice Village* resort, rows of Manna women sift through heaps of fragrant green pods using heart-shaped baskets.

Arrival and information

Buses from Kottayam (every 30min; 4hr), Ernakulam (10 daily; 6hr) and Madurai in Tamil Nadu (at least hourly; 5hr 30min) pull in to the scruffy bus stand east of the main bazaar. **Auto-rickshaws** will run you from here to the visitor centre inside the park for around Rs50–60, stopping at the park entrance at Thekkady for you to pay the fee (see p.1054).

To book any of the Periyar Tiger Reserve's popular **eco-tourism tours** (see p.1056), you'll have to walk down the Thekkady Road to the **eco-tourism centre** on Ambadi Junction (daily 9am–8pm, last tickets sold at 7.30pm; ⓣ04869/224571) – or better still, book in advance.

Both the State Bank of Travancore (which has an ATM), near the bus stand, and the Thekkady Bankers in the main bazaar can **change currency** and travellers' cheques. **Internet** facilities are available around Thekkady Junction for about Rs40 per hour.

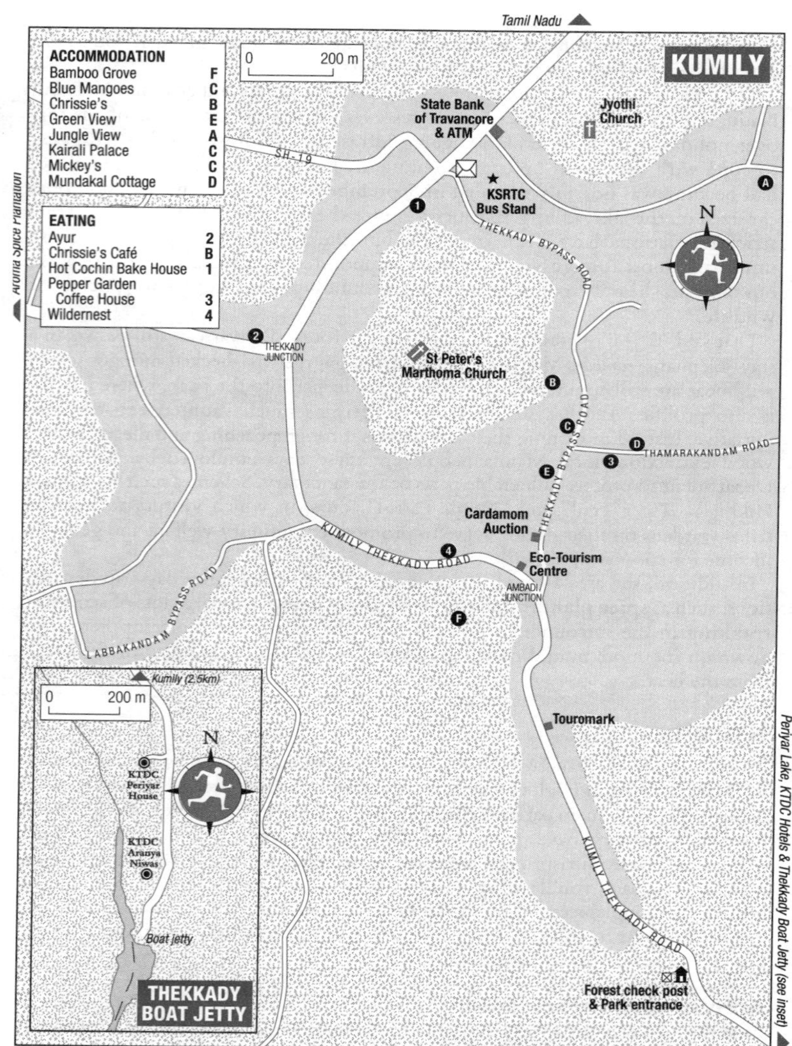

Tours and treks around Kumily

As well as the attraction of the wildlife sanctuary, **tea factory** and **spice plantation tours** are offered by almost every hotel and tourist agency in Kumily. Unfortunately, many places have become heavily commercialized, so it's worth shopping around; often the best way to organize a tour is to ask at your hotel. The only certified organic spice garden in the area, and a particularly enjoyable one to visit, is the Aroma at Chelimada, a short walk west of Kumily on the Kottayam road; contact the owner, Mr Sebastian ("Baby"), on his cell phone ⓣ 9495 367837. Most of the plantations charge around Rs300–500 per person for a three-hour tour with guide and vehicle.

The windy, grassy ridgetops and forests around Periyar afford many fine **treks**, with superb views over the High Range guaranteed. One especially rewarding half-day trip is the hike up **Kurusamalai** (3hr), the peak towering to the northwest of Kumily, whose summit is crowned with a Holy Cross. As the summit falls within the national park boundaries, you're only permitted to hike to it under the auspices of the eco-tourism centre (see p.1051), who market it as their "Cloud Walk" (Rs300). Although hilly, this area is also good **cycling** territory; you can **rent bikes** from stalls in the market, and Touromark (Ⓣ04869/224332, Ⓦwww.touromark.com), midway between Kumily and Thekkady, have imported 21-speed **mountain bikes** for rent. They also offer guided trips, ranging from four-hour/fifteen-kilometre hacks through local spice gardens, coffee plantations and woodlands to a three-night/four-day ride across the Cardamom Hills to Munnar.

The Forest Department runs **village tours** (6am–2.30pm; Rs750) from the eco-tourism centre to a remote tribal settlement on the Tamil Nadu side of the mountains bordering Periyar. You're transported 10km by taxi to the start of the route, which is covered by **bullock cart** and **coracle** through a variety of different habitats and farmland. Profits go to the development of the local community.

Accommodation

Kumily has **accommodation** to suit all pockets, with a number of small homestay guesthouses on the fringes of the village offering particularly good value. The three government-run places actually inside the park are either ludicrously expensive or shabby, or both, and thus not listed here.

Bamboo Grove Ⓣ04869/224571, Ⓦwww.periyartigerreserve.org. Part of the Forest Department's eco-tourism project, this eco-lodge between Kumily bazaar and the park gates offers spacious en-suite huts made of renewable, natural materials, serviced by staff drawn from local *adivasi* minorities. The location isn't nearly as inspiring as the brochure shots suggest, but rates do include breakfast, jungle treks and boat trips, making this a good all-in deal. ❺

Blue Mangoes Bypass Rd Ⓣ04869/224603 or Ⓣ9744 995253. Simple en-suite rooms (with sitouts and balconies) in an impeccably clean modern block, with a larger family "cottage". Rock-bottom rates, but good bedding and a quiet location. Owner Bobby speaks excellent English. ❷–❸

Chrissie's Bypass Rd Ⓣ04869/224155 or Ⓣ9447 601304, Ⓦwww.chrissies.in. Smart four-storey hotel below the bazaar, run by expats Chrissie (from the UK) and Adel (from Egypt). It's pricier than most homestays in the area, but you get more privacy and better views, and relaxing, homely interiors. There's also a great yoga *shala* on the rooftop, and popular little café-restaurant on the ground floor (see p.1054). ❺–❻

Green View Bypass Rd Ⓣ04869/211015 or Ⓣ9447 432008, Ⓦwww.sureshgreenview.com. One of Kumily's most popular homestays, in a newish house just off the Thekkady Road. The 17 rooms range from basic Rs350 options with bucket hot water to large en-suite ones with solar-heated showers and balconies looking across the valley to Kurusamalai mountain. A lovely rear garden attracts lots of wild birds. If it's full, try the identically priced *Rose Garden* next door (Ⓣ04869/223146). ❸–❺

Jungle View On the eastern edge of town Ⓣ04869/223582 or Ⓣ9446 136407, Ⓔjungleview8@yahoo.com. The best-value budget homestay in Kumily, a 10min plod (or short auto-rickshaw ride) from the bus stand – literally on the Tamil Nadu–Kerala border. The clean, bright, attached bedrooms are all comfortably furnished; those on the upper storey open onto a marble-floored veranda just metres away from jungle. Nocturnal wildlife-spotting walks into the adjacent forest are offered for free by welcoming host, Mr Ramachandran. ❹–❺

Kairali Palace Bypass Rd Ⓣ04869/224604 or Ⓣ9895 187789. Outstandingly attractive homestay in a fusion building that blends traditional and modern styles, with gabled roofs, and wooden railings wrapped around the airy first-floor terrace. Its en-suite rooms are well furnished for the price. ❹

Mickey's Bypass Rd Ⓣ04869/222196 or Ⓣ9447 284160. One of the oldest guesthouses in Kumily, whose smiling owner, Sujata, offers a range of rooms and cottages, all with balconies or sitouts littered with relaxing cane furniture. ❸–❹

Mundakal Cottage Thamarakandam Rd ⑦04869/223317 or ⑦9447 980924. Philip and Mariyamma Mundakal's budget travellers' homestay, up a side lane off Bypass Rd, comprises six squeaky-clean rooms in a peaceful spot well away from the bustle of the bazaar. The best are in a newish block fitted with comfy wooden beds, quality mattresses and tiled floors. ❸–❹

Eating

You're more likely to take **meals** at your guesthouse or hotel than eat out in Kumily, but for a change of scene the following are the best options within walking distance of the bazaar.

Ayur West side of the main bazaar. Quality south Indian thali "meals" (Rs75), freshly made each day and served on banana leaves from a buffet. It's more hygienic (and less manic) than the competition further down the main street. *Ginger*, upstairs, is a swisher a/c alternative offering an exhaustive Indian-Chinese-Continental menu.

Chrissie's Café Bypass Rd. This relaxing expat-run café, on the ground floor of *Chrissie's* hotel, pulls in a steady stream of foreigners throughout the day and evening for its delicious pizzas (Rs150–200), made with Kodai mozzarella; check out the specials board. They also do healthy breakfasts of muesli with fresh fruit, crunchy cereal, toast with home-made bread and cakes, and proper coffee. Count on Rs300 per head.

Hot Cochin Bake House Main bazaar. The best of a pretty unimpressive batch of "meals" places on the east side of the main street, close to the bus stand. Most people come at lunchtime for the tasty fish curry thali, with optional *avioli* (pearlspot) masala fry, served on china plates instead of the usual tin trays or leaves.

Pepper Garden Coffee House Thamarkandam Rd. In a garden filled with cardamom bushes behind a prettily painted blue-and-green house, a former park guide and his wife whip up tempting travellers' breakfasts (date and raisin pancakes, porridge with jungle honey, fresh coffee and Nilgiri tea), in addition to home-cooked lunches of veg fried rice, curry and dhal, using mostly local organic produce. Mains Rs35–100.

Wildernest Thekkady Rd. Filling Continental buffet breakfasts (fruit, juices, cereals, eggs, toast, peanut butter, home-made jams and freshly ground coffee; Rs130) served in the ground-floor café of a stylish small hotel. They also serve afternoon tea and cakes (including a delicious, very British warm plum cake).

The sanctuary

Centred on a vast artificial **lake** created by the British in 1895 to supply water to the drier parts of neighbouring Tamil Nadu, the Periyar Wildlife Sanctuary lies at altitudes of between 900m and 1800m, and is correspondingly cool: temperatures range from 15°C to 30°C. The royal family of Travancore, anxious to preserve favourite hunting grounds from the encroachment of tea plantations, declared it a forest reserve, and built the Edapalayam Lake Palace to accommodate their guests in 1899. It expanded as a wildlife reserve in 1933, and once again when it became part of **Project Tiger** (see p.1178) in 1979.

Seventy percent of the protected area, which is divided into core, buffer and tourist zones, is covered with evergreen and semi-evergreen forest. The **tourist zone** – logically enough, the part accessible to casual visitors – surrounds the lake, and consists mostly of semi-evergreen and deciduous woodland interspersed with grassland, both on hilltops and in the valleys. Although excursions on the lake (either by diesel-powered launch or paddle-powered bamboo raft) are the standard ways to experience the park, you can get much more out of a visit by **walking** with a local guide in a small group away from the crowd. However, avoid the period immediately after the monsoons, when **leeches** make hiking virtually impossible. The **best time to visit** is from December until April, when the dry weather draws animals from the forest to drink at the lakeside.

Park practicalities

The **entrance fee**, payable at the park entrance on the Kumily–Thekkady road, is Rs300 [Rs100]. By far the best option for wildlife-viewing from the lake is

Accommodation

Munnar's **accommodation** costs significantly more than elsewhere in the High Range region, reflecting the high demand for beds from middle-class tourists from the big cities. Rooms at the low end of the scale are in particularly short supply; the few that exist are blighted by racket from the bus stand and bazaar, and are thus not listed below. Included here are options outside town, which would suit travellers with their own transport.

British County ET City Rd, Anachal, 12km from Munnar ⓣ0484/236 9811 or ⓣ9744 128761. On a ridge enjoying a vast valley view, this property run by the Tourist Desk in Kochi (see p.1061) has just four simply furnished rooms. They're clean and comfortable enough, but the real attraction here is the terrace, disturbed by nothing but bird calls and the wind in the trees. Cook Ranjit rustles up tasty Indian food; rates cover full board. ❺

Green View Sri Parvati Amman Kovil St, near the KSRTC bus stand ⓣ04865/230189 or ⓣ9447 825447. Clean and friendly budget guesthouse on the valley floor, down a side road just off the main drag, with rooms of various sizes – the best of them, #402, is a tiny double with big windows and hill views. Pitched squarely at foreign backpackers, it's run by an enthusiastic, competent young crew who do a sideline in guided day-treks (see p.1058). ❷–❹

High Range Club Kanan Devan Hills Rd ⓣ04865/230253, ⓦwww.highrangeclubmunnar.com. This old Raj-era club, founded by British planters in 1909, must have been a nightmare of stuffiness and racism in its heyday. But now the faded colonial ambience, with turbaned bearers politely greeting guests in lounges filled with 1940s furniture and moth-eaten hunting trophies, feels undeniably quaint. The club's guest wing holds three kinds of rooms and cottages, varying in size and comfort. Rates include obligatory full board. ❻–❼

Hillview Kanan Devan Hills Rd ⓣ04865/230567 or ⓣ9447 740883, ⓦhillviewmunnar.com. A big red block on the southern edge of town, it's not much to look at from the outside, but the interiors boast stripped wood floors and traditional carved wall panels. A dependable mid-range choice, despite its rough edges. ❻

JJ Cottage Sri Parvati Amman Kovil St, near the KSRTC bus stand ⓣ04865/230104. Next door to *Green View*, and very much in the same mould, though it's been open longer, charges higher rates and tends to get booked up earlier. Like its neighbour, the nicest of its clean, variously sized rooms is the one at the top (frontside), which has wood-panelled walls and fine views. A warm family welcome is guaranteed. ❸–❹

Royal Retreat Kanan Devan Hills Rd ⓣ04865/230240, ⓦwww.royalretreat.co.in. Pleasant, efficiently run roadside motel at the south end of town. Go for a "super-deluxe" room if possible: they're south-facing, have brick fireplaces and cane furniture, and are fronted by a cheerful little flower garden. ❺–❼

Zina Cottage Kad ⓣ04865/230349 or ⓣ9447 190954. British-era stone bungalow, nestled amid tea gardens high on the hillside above Munnar. Its flower-filled front terrace has magnificent views across the town to Ana Mudi, and host Joseph Iype (see opposite) will fill you in on local walks over flasks of hot tea in his sitting room. The basic, gloomy rooms lack outlook, and you'll probably need a pile of blankets at night, but all have their own entrances and bathrooms. Come here less for creature comforts than for atmosphere, of which it has plenty. ❹

The Town

Clustered around the confluence of three mountain streams, Munnar town is a typical hill bazaar of haphazard buildings and congested market streets, which you'll probably want to escape at the first opportunity. The one sight of note is the **Tea Museum** (Tues–Sun 9am–4pm; Rs50), 2km northwest of the centre on Nallathany Road, which houses various pieces of old machinery and an exhibition of photos of the area's tea industry.

The social hub of the colonial period, and an important cultural icon in Munnar, the famous **High Range Club** is perched on a balcony overlooking the river on the southeastern edge of town. Indians were only officially permitted to enter the premises as recently as 1948, but these days non-members of any race are welcome to visit the typically Raj-era building for a round of golf, or to enjoy a G&T

served on the lawns by liveried retainers. In the men-only bar, the walls are hung with rows of hunting trophies and topees. Stiff-upper-lipped dress codes apply throughout: no T-shirts or sandals, and formal evening wear after 7pm on Saturdays.

Eating

The **thattukada** (hot food stall market) just south of the main bazaar, opposite the taxi stand, gets into its stride around 7.30pm and runs through the night, serving delicious, piping-hot Keralan food – dosas, *parottas*, *iddiappam*, green-bean curry, egg masala – ladled onto tin plates and eaten on rough wood tables in the street. The most hygienic option in the main bazaar is *Food Count*, on the ground floor of the *Munnar Inn*, serving samosas, veg cutlets, sandwiches and light meals. *Guru Bhavan*, Mutapatty Road, Ikka Nagar, is the most dependable of Munnar's local south Indian "meals" joints. It's a ten-minute walk north of the main bazaar, but worth the effort, with a daily changing menu of delicious Keralan vegetarian dishes, in addition to hot *parottas*, stupendously crunchy paper dosas and other *udipi* snacks.

Around Munnar

Several of the summits towering above the town may be reached on day-**treks** through the tea gardens. A good first stop for information is the *Green View* guesthouse, on the south side of town (see p.1057), whose owner, Deepak (Ⓣ04865/230940, Ⓦwww.munnartrekking.com), heads a team of enthusiastic young guides. Rates range from Rs400–500 per person for soft treks to Rs500–800 for longer, more challenging outings, transport to and from the trail-heads included. The **Kerala Forest Development Corporation** (**KFDC**; Ⓦwww.kfdc.org/ecotourism.asp) also runs guided treks around Munnar, ranging from the one-day walk (8am– 5pm; Rs300) to longer routes involving nights under canvas (Rs1000–3000/head, including meals and camping). You should also budget for travel to and from the trailhead, which can also be arranged through KFDC. These walks are extremely popular and sell out quickly, so book as far in advance as possible through KFDC's office in Munnar (Ⓣ04865/230332).

One of the most popular **excursions** from Munnar is the 34-kilometre climb through some of the Subcontinent's highest tea estates to **TOP STATION**, a tiny hamlet on the Kerala–Tamil Nadu border which, at 1600m, is the highest point on the interstate road. The settlement takes its name from the old aerial **ropeway** that used to connect it with the valley floor, the ruins of which can still be seen in places. Apart from the marvellous views over the Tamil plains, Top Station is renowned for the very rare **Neelakurunji plant** (*Strobilatanthes*), which grows on the mountainsides but only flowers once every twelve years, when huge crowds climb up to admire the cascades of violet blossom spilling down the slopes (the next flowering is due in Oct/Nov 2018). You can get here by **bus** from Munnar (10 daily from 5.30am; 1hr 30min), and Jeep-taxis do the return trip for Rs900. Views are best before the mist builds at 9am.

Wildlife sanctuaries

Encompassing 100 square kilometres of moist evergreen forest and grassy hilltops in the Western Ghats, the **Eravikulam National Park** (daily 7am–6pm; Rs200 [Rs40]; Ⓦwww.eravikulam.org), 13km northeast of Munnar, is the last stronghold of one of the world's rarest mountain goats, the **Nilgiri tahr**. Its innate friendliness made the tahr pathetically easy prey during the hunting frenzy of the colonial era. Today, however, numbers are healthy, and the animals have regained and qualified guides for visitors, is inconveniently situated on Willingdon Island, between the *Taj Malabar Hotel* and Tourist Office Jetty; they also have a desk at the airport. KTDC's **reception centre**, on Shanmugham Road, Ernakulam (daily 8am–7pm; ⓣ0484/235 3234, ⓦwww.ktdc.com), books rooms in their hotel chain and organizes sightseeing and backwater tours; they too have a counter at the airport. For general advice the two most convenient sources are the **Kerala Department of Tourism**'s office next to the Government Jetty in Fort Cochin (Mon–Sat 10.15am–5pm; no phone, ⓦwww.keralatourism.com), and the tiny, independently run **Tourist Desk** (daily 8am–6.30pm; ⓣ0484/237 1761, ⓔmail@touristdesk.in) at the entrance to the Main Boat Jetty in Ernakulam (with a subsidiary office on Tower Road in Fort Cochin; same hours; ⓣ0484/221 6129). Both hand out maps of the town and backwaters – and **walking-tour maps** and guides to Fort Cochin – but the latter is more helpful when it comes to checking ferry and bus times.

Tours and backwater trips

If you are pushed for time, KTDC's half-day **Kochi boat cruise** (daily 9am–12.30pm & 2–5.30pm; Rs100) is a good way to orient yourself, but it doesn't stop long in either Mattancherry or Fort Cochin. Book at the reception Centre on Shanmugham Road (see above). They also offer day-trips into the backwaters south of Kochi, but they're not as good as those run by the **Tourist Desk** (daily 8.30am–6.30pm; Rs550; book at their counters in Fort Cochin and Ernakulam). The cost includes hotel pick-up, transfer to the departure point near **Vaikom**, 30km south, a morning cruise (in a motorized boat) on the open backwaters, a village tour, a Keralan lunch buffet on board the *kettu vallam* and an afternoon trip through narrow waterways in a much smaller punted canoe.

Accommodation

Most foreign visitors opt to stay in **Fort Cochin**, which, with its uncongested backstreets and charming colonial-era architecture, holds considerably more appeal than the mayhem of modern Ernakulam. There are, however, drawbacks: room rates are grossly inflated (especially over Christmas and New Year), with few options at the budget end of the scale, and the tourist crowds can be disconcerting. **Ernakulam** may lack historic ambience, but it's far more convenient for travel connections, and offers lots of choice, and far better value, in all categories. Wherever you choose to stay, book well in advance – particularly for the weekend.

Places to stay in Ernakulam and Fort Cochin are marked on their respective **maps** (p.1066 & p.1064).

Ernakulam

Budget

Biju's Tourist Home Corner of Cannonshed and Market roads ⓣ0484/238 1881, ⓦwww.bijustouristhome.com. The pick of the budget bunch: a friendly, efficiently run block 2min walk from the boat jetty, with thirty spotless, well-aired and generous rooms ranged over four storeys. It has its own clean water supply and offers a cheap same-day laundry service. Phone reservations accepted. ❹–❺

Maple Regency XL/1511 Cannonshed Rd ⓣ0484/235 5156 or 237 1711, ⓔmapleregency@airtelmail.in. The best of the few rock-bottom options in the streets immediately east of the Main Boat Jetty, with 30 cheap, clean, non-a/c rooms. To the rear of the main building, a couple of old ancestral bungalows, dating from 1891, have been converted into pleasant chalet-style "cottages", with red tiled floors, long pillared verandas and a lot more charm than anything else in this price bracket. Free internet (for guests) in the lobby. ❷–❹

Park View Residency Cannonshed Rd ⓣ0484/236 2945. The cheapest rooms in the city, and well scrubbed, with only a few smudges on the walls (though the bathrooms can be fusty). A bargain all the same, with rooms for less than Rs300. ❶–❷

Saas Tower Cannonshed Rd ⓣ0484/236 5319, ⓦwww.saastower.com. Since its refit, this tower-block hotel, with 72 well-furnished rooms, has begun to rival nearby *Biju's* for quality and price at the upper end of the budget category. Singles from Rs300, and also some a/c options. ❸–❺

Mid-range & luxury

Government Guesthouse Marine Drive ⓣ0484/236 0502. The maharaja of Kerala's great-value *Government Guesthouses*, in a shiny eight-storey tower overlooking the harbour. Centred on a vast atrium lobby, its rooms offer comfort comparable to a four-star business-class hotel, only at amazingly low rates (Rs1500/double, and they do single occupancy). Advance reservation, as with all Kerala state guesthouses, can be hit-and-miss, with priority given to government officials. ❺

Grand MG Rd ⓣ0484/238 2061, ⓦwww.grandhotelkerala.com. This is the most classically glamorous place to stay in central Ernakulam. Spread over three floors of a 1960s building, its relaxing a/c rooms are done in retro-colonial style, with varnished wood floors and split-cane blinds. Surprisingly low rates given the level of comfort and location. ❻–❼

Travancore Court Warriam Rd ⓣ0484/235 1120, ⓦwww.travancorecourt.com. Modern, international-standard high-rise hotel close to the station that's popular with visiting tour groups thanks to its competitive rates and facilities, which include a splendid rooftop pool and wooden sun deck. It's also famous locally for being owned by Malayali screen legend, Mohanlal. ❼–❽

Yuvarani Residency Jos Junction, MG Rd ⓣ0484/237 7040, ⓦwww.yuvaraniresidency.com. Comfortable, central and well-managed three-star with a choice of carpeted or tiled rooms – and especially good showers. The popular Keralan seafood restaurant hosts live music recitals daily (except Tues), and there's a bar and a coffee shop. ❺–❻

Fort Cochin

Budget

Adam's Old Inn 1/430 Burgher St ⓣ0484/221 8870, ⓦwww.adamsoldinn.com. Since its recent makeover, *Adam's* has established itself as the best budget option in the Fort district, with well-scrubbed little en suite rooms opening onto a central corridor – only the "deluxe" one to the rear has a terrace. There's a helpful travel agent on the ground floor. ❷–❸

Oy's Burgher St ⓣ9947 594903, ⓦoys.co.in. Pleasant, clean and friendly backpackers' hideaway, with just three cosy rooms, down the lane from *Kashi Arts Café*. Barred windows look onto a little raised terrace and there's a hip travellers' café on the ground floor. ❸–❹

Santa Cruz Peter Celli St ⓣ0484/221 6250 or ⓣ9847 518598. Half of the rooms in this small guesthouse behind St Francis' Church have windows opening onto an enclosed corridor, but the others are well ventilated – and they're all impeccably clean, neatly tiled and freshly painted, with new beds. A/c for an extra Rs600. Good value. ❷–❸

Sonnetta Residency 1/387 Princess St ⓣ0484/221 5744 or ⓣ9895 543555, ⓔmail@sonnettaresidency.com. This small guesthouse has to be one of the cleanest places to stay in Kerala: the surfaces are gleaming, bed linen boil-washed and bathrooms polished. It lacks character, and has no outside sitting space, but is efficiently run and provides a secure, convenient base, with some of the cheapest a/c rooms in the district. ❹–❺

Spencer Home 1/298 Parade Rd ⓣ0484/221 5049. Warm-toned wood pillars and gleaming ceramic tiled floors line the verandas fronting this Portuguese-era house's eleven immaculate rooms, which open onto a painstakingly kept garden. Peaceful and good value for the area. A/c Rs500 extra. ❹

Mid-range

Chiramel Residency 1/296 Lilly St ⓣ0484/221 7310, ⓦwww.chiramelhomestay.com. A great seventeenth-century heritage homestay, with welcoming owners and five lofty and carefully restored non-a/c rooms set around a fancily furnished communal sitting room. All have big wooden beds, teak floors and modern bathrooms. ❺–❻

Delight Ridsdale Rd, opposite the parade ground ⓣ0484/221 7658 or ⓣ9846 121421, ⓦwww.delightfulhomestay.com. Occupying an annexe tacked onto a splendid 300-year-old Portuguese mansion, David and Flowery's homestay holds seven spacious, comfortable and well-aired rooms, all equipped with new bathrooms and quiet ceiling fans. Some open onto a lovely courtyard garden; another has a long veranda overlooking the parade ground. Breakfast available. ❺–❼

Fort House 2/6A Calvathy Rd ⓣ0484/221 7103, ⓦwww.forthousecochin.com. Stylishly simple rooms ranged along the sides of a sandy courtyard littered with pot plants and votive terracotta statues. Those in the better block (rooms #1–6) have white walls and red-oxide floors, comfy king-sized beds with lathe-turned legs and good showers in their chic wet-room bathrooms – though the a/c units can be noisy. Avoid the older budget block on the west side. Rates include breakfast. 6–7

Kapithan Inn 1/931 KL Bernard Rd ⓣ0484/221 6560, ⓦwww.kapithaninn.com. Scrupulously clean, very nicely furnished rooms in a friendly homestay behind Santa Cruz Basilica, with four smarter, larger a/c cottages to the rear (large enough for families). Bargain rates for the level of comfort. 3–6

The Old Courtyard 1/371–2 Princess St ⓣ0484/221 6302, ⓦwww.oldcourtyard.com. A gem of a heritage hotel, whose eight rooms flank a seventeenth-century courtyard framed by elegant Portuguese arches and bands of original azulejo tiles. For once the decor and antique furnishings (including romantic four-posters) are in keeping with the building – though some may find them dark and lacking mod cons. Upper-storey rooms are less disturbed by noise from the courtyard restaurant (see p.1068). 8–9

Raintree 1/618 Peter Celli St ⓣ0484/325 1489 or ⓣ9847 029000, ⓦwww.fortcochin.com. Five outstandingly smart rooms furnished in modern style (two of them with tiny balconies) in a cosy guesthouse that's within easy walking distance of the sights, but still tucked away. The really nice thing about this place is its plant-filled roof terrace, which has panoramic views. 6

Walton's Homestay 1/39 Princess St ⓣ0484/221 5309 or ⓣ9249 721935, ⓦwww.waltonshomestay.com. Among Cochin's most characterful homestays, run by philosopher and local historian Mr Christopher Edward Walton, in a centuries-old Dutch house. The rooms, many of which open onto a delightful rear garden busy with birdlife, have been beautifully renovated, with modern bathrooms, solar-powered hot water and comfy beds; all have the option of a/c (Rs400 extra). Facilities include a book-swap library and yoga classes; breakfast (included in tariff) is served on a terrace. 5–6

Luxury

Secret Garden 11/745 Bishop Garden Lane 2, near Pattalam Market ⓣ9895 581489, ⓦwww.secretgarden.in. Buried in a maze of narrow back lanes, this is a hidden gem, run by Icelandic architect, Thóra Guðmundsdóttir. The four white-walled rooms, which have high wooden ceilings, hand-carved beds and traditional terra-cotta tiled floors, all open onto balconies fronting an exotic garden with a good-size pool. Rates (Rs5500–6000 in high season) include (optional) morning yoga, and use of the house computer, books and bicycles. 8

The Tower House 1/320-321 Tower St ⓣ0484/221 6960, ⓦwww.neemranahotels.com. The French-run *Neemrana* chain does heritage hotels better than anyone else in India, and this latest venture – which describes itself as a "Non-Hotel Hotel" – doesn't disappoint. The location, in a graceful period house opposite the Chinese fishing nets, is perfect, the airy interiors are scrupulously in period, and there's a secluded pool. Don't expect the slick service of other places in this bracket, nor Fort Cochin's usual exorbitant rates – doubles Rs5000–8000 ($110–175). 8–9

Old Kochi: Fort Cochin and Mattancherry

Old Kochi, the thumb-shaped peninsula whose northern tip presides over the entrance to the city's harbour, formed the focus of European trading activities from the sixteenth century onwards. With high-rise development restricted to Ernakulam across the water, its twin districts of **Fort Cochin**, in the west, and **Mattancherry**, on the headland's eastern side, have preserved an extraordinary wealth of early colonial architecture, spanning the Portuguese, Dutch and British eras – a crop unparalleled in India. Approaching by ferry, the waterfront, with its sloping red-tiled roofs and ranks of peeling, pastel-coloured *godowns* (warehouses), offers a view that can have changed little in centuries.

Closer up, however, Old Kochi's historic patina has started to show some ugly cracks. The spice trade that fuelled the town's original rise is still very much in evidence. But over the past decade, an extraordinary rise in visitor numbers has had a major impact. Thousands of tourists pour through daily during the winter, and with no planning or preservation authority to take control, the resulting rash of new building threatens to destroy the very atmosphere people come here to experience. That said, tourism has also brought some benefits, inspiring renovation work to buildings that would otherwise have been left to rot.

Fort Cochin

Fort Cochin, the grid of venerable old streets at the northwest tip of the peninsula, is where the Portuguese erected their first walled citadel, Fort Immanuel. Only a few fragments of the former battlements remain, crumbling into the sea beside Cochin's iconic Chinese fishing nets. But dozens of other evocative Lusitanian, Dutch and British monuments survive.

A good way to get to grips with Fort Cochin's many-layered history is to pick up the free **walking-tour maps** produced by Kerala Tourism and the privately run Tourist Desk (see p.1061). They lead you around some of the district's more significant landmarks, including the early eighteenth-century Dutch Cemetery, Vasco da Gama's supposed house and several traders' residences.

Chinese fishing nets

The huge, elegant **Chinese fishing nets** lining the northern shore of Fort Cochin add grace to the waterfront view, and are probably the single most familiar photographic image of Kerala. Traders from the court of Kublai Khan are said to have introduced them to the Malabar region. Known in Malayalam as *cheena vala*, they can also be seen throughout the backwaters further south. The nets, which are suspended from poles and operated by levers and weights, require at least four men to control them.

St Francis church and around

South of the Chinese fishing nets on Church Road (the continuation of River Rd) is the large, typically English **Parade Ground**. Overlooking it, the **Church of St Francis** (daily 8.30am–6.30pm) was the first built by Europeans in India. Its exact

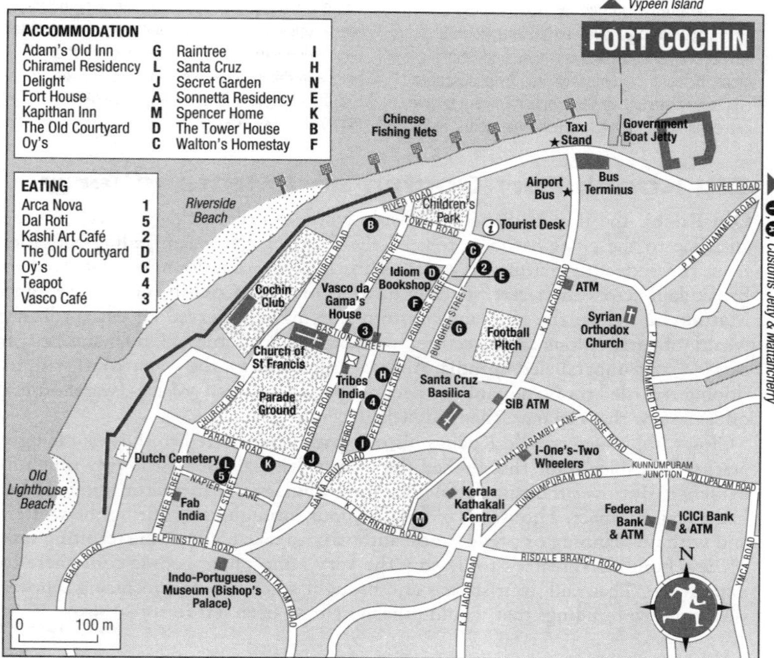

age is not known, though the stone structure is thought to date back to the early sixteenth century. The facade, meanwhile, became the model for most Christian churches in India. Vasco da Gama was buried here in 1524, but his body was later removed to Portugal. Under the Dutch, the church was renovated and became Protestant in 1663, then Anglican with the advent of the British in 1795. Inside, the earliest of various tombstone inscriptions placed in the walls dates from 1562.

Mattancherry

Mattancherry, the old district of red-tiled riverfront wharves and houses occupying the northeastern tip of the headland, was once the colonial capital's main market area – the epicentre of the Malabar's spice trade, and home to its wealthiest Jewish and Jain merchants. Like Fort Cochin, its once grand buildings have lapsed into advanced states of disrepair, with most of their original owners working overseas. When Mattancherry's Jews emigrated en masse to Israel in the 1940s, their furniture and other un-portable heirlooms ended up in the **antique shops** for which the area is now renowned – though these days genuine pieces are few and far between.

The sight at the top of most itineraries is **Mattancherry Palace** (daily except Fri 10am–5pm; Rs2), on the roadside a short walk from the Mattancherry Jetty, 1km or so southeast of Fort Cochin. Known locally as the Dutch Palace, the two-storey building was actually erected by the Portuguese, as a gift to the Raja of Cochin, Vira Keralavarma (1537–61) – though the Dutch did add to the complex. While its squat exterior is not particularly striking, the interior is captivating, with some of the finest examples of Kerala's underrated school of **mural** painting, along with Dutch maps of old Cochin, coronation robes belonging to past maharajas, royal palanquins, weapons and furniture.

Jew Town

The road heading south from Mattancherry Jetty leads into the district known as **Jew Town**, home of a once-thriving Jewish community whose main place of worship, until most of them emigrated to Israel, was the **Pardesi (White Jew) Synagogue** (daily except Sat 10am–noon & 3–5pm; Rs2). Founded in 1568 and rebuilt in 1664, the building is best known for its interior, an incongruous hotch-potch paved with hand-painted eighteenth-century blue-and-white tiles from Canton. An elaborately carved Ark houses four scrolls of the Torah, on which sit gold crowns presented by the maharajas of Travancore and Cochin, testifying to good relations with the Jewish community. The synagogue's oldest artefact is a fourth-century copperplate inscription from the Raja of Cochin.

Ernakulam and south of the centre

ERNAKULAM presents the modern face of Kerala, studded with flashy gold emporia and with more of a big-city feel than Thiruvananthapuram – despite the fact it's marginally smaller. Other than the contemporary art on display at the small **Durbar Hall Art Gallery** (daily 11am–7pm; free) on Durbar Hall Road, and the remarkable **folklore museum** (see p.1066) on the southern outskirts, there's little in the way of sights – if you spend any time here, it'll probably be to eat at one of the area's famous Keralan **restaurants**.

Running parallel to the seafront, roughly 500m inland, **Mahatma Gandhi (MG) Road** is its main thoroughfare, where you'll find some of the largest textile stores, jewellery shops and hotels. Prime leisure destinations for the city's well-heeled middle classes are the massive **shopping malls** 7km north of the centre around Edapally Junction. Spread over six storeys, the **Oberon**

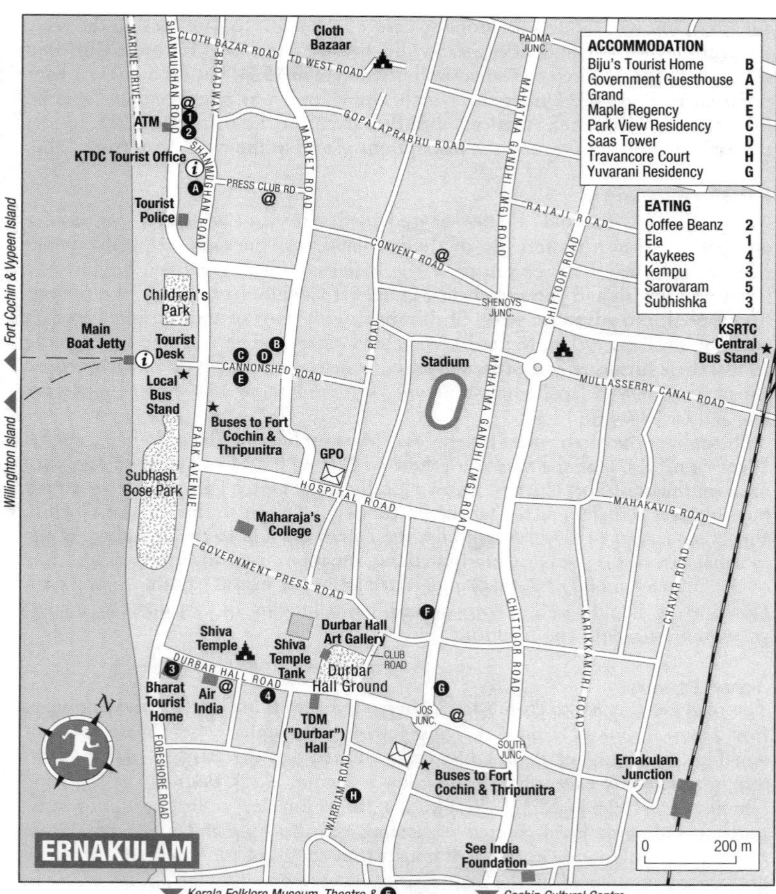

(daily 10am–10pm) used to be the high temple of modern Keralan consumerism until it was usurped by the colossal **LuLu Mall** (same hours; ⓦwww.luluindia.com), a 16-acre complex with a seven-screen multiplex, 18 food outlets and parking for three thousand cars.

Ernakulam's one outstanding visitor attraction is the **Kerala Folklore Museum** (daily 9.30am–7pm, ⓣ0484/266 5452; Rs200), on the distant southeast fringes of the city. Housed in a multi-storey laterite building encrusted with traditional wood- and tile-work, the collection of antiques includes dance-drama masks and costumes, ritual paraphernalia, musical instruments, pieces of temple architecture, Thanjavur paintings, cooking utensils, portraits and ancestral photographs – to name but a few. Its crowning glory is an exquisitely decorated **theatre** on the top floor, where evening performances of *kathakali* and *theyyem* are given against a backdrop of swirling Keralan temple murals and dark wooden pillars (see p.1069). Auto-rickshaws charge around Rs75 for the trip out to the museum from the Main Boat Jetty in Ernakulam – ask for Theyvara (aka "Shantinagar") Junction, or Kundulur Bridge.

Eating

Until recently, the quintessential Kochi dining experience was buying a fish straight from the **Chinese fishing nets** in the Fort, then having it grilled at one of the stalls nearby. Alas, the authorities recently closed the stalls down, and these days foreign tourists tend to congregate at the pavement joints along the nearby **Tower Road**, drinking warm beer disguised in tea pots to circumvent local liquor licensing laws. The food served in these cafés, however, is notoriously unhygienic, regularly causing stomach upsets.

As with everything else in Fort Cochin, upmarket **restaurants** generally tend to be pricier, and smarter, than those across the water in **Ernakulam**, which serve some of the best traditional food in all South India. Unless otherwise stated, restaurants under the "Ernakulam" and "Fort Cochin" headings below are shown on their relevant **maps** (see opposite & p.1064).

Ernakulam

Coffee Beanz Shanmugham Rd. Trendy a/c cappuccino bar, patronized mainly by well-heeled students from the local management college shrieking into their mobiles over a full-on MTV soundtrack. The din notwithstanding, it's a good spot to beat the heat and grab a quick meal (burgers, fries, grilled sandwiches, dosas, fish curries, *appam* and samosas). The coffee's freshly ground and delicious, though the service is far less snappy than the fast-food uniforms.

Ela Shanmugham Rd. Great value, a/c Keralan speciality place where nothing costs more than Rs100. The vibe is upbeat and trendy, but the non-veg food's very trad: *meen pollichathu*, deliciously rich Syrian-Christian vegetable stew, lamb-coconut curry and light, spongy *appam*s to soak it all up. Lots of old-style desserts, too, including *payasam* and more-ish banana fritters.

Kaykees Durbar Hall Rd. The city's most famous Muslim restaurant (pronounced "Kai-ka's") has two branches: an old-style place over in Mattancherry, and this much more salubrious, modern dining hall in the heart of the downtown area, with an a/c section on the first floor. They've recently added all kinds of items to the menu, but everyone comes for the Malabari biriyanis (veg, chicken or mutton), served with *Kaykees*' mellow palm-date pickle and Arabian tea. It gets packed at lunchtime, and there are always long queues on Sundays. Pay for your meal token in advance.

Kempu *Bharat Tourist Home*, Durbar Hall Rd. This relaxed coffee shop on the ground floor of *BTH* is a great place to chill between bursts of shopping on nearby MG Rd. The decor – terracotta murals, thick stone floors and dark Keralan wood – is soothing, and the south Indian bites, prepared in an open kitchen, dependably good. Try their *bonda* – spicy vegetable and peanut balls, served with coconut-and-green-chilli *chatni* that's so thick you have to spread it with a knife.

Subhishka *Bharat Tourist Home*, Durbar Hall Rd. You won't find better Keralan vegetarian food in the city centre than the meals served on banana leaves in this popular local hotel restaurant. They're pricier than average (Rs80, unlimited), and the contemporary decor and muzak are incongruous, but the cooking is painstakingly traditional – and it's a great place for crowd-watching. If you can, come on a Sunday when everyone dons their best saris and shirts for the big family meal.

Fort Cochin

Arca Nova *Fort House* hotel, 2/6A Calvathy Rd. One of the Fort's hidden gems: carefully prepared Keralan specialities – including delicious *karimeen pollichathu* or a grilled fish steak – served on a romantic, candle-lit jetty. The food is consistently good, and not too pricey (most mains Rs250–300), and the location's perfect for watching the ships chugging in and out of the docks.

Dal Roti 1/293 Lilly St. In the short time it's been open, *Dal Roti* has become the first choice among Fort Cochin's hungry travellers, both Indian and Western – despite the generally grubby state of its walls, erratic service and shortage of tables. You'll know why as soon as you taste their signature *kati* rolls – deliciously flaky wraps filled with egg, chicken or vegetables – or good value thalis (Rs170 for the works). The food is authentic north Indian, inspired by the village cooking of UP, Madhya Pradesh, Orissa and Punjab – hence full of smoky, spicy flavours you don't get to enjoy that often in Kerala. And the prices are as refreshingly honest as the cooking.

Kashi Art Café Burgher St. Chichi gallery café, patronized almost exclusively by Westerners, and with a menu to match. Freshly ground espresso is the big draw, along with their famous house cakes (the chocolate gateau is legendary), but they also do light meals and savoury snacks: check the specials board.

The Old Courtyard 1/371–2 Princess St. Few places capture the feel of old-world Cochin as vividly as this courtyard restaurant, where candle-lit tables are laid out beneath Portuguese vaulted arches. The food is as fine as the location (hallmark dishes include baked seafood spaghetti and fish grilled with coriander butter) – and the *patronne*-chef is a dessert wizard. Frequent live Carnatic music 7.30–9pm. It's also a nice spot for breakfast, with a wide choice of local and Western options. Most dinner mains Rs325–350.

Oy's Burgher St. Chilled, friendly café, popular with young backpackers, where you can enjoy travellers' breakfasts and inexpensive north and south Indian dishes, including tasty fish *moillee*, seated on low-slung sofas under the gaze of Bob Marley posters.

Teapot Peter Celli St. With its massive collection of teapots from around the world, shabby-chic colour-washed wood floors, tea-chest tables and funky little mezzanine floor, this backstreet tearoom has been giving *Kashi* some much-needed competition. Quality teas and coffees are the mainstay, but they also do light meals and delicious home-made cakes (including a stupendous Death by Chocolate).

Vasco Café Bastion St. Tiny budget travellers' breakfast joint in the heart of the tourist enclave, with wood tables and a huge bell-metal bowl in its barred window. The food – toasties, omelettes, muesli, fruit salad with curd, pancakes, juices and the like – is prepared to order, tasty and inexpensive.

Listings

Airlines, domestic Air India, Durbar Hall Rd ⓣ0484/237 1141, airport ⓣ0484/261 0041; Go Air, c/o UAE Travel Services, Chettupuzha Towers, PT Usha Rd Junction ⓣ0484/235 5522; Jet Airways/JetLite, 39/4158 Elmar Square Bldg, MG Rd ⓣ0484/235 9212, airport ⓣ0484/261 0037; Kingfisher Airlines, K.B. Oxford Business Center, 39/4013, Free Kandath Rd, MG Rd ⓣ0484/235 1144; Paramount Airways, airport ⓣ0484/261 0404.

Airlines, international Air India, Collis Estate, MG Rd ⓣ0484/238 1874, airport ⓣ0484/261 0070; Air India Express, Collis Estate, MG Rd ⓣ0484/238 1885, airport ⓣ0484/261 0050; Emirates, Plot No. 696-A, opposite Wyte Fort Hotel, NH-47 Bypass, Maradu ⓣ0484/408 4444, airport ⓣ0484/261 1194; Gulf Air, Room 201, Travancore Court Hotel, Warriam Rd, ⓣ1-800/221122, airport ⓣ0484/261 1346; Kuwait Airways, Room 35, International Terminal, Nedumbassery Airport ⓣ0484/261 0251; Qatar Airways, Hotel Le Meridien, Mezzanine Floor, Maradu ⓣ0484/261 1305; SriLankan Airlines, 70–71 DD Vyapar Bhavan, K.P. Vallon Rd, Kadavanthara, Ernakulam ⓣ0484/232 0372, airport ⓣ0484/261 1313.

Banks All the major south Indian banks have branches on MG Rd in Ernakulam. To exchange travellers' cheques, the best place is Thomas Cook (Mon–Sat 9.30am–6pm), near the Air India Building at Palal Towers, also on MG Rd. ATMs can be found all over the centre of Ernakulam. In Fort Cochin, the Canara Bank has an ATM on Kanumpuram Junction.

Bookshops The two branches of Idiom (opposite the Dutch Palace, Jew Town, Mattancherry; and on Bastion St near Princess St, Fort Cochin) are wonderful places to browse for books on travel, Indian and Keralan culture, flora and fauna, religion and art; they also have an excellent range of fiction.

Cinemas The multiplex at LuLu Mall (ⓦwww.luluindia.com), 7km north of the centre (see p.1066), hosts regular screenings of English-language movies as well as Malluwood and Bollywood releases.

Dentist The Emmanuel Dental Centre, Noble Square, Kadavanthara (ⓣ0484/220 7544, ⓦwww.cosmeticdentalcentre.com) is an international-standard practice that does routine dental procedures as well as more advanced cosmetic work.

Hospitals The 600-bed Medical Trust Hospital on MG Rd (ⓣ0484/235 8001, ⓦwww.medicaltrusthospital.com) is one of the state's most advanced private hospitals and has a 24hr casualty unit and ambulance service.

Internet access There are plenty of small internet places around Fort Cochin, charging Rs40/hr or thereabouts. In Ernakulam, convenient options include Net Park on Convent Rd and Mathsons on Durbar Hall Rd (both Rs30/hr).

Motorcycle rental I-One's-Two Wheelers, at 1/946-A Njaliparambu (the lane opposite the entrance to the Kerala Kathakali Centre, near the Basilica in Fort Cochin) has Enfields for rent, as well as a few automatic Honda Activas. You'll need to leave your passport as security. Contact Ivan Joseph on ⓣ9847 155306, ⓦwww.rentabikecochin.com.

Kathakali in Kochi

Kochi is the only city in Kerala where you are guaranteed the chance to see live **kathakali**, the state's unique form of ritualized theatre (see p.1024). Whether in its authentic setting, in temple festivals held in winter, or at the shorter tourist-oriented shows that take place year-round, these mesmerizing dance dramas – depicting the struggles of gods and demons – are an unmissable feature of Kochi's cultural life.

Five venues in the city currently hold daily shows, each preceded by an introductory talk at around 6.30pm. You can watch the dancers being made up if you arrive an hour or so beforehand; keen photographers should turn up well before the start to ensure a front-row seat. Tickets (usually Rs100–150) can be bought at the door. Most visitors only attend one performance, but you'll gain a much better sense of what **kathakali** is all about if you take in at least a couple. The next step is an all-night recital at a temple festival, or one of the performances given by the top-notch Ernakulam Kathakali Club, which stages night-long plays by Kerala's leading actors once a month, either at the TDM Hall in Ernakulam or at the Ernakulathappan Hall in the city's main Shiva temple. For details phone ⓣ0484/236 9357, or drop in at the Tourist Desk at the Main Boat Jetty, Ernakulam (see p.1061).

Dr Devan's Kathakali See India Foundation, Kalathiparambil Cross Rd, near Ernakulam Junction railway station ⓣ0484/236 6471. The oldest tourist show in the city, introduced by the inimitable Dr Devan, who starts the show with a lengthy discourse on Indian philosophy and mythology. 6.45–8pm (make-up 6pm).

Folklore Museum Bypass Rd, southeastern edge of Ernakulam. The most atmospheric venue – an a/c theatre decorated with wonderful Keralan murals and traditional wooden architecture – though it's quite pricey (Rs350), and a long trek across town if you're staying in Fort Cochin. Try to combine a performance with a tour of the museum downstairs (see p.1066), and maybe a meal at nearby *Sarovaram* (see map, p.1066). Taxis charge Rs75–100 from central Ernakulam.

Kairali Kathakali River Rd, opposite *Brunton Boatyard Hotel*, Fort Cochin. The smallest and most intimate venue, in an old-fashioned hessian-roofed structure. Show daily 6–7.30pm (make-up 5pm); Carnatic music from 9pm.

Kerala Kathakali Centre Bernard Master Lane, near Santa Cruz Basilica, just off KB Jacob Rd, Fort Cochin ⓣ0484/221 7552. Popular performances in a dedicated a/c theatre by a company of graduates of the renowned Kalamandalam academy. You usually get to see three characters, and the music is live. Shows 6–7.30pm (make-up 5pm), plus *kalarippayat* (4–5pm), and live Carnatic music (8.30pm).

Rhythms Theatre (Greenix) Opposite *Fort House*, Fort Cochin. Costing Rs450, this is the priciest show, but combines excerpts from *kathakali* plays with displays of *mohiniyattam* dance, *kalarippayat* martial art and, on Sundays, *theyyem*, set against a combination of live and pre-recorded music. Performances aren't of the highest standard, but the evening is more likely to appeal to kids, as costumes and acts change in quick succession.

Music shops Music World, MKV Building, near *Shenoy's Theatre* on MG Rd is Kochi's answer to a music superstore, with Western pop, classical, compilations, world music and Indian filmi music. Sound of Melody, DH Rd, near the Ernakulam Junction station, has a good selection of traditional South Indian and contemporary Western music.

Police The city's tourist police have counters at Ernakulam Junction railway station and next to the KTDC Tourist Office at the southern end of Shanmugham Rd.

Post office The GPO is on Hospital Rd, not far from the Main Jetty; the city's poste restante is at the post office behind St Francis Church in Fort Cochin.

Taxis Ashik Taxis ⓣ9288 157145 or ⓣ9656 798481 cover the entire state, and offer day-trips at fair prices.

The Lakshadweep Islands

Visitors for whom Kerala's beaches come as a disappointment may well find what they're looking for in **LAKSHADWEEP** (Ⓦwww.lakshadweep.nic.in), a coral archipelago lying between 200km and 400km offshore in the Arabian Sea. The smallest Union Territory in India, Lakshadweep's 27 tiny, coconut-palm-covered **islands** are a text-book tropical hideaway, edged with pristine white sands and surrounded by calm lagoons where the average water the temperature stays around 26°C all year. Beyond the lagoons lie coral **reefs**, home to sea turtles, dolphins, eagle rays, lionfish, parrotfish, octopus, barracudas and sharks. Devoid of animal and bird life, only ten of the islands are inhabited, with a total population of just over fifty thousand, the majority of whom are Malayalam-speaking Sunni Muslims said to be descended from seventh-century Keralan Hindus who converted to Islam. Concerted attempts are being made to minimize the ecological impact of tourism in Lakshadweep. Accommodation is available for **non-Indians** on only two of the islands – Bangaram and Kadmat. Indian tourists only are also allowed to visit the neighbouring islands of Kavaratti and Minicoy.

Visiting the islands

All visits to **Kadmat** must be arranged in Kochi through the Society for Promotion of Nature Tourism and Sports on IG Rd, Willingdon Island (Ⓣ0484/266 8387, Ⓦwww.lakshadweeptourism.com). They offer a five-day package **cruise** to Kavaratti, Kalpeni and Minicoy islands ($450/person).

The uninhabited, teardrop-shaped half-square-kilometre islet of **Bangaram** welcomes a limited number of foreign tourists at any one time. At present, the only way for foreigners to reach the islet is from Kochi, on small aircraft run by Indian Airlines and Kingfisher Airlines (1–2 daily except Sun; 1hr–1hr 35min; $300). Flights arrive on the island of **Agatti**, 8km southwest of Bangaram; a boat (2hr) – or, during the monsoon (May 16–Sept 15), a helicopter – connects to Bangaram. All arrangements, including flights, accommodation and the necessary entry permit, are handled by CGH Earth, on Willlingdon Island. Their luxury eco-retreat, the *Bangaram Island Resort* (Ⓦwww.cghearth.com; ⑨), accommodates up to thirty couples in thatched rooms a stone's throw away from the water's edge. There's no a/c, TV, radio, telephone, newspapers or shops, let alone discos. The price of such remoteness, however, is steep: $300–550 per night, full board, not including flights and boat transfers.

A British-run diving firm based in Goa also operates diving holidays in Lakshadweep; a full rundown of prices and booking conditions appears online at Ⓦwww.goadiving.com.

Tour and travel agents For air tickets, Kapithan Air Travel and Tours at 1/430 Burgher St in Fort Cochin (on the ground floor of *Adam's Old Inn*) is the Fort's only IATA-bonded agent. The Tourist Desk at the Main Jetty in Ernakulam (Ⓣ0484/237 1761) and Tower Rd in Fort Cochin runs elephant-spotting tours to Wayanad, and beach and backwater stays in its own guesthouses around Kannur.

Moving on from Kochi/Ernakulam

The international **airport** (Ⓣ0484/261 0113, Ⓦwww.cochinairport.com) at **Nedumbassery**, near Alwaye (aka Alua), is 29km north of Ernakulam and serves as Kerala's main gateway to and from the Gulf. Snazzy new a/c airport buses run there from the terminus in Fort Cochin (9 daily; 1hr 30min; Rs70).

Buses leave Ernakulam's KSRTC **Central bus stand** for virtually every town in Kerala, and some beyond; most, but not all, are bookable in advance at the bus

Recommended trains from Kochi/Ernakulam

The trains listed below are recommended as the fastest and/or most convenient services from Kochi. If you're heading to **Alappuzha** for the backwater trip to Kollam, take the bus, as the only train that can get you there in time invariably arrives late.

Destination	Name	No.	Station	Departs	Total time
Bengaluru (Bangalore)	*Kanyakumari–Bangalore Express*	#6525	ET	daily 5.55pm	13hr
Chennai	*Trivandrum–Chennai Mail*	#2624	ET	daily 7pm	11hr 45min
Kozhikode (Calicut)	*Netravati Express*	#6346	EJ	daily 2.05pm	5hr
Madgaon/ Margao (Goa)	*Rajdhani Express**	#2431	EJ	Tues & Thurs 10.35pm	11hr 40min
	Gandhidam Express	#6336	ET	daily 8pm	14hr 45min
Madurai	*Guruvayur–Chennai Express*	#6128	EJ	daily 11.15pm	11hr 45min
Mangalore	*Malabar Express*	#6629	ET	daily 11.50pm	10hr 10min
Mumbai	*Netravati Express*	#6346	EJ	daily 2.05pm	26hr 35min
Thiruvananthapuram	*Netravati Express*	#6345	ET	daily 2.15pm	4hr 25min
Varkala	*Malabar Express*	#6330	ET	daily 3.45pm	4hr

EJ = Ernakulam Junction
ET = Ernakulam Town
* = a/c only, meals included

station. However, for destinations further afield, you're generally much better off taking the train.

Kochi lies on Kerala's main **broad-gauge line** and sees frequent services down the coast to Thiruvananthapuram via Kottayam, Kollam and Varkala. Heading north, there are plenty of trains to Thrissur, and thence northeast across Tamil Nadu to Chennai, but only a couple run direct to Mangalore. Since the opening of the Konkan Railway, a few express trains travel along the coast all the way to Goa and Mumbai, stopping close to Mangalore. Although most long-distance express and mail trains depart from **Ernakulam Junction**, a couple of key services leave from **Ernakulam Town**. To confuse matters further, a few also start at Cochin Harbour station, so be sure to check the departure point when you book your ticket. The main reservation office, good for trains leaving all the stations, is at Ernakulam Junction.

Around Kochi and Ernakulam

Some 12km southeast of Ernakulam and a short bus or auto-rickshaw ride from the bus stand just south of Jos Junction on MG Road, the small suburban town of **THRIPUNITRA** is worth a visit for its dilapidated colonial-style **Hill Palace** (Tues–Sun 9am–5pm; Rs10), now an eclectic museum. The royal family of

Cochin at one time maintained around forty palaces – this one was confiscated by the state government after Independence, and has slipped into dusty decline over the past decade. One of the museum's finest exhibits is an early seventeenth-century wooden *mandapa* (hall) featuring carvings of episodes from the Ramayana. Of interest too are the silver filigree jewel boxes, gold and silver ornaments, and ritual objects associated with grand ceremonies. Artefacts in the **bronze gallery** include a *kingini katti* knife, whose decorative bells belie the fact that it was used for beheading, and a body-shaped cage in which condemned prisoners would be hung while birds pecked them to death.

Performances of theatre, classical music and dance, including all-night **kathakali** performances, are held over a period of eight days during the annual **Vrishikolsavam** festival (Oct/Nov) at the **Sri Purnathrayisa Temple** on the way to the palace. Inside the temple compound, both in the morning and at night, massed drum orchestras perform *chenda melam* in procession with fifteen caparisoned elephants.

Cherai beach

The closest decent beach to Kochi is **Cherai**, 25km north on Vypeen Island. A three-kilometre strip of golden sand and thumping surf, it's sandwiched on a narrow strip of land between the sea and a very pretty backwater area of glassy lagoons. Despite the fact the sand is no more than a few metres wide at high tide, Cherai is gaining in popularity each year, and a row of small, overpriced resorts and guesthouses has sprung up to accommodate the trickle of mainly foreign travellers who find their way up here from Kochi. The best of them by far is *Ocean Breath* (Ⓣ9847 635206, Ⓦwww.beachandbackwater.com; ❹); set back across the road from the sea wall, it lacks views but the rooms are pleasant, with high, traditional Keralan ceilings and carved gables, shiny ceramic floors and small sitouts.

To get to Cherai, you can either jump on the car ferry across to Vypeen Island from the jetty next to *Brunton Boatyard* in Fort Cochin, then transfer onto the hourly bus waiting on the other side, or catch one of the more frequent buses from opposite the High Court Jetty in Ernakulam. Alternatively, rent a scooter (see p.1068) and ride up – in which case, a preferable route to the main road is the more picturesque coastal lane hugging the sea wall; you can pick it up by turning west (left) down a bumpy backroad at **Nayarambalam**, 1km north of **Narakkal**, or via any of the lanes peeling left further on.

Thrissur and around

THRISSUR (Trichur), a bustling market hub and temple town roughly midway between Kochi (74km south) and Palakkad (79km northeast) on the NH-47, is a convenient base for exploring the cultural riches of central Kerala. Close to the Palghat (Palakkad) Gap – an opening in the natural border made by the Western Ghat mountains – it presided over the main trade route into the region from Tamil Nadu and Karnataka. For years Thrissur was the capital of Cochin state, controlled at various times by both the Zamorin of Kozhikode and Tipu Sultan of Mysore.

Today, Thrissur derives most of its income from remittance cheques sent by expatriates in the Gulf – hence the predominance of ostentatious modern houses in the surrounding villages. As the home of several influential art institutions, the town also prides itself on being the cultural capital of Kerala. The state's largest temple, **Vadukkunnathan**, is here too, at the centre of a huge circular maidan that hosts all kinds of public gatherings, not least Kerala's most extravagant, noisy and sumptuous festival, **Puram**.

Arrival and information

The principal point of orientation in Thrissur is the **Round**, a road (subdivided into North, South, East and West) which circles the Vadukkunnathan temple complex and maidan in the town centre. On the main line to Chennai and other points in neighbouring Tamil Nadu, and with good connections to Kochi and Thiruvananthapuram, the **railway station** is 1km southwest, opposite the **KSRTC long-distance bus stand**. **Priya Darshini bus stand** (also known as "North", "Shoranur" and "Wadakkancheri" stand), close to Round North, serves Shoranur (for the Kalamanadalam academy). The **Shakthan Thampuran bus stand**, on TB Road, around 1km from Round South, serves local destinations south such as Irinjalakuda, Kodungallur and Guruvayur.

The primary purpose of the volunteer-run DTPC **tourist office** (Mon–Sat 10am–5pm; ⓣ0487/232 0800), on Palace Road opposite the Town Hall (five minutes' walk off Round East), is to promote the Puram festival, but they also give out maps of Thrissur. The best place to **change money** and travellers' cheques is the UTI Bank in the City Centre Shopping building (Mon–Fri 9.30am–3.30pm, Sat 9.30am–1.30pm) on Round West. The UAE Exchange & Financial Services (Mon–Sat 9.30am–6pm, Sun 9.30am–1.30pm) in the basement of the *Casino Hotel* building also changes currency and travellers' cheques. Both of the above, and a dozen or so other banks around the centre, have ATMs. The **main post office** is on the southern edge of town, just off Round South. **Internet** (around Rs30/hr) is available at Hugues Net on the top floor of the City Centre Shopping building and at SS Consultants next to the *Luciya Palace* hotel.

Accommodation

Thrissur has plenty of competetively priced mid-scale **hotels**, but only a couple of decent budget places – the best of them the splendid *Ramanilayam Government Guesthouse*. If you're planning to be here during **Puram**, book well in advance and bear in mind that room rates soar – some of the more upmarket hotels, and those overlooking the Round, charge up to ten times their usual prices.

Ashoka Inn TB Rd ⓣ0487/244 4333, ⓦwww.ashokainn.co.in. Best value among the business-oriented three-stars in the Shakthan Thampuran bus stand district, in a spanking new, glass-sided tower block with spacious, impeccably clean rooms. ❺

Elite International Chembottil Lane, off Round South ⓣ0487/242 1033, ⓔmail@hotelelite international.com. Pronounced "Ee-light", this massive gun-metal-grey tower block in the centre of town has some rooms with balconies overlooking the green. They're huge for the price, but dowdy. Rates include breakfast. ❸–❹

Gurukripa Lodge Chembottil Lane ⓣ0487/242 1895. Run with great efficiency by the venerable Mr Venugopal, the *Gurukripa*, just off Round South, offers a variety of simple en-suite rooms, (including several great-value singles) ranged around a long inner courtyard. Some a/c. ❶–❷

Kuruppath Mannadiara Lane, off Kuruppam Rd ⓣ09495/260000, ⓦwww.paithrukam.com. An impeccably restored heritage bungalow, cowering amid the highrise tower blocks in the heart of town, just a stone's throw from Round South. Filled with dark wood and antique tiles, the interiors are light, well-aired, cool and amazingly peaceful considering the location, while the master bedroom on the first floor has a gigantic bathroom. Rates include meals. ❼

Pathan's Round South ⓣ0487/242 5620, ⓦwww.pathansresidentialhotel.com. Budget place on the Round holding just twenty rooms, all with larger than average bathrooms and generous outside sitting space. The deluxe rooms are worn, but the a/c ones are smarter, bigger, better kept and afford grandstand views over the Round. Minimum two-night stay during Puram, when prices rise tenfold (though you're allowed to cram four people in for the price). ❷–❹

Ramanilayam Government Guesthouse Palace Rd ☎0471/233 2016. Star-hotel comfort at economy lodge rates, in palatial suites with balconies, or smaller doubles (some a/c), set in manicured gardens on the northeast side of town near the zoo and museum. As with all *Government Guesthouses*, officials get priority (even at the last minute), which can make a mockery of advance bookings. ❷–❸

The Town

The mighty **Vadukkunnathan Temple**, in the centre of the Round, may be closed to non-Hindus, but you can gain a sense of how ancient its roots are at the nearby **Vadakka Madham Brahmaswam** (daily 7.30am–2.30pm; free), five minutes' walk west of the temple off MG Rd, where young Namboodiri Brahmin boys attend **chanting** classes at a traditional *madham* or college. Wearing traditional white *mundu*, sacred threads and ash marks on their skin, the students sit cross-legged in traditional Keralan halls while they repeat verses from 3000-year-old texts modelled for them by their gurus. If you'd like to visit, telephone (☎0487/244 0877 or 6126) to ensure classes will be in progress; donations towards the *madham*'s activities are welcome.

Thrissur Puram

Thrissur is best known to outsiders as the venue for Kerala's biggest annual festival, **Puram**, which takes place on one day in the Hindu month of Medam (April–May; ask at a tourist office or check online for the exact date). Inaugurated by Shaktan Tampuran, the Raja of Cochin, between 1789 and 1803, the event is the culmination of eight days of festivities spread over nine different temples to mark obeisance to Lord Shiva, at the peak of the summer's heat. Like temple festivals across Kerala, it involves the stock ingredients of caparisoned elephants, massed drum orchestras and firework displays, but on a scale, and performed with an intensity, unmatched by any other.

Puram's grand stage is the long, wide path leading to the southern entrance of **Vadukkunnathan Temple** on the Round. Shortly after dawn, a sea of onlookers gathers here to watch the first phase of the 36-hour marathon – the **kudammattom**, or "Divine Durbar" – in which two majestic **elephant processions**, representing Thrissur's Tiruvambadi and Paramekkavu temples, advance towards each other down the walkway, like armies on a medieval battlefield, preceded by ranks of drummers and musicians. Both sides present thirteen tuskers sumptuously decorated with gold caparisons (*nettipattom*), each ridden by three young Brahmins clutching objects symbolizing royalty: silver-handled whisks of yak hair, circular peacock-feather fans and colourful silk umbrellas fringed with silver pendants. At the centre of the opposing lines, the principal elephant carries an image of the temple's presiding deity. Swaying gently, the elephants stand still much of the time, ears flapping, seemingly oblivious to the crowds and huge orchestra that plays in front of them, competing to create the most noise and greatest spectacle. When the music reaches its peak around sunset, the two groups set off towards different districts of town. This signals the start of a spectacular **firework display** that begins with a series of deafening explosions and lasts through the night, with the teams once again trying to outdo each other to put on the most impressive show.

If you venture to Thrissur for Puram, be prepared for packed buses and trains, and book **accommodation** well in advance. As is usual for temple festivals, many men use the event as an excuse to get hopelessly drunk. Women are thus advised to dress conservatively and only to go to the morning session, or to watch with a group of Indian women – and at all times avoid the area immediately in front of the drummers, where the "rhythm madmen" congregate.

Not to be outdone by the scale of the Hindu temple across town, the vast Indo-Gothic **Basilica of Our Lady of Dolours** (Puthan Pally in Malayalam) dominates the skyline southeast of the Round, thanks to its gigantic 79m bellfry – allegedly the largest church tower in Asia. You can scale the mighty edifice (Tues–Fri 10am–1pm & 2–6pm, Sat & Sun 10am–1pm & 2–7.30pm; Rs15), either via a lift or 350-step staircase, from the top of which superb views extend across the palm forest surrounding Thrissur.

Of the town's **museums**, grouped to the north of the Round, the only one worth visiting – not least for the splendid Keralan architecture of the former palace it's housed in – is the **Archeological Museum** (Tues–Sun 9.30am–1pm & 2–4.30pm; Rs10), opposite the Priya Darshini bus stand, a five-minute walk north of the Round. Former residence of the Cochin royal family, the 200-year-old Shaktan Thampuran Palace is beautifully decorated with intricate wood- and tile-work. Exhibits include fifteenth- and eighteenth-century hero stones, a fearsome selection of beheading axes, and a massive iron-studded treasury box.

It's worth enquiring to see if there's anything on at the the **Sangeet Natak Akademi** (Ⓣ0487/233 2134, Ⓦwww.sangeetnatak.org) on Stadium Road, whose large auditorium hosts occasional music and dance concerts. Around the corner stands the **Lalit Kala Akademi** (Mon–Fri 11am–7pm; Ⓣ0487/233 3773, Ⓦwww.lalitkala.gov.in) where contemporary *adivasi* (tribal) art is exhibited in a light, cool building designed by British architect Laurie Baker.

Eating and drinking

There are plenty of dependable places to eat in Thrissur, with many hotels and busy "meals" joints lining the Round. From 8.30pm, you can also join the auto-rickshaw-wallahs, hospital visitors, itinerant mendicants, Ayappa devotees and students who congregate at the popular **thattukada** hot food market on the corner of Round South and Round East, opposite the Medical College Hospital. The rustic Keralan cooking – omelettes, dosas, *parottas*, *iddiappam*, bean curries and egg masala – is freshly prepared, delicious and unbelievably cheap.

Akshaya *Luciya Palace*, Marar Rd, just off the southwest corner of the Round. Hotel restaurant where waiters in bow ties serve quality Keralan meals at lunchtime (Rs90) in a blissfully cold a/c dining hall. From 7.30pm you can order from an exhaustive multi-cuisine menu, sitting outside in a pleasant garden illuminated by fairy lights. Beer is permitted with meals.

Bharath Hotel Chembottil Lane, 50m down the road from the *Elite Hotel*. Thrissur's top pure-veg place, packed from 7.30am onwards. The food is unfailingly fresh and delicious. Try their tangy curd *vada*, crammed with a hundred different flavours, or traditional lunchtime thali (Rs35), for which the queues stretch out the door on weekends, and be sure to leave room for the *ada*, a mix of sugar cane, coconut and rice steamed in a banana leaf (which tastes disconcertingly like old-fashioned British treacle pudding).

Indian Coffee House Round South. The usual cheap and popular *ICH* range of South Indian snacks, as well as strong chai and weak coffee, served by waiters whose serious demeanour is undermined by their old-school turbans and curry-stained tunics.

Pathans Round South. Much dingier than the *Bharath*, but with an equally devoted following. Its lunchtime meals (Rs45) are as good as any in the district, and they also do the full range of *udipi* standards, as well as some tasty Sri Lankan specialities.

Around Thrissur

CHERUTHURUTHY, on the banks of the Bharatpuzha (aka "Nila") River 32km north of Thrissur, is internationally famous as the home of **Kerala Kalamandalam**, the state's flagship training school for *kathakali* and other indigenous Keralan performing arts. The academy was founded in 1927 by the revered Keralan poet Vallathol (1878–1957), and has since been instrumental in the large-scale revival of interest in unique Keralan art forms. Non-Hindus are welcome to attend performances of *kathakali*, *kudiyattam* and *mohiniyattam* performed in the school's wonderful **theatre**, which replicates the style of the wooden, sloping-roofed traditional *kuttambalam* auditoria found in Keralan temples. You can also sit in on classes, watch demonstrations of mural painting, and visit exhibitions of costumes by signing up for the fascinating "**a day with the masters**" cultural programme (Mon–Sat 9.30am–1.30pm; $20, including lunch).

Buses heading to Shoranur from Thrissur's Priya Darshini (aka "Wadakkancheri") stand pass through Cheruthuruthy; the nearest mainline **railway station** is Shoranur Junction, 3km south, served by express trains to and from Mangalore, Chennai and Kochi. **Accommodation** is limited to the luxurious *River Retreat Heritage Ayurvedic Resort* (Ⓣ04884/262244; Ⓦwww.riverretreat.in; ❻–❽), 2km from Kalamandalan. The former palace of the Raja of Cochin, the three-star hotel and ayurveda spa occupies an idyllic position on the banks of the Nila, where you can admire a crystalline pool, partly shaded by coconut palms.

GURUVAYUR, 19km west of Thrissur, is the site of South India's most revered Krishna temple, with hundreds of thousands of Hindu pilgrims pouring in year round to worship at the shrine. As usual, non-Hindus are barred from entering, but it's still worth coming on a day-trip to visit the **Punnathur Kotta Elephant Camp** (daily 8am–6pm; Rs5, camera Rs25), 4km north of town, where the temple's elephants reside. Some 67 pachyderms, aged from 8 to 95, live in the park, munching for most of the day on specially imported piles of fodder. They're cared for by their personal *mahout*s, who wash and scrub them several times a week in the sanctuary pond. As with domestic elephants everywhere, only approach an animal if the wardens allow you, as they can be unpredictable and dangerous.

Kozhikode (Calicut)

Formerly one of Asia's most prosperous trading capitals, the busy coastal city of **KOZHIKODE** (Calicut), 225km north of Kochi, occupies an extremely important place in Keralan legend and history. It's also significant in the chronicles of European involvement on the Subcontinent, as Vasco da Gama landed at nearby Kappad beach in 1498. After centuries of decline following the Portuguese destruction of the city, Kozhikode is once again prospering thanks to the flow of remittance cheques from the Gulf – a legacy of its powerful, Moppila-Muslim merchant community, who ran the local ruler's (zamorin's) navy and trade. The recent building boom has swept aside most monuments dating from the golden age, but a few survive, notably a handful of splendid Moppila **mosques**, distinguished by their typically Keralan, multi-tiered roofs. The three most impressive specimens lie off a backroad running through the **Muslim** quarter of **Thekkepuram**, 2km southwest of the maidan (the auto-rickshaw-wallahs will know how to find them). Start at the 1100-year-old **Macchandipalli Masjid**, between Francis Road and the Kuttichira Tank, whose ceilings are covered in beautiful polychrome stucco and intricate Koranic script. A couple of hundred metres further north, the eleventh-century **Jama Masjid**'s main prayer hall, large enough for a congregation of twelve hundred worshippers, holds another elaborately carved ceiling. The most magnificent of the trio of mosques, however, is the **Mithqalpalli** (aka **Jama'atpalli**) **Masjid**, hidden down a lane behind Kuttichira tank. Resting on 24 wooden pillars, its four-tier roof and turquoise walls were built more than seven hundred years ago.

Arrival and information

The **railway station** (☎0495/270 1234), near the centre of town, is served by coastal expresses, slower passenger trains, and superfast express trains from Delhi, Mumbai, Kochi and Thiruvananthapuram. There are three **bus stands**. Government-run services pull in at the **KSRTC bus stand**, on Mavoor Road (aka Indira Gandhi Rd). Private long-distance – mainly overnight – buses stop at the **New Moffussil private stand**, 500m away on the other side of Mavoor Road. The **Palayam bus stand**, off MM Ali Road, just serves the city.

Kozhikode's international **airport** (Ⓦwww.calicutairport.com), at Karippur, 23km south of the city, is primarily a gateway for emigrant workers flying to and from the Gulf, but also has direct flights to other Indian cities. A taxi from the airport into town costs around Rs500. KTDC's **tourist information** booth (officially daily 9am–7.30pm; ☎0495/270 0097) at the railway station has information on travel connections and sights, but opening hours are erratic. The main KTDC tourist office (☎0495/272 2391), in the *Malabar Mansion* hotel at the corner of SM Street, can supply only limited information about the town and area. The UAE Exchange on Bank Road, next to *Hyson Heritage* (Mon–Sat 9.30am–1.30pm & 2–6pm, Sun 9.30am–1.30pm) changes **cash and travellers' cheques**, while the Union Bank of India and the State Bank of India, opposite each other on MM Ali Road, are two of many large branches with ATMs. **Internet** access is available at the Hub, on the first floor of the block to the right of *Nandhinee Sweets*, MM Ali Road, and at Internet Zone, near KTDC *Malabar Mansion* (both Rs30/hr).

Accommodation

Hotels in Kozhikode are plentiful, except at the bottom end of the range, where decent places are few and far between. This is one city where travellers on tighter budgets might be tempted to upgrade. Most establishments operate 24hr check-outs; because of the amount of traffic to and from the airport, the better-value ones rarely have vacancies at short notice so **reserve well ahead**.

Beach Heritage Beach Rd, 2km west of the centre ☎0495/276 2055, Ⓦwww.beachheritage.com. Dating from 1890, the premises of the colonial-era Malabar English Club, with its closely cropped lawns and high-pitched tiled roofs, now house a delightful heritage hotel retaining plenty of period feel. There are only six rooms, all with a/c units, balconies or private patios, split-cane blinds and paddle fans. Those on the upper floor are larger and have the best sea views. Good value. ❻

Calicut Tower Markaz Complex, off Mavoor Rd ☎0495/272 3202, Ⓔcalicuttower@yahoo.com. This 90-room tower block, tucked away down a quiet side-street off the main drag and popular mainly with visiting Gulf Arabs, offers by far the best value in Kozhikode's lower-mid-range bracket. Impeccably clean, with shiny tiled floors and well-scrubbed bathrooms, its "standard a/c" rooms (just Rs200 pricier than the stuffier non-a/c options) are huge for the price. Strictly no alcohol. ❹–❺

Kaza Marina Elathur, 10km north ☎0495/246 2162. This large wood-and-brick property sits next to the waves, on the fringe of a esidential area half an hour's drive north of the city – a perfect overnight pitstop if you're travelling with your own transport between Cochin and the far north of Kerala. The best of its three rooms has a huge balcony offering unimpeded sea views; the other two are smaller and more sparely furnished, but impeccably clean and comfortable. Home-cooked meals available on request. ❺

NCK Tourist Home Mavoor/IG Rd ☎0495/272 3530. An enormous, lime-green-painted budget lodge slap in the city centre. Set back from the main road, it's marginally quieter and cleaner than the competition, and there's a bustling *Indian Coffee House* on the ground floor. Limited a/c available for Rs800. ❶–❷

Sasthapuri MM Ali Rd ☎0495/272 3281, Ⓦwww.sasthapuri.com. Compact lodge on four storeys, close to the Palayam bus stand and market, and the only commendable budget place on the south side of the centre. There's a rooftop restaurant and an internet room for guests. ❷–❹

Sea Queen Beach Rd ⓣ0495/236 6604, ⓦwww.seaqueenhotel.com. Bright yellow-and-blue brick building next to a lorry park on the seafront, entirely refurbished a few years back. It's a good option if your budget can stretch to one of the pleasant, spacious a/c rooms, the best of which is the sea-facing "a/c-deluxe" (no. 213). The non-a/c rooms are fusty and not nearly as nice. Breakfast, served alfresco on the rooftop, is included in the price. ❺–❻

Eating

Kozhikode is famous for its **Moppila cuisine**, which has its roots in the culinary traditions of the city's former Arab traders. Fragrant chicken biriyanis and seafood curries with distinctive Malabari blends of spices crop up on most non-veg restaurant menus, but to sample the definitive versions you should aim to have a least one meal in *Paragon*, *Sagar* or *Zain's* (or preferably all three). **Mussels** are also big news here; deep-fried in their shells in crunchy, spicy millet coatings, they're served everywhere during the season, from October to December (at any other time, they'll have been imported and won't be as fresh). Finally, no Kozhikode feast is complete without a serving of the city's legendary **halwa**: a sticky Malabari sweet made from rice flour, coconut, jaggery (unrefined sugar) and ghee. It comes in a dazzling variety of colours and flavours. A favourite place to sample it on the south side of town is the *Grand* (aka *Nandhinee Sweets*) on MM Ali Rd, just down from the Palayam bus stand. Up on Mavoor/IG Rd, *Cool Bakery* and the adjacent *Aishwarya* have even more impressive displays.

Paragon Off the Kannur Rd. *Paragon* has been a city institution since it opened in 1939. Don't be put off by the gloomy setting beneath a flyover: the Malabari cooking here is as good as you'll find anywhere. Seafood dishes are the house speciality – especially fish tamarind, fish-mango curry, *pollichathu*, *moillee* – but there are dozens of alternatives. Whatever you order, make sure it's accompanied by their famously light *appam* and *parotta* combo. Opens at 8am for breakfast. Most mains Rs90–125.

Sagar Mavoor/IG Rd. Another old favourite of Calicut's middle classes, now with two branches. Both are housed in distinctive laterite buildings, with non-a/c on the ground floor, and brighter a/c "family" dining halls on the floors above. Ignore the generic north Indian-Chinese-multi-cuisine menu. Everyone comes for the Malabari dishes such as egg curry, fish korma and, best of all, the flavour-packed chicken *pollichathu* – boneless chicken pieces marinated in ginger, garlic, green chillies and curry leaves, and then crisp fried.

Sanjeevanam MN's Ave, near 4th Railway Gate, off PT Usha Rd. The perfect, pure-veg antidote to all those rich Malabari meals across town, *Sanjeevanam* specializes in healthy, additive-free, Satvic cooking. Their sumptuous lunchtime thali, "rajakeeam" (noon–3pm; Rs110), is out of this world, featuring twenty or more items. They also do lots of equally healthy Chinese and north Indian dishes, plus the full range of *udipi* snacks.

Sopanam Delma Complex, Mavoor/IG Rd. Cheapest and most popular of the pure-veg *udipi* joints along the city's main road. It gets packed out from breakfast time for huge, crunchy dosas, *iddli-vada* plates and delicious coconut korma with *parotta*.

Zain's Convent Cross Rd. An unassuming, green-painted family house down a dingy lane in the west end of town is hardly what you'd expect the Holy Grail of Moppila cuisine to look like, but people travel from across the city to eat here. For the benefit of the uninitiated, the dishes of the day are displayed in a glass cabinet. There's generally a choice of biriyanis (fish, chicken or mutton; Rs80–100), various fiery seafood curries, and a range of different *pathiris* – the definitive Malabari rice-flour bread. Most mains Rs100–125.

Wayanad

The seven mountains encircling the hill district of **Wayanad**, 70km inland from Kozhikode, enfold some of the most dramatic scenery in all of South India. With landscapes varying from semi-tropical savanna to misty tea and coffee plantations, and steep slopes that rise through dense forest to distinctive, angular summits of exposed grassland, the region ranges over altitudes of between 750m and 2100m. Even at the base of the plateau, scattered with typically ramshackle Indian hill bazaars, it's noticeably cooler than down on the plains.

The main Mysore–Kozhikode highway, NH-17, slices through Wayanad. Since the late 1990s, it has been the source of new income in the form of over-stressed dot-com executives and their families from Bangalore and Delhi, with numerous high-end resorts, eco-hideaways and plantation stays springing up to service the screen-weary. Even if you can't afford to stay in one of these bijou retreats, however, there are plenty of reasons to venture up here. Abutting the Tamil Nadu and Karnatakan borders, the twin reserves of **Muthanga** in the southeast, and **Tholpetty** in the north, collectively comprise the **Wayanad Wildlife Sanctuary** – part of the world-famous Nilgiri Biosphere and one of the best places in India to spot wild **elephant**.

Most of the affordable accommodation is concentrated around **Kalpetta**, the district headquarters on the highway. The town is a convenient, if uncharismatic, springboard from which to explore the south of the region, but if you want to head into the remote northern jungles, consider basing yourself in **Tholpetty**, 52km north on the Karnatakan border.

Kalpetta and southern Wayanad

If you're travelling on all but the most flexible of budgets, you'll have to base yourself in the district's capital, **KALPETTA**. A hectic market hub straddling the main road, the town has little to commend it as a place to hang out, but does have the only budget accommodation in the area, as well as good transport connections to points east, notably the **Muthanga Wildlife Sanctuary** (daily 6–10am & 3–5pm; Rs110, camera Rs25), the southern portion of the Wayanad reserve. Some 40km east of town, the park is noted primarily for its elephants, but also shelters Indian bison (gaur), deer, wild boar, bear and a handful of tigers. **Trekking** in the sanctuary is only allowed during the morning slot; guides for the three-hour route charge Rs150. If you opt for the two-hour, 22km Jeep trip, you'll also have to pay for a guide (Rs100) and the vehicle's rental (Rs300) and entry fee (Rs50).

Buses bound for Mysore and Bangalore (Bengaluru) from Kalpetta run past the park gates, as do local services heading towards Ponkuzhy. The state **bus stand** in the centre of town has frequent services to Kozhikode (72km; 2hr) and Mananthavady, for the Tholpetty reserve (27km; 1hr). **Auto-rickshaws** and **Jeeps** are also available for local destinations. **Kerala Tourism**'s office (Mon–Sat 10am–5pm, closed 2nd Sat of each month; ⓣ04936/204441) is in Kalpetta North, 1km from the bus stand, in a building sharing space with the local DTPC information desk. Helpful staff can assist with hiring forest guides and Jeeps for those going to Muthanga. Numerous small **internet** cafés are dotted around town, and there are plenty of 24hr **ATMs**, as well as a UAE Foreign Exchange outlet where you can cash travellers' cheques and **change currency**.

Accommodation and eating

A number of run-of-the-mill **hotels**, motels and lodges are dotted along, or just off, the main street. The surrounding hills also shelter many swanky plantation stays and eco-resorts, but only *Aranyakam* offers reasonable value. If you're just passing through and after a quick pit-stop, *Swamy's Udipi*, on the ground floor of the *Affas* hotel at the south end of Kalpetta, serves the usual tasty south Indian snacks and rice-based meals.

Affas Kalpetta ⓣ04936/205185 or ⓣ9447/234034, ⓦwww.hotelaffas.com. Multi-storey budget motel in the centre of town. Its en-suite rooms are clean, and the town's best *udipi* joint sits on the ground floor, but book ahead on weekends when it gets swamped by visiting students. 4

Aranyakam Valathur–Rippon, Meppadi ⓣ04936/280261 or ⓣ9447/781203, ⓦwww.aranyakam.com. Rooms in a handsome Keralan-style bungalow, with wood floors and verandas on both sides, the rear ones a stone's throw from the coffee bushes. If you can stretch to it, go for one of their two huts, which look across a spectacular wilderness of pristine forest and mountain. Rates include all meals. 6–8

Chandragiri Main Rd, Kalpetta ⓣ04936/203049. The best cheapie in town, in a modern block in the centre, and the only place with beds under Rs600 that you'd want to sleep in. Its three kinds of room vary from tiny to small, but they're well scrubbed and well aired. 3–4

Green Gates TB Rd, Kalpetta North ⓣ04936/202001, ⓦwww.greengateshotel.com. Modern three-star, tucked away in its own lush grounds 300m north of the tourist office, offering a variety of rooms in the main multi-storey block, and more private cottages to its rear. There's a pool, plenty of chill-out space in the gardens, and an ayurveda centre. 6–8

Woodlands Kalpetta ⓣ04936/202547, ⓦwww.thewoodlandshotel.com. Dependable mid-range place on the main drag, at the north end of town. Rooms are a little worn, but comfortable enough for a night and the staff are unfailingly courteous; there's secure parking, and veg and non-veg restaurants. 4–5

North Wayanad: Tholpetty

The teak forest takes over completely as you climb towards the northern limits of Wayanad, tracked by the savanna grass summits of the Brahmagiri massif. Some travellers use the pot-holed trunk road cutting north towards Mysore to reach the Nagarhole National Park or the Kodagu (Coorg) district in neighbouring Karnataka. But the majority of people who venture up here do so for a glimpse of wild elephants at the **Tholpetty Wildlife Sanctuary**, close to the state boundary. You'll see plenty of pachyderms at temple festivals down at sea level, but viewing them in the wild, foraging amid buttressed tree roots and stands of giant bamboo, is quite another thing.

Hourly buses run to Tholpetty from the town of Mananthavady, 25km southwest, itself reachable by frequent KSRTC services from Kalpetta. From the park gate itself, the Forest Department runs 24-kilometre **Jeep safaris** (daily 7–9am & 3–5pm; 90min) along a network of tracks. The cost varies according to numbers – reckon on Rs250–300 per head. You can also join guided **treks** (daily 8am–1pm; Rs800 for up to four people), though be warned that the pace can be brisk, and stops few and far between.

Accommodation

Pachyderm Palace Near the Tholpetty Forest Check Post; book through the Tourist Desk in Kochi on ⓣ0484/237 1761. Traditional Keralan bungalow with five simple rooms and garden hut on stilts rented on an all-inclusive basis. On arrival, many guests are surprised by how basic their room is for the price, but are invariably won over by the authentic Keralan cuisine and friendly welcome of host, Mr Venu. Jeeps for wildlife drives can be arranged here, along with guides for treks into the nearby Brahmagiri range. 6

Udayagiri 3.5km from the Tholpetty Forest Check Post ⓣ04935/250945 or ⓣ9539 840303, ⓦwww.ayurvedayogavilla.com. On a coffee plantation high in the hills overlooking the Tholpetty reserve, these two Keralan-style chalets boast magnificent views from their traditional slatted verandas. The interiors are a touch chintzy, but the location can't be beaten – great for lazing or as a base for forest and plantation walks. Rates include all meals (veg; no alcohol). 6

Wildlife Resort 500m from the Tholpetty Forest Check Post ⓣ09656/566977 or ⓣ9744 770500, ⓦwww.wildliferesort.in. The most comfortable option within easy walking distance of the Tholpetty park gate. Its recently built laterite, red-tiled "cottages", set in steeply sloping gardens just off the main road, are bland, and a tad overpriced, but well furnished (with good mattresses) and private sitouts. ❼

The far north

The beautiful coast **north of Kozhikode** is a seemingly endless stretch of coconut palms, wooded hills and virtually deserted beaches. The small fishing towns ranged along it hold little of interest for visitors, most of whom bypass the area completely – missing out on the chance to see **theyyem**, the extraordinary masked trance dances that take place in villages throughout the region between November and May.

Kannur (Cannanore)

KANNUR (Cannanore), a large, predominantly Moppila Muslim fishing and market town 92km north of Kozhikode, was for many centuries the capital of the Kolathiri rajas, who prospered from the maritime spice-trade through its port. India's first Portuguese Viceroy, Francisco de Almeida, took the stronghold in 1505, leaving in his wake an imposing triangular bastion, **St Angelo's Fort**. This was taken in the seventeenth century by the Dutch, who sold it a hundred or so years later to the Arakkal rajas, Kerala's only ruling Muslim dynasty. You can still clamber up the ramparts, littered with British cannon, for views over the town's fishing anchorage.

The unexploited **beaches** around Kannur are spectacular enough, but most visitors come to the town to search out **theyyem** (see p.1082). Throughout the festival season, the daily *Malayala Manorama* newspaper lists performances at the top left of the second page, though you will have to ask someone to translate. For anyone short of time, the daily rituals at **Parassinikadavu**, or the Sri Muthappam Temple next to the railway station (daily 4pm), are worthwhile alternatives.

Arrival and information

Straddling the main coastal transport artery between Mangalore and Kochi/Thiruvananthapuram, Kannur is well connected by **bus** and **train** to most major towns and cities in Kerala, as well as Mangalore in Karnataka. Buses also travel from here to Mysore, climbing the beautiful wooded Ghats to Virajpet in Kodagu. The **railway station** is just over five minutes' walk southwest of the bus stand. The State Bank of India on Fort Road will **change money** and travellers' cheques, as will UAE Exchange in the City Centre Shopping complex (Mon–Sat 9.30am–1.30pm & 2–6pm), 500m east of the bus stand. There's a **tourist information centre** at the railway station (Mon–Sat 10am–5pm; ⓣ0497/270 3121) and **internet** access is widely available.

Accommodation and eating

Kannur's noisy and congested centre is jammed with **hotels**, but you'll find better options further east in the cantonment district behind **Baby Beach**, and further north at **Palliyamoola Beach** (a Rs50–75 ride away), where a number of small resorts and homestays stand close to the sea. Southeast of town down the coast, a string of four spectacular beaches hold even more desirable places to stay.

Theyyem

Theyyem (or *theyyam*) – the dramatic spirit-possession ceremonies held at village shrines throughout the northern Malabar region in the winter – rank among Kerala's most extraordinary spectacles. Over four hundred different manifestations of this arcane ritual exist in the area around Kannur alone, each with its own distinctive costumes, elaborate jewellery, body paints, face make-up and, above all, gigantic headdresses (*mudi*).

Unlike in *kathakali* and *kudiyattam*, where actors impersonate goddesses or gods, here the performers actually become the deity being invoked, acquiring their magical powers. These allow them to perform superhuman feats, such as rolling in hot ashes or dancing with a crown that rises to the height of a coconut tree. By watching the *theyyem*, members of the audience believe they can partake of the deity's powers – to cure illness, conceive a child or get lucky in a business venture.

Traditionally staged in small clearings (*kaavus*) attached to village shrines, *theyyem* rituals are always performed by members of the lowest castes; Namboodiri and other high-caste people may attend, but they do so to venerate the deity – a unique inversion of the normal social hierarchy. Performances generally have three distinct phases: the *thottam*, where the dancer, wearing a small red headdress, recites a simple devotional song accompanied by the temple musicians; the *vellattam*, in which he runs through a series of more complicated rituals and slower, elegant poses; and the *mukhathezhuttu*, the main event, when he appears in full costume in front of the shrine. From this point on until the end of the performance, which may last all night, the *theyyem* is manifest and empowered, dancing around the arena in graceful, rhythmic steps that grow quicker and more energetic as the night progresses, culminating in a frenzied outburst just before dawn, when it isn't uncommon for the dancer to be struck by a kind of spasm.

Increasing numbers of visitors are making the journey up to Kannur to experience *theyyem*, but **finding rituals** requires time, patience and stamina. The best sources of advice are local guesthouse owners, who can check the Malayalai newspapers for notices; **websites** such as ⓦwww.theyyemcalendar.com can also point you in the right direction. Anyone pushed for time might consider a trip out to **Parassinikadavu** (see opposite), where a form of *theyyem* is staged daily.

Packed with commuters and travellers in transit, the best traditional *udipi* **restaurant** in town is the diminutive *Komala Vilas*, tucked down a sidestreet opposite the railway station exit, which serves the usual range of south Indian *iddli-vada*, dosas and rice meals for next to nothing. There's also a good *Indian Coffee House* on Fort Rd, 50m south of the City Centre shopping mall.

Costa Malabari 10km south near Thottada village; book through the Tourist Desk, Main Jetty, Kochi ⓣ0484/237 1761, ⓦwww.costamalabari.com. Three traditional Keralan bungalows, surrounded cashew and coconut groves on the bluff above Thottada Beach. *Costa Malabari II* is the pick of the crop, perched on a clifftop where a flight of rickety wooden steps takes you down to the most glorious golden sand cove. The food gets rave reviews, too. Pick-up from Kannur by prior arrangement. ❻–❼

Ezhara Beach House House 7/347, near Ezhara Moppila School, Ezhara Kadappuram, Kuttikkagam ⓣ0497/283 5022 or ⓣ9846 819941, ⓦwww.ezharabeachhouse.com. Tucked under the palms on the edge of a traditional Moppila quarter, this old, blue-painted bungalow is a great place to experience village life at close quarters. It's only a stone's throw from the sand, and within easy walking distance of long, empty beaches and owners Hyacinth and Georgio are great hosts. ❺

Government Guesthouse Cantonment area ⓣ0497/270 6426. Superb-value government-run place on a clifftop at the edge of Kannur, with huge, simple a/c and non-a/c rooms whose huge balconies have uninterrupted sea views. As ever, advance booking can be a problem; ring ahead when you arrive. Inexpensive veg meals on request. ❷

Palmgrove Heritage Mill Rd, near *Government Guesthouse* ⓣ0497/270 3182,

Ⓦ www.palmgroveheritageretreat.com. Dating from the 1930s, this former palace once belonged to the last raja of Arikkal but now accommodates an offbeat little heritage hotel, with a choice of bargain rooms or threadbare suites in the old portion, and large, modern, good-value doubles (some a/c) in the two adajcent, multi-storey blocks. ❸–❺

Pranav Beach Rd, Palliyamoola Ⓣ 0497/274 1148 or Ⓣ 9986 603756, Ⓦ www.pranavbeachresort.in. A well-run little resort, in a lawned palm grove a stone's throw from the beach to the north of town, which offers a wide range of accommodation, from attractive a/c laterite cottages with pillared sitouts to smaller cabins made of palm wood. They also offer bargain rooms with shared toilets in a beautiful old mansion – small and simply furnished, but with a huge traditional veranda. Fabulous Malabari meals are included in the price. ❸–❻

Kannur Beach House Thottada Ⓣ 9847 186330 or Ⓣ 9847 184535, Ⓦ www.kannurbeachhouse.com. Sandwiched on a slither of land between a river and the beach, the location of this friendly little guesthouse is sublime and the rooms, with their antique wooden doors and windows, luminous interiors and lovely verandas, perfect havens. Rates include meals served around a communal dining table. Trips out to *theyyem* run most evenings. If they're full, try the *Shoreline* nearby (Ⓣ 9496 55444 or Ⓣ 9746 376680, Ⓦ www.shorelinegarden.com; ❻). ❻

Parassinikadavu

The only place you can be almost guaranteed a glimpse of *theyyem* is the village of **PARASSINIKADAVU**, 20km north of Kannur, beside the River Valapatanam, where the head priest, or *madayan*, of the **Parassini Madammpura** temple performs twice a day during winter (6.30–8.30am & 5.45–8.30pm) before assembled worshippers. Elaborately dressed and accompanied by a traditional drum group, he becomes possessed by the temple's presiding deity – Lord Muthappan, Shiva, in the form of a *kiratha*, or hunter – and enacts a series of complex offerings. The two-hour ceremony culminates when the priest/deity dances forward to bless individual members of the congregation. Even by Keralan standards, it is an extraordinary spectacle, and well worth taking time out of a journey along the coast for.

Regular local **buses** leave Kannur for Parassinikadavu from around 7am, dropping passengers at the top of the village. If you want to get here in time for the earliest *theyyem*, however, you'll have to splash out on one of the Ambassador taxis that line up outside Kannur bus stand (around Rs400 return). Cabbies sleep in their cars, so you can arrange the trip on the spot by waking one up; taxis may also be arranged through most hotels. Either way, you'll have to leave around 4.30am. Alternatively, **stay** in the conveniently located *Thai Resort* (Ⓣ 0497/278 4242; ❺) 80m from the temple. Shaded by coconut trees, seven circular stone cottages are dotted around a well-kept garden, with cool, comfortable rooms.

22

Karnataka

* **Bengaluru** Booming silicon city offers the best shopping, nightlife and dining this side of Mumbai, not to mention a few great parks. See p.1088

* **Mysore** The sandalwood city oozes relaxed, old-world charm and has lots to see, including the opulent Maharaja's Palace. See p.1098

* **Halebid & Belur** Two wonderfully ornate Hoysala temples set deep in the slow-paced Karnataka countryside. See p.1109 & p.1110

* **Gokarna** This vibrant Hindu holy town is blessed with exquisite crescent beaches and is ideal for serious unwinding. See p.1123

* **Hampi** The crumbling remains of the Vijayanagar kingdom, scattered among a stunning boulder-strewn landscape bisected by the Tungabhadra River. See p.1129

* **Bijapur** Known as the "Agra of the South" for its splendid Islamic architecture, most famously the vast dome of the Golgumbaz. See p.1141

* **Bidar** Rarely visited Muslim outpost in the remote northeast of the state, famed for *bidri* metalwork and magnificent medieval monuments. See p.1146

▲ The Maharaja's Palace, Mysore

Created in 1956 from the princely state of Mysore, **KARNATAKA** – a derivation of the name of the local language, Kannada, spoken by virtually all of its 53 million inhabitants, known as Kannadigas – marks a transition zone between central India and the Dravidian deep south. Along its border with Maharashtra and Andhra Pradesh, a string of medieval walled towns, studded with domed mausoleums and minarets, recall the era when this part of the Deccan was a Muslim stronghold. The coastal and hill districts that dovetail with Kerala are quintessential Hindu south India, lush with tropical vegetation and soaring temple *gopuras*. In between are scattered several extraordinary sites, notably the ruined Vijayanagar city at Hampi, whose lost temples and derelict palaces stand amid an arid, boulder-strewn landscape of surreal beauty.

Coastal Karnataka is one of the wettest regions in India, its **climate** dominated by the seasonal monsoon, which sweeps in from the southwest in June, dumping an average of 4m of rain on the coast before it peters out in late September. Running in an unbroken line along the state's palm-fringed coast, the **Western Ghats**, draped in dense deciduous forests, impede the path of the rain clouds east. As a result, the landscape of the interior – comprising the southern apex of the triangular Deccan trap, known here as the **Mysore plateau** – is considerably drier, with dark volcanic soils in the north, and poor quartzite-granite country to the south. Two of India's most sacred rivers, the Tungabhadra and Krishna, flow across this sun-baked terrain, draining east to the Bay of Bengal.

Karnataka's principal attractions are concentrated at opposite ends of the state, with a handful of lesser-visited places dotted along the coast between Goa and Kerala. Road and rail routes dictate that most itineraries take in the brash state capital, **Bengaluru**, a go-ahead, modern city that epitomizes the aspirations of the country's new middle classes, with glittering malls, fast-food outlets and a nightlife unrivalled outside Mumbai. The state's second city, **Mysore**, appeals more for its Raj-era ambience, nineteenth-century palaces and vibrant produce and incense markets. It also lies within easy reach of several important historical monuments.

A clutch of unmissable sights lie further northeast, dotted around the dull railway town of **Hassan**. Around nine centuries ago, the Hoysala kings sited their grand dynastic capitals here, at the now middle-of-nowhere villages of **Belur** and **Halebid**, where several superbly crafted temples survive intact. More impressive still, and one of India's most extraordinary sacred sites, is the eighteen-metre Jain colossus at **Sravanabelagola**, which stares serenely over idyllic Deccani countryside.

West of Mysore, the Ghats rise in a wall of thick jungle cut by deep ravines and isolated valleys. Within, the coffee- and spice-growing region of **Kodagu (Coorg)** offers an entrancing, unique culture and lush, misty vistas. Most Coorgi agricultural produce is shipped out of **Mangalore**, an uninspiring place to pause on the journey along Karnataka's beautiful **Karavali coast**. Interrupted by countless mangrove-lined estuaries, the state's 320-kilometre-long, reddish-coloured coast contains plenty of fine beaches, mostly devoid of facilities. Few Western tourists visit the famous Krishna temple at **Udupi**, an important Vaishnavite pilgrimage centre, and fewer still venture into the mountains to see India's highest waterfall at **Jog Falls**, set amid some of the region's most spectacular scenery. However, the atmospheric Hindu pilgrimage town of **Gokarna**, further north up the coast, is an increasingly popular hideaway for budget travellers, owing to its string of exquisite beaches.

Winding inland from the mountainous Goan border, NH-4A and the rail line comprise sparsely populated **northern Karnataka**'s main transport artery and lean towards this region's undisputed highlight, the ghost city of Vijayanagar, better known as **Hampi**. Scattered around boulder hills on the south banks of the

KARNATAKA
Nizamabad
Mumbai
Panjim
Vijayawada
Chennai
Ernakulam/ Kochi
MAHARASHTRA
ANDHRA PRADESH
GOA
KERALA
TAMIL NADU
K A R N A T A K A
ARABIAN SEA
KODAGU
Bidar
Humnabad
NH-9
Sholapur
Gulbarga
Hyderabad
Gangapur
Bhima
Wadi
Bijapur
Basavana Bagevadi
Shorapur
Krishna
NH-4
Ghatprabha
Gokak
Hatti
Raichur
Mudgal
Aihole
Badami
Pattadakal
Maski
Belgaum
Saundatti
NH-13
Kittur
Hampi (Vijaynagar)
NH-7
NH-4A
Dharwar
Gadag
Hubli
Lakkundi
Hospet
Dandeli
Bellary
Guntakal
Mundgod
Tungabhadra Reservoir
Kotturu
Karwar
Ankola
Gokarna
Yana
Sirsi
Banvasi
Davangere
Kumta
Talguppa
Honavar
Jog Falls
Sagar
Chitradurga
Bhatkal
Shimoga
Vedavati
Bhadravati
NH-17
Hosdurga
NH-240
Sringeri
Udupi
Karkal
Ariskere
Nandi Hills
Mudabidri
Belur
Halebid
Kyatsandra
Dharamastala
Channarayapatna
Kolar
Mangalore
Hassan
NH-48
Yadiyur
Bengaluru
Kolar Gold Fields
Sravanabelgola
Subrahmanya
Madikeri (Mercara)
Srirangapatnam
KONKAN RAILWAY
Kushalnagar
Mysore
Kaveri
Hogenekal Falls
NAGARHOLE NATIONAL PARK
Somnathpur
Chamrajnagar
N
Kharapur
BANDIPUR NATIONAL PARK
MUDUMALAI WILDLIFE SANCTUARY
Salem
Udhagamandalam
0
100 km

Tungabhadra River, the ruins of this once splendid capital occupy a magical site and make a great spot to hole up in. The jumping-off place for Hampi is **Hospet**, from where buses leave for the bumpy journey north across the rolling Deccani plains to **Badami**, **Aihole** and UNESCO World Heritage Site **Pattadakal**. Now lost in countryside, these tiny villages – once capitals of the **Chalukya** dynasty – remain littered with ancient rock-cut caves and finely carved stone temples.

Further north still, in one of Karnataka's most remote and poorest districts, craggy hilltop citadels and crumbling wayside tombs herald the formerly troubled buffer-zone between the Muslim-dominated northern Deccan and the Dravidian-Hindu south. **Bijapur**, capital of the Bahmanis, harbours south India's finest collection of Islamic architecture, including the world's second-largest freestanding dome, the Golgumbaz. The first Bahmani capital, **Gulbarga**, site of a famous Muslim shrine and theological college, has retained little of its former splendour but the more isolated **Bidar**, where the Bahmanis moved in the sixteenth century, deserves a detour en route to or from Hyderabad. Perched on a rocky escarpment, its crumbling red ramparts include Persian-style mosaic-fronted mosques, mausoleums and a sprawling fort complex evocative of Samarkand on the Silk Route.

Some history

Like much of southern India, Karnataka has been ruled by successive Buddhist, Hindu and Muslim dynasties. The influence of Jainism has also been marked; India's very first emperor, **Chandragupta Maurya**, is believed to have converted to Jainism in the fourth century BC, renounced his throne and fasted to death at Sravanabelagola, now one of the most visited Jain pilgrimage centres in the country.

During the first millennium AD, this whole region was dominated by power struggles between the various kingdoms controlling the western Deccan. From the sixth to the eighth centuries, the **Chalukya** kingdom included Maharashtra, the Konkan coast on the west and the whole of Karnataka. The **Cholas** were powerful in the east of the region from about 870 until the thirteenth century, when the Deccan kingdoms were overwhelmed by General Malik Kafur, a convert to Islam.

By the medieval era Muslim incursions from the north had forced the hitherto warring and fractured Hindu states of the south into close alliance, with the mighty **Vijayanagars** emerging as overlords. Their lavish capital, Vijayanagar, ruled an empire stretching from the Bay of Bengal to the Arabian Sea and south to Cape Comorin. Yet the Muslims' superior military strength triumphed in 1565 at the Battle of Talikota, when the **Bahmanis** laid siege to Vijayanagar, reducing it to rubble and plundering its opulent palaces and temples.

Thereafter, a succession of Muslim sultans held sway over the north, while in the south of the state, the independent **Wadiyar rajas** of Mysore, whose territory was comparatively small, successfully fought off the Marathas. In 1761, the brilliant Muslim campaigner Haider Ali, with French support, seized the throne. His son, Tipu Sultan, turned Mysore into a major force in the south before he was killed by the British at the **battle of Srirangapatnam** in 1799. Following Tipu's defeat, the British restored the Wadiyar family to the throne. Apart from a further half century of colonial rule in the mid-nineteenth century, they kept it until Karnataka was created by the merging of the states of Mysore and the Madras Presidencies in 1956.

Since Independence, the political scene was dominated by the **Congress** party, with the exception of some Janata Dal administrations in the 1980s, until, following an unstable period of President's rule, the **BJP** took control in May 2008.

Bengaluru (Bangalore) and around

The political hub of the region, **BENGALURU** is a world apart from the rest of the state and in many ways India's most westernized urban centre. From a charming, verdant "Garden City" of just over 600,000 at Independence, Bengaluru has been completely transformed by the technology boom into both a trendy, high-speed business hub and a bustling, smog-choked megalopolis of eight million. These days, signs of the West are thick on the ground: *Starbucks*-like *Café Coffee Days* on nearly every corner, a flash new airport and ultra-modern metro (set for completion in 2011) and legions of hard-working, free-spending twenty- and thirty-somethings in designer T-shirts and mini-skirts.

Bengaluru's few attractions are no match for those elsewhere in the state, and the city's comparative local advantages are ten-a-penny in the West. That said, it's an efficient transport hub, well served by plane and bus, and at nearly 1000m the climate is relatively mild. Paired with first-rate shopping, dining and nightlife, this vibrant city can still deliver a few days' respite from south India's more taxing inconveniences.

Some history

A stone inscription near a tenth-century temple in the eastern part of the city describes a battle fought on this ground in 890, in a placed called "Bengavaluru," or the "City of Guards." This marks the earliest historical reference to the city that was **renamed** Bengaluru in 2006. The city was established more firmly in 1537 when Magadi **Kempe Gowda**, a devout Hindu and feudatory chief of the Vijayanagar empire, built a mud fort and erected four watchtowers outside the village, predicting that it would one day extend that far (the city now stretches far beyond). During the first half of the seventeenth century, Bangalore fell to the Muslim sultanate of Bijapur and changed hands several times before being returned to Hindu rule under the Mysore Wadiyar rajas. In 1758, Chikka Krishnaraja Wadiyar II was deposed by the military genius Haider Ali, who set up arsenals here to produce muskets, rockets and other weapons for his formidable anti-British campaigns. He and his son, **Tipu**

Bengaluru backlash?

In recent decades Bengaluru has experienced a **seismic societal shift**, predominantly due to the endless job opportunities presented by computer software and back-office services. The population grew nearly forty percent to 5.7 million in the decade ending in 2001, and is now approaching eight million. By late 2007 every fifth city resident hailed from a different state and Bengaluru's **software industry** had become a US$8 billion behemoth.

Many locals blame IT professionals for skyrocketing living costs, choking **pollution** and the rise of a liberal, West-leaning bar and disco culture, not to mention **traffic jams**, regular power failures and crippling seasonal **water shortages**. In addition, due to higher salaries and bright futures, IT professionals are favoured in the competitive marriage market, creating further tension.

Yet hope springs eternal. After more than two decades of hand-wringing and debate, work recently began on a much-needed **subway system** to alleviate the city's infamous traffic jams. The new **international airport**, opened in early 2008, should smooth the increase of business and tourist visitors. Longtime residents may never regain their urban idyll, but with compromise and elbow grease Bengaluru may yet inspire civic pride.

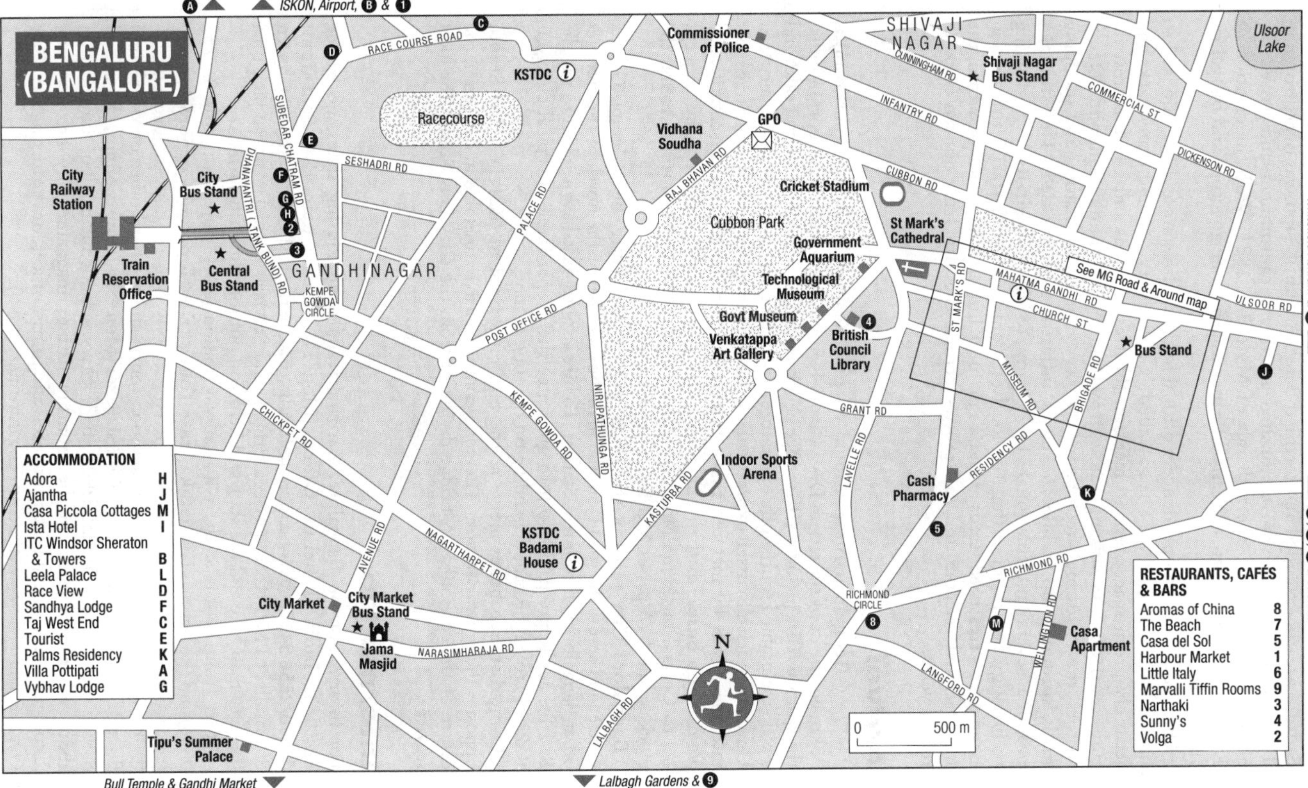
BENGALURU (BANGALORE)
ACCOMMODATION
Adora H
Ajantha J
Casa Piccola Cottages M
Ista Hotel I
ITC Windsor Sheraton & Towers B
Leela Palace L
Race View D
Sandhya Lodge F
Taj West End C
Tourist E
Palms Residency K
Villa Pottipati A
Vybhav Lodge G
RESTAURANTS, CAFÉS & BARS
Aromas of China 8
The Beach 7
Casa del Sol 5
Harbour Market 1
Little Italy 6
Marvalli Tiffin Rooms 9
Narthaki 3
Sunny's 4
Volga 2
ISKON, Airport, B & 1
Whitefield Ashram & I
L, 6, 7 & Chennai
Mysore
Bull Temple & Gandhi Market
Lalbagh Gardens & 9
SHIVAJI NAGAR
GANDHINAGAR
Ulsoor Lake
Racecourse
Cubbon Park
City Railway Station
Train Reservation Office
City Bus Stand
Central Bus Stand
KEMPE GOWDA CIRCLE
KSTDC
Commissioner of Police
Shivaji Nagar Bus Stand
Vidhana Soudha
GPO
Cricket Stadium
St Mark's Cathedral
Government Aquarium
Technological Museum
Govt Museum
Venkatappa Art Gallery
British Council Library
Indoor Sports Arena
Cash Pharmacy
Bus Stand
See MG Road & Around map
KSTDC Badami House
City Market
City Market Bus Stand
Jama Masjid
Tipu's Summer Palace
Casa Apartment
RICHMOND CIRCLE
RACE COURSE ROAD
SUBEDAR CHATRAM RD
DHANAVANTRI (TANK BUND) RD
SESHADRI RD
PALACE RD
RAJ BHAVAN RD
CUNNINGHAM RD
INFANTRY RD
COMMERCIAL ST
DICKENSON RD
CUBBON RD
MAHATMA GANDHI RD
CHURCH ST
ULSOOR RD
ST MARK'S RD
MUSEUM RD
BRIGADE RD
POST OFFICE RD
KEMPE GOWDA RD
NIRUPATHUNGA RD
GRANT RD
LAVELLE RD
RESIDENCY RD
KASTURBA RD
CHICKPET RD
AVENUE RD
NAGARTHARPET RD
NARASIMHARAJA RD
RICHMOND RD
WELLINGTON RD
LANGFORD RD
LALBAGH RD
N
0 500 m

Sultan, greatly extended and fortified Bangalore until Tipu was overthrown in 1799 by the British, who established a military cantonment and passed the administration over to the maharaja of Mysore in 1881. With the creation of Karnataka state in 1956, the erstwhile maharaja became governor and Bangalore the capital.

Until well after Independence, political leaders, film stars and VIPs flocked to buy or build homes here. The so-called "Garden City" offered many parks and leisurely green spaces, not to mention theatres, cinemas and a lack of restrictions on alcohol. Following a slow growth in the communications and defence sectors, the 1990s high-tech boom saw skyscrapers, swish stores and shopping malls springing up, while the city's infrastructure buckled. The stumbles prodded several multinationals to decamp to Hyderabad, itself a growing technology centre, upsetting the local economy and temporarily threatening Bengaluru's treasured status as India's main IT hub. Led by rapid growth in the international telecom and call-centre sectors, the city has bounced back in recent years.

Arrival

The new **Bengaluru International Airport** (Ⓦwww.bengaluruairport.com) is 35km northeast of the city in Devanahalli. Reportedly the priciest airport in India, the spacious BIA includes self-service check-in kiosks, high-end bars and cafés and a well-maintained tourist office – features that are a cut above most Indian airports. Until the much-discussed express rail is up and running, the only ground transport into the city is by metered **taxis** (Rs550–700) or the efficient air-conditioned **Vayu Vajra buses**; of their ten routes, the most useful to visitors is the frequent #9 to Central bus stand (45min–1hr 15min; Rs140), which operates round the clock, while #7A passes MG Road twice a day.

Bangalore City railway station is west of the centre, near Kempe Gowda Circle, and across the road from the main bus stands; for the north of the city, get off at Bangalore Cantonment Station. To hire an auto-rickshaw it is best to pay the Rs1 fee at the pre-paid booth to guarantee the proper fare – a typical charge is Rs25–40 to MG Road, depending on the time of day.

Long-distance buses arrive at the big, busy **Central** (KSRTC) **Bus Stand**, opposite the railway station. There is a comprehensive timetable in English in the centre of the concourse. A bridge divides it from the **City Bus Stand**, for local services.

Information

For information on Bangalore, Karnataka and neighbouring states, go to the excellent **India Tourism Office** (Mon–Fri 9.30am–6pm, Sat 9am–1pm; Ⓣ080/2558 5417, Ⓦwww.incredibleindia.org), in the KSFC Building, 48 Church St (parallel to MG Road between Brigade and St Mark's roads). You can pick up a free city map here and the staff will help you put together itineraries.

Apart from booths at the City railway station (daily 7am–8pm; Ⓣ080/2287 0068) and the airport, **Karnataka State Tourist Development Corporation** also has two city offices: one at Badami House, NR Square (daily 6.30am–10pm; Ⓣ080/2227 5883), where you can book tours; and the head office on the second floor of Khanija Bhavan, Race Course Road (Mon–Sat 10am–5.30pm, closed 2nd Sat of month; Ⓣ080/2235 2901 to 3, Ⓦwww.kstdc.nic.in). For information about **what's on**, pick up the monthly listings magazine *City Info* (Ⓦwww.explocity.com), available at most hotels and tourist offices, or the fortnightly *Time Out Bengaluru* (Ⓦwww.timeoutbengaluru.net; Rs40).

Moving on from Bengaluru

Bengaluru is south India's principal transport hub. Fast and efficient computerised booking facilities make moving on straightforward, although the availability of seats should never be taken for granted; book as far in advance as possible. Bengaluru's **airport** is the busiest in south India, with more than a dozen daily flights to **Mumbai**, **Chennai** and **Hyderabad**, plus services to numerous other destinations.

Most of the wide range of long-distance **buses** from **Central Bus Stand** can be booked in advance at the computerized counters near Bay 13 (7.30am–7.30pm daily). As well as Karnataka's state bus corporation (KSRTC), government-run services from Andhra Pradesh, Kerala, Maharashtra, Tamil Nadu and Goa also operate from Bengaluru. Timings and ticket availability for the forthcoming week are posted on a large board to the left of the main entrance. For general enquiries, call ⓣ080/2287 3377.

Several **private bus companies** run luxury coaches to destinations such as Mysore, Bijapur, Ooty, Chennai, Kochi/Ernakulam, Thrissur, Kollam and Thiruvananthapuram. Tickets can be bought from the agencies on Tank Bund Road, opposite the bus stand; operators include Sharma (ⓣ080/2670 2447), National (ⓣ080/2660 3112) and Shama (ⓣ080/2670 5855), each of which advertise overnight **sleeper coaches** to **Goa** and sleeper coaches and services to **Mumbai** and **Chennai**. The most reliable of the private bus companies is Vijayanand Travels (ⓣ080/2297 1257), who also have an office on Tank Bund Road; their distinctive yellow-and-black luxury coaches run to destinations such as Mangalore, Gokarna/Goa, and Hospet for Hampi.

Bengaluru's **City railway station**'s reservations office (Mon–Sat 8am–2pm & 2.15–8pm, Sun 8am–2pm; ⓣ132) is in a separate building, east of the main station (to the left as you approach). Counter 14 is for foreigners. If you have an Indrail Pass, go to the Chief Reservations Supervisor's Office on the first floor, where "reservations are guaranteed". Trains to **Goa** and a handful of trains to other destinations depart from Yeshwanthpur railway station (ⓣ080/2337 7161) in the north of the city.

Recommended trains from Bengaluru

The following trains are recommended as the fastest and/or most convenient from Bengaluru.

Destination	Name	No.	Departs	Total time
Chennai	*Shatabdi Express**	#2008	daily except Tues 4.20pm	5hr 5min
	Lalbagh Express	#2608	daily 6.30am	5hr 45min
Delhi	*Karnataka Express*	#2627	daily 7.20pm	39hr 20min
Ernakulam (for Kochi)	*Kanniyakumari Express*	#6526	daily 9.40pm	12hr 20min
Hospet (for Hampi)	*Hampi Express*	#6592	daily 10.30pm	8hr 55min
Mumbai	*Udyan Express*	#6530	daily 8.10pm	23hr 40min
Mysore	*Shatabdi Express**	#2007	daily except Tues 11am	2hr
	Tippu Express	#2614	daily 3pm	2hr 30min
	Chamundi Express	#6216	daily 6.15pm	2hr 55min
Secunderabad (Hyderabad)	*Rajdhani Express**	#2429	4 weekly 8.20pm	10hr 45min
Thiruvananthapuram	*Kanniyakumari Express*	#6526	daily 9.40pm	17hr 25min

*= a/c only

For information on any of Karnataka's **national parks**, call at the Wildlife Office, Forest Department, Aranya Bhavan, Malleswaram (Ⓣ080/2334 1993), or try Jungle Lodges & Resorts, Floor 2, Shrungar Shopping Centre, off MG Road (Ⓣ080/2559 7021, Ⓦwww.junglelodges.com). The latter, a quasi-government body, promotes ecotourism through a number of upmarket forest lodges including the much-lauded *Kabini River Lodge* (see p.1107) near Nagarhole.

City transport

Until the metro opens (expected to be in 2011), the easiest way of getting around Bengaluru is by metered **auto-rickshaw**; fares start at Rs10 for the first kilometre and Rs5 per kilometre thereafter. Most meters do work and drivers are usually willing to use them, although you will occasionally be asked for a flat fare, especially during rush hour.

Bengaluru's extensive **bus** system radiates from the City Bus Stand (Ⓣ080/222 2542), near the railway station. Most buses from platform 17 travel past MG Road. Along with regular buses, BMTC also operates a deluxe express service, Pushpak, on a number of set routes (#P109 terminates at Whitefield ashram) as well as a handful of night buses. Other important city bus stands include the City Market Bus Stand (Ⓣ080/670 2177) to the south of the railway station and Shivaji Nagar (Ⓣ080/286 5332) to the north of Cubbon Park – the #P2 Jayanagar service from here is handy for the Lalbagh Botanical Gardens.

You can book **chauffeur-driven cars and taxis** through several agencies including the Cab Service, Sabari Complex, 24 Residency Rd (Ⓣ080/2558 6121), and the 24-hour Dial-a-Car service (Ⓣ080/2526 1737, Ⓔdialacar@hotmail.com).

Accommodation

Due to the great number of business visitors it receives, Bengaluru offers a wealth of up-market lodgings, as well as serviced apartments. Decent **budget accommodation** is also available, mostly concentrated around the Central Bus Stand and railway station.

Around the railway station and Central Bus Stand

Hotel Adora 47 SC Rd Ⓣ080/2287 2280. Above a quality south Indian veg restaurant, this is a top budget place. Though bland, the rooms are clean and good sized; a popular choice for backpackers. ❷–❸

Sandhya Lodge 70 SC Rd Ⓣ080/2287 4071, Ⓔsandhyalodge@gmail.com. Tall concrete block with spacious rooms, all with cable TV, some with a/c. Gradually being upgraded with marble fittings and smart furniture. ❸–❺

Tourist Ananda Rao Circle Ⓣ080/2226 2381–8. One of Bengaluru's best all-round budget lodges, just a short walk from the station. Small rooms, long verandas, friendly family management and no reservations, so it fills up fast. ❶

Vybhav Lodge 60 SC Rd Ⓣ080/2287 3997. A tad grubby and frayed at the edges but not a bad fallback. Cell-like attached singles with TV cost only Rs250. ❶

Around the racecourse and Cubbon Park

ITC Windsor Sheraton & Towers 25 Golf Course Rd Ⓣ080/2226 9898, Ⓦwww.sheraton.com. Ersatz palace now a luxurious five-star, mainly for overseas businesspeople with rates from around $250. Facilities include broadband, gym, pool, Jacuzzi, a fine restaurant and popular Irish pub. ❾

Race View 25 Race Course Rd Ⓣ080/4069 6111. Large business hotel with sizeable wood-panelled rooms. Those at the front do overlook the racecourse but also the busy road. Good value a/c rooms. ❹–❺

Taj West End Race Course Rd Ⓣ080/2225 5055, Ⓦwww.tajhotels.com. Begun as a British-run boarding house in 1887, these lodgings were upgraded with fabulous gardens and long colonnaded walkways. The old wing is bursting with character, with broad verandas overlooking acres of grounds. Online room rates start at $280 a night. ❾

Villa Pottipati 142 4th Main, 8th Cross, Malleswaram ⓣ080/2336 0777, ⓦwww.neemranahotels.com A heritage hotel in the northwestern suburbs, wrapped in a garden of jacaranda trees and flowering shrubs. Its rooms ooze old-world style, with pillared verandas, deep bathtubs and direct access to an outdoor swimming pool. Part of the *Neemrana* chain, so the highest standards of service are guaranteed. Gourmet meals, prepared by a French chef, are also served. ❽

MG Road and around

Ajantha 22-A MG Rd (see map, p.1089) ⓣ080/2558 4321, ⓕ2558 4780. Best value in this area, with basic but larger than average attached rooms and some spacious, three-room cottages, located at the end of a quiet lane but near shops. Veg restaurant, internet, bakery, travel agent and sundries shop all on site. Often full, in which case try the pricier *Ashley Inn* (ⓣ080/4123 3415; ❻–❼) almost next door. ❹–❺

Brindavan 40 MG Rd ⓣ080/2558 4000. With mostly quiet and charming rooms set slightly off the main road, this is still a backpacker's favourite, though overpriced these days. Book ahead. ❹–❻

Casa Piccola Cottages No. 2, Clapham St, off Richmond Rd ⓣ080/2227 0754, ⓦwww.casapiccola.com. Tranquillity awaits at these cottages, set in well-maintained grounds just over a kilometre south of MG Road. The cottages and apartments are enormous, comfortable and well-appointed, and the free breakfasts are excellent; wi-fi is also available. If full, request lodging at similarly-priced *Casa Piccola Apartments* around the corner (A-002 Wellington Park on Wellington St). ❻–❼

Empire International 36 Church St ⓣ080/2559 3743, ⓦwww.hotelempire.in. Smart new hotel with popular restaurant and very comfortable rooms boasting modern decor and good facilities. Sister concern *Hotel Empire* (❹–❺), similar but without the finer touches, is a few blocks north of MG Rd. ❺–❻

Ista Hotel 1/1 Sami Vivekananda Rd, ⓣ080/2555 8888, ⓦwww.istahotels.com. This gorgeous new ultra-luxury hotel, with breezy, safari-themed bar, infinity pool, jacuzzi and gym, is a secluded sanctuary. Some of the spacious rooms have marble baths and views of Ulsoor Lake; suites have large garden balconies. Internet rates from $175. ❾

Leela Palace 23 Airport Rd ⓣ080/2521 1234, ⓦwww.theleela.com. This enormous gold-domed palace on nine acres of jungle lagoon, 5km southeast of town, has a spa and lodgings fit for a king. The 256 rooms (from $435), most with balconies overlooking the lush grounds, are enormous and gorgeously appointed, while the *Royal Club* serves truffles, fine French cheese and perfectly-aged Scotch whisky. ❾

Palms Residency 125 Brigade Rd, opposite Brigade Towers ⓣ080/2554 7807, ⓦwww.palmsresidency.com. A solid deal for this area, with clean, good-sized rooms, all with TV and some a/c. If full, check out similarly-priced *Vellara* just down the road at #283 (ⓣ080/2536 9116). ❹–❺

Shangrila 182 Brigade Rd ⓣ080/5112 1622, ⓔshangrila_htl@yahoo.co.in. Tibetan-run lodge right in the thick of things but welcoming; the comfy standard rooms are decent value and a/c ones a great deal. ❹

The City

The centre of modern Bengaluru lies about 4km east of Kempe Gowda Circle (and the bus and railway stations), near **MG Road**, where you'll find most of the mid-range accommodation, restaurants, shops, tourist information and banks. Leafy **Cubbon Park**, and its less than exciting museums, lie on its eastern edge, while the oldest, most "Indian" part of the city extends south from the railway station, a warren of winding streets at their most dynamic in the hubbub of the **City** and **Gandhi markets**. Bengaluru's tourist attractions are spread out: monuments such as **Tipu's Summer Palace** and the **Bull Temple** are some way south of the centre. Most, if not all, can be seen on a half-day tour, but if you explore on foot, be warned that Bengaluru has some of the worst pavements in India.

Cubbon Park and museums

A welcome green space in the heart of the city, shaded by massive clumps of bamboo, **Cubbon Park** is entered from the western end of MG Road, presided over by a statue of Queen Victoria. On Kasturba Road, which runs along its

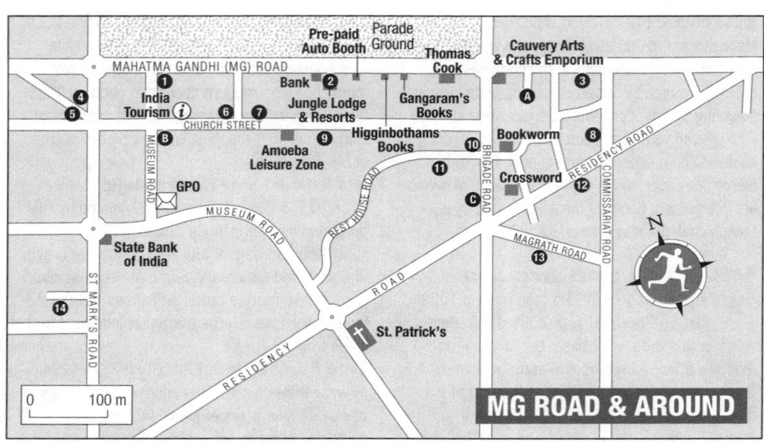

ACCOMMODATION		RESTAURANTS & BARS					
Brindavan	A	13th Floor	2	Fuga	13	Kaati Zone	6
Empire International	B	Barista	2	Green Onion	8	Koshy's	5
Shangrila	C	Coconut Grove	7	Guzzlers Inn	11	Pecos	10
		Couch	1	Hard Rock Café	4	The Pub World	12
		Friends & Bucchus	14	Indian Coffee House	9	Ulla's	3

southern edge, the poorly labelled and maintained **Government Museum** (Tues–Sun 10am–5pm; Rs5) features prehistoric artefacts, Vijayanagar, Hoysala and Chalukya sculpture, musical instruments, Thanjavur paintings and Deccani and Rajasthani miniatures. It includes the adjacent **Venkatappa Art Gallery**, which exhibits twentieth-century landscapes, portraits, abstract art, wood sculpture and occasional temporary art shows.

Vidhana Soudha

Built in 1956, Bangalore's vast State Secretariat, **Vidhana Soudha**, northwest of Cubbon Park, is the largest civic structure of its kind in the country. Kengal Hanumanthaiah, chief minister at the time, wanted a "people's palace" that, following the transfer of power from the royal Wadiyar dynasty to a legislature, would "reflect the power and dignity of the people". In theory its design is entirely Indian, but its overall effect is not unlike the bombastic colonial architecture built in the so-called Indo-Saracenic style.

Lalbagh Botanical Gardens

Inspired by the splendid gardens of the Mughals and the French botanical gardens at Puducherry in Tamil Nadu (see p.977), Sultan Haider Ali set to work in 1760 laying out the **Lalbagh Botanical Gardens** (daily 6am–8pm; Rs5; 9am–6pm), 4km south of the centre. Originally covering forty acres, just beyond his fort – where one of Kempe Gowda's original watchtowers can still be seen – the gardens were expanded under Ali's son Tipu, who introduced numerous exotic species of plants, and today the gardens house an extensive horticultural seedling centre. The British brought in gardeners from Kew in 1856 and built a military bandstand and a glasshouse, based on London's Crystal Palace, which hosts wonderful flower shows. Now spreading over 240 acres, the gardens are pleasant to visit during the day, but tend to attract unsavoury characters after 6pm. Great sunsets and city views can be had from the central hill, which is topped by a small shrine.

Jama Masjid and Tipu's Summer Palace

Just southeast of the City Market is the fairytale-like **Jama Masjid**, whitewashed and rambling and still in regular use. Nearby is **Tipu's Summer Palace**, a two-storey, mostly wooden structure built in 1791 (daily 9am–5pm; Rs100 [Rs5]). Similar in style to the Daria Daulat Palace at Srirangapatnam (see p.1105), the palace is in a far worse state, with most of its painted decoration destroyed. Next door, the **Venkataramanaswamy Temple**, dating from the early eighteenth century, was built by the Wadiyar rajas. The *gopura* entranceway was erected in 1978.

Bull Temple

Lying 6km south of the City Bus Stand (bus #34 & #37), in the Basavanagudi area, Kempe Gowda's sixteenth-century **Bull Temple** (daily 7.30am–1.30pm & 2.30–8.30pm) houses a massive monolithic Nandi bull, its grey granite made black by the application of charcoal and oil. The temple is approached along a path lined with mendicants and snake charmers; inside, for a few rupees, the priest will offer you a string of fragrant jasmine flowers.

ISKCON temple

A hybrid of ultramodern glass and vernacular south Indian temple architecture, ISKCON's (International Society of Krishna Consciousness) gleaming temple – **Sri Radha Krishna Mandir**, Hare Krishna Hill, Chord Road (daily 7.15am–1pm & 4.15–8.30pm), 8km north of the centre, is a lavish showpiece crowned by a gold-plated dome. Barriers guide visitors on a one-way journey through the huge, well-organized complex to the inner sanctum with its images of the god Krishna and his consort Radha. Collection points throughout, and inescapable merchandizing on the way out, are evidence of the organization's highly successful commercialization. Regular **buses** to the temple depart from both the City and Shivaji Nagar bus stands.

Eating

With unmissable sights thin on the ground but tempting cafés and restaurants on every corner, you could easily spend most of your time in Bengaluru **eating**. Nowhere else in south India will you find such gastronomic variety. Around **MG Road**, pizzerias, ritzy ice-cream parlours and gourmet French restaurants stand cheek by jowl with regional cuisine from Andhra Pradesh and Kerala, Mumbai *chaat* cafés and snack bars. Places below are marked on the MG Road map on opposite unless stated otherwise.

Aromas of China G3–4 Shiva Shankar Plaza, 19 Lalbagh Rd, Richmond Circle. See map, p.1089. Among the city's top Chinese restaurants, delicacies here include dim sum, duck and sharkfin soup, as well as above-average versions of all the favourites. Around Rs150–300 for a main course.

Barista Base of Ivory Tower, MG Rd. Pleasant, expansive terrace tucked behind a row of leafy plants. Along with fine coffees and teas, serves sandwiches, baked goods, and delicious slushies.

Casa del Sol 3rd floor, Devatha Plaza, 131 Residency Rd. See map, p.1089. The Rs200 lunch buffet is worth every paise and the Sunday brunches are festive, all-you-can-drink affairs. An evening cocktail on the cool, comfortable terrace is a real treat.

Coconut Grove Church St. Mouthwatering and moderately priced gourmet Keralan, Chettinad and Coorg cuisine. Veg, fish and meat preparations are served in traditional copper thalis on a leafy terrace, and there's a wide range of seafood dishes. Main dishes Rs200–300 and plain rice a whopping Rs100. Its *Coco Grove* cocktail bar is a good spot for a drink.

Green Onion Residency Rd Cross. No-nonsense first-floor Chinese canteen serving all the usual favourites, a few Thai dishes and Tibetan veg *momos*. Mains cost Rs60–110.

Harbour Market 37 Crescent Rd, in *Hotel 37th Crescent*, off Race Course Rd. See map, p.1089. ⓣ080/4113 6262. Excellent selection of Goan, Keralan, and Mangalorean seafood along with pastas and Japanese selections in a smart, elegant space. The crunchy fried prawns are particularly special. Reservations recommended.

Indian Coffee House MG Rd. Now occupying incongruous new premises but still old-fashioned at heart, with turbaned waiters serving tasty finger foods (Rs 20–70) and fine filtered coffee. The perfectly fluffy scrambled eggs are top-notch.

Kaati Zone Church St. Fast, clean and cheap, with *kaati* rolls (Rs40–60) almost as good as those you get in Kolkata (Calcutta).

Koshy's St Mark's Rd, at Church. Spacious old-style café with cane blinds, pewter teapots and cotton-clad waiters. It serves tasty Indian specialities and international favourites like fish and chips for Rs100–200. Its adjacent sister establishment, *Jewel Box*, is much more upmarket.

Little Italy 1135 100 Feet Rd, Indiranagar. See map, p.1089. ⓣ080/2528 9126. Whether on the bamboo-bordered terrace or the elegant dining room, you'll get fantastic Italian food here, particularly the risottos and tomato-based pasta dishes. There's also an extensive wine list.

Marvalli Tiffin Rooms Lalbagh Rd. See map, p.1089. Top-notch south Indian food served cafeteria-style in an ageing, bare-bones canteen. Middle-aged waiters in white *lunghis* and striped shirts serve twelve-course set thali meals to hordes of locals at shared tables. Kudos for sticking it out to the menthol-cool, post-dessert paan.

Narthaki Just off SC Rd. See map, p.1089. The best restaurant in the station/bus stand area. Filling meals are served on the first floor, while on the second there is a restaurant-bar with a full menu of Indian and Chinese dishes. The chicken chilli is a belter.

Sunny's 34 Vittal Mallya Rd. See map, p.1089. Bracingly fresh, well-prepared ingredients, tasty Western specialities like BBQ chicken and an elegant yet leafy and casual indoor/outdoor setting. This could be Los Angeles and indeed it's popular with expats and very pricey (Rs275–600).

Ullas Above cinema, MG Rd. Superb pure-veg restaurant, with a terrace and indoor section. Excellent lunchtime thalis (Rs40–90) and a good choice of curries (around Rs60).

Volga 42 SC Rd. See map, p.1089. Good solid Indian and Chinese cuisine, mostly under Rs100, plus excellent juices. There's an open terrace above the main dining hall.

Nightlife

Bengaluru's hordes of bright young things have money to burn and a thriving **nightlife** in which to do it. A night on the town generally kicks off with a bar crawl along **Brigade Road**, **Residency Road** or **Church Street** (see map, p.1094), where there are scores of swish **pubs**. Drinking alcohol does not have the seedy connotations it does elsewhere in India; you'll even see young Indian women enjoying a beer with their mates. Note that most clubs operate a couples-only policy. For a quiet, more elegant tipple head for the bars of five-star **hotels**.

Bengaluru is a major **cinema** centre, with a booming industry and dozens of theatres showing the latest releases from India and abroad. Check the *Deccan Herald* or *Time Out* to find out what's on. To arrange a visit to a **movie studio** phone Chamundeshwari Studio (ⓣ080/2226 8642).

Bars and clubs

All on p.1094 map, exert The Beach on p.1089

13th Floor 13th Floor, Ivory Tower, 84 MG Rd. Lean over the outward facing bar, cool cocktail in hand, and enjoy the hubbub of the city from a bird's-eye view. Classy and cosmopolitan, with stunning city and sunset views and cool post-modern decor, *13th Floor* is an absolute must, but come early because it fills up fast.

The Beach 1211 100 Feet Rd, Indiranagar ⓣ080/4126 1114. The music can get rather loud on weekends, but you might not mind so much while sipping expertly made *mojitos* with your feet in the sand.

Couch 1st Floor, SAI Complex, west end of MG Rd, near corner of Museum Rd. Cool and cavernous bi-level lounge with stone floors and stylishly mismatched retro furnishings. Grab a booth near the front windows and enjoy a well-made cocktail or two as life zooms by below. Also offers a full international menu; open daily 11am–11pm.

Friends & Bacchus St Mark's Rd. The bar in this startingly designed establishment features four distinct spaces with cantilevered platforms, and hosts theme nights, including gigs, comedy, drinking games and wine tastings.

Fuga 1 Castle St, just off south end of Brigade Rd. A glowing marble bar, black and white leather banquettes, renowned guest DJs, and absinthe make this Bengaluru's swankiest club.

Guzzlers Inn 48 Rest House Rd, off Brigade Rd. A decent Indian stab at an English pub offering MTV, Star Sport, snooker, pool and good draught beer.

Hard Rock Café 40 St Mark's Rd, at Church ⓣ080/4124 2222. Upon opening in early 2008 this gorgeous, multi-room space inside an old stone library quickly became the buzzing nexus of Bengaluru nightlife, not to mention the finest bar and grill in town. With high, vaulted ceilings, grey stone walls and subtle accents, it feels both lived in and new.

Pecos Rest House Rd, off Brigade Rd. Three dank levels of rock posters and ageing wood make up the definitive Bangalore dive. The tunes are hard-driving, the beer's cheap and the Indian grub ain't half bad.

Pub World Opposite Galaxy Cinema, Residency Rd. The city's second oldest pub, this stylish place has lots of TVs and semi-private booths with crimson couches, popular with trendy young professionals.

Listings

Airlines, domestic Air India ⓣ080/2554 8888; Indian Airlines c/o Air India; Indigo ⓣ080/2224 4622; Jet Airways, ⓣ080/2522 1929, airport ⓣ080/2521 6579; JetLite ⓣ080/3989 9999; Kingfisher ⓣ080/4197 9797; Paramount ⓣ080/4115 4666; SpiceJet ⓣ080/2522 9791.

Airlines, international American ⓣ1-800/180 7300; British Airways ⓣ080/4147 3951; Delta ⓣ080/2221 9820; KLM/Northwest Airlines ⓣ080/2226 9854; Lufthansa ⓣ080/2506 0800; Malaysia Airlines ⓣ080/2212 2991; Qantas ⓣ080/2226 4719; Singapore Airlines ⓣ080/2286 7868; Thai Airways ⓣ080/4112 4333; United Airlines ⓣ080/2224 4620.

Banks and exchange Thomas Cook, 55 MG Rd; LKP Forex, 44/45 Residency Rd Cross; and Weizmann Forex Ltd, 56 Residency Rd (all Mon–Sat 9.30am–6pm). Banks have better rates; the State Bank of Mysore on MG Rd is most convenient. There are many ATMs dotted around the city, especially in the MG Rd area.

Bookshops There are a half-dozen decent bookshops along MG Rd and Church St, and the latter offers two fine newsstands. Crossword (ACR Towers, 32 Residency Rd, behind car dealership) has all the latest titles along with music, movies, a great magazine selection and a *Café Coffee Day*. Motilal Banarsidas, 16 St Mark's Rd, close to the junction with MG Rd, offers a superb selection of heavyweight Indology and philosophy titles.

Car rental Avis, the *Oberoi* hotel, 37–39 MG Rd ⓣ080/2558 5858, ⓦwww.avis.com; and Hertz, Unit 12 Raheja Plaza, 17 Commissariat Rd ⓣ080/2559 9408, ⓦwww.hertz.com both have airport outlets. For long-distance car rental and tailor-made itineraries, try Gullivers Tours & Travels, South Black 201/202 Manipal Centre, 47 Dickenson Rd ⓣ080/2558 8001; Clipper Holidays, 406 Regency Enclave, 4 Magrath Rd ⓣ080/2559 9032; any KSTDC office; and the ITDC booth at the railway station.

Hospitals Victoria, near City Market ⓣ080/2670 1150; Sindhi Charitable, 3rd Main St, SR Nagar ⓣ080/2223 7318. Dr. Suresh Nao ⓣ9845 021614, a family practice physician based in central Bengaluru, can recommend treatments and/ or closest hospital.

Internet Internet cafés are widely available across the city, generally charge Rs10–30/hr and are open until 9pm or later. The Cyber Café, 13–15 Brigade Rd, is one of the most convenient.

Libraries The British Council (English-language) library, 23 Kasturba Rd Cross (Mon–Sat 10.30am–6.30pm; ⓣ080/2221 3485), has newspapers and magazines which visitors are welcome to peruse in a/c comfort.

Music stores The best music shops in the city centre, selling Indian, Western and world music, are Music World and Planet M, both on Brigade Rd, or Rhythms, at 14 St Mark's Rd, beneath the *Nahar Heritage* hotel.

Pharmacies Al-Siddique Pharma Centre, opposite Jama Masjid near City Market, and Janata Bazaar, in the Victoria Hospital, near City Market are open all night.

Police ⓣ100.

Post office On the corner of Raj Bhavan Rd and Cubbon Rd, at the northern tip of Cubbon Park, about a 10min walk from MG Rd (Mon–Sat 10am–7pm, Sun 10.30am–1.30pm).

Shopping Cauvery Arts and Crafts Emporium, on the corner of MG and Brigade roads, is a government-run outlet shop selling all variety of wooden toys and gadgets, sandalwood sculptures, inlaid rosewood coffee-tables and hundreds of other gift items. Lots of new malls along the main section of MG Rd sell western designer goods a little cheaper than in the West, as well as quality Indian clothing and accessories.

Travel agents For flight booking and reconfirmation, and other travel necessities, try Via, on MG Rd next to *Hotel Brindavan*; Sahara Global, Unit G2, 35 Church St, next to *Empire International* ⓣ080/6535 0001; Gullivers Tours & Travels, South Black 201–202 Manipal Centre, Dickenson Rd, just north of MG Rd ⓣ080/2558 8001.

Around Bengaluru

Many visitors to Bengaluru are on their way to or from Mysore. The **Janapada Loka Folk Arts Museum** (daily 9am–5.30pm; Rs10; ⓦwww.janapadaloka.org), 53km southwest of Bengaluru on the Mysore road, gives a fascinating insight into Karnatakan culture. It includes an amazing array of Karnatakan agricultural, hunting and fishing implements, weapons, ingenious household gadgets, masks, dolls and shadow puppets, carved wooden *bhuta* (spirit) sculptures and larger-than-life temple procession figures, manuscripts, musical instruments and *yakshagana* theatre costumes. In addition, there is a **video show** (Rs5) of musicians, dancers and rituals from the state, and **boating** facilities (Rs5), while a small **restaurant** serves simple food. Any Bangalore to Mysore bus will put you down here, as long as it's not a non-stop express.

Anyone wishing to see or study classical dance in a rural environment should check out **Nrityagram Dance Village** (Tues–Sat 10am–2pm; Rs20), a delightful, purpose-built model village, 30km west of Bengaluru, designed by the award-winning architect Gerard de Cunha and founded by the late Protima Gauri. Gauri had a colourful career in media and film, and eventually came to be renowned as an exponent of Odissi dance (see p.898). The school continues without her and attracts pupils from all over the world. It hosts regular performances and lectures on Indian mythology and art, and also offers courses in different forms of Indian dance. **Guided tours** of the complex cost Rs850 per person (minimum six), including lunch and a demonstration. **Accommodation** for longer stays promises "no TV, telephones, newspapers or noise". Contact its Bengaluru office (ⓣ080/2846 6313, ⓦwww.nrityagram.org; ❼).

Mysore

A centre of sandalwood-carving, silk and incense production, **MYSORE** is one of south India's more appealing cities. Nearly 160km southwest of Bengaluru, the erstwhile capital of the Wadiyar rajas can be disappointing at first blush considering the compliments often heaped on it: upon stumbling off a bus or train one is not so much embraced by the scent of jasmine blossoms or gentle wafts of sandalwood as smacked by a cacophony of tooting, careering buses, bullock carts, motorbikes, and tongas. The city was recently ranked by a national magazine as one of India's best for business and is Karnataka's most popular tourist destination by a long shot, attracting about 2.5 million each year. Nevertheless, Mysore remains a charming, old-fashioned and undaunting town, changed by neither an IT boom nor its newfound status as a top international yoga destination. Give it a few days and Mysore will cast a spell on you.

In the tenth century Mysore was known as Mahishur – "the town where the demon buffalo was slain" (by the goddess Durga). Presiding over a district of many villages, the city was ruled from about 1400 until Independence by the Hindu **Wadiyars**. Their rule was only broken from 1761, when the Muslim Haider Ali and his son Tipu Sultan took over. Two years later, the new rulers demolished the labyrinthine old city to replace it with the elegant grid of sweeping, leafy streets and public gardens that survive today. However, following Tipu Sultan's defeat in 1799 by the British colonel Arthur Wellesley (later the Duke of Wellington), Wadiyar power was restored. As the capital of Mysore state, the city thereafter dominated a major part of southern India. In 1956, when Bangalore became capital of newly formed Karnataka, its maharaja was appointed governor.

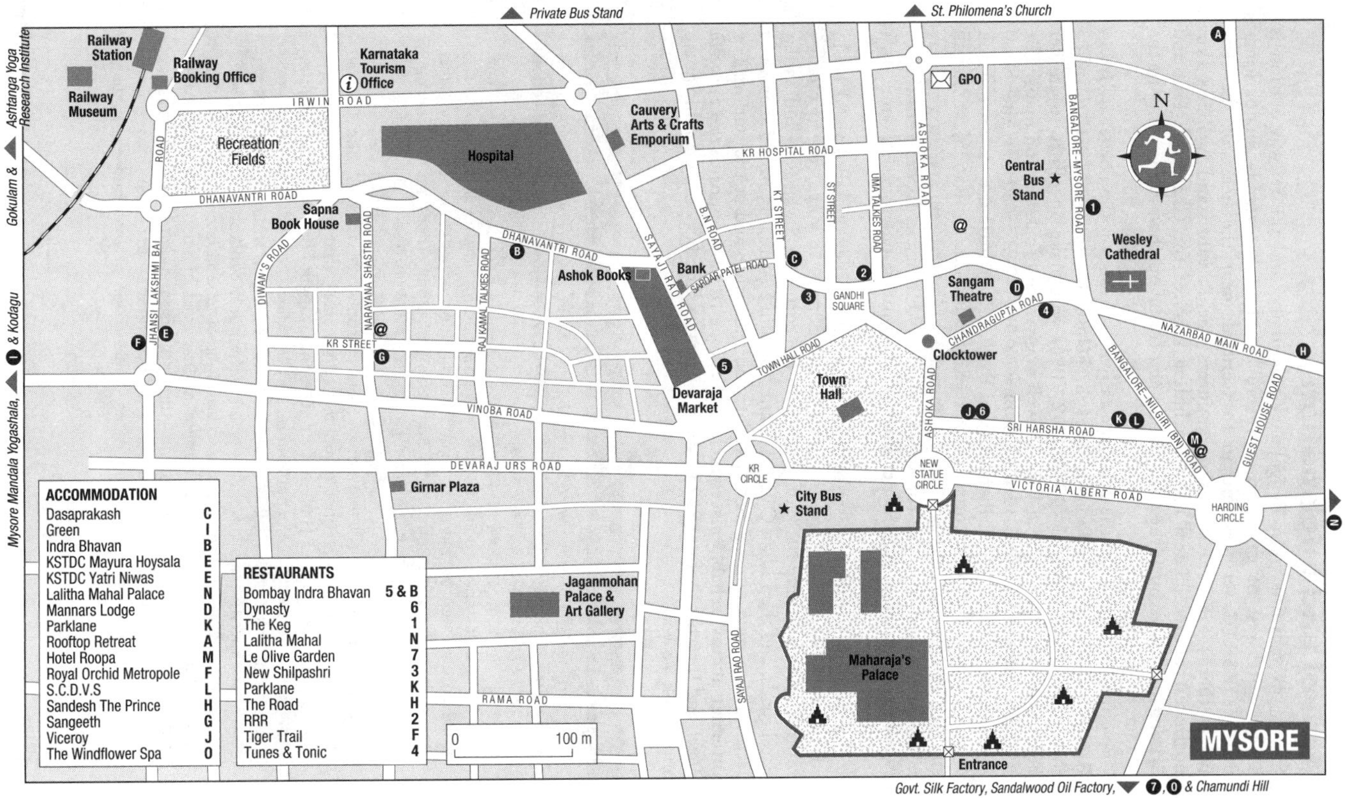

MYSORE

ACCOMMODATION

Dasaprakash	C
Green	I
Indra Bhavan	B
KSTDC Mayura Hoysala	E
KSTDC Yatri Niwas	E
Lalitha Mahal Palace	N
Mannars Lodge	D
Parklane	K
Rooftop Retreat	A
Hotel Roopa	M
Royal Orchid Metropole	F
S.C.D.V.S	L
Sandesh The Prince	H
Sangeeth	G
Viceroy	J
The Windflower Spa	O

RESTAURANTS

Bombay Indra Bhavan	5 & B
Dynasty	6
The Keg	1
Lalitha Mahal	N
Le Olive Garden	7
New Shilpashri	3
Parklane	K
The Road	H
RRR	2
Tiger Trail	F
Tunes & Tonic	4

Private Bus Stand
St. Philomena's Church
Ashtanga Yoga Research Institute
Gokulam &
Mysore Mandala Yogashala, I & Kodagu
Govt. Silk Factory, Sandalwood Oil Factory, 7, O & Chamundi Hill
N
Railway Station
Railway Booking Office
Railway Museum
Karnataka Tourism Office
Recreation Fields
Hospital
Cauvery Arts & Crafts Emporium
GPO
Central Bus Stand
Wesley Cathedral
Sapna Book House
Ashok Books
Bank
Gandhi Square
Sangam Theatre
Clocktower
Town Hall
Devaraja Market
KR Circle
New Statue Circle
Harding Circle
City Bus Stand
Girnar Plaza
Jaganmohan Palace & Art Gallery
Maharaja's Palace
Entrance
IRWIN ROAD
ROAD
DHANAVANTRI ROAD
KR HOSPITAL ROAD
ASHOKA ROAD
BANGALORE-MYSORE ROAD
ST STREET
UMA TALKIES ROAD
KT STREET
B.N ROAD
SAYAJI RAO ROAD
SARDAR PATEL ROAD
DIWAN'S ROAD
NARAYANA SHASTRI ROAD
RAJ KAMAL TALKIES ROAD
KR STREET
JHANSI LAKSHMI BAI
VINOBA ROAD
DEVARAJ URS ROAD
TOWN HALL ROAD
CHANDRAGUPTA ROAD
NAZARBAD MAIN ROAD
BANGALORE-NILGIRI (BN) ROAD
SRI HARSHA ROAD
GUEST HOUSE ROAD
VICTORIA ALBERT ROAD
RAMA ROAD
0 100 m

Arrival and information

Six or seven **trains** from Bengaluru arrive daily, and the railway station is 1.5km northwest of the centre. Mysore has three bus stands: major long-distance KSRTC services pull in to **Central**, near the heart of the city, where there's a KSTDC booking counter. The Private stand is about 1km northwest of here. Local buses, including services for Chamundi Hill and Srirangapatnam, stop at the **City** stand, next to the northwestern corner of the Maharaja's Palace.

Five minutes' walk southeast of the railway station, on the corner of Irwin Road in the Old Exhibition Building, the helpful **Karnataka Tourism office** (Mon–Sat 10am–5.30pm; ⓣ0821/242 2096) will make an effort to answer queries and can arrange transport, as well as give out brochures and maps. The **KSTDC office** (daily 6.30am–8.30pm; ⓣ0821/242 3652) at the hotel KSTDC *Mayura Hoysala*, 2 Jhansi Laxmi Bai Rd, is of little use except to book one of its marathon city **tours** (7.15am–11pm; Rs525, a/c Rs675). It hits all city sights and only leaves with a minimum of ten passengers, so you may not be sure whether it will run when you buy your ticket. Its **car rental** rates (with driver) start at Rs7.50 per km, if you want to put together your own itinerary.

The main **post office** (poste restante) is on the corner of Ashoka and Irwin roads (Mon–Sat 10am–7pm, Sun 10.30am–1.30pm). If you need to **change money**, there's a State Bank of Mysore on the corner of Sayaji Rao and Sardar Patel roads, and the Indian Overseas Bank, Gandhi Square, opposite *Dasaprakash Hotel*. There are a number of **ATMs** around the centre and at the station. For **internet access**, reliable places include Netzone (Rs20), opposite the *Sangeeth Hotel*, and Internet Online (Rs25), above a sundries shop between Gandhi Square and Clock Tower.

Moving on from Mysore

For long hauls, the best way to travel is by **train**, usually with a change at **Bengaluru**. The fastest of the half dozen daily services, the air-conditioned *Shatabdi Express* #2008 (daily except Tues 2.15pm; 1hr 55min), continues on to Chennai (7hr 10min); most of the others terminate in Bengaluru, where you can pick up long-distance connections to a wide range of Indian cities (see p.1091). **Reservations** can be made at Mysore's computerized booking hall inside the station (Mon–Sat 8am–2pm & 2.15–8pm, Sun 8am–2pm). There are four services daily to **Hassan**, of which the *Shimoga Express* #268 (10.15am; 2hr 5min) is the fastest.

Most other destinations within a day's travel can only be reached by **bus**. Central Bus Stand, where you can book computerized tickets up to three days in advance, has state-run services to **Hassan** (3hr), Channarayapatna (for **Sravanabelagola**; 2hr 30min) and **Hubli** (for Hospet/**Hampi**; 9hr). Heading south to **Ooty** (5hr), there's a choice of eight buses, all of which stop at **Bandipur National Park.** Direct services to several cities in Kerala, including **Kannur**, **Kozhikode** and **Kochi**, also operate from Mysore. The only way to travel direct to **Goa** is on the 4pm or 5pm overnight buses that arrive at **Panjim** at 9am and 10am, respectively. Most Mangalore-bound buses (every 30min–1hr; 7hr) pass through **Madikeri** (3hr). For details of services to **Somnathpur** and **Srirangapatnam**, see the relevant accounts. A host of agents can make booking for **private buses** to many destinations.

Accommodation

Finding a room is only a problem during Dussehra (see p.1102) and the Christmas/New Year period, when the popular places are booked up weeks in advance and prices predictably soar.

Dasaprakash Gandhi Square ⓣ0821/244 2444, ⓦwww.mysoredasaprakashgroup.com. Large, crumbling yet charming hotel complex arranged around a spacious paved courtyard. It's busy, clean and efficient, and has some a/c rooms, cheap singles and an excellent veg restaurant. ❸–❹

Green Chittaranjan Palace, 2270 Vinoba Rd, Jayalakshmipuram ⓣ0821/251 2536, ⓦwww.greenhotelindia.com. This former royal palace on the western outskirts has been refurbished as an elegant, eco-conscious two-star hotel among landscaped gardens. The rooms are a decent size, and facilities include lounges, verandas, a croquet lawn and well-stocked library. All profits go to charities and environmental projects, and their auto-rickshaw will pick you up by prior arrangement. Book in advance. ❼–❽

Indra Bhavan Dhanavantri Rd ⓣ0821/242 3933, ⓔhotelindrabhavan@rediffmail.com. Dilapidated old lodge full of character, with attached singles and doubles and popular with Tibetans. The "ordinary" rooms are a little grubby, but the good-value "deluxe" have clean tiled floors and open onto a wide common veranda. ❶

KSTDC Mayura Hoysala 2 Jhansi Lakshmi Bai Rd ⓣ0821/242 5349, ⓦwww.kstdc.nic.in. Reasonably priced rooms and suites in a colonial-era mansion. There's a terrace restaurant and beer garden, which is good value, but the food is uninspiring. ❹–❺

KSTDC Yatri Niwas 2 Jhansi Lakshmi Bai Rd ⓣ0821/242 3492, ⓦwww.kstdc.nic.in. The economy wing of the government-run *Mayura Hoysala*, with simple rooms around a central garden and dorms for large groups only. ❸

Lalitha Mahal Palace T Narasipur Rd ⓣ0821/252 6100, ⓦwww.lalithamahalpalace.in. On a slope overlooking the city in the distance, this white, Neoclassical palace was built in 1931 to accommodate the maharaja's foreign guests. Now it's a Raj-style fantasy, decked with stunning period furniture and popular with tour groups. Rooms range from the cute turret rooms (Rs4000) to the "Viceroy Suite" (Rs30,000). The tea lounge, restaurant (see p.1104) and pool are open to non-residents (Rs225). ❽–❾

Mannars Lodge Chandragupta Rd ⓣ0821/244 8060. Budget hotel near the Central Bus Stand and Gandhi Square. No frills, though the "deluxe" rooms have TV. Deservedly popular with backpackers but no advance booking. ❶–❷

Parklane 2720 Sri Harsha Rd ⓣ0821/243 0400, ⓦwww.parklanemysore.com. A complete overhaul has transformed the *Parklane* into a swish yet affordable boutique hotel. Appealingly misshapen rooms, all with contemporary furnishings and most with balconies, encircle a skylit atrium; wi-fi available. For restaurant review see p.1104. ❹–❻

Hotel Roopa 2724-C Bangalore–Nilgiri Rd ⓣ0821/244 3770, ⓦwww.hotelroopa.com. Bright modern hotel block with compact but comfy rooms at surprisingly reasonable prices. Very handy for the palace. ❹–❻

Rooftop Retreat 2.5km from bus stand in Gayathripuram, ⓣ0821/245 0483, ⓦwww.coconutcastle.com. This delightful apartment homestay in a tranquil neighbourhood offers an Indian twist on the B&B experience. Bright blues and cosy creams dominate the mostly wood furnishings, and you can enjoy delightful mornings and evenings on the rooftop patio. Divya Damodaran is a welcoming hostess and, along with her sister, an excellent cook. Must reserve in advance. ❸

Royal Orchid Metropole 5 Jhansi Lakshmi Bai Rd ⓣ0821/425 5566, ⓦwww.royalorchidhotels.com. Luxurious heritage hotel built in 1920 by the Maharaja of Mysore amid pleasant gardens. Rooms (all well under $200) have high ceilings and a sense of grandeur. There's also a small outdoor pool and gym, plus the fine *Tiger Trail* multi-cuisine restaurant (see p.1104) in the central courtyard. ❽–❾

S.C.D.V.S. Sri Harsha Rd ⓣ0821/242 1379, ⓕ242 7580. Friendly modern lodge with some a/c rooms and cable TV in most. Some higher doubles have balconies overlooking the palace. ❸–❹

Sandesh The Prince 3 Nazarbad Main Rd ⓣ0821/243 6777, ⓦwww.sandeshtheprince.com. Smart, stylish 4-star with comfortable, well-furnished rooms and an impressive, skylit foyer. Facilities include travel desk, foreign exchange, outdoor pool with BBQ, and an excellent Ayurvedic centre and beauty parlour. Request a top-floor room with balcony if possible. ❼–❾

Sangeeth 1966 Narayana Shastri Rd, near the Udipi Krishna temple ⓣ0821/242 4693. One of Mysore's best all-round budget deals: bland and a bit boxed in, but friendly and very good value, with a new rooftop restaurant. ❷

Viceroy Sri Harsha Rd ⓣ0821/242 4001, ⓦwww.theviceroygroup.com. Business-oriented hotel, with most mod cons and two good restaurants. Rooms are rather overpriced but all a/c and the front ones have palace views. ❻–❽

The Windflower Spa Maharanapratap Rd, 3km southeast of town ⓣ0821/252 2500, ⓦwww.thewindflower.com. Whitewashed Balinese-style cottages surround a small lagoon on these gorgeous, sprawling grounds at the base of Chamundi Hill. Amenities include spa and massage, billiards and foosball, an elegant bar, lagoon restaurant (see p.1104) and an outdoor pool with waterfall. ❽–❾

The City

In addition to its official tourist attractions, chief among them the **Maharaja's Palace**, Mysore is a great city simply to stroll around. The evocative, if dilapidated, pre-Independence buildings lining market areas such as **Ashok Road** and **Sayaji Rao Road** lend an air of faded grandeur to the busy centre, teeming with vibrant street life. Souvenir stores spill over with the famous **sandalwood**; the best place to get a sense of what's on offer is the Government Cauvery Arts and Crafts Emporium on Sayaji Rao Road (closed Thurs), which stocks a wide range of local crafts that can be shipped overseas. The city's famous **Devaraja Market** on Sayaji Rao Road is one of south India's most atmospheric produce markets: a giant complex of covered stalls groaning with bananas (the delicious *nanjangod* variety), luscious mangoes, blocks of sticky *jaggery* and conical heaps of lurid *kumkum* powder.

Maharaja's Palace

Mysore's centre is dominated by the walled **Maharaja's Palace** (daily 10am–5.30pm; Rs200 [Rs20]), a fairytale spectacle topped with a shining brass-plated dome. It's especially magnificent on Sunday nights and during festivals, when it is illuminated by nearly 100,000 lightbulbs. It was completed in 1912 for the twenty-fourth Wadiyar raja, on the site of the old wooden palace that had been destroyed by fire in 1897. In 1998, after a lengthy judicial tussle, the courts decided in favour of formally placing the main palace in the hands of the Karnataka state government but the royal family, who still hold a claim, have lodged an appeal which is ongoing. Twelve temples surround the palace, some of them of much earlier origin. Although there are six gates in the perimeter wall, entrance is on the south side only. Shoes and cameras must be left at the cloakroom inside.

An extraordinary amalgam of styles from India and around the world crowds the lavish **interior**. Entry is through the Gombe Thotti or **Dolls' Pavilion**, once a showcase for the figures featured in the city's lively Dussehra celebrations and now a gallery of European and Indian sculpture and ceremonial objects. Halfway along, the brass **Elephant Gate** forms the main entrance to the centre of the palace, through which the maharaja would drive to his car park. Decorated with floriate designs, it bears the Mysore royal symbol of a double-headed eagle, now the state emblem. To the north, past the gate, stands a ceremonial wooden elephant *howdah*.

Mysore Dussehra festival

Following the tradition set by the Vijayanagar kings, the ten-day festival of **Dussehra** (Sept/Oct), to commemorate the goddess Durga's slaying of the demon buffalo, Mahishasura, is celebrated in grand style at Mysore. Scores of cultural events include concerts of south Indian classical (Carnatic) music and dance performances in the great Durbar Hall of the **Maharaja's Palace**. On Vijayadasmi, the tenth and last day of the festival, a magnificent procession of mounted guardsmen on horseback and caparisoned elephants – one carrying the palace deity, Chaamundeshwari, on a gold *howdah* – marches 5km from the palace to Banni Mantap. There's also a floating festival in the temple tank at the foot of **Chamundi Hill**, and a procession of chariots around the temple at the top. A torchlit parade takes place in the evening, followed by a massive firework display and much jubilation on the streets.

Elaborately decorated with 84kg of 24-carat gold, it appears to be inlaid with red and green gems – in fact the twinkling lights are battery-powered signals that let the *mahout* know when the maharaja wished to stop or go.

Walls leading into the octagonal **Kalyana Mandapa**, the royal wedding hall, are lined with a meticulously detailed frieze of oil paintings, executed over a period of fifteen years by four Indian artists, illustrating the great Mysore Dussehra festival (see box opposite) of 1930. The hall itself is magnificent, a cavernous space featuring cast-iron pillars from Glasgow, Bohemian chandeliers and multicoloured Belgian stained glass arranged in peacock designs in the domed ceiling.

Climbing a staircase with Italian marble balustrades, past an unnervingly realistic life-size plaster-of-Paris figure of Krishnaraja Wadiyar IV, lounging comfortably with his bejewelled feet on a stool, you come into the **Public Durbar Hall**, an orientalist fantasy like something from *A Thousand and One Nights*. A vision of brightly painted and gilded colonnades, open on one side, the massive hall affords views out across the parade ground and gardens to Chamundi Hill. The maharaja gave audience from here, seated on a throne made from 280kg of solid Karnatakan gold. These days, the hall is only used during the Dussehra festival, when it hosts classical concerts. The smaller **Private Durbar Hall** features especially beautiful stained glass and gold-leaf painting. Before leaving you pass two embossed silver doors – all that remains of the old palace.

Jaganmohan Palace: Jayachamarajendra Art Gallery

Built in 1861, the **Jaganmohan Palace** (daily 8am–5pm; Rs100 [Rs20]; no cameras), 300m west of the Maharaja's Palace, was used as a royal residence until 1915, when it was turned into a picture gallery and museum by Maharaja Krishnaraja Wadiyar IV. Most of the "contemporary" art on show dates from the 1930s, when a revival of Indian painting was spearheaded by E.B. Havell and the Tagore brothers, Rabindranath and Gaganendranath, in Bengal.

Nineteenth- and twentieth-century **paintings** dominate the first floor; among them the work of the pioneering oil painter Raja Ravi Varma who, although not everyone's cup of tea, has been credited for introducing modern techniques to Indian art. Games on the upper floor include circular *ganjifa* playing cards illustrated with portraits of royalty or deities, and board games delicately inlaid with ivory. There's also a cluster of musical instruments, among them a brass *jaltarang* set and glass xylophone. Another gallery, centring on a large wooden Ganesh seated on a tortoise, is lined with paintings, including Krishnaraja Wadiyar sporting with the "inmates" of his zenana during Holi.

Chamundi Hill

Chamundi Hill, 3km southeast of the city, is topped with a temple to the chosen deity of the Mysore rajas – the goddess Chamundi, or Durga, who slew the demon buffalo Mahishasura. It's a pleasant, easy bus trip (#201 from the City stand) to the top; the walk down, past a huge Nandi, Shiva's bull, takes about thirty minutes. Take drinking water to sustain you, especially in the middle of the day – the walk isn't very demanding, but by the end of it, after more than a thousand steps, your legs are likely to be a bit wobbly.

Inside the twelfth-century **temple** (daily 7am–2pm, 3.30–6pm & 7–9pm), which is open to non-Hindus, is a solid gold Chamundi figure. Outside, in the courtyard, stands a fearsome, if gaily coloured, statue of the demon Mahishasura. Overlooking the path down the hill, the magnificent five-metre **Nandi**, carved from a single piece of black granite in 1659, is an object of worship himself, adorned with bells and garlands and tended by his own priest. Minor shrines, dedicated to Chamundi and the monkey god Hanuman, among others, line the side of the path; at the bottom, a little shrine to Ganesh lies near a chai shop. From here it's usually possible to pick up an auto-rickshaw or bus back into the city, but at weekends the latter are often full. If you walk on towards the city, passing a temple on the left with a big water tank (the site of the floating festival during Dussehra), you come after ten minutes to the main road between the *Lalitha Mahal Palace* and the city; there's a bus stop, and often auto-rickshaws, at the junction.

Eating and drinking

Mysore has scores of **places to eat**, from numerous south Indian "meals" joints dotted around the market to the opulent *Lalita Mahal Palace*, where you can work up an appetite for a gourmet meal by swimming a few lengths of the pool. To sample the renowned Mysore *pak*, a sweet, rich crumbly mixture made of ghee and maize flour, queue at Guru Sweet Mart, a small stall at KR Circle considered the best sweetshop in the city. Another speciality from this part of the world is *malligi iddli*, a delicate jasmine-flavored *iddli* usually served in the mornings and at lunch.

Bombay Indra Bhavan Sayaji Rao Rd. Comfortable and popular veg restaurant that serves both south and north Indian cuisine and sweets. Its other branch on Dhanavantri Rd is equally, if not more, popular and also has an a/c section.

Dynasty *Palace Plaza* hotel, Sri Harsha Rd. Classy ground-floor dining room complemented in evenings by a breezy covered rooftop restaurant with a broad menu (mains Rs100–150), full bar, and pleasant decor.

The Keg Maharaja Shopping Complex, Bangalore-Mysore Rd. This dark, tiny pub has excellent Kingfisher on tap for Rs140 a pitcher all day.

Lalitha Mahal Palace T Narasipur Rd. Sample the charms of this palatial five-star hotel with a hot drink in the atmospheric tea lounge, or an à la carte lunch in the grand dining hall, accompanied by live sitar music. Buffet dinners (Rs850) on special occasions. The old-style bar also boasts a full-size billiards table.

Le Olive Garden *Windflower Spa*. Excellent, reasonably-priced Indian, Chinese and Western dishes served to the sound of falling water and croaking frogs at this jungle hideaway.

New Shilpashri Gandhi Square. Encircled by leafy potted plants, this rooftop terrace is one of the best spots in the city to enjoy a sun-dipped egg and toast breakfast or a cool evening cocktail. Quality north Indian food (Rs60–90), with particularly tasty tandoori – try the chicken tikka. Plenty of good veg options, too, including lots of dhals.

Parklane Sri Harsha Rd. Congenial courtyard restaurant-cum-beer balcony, with moderately priced veg and non-veg (meat sizzlers are a speciality), fake trees and live Indian classical music every evening. The hotel rooftop space is a real stunner, with full bar, pool and fantastic views. Popular with travellers and locals alike.

The Road *Sandesh The Prince*. Lined with plush booths – several of which are inside faux classic cars – this upmarket, American road trip-themed restaurant/club serves a quality buffet lunch and fine multi-cuisine dinner before plates are cleared and patrons take to the circular wooden dancefloor, usually to guest DJs. The kebabs and tandoori specialities are top-notch. Rs300–400 cover at weekends.

RRR Gandhi Square. Superb Andhra canteen with a small but plush a/c room at the back. Gets packed at lunchtimes and at weekends, but well worth the wait for its excellent chicken biriyani, fried fish and set menus served on banana leaves.

Tiger Trail *Royal Orchid Metropole*. Cool and tranquil courtyard garden with excellent Indian dinners and great Western-style breakfast buffets that include bacon, sausage, omelettes, fresh fruit and croissants for around Rs200.

Tunes & Tonic *Hotel Adhi Manor*, Chandragupta Rd. With black tables and banquettes, red accents and posters of musicians plastered all over, the young, well-travelled Coorgi owner has created Mysore's most stylish lounge. The service and cocktails are excellent.

Yoga

Despite the passing in 2009 of its founder, Sri Pattahbi Jois, the world-renowned **Ashtanga Yoga Insitute** (Ⓦwww.kpjayi.org), 2.5km northwest of town, is still a revered pilgrimage destination for devotees. The surrounding neighbourhood has in recent years turned into a bustling expat haven, filled with cafés, guesthouses, restaurants and internet cafés. The institute doesn't offer drop-in classes;

students must register for a minimum of one month (Rs27,000, Rs19,000 every additional month), and book at least two months in advance.

In contrast, **Mysore Mandala Yogashala**, 581 Dewans Rd, Laxmipuram (closed Sat & Mon; ⓣ0821/425 6277, ⓦwww.mandala.ashtanga.org), is a self-contained retreat, offering excellent instruction, an organic café, well-tended garden, cultural events and, uniquely in Mysore, drop-in classes. Ashtanga classes (Rs400) run at 6am and 5pm, with the slightly less strenuous Hata classes (Rs350) at 8:15am.

Around Mysore

Mysore is a jumping-off point for some of Karnataka's most popular destinations. At **Srirangapatnam**, the fort, palace and mausoleum date from the era of Tipu Sultan, the "Tiger of Mysore", while the superb Hoysala temple (see p.1111) of **Somnathpur** is an architectural masterpiece. If you're heading south towards Ooty, **Bandipur National Park** pales in comparison to Mudumalai across the Tamil Nadu border, although **Nagarhole National Park**, three hours southwest of Mysore towards the Kerala border, can be more rewarding.

Srirangapatnam

The island of **Srirangapatnam**, in the River Kaveri, 14km northeast of Mysore, measures 5km by 1km. Long a site of Hindu pilgrimage, it is named after its tenth-century Sriranganathaswamy Vishnu temple. The Vijayanagars built a fort here in 1454, and in 1616 it became the capital of the Mysore Wadiyar rajas. However, Srirangapatnam is more famously associated with **Haider Ali**, who deposed the Wadiyars in 1761, and even more so with his son **Tipu Sultan**. During his seventeen-year reign – which ended with his death in 1799, when the future Duke of Wellington took the fort at the bloody battle of "Seringapatnam" – Tipu posed a greater threat than any other Indian ruler to British plans to dominate India. Born in 1750, of a Hindu mother, he inherited his father Haider Ali's considerable military skills, but was also an educated, cultured man, whose lifelong desire to rid India of the hated British invaders naturally brought him an ally in the French. He obsessively embraced his popular name of the **Tiger of Mysore**, surrounding himself with symbols and images of tigers; much of his memorabilia is decorated with the animal or its stripes, and, like the Romans, he is said to have kept tigers for the punishment of criminals.

The former summer palace, the **Daria Daulat Bagh** (daily except Fri 9am–5pm; Rs100 [Rs5]), literally "wealth of the sea", was used to entertain Tipu's guests. At first sight, this low, wooden colonnaded building set in an attractive formal garden fails to impress. But the superbly preserved interior, with its ornamental arches, tiger-striped columns and floral decoration on every inch of the teak walls and ceiling, is remarkable. A much-repainted mural on the west wall relishes every detail of Haider Ali's victory over the British at Pollilore in 1780.

An avenue of cypresses leads from an intricately carved gateway to the **Gumbaz mausoleum** (daily except Fri 9am–5pm; free), 3km further east. Built by Tipu Sultan in 1784 to commemorate Haider Ali, and later also to serve as his own resting place, the lower half of the grey-granite edifice is crowned by a dome of whitewashed brick and plaster, spectacular against the blue sky. Ivory-inlaid rosewood doors lead to the tombs of Haider Ali and Tipu, each covered by a pall (tiger stripes for Tipu), and an Urdu tablet records Tipu's martyrdom.

At the heart of the fortress, the great temple of **Sriranganathaswamy** (daily 8am–1pm & 4–8pm) still stands proud and virtually untouched by the turbulent history that has flowed around it, and remains, for many devotees, the prime draw. Developed by succeeding dynasties, the temple consists of three distinctive sanctuaries and is entered via an impressive five-storeyed gateway and a hall that was built by Haider Ali. The innermost sanctum, the oldest part of the temple, contains an image of the reclining Vishnu.

Practicalities

Frequent **buses** from Mysore City Bus Stand (including #313 & #316) and all the Mysore–Bangalore **trains** pull in near the temple and fort. Srirangapatnam is a small island, but places of interest are quite spread out; tongas, auto-rickshaws and bicycles are available on the main road near the bus stand. The KSTDC **hotel**-cum-restaurant, *Mayura River View* (Ⓣ08236/252114; ❺), occupies a pleasant spot beside the River Kaveri, 3km from the bus stand; another good option is the smart and elegant *Fort View Resorts* (Ⓣ08236/252777; ❹–❻), set in its own grounds not far from the fort entrance.

Somnathpur

Built in 1268, the exquisite **Keshava Vishnu temple** (daily 9am–5pm; Rs100 [Rs5]), in the sleepy hamlet of **SOMNATHPUR**, was the last important temple to be constructed by the Hoysalas; it is also the most complete and, in many respects, the finest example of this singular style (see p.1111). Somnathpur itself, just ninety minutes from Mysore by road, is little more than a few neat tracks and some attractive simple houses with pillared verandas.

Like other Hoysala temples, the Keshava was built on a star-shaped plan. ASI staff can show you around and also grant permission to clamber on the enclosure walls, so you can get a marvellous bird's-eye view of the modestly proportioned structure. It's best to do this as early as possible, as the black-coloured stone gets very hot to walk on in bare feet later in the day. The temple is a *trikutachala*, "three-peaked hills" type, with a tower on each shrine. Its high plinth (*jagati*) provides an upper ambulatory, which on its outer edge allows visitors to approach the upper registers of the profusely decorated walls. Among the many superb images here are an unusually high proportion of Shaivite figures for a Vishnu temple. As at Halebid, a lively frieze details countless episodes from the Ramayana, Bhagavata Purana and Mahabharata. Intended to accompany circumambulation, the panels are "read" (there is no text) in a clockwise direction. Unusually, the temple is autographed; all its sculpture was the work of one man, named Malitamba. Outside the temple stands a *dvajastambha* column, which may originally have been surmounted by a figure of Vishnu's bird vehicle Garuda.

Practicalities

There are no direct **buses** from Mysore to Somnathpur. Buses from the Private stand run to Tirumakudal Narasipur (1hr), from where there are regular buses to Somnathpur (20min). Everyone will know where you want to go, and someone will show you which scrum to join. Alternatively, join one of KSTDC's guided tours from Mysore (see p.1100).

There is nowhere to stay near the temple and the only **food** available is biscuits or maybe a samosa or fruit from a street-seller. Tucked in the backwaters of a dammed section of the Cauvery, a further 25km southeast, the exquisite *Talakadu Jaladhana* resort (Ⓣ08227/271196, Ⓔjaladhana@hotmail.com; ❽) offers secluded cottages, some with rooftop hot tubs and herb gardens. Boating and sports activities are available and the resort can be reached by direct private bus from Mysore.

Nagarhole National Park

NAGARHOLE ("Snake River") **NATIONAL PARK** (Rs200 [Rs75], camera Rs20), together with Bandipur (see p.1100 "Moving on…") and Tamil Nadu's Mudumalai, forms the **Nilgiri Biosphere Reserve**, one of India's most extensive tracts of protected forest. The park extends 640 square kilometres north from the River Kabini, which has been dammed to form a picturesque artificial lake. During the dry season (Feb–June), this perennial water source attracts large numbers of animals, making it a potentially prime spot for sighting wildlife. The forest here is of the moist deciduous type – thick jungle with a 30m-high canopy – and more impressive than Bandipur's drier scrub.

However, disaster struck Nagarhole in 1992, when friction between local pastoralist "tribals" and the park wardens over grazing rights and poaching erupted into a spate of arson attacks. Thousands of acres of forest were burned to the ground. The trees have grown back in places, but it will be years before animal numbers completely recover. An added threat to the fragile jungle tracts of the region is a notorious female gang of wood smugglers from Kerala, who have developed a fearsome and almost mythical reputation. Consequently, Nagarhole is most worth visiting at the height of the dry season, when its muddy riverbanks and grassy swamps, or *hadlus*, offer decent chances of sighting gaur (Indian bison), elephant, *dhole* (wild dog), deer, boar, and even the odd tiger or leopard.

Practicalities

Nagarhole is open year-round, but avoid the monsoons, when floods wash out most of its dirt tracks and leeches make hiking impossible. To get here from Mysore, catch one of the two daily **buses** from the Central stand to **Hunsur** (3hr), 10km from the park's north gate, where you can find transport to the Forest Department's two resthouses (❷–❹). The **resthouses** have to be booked well in advance through the Forest Department offices in Mysore (ⓣ0821/248 0901) or Bengaluru (ⓣ080/2334 1993). It is also essential to arrive at the park gates well before dusk, as the road through the reserve to the lodges closes at 6pm, and is prone to "elephant blocks". The Nagarhole **visitor centre** organizes elephant rides (Rs50) and schedules bus tours round the sanctuary (6–9am & 3.30–6pm; Rs50).

Other **accommodation** around Nagarhole includes the highly acclaimed and luxurious *Kabini River Lodge* (book through Jungle Lodges & Resorts; ⓦwww.junglelodges.com, ⓣ080/2559 7021; ❼–❽), approached via the village of Karapura, 3km from the park's south entrance. Set in its own leafy compound on the lakeside, this former maharaja's hunting lodge offers all-in deals that include meals and transport around the park with expert guides. It's impossible to reach by public transport, so you'll need to rent a car to get here and you will also have to book well in advance. Another upmarket option, though not quite in the same league, is the *Jungle Inn* at Veerana Hosahalli (ⓣ08222/246022, ⓦwww.jungleinn.in; ❻–❼), which is close to the park entrance and arranges wildlife safaris.

Hassan and around

The unprepossessing town of **HASSAN**, 118km northwest of Mysore, is visited in large numbers because of its proximity to the Hoysala temples at **Belur** and **Halebid**, both northwest of the town, and the Jain pilgrimage site of **Sravanabelagola** to the southeast. Some travellers end up staying a couple of nights but with a little forward planning you shouldn't have to linger for long. Set deep in the serene Karnatakan countryside, Belur, Halebid and Sravanabelagola offer considerably more appealing surroundings.

Arrival and information

Hassan's **KSRTC Bus Stand** is in the centre of town, at the northern end of Bus Stand Road, which runs south past the post office to **Narsimharaja Circle**. Apart from the smattering of ATMs, you can **change money** at Shenoy Tours & Travels (Ⓣ08172/269729), near the bus stand. Local auto-rickshaws operate without meters and charge a minimum of Rs20. The friendly and informative **tourist office** is under five minutes' walk from the bus stand at AVK College Road (Mon–Sat 10am–5.30pm; Ⓣ08172/268862). The **railway station**, served by one express and three slow passenger trains a day from Mysore (2–3hr), is a further 2km down BM Road. There are two trains to Mangalore, one of them overnight.

Apart from taking a **tour**, the only way to see Sravanabelagola (53km), Belur (37km) and Halebid (30km) in one day is **by car**, which some visitors share; most of the hotels can fix this up (around Rs1800/day or Rs6.50/km for a minimum of 250km). Travelling **by bus**, you'll need at least two days. Belur and Halebid can be comfortably covered in one day; it's best to take one of the earliest hourly buses to Halebid (1hr) and move on to Belur (30min; 16km), from where services back to Hassan are more frequent (6.30am–6.15pm; 1hr 10min). **Sravanabelagola**, however, is in the opposite direction, and not served by direct buses; you have to head to **Channarayapatna**, aka "CR Patna", (from 6.30am; 1hr) on the main Bengaluru highway and pick up one of the regular buses (30min) or any number of minibuses from there.

Accommodation

Wherever you decide to stay, it's best to call ahead, as hotels tend to be full by early evening.

The Ashok Hassan 121 BM Rd Ⓣ08172/268731, Ⓦwww.hassanashok.com. Hassan lodging has reached a new peak in this lush garden compound and whitewashed hotel building. The rooms are large with sharp modern furnishings, and there's a top-notch restaurant and bar. ❼–❾

DR Karigowda Residency BM Rd, Under 1km from railway station Ⓣ08172/264506. Immaculate budget hotel: friendly, comfortable and amazing value. Single occupancy possible; a/c good value. ❷–❸

Hoysala Village Resort Belur Rd, 6km northwest of the centre Ⓣ08172/256065. Government-run luxury cottages in a quiet rural setting. Multi-cuisine restaurant and a pool which is open to nonresidents (Rs75/hr). ❽

Southern Star BM Rd, 500m from the train station Ⓣ08172/251816, Ⓦwww.ushalexushotels.com. New hotel with all mod cons, but better value than most and the *Karwar* restaurant is excellent. ❼–❽

Suvarna Regency PB 97, BM Rd Ⓣ08172/264006. Swish place with lots of lights, shiny marble lobby, comfortable rooms and one of the most popular restaurants in town. Great value. ❹–❺

Vaishnavi Lodging Harsha Mahal Rd Ⓣ08172/263885. Hassan's best budget lodge, with big clean rooms (all with phone and TV) and a veg restaurant. Reservations recommended; for a bit of quiet, ask for a room in the back. ❷

Eating

Cocktails BM Rd near *Suvarna Regency*. Tri-level restaurant and bar with breezy rooftop. Skip the grub and enjoy an evening drink in the open air.

Harsha Mahal Below *Harsha Mahal Lodge*, Harsha Mahal Rd. Excellent veg canteen that serves freshly cooked *iddli* and stunningly good dosas from 7.30am.

Hotel GRR Opposite the bus stand. Broad veg and non-veg range of excellent, spicy Andhra "mini-meals" served on banana leaves. Tasty ice creams, too, all for paise.

Swarna Gate *Suvarna Regency*, PB 97, BM Rd. This plush non-veg restaurant and bar with a few tables overlooking the garden is one of Hassan's finest. The varied menu is not cheap, with most curries going for around Rs200.

Upper Deck Harsha Mahal Rd. Small, modern terrace café offers coffees, ice creams and tasty *chaats* on first-floor balcony. Popular with students.

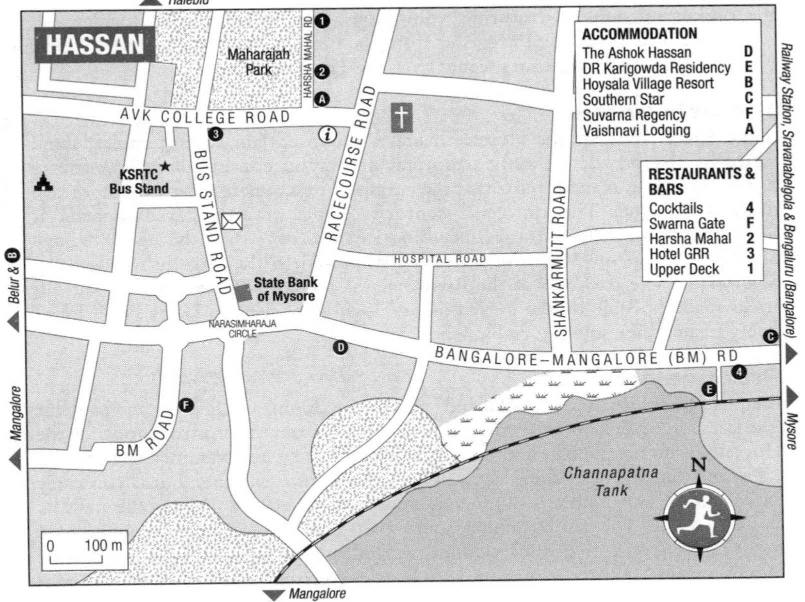

Halebid

Now little more than a scruffy village of brick houses and chai stalls, **HALEBID**, 32km northwest of Hassan, was once the capital of the powerful Hoysala dynasty, who held sway over south Karnataka from the eleventh until the early fourteenth centuries. Once known as **Dora Samudra**, the city was renamed *Hale-bidu*, or "Dead City", in 1311 when Delhi sultanate forces under the command of Ala-ud-Din-Khalji swept through and reduced it to rubble. Despite the sacking, several large Hoysala temples (see p.1111) survive, two of which, the **Hoysaleshvara** and **Kedareshvara**, are superb, covered in exquisite carvings. A small **archeological museum** (daily except Fri 10am–5pm), next to the Hoysaleshvara temple, houses a collection of Hoysala art and other finds from the area.

The Hoysaleshvara temple

The **Hoysaleshvara** temple (daily sunrise to sunset; free) was started in 1141, and after some forty years of work remained incomplete; this possibly accounts for the absence here of the type of towers that feature at Somnathpur, for example. It is no longer known which deities were originally worshipped, though the double shrine is thought to have been devoted at one time to Shiva and his consort. In any event, both shrines contain *shivalinga* and are adjoined by two linked, partly enclosed *mandapa* hallways in which stand Nandi bulls.

Hoysaleshvara also features many Vaishnavite images. The **sculptures**, which have a fluid quality lacking in the earlier work at Belur (see p.1110), include Brahma aboard his goose vehicle Hamsa, Krishna holding up Mount Govardhana, another where he plays the flute and Vishnu (Trivikrama) bestriding the world in three steps. One of the most remarkable images is of the demon king **Ravana** shaking Shiva's mountain abode, Mount Kailash, populated by numerous animals and figures with Shiva and Parvati seated atop. Secular characters, among them dancers and musicians, occupy the same register as the gods, and you'll come across the odd erotic tableau featuring voluptuous, heavily bejewelled maidens. A narrative frieze, on the sixth register from the bottom, follows the length of the Nandi *mandapas* and illustrates scenes from the Hindu epics.

The Jain bastis

Some 600m south of the Hoysaleshvara, a group of Jain *basti*s (temples) stand virtually unadorned; the only sculptural decoration consists of ceiling friezes inside the *mandapa*s and elephants at the entrance steps, where there's an impressive donatory plaque. The thirteenth-century temple of **Adi Parshwanatha** is dedicated to the twenty-third *tirthankara*, Parshvanath, while the newer **Vijayanatha** built in the sixteenth century is dedicated to the sixteenth *tirthankara*, Shantinath. The *chowkidar* at the Parshwanatha temple will demonstrate various tricks made possible by the carved pillars' highly polished surfaces; some are so finely turned they sound metallic when struck.

Practicalities

Frequent **buses** run between Halebid (the last at 8.30pm) and Hassan, and to Belur (the last at 8pm). The private **minibuses** that leave from the crossroads outside the Hoysaleshvara temple take a lot longer and only leave when crammed to bursting.

The monuments lie within easy walking distance of each other, but if you fancy exploring the surrounding countryside, rent a **bicycle** (Rs3/hr) from the stalls by the bus stand. The road running south past the temples leads through some beautiful scenery, with possible side-hikes to hilltop shrines, while the road to Belur (16km) makes for another pleasant bicycle ride. **Accommodation** in the village is limited to the KSTDC *Mayura Shantala* (Ⓣ08177/773224; ❶–❷) opposite the main temple and set in a small garden by the road. It offers three comfortable doubles with verandas, plus a four-bed room – all should be booked in advance. This is also the only place to eat after 6pm, when the chai stalls at the crossroads have closed.

Belur

BELUR, 37km northwest of Hassan, on the banks of the Yagachi River, was the Hoysala capital prior to Halebid, during the eleventh and twelfth centuries. Still active, the **Chennakeshava temple** (daily 7.30am–8.30pm; free) is a fine and early example of the singular Hoysala style, built by King Vishnuvardhana in 1117 to celebrate his conversion from Jainism, victory over Chola forces at Talakad and his independence from the Chalukyas. Today, its grey-stone *gopura*, or gateway tower, soars above a small, bustling market town – a popular pilgrimage site from October to December, when busloads of Ayappan devotees stream through en route to Sabarimala (see p.1055). The **Car festival** held around March or April takes place over twelve days and has a pastoral feel, attracting farmers from the surrounding countryside who conduct a bullock cart procession through the streets to the temple. If you have time to linger, Belur, with much better facilities than those found at Halebid, is a far better place to base yourself in order to explore the Hoysala region.

Arrival and information

Buses from Hassan and Halebid arrive at the small bus stand in the middle of town, ten minutes' walk along the main street from the temple, or sometimes drop people off on the highway next to the bus stand. There are auto-rickshaws available, but a good way to explore the area, including Halebid, is to rent a **bicycle** (Rs3/hr) from one of the stalls around the bus stand. The **tourist office** (Mon–Sat 10am–5pm) is located within the KSTDC *Mayuri Velapuri* compound on Temple Road. It has all the local bus times, and sometimes the tourist officer is available as a guide.

Accommodation and eating

The KSTDC *Mayuri Velapuri* (Ⓣ08177/222209; ❹–❺) is the best **place to stay**, with ten clean non-air-conditioned and three air-conditioned rooms; breakfast is included. The two dorms (Rs100/bed) are rarely occupied, other than between March and May, when pilgrims tend to block book the hotel. A little further towards the temple the *Sumukha Residency* (Ⓣ08177/222039; ❷–❸) is fairly modern and comfortable. Of the hotels around the bus stand, the *Vishnu Lodge* (Ⓣ08177/222263, Ⓕ230310; ❷–❸) above a restaurant and sweetshop, is the best bet, with sizeable rooms (some with TV) but tiny attached bathrooms where hot water is only available in the mornings.

The best **place to eat** is the veg restaurant below the *Vishnu Lodge*, followed by the *Mayuri Velapuri*'s canteen, whose menu is limited but does include chicken. There are plenty of veg *dhabas* near the temple, while the *Kalpavriksha*, just off Temple Road, serves meat and beer.

Chennakeshava temple

Chennakeshava stands in a huge walled courtyard, surrounded by smaller shrines and columned *mandapa* hallways. Lacking any form of superstructure, it appears to have a flat roof. If it ever had a tower, it would have disappeared by the Vijayanagar (sixteenth-century) period. Both the sanctuary and *mandapa* are raised on the usual plinth (*jagati*). Double flights of steps, flanked by minor towered shrines, afford entry to the *mandapa* on three sides; this hallway was originally open, but in the 1200s, pierced stone screens, carved with geometric designs and scenes from the Puranas, were inserted between the lathe-turned pillars. The main shrine opens four times a day for worship (8.30–10am, 11am–1pm, 2.30–5pm & 6.30–8.30pm) and it's worth considering using one of the guides (Rs200 for 1–4) who offer their services at the gates to explain the intricacies of the carvings. The quantity of **sculptural decoration**, if less mature than in later Hoysala temples, is staggering.

Hoysala temples

The **Hoysala** dynasty, who ruled southwestern Karnataka between the eleventh and thirteenth centuries, built a series of distinctive temples centred primarily at three sites: **Belur** and **Halebid**, close to modern Hassan, and **Somnathpur**, near Mysore. At first sight, and from a distance, the buildings, all based on a star-shaped plan, appear to be modest structures, compact and even squat. Yet on closer inspection, their profusion of fabulously detailed and sensuous sculpture, covering every inch of the exterior, is astonishing. Detractors often class Hoysala art as decadent and overly fussy, but anyone with an eye for craftsmanship will likely marvel at these jewels of Karnatakan art.

The intricacy of the carvings was made possible by the material used in construction: a soft **soapstone** that on oxidization hardens to a glassy, highly polished surface. The level of detail, similar to that seen in sandalwood and ivory-work, became increasingly freer and more fluid as the style developed, and reached its highest point at Somnathpur. Beautiful bracket figures, often delicate portrayals of voluptuous female subjects, were placed under the eaves, fixed by pegs top and bottom. A later addition (except possibly in the Somnathpur temple), these serve no structural function.

Another technique more usually associated with wood is the unusual treatment of the massive stone **pillars**: lathe-turned, they resemble those of the wooden temples of Kerala. They were probably turned on a horizontal plane, pinned at each end, and rotated with the use of a rope. It may be no coincidence that, to this day, wood turning is still a local speciality.

Within the same enclosure, the **Kappe Channigaraya temple** has some finely carved niche images and a depiction of Narasimha (Vishnu as man-lion) killing the demon Hiranyakashipu. Further west, fine sculptures in the smaller **Viranarayana** shrine include a scene from the Mahabharata of Bhima killing the demon Bhaga.

Sravanabelagola

The sacred Jain site of **SRAVANABELAGOLA**, 49km southeast of Hassan and 93km north of Mysore, consists of two hills and a large tank. On one of the hills, Indragiri (also known as Vindhyagiri), stands an extraordinary eighteen-metre-high monolithic statue of a naked male figure, **Gomateshvara**. Said to be the largest freestanding sculpture in India, this tenth-century colossus, visible for miles around, makes Sravanabelagola a key pilgrimage centre, though surprisingly few Western travellers find their way out here. Spend a night or two in the village, however, and you can climb Indragiri Hill before dawn to enjoy the serene spectacle of the sun rising over the sugar cane fields and outcrops of lumpy granite that litter the surrounding plains – an unforgettable sight.

Sravanabelagola is linked in tradition with the Mauryan emperor Chandragupta, who is said to have starved himself to death on the second hill in around 300 BC, in accordance with a Jain practice. The hill was renamed Chandragiri, marking the arrival of Jainism in southern India. At the same time, a controversy regarding the doctrines of Mahavira, the last of the 24 Jain **tirthankaras** (literally "crossing-makers", who assist the aspirant to cross the "ocean of rebirth"), split Jainism into two separate branches – *svetambara*, "white-clad" Jains, are more common in north India, while *digambara*, "sky-clad", are usually associated with the south. Truly ascetic *digambara* devotees go naked, though few do so away from sacred sites.

The monuments at Sravanabelagola probably date from no earlier than the tenth century, when a General Chamundaraya is said to have visited Chandragiri in search of a Mauryan statue of Gomateshvara. Failing to find it, he decided to have one made. From the top of Chandragiri he fired an arrow across to Indragiri Hill; where the arrow landed he had a new Gomateshvara sculpted from a single rock.

Indragiri Hill

Gomateshvara is approached from the tank between the two hills by 620 steps, cut into the granite of **Indragiri Hill**, which pass numerous rock inscriptions on the way up to a walled enclosure. Shoes must be deposited at the stall to the left of the steps, and you can leave bags at the site office nearby. Take plenty of water if it's hot, as there is none available on the hill. Entered through a small wagon-vaulted *gopura*, the **temple** is entirely dominated by the towering figure of Gomateshvara. With elongated arms and exaggeratedly wide shoulders, his proportions are decidedly non-naturalistic. The sensuously smooth surface of the white granite is finely carved: particularly the hands, hair and serene face. As in legend, ant-hills and snakes sit at his feet and creepers appear to grow on his limbs.

Bhandari Basti and monastery (math)

The road east from the foot of the steps at Chandragiri leads to two interesting Jain buildings in town. To the right, the Bhandari **Basti** (1159), housing a shrine with images of the 24 *tirthankaras*, was built by Hullamaya, treasurer of the Hoysala raja Narasimha. Two *mandapa* hallways, where naked *digambara* Jains may sometimes be seen discoursing with devotees clad in white, lead to the shrine at the back.

At the end of the street, the *math* (monastery) was the residence of Sravanabelagola's senior *acharya*, or guru. Thirty male and female monks, who also "go wandering in every direction", are attached to the *math*; normally a member of staff will be happy to show visitors around. Among the rare palm-leaf manuscripts in the library, some more than a millennium old, are works on mathematics and geography, and the Mahapurana, hagiographies of the *tirthankaras*. Next door, a covered walled courtyard is edged by a high platform on three sides, on which a chair is placed for the *acharya*. A collection of tenth-century bronze *tirthankara* images is housed here, and vibrant murals detail the various lives of Parshvanath. The hills where the *tirthankaras* stood to gain *moksha* are represented in a model, somewhat resembling a jelly mould, with tacked-on footprints.

Chandragiri Hill

Leaving your shoes with the keeper at the bottom, take the rock-cut steps to the top of the smaller **Chandragiri Hill**. Fine views stretch south to Indragiri and, from the north on the far side, across to a river, paddy and sugar cane fields, palms and the village of **Jinanathapura**, where there's another ornate Hoysala temple, the Shantishvara *basti*.

Rather than a single large shrine, as at Indragiri, Chandragiri holds a group of *bastis* in late Chalukya Dravida style, within a walled enclosure. Caretakers will take you around and open up the closed shrines. Save for pilasters and elaborate parapets, all the temples have plain exteriors. Named after its patron, the tenth-century **Chamundaraya** is the largest of the group, dedicated to Parshvanath. Inside the **Chandragupta** (twelfth century), superb carved panels in a small shrine tell the story of Chandragupta and his teacher Bhadrabahu. Traces of painted geometric designs survive and the pillars feature detailed carving. Elsewhere in the enclosure stands a 24m-high *manastambha*, "pillar of fame", decorated with images of spirits, *yakshis* and a *yaksha*. No fewer than 576 inscriptions dating from the sixth to the nineteenth centuries are dotted around the site, on pillars and on the rock itself.

Practicalities

Sravanabelagola, along with Belur and Halebid, features on **tours** from Bengaluru and Mysore (see p.1090 & p.1100). However, if you want to look around at a civilized pace, it's best to come independently. The **tourist office** (Mon–Sat 10am–5.30pm; ⓣ08176/657254) at the bottom of the stairs has little to offer and the management committee office next door only serves to collect donations and hand out tickets for the *dolis*.

There are plenty of **dharamshalas** to choose from if you want to stay, managed by the temple authorities and offering simple, scrupulously clean rooms, many with their own bathrooms and sitouts, ranged around gardens and courtyards, and most costing under Rs200 per night. The 24-hour accommodation office (ⓣ08176/657258), located inside the *SP Guest House* next to the bus stand (look for the clock-tower), will allocate you a room. *Hotel Raghu*, opposite the main tank, houses the best of the many small local **restaurants**.

Crisscrossed by winding back roads, the idyllic countryside around Sravanabelagola is mostly flat and thus perfect cycling terrain. **Bicycles** are available for rent (Rs3/hr) at Saleem Cycle Mart, on Masjid Road, opposite the northeast corner of the tank. See p.1108 for transport to and from the site.

Kodagu (Coorg)

The hill region of **Kodagu**, formerly known as **Coorg**, lies 100km west of Mysore in the Western Ghats, its eastern fringes merging with the Mysore plateau. Rugged mountain terrain interspersed with cardamom jungle, coffee plantations and fields of lush rice paddy, it's one of south India's most beautiful areas. Little has changed since Dervla Murphy spent a few months here with her daughter in the

1970s (the subject of her classic travelogue, *On a Shoestring to Coorg*) and was entranced by the landscape and people, whose customs, language and appearance set them apart from their neighbours (see p.1116).

If you plan to cross the Ghats between Mysore and the coast, the route through Kodagu is definitely worth considering. Some coffee-plantation owners open their doors to visitors – to find out more contact the Codagu Planters Association, Mysore Road, Madikeri (☎08272/229873). A good time to visit is during the festival season in early December or during the **Blossom Showers** around March and April when the coffee plants bloom with white flowers – some people find the strong scent overpowering.

Kodagu is relatively undeveloped apart from a new crop of homestays and "sights" are few but the countryside is idyllic and the climate refreshingly cool, even in summer. Many visitors **trek** through the unspoilt forest tracts and ridges that fringe the district. On the eastern borders of Kodagu around Kushalnagar, large **Tibetan settlements** have transformed a once barren countryside into fertile farmland dotted with busy monasteries, some housing thousands of monks.

Some history

The first concrete evidence of the kingdom dates from the eighth century, when it prospered from the salt trade passing between the coast and the cities on the Deccan. Under the Hindu **Haleri rajas**, the state repulsed invasions by its more powerful neighbours, including Haider Ali and his son Tipu Sultan (see p.1105). A combination of hilly terrain, absence of roads (a deliberate policy on the part of defence-conscious Kodagu kings) and the tenacity of its highly trained army ensured Kodagu was the only Indian kingdom never to be conquered.

In 1834, after ministers appealed to the British to help depose their despotic king, Vira Rajah, Kodagu became a princely state with nominal independence, which it retained until the creation of Karnataka in 1956. **Coffee** was introduced during the Raj and, despite plummeting prices on the international market, this continues to be the linchpin of the local economy, along with pepper and cardamom. Although Kodagu is Karnataka's wealthiest region, and provides the highest tax revenue, it does not reap the rewards – some villages are still without electricity – and this, coupled with the distinct identity and fiercely independent nature of the Kodavas, has given rise to an autonomy movement known as **Kodagu Rajya Mukti Morcha**. Methods used by the KRMM include cultural programmes and occasional strikes; violence is very rare.

Madikeri and around

Nestling beside a curved stretch of craggy hills, **MADIKERI**, capital of Kodagu, undulates around 1300m up in the Western Ghats, roughly midway between Mysore and the coastal city of Mangalore. The gradually increasing number of foreigners who travel up here find it a pleasant enough town, with red-tiled buildings and undulating roads that converge on a bustling bazaar, but most move on to home- and plantation stays in the verdant Coorg countryside within a couple of days.

Arrival and information

You can only reach Madikeri by road, but it's a scenic three-hour **bus** ride via **Kushalnagar** from **Mysore**, 120km southeast (avoid buses that go via Siddapura, as they take more than an hour longer). Regular services, including deluxe buses, also connect Madikeri with **Mangalore** (4hr), 135km northwest across the Ghats, and Hassan (4 daily; 4hr). The KSTRC state **bus stand** is at the bottom of town, below the main bazaar; private buses from villages around the region pull into a parking lot at the end of the main street.

The small local **tourist office** (Mon–Sat 10.30am–5.30pm, closed 2nd Sat of month; ⓣ08272/228580) stands five minutes' walk along the Mysore road below Thimaya Circle, next to the PWD *Travellers' Bungalow*, and can suggest itineraries, but is otherwise quite limited. If you're thinking of **trekking** in Kodagu, contact Ganesh Aiyanna at the *Hotel Cauvery* (see below), who is very helpful and organizes itineraries and trips for various budgets. Coorg Travels, next to *Rajdarshan Lodge*, (ⓣ08272/225817) arranges treks, tours and homestays, as does Travel Coorg (ⓣ9448 721252, ⓦwww.coorgtravelcoorg.com), right by the bus stand. For information on Kodagu's **forests** and forest bungalows contact the Conservator of Forests, Deputy Commissioner's Office at the fort (ⓣ08272/225708). If you don't make it out to the plantations, *Athithi Coffee Works*, just off Indira Gandhi Chowk, offers fresh Coorg coffee (Rs250–170/kg) and other local delicacies.

Accommodation and eating

Accommodation in Madikeri is rarely hard to come by, except occasionally in the budget range, most of which is concentrated around the bazaar and bus stand. The nicer hotels generally have **restaurants** and some have bars. The *Choice Hotel* on School Road is a restaurant only, serving breakfast items and a decent range of veg and meat dishes. *Tao*, up near the fort, is an authentic Chinese place, while the adjacent *Sri Ambica* serves wholesome veg snacks and meals.

Anchorage Guest House Kohinoor Rd ⓣ08272/228939. On a quiet side-street, close to the bus stand; the no-frills rooms are all attached. ❷

Cauvery School Rd ⓣ08272/225492. Below the private bus stand, this large and friendly place is almost hidden behind their excellent *Capitol* restaurant, where local delicacy *pondhi* (pork) curry is served good and spicy. They also run the *Capitol Village* resort, 5km east of town. ❹

Chitra School Rd ⓣ08272/225372. Best value in town, with neat well-kept rooms, the slightly pricier ones with cable TV. Excellent non-veg restaurant-cum-bar downstairs. ❸

Coorg International Convent Rd ⓣ08272/228071, ⓦwww.coorginternational.com. 10min by rickshaw west of the centre, this is one of the few upmarket options. It's a large but slightly characterless hotel with comfortable Western-style rooms, a multi-cuisine restaurant, exchange facilities, and shops. ❼–❽

East End General Thimaya Rd (aka Mysore Rd) ⓣ08272/229996. A large, plain, tiled-roof colonial bungalow turned into a hotel with a hint of character, but more renowned for its popular bar and restaurant. ❹

KSTDC Hotel Mayura Valley View Raja Rd ⓣ08272/228387. Well away from the main road, past Raja's Seat, the rooms here are enormous and many have excellent views. The restaurant serves booze and has an open terrace with epic views. Tough 20min uphill walk from the bus stand. ❺–❻

Mojo Rainforest Retreat 13km north of Madikeri, near Galibeedu village ⓣ08272/265636, ⓦwww.rainforestours.com. Informed hosts Sujata and Annu Goel have carved a thrumming idyll out of their little wedge of Kodagu plantation, with excellent organic meals (included) and warmly furnished cottages and tents set amid lush rainforest. All profits go to their NGO, which fosters environmental awareness and sustainable agriculture in the region. ❺–❼

The School Estate 15 km from Madikeri ⓣ08274/258358, ⓦschoolestate.in. Set amid beautifully landscaped grounds surrounded by coffee, cardamom and vanilla plantations, *School Estate* is an absolute charmer. Owner Rani Aiyapa is an excellent chef, and leads weekly cooking classes. The rooms are enormous, with rosewood beds and a number of homely touches that lend a refined English bed-and-breakfast feel, and the grounds are gorgeous ❼–❾

The Town and around

The **Omkareshwara Shiva** temple, built in 1820, features an unusual combination of red-tiled roofs, Keralan Hindu architecture, Gothic elements and Islamic-influenced domes. The fort and palace, worked over by Tipu Sultan in 1781 and rebuilt in the nineteenth century, now serve as offices and a prison. Within the complex, **St Mark's Church** holds a small **museum** (Tues–Sun

The Kodavas

Theories abound as to the origins of the **Kodavas**, or **Coorgis**, who today comprise less than one sixth of the hill region's population. Fair-skinned and with their own language and customs, they are thought to have migrated to southern India from Kurdistan, Kashmir or even Greece, though no one knows exactly why or when. One popular belief holds that this staunchly martial people, who since Independence have produced some of India's leading military brains, are descended from Roman mercenaries who fled here following the collapse of the Pandyan dynasty in the eighth century; some even claim connections with Alexander the Great's invading army. Whatever their origins, the Kodavas have managed to retain a distinct identity apart from the freed plantation slaves, Moplah Muslim traders and other immigrants who have settled here. More akin to Tamil than Kannada, their language is Dravidian, yet their religious practices, based on ancestor veneration and worship of nature spirits and the river, differ markedly from those of mainstream Hinduism. Land tenure in Kodagu is also quite distinctive: women have a right to inheritance and ownership and are also allowed to remarry.

Spiritual and social life for traditional Kodavas revolves around the **ain mane**, or ancestral homestead. Built on raised platforms to overlook the family land, these large, detached houses, with their beautiful carved wood doors and beaten-earth floors, generally have four wings and courtyards to accommodate various branches of the extended family, as well as shrine rooms, or **Karona Kalas**, dedicated to the clan's most important forebears. Key religious rituals and rites of passage are always conducted in the *ain mane*, rather than the local temple. However, you could easily travel through Kodagu without ever seeing one, as they are invariably away from roads, shrouded in thick forest.

9am–5pm, except 2nd Sat; free) of British memorabilia, Jain, Hindu and village deity figures and weapons. Also worth a look are the huge square **tombs of the rajas** which, with their Islamic-style gilded domes and minarets, dominate the town's skyline.

The early eighteenth-century Kodagu king was no dummy – he chose one of the best sunset vantage points in south India for **Raja's Seat** (dawn to 8pm; Rs2). On the western edge of town near *Hotel Valley View*, this is a popular grassy park and garden that fills up just before dusk. At 7pm a kitschy water and light show set to Bollywood tunes dazzles the locals.

Madikeri is the centre of the lucrative coffee trade, and although auto-rickshaws will take you there and back for around Rs200, a walk to **Abbi Falls** (8km) is a good introduction to coffee-growing country. The pleasant road, devoid of buses, winds through the hill country past plantations and makes for a good day's outing. At the litter-strewn car park at the end of the road, a gate leads through a private coffee plantation, sprinkled with cardamom sprays and pepper vines, to the bottom of the large stepped falls that are most impressive during and straight after the monsoons.

Mangalore

Many visitors only come to **MANGALORE** on their way somewhere else. As well as being fairly close to the Kodagu (Coorg) hill region, it's also a stopping-off point between Goa and Kerala, and is the nearest coastal town to the Hoysala and Jain monuments near Hassan, 172km east.

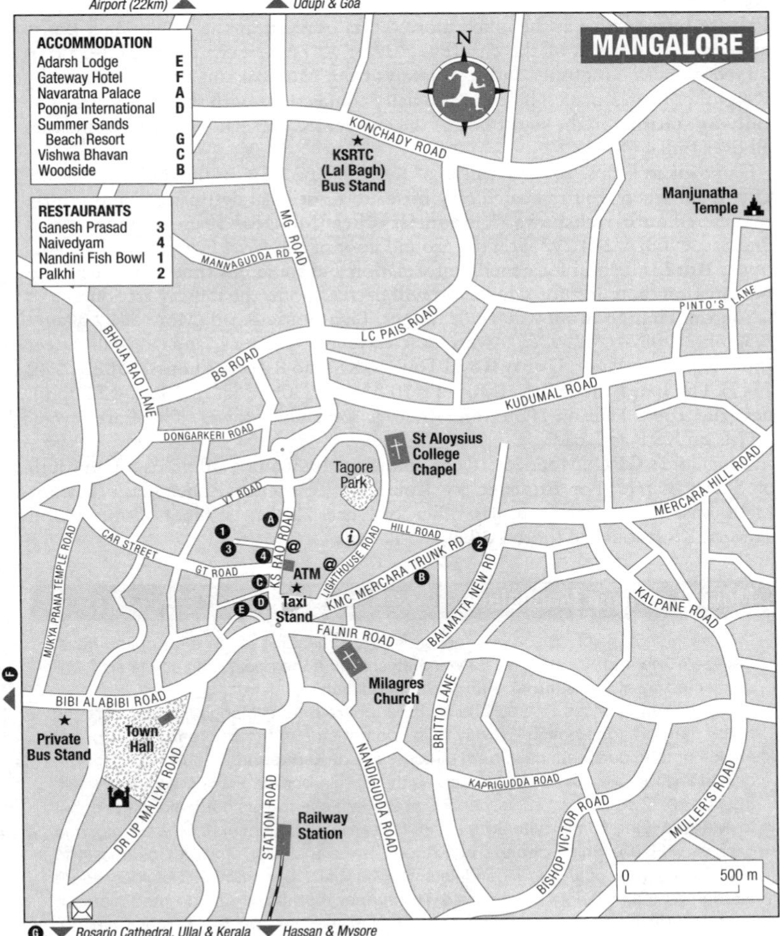

Mangalore was one of the most famous ports of south India. It was already well-known overseas in the sixth century, as a major source of pepper, and the fourteenth-century Muslim writer Ibn Battuta noted its trade in pepper and ginger and the presence of merchants from Persia and Yemen. In the mid-1400s, the Persian ambassador Abdu'r-Razzaq saw Mangalore as the "frontier town" of the Vijayanagar empire (see p.1130), which was why the Portuguese captured it in 1529. Nowadays, the modern port, 10km north of the city proper, is principally known for the processing and export of coffee and cocoa (mostly from Kodagu), and cashew nuts (from Kerala). It is also a centre for the production of *beedi* cigarettes.

Arrival and information

Mangalore's busy KSRTC **Bus Stand** (known locally as the "Lal Bagh" Bus Stand) is 2km north of the town centre, Hampankatta, at the bottom of Kadri Hill.

Private buses arrive at the much more central stand near the Town Hall. **Bajpe airport**, 22km north of the city (bus #22 or #47A or taxis for Rs300–350), is served by both Kingfisher and Jet Airways from Mumbai and Bengaluru, and by Kingfisher from Kochi. There are also daily connections with the Gulf states. The **railway station**, on the south side of the city centre, sees daily services from cities all over India.

Hampankatta, close to the facilities of KS Rao Road, acts as the traffic hub of the city, from where you can catch **city buses** to most local destinations and mostly unmetered **auto-rickshaws**. The **tourist office** (Mon–Sat 10am–5.30pm, closed 2nd Sat; ⓣ0824/244 2926) on the ground floor of the *Hotel Indraprashta* on Lighthouse Road is helpful for general information and some bus times, but carries no information on trains, for which you will need to go to the railway station.

You can **change money** at Trade Wings, Lighthouse Road (Mon–Sat 9.30am–5.30pm; ⓣ0824/242 6225), who cash travellers' cheques, and at Wall Street Interchange, 1st Floor, Utility Royal Towers, KS Rao Rd (same hours; ⓣ0824/242 1717). The State Bank of India (Mon–Fri 10.30am–2.30pm, Sat 10.30am–12.30pm), near the Town Hall on Hamilton Circle, is somewhat slower. There are several ATMs on KS Rao Road.

Mangalore's **GPO** (Mon–Sat 10am–7pm, Sun 10.30am–1.30pm) is 500m south of Shetty Circle. For **internet** try Kohinoor Computer Zone, Plaza Towers, Lighthouse Road, near the tourist office, or Cyber Zoom, 1st Floor, Utility Royal Towers, KS Rao Road (both 20/hr).

Moving on from Mangalore

Mangalore is a major crossroads for tourist traffic heading along the Konkan coast between **Goa** and **Kerala**, and between Mysore and the coast. The city is also well connected **by air** to **Mumbai**, **Bangalore** and **Kochi**.

Though **rail** services to Goa and Mumbai operate from Mangalore, it should be noted that through Konkan Railway trains do not stop at the city terminus. A better choice of train connections in both directions is at **Kankanadi**, around 10km north, or **Kasargode**, an easy bus ride across the Kerala border. From Mangalore itself, the fast #KR2 *Verna Passenger* departs at 6.50am and travels north along the coast to **Margao** (6hr 10min) via Udupi and **Gokarna** (3hr 50min). The *Matsyaganda Express* (#2620), which departs at 2.40pm, takes a similar time to Gokarna (4hr) and Panjim (6hr 5min) and continues to Mumbai (13hr 55min). Services south through all major points in Kerala to **Thiruvananthapuram** include the *Parsuram Express* (#6350; departs 4.15am; 14hr 15min) and the *Malabar Express* (#6630; departs 6.15pm; 15hr).

With the advent of the Konkan Railway, there is no point in travelling through to Goa by **bus**. The only direct bus to Gokarna leaves Mangalore at 1.30pm, otherwise change at Kumta. There are plenty of state buses heading north to **Udupi** and south along the coast into northern **Kerala**, though it is easier to pick up the more numerous private services to those places.

Mysore and **Bengaluru** can be reached by train via Hassan or directly by hourly buses. **Madikeri** is only reachable by road: the hourly buses to Mysore stop there, as do some luxury services to Bengaluru. The best private bus service to Bengaluru is the distinctive yellow luxury coaches of VRL; two buses leave at night (10pm; 7–8hr; Rs300) and tickets are available through Vijayananda Travels, PVS Centenary Building, Kodiyalbail, Kudmulranga Rao Road (ⓣ0824/249 3536). Agents along Falnir Road include Anand Travels (ⓣ0824/244 6737) and Ideal Travels (ⓣ0824/242 4899), which also runs luxury buses to Bengaluru (7–8hr; Rs 300) and two buses to **Ernakulam** (8 & 9pm; 9–10hr; Rs340).

Accommodation

The main area for hotels, **KS Rao Road**, runs south from the bus stand and has an ample choice to suit most pockets. You can also stay out of town by the beach in **Ullal**, 10km south of the city.

Adarsh Lodge Market Rd ⓣ0824/244 0878. Good value, especially the Rs160 singles, with compact but clean rooms, all attached. ❶–❷

The Gateway Hotel Old Port Rd ⓣ0824/666 0420, ⓦwww.thegatewayhotels.com. Modern Taj group business hotel; all rooms are a/c and some have a view of the river joining the sea. Travel desk, exchange, pool, bar, two classy restaurants and 24hr coffee shop. ❻–❼

Navaratna Palace KS Rao Rd ⓣ0824/244 1104, ⓔnish77772000@yahoo.com. Preferable to its adjacent older sister, *Navaratna*, with better rooms (some a/c) for little extra cost. Also two good a/c restaurants: *Heera Panna* and *Palimar* (pure veg). ❸–❺

Poonja International KS Rao Rd ⓣ0824/244 0171, ⓦwww.hotelpoonjainternational.com. Smart mostly a/c high-rise with all facilities and stunning views from the upper floors. South Indian buffet breakfast included. ❹–❺

Summer Sands Beach Resort Chota Mangalore, Ullal ⓣ0824/246 7690, ⓦwww.summersands.in. Near the beach, with a pool and a bar-restaurant serving local specialities, Indian and Chinese food. Unfortunately the spacious rooms and cottages are rather run down. Foreign exchange for guests. ❺–❽

Vishwa Bhavan KS Rao Rd ⓣ0824/244 0822. Cheap, plain rooms, some with attached baths, arranged around a courtyard close to all amenities. Best of the real cheapies. ❶

Woodside KMC Mercara Trunk Rd ⓣ0824/244 0296. Now occupying a sparkling new building nearly 1km from its former location, the hotel offers some of the best-value rooms (some a/c) and a good veg restaurant, *Xanadu*. ❹–❺

The City and beaches

Mangalore's strong Christian influence can be traced back to the arrival further south of St Thomas (see p.1175). Some 1400 years later, in 1526, the Portuguese founded one of the earliest churches on the coast. Today's **Rosario Cathedral**, however, with a dome based on St Peter's in Rome, dates only from 1910. Closer to the centre, on Lighthouse Road, fine restored fresco, tempera and oil murals by an Italian artist, Antonio Moscheni, adorn the Romanesque-style **St Aloysius College Chapel**, built in 1885.

At the foot of Kadri Hill, 3km north of the centre, Mangalore's tenth-century **Manjunatha temple** is an important centre of the Shaivite and tantric **Natha-Pantha cult**. Thought to be an outgrowth of Vajrayana Buddhism, the cult is a divergent species of Hinduism, similar to certain cults in Nepal. Enshrined in the sanctuary are a number of superb **bronzes,** including a 1.5m-high seated Lokeshvara (Matsyendranatha), made in 958 AD and considered the finest southern bronze outside Tamil Nadu. To see it close up, visit at *darshan* times (6am–1pm & 4–8pm), although the bronzes can be glimpsed through the wooden slats on the side of the sanctuary. If possible, time your visit to coincide with *mahapooja* (8am, noon & 8pm) when the priests give a fire blessing to the accompaniment of raucous music. Opposite the east entrance, steps lead via a reddish-coloured path to a curious group of minor shrines. Beyond this complex stands the **Shri Yogishwar Math**, a hermitage of tantric sadhus set round two courtyards.

If you're looking to escape the city for a few hours, head out to the village of **ULLAL**, 10km south, whose long sandy **beach**, backed by wispy fir trees, stretches for miles in both directions. It's a deservedly popular place for a stroll, particularly in the evening when Mangaloreans come out to watch the sunset, but a strong undertow makes swimming difficult, and at times unsafe. You're better off using the pool at the *Summer Sands Beach Resort* (see above), immediately behind the beach (Rs100 for non-residents). Towards the centre of Ullal, and around 700m from the main bus stand, is the *dargah* of **Seyyid Mohammad Shareeful Madani**, a sixteenth-century saint who is said to have come from Medina in Arabia, floating across the sea on a handkerchief. The extraordinary nineteenth-century building with garish onion domes houses the saint's tomb, which is one of the most important Sufi shrines in southern India. Visitors are advised to follow custom and cover their heads and limbs and wash their feet before entering. Local **buses** (#44A) run to Ullal from the junction at the south end of KS Rao Road.

Eating

The best **places to eat** are in the bigger hotels. If you're on a tight budget, try one of the inexpensive *dhabas* opposite the bus stand, or the excellent canteen inside the bus stand itself. Also recommended for delicious, freshly cooked and inexpensive "meals", down a lane running off KS Rao Road from the *Vasanth Mahal*, is the *Ganesh Prasad*, while just beyond it the *Nandini Fish Bowl* rustles up tasty fish and chicken. The rooftop *Palkhi* on Mercara Trunk Road is an airy family restaurant with a wide menu. One of the best of the hotel restaurants is the pure-veg *Naivedyam* at the *Mangalore International*, on KS Rao Road, which has a plush air-conditioned section.

North of Mangalore: coastal Karnataka

Whether you travel the **Karnatakan (Karavali) coast** on the Konkan Railway or along the busy NH-14, southern India's smoothest highway, the route between Goa and Mangalore ranks among the most scenic anywhere in the country. Crossing countless palm- and mangrove-fringed estuaries, the railway line stays fairly flat, while the recently upgraded road, dubbed by the local tourist board as "The Sapphire Route", scales several spurs of the Western Ghats, which here creep to within a stone's throw of the sea, with spellbinding views over long, empty

Kambla

If you're anywhere between Mangalore and Bhatkal from October to April and come across a crowd gathering around a waterlogged paddy field, pull over and spend a day at the races – Karnatakan style. Few Westerners ever experience it, but the spectacular rural sport of **Kambla**, or **bull racing**, played in the southernmost district of coastal Karnataka (known as Dakshina Kannada), is well worth seeking out.

Two contestants, usually local rice farmers, take part in each race, riding on a wooden plough-board tethered to a pair of prize bullocks. The object is to reach the opposite end of the field first, but points are also awarded for style, and riders gain extra marks – and roars of approval from the crowd – if the muddy spray kicked up from the plough-board splashes the special white banners, or *thoranam*, strung across the course at a height of six to eight metres.

Generally, race days are organized by wealthy landowners on fields specially set aside for the purpose. Villagers flock in from all over the region, as much for the fair, or *shendi*, as the races themselves: men huddle in groups to watch cockfights (*korikatta*), women haggle with bangle sellers and kids roam around sucking sticky *kathambdi goolay*, the local bonbons. It is considered highly prestigious to be able to throw such a party, especially if your bulls win any events or, better still, come away as champions. Known as *yeru* in Kannada, racing bulls are thoroughbreds who are rarely, if ever, put to work. Pampered by their doting owners, they are massaged, oiled and blessed by priests before big events, during which large sums of money are often won and lost.

beaches and deep blue bays. Highlights are the pilgrim town of **Udupi**, site of a famous Krishna temple, and **Gokarna**, another important Hindu centre that provides access to exquisite unexploited beaches. A recently upgraded inland road winds through the mountains to **Jog Falls**, India's biggest waterfall, which can also be approached from the east.

Udupi

UDUPI (also spelt Udipi), on the west coast, 60km north of Mangalore, is one of south India's holiest Vaishnavite centres. The Hindu saint **Madhva** (1238–1317) was born here, and the **Krishna temple** and *maths* (monasteries) he founded are visited by hundreds of thousands of pilgrims each year. The largest numbers congregate during the late winter, when the town hosts a series of spectacular **car festivals** and gigantic, bulbous-domed chariots are hauled through the streets around the temple. Even if your visit doesn't coincide with a festival, Udupi is a good place to break the journey along the Karavali coast. Thronging with *pujaris* and pilgrims, its small sacred enclave is wonderfully atmospheric.

Arrival and information

Udupi's three **bus stands** are dotted around the amorphous square in the centre of town: the KSRTC and private stands form a practically indistinguishable gathering spot for the numerous services to Mangalore and more long-distance buses to Mysore, Bengaluru and between northern Kerala and Goa. There are hardly any direct buses to Gokarna or Jog Falls, so you usually have to change at Kumta for both. The City stand is down some steps to the north and handles private services to local villages. Udupi's **railway station** is at Indrali on Manipal Road, 3km from the centre, and there are at least five trains in each direction daily. The tourist office is near the temple in the Krishna Building, on Car Street (Mon–Sat 10am–5.30pm; ⓣ0820/252 9718). Money can be **exchanged** at the KM Dutt branch of Canara Bank (on the main road just south of the bus stands). **Internet** facilities are available at nearby Netpoint (Rs30/hr), one of several such outlets.

Accommodation

As a busy pilgrimage town, there is ample inexpensive **accommodation**, which is only likely to near capacity during a major festival.

Durga International Just west of City Bus Stand ⓣ0820/253 6971, ⓔdurga-hotel@yahoo.com. Airy and efficient lodge with a variety of attached rooms, all with TV and some a/c, on the upper storeys of a modern block. ❷–❹

Janardhana South of the KSRTC Bus Stand ⓣ0820/252 3880, ⓕ252 3887. Fairly mundane hotel with simple attached rooms of different sizes, most with cable TV. ❷–❹

Sriram Residency Opposite the GPO ⓣ0820/253 0761, ⓔsriramresidency@indiatimes.com. Plushest place in the centre with a smart lobby, comfortable a/c rooms, two restaurants and a bar. ❸–❼

Sri Vidyasamudra Choultry Opposite Krishna temple ⓣ0820/252 0820. Foreigners are welcome in this ultra-basic lodge for pilgrims. The front rooms overlooking the temple and bathing tank are incredibly atmospheric. ❶

Vyavahar Lodge Kankads Rd ⓣ0820/252 2568. Basic but friendly and clean lodge between the bus stands and temple. ❶–❷

The Krishna temple and maths

Udupi's **Krishna temple** lies five minutes' walk east of the main street, surrounded by the eight **maths** founded by Madhva in the thirteenth century. Legend has it that the idol enshrined within was discovered by the saint himself after he prevented a shipwreck. The grateful captain of the vessel offered Madhva his precious cargo as a reward, but the holy man asked instead for a block of ballast, which he broke open to expose a perfectly formed image of Krishna. Believed to contain the essence (*sannidhya*) of the god, this deity draws a steady stream of pilgrims, and is the focus of almost constant ritual activity. It is cared for by *acharyas*, or pontiffs, from one or other of the *maths*. They perform pujas (5.30am–8.45pm) that are open to non-Hindus; men are only allowed into the main shrine bare-chested.

At the **Regional Resources Centre for the Performing Arts** in the MGM College, staff can tell you about local festivals and events that are well off the tourist trail; the collection includes film, video and audio archives. The pamphlet *Udupi: an Introduction*, on sale in the stalls around the sacred enclave, is another rich source of background detail on the temple and its complex rituals.

Eating

As you might expect of the **masala dosa**'s birthplace, there are many fine, simple south Indian **restaurants** where you can sample these and other veg favourites, such as *Adarsha*, below the *Janardhana*. For non-veg or alcohol, you'll have to try a posh hotel restaurant, such as the *Pisces* at the *Sriram Residency*.

Jog Falls

Hidden in a remote, thickly forested corner of the Western Ghats, **Jog Falls**, 240km northeast of Mangalore, are the highest **waterfalls** in India. Yet today, they are rarely as spectacular as they were before the construction of a large dam upriver, which impedes the flow of the River Sharavati over the sheer red-brown sandstone cliffs. Still, the surrounding scenery is gorgeous, with dense scrub and jungle carpeting sparsely populated, mountainous terrain. The views of the falls from the opposite side of the gorge is also impressive, unless, that is, you come here during the monsoons, when mist and rain clouds envelop the cascades. Another reason not to come here during the wet season is that the extra water, and abundance of leeches at this time, make the excellent **hike** to the floor valley a trial; if you can, head up here between October and January. The trail starts just below the bus park and winds steeply down to the water, where you can enjoy a refreshing dip. The whole patch opposite the falls has been landscaped for appealing viewing, with its own impressive entrance gate (vehicle entry fee varies) and attractively designed reception centre.

Arrival and information

Getting to and from Jog Falls by **bus** is now a lot easier thanks to the completion of the NH-206 across the Ghats, which has cut the journey time to **Honavar** (4–6 daily; 2hr 30min), on the Konkan Railway, and on to **Kumta** (2 daily; 3hr), where you can connect to Gokarna. Currently there is only one direct night bus from the Falls to **Udupi** and on to **Mangalore** (9hr), otherwise change at Honavar. A service to **Panaji** pulls through Jog Falls around midnight. There are hourly services to **Shimoga**, from where you can change onto buses for Hospet and Hampi. Better connections can be had at nearby Sagar (30km southeast) with buses to Shimoga, Udupi, Mysore, Hassan and Bangalore. With a car or motorbike, you can approach the falls from the coast along one of several scenic routes through the Ghats. The **tourist office** (Mon–Sat 10am–1.30pm & 2.30–5.30pm), upstairs at the new reception centre, opens rather erratically but can supply information on transport and vehicle rental.

Accommodation and eating

Accommodation is limited in the settlement and largely a KSTDC monopoly (Ⓣ08186/244732); it runs the ugly concrete *Mayura Sharavathi* (❸), whose vast rooms are old-fashioned but comfortable with good views, and the humbler

Tunga Tourist Home nearer the reception centre, with basic attached doubles (❷) and a Rs100 dorm. On the opposite side of the road the Karnataka Power Corporation also lets out four comfy air-conditioned rooms (☎08186/244742; ❹) when available, as does the Shimoga District PWD *Inspection Bungalow* (☎08186/244333; ❸), whose air-conditioned rooms are nicely situated on a hillock about 400m west. The youth hostel (☎08186/244251; ❶), ten minutes' walk down the Shimoga road, is very basic and tatty.

Apart from the KSTDC *Mayura* canteen next to the *Tunga Tourist Home*, which offers the usual adequate but uninspiring fare, the only other **food** options are at the enclave of small chai stalls and shops that have been relocated to the reception centre – *Hotel Rashmita* is the best of the bunch.

Gokarna

Among India's most scenically situated sacred sites, **GOKARNA** lies between a broad white-sand beach and the verdant foothills of the Western Ghats, six hours north of Mangalore by bus. Yet this compact little coastal town – a Shaivite centre for more than two millennia – remained largely "undiscovered" by Western tourists until the early 1990s, when it began to attract dreadlocked and didgeridoo-toting neo-hippies fleeing the commercialization of Goa. Now it's firmly on the tourist map, although the town retains a charming local character, as the Hindu pilgrims pouring through still far outnumber the foreigners who flock here in winter.

Arrival and information

The KSRTC **Bus Stand**, 300m from Car Street, is within easy walking distance of Gokarna's limited accommodation. Gokarna Road **railway station**, served by at least two daily trains in each direction, is 9km inland but buses, taxis and auto-rickshaws (Rs150) are available to take you into town.

You can **change money** at the *Om Hotel* near the bus stand but the best rates to be had are at the Pai STD booth on the road into town near the bus stand, one of several licensed dealers. There are a couple of ATMs, including Karnataka Bank's, opposite the bus stand. **Joya Tours and Travels**, behind the bus stand and opposite *Ram Dev Lodge*, will book **train tickets** and **provide cash** for MasterCard and Visa for a very fair two-percent fee. Numerous **internet** joints (all Rs40/hr) are dotted along Car Street and even on the beaches. **Bicycles** are available for rent from a stall next to the *Pai Restaurant*, for Rs5 per hour or Rs50 for a full day. Auto-rickshaws and taxis cost Rs100–150 to Om Beach. The **post office** is at the east end of Car Street, above a small produce market. Just east of the beach, a small, well-stocked bookshop, Sri Radhakrisna, contains good Indian, spiritual and fiction sections. If you need a doctor, English-speaking Dr Shastri (☎08386/256220) is highly recommended by long-stay visitors.

Moving on from Gokarna

Gokarna is well connected by direct daily **bus** to **Goa** (5hr), and several towns in Karnataka, including Bengaluru (13hr), Hospet/Hampi (10hr) and Mysore (14hr), via Mangalore (7hr) and Udupi (6hr). You can change at Ankola on the main highway for more services north into Goa. For more buses to Hospet and Hampi and the best connections to Jog Falls, change at Kumta.

Gokarna Road now has at least two **daily trains** in each direction. Trains to Mangalore depart at 4pm and 1:45am (4.5hrs), and trains north to Goa and Mumbai depart at 7pm and 10:45am. A couple of weekly expresses also call here, but regular **express connections** can be found in either Kumta or Ankola.

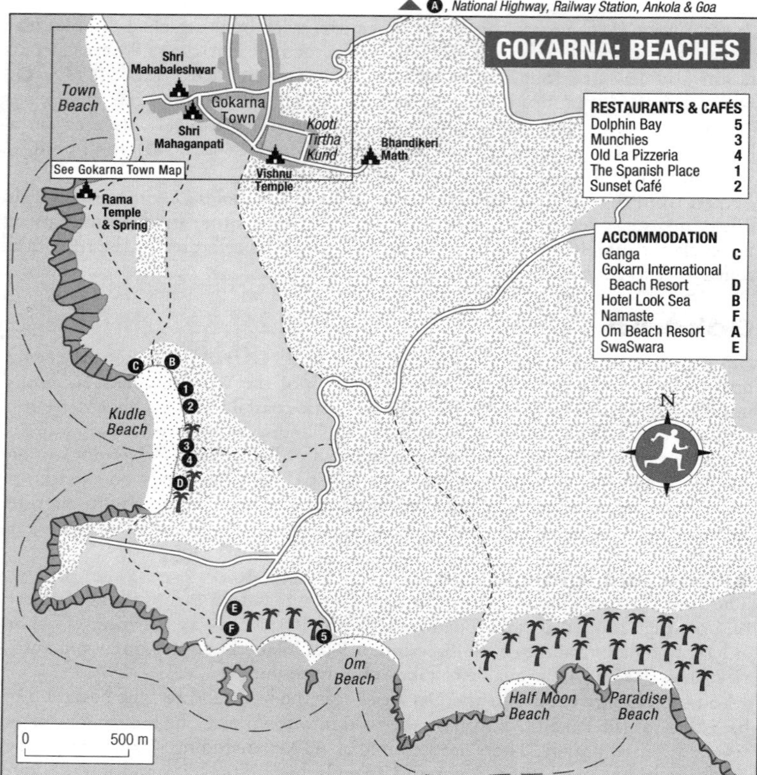

Accommodation

Gokarna has a few bona fide **hotels** and a small but reasonable choice of **guest-houses**. As a last resort, you can nearly always find a bed in one of the pilgrims' hostels, or **dharamshalas**, dotted around town. With dorms, bare, cell-size rooms and basic washing facilities, these are intended mainly for Hindus, but Western tourists are welcome. There are an increasing number of options at the **beaches**, from basic huts to a couple of new resorts. Prices can double over the Christmas/New Year period.

Ganga North end of Kudlee Beach ☎08386/257195. One of the more established beach joints with simple huts, an excellent terrace restaurant and Kudlee's fastest internet connection. ❶

Gokarn International On the main road into town ☎08386/256622, ⓔhotelgokarn@yahoo.com. Popular mid-scale place in a four-storey block on the edge of town, offering good value, from no-frills singles to deluxe, carpeted a/c doubles. The better ones have balconies overlooking the palm tops. Restaurant and bar on the premises. ❷–❹

Gokarn International Beach Resort Kudlee Beach ☎08386/257843, ⓔhotelgokarn@yahoo.com. Set back from the sands in its own small garden, this compact, newly constructed hotel offers comfortable mid-price rooms with small kitchenettes and verandas, some of them sea-facing. ❹

Hotel Look Sea Kudlee Beach ☎08386/657521. Basic shared-bath huts and rooms, many with excellent beach views. Fine muesli in the morning; football matches on the telly and beer in the evening. ❶

Namaste Northwest end of Om Beach Ⓣ08386/257141. One of the more popular beach options, with well-built attached rooms. Each has a different theme: in one, everything is round (including the bed); another resembles a rustic log cabin. Phone and internet connection on-site, along with a pleasant, shaded restaurant. ❷–❸

New Prasad Nilay On lane near the bus stand Ⓣ08386/257135. Very clean budget place with helpful management. The pricier rooms have cable TV and balconies. ❶–❷

Nimmu House Gokarna town, just south of main road, towards Kudlee beach Ⓣ08386/256730, Ⓔnimmuhouse@yahoo.com. Foreigners' favourite run by the friendly and helpful woman whose name it bears. Double rooms in the attractive modern block are well maintained and have decent mattresses, but avoid the grungier old wing. Many upper rooms have balconies with fine beach and sea views and there's a peaceful yard to sit in. ❶–❹

Om Beach Resort 1.5km east of town Ⓣ9448 579395, Ⓦwww.ombeachresort.com. Not actually near Om beach but nearer town on a high bluff with good views. Designed primarily as an Ayurvedic spa, its dozen or so colonial-style chalets are spacious and nicely furnished. Breakfast included. ❼

Shastri Guest House 100m east of the bus stand Ⓣ08386/256220, Ⓔshastriguesthouse@gmail.com. Tucked behind the Shastri Clinic on the main road, this quiet place offers some attached rooms and rock-bottom single rates. Only Rs50 more in high season. ❶

SwaSwara Above Om beach Ⓣ0484/301 1711, Ⓦwww.swaswara.com. The first luxury resort in Gokarna, this CGH Earth property offers beautifully designed wood villas spread over terraces on a hillside overlooking the bay. There's a pool, yoga dome and an Ayurvedic treatment centre, all set in extensive gardens. Minimum five-day stay; all-inclusive packages cost approximately US$2275 per villa. ❾

Vaibhav Nivas Off the main road, less than 5min from the bus stand Ⓣ08386/256714. Friendly, cheap and justifiably popular guesthouse pitched at foreigners, with a rooftop café-restaurant; all rooms are attached. ❶

The Town

Gokarna **town**, a hotchpotch of wood-fronted houses and red terracotta roofs, is clustered around a long L-shaped bazaar, its broad main road – known as **Car Street** – running west to the town beach, a sacred site in its own right. Hindu mythology identifies it as the place where Rudra (another name for Shiva) was reborn through the ear of a cow from the underworld after a period of penance. Gokarna is also the home of one of India's most powerful *shivalinga* – the **pranalingam**, which came to rest here after being carried off by Ravana, the evil king of Lanka, from Shiva's home on Mount Kailash in the Himalayas.

The *pranalingam* resides in Gokarna to this day, enshrined in the medieval **Shri Mahabaleshwar temple**, at the far west end of the bazaar. It is regarded as so auspicious that a mere glimpse of it will absolve a hundred sins, even the murder of a brahmin. Pilgrims shave their heads, fast and take a ritual dip in the sea before *darshan*. For this reason, the tour of Gokarna traditionally begins at the beach, followed by a puja at the **Shri Mahaganpati temple**, a stone's throw east of Shri Mahabaleshwar, to propitiate the elephant-headed god Ganesh. Sadly, owing to some ugly incidents involving insensitive behaviour by a minority of foreigners, tourists are now banned from the main temples, though you can still get a good view of proceedings in the smaller Shri Mahaganpati from the entrance. One interesting holy place you can visit is **Bhandikeri Math**, a short way east of the bathing tank. This 300-year-old temple and learning centre has shrines to the deities Bhavani Shankar, Uma Maheshwar and Maruthi.

The beaches

Notwithstanding Gokarna's numerous temples, shrines and tanks, most Western tourists come here for the beautiful **beaches** to the south of the more crowded town beach, beyond the lumpy, reddish-coloured headland that overlooks the town. Many lounge for weeks, taking advantage of lax attitudes and imbibing potent bhang lassis.

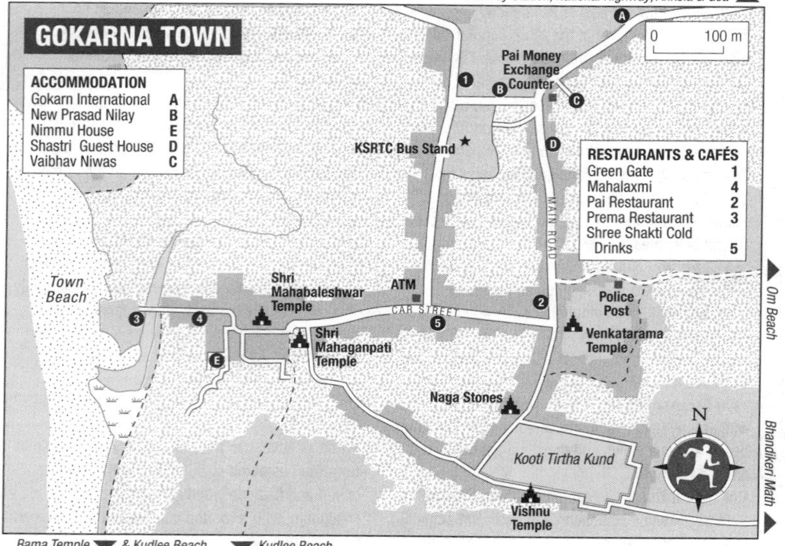

To pick up the trail, take a left off Car Street beside the Shri Mahaganapati temple and follow the newly cemented path for twenty minutes uphill and across a rocky plateau to **Kudlee Beach**. This wonderful kilometre-long sweep of golden-white sand sheltered by a pair of steep-sided promontories is now punctuated by around fifteen restaurant-cum-hut ventures and one proper hotel. This is the longest and broadest of Gokarna's beaches, and with decent surf too, though the water can be dangerous.

It takes around twenty minutes more to hike over the headland from Kudlee to exquisite **Om Beach**, so named because its distinctive twin crescent-shaped bays resemble the auspicious Om symbol. Apart from the luxury resort set well back from the beach, largely flimsy huts and the odd hammock still populate the palm groves, usually belonging to restaurants that offer a constantly expanding range of cuisine.

Gokarna's two most remote beaches lie another half-hour walk/climb over the rocky hills. **Half-Moon** and **Paradise** beaches, are, despite the presence of a few chai shops and extremely basic lodgings on each, mainly for intrepid sun-lovers happy to pack in their own supplies. If you're looking for near-total isolation, this is your best bet.

Eating and drinking

Gokarna town offers a good choice of **places to eat**, with a string of busy "meals" joints along Car Street and the main road. The beaches have a string of places offering travellers' favourites. Look out for the local sweet speciality *gadbad*, several layers of different ice creams mixed with chopped nuts and chewy dried fruit.

Dolphin Bay Southeastern Om Beach. Typically laidback place at the back of the beach, offering Western and Indian food, plus a fine range of lassis.

Green Gate *Om Hotel*, near the new bus stand. The more pleasant of this hotel's two restaurants offers a range of Mexican, Italian and Israeli dishes, as well as fish and sizzlers for around Rs100. The bar downstairs has a small garden area.

Mahalaxmi At the beach end of Car St. Service can be rather slow but there's no need to hurry while waiting for banana pancakes, delicious dosas and tasty veg curries up on this soothing, rooftop perch with a sea view.

Munchies South-central Kudlee Beach. One of the newer spots on Kudlee, with pleasant shady seating and tasty grilled seafood and curries.

Old La Pizzeria Kudlee Beach. A few tables on the sand and a cozy atmosphere within make this one of the better beach dining spots, with some of the best pizzas (Rs100–120) in south India.

Pai Restaurant Main Rd. Excellent spot for fresh and tasty veg thalis, masala dosas, crisp *vadas*, teas and coffees until late. All items under Rs50.

Prema Restaurant At the beach end of Car St. Welcoming veg canteen with delicious dosas, superb toasted English muffin sandwiches, and the best *gadbad* (rich local ice cream) in town.

Shree Shakti Cold Drinks Car St. Tasty home-made peanut butter and fresh cheese, both made to American recipes, the latter served with rolls, garlic and tomato. Also available are filling toasties, ice cream and creamy lassis.

The Spanish Place North-central Kudlee Beach. Good pasta, sandwiches, sweets and creamy lassis in a relaxed atmosphere.

Sunset Café Midway down Kudlee Beach. Very popular restaurant offering a range of veg, chicken and seafood dishes for around Rs60–150, as well as a prime sunset-viewing locale buffeted by Arabian Sea breezes.

Hubli and around

Karnataka's second most industrialized city, **HUBLI**, 418km northwest of Bengaluru, has little to offer tourists except for its transport connections to Mumbai, Goa, the coast of Uttar Kanada (Northern Karnataka), Hampi and other points in the interior.

Arrival and information

Hubli's **railway station**, close to the town centre and within walking distance of several of the hotels, is well connected to Bengaluru, Mumbai, Pune, Hassan and Hospet. Hubli's efficient **KSRTC Bus Stand** is 2km south of town, and can be reached by bus from the railway station or the chaotic City Bus Stand, about 1km west. The best way of getting around the city is by metered **auto-rickshaw**; there's also an efficient pre-paid booth outside the railway station. ICICI Bank has an **ATM** at the railway station and another one halfway along Lamington Road to the City Bus Stand. For **internet** access, head to JC Nagar Road, where both I-way, almost opposite the *Ajanta*, and the Cybercafé in the Sri Naradmuni complex, charges Rs20 per hour.

Accommodation and eating

Accommodation around the railway station includes the huge *Hotel Ajanta* on JC Nagar Road (Ⓣ0836/236 2216; ❶–❸), which has a range of rooms, including very cheap singles with shared bathroom. Opposite the City Bus Stand, the large and well-organized *Shri Renuka Lodge* (Ⓣ0836/225 3615; ❷–❹) offers a good range of reasonable rooms, some with air conditioning, and has its own veg restaurant. There are a few hotels between the railway station and the bus stand on Lamington Road, including the pleasant *Kailash* (Ⓣ0836/235 2732; ❷–❹), an

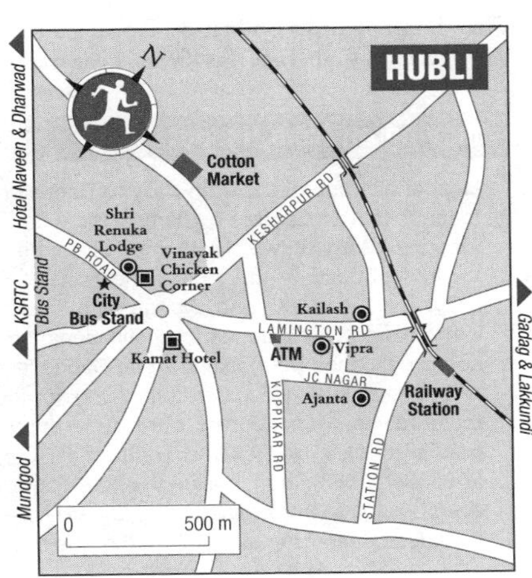

efficient business hotel with good-value air-conditioned rooms and a decent restaurant, and the *Vipra*, opposite, which has simple rooms (ⓣ0836/236 2336, ⓔvipratravels@satyam.net.in; ❶–❷).

Most hotels have their own **restaurants** – the *Shri Renuka*, for example, has two sections, one serving south Indian veg food and the other Chinese and north Indian cuisine. The best of the independent restaurants is the *Kamat Hotel*, by the traffic island at the bus stand end of Lamington Road; there's another branch opposite the railway station. *Vinayak Chicken Corner*, opposite the City Bus Stand, is a good spot for inexpensive non-veg food and beer.

Hospet

Charmless **HOSPET**, about ten hours from both Bengaluru and Goa, is of little interest except as the jumping-off place for the extraordinary ruined city of Hampi (Vijayanagar), 13km northeast. If you arrive late, or want a more upmarket hotel, it makes sense to stay here and catch a bus or taxi out to the ruins the following morning.

Arrival and information

Hospet's **railway station** is 1500m north of the centre. Auto-rickshaws are plentiful or you can get into town on foot if unencumbered. The **bus stand** is in the centre, just off MG (Station) Road, which runs south from the railway station. **Bookings** for long-distance routes can be made at the ticket office on the bus-stand concourse (daily 8am–noon & 3–6pm), where there's also a **left-luggage** facility. Regular buses run the half-hour **route to Hampi**, some via Kamalapuram, until around 7.30pm. Alternatively, you can take an auto-rickshaw for Rs80–100; you will probably be asked for more, so bargain hard. Enfield motorbikes are available for rent (or sale) from Bharat Motors (ⓣ08394/224704) near Rama Talkies.

The **tourist office** at the Rotary Circle (Mon–Sat: June–March 10am–5.30pm; April & May 8am–1.30pm; ⓣ08394/228537) offers limited information and sells tickets for KSTDC conducted tours of Hampi. You can **exchange** travellers' cheques and cash at the State Bank of Mysore, next to the tourist office, and cash only at the State Bank of India on Station Road. Full exchange facilities are also available at the *Hotel Malligi*. Cybernet (Rs40/hr), near the bus stand, can get you online.

Moving on from Hospet

Hospet has one direct **train** daily to Bengaluru, the overnight *Hampi Express* #6592 (departs 8.10pm, arrives 6.10am) and the daily *Haripriya Express* #7416 to Hyderabad (departs 10pm, arrives 10.30am). For connections to the coast and Goa, head west to Hubli (4 daily; 3–4hr). For connections to Badami and Bijapur, travel to Gadag (4 daily; 1hr 20min–2hr) and change onto the slow single track running north.

There are KSRTC **buses** to destinations throughout the state but journeys are slow so the only ones worth taking are to Gadag (every 30min; 2hr), Hubli (every 30min; 3hr) or Guntakal (every hour; 2hr 30min–3hr), for the improved rail and road connections in those towns. Many tourists opt for the apparently easy option of a private **sleeper coach** to Goa or Gokarna (7–8pm; 9–10hr; Rs600), operated by Paulo Travels (ⓣ08394/225867) from beside the hotel *Priyadarshini*. Unfortunately, these are usually overbooked, overcrowded and if you are travelling to Gokarna, you will be offloaded for a dubious transfer at Ankola in the wee hours, whatever you are told to the contrary.

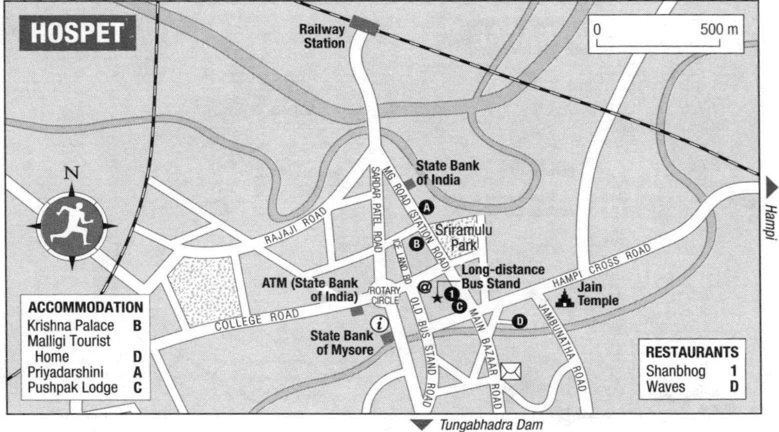

Accommodation and eating

Many of the hotels have good **dining rooms**, but in the evening, the *Malligi*'s upscale (though affordable) indoor restaurant *Temptations* and its terrace *Waves* bar serve good tandoori and chilled beer. *Shanbhog*, an excellent little Udupi restaurant next to the bus station, is a perfect pit-stop before heading to Hampi, and opens early for breakfast.

Krishna Palace MG Rd ⓣ08394/294300, ⓦwww.krishnapalacehotel.com. Snazzy new centrally air-conditioned hotel, with smartly furnished rooms and an ostentatious lobby. Popular with eastern Europeans. ⑦–⑧

Malligi Tourist Home 6/143 Jambunatha Rd, a 2min walk east of MG Rd (look for the signs) and the bus stand ⓣ08394/228101, ⓦwww.malligihotels.com. Now completely refurbished with several blocks of luxurious a/c rooms and suites separated by manicured lawns. There is also a large outdoor swimming pool (Rs50/hr for non-residents), plus billiards and massage facilities, in addition to a small bookshop, internet access, and an efficient travel service. ⑦

Priyadarshini MG Rd ⓣ08394/228838. Large and bland, but spotless and decent value, especially the a/c rooms (some with balconies). Two good restaurants: the veg *Naivedyam* and, in the garden, the excellent non-veg *Manasa*, which has a bar. ⑤

Pushpak Lodge MG Rd ⓣ08394/421380. With basic but clean attached rooms, this is the best rock-bottom lodge in town and right by the bus stand. ②

Hampi (Vijayanagar)

Among a surreal landscape of golden-brown boulders and leafy banana fields, the ruined "City of Victory," **Vijayanagar**, better known as **HAMPI** (the name of the main local village), spills from the south bank of the River Tungabhadra.

This once dazzling Hindu capital was devastated by a six-month Muslim siege in the second half of the sixteenth century. Only stone, brick and stucco structures survived the ensuing sack – monolithic deities, crumbling houses and abandoned temples dominated by towering *gopuras* – as well as the sophisticated irrigation system that channelled water to huge tanks and temples.

Thus, most of Hampi's monuments are in disappointingly poor shape, appearing a lot older than their four or five hundred years. Yet the serene riverside setting and air of magic that lingers over the site, sacred for centuries before a city was founded here, make it one of India's most extraordinary locations. Many find it

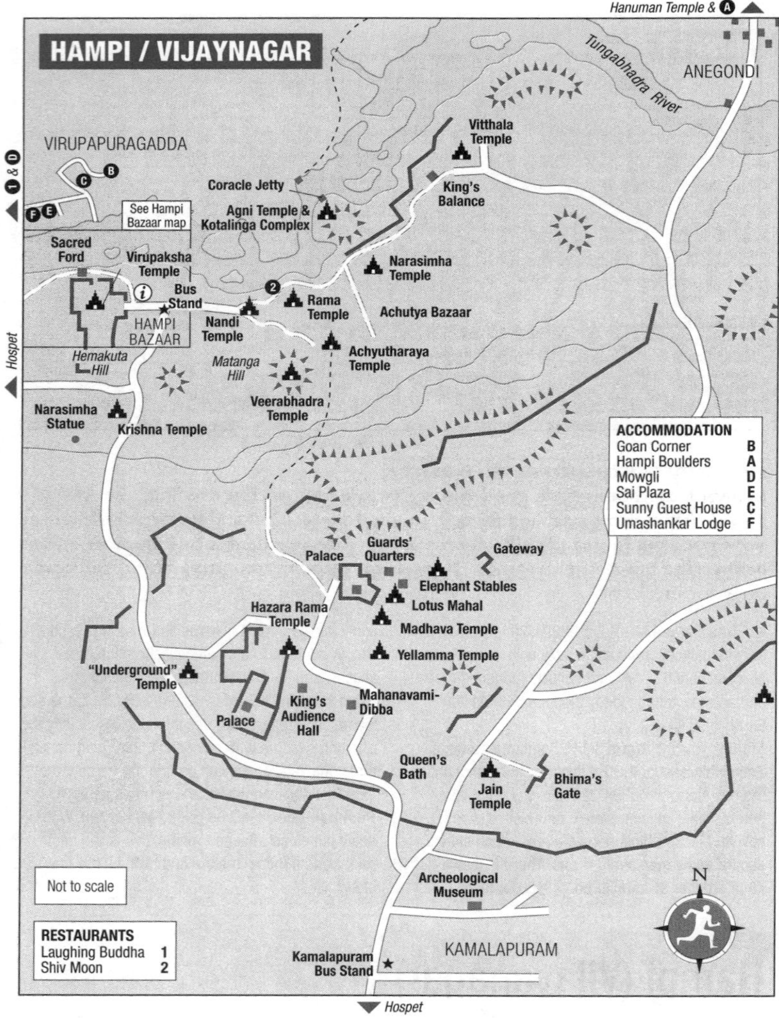

difficult to leave and spend weeks chilling out in cafés, wandering to whitewashed hilltop temples and gazing at the spectacular sunsets.

Some history

According to the Ramayana, the settlement began its days as Kishkinda, ruled by the monkey kings Bali and Sugriva and their ambassador, Hanuman. The unpredictably-placed rocks – some balanced in perilous arches, others heaped in colossal, hill-sized piles – are said to have been flung down by their armies in a show of strength.

The rise of the **Vijayanagar empire** seems to have been a direct response, in the first half of the fourteenth century, to the expansionist aims of Muslims from the north, most notably Malik Kafur and Mohammed-bin-Tughluq. Two Hindu brothers from Andhra Pradesh, Harihara and Bukka, who had been employed as treasury officers in Kampila, 19km east of Hampi, were captured by the Tughluqs and taken to Delhi, where they supposedly converted to Islam. Assuming them to be suitably tamed, the Delhi sultan despatched them to quell civil disorder in Kampila, which they duly did, only to abandon both Islam and allegiance to Delhi shortly afterwards, preferring to establish their own independent Hindu kingdom. Within a few years they controlled vast tracts of land from coast to coast. In 1343 their new capital, Vijayanagar, was founded on the southern banks of the River Tungabhadra, a location long considered sacred by Hindus. The city's most glorious period was under the reign of **Krishna Deva Raya** (1509–29), when it enjoyed a near monopoly of the lucrative trade in Arabian horses and Indian spices passing through the coastal ports and was the most powerful Hindu capital in the Deccan. Travellers such as the Portuguese chronicler Domingo Paez, who stayed for two years after 1520, were astonished by its size and wealth, telling tales of markets full of silk and precious gems, beautiful, bejewelled courtesans, ornate palaces and fantastic festivities.

Thanks to its natural features and massive fortifications, Vijayanagar was virtually impregnable. Yet in 1565, following his interference in the affairs of local Muslim sultanates, the regent Rama Raya was drawn into a battle with a confederacy of Muslim forces to the north and ultimately defeated. Rama Raya was captured and suffered a grisly death at the hands of the **sultan of Ahmadnagar**. Vijayanagar then fell victim to a series of destructive raids, and its days of splendour were brought to an abrupt end.

Arrival and information

Buses from Hospet terminate close to where the road joins the main street in Hampi Bazaar, halfway along its dusty length. A little further towards the Virupaksha temple, the **tourist office** (daily except Fri 10am–5.30pm; ⓣ08394/241339) can put you in touch with a **guide** for Rs800 per day but not much else.

Rented **bicycles** are available from stalls near the lodges (Rs10/hr, Rs40–50/day). Pedal bikes can be hard work on the bumpy roads so consider a motorized two-wheeler. The Raju stall, round the corner from the tourist office, has motorbikes and scooters for hire (around Rs150/day). Sneha Travels, whose main office is at D131/11 Main St (daily 9am–9pm; ⓣ08394/241590), can **change money** (albeit at lowish rates) and advance cash on credit cards. They can also book tickets for planes, trains and **sleeper coaches** to Goa and Gokarna, though you have to pick them up from Hospet (see p.1128).

Accommodation

Hampi Bazaar remains the best place to stay for access to the sites, choice of restaurants and other facilities. There are no fancy hotels but around forty guesthouses of varying size and calibre. Some travellers, especially Israelis, prefer to stay across the river in **Virupapuragadda**, which is fast developing and has caught up in price. Prices are pretty low most of the year apart from the Christmas to mid-February peak, when they at least double.

Hampi Bazaar

Archana Towards river from village centre ⓣ08394/241547, ⓔaddihampi@yahoo.com. The best rooms here are in the river-facing block, which has shared balconies with swinging baskets and a roof terrace. ❷

Garden Paradise Far northeast end of village ⓣ08394/652539. Five attached and seven non-attached huts in an excellent riverside location. Also a chilled-out restaurant area. ❶

Gopi Centre of village Ⓣ08394/241695, Ⓔkirangopi2002@yahoo.com. One of the more established places with small, simple rooms. Offers free yoga classes to residents. ❶–❷

Kiran Beside river Ⓣ08394/204159, Ⓔgowdakiran96@yahoo.co.in. The basic rooms here are compact but clean enough. The rooftop restaurant has fine views of the river and the temple. ❶

Shanti Guest House Just north of the Virupaksha temple Ⓣ08394/241568. This is a real favourite, comprising a dozen or so twin-bedded rooms arranged on two storeys around a leafy inner courtyard. It's basic (showers and toilets are shared), but spotless, and all rooms have fans and windows. ❶

Sudha Northeast end of village Ⓣ9481 042336. One of the nicest, friendliest places to stay. The rooms have been renovated and some of the new ones are spacious for Hampi. Rooftop Tibetan restaurant. ❶–❸

Vicky's 100m north of tourist office Ⓣ08394/241694. Small clean rooms, some attached. Friendly and popular for its rooftop restaurant. ❷

Across the river

Goan Corner 500m inland and east of boat crossing, Virupapuragadda Ⓣ9448 718951. Large complex amid paddy fields and near the rocks with a range of rooms and huts, some with attached bathrooms. Lively restaurant. ❶–❷

Hampi Boulders Narayanpet, Bandi Harlur Ⓣ08539/265939. Overlooking a bend in the River Tungabhadra, this small, quirky resort hotel is the best upscale option, reached via coracle crossing and a 6km walk, or by a 30min car ride from Hampi bazaar. There are two grades of cottages, moulded around giant boulder outcrops, with palms, mango trees and brakes of bamboo for shade. Meals are so-so Indian buffets and they have a natural rock-cut swimming pool. ❽–❾

Mowgli Far west end of main road, Virupapuragadda Ⓣ08394/329844, Ⓔhampimowgli@hotmail.com. A range of rooms with comfy sitouts and private balconies, some with fantastic views, as well as a welcoming restaurant, set against a gorgeous paddy and river backdrop, and full tourist services make this the best-value lodgings in Viru. Book ahead. ❶–❹

Sai Plaza Virupapuragadda Ⓣ08533/287017, Ⓔsantoshgvt@yahoo.com. These fifteen bungalows enclosing an attractive courtyard garden are relaxed and welcoming. The restaurant has delicious lassis and sandwiches and excellent views across the river. ❶

Sunny Guesthouse Virupapuragadda Ⓣ08533/287005. Nicely landscaped gardens with brightly painted bungalows and a row of compact rooms. The *Sheesh Besh* restaurant is a popular hangout. ❶–❷

Umashankar Lodge Virupapuragadda Ⓣ08533/287067. Cosy, popular spot with small but clean attached rooms (the upstairs ones rather overpriced) set round a leafy courtyard. ❶–❷

The ruins

Although spread over 26 square kilometres, the ruins of Vijayanagar are mostly concentrated in two distinct groups: the first lies in and around **Hampi Bazaar** and the nearby riverside area, encompassing the city's most sacred enclave of temples and *ghats*; the second centres on the **royal enclosure** – 3km south of the river, just northwest of **Kamalapuram** village – which holds the remains of palaces, pavilions, elephant stables, guardhouses and temples. Between the two stretches a long boulder-choked hill and scores of banana plantations, fed by ancient irrigation canals.

Hampi Bazaar, the Virupaksha temple and riverside

Lining Hampi's long, straight main street, **Hampi Bazaar**, which runs east from the eastern entrance of the Virupaksha temple, you can still make out the remains of Vijayanagar's ruined, columned bazaar, partly inhabited by today's lively market. Landless labourers live in many of the crumbling 500-year-old buildings.

Dedicated to a local form of Shiva known as Virupaksha or Pampapati, the functioning **Virupaksha temple** (daily 6.30am–12.30pm & 2–8.30pm; Rs2) dominates the village, drawing a steady flow of pilgrims from all over southern

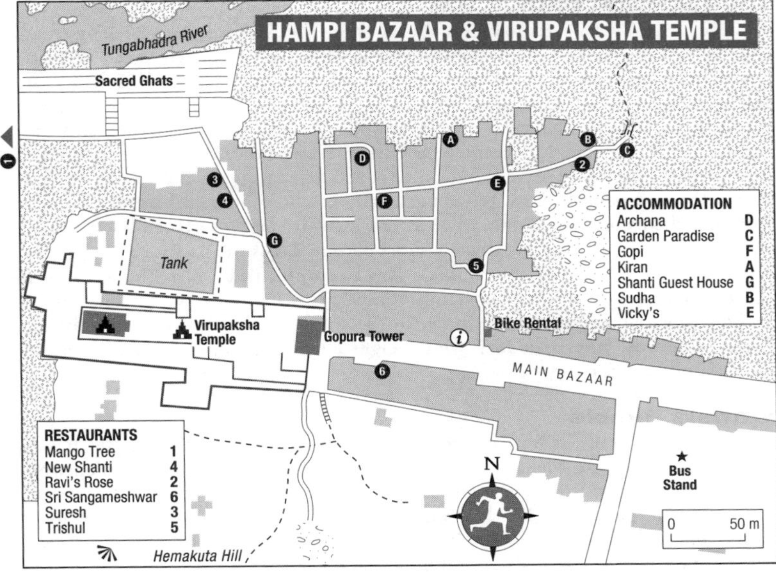

India. Also known as **Sri Virupaksha Swami**, the temple is at its liveliest and most atmospheric during *arati* (daily 6.30–8am & 6.30–8.30pm). The complex consists of two courts, each entered through a towered *gopura*.

A colonnade surrounds the inner court, usually filled with pilgrims dozing and singing religious songs. On entering, if the temple elephant, Lakshmi, is around, you can get her to bless you by placing a rupee in her trunk. In the middle the principal temple is approached through a *mandapa* hallway whose carved columns feature rearing animals. Rare Vijayanagar-era paintings on the *mandapa* ceiling include aspects of Shiva, a procession with the sage Vidyaranya, the ten incarnations of Vishnu and scenes from the Mahabharata.

The sacred **ford** in the river is reached from the Virupaksha's north *gopura*; you can also get there by following the lane around the impressive temple **tank**. A *mandapa* overlooks the steps that originally led to the river, now some distance away. A small **motor boat** plies from this part of the bank, ferrying villagers to the fields and tourists to the increasingly popular enclave of **Virupapuragadda**. The road left through the village eventually loops back towards the hilltop Hanuman temple, about 5km east, and on to Anegondi – a recommended round walk.

Matanga Hill

The place to head for sunrise is the boulder hill immediately east of Hampi Bazaar. From the end of the main street, an ancient paved pathway winds up a rise, at the top of which the magnificent Achyutharaya temple (see p.1134) is revealed. The views improve as you progress up **Matanga Hill**, and a small stone temple (named Veerabhadra) at its summit provides an extraordinary vantage point. The problem of muggings early in the morning along this path seems to have waned but it's probably still a good idea to be vigilant if there are only one or two of you.

The riverside path

To reach the Vitthala temple, walk east from the Virupaksha, the length of Hampi Bazaar, where a huge monolithic **Nandi** statue gazes across at the main temple from its shrine. Just before you reach these, a path on the left, staffed at regular intervals by conch-blowing sadhus and an assortment of other ragged mendicants, follows the river past a couple of cafés and numerous shrines, including a Rama temple – home to hordes of fearless monkeys. Beyond at least four Vishnu shrines, a paved and colonnaded **bazaar** leads due south to the **Achyutharaya temple** (aka Tiruvengalanatha), whose beautiful stone carvings – among them some of Hampi's famed erotica – are being restored by the ASI. Back on the main path again, make a short detour across the rocks leading to the river to see the little-visited waterside **Agni temple**; next to it, the Kotalinga complex consists of 108 (an auspicious number) tiny *linga*s, carved on a flat rock. As you approach the Vitthala temple, to the south is an archway known as the **King's Balance**, where the rajas were weighed against gold, silver and jewels to be distributed to the city's priests.

Vitthala temple

Although the area of the **Vitthala temple** (daily 6am–6pm; Rs250 [Rs10]; ticket also valid for the Lotus Mahal on the same day) does not show the same evidence of early cult worship as Virupaksha, the ruined bridge to the west probably dates from before Vijayanagar times. The bathing *ghat* may be from the Chalukya or Ganga period, but as the temple has fallen into disuse it seems that the river crossing (*tirtha*) here has not had the same sacred significance as the Virupaksha site. Now part of a UNESCO World Heritage Site, the Vitthala temple was built for Vishnu, who according to legend was too embarrassed by its ostentation to live here.

The open *mandapa* features slender monolithic granite musical **pillars** which were constructed so as to sound the notes of the scale when struck. Today, due to vandalism and erosion from being repeatedly beaten, heavy security makes sure that no one is allowed to touch them. Guides, however, will happily demonstrate the musical resonance of other pillars on an adjacent structure. Outer columns sport characteristic Vijayanagar rearing horses, while friezes of lions, elephants and horses on the moulded basement display sculptural trickery – you can transform one beast into another simply by masking one portion of the image.

In front of the temple, to the east, a stone representation of a wooden processional **rath**, or chariot, houses an image of Garuda, Vishnu's bird vehicle. Now cemented, at one time the chariot's wheels revolved.

Anegondi and beyond

With more time, and a sense of adventure, you can head across the River Tungabhadra to **ANEGONDI**, a fortress town predating Vijayanagar, and its fourteenth-century headquarters. The most pleasant way to get here is to take a coracle from the ford 1500m east of the Vitthala temple; these circular rush baskets, which are today reinforced with plastic sheets, also carry bicycles, which are a good way to visit Hampi's many monuments. A bridge had been constructed at this point but it collapsed and there are no plans to rebuild.

Forgotten temples and fortifications litter Anegondi village and its quiet surroundings. The ruined **Huchchappa-matha temple**, near the river gateway, is worth a look for its black stone lathe-turned pillars and fine panels of dancers. **Aramani**, a ruined palace in the centre, stands opposite the home of the descendants of the royal family; also in the centre, the **Ranganatha temple** is still active. A huge wooden temple chariot stands in the village square. The only **accommodation** here is in village houses and you can get basic snacks at the *Hoova Café* .

To complete a five-kilometre loop back to Hampi from here (the simplest route if you have wheels), head left (west) along the turning just north of the village, which winds through sugar cane fields and eventually comes out near Virupapuragadda. En route you can visit the sacred **Pampla Sarovar**, signposted down a dirt lane to the left. The small temple above this square bathing tank, tended by a *swami* who will proudly show you photos of his pilgrimage to Mount Kailash, is dedicated to the goddess Lakshmi and holds a cave containing a footprint of Vishnu. If you are staying around Anegondi, this quiet and atmospheric spot is best visited early in the evening during *arati* (worship).

Another worthwhile detour from the road is the hike up to the tiny whitewashed **Hanuman temple**, perched on a rocky hilltop north of the river, from where you gain superb views over Hampi, especially at sunrise and sunset. The steep climb up to it takes around half an hour. An alternative walking route back involves following the path a further 2km until you reach an impressive old **stone bridge** dating from Vijayanagar times. The bridge no longer spans the river but just beyond it, to the west, another coracle crossing returns you to a point about halfway between the Vitthala temple and Hampi Bazaar.

Hemakuta Hill and around

Directly above Hampi Bazaar, **Hemakuta Hill** is dotted with pre-Vijayanagar temples that probably date from between the ninth and eleventh centuries. Aside from the architecture, the main reason to clamber up here is to admire the **views** of the ruins and surrounding countryside. Looking across the boulder-covered terrain and banana plantations, the sheer western edge of the hill is Hampi's number-one sunset spot, attracting a crowd of blissed-out tourists most evenings, along with a couple of entrepreneurial chai-wallahs and little boys posing for photos in Hanuman costumes.

A couple of interesting monuments lie on the road leading south towards the main, southern group of ruins. The first of these, a walled **Krishna temple complex** to the west of the road, dates from 1513. Although dilapidated in parts, it features some fine carving and shrines.

Hampi's most-photographed monument stands just south of the Krishna temple in its own enclosure. Depicting Vishnu in his incarnation as the Man-Lion, the monolithic **Narasimha** statue, with its bulging eyes and crossed legs strapped into yogic pose, is one of Vijayanagar's greatest treasures.

The southern and royal monuments

The most impressive remains of Vijayanagar, the city's **royal monuments**, lie some 3km south of Hampi Bazaar, spread over a large expanse of open ground. Before tackling the ruins proper, it's a good idea to get your bearings with a visit to the small **Archeological Museum** (daily except Fri 10am–5pm; free) at Kamalapuram, which can be reached by bus from Hospet or Hampi. Among the sculpture, weapons, palm-leaf manuscripts and painting from Vijayanagar and Anegondi, the highlight is a superb scale model of the city, giving an excellent bird's-eye view of the entire site.

Bhima's Gate, Queen's Bath, Mahanavami-Dibba and King's Audience Hall

The route to the monuments is well signposted. After 200m or so you reach the partly ruined massive **inner city wall**, made from granite slabs, which runs 32km around the city, in places as high as 10m. Just beyond the wall, the **citadel area** was once enclosed by another wall and gates, of which only traces remain. To the east, the small *ganigitti* ("oil-woman's") fourteenth-century **Jain temple** features a simple stepped pyramidal tower of undecorated horizontal slabs. Beyond it is **Bhima's Gate**, once one of the principal entrances to the city, named after the Titan-like Pandava prince and hero of the Mahabharata. Like many of the gates, it is "bent", a form of defence that meant anyone trying to get in had to make two 90° turns. Bas-reliefs depict such episodes as Bhima avenging the honour of his wife, Draupadi, by killing the general Dushasana. Draupadi vowed she would not dress her hair until Dushasana was dead; one panel shows her tying up her locks, the vow fulfilled.

Back on the path, to the west, the plain facade of the fifteen-metre-square **Queen's Bath** belies its glorious interior, open to the sky and surrounded by corridors with 24 different domes. Eight projecting balconies overlook where once was water; traces of Islamic-influenced stucco decoration survive. Women from the royal household would bathe here and umbrellas were placed in shafts in the tank floor to protect them from the sun. The water supply channel can be seen outside.

Continuing northwest brings you to **Mahanavami-Dibba** or "House of Victory", built to commemorate a successful campaign in Orissa. A twelve-metre pyramidal structure with a square base, it is said to have been where the king gave and received honours and gifts. From here he watched the magnificent parades, music and dance performances, martial arts displays, elephant fights and animal sacrifices that made celebration of the ten-day Dussehra festival famed throughout the land. Carved reliefs decorate the sides of the platform. To the west, another platform – the largest at Vijayanagar – is thought to be the basement of the **King's Audience Hall**. Stone bases of a hundred pillars remain, in an arrangement that has caused speculation as to how the building could have been used; there are no passageways or open areas.

Lotus Mahal and Hazra Rama temple

The two-storey **Lotus Mahal** (daily 6am–6pm; Rs 250 [Rs10]; ticket also valid for the Vitthala temple on the same day), a little further north and part of the **zenana enclosure**, or women's quarters, was designed for the pleasure of Krishna Deva Raya's queen: a place where she could relax, particularly in summer. Displaying a strong Indo-Islamic influence, the pavilion is open on the ground floor, whereas the inaccessible upper level contains windows and balcony seats. A moat surrounding the building is thought to have provided water-cooled air via tubes.

Beyond the Lotus Mahal, the **Elephant Stables**, a series of high-ceilinged, domed chambers, entered through arches, are the most substantial surviving secular buildings at Vijayanagar – a reflection of the high status accorded to elephants, both ceremonial and in battle.

Walking west of the Lotus Mahal, you pass two temples before reaching the road to Hemakuta Hill. The rectangular enclosure wall of the small **Hazara Rama** ("One thousand Ramas") temple, thought to have been the private palace shrine, features a series of medallion figures and bands of detailed friezes showing scenes from the Ramayana.

Eating

Hampi has a plethora of traveller-oriented **restaurants**, delivering safe options rather than haute cuisine. Many of the most popular are attached to guesthouses in the bazaar, or among the growing row of joints in Virupapuragadda. As a holy site, the whole village is supposed to be strictly vegetarian, and alcohol-free, but one or two places bend the rules. There are no such restrictions on the other side of the river.

Laughing Buddha Virupapuragadda. Good for meat dishes such as schnitzel and has a generally relaxed atmosphere. Films shown every evening.

Mango Tree 300m beyond Sacred Ford. Wonderfully relaxed riverside hangout on a series of stone terraces. It would be a far better place to linger over a simple snack or drink but for hordes of pesky flies.

New Shanti On the path from Virupaksha temple down to the river. Best known for its delicious cakes and breads but also does standard Indian and continental dishes.

Ravi's Rose East end of village. Small rooftop joint that can actually come up with genuinely spicy dishes on request. Good sound system and lassis.

Shiv Moon Riverside path, east of the village. Good place to break the journey to or from the Vitthala temple, serving pastas and standard curries.

Sri Sangameshwar Main Bazaar. One of the more genuine Indian places, where you can get the best thalis and masala dosas, as well as the odd Western snack.

Suresh On the path from Virupaksha temple down to the river. Established joint which specializes in tuna, Goan dishes and *momos* (Tibetan dumplings).

Trishul On the lane from beside the tourist office. Offers one of Hampi's widest menus, featuring chicken, tuna, lasagne, pizza and desserts such as scrumptious apple crumble. Beer is occasionally available.

Monuments of the Chalukyas

Now quiet villages, **Badami**, **Aihole** and **Pattadakal**, the last a UNESCO World Heritage Site, were once the capital cities of the **Chalukyas**, who ruled much of the Deccan between the fourth and eighth centuries. The astonishing profusion of **temples** in the area beggars belief. Badami's and Aihole's cave temples, stylistically related to those at Ellora (see p.641), are some of the most important of their type. Among the many freestanding temples are some of the earliest in India, and uniquely, it is possible to see both northern (*nagari*) and southern (Dravida) architectural styles side by side.

Badami

Surrounded by a yawning expanse of flat farmland, **BADAMI**, capital of the Chalukyas from 543 AD to 757 AD, extends east into a gorge between two red sandstone hills, topped by two ancient fort complexes. The south is riddled with cave temples, and on the north stand early structural temples. Beyond the village, to the east, is an artificial lake, Agastya, said to date from the fifth century. Badami's small selection of hotels and restaurants makes it an ideal base from which to explore the Chalukyan remains at Aihole and Pattadakal as well. The whole Badami area is also home to numerous troupes of monkeys, especially around the monuments, and you are likely to find the cheeky characters all over you if you produce any food.

Arrival and information

Badami **bus stand** – in the centre of the village on Main Station Road – sees frequent daily services to Gadag (2hr), Hubli (3hr) and Bijapur (4hr), as well as local buses to Aihole and Pattadakal. The direct Hospet buses all leave by 8.30am (5hr); at other times change in Gadag. The **railway station** is 5km north, along a road lined with neem trees; tongas (Rs30 or Rs5/head shared) as well as buses and auto-rickshaws are usually available for the journey into town. The line from Bijapur to Gadag via Badami carries two daily trains in each direction.

The friendly but erratically opening **tourist office** (Mon–Sat: April–May 8am–1pm; June–March 10am–5.30pm; ⓣ08357/220414), located inside the KSTDC *Hotel Mayura Chalukya* (see p.1138), can help you find a **guide**. There are a couple of **ATMs** in town: the Syndicate Bank opposite the bus stand and SBI towards the tourist office. Ambika Tours & Travels at *Mookambika Deluxe* runs **tours** taking in Badami, Aihole and Pattadakal in Ambassador taxis for a reasonable Rs1100.

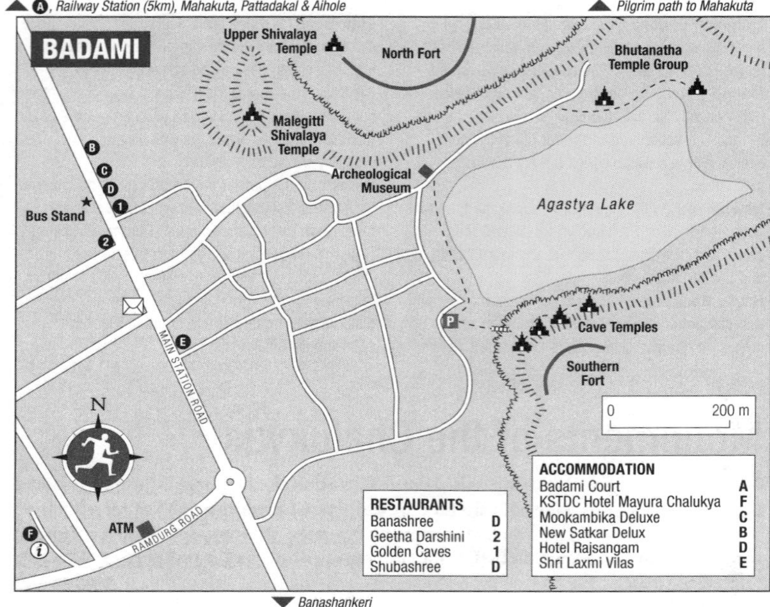

Accommodation and eating

Apart from the hotel restaurants listed below, the *Geetha Darshini* (closed Sun), 100m south of the bus stand, is a top south Indian joint whose *iddlis*, *vadas* and dosas are out of this world. Just south of the *Hotel Rajsangam*, the *Golden Caves* restaurant serves good inexpensive non-veg Indian and Chinese food.

Badami Court 2km north of town ⓣ08357/220230. Ranged around a garden, its 27 attached rooms are plain but spacious. The restaurant serves meals and expensive beer, while the swimming pool is open to non-residents for Rs80/hr. ❹–❼

KSTDC Mayura Chalukya Ramdurg Rd ⓣ08357/220046. This renovated government hotel has ten sizeable rooms, pleasant gardens and a standard restaurant. ❸–❹

Mookambika Deluxe Opposite the bus stand ⓣ08357/220067, ⓔhotelmookambika@yahoo.com. Functional mid-range hotel with simple doubles on the ground floor and comfortable new air-conditioned rooms upstairs. ❹–❻

New Satkar Delux Just north of the bus stand ⓣ08357/220417. Friendly lodge with decent rooms, particularly the cleaner and more spacious ones on the first floor. Also a back-garden restaurant, which serves excellent food such as chicken Mughlai. ❷–❺

Hotel Rajsangam Opposite the bus stand ⓣ08357/221991. The priciest in-town option offers spacious singles, deluxe doubles, and suites with balconies. It also has two good restaurants: the *Banashree* serves pure-veg food and the *Shubashree* is non-veg and has a bar. Complimentary breakfast. ❹–❼

Shri Laxmi Vilas 200m south of the bus stand ⓣ08357/220077. Simple lodge with very basic rooms and a reasonable veg restaurant. ❶

Southern Fort cave temples

Badami's earliest monuments, in the Southern Fort area, are a group of sixth-century **caves** (daily sunrise to sunset; Rs100 [Rs5]) cut into the hill's red sandstone, each connected by steps leading up the hillside.

About 15m up the face of the rock, **Cave 1**, a Shiva temple, is probably the earliest. Entrance is through a triple opening into a long porch raised on a plinth decorated with images of Shiva's dwarf attendants, the *ganas*. Outside, to the left of the porch, a *dvarpala* door guardian stands beneath a Nandi bull. On the right is a striking 1.5m-high image of a sixteen-armed dancing Shiva. He carries a stick-zither-type *vina*, which may or may not be a *yal*, a now-extinct musical instrument, on which the earliest Indian classical music theory is thought to have been developed.

A little higher, the similar **Cave 2**, a Vishnu shrine, holds some impressive sculpture and painting. Steps and slopes lead on upwards, past a natural cave containing a smashed image of the Buddhist *bodhisattva*, Padmapani (he who holds the lotus), and steps on the right in a cleft in the rock lead up to the fort. **Cave 3** (578 AD) stands beneath a 30m-high perpendicular bluff. The largest of the group, with a facade measuring 21m from north to south, it is also considered to be the finest, for the quality of its sculptural decoration. Treatment of the pillars is extremely elaborate, featuring male and female bracket figures, lotus motifs and medallions portraying amorous couples.

To the east of the others, a Jain temple, **Cave 4**, overlooks Agastya Lake and the town. It's a much simpler shrine, dating from the sixth century. Figures, both seated and standing, of the 24 *tirthankaras*, mostly without their identifying emblems, line the walls. Here, the rock is striped.

After seeing the caves it is possible to climb up to the fort and walk east where, hidden in the rocks, a carved panel shows Vishnu reclining on the serpent Adisesha, attended by a profusion of gods and sages. Continuing, you can skirt the gorge and descend on the east to the Bhutanatha temples at the lakeside.

North Fort

North of Agastya Lake, a number of structural temples can be reached by steps. The small **Archeological Museum** (daily except Fri 10am–5pm; Rs2) contains sculpture from the region. Although now dilapidated, the **Upper Shivalaya temple** is one of the earliest Chalukyan buildings. Scenes from the life of Krishna decorate the base and various images of him can be seen between pilasters on the walls. Only the sanctuary and tower of the **Lower Shivalaya** survive. Perched on a rock, the **Malegitti Shivalaya** (late seventh century) is the finest southern-style early Chalukyan temple. Its shrine is adjoined by a pillared hallway with small pierced stones and a single image on each side: Vishnu on the north and Shiva on the south.

Aihole

No fewer than 125 temples, dating from the Chalukyan and the later Rashtrakuta periods (sixth to twelfth centuries), are found in the tiny village of **AIHOLE** (Aivalli), near the banks of the River Malaprabha. Lying in clusters within the village, in surrounding fields and on rocky outcrops, many of the temples are remarkably well preserved, despite being used as dwellings and cattle sheds. Reflecting both its geographical position and spirit of architectural experimentation, Aihole boasts northern (*nagari*) and southern (Dravida) temples, as well as variants that failed to survive subsequent stylistic developments.

Two of the temples are **rock-cut caves** dating from the sixth century. The Hindu **Ravanaphadigudi**, northeast of the centre, a Shiva shrine with a triple entrance, contains fine sculptures of Mahishasuramardini, a ten-armed Nateshan (the precursor of Shiva Nataraja) dancing with Parvati, Ganesh and the Sapta Matrikas ("seven mothers"). A two-storey cave, plain save for decoration at the entrances and a panel image of Buddha in its upper veranda, can be found partway up the hill to the southeast, overlooking the village. At the top of that hill, the Jain **Meguti** temple, which may never have been completed, bears an inscription on an outer wall dating it to 634 AD. You can climb up to the first floor for fine views of Aihole and the surrounding country.

The late seventh- to early eighth-century **Durga temple** (daily 6am–6pm; Rs 100 [Rs5]), – one of the most unusual, elaborate and large in Aihole, – stands close to others on open ground in the Archeological Survey compound, near the centre of the village. It derives its name not from the goddess Durga but from the Kannada *durgadagudi*, meaning "temple near the fort". A series of pillars – many featuring amorous couples – forming an open ambulatory continue from the porch around the whole building. Other sculptural highlights include the decoration on the entrance to the *mandapa* hallway and niche images on the outer walls of the now-empty semicircular sanctum. Nearby, a small **Archeological Museum** (daily except Fri 10am–5pm; free) displays early Chalukyan sculpture and sells the booklet *Glorious Aihole*, which includes a site map and accounts of the monuments.

Further south, beyond several other temples, the **Ladh Khan** (the name of a Muslim who made it his home) is perhaps the best known of all at Aihole. Now thought to have been constructed at some point between the end of the sixth century and the eighth, it was originally seen as one of the country's temple prototypes. Inside stands a Nandi bull and a small sanctuary containing a *shivalingam* is next to the back wall. Both may have been later additions, with the original inner sanctum located at the centre.

Practicalities

Six daily **buses** run to Aihole from Badami (1hr 30min) via Pattadakal (45min) from 5.30am to 9pm; the last bus returns around 6pm. The only place to **stay and eat** (apart from a few chai shops) in Aihole is the small, clean and spartan KSTDC *Tourist Rest House* (Ⓣ08351/234541; ❷) about five minutes' walk up the main road north out of the village, next to the ASI offices. Simple, tasty food is available by arrangement – and by candlelight during frequent power cuts. The *Kiran Bar* on the same road, but in the village, serves beer and spirits and has a restaurant.

Pattadakal

The village of **PATTADAKAL**, on a bend in the River Malaprabha 22km from Badami, served as the site of Chalukyan coronations between the seventh and eighth centuries; in fact it may only have been used for such ceremonials. Like Badami and Aihole, the area boasts fine Chalukyan architecture, with particularly large mature examples; as at Aihole, both northern and southern styles can be seen. Pattadakal's main group of monuments (daily 6am–6pm; Rs250 [Rs10]) stand together in a well-maintained compound, next to the village, and have been designated a UNESCO World Heritage Site.

Earliest among the temples, the **Sangameshvara**, also known as **Shri Vijayeshvara** (a reference to its builder, Vijayaditya Satyashraya; 696–733), shows typical southern features. To the south, both the **Mallikarjuna** and the enormous **Virupaksha**, side by side, are in the southern style, built by two sisters who were successively the queens of Vikramaditya II (733–46). Along with the Kanchipuram temple in Tamil Nadu, the Virupaksha was probably one of the largest and most elaborate in India at the time. Interior pillars are carved with scenes from the Ramayana and Mahabharata, while in the Mallikarjuna the stories are from the life of Krishna.

The largest northern-style temple, the **Papanatha**, further south, was probably built after the Virupaksha in the eighth century. Outside walls feature reliefs (some of which, unusually, bear the sculptors' autographs) from the Ramayana, including, on the south wall, Hanuman's monkey army.

Pattadakal is connected by regular state **buses** and hourly private buses to Badami (45min) and Aihole (45min). Aside from a few teashops, cold drinks and coconut stalls, there are no facilities. For three days at the end of January, Pattadakal hosts an annual **dance festival** featuring dancers from across India.

Bijapur and the north

Boasting some of the Deccan's finest Muslim monuments, **BIJAPUR** is often billed as "The Agra of the South". The comparison is partly justified: for more than three hundred years, this was the capital of a succession of powerful rulers, whose domed mausoleums, mosques, colossal civic buildings and fortifications recall a lost golden age of unrivalled prosperity and artistic refinement. Yet there the similarities between the two cities end. A provincial market town of just 210,000 inhabitants, modern Bijapur is a world away from the urban frenzy of Agra. With the exception of the mighty **Golgumbaz**, which attracts busloads of day-trippers, its historic sites see only a slow trickle of tourists, while the ramshackle town centre is surprisingly laidback, dotted with peaceful green spaces and colonnaded mosque courtyards. In the first week of February the town hosts an annual **music festival** which attracts several renowned musicians from both the Carnatic (south Indian) and the Hindustani (north Indian) classical music traditions.

Some history

Bijapur began life in the tenth century as **Vijayapura**, the Chalukyas' "City of Victory". Taken by the Vijayanagars, it passed into Muslim hands for the first time in the thirteenth century with the arrival of the sultans of Delhi. The Bahmanis administered the area for a time, but it was only after the local rulers, the **Adil Shahis**, won independence from Bidar by expelling the Bahmani garrison and declaring this their capital that Bijapur's rise to prominence began.

Burying their differences for a brief period in the late sixteenth century, the five Muslim dynasties that issued from the breakdown of Bahmani rule – based at Golconda, Ahmednagar, Bidar and Gulbarga – formed a military alliance to defeat the Vijayanagars. The spoils of this campaign, which saw the total destruction of Vijayanagar (Hampi), funded a two-hundred-year building boom in Bijapur during which the city's most impressive monuments were built. However, old enmities between rival Muslim sultanates on the Deccan soon resurfaced, and the Adil Shahis'

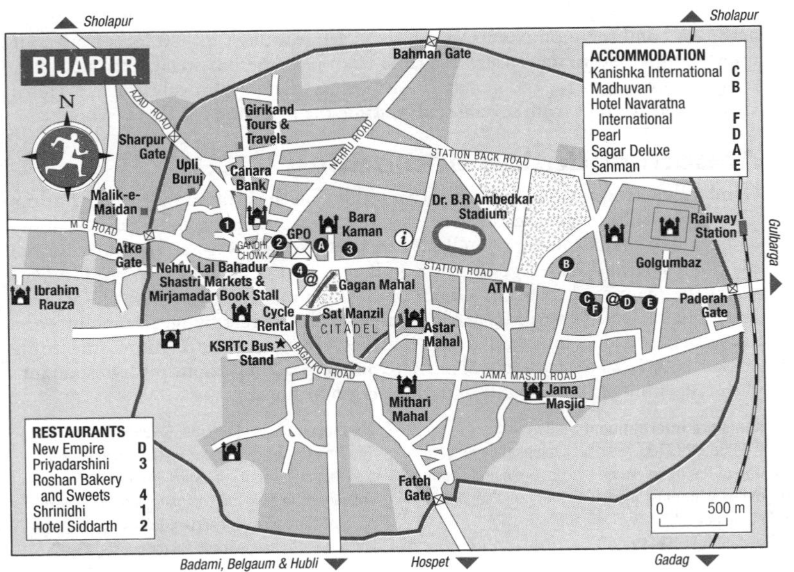

royal coffers were gradually squandered on fruitless and protracted wars. By the time the British arrived on the scene in the eighteenth century, the Adil Shahis were a spent force, locked into a decline from which they and their capital never recovered.

Arrival and information

Just a stone's throw away from the Golgumbaz, outside the old city walls, the **railway station**, 3km northeast of the bus stand, is the most inspiring point of arrival. There are three trains weekly from both Mumbai and Yesvantpur (Bengaluru), as well as a daily passenger service to Hyderabad and two more north to Solapur and south to Gadag, via Badami.

State and interstate **buses** from as far afield as Mumbai and Aurangabad pull into the KSRTC Bus Stand on the southwest edge of the town centre; ask at the enquiries desk for exact timings, as the timetables are all in Kannada. KSRTC run deluxe buses to Bengaluru, Hubli, Mumbai and Hyderabad. Heading to Badami, it is often quicker to take the first bus to Bagalkot and change there. VRL, recognizable by its distinctive yellow-and-black livery, runs **private services** to Bengaluru (3 buses from 7pm) and operates other overnight buses to Mangalore via Udupi and Mumbai. These can be booked through Vijayanand Travel, Terrace floor, Shastri Market, Gandhi Circle (Ⓣ08352/251000) or its other branch just south of the bus stand.

The **tourist office** (Mon–Sat 10am–5.30pm; Ⓣ08352/250359) behind the *Hotel Adil Shahi* annexe on Station Road, can help with arranging itineraries and guides. For **changing cash** (or travellers' cheques), the most reliable service is at Girikand Tours and Travels (Ⓣ08352/220510) on the first floor at Nishant Plaza, Rama Mandir Road; you can also use the Canara Bank, on nearby Azad Road. There are a couple of ATMs on Station Road. **Internet** services are available at the adjacent Friends Cyber Zone and Cyber Park (both Rs20/hr), opposite the post office.

City transport

Auto-rickshaws don't have meters and charge a minimum of Rs10; although most of Bijapur is covered by a fare of Rs30, they are a much more expensive way of getting around the monuments, when they charge at least Rs200 for a four-hour tour. **Tongas** and **taxis** are also available from near the bus stand. Bijapur is flat, relatively uncongested, and generally easy to negotiate by **bicycle**; rickety Heros are available for rent from several stalls outside the bus stand for Rs3 per hour.

Accommodation and eating

Good-value **accommodation** is relatively thick on the ground in Bijapur. **Eating** is largely confined to the hotels – try the *New Empire* at the *Pearl*. At most independent establishments you'll be restricted to pure-veg; at Gandhi Chowk, the *Shrinidhi Hotel* serves good south Indian veg food, as does the *Priyadarshini*, across the main road from the Gagan Mahal. Among other goodies, the popular *Roshan Bakery and Sweets*, MG Road, whips up the perfect budget brunch to-go: flaky, rich and delicious boiled egg and veg croissants (Rs6). Above the main market is *Hotel Siddarth* (Ⓣ08352/220338), a sprawling rooftop bar-restaurant, with tasty non-veg Indian and a good selection of booze.

Kanishka International Station Rd Ⓣ08352/223788, Ⓦwww.kanishkabijapur.com. One of the better-value places, providing comfy rooms with most mod cons and good service at decent rates. Fine veg and non-veg restaurants. ❸–❺

Madhuvan Station Rd Ⓣ08352/255571, Ⓕ256201. The smartest place in town, with a bright yellow exterior and a variety of rooms, from overpriced ordinary doubles to more comfortable a/c "deluxe" options. The restaurant serves good-value thalis at lunchtime. Exchange available for guests. ❹–❺

Hotel Navaratna International Just off Station Rd ⓣ08352/222771, ⓕ222772. The huge, shiny-tiled rooms at this quiet hotel are great value for this price. Good service, veg and non-veg restaurants and a popular palm-shaded dining (and drinking) area. ❸–❹

Pearl Station Rd ⓣ08352/256002, ⓕ243606. Bright modern hotel with clean, sizeable rooms. The front ones have balconies and those at the top views of Golgumbaz. Better value than the *Madhuvan* and with an excellent restaurant. ❸–❹

Sagar Deluxe Near Bara Kaman ⓣ08352/259234. Fine budget option, close to the action but on a quiet side street. Simple but adequate rooms, including Rs100 singles. ❶–❸

Sanman Station Rd ⓣ08352/251866, ⓕ222772. Best value among the budget places, and well placed for the railway station. Clean, good-sized rooms, some with a/c, and a rooftop restaurant/bar with excellent evening views of the mausoleum. ❶–❷

The town and monuments

Unlike most medieval Muslim strongholds, Bijapur lacked natural rock defences and had to be strengthened by the Adil Shahis with huge **fortified walls**. Extending some 10km around the town, these ramparts, studded with cannon emplacements (*burjes*) and watchtowers, are breached in five points by *darwazas*, or strong gateways, and several smaller postern gates (*didis*). In the middle of the town, a further hoop of crenellated battlements encircled Bijapur's **citadel**, site of the sultans' apartments and durbar hall, of which only fragments remain. The Adil Shahis' **tombs** are scattered around the outskirts, while most of the important **mosques** lie southeast of the citadel.

The Golgumbaz

The vast **Golgumbaz** mausoleum (daily 6am–6pm; Rs100 [Rs5]), Bijapur's most famous building, soars above the town's east walls, visible for miles in every direction. Built towards the end of the Adil Shahis' reign, the building is a fitting monument to a dynasty on its last legs – pompous, decadent and ill-proportioned, but conceived on an irresistibly awesome scale.

The cubic tomb, enclosing a 170-square-metre hall, is crowned with a single hemispherical **dome**, the largest in the world after St Peter's in Rome (which is only 5m wider). Spiral staircases wind up the four seven-storey octagonal towers that buttress the building to the famous **Whispering Gallery**, a 3m-wide passage encircling the interior base of the dome from where, looking carefully down, you can get a real feel of the sheer size of the building. Arrive here just after opening time to avoid the bus tours and experiment with the extraordinary acoustics. The **view** from the mausoleum's ramparts, which overlook the town and its monuments to the dark-soiled Deccan countryside beyond, is superb .

Set on a plinth in the centre of the hall below are the gravestones of the ruler who built the Golgumbaz, **Mohammed Adil Shah**, along with those of his wife, daughter, grandson and favourite courtesan, Rambha. At one corner of the grounds stands the simple gleaming white shrine to a Sufi saint of the Adil Shahi period, **Hashim Pir** which, around February, attracts *qawwals* (singers of devotional *qawwali* music) to the annual *urs*, which lasts for three days.

The Jama Masjid

A little under 1km southwest of the Golgumbaz, the **Jama Masjid** presides over the quarter that formed the centre of the city during Bijapur's nineteenth-century nadir under the Nizam of Hyderabad. It was commissioned by Ali Adil Shah, the ruler credited with constructing the city walls and complex water supply system, as a monument to his victory over the Vijayanagars at the battle of Talikota in 1565, and is widely regarded as one of the finest mosques in India. As it is a living place of worship, you should not enter improperly dressed (no shorts or skirts).

Simplicity and restraint are the essence of the colonnaded prayer hall below, divided by gently curving arches and rows of thick plaster-covered pillars. Aside from the odd geometric design and trace of yellow, blue and green tile-work, the only ornamentation is found in the mihrab, or west- (Mecca-) facing prayer niche, which is smothered in gold leaf and elaborate calligraphy. The marble floor of the hall features a grid of twenty five hundred rectangles, known as *musallahs* (after the *musallah* prayer mats brought to mosques by worshippers). These were added by the Mughal emperor Aurangzeb, allegedly as recompense for making off with the velvet carpets, long golden chain and other valuables that originally filled the prayer hall.

The Mithari and Astar Mahals

Continuing west from the Jama Masjid, the first monument of note is a small, ornately carved gatehouse on the south side of the road. Although of modest size, the delicate three-storey structure, known as the **Mithari Mahal**, is one of Bijapur's most beautiful buildings, with ornate projecting windows and minarets crowning its corners. Once again, Ali Adil Shah erected it, along with the mosque behind, using gifts presented to him during a state visit to Vijayanagar.

The lane running north from opposite the Mithari Mahal brings you to the dilapidated **Astar Mahal**, a large open-fronted hall fronted by a large stagnant step-well. Built in 1646 by Mohammed Adil Shah as a hall of justice, it was later chosen to house hairs from the Prophet's beard, thereby earning the title **Asar-i-Sharif**, or "place of illustrious relics". In theory, women are not permitted inside to view the upper storey, where fifteen niches are decorated with mediocre, Persian-style pot-and-foliage murals, but for a little baksheesh, one of the girls who hang around the site will unlock the doors for you.

The citadel

Bijapur's **citadel** stands in the middle of town, hemmed in on all but its north side by battlements. Most of the buildings inside have collapsed, or have been converted into government offices, but enough remain to give a sense of how imposing this royal enclave must once have been.

The best-preserved monuments lie along, or near, the citadel's main north–south artery, Anand Mahal Road, reached by skirting the southeast wall from the Astar Mahal. The latter route brings you first to the **Gagan Mahal**. Originally Ali Adil Shah's "Heavenly Palace", this now-ruined hulk later served as a durbar hall for the sultans, who would sit in state on the platform at the open-fronted north side, watched by crowds gathered in the grounds opposite. West off Anand Mahal Road, the five-storeyed **Sat Manzil** was the pleasure palace of the courtesan Rambha, entombed with Mohammed Adil Shah and his family in the Golgumbaz. In front stands an ornately carved water pavilion, the **Jal Mandir**, now left high and dry in an empty tank.

Malik-e-Maidan and Upli Buruj

Guarding the principal western entrance to the city is one of several bastions that punctuate Bijapur's battlements. This one, the Burj-i-Sherza ("Lion Gate") sports a colossal cannon, known as the **Malik-e-Maidan**, literally "Lord of the Plains". It was brought here as war booty in the sixteenth century, and needed four hundred bullocks, ten elephants and an entire battalion to haul it up the steps to the emplacement. Inscriptions record that the cannon, whose muzzle features a relief of a monster swallowing an elephant, was cast in Ahmednagar in 1551.

A couple more discarded cannons lie atop the watchtower visible a short walk northwest. Steps wind around the outside of the oval-shaped **Upli Buruj**, or "Upper Bastion", to a gun emplacement that affords unimpeded views over the city and plains.

The Ibrahim Rauza

Set in its own walled compound less than 1km west of the ramparts, the **Ibrahim Rauza** represents the high-water mark of Bijapuri architecture (daily 6am–6pm; Rs100 [Rs5]). Whereas the Golgumbaz impresses primarily by its scale, the appeal of this tomb complex lies in its grace and simplicity. Beyond the reach of most bus parties, it's also a haven of peace, with cool colonnaded verandas and flocks of iridescent parakeets careening between the mildewed domes, minarets and gleaming golden finials.

Opinions differ over whether the tomb was commissioned by Ibrahim Adil Shah (1580–1626), or his favourite wife, Taj Sultana, but the former was the first to be interred here, in a gloomy chamber whose only light enters via a series of exquisite pierced-stone windows. Made up of elaborate Koranic inscriptions, these are the finest examples of their kind in India. More amazing stonework decorates the exterior of the mausoleum, and the equally beautiful **mosque** opposite, the cornice of whose facade features a stone chain carved from a single block. The two buildings, bristling with minarets and cupolas, face each other from opposite sides of a rectangular raised plinth, divided by a small reservoir and fountains. Viewed from on top of the walls that enclose the complex, you can see why its architect, Malik Sandal, added a self-congratulatory inscription in his native Persian over the tomb's south doorway, describing his masterpiece as "...A beauty of which Paradise stood amazed".

Gulbarga

GULBARGA, 165km northeast of Bijapur, was the founding capital of the Bahmani dynasty and the region's principal city before the court moved to Bidar in 1424. Later captured by the Adil Shahis and Mughals, it has remained a staunchly Muslim town, and bulbous onion domes and mosque minarets still soar prominently above its ramshackle concrete-box skyline. The town is also famous as the birthplace of the *chishti*, or saint, Hazrat Bandah Nawaz Gesu Daraz (1320–1422), whose tomb, situated next to one of India's foremost Islamic theological colleges, is a major shrine.

In spite of Gulbarga's religious and historical significance, its **monuments** pale in comparison with those at Bijapur, and even Bidar. Unless you're particularly interested in medieval Muslim architecture, few are worth breaking a journey to see. The one exception is the tomb complex on the northeast edge of town, known as **the Dargah**. Approached via a broad bazaar, this marble-lined enclosure centres on the tomb of Hazrat Gesu Daraz, affectionately known to his devotees as **Bandah Nawaz**, or "the long-haired one who brings comfort to others". The saint was spiritual mentor to the Bahmani rulers, and it was they who erected his beautiful double-storeyed mausoleum, now visited by hundreds of thousands of Muslim pilgrims each year. Women are not allowed inside, and men must wear long trousers. The same applies to the neighbouring tomb, whose interior has retained its exquisite Persian paintings. The Dargah's other important building, open to both sexes, is the **madrasa**, founded by Bandah Nawaz and enlarged during the two centuries after his death.

After mingling with the crowds at the Dargah, escape across town to Gulbarga's deserted **fort**. Encircled by sixteen-metre-thick crenellated walls, fifteen watchtowers and an evil-smelling stagnant moat, the great citadel now lies in ruins behind the town's large artificial lake. Its only surviving building is the beautiful fourteenth-century **Jama Masjid**. Thought to have been modelled by a Moorish architect on the great Spanish mosque of Cordoba, it is unique in India for having an entirely domed prayer hall.

Arrival and information

Daily KSRTC **buses** from Bijapur, Bidar and beyond pull in to the State Bus Stand on the southwest edge of town. Private minibuses work from the roadside opposite. Don't be tempted to take one of these to Bidar; they only run as far as the fly-blown junction of Humnabad, 40km short, where you may get stranded. Gulbarga's mainline **railway station**, with services to and from Mumbai, Pune, Hyderabad, Bangalore and Chennai, lies 1.5km east of the bus stand, along Mill Road. Station Road, the town's other main artery, runs due north of here past the lake to the busy Chowk crossroads, at the heart of the bazaar.

Gulbarga's main sights are well spread out, so you'll need to get around by **auto-rickshaw**; fix fares in advance. There are **ATMs** at the station and both main roads, as well as several places to get online.

Accommodation and eating

All the hotels listed below have **restaurants**, mostly pure-veg places with a no-alcohol rule. *Kamat*, the chain restaurant, has several branches in Gulbarga including a pleasant one at Station Chowk, specializing in veg "meals" as well as *iddlis* and dosas; try *joleata roti*, a local bread cooked either hard and crisp or soft like a chapatti. On the road up from the station several hole-in-the-wall spots sell freshly fried chicken and fish.

Central Park Station Rd, nearly 1km north of station ⓣ08472/273231, ⓦwww.centralparkgulbarga.com. Clean modern business hotel whose simple but smart rooms all have TV and wi-fi connections. Good non-veg restaurant. ❸–❺

Hotel Prashant First lane on the right leaving the station ⓣ08472/221456. Decent rooms of varying sized and amenities, surprisingly quiet. ❷–❹

Preetam Lodge Mill Rd ⓣ08472/221673. Head and shoulders above the other places around the bus stand, with clean, spacious rooms in a newish block. ❷–❹

Raj Rajeshwari Vasant Nagar, Mill Rd ⓣ08472/225881. Just 5min from the bus stand, this friendly hotel is set in a well-maintained modern building with large attached rooms with balconies, plus a reasonable veg restaurant. Strictly no alcohol. ❸–❹

Southern Star Near the Fort, Super Market ⓣ08472/224093. Pricey rooms, some with fort views, but the vast side-courtyard offers relaxing alfresco dining and is a great spot to watch the sunset behind the fort while nursing a beer. ❸–❻

Bidar

Lost in the far northeast of Karnataka, **BIDAR**, 284km northeast of Bijapur, is nowadays a provincial backwater, better known for its fighter-pilot training base than the gently decaying monuments nearby. Yet the town, half of whose 140,000 population is still Muslim, has a gritty charm, with narrow red-dirt streets ending at arched gates and open vistas across the plains. Littered with tile-fronted tombs, rambling fortifications and old mosques, it merits a visit if you're travelling between Hyderabad (150km east) and Bijapur, although expect little in the way of Western comforts, and a higher level of curious approaches from locals.

In 1424, following the break-up of the Bahmani dynasty into five rival factions, **Ahmad Shah I** shifted his court from Gulbarga to a less constricted site at Bidar. Revamping the town with a new fort, splendid palaces, mosques and ornamental gardens, the Bahmanis ruled from here until 1487, when the Barid Shahis took control. They were succeeded by the Adil Shahis from Bijapur, and later the Mughals under Aurangzeb, who annexed the region in 1656, before the Nizam of Hyderabad acquired the territory in the early eighteenth century.

Bidar's sights are too spread out to be comfortably explored on foot. However, auto-rickshaws tend to be thin on the ground away from the main streets, and are reluctant to wait while you look around, so it's a good idea to rent a bicycle for the day (Rs3/hr) from Rouf's, only 50m east of the bus stand, next to the excellent *Karnatak Juice Centre*.

Arrival and information

Bidar lies on a branch line of the main Mumbai–Secunderabad–Chennai rail route, and can only be reached by slow passenger **train**. The few visitors that come here invariably arrive **by bus**, arriving at the KSRTC Bus Stand on the far northwestern edge of town. There is no tourist office but there are several **internet** outlets such as Cyber Park (Rs15/hr), 100m southeast of the bus stand on Udgir Road.

Accommodation and eating

Hotel Mayura (Ⓣ08482/228142; ❷–❹) opposite the bus stand, has large rooms with optional air-conditioning. Its older sister, the *Ashoka* (Ⓣ08482/227621; ❷–❹), 1500m from the bus stand past Dr Ambedkar Chowk, is comfortable with good-value deluxe rooms, some with air-conditioning. *Sapna International* (Ⓣ08482/220991, ❸–❹), 300m north of the bus stand, offers Bidar's nicest lodgings, with big, clean rooms and a good non-veg restaurant. If you don't mind some grubbiness, a real budget option is *Hotel Kailash* (Ⓣ08482/227727; ❶) on Udgir Road, in the centre of town.

Finding somewhere good to **eat** is not a problem in Bidar, thanks to the restaurants at the *Mayura* and *Ashoka*, which both offer a varied selection of north Indian veg and meat dishes (try the *Mayura*'s pepper chicken) and serve cold beer. Also recommended, and much cheaper, is the popular *Udupi Krishna* restaurant, overlooking the chowk, which serves up unlimited pure-veg thalis for lunch and south Indian breakfasts. The *Jyothi Udupi*, opposite the new bus stand, also serves big, delicious dosas and tasty thalis.

The old town

The heart of Bidar is its medieval **old town**, encircled by crenellated ramparts and eight imposing gateways (*darwazas*). This predominantly Muslim quarter holds many Bahmani-era mosques, havelis and *khanqahs* – "monasteries" set up by the local rulers for Muslim cleric-mystics and their disciples – but its real highlight is the impressive ruins of **Mahmud Gawan's madrasa**, whose single minaret soars high above the city centre. The distinctively Persian-style building, originally surmounted by large bulbous domes, once housed a world-famous library. However, this burnt down after being struck by lightning in 1696, while several of the walls and domes were blown away when gunpowder stored here by Aurangzeb's occupying army caught fire and exploded. Today, the madrasa is little

Bidri

Bidar is renowned as the home of a unique damascene metalwork technique known as **bidri**, developed by the Persian silversmiths who came to the area with the Bahmani court in the fifteenth century. These highly skilled artisans engraved and inlaid their traditional Iranian designs onto a metal alloy composed of lead, copper, zinc and tin, which they blackened and polished. The resulting effect – swirling silver floral motifs framed by geometric patterns and set against black backgrounds – has since become the hallmark of Muslim metalwork in India.

Bidri objets d'art are displayed in museums and galleries all over the country. But if you want to see pukka *bidri*-wallahs at work, take a walk down Bidar's **Siddiq Talim Road**, which cuts across the south side of the old town, where skull-capped artisans tap and burnish vases, goblets, plates, spice boxes, betel-nut tins and ornamental hookah pipes, as well as less traditional objects – coasters, ashtrays and bangles – that crop up (at vastly inflated prices) in silver emporiums as far away as Delhi and Kolkata.

more than a shell, although its elegant arched facade has retained large patches of the vibrant Persian glazed tile-work that once covered most of the exterior surfaces.

The Fort

A rambling, crumbling monument valley to the fifteenth-century Bahmani Empire, the Bidar **Fort**, at the far north end of the street running past the madrasa, retains a serene, austere beauty. Though locals have incorporated the vast rolling spaces into their lives – young boys play cricket in the grassy turf, terraces are planted with rice, and scooters and small trucks ply its roads – its appeal remains undiminished.

The fort was founded by the Hindu Chalukyas and strengthened by the Bahmanis in the early fifteenth century. Despite repeated sieges, it remains largely intact, encircled by 10km of ramparts that drop away in the north and west to 300-metre cliffs. The main southern entrance is protected by equally imposing man-made defences: gigantic fortified gates and a triple moat formerly crossed by a series of drawbridges. Once inside, the first building of note (on the left after the third and final gateway) is the exquisite **Rangin Mahal**. Mahmud Shah built this modest "Coloured Palace" after an unsuccessful uprising of Abyssinian slaves in 1487 forced him to relocate to a safer site inside the citadel. The palace's relatively modest proportions reflect the Bahmanis' declining fortunes, but its interior comprises some of the finest surviving Islamic art in the Deccan, with superb woodcarving above the door arches and Persian-style mother-of-pearl inlay on polished black granite surfaces. If the doors to the palace are locked, ask for the keys at the nearby ASI **museum** (daily 8am–1pm & 2–5pm; free), which houses a missable collection of Hindu temple sculpture, weapons and Stone Age artefacts.

Opposite the museum, an expanse of gravel is all that remains of the royal gardens. This is overlooked by the austere **Solah Khamb** mosque (1327), Bidar's oldest Muslim monument, whose most outstanding feature is the intricate pierced-stone calligraphy around its central dome. From here, continue west through the ruins of the former royal enclosure – a rambling complex of half-collapsed palaces, baths, zenanas and assembly halls – to the fort's west walls. You can complete the round of **the ramparts** in ninety minutes, taking time out to enjoy the views over the red cliffs and across the plains.

Ashtur: the Bahmani tombs

As you look from the fort's east walls, a cluster of eight bulbous white domes floats alluringly above the trees in the distance. Dating from the fifteenth century, the mausoleums at **Ashtur**, 3km east of Bidar (leave the old town via Dulhan Darwaza gate), are the final resting-places of the Bahmani sultans and their families, including the son of the ruler who first decamped from Gulbarga, Ala-ud-Din Shah I. His remains by far the most impressive tomb, with patches of coloured glazed tiles on its arched facade, and a large dome whose interior surfaces writhe with sumptuous Persian paintings. Reflecting sunlight onto the ceiling with a small pocket mirror, the *chowkidar* picks out the highlights, among them a diamond, barely visible among the bat droppings.

The tomb of Ala-ud-Din's father, the ninth and most illustrious Bahmani Sultan, Ahmad Shah I, stands beside that of his son, decorated with Persian inscriptions. Beyond this are two more minor mausoleums, followed by the partially collapsed tomb of Humayun the Cruel (1458–61), cracked open by a bolt of lightning. Continuing along the line, you can chart the gradual decline of the Bahmanis as the mausoleums diminish in size, ending with a sad handful erected in the early sixteenth century, when the sultans were no more than puppet rulers of the Badrid Shahis.

Contexts

History

India's history is as complex and as multifaceted as you would expect from such a huge, populous and culturally varied country – a place which was home to one of the world's earliest civilizations, the birthplace of four major global religions, as well as having spawned more dynasties, monarchs and kingdoms than even the most determined historian can keep track of. Broadly speaking, the history of India divides into two parts: the history of the Aryan **north**, heavily influenced by successive waves of invaders from the uplands of Central Asia, and the much more self-contained history of the Dravidian **south**.

The Indus Valley civilization

The earliest human presence in the Indian subcontinent can be traced back to the Early, Middle and Late **Stone Ages** (400,000–200,000 BC), when the country was first settled by semi-nomadic hunters and gatherers. Village settlements gradually developed over the next four thousand years across the Indus Valley as their inhabitants began to use copper and bronze, domesticate animals, make pottery and trade with their neighbours.

By around 2500 BC, the village settlements of the Indus Valley had begun to develop into one of the world's earliest civilizations – roughly contemporary with those of Sumer and ancient Egypt. Known variously as the **Indus Valley civilization** or the **Harappan Civilization**, this first great Subcontinental culture spread across a sizeable proportion of what is now southern Pakistan and the periphery of western India. Much of what is known about it comes from the remains of two great cities on the Indus, **Harappa** in the north and **Mohenjo Daro** in the south (both in present-day Pakistan). Laid out on a grid, both cities boasted large houses made from uniformly sized baked bricks, an elaborate system of covered drains (the world's first urban sanitation system) and large granaries. The absence of royal palaces and the large numbers of religious figurines found at both sites suggest that the Indus Valley civilization was a theocratic state of priests, merchants and farmers.

The Indus Valley civilization displayed remarkable longevity, surviving for a thousand years until its sudden demise around 1700 BC, probably caused by a catastrophic series of floods.

The Vedic Age (1500–600 BC)

The written history of India begins with the invasions of the charioteering **Indo-European** or **Aryan** tribes, which dealt the final death blow to the enfeebled Indus civilization. The arrival of the Aryans marks the beginning of the so-called **Vedic Age**, named after the earliest Indian literature, the Vedas (see p.1068). The Aryans were one of the various nomadic tribes who emerged out of the vast steppes of Central Asia, marauding and eventually colonizing Europe, the Middle East and the Indian subcontinent.

Aryan culture was diametrically opposed to that of the Indus civilization. Semi-nomadic hunters and pastoralists when they first reached the Subcontinent, the Aryans gradually adopted the farming techniques learned from the peoples they conquered as they spread eastwards into India.

The Aryans' hymns, written down in the Vedas, describe the inter-tribal conflicts characteristic of the period, but also express an underlying sense of solidarity against the indigenous peoples, whom the Aryans referred to as **Dasas**. Originally a general term for "enemies", it came to denote "subjects" as they were colonized within the expanding land of the Aryans. The Aryans began to emphasize purity of blood as they settled among the darker aboriginals, and their original class divisions of nobility and ordinary tribesmen were hardened to exclude the Dasas. At the same time, the priests, the sole custodians of the increasingly complex religion and sacrificial rituals, began to claim high privileges for their skill and training. By 1000 BC, Aryan society had become divided into four classes, or **varnas** (literally "colour"): priests (brahmins), warriors (*kshatriya*), peasants (*vaishya*) and serfs (*shudra*), a division that still survives today. The first three classes covered the main divisions within the Aryan tribes; the Dasas and other non-Aryan subjects became the *shudras*, who served the three higher classes. Many of India's most important religious texts and epics also date from this period, including the Sama, Yajur and Atharva Vedas, Brahmanas and the Upanishads (see p.1068), while the **Mahabharata** and the **Ramayana** (see p.1069) also claim to relate to this era.

During the later Vedic period, between 1000 and 600 BC, the centre of Aryan power shifted eastwards from the Punjab to the Doab, the region between the Ganges and Yamuna rivers. By 600 BC, at least sixteen separate republics and monarchies, known as **mahajanapadas**, had been established across northern India. The concept of divinely ordained kings tended to preserve the status quo in the monarchies, while the republics provided an atmosphere in which unorthodox views increasingly flourished – the founders of the new religions of Buddhism and Jainism were both born in small republics of this kind. The consolidation of the *mahajanapadas* was based on the growth of a stable agrarian economy and the increasing importance of trade, which led to the use of coins, the development of the **Brahmi script** (from which the current scripts of India, Sri Lanka, Tibet, Java and Myanmar derive) and the emergence of new towns. The resultant prosperity stimulated conflict, however, and by the fifth century BC the scattered states of north India had been consolidated into five great kingdoms: Magadha, Kashi, Koshala, Vatsa, and the republic of the Vrijjis.

Eventually, **Magadha** emerged supreme, under Bimbisara (543–491 BC), who was also, according to legend, a personal friend and great patron of the **Buddha**, his almost exact contemporary. Bimbisara's son and successor Ajatashatru (491–461 BC) moved the capital of Magadha to **Pataliputra** (the forerunner of modern Patna) and either annihilated the other kingdoms in the Ganges valley or reduced them to the status of vassals. In the middle of the fourth century BC, the **Nanda** dynasty usurped the Magadhan throne; Mahapadma Nanda conquered Kalinga (Orissa and the northern coastal strip of Andhra Pradesh) and gained control of parts of the Deccan. The disputed succession after his death coincided with significant events in the northwest; out of this confusion the first of India's empires was born.

The Mauryan Empire (320–184 BC)

North India's burgeoning prosperity was by now beginning to attract the attention of ambitious rulers in Central Asia – something that was to become a recurrent theme in Indian history over the next thousand years. **Darius I**, the third Achaemenid emperor of Persia, had already conquered the kingdom of Gandhara (in what is now northern Pakistan and eastern Afghanistan) around 520 BC. Far more significant, however, was the later invasion by **Alexander the Great**, who defeated Darius III, the last Achaemenid, crossed the Indus in 326 BC, and then overran the Punjab. Alexander was in India for just two years, and although he left garrisons and appointed satraps to govern the conquered territories, their position following his death in 323 BC became increasingly untenable.

The disruption caused by Alexander's brief incursion was seized upon by **Chandragupta Maurya**, the ruler of Magadha, who had overthrown the last of the Nanda dynasty in around 320 BC. Chandragupta is said to have met Alexander the Great and was probably inspired by his exploits; his 500,000-strong army drove out the Greek garrisons in the northwest and annexed all the lands east of the Indus.

From about 297 BC onwards, Chandragupta's son Bindusara extended the empire as far south as Mysore, before being succeeded in around 269 BC by his son, **Ashoka**, the most famous of India's early rulers. Ashoka ruthlessly consolidated his power for the first eight years of his reign, but then – allegedly sickened by the terrible carnage caused by his conquests – abruptly converted to Buddhism and renounced the use of violence in favour of the law of moral righteousness, or *dharma*. His adoption of Buddhism, however, did not interfere with his imperial pragmatism, and he continued to govern the newly acquired territory with a firm military hand, and by the end of his reign, Ashoka's empire stretched from Assam to Afghanistan and from Kashmir to Mysore; only the three Dravidian kingdoms of the Cholas, Cheras and Pandyas in the southernmost tip of the Subcontinent remained independent. After Ashoka's death in 232 BC, the empire began to fall apart, and in 184 BC the last of the Mauryans, Brihadratha, was assassinated by one of his generals, bringing to an end nearly 140 years of Mauryan rule.

The age of invasions (184 BC–320 AD)

The five hundred years following the collapse of the Mauryan Empire are the most complex and confusing in Subcontinental history, marked by political fragmentation and a new and seemingly endless series of **invasions** from the northwest. The period is sometimes referred to as India's "Dark Age", although despite the lack of any unified central power it was also one of economic dynamism and considerable cultural achievement.

The first invaders were the **Bactrian Greeks** of Gandhara, part of the enormous swathe of territories conquered by Alexander the Great that had subsequently become part of the Seleucid Empire under his successor, Seleucus. Around 180 BC the Bactrian Greeks declared independence from the Seleucid imperium, and shortly afterwards descended on India to carve out small fiefdoms of their own, occupying the Punjab and extending their power as far as Mathura in Uttar Pradesh.

Yet the arrival of newcomers from Central Asia soon threatened the Greek position in Bactria. Large-scale movements of central Asian Yueh-Chi nomads had precipitated the migration of the **Shakas** (Scythians), from the Aral Sea area, who displaced the **Parthians** (Pahlavas) from Iran, who in turn wrested control of Bactria from the Greeks (who henceforth administered their Indian territories from a new capital in Kabul). The finer details of these various population movements remain unclear, and they were probably more in the nature of migrations than invasions. Whatever the details, both the Yueh-Chi and Shakas continued to drift slowly in the direction of India, finally arriving during the first century AD. The Shakas were the first to arrive, establishing themselves in northwestern India until the coming of the **Kushan** branch of the Yueh-Chi, who drove the Shakas off into Gujarat and Malwa (the area around Ujjain).

Despite the disintegration of the Mauryan Empire and the proliferation of rival kingdoms, the period from 200 BC to 300 AD was also one of unprecedented economic wealth and cultural development. Urban centres began to develop all over India, while external trade, both overland and maritime, opened up lines of communication with the outside world stretching as far as Arabia and southeast Asia by sea, and China and the Mediterranean by land via the **Silk Route**.

The rise of the south

Meanwhile, the first great kingdom of southern India was flexing its muscles. Between the second century BC and the second century AD the **Andhra** or **Satavahana** dynasty, which originated in the region between the Godavari and Krishna rivers (modern-day Andhra Pradesh and Maharashtra), began to make inroads into much of south and central India, creating capitals at Paithan on the Godavari and at Amaravati on the Krishna. The dynasty survived until the middle of the third century, when its territories were carved up by rival dynasties including the Pallavas (see p.947), who took control of their territories in Andhra Pradesh.

Further south, the three kingdoms of the **Cheras** on the Malabar Coast in the west, the **Pandyas** in the central southern tip of the peninsula, and the **Cholas** on the east coast of Coromandel – together comprising much of present-day Tamil Nadu and Kerala – had been developing almost completely independently of north India. Society was divided into groups based on the geographical domains of hills, plains, forest, coast and desert rather than class or *varna*, though Brahmins did command high status. Although agriculture, pastoralism and fishing were the main occupations, trade in spices, gold and jewels with Rome and southeast Asia underpinned the region's prosperity.

From the middle of the first century BC, however, conflicts between the three states intensified. This enervating warfare rendered them vulnerable; early in the fourth century AD, the **Pallavas** overran the Chola capital of Kanchipuram, and by 325 AD had taken control of Tamil Nadu. The Pallavas remained a dominant power in the south until the ninth century AD, and thus became one of the longest ruling dynasties in Indian history.

The Guptas (320–650)

During the fourth century AD, a second great Indian empire began to emerge in the north: the **Guptas**. The parallels with the earlier Mauryan Empire are striking. Both were founded in the year 320 (BC and AD respectively) by a king named Chandragupta (though the later king is usually written as two words, Chandra Gupta), and both emerged from within the famous old kingdom of Magadha. **Chandra Gupta** (reigned *c*.320–335) appears to have been the ruler of a minor statelet within the old Magadhan kingdom, who acquired considerable new territory through intermarriage with the famous Licchavi clan, one of the Mauryas' principal enemies six hundred years previously. Chandra Gupta thus found himself master of a powerful kingdom in the Gangetic plain, which controlled the vital east–west trade route. His son and heir, **Samudra Gupta** (c.335–376 AD), expanded the frontiers of his realm from Punjab to Assam, while the empire reached its apogee under his successor, **Chandra Gupta II** (376–415 AD), who subjugated the Shakas in Gujarat and reunified the whole of northern India, with the exception of the northwest.

The era of these three imperial Guptas, along with the subsequent reign of Harsha Vardhana (606–647 AD) of Kanauj (see p.1154), is generally seen as the **Classical Age** of Indian history, one of cultural and artistic brilliance, religious ferment and political stability. Secular **Sanskrit literature** reached its perfection in the works of Kalidasa, the greatest Indian poet and dramatist, who was a member of Chandra Gupta II's court. The cave paintings of **Ajanta** and **Ellora** inspired Buddhist artists throughout Asia, and Yashodhara's detailed analysis of painting in the fifth century prescribed the classical conventions for the new art form. In **sculpture**, the images of the Buddha produced in Sarnath and Mathura embodied the simple and serene quality of classicism. In **architecture**, the Gupta era saw the birth of a new style of **Hindu temple** which would became India's classic architectural form. The era of the Guptas produced great thinkers as well: six systems of **philosophy** evolved, which refuted Buddhism and Jainism. One of them, **Vedanta**, has continued as the basis of all philosophical studies in India to this day.

The Guptas performed Vedic sacrifices to legitimize their rule, and patronized popular forms of Hinduism, such as devotional religion (*bhakti*) and the worship in temples of images of Vishnu, Shiva and the goddess Shakti, deities who were attracting increasing numbers of devotees during this era. Buddhism continued to thrive, however, with thousands of monks dwelling at Mathura as well as hundreds in Pataliputra itself.

The Gupta Empire remained relatively peaceful during the long reign of Kumara Gupta (c.415–455), who succeeded Chandra Gupta II, but by the time Skanda Gupta (c.455–467) came to the throne, western India was again threatened by invasions from Central Asia, this time by the **White Huns**, nomads from Central Asia who had already established themselves in Bactria. Skanda managed to repel White Hun raids, but after his death their disruption of central Asian trade seriously destabilized the empire. By the end of the fifth century, the Huns had wrested the Punjab from Gupta control, and further incursions early in the sixth century dealt a death blow to the Gupta Empire, which had completely disintegrated by 550 AD.

After the demise of the Guptas, northern India again split into rival kingdoms, but the Pushpabhutis of Sthanvishvara (Thanesar, north of Delhi) had established supremacy by the time **Harsha Vardhana** came to the throne in 606 AD. He reigned for 41 years over an empire that ranged from Gujarat to Bengal, including the Punjab, Kashmir and Nepal, and moved his capital to **Kanauj** (northwest of modern Kanpur in Uttar Pradesh). Harsha's empire was essentially feudal, with most of the defeated kings retaining their thrones as vassals; when he died without heirs in 647 AD, north India once again fragmented into independent kingdoms.

Kingdoms of central and south India (500–1250)

Meanwhile, significant events were taking place in central and south India. The history of the period was dominated by three major kingdoms: the **Pallavas**, who had supplanted the Satavahanas in the Andhra region and made Kanchipuram their capital back in the fourth century; the **Pandyas** of Madurai, who had established their own regional kingdom by the sixth century; and the **Chalukyas** of Vatapi (Badami in Karnataka), who had expanded into the Deccan in the middle of the sixth century. All three kingdoms intermittently fought one another, but their military strength was so evenly matched that none was able to gain ascendancy.

The Chalukyas were eventually overthrown in 753 by Dantidurga, the founder of the **Rashtrakuta** kingdom (whose rulers also tried their luck in the north, briefly gaining possession of Kanauj). The Pallavas survived their arch-enemies by about a hundred years, then succumbed to a combined attack of the Pandyas and the **Cholas**. The Cholas were a major new force in Tamil Nadu, conquering the Thanjavur region in the ninth century and taking Madurai from the Pandyas in 907, before being defeated by the Rashtrakutas in the middle of the tenth century, who were themselves replaced by the revived Chalukyas in 973 AD.

Ultimately, the chief beneficiaries of these dynastic toings-and-froings were the Cholas, who were able to regain lost territories and expand further during the eleventh and twelfth centuries. The great Chola kings **Rajaraja I** (985–1014) and **Rajendra I** (1014–1044), launched a series of campaigns against the Cheras, Pandyas and Chalukyas, and by the end of the eleventh century the Cholas were supreme in the south, although incessant campaigning had exhausted their resources. Ironically, their destruction of the Chalukyas laid the seeds of their own downfall. Former Chalukya feudatories, such as the **Yadavas** of Devagiri in the northern Deccan and the **Hoysalas**, around modern Mysore, set up their own kingdoms; the latter attacked the Cholas from the west while the Pandyas directed a new offensive from the south. By the thirteenth century, the **Pandyas** had superseded the Cholas as south India's major power, while the Yadavas and Hoysalas controlled the Deccan until the advent of the Delhi sultans in the fourteenth century.

Despite constant political and military conflicts, this period was very much the classical age of the south. The ascendancy of the Cholas was complemented by the crystallization of Tamil culture; the religious, artistic, and institutional patterns of this period dominated the culture of the south and influenced developments elsewhere in the Subcontinent. In the sphere of religion for instance, the great philosophers Shankara and Ramanuja, as well as the Tamil and Maharashtrian saints, had a significant impact on Hinduism in north India.

Kingdoms in north India (650–1250)

In north India, Harsha Vardhana's death was followed by a century of confusion, with assorted kingdoms competing to control the Gangetic valley. In time, the **Pratihara-Gurjaras**, from western India, and the **Palas**, of Bihar and Bengal, emerged as the main rivals, although both were weakened by repeated incursions from the Deccan by the **Rashtrakutas**, who briefly occupied Kanauj in 916. The Pratiharas regained their capital, but the tripartite struggle sapped their strength and they were unable to repel the invasion of Kanauj by Mahmud of Ghazni (see below) in 1018. The struggle for possession of Kanauj depleted the resources of all three competing powers and resulted in their almost simultaneous decline, while various smaller feudatory kingdoms began to assert their independence. Kingdoms emerged in Nepal, Kamarupa (Assam), Kashmir and Orissa, all with their own cultural identities, customs, literatures and histories. The Eastern Gangas of **Kalinga** (roughly equivalent to modern Orissa) also achieved political independence and unity in the twelfth century.

Meanwhile, in the west, the celebrated **Rajputs** began to emerge as a new element within Indian society. Their origins remain the subject of considerable speculation, although they probably descended from the various invaders who arrived in India between the third and sixth centuries, including the Pratihara-Gurjaras, Huns and Shakas and perhaps others. Whatever their origins, they acquired respectable Hindu genealogies and were given *kshatriya* status. By the tenth century, the most important Rajput clans, like the Chauhans of Ajmer, the Guhilas of Chittaurgarh, the Chandellas of Bundelkhand, and the Tomaras of Haryana (who founded modern Delhi in 1060), had all established small regional kingdoms spread across modern-day Rajasthan, Gujarat, Madhya Pradesh and other parts of the north.

The Rajputs fought among each other incessantly, however, and failed to grasp the significance of a new factor, which entered the politics of north India at the start of the eleventh century. **Mahmud of Ghazni** (971–1030), a Turkish chieftain who had established the powerful Ghaznavid kingdom at Ghazni in Afghanistan, made seventeen plundering raids into India between 1000 and 1027, looting Mathura, Kanauj and Somnath, among other places. The powerful Rajput clans of northern India were still busy fighting one another almost two centuries later when **Muhammad of Ghor** (1162–1206) seized Ghaznavid possessions in the Punjab at the end of the twelfth century, and then turned his attention towards the wealthy lands further east. **Prithviraj III**, the legendary hero of the Chauhans of Ajmer, patched together an alliance to defeat the Turkish warlord at Tarain (north of Delhi) in 1191; but Muhammad returned the next year with a superior force and defeated the Rajputs. He had Prithviraj executed before returning home, leaving his generals to complete his conquest.

The Delhi Sultanate (1206–1526)

Muhammad of Ghor was assassinated in 1206 and his empire immediately disintegrated, leaving his Turkish general **Qutb-ud-Din-Aiback**, a former slave, as the autonomous ruler of Muhammad's former Indian territories. Aiback thus became the founder of the so-called "Slave Dynasty", the first part of which would eventually come to be known as the **Delhi Sultanate**, which would remain the major political force in the north until the early sixteenth century. The sultanate marked an important turning-point in Indian history. Islam rather than Hinduism suddenly became the religion of the country's rulers, while Delhi, rather than Kanauj or Pataliputra, became the most important city in the north.

Aiback's son-in-law **Iltutmish** (1211–36) extended the sultanate's territories from the Sind to Bengal by the time he died, but a period of confusion followed, with five different rulers in just six years. Not until **Ghiyas-ud-Din Balban**, took effective control in 1246 did the sultanate attain any degree of stability, despite repeated threats from yet another set of foreign interlopers, the **Mongols**, who had been launching raids into western India from around 1220 and continued to attack the edges of the sultanate.

Ghiyas-ud-Din's death in 1287 was followed by the inevitable period of dynastic mayhem that only ended in 1290, when Aiback's Slave Dynasty came to an end, replaced by the **Khalji** dynasty. The Khalji family had entered India with Muhammad of Ghor, and subsequently carved out their own Muslim fiefdom in Bengal and Bihar. The first Khalji sultan, the elderly Feroz Shah I, was soon done away with by the implacable **Ala-ud-Din Khalji** (1296–1315), one of the most fearsome of all Indian rulers. A hard man for hard times, Ala-ud-Din was faced immediately by a series of further Mongol attacks. Delhi was besieged twice and its hinterlands plundered before the invaders suffered a resounding defeat at the hands of the new sultan in 1300, after which they left him alone. Having seen off the Mongols, Ala-ud-Din set out to conquer Gujarat and Rajasthan in a series of expeditions between 1299 and 1311, before turning his attention to the Deccan and the south. Even so, his military campaigns were more a question of exacting tribute and raising funds than of building a stable empire.

A fresh imperial impetus came from the **Tughluq** dynasty, which succeeded the Khaljis in 1320. Under **Mohammed bin Tughluq** (1325–51), the sultanate reached its largest extent, comparable in size to Ashoka's empire, although the onerous taxes required to finance Mohammed's military campaigns provoked a series of revolts, while the new Hindu kingdom of **Vijayanagar** took advantage of the decline of the sultanate's authority to extend its influence from its capital near **Hampi**. **Firoz Shah Tughluq** (1351–88) reversed the fortunes of the sultanate to some extent, thanks to the comparative mildness of his rule, but arguments over the succession after his death in 1388 further weakened the sultanate, as did an attack by the ruthless **Timur**, the Central Asian despot known to the West as Tamerlane, who sacked Delhi in 1398. By the end of the fourteenth century, the Delhi Sultanate had been reduced to just one of several competing Muslim states in northern India.

The greatly weakened sultanate was next taken over by the Afghan-descended Khizr Khan (1414–21), whose **Sayyid** dynasty ruled until 1444, to be succeded by the **Lodis**, under whom the sultanate experienced a modest revival. **Sikander Lodi** (1489–1517) was particularly energetic and successful, annexing Jaunpur and Bihar, but his successor, Ibrahim, was unable to quell dissension among his Afghan feudatories, one of whom enlisted the support of Babur, the ruler of Kabul, who defeated Ibrahim at Panipat in 1526.

The early Mughal Empire (1526–1605)

For Babur – the founder of India's most famous dynasty, the **Mughals** – India appears to have been something of an afterthought. A direct descendant of Timur (and also distantly related to Genghis Khan), Babur was born in Uzbekistan and spent most of his life in Afghanistan, where he seized control of Kabul. It was only relatively late in life, hearing of the military weakness of the Lodis, that he decided to attack India.

His battle-hardened forces easily routed the very last Delhi sultan, Ibrahim Lodi, at the Battle of Panipat in 1526, which gave him tenuous control of Delhi and Agra, although his position remained unsafe until his troops had first defeated a far stronger Rajput force led by Rana Sanga of Mewar, at the battle of Kanwaha in 1527, and then the allied forces of assorted Afghan chiefs. Shortly afterwards, his failing health forced him to retire to Agra, where he died in 1530.

Humayun, his son and successor, was by contrast a volatile character, alternating between bursts of energetic activity and indolence. He subdued Malwa and Gujarat, only to lose both while he "took his pleasure" in Agra. The Afghan-descended **Sher Shah Suri** (also known as Sher Khan or Sher Khan Sur) of south Bihar soon assumed the leadership of the Afghan opposition and, after two resounding defeats, Humayun was forced to seek refuge in Persia in 1539. A much cleverer politician than the hot-headed Humayun, Sher Shah later subjugated several of the Rajput dynasties, although his career was brought to a premature end in 1545 when he was killed during a siege at Kalinjar. Sher Shah was succeded by his son, Islam Shah Sur, but when he died in 1553 the Sur territories fell into chaos as three rival claimants battled for the throne. Judging the moment ripe for return, Humayun led his armies back into India. In 1555 Humayun's forces annihilated those of Sikander Sur, the most powerful of the three pretenders to the throne, at Sirhund in the Punjab, and then marched into Delhi virtually unopposed. Humayun died the following year after a fall in the Purana Qila in Delhi, leaving his 13-year-old son **Akbar**, to succeed to the throne.

Fortunately for the young emperor, Humayun's experienced general **Bairam Khan** was on hand to serve as guardian and regent to help him through the difficult early years of his reign. Bairam first overcame the challenge of the Hindu general Hemu at the second battle of Panipat in 1556, recovered Gwalior and Jaunpur, and handed over a consolidated kingdom of north India to Akbar in 1560. Akbar's own first military campaigns were against the **Rajputs**; and within a decade he had subdued all the Rajput domains except Mewar (Udaipur) by a clever combination of diplomacy and force. He then turned his attentions to Bengal, the richest province, which he secured by 1576. By the end of his reign in 1605 he controlled a broad sweep of territory stretching from the Bay of Bengal to Kandahar in Afghanistan.

In 1565, Akbar had the small fort built by Sikander Lodi in **Agra** demolished and replaced by the magnificent new Agra Fort, the centrepiece of a newly revitalized city that would henceforth rival Delhi as the major centre of Mughal power. Not content with this, in the early 1570s he embarked on the creation of an entire new city, the remarkable but short-lived **Fatehpur Sikri**, which served for a brief period as the capital of the empire.

Akbar was as clever a politician and administrator as he was a successful general. In addition to involving Hindu landowners and nobles in political life, Akbar adopted a conscious policy of religious toleration aimed at widening his power base, abolishing the despised poll tax on non-Muslims (*jizya*) and tolls on Hindu pilgrimages.

The later Mughals (1605–1761)

The reign of **Jahangir** (1605–27) was a time of brisk economic and expansionist activity conjoined with artistic and architectural brilliance. Jahangir himself was a contradictory character: an alcoholic and a sadist, but also a notable connoisseur of art as well as an able and determined military commander who succeeded in extending the bounds of the already very considerable domains bequeathed to him by Akbar.

Jahangir's son **Shah Jahan** came to power in 1628, having already proved himself an outstanding commander during his father's reign. Despite his considerable military abilities, however, it is as perhaps the greatest patron of architecture the world has ever known that Shah Jahan is best remembered. In 1648 he officially moved the Mughal capital from Agra back to Delhi, celebrating the translocation with the construction of the new city of **Shahjahanabad** (now better known as Old Delhi), though it was in Agra that he left his greatest mark, with his myriad embellishments to the city's fort and, pre-eminently, in the creation of the **Taj Mahal**.

Shah Jahan's reign witnessed the entry of a new force into Indian history: the **Marathas**, a potent military power in central India. A group of militant Hindus from Maharashtra in central India, the Marathas had carved out a kingdom of their own under their inspirational chief, **Shivaji**, and soon began to turn their attentions northwards. Shah Jahan had responded to the Maratha threat by sending his third son, the ambitious young **Aurangzeb**, to the Deccan to take charge of Mughal interests in the region, although his military successes were repeatedly undermined by Shah Jahan's oldest son and preferred heir **Dara Shikoh**, who was anxious to destabilize Aurangzeb's military exploits lest they create a threat to his own prestige. The anticipated struggle between the two brothers erupted in 1658 when Shah Jahan fell suddenly and seriously ill. Shah Jahan recovered, but not before Aurangzeb had seen off Dara Shikoh, wiping out his army in a series of encounters that culminated in a rout at Ajmer. The thirty-year reign of the ailing emperor ended ignominiously. Aurangzeb had him incarcerated in Agra Fort, where he remained until his death in 1666.

Though lacking the charisma of Akbar or Babur, Aurangzeb evoked an awe of his own and proved to be a firm and capable administrator, who retained his grip on the increasingly unsettled empire until his death at the age of 88. In contrast to the extravagance of the other Mughals, Aurangzeb's lifestyle was pious and disciplined. However, his religious dogmatism ultimately alienated the Hindu community whose leaders had been so carefully cultivated by Akbar. Hindu places of worship were again the object of iconoclasm and the *jizya* tax on non-Muslims was reintroduced.

The chief threat to Mughal rule in this period came from the Maratha chief, Shivaji, who established a compact and well-organized kingdom in western India, while the nearby Muslim kingdoms of Bijapur and Golconda allied themselves with him. Meanwhile, Guru Tegh Bahadur, the leader of the important new **Sikh** religion, was executed in 1675 for refusing to embrace Islam; his son, Guru Gobind, transformed the religious community into a military sect that became increasingly powerful in the Punjab. Aurangzeb's confrontation with the Rajputs over the Jodhpur succession in 1678 resulted in another war, and the alienation of most of his Rajput partners in the empire.

Aurangzeb's attention, however, was turning steadily south. In 1681 he transferred his base to the Deccan, where he spent the rest of his extremely long life overseeing the subjugation of the Bijapur and Golconda kingdoms and trying to contain the increasingly belligerent Marathas. In 1689, he succeeded in capturing and executing Shivaji's son, and by 1698 the Mughals had overrun almost the whole of the peninsula.

Aurangzeb's son, Bahadur Shah, succeeded in 1707 but reigned for only five years. His death in 1712 marked the beginning of the end for the Mughals, as their empire disintegrated. By the 1720s the rulers of Hyderabad, Avadh (Lucknow) and Bengal were effectively independent; the Marathas overwhelmed the rich province of Malwa in 1738; Hindu landholders everywhere were in revolt; and **Nadir Shah** of Persia dealt a serious blow to the empire's prestige when he invaded India, defeated the Mughal army and sacked Delhi in 1739.

The East India Company (1600–1857)

India's trading potential had attracted European interest ever since 1498, when Vasco da Gama landed on the Malabar (Keralan) Coast. During the ensuing century Portuguese, Dutch, English, French and Danish companies had all set up coastal trading centres, exporting textiles, sugar and indigo. British interests in India were formalized by the creation of the **East India Company**, granted a royal charter by Elizabeth I in 1600, whose representatives arrived at Surat in Gujarat in 1608, quickly establishing 27 trading posts around the country, including Fort George and Fort William (out of which the cities of Madras and Calcutta would subsequently develop), as well as at the fledgling settlement of Bombay.

It was in the south that European trading initiatives first took on a political significance, after the onset of the War of the Austrian Succession in 1740. Armed conflict between French and English trading companies along the south Indian coast soon developed into a minor war over the succession of the nizam of Hyderabad. Sporadic fighting continued until the end of the Seven Years' War in Europe and the Treaty of Paris in 1763 put an effective end to French ambitions in India. Meanwhile, **Robert Clive**'s defeat of the rebellious young nawab of Bengal at Plassey in 1757 had decisively augmented British power; by 1765 the enervated Mughal emperor legally recognized the Company by granting it the revenue management of Bengal, Bihar and Orissa.

For the next thirty years, the British in India contented themselves with developing trade and repulsing Indian offensives against their three major settlements in Calcutta, Bombay and Madras, though by the end of the century the defeat of **Tipu Sultan** of Mysore, the Company's best-organized and most resolute enemy, and the subjugation of the nizam of Hyderabad resulted in the annexation of considerable territories, and by 1805 nearly all the other rulers in India recognized British suzerainty. A long-drawn-out series of conflicts between the British and Marathas (the so-called three "Maratha Wars" of 1774–1818) finally extinguished the Marathas as an effective military threat.

Following the subjugation of the Marathas, the British established a series of treaties with the rulers of Rajasthan and with most of India's other surviving independent kingdoms, collectively known as the so-called **princely states**, stretching from Hyderabad in the south to Kashmir in the north. Under these treaties, the various kingdoms retained their autonomy more or less intact and received a guarantee of military protection in exchange for pledging their loyalty to the British Crown and agreeing to certain political, mercantile and financial concessions. The much-abused city of Delhi, the traditional capital of north India, fared less well, as the British established their capital at the burgeoning new city of **Calcutta**. Not until 1911 would Delhi recapture its mantle as the north's imperial city.

The 1857 uprising

The new British **colony**, however, was in a state of social and economic collapse as a result of the almost incessant conflicts of the previous hundred years. The controversial "Doctrine of Lapse", whereby autonomous states were gradually annexed, was widely resented. In addition, the Company's policy, after 1835, of promoting European literature and science (with English replacing Persian as the official state language), the suppression of local customs such as *sati* and child marriage, and the deployment of Indian troops overseas (resulting in loss of caste) were increasingly perceived as part of a covert British attack on traditional Hindu and Muslim religious and cultural practices.

The final spark which ignited a full-blown uprising by the Indian army was supplied when troops were issued with cartridges for a new Enfield rifle smeared in cows' and pigs' grease (polluting to both Hindus and Muslims). The resultant **1857 uprising** (traditionally referred to by the British as the "Indian Mutiny" or "Sepoy Rebellion", and by Indian historians as the "First War of Independence") began with a rebellion of Indian troops (sepoys) at Meerut on May 10, 1857, and Delhi was seized the next day. The rebellion quickly spread across most of central northern India, where mutineers seized Lucknow and Kanpur. The British authorities were caught by surprise, though control was gradually reasserted. Delhi and Kanpur were both retaken in September, and the final recapture of Lucknow in March 1858 effectively signalled the end of the uprising.

The Raj and Indian nationalism (1857–1947)

The uprising had important consequences for subsequent British rule in the Subcontinent. The governing powers of the East India Company were abolished and the British Crown assumed the direct administration of India in the same year. Henceforth, British India was no longer merely a massive trade operation, but a fully-fledged independent kingdom, or **Raj**, as the period of British rule in the Subcontinent subsequently became known.

As a British colony, India assumed a new position in the world economy. Its trade benefited from the railways developed by the British, and Indian businessmen began to invest in a range of manufacturing industries. However, India subsidized the British economy as a source of cheap raw materials and as a market for manufactured goods, and its own economy and agriculture remained underdeveloped. British civil servants dominated the higher echelons of the administration, often introducing policies contrary to Indian interests and cultural traditions. Public demonstrations eventually forced the British to sanction the creation of the **Indian National Congress** party (usually known simply as "Congress") in 1885, and by 1905 Congress had adopted self-government as a political aim. In 1906, concerns about the predominantly Hindu Congress led to the foundation of the **All-India Muslim League** to represent the country's Muslims.

The Morley-Minto Reforms of 1909 paved the way for Indian participation in provincial executive councils and made allowance for separate Muslim representation. At the **Great Durbar** of 1911, held in honour of the new king, George V, the capital was moved back to **Delhi**, with the construction of yet another imperial city, so-called "New" Delhi, to celebrate the relocation (though it wasn't finished until 1931). A few years later, the Royal Proclamation of 1917 promised a gradual development of dominion-style self-government; and two years later the Montagu-Chelmsford Reforms attempted to implement the declaration.

At this point an England-educated lawyer, **Mohandas Karamchand Gandhi** (see p.567) – better known as the Mahatma, or "Great Soul" – took up the initiative, espousing a political philosophy based on nonviolence and the championing of the untouchables, whom he renamed the Children of God (Harijan). Gandhi began by organizing India-wide one-day strikes and protests, though these were mercilessly crushed by the government – as in the infamous incident (see p.534) in 1919 when troops under General Dyer dispersed a meeting at Jallianwalla Bagh in Amritsar by firing on the unarmed crowd, killing 379 and wounding 1200.

By 1928 Congress was demanding complete independence. The government offered talks, but the more radical elements in Congress, now led by the young **Jawaharlal Nehru**, were in a confrontational mood. Gandhi, in turn, led a well-publicized 240-mile "salt march" from his ashram in Sabarmati to make salt illegally at Dandi in Gujarat in defiance of a particularly unpopular British tax. This demonstration of nonviolent civil disobedience (*satyagraha*) fired the popular imagination, leading to more processions, strikes, and mass imprisonments over the next few years, which in turn led to the formulation of the new **Government of India Act** in 1935, although this still fell short of offering the country complete independence. Congress remained suspicious of British intentions, and despite Gandhi's overtures refused to accommodate Muslim demands for representation. **Mohammed Ali Jinnah**, who assumed the leadership of the Muslim League in 1935, initially promoted Muslim–Hindu cooperation, but he soon despaired of influencing Congress and by 1940 the League passed a resolution demanding an independent Pakistan.

Confrontations between the government, Congress and the Muslim League continued throughout World War II, despite the promise, in 1942, by a Britain increasingly reliant on Indian troops, of postwar Independence. Gandhi introduced the **Quit India** slogan and proposed another campaign of civil disobedience; Jinnah, meanwhile, preached his "two nations" theory and inspired mass Muslim support with his rhetoric against "Hinduization". A spate of terrorist activities across the country left one thousand dead and sixty thousand imprisoned. By the end of the war, the British government accepted that complete independence for India could no longer be postponed.

Unfortunately, British attempts to find a solution that would preserve a united India while allaying Muslim fears disintegrated in the face of continued intransigence from both sides, and they gradually realized that the division – or so-called **Partition** – of the existing country of India into separate Muslim and Hindu states was inevitable. **Lord Mountbatten** was appointed viceroy to supervise the handover of power. The Subcontinent was **partitioned** on August 15, 1947, and Pakistan came into existence. The new boundaries cut through both Bengal and the Punjab; Sikhs, Muslims and Hindus who had been neighbours became enemies overnight. Five million Hindus and Sikhs from Pakistan, and a similar number of Muslims from India, were involved in the ensuing two-way exodus, and the atrocities cost half a million lives. Mahatma Gandhi, who had devoted himself to ending the communal violence after Partition, was **assassinated** in January 1948 by Hindu extremists antagonized by his defence of Muslims.

India under Nehru (1947–1964)

Jawaharlal Nehru, India's first and longest-serving prime minister, proved to be a dynamic and extremely popular leader during his seventeen years in office, building the foundations of a democratic secular nation, and guiding the first stages of its agricultural and industrial development. The franchise was made universal for all adults and, with 173 million eligible to vote, in 1951 India became the **world's largest democracy**.

Despite Independence, there was still the problem of the 562 **princely states** within India, covering no less than two-fifths of the country's total area, and which remained technically autonomous under the terms of ongoing British treaties. At Independence rulers of several of these states had yet to decide whether they were going to join India or Pakistan. Nehru's able deputy prime minister, Sardar Vallabhai Patel, was made responsible for encouraging the rulers of the recalcitrant statelets to join the new India, including sending a detachment of Indian troops into the territory of the Muslim nizam of **Hyderabad**, who had resisted joining the union even though the majority of his state's population was Hindu. Some parts of the Subcontinent retained their independence for even longer. The **French** enclaves at Pondicherry and Chandernagar were not incorporated until the 1950s, while the Portuguese refused to accept the new situation, until in 1961 Nehru finally sent in the army to annex **Goa**.

The most serious legacy of Partition concerned the Himalayan state of **Kashmir**. At Independence, Kashmir's Hindu maharaja Hari Singh remained undecided as to which of the two new countries he wished to join. Jinnah naturally assumed Kashmir would join Pakistan, given three-quarters of its inhabitants were Muslims; Nehru was equally determined to keep it for India. Meanwhile, the maharaja continued to prevaricate. Events reached a head in October 1947, when Islamic partisans from Pakistan's tribal areas suddenly arrived in the Kashmir valley to encourage the maharaja to join with Pakistan. Hari Singh, fearing he was about to be overthrown, immediately determined to join India instead. Shortly afterwards Indian troops were airlifted into the valley, and began to battle with the Islamic insurgents. Although war was never officially declared, and no regular Pakistani military units were involved, the fighting is usually described as the **First Indo-Pakistan War**. By the time the UN brokered a ceasefire in 1948, Pakistani insurgents had secured a sizeable slice of Kashmiri territory, which Pakistan retains to this day.

Elsewhere in the region, Nehru attempted to promote Asian unity by following a policy of peaceful **nonalignment**, although this was repeatedly threatened by **Chinese aggression**. The Chinese invasion of Tibet in 1950 brought the Chinese right up to India's border (and a flood of refugees into India itself, including the Dalai Lama, who arrived in 1959), while in 1962 Chinese troops brushed aside Indian border patrols and began to move down into Assam. This "invasion" (although it was really more a show of force) ended soon afterwards, and while the humiliating inability of the Indian army to repel the interlopers did not officially spell the end of India's policy of non-alignment (it continues to this day), Nehru immediately signed a defence treaty with the US, and the Chinese retained small areas of Indian territory in Kashmir and Assam which they still hold.

Indira Gandhi (1966–1984)

The whole nation mourned Nehru's death in 1964, which prevented him from witnessing the restoration of India's military prestige in the **Second Indo-Pakistan War** of 1965. Pakistani leader General Ayub Khan, perhaps wishing to test the resolve of new Indian premier **Lal Bahadur Shastri**, launched a series of skirmishes into disputed areas of Gujarat, and followed this up with attempts to infiltrate Kashmir and provoke a pro-Pakistani uprising. Full-scale fighting broke out in Kashmir and to the south, and the Indian army responded by driving Pakistani forces back to within five kilometres of a virtually defenceless Lahore before a ceasefire was agreed, with both sides returning to their previous borders. Despite this triumph, Lal Bahadur Shastri died shortly afterwards, in January 1966, leaving Nehru's daughter **Indira Gandhi** to establish herself as the new leader of Congress.

The 49-year-old Indira – or "Mrs Gandhi", as she is often called (though no relation to the Mahatma; she acquired her surname through marriage to a Parsi named Feroze Gandhi, who had died in 1960) – was initially chosen as a popular but easily manipulated figurehead by Congress chiefs. Gandhi herself had different plans. She moved rapidly to shore up her own power, and then – after consolidating her mandate in fresh elections in 1971 – launched Congress along a populist socialist path, nationalizing the banks, abolishing the former maharajas' privy purses, and introducing new legislation on corporate profits and land holdings. By this time, India was experiencing massive industrial growth and had also made a spectacular agricultural breakthrough with its **Green Revolution**, becoming self-sufficient in food by the early 1970s thanks to the introduction of high-yield grains.

Gandhi also had to deal with the increasingly chaotic situation in **East Pakistan** (present-day Bangladesh), which had declared independence from (West) Pakistan in 1971. Pakistani troops had been sent in to bring the East Pakistanis back into line, causing a mass exodus of refugees into India. Gandhi astutely waited until she had the moral support of the international community before launching simultaneous attacks in West and East Pakistan on December 4. By December 15, Pakistani forces in Bangladesh had capitulated.

Back at home, Gandhi was proving less successful. After widespread agrarian and industrial unrest against the rate of inflation and corruption within the Congress Party, she declared a **State of Emergency** on June 26, 1975, suspending all civil rights, censoring the press and imprisoning some twenty thousand of her opponents, real or imagined. The "Emergency" lasted eighteen months, characterized by the enforced sterilization of men and brutal slum-clearances in Delhi and elsewhere. When she finally released her opponents and called off the Emergency in January 1977, the bitterness she had engendered resulted in her ignominious defeat in the March elections. The ensuing **Janata** coalition under Morarji Desai fell apart within two years, and his premiership was terminated by a vote of no confidence in 1979. Gandhi, now apparently forgiven, swept back into office in January 1980.

Four years afterwards, Gandhi made the second, fatal, mistake of her career. A group of rebels demanding a separate Sikh nation – Khalistan – took control of the **Golden Temple** in Amritsar early in 1984, from where they organized a campaign of violence, killing hundreds of Hindus and moderate Sikhs. Gandhi sent in the tanks in June 1984, but two days of raging combat desecrated the Sikhs' holiest shrine as well as giving Khalistan its first martyrs. In October that year, Gandhi's Sikh bodyguards took revenge by assassinating her at her house in Delhi. The city was then engulfed in massive communal **rioting**, during which Hindu mobs went about Delhi systematically murdering Sikhs – according to some reports locating their victims with the help of electoral rolls supplied by Congress politicians.

Communal conflict (1984–1995)

Following Gandhi's death, it was left to her sole surviving son, **Rajiv Gandhi** (a former airline pilot) to take up leadership of Congress. He came to power in December 1984 on a wave of sympathy boosted by his reputation as "Mr Clean", an image given added meaning by the **Bhopal** gas tragedy (see p.351) just two weeks before the elections. The opposition subsequently rallied under the leadership of **V.P. Singh**. Elections in 1989 did not give Singh's Janata Party a majority, but he managed to form a coalition government with the support of the "Hindu first" Bharatiya Janata Party, or **BJP**, led by **L.K. Advani**.

Singh was immediately confronted by problems in the Punjab and Kashmir, but it was an even more emotive issue that brought down his government in less than a year. Advani's populist BJP were demanding that the Babri Masjid mosque in **Ayodhya**, built by Babur on the supposed site of the birthplace of Rama, god-hero of the Ramayana, should be replaced by a Hindu temple. Advani set off towards Ayodhya in October 1990, accompanied by thousands of supporters, with the avowed intention of destroying the mosque. Singh ordered Advani's arrest, and the inevitable withdrawal of the BJP from his coalition government resulted in a vote of no confidence.

New elections were called. Shortly afterwards, while campaigning in Tamil Nadu in May 1991, Rajiv Gandhi was assassinated by Tamil Tigers seeking revenge for India's military opposition to their "freedom fight" in Sri Lanka. It was left to **P.V. Narasimha Rao** to steer Congress through the elections and form a new coalition government, which immediately embarked on a far-reaching programme of **economic liberalization**, dismantling trade barriers and allowing multinationals such as Coca-Cola, Pepsi and KFC to enter the Indian market for the first time.

At the same time, the BJP increased its seats in the Lok Sabha (the Lower House of Parliament) from 80 to 120 and Advani became leader of the opposition, amid growing popular support for the rebuilding of Rama's temple in Ayodhya. The situation finally came to a head in December 1992, as Hindu extremists incited crowds of fanatical devotees to tear down the Babri Masjid at Ayodhya in a blaze of publicity. The demolition was followed by terrible **riots** in many parts of the country, especially Bombay and Gujarat, where Muslim families and businesses were targeted. A few months later, a massive series of bomb blasts ripped through **Bombay**, killing 260 people and destroying some of the city's most important commercial buildings. No one claimed responsibility, though the attacks were thought to have been orchestrated by Islamic groups in retaliation for Hindu violence against their fellow Muslims.

National morale during this post-Ayodhya period was shaky. After a year blighted by bomb blasts, riots and the rise of religious extremism, it seemed as if India's secular constitution was doomed. To rub salt in the wounds, fifteen thousand people died in a massive **earthquake** around the northwestern Maharashtrian city of Latur, and soon after, Surat, in southern Gujarat, was at the centre of an outbreak of a disease ominously resembling bubonic **plague**.

Against this backdrop of uncertainty, the rise of right-wing Hindu-fundamentalist parties gathered pace. The BJP took advantage of the power struggle in the Congress Party to rekindle regional support. Their new rallying cry was **Swadeshi** – a campaign against the Congress-led programme of economic liberalization and, in particular, the activities of newly arrived companies such as Coca-Cola, Pepsi and KFC (one of whose branches was forced to close by the BJP-controlled Delhi municipality).

The rise of the BJP (1996–1999)

The BJP emerged from the **general election** of May 1996 as the single largest party but were unable to muster a majority and were ousted a couple of weeks later by the hastily formed **Unified Front** (UF) coalition. The UF soldiered on until March 1998, after which the **BJP** finally struggled to power as the head of a new conservative coalition government under **Atal Bihari Vajpayee**.

This time, the party managed to stay in office for thirteen months, as opposed to the thirteen days of its previous spell in government. The BJP had promised change and the restoration of national pride, and one of its early acts in government was to conduct five underground **nuclear tests** in May 1998, provoking Pakistan to respond in kind. There was a chorus of world criticism, and US-led financial **sanctions** were imposed on both nations.

Ongoing tensions in **Kashmir** did little to calm local and international fears. In May 1999, at least eight hundred Pakistani-backed mujahideen crept across the so-called Line of Control (the de facto border) overlooking the Srinagar–Leh road near **Kargil** and began to occupy Indian territory. India moved thousands of troops into the area, and within days the two countries were poised on the brink of all-out war. In the event the conflict was contained, and by July 1999 the Indian army had retaken all the ground previously lost to the militants.

Shortly afterwards, the Congress Party, reinvigorated under the leadership of **Sonia Gandhi**, the Italian-born widow of the former prime minister Rajiv, collaborated with the Jayalalitha's AIADMK (see p.949) to bring about the downfall of the BJP government. At the start of the campaign, Congress hopes were high that, with a Gandhi once again as party leader, it could revive the popular support lost after years of infighting and corruption scandals. Unfortunately for them, the wave of **patriotism** that swept India after the Kargil victory in Kashmir was a godsend for Vajpayee (cynics argued it may well have been the hidden policy behind the army's uncompromising response to the crisis). Riding high on the feel-good factor, his party inflicted the biggest defeat Congress had sustained since 1947.

The new millennium

India's political problems were temporarily eclipsed by a succession of catastrophic **natural disasters**. In the arid zones of Rajasthan and Gujarat, high May temperatures in 2000 compounded the third failure of the monsoons in as many years, forcing tens of thousands of poor farming families off their land in search of food and water. While the monsoon, when it finally broke, made little impact on the parched northwest, **record rainfalls** wreaked havoc in Andhra Pradesh, West Bengal and low-lying areas of Uttar Pradesh. An estimated twelve million were left marooned or homeless as river levels rose by as much as four metres in places. An even worse tragedy lay in store for millions of Gujaratis when, in the morning of January 26, 2001 – Indian Republic Day – a massive **earthquake** measuring 7.9 on the Richter scale levelled a vast area in the northwest of the state (see p.555).

Meanwhile in Delhi, a string of **corruption scandals** was piling pressure onto the fractious BJP-led coalition. Vajpayee's party also came in for more flak for yielding ground to its regionalist coalition partners when the prime minister announced the **creation of three new states**: Jharkhand, Chhattisgarh and Uttaranchal (later changing its name to Uttarakhand), made up of remote parts of Bihar, Madhya Pradesh and Uttar Pradesh respectively.

That there was much more to India at the turn of the millennium than natural disasters and corruption scandals, however, was proved by south India's burgeoning **hi-tech revolution**, centred on the cities of Bangalore and Hyderabad. **Bangalore** had led the way in the early 1980s, and by the mid-1990s had become a major player in the international software market. Yet by the turn of the millennium its pre-eminence was being challenged by the even more spectacular emergence of **Hyderabad** (quickly nicknamed "Cyberabad"), which thanks to massive state subsidies had begun to attract leading global players including Microsoft and Dell – although the rural poor of southern India saw very little of this newly generated wealth, further exacerbating the gap between rich and poor, which commentators quickly rechristened the "digital divide".

To the brink of war

During late 2001, **Indo-Pak relations** and the **Kashmir** question returned to the fore as India entered one of the most volatile periods in its modern history. In October, the **State Assembly building in Srinagar** was destroyed by Islamist suicide car-bombers, while in December, three Muslim gunmen stormed the **Parliament Building** in New Delhi, killing several police guards, before they were picked off by army marksmen. Pakistani involvement was inevitably suspected. Then, in early 2002, a Muslim mob in **Godhra**, Gujarat, attacked a trainload of Hindu pilgrims returning from Ayodhya: 38 died and 74 were injured, although this paled in comparison with the reprisal killings that followed, in which around two thousand people (mostly Muslims) were slaughtered.

Anti-Muslim sentiment in India was further fuelled only a month after Godhra when an Islamist suicide squad commandeered a tourist bus and used it to attack the **Kaluchak** army cantonment near Jammu. Coming only four months after the attack on the Indian parliament, and hot on the heels of yet another promise by Pakistan to clamp down on cross-border militancy, the atrocity provoked outrage in Delhi. Vajpayee, bowing to the hawks on the right of his own party, called for a "decisive battle", initiating a massive build-up of troops on the border. An estimated million men at arms were involved in the ensuing stand-off as India and Pakistan edged to the brink of all-out **war**. Once again, however, US diplomacy diffused the crisis and the armies stood down.

In 2003, the Archeological Survey of India released its long-awaited **report on Ayodhya**. To no one's surprise, the ASI panel of "experts", appointed by the right-wing BJP government, declared they'd found evidence to show there had been a temple, in effect condoning the tearing down of the mosque. Rubbing salt in old wounds, the ruling did little to quell post-Godhra tensions; and when, on August 25, 2003 (the day after the Ayodhya report was published), two **bombs** ripped through the centre of downtown Mumbai, commentators were quick to identify the Babri Masjid dispute as the provocation.

The return of Congress

Despite continuing sectarian troubles, with India booming as never before, Vajpayee and his BJP-led coalition decided to cash in on the perceived feel-good factor and call a snap **election** in **May 2004**, although far from increasing his majority as he'd expected, Vajpayee and his government were thrown out in the most dramatic political turnaround of recent times. Congress gained the largest share of the vote and **Sonia Gandhi** was duly invited to form a government. However, she stunned supporters by "humbly declining" the invitation and stepped down. Eventually, former finance minister, 71-year-old **Manmohan Singh**, stepped into the breach and was named as prime minister, the first Sikh ever to lead the country.

As the architect of the important liberalizing economic reforms enacted during the early 1990s, Singh seemed like the perfect candidate to oversee India's continuing economic and technological growth (as Singh himself once put it, "India happens to be a rich country inhabited by very poor people"). In April 2007 the country launched its first commercial space rocket, and the following month saw the government announce the strongest economic growth figures (an impressive 9.4 percent) for twenty years. India's technological and economic transformation continues apace. The country is now the world's second-largest exporter of computer software after the US, generating sales of around a billion dollars a year, focused on the southern cities of Bangalore and Hyderabad, which have also become home to innumerable international call centres thanks to the cities' educated, English-speaking workforce.

Yet such spectacular developments have had little effect on the lives of India's rural poor. In an attempt to address the ever-widening divide between the nation's increasingly affluent middle classes and the rest of the country, Singh's coalition government launched the nation's largest-ever rural jobs scheme in February 2006 with the aim of freeing around sixty million families from poverty, although this promised "New Deal" has yet to bear fruit. Progress has also been made on the looming **nuclear threat** hanging over the Subcontinent, with agreements now in place with the US and Pakistan.

Terrorist violence continues to plague the country, even so, including many attacks by Pakistan-based Islamic militants designed to derail the ongoing peace process in Kashmir, or to avenge attacks by Hindu mobs against Muslims in India. Bomb attacks in October 2005 and September 2008 killed almost a hundred people in Delhi, while in February 2007, 68 passengers (ironically, most of them Pakistani) were killed by bomb blasts on a train travelling from New Delhi to Lahore. Even the normally peaceful city of Jaipur became a target in May 2008, when seven bombs exploded in various busy streets around the Pink City, killing 63 people. It is **Mumbai**, however, which has suffered the worst from terrorist atrocities. In July 2006 a series of bombs blasts exploded almost simultaneously on seven commuter trains, leaving over two hundred dead, while the horrific wave of coordinated attacks by Pakistani gunmen in **November 2008** (see p.593) brought the city to its knees, temporarily at least. Images of the burning Taj Palace hotel and the blood-spattered concourse of CST station were beamed live around the world, producing a sense of global compassion and outrage, while also raising alarming questions about India's security and economic prospects.

Challenges and potential

Despite these various setbacks, **elections in 2009** saw an unexpected landslide victory for the Congress-led coalition, with Manmohan Singh becoming the first Indian leader since Nehru in 1952 to be returned directly to power after a five-year term. Despite opposition carping, Singh's low-key and scandal-free leadership, concentrating on economic fundamentals, the alleviation of poverty and improving relationships with Pakistan, has proved popular in a country which had enjoyed more than its fair share of big-talking but ineffective politicos.

In many ways Singh's business-oriented but socially conscious leadership provides the perfect template for how India will hope to develop in the coming decades. Many of India's citizens are enjoying increasing levels of affluence, while the country's **economy** (which has grown at an average rate of over seven percent for the past decade) continues to boom thanks to its increasingly skilled and educated workforce, as well as rocketing levels of foreign investment. All of which raises the genuine possibility that India will shortly become one of the global economic superpowers of the 21st century; according to estimates by Goldman Sachs, the country is on course to overtake France, Germany and former colonial masters Britain by around 2015, and to become the world's third-largest economy (after the USA and China) by 2035.

Still, huge **challenges** remain. The most obvious is the simple fact that, for all India's spectacular economic progress, millions of its inhabitants continue to live in abject poverty, while rampant development is placing increasing strains on the country's outdated infrastructure. The always volatile relationship with Pakistan is another source of uncertainty, while the spectre of home-grown Hindu fundamentalism – as well as threats from Islamic militants from abroad – is still very much alive and well. Meanwhile, a string of violent regional movements continue to sporadically challenge the authority of central and state governments; these range from Islamic jihadis in Kashmir and tribal insurgents in the northeastern hill states to the neo-Marxist Naxalite revolutionaries who continue to disrupt life in the impoverished eastern states of Chhattisgarh, Orissa, Bihar and Jharkhand.

Yet for the time being India continues to evolve at a breathtaking rate. Whether the country can continue to ride the economic wave – while simultaneously matching the aspirations of its middle classes and meeting the basic needs of its marginalized poor – will determine the speed and success with which it manages to achieve its rightful position on the global stage.

Religion

Four out of five Indians are Hindus, and Hinduism permeates every aspect of life in the country, from the commonplace details of daily life up to national politics. After Hindus, **Muslims** are the largest religious group, and have been an integral part of Indian society since the twelfth century. The more recently established **Sikh** faith was founded in reaction to the caste laws and ritual observances of Hinduism and now boasts millions of adherents. The far older **Jain** religion also still commands a sizeable following, and there are also small communities of **Buddhists**, **Christians**, and Iranian-descended Zoroastrians, or **Parsis**.

Hinduism

Hinduism is the product of several thousand years of evolution and assimilation. It has no founder or prophet, no single creed, and no single prescribed practice or doctrine; it takes in hundreds of gods, goddesses, beliefs and practices, and widely variant cults and philosophies. Some are recognized by only two or three villages, others are popular right across the Subcontinent. Hindus call their beliefs and practices **dharma**, which defines a way of living in harmony with natural and moral law while fulfilling personal goals and meeting the requirements of society.

The Vedic age

The origins of Hinduism date back to the arrival of the **Aryans** (see p.1150). The Aryans believed in a number of gods associated with the elements, including **Agni**, the god of fire, **Surya**, the sun god, and **Indra**, the chief god. Most of these deities faded in importance in later times, but Indra is still regarded as the father of the gods, and Surya was widely worshipped until the medieval period.

Aryan religious beliefs were first set down in a series of four books, the **Vedas** (from the Sanskrit word veda, meaning "knowledge"). Transmitted orally for centuries, the Vedas were finally written down, in Sanskrit, between 1000 BC and 500 AD. The earliest and most important of the four Vedas, the **Rig Veda**, contains over a thousand hymns to various deities, while the other three (the *Yajur* Veda, Sama Veda and Atharva Veda) contain further prayers, chants and instructions for performing the complex sacrificial rituals associated with this early Vedic religion.

The Vedas were followed by further religious texts, including the **Brahmanas**, a series of commentaries on the Vedas for the use of priests (brahmins) and, more importantly, the **Upanishads**, which describe in beautiful and emotive verse the mystic experience of unity of the soul (*atman*) with Brahma, the absolute creator of the universe, ideally attained through asceticism, renunciation of worldly values and meditation. In the Upanishads the concepts of **samsara**, a cyclic round of death and rebirth characterized by suffering and perpetuated by desire, and **moksha**, liberation from *samsara*, became firmly rooted. As fundamental aspects of the Hindu world view, both are accepted by all but a handful of Hindus today, along with the belief in **karma**, the certainty that one's present position in society is determined by the effect of one's previous actions in this and past lives.

Hindu society

The stratification of Hindu society is rooted in the **Dharma Sutras**, a further collection of scriptures written at roughly the same time as the later Vedas. These defined four hierarchical classes, or **varnas** (from *varna*, meaning "colour", perhaps

The Mahabharata and the Ramayana

Eight times as long as the *Iliad* and *Odyssey* combined, the **Mahabharata** was written around 400 AD and tells of a feuding *kshatriya* family in northern India during the fourth millennium BC. The chief character is **Arjuna**, who, with his four brothers, represents the **Pandava** clan, supreme fighters and upholders of righteousness. The Pandava clan are resented by their cousins, the evil **Kauravas**, led by Duryodhana, the eldest son of Dhrtarashtra, ruler of the Kuru kingdom.

When Dhrtarashtra hands his kingdom over to the Pandavas, the Kauravas are understandably less than overjoyed. The subsequent battle between the Pandavas and Kauravas is described in the sixth book, the famous **Bhagavad Gita**. Krishna steps into battle as Arjuna's charioteer. Arjuna is in a dilemma, unable to justify the killing of his own kin in pursuit of a rightful kingdom. Krishna consoles him, reminding him that his principal duty is as a warrior, and convincing him that by fulfilling his dharma he not only upholds law and order by saving the kingdom from the grasp of unrighteous rulers, he also serves the gods in the spirit of devotion, and thus guarantees himself eternal union with the divine in the blissful state of *moksha*.

The Pandavas finally win the battle and Yudhishtra, one of the five Pandava brothers, is crowned king. Eventually Arjuna's grandson, Pariksit, inherits the throne, and the Pandavas trek to Mount Meru, the mythical centre of the universe and the abode of the gods, where Arjuna finds Krishna's promised *moksha*.

The Ramayana

The Ramayana tells the story of **Rama**, the seventh of Vishnu's eight incarnations. Rama is the oldest of four sons born to Dasaratha, the king of Ayodhya, and heir to the throne. When the time comes for Rama's coronation, Dasaratha's scheming third wife Kaikeyi has her own son Bharata crowned instead, and has Rama banished to the forest for fourteen years. In an exemplary show of filial piety, Rama accepts the loss of his throne and leaves the city with his wife Sita and brother Laksmana.

One day, Suparnakhi, the sister of the demon **Ravana**, spots Rama in the woods and instantly falls in love with him. Being a virtuous husband, Rama rebuffs her advances, while Laksmana cuts off her nose and ears in retaliation. In revenge, Ravana kidnaps Sita, who is borne away to one of Ravana's palaces on the island of **Lanka**.

Determined to find Sita, Rama enlists the help of the monkey god **Hanuman**, and the two of them gather an army and prepare to attack. After much fighting, Sita is rescued and reunited with her husband. On the long journey back to Ayodhya, Sita's honour is brought into question. To prove her innocence, she asks Laksmana to build a funeral pyre and steps into the flames, praying to Agni, the fire god. Agni walks her through the fire into the arms of a delighted Rama. They march into Ayodhya guided by a trail of lights laid out by the local people. Today, this illuminated homecoming is commemorated by Hindus all over the world during **Diwali**, the festival of lights. At the end of the epic, Rama's younger brother gladly steps down, allowing Rama to be crowned as the rightful king.

a reference to difference in appearance between the lighter-skinned Aryans and the darker indigenous Dravidian population). Each *varna* was assigned specific religious and social duties, with Aryans established as the highest social class. In descending order the *varnas* are: **brahmins** (priests and teachers), **kshatriyas** (rulers and warriors), **vaishyas** (merchants and cultivators) and **shudras** (menials). The first three classes, known as "twice-born", are distinguished by a sacred thread worn from the time of initiation, and are granted full access to religious texts and rituals. Below all four categories, groups whose jobs involve contact with dirt or death (such as undertakers, leather-workers and cleaners) were classified as

untouchables. Though discrimination against untouchables is now a criminal offence, in part thanks to the campaigns of Gandhi, the lowest stratum of society has by no means disappeared.

Within the four *varnas*, social status is further defined by **jati**, classifying each individual in terms of their family and job (for example, a *vaishya* may be a jewellery seller, cloth merchant, cowherd or farmer). A person's *jati* determines his **caste**, and lays restrictions on all aspects of life from what sort of food he can eat, religious obligations and contact with other castes, to the choice of marriage partners. There are almost three thousand *jatis*; the divisions and restrictions they have enforced have repeatedly been the target of reform movements and critics.

A Hindu has three **aims in life**: to fulfil his social and religious duties (*dharma*); to follow the correct path in his work and actions (*karma*); and to gain material wealth (*artha*). These goals are linked with the four traditional stages in life. The first is as a child and student, devoted to learning from parents and guru. Next comes the stage of householder, expected to provide for a family and raise children. That accomplished, he may then take up a life of celibacy and retreat into the forest to meditate alone, and finally renounce all possessions to become a homeless ascetic, hoping to achieve the ultimate goal of *moksha*. The small number

Hindu gods and goddesses

Vishnu

With four arms holding a conch, discus, lotus and mace, **Vishnu** is blue-skinned, and often shaded by a serpent, or resting on its coils, afloat on an ocean. He is usually seen alongside his half-man-half-eagle vehicle, Garuda. **Vaishnavites**, often distinguishable by two vertical lines of paste on their foreheads, recognize Vishnu as supreme lord, and hold that he has manifested himself on earth nine times. The most important avatars are Rama (see p.1169) and **Krishna**, the hero of the *Bhagavad Gita*. The cult of Krishna evolved into the popular *bhakti* movement – the attempt to achieve *moksha* through devotion to god, and without the intercession of officiating Brahmin priests, finding expression in emotional songs concerning the quest for union with the divine. Krishna is represented in various ways: most popularly he is shown as the playful cowherd who seduces and dances with cowgirls (*gopis*), giving each the illusion that she is his only lover. He is also pictured as a small, chubby, mischievous baby, known for his butter-stealing exploits. Like Vishnu, Krishna is blue, and often shown dancing and playing the flute.

Shiva

Shaivism, the cult of **Shiva**, was also inspired by *bhakti*, requiring selfless love from devotees in a quest for divine communion, but Shiva has never been incarnate on earth. He is presented in many different aspects, such as **Nataraja**, Lord of the Dance, **Mahadev**, Great God, and **Maheshvar**, Divine Lord, source of all knowledge. Though he does have several terrible forms, his role extends beyond that of destroyer, and he is revered as the source of the whole universe.

Shiva is often depicted with four or more faces, holding a trident, draped with serpents, and bearing a third eye in his forehead. In temples, he is identified with the lingam, or phallic symbol, resting in the yoni, a representation of female sexuality. Whether as statue or lingam, Shiva is accompanied by his bull-mount, Nandi, and often by a consort, who also assumes various forms, and is looked upon as the vital energy, **shakti**, that empowers him.

While Shiva is the object of popular devotion all over India, as the terrible **Bhairav** he is also the god of the Shaivite **ascetics**, who renounce family and caste ties and perform extreme meditative and yogic practices.

of Hindus who follow this ideal life assume the final stage as saffron-clad **sadhus** who wander throughout India, begging for food and retreating to isolated caves, forests and hills to meditate. They're a common feature in most Indian towns and many stay for long periods in particular temples. Not all have raised families: some assume the life of a sadhu at an early age as *chellas*, pupils of an older sadhu.

The main deities

Alongside the Vedas and Upanishads, the most important Hindu religious texts are the **Puranas** – long mythological stories about the Vedic gods – and the two great epics, the **Mahabharata** and **Ramayana** (see p.1169) thought to have been completed by the first century AD, though subsequently retold, modified and embellished on numerous occasions and in various different regional languages. The Puranas and the two great epics helped crystallize the basic framework of Hindu religious belief, which survives to this day, based on a supreme triumvirate of deities. **Brahma**, the original Aryan godhead, or "creator", was joined by two gods who had begun to achieve increasing significance in the evolving Hindu world-view. The first, **Vishnu**, "the preserver", was seen as the force responsible for maintaining the balance of the cosmos whenever it was threatened by

Other gods and goddesses

Chubby and smiling, elephant-headed **Ganesh**, the first son of Shiva and Parvati, is invoked before every undertaking (except funerals). Seated on a throne or lotus, his image is often placed above temple gateways, in shops and houses; in his four arms he holds a conch, discus, bowl of sweets (or club) and a water lily, and he's always attended by his vehicle, a rat. Ganesh is regarded by many as the god of learning, the lord of success, prosperity and peace.

Durga, the fiercest of the female deities, is an aspect of Shiva's more conservative consort, Parvati (also known as Uma), who is remarkable only for her beauty and fidelity. Among Durga's many aspects, each a terrifying goddess eager to slay demons, are Chamunda, Kali and Muktakeshi, but in all her forms she is Mahadevi (Great Goddess). Statues show her with ten arms, holding the head of a demon, a spear and other weapons; she tramples demons underfoot, or dances upon Shiva's body.

The comely goddess **Lakshmi**, Vishnu's consort, is usually shown sitting or standing on a lotus flower, and sometimes called Padma (lotus). Lakshmi is the embodiment of loveliness and grace, and the goddess of prosperity and wealth. She appears in different aspects alongside each of Vishnu's avatars, including Sita, wife of Rama, and Radha, Krishna's favourite *gopi*. In many temples she is shown as one with Vishnu, in the form of Lakshmi Narayan.

India's great monkey god, **Hanuman**, features in the Ramayana as Rama's chief aide in the fight against the demon-king of Lanka. Depicted as a giant monkey clasping a mace, Hanuman is seen as Rama and Sita's greatest devotee – as his representatives, monkeys find sanctuary in temples all over India.

The most beautiful Hindu goddess, **Saraswati**, the wife of Brahma, with her flawless milk-white complexion, sits or stands on a water lily or peacock, playing a lute, sitar or *vina*. She is revered as the goddess of music, creativity and learning.

Closely linked with the planet Saturn, **Shani** is feared for his destructive powers. His image, a black statue with protruding blood-red tongue, is often found on street corners; strings of green chillies and lemon are hung in shops and houses each Saturday (*Saniwar*) to ward off his evil influences.

disruptive forces, incarnating himself on earth nine times in various animal and human forms, or avatars, to fight the forces of evil and chaos, most famously as Rama (the god-hero whose exploits are described in the Ramayana) and as Krishna (who appears at the most significant juncture of the Mahabharata). The second, **Shiva**, "the destroyer" (a development of the Aryan god Rudra, who had played a minor role in the Vedas), was charged with destroying and renewing the universe at periodic intervals, though his powers are not merely destructive, and he is worshipped in myriad forms with various attributes (see p.1170). The three supreme gods are often depicted in a trinity, or *trimurti*, though in time Brahma's importance declined, and Shiva and Vishnu became the most popular deities – the famous Brahma temple at Pushkar is now one of the few in India dedicated to this venerable but rather esoteric god.

Depicted in human or semi-human form and accompanied by an animal "vehicle", other gods and goddesses who came alive in the mythology of the Puranas are still venerated across India. River goddesses, ancestors, guardians of particular places and protectors against disease and natural disaster are as central to village life as the major deities.

Practice and pilgrimage

In most Hindu homes, a chosen deity is worshipped daily in a shrine room. Outside the home, worship takes place in temples and consists of **puja** – sometimes a simple act of prayer, but more commonly a complex process when the god's image is circumambulated, offered flowers, rice, sugar and incense, and anointed with water, milk or sandalwood paste (which is usually done on behalf of the devotee by the temple priest). The aim in puja is to take **darshan** – glimpse the god – and thus receive his or her blessing. Worshippers leave the temple with *prasad*, an offering of food or flowers taken from the holy sanctuary. **Temple ceremonies** are conducted by priests who tend the image in daily rituals in which the god is symbolically woken, bathed, fed, dressed and, at the end of each day, put back to bed. In many villages, shrines to *devata*s, village deities who function as protectors, are more important than temples.

Strict rules address **purity and pollution**, the most obvious of them requiring high-caste Hindus to limit their contact with potentially polluting lower castes. Above all else, **water** is the agent of purification, used in ablutions before prayer and revered in all rivers, especially Ganga (the Ganges). *Ghat*s, steps leading to the water's edge, are common in all river- or lakeside towns, used for bathing, washing clothes and performing religious rituals.

India also has a wealth of **pilgrimage** sites visited by devotees eager to receive *darshan* and attain merit – see the "Sacred spaces and pilgrimage places" colour insert.

Islam

Muslims – some thirteen percent of the population – form a significant presence in almost every town, city and village. The belief in only one god, Allah, the condemnation of idol worship and the observance of their own strict dietary laws and specific festivals all set Muslims apart from their Hindu neighbours, with whom they have coexisted, not always peacefully, for centuries.

The first Muslims to settle in India were traders who arrived on the southwest coast in the seventh century. Much more significant was the invasion of north India under **Mahmud of Ghazni** (see p.1155), while more raids from Central Asia followed in the twelfth century, resulting in the partial colonization of India, while the invading Muslims set themselves up in Delhi as sultans.

Many Muslims who settled in India intermarried with Hindus, Buddhists and Jains, and the community spread. A further factor in its growth was missionary activity by **Sufis**, who stressed the attainment of inner knowledge of God through meditation and mystical experience. Their use of music (particularly *qawwali* singing – see p.114) and dance, shunned by orthodox Muslims, appealed to Hindus, for whom singing played an important role in religious practice. Muslims are enjoined to pray five times daily. They may do this at home or in a **mosque** – always full at noon on Friday, for communal prayer (the only exception being the Druze of Mumbai, who hold communal prayers on Thurs).

The position of **women** in Islam is a subject of great debate. It's customary for women to be veiled – though in larger cities many women don't cover their heads – and in strictly orthodox communities most wear a *burqa*, usually black, that covers them from head to toe. Like other Indian women, Muslim women take second place to men in public, but in the home they wield great influence. Contrary to popular belief, polygamy is not widespread; while it does occur (Mohammed himself had several wives), many Muslims prefer monogamy and several sects actually stress it as a duty. In marriage, women receive a dowry as financial security.

Buddhism

Buddhism was born in the Indian subcontinent, developing as an offshoot of – and a reaction to – Hinduism, with which it shares many assumptions about the nature of existence. For a time it became the dominant religion in the country, though from around the fourth century AD onwards it was gradually eclipsed by a resurgent Hinduism (which cleverly reappropriated the Buddha, claiming him to be an incarnation of Vishnu), and the subsequent arrival of Islam more or less finished it off. Today Buddhists make up only a tiny fraction of the population – outside north India's numerous Tibetan refugee camps, only Ladakh and Sikkim now preserve a significant Buddhist presence.

The founder of Buddhism, **Siddhartha Gautama**, known as the **Buddha** ("awakened one"), was born into a wealthy *kshatriya* family in Lumbini, north of the Gangetic plain in present-day Nepal, around 566 BC. Brought up in luxury as a prince, he married at an early age, but renounced family life when he was thirty. Unsatisfied with the explanations of worldly suffering proposed by religious gurus, and convinced that asceticism did not lead to spiritual realization, Siddhartha spent years wandering the countryside and meditating. His enlightenment is said to have taken place under a *bodhi* tree in **Bodhgaya** (Bihar). Soon afterwards he gave his first sermon in **Sarnath**, near Varanasi. For the rest of his life he taught, expounding **dharma**, the true nature of the world, human life and spiritual attainment. Before his death (c.486 BC) in Kushinagara (UP), he had established the **Sangha**, a community of monks and nuns who continued his teachings.

The Buddha's world-view incorporated the Hindu concept of *samsara*, and *karma* and *moksha*, which Buddhists call **nirvana** (literally "no wind"). The most important concept outlined by the Buddha was that all things are subject to the inevitability of **impermanence**. There is no independent inherent self due to the interconnectedness of all things, and our egos are the biggest obstacles on the road to enlightenment.

Tibetan Buddhism

Buddhism was introduced to **Tibet** in the seventh century AD, and integrated to a certain extent with the indigenous **Bon** cult. Practised largely in Ladakh, along with parts of Himachal Pradesh and Sikkim, Tibetan Buddhism recognizes the historical Buddha alongside a host of other Buddhas past and to come, and incorporates elaborate rituals into its worship. There is also a heavy emphasis on teachers, known as lamas, and reincarnated teachers, known as *tulkus*. The **Dalai Lama**, the head of Tibetan Buddhism, is the fourteenth in a succession of incarnate *bodhisattvas*, the representative of Avalokitesvara (the *bodhisattva* of compassion), and the leader of the exiled Tibetan community based in Dharamsala. With over 100,000 Tibetan **refugees** now living in India, including the Dalai Lama and the Tibetan government in exile, Tibetan Buddhism is probably the most accessible and flourishing form of Buddhism in India, and there are numerous opportunities for study (see p.437). Tibetan Buddhist devotees hang prayer flags, turn prayer wheels, and set stones carved with mantras (religious verses) in rivers, thus sending the word of the Buddha with wind and water to all corners of the earth.

Jainism

The number of **Jains** in India is small – accounting for less than one percent of the population – but has been tremendously influential for at least 2500 years. A large proportion of Jains live in Gujarat, and all over India they are commonly found working as merchants and traders. Similarities to Hinduism, and a shared respect for nature and nonviolence, have contributed to the decline of the Jain community through conversion to Hinduism, but there is no antagonism between the two religions.

Focused on the practice of **ahimsa** (nonviolence), Jains follow a rigorous discipline to avoid harm to all **jivas**, or "souls", which exist in humans, animals, plants, water, fire, earth and air. They assert that every *jiva* is pure and capable of achieving liberation from existence in this universe. However, *jiva*s are obscured by **karma**, a form of subtle matter that clings to the soul, which is born of action and binds the *jiva* to physical existence. For the most orthodox Jain, the only way to dissociate *karma* from the *jiva* is to follow the path of asceticism and meditation, rejecting passion, attachment and impure action.

The Jain doctrine is based upon the teachings of **Mahavira**, or "Great Hero", the last in a succession of 24 **tirthankaras** ("crossing-makers") said to appear on earth every 300 million years. Mahavira (c.599–527 BC) was born as Vardhamana Jnatrputra into a *kshatriya* family near modern Patna. Like his near-contemporary the Buddha, Mahavira rejected family life at the age of thirty and spent years wandering as an ascetic in an attempt to conquer attachment to worldly values.

His teachings were written down in the first millennium BC and Jainism prospered throughout India. Not long after, there was a schism. On the one hand the **Digambaras** ("sky-clad") believed that nudity was an essential part of world renunciation, and that women are incapable of achieving liberation from worldly existence. The **Svetambaras** ("white-clad"), however, disregarded the extremes of nudity, incorporated nuns into monastic communities and even acknowledged a female *tirthankara*. Today the two sects worship at different temples, but the number of naked Digambaras is minimal. Many Svetambara monks and nuns wear white masks to avoid breathing in insects, and carry a "fly-whisk", sometimes used to brush their path; none will use public transport and they often spend days or weeks walking barefoot to a pilgrimage site.

Sikhism

Sikhism, India's youngest religion, remains dominant in the Punjab, while its adherents have spread throughout northern India. The movement was founded by

Guru Nanak (1469–1539), who was born into an orthodox Hindu *kshatriya* family near Lahore. Nanak was among many sixteenth-century poet-philosophers, sometimes referred to as *sants*, who formed emotional cults, drawing elements from both Hinduism and Islam. Nanak declared that "God is neither Hindu nor Muslim and the path which I follow is God's"; he regarded God as **Sat**, or truth, who makes himself known through gurus. Though he condemned the rituals of Brahmins, Nanak did not attack Islam or Hinduism – he simply regarded the many deities as names for one supreme God, and encouraged his followers to shift religious emphasis from ritual to meditation. In common with Hindus, Nanak believed in a cyclic process of death and rebirth (*samsara*), but asserted that liberation (*moksha*) was attainable in this life by all women and men regardless of caste, and that religious practice could and should be integrated into everyday practical living.

Guru Nanak was succeeded by **Guru Angad**, who continued to lead the community of Sikhs (literally, "disciples"), the so-called **Sikh Panth**, and wrote his own and Nanak's hymns in a new script, **Gurumukhi**, which is today used as the script of written Punjabi. Eight further gurus successively led the Sikh Panth after Guru Angad's death in 1552, gradually developing Sikhism into a powerful independent religious movement. **Guru Ram Das** (1552–74) founded the sacred city of **Amritsar**; his successor, **Guru Arjan Dev**, compiled the gurus' hymns in a book called the **Adi Granth**, built the Golden Temple to house it and also became Sikhism's first martyr when Jahangir executed him. Throughout their history, the Sikhs have had to battle to protect their faith and their people, especially against the Mughals; Aurangzeb had **Guru Teg Bahadur** beheaded in 1675, an event that heralded the era of his son and successor, **Guru Gobind Singh**, who was to revolutionize the entire movement.

Gobind Singh, the last leader, was largely responsible for moulding the community as it exists today. In 1699, he founded the brotherhood of the **Khalsa**. The aims of the Khalsa are to assist the poor and fight oppression; to have faith in one god and to abandon superstition and dogma; to worship god; and to protect the faith with steel. The Khalsa requires members to renounce tobacco, halal meat and sexual relations with Muslims, and to adopt the **five Ks**: *kangha* (comb), *kirpan* (sword), *kara* (steel bracelet), *kachcha* (short trousers) and *kesh* (unshorn hair) – the last requirement means that Sikh men are usually instantly recognizable thanks to their luxuriant beards and distinctive turbans. Less visibly, Guru Gobind Singh replaced traditional caste names with Singh for men (meaning "lion" – although this name is not unique to Sikhs, being a common Hindu surname as well) and Kaur ("princess") for women. Finally, Guru Gobind Singh also compiled a standardized version of the Adi Granth, which contains the hymns of the first nine gurus as well as poems written by Hindus and Muslims, and installed it as his successor, naming it **Guru Granth Sahib**. This became the Sikh's spiritual guide, while political authority rested with the Khalsa.

Demands for a separate Sikh state – **Khalistan** – and fighting in the eighteenth century, and later after Independence, have burdened Sikhs with a reputation as military activists, and their bravery and martial traditions mean that they continue to make up an important part of the Indian army. Despite this, Sikhs regard their religion as one devoted to egalitarianism, democracy and social awareness. Though to die fighting for the cause of religious freedom is considered to lead to liberation, the use of force is officially sanctioned only when other methods have failed.

Christianity

The **Apostle Thomas** is said to have arrived in Kerala in 54 AD, and according to popular tradition the Church of San Thome is the oldest Christian denomination in the world, with many tales of miracles by "Mar Thoma", as Thomas is known in Malayalam. According to tradition, Thomas was martyred in 72 AD at Mylapore in **Madras**. The tomb has since become a major place of pilgrimage, while the Portuguese added the Gothic **San Thome Cathedral** to the site in the late nineteenth century.

From the sixteenth century onwards, the history of the Church in India is linked to the spread of foreign Christians across the Subcontinent. In 1552, St Francis Xavier arrived in the Portuguese trading colony of **Goa** to establish missions to reach out to the Hindu "untouchables". In 1559, at the behest of the Portuguese king, the Inquisition arrived in Goa. Jesuit missionaries carried out a bloody and brutal campaign to "cleanse" the small colony of Hindu and Muslim religious practice. Early British incomers took the attitude that the Subcontinent was a heathen and polytheistic civilization waiting to be proselytized and made significant numbers of converts – as Christianity is intended to be free of caste stigmas, it can be attractive to those seeking social advancement, and of the two million Christians in present-day India, most are *adivasi* (tribal) and *dalit* (untouchable) people.

The position of Christians in Indian society remains uncertain. In early 1999, Christian communities in some areas, notably in Gujarat and Orissa, were subject to forced "reconversions" and attacks. These were allegedly carried out by Hindu extremists incensed by proselytizing evangelists targeting low-caste Hindus. Following an international outcry, some states passed laws banning "forced conversions", but in December 2002, a riot was only narrowly averted after police acted to prevent 1500 Dalit ("Untouchable") people from attending a mass-conversion in Chennai (Madras).

The **Hindu influence** on Christianity remains marked, in any case, and in many churches you can see devotees offering the Hindu *arati* (a plate of coconut, sweets and rice), and women wearing *tilak* dots on their foreheads. In the same way that Hindus and Muslims consider pilgrimage to be an integral part of life's journey, Indian Christians have numerous devotional sites, including St Jude's Shrine in **Jhansi** and the Temple of Mother Mary in **Mathura**. This sharing of traditions works both ways. At Christmas, for instance, you can't fail to notice the brightly coloured paper stars and small Nativity scenes glowing and flashing outside schools, houses, shops and churches throughout India.

Zoroastrianism

Of all India's religious communities, Western visitors are least likely to come across – or recognize – **Zoroastrians**, who have no distinctive dress and few houses of worship. Most live in Mumbai, where they are known as **Parsis** (Persians) and are active in business, education and politics. Zoroastrian numbers – roughly ninety thousand – are rapidly dwindling due to a falling birth rate and absorption into wider communities.

The religion's founder, **Zarathustra** (Zoroaster), lived in Iran around the sixth or seventh century BC, and was the first religious prophet to expound a dualistic philosophy, based on the opposing powers of good and evil. For him, the absolute, wholly good and wise God, **Ahura Mazda**, together with his holy spirit and six emanations present in earth, water, the sky, animals, plants and fire, is constantly at odds with an evil power, **Angra Mainyu**, who is aided by **daevas**, or evil spirits. Five daily prayers, usually hymns, uttered by Zarathustra and standardized in the **Avesta**, the main Zoroastrian text, are said in the home or in a temple, before a fire, which symbolizes truth, righteousness and order. For this reason, Zoroastrians are often, incorrectly, called "fire-worshippers".

Wildlife

India's vast range of habitats support a staggering range of wildlife, with around 65,000 species of fauna including 1200 birds and 340 mammals (India is the only country in the world where you can see both wild lions and tigers) plus a staggering 13,000 varieties of flowering plant. The lush deodar and rhododendron forests of the lower **Himalayas** are home to bears and black bucks, while the fabled snow leopard and yak inhabit the higher mountains. Down on the **Gangetic plain**, the warm climate, forests and numerous lakes and rivers support a rich array of birdlife, while the **Sunderbans** mangrove swamps in the east are famous for their population of unusual swimming tigers. Camels, both wild and domesticated, can be found in the deserts of **Rajasthan**, while elsewhere in the west the dry climate supports spotted deer, leopards and the famous Asiatic lion. Further south, the dry **Deccan plateau** is thick with sandalwood forests, the home of wild elephants, while at the very **southern tip** of India you'll find elephants, butterflies and jewel-like birds under the canopy of the teak and rosewood rainforest.

Mammals

The Indian **elephant**, distinguished from its African cousin by its long front legs and smaller ears and body, is still widely used as a beast of burden in many parts of the country. Elephants have worked and been tamed in India for three thousand years, and there is still a sizeable population of wild elephants across the country. Another pachyderm, the lumbering **one-horned rhinoceros**, retains a tenuous foothold in the northeast of the country, with around eleven hundred living in the protected Manas and Kaziranga wildlife sanctuaries in Assam.

Indian **tigers** are fast becoming extinct in the wild (see p.1178), but you still stand a reasonable chance of coming across one in a national park – for the next few years at least. The other **big cats** have fared even worse than the tiger. The **Asiatic lion** (see p.573) now clings on in just one tiny patch of Gujarat, while the ghostly grey- and black-spotted **snow leopard** of the Himalayas is so rare as to be almost legendary. Only the plains-dwelling **leopard** (also known as the panther) can still be commonly found, especially in forested places near human settlement where domestic animals make easy prey. Other indigenous felines include the rare multicoloured marbled cat, the miniature leopard cat, the jungle cat, the fishing cat, and a kind of lynx called the caracal.

Deer and antelope, the larger cats' prey, are much more abundant. The often solitary *sambar* is the largest of the **deer**. Smaller and more gregarious are chital (spotted deer), while other deer include the elusive mountain-loving muntjac (barking deer) and the para (hog deer). The smallest deer in India is the nocturnal chevrotain, known from its size (only 30cm high) as the mouse deer. **Antelopes** include the nilgai ("blue cow"); the endangered black buck; and the unique forest-dwelling four-horned chowsingha (swamp deer). The desert-loving gazelle is known as the *chinkara* ("the one who sneezes") due to the sneeze-like alarm call it makes.

The most common **monkeys** are the feisty red-bottomed rhesus macaque and the black-faced "Hanuman" langurs, often found around temples. Wild monkeys include the Assamese macaque and pig-tailed macaque in the northern hills, and the bonnet macaque in the steamy tropical jungles of the south.

The shaggy **sloth bear** is hard to spot in the wild, although you may see captive bears being forced to dance near tourist sites; other bears include the black and

The Indian tiger: survival or extinction?

Few animals command such universal fascination as the **tiger**, and India is one of the very few places where this rare and enigmatic big cat can still be glimpsed in the wild, stalking through the teak forests and terai grass – a solitary predator, with no natural enemies save one.

As recently as the beginning of the twentieth century, up to 100,000 tigers still roamed the Subcontinent, even though tiger hunting had long been the "sport of kings". It was the trigger-happy British who brought tiger hunting to its most gratuitous excesses, however. Photographs of pith-helmeted, bare-kneed *burra-sahibs* posing behind mountains of striped carcasses became a hackneyed image of the Raj.

In the years following Independence, **demographic pressures** nudged the Indian tiger perilously close to extinction. As the human population increased in rural districts, more and more forest was cleared for farming, depriving large carnivores of their main source of game and of the cover they needed to hunt. Forced to turn on farm cattle as an alternative, tigers were drawn into direct conflict with humans; some animals, out of sheer desperation, even turned man-eater and attacked human settlements. **Poaching** has taken an even greater toll. The black market has always paid high prices for dead animals – a tiger pelt alone can fetch $12,500 in China – and for the various body parts believed to hold magical or medicinal properties.

Numbers had plummeted to under two thousand by 1973, the year in which India's ambitious **Project Tiger** was inaugurated. Nine areas of pristine forest were set aside for the remaining tigers. Demand for tiger parts did not end with Project Tiger, however, and the poachers remained in business, aided by organised smuggling rings. India's worst-case conservation scenario was finally played out in 2005, when it was discovered that the entire population of big cats at Sariska Tiger Reserve had mysteriously vanished at the hands of poachers.

Well-organised guerrilla groups operate with virtual impunity out of remote national parks, where inadequate numbers of poorly armed and poorly paid wardens offer little more than token resistance. Project Tiger officials are understandably reluctant to jeopardise lucrative tourist traffic by admitting that sightings are getting rarer, but the prognosis looks very gloomy indeed.

Today, though there are 23 Project Tiger sites, numbers continue to fall. Official figures optimistically claim a **population** of 3000 to 3500, but independent evidence is more pessimistic – a survey in 2008 suggested that numbers had fallen to just 1411, down from 3642 at the last major survey in 2002. Estimates claim that one tiger is being poached every day in India, and the most pessimistic experts believe that India's most exotic animal could face extinction in the wild within less than a decade.

brown varieties. Of the **canines**, the scavenging striped hyena and the small pest-eating Indian fox are fairly common, though the desert-dwelling Indian wolf is under threat of extinction.

The wild **buffalo** has a close genetic relationship with the domesticated water buffalo. More exotic members of the cow family are the hill-loving **gaur**, an Indian bison which stands 2m across at the shoulders, and the nimble, mountain-dwelling **yak**.

Reptiles

The 238 species of **snake** in India (of which fifty are poisonous) extend from the 10cm-long worm snake to nest-building king cobras and massive pythons. Poisonous snakes include the majestically hooded cobra, the yellow-brown

Russel's viper, the small krait and the saw-scaled viper. **Lizards** are also common, with every hotel room seeming to have a resident gecko to keep the place free of insects. The colourful garden lizard and Sita's lizard are both found throughout India. Olive Ridley marine turtles (see p.710 & p.885) nest at remote beaches along the east and southwest coasts. **Crocodiles** are common throughout the Subcontinent.

Birds

You don't have to be an aficionado to enjoy India's abundant **birdlife**, with a spectacular array of resident avifauna, while its geographical location also attracts many migratory species from colder countries to the north during the winter months.

Three common species of **kingfisher** frequently crop up amid the paddy fields and wetlands of the coastal plains. Other common and brightly coloured species include the grass-green, blue and yellow **bee-eaters**, the stunning **golden oriole** and the brilliant-blue **Indian roller**. **Hoopoes**, recognizable by their elegant black-and-white tipped crests, also flit around fields and villages, as do several kinds of **bulbuls**, **babblers** and **drongos**. Paddy fields and ponds often teem with water birds. The most ubiquitous of these is the snowy white **cattle egret**, which can often be seen riding on the backs of cows and buffalo. Look out too for the mud-brown **paddy bird**, India's most common heron, distinguished by its pale green legs, speckled breast and hunched posture.

Common birds of prey such as the **brahminy kite** and the **pariah kite** are widespread around towns and fishing villages, where they vie with raucous gangs of house **crows** and **white-eyed jackdaws** for scraps. Pink-headed **king vultures** and the **white-backed vulture**, which has a white ruff around its bare neck and head, also show up whenever there are carcasses to pick clean. A bird whose call is a regular feature of the Western Ghat forests is the wild ancestor of the domestic chicken – the **jungle fowl**. Finally, among India's abundant **forest birds**, one species every enthusiast hopes to glimpse is the magnificent **hornbill**, with its huge yellow beak sporting a long curved casque on top.

Music

India is home to a staggering variety of different musical traditions, both ancient and modern, ranging from archaic styles of Hindu devotional chanting to the eclectic sounds of contemporary film scores. For many outsiders, the country's aural signature is provided by **north Indian classical music**, one of the world's most instantly recognizable sounds, with its twanging tanpuras and complex tabla beats. There's also Bollywood's huge treasury of film songs, or **filmi**, to explore, as well as a rich folk music tradition.

Indian classical music: ragas and talas

Underlying all Indian classical music is the concept of the **raga** (or *raag*, from the Sanskrit word meaning "colour"). Put simplistically, a raga is simply a musical scale or mode (loosely equivalent to the "key" of a piece of Western music), determining which notes can and can't be played during a particular piece. The raga defines the basic musical material and expressive content of each particular piece, meaning that while Indian classical musicians are renowned for their **improvisation**, this only takes place within strictly defined limits – the mark of a good performer is his or her ability to improvise extensively without stepping outside the boundaries of the chosen raga.

Just as the raga organizes melody, so the rhythm of a piece is organised using metric cycles known as **talas**. A *tala* is made up of a number of beats, with each beat being defined by a combination of rhythm pattern and timbre. There are literally hundreds of *talas*, the most common being the sixteen-beat *teen tala* (four times four beats).

The performance of a raga follows a set pattern. First comes the **alap**, a slow, meditative introduction in free rhythm which explores the chosen raga, carefully introducing its constituent notes one by one. In the next two sections, the **jor** and the **jhala**, the instrumentalist introduces a rhythmic element, developing the raga through a series of increasingly complex variations. Only in these and the final section, the **gat**, does the percussion instrument – usually the tabla or (in south India) the *mridangam* – enter. The soloist introduces a short, fixed phrase (known as "the composition") to which he returns between flights of improvisation. In this section rhythm is an important structural element. Both percussionist and soloist improvise, at times echoing each other and sometimes pursuing individual variations of rhythmic counterpoint, regularly punctuated by unison statements of "the composition". The *gat* itself is subdivided into three sections: a slow tempo passage known as *vilambit*, increasing to a medium tempo section called *madhya*, and leading finally to the fast concluding *drut*.

Musical instruments

The best-known Indian instrument is the **sitar**. This has six or seven main strings, plucked with a plectrum, along with between eleven and nineteen sympathetic strings. The curved neck allows the player to alter the pitch by pulling strings sideways across the fret to provide the pitch-bends so characteristic of Indian music. The **surbahar**, effectively a bass sitar, is played in the same way. Smaller than a sitar, the **sarod** has two resonating chambers connected by a metal fingerboard, and ten metal strings, plucked with a fragment of coconut shell (plus a further fifteen sympathetic strings underneath).

Indian classical masters on CD

There's a huge variety of Indian – especially north Indian – classical music available on CD, including recordings by many of the country's leading virtuosos of the past fifty years. Perhaps the best-known and most recorded Indian classical artist is sitar player **Ravi Shankar** (b.1920), who has made numerous solo recordings, as well as duetting with artists ranging from Ali Akbar Khan (see below) to Yehudi Menuhin. Other legendary sitar players include **Nikhil Banerjee** (1931–1986) and **Vilayat Khan** (1928–2004), while it's also worth searching out recordings by **Imrat Khan** (b.1935, and younger brother of Vilayat), the acknowledged master of the soulful *surbahar* (bass sitar).

Rivalling Ravi Shankar for recorded legacy is the internationally revered *sarod* virtuoso **Ali Akbar Khan** (1922–2009), while the hauntingly atmospheric music of **Hariprasad Chaurasia** (b.1938), India's leading master of the *bansuri* (bamboo flute), is also essential listening for anyone with even a passing interest in Subcontinental music. Less well-known, but equally rewarding, are the recorded performances of **Sultan Khan** (b.1940) and **Ram Narayan** (b.1927), two of modern India's greatest masters of the *sarangi*, while recordings by leading *shehnai* virtuoso **Bismillah Khan** (1916–2006) are also worth looking out for – albeit the instrument is something of an acquired taste. Many notable recordings also feature **Alla Rakha** (1919–2000), perhaps the finest tabla virtuoso of recent years. For **Carnatic** music, try some of the many recordings by violin wizard L. Subramanian, or look out for the much rarer recordings by **Sundaram Balachander** (1927–1990), one of the twentieth century's leading exponents of the soulful *veena*.

The **sarangi** is a fretless bowed instrument with a very broad fingerboard and three or four main strings of gut, plus anything up to forty sympathetic metal strings. Some claim it is the most difficult musical instrument to play in the world. The *sarangi* is capable of a wide range of timbres and its sound is likened to that of the human voice, meaning that it is often used to accompany vocal recitals. The word **bansuri** refers to a wide variety of bamboo (*banse*) flutes, either end-blown or side-blown. The **shehnai**, traditionally used for wedding music, is a double-reed, oboe-type instrument with up to nine finger holes.

The **tabla** is a set of two small drums, tuned to the tonic, dominant or subdominant notes of the raga and played with the palms and fingertips to produce an incredible variety of sounds and timbres. Predating the tabla, the **pakhavaj** is nearly a metre long and was traditionally made of clay, although wood is now more popular. It has two parchment heads, each tuned to a different pitch.

The instruments of **Carnatic music** (see p.1182) include the **vina**, which resembles the sitar but has no sympathetic strings; the **mridangam** double-headed drum; and the enormous **nadaswaram** (or *nagaswaram*), a kind of metre-long oboe, commonly used during temple ceremonies. The **violin** (slightly modified to suit Indian musical requirements) is also widely used.

Finally, perhaps the most ubiquitous but self-effacing of all Indian musical instruments is the **tanpura** (or *tambura*), a type of fretless lute with (usually) four or five wire strings. It's the tanpura that supplies the instantly recognizable, buzzing drone which underpins all Indian classical music. The tanpura is traditionally played by an advanced student of the lead performer – considered a rare and special honour for the pupil concerned.

Classical vocal music

Dhrupad is the oldest and most austere form of north Indian classical music. *Dhrupads* typically consist of two sections: a long and entirely wordless introductory *alap* during which the singer(s) vocalize a sequence of syllables deriving from the mantra "Hari Om Narayana Taan Tarana Tum", followed by a much shorter and faster section sung to the accompaniment of a *pakhavaj* drum. During the eighteenth century the rather severe *dhrupad* was largely displaced by the much more flamboyant **khayal** – described as the "bel canto of Indian music" – a form which allows for far greater displays of virtuosity. *Khayal* is typically accompanied by tabla and harmonium, along with a bowed instrument such as a *sarangi* or violin, which mirrors the vocal line.

Thumri are essentially love songs, written from a female perspective and sung in a language known as Braj Bhasha, a literary dialect of Hindi particularly associated with Lucknow. The singer is always accompanied by the tabla, as well perhaps as the tanpura, the *sarangi* or the *surmandal*, and sometimes the violin or harmonium. Still more song-like than the *thumri* is the **ghazal**. In some ways the Urdu counterpart of *thumri*, the *ghazal* was introduced to India by Persian Muslims and is a poetic rather than a musical form – many favourite *ghazals* are drawn from the works of great Urdu poets.

Carnatic music

Southern India's classical music – known as **Carnatic** (or "Karnatak") music – is essentially similar to Hindustani classical music in its overall concept but differs in many details, usually ascribed to the far greater Islamic influence in the north. To the Western ear, Carnatic music is emotionally direct and impassioned, without the restraint that characterizes much of the north's music.

Song is at the root of south Indian music, and forms based on song are paramount, even when the performance is purely instrumental. The vast majority of the texts are religious, and the temple is frequently the venue for performance. The most important form is the *kriti*, a devotional song, hundreds of which were written by the most influential figure in the development of Carnatic music, the singer **Thyagaraja** (1767–1847).

Folk music

There are many kinds of **Indian folk music** (*Lok Sangeet*), but the main regional strands are those of Rajasthan, the Punjab (spread across both India and Pakistan), and Bengal. In **Rajasthan**, music is always played for weddings and theatre performances, and often at local markets or gatherings. There is a whole cast of professional musicians who perform this function, and a wonderful assortment of earthy-sounding stringed instruments like the *kamayacha* and *ravanhata* that accompany their songs.

Bengal is best known for the music of the **Bauls**, an order of wandering mystics and musicians who subscribe to a syncretic mix of Sufi and *bhakti* Hindu mystical beliefs expressed primarily through song, typically accompanied by the *ektara*, a one-stringed drone instrument.

The **Punjab** is most closely associated with **bhangra**. This was originally a kind of folk dance, traditionally performed as part of harvest festival celebrations and accompanied by music on the *dhol* and *dholki* drums, *ektara* and *tumbi* (a kind of single-string guitar), but since the 1980s has become a global pop phenomenon both in its traditional form and in contemporary dance, house and hip-hop fusions, mainly created by Asian musicians in the UK.

Filmi

Indian **popular music** is intimately bound up with the country's massive film industry. Music plays a crucial role in Bollywood movies (see the "Bollywood and beyond" colour insert) and up until the 1990s virtually all Indian popular music consisted of songs, known as **filmi**, taken from the soundtracks to these movies. The most striking feature of these Bollywood *filmi* is their incredibly eclectic style, offering a fascinating snapshot of changing musical fashions over the past five decades, all seen from a uniquely Indian point of view.

Early film scores tended to be rooted in Indian folk and classical music, but from the 1960s onwards Bollywood film composers such as the famous **RD Burman** began to soak up an incredible range of musical influences in their work, from big band rock'n'roll to the techno and electronic creations of the innovative **AR Rahman**. Bollywood *filmi* are performed by so-called **playback singers**, the invisible artists who record the songs which the film's actors and actresses then mime along to. Many of these singers have achieved massive fame in their own right, including the legendary Asha Bhosle and her sister Lata Mangeshkar, along with male singers such as Kishore Kumar and Mohammed Rafi.

Books

India is one of the most written-about places on earth, and there are a bewildering number of titles available covering virtually every aspect of the country, ranging from scholarly historical dissertations to racy travelogues. Books marked ★ are particularly recommended.

History, society and reportage

Charles Allen *Plain Tales from the Raj*. First-hand accounts from erstwhile *sahibs* and *memsahibs* of everyday British India, organized thematically.

A.L. Basham *The Wonder That Was India*. This veritable encyclopedia by one of India's foremost historical authorities positively bristles with erudition.

★ **Elizabeth Bumiller** *May You Be the Mother of a Hundred Sons*. Lucid exploration of the Indian woman's lot, drawn from dozens of first-hand encounters.

David Burton *The Raj at Table*. Vividly evokes the quirky world of British India – commendable both for its extraordinary recipes and as a marvellous piece of social history.

Liz Collingham *Curry*. Original and entertaining account of Indian history seen through its food, from Mughal biriyanis to Mulligatawny soup.

Larry Collins and Dominique Lapierre *Freedom at Midnight*. Readable, if shallow, account of Independence, highly sympathetic to the British and, particularly, to Mountbatten, who was the authors' main source of information.

★ **William Dalrymple** *The Last Mughal*. Masterful account of Delhi's part in the 1857 uprising. Using Urdu as well as English sources, Dalrymple tells us what it was like for the insurgents, the British, the Mughal court and – most importantly – the ordinary people of Delhi.

★ **William Dalrymple** *White Mughals*. Compelling account of the previously forgotten story of British political officer James Achilles Kirkpatrick's marriage to the great-niece of the nizam of Hyderabad's prime minister.

Louis Fischer *The Life of Mahatma Gandhi*. Veteran American journalist Louis Fischer knew his subject personally, and his book provides an engaging account of Gandhi as a man, politician and propagandist.

Patrick French *Liberty or Death*. The definitive account (and a damning indictment) of the last years of the British Raj.

★ **M.K. Gandhi** *The Story of My Experiments with Truth*. Gandhi's fascinating record of his life, including his spiritual and moral quests and gradual emergence to the fore of national politics.

Bamber Gascoigne *The Great Mughals*. Concise, entertaining and eminently readable account of the lives of the first six great Mughals.

Christopher Hibbert *The Great Mutiny*. Account of the 1857 uprising, told entirely from the British point of view, in easy prose and with some excellent first-hand material from the British side.

John Keay *The Honourable Company: A History of the English East India Company*. Readable and balanced account of the East India Company and its strange role in Subcontinental history.

John Keay *India: A History*. The best single-volume history currently in print. Keay manages to coax clear, impartial and highly readable narrative from five thousand years of fragmented events, enlivened with plenty of quirky asides.

John Keay *Into India*. As an all-round introduction to India, this book – originally written in 1973 but reissued in 1999 – is the one most often recommended by old hands, presenting a wide spread of history and cultural background, interspersed with lucid personal observations.

Dominique Lapierre and Javier Moro *Five Past Midnight in Bhopal*. The definitive account of the world's worst industrial disaster, weaving the portraits of its victims together into an outstanding piece of investigative journalism.

Sarah Lloyd *An Indian Attachment*. Life in a Punjabi plains village through the eyes of a young Western woman, whose relationship with an opium-addicted Sikh forms the essence of this honest and enlightening book.

Edward Luce *In Spite of the Gods*. The most authoritative account of the state of the nation currently in print, packed full of sobering statistics and myth-busting facts that challenge common misconceptions about the country.

Suketu Mehta *Maximum City: Bombay Lost and Found*. Acclaimed portrait of India's largest city, mixing memoir and travelogue, along with penetrating insights into the history, society and people of Mumbai.

Geoffrey Moorhouse *India Britannica*. A balanced, lively survey of the rise and fall of the British Raj.

Palagummi Sainath *Everybody Loves a Good Drought*. A classic report on India's poorest districts, telling the stories of individual villages that are usually lost in a maze of development statistics.

Amartya Sen *The Argumentative Indian*. A provocative and sharply written collection of essays on identity, religion, history, philosophy and – above all – what it means to be Indian.

Mala Sen *Death By Fire*. Later made into a controversial movie, this book uses the infamous Roop Kanwar case as a springboard to explore some of the wider issues affecting women in contemporary Indian society.

Mark Tully *No Full Stops in India*. Earnest dissection of contemporary India by the former BBC correspondent. His subsequent books, *India in Slow Motion* and *India's Unending Journey*, cover a similarly diverse range of subjects, from Hindu extremism to child labour.

Travel

James Cameron *An Indian Summer*. Affectionate and humorous description of the veteran British journalist's visit to India in 1972, and his marriage to an Indian woman.

William Dalrymple *City of Djinns*. Dalrymple's account of a year in Delhi sifts through successive layers of the city's past using a blend of inspired historical sleuth-work and interviews with a cast of characters ranging from Urdu calligraphers to local pigeon fanciers. The *Age of Kali* (published in India as In the *Court of the Fish-Eyed Goddess*) is a collection of essays drawn from ten years' travel in India.

Trevor Fishlock *Cobra Road*. Former *Times* correspondent Fishlock's 1999 account of a journey from the Khyber to Cape Comorin – a classic all-round introduction to the Subcontinent.

Alexander Frater *Chasing the Monsoon*. Frater's wet-season jaunt up the west coast and across to Shillong took him through an India of muddy puddles and grey skies: an evocative account of the country as few visitors see it, now something of a classic.

Justine Hardy *Bollywood Boy*. Chick-lit-style travelogue featuring a lurid cast of has-been movie stars, Grant Road prostitutes, and some formidable regulars at her local beauty salon.

Norman Lewis *A Goddess in the Stones*. Veteran English travel writer's typically idiosyncratic account of his trip to Kolkata and around the backwaters of Bihar and Orissa.

Tim Mackintosh-Smith *The Hall of a Thousand Columns*. Quirky, learned and entertaining travelogue following the footsteps of Ibn Battuta through the Delhi of the Tughluq sultan Muhammad Shah and thence south to Kerala, with lashings of offbeat Subcontinental Islamic history en route.

Geoffrey Moorhouse *Om*. An account of Moorhouse's travels around south India's key spiritual centres, providing typically well-informed asides on history, politics, contemporary culture and religion.

Dervla Murphy *On a Shoestring to Coorg*. Murphy stays with her young daughter in the little-visited tropical mountains of Coorg, Karnataka. A compelling manifesto for single-parent budget travel.

Tahir Shah *Sorcerer's Apprentice*. A journey through the weird underworld of occult India. Travelling as an apprentice to a master conjurer and illusionist, Shah encounters hangmen, baby renters, skeleton dealers, sadhus and charlatans.

Mark Shand *Travels on My Elephant*. Award-winning account of a 600-mile ride on an elephant from Konarak in Orissa to Bihar, and full of incident, humour and pathos. For the sequel, *Queen of the Elephants*, Shand teams up with an Assamese princess who's the country's leading elephant-handler.

Eric Shipton and H.W. Tilman *Nanda Devi: Exploration and Ascent*. Two classics of Himalayan mountaineering literature published in a single volume, recounting the famous expeditions of 1934 and 1936. Shipton's work, in particular, is a masterpiece of the genre: beautifully written and enthralling from start to finish.

Fiction

Aravind Adiga *The White Tiger*. Brilliantly dark satire on the "New" India, set largely in Delhi and featuring the relationship between a wealthy employer and his impecunious but murderously ambitious servant.

Mulk Raj Anand *Untouchable* and *Coolie*. First published in 1935, *Untouchable* gives a memorable worm's-eye view of the brutal life of an untouchable sweeper, while the subsequent *Coolie* (1936) describes the death of a 15-year-old child labourer.

Anita Desai *Fasting, Feasting*. One of India's leading female authors' eloquent portrayal of the frustration of a sensitive young woman stuck in the stifling atmosphere of home while her spoilt brother is packed off to study in America.

Kiran Desai *The Inheritance of Loss*. Warm, wise and beautifully told family tale straddling India and the US, set in the 1980s, with most of the action unfolding near Kalimpong against a backdrop of Nepalese insurgency.

E.M. Forster *A Passage to India*. Set in the 1920s, this withering critique of colonialism is memorable as much for its sympathetic portrayal of middle-class Indian life as for its insights into cultural misunderstandings.

Rudyard Kipling *Kim*. Cringingly colonialist at times, of course, but the atmosphere of India and Kipling's love of it shine through in this subtle story of an orphaned white boy. Kipling's other key works on India are two books of short stories: *Soldiers Three* and *In Black and White*.

Rohinton Mistry *A Fine Balance*. Compelling novel focusing on two friends who leave their lower-caste rural lives for the urban opportunities of the big smoke (in this case a fictionalized Mumbai). Mistry's *Such a Long Journey* is an acclaimed account of a Bombay Parsi's struggle to maintain personal integrity in the face of betrayals and disappointment.

V.S. Naipaul *An Area of Darkness*. One of the finest (and bleakest) books ever written about India: a darkly comic portrait of the country based on a year of travel around the Subcontinent in the early 1960s – dated, but still essential reading. Naipaul followed this up with *India: A Wounded Civilisation*, a damning analysis of Indian society written during the Emergency of 1975–77, and the altogether sunnier *India: A Million Mutinies Now*, published in 1990.

R.K. Narayan *Gods, Demons and Others*. Classic Indian folk tales and popular myths told through the voice of a village storyteller. Many of Narayan's beautifully crafted books, full of touching characters and subtle humour, are set in the fictional south Indian territory of Malgudi.

Gregory David Roberts *Shantaram*. Entertaining, albeit rather over-long, semi-autobiographical account of an escaped Australian convict taking refuge in India (mainly Mumbai), with memorable, if occasionally clichéd, depictions of the country and its people.

Arundhati Roy *The God of Small Things*. Haunting Booker Prize-winner about a well-to-do south Indian family caught between the snobberies of high-caste tradition, a colonial past and the diverse personal histories of its members.

Salman Rushdie *Midnight's Children*. This story of a man born at the very moment of Independence, whose life mirrors that of modern India itself, won Rushdie the Booker Prize and the enmity of Indira Gandhi, who had it banned in India. Set in Kerala and Bombay, *The Moor's Last Sigh* was the subject of a defamation case brought by Shiv Sena leader Bal Thackeray.

Vikram Seth *A Suitable Boy*. Vast, all-embracing tome set in UP shortly after Independence; wonderful characterization and an impeccable sense of place and time make this an essential read for long train journeys.

William Sutcliffe *Are You Experienced?* Hilarious novel sending up the backpacker scene in India. Wickedly perceptive and very readable.

Tarun J. Tejpal *The Alchemy of Desire*. Set mainly in the Himalayas, this sensuous contemporary tale focuses on two lovers, mixing its exploration of human relationships with wider reflections on India in the twentieth century.

Art, architecture and religion

Roy Craven *Indian Art*. Concise general introduction to Indian art, from Harappan seals to Mughal miniatures.

Diana L. Eck *Banaras – City of Light*. Thorough disquisition on the religious significance of Varanasi, and a good introduction to the practice of Hindu cosmology.

Dorf Hartsuiker *Sadhus: Holy Men of India*. The weird world of India's itinerant ascetics exposed in glossy colour photographs and erudite but accessible text.

Stephen P. Huyler *Meeting God*. Unrivalled overview of the beliefs and practices of contemporary Hinduism, accompanied by sublime photographs.

George Michell *The Hindu Temple*. A reasonable primer, introducing Hindu temples, their significance, and architectural development.

Wendy O'Flaherty (transl) *Hindu Myths*. Translations of key myths from the original Sanskrit texts, providing an insight into the foundations of Hinduism.

Paramahansa Yogananda *Autobiography of a Yogi*. Uplifting account of religious awakening and spiritual development by one of the most internationally influential Hindu masters.

Language

Language

No fewer than **eighteen major languages** are officially recognized by the Indian constitution, while numerous minor ones and over a thousand dialects are also spoken across the country. When independent India was organized, the present-day states were largely created along linguistic lines, which helps the traveller make some sense of the complex situation. Considering the continuing prevalence of **English**, there is rarely any necessity to speak a local language, but some theoretical knowledge of the background and learning at least a few words of one or two can only enhance your visit.

The main languages of northern India, including the country's eastern and western extremities, are all **Indo-Aryan**, the easternmost subgroup of the Indo-European family that is thought to have originated somewhere between Europe and Central Asia several millennia BC, before tribal movements spread its progeny in all directions. The oldest extant Subcontinental language is Sanskrit, one of the three "big sisters" (along with Latin and Greek) upon which philologists have created the model of proto-Indo-European language. It's known to have been spoken early in the second millennium BC, although it was not written down until much later, and is the vehicle for all the sacred texts of Hinduism. Sanskrit remained the language of the educated until around 1000 AD and gradually developed into the modern tongues of northern India: Hindi, Urdu, Bengali, Gujarati, Marathi, Kashmiri, Punjabi and Oriya.

North India

Hindi is the pre-eminent language in the north, and the main language in the states of Uttar Pradesh, Madhya Pradesh, Rajasthan, Haryana, Bihar and Himachal Pradesh, as well as being widely used as a second language in other states. Hindi is very closely related to **Urdu**, the main language of Pakistan. Both Hindi and Urdu developed in tandem around the markets and army camps of Delhi (the term Urdu derives from the Turkish word for "camp") during the establishment of Muslim rule around the start of the second millennium AD. Whereas Hindi later returned to the Sanskrit roots of its Hindu speakers, however, and adopted the classical **Devanagari** script, Urdu became culturally more closely linked with Islam and is written in **Perso-Arabic** script. The vocabulary of each also reflects these cultural and religious ties. The scripts of Punjabi, Bengali and Gujarati are among those that have developed out of Devanagari and still bear some resemblance to it.

Other important languages spoken in north India include **Bengali** (West Bengal and Tripura), **Nepali** (West Bengal and Sikkim), **Gujarati** (Gujarat), **Punjabi** (Punjab, Delhi), **Kashmiri** and **Dogri** (Kashmir), **Assamese** and **Bodo** (Assam), **Oriya** (Orissa) and **Maithili** (Bihar).

South India

The four most widely spoken south Indian languages, **Tamil** (Tamil Nadu), **Telugu** (Andhra Pradesh), **Kannada** (Karnataka) and **Malayalam** (Kerala) all belong to the Dravidian family, the world's fourth largest group of languages.

These and related minor languages grew up quite separately among the non-Aryan peoples of southern India over thousands of years, and the earliest written records of Tamil date back to the third century AD. The exact origins of the Dravidian group have not been established, but it is possible that proto-Dravidian was spoken further north in prehistoric times before the people were driven south by the Aryan invaders.

Language in India since Independence

With **Independence** it was decided by the government in Delhi that Hindi should become the **official language** of the newly created country. A drive to teach Hindi in all schools followed and over half the country's population are now reckoned to have a decent working knowledge of the language. However, there has always been strong **resistance** to the imposition of Hindi in certain areas, especially the **Tamil-led** Dravidian south, and the vast majority of people living below the Deccan plateau have little or no knowledge of it.

This is where **English**, the language of the ex-colonists, becomes an important means of communication. Not surprisingly, given India's rich linguistic diversity, **English** remains a **lingua franca** for many people. It is still the preferred language of law, higher education, much of commerce and the media, and to some degree political dialogue; and for many educated Indians, not just those living abroad, it is actually their first language. All this explains why the Anglophone visitor can often soon feel surprisingly at home despite the huge cultural differences. It is not unusual to overhear everyday contact between Indians from different parts of the country being conducted in English, and stimulating conversations can often be had, not only with students or businesspeople, but also with chai-wallahs and shoeshine boys.

Indian English

During the British Raj, Indian English developed its own characteristics, which have survived to the present day. It was during this period that many Indian words entered the vocabulary of everyday English, including words like veranda, bungalow, sandal, pyjamas, shampoo, jungle, turban, caste, chariot, chilli, cardamom, pundit and yoga. The traveller to India soon becomes familiar with other terms in common usage that have not spread so widely outside the Subcontinent: *dacoit*, *dhoti*, *panchayat*, *lakh* and *crore* are but a few – a full list of Anglo-Indianisms can be found in the famous Hobson-Jobson Anglo-Indian dictionary.

Perhaps the most endearing aspect of Indian English is the way it has preserved forms now regarded as highly old-fashioned in Britain. Addresses such as "Good sir" and questions like "May I know your good name?" are commonplace, as are terms like "tiffin" and "cantonment". This type of usage reaches its apogee in the more flowery expressions of the media, which regularly feature in the vast array of daily newspapers published in English. Thus headlines often appear such as "37 perish in mishap", referring to a train crash, or passages like this splendid report of a bank robbery: "The miscreants absconded with the loot in great haste. They repaired immediately to their hideaway, whereupon they divided the iniquitous spoils before vanishing into thin air."

Useful Hindi words and phrases

Greetings

Hello (slightly formal; not used for Muslims)	Namaste/Namaskar
Hello (formal; to a Muslim)	As salaam alaykum (in reply) Alaykum as salaam
Goodbye	Namaste
See you later	Phir mileynge
Goodbye (to a Muslim)	Khudaa haafiz
How are you? (formal)	Aap kaise hai?
How are you? (familiar)	Kya hal hai?
brother (informal; not to be used to older men)	bhaaii
sister (informal; not to be used to older women)	diidi
sir	sahib
sir	hazur (Muslims only)

Basic words

yes (informal/more formal)	haa/ji haa
no (informal/more formal)	nahi/ji nahi
OK	acha/tiik hai
I/me	mai
you (formal)	aap
you (familiar; and to children)	tum
and/more	aur
how?	kaise?
How much?	Kitna?
thank you (formal; Indians don't usually say thank you during everyday transactions. There's no direct Hindi equivalent to the English word "please"	dhanyavad/shukriya
good	acha
very good	bahut acha
bad	buraa
big	barra
small	chhota
hot	garam
hot (spicy)	mirchi
cold	thanda
clean	saaf
dirty	gandaa
open	khulaa
expensive	mehngaa
please come	aiiye
go	jao
run (also "take a run" or "scram")	bhaago
enough	bas

Basic phrases

My name is…	Mera naam…hai
What is your name? (formal)	Aapka naam kya hai?
What is your name? (familiar, and to children)	Tumhara naam kya hai?
I'm from…	Mai…se hu
We're from…	Hum…se hai
Where do you come from?	Aap kaha se aate hai?
I understand	Samaj gayaa
I don't understand	Samaj nahin aayaa
I don't know	Maluum nahi
I don't speak Hindi	Mai Hindi nahi bol sakta hu
Please speak slowly	Dhiire boliye
Sorry	Ma'af kiijiye
It is OK?	Tiik hai?
How much?	Kitna paisa?
How much is this?	Yeh kitne ka hai?
I don't need it (literally "not needed"); useful response to persistent touts	Nahi chai'iya
Do you have…?	…hai?

I/we like it	Acha lugta hai
How are you?	Kya haal hai?
I'm fine	Tiik hai
What work do you do?	Kya kam karte hai?
Do you have any brothers or sisters?	Bhaai behan hai?
Oh dear!	Arey!

Getting around

Where is the...?	...kaha hai?
I want to go to...	Mai...jaana chaata hu
Where is it?	Kaha hai?
How far?	Kitna duur?
Which is the bus for Agra?	Agra ki bas kaha hai?
What time does the train leave?	Gaarii kab jayegi?
Stop!	Ruko!
Wait!	Thehero!

Accommodation

I need a room	Mujhe kamra chai'eeye
How much is the room?	Kamra kitne ka hai?
I am staying for one night	Mai ek raat ke liiye theheroonga

Health

I have a headache	Sir me dard hai
I have a pain in my stomach	Mere pate me dard hai
The pain is here	Dard yaha hai
Where is the doctor's clinic?	Daktar ka clinic kaha hai?
Where is the hospital?	Haspital kaha hai?
Where is the pharmacy?	Dawaaii khana kaha hai?
medicine	dawaaii
ill	bimar
pain	dard
stomach	pate
eye	aankh
nose	naak
ear	kaan
back	piith
foot	paao

Numbers and time

zero	shunya
one	ek
two	do
three	tiin
four	char
five	paanch
six	che
seven	saat
eight	aath
nine	nau
ten	das
eleven	gyaarah
twelve	baarah
thirteen	terah
fourteen	chaudah
fifteen	pandrah
sixteen	solah
seventeen	satrah
eighteen	ataarah
nineteen	unniis
twenty	biis
thirty	tiis
forty	chaaliis
fifty	pachaas
sixty	saath
seventy	sattar
eighty	assii
ninety	nabbe
one hundred	ek sau
one thousand	ek hazaar
one hundred thousand	ek lakh
ten million	ek crore
today	aaj
tomorrow/ yesterday	kal
day	din
afternoon	dopahar
evening	shaam
night	raat
week	haftaah
month	mahiinaa

year	saal	**Thursday**	viirvaar
Monday	somvaar	**Friday**	shukravaar
Tuesday	mangalvaar	**Saturday**	shanivaar
Wednesday	budhvaar	**Sunday**	ravivaar

Food and drink glossary

Basics

khaana	food
chawaal	rice
chamach	spoon
chhoori	knife
kanta	fork
plate	plate
chini	sugar
chini nahi	no sugar (eg in tea)
kali mirch	black pepper
gur	jaggery (unrefined sugar
namak	salt
mirch	pepper
mirchi	chilli hot
mirchi kam	less hot
garam	hot
thanda	cold
dahi	yoghurt
dhal	curried lentils, some times reduced to a kind of broth; traditionally served as an accompaniment to all Indian meals
garam masala	spice mix (literally "hot spices") added to dishes as hot seasoning
ghee	clarified butter; often used instead of cooking oil, or to flavour food
gravy	any kind of curry sauce; nothing to do with British gravy
jeera	cumin
lal mirch	red pepper
masala	generic term indicating either a spice mixture or something spicy
methi	fenugreek
paan	digestif; see p.84
paneer	unfermented cheese
sabji	any vegetable

Drinks

bhang lassi	lassi flavoured with bhang (cannabis)
botal vaala paani	mineral water
chai	tea
doodh	milk
falooda	traditional Mughlai dessert, usually made with milk, ice cream, nuts and sweets
kaapi or **kaafi**	coffee
lassi	yoghurt drink, served either plain or flavoured with salt or fruit
pani	water
peenay ka pani	drinking water (not mineral water)

Meat and fish

chingri	prawns
gosht	meat, usually mutton
keema	minced meat
macchi	fish
murg	chicken

Vegetables and fruit

aam	mango
alu	potatoes
baingan	eggplant (aubergine) or brinjal

bhindi	okra (ladies' fingers)
chana	chickpeas
gaajar	carrot
gobi	cauliflower
kaddoo	pumpkin
kela	banana
palak	spinach
piaz	onions
sabji	vegetables (literally, "greens")
santaraa	orange
seb	apple
sag	spinach
tamatar	tomato

Dishes and cooking terms

alu baingan	potato and aubergine; usually mild to medium
alu gobi	potato and cauliflower; usually mild
alu methi	potato with fenugreek leaves, usually medium-hot
alu muttar	potato and pea curry; usually mild
baingan bharta	baked and mashed aubergine mixed with onion
bhindi bhaji	gently spiced fried okra
bhuna	roasted and then thickened-down medium-hot curry sauce
biriyani	rice baked with saffron or turmeric, whole spices and meat (sometimes vegetables), and often hard-boiled egg; rich
chana masala	spicy chickpeas; usually medium-hot
cutlet	fried cutlet of minced meat or chopped vegetables
dhal gosht	meat cooked in lentils; usually hot
dhal makhani	lentils cooked with cream
dhansak	curry sauce made from reduced lentils; usually medium-hot
dopiaza	onion-based sauce; medium-mild
dum	steamed in a casserole; the most common dish is dum aloo, with potatoes
jalfrezi	dish cooked with tomatoes and green chilli; medium-hot to hot
karahi	cast-iron wok which has given its name to a method of cooking with dry spices to create dishes of medium strength
karhi	dhal-like dish made from dahi and gram flour
kofta	balls of minced vegetables or meat in a curried sauce
korma	mild sauce made with curd (and perhaps cream)
malai kofta	vegetable balls in a rich cream sauce; usually medium-mild
momo	Tibetan dumplings
mughlai masala	Mughal-style mild, creamy sauce
mulligatawny	classic Anglo-Indian–style vegetable soup; moderately spicy
murg makhani	butter chicken
muttar paneer	paneer and peas curry
palak paneer	paneer and spinach
pathia	thickened curry with lemon juice; hot
pomfret	a flatfish popular in Mumbai and Kolkata
pongal	spicy rice and dhal
pulau	rice, gently spiced and pre-fried

raita	chilled yoghurt flavoured with mild spices, sometimes with the addition of small pieces of cucumber and tomato; usually eaten as an accompaniment to a main course
rasam	south Indian-style spicy soup
rogan josh	deep-red lamb curry, a classic Mughlai dish; medium-hot
sambar	soupy lentil and vegetable curry with asafoetida and tamarind
shahi paneer	"royal" paneer; slightly more elaborate version of standard paneer curry, sometimes including fruit and nuts
seekh kebab	minced lamb grilled on a skewer
shami kebab	small minced lamb cutlets
tarka dhal	lentils with a masala of fried garlic, onions and spices
thali	combination of vegetarian dishes, chutneys, pickles, rice and bread served as an all-in-one meal
vindaloo	Goan vinegared meat (sometimes fish) curry, originally pork; very hot

Breads and pancakes

appam*	south Indian-style rice pancake speckled with holes, soft in the middle
bhatura	soft bread made of white flour and traditionally accompanying chana; common in Delhi
chapatti	unleavened bread made of wholewheat flour
dosa*	crispy south Indian rice pancake; can be served in various forms, the best known of which is the masala dosa, when the dosa is wrapped around a filling of spicy potato curry
iddli*	south Indian steamed rice cake, usually served with sambar
kaathi	filled wraps
kachori	small thick cakes of salty deep-fried bread
loochi	delicate puri often mixed with white flour; cooked in Bengal
Mughlai paratha	paratha with egg
naan	white leavened bread kneaded with yoghurt and baked in a tandoor
papad or **poppadum***	crisp, thin, chickpea-flour cracker
paratha or **parantha**	wholewheat bread made with butter, rolled thin and griddle-fried; a little bit like a chewy pancake, sometimes stuffed with meat or vegetables
puri	crispy, puffed-up, deep-fried whole wheat bread

roti loosely used term; often just another name for chapatti, though it should be thicker, chewier, and baked in a tandoor

uttapam* thick, south Indian-style rice pancake often cooked with onions

Snacks (chaat), sweets and desserts

barfi or **burfi** traditional sweet made with milk; a bit like fudge

bhaji or **bhajia** pieces of vegetable deep-fried in chickpea batter, served as a main course or a street snack

bhel puri mix of puffed rice, potato and crunchy puri with tamarind sauce; a Mumbai speciality, though now popular nationwide

gulab jamun classic Indian sweet made from deep-fried dough balls served in syrup

halwa traditional sweet made from lentils, nuts and fruit, baked in a large tray and cut into small squares

jalebi flour batter, which is deep fried and soaked in sugar syrup

raj kachori a crisp puri usually filled with chickpeas and doused in curd and sauce

kheer delicate, Mughal-style rice pudding

kulfi Indian-style ice cream, often flavoured with pistachio

ladoo (or ladu) sweets made from small balls of gram flour and semolina

pakora pieces of vegetable deep-fried in chickpea batter; a popular street snack

rasgulla curd cheese balls flavoured with rosewater; a popular dessert

samosa parcels of vegetable and potato (and sometimes meat) wrapped up in triangles of pastry and deep-fried

vada* doughnut-shaped, deep-fried lentil cake (also spelt vadai, vade, wadi, etc)

vada pao* a vada served in a bun with chutney

**south Indian terminology; all other terms are either in Hindi or refer to north Indian cuisine.*

Glossary

aarti evening temple puja of lights

adivasi official term for tribal person

ahimsa nonviolence

amrita nectar of immortality

anda literally "egg": the spherical part of a stupa

angrez general term for Westerners

apsara heavenly nymph

arak liquor distilled from rice or coconut

asana yogic seating posture; small mat used in prayer and meditation

ashram centre for spiritual learning and religious practice

asura demon

atman soul

avatar reincarnation of Vishnu on earth, in human or animal form

ayah nursemaid

Ayurveda ancient system of medicine employing herbs, minerals and massage

baba respectful term for a sadhu or an old man

bagh garden, park

baithak reception area in private house

baksheesh tip, donation or alms

bandh general strike

bandhani tie-dye

baniya another word for shopkeeper/trader/merchant

banyan vast fig tree, used traditionally as a meeting place, or shade for teaching and meditating

baniyan a cotton vest

baoli or **baori** step-well

bastee or **bustee** slum area

beedi Indian-style cigarette, with tobacco rolled in a leaf

begum a Muslim woman of high status

betel leaf chewed in paan, with the nut of the areca tree; also loosely applies to the nut

bhajan song in praise of god

bhakti religious devotion expressed in a personalized or emotional relationship with the deity

bhang pounded marijuana leaf, often mixed in lassi

bharat Hindi name for India

bharat mata literally "Mother India"; a representation of India personified as a maternal goddess

bhawan or **bhavan** building, house, palace or residence

bhotia Himalayan people of Tibetan origin

bhumi earth

bindu seed, or the red dot (also bindi) worn by women on their foreheads as decoration

bodhi enlightenment

bodhi tree or **bo tree** peepal tree (*ficus religiosa*), associated with the Buddha's enlightenment

bodhisattva in Buddhism an enlightened being

brahmin priest; a member of the highest caste group

burj tower or bastion

burqa a loose rob worn by orthodox Muslim women that covers the entire body

burra sahib colonial official, boss, or a man of great importance

cantonment area of town occupied by military quarters

caste social status acquired at birth

cella chamber, often housing the image of a deity

cenotaph ornate tomb

chaat snack

chaddar literally a sheet, can also mean a shawl

chaitya Buddhist temple or stupa

chajja sloping dripstone eave

chakra discus; focus of power; energy point in the body; wheel, often representing the cycle of death and rebirth

chandan sandalwood paste

chandra moon

chang Ladakhi beer made from fermented millet, wheat or rice

chappal sandals or flip-flops (thongs)

charas hashish

charbagh Persian-style garden divided into quadrants

charpoy traditional Indian bed; wooden-framed, with rope stretched across it

chhatri domed stone pavilion, often erected over a tomb

chillum cylindrical clay or wood pipe for smoking charas or ganja

chisthti a follower of the Sufi saint Khwaja Muin-ud-Din Chishti of Ajmer

choli short, tight-fitting blouse worn with a sari

chor robber

chorten monument, often containing prayers, texts or relics, erected as a sign of faith by Tibetan Buddhists

choultry quarters for pilgrims adjoined to south Indian temples

chowk crossroads or courtyard

chowki police post

chowkidar watchman/caretaker

coolie porter/labourer

crore ten million

cupola small dome

dabba box; lunch box

dacoit bandit

dalit "oppressed", "out-caste". The term is preferred by so-called "untouchables" as a description of their social position

dargah tomb of a Muslim saint

darshan vision of a deity or saint; receiving religious teachings

darwaza gateway; door

dawan servant

deg cauldron for food offerings, often found in dargahs

deul Orissan temple or sanctuary

deva god

devadasi temple dancer

devi goddess

devta deity

dhaba food hall selling local dishes

dham important religious site, or a theological college

dharamshala resthouse for pilgrims

dharma sense of religious and social duty (Hindu); the law of nature, teachings, truth (Buddhist)

dhobi laundryman

dholak double-ended drum

dhoop thick pliable block of strong incense

dhoti white ankle-length cloth worn by males, tied around the waist, and hitched up through the legs

dhurrie woollen rug

digambara literally "sky-clad": a Jain sect, known for the habit of nudity among monks, though this is no longer commonplace

diwan (dewan) chief minister

diwan-i-am public audience hall

diwan-i-khas hall of private audience

Dravidian of the south, but usually related to the family of languages used by aboriginal races of India who were pushed south

du-khang main temple in a gompa

dukka tank and fountain in courtyard of mosque

dupatta veil worn by Hindu and Muslim women with salwar kameez

durbar royal audience or council of state

dvarpala guardian image placed at sanctuary door

dzo domesticated half-cow half-yak

Eve-teasing sexual harassment of women, either physical or verbal

fakir ascetic Muslim mendicant

feni Goan spirit, distilled from coconut or cashew fruits

finial capping motif on temple pinnacle

gandharvas Indra's heavenly musicians

ganj area or neigbourhood

ganja marijuana buds

garbhagriha temple sanctuary, literally "womb-chamber"

garh fort

gari vehicle or car

ghat mountain, landing platform, or steps leading to water

ghazal melancholy Urdu songs

godown warehouse

go-khang temple in a gompa devoted to protector (gon) deities

gompa Tibetan, or Ladakhi, Buddhist monastery

goonda ruffian

gopi young cattle-tending maidens who feature as Krishna's playmates and lovers in popular mythology

gopura towered temple gateway, common in south India

guru teacher of religion, music, dance, astrology etc

gurudwara Sikh place of worship

haj Muslim pilgrimage to Mecca

hajji Muslim engaged upon, or who has performed, the haj

hammam sunken Persian-style bath

Harijan title – "Children of God" – given to "untouchables" by Gandhi

hartal strike

haveli elaborately decorated mansion

hijra eunuch or transvestite

Hinayana literally "lesser vehicle": the name given to the original school of Buddhism by later sects

hookah water pipe for smoking strong tobacco or marijuana

howdah bulky elephant-saddle, sometimes made of pure silver, and often shaded by a canopy

hypostyle a building or room in which the roof is supported by columns (usually numerous) rather than walls, arches or vaulting

idgah area laid aside in the west of town for prayers during the Muslim festival Id-ul-zuha

imam Muslim leader or teacher

imambara tomb of a Shi'ite saint

Indo-Saracenic overblown Raj-era architecture that combines Muslim, Hindu, Jain and Western elements

ishwara god

iwan the main (often central) arch in a mosque

jagirdar landowner

jali latticework in stone, or a pierced screen

jama or **jami** Friday, as in Jama Masjid, or "Friday mosque"

janapadas small republics and monarchies; literally "territory of the clan"

jangha the body of a temple

jarokha small canopied balcony, often containing a window seat

Jat major north Indian ethnic group; particularly numerous in eastern Rajasthan around Bharatpur

jataka popular tales about the Buddha's life and teachings

jati caste, determined by family and occupation

jawab a building constructed to mirror another building opposite it, thus creating symmetry

jawan soldier

jhuta soiled by lips: food or drink polluted by touch

-ji suffix added to names as a term of respect

jihad striving by Muslims, through battle, to spread their faith

johar old practice of self-immolation by women in times of war

jyotirlinga twelve sacred sites associated with Shiva's unbounded lingam of light

Kailasa or **Kailash** mountain in western Tibet: Shiva's abode and the traditional source of the Ganges and Brahmaputra; the earthly manifestation of the "world pillar", Mount Meru

kalasha pot-like capping stone characteristic of south Indian temples

kama satisfaction

karma weight of good and bad actions that determine status of rebirth

katcha raw, crude, unsound, weak

kavad small decorated box that unfolds to serve as a travelling temple

khadi home-spun cotton; Gandhi's symbol of Indian self-sufficiency

khan honorific Muslim title

khana dwelling or house

khejri small tree found throughout the desert regions of Rajasthan

kirtan hymn-singing

kot fort

kothi residence

kotla citadel

kotwali police station

kovil term for a Tamil Nadu temple

kshatriya the warrior and ruling caste

kumkum red mark on a Hindu woman's forehead (widows are not supposed to wear it)

kund tank, lake, reservoir

kurta long men's shirt worn over baggy pajamas

lakh one hundred thousand

lama Tibetan Buddhist monk and teacher

lathi heavy stick that can be used for support or as a weapon

lingam phallic symbol in places of worship representing the god Shiva

liwan prayer hall or covered area of a mosque

loka realm or world, eg devaloka, world of the gods

lunghi male garment; long wraparound cloth worn tucked in around the waist flowing down to the ankles

madrasa Islamic school

maha- great or large

mahadeva literally "great god", and a common epithet for Shiva

mahal palace; mansion

mahant in Hinduism, a high-ranking pandit; in Sikhism, the manger of a gurudwara

maharaja (maharana, Maharawal) prince, especially one who rules

maharani the wife of a maharaja, or the woman holding the rank of maharaja

mahatma great soul

Mahayana "Great Vehicle": a Buddhist school that has spread throughout Southeast Asia

mahout elephant driver or keeper

maidan large open space or field

makara crocodile-like animal featuring on temple doorways and symbolizing the river Ganges. Also the vehicle of Varuna, the Vedic god of the sea

mala necklace, garland or rosary

mandala religious diagram

mandapa hall, often with many pillars, used for various purposes such as weddings or dances

mandi market

mandir temple

mantra sacred verse, often repeated as an aid to meditation

mardana area for use of men in a haveli or palace

marg road

masjid mosque

mataji means 'mother', it is also used as a polite form of address to an older woman or a female sadhu

math or **mutt** Hindu or Jain monastery

mayur peacock

medhi terrace

mehendi henna

mela festival

memsahib respectful address to European women

mihrab niche in the wall of a mosque indicating the direction of Mecca

minaret high slender tower, characteristic of mosques

minbar pulpit in a mosque from which the Friday sermon is read

mithuna amorous couples in Hindu and Buddhist figurative art

mohalla neighbourhood

moksha blissful state of freedom from rebirth aspired to by Hindus, Sikhs and Jains

mudra symbolic hand gestures used in meditation and dance that also feature in Hindu, Buddhist and Jain art

muezzin man behind the voice calling Muslims to prayer from a mosque

mullah Muslim teacher and scholar

muqarna a style of Islamic moulded vaulting

nadi river

naga mythical serpent; alternatively, a person from Nagaland

nala gorge cut by a seasonal stream

natak drama

natya dance

nautch dance

nawab Muslim landowner or prince

nilgai blue bull

nirvana (or, in Pali, *nibbana*) Buddhist equivalent of moksha

nizam title of Hyderabad rulers

NRI nonresident Indian, someone entitled to Indian nationality but resident abroad

nullah stream gorge in the mountains

om (or **aum**) symbol denoting the origin of all things, and ultimate divine essence, used in meditation by Hindus and Buddhists

paan betel nut, lime, calcium and aniseed wrapped in a leaf and chewed as a digestive. Mildly addictive

pada foot, or base, also a poetic metre

padma lotus; another name for the goddess Lakshmi

pagoda multistoreyed Buddhist monument

paisa There are a hundred paisa in a rupee

pali original language of early Buddhist texts

panchayat village council

parikrama ritual circumambulation around a temple, shrine or mountain

Parsi Zoroastrian

pietra dura inlay work, traditionally consisting of semiprecious stones set in marble; particularly associated with Agra

pir Muslim holy man

pol fortified gate

pradakshina patha processional path circling a monument or sanctuary

prakara enclosure or courtyard in a south Indian temple

pranayama breath control, used in meditation

prasad food blessed in temple sanctuaries and shared among devotees

prayag auspicious confluence of two or more rivers

puja worship

pujari priest

pukka ripe, mature, firm and stable also correct and acceptable, in the very English sense of "proper"

punkah type of manually operated ceiling fan, widely used during the Raj era, hand-pulled by a so-called "punkah-wallah"

punya religious merit

purdah literally "curtain": the enforced segregation and isolation of women within a haveli or palace or, more figuratively, within society in general. General term for wearing a veil

purnima full moon

pyjama men's baggy trousers

qawwali devotional singing popular among Sufis

qibla wall in a mosque indicating the direction of Mecca

qila fort

raag or **raga** series of notes forming the basis of a melody

Raj rule; monarchy; in particular the period of British imperial rule 1857–1947

raja a ruler or landlord

Rajput princely rulers who once dominated much of north and west India

rakshasa demon

rangoli geometrical pattern of rice powder laid before houses and temples

rani a queen or princess of a raja

rath chariot

rawal chieftain or ruler of a minor principality

rekha deul Orissan towered sanctuary

rinpoche literally "precious one", a highly revered Tibetan Buddhist lama, considered to be a reincarnation of a previous teacher

rishi "seer"; philosophical sage or poet

rudraksha beads used to make Shiva rosaries

rumal handkerchief, particularly finely embroidered in Chamba state (HP)

sadar "main"; eg Sadar Bazaar

sadhak a person who is engaged in an all-encompassing course in spirituality to achieve realization of the self and God

sadhu Hindu holy man with no caste or family ties

sagar lake

sahib respectful title for gentlemen; general term of address for European men

salwar kameez long shirt and baggy ankle-hugging trousers worn by Indian women

samadhi final enlightenment; a site of death or burial of a saint

sambar species of Asian deer

samsara cyclic process of death and rebirth

sangam sacred confluence of two or more rivers, or an academy

sangeet music

sannyasi homeless, possessionless ascetic (Hindu)

sarai resting place for caravans and travellers who once followed the trade routes through Asia

sari usual dress for Indian women: a length of cloth wound around the waist and draped over one shoulder

sati one who sacrifices her life on her husband's funeral pyre in emulation of Shiva's wife. No longer a common practice, and officially illegal

satyagraha Gandhi's campaign of nonviolent protest, literally "grasping truth"

scheduled castes official name for "untouchables"

sepoy infantry private, an Indian soldier in the British army during the colonial period

seva voluntary service in a temple or community

shaikh Muslim holy man or saint

Shaivite Hindu recognizing Shiva as the supreme god

shankha conch, symbol of Vishnu

shastra treatise

sheesh mahal "glass palace"; usually a small room or apartment decorated with mirrorwork mosaics

shikar hunting

shikhara temple tower or spire common in northern Indian architecture

shloka verse from a Sanskrit text

shri (or **sri**) respectful prefix; another name for Lakshmi

shudra the lowest of the four varnas; servant

singh or **singha** lion

sitout veranda

soma medicinal herb with hallucinogenic properties used in early Vedic and Zoroastrian rituals

stambha pillar, or flagstaff

sthala site sacred for its association with legendary events

stupa large hemispherical mound, representing the Buddha's presence, and often protecting relics of the Buddha or a Buddhist saint

suchalaya toilet

sulabh convenient toilet

surma black eyeliner, also known as kohl

Surya the sun, or sun god

sutra (aka **sutta**) verse in Sanskrit and Pali texts (literally "thread")

svetambara "white-clad" sect of Jainism that accepts nuns and shuns nudity

swami master; title for a holy man

swaraj "self-rule"; synonym for independence, coined by Gandhi

tala rhythmic cycle in classical music; in sculpture a tala signifies one face-length

tandoor clay oven

tank square or rectangular water pool in a temple complex, for ritual bathing

tanpura the instrument producing the drone which accompanies all Indian classical music

tempo three-wheeled taxi

terma precious manuscript (Tibetan Buddhist term)

thakur usually Rajput landowner

thangka Tibetan religious scroll painting

Theravada "Doctrine of the Elders": the original name for early Buddhism, which persists today in Sri Lanka and Thailand

thug member of a north Indian cult of professional robbers and murderers

tiffin light meal

tiffin carrier stainless-steel set of tins used for carrying meals

tilak red dot smeared on the forehead during worship, and often used cosmetically

tirtha river crossing considered sacred by Hindus, or the transition from the mundane world to heaven; a place of pilgrimage for Jains

tirthankara "ford-maker" or "crossing-maker": an enlightened Jain teacher who is deified – 24 appear every 300 million years

tola the weight of a silver rupee: 180 grains, or approximately 11.6g

tonga two-wheeled horse-drawn cart

topi cap

torana arch, or freestanding gateway of two pillars linked by an elaborate arch

trimurti the Hindu trinity

trishula Shiva's trident

tuk fortified enclosure of Jain shrines or temples

tulku reincarnated teacher of Tibetan Buddhism

untouchables members of the lowest strata of society, considered polluting to all higher castes

urs Muslim saint's-day festival

vahana the "vehicle" of a deity: the bull Nandi is Shiva's vahana

vaishya member of the merchant and trading caste group

varna literally "colour"; one of four hierarchical social categories: Brahmins, kshatriyas, vaishyas and shudras

vav step-well, common in Gujarat

Vedas sacred texts of early Hinduism

vedika railing around a stupa

vihara Jain or Buddhist monastery

vimana tower over temple sanctuary

waddo south Indian term meaning ward or subdivision of a district

-wallah suffix implying occupation, eg rickshaw-wallah

wazir chief minister to the king

yagna Vedic sacrificial ritual

yaksha pre-Vedic folklore figure connected with fertility and incorporated into later Hindu iconography

yakshi female yaksha

yali mythical lion

yantra cosmological pictogram, or instrument used in an observatory

yatra pilgrimage

yatri pilgrim

yogi sadhu or priestly figure possessing occult powers gained through the practice of yoga (female: yogini)

yoni symbol of the female sexual organ, set around the base of the lingam in temple shrines

yuga aeon: the present age is the last in a cycle of four yugas, kali-yuga, a "black-age" of degeneration and spiritual decline

zamindar landowner

zenana women's quarters; segregated area for women in a mosque, haveli or palace

Small print and

Index

A Rough Guide to Rough Guides

Published in 1982, the first Rough Guide – to Greece – was a student scheme that became a publishing phenomenon. Mark Ellingham, a recent graduate in English from Bristol University, had been travelling in Greece the previous summer and couldn't find the right guidebook. With a small group of friends he wrote his own guide, combining a highly contemporary, journalistic style with a thoroughly practical approach to travellers' needs.

The immediate success of the book spawned a series that rapidly covered dozens of destinations. And, in addition to impecunious backpackers, Rough Guides soon acquired a much broader and older readership that relished the guides' wit and inquisitiveness as much as their enthusiastic, critical approach and value-for-money ethos.

These days, Rough Guides include recommendations from shoestring to luxury and cover more than 200 destinations around the globe, including almost every country in the Americas and Europe, more than half of Africa and most of Asia and Australasia. Our ever-growing team of authors and photographers is spread all over the world, particularly in Europe, the US and Australia.

In the early 1990s, Rough Guides branched out of travel, with the publication of Rough Guides to World Music, Classical Music and the Internet. All three have become benchmark titles in their fields, spearheading the publication of a wide range of books under the Rough Guide name.

Including the travel series, Rough Guides now number more than 350 titles, covering: phrasebooks, waterproof maps, music guides from Opera to Heavy Metal, reference works as diverse as Conspiracy Theories and Shakespeare, and popular culture books from iPods to Poker. Rough Guides also produce a series of more than 120 World Music CDs in partnership with World Music Network.

Visit www.roughguides.com to see our latest publications.

Rough Guide credits

Text editor: Ros Belford, Róisín Cameron, Samantha Cook, Brendon Griffin, Kathryn Lane, Alison Roberts, Harry Wilson
Layout: Anita Singh
Cartography: Rajesh Chhibber, Deshpal Dabas
Picture editor: Michelle Bhatia
Production: Rebecca Short
Proofreader: Stewart Wild
Cover design: Nicole Newman, Dan May
Photographer: Tim Draper, Simon Bracken, Dave Abram
Indian factchecker: Padmanbhan Iyer
Editorial: **London** Andy Turner, Keith Drew, Edward Aves, Alice Park, Lucy White, Jo Kirby, James Smart, Natasha Foges, James Rice, Lara Kavanagh, Emma Beatson, Emma Gibbs, Monica Woods, Mani Ramaswamy, Lucy Cowie, Eleanor Aldridge, Ian Blenkinsop, Joe Staines, Matthew Milton, Tracy Hopkins, Ruth Tidball **Delhi** Madhavi Singh, Lubna Shaheen, Jalpreen Kaur Chhatwal
Design & Pictures: **London** Scott Stickland, Dan May, Diana Jarvis, Mark Thomas, Nicole Newman, Sarah Cummins, Emily Taylor; **Delhi** Umesh Aggarwal, Ajay Verma, Jessica Subramanian, Ankur Guha, Pradeep Thapliyal, Sachin Tanwar, Nikhil Agarwal, Sachin Gupta
Production: Liz Cherry, Louise Daly, Erika Pepe
Cartography: **London** Ed Wright, Katie Lloyd-Jones; **Delhi** Ashutosh Bharti, Rajesh Mishra, Animesh Pathak, Jasbir Sandhu, Karobi Gogoi, Swati Handoo, Lokamata Sahu
Online: **London** Faye Hellon, Jeanette Angell, Fergus Day, Justine Bright, Clare Bryson, Aine Fearon, Adrian Low, Ezgi Celebi; **Delhi** Amit Verma, Rahul Kumar, Narender Kumar, Ravi Yadav, Debojit Borah, Rakesh Kumar, Ganesh Sharma, Shisir Basumatari
Marketing & Publicity: **London** Liz Statham, Jess Carter, Vivienne Watton, Anna Paynton, Rachel Sprackett, Laura Vipond; **New York** Katy Ball; **Delhi** Aman Arora
Digital Travel Publisher: Peter Buckley
Reference Director: Andrew Lockett
Operations Assistant: Becky Doyle
Operations Manager: Helen Atkinson
Publishing Director (Travel): Clare Currie
Commercial Manager: Gino Magnotta
Managing Director: John Duhigg

Publishing information

This eighth edition published January 2011 by
Rough Guides Ltd,
80 Strand, London WC2R 0RL
11, Community Centre, Panchsheel Park, New Delhi 110017, India
Distributed by the Penguin Group
Penguin Books Ltd,
80 Strand, London WC2R 0RL
Penguin Group (USA)
375 Hudson Street, NY 10014, USA
Penguin Group (Australia)
250 Camberwell Road, Camberwell,
Victoria 3124, Australia
Penguin Group (NZ)
67 Apollo Drive, Mairangi Bay, Auckland 1310, New Zealand
This paperback edition published in Canada in 2010. Rough Guides is represented in Canada by Tourmaline Editions Inc., 662 King Street West, Suite 304, Toronto, Ontario, M5V 1M7
Cover concept by Peter Dyer.
Typeset in Bembo and Helvetica to an original design by Henry Iles.
Printed in Malaysia by Vivar Printing Sdn Bhd.

1224pp includes index
A catalogue record for this book is available from the British Library
ISBN: 978-1-84836-563-6

3 5 7 9 8 6 4 2

Help us update

We've gone to a lot of effort to ensure that the eighth edition of **The Rough Guide to India** is accurate and up-to-date. However, things change – places get "discovered", opening hours are notoriously fickle, restaurants and rooms raise prices or lower standards. If you feel we've got it wrong or left something out, we'd like to know, and if you can remember the address, the price, the hours, the phone number, so much the better.

Please send your comments with the subject line "**Rough Guide India Update**" to ⓔmail @roughguides.com. We'll credit all contributions and send a copy of the next edition (or any other Rough Guide if you prefer) for the very best emails.

Find more travel information, connect with fellow travellers and book your trip on ⓦwww .roughguides.com

Acknowledgements

David Abram: thanks for their help during the research for the Kerala and Goa chapters: PJ Sinna, Mr and Mrs C & F Moosa, Victor, Rajini, Ajay and Nisha in Wayanad; Sajeev, PJ Varghese, Fiona Jeffry, Paul Gray, Mrs Amrit Singh, Viriam Kaur, Shelly, Teresa, Royston and Willy, Mariketty, Joanna Thornycroft, Simon Hayward, Jazz KoKo and Fiona Spiral. Thanks also to editors Brendon Griffin and Sam Cook, for doing such a splendid job on our Goa and Kerala chapters, respectively.

Edward Aves: I'm hugely indebted to the indefatigable Professor Chandrashekhar Jaiswal at MTDC in Aurangabad, my Maharashtran Mr Fix It, for his help and insight. Warm thanks too to the inimitable Lords in Matheran, and to the wonderful owners of the Hotel Plaza in Jalgaon for their advice and hospitality. Thanks also to Sandeep Ghosh at the Lemon Tree and Sanjay Dabhade at The Meadows in Aurangabad, Gajanan Kharat in Lonar, and all at The Duke's Retreat in Khandala. And finally, back in London, a big shout out – and a pint or two – to Keith for packing me off to India in the first place, and to Harry for his encouraging words and spot-on editing.

Nick Edwards conveys the warmest thanks to his old friend Manzoor Chachoo for setting things up for the Kashmir visit and to Gulam and Altaf in Srinagar. Many thanks also to Nimmu and family in Gokarna and once again to Benny & Lynda on Havelock. For help in gathering remote info, many thanks to Micah Hanson and Sylvia Eyzaguirre, companions in the Kinnaur avalanche episodes, Chris Scott for the latest on Manali-Leh, and Kevin Telfer on the Andamans. For fine company in the mountains, many cheers to Mike Watkins, and for shared frolics in Gokarna, to Chris and Jamie Coe. Finally, heartfelt hugs to my dearest Maria for joining in on Karnataka and being a trooper in the face of adversity.

Daniel Jacobs thanks Mahendra Dan (Mount Abu), Ratindi Pandey (UP Tourism, Lucknow), Kumar Gaurav (India Tourism, Patna), and the staff at Chandigarh Tourism; special thanks to Ramesh Wadhwa (Tourists Rest House, Agra), and to Rajesh and Anil, and Ashok, Sabir and all the staff at the Tourists Rest House, and also to everyone at Rough Guides in Delhi, and in particular Madhavi Singh, for their invaluable help and advice.

Shafik Meghji thanks the many travellers and locals who offered their help, recommendations and – from time to time – horror stories. A special dhanyavad must go to: my fellow authors for all their advice and support; Keith Drew, Róisín Cameron and Harry Wilson at Rough Guides in London; Francisco in Diu; Mr Sorathia in Junagadh; Pramod Jethi in Bhuj for sharing his expertise on Kutch; Sanjay Malhotra of MP Tourism in Orchha; Ajit Pal Singh of India Tourism in Khajuraho; Katie and Jehan Bhujwala and all the staff at Shergarh in Mukki; the AP Tourism office in Hyderabad; Sarat Achyra of Discover Tours in Bhubaneswar; James Perry of Cultural Pursuits in Shillong for his help with permits; Rahul and Dave at Travel the Unknown for their insight into the Northeast; Jean, Nizar and Nina Meghji; and Sioned Jones for a wonderful week in MP, and all her love, support and encouragement.

Gavin Thomas offers massive thanks, once again, to the mighty Satinder Pal Singh for all his help and kindness, and to everyone at the Pearl Palace Hotel in Jaipur for making my stay so comfortable (particularly Bidyut Tarafdav for driving my passport all the way to Nawalgarh). Grateful thanks also to Abhinav Wadhwa at the Sundar Palace Hotel for further information, insights and assistance, and for providing such enjoyable company during my visits to the city. A big vote of thanks also to Indar Ujjawal at Adventure Travel in Jaisalmer; Jaggi and Sohel at the Govind Hotel in Johdpur; Rahul and Abher at the Tiger Safari Hotel in Ranthambore; and to Sanjay Sain, for driving me from Jaipur to Ranthambore with unfailing patience and courtesy, despite my frequently incomprehensible meanderings. And, of course, to Allison, Laura and Jamie, for keeping the home fires burning, once again.

Readers' letters

Thanks to all the readers who have taken the time to write in with comments and suggestions (and apologies if we've inadvertently omitted or misspelt anyone's name):

Erika Abrams; Anna Adam; Joan Alawoya; Elaine Almén; Jonni Aromaa; Sam Athol-Murray; Barry Atkinson; Louise Attwood; Sam Barfoot; Kathryn Barley; Wolfgang Bartels; Chris Baumann; Derek Bedlow; Pippa Behr; Sophie Broadbent; Beth & Steve Brown; Andre Burney; Jane Butterfield; Eric & Sylvia Castaldi; Peter Castro; Bill Clark; Malcolm Clark; Karein Davie; Lydia Dawson; Ann Day; Rev. Fr Ynte de Groot; Theresa Durso; Mylene Evered; Stuart Forster; Christine Foster; Aaron Fox; Sharon "Shazbaz" Foxwell; Peter Frank & Meryl D'Souza-Frank; Janet Giaretta; Stuart Graham and Beryl Jackson; Geoff Hill; John Kehoe; Sonia Khan and John Hendry; Geoffrey Kremer; Anne-Flore Laloë; Judith and Bill Landles; Roger & Denise Lawrence; Ryan Leeward; Lynne Le Gros; Emil Malmborg; Amy Marsh; Hannah McKerchar; Carol Miller; Clare Mooney; Sophie Morris; Julia Morton; Rose Murphy; Andrew Mutter; Zak Nields; Joe Norman; Clare Oakland; Karyn Olden; Berl Peck; Stephen Phelps; Graham Poole; Robin Pritchard; GS Rajmohan; Dawn Richardson; Tino Rochez; Adam Rowland; Pia Russo; Anthony Schlesinger; Hans Dieter Schmitt; Minesh Shah; Noori Siddiqui; Natasa Stankovic; Tom Stuart; Michelle Superle; David Trelawny-Ross; Geke van der A; Roland Weilguny; Bob Wiggins; Jackie Williams; Bradley Young.

Photo credits

All photos © Rough Guides except the following:

Title page
Women sorting peppers, Orissa © Floris Leeuwenberg/Corbis

Full page
Pilgrims at Sabarimala, Kerala © Jean-Baptiste Rabouan/Corbis

Introduction
Elephant trunk © Travel Ink/Getty Images/Gallo Images
Jaisalmer Palace © Douglas Pearson/Corbis
Kolkata flower market © Peter Adams/Getty Images
Prayer flags, Ladakh © Dieter Mendzigall/Corbis
Priest and statue © Hemis/Alamy

Things not to miss
01 Durga Puja © Amit Bhargava/Corbis
02 Fatehpur Sikri © Blaine Harrington III/Corbis
04 Ajanta painting © Luca Tettoni/Corbis
06 Phuktal monastery, Zanskar © Jacques Ducoin/Sygma/Corbis
07 Gosain Narain taking poison in the presence of Emperor Jahangir © Angelo Hornak/Corbis
08 Pushkar camel mela © Frédéric Soltan/Corbis
09 Khajuraho © Hal Beral/Corbis
10 Gangotri © Christophe Boisvieux/Corbis
11 Sadhus, Orchha © Frédéric Soltan/Corbis
12 Jaisalmer Fort © Nicholas Reuss Getty Images/Lonely Planet Images
13 Manali-Leh road © Daniel H. Bailey/Alamy
14 Prayer wheels, Dharamsala © Pep Roig/Alamy
16 Keoladeo National Park © Harish Tyagi/epa/Corbis
18 Om Beach, Gokarna © Franck Guiziou/Hemis/Corbis
19 Rath Yatra, Puri © STR/epa/Corbis
20 Konarak temple, Orissa © Wang Ye/Corbis
21 Meenakshi Amman temple, Madurai © Frédéric Soltan Sygma/Corbis
22 Tiger © Thorsten Milse Robert Harding World Imagery/Corbis
24 Ellora caves © Richard A. Cooke/Corbis
25 Bracelets © Catherine Karnow/Corbis
26 Bathers, Varanasi © Bob Krist/Corbis
27 Varkala, Kerala © Michele Falzone Getty Images
29 Mamallapuram, Tamil Nadu © Beate Schleep/Corbis
30 Tikse monastery © Destinations/Corbis
33 City Palace, Lake Pichola, Udaipur © Martin Harvey/Corbis
34 Golden Temple, Amritsar © Raminder Pal Singh/epa/Corbis

Crafts to go colour section
Puppets © Jon Arnold Images Ltd/Alamy
Miniature painting school © Frédéric Soltan/Corbis
Meenakari © Dinodia/photolibrary.com
Carpets and tapestries © Blaine Harrington III/Corbis
Sandals © Aurora Photos/Alamy
Tailor © Michael Sparrow/Alamy
Umbrellas © Keren Su/Getty Images

Bollywood and beyond colour section
Dancer © DreamPictures/GettyImages
My Name is Khan poster © STR/epa/Corbis
Dancers and poster © Stuart Freedman/Corbis
Actors dancing © DreamPictures/Getty Images
Amitabh Bachchan © Vijay Mathur/Reuters/Corbis
Aishwarya Rai © Stephane Reix/Corbis
Lagaan © MovieStore Collection
Mother India © MovieStore Collection
Salaam Bombay © MovieStore Collection

Sacred spaces colour section
Pilgrim bathing © Kazuyoshi Nomachi/Corbis
Pilgrims walking © Fredrik Renander/Alamy
Bathing at Varanasi © Peter Adams/Corbis
Monks reading © photolibrary.com
Sadhu © Raj Patidar/Corbis
Kumbh Mela © Anindito Mukherjee/Corbis
Jagannath temple © photolibrary.com
Temple, Shatrunjaya © Hans Georg Roth/Corbis
Ramanathaswamy temple © photolibrary.com

Black and whites
p.242 Ghat and boats, Varanasi © John Hicks/Corbis
p.301 Sadhu, Rishikesh © Frédéric Soltan Sygma/Corbis
p.343 Jagadambi Devi temple, Khajuraho © Jose Fuste Raga/Corbis
p.407 Spiti, Kumzum-La Road Pass © David Samuel Robbins/Corbis
p.470 Dal Lake, Srinagar, Kashmir © Pep Roig/Alamy
p.519 Golden Temple © Raminder Pal Singh/Corbis
p.536 Embroidery work, Kutch © Jean-Baptiste Rabouan Hemis/Corbis
p.628 Ellora Caves © Frédéric Soltan/Corbis
p.732 Tea harvesters, Darjeeling © Macduff Everton/Corbis
p.791 Mahabodhi Temple, Bodhgaya © Robert Nickelsberg/Getty Images
p.807 Monks in Rumtek, Sikkim © Earl & Nazima Kowall/Corbis
p.836 Rhinoceros, Kaziranga National Park © James Warwick/Getty Images
p.871 Konark sun temple © Wang Ye/XinHua/Xinhua Press/Corbis
p.903 Charminar, Hyderabad © Jon Hicks/Corbis
p.922 Havelock Island © Neil McAllister/Alamy
p.944 Brihadishwara temple, Thanjavur © Frédéric Soltan Sygma/Corbis
p.1084 Maharaja's Palace, Mysore © Michael Melford/National Geographic Society/Corbis

Index

Map entries are in colour.

State and Union Territory (UT) abbreviations

AN Andaman and Nicobar (UT)
AP Andhra Pradesh
AR Arunachal Pradesh
AS Assam
BR Bihar
CH Chandigarh (UT)
CT Chattisgarh
DD Daman and Diu (UT)
DL Delhi (Capital Territory)
DN Dadra and Nagar Haveli (UT)
GA Goa
GJ Gujarat
HP Himachal Pradesh
HR Haryana
JH Jharkhand
JK Jammu and Kashmir
KA Karnataka
KE Kerala
LD Lakshadweep (UT)
MH Maharashtra
ML Meghalaya
MN Manipur
MP Madhya Pradesh
MZ Mizoram
NL Nagaland
OR Orissa
PB Punjab
PY Puducherry (UT)
RJ Rajasthan
SK Sikkim
TN Tamil Nadu
TR Tripura
UP Uttar Pradesh
UA Uttarakhand
WB West Bengal

A

B

D

E

F

G

H

I

J

K

L

M

N

O

P

Q

R

S

W

Y

Z

Map symbols

maps are listed in the full index using coloured text

REGIONAL MAPS

- Motorway
- Major road
- Minor road
- Unpaved road
- Railway
- Track/trail
- Coastline/river
- Ferry
- International boundary
- State/provincial boundary
- Chapter division boundary
- Mountain range
- Peak
- Rocks/reefs
- Caves
- Pass
- Waterfall
- Viewpoint
- Airport
- Domestic airport
- Point of interest
- Church
- Mountain refuge/lodge
- Lighthouse
- Palm trees
- Swamp
- Synagogue
- Camps
- Country park
- Fortress
- Boulders
- Glacier
- Forest
- Mudflats

STREET MAPS

- Main road
- Secondary road
- Track
- Steps
- Railway
- Path
- Bridge
- Wall
- Gate
- Information office
- Post office
- Internet
- Fuel station
- Hospital
- Bus/taxi stand
- Metro station
- Stadium
- Accommodation
- Restaurant
- Cliff
- Pagoda
- Parking
- Helipad
- Springs
- Statue
- Boat
- Escarpment
- Golf course
- Cascade
- Market
- Building
- Church
- Cemetery
- Muslim cemetery

COMMON SYMBOLS

- Mosque/Muslim monument
- Buddhist temple
- Hindu/Jain temple
- Chinese temple
- Palace
- Shrine
- Monastery
- Ghat
- Haveli
- Park
- Beach